Ron Larson, Ph.D., is well known as the lead author of a comprehensive program for mathematics that spans middle school, high school, and college courses. He holds the distinction of Professor Emeritus from Penn State Erie, The Behrend College, where he taught for nearly 40 years. He received his Ph.D. in mathematics from the University of Colorado. Dr. Larson's numerous professional activities keep him actively involved in the mathematics education community and allow him to fully understand the needs of students, teachers, supervisors, and administrators.

Ron Larson

Laurie Boswell, Ed.D., is the Head of School and a mathematics teacher at the Riverside School in Lyndonville, Vermont. Dr. Boswell is a recipient of the Presidential Award for Excellence in Mathematics Teaching and has taught mathematics to students at all levels, from elementary through college. Dr. Boswell was a Tandy Technology Scholar and served on the NCTM Board of Directors from 2002 to 2005. She currently serves on the board of NCSM and is a popular national speaker.

Laurie Boswell

Dr. Ron Larson and **Dr. Laurie Boswell** began writing together in 1992. Since that time, they have authored over two dozen textbooks. In their collaboration, Ron is primarily responsible for the student edition while Laurie is primarily responsible for the teaching edition.

For the Student

Welcome to *Big Ideas Math Geometry*. From start to finish, this program was designed with you, the learner, in mind.

As you work through the chapters in your Geometry course, you will be encouraged to think and to make conjectures while you persevere through challenging problems and exercises. You will make errors—and that is ok! Learning and understanding occur when you make errors and push through mental roadblocks to comprehend and solve new and challenging problems.

In this program, you will also be required to explain your thinking and your analysis of diverse problems and exercises. Being actively involved in learning will help you develop mathematical reasoning and use it to solve math problems and work through other everyday challenges.

We wish you the best of luck as you explore Geometry. We are excited to be a part of your preparation for the challenges you will face in the remainder of your high school career and beyond.

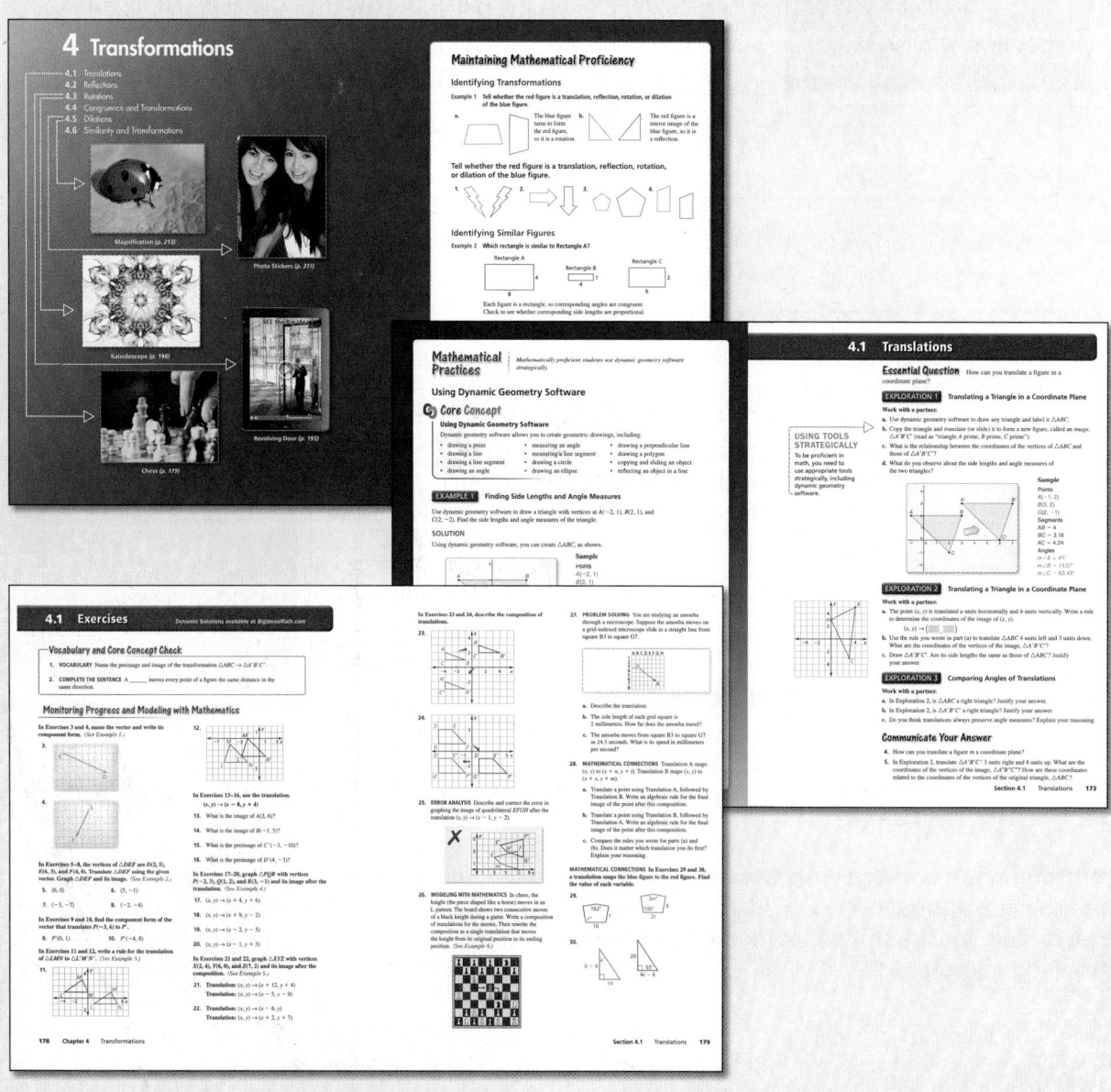

Big Ideas Math
High School Research

Big Ideas Math Algebra 1, *Geometry*, and *Algebra 2* is a research-based program providing a rigorous, focused, and coherent curriculum for high school students. Ron Larson and Laurie Boswell utilized their expertise as well as the body of knowledge collected by additional expert mathematicians and researchers to develop each course.

The pedagogical approach to this program follows the best practices outlined in the most prominent and widely-accepted educational research and standards, including:

Achieve, ACT, and The College Board

Adding It Up: Helping Children Learn Mathematics
National Research Council ©2001

Common Core State Standards for Mathematics
National Governors Association Center for Best Practices and the Council of Chief State
    School Officers ©2010

Curriculum Focal Points and the *Principles and Standards for School Mathematics* ©2000
National Council of Teachers of Mathematics (NCTM)

Project Based Learning
The Buck Institute

Rigor/Relevance Framework™
International Center for Leadership in Education

Universal Design for Learning Guidelines
CAST ©2011

Big Ideas Math would like to express our gratitude to the mathematics education and instruction experts who served as consultants during the writing of *Big Ideas Math Algebra 1*, *Geometry*, and *Algebra 2*. Their input was an invaluable asset during the development of this program.

Kristen Karbon
Curriculum and Assessment Coordinator
Troy School District
Troy, Michigan

Bonnie Spence
Differentiated Instruction Consultant
Mathematics Lecturer, The University of Montana
Missoula, Montana

Jean Carwin
Math Specialist/TOSA
Snohomish School District
Snohomish, Washington

Connie Schrock, Ph.D.
Performance Tasks Consultant
Mathematics Professor, Emporia State University
Emporia, Kansas

Carolyn Briles
Performance Tasks Consultant
Mathematics Teacher, Loudoun County Public Schools
Leesburg, Virginia

We would also like to thank all of our reviewers who took the time to provide feedback during the final development phases. For a complete list of the *Big Ideas Math* program reviewers, please visit *www.BigIdeasLearning.com*.

Common Core State Standards for Mathematical Practice

Make sense of problems and persevere in solving them.

- *Essential Questions* help students focus on core concepts as they analyze and work through each *Exploration*.
- Section opening *Explorations* allow students to struggle with new mathematical concepts and explain their reasoning in the *Communicate Your Answer* questions.

Reason abstractly and quantitatively.

- *Reasoning, Critical Thinking, Abstract Reasoning,* and *Problem Solving* exercises challenge students to apply their acquired knowledge and reasoning skills to solve each problem.
- *Thought Provoking* exercises test the reasoning skills of students as they analyze and interpret perplexing scenarios.

Construct viable arguments and critique the reasoning of others.

- Students must justify their responses to each *Essential Question* in the *Communicate Your Answer* questions at the end of each *Exploration* set.
- Students are asked to construct arguments and critique the reasoning of others in specialized exercises, including *Making an Argument, How Do You See It?, Drawing Conclusions, Reasoning, Error Analysis, Problem Solving,* and *Writing*.

Model with mathematics.

- Real-life scenarios are utilized in *Explorations, Examples, Exercises,* and *Assessments* so students have opportunities to apply the mathematical concepts they have learned to realistic situations.
- *Modeling with Mathematics* exercises allow students to interpret a problem in the context of a real-life situation, often utilizing tables, graphs, visual representations, and formulas.

Use appropriate tools strategically.

- Students are provided opportunities for selecting and utilizing the appropriate mathematical tool in *Using Tools* exercises. Students work with graphing calculators, dynamic geometry software, models, and more.
- A variety of tool papers and manipulatives are available for students to use in problems as strategically appropriate.

Attend to precision.

- *Vocabulary and Core Concept Check* exercises require students to use clear, precise mathematical language in their solutions and explanations.
- The many opportunities for cooperative learning in this program, including working with partners for each *Exploration*, support precise, explicit mathematical communication.

Look for and make use of structure.

- *Using Structure* exercises provide students with the opportunity to explore patterns and structure in mathematics.
- *Proof* exercises require students to understand and apply the structure of geometric theorems to solve each problem.

Look for and express regularity in repeated reasoning.

- Students are continually encouraged to evaluate the reasonableness of their solutions and their steps in the problem-solving process.
- Stepped-out *Examples* encourage students to maintain oversight of their problem-solving process and pay attention to the relevant details in each step.

Go to *BigIdeasLearning.com* for more information on the
Common Core State Standards for Mathematical Practice.

Common Core State Standards for Mathematical Content for Geometry

Chapter Coverage for Standards

1 2 3 4 5 6 7 8 9 10 11 12

Conceptual Category Geometry

○ Congruence

1 2 3 **4 5** 6 **7 8 9** 10 11 12

Conceptual Category Geometry

○ Similarity, Right Triangles, and Trigonometry

1 2 3 4 5 **6** 7 8 9 **10 11** 12

Conceptual Category Geometry

○ Circles

1 2 **3** 4 **5** 6 7 **8** 9 **10** 11 12

Conceptual Category Geometry

○ Expressing Geometric Properties with Equations

1 2 3 4 5 6 7 8 9 10 **11** 12

Conceptual Category Geometry

○ Geometric Measurement and Dimension

1 2 3 4 5 6 7 8 9 10 11 **12**

Conceptual Category Statistics and Probability

○ Probability

Go to *BigIdeasLearning.com* for more information on the
Common Core State Standards for Mathematical Content.

1 Basics of Geometry

See the Big Idea
Learn how bridges are designed using
compression and tension.

Reasoning and Proofs 2

Laurie's Notes

See the Big Idea
Tigers and humans display obvious differences
between males and females. Use logic to
determine whether other mammals do.

3 Parallel and Perpendicular Lines

See the Big Idea
Discover why parallel lines and reference
points are so important to builders.

Transformations 4

Laurie's Notes

See the Big Idea
Investigate the rotational symmetry of revolving doors and discover why this technology allows skyscrapers to be built.

5 Congruent Triangles

See the Big Idea
Learn how to use triangle congruence
in a model hang glider challenge.

Relationships Within Triangles 6

See the Big Idea
Discover why triangles are used in building for strength.

7 Quadrilaterals and Other Polygons

Laurie's Notes

See the Big Idea
Explore what the refractive index, reflected light, and light dispersion have to do with diamonds.

Similarity 8

See the Big Idea
Discover how many different ways you can scale a model.

9 Right Triangles and Trigonometry

See the Big Idea
Test the accuracy of two measurement
methods and discover which one prevails.

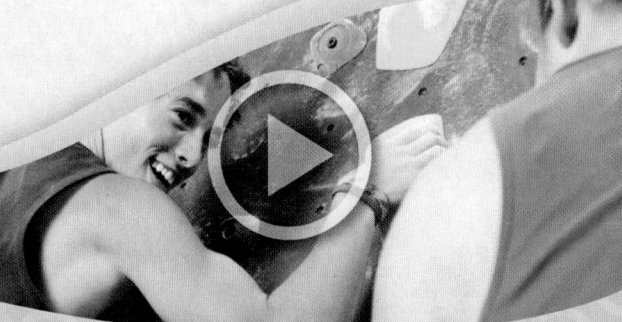

Circles 10

Laurie's Notes

See the Big Idea
Utilize trilateration to find the epicenters of historical earthquakes and discover where they lie on known fault lines.

11 Circumference, Area, and Volume

Laurie's Notes

See the Big Idea
Analyze the population density in various parts of Los Angeles—as viewed from an observation point high in the hills of Santa Monica.

Probability 12

Laurie's Notes

See the Big Idea
Learn about caring for trees at an arboretum.

How to Use Your Math Book

Get ready for each chapter by **Maintaining Mathematical Proficiency** and reviewing the **Mathematical Practices**. Begin each section by working through the **EXPLORATIONS** to **Communicate Your Answer** to the **Essential Question**. Each **Lesson** will explain **What You Will Learn** through **EXAMPLES**, **Core Concepts**, and **Core Vocabulary**. Answer the **Monitoring Progress** questions as you work through each lesson. Look for STUDY TIPS, COMMON ERRORS, and suggestions for looking at a problem ANOTHER WAY throughout the lessons. We will also provide you with guidance for accurate mathematical READING and concept details you should REMEMBER.

Sharpen your newly acquired skills with **Exercises** at the end of every section. Halfway through each chapter you will be asked **What Did You Learn?** and you can use the Mid-Chapter **Quiz** to check your progress. You can also use the **Chapter Review** and **Chapter Test** to review and assess yourself after you have completed a chapter.

Apply what you learned in each chapter to a **Performance Task** and build your confidence for taking standardized tests with each chapter's **Cumulative Assessment**.

For extra practice in any chapter, use your *Online Resources*, *Skills Review Handbook*, or your *Student Journal*.

Program Overview

Program Philosophy: Rigor and Balance with Real-Life Applications

The *Big Ideas Math*® program balances conceptual understanding with procedural fluency. Real-life applications help turn mathematical learning into an engaging and meaningful way to see and explore the real world.

Essential Question How can you reflect a figure in a coordinate plane?

EXPLORATION 1 **Reflecting a Triangle Using a Reflective Device**

Work with a partner. Use a straightedge to draw any triangle on paper. Label it $\triangle ABC$.

a. Use the straightedge to draw a line that does not pass through the triangle. Label it m.

b. Place a reflective device on line m.

c. Use the reflective device to plot the images of the vertices of $\triangle ABC$. Label the images of vertices A, B, and C as A', B', and C', respectively.

d. Use a straightedge to draw $\triangle A'B'C'$ by connecting the vertices.

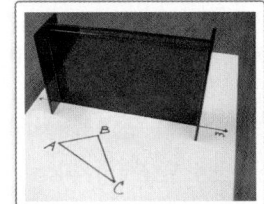

> Explorations and guiding *Essential Questions* encourage **conceptual understanding**.

4.2 Lesson

Core Vocabulary

reflection, *p. 182*
line of reflection, *p. 182*
glide reflection, *p. 184*
line symmetry, *p. 185*
line of symmetry, *p. 185*

What You Will Learn

▶ Perform reflections.
▶ Perform glide reflections.
▶ Identify lines of symmetry.
▶ Solve real-life problems involving reflections.

Performing Reflections

Core Concept

Reflections

A **reflection** is a transformation that uses a line like a mirror to reflect a figure. The mirror line is called the **line of reflection**.

A reflection in a line m maps every point P in the plane to a point P', so that for each point one of the following properties is true.

- If P is not on m, then m is the perpendicular bisector of $\overline{PP'}$, or
- If P is on m, then $P = P'$.

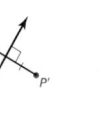

point P not on m point P on m

EXAMPLE 1 **Reflecting in Horizontal and Vertical Lines**

Graph $\triangle ABC$ with vertices $A(1, 3)$, $B(5, 2)$, and $C(2, 1)$ and its image after the reflection described.

a. In the line n: $x = 3$ **b.** In the line m: $y = 1$

SOLUTION

a. Point A is 2 units left of line n, so its reflection A' is 2 units right of line n at $(5, 3)$. Also, B' is 2 units left of line n at $(1, 2)$, and C' is 1 unit right of line n at $(4, 1)$.

b. Point A is 2 units abo A' is 2 units below li Also, B' is 1 unit bel $(5, 0)$. Because point you know that $C = C$

> Direct instruction lessons allow for **procedural fluency** and provide the opportunity to use clear, precise mathematical language.

> Real-life applications provide students with opportunities to connect classroom lessons to realistic scenarios.

Solving Real-Life Problems

EXAMPLE 6 **Finding a Minimum Distance**

You are going to buy books. Your friend is going to buy CDs. Where should you park to minimize the distance you both will walk?

SOLUTION

Reflect B in line m to obtain B'. Then draw $\overline{A'B'}$. Label the intersection of $\overline{AB'}$ and m as C. Because $\overline{AB'}$ is the shortest distance between A and B' and $BC = B'C$, park at point C to minimize the combined distance, $AC + BC$, you both have to walk.

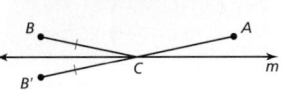

> Chapter openers focused on **Maintaining Mathematical Proficiency** promote the development of the habits of mind mathematically proficient students demonstrate.

> The Standards for Mathematical Practice are woven into every chapter, including a full page dedicated to mastering one of the **Mathematical Practices**.

Maintaining Mathematical Proficiency

Identifying Transformations

Example 1   Tell whether the red figure is a translation, reflection, rotation, or dilation of the blue figure.

a. 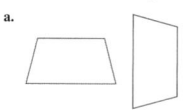 The blue figure turns to form the red figure, so it is a rotation.

b. 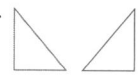 The red figure is a mirror image of the blue figure, so it is a reflection.

Tell whether the red figure is a translation, reflection, rotation, or dilation of the blue figure.

1.    2.   3. 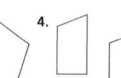   4.

Identifying Similar Figures

Example 2   Which rectangle is similar to Rectangle A?

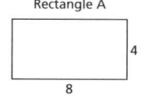

Rectangle A   8, 4   Rectangle B   4, 1   Rectangle C   6, 3

Each figure is a rectangle, so corresponding angles are congruent. Check to see whether corresponding side lengths are proportional.

Rectangle A and Rectangle B

$\dfrac{\text{Length of A}}{\text{Length of B}} = \dfrac{8}{4} = 2$ $\dfrac{\text{Width of A}}{\text{Width of B}} = \dfrac{4}{1} = 4$

not proportional

Rectangle A and Rectangle C

$\dfrac{\text{Length of A}}{\text{Length of C}} = \dfrac{8}{6} = \dfrac{4}{3}$ $\dfrac{\text{Width of A}}{\text{Width of C}} = \dfrac{4}{3}$

proportional

...o, Rectangle C is similar to Rectangle A.

...ether the two figures are similar. Explain your reasoning.

 12, 14   6. 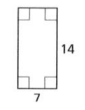 8, 10, 7, 6   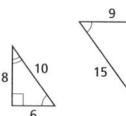 9, 15, 12, 6   7. 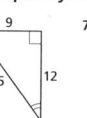 10 5, 3

...TRACT REASONING Can you draw two squares that are not similar? Explain your reasoning.

Mathematical Practices

Mathematically proficient students use dynamic geometry software strategically.

Using Dynamic Geometry Software

Core Concept

Using Dynamic Geometry Software

Dynamic geometry software allows you to create geometric drawings, including:

- drawing a point
- drawing a line
- drawing a line segment
- drawing an angle
- measuring an angle
- measuring a line segment
- drawing a circle
- drawing an ellipse
- drawing a perpendicular line
- drawing a polygon
- copying and sliding an object
- reflecting an object in a line

EXAMPLE 1   Finding Side Lengths and Angle Measures

Use dynamic geometry software to draw a triangle with vertices at $A(-2, 1)$, $B(2, 1)$, and $C(2, -2)$. Find the side lengths and angle measures of the triangle.

SOLUTION

Using dynamic geometry software, you can create $\triangle ABC$, as shown.

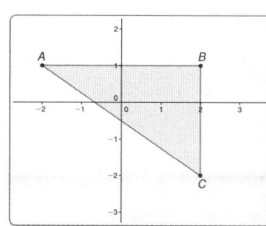

Sample

Points
$A(-2, 1)$
$B(2, 1)$
$C(2, -2)$

Segments
$AB = 4$
$BC = 3$
$AC = 5$

Angles
$m\angle A = 36.87°$
$m\angle B = 90°$
$m\angle C = 53.13°$

▶ From the display, the side lengths are $AB = 4$ units, $BC = 3$ units, and $AC = 5$ units. The angle measures, rounded to two decimal places, are $m\angle A \approx 36.87°$, $m\angle B \approx 90°$, and $m\angle C \approx 53.13°$.

Monitoring Progress

Use dynamic geometry software to draw the polygon with the given vertices. Use the software to find the side lengths and angle measures of the polygon. Round your answers to the nearest hundredth.

1. $A(0, 2), B(3, -1), C(4, 3)$
2. $A(-2, 1), B(-2, -1), C(3, 2)$
3. $A(1, 1), B(-3, 1), C(-3, -2), D(1, -2)$
4. $A(1, 1), B(-3, 1), C(-2, -2), D(2, -2)$
5. $A(-3, 0), B(0, 3), C(3, 0), D(0, -3)$
6. $A(0, 0), B(4, 0), C(1, 1), D(0, 3)$

> **Monitoring Progress** problems allow students to practice and sharpen their skills as they work toward mathematical understanding.

Personalized Learning

The *Big Ideas Math* program offers teachers and students many ways to personalize and enrich the learning experience of all levels of learners.

Dynamic Student Edition

This unique tool, available online or as an eBook App, provides students with embedded 21st century learning resources. Students have the opportunity to interact with the underlying mathematics in a number of ways, including engaging tutorials, interactive manipulatives, flashcards, vocabulary support, and games that enhance the learning experience and promote mathematical understanding.

Dynamic Assessment & Progress Monitoring Tool

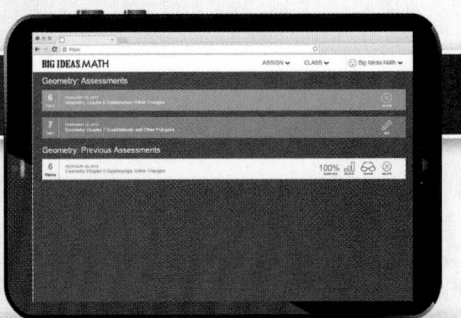

This tool allows teachers to provide customizable homework directly related to the *Big Ideas Math* program. Question types include technology enhanced items such as drag and drop, graphing, point plotting, multiple select, and fill in the blank using math expressions. Assignments are automatically scored and students have access to immediate remediation on homework questions.

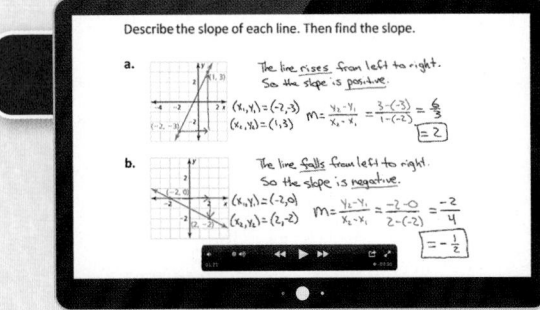

Online Lesson Tutorials

Two- to three-minute lesson tutorial videos provide video and audio support for every example in the textbook. These are valuable for students who miss a class, need a second explanation, or need extra assistance with a homework assignment. Parents can also utilize the tutorials to stay connected or to provide additional help at home.

Differentiated Instruction

Through print and digital resources, the *Big Ideas Math* program completely supports the 3-Tier Response to Intervention model. Using research-based strategies, teachers can reach, challenge, and motivate each student with high-quality instruction targeted to individual needs.

Customized Learning Intervention

- *Big Ideas Math* Middle School program at *BigIdeasMath.com*

3 Tier

Strategic Intervention

- Lesson Tutorials
- Game Closet
- Skills Review Handbook
- Differentiated Instruction
- Dynamic Assessment and Progress Monitoring Tool

2 Tier

Daily Intervention

- Student Journal
- Vocabulary Support
- Lesson Tutorials
- Communicate Your Answer
- Monitoring Progress
- Maintaining Mathematical Proficiency
- Dynamic Assessment and Progress Monitoring Tool

1 Tier

Big Ideas Math
Dynamic Technology

The Dynamic Assessment and Progress Monitoring Tool

The **Dynamic Assessment and Progress Monitoring Tool** allows teachers to track and evaluate their students' advancement through the curriculum. Developed exclusively for *Big Ideas Math*, this technology provides teachers and students an intuitive and state-of-the-art tool to help students effectively learn mathematics. Built for ease of use, the tool is available on a wide range of devices.

Homework and Assessment

- Includes multiple assignments available for each chapter that are customizable
- Allows you to assign homework and assessments for the entire class or a select group of students
- Offers progress monitoring assessments for an adaptive testing experience

Direct Ties to Remediation

- Includes direct links to Lesson Tutorial Videos and relevant lesson sections

All-In-One Reporting

- Offers real-time reporting at both the class and student level
- Tracks progress through Item Analysis, Standard Analysis, or Remediation reports

Assessment Delivery

- Provides embedded tools for students
- Includes auto-scored technology enhanced items such as drag and drop, graphing, point plotting, multiple select, and fill in the blank using math expressions
- Allows you to include reminders or notes to students

Intuitive Design

- Operates on a wide range of devices with large and clear icons for visibility
- Allows for multiple reporting views through toggle options
- Includes intelligent presets and easy navigation

Dynamic Student Edition

Through the **Dynamic Student Edition eBook App**, students not only have access to the complete textbook, but they can also explore robust interactive digital resources embedded within each lesson. There is audio support for the text and Lesson Tutorial Videos in both English and Spanish. Interactive investigations, direct links to remediation, and additional resources are linked right to the lesson.

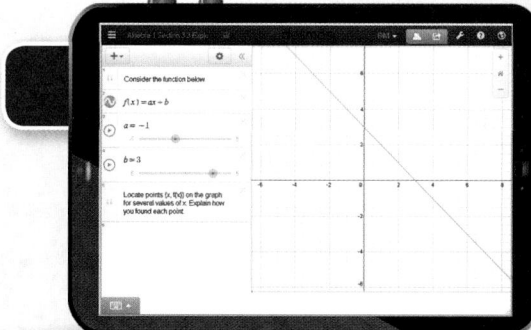

Dynamic Investigations

Dynamic Investigations in the *Big Ideas Math* program are powered by Desmos® and GeoGebra®. Teachers and students can integrate these investigations into their discovery learning to interact with the Explorations in the Student Edition.

Real-Life STEM Videos

Science - Technology - Engineering - Mathematics

Every chapter in the *Big Ideas Math* program contains a Real-Life STEM Video allowing students to further engage with mathematical concepts. Students learn about the speed of light, natural disasters, solar power, and more!

Teaching Support

Lesson Planning Support

Online Lesson Plans

Complete, editable Lesson Plans are included for every lesson in the program.

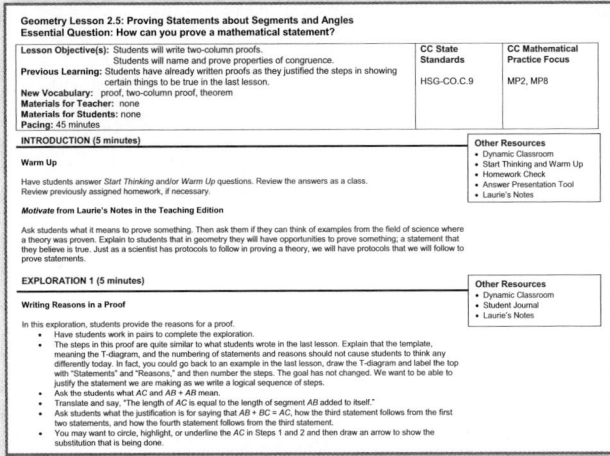

Laurie's Notes

Laurie Boswell provides comprehensive teaching support for every student page in the Teaching Edition.

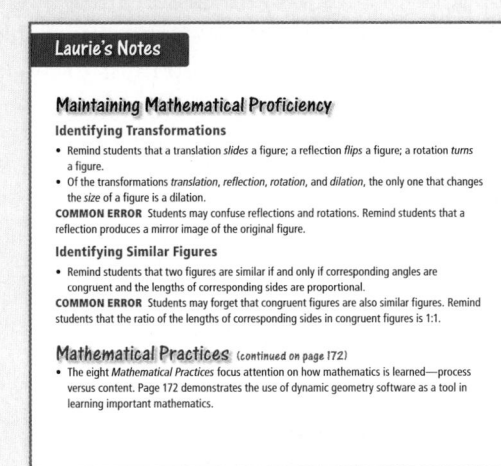

Lesson Presentation Support

Dynamic Classroom

This online tool contains a collection of interactive resources for presenting lessons.

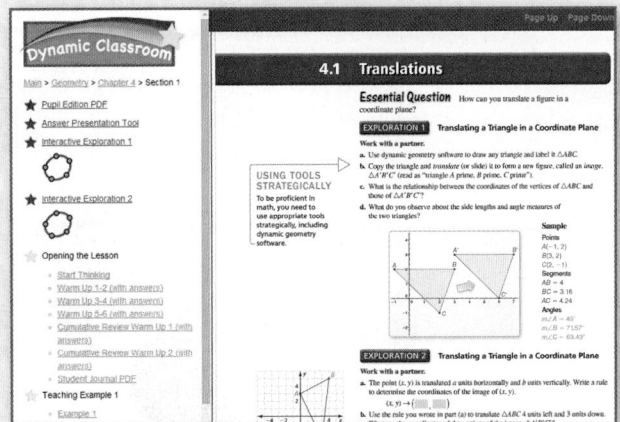

Interactive Whiteboard Lesson Library

Standard or customizable lessons are provided for SMART®, Promethean®, and Mimeo® interactive whiteboards.

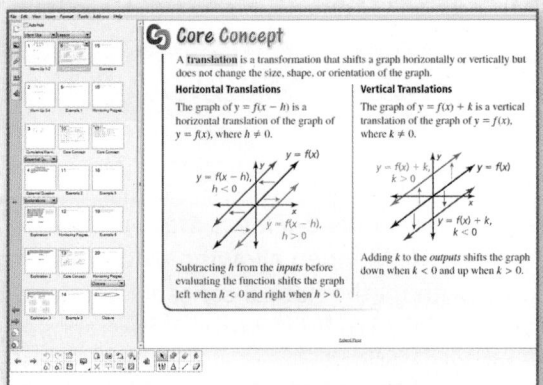

Program Resources

Print

Student Edition

Teaching Edition
- Laurie's Notes

Student Journal
Available in English and Spanish

Resources by Chapter
- Start Thinking
- Warm-Up
- Cumulative Review Warm-Up
- Practice A and B
- Enrichment and Extension
- Puzzle Time
- Family Communication Letters
  Available in English and Spanish

Assessment Book
- Performance Tasks
- Prerequisite Skills Tests with Item Analysis
- Cumulative Test
- Quizzes
- Chapter Tests
- Alternative Assessments with Scoring Rubrics
- Pre-Course Test with Item Analysis
- Post-Course Test with Item Analysis

Technology

Student Edition
With complete English and Spanish audio
- Dynamic eBook App
  - Lesson Tutorial Videos
  - Dynamic Investigations
- Online Home Edition
  - Multi-Language Glossary
  - Skills Review Handbook
- Dynamic Solutions Tool

Dynamic Classroom
- Interactive Manipulatives
- Answer Presentation Tool
- Extra Examples
- Mini-Assessment

Dynamic Teaching Tools
- Interactive Whiteboard Lesson Library
  - Includes standard and customizable lessons.
  - Compatible with SMART®, Promethean®, and Mimio® technology
- ExamView
- Real-Life STEM Videos
- Editable Online Resources
  - Lesson Plans
  - Pacing Guides
  - Assessment Book
  - Resources by Chapter

Dynamic Assessment and Progress Monitoring Tool
- Homework and Assessment Creation
- Progress Monitoring
- Direct Ties to Remediation
- All-In-One Reporting
- Online Chat Tutor

Correlation from Geometry to Common Core State Standards for Mathematical Content

Lesson	Standard(s)
Chapter 1: Basics of Geometry	
1.1 Points, Lines, and Planes	HSG-CO.A.1
1.2 Measuring and Constructing Segments	HSG-CO.A.1, HSG-CO.D.12
1.3 Using Midpoint and Distance Formulas	HSG-CO.D.12, HSG-GPE.B.7
1.4 Perimeter and Area in the Coordinate Plane	HSG-GPE.B.7, HSG-MG.A.1
1.5 Measuring and Constructing Angles	HSG-CO.A.1, HSG-CO.D.12
1.6 Describing Pairs of Angles	HSG-CO.A.1
Chapter 2: Reasoning and Proofs	
2.1 Conditional Statements	HSG-CO.C.9, HSG-CO.C.10, HSG-CO.C.11, HSG-SRT.B.4
2.2 Inductive and Deductive Reasoning	HSG-CO.C.9, HSG-CO.C.10, HSG-CO.C.11, HSG-SRT.B.4
2.3 Postulates and Diagrams	HSG-CO.C.9, HSG-CO.C.10, HSG-CO.C.11, HSG-SRT.B.4
2.4 Algebraic Reasoning	HSG-CO.C.9, HSG-CO.C.10, HSG-CO.C.11, HSG-SRT.B.4
2.5 Proving Statements about Segments and Angles	HSG-CO.C.9
2.6 Proving Geometric Relationships	HSG-CO.C.9
Chapter 3: Parallel and Perpendicular Lines	
3.1 Pairs of Lines and Angles	HSG-CO.A.1
3.2 Parallel Lines and Transversals	HSG-CO.C.9
3.3 Proofs with Parallel Lines	HSG-CO.C.9, HSG-CO.D.12
3.4 Proofs with Perpendicular Lines	HSG-CO.C.9, HSG-CO.D.12
3.5 Equations of Parallel and Perpendicular Lines	HSG-GPE.B.5, HSG-GPE.B.6

Correlation from Geometry to Common Core State Standards for Mathematical Content *(continued)*

Lesson	Standard(s)
Chapter 7: Quadrilaterals and Other Polygons	
7.1 Angles of Polygons	HSG-CO.C.11
7.2 Properties of Parallelograms	HSG-CO.C.11, HSG-SRT.B.5
7.3 Proving That a Quadrilateral is a Parallelogram	HSG-CO.C.11, HSG-SRT.B.5, HSG-MG.A.1
7.4 Properties of Special Parallelograms	HSG-CO.C.11, HSG-SRT.B.5, HSG-MG.A.1, HSG-MG.A.3
7.5 Properties of Trapezoids and Kites	HSG-SRT.B.5, HSG-MG.A.1
Chapter 8: Similarity	
8.1 Similar Polygons	HSG-SRT.A.2, HSG-MG.A.3
8.2 Proving Triangle Similarity by AA	HSG-SRT.A.3, HSG-SRT.B.5
8.3 Proving Triangle Similarity by SSS and SAS	HSG-SRT.B.4, HSG-SRT.B.5, HSG-GPE.B.5, HSG-MG.A.1
8.4 Proportionality Theorems	HSG-SRT.B.4, HSG-SRT.B.5, HSG-GPE.B.6
Chapter 9: Right Triangles and Trigonometry	
9.1 The Pythagorean Theorem	HSG-SRT.B.4, HSG-SRT.C.8
9.2 Special Right Triangles	HSG-SRT.C.8, HSG-MG.A.1
9.3 Similar Right Triangles	HSG-SRT.B.5
9.4 The Tangent Ratio	HSG-SRT.C.6, HSG-SRT.C.8
9.5 The Sine and Cosine Ratios	HSG-SRT.C.6, HSG-SRT.C.7, HSG-SRT.C.8
9.6 Solving Right Triangles	HSG-SRT.C.8, HSG-MG.A.1, HSG-MG.A.3
9.7 Law of Sines and Law of Cosines	HSG-SRT.D.9, HSG-SRT.D.10, HSG-SRT.D.11, HSG-MG.A.3

Common Core State Standards for Mathematical Content Correlated to Algebra 1, Geometry, and Algebra 2

Standard	Descriptor	Algebra 1	Geometry	Algebra 2
Number and Quantity				
HSN-RN.A.1	Explain how the definition of the meaning of rational exponents follows from extending the properties of integer exponents to those values, allowing for a notation for radicals in terms of rational exponents.	**6.2**		**5.1**
HSN-RN.A.2	Rewrite expressions involving radicals and rational exponents using the properties of exponents.	**6.1, 6.2, 9.1,** 10.3		**5.1, 5.2,** 5.3, 5.4, 5.5, 6.1, 6.2, 6.6, 6.7
HSN-RN.B.3	Explain why the sum or product of two rational numbers is rational; that the sum of a rational number and an irrational number is irrational; and that the product of a nonzero rational number and an irrational number is irrational.	**9.1**		
HSN-Q.A.1	Use units as a way to understand problems and to guide the solution of multi-step problems; choose and interpret units consistently in formulas; choose and interpret the scale and the origin in graphs and data displays.	**1.2,** 1.5, 3.4		
HSN-Q.A.2	Define appropriate quantities for the purpose of descriptive modeling.	3.3, 4.1, 5.1, 5.2, 5.3, 5.5, 6.6, 7.7, 8.2, 8.3, 8.6, 9.2, 9.4, 9.5, 10.2, 10.3		1.3, 2.2, 2.4, 3.1, 3.3, 3.4, 4.4, 9.6
HSN-Q.A.3	Choose a level of accuracy appropriate to limitations on measurement when reporting quantities.	4.5, 6.2, 6.4, 8.6, 9.3, 10.1, 10.2		
HSN-CN.A.1	Know there is a complex number i such that $i^2 = -1$, and every complex number has the form $a + bi$ with a and b real.			**3.2**
HSN-CN.A.2	Use the relation $i^2 = -1$ and the commutative, associative, and distributive properties to add, subtract, and multiply complex numbers.			**3.2,** 3.4, 4.6
HSN-CN.C.7	Solve quadratic equations with real coefficients that have complex solutions.			**3.2, 3.3, 3.4,** 4.6
HSN-CN.C.8	Extend polynomial identities to the complex numbers.			3.2, **4.6**
HSN-CN.C.9	Know the Fundamental Theorem of Algebra; show that it is true for quadratic polynomials.			**4.6**
Algebra				
HSA-SSE.A.1	Interpret expressions that represent a quantity in terms of its context.			
	a. Interpret parts of an expression, such as terms, factors, and coefficients.	3.2, 3.3, 3.5, 7.1		1.3, 2.2, 2.4, 3.1, 3.3, 3.4, 4.4, 9.6
	b. Interpret complicated expressions by viewing one or more of their parts as a single entity.	1.2, 6.4, 7.4		3.1, 4.4, 4.5, 6.1, 6.2

Boldface indicates a lesson in which the standard is a primary focus.

Standard	Descriptor	Algebra 1	Geometry	Algebra 2
HSA-SSE.A.2	Use the structure of an expression to identify ways to rewrite it.	**7.5, 7.6, 7.7, 7.8**		**3.1**, 3.3, 3.4, 3.5, 3.6, **4.4**, 4.5, 4.6, 5.4, 6.1, 6.2, 6.3, **6.5**, 6.6, 6.7, 7.2, 7.3, 7.4, 7.5, 9.7, 9.8
HSA-SSE.B.3	Choose and produce an equivalent form of an expression to reveal and explain properties of the quantity represented by the expression.			
	a. Factor a quadratic expression to reveal the zeros of the function it defines.	**7.5, 7.6, 7.7, 7.8, 8.5**		
	b. Complete the square in a quadratic expression to reveal the maximum or minimum value of the function it defines.	**9.4**		
	c. Use the properties of exponents to transform expressions for exponential functions.	**6.4**		**6.1**, 6.2, 6.7
HSA-SSE.B.4	Derive the formula for the sum of a finite geometric series (when the common ratio is not 1), and use the formula to solve problems.			**8.3, 8.4**
HSA-APR.A.1	Understand that polynomials form a system analogous to the integers, namely, they are closed under the operations of addition, subtraction, and multiplication; add, subtract, and multiply polynomials.	**7.1, 7.2, 7.3**		**4.2**, 4.3, 4.5, 4.6, 7.3, 7.4, 7.5
HSA-APR.B.2	Know and apply the Remainder Theorem: For a polynomial $p(x)$ and a number a, the remainder on division by $x - a$ is $p(a)$, so $p(a) = 0$ if and only if $(x - a)$ is a factor of $p(x)$.			**4.3, 4.4**, 4.5
HSA-APR.B.3	Identify zeros of polynomials when suitable factorizations are available, and use the zeros to construct a rough graph of the function defined by the polynomial.	**7.4**, 7.5, 7.6, 7.7, 7.8, **8.5**, 9.2		**2.2**, 3.1, 3.6, **4.4, 4.5, 4.6**, **4.8**
HSA-APR.C.4	Prove polynomial identities and use them to describe numerical relationships.			**4.2**
HSA-APR.C.5	Know and apply the Binomial Theorem for the expansion of $(x + y)^n$ in powers of x and y for a positive integer n, where x and y are any numbers, with coefficients determined for example by Pascal's Triangle.			**4.2, 10.5**
HSA-APR.D.6	Rewrite simple rational expressions in different forms; write $a(x)/b(x)$ in the form $q(x) + r(x)/b(x)$, where $a(x)$, $b(x)$, $q(x)$, and $r(x)$ are polynomials with the degree of $r(x)$ less than the degree of $b(x)$, using inspection, long division, or, for the more complicated examples, a computer algebra system.			**4.3, 7.2, 7.3, 7.4**
HSA-APR.D.7	Understand that rational expressions form a system analogous to the rational numbers, closed under addition, subtraction, multiplication, and division by a nonzero rational expression; add, subtract, multiply, and divide rational expressions.			**7.3, 7.4**

Boldface indicates a lesson in which the standard is a primary focus.

Common Core State Standards for Mathematical Content Correlated to Algebra 1, Geometry, and Algebra 2 (continued)

Standard	Descriptor	Algebra 1	Geometry	Algebra 2
HSA-CED.A.1	Create equations and inequalities in one variable and use them to solve problems.	**1.1, 1.2, 1.3, 1.4, 2.1, 2.2, 2.3, 2.4, 2.5, 2.6, 6.5,** 7.5, 7.6, 7.7, 7.8, **9.3, 9.4, 9.5,** 9.6, **10.3**		1.3, 2.4, 3.1, 3.3, 3.4, **3.6,** 4.5, 5.1, 5.3, 6.1, 6.2, 6.5, 6.6, 6.7, **7.1,** 7.3, 7.5, 9.1
HSA-CED.A.2	Create equations in two or more variables to represent relationships between quantities; graph equations on coordinate axes with labels and scales.	**3.2, 3.3, 3.4, 3.5, 3.7, 4.1, 4.2, 4.3, 4.7,** 5.1, 5.2, 5.3, 5.4, **6.3, 6.4, 8.1, 8.2, 8.3, 8.4, 8.5,** 8.6, **10.1, 10.2,** 10.4		1.2, **1.3,** 1.4, 2.1, 2.3, **2.4,** 3.1, 3.4, 4.7, **4.9,** 5.3, 5.6, 6.1, 6.4, **6.7, 7.1,** 7.2, 7.3, 7.5, **9.6**
HSA-CED.A.3	Represent constraints by equations or inequalities, and by systems of equations and/or inequalities, and interpret solutions as viable or nonviable options in a modeling context.	**5.1, 5.2, 5.3, 5.4, 5.5, 5.6,** 5.7		1.3, **1.4,** 3.1, 3.4, **3.5, 3.6,** 4.6, 5.4, 6.6, **7.1,** 7.2
HSA-CED.A.4	Rearrange formulas to highlight a quantity of interest, using the same reasoning as in solving equations.	**1.5, 9.3**		1.3, 5.4, **5.6,** 6.6, **7.5**
HSA-REI.A.1	Explain each step in solving a simple equation as following from the equality of numbers asserted at the previous step, starting from the assumption that the original equation has a solution. Construct a viable argument to justify a solution method.	**1.1,** 1.2, 1.3, 1.4, **6.5,** 9.3, 9.4, 9.5, 10.3		5.1, **5.4, 6.6, 7.5,** 8.2, 8.3, 9.1
HSA-REI.A.2	Solve simple rational and radical equations in one variable, and give examples showing how extraneous solutions may arise.			**5.4, 7.5**
HSA-REI.B.3	Solve linear equations and inequalities in one variable, including equations with coefficients represented by letters.	**1.1, 1.2, 1.3, 1.4, 2.2, 2.3, 2.4, 2.5, 2.6**		
HSA-REI.B.4	Solve quadratic equations in one variable.			
	a. Use the method of completing the square to transform any quadratic equation in x into an equation of the form $(x - p)^2 = q$ that has the same solutions. Derive the quadratic formula from this form.	**9.4, 9.5**		
	b. Solve quadratic equations by inspection (e.g., for $x^2 = 49$), taking square roots, completing the square, the quadratic formula and factoring, as appropriate to the initial form of the equation. Recognize when the quadratic formula gives complex solutions and write them as $a \pm bi$ for real numbers a and b.	**7.4,** 7.5, 7.6, 7.7, 7.8, **9.3, 9.4, 9.5**		**3.1, 3.2, 3.3, 3.4,** 3.5, 3.6, 4.5, 4.6, 5.4, 6.6, 7.5

Boldface indicates a lesson in which the standard is a primary focus.

Standard	Descriptor	Algebra 1	Geometry	Algebra 2
HSA-REI.C.5	Prove that, given a system of two equations in two variables, replacing one equation by the sum of that equation and a multiple of the other produces a system with the same solutions.	**5.3**		
HSA-REI.C.6	Solve systems of linear equations exactly and approximately (e.g., with graphs), focusing on pairs of linear equations in two variables.	**5.1, 5.2, 5.3, 5.4**		**1.4**, 2.4, 8.2, 8.3
HSA-REI.C.7	Solve a simple system consisting of a linear equation and a quadratic equation in two variables algebraically and graphically.	**9.6**		**3.5**, 5.4
HSA-REI.D.10	Understand that the graph of an equation in two variables is the set of all its solutions plotted in the coordinate plane, often forming a curve (which could be a line).	**3.2, 3.7, 4.7,** 6.3, 8.1, 8.3, 10.1, 10.2		
HSA-REI.D.11	Explain why the x-coordinates of the points where the graphs of the equations $y = f(x)$ and $y = g(x)$ intersect are the solutions of the equation $f(x) = g(x)$; find the solutions approximately, e.g., using technology to graph the functions, make tables of values, or find successive approximations. Include cases where $f(x)$ and/or $g(x)$ are linear, polynomial, rational, absolute value, exponential, and logarithmic functions.	**5.5, 6.5, 9.2, 9.6, 8.6, 10.3**		**3.5**, 4.5, 5.4, 6.6, 7.5
HSA-REI.D.12	Graph the solutions to a linear inequality in two variables as a half-plane (excluding the boundary in the case of a strict inequality), and graph the solution set to a system of linear inequalities in two variables as the intersection of the corresponding half-planes.	**5.6, 5.7**		
Functions				
HSF-IF.A.1	Understand that a function from one set (called the domain) to another set (called the range) assigns to each element of the domain exactly one element of the range. If f is a function and x is an element of its domain, then $f(x)$ denotes the output of f corresponding to the input x. The graph of f is the graph of the equation $y = f(x)$.	**3.1, 3.3**		
HSF-IF.A.2	Use function notation, evaluate functions for inputs in their domains, and interpret statements that use function notation in terms of a context.	**3.3**		
HSF-IF.A.3	Recognize that sequences are functions, sometimes defined recursively, whose domain is a subset of the integers.	**4.6, 6.6, 6.7**		**8.1, 8.2, 8.3, 8.5**
HSF-IF.B.4	For a function that models a relationship between two quantities, interpret key features of graphs and tables in terms of the quantities, and sketch graphs showing key features given a verbal description of the relationship.	3.3, **3.5, 6.3,** 8.4, 8.5, 9.2, **10.1, 10.2**		1.3, **2.2, 2.3, 4.1,** 4.4, **4.8,** 6.1, 6.2, 6.3, 7.2, 8.4, 8.5, 9.4, 9.5
HSF-IF.B.5	Relate the domain of a function to its graph and, where applicable, to the quantitative relationship it describes.	**3.2**, 3.4		1.1, 1.3, 2.2, 2.4, 3.6, 4.1, 4.6, 5.3, 5.5, 5.6, 6.1, 6.3, 7.2, 9.4, 9.5

Boldface indicates a lesson in which the standard is a primary focus.

Common Core State Standards for Mathematical Content Correlated to Algebra 1, Geometry, and Algebra 2 (continued)

Standard	Descriptor	Algebra 1	Geometry	Algebra 2
HSF-IF.B.6	Calculate and interpret the average rate of change of a function (presented symbolically or as a table) over a specified interval. Estimate the rate of change from a graph.	6.4, **8.6, 10.1, 10.2**		1.3, **2.4**, 4.1, 5.3, 6.1, 6.2, 6.3, 7.2, 9.4, 9.5
HSF-IF.C.7	Graph functions expressed symbolically and show key features of the graph, by hand in simple cases and using technology for more complicated cases.			
	a. Graph linear and quadratic functions and show intercepts, maxima, and minima.	**3.2, 3.3, 3.4, 3.5, 3.6, 8.1, 8.2, 8.3, 9.2**		
	b. Graph square root, cube root, and piecewise-defined functions, including step functions and absolute value functions.	**3.7, 4.7, 10.1,** 10.2		**5.3**, 5.4, 5.5, 5.6
	c. Graph polynomial functions, identifying zeros when suitable factorizations are available, and showing end behavior.			2.1, 2.2, 2.3, 3.1, 3.6, **4.1**, 4.5, **4.7, 4.8**, 4.9
	e. Graph exponential and logarithmic functions, showing intercepts and end behavior, and trigonometric functions, showing period, midline, and amplitude.	6.3, 6.4		**6.1, 6.2, 6.3, 6.4, 9.4, 9.5**
HSF-IF.C.8	Write a function defined by an expression in different but equivalent forms to reveal and explain different properties of the function.			
	a. Use the process of factoring and completing the square in a quadratic function to show zeros, extreme values, and symmetry of the graph, and interpret these in terms of a context.	8.5, 9.4		3.1, 3.3
	b. Use the properties of exponents to interpret expressions for exponential functions.	6.4		**6.1**, 6.2, 6.7
HSF-IF.C.9	Compare properties of two functions each represented in a different way (algebraically, graphically, numerically in tables, or by verbal descriptions).	**3.3, 4.2, 6.3, 8.3, 10.1, 10.2**		1.3, 2.2, 4.9, 5.3, 6.1, 6.2, 6.3, 7.2, 9.5, 9.6
HSF-BF.A.1	Write a function that describes a relationship between two quantities.			
	a. Determine an explicit expression, a recursive process, or steps for calculation from a context.	**4.1, 4.2, 4.4, 4.6, 6.3, 6.4, 6.7, 8.4, 8.5, 8.6**		1.3, **2.4**, 3.1, 3.4, **4.9**, 6.1, **6.7**, 7.1, 7.3, **8.5**, 9.6
	b. Combine standard function types using arithmetic operations.	6.4, 8.2		**5.5**, 6.6, 7.3
HSF-BF.A.2	Write arithmetic and geometric sequences both recursively and with an explicit formula, use them to model situations, and translate between the two forms.	**4.6, 6.6, 6.7**		**8.2, 8.3, 8.5**

Boldface indicates a lesson in which the standard is a primary focus.

Standard	Descriptor	Algebra 1	Geometry	Algebra 2
HSF-BF.B.3	Identify the effect on the graph of replacing $f(x)$ by $f(x) + k$, $kf(x)$, $f(kx)$, and $f(x + k)$ for specific values of k (both positive and negative); find the value of k given the graphs. Experiment with cases and illustrate an explanation of the effects on the graph using technology. Include recognizing even and odd functions from their graphs and algebraic expressions for them.	**3.6, 3.7, 6.3, 8.1, 8.2, 8.4**		**1.1, 1.2, 2.1, 4.7, 4.8, 5.3, 6.4, 7.2,** 7.4, **9.4, 9.5,** 9.7
HSF-BF.B.4	Find inverse functions.			
	a. Solve an equation of the form $f(x) = c$ for a simple function f that has an inverse and write an expression for the inverse.	**10.4**		**5.6, 6.3,** 7.5
HSF-LE.A.1	Distinguish between situations that can be modeled with linear functions and with exponential functions.			
	a. Prove that linear functions grow by equal differences over equal intervals, and that exponential functions grow by equal factors over equal intervals.	3.5, **6.3**		
	b. Recognize situations in which one quantity changes at a constant rate per unit interval relative to another.	**3.2, 4.1, 4.2,** 8.6		
	c. Recognize situations in which a quantity grows or decays by a constant percent rate per unit interval relative to another.	6.3, **6.4,** 8.6		
HSF-LE.A.2	Construct linear and exponential functions, including arithmetic and geometric sequences, given a graph, a description of a relationship, or two input-output pairs (include reading these from a table).	**4.1, 4.2, 4.3, 4.6, 6.3, 6.4, 6.6, 6.7**		**1.3, 6.1, 6.7, 8.2, 8.3**
HSF-LE.A.3	Observe using graphs and tables that a quantity increasing exponentially eventually exceeds a quantity increasing linearly, quadratically, or (more generally) as a polynomial function.	8.6		
HSF-LE.A.4	For exponential models, express as a logarithm the solution to $ab^{ct} = d$ where a, c, and d are numbers and the base b is 2, 10, or e; evaluate the logarithm using technology.			**6.3, 6.5, 6.6**
HSF-LE.B.5	Interpret the parameters in a linear or exponential function in terms of a context.	**3.5, 4.4, 4.5,** 6.4		**6.1, 6.2**
HSF-TF.A.1	Understand radian measure of an angle as the length of the arc on the unit circle subtended by the angle.			9.1, **9.2,** 9.3
HSF-TF.A.2	Explain how the unit circle in the coordinate plane enables the extension of trigonometric functions to all real numbers, interpreted as radian measures of angles traversed counterclockwise around the unit circle.			9.1, **9.3,** 9.4, 9.5
HSF-TF.B.5	Choose trigonometric functions to model periodic phenomena with specified amplitude, frequency, and midline.			9.1, **9.6**
HSF-TF.C.8	Prove the Pythagorean identity $\sin^2(\theta) + \cos^2(\theta) = 1$ and use it to find $\sin(\theta)$, $\cos(\theta)$, or $\tan(\theta)$ given $\sin(\theta)$, $\cos(\theta)$, or $\tan(\theta)$ and the quadrant of the angle.			9.1, **9.7**

Boldface indicates a lesson in which the standard is a primary focus.

Common Core State Standards for Mathematical Content Correlated to Algebra 1, Geometry, and Algebra 2 *(continued)*

Standard	Descriptor	Algebra 1	Geometry	Algebra 2
HSF-TF.C.9	Prove the addition and subtraction formulas for sine, cosine, and tangent and use them to solve problems.			**9.8**
Geometry				
HSG-CO.A.1	Know precise definitions of angle, circle, perpendicular line, parallel line, and line segment, based on the undefined notions of point, line, distance along a line, and distance around a circular arc.		**1.1, 1.2**, 1.3, **1.5, 1.6**, 2.5, 2.6, **3.1, 10.1, 11.1**	
HSG-CO.A.2	Represent transformations in the plane using, e.g., transparencies and geometry software; describe transformations as functions that take points in the plane as inputs and give other points as outputs. Compare transformations that preserve distance and angle to those that do not (e.g., translation versus horizontal stretch).		**4.1, 4.2, 4.3, 4.5**	
HSG-CO.A.3	Given a rectangle, parallelogram, trapezoid, or regular polygon, describe the rotations and reflections that carry it onto itself.		**4.2, 4.3**	
HSG-CO.A.4	Develop definitions of rotations, reflections, and translations in terms of angles, circles, perpendicular lines, parallel lines, and line segments.		**4.1, 4.2, 4.3**	
HSG-CO.A.5	Given a geometric figure and a rotation, reflection, or translation, draw the transformed figure using, e.g., graph paper, tracing paper, or geometry software. Specify a sequence of transformations that will carry a given figure onto another.		**4.1, 4.2, 4.3, 4.4, 4.6, 5.3, 5.5, 5.6**	
HSG-CO.B.6	Use geometric descriptions of rigid motions to transform figures and to predict the effect of a given rigid motion on a given figure; given two figures, use the definition of congruence in terms of rigid motions to decide if they are congruent.		**4.1, 4.2, 4.3, 4.4**	
HSG-CO.B.7	Use the definition of congruence in terms of rigid motions to show that two triangles are congruent if and only if corresponding pairs of sides and corresponding pairs of angles are congruent.		**5.2**	
HSG-CO.B.8	Explain how the criteria for triangle congruence (ASA, SAS, and SSS) follow from the definition of congruence in terms of rigid motions.		**5.3, 5.5, 5.6**	
HSG-CO.C.9	Prove theorems about lines and angles.		2.1, 2.2, 2.3, 2.4, **2.5, 2.6, 3.2, 3.3, 3.4, 4.1, 6.1**	
HSG-CO.C.10	Prove theorems about triangles.		2.1, 2.2, 2.3, 2.4, **5.1, 5.4, 6.2, 6.3, 6.4, 6.5, 6.6**	

Boldface indicates a lesson in which the standard is a primary focus.

Standard	Descriptor	Algebra 1	Geometry	Algebra 2
HSG-CO.C.11	Prove theorems about parallelograms.		2.1, 2.2, 2.3, 2.4, 7.1, **7.2**, **7.3**, **7.4**	
HSG-CO.D.12	Make formal geometric constructions with a variety of tools and methods (compass and straightedge, string, reflective devices, paper folding, dynamic geometric software, etc.).		**1.2**, **1.3**, **1.5**, **3.3**, **3.4**, **4.4**, **6.2**, **10.1**	
HSG-CO.D.13	Construct an equilateral triangle, a square, and a regular hexagon inscribed in a circle.		**1.5**, **3.4**, **5.4**, **10.4**	
HSG-SRT.A.1	Verify experimentally the properties of dilations given by a center and a scale factor:			
	a. A dilation takes a line not passing through the center of the dilation to a parallel line, and leaves a line passing through the center unchanged.		**4.5**	
	b. The dilation of a line segment is longer or shorter in the ratio given by the scale factor.		**4.5**	
HSG-SRT.A.2	Given two figures, use the definition of similarity in terms of similarity transformations to decide if they are similar; explain using similarity transformations the meaning of similarity for triangles as the equality of all corresponding pairs of angles and the proportionality of all corresponding pairs of sides.		**4.6**, **8.1**	
HSG-SRT.A.3	Use the properties of similarity transformations to establish the AA criterion for two triangles to be similar.		**8.2**	
HSG-SRT.B.4	Prove theorems about triangles.		2.1, 2.2, 2.3, 2.4, **8.3**, **8.4**, **9.1**	
HSG-SRT.B.5	Use congruence and similarity criteria for triangles to solve problems and to prove relationships in geometric figures.		5.7, 6.1, 6.3, **7.2**, **7.3**, **7.4**, **7.5**, **8.2**, **8.3**, **9.3**	
HSG-SRT.C.6	Understand that by similarity, side ratios in right triangles are properties of the angles in the triangle, leading to definitions of trigonometric ratios for acute angles.		**9.4**, **9.5**	
HSG-SRT.C.7	Explain and use the relationship between the sine and cosine of complementary angles.		**9.5**	
HSG-SRT.C.8	Use trigonometric ratios and the Pythagorean Theorem to solve right triangles in applied problems.		9.1, 9.2, **9.4**, **9.5**, **9.6**	
HSG-SRT.D.9	Derive the formula $A = (1/2)\, ab \sin(C)$ for the area of a triangle by drawing an auxiliary line from a vertex perpendicular to the opposite side.		**9.7**	
HSG-SRT.D.10	Prove the Laws of Sines and Cosines and use them to solve problems.		**9.7**	

Boldface indicates a lesson in which the standard is a primary focus.

Common Core State Standards for Mathematical Content Correlated to Algebra 1, Geometry, and Algebra 2 *(continued)*

Standard	Descriptor	Algebra 1	Geometry	Algebra 2
HSG-SRT.D.11	Understand and apply the Law of Sines and the Law of Cosines to find unknown measurements in right and non-right triangles (e.g., surveying problems, resultant forces).		**9.7**	
HSG-C.A.1	Prove that all circles are similar.		**10.2**	
HSG-C.A.2	Identify and describe relationships among inscribed angles, radii, and chords.		**10.1, 10.2, 10.3, 10.4, 10.5, 10.6**	
HSG-C.A.3	Construct the inscribed and circumscribed circles of a triangle, and prove properties of angles for a quadrilateral inscribed in a circle.		**6.2, 10.4**	
HSG-C.A.4	Construct a tangent line from a point outside a given circle to the circle.		**10.1**	
HSG-C.B.5	Derive using similarity the fact that the length of the arc intercepted by an angle is proportional to the radius, and define the radian measure of the angle as the constant of proportionality; derive the formula for the area of a sector.		**11.1, 11.2**	
HSG-GPE.A.1	Derive the equation of a circle of given center and radius using the Pythagorean Theorem; complete the square to find the center and radius of a circle given by an equation.		**10.7**	
HSG-GPE.A.2	Derive the equation of a parabola given a focus and directrix.			**2.3**
HSG-GPE.B.4	Use coordinates to prove simple geometric theorems algebraically.		**5.8, 6.4, 10.7**	
HSG-GPE.B.5	Prove the slope criteria for parallel and perpendicular lines and use them to solve geometric problems (e.g., find the equation of a line parallel or perpendicular to a given line that passes through a given point).	**4.3**	**3.5, 8.3**	
HSG-GPE.B.6	Find the point on a directed line segment between two given points that partitions the segment in a given ratio.		**3.5, 8.4**	
HSG-GPE.B.7	Use coordinates to compute perimeters of polygons and areas of triangles and rectangles, e.g., using the distance formula.		**1.3, 1.4**	
HSG-GMD.A.1	Give an informal argument for the formulas for the circumference of a circle, area of a circle, volume of a cylinder, pyramid, and cone.		**11.1, 11.2, 11.5, 11.6, 11.7**	
HSG-GMD.A.2	Give an informal argument using Cavalieri's principle for the formulas for the volume of a sphere and other solid figures.		**11.5, 11.8**	
HSG-GMD.A.3	Use volume formulas for cylinders, pyramids, cones, and spheres to solve problems.		**11.3, 11.5, 11.6, 11.7, 11.8**	

Boldface indicates a lesson in which the standard is a primary focus.

Standard	Descriptor	Algebra 1	Geometry	Algebra 2
HSG-GMD.B.4	Identify the shapes of two-dimensional cross-sections of three-dimensional objects, and identify three-dimensional objects generated by rotations of two-dimensional objects.		**11.4**	
HSG-MG.A.1	Use geometric shapes, their measures, and their properties to describe objects (e.g., modeling a tree trunk or a human torso as a cylinder).		1.4, 5.1, 5.3, 5.4, 5.5, 6.1, 6.2, 6.4, 7.3, 7.4, 7.5, 8.3, 9.2, 9.6, 10.6, 11.5, 11.6, 11.8	
HSG-MG.A.2	Apply concepts of density based on area and volume in modeling situations (e.g., persons per square mile, BTUs per cubic foot).		11.2, 11.5	
HSG-MG.A.3	Apply geometric methods to solve design problems (e.g., designing an object or structure to satisfy physical constraints or minimize cost; working with typographic grid systems based on ratios).		4.2, 5.5, 6.2, 7.4, 8.1, 9.6, 9.7, 10.3, 11.5	
Statistics and Probability				
HSS-ID.A.1	Represent data with plots on the real number line (dot plots, histograms, and box plots).	11.2, 11.3, 11.5		
HSS-ID.A.2	Use statistics appropriate to the shape of the data distribution to compare center (median, mean) and spread (interquartile range, standard deviation) of two or more different data sets.	11.3		
HSS-ID.A.3	Interpret differences in shape, center, and spread in the context of the data sets, accounting for possible effects of extreme data points (outliers).	11.1, 11.2, 11.3		
HSS-ID.A.4	Use the mean and standard deviation of a data set to fit it to a normal distribution and to estimate population percentages. Recognize that there are data sets for which such a procedure is not appropriate. Use calculators, spreadsheets, and tables to estimate areas under the normal curve.			11.1
HSS-ID.B.5	Summarize categorical data for two categories in two-way frequency tables. Interpret relative frequencies in the context of the data (including joint, marginal, and conditional relative frequencies). Recognize possible associations and trends in the data.	11.4		
HSS-ID.B.6	Represent data on two quantitative variables on a scatter plot, and describe how the variables are related.			
	a. Fit a function to the data; use functions fitted to data to solve problems in the context of the data.	4.4, 4.5		1.3, **2.4**, 4.9, 6.7, 9.6
	b. Informally assess the fit of a function by plotting and analyzing residuals.	4.5		
	c. Fit a linear function for a scatter plot that suggests a linear association.	4.4, 4.5		

Boldface indicates a lesson in which the standard is a primary focus.

Common Core State Standards for Mathematical Content Correlated to Algebra 1, Geometry, and Algebra 2 (continued)

Standard	Descriptor	Algebra 1	Geometry	Algebra 2
HSS-ID.C.7	Interpret the slope (rate of change) and the intercept (constant term) of a linear model in the context of the data.	**4.4, 4.5**		
HSS-ID.C.8	Compute (using technology) and interpret the correlation coefficient of a linear fit.	**4.5**		
HSS-ID.C.9	Distinguish between correlation and causation.	**4.5**		
HSS-IC.A.1	Understand statistics as a process for making inferences about population parameters based on a random sample from that population.			**11.2, 11.3, 11.4**
HSS-IC.A.2	Decide if a specified model is consistent with results from a given data-generating process, e.g., using simulation.			11.2, **11.5, 11.6**
HSS-IC.B.3	Recognize the purposes of and differences among sample surveys, experiments, and observational studies; explain how randomization relates to each.			**11.3, 11.4**
HSS-IC.B.4	Use data from a sample survey to estimate a population mean or proportion; develop a margin of error through the use of simulation models for random sampling.			**11.5**
HSS-IC.B.5	Use data from a randomized experiment to compare two treatments; use simulations to decide if differences between parameters are significant.			**11.6**
HSS-IC.B.6	Evaluate reports based on data.			**11.4, 11.5, 11.6**
HSS-CP.A.1	Describe events as subsets of a sample space (the set of outcomes) using characteristics (or categories) of the outcomes, or as unions, intersections, or complements of other events ("or," "and," "not").		**12.1, 12.2, 12.4**	**10.1, 10.2, 10.4**
HSS-CP.A.2	Understand that two events A and B are independent if the probability of A and B occurring together is the product of their probabilities, and use this characterization to determine if they are independent.		**12.2**	**10.2**
HSS-CP.A.3	Understand the conditional probability of A given B as $P(A \text{ and } B)/P(B)$, and interpret independence of A and B as saying that the conditional probability of A given B is the same as the probability of A, and the conditional probability of B given A is the same as the probability of B.		**12.2, 12.4**	**10.2, 10.4**
HSS-CP.A.4	Construct and interpret two-way frequency tables of data when two categories are associated with each object being classified. Use the two-way table as a sample space to decide if events are independent and to approximate conditional probabilities.		**12.3**	**10.3**
HSS-CP.A.5	Recognize and explain the concepts of conditional probability and independence in everyday language and everyday situations.		**12.2, 12.3**	**10.2, 10.3**

Boldface indicates a lesson in which the standard is a primary focus.

Standard	Descriptor	Algebra 1	Geometry	Algebra 2
HSS-CP.B.6	Find the conditional probability of A given B as the fraction of B's outcomes that also belong to A, and interpret the answer in terms of the model.		**12.2**	**10.2**
HSS-CP.B.7	Apply the Addition Rule, $P(A \text{ or } B) = P(A) + P(B) - P(A \text{ and } B)$, and interpret the answer in terms of the model.		**12.4**, 12.6	**10.4**, 10.6
HSS-CP.B.8	Apply the general Multiplication Rule in a uniform probability model, $P(A \text{ and } B) = P(A)P(B \mid A) = P(B)P(A \mid B)$, and interpret the answer in terms of the model.		**12.2**	**10.2**
HSS-CP.B.9	Use permutations and combinations to compute probabilities of compound events and solve problems.		**12.5, 12.6**	**10.5, 10.6**
HSS-MD.B.6	Use probabilities to make fair decisions (e.g., drawing by lots, using a random number generator).		12.2, 12.3, 12.4	10.2, 10.3, 10.4
HSS-MD.B.7	Analyze decisions and strategies using probability concepts (e.g., product testing, medical testing, pulling a hockey goalie at the end of a game).		12.2, 12.3, 12.4	10.2, 10.3, 10.4

Boldface indicates a lesson in which the standard is a primary focus.

Pacing Guide

Chapters 1–12   160 Days

Chapter 1   (12 Days)

Chapter Opener/ Mathematical Practices	0.5 Day
Section 1	1.5 Days
Section 2	1 Day
Section 3	1 Day
Quiz	0.5 Day
Section 4	1.5 Days
Section 5	2 Days
Section 6	2 Days
Chapter Review/Chapter Tests	2 Days
Year-to-Date	**12 Days**

Chapter 2   (12 Days)

Chapter Opener/ Mathematical Practices	0.5 Day
Section 1	1.5 Days
Section 2	2 Days
Section 3	1 Day
Quiz	0.5 Day
Section 4	1.5 Days
Section 5	1 Day
Section 6	2 Days
Chapter Review/Chapter Tests	2 Days
Year-to-Date	**24 Days**

Chapter 3   (12 Days)

Chapter Opener/ Mathematical Practices	0.5 Day
Section 1	1.5 Days
Section 2	2 Days
Section 3	2 Days
Quiz	0.5 Day
Section 4	1.5 Days
Section 5	2 Days
Chapter Review/Chapter Tests	2 Days
Year-to-Date	**36 Days**

Chapter 4   (12 Days)

Chapter Opener/ Mathematical Practices	0.5 Day
Section 1	1.5 Days
Section 2	1 Day
Section 3	2 Days
Quiz	0.5 Day
Section 4	1.5 Days
Section 5	2 Days
Section 6	1 Day
Chapter Review/Chapter Tests	2 Days
Year-to-Date	**48 Days**

Chapter 5   (15 Days)

Chapter Opener/ Mathematical Practices	0.5 Day
Section 1	1.5 Days
Section 2	1 Day
Section 3	1 Day
Section 4	2 Days
Quiz	0.5 Day
Section 5	1.5 Days
Section 6	2 Days
Section 7	1 Day
Section 8	2 Days
Chapter Review/Chapter Tests	2 Days
Year-to-Date	**63 Days**

Chapter 6   (13 Days)

Chapter Opener/ Mathematical Practices	0.5 Day
Section 1	1.5 Days
Section 2	2 Days
Section 3	2 Days
Quiz	0.5 Day
Section 4	1.5 Days
Section 5	2 Days
Section 6	1 Day
Chapter Review/Chapter Tests	2 Days
Year-to-Date	**76 Days**

Chapter 7 (12 Days)

Chapter Opener/ Mathematical Practices	0.5 Day
Section 1	1.5 Days
Section 2	2 Days
Section 3	2 Days
Quiz	0.5 Day
Section 4	1.5 Days
Section 5	2 Days
Chapter Review/Chapter Tests	2 Days
Year-to-Date	**88 Days**

Chapter 8 (10 Days)

Chapter Opener/ Mathematical Practices	0.5 Day
Section 1	1.5 Days
Section 2	2 Days
Quiz	0.5 Day
Section 3	1.5 Days
Section 4	2 Days
Chapter Review/Chapter Tests	2 Days
Year-to-Date	**98 Days**

Chapter 9 (15 Days)

Chapter Opener/ Mathematical Practices	0.5 Day
Section 1	1.5 Days
Section 2	1 Day
Section 3	2 Days
Quiz	0.5 Day
Section 4	1.5 Days
Section 5	2 Days
Section 6	2 Days
Section 7	2 Days
Chapter Review/Chapter Tests	2 Days
Year-to-Date	**113 Days**

Chapter 10 (16 Days)

Chapter Opener/ Mathematical Practices	0.5 Day
Section 1	1.5 Days
Section 2	2 Days
Section 3	2 Days
Quiz	0.5 Day
Section 4	1.5 Days
Section 5	2 Days
Section 6	2 Days
Section 7	2 Days
Chapter Review/Chapter Tests	2 Days
Year-to-Date	**129 Days**

Chapter 11 (17 Days)

Chapter Opener/ Mathematical Practices	0.5 Day
Section 1	1.5 Days
Section 2	2 Days
Section 3	2 Days
Section 4	1 Day
Quiz	0.5 Day
Section 5	1.5 Days
Section 6	2 Days
Section 7	2 Days
Section 8	2 Days
Chapter Review/Chapter Tests	2 Days
Year-to-Date	**146 Days**

Chapter 12 (14 Days)

Chapter Opener/ Mathematical Practices	0.5 Day
Section 1	1.5 Days
Section 2	2 Days
Section 3	2 Days
Quiz	0.5 Day
Section 4	1.5 Days
Section 5	2 Days
Section 6	2 Days
Chapter Review/Chapter Tests	2 Days
Year-to-Date	**160 Days**

Additional Topic

Additional Topic Section	2 Days

1 Basics of Geometry

Chapter 1 Pacing Guide	
Chapter Opener/ Mathematical Practices	0.5 Day
Section 1	1.5 Days
Section 2	1 Day
Section 3	1 Day
Quiz	0.5 Day
Section 4	1.5 Days
Section 5	2 Days
Section 6	2 Days
Chapter Review/ Chapter Tests	2 Days
Total Chapter 1	12 Days
Year-to-Date	12 Days

SEE the Big Idea
Alamillo Bridge (p. 53)

Soccer (p. 49)

Shed (p. 33)

Skateboard (p. 20)

Sulfur Hexafluoride (p. 7)

Chapter Summary

Welcome to a new school year, and for some students, a new school. There is always great excitement, and students are anxious to start anew. As teachers, we need to capitalize on the opportunity, establishing norms and routines for student discourse and classroom climate. In this book, students are expected to work together on explorations, to make conjectures, to construct viable arguments, and to critique the reasoning of others. Take time in this first chapter to make explicit what classroom productive dialogue sounds like. Listen for students explaining their thinking, not just their process.

- Chapter 1 presents a great deal of vocabulary, basic concepts, and the beginning of building an axiomatic system by establishing definitions, undefined terms, and postulates. Take time to consider how you will have students keep track of definitions, postulates, and theorems. Will it be their responsibility to keep a list in their notebook? Will they keep an electronic file? Will you be providing a list? Additionally, how will students reference the definitions, postulates, and theorems when using them in an argument (proof)? For instance, will you expect them to write the entire definition of linear pairs when used in a proof or simply state that two angles form a linear pair? While students will not be writing a proof in this chapter, these are decisions that are best made now so that students will be able to organize new information in a useful way.
- The first lesson establishes the building blocks of geometry. The next three lessons deal with linear measurement and extend this to finding area. These concepts are explored synthetically and also in a coordinate system. The last two lessons deal with angle measurement and relationships between pairs of angles.

COMMON CORE PROGRESSION

Middle School
- Draw polygons in the coordinate plane given coordinates for the vertices.
- Use coordinates and absolute value to find distances between points with the same first coordinate or the same second coordinate.
- Find areas of triangles and quadrilaterals.
- Apply the Pythagorean Theorem to find unknown side lengths in right triangles and the distance between two points in a coordinate plane.

Algebra 1
- Write equations in one variable and use them to solve problems.
- Solve multistep linear equations using inverse operations.

Geometry
- Name points, lines, planes, segments, and rays.
- Find segment lengths using the Ruler Postulate, the Segment Addition Postulate, midpoints, segment bisectors, and the Distance Formula.
- Classify polygons and angles.
- Find perimeters and areas of polygons in the coordinate plane.
- Construct congruent segments and angles, and bisect segment and angles.

Dynamic Teaching Tools
- Dynamic Assessment & Progress Monitoring Tool
- Lesson Planning Tool
- Interactive Whiteboard Lesson Library
- Dynamic Classroom with Dynamic Investigations
- Real-Life STEM Videos

Scaffolding in the Classroom
Graphic Organizers: Concept Circle
A Concept Circle can be used to organize information about a concept. Students write the concept above the circle. Then students write associated information in the sectors of the circle. Associated information can include (an explanation of the) *Concept, Apply, Solve, Check, Example,* and *Justify.* Concept Circles can have any number of sectors. Students can place their concept circles on note cards to use as a quick study reference.

Standards Summary

Section	Common Core State Standards	
1.1	Learning	HSG-CO.A.1
1.2	Learning	HSG-CO.A.1, HSG-CO.D.12
1.3	Learning Preparing	HSG-CO.D.12 HSG-GPE.B.7
1.4	Learning	HSG-GPE.B.7, HSG-MG.A.1
1.5	Learning	HSG-CO.A.1, HSG-CO.D.12
1.6	Learning	HSG-CO.A.1

Questioning in the Classroom
Share ideas.

Have students discuss closure questions or start thinking questions in small groups and then share their answers using a document camera, chart paper, etc. Have different students from each group support their answer.

Laurie's Notes

Maintaining Mathematical Proficiency

Finding Absolute Value

- Remind students that the absolute value of a number is its *distance* from 0 on a number line. Distance is always a positive value, so the absolute value of a number is never negative.

COMMON ERROR Absolute value signs are grouping symbols. Students should simplify the expression within the absolute value signs *before* finding the absolute value. For example, $|3 + (-4)| \neq |3| + |-4|$.

Finding the Area of a Triangle

- Review the formula for the area of a triangle, $A = \frac{1}{2}bh$, where b represents the length of a base and h represents the height. The height of a triangle is the length of the altitude to that base. An altitude is the perpendicular segment from a vertex to the line containing the opposite side.

COMMON ERROR Students may forget to include units when they write their answers to area computations. Remind students that area is measured in *square units*.

Mathematical Practices (continued on page 2)

- The eight Common Core State Standards for Mathematical Practices focus attention on how mathematics is learned—process versus content. Page 2 demonstrates that focusing on the unit analysis that leads to labeling answers with correct units of measures provides an entry point into solving problems.

If students need help...	If students got it...
Student Journal • Maintaining Mathematical Proficiency	Game Closet at *BigIdeasMath.com*
Lesson Tutorials	Start the *next* Section
Skills Review Handbook	

Maintaining Mathematical Proficiency

Finding Absolute Value

Example 1 Simplify $|-7 - 1|$.

$$|-7 - 1| = |-7 + (-1)| \qquad \text{Add the opposite of 1.}$$
$$= |-8| \qquad \text{Add.}$$
$$= 8 \qquad \text{Find the absolute value.}$$

▶ $|-7 - 1| = 8$

Simplify the expression.

1. $|8 - 12|$
2. $|-6 - 5|$
3. $|4 + (-9)|$

4. $|13 + (-4)|$
5. $|6 - (-2)|$
6. $|5 - (-1)|$

7. $|-8 - (-7)|$
8. $|8 - 13|$
9. $|-14 - 3|$

Finding the Area of a Triangle

Example 2 Find the area of the triangle.

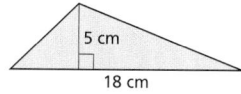

$$A = \tfrac{1}{2}bh \qquad \text{Write the formula for area of a triangle.}$$
$$= \tfrac{1}{2}(18)(5) \qquad \text{Substitute 18 for } b \text{ and 5 for } h.$$
$$= \tfrac{1}{2}(90) \qquad \text{Multiply 18 and 5.}$$
$$= 45 \qquad \text{Multiply } \tfrac{1}{2} \text{ and 90.}$$

▶ The area of the triangle is 45 square centimeters.

Find the area of the triangle.

10.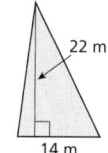

11.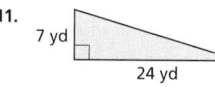

12.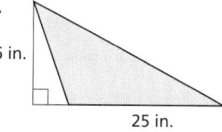

13. **ABSTRACT REASONING** Describe the possible values for x and y when $|x - y| > 0$. What does it mean when $|x - y| = 0$? Can $|x - y| < 0$? Explain your reasoning.

Common Core State Standards

6.NS.C.7c Understand the absolute value of a rational number as its distance from 0 on the number line; …

7.NS.A.3 Solve … mathematical problems involving … operations with rational numbers.

6.G.A.1 Find the area of right triangles, other triangles, …

ANSWERS

1. 4
2. 11
3. 5
4. 9
5. 8
6. 6
7. 1
8. 5
9. 17
10. 154 m^2
11. 84 yd^2
12. 200 in.^{2}
13. x and y can be any real number, $x \neq y$; $x = y$; no; Absolute value is never negative.

Vocabulary Review

Have students make a Notetaking Organizer for the formula for the area of a triangle. Include the following words.

- Base
- Height

MONITORING PROGRESS ANSWERS

1. about 0.31 in.²
2. about 32.26 cm²
3. about 193 km

Mathematical Practices

Mathematically proficient students carefully specify units of measure.

Specifying Units of Measure

Core Concept

Customary Units of Length	**Metric Units of Length**
1 foot = 12 inches	1 centimeter = 10 millimeters
1 yard = 3 feet	1 meter = 1000 millimeters
1 mile = 5280 feet = 1760 yards	1 kilometer = 1000 meters

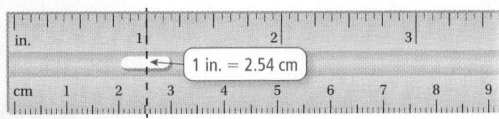

1 in. = 2.54 cm

EXAMPLE 1 **Converting Units of Measure**

Find the area of the rectangle in square centimeters. Round your answer to the nearest hundredth.

2 in.

6 in.

SOLUTION

Use the formula for the area of a rectangle. Convert the units of length from customary units to metric units.

Area = (Length)(Width)	Formula for area of a rectangle
= (6 in.)(2 in.)	Substitute given length and width.
$= \left[(6 \text{ in.})\left(\dfrac{2.54 \text{ cm}}{1 \text{ in.}}\right) \right]\left[(2 \text{ in.})\left(\dfrac{2.54 \text{ cm}}{1 \text{ in.}}\right) \right]$	Multiply each dimension by the conversion factor.
= (15.24 cm)(5.08 cm)	Multiply.
≈ 77.42 cm²	Multiply and round to the nearest hundredth.

▶ The area of the rectangle is about 77.42 square centimeters.

Monitoring Progress

Find the area of the polygon using the specified units. Round your answer to the nearest hundredth.

1. triangle (square inches)

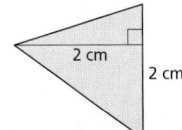

2 cm

2 cm

2. parallelogram (square centimeters)

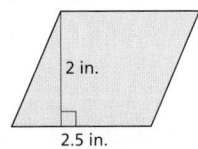

2 in.

2.5 in.

3. The distance between two cities is 120 miles. What is the distance in kilometers? Round your answer to the nearest whole number.

Laurie's Notes Mathematical Practices (continued from page T-1)

- Use the *Mathematical Practices* page to help students develop mathematical habits of mind—how mathematics can be explored and how mathematics is thought about.
- Quickly review the common conversion facts and the conversion factor relating inches and centimeters.
- **MP6 Attend to Precision:** In Example 1, students see dimensional analysis used to convert from inches to centimeters. This representation should be helpful when students work Question 3, converting from miles to kilometers.
- Students could work with partners or in groups on *Monitoring Progress*. Allow private think time before dialogue begins.

Dynamic Teaching Tools

Dynamic Assessment & Progress Monitoring Tool
Lesson Planning Tool
Interactive Whiteboard Lesson Library
Dynamic Classroom with Dynamic Investigations

Laurie's Notes

Overview of Section 1.1

Introduction

- Students will be familiar with the basic geometric terms of *point, line, segment, ray,* and *plane.* They should also be familiar with how each is represented, meaning the notation used to identify these geometric objects.
- Sketching geometric relationships is challenging for many students. Specific steps are given in the lesson to help students.
- To keep the lesson interesting, be sure to have lots of common objects around the room for students to reference when, for example, they are asked to describe the intersection of two lines, or the intersection of a line and a plane.

Resources

- Have materials available that represent (model) lines and planes: coffee stirrers, straws, spaghetti (not thin—it breaks too easily!), wooden dowels, chopsticks, file folders, cardboard dividers from a box, and poster board.

Formative Assessment Tips

- **Turn and Talk:** This technique allows all students in the class to have a voice. Using a 3-foot voice, students turn and talk to their partners about a problem or to discuss a question. There may be different roles that I ask partners to assume, so I refer to partner A and partner B. In discussing a procedure or explaining an answer, I might ask partner A to talk uninterrupted for a fixed period of time. Then partner B might be asked to repeat back what he/she heard or to ask a question about what has been shared.
  Example: *Turn and Talk* so that partner A explains the intersection possibilities for a line and a plane.
- It is important to establish norms: 3-foot voices should be expected when students are doing partner work. Discuss with students the difference between *authentic listening* and being quiet while your partners are speaking.

Another Way

- If computers are not available for use on the first day, the goal of the explorations on page 3 could be achieved in an alternate fashion. Place an assortment of common objects in view of all students (or give 2–3 objects to each group of students). Ask students to describe the objects using geometric terms with which they are familiar. The collection of objects could be enlarged by capturing screen images and then displaying them for all students to see.

Pacing Suggestion

- If you believe that students are familiar with the basic geometric terms and the correct notations, you might have students do *Monitoring Progress* Questions 1–3 on pages 4 and 5 and spend the remaining class time on sketching (Examples 3 and 4) and applying (Example 5).

Laurie's Notes

Exploration

Motivate

- Write two lists of words on the board—those beginning with "geo-" and those ending with "-metry."
  - geothermal, geopolitics, geophysical, geology, geoid, geometry
  - asymmetry, symmetry, trigonometry, optometry, densitometry, geometry
- Ask students to discuss the two lists with partners, specifically deciding what the prefix "geo-" means and the suffix "-metry" means.
- The prefix "geo-" is derived from the Greek word *geo,* which means earth.
- The suffix "-metry" means the process or science of measuring. It is derived from the Greek word *metria,* which means to measure.

For Your Information

- Often there are things that need to be done on the first day of school that take up teaching time. These first three explorations can be used to facilitate conversation about what geometry is and what the experience will be like for students this year. It provides an opportunity for students to become familiar with whatever dynamic geometry software they will be using.

Exploration 1

- Students should be familiar with the terms *point, segment, ray,* and *line.* The goal is for students to familiarize themselves with the software.
- **?** "Could these geometric objects be drawn without the coordinate grid?" yes
- Discuss the difference between synthetic and coordinate geometry. Geometry will be explored in both environments this year.
- Depending on time, you might have students spend a little time with Exploration 3 next and finish the period with Exploration 2.

Exploration 2

- The goal of this exploration is to get students talking and observing the geometry around them.
- In addition to the physical components of the classroom, you should have available items that can serve as models of lines and planes. For lines, you could use coffee stirrers, straws, spaghetti, wooden dowels, or chopsticks. For planes, you could use file folders, cardboard dividers from a box, or poster board.
- Ask for volunteers in each group to model the various possibilities.

Exploration 3

- If time permits, allow students to use the software to explore terms with which they might not be familiar.

Communicate Your Answer

- You could extend this question to include the objects and physical components of the classroom.

Connecting to Next Step

- Students have now had the opportunity to use geometric vocabulary. In the formal lesson, students will be presented with definitions and notations for simple geometric objects.

1.1 Points, Lines, and Planes

Essential Question How can you use dynamic geometry software to visualize geometric concepts?

EXPLORATION 1 Using Dynamic Geometry Software

Work with a partner. Use dynamic geometry software to draw several points. Also, draw some lines, line segments, and rays. What is the difference between a line, a line segment, and a ray?

Sample

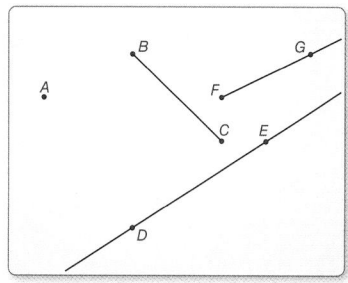

EXPLORATION 2 Intersections of Lines and Planes

Work with a partner.

a. Describe and sketch the ways in which two lines can intersect or not intersect. Give examples of each using the lines formed by the walls, floor, and ceiling in your classroom.

b. Describe and sketch the ways in which a line and a plane can intersect or not intersect. Give examples of each using the walls, floor, and ceiling in your classroom.

c. Describe and sketch the ways in which two planes can intersect or not intersect. Give examples of each using the walls, floor, and ceiling in your classroom.

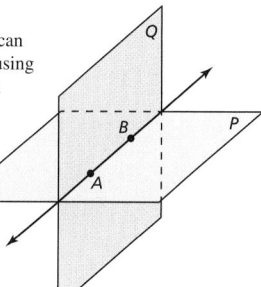

UNDERSTANDING MATHEMATICAL TERMS

To be proficient in math, you need to understand definitions and previously established results. An appropriate tool, such as a software package, can sometimes help.

EXPLORATION 3 Exploring Dynamic Geometry Software

Work with a partner. Use dynamic geometry software to explore geometry. Use the software to find a term or concept that is unfamiliar to you. Then use the capabilities of the software to determine the meaning of the term or concept.

Communicate Your Answer

4. How can you use dynamic geometry software to visualize geometric concepts?

Section 1.1   Points, Lines, and Planes   **3**

ANSWERS

1. A line extends infinitely in each direction, a line segment has two endpoints, and a ray has one endpoint and extends infinitely in one direction.

2. See Additional Answers.

3. *Sample answer:* A segment bisector is a point, ray, line, line segment, or plane that intersects the segment at its midpoint.

4. You can draw geometric shapes and figures and explore their characteristics.

Differentiated Instruction

Kinesthetic

Have students draw a rectangle on a piece of paper. Label the vertices *A*, *B*, *C*, and *D*. Ask them whether points *A*, *B*, *C*, and *D* are collinear (no); coplanar (yes). Then have them fold the paper so that points *A*, *B*, *C*, and *D* are not coplanar.

Extra Example 1

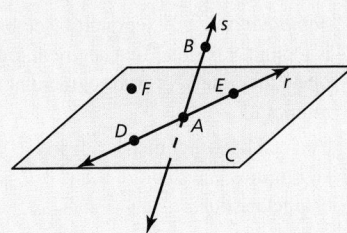

a. Give two other names for $\overleftrightarrow{DE}$ and plane *C*. *Sample answer:* line *r*, $\overleftrightarrow{ED}$; *Sample answer:* plane *DEF*, plane *AEF*

b. Name three points that are collinear. Name four points that are coplanar.
D, A, E; *D, A, E, F*

MONITORING PROGRESS ANSWER

1. $\overleftrightarrow{PT}$, line *m*; *V*

1.1 Lesson

Core Vocabulary

undefined terms, p. 4
point, p. 4
line, p. 4
plane, p. 4
collinear points, p. 4
coplanar points, p. 4
defined terms, p. 5
line segment, or segment, p. 5
endpoints, p. 5
ray, p. 5
opposite rays, p. 5
intersection, p. 6

What You Will Learn

▶ Name points, lines, and planes.
▶ Name segments and rays.
▶ Sketch intersections of lines and planes.
▶ Solve real-life problems involving lines and planes.

Using Undefined Terms

In geometry, the words *point*, *line*, and *plane* are **undefined terms**. These words do not have formal definitions, but there is agreement about what they mean.

Core Concept

Undefined Terms: Point, Line, and Plane

Point A **point** has no dimension. A dot represents a point.

point *A*

Line A **line** has one dimension. It is represented by a line with two arrowheads, but it extends without end.

Through any two points, there is exactly one line. You can use any two points on a line to name it.

line ℓ, line *AB* ($\overleftrightarrow{AB}$), or line *BA* ($\overleftrightarrow{BA}$)

Plane A **plane** has two dimensions. It is represented by a shape that looks like a floor or a wall, but it extends without end.

Through any three points not on the same line, there is exactly one plane. You can use three points that are not all on the same line to name a plane.

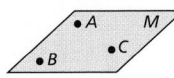
plane *M*, or plane *ABC*

Collinear points are points that lie on the same line. **Coplanar points** are points that lie in the same plane.

EXAMPLE 1   Naming Points, Lines, and Planes

a. Give two other names for $\overleftrightarrow{PQ}$ and plane *R*.

b. Name three points that are collinear. Name four points that are coplanar.

SOLUTION

a. Other names for $\overleftrightarrow{PQ}$ are $\overleftrightarrow{QP}$ and line *n*. Other names for plane *R* are plane *SVT* and plane *PTV*.

b. Points *S*, *P*, and *T* lie on the same line, so they are collinear. Points *S*, *P*, *T*, and *V* lie in the same plane, so they are coplanar.

Monitoring Progress 🔊 Help in English and Spanish at *BigIdeasMath.com*

1. Use the diagram in Example 1. Give two other names for $\overleftrightarrow{ST}$. Name a point that is *not* coplanar with points *Q*, *S*, and *T*.

Laurie's Notes   Teacher Actions

- Introduce the *undefined terms—point, line,* and *plane*.
- ❓ "How many lines can be drawn through one point?" infinitely many "How many lines can be drawn through two points?" one
- ❓ "How many planes can be drawn through one point?" infinitely many "How many planes can be drawn through two points?" infinitely many "How many planes can be drawn through three points not on the same line?" one
- Use these questions to help students visualize geometric relationships and to understand necessary conditions to establish a line and a plane.
- **MP4 Model with Mathematics:** Make a three-dimensional physical model for Example 1. Use a file folder for the plane and wooden dowel for line *n*.

Using Defined Terms

In geometry, terms that can be described using known words such as *point* or *line* are called **defined terms**.

Core Concept

Defined Terms: Segment and Ray

The definitions below use line AB (written as $\overleftrightarrow{AB}$) and points A and B.

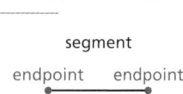
line

Segment The **line segment** AB, or **segment** AB, (written as $\overline{AB}$) consists of the **endpoints** A and B and all points on $\overleftrightarrow{AB}$ that are between A and B. Note that $\overline{AB}$ can also be named $\overline{BA}$.

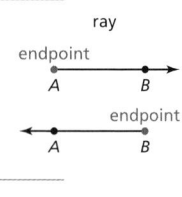
segment
endpoint   endpoint
A   B

Ray The **ray** AB (written as $\overrightarrow{AB}$) consists of the endpoint A and all points on $\overleftrightarrow{AB}$ that lie on the same side of A as B.

Note that $\overrightarrow{AB}$ and $\overrightarrow{BA}$ are different rays.

ray
endpoint
A   B

endpoint
A   B

Opposite Rays If point C lies on $\overleftrightarrow{AB}$ between A and B, then $\overrightarrow{CA}$ and $\overrightarrow{CB}$ are **opposite rays**.

A   C   B

Segments and rays are collinear when they lie on the same line. So, opposite rays are collinear. Lines, segments, and rays are coplanar when they lie in the same plane.

EXAMPLE 2 Naming Segments, Rays, and Opposite Rays

a. Give another name for $\overline{GH}$.
b. Name all rays with endpoint J. Which of these rays are opposite rays?

SOLUTION

a. Another name for $\overline{GH}$ is $\overline{HG}$.

b. The rays with endpoint J are $\overrightarrow{JE}$, $\overrightarrow{JG}$, $\overrightarrow{JF}$, and $\overrightarrow{JH}$. The pairs of opposite rays with endpoint J are $\overrightarrow{JE}$ and $\overrightarrow{JF}$, and $\overrightarrow{JG}$ and $\overrightarrow{JH}$.

COMMON ERROR

In Example 2, $\overrightarrow{JG}$ and $\overrightarrow{JF}$ have a common endpoint, but they are not collinear. So, they are *not* opposite rays.

Monitoring Progress Help in English and Spanish at *BigIdeasMath.com*

Use the diagram.

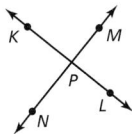

2. Give another name for $\overline{KL}$.

3. Are $\overrightarrow{KP}$ and $\overrightarrow{PK}$ the same ray? Are $\overrightarrow{NP}$ and $\overrightarrow{NM}$ the same ray? Explain.

English Language Learners

Notebook Development
Have students record new vocabulary in their notebooks. Include the terms *point*, *line*, *plane*, *segment*, *ray*, and *opposite rays*. For each term, include a labeled sketch.

Extra Example 2

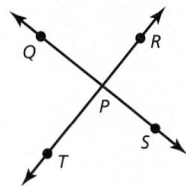

a. Give another name for $\overleftrightarrow{TR}$. $\overleftrightarrow{RT}$
b. Name all rays with endpoint P. Which of these rays are opposite rays? $\overrightarrow{PQ}$, $\overrightarrow{PR}$, $\overrightarrow{PS}$, $\overrightarrow{PT}$; $\overrightarrow{PQ}$ and $\overrightarrow{PS}$, $\overrightarrow{PT}$ and $\overrightarrow{PR}$

MONITORING PROGRESS ANSWERS

2. $\overline{LK}$

3. no; yes; $\overrightarrow{KP}$ and $\overrightarrow{PK}$ have different endpoints and are going in different directions. $\overrightarrow{NP}$ and $\overrightarrow{NM}$ have the same endpoint and are going in the same direction.

Laurie's Notes   Teacher Actions

- Introduce the *defined terms*—segment and ray—and how each is represented.
- **Common Misconception:** For the diagram shown, be sure students understand that $\overrightarrow{AB}$ and $\overrightarrow{BA}$ are *not* the same ray, but $\overleftrightarrow{BA}$ and $\overleftrightarrow{AB}$ are the same ray. However, it is *not* common to write $\overleftrightarrow{BA}$ as $\overleftrightarrow{AB}$.
- Use physical models to aid discussion of the terms.

Extra Example 3

a. Sketch two intersecting lines *a* and *b* that lie in plane *W*.

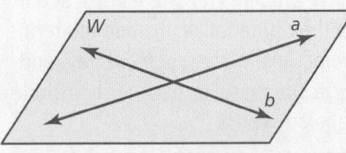

b. Sketch line *d* that intersects plane *D* in only one point. Label the point *A*.

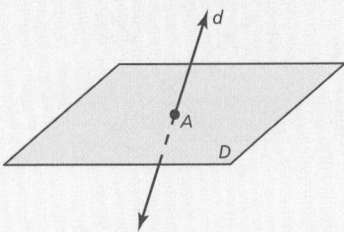

c. Sketch a plane *X* that contains $\overleftrightarrow{PQ}$ and a point *B* not on $\overleftrightarrow{PQ}$.

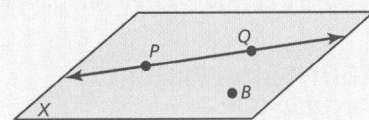

Extra Example 4

Sketch two planes *R* and *S* that intersect in line $\overleftrightarrow{AB}$.

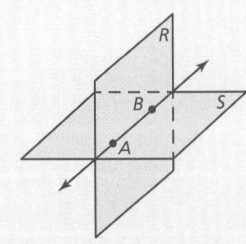

MONITORING PROGRESS ANSWERS

4. *Sample answer:*

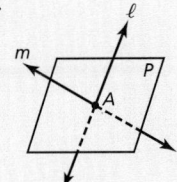

5. *M*
6. line *k*
7. line *k*

Sketching Intersections

Two or more geometric figures *intersect* when they have one or more points in common. The **intersection** of the figures is the set of points the figures have in common. Some examples of intersections are shown below.

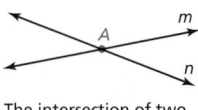

The intersection of two different lines is a point.

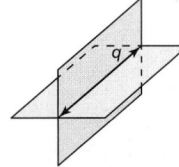

The intersection of two different planes is a line.

EXAMPLE 3   Sketching Intersections of Lines and Planes

a. Sketch a plane and a line that is in the plane.

b. Sketch a plane and a line that does not intersect the plane.

c. Sketch a plane and a line that intersects the plane at a point.

SOLUTION

a.
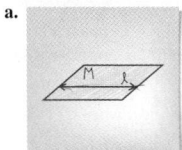

b.
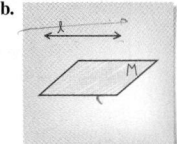

c.
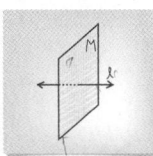

EXAMPLE 4   Sketching Intersections of Planes

Sketch two planes that intersect in a line.

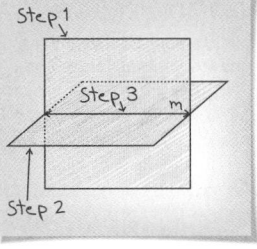

SOLUTION

Step 1 Draw a vertical plane. Shade the plane.

Step 2 Draw a second plane that is horizontal. Shade this plane a different color. Use dashed lines to show where one plane is hidden.

Step 3 Draw the line of intersection.

Monitoring Progress 🔊 Help in English and Spanish at *BigIdeasMath.com*

4. Sketch two different lines that intersect a plane at the same point.

Use the diagram.

5. Name the intersection of $\overleftrightarrow{PQ}$ and line *k*.

6. Name the intersection of plane *A* and plane *B*.

7. Name the intersection of line *k* and plane *A*.

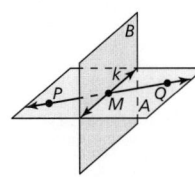

Laurie's Notes   Teacher Actions

- Sketching intersections of lines and planes can be challenging for students. Share the explicit steps for sketching. Offer colored pencils for shading if available.

- **MP4 and MP5 Use Appropriate Tools Strategically:** For each case, the student should use the tools to model the intersection. Modeling with physical objects is easier than sketching!

? Hand a file folder (model of a plane) and a wooden dowel (model of a line) to a student. "What are the intersection possibilities for a line and a plane?" no points, one point, or infinitely many points of intersection

- Students should notice that the non-rectangular parallelogram is used in sketching planes. It gives the perspective of continuing to cover the plane in a way that a rectangle does not.

- **Turn and Talk:** Have students discuss *Monitoring Progress* Questions 5–7.

Solving Real-Life Problems

EXAMPLE 5 Modeling with Mathematics

The diagram shows a molecule of sulfur hexafluoride, the most potent greenhouse gas in the world. Name two different planes that contain line r.

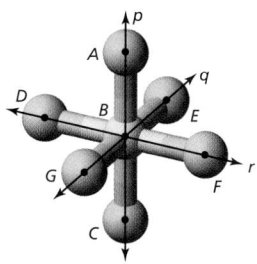

Electric utilities use sulfur hexafluoride as an insulator. Leaks in electrical equipment contribute to the release of sulfur hexafluoride into the atmosphere.

SOLUTION

1. **Understand the Problem** In the diagram, you are given three lines, p, q, and r, that intersect at point B. You need to name two different planes that contain line r.

2. **Make a Plan** The planes should contain two points on line r and one point not on line r.

3. **Solve the Problem** Points D and F are on line r. Point E does not lie on line r. So, plane DEF contains line r. Another point that does not lie on line r is C. So, plane CDF contains line r.

   Note that you cannot form a plane through points D, B, and F. By definition, three points that do not lie on the same line form a plane. Points D, B, and F are collinear, so they do *not* form a plane.

4. **Look Back** The question asks for two *different* planes. You need to check whether plane DEF and plane CDF are two unique planes or the same plane named differently. Because point C does not lie on plane DEF, plane DEF and plane CDF are different planes.

Monitoring Progress Help in English and Spanish at *BigIdeasMath.com*

Use the diagram that shows a molecule of phosphorus pentachloride.

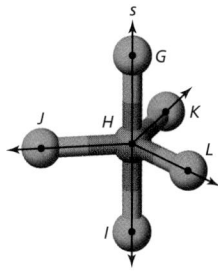

8. Name two different planes that contain line s.
9. Name three different planes that contain point K.
10. Name two different planes that contain $\overleftrightarrow{HJ}$.

Extra Example 5
The diagram shows a juice box. Name two different planes that contain $\overleftrightarrow{QP}$.

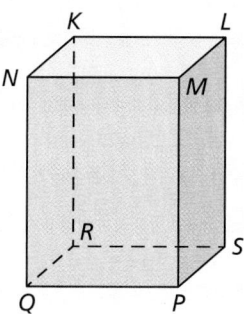

Sample answer: plane *QPR*, plane *QPN*

MONITORING PROGRESS ANSWERS

8. *Sample answer:* plane *GHL*, plane *GHK*

9. *Sample answer:* plane *GHK*, plane *KHL*, plane *JHK*

10. *Sample answer:* plane *GHJ*, plane *JHK*

Laurie's Notes   Teacher Actions

- **FYI:** Sulfur hexafluoride is a non-toxic, invisible gas that you can use to perform interesting chemistry demonstrations. Breathe it in and make your voice much deeper when you talk. Pour it into a container and float light objects on "nothing."
- If time permits, search the Internet for "sulfur hexafluoride" and show a quick video demonstrating properties of sulfur hexafluoride.
- Display an image of the sulfur hexafluoride molecule and pose the problem.

- In *Make a Plan*, ask students why the plane must contain line r and a point not on line r.

Closure
- Sketch and label the cube as shown. Ask students to identify segments, intersecting lines, intersecting planes, a line not on a plane, and so on.

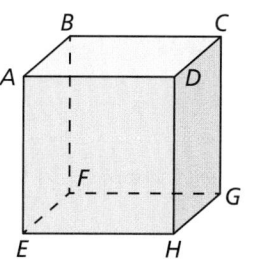

Assignment Guide and Homework Check

ASSIGNMENT

Basic: 1, 2, 3–19 odd, 25–43 odd, 50, 55, 65–72

Average: 1, 2, 10–46 even, 50–54 even, 55, 65–72

Advanced: 1, 2, 12, 18, 24, 26, 34–54 even, 55, 56–64 even, 65–72

HOMEWORK CHECK

Basic: 7, 9, 15, 19, 33

Average: 10, 16, 18, 30, 40

Advanced: 18, 34, 44, 54, 62

ANSWERS

1. Collinear points lie on the same line. Coplanar points lie on the same plane.

2. plane *CDE*; Planes have two dimensions. Lines, line segments, and rays have one dimension.

3. *Sample answer:* A, B, D, E

4. $\overleftrightarrow{DE}$, $\overleftrightarrow{BC}$

5. plane *S*

6. plane *T*

7. $\overleftrightarrow{QW}$, line *g*

8. *Sample answer:* plane *RST*

9. R, Q, S; *Sample answer:* T

10. W

11. $\overline{DB}$

12. $\overleftrightarrow{CA}$

13. $\overrightarrow{AC}$

14. $\overrightarrow{EB}$, $\overrightarrow{EC}$, $\overrightarrow{ED}$, $\overrightarrow{EA}$

15. $\overrightarrow{EB}$ and $\overrightarrow{ED}$, $\overrightarrow{EA}$ and $\overrightarrow{EC}$

16. *Sample answer:* $\overrightarrow{EC}$ and $\overrightarrow{ED}$

17. *Sample answer:*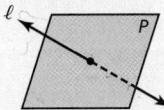

18. *Sample answer:*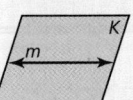

19. *Sample answer:*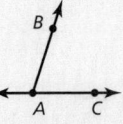

20. *Sample answer:*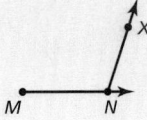

Vocabulary and Core Concept Check

1. **WRITING** Compare collinear points and coplanar points.

2. **WHICH ONE DOESN'T BELONG?** Which term does *not* belong with the other three? Explain your reasoning.

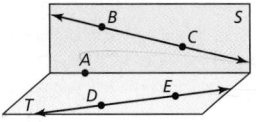

Monitoring Progress and Modeling with Mathematics

In Exercises 3–6, use the diagram.

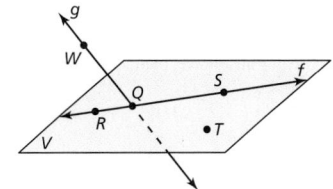

3. Name four points.

4. Name two lines.

5. Name the plane that contains points *A*, *B*, and *C*.

6. Name the plane that contains points *A*, *D*, and *E*.

In Exercises 7–10, use the diagram. *(See Example 1.)*

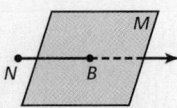

7. Give two other names for $\overleftrightarrow{WQ}$.

8. Give another name for plane *V*.

9. Name three points that are collinear. Then name a fourth point that is not collinear with these three points.

10. Name a point that is not coplanar with *R*, *S*, and *T*.

In Exercises 11–16, use the diagram. *(See Example 2.)*

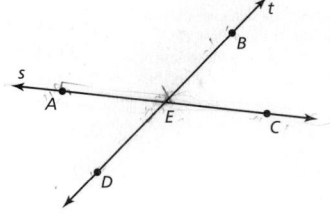

11. What is another name for $\overline{BD}$?

12. What is another name for $\overleftrightarrow{AC}$?

13. What is another name for ray $\overrightarrow{AE}$?

14. Name all rays with endpoint *E*.

15. Name two pairs of opposite rays.

16. Name one pair of rays that are not opposite rays.

In Exercises 17–24, sketch the figure described. *(See Examples 3 and 4.)*

17. plane *P* and line ℓ intersecting at one point

18. plane *K* and line *m* intersecting at all points on line *m*

19. $\overrightarrow{AB}$ and $\overrightarrow{AC}$

20. $\overrightarrow{MN}$ and $\overrightarrow{NX}$

21. plane *M* and $\overrightarrow{NB}$ intersecting at *B*

22. plane *M* and $\overrightarrow{NB}$ intersecting at *A*

23. plane *A* and plane *B* not intersecting

24. plane *C* and plane *D* intersecting at $\overleftrightarrow{XY}$

21. *Sample answer:*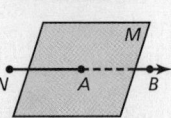

22. *Sample answer:*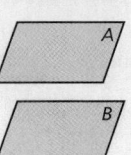

23. *Sample answer:*

24. *Sample answer:*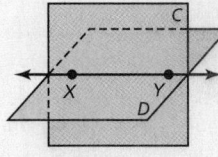

ERROR ANALYSIS In Exercises 25 and 26, describe and correct the error in naming opposite rays in the diagram.

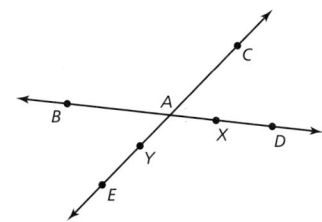

25.

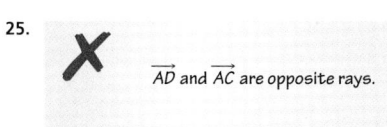

$\overrightarrow{AD}$ and $\overrightarrow{AC}$ are opposite rays.

26.

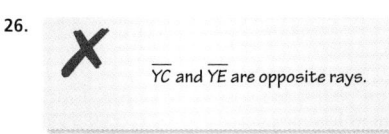

$\overrightarrow{YC}$ and $\overrightarrow{YE}$ are opposite rays.

In Exercises 27–34, use the diagram.

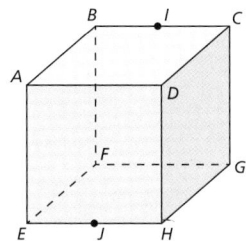

27. Name a point that is collinear with points E and H.

28. Name a point that is collinear with points B and I.

29. Name a point that is not collinear with points E and H.

30. Name a point that is not collinear with points B and I.

31. Name a point that is coplanar with points D, A, and B.

32. Name a point that is coplanar with points C, G, and F.

33. Name the intersection of plane AEH and plane FBE.

34. Name the intersection of plane BGF and plane HDG.

In Exercises 35–38, name the geometric term modeled by the object.

35.

36.

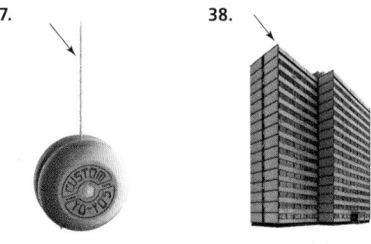

37.   **38.**

In Exercises 39–44, use the diagram to name all the points that are not coplanar with the given points.

39. N, K, and L

40. P, Q, and N

41. P, Q, and R

42. R, K, and N

43. P, S, and K

44. Q, K, and L

45. CRITICAL THINKING Given two points on a line and a third point not on the line, is it possible to draw a plane that includes the line and the third point? Explain your reasoning.

46. CRITICAL THINKING Is it possible for one point to be in two different planes? Explain your reasoning.

ANSWERS

25. $\overrightarrow{AD}$ and $\overrightarrow{AC}$ are not opposite rays because A, C, and D are not collinear; $\overrightarrow{AD}$ and $\overrightarrow{AB}$ are opposite rays because A, B, and D are collinear, and A is between B and D.

26. $\overline{YC}$ and $\overline{YE}$ are segments; $\overrightarrow{YC}$ and $\overrightarrow{YE}$ are opposite rays.

27. J

28. C

29. *Sample answer:* D

30. *Sample answer:* A

31. *Sample answer:* C

32. *Sample answer:* B

33. $\overleftrightarrow{AE}$

34. $\overleftrightarrow{CG}$

35. point

36. plane

37. segment

38. point

39. P, Q, R, S

40. K, L, R, S

41. K, L, M, N

42. L, M, P, S

43. L, M, Q, R

44. M, N, R, S

45. yes; Use the point not on the line and two points on the line to draw the plane.

46. yes; Infinitely many planes can intersect any given point.

ANSWERS

47. Three legs of the chair will meet on the floor to define a plane, but the point at the bottom of the fourth leg may not be in the same plane. When the chair tips so that this leg is on the floor, the plane defined by this leg and the two legs closest to it now lies in the plane of the floor; no; Three points define a plane, so the legs of the three-legged chair will always meet in the flat plane of the floor.

48. See Additional Answers.

49. 6; The first two lines intersect at one point. The third line could intersect each of the first two lines. The fourth line can be drawn to intersect each of the first 3 lines. Then the total is $1 + 2 + 3 = 6$.

50–72. See Additional Answers.

Mini-Assessment

Use the diagram that shows a molecule of phosphorus pentachloride.

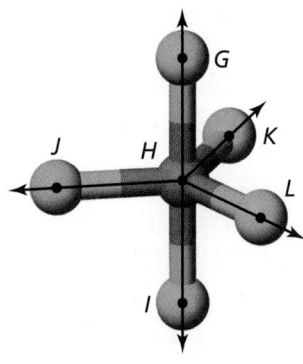

1. Name three points that are not collinear. *Sample answer: J, H, L*

2. Name two opposite rays. $\overrightarrow{HG}$, $\overrightarrow{HI}$

3. Give another name for $\overleftrightarrow{JH}$. $\overleftrightarrow{HJ}$

4. Name two different planes that contain $\overrightarrow{HL}$. *Sample answer: plane HKL, plane HLI*

5. Sketch two planes A and B that intersect in line p.

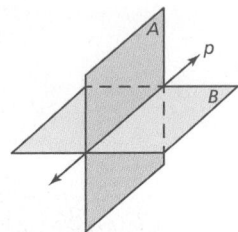

10   Chapter 1

---

47. REASONING Explain why a four-legged chair may rock from side to side even if the floor is level. Would a three-legged chair on the same level floor rock from side to side? Why or why not?

48. THOUGHT PROVOKING You are designing the living room of an apartment. Counting the floor, walls, and ceiling, you want the design to contain at least eight different planes. Draw a diagram of your design. Label each plane in your design.

49. LOOKING FOR STRUCTURE Two coplanar intersecting lines will always intersect at one point. What is the greatest number of intersection points that exist if you draw four coplanar lines? Explain.

50. HOW DO YOU SEE IT? You and your friend walk in opposite directions, forming opposite rays. You were originally on the corner of Apple Avenue and Cherry Court.

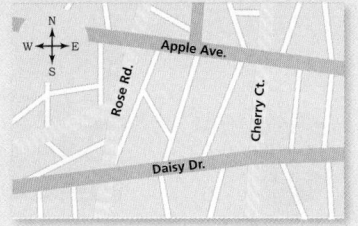

a. Name two possibilities of the road and direction you and your friend may have traveled.

b. Your friend claims he went north on Cherry Court, and you went east on Apple Avenue. Make an argument as to why you know this could not have happened.

MATHEMATICAL CONNECTIONS In Exercises 51–54, graph the inequality on a number line. Tell whether the graph is a *segment*, a *ray* or *rays*, a *point*, or a *line*.

51. $x \le 3$ **52.** $-7 \le x \le 4$

Maintaining Mathematical Proficiency
Reviewing what you learned in previous grades and lessons

Find the absolute value. *(Skills Review Handbook)*

65. $|6 + 2|$ **66.** $|3 - 9|$ **67.** $|-8 - 2|$ **68.** $|7 - 11|$

Solve the equation. *(Skills Review Handbook)*

69. $18 + x = 43$ **70.** $36 + x = 20$ **71.** $x - 15 = 7$ **72.** $x - 23 = 19$

10   Chapter 1   Basics of Geometry

---

53. $x \ge 5$ or $x \le -2$ **54.** $|x| \le 0$

55. MODELING WITH MATHEMATICS Use the diagram.

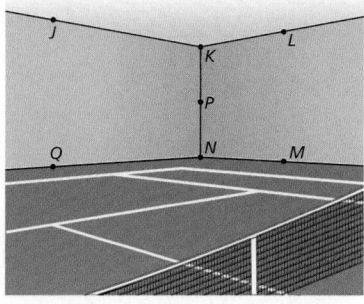

a. Name two points that are collinear with P.

b. Name two planes that contain J.

c. Name all the points that are in more than one plane.

CRITICAL THINKING In Exercises 56–63, complete the statement with *always*, *sometimes*, or *never*. Explain your reasoning.

56. A line _____ has endpoints.

57. A line and a point _____ intersect.

58. A plane and a point _____ intersect.

59. Two planes _____ intersect in a line.

60. Two points _____ determine a line.

61. Any three points _____ determine a plane.

62. Any three points not on the same line _____ determine a plane.

63. Two lines that are not parallel _____ intersect.

64. ABSTRACT REASONING Is it possible for three planes to never intersect? intersect in one line? intersect in one point? Sketch the possible situations.

If students need help...	If students got it...
Resources by Chapter • Practice A and Practice B • Puzzle Time	Resources by Chapter • Enrichment and Extension • Cumulative Review
Student Journal • Practice	Start the *next* Section
Differentiating the Lesson Skills Review Handbook	

Overview of Section 1.2

Introduction
- This lesson is about measuring and copying segments.
- Share expectations with students about how they should record postulates and theorems in their notes and how the postulate or theorem should be referenced, meaning by name rather than by number.
- The two postulates in this lesson can be confusing to students, mainly because they seem so obvious. The Ruler Postulate establishes how to measure a segment on a number line. The Segment Addition Postulate says that when a point is between two other points, the measures of the two shorter segments add to the measure of the longer segment.
- Notation for the measure of a segment is introduced.

Resources
- Tools such as Google Earth can be used to demonstrate the Ruler Postulate. In Example 4, students look at the straight-line distances between Lubbock, Texas; Tulsa, Oklahoma; and St. Louis, Missouri. While the roads between these cities are not straight lines, there is a straight-line map distance.

Formative Assessment Tips
- **Thumbs Up:** This technique asks students to indicate the extent to which they understand a concept, procedure, or even the directions for an activity.

| I get it. | I don't get it. | I'm not sure. |

- Use this technique to assess students' understanding of directions for an exploration, getting started with a problem, or in response to a peer's explanation of a problem.

Pacing Suggestion
- If you believe that students are secure with measuring and copying a segment, state the Ruler Postulate and begin the lesson with Example 2.

Dynamic Teaching Tools

Dynamic Assessment & Progress Monitoring Tool

Lesson Planning Tool

Interactive Whiteboard Lesson Library

Dynamic Classroom with Dynamic Investigations

Common Core
State Standards

HSG-CO.A.1 Know precise definitions of … line segment, based on the undefined notions of point, line, distance along a line, …

HSG-CO.D.12 Make formal geometric constructions with a variety of tools and methods (compass and straightedge, …). …

Laurie's Notes

Exploration

Motivate
- Display four items at the front of the room, such as a standard paper clip, an unsharpened pencil, a marker, and an empty 1-liter bottle.
- Divide the class into four groups. Each group is assigned one of the objects and asked to estimate the length of one classroom wall using their nonstandard unit.
- Gather estimates and record. Do a quick vote to decide on the best estimate.
- **?** "Is it possible to measure the wall using any of the four objects as the unit of measure?" yes
- It would take quite some time to perform the actual estimates, so do this in advance using the efficient method of measuring in inches and doing a conversion. Share results.

Discuss
- The goal of the exploration is to help students recognize that we have standard and metric units of measures that many are familiar with; however, any length could be established as the base of a measurement system.
- The challenge, of course, is that if you use a nonstandard unit of measure—say a paper clip—not everyone would be familiar with it. In the world of commerce, it is necessary to communicate in units that are understood by all.

Exploration 1
- Students should have sharp pencils when measuring a segment with paper clips.
- Most students will have a measure of 1.25″ for 1 paper clip. This conversion factor, like any conversion factor, can be written two ways: 1.25 inches = 1 paper clip or 1 inch = 0.8 paper clip.
- **Thumbs Up:** Determine whether students understand the problem posed in part (d). It may not be obvious to students that they should use the straightedge to start with a segment they know looks longer than 6 inches.

Exploration 2
- If you do not have 3-inch by 5-inch index cards available, you could use a different sized index card or cut scrap paper to a 3-inch by 5-inch size.
- **MP6 Attend to Precision:** The exact length of the diagonal is $\sqrt{34}$ inches, which is approximately 5.83 inches.
- **?** "Approximately what fraction of an inch is 0.83 inch?" $\frac{13}{16}$ inch
- In part (d), students will recognize that while the Pythagorean Theorem works for any nonstandard unit of measure, it is difficult to be accurate when measuring with paper clips!

Exploration 3
- **MP2 Reason Abstractly and Quantitatively:** Students will likely convert their known height in inches to a new unit called 1 diag. Ask volunteers to explain how they found their height in diags.

Communicate Your Answer
- Listen for students to describe the use of standard and nonstandard units of measure.

Connecting to Next Step
- Measuring in nonstandard units, students have used the Ruler Postulate and the Segment Addition Postulate.

1.2 Measuring and Constructing Segments

Essential Question How can you measure and construct a line segment?

EXPLORATION 1 Measuring Line Segments Using Nonstandard Units

Work with a partner.

a. Draw a line segment that has a length of 6 inches.

b. Use a standard-sized paper clip to measure the length of the line segment. Explain how you measured the line segment in "paper clips."

> **MAKING SENSE OF PROBLEMS**
> To be proficient in math, you need to explain to yourself the meaning of a problem and look for entry points to its solution.

c. Write conversion factors from paper clips to inches and vice versa.

1 paper clip = ▢ in.

1 in. = ▢ paper clip

d. A *straightedge* is a tool that you can use to draw a straight line. An example of a straightedge is a ruler. Use only a pencil, straightedge, paper clip, and paper to draw another line segment that is 6 inches long. Explain your process.

EXPLORATION 2 Measuring Line Segments Using Nonstandard Units

Work with a partner.

a. Fold a 3-inch by 5-inch index card on one of its diagonals.

b. Use the Pythagorean Theorem to algebraically determine the length of the diagonal in inches. Use a ruler to check your answer.

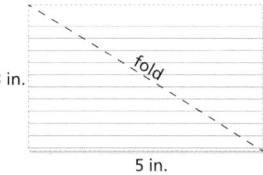

3 in.

fold

5 in.

c. Measure the length and width of the index card in paper clips.

d. Use the Pythagorean Theorem to algebraically determine the length of the diagonal in paper clips. Then check your answer by measuring the length of the diagonal in paper clips. Does the Pythagorean Theorem work for any unit of measure? Justify your answer.

EXPLORATION 3 Measuring Heights Using Nonstandard Units

Work with a partner. Consider a unit of length that is equal to the length of the diagonal you found in Exploration 2. Call this length "1 diag." How tall are you in diags? Explain how you obtained your answer.

Communicate Your Answer

4. How can you measure and construct a line segment?

Section 1.2 Measuring and Constructing Segments **11**

ANSWERS

1. **a.** Check students' work.

   b. $4\frac{4}{5}$ paper clips; Sliding the paper clip end-to-end, the 6-inch segment is just less than 5 lengths of the paper clip.

   c. $1\frac{1}{4}$; $\frac{4}{5}$

   d. Use the pencil and straightedge to draw a segment longer than 6 inches. Starting at one end, measure about $4\frac{4}{5}$ paper clips. Mark the endpoint.

2. **a.** Check students' work.

   b. about 5.8 in.

   c. $2\frac{2}{5} \times 4$ paper clips

   d. about 4.7 paper clips; yes; The Pythagorean Theorem states a relationship between lengths, regardless of how they are measured.

3. *Sample answer:* for a height of 60 inches, about 10.3 diags; Divide the height in inches by 5.8.

4. Use a ruler or a straightedge and a measuring tool.

Extra Example 1

Measure the length of $\overline{AB}$ to the nearest tenth of a centimeter.

about 2.6 centimeters

MONITORING PROGRESS ANSWERS

1. $1\frac{5}{8}$ in.

2. $1\frac{3}{8}$ in.

3. $\frac{7}{8}$ in.

4. $1\frac{1}{4}$ in.

1.2 Lesson

Core Vocabulary

postulate, *p. 12*
axiom, *p. 12*
coordinate, *p. 12*
distance, *p. 12*
construction, *p. 13*
congruent segments, *p. 13*
between, *p. 14*

What You Will Learn

▶ Use the Ruler Postulate.
▶ Copy segments and compare segments for congruence.
▶ Use the Segment Addition Postulate.

Using the Ruler Postulate

In geometry, a rule that is accepted without proof is called a **postulate** or an **axiom**. A rule that can be proved is called a *theorem*, as you will see later. Postulate 1.1 shows how to find the distance between two points on a line.

🔄 Postulate

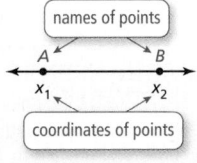

Postulate 1.1   Ruler Postulate

The points on a line can be matched one to one with the real numbers. The real number that corresponds to a point is the **coordinate** of the point.

The **distance** between points *A* and *B*, written as *AB*, is the absolute value of the difference of the coordinates of *A* and *B*.

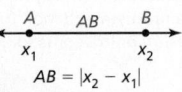

$$AB = |x_2 - x_1|$$

EXAMPLE 1   Using the Ruler Postulate

Measure the length of $\overline{ST}$ to the nearest tenth of a centimeter.

SOLUTION

Align one mark of a metric ruler with *S*. Then estimate the coordinate of *T*. For example, when you align *S* with 2, *T* appears to align with 5.4.

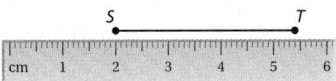

$$ST = |5.4 - 2| = 3.4 \qquad \text{Ruler Postulate}$$

▶ So, the length of $\overline{ST}$ is about 3.4 centimeters.

Monitoring Progress 🔊 Help in English and Spanish at *BigIdeasMath.com*

Use a ruler to measure the length of the segment to the nearest $\frac{1}{8}$ inch.

1.

2.

3.

4.

Laurie's Notes   Teacher Actions

? "What does the verb *postulate* mean?"   Answers will vary. The definition is to claim or assume the existence or truth of, especially as a basis for reasoning or arguing.

? "What does the noun *postulate* mean?"   Answers will vary. The definition is something taken as self-evident or assumed without proof as a basis for reasoning.

• Discuss the difference between *AB* and $\overline{AB}$.

• If you are confident that students can measure accurately, you may want to omit Example 1 and Questions 1–4.

Constructing and Comparing Congruent Segments

A **construction** is a geometric drawing that uses a limited set of tools, usually a *compass* and *straightedge*.

CONSTRUCTION	Copying a Segment

Use a compass and straightedge to construct a line segment that has the same length as $\overline{AB}$.

SOLUTION

Step 1

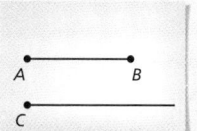

Draw a segment Use a straightedge to draw a segment longer than $\overline{AB}$. Label point C on the new segment.

Step 2

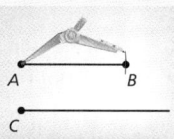

Measure length Set your compass at the length of $\overline{AB}$.

Step 3

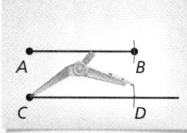

Copy length Place the compass at C. Mark point D on the new segment. So, $\overline{CD}$ has the same length as $\overline{AB}$.

Core Concept

READING

In the diagram, the red tick marks indicate $\overline{AB} \cong \overline{CD}$. When there is more than one pair of congruent segments, use multiple tick marks.

Congruent Segments

Line segments that have the same length are called **congruent segments**. You can say "the length of $\overline{AB}$ is equal to the length of $\overline{CD}$," or you can say "$\overline{AB}$ is *congruent to* $\overline{CD}$." The symbol $\cong$ means "is congruent to."

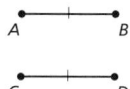
A B

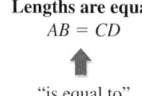
C D

Lengths are equal.
$AB = CD$
⬆
"is equal to"

Segments are congruent.
$\overline{AB} \cong \overline{CD}$
⬆
"is congruent to"

EXAMPLE 2	Comparing Segments for Congruence

Plot $J(-3, 4)$, $K(2, 4)$, $L(1, 3)$, and $M(1, -2)$ in a coordinate plane. Then determine whether $\overline{JK}$ and $\overline{LM}$ are congruent.

SOLUTION

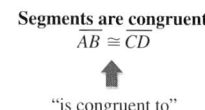

Plot the points, as shown. To find the length of a horizontal segment, find the absolute value of the difference of the x-coordinates of the endpoints.

$JK = |2 - (-3)| = 5$ Ruler Postulate

To find the length of a vertical segment, find the absolute value of the difference of the y-coordinates of the endpoints.

$LM = |-2 - 3| = 5$ Ruler Postulate

▶ $\overline{JK}$ and $\overline{LM}$ have the same length. So, $\overline{JK} \cong \overline{LM}$.

Monitoring Progress Help in English and Spanish at BigIdeasMath.com

5. Plot $A(-2, 4)$, $B(3, 4)$, $C(0, 2)$, and $D(0, -2)$ in a coordinate plane. Then determine whether $\overline{AB}$ and $\overline{CD}$ are congruent.

Extra Example 2

Plot the points $P(-4, 3)$, $Q(3, 3)$, $R(-1, 4)$, and $S(-1, -2)$ in a coordinate plane. Then determine whether $\overline{PQ}$ and $\overline{RS}$ are congruent.

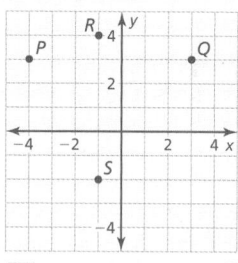

$\overline{PQ}$ is not congruent to $\overline{RS}$.

MONITORING PROGRESS ANSWER

5.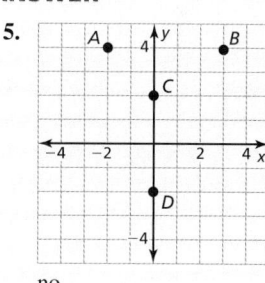

no

Laurie's Notes   Teacher Actions

- Have students draw a segment and construct a copy of the segment.
- Copy and discuss the *Core Concept*. Students should be familiar with congruent segments (and angles) from middle school.
- In Example 2, finding the length of a horizontal segment involves using the x-coordinates. Finding the length of a vertical segment involves using the y-coordinates.
- **?** "How can you find the measure of a diagonal segment?" Answers will vary, but some may allude to the Pythagorean Theorem.

Extra Example 3

a. Find *XZ*.

41

b. Find *CD*.

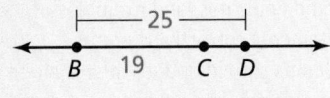

6

MONITORING PROGRESS ANSWERS

6. 73

7. no; Point *Y* is not between points *W* and *Z*.

8. 107

Using the Segment Addition Postulate

When three points are collinear, you can say that one point is **between** the other two.

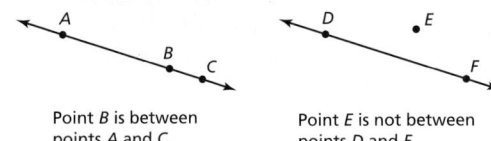

Point *B* is between points *A* and *C*.

Point *E* is not between points *D* and *F*.

Postulate

Postulate 1.2   Segment Addition Postulate

If *B* is between *A* and *C*, then $AB + BC = AC$.

If $AB + BC = AC$, then *B* is between *A* and *C*.

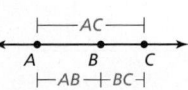

EXAMPLE 3   Using the Segment Addition Postulate

a. Find *DF*.

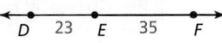

b. Find *GH*.

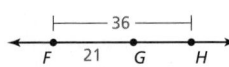

SOLUTION

a. Use the Segment Addition Postulate to write an equation. Then solve the equation to find *DF*.

$DF = DE + EF$	Segment Addition Postulate
$DF = 23 + 35$	Substitute 23 for *DE* and 35 for *EF*.
$DF = 58$	Add.

b. Use the Segment Addition Postulate to write an equation. Then solve the equation to find *GH*.

$FH = FG + GH$	Segment Addition Postulate
$36 = 21 + GH$	Substitute 36 for *FH* and 21 for *FG*.
$15 = GH$	Subtract 21 from each side.

Monitoring Progress   Help in English and Spanish at *BigIdeasMath.com*

Use the diagram at the right.

6. Use the Segment Addition Postulate to find *XZ*.

7. In the diagram, $WY = 30$. Can you use the Segment Addition Postulate to find the distance between points *W* and *Z*? Explain your reasoning.

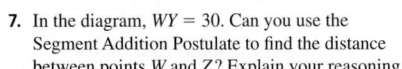

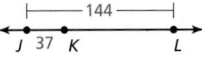

8. Use the diagram at the left to find *KL*.

Laurie's Notes   Teacher Actions

- Copy and discuss the Segment Addition Postulate. Draw a sketch to show what it would mean if point *B* is not between point *A* and point *C*.
- **MP5 Use Appropriate Tools Strategically:** Demonstrate examples, such as Example 3, using dynamic geometry software.

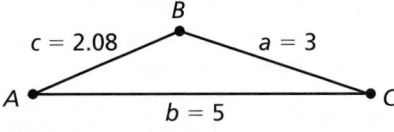

EXAMPLE 4 Using the Segment Addition Postulate

The cities shown on the map lie approximately in a straight line. Find the distance from Tulsa, Oklahoma, to St. Louis, Missouri.

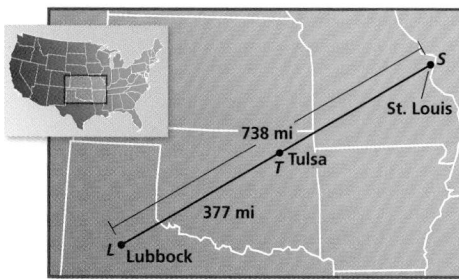

SOLUTION

1. **Understand the Problem** You are given the distance from Lubbock to St. Louis and the distance from Lubbock to Tulsa. You need to find the distance from Tulsa to St. Louis.

2. **Make a Plan** Use the Segment Addition Postulate to find the distance from Tulsa to St. Louis.

3. **Solve the Problem** Use the Segment Addition Postulate to write an equation. Then solve the equation to find TS.

$LS = LT + TS$	Segment Addition Postulate
$738 = 377 + TS$	Substitute 738 for LS and 377 for LT.
$361 = TS$	Subtract 377 from each side.

   ▶ So, the distance from Tulsa to St. Louis is about 361 miles.

4. **Look Back** Does the answer make sense in the context of the problem? The distance from Lubbock to St. Louis is 738 miles. By the Segment Addition Postulate, the distance from Lubbock to Tulsa plus the distance from Tulsa to St. Louis should equal 738 miles.

   $$377 + 361 = 738 \ \checkmark$$

Monitoring Progress 🔊 Help in English and Spanish at *BigIdeasMath.com*

9. The cities shown on the map lie approximately in a straight line. Find the distance from Albuquerque, New Mexico, to Provo, Utah.

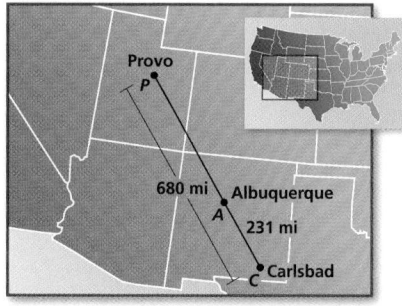

Extra Example 4
The cities shown on the map lie approximately in a straight line. Find the distance from Sacramento, California, to San Bernardino, California.

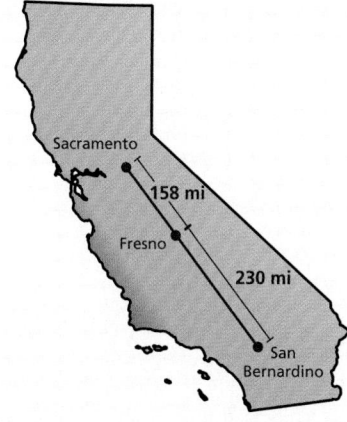

388 miles

MONITORING PROGRESS ANSWER
9. 449 mi

Laurie's Notes | **Teacher Actions**

• Example 4 suggests that the three cities lie approximately in a straight line. This does not mean that vehicular travel would be a straight line, but weather fronts could be.

• Use actual maps or electronic maps to demonstrate the Segment Addition Postulate.

Closure

• **Writing Prompt:**
A postulate is … *Sample answer:* a rule that is accepted without proof.
An example of a postulate is … *Sample answer:* the Segment Addition Postulate. If B is between A and C, then $AB + BC = AC$.

Assignment Guide and Homework Check

ASSIGNMENT

Basic: 1, 2, 3–25 odd, 32, 34, 38–45

Average: 1, 2–28 even, 32, 34, 38–45

Advanced: 1, 2, 6, 8, 12, 14, 20–28 even, 29–45

HOMEWORK CHECK

Basic: 7, 9, 13, 21, 32

Average: 12, 20, 26, 28, 32

Advanced: 14, 22, 32, 33, 37

ANSWERS

1. $\overline{XY}$ represents the segment XY, while XY represents the distance between points X and Y (the length of $\overline{XY}$).

2. Find $BC - AC$.; 4; 10

3. 3.5 cm

4. 6 cm

5. 4.5 cm

6. 7 cm

7.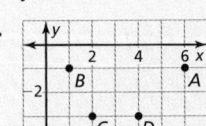

8. See Additional Answers.

9.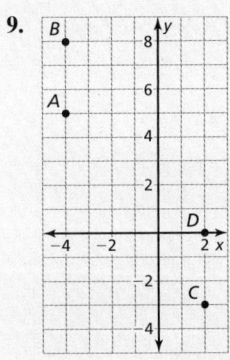
yes

10.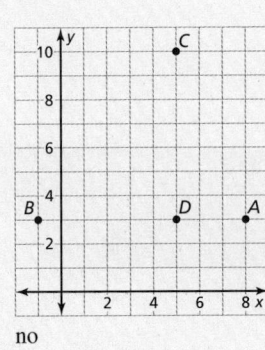
no

11.
no

Vocabulary and Core Concept Check

1. **WRITING** Explain how $\overline{XY}$ and XY are different.

2. **DIFFERENT WORDS, SAME QUESTION** Which is different? Find "both" answers.

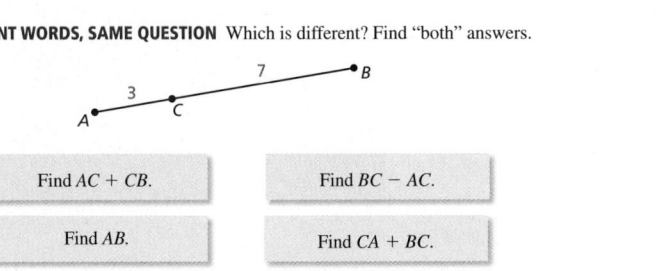

Find $AC + CB$.   Find $BC - AC$.

Find AB.   Find $CA + BC$.

Monitoring Progress and Modeling with Mathematics

In Exercises 3–6, use a ruler to measure the length of the segment to the nearest tenth of a centimeter. *(See Example 1.)*

3. ●————————●

4. ●——————————————●

5. ●——————————●

6. ●————————————————————●

CONSTRUCTION In Exercises 7 and 8, use a compass and straightedge to construct a copy of the segment.

7. Copy the segment in Exercise 3.

8. Copy the segment in Exercise 4.

In Exercises 9–14, plot the points in a coordinate plane. Then determine whether $\overline{AB}$ and $\overline{CD}$ are congruent. *(See Example 2.)*

9. $A(-4, 5), B(-4, 8), C(2, -3), D(2, 0)$

10. $A(6, -1), B(1, -1), C(2, -3), D(4, -3)$

11. $A(8, 3), B(-1, 3), C(5, 10), D(5, 3)$

12. $A(6, -8), B(6, 1), C(7, -2), D(-2, -2)$

13. $A(-5, 6), B(-5, -1), C(-4, 3), D(3, 3)$

14. $A(10, -4), B(3, -4), C(-1, 2), D(-1, 5)$

In Exercises 15–22, find *FH*. *(See Example 3.)*

15.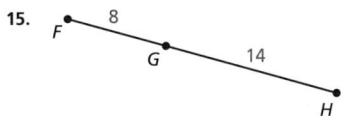

16.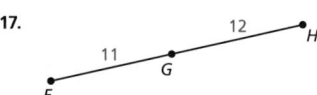

17.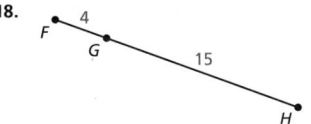

18.

19.
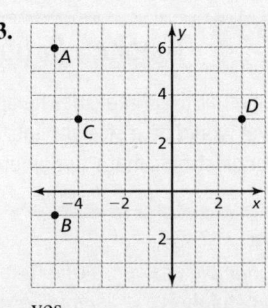

12.
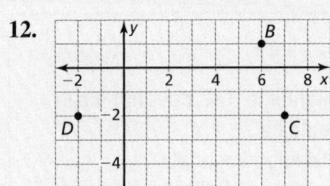
yes

13.
yes

14–19. See Additional Answers.

20.

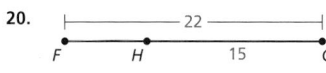

21.

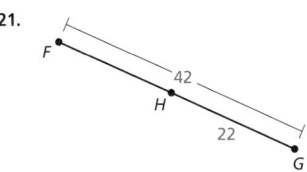

22.

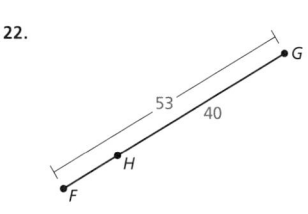

ERROR ANALYSIS In Exercises 23 and 24, describe and correct the error in finding the length of $\overline{AB}$.

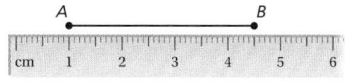

23.

 $AB = 1 - 4.5 = -3.5$

24.

$AB = |1 + 4.5| = 5.5$

25. ATTENDING TO PRECISION The diagram shows an insect called a walking stick. Use the ruler to estimate the length of the abdomen and the length of the thorax to the nearest $\frac{1}{4}$ inch. How much longer is the walking stick's abdomen than its thorax? How many times longer is its abdomen than its thorax?

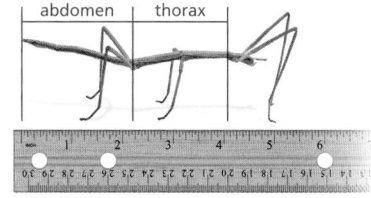

26. MODELING WITH MATHEMATICS In 2003, a remote-controlled model airplane became the first ever to fly nonstop across the Atlantic Ocean. The map shows the airplane's position at three different points during its flight. Point *A* represents Cape Spear, Newfoundland, point *B* represents the approximate position after 1 day, and point *C* represents Mannin Bay, Ireland. The airplane left from Cape Spear and landed in Mannin Bay. *(See Example 4.)*

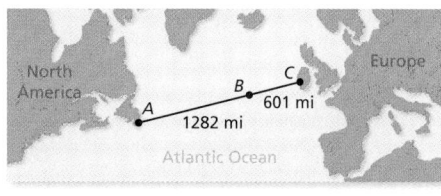

a. Find the total distance the model airplane flew.

b. The model airplane's flight lasted nearly 38 hours. Estimate the airplane's average speed in miles per hour.

27. USING STRUCTURE Determine whether the statements are true or false. Explain your reasoning.

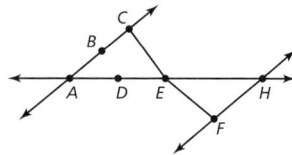

a. *B* is between *A* and *C*.

b. *C* is between *B* and *E*.

c. *D* is between *A* and *H*.

d. *E* is between *C* and *F*.

28. MATHEMATICAL CONNECTIONS Write an expression for the length of the segment.

a. $\overline{AC}$

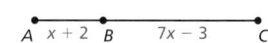

b. $\overline{QR}$

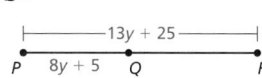

ANSWERS

20. 7

21. 20

22. 13

23. The absolute value should have been taken; $AB = |1 - 4.5| = 3.5$

24. The difference should have been taken; $AB = |1 - 4.5| = 3.5$

25. $2\frac{1}{4}$ in., $1\frac{3}{4}$ in.; $\frac{1}{2}$ in.; $1\frac{2}{7}$

26. a. 1883 mi

b. about 50 mi/h

27. a. true; *B* is on $\overleftrightarrow{AC}$ between *A* and *C*.

b. false; *B*, *C*, and *E* are not collinear.

c. true; *D* is on $\overleftrightarrow{AH}$ between *A* and *H*.

d. false; *C*, *E*, and *F* are not collinear.

28. a. $8x - 1$

b. $5y + 20$

ANSWERS

29. **a.** $3x + 6 = 21$; $x = 5$; $RS = 20$;
   $ST = 1$; $RT = 21$

   b. $7x - 24 = 60$; $x = 12$; $RS = 20$;
   $ST = 40$; $RT = 60$

   c. $2x + 3 = x + 10$; $x = 7$; $RS = 6$;
   $ST = 11$; $RT = 17$

   d. $4x + 10 = 8x - 14$; $x = 6$;
   $RS = 15$; $ST = 19$; $RT = 34$

30. See Additional Answers.

31. **a.** 64 ft

   b. about 0.24 min

   c. You might walk slower if other people are in the hall.

32. cousin; If you do not line up an object at zero, then take the absolute value of the difference of the measurements at both ends of the object.

33. 296.5 mi; If the round-trip distance is 647 miles, then the one-way distance is 323.5 miles. $323.5 - 27 = 296.5$

34. The number of wins plus the number of losses equals the number of games played each year.

35. $|a - c| = |e - f|$; b and d are not used because when the x-values are the same, you subtract the y-values to find the length of the segment, and vice versa.

36–45. See Additional Answers.

Mini-Assessment

Use $\overline{ST}$.

1. Measure the length of $\overline{ST}$ to the nearest $\frac{1}{8}$ inch. $1\frac{1}{8}$ inches

2. Construct a segment congruent to $\overline{ST}$ using a compass and straightedge. Check students' work.

3. Plot $A(-2, -3)$, $B(5, -3)$, $C(6, -1)$, and $D(1, -1)$ in a coordinate plane. Then determine whether $\overline{AB}$ and $\overline{CD}$ are congruent. $\overline{AB}$ is not congruent to $\overline{CD}$.

4. Find FG.

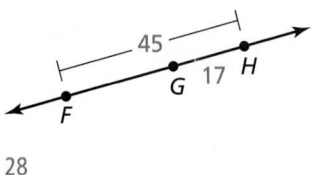

28

---

29. **MATHEMATICAL CONNECTIONS** Point S is between points R and T on $\overline{RT}$. Use the information to write an equation in terms of x. Then solve the equation and find RS, ST, and RT.

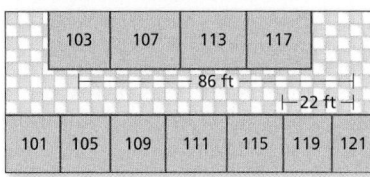

   a. $RS = 2x + 10$ **b.** $RS = 3x - 16$
   $ST = x - 4$ $ST = 4x - 8$
   $RT = 21$ $RT = 60$

   c. $RS = 2x - 8$ **d.** $RS = 4x - 9$
   $ST = 11$ $ST = 19$
   $RT = x + 10$ $RT = 8x - 14$

30. **THOUGHT PROVOKING** Is it possible to design a table where no two legs have the same length? Assume that the endpoints of the legs must all lie in the same plane. Include a diagram as part of your answer.

31. **MODELING WITH MATHEMATICS** You have to walk from Room 103 to Room 117.

103	107	113	117

86 ft
22 ft

101	105	109	111	115	119	121

   a. How many feet do you travel from Room 103 to Room 117?

   b. You can walk 4.4 feet per second. How many minutes will it take you to get to Room 117?

   c. Why might it take you longer than the time in part (b)?

32. **MAKING AN ARGUMENT** Your friend and your cousin discuss measuring with a ruler. Your friend says that you must always line up objects at the zero on a ruler. Your cousin says it does not matter. Decide who is correct and explain your reasoning.

Maintaining Mathematical Proficiency
Reviewing what you learned in previous grades and lessons

Simplify. *(Skills Review Handbook)*

38. $\dfrac{-4 + 6}{2}$ 39. $\sqrt{20 + 5}$ 40. $\sqrt{25 + 9}$ 41. $\dfrac{7 + 6}{2}$

Solve the equation. *(Skills Review Handbook)*

42. $5x + 7 = 9x - 17$ 43. $\dfrac{3 + y}{2} = 6$ 44. $\dfrac{-5 + x}{2} = -9$ 45. $-6x - 13 = -x - 23$

18   **Chapter 1**   Basics of Geometry

---

33. **REASONING** You travel from City X to City Y. You know that the round-trip distance is 647 miles. City Z, a city you pass on the way, is 27 miles from City X. Find the distance from City Z to City Y. Justify your answer.

34. **HOW DO YOU SEE IT?** The bar graph shows the win-loss record for a lacrosse team over a period of three years. Explain how you can apply the Ruler Postulate (Post. 1.1) and the Segment Addition Postulate (Post. 1.2) when interpreting a stacked bar graph like the one shown.

35. **ABSTRACT REASONING** The points (a, b) and (c, b) form a segment, and the points (d, e) and (d, f) form a segment. Create an equation assuming the segments are congruent. Are there any letters not used in the equation? Explain.

36. **MATHEMATICAL CONNECTIONS** In the diagram, $\overline{AB} \cong \overline{BC}$, $\overline{AC} \cong \overline{CD}$, and $AD = 12$. Find the lengths of all segments in the diagram. Suppose you choose one of the segments at random. What is the probability that the measure of the segment is greater than 3? Explain your reasoning.

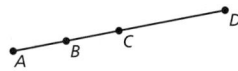

37. **CRITICAL THINKING** Is it possible to use the Segment Addition Postulate (Post. 1.2) to show $FB > CB$ or that $AC > DB$? Explain your reasoning.

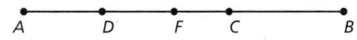

If students need help...	If students got it...
Resources by Chapter • Practice A and Practice B • Puzzle Time	Resources by Chapter • Enrichment and Extension • Cumulative Review
Student Journal • Practice	Start the *next* Section
Differentiating the Lesson Skills Review Handbook	

18   **Chapter 1**

Overview of Section 1.3

Dynamic Teaching Tools
Dynamic Assessment & Progress Monitoring Tool
Lesson Planning Tool
Interactive Whiteboard Lesson Library
Dynamic Classroom with Dynamic Investigations

Introduction

- This lesson presents two formulas that are useful in the study of geometry, the Midpoint Formula and the Distance Formula. When figures are drawn in the coordinate plane, it will be possible to determine midpoints of sides and lengths of segments, both helpful when doing a coordinate proof.
- The two explorations provide an opportunity for students to make sense of, and to derive, the formulas. Having made sense of the formulas, students are then able to apply them. If students are secure with their computations and symbolic manipulations, then time can be spent on higher cognitive-demand problems.

Common Misconceptions

- Students recall that in working with the slope formula, the order in which the subtraction is performed matters, meaning whichever ordered pair you begin with in the numerator, you must do the same in the denominator.
- With the Distance Formula, it does not matter because the quantity is then squared. The result is the same whether we do $\sqrt{(x_2 - x_1)^2 + (y_2 - y_1)^2}$ or $\sqrt{(x_2 - x_1)^2 + (y_1 - y_2)^2}$. I am not advocating for students to change the order, but they should be able to reason quantitatively about the formula.

Formative Assessment Tips

- **I Used to Think ... But Now I Know:** This technique asks students to consider how their thinking about a concept or skill has changed from the beginning of instruction to the end of instruction. This can be done orally or in writing. It is important for students to be able to self-assess and reflect on their own learning.
- Use this technique at the end of the formal lesson. If time permits, have students discuss with one another or the whole class how their understanding developed and/or changed. They may be able to identify the example or class discussion that helped to promote the learning.

Another Way

- Each of the formulas in this lesson can be investigated using dynamic geometry software. Instead of doing the explorations with paper and straightedge, have students use the software.

Pacing Suggestion

- If students derive both formulas during the explorations, check for understanding with the *Monitoring Progress* Questions 1–8, and have them do Example 4 and spend time with the applications in the exercises.

HSG-CO.D.12 Make formal geometric constructions with a variety of tools and methods ... paper folding, ...

HSG-GPE.B.7 Use coordinates to compute perimeters of polygons and areas of triangles and rectangles, e.g., using the distance formula.

Laurie's Notes

Exploration

Motivate

? "What are some common distances that you know?" Answers may include:
conversion facts (i.e., 1 mile = 5280 feet)
exact distances (i.e., pitcher's mound to home plate is 60 feet, 6 inches)
approximate distances (i.e., circumference of Earth is about 24,900 miles)
local distances (i.e., home to school is 2.5 miles)

- Discuss what it means to find a distance: for instance, not all of the examples above are segments.

Exploration 1

- The goal of this exploration is for students to discover how to determine the midpoint of a segment when the coordinates of the endpoints are known.
- Solicit answers in part (b) as to how students bisected the segment. Some students may fold their paper. Others may use a slope approach and say, "Starting at point *B* go right 4, up 3, and repeat again to get to point *A*." Listen for valid approaches.
- **Turn and Talk:** Ask partner A to explain, "How are the coordinates of point *M* related to the coordinates of points *A* and *B*?" Ask a partner B to state the relationship to the class.

Exploration 2

? What is the relationship between point *C* and points *A* and *B*?" Segment *CA* is vertical and segment *BC* is horizontal. The two segments form a right angle.

COMMON ERROR If students use a scale of 2 units as shown in the diagram, they may incorrectly say that the length of *AC* is 12 instead of 6. This is especially true if students count lattice points (points at the intersections of grid lines) on the graph paper between points *A* and *C*.

? Extension: "What other point(s) could be used to form a right triangle with segment *BA* as the hypotenuse?" (−5, 4)

Communicate Your Answer

- **Turn and Talk:** Ask partner B to explain how to find the midpoint and length of a line segment in the coordinate plane. Ask a partner A to summarize for the class.

Connecting to Next Step

- If you are confident that students are able to use the Midpoint and Distance Formulas, practice a few *Monitoring Progress* questions in the formal lesson and spend time with applications.

1.3 Using Midpoint and Distance Formulas

Essential Question How can you find the midpoint and length of a line segment in a coordinate plane?

EXPLORATION 1 Finding the Midpoint of a Line Segment

Work with a partner. Use centimeter graph paper.

a. Graph $\overline{AB}$, where the points A and B are as shown.

b. Explain how to *bisect* $\overline{AB}$, that is, to divide $\overline{AB}$ into two congruent line segments. Then bisect $\overline{AB}$ and use the result to find the *midpoint M* of $\overline{AB}$.

c. What are the coordinates of the midpoint M?

d. Compare the x-coordinates of A, B, and M. Compare the y-coordinates of A, B, and M. How are the coordinates of the midpoint M related to the coordinates of A and B?

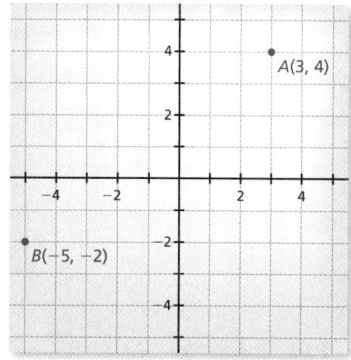

MAKING SENSE OF PROBLEMS

To be proficient in math, you need to check your answers and continually ask yourself, "Does this make sense?"

EXPLORATION 2 Finding the Length of a Line Segment

Work with a partner. Use centimeter graph paper.

a. Add point C to your graph as shown.

b. Use the Pythagorean Theorem to find the length of $\overline{AB}$.

c. Use a centimeter ruler to verify the length you found in part (b).

d. Use the Pythagorean Theorem and point M from Exploration 1 to find the lengths of $\overline{AM}$ and $\overline{MB}$. What can you conclude?

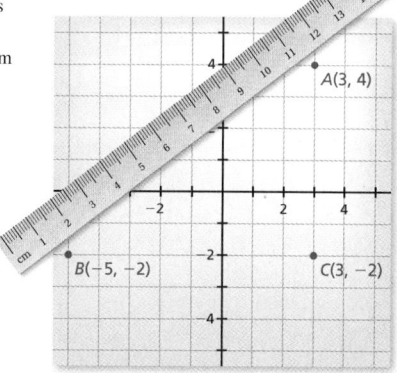

Communicate Your Answer

3. How can you find the midpoint and length of a line segment in a coordinate plane?

4. Find the coordinates of the midpoint M and the length of the line segment whose endpoints are given.

   a. $D(-10, -4)$, $E(14, 6)$ b. $F(-4, 8)$, $G(9, 0)$

3. *Sample answer:* Find the averages of the x-coordinates and the y-coordinates; Use the Pythagorean Theorem.

4. a. $M(2,1)$, $DE = 26$
   b. $M\left(\frac{5}{2}, 4\right)$, $FG = \sqrt{233}$

Dynamic Teaching Tools

Dynamic Assessment & Progress Monitoring Tool

Lesson Planning Tool

Interactive Whiteboard Lesson Library

Dynamic Classroom with Dynamic Investigations

ANSWERS

1. a.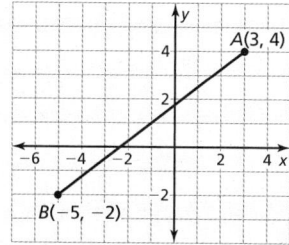

   b. *Sample answer:* Fold the graph paper diagonally so that B is on top of A and both halves of $\overline{AB}$ overlap. Unfold the paper and label point M where the crease intersects $\overline{AB}$.

   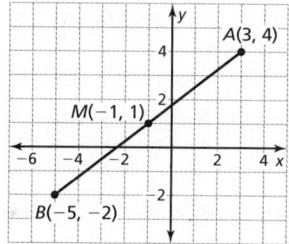

   c. $(-1, 1)$

   d. The x-coordinate of M is halfway between the x-coordinates of B and A. The y-coordinate of M is halfway between the y-coordinates of B and A. The x-coordinate of M equals the average of the x-coordinates of B and A. The y-coordinate of M equals the average of the y-coordinates of B and A.

2. a.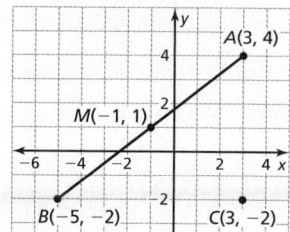

   b. 10 cm

   c. 10 cm

   d. $AM = MB = 5$; *Sample answer:* The Pythagorean Theorem can be used to find the length of any line segment on the coordinate plane.

Extra Example 1

In the figure, $PM = 1.8$ mm. Identify the segment bisector of $\overline{PQ}$. Then find PQ.

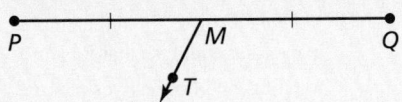

$\overrightarrow{MT}$; 3.6 millimeters

MONITORING PROGRESS ANSWERS

1. $\overrightarrow{MN}$; $3\frac{3}{4}$
2. M; $4\frac{4}{7}$

1.3 Lesson

READING

The word *bisect* means "to cut into two equal parts."

What You Will Learn

▶ Find segment lengths using midpoints and segment bisectors.
▶ Use the Midpoint Formula.
▶ Use the Distance Formula.

Midpoints and Segment Bisectors

Core Concept

Midpoints and Segment Bisectors

The **midpoint** of a segment is the point that divides the segment into two congruent segments.

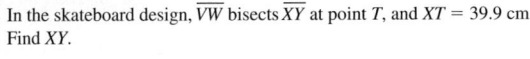

M is the midpoint of $\overline{AB}$.
So, $\overline{AM} \cong \overline{MB}$ and $AM = MB$.

A **segment bisector** is a point, ray, line, line segment, or plane that intersects the segment at its midpoint. A midpoint or a segment bisector *bisects* a segment.

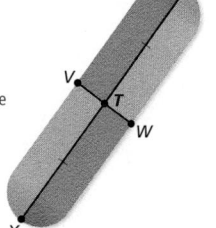

$\overleftrightarrow{CD}$ is a segment bisector of $\overline{AB}$.
So, $\overline{AM} \cong \overline{MB}$ and $AM = MB$.

EXAMPLE 1 Finding Segment Lengths

In the skateboard design, $\overline{VW}$ bisects $\overline{XY}$ at point T, and $XT = 39.9$ cm. Find XY.

SOLUTION

Point T is the midpoint of $\overline{XY}$. So, $XT = TY = 39.9$ cm.

$$XY = XT + TY \quad \text{Segment Addition Postulate (Postulate 1.2)}$$
$$= 39.9 + 39.9 \quad \text{Substitute.}$$
$$= 79.8 \quad \text{Add.}$$

▶ So, the length of $\overline{XY}$ is 79.8 centimeters.

Monitoring Progress 🔊 Help in English and Spanish at *BigIdeasMath.com*

Identify the segment bisector of $\overline{PQ}$. Then find PQ.

1.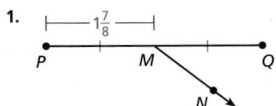

2.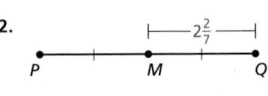

Laurie's Notes   Teacher Actions

? "What do *midpoints* and *segment bisectors* have in common and how are they different?" They both involve the midpoint of a segment. The segment bisector is the geometric figure that passes through the midpoint.

? "Can a segment have more than one midpoint?" no "Can a segment have more than one bisector?" yes "Can a line have more than one midpoint?" A line does not have any midpoint because it continues infinitely in both directions.

- **Monitoring Progress:** Students should be secure with fraction addition!

 **EXAMPLE 2** **Using Algebra with Segment Lengths**

Point M is the midpoint of $\overline{VW}$. Find the length of $\overline{VM}$.

$$\underset{V}{\bullet} \overset{4x-1}{\rule{0pt}{0pt}} \underset{M}{|} \overset{3x+3}{\rule{0pt}{0pt}} \underset{W}{\bullet}$$

SOLUTION

Step 1 Write and solve an equation. Use the fact that $VM = MW$.

$VM = MW$	Write the equation.
$4x - 1 = 3x + 3$	Substitute.
$x - 1 = 3$	Subtract $3x$ from each side.
$x = 4$	Add 1 to each side.

Step 2 Evaluate the expression for VM when $x = 4$.

$$VM = 4x - 1 = 4(4) - 1 = 15$$

▶ So, the length of $\overline{VM}$ is 15.

Check

Because $VM = MW$, the length of $\overline{MW}$ should be 15.

$MW = 3x + 3 = 3(4) + 3 = 15$ ✓

Monitoring Progress Help in English and Spanish at *BigIdeasMath.com*

3. Identify the segment bisector of $\overline{PQ}$. Then find MQ.

4. Identify the segment bisector of $\overline{RS}$. Then find RS.

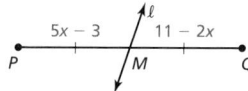

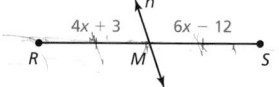

CONSTRUCTION **Bisecting a Segment**

Construct a segment bisector of $\overline{AB}$ by paper folding. Then find the midpoint M of $\overline{AB}$.

SOLUTION

Step 1	Step 2	Step 3
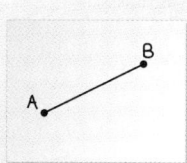		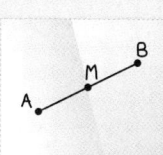
Draw the segment Draw $\overline{AB}$ on a piece of paper.	**Fold the paper** Fold the paper so that B is on top of A.	**Label the midpoint** Label point M. Compare AM, MB, and AB. $AM = MB = \frac{1}{2}AB$

Section 1.3   Using Midpoint and Distance Formulas   **21**

Extra Example 2
Point M is the midpoint of $\overline{AB}$. Find the length of $\overline{AB}$.

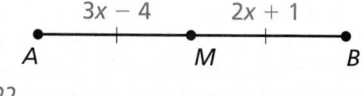

$$\underset{A}{\bullet} \overset{3x-4}{\rule{0pt}{0pt}} \underset{M}{|} \overset{2x+1}{\rule{0pt}{0pt}} \underset{B}{\bullet}$$

22

MONITORING PROGRESS ANSWERS
3. line ℓ; 7
4. line n; 66

Laurie's Notes   Teacher Actions

- Pose the problem and have students work with their partners to solve. Solving an equation with variables on both sides should be a secure skill for students.
- **MP2 Reason Abstractly and Quantitatively:** If students have paper-folded to find the midpoint in Exploration 1, change the context. You want to find the midpoint of something that cannot be folded, like the diagonal of a picture frame. You have a straightedge (not a ruler) and paper. Explain how to find the midpoint.

Extra Example 3

a. The endpoints of $\overline{AB}$ are $A(-8, 7)$ and $B(5, 1)$. Find the coordinates of the midpoint M. $(-1.5, 4)$

b. The midpoint of $\overline{PQ}$ is $M(2, -3)$. One endpoint is $P(4, 1)$. Find the coordinates of endpoint Q. $(0, -7)$

MONITORING PROGRESS ANSWERS

5. $(4, 5)$
6. $(-5, 4)$
7. $(3, 7)$
8. $(-6, -8)$

Using the Midpoint Formula

You can use the coordinates of the endpoints of a segment to find the coordinates of the midpoint.

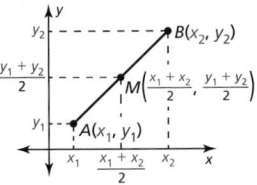

⟳ Core Concept

The Midpoint Formula

The coordinates of the midpoint of a segment are the averages of the x-coordinates and of the y-coordinates of the endpoints.

If $A(x_1, y_1)$ and $B(x_2, y_2)$ are points in a coordinate plane, then the midpoint M of $\overline{AB}$ has coordinates

$$\left(\frac{x_1 + x_2}{2}, \frac{y_1 + y_2}{2} \right).$$

EXAMPLE 3 Using the Midpoint Formula

a. The endpoints of $\overline{RS}$ are $R(1, -3)$ and $S(4, 2)$. Find the coordinates of the midpoint M.

b. The midpoint of $\overline{JK}$ is $M(2, 1)$. One endpoint is $J(1, 4)$. Find the coordinates of endpoint K.

SOLUTION

a. Use the Midpoint Formula.

$$M\left(\frac{1 + 4}{2}, \frac{-3 + 2}{2} \right) = M\left(\frac{5}{2}, -\frac{1}{2} \right)$$

▶ The coordinates of the midpoint M are $\left(\frac{5}{2}, -\frac{1}{2} \right)$.

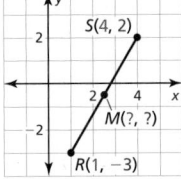

b. Let (x, y) be the coordinates of endpoint K. Use the Midpoint Formula.

Step 1 Find x.
$$\frac{1 + x}{2} = 2$$
$$1 + x = 4$$
$$x = 3$$

Step 2 Find y.
$$\frac{4 + y}{2} = 1$$
$$4 + y = 2$$
$$y = -2$$

▶ The coordinates of endpoint K are $(3, -2)$.

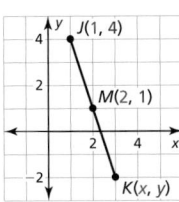

Monitoring Progress ◀ᴺ)) Help in English and Spanish at *BigIdeasMath.com*

5. The endpoints of $\overline{AB}$ are $A(1, 2)$ and $B(7, 8)$. Find the coordinates of the midpoint M.

6. The endpoints of $\overline{CD}$ are $C(-4, 3)$ and $D(-6, 5)$. Find the coordinates of the midpoint M.

7. The midpoint of $\overline{TU}$ is $M(2, 4)$. One endpoint is $T(1, 1)$. Find the coordinates of endpoint U.

8. The midpoint of $\overline{VW}$ is $M(-1, -2)$. One endpoint is $W(4, 4)$. Find the coordinates of endpoint V.

Laurie's Notes | Teacher Actions

• Write the *Core Concept*. Note the use of the word *average* in describing the coordinates of the midpoint.

COMMON ERROR Students may take the absolute value of coordinates that are negative. Finding distance involves absolute value but determining the midpoint does not.

• If students are secure with the Midpoint Formula, you may want to omit Example 3 and check for understanding with *Monitoring Progress* Questions 5 and 7, or 6 and 8.

Using the Distance Formula

You can use the Distance Formula to find the distance between two points in a coordinate plane.

 Core Concept

The Distance Formula

READING
The red mark at the corner of the triangle that makes a right angle indicates a right triangle.

If $A(x_1, y_1)$ and $B(x_2, y_2)$ are points in a coordinate plane, then the distance between A and B is

$$AB = \sqrt{(x_2 - x_1)^2 + (y_2 - y_1)^2}.$$

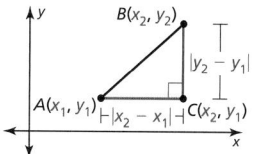

The Distance Formula is related to the *Pythagorean Theorem*, which you will see again when you work with right triangles.

Distance Formula

$$(AB)^2 = (x_2 - x_1)^2 + (y_2 - y_1)^2$$

Pythagorean Theorem

$$c^2 = a^2 + b^2$$

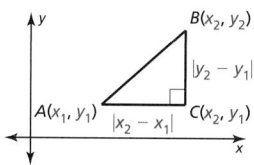
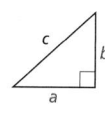

EXAMPLE 4 Using the Distance Formula

Your school is 4 miles east and 1 mile south of your apartment. A recycling center, where your class is going on a field trip, is 2 miles east and 3 miles north of your apartment. Estimate the distance between the recycling center and your school.

SOLUTION

You can model the situation using a coordinate plane with your apartment at the origin $(0, 0)$. The coordinates of the recycling center and the school are $R(2, 3)$ and $S(4, -1)$, respectively. Use the Distance Formula. Let $(x_1, y_1) = (2, 3)$ and $(x_2, y_2) = (4, -1)$.

READING
The symbol $\approx$ means "is approximately equal to."

$$RS = \sqrt{(x_2 - x_1)^2 + (y_2 - y_1)^2} \qquad \text{Distance Formula}$$
$$= \sqrt{(4 - 2)^2 + (-1 - 3)^2} \qquad \text{Substitute.}$$
$$= \sqrt{2^2 + (-4)^2} \qquad \text{Subtract.}$$
$$= \sqrt{4 + 16} \qquad \text{Evaluate powers.}$$
$$= \sqrt{20} \qquad \text{Add.}$$
$$\approx 4.5 \qquad \text{Use a calculator.}$$

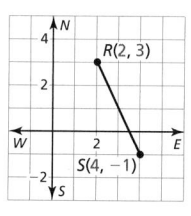

▶ So, the distance between the recycling center and your school is about 4.5 miles.

Monitoring Progress Help in English and Spanish at *BigIdeasMath.com*

9. In Example 4, a park is 3 miles east and 4 miles south of your apartment. Find the distance between the park and your school.

Extra Example 4
Use the information in Example 4. You bicycle 5 miles east and then 2 miles north from your apartment to a friend's house. Estimate the distance between your friend's house and your school. about 3.2 miles

MONITORING PROGRESS ANSWER
9. about 3.2 mi

Laurie's Notes   Teacher Actions

- **Big Idea:** From Exploration 2, students should see the connection between the Pythagorean Theorem and finding the length of a segment.
- ❓ **Turn and Talk:** Have partner A explain the connection between the Pythagorean Theorem and the Distance Formula. Choose a partner B to explain the connection to the class.
- **MP5 Use Appropriate Tools Strategically:** Choosing to locate your apartment at the origin is a convenient way to draw a model for Example 4.

Closure

- **I Used to Think … But Now I Know:** Take time for students to reflect on their current understanding of the Pythagorean Theorem and the Distance Formula.
- **Exit Ticket:** Given $A(-3, 5)$ and $B(4, -1)$, find the coordinates of the midpoint of $\overline{AB}$ and the length of segment AB. midpoint: $\left(\frac{1}{2}, 2\right)$; length: $\sqrt{85} \approx 9.2$

Assignment Guide and Homework Check

ASSIGNMENT

Basic: 1, 2, 3–33 odd, 40, 42, 46–53

Average: 1, 2, 4–12 even, 16–34 even, 37, 40, 42, 46–53

Advanced: 1, 2, 10, 14, 16, 22, 28–34 even, 35–53

HOMEWORK CHECK

Basic: 3, 9, 13, 19, 27

Average: 10, 20, 26, 37, 42

Advanced: 10, 16, 22, 30, 37, 45

ANSWERS

1. It bisects the segment.
2. Distance Formula
3. line k; 34
4. $\overrightarrow{MA}$; 18
5. M; 44
6. line s; 24
7. M; 40
8. line ℓ; 9
9. $\overrightarrow{MN}$; 32
10. line n; 6

Vocabulary and Core Concept Check

1. **VOCABULARY** If a point, ray, line, line segment, or plane intersects a segment at its midpoint, then what does it do to the segment?

2. **COMPLETE THE SENTENCE** To find the length of $\overline{AB}$, with endpoints $A(-7, 5)$ and $B(4, -6)$, you can use the _____.

Monitoring Progress and Modeling with Mathematics

In Exercises 3–6, identify the segment bisector of $\overline{RS}$. Then find *RS*. *(See Example 1.)*

3.
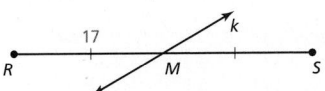

4.
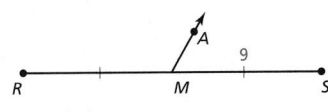

5.
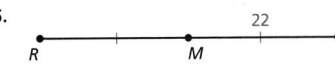

6.
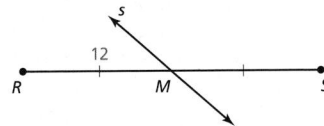

In Exercises 7 and 8, identify the segment bisector of $\overline{JK}$. Then find *JM*. *(See Example 2.)*

7.
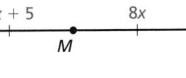

8.
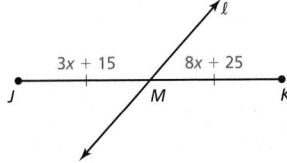

In Exercises 9 and 10, identify the segment bisector of $\overline{XY}$. Then find *XY*. *(See Example 2.)*

9.
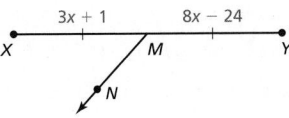

10.
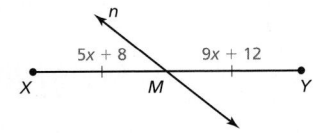

CONSTRUCTION In Exercises 11–14, copy the segment and construct a segment bisector by paper folding. Then label the midpoint *M*.

11.
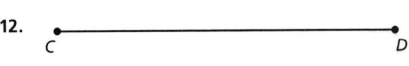

12.

13.
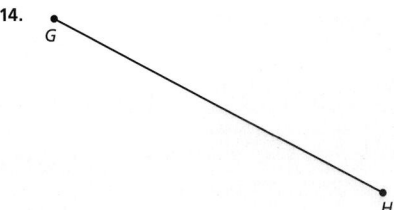

14.

11.
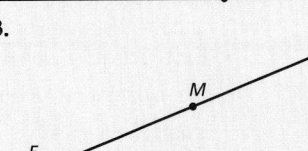

12.

13.

14.
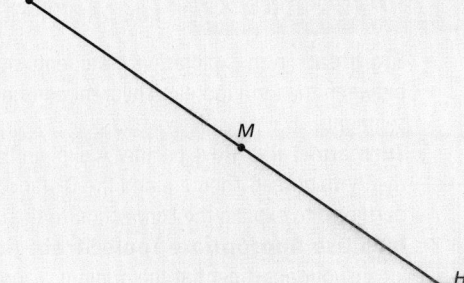

In Exercises 15–18, the endpoints of $\overline{CD}$ are given. Find the coordinates of the midpoint M. *(See Example 3.)*

15. $C(3, -5)$ and $D(7, 9)$

16. $C(-4, 7)$ and $D(0, -3)$

17. $C(-2, 0)$ and $D(4, 9)$

18. $C(-8, -6)$ and $D(-4, 10)$

In Exercises 19–22, the midpoint M and one endpoint of $\overline{GH}$ are given. Find the coordinates of the other endpoint. *(See Example 3.)*

19. $G(5, -6)$ and $M(4, 3)$ **20.** $H(-3, 7)$ and $M(-2, 5)$

21. $H(-2, 9)$ and $M(8, 0)$

22. $G(-4, 1)$ and $M\left(-\frac{13}{2}, -6\right)$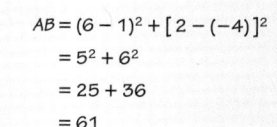

In Exercises 23–30, find the distance between the two points. *(See Example 4.)*

23. $A(13, 2)$ and $B(7, 10)$ **24.** $C(-6, 5)$ and $D(-3, 1)$

25. $E(3, 7)$ and $F(6, 5)$ **26.** $G(-5, 4)$ and $H(2, 6)$

27. $J(-8, 0)$ and $K(1, 4)$ **28.** $L(7, -1)$ and $M(-2, 4)$

29. $R(0, 1)$ and $S(6, 3.5)$ **30.** $T(13, 1.6)$ and $V(5.4, 3.7)$

ERROR ANALYSIS In Exercises 31 and 32, describe and correct the error in finding the distance between $A(6, 2)$ and $B(1, -4)$.

31.

✗
$$AB = (6 - 1)^2 + [2 - (-4)]^2$$
$$= 5^2 + 6^2$$
$$= 25 + 36$$
$$= 61$$

32.

✗
$$AB = \sqrt{(6 - 2)^2 + [1 - (-4)]^2}$$
$$= \sqrt{4^2 + 5^2}$$
$$= \sqrt{16 + 25}$$
$$= \sqrt{41}$$
$$\approx 6.4$$

COMPARING SEGMENTS In Exercises 33 and 34, the endpoints of two segments are given. Find each segment length. Tell whether the segments are congruent. If they are not congruent, state which segment length is greater.

33. $\overline{AB}$: $A(0, 2)$, $B(-3, 8)$ and $\overline{CD}$: $C(-2, 2)$, $D(0, -4)$

34. $\overline{EF}$: $E(1, 4)$, $F(5, 1)$ and $\overline{GH}$: $G(-3, 1)$, $H(1, 6)$

35. WRITING Your friend is having trouble understanding the Midpoint Formula.

  a. Explain how to find the midpoint when given the two endpoints in your own words.

  b. Explain how to find the other endpoint when given one endpoint and the midpoint in your own words.

36. PROBLEM SOLVING In baseball, the strike zone is the region a baseball needs to pass through for the umpire to declare it a strike when the batter does not swing. The top of the strike zone is a horizontal plane passing through the midpoint of the top of the batter's shoulders and the top of the uniform pants when the player is in a batting stance. Find the height of T. *(Note: All heights are in inches.)*

37. MODELING WITH MATHEMATICS The figure shows the position of three players during part of a water polo match. Player A throws the ball to Player B, who then throws the ball to Player C.

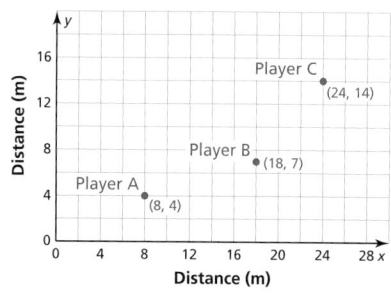

  a. How far did Player A throw the ball? Player B?

  b. How far would Player A have to throw the ball to throw it directly to Player C?

ANSWERS

15. $(5, 2)$

16. $(-2, 2)$

17. $\left(1, \frac{9}{2}\right)$

18. $(-6, 2)$

19. $(3, 12)$

20. $(-1, 3)$

21. $(18, -9)$

22. $(-9, -13)$

23. 10

24. 5

25. $\sqrt{13}$, or about 3.6

26. $\sqrt{53}$, or about 7.3

27. $\sqrt{97}$, or about 9.8

28. $\sqrt{106}$, or about 10.3

29. 6.5

30. $\sqrt{62.17}$, or about 7.9

31. The square root should have been taken. $\sqrt{61} \approx 7.8$

32. The difference of the x-values and the difference of the y-values should be used.
$$AB = \sqrt{(6 - 1)^2 + [2 - (-4)]^2}$$
$$= \sqrt{5^2 + 6^2}$$
$$= \sqrt{25 + 36}$$
$$= \sqrt{61}$$
$$\approx 7.8$$

33. about 6.7, about 6.3; no; $AB > CD$

34. 5, about 6.4; no; $GH > EF$

35. a. To find the x-coordinate of the midpoint, add the x-coordinates of the endpoints, and divide by 2. To find the y-coordinate of the midpoint, add the y-coordinates of the endpoints, and divide by 2.

  b. To find the x-coordinate of the other endpoint, multiply the x-coordinate of the midpoint by 2, and subtract the x-coordinate of the given endpoint. To find the y-coordinate of the other endpoint, multiply the y-coordinate of the midpoint by 2, and subtract the y-coordinate of the given endpoint.

36. 51 in.

37. a. about 10.4 m; about 9.2 m

  b. about 18.9 m

ANSWERS

38. about 3.5 mi

39. a. about 191 yd

  b. about 40 yd

  c. about 1.5 min; $MR \approx 40$ yd,
    total distance $\approx 40 + 40 + 40 + 70 + 40 = 230$ yd, $\frac{230}{150} \approx 1.5$ min

40. no; You have to take the absolute value of the difference.

41. $\left(\dfrac{a + b}{2}, c\right)$, $|b - a|$

42. a. $AM = MB$; M is the midpoint of $\overline{AB}$.

  b. $AC < MB$; C is between A and M, so $AC < AM$. Because $AM = MB$, $AC < MB$.

  c. impossible to tell; The problem does not provide any information about whether C or D is closer to M.

  d. $MB > DB$; D is between M and B, so $MB > DB$.

43. location D for lunch; The total distance traveled if you return home is $AM + AM + AB + AB$. The total distance traveled if you go to location D for lunch is $AB + DB + DB + AB$. Because $DB < AM$, the second option involves less traveling.

44–53. See Additional Answers.

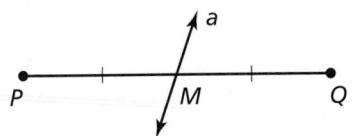
---

38. **MODELING WITH MATHEMATICS** Your school is 20 blocks east and 12 blocks south of your house. The mall is 10 blocks north and 7 blocks west of your house. You plan on going to the mall right after school. Find the distance between your school and the mall assuming there is a road directly connecting the school and the mall. One block is 0.1 mile.

39. **PROBLEM SOLVING** A path goes around a triangular park, as shown.

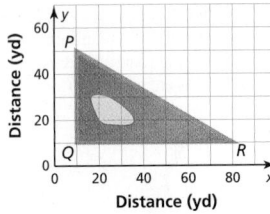

  a. Find the distance around the park to the nearest yard.

  b. A new path and a bridge are constructed from point Q to the midpoint M of $\overline{PR}$. Find QM to the nearest yard.

  c. A man jogs from P to Q to M to R to Q and back to P at an average speed of 150 yards per minute. About how many minutes does it take? Explain your reasoning.

40. **MAKING AN ARGUMENT** Your friend claims there is an easier way to find the length of a segment than the Distance Formula when the x-coordinates of the endpoints are equal. He claims all you have to do is subtract the y-coordinates. Do you agree with his statement? Explain your reasoning.

41. **MATHEMATICAL CONNECTIONS** Two points are located at (a, c) and (b, c). Find the midpoint and the distance between the two points.

42. **HOW DO YOU SEE IT?** $\overline{AB}$ contains midpoint M and points C and D, as shown. Compare the lengths. If you cannot draw a conclusion, write *impossible to tell*. Explain your reasoning.

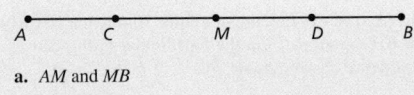

  a. AM and MB

  b. AC and MB

  c. MC and MD

  d. MB and DB

43. **ABSTRACT REASONING** Use the diagram in Exercise 42. The points on $\overline{AB}$ represent locations you pass on your commute to work. You travel from your home at location A to location M before realizing that you left your lunch at home. You could turn around to get your lunch and then continue to work at location B. Or you could go to work and go to location D for lunch today. You want to choose the option that involves the least distance you must travel. Which option should you choose? Explain your reasoning.

44. **THOUGHT PROVOKING** Describe three ways to divide a rectangle into two congruent regions. Do the regions have to be triangles? Use a diagram to support your answer.

45. **ANALYZING RELATIONSHIPS** The length of $\overline{XY}$ is 24 centimeters. The midpoint of $\overline{XY}$ is M, and C is on $\overline{XM}$ so that XC is $\frac{2}{3}$ of XM. Point D is on $\overline{MY}$ so that MD is $\frac{3}{4}$ of MY. What is the length of $\overline{CD}$?

Maintaining Mathematical Proficiency
Reviewing what you learned in previous grades and lessons

Find the perimeter and area of the figure. *(Skills Review Handbook)*

46. 5 cm (square)

47. 10 ft, 3 ft

48. 3 m, 5 m, 4 m (triangle)

49. 13 yd, 12 yd, 5 yd + 5 yd (triangle)

Solve the inequality. Graph the solution. *(Skills Review Handbook)*

50. $a + 18 < 7$

51. $y - 5 \geq 8$

52. $-3x > 24$

53. $\frac{z}{4} \leq 12$

Core Vocabulary

undefined terms, *p. 4*
point, *p. 4*
line, *p. 4*
plane, *p. 4*
collinear points, *p. 4*
coplanar points, *p. 4*
defined terms, *p. 5*

line segment, or segment, *p. 5*
endpoints, *p. 5*
ray, *p. 5*
opposite rays, *p. 5*
intersection, *p. 6*
postulate, *p. 12*
axiom, *p. 12*

coordinate, *p. 12*
distance, *p. 12*
construction, *p. 13*
congruent segments, *p. 13*
between, *p. 14*
midpoint, *p. 20*
segment bisector, *p. 20*

Core Concepts

Section 1.1

Undefined Terms: Point, Line, and Plane, *p. 4*
Defined Terms: Segment and Ray, *p. 5*

Intersections of Lines and Planes, *p. 6*

Section 1.2

Postulate 1.1 Ruler Postulate, *p. 12*
Congruent Segments, *p. 13*

Postulate 1.2 Segment Addition Postulate, *p. 14*

Section 1.3

Midpoints and Segment Bisectors, *p. 20*
The Midpoint Formula, *p. 22*

The Distance Formula, *p. 23*

Mathematical Practices

1. Sketch an example of the situation described in Exercise 49 on page 10 in a coordinate plane. Label your figure.

2. Explain how you arrived at your answer for Exercise 35 on page 18.

3. What assumptions did you make when solving Exercise 43 on page 26?

- - - - - - - - - - Study Skills - - - - - - - - - -

Keeping Your Mind Focused

- Keep a notebook just for vocabulary, formulas, and core concepts.
- Review this notebook before completing homework and before tests.

27

ANSWERS

1. *Sample answer:*

2. To find the length of a segment when the *y*-values of two endpoints are the same, find the absolute value of the difference of the *x*-values. When the *x*-values are the same, find the absolute value of the difference of the *y*-values. Because the segments are congruent, you set these two quantities equal to each other.

3. Assume that all of the locations lie on a straight line and that *D* is between *M* and *B*. So, you can assume that *DB* < *MB*. Based on the definition of midpoint, *AM* = *MB*, so *DB* < *AM*.

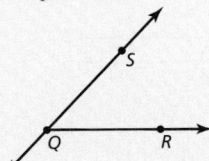
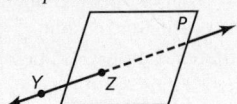
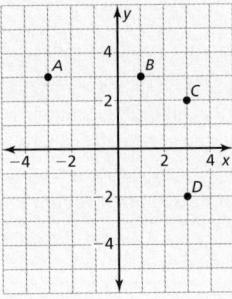
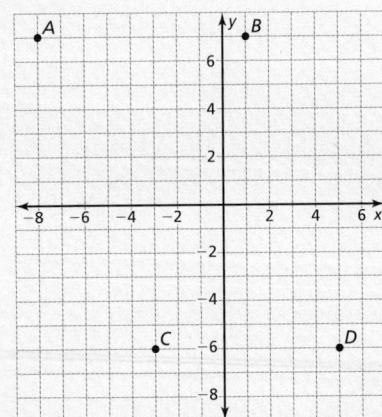
Use the diagram. *(Section 1.1)*

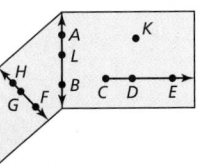

1. Name four points.
2. Name three collinear points.
3. Name two lines.
4. Name three coplanar points.
5. Name the plane that is shaded green.
6. Give two names for the plane that is shaded blue.
7. Name three line segments.
8. Name three rays.

Sketch the figure described. *(Section 1.1)*

9. $\overrightarrow{QR}$ and $\overrightarrow{QS}$
10. plane P intersecting $\overleftrightarrow{YZ}$ at Z

Plot the points in a coordinate plane. Then determine whether $\overline{AB}$ and $\overline{CD}$ are congruent. *(Section 1.2)*

11. A(−3, 3), B(1, 3), C(3, 2), D(3, −2)
12. A(−8, 7), B(1, 7), C(−3, −6), D(5, −6)

Find AC. *(Section 1.2)*

13.
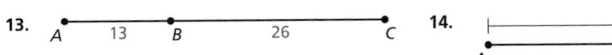

14.

Find the coordinates of the midpoint M and the distance between the two points. *(Section 1.3)*

15. J(4, 3) and K(2, −3)
16. L(−4, 5) and N(5, −3)
17. P(−6, −1) and Q(1, 2)

18. Identify the segment bisector of $\overline{RS}$. Then find RS. *(Section 1.3)*

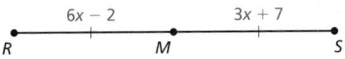

19. The midpoint of $\overline{JK}$ is M(0, 1). One endpoint is J(−6, 3). Find the coordinates of endpoint K. *(Section 1.3)*

20. Your mom asks you to run some errands on your way home from school. She wants you to stop at the post office and the grocery store, which are both on the same straight road between your school and your house. The distance from your school to the post office is 376 yards, the distance from the post office to your house is 929 yards, and the distance from the grocery store to your house is 513 yards. *(Section 1.2)*

   a. Where should you stop first?
   b. What is the distance from the post office to the grocery store?
   c. What is the distance from your school to your house?
   d. You walk at a speed of 75 yards per minute. How long does it take you to walk straight home from school? Explain your answer.

21. The figure shows a coordinate plane on a baseball field. The distance from home plate to first base is 90 feet. The pitching mound is the midpoint between home plate and second base. Find the distance from home plate to second base. Find the distance between home plate and the pitching mound. Explain how you found your answers. *(Section 1.3)*

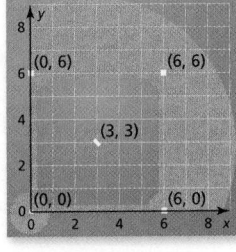

Dynamic Teaching Tools

Dynamic Assessment & Progress Monitoring Tool

Lesson Planning Tool

Interactive Whiteboard Lesson Library

Dynamic Classroom with Dynamic Investigations

Overview of Section 1.4

Introduction

- The goal of this lesson is to find the perimeter and area of figures that are drawn in the coordinate plane, applying knowledge from the previous lesson. In addition, the names of polygons are reviewed, and students classify the polygons as being convex or concave.

- The explorations and lesson allow for students to be engaged in conversation with partners. Pose problems, ask questions, and let students work. You will find that students may have alternate ways of reaching an answer than what you might have anticipated. Be pleased that students are thinking and solving problems!

Resources

- Centimeter grid paper, straightedges, and colored pencils are helpful in working the problems in the explorations and lesson.

Formative Assessment Tips

- **Popsicle Sticks:** This technique ensures that *any* student can be called on during questioning time in class. Write the name of each student on a Popsicle stick. Place the sticks in a cup (or can). When questions are posed in class during *No-Hands Questioning**, each student should think and be prepared to answer. If you only call on students who raise their hands, students can then opt out of being engaged. All students think they have an equal chance of being called on when a stick is pulled randomly, so they engage more in the lesson.

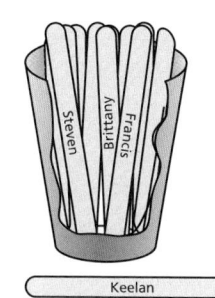

- If there are certain students that you want to hear from, the cup could have an inner cylinder where *select* sticks are placed. It will appear that the process is still random, and the voices you have not heard much from will still have the opportunity to prepare and formulate their answer.

* See Section 2.4 for a description of *No-Hands Questioning*.

Another Way

- If you wish students to become familiar with dynamic geometry software, this lesson should provide time to investigate drawing polygons in the coordinate plane and determining the perimeter and area. The results should confirm work done with paper and pencil.

Pacing Suggestion

- The problems students will work in the explorations are similar to the lesson examples. You could have students complete the explorations, check understanding of classifying polygons, and then have them work Exercises 17–24 on page 34.

Common Core State Standards

HSG-GPE.B.7 Use coordinates to compute perimeters of polygons and areas of triangles and rectangles, e.g., using the distance formula.

HSG-MG.A.1 Use geometric shapes, their measures, and their properties to describe objects (e.g., modeling a tree trunk or a human torso as a cylinder).

Laurie's Notes

Exploration

Motivate

- Draw a parallelogram and divide it into a rectangle and two triangles, as shown. Ask students to show how they could divide a hexagon and octagon into familiar polygons.

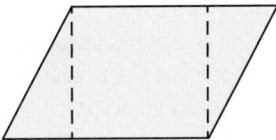

Exploration 1

- This exploration is an application of the Distance Formula from the last lesson and so students should need little guidance in finding the perimeter.
- **?** "How can you tell whether adjacent sides are perpendicular?" If the slopes of adjacent sides are opposite reciprocals, then the sides are perpendicular.
- **?** "If you find one right angle, meaning a pair of adjacent sides are perpendicular, will you know that all of the angles are right angles?" not necessarily; You will need to find at least 3 right angles.
- It is quite possible that instead of subtracting coordinates to find the vertical and horizontal distances, students will count with their fingers on the diagram.
- **Popsicle Sticks:** Select a student to share his/her justification for part (d).
- **MP3 Construct Viable Arguments and Critique the Reasoning of Others:** Is the quadrilateral a square?

Exploration 2

- If students have worked with geoboards or dot paper, deconstructing the quadrilateral into four triangles and a square will seem familiar.
- Students should recognize the 3-4-5 right triangles in this diagram. Students may also have the spatial skills to see that two of the triangles could be transformed to form a 3-by-4 rectangle.
- **?** "Is the sum you found for quadrilateral *ABCD* the same as your answer in the previous exploration?" yes

Communicate Your Answer

- To find the perimeter of a polygon in the coordinate plane, you need to find the length of each side. To find the area of a polygon, it is necessary to deconstruct the polygon into polygons of which you know how to find the area.
- **?** "Can you think of a polygon that you could not deconstruct into simpler polygons?" Answers will vary.
- **Note:** While the polygon might be decomposed into simpler polygons, the vertices of the new polygons might not be obvious or easily found.

Connecting to Next Step

- Students have used the Distance Formula to find the perimeter and area of a quadrilateral. In the formal lesson, perimeter and area of other polygons are explored.

Perimeter and Area in the Coordinate Plane

Essential Question How can you find the perimeter and area of a polygon in a coordinate plane?

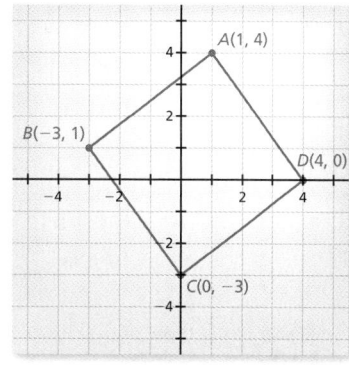

EXPLORATION 1 Finding the Perimeter and Area of a Quadrilateral

Work with a partner.

a. On a piece of centimeter graph paper, draw quadrilateral *ABCD* in a coordinate plane. Label the points $A(1, 4)$, $B(-3, 1)$, $C(0, -3)$, and $D(4, 0)$.

b. Find the perimeter of quadrilateral *ABCD*.

c. Are adjacent sides of quadrilateral *ABCD* perpendicular to each other? How can you tell?

d. What is the definition of a square? Is quadrilateral *ABCD* a square? Justify your answer. Find the area of quadrilateral *ABCD*.

LOOKING FOR STRUCTURE

To be proficient in math, you need to visualize single objects as being composed of more than one object.

EXPLORATION 2 Finding the Area of a Polygon

Work with a partner.

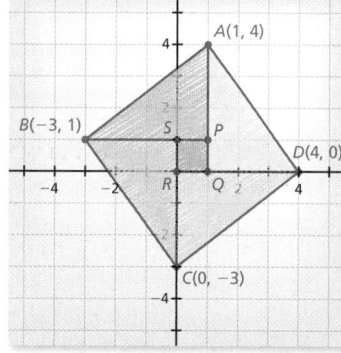

a. Partition quadrilateral *ABCD* into four right triangles and one square, as shown. Find the coordinates of the vertices for the five smaller polygons.

b. Find the areas of the five smaller polygons.

Area of Triangle *BPA*: ▒

Area of Triangle *AQD*: ▒

Area of Triangle *DRC*: ▒

Area of Triangle *CSB*: ▒

Area of Square *PQRS*: ▒

c. Is the sum of the areas of the five smaller polygons equal to the area of quadrilateral *ABCD*? Justify your answer.

Communicate Your Answer

3. How can you find the perimeter and area of a polygon in a coordinate plane?

4. Repeat Exploration 1 for quadrilateral *EFGH*, where the coordinates of the vertices are $E(-3, 6)$, $F(-7, 3)$, $G(-1, -5)$, and $H(3, -2)$.

Section 1.4 Perimeter and Area in the Coordinate Plane **29**

ANSWERS

1. a. Check students' work.

   b. 20 cm

   c. yes; The slopes of $\overline{AB}$ and $\overline{CD}$ are $\frac{3}{4}$, and the slopes of $\overline{BC}$ and $\overline{AD}$ are $-\frac{4}{3}$. Because $\frac{3}{4}\left(-\frac{4}{3}\right) = -1$, the sides are perpendicular.

   d. a quadrilateral with four congruent sides and four right angles; yes; $AB = BC = CD = DA = 5$, and all four angles are right angles; $A = 25$ cm²

2. a. *BPA*: $B(-3, 1)$, $P(1, 1)$, $A(1, 4)$
      AQD: $A(1, 4)$, $Q(1, 0)$, $D(4, 0)$
      DRC: $D(4, 0)$, $R(0, 0)$, $C(0, -3)$
      CSB: $C(0, -3)$, $S(0, 1)$, $B(-3, 1)$
      PQRS: $P(1, 1)$, $Q(1, 0)$, $R(0, 0)$, $S(0, 1)$

   b. 6 cm²; 6 cm²; 6 cm²; 6 cm²; 1 cm²

   c. yes; $6 + 6 + 6 + 6 + 1 = 25$ cm²

3. Use the Distance Formula to find the lengths of the sides and add the lengths together. Use the appropriate area formula and the dimensions of the figure, or partition the figure into shapes that have easily determined areas and add the areas together.

4. a.

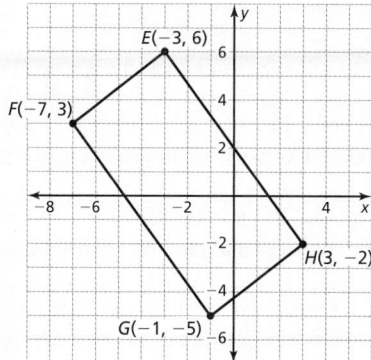

   b. 30 cm

   c. yes; The slopes of $\overline{EF}$ and $\overline{GH}$ are $\frac{3}{4}$, and the slopes of $\overline{FG}$ and $\overline{EH}$ are $-\frac{4}{3}$. Because $\frac{3}{4}\left(-\frac{4}{3}\right) = -1$, the sides are perpendicular.

   d. a quadrilateral with four congruent sides and four right angles; no; All four sides are not congruent; $A = 50$ cm²

Extra Example 1

Classify each polygon by the number of sides. Tell whether it is *convex* or *concave*.

a.

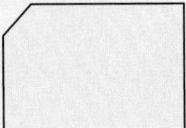

pentagon; convex

b.

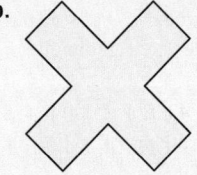

dodecagon; concave

MONITORING PROGRESS ANSWERS

1. pentagon; concave
2. heptagon; convex

1.4 Lesson

Core Vocabulary

Previous
polygon
side
vertex
n-gon
convex
concave

What You Will Learn

▶ Classify polygons.
▶ Find perimeters and areas of polygons in the coordinate plane.

Classifying Polygons

Core Concept

Polygons

In geometry, a figure that lies in a plane is called a plane figure. Recall that a *polygon* is a closed plane figure formed by three or more line segments called *sides*. Each side intersects exactly two sides, one at each *vertex*, so that no two sides with a common vertex are collinear. You can name a polygon by listing the vertices in consecutive order.

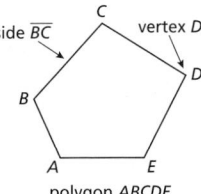

polygon *ABCDE*

The number of sides determines the name of a polygon, as shown in the table.

You can also name a polygon using the term *n*-gon, where *n* is the number of sides. For instance, a 14-gon is a polygon with 14 sides.

Number of sides	Type of polygon
3	Triangle
4	Quadrilateral
5	Pentagon
6	Hexagon
7	Heptagon
8	Octagon
9	Nonagon
10	Decagon
12	Dodecagon
n	*n*-gon

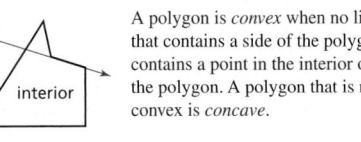

convex polygon   concave polygon

A polygon is *convex* when no line that contains a side of the polygon contains a point in the interior of the polygon. A polygon that is not convex is *concave*.

EXAMPLE 1   **Classifying Polygons**

Classify each polygon by the number of sides. Tell whether it is *convex* or *concave*.

a.

b.

SOLUTION

a. The polygon has four sides. So, it is a quadrilateral. The polygon is concave.

b. The polygon has six sides. So, it is a hexagon. The polygon is convex.

Monitoring Progress Help in English and Spanish at *BigIdeasMath.com*

Classify the polygon by the number of sides. Tell whether it is *convex* or *concave*.

1.

2.
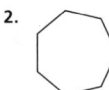

Laurie's Notes   Teacher Actions

- The (mostly Greek) numerical prefixes for polygons are likely familiar to students. They may have heard the 7-sided polygon called a *septagon,* from the Latin prefix "septua-." "Hepta-" is the Greek prefix for *seven.* The suffix "-gon" is from the Greek meaning *angles.* Interestingly, *trilateral* and *quadrilateral* are Latin.
- Note concave polygons are defined as *not* being convex. This may be students' first experience with a definition that, instead of defining what it is, defines what it is not. Students should be familiar with concave lenses and spoons.
- To quickly check for understanding, ask students to sketch a convex hexagon, concave octagon, and concave triangle (not possible). Use *Popsicle Sticks* to select students to share their work at the board.

Finding Perimeter and Area in the Coordinate Plane

You can use the formulas given below and the Distance Formula to find the perimeters and areas of polygons in the coordinate plane.

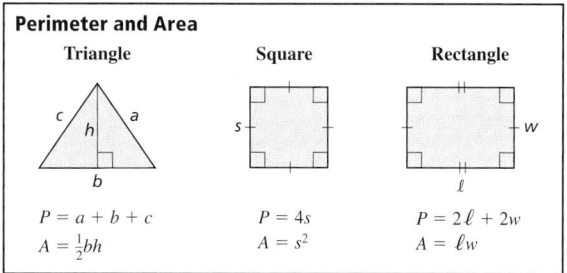

Perimeter and Area

Triangle	Square	Rectangle

$$P = a + b + c$$
$$A = \frac{1}{2}bh$$

$$P = 4s$$
$$A = s^2$$

$$P = 2\ell + 2w$$
$$A = \ell w$$

EXAMPLE 2   Finding Perimeter in the Coordinate Plane

Find the perimeter of △ABC with vertices $A(-2, 3)$, $B(3, -3)$, and $C(-2, -3)$.

SOLUTION

Step 1   Draw the triangle in a coordinate plane. Then find the length of each side.

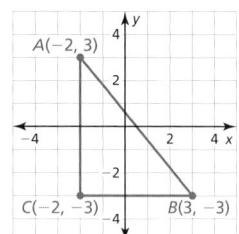

Side $\overline{AB}$

$$AB = \sqrt{(x_2 - x_1)^2 + (y_2 - y_1)^2}$$ Distance Formula

$$= \sqrt{[3 - (-2)]^2 + (-3 - 3)^2}$$ Substitute.

$$= \sqrt{5^2 + (-6)^2}$$ Subtract.

$$= \sqrt{61}$$ Simplify.

$$\approx 7.81$$ Use a calculator.

Side $\overline{BC}$

$$BC = |-2 - 3| = 5$$ Ruler Postulate (Postulate 1.1)

Side $\overline{CA}$

$$CA = |3 - (-3)| = 6$$ Ruler Postulate (Postulate 1.1)

Step 2   Find the sum of the side lengths.

$$AB + BC + CA \approx 7.81 + 5 + 6 = 18.81$$

▶ So, the perimeter of △ABC is about 18.81 units.

Monitoring Progress Help in English and Spanish at *BigIdeasMath.com*

Find the perimeter of the polygon with the given vertices.

3. $D(-3, 2)$, $E(4, 2)$, $F(4, -3)$ **4.** $G(-3, 2)$, $H(2, 2)$, $J(-1, -3)$

5. $K(-1, 1)$, $L(4, 1)$, $M(2, -2)$, $N(-3, -2)$

6. $Q(-4, -1)$, $R(1, 4)$, $S(4, 1)$, $T(-1, -4)$

Extra Example 2

Find the perimeter of △PQR with vertices $P(-1, 4)$, $Q(2, 4)$, and $R(2, -1)$.
about 13.83 units

MONITORING PROGRESS ANSWERS

3. about 20.60 units
4. about 16.22 units
5. about 17.22 units
6. about 22.62 units

Laurie's Notes   Teacher Actions

? "Can you sketch a rectangle with area of 8 inches?"   no; Area must be measured in square units.

• Example 2 is similar to Explorations 1 and 2, except that a calculated distance is irrational.

• **MP6 Attend to Precision:** Discuss the difference between exact measures $\left(\sqrt{61}\right)$ and approximate measures (7.81).

• **Monitoring Progress:** You might assign odds to some students and evens to the rest of the students.

Extra Example 3

Find the area of △*ABC* with vertices
A(1, 3), *B*(3, −3), and *C*(−2, −3).

15 square units

MONITORING PROGRESS
ANSWERS

7. 7.5 square units

8. 9 square units

9. 12 square units

10. 24 square units

EXAMPLE 3 **Finding Area in the Coordinate Plane**

Find the area of △*DEF* with vertices *D*(1, 3), *E*(4, −3), and *F*(−4, −3).

SOLUTION

Step 1 Draw the triangle in a coordinate plane by plotting the vertices and connecting them.

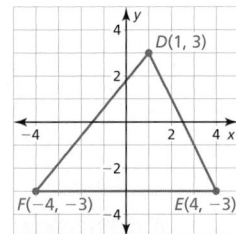

Step 2 Find the lengths of the base and height.

Base

The base is $\overline{FE}$. Use the Ruler Postulate (Postulate 1.1) to find the length of $\overline{FE}$.

$$FE = |4 - (-4)| \qquad \text{Ruler Postulate (Postulate 1.1)}$$
$$= |8| \qquad \text{Subtract.}$$
$$= 8 \qquad \text{Simplify.}$$

So, the length of the base is 8 units.

Height

The height is the distance from point *D* to line segment $\overline{FE}$. By counting grid lines, you can determine that the height is 6 units.

Step 3 Substitute the values for the base and height into the formula for the area of a triangle.

$$A = \tfrac{1}{2}bh \qquad \text{Write the formula for area of a triangle.}$$
$$= \tfrac{1}{2}(8)(6) \qquad \text{Substitute.}$$
$$= 24 \qquad \text{Multiply.}$$

▶ So, the area of △*DEF* is 24 square units.

Monitoring Progress Help in English and Spanish at *BigIdeasMath.com*

Find the area of the polygon with the given vertices.

7. *G*(2, 2), *H*(3, −1), *J*(−2, −1)

8. *N*(−1, 1), *P*(2, 1), *Q*(2, −2), *R*(−1, −2)

9. *F*(−2, 3), *G*(1, 3), *H*(1, −1), *J*(−2, −1)

10. *K*(−3, 3), *L*(3, 3), *M*(3, −1), *N*(−3, −1)

32 **Chapter 1** Basics of Geometry

Laurie's Notes   Teacher Actions

- **Turn and Talk:** "In Example 3, what information will you need to find the area of the triangle?" Listen as partners decide which side of the triangle to use as a base and how to determine the height to that base.
- You may also hear other students discuss how the triangle could be rearranged to form a rectangle. One possibility is shown at the right. Left alone, students may follow different routes!

- **MP1 Make Sense of Problems and Persevere in Solving Them:** Allow time for different solution methods to be shown.
- **Monitoring Progress:** You might assign odds to some students and evens to the rest of the students.

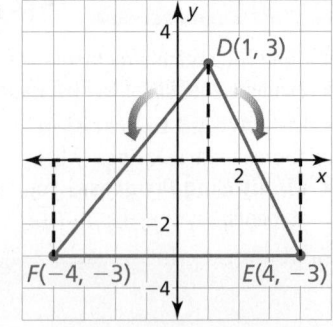

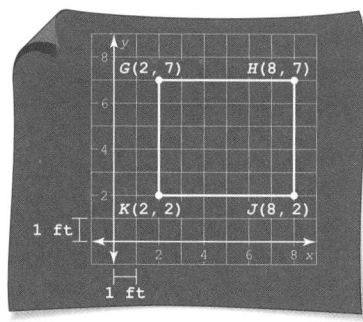

EXAMPLE 4 **Modeling with Mathematics**

You are building a shed in your backyard. The diagram shows the four vertices of the shed. Each unit in the coordinate plane represents 1 foot. Find the area of the floor of the shed.

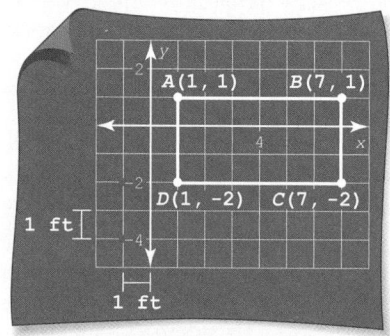

SOLUTION

1. **Understand the Problem** You are given the coordinates of a shed. You need to find the area of the floor of the shed.

2. **Make a Plan** The shed is rectangular, so use the coordinates to find the length and width of the shed. Then use a formula to find the area.

3. **Solve the Problem**

   Step 1 Find the length and width.

   Length $GH = |8 - 2| = 6$ Ruler Postulate (Postulate 1.1)

   Width $GK = |7 - 2| = 5$ Ruler Postulate (Postulate 1.1)

   The shed has a length of 6 feet and a width of 5 feet.

   Step 2 Substitute the values for the length and width into the formula for the area of a rectangle.

   $A = \ell w$ Write the formula for area of a rectangle.

   $= (6)(5)$ Substitute.

   $= 30$ Multiply.

   ▶ So, the area of the floor of the shed is 30 square feet.

4. **Look Back** Make sure your answer makes sense in the context of the problem. Because you are finding an area, your answer should be in square units. An answer of 30 square feet makes sense in the context of the problem. ✔

Monitoring Progress 🔊 Help in English and Spanish at *BigIdeasMath.com*

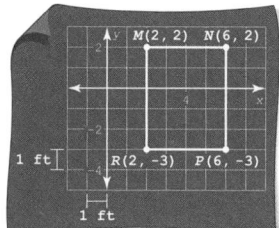

11. You are building a patio in your school's courtyard. In the diagram at the left, the coordinates represent the four vertices of the patio. Each unit in the coordinate plane represents 1 foot. Find the area of the patio.

Extra Example 4

You are making a banner for the school basketball game. The diagram shows the four vertices of the banner. Each unit in the coordinate plane represents 1 foot. Find the area of the banner.

18 square feet

MONITORING PROGRESS ANSWER

11. 20 ft^2

Laurie's Notes | **Teacher Actions**

- Students should have little difficulty finding the area of the rectangle in Example 4. Differentiate instruction for this example by having different polygons of which students find the area. Parallelograms, hexagons, and octagons should provide an appropriate challenge for students.

Closure

- **I Used to Think ... But Now I Know:** Summarize the skills and strategies you are confident in as a result of today's lesson.

ANSWERS

1. $4s$
2. $A = \frac{1}{2}bh$, Distance Formula
3. quadrilateral; concave
4. triangle; convex
5. pentagon; convex
6. hexagon; concave
7. 22 units
8. 16 units
9. about 22.43 units
10. about 14.47 units
11. about 16.93 units
12. about 16.94 units
13. 7.5 square units
14. 24.5 square units
15. 9 square units
16. 10 square units
17. about 9.66 units
18. about 16.98 units
19. about 12.17 units
20. about 27.49 units
21. 4 square units
22. 16 square units
23. 6 square units
24. 26 square units

Vocabulary and Core Concept Check

1. **COMPLETE THE SENTENCE** The perimeter of a square with side length s is $P =$ _____.

2. **WRITING** What formulas can you use to find the area of a triangle in a coordinate plane?

Monitoring Progress and Modeling with Mathematics

In Exercises 3–6, classify the polygon by the number of sides. Tell whether it is *convex* or *concave*. *(See Example 1.)*

3.

4.

5.

6.

In Exercises 7–12, find the perimeter of the polygon with the given vertices. *(See Example 2.)*

7. $G(2, 4), H(2, -3), J(-2, -3), K(-2, 4)$

8. $Q(-3, 2), R(1, 2), S(1, -2), T(-3, -2)$

9. $U(-2, 4), V(3, 4), W(3, -4)$

10. $X(-1, 3), Y(3, 0), Z(-1, -2)$

11.
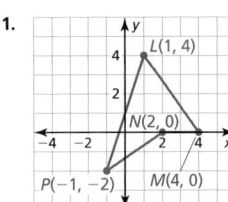

12.
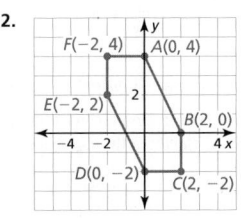

In Exercises 13–16, find the area of the polygon with the given vertices. *(See Example 3.)*

13. $E(3, 1), F(3, -2), G(-2, -2)$

14. $J(-3, 4), K(4, 4), L(3, -3)$

15. $W(0, 0), X(0, 3), Y(-3, 3), Z(-3, 0)$

16. $N(-2, 1), P(3, 1), Q(3, -1), R(-2, -1)$

In Exercises 17–24, use the diagram.

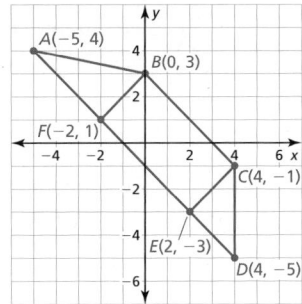

17. Find the perimeter of $\triangle CDE$.

18. Find the perimeter of rectangle $BCEF$.

19. Find the perimeter of $\triangle ABF$.

20. Find the perimeter of quadrilateral $ABCD$.

21. Find the area of $\triangle CDE$.

22. Find the area of rectangle $BCEF$.

23. Find the area of $\triangle ABF$.

24. Find the area of quadrilateral $ABCD$.

ERROR ANALYSIS In Exercises 25 and 26, describe and correct the error in finding the perimeter or area of the polygon.

25.

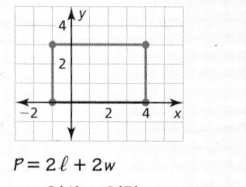

$P = 2\ell + 2w$
$= 2(4) + 2(3)$
$= 14$
The perimeter is 14 units.

26.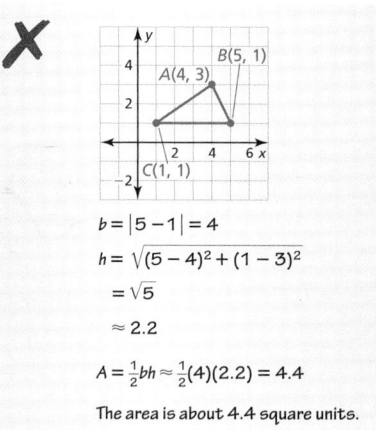

$b = |5 - 1| = 4$
$h = \sqrt{(5-4)^2 + (1-3)^2}$
$= \sqrt{5}$
≈ 2.2
$A = \frac{1}{2}bh \approx \frac{1}{2}(4)(2.2) = 4.4$
The area is about 4.4 square units.

In Exercises 27 and 28, use the diagram.

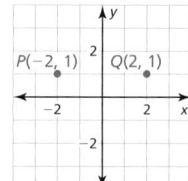

27. Determine which point is the remaining vertex of a triangle with an area of 4 square units.

(A) $R(2, 0)$

(B) $S(-2, -1)$

(C) $T(-1, 0)$

(D) $U(2, -2)$

28. Determine which points are the remaining vertices of a rectangle with a perimeter of 14 units.

(A) $A(2, -2)$ and $B(2, -1)$

(B) $C(-2, -2)$ and $D(-2, 2)$

(C) $E(-2, -2)$ and $F(2, -2)$

(D) $G(2, 0)$ and $H(-2, 0)$

29. **USING STRUCTURE** Use the diagram.

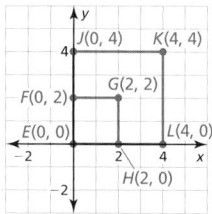

a. Find the areas of square $EFGH$ and square $EJKL$. What happens to the area when the perimeter of square $EFGH$ is doubled?

b. Is this true for every square? Explain.

30. **MODELING WITH MATHEMATICS** You are growing zucchini plants in your garden. In the figure, the entire garden is rectangle $QRST$. Each unit in the coordinate plane represents 1 foot. *(See Example 4.)*

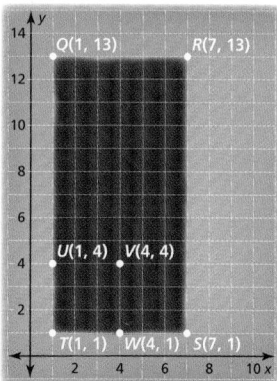

a. Find the area of the garden.

b. Zucchini plants require 9 square feet around each plant. How many zucchini plants can you plant?

c. You decide to use square $TUVW$ to grow lettuce. You can plant four heads of lettuce per square foot. How many of each vegetable can you plant? Explain.

ANSWERS

25. The length should be 5 units;
$P = 2\ell + 2w = 2(5) + 2(3) = 16$;
The perimeter is 16 units.

26. The height should be the distance from A to $\overline{BC}$; $h = |3 - 1| = 2$,
$A = \frac{1}{2}bh = \frac{1}{2}(4)(2) = 4$; The area is 4 square units.

27. B

28. C

29. a. 4 square units; 16 square units; It is quadrupled.

b. yes; If you double the perimeter of the square, which is the same as doubling the side length, then the new area will be $2^2 = 4$ times as big.

30. a. 72 ft²

b. 8 zucchini plants

c. 36 heads of lettuce, 7 zucchini plants; $3^2 = 9$ ft² for lettuce, $4(9) = 36$ heads of lettuce; An area of 9 square feet is used for lettuce, so there can be $8 - 1 = 7$ zucchini plants.

31. **a.**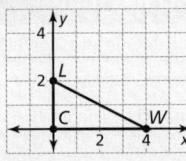

b. about 10.47 mi

c. about 17.42 mi

32. rectangle; rectangle; The base and height are the same length for each. So, the triangle's area will be half of the rectangle's area. For perimeter, two of the dimensions are the same, and the triangle's third side is shorter than the total of the rectangle's remaining two sides.

33. **a.** y_1 and y_3

b. $(0, 4), (4, 2), (2, -2)$

c. about 15.27 units, 10 square units

34. See Additional Answers.

35. **a.** 16 units, 16 square units

b. yes; The sides are all the same length because each one is the hypotenuse of a right triangle with legs that are each 2 units long. Because the slopes of the lines of each side are either 1 or -1, they are perpendicular.

c. about 11.31 units, 8 square units; It is half of the area of the larger square.

36. no; triangle: $P = 12$ units and $A = 6$ square units; A rectangle that is 1×5 will have the same perimeter as the triangle (12 units) but not the same area (5 square units).

37–44. See Additional Answers.

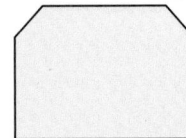
---

31. **MODELING WITH MATHEMATICS** You are going for a hike in the woods. You hike to a waterfall that is 4 miles east of where you left your car. You then hike to a lookout point that is 2 miles north of your car. From the lookout point, you return to your car.

a. Map out your route in a coordinate plane with your car at the origin. Let each unit in the coordinate plane represent 1 mile. Assume you travel along straight paths.

b. How far do you travel during the entire hike?

c. When you leave the waterfall, you decide to hike to an old wishing well before going to the lookout point. The wishing well is 3 miles north and 2 miles west of the lookout point. How far do you travel during the entire hike?

32. **HOW DO YOU SEE IT?** Without performing any calculations, determine whether the triangle or the rectangle has a greater area. Which one has a greater perimeter? Explain your reasoning.

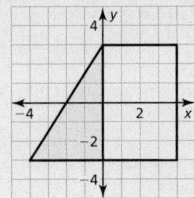

33. **MATHEMATICAL CONNECTIONS** The lines $y_1 = 2x - 6$, $y_2 = -3x + 4$, and $y_3 = -\frac{1}{2}x + 4$ are the sides of a right triangle.

a. Use slopes to determine which sides are perpendicular.

b. Find the vertices of the triangle.

c. Find the perimeter and area of the triangle.

Maintaining Mathematical Proficiency
Reviewing what you learned in previous grades and lessons

Solve the equation. *(Skills Review Handbook)*

38. $3x - 7 = 2$

39. $5x + 9 = 4$

40. $x + 4 = x - 12$

41. $4x - 9 = 3x + 5$

42. $11 - 2x = 5x - 3$

43. $\dfrac{x + 1}{2} = 4x - 3$

44. Use a compass and straightedge to construct a copy of the line segment. *(Section 1.2)*

---

34. **THOUGHT PROVOKING** Your bedroom has an area of 350 square feet. You are remodeling to include an attached bathroom that has an area of 150 square feet. Draw a diagram of the remodeled bedroom and bathroom in a coordinate plane.

35. **PROBLEM SOLVING** Use the diagram.

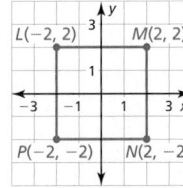

a. Find the perimeter and area of the square.

b. Connect the midpoints of the sides of the given square to make a quadrilateral. Is this quadrilateral a square? Explain your reasoning.

c. Find the perimeter and area of the quadrilateral you made in part (b). Compare this area to the area you found in part (a).

36. **MAKING AN ARGUMENT** Your friend claims that a rectangle with the same perimeter as $\triangle QRS$ will have the same area as the triangle. Is your friend correct? Explain your reasoning.

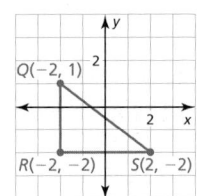

37. **REASONING** Triangle ABC has a perimeter of 12 units. The vertices of the triangle are $A(x, 2)$, $B(2, -2)$, and $C(-1, 2)$. Find the value of x.

Overview of Section 1.5

Introduction

- There is content in the lesson that should be familiar to students from earlier grades, namely measuring and classifying angles, which are presented in the explorations. Also used in the explorations are the two postulates presented formally in the lesson.
- The two postulates in this lesson can be confusing to students, mainly because they seem so obvious. The Protractor Postulate establishes how an angle measure is matched with a real number from 0 to 180. The Angle Addition Postulate says that when a ray is between two other rays and they share the same vertex, the measures of the two smaller angles add to the measure of the larger angle.
- Two constructions are introduced in this lesson: copying an angle and bisecting an angle.

Resources

- Scissors, straightedges, compasses, protractors, and heavyweight paper are helpful in working the explorations and examples.

Common Misconceptions

- The 0° and 180° marks on many protractors are not flush with the edge of the protractor. Students need to be careful in using this tool and pay attention to its design. A similar error can be found on some rulers that do not begin with 0 at the edge.

Formative Assessment Tips

- **Whiteboarding:** Whiteboards can be used to provide individual responses, or used with small groups to encourage student collaboration and consensus on a problem or solution method. Whiteboards can be used at the beginning of class for warm-ups or throughout the lesson to elicit student responses. Unlike writing on scrap paper (individual response) or chart paper (group response), responses can be erased and modified easily. As understanding progresses, responses can reflect this growth.
- Use boards for more than quick responses. Sizable boards can be used to communicate thinking, providing evidence of how a problem was solved. When students display their whiteboards in the front of the room, classmates can critique their reasoning or method of solution.

Extensions

- Students are often curious about angles that measure more than 180° or less than 0°. Students have heard about "doing a 360," so it is important to acknowledge these angles exist. You could talk about reflex angles (more than 180° but less than 360°) and negative angles that students will encounter in trigonometry.

Pacing Suggestion

- The lesson contains two postulates and two constructions, so you may want to omit examples that you feel students are secure with, after completing the explorations.

HSG-CO.A.1 Know precise definitions of
angle, … based on the undefined notions
of point, line, …

HSG-CO.D.12 Make formal geometric
constructions with a variety of
tools and methods (compass and
straightedge, …). …

Laurie's Notes

Exploration

Motivate
- Draw and label $\overrightarrow{YX}$ and $\overrightarrow{YZ}$ with an angle of about 80° on the board. Label $\angle XYZ$.
- **?** "What is the measure of $\angle XYZ$?" Students should estimate.
- **?** "How do you know for sure what the measure is?" Measure the angle using a protractor.
- **?** Extend one ray of the angle. "What is the measure of the angle now?" Hopefully students will know that the measure has not changed!
- Model how to use a protractor and measure the angle.

Discuss
COMMON ERROR The common error or confusion that students have in using a protractor is reading the wrong scale.
- A relatively simple strategy is to think first about whether the angle is acute or obtuse!
- Certainly looking at which scale reads 0° when one ray of the angle is aligned with the edge of the protractor is another strategy.

Exploration 1
- **MP5 Use Appropriate Tools Strategically** and **MP6 Attend to Precision:** These problems serve as a quick review of reading a protractor to find the measure of an angle. You will also hear students use the vocabulary associated with angles.
- **Popsicle Sticks:** Solicit answers for each of the angles listed.

Exploration 2
- You should have scissors and heavyweight paper available for students to use.
- If students are accurate with their tracing, they should end up with a regular hexagon.
- Students found the sum of the interior angles of a polygon in grade 8. They also found the exterior angles sum as well.
- **Big Idea:** The *Big Idea* in this exploration is that when a polygon is decomposed into smaller polygons, the interior angle sums still add up to the expected sum. For instance, when the hexagon is decomposed into two trapezoids, four of the angles are still 120°. Two of the 120° angles have each been bisected into two 60° angles. Note that $4(120°) + 4(60°) = 720°$.

COMMON ERROR When the regular hexagon is decomposed into six equilateral triangles, you cannot find the sum of the interior angles of the hexagon by multiplying 6(180°). There are six 60° angles at the center of the hexagon that must be subtracted from the sum because they are not part of the interior angles of the hexagon.

Communicate Your Answer
- Students should be comfortable using the protractor to measure angles and then classify them.

Connecting to Next Step
- Students have used the Protractor Postulate in completing these explorations and have classified angles. You may want to omit Example 2 in the formal lesson.

1.5 Measuring and Constructing Angles

Essential Question How can you measure and classify an angle?

EXPLORATION 1   Measuring and Classifying Angles

Work with a partner. Find the degree measure of each of the following angles. Classify each angle as acute, right, or obtuse.

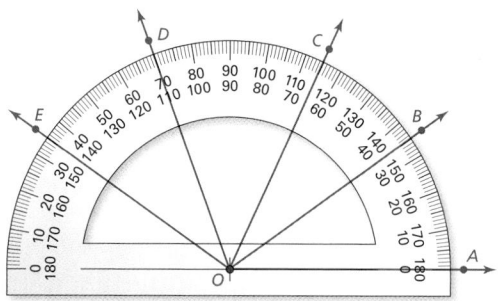

a. ∠AOB   b. ∠AOC   c. ∠BOC   d. ∠BOE
e. ∠COE   f. ∠COD   g. ∠BOD   h. ∠AOE

EXPLORATION 2   Drawing a Regular Polygon

Work with a partner.

a. Use a ruler and protractor to draw the triangular pattern shown at the right.

b. Cut out the pattern and use it to draw three regular hexagons, as shown below.

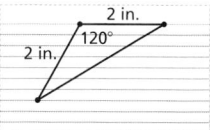

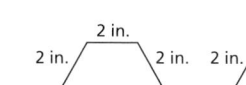

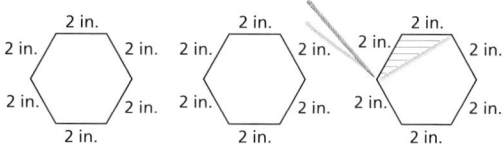

ATTENDING TO PRECISION

To be proficient in math, you need to calculate and measure accurately and efficiently.

c. The sum of the angle measures of a polygon with n sides is equal to $180(n - 2)°$. Do the angle measures of your hexagons agree with this rule? Explain.

d. Partition your hexagons into smaller polygons, as shown below. For each hexagon, find the sum of the angle measures of the smaller polygons. Does each sum equal the sum of the angle measures of a hexagon? Explain.

Communicate Your Answer

3. How can you measure and classify an angle?

Section 1.5   Measuring and Constructing Angles   **37**

Dynamic Teaching Tools

Dynamic Assessment & Progress Monitoring Tool
Lesson Planning Tool
Interactive Whiteboard Lesson Library
Dynamic Classroom with Dynamic Investigations

ANSWERS

1.   a.   35°; acute
     b.   65°; acute
     c.   30°; acute
     d.   110°; obtuse
     e.   80°; acute
     f.   45°; acute
     g.   75°; acute
     h.   145°; obtuse

2.   a.   Check students' work.
     b.   Check students' work.
     c.   yes; $180(6 - 2) = 180(4) = 720°$ and $120(6) = 720°$
     d.   720°, 720°, 1080°; no; the first two hexagons split up angles in the hexagon, but the third hexagon adds six angles in the center of the hexagon.

3.   Use a protractor; When the measure is greater than 0° and less than 90°, the angle is acute. When the measure is equal to 90°, the angle is right. When the measure is greater than 90° and less than 180°, the angle is obtuse. When the measure is equal to 180°, the angle is straight.

Extra Example 1
Write three names for the angle.

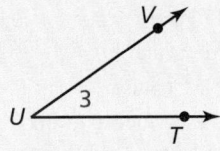

Sample answer: ∠3, ∠U, ∠TUV

MONITORING PROGRESS ANSWERS
1. ∠Q, ∠PQR, ∠RQP
2. ∠1, ∠Y, ∠XYZ (or ∠ZYX)
3. ∠2, ∠E, ∠DEF (or ∠FED)

1.5 Lesson

Core Vocabulary
angle, *p. 38*
vertex, *p. 38*
sides of an angle, *p. 38*
interior of an angle, *p. 38*
exterior of an angle, *p. 38*
measure of an angle, *p. 39*
acute angle, *p. 39*
right angle, *p. 39*
obtuse angle, *p. 39*
straight angle, *p. 39*
congruent angles, *p. 40*
angle bisector, *p. 42*

Previous
protractor
degrees

What You Will Learn
▶ Name angles.
▶ Measure and classify angles.
▶ Identify congruent angles.
▶ Use the Angle Addition Postulate to find angle measures.
▶ Bisect angles.

Naming Angles
An **angle** is a set of points consisting of two different rays that have the same endpoint, called the **vertex**. The rays are the **sides** of the angle.

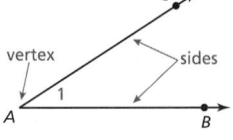

You can name an angle in several different ways.

• Use its vertex, such as ∠A.
• Use a point on each ray and the vertex, such as ∠BAC or ∠CAB.
• Use a number, such as ∠1.

The region that contains all the points between the sides of the angle is the **interior of the angle**. The region that contains all the points outside the angle is the **exterior of the angle**.

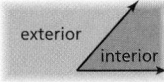

EXAMPLE 1   Naming Angles

A lighthouse keeper measures the angles formed by the lighthouse at point *M* and three boats. Name three angles shown in the diagram.

SOLUTION
∠JMK or ∠KMJ

∠KML or ∠LMK

∠JML or ∠LMJ

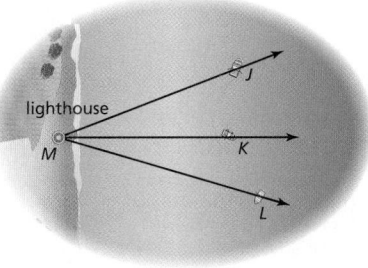

Monitoring Progress 🔊 Help in English and Spanish at *BigIdeasMath.com*
Write three names for the angle.

1.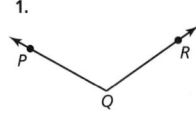

2.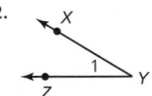

3.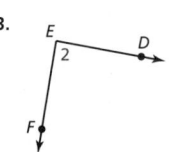

Laurie's Notes   Teacher Actions

• **Turn and Talk:** Sketch a figure similar to Example 1. Have partner A share what he/she knows about naming angles. Use *Popsicle Sticks* and ask a partner B to share with the class how to name angles.
• Discuss the common technique of using numbers in the interior of an angle. When a diagram includes several rays, numbers are a convenient way to refer to various angles.

Measuring and Classifying Angles

A protractor helps you approximate the *measure* of an angle. The measure is usually given in *degrees*.

COMMON ERROR

Most protractors have an inner and an outer scale. When measuring, make sure you are using the correct scale.

⑤ Postulate

Postulate 1.3 Protractor Postulate

Consider $\overrightarrow{OB}$ and a point A on one side of $\overleftrightarrow{OB}$. The rays of the form $\overrightarrow{OA}$ can be matched one to one with the real numbers from 0 to 180.

The **measure** of $\angle AOB$, which can be written as $m\angle AOB$, is equal to the absolute value of the difference between the real numbers matched with $\overrightarrow{OA}$ and $\overrightarrow{OB}$ on a protractor.

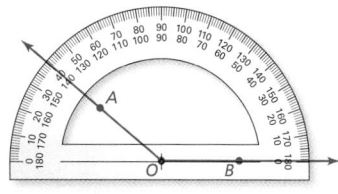

You can classify angles according to their measures.

⑤ Core Concept

Types of Angles

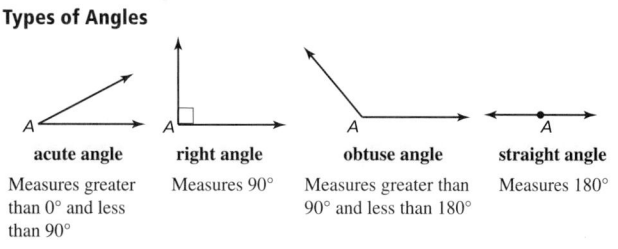

acute angle	right angle	obtuse angle	straight angle
Measures greater than 0° and less than 90°	Measures 90°	Measures greater than 90° and less than 180°	Measures 180°

EXAMPLE 2 **Measuring and Classifying Angles**

Find the measure of each angle. Then classify each angle.

a. $\angle GHK$ **b.** $\angle JHL$ **c.** $\angle LHK$

SOLUTION

a. $\overrightarrow{HG}$ lines up with 0° on the outer scale of the protractor. $\overrightarrow{HK}$ passes through 125° on the outer scale. So, $m\angle GHK = 125°$. It is an *obtuse* angle.

b. $\overrightarrow{HJ}$ lines up with 0° on the inner scale of the protractor. $\overrightarrow{HL}$ passes through 90°. So, $m\angle JHL = 90°$. It is a *right* angle.

c. $\overrightarrow{HL}$ passes through 90°. $\overrightarrow{HK}$ passes through 55° on the inner scale. So, $m\angle LHK = |90 - 55| = 35°$. It is an *acute* angle.

Monitoring Progress 🔊 Help in English and Spanish at *BigIdeasMath.com*

Use the diagram in Example 2 to find the angle measure. Then classify the angle.

4. $\angle JHM$ **5.** $\angle MHK$ **6.** $\angle MHL$

Extra Example 2

Find the measure of each angle. Then classify each angle.

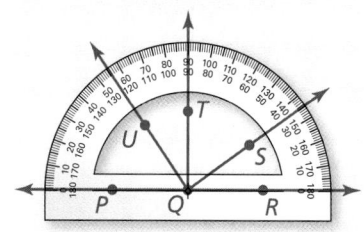

a. $\angle RQU$ 125°; obtuse
b. $\angle TQU$ 35°; acute
c. $\angle UQS$ 90°; right

MONITORING PROGRESS ANSWERS

4. 145°; obtuse
5. 90°; right
6. 55°; acute

Laurie's Notes   Teacher Actions

- **Common Misconception:** The lengths of the rays forming the angle have no bearing on the measure of the angle. Refer to the *Motivate*.
- Write the Protractor Postulate and connect it to the work students did in the explorations.
- If students completed the explorations, you may want to omit Example 2.

Extra Example 3

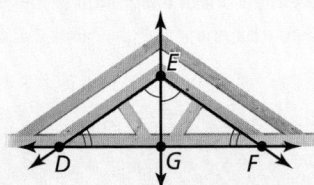

a. Identify the congruent angles in the roof frame. *Sample answer:* $\angle DEG \cong \angle FEG$, $\angle EDG \cong \angle EFG$

b. $m\angle EDG = 40°$. What is $m\angle EFG$? $40°$

MONITORING PROGRESS ANSWER

7. no; $\angle DAB$ appears to be a right angle and $\angle FEH$ is obtuse.

Identifying Congruent Angles

You can use a compass and straightedge to construct an angle that has the same measure as a given angle.

CONSTRUCTION Copying an Angle

Use a compass and straightedge to construct an angle that has the same measure as $\angle A$. In this construction, the *center* of an arc is the point where the compass point rests. The *radius* of an arc is the distance from the center of the arc to a point on the arc drawn by the compass.

SOLUTION

Step 1	Step 2	Step 3	Step 4
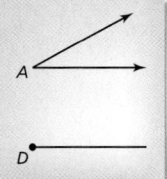	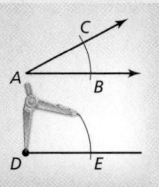	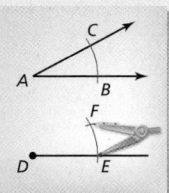	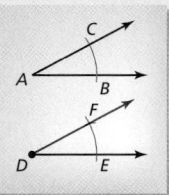
Draw a segment Draw an angle such as $\angle A$, as shown. Then draw a segment. Label a point D on the segment.	**Draw arcs** Draw an arc with center A. Using the same radius, draw an arc with center D.	**Draw an arc** Label B, C, and E. Draw an arc with radius BC and center E. Label the intersection F.	**Draw a ray** Draw $\overrightarrow{DF}$. $\angle EDF \cong \angle BAC$.

Two angles are **congruent angles** when they have the same measure. In the construction above, $\angle A$ and $\angle D$ are congruent angles. So,

$\qquad m\angle A = m\angle D$ The measure of angle A is *equal to* the measure of angle D.

and

$\qquad \angle A \cong \angle D$.   Angle A is *congruent* to angle D.

EXAMPLE 3 Identifying Congruent Angles

a. Identify the congruent angles labeled in the quilt design.

b. $m\angle ADC = 140°$. What is $m\angle EFG$?

SOLUTION

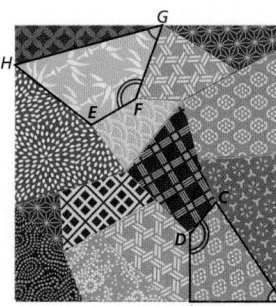

a. There are two pairs of congruent angles:

$\qquad \angle ABC \cong \angle FGH$ and $\angle ADC \cong \angle EFG$.

b. Because $\angle ADC \cong \angle EFG$, $m\angle ADC = m\angle EFG$.

So, $m\angle EFG = 140°$.

> **READING**
>
> In diagrams, matching arcs indicate congruent angles. When there is more than one pair of congruent angles, use multiple arcs.

Monitoring Progress Help in English and Spanish at *BigIdeasMath.com*

7. Without measuring, is $\angle DAB \cong \angle FEH$ in Example 3? Explain your reasoning. Use a protractor to verify your answer.

Laurie's Notes   Teacher Actions

- Work through the steps in copying an angle. The construction can be proven valid by the Side-Side-Side Congruence Theorem. You may wish to refer back to this construction in Section 5.5.
- Discuss how to represent the fact that two angles have the same measure and that two angles are congruent.

Using the Angle Addition Postulate

🔄 Postulate

Postulate 1.4   Angle Addition Postulate

Words   If *P* is in the interior of
∠*RST*, then the measure of ∠*RST* is
equal to the sum of the measures of
∠*RSP* and ∠*PST*.

Symbols   If *P* is in the interior of
∠*RST*, then

$$m\angle RST = m\angle RSP + m\angle PST.$$

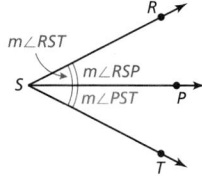

EXAMPLE 4   **Finding Angle Measures**

Given that $m\angle LKN = 145°$,
find $m\angle LKM$ and $m\angle MKN$.

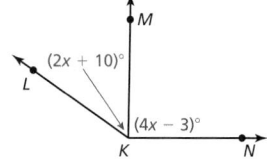

SOLUTION

Step 1   Write and solve an equation to find the value of *x*.

$m\angle LKN = m\angle LKM + m\angle MKN$	Angle Addition Postulate
$145° = (2x + 10)° + (4x - 3)°$	Substitute angle measures.
$145 = 6x + 7$	Combine like terms.
$138 = 6x$	Subtract 7 from each side.
$23 = x$	Divide each side by 6.

Step 2   Evaluate the given expressions when $x = 23$.

$$m\angle LKM = (2x + 10)° = (2 \cdot 23 + 10)° = 56°$$
$$m\angle MKN = (4x - 3)° = (4 \cdot 23 - 3)° = 89°$$

▶ So, $m\angle LKM = 56°$, and $m\angle MKN = 89°$.

Monitoring Progress 🔊 Help in English and Spanish at *BigIdeasMath.com*

Find the indicated angle measures.

8. Given that ∠*KLM* is a straight angle,
find $m\angle KLN$ and $m\angle NLM$.

9. Given that ∠*EFG* is a right angle,
find $m\angle EFH$ and $m\angle HFG$.

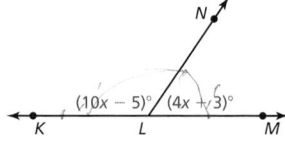

Extra Example 4
Given that $m\angle PQR = 102°$, find $m\angle SQR$
and $m\angle PQS$.

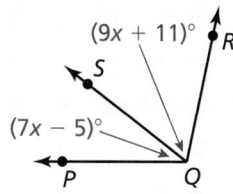

$m\angle SQR = 65°, m\angle PQS = 37°$

**MONITORING PROGRESS
ANSWERS**

8. 125°, 55°

9. 60°, 30°

Laurie's Notes   Teacher Actions

- The Angle Addition Postulate is similar to the Segment Addition Postulate. Ask a student to summarize what the postulate means. Listen for something like, "When a ray is drawn in the interior of an angle and has an endpoint at the vertex, the measures of the two smaller angles add to the measure of the larger angle."

- **Whiteboarding:** Have partners solve Example 4 and quickly check for understanding. Then have some students solve Question 8 and other students Question 9. Ask two volunteers to share their work at the front of the class.

- **Extension:** "What is the relationship between the two angles in Question 8?" They are supplementary. "What is the relationship between the two angles in Question 9?" They are complementary.

Extra Example 5

$\overrightarrow{VB}$ bisects $\angle AVC$ and $m\angle AVC = 158°$. Find $m\angle BVC$. 79°

MONITORING PROGRESS ANSWER

10.

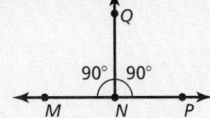

Bisecting Angles

An **angle bisector** is a ray that divides an angle into two angles that are congruent. In the figure, $\overrightarrow{YW}$ bisects $\angle XYZ$, so $\angle XYW \cong \angle ZYW$.

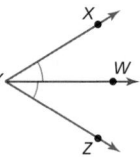

You can use a compass and straightedge to bisect an angle.

CONSTRUCTION   Bisecting an Angle

Construct an angle bisector of $\angle A$ with a compass and straightedge.

SOLUTION

Step 1	Step 2	Step 3
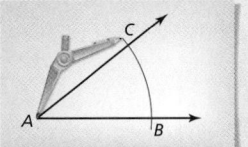	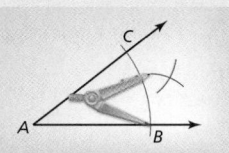	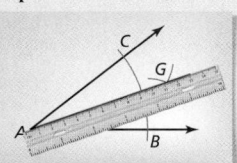
Draw an arc Draw an angle such as $\angle A$, as shown. Place the compass at A. Draw an arc that intersects both sides of the angle. Label the intersections B and C.	**Draw arcs** Place the compass at C. Draw an arc. Then place the compass point at B. Using the same radius, draw another arc.	**Draw a ray** Label the intersection G. Use a straightedge to draw a ray through A and G. $\overrightarrow{AG}$ bisects $\angle A$.

EXAMPLE 5   Using a Bisector to Find Angle Measures

$\overrightarrow{QS}$ bisects $\angle PQR$, and $m\angle PQS = 24°$. Find $m\angle PQR$.

SOLUTION

Step 1 Draw a diagram.

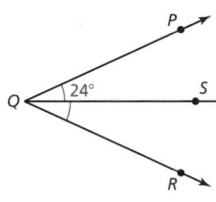

Step 2 Because $\overrightarrow{QS}$ bisects $\angle PQR$, $m\angle PQS = m\angle RQS$. So, $m\angle RQS = 24°$. Use the Angle Addition Postulate to find $m\angle PQR$.

$m\angle PQR = m\angle PQS + m\angle RQS$	Angle Addition Postulate
$= 24° + 24°$	Substitute angle measures.
$= 48°$	Add.

▶ So, $m\angle PQR = 48°$.

Monitoring Progress Help in English and Spanish at *BigIdeasMath.com*

10. Angle MNP is a straight angle, and $\overrightarrow{NQ}$ bisects $\angle MNP$. Draw $\angle MNP$ and $\overrightarrow{NQ}$. Use arcs to mark the congruent angles in your diagram. Find the angle measures of these congruent angles.

Laurie's Notes   Teacher Actions

- There are several figures that can bisect a segment. Rays bisect angles.
- Work through the steps in bisecting an angle. The construction can be proven valid by the Side-Side-Side Congruence Theorem in Section 5.5 and corresponding parts of congruent triangles in Section 5.7.
- **Extension:** Have students paper-fold the angle bisector of an angle.
- **?** "When you bisect an obtuse angle, the result will (*always, sometimes, never*) be two obtuse angles? Explain."

never; An obtuse angle measures between 90° and 180° (exclusive), and when you divide by two, you have angles between 45° and 90° (exclusive).

Closure

- **Exit Ticket:** Given that $m\angle ABC = 143°$, find $m\angle ABD$ and $m\angle DBC$. $m\angle ABD = 24°$; $m\angle DBC = 119°$

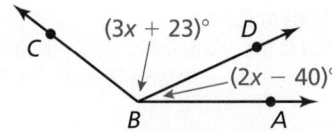

Vocabulary and Core Concept Check

1. **COMPLETE THE SENTENCE** Two angles are _____ angles when they have the same measure.

2. **WHICH ONE DOESN'T BELONG?** Which angle name does *not* belong with the other three? Explain your reasoning.

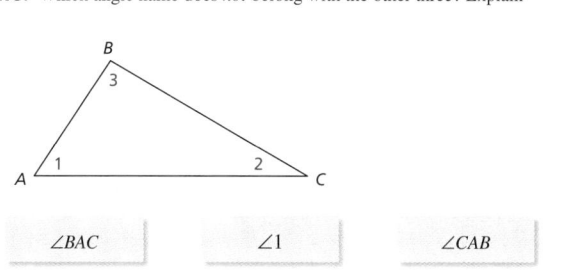

| ∠BCA | ∠BAC | ∠1 | ∠CAB |

Monitoring Progress and Modeling with Mathematics

In Exercises 3–6, write three names for the angle.
(See Example 1.)

3.
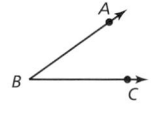

4.
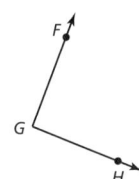

5.
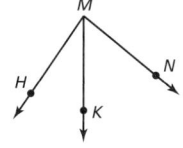

6.
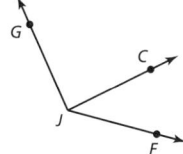

In Exercises 7 and 8, name three different angles in the diagram. *(See Example 1.)*

7.

8.

In Exercises 9–12, find the angle measure. Then classify the angle. *(See Example 2.)*

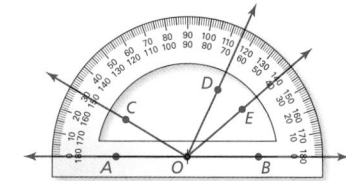

9. *m*∠*AOC*

10. *m*∠*BOD*

11. *m*∠*COD*

12. *m*∠*EOD*

ERROR ANALYSIS In Exercises 13 and 14, describe and correct the error in finding the angle measure. Use the diagram from Exercises 9–12.

13.

m∠*BOC* = 30°

14.
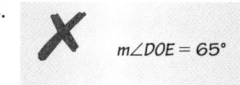

m∠*DOE* = 65°

Assignment Guide and Homework Check

ASSIGNMENT

Basic: 1, 2, 3–27 odd, 52, 54, 58–65

Average: 1, 2, 6–16 even, 24–44 even, 49, 52, 54, 58–65

Advanced: 1, 2, 6, 14, 16, 28–32 even, 40–44 even, 47–49, 52, 54, 56, 58–65

HOMEWORK CHECK

Basic: 5, 9, 11, 23, 27

Average: 8, 14, 28, 38, 42

Advanced: 28, 40, 42, 47, 48

ANSWERS

1. congruent

2. ∠BCA; The other three names refer to the same angle.

3. ∠B, ∠ABC, ∠CBA

4. ∠G, ∠FGH, ∠HGF

5. ∠1, ∠K, ∠JKL (or ∠LKJ)

6. ∠8, ∠R, ∠QRS (or ∠SRQ)

7. ∠HMK, ∠KMN, ∠HMN

8. ∠CJF, ∠CJG, ∠FJG

9. 30°; acute

10. 65°; acute

11. 85°; acute

12. 25°; acute

13. The outer scale was used, but the inner scale should have been used because $\overrightarrow{OB}$ passes through 0° on the inner scale; 150°

14. Because neither side passes through 0°, the measure of the angle should be calculated as the absolute value of the difference between the numbers on the protractor that are matched with the sides; $|65 - 40| = 25°$

ANSWERS

15.

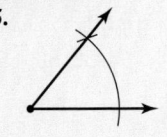

16.

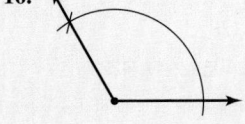

17. ∠ADE, ∠BDC, ∠BCD

18. ∠ADB, ∠CBD

19. 34°

20. 112°

21. 58°

22. 108°

23. 42°

24. 101°

25. 37°, 58°

26. 32°, 85°

27. 77°, 103°

28. 112°, 68°

29. 32°, 58°

30. 39°, 51°

CONSTRUCTION In Exercises 15 and 16, use a compass and straightedge to copy the angle.

15.

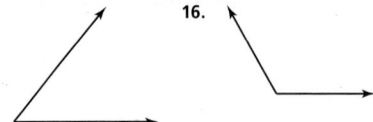

16.

In Exercises 17–20, $m\angle AED = 34°$ **and** $m\angle EAD = 112°$.
(See Example 3.)

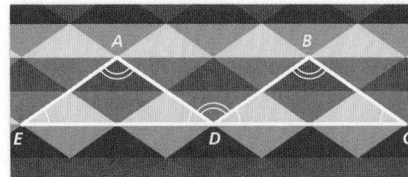

17. Identify the angles congruent to ∠AED.

18. Identify the angles congruent to ∠EAD.

19. Find $m\angle BDC$.

20. Find $m\angle ADB$.

In Exercises 21–24, find the indicated angle measure.

21. Find $m\angle ABC$.

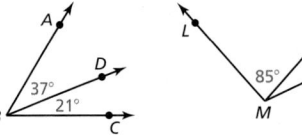

22. Find $m\angle LMN$.

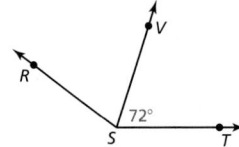

23. $m\angle RST = 114°$. Find $m\angle RSV$.

24. ∠GHK is a straight angle. Find $m\angle LHK$.

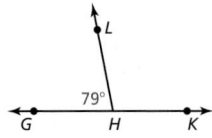

In Exercises 25–30, find the indicated angle measures.
(See Example 4.)

25. $m\angle ABC = 95°$. Find $m\angle ABD$ and $m\angle DBC$.

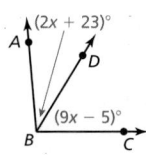

26. $m\angle XYZ = 117°$. Find $m\angle XYW$ and $m\angle WYZ$.

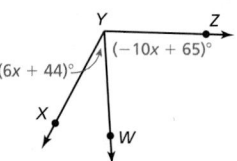

27. ∠LMN is a straight angle. Find $m\angle LMP$ and $m\angle NMP$.

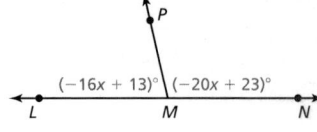

28. ∠ABC is a straight angle. Find $m\angle ABX$ and $m\angle CBX$.

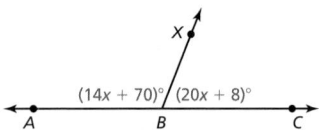

29. Find $m\angle RSQ$ and $m\angle TSQ$.

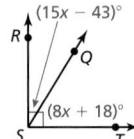

30. Find $m\angle DEH$ and $m\angle FEH$.

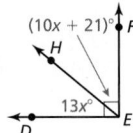

CONSTRUCTION In Exercises 31 and 32, copy the angle. Then construct the angle bisector with a compass and straightedge.

31.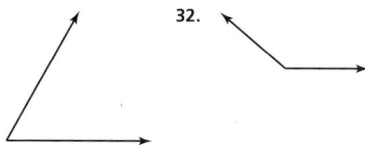

32.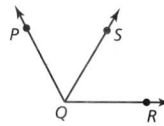

In Exercises 33–36, $\overrightarrow{QS}$ bisects $\angle PQR$. Use the diagram and the given angle measure to find the indicated angle measures. *(See Example 5.)*

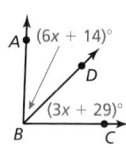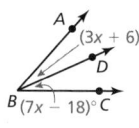

33. $m\angle PQS = 63°$. Find $m\angle RQS$ and $m\angle PQR$.

34. $m\angle RQS = 71°$. Find $m\angle PQS$ and $m\angle PQR$.

35. $m\angle PQR = 124°$. Find $m\angle PQS$ and $m\angle RQS$.

36. $m\angle PQR = 119°$. Find $m\angle PQS$ and $m\angle RQS$.

In Exercises 37–40, $\overrightarrow{BD}$ bisects $\angle ABC$. Find $m\angle ABD$, $m\angle CBD$, and $m\angle ABC$.

37.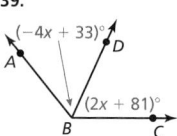

38.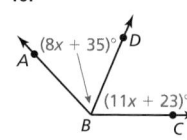

39.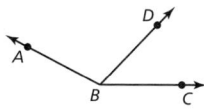

40.

41. **WRITING** Explain how to find $m\angle ABD$ when you are given $m\angle ABC$ and $m\angle CBD$.

42. **ANALYZING RELATIONSHIPS** The map shows the intersections of three roads. Malcom Way intersects Sydney Street at an angle of 162°. Park Road intersects Sydney Street at an angle of 87°. Find the angle at which Malcom Way intersects Park Road.

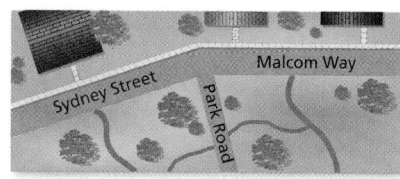

43. **ANALYZING RELATIONSHIPS** In the sculpture shown in the photograph, the measure of $\angle LMN$ is 76° and the measure of $\angle PMN$ is 36°. What is the measure of $\angle LMP$?

USING STRUCTURE In Exercises 44–46, use the diagram of the roof truss.

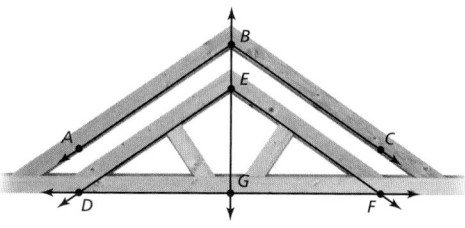

44. In the roof truss, $\overrightarrow{BG}$ bisects $\angle ABC$ and $\angle DEF$, $m\angle ABC = 112°$, and $\angle ABC \cong \angle DEF$. Find the measure of each angle.

   a. $m\angle DEF$ b. $m\angle ABG$

   c. $m\angle CBG$ d. $m\angle DEG$

45. In the roof truss, $\angle DGF$ is a straight angle and $\overrightarrow{GB}$ bisects $\angle DGF$. Find $m\angle DGE$ and $m\angle FGE$.

46. Name an example of each of the four types of angles according to their measures in the diagram.

31.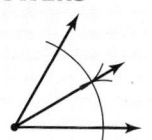

32.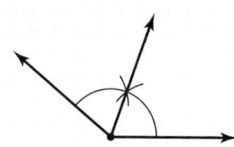

33. 63°, 126°

34. 71°, 142°

35. 62°, 62°

36. 59.5°, 59.5°

37. 44°, 44°, 88°

38. 24°, 24°, 48°

39. 65°, 65°, 130°

40. 67°, 67°, 134°

41. Subtract $m\angle CBD$ from $m\angle ABC$ to find $m\angle ABD$.

42. 75°

43. 40°

44. a. 112°
   b. 56°
   c. 56°
   d. 56°

45. 90°, 90°

46. *Sample answer:* acute: $\angle ABG$, right: $\angle DGE$, obtuse: $\angle ABC$, straight: $\angle DGF$

47. a.

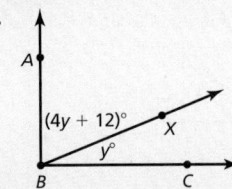

b. $4y + 12 + y = 92$, $76°$, $16°$

48. *Sample answer:* 3:00 or 9:00; The hour hand will be pointing at the 3 or 9 exactly, and the minute hand will be on the 12 exactly.

49. a. acute

   b. acute

   c. acute

   d. right

50–65. See Additional Answers.

Mini-Assessment

Use the figure below.

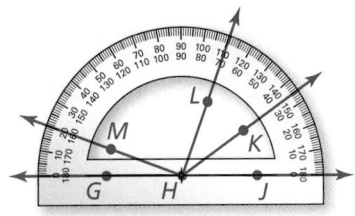

1. Write another name for $\angle GHM$.
   $\angle MHG$

2. Name a right angle.
   Sample answer: $\angle MHL$

3. Identify a pair of congruent angles and find their measures. *Sample answer:* $\angle LHK \cong \angle KHJ$; 35°

Use the figure below.

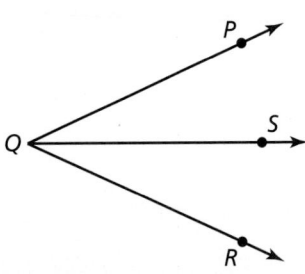

4. Given that $m\angle PQS = 28°$ and $m\angle RQS = 25°$, find $m\angle PQR$. 53°

5. $\overrightarrow{QS}$ bisects $\angle PQR$ and $m\angle PQR = 57°$. Find $m\angle PQS$. 28.5°

---

47. MATHEMATICAL CONNECTIONS In $\angle ABC$, $\overrightarrow{BX}$ is in the interior of the angle, $m\angle ABX$ is 12 more than 4 times $m\angle CBX$, and $m\angle ABC = 92°$.

   a. Draw a diagram to represent the situation.

   b. Write and solve an equation to find $m\angle ABX$ and $m\angle CBX$.

48. THOUGHT PROVOKING The angle between the minute hand and the hour hand of a clock is 90°. What time is it? Justify your answer.

49. ABSTRACT REASONING Classify the angles that result from bisecting each type of angle.

   a. acute angle   **b.** right angle

   c. obtuse angle   **d.** straight angle

50. ABSTRACT REASONING Classify the angles that result from drawing a ray in the interior of each type of angle. Include all possibilities and explain your reasoning.

   a. acute angle   **b.** right angle

   c. obtuse angle   **d.** straight angle

51. CRITICAL THINKING The ray from the origin through $(4, 0)$ forms one side of an angle. Use the numbers below as x- and y-coordinates to create each type of angle in a coordinate plane.

−2	−1	0	1	2

   a. acute angle   **b.** right angle

   c. obtuse angle   **d.** straight angle

52. MAKING AN ARGUMENT Your friend claims it is possible for a straight angle to consist of two obtuse angles. Is your friend correct? Explain your reasoning.

53. CRITICAL THINKING Two acute angles are added together. What type(s) of angle(s) do they form? Explain your reasoning.

54. HOW DO YOU SEE IT? Use the diagram.

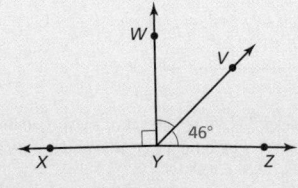

   a. Is it possible for $\angle XYZ$ to be a straight angle? Explain your reasoning.

   b. What can you change in the diagram so that $\angle XYZ$ is a straight angle?

55. WRITING Explain the process of bisecting an angle in your own words. Compare it to bisecting a segment.

56. ANALYZING RELATIONSHIPS $\overrightarrow{SQ}$ bisects $\angle RST$, $\overrightarrow{SP}$ bisects $\angle RSQ$, and $\overrightarrow{SV}$ bisects $\angle RSP$. The measure of $\angle VSP$ is 17°. Find $m\angle TSQ$. Explain.

57. ABSTRACT REASONING A bubble level is a tool used to determine whether a surface is horizontal, like the top of a picture frame. If the bubble is not exactly in the middle when the level is placed on the surface, then the surface is not horizontal. What is the most realistic type of angle formed by the level and a horizontal line when the bubble is not in the middle? Explain your reasoning.

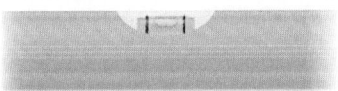

Maintaining Mathematical Proficiency *Reviewing what you learned in previous grades and lessons*

Solve the equation. *(Skills Review Handbook)*

58. $x + 67 = 180$

59. $x + 58 = 90$

60. $16 + x = 90$

61. $109 + x = 180$

62. $(6x + 7) + (13x + 21) = 180$

63. $(3x + 15) + (4x - 9) = 90$

64. $(11x - 25) + (24x + 10) = 90$

65. $(14x - 18) + (5x + 8) = 180$

If students need help...	If students got it...
Resources by Chapter • Practice A and Practice B • Puzzle Time	Resources by Chapter • Enrichment and Extension • Cumulative Review
Student Journal • Practice	Start the *next* Section
Differentiating the Lesson Skills Review Handbook	

Overview of Section 1.6

Introduction

- Many of the angle pair relationships presented in this lesson should be familiar to students. The relationships were first introduced in middle school. (7.G.5: Use facts about supplementary, complementary, vertical, and adjacent angles in a multi-step problem to write and solve simple equations for an unknown angle in a figure.) While students may mix up the vocabulary (complementary and supplementary), the concepts are not new.
- **MP6 Attend to Precision:** While students may be familiar with the concepts, they need to be aware of the definitions. For instance, adjacent angles share a common vertex and common side, but have no interior points in common, meaning the angles cannot overlap.
- Pairs of angles can share more than one relationship, and throughout the lesson this will become evident. For instance, complementary angles can be congruent, or both acute, or adjacent.

Common Misconceptions

- Students often believe that complementary and supplementary angles are adjacent. They are often drawn this way and in real-life applications they are adjacent, but the relationship does not make it a condition. Be explicit in stating this.

Formative Assessment Tips

- **Concept Card Mapping:** This strategy is related to concept mapping where relationships between concepts are depicted graphically. In this variation, students are presented with cards that state the concept. They create the linkages that describe the relationship between the concepts. The cards are moveable, thus allowing students to think about different ways in which the concepts can be linked.
- *Sample:* Make a set of concept cards relating to angle relationships.

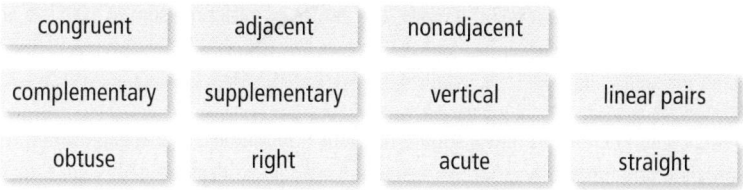

- Students work with partners or in groups to arrange the cards on a paper (or whiteboard). The lines drawn between the cards state the linkage of the concepts. For instance, they may link *vertical* with *congruent* and state a property they believe is true for vertical angles, while another group may link *vertical* with *nonadjacent* because it is part of the definition. You should allow for concepts to be linked to more than one other card. You may also want to allow linkages for three cards.
- This technique can be used at the beginning of a unit of instruction to determine what conceptions and knowledge students have. It can also be used at the end of instruction for students to reflect on how a group of concepts are connected.

Extensions

- Create a photo collage or album of angle relationships. Display the photos to students and ask them to identify the relationships they see.

Pacing Suggestion

- Once students have worked the explorations, continue with the formal lesson.

Dynamic Teaching Tools

Dynamic Assessment & Progress Monitoring Tool
Lesson Planning Tool
Interactive Whiteboard Lesson Library
Dynamic Classroom with Dynamic Investigations

Common Core State Standards

HSG-CO.A.1 Know precise definitions of angle, ... based on the undefined notions of point, line, ...

Laurie's Notes

Exploration

Motivate

- Show an aerial view of the runways at an airport. Number the angles formed by different runways to facilitate students being able to reference them more easily. Ask students to make a list of pairs of angles and then state the relationships between each pair of angles. Do not specify the measures of the angles.
- You should have a sense of what relationships students recall and are familiar with.

Exploration Note

- Students should be familiar (from middle school) with many of the angle pairs presented in this lesson. For that reason, the explorations are an interesting presentation of the relationships and will give you information as to what your students recall.
- The proofs of vertical angles being congruent, or the base angles of an isosceles triangle being congruent, were likely presented in an informal manner in middle school. Justification (formal proof) is presented in this course.
- The new relationship presented in the formal lesson is *linear pairs*.

Exploration 1

- The measure of one interior angle of a regular pentagon is given. That is all that will be needed in order for students to determine the remaining angles.
- The important part of this exploration is hearing students give their explanations. Often students will use eyesight to state the angle measure, versus being able to state the underlying relationship.
- **MP3 Construct Viable Arguments and Critique the Reasoning of Others:** A sample explanation might be, "Angle x is supplementary to the 108° angle, so it measures 72°. Angle z would be 72° for the same reason. Angle y is supplementary to angles x and z, so it is 108°. It is also a vertical angle. Angle w is supplementary to another interior angle of the regular pentagon, so it is 72°. Finally, the angles of a triangle sum to 180°, so angle $v = 180° - 2(72°) = 36°$."

Exploration 2

- Students come in knowing that a square has four right angles. In this exploration, what you are listening for is how students describe the angle pair relationships. Do they have the vocabulary to describe an angle being bisected? Two angles being congruent? Two angles being vertical or supplementary?

Communicate Your Answer

- Listen for student understanding of common angle pair relationships such as complementary, supplementary, and vertical.

Connecting to Next Step

- The explorations should be a review of common angle pair relationships. Quickly transition to the formal lesson.

1.6 Describing Pairs of Angles

Essential Question
How can you describe angle pair relationships and use these descriptions to find angle measures?

EXPLORATION 1 — Finding Angle Measures

Work with a partner. The five-pointed star has a regular pentagon at its center.

a. What do you notice about the following angle pairs?

$x°$ and $y°$

$y°$ and $z°$

$x°$ and $z°$

b. Find the values of the indicated variables. Do not use a protractor to measure the angles.

$x =$

$y =$

$z =$

$w =$

$v =$

Explain how you obtained each answer.

EXPLORATION 2 — Finding Angle Measures

Work with a partner. A square is divided by its diagonals into four triangles.

a. What do you notice about the following angle pairs?

$a°$ and $b°$

$c°$ and $d°$

$c°$ and $e°$

b. Find the values of the indicated variables. Do not use a protractor to measure the angles.

$c =$

$d =$

$e =$

Explain how you obtained each answer.

ATTENDING TO PRECISION

To be proficient in math, you need to communicate precisely with others.

Communicate Your Answer

3. How can you describe angle pair relationships and use these descriptions to find angle measures?

4. What do you notice about the angle measures of complementary angles, supplementary angles, and vertical angles?

Section 1.6   Describing Pairs of Angles   **47**

ANSWERS

1. a. $x°$ and $y°$ make a straight angle together; $y°$ and $z°$ make a straight angle together; $x°$ and $z°$ appear to be congruent.

   b. 72; 108; 72; 72; 36;
   $x = 180 - 108 = 72$;
   $y = 180 - 72 = 108$;
   $z = 180 - 108 = 72$;
   $w = 180 - 108 = 72$;
   $v = 180 - (72 + 72) = 36$

2. a. $a°$ and $b°$ make a right angle together; $c°$ and $d°$ make a straight angle together; $c°$ and $e°$ appear to be congruent.

   b. 90; 90; 90;
   $c = 180 - 90 = 90$;
   $d = 180 - c = 180 - 90 = 90$;
   $e = 180 - 90 = 90$

3. When two lines intersect, four angles and two pairs of opposite rays are formed. The angles that are next to each other have measures that add up to 180°. The angles that are across from each other are congruent and have the same measure.

4. Complementary angle measures add up to 90°; Supplementary angle measures add up to 180°; Vertical angles have the same measure.

Extra Example 1

In the figure, name a pair of complementary angles, a pair of supplementary angles, and a pair of adjacent angles.

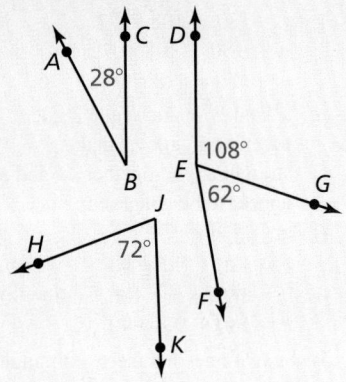

Sample answer: ∠ABC and ∠GEF, ∠DEG and ∠HJK, ∠DEG and ∠GEF

1.6 Lesson

Core Vocabulary

complementary angles, *p. 48*
supplementary angles, *p. 48*
adjacent angles, *p. 48*
linear pair, *p. 50*
vertical angles, *p. 50*

Previous
vertex
sides of an angle
interior of an angle
opposite rays

What You Will Learn

▶ Identify complementary and supplementary angles.
▶ Identify linear pairs and vertical angles.

Using Complementary and Supplementary Angles

Pairs of angles can have special relationships. The measurements of the angles or the positions of the angles in the pair determine the relationship.

Core Concept

Complementary and Supplementary Angles

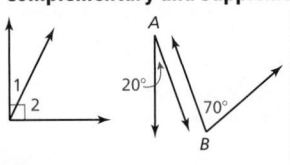 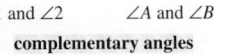 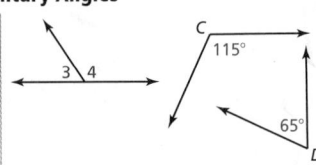

∠1 and ∠2	∠A and ∠B	∠3 and ∠4	∠C and ∠D
complementary angles		**supplementary angles**	

Two positive angles whose measures have a sum of 90°. Each angle is the *complement* of the other.

Two positive angles whose measures have a sum of 180°. Each angle is the *supplement* of the other.

Adjacent Angles

Complementary angles and supplementary angles can be *adjacent angles* or *nonadjacent angles*. **Adjacent angles** are two angles that share a common vertex and side, but have no common interior points.

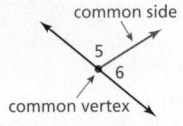 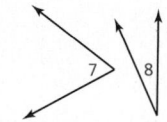

∠5 and ∠6 are adjacent angles.   ∠7 and ∠8 are nonadjacent angles.

EXAMPLE 1   Identifying Pairs of Angles

In the figure, name a pair of complementary angles, a pair of supplementary angles, and a pair of adjacent angles.

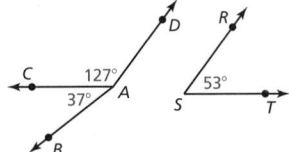

SOLUTION

Because 37° + 53° = 90°, ∠BAC and ∠RST are complementary angles.

Because 127° + 53° = 180°, ∠CAD and ∠RST are supplementary angles.

Because ∠BAC and ∠CAD share a common vertex and side, they are adjacent angles.

Laurie's Notes   Teacher Actions

- Write the *Core Concept* and draw sketches to support the definitions.
- Note that *complementary* and *supplementary* angles do not need to be adjacent. Their relationship is a matter of measurement, not position.
- **?** "What is the supplement of a 72° angle?" 108° "What is the complement of a 72° angle?" 18° "What is the supplement of a 142° angle?" 38° "What is the complement of a 142° angle?" An angle of 142° does not have a complement.
- Note the *Common Error* in the sidebar column.

EXAMPLE 2 **Finding Angle Measures**

a. ∠1 is a complement of ∠2, and $m\angle 1 = 62°$. Find $m\angle 2$.

b. ∠3 is a supplement of ∠4, and $m\angle 4 = 47°$. Find $m\angle 3$.

SOLUTION

a. Draw a diagram with complementary adjacent angles to illustrate the relationship.

$$m\angle 2 = 90° - m\angle 1 = 90° - 62° = 28°$$

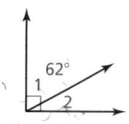

b. Draw a diagram with supplementary adjacent angles to illustrate the relationship.

$$m\angle 3 = 180° - m\angle 4 = 180° - 47° = 133°$$

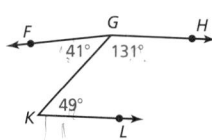

Monitoring Progress Help in English and Spanish at *BigIdeasMath.com*

In Exercises 1 and 2, use the figure.

1. Name a pair of complementary angles, a pair of supplementary angles, and a pair of adjacent angles.

2. Are ∠KGH and ∠LKG adjacent angles? Are ∠FGK and ∠FGH adjacent angles? Explain.

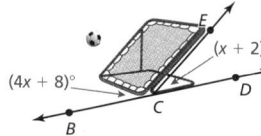

3. ∠1 is a complement of ∠2, and $m\angle 2 = 5°$. Find $m\angle 1$.

4. ∠3 is a supplement of ∠4, and $m\angle 3 = 148°$. Find $m\angle 4$.

EXAMPLE 3 **Real-Life Application**

When viewed from the side, the frame of a ball-return net forms a pair of supplementary angles with the ground. Find $m\angle BCE$ and $m\angle ECD$.

SOLUTION

Step 1 Use the fact that the sum of the measures of supplementary angles is 180°.

$m\angle BCE + m\angle ECD = 180°$	Write an equation.
$(4x + 8)° + (x + 2)° = 180°$	Substitute angle measures.
$5x + 10 = 180$	Combine like terms.
$x = 34$	Solve for x.

Step 2 Evaluate the given expressions when $x = 34$.

$$m\angle BCE = (4x + 8)° = (4 \cdot 34 + 8)° = 144°$$

$$m\angle ECD = (x + 2)° = (34 + 2)° = 36°$$

▶ So, $m\angle BCE = 144°$ and $m\angle ECD = 36°$.

Monitoring Progress  Help in English and Spanish at *BigIdeasMath.com*

5. ∠LMN and ∠PQR are complementary angles. Find the measures of the angles when $m\angle LMN = (4x - 2)°$ and $m\angle PQR = (9x + 1)°$.

Extra Example 2

a. ∠5 is a complement of ∠3, and $m\angle 3 = 53°$. Find $m\angle 5$. 37°

b. ∠4 is a supplement of ∠2, and $m\angle 4 = 29°$. Find $m\angle 2$. 151°

Extra Example 3

The veins in a leaf form a pair of supplementary angles. Find the measures of the angles when $m\angle 1 = (7x + 13)°$ and $m\angle 2 = (25x + 7)°$.

$m\angle 1 = 48°, m\angle 2 = 132°$

MONITORING PROGRESS ANSWERS

1. ∠FGK and ∠LKG, ∠KGH and ∠LKG, ∠FGK and ∠KGH

2. no; no; ∠KGH and ∠LKG do not share a common side; ∠FGK and ∠FGH share common interior points.

3. 85°

4. 32°

5. $m\angle LMN = 26°$; $m\angle PQR = 64°$

Laurie's Notes **Teacher Actions**

• Example 2 could be done by asking students to sketch or use a protractor to draw each of the angle pairs.

• A ball-return net may not be familiar to all students. Ask for examples of similar structures: ramps, mousetraps, windshield wipers, diagonal paths off a sidewalk, and so on.

• **Whiteboarding:** Have students work with their partners on Example 3, followed by completing Question 5.

Extra Example 4

Identify all of the linear pairs and all of the vertical angles in the figure.

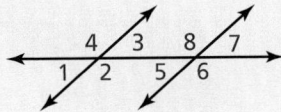

∠1 and ∠2, ∠2 and ∠3, ∠3 and ∠4, ∠4 and ∠1, ∠5 and ∠6, ∠6 and ∠7, ∠7 and ∠8, ∠8 and ∠5; ∠1 and ∠3, ∠2 and ∠4, ∠5 and ∠7, ∠6 and ∠8

Extra Example 5

Two angles form a linear pair. The measure of one angle is eight times the measure of the other angle. Find the measure of each angle. 20°, 160°

Using Other Angle Pairs

🔁 Core Concept

Linear Pairs and Vertical Angles

Two adjacent angles are a **linear pair** when their noncommon sides are opposite rays. The angles in a linear pair are supplementary angles.

Two angles are **vertical angles** when their sides form two pairs of opposite rays.

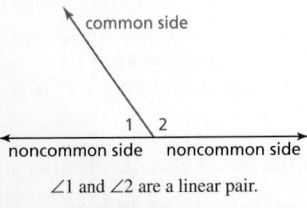

common side

1 2

noncommon side   noncommon side

∠1 and ∠2 are a linear pair.

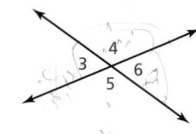

∠3 and ∠6 are vertical angles.
∠4 and ∠5 are vertical angles.

EXAMPLE 4   **Identifying Angle Pairs**

Identify all the linear pairs and all the vertical angles in the figure.

SOLUTION

To find vertical angles, look for angles formed by intersecting lines.

▶   ∠1 and ∠5 are vertical angles.

To find linear pairs, look for adjacent angles whose noncommon sides are opposite rays.

▶   ∠1 and ∠4 are a linear pair. ∠4 and ∠5 are also a linear pair.

COMMON ERROR

In Example 4, one side of ∠1 and one side of ∠3 are opposite rays. But the angles are not a linear pair because they are *nonadjacent.*

EXAMPLE 5   **Finding Angle Measures in a Linear Pair**

Two angles form a linear pair. The measure of one angle is five times the measure of the other angle. Find the measure of each angle.

SOLUTION

Step 1   Draw a diagram. Let $x°$ be the measure of one angle. The measure of the other angle is $5x°$.

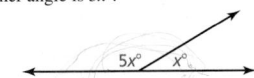

$5x°$ $x°$

Step 2   Use the fact that the angles of a linear pair are supplementary to write an equation.

$x° + 5x° = 180°$	Write an equation.
$6x = 180$	Combine like terms.
$x = 30$	Divide each side by 6.

▶   The measures of the angles are $30°$ and $5(30°) = 150°$.

Laurie's Notes   Teacher Actions

- Write the *Core Concept*. Students should be familiar with *vertical angles*, but have likely not heard the phrase *linear pairs*.
- **?** "What is the relationship between linear pairs and supplementary angles?" Linear pairs are supplementary, but not all supplementary angles are linear pairs.
- A common question from students will be why *vertical angles* are called *vertical* instead of *opposite*. Also confusing to students is the use of *vertical* to describe the orientation of being upright, and yet the position of vertical angles can be horizontal! Searching online or in math history books, there are different explanations for the origin of the term *vertical angles*.

6. Do any of the numbered angles in the figure form a linear pair? Which angles are vertical angles? Explain your reasoning.

7. The measure of an angle is twice the measure of its complement. Find the measure of each angle.

8. Two angles form a linear pair. The measure of one angle is $1\frac{1}{2}$ times the measure of the other angle. Find the measure of each angle.

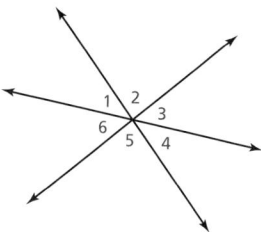

MONITORING PROGRESS ANSWERS

6. no; $\angle 1$ and $\angle 4$, $\angle 2$ and $\angle 5$, $\angle 3$ and $\angle 6$; There are no numbered adjacent angles whose noncommon sides are opposite rays; The sides form two pairs of opposite rays.

7. $30°$, $60°$

8. $72°$, $108°$

Concept Summary

Interpreting a Diagram

There are some things you can conclude from a diagram, and some you cannot. For example, here are some things that you *can* conclude from the diagram below.

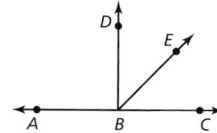

YOU CAN CONCLUDE

- All points shown are coplanar.
- Points A, B, and C are collinear, and B is between A and C.
- $\overleftrightarrow{AC}$, $\overrightarrow{BD}$, and $\overrightarrow{BE}$ intersect at point B.
- $\angle DBE$ and $\angle EBC$ are adjacent angles, and $\angle ABC$ is a straight angle.
- Point E lies in the interior of $\angle DBC$.

Here are some things you *cannot* conclude from the diagram above.

YOU CANNOT CONCLUDE

- $\overline{AB} \cong \overline{BC}$.
- $\angle DBE \cong \angle EBC$.
- $\angle ABD$ is a right angle.

To make such conclusions, the following information must be given.

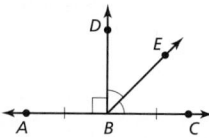

Laurie's Notes Teacher Actions

- The *Monitoring Progress* questions integrate skills from algebra. Students are expected to translate words into symbols.
- **Whiteboarding:** Draw the diagram in the *Concept Summary* and ask pairs of students to make a list of those things that they can conclude from the diagram and those which they cannot conclude.
- **MP3:** Share as a whole class and have students give explanations for what statements were written for each list.

Closure

- **Concept Card Mapping:** See the description of this activity on page T-46.

ANSWERS

1. Adjacent angles share a common side, and are next to each other. Vertical angles form two pairs of opposite rays, and are across from each other.

2. linear pair with ∠3 and ∠4; This pair of angles is supplementary, but the other ones show complementary angles.

3. ∠LJM, ∠MJN

4. ∠KJM, ∠MJN (or ∠KJL, ∠LJN)

5. ∠EGF, ∠NJP

6. ∠FGH, ∠LJM

7. 67°

8. 44°

9. 102°

10. 71°

11. $m\angle QRT = 47°$, $m\angle TRS = 133°$

12. $m\angle BAC = 58°$, $m\angle CAD = 32°$

13. $m\angle UVW = 12°$, $m\angle XYZ = 78°$

14. $m\angle EFG = 161°$, $m\angle LMN = 19°$

15. ∠1 and ∠5

16. ∠7 and ∠6, ∠7 and ∠8

17. yes; The sides form two pairs of opposite rays.

18. no; Only one pair of opposite rays is formed by these two angles.

19. 60°, 120°

20. 45°, 135°

21. 9°, 81°

Vocabulary and Core Concept Check

1. **WRITING** Explain what is different between adjacent angles and vertical angles.

2. **WHICH ONE DOESN'T BELONG?** Which one does *not* belong with the other three? Explain your reasoning.

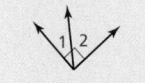 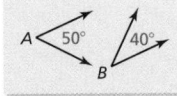 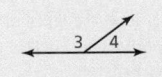 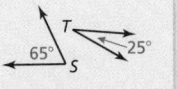

Monitoring Progress and Modeling with Mathematics

In Exercises 3–6, use the figure. *(See Example 1.)*

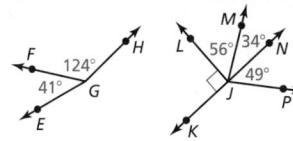

3. Name a pair of adjacent complementary angles.

4. Name a pair of adjacent supplementary angles.

5. Name a pair of nonadjacent complementary angles.

6. Name a pair of nonadjacent supplementary angles.

In Exercises 7–10, find the angle measure. *(See Example 2.)*

7. ∠1 is a complement of ∠2, and $m\angle 1 = 23°$. Find $m\angle 2$.

8. ∠3 is a complement of ∠4, and $m\angle 3 = 46°$. Find $m\angle 4$.

9. ∠5 is a supplement of ∠6, and $m\angle 5 = 78°$. Find $m\angle 6$.

10. ∠7 is a supplement of ∠8, and $m\angle 7 = 109°$. Find $m\angle 8$.

In Exercises 11–14, find the measure of each angle. *(See Example 3.)*

11.

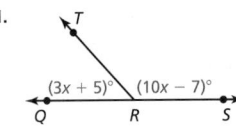

12.

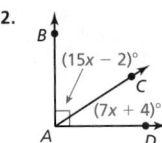

13. ∠UVW and ∠XYZ are complementary angles, $m\angle UVW = (x - 10)°$, and $m\angle XYZ = (4x - 10)°$.

14. ∠EFG and ∠LMN are supplementary angles, $m\angle EFG = (3x + 17)°$, and $m\angle LMN = \left(\frac{1}{2}x - 5\right)°$.

In Exercises 15–18, use the figure. *(See Example 4.)*

15. Identify the linear pair(s) that include ∠1.

16. Identify the linear pair(s) that include ∠7.

17. Are ∠6 and ∠8 vertical angles? Explain your reasoning.

18. Are ∠2 and ∠5 vertical angles? Explain your reasoning.

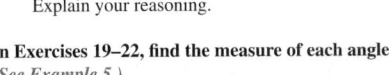

In Exercises 19–22, find the measure of each angle. *(See Example 5.)*

19. Two angles form a linear pair. The measure of one angle is twice the measure of the other angle.

20. Two angles form a linear pair. The measure of one angle is $\frac{1}{3}$ the measure of the other angle.

21. The measure of an angle is nine times the measure of its complement.

22. The measure of an angle is $\frac{1}{4}$ the measure of its complement.

ERROR ANALYSIS In Exercises 23 and 24, describe and correct the error in identifying pairs of angles in the figure.

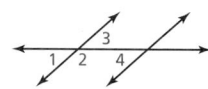

23.

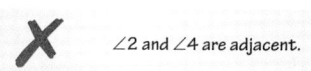

∠2 and ∠4 are adjacent.

24.

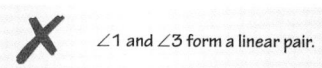

∠1 and ∠3 form a linear pair.

In Exercises 25 and 26, the picture shows the Alamillo Bridge in Seville, Spain. In the picture, $m\angle 1 = 58°$ and $m\angle 2 = 24°$.

25. Find the measure of the supplement of ∠1.

26. Find the measure of the supplement of ∠2.

27. PROBLEM SOLVING The arm of a crossing gate moves 42° from a vertical position. How many more degrees does the arm have to move so that it is horizontal?

A. 42°   **B.** 138°

C. 48°   **D.** 90°

28. REASONING The foul lines of a baseball field intersect at home plate to form a right angle. A batter hits a fair ball such that the path of the baseball forms an angle of 27° with the third base foul line. What is the measure of the angle between the first base foul line and the path of the baseball?

29. CONSTRUCTION Construct a linear pair where one angle measure is 115°.

30. CONSTRUCTION Construct a pair of adjacent angles that have angle measures of 45° and 97°.

31. PROBLEM SOLVING $m\angle U = 2x°$, and $m\angle V = 4m\angle U$. Which value of x makes ∠U and ∠V complements of each other?

    A. 25   **B.** 9   **C.** 36   **D.** 18

MATHEMATICAL CONNECTIONS In Exercises 32–35, write and solve an algebraic equation to find the measure of each angle based on the given description.

32. The measure of an angle is 6° less than the measure of its complement.

33. The measure of an angle is 12° more than twice the measure of its complement.

34. The measure of one angle is 3° more than $\frac{1}{2}$ the measure of its supplement.

35. Two angles form a linear pair. The measure of one angle is 15° less than $\frac{2}{3}$ the measure of the other angle.

CRITICAL THINKING In Exercises 36–41, tell whether the statement is *always*, *sometimes*, or *never* true. Explain your reasoning.

36. Complementary angles are adjacent.

37. Angles in a linear pair are supplements of each other.

38. Vertical angles are adjacent.

39. Vertical angles are supplements of each other.

40. If an angle is acute, then its complement is greater than its supplement.

41. If two complementary angles are congruent, then the measure of each angle is 45°.

42. WRITING Explain why the supplement of an acute angle must be obtuse.

43. WRITING Explain why an obtuse angle does not have a complement.

Section 1.6   Describing Pairs of Angles   **53**

ANSWERS

22. 18°, 72°

23. They do not share a common side, so they are not adjacent; ∠1 and ∠2 are adjacent.

24. They are not adjacent, so they cannot form a linear pair; ∠1 and ∠3 are vertical angles.

25. 122°

26. 156°

27. C

28. 63°

29.

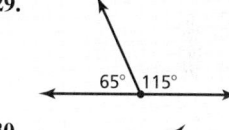

65°   115°

30.

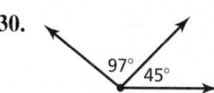

97°   45°

31. B

32. $x + (x - 6) = 90$; 48° and 42°

33. $x + (2x + 12) = 90$; 26° and 64°

34. $x + \left(\frac{1}{2}x + 3\right) = 180$; 118° and 62°

35. $x + \left(\frac{2}{3}x - 15\right) = 180$; 117° and 63°

36. sometimes; The angles could share a common side and make a right angle.

37. always; A linear pair forms a straight angle, which is 180°.

38. never; Vertical angles are formed by two pairs of opposite rays.

39. sometimes; This is possible if the lines are perpendicular.

40. never; Its complement will be acute, and its supplement will be obtuse.

41. always; 45 + 45 = 90

42. If two angles add up to 180° and one is less than 90°, then the other has to be greater than 90°.

43. The measure of an obtuse angle is greater than 90°. So, you cannot add it to the measure of another angle and get 90°.

ANSWERS

44. *Sample answer:*

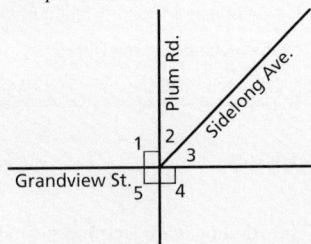

supplementary: ∠4 and ∠5, ∠4 and
∠1, ∠5 and ∠1; complementary:
∠2 and ∠3; vertical: ∠1 and ∠4

45. a. 50°, 40°, 140°

b. $\frac{1}{3}$; Because all 4 angles have
supplements, the first paper
can be any angle. Then there is
a 1 in 3 chance of drawing its
supplement.

46. a. yes; They are marked as
congruent.

b. yes; Point A lies on $\overleftrightarrow{CF}$.

c. no; They do not have a special
relationship, and their angle
measurements are unknown.

d. no; They are not marked as
congruent.

46e–59. See Additional Answers.

Mini-Assessment

Use the figure.

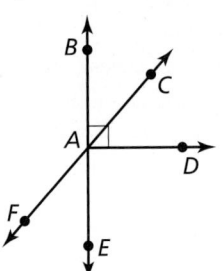

1. Name a pair of adjacent
   complementary angles.
   Sample answer: ∠CAB, ∠CAD

2. $m\angle CAB = 42°$. Find $m\angle CAD$. 48°

3. Name a pair of acute vertical angles.
   Sample answer: ∠CAB, ∠EAF

4. Name two angles that form a linear
   pair with ∠BAF. *Sample answer:*
   ∠BAC, ∠FAE

5. $m\angle BAC = \frac{1}{2} m\angle BAF$. Find $m\angle BAF$.
   120°

54   Chapter 1

---

44. THOUGHT PROVOKING Sketch an intersection of
roads. Identify any supplementary, complementary,
or vertical angles.

45. ATTENDING TO PRECISION Use the figure.

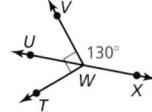

a. Find $m\angle UWV$, $m\angle TWU$, and $m\angle TWX$.

b. You write the measures of ∠TWU, ∠TWX, ∠UWV,
and ∠VWX on separate pieces of paper and place
the pieces of paper in a box. Then you pick two
pieces of paper out of the box at random. What is
the probability that the angle measures you choose
are supplementary? Explain your reasoning.

46. HOW DO YOU SEE IT? Tell whether you can
conclude that each statement is true based on the
figure. Explain your reasoning.

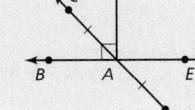

a. $\overline{CA} \cong \overline{AF}$.

b. Points C, A, and
F are collinear.

c. $\angle CAD \cong \angle EAF$.

d. $\overline{BA} \cong \overline{AE}$.

e. $\overleftrightarrow{CF}$, $\overleftrightarrow{BE}$, and $\overleftrightarrow{AD}$ intersect at point A.

f. ∠BAC and ∠CAD are complementary angles.

g. ∠DAE is a right angle.

47. REASONING ∠KJL and ∠LJM
are complements, and ∠MJN
and ∠LJM are complements.
Can you show that
∠KJL ≅ ∠MJN?
Explain your reasoning.

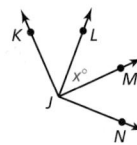

48. MAKING AN ARGUMENT Light from a flashlight
strikes a mirror and is reflected so that the angle of
reflection is congruent to the angle of incidence. Your
classmate claims that ∠QPR is congruent to ∠TPU
regardless of the measure of ∠RPS. Is your classmate
correct? Explain your reasoning.

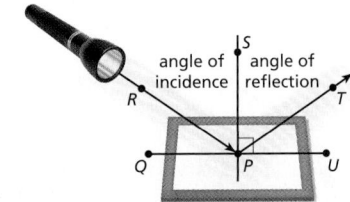

49. DRAWING CONCLUSIONS Use the figure.

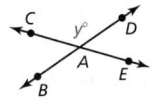

a. Write expressions for the measures of ∠BAE,
∠DAE, and ∠CAB.

b. What do you notice about the measures of vertical
angles? Explain your reasoning.

50. MATHEMATICAL CONNECTIONS Let $m\angle 1 = x°$,
$m\angle 2 = y_1°$, and $m\angle 3 = y_2°$. ∠2 is the complement of
∠1, and ∠3 is the supplement of ∠1.

a. Write equations for y_1 as a function of x and for
y_2 as a function of x. What is the domain of each
function? Explain.

b. Graph each function and describe its range.

51. MATHEMATICAL CONNECTIONS The sum of the
measures of two complementary angles is 74° greater
than the difference of their measures. Find the
measure of each angle. Explain how you found the
angle measures.

Maintaining Mathematical Proficiency   Reviewing what you learned in previous grades and lessons

Determine whether the statement is *always*, *sometimes*, or *never* true. Explain your reasoning.
(Skills Review Handbook)

52. An integer is a whole number.

53. An integer is an irrational number.

54. An irrational number is a real number.

55. A whole number is negative.

56. A rational number is an integer.

57. A natural number is an integer.

58. A whole number is a rational number.

59. An irrational number is negative.

54   Chapter 1   Basics of Geometry

If students need help...	If students got it...
Resources by Chapter • Practice A and Practice B • Puzzle Time	Resources by Chapter • Enrichment and Extension • Cumulative Review
Student Journal • Practice	Start the *next* Section
Differentiating the Lesson Skills Review Handbook	

Core Vocabulary

angle, *p. 38*
vertex, *p. 38*
sides of an angle, *p. 38*
interior of an angle, *p. 38*
exterior of an angle, *p. 38*
measure of an angle, *p. 39*

acute angle, *p. 39*
right angle, *p. 39*
obtuse angle, *p. 39*
straight angle, *p. 39*
congruent angles, *p. 40*
angle bisector, *p. 42*

complementary angles, *p. 48*
supplementary angles, *p. 48*
adjacent angles, *p. 48*
linear pair, *p. 50*
vertical angles, *p. 50*

Core Concepts

Section 1.4

Classifying Polygons, *p. 30*
Finding Perimeter and Area in the Coordinate Plane, *p. 31*

Section 1.5

Postulate 1.3 Protractor Postulate, *p. 39*
Types of Angles, *p. 39*
Postulate 1.4 Angle Addition Postulate, *p. 41*
Bisecting Angles, *p. 42*

Section 1.6

Complementary and Supplementary Angles, *p. 48*
Adjacent Angles, *p. 48*
Linear Pairs and Vertical Angles, *p. 50*
Interpreting a Diagram, *p. 51*

Mathematical Practices

1. How could you explain your answers to Exercise 33 on page 36 to a friend who is unable to hear?

2. What tool(s) could you use to verify your answers to Exercises 25–30 on page 44?

3. Your friend says that the angles in Exercise 28 on page 53 are supplementary angles. Explain why you agree or disagree.

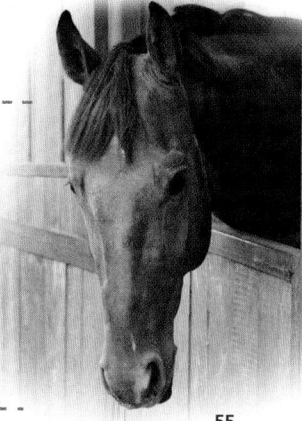

Performance Task

Comfortable Horse Stalls

The plan for a new barn includes standard, rectangular horse stalls. The architect is sure that this will provide the most comfort for your horse because it is the greatest area for the stall. Is that correct? How can you investigate to find out?

To explore the answers to this question and more, go to *BigIdeasMath.com*.

55

Dynamic Teaching Tools

Dynamic Assessment & Progress Monitoring Tool
Interactive Whiteboard Lesson Library
Dynamic Classroom with Dynamic Investigations

ANSWERS

1. See Additional Answers.
2. protractor
3. disagree; The angles are complementary because they form a right angle, and the sum of their measures is 90°.

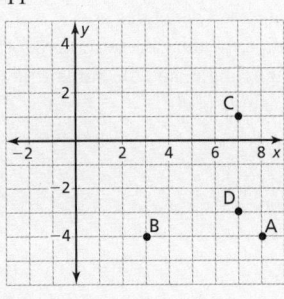
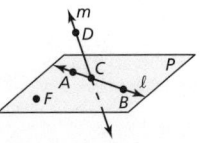

1.1 Points, Lines, and Planes *(pp. 3–10)*

Use the diagram at the right. Give another name for plane *P*. Then name a line in the plane, a ray, a line intersecting the plane, and three collinear points.

You can find another name for plane *P* by using any three points in the plane that are not on the same line. So, another name for plane *P* is plane *FAB*.

A line in the plane is $\overleftrightarrow{AB}$, a ray is $\overrightarrow{CB}$, a line intersecting the plane is $\overleftrightarrow{CD}$, and three collinear points are *A*, *C*, and *B*.

Use the diagram.

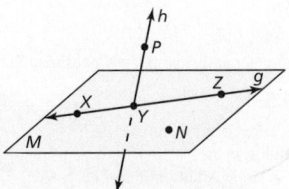

1. Give another name for plane *M*.
2. Name a line in the plane.
3. Name a line intersecting the plane.
4. Name two rays.
5. Name a pair of opposite rays.
6. Name a point not in plane *M*.

1.2 Measuring and Constructing Segments *(pp. 11–18)*

a. **Find *AC*.**

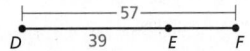

$$AC = AB + BC \qquad \text{Segment Addition Postulate (Postulate 1.2)}$$
$$= 12 + 25 \qquad \text{Substitute 12 for } AB \text{ and 25 for } BC.$$
$$= 37 \qquad \text{Add.}$$

▶ So, $AC = 37$.

b. **Find *EF*.**

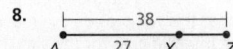

$$DF = DE + EF \qquad \text{Segment Addition Postulate (Postulate 1.2)}$$
$$57 = 39 + EF \qquad \text{Substitute 57 for } DF \text{ and 39 for } DE.$$
$$18 = EF \qquad \text{Subtract 39 from each side.}$$

▶ So, $EF = 18$.

Find *XZ*.

7. $X \quad 17 \quad Y \quad 24 \quad Z$

8. $\overset{\displaystyle 38}{A \quad 27 \quad X \quad Z}$

9. Plot $A(8, -4)$, $B(3, -4)$, $C(7, 1)$, and $D(7, -3)$ in a coordinate plane. Then determine whether $\overline{AB}$ and $\overline{CD}$ are congruent.

ANSWERS

10. $\left(\frac{1}{2}, \frac{13}{2}\right)$; about 7.1

11. $\left(\frac{13}{2}, -\frac{5}{2}\right)$; about 1.4

12. $(-2, -3)$

13. 40

14. 20 units, 21 square units

15. about 23.9 units, 24.5 square units

1.3 Using Midpoint and Distance Formulas *(pp. 19–26)*

The endpoints of $\overline{AB}$ are $A(6, -1)$ and $B(3, 5)$. Find the coordinates of the midpoint M. Then find the distance between points A and B.

Use the Midpoint Formula.

$$M\left(\frac{6 + 3}{2}, \frac{-1 + 5}{2}\right) = M\left(\frac{9}{2}, 2\right)$$

Use the Distance Formula.

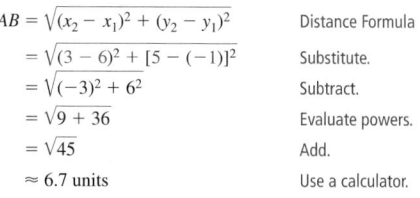

$$AB = \sqrt{(x_2 - x_1)^2 + (y_2 - y_1)^2}$$ Distance Formula

$$\quad = \sqrt{(3 - 6)^2 + [5 - (-1)]^2}$$ Substitute.

$$\quad = \sqrt{(-3)^2 + 6^2}$$ Subtract.

$$\quad = \sqrt{9 + 36}$$ Evaluate powers.

$$\quad = \sqrt{45}$$ Add.

$$\quad \approx 6.7 \text{ units}$$ Use a calculator.

▶ So, the midpoint is $M\left(\frac{9}{2}, 2\right)$, and the distance is about 6.7 units.

Find the coordinates of the midpoint M. Then find the distance between points S and T.

10. $S(-2, 4)$ and $T(3, 9)$ 11. $S(6, -3)$ and $T(7, -2)$

12. The midpoint of $\overline{JK}$ is $M(6, 3)$. One endpoint is $J(14, 9)$. Find the coordinates of endpoint K.

13. Point M is the midpoint of $\overline{AB}$ where $AM = 3x + 8$ and $MB = 6x - 4$. Find AB.

1.4 Perimeter and Area in the Coordinate Plane *(pp. 29–36)*

Find the perimeter and area of rectangle $ABCD$ with vertices $A(-3, 4)$, $B(6, 4)$, $C(6, -1)$, and $D(-3, -1)$.

Draw the rectangle in a coordinate plane. Then find the length and width using the Ruler Postulate (Postulate 1.1).

Length $AB = |-3 - 6| = 9$

Width $BC = |4 - (-1)| = 5$

Substitute the values for the length and width into the formulas for the perimeter and area of a rectangle.

$P = 2\ell + 2w$ $A = \ell w$

$\quad = 2(9) + 2(5)$ $\quad = (9)(5)$

$\quad = 18 + 10$ $\quad = 45$

$\quad = 28$

▶ So, the perimeter is 28 units, and the area is 45 square units.

Find the perimeter and area of the polygon with the given vertices.

14. $W(5, -1)$, $X(5, 6)$, $Y(2, -1)$, $Z(2, 6)$ 15. $E(6, -2)$, $F(6, 5)$, $G(-1, 5)$

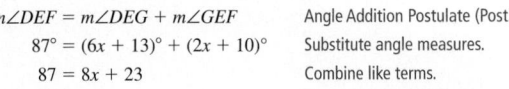

Given that $m\angle DEF = 87°$, find $m\angle DEG$ and $m\angle GEF$.

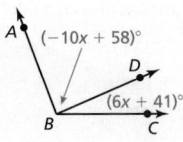

Step 1 Write and solve an equation to find the value of x.

$m\angle DEF = m\angle DEG + m\angle GEF$	Angle Addition Postulate (Post. 1.4)
$87° = (6x + 13)° + (2x + 10)°$	Substitute angle measures.
$87 = 8x + 23$	Combine like terms.
$64 = 8x$	Subtract 23 from each side.
$8 = x$	Divide each side by 8.

Step 2 Evaluate the given expressions when $x = 8$.

$m\angle DEG = (6x + 13)° = (6 \cdot 8 + 13)° = 61°$

$m\angle GEF = (2x + 10)° = (2 \cdot 8 + 10)° = 26°$

▶ So, $m\angle DEG = 61°$, and $m\angle GEF = 26°$.

Find $m\angle ABD$ and $m\angle CBD$.

16. $m\angle ABC = 77°$

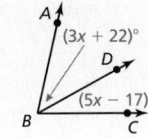

17. $m\angle ABC = 111°$

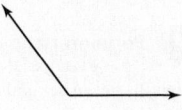

18. Find the measure of the angle using a protractor.

a. $\angle 1$ is a complement of $\angle 2$, and $m\angle 1 = 54°$. Find $m\angle 2$.

Draw a diagram with complementary adjacent angles to illustrate the relationship.

$m\angle 2 = 90° - m\angle 1 = 90° - 54° = 36°$

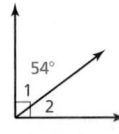

b. $\angle 3$ is a supplement of $\angle 4$, and $m\angle 4 = 68°$. Find $m\angle 3$.

Draw a diagram with supplementary adjacent angles to illustrate the relationship.

$m\angle 3 = 180° - m\angle 4 = 180° - 68° = 112°$

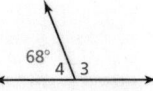

$\angle 1$ and $\angle 2$ are complementary angles. Given $m\angle 1$, find $m\angle 2$.

19. $m\angle 1 = 12°$ 20. $m\angle 1 = 83°$

$\angle 3$ and $\angle 4$ are supplementary angles. Given $m\angle 3$, find $m\angle 4$.

21. $m\angle 3 = 116°$ 22. $m\angle 3 = 56°$

1 Chapter Test

Find the length of $\overline{QS}$. Explain how you found your answer.

1.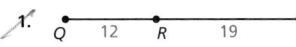

2.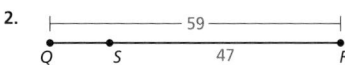

Find the coordinates of the midpoint M. Then find the distance between the two points.

3. $A(-4, -8)$ and $B(-1, 4)$

4. $C(-1, 7)$ and $D(-8, -3)$

5. The midpoint of $\overline{EF}$ is $M(1, -1)$. One endpoint is $E(-3, 2)$. Find the coordinates of endpoint F.

Use the diagram to decide whether the statement is true or false.

6. Points A, R, and B are collinear.

7. $\overleftrightarrow{BW}$ and $\overleftrightarrow{AT}$ are lines.

8. $\overrightarrow{BR}$ and $\overrightarrow{RT}$ are opposite rays.

9. Plane D could also be named plane ART.

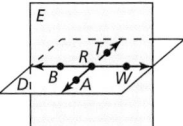

Find the perimeter and area of the polygon with the given vertices. Explain how you found your answer.

10. $P(-3, 4)$, $Q(1, 4)$, $R(-3, -2)$, $S(3, -2)$

11. $J(-1, 3)$, $K(5, 3)$, $L(2, -2)$

12. In the diagram, $\angle AFE$ is a straight angle and $\angle CFE$ is a right angle. Identify all supplementary and complementary angles. Explain. Then find $m\angle DFE$, $m\angle BFC$, and $m\angle BFE$.

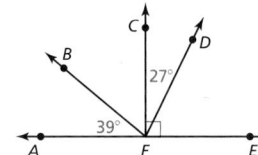

13. Use the clock at the left.

    a. What is the measure of the acute angle created when the clock is at 10:00?

    b. What is the measure of the obtuse angle created when the clock is at 5:00?

    c. Find a time where the hour and minute hands create a straight angle.

14. Sketch a figure that contains a plane and two lines that intersect the plane at one point.

15. Your parents decide they would like to install a rectangular swimming pool in the backyard. There is a 15-foot by 20-foot rectangular area available. Your parents request a 3-foot edge around each side of the pool. Draw a diagram of this situation in a coordinate plane. What is the perimeter and area of the largest swimming pool that will fit?

16. The picture shows the arrangement of balls in a game of boccie. The object of the game is to throw your ball closest to the small, white ball, which is called the *pallino*. The green ball is the midpoint between the red ball and the pallino. The distance between the green ball and the red ball is 10 inches. The distance between the yellow ball and the pallino is 8 inches. Which ball is closer to the pallino, the green ball or the yellow ball? Explain.

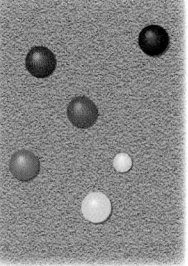

If students need help...	If students got it...
Lesson Tutorials	Resources by Chapter • Enrichment and Extension • Cumulative Review
Skills Review Handbook	Performance Task
BigIdeasMath.com	Start the *next* Section

ANSWERS

1. 31; Segment Addition Postulate (Post. 1.2): $QR + RS = QS$, so $QS = 12 + 19 = 31$

2. 12; Segment Addition Postulate (Post. 1.2): $QS + SR = QR$, so $QS = QR - SR = 59 - 47 = 12$

3. $\left(-\frac{5}{2}, -2\right)$; about 12.4

4. $\left(-\frac{9}{2}, 2\right)$; about 12.2

5. $(5, -4)$

6. false

7. true

8. false

9. false

10. about 22.3 units, 30 square units; $PQRS$ is a trapezoid, $PQ = |-3 - 1| = 4$, $RS = |3 - (-3)| = 6$, and $RP = |-2 - 4| = 6$ by the Ruler Postulate (Post. 1.1), $QS = \sqrt{(3-1)^2 + (-2-4)^2} \approx 6.3$ by the Distance Formula, perimeter $\approx 6 + 6 + 4 + 6.3 = 22.3$ units, area $= \frac{1}{2}(6)(4 + 6) = 30$ square units

11. about 17.66 units, 15 square units; JKL is a triangle, $JK = |5 - (-1)| = 6$ by the Ruler Postulate (Post. 1.1), $KL = \sqrt{(5-2)^2 + (3-(-2))^2} \approx 5.83$ and $LJ = \sqrt{(-1-2)^2 + (3-(-2))^2} \approx 5.83$ by the Distance Formula, the height h of the triangle $= |3 - (-2)| = 5$ by the Ruler Postulate (Post. 1.1), perimeter $\approx 6 + 5.83 + 5.83 = 17.66$ units, area $= \frac{1}{2}bh = \frac{1}{2}(6)(5) = 15$ square units

12. supplementary: $\angle AFB$ and $\angle BFE$, $\angle AFC$ and $\angle CFE$, $\angle AFD$ and $\angle DFE$; complementary: $\angle AFB$ and $\angle BFC$, $\angle CFD$ and $\angle DFE$; The pairs of supplementary angles each form a linear pair. The pairs of complementary angles each form a right angle; $m\angle DFE = 63°$, $m\angle BFC = 51°$, $m\angle BFE = 141°$

13. **a.** $60°$
    b. $150°$
    c. *Sample answer:* 6:00

14. *Sample answer:*

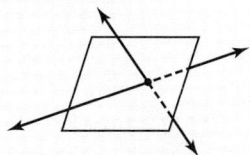

15–16. See Additional Answers.

1. $\overline{EF} \cong \overline{KL} \cong \overline{PQ}$ and $\overline{CD} \cong \overline{MN}$

2. point, segment, ray, line, plane

3. B

4. about 24.6 units; 36 square units

5.

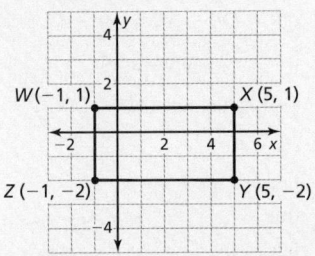

rectangle; yes; If each unit on the coordinate plane represents 15 feet on the basketball court, then each square unit represents $15^2 = 225$ square feet. The rectangle on the coordinate plane that is 3 units by 6 units makes a good model of a basketball court that is 45 feet by 90 feet with the given perimeter and area.

1 Cumulative Assessment

1. Use the diagram to determine which segments, if any, are congruent. List all congruent segments.

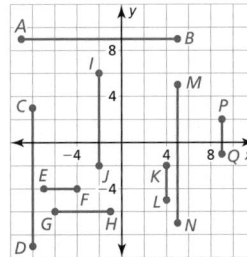

2. Order the terms so that each consecutive term builds off the previous term.

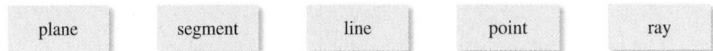

plane   segment   line   point   ray

3. The endpoints of a line segment are $(-6, 13)$ and $(11, 5)$. Which choice shows the correct midpoint and distance between these two points?

Ⓐ $\left(\frac{5}{2}, 4\right)$; 18.8 units

Ⓑ $\left(\frac{5}{2}, 9\right)$; 18.8 units

Ⓒ $\left(\frac{5}{2}, 4\right)$; 9.4 units

Ⓓ $\left(\frac{5}{2}, 9\right)$; 9.4 units

4. Find the perimeter and area of the figure shown.

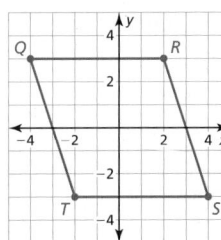

5. Plot the points $W(-1, 1)$, $X(5, 1)$, $Y(5, -2)$, and $Z(-1, -2)$ in a coordinate plane. What type of polygon do the points form? Your friend claims that you could use this figure to represent a basketball court with an area of 4050 square feet and a perimeter of 270 feet. Do you support your friend's claim? Explain.

6. Use the steps in the construction to explain how you know that $\overrightarrow{AG}$ is the angle bisector of $\angle CAB$.

Step 1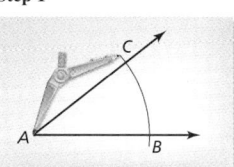

Step 2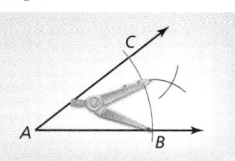

Step 3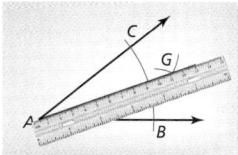

7. The picture shows an aerial view of a city. Use the streets highlighted in red to identify all congruent angles. Assume all streets are straight angles.

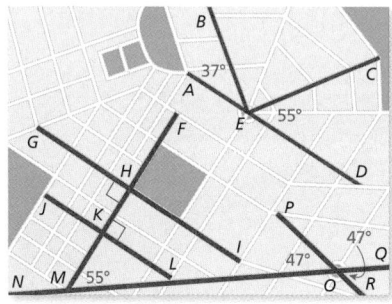

8. Three roads come to an intersection point that the people in your town call Five Corners, as shown in the figure.

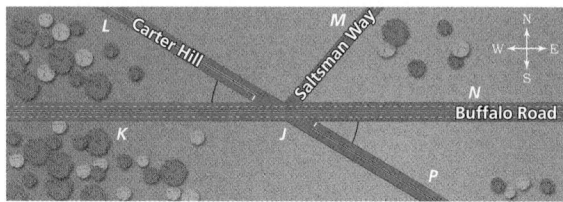

    a. Identify all vertical angles.

    b. Identify all linear pairs.

    c. You are traveling east on Buffalo Road and decide to turn left onto Carter Hill. Name the angle of the turn you made.

| $\angle KJL$ | $\angle KJM$ | $\angle KJN$ | $\angle KJP$ | $\angle LJM$ |

| $\angle LJN$ | $\angle LJP$ | $\angle MJN$ | $\angle MJP$ | $\angle NJP$ |

ANSWERS

6. In step 1, a compass is used to draw an arc. The two points (C and B) where this arc intersects the sides of the angle are the same distance from vertex A. In step 2, the compass is used to draw an arc of points equidistant from B and a separate arc of points equidistant from C. The point where these two arcs intersect is a point that is equidistant from each side of the angle. In step 3, a straightedge is used to draw the angle bisector, a ray that has an endpoint at the vertex and that passes through the point that is equidistant from each side of the angle.

7. $\angle NMK \cong \angle AEC$, $\angle KMO \cong \angle CED$, $\angle MOP \cong \angle QOR$, $\angle POQ \cong \angle MOR$; right angles: $\angle MKJ \cong \angle MKL \cong \angle LKH \cong \angle HKJ \cong \angle KHG \cong \angle GHF \cong \angle FHI \cong \angle KHI$; straight angles: $\angle NMO \cong \angle MOQ \cong \angle POR \cong \angle MKH \cong \angle KHF \cong \angle JKL \cong \angle GHI \cong \angle AED$

8. a. $\angle KJL$ and $\angle NJP$, $\angle KJP$ and $\angle LJN$

    b. $\angle KJL$ and $\angle LJN$, $\angle KJM$ and $\angle MJN$, $\angle LJM$ and $\angle MJP$, $\angle LJN$ and $\angle NJP$, $\angle NJP$ and $\angle KJP$, $\angle KJL$ and $\angle KJP$

    c. $\angle KJL$

2 Reasoning and Proofs

2.1 Conditional Statements
2.2 Inductive and Deductive Reasoning
2.3 Postulates and Diagrams
2.4 Algebraic Reasoning
2.5 Proving Statements about Segments and Angles
2.6 Proving Geometric Relationships

Airport Runway *(p. 108)*

Sculpture *(p. 104)*

City Street *(p. 95)*

SEE the Big Idea

Tiger *(p. 81)*

Guitar *(p. 67)*

Chapter Summary

- Geometry is often thought of as the high school course in which students are taught how to reason and construct logical arguments. In theory, this should be happening in every mathematics course in high school. Geometry is also remembered, without great fondness, as the class in which you had to write the dreaded proofs. Again, reasoning should permeate the high school curriculum.

- In this chapter, students are introduced to inductive and deductive reasoning as well as conditional statements written in if-then form. Students examine when conditional statements are true and false.

- In the middle of the chapter, connections are made to the reasoning students did in an algebra setting when solving equations. There is always justification for the steps taken in solving an equation, although we do not always write them.

- The last lessons in the chapter introduce students to two-column, flowchart, and paragraph proofs. These different formats are practiced while proving statements about segments and angles.

 COMMON CORE PROGRESSION

Middle School
- Solve linear equations in one variable.
- Use the distributive property.
- Use informal arguments to establish facts about angles.

Algebra 1
- Solve literal equations.
- Solve multi-step linear equations.
- Identify and extend arithmetic and geometric sequences.

Geometry
- Write conditional and biconditional statements.
- Use inductive and deductive reasoning.
- Use properties of equality to justify the steps in solving equations and to find segment lengths and angle measures.
- Write two-column proofs, flowchart proofs, and paragraph proofs.

Dynamic Teaching Tools

Dynamic Assessment & Progress Monitoring Tool
Lesson Planning Tool
Interactive Whiteboard Lesson Library
Dynamic Classroom with Dynamic Investigations
Real-Life STEM Videos

Scaffolding in the Classroom

Begin with a worked-out problem and work backwards.
Ask students to explain what happened in step 5 to get to step 6. Then ask what happened in step 4 to get to step 5, etc.

Standards Summary		
Section	**Common Core State Standards**	
2.1	Preparing	HSG-CO.C.9, HSG-CO.C.10, HSG-CO.C.11, HSG-SRT.B.4
2.2	Preparing	HSG-CO.C.9, HSG-CO.C.10, HSG-CO.C.11, HSG-SRT.B.4
2.3	Preparing	HSG-CO.C.9, HSG-CO.C.10, HSG-CO.C.11, HSG-SRT.B.4
2.4	Preparing	HSG-CO.C.9, HSG-CO.C.10, HSG-CO.C.11, HSG-SRT.B.4
2.5	Learning	HSG-CO.C.9
2.6	Learning	HSG-CO.C.9

Questioning in the Classroom
One thing leads to another.
Try to build questions from the responses given. This requires students to listen to other students' responses.

Laurie's Notes

Maintaining Mathematical Proficiency

Finding the *n*th Term of an Arithmetic Sequence

- Remind students that the terms of an arithmetic sequence differ by a *common difference*.
- Discuss the **Equation of an Arithmetic Sequence**: $a_n = a_1 + (n - 1)d$.
- Define each term: a_n represents the value of the *n*th term, a_1 is the value of the first term, *n* is the term number, and *d* is the common difference. Have students generate some arithmetic sequences.
- As needed, review the Distributive Property and rules for combining like terms.

COMMON ERROR Students may not realize that the common difference can be either positive or negative. When the terms of a sequence increase, the common difference is positive. When the terms decrease, the common difference is negative.

Rewriting Literal Equations

- Remind students that a literal equation is any equation with two or more variables.
- Discuss the steps for solving equations in one variable, and remind students that the steps for solving literal equations are the same.

COMMON ERROR Students may be intimidated by equations with more than one variable. Have students solve equations in one variable only, simplifying their work on the side of the equation where they are isolating the variable. Explain that the same steps are used for solving literal and single-variable equations.

Mathematical Practices (continued on page 64)

- The eight *Mathematical Practices* focus attention on how mathematics is learned—process versus content. Page 64 demonstrates that the reasoning used by students as they make statements about the mathematics they are learning must be correct, and students' logic must not be flawed.
- Use the *Mathematical Practices* page to help students develop mathematical habits of mind—how mathematics can be explored and how mathematics is thought about.
- Discuss the *Core Concept* and have students pair with partners to write an example of what they consider *deductive reasoning*. The example might relate to students' daily routines, events that happen in nature or in business, or other activities that interest students. Share students' examples and decide whether the conclusions follow from the stated premises. This pattern of reasoning is called a syllogism.

If students need help...	If students got it...
Student Journal • Maintaining Mathematical Proficiency	Game Closet at *BigIdeasMath.com*
Lesson Tutorials	Start the *next* Section
Skills Review Handbook	

Maintaining Mathematical Proficiency

Finding the nth Term of an Arithmetic Sequence

Example 1 Write an equation for the nth term of the arithmetic sequence 2, 5, 8, 11, ... Then find a_{20}.

The first term is 2, and the common difference is 3.

$a_n = a_1 + (n - 1)d$ Equation for an arithmetic sequence

$a_n = 2 + (n - 1)3$ Substitute 2 for a_1 and 3 for d.

$a_n = 3n - 1$ Simplify.

Use the equation to find the 20th term.

$a_n = 3n - 1$ Write the equation.

$a_{20} = 3(20) - 1$ Substitute 20 for n.

$= 59$ Simplify.

▶ The 20th term of the arithmetic sequence is 59.

Write an equation for the nth term of the arithmetic sequence. Then find a_{50}.

1. 3, 9, 15, 21, . . .   **2.** $-29, -12, 5, 22, . . .$ **3.** 2.8, 3.4, 4.0, 4.6, . . .

4. $\frac{1}{3}, \frac{1}{2}, \frac{2}{3}, \frac{5}{6}, . . .$ **5.** 26, 22, 18, 14, . . .   **6.** $8, 2, -4, -10, . . .$

Rewriting Literal Equations

Example 2 Solve the literal equation $3x + 6y = 24$ for y.

$3x + 6y = 24$ Write the equation.

$3x - 3x + 6y = 24 - 3x$ Subtract $3x$ from each side.

$6y = 24 - 3x$ Simplify.

$\dfrac{6y}{6} = \dfrac{24 - 3x}{6}$ Divide each side by 6.

$y = 4 - \dfrac{1}{2}x$ Simplify.

▶ The rewritten literal equation is $y = 4 - \frac{1}{2}x$.

Solve the literal equation for x.

7. $2y - 2x = 10$ **8.** $20y + 5x = 15$ **9.** $4y - 5 = 4x + 7$

10. $y = 8x - x$ **11.** $y = 4x + zx + 6$ **12.** $z = 2x + 6xy$

13. ABSTRACT REASONING Can you use the equation for an arithmetic sequence to write an equation for the sequence 3, 9, 27, 81, . . . ? Explain your reasoning.

Common Core State Standards

HSF-BF.A.2 Write arithmetic and geometric sequences both recursively and with an explicit formula, use them to model situations, and translate between the two forms.

HSA-CED.A.4 Rearrange formulas to highlight a quantity of interest, using the same reasoning as in solving equations.

ANSWERS

1. $a_n = 6n - 3; a_{50} = 297$
2. $a_n = 17n - 46; a_{50} = 804$
3. $a_n = 0.6n + 2.2; a_{50} = 32.2$
4. $a_n = \frac{1}{6}n + \frac{1}{6}; a_{50} = \frac{17}{2}$, or $8\frac{1}{2}$
5. $a_n = -4n + 30; a_{50} = -170$
6. $a_n = -6n + 14; a_{50} = -286$
7. $x = y - 5$
8. $x = -4y + 3$
9. $x = y - 3$
10. $x = \dfrac{y}{7}$
11. $x = \dfrac{y - 6}{z + 4}$
12. $x = \dfrac{z}{6y + 2}$
13. no; The sequence does not have a common difference.

Vocabulary Review

Have students make a Notetaking Organizer for the Equation for an Arithmetic Sequence. Include the following items.

- nth term
- 1st term
- Term number
- Common difference

Mathematical Practices

Mathematically proficient students distinguish correct reasoning from flawed reasoning.

Using Correct Reasoning

Core Concept

Deductive Reasoning

When you use *deductive reasoning*, you start with two or more true statements and *deduce* or *infer* the truth of another statement. Here is an example.

1. Premise: If a polygon is a triangle, then the sum of its angle measures is 180°.
2. Premise: Polygon *ABC* is a triangle.
3. Conclusion: The sum of the angle measures of polygon *ABC* is 180°.

This pattern for deductive reasoning is called a *syllogism*.

EXAMPLE 1   **Recognizing Flawed Reasoning**

The syllogisms below represent common types of *flawed reasoning*. Explain why each conclusion is not valid.

a. When it rains, the ground gets wet.
   The ground is wet.
   Therefore, it must have rained.

b. If $\triangle ABC$ is equilateral, then it is isosceles.
   $\triangle ABC$ is not equilateral.
   Therefore, it must not be isosceles.

c. All squares are polygons.
   All trapezoids are quadrilaterals.
   Therefore, all squares are quadrilaterals.

d. No triangles are quadrilaterals.
   Some quadrilaterals are not squares.
   Therefore, some squares are not triangles.

SOLUTION

a. The ground may be wet for another reason.

b. A triangle can be isosceles but not equilateral.

c. All squares are quadrilaterals, but not because all trapezoids are quadrilaterals.

d. No squares are triangles.

Monitoring Progress

Decide whether the syllogism represents correct or flawed reasoning. If flawed, explain why the conclusion is not valid.

1. All triangles are polygons.
   Figure *ABC* is a triangle.
   Therefore, figure *ABC* is a polygon.

2. No trapezoids are rectangles.
   Some rectangles are not squares.
   Therefore, some squares are not trapezoids.

3. If polygon *ABCD* is a square, then it is a rectangle.
   Polygon *ABCD* is a rectangle.
   Therefore, polygon *ABCD* is a square.

4. If polygon *ABCD* is a square, then it is a rectangle.
   Polygon *ABCD* is not a square.
   Therefore, polygon *ABCD* is not a rectangle.

Laurie's Notes   Mathematical Practices (continued from page T-63)

- Read each of the statements in Example 1, and ask students to decide whether the logic is correct or flawed.

- **?** "Why is it important to distinguish correct logic from that which is flawed?" Listen for students to explain that when people make statements you need to be able to judge whether the logic is flawed. Decisions are made and thoughts are formed based on statements made by people. You need to know whether the statements are even logical.

- Throughout this course you want students to develop the habit of distinguishing correct logic or reasoning from that which is flawed.

- Students could work with partners or in groups on *Monitoring Progress*. Allow private think time before dialogue begins.

Overview of Section 2.1

Introduction

- This lesson will introduce students to language used in geometry to describe different statements. These statements will include definitions, postulates, and theorems.
- *Conditional statements* are composed of two parts, the *hypothesis* and the *conclusion*. Students should be able to identify these two parts even when the statements are not written in *if-then form*. Students will have the chance to practice writing definitions in *if and only if form*.
- The last part of the lesson introduces different forms of a conditional statement and evaluates the truth table for each form. The result is recognition that a conditional statement and the contrapositive are equivalent, and the converse and inverse are equivalent.

Formative Assessment Tips

- **Learning Goals Inventory:** At the beginning of a chapter or unit of study, it is important for students to identify their level of understanding or knowledge of the learning intentions (goals) for the chapter. Taking an inventory of the explicit goals for the chapter informs students what you want them to learn—they know the target. On one side of a sheet of paper, I type the assignment guide for the chapter. On the other side, I list the learning intentions for the chapter and ask students to do a self-assessment for each learning goal.

    0—no knowledge, understanding, or ability   2—feeling okay

    1—beginning to get it   3—very confident
- Students return to the *Learning Goals Inventory* midway through the chapter and after the chapter assessment. Students recognize their own growth in completing the inventory multiple times.

Extensions

- You can find additional resources online or in print materials if you wish to have your students construct more involved truth tables. The focus might be on determining whether a statement is a tautology, meaning all forms of the statement are true.

Pacing Suggestion

- The explorations provide an interesting introduction to conditional statements to help launch the lesson. Transition to the formal lesson as soon as students have discussed each exploration.

Laurie's Notes

Exploration

Motivate

? "What is a *conditional statement*?" Answers will vary. Students will likely mention something about a condition being made.

? "How do you judge whether a conditional statement is true or not? For instance, is the following conditional statement true or false? If there is paper on the floor, then someone dropped the paper." For the argumentative students in the class, this should prompt a variety of scenarios about how the paper ended up on the floor. Refocus attention on whether they believe the statement is true or false.

• There have to be established conditions of when a conditional statement is true or false, and that is addressed in this lesson.

Exploration Note

• **MP3 Construct Viable Arguments and Critique the Reasoning of Others:** The focus of the explorations is for students to provide logical arguments to support their conclusions. The evidence they provide must be valid.

Exploration 1

• Be sure that students read the directions and the introduction. They should note that for a *conditional statement* to be true, the *hypothesis* and *conclusion* do not necessarily both have to be true. This is a difficult concept for students to grasp. They will learn that the only time a conditional statement is false is when the hypothesis is true and the conclusion is false.

• The statement that students will have the most difficulty with is part (d). The hypothesis is false and the conclusion is false. Do not get hung up on this statement. On page 70, the truth of a conditional statement will be addressed. You might also refer back to part (a). Say, "Today (in class) it is a Monday. The hypothesis would be false and the conclusion would be false, and yet the conditional statement is still true."

Exploration 2

• This exploration could be completed with dynamic geometry software. Students would still need to provide evidence for their answers. For instance, in part (a), students would either need to measure the angles and see that $\angle B$ is a right angle, or they could find the slopes and see that segment BC has a slope of 0 (horizontal) and segment AB has an undefined slope (vertical) and so the segments are perpendicular and $\triangle ABC$ is a right triangle.

• Instead of having all students answer all five questions, assign one or two questions to each pair of students. Again, the focus is on evidence. How do they know they are correct?

Exploration 3

• The conditional statements made are either true or false. Students should use known information to justify their answers.

Communicate Your Answer

• It is common for students to say that a conditional statement is true "when it is true" and to have difficulty thinking about the two parts of the conditional statement, the hypothesis and the conclusion.

• Many of the theorems stated in geometry are written as conditional statements, or they could be written as conditional statements. It will be important for students to be able to determine when conditional statements or theorems are true.

Connecting to Next Step

• Once students have worked the explorations, continue with the formal lesson.

2.1 Conditional Statements

Essential Question When is a conditional statement true or false?

A *conditional statement*, symbolized by $p \rightarrow q$, can be written as an "if-then statement" in which *p* is the *hypothesis* and *q* is the *conclusion*. Here is an example.

If a polygon is a triangle, then the sum of its angle measures is 180°.

hypothesis, *p*   conclusion, *q*

EXPLORATION 1 Determining Whether a Statement Is True or False

Work with a partner. A hypothesis can either be true or false. The same is true of a conclusion. For a conditional statement to be true, the hypothesis and conclusion do not necessarily both have to be true. Determine whether each conditional statement is true or false. Justify your answer.

a. If yesterday was Wednesday, then today is Thursday.

b. If an angle is acute, then it has a measure of 30°.

c. If a month has 30 days, then it is June.

d. If an even number is not divisible by 2, then 9 is a perfect cube.

EXPLORATION 2 Determining Whether a Statement Is True or False

Work with a partner. Use the points in the coordinate plane to determine whether each statement is true or false. Justify your answer.

a. $\triangle ABC$ is a right triangle.

b. $\triangle BDC$ is an equilateral triangle.

c. $\triangle BDC$ is an isosceles triangle.

d. Quadrilateral *ABCD* is a trapezoid.

e. Quadrilateral *ABCD* is a parallelogram.

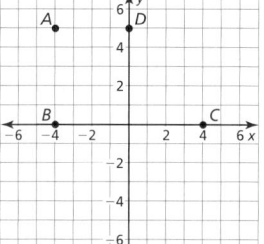

CONSTRUCTING VIABLE ARGUMENTS

To be proficient in math, you need to distinguish correct logic or reasoning from that which is flawed.

EXPLORATION 3 Determining Whether a Statement Is True or False

Work with a partner. Determine whether each conditional statement is true or false. Justify your answer.

a. If $\triangle ADC$ is a right triangle, then the Pythagorean Theorem is valid for $\triangle ADC$.

b. If $\angle A$ and $\angle B$ are complementary, then the sum of their measures is 180°.

c. If figure *ABCD* is a quadrilateral, then the sum of its angle measures is 180°.

d. If points *A*, *B*, and *C* are collinear, then they lie on the same line.

e. If $\overleftrightarrow{AB}$ and $\overleftrightarrow{BD}$ intersect at a point, then they form two pairs of vertical angles.

Communicate Your Answer

4. When is a conditional statement true or false?

5. Write one true conditional statement and one false conditional statement that are different from those given in Exploration 3. Justify your answer.

Section 2.1   Conditional Statements   **65**

ANSWERS

1. a. true; Thursday always follows Wednesday.

  b. false; 30° is only one example of an acute angle.

  c. false; June is only one of the months that has 30 days.

  d. true; All even numbers are divisible by 2, and 9 is not a perfect cube. Because both the hypothesis and conclusion are false, the conditional statement is true.

2. a. true; $\overline{AB}$ is a vertical segment, and $\overline{BC}$ is a horizontal segment. So, they are perpendicular.

  b. false; $\overline{BC}$ is longer than the other two sides.

  c. true; $BD = CD$ because both have endpoints that are the same distance from the origin.

  d. true; $\overline{AD} \parallel \overline{BC}$ because they are both horizontal segments.

  e. false; $\overline{AB}$ is vertical, but $\overline{CD}$ is not. So, they are not parallel.

3. a. true; The Pythagorean Theorem is valid for all right triangles.

  b. false; Two angles are complementary when the sum of their measures is 90°.

  c. false; The sum of the angle measures of a quadrilateral is always 360°.

  d. true; This is the definition of collinear.

  e. true; Every pair of intersecting lines forms two pairs of opposite rays and therefore two pairs of vertical angles.

4. A conditional statement is only false when a true hypothesis produces a false conclusion. Otherwise, it is true.

5. *Sample answer:* If the measure of an angle is greater than 0° and less than 90°, then it is an acute angle; If polygon *ABCD* is a trapezoid, then it is a rectangle; The first statement is true because it is the definition of an acute angle. The second statement is false because trapezoids only have one pair of parallel sides, but rectangles have two pairs of parallel sides.

Section 2.1   **65**

Extra Example 1

Use (H) to identify the hypothesis and (C) to identify the conclusion. Then rewrite each conditional in if-then form.

a. $x > 5$ if $x > 3$. (H) $x > 3$, (C) $x > 5$; If $x > 3$, then $x > 5$.

b. All members of the soccer team have practice today. (H) a person is a member of the soccer team, (C) a person has practice today; If a person is a member of the soccer team, then he or she has practice today.

Extra Example 2

Write the negation of each statement.

a. The car is white. The car is not white.

b. It is not snowing. It is snowing.

MONITORING PROGRESS ANSWERS

1. hypothesis: All 30° angles; conclusion: acute angles; If an angle measures 30°, then it is an acute angle.

2. hypothesis: $x = -3$; conclusion: $2x + 7 = 1$; If $x = -3$, then $2x + 7 = 1$.

2.1 Lesson

What You Will Learn

▶ Write conditional statements.
▶ Use definitions written as conditional statements.
▶ Write biconditional statements.
▶ Make truth tables.

Core Vocabulary

conditional statement, *p. 66*
if-then form, *p. 66*
hypothesis, *p. 66*
conclusion, *p. 66*
negation, *p. 66*
converse, *p. 67*
inverse, *p. 67*
contrapositive, *p. 67*
equivalent statements, *p. 67*
perpendicular lines, *p. 68*
biconditional statement, *p. 69*
truth value, *p. 70*
truth table, *p. 70*

Writing Conditional Statements

Core Concept

Conditional Statement

A **conditional statement** is a logical statement that has two parts, a *hypothesis p* and a *conclusion q*. When a conditional statement is written in **if-then form**, the "if" part contains the **hypothesis** and the "then" part contains the **conclusion**.

Words   If p, then q.   **Symbols** $p \rightarrow q$ (read as "p implies q")

EXAMPLE 1   Rewriting a Statement in If-Then Form

Use red to identify the hypothesis and blue to identify the conclusion. Then rewrite the conditional statement in if-then form.

a. All birds have feathers.   b. You are in Texas if you are in Houston.

SOLUTION

a. All birds have feathers.   b. You are in Texas if you are in Houston.

   ▶ If an animal is a bird,   ▶ If you are in Houston,
     then it has feathers.   then you are in Texas.

Monitoring Progress Help in English and Spanish at *BigIdeasMath.com*

Use red to identify the hypothesis and blue to identify the conclusion. Then rewrite the conditional statement in if-then form.

1. All 30° angles are acute angles.   2. $2x + 7 = 1$, because $x = -3$.

Core Concept

Negation

The **negation** of a statement is the *opposite* of the original statement. To write the negation of a statement p, you write the symbol for negation ($\sim$) before the letter. So, "not p" is written $\sim p$.

Words   not p **Symbols** $\sim p$

EXAMPLE 2   Writing a Negation

Write the negation of each statement.

a. The ball is red.   b. The cat is *not* black.

SOLUTION

a. The ball is *not* red.   b. The cat is black.

Laurie's Notes   Teacher Actions

- Write the *Core Concept*, paying attention to the words and the symbols.
- Example 1 demonstrates that the words "if" and "then" are not part of the hypothesis or conclusion. Two statements, called the *hypothesis* and *conclusion*, are joined using the words "if" and "then" to make the conditional statement.
- Discuss the *negation* of a statement.
- **Extension:** Ask students what a double negative is and to give examples. They should also state what the double negative means when simplified. *Example:* "I am not going to not eat" means "I am going to eat."

 Core Concept

Related Conditionals

Consider the conditional statement below.

Words   If p, then q.   **Symbols** $p \rightarrow q$

Converse   To write the **converse** of a conditional statement, exchange the hypothesis and the conclusion.

Words   If q, then p.   **Symbols** $q \rightarrow p$

Inverse   To write the **inverse** of a conditional statement, negate both the hypothesis and the conclusion.

Words   If not p, then not q.   **Symbols** $\sim p \rightarrow \sim q$

Contrapositive   To write the **contrapositive** of a conditional statement, first write the converse. Then negate both the hypothesis and the conclusion.

Words   If not q, then not p.   **Symbols** $\sim q \rightarrow \sim p$

A conditional statement and its contrapositive are either both true or both false. Similarly, the converse and inverse of a conditional statement are either both true or both false. In general, when two statements are both true or both false, they are called **equivalent statements**.

COMMON ERROR

Just because a conditional statement and its contrapositive are both true does not mean that its converse and inverse are both false. The converse and inverse could also both be true.

EXAMPLE 3   Writing Related Conditional Statements

Let p be "you are a guitar player" and let q be "you are a musician." Write each statement in words. Then decide whether it is *true* or *false*.

a. the conditional statement $p \rightarrow q$

b. the converse $q \rightarrow p$

c. the inverse $\sim p \rightarrow \sim q$

d. the contrapositive $\sim q \rightarrow \sim p$

SOLUTION

a. Conditional: If you are a guitar player, then you are a musician.
true; Guitar players are musicians.

b. Converse: If you are a musician, then you are a guitar player.
false; Not all musicians play the guitar.

c. Inverse: If you are not a guitar player, then you are not a musician.
false; Even if you do not play a guitar, you can still be a musician.

d. Contrapositive: If you are not a musician, then you are not a guitar player.
true; A person who is not a musician cannot be a guitar player.

Monitoring Progress Help in English and Spanish at *BigIdeasMath.com*

In Exercises 3 and 4, write the negation of the statement.

3. The shirt is green.   **4.** The shoes are *not* red.

5. Repeat Example 3. Let p be "the stars are visible" and let q be "it is night."

Extra Example 3

Let p be "you are in New York City" and let q be "you are in the United States." Write each statement in words and decide whether it is *true* or *false*.

a. the conditional statement $p \rightarrow q$
If you are in New York City, then you are in the United States. True.

b. the converse $q \rightarrow p$ If you are in the United States, then you are in New York City. False.

c. the inverse $\sim p \rightarrow \sim q$ If you are not in New York City, then you are not in the United States. False.

d. the contrapositive $\sim q \rightarrow \sim p$
If you are not in the United States, then you are not in New York City. True.

MONITORING PROGRESS ANSWERS

3. The shirt is not green.

4. The shoes are red.

5. a. conditional: If the stars are visible, then it is night; true

   b. converse: If it is night, then the stars are visible; false

   c. inverse: If the stars are not visible, then it is not night; false

   d. contrapositive: If it is not night, then the stars are not visible; true

---

Laurie's Notes   Teacher Actions

COMMON ERROR People use the words *converse* and *inverse* in common language, and these words are not always used correctly!

• Write the *Core Concept*, discussing each of the related conditionals.

? "What are equivalent equations?" Two equations that have the same solution(s).

? "What are equivalent statements?" Listen for students to say something like "statements that mean the same thing, and they are both true or they are both false."

• State Example 3 and ask students to work with their partners to write the conditional statement and the related conditional statements, along with deciding whether the statements are true or false.

Extra Example 4

Decide whether each statement about the diagram is true. Explain your answer using the definitions you have learned.

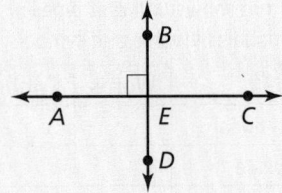

a. $m\angle AEB = 90°$ True. The right angle symbol in the diagram indicates that $\angle AEB$ is a right angle. The measure of a right angle is 90°.

b. *Points A, C,* and *D* are collinear. False. Point *D* does not lie on the same line as *A* and *C*.

c. $\overrightarrow{AC}$ and $\overrightarrow{CA}$ are opposite rays. False. Opposite rays must have a common endpoint, but *A* is the endpoint of $\overrightarrow{AC}$ and *C* is the endpoint of $\overrightarrow{CA}$.

MONITORING PROGRESS ANSWERS

6. true; The diagram shows that $\angle JMF$ and $\angle FMG$ are a linear pair. By definition, angles that form a linear pair are supplementary.

7. false; The midpoint cannot be assumed from a diagram without markings that indicate $FM = MH$.

8. true; Because *M* lies on $\overleftrightarrow{FH}$ and $\overleftrightarrow{JG}$, two pairs of opposite rays are formed.

9. false; Right angles and perpendicular lines cannot be assumed from a diagram without being marked as such.

Using Definitions

You can write a definition as a conditional statement in if-then form or as its converse. Both the conditional statement and its converse are true for definitions. For example, consider the definition of *perpendicular lines.*

If two lines intersect to form a right angle, then they are **perpendicular lines**.

You can also write the definition using the converse: If two lines are perpendicular lines, then they intersect to form a right angle.

You can write "line ℓ is perpendicular to line *m*" as $\ell \perp m$.

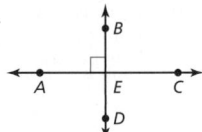

EXAMPLE 4   Using Definitions

Decide whether each statement about the diagram is true. Explain your answer using the definitions you have learned.

a. $\overleftrightarrow{AC} \perp \overleftrightarrow{BD}$

b. $\angle AEB$ and $\angle CEB$ are a linear pair.

c. $\overrightarrow{EA}$ and $\overrightarrow{EB}$ are opposite rays.

SOLUTION

a. This statement is *true*. The right angle symbol in the diagram indicates that the lines intersect to form a right angle. So, you can say the lines are perpendicular.

b. This statement is *true*. By definition, if the noncommon sides of adjacent angles are opposite rays, then the angles are a linear pair. Because $\overrightarrow{EA}$ and $\overrightarrow{EC}$ are opposite rays, $\angle AEB$ and $\angle CEB$ are a linear pair.

c. This statement is *false*. Point *E* does not lie on the same line as *A* and *B*, so the rays are not opposite rays.

Monitoring Progress 🔊 Help in English and Spanish at *BigIdeasMath.com*

Use the diagram. Decide whether the statement is true. Explain your answer using the definitions you have learned.

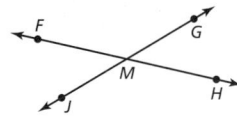

6. $\angle JMF$ and $\angle FMG$ are supplementary.

7. Point *M* is the midpoint of $\overline{FH}$.

8. $\angle JMF$ and $\angle HMG$ are vertical angles.

9. $\overleftrightarrow{FH} \perp \overleftrightarrow{JG}$

Laurie's Notes   Teacher Actions

- Definitions are generally not written as conditional statements. In fact, definitions are biconditional, which means that the statement and its converse are both true when you have a definition. Biconditionals are introduced on page 69. Discuss the definition of perpendicular lines. You could use other examples, such as prime numbers, complementary angles, or equivalent fractions.
- **Turn and Talk:** Pose Example 4 and then ask partners to *Turn and Talk*. Speakers should alternate between partner A and partner B so that one person is not doing all of the talking.
- **Monitoring Progress:** Listen for students' understanding of particular definitions.

Writing Biconditional Statements

 **Core** Concept

Biconditional Statement

When a conditional statement and its converse are both true, you can write them as a single *biconditional statement*. A **biconditional statement** is a statement that contains the phrase "if and only if."

Words *p* if and only if *q*   **Symbols** $p \leftrightarrow q$

Any definition can be written as a biconditional statement.

EXAMPLE 5   **Writing a Biconditional Statement**

Rewrite the definition of perpendicular lines as a single biconditional statement.

Definition If two lines intersect to form a right angle, then they are perpendicular lines.

SOLUTION

Let *p* be "two lines intersect to form a right angle" and let *q* be "they are perpendicular lines." Use red to identify *p* and blue to identify *q*. Write the definition $p \rightarrow q$.

Definition If two lines intersect to form a right angle, then they are perpendicular lines.

Write the converse $q \rightarrow p$.

Converse If two lines are perpendicular lines, then they intersect to form a right angle.

Use the definition and its converse to write the biconditional statement $p \leftrightarrow q$.

▶ **Biconditional** Two lines intersect to form a right angle if and only if they are perpendicular lines.

(figure showing lines s and t intersecting at a right angle; $s \perp t$)

Monitoring Progress 🔊 Help in English and Spanish at *BigIdeasMath.com*

10. Rewrite the definition of a right angle as a single biconditional statement.

   Definition If an angle is a right angle, then its measure is 90°.

11. Rewrite the definition of congruent segments as a single biconditional statement.

   Definition If two line segments have the same length, then they are congruent segments.

12. Rewrite the statements as a single biconditional statement.

   If Mary is in theater class, then she will be in the fall play. If Mary is in the fall play, then she must be taking theater class.

13. Rewrite the statements as a single biconditional statement.

   If you can run for President, then you are at least 35 years old. If you are at least 35 years old, then you can run for President.

Extra Example 5

Rewrite the definition of complementary angles as a single biconditional statement.
Definition: If two angles are complementary, then the sum of the measures of the angles is 90°.
Two angles are complementary if and only if the sum of their measures is 90°.

MONITORING PROGRESS ANSWERS

10. An angle is a right angle if and only if its measure is 90°.

11. Two line segments have the same length if and only if they are congruent segments.

12. Mary is in the fall play if and only if she is taking theater class.

13. You can run for President if and only if you are at least 35 years old.

Laurie's Notes   Teacher Actions

- Write the *Core Concept*, noting the *if and only if* language and notation.
- Work through Example 5 as shown.
- **?** Give students time to consider the question, "Are all definitions biconditional?" This is when I like to discuss what it means to write a good definition. Writing a good definition of a square means it should be biconditional and it should not list all of the properties of a square.
- Students have fun thinking of additional *if and only if* statements.

Extra Example 6

Make a truth table for the conditional statement $\sim(\sim p \rightarrow q)$.

p	q	$\sim p$	$\sim p \rightarrow q$	$\sim(\sim p \rightarrow q)$
T	T	F	T	F
T	F	F	T	F
F	T	T	T	F
F	F	T	F	T

MONITORING PROGRESS ANSWERS

14.

p	q	$\sim q$	$p \rightarrow \sim q$
T	T	F	F
T	F	T	T
F	T	F	T
F	F	T	T

15.

p	q	$p \rightarrow q$	$\sim(p \rightarrow q)$
T	T	T	F
T	F	F	T
F	T	T	F
F	F	T	F

Making Truth Tables

The **truth value** of a statement is either true (T) or false (F). You can determine the conditions under which a conditional statement is true by using a **truth table**. The truth table below shows the truth values for hypothesis p and conclusion q.

Conditional		
p	q	$p \rightarrow q$
T	T	T
T	F	F
F	T	T
F	F	T

The conditional statement $p \rightarrow q$ is only false when a true hypothesis produces a false conclusion.

Two statements are *logically equivalent* when they have the same truth table.

EXAMPLE 6   Making a Truth Table

Use the truth table above to make truth tables for the converse, inverse, and contrapositive of a conditional statement $p \rightarrow q$.

SOLUTION

The truth tables for the converse and the inverse are shown below. Notice that the converse and the inverse are logically equivalent because they have the same truth table.

Converse		
p	q	$q \rightarrow p$
T	T	T
T	F	T
F	T	F
F	F	T

Inverse				
p	q	$\sim p$	$\sim q$	$\sim p \rightarrow \sim q$
T	T	F	F	T
T	F	F	T	T
F	T	T	F	F
F	F	T	T	T

The truth table for the contrapositive is shown below. Notice that a conditional statement and its contrapositive are logically equivalent because they have the same truth table.

Contrapositive				
p	q	$\sim q$	$\sim p$	$\sim q \rightarrow \sim p$
T	T	F	F	T
T	F	T	F	F
F	T	F	T	T
F	F	T	T	T

Monitoring Progress Help in English and Spanish at *BigIdeasMath.com*

14. Make a truth table for the conditional statement $p \rightarrow \sim q$.

15. Make a truth table for the conditional statement $\sim(p \rightarrow q)$.

Laurie's Notes   Teacher Actions

- Students find it challenging to think about what a truth table represents. When you have two statements, there are four possible situations as established in the truth table.
- **Big Idea:** The *Big Idea* for students to grasp is that the conditional statement is only false when the hypothesis is true and the conclusion is false.
- In Example 6, be sure that students look at the labels at the top of each table. For instance, when making a truth table for the converse of a statement, the last column is labeled $q \rightarrow p$. To decide the truth value, the second column (q) represents the hypothesis and the first column (p) represents the conclusion.

? "Which truth tables have the same truth values?" the original statement and the contrapositive; the converse and the inverse

Closure

- Let p be "snow is falling" and let q be "it is winter." Write the conditional statement ($p \rightarrow q$), converse, inverse, and contrapositive in words. Conditional statement: If snow is falling, then it is winter.
Converse: If it is winter, then snow is falling.
Inverse: If snow is not falling, then it is not winter.
Contrapositive: If it is not winter, then snow is not falling.

Assignment Guide and Homework Check

ASSIGNMENT

Basic: 1, 2, 3—43 odd, 46, 58, 64—69

Average: 1, 2, 4—48 even, 55, 58, 61, 64—69

Advanced: 1, 2, 10, 16, 17, 20, 28, 32—58 even, 59, 64—69

HOMEWORK CHECK

Basic: 3, 7, 19, 33, 39

Average: 14, 20, 28, 36, 40

Advanced: 16, 20, 28, 42, 58

Vocabulary and Core Concept Check

1. **VOCABULARY** What type of statements are either both true or both false?

2. **WHICH ONE DOESN'T BELONG?** Which statement does *not* belong with the other three? Explain your reasoning.

If today is Tuesday, then tomorrow is Wednesday.	If it is Independence Day, then it is July.
If an angle is acute, then its measure is less than 90°.	If you are an athlete, then you play soccer.

Monitoring Progress and Modeling with Mathematics

In Exercises 3–6, copy the conditional statement. Underline the hypothesis and circle the conclusion.

3. If a polygon is a pentagon, then it has five sides.

4. If two lines form vertical angles, then they intersect.

5. If you run, then you are fast.

6. If you like math, then you like science.

In Exercises 7–12, rewrite the conditional statement in if-then form. *(See Example 1.)*

7. $9x + 5 = 23$, because $x = 2$.

8. Today is Friday, and tomorrow is the weekend.

9. You are in a band, and you play the drums.

10. Two right angles are supplementary angles.

11. Only people who are registered are allowed to vote.

12. The measures of complementary angles sum to 90°.

In Exercises 13–16, write the negation of the statement. *(See Example 2.)*

13. The sky is blue.   14. The lake is cold.

15. The ball is *not* pink.   16. The dog is *not* a Lab.

In Exercises 17–24, write the conditional statement $p \rightarrow q$**, the converse** $q \rightarrow p$**, the inverse** $\sim p \rightarrow \sim q$**, and the contrapositive** $\sim q \rightarrow \sim p$ **in words. Then decide whether each statement is true or false.** *(See Example 3.)*

17. Let p be "two angles are supplementary" and let q be "the measures of the angles sum to 180°."

18. Let p be "you are in math class" and let q be "you are in Geometry."

19. Let p be "you do your math homework" and let q be "you will do well on the test."

20. Let p be "you are not an only child" and let q be "you have a sibling."

21. Let p be "it does not snow" and let q be "I will run outside."

22. Let p be "the Sun is out" and let q be "it is daytime."

23. Let p be "$3x - 7 = 20$" and let q be "$x = 9$."

24. Let p be "it is Valentine's Day" and let q be "it is February."

In Exercises 25–28, decide whether the statement about the diagram is true. Explain your answer using the definitions you have learned. *(See Example 4.)*

25. $m\angle ABC = 90°$ 26. $\overrightarrow{PQ} \perp \overrightarrow{ST}$

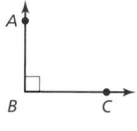

27. $m\angle 2 + m\angle 3 = 180°$ 28. M is the midpoint of $\overline{AB}$.

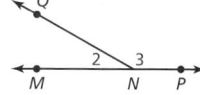

18. conditional: If you are in math class, then you are in Geometry; false

converse: If you are in Geometry, then you are in math class; true

inverse: If you are not in math class, then you are not in Geometry; true

contrapositive: If you are not in Geometry, then you are not in math class; false

19. conditional: If you do your math homework, then you will do well on the test; false

converse: If you do well on the test, then you did your math homework; false

inverse: If you do not do your math homework, then you will not do well on the test; false

contrapositive: If you do not do well on the test, then you did not do your math homework; false

20–28. See Additional Answers.

ANSWERS

1. a conditional statement and its contrapositive, as well as the converse and inverse of a conditional statement

2. If you are an athlete, then you play soccer; This statement is false, but the other 3 are true.

3. If <u>a polygon is a pentagon</u>, then (it has five sides.)

4. If <u>two lines form vertical angles</u>, then (they intersect.)

5. If <u>you run</u>, then (you are fast.)

6. If <u>you like math</u>, then (you like science.)

7. If $x = 2$, then $9x + 5 = 23$.

8. If today is Friday, then tomorrow is the weekend.

9. If you are in a band, then you play the drums.

10. If two angles are right angles, then they are supplementary.

11. If you are registered, then you are allowed to vote.

12. If two angles are complementary, then their measures sum to 90°.

13. The sky is not blue.

14. The lake is not cold.

15. The ball is pink.

16. The dog is a Lab.

17. conditional: If two angles are supplementary, then the measures of the angles sum to 180°; true

converse: If the measures of two angles sum to 180°, then they are supplementary; true

inverse: If the two angles are not supplementary, then their measures do not sum to 180°; true

contrapositive: If the measures of two angles do not sum to 180°, then they are not supplementary; true

ANSWERS

29. A point is the midpoint of a segment if and only if it is the point that divides the segment into two congruent segments.

30. Two angles are vertical angles if and only if their sides form two pairs of opposite rays.

31. Two angles are adjacent angles if and only if they share a common vertex and side, but have no common interior points.

32. Two angles are supplementary angles if and only if the sum of their measures is 180°.

33. A polygon has three sides if and only if it is a triangle.

34. A polygon is a quadrilateral if and only if it has four sides.

35. An angle is a right angle if and only if it measures 90°.

36. An angle has a measure between 90° and 180° if and only if it is obtuse.

37. Taking four English courses is a requirement regardless of how many courses the student takes total, and the courses do not have to be taken simultaneously; If students are in high school, then they will take four English courses before they graduate.

38. The inverse was used instead of the converse; If I bring an umbrella, then it is raining.

39.

p	q	$\sim p$	$\sim p \to q$
T	T	F	T
T	F	F	T
F	T	T	T
F	F	T	F

40.

p	q	$\sim q$	$\sim q \to p$
T	T	F	T
T	F	T	T
F	T	F	T
F	F	T	F

41–42. See Additional Answers.

In Exercises 29–32, rewrite the definition of the term as a biconditional statement. *(See Example 5.)*

29. The *midpoint* of a segment is the point that divides the segment into two congruent segments.

30. Two angles are *vertical angles* when their sides form two pairs of opposite rays.

31. *Adjacent angles* are two angles that share a common vertex and side but have no common interior points.

32. Two angles are *supplementary angles* when the sum of their measures is 180°.

In Exercises 33–36, rewrite the statements as a single biconditional statement. *(See Example 5.)*

33. If a polygon has three sides, then it is a triangle.
    If a polygon is a triangle, then it has three sides.

34. If a polygon has four sides, then it is a quadrilateral.
    If a polygon is a quadrilateral, then it has four sides.

35. If an angle is a right angle, then it measures 90°.
    If an angle measures 90°, then it is a right angle.

36. If an angle is obtuse, then it has a measure between 90° and 180°.
    If an angle has a measure between 90° and 180°, then it is obtuse.

37. **ERROR ANALYSIS** Describe and correct the error in rewriting the conditional statement in if-then form.

> **Conditional statement**
> All high school students take four English courses.
>
> **If-then form**
> If a high school student takes four courses, then all four are English courses.

38. **ERROR ANALYSIS** Describe and correct the error in writing the converse of the conditional statement.

> **Conditional statement**
> If it is raining, then I will bring an umbrella.
>
> **Converse**
> If it is not raining, then I will not bring an umbrella.

In Exercises 39–44, create a truth table for the logical statement. *(See Example 6.)*

39. $\sim p \to q$

40. $\sim q \to p$

41. $\sim(\sim p \to \sim q)$

42. $\sim(p \to \sim q)$

43. $q \to \sim p$

44. $\sim(q \to p)$

45. **USING STRUCTURE** The statements below describe three ways that rocks are formed.

Igneous rock is formed from the cooling of molten rock.

Sedimentary rock is formed from pieces of other rocks.

Metamorphic rock is formed by changing temperature, pressure, or chemistry.

a. Write each statement in if-then form.

b. Write the converse of each of the statements in part (a). Is the converse of each statement true? Explain your reasoning.

c. Write a true if-then statement about rocks that is different from the ones in parts (a) and (b). Is the converse of your statement true or false? Explain your reasoning.

46. **MAKING AN ARGUMENT** Your friend claims the statement "If I bought a shirt, then I went to the mall" can be written as a true biconditional statement. Your sister says you cannot write it as a biconditional. Who is correct? Explain your reasoning.

47. **REASONING** You are told that the contrapositive of a statement is true. Will that help you determine whether the statement can be written as a true biconditional statement? Explain your reasoning.

43.

p	q	$\sim p$	$q \to \sim p$
T	T	F	F
T	F	F	T
F	T	T	T
F	F	T	T

44.

p	q	$q \to p$	$\sim(q \to p)$
T	T	T	F
T	F	T	F
F	T	F	T
F	F	T	F

45. See Additional Answers.

46. your sister; It is possible to go to the mall without buying a shirt. So, the converse is not true.

47. no; The contrapositive is equivalent to the original conditional statement. In order to write a conditional statement as a true biconditional statement, you must know that the converse (or inverse) is true.

48. **PROBLEM SOLVING** Use the conditional statement to identify the if-then statement as the converse, inverse, or contrapositive of the conditional statement. Then use the symbols to represent both statements.

> **Conditional statement**
> If I rode my bike to school, then I did not walk to school.
>
> **If-then statement**
> If I did not ride my bike to school, then I walked to school.

| p | q | $\sim$ | $\rightarrow$ | $\leftrightarrow$ |

USING STRUCTURE In Exercises 49–52, rewrite the conditional statement in if-then form. Then underline the hypothesis and circle the conclusion.

49.

> *If you tell the truth, you don't have to remember anything.*
> *Mark Twain*

50.
> You have to expect things of yourself before you can do them.
> Michael Jordan

51.
> If one is lucky, a solitary fantasy can totally transform one million realities.
> Maya Angelou

52.
> Whoever is happy will make others happy too.
> Anne Frank

53. **MATHEMATICAL CONNECTIONS** Can the statement "If $x^2 - 10 = x + 2$, then $x = 4$" be combined with its converse to form a true biconditional statement?

54. **CRITICAL THINKING** The largest natural arch in the United States is Landscape Arch, located in Thompson, Utah. It spans 290 feet.

   a. Use the information to write at least two true conditional statements.

   b. Which type of related conditional statement must also be true? Write the related conditional statements.

   c. What are the other two types of related conditional statements? Write the related conditional statements. Then determine their truth values. Explain your reasoning.

55. **REASONING** Which statement has the same meaning as the given statement?

> **Given statement**
> You can watch a movie after you do your homework.

   Ⓐ If you do your homework, then you can watch a movie afterward.

   Ⓑ If you do not do your homework, then you can watch a movie afterward.

   Ⓒ If you cannot watch a movie afterward, then do your homework.

   Ⓓ If you can watch a movie afterward, then do not do your homework.

56. **THOUGHT PROVOKING** Write three conditional statements, where one is always true, one is always false, and one depends on the person interpreting the statement.

ANSWERS

48. inverse; $p \rightarrow q$; $\sim p \rightarrow \sim q$

49. If <u>you tell the truth</u>, then ⟨you don't have to remember anything.⟩

50. If <u>you expect things of yourself</u>, then ⟨you can do them.⟩

51. If <u>one is lucky</u>, then ⟨a solitary fantasy can totally transform one million realities.⟩

52. If <u>you are happy</u>, then ⟨you will make others happy too.⟩

53. no; "If $x^2 - 10 = x + 2$, then $x = 4$" is a false statement because $x = -3$ is also possible. The converse, however, of the original conditional statement is true. In order for a biconditional statement to be true, both the conditional statement and its converse must be true.

54. a. *Sample answer:* If a natural arch is the largest in the United States, then it is the Landscape Arch. If a natural arch is the Landscape Arch, then it spans 290 feet.

   b. contrapositive; If a natural arch is not the Landscape Arch, then it is not the largest in the United States. If a natural arch does not span 290 feet, then it is not the Landscape Arch.

   c. converse, inverse; converse: If a natural arch is the Landscape Arch, then it is the largest in the United States. inverse: If a natural arch is not the largest in the United States, then it is not the Landscape Arch; Both of these statements are true because there is only one arch that fits both criteria.

   converse: If a natural arch spans 290 feet, then it is the Landscape Arch. inverse: If a natural arch is not the Landscape Arch, then it does not span 290 feet; Both of these statements are false because it is possible for a natural arch in another country to span 290 feet.

55. A

56. *Sample answer:* If today is Monday, then tomorrow is Tuesday; If the measure of an angle is 85°, then it is obtuse; If today is sunny, then I will go for a walk.

Mini-Assessment

1. Make a truth table for $\sim(\sim p.)$

p	$\sim p$	$\sim(\sim p)$
T	F	T
F	T	F

2. Let p be "$x^2 = 4$." Let q be "$x = 2$." Write the contrapositive $\sim q \rightarrow \sim p$ in words and decide whether it is true or false. If $x \neq 2$, then $x^2 \neq 4$; False.

3. Rewrite the definition as a single biconditional:

If two angles are congruent, then they have equal measures.

Two angles are congruent if and only if they have equal measures.

4. Decide whether the statement is true and explain your answer. $\angle JMH$ and $\angle HMG$ are a linear pair.

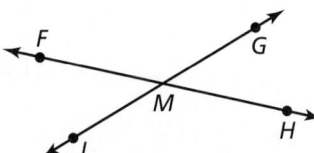

True. The noncommon sides of the two adjacent angles are opposite rays, so by definition the angles are a linear pair.

---

57. **CRITICAL THINKING** One example of a conditional statement involving dates is "If today is August 31, then tomorrow is September 1." Write a conditional statement using dates from two different months so that the truth value depends on when the statement is read.

58. **HOW DO YOU SEE IT?** The Venn diagram represents all the musicians at a high school. Write three conditional statements in if-then form describing the relationships between the various groups of musicians.

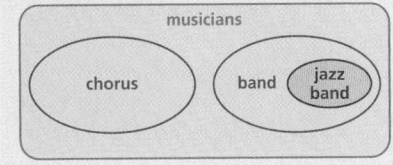

59. **MULTIPLE REPRESENTATIONS** Create a Venn diagram representing each conditional statement. Write the converse of each conditional statement. Then determine whether each conditional statement and its converse are true or false. Explain your reasoning.

   a. If you go to the zoo to see a lion, then you will see a cat.

   b. If you play a sport, then you wear a helmet.

   c. If this month has 31 days, then it is not February.

60. **DRAWING CONCLUSIONS** You measure the heights of your classmates to get a data set.

   a. Tell whether this statement is true: If x and y are the least and greatest values in your data set, then the mean of the data is between x and y.

   b. Write the converse of the statement in part (a). Is the converse true? Explain your reasoning.

   c. Copy and complete the statement below using *mean*, *median*, or *mode* to make a conditional statement that is true for any data set. Explain your reasoning.

     If a data set has a mean, median, and a mode, then the _____ of the data set will always be a data value.

61. **WRITING** Write a conditional statement that is true, but its converse is false.

62. **CRITICAL THINKING** Write a series of if-then statements that allow you to find the measure of each angle, given that $m\angle 1 = 90°$. Use the definition of linear pairs.

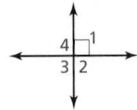

63. **WRITING** Advertising slogans such as "Buy these shoes! They will make you a better athlete!" often imply conditional statements. Find an advertisement or write your own slogan. Then write it as a conditional statement.

Maintaining Mathematical Proficiency   *Reviewing what you learned in previous grades and lessons*

Find the pattern. Then draw the next two figures in the sequence.   *(Skills Review Handbook)*

64.

65.

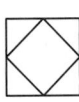 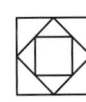

Find the pattern. Then write the next two numbers.   *(Skills Review Handbook)*

66. $1, 3, 5, 7, \ldots$ **67.** $12, 23, 34, 45, \ldots$

68. $2, \frac{4}{3}, \frac{8}{9}, \frac{16}{27}, \ldots$ **69.** $1, 4, 9, 16, \ldots$

If students need help...	*If students got it...*
Resources by Chapter • Practice A and Practice B • Puzzle Time	Resources by Chapter • Enrichment and Extension • Cumulative Review
Student Journal • Practice	Start the *next* Section
Differentiating the Lesson Skills Review Handbook	

Laurie's Notes

Overview of Section 2.2

Introduction

- This lesson presents opportunities for students to reason inductively and deductively. The amount of vocabulary in the lesson can be challenging for students. Be prepared to offer additional examples.
- *Inductive reasoning* means that observations are made and then a *conjecture* is stated. To prove a conjecture, it must be proven for all cases. To disprove a conjecture, only one *counterexample* is needed.
- *Deductive reasoning* uses known facts, definitions, accepted properties, and the laws of logic to form a logical argument. The two laws of logic presented are the *Law of Detachment* and the *Law of Syllogism*.

Common Misconceptions

- Students will sometimes question why inductive reasoning is not sufficient, asking, "Why not simply observe patterns and make a conjecture?" You need to have a problem in which the observation falls apart at some point. There are classic problems that make this point nicely.

Formative Assessment Tips

- **Think-Pair-Share:** This technique allows students to share their thinking about a problem with their partners after they have had time to consider the problem alone. Once partners have discussed the problem, small groups or the whole class should discuss the problem.
- The initial time working alone is important for students to develop their own understanding of the mathematics. "Private think time" is what I call it. Once students have engaged in the problem, sharing with partners helps confirm their understanding or perhaps the need to modify their thinking. Sharing your thinking with the whole class is more comfortable for students when they have had the chance to discuss their thinking with partners.
- **MP3 Construct Viable Arguments and Critique the Reasoning of Others:** Using this formative assessment technique allows you to check students' conceptual knowledge and their ability to construct a viable argument.

Extensions

- Search for "logic puzzles" on the Internet and you will find lots of sample problems in which students can use the two *Laws of Logic* presented in this lesson.

Pacing Suggestion

- Students should work through at least Explorations 1 and 2 before you proceed with the formal lesson.

Common Core State Standards

HSG-CO.C.9 Prove theorems about lines and angles.

HSG-CO.C.10 Prove theorems about triangles.

HSG-CO.C.11 Prove theorems about parallelograms.

HSG-SRT.B.4 Prove theorems about triangles.

Laurie's Notes

Exploration

Motivate

- Make a Venn diagram showing at least two intersecting sets of students. You could use yarn to form regions on the floor of the classroom for students to step into, or you could draw the diagram on the board. Select properties for which you know there will be elements (students) in each region.
- Students should either step into the yarn or write their names in the Venn diagram. Ask questions about the different regions in the form of a conditional statement. (See Exploration 2.)

Discuss

- Students should be familiar with the word *conjecture,* but they may not be. You could model what it means to make a conjecture by making observations of students in the classroom. For instance, you observe that the first three people you look at are wearing sneakers, so you conclude (make a conjecture) that students in geometry class wear sneakers. You have made an unproven statement based on observations.

Exploration 1

- Students generally like this type of problem. It tends to be nonthreatening, and visual patterns sometimes seem easier to figure out than numeric patterns.
- When students have made a conjecture, use *Popsicle Sticks* to solicit answers.

Exploration 2

- Students may be confused by what Property A, B, and C mean. They could be any property or attribute that elements in a set would have. The *Motivate* could be an example.
- In answering the questions, students should have a particular region of the Venn diagram in mind.
- **MP3:** The justification is being able to point to the region that shows that the statement is or is not satisfied. Students do not need to know what the properties are in order to answer the questions.

Exploration 3

- If you feel your students are knowledgeable enough about quadrilaterals, continue with this exploration. If not, you may want to skip this exploration and begin the formal lesson.

Communicate Your Answer

- Students may not be able to articulate how they use reasoning to solve a problem. Share a personal example, give students additional think time, and then ask again.

Connecting to Next Step

- You may consider omitting Example 1 as it is very similar to Exploration 1.

2.2 Inductive and Deductive Reasoning

Essential Question How can you use reasoning to solve problems?

A **conjecture** is an unproven statement based on observations.

EXPLORATION 1   Writing a Conjecture

Work with a partner. Write a conjecture about the pattern. Then use your conjecture to draw the 10th object in the pattern.

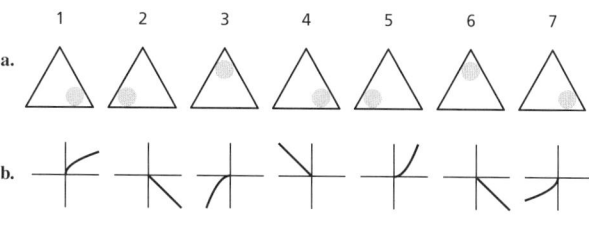

CONSTRUCTING VIABLE ARGUMENTS

To be proficient in math, you need to justify your conclusions and communicate them to others.

EXPLORATION 2   Using a Venn Diagram

Work with a partner. Use the Venn diagram to determine whether the statement is true or false. Justify your answer. Assume that no region of the Venn diagram is empty.

a. If an item has Property B, then it has Property A.

b. If an item has Property A, then it has Property B.

c. If an item has Property A, then it has Property C.

d. Some items that have Property A do not have Property B.

e. If an item has Property C, then it does not have Property B.

f. Some items have both Properties A and C.

g. Some items have both Properties B and C.

EXPLORATION 3   Reasoning and Venn Diagrams

Work with a partner. Draw a Venn diagram that shows the relationship between different types of quadrilaterals: squares, rectangles, parallelograms, trapezoids, rhombuses, and kites. Then write several conditional statements that are shown in your diagram, such as "If a quadrilateral is a square, then it is a rectangle."

Communicate Your Answer

4. How can you use reasoning to solve problems?

5. Give an example of how you used reasoning to solve a real-life problem.

Section 2.2   Inductive and Deductive Reasoning   **75**

ANSWERS

1. a. The circle is rotating from one vertex in the triangle to the next in a clockwise direction.

b. The pattern alternates between a curve in an odd quadrant and a line segment with a negative slope in an even quadrant. The quadrants with a curve or a line segment follow the pattern I, IV, III, II, and the curves follow the pattern of two concave down and two concave up.

c. The pattern alternates between the first three arrangements, then their respective mirror images.

2. a. true; Because all of Property B is inside Property A, all items with Property B must also have Property A.

b. false; There is a region for items that have Property A but not B.

c. false; There is a region for items that have Property A but not C.

d. true; There is a region for items that have Property A but not B.

e. true; There is no intersection of the regions for Properties C and B.

f. true; There is a region that is the intersection of Properties A and C.

g. false; There is no intersection of the regions for Properties B and C.

3.

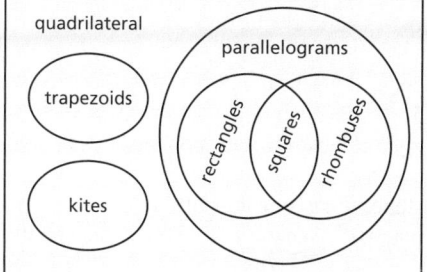

Sample answer: If a quadrilateral is a kite, then it is not a trapezoid. If a quadrilateral is a rectangle, then it is a parallelogram. If a quadrilateral is a square, then it is a rhombus, a rectangle, and a parallelogram. If a polygon is a rhombus, then it is a quadrilateral.

4. You can look for a pattern and then use a "rule" based on that pattern to predict what will happen if the pattern continues.

5. *Sample answer:* You noticed that you did much better on your math tests when you were able to study for at least one hour the night before as opposed to when you were only able to study for less than an hour. So now you make sure that you study for at least one hour the night before a test.

Extra Example 1
Describe how to sketch the fifth figure in the pattern. Then sketch the fifth figure.

Figure 1   Figure 2

Figure 3   Figure 4

Each figure has length and width of as many squares as the figure number. Sketch the fifth figure by adding a fifth square to the end of each set of squares.

Figure 5

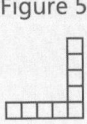

MONITORING PROGRESS ANSWERS
1.
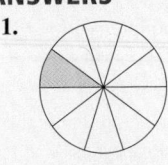

2.
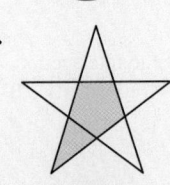

3.
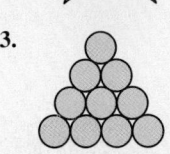

2.2 Lesson

What You Will Learn
▶ Use inductive reasoning.
▶ Use deductive reasoning.

Using Inductive Reasoning

🔁 Core Concept

Inductive Reasoning
A **conjecture** is an unproven statement that is based on observations. You use **inductive reasoning** when you find a pattern in specific cases and then write a conjecture for the general case.

EXAMPLE 1 **Describing a Visual Pattern**

Describe how to sketch the fourth figure in the pattern. Then sketch the fourth figure.

Figure 1   Figure 2   Figure 3

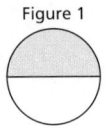 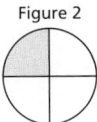 

SOLUTION

Each circle is divided into twice as many equal regions as the figure number. Sketch the fourth figure by dividing a circle into eighths. Shade the section just above the horizontal segment at the left.

Figure 4

Monitoring Progress Help in English and Spanish at *BigIdeasMath.com*

1. Sketch the fifth figure in the pattern in Example 1.

Sketch the next figure in the pattern.

2.

3.

Laurie's Notes   Teacher Actions

? "What does it mean to deduce something?" In logic, it means to reach a conclusion from something known or assumed.

? "What does it mean to induce something?" In logic, it means to assert on the basis of observations or a number of particular facts.

• In addition to sketching the fourth figure, have students describe the pattern.

? "Is it possible to determine a pattern from two figures?" Generally no; at least three terms are needed.

• **Extension:** Have students create a visual pattern and share it with their partners to solve.

EXAMPLE 2 Making and Testing a Conjecture

Numbers such as 3, 4, and 5 are called *consecutive integers*. Make and test a conjecture about the sum of any three consecutive integers.

SOLUTION

Step 1 Find a pattern using a few groups of small numbers.

$$3 + 4 + 5 = 12 = 4 \cdot 3 \qquad 7 + 8 + 9 = 24 = 8 \cdot 3$$
$$10 + 11 + 12 = 33 = 11 \cdot 3 \qquad 16 + 17 + 18 = 51 = 17 \cdot 3$$

Step 2 Make a conjecture.

Conjecture The sum of any three consecutive integers is three times the second number.

Step 3 Test your conjecture using other numbers. For example, test that it works with the groups −1, 0, 1 and 100, 101, 102.

$$-1 + 0 + 1 = 0 = 0 \cdot 3 \checkmark$$
$$100 + 101 + 102 = 303 = 101 \cdot 3 \checkmark$$

 Core Concept

Counterexample

To show that a conjecture is true, you must show that it is true for all cases. You can show that a conjecture is false, however, by finding just one *counterexample*. A **counterexample** is a specific case for which the conjecture is false.

EXAMPLE 3 Finding a Counterexample

A student makes the following conjecture about the sum of two numbers. Find a counterexample to disprove the student's conjecture.

Conjecture The sum of two numbers is always more than the greater number.

SOLUTION

To find a counterexample, you need to find a sum that is less than the greater number.

$$-2 + (-3) = -5$$
$$-5 \not> -2$$

▶ Because a counterexample exists, the conjecture is false.

Monitoring Progress Help in English and Spanish at *BigIdeasMath.com*

4. Make and test a conjecture about the sign of the product of any three negative integers.

5. Make and test a conjecture about the sum of any five consecutive integers.

Find a counterexample to show that the conjecture is false.

6. The value of x^2 is always greater than the value of x.

7. The sum of two numbers is always greater than their difference.

Extra Example 2
Make and test a conjecture about the product of a negative integer and a positive integer. The product of a negative integer and a positive integer is negative.
Sample answer: $(6)(-7) = -42$; $(-8)(3) = -24$; $(-14)(13) = -182$

Extra Example 3
A student makes a conjecture about absolute values. Find a counterexample to disprove the student's conjecture.
Conjecture: The absolute value of the sum of two numbers is equal to the sum of the two numbers.
Sample answer: $3 + (-5) = -2$, and $|3 + (-5)| = |-2| = 2$

MONITORING PROGRESS ANSWERS

4. The product of any three negative integers will be a negative integer. Tests: $-5(-2)(-1) = -10$; $-7(-3)(-5) = -105$; $-50(-10)(-5) = -2500$

5. The sum of any five consecutive integers is five times the middle (third) number. Tests: $2 + 3 + 4 + 5 + 6 = 20 = 5(4)$; $-2 + (-1) + 0 + 1 + 2 = 0 = 5(0)$; $-10 + (-9) + (-8) + (-7) + (-6) = -40 = 5(-8)$

6. *Sample answer:* $0^2 = 0$, $0 \not> 0$

7. *Sample answer:* $-5 + (-3) = -8$ and $-5 - (-3) = -2$, $-8 \not> -2$

Laurie's Notes **Teacher Actions**

• Example 2 demonstrates how to make and test a conjecture.
• **Think-Pair-Share:** Pose Example 2 to students saying, "Make and test a conjecture about the sum of any three consecutive integers." Give students time to explore. It is possible that besides stating the conjecture that the sum will be 3 times the second number, students may say that the sum is divisible by 3 or that the average of the numbers will be the second number.
? "Your conjecture is that the sum of three consecutive numbers is an even number. Is this true?" no; If the first number is even, then the sum will be odd. Explain that this is a counterexample.
• Discuss the *Core Concept*. Showing that a conjecture is true means you must show that it is true for all cases. Showing that a conjecture is false means you only need one counterexample.

Extra Example 4
If a figure is a square, then it is a rectangle. You know that quadrilateral *ABCD* is a square. Using the Law of Detachment, what statement can you make? Quadrilateral *ABCD* is a rectangle.

Extra Example 5
If possible, use the Law of Syllogism to write a new conditional statement that follows from the pair of true statements.
a. If soccer practice is cancelled, then you can go to the mall after school. If it is raining today, then soccer practice is cancelled. If it is raining today, then you can go to the mall after school.
b. If a figure is a rectangle, then all interior angles are right angles. If a figure is a square, then all interior angles are right angles. Not possible

---

Using Deductive Reasoning

Core Concept

Deductive Reasoning

Deductive reasoning uses facts, definitions, accepted properties, and the laws of logic to form a logical argument. This is different from *inductive reasoning*, which uses specific examples and patterns to form a conjecture.

Laws of Logic

Law of Detachment

If the hypothesis of a true conditional statement is true, then the conclusion is also true.

Law of Syllogism

If hypothesis p, then conclusion q.
If hypothesis q, then conclusion r.   ⟩ If these statements are true,

If hypothesis p, then conclusion r.   ← then this statement is true.

EXAMPLE 4 Using the Law of Detachment

If two segments have the same length, then they are congruent. You know that $BC = XY$. Using the Law of Detachment, what statement can you make?

SOLUTION

Because $BC = XY$ satisfies the hypothesis of a true conditional statement, the conclusion is also true.

▶ So, $\overline{BC} \cong \overline{XY}$.

EXAMPLE 5 Using the Law of Syllogism

If possible, use the Law of Syllogism to write a new conditional statement that follows from the pair of true statements.

a. If $x^2 > 25$, then $x^2 > 20$.
   If $x > 5$, then $x^2 > 25$.

b. If a polygon is regular, then all angles in the interior of the polygon are congruent.
   If a polygon is regular, then all its sides are congruent.

SOLUTION

a. Notice that the conclusion of the second statement is the hypothesis of the first statement. The order in which the statements are given does not affect whether you can use the Law of Syllogism. So, you can write the following new statement.

   ▶ If $x > 5$, then $x^2 > 20$.

b. Neither statement's conclusion is the same as the other statement's hypothesis.

   ▶ You cannot use the Law of Syllogism to write a new conditional statement.

Laurie's Notes   Teacher Actions

- The first law, *Law of Detachment,* is easier to state than to understand for most students. Symbolically, it says if $p \rightarrow q$ is true and p is true, then you conclude that q is true. The *Law of Syllogism* says if $p \rightarrow q$ is true and $q \rightarrow r$ is true, then you conclude that $p \rightarrow r$ is true.
- **?** "If two segments have the same length, then they are congruent. ($p \rightarrow q$) Why is this true?" definition of congruent segments
- **?** "You are told $BC = XY$. (p is true.) What can you conclude?" $\overline{BC} \cong \overline{XY}$ (q is true.)
- Students may need to change the order of the statements in Example 5(a) to see that the conclusion of one conditional statement is the hypothesis of the other conditional statement.

EXAMPLE 6 Using Inductive and Deductive Reasoning

What conclusion can you make about the product of an even integer and any other integer?

SOLUTION

Step 1 Look for a pattern in several examples. Use inductive reasoning to make a conjecture.

$$(-2)(2) = -4 \qquad (-1)(2) = -2 \qquad 2(2) = 4 \qquad 3(2) = 6$$
$$(-2)(-4) = 8 \qquad (-1)(-4) = 4 \qquad 2(-4) = -8 \qquad 3(-4) = -12$$

Conjecture Even integer • Any integer = Even integer

Step 2 Let n and m each be any integer. Use deductive reasoning to show that the conjecture is true.

$2n$ is an even integer because any integer multiplied by 2 is even.

$2nm$ represents the product of an even integer $2n$ and any integer m.

$2nm$ is the product of 2 and an integer nm. So, $2nm$ is an even integer.

▶ The product of an even integer and any integer is an even integer.

MAKING SENSE OF PROBLEMS

In geometry, you will frequently use inductive reasoning to make conjectures. You will also use deductive reasoning to show that conjectures are true or false. You will need to know which type of reasoning to use.

EXAMPLE 7 Comparing Inductive and Deductive Reasoning

Decide whether inductive reasoning or deductive reasoning is used to reach the conclusion. Explain your reasoning.

a. Each time Monica kicks a ball up in the air, it returns to the ground. So, the next time Monica kicks a ball up in the air, it will return to the ground.

b. All reptiles are cold-blooded. Parrots are not cold-blooded. Sue's pet parrot is not a reptile.

SOLUTION

a. Inductive reasoning, because a pattern is used to reach the conclusion.

b. Deductive reasoning, because facts about animals and the laws of logic are used to reach the conclusion.

Monitoring Progress 🔊 Help in English and Spanish at *BigIdeasMath.com*

8. If $90° < m\angle R < 180°$, then $\angle R$ is obtuse. The measure of $\angle R$ is 155°. Using the Law of Detachment, what statement can you make?

9. Use the Law of Syllogism to write a new conditional statement that follows from the pair of true statements.

   If you get an A on your math test, then you can go to the movies.
   If you go to the movies, then you can watch your favorite actor.

10. Use inductive reasoning to make a conjecture about the sum of a number and itself. Then use deductive reasoning to show that the conjecture is true.

11. Decide whether inductive reasoning or deductive reasoning is used to reach the conclusion. Explain your reasoning.

    All multiples of 8 are divisible by 4.
    64 is a multiple of 8.
    So, 64 is divisible by 4.

Section 2.2   Inductive and Deductive Reasoning   **79**

Extra Example 6
The table shows the sum of the measures of the interior angles in various polygons.

Polygon	Number of sides	Sum of interior angles
Triangle	3	180°
Quadrilateral	4	360°
Pentagon	5	540°
Hexagon	6	720°

What conclusion can you make about the sum of the interior angles in an n-sided polygon? The sum of the measures of the interior angles is $180(n - 2)°$.

Extra Example 7
Decide whether inductive reasoning or deductive reasoning is used to reach the conclusion. Explain your reasoning.

a. If the sum of the digits of a number is divisible by 3, then the number is divisible by 3. The sum of the digits of the number 147 is 12. So, the number 147 is divisible by 3. Deductive reasoning, because facts are used.

b. Each time you forget to do your math homework, your parents take away your phone privileges for a day. So, the next time your forget to do your math homework, you will lose your phone privileges. Inductive reasoning, because a pattern is used.

MONITORING PROGRESS ANSWERS

8. $\angle R$ is obtuse.

9. If you get an A on your math test, then you can watch your favorite actor.

10. The sum of a number and itself is two times the number; $n + n = 2n$

11. deductive reasoning; The Law of Detachment is used to reach the conclusion.

Laurie's Notes   Teacher Actions

- Example 6 helps students see the difference between inductive reasoning and deductive reasoning. You may need to explain that even integers include positive and negative even integers.
- **Think-Pair-Share:** Pose Example 7 and give time for students to discuss with their neighbors. Solicit responses by using *Popsicle Sticks*.

Closure
- **Writing Prompt:** Compare and contrast inductive reasoning and deductive reasoning.

ANSWERS

1. The prefix *counter-* means "opposing." So, a counterexample opposes the truth of the statement.

2. Inductive reasoning uses patterns to write a conjecture. Deductive reasoning uses facts, definitions, accepted properties, and the laws of logic to form a logical argument.

3. The absolute value of each number in the list is 1 greater than the absolute value of the previous number in the list, and the signs alternate from positive to negative; $-6, 7$

4. The numbers are increasing by successive multiples of 2; 30, 42

5. The list items are letters in backward alphabetical order; U, T

6. Each letter is the first letter of a month of the year, and they are in the order of the months; J, J

7. This is a sequence of regular polygons, each polygon having one more side than the previous polygon.

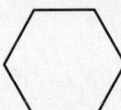 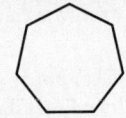

8. See Additional Answers.

9. The product of any two even integers is an even integer. *Sample answer:* $-2(4) = -8, 6(12) = 72,$ $8(10) = 80$

10. The sum of an even integer and an odd integer is an odd integer. *Sample answer:* $2 + 5 = 7, -4 + 9 = 5,$ $10 + 7 = 17$

Vocabulary and Core Concept Check

1. **VOCABULARY** How does the prefix "counter-" help you understand the term counterexample?

2. **WRITING** Explain the difference between inductive reasoning and deductive reasoning.

Monitoring Progress and Modeling with Mathematics

In Exercises 3–8, describe the pattern. Then write or draw the next two numbers, letters, or figures. *(See Example 1.)*

3. $1, -2, 3, -4, 5, \ldots$

4. $0, 2, 6, 12, 20, \ldots$

5. Z, Y, X, W, V, . . .

6. J, F, M, A, M, . . .

7.

8.

In Exercises 9–12, make and test a conjecture about the given quantity. *(See Example 2.)*

9. the product of any two even integers

10. the sum of an even integer and an odd integer

11. the quotient of a number and its reciprocal

12. the quotient of two negative integers

In Exercises 13–16, find a counterexample to show that the conjecture is false. *(See Example 3.)*

13. The product of two positive numbers is always greater than either number.

14. If n is a nonzero integer, then $\dfrac{n + 1}{n}$ is always greater than 1.

15. If two angles are supplements of each other, then one of the angles must be acute.

16. A line s divides $\overline{MN}$ into two line segments. So, the line s is a segment bisector of $\overline{MN}$.

In Exercises 17–20, use the Law of Detachment to determine what you can conclude from the given information, if possible. *(See Example 4.)*

17. If you pass the final, then you pass the class. You passed the final.

18. If your parents let you borrow the car, then you will go to the movies with your friend. You will go to the movies with your friend.

19. If a quadrilateral is a square, then it has four right angles. Quadrilateral *QRST* has four right angles.

20. If a point divides a line segment into two congruent line segments, then the point is a midpoint. Point P divides $\overline{LH}$ into two congruent line segments.

In Exercises 21–24, use the Law of Syllogism to write a new conditional statement that follows from the pair of true statements, if possible. *(See Example 5.)*

21. If $x < -2$, then $|x| > 2$. If $x > 2$, then $|x| > 2$.

22. If $a = 3$, then $5a = 15$. If $\frac{1}{2}a = 1\frac{1}{2}$, then $a = 3$.

23. If a figure is a rhombus, then the figure is a parallelogram. If a figure is a parallelogram, then the figure has two pairs of opposite sides that are parallel.

24. If a figure is a square, then the figure has four congruent sides. If a figure is a square, then the figure has four right angles.

In Exercises 25–28, state the law of logic that is illustrated.

25. If you do your homework, then you can watch TV. If you watch TV, then you can watch your favorite show.

    If you do your homework, then you can watch your favorite show.

---

11. The quotient of a number and its reciprocal is the square of that number. *Sample answer:* $9 \div \frac{1}{9} = 9 \cdot 9 = 9^2, \frac{2}{3} \div \frac{3}{2} = \frac{2}{3} \cdot \frac{2}{3} = \left(\frac{2}{3}\right)^2,$ $\frac{1}{7} \div 7 = \frac{1}{7} \cdot \frac{1}{7} = \left(\frac{1}{7}\right)^2$

12. The quotient of two negative integers is a positive rational number. *Sample answer:* $\frac{-4}{-5} = \frac{4}{5}, \frac{-14}{-7} = 2, \frac{-21}{-5} = \frac{21}{5}$

13. *Sample answer:* $1 \cdot 5 = 5, 5 \not> 5$

14. *Sample answer:* Let $n = -2$. $\frac{-2 + 1}{-2} = \frac{1}{2}, \frac{1}{2} \not> 1$

15. They could both be right angles. Then, neither are acute.

16. If line s intersects $\overline{MN}$ at any point other than the midpoint, it is not a segment bisector.

17. You passed the class.

18. not possible

19. not possible

20. Point P is the midpoint of $\overline{LH}$.

21. not possible

22. If $\frac{1}{2}a = 1\frac{1}{2}$, then $5a = 15$.

23. If a figure is a rhombus, then the figure has two pairs of opposite sides that are parallel.

24. not possible

25. Law of Syllogism

26. If you miss practice the day before a game, then you will not be a starting player in the game.

You miss practice on Tuesday. You will not start the game Wednesday.

27. If $x > 12$, then $x + 9 > 20$. The value of x is 14.

So, $x + 9 > 20$.

28. If $\angle 1$ and $\angle 2$ are vertical angles, then $\angle 1 \cong \angle 2$. If $\angle 1 \cong \angle 2$, then $m\angle 1 = m\angle 2$.

If $\angle 1$ and $\angle 2$ are vertical angles, then $m\angle 1 = m\angle 2$.

In Exercises 29 and 30, use inductive reasoning to make a conjecture about the given quantity. Then use deductive reasoning to show that the conjecture is true. (*See Example 6.*)

29. the sum of two odd integers

30. the product of two odd integers

In Exercises 31–34, decide whether inductive reasoning or deductive reasoning is used to reach the conclusion. Explain your reasoning. (*See Example 7.*)

31. Each time your mom goes to the store, she buys milk. So, the next time your mom goes to the store, she will buy milk.

32. Rational numbers can be written as fractions. Irrational numbers cannot be written as fractions. So, $\frac{1}{2}$ is a rational number.

33. All men are mortal. Mozart is a man, so Mozart is mortal.

34. Each time you clean your room, you are allowed to go out with your friends. So, the next time you clean your room, you will be allowed to go out with your friends.

ERROR ANALYSIS In Exercises 35 and 36, describe and correct the error in interpreting the statement.

35. If a figure is a rectangle, then the figure has four sides. A trapezoid has four sides.

> Using the Law of Detachment, you can conclude that a trapezoid is a rectangle.

36. Each day, you get to school before your friend.

> Using deductive reasoning, you can conclude that you will arrive at school before your friend tomorrow.

37. REASONING The table shows the average weights of several subspecies of tigers. What conjecture can you make about the relation between the weights of female tigers and the weights of male tigers? Explain your reasoning.

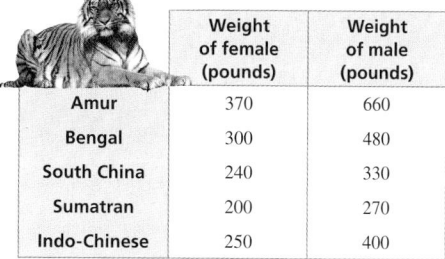

	Weight of female (pounds)	Weight of male (pounds)
Amur	370	660
Bengal	300	480
South China	240	330
Sumatran	200	270
Indo-Chinese	250	400

38. HOW DO YOU SEE IT? Determine whether you can make each conjecture from the graph. Explain your reasoning.

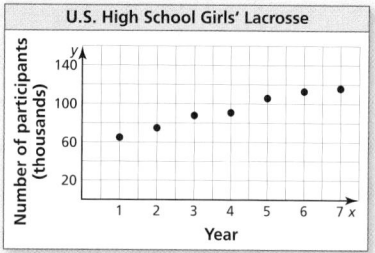

U.S. High School Girls' Lacrosse

a. More girls will participate in high school lacrosse in Year 8 than those who participated in Year 7.

b. The number of girls participating in high school lacrosse will exceed the number of boys participating in high school lacrosse in Year 9.

39. MATHEMATICAL CONNECTIONS Use inductive reasoning to write a formula for the sum of the first n positive even integers.

40. FINDING A PATTERN The following are the first nine *Fibonacci numbers*.

$$1, 1, 2, 3, 5, 8, 13, 21, 34, \ldots$$

a. Make a conjecture about each of the Fibonacci numbers after the first two.

b. Write the next three numbers in the pattern.

c. Research to find a real-world example of this pattern.

ANSWERS

26. Law of Detachment

27. Law of Detachment

28. Law of Syllogism

29. The sum of two odd integers is an even integer; Let m and n be integers. Then $(2m + 1)$ and $(2n + 1)$ are odd integers. $(2m + 1) + (2n + 1) = 2m + 2n + 2 = 2(m + n + 1)$; $2(m + n + 1)$ is divisible by 2 and is therefore an even integer.

30. The product of two odd integers is an odd integer; Let m and n be integers. Then $(2m + 1)$ and $(2n + 1)$ are odd integers. $(2m + 1)(2n + 1) = 4mn + 2m + 2n + 1 = 2(2mn + m + n) + 1$; $2(2mn + m + n)$ is divisible by 2 and is therefore an even integer. An even integer plus one is an odd integer.

31. inductive reasoning; The conjecture is based on the assumption that a pattern, observed in specific cases, will continue.

32. deductive reasoning; The conclusion is based on mathematical definitions and properties.

33. deductive reasoning; Laws of nature and the Law of Syllogism were used to draw the conclusion.

34. inductive reasoning; The conjecture is based on the assumption that a pattern, observed in specific cases, will continue.

35. The Law of Detachment cannot be used because the hypothesis is not true; *Sample answer:* Using the Law of Detachment, because a square is a rectangle, you can conclude that a square has four sides.

36. The conjecture was based on a pattern in specific cases, not rules or laws about the general case; Using inductive reasoning, you can make a conjecture that you will arrive at school before your friend tomorrow.

37. Using inductive reasoning, you can make a conjecture that male tigers weigh more than female tigers because this was true in all of the specific cases listed in the table.

38. a. yes; Based on inductive reasoning, the pattern in all of the years shown is that the number of girls participating is more than the year before.

b. no; There is no information in the graph about how the number of girl participants compares with the number of boy participants.

39. $n(n + 1)$ = the sum of first n positive even integers

40. a. Each number in the sequence is the sum of the previous two numbers in the sequence.

b. 55, 89, 144

c. *Sample answer:* A spiral can be drawn by connecting the opposite corners of squares with side lengths that follow the Fibonacci sequence. This spiral is similar to the spiral seen on nautilus shells. It is also similar to the golden spiral, which is sometimes found in spiraling galaxies.

ANSWERS

41. Argument 2; This argument uses the Law of Detachment to say that when the hypothesis is met, the conclusion is true.

42. *Sample answer:* Each term in the sequence is twice the previous term, $\frac{1}{4}$, $\frac{1}{2}$, 1, 2, 4; Each term is $\frac{1}{4}$ more than the previous term, $\frac{1}{4}$, $\frac{1}{2}$, $\frac{3}{4}$, 1, $\frac{5}{4}$; Multiply each term by half the reciprocal of the previous term; $\frac{1}{4}$, $\frac{1}{2}$, $\frac{1}{2}$, $\frac{1}{2}$, $\frac{1}{2}$

43. The value of y is 2 more than three times the value of x; $y = 3x + 2$; *Sample answer:* If $x = 10$, then $y = 3(10) + 2 = 32$; If $x = 72$, then $y = 3(72) + 2 = 218$.

44. **a.** 4, 8, 12, 16, 20; The perimeter is equal to the product of 4 and the figure number.
    b. 80

45–46. See Additional Answers.

47. Segment Addition Postulate (Post. 1.2)

48. Angle Addition Postulate (Post. 1.4)

49. Ruler Postulate (Post. 1.1)

50. Protractor Postulate (Post. 1.3)

---

41. **MAKING AN ARGUMENT** Which argument is correct? Explain your reasoning.

    Argument 1: If two angles measure 30° and 60°, then the angles are complementary. $\angle 1$ and $\angle 2$ are complementary. So, $m\angle 1 = 30°$ and $m\angle 2 = 60°$.

    Argument 2: If two angles measure 30° and 60°, then the angles are complementary. The measure of $\angle 1$ is 30° and the measure of $\angle 2$ is 60°. So, $\angle 1$ and $\angle 2$ are complementary.

42. **THOUGHT PROVOKING** The first two terms of a sequence are $\frac{1}{4}$ and $\frac{1}{2}$. Describe three different possible patterns for the sequence. List the first five terms for each sequence.

43. **MATHEMATICAL CONNECTIONS** Use the table to make a conjecture about the relationship between x and y. Then write an equation for y in terms of x. Use the equation to test your conjecture for other values of x.

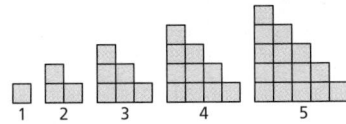

x	0	1	2	3	4
y	2	5	8	11	14

44. **REASONING** Use the pattern below. Each figure is made of squares that are 1 unit by 1 unit.

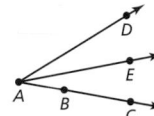

    a. Find the perimeter of each figure. Describe the pattern of the perimeters.
    b. Predict the perimeter of the 20th figure.

45. **DRAWING CONCLUSIONS** Decide whether each conclusion is valid. Explain your reasoning.

    • Yellowstone is a national park in Wyoming.
    • You and your friend went camping at Yellowstone National Park.
    • When you go camping, you go canoeing.
    • If you go on a hike, your friend goes with you.
    • You go on a hike.
    • There is a 3-mile-long trail near your campsite.

    a. You went camping in Wyoming.
    b. Your friend went canoeing.
    c. Your friend went on a hike.
    d. You and your friend went on a hike on a 3-mile-long trail.

46. **CRITICAL THINKING** Geologists use the Mohs' scale to determine a mineral's hardness. Using the scale, a mineral with a higher rating will leave a scratch on a mineral with a lower rating. Testing a mineral's hardness can help identify the mineral.

Mineral	Talc	Gypsum	Calcite	Fluorite
Mohs' rating	1	2	3	4

    a. The four minerals are randomly labeled A, B, C, and D. Mineral A is scratched by Mineral B. Mineral C is scratched by all three of the other minerals. What can you conclude? Explain your reasoning.
    b. What additional test(s) can you use to identify *all* the minerals in part (a)?

Maintaining Mathematical Proficiency
Reviewing what you learned in previous grades and lessons

Determine which postulate is illustrated by the statement.   *(Section 1.2 and Section 1.5)*

47. $AB + BC = AC$

48. $m\angle DAC = m\angle DAE + m\angle EAB$

49. AD is the absolute value of the difference of the coordinates of A and D.

50. $m\angle DAC$ is equal to the absolute value of the difference between the real numbers matched with $\overrightarrow{AD}$ and $\overrightarrow{AC}$ on a protractor.

Overview of Section 2.3

Introduction

- This lesson presents a list of the postulates about points, lines, and planes. The postulates make sense to students—common sense as some students will say.
- You will want to discuss each postulate and draw an illustration. As part of the discussion, ask students what the consequences would be if the postulate were not true.
- Sketching relationships between points, lines, and planes is not taught explicitly in this lesson, but it may be a skill you wish to include.

Resources

- You could use actual models to demonstrate the postulates: wooden skewers for lines, paper or cardboard for planes, and interlocking cardboard pieces for intersecting planes. Use the dividers that come in boxes used to ship bottles for the interlocking cardboard pieces.

Formative Assessment Tips

- **Exit Ticket:** This technique asks students to respond to a question at the end of the lesson, activity, or learning experience. The *Exit Ticket* allows you to collect evidence of student learning. I cut scrap paper into smaller pieces so that "exit tickets" can be distributed quickly to students.
- The *Exit Ticket* is helpful in planning instruction. During the class, there may be students who you have not heard from. They may not have raised their hands, or they may have been less vocal when working with partners. The *Exit Ticket* helps you gauge the ability of all students to answer a particular type of question.
- Students write their names on the exit tickets, which are then collected.
- If a subset of students has difficulty with the skill addressed by the *Exit Ticket*, instruction for the following day should address this problem.

Pacing Suggestion

- Once students have worked the explorations, continue with the formal lesson.

HSG-CO.C.9 Prove theorems about lines
and angles.

HSG-CO.C.10 Prove theorems about
triangles.

HSG-CO.C.11 Prove theorems about
parallelograms.

HSG-SRT.B.4 Prove theorems about
triangles.

Laurie's Notes

Exploration

Motivate
• Show several examples of optical illusions. Two very common ones are shown. Can you trust your eyes?

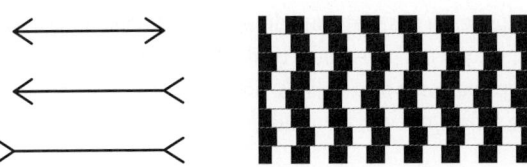

Exploration 1
• The point of this exploration is that the diagrams need to be labeled. You cannot conclude that two lines are perpendicular just because they appear to be perpendicular.
• Students should be looking at different elevations. If their eyes are in the same plane as the lines, then they will not see much!

Exploration 2
• **MP6 Attend to Precision:** Discuss with students that when they make a drawing, or view a drawing, information is being communicated. We label units of measure when we state solutions because we are communicating information. The same will be true about diagrams in geometry.
• **MP3 Construct Viable Arguments and Critique the Reasoning of Others:** These are not simply true-false questions. Be sure that students are writing explanations for their answers.
• Question (i) may be disputed by students. In the diagram, the lines do not intersect. If the lines are not parallel, then the lines will intersect at some point not shown in the diagram.

Communicate Your Answer
• Make a list of the things that students believe can be assumed in a diagram and those that cannot be assumed.

Connecting to Next Step
• The explorations will help prepare students to think carefully about assumptions. The formal lesson presents a list of postulates that establish basic relationships about points, lines, and planes.

2.3 Postulates and Diagrams

Essential Question
In a diagram, what can be assumed and what needs to be labeled?

EXPLORATION 1 Looking at a Diagram

Work with a partner. On a piece of paper, draw two perpendicular lines. Label them $\overleftrightarrow{AB}$ and $\overleftrightarrow{CD}$. Look at the diagram from different angles. Do the lines appear perpendicular regardless of the angle at which you look at them? Describe *all* the angles at which you can look at the lines and have them appear perpendicular.

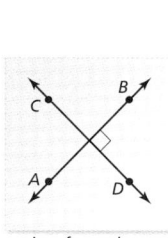

view from above

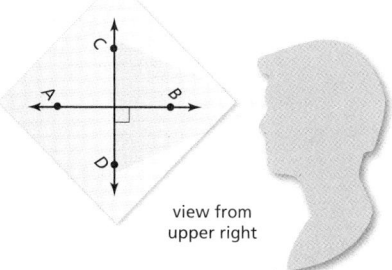

view from upper right

ATTENDING TO PRECISION

To be proficient in math, you need to state the meanings of the symbols you choose.

EXPLORATION 2 Interpreting a Diagram

Work with a partner. When you draw a diagram, you are communicating with others. It is important that you include sufficient information in the diagram. Use the diagram to determine which of the following statements you can assume to be true. Explain your reasoning.

a. All the points shown are coplanar.

b. Points D, G, and I are collinear.

c. Points A, C, and H are collinear.

d. $\overleftrightarrow{EG}$ and $\overleftrightarrow{AH}$ are perpendicular.

e. $\angle BCA$ and $\angle ACD$ are a linear pair.

f. $\overleftrightarrow{AF}$ and $\overleftrightarrow{BD}$ are perpendicular.

h. $\overleftrightarrow{AF}$ and $\overleftrightarrow{BD}$ are coplanar.

j. $\overleftrightarrow{AF}$ and $\overleftrightarrow{BD}$ intersect.

l. $\angle ACD$ and $\angle BCF$ are vertical angles.

g. $\overleftrightarrow{EG}$ and $\overleftrightarrow{BD}$ are parallel.

i. $\overleftrightarrow{EG}$ and $\overleftrightarrow{BD}$ do not intersect.

k. $\overleftrightarrow{EG}$ and $\overleftrightarrow{BD}$ are perpendicular.

m. $\overleftrightarrow{AC}$ and $\overleftrightarrow{FH}$ are the same line.

Communicate Your Answer

3. In a diagram, what can be assumed and what needs to be labeled?

4. Use the diagram in Exploration 2 to write two statements you can assume to be true and two statements you cannot assume to be true. Your statements should be different from those given in Exploration 2. Explain your reasoning.

ANSWERS

1. The lines appear perpendicular from all angles, including when you look at the lines from a view that is perpendicular to both lines.

2. **a.** true; They all lie in the same plane.

   b. false; There is not a line shown that connects all three of them.

   c. true; All three points are on $\overleftrightarrow{AH}$.

   d. true; $\angle GFH$ is marked as a right angle.

   e. true; These two angles are adjacent and form a straight angle.

   f. false; The angles formed by these two lines are not marked. So, you do not know whether or not the lines are perpendicular.

   g. false; Even though they appear to be parallel, you cannot tell for sure.

   h. true; Both lines are in the same plane.

   i. false; Even though they appear to be parallel, you cannot tell for sure.

   j. true; They intersect in point C.

   k. false; $\overleftrightarrow{EG}$ is perpendicular to $\overleftrightarrow{AH}$, and it could not be perpendicular to two different lines that intersect.

   l. true; These angles form two pairs of opposite rays.

   m. true; Points A, C, F, and H are all on the same line, which can be named using any two points on the line.

3. You can assume intersecting lines, opposite rays, vertical angles, linear pairs, adjacent angles, coplanar (points, lines, rays, etc.), collinear points, which point is between two other points, and which points are in the interior of an angle. You have to have a label for identifying angle measures, segment lengths, perpendicular lines, parallel lines, and congruent segments or angles.

4. *Sample answer:* $\angle ACD$ and $\angle DCF$ form a linear pair, because these angles share a vertex and a side but no common interior points and $\angle ACF$ is a straight angle. $\angle CFE$ and $\angle GFH$ are vertical angles, because $\overrightarrow{FG}$ and $\overrightarrow{FE}$ are opposite rays as well as $\overrightarrow{FC}$ and $\overrightarrow{FH}$; $\angle DCF$ is a right angle, which cannot be assumed because angle measurements have to be marked. $\overline{BC} \cong \overline{CD}$, which cannot be assumed because lengths of segments have to be labeled.

2.3 Lesson

Core Vocabulary

line perpendicular to a plane, *p. 86*

Previous
postulate
point
line
plane

What You Will Learn

▶ Identify postulates using diagrams.

▶ Sketch and interpret diagrams.

Identifying Postulates

Here are seven more postulates involving points, lines, and planes.

🔄 Postulates

Point, Line, and Plane Postulates

Postulate	Example	
2.1 Two Point Postulate Through any two points, there exists exactly one line.	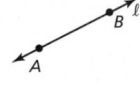	Through points *A* and *B*, there is exactly one line ℓ. Line ℓ contains at least two points.
2.2 Line-Point Postulate A line contains at least two points.		
2.3 Line Intersection Postulate If two lines intersect, then their intersection is exactly one point.	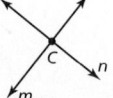	The intersection of line *m* and line *n* is point *C*.
2.4 Three Point Postulate Through any three noncollinear points, there exists exactly one plane.	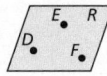	Through points *D*, *E*, and *F*, there is exactly one plane, plane *R*. Plane *R* contains at least three noncollinear points.
2.5 Plane-Point Postulate A plane contains at least three noncollinear points.		
2.6 Plane-Line Postulate If two points lie in a plane, then the line containing them lies in the plane.	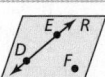	Points *D* and *E* lie in plane *R*, so $\overleftrightarrow{DE}$ lies in plane *R*.
2.7 Plane Intersection Postulate If two planes intersect, then their intersection is a line.	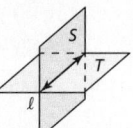	The intersection of plane *S* and plane *T* is line ℓ.

Laurie's Notes Teacher Actions

• Decide how you want to present the postulates. You could present the entire list of seven postulates and ask students to consider what it would mean if each postulate were not true. For instance, if the Two Point Postulate (Post. 2.1) were not true, then you would be able to draw two different "lines" through the two points, meaning the lines would need to bend as shown.

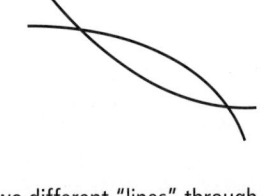

• I refer to the Three Point Postulate (Post. 2.4) as the tripod postulate. There are three legs on the tripod that define a plane, and the tripod is stable even when the legs are different lengths. When you add a fourth leg, like to a table or chair, the object can become tippy because the fourth point may not be in the same plane as the first three points.

• **MP4 Model with Mathematics:** Draw sketches of each postulate to help students make sense of the words.

EXAMPLE 1 **Identifying a Postulate Using a Diagram**

State the postulate illustrated by the diagram.

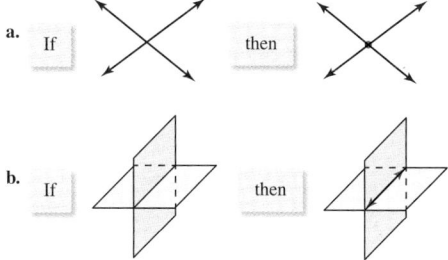

a. If   then

b. If   then

SOLUTION

a. Line Intersection Postulate If two lines intersect, then their intersection is exactly one point.

b. Plane Intersection Postulate If two planes intersect, then their intersection is a line.

EXAMPLE 2 **Identifying Postulates from a Diagram**

Use the diagram to write examples of the Plane-Point Postulate and the Plane-Line Postulate.

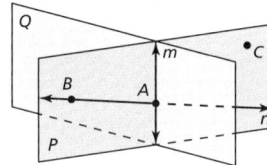

SOLUTION

Plane-Point Postulate Plane P contains at least three noncollinear points, A, B, and C.

Plane-Line Postulate Point A and point B lie in plane P. So, line n containing points A and B also lies in plane P.

Monitoring Progress 🔊 Help in English and Spanish at *BigIdeasMath.com*

1. Use the diagram in Example 2. Which postulate allows you to say that the intersection of plane P and plane Q is a line?

2. Use the diagram in Example 2 to write an example of the postulate.

   a. Two Point Postulate

   b. Line-Point Postulate

   c. Line Intersection Postulate

Extra Example 1
State the postulate illustrated by the diagram.

a.

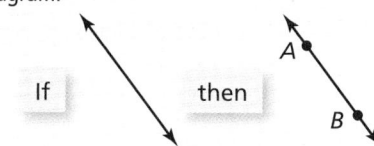

If   then

Line-Point Postulate (Post. 2.2): A line contains at least two points.

b.

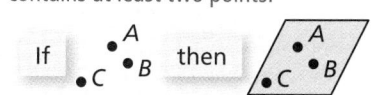

If   then

Three Point Postulate (Post. 2.4): Through any three noncollinear points, there exists exactly one plane.

Extra Example 2

Use the diagram in Example 2 to write an example of the Three Point Postulate (Post. 2.4). Points A, B, and C are noncollinear, so there is exactly one plane, plane P, that contains them.

MONITORING PROGRESS ANSWERS

1. Plane Intersection Postulate (Post. 2.7)

2. a. Line n passes through points A and B.

   b. Line n contains points A and B.

   c. Line n and line m intersect at point A.

Laurie's Notes   **Teacher Actions**

• **MP4:** Example 1 shows how the Line Intersection Postulate (Post. 2.3) and the Plane Intersection Postulate (Post. 2.7) could be illustrated.

• Note the shading of the planes to help students recognize the three dimensions of the diagram. The dotted lines represent segments that could not be seen from the perspective chosen.

• **Common Misconception:** In Example 2, it is difficult for all students to interpret the diagram correctly. Some students may see $\overrightarrow{AB}$ as lying in plane Q versus plane P.

Extra Example 3

Sketch a diagram showing $\overrightarrow{VX}$ intersecting $\overleftrightarrow{UW}$ at V so that $\overrightarrow{VX}$ is perpendicular to $\overleftrightarrow{UW}$ and U, V, and W are collinear.

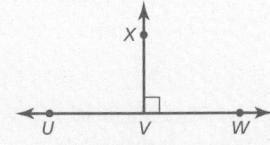

Extra Example 4

Use the diagram in Example 4. Which statements *cannot* be assumed from the diagram?

- There exists a plane that contains points A, D, and E.
- $AB = BF$.

You cannot assume $AB = BF$.

MONITORING PROGRESS ANSWERS

3. Put double tick marks on each of them.

4. *Sample answer:* $\angle PWT$ and $\angle TWQ$; They form a linear pair.

5. yes

6. $\overleftrightarrow{AB}$ is perpendicular to plane S, and $\overleftrightarrow{BC}$ is on plane S and intersects $\overleftrightarrow{AB}$ at B.

Sketching and Interpreting Diagrams

EXAMPLE 3   Sketching a Diagram

Sketch a diagram showing $\overleftrightarrow{TV}$ intersecting $\overleftrightarrow{PQ}$ at point W, so that $\overline{TW} \cong \overline{WV}$.

SOLUTION

Step 1   Draw $\overleftrightarrow{TV}$ and label points T and V.

Step 2   Draw point W at the midpoint of $\overline{TV}$. Mark the congruent segments.

Step 3   Draw $\overleftrightarrow{PQ}$ through W.

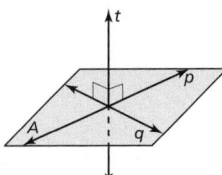

ANOTHER WAY

In Example 3, there are many ways you can sketch the diagram. Another way is shown below.

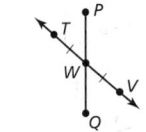

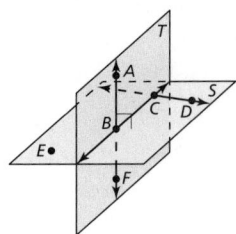

A line is a **line perpendicular to a plane** if and only if the line intersects the plane in a point and is perpendicular to every line in the plane that intersects it at that point.

In a diagram, a line perpendicular to a plane must be marked with a right angle symbol, as shown.

EXAMPLE 4   Interpreting a Diagram

Which of the following statements *cannot* be assumed from the diagram?

Points A, B, and F are collinear.

Points E, B, and D are collinear.

$\overleftrightarrow{AB} \perp$ plane S

$\overleftrightarrow{CD} \perp$ plane T

$\overleftrightarrow{AF}$ intersects $\overleftrightarrow{BC}$ at point B.

SOLUTION

No drawn line connects points E, B, and D. So, you cannot assume they are collinear. With no right angle marked, you cannot assume $\overleftrightarrow{CD} \perp$ plane T.

Monitoring Progress 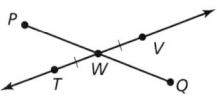 Help in English and Spanish at *BigIdeasMath.com*

Refer back to Example 3.

3. If the given information states that $\overline{PW}$ and $\overline{QW}$ are congruent, how can you indicate that in the diagram?

4. Name a pair of supplementary angles in the diagram. Explain.

Use the diagram in Example 4.

5. Can you assume that plane S intersects plane T at $\overleftrightarrow{BC}$?

6. Explain how you know that $\overleftrightarrow{AB} \perp \overleftrightarrow{BC}$.

Laurie's Notes   Teacher Actions

- **MP4:** Use a wooden skewer and paper to model a line perpendicular to a plane.
- Many students will need help drawing intersecting planes, which is a good exercise before looking at Example 4. Explain that nonrectangular parallelograms are used to give the sense of perspective, with the plane continuing in all directions.
- **Think-Pair-Share:** Show the diagram for Example 4. Students should have time for private thought before sharing their thinking with neighbors and then with the whole class.
- Check for understanding by having students answer the *Monitoring Progress* questions.

Closure

- **Exit Ticket:** Select two postulates from this lesson. State each postulate and sketch a diagram that illustrates the postulate.

Vocabulary and Core Concept Check

1. **COMPLETE THE SENTENCE** Through any _____ noncollinear points, there exists exactly one plane.

2. **WRITING** Explain why you need at least three noncollinear points to determine a plane.

Monitoring Progress and Modeling with Mathematics

In Exercises 3 and 4, state the postulate illustrated by the diagram. *(See Example 1.)*

3.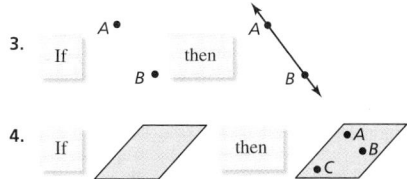

4.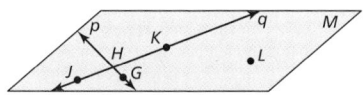

In Exercises 5–8, use the diagram to write an example of the postulate. *(See Example 2.)*

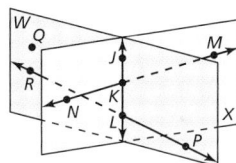

5. Line-Point Postulate (Postulate 2.2)

6. Line Intersection Postulate (Postulate 2.3)

7. Three Point Postulate (Postulate 2.4)

8. Plane-Line Postulate (Postulate 2.6)

In Exercises 9–12, sketch a diagram of the description. *(See Example 3.)*

9. plane *P* and line *m* intersecting plane *P* at a 90° angle

10. $\overline{XY}$ in plane *P*, $\overline{XY}$ bisected by point *A*, and point *C* not on $\overline{XY}$

11. $\overline{XY}$ intersecting $\overline{WV}$ at point *A*, so that $XA = VA$

12. $\overline{AB}$, $\overline{CD}$, and $\overline{EF}$ are all in plane *P*, and point *X* is the midpoint of all three segments.

In Exercises 13–20, use the diagram to determine whether you can assume the statement. *(See Example 4.)*

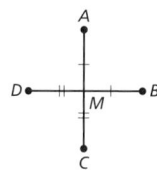

13. Planes *W* and *X* intersect at $\overleftrightarrow{KL}$.

14. Points *K*, *L*, *M*, and *N* are coplanar.

15. Points *Q*, *J*, and *M* are collinear.

16. $\overleftrightarrow{MN}$ and $\overleftrightarrow{RP}$ intersect.

17. $\overleftrightarrow{JK}$ lies in plane *X*. 18. ∠*PLK* is a right angle.

19. ∠*NKL* and ∠*JKM* are vertical angles.

20. ∠*NKJ* and ∠*JKM* are supplementary angles.

ERROR ANALYSIS In Exercises 21 and 22, describe and correct the error in the statement made about the diagram.

21.
> ✗ *M* is the midpoint of $\overline{AC}$ and $\overline{BD}$.

22.
> ✗ $\overline{AC}$ intersects $\overline{BD}$ at a 90° angle, so $\overline{AC} \perp \overline{BD}$.

15. no
16. no
17. yes
18. no
19. yes
20. yes
21. In order to determine that *M* is the midpoint of $\overline{AC}$ or $\overline{BD}$, the segments that would have to be marked as congruent are $\overline{AM}$ and $\overline{MC}$ or $\overline{DM}$ and $\overline{MB}$, respectively; Based on the diagram and markings, you can assume $\overline{AC}$ and $\overline{DB}$ intersect at point *M*, such that $\overline{AM} \cong \overline{MB}$ and $\overline{DM} \cong \overline{MC}$.

22. In order to assume that an angle measures 90°, the angle must be marked as such; Based on the diagram, you can assume two pairs of vertical angles, ∠*DMC* and ∠*AMB* or ∠*DMA* and ∠*CMB*, and you can assume linear pairs, such as ∠*DMC* and ∠*CMB*.

Assignment Guide and Homework Check

ASSIGNMENT

Basic: 1, 2, 3–21 odd, 24, 31, 32, 35–38

Average: 1, 2, 4, 6, 12–24 even, 26, 29, 31, 32, 35–38

Advanced: 1, 2, 6, 12–22 even, 23–26, 31–38

HOMEWORK CHECK

Basic: 3, 5, 19, 21, 31

Average: 12, 18, 22, 29, 31

Advanced: 18, 24, 25, 31, 34

ANSWERS

1. three

2. Two points determine a line, which could be on infinitely many planes, but only one plane will go through those two points and a third noncollinear point.

3. Two Point Postulate (Post. 2.1)

4. Plane-Point Postulate (Post. 2.5)

5. *Sample answer:* Line *q* contains points *J* and *K*.

6. *Sample answer:* The intersection of line *p* and line *q* is point *H*.

7. *Sample answer:* Through points *K*, *H*, and *L*, there is exactly one plane, which is plane *M*.

8. *Sample answer:* Points *H* and *G* lie in plane *M*, so line *p* lies in plane *M*.

9.

10.

11.

12.

13. yes
14. yes

ANSWERS

23. C, D, F, H

24. one; Based on the Line-Point Postulate (Post. 2.2), line *m* contains at least two points; Because these two points are noncollinear with point *C*, based on the Three Point Postulate (Post. 2.4), there is exactly one plane that goes through line *m* and point *C*.

25. Two-Point Postulate (Post. 2.1)

26–38. See Additional Answers.

Mini-Assessment

1. Use the diagram to write an example of the Plane-Line Postulate (Post. 2.6).

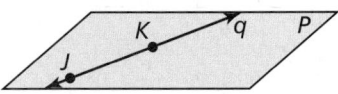

Points *J* and *K* lie in plane *P*, so line *q* containing *J* and *K* lies in plane *P*.

2. Sketch a diagram showing $\overline{AC}$ and $\overline{BD}$ bisecting each other, but $AC \neq BD$.

Sample answer:

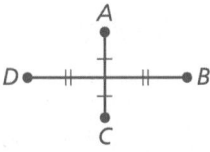

3. Which of the following statements *cannot* be assumed from the figure?

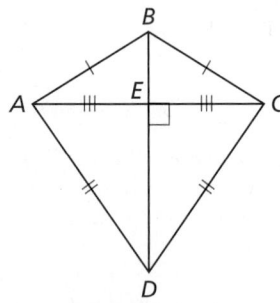

   a. Points *A*, *B*, and *C* are collinear.

   b. Point *E* is the midpoint of $\overline{BD}$.

   c. $\overline{AC} \perp \overline{BD}$

   d. *AD = CD*   a and b

---

23. **ATTENDING TO PRECISION** Select all the statements about the diagram that you *cannot* conclude.

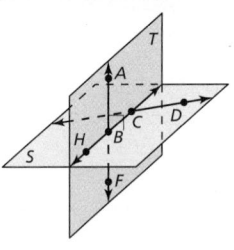

   Ⓐ *A*, *B*, and *C* are coplanar.

   Ⓑ Plane *T* intersects plane *S* in $\overleftrightarrow{BC}$.

   Ⓒ $\overleftrightarrow{AB}$ intersects $\overleftrightarrow{CD}$.

   Ⓓ *H*, *F*, and *D* are coplanar.

   Ⓔ Plane *T* ⊥ plane *S*.

   Ⓕ Point *B* bisects $\overline{HC}$.

   Ⓖ ∠*ABH* and ∠*HBF* are a linear pair.

   Ⓗ $\overleftrightarrow{AF} \perp \overleftrightarrow{CD}$.

24. **HOW DO YOU SEE IT?** Use the diagram of line *m* and point *C*. Make a conjecture about how many planes can be drawn so that line *m* and point *C* lie in the same plane. Use postulates to justify your conjecture.

25. **MATHEMATICAL CONNECTIONS** One way to graph a linear equation is to plot two points whose coordinates satisfy the equation and then connect them with a line. Which postulate guarantees this process works for any linear equation?

26. **MATHEMATICAL CONNECTIONS** A way to solve a system of two linear equations that intersect is to graph the lines and find the coordinates of their intersection. Which postulate guarantees this process works for any two linear equations?

In Exercises 27 and 28, (a) rewrite the postulate in if-then form. Then (b) write the converse, inverse, and contrapositive and state which ones are true.

27. Two Point Postulate (Postulate 2.1)

28. Plane-Point Postulate (Postulate 2.5)

29. **REASONING** Choose the correct symbol to go between the statements.

number of points to determine a line   number of points to determine a plane

  =

30. **CRITICAL THINKING** If two lines intersect, then they intersect in exactly one point by the Line Intersection Postulate (Postulate 2.3). Do the two lines have to be in the same plane? Draw a picture to support your answer. Then explain your reasoning.

31. **MAKING AN ARGUMENT** Your friend claims that even though two planes intersect in a line, it is possible for three planes to intersect in a point. Is your friend correct? Explain your reasoning.

32. **MAKING AN ARGUMENT** Your friend claims that by the Plane Intersection Postulate (Post. 2.7), any two planes intersect in a line. Is your friend's interpretation of the Plane Intersection Postulate (Post. 2.7) correct? Explain your reasoning.

33. **ABSTRACT REASONING** Points *E*, *F*, and *G* all lie in plane *P* and in plane *Q*. What must be true about points *E*, *F*, and *G* so that planes *P* and *Q* are different planes? What must be true about points *E*, *F*, and *G* to force planes *P* and *Q* to be the same plane? Make sketches to support your answers.

34. **THOUGHT PROVOKING** The postulates in this book represent Euclidean geometry. In spherical geometry, all points are points on the surface of a sphere. A line is a circle on the sphere whose diameter is equal to the diameter of the sphere. A plane is the surface of the sphere. Find a postulate on page 84 that is not true in spherical geometry. Explain your reasoning.

┌─ **Maintaining Mathematical Proficiency**   Reviewing what you learned in previous grades and lessons

Solve the equation. Tell which algebraic property of equality you used.   *(Skills Review Handbook)*

35. $t - 6 = -4$ **36.** $3x = 21$ **37.** $9 + x = 13$ **38.** $\frac{x}{7} = 5$

If students need help...	If students got it...
Resources by Chapter • Practice A and Practice B • Puzzle Time	Resources by Chapter • Enrichment and Extension • Cumulative Review
Student Journal • Practice	Start the *next* Section
Differentiating the Lesson Skills Review Handbook	

Core Vocabulary

conditional statement, *p. 66*	inverse, *p. 67*	truth table, *p. 70*
if-then form, *p. 66*	contrapositive, *p. 67*	conjecture, *p. 76*
hypothesis, *p. 66*	equivalent statements, *p. 67*	inductive reasoning, *p. 76*
conclusion, *p. 66*	perpendicular lines, *p. 68*	counterexample, *p. 77*
negation, *p. 66*	biconditional statement, *p. 69*	deductive reasoning, *p. 78*
converse, *p. 67*	truth value, *p. 70*	line perpendicular to a plane, *p. 86*

Core Concepts

Section 2.1

Conditional Statement, *p. 66*   Biconditional Statement, *p. 69*
Negation, *p. 66*   Making a Truth Table, *p. 70*
Related Conditionals, *p. 67*

Section 2.2

Inductive Reasoning, *p. 76*   Deductive Reasoning, *p. 78*
Counterexample, *p. 77*   Laws of Logic, *p. 78*

Section 2.3

Postulates 2.1–2.7 Point, Line, and Plane Postulates, *p. 84*
Identifying Postulates, *p. 85*
Sketching and Interpreting Diagrams, *p. 86*

Mathematical Practices

1. Provide a counterexample for each *false* conditional statement in Exercises 17–24 on page 71. (You do not need to consider the converse, inverse, and contrapositive statements.)

2. Create a truth table for each of your answers to Exercise 59 on page 74.

3. For Exercise 32 on page 88, write a question you would ask your friend about his or her interpretation.

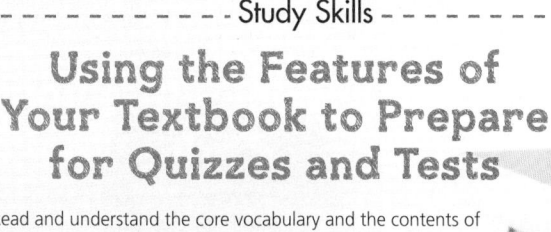

--- Study Skills ---

Using the Features of Your Textbook to Prepare for Quizzes and Tests

- Read and understand the core vocabulary and the contents of the Core Concept boxes.
- Review the Examples and the Monitoring Progress questions. Use the tutorials at *BigIdeasMath.com* for additional help.
- Review previously completed homework assignments.

89

Dynamic Teaching Tools

Dynamic Assessment & Progress Monitoring Tool

Interactive Whiteboard Lesson Library

Dynamic Classroom with Dynamic Investigations

ANSWERS

1. For "If you are in math class, then you are in Geometry," a counterexample would be that you are in Algebra class. For "If you do your math homework, then you will do well on the test," a counterexample would be that you did your homework incorrectly and then made the same mistakes on the test. For "If it does not snow, then I will run outside," a counterexample would be a day when it is not snowing but you feel too sick to run outside.

2. If you see a cat (q), then you went to the zoo to see a lion (p).

p	q	$q{\rightarrow}p$
T	T	T
T	F	F
F	T	T
F	F	T

If you wear a helmet (q), then you play a sport (p).

p	q	$q{\rightarrow}p$
T	T	T
T	F	F
F	T	T
F	F	T

If this month is not February (q), then it has 31 days (p).

p	q	$q{\rightarrow}p$
T	T	T
T	F	F
F	T	T
F	F	T

3. *Sample answer:* What about planes that will never intersect, such as the ceiling and floor of your bedroom?

1. conditional: If the measure of an angle is 167°, then it is an obtuse angle; true

   converse: If an angle is obtuse, then the measure of the angle is 167°; false

   inverse: If the measure of an angle is not 167°, then it is not an obtuse angle; false

   contrapositive: If an angle is not obtuse, then the measure of the angle is not 167°; true

2. conditional: If you are in physics class, then you always have homework; true

   converse: If you always have homework, then you are in physics class; false

   inverse: If you are not in physics class, then you do not always have homework; false

   contrapositive: If you do not always have homework, then you are not in physics class; true

3. conditional: If I take my driving test, then I will get my driver's license; false

   converse: If I get my driver's license, then I took my driving test; true

   inverse: If I do not take my driving test, then I will not get my driver's license; true

   contrapositive: If I do not get my driver's license, then I did not take my driving test; false

4. *Sample answer:* $2 + (-5) = -3$

5. *Sample answer:* trapezoid

6. The sum of two negative integers is a negative integer; When you add two integers with the same sign, the rule is to first add the absolute values, and then give the sum with the same sign as the addends. So, the sum will be negative.

7. The difference of two even integers is an even integer; Let n and m be any integer. Then, $2n$ and $2m$ are even integers because they are the product of 2 and an integer. $2n - 2m$ represents the difference of the two even integers. By the Distributive Property, $2n - 2m = 2(n - m)$, and $2(n - m)$ is an even integer because it is the product of 2 and an integer, $(n - m)$.

8. yes

9. no

10. yes

11. yes

Rewrite the conditional statement in if-then form. Then write the converse, inverse, and contrapositive of the conditional statement. Decide whether each statement is true or false. *(Section 2.1)*

1. An angle measure of 167° is an obtuse angle.

2. You are in a physics class, so you always have homework.

3. I will take my driving test, so I will get my driver's license.

Find a counterexample to show that the conjecture is false. *(Section 2.2)*

4. The sum of a positive number and a negative number is always positive.

5. If a figure has four sides, then it is a rectangle.

Use inductive reasoning to make a conjecture about the given quantity. Then use deductive reasoning to show that the conjecture is true. *(Section 2.2)*

6. the sum of two negative integers

7. the difference of two even integers

Use the diagram to determine whether you can assume the statement. *(Section 2.3)*

8. Points D, B, and C are coplanar.

9. Plane EAF is parallel to plane DBC.

10. Line m intersects line $\overleftrightarrow{AB}$ at point A.

11. Line $\overleftrightarrow{DC}$ lies in plane DBC.

12. $m\angle DBG = 90°$

13. You and your friend are bowling. Your friend claims that the statement "If I got a strike, then I used the green ball" can be written as a true biconditional statement. Is your friend correct? Explain your reasoning. *(Section 2.1)*

Females	Males
06:43	05:41
07:22	06:07
07:04	05:13
06:39	05:21
06:56	06:01

14. The table shows the 1-mile running times of the members of a high school track team. *(Section 2.2)*

   a. What conjecture can you make about the running times of females and males?

   b. What type of reasoning did you use? Explain.

15. List five of the seven Point, Line, and Plane Postulates on page 84 that the diagram of the house demonstrates. Explain how the postulate is demonstrated in the diagram. *(Section 2.3)*

---

12. no

13. no; The converse would be, "If I used the green ball, then I got a strike," and only one counterexample of using the green ball and not getting a strike or getting a strike with another color ball would be all you need to disprove the biconditional statement for the given conditional statement.

14. a. Female high school track members have longer 1-mile running times than male high school track members.

   b. Inductive reasoning was used, because the conjecture was based on the specific cases represented in the table.

15. *Sample answer:* Two Point Postulate (Post. 2.1): Through points C and D there exists exactly one line, $\overleftrightarrow{CD}$. Line Intersection Postulate (Post. 2.3): Line m and n intersect in exactly one point, G. Three Point Postulate (Post. 2.4): Through points A, B, and C there exists exactly one plane, X. Plane-Line Postulate (Post. 2.6): Because points C and D both lie in plane Y (or X), $\overleftrightarrow{CD}$ lies in plane Y (or X). Plane Intersection Postulate (Post. 2.7): Plane Y and plane X intersect in $\overleftrightarrow{CD}$.

Overview of Section 2.4

Introduction

- This lesson reviews the properties of equality introduced in middle school when students were first solving equations. A few new properties of equality are presented: substitution, reflexive, symmetric, and transitive. Students are asked to justify the steps in solving an equation. This same style of justification is applied to a geometric context.
- **Connection:** The measures of angles and the lengths of segments are real numbers and as such they can be operated on and substitutions can be made. Instead of saying, "If $x = 4$, then $x + 2 = 4 + 2$," we will say, "If $AB = CD$, then $AB + EF = CD + EF$."
- The focus is on justifying the steps we are writing.

Common Misconceptions

- Students often forget that angle measures and segment lengths are real numbers. In talking about $m\angle A$, remind students that this notation represents a number; we are not referring to a term that has two variables (m and A) with a symbol ($\angle$) between the variables.

Formative Assessment Tips

- **No-Hands Questioning:** Typically, when you ask a question, there are hands that immediately go up—often the same hands each time. Some students need a longer time to process a question and think through their response. This technique instructs students not to put their hands in the air when the question is posed. *Wait Time** is exercised.
- This technique encourages all students to be active and engaged in the lesson. Students who need additional think time are provided that opportunity. Teachers can then use *Popsicle Sticks* to call on students for a response, or they can purposely call on those students whose voices they do not hear enough.
- To be effective, the question(s) posed during *No-Hands Questioning* have to require more than a simple response.

*See Section 2.5 for a description of *Wait Time*.

Pacing Suggestion

- The two explorations are similar to Example 1 in the formal lesson. If students recall prior work with properties of equality, you may want to omit the explorations and start with Example 1. Alternatively, do both explorations and omit Example 1.

Dynamic Teaching Tools

Dynamic Assessment & Progress Monitoring Tool

Lesson Planning Tool

Interactive Whiteboard Lesson Library

Dynamic Classroom with Dynamic Investigations

HSG-CO.C.9 Prove theorems about lines and angles.

HSG-CO.C.10 Prove theorems about triangles.

HSG-CO.C.11 Prove theorems about parallelograms.

HSG-SRT.B.4 Prove theorems about triangles.

Laurie's Notes

Exploration

Motivate

? "Can you sketch what it looks like when a light beam reflects off a mirror?" Give students time to discuss with their partners, and then ask for a volunteer. Students should sketch something similar to the diagram shown.

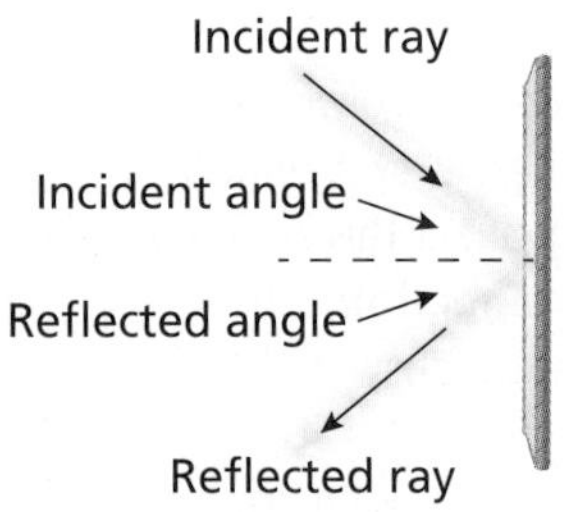

- Refer to the incident angle and reflected angle. These are congruent, and they will be discussed in an example in the lesson.
- If time permits, search the Internet (reflection of light in a plane mirror) and show a quick video that demonstrates angle of incidence = angle of reflection.

Incident ray
Incident angle
Reflected angle
Reflected ray

Exploration Note

- The two explorations will take little time, yet they help make the connection between justifying the steps in solving an algebraic equation and justifying the steps in a geometric proof.

Exploration 1

- Students should work with their partners to state the properties that justify the steps in the solution.
- Use *Popsicle Sticks* to solicit properties for the steps in the solution.

Exploration 2

? "How did you decide which operation to match to each symbol?" Answers will vary.

? "Were you able to answer the questions in order? Explain." no; I had to figure out what each symbol represented first.

Communicate Your Answer

- Students will recognize that the algebraic properties justify the steps.
- In geometry, students will write properties, theorems, and definitions to justify steps in a formal proof.

Connecting to Next Step

- If you feel students are comfortable with naming the properties that justify the steps, you may want to omit Example 1. Select one of the questions in *Monitoring Progress* and move to Example 2.

2.4 Algebraic Reasoning

Essential Question

How can algebraic properties help you solve an equation?

EXPLORATION 1 Justifying Steps in a Solution

Work with a partner. In previous courses, you studied different properties, such as the properties of equality and the Distributive, Commutative, and Associative Properties. Write the property that justifies each of the following solution steps.

Algebraic Step	Justification
$2(x + 3) - 5 = 5x + 4$	Write given equation.
$2x + 6 - 5 = 5x + 4$	
$2x + 1 = 5x + 4$	
$2x - 2x + 1 = 5x - 2x + 4$	
$1 = 3x + 4$	
$1 - 4 = 3x + 4 - 4$	
$-3 = 3x$	
$\frac{-3}{3} = \frac{3x}{3}$	
$-1 = x$	
$x = -1$	

LOOKING FOR STRUCTURE

To be proficient in math, you need to look closely to discern a pattern or structure.

EXPLORATION 2 Stating Algebraic Properties

Work with a partner. The symbols ♦ and • represent addition and multiplication (not necessarily in that order). Determine which symbol represents which operation. Justify your answer. Then state each algebraic property being illustrated.

Example of Property	Name of Property
5 ♦ 6 = 6 ♦ 5	
5 • 6 = 6 • 5	
4 ♦ (5 ♦ 6) = (4 ♦ 5) ♦ 6	
4 • (5 • 6) = (4 • 5) • 6	
0 ♦ 5 = 0	
0 • 5 = 5	
1 ♦ 5 = 5	
4 ♦ (5 • 6) = 4 ♦ 5 • 4 ♦ 6	

Communicate Your Answer

3. How can algebraic properties help you solve an equation?
4. Solve $3(x + 1) - 1 = -13$. Justify each step.

Dynamic Teaching Tools

- Dynamic Assessment & Progress Monitoring Tool
- Lesson Planning Tool
- Interactive Whiteboard Lesson Library
- Dynamic Classroom with Dynamic Investigations

ANSWERS

1. Distributive Property; Simplify; Subtraction Property of Equality; Simplify; Subtraction Property of Equality; Simplify; Division Property of Equality; Simplify; Symmetric Property of Equality
2. The diamond represents multiplication, because $0 \times 5 = 0$; The circle represents addition, because $0 + 5 = 5$; Commutative Property of Multiplication; Commutative Property of Addition; Associative Property of Multiplication; Associative Property of Addition; Zero Property of Multiplication; Identity Property of Addition; Identity Property of Multiplication; Distributive Property
3. Algebraic properties are used to isolate the variable on one side of the equation.
4. See Additional Answers.

Extra Example 1

Solve $2x - 5 = 13$. Justify each step.

$2x - 5 = 13$	Given
$2x - 5 + 5 = 13 + 5$	Add. Prop. =
$2x = 18$	Simplify.
$\dfrac{2x}{2} = \dfrac{18}{2}$	Div. Prop. =
$x = 9$	Simplify.

MONITORING PROGRESS ANSWERS

1–3. See Additional Answers.

2.4 Lesson

Core Vocabulary

Previous
equation
solve an equation
formula

What You Will Learn

▶ Use Algebraic Properties of Equality to justify the steps in solving an equation.

▶ Use the Distributive Property to justify the steps in solving an equation.

▶ Use properties of equality involving segment lengths and angle measures.

Using Algebraic Properties of Equality

When you *solve an equation*, you use properties of real numbers. Segment lengths and angle measures are real numbers, so you can also use these properties to write logical arguments about geometric figures.

Core Concept

Algebraic Properties of Equality

Let a, b, and c be real numbers.

Addition Property of Equality	If $a = b$, then $a + c = b + c$.
Subtraction Property of Equality	If $a = b$, then $a - c = b - c$.
Multiplication Property of Equality	If $a = b$, then $a \cdot c = b \cdot c, c \neq 0$.
Division Property of Equality	If $a = b$, then $\dfrac{a}{c} = \dfrac{b}{c}, c \neq 0$.
Substitution Property of Equality	If $a = b$, then a can be substituted for b (or b for a) in any equation or expression.

REMEMBER

Inverse operations "undo" each other. Addition and subtraction are inverse operations. Multiplication and division are inverse operations.

EXAMPLE 1   **Justifying Steps**

Solve $3x + 2 = 23 - 4x$. Justify each step.

SOLUTION

Equation	Explanation	Reason
$3x + 2 = 23 - 4x$	Write the equation.	Given
$3x + 2 + 4x = 23 - 4x + 4x$	Add $4x$ to each side.	Addition Property of Equality
$7x + 2 = 23$	Combine like terms.	Simplify.
$7x + 2 - 2 = 23 - 2$	Subtract 2 from each side.	Subtraction Property of Equality
$7x = 21$	Combine constant terms.	Simplify.
$x = 3$	Divide each side by 7.	Division Property of Equality

▶ The solution is $x = 3$.

Monitoring Progress Help in English and Spanish at *BigIdeasMath.com*

Solve the equation. Justify each step.

1. $6x - 11 = -35$ **2.** $-2p - 9 = 10p - 17$ **3.** $39 - 5z = -1 + 5z$

Laurie's Notes   Teacher Actions

• Discuss the properties in the *Core Concept*. The one property that may be unfamiliar is the Substitution Property of Equality. This property was used when solving systems of equations in algebra.

• **Think-Pair-Share:** Students could do a *Think-Pair-Share* to work on Example 1.

Using the Distributive Property

Core Concept

Distributive Property

Let a, b, and c be real numbers.

Sum $a(b + c) = ab + ac$ **Difference** $a(b - c) = ab - ac$

EXAMPLE 2   Using the Distributive Property

Solve $-5(7w + 8) = 30$. Justify each step.

SOLUTION

Equation	Explanation	Reason
$-5(7w + 8) = 30$	Write the equation.	Given
$-35w - 40 = 30$	Multiply.	Distributive Property
$-35w = 70$	Add 40 to each side.	Addition Property of Equality
$w = -2$	Divide each side by -35.	Division Property of Equality

▶ The solution is $w = -2$.

EXAMPLE 3   Solving a Real-Life Problem

You get a raise at your part-time job. To write your raise as a percent, use the formula $p(r + 1) = n$, where p is your previous wage, r is the percent increase (as a decimal), and n is your new wage. Solve the formula for r. What is your raise written as a percent when your hourly wage increases from $7.25 to $7.54 per hour?

SOLUTION

Step 1 Solve for r in the formula $p(r + 1) = n$.

Equation	Explanation	Reason
$p(r + 1) = n$	Write the equation.	Given
$pr + p = n$	Multiply.	Distributive Property
$pr = n - p$	Subtract p from each side.	Subtraction Property of Equality
$r = \dfrac{n - p}{p}$	Divide each side by p.	Division Property of Equality

Step 2 Evaluate $r = \dfrac{n - p}{p}$ when $n = 7.54$ and $p = 7.25$.

$$r = \frac{n - p}{p} = \frac{7.54 - 7.25}{7.25} = \frac{0.29}{7.25} = 0.04$$

REMEMBER

When evaluating expressions, use the order of operations.

▶ Your raise is 4%.

Monitoring Progress Help in English and Spanish at *BigIdeasMath.com*

Solve the equation. Justify each step.

4. $3(3x + 14) = -3$

5. $4 = -10b + 6(2 - b)$

6. Solve the formula $A = \frac{1}{2}bh$ for b. Justify each step. Then find the base of a triangle whose area is 952 square feet and whose height is 56 feet.

English Language Learners

Notebook Development
Have students create a page in their notebooks for Algebraic Properties in this section. Include the Addition, Subtraction, Multiplication, Division, Substitution, Reflexive, Symmetric, and Transitive Properties of Equality, and the Distributive Property.

Extra Example 2
Solve $2(x + 1) = -4$. Justify each step.

$2(x + 1) = -4$	Given
$2x + 2 = -4$	Distrib. Prop.
$2x = -6$	Subtr. Prop. =
$x = -3$	Div. Prop. =

Extra Example 3
Use the formula $p(1 + rt) = a$ to find the value a of an investment, where p is the original principal invested, r is the rate of simple interest (as a decimal), and t is the time in years the money is invested. Solve the formula for t. How many years will it take until a principal of $250 grows to a value of $285 when the simple interest rate is 2%? $t = \dfrac{a - p}{pr}$; 7 years

MONITORING PROGRESS ANSWERS
4–6. See Additional Answers.

Laurie's Notes   Teacher Actions

- Work through Example 2 as shown. Ask, "Is there another approach that could be taken to solve this equation?" Students may recognize that the first step could be dividing both sides of the equation by -5. When this is the first step, the result is solving $7w + 8 = -6$. The solution to the equation is still $w = -2$.
- Ask students if they have had a part-time job. Discuss salary (hourly, tips, by the job) and how students were paid (weekly, bimonthly, monthly).
- ? **No-Hands Questioning:** Explain what the variables represent in the equation $p(r + 1) = n$. "Why is 1 added to r?" Wait an appropriate amount of time and ask for an answer. The 1 represents 100% as a decimal, added to the r as a decimal (percent increase in wage). "Why is p multiplied by $(r + 1)$?" Multiplying the current salary p by the factor $(r + 1)$ will give the new hourly wage.

Extra Example 4

You bounce a pool ball off the wall of a pool table, as shown. Determine whether $m\angle RTP = m\angle STQ$.

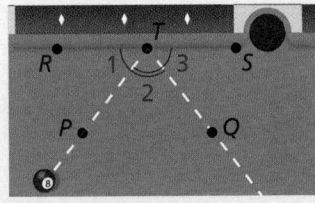

$m\angle RTQ = m\angle PTS$ (Given)

$m\angle RTQ = m\angle 1 + m\angle 2$ (Angle Add. Post. 1.4)

$m\angle PTS = m\angle 3 + m\angle 2$ (Angle Add. Post. 1.4)

$m\angle 1 + m\angle 2 = m\angle 3 + m\angle 2$ (Substit. Prop. =)

$m\angle 1 = m\angle 3$ (Subtr. Prop. =)

MONITORING PROGRESS ANSWERS

7. Symmetric Property of Equality
8. Reflexive Property of Equality
9. Transitive Property of Equality

Using Other Properties of Equality

The following properties of equality are true for all real numbers. Segment lengths and angle measures are real numbers, so these properties of equality are true for all segment lengths and angle measures.

Core Concept

Reflexive, Symmetric, and Transitive Properties of Equality

	Real Numbers	Segment Lengths	Angle Measures
Reflexive Property	$a = a$	$AB = AB$	$m\angle A = m\angle A$
Symmetric Property	If $a = b$, then $b = a$.	If $AB = CD$, then $CD = AB$.	If $m\angle A = m\angle B$, then $m\angle B = m\angle A$.
Transitive Property	If $a = b$ and $b = c$, then $a = c$.	If $AB = CD$ and $CD = EF$, then $AB = EF$.	If $m\angle A = m\angle B$ and $m\angle B = m\angle C$, then $m\angle A = m\angle C$.

EXAMPLE 4 **Using Properties of Equality with Angle Measures**

You reflect the beam of a spotlight off a mirror lying flat on a stage, as shown. Determine whether $m\angle DBA = m\angle EBC$.

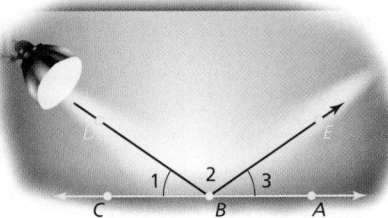

SOLUTION

Equation	Explanation	Reason
$m\angle 1 = m\angle 3$	Marked in diagram.	Given
$m\angle DBA = m\angle 3 + m\angle 2$	Add measures of adjacent angles.	Angle Addition Postulate (Post. 1.4)
$m\angle DBA = m\angle 1 + m\angle 2$	Substitute $m\angle 1$ for $m\angle 3$.	Substitution Property of Equality
$m\angle 1 + m\angle 2 = m\angle EBC$	Add measures of adjacent angles.	Angle Addition Postulate (Post. 1.4)
$m\angle DBA = m\angle EBC$	Both measures are equal to the sum $m\angle 1 + m\angle 2$.	Transitive Property of Equality

Monitoring Progress Help in English and Spanish at *BigIdeasMath.com*

Name the property of equality that the statement illustrates.

7. If $m\angle 6 = m\angle 7$, then $m\angle 7 = m\angle 6$.

8. $34° = 34°$

9. $m\angle 1 = m\angle 2$ and $m\angle 2 = m\angle 5$. So, $m\angle 1 = m\angle 5$.

Laurie's Notes   Teacher Actions

- **Discuss:** Angle measures and segment lengths are real numbers and as such will be operated on like any real number.
- Write the *Core Concept*. Note the use of equality and not congruency.
- **FYI:** The angles marked congruent, $\angle 1$ and $\angle 3$, are complements of the angle of incidence and angle of reflection. See the *Motivate* on page T-91.
- **?** Draw the diagram for Example 4 and allow think time. "How might we show that the two greater angles have the same measure when we know $m\angle 1 = m\angle 3$?" Listen for the suggestion of adding $m\angle 2$ to each of the smaller angles. Work through the steps in the solution.

EXAMPLE 5 Modeling with Mathematics

A park, a shoe store, a pizza shop, and a movie theater are located in order on a city street. The distance between the park and the shoe store is the same as the distance between the pizza shop and the movie theater. Show that the distance between the park and the pizza shop is the same as the distance between the shoe store and the movie theater.

SOLUTION

1. **Understand the Problem** You know that the locations lie in order and that the distance between two of the locations (park and shoe store) is the same as the distance between the other two locations (pizza shop and movie theater). You need to show that two of the other distances are the same.

2. **Make a Plan** Draw and label a diagram to represent the situation.

park   shoe   pizza   movie
         store   shop   theater

Modify your diagram by letting the points P, S, Z, and M represent the park, the shoe store, the pizza shop, and the movie theater, respectively. Show any mathematical relationships.

P   S   Z   M

Use the Segment Addition Postulate (Postulate 1.2) to show that $PZ = SM$.

3. **Solve the Problem**

Equation	Explanation	Reason
$PS = ZM$	Marked in diagram.	Given
$PZ = PS + SZ$	Add lengths of adjacent segments.	Segment Addition Postulate (Post. 1.2)
$SM = SZ + ZM$	Add lengths of adjacent segments.	Segment Addition Postulate (Post. 1.2)
$PS + SZ = ZM + SZ$	Add SZ to each side of $PS = ZM$.	Addition Property of Equality
$PZ = SM$	Substitute PZ for $PS + SZ$ and SM for $ZM + SZ$.	Substitution Property of Equality

4. **Look Back** Reread the problem. Make sure your diagram is drawn precisely using the given information. Check the steps in your solution.

Monitoring Progress 🔊 Help in English and Spanish at *BigIdeasMath.com*

Name the property of equality that the statement illustrates.

10. If $JK = KL$ and $KL = 16$, then $JK = 16$.

11. $PQ = ST$, so $ST = PQ$.

12. $ZY = ZY$

13. In Example 5, a hot dog stand is located halfway between the shoe store and the pizza shop, at point H. Show that $PH = HM$.

Extra Example 5

There are two exits from Theater 10 at the local cinema. The cinema manager wants to put a trash can along the wall, the same distance from each of the two exits. Create a diagram to model this problem. Show that the distance from the trash can to the left exit is half the distance between the two exits.

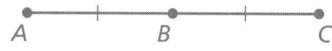

A   B   C

A and C represent exits, and B represents the can.

$AB = BC$	Given
$AB + BC = AC$	Seg. Add. Post. (1.2)
$AB + AB = AC$	Substit. Prop $=$
$2(AB) = AC$	Simplify.
$AB = \dfrac{AC}{2}$	Div. Prop. $=$

MONITORING PROGRESS ANSWERS

10. Transitive Property of Equality

11. Symmetric Property of Equality

12. Reflexive Property of Equality

13. See Additional Answers.

Laurie's Notes   Teacher Actions

Teacher Actions

- **MP4 Model with Mathematics:** Mathematically proficient students read the problem and then draw a diagram to help show the relationship between the locations.
- **MP7 Look For and Make Use of Structure:** Give time for partners to work through the example. Students should recognize that this example is structurally the same as the previous example, only with segment lengths versus angle measures.
- Use *Popsicle Sticks* to solicit a solution.

Closure

- **Exit Ticket:** State the Property of Equality each statement illustrates.

  a. If $AB = CD$, then $AB + FE = CD + FE$.
     Addition Property of Equality

  b. If $m\angle 2 = m\angle 4$ and $m\angle 4 = m\angle 6$, then $m\angle 2 = m\angle 6$.
     Transitive Property of Equality

  c. If $XY = AB$, then $AB = XY$.
     Symmetric Property of Equality

ASSIGNMENT

Basic: 1, 2, 3–41 odd, 45, 46, 52, 57–60

Average: 1, 2, 4, 12, 14, 16–46 even, 50–53, 57–60

Advanced: 1, 2, 4, 12, 18, 24, 30–42, 45–47, 50–60

HOMEWORK CHECK

Basic: 3, 13, 19, 29, 45

Average: 12, 18, 46, 50, 53

Advanced: 12, 18, 24, 46, 51

ANSWERS

1. Reflexive Property of Equality

2. If $e = f$ and $f = g$, then $e = g$; Transitive Property of Equality; Symmetric Property of Equality

3. Subtraction Property of Equality; Addition Property of Equality; Division Property of Equality

4. Distributive Property; Subtraction Property of Equality; Addition Property of Equality

5–24. See Additional Answers.

25. Multiplication Property of Equality

26. Addition Property of Equality

27. Reflexive Property of Equality

28. Symmetric Property of Equality

29. Reflexive Property of Equality

30. Substitution Property of Equality

31. Symmetric Property of Equality

32. Transitive Property of Equality

2.4 Exercises

Dynamic Solutions available at *BigIdeasMath.com*

Vocabulary and Core Concept Check

1. **VOCABULARY** The statement "The measure of an angle is equal to itself" is true because of what property?

2. **DIFFERENT WORDS, SAME QUESTION** Which is different? Find both answers.

   What property justifies the following statement?

   If $c = d$, then $d = c$.   If $JK = LM$, then $LM = JK$.

   If $e = f$ and $f = g$, then $e = g$.   If $m\angle R = m\angle S$, then $m\angle S = m\angle R$.

Monitoring Progress and Modeling with Mathematics

In Exercises 3 and 4, write the property that justifies each step.

3. $3x - 12 = 7x + 8$ Given

   $-4x - 12 = 8$ _____

   $-4x = 20$ _____

   $x = -5$ _____

4. $5(x - 1) = 4x + 13$ Given

   $5x - 5 = 4x + 13$ _____

   $x - 5 = 13$ _____

   $x = 18$ _____

In Exercises 5–14, solve the equation. Justify each step. *(See Examples 1 and 2.)*

5. $5x - 10 = -40$ 6. $6x + 17 = -7$

7. $2x - 8 = 6x - 20$ 8. $4x + 9 = 16 - 3x$

9. $5(3x - 20) = -10$

10. $3(2x + 11) = 9$

11. $2(-x - 5) = 12$

12. $44 - 2(3x + 4) = -18x$

13. $4(5x - 9) = -2(x + 7)$

14. $3(4x + 7) = 5(3x + 3)$

In Exercises 15–20, solve the equation for y. Justify each step. *(See Example 3.)*

15. $5x + y = 18$ 16. $-4x + 2y = 8$

17. $2y + 0.5x = 16$ 18. $\frac{1}{2}x - \frac{3}{4}y = -2$

19. $12 - 3y = 30x + 6$ 20. $3x + 7 = -7 + 9y$

In Exercises 21–24, solve the equation for the given variable. Justify each step. *(See Example 3.)*

21. $C = 2\pi r$; r 22. $I = Prt$; P

23. $S = 180(n - 2)$; n 24. $S = 2\pi r^2 + 2\pi rh$; h

In Exercises 25–32, name the property of equality that the statement illustrates.

25. If $x = y$, then $3x = 3y$.

26. If $AM = MB$, then $AM + 5 = MB + 5$.

27. $x = x$

28. If $x = y$, then $y = x$.

29. $m\angle Z = m\angle Z$

30. If $m\angle A = 29°$ and $m\angle B = 29°$, then $m\angle A = m\angle B$.

31. If $AB = LM$, then $LM = AB$.

32. If $BC = XY$ and $XY = 8$, then $BC = 8$.

In Exercises 33–40, use the property to copy and complete the statement.

33. Substitution Property of Equality:
    If $AB = 20$, then $AB + CD =$ ____.

34. Symmetric Property of Equality:
    If $m\angle 1 = m\angle 2$, then ____.

35. Addition Property of Equality:
    If $AB = CD$, then $AB + EF =$ ____.

36. Multiplication Property of Equality:
    If $AB = CD$, then $5 \cdot AB =$ ____.

37. Subtraction Property of Equality:
    If $LM = XY$, then $LM - GH =$ ____.

38. Distributive Property:
    If $5(x + 8) = 2$, then ____ + ____ = 2.

39. Transitive Property of Equality:
    If $m\angle 1 = m\angle 2$ and $m\angle 2 = m\angle 3$, then ____.

40. Reflexive Property of Equality:
    $m\angle ABC =$ ____.

ERROR ANALYSIS In Exercises 41 and 42, describe and correct the error in solving the equation.

41.
$$
\begin{array}{ll}
7x = x + 24 & \text{Given} \\
8x = 24 & \text{Addition Property of Equality} \\
x = 3 & \text{Division Property of Equality}
\end{array}
$$

42.
$$
\begin{array}{ll}
6x + 14 = 32 & \text{Given} \\
6x = 18 & \text{Division Property of Equality} \\
x = 3 & \text{Simplify.}
\end{array}
$$

43. **REWRITING A FORMULA** The formula for the perimeter P of a rectangle is $P = 2\ell + 2w$, where ℓ is the length and w is the width. Solve the formula for ℓ. Justify each step. Then find the length of a rectangular lawn with a perimeter of 32 meters and a width of 5 meters.

44. **REWRITING A FORMULA** The formula for the area A of a trapezoid is $A = \frac{1}{2}h(b_1 + b_2)$, where h is the height and b_1 and b_2 are the lengths of the two bases. Solve the formula for b_1. Justify each step. Then find the length of one of the bases of the trapezoid when the area of the trapezoid is 91 square meters, the height is 7 meters, and the length of the other base is 20 meters.

45. **ANALYZING RELATIONSHIPS** In the diagram, $m\angle ABD = m\angle CBE$. Show that $m\angle 1 = m\angle 3$. *(See Example 4.)*

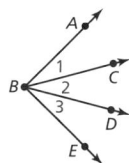

46. **ANALYZING RELATIONSHIPS** In the diagram, $AC = BD$. Show that $AB = CD$. *(See Example 5.)*

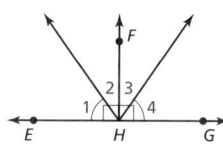

47. **ANALYZING RELATIONSHIPS** Copy and complete the table to show that $m\angle 2 = m\angle 3$.

Equation	Reason
$m\angle 1 = m\angle 4$, $m\angle EHF = 90°$, $m\angle GHF = 90°$	Given
$m\angle EHF = m\angle GHF$	
$m\angle EHF = m\angle 1 + m\angle 2$ $m\angle GHF = m\angle 3 + m\angle 4$	
$m\angle 1 + m\angle 2 = m\angle 3 + m\angle 4$	
	Substitution Property of Equality
$m\angle 2 = m\angle 3$	

48. **WRITING** Compare the Reflexive Property of Equality with the Symmetric Property of Equality. How are the properties similar? How are they different?

ANSWERS

33. $20 + CD$

34. $m\angle 2 = m\angle 1$

35. $CD + EF$

36. $5 \cdot CD$

37. $XY - GH$

38. $5x + 40$

39. $m\angle 1 = m\angle 3$

40. $m\angle ABC$

41. The Subtraction Property of Equality should be used to subtract x from each side of the equation in order to get the second step.

$$
\begin{array}{ll}
7x = x + 24 & \text{Given} \\
6x = 24 & \text{Subtraction Property of Equality} \\
x = 4 & \text{Division Property of Equality}
\end{array}
$$

42. The reasons for the second and third equations are incorrect.

$$
\begin{array}{ll}
6x + 14 = 32 & \text{Given} \\
6x = 18 & \text{Subtraction Property of Equality} \\
x = 3 & \text{Division Property of Equality}
\end{array}
$$

43–46. See Additional Answers.

47. Transitive Property of Equality; Angle Addition Postulate (Post. 1.4); Transitive Property of Equality; $m\angle 1 + m\angle 2 = m\angle 3 + m\angle 1$; Subtraction Property of Equality

48. Both properties state basic ideas about equality. The Reflexive Property of Equality states that something is equal to itself. So, both sides of the equal sign are identical. The Symmetric Property of Equality states that you can switch the two sides of an equation. So, two equations are equivalent if they have the same two expressions set equal to each other, but the expressions are on different sides of the equal sign.

ANSWERS

49–50. See Additional Answers.

51. $ZY = XW = 9$

52. *Sample answer:* Reflexive: Employee 1 worked the same number of hours as Employee 1. Symmetric: If Employee 4 worked the same number of hours as Employee 5, then Employee 5 worked the same number of hours as Employee 4. Transitive: If Employee 2 worked the same number of hours as Employee 4, and Employee 4 worked the same number of hours as Employee 5, then Employee 2 worked the same number of hours as Employee 5.

53. A, B, F

54–56. See Additional Answers.

57. Segment Addition Postulate (Post. 1.2)

58. angle bisector

59. midpoint

60. Angle Addition Postulate (Post. 1.4)

Mini-Assessment

Solve each equation. Justify each step.

1. $9 - 4y = 13$

$9 - 4y = 13$	Given
$9 - 9 - 4y = 13 - 9$	Subt. Prop. =
$-4y = 4$	Simplify.
$\dfrac{-4y}{-4} = \dfrac{4}{-4}$	Div. Prop. =
$y = -1$	Simplify.

2. $4(3 + 4x) = 52 - 4x$

$4(3 + 4x) = 52 - 4x$	Given
$12 + 16x = 52 - 4x$	Dist. Prop.
$12 + 20x = 52$	Add. Prop. =
$20x = 40$	Subt. Prop. =
$x = 2$	Div. Prop. =

3. Solve the formula $P = 2(\ell + w)$ for w. What is the width of a rectangle when the perimeter is 88 feet and the length is 28 feet?
$\dfrac{P - 2\ell}{2} = w$; 16 feet

4. Name the property of equality the statement illustrates.
If $m\angle 1 = m\angle 2$, then $m\angle 2 = m\angle 1$.
Symmetric Property of Equality

REASONING In Exercises 49 and 50, show that the perimeter of $\triangle ABC$ is equal to the perimeter of $\triangle ADC$.

49.

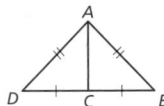

50.

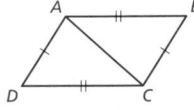

51. **MATHEMATICAL CONNECTIONS** In the figure, $\overline{ZY} \cong \overline{XW}$, $ZX = 5x + 17$, $YW = 10 - 2x$, and $YX = 3$. Find ZY and XW.

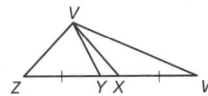

52. **HOW DO YOU SEE IT?** The bar graph shows the number of hours each employee works at a grocery store. Give an example of the Reflexive, Symmetric, and Transitive Properties of Equality.

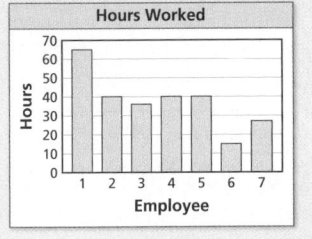

53. **ATTENDING TO PRECISION** Which of the following statements illustrate the Symmetric Property of Equality? Select all that apply.

Ⓐ If $AC = RS$, then $RS = AC$.

Ⓑ If $x = 9$, then $9 = x$.

Ⓒ If $AD = BC$, then $DA = CB$.

Ⓓ $AB = BA$

Ⓔ If $AB = LM$ and $LM = RT$, then $AB = RT$.

Ⓕ If $XY = EF$, then $FE = XY$.

54. **THOUGHT PROVOKING** Write examples from your everyday life to help you remember the Reflexive, Symmetric, and Transitive Properties of Equality. Justify your answers.

55. **MULTIPLE REPRESENTATIONS** The formula to convert a temperature in degrees Fahrenheit (°F) to degrees Celsius (°C) is $C = \frac{5}{9}(F - 32)$.

a. Solve the formula for F. Justify each step.

b. Make a table that shows the conversion to Fahrenheit for each temperature: 0°C, 20°C, 32°C, and 41°C.

c. Use your table to graph the temperature in degrees Fahrenheit as a function of the temperature in degrees Celsius. Is this a linear function?

56. **REASONING** Select all the properties that would also apply to inequalities. Explain your reasoning.

Ⓐ Addition Property

Ⓑ Subtraction Property

Ⓒ Substitution Property

Ⓓ Reflexive Property

Ⓔ Symmetric Property

Ⓕ Transitive Property

Maintaining Mathematical Proficiency
Reviewing what you learned in previous grades and lessons

Name the definition, property, or postulate that is represented by each diagram.
(Section 1.2, Section 1.3, and Section 1.5)

57.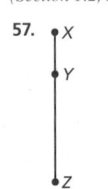
$XY + YZ = XZ$

58.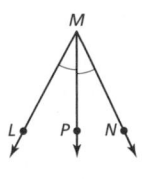

59.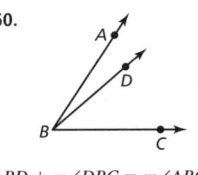

60.

$m\angle ABD + m\angle DBC = m\angle ABC$

If students need help...	If students got it...
Resources by Chapter • Practice A and Practice B • Puzzle Time	Resources by Chapter • Enrichment and Extension • Cumulative Review
Student Journal • Practice	Start the *next* Section
Differentiating the Lesson Skills Review Handbook	

Overview of Section 2.5

Introduction

- This lesson presents the first formal two-column proofs, though students have already written proofs as they justified the steps in showing certain things to be true in the last lesson. Now the template or structure of a two-column proof is introduced using examples very similar to the last lesson.

- It would be helpful to give students an overview of your expectations regarding the writing of proofs if you have not already. What is expected for the reasons? Should students write out what the postulate (theorem or definition) says or simply reference the name of the postulate (theorem or definition)? Are abbreviations acceptable? Will there be a list of reasons students can reference or will they need to remember them?

- Properties of congruence, which follow from properties of equality, are also introduced in this lesson.

Formative Assessment Tips

- **Wait Time:** Wait time is the interval between a question being posed and a student (or the teacher) response. Silence can be uncomfortable in a classroom, but research has shown that increasing wait time increases class participation and answers are more detailed. For complex, higher-order thinking questions, increased wait time is necessary.

- **MP2 Reason Abstractly and Quantitatively** and **MP3 Construct Viable Arguments and Critique the Reasoning of Others:** If we want students to reason abstractly and quantitatively, and to construct viable arguments, then we need to first pose complex questions. Students then need additional *Wait Time* to allow for thinking and formulation of responses. With increased participation, teachers can learn more about students' progress and their learning.

Another Way

- There are different formats for writing a proof. In this lesson, the two-column format is used, and in the next lesson, the flowchart proof is used. In addition, a proof could be written in paragraph form, or it might be done as a coordinate proof. Different styles of proof will be used this year.

Pacing Suggestion

- Have students work through each of the problems in the explorations. These serve as an introduction to a discussion of proof as you begin the formal lesson.

Laurie's Notes

Exploration

Motivate

? "What does it mean to prove something?" Answers will vary.

? "Can you think of examples from the field of science where a theory was proven?" Answers will vary.

• Explain to students that in geometry they will have opportunities to prove something; a statement that they believe is true. Just as a scientist has protocols to follow in proving a theory, we will have protocols that we will follow to prove statements.

Exploration 1

• The steps in this proof are quite similar to what students wrote in the last lesson. Explain that the template, meaning the T-diagram, and the numbering of statements and reasons should not cause students to think any differently today. In fact, you could go back to an example in the last lesson, draw the T-diagram and label the top with "Statements" and "Reasons," and then number the steps. The goal has not changed. We want to be able to justify the statement we are making as we write a logical sequence of steps.

? "What does AC mean?" The length of segment AC.

? "What does $AB + AB$ mean?" The length of segment AB added to itself.

• Translate and say, "The length of AC is equal to the length of segment AB added to itself."

? "What is the justification for saying that $AB + BC = AC$?" Segment Addition Postulate

? "How does the third statement follow from the first two statements?" substitution; $AB + AB$ is substituted for AC.

? "How does the fourth statement follow from the third statement?" The length of segment AB is subtracted from each side of the equation.

• **Teaching Tip:** You may want to circle, highlight, or underline the AC in Steps 1 and 2 and then draw an arrow to show the substitution that is being done.

Exploration 2

• **Connection:** This is the same problem as Example 4 on page 94. Now the steps are being put in a proof template, or T-diagram, but the steps are the same. The same logical process is followed.

• **Wait Time:** Give partners time to write the statements for this example. Do not rush in to answer questions. Refer students back to page 94.

Communicate Your Answer

• Listen for students to describe the process of writing logical statements and being able to justify each one.

Connecting to Next Step

• Discuss the process of writing statements and justifications for the steps. This will lead to a discussion of proof in the formal lesson.

2.5 Proving Statements about Segments and Angles

Essential Question How can you prove a mathematical statement?

A **proof** is a logical argument that uses deductive reasoning to show that a statement is true.

EXPLORATION 1 Writing Reasons in a Proof

REASONING ABSTRACTLY
To be proficient in math, you need to know and be able to use algebraic properties.

Work with a partner. Four steps of a proof are shown. Write the reasons for each statement.

Given $AC = AB + AB$

Prove $AB = BC$

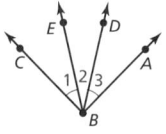

STATEMENTS	REASONS
1. $AC = AB + AB$	**1.** Given
2. $AB + BC = AC$	**2.**
3. $AB + AB = AB + BC$	**3.**
4. $AB = BC$	**4.**

EXPLORATION 2 Writing Steps in a Proof

Work with a partner. Six steps of a proof are shown. Complete the statements that correspond to each reason.

Given $m\angle 1 = m\angle 3$

Prove $m\angle EBA = m\angle CBD$

STATEMENTS	REASONS
1.	**1.** Given
2. $m\angle EBA = m\angle 2 + m\angle 3$	**2.** Angle Addition Postulate (Post.1.4)
3. $m\angle EBA = m\angle 2 + m\angle 1$	**3.** Substitution Property of Equality
4. $m\angle EBA =$	**4.** Commutative Property of Addition
5. $m\angle 1 + m\angle 2 =$	**5.** Angle Addition Postulate (Post.1.4)
6.	**6.** Transitive Property of Equality

Communicate Your Answer

3. How can you prove a mathematical statement?

4. Use the given information and the figure to write a proof for the statement.

Given B is the midpoint of $\overline{AC}$.
C is the midpoint of $\overline{BD}$.

Prove $AB = CD$

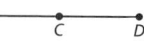

ANSWERS

1. Segment Addition Postulate (Post. 1.2); Transitive Property of Equality; Subtraction Property of Equality

2. $m\angle 1 = m\angle 3$; $m\angle 1 + m\angle 2$; $m\angle CBD$; $m\angle EBA = m\angle CBD$

3. You can use deductive reasoning to make statements about a given situation and use math definitions, postulates, and theorems as your reason or justification for each statement.

4. STATEMENTS	REASONS
1. B is the midpoint of $\overline{AC}$. C is the midpoint of $\overline{BD}$.	**1.** Given
2. $\overline{AB} \cong \overline{BC}$, $\overline{BC} \cong \overline{CD}$	**2.** Definition of midpoint
3. $AB = BC$, $BC = CD$	**3.** Definition of congruent segments
4. $AB = CD$	**4.** Transitive Property of Equality

Extra Example 1

Write a two-column proof.

Given $\angle 1$ is supplementary to $\angle 3$.
$\angle 2$ is supplementary to $\angle 3$.

Prove $\angle 1 \cong \angle 2$

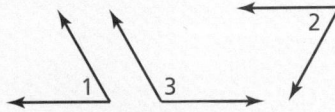

Statements (Reasons)

1. $\angle 1$ is supplementary to $\angle 3$. (Given)
2. $m\angle 1 + m\angle 3 = 180°$ (Def. supp $\angle$s)
3. $\angle 2$ is supplementary to $\angle 3$. (Given)
4. $m\angle 2 + m\angle 3 = 180°$ (Def. supp $\angle$s)
5. $m\angle 1 + m\angle 3 = m\angle 2 + m\angle 3$ (Subst. Prop $=$)
6. $m\angle 1 = m\angle 2$ (Subtr. Prop. $=$)
7. $\angle 1 \cong \angle 2$ (Def. congruent $\angle$s)

MONITORING PROGRESS ANSWER

1. Given; Substitution Property of Equality; $4x = 20$; Division Property of Equality

---

2.5 Lesson

Core Vocabulary

proof, *p. 100*
two-column proof, *p. 100*
theorem, *p. 101*

What You Will Learn

▶ Write two-column proofs.
▶ Name and prove properties of congruence.

Writing Two-Column Proofs

A **proof** is a logical argument that uses deductive reasoning to show that a statement is true. There are several formats for proofs. A **two-column proof** has numbered statements and corresponding reasons that show an argument in a logical order.

In a two-column proof, each statement in the left-hand column is either given information or the result of applying a known property or fact to statements already made. Each reason in the right-hand column is the explanation for the corresponding statement.

EXAMPLE 1   Writing a Two-Column Proof

Write a two-column proof for the situation in Example 4 from the Section 2.4 lesson.

Given $m\angle 1 = m\angle 3$

Prove $m\angle DBA = m\angle EBC$

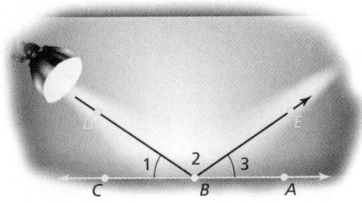

STATEMENTS	REASONS
1. $m\angle 1 = m\angle 3$	1. Given
2. $m\angle DBA = m\angle 3 + m\angle 2$	2. Angle Addition Postulate (Post.1.4)
3. $m\angle DBA = m\angle 1 + m\angle 2$	3. Substitution Property of Equality
4. $m\angle 1 + m\angle 2 = m\angle EBC$	4. Angle Addition Postulate (Post.1.4)
5. $m\angle DBA = m\angle EBC$	5. Transitive Property of Equality

Monitoring Progress   Help in English and Spanish at *BigIdeasMath.com*

1. Six steps of a two-column proof are shown. Copy and complete the proof.

   Given T is the midpoint of $\overline{SU}$.

   S —— $7x$ —— T —— $3x + 20$ —— U

   Prove $x = 5$

STATEMENTS	REASONS
1. T is the midpoint of $\overline{SU}$.	1. _____
2. $\overline{ST} \cong \overline{TU}$	2. Definition of midpoint
3. $ST = TU$	3. Definition of congruent segments
4. $7x = 3x + 20$	4. _____
5. _____	5. Subtraction Property of Equality
6. $x = 5$	6. _____

Laurie's Notes   Teacher Actions

- Begin with a discussion of *proof* and a reminder of what deductive reasoning is. Explain that statements are either given information or they result from applying a known property or fact to statements already made. Reasons are the explanations for the corresponding statements.
- The first example is a previously proven statement (Example 4, page 94), now written in a *two-column format*.
- **Proof Strategy:** Mark the diagram with given information. In this case, mark $\angle 1 \cong \angle 3$ on the diagram because these angle measures are equal.
- Be sure that students see where the substitution has occurred.
- **Wait Time:** Give partners time to write the statements or reasons in the *Monitoring Progress*. Do not rush in to answer questions.

Using Properties of Congruence

The reasons used in a proof can include definitions, properties, postulates, and *theorems*. A **theorem** is a statement that can be proven. Once you have proven a theorem, you can use the theorem as a reason in other proofs.

↻ Theorems

Theorem 2.1   Properties of Segment Congruence

Segment congruence is reflexive, symmetric, and transitive.

Reflexive   For any segment AB, $\overline{AB} \cong \overline{AB}$.

Symmetric   If $\overline{AB} \cong \overline{CD}$, then $\overline{CD} \cong \overline{AB}$.

Transitive   If $\overline{AB} \cong \overline{CD}$ and $\overline{CD} \cong \overline{EF}$, then $\overline{AB} \cong \overline{EF}$.

Proofs Ex. 11, p. 103; Example 3, p. 101; Chapter Review 2.5 Example, p. 118

Theorem 2.2   Properties of Angle Congruence

Angle congruence is reflexive, symmetric, and transitive.

Reflexive   For any angle A, $\angle A \cong \angle A$.

Symmetric   If $\angle A \cong \angle B$, then $\angle B \cong \angle A$.

Transitive   If $\angle A \cong \angle B$ and $\angle B \cong \angle C$, then $\angle A \cong \angle C$.

Proofs Ex. 25, p. 118; 2.5 Concept Summary, p. 102; Ex. 12, p. 103

EXAMPLE 2   **Naming Properties of Congruence**

Name the property that the statement illustrates.

a. If $\angle T \cong \angle V$ and $\angle V \cong \angle R$, then $\angle T \cong \angle R$.

b. If $\overline{JL} \cong \overline{YZ}$, then $\overline{YZ} \cong \overline{JL}$.

SOLUTION

a. Transitive Property of Angle Congruence

b. Symmetric Property of Segment Congruence

In this lesson, most of the proofs involve showing that congruence and equality are equivalent. You may find that what you are asked to prove seems to be obviously true. It is important to practice writing these proofs to help you prepare for writing more-complicated proofs in later chapters.

> **STUDY TIP**
>
> When writing a proof, organize your reasoning by copying or drawing a diagram for the situation described. Then identify the **Given** and **Prove** statements.

EXAMPLE 3   **Proving a Symmetric Property of Congruence**

Write a two-column proof for the Symmetric Property of Segment Congruence.

Given $\overline{LM} \cong \overline{NP}$

Prove $\overline{NP} \cong \overline{LM}$

STATEMENTS	REASONS
1. $\overline{LM} \cong \overline{NP}$	**1.** Given
2. $LM = NP$	**2.** Definition of congruent segments
3. $NP = LM$	**3.** Symmetric Property of Equality
4. $\overline{NP} \cong \overline{LM}$	**4.** Definition of congruent segments

Extra Example 2

Name the property that the statement illustrates.

a. $\angle A \cong \angle A$ Reflexive Property of Angle Congruence (Thm. 2.2)

b. If $\overline{PQ} \cong \overline{JG}$ and $\overline{JG} \cong \overline{XY}$, then $\overline{PQ} \cong \overline{XY}$. Transitive Property of Segment Congruence (Thm. 2.1)

Extra Example 3

Write a two-column proof for the Reflexive Property of Angle Congruence.

Given $\angle A$

Prove $\angle A \cong \angle A$

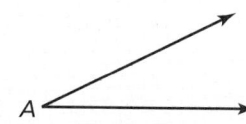

Statements (Reasons)

1. $m\angle A = m\angle A$ (Reflexive Prop. $=$)

2. $\angle A \cong \angle A$ (Def. of $\cong$ $\angle$s)

Laurie's Notes   Teacher Actions

- Define *theorem* and explain how theorems will be used.
- **MP8 Look For and Express Regularity in Repeated Reasoning:** Once a theorem is proven, it can be used in subsequent proofs and the steps do not need to be repeated. The proven theorem is then a tool, or strategy, that helps in proving a new statement.
- ❓ "What is the definition of congruent segments?" Two segments are congruent if and only if they have the same length. Repeat with a similar question for congruent angles.
- State that Reflexive, Symmetric, and Transitive Properties are true for congruence just as they were for equal measures. The Symmetric Property of Congruence is proven in Example 3.
- Some of the proofs may seem obvious to students, and students may be confused as to why there is a need to prove something that is obvious. Students practiced representing the steps in solving $2x - 7 = 15$ in preparation for long, more involved equations. Such is the case with proofs.

Extra Example 4

Write a two-column proof.

Given $\overrightarrow{MP}$ bisects $\angle LMN$.

Prove $2(m\angle LMP) = m\angle LMN$

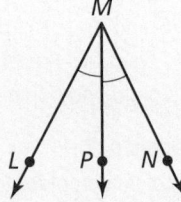

Statements (Reasons)

1. $\overrightarrow{MP}$ bisects $\angle LMN$. (Given)
2. $\angle LMP \cong \angle NMP$ (Def. $\angle$ bisector)
3. $m\angle LMP = m\angle NMP$ (Def. $\cong \angle$s)
4. $m\angle LMP + m\angle NMP = m\angle LMN$ (Angle Add. Post. 1.4)
5. $m\angle LMP + m\angle LMP = m\angle LMN$ (Substitution Prop. =)
6. $2(m\angle LMP) = m\angle LMN$ (Distr. Prop.)

MONITORING PROGRESS ANSWERS

2. Reflexive Property of Segment Congruence (Thm. 2.1)

3. Symmetric Property of Angle Congruence (Thm. 2.2)

4. In Steps 5, 6, and 7, *AM* would be replaced by *MB*.

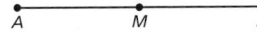 **Writing a Two-Column Proof**

Prove this property of midpoints: If you know that *M* is the midpoint of $\overline{AB}$, prove that *AB* is two times *AM* and *AM* is one-half *AB*.

Given *M* is the midpoint of $\overline{AB}$.

Prove $AB = 2AM$, $AM = \frac{1}{2}AB$

STATEMENTS	REASONS
1. *M* is the midpoint of $\overline{AB}$.	1. Given
2. $\overline{AM} \cong \overline{MB}$	2. Definition of midpoint
3. $AM = MB$	3. Definition of congruent segments
4. $AM + MB = AB$	4. Segment Addition Postulate (Post. 1.2)
5. $AM + AM = AB$	5. Substitution Property of Equality
6. $2AM = AB$	6. Distributive Property
7. $AM = \frac{1}{2}AB$	7. Division Property of Equality

Monitoring Progress 🔊 Help in English and Spanish at *BigIdeasMath.com*

Name the property that the statement illustrates.

2. $\overline{GH} \cong \overline{GH}$ 3. If $\angle K \cong \angle P$, then $\angle P \cong \angle K$.

4. Look back at Example 4. What would be different if you were proving that $AB = 2 \cdot MB$ and that $MB = \frac{1}{2}AB$ instead?

Concept Summary

Writing a Two-Column Proof

In a proof, you make one statement at a time until you reach the conclusion. Because you make statements based on facts, you are using deductive reasoning. Usually the first statement-and-reason pair you write is given information.

Proof of the Symmetric Property of Angle Congruence

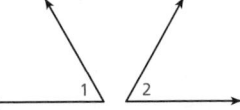

Given $\angle 1 \cong \angle 2$

Prove $\angle 2 \cong \angle 1$

statements based on facts that you know or on conclusions from deductive reasoning →

STATEMENTS	REASONS
1. $\angle 1 \cong \angle 2$	1. Given
2. $m\angle 1 = m\angle 2$	2. Definition of congruent angles
3. $m\angle 2 = m\angle 1$	3. Symmetric Property of Equality
4. $\angle 2 \cong \angle 1$	4. Definition of congruent angles

← definitions, postulates, or proven theorems that allow you to state the corresponding statement

The number of statements will vary.

Remember to give a reason for the last statement.

Copy or draw diagrams and label given information to help develop proofs. Do not mark or label the information in the Prove statement on the diagram.

Laurie's Notes Teacher Actions

- Students may ask why it is necessary to prove these statements. "It is obvious," they will say. Ask them the definition of *midpoint*. The definition says that the midpoint divides the segment into two congruent segments, which is different from what is being asked.
- Work through the steps of the proof as shown.
- **MP8:** Remind students that now that this has been proven, they can use it in other proofs even though it was not given a theorem name. In fact, it could be called a theorem, like Laurie's Theorem, except that does not describe what the theorem is about. Perhaps "Midpoint Theorem" would be better.

- Discuss the *Concept Summary*.

Closure

- Prove the Reflexive Property of Segment Congruence. (See Exercise 11.)

Given $\overline{AB}$ is a line segment.

Prove $\overline{AB} \cong \overline{AB}$

STATEMENTS	REASONS
1. $\overline{AB}$ is a line segment.	1. Given
2. *AB* is the length of $\overline{AB}$.	2. Ruler Postulate (Post. 1.1)
3. $AB = AB$	3. Reflexive Property of Equality
4. $\overline{AB} \cong \overline{AB}$	4. Definition of congruent segments

Vocabulary and Core Concept Check

1. **WRITING** How is a theorem different from a postulate?

2. **COMPLETE THE SENTENCE** In a two-column proof, each _____ is on the left and each _____ is on the right.

Monitoring Progress and Modeling with Mathematics

In Exercises 3 and 4, copy and complete the proof. *(See Example 1.)*

3. **Given** $PQ = RS$

   Prove $PR = QS$

STATEMENTS	REASONS
1. $PQ = RS$	**1.** _____
2. $PQ + QR = RS + QR$	**2.** _____
3. _____	**3.** Segment Addition Postulate (Post. 1.2)
4. $RS + QR = QS$	**4.** Segment Addition Postulate (Post. 1.2)
5. $PR = QS$	**5.** _____

4. **Given** $\angle 1$ is a complement of $\angle 2$.
   $\angle 2 \cong \angle 3$

   Prove $\angle 1$ is a complement of $\angle 3$.

   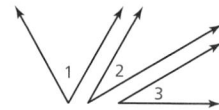

STATEMENTS	REASONS
1. $\angle 1$ is a complement of $\angle 2$.	**1.** Given
2. $\angle 2 \cong \angle 3$	**2.** _____
3. $m\angle 1 + m\angle 2 = 90°$	**3.** _____
4. $m\angle 2 = m\angle 3$	**4.** Definition of congruent angles
5. _____	**5.** Substitution Property of Equality
6. $\angle 1$ is a complement of $\angle 3$.	**6.** _____

In Exercises 5–10, name the property that the statement illustrates. *(See Example 2.)*

5. If $\overline{PQ} \cong \overline{ST}$ and $\overline{ST} \cong \overline{UV}$, then $\overline{PQ} \cong \overline{UV}$.

6. $\angle F \cong \angle F$

7. If $\angle G \cong \angle H$, then $\angle H \cong \angle G$.

8. $\overline{DE} \cong \overline{DE}$

9. If $\overline{XY} \cong \overline{UV}$, then $\overline{UV} \cong \overline{XY}$.

10. If $\angle L \cong \angle M$ and $\angle M \cong \angle N$, then $\angle L \cong \angle N$.

PROOF In Exercises 11 and 12, write a two-column proof for the property. *(See Example 3.)*

11. Reflexive Property of Segment Congruence (Thm. 2.1)

12. Transitive Property of Angle Congruence (Thm. 2.2)

PROOF In Exercises 13 and 14, write a two-column proof. *(See Example 4.)*

13. **Given** $\angle GFH \cong \angle GHF$

    Prove $\angle EFG$ and $\angle GHF$ are supplementary.

    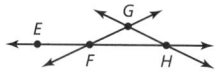

14. **Given** $\overline{AB} \cong \overline{FG}$,
    $\overleftrightarrow{BF}$ bisects $\overline{AC}$ and $\overline{DG}$.

    Prove $\overline{BC} \cong \overline{DF}$

    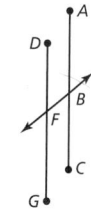

11.

STATEMENTS	REASONS
1. A segment exists with endpoints A and B.	**1.** Given
2. AB equals the length of the segment with endpoints A and B.	**2.** Ruler Postulate (Post. 1.1)
3. $AB = AB$	**3.** Reflexive Property of Equality
4. $\overline{AB} \cong \overline{AB}$	**4.** Definition of congruent segments

12.

STATEMENTS	REASONS
1. $\angle 1 \cong \angle 2$; $\angle 2 \cong \angle 3$	**1.** Given
2. $m\angle 1 = m\angle 2$; $m\angle 2 = m\angle 3$	**2.** Definition of congruent angles
3. $m\angle 1 = m\angle 3$	**3.** Transitive Property of Equality
4. $\angle 1 \cong \angle 3$	**4.** Definition of congruent angles

13–14. See Additional Answers.

Assignment Guide and Homework Check

ASSIGNMENT

Basic: 1, 2, 3–15 odd, 18, 20, 24–26

Average: 1, 2, 4–14 even, 15, 16–20 even, 23–26

Advanced: 1, 2, 4–14 even, 15, 16, 18–26

HOMEWORK CHECK

Basic: 3, 5, 13, 15, 20

Average: 4, 14, 15, 20, 23

Advanced: 12, 14, 15, 20, 22

ANSWERS

1. A postulate is a rule that is accepted to be true without proof, but a theorem is a statement that can be proven.

2. statement; reason

3. Given; Addition Property of Equality; $PQ + QR = PR$; Transitive Property of Equality

4. Given; Definition of complementary angles; $m\angle 1 + m\angle 3 = 90°$; Definition of complement

5. Transitive Property of Segment Congruence (Thm. 2.1)

6. Reflexive Property of Angle Congruence (Thm. 2.2)

7. Symmetric Property of Angle Congruence (Thm. 2.2)

8. Reflexive Property of Segment Congruence (Thm. 2.1)

9. Symmetric Property of Segment Congruence (Thm. 2.1)

10. Transitive Property of Angle Congruence (Thm. 2.2)

ANSWERS

15. The Transitive Property of Segment Congruence (Thm. 2.1) should have been used; Because if $\overline{MN} \cong \overline{LQ}$ and $\overline{LQ} \cong \overline{PN}$, then $\overline{MN} \cong \overline{PN}$ by the Transitive Property of Segment Congruence (Thm. 2.1).

16–26. See Additional Answers.

Mini-Assessment

1. Name the property that the statement illustrates: If $\angle B \cong \angle D$, then $\angle D \cong \angle B$.
   Symmetric Property of Angle Congruence (Thm. 2.2)

2. Write a two-column proof.
   Given M is the midpoint of $\overline{GH}$.
   Prove $x = 2$

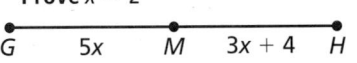

Statements (Reasons)
1. M is the midpoint of $\overline{GH}$. (Given)
2. $\overline{GM} \cong \overline{MH}$ (Def. midpoint)
3. $GM = MH$ (Def. $\cong$ segments)
4. $5x = 3x + 4$ (Substit. Prop. =)
5. $2x = 4$ (Subtr. Prop. =)
6. $x = 2$ (Div. Prop. =)

3. Write a two-column proof.
   Given $\overrightarrow{BD}$ bisects $\angle ABC$.
   Prove $m\angle DBA = \frac{1}{2}m\angle ABC$

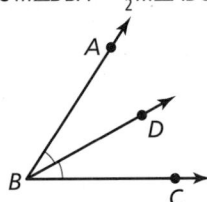

Statements (Reasons)
1. $\overrightarrow{BD}$ bisects $\angle ABC$. (Given)
2. $\angle DBC \cong \angle DBA$ (Def. $\angle$ bisector)
3. $m\angle DBC = m\angle DBA$ (Def. $\cong$ $\angle$s)
4. $m\angle DBC + m\angle DBA = m\angle ABC$ (Angle Add. Post. 1.4)
5. $m\angle DBA + m\angle DBA = m\angle ABC$ (Substit. Prop =)
6. $2(m\angle DBA) = m\angle ABC$ (Distr. Prop.)
7. $m\angle DBA = \frac{1}{2}(m\angle ABC)$ (Div. Prop. =)

---

15. **ERROR ANALYSIS** In the diagram, $\overline{MN} \cong \overline{LQ}$ and $\overline{LQ} \cong \overline{PN}$. Describe and correct the error in the reasoning.

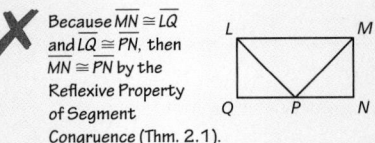

16. **MODELING WITH MATHEMATICS** The distance from the restaurant to the shoe store is the same as the distance from the café to the florist. The distance from the shoe store to the movie theater is the same as the distance from the movie theater to the cafe, and from the florist to the dry cleaners.

restaurant shoe store movie theater café florist dry cleaners

Use the steps below to prove that the distance from the restaurant to the movie theater is the same as the distance from the café to the dry cleaners.

a. State what is given and what is to be proven for the situation.

b. Write a two-column proof.

17. **REASONING** In the sculpture shown, $\angle 1 \cong \angle 2$ and $\angle 2 \cong \angle 3$. Classify the triangle and justify your answer.

18. **MAKING AN ARGUMENT** In the figure, $\overline{SR} \cong \overline{CB}$ and $\overline{AC} \cong \overline{QR}$. Your friend claims that, because of this, $\overline{CB} \cong \overline{AC}$ by the Transitive Property of Segment Congruence (Thm. 2.1). Is your friend correct? Explain your reasoning.

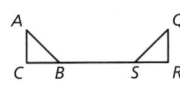

19. **WRITING** Explain why you do not use inductive reasoning when writing a proof.

20. **HOW DO YOU SEE IT?** Use the figure to write Given and Prove statements for each conclusion.

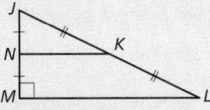

a. The acute angles of a right triangle are complementary.

b. A segment connecting the midpoints of two sides of a triangle is half as long as the third side.

21. **REASONING** Fold two corners of a piece of paper so their edges match, as shown.

a. What do you notice about the angle formed at the top of the page by the folds?

b. Write a two-column proof to show that the angle measure is always the same no matter how you make the folds.

22. **THOUGHT PROVOKING** The distance from Springfield to Lakewood City is equal to the distance from Springfield to Bettsville. Janisburg is 50 miles farther from Springfield than Bettsville. Moon Valley is 50 miles farther from Springfield than Lakewood City is. Use line segments to draw a diagram that represents this situation.

23. **MATHEMATICAL CONNECTIONS** Solve for x using the given information. Justify each step.
   Given $\overline{QR} \cong \overline{PQ}$, $\overline{RS} \cong \overline{PQ}$

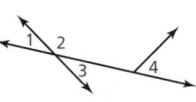

Maintaining Mathematical Proficiency   Reviewing what you learned in previous grades and lessons

Use the figure.   *(Section 1.6)*

24. $\angle 1$ is a complement of $\angle 4$, and $m\angle 1 = 33°$. Find $m\angle 4$.

25. $\angle 3$ is a supplement of $\angle 2$, and $m\angle 2 = 147°$. Find $m\angle 3$.

26. Name a pair of vertical angles.

If students need help...	If students got it...
Resources by Chapter • Practice A and Practice B • Puzzle Time	Resources by Chapter • Enrichment and Extension • Cumulative Review
Student Journal • Practice	Start the *next* Section
Differentiating the Lesson Skills Review Handbook	

Overview of Section 2.6

Introduction

- This lesson presents five of the angle theorems or postulates that will be used in proving statements in subsequent chapters. You will want students to be familiar with these: all right angles are congruent; angles supplementary to the same angle (or congruent angles) are congruent; angles complementary to the same angle (or congruent angles) are congruent; the Linear Pair Postulate; and vertical angles are congruent.

- The angle relationships are proven using two alternative proof styles, the flowchart proof and the paragraph proof. Be clear with students about your expectations for writing proofs. Can they use any format? How specific must the reasons be?

- Do not rush in this lesson. Take time for students to become familiar with what constitutes a deductive proof. Seeing the proof done in more than one format is helpful to students.

Teaching Strategy

- A *flowchart proof*, or simply *flow proof*, is another format for writing a proof. A flowchart proof is a graphical representation of a two-column proof. Sets of statements and reasons are recorded in boxes, and arrows are drawn from one step to the next. A flowchart proof is used to show the logical flow of information and how different ideas are brought together to formulate the proof.

- You may find that some students are able to follow the reasoning in a proof more easily when it is presented in a flowchart proof format than when written linearly in a two-column format. How particular steps fit together, or how one statement is a result of previous statement(s), seems more evident in a flowchart proof to some students.

- A second alternative proof format is the *paragraph proof*. Some students like to write in sentence format what the logical flow of an argument is. A paragraph proof is a readable narrative that presents the statements and reasons of a proof as sentences in a paragraph.

- Flowchart proofs and paragraph proofs are just as valid as forms of a deductive proof as a two-column proof is. Providing alternative approaches for students can only improve their success with formal proofs.

Pacing Suggestion

- The formal lesson is long; however, experience with the explorations helps students see the connection between two-column proofs and flowchart proofs. Have students complete the two explorations, and then begin with Example 1 in the formal lesson.

Laurie's Notes

Exploration

Motivate

? Show students a picture of a staircase with a balustrade (handrail, balusters, and newel posts) and ask, "Are there pairs of angles in this picture that you know are congruent without measuring?" Answers will vary.

• Explain to students that in this lesson they will study theorems that will answer this question.

Exploration Note

• The two explorations are the same as the explorations in Section 2.5. The focus is on the proof format, in this case a flowchart proof. Instead of doing two new proofs, the same proofs are repeated so that the contrast between proof styles can be made.

Exploration 1

• Explain to students that they have seen this proof before. Instead of writing the steps in a two-column format, the statements are written in boxes with arrows showing how to follow the reasoning. The justification for each statement is written below the box.

• Because students have seen this proof before, matching the reasons with the steps should not be difficult.

• **Note:** When two arrows point to the same box, it means that this statement logically follows from two prior statements.

Exploration 2

• Give partners sufficient time to match the reasons with the statements.

• Ask volunteers to share their thinking.

Communicate Your Answer

• Students should describe the structure of a flowchart proof.

Connecting to Next Step

• The two flowchart proofs should not take long for students to complete. The explorations serve as an introduction to this style of proof. Begin with Example 1 in the formal lesson.

2.6 Proving Geometric Relationships

Essential Question
How can you use a flowchart to prove a mathematical statement?

EXPLORATION 1 Matching Reasons in a Flowchart Proof

Work with a partner. Match each reason with the correct step in the flowchart.

Given $AC = AB + AB$

Prove $AB = BC$

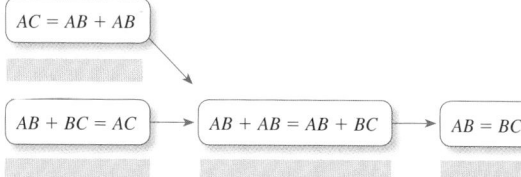

$AC = AB + AB$

$AB + BC = AC$ → $AB + AB = AB + BC$ → $AB = BC$

A. Segment Addition Postulate (Post. 1.2) **B.** Given

C. Transitive Property of Equality **D.** Subtraction Property of Equality

MODELING WITH MATHEMATICS

To be proficient in math, you need to map relationships using such tools as diagrams, two-way tables, graphs, flowcharts, and formulas.

EXPLORATION 2 Matching Reasons in a Flowchart Proof

Work with a partner. Match each reason with the correct step in the flowchart.

Given $m\angle 1 = m\angle 3$

Prove $m\angle EBA = m\angle CBD$

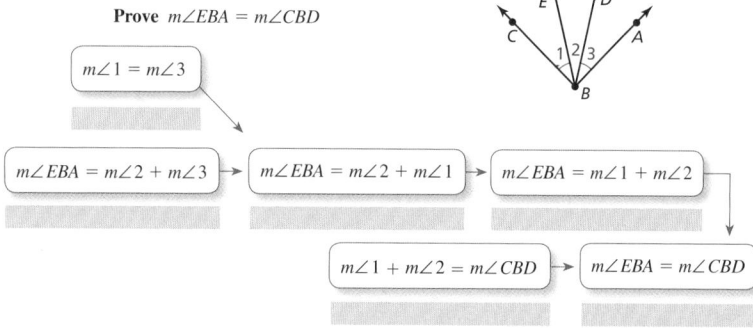

$m\angle 1 = m\angle 3$

$m\angle EBA = m\angle 2 + m\angle 3$ → $m\angle EBA = m\angle 2 + m\angle 1$ → $m\angle EBA = m\angle 1 + m\angle 2$

$m\angle 1 + m\angle 2 = m\angle CBD$ → $m\angle EBA = m\angle CBD$

A. Angle Addition Postulate (Post. 1.4) **B.** Transitive Property of Equality

C. Substitution Property of Equality **D.** Angle Addition Postulate (Post. 1.4)

E. Given **F.** Commutative Property of Addition

Communicate Your Answer

3. How can you use a flowchart to prove a mathematical statement?

4. Compare the flowchart proofs above with the two-column proofs in the Section 2.5 Explorations. Explain the advantages and disadvantages of each.

Section 2.6 Proving Geometric Relationships **105**

ANSWERS

1. B; A; C; D

2. E; A or D; C; F; A or D; B

3. Use boxes and arrows to show the flow of a logical argument.

4. The flowchart proof, unlike the two-column proof, allows you to show explicitly which statement leads to which, but the two-column proof has a uniform, predictable shape and style and has each statement right below the previous one to allow for easy comparison. Both allow you to provide a logical argument and justification for why something is true.

Extra Example 1

Use the given flowchart proof to write a two-column proof.

Given $\overline{AB} \perp \overline{BC}, \overline{AD} \perp \overline{DC}$

Prove $\angle B \cong \angle D$

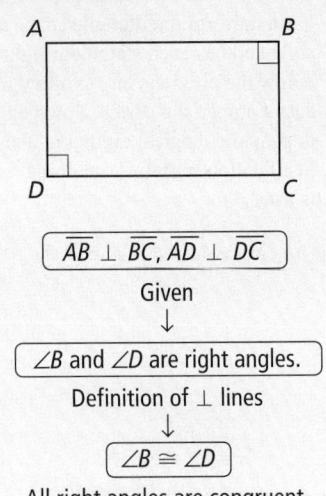

$\boxed{\overline{AB} \perp \overline{BC}, \overline{AD} \perp \overline{DC}}$

Given
↓

$\boxed{\angle B \text{ and } \angle D \text{ are right angles.}}$

Definition of ⊥ lines
↓

$\boxed{\angle B \cong \angle D}$

All right angles are congruent.

Statements (Reasons)

1. $\overline{AB} \perp \overline{BC}, \overline{AD} \perp \overline{DC}$ (Given)
2. $\angle B$ and $\angle D$ are right angles. (Def. ⊥ lines)
3. $\angle B \cong \angle D$ (All rt. ⊿ are ≅.)

MONITORING PROGRESS ANSWER

1. See Additional Answers.

2.6 Lesson

Core Vocabulary

flowchart proof, or flow proof, *p. 106*
paragraph proof, *p. 108*

STUDY TIP

When you prove a theorem, write the hypothesis of the theorem as the **Given** statement. The conclusion is what you must **Prove**.

What You Will Learn

▶ Write flowchart proofs to prove geometric relationships.
▶ Write paragraph proofs to prove geometric relationships.

Writing Flowchart Proofs

Another proof format is a **flowchart proof**, or **flow proof**, which uses boxes and arrows to show the flow of a logical argument. Each reason is below the statement it justifies. A flowchart proof of the *Right Angles Congruence Theorem* is shown in Example 1. This theorem is useful when writing proofs involving right angles.

⟳ Theorem

Theorem 2.3   Right Angles Congruence Theorem

All right angles are congruent.

Proof Example 1, p. 106

EXAMPLE 1   **Proving the Right Angles Congruence Theorem**

Use the given flowchart proof to write a two-column proof of the Right Angles Congruence Theorem.

Given $\angle 1$ and $\angle 2$ are right angles.

Prove $\angle 1 \cong \angle 2$

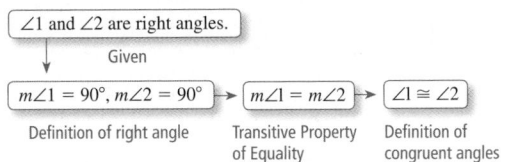

Flowchart Proof

$\boxed{\angle 1 \text{ and } \angle 2 \text{ are right angles.}}$

Given
↓

$\boxed{m\angle 1 = 90^\circ, m\angle 2 = 90^\circ} \rightarrow \boxed{m\angle 1 = m\angle 2} \rightarrow \boxed{\angle 1 \cong \angle 2}$

Definition of right angle   Transitive Property   Definition of
                              of Equality   congruent angles

Two-Column Proof

STATEMENTS	REASONS
1. $\angle 1$ and $\angle 2$ are right angles.	1. Given
2. $m\angle 1 = 90^\circ, m\angle 2 = 90^\circ$	2. Definition of right angle
3. $m\angle 1 = m\angle 2$	3. Transitive Property of Equality
4. $\angle 1 \cong \angle 2$	4. Definition of congruent angles

Monitoring Progress   Help in English and Spanish at *BigIdeasMath.com*

1. Copy and complete the flowchart proof. Then write a two-column proof.

   Given $\overline{AB} \perp \overline{BC}, \overline{DC} \perp \overline{BC}$

   Prove $\angle B \cong \angle C$

   $\boxed{\overline{AB} \perp \overline{BC}, \overline{DC} \perp \overline{BC}} \rightarrow \boxed{} \rightarrow \boxed{\angle B \cong \angle C}$

   Given   Definition of ⊥ lines

Laurie's Notes | Teacher Actions

- Students have been introduced to the flowchart proof in the explorations.
- **?** "What is the definition of perpendicular lines (or segments)?" The lines (or segments) intersect at right angles.
- The first theorem in this lesson provides practice in writing a flowchart proof. Have students compare and contrast the two proof formats.
- **MP8 Look For and Express Regularity in Repeated Reasoning:** This is a theorem that will be referenced in many subsequent proofs. Once proven, this theorem is then used as a justification without repeating all of the steps in this proof.
- **Think-Pair-Share:** Have students complete the proof in *Monitoring Progress* and compare with their neighbors.

⑤ Theorems

Theorem 2.4 Congruent Supplements Theorem

If two angles are supplementary to the same angle
(or to congruent angles), then they are congruent.

If ∠1 and ∠2 are supplementary and ∠3 and ∠2
are supplementary, then ∠1 ≅ ∠3.

Proof Example 2, p. 107 (case 1); Ex. 20, p. 113 (case 2)

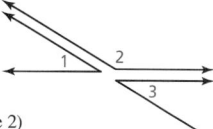

Theorem 2.5 Congruent Complements Theorem

If two angles are complementary to the same
angle (or to congruent angles), then they
are congruent.

If ∠4 and ∠5 are complementary and ∠6
and ∠5 are complementary, then ∠4 ≅ ∠6.

Proof Ex. 19, p. 112 (case 1); Ex. 22, p. 113 (case 2)

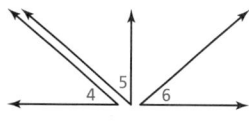

To prove the Congruent Supplements Theorem, you must prove two cases: one
with angles supplementary to the same angle and one with angles supplementary to
congruent angles. The proof of the Congruent Complements Theorem also requires
two cases.

EXAMPLE 2 Proving a Case of Congruent Supplements Theorem

Use the given two-column proof to write a flowchart proof that proves that two angles
supplementary to the same angle are congruent.

Given ∠1 and ∠2 are supplementary.
      ∠3 and ∠2 are supplementary.
Prove ∠1 ≅ ∠3

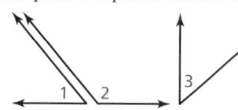

Two-Column Proof

STATEMENTS	REASONS
1. ∠1 and ∠2 are supplementary. ∠3 and ∠2 are supplementary.	1. Given
2. $m\angle 1 + m\angle 2 = 180°$, $m\angle 3 + m\angle 2 = 180°$	2. Definition of supplementary angles
3. $m\angle 1 + m\angle 2 = m\angle 3 + m\angle 2$	3. Transitive Property of Equality
4. $m\angle 1 = m\angle 3$	4. Subtraction Property of Equality
5. ∠1 ≅ ∠3	5. Definition of congruent angles

Flowchart Proof

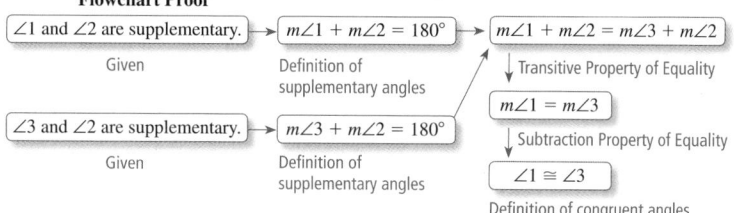

Section 2.6   Proving Geometric Relationships   **107**

Extra Example 2

Write a flowchart proof.
Given ∠1 and ∠2 are supplementary.
      ∠1 and ∠3 are supplementary.
Prove ∠2 ≅ ∠3

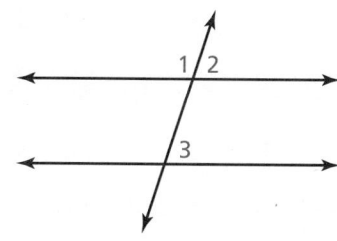

∠1 and ∠2 are supplementary.
Given
↓
$m\angle 1 + m\angle 2 = 180°$
Definition of supplementary angles
↓
∠1 and ∠3 are supplementary.
Given
↓
$m\angle 1 + m\angle 3 = 180°$
Definition of supplementary angles
↓
$m\angle 1 + m\angle 2 = m\angle 1 + m\angle 3$
Transitive Property of Equality
↓
$m\angle 2 = m\angle 3$
Subtraction Property of Equality
↓
∠2 ≅ ∠3
Definition of congruent angles

Extra Example 3

Use the diagram and the given angle measure to find the other three angle measures.

$m\angle 3 = 128°$

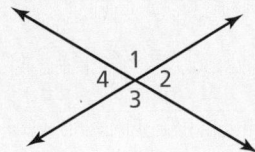

$m\angle 1 = 128°$, $m\angle 2 = 52°$, $m\angle 4 = 52°$

Writing Paragraph Proofs

Another proof format is a **paragraph proof**, which presents the statements and reasons of a proof as sentences in a paragraph. It uses words to explain the logical flow of the argument.

Two intersecting lines form pairs of vertical angles and linear pairs. The *Linear Pair Postulate* formally states the relationship between linear pairs. You can use this postulate to prove the *Vertical Angles Congruence Theorem*.

🔁 Postulate and Theorem

Postulate 2.8 Linear Pair Postulate

If two angles form a linear pair, then they are supplementary.

$\angle 1$ and $\angle 2$ form a linear pair, so $\angle 1$ and $\angle 2$ are supplementary and $m\angle 1 + m\angle 2 = 180°$.

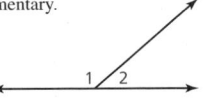

Theorem 2.6 Vertical Angles Congruence Theorem

Vertical angles are congruent.

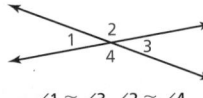

Proof Example 3, p. 108 $\angle 1 \cong \angle 3$, $\angle 2 \cong \angle 4$

EXAMPLE 3   **Proving the Vertical Angles Congruence Theorem**

Use the given paragraph proof to write a two-column proof of the Vertical Angles Congruence Theorem.

Given $\angle 5$ and $\angle 7$ are vertical angles.

Prove $\angle 5 \cong \angle 7$

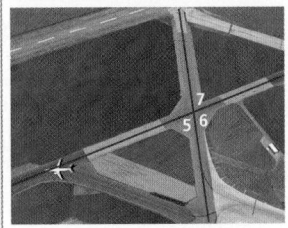

STUDY TIP

In paragraph proofs, *transitional words* such as *so*, *then*, and *therefore* help make the logic clear.

Paragraph Proof

$\angle 5$ and $\angle 7$ are vertical angles formed by intersecting lines. As shown in the diagram, $\angle 5$ and $\angle 6$ are a linear pair, and $\angle 6$ and $\angle 7$ are a linear pair. Then, by the Linear Pair Postulate, $\angle 5$ and $\angle 6$ are supplementary and $\angle 6$ and $\angle 7$ are supplementary. So, by the Congruent Supplements Theorem, $\angle 5 \cong \angle 7$.

JUSTIFYING STEPS

You can use information labeled in a diagram in your proof.

Two-Column Proof

STATEMENTS	REASONS
1. $\angle 5$ and $\angle 7$ are vertical angles.	1. Given
2. $\angle 5$ and $\angle 6$ are a linear pair. $\angle 6$ and $\angle 7$ are a linear pair.	2. Definition of linear pair, as shown in the diagram
3. $\angle 5$ and $\angle 6$ are supplementary. $\angle 6$ and $\angle 7$ are supplementary.	3. Linear Pair Postulate
4. $\angle 5 \cong \angle 7$	4. Congruent Supplements Theorem

Laurie's Notes Teacher Actions

- Review linear pairs and vertical angles. Tell students that the Linear Pair Postulate (Post. 2.8) is used to prove the Vertical Angles Congruence Theorem (Thm. 2.6). Have partners work together, using any format, to prove this theorem. Compare students' work with Example 3.

? "Is the converse of the Vertical Angles Congruence Theorem (Thm. 2.6) true? Explain." no; Just because two angles are congruent, it does not mean they have to be vertical angles.

? "Is the converse of the Linear Pair Postulate (Post. 2.8) true? Explain." no; Just because two angles are supplementary, it does not mean they have to be a linear pair.

Monitoring Progress  Help in English and Spanish at *BigIdeasMath.com*

2. Copy and complete the two-column proof. Then write a flowchart proof.

Given $AB = DE, BC = CD$

Prove $\overline{AC} \cong \overline{CE}$

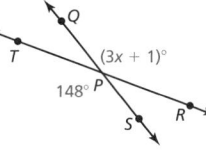

STATEMENTS	REASONS
1. $AB = DE, BC = CD$	**1.** Given
2. $AB + BC = BC + DE$	**2.** Addition Property of Equality
3. _____	**3.** Substitution Property of Equality
4. $AB + BC = AC, CD + DE = CE$	**4.** _____
5. _____	**5.** Substitution Property of Equality
6. $\overline{AC} \cong \overline{CE}$	**6.** _____

3. Rewrite the two-column proof in Example 3 without using the Congruent Supplements Theorem. How many steps do you save by using the theorem?

EXAMPLE 4 Using Angle Relationships

Find the value of x.

SOLUTION

$\angle TPS$ and $\angle QPR$ are vertical angles. By the Vertical Angles Congruence Theorem, the angles are congruent. Use this fact to write and solve an equation.

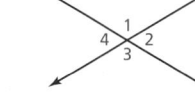

$m\angle TPS = m\angle QPR$	Definition of congruent angles
$148° = (3x + 1)°$	Substitute angle measures.
$147 = 3x$	Subtract 1 from each side.
$49 = x$	Divide each side by 3.

▶ So, the value of x is 49.

Monitoring Progress 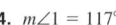 Help in English and Spanish at *BigIdeasMath.com*

Use the diagram and the given angle measure to find the other three angle measures.

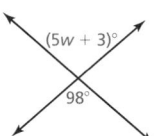

4. $m\angle 1 = 117°$

5. $m\angle 2 = 59°$

6. $m\angle 4 = 88°$

7. Find the value of w.

Extra Example 4
Find the value of x.

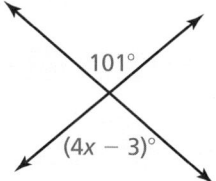

$x = 26$

MONITORING PROGRESS ANSWERS

2–3. See Additional Answers.

4. $m\angle 2 = 63°$; $m\angle 3 = 117°$; $m\angle 4 = 63°$

5. $m\angle 1 = 121°$; $m\angle 3 = 121°$; $m\angle 4 = 59°$

6. $m\angle 1 = 92°$; $m\angle 2 = 88°$; $m\angle 3 = 92°$

7. $w = 19$

Laurie's Notes Teacher Actions

- *Monitoring Progress* Question 3 demonstrates that it is not wrong to repeat the steps of a previously proven theorem in a proof; it simply takes more steps!
- Example 4 may be a relief for students—instead of doing a proof, they are solving an algebraic equation! Point out to students that each of the statements in the solution has a reason (justification) associated with it.

Extra Example 5

Write a paragraph proof.

Given $\angle 1 \cong \angle 4$

Prove $\angle 2 \cong \angle 3$

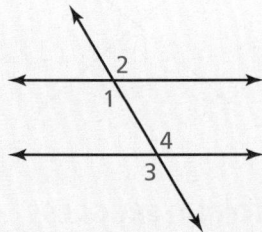

$\angle 1$ is congruent to $\angle 4$. By the Vertical Angles Congruence Theorem (Thm. 2.6), $\angle 1 \cong \angle 2$. By the Transitive Property of Congruence (Thm. 2.2), $\angle 2 \cong \angle 4$. By the Vertical Angles Congruence Theorem (Thm. 2.6), $\angle 3 \cong \angle 4$. By the Transitive Property of Congruence (Thm. 2.2), $\angle 2 \cong \angle 3$.

MONITORING PROGRESS ANSWER

8. $\angle 1$ is a right angle, and by the definition of a right angle, $m\angle 1 = 90°$. In the diagram, $\angle 1$ and $\angle 2$ form a linear pair. So, by the Linear Pair Postulate (Post. 2.8), $\angle 1$ and $\angle 2$ are supplementary and $m\angle 1 + m\angle 2 = 180°$. Using both of these statements and the Substitution Property of Equality, $90° + m\angle 2 = 180°$. By the Subtraction Property of Equality, $m\angle 2 = 90°$. So, by definition, $\angle 2$ is a right angle.

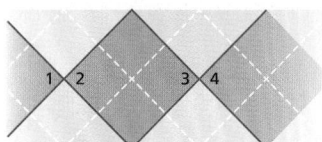 **Using the Vertical Angles Congruence Theorem**

Write a paragraph proof.

Given $\angle 1 \cong \angle 4$

Prove $\angle 2 \cong \angle 3$

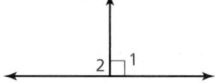

Paragraph Proof

$\angle 1$ and $\angle 4$ are congruent. By the Vertical Angles Congruence Theorem, $\angle 1 \cong \angle 2$ and $\angle 3 \cong \angle 4$. By the Transitive Property of Angle Congruence (Theorem 2.2), $\angle 2 \cong \angle 4$. Using the Transitive Property of Angle Congruence (Theorem 2.2) once more, $\angle 2 \cong \angle 3$.

Monitoring Progress 🔊 Help in English and Spanish at *BigIdeasMath.com*

8. Write a paragraph proof.

    Given $\angle 1$ is a right angle.

    Prove $\angle 2$ is a right angle.

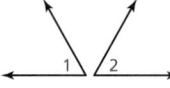

Concept Summary

Types of Proofs

Symmetric Property of Angle Congruence (Theorem 2.2)

    Given $\angle 1 \cong \angle 2$

    Prove $\angle 2 \cong \angle 1$

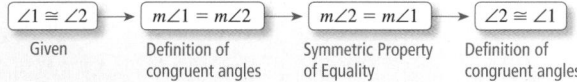

Two-Column Proof

STATEMENTS	REASONS
1. $\angle 1 \cong \angle 2$	1. Given
2. $m\angle 1 = m\angle 2$	2. Definition of congruent angles
3. $m\angle 2 = m\angle 1$	3. Symmetric Property of Equality
4. $\angle 2 \cong \angle 1$	4. Definition of congruent angles

Flowchart Proof

$\angle 1 \cong \angle 2$	$\to$	$m\angle 1 = m\angle 2$	$\to$	$m\angle 2 = m\angle 1$	$\to$	$\angle 2 \cong \angle 1$
Given		Definition of congruent angles		Symmetric Property of Equality		Definition of congruent angles

Paragraph Proof

$\angle 1$ is congruent to $\angle 2$. By the definition of congruent angles, the measure of $\angle 1$ is equal to the measure of $\angle 2$. The measure of $\angle 2$ is equal to the measure of $\angle 1$ by the Symmetric Property of Equality. Then by the definition of congruent angles, $\angle 2$ is congruent to $\angle 1$.

Laurie's Notes | Teacher Actions

? Do you know what this design is called?" an argyle pattern

- **Whiteboarding:** Pose the problem to students and then give time for them to write a paragraph proof.
- **MP3:** Ask several students to read their proofs, and critique their work.

Closure

- **I Used to Think … But Now I Know:** Have students reflect on their current understanding of the different styles of proof.

Vocabulary and Core Concept Check

1. **WRITING** Explain why all right angles are congruent.

2. **VOCABULARY** What are the two types of angles that are formed by intersecting lines?

Monitoring Progress and Modeling with Mathematics

In Exercises 3–6, identify the pair(s) of congruent angles in the figures. Explain how you know they are congruent. *(See Examples 1, 2, and 3.)*

3.
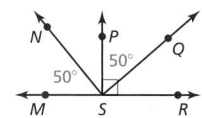

4.
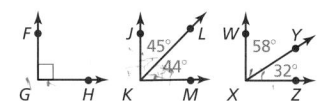

5.
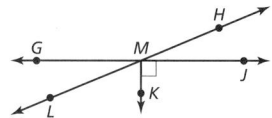

6. ∠ABC is supplementary to ∠CBD.
   ∠CBD is supplementary to ∠DEF.

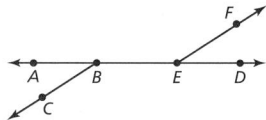

In Exercises 7–10, use the diagram and the given angle measure to find the other three measures. *(See Example 3.)*

7. m∠1 = 143°

8. m∠3 = 159°

9. m∠2 = 34°

10. m∠4 = 29°

In Exercises 11–14, find the values of x and y. *(See Example 4.)*

11.
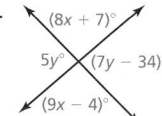

12.
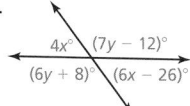

13.
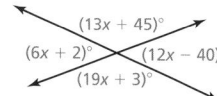

14.
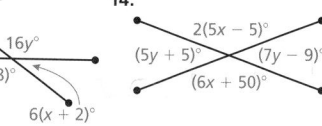

ERROR ANALYSIS In Exercises 15 and 16, describe and correct the error in using the diagram to find the value of x.

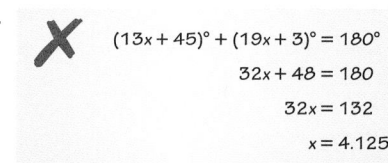

15.
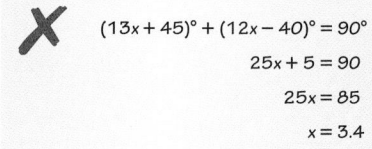
$$(13x + 45)° + (19x + 3)° = 180°$$
$$32x + 48 = 180$$
$$32x = 132$$
$$x = 4.125$$

16.
$$(13x + 45)° + (12x - 40)° = 90°$$
$$25x + 5 = 90$$
$$25x = 85$$
$$x = 3.4$$

Assignment Guide and Homework Check

ASSIGNMENT

Basic: 1, 2, 3–19 odd, 25, 30–36

Average: 1, 2, 6–22 even, 25, 27, 29–36

Advanced: 1, 2, 4, 6, 12–24 even, 25–36

HOMEWORK CHECK

Basic: 3, 7, 11, 17, 19

Average: 6, 14, 18, 20, 22

Advanced: 14, 18, 20, 22, 30

ANSWERS

1. All right angles have the same measure, 90°, and angles with the same measure are congruent.

2. supplementary, vertical

3. ∠MSN ≅ ∠PSQ by definition because they have the same measure; ∠MSP ≅ ∠PSR by the Right Angles Congruence Theorem (Thm. 2.3). They form a linear pair, which means they are supplementary by the Linear Pair Postulate (Post. 2.8), and because one is a right angle, so is the other by the Subtraction Property of Equality; ∠NSP ≅ ∠QSR by the Congruent Complements Theorem (Thm. 2.5) because they are complementary to congruent angles.

4. ∠FGH ≅ ∠WXZ, because m∠WXZ = 90° by the Angle Addition Postulate (Post. 1.4), which means that it is a right angle, and so, ∠FGH and ∠WXZ are congruent by the Right Angles Congruence Theorem (Thm. 2.3).

5. ∠GML ≅ ∠HMJ and ∠GMH ≅ ∠LMJ by the Vertical Angles Congruence Theorem (Thm. 2.6); ∠GMK ≅ ∠JMK by the Right Angles Congruence Theorem (Thm. 2.3). They form a linear pair, which means they are supplementary by the Linear Pair Postulate (Post. 2.8), and because one is a right angle, so is the other by the Subtraction Property of Equality.

6. ∠ABC ≅ ∠DEF by the Congruent Supplements Theorem (Thm. 2.4); ∠CBD ≅ ∠FEA by the Congruent Supplements Theorem (Thm. 2.4). ∠DEF and ∠FEA are supplementary, because they form a linear pair, and because ∠CBD and ∠FEA are supplementary to congruent angles, they are also congruent to each other.

7. m∠2 = 37°, m∠3 = 143°, m∠4 = 37°

8. m∠1 = 159°, m∠2 = 21°, m∠4 = 21°

9. m∠1 = 146°, m∠3 = 146°, m∠4 = 34°

10. m∠1 = 151°, m∠2 = 29°, m∠3 = 151°

11. x = 11, y = 17

12. x = 13, y = 20

13. x = 4, y = 9

14. x = 15, y = 7

15. The expressions should have been set equal to each other because they represent vertical angles;
$$(13x + 45)° = (19x + 3)°$$
$$-6x + 45 = 3$$
$$-6x = -42$$
$$x = 7$$

16. See Additional Answers.

ANSWERS

17–19. See Additional Answers.

17. **PROOF** Copy and complete the flowchart proof. Then write a two-column proof. *(See Example 1.)*

Given $\angle 1 \cong \angle 3$

Prove $\angle 2 \cong \angle 4$

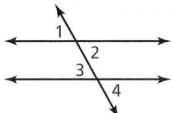

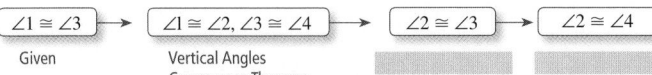

18. **PROOF** Copy and complete the two-column proof. Then write a flowchart proof. *(See Example 2.)*

Given $\angle ABD$ is a right angle.
$\angle CBE$ is a right angle.

Prove $\angle ABC \cong \angle DBE$

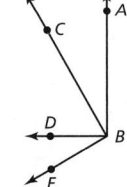

STATEMENTS	REASONS
1. $\angle ABD$ is a right angle. $\angle CBE$ is a right angle.	1. _____
2. $\angle ABC$ and $\angle CBD$ are complementary.	2. Definition of complementary angles
3. $\angle DBE$ and $\angle CBD$ are complementary.	3. _____
4. $\angle ABC \cong \angle DBE$	4. _____

19. **PROVING A THEOREM** Copy and complete the paragraph proof for the Congruent Complements Theorem (Theorem 2.5). Then write a two-column proof. *(See Example 3.)*

Given $\angle 1$ and $\angle 2$ are complementary.
$\angle 1$ and $\angle 3$ are complementary.

Prove $\angle 2 \cong \angle 3$

$\angle 1$ and $\angle 2$ are complementary, and $\angle 1$ and $\angle 3$ are complementary. By the definition of _____ angles, $m\angle 1 + m\angle 2 = 90°$ and _____ $= 90°$. By the _____, $m\angle 1 + m\angle 2 = m\angle 1 + m\angle 3$. By the Subtraction Property of Equality, _____. So, $\angle 2 \cong \angle 3$ by the definition of _____.

20. PROVING A THEOREM Copy and complete the two-column proof for the Congruent Supplement Theorem (Theorem 2.4). Then write a paragraph proof. *(See Example 5.)*

Given $\angle 1$ and $\angle 2$ are supplementary.
$\angle 3$ and $\angle 4$ are supplementary.
$\angle 1 \cong \angle 4$

Prove $\angle 2 \cong \angle 3$

STATEMENTS	REASONS
1. $\angle 1$ and $\angle 2$ are supplementary. $\angle 3$ and $\angle 4$ are supplementary. $\angle 1 \cong \angle 4$	**1.** Given
2. $m\angle 1 + m\angle 2 = 180°$, $m\angle 3 + m\angle 4 = 180°$	**2.** _____
3. _____ $= m\angle 3 + m\angle 4$	**3.** Transitive Property of Equality
4. $m\angle 1 = m\angle 4$	**4.** Definition of congruent angles
5. $m\angle 1 + m\angle 2 - $ _____	**5.** Substitution Property of Equality
6. $m\angle 2 = m\angle 3$	**6.** _____
7. _____	**7.** _____

PROOF In Exercises 21–24, write a proof using any format.

21. Given $\angle QRS$ and $\angle PSR$ are supplementary.
Prove $\angle QRL \cong \angle PSR$

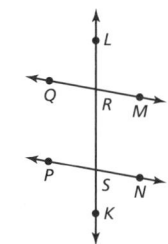

22. Given $\angle 1$ and $\angle 3$ are complementary.
$\angle 2$ and $\angle 4$ are complementary.
Prove $\angle 1 \cong \angle 4$

23. Given $\angle AEB \cong \angle DEC$
Prove $\angle AEC \cong \angle DEB$

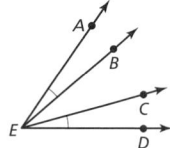

24. Given $\overline{JK} \perp \overline{JM}$, $\overline{KL} \perp \overline{ML}$, $\angle J \cong \angle M$, $\angle K \cong \angle L$
Prove $\overline{JM} \perp \overline{ML}$ and $\overline{JK} \perp \overline{KL}$

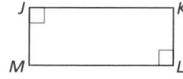

25. MAKING AN ARGUMENT You overhear your friend discussing the diagram shown with a classmate. Your classmate claims $\angle 1 \cong \angle 4$ because they are vertical angles. Your friend claims they are not congruent because he can tell by looking at the diagram. Who is correct? Support your answer with definitions or theorems.

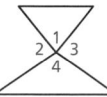

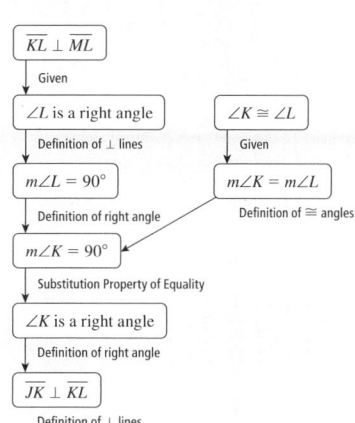

Section 2.6   Proving Geometric Relationships   **113**

24.

$\overline{JK} \perp \overline{JM}$
↓ Given
$\angle J$ is a right angle
↓ Definition of $\perp$ lines
$m\angle J = 90°$
↓ Definition of right angle

$\angle J \cong \angle M$
↓ Given
$m\angle J = m\angle M$
↓ Definition of $\cong$ angles

$m\angle M = 90°$
↓ Substitution Property of Equality
$\angle M$ is a right angle
↓ Definition of right angle
$\overline{JM} \perp \overline{ML}$
Definition of $\perp$ lines

$\overline{KL} \perp \overline{ML}$
↓ Given
$\angle L$ is a right angle
↓ Definition of $\perp$ lines
$m\angle L = 90°$
↓ Definition of right angle

$\angle K \cong \angle L$
↓ Given
$m\angle K = m\angle L$
↓ Definition of $\cong$ angles

$m\angle K = 90°$
↓ Substitution Property of Equality
$\angle K$ is a right angle
↓ Definition of right angle
$\overline{JK} \perp \overline{KL}$
Definition of $\perp$ lines

Mini-Assessment

1. Write a flowchart proof.

Given ∠1 and ∠2 are supplementary.

∠2 and ∠3 are a linear pair.

Prove ∠1 ≅ ∠3

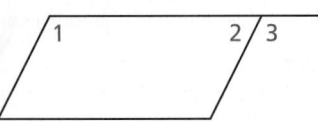

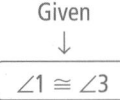

$\boxed{∠2 \text{ and } ∠3 \text{ are a linear pair.}}$

Given

↓

$\boxed{∠2 \text{ and } ∠3 \text{ are supplementary.}}$

Linear Pair Postulate (Post. 2.8)

↓

$\boxed{∠1 \text{ and } ∠2 \text{ are supplementary.}}$

Given

↓

$\boxed{∠1 ≅ ∠3}$

Congruent Suppl. Theorem (Thm. 2.4)

2. Write a paragraph proof.

Given ∠2 ≅ ∠3, ∠4 ≅ ∠5

Prove ∠1 ≅ ∠5

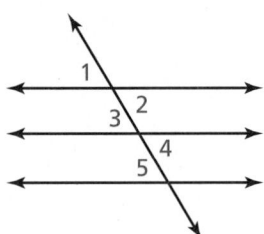

See Additional Answers.

3. Find the values of *x* and *y*.

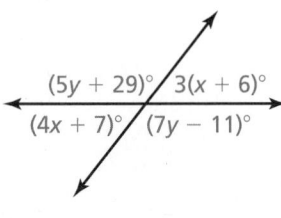

$(5y + 29)°$ $3(x + 6)°$
$(4x + 7)°$ $(7y − 11)°$

$x = 11, y = 20$

---

26. **THOUGHT PROVOKING** Draw three lines all intersecting at the same point. Explain how you can give two of the angle measures so that you can find the remaining four angle measures.

27. **CRITICAL THINKING** Is the converse of the Linear Pair Postulate (Postulate 2.8) true? If so, write a biconditional statement. Explain your reasoning.

28. **WRITING** How can you save time writing proofs?

29. **MATHEMATICAL CONNECTIONS** Find the measure of each angle in the diagram.

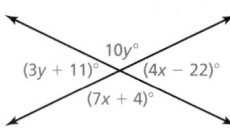

$10y°$
$(3y + 11)°$ $(4x − 22)°$
$(7x + 4)°$

30. **HOW DO YOU SEE IT?** Use the student's two-column proof.

Given ∠1 ≅ ∠2

∠1 and ∠2 are supplementary.

Prove _____

STATEMENTS	REASONS
1. ∠1 ≅ ∠2 ∠1 and ∠2 are supplementary.	**1.** Given
2. $m∠1 = m∠2$	**2.** Definition of congruent angles
3. $m∠1 + m∠2 = 180°$	**3.** Definition of supplementary angles
4. $m∠1 + m∠1 = 180°$	**4.** Substitution Property of Equality
5. $2m∠1 = 180°$	**5.** Simplify.
6. $m∠1 = 90°$	**6.** Division Property of Equality
7. $m∠2 = 90°$	**7.** Transitive Property of Equality
8. _____	**8.** _____

a. What is the student trying to prove?

b. Your friend claims that the last line of the proof should be ∠1 ≅ ∠2, because the measures of the angles are both 90°. Is your friend correct? Explain.

Maintaining Mathematical Proficiency

Reviewing what you learned in previous grades and lessons

Use the cube. *(Section 1.1)*

31. Name three collinear points.

32. Name the intersection of plane *ABF* and plane *EHG*.

33. Name two planes containing $\overline{BC}$.

34. Name three planes containing point *D*.

35. Name three points that are not collinear.

36. Name two planes containing point *J*.

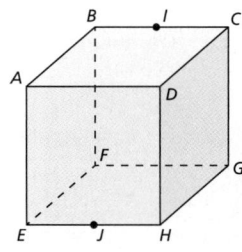

If students need help...	If students got it...
Resources by Chapter • Practice A and Practice B • Puzzle Time	Resources by Chapter • Enrichment and Extension • Cumulative Review
Student Journal • Practice	Start the *next* Section
Differentiating the Lesson Skills Review Handbook	

Core Vocabulary

proof, *p. 100*
two-column proof, *p. 100*
theorem, *p. 101*

flowchart proof, or flow proof, *p. 106*
paragraph proof, *p. 108*

Core Concepts

Section 2.4

Algebraic Properties of Equality, *p. 92*
Distributive Property, *p. 93*

Reflexive, Symmetric, and Transitive Properties
of Equality, *p. 94*

Section 2.5

Writing Two-Column Proofs, *p. 100*
Theorem 2.1 Properties of Segment Congruence Theorem, *p. 101*
Theorem 2.2 Properties of Angle Congruence Theorem, *p. 101*

Section 2.6

Writing Flowchart Proofs, *p. 106*
Theorem 2.3 Right Angles Congruence Theorem,
  p. 106
Theorem 2.4 Congruent Supplements Theorem,
  p. 107

Theorem 2.5 Congruent Complements Theorem, *p. 107*
Writing Paragraph Proofs, *p. 108*
Postulate 2.8 Linear Pair Postulate, *p. 108*
Theorem 2.6 Vertical Angles Congruence Theorem,
  p. 108

Mathematical Practices

1. Explain the purpose of justifying each step in Exercises 5–14 on page 96.

2. Create a diagram to model each statement in Exercises 5–10 on page 103.

3. Explain why you would not be able to prove the statement in Exercise 21 on page 113 if you were not
    provided with the given information or able to use any postulates or theorems.

Performance Task

Induction and the Next Dimension

Before you took Geometry, you could find the midpoint of a segment on a number line (a one-dimensional system). In Chapter 1, you learned how to find the midpoint of a segment in a coordinate plane (a two-dimensional system). How would you find the midpoint of a segment in a three-dimensional system?

To explore the answers to this question and more, go to *BigIdeasMath.com*.

115

ANSWERS

1. Even though the process for solving
    an equation may be almost automatic,
    when you have to justify each step,
    you have to think about the rules
    you are using and why you do each
    step in the process. When you think
    carefully about the rules and steps,
    you will make fewer mistakes, and
    this is how you know that your
    solution is a true statement for the
    given equation.

2. See Additional Answers.

3. $\overleftrightarrow{MQ}$ and $\overleftrightarrow{NP}$ could be meeting $\overleftrightarrow{LK}$
    at different angles. So, unless $\overleftrightarrow{MQ}$
    and $\overleftrightarrow{NP}$ are parallel, $\angle QRL$ is not
    congruent to $\angle PSR$.

1. conditional: If two lines intersect, then their intersection is a point.

   converse: If two lines intersect in a point, then they are intersecting lines.

   inverse: If two lines do not intersect, then they do not intersect in a point.

   contrapositive: If two lines do not intersect in a point, then they are not intersecting lines.

   biconditional: Two lines intersect if and only if their intersection is a point.

2. conditional: If $4x + 9 = 21$, then $x = 3$.

   converse: If $x = 3$, then $4x + 9 = 21$.

   inverse: If $4x + 9 \neq 21$, then $x \neq 3$.

   contrapositive: If $x \neq 3$, then $4x + 9 \neq 21$.

   biconditional: $4x + 9 = 21$ if and only if $x = 3$.

3. conditional: If angles are supplementary, then they sum to $180°$.

   converse: If angles sum to $180°$, then they are supplementary.

   inverse: If angles are not supplementary, then they do not sum to $180°$.

   contrapositive: If angles do not sum to $180°$, then they are not supplementary.

   biconditional: Angles are supplementary if and only if they sum to $180°$.

4. conditional: If an angle is a right angle, then it measures $90°$.

   converse: If an angle measures $90°$, then it is a right angle.

   inverse: If an angle is not a right angle, then it does not measure $90°$.

   contrapositive: If an angle does not measure $90°$, then it is not a right angle.

   biconditional: An angle is a right angle if and only if it measures $90°$.

5. The difference of any two odd integers is an even integer.

6. The product of an even and an odd integer is an even integer.

7. $m\angle B = 90°$

8. If $4x = 12$, then $2x = 6$.

2.1 Conditional Statements (pp. 65–74)

Write the if-then form, the converse, the inverse, the contrapositive, and the biconditional of the conditional statement "A leap year is a year with 366 days."

If-then form: If it is a leap year, then it is a year with 366 days.

Converse: If it is a year with 366 days, then it is a leap year.

Inverse: If it is not a leap year, then it is not a year with 366 days.

Contrapositive: If it is not a year with 366 days, then it is not a leap year.

Biconditional: It is a leap year if and only if it is a year with 366 days.

Write the if-then form, the converse, the inverse, the contrapositive, and the biconditional of the conditional statement.

1. Two lines intersect in a point.
2. $4x + 9 = 21$ because $x = 3$.
3. Supplementary angles sum to $180°$.
4. Right angles are $90°$.

2.2 Inductive and Deductive Reasoning (pp. 75–82)

What conclusion can you make about the sum of any two even integers?

Step 1 Look for a pattern in several examples. Use inductive reasoning to make a conjecture.

$$2 + 4 = 6 \qquad 6 + 10 = 16 \qquad 12 + 16 = 28$$
$$-2 + 4 = 2 \qquad 6 + (-10) = -4 \qquad -12 + (-16) = -28$$

Conjecture Even integer + Even integer = Even integer

Step 2 Let n and m each be any integer. Use deductive reasoning to show that the conjecture is true.

$2n$ and $2m$ are even integers because any integer multiplied by 2 is even.

$2n + 2m$ represents the sum of two even integers.

$2n + 2m = 2(n + m)$ by the Distributive Property.

$2(n + m)$ is the product of 2 and an integer $(n + m)$.
So, $2(n + m)$ is an even integer.

▶ The sum of any two even integers is an even integer.

5. What conclusion can you make about the difference of any two odd integers?
6. What conclusion can you make about the product of an even and an odd integer?
7. Use the Law of Detachment to make a valid conclusion.
   If an angle is a right angle, then the angle measures $90°$. $\angle B$ is a right angle.
8. Use the Law of Syllogism to write a new conditional statement that follows from the pair of true statements: If $x = 3$, then $2x = 6$. If $4x = 12$, then $x = 3$.

2.3 **Postulates and Diagrams** *(pp. 83–88)*

Use the diagram to make three statements that can be concluded and three statements that *cannot* **be concluded. Justify your answers.**

You can conclude:

1. Points *A*, *B*, and *C* are coplanar because they lie in plane *M*.

2. $\overrightarrow{FG}$ lies in plane *P* by the Plane-Line Postulate (Post. 2.6).

3. $\overleftrightarrow{CD}$ and $\overleftrightarrow{FH}$ intersect at point *H* by the Line Intersection Postulate (Post. 2.3).

You *cannot* conclude:

1. $\overleftrightarrow{CD} \perp$ to plane *P* because no right angle is marked.

2. Points *A*, *F*, and *G* are coplanar because point *A* lies in plane *M* and point *G* lies in plane *P*.

3. Points *G*, *D*, and *J* are collinear because no drawn line connects the points.

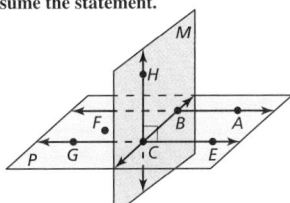

Use the diagram at the right to determine whether you can assume the statement.

9. Points *A*, *B*, *C*, and *E* are coplanar.
10. $\overleftrightarrow{HC} \perp \overleftrightarrow{GE}$
11. Points *F*, *B*, and *G* are collinear.
12. $\overleftrightarrow{AB} \parallel \overleftrightarrow{GE}$

Sketch a diagram of the description.

13. ∠*ABC*, an acute angle, is bisected by $\overrightarrow{BE}$.
14. ∠*CDE*, a straight angle, is bisected by $\overrightarrow{DK}$.
15. Plane *P* and plane *R* intersect perpendicularly in $\overleftrightarrow{XY}$. $\overline{ZW}$ lies in plane *P*.

2.4 **Algebraic Reasoning** *(pp. 91–98)*

Solve $2(2x + 9) = -10$**. Justify each step.**

Equation	Explanation	Reason
$2(2x + 9) = -10$	Write the equation.	Given
$4x + 18 = -10$	Multiply.	Distributive Property
$4x = -28$	Subtract 18 from each side.	Subtraction Property of Equality
$x = -7$	Divide each side by 4.	Division Property of Equality

▶ The solution is $x = -7$.

Solve the equation. Justify each step.

16. $-9x - 21 = -20x - 87$
17. $15x + 22 = 7x + 62$
18. $3(2x + 9) = 30$
19. $5x + 2(2x - 23) = -154$

Name the property of equality that the statement illustrates.

20. If *LM* = *RS* and *RS* = 25, then *LM* = 25.
21. *AM* = *AM*

9. yes
10. yes
11. no
12. no
13. *Sample answer:*

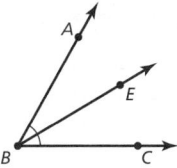

14. *Sample answer:*

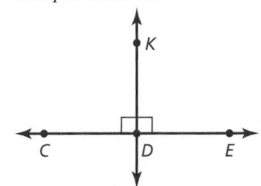

15. *Sample answer:*

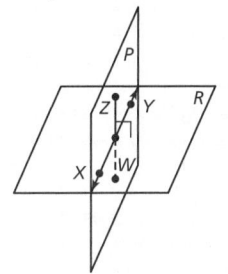

16–19. See Additional Answers.
20. Transitive Property of Equality
21. Reflexive Property of Equality

22. Symmetric Property of Angle
    Congruence (Thm. 2.2)

23. Reflexive Property of Angle
    Congruence (Thm. 2.2)

24. Transitive Property of Equality

25–26. See Additional Answers.

2.5 **Proving Statements about Segments and Angles** *(pp. 99–104)*

Write a two-column proof for the Transitive Property of Segment Congruence (Theorem 2.1).

Given $\overline{AB} \cong \overline{CD}, \overline{CD} \cong \overline{EF}$

Prove $\overline{AB} \cong \overline{EF}$

STATEMENTS	REASONS
1. $\overline{AB} \cong \overline{CD}, \overline{CD} \cong \overline{EF}$	1. Given
2. $AB = CD, CD = EF$	2. Definition of congruent segments
3. $AB = EF$	3. Transitive Property of Equality
4. $\overline{AB} \cong \overline{EF}$	4. Definition of congruent segments

Name the property that the statement illustrates.

22. If $\angle DEF \cong \angle JKL$, then $\angle JKL \cong \angle DEF$.

23. $\angle C \cong \angle C$

24. If $MN = PQ$ and $PQ = RS$, then $MN = RS$.

25. Write a two-column proof for the Reflexive Property of Angle Congruence (Thm. 2.2).

2.6 **Proving Geometric Relationships** *(pp. 105–114)*

Rewrite the two-column proof into a paragraph proof.

Given $\angle 2 \cong \angle 3$

Prove $\angle 3 \cong \angle 6$

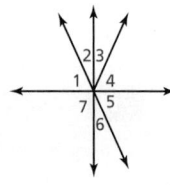

Two-Column Proof

STATEMENTS	REASONS
1. $\angle 2 \cong \angle 3$	1. Given
2. $\angle 2 \cong \angle 6$	2. Vertical Angles Congruence Theorem (Thm. 2.6)
3. $\angle 3 \cong \angle 6$	3. Transitive Property of Angle Congruence (Thm. 2.2)

Paragraph Proof

$\angle 2$ and $\angle 3$ are congruent. By the Vertical Angles Congruence Theorem (Theorem 2.6), $\angle 2 \cong \angle 6$. So, by the Transitive Property of Angle Congruence (Theorem 2.2), $\angle 3 \cong \angle 6$.

26. Write a proof using any format.

   Given $\angle 3$ and $\angle 2$ are complementary.
   $m\angle 1 + m\angle 2 = 90°$

   Prove $\angle 3 \cong \angle 1$

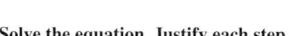

2 Chapter Test

Use the diagram to determine whether you can assume the statement. Explain your reasoning.

1. $\overleftrightarrow{AB} \perp$ plane M

2. Points F, G, and A are coplanar.

3. Points E, C, and G are collinear.

4. Planes M and P intersect at $\overrightarrow{BC}$.

5. $\overleftrightarrow{FA}$ lies in plane P.

6. $\overleftrightarrow{FG}$ intersects $\overleftrightarrow{AB}$ at point B.

Solve the equation. Justify each step.

7. $9x + 31 = -23 + 3x$ 8. $26 + 2(3x + 11) = -18$ 9. $3(7x - 9) - 19x = -15$

Write the if-then form, the converse, the inverse, the contrapositive, and the biconditional of the conditional statement.

10. Two planes intersect at a line.

11. A relation that pairs each input with exactly one output is a function.

Use inductive reasoning to make a conjecture about the given quantity. Then use deductive reasoning to show that the conjecture is true.

12. the sum of three odd integers

13. the product of three even integers

14. Give an example of two statements for which the Law of Detachment does not apply.

15. The formula for the area A of a triangle is $A = \frac{1}{2}bh$, where b is the base and h is the height. Solve the formula for h and justify each step. Then find the height of a standard yield sign when the area is 558 square inches and each side is 36 inches.

16. You visit the zoo and notice the following.
    - The elephants, giraffes, lions, tigers, and zebras are located along a straight walkway.
    - The giraffes are halfway between the elephants and the lions.
    - The tigers are halfway between the lions and the zebras.
    - The lions are halfway between the giraffes and the tigers.

    Draw and label a diagram that represents this information. Then prove that the distance between the elephants and the giraffes is equal to the distance between the tigers and the zebras. Use any proof format.

17. Write a proof using any format.

    Given $\angle 2 \cong \angle 3$
    $\overrightarrow{TV}$ bisects $\angle UTW$.

    Prove $\angle 1 \cong \angle 3$

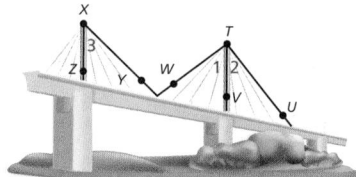

If students need help...	If students got it...
Lesson Tutorials	Resources by Chapter • Enrichment and Extension • Cumulative Review
Skills Review Handbook	Performance Task
BigIdeasMath.com	Start the *next* Section

ANSWERS

1. no; No right angle is marked on $\overleftrightarrow{AB}$.

2. yes; They all lie in plane P.

3. yes; They all are on $\overleftrightarrow{GC}$.

4. yes; The intersection of two planes is a line by the Plane Intersection Postulate (Post. 2.7).

5. yes; Both points lie in plane P. So, the line connecting them lies in the same plane.

6. no; $\overleftrightarrow{FG}$ is not drawn. So, you cannot be sure about where it intersects $\overleftrightarrow{AB}$.

7–9. See Additional Answers.

10. conditional: If two planes intersect, then their intersection is a line.

    converse: If two planes intersect in a line, then they are intersecting planes.

    inverse: If two planes do not intersect, then they do not intersect in a line.

    contrapositive: If two planes do not intersect in a line, then they are not intersecting planes.

    biconditional: Two planes intersect if and only if their intersection is a line.

11. conditional: If a relation pairs each input with exactly one output, then the relation is a function.

    converse: If a relation is a function, then each input is paired with exactly one output.

    inverse: If a relation does not pair each input with exactly one output, then the relation is not a function.

    contrapositive: If a relation is not a function, then each input is not paired with exactly one output.

    biconditional: A relation pairs each input with exactly one output if and only if the relation is a function.

12. The sum of three odd integers is an odd integer; Let m, n, and p be integers. Then, $2m + 1$, $2n + 1$, and $2p + 1$ represent three odd integers because they are each 1 more than an even integer. The sum would be $(2m + 1) + (2n + 1) + (2p + 1)$, which equals $2m + 2n + 2p + 3$ when it is simplified using the Associative and Commutative Properties of Equality. According to the Distributive Property, $2m + 2n + 2p + 3 = 2(m + n + p + 1) + 1$. Because this is 1 more than an even integer [the product of 2 and $(m + n + p + 1)$], the sum is an odd integer.

13–17. See Additional Answers.

1. a. Through points C and D, there exists exactly one line, $\overleftrightarrow{CD}$.

b. The intersection of $\overleftrightarrow{AF}$ and $\overleftrightarrow{BC}$ is point B.

c. Through points C, D, and E, there exists exactly one plane S.

d. Points A and F lie in plane T, so $\overleftrightarrow{AF}$ also lies in plane T.

e. Plane T and plane S intersect, and their intersection is $\overleftrightarrow{BC}$.

2. Definition of congruent segments; Definition of congruent segments; Segment Addition Postulate (Post. 1.2); Segment Addition Postulate (Post. 1.2); Substitution Property of Equality; Substitution Property of Equality; Definition of congruent segments

3. a. biconditional

b. inverse

c. converse

d. contrapositive

4. line ℓ bisects $\overline{BD}$, line n bisects $\overline{DF}$, line m bisects $\overline{AF}$

2 Cumulative Assessment

1. Use the diagram to write an example of each postulate.

a. **Two Point Postulate (Postulate 2.1)** Through any two points, there exists exactly one line.

b. **Line Intersection Postulate (Postulate 2.3)** If two lines intersect, then their intersection is exactly one point.

c. **Three Point Postulate (Postulate 2.4)** Through any three noncollinear points, there exists exactly one plane.

d. **Plane-Line Postulate (Postulate 2.6)** If two points lie in a plane, then the line containing them lies in the plane.

e. **Plane Intersection Postulate (Postulate 2.7)** If two planes intersect, then their intersection is a line.

2. Enter the reasons in the correct positions to complete the two-column proof.

Given $\overline{AX} \cong \overline{DX}, \overline{XB} \cong \overline{XC}$
Prove $\overline{AC} \cong \overline{BD}$

STATEMENTS	REASONS
1. $\overline{AX} \cong \overline{DX}$	**1.** Given
2. $AX = DX$	**2.** _____
3. $\overline{XB} \cong \overline{XC}$	**3.** Given
4. $XB = XC$	**4.** _____
5. $AX + XC = AC$	**5.** _____
6. $DX + XB = DB$	**6.** _____
7. $AC = DX + XB$	**7.** _____
8. $AC = BD$	**8.** _____
9. $\overline{AC} \cong \overline{BD}$	**9.** _____

Segment Addition Postulate (Postulate 1.2)

Definition of congruent segments

Substitution Property of Equality

3. Classify each related conditional statement, based on the conditional statement "If I study, then I will pass the final exam."

a. I will pass the final exam if and only if I study.

b. If I do not study, then I will not pass the final exam.

c. If I pass the final exam, then I studied.

d. If I do not pass the final exam, then I did not study.

4. List all segment bisectors given $x = 3$.

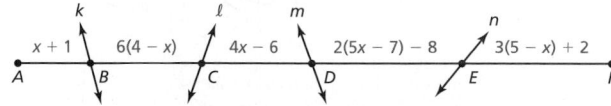

5. You are given $m\angle FHE = m\angle BHG = m\angle AHF = 90°$. Choose the symbol that makes each statement true. State which theorem or postulate, if any, supports your answer.

    a. $\angle 3$ ___ $\angle 6$ **b.** $m\angle 4$ ___ $m\angle 7$

    c. $m\angle FHE$ ___ $m\angle AHG$ **d.** $m\angle AHG + m\angle GHE$ ___ $180°$

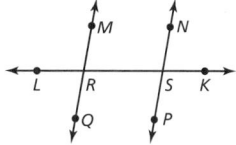

$=$	$\cong$	$\neq$

6. Find the distance between each pair of points. Then order each line segment from longest to shortest.

    a. $A(-6, 1), B(-1, 6)$ **b.** $C(-5, 8), D(5, 8)$

    c. $E(2, 7), F(4, -2)$ **d.** $G(7, 3), H(7, -1)$

    e. $J(-4, -2), K(1, -5)$ **f.** $L(3, -8), M(7, -5)$

7. The proof shows that $\angle MRL$ is congruent to $\angle NSR$. Select all other angles that are also congruent to $\angle NSR$.

    Given $\angle MRS$ and $\angle NSR$ are supplementary.
    Prove $\angle MRL \cong \angle NSR$

STATEMENTS	REASONS
1. $\angle MRS$ and $\angle NSR$ are supplementary.	**1.** Given
2. $\angle MRL$ and $\angle MRS$ are a linear pair.	**2.** Definition of linear pair, as shown in the diagram
3. $\angle MRL$ and $\angle MRS$ are supplementary.	**3.** Linear Pair Postulate (Postulate 2.8)
4. $\angle MRL \cong \angle NSR$	**4.** Congruent Supplements Theorem (Theorem 2.4)

$\angle PSK$	$\angle KSN$	$\angle PSR$	$\angle QRS$	$\angle QRL$

8. Your teacher assigns your class a homework problem that asks you to prove the Vertical Angles Congruence Theorem (Theorem 2.6) using the picture and information given at the right. Your friend claims that this can be proved without using the Linear Pair Postulate (Postulate 2.8). Is your friend correct? Explain your reasoning.

    Given $\angle 1$ and $\angle 3$ are vertical angles.
    Prove $\angle 1 \cong \angle 3$

3 Parallel and Perpendicular Lines

Bike Path *(p. 161)*

Crosswalk *(p. 154)*

Kiteboarding *(p. 143)*

SEE the Big Idea

Gymnastics *(p. 130)*

Tree House *(p. 130)*

Chapter Summary

- Students have been introduced to the idea of an axiomatic system and have a growing list of theorems, postulates, definitions, and properties. In this chapter, the list will grow some more, and students will continue to develop their deductive skills.
- The chapter begins with line relationships (parallel, skew, coplanar, intersecting) and angle-pair relationships (corresponding, alternate interior, alternate exterior, and consecutive interior).
- Statements about parallel lines cut by a transversal and the relationships between the pairs of angles formed are presented in Section 3.2. The converse of each statement is explored in Section 3.3.
- There is a greater focus on proofs in the middle sections. It is here that students often use circular reasoning, using a theorem in the process of trying to prove the theorem.
- The last lesson connects skills from algebra, allowing for a coordinate approach to justifying that two lines are parallel or two lines are perpendicular.
- Throughout the chapter, students should not lose sight of the bigger picture with regard to writing proofs. The goal is to write a logical argument based on known information or information that can be deduced from given information.

Scaffolding in the Classroom

Graphic Organizers: Information Frame

An Information Frame can be used to help students organize and remember concepts. Students write the topic in the middle rectangle. Then students write related concepts in the spaces around the rectangle. Related concepts can include *Words, Numbers, Algebra, Definition, Example, Non-Example, Visual, Procedure, Details,* and *Vocabulary*. Students can place their Information Frames on note cards to use as a quick study reference.

COMMON CORE PROGRESSION

Middle School
- Solve linear equations in one variable.
- Find distance between points with the same x- or y-coordinate.
- Use the Pythagorean Theorem to find missing measures in two dimensions.
- Establish facts about angles formed by parallel lines and a transversal.

Algebra 1
- Solve systems of linear equations.
- Find the slope of a line, and write equations in slope-intercept form.
- Graph linear equations.
- Identify and write equations of parallel and perpendicular lines.
- Use parallel and perpendicular lines in real-life problems.

Geometry
- Identify planes, pairs of angles formed by transversals, parallel lines, and perpendicular lines.
- Use properties and theorems of parallel lines.
- Prove theorems about parallel lines and about perpendicular lines.
- Write equations of parallel lines and perpendicular lines.
- Find the distance from a point to a line.

Standards Summary		
Section	**Common Core State Standards**	
3.1	Learning	HSG-CO.A.1
3.2	Learning	HSG-CO.C.9
3.3	Learning	HSG-CO.C.9, HSG-CO.D.12
3.4	Learning	HSG-CO.C.9, HSG-CO.D.12
3.5	Learning	HSG-GPE.B.5, HSG-GPE.B.6

Maintaining Mathematical Proficiency

Finding the Slope of a Line

• Review the slope-intercept form of the equation of a line, $y = mx + b$, where m is the slope of the line and b is the y-intercept.

COMMON ERROR Students may make a sign error when computing the slope. Remind them that they can use a graph of the equation to visually verify whether the slope is positive or negative. A line that rises from left to right has a *positive* slope. A line that falls from left to right has a *negative* slope.

Writing Equations of Lines

• Remind students that the slope of the line is represented by m and describes the steepness of the line. The y-intercept is represented by b, and it is the y-coordinate of the point where the line intersects the y-axis.

COMMON ERROR When solving for b, students may be confused about which coordinate to substitute for x and for y. Have them highlight the x-coordinate and the variable x in the same color to remind them which number should be substituted for which variable.

Mathematical Practices (continued on page 124)

• The eight *Mathematical Practices* focus attention on how mathematics is learned—process versus content. Page 124 demonstrates that the graphing calculator can be used as a tool to display the graph of a function using a true perspective.

• Use the *Mathematical Practices* page to help students develop mathematical habits of mind—how mathematics can be explored and how mathematics is thought about.

If students need help...	If students got it...
Student Journal • Maintaining Mathematical Proficiency	Game Closet at *BigIdeasMath.com*
Lesson Tutorials	Start the *next* Section
Skills Review Handbook	

Maintaining Mathematical Proficiency

Finding the Slope of a Line

Example 1 Find the slope of the line shown.

Let $(x_1, y_1) = (-2, -2)$ and $(x_2, y_2) = (1, 0)$.

$$\text{slope} = \frac{y_2 - y_1}{x_2 - x_1} \qquad \text{Write formula for slope.}$$

$$= \frac{0 - (-2)}{1 - (-2)} \qquad \text{Substitute.}$$

$$= \frac{2}{3} \qquad \text{Simplify.}$$

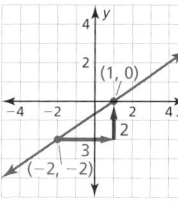

Find the slope of the line.

1.
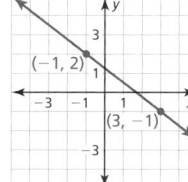

2.
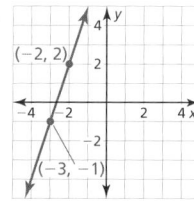

3.
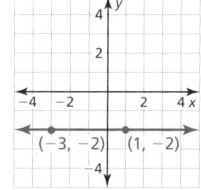

Writing Equations of Lines

Example 2 Write an equation of the line that passes through the point $(-4, 5)$ and has a slope of $\frac{3}{4}$.

$$y = mx + b \qquad \text{Write the slope-intercept form.}$$

$$5 = \frac{3}{4}(-4) + b \qquad \text{Substitute } \frac{3}{4} \text{ for } m, -4 \text{ for } x, \text{ and } 5 \text{ for } y.$$

$$5 = -3 + b \qquad \text{Simplify.}$$

$$8 = b \qquad \text{Solve for } b.$$

▶ So, an equation is $y = \frac{3}{4}x + 8$.

Write an equation of the line that passes through the given point and has the given slope.

4. $(6, 1)$; $m = -3$
5. $(-3, 8)$; $m = -2$
6. $(-1, 5)$; $m = 4$
7. $(2, -4)$; $m = \frac{1}{2}$
8. $(-8, -5)$; $m = -\frac{1}{4}$
9. $(0, 9)$; $m = \frac{2}{3}$

10. **ABSTRACT REASONING** Why does a horizontal line have a slope of 0, but a vertical line has an undefined slope?

Common Core State Standards

HSF-IF.B.6 Calculate and interpret the average rate of change of a function (presented symbolically ...) over a specified interval. Estimate the rate of change from a graph.

HSA-CED.A.2 Create equations in two or more variables to represent relationships between quantities; ...

ANSWERS

1. $m = -\frac{3}{4}$
2. $m = 3$
3. $m = 0$
4. $y = -3x + 19$
5. $y = -2x + 2$
6. $y = 4x + 9$
7. $y = \frac{1}{2}x - 5$
8. $y = -\frac{1}{4}x - 7$
9. $y = \frac{2}{3}x + 9$
10. When calculating the slope of a horizontal line, the vertical change is zero. This is the numerator of the fraction, and zero divided by any number is zero. When calculating the slope of a vertical line, the horizontal change is zero. This is the denominator of the fraction, and any number divided by zero is undefined.

Vocabulary Review

Have students make a Process Diagram to show the steps in writing an equation of a line that passes through a given point and has a given slope. Include the following terms.

- Slope-intercept form
- Slope
- *y*-intercept

1.

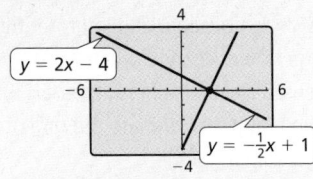

$y = 2x - 4$

$y = -\frac{1}{2}x + 1$

perpendicular; They have slopes of $m_1 = -\frac{1}{2}$ and $m_2 = 2$.

2.

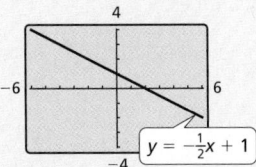

$y = -\frac{1}{2}x + 1$

coincident; Their equations are equivalent.

3.

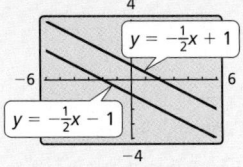

$y = -\frac{1}{2}x + 1$

$y = -\frac{1}{2}x - 1$

parallel; Each line has a slope of $m = -\frac{1}{2}$.

4.

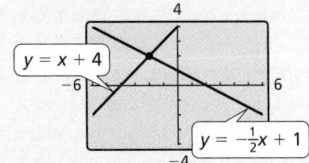

$y = x + 4$

$y = -\frac{1}{2}x + 1$

nonperpendicular intersecting lines; Their slopes are $m_1 = -\frac{1}{2}$ and $m_2 = 1$, so they are neither parallel nor perpendicular, and they intersect at $(-2, 2)$.

Mathematical Practices

Mathematically proficient students use technological tools to explore concepts.

Characteristics of Lines in a Coordinate Plane

⟲ Core Concept

Lines in a Coordinate Plane

1. In a coordinate plane, two lines are *parallel* if and only if they are both vertical lines or they both have the same slope.

2. In a coordinate plane, two lines are *perpendicular* if and only if one is vertical and the other is horizontal or the slopes of the lines are negative reciprocals of each other.

3. In a coordinate plane, two lines are *coincident* if and only if their equations are equivalent.

EXAMPLE 1   **Classifying Pairs of Lines**

Here are some examples of pairs of lines in a coordinate plane.

a. $2x + y = 2$ These lines are not parallel
     $x - y = 4$ or perpendicular. They
               intersect at $(2, -2)$.

b. $2x + y = 2$ These lines are coincident
     $4x + 2y = 4$ because their equations
                are equivalent.

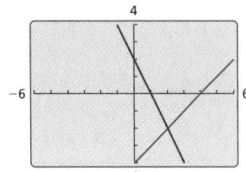

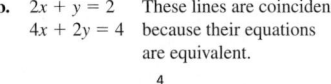
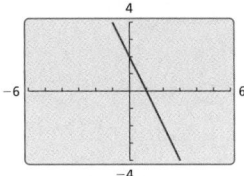

c. $2x + y = 2$ These lines are parallel.
     $2x + y = 4$ Each line has a slope
                of $m = -2$.

d. $2x + y = 2$ These lines are perpendicular.
     $x - 2y = 4$ They have slopes of $m_1 = -2$
                and $m_2 = \frac{1}{2}$.

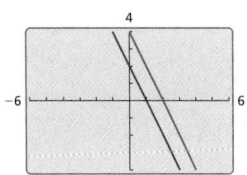

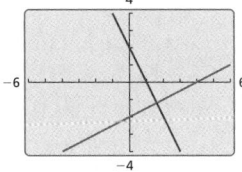

Monitoring Progress

Use a graphing calculator to graph the pair of lines. Use a square viewing window. Classify the lines as parallel, perpendicular, coincident, or nonperpendicular intersecting lines. Justify your answer.

1. $x + 2y = 2$
     $2x - y = 4$

2. $x + 2y = 2$
     $2x + 4y = 4$

3. $x + 2y = 2$
     $x + 2y = -2$

4. $x + 2y = 2$
     $x - y = -4$

Laurie's Notes   Mathematical Practices (continued from page T-123)

- Discuss the *Core Concept* and ask questions about each statement.
- **?** "Why are vertical lines a special case for parallel lines?"   Vertical lines have undefined slope.
- **?** "Why is there a special case for a vertical line and a horizontal line being perpendicular?" Vertical lines have undefined slope and horizontal lines have 0 slope. So they are not negative reciprocals of one another, but they are perpendicular.
- Students will be working with parallel and perpendicular lines in this chapter, extending what they already know about these concepts in the Cartesian plane.
- In answering the *Monitoring Progress* questions, students' evidence (justification) needs to be more than eyesight!

Overview of Section 3.1

Introduction

- This short lesson introduces the vocabulary and concepts associated with *parallel lines* and *parallel planes*. While much of the vocabulary is not new to students, do not presume that their spatial skills are such that they can interpret pictures and/or sketch the relationships they are studying. Physical models are very helpful.

- The lesson introduces *parallel lines* and *skew lines*. The Parallel Postulate (Post. 3.1) and the Perpendicular Postulate (Post. 3.2) are stated. If time permits, you may wish to have a discussion about non-Euclidean geometry.

- The second part of the lesson presents the pairs of angles formed when two lines are intersected by a transversal.

Resources

- Uncooked spaghetti, chopsticks, transparencies, cardboard dividers, and rectangular prisms are helpful models to have available for this lesson.

Formative Assessment Tips

- **Opposing Views:** This technique allows students to compare two or more solutions or ways of thinking about a problem, or as is the case in the first lesson, what is a sufficient definition for skew lines? Skew lines are non-coplanar versus skew lines are non-coplanar lines that do not intersect. Another way to ask the question is, "Is it a sufficient definition to simply say that skew lines are non-coplanar lines?"

- To be informative, students must present more than yes/no answers. Students must be able to explain their reasoning for classmates to hear. Once the different views are presented, all students should decide which view most closely reflects their own and give justification for their thinking. Students can respond in writing or you can solicit viewpoints as a discussion prompt.

- **MP3 Construct Viable Arguments and Critique the Reasoning of Others:** Using this formative assessment technique allows you to check students' conceptual knowledge and their ability to construct a viable argument.

Extensions

- Postulate 3.1 in this lesson is called the Parallel Postulate, and historically, it is known at Euclid's Fifth Postulate. Because a postulate is a statement assumed to be true but not proven, when you assume that it is not true, it leads to a branch of mathematics known as non-Euclidean geometry.

- The negation of Euclid's Fifth Postulate can be done in two ways. Given a line and a point not on the line, there are no lines (elliptic geometry) parallel to the given line, or there is more than one line (hyperbolic geometry) parallel to the given line.

- This is a model of the plane in elliptic geometry. Lines are defined as great circles and will always intersect at two points. The sum of the angle measures of a triangle is greater than 180°.

- This is a model of the plane in hyperbolic geometry, where the sum of the angle measures of a triangle is less than 180°.

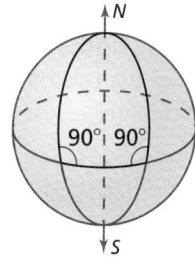

Plane in elliptic geometry

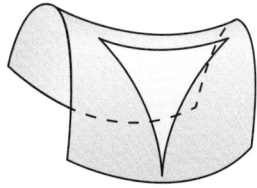

Plane in hyperbolic geometry

Pacing Suggestion

- Once students have worked the explorations, continue with the formal lesson.

Dynamic Teaching Tools

Dynamic Assessment & Progress Monitoring Tool
Lesson Planning Tool
Interactive Whiteboard Lesson Library
Dynamic Classroom with Dynamic Investigations

Common Core State Standards

HSG-CO.A.1 Know precise definitions of angle, …, perpendicular line, parallel line, and line segment, based on the undefined notions of point, line, distance along a line, …

Laurie's Notes

Exploration

Motivate
- Hold up three pieces of uncooked spaghetti or three chopsticks.
- **? Turn and Talk:** "How might these three coplanar lines be related in terms of intersection possibilities?

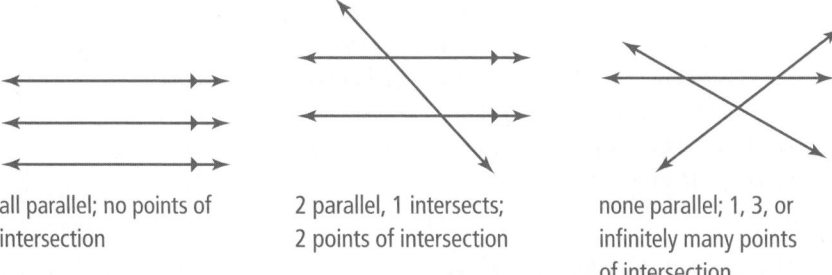

all parallel; no points of intersection

2 parallel, 1 intersects; 2 points of intersection

none parallel; 1, 3, or infinitely many points of intersection

- **?** "How might these three lines be related when they are not coplanar?" Listen for possibilities.

Exploration 1
- Students should recall the term "coincident" from systems of equations in Algebra 1.
- **Connection:** 0, 1, and infinitely many points of intersection are the three cases when solving systems of equations.

Exploration 2
- Some students will find it helpful to hold a cube or prism in their hands as they answer these questions. Remind students that the dotted lines mean that the edges are not visible from the given perspective.
- Discuss the definition of *skew lines*.
- **? Opposing Views:** Ask the *Probing Question*, "Would it be sufficient to define skew lines as simply lines that are not coplanar? Explain." Give students time to consider their answer. Some students will say yes, some will say no, and some will be uncertain. Ask a few students from each viewpoint to share their thinking. The class should decide that lines that are not coplanar are skew lines.
- **Big Idea:** The *Big Idea* is that if lines are not coplanar, then they cannot intersect.
- Be sure students give a reason for their classification.

Exploration 3
- The red directed arrows denote that the lines are parallel. Students should quickly identify vertical angles and linear pairs of angles.

Communicate Your Answer
- Students should correctly define parallel, skew, and coincident lines.
- Having a prism to hold is helpful as students answer Question 5.

Connecting to Next Step
- If students have been successful in identifying types of lines, you may want to omit Example 1 in the formal lesson.

3.1 Pairs of Lines and Angles

Essential Question
What does it mean when two lines are parallel, intersecting, coincident, or skew?

Dynamic Teaching Tools

Dynamic Assessment & Progress Monitoring Tool

Lesson Planning Tool

Interactive Whiteboard Lesson Library

Dynamic Classroom with Dynamic Investigations

EXPLORATION 1 Points of Intersection

Work with a partner. Write the number of points of intersection of each pair of coplanar lines.

a. parallel lines

b. intersecting lines

c. coincident lines

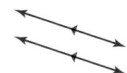  

EXPLORATION 2 Classifying Pairs of Lines

Work with a partner. The figure shows a *right rectangular prism*. All its angles are right angles. Classify each of the following pairs of lines as *parallel, intersecting, coincident,* or *skew*. Justify your answers. (Two lines are **skew lines** when they do not intersect and are not coplanar.)

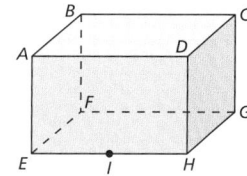

Pair of Lines	Classification	Reason
a. $\overleftrightarrow{AB}$ and $\overleftrightarrow{BC}$		
b. $\overleftrightarrow{AD}$ and $\overleftrightarrow{BC}$		
c. $\overrightarrow{EI}$ and $\overrightarrow{IH}$		
d. $\overleftrightarrow{BF}$ and $\overleftrightarrow{EH}$		
e. $\overrightarrow{EF}$ and $\overrightarrow{CG}$		
f. $\overleftrightarrow{AB}$ and $\overleftrightarrow{GH}$		

CONSTRUCTING VIABLE ARGUMENTS

To be proficient in math, you need to understand and use stated assumptions, definitions, and previously established results.

EXPLORATION 3 Identifying Pairs of Angles

Work with a partner. In the figure, two parallel lines are intersected by a third line called a *transversal*.

a. Identify all the pairs of vertical angles. Explain your reasoning.

b. Identify all the linear pairs of angles. Explain your reasoning.

Communicate Your Answer

4. What does it mean when two lines are parallel, intersecting, coincident, or skew?

5. In Exploration 2, find three more pairs of lines that are different from those given. Classify the pairs of lines as *parallel, intersecting, coincident,* or *skew.* Justify your answers.

Section 3.1   Pairs of Lines and Angles   **125**

ANSWERS

1. a. zero

   b. one

   c. infinitely many

2. a. intersecting; They intersect at point *B*.

   b. parallel; They are coplanar and will never intersect.

   c. coincident; Points *E*, *I*, and *H* are collinear.

   d. skew; They are not coplanar and will never intersect.

   e. skew; They are not coplanar and will never intersect.

   f. parallel; They both lie on plane *ABG*, which is not drawn, and they will never intersect.

3. a. ∠1 and ∠3, ∠2 and ∠4, ∠5 and ∠7, ∠6 and ∠8; Two pairs of opposite rays are formed by each of these pairs of angles.

   b. ∠1 and ∠2, ∠2 and ∠3, ∠3 and ∠4, ∠1 and ∠4, ∠5 and ∠6, ∠6 and ∠7, ∠7 and ∠8, ∠5 and ∠8; One pair of opposite rays is formed by each of these pairs of angles.

4. Parallel lines are coplanar and never intersect. Intersecting lines are coplanar and intersect at exactly one point. Coincident lines are coplanar and share all the same points because they are the same line. Skew lines are not coplanar and never intersect.

5. *Sample answer:* $\overleftrightarrow{DH}$ and $\overleftrightarrow{CG}$ are parallel because they are coplanar and will never intersect. $\overleftrightarrow{BF}$ and $\overleftrightarrow{AB}$ are intersecting because they intersect at point *B*. $\overleftrightarrow{FG}$ and $\overleftrightarrow{AE}$ are skew because they are in different planes and will never intersect.

Extra Example 1

Think of each segment in the figure as part of a line. Which line(s) or plane(s) appear to fit the description?

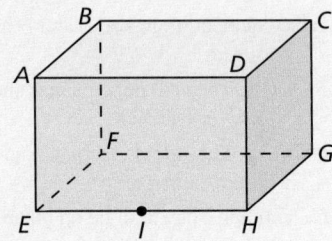

a. line(s) parallel to $\overleftrightarrow{GH}$ and containing point F $\overleftrightarrow{EF}$

b. line(s) skew to $\overleftrightarrow{GH}$ and containing point F $\overleftrightarrow{BF}$

c. line(s) perpendicular to $\overleftrightarrow{GH}$ and containing point F $\overleftrightarrow{FG}$

d. plane(s) parallel to plane GHD and containing point F plane ABF

MONITORING PROGRESS ANSWER

1. $\overleftrightarrow{CF}$

Core Vocabulary

parallel lines, *p. 126*
skew lines, *p. 126*
parallel planes, *p. 126*
transversal, *p. 128*
corresponding angles,
   p. 128
alternate interior angles,
   p. 128
alternate exterior angles,
   p. 128
consecutive interior angles,
   p. 128

Previous
perpendicular lines

What You Will Learn

▶ Identify lines and planes.

▶ Identify parallel and perpendicular lines.

▶ Identify pairs of angles formed by transversals.

Identifying Lines and Planes

Core Concept

Parallel Lines, Skew Lines, and Parallel Planes

Two lines that do not intersect are either *parallel lines* or *skew lines*. Two lines are **parallel lines** when they do not intersect and are coplanar. Two lines are **skew lines** when they do not intersect and are not coplanar. Also, two planes that do not intersect are **parallel planes**.

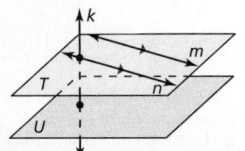

Lines m and n are parallel lines ($m \parallel n$).

Lines m and k are skew lines.

Planes T and U are parallel planes ($T \parallel U$).

Lines k and n are intersecting lines, and there is a plane (not shown) containing them.

Small directed arrows, as shown in red on lines m and n above, are used to show that lines are parallel. The symbol $\parallel$ means "is parallel to," as in $m \parallel n$.

Segments and rays are parallel when they lie in parallel lines. A line is parallel to a plane when the line is in a plane parallel to the given plane. In the diagram above, line n is parallel to plane U.

REMEMBER

Recall that if two lines intersect to form a right angle, then they are perpendicular lines.

EXAMPLE 1   **Identifying Lines and Planes**

Think of each segment in the figure as part of a line. Which line(s) or plane(s) appear to fit the description?

a. line(s) parallel to $\overleftrightarrow{CD}$ and containing point A

b. line(s) skew to $\overleftrightarrow{CD}$ and containing point A

c. line(s) perpendicular to $\overleftrightarrow{CD}$ and containing point A

d. plane(s) parallel to plane EFG and containing point A

SOLUTION

a. $\overleftrightarrow{AB}$, $\overleftrightarrow{HG}$, and $\overleftrightarrow{EF}$ all appear parallel to $\overleftrightarrow{CD}$, but only $\overleftrightarrow{AB}$ contains point A.

b. Both $\overleftrightarrow{AG}$ and $\overleftrightarrow{AH}$ appear skew to $\overleftrightarrow{CD}$ and contain point A.

c. $\overleftrightarrow{BC}$, $\overleftrightarrow{AD}$, $\overleftrightarrow{DE}$, and $\overleftrightarrow{FC}$ all appear perpendicular to $\overleftrightarrow{CD}$, but only $\overleftrightarrow{AD}$ contains point A.

d. Plane ABC appears parallel to plane EFG and contains point A.

Monitoring Progress 🔊 Help in English and Spanish at *BigIdeasMath.com*

1. Look at the diagram in Example 1. Name the line(s) through point F that appear skew to $\overleftrightarrow{EH}$.

Laurie's Notes | Teacher Actions

- **Probing Statement:** "If two lines do not intersect, then they are parallel." Ask for comments. Do students recognize that lines could be skew versus parallel? This is connected to the definition of *parallel lines* and why the lines are said to be nonintersecting coplanar lines.
- You may want to take time for students to practice sketching parallel planes. Explain that three letters are used to identify a plane.
- **Turn and Talk:** Have students discuss Example 1 with their partners.

Identifying Parallel and Perpendicular Lines

Two distinct lines in the same plane either are parallel, like line ℓ and line *n*, or intersect in a point, like line *j* and line *n*.

Through a point not on a line, there are infinitely many lines. Exactly one of these lines is parallel to the given line, and exactly one of them is perpendicular to the given line. For example, line *k* is the line through point *P* perpendicular to line ℓ, and line *n* is the line through point *P* parallel to line ℓ.

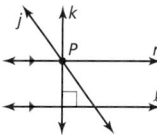

🔄 Postulates

Postulate 3.1   Parallel Postulate

If there is a line and a point not on the line, then there is exactly one line through the point parallel to the given line.

There is exactly one line through *P* parallel to ℓ.

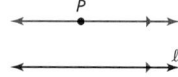

Postulate 3.2   Perpendicular Postulate

If there is a line and a point not on the line, then there is exactly one line through the point perpendicular to the given line.

There is exactly one line through *P* perpendicular to ℓ.

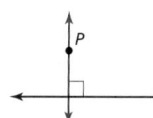

EXAMPLE 2   Identifying Parallel and Perpendicular Lines

The given line markings show how the roads in a town are related to one another.

a. Name a pair of parallel lines.

b. Name a pair of perpendicular lines.

c. Is $\overleftrightarrow{FE} \parallel \overleftrightarrow{AC}$? Explain.

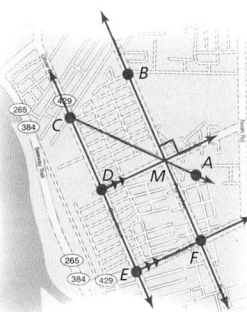

SOLUTION

a. $\overleftrightarrow{MD} \parallel \overleftrightarrow{FE}$

b. $\overleftrightarrow{MD} \perp \overleftrightarrow{BF}$

c. $\overleftrightarrow{FE}$ is not parallel to $\overleftrightarrow{AC}$, because $\overleftrightarrow{MD}$ is parallel to $\overleftrightarrow{FE}$, and by the Parallel Postulate, there is exactly one line parallel to $\overleftrightarrow{FE}$ through *M*.

Monitoring Progress 🔊 Help in English and Spanish at *BigIdeasMath.com*

2. In Example 2, can you use the Perpendicular Postulate to show that $\overleftrightarrow{AC}$ is *not* perpendicular to $\overleftrightarrow{BF}$? Explain why or why not.

Extra Example 2

The given line markings show how the roads in a town are related to each other.

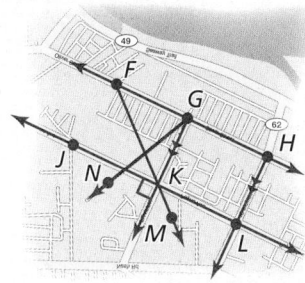

a. Name a pair of parallel lines. $\overleftrightarrow{GK} \parallel \overleftrightarrow{HL}$

b. Name a pair of perpendicular lines. $\overleftrightarrow{GK} \perp \overleftrightarrow{JL}$

c. Is $\overleftrightarrow{GN} \perp \overleftrightarrow{JL}$? Explain. $\overleftrightarrow{GN}$ is not perpendicular to $\overleftrightarrow{JL}$, because $\overleftrightarrow{GK} \perp \overleftrightarrow{JL}$. By the Perpendicular Postulate, there is exactly one line through *G* that is perpendicular to $\overleftrightarrow{JL}$.

MONITORING PROGRESS ANSWER

2. yes; Because $\overleftrightarrow{DM}$ is perpendicular to $\overleftrightarrow{BF}$ at *M*, no other line could also be perpendicular to the same line through the same point according to the Perpendicular Postulate (Post. 3.2).

Laurie's Notes   Teacher Actions

? Draw a line *AB* and a point *P* not on the line. Ask, "How many lines can you draw through point *P*?" infinitely many "How many of the lines are parallel to line *AB*?" one "Could there be more than one?" no

- State the Parallel Postulate (Post. 3.1) and the Perpendicular Postulate (Post. 3.2). If time permits, tell a little about non-Euclidean geometry. See page T-124.

- **Extension:** Import a local street map for your location. Use dynamic geometry software to identify parallel and perpendicular streets.

Extra Example 3

Identify all pairs of angles of the given type.

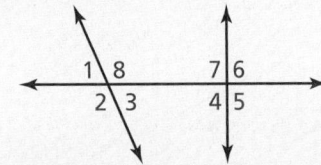

a. consecutive interior ∠3 and ∠4, ∠7 and ∠8
b. alternate exterior ∠1 and ∠5, ∠2 and ∠6
c. corresponding ∠1 and ∠7, ∠2 and ∠4, ∠3 and ∠5, ∠8 and ∠6
d. alternate interior ∠3 and ∠7, ∠4 and ∠8

MONITORING PROGRESS ANSWERS

3. corresponding
4. alternate exterior
5. alternate interior

Identifying Pairs of Angles

A **transversal** is a line that intersects two or more coplanar lines at different points.

Core Concept

Angles Formed by Transversals

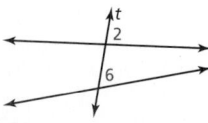

Two angles are **corresponding angles** when they have corresponding positions. For example, ∠2 and ∠6 are above the lines and to the right of the transversal *t*.

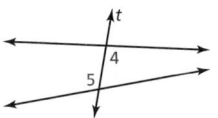

Two angles are **alternate interior angles** when they lie between the two lines and on opposite sides of the transversal *t*.

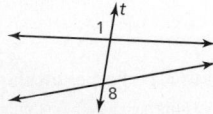

Two angles are **alternate exterior angles** when they lie outside the two lines and on opposite sides of the transversal *t*.

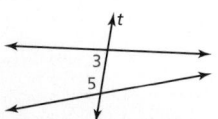

Two angles are **consecutive interior angles** when they lie between the two lines and on the same side of the transversal *t*.

EXAMPLE 3 Identifying Pairs of Angles

Identify all pairs of angles of the given type.

a. corresponding
b. alternate interior
c. alternate exterior
d. consecutive interior

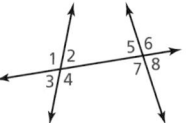

SOLUTION

a. ∠1 and ∠5
   ∠2 and ∠6
   ∠3 and ∠7
   ∠4 and ∠8

b. ∠2 and ∠7
   ∠4 and ∠5

c. ∠1 and ∠8
   ∠3 and ∠6

d. ∠2 and ∠5
   ∠4 and ∠7

Monitoring Progress Help in English and Spanish at *BigIdeasMath.com*

Classify the pair of numbered angles.

3.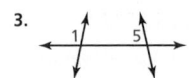

4.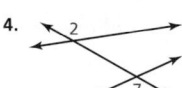

5.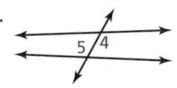

Laurie's Notes Teacher Actions

- In grade 8, students were introduced to the angles formed when a transversal intersects two other lines.
- The *Core Concept* only names the angle pairs. The lines intersected by the transversal do not need to be parallel.
- When going over Example 3, include identification of vertical angles.

Closure

- **Exit Ticket:** Sketch a right triangular prism with the vertices labeled. Identify:

  a pair of parallel lines *Sample answer:* $\overleftrightarrow{VW}$ and $\overleftrightarrow{YZ}$

  a pair of perpendicular lines *Sample answer:* $\overleftrightarrow{UX}$ and $\overleftrightarrow{XY}$

  a pair of skew lines *Sample answer:* $\overleftrightarrow{UW}$ and $\overleftrightarrow{YZ}$

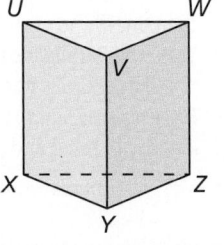

Vocabulary and Core Concept Check

1. **COMPLETE THE SENTENCE** Two lines that do not intersect and are also not parallel are _____ lines.

2. **WHICH ONE DOESN'T BELONG?** Which angle pair does *not* belong with the other three? Explain your reasoning.

   ∠2 and ∠3   ∠4 and ∠5

   ∠1 and ∠8   ∠2 and ∠7

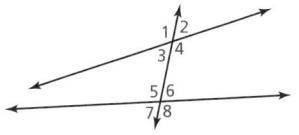

Monitoring Progress and Modeling with Mathematics

In Exercises 3–6, think of each segment in the diagram as part of a line. All the angles are right angles. Which line(s) or plane(s) contain point *B* and appear to fit the description? *(See Example 1.)*

3. line(s) parallel to $\overleftrightarrow{CD}$

4. line(s) perpendicular to $\overleftrightarrow{CD}$

5. line(s) skew to $\overleftrightarrow{CD}$

6. plane(s) parallel to plane *CDH*

In Exercises 7–10, use the diagram. *(See Example 2.)*

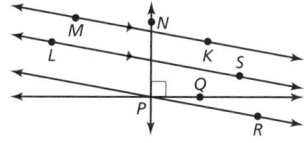

7. Name a pair of parallel lines.

8. Name a pair of perpendicular lines.

9. Is $\overleftrightarrow{PN} \parallel \overleftrightarrow{KM}$? Explain.

10. Is $\overrightarrow{PR} \perp \overleftrightarrow{NP}$? Explain.

In Exercises 11–14, identify all pairs of angles of the given type. *(See Example 3.)*

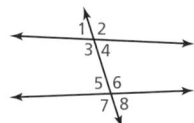

11. corresponding

12. alternate interior

13. alternate exterior

14. consecutive interior

USING STRUCTURE In Exercises 15–18, classify the angle pair as *corresponding*, *alternate interior*, *alternate exterior*, or *consecutive interior* angles.

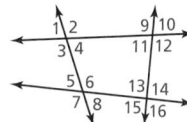

15. ∠5 and ∠1   16. ∠11 and ∠13

17. ∠6 and ∠13   18. ∠2 and ∠11

Section 3.1   Pairs of Lines and Angles   **129**

Assignment Guide and Homework Check

ASSIGNMENT

Basic: 1, 2, 3–21 odd, 24, 29–31

Average: 1, 2–20 even, 24–31

Advanced: 1, 2, 4, 10, 12, 16–31

HOMEWORK CHECK

Basic: 5, 11, 17, 19, 24

Average: 4, 10, 12, 18, 24

Advanced: 4, 16, 19, 22, 29

ANSWERS

1. skew

2. ∠2 and ∠3; They are vertical angles formed by one pair of intersecting lines and one point of intersection. The others are either alternate interior or alternate exterior, and are formed by three lines and two points of intersection.

3. $\overleftrightarrow{AB}$

4. $\overleftrightarrow{BC}$

5. $\overleftrightarrow{BF}$

6. plane *ABF*

7. $\overleftrightarrow{MK}$ and $\overleftrightarrow{LS}$

8. $\overleftrightarrow{NP}$ and $\overleftrightarrow{PQ}$

9. no; They are intersecting lines.

10. no; By the Perpendicular Postulate (Post. 3.2), only one line can be perpendicular to $\overleftrightarrow{NP}$ at point *P*. Because $\overrightarrow{PQ}$ is marked as perpendicular to $\overleftrightarrow{NP}$, $\overrightarrow{PR}$ cannot be perpendicular to $\overleftrightarrow{NP}$.

11. ∠1 and ∠5; ∠2 and ∠6; ∠3 and ∠7; ∠4 and ∠8

12. ∠3 and ∠6; ∠4 and ∠5

13. ∠1 and ∠8; ∠2 and ∠7

14. ∠3 and ∠5; ∠4 and ∠6

15. corresponding

16. consecutive interior

17. consecutive interior

18. alternate interior

ANSWERS

19. Lines that do not intersect could also be skew; If two coplanar lines do not intersect, then they are parallel.

20–29. See Additional Answers.

30. $m\angle 2 = 104°$, $m\angle 3 = 76°$, $m\angle 4 = 104°$

31. $m\angle 1 = 21°$, $m\angle 3 = 21°$, $m\angle 4 = 159°$

Mini-Assessment

1. Which line(s) or plane(s) appear to fit the description?

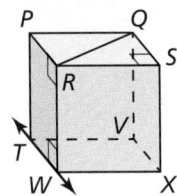

a. line(s) parallel to $\overleftrightarrow{TW}$
   $\overleftrightarrow{PR}$, $\overleftrightarrow{QS}$, $\overleftrightarrow{VX}$

b. line(s) skew to $\overleftrightarrow{TW}$ and containing point S $\overleftrightarrow{RS}$, $\overleftrightarrow{SX}$

c. line(s) perpendicular to $\overleftrightarrow{TW}$ and containing point R $\overleftrightarrow{RW}$

d. plane(s) parallel to plane RPT and containing point Q
   plane QVX

Use the figure to identify pairs of lines and angles.

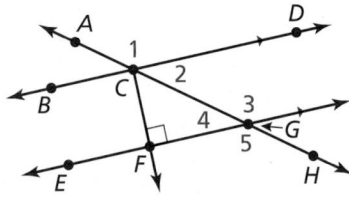

2. a pair of parallel lines $\overleftrightarrow{BD} \parallel \overleftrightarrow{EG}$

3. a pair of perpendicular lines
   $\overleftrightarrow{CF} \perp \overleftrightarrow{EG}$

4. a pair of corresponding angles that are numbered $\angle 1$ and $\angle 3$

5. a pair of alternate interior angles that are numbered $\angle 2$ and $\angle 4$

ERROR ANALYSIS In Exercises 19 and 20, describe and correct the error in the conditional statement about lines.

19.   If two lines do not intersect, then they are parallel.

20.   If there is a line and a point not on the line, then there is exactly one line through the point that intersects the given line.

21. **MODELING WITH MATHEMATICS** Use the photo to decide whether the statement is true or false. Explain your reasoning.

a. The plane containing the floor of the tree house is parallel to the ground.

b. The lines containing the railings of the staircase, such as $\overleftrightarrow{AB}$, are skew to all lines in the plane containing the ground.

c. All the lines containing the balusters, such as $\overleftrightarrow{CD}$, are perpendicular to the plane containing the floor of the tree house.

22. **THOUGHT PROVOKING** If two lines are intersected by a third line, is the third line necessarily a transversal? Justify your answer with a diagram.

23. **MATHEMATICAL CONNECTIONS** Two lines are cut by a transversal. Is it possible for all eight angles formed to have the same measure? Explain your reasoning.

Maintaining Mathematical Proficiency   Reviewing what you learned in previous grades and lessons

Use the diagram to find the measures of all the angles. (Section 2.6)

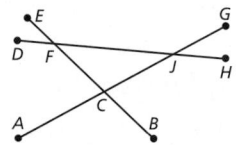

30. $m\angle 1 = 76°$

31. $m\angle 2 = 159°$

---

24. **HOW DO YOU SEE IT?** Think of each segment in the figure as part of a line.

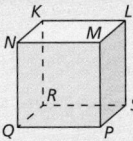

a. Which lines are parallel to $\overleftrightarrow{NQ}$?

b. Which lines intersect $\overleftrightarrow{NQ}$?

c. Which lines are skew to $\overleftrightarrow{NQ}$?

d. Should you have named all the lines on the cube in parts (a)–(c) except $\overleftrightarrow{NQ}$? Explain.

In Exercises 25–28, copy and complete the statement. List all possible correct answers.

25. $\angle BCG$ and ____ are corresponding angles.

26. $\angle BCG$ and ____ are consecutive interior angles.

27. $\angle FCJ$ and ____ are alternate interior angles.

28. $\angle FCA$ and ____ are alternate exterior angles.

29. **MAKING AN ARGUMENT** Your friend claims the uneven parallel bars in gymnastics are not really parallel. She says one is higher than the other, so they cannot be in the same plane. Is she correct? Explain.

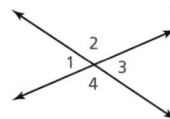

Overview of Section 3.2

Introduction

- The lesson looks at the relationship of different angle pairs when two parallel lines are cut by a transversal. The results are not surprising to students. What is challenging for students is being able to string a series of reasons together to give a logical explanation of why angles have a particular measure.
- The visual experience of seeing a dynamic presentation of parallel lines cut by transversals is helpful in developing spatial skills.

Common Misconceptions

- Students sometimes believe that the angle relationships in this lesson only apply for parallel lines and not for parallel segments. Help students understand that when the segments lie in lines that are parallel, the segments are parallel. When the segments are parallel, the theorems in this lesson apply. For instance, the vertical edges of this podium are parallel, and the consecutive interior angles are supplementary.

Teaching Strategy

- If you do not have access to dynamic geometry software, you can still model the relationship between the various angle pairs.
- **MP4 Model with Mathematics:** Cut long strips of clear transparency. Draw a line on each strip. To make the model, punch a hole in the transparencies where the lines intersect and attach the strips with brass fasteners or sewing snaps. Manipulating the strips allows students to see how the angles change as the lines are made to be parallel.

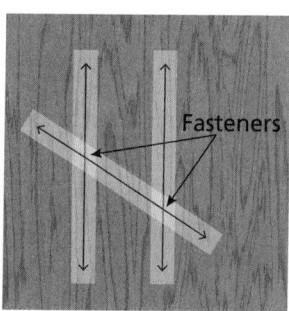

Fasteners

Applications

- Search the Internet (rainbow + "angle of sun") to find articles and images that explain in greater depth the relationship between the angle of the sun and the angle of the viewer and what colors we see in a rainbow.

Pacing Suggestion

- Once students have worked the explorations, they will be ready to begin with Example 1 in the formal lesson.

Laurie's Notes

Exploration

Motivate

- Show students an image that contains many parallel lines (segments) and a transversal that intersects them, perhaps the 2-by-4 framing of a house. Identify several angles and ask students what they notice.

Exploration Note

- In the first exploration, students will construct two parallel lines and a transversal. Be sure that students construct the transversal so that it is dynamic, meaning it can be rotated and thus all eight angles will change measure.

Exploration 1

- The construction should not take long to perform. Students will recognize vertical angles and linear pairs, and therefore they may not actually measure all eight angles. Encourage students to verify their hunches.
- **? Popsicle Sticks:** "What can you conclude from your measurements?" Answers will vary. There should be many conclusions.

Exploration 2

- Remind students that conjectures are unproven statements that are based on observations.
- **MP6 Attend to Precision:** If students make the conjecture that corresponding angles are congruent, ask a *Probing Question*. "Are corresponding angles always congruent?" only when the lines are parallel
- Each hypothesis needs to include the condition of the lines being parallel.
- **Extension:** Ask students to write a conjecture about exterior angles on the same side of the transversal.

Communicate Your Answer

- Students should mention corresponding angles, alternate interior angles, and alternate exterior angles as being congruent when parallel lines are intersected by a transversal. Students should not include vertical angles as being congruent. Vertical angles are formed when two lines intersect, *not* when parallel lines are intersected by a transversal.

Connecting to Next Step

- The conjectures students have written are stated as theorems. Students should be ready to begin with Example 1 in the formal lesson.

3.2 Parallel Lines and Transversals

Essential Question
When two parallel lines are cut by a transversal, which of the resulting pairs of angles are congruent?

EXPLORATION 1 — Exploring Parallel Lines

Work with a partner.
Use dynamic geometry software to draw two parallel lines. Draw a third line that intersects both parallel lines. Find the measures of the eight angles that are formed. What can you conclude?

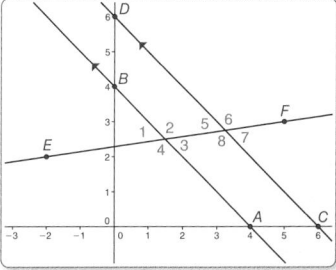

ATTENDING TO PRECISION

To be proficient in math, you need to communicate precisely with others.

EXPLORATION 2 — Writing Conjectures

Work with a partner. Use the results of Exploration 1 to write conjectures about the following pairs of angles formed by two parallel lines and a transversal.

a. corresponding angles

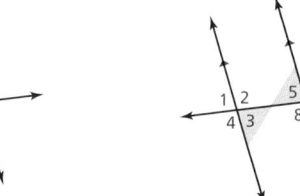

b. alternate interior angles

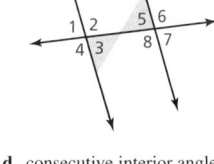

c. alternate exterior angles

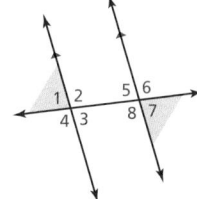

d. consecutive interior angles

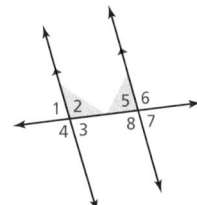

Communicate Your Answer

3. When two parallel lines are cut by a transversal, which of the resulting pairs of angles are congruent?

4. In Exploration 2, $m\angle 1 = 80°$. Find the other angle measures.

Dynamic Teaching Tools

Dynamic Assessment & Progress Monitoring Tool

Lesson Planning Tool

Interactive Whiteboard Lesson Library

Dynamic Classroom with Dynamic Investigations

ANSWERS

1. $m\angle 1 = m\angle 3 = m\angle 5 = m\angle 7$, $m\angle 2 = m\angle 4 = m\angle 6 = m\angle 8$, and any odd-numbered angle is supplementary to any even-numbered angle.

2. **a.** Corresponding angles are congruent when they are formed by two parallel lines and a transversal.

   b. Alternate interior angles are congruent when they are formed by two parallel lines and a transversal.

   c. Alternate exterior angles are congruent when they are formed by two parallel lines and a transversal.

   d. Consecutive interior angles are supplementary when they are formed by two parallel lines and a transversal.

3. corresponding angles, alternate interior angles, and alternate exterior angles

4. $m\angle 2 = 100°$, $m\angle 3 = 80°$, $m\angle 4 = 100°$, $m\angle 5 = 80°$, $m\angle 6 = 100°$, $m\angle 7 = 80°$, $m\angle 8 = 100°$

Extra Example 1

The measures of three of the numbered angles are 75°. Identify the angles. Explain your reasoning.

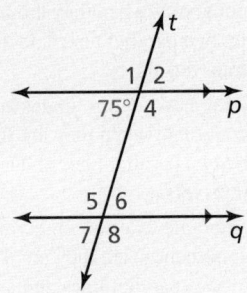

$\angle 2$, $\angle 6$, $\angle 7$; *Sample answer:* By the Vertical Angles Congruence Theorem (Thm. 2.6), $m\angle 2 = 75°$. By the Alternate Interior Angles Theorem (Thm. 3.2), $m\angle 6 = 75°$. By the Corresponding Angles Theorem (Thm. 3.1), $m\angle 7 = 75°$.

3.2 Lesson

Core Vocabulary

Previous
corresponding angles
parallel lines
supplementary angles
vertical angles

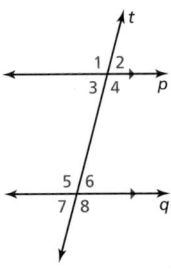

ANOTHER WAY

There are many ways to solve Example 1. Another way is to use the Corresponding Angles Theorem to find $m\angle 5$ and then use the Vertical Angles Congruence Theorem (Theorem 2.6) to find $m\angle 4$ and $m\angle 8$.

What You Will Learn

▶ Use properties of parallel lines.
▶ Prove theorems about parallel lines.
▶ Solve real-life problems.

Using Properties of Parallel Lines

🌀 Theorems

Theorem 3.1 Corresponding Angles Theorem

If two parallel lines are cut by a transversal, then the pairs of corresponding angles are congruent.

Examples In the diagram at the left, $\angle 2 \cong \angle 6$ and $\angle 3 \cong \angle 7$.

Proof Ex. 36, p. 180

Theorem 3.2 Alternate Interior Angles Theorem

If two parallel lines are cut by a transversal, then the pairs of alternate interior angles are congruent.

Examples In the diagram at the left, $\angle 3 \cong \angle 6$ and $\angle 4 \cong \angle 5$.

Proof Example 4, p. 134

Theorem 3.3 Alternate Exterior Angles Theorem

If two parallel lines are cut by a transversal, then the pairs of alternate exterior angles are congruent.

Examples In the diagram at the left, $\angle 1 \cong \angle 8$ and $\angle 2 \cong \angle 7$.

Proof Ex. 15, p. 136

Theorem 3.4 Consecutive Interior Angles Theorem

If two parallel lines are cut by a transversal, then the pairs of consecutive interior angles are supplementary.

Examples In the diagram at the left, $\angle 3$ and $\angle 5$ are supplementary, and $\angle 4$ and $\angle 6$ are supplementary.

Proof Ex. 16, p. 136

EXAMPLE 1   **Identifying Angles**

The measures of three of the numbered angles are 120°. Identify the angles. Explain your reasoning.

SOLUTION

By the Alternate Exterior Angles Theorem, $m\angle 8 = 120°$.

$\angle 5$ and $\angle 8$ are vertical angles. Using the Vertical Angles Congruence Theorem (Theorem 2.6), $m\angle 5 = 120°$.

$\angle 5$ and $\angle 4$ are alternate interior angles. By the Alternate Interior Angles Theorem, $\angle 4 = 120°$.

▶ So, the three angles that each have a measure of 120° are $\angle 4$, $\angle 5$, and $\angle 8$.

Laurie's Notes   Teacher Actions

- Write the theorems.
- **❓ Probing Question:** "Will there always be four acute and four obtuse angles when the transversal intersects the two parallel lines? Explain." no; There could be eight right angles if the transversal is perpendicular to the parallel lines.
- **MP3 Construct Viable Arguments and Critique the Reasoning of Others:** Students need to justify why each angle has a measure of 120° in Example 1. There are different trains of logic that students may follow. Give time for partners to discuss before having the whole-class discussion.

EXAMPLE 2   Using Properties of Parallel Lines

Find the value of *x*.

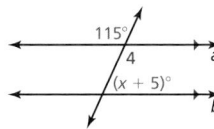

SOLUTION

By the Vertical Angles Congruence Theorem (Theorem 2.6), $m\angle 4 = 115°$. Lines *a* and *b* are parallel, so you can use the theorems about parallel lines.

$m\angle 4 + (x + 5)° = 180°$	Consecutive Interior Angles Theorem
$115° + (x + 5)° = 180°$	Substitute 115° for $m\angle 4$.
$x + 120 = 180$	Combine like terms.
$x = 60$	Subtract 120 from each side.

▶ So, the value of *x* is 60.

Check

$115° + (x + 5)° = 180°$

$115 + (60 + 5) \overset{?}{=} 180$

$180 = 180$ ✓

EXAMPLE 3   Using Properties of Parallel Lines

Find the value of *x*.

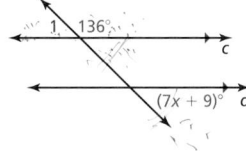

SOLUTION

By the Linear Pair Postulate (Postulate 2.8), $m\angle 1 = 180° - 136° = 44°$. Lines *c* and *d* are parallel, so you can use the theorems about parallel lines.

$m\angle 1 = (7x + 9)°$	Alternate Exterior Angles Theorem
$44° = (7x + 9)°$	Substitute 44° for $m\angle 1$.
$35 = 7x$	Subtract 9 from each side.
$5 = x$	Divide each side by 7.

▶ So, the value of *x* is 5.

Check

$44° = (7x + 9)°$

$44 \overset{?}{=} 7(5) + 9$

$44 = 44$ ✓

Monitoring Progress 🔊 Help in English and Spanish at *BigIdeasMath.com*

Use the diagram.

1. Given $m\angle 1 = 105°$, find $m\angle 4$, $m\angle 5$, and $m\angle 8$. Tell which theorem you use in each case.

2. Given $m\angle 3 = 68°$ and $m\angle 8 = (2x + 4)°$, what is the value of *x*? Show your steps.

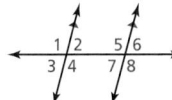

Extra Example 2
Find the value of *x*.

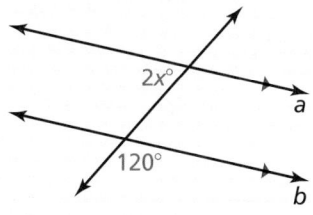

$x = 30$

Extra Example 3
Find the value of *y*.

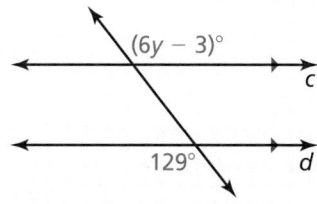

$y = 22$

MONITORING PROGRESS ANSWERS

1. $m\angle 4 = 105°$ by Vertical Angles Congruence Theorem (Thm. 2.6); $m\angle 5 = 105°$ by Corresponding Angles Theorem (Thm. 3.1); $m\angle 8 = 105°$ by Alternate Exterior Angles Theorem (Thm. 3.3)

2. 54; $m\angle 7 = m\angle 3$

$$m\angle 3 + m\angle 8 = 180°$$
$$68° + (2x + 4)° = 180°$$
$$2x + 72 = 180$$
$$2x = 108$$
$$x = 54$$

Laurie's Notes   **Teacher Actions**

• Students recognize that when parallel lines are given, angle pairs are going to be supplementary or congruent. Still, expect justification for how the problem is set up. In Example 2, the angles are supplementary because a vertical angle is substituted for a consecutive interior angle.

? MP3: "In Example 3, what is the relationship between the given angles? Explain." Students need to label an additional angle. In the diagram, $\angle 1$ is a linear pair with the angle labeled 136° and is the alternate exterior angle with the angle labeled $(7x + 9)°$. Students may label a different angle and still give a valid explanation.

Extra Example 4

Prove the Alternate Interior Angles Theorem without using the Corresponding Angles Theorem.

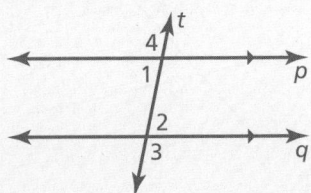

Given $p \parallel q$

Prove $\angle 1 \cong \angle 2$

Statements (Reasons)

1. $p \parallel q$ (Given)
2. $\angle 1$ is supplementary to $\angle 4$. (Linear Pair Post. 2.8)
3. $\angle 2$ is supplementary to $\angle 3$. (Linear Pair Post. 2.8)
4. $\angle 4 \cong \angle 3$ (Alt. Ext. $\angle$s Thm. 3.3)
5. $\angle 1 \cong \angle 2$ (Congr. Suppl. Thm. 2.4)

Extra Example 5

A balloonist sees a car at a 37° angle of depression from horizontal. In the diagram, $m\angle 1 = 37°$. What is $m\angle 2$? How do you know?

$m\angle 2 = 37°$; Alt. Int. $\angle$s Thm. 3.2

MONITORING PROGRESS ANSWERS

3. yes; The congruence of $\angle 3$ and $\angle 2$ is not dependent on the congruence of $\angle 1$ and $\angle 3$, so the order does not matter.

4. 41°; Because the Sun's rays are parallel, $\angle 1$ and $\angle 2$ are alternate interior angles. By the Alternate Interior Angles Theorem (Thm. 3.2), $\angle 1 \cong \angle 2$. So, by the definition of congruent angles, $m\angle 1 = m\angle 2 = 41°$.

Proving Theorems about Parallel Lines

EXAMPLE 4   Proving the Alternate Interior Angles Theorem

Prove that if two parallel lines are cut by a transversal, then the pairs of alternate interior angles are congruent.

SOLUTION

Draw a diagram. Label a pair of alternate interior angles as $\angle 1$ and $\angle 2$. You are looking for an angle that is related to both $\angle 1$ and $\angle 2$. Notice that one angle is a vertical angle with $\angle 2$ and a corresponding angle with $\angle 1$. Label it $\angle 3$.

STUDY TIP

Before you write a proof, identify the **Given** and **Prove** statements for the situation described or for any diagram you draw.

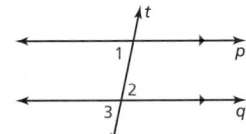

Given $p \parallel q$

Prove $\angle 1 \cong \angle 2$

STATEMENTS	REASONS
1. $p \parallel q$	1. Given
2. $\angle 1 \cong \angle 3$	2. Corresponding Angles Theorem
3. $\angle 3 \cong \angle 2$	3. Vertical Angles Congruence Theorem (Theorem 2.6)
4. $\angle 1 \cong \angle 2$	4. Transitive Property of Congruence (Theorem 2.2)

Monitoring Progress Help in English and Spanish at *BigIdeasMath.com*

3. In the proof in Example 4, if you use the third statement before the second statement, could you still prove the theorem? Explain.

Solving Real-Life Problems

EXAMPLE 5   Solving a Real-life Problem

When sunlight enters a drop of rain, different colors of light leave the drop at different angles. This process is what makes a rainbow. For violet light, $m\angle 2 = 40°$. What is $m\angle 1$? How do you know?

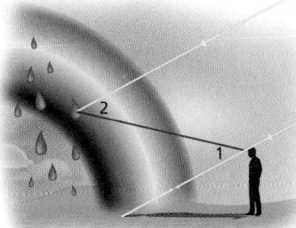

SOLUTION

Because the Sun's rays are parallel, $\angle 1$ and $\angle 2$ are alternate interior angles. By the Alternate Interior Angles Theorem, $\angle 1 \cong \angle 2$.

▶ So, by the definition of congruent angles, $m\angle 1 = m\angle 2 = 40°$.

Monitoring Progress Help in English and Spanish at *BigIdeasMath.com*

4. **WHAT IF?** In Example 5, yellow light leaves a drop at an angle of $m\angle 2 = 41°$. What is $m\angle 1$? How do you know?

Laurie's Notes   Teacher Actions

- In proving the Alternate Interior Angles Theorem (Thm. 3.2), any previously stated postulate, theorem, or definition may be used.
- **Whiteboarding:** Have partners work on the proof together. Ask for volunteers to share their work. Continue to ask, "How do you know?"

Closure

- Imagine a friend was absent today. What are the *Big Ideas* of the lesson you would tell your friend?

Vocabulary and Core Concept Check

1. **WRITING** How are the Alternate Interior Angles Theorem (Theorem 3.2) and the Alternate Exterior Angles Theorem (Theorem 3.3) alike? How are they different?

2. **WHICH ONE DOESN'T BELONG?** Which pair of angle measures does *not* belong with the other three? Explain.

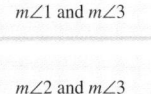 $m\angle 1$ and $m\angle 3$

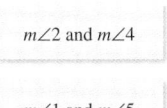 $m\angle 2$ and $m\angle 4$

$m\angle 2$ and $m\angle 3$

$m\angle 1$ and $m\angle 5$

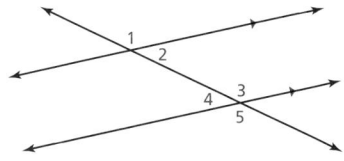

Monitoring Progress and Modeling with Mathematics

In Exercises 3–6, find $m\angle 1$ and $m\angle 2$. Tell which theorem you use in each case. *(See Example 1.)*

3.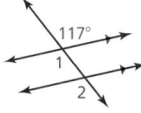

4.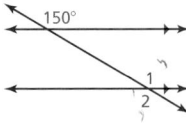

5.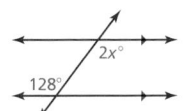

6.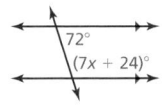

In Exercises 7–10, find the value of x. Show your steps. *(See Examples 2 and 3.)*

7.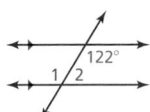

8.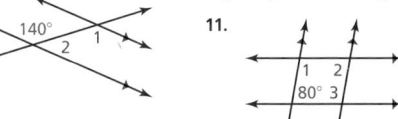

9.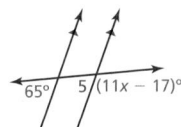

10.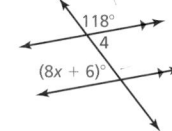

In Exercises 11 and 12, find $m\angle 1$, $m\angle 2$, and $m\angle 3$. Explain your reasoning.

11.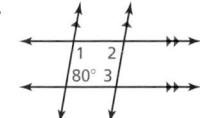

12.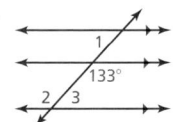

13. **ERROR ANALYSIS** Describe and correct the error in the student's reasoning.

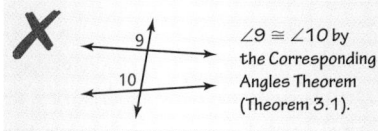

$\angle 9 \cong \angle 10$ by the Corresponding Angles Theorem (Theorem 3.1).

9. 12; $m\angle 5 = 65°$
$$65° + (11x - 17)° = 180°$$
$$11x + 48 = 180$$
$$11x = 132$$
$$x = 12$$

10. 7; $118° + (8x + 6)° = 180°$
$$8x + 124 = 180$$
$$8x = 56$$
$$x = 7$$

11. $m\angle 1 = 100°$, $m\angle 2 = 80°$, $m\angle 3 = 100°$; Because the 80° angle is a consecutive interior angle with both $\angle 1$ and $\angle 3$, they are supplementary by the Consecutive Interior Angles Theorem (Thm. 3.4). Because $\angle 1$ and $\angle 2$ are consecutive interior angles, they are supplementary by the Consecutive Interior Angles Theorem (Thm. 3.4).

12–13. See Additional Answers.

Assignment Guide and Homework Check

ASSIGNMENT

Basic: 1, 2, 3–13 odd, 14, 15, 23, 25–28

Average: 1, 2–12 even, 13–17, 23, 25–28

Advanced: 1, 2, 4, 8, 12, 13–20, 23–28

HOMEWORK CHECK

Basic: 3, 9, 11, 13, 14

Average: 10, 12, 13, 14, 23

Advanced: 8, 12, 14, 19, 24

ANSWERS

1. Both theorems refer to two pairs of congruent angles that are formed when two parallel lines are cut by a transversal, and the angles that are congruent are on opposite sides of the transversal. However with the Alternate Interior Angles Theorem (Thm. 3.2), the congruent angles lie between the parallel lines, and with the Alternate Exterior Angles Theorem (Thm. 3.3), the congruent angles lie outside the parallel lines.

2. $m\angle 2$ and $m\angle 3$; These are consecutive interior angles, which are supplementary. The other three are pairs of congruent angles.

3. $m\angle 1 = 117°$ by Vertical Angles Congruence Theorem (Thm. 2.6); $m\angle 2 = 117°$ by Alternate Exterior Angles Theorem (Thm. 3.3)

4. $m\angle 1 = 150°$ by Corresponding Angles Theorem (Thm. 3.1); $m\angle 2 = 150°$ by Alternate Exterior Angles Theorem (Thm. 3.3)

5. $m\angle 1 = 122°$ by Alternate Interior Angles Theorem (Thm. 3.2); $m\angle 2 = 58°$ by Consecutive Interior Angles Theorem (Thm. 3.4)

6. $m\angle 1 = 140°$ by Alternate Interior Angles Theorem (Thm. 3.2); $m\angle 2 = 40°$ by Consecutive Interior Angles Theorem (Thm. 3.4)

7. 64; $2x° = 128°$
$$x = 64$$

8. 12; $72° + (7x + 24)° = 180°$
$$7x + 96 = 180$$
$$7x = 84$$
$$x = 12$$

Dynamic Teaching Tools

Dynamic Assessment & Progress Monitoring Tool

Interactive Whiteboard Lesson Library

Dynamic Classroom with Dynamic Investigations

ANSWERS

14. a. $\angle ADB \cong \angle CBD$ and $\angle CAD \cong \angle ACB$ by the Alternate Interior Angles Theorem (Thm. 3.2).

b. $\angle BAD$ and $\angle CDA$ are supplementary, as well as $\angle ABC$ and $\angle DCB$, by the Consecutive Interior Angles Theorem (Thm. 3.4).

15–16. See Additional Answers.

17. $m\angle 2 = 104°$; Because the trees form parallel lines, and the rope is a transversal, the 76° angle and $\angle 2$ are consecutive interior angles. So, they are supplementary by the Consecutive Interior Angles Theorem (Thm. 3.4).

18–28. See Additional Answers.

Mini-Assessment

Use the diagram.

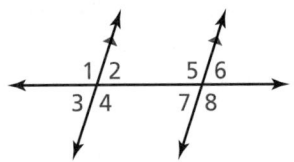

1. Given $m\angle 7 = 72°$, find $m\angle 2$ and $m\angle 5$. $m\angle 2 = 72°$; $m\angle 5 = 108°$

2. Given $m\angle 8 = 115°$ and $m\angle 2 = (2x - 3)°$. Find the value of x. 34

3. A bicycle path divides a rectangular park. The path makes a 42° angle with the top border of the park, so $m\angle 1 = 42°$. What is $m\angle 2$? How do you know?

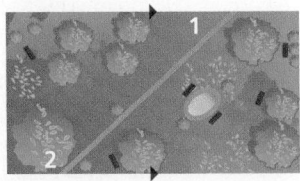

$m\angle 2 = 138°$; Consec. Int. $\angle s$ Theorem (Thm. 3.4)

136   Chapter 3

---

14. HOW DO YOU SEE IT? Use the diagram.

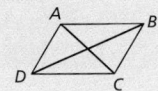

a. Name two pairs of congruent angles when $\overline{AD}$ and $\overline{BC}$ are parallel. Explain your reasoning.

b. Name two pairs of supplementary angles when $\overline{AB}$ and $\overline{DC}$ are parallel. Explain your reasoning.

PROVING A THEOREM In Exercises 15 and 16, prove the theorem. *(See Example 4.)*

15. Alternate Exterior Angles Theorem (Thm. 3.3)

16. Consecutive Interior Angles Theorem (Thm. 3.4)

17. PROBLEM SOLVING A group of campers tie up their food between two parallel trees, as shown. The rope is pulled taut, forming a straight line. Find $m\angle 2$. Explain your reasoning. *(See Example 5.)*

18. DRAWING CONCLUSIONS You are designing a box like the one shown.

a. The measure of $\angle 1$ is 70°. Find $m\angle 2$ and $m\angle 3$.

b. Explain why $\angle ABC$ is a straight angle.

c. If $m\angle 1$ is 60°, will $\angle ABC$ still be a straight angle? Will the opening of the box be *more steep* or *less steep*? Explain.

Maintaining Mathematical Proficiency   Reviewing what you learned in previous grades and lessons

Write the converse of the conditional statement. Decide whether it is true or false. *(Section 2.1)*

25. If two angles are vertical angles, then they are congruent.

26. If you go to the zoo, then you will see a tiger.

27. If two angles form a linear pair, then they are supplementary.

28. If it is warm outside, then we will go to the park.

136   Chapter 3   Parallel and Perpendicular Lines

---

19. CRITICAL THINKING Is it possible for consecutive interior angles to be congruent? Explain.

20. THOUGHT PROVOKING The postulates and theorems in this book represent Euclidean geometry. In spherical geometry, all points are points on the surface of a sphere. A line is a circle on the sphere whose diameter is equal to the diameter of the sphere. In spherical geometry, is it possible that a transversal intersects two parallel lines? Explain your reasoning.

MATHEMATICAL CONNECTIONS In Exercises 21 and 22, write and solve a system of linear equations to find the values of x and y.

21. 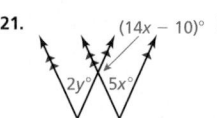   **22.**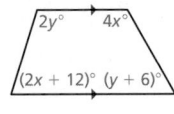

23. MAKING AN ARGUMENT During a game of pool, your friend claims to be able to make the shot shown in the diagram by hitting the cue ball so that $m\angle 1 = 25°$. Is your friend correct? Explain your reasoning.

24. REASONING In the diagram, $\angle 4 \cong \angle 5$ and $\overline{SE}$ bisects $\angle RSF$. Find $m\angle 1$. Explain your reasoning.

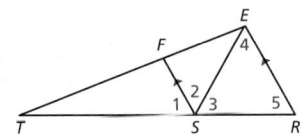

Overview of Section 3.3

Introduction

- This lesson presents a total of five methods for showing that two lines are parallel. The first four methods are converses of statements from the previous lesson. The last method is the Transitive Property of Parallel Lines (Thm. 3.9).
- I find that at about this point it is wise to spiral back to a discussion about deductive reasoning and proof. The list of properties, definitions, theorems, and postulates is starting to get long, and these are the tools available to students in constructing a logical argument.

Common Misconceptions

- **MP3 Construct Viable Arguments and Critique the Reasoning of Others:** Students often use circular reasoning. They will state that two angles are congruent because the lines are parallel, and then they will state that the lines are parallel because the pair of angles is congruent.
- When writing proofs, it is helpful for students to identify the lines that are parallel $\left(\overleftrightarrow{AB} \parallel \overleftrightarrow{CD}\right)$ if they are going to use that relationship to say that $\angle 1 \cong \angle 2$ because they are corresponding angles. That way, when the next step is to conclude that the lines are parallel $\left(\overleftrightarrow{AB} \parallel \overleftrightarrow{CD}\right)$ because corresponding angles are congruent ($\angle 1 \cong \angle 2$), the circular reasoning is more obvious.

Formative Assessment Tips

- **Writing Prompt:** This technique asks students to give feedback at the end of the lesson, activity, or learning experience. The *Writing Prompt* allows you to collect feedback in a short period of time (two minutes) on student learning.
- Used at the end of the class, a *Writing Prompt* is similar to an *Exit Ticket*. The written responses give students time to reflect on their learning, how well they believe they understand the concept or skill, and where they are still uncertain.
- It is important on the following day to share responses with students and let them know how the lesson has been adjusted to reflect their responses. Students need to know that you value their responses and that instruction is modified accordingly. Students will take the writing prompts more seriously when they are valued and used.

Extensions

- Example 4 about the flag of the United States presents an opportunity to integrate historical information into the class. Students love it when I share trivia or "did you know?" information. It is likely there are students in the class who can add to any information that you share.

Pacing Suggestion

- Take time for students to write and discuss the converses in the exploration, and then begin with Example 1 in the formal lesson.

Dynamic Teaching Tools
Dynamic Assessment & Progress Monitoring Tool
Lesson Planning Tool
Interactive Whiteboard Lesson Library
Dynamic Classroom with Dynamic Investigations

Common Core State Standards

HSG-CO.C.9 Prove theorems about lines and angles.

HSG-CO.D.12 Make formal geometric constructions with a variety of tools and methods (compass and straightedge, …).

Laurie's Notes

Exploration

Motivate

? "Given a conditional statement, how do you write the converse?" Interchange the hypothesis and the conclusion. $p \rightarrow q$ becomes $q \rightarrow p$.

- Discuss with partners the converse of each statement. Decide whether the original statement is *true* or *false,* and decide whether the converse is *true* or *false.*

    If today is Tuesday, then tomorrow is Wednesday. statement: true, converse: true
    If $x = 4$, then $x^2 = 16$. statement: true, converse: false
    If you live in California, then you live in San Francisco. statement: false, converse: true
    If $2x + 7 = 11$, then $x = 3$. statement: false, converse: false

    Discuss with students that a statement and its converse may both be true, or not!

Exploration 1

- The converse of a true statement is not always true, as students will recognize in the *Motivate.*
- Students should not have difficulty writing the converse of each statement, and they will likely believe that each converse is true. Justifying their conclusion is where they may struggle. You are listening for reasoning that is more than "the lines look parallel" or "the lines have to be parallel."
- One possibility is to have students construct the diagram using dynamic geometry software. The construction is similar to the compass construction on page 139. The construction involves the following:
    1. Draw a line through two points (A and B).
    2. Draw a transversal through one of the points (B), and label a third point on the transversal (C).
    3. Measure $\angle ABC$.
    4. Now copy the measure of $\angle ABC$ so that the new angle with vertex C is a corresponding angle to $\angle ABC$ (or is an alternate interior angle to $\angle ABC$).
- Students now need to convince themselves that the two lines are parallel. Using a construction tool of the software, they might construct the line through C parallel to $\overleftrightarrow{AB}$ to see that it is the same line as previously constructed.

Communicate Your Answer

- Students should be convinced that all four of the converses are true statements.

Connecting to Next Step

- Now that students have written the converses on their own and are satisfied that they are true statements, they will see the four converses stated as theorems in the formal lesson.

3.3 Proofs with Parallel Lines

Essential Question
For which of the theorems involving parallel lines and transversals is the converse true?

EXPLORATION 1   Exploring Converses

Work with a partner. Write the converse of each conditional statement. Draw a diagram to represent the converse. Determine whether the converse is true. Justify your conclusion.

a. Corresponding Angles Theorem (Theorem 3.1)
If two parallel lines are cut by a transversal, then the pairs of corresponding angles are congruent.

Converse

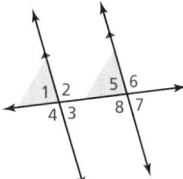

b. Alternate Interior Angles Theorem (Theorem 3.2)
If two parallel lines are cut by a transversal, then the pairs of alternate interior angles are congruent.

Converse

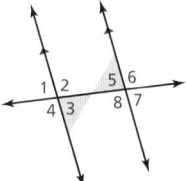

c. Alternate Exterior Angles Theorem (Theorem 3.3)
If two parallel lines are cut by a transversal, then the pairs of alternate exterior angles are congruent.

Converse

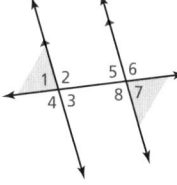

d. Consecutive Interior Angles Theorem (Theorem 3.4)
If two parallel lines are cut by a transversal, then the pairs of consecutive interior angles are supplementary.

Converse

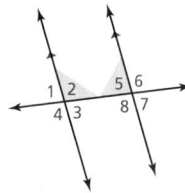

Communicate Your Answer

2. For which of the theorems involving parallel lines and transversals is the converse true?

3. In Exploration 1, explain how you would prove any of the theorems that you found to be true.

ANSWERS

1. **a.** If two lines are cut by a transversal so that the corresponding angles are congruent, then the lines are parallel; The converse is true; Answers will vary.

    b. If two lines are cut by a transversal so that the alternate interior angles are congruent, then the lines are parallel; The converse is true; Answers will vary.

    c. If two lines are cut by a transversal so that the alternate exterior angles are congruent, then the lines are parallel; The converse is true; Answers will vary.

    d. If two lines are cut by a transversal so that the consecutive interior angles are supplementary, then the lines are parallel; The converse is true; Answers will vary.

2. The converse is true for all four of these theorems.

3. If you assume the converse of the Corresponding Angles Theorem (Thm. 3.1), then you can use it to prove the converse of the other three theorems.

Extra Example 1

Find the value of x that makes $m \parallel n$.

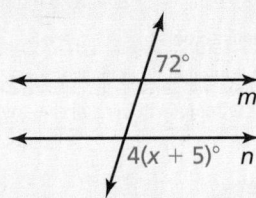

$x = 22$

MONITORING PROGRESS ANSWERS

1. yes; The angle that is corresponding with the 75° angle also forms a linear pair with the 105° angle. So, it must be $180° - 105° = 75°$ by the Linear Pair Postulate (Post. 2.8). Because the corresponding angles have the same measure, they are congruent by definition. So, $m \parallel n$ by the Corresponding Angles Converse (Thm. 3.5).

2. The hypothesis and conclusion of the Corresponding Angles Converse (Thm. 3.5) are the reverse of the Corresponding Angles Theorem (Thm. 3.1).

3.3 Lesson

Core Vocabulary

Previous
converse
parallel lines
transversal
corresponding angles
congruent
alternate interior angles
alternate exterior angles
consecutive interior angles

What You Will Learn

▶ Use the Corresponding Angles Converse.
▶ Construct parallel lines.
▶ Prove theorems about parallel lines.
▶ Use the Transitive Property of Parallel Lines.

Using the Corresponding Angles Converse

Theorem 3.5 below is the converse of the Corresponding Angles Theorem (Theorem 3.1). Similarly, the other theorems about angles formed when parallel lines are cut by a transversal have true converses. Remember that the converse of a true conditional statement is not necessarily true, so you must prove each converse of a theorem.

Theorem

Theorem 3.5   Corresponding Angles Converse

If two lines are cut by a transversal so the corresponding angles are congruent, then the lines are parallel.

Proof Ex. 36, p. 180

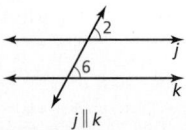

$j \parallel k$

EXAMPLE 1   Using the Corresponding Angles Converse

Find the value of x that makes $m \parallel n$.

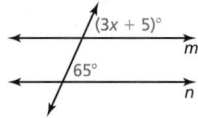

SOLUTION

Lines m and n are parallel when the marked corresponding angles are congruent.

$(3x + 5)° = 65°$	Use the Corresponding Angles Converse to write an equation.
$3x = 60$	Subtract 5 from each side.
$x = 20$	Divide each side by 3.

▶ So, lines m and n are parallel when $x = 20$.

Monitoring Progress 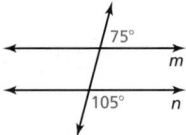 Help in English and Spanish at *BigIdeasMath.com*

1. Is there enough information in the diagram to conclude that $m \parallel n$? Explain.

2. Explain why the Corresponding Angles Converse is the converse of the Corresponding Angles Theorem (Theorem 3.1).

Laurie's Notes   Teacher Actions

• The converse of the Corresponding Angles Theorem (Thm. 3.1) from the previous lesson is also a theorem, the Corresponding Angles Converse (Thm. 3.5). The converses of the other angle theorems are also theorems and are proven to be true using the Corresponding Angles Converse.

? Turn and Talk: "Explain what it means to find a value of x that makes $m \parallel n$." There is one value of x that makes the expression $3x + 5$ equal to 65. If the corresponding angles are congruent, then $m \parallel n$ by the Corresponding Angles Converse.

Constructing Parallel Lines

The Corresponding Angles Converse justifies the construction of parallel lines, as shown below.

CONSTRUCTION **Constructing Parallel Lines**

Use a compass and straightedge to construct a line through point P that is parallel to line m.

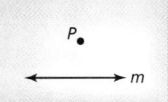

SOLUTION

Step 1	Step 2	Step 3	Step 4
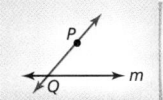	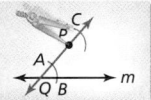	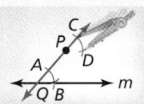	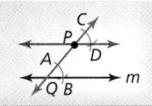
Draw a point and line Start by drawing point P and line m. Choose a point Q anywhere on line m and draw $\overleftrightarrow{QP}$.	**Draw arcs** Draw an arc with center Q that crosses $\overleftrightarrow{QP}$ and line m. Label points A and B. Using the same compass setting, draw an arc with center P. Label point C.	**Copy angle** Draw an arc with radius AB and center A. Using the same compass setting, draw an arc with center C. Label the intersection D.	**Draw parallel lines** Draw $\overleftrightarrow{PD}$. This line is parallel to line m.

Theorems

Theorem 3.6   Alternate Interior Angles Converse

If two lines are cut by a transversal so the alternate interior angles are congruent, then the lines are parallel.

Proof Example 2, p. 140

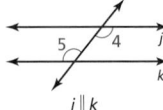

$j \parallel k$

Theorem 3.7   Alternate Exterior Angles Converse

If two lines are cut by a transversal so the alternate exterior angles are congruent, then the lines are parallel.

Proof Ex. 11, p. 142

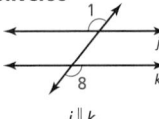

$j \parallel k$

Theorem 3.8   Consecutive Interior Angles Converse

If two lines are cut by a transversal so the consecutive interior angles are supplementary, then the lines are parallel.

Proof Ex. 12, p. 142

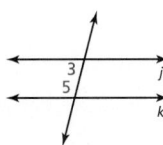

If $\angle 3$ and $\angle 5$ are supplementary, then $j \parallel k$.

Section 3.3   Proofs with Parallel Lines   **139**

Laurie's Notes   Teacher Actions

? "What evidence is needed for you to know that constructed lines are parallel?" Corresponding angles will have to be congruent.

- Make a note of the names for these theorems. They are all converses of previously proven theorems. In the original theorems, lines were parallel and we concluded a relationship about angles. In the converses, the angle relationship is known and we conclude the lines are parallel.

Extra Example 2

Prove the Alternate Interior Angles Converse without using the Vertical Angles Congruence Theorem.

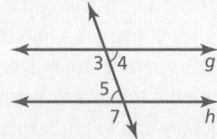

Given $\angle 4 \cong \angle 5$
Prove $g \parallel h$
Statements (Reasons)
1. $\angle 4 \cong \angle 5$ (Given)
2. $\angle 4$ is supplementary to $\angle 3$. (Linear Pair Post. 2.8)
3. $\angle 5$ is supplementary to $\angle 7$. (Linear Pair Post. 2.8)
4. $\angle 3 \cong \angle 7$ (Congr. Suppl. Thm. 2.4)
5. $g \parallel h$ (Corr. $\angle$s Converse 3.5)

Extra Example 3

In the diagram, $p \parallel q$ and $\angle 1$ is supplementary to $\angle 2$. Prove $r \parallel s$ using a paragraph proof.

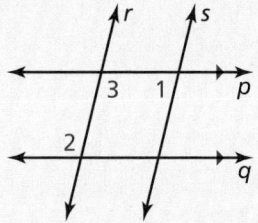

It is given that $\angle 1$ is supplementary to $\angle 2$. So $m\angle 1 + m\angle 2 = 180°$ by the definition of supp. $\angle$s. It is given that $p \parallel q$, so by the Alternate Interior Angles Theorem (Thm.3.2), $\angle 2 \cong \angle 3$. By the def. of $\cong$ $\angle$s, $m\angle 2 = m\angle 3$. By the Substitution Prop., $m\angle 1 + m\angle 3 = 180°$. So $\angle 1$ and $\angle 3$ are supplementary by the def. of supp. $\angle$s. Then, by the Consecutive Interior Angles Converse (Thm. 3.8), $r \parallel s$.

Proving Theorems about Parallel Lines

EXAMPLE 2   **Proving the Alternate Interior Angles Converse**

Prove that if two lines are cut by a transversal so the alternate interior angles are congruent, then the lines are parallel.

SOLUTION

Given $\angle 4 \cong \angle 5$
Prove $g \parallel h$

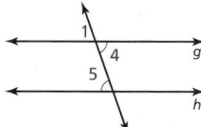

STATEMENTS	REASONS
1. $\angle 4 \cong \angle 5$	1. Given
2. $\angle 1 \cong \angle 4$	2. Vertical Angles Congruence Theorem (Theorem 2.6)
3. $\angle 1 \cong \angle 5$	3. Transitive Property of Congruence (Theorem 2.2)
4. $g \parallel h$	4. Corresponding Angles Converse

EXAMPLE 3   **Determining Whether Lines Are Parallel**

In the diagram, $r \parallel s$ and $\angle 1$ is congruent to $\angle 3$. Prove $p \parallel q$.

SOLUTION

Look at the diagram to make a plan. The diagram suggests that you look at angles 1, 2, and 3. Also, you may find it helpful to focus on one pair of lines and one transversal at a time.

Plan for Proof   **a.** Look at $\angle 1$ and $\angle 2$. $\angle 1 \cong \angle 2$ because $r \parallel s$.
                     b. Look at $\angle 2$ and $\angle 3$. If $\angle 2 \cong \angle 3$, then $p \parallel q$.

Plan for Action   **a.** It is given that $r \parallel s$, so by the Corresponding Angles Theorem (Theorem 3.1), $\angle 1 \cong \angle 2$.
                     b. It is also given that $\angle 1 \cong \angle 3$. Then $\angle 2 \cong \angle 3$ by the Transitive Property of Congruence (Theorem 2.2).

▶   So, by the Alternate Interior Angles Converse, $p \parallel q$.

Monitoring Progress Help in English and Spanish at *BigIdeasMath.com*

3. If you use the diagram below to prove the Alternate Exterior Angles Converse, what **Given** and **Prove** statements would you use?

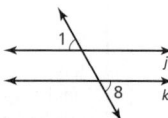

4. Copy and complete the following paragraph proof of the Alternate Interior Angles Converse using the diagram in Example 2.

It is given that $\angle 4 \cong \angle 5$. By the _____, $\angle 1 \cong \angle 4$. Then by the Transitive Property of Congruence (Theorem 2.2), _____. So, by the _____, $g \parallel h$.

Laurie's Notes   Teacher Actions

- **MP3:** To prove the Alternate Interior Angles Converse (Thm. 3.6), the only method available is to use the Corresponding Angles Converse (Thm 3.5). Once proven, there are two methods available to use as justification. Proofs of the remaining theorems are left for the exercise set.
- In Example 3, labeling $\angle 2$ is a hint that you may want to eliminate for some students.
- **? Teaching Tip:** Cover the top part of the diagram so that line p is not seen. "What do you know about $\angle 1$ when $r \parallel s$?" $\angle 1 \cong \angle 2$
- **Think-Pair-Share:** Have students work on *Monitoring Progress* and then check with their partners.

Using the Transitive Property of Parallel Lines

⟳ Theorem

Theorem 3.9   Transitive Property of Parallel Lines

If two lines are parallel to the same line,
then they are parallel to each other.

Proof Ex. 39, p. 144; Ex. 48, p. 162

If $p \parallel q$ and $q \parallel r$, then $p \parallel r$.

EXAMPLE 4   Using the Transitive Property of Parallel Lines

The flag of the United States has 13 alternating red and white stripes. Each stripe is parallel to the stripe immediately below it. Explain why the top stripe is parallel to the bottom stripe.

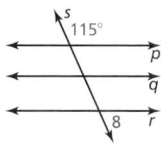

SOLUTION

You can name the stripes from top to bottom as $s_1, s_2, s_3, \ldots, s_{13}$. Each stripe is parallel to the one immediately below it, so $s_1 \parallel s_2$, $s_2 \parallel s_3$, and so on. Then $s_1 \parallel s_3$ by the Transitive Property of Parallel Lines. Similarly, because $s_3 \parallel s_4$, it follows that $s_1 \parallel s_4$. By continuing this reasoning, $s_1 \parallel s_{13}$.

▶   So, the top stripe is parallel to the bottom stripe.

Monitoring Progress 🔊 Help in English and Spanish at *BigIdeasMath.com*

5. Each step is parallel to the step immediately above it. The bottom step is parallel to the ground. Explain why the top step is parallel to the ground.

6. In the diagram below, $p \parallel q$ and $q \parallel r$. Find $m\angle 8$. Explain your reasoning.

Extra Example 4

Each parking space in a lot is defined by two parallel lines and shares a common line with the next adjacent space. Explain why the left line in space 02 is parallel to the right line in space 08.

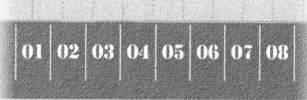

The left and right sides of space 02 are parallel. The right side of space 02 is parallel to the right side of space 03, which is parallel to the right side of 04, and so on. By the Transitive Property of Parallel Lines (Thm. 3.9), the left line in space 02 is parallel to the right line in space 08.

MONITORING PROGRESS ANSWERS

5. Using the Transitive Property of Parallel Lines (Theorem 3.9) over and over again, you can show that the ground is parallel to the step above it and the one above that, and so on, until you have stated that the line formed by the ground is parallel to the line formed by the top step.

6. $m\angle 8 = 65°$; By the Transitive Property of Parallel Lines (Thm. 3.9), $p \parallel r$. By the Corresponding Angles Theorem (Thm 3.1), the angle at the intersection of line r and line s that is corresponding with the 115° angle would also have a measure of 115°. This angle also forms a linear pair with $\angle 8$. So, by the Linear Pair Postulate (Post. 2.8), $m\angle 8 = 180° - 115° = 65°$.

ASSIGNMENT

Basic: 1, 2, 3–27 odd, 33, 37, 38, 41–44

Average: 1, 2–30 even, 35, 37, 38, 41–44

Advanced: 1, 2, 8, 12, 16–34 even, 36–38, 40–44

HOMEWORK CHECK

Basic: 1, 3, 9, 15, 21

Average: 8, 18, 24, 28, 35

Advanced: 8, 20, 28, 36, 40

Vocabulary and Core Concept Check

1. **VOCABULARY** Two lines are cut by a transversal. Which angle pairs must be congruent for the lines to be parallel?

2. **WRITING** Use the theorems from Section 3.2 and the converses of those theorems in this section to write three biconditional statements about parallel lines and transversals.

Monitoring Progress and Modeling with Mathematics

In Exercises 3–8, find the value of *x* that makes *m* ∥ *n*. Explain your reasoning. *(See Example 1.)*

3.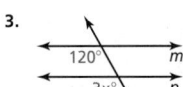

4.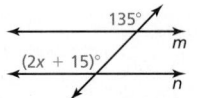

5.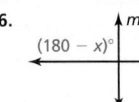

6.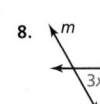

7.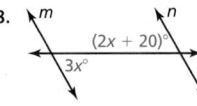

8.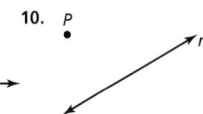

In Exercises 9 and 10, use a compass and straightedge to construct a line through point *P* that is parallel to line *m*.

9. *P*
    •

    m ←——————→

10. *P*
    •   ↗ *m*

PROVING A THEOREM In Exercises 11 and 12, prove the theorem. *(See Example 2.)*

11. Alternate Exterior Angles Converse (Theorem 3.7)

12. Consecutive Interior Angles Converse (Theorem 3.8)

In Exercises 13–18, decide whether there is enough information to prove that *m* ∥ *n*. If so, state the theorem you would use. *(See Example 3.)*

13.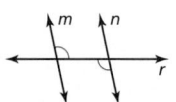

14.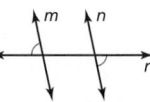

15.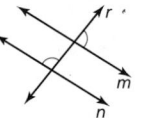

16.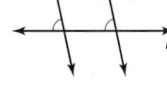

17.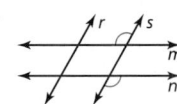

18.

ERROR ANALYSIS In Exercises 19 and 20, describe and correct the error in the reasoning.

19.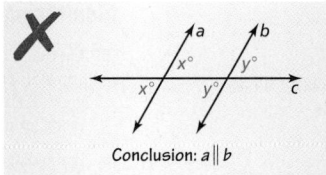

    Conclusion: *a* ∥ *b*

20.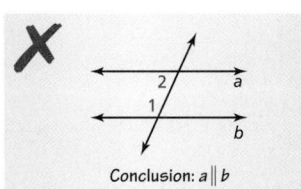

    Conclusion: *a* ∥ *b*

142   Chapter 3   Parallel and Perpendicular Lines

1. corresponding, alternate interior, alternate exterior

2. *Sample answer:* Two lines cut by a transversal are parallel if and only if the corresponding angles are congruent. Two lines cut by a transversal are parallel if and only if the alternate interior angles are congruent. Two lines cut by a transversal are parallel if and only if the consecutive interior angles are supplementary.

3. $x = 40$; Lines *m* and *n* are parallel when the marked corresponding angles are congruent.

    $3x° = 120°$

    $x = 40$

4. $x = 60$; Lines *m* and *n* are parallel when the marked corresponding angles are congruent.

    $(2x + 15)° = 135°$

    $2x = 120$

    $x = 60$

5. $x = 15$; Lines *m* and *n* are parallel when the marked consecutive interior angles are supplementary.

    $(3x - 15)° + 150° = 180°$

    $3x + 135 = 180$

    $3x = 45$

    $x = 15$

6. $x = 90$; Lines *m* and *n* are parallel when the marked alternate exterior angles are congruent.

    $(180 - x)° = x°$

    $180 = 2x$

    $90 = x$

7. $x = 60$; Lines *m* and *n* are parallel when the marked consecutive interior angles are supplementary.

    $2x° + x° = 180°$

    $3x = 180$

    $x = 60$

8. $x = 20$; Lines *m* and *n* are parallel when the marked alternate interior angles are congruent.

    $(2x + 20)° = 3x°$

    $20 = x$

9.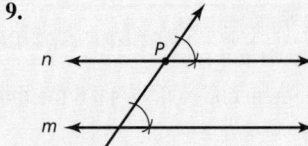

10.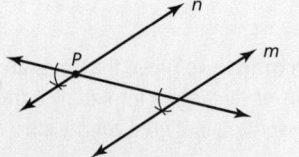

11–20. See Additional Answers.

In Exercises 21–24, are $\overleftrightarrow{AC}$ and $\overleftrightarrow{DF}$ parallel? Explain your reasoning.

21.
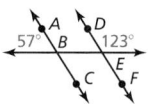

22.
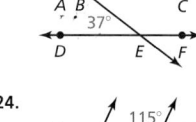

23.
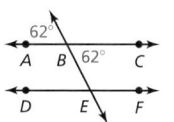

24.
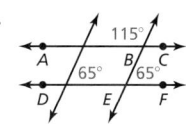

25. **ANALYZING RELATIONSHIPS** The map shows part of Denver, Colorado. Use the markings on the map. Are the numbered streets parallel to one another? Explain your reasoning. *(See Example 4.)*

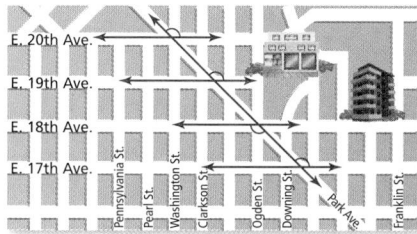

26. **ANALYZING RELATIONSHIPS** Each rung of the ladder is parallel to the rung directly above it. Explain why the top rung is parallel to the bottom rung.

27. **MODELING WITH MATHEMATICS** The diagram of the control bar of the kite shows the angles formed between the control bar and the kite lines. How do you know that n is parallel to m?

28. **REASONING** Use the diagram. Which rays are parallel? Which rays are not parallel? Explain your reasoning.

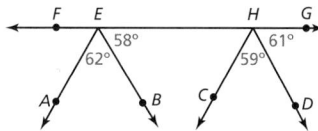

29. **ATTENDING TO PRECISION** Use the diagram. Which theorems allow you to conclude that $m \parallel n$? Select all that apply. Explain your reasoning.

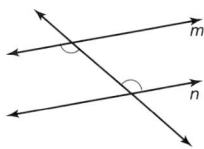

- Ⓐ Corresponding Angles Converse (Thm. 3.5)
- Ⓑ Alternate Interior Angles Converse (Thm. 3.6)
- Ⓒ Alternate Exterior Angles Converse (Thm. 3.7)
- Ⓓ Consecutive Interior Angles Converse (Thm. 3.8)

30. **MODELING WITH MATHEMATICS** One way to build stairs is to attach triangular blocks to an angled support, as shown. The sides of the angled support are parallel. If the support makes a 32° angle with the floor, what must $m\angle 1$ be so the top of the step will be parallel to the floor? Explain your reasoning.

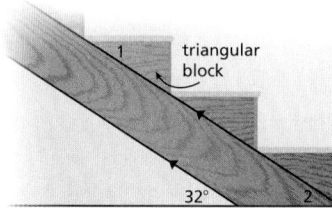

31. **ABSTRACT REASONING** In the diagram, how many angles must be given to determine whether $j \parallel k$? Give four examples that would allow you to conclude that $j \parallel k$ using the theorems from this lesson.

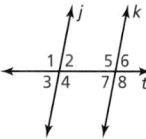

28. $\overrightarrow{EA} \parallel \overrightarrow{HC}$ by the Corresponding Angles Converse (Thm. 3.5).
$\angle AEH \cong \angle CHG$ by definition because $m\angle AEH = 62° + 58° = 120°$ and $m\angle CHG = 59° + 61° = 120°$.
However, $\overrightarrow{EB}$ is not parallel to $\overrightarrow{HD}$ because corresponding angles $\angle BEH$ and $\angle DHG$ do not have the same measure and are therefore not congruent.

29. See Additional Answers.

30. $m\angle 1 = 32°$; The 32° angle that is marked is corresponding with $\angle 2$. So, $m\angle 2 = 32°$ by the Corresponding Angles Theorem (Thm. 3.1). Considering the line formed by the top of the step and the line formed by the floor, $\angle 1$ and $\angle 2$ are alternate interior angles. So, if $\angle 1 \cong \angle 2$, then the top of the step will be parallel to the floor by the Alternate Interior Angles Converse (Thm. 3.6).

31. two; *Sample answer:* $\angle 1 \cong \angle 5$, $\angle 2 \cong \angle 7$, $\angle 3 \cong \angle 6$, $\angle 4$ and $\angle 7$ are supplementary

ANSWERS

21. yes; $m\angle DEB = 180° - 123° = 57°$ by the Linear Pair Postulate (Post. 2.8). So, by definition, a pair of corresponding angles are congruent, which means that $\overleftrightarrow{AC} \parallel \overleftrightarrow{DF}$ by the Corresponding Angles Converse (Thm. 3.5).

22. yes; $m\angle BEF = 180° - 37° = 143°$ by the Linear Pair Postulate (Post. 2.8). So, by definition, a pair of corresponding angles are congruent, which means that $\overleftrightarrow{AC} \parallel \overleftrightarrow{DF}$ by the Corresponding Angles Converse (Thm. 3.5).

23. cannot be determined; The marked angles are vertical angles. You do not know anything about the angles formed by the intersection of $\overleftrightarrow{DF}$ and $\overleftrightarrow{BE}$.

24. yes; $m\angle EBC = 115°$ by the Vertical Angles Congruence Theorem (Thm. 2.6). Because $m\angle EBC + m\angle FEB = 115° + 65° = 180°$, $\angle EBC$ and $\angle FEB$ are supplementary by definition, which means that $\overleftrightarrow{AC} \parallel \overleftrightarrow{DF}$ by the Consecutive Interior Angles Converse (Thm. 3.8).

25. yes; E. 20th Ave. is parallel to E. 19th Ave. by the Corresponding Angles Converse (Thm. 3.5). E. 19th Ave. is parallel to E. 18th Ave. by the Alternate Exterior Angles Converse (Thm. 3.7). E. 18th Ave. is parallel to E. 17th Ave. by the Alternate Interior Angles Converse (Thm. 3.6). So, they are all parallel to each other by the Transitive Property of Parallel Lines (Thm. 3.9).

26. All of the rungs are parallel to each other by the Transitive Property of Parallel Lines (Thm. 3.9).

27. The two angles marked as 108° are corresponding angles. Because they have the same measure, they are congruent to each other. So, $m \parallel n$ by the Corresponding Angles Converse (Thm. 3.5).

ANSWERS

32–44. See Additional Answers.

Mini-Assessment

1. Find the value of x that makes $m \parallel n$.

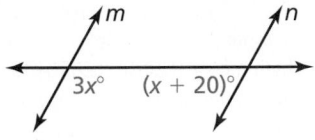

$x = 40$

2. Sketch a horizontal line m with point P below m. Construct a line through P that is parallel to line m.

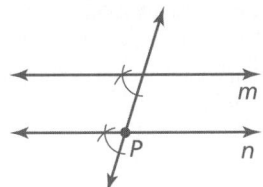

3. Write a two-column proof.
   Given $\angle 1 \cong \angle 3$
   Prove $j \parallel k$

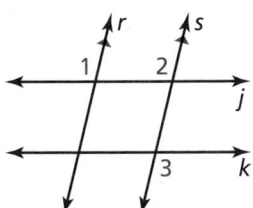

Statements (Reasons)
1. $\angle 1 \cong \angle 3$ (Given)
2. $\angle 1 \cong \angle 2$ (Corr. $\angle$s Thm. 3.1)
3. $\angle 2 \cong \angle 3$ (Trans. Prop. $\cong$ 2.2)
4. $j \parallel k$ (Alt. Ext. $\angle$s Conv. Thm. 3.7)

4. In the diagram, $p \parallel q$ and $q \parallel r$. Find the value of x. Explain your reasoning.

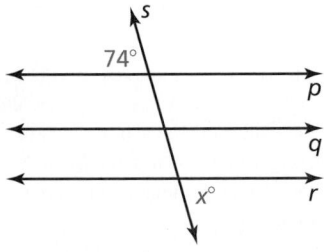

$x = 74$; by the Trans. Prop. of Parallel Lines (Thm. 3.9), $p \parallel r$. By the Alt. Ext. $\angle$s Theorem (Thm. 3.3), $x = 74$.

---

32. **THOUGHT PROVOKING** Draw a diagram of at least two lines cut by at least one transversal. Mark your diagram so that it cannot be proven that any lines are parallel. Then explain how your diagram would need to change in order to prove that lines are parallel.

PROOF In Exercises 33–36, write a proof.

33. **Given** $m\angle 1 = 115°$, $m\angle 2 = 65°$
    Prove $m \parallel n$

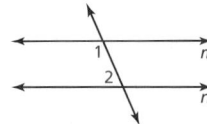

34. **Given** $\angle 1$ and $\angle 3$ are supplementary.
    Prove $m \parallel n$

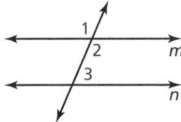

35. **Given** $\angle 1 \cong \angle 2$, $\angle 3 \cong \angle 4$
    Prove $\overline{AB} \parallel \overline{CD}$

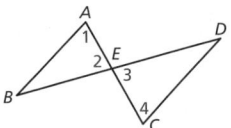

36. **Given** $a \parallel b$, $\angle 2 \cong \angle 3$
    Prove $c \parallel d$

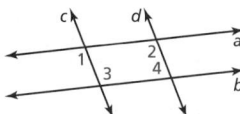

37. **MAKING AN ARGUMENT** Your classmate decided that $\overrightarrow{AD} \parallel \overrightarrow{BC}$ based on the diagram. Is your classmate correct? Explain your reasoning.

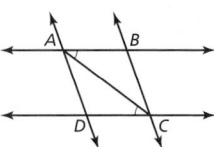

38. **HOW DO YOU SEE IT?** Are the markings on the diagram enough to conclude that any lines are parallel? If so, which ones? If not, what other information is needed?

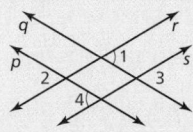

39. **PROVING A THEOREM** Use these steps to prove the Transitive Property of Parallel Lines Theorem (Theorem 3.9).

    a. Copy the diagram with the Transitive Property of Parallel Lines Theorem on page 141.

    b. Write the **Given** and **Prove** statements.

    c. Use the properties of angles formed by parallel lines cut by a transversal to prove the theorem.

40. **MATHEMATICAL CONNECTIONS** Use the diagram.

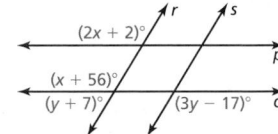

    a. Find the value of x that makes $p \parallel q$.

    b. Find the value of y that makes $r \parallel s$.

    c. Can r be parallel to s and can p be parallel to q at the same time? Explain your reasoning.

Maintaining Mathematical Proficiency
Reviewing what you learned in previous grades and lessons

Use the Distance Formula to find the distance between the two points. *(Section 1.3)*

41. $(1, 3)$ and $(-2, 9)$

42. $(-3, 7)$ and $(8, -6)$

43. $(5, -4)$ and $(0, 8)$

44. $(13, 1)$ and $(9, -4)$

If students need help...	If students got it...
Resources by Chapter • Practice A and Practice B • Puzzle Time	**Resources by Chapter** • Enrichment and Extension • Cumulative Review
Student Journal • Practice	Start the *next* Section
Differentiating the Lesson Skills Review Handbook	

Core Vocabulary

parallel lines, *p. 126*
skew lines, *p. 126*
parallel planes, *p. 126*
transversal, *p. 128*

corresponding angles, *p. 128*
alternate interior angles, *p. 128*
alternate exterior angles, *p. 128*
consecutive interior angles, *p. 128*

Core Concepts

Section 3.1

Parallel Lines, Skew Lines, and Parallel Planes, *p. 126*
Postulate 3.1 Parallel Postulate, *p. 127*

Postulate 3.2 Perpendicular Postulate, *p. 127*
Angles Formed by Transversals, *p. 128*

Section 3.2

Theorem 3.1 Corresponding Angles Theorem, *p. 132*
Theorem 3.2 Alternate Interior Angles Theorem, *p. 132*

Theorem 3.3 Alternate Exterior Angles Theorem,
  p. 132
Theorem 3.4 Consecutive Interior Angles Theorem,
  p. 132

Section 3.3

Theorem 3.5 Corresponding Angles Converse, *p. 138*
Theorem 3.6 Alternate Interior Angles Converse,
  p. 139
Theorem 3.7 Alternate Exterior Angles Converse,
  p. 139

Theorem 3.8 Consecutive Interior Angles Converse,
  p. 139
Theorem 3.9 Transitive Property of Parallel Lines,
  p. 141

Mathematical Practices

1. Draw the portion of the diagram that you used to answer Exercise 26 on page 130.

2. In Exercise 40 on page 144, explain how you started solving the problem and why you started that way.

- - - - - - - - Study Skills - - - - - - - -

Analyzing Your Errors

Misreading Directions

- **What Happens:** You incorrectly read or do not understand directions.

- **How to Avoid This Error:** Read the instructions for exercises at least twice and make sure you understand what they mean. Make this a habit and use it when taking tests.

145

Dynamic Teaching Tools

Dynamic Assessment & Progress Monitoring Tool

Interactive Whiteboard Lesson Library

Dynamic Classroom with Dynamic Investigations

ANSWERS

1.
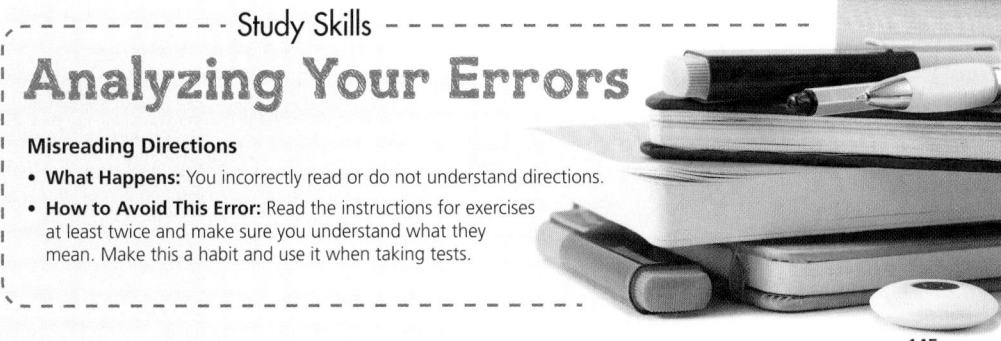

2. For part (a), start by writing the equation $(2x + 2)° = (x + 56)°$, because the angles represented by these two expressions are corresponding angles with respect to lines p and q. So, in order for lines p and q to be parallel by the Corresponding Angles Theorem (Thm. 3.1), the expressions must be equal to each other. For part (b), start by writing the equation $(y + 7)° + (3y − 17)° = 180°$. In order for lines r and s to be parallel, the angles represented by these two expressions must be supplementary because each one forms a linear pair with one of the consecutive interior angles formed by lines r and s and transversal q.

ANSWERS

1. $\overleftrightarrow{HG}$
2. $\overrightarrow{FG}$
3. $\overleftrightarrow{CG}$
4. plane BCG
5. $\angle 3$ and $\angle 5$, $\angle 4$ and $\angle 6$
6. $\angle 3$ and $\angle 6$, $\angle 4$ and $\angle 5$
7. $\angle 1$ and $\angle 5$, $\angle 2$ and $\angle 6$, $\angle 3$ and $\angle 7$, $\angle 4$ and $\angle 8$
8. $\angle 1$ and $\angle 8$, $\angle 2$ and $\angle 7$
9. $m\angle 1 = 42°$ by the Linear Pair Postulate (Post. 2.8); $m\angle 2 = 42°$ by the Alternate Exterior Angles Theorem (Thm. 3.3).
10. $m\angle 1 = 123°$ by the Corresponding Angles Theorem (Thm. 3.1); $m\angle 2 = 123°$ by the Vertical Angles Congruence Theorem (Thm. 2.6).
11. $m\angle 1 = 123°$ by the Linear Pair Postulate (Post. 2.8); $m\angle 2 = 57°$ by the Alternate Interior Angles Theorem (Thm. 3.2).
12. yes; Consecutive Interior Angles Converse (Thm. 3.8)
13. no
14. yes; Transitive Property of Parallel Lines (Thm 3.9)
15. a. All of the bars are parallel to each other by the Transitive Property of Parallel Lines (Thm. 3.9).
    b. $m\angle 2 = 58°$
16. a. *Sample answer:* $p \parallel q, k \parallel m$
    b. *Sample answer:* $k \perp n, n \perp m$
    c. *Sample answer:* lines q and m, lines ℓ and k
    d. Because $m \parallel k$, $\angle 1 \cong \angle 2$ by the Alternate Exterior Angles Theorem (Thm. 3.3).

Think of each segment in the diagram as part of a line. Which line(s) or plane(s) contain point G and appear to fit the description? *(Section 3.1)*

1. line(s) parallel to $\overleftrightarrow{EF}$
2. line(s) perpendicular to $\overleftrightarrow{EF}$
3. line(s) skew to $\overleftrightarrow{EF}$
4. plane(s) parallel to plane ADE

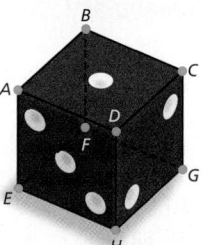

Identify all pairs of angles of the given type. *(Section 3.1)*

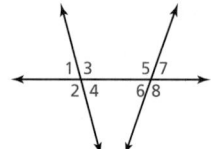

5. consecutive interior
6. alternate interior
7. corresponding
8. alternate exterior

Find $m\angle 1$ and $m\angle 2$. Tell which theorem you use in each case. *(Section 3.2)*

9.
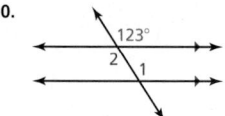

10.
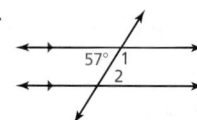

11.
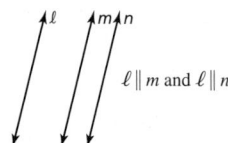

Decide whether there is enough information to prove that $m \parallel n$. If so, state the theorem you would use. *(Section 3.3)*

12.
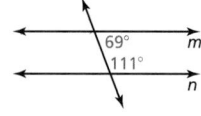

13.
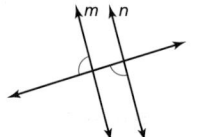

14.
$\ell \parallel m$ and $\ell \parallel n$

15. Cellular phones use bars like the ones shown to indicate how much signal strength a phone receives from the nearest service tower. Each bar is parallel to the bar directly next to it. *(Section 3.3)*
    a. Explain why the tallest bar is parallel to the shortest bar.
    b. Imagine that the left side of each bar extends infinitely as a line. If $m\angle 1 = 58°$, then what is $m\angle 2$?

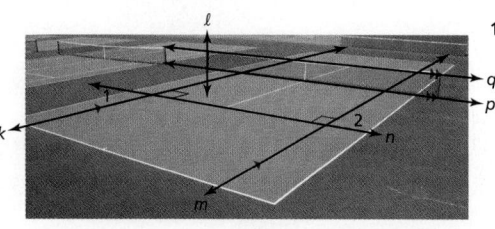

16. The diagram shows lines formed on a tennis court. *(Section 3.1 and Section 3.3)*
    a. Identify two pairs of parallel lines so that each pair is in a different plane.
    b. Identify two pairs of perpendicular lines.
    c. Identify two pairs of skew lines.
    d. Prove that $\angle 1 \cong \angle 2$.

Laurie's Notes

Overview of Section 3.4

Introduction

- This lesson presents three theorems, two constructions, and a definition—all related to perpendicular lines. There is an additional construction in the explorations. Similar to the previous lesson, the goal is to consider under what conditions two lines will be perpendicular.
- The lesson begins with finding the distance from a point to a line, requiring students to recall the Distance Formula.
- In performing the constructions, it is helpful to remind students that they are making congruent segments when an arc intersects a line in two locations. This is not obvious because the congruent segments are not drawn.
- The three theorems about perpendicular lines will take time to discuss, sketch, and prove.

Common Misconceptions

- **MP3 Construct Viable Arguments and Critique the Reasoning of Others:** Students often use circular reasoning. In Example 2, when you ask students how they can prove two lines are perpendicular, they may say by using the Perpendicular Transversal Theorem (Thm 3.11). This is the theorem they are trying to prove!

Formative Assessment Tips

- **Point of Most Significance:** This technique asks students to identify the most significant idea, learning, or concept they gained in the lesson today. Students reflect on the lesson and are asked to identify the key example, problem, or point that was significant in their learning today. If the goal or learning intention was identified at the beginning of the class, students assess what contributed to their attainment of the goal.
- It is important for teachers to know whether the lesson as designed helped move learning forward for students or whether the lesson needs to be modified. Share with students what you learned from their reflections. Students will take the reflections more seriously when they are valued and used.

Another Way

- Students may feel that Example 2 is a tedious theorem to prove. There is a need to change from angles being congruent to angle measures being equal. Statements 2 and 4 are what allow statement 5 to be made. This is a proof for which a paragraph or flowchart proof might make more sense to students.

Pacing Suggestion

- The explorations will not take long for students to do and then discuss. If you wish, you could wait and do Exploration 3, a construction, in the formal lesson when other constructions are done.

**Common Core
State Standards**

HSG-CO.C.9 Prove theorems about lines and angles.

HSG-CO.D.12 Make formal geometric constructions with a variety of tools and methods (compass and straightedge, ... paper folding, ...)

Exploration

Motivate
- Borrow a plumb line from the custodial staff. Stand on a chair and hold the plumb line extended from your body.
- **?** *"What is a plumb line, and what is it used for?"* You should hear a variety of purposes for the plumb line, all of them related to finding a true vertical.
- Hold the plumb line next to a wall and demonstrate how to draw a vertical line to the floor, one that should be perpendicular to the edge of the floor!
- There are online videos if you prefer not to do the demonstration yourself.
- The goal is to have a discussion of the word *perpendicular* and how you know whether two lines or two segments are perpendicular.

Exploration 1
- Use scrap paper and have partners make the folds and answer the questions. Students will say that segments $\overline{AB}$ and $\overline{CD}$ are perpendicular and that $\overline{AO}$ and $\overline{OB}$ have the same length.
- **Popsicle Sticks:** Ask students how they justified their conjectures. For the perpendicular segments, they may say something about the right angles formed when there were four layers of paper. They may use a protractor. They may also refer to the edges of the rectangular paper. Not all justifications will be valid! To justify why the segments have the same length, students may show how one segment folds on top of the other when creased. They may even use the word *reflected*.
- **MP3:** The goal is for students to develop the ability to construct viable arguments and not simply say, "Because they look perpendicular."

Exploration 2
- The exploration is the same as the last, but it is not as easy for students to visualize. It differs in that there are no longer edges of the paper for students to refer to in their justifications.
- Students may again refer to the four layers of paper and the four congruent angles so that each angle is 90°.
- The conjecture that is not as obvious is that a segment has been bisected. The second crease is the perpendicular bisector of $\overline{AB}$.

Exploration 3
- The last exploration is the construction of a perpendicular bisector. While the proof of this construction depends on congruent triangles, students should still be able to write a conjecture and also offer thoughts as to why their conjecture is valid.

Communicate Your Answer
- Students should mention that perpendicular lines form four right angles and bisectors divide a segment into two congruent segments.

Connecting to Next Step
- The explorations give students time to explore relationships about perpendicular lines. Once explored, students will be better able to consider deductive proofs about perpendicular lines.

3.4 Proofs with Perpendicular Lines

Essential Question What conjectures can you make about perpendicular lines?

EXPLORATION 1 Writing Conjectures

Work with a partner. Fold a piece of paper in half twice. Label points on the two creases, as shown.

a. Write a conjecture about $\overline{AB}$ and $\overline{CD}$. Justify your conjecture.

b. Write a conjecture about $\overline{AO}$ and $\overline{OB}$. Justify your conjecture.

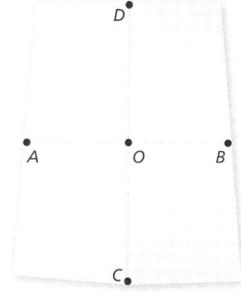

EXPLORATION 2 Exploring a Segment Bisector

Work with a partner. Fold and crease a piece of paper, as shown. Label the ends of the crease as A and B.

a. Fold the paper again so that point A coincides with point B. Crease the paper on that fold.

b. Unfold the paper and examine the four angles formed by the two creases. What can you conclude about the four angles?

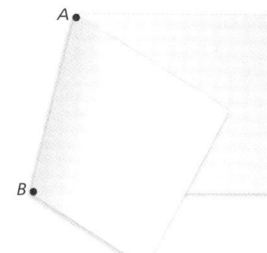

EXPLORATION 3 Writing a Conjecture

Work with a partner.

a. Draw $\overline{AB}$, as shown.

b. Draw an arc with center A on each side of $\overline{AB}$. Using the same compass setting, draw an arc with center B on each side of $\overline{AB}$. Label the intersections of the arcs C and D.

c. Draw $\overline{CD}$. Label its intersection with $\overline{AB}$ as O. Write a conjecture about the resulting diagram. Justify your conjecture.

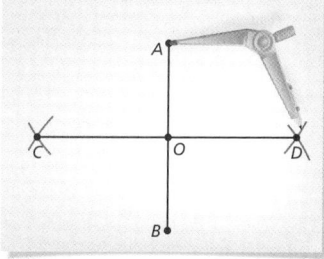

CONSTRUCTING VIABLE ARGUMENTS

To be proficient in math, you need to make conjectures and build a logical progression of statements to explore the truth of your conjectures.

Communicate Your Answer

4. What conjectures can you make about perpendicular lines?

5. In Exploration 3, find AO and OB when $AB = 4$ units.

ANSWERS

1. a. $\overline{AB} \perp \overline{CD}$; $\overline{AB}$ is parallel to the horizontal edge of the paper because points A, O, and B are all the same distance from the edge. Similarly, $\overline{CD}$ is parallel to the vertical edge of the paper because points C, O, and D are the same distance from the edge. The horizontal and vertical edges form right angles in the corners. So, lines parallel to them will also be perpendicular.

   b. $\overline{AO} \cong \overline{OB}$; Point O must be the midpoint of $\overline{AB}$ because the paper was folded in half. So, $\overline{AO}$ and $\overline{OB}$ are congruent by definition of midpoint.

2. a. Check students' work.

   b. They are all right angles.

3. a. Check students' work.

   b. Check students' work.

   c. Check students' work; $\overline{CD}$ is perpendicular to $\overline{AB}$, and point O is the midpoint of $\overline{AB}$. Point C is the same distance from A as it is from B, and D is the same distance from A as it is from B. So, the segment connecting C and D contains all the points that are equidistant from points A and B.

4. *Sample answer:* If you have a segment, and you fold it in half so that both halves match, the fold will be perpendicular to the segment. When lines are perpendicular, all four angles are right angles. If two lines intersect to form a linear pair of congruent angles, then the lines are perpendicular. In a plane, if a transversal is perpendicular to one of the two parallel lines, then it is perpendicular to the other line. Finally, in a plane, if two lines are perpendicular to the same line, then they are parallel to each other.

5. $AO = OB = 2$ units

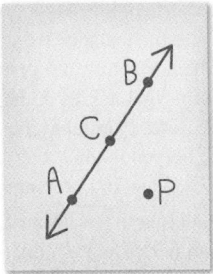
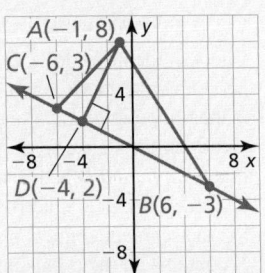
3.4 Lesson

Core Vocabulary

distance from a point to a line, *p. 148*
perpendicular bisector, *p. 149*

REMEMBER

Recall that if $A(x_1, y_1)$ and $C(x_2, y_2)$ are points in a coordinate plane, then the distance between A and C is
$$AC = \sqrt{(x_2 - x_1)^2 + (y_2 - y_1)^2}.$$

What You Will Learn

▶ Find the distance from a point to a line.
▶ Construct perpendicular lines.
▶ Prove theorems about perpendicular lines.
▶ Solve real-life problems involving perpendicular lines.

Finding the Distance from a Point to a Line

The **distance from a point to a line** is the length of the perpendicular segment from the point to the line. This perpendicular segment is the shortest distance between the point and the line. For example, the distance between point A and line k is AB.

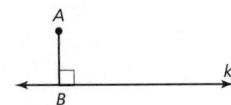

distance from a point to a line

EXAMPLE 1 Finding the Distance from a Point to a Line

Find the distance from point A to $\overleftrightarrow{BD}$.

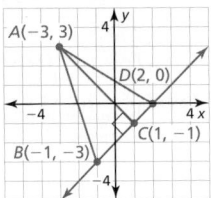

SOLUTION

Because $\overline{AC} \perp \overleftrightarrow{BD}$, the distance from point A to $\overleftrightarrow{BD}$ is AC. Use the Distance Formula.

$$AC = \sqrt{(-3 - 1)^2 + [3 - (-1)]^2} = \sqrt{(-4)^2 + 4^2} = \sqrt{32} \approx 5.7$$

▶ So, the distance from point A to $\overleftrightarrow{BD}$ is about 5.7 units.

Monitoring Progress Help in English and Spanish at *BigIdeasMath.com*

1. Find the distance from point E to $\overleftrightarrow{FH}$.

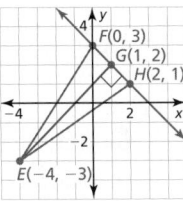

Laurie's Notes Teacher Actions

- **Connection:** Discuss the altitude of an airplane or the altitude of a triangle. The distance from a point to a line will be perpendicular.
- **? Assessing Question:** "How do you find the distance between a line and point not on the line?" Find the distance perpendicularly from the point to the line.
- In Example 1, $\overline{AC}$ is a perpendicular segment. Remind students of the Distance Formula if they have forgotten.
- **Extension:** To find the distance from a point (x_0, y_0) to the line $Ax + By = C$:
$$d = \frac{|Ax_0 + By_0 + C|}{\sqrt{A^2 + B^2}}.$$

Constructing Perpendicular Lines

CONSTRUCTION **Constructing a Perpendicular Line**

Use a compass and straightedge to construct a line
perpendicular to line *m* through point *P*, which is
not on line *m*.

SOLUTION

Step 1	Step 2	Step 3
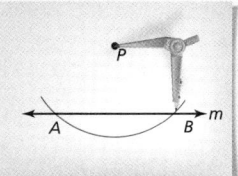	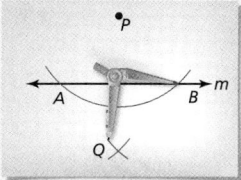	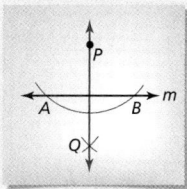
Draw arc with center *P* Place the compass at point *P* and draw an arc that intersects the line twice. Label the intersections *A* and *B*.	**Draw intersecting arcs** Draw an arc with center *A*. Using the same radius, draw an arc with center *B*. Label the intersection of the arcs *Q*.	**Draw perpendicular line** Draw $\overleftrightarrow{PQ}$. This line is perpendicular to line *m*.

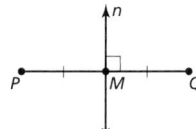

The **perpendicular bisector** of a line segment $\overline{PQ}$ is the line *n* with the following
two properties.

- $n \perp \overline{PQ}$

- *n* passes through the midpoint *M* of $\overline{PQ}$.

CONSTRUCTION **Constructing a Perpendicular Bisector**

Use a compass and straightedge to construct
the perpendicular bisector of $\overline{AB}$.

SOLUTION

Step 1	Step 2	Step 3
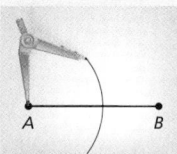	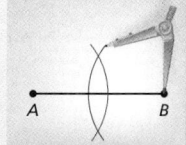	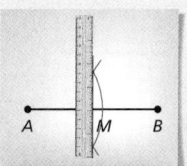
Draw an arc Place the compass at *A*. Use a compass setting that is greater than half the length of $\overline{AB}$. Draw an arc.	**Draw a second arc** Keep the same compass setting. Place the compass at *B*. Draw an arc. It should intersect the other arc at two points.	**Bisect segment** Draw a line through the two points of intersection. This line is the perpendicular bisector of $\overline{AB}$. It passes through *M*, the midpoint of $\overline{AB}$. So, $AM = MB$.

Section 3.4   Proofs with Perpendicular Lines   **149**

Laurie's Notes   Teacher Actions

- In the explorations, students constructed the perpendicular bisector of a segment. Here they are constructing a perpendicular to a line. Again, the justification for this construction has to do with proving triangles congruent.
- **Note:** A perpendicular bisector can be a line, a segment, a ray, or a plane. It is shown as a line on this page.
- **Extension:** The constructions on this page can be simulated using dynamic geometry software by constructing circles.

Prove the Perpendicular Transversal Theorem using the diagram and the Alternate Interior Angles Theorem (Theorem 3.2).

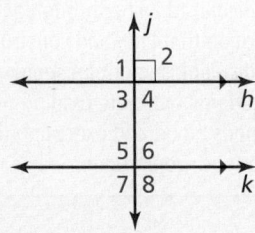

Given $h \parallel k, j \perp h$
Prove $j \perp k$
Statements (Reasons)
1. $h \parallel k, j \perp h$ (Given)
2. $m\angle 2 = 90°$ (Def. of $\perp$ lines)
3. $\angle 3 \cong \angle 2$ (Vert. $\angle$s $\cong$ Thm. 2.6)
4. $\angle 3 \cong \angle 6$ (Alt. Int. $\angle$s Thm. 3.2)
5. $\angle 2 \cong \angle 6$ (Trans. Prop. $\cong$ 2.2)
6. $m\angle 2 = m\angle 6$ (Def. of $\cong$ $\angle$s)
7. $m\angle 6 = 90°$ (Trans. Prop. =)
8. $j \perp k$ (Def. of $\perp$ lines)

MONITORING PROGRESS ANSWER
2. See Additional Answers.

Proving Theorems about Perpendicular Lines

🔁 Theorems

Theorem 3.10   Linear Pair Perpendicular Theorem

If two lines intersect to form a linear pair of congruent angles, then the lines are perpendicular.

If $\angle 1 \cong \angle 2$, then $g \perp h$.

Proof Ex. 13, p. 153

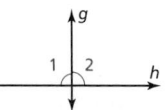

Theorem 3.11   Perpendicular Transversal Theorem

In a plane, if a transversal is perpendicular to one of two parallel lines, then it is perpendicular to the other line.

If $h \parallel k$ and $j \perp h$, then $j \perp k$.

Proof Example 2, p. 150; Question 2, p. 150

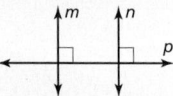

Theorem 3.12   Lines Perpendicular to a Transversal Theorem

In a plane, if two lines are perpendicular to the same line, then they are parallel to each other.

If $m \perp p$ and $n \perp p$, then $m \parallel n$.

Proof Ex. 14, p. 153; Ex. 47, p. 162

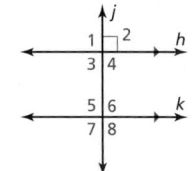

EXAMPLE 2   **Proving the Perpendicular Transversal Theorem**

Use the diagram to prove the Perpendicular Transversal Theorem.

SOLUTION

Given $h \parallel k, j \perp h$

Prove $j \perp k$

STATEMENTS	REASONS
1. $h \parallel k, j \perp h$	**1.** Given
2. $m\angle 2 = 90°$	**2.** Definition of perpendicular lines
3. $\angle 2 \cong \angle 6$	**3.** Corresponding Angles Theorem (Theorem 3.1)
4. $m\angle 2 = m\angle 6$	**4.** Definition of congruent angles
5. $m\angle 6 = 90°$	**5.** Transitive Property of Equality
6. $j \perp k$	**6.** Definition of perpendicular lines

Monitoring Progress 🔊 Help in English and Spanish at *BigIdeasMath.com*

2. Prove the Perpendicular Transversal Theorem using the diagram in Example 2 and the Alternate Exterior Angles Theorem (Theorem 3.3).

Laurie's Notes   Teacher Actions

- The three theorems need to be read carefully.
- ❓ To introduce the first one ask, "When two lines intersect to form congruent adjacent angles, what do you know?" The lines are perpendicular.
- ❓ **Probing Question:** "In the Perpendicular Transversal Theorem (Thm. 3.11), why is it necessary for the lines to be coplanar?" If the perpendicular line were not in the same plane as the parallel lines, then it would be perpendicular to only one of the parallel lines.
- The third theorem demonstrates why there is no transitive property for perpendicular lines!

Solving Real-Life Problems

EXAMPLE 3 Proving Lines Are Parallel

The photo shows the layout of a neighborhood. Determine which lines, if any, must be parallel in the diagram. Explain your reasoning.

SOLUTION

Lines p and q are both perpendicular to s, so by the Lines Perpendicular to a Transversal Theorem, $p \parallel q$. Also, lines s and t are both perpendicular to q, so by the Lines Perpendicular to a Transversal Theorem, $s \parallel t$.

▶ So, from the diagram you can conclude $p \parallel q$ and $s \parallel t$.

Monitoring Progress Help in English and Spanish at *BigIdeasMath.com*

Use the lines marked in the photo.

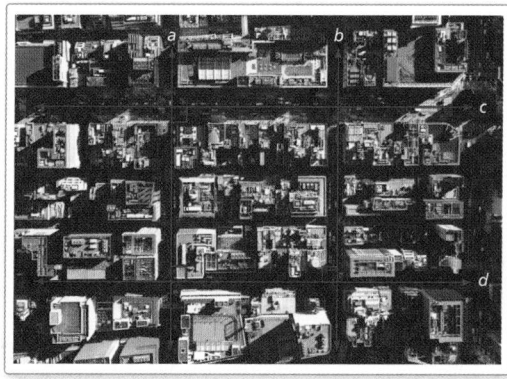

3. Is $b \parallel a$? Explain your reasoning.

4. Is $b \perp c$? Explain your reasoning.

Extra Example 3

The diagram shows the layout of walking paths in a town park. Determine which lines, if any, must be parallel in the diagram. Explain your reasoning.

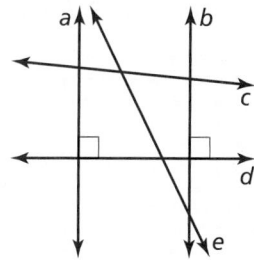

$a \parallel b$; Lines a and b are both perpendicular to d. So by the Lines Perpendicular to a Transversal Theorem (Thm. 3.12), $a \parallel b$.

MONITORING PROGRESS ANSWERS

3. yes; Because $a \perp d$ and $b \perp d$, we can conclude that $b \parallel a$ by the Lines Perpendicular to a Transversal Theorem (Thm. 3.12).

4. yes; Because $b \perp d$ and $c \parallel d$, we can conclude that $b \perp c$ by the Perpendicular Transversal Theorem (Thm. 3.11).

Laurie's Notes | Teacher Actions

? Show Example 3 and ask, "What lines are parallel and how do you know?" Listen for valid justification.

• **Extension:** "Why do you think cities are often designed in a grid fashion with streets running parallel and perpendicular?" Answers will vary. "What do the cities where there is not a grid design have in common?" Many of them are older cities in which horse and carriage was the main mode of travel.

Closure

• **Point of Most Significance:** Ask students to identify, aloud or on a paper to be collected, the most significant point (or part) in the lesson that aided their learning.

Assignment Guide and Homework Check

ASSIGNMENT

Basic: 1, 2, 3–11 odd, 15, 17, 24, 26, 34–41

Average: 1, 2–26 even, 27, 34–41

Advanced: 1, 2, 4, 10, 12, 16, 22–28, 30–32, 34–41

HOMEWORK CHECK

Basic: 3, 9, 11, 15, 17

Average: 4, 6, 12, 16, 27

Advanced: 4, 12, 23, 25, 27

ANSWERS

1. midpoint, right

2. Find *XZ*; about 7.1 units; about 6.3 units

3. about 3.2 units

4. about 4.1 units

5.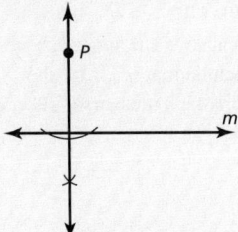

6.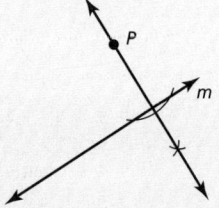

7.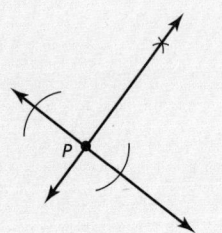

8.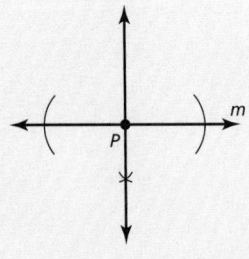

Vocabulary and Core Concept Check

1. **COMPLETE THE SENTENCE** The perpendicular bisector of a segment is the line that passes through the _____ of the segment at a _____ angle.

2. **DIFFERENT WORDS, SAME QUESTION** Which is different? Find "both" answers.

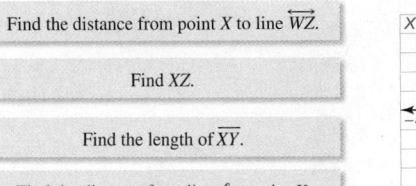

Find the distance from point *X* to line $\overleftrightarrow{WZ}$.

Find *XZ*.

Find the length of $\overline{XY}$.

Find the distance from line ℓ to point *X*.

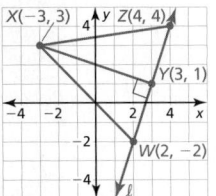

Monitoring Progress and Modeling with Mathematics

In Exercises 3 and 4, find the distance from point *A* to $\overleftrightarrow{XZ}$. (*See Example 1.*)

3.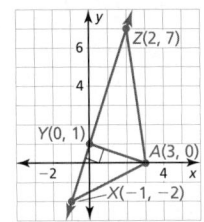

4.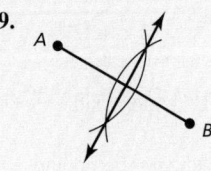

CONSTRUCTION In Exercises 5–8, trace line *m* and point *P*. Then use a compass and straightedge to construct a line perpendicular to line *m* through point *P*.

5.

6.

7.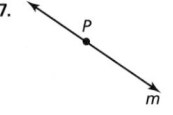

8.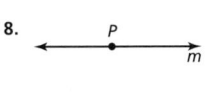

CONSTRUCTION In Exercises 9 and 10, trace $\overline{AB}$. Then use a compass and straightedge to construct the perpendicular bisector of $\overline{AB}$.

9.

10.

9.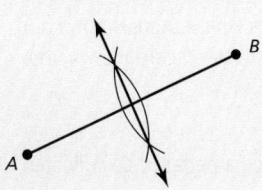

10.

ERROR ANALYSIS In Exercises 11 and 12, describe and correct the error in the statement about the diagram.

11.

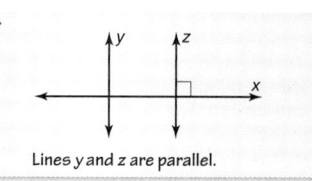

Lines *y* and *z* are parallel.

12.

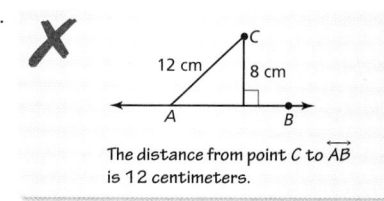

The distance from point *C* to $\overrightarrow{AB}$ is 12 centimeters.

PROVING A THEOREM In Exercises 13 and 14, prove the theorem. *(See Example 2.)*

13. Linear Pair Perpendicular Theorem (Thm. 3.10)

14. Lines Perpendicular to a Transversal Theorem (Thm. 3.12)

PROOF In Exercises 15 and 16, use the diagram to write a proof of the statement.

15. If two intersecting lines are perpendicular, then they intersect to form four right angles.

   Given $a \perp b$
   Prove $\angle 1$, $\angle 2$, $\angle 3$, and $\angle 4$ are right angles.

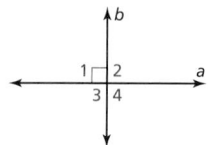

16. If two sides of two adjacent acute angles are perpendicular, then the angles are complementary.

   Given $\overrightarrow{BA} \perp \overrightarrow{BC}$
   Prove $\angle 1$ and $\angle 2$ are complementary.

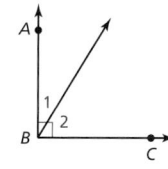

In Exercises 17–22, determine which lines, if any, must be parallel. Explain your reasoning. *(See Example 3.)*

17.
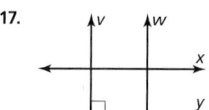

18.
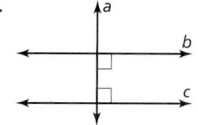

19.
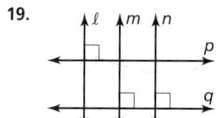

20.
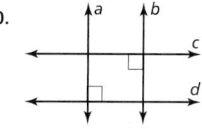

21.
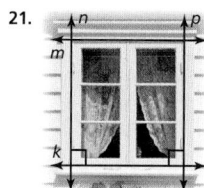

22.
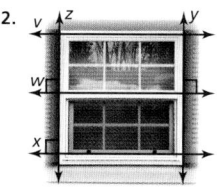

23. **USING STRUCTURE** Find all the unknown angle measures in the diagram. Justify your answer for each angle measure.

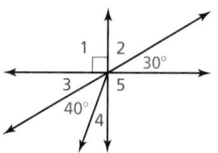

24. **MAKING AN ARGUMENT** Your friend claims that because you can find the distance from a point to a line, you should be able to find the distance between any two lines. Is your friend correct? Explain your reasoning.

25. **MATHEMATICAL CONNECTIONS** Find the value of *x* when $a \perp b$ and $b \parallel c$.

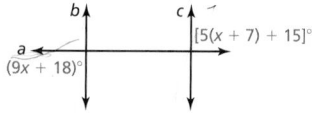

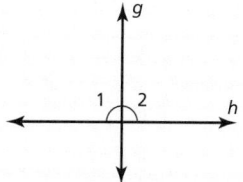

Dynamic Teaching Tools

Dynamic Assessment & Progress Monitoring Tool

Interactive Whiteboard Lesson Library

Dynamic Classroom with Dynamic Investigations

ANSWERS

11. In order to claim parallel lines by the Lines Perpendicular to a Transversal Theorem (Thm. 3.12), *both* lines must be marked as perpendicular to the transversal; Lines *x* and *z* are perpendicular.

12. The length of the perpendicular segment should be used; The distance from point *C* to $\overline{AB}$ is 8 centimeters.

13.

Because $\angle 1 \cong \angle 2$ by definition, $m\angle 1 = m\angle 2$. Also, by the Linear Pair Postulate (Post. 2.8), $m\angle 1 + m\angle 2 = 180°$. Then, by the Substitution Property of Equality, $m\angle 1 + m\angle 1 = 180°$, and $2(m\angle 1) = 180°$ by the Distributive Property. So, by the Division Property of Equality, $m\angle 1 = 90°$. Finally, $g \perp h$ by the definition of perpendicular lines.

14–16. See Additional Answers.

17. none; The only thing that can be concluded in this diagram is that $v \perp y$. In order to say that lines are parallel, you need to know something about both of the intersections between the transversal and the two lines.

18. $b \parallel c$; Because $a \perp b$ and $a \perp c$, lines *b* and *c* are parallel by the Lines Perpendicular to a Transversal Theorem (Thm. 3.12).

19. $m \parallel n$, Because $m \perp q$ and $n \perp q$, lines *m* and *n* are parallel by the Lines Perpendicular to a Transversal Theorem (Thm. 3.12). The other lines may or may not be parallel.

---

20. none; The only things that can be concluded in this diagram are that $a \perp d$ and $b \perp c$. In order to say that lines are parallel, you need to know something about both of the intersections between the transversal and the two lines.

21. $n \parallel p$; Because $k \perp n$ and $k \perp p$, lines *n* and *p* are parallel by the Lines Perpendicular to a Transversal Theorem (Thm. 3.12).

22. $y \parallel z$ and $w \parallel x$; Because $w \perp y$ and $w \perp z$, lines *y* and *z* are parallel by the Lines Perpendicular to a Transversal Theorem (Thm. 3.12). Because $w \perp z$ and $x \perp z$, lines *w* and *x* are parallel by the Lines Perpendicular to a Transversal Theorem (Thm. 3.12).

23–25. See Additional Answers.

ANSWERS

26. point *C*; Because $\overline{AC}$ appears to be perpendicular to the water's edge, it would represent the shortest distance from point *A* to the line formed by the opposite edge of the stream.

27. A, C, D, E

28. 8; Because two lines always intersect in two points, and each intersection creates four right angles, there will be eight right angles formed by two perpendicular lines.

29–41. See Additional Answers.

Mini-Assessment

1. Find the distance from point *P* to $\overleftrightarrow{QS}$.

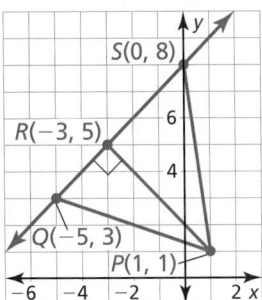

$\sqrt{32}$; about 5.7 units

2. Sketch a vertical line segment *AB*. Construct the perpendicular bisector of $\overline{AB}$.

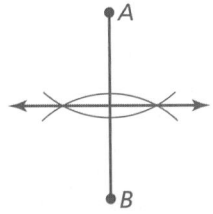

3. The diagram shows the outline of the foundation of a garage. Is $\overleftrightarrow{RS} \perp \overleftrightarrow{TS}$? Explain your reasoning.

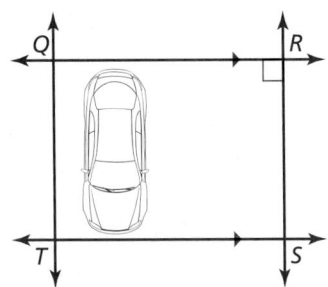

Yes; The diagram shows $\overleftrightarrow{QR} \parallel \overleftrightarrow{TS}$ and $\overleftrightarrow{QR} \perp \overleftrightarrow{RS}$. So, by the Perpendicular Transversal Theorem (Thm. 3.11), $\overleftrightarrow{RS} \perp \overleftrightarrow{TS}$.

154   **Chapter 3**

---

26. **HOW DO YOU SEE IT?** You are trying to cross a stream from point *A*. Which point should you jump to in order to jump the shortest distance? Explain your reasoning.

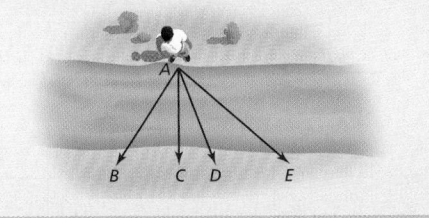

27. **ATTENDING TO PRECISION** In which of the following diagrams is $\overline{AC} \parallel \overline{BD}$ and $\overline{AC} \perp \overline{CD}$? Select all that apply.

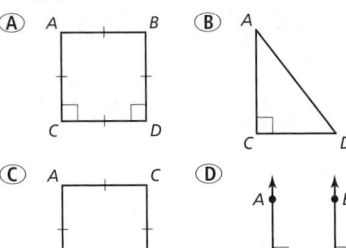

28. **THOUGHT PROVOKING** The postulates and theorems in this book represent Euclidean geometry. In spherical geometry, all points are points on the surface of a sphere. A line is a circle on the sphere whose diameter is equal to the diameter of the sphere. In spherical geometry, how many right angles are formed by two perpendicular lines? Justify your answer.

29. **CONSTRUCTION** Construct a square of side length *AB*.

30. **ANALYZING RELATIONSHIPS** The painted line segments that form the path of a crosswalk are usually perpendicular to the crosswalk. Sketch what the segments in the photo would look like if they were perpendicular to the crosswalk. Which type of line segment requires less paint? Explain your reasoning.

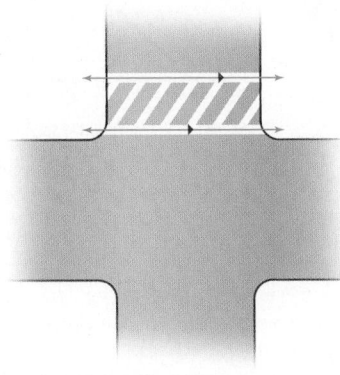

31. **ABSTRACT REASONING** Two lines, *a* and *b*, are perpendicular to line *c*. Line *d* is parallel to line *c*. The distance between lines *a* and *b* is *x* meters. The distance between lines *c* and *d* is *y* meters. What shape is formed by the intersections of the four lines?

32. **MATHEMATICAL CONNECTIONS** Find the distance between the lines with the equations $y = \frac{3}{2}x + 4$ and $-3x + 2y = -1$.

33. **WRITING** Describe how you would find the distance from a point to a plane. Can you find the distance from a line to a plane? Explain your reasoning.

Maintaining Mathematical Proficiency   Reviewing what you learned in previous grades and lessons

Simplify the ratio. *(Skills Review Handbook)*

34. $\dfrac{6-(-4)}{8-3}$ 35. $\dfrac{3-5}{4-1}$ 36. $\dfrac{8-(-3)}{7-(-2)}$ 37. $\dfrac{13-4}{2-(-1)}$

Identify the slope and the y-intercept of the line. *(Skills Review Handbook)*

38. $y = 3x + 9$ 39. $y = -\frac{1}{2}x + 7$ 40. $y = \frac{1}{6}x - 8$ 41. $y = -8x - 6$

If students need help...	If students got it...
Resources by Chapter • Practice A and Practice B • Puzzle Time	Resources by Chapter • Enrichment and Extension • Cumulative Review
Student Journal • Practice	Start the *next* Section
Differentiating the Lesson Skills Review Handbook	

Overview of Section 3.5

Introduction

- This lesson uses skills learned in Algebra 1 as lines and segments are drawn in the coordinate plane. Students will be writing the equations of lines parallel and perpendicular to a given line and passing through a given point. These skills provide another means by which you can determine whether two lines are parallel or whether they are perpendicular. It also allows for coordinate proofs to be used as a means of justification.
- The lesson begins with partitioning a *directed line segment* into two segments of a specified ratio. The outcome is an ordered pair on the line segment.
- The lesson ends with another look at finding the distance from a point to a line. Students must first find the equation of the perpendicular to the line, determine the point of intersection, and then find the distance between the ordered pairs.

Teaching Strategy

- **Selective Responses:** When students are working alone or with partners on a problem, teachers have the opportunity to circulate about the room to see different approaches. Students' work varies, revealing their thinking and conceptions about the mathematics. Discourse about the mathematics and student comprehension can both be improved if we are thoughtful in how responses (students' work) are displayed.
- I carry a clipboard with me as I circulate so that I can make notes about the order in which I want to call on students. If I leave it to chance when I call on students to share their solutions, I lose the ability to control the sequence of responses. I do not want the first response to be the most polished, efficient, or eloquent. Knowing the outcome(s) I want from the activity or problem, I look for particular work that clearly demonstrates the outcome. If there is a particular *Mathematical Practice* that is evident in the students' work, I also want to highlight that.

Pacing Suggestion

- You might select only two problems from the first exploration for students to do, one of each type, where the y-intercepts are not given as the ordered pair. This should provide the needed review so that students are ready to begin the formal lesson.

HSG-GPE.B.5 Prove the slope criteria for parallel and perpendicular lines and use them to solve geometric problems (e.g., find the equation of a line parallel or perpendicular to a given line that passes through a given point).

HSG-GPE.B.6 Find the point on a directed line segment between two given points that partitions the segment in a given ratio.

Laurie's Notes

Exploration

Motivate
- Before students arrive, make three sets of cards with equations written on them. The first set, labeled A, has an equation of a line. Each equation in Set B is parallel to one of the equations in Set A. Each equation in Set C is perpendicular to one of the equations in Set A. All of the equations can be written in slope-intercept or standard form, allowing you to differentiate for students in your class.
- Hand each student a card. The goal is for students to find their matches so that a set of three students will have an A, B, and C card.

Exploration Note
- In Algebra 1, students learned that parallel lines have the same slope, and perpendicular lines have slopes that are negative reciprocals. These two relationships are stated as theorems in geometry. Students also learned to write the equation of a line when given a point and a slope.
- You will need to judge how much review is necessary for your students to be successful with these problems. They will be writing equations in the formal lesson. Having students recall content while working with partners in writing equations may give you a better assessment of what your students recall from Algebra 1 than presenting it in a formal lesson.

Exploration 1
- Students can read the equation and the ordered pair from each graph. Because the equation is given in slope-intercept form, the slope is known.
- ❓ "How can you write the equation of a line when you know the slope and a point on the line?"
  Use the point-slope formula.
- ❓ "How can you use your graphing calculators to verify that your answers are correct?"
  Students should mention looking at the table of values to verify that their line contains the point given.

Exploration 2
- This exploration requires students to read ordered pairs from the graphs. From the ordered pairs, the slopes can be found.
- **Selective Responses:** As you circulate around you may observe different strategies for determining the equations of the lines. For instance, some students may compute the slope from the graph by finding the rise and run. They will have little work written! Some students may select the y-intercept as the point to work with and will write the equation immediately in the form $y = mx + b$ without using the point-slope formula. Make a note of the different strategies, and be purposeful with the order in which you call on students to share their work.

Communicate Your Answer
- Question 4 could be an *Exit Ticket* if it is toward the end of the period.

Connecting to Next Step
- The algebraic skills reviewed in these explorations are necessary in the formal lesson. You may decide more or less review is needed.

Equations of Parallel and Perpendicular Lines

Dynamic Teaching Tools

Dynamic Assessment & Progress Monitoring Tool

Lesson Planning Tool

Interactive Whiteboard Lesson Library

Dynamic Classroom with Dynamic Investigations

Essential Question How can you write an equation of a line that is parallel or perpendicular to a given line and passes through a given point?

EXPLORATION 1 Writing Equations of Parallel and Perpendicular Lines

Work with a partner. Write an equation of the line that is parallel or perpendicular to the given line and passes through the given point. Use a graphing calculator to verify your answer. What is the relationship between the slopes?

a.
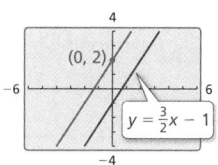

b.
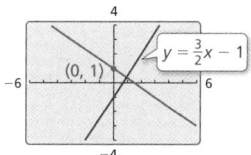

c.
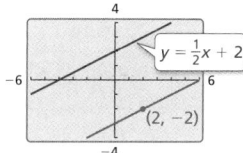

d.
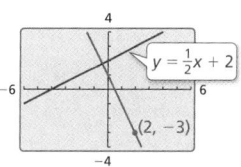

e.
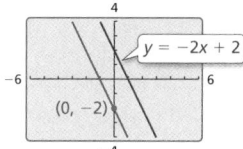

f.
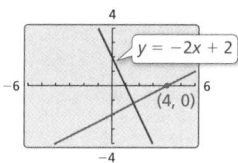

EXPLORATION 2 Writing Equations of Parallel and Perpendicular Lines

Work with a partner. Write the equations of the parallel or perpendicular lines. Use a graphing calculator to verify your answers.

a.
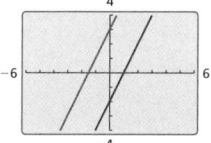

b.
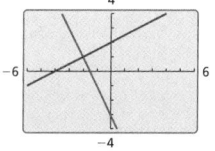

MODELING WITH MATHEMATICS

To be proficient in math, you need to analyze relationships mathematically to draw conclusions.

Communicate Your Answer

3. How can you write an equation of a line that is parallel or perpendicular to a given line and passes through a given point?

4. Write an equation of the line that is (a) parallel and (b) perpendicular to the line $y = 3x + 2$ and passes through the point $(1, -2)$.

Section 3.5   Equations of Parallel and Perpendicular Lines   **155**

ANSWERS

1. **a.** $y = \frac{3}{2}x + 2$; The slopes are equal.
   b. $y = -\frac{2}{3}x + 1$; The slopes are opposite reciprocals and have a product of -1.
   c. $y = \frac{1}{2}x - 3$; The slopes are equal.
   d. $y = -2x + 1$; The slopes are opposite reciprocals and have a product of -1.
   e. $y = -2x - 2$; The slopes are equal.
   f. $y = \frac{1}{2}x - 2$; The slopes are opposite reciprocals and have a product of -1.

2. **a.** $y = 2x + 3$; $y = 2x - 2$
   b. $y = \frac{1}{2}x + 2$; $y = -2x - 3$

3. For a line parallel to a given line, the slopes will be the same. For a line perpendicular to the given line, the slopes will be opposite reciprocals. Find the y-intercept of a line by substituting the slope and the given point into the slope-intercept form of a line, $y = mx + b$, and solving for b. Once you know the slope and y-intercept of a line, you can get the equation of the line by substituting them into $y = mx + b$.

4. **a.** $y = 3x - 5$
   b. $y = -\frac{1}{3}x - \frac{5}{3}$

Extra Example 1

Find the coordinates of point *F* along the directed line segment *CD* so that the ratio of *CF* to *FD* is 3 to 5.

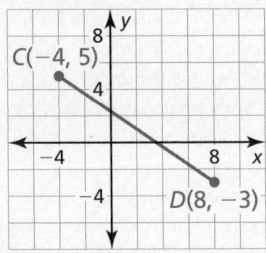

$F(0.5, 2)$

MONITORING PROGRESS ANSWERS

1. $P(6.6, 3.8)$
2. $P(-0.2, 2.2)$

3.5 Lesson

Core Vocabulary

directed line segment, *p. 156*

Previous
slope
slope-intercept form
y-intercept

What You Will Learn

▶ Use slope to partition directed line segments.
▶ Identify parallel and perpendicular lines.
▶ Write equations of parallel and perpendicular lines.
▶ Use slope to find the distance from a point to a line.

Partitioning a Directed Line Segment

A **directed line segment** *AB* is a segment that represents moving from point *A* to point *B*. The following example shows how to use slope to find a point on a directed line segment that partitions the segment in a given ratio.

EXAMPLE 1 **Partitioning a Directed Line Segment**

Find the coordinates of point *P* along the directed line segment *AB* so that the ratio of *AP* to *PB* is 3 to 2.

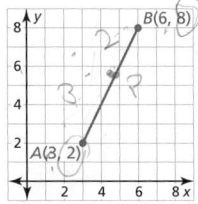

SOLUTION

In order to divide the segment in the ratio 3 to 2, think of dividing, or *partitioning*, the segment into $3 + 2$, or 5 congruent pieces.

Point *P* is the point that is $\frac{3}{5}$ of the way from point *A* to point *B*.

Find the rise and run from point *A* to point *B*. Leave the slope in terms of rise and run and do not simplify.

$$\text{slope of } \overline{AB}: \quad m = \frac{8 - 2}{6 - 3} = \frac{6}{3} = \frac{\text{rise}}{\text{run}}$$

To find the coordinates of point *P*, add $\frac{3}{5}$ of the run to the *x*-coordinate of *A*, and add $\frac{3}{5}$ of the rise to the *y*-coordinate of *A*.

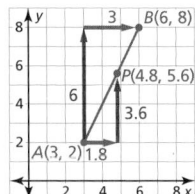

run: $\frac{3}{5}$ of $3 = \frac{3}{5} \cdot 3 = 1.8$

rise: $\frac{3}{5}$ of $6 = \frac{3}{5} \cdot 6 = 3.6$

▶ So, the coordinates of *P* are

$$(3 + 1.8, 2 + 3.6) = (4.8, 5.6).$$

The ratio of *AP* to *PB* is 3 to 2.

Monitoring Progress 🔊 Help in English and Spanish at *BigIdeasMath.com*

Find the coordinates of point *P* along the directed line segment *AB* so that *AP* to *PB* is the given ratio.

1. $A(1, 3)$, $B(8, 4)$; 4 to 1
2. $A(-2, 1)$, $B(4, 5)$; 3 to 7

Laurie's Notes   Teacher Actions

- **Turn and Talk:** Define a *directed line segment* and pose Example 1. Give time for partners to discuss strategies. If students are getting nowhere, ask a *Probing Question*: "How would you proceed if the segment were horizontal or vertical?" Walk away. Do not solve it for students at this point.
- **MP1 Make Sense of Problems and Persevere in Solving Them:** Trust that students have the tools to solve the problem when they persevere.
- **Monitoring Progress:** You may want to have some students do Question 1 and others Question 2.

Identifying Parallel and Perpendicular Lines

In the coordinate plane, the *x*-axis and the *y*-axis are perpendicular. Horizontal lines are parallel to the *x*-axis, and vertical lines are parallel to the *y*-axis.

🗘 Theorems

Theorem 3.13   Slopes of Parallel Lines

In a coordinate plane, two distinct nonvertical lines are parallel if and only if they have the same slope.

Any two vertical lines are parallel.

Proof p. 439; Ex. 41, p. 444

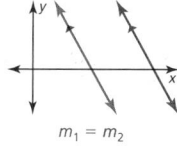

$m_1 = m_2$

READING

If the product of two numbers is −1, then the numbers are called *negative reciprocals*.

Theorem 3.14   Slopes of Perpendicular Lines

In a coordinate plane, two nonvertical lines are perpendicular if and only if the product of their slopes is −1.

Horizontal lines are perpendicular to vertical lines.

Proof p. 440; Ex. 42, p. 444

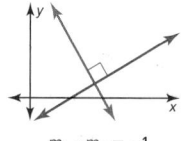

$m_1 \cdot m_2 = -1$

EXAMPLE 2   Identifying Parallel and Perpendicular Lines

Determine which of the lines are parallel and which of the lines are perpendicular.

SOLUTION

Find the slope of each line.

Line *a*: $m = \dfrac{3-2}{0-(-3)} = \dfrac{1}{3}$

Line *b*: $m = \dfrac{0-(-1)}{2-0} = \dfrac{1}{2}$

Line *c*: $m = \dfrac{-4-(-5)}{1-(-1)} = \dfrac{1}{2}$

Line *d*: $m = \dfrac{2-0}{-3-(-2)} = -2$

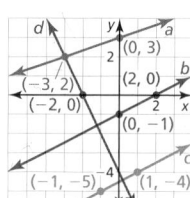

▶ Because lines *b* and *c* have the same slope, lines *b* and *c* are parallel. Because $\dfrac{1}{2}(-2) = -1$, lines *b* and *d* are perpendicular and lines *c* and *d* are perpendicular.

Monitoring Progress 🔊 Help in English and Spanish at *BigIdeasMath.com*

3. Determine which of the lines are parallel and which of the lines are perpendicular.

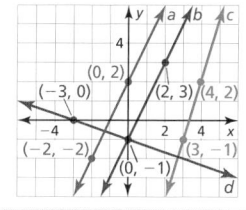

Extra Example 2

Determine which of the lines are parallel and which of the lines are perpendicular.

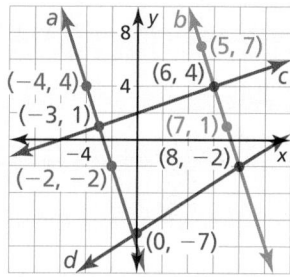

$a \parallel b, b \perp c, a \perp c$

MONITORING PROGRESS ANSWER

3. $a \parallel b, c \perp d$

Laurie's Notes   Teacher Actions

? Probing Question: "Why do you think it is necessary to state that horizontal lines are perpendicular to vertical lines?" Vertical lines have undefined slope, and horizontal lines have a slope of 0. Their product will not equal −1.

- The theorems will be familiar to students. Discuss the *Reading* note: A product of −1 means the slopes are negative reciprocals.
- **Turn and Talk:** Have students work through Example 2 with their partners.

Extra Example 3

Write an equation of the line passing through the point $(-4, 6)$ that is parallel to the line $y = 3x - 4$. $y = 3x + 18$

Extra Example 4

Write an equation of the line passing through the point $(-12, 6)$ that is perpendicular to the line $y = \frac{2}{3}x - 10$. $y = -\frac{3}{2}x - 12$

MONITORING PROGRESS ANSWERS

4. a. $y = 3x + 2$
   b. $y = -\frac{1}{3}x + \frac{16}{3}$

5. Line $x = 4$ is a vertical line, and line $y = 2$ is a horizontal line. So, they are perpendicular by the Slopes of Perpendicular Lines Theorem (Thm. 3.14).

Writing Equations of Parallel and Perpendicular Lines

You can apply the Slopes of Parallel Lines Theorem and the Slopes of Perpendicular Lines Theorem to write equations of parallel and perpendicular lines.

EXAMPLE 3 Writing an Equation of a Parallel Line

Write an equation of the line passing through the point $(-1, 1)$ that is parallel to the line $y = 2x - 3$.

SOLUTION

Step 1 Find the slope m of the parallel line. The line $y = 2x - 3$ has a slope of 2. By the Slopes of Parallel Lines Theorem, a line parallel to this line also has a slope of 2. So, $m = 2$.

Step 2 Find the y-intercept b by using $m = 2$ and $(x, y) = (-1, 1)$.

$y = mx + b$	Use slope-intercept form.
$1 = 2(-1) + b$	Substitute for m, x, and y.
$3 = b$	Solve for b.

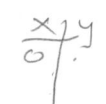

▶ Because $m = 2$ and $b = 3$, an equation of the line is $y = 2x + 3$. Use a graph to check that the line $y = 2x - 3$ is parallel to the line $y = 2x + 3$.

Check

EXAMPLE 4 Writing an Equation of a Perpendicular Line

Write an equation of the line passing through the point $(2, 3)$ that is perpendicular to the line $2x + y = 2$.

SOLUTION

Step 1 Find the slope m of the perpendicular line. The line $2x + y = 2$, or $y = -2x + 2$, has a slope of -2. Use the Slopes of Perpendicular Lines Theorem.

$-2 \cdot m = -1$	The product of the slopes of $\perp$ lines is -1.
$m = \frac{1}{2}$	Divide each side by -2.

Step 2 Find the y-intercept b by using $m = \frac{1}{2}$ and $(x, y) = (2, 3)$.

$y = mx + b$	Use slope-intercept form.
$3 = \frac{1}{2}(2) + b$	Substitute for m, x, and y.
$2 = b$	Solve for b.

Check

▶ Because $m = \frac{1}{2}$ and $b = 2$, an equation of the line is $y = \frac{1}{2}x + 2$. Check that the lines are perpendicular by graphing their equations and using a protractor to measure one of the angles formed by their intersection.

Monitoring Progress 🔊 Help in English and Spanish at *BigIdeasMath.com*

4. Write an equation of the line that passes through the point $(1, 5)$ and is (a) parallel to the line $y = 3x - 5$ and (b) perpendicular to the line $y = 3x - 5$.

5. How do you know that the lines $x = 4$ and $y = 2$ are perpendicular?

> **REMEMBER**
>
> The linear equation $y = 2x - 3$ is written in slope-intercept form $y = mx + b$, where m is the slope and b is the y-intercept.

Laurie's Notes Teacher Actions

- You may wish to skip Example 3 if students have worked the explorations.

COMMON ERROR In Example 4, students often say the slope is 2. Remind them that the equation is not in slope-intercept form. Rewriting the equation first, the slope is -2.

- **Think-Pair-Share:** Have students work to solve the questions in *Monitoring Progress*.

Finding the Distance from a Point to a Line

Recall that the distance from a point to a line is the length of the perpendicular segment from the point to the line.

EXAMPLE 5 **Finding the Distance from a Point to a Line**

Find the distance from the point $(1, 0)$ to the line $y = -x + 3$.

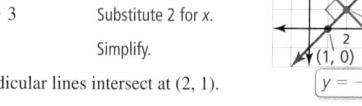

SOLUTION

Step 1 Find an equation of the line perpendicular to the line $y = -x + 3$ that passes through the point $(1, 0)$.

First, find the slope m of the perpendicular line. The line $y = -x + 3$ has a slope of -1. Use the Slopes of Perpendicular Lines Theorem.

$-1 \cdot m = -1$ The product of the slopes of $\perp$ lines is -1.

$m = 1$ Divide each side by -1.

Then find the y-intercept b by using $m = 1$ and $(x, y) = (1, 0)$.

$y = mx + b$ Use slope-intercept form.

$0 = 1(1) + b$ Substitute for x, y, and m.

$-1 = b$ Solve for b.

Because $m = 1$ and $b = -1$, an equation of the line is $y = x - 1$.

Step 2 Use the two equations to write and solve a system of equations to find the point where the two lines intersect.

$y = -x + 3$ Equation 1

$y = x - 1$ Equation 2

Substitute $-x + 3$ for y in Equation 2.

$y = x - 1$ Equation 2

$-x + 3 = x - 1$ Substitute $-x + 3$ for y.

$x = 2$ Solve for x.

Substitute 2 for x in Equation 1 and solve for y.

$y = -x + 3$ Equation 1

$y = -2 + 3$ Substitute 2 for x.

$y = 1$ Simplify.

So, the perpendicular lines intersect at $(2, 1)$.

Step 3 Use the Distance Formula to find the distance from $(1, 0)$ to $(2, 1)$.

$$\text{distance} = \sqrt{(1 - 2)^2 + (0 - 1)^2} = \sqrt{(-1)^2 + (-1)^2} = \sqrt{2} \approx 1.4$$

▶ So, the distance from the point $(1, 0)$ to the line $y = -x + 3$ is about 1.4 units.

REMEMBER

Recall that the solution of a system of two linear equations in two variables gives the coordinates of the point of intersection of the graphs of the equations.

There are two special cases when the lines have the same slope.

- When the system has no solution, the lines are parallel.
- When the system has infinitely many solutions, the lines coincide.

Monitoring Progress ◀)) Help in English and Spanish at *BigIdeasMath.com*

6. Find the distance from the point $(6, 4)$ to the line $y = x + 4$.

7. Find the distance from the point $(-1, 6)$ to the line $y = -2x$.

Section 3.5   Equations of Parallel and Perpendicular Lines   **159**

Extra Example 5

Find the distance from the point $(6, -2)$ to the line $y = 2x - 4$.

$\sqrt{20}$, or about 4.5 units

MONITORING PROGRESS ANSWERS

6. about 4.2 units

7. about 1.8 units

Laurie's Notes   Teacher Actions

- **Turn and Talk:** Pose Example 5 and give time for students to discuss strategies with their partners. Discuss as a class.
- **Selective Responses:** This is a problem for which students may use different strategies. Allow ample work time before asking selected students to share their approach.

Closure

- **Exit Ticket:** Write an equation of the line that is (a) parallel and (b) perpendicular to the line $y = -3x - 2$ and passing through $(3, -1)$. (a) $y = -3x + 8$ (b) $y = \frac{1}{3}x - 2$

ANSWERS

1. directed

2. Because their product equals -1, they must have opposite signs and be reciprocals of each other.

3. $P(7, -0.4)$

4. $P(2.8, -1)$

5. $P(-1.5, -1.5)$

6. $P(-1, 0.5)$

7. $a \parallel c, b \perp d$

8. $c \parallel d, b \perp c, b \perp d$

9. perpendicular; Because
$m_1 \cdot m_2 = \left(\frac{2}{3}\right)\left(-\frac{3}{2}\right) = -1$, lines 1 and 2 are perpendicular by the Slopes of Perpendicular Lines Theorem (Thm. 3.14).

10. neither; Because the slopes, $m_1 = \frac{3}{4}$ and $m_2 = \frac{5}{6}$, are not equal, and their product is not -1, they are neither parallel nor perpendicular.

11. perpendicular; Because
$m_1 \cdot m_2 = 1(-1) = -1$, lines 1 and 2 are perpendicular by the Slopes of Perpendicular Lines Theorem (Thm. 3.14).

12. parallel; Because $m_1 = m_2 = -\frac{2}{9}$, lines 1 and 2 are parallel by the Slopes of Parallel Lines Theorem (Thm. 3.13).

13. $y = -2x - 1$

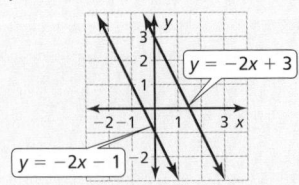

Vocabulary and Core Concept Check

1. **COMPLETE THE SENTENCE** A _____ line segment AB is a segment that represents moving from point A to point B.

2. **WRITING** How are the slopes of perpendicular lines related?

Monitoring Progress and Modeling with Mathematics

In Exercises 3–6, find the coordinates of point P along the directed line segment AB so that AP to PB is the given ratio. *(See Example 1.)*

3. $A(8, 0), B(3, -2)$; 1 to 4

4. $A(-2, -4), B(6, 1)$; 3 to 2

5. $A(1, 6), B(-2, -3)$; 5 to 1

6. $A(-3, 2), B(5, -4)$; 2 to 6

In Exercises 7 and 8, determine which of the lines are parallel and which of the lines are perpendicular. *(See Example 2.)*

7.
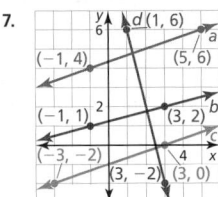

8.
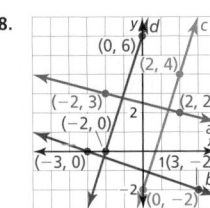

In Exercises 9–12, tell whether the lines through the given points are *parallel*, *perpendicular*, or *neither*. Justify your answer.

9. **Line 1:** $(1, 0), (7, 4)$
   Line 2: $(7, 0), (3, 6)$

10. **Line 1:** $(-3, 1), (-7, -2)$
    Line 2: $(2, -1), (8, 4)$

11. **Line 1:** $(-9, 3), (-5, 7)$
    Line 2: $(-11, 6), (-7, 2)$

12. **Line 1:** $(10, 5), (-8, 9)$
    Line 2: $(2, -4), (11, -6)$

In Exercises 13–16, write an equation of the line passing through point P that is parallel to the given line. Graph the equations of the lines to check that they are parallel. *(See Example 3.)*

13. $P(0, -1), y = -2x + 3$

14. $P(3, 8), y = \frac{1}{5}(x + 4)$

15. $P(-2, 6), x = -5$ 16. $P(4, 0), -x + 2y = 12$

In Exercises 17–20, write an equation of the line passing through point P that is perpendicular to the given line. Graph the equations of the lines to check that they are perpendicular. *(See Example 4.)*

17. $P(0, 0), y = -9x - 1$

18. $P(4, -6), y = -3$

19. $P(2, 3), y - 4 = -2(x + 3)$

20. $P(-8, 0), 3x \quad 5y = 6$

In Exercises 21–24, find the distance from point A to the given line. *(See Example 5.)*

21. $A(-1, 7), y = 3x$

22. $A(-9, -3), y = x - 6$

23. $A(15, -21), 5x + 2y = 4$

24. $A\left(-\frac{1}{4}, 5\right), -x + 2y = 14$

14. $y = \frac{1}{5}x + \frac{37}{5}$

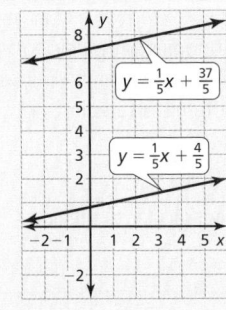

15. $x = -2$

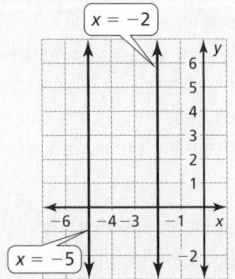

16–24. See Additional Answers.

25. **ERROR ANALYSIS** Describe and correct the error in determining whether the lines are parallel, perpendicular, or neither.

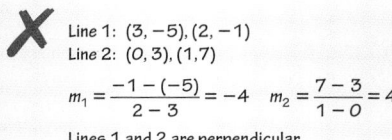

> Line 1: $(3, -5), (2, -1)$
> Line 2: $(0, 3), (1, 7)$
> $m_1 = \dfrac{-1 - (-5)}{2 - 3} = -4 \quad m_2 = \dfrac{7 - 3}{1 - 0} = 4$
> Lines 1 and 2 are perpendicular.

26. **ERROR ANALYSIS** Describe and correct the error in writing an equation of the line that passes through the point $(3, 4)$ and is parallel to the line $y = 2x + 1$.

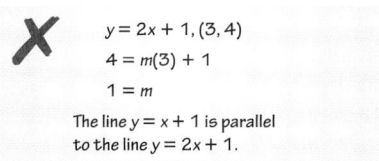

> $y = 2x + 1, (3, 4)$
> $4 = m(3) + 1$
> $1 = m$
> The line $y = x + 1$ is parallel to the line $y = 2x + 1$.

In Exercises 27–30, find the midpoint of $\overline{PQ}$. Then write an equation of the line that passes through the midpoint and is perpendicular to $\overline{PQ}$. This line is called the *perpendicular bisector*.

27. $P(-4, 3), Q(4, -1)$ 28. $P(-5, -5), Q(3, 3)$

29. $P(0, 2), Q(6, -2)$ 30. $P(-7, 0), Q(1, 8)$

31. **MODELING WITH MATHEMATICS** Your school lies directly between your house and the movie theater. The distance from your house to the school is one-fourth of the distance from the school to the movie theater. What point on the graph represents your school?

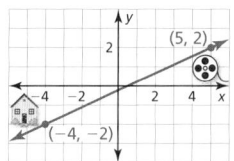

32. **REASONING** Is quadrilateral $QRST$ a parallelogram? Explain your reasoning.

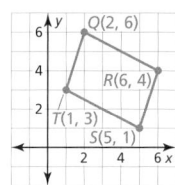

33. **REASONING** A triangle has vertices $L(0, 6)$, $M(5, 8)$, and $N(4, -1)$. Is the triangle a right triangle? Explain your reasoning.

34. **MODELING WITH MATHEMATICS** A new road is being constructed parallel to the train tracks through point V. An equation of the line representing the train tracks is $y = 2x$. Find an equation of the line representing the new road.

35. **MODELING WITH MATHEMATICS** A bike path is being constructed perpendicular to Washington Boulevard through point $P(2, 2)$. An equation of the line representing Washington Boulevard is $y = -\frac{2}{3}x$. Find an equation of the line representing the bike path.

36. **PROBLEM SOLVING** A gazebo is being built near a nature trail. An equation of the line representing the nature trail is $y = \frac{1}{3}x - 4$. Each unit in the coordinate plane corresponds to 10 feet. Approximately how far is the gazebo from the nature trail?

37. **CRITICAL THINKING** The slope of line ℓ is greater than 0 and less than 1. Write an inequality for the slope of a line perpendicular to ℓ. Explain your reasoning.

ANSWERS

25. Because the slopes are opposites but not reciprocals, their product does not equal -1. Lines 1 and 2 are neither parallel nor perpendicular.

26. Parallel lines have the same slope, not the same y-intercept.
$$y = 2x + 1, \quad (3, 4)$$
$$4 = 2(3) + b$$
$$-2 = b$$
The line $y = 2x - 2$ is parallel to the line $y = 2x + 1$.

27. $(0, 1); y = 2x + 1$

28. $(-1, -1); y = -x - 2$

29. $(3, 0); y = \frac{3}{2}x - \frac{9}{2}$

30. $(-3, 4); y = -x + 1$

31. $\left(-\frac{11}{5}, -\frac{6}{5}\right)$

32. yes; $\overline{QT} \parallel \overline{RS}$ because they have the same slope $(m = 3)$, and $\overline{ST} \parallel \overline{QR}$ because they have the same slope $\left(m = -\frac{1}{2}\right)$.

33. no; $m_{\overline{LM}} = \frac{2}{5}$, $m_{\overline{LN}} = -\frac{7}{4}$, and $m_{\overline{MN}} = 9$. None of these can pair up to make a product of -1, so none of the segments are perpendicular.

34. $y = 2x + 7$

35. $y = \frac{3}{2}x - 1$

36. about 95 ft

37. $m < -1$; The slope of a line perpendicular to ℓ must be the opposite reciprocal of the slope of line ℓ. So, it must be negative, and have an absolute value greater than 1.

38. yes; The angles are all right angles because the sides are all formed by horizontal or vertical lines. Also, the length of each side is the same.

39. It will be the same point.

40. yes; If two lines have the same y-intercept, then they intersect at that point. But parallel lines do not intersect.

41. a. no solution; The lines do not intersect, so they are parallel.

 b. $(7, -4)$; The lines intersect at one point.

 c. infinitely many solutions; The lines are the same line.

42. See Additional Answers

43. $k = 4$

44. $k = 5$

45–57. See Additional Answers

Mini-Assessment

1. $\overline{QR}$ has endpoints $Q(8, 4)$ and $R(-2, -1)$. Find the coordinates of point P along $\overline{QR}$ so that the ratio of QP to PR is 1 to 4. $P(6, 3)$

2. Tell whether the lines through the given points are *parallel*, *perpendicular*, or *neither*.

 a. Line 1: $(2, -3)$, $(-4, -6)$
  Line 2: $(-3, 2)$, $(2, -8)$
  perpendicular

 b. Line 1: $(-4, -5)$, $(4, 1)$
  Line 2: $(6, 10)$, $(-3, -2)$
  neither

 c. Line 1: $(0, -4)$, $(-2, -8)$
  Line 2: $(-1, 5)$, $(1, 9)$
  parallel

3. Write an equation of the line passing through the point $(-8, 6)$ that is parallel to the line $y = -4x - 1$. $y = -4x - 26$

4. Write an equation of the line passing through the point $(-20, 4)$ that is perpendicular to the line $2x + 5y = 10$. $y = \frac{5}{2}x + 54$

5. Find the distance from the point $(0, -3)$ to the line $y = x - 1$. $\sqrt{2}$, or about 1.4 units

---

38. HOW DO YOU SEE IT? Determine whether quadrilateral $JKLM$ is a square. Explain your reasoning.

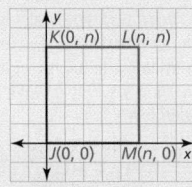

39. CRITICAL THINKING Suppose point P divides the directed line segment XY so that the ratio of XP to PY is 3 to 5. Describe the point that divides the directed line segment YX so that the ratio of YP to PX is 5 to 3.

40. MAKING AN ARGUMENT Your classmate claims that no two nonvertical parallel lines can have the same y-intercept. Is your classmate correct? Explain.

41. MATHEMATICAL CONNECTIONS Solve each system of equations algebraically. Make a conjecture about what the solution(s) can tell you about whether the lines intersect, are parallel, or are the same line.

 a. $y = 4x + 9$
  $4x - y = 1$

 b. $3y + 4x = 16$
  $2x - y = 18$

 c. $y = -5x + 6$
  $10x + 2y = 12$

42. THOUGHT PROVOKING Find a formula for the distance from the point (x_0, y_0) to the line $ax + by = 0$. Verify your formula using a point and a line.

Maintaining Mathematical Proficiency
Reviewing what you learned in previous grades and lessons

Plot the point in a coordinate plane. *(Skills Review Handbook)*

52. $A(3, 6)$

53. $B(0, -4)$

54. $C(5, 0)$

55. $D(-1, -2)$

Copy and complete the table. *(Skills Review Handbook)*

56.

x	-2	-1	0	1	2
$y = x + 9$					

57.

x	-2	-1	0	1	2
$y = x - \frac{3}{4}$					

MATHEMATICAL CONNECTIONS In Exercises 43 and 44, find a value for k based on the given description.

43. The line through $(-1, k)$ and $(-7, -2)$ is parallel to the line $y = x + 1$.

44. The line through $(k, 2)$ and $(7, 0)$ is perpendicular to the line $y = x - \frac{28}{5}$.

45. ABSTRACT REASONING Make a conjecture about how to find the coordinates of a point that lies beyond point B along $\overrightarrow{AB}$. Use an example to support your conjecture.

46. PROBLEM SOLVING What is the distance between the lines $y = 2x$ and $y = 2x + 5$? Verify your answer.

PROVING A THEOREM In Exercises 47 and 48, use the slopes of lines to write a paragraph proof of the theorem.

47. Lines Perpendicular to a Transversal Theorem (Theorem 3.12): In a plane, if two lines are perpendicular to the same line, then they are parallel to each other.

48. Transitive Property of Parallel Lines Theorem (Theorem 3.9): If two lines are parallel to the same line, then they are parallel to each other.

49. PROOF Prove the statement: If two lines are vertical, then they are parallel.

50. PROOF Prove the statement: If two lines are horizontal, then they are parallel.

51. PROOF Prove that horizontal lines are perpendicular to vertical lines.

If students need help...	If students got it...
Resources by Chapter • Practice A and Practice B • Puzzle Time	Resources by Chapter • Enrichment and Extension • Cumulative Review
Student Journal • Practice	Start the *next* Section
Differentiating the Lesson Skills Review Handbook	

Core Vocabulary

distance from a point to a line, *p. 148*
perpendicular bisector, *p. 149*
directed line segment, *p. 156*

Core Concepts

Section 3.4

Finding the Distance from a Point to a Line, *p. 148*
Constructing Perpendicular Lines, *p. 149*
Theorem 3.10 Linear Pair Perpendicular Theorem, *p. 150*
Theorem 3.11 Perpendicular Transversal Theorem, *p. 150*
Theorem 3.12 Lines Perpendicular to a Transversal Theorem, *p. 150*

Section 3.5

Partitioning a Directed Line Segment, *p. 156*
Theorem 3.13 Slopes of Parallel Lines, *p. 157*
Theorem 3.14 Slopes of Perpendicular Lines, *p. 157*
Writing Equations of Parallel and Perpendicular Lines, *p. 158*
Finding the Distance from a Point to a Line, *p. 159*

Mathematical Practices

1. Compare the effectiveness of the argument in Exercise 24 on page 153 with the argument "You can find the distance between any two parallel lines." What flaw(s) exist in the argument(s)? Does either argument use correct reasoning? Explain.

2. Look back at your construction of a square in Exercise 29 on page 154. How would your construction change if you were to construct a rectangle?

3. In Exercise 31 on page 161, a classmate tells you that your answer is incorrect because you should have divided the segment into four congruent pieces. Respond to your classmate's argument by justifying your original answer.

------- Performance Task -------

Navajo Rugs

Navajo rugs use mathematical properties to enhance their beauty. How can you describe these creative works of art with geometry? What properties of lines can you see and use to describe the patterns?

To explore the answers to this question and more, go to *BigIdeasMath.com*.

163

ANSWERS

1. You can find the distance between two lines only if the two lines are parallel. If you choose a point on one line and find the distance from that point to the other line, then the answer will always be the same when the lines are parallel. If the lines are not parallel, then the answer will be different for every point on the line.

2. After drawing the perpendicular lines through each endpoint of the given segment, you could pick an arbitrary point on one of the perpendicular lines. Then set the compass to the distance from this point to the corresponding endpoint, and use the same compass setting to mark a point on the other perpendicular line that is the same distance from the other endpoint. Connect these two points to construct the fourth segment of the rectangle. This segment should be congruent and parallel to the original segment and perpendicular to the other two constructed segments.

3. Because the distance from your house to the school is one-fourth of the distance from the school to the movie theater, you have to use five congruent segments. Four of the segments are between your school and the movie theater and one is between your house and your school.

3 Chapter Review

Dynamic Solutions available at *BigIdeasMath.com*

3.1 Pairs of Lines and Angles (pp. 125–130)

Think of each segment in the figure as part of a line.

a. Which line(s) appear perpendicular to $\overleftrightarrow{AB}$?

▶ $\overleftrightarrow{BD}$, $\overleftrightarrow{AC}$, $\overleftrightarrow{BH}$, and $\overleftrightarrow{AG}$ appear perpendicular to $\overleftrightarrow{AB}$.

b. Which line(s) appear parallel to $\overleftrightarrow{AB}$?

▶ $\overleftrightarrow{CD}$, $\overleftrightarrow{GH}$, and $\overleftrightarrow{EF}$ appear parallel to $\overleftrightarrow{AB}$.

c. Which line(s) appear skew to $\overleftrightarrow{AB}$?

▶ $\overleftrightarrow{CF}$, $\overleftrightarrow{CE}$, $\overleftrightarrow{DF}$, $\overleftrightarrow{FH}$, and $\overleftrightarrow{EG}$ appear skew to $\overleftrightarrow{AB}$.

d. Which plane(s) appear parallel to plane ABC?

▶ Plane EFG appears parallel to plane ABC.

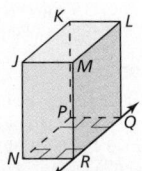

Think of each segment in the figure as part of a line. Which line(s) or plane(s) appear to fit the description?

1. line(s) perpendicular to $\overleftrightarrow{QR}$
2. line(s) parallel to $\overleftrightarrow{QR}$
3. line(s) skew to $\overleftrightarrow{QR}$
4. plane(s) parallel to plane LMQ

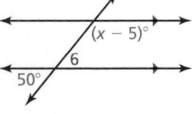

3.2 Parallel Lines and Transversals (pp. 131–136)

Find the value of x.

By the Vertical Angles Congruence Theorem (Theorem 2.6), $m\angle 6 = 50°$.

$(x - 5)° + m\angle 6 = 180°$	Consecutive Interior Angles Theorem (Thm. 3.4)
$(x - 5)° + 50° = 180°$	Substitute 50° for $m\angle 6$.
$x + 45 = 180$	Combine like terms.
$x = 135$	Subtract 45 from each side.

▶ So, the value of x is 135.

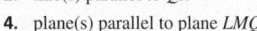

Find the values of x and y.

5.

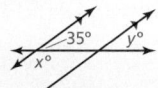

6.

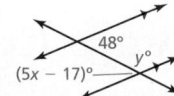

7.

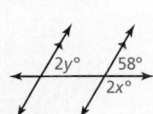

8.

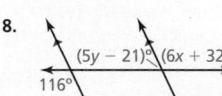

3.3 Proofs with Parallel Lines (pp. 137–144)

Find the value of *x* that makes *m* ∥ *n*.

By the Alternate Interior Angles Converse (Theorem 3.6), *m* ∥ *n* when the marked angles are congruent.

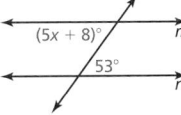

$$(5x + 8)° = 53°$$
$$5x = 45$$
$$x = 9$$

▶ The lines *m* and *n* are parallel when *x* = 9.

Find the value of *x* that makes *m* ∥ *n*.

9.

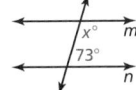

10.

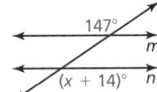

11.

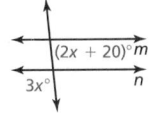

12.

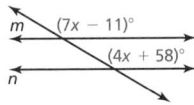

3.4 Proofs with Perpendicular Lines (pp. 147–154)

Determine which lines, if any, must be parallel. Explain your reasoning.

Lines *a* and *b* are both perpendicular to *d*, so by the Lines Perpendicular to a Transversal Theorem (Theorem 3.12), *a* ∥ *b*.

Also, lines *c* and *d* are both perpendicular to *b*, so by the Lines Perpendicular to a Transversal Theorem (Theorem 3.12), *c* ∥ *d*.

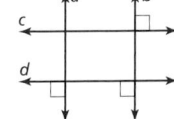

Determine which lines, if any, must be parallel. Explain your reasoning.

13.

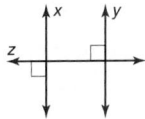

14.

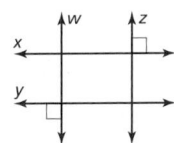

15.

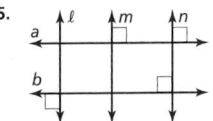

16.

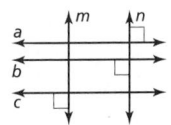

ANSWERS

9. $x = 107$

10. $x = 133$

11. $x = 32$

12. $x = 23$

13. $x \parallel y$; Because $x \perp z$ and $y \perp z$, lines *x* and *y* are parallel by the Lines Perpendicular to a Transversal Theorem (Thm. 3.12).

14. none; The only thing that can be concluded in this diagram is that $x \perp z$ and $w \perp y$. In order to say that lines are parallel, you need to know something about *both* of the intersections between the two lines and a transversal.

15. $\ell \parallel m \parallel n$, $a \parallel b$; Because $a \perp n$ and $b \perp n$, lines *a* and *b* are parallel by the Lines Perpendicular to a Transversal Theorem (Thm. 3.12). Because $m \perp a$ and $n \perp a$, lines *m* and *n* are parallel by the Lines Perpendicular to a Transversal Theorem (Thm. 3.12). Because $\ell \perp b$ and $n \perp b$, lines ℓ and *n* are parallel by the Lines Perpendicular to a Transversal Theorem (Thm. 3.12). Because $\ell \parallel n$ and $m \parallel n$, lines ℓ and *m* are parallel by the Transitive Property of Parallel Lines (Thm. 3.9).

16. $a \parallel b$; Because $a \perp n$ and $b \perp n$, lines *a* and *b* are parallel by the Lines Perpendicular to a Transversal Theorem (Thm. 3.12).

17. $y = -x - 1$
18. $y = \frac{1}{2}x + 8$
19. $y = 3x - 6$
20. $y = \frac{1}{3}x - 2$
21. $y = \frac{1}{2}x - 4$
22. $y = 2x + 3$
23. $y = -\frac{1}{4}x + 4$
24. $y = -7x - 2$
25. about 2.1 units
26. about 2.7 units

3.5 **Equations of Parallel and Perpendicular Lines** *(pp. 155–162)*

a. **Write an equation of the line passing through the point $(-2, 4)$ that is parallel to the line $y = 5x - 7$.**

Step 1 Find the slope m of the parallel line. The line $y = 5x - 7$ has a slope of 5. By the Slopes of Parallel Lines Theorem (Theorem 3.13), a line parallel to this line also has a slope of 5. So, $m = 5$.

Step 2 Find the y-intercept b by using $m = 5$ and $(x, y) = (-2, 4)$.

$y = mx + b$ Use slope-intercept form.

$4 = 5(-2) + b$ Substitute for m, x, and y.

$14 = b$ Solve for b.

▶ Because $m = 5$ and $b = 14$, an equation of the line is $y = 5x + 14$.

b. **Write an equation of the line passing through the point $(6, 1)$ that is perpendicular to the line $3x + y = 9$.**

Step 1 Find the slope m of the perpendicular line. The line $3x + y = 9$, or $y = -3x + 9$, has a slope of -3. Use the Slopes of Perpendicular Lines Theorem (Theorem 3.14).

$-3 \cdot m = -1$ The product of the slopes of ⊥ lines is -1.

$m = \frac{1}{3}$ Divide each side by -3.

Step 2 Find the y-intercept b by using $m = \frac{1}{3}$ and $(x, y) = (6, 1)$.

$y = mx + b$ Use slope-intercept form.

$1 = \frac{1}{3}(6) + b$ Substitute for m, x, and y.

$-1 = b$ Solve for b.

▶ Because $m = \frac{1}{3}$ and $b = -1$, an equation of the line is $y = \frac{1}{3}x - 1$.

Write an equation of the line passing through the given point that is parallel to the given line.

17. $A(3, -4)$, $y = -x + 8$ 18. $A(-6, 5)$, $y = \frac{1}{2}x - 7$

19. $A(2, 0)$, $y = 3x - 5$ 20. $A(3, -1)$, $y = \frac{1}{3}x + 10$

Write an equation of the line passing through the given point that is perpendicular to the given line.

21. $A(6, -1)$, $y = -2x + 8$ 22. $A(0, 3)$, $y = -\frac{1}{2}x - 6$

23. $A(8, 2)$, $y = 4x - 7$ 24. $A(-1, 5)$, $y = \frac{1}{7}x + 4$

Find the distance from point A to the given line.

25. $A(2, -1)$, $y = -x + 4$ 26. $A(-2, 3)$, $y = \frac{1}{2}x + 1$

3 Chapter Test

Find the values of _x_ and _y_. State which theorem(s) you used.

1.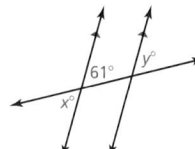

2.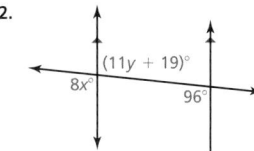

3.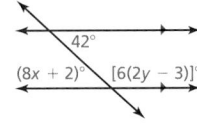

Find the distance from point _A_ to the given line.

4. $A(3, 4), y = -x$

5. $A(-3, 7), y = \frac{1}{3}x - 2$

Find the value of _x_ that makes $m \parallel n$.

6.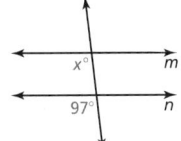

7.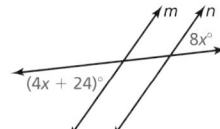

8.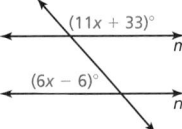

Write an equation of the line that passes through the given point and is (a) parallel to and (b) perpendicular to the given line.

9. $(-5, 2), y = 2x - 3$

10. $(-1, -9), y = -\frac{1}{3}x + 4$

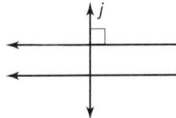

11. A student says, "Because $j \perp k, j \perp \ell$." What missing information is the student assuming from the diagram? Which theorem is the student trying to use?

12. You and your family are visiting some attractions while on vacation. You and your mom visit the shopping mall while your dad and your sister visit the aquarium. You decide to meet at the intersection of lines _q_ and _p_. Each unit in the coordinate plane corresponds to 50 yards.

   a. Find an equation of line _q_.

   b. Find an equation of line _p_.

   c. What are the coordinates of the meeting point?

   d. What is the distance from the meeting point to the subway?

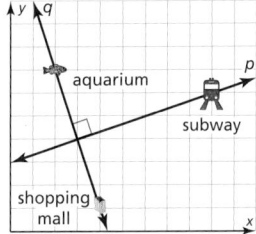

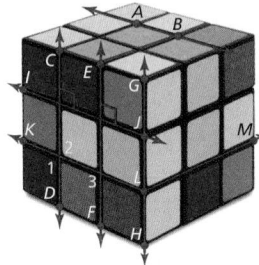

13. Identify an example on the puzzle cube of each description. Explain your reasoning.

   a. a pair of skew lines

   b. a pair of perpendicular lines

   c. a pair of parallel lines

   d. a pair of congruent corresponding angles

   e. a pair of congruent alternate interior angles

ANSWERS

1. $x = 61, y = 61$; $x° = 61°$ by the Vertical Angles Congruence Theorem (Thm. 2.6). $y° = x° = 61°$ by the Alternate Exterior Angles Theorem (Thm. 3.3).

2. $x = 12, y = 7$; $8x° = 96°$ by the Corresponding Angles Theorem (Thm. 3.1). $(11y + 19)° = 96°$ by the Alternate Interior Angles Theorem (Thm. 3.2).

3. $x = 5, y = 13$; $(8x + 2)° = 42°$ by the Alternate Interior Angles Theorem (Thm. 3.2). $[6(2y - 3)]° + 42° = 180°$ by the Consecutive Interior Angles Theorem (Thm. 3.4).

4. about 4.9 units

5. about 9.5 units

6. $x = 97$

7. $x = 6$

8. $x = 9$

9. **a.** $y = 2x + 12$
   b. $y = -\frac{1}{2}x - \frac{1}{2}$

10. **a.** $y = -\frac{1}{3}x - \frac{28}{3}$
    b. $y = 3x - 6$

11. $k \parallel \ell$; Perpendicular Transversal Theorem (Thm. 3.11)

12. **a.** $y = -3x + 650$
    b. $y = \frac{1}{3}x + 150$
    c. $(150, 200)$
    d. about 316 yd

13. **a.** *Sample answer:* $\overleftrightarrow{AB}$ and $\overleftrightarrow{GH}$; non-intersecting, non-coplanar, non-parallel lines
    b. *Sample answer:* $\overleftrightarrow{IJ}$ and $\overleftrightarrow{CD}$; lines intersect at right angle
    c. $\overleftrightarrow{CD}$ and $\overleftrightarrow{EF}$; lines are perpendicular to same transversal
    d. $\angle 1$ and $\angle 3$; angles are corresponding and $\overleftrightarrow{CD} \parallel \overleftrightarrow{EF}$
    e. $\angle 2$ and $\angle 3$; angles are alternate interior and $\overleftrightarrow{CD} \parallel \overleftrightarrow{EF}$

If students need help...	If students got it...
Lesson Tutorials	Resources by Chapter • Enrichment and Extension • Cumulative Review
Skills Review Handbook	Performance Task
BigIdeasMath.com	Start the *next* Section

ANSWERS

1. Every point on the red arc in Step 1 is the same distance from point A. Because the same compass setting is used, every point on the red arc in Step 2 is the same distance from point B as all of the points in the blue arc are from point A. Also, $\overleftrightarrow{CD} \perp \overline{AB}$ because the shortest distance from a point to a line is the perpendicular segment that connects the point to that line. So, points C and D and every point on $\overleftrightarrow{CD}$ are equidistant from points A and B, which means that M is the midpoint of $\overline{AB}$ by definition.

2. **a.** $y = -\frac{1}{2}x - 3$
   b. $y = 2x - 5$

3. **a.** supplementary
   b. adjacent
   c. vertical
   d. complementary

4. **a.** 360 ft
   b. 1040 ft
   c. no

1. Use the steps in the construction to explain how you know that $\overleftrightarrow{CD}$ is the perpendicular bisector of $\overline{AB}$.

Step 1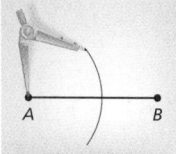

Step 2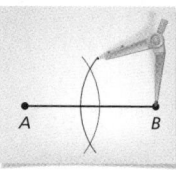

Step 3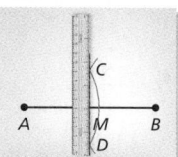

2. The equation of a line is $x + 2y = 10$.

   a. Use the numbers and symbols to create the equation of a line in slope-intercept form that passes through the point $(4, -5)$ and is parallel to the given line.

   b. Use the numbers and symbols to create the equation of a line in slope-intercept form that passes through the point $(2, -1)$ and is perpendicular to the given line.

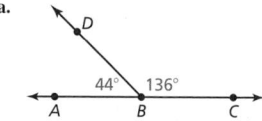
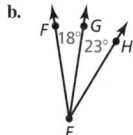

3. Classify each pair of angles whose measurements are given.

   a.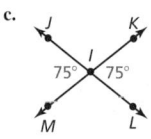

   b.

   c.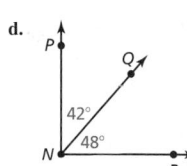

   d.

4. Your school is installing new turf on the football field. A coordinate plane has been superimposed on a diagram of the football field where 1 unit = 20 feet.

   a. What is the length of the field?

   b. What is the perimeter of the field?

   c. Turf costs $2.69 per square foot. Your school has a $150,000 budget. Does the school have enough money to purchase new turf for the entire field?

168 **Chapter 3** Parallel and Perpendicular Lines

5. Enter a statement or reason in each blank to complete the two-column proof.

Given ∠1 ≅ ∠3

Prove ∠2 ≅ ∠4

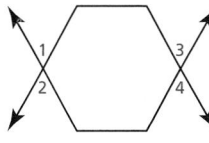

STATEMENTS	REASONS
1. ∠1 ≅ ∠3	1. Given
2. ∠1 ≅ ∠2	2. _____
3. ∠2 ≅ ∠3	3. _____
4. _____	4. Vertical Angles Congruence Theorem (Thm. 2.6)
5. ∠2 ≅ ∠4	5. _____

6. Your friend claims that lines *m* and *n* are parallel. Do you support your friend's claim? Explain your reasoning.

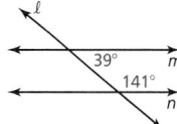

7. Which of the following is true when $\overleftrightarrow{AB}$ and $\overleftrightarrow{CD}$ are skew?

Ⓐ $\overleftrightarrow{AB}$ and $\overleftrightarrow{CD}$ are parallel.

Ⓑ $\overleftrightarrow{AB}$ and $\overleftrightarrow{CD}$ intersect.

Ⓒ $\overleftrightarrow{AB}$ and $\overleftrightarrow{CD}$ are perpendicular.

Ⓓ *A*, *B*, and *C* are noncollinear.

8. Select the angle that makes the statement true.

a. ∠4 ≅ ___ by the Alternate Interior Angles Theorem (Thm. 3.2).

b. ∠2 ≅ ___ by the Corresponding Angles Theorem (Thm. 3.1).

c. ∠1 ≅ ___ by the Alternate Exterior Angles Theorem (Thm. 3.3).

d. *m*∠6 + *m* _____ = 180° by the Consecutive Interior Angles Theorem (Thm. 3.4).

9. You and your friend walk to school together every day. You meet at the halfway point between your houses first and then walk to school. Each unit in the coordinate plane corresponds to 50 yards.

a. What are the coordinates of the midpoint of the line segment joining the two houses?

b. What is the distance that the two of you walk together?

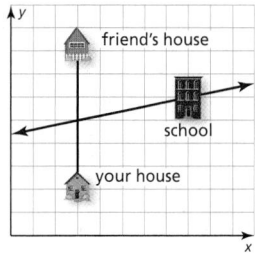

5. Vertical Angles Congruence Theorem (Thm. 2.6); Transitive Property of Congruence (Thm. 2.2); ∠3 ≅ ∠4; Transitive Property of Congruence (Thm. 2.2)

6. yes; Because 141° + 39° = 180°, the marked angles are supplementary. They are consecutive interior angles, so *m* ∥ *n* by the Consecutive Angles Converse (Thm. 3.5).

7. D

8. a. ∠5

   b. ∠6

   c. ∠8

   d. ∠4

9. a. (150, 250)

   b. about 255 yd

Chapter 4 Pacing Guide	
Chapter Opener/ Mathematical Practices	0.5 Day
Section 1	1.5 Days
Section 2	1 Day
Section 3	2 Days
Quiz	0.5 Day
Section 4	1.5 Days
Section 5	2 Days
Section 6	1 Day
Chapter Review/ Chapter Tests	2 Days
Total Chapter 4	12 Days
Year-to-Date	48 Days

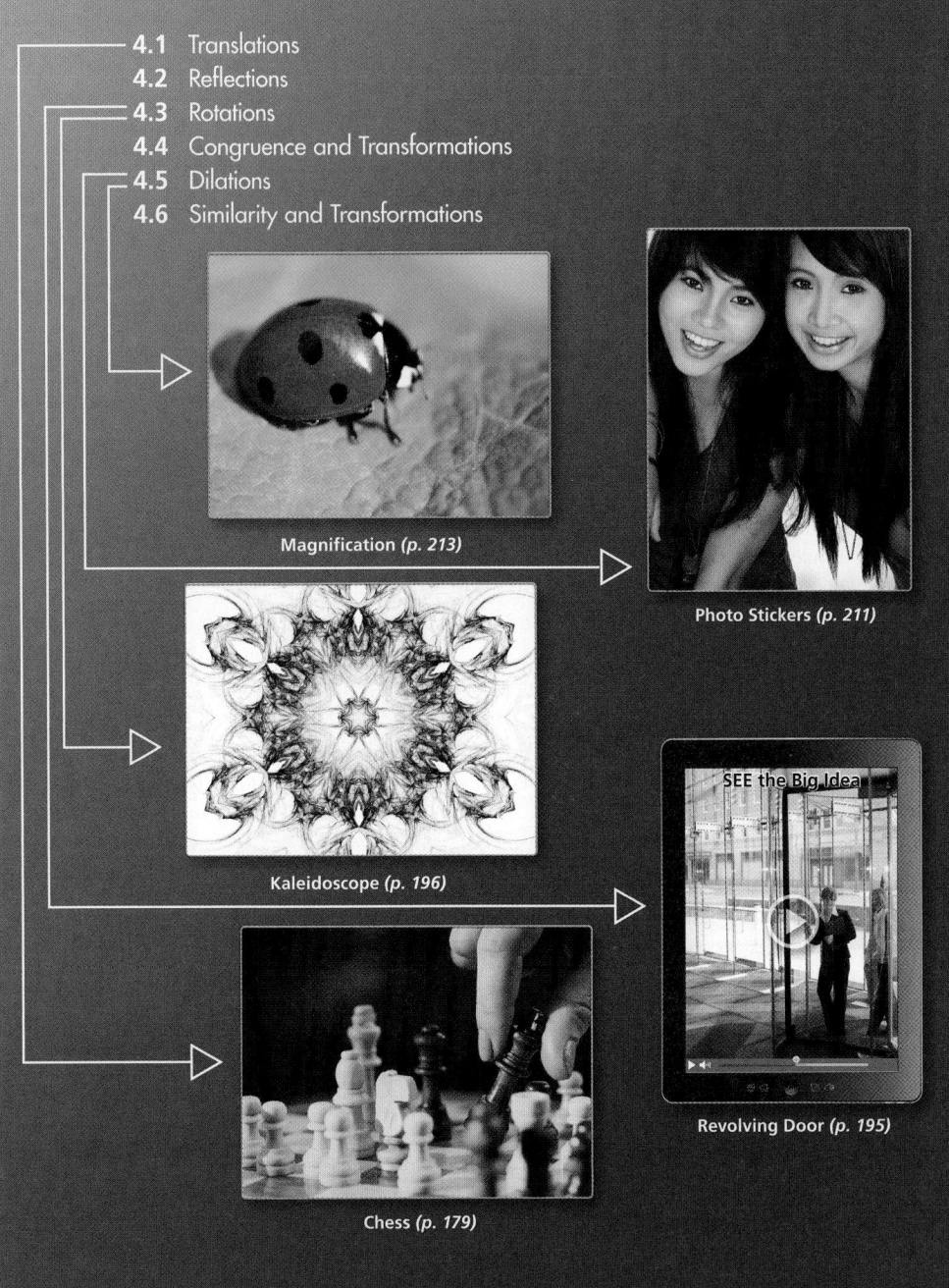

Magnification (p. 213)

Photo Stickers (p. 211)

Kaleidoscope (p. 196)

SEE the Big Idea

Revolving Door (p. 195)

Chess (p. 179)

Chapter Summary

- Students should have a conceptual understanding of transformations from middle school, where they studied translations, reflections, and rotations. Some may also have been introduced to glide reflections.

- The focus on plane transformations in the Common Core State Standards makes sense in terms of the continuity from middle school to high school. In middle school, the conditions for triangle congruence were informally explored. In high school, "once these triangle congruence criteria (ASA, SAS, and SSS) are established using rigid motions, they can be used to prove theorems about triangles, quadrilaterals, and other geometric figures." The criteria for triangle similarity are established through similarity transformations.

- In this chapter, key postulates and theorems relating to rigid motions are presented. Translations, reflections, glide reflections, and rotations are all postulated to be rigid motions. While all could be proven and established as theorems, we have chosen to treat them as postulates in this book.

- Dilations are introduced as nonrigid transformations where the scale factor k results in an enlargement ($k > 1$) or a reduction ($0 < k < 1$). The composition of a dilation with rigid motions results in a similarity transformation. In the last lesson, similar figures are defined in terms of similarity transformations.

- The use of dynamic geometry software for the explorations and formal lessons is highly encouraged. This tool provides students the opportunity to explore and make conjectures, mathematical practices we want to develop in all students.

Scaffolding in the Classroom

How do you solve that?

Verbally state the thought processes you use to solve a problem. What questions do you ask yourself? Help the students develop their own set of questions.

COMMON CORE PROGRESSION

Middle School
- Draw polygons in the coordinate plane given the vertices, and find lengths of sides.
- Identify congruent figures and similar figures.
- Verify the properties of rotations, reflections, and translations.

Algebra 1
- Translate, reflect, stretch, and shrink graphs of functions.
- Combine transformations of graphs of functions.
- Use slope to solve real-life problems.

Geometry
- Perform translations, reflections, rotations, dilations, and compositions of transformations.
- Solve real-life problems involving transformations.
- Identify lines of symmetry and rotational symmetry.
- Describe and perform congruence transformations and similarity transformations.

Standards Summary		
Section		Common Core State Standards
4.1	Learning	HSG-CO.A.2, HSG-CO.A.4, HSG-CO.A.5, HSG-CO.B.6
4.2	Learning	HSG-CO.A.2, HSG-CO.A.3, HSG-CO.A.4, HSG-CO.A.5, HSG-CO.B.6, HSG-MG.A.3
4.3	Learning	HSG-CO.A.2, HSG-CO.A.3, HSG-CO.A.4, HSG-CO.A.5, HSG-CO.B.6
4.4	Learning	HSG-CO.A.5, HSG-CO.B.6
4.5	Learning	HSG-CO.A.2, HSG-SRT.A.1a, HSG-SRT.A.1b
4.6	Learning	HSG-CO.A.5, HSG-SRT.A.2

All students need to participate.
When a small group of students continually answers the questions in your classroom, no one else has to think. Try asking a different student whether they agree with the answer given and then follow up with why or why not.

Laurie's Notes

Maintaining Mathematical Proficiency

Identifying Transformations

- Remind students that a translation *slides* a figure; a reflection *flips* a figure; a rotation *turns* a figure.
- Of the transformations *translation*, *reflection*, *rotation*, and *dilation*, the only one that changes the *size* of a figure is a dilation.

COMMON ERROR Students may confuse reflections and rotations. Remind students that a reflection produces a mirror image of the original figure.

Identifying Similar Figures

- Remind students that two figures are similar if and only if corresponding angles are congruent and the lengths of corresponding sides are proportional.

COMMON ERROR Students may forget that congruent figures are also similar figures. Remind students that the ratio of the lengths of corresponding sides in congruent figures is 1:1.

Mathematical Practices (continued on page 172)

- The eight *Mathematical Practices* focus attention on how mathematics is learned—process versus content. Page 172 demonstrates the use of dynamic geometry software as a tool in learning important mathematics.

If students need help...	*If students got it...*
Student Journal • Maintaining Mathematical Proficiency	Game Closet at *BigIdeasMath.com*
Lesson Tutorials	Start the *next* Section
Skills Review Handbook	

Maintaining Mathematical Proficiency

Identifying Transformations

Example 1 Tell whether the red figure is a translation, reflection, rotation, or dilation of the blue figure.

a. 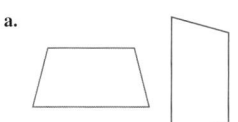 The blue figure turns to form the red figure, so it is a rotation.

b. 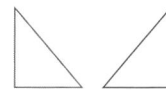 The red figure is a mirror image of the blue figure, so it is a reflection.

Tell whether the red figure is a translation, reflection, rotation, or dilation of the blue figure.

1.

2.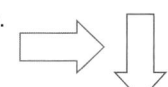

3.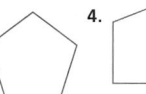

4. (figure)

Identifying Similar Figures

Example 2 Which rectangle is similar to Rectangle A?

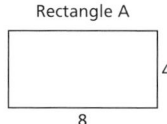

Rectangle A — 4, 8

Rectangle B — 1, 4

Rectangle C — 3, 6

Each figure is a rectangle, so corresponding angles are congruent. Check to see whether corresponding side lengths are proportional.

Rectangle A and Rectangle B

$$\frac{\text{Length of A}}{\text{Length of B}} = \frac{8}{4} = 2 \qquad \frac{\text{Width of A}}{\text{Width of B}} = \frac{4}{1} = 4$$

not proportional

Rectangle A and Rectangle C

$$\frac{\text{Length of A}}{\text{Length of C}} = \frac{8}{6} = \frac{4}{3} \qquad \frac{\text{Width of A}}{\text{Width of C}} = \frac{4}{3}$$

proportional

▶ So, Rectangle C is similar to Rectangle A.

Tell whether the two figures are similar. Explain your reasoning.

5. 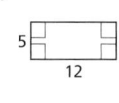 5, 12, 14, 7

6. 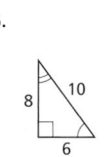 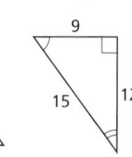 8, 10, 6, 9, 15, 12

7. 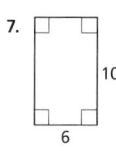 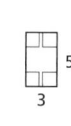 10, 5, 6, 3

8. ABSTRACT REASONING Can you draw two squares that are not similar? Explain your reasoning.

Common Core State Standards

8.G.A.1 Verify experimentally the properties of rotations, reflections, and translations.

8.G.A.4 Understand that a two-dimensional figure is similar to another if the second can be obtained from the first by a sequence of rotations, reflections, translations, and dilations; given two similar two-dimensional figures, describe a sequence that exhibits the similarity between them.

ANSWERS

1. reflection

2. rotation

3. dilation

4. translation

5. no; $\frac{12}{14} = \frac{6}{7} \neq \frac{5}{7}$, The sides are not proportional.

6. yes; The corresponding angles are congruent and the corresponding side lengths are proportional.

7. yes; The corresponding angles are congruent and the corresponding side lengths are proportional.

8. no; Squares have four right angles, so the corresponding angles are always congruent. Because all four sides are congruent, the corresponding sides will always be proportional.

Vocabulary Review

Have students make an Example and Non-Example Chart for the following terms.

- Translation
- Reflection
- Rotation
- Dilation

1.

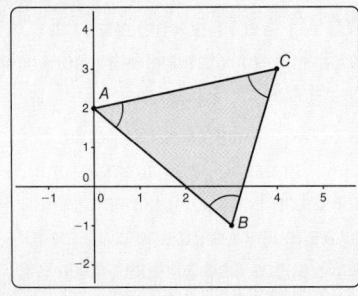

$AB \approx 4.24$; $BC \approx 4.12$; $AC \approx 4.12$;
$m\angle A \approx 59.04°$;
$m\angle B \approx 59.04°$; $m\angle C \approx 61.93°$

2.

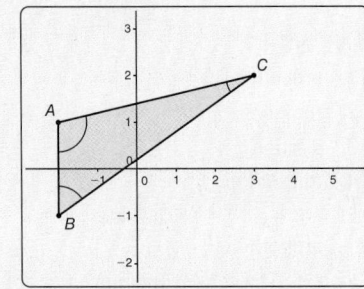

$AB = 2$; $BC \approx 5.83$; $AC \approx 5.10$;
$m\angle A \approx 101.31°$;
$m\angle B \approx 59.04°$; $m\angle C \approx 19.65°$

3.

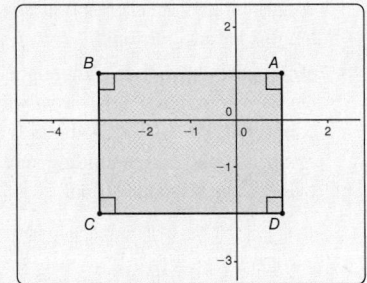

$AB = 4$; $BC = 3$; $CD = 4$; $AD = 3$;
$m\angle A = 90°$; $m\angle B = 90°$;
$m\angle C = 90°$; $m\angle D = 90°$

4.

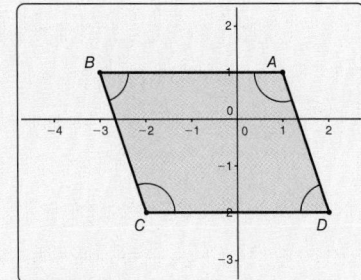

$AB = 4$; $BC \approx 3.16$; $CD = 4$;
$AD \approx 3.16$; $m\angle A \approx 108.43°$;
$m\angle B \approx 71.57°$; $m\angle C \approx 108.43°$;
$m\angle D \approx 71.57°$

5–6. See Additional Answers.

Mathematical Practices

Mathematically proficient students use dynamic geometry software strategically.

Using Dynamic Geometry Software

⟳ Core Concept

Using Dynamic Geometry Software

Dynamic geometry software allows you to create geometric drawings, including:

- drawing a point
- drawing a line
- drawing a line segment
- drawing an angle

- measuring an angle
- measuring a line segment
- drawing a circle
- drawing an ellipse

- drawing a perpendicular line
- drawing a polygon
- copying and sliding an object
- reflecting an object in a line

EXAMPLE 1   Finding Side Lengths and Angle Measures

Use dynamic geometry software to draw a triangle with vertices at $A(-2, 1)$, $B(2, 1)$, and $C(2, -2)$. Find the side lengths and angle measures of the triangle.

SOLUTION

Using dynamic geometry software, you can create $\triangle ABC$, as shown.

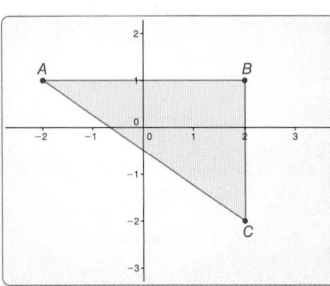

Sample

Points
$A(-2, 1)$
$B(2, 1)$
$C(2, -2)$
Segments
$AB = 4$
$BC = 3$
$AC = 5$
Angles
$m\angle A = 36.87°$
$m\angle B = 90°$
$m\angle C = 53.13°$

▶ From the display, the side lengths are $AB = 4$ units, $BC = 3$ units, and $AC = 5$ units. The angle measures, rounded to two decimal places, are $m\angle A \approx 36.87°$, $m\angle B = 90°$, and $m\angle C \approx 53.13°$.

Monitoring Progress

Use dynamic geometry software to draw the polygon with the given vertices. Use the software to find the side lengths and angle measures of the polygon. Round your answers to the nearest hundredth.

1. $A(0, 2)$, $B(3, -1)$, $C(4, 3)$

2. $A(-2, 1)$, $B(-2, -1)$, $C(3, 2)$

3. $A(1, 1)$, $B(-3, 1)$, $C(-3, -2)$, $D(1, -2)$

4. $A(1, 1)$, $B(-3, 1)$, $C(-2, -2)$, $D(2, -2)$

5. $A(-3, 0)$, $B(0, 3)$, $C(3, 0)$, $D(0, -3)$

6. $A(0, 0)$, $B(4, 0)$, $C(1, 1)$, $D(0, 3)$

Laurie's Notes   Mathematical Practices *(continued from page T-171)*

- Use the *Mathematical Practices* page to help students develop mathematical habits of mind—how mathematics can be explored and how mathematics is thought about.
- Refer to the *Core Concept*, and then have students explore the home screen of the software they will use in this chapter if they have not done so earlier in the year.
- In Example 1, make sure students know how to measure lengths and angles.
- Throughout this course, you want students to develop the habit of using the dynamic geometry software as a tool to investigate mathematics and develop understanding of geometric properties and relationships.
- Students should try at least one triangle and one quadrilateral, perhaps Questions 1 and 6.

Overview of Section 4.1

Introduction

- Students are familiar with translations (slides) from middle school. They learned to translate figures in the plane and represent a translation using coordinate notation.
- The explorations provide an opportunity for students to become familiar with the dynamic geometry software if they are not already. They need to know how to draw a polygon and translate it by some vector. Students will also verify that a translation preserves the segment length of the preimage for a specific case.
- The formal lesson introduces a key postulate and a key theorem relating to rigid motions. Stating that a translation is a rigid motion is the first postulate of the chapter. The rigid motions, reflection and rotation, are postulated in later lessons. An important and useful theorem presented in this lesson is the *Composition Theorem* (Thm. 4.1).
- Translations are represented most often in this lesson using coordinate notation, though vector notation is also used. When working with dynamic geometry software, students will need to be familiar with vector notation.

Resources

- **MP5 Use Appropriate Tools Strategically:** Dynamic geometry software, graph paper, and tracing paper are all tools that will be helpful for students to make sense of translations. Transparencies (overhead projector) and interactive whiteboards are useful tools for teachers.

Common Misconceptions

- Students sometimes think that just a few points are translated, such as the endpoints of segments or vertices of a polygon. Help students to understand that a translation is a function that maps all points of the preimage in the plane to a new location called the image.

Formative Assessment Tips

- **Always-Sometimes-Never True (AT-ST-NT):** This strategy is useful in assessing whether students over-generalize or under-generalize a particular concept.
- **MP2 Reason Abstractly and Quantitatively** and **MP3 Construct Viable Arguments and Critique the Reasoning of Others:** When answering, a student should be asked to justify his or her answer (MP2), and other students listening to the justification should critique the reasoning (MP3).
- *AT-ST-NT* statements help students practice the habit of checking validity when a statement (conjecture) is made. Are there different cases that need to be checked? Is there a counterexample that would show the conjecture to be false?
- Using *AT-ST-NT* statements encourages discourse. To develop these statements for a lesson, consider the common errors or misconceptions that students have relating to the goal(s) of the lesson. Allow private think time before students share their thinking with partners or the whole class.

Pacing Suggestion

- The formal lesson is long; however, experience with the explorations helps students develop essential understanding of translations. Students should work through Examples 2–4 more quickly as a result of the explorations.

HSG-CO.A.2 Represent transformations
in the plane using, e.g., ... geometry
software; describe transformations as
functions that take points in the plane
as inputs and give other points as
outputs ... .

HSG-CO.A.4 Develop definitions of ...
translations in terms of angles, ... parallel
lines, and line segments.

HSG-CO.A.5 Given a geometric
figure and a ... translation, draw the
transformed figure using, e.g., graph
paper, ... or geometry software. Specify a
sequence of transformations that will carry
a given figure onto another.

HSG-CO.B.6 Use geometric descriptions
of rigid motions to transform figures
and to predict the effect of a given rigid
motion on a given figure; ...

Laurie's Notes

Exploration

Motivate
- Ask for four volunteers. Hand them a piece of yarn or rope at least 12 feet long that has been knotted to form a loop. Have students form the yarn in the shape of a rectangle by holding the vertices.
- Tell students that you are going to give them instructions to move and that on the word "go" they will all move at the same time.
- Examples: "Take two steps to the front of the classroom. Go."
  "Take three steps toward the door. Go."
- Discuss the results of each instruction. In particular, what happened to the rectangle? The rectangle should have remained the same—congruent.
- Repeat with four new students and ask them to form a trapezoid. Tap three of the students on the shoulder and tell them to follow your instructions. The remaining student is to ignore your instructions.
- When you give the first instruction, it is clear that unless all four students move at the same time and in the same direction, the trapezoid is going to change shape!

Exploration 1
- This first exploration serves to familiarize students with the *translate* and *copy* commands in the dynamic geometry software. It also uses the language and notation of transformations, both of which should be familiar from middle school.
- Students should observe that the side lengths and angle measures of the copied triangle are the same as the measures in the original triangle.

Exploration 2
- Students complete this exploration with paper and pencil. Expect that students recall how to write the rule for translating an ordered pair using coordinate notation. (The software uses vector notation: $<a, b>$.)
- None of the sides of $\triangle ABC$ are vertical or horizontal. Finding the lengths of the sides requires students to use the *Distance Formula*.
- **? Always-Sometimes-Never True:** "When a segment is translated, the length of the image is congruent to the original segment." always

Exploration 3
- **? Assessing Question:** "How can you determine whether a triangle in the coordinate plane is a right triangle?" Find the slopes of the two sides that form the right angle and see whether their product is -1.
- **? Always-Sometimes-Never True:** "When an angle is translated, the resulting angle is congruent to the original angle." always

Communicate Your Answer
- **Neighbor Check:** Have students work independently, and then have their neighbors check their work. Have students discuss any discrepancies.

Connecting to Next Step
- Students have now been introduced to translations. In the formal lesson, students will perform translations using vector notation.

4.1 Translations

Essential Question
How can you translate a figure in a coordinate plane?

EXPLORATION 1 — Translating a Triangle in a Coordinate Plane

Work with a partner.

a. Use dynamic geometry software to draw any triangle and label it △ABC.

b. Copy the triangle and *translate* (or slide) it to form a new figure, called an *image*, △A′B′C′ (read as "triangle A prime, B prime, C prime").

c. What is the relationship between the coordinates of the vertices of △ABC and those of △A′B′C′?

d. What do you observe about the side lengths and angle measures of the two triangles?

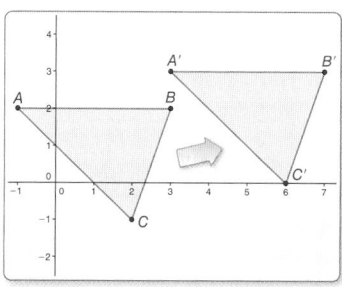

Sample

Points
A(−1, 2)
B(3, 2)
C(2, −1)

Segments
AB = 4
BC = 3.16
AC = 4.24

Angles
m∠A = 45°
m∠B = 71.57°
m∠C = 63.43°

USING TOOLS STRATEGICALLY
To be proficient in math, you need to use appropriate tools strategically, including dynamic geometry software.

EXPLORATION 2 — Translating a Triangle in a Coordinate Plane

Work with a partner.

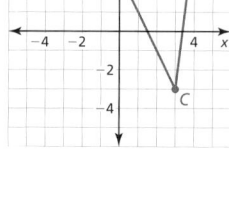

a. The point (x, y) is translated a units horizontally and b units vertically. Write a rule to determine the coordinates of the image of (x, y).

$$(x, y) \rightarrow (\boxed{}, \boxed{})$$

b. Use the rule you wrote in part (a) to translate △ABC 4 units left and 3 units down. What are the coordinates of the vertices of the image, △A′B′C′?

c. Draw △A′B′C′. Are its side lengths the same as those of △ABC? Justify your answer.

EXPLORATION 3 — Comparing Angles of Translations

Work with a partner.

a. In Exploration 2, is △ABC a right triangle? Justify your answer.

b. In Exploration 2, is △A′B′C′ a right triangle? Justify your answer.

c. Do you think translations always preserve angle measures? Explain your reasoning.

Communicate Your Answer

4. How can you translate a figure in a coordinate plane?

5. In Exploration 2, translate △A′B′C′ 3 units right and 4 units up. What are the coordinates of the vertices of the image, △A″B″C″? How are these coordinates related to the coordinates of the vertices of the original triangle, △ABC?

Dynamic Teaching Tools

Dynamic Assessment & Progress Monitoring Tool

Lesson Planning Tool

Interactive Whiteboard Lesson Library

Dynamic Classroom with Dynamic Investigations

ANSWERS

1. a. Check students' work.

   b. Check students' work.

   c. The *x*-values of each of the three vertices in the image can be attained by adding the same amount (positive or negative) to the corresponding *x*-values of the vertices in the original figure. The same is true for the *y*-values.

   d. The side lengths and angle measures of the original figure are equal to the corresponding side lengths and angle measures of the image.

2. a. $x + a; y + b$

   b. $A'(-4, 0), B'(0, 2), C'(-1, -6)$

   c.

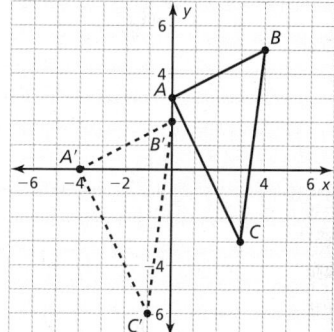

   yes; Use the Distance Formula to find the lengths.

3. a. yes; $(AB)^2 + (AC)^2 = (BC)^2$

   b. yes; The side lengths of the image are the same as the original figure.

   c. yes; The image is congruent to the original figure, so the corresponding angles will be congruent.

4. Move each vertex the same number of units left or right, and up or down. Connect the vertices with a straightedge.

5. $A''(-1, 4), B''(3, 6), C''(2, -2)$; Each vertex of the image is 1 unit left and 1 unit up from the corresponding vertex in the original triangle.

Extra Example 1

Name the vector and write its component form.

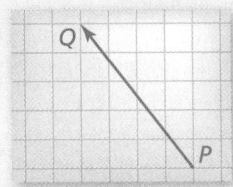

$\overrightarrow{PQ}$; $\langle -4, 5 \rangle$

4.1 Lesson

Core Vocabulary

vector, *p. 174*
initial point, *p. 174*
terminal point, *p. 174*
horizontal component, *p. 174*
vertical component, *p. 174*
component form, *p. 174*
transformation, *p. 174*
image, *p. 174*
preimage, *p. 174*
translation, *p. 174*
rigid motion, *p. 176*
composition of
    transformations, *p. 176*

What You Will Learn

▶ Perform translations.
▶ Perform compositions.
▶ Solve real-life problems involving compositions.

Performing Translations

A **vector** is a quantity that has both direction and *magnitude*, or size, and is represented in the coordinate plane by an arrow drawn from one point to another.

🅖 Core Concept

Vectors

The diagram shows a vector. The **initial point**, or starting point, of the vector is P, and the **terminal point**, or ending point, is Q. The vector is named $\overrightarrow{PQ}$, which is read as "vector PQ." The **horizontal component** of $\overrightarrow{PQ}$ is 5, and the **vertical component** is 3. The **component form** of a vector combines the horizontal and vertical components. So, the component form of $\overrightarrow{PQ}$ is $\langle 5, 3 \rangle$.

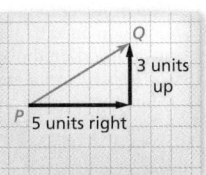

EXAMPLE 1 Identifying Vector Components

In the diagram, name the vector and write its component form.

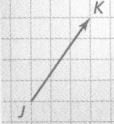

SOLUTION

The vector is $\overrightarrow{JK}$. To move from the initial point J to the terminal point K, you move 3 units right and 4 units up. So, the component form is $\langle 3, 4 \rangle$.

A **transformation** is a function that moves or changes a figure in some way to produce a new figure called an **image**. Another name for the original figure is the **preimage**. The points on the preimage are the inputs for the transformation, and the points on the image are the outputs.

🅖 Core Concept

Translations

A **translation** moves every point of a figure the same distance in the same direction. More specifically, a translation *maps*, or moves, the points P and Q of a plane figure along a vector $\langle a, b \rangle$ to the points P' and Q', so that one of the following statements is true.

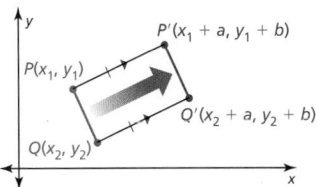

> **STUDY TIP**
> You can use *prime notation* to name an image. For example, if the preimage is point P, then its image is point P', read as "point P *prime*."

• $PP' = QQ'$ and $\overline{PP'} \parallel \overline{QQ'}$, or
• $PP' = QQ'$ and $\overline{PP'}$ and $\overline{QQ'}$ are collinear.

Translations map lines to parallel lines and segments to parallel segments. For instance, in the figure above, $\overline{PQ} \parallel \overline{P'Q'}$.

Laurie's Notes   Teacher Actions

• Vectors were introduced when using dynamic geometry software and are formally defined here. Later you will make the connection between representing translations using vector notation and coordinate notation.
• **Big Idea:** Note that points on the preimage are inputs and points on the image are outputs. Transformations are functions in the plane.

• Write the *Core Concept, Translations,* and spend time discussing the two bullets. $PP' = QQ'$ means that the length of the two segments is the same. $\overline{PP'} \parallel \overline{QQ'}$ means that the segments are parallel. All points of $\overline{PQ}$ are translated the same distance in the same direction.
• Do not become so preoccupied with notation that students fail to see the simplicity of translations.

EXAMPLE 2 **Translating a Figure Using a Vector**

The vertices of △ABC are A(0, 3), B(2, 4), and C(1, 0). Translate △ABC using the vector ⟨5, −1⟩.

SOLUTION

First, graph △ABC. Use ⟨5, −1⟩ to move each vertex 5 units right and 1 unit down. Label the image vertices. Draw △A′B′C′. Notice that the vectors drawn from preimage vertices to image vertices are parallel.

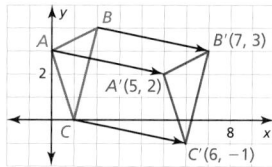

You can also express a translation along the vector ⟨a, b⟩ using a rule, which has the notation $(x, y) \rightarrow (x + a, y + b)$.

EXAMPLE 3 **Writing a Translation Rule**

Write a rule for the translation of △ABC to △A′B′C′.

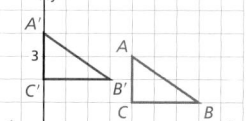

SOLUTION

To go from A to A′, you move 4 units left and 1 unit up, so you move along the vector ⟨−4, 1⟩.

▶ So, a rule for the translation is $(x, y) \rightarrow (x − 4, y + 1)$.

EXAMPLE 4 **Translating a Figure in the Coordinate Plane**

Graph quadrilateral ABCD with vertices A(−1, 2), B(−1, 5), C(4, 6), and D(4, 2) and its image after the translation $(x, y) \rightarrow (x + 3, y − 1)$.

SOLUTION

Graph quadrilateral ABCD. To find the coordinates of the vertices of the image, add 3 to the x-coordinates and subtract 1 from the y-coordinates of the vertices of the preimage. Then graph the image, as shown at the left.

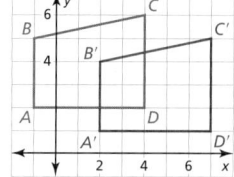

$$(x, y) \rightarrow (x + 3, y − 1)$$
$$A(−1, 2) \rightarrow A′(2, 1)$$
$$B(−1, 5) \rightarrow B′(2, 4)$$
$$C(4, 6) \rightarrow C′(7, 5)$$
$$D(4, 2) \rightarrow D′(7, 1)$$

Monitoring Progress Help in English and Spanish at *BigIdeasMath.com*

1. Name the vector and write its component form.

2. The vertices of △LMN are L(2, 2), M(5, 3), and N(9, 1). Translate △LMN using the vector ⟨−2, 6⟩.

3. In Example 3, write a rule to translate △A′B′C′ back to △ABC.

4. Graph △RST with vertices R(2, 2), S(5, 2), and T(3, 5) and its image after the translation $(x, y) \rightarrow (x + 1, y + 2)$.

English Language Learners

Class Activity
Create a sheet with two columns. In the first column, show the graphs of four translations. In the second column, show the rules for the four translations—out of order. Have students match each graph with its rule and explain their choices.

Extra Example 2
The vertices of △ABC are A(0, 3), B(2, 4), and C(1, 0). Translate △ABC using the vector ⟨−1, −2⟩. A′(−1, 1), B′(1, 2), C′(0, −2)

Extra Example 3
Write a rule for the translation of △ABC to △A′B′C′.

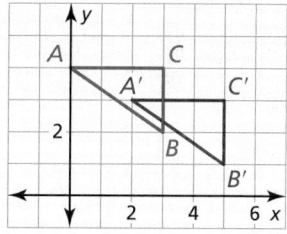

$(x, y) \rightarrow (x + 2, y − 1)$

Extra Example 4
Graph quadrilateral ABCD with vertices A(1, −2), B(2, 1), C(4, 1), and D(4, −2) and its image after the translation $(x, y) \rightarrow (x − 1, y + 4)$.

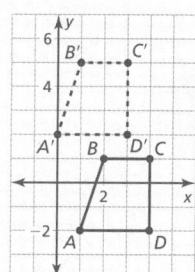

MONITORING PROGRESS ANSWERS

1. $\overrightarrow{BK}$, ⟨−5, 2⟩

2. L′(0, 8), M′(3, 9), N′(7, 7)

3. $(x, y) \rightarrow (x + 4, y − 1)$

4. See Additional Answers.

Laurie's Notes **Teacher Actions**

- Examples 2 and 3 make the connection between vector notation and coordinate notation.
- **Connection:** Students will often comment that the translation arrows make the figure look three-dimensional. The edges of a prism are parallel, so this should be the case.
- **Alternate Approach:** In Example 4, some students will find it easier to plot the vertices of the image using a strategy of "right 3 and down 1" and then recording the coordinates of the new vertices. The technique shown is to apply the translation rule to find the coordinates of the new vertices, and then those vertices are plotted.
- **Monitoring Progress:** Use *Think-Pair-Share* to assess student understanding.

Extra Example 5

Graph $\overline{RS}$ with endpoints $R(-8, 5)$ and $S(-6, 8)$. Graph its image after the composition.

Translation: $(x, y) \rightarrow (x - 1, y + 4)$
Translation: $(x, y) \rightarrow (x + 4, y - 6)$

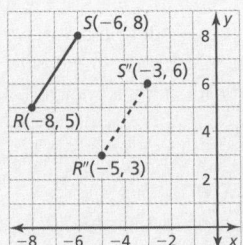

Performing Compositions

A **rigid motion** is a transformation that preserves length and angle measure. Another name for a rigid motion is an *isometry*. A rigid motion maps lines to lines, rays to rays, and segments to segments.

Postulate

Postulate 4.1   Translation Postulate

A translation is a rigid motion.

Because a translation is a rigid motion, and a rigid motion preserves length and angle measure, the following statements are true for the translation shown.

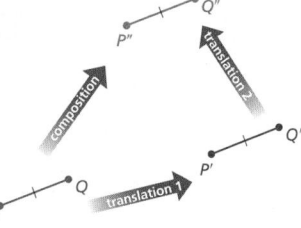

- $DE = D'E'$, $EF = E'F'$, $FD = F'D'$
- $m\angle D = m\angle D'$, $m\angle E = m\angle E'$, $m\angle F = m\angle F'$

When two or more transformations are combined to form a single transformation, the result is a **composition of transformations**.

Theorem

Theorem 4.1   Composition Theorem

The composition of two (or more) rigid motions is a rigid motion.

Proof   Ex. 35, p. 180

The theorem above is important because it states that no matter how many rigid motions you perform, lengths and angle measures will be preserved in the final image. For instance, the composition of two or more translations is a translation, as shown.

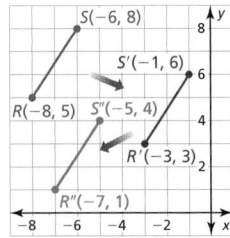

EXAMPLE 5   **Performing a Composition**

Graph $\overline{RS}$ with endpoints $R(-8, 5)$ and $S(-6, 8)$ and its image after the composition.

Translation: $(x, y) \rightarrow (x + 5, y - 2)$
Translation: $(x, y) \rightarrow (x - 4, y - 2)$

SOLUTION

Step 1 Graph $\overline{RS}$.

Step 2 Translate $\overline{RS}$ 5 units right and 2 units down. $\overline{R'S'}$ has endpoints $R'(-3, 3)$ and $S'(-1, 6)$.

Step 3 Translate $\overline{R'S'}$ 4 units left and 2 units down. $\overline{R''S''}$ has endpoints $R''(-7, 1)$ and $S''(-5, 4)$.

Laurie's Notes   Teacher Actions

- The definition of a rigid motion (isometry) is simple to state and it says a lot! Remind students that a transformation moves points in the plane, and when the length and angle measure are preserved, it is called a *rigid motion*. Recall the *Motivate* when only three of the four students followed directions. Length and angle measure were not preserved and, hence, the transformation was not rigid. Students will learn that there are only three rigid motions in the plane. The *Translation Postulate* (Post. 4.1) identifies the first rigid motion.

- **Connection:** Students have done composition of functions in algebra. If $f(x) = x^2$ and $g(x) = x + 2$, then $g(f(x)) = x^2 + 2$.
- The statement of the *Composition Theorem* (Thm. 4.1) is simple, yet its importance is enormous. As figures in the plane are mapped onto new figures, regardless of the number of times, segment lengths and angle measures are preserved. The final image is congruent to the preimage.
- **Alternate Approach:** Students should have graph paper or dynamic geometry software available for Example 5.

Solving Real-Life Problems

EXAMPLE 6   Modeling with Mathematics

You are designing a favicon for a golf website. In an image-editing program, you move the red rectangle 2 units left and 3 units down. Then you move the red rectangle 1 unit right and 1 unit up. Rewrite the composition as a single translation.

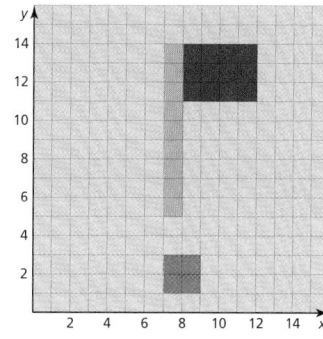

SOLUTION

1. **Understand the Problem** You are given two translations. You need to rewrite the result of the composition of the two translations as a single translation.

2. **Make a Plan** You can choose an arbitrary point (x, y) in the red rectangle and determine the horizontal and vertical shift in the coordinates of the point after both translations. This tells you how much you need to shift each coordinate to map the original figure to the final image.

3. **Solve the Problem** Let $A(x, y)$ be an arbitrary point in the red rectangle. After the first translation, the coordinates of its image are

   $A'(x - 2, y - 3)$.

   The second translation maps $A'(x - 2, y - 3)$ to

   $A''(x - 2 + 1, y - 3 + 1) = A''(x - 1, y - 2)$.

   The composition of translations uses the original point (x, y) as the input and returns the point $(x - 1, y - 2)$ as the output.

   ▶ So, the single translation rule for the composition is $(x, y) \to (x - 1, y - 2)$.

4. **Look Back** Check that the rule is correct by testing a point. For instance, $(10, 12)$ is a point in the red rectangle. Apply the two translations to $(10, 12)$.

   $(10, 12) \to (8, 9) \to (9, 10)$

   Does the final result match the rule you found in Step 3?

   $(10, 12) \to (10 - 1, 12 - 2) = (9, 10)$ ✓

Monitoring Progress Help in English and Spanish at *BigIdeasMath.com*

5. Graph $\overline{TU}$ with endpoints $T(1, 2)$ and $U(4, 6)$ and its image after the composition.

   Translation: $(x, y) \to (x - 2, y - 3)$
   Translation: $(x, y) \to (x - 4, y + 5)$

6. Graph $\overline{VW}$ with endpoints $V(-6, -4)$ and $W(-3, 1)$ and its image after the composition.

   Translation: $(x, y) \to (x + 3, y + 1)$
   Translation: $(x, y) \to (x - 6, y - 4)$

7. In Example 6, you move the gray square 2 units right and 3 units up. Then you move the gray square 1 unit left and 1 unit down. Rewrite the composition as a single transformation.

Extra Example 6

Another graphic artist is designing an alternate icon for the one in the graph in Example 6. She moves the red rectangle 3 units right and 1 unit down. Then she moves the red rectangle 1 unit left and 4 units up. Rewrite the composition as a single transformation.

$(x, y) \to (x + 2, y + 3)$

MONITORING PROGRESS ANSWERS

5.

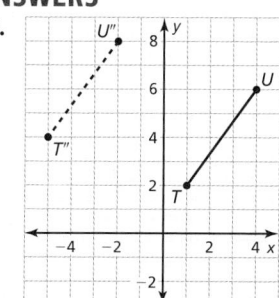

6.

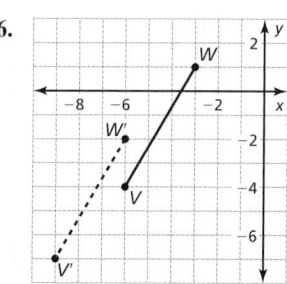

7. $(x, y) \to (x + 1, y + 2)$

Laurie's Notes   Teacher Actions

❓ "Does anyone know what a favicon is? Explain." Answers will vary.

- **FYI:** A favicon is a custom icon associated with a webpage or website that appears next to the http address in the URL window of a browser. It will also occupy open tabs in tab-enabled browsers, and it will display next to bookmarked links. The term combines the words "favorites" and "icon."

- The problem posed is not difficult to solve with mental math. The point is not that you can solve the problem mentally. The practice

you want to provide students is the opportunity to read a problem, make sense of the context, and translate words into symbols. This is a building block for future problems. I ask a volunteer to read Steps 1 and 2 in the problem-solving plan.

Closure

- Draw a triangle in Quadrant I. Have students identify a translation that would map the triangle entirely to Quadrant III. Write the translation using coordinate notation and vector notation.

ANSWERS

1. $\triangle ABC$ is the preimage, and $\triangle A'B'C'$ is the image.

2. translation

3. $\overrightarrow{CD}, \langle 7, -3 \rangle$

4. $\overrightarrow{ST}, \langle -2, -4 \rangle$

5.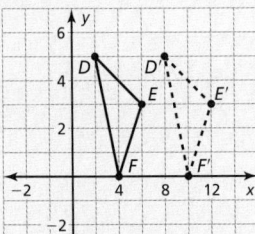

6.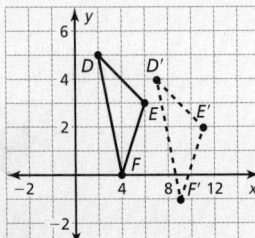

7.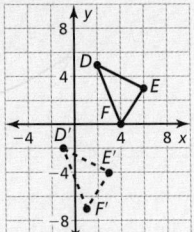

8.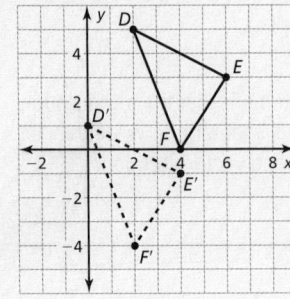

Vocabulary and Core Concept Check

1. **VOCABULARY** Name the preimage and image of the transformation $\triangle ABC \rightarrow \triangle A'B'C'$.

2. **COMPLETE THE SENTENCE** A _____ moves every point of a figure the same distance in the same direction.

Monitoring Progress and Modeling with Mathematics

In Exercises 3 and 4, name the vector and write its component form. *(See Example 1.)*

3.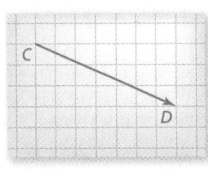

4.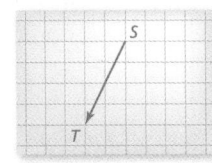

In Exercises 5–8, the vertices of $\triangle DEF$ are $D(2, 5)$, $E(6, 3)$, and $F(4, 0)$. Translate $\triangle DEF$ using the given vector. Graph $\triangle DEF$ and its image. *(See Example 2.)*

5. $\langle 6, 0 \rangle$

6. $\langle 5, -1 \rangle$

7. $\langle -3, -7 \rangle$

8. $\langle -2, -4 \rangle$

In Exercises 9 and 10, find the component form of the vector that translates $P(-3, 6)$ to P'.

9. $P'(0, 1)$

10. $P'(-4, 8)$

In Exercises 11 and 12, write a rule for the translation of $\triangle LMN$ to $\triangle L'M'N'$. *(See Example 3.)*

11.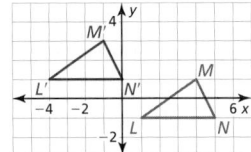

12.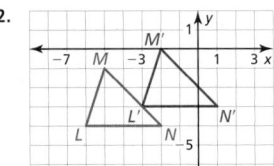

In Exercises 13–16, use the translation.

$$(x, y) \rightarrow (x - 8, y + 4)$$

13. What is the image of $A(2, 6)$?

14. What is the image of $B(-1, 5)$?

15. What is the preimage of $C'(-3, -10)$?

16. What is the preimage of $D'(4, -3)$?

In Exercises 17–20, graph $\triangle PQR$ with vertices $P(-2, 3)$, $Q(1, 2)$, and $R(3, -1)$ and its image after the translation. *(See Example 4.)*

17. $(x, y) \rightarrow (x + 4, y + 6)$

18. $(x, y) \rightarrow (x + 9, y - 2)$

19. $(x, y) \rightarrow (x - 2, y - 5)$

20. $(x, y) \rightarrow (x - 1, y + 3)$

In Exercises 21 and 22, graph $\triangle XYZ$ with vertices $X(2, 4)$, $Y(6, 0)$, and $Z(7, 2)$ and its image after the composition. *(See Example 5.)*

21. Translation: $(x, y) \rightarrow (x + 12, y + 4)$
    Translation: $(x, y) \rightarrow (x - 5, y - 9)$

22. Translation: $(x, y) \rightarrow (x - 6, y)$
    Translation: $(x, y) \rightarrow (x + 2, y + 7)$

9. $\langle 3, -5 \rangle$

10. $\langle -1, 2 \rangle$

11. $(x, y) \rightarrow (x - 5, y + 2)$

12. $(x, y) \rightarrow (x + 3, y + 1)$

13. $A'(-6, 10)$

14. $B'(-9, 9)$

15. $C(5, -14)$

16. $D(12, -7)$

17.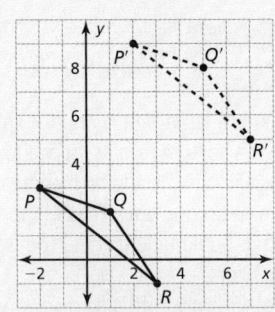

18–22. See Additional Answers.

In Exercises 23 and 24, describe the composition of translations.

23.

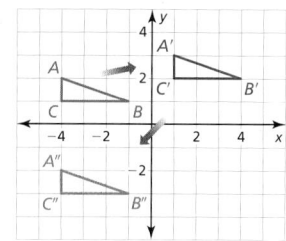

24.

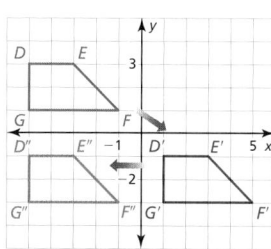

25. **ERROR ANALYSIS** Describe and correct the error in graphing the image of quadrilateral *EFGH* after the translation $(x, y) \rightarrow (x - 1, y - 2)$.

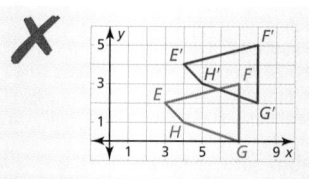

26. **MODELING WITH MATHEMATICS** In chess, the knight (the piece shaped like a horse) moves in an L pattern. The board shows two consecutive moves of a black knight during a game. Write a composition of translations for the moves. Then rewrite the composition as a single translation that moves the knight from its original position to its ending position. *(See Example 6.)*

27. **PROBLEM SOLVING** You are studying an amoeba through a microscope. Suppose the amoeba moves on a grid-indexed microscope slide in a straight line from square B3 to square G7.

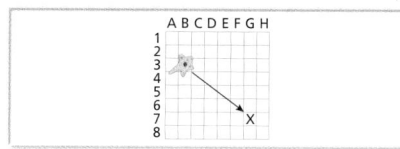

   a. Describe the translation.

   b. The side length of each grid square is 2 millimeters. How far does the amoeba travel?

   c. The amoeba moves from square B3 to square G7 in 24.5 seconds. What is its speed in millimeters per second?

28. **MATHEMATICAL CONNECTIONS** Translation A maps (x, y) to $(x + n, y + t)$. Translation B maps (x, y) to $(x + s, y + m)$.

   a. Translate a point using Translation A, followed by Translation B. Write an algebraic rule for the final image of the point after this composition.

   b. Translate a point using Translation B, followed by Translation A. Write an algebraic rule for the final image of the point after this composition.

   c. Compare the rules you wrote for parts (a) and (b). Does it matter which translation you do first? Explain your reasoning.

MATHEMATICAL CONNECTIONS In Exercises 29 and 30, a translation maps the blue figure to the red figure. Find the value of each variable.

29.

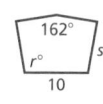 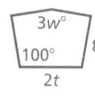

30.

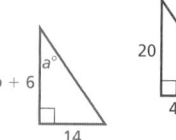

ANSWERS

23. translation: $(x, y) \rightarrow (x + 5, y + 1)$,
    translation: $(x, y) \rightarrow (x - 5, y - 5)$

24. translation: $(x, y) \rightarrow (x + 6, y - 4)$,
    translation: $(x, y) \rightarrow (x - 6, y)$

25. The quadrilateral should have been translated left and down;

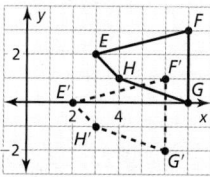

26. translation: $(x, y) \rightarrow (x + 2, y - 1)$,
    translation: $(x, y) \rightarrow (x + 1, y - 2)$;
    $(x, y) \rightarrow (x + 3, y - 3)$

27. a. The amoeba moves right 5 squares and down 4 squares.

    b. about 12.8 mm

    c. about 0.52 mm/sec

28. a. $(x, y) \rightarrow (x + n + s, y + t + m)$

    b. $(x, y) \rightarrow (x + s + n, y + m + t)$

    c. no; Each image will end up in the same place.

29. $r = 100, s = 8, t = 5, w = 54$

30. $a = 35, b = 14, c = 5$

31. $E'(-3, -4)$, $F'(-2, -5)$, $G'(0, -1)$
32. figures 5 and 7; To go from figure 5 to figure 7, you move 4 units right and 8 units up.
33. $(x, y) \rightarrow (x - m, y - n)$; You must go back the same number of units in the opposite direction.
34–50. See Additional Answers.

Mini-Assessment

1. The vertices of $\triangle ABC$ are $A(0, 3)$, $B(2, 4)$, and $C(1, 0)$. Translate $\triangle ABC$ using the vector $\langle -4, 3 \rangle$. $A'(-4, 6)$, $B'(-2, 7)$, $C'(-3, 3)$

2. Graph $\overline{RS}$ with endpoints $R(-4, 2)$ and $S(2, -2)$ and its image after the translation $(x, y) \rightarrow (x + 5, y - 1)$.

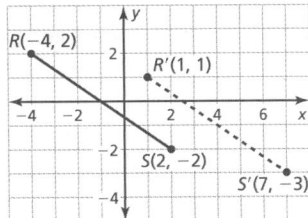

3. Graph quadrilateral $ABCD$ with vertices $A(1, -2)$, $B(2, 1)$, $C(4, 1)$, and $D(4, -2)$ and its image after the composition.

   Translation:
   $(x, y) \rightarrow (x - 2, y + 1)$
   Translation:
   $(x, y) \rightarrow (x + 1, y - 3)$

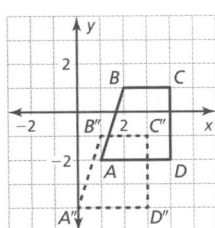

4. A gardener transplants a small bush, moving it 3 feet east and 10 feet south of its original position. She realizes that the plant is not getting enough sunlight, so she moves it 8 feet west and 2 feet north. Using addition to represent moves east or north and subtraction to represent moves west or south, write the composition as a single translation. $(x, y) \rightarrow (x - 5, y - 8)$

---

31. **USING STRUCTURE** Quadrilateral $DEFG$ has vertices $D(-1, 2)$, $E(-2, 0)$, $F(-1, -1)$, and $G(1, 3)$. A translation maps quadrilateral $DEFG$ to quadrilateral $D'E'F'G'$. The image of D is $D'(-2, -2)$. What are the coordinates of E', F', and G'?

32. **HOW DO YOU SEE IT?** Which two figures represent a translation? Describe the translation.

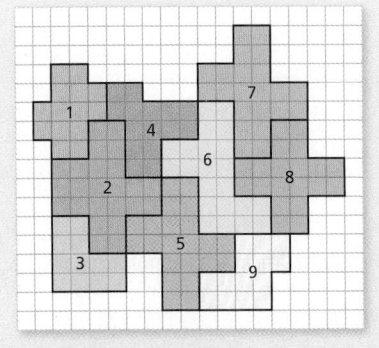

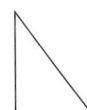

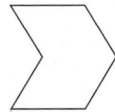

33. **REASONING** The translation $(x, y) \rightarrow (x + m, y + n)$ maps $\overline{PQ}$ to $\overline{P'Q'}$. Write a rule for the translation of $\overline{P'Q'}$ to $\overline{PQ}$. Explain your reasoning.

34. **DRAWING CONCLUSIONS** The vertices of a rectangle are $Q(2, -3)$, $R(2, 4)$, $S(5, 4)$, and $T(5, -3)$.
    a. Translate rectangle $QRST$ 3 units left and 3 units down to produce rectangle $Q'R'S'T'$. Find the area of rectangle $QRST$ and the area of rectangle $Q'R'S'T'$.
    b. Compare the areas. Make a conjecture about the areas of a preimage and its image after a translation.

35. **PROVING A THEOREM** Prove the Composition Theorem (Theorem 4.1).

36. **PROVING A THEOREM** Use properties of translations to prove each theorem.
    a. Corresponding Angles Theorem (Theorem 3.1)
    b. Corresponding Angles Converse (Theorem 3.5)

37. **WRITING** Explain how to use translations to draw a rectangular prism.

38. **MATHEMATICAL CONNECTIONS** The vector $PQ = \langle 4, 1 \rangle$ describes the translation of $A(-1, w)$ onto $A'(2x + 1, 4)$ and $B(8y - 1, 1)$ onto $B'(3, 3z)$. Find the values of w, x, y, and z.

39. **MAKING AN ARGUMENT** A translation maps $\overline{GH}$ to $\overline{G'H'}$. Your friend claims that if you draw segments connecting G to G' and H to H', then the resulting quadrilateral is a parallelogram. Is your friend correct? Explain your reasoning.

40. **THOUGHT PROVOKING** You are a graphic designer for a company that manufactures floor tiles. Design a floor tile in a coordinate plane. Then use translations to show how the tiles cover an entire floor. Describe the translations that map the original tile to four other tiles.

41. **REASONING** The vertices of $\triangle ABC$ are $A(2, 2)$, $B(4, 2)$, and $C(3, 4)$. Graph the image of $\triangle ABC$ after the transformation $(x, y) \rightarrow (x + y, y)$. Is this transformation a translation? Explain your reasoning.

42. **PROOF** $\overline{MN}$ is perpendicular to line ℓ. $\overline{M'N'}$ is the translation of $\overline{MN}$ 2 units to the left. Prove that $\overline{M'N'}$ is perpendicular to ℓ.

Maintaining Mathematical Proficiency   Reviewing what you learned in previous grades and lessons

Tell whether the figure can be folded in half so that one side matches the other.
(Skills Review Handbook)

43.   44.   45.   46.

Simplify the expression.   *(Skills Review Handbook)*
47. $-(-x)$ 48. $-(x + 3)$ 49. $x - (12 - 5x)$ 50. $x - (-2x + 4)$

If students need help...	If students got it...
Resources by Chapter • Practice A and Practice B • Puzzle Time	Resources by Chapter • Enrichment and Extension • Cumulative Review
Student Journal • Practice	Start the *next* Section
Differentiating the Lesson Skills Review Handbook	

Dynamic Teaching Tools

Dynamic Assessment & Progress Monitoring Tool

Lesson Planning Tool

Interactive Whiteboard Lesson Library

Dynamic Classroom with Dynamic Investigations

Overview of Section 4.2

Introduction

- Students worked with reflections of polygons in middle school. In algebra, they explored the transformation of $y = x^2$ to $y = -x^2$ as a reflection in the x-axis.
- The explorations provide an opportunity for students to become familiar with using dynamic geometry software to perform reflections. Inductively, students will develop rules for reflections in the x- and y-axes. They also explore preservation of segment length using the *Distance Formula*.
- The formal lesson includes the definitions of *reflection* and *glide reflection*. The coordinate rules for reflections in the x- and y-axes and in the lines $y = x$ and $y = -x$ are also developed. Once the postulate stating that a reflection is a rigid motion is given, glide reflections are introduced as the composition of a translation followed by a reflection; hence, it too is a rigid motion by the *Composition Theorem* (Thm. 4.1).
- Students may forget that the line of reflection is the perpendicular bisector of the segment connecting a point on the preimage and its corresponding point on the image, when the point is not on the line of reflection. Recalling this property will be helpful in later lessons.

Resources

- **MP5 Use Appropriate Tools Strategically:** In addition to dynamic geometry software, graph paper, and tracing paper mirrors, there are other tools that will be helpful for students to make sense of reflections. Exploration 1 is designed to use a reflective device.

Formative Assessment Tips

- **Fact-First Questioning:** This is a higher-order questioning technique that goes beyond asking straight recall questions. Instead, this strategy allows you to assess students' growing understanding of a concept or skill.
- First, state a fact. Then ask students why, or how, or to explain. Student thinking is activated, and you gain insight into the depth of students' conceptual understanding.
- Example: State the fact, "All squares are rectangles." Then ask, "Why is this true?"

Applications

- There are particular occupations that come to mind in which the ability to work with reflections is absolutely essential. Dentists see a reflection of your teeth as they do their work. A driver backing up and using his or her side or rearview mirrors is working with a reflected image.

Pacing Suggestion

- Once students have worked through the explorations, you could assign Exercises 3–12 on page 186. You may consider omitting Example 1 and *Monitoring Progress* Questions 1–4.

HSG-CO.A.2 Represent transformations in the plane using, e.g., ... geometry software; describe transformations as functions that take points in the plane as inputs and give other points as outputs. ...

HSG-CO.A.3 Given a rectangle, parallelogram, trapezoid, or regular polygon, describe the ... reflections that carry it onto itself.

HSG-CO.A.4 Develop definitions of ... reflections, ... in terms of angles, ... perpendicular lines, parallel lines, and line segments.

HSG-CO.A.5 Given a geometric figure and a ... reflection, ... draw the transformed figure using, e.g., graph paper, ... or geometry software. Specify a sequence of transformations that will carry a given figure onto another.

HSG-CO.B.6 Use geometric descriptions of rigid motions to transform figures and to predict the effect of a given rigid motion on a given figure; ...

HSG-MG.A.3 Apply geometric methods to solve design problems (e.g., designing an object or structure to satisfy physical constraints or minimize cost; working with typographic grid systems based on ratios).

Laurie's Notes

Exploration

Motivate

- **60-Second Write:** Tell students that they have 60 seconds to make a list of words that can be reflected in a vertical or horizontal line and the result is the same word or a new word.
- Example: When the word MOM is reflected in a vertical line, it is still MOM. When it is reflected in a horizontal line, it becomes WOW.
- Share word lists after 60 seconds. The list should contain letters that have line symmetry themselves: A, B, C, D, E, H, I, K, M, O, T, V, W, X, and Y.
- Explain that reflections and line symmetry are studied in this lesson.

Exploration 1

- If you have reflective devices, have students complete the construction of the reflected triangle.
- **?** "Which point of the preimage is closest to line *m*?" Answers vary. "Which point of the image is closest to line *m*?" Answers vary, but for every student the two answers are related.

Exploration 2

- This exploration serves to familiarize students with the *reflect* command in the dynamic geometry software. In using the software, students will learn that they must select a polygon, in this case the triangle, and also the line in which the reflection will be done.
- Encourage students to draw a scalene triangle so that the correspondence of sides will be easier to see following the reflection.
- Students should observe that the side lengths and angle measures of the reflected triangle are the same as the measures in the original triangle. They should also observe a relationship between the coordinates of corresponding vertices. Using lattice points (points at the intersections of grid lines) for vertices will help students recognize a pattern.
- The generalizations students should recognize are the coordinate representations of (x, y) when a point is reflected in the y-axis and in the x-axis.
- **?** **Always-Sometimes-Never True:** "When an ordered pair is reflected in the x-axis, the y-coordinate of the image is negative." sometimes true; When the y-coordinate is positive, it will be negative when reflected in the x-axis. When the y-coordinate is negative, it will be positive when reflected in the x-axis. When the y-coordinate is 0, it will be 0 when reflected in the x-axis.
- **Extension:** Use software to reflect a triangle in any horizontal or vertical line. Ask students to develop a rule for reflecting (x, y) in the line $y = x$ or $y = -x$.

Communicate Your Answer

- Expect students to refer to reflections in the x- or y-axis in Question 3.

Connecting to Next Step

- If students complete both explorations, skip Example 1 in the formal lesson and check for understanding with *Monitoring Progress Questions* 1–4.

4.2 Reflections

Essential Question
How can you reflect a figure in a coordinate plane?

EXPLORATION 1 **Reflecting a Triangle Using a Reflective Device**

Work with a partner. Use a straightedge to draw any triangle on paper. Label it △ABC.

a. Use the straightedge to draw a line that does not pass through the triangle. Label it *m*.

b. Place a reflective device on line *m*.

c. Use the reflective device to plot the images of the vertices of △ABC. Label the images of vertices A, B, and C as A′, B′, and C′, respectively.

d. Use a straightedge to draw △A′B′C′ by connecting the vertices.

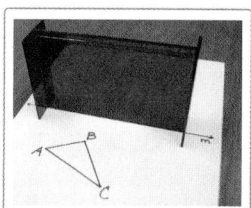

LOOKING FOR STRUCTURE
To be proficient in math, you need to look closely to discern a pattern or structure.

EXPLORATION 2 **Reflecting a Triangle in a Coordinate Plane**

Work with a partner. Use dynamic geometry software to draw any triangle and label it △ABC.

a. Reflect △ABC in the *y*-axis to form △A′B′C′.

b. What is the relationship between the coordinates of the vertices of △ABC and those of △A′B′C′?

c. What do you observe about the side lengths and angle measures of the two triangles?

d. Reflect △ABC in the *x*-axis to form △A′B′C′. Then repeat parts (b) and (c).

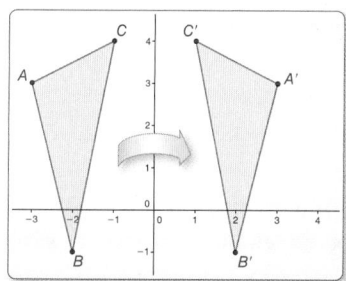

Sample

Points
A(−3, 3)
B(−2, −1)
C(−1, 4)
Segments
AB = 4.12
BC = 5.10
AC = 2.24
Angles
m∠A = 102.53°
m∠B = 25.35°
m∠C = 52.13°

Communicate Your Answer

3. How can you reflect a figure in a coordinate plane?

Section 4.2   Reflections   **181**

---

3. If a figure is reflected in the *y*-axis, then each pair of corresponding vertices will have the same *y*-value and opposite *x*-values. If a figure is reflected in the *x*-axis, then each pair of corresponding vertices will have the same *x*-value and opposite *y*-values.

Dynamic Teaching Tools
- Dynamic Assessment & Progress Monitoring Tool
- Lesson Planning Tool
- Interactive Whiteboard Lesson Library
- Dynamic Classroom with Dynamic Investigations

ANSWERS

1. a. Check students' work.

b. Check students' work.

c. *Sample answer:*

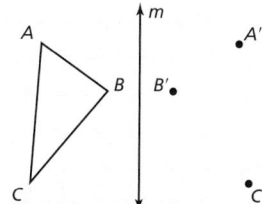

d. *Sample answer:*

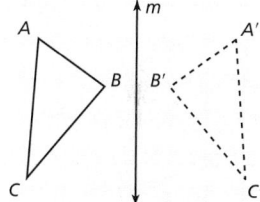

2. a. Check students' work.

b. Each vertex of △A′B′C′ has the same *y*-value as its corresponding vertex of △ABC. The *x*-value of each vertex of △A′B′C′ is the opposite of the *x*-value of its corresponding vertex of △ABC.

c. The corresponding sides and corresponding angles are congruent.

d. *Sample answer:*

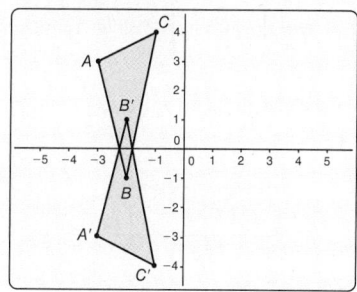

Each vertex of △A′B′C′ has the same *x*-value as its corresponding vertex of △ABC. The *y*-value of each vertex of △A′B′C′ is the opposite of the *x*-value of its corresponding vertex of △ABC; The corresponding sides and corresponding angles are congruent.

Extra Example 1

Graph △ABC with vertices A(1, 3), B(5, 2), and C(2, 1) and its image after the reflection described.

a. In the line n: $x = -1$

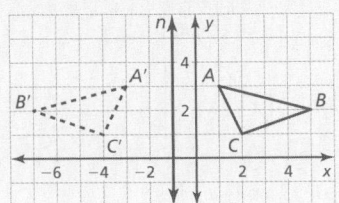

b. In the line m: $y = 3$

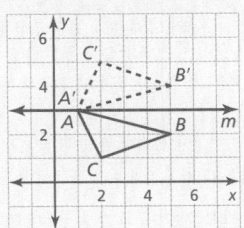

MONITORING PROGRESS ANSWERS

1.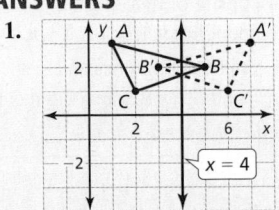

2. See Additional Answers.

3.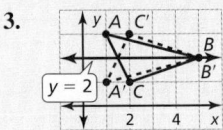

4.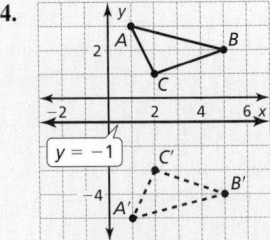

4.2 Lesson

Core Vocabulary

reflection, *p. 182*
line of reflection, *p. 182*
glide reflection, *p. 184*
line symmetry, *p. 185*
line of symmetry, *p. 185*

What You Will Learn

▶ Perform reflections.
▶ Perform glide reflections.
▶ Identify lines of symmetry.
▶ Solve real-life problems involving reflections.

Performing Reflections

Core Concept

Reflections

A **reflection** is a transformation that uses a line like a mirror to reflect a figure. The mirror line is called the **line of reflection**.

A reflection in a line *m* maps every point *P* in the plane to a point *P′*, so that for each point one of the following properties is true.

- If *P* is not on *m*, then *m* is the perpendicular bisector of $\overline{PP'}$, or
- If *P* is on *m*, then $P = P'$.

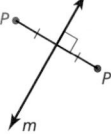

point *P* not on *m*

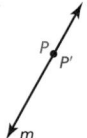

point *P* on *m*

EXAMPLE 1   **Reflecting in Horizontal and Vertical Lines**

Graph △ABC with vertices A(1, 3), B(5, 2), and C(2, 1) and its image after the reflection described.

a. In the line n: $x = 3$ **b.** In the line m: $y = 1$

SOLUTION

a. Point A is 2 units left of line n, so its reflection A′ is 2 units right of line n at (5, 3). Also, B′ is 2 units left of line n at (1, 2), and C′ is 1 unit right of line n at (4, 1).

b. Point A is 2 units above line m, so A′ is 2 units below line m at (1, −1). Also, B′ is 1 unit below line m at (5, 0). Because point C is on line m, you know that C = C′.

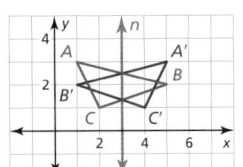

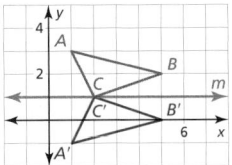

Monitoring Progress 🔊 Help in English and Spanish at *BigIdeasMath.com*

Graph △ABC from Example 1 and its image after a reflection in the given line.

1. $x = 4$ 2. $x = -3$

3. $y = 2$ 4. $y = -1$

Laurie's Notes   Teacher Actions

- Write the *Core Concept*. Distinguish the two cases related to the two bullets.
- **Teaching Tip:** Draw two points on scrap paper. Crease the paper to form the *line of reflection* for the points. Draw the segment that connects the two points. Use this model to highlight the property of the line of reflection being the perpendicular bisector of the segment joining the two points.
- Students have little difficulty reflecting a point in a horizontal ($x = k$) or vertical line ($y = k$). Their spatial skills may make them less able to correctly reflect in a diagonal line.

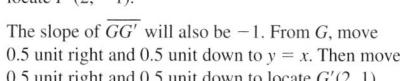 **EXAMPLE 2** **Reflecting in the Line y = x**

Graph $\overline{FG}$ with endpoints $F(-1, 2)$ and $G(1, 2)$ and its image after a reflection in the line $y = x$.

SOLUTION

The slope of $y = x$ is 1. The segment from F to its image, $\overline{FF'}$, is perpendicular to the line of reflection $y = x$, so the slope of $\overline{FF'}$ will be -1 (because $1(-1) = -1$). From F, move 1.5 units right and 1.5 units down to $y = x$. From that point, move 1.5 units right and 1.5 units down to locate $F'(2, -1)$.

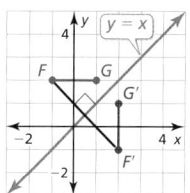

The slope of $\overline{GG'}$ will also be -1. From G, move 0.5 unit right and 0.5 unit down to $y = x$. Then move 0.5 unit right and 0.5 unit down to locate $G'(2, 1)$.

REMEMBER

The product of the slopes of perpendicular lines is -1.

You can use coordinate rules to find the images of points reflected in four special lines.

🔎 Core Concept

Coordinate Rules for Reflections

- If (a, b) is reflected in the x-axis, then its image is the point $(a, -b)$.
- If (a, b) is reflected in the y-axis, then its image is the point $(-a, b)$.
- If (a, b) is reflected in the line $y = x$, then its image is the point (b, a).
- If (a, b) is reflected in the line $y = -x$, then its image is the point $(-b, -a)$.

EXAMPLE 3 **Reflecting in the Line y = −x**

Graph $\overline{FG}$ from Example 2 and its image after a reflection in the line $y = -x$.

SOLUTION

Use the coordinate rule for reflecting in the line $y = -x$ to find the coordinates of the endpoints of the image. Then graph $\overline{FG}$ and its image.

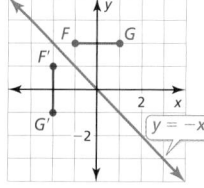

$$(a, b) \rightarrow (-b, -a)$$
$$F(-1, 2) \rightarrow F'(-2, 1)$$
$$G(1, 2) \rightarrow G'(-2, -1)$$

Monitoring Progress 🔊 Help in English and Spanish at *BigIdeasMath.com*

The vertices of $\triangle JKL$ are $J(1, 3)$, $K(4, 4)$, and $L(3, 1)$.

5. Graph $\triangle JKL$ and its image after a reflection in the x-axis.

6. Graph $\triangle JKL$ and its image after a reflection in the y-axis.

7. Graph $\triangle JKL$ and its image after a reflection in the line $y = x$.

8. Graph $\triangle JKL$ and its image after a reflection in the line $y = -x$.

9. In Example 3, verify that $\overline{FF'}$ is perpendicular to $y = -x$.

Extra Example 2
Graph $\overline{AB}$ with endpoints $A(3, -1)$ and $B(3, 2)$ and its image after a reflection in the line $y = x$.

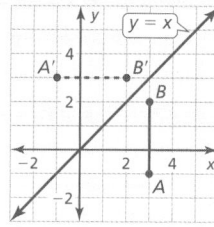

Extra Example 3
Graph $\overline{AB}$ with endpoints $A(3, -1)$ and $B(3, 2)$ and its image after a reflection in the line $y = -x$.

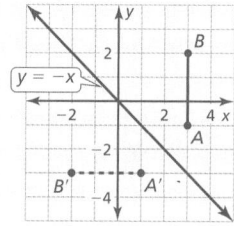

MONITORING PROGRESS ANSWERS

5.
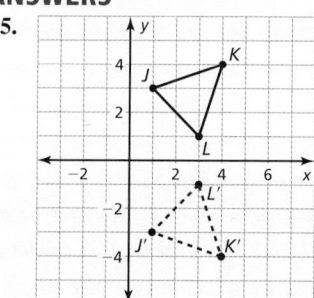

6.
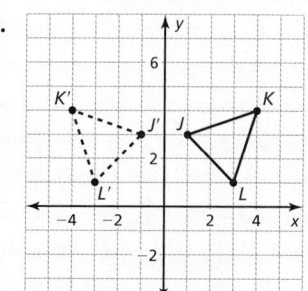

7.
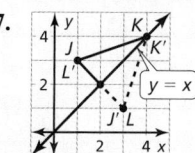

8–9. See Additional Answers.

Laurie's Notes   Teacher Actions

- One strategy students use to reflect in the line $y = x$ is to rotate their graph paper so that the line of reflection is horizontal. It is easier for many students to then reflect the endpoints of $\overline{FG}$ in a vertical direction. Work through the Example 2 solution that involves the slopes of perpendicular lines.
- Before stating the *Core Concept* that summarizes the rules for four common reflections, try the formative assessment tip, *Fact-First Question*.
- **❓ Fact-First Question:** "The reflection of (x, y) in the line $y = x$ is (y, x). Why are the coordinates interchanged, or reversed, when a point is reflected in the line $y = x$?" Listen for explanations involving the slope between (x, y) and (y, x) being -1.
- **Think-Pair-Share:** Have students work Example 3 and then compare work with their partners.

Extra Example 4

Graph △ABC with vertices A(3, 2), B(6, 3), and C(7, 1) and its image after the glide reflection.

Translation: $(x, y) \rightarrow (x, y - 6)$
Reflection: in the y-axis

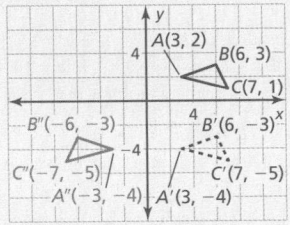

MONITORING PROGRESS ANSWERS

10.

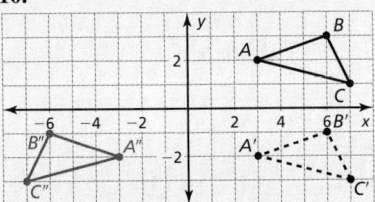

11. translation: $(x, y) \rightarrow (x + 12, y)$, reflection: in the x-axis

---

Postulate

Postulate 4.2 Reflection Postulate

A reflection is a rigid motion.

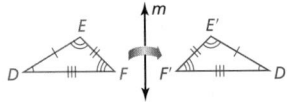

Because a reflection is a rigid motion, and a rigid motion preserves length and angle measure, the following statements are true for the reflection shown.

- $DE = D'E'$, $EF = E'F'$, $FD = F'D'$
- $m\angle D = m\angle D'$, $m\angle E = m\angle E'$, $m\angle F = m\angle F'$

Because a reflection is a rigid motion, the Composition Theorem (Theorem 4.1) guarantees that any composition of reflections and translations is a rigid motion.

A **glide reflection** is a transformation involving a translation followed by a reflection in which every point P is mapped to a point P'' by the following steps.

Step 1 First, a translation maps P to P'.

Step 2 Then, a reflection in a line k parallel to the direction of the translation maps P' to P''.

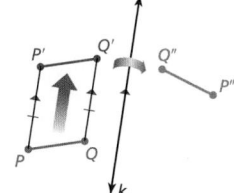

STUDY TIP

The line of reflection must be parallel to the direction of the translation to be a glide reflection.

EXAMPLE 4 Performing a Glide Reflection

Graph △ABC with vertices A(3, 2), B(6, 3), and C(7, 1) and its image after the glide reflection.

Translation: $(x, y) \rightarrow (x - 12, y)$
Reflection: in the x-axis

SOLUTION

Begin by graphing △ABC. Then graph △A'B'C' after a translation 12 units left. Finally, graph △A″B″C″ after a reflection in the x-axis.

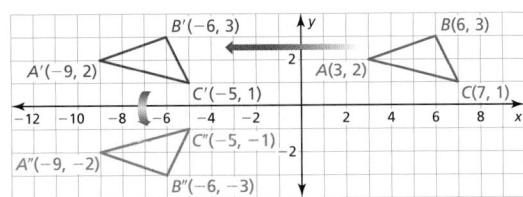

Monitoring Progress Help in English and Spanish at BigIdeasMath.com

10. WHAT IF? In Example 4, △ABC is translated 4 units down and then reflected in the y-axis. Graph △ABC and its image after the glide reflection.

11. In Example 4, describe a glide reflection from △A″B″C″ to △ABC.

Identifying Lines of Symmetry

A figure in the plane has **line symmetry** when the figure can be mapped onto itself by a reflection in a line. This line of reflection is a **line of symmetry**, such as line m at the left. A figure can have more than one line of symmetry.

EXAMPLE 5 Identifying Lines of Symmetry

How many lines of symmetry does each hexagon have?

a.  b.  c.

SOLUTION

a. 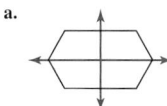 b.  c.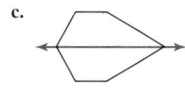

Monitoring Progress Help in English and Spanish at *BigIdeasMath.com*

Determine the number of lines of symmetry for the figure.

12.    13. 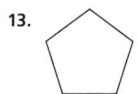   14.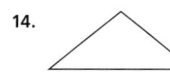

15. Draw a hexagon with no lines of symmetry.

Solving Real-Life Problems

EXAMPLE 6 Finding a Minimum Distance

You are going to buy books. Your friend is going to buy CDs. Where should you park to minimize the distance you both will walk?

SOLUTION

Reflect B in line m to obtain B'. Then draw $\overline{AB'}$. Label the intersection of $\overline{AB'}$ and m as C. Because AB' is the shortest distance between A and B' and $BC = B'C$, park at point C to minimize the combined distance, $AC + BC$, you both have to walk.

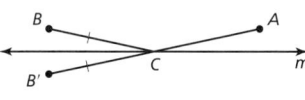

Monitoring Progress Help in English and Spanish at *BigIdeasMath.com*

16. Look back at Example 6. Answer the question by using a reflection of point A instead of point B.

How many lines of symmetry does the triangle have?

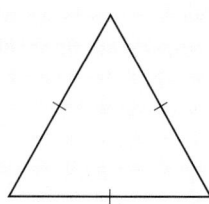

3

Extra Example 6
Use the picture in Example 6. You are going to the music store. Your friend is going to buy craft supplies. Where should you park to minimize the distance you both will walk?

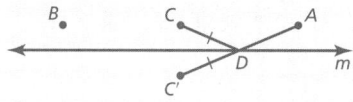

Let point C be in front of the Arts and Crafts store, on the same line as $\overline{AB}$. You should park at point D.

MONITORING PROGRESS ANSWERS

12. 2
13. 5
14. 1
15. *Sample answer:*

16. Reflect A in line m to obtain A'. Then draw $\overline{BA'}$. Label the intersection of $\overline{BA'}$ and m as C. Because BA' is the shortest distance between B and A' and $AC = A'C$, park at point C.

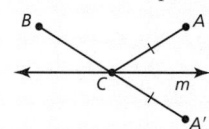

Laurie's Notes   Teacher Actions

- *Line symmetry* should be familiar to students from middle school geometry.
- **Alternate Approach:** If you are confident of students' knowledge of line symmetry, skip Example 5 and *Monitoring Progress* Questions 12–15 and instead ask students to work with partners to draw hexagons with the following lines of symmetry: 0, 1, 2, 3, 4, 5, and 6. *Note:* It is not possible to draw a hexagon with exactly 4 or 5 lines of symmetry.
- **MP1 Make Sense of Problems and Persevere in Solving Them:** Example 6 is a classic problem that can be posed using

a variety of different contexts. (See Exercise 27.) Consider posing the problem for students to explore with partners in class, or for homework. In either scenario, the example can be done with or without dynamic geometry software.

Closure
? Fact-First Questioning: "The reflection of △CAT is △C'A'T', and the two triangles have the same perimeter. Why should the triangles have the same perimeter?" Reflection is a rigid motion that preserves length (and angles), so the perimeter of △CAT is the same length as the perimeter of △C'A'T'.

ASSIGNMENT

Basic: 1–4, 5–25 odd, 26, 27, 34, 40–49

Average: 1, 2, 4–32 even, 33, 34, 39, 40–49

Advanced: 1, 2, 10, 12, 16, 20–26 even, 27–29, 32–34, 37–49

HOMEWORK CHECK

Basic: 7, 15, 17, 23, 34

Average: 12, 16, 20, 22, 34

Advanced: 12, 16, 20, 32, 34

ANSWERS

1. translation and reflection

2.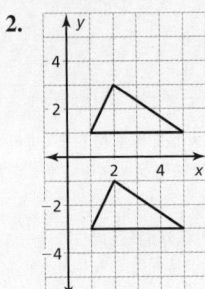

It is a translation, and the other three are reflections.

3. y-axis

4. neither

5. neither

6. x-axis

7.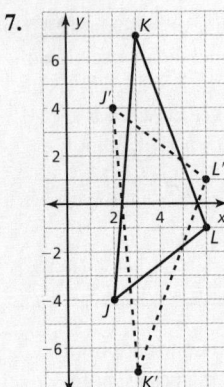

8.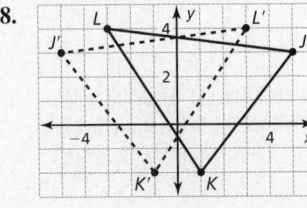

4.2 Exercises

Dynamic Solutions available at *BigIdeasMath.com*

Vocabulary and Core Concept Check

1. **VOCABULARY** A glide reflection is a combination of which two transformations?

2. **WHICH ONE DOESN'T BELONG?** Which transformation does *not* belong with the other three? Explain your reasoning.

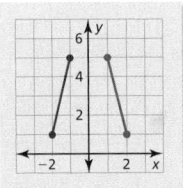 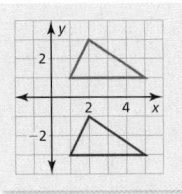 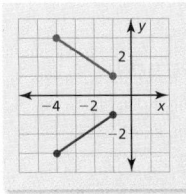 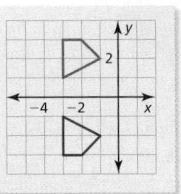

Monitoring Progress and Modeling with Mathematics

In Exercises 3–6, determine whether the coordinate plane shows a reflection in the *x-axis*, *y-axis*, or *neither*.

3.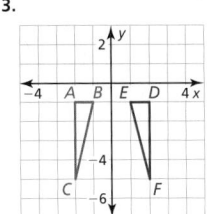

4.

5.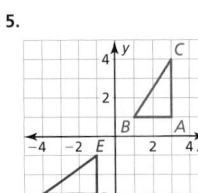

6.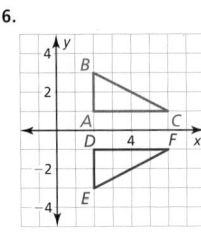

In Exercises 7–12, graph △*JKL* and its image after a reflection in the given line. *(See Example 1.)*

7. J(2, −4), K(3, 7), L(6, −1); x-axis

8. J(5, 3), K(1, −2), L(−3, 4); y-axis

9. J(2, −1), K(4, −5), L(3, 1); x = −1

10. J(1, −1), K(3, 0), L(0, −4); x = 2

11. J(2, 4), K(−4, −2), L(−1, 0); y = 1

12. J(3, −5), K(4, −1), L(0, −3); y = −3

In Exercises 13–16, graph the polygon and its image after a reflection in the given line. *(See Examples 2 and 3.)*

13. y = x

14. y = x

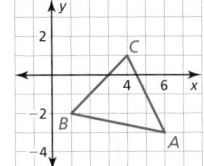 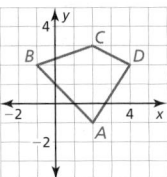

15. y = −x

16. y = −x

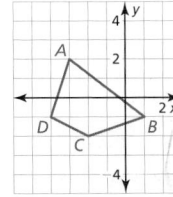 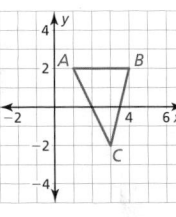

9.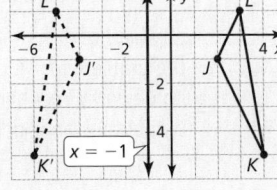

10.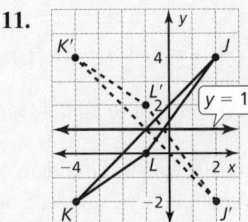

11.

12–16. See Additional Answers.

In Exercises 17–20, graph $\triangle RST$ with vertices $R(4, 1)$, $S(7, 3)$, and $T(6, 4)$ and its image after the glide reflection. *(See Example 4.)*

17. **Translation:** $(x, y) \rightarrow (x, y - 1)$
    Reflection: in the y-axis

18. **Translation:** $(x, y) \rightarrow (x - 3, y)$
    Reflection: in the line $y = -1$

19. **Translation:** $(x, y) \rightarrow (x, y + 4)$
    Reflection: in the line $x = 3$

20. **Translation:** $(x, y) \rightarrow (x + 2, y + 2)$
    Reflection: in the line $y = x$

In Exercises 21–24, determine the number of lines of symmetry for the figure. *(See Example 5.)*

21.

22.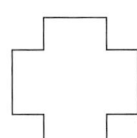

23.

24.

25. **USING STRUCTURE** Identify the line symmetry (if any) of each word.
    a. LOOK
    b. MOM
    c. OX
    d. DAD

26. **ERROR ANALYSIS** Describe and correct the error in describing the transformation.

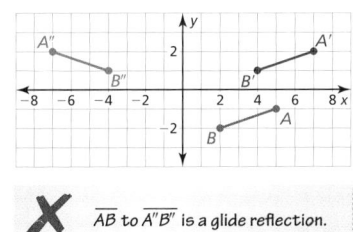

$\overline{AB}$ to $\overline{A''B''}$ is a glide reflection.

27. **MODELING WITH MATHEMATICS** You park at some point K on line n. You deliver a pizza to House H, go back to your car, and deliver a pizza to House J. Assuming that you can cut across both lawns, how can you determine the parking location K that minimizes the distance $HK + KJ$? *(See Example 6.)*

28. **ATTENDING TO PRECISION** Use the numbers and symbols to create the glide reflection resulting in the image shown.

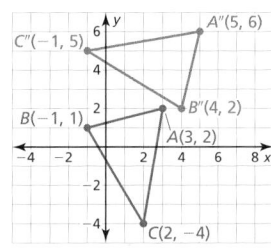

Translation: $(x, y) \rightarrow \left(\rule{1cm}{0.3mm} , \rule{1cm}{0.3mm} \right)$
Reflection: in $y = x$

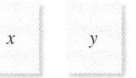  

In Exercises 29–32, find point C on the x-axis so $AC + BC$ is a minimum.

29. $A(1, 4)$, $B(6, 1)$

30. $A(4, -5)$, $B(12, 3)$

31. $A(-8, 4)$, $B(-1, 3)$

32. $A(-1, 7)$, $B(5, -4)$

33. **MATHEMATICAL CONNECTIONS** The line $y = 3x + 2$ is reflected in the line $y = -1$. What is the equation of the image?

26. The line of reflection has to be *parallel* to the direction of the translation for it to be a guide reflection; translation $(x, y) \rightarrow (x + 2, y + 3)$, reflection: in the y-axis

27. Reflect H in line n to obtain H'. Then draw $\overline{JH'}$. Label the intersection of $\overline{JH'}$ and n as K. Because $\overline{JH'}$ is the shortest distance between J and H' and $HK = H'K$, park at point K.

28. $x + 3$, $y + 3$

29. $C(5, 0)$

30. $C(9, 0)$

31. $C(-4, 0)$

32. $C\left(\frac{31}{11}, 0\right)$

33. $y = -3x - 4$

ANSWERS

17.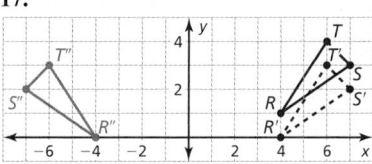

18.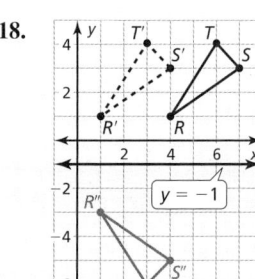

19.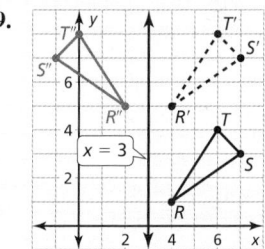

20.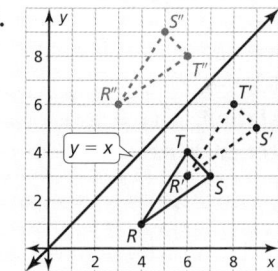

21. 1

22. 4

23. 0

24. 5

25. a. none
    b.
    c. OX
    d. none

ANSWERS

34–38. See Additional Answers.

39. $y = x + 1$

40. 60°

41. 130°

42. 20°

43. 160°

44. 70°

45. 30°

46. 100°

47. 180°

48. 120°

49. 50°

Mini-Assessment

$\triangle ABC$ has vertices $A(1, 3)$, $B(4, 1)$, and $C(1, 1)$.

1. Graph $\triangle ABC$ and its image after a reflection in the line $y = x$.

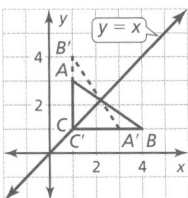

2. Graph $\triangle ABC$ and its image after the glide reflection.
Translation: $(x, y) \rightarrow (x - 4, y)$
Reflection: in the x-axis

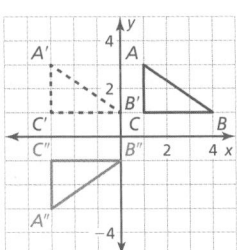

3. How many lines of symmetry does the figure have?

1

188   **Chapter 4**

---

34. **HOW DO YOU SEE IT?** Use Figure A.

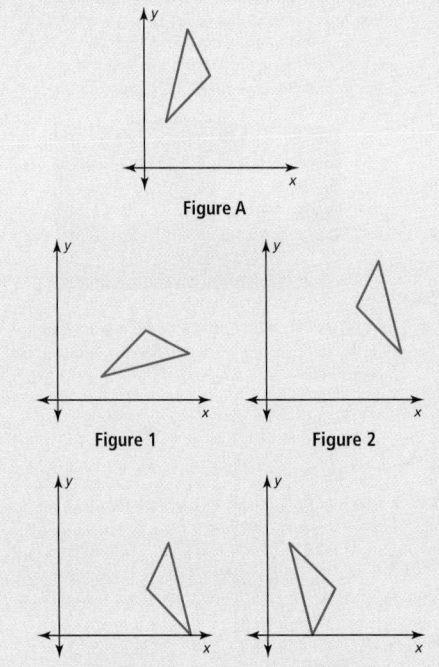

Figure A

Figure 1   Figure 2

Figure 3   Figure 4

a. Which figure is a reflection of Figure A in the line $x = a$? Explain.

b. Which figure is a reflection of Figure A in the line $y = b$? Explain.

c. Which figure is a reflection of Figure A in the line $y = x$? Explain.

d. Is there a figure that represents a glide reflection? Explain your reasoning.

---

35. **CONSTRUCTION** Follow these steps to construct a reflection of $\triangle ABC$ in line m. Use a compass and straightedge.

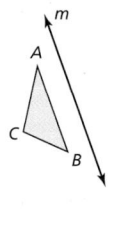

Step 1 Draw $\triangle ABC$ and line m.

Step 2 Use one compass setting to find two points that are equidistant from A on line m. Use the same compass setting to find a point on the other side of m that is the same distance from these two points. Label that point as A'.

Step 3 Repeat Step 2 to find points B' and C'. Draw $\triangle A'B'C'$.

36. **USING TOOLS** Use a reflective device to verify your construction in Exercise 35.

37. **MATHEMATICAL CONNECTIONS** Reflect $\triangle MNQ$ in the line $y = -2x$.

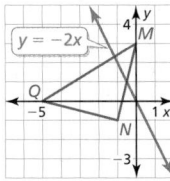

38. **THOUGHT PROVOKING** Is the composition of a translation and a reflection commutative? (In other words, do you obtain the same image regardless of the order in which you perform the transformations?) Justify your answer.

39. **MATHEMATICAL CONNECTIONS** Point $B'(1, 4)$ is the image of $B(3, 2)$ after a reflection in line c. Write an equation for line c.

Maintaining Mathematical Proficiency   Reviewing what you learned in previous grades and lessons

Use the diagram to find the angle measure. *(Section 1.5)*

40. $m\angle AOC$ **41.** $m\angle AOD$

42. $m\angle BOE$ **43.** $m\angle AOE$

44. $m\angle COD$ **45.** $m\angle EOD$

46. $m\angle COE$ **47.** $m\angle AOB$

48. $m\angle COB$ **49.** $m\angle BOD$

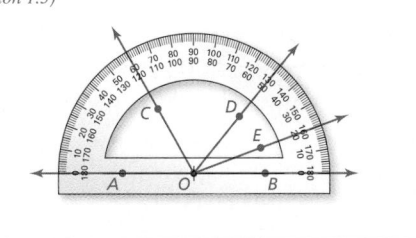

188   **Chapter 4**   Transformations

If students need help...	If students got it...
Resources by Chapter • Practice A and Practice B • Puzzle Time	Resources by Chapter • Enrichment and Extension • Cumulative Review
Student Journal • Practice	Start the *next* Section
Differentiating the Lesson Skills Review Handbook	

Overview of Section 4.3

Introduction

- Students worked with rotation of polygons in middle school; however, it is unlikely that they developed coordinate rules for the benchmark rotations.
- The explorations provide an opportunity for students to become familiar with using dynamic geometry software to perform rotations. Inductively, students will develop rules for rotations of 90° and 180° about the origin.
- The formal lesson presents the definition of a rotation and then students use a protractor and compass to draw a rotation. The coordinate rules for rotations about benchmark angles are developed, and this can be a muddy point for students. The rules make sense when looking at an example, but students find them hard to remember. Encourage students to focus on a single point such as (3, 1) and try to visualize the image.
- **Big Idea:** Students will see that the order in which transformations are performed generally does matter. The Composition Theorem (Thm. 4.1) states that the result of composing two or more rigid motions will be a rigid motion. That is different from the question of the order in which the compositions are done.

Resources

- **MP5 Use Appropriate Tools Strategically:** Dynamic geometry software, graph paper, and tracing paper are all tools that will be helpful for students to make sense of rotations. Transparencies (overhead projector) and interactive whiteboards are useful tools for teachers.

Teaching Strategy

- Students can generally visualize and sketch the translation or reflection of a figure. This is not true for rotations. The rotation is the most difficult transformation for students to visualize and to sketch. The difficulty is that all points in the preimage turn through the same number of degrees but they do not move the same distance.
- **MP4 Model with Mathematics and MP5:** To help students visualize the rotation, it is very helpful for them to have tracing paper. For demonstration purposes, it is helpful to have a transparency or a projecting device that allows students to see the fixed point (center of rotation) and the movement of the figure from the initial state (preimage) to the final state (image).
- Use the *Motivate* to help students visualize rotations.

Pacing Suggestion

- Take time for students to work through all three explorations, and then begin the formal lesson. Alternatively, you may integrate the explorations at point of use in the formal lesson: Do Exploration 1 followed by Example 1. Do Explorations 2 and 3 and then complete the formal lesson.

Dynamic Teaching Tools
Dynamic Assessment & Progress Monitoring Tool
Lesson Planning Tool
Interactive Whiteboard Lesson Library
Dynamic Classroom with Dynamic Investigations

Common Core State Standards

HSG-CO.A.2 Represent transformations in the plane using, e.g., ... geometry software; describe transformations as functions that take points in the plane as inputs and give other points as outputs... .

HSG-CO.A.3 Given a rectangle, parallelogram, trapezoid, or regular polygon, describe the rotations ... that carry it onto itself.

HSG-CO.A.4 Develop definitions of rotations, ... in terms of angles, circles, ... and line segments.

HSG-CO.A.5 Given a geometric figure and a rotation, ... draw the transformed figure using, e.g., graph paper, tracing paper, or geometry software. Specify a sequence of transformations that will carry a given figure onto another.

HSG-CO.B.6 Use geometric descriptions of rigid motions to transform figures and to predict the effect of a given rigid motion on a given figure; ...

Laurie's Notes

Exploration

Motivate

- A windshield wiper blade is a useful model in this lesson. The next time you change blades, keep a used blade for a model in teaching this lesson!
- Hold the blade at one end of the wiper (point A). Without saying anything, pretend to use the blade for wiping a windshield (rotating about point A).
- **?** "Do all points on the blade travel the same distance?" no
- **?** "Are there any points that are not moving?" yes; point A
- **?** "Is there anything that is true about all points on the blade?" yes; They all turn the same number of degrees.
- Now tape the blade to a meterstick and explain, "The blade on a car is attached to an arm." Model the movement of the blade now and ask questions similar to before. The difference now is that point A is no longer the center of the rotation, so it is moving.

Exploration 1

- This first exploration serves to familiarize students with the *rotate* command in the dynamic geometry software. In using the software, students will learn that they must select a polygon, a point of rotation, and the number of degrees the figure will be rotated.
- Encourage students to draw a scalene triangle so that the correspondence of sides will be easier to see after the rotation.
- Students should observe that the side lengths and angle measures of the rotated triangle are the same as the measures in the original triangle. They should also observe a relationship between the coordinates of corresponding vertices. Using lattice points (points at intersections of grid lines) for vertices will help students recognize a pattern.

Exploration 2

- Students should use the results of Exploration 1 to write the rule for a rotation of 90° counterclockwise about the origin. If the pattern is not obvious, then suggest that students try additional triangles in Exploration 1.
- None of the sides of $\triangle ABC$ are vertical or horizontal. Finding the lengths of the sides requires students to use the *Distance Formula*.

Exploration 3

- A rotation of 180° can be investigated using the software. Students should observe that it is not necessary to specify clockwise or counterclockwise when the angle measure is 180°.

Communicate Your Answer

- Expect students to mention needing a center of rotation and an angle measure.
- **Popsicle Sticks:** Select a student to explain Question 5.

Connecting to Next Step

- Now that students have developed some spatial abilities by using the software, move to the formal lesson, where a protractor and compass are used to construct a rotation.

4.3 Rotations

Essential Question
How can you rotate a figure in a coordinate plane?

EXPLORATION 1   Rotating a Triangle in a Coordinate Plane

Work with a partner.

a. Use dynamic geometry software to draw any triangle and label it $\triangle ABC$.

b. *Rotate* the triangle $90°$ counterclockwise about the origin to form $\triangle A'B'C'$.

c. What is the relationship between the coordinates of the vertices of $\triangle ABC$ and those of $\triangle A'B'C'$?

d. What do you observe about the side lengths and angle measures of the two triangles?

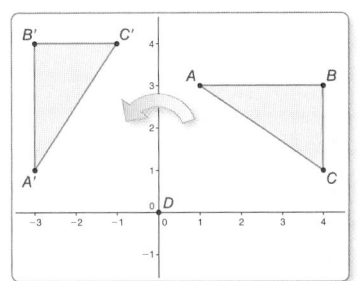

Sample

Points
$A(1, 3)$
$B(4, 3)$
$C(4, 1)$
$D(0, 0)$
Segments
$AB = 3$
$BC = 2$
$AC = 3.61$
Angles
$m\angle A = 33.69°$
$m\angle B = 90°$
$m\angle C = 56.31°$

CONSTRUCTING VIABLE ARGUMENTS

To be proficient in math, you need to use previously established results in constructing arguments.

EXPLORATION 2   Rotating a Triangle in a Coordinate Plane

Work with a partner.

a. The point (x, y) is rotated $90°$ counterclockwise about the origin. Write a rule to determine the coordinates of the image of (x, y).

b. Use the rule you wrote in part (a) to rotate $\triangle ABC$ $90°$ counterclockwise about the origin. What are the coordinates of the vertices of the image, $\triangle A'B'C'$?

c. Draw $\triangle A'B'C'$. Are its side lengths the same as those of $\triangle ABC$? Justify your answer.

EXPLORATION 3   Rotating a Triangle in a Coordinate Plane

Work with a partner.

a. The point (x, y) is rotated $180°$ counterclockwise about the origin. Write a rule to determine the coordinates of the image of (x, y). Explain how you found the rule.

b. Use the rule you wrote in part (a) to rotate $\triangle ABC$ (from Exploration 2) $180°$ counterclockwise about the origin. What are the coordinates of the vertices of the image, $\triangle A'B'C'$?

Communicate Your Answer

4. How can you rotate a figure in a coordinate plane?

5. In Exploration 3, rotate $\triangle A'B'C'$ $180°$ counterclockwise about the origin. What are the coordinates of the vertices of the image, $\triangle A''B''C''$? How are these coordinates related to the coordinates of the vertices of the original triangle, $\triangle ABC$?

ANSWERS

1. a. Check students' work.

   b. Check students' work.

   c. The x-value of each vertex of $\triangle A'B'C'$ is the opposite of the y-value of its corresponding vertex in $\triangle ABC$. The y-value of each vertex of $\triangle A'B'C'$ is equal to the x-value of its corresponding vertex in $\triangle ABC$.

   d. The side lengths and angle measures of the original figure are equal to the corresponding side lengths and angle measures of the image. For example, $AB = A'B'$ and $m\angle A = m\angle A'$.

2. a. $(x, y) \to (-y, x)$

   b. $A'(-3, 0)$, $B'(-5, 4)$, $C'(3, 3)$

   c.

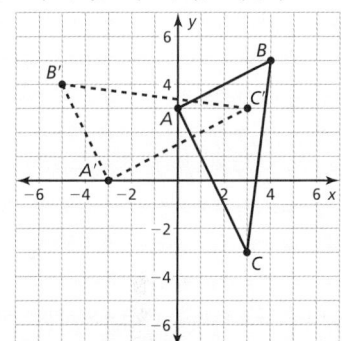

   yes; Use the Distance Formula to find the lengths.

3. a. $-x$; $-y$; When a point is rotated $180°$, the x-value and y-value of the image are the opposite of the x-value and y-value of the original point.

   b. $A'(0, -3)$, $B'(-4, -5)$, $C'(-3, 3)$

4. *Sample answer:* Put your pencil on the origin and rotate the graph the given number of degrees. Record the coordinates of the image in this orientation. Then return the coordinate plane to its original orientation, and draw the image using the coordinates you recorded.

5. $A''(0, 3)$, $B''(4, 5)$, $C''(3, -3)$; The coordinates of each vertex are the same as the corresponding vertex of the original triangle.

Extra Example 1

Use the diagram in Example 1. Draw a 60° rotation of △ABC about point P.

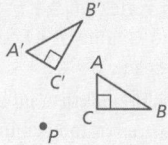

4.3 Lesson

What You Will Learn

▶ Perform rotations.
▶ Perform compositions with rotations.
▶ Identify rotational symmetry.

Performing Rotations

🌀 Core Concept

Rotations

A **rotation** is a transformation in which a figure is turned about a fixed point called the **center of rotation**. Rays drawn from the center of rotation to a point and its image form the **angle of rotation**.

A rotation about a point P through an angle of $x°$ maps every point Q in the plane to a point Q' so that one of the following properties is true.

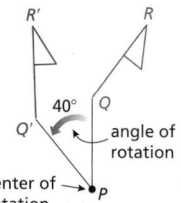

- If Q is not the center of rotation P, then $QP = Q'P$ and $m\angle QPQ' = x°$, or

- If Q is the center of rotation P, then $Q = Q'$.

Direction of rotation

clockwise

counterclockwise

The figure above shows a 40° counterclockwise rotation. Rotations can be *clockwise* or *counterclockwise*. In this chapter, all rotations are counterclockwise unless otherwise noted.

EXAMPLE 1 **Drawing a Rotation**

Draw a 120° rotation of △ABC about point P.

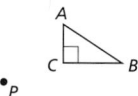

SOLUTION

Step 1 Draw a segment from P to A.

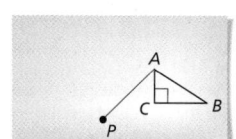

Step 2 Draw a ray to form a 120° angle with $\overline{PA}$.

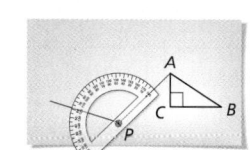

Step 3 Draw A' so that $PA' = PA$.

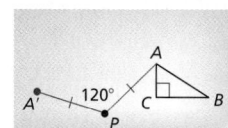

Step 4 Repeat Steps 1–3 for each vertex. Draw △A′B′C′.

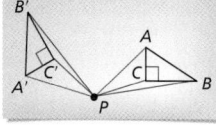

Laurie's Notes   Teacher Actions

- Write the *Core Concept*. Note how the *angle of rotation* is defined. Again, differentiate between the two bullets.
- **Teaching Tip:** Use a transparency at the overhead or document camera, or use an electronic model that allows the *center of rotation* to be visible as the rotation is occurring.
- ❓ "If you want to perform a rotation, what do you need to know?" the figure to be rotated, the center of rotation, and how many degrees the figure is rotated
- Mention the convention that rotations in this book will be counterclockwise unless otherwise noted.
- Go through the steps necessary for drawing a *rotation*.
- ❓ **Turn and Talk:** "Is it necessary to find the image of all three vertices to rotate a triangle? Explain." Discuss as a class.

You can rotate a figure more than 180°. The diagram shows rotations of point A 130°, 220°, and 310° about the origin. Notice that point A and its images all lie on the same circle. A rotation of 360° maps a figure onto itself.

You can use coordinate rules to find the coordinates of a point after a rotation of 90°, 180°, or 270° about the origin.

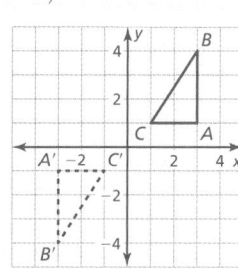

USING
ROTATIONS
You can rotate a figure
more than 360°. The
effect, however, is the
same as rotating the
figure by the angle
minus 360°.

Core Concept

Coordinate Rules for Rotations about the Origin

When a point (a, b) is rotated counterclockwise about the origin, the following are true.

- For a rotation of 90°,
  $(a, b) \rightarrow (-b, a)$.

- For a rotation of 180°,
  $(a, b) \rightarrow (-a, -b)$.

- For a rotation of 270°,
  $(a, b) \rightarrow (b, -a)$.

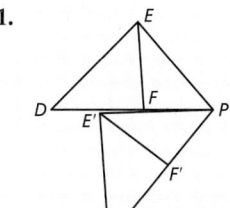

EXAMPLE 2 Rotating a Figure in the Coordinate Plane

Graph quadrilateral $RSTU$ with vertices $R(3, 1)$, $S(5, 1)$, $T(5, -3)$, and $U(2, -1)$ and its image after a 270° rotation about the origin.

SOLUTION

Use the coordinate rule for a 270° rotation to find the coordinates of the vertices of the image. Then graph quadrilateral $RSTU$ and its image.

$$(a, b) \rightarrow (b, -a)$$

$R(3, 1) \rightarrow R'(1, -3)$

$S(5, 1) \rightarrow S'(1, -5)$

$T(5, -3) \rightarrow T'(-3, -5)$

$U(2, -1) \rightarrow U'(-1, -2)$

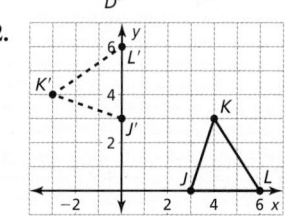

Monitoring Progress 🔊 Help in English and Spanish at BigIdeasMath.com

1. Trace $\triangle DEF$ and point P. Then draw a 50° rotation of $\triangle DEF$ about point P.

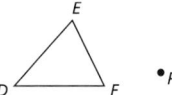

2. Graph $\triangle JKL$ with vertices $J(3, 0)$, $K(4, 3)$, and $L(6, 0)$ and its image after a 90° rotation about the origin.

Extra Example 2

Graph $\triangle ABC$ with vertices $A(3, 1)$, $B(3, 4)$, and $C(1, 1)$ and its image after a 180° rotation about the origin.

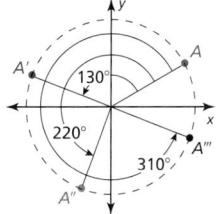

MONITORING PROGRESS ANSWERS

1.

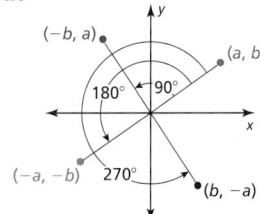

2.

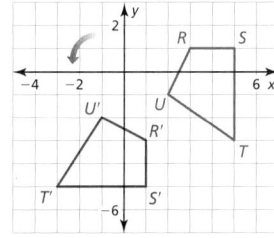

Laurie's Notes Teacher Actions

? "Have you heard of angle measures greater than 360°? Explain." Students should quickly mention contexts such as skateboarding and snowboarding where multiples of 180° are common.

- **MP8 Look For and Express Regularity in Repeated Reasoning:** Use dynamic geometry software or a transparency with grid paper to model rotations of 90°, 180°, and 270°. Rotating just one point (which is not near $y = x$ or $y = -x$) is all that is necessary. For example, using point $A(3, 1)$, the 90° rotation is $(-1, 3)$, the 180° rotation is $(-3, -1)$, and the 270° rotation

is $(1, -3)$. This simple activity will help convince students of the rules that follow.

- Write the coordinate rules for benchmark rotations about the origin. Confirm that the rules work for the example with $A(3, 1)$.

- **Whiteboarding:** Pose Example 2 and give partners time to work the example. Circulate and ask advancing questions as needed to assist students in making progress.

Extra Example 3

Graph $\overline{RS}$ with endpoints $R(1, -3)$ and $S(2, -6)$ and its image after the composition.

Rotation: 180° about the origin

Reflection: in the y-axis

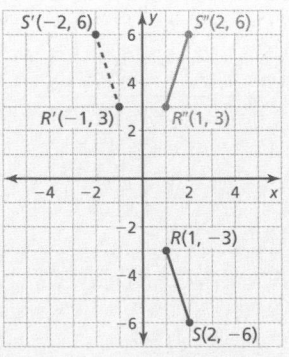

MONITORING PROGRESS ANSWERS

3.

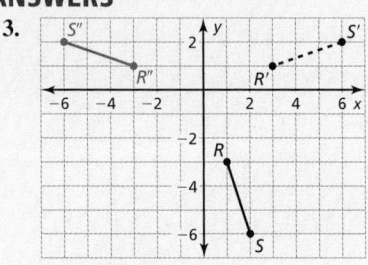

yes; The image is in Quadrant I, not Quadrant IV.

4.

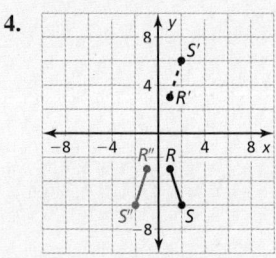

5–6. See Additional Answers.

Performing Compositions with Rotations

⟳ Postulate

Postulate 4.3   Rotation Postulate

A rotation is a rigid motion.

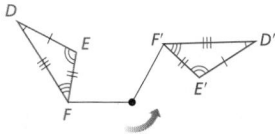

Because a rotation is a rigid motion, and a rigid motion preserves length and angle measure, the following statements are true for the rotation shown.

- $DE = D'E'$, $EF = E'F'$, $FD = F'D'$
- $m\angle D = m\angle D'$, $m\angle E = m\angle E'$, $m\angle F = m\angle F'$

Because a rotation is a rigid motion, the Composition Theorem (Theorem 4.1) guarantees that compositions of rotations and other rigid motions, such as translations and reflections, are rigid motions.

EXAMPLE 3   Performing a Composition

Graph $\overline{RS}$ with endpoints $R(1, -3)$ and $S(2, -6)$ and its image after the composition.

> **Reflection:** in the y-axis
>
> **Rotation:** 90° about the origin

COMMON ERROR

Unless you are told otherwise, perform the transformations in the order given.

SOLUTION

Step 1 Graph $\overline{RS}$.

Step 2 Reflect $\overline{RS}$ in the y-axis. $\overline{R'S'}$ has endpoints $R'(-1, -3)$ and $S'(-2, -6)$.

Step 3 Rotate $\overline{R'S'}$ 90° about the origin. $\overline{R''S''}$ has endpoints $R''(3, -1)$ and $S''(6, -2)$.

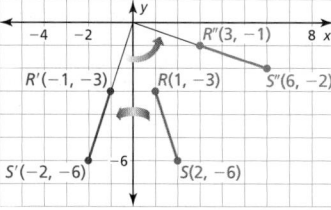

Monitoring Progress 🔊 Help in English and Spanish at BigIdeasMath.com

3. Graph $\overline{RS}$ from Example 3. Perform the rotation first, followed by the reflection. Does the order of the transformations matter? Explain.

4. **WHAT IF?** In Example 3, $\overline{RS}$ is reflected in the x-axis and rotated 180° about the origin. Graph $\overline{RS}$ and its image after the composition.

5. Graph $\overline{AB}$ with endpoints $A(-4, 4)$ and $B(-1, 7)$ and its image after the composition.

> **Translation:** $(x, y) \rightarrow (x - 2, y - 1)$
>
> **Rotation:** 90° about the origin

6. Graph $\triangle TUV$ with vertices $T(1, 2)$, $U(3, 5)$, and $V(6, 3)$ and its image after the composition.

> **Rotation:** 180° about the origin
>
> **Reflection:** in the x-axis

Laurie's Notes   Teacher Actions

- Write the *Rotation Postulate* (Post. 4.3) and ask students to interpret what it means. When rigid motions or isometries are referred to, students should be thinking about segment lengths and angle measures being preserved.
- Interpret the postulate for $\triangle DEF$ rotated about point P.
- **Alternate Approach:** Students could do the composition using software.
- ❓ **Always-Sometimes-Never True:** "The order in which you perform two transformations does not matter." Give partners time to consider the validity of this statement. They think of it as a question of commutativity. The statement is *sometimes true* for special cases (i.e., the preimage is a point on the line of reflection), but in general it is not true. *Monitoring Progress* Question 3 explores this.

Identifying Rotational Symmetry

A figure in the plane has **rotational symmetry** when the figure can be mapped onto itself by a rotation of 180° or less about the center of the figure. This point is the **center of symmetry**. Note that the rotation can be either clockwise or counterclockwise.

For example, the figure below has rotational symmetry, because a rotation of either 90° or 180° maps the figure onto itself (although a rotation of 45° does not).

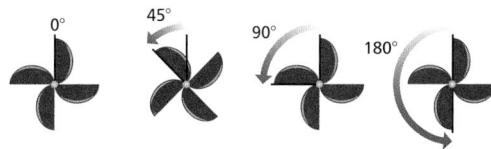

The figure above also has *point symmetry*, which is 180° rotational symmetry.

EXAMPLE 4   **Identifying Rotational Symmetry**

Does the figure have rotational symmetry? If so, describe any rotations that map the figure onto itself.

a. parallelogram   b. regular octagon   c. trapezoid

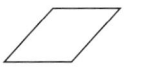

SOLUTION

a. The parallelogram has rotational symmetry. The center is the intersection of the diagonals. A 180° rotation about the center maps the parallelogram onto itself.

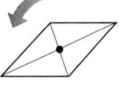

b. The regular octagon has rotational symmetry. The center is the intersection of the diagonals. Rotations of 45°, 90°, 135°, or 180° about the center all map the octagon onto itself.

c. The trapezoid does not have rotational symmetry because no rotation of 180° or less maps the trapezoid onto itself.

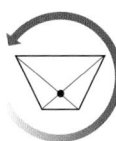

Monitoring Progress Help in English and Spanish at *BigIdeasMath.com*

Determine whether the figure has rotational symmetry. If so, describe any rotations that map the figure onto itself.

7. rhombus   8. octagon   9. right triangle

   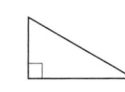

Differentiated Instruction

Kinesthetic

Have students draw and cut out a rectangle and a parallelogram that is not a rectangle. Have them identify the center of each figure by finding the intersection of the diagonals. Ask students to place a pin through the center of each figure, and then rotate the figures about the pins to test for rotational symmetry.

Extra Example 4

Does the figure have rotational symmetry? If so, describe any rotations that map the figure onto itself.

a.

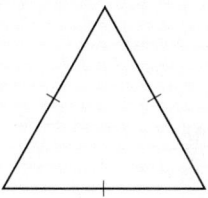

yes, 120°

b.

no

c.

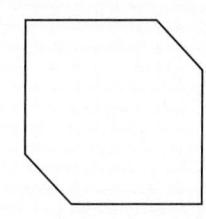

yes, 180°

MONITORING PROGRESS ANSWERS

7. yes; The center is the intersection of the diagonals. A rotation of 180° about the center maps the rhombus onto itself.

8. yes; The center is the intersection of the diagonals. Rotations of 90° and 180° about the center map the octagon onto itself.

9. no

Laurie's Notes   Teacher Actions

- *Rotational symmetry* should be familiar to students from middle school geometry.
- **Teaching Tip:** Provide tracing paper for students to use.
- **Extension:** Draw a hexagon with 60° rotational symmetry.

Closure

- **Muddiest Point:** Ask students to identify, aloud or on a paper to be collected, the muddiest point(s) about the lesson. What was difficult to understand?

Assignment Guide and Homework Check

ASSIGNMENT

Basic: 1, 2, 3–25 odd, 30, 38, 40, 41

Average: 1, 2, 4–32 even, 35, 38, 40, 41

Advanced: 1, 2, 6, 10, 15, 24–34, 36–41

HOMEWORK CHECK

Basic: 2, 7, 13, 17, 25

Average: 2, 10, 16, 26, 32

Advanced: 10, 15, 29, 34, 36

ANSWERS

1. 270°

2. What are the coordinates of the vertices of the image after a 270° counterclockwise rotation about the origin?;
   $A'(2, -1)$, $B'(4, -2)$, $C'(2, -4)$; $A'(-2, 1)$, $B'(-4, 2)$, $C'(-2, 4)$

3.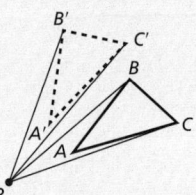

4.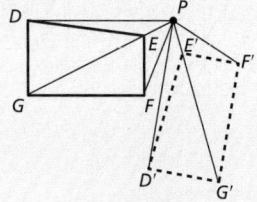

5.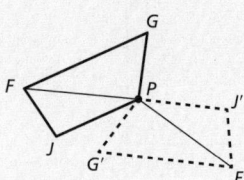

6.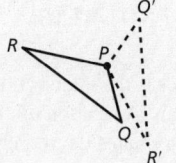

Vocabulary and Core Concept Check

1. **COMPLETE THE SENTENCE** When a point (a, b) is rotated counterclockwise about the origin, $(a, b) \rightarrow (b, -a)$ is the result of a rotation of _____.

2. **DIFFERENT WORDS, SAME QUESTION** Which is different? Find "both" answers.

   What are the coordinates of the vertices of the image after a 90° counterclockwise rotation about the origin?

   What are the coordinates of the vertices of the image after a 270° clockwise rotation about the origin?

   What are the coordinates of the vertices of the image after turning the figure 90° to the left about the origin?

   What are the coordinates of the vertices of the image after a 270° counterclockwise rotation about the origin?

   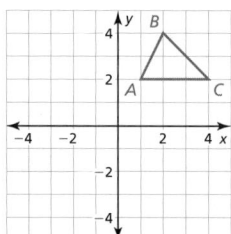

Monitoring Progress and Modeling with Mathematics

In Exercises 3–6, trace the polygon and point P. Then draw a rotation of the polygon about point P using the given number of degrees. *(See Example 1.)*

3. 30°

4. 80°

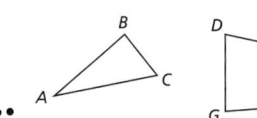

5. 150°

6. 130°

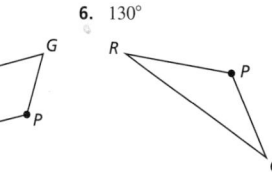

In Exercises 7–10, graph the polygon and its image after a rotation of the given number of degrees about the origin. *(See Example 2.)*

7. 90°

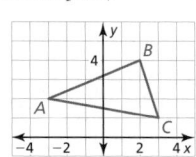

8. 180°

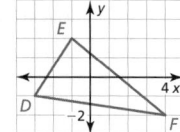

9. 180°

10. 270°

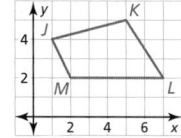

In Exercises 11–14, graph $\overline{XY}$ with endpoints $X(-3, 1)$ and $Y(4, -5)$ and its image after the composition. *(See Example 3.)*

11. **Translation:** $(x, y) \rightarrow (x, y + 2)$
    Rotation: 90° about the origin

12. **Rotation:** 180° about the origin
    Translation: $(x, y) \rightarrow (x - 1, y + 1)$

13. **Rotation:** 270° about the origin
    Reflection: in the y-axis

14. **Reflection:** in the line $y = x$
    Rotation: 180° about the origin

7.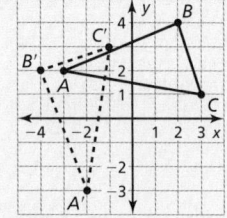

8.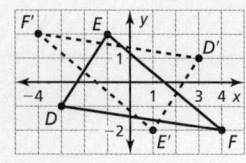

9.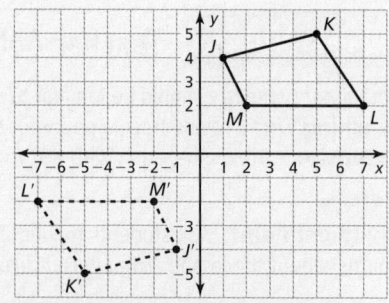

10–14. See Additional Answers.

In Exercises 15 and 16, graph △LMN with vertices
L(1, 6), M(−2, 4), and N(3, 2) and its image after the
composition. *(See Example 3.)*

15. Rotation: 90° about the origin
Translation: $(x, y) \rightarrow (x - 3, y + 2)$

16. Reflection: in the *x*-axis
Rotation: 270° about the origin

In Exercises 17–20, determine whether the figure has
rotational symmetry. If so, describe any rotations that
map the figure onto itself. *(See Example 4.)*

17.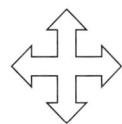

18.

19.

20.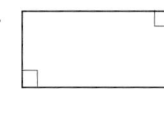

REPEATED REASONING In Exercises 21–24, select the
angles of rotational symmetry for the regular polygon.
Select all that apply.

(A) 30° (B) 45° (C) 60° (D) 72°
(E) 90° (F) 120° (G) 144° (H) 180°

21.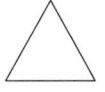

22.

23.

24.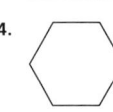

ERROR ANALYSIS In Exercises 25 and 26, the endpoints
of $\overline{CD}$ are C(−1, 1) and D(2, 3). Describe and correct
the error in finding the coordinates of the vertices of the
image after a rotation of 270° about the origin.

25.

$$C(-1, 1) \rightarrow C'(-1, -1)$$
$$D(2, 3) \rightarrow D'(2, -3)$$

26.

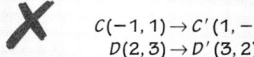
$$C(-1, 1) \rightarrow C'(1, -1)$$
$$D(2, 3) \rightarrow D'(3, 2)$$

27. CONSTRUCTION Follow these steps to construct a
rotation of △ABC by angle D around a point O. Use
a compass and straightedge.

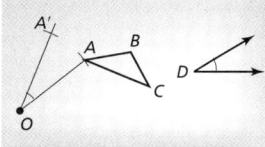

Step 1 Draw △ABC, ∠D, and O, the center
of rotation.

Step 2 Draw $\overline{OA}$. Use the construction for copying
an angle to copy ∠D at O, as shown. Then
use distance OA and center O to find A′.

Step 3 Repeat Step 2 to find points B′ and C′. Draw
△A′B′C′.

28. REASONING You enter the revolving door at a hotel.

a. You rotate the door 180°.
What does this mean in the
context of the situation?
Explain.

b. You rotate the door 360°.
What does this mean in the
context of the situation?
Explain.

29. MATHEMATICAL CONNECTIONS Use the graph of
$y = 2x - 3$.

a. Rotate the line 90°, 180°,
270°, and 360° about the
origin. Write the equation
of the line for each image.
Describe the relationship
between the equation of the
preimage and the equation
of each image.

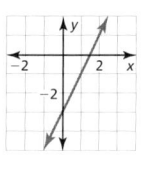

b. Do you think that the relationships you
described in part (a) are true for any line?
Explain your reasoning.

30. MAKING AN ARGUMENT Your friend claims that
rotating a figure by 180° is the same as reflecting a
figure in the *y*-axis and then reflecting it in the *x*-axis.
Is your friend correct? Explain your reasoning.

28. a. If you were outside, you are now inside,
or vice versa, because you have made
half of a rotation.

b. You are back where you started because
you have made a full rotation.

29. See Additional Answers.

30. yes; Reflection in the *y*-axis and then in the
x-axis yields $(x, y) \rightarrow (-x, y) \rightarrow (-x, -y)$.
A 180° rotation yields the same result:
$(x, y) \rightarrow (-x, -y)$.

ANSWERS

15.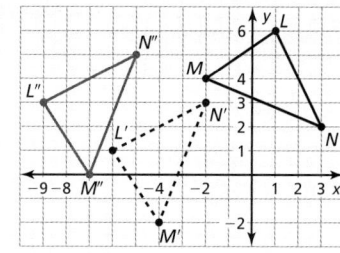

16.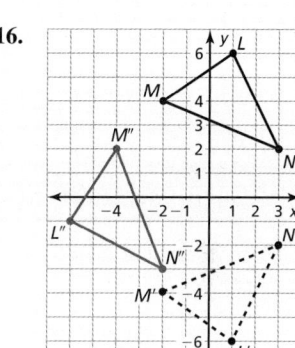

17. yes; Rotations of 90° and 180° about
the center map the figure onto itself.

18. yes; Rotations of 72° and 144° about
the center map the figure onto itself.

19. yes; Rotations of 45°, 90°, 135°, and
180° about the center map the figure
onto itself.

20. yes; A 180° rotation about the center
maps the rectangle onto itself.

21. F

22. E, H

23. D, G

24. C, F, H

25. The rule for a 270° rotation,
$(x, y) \rightarrow (y, -x)$, should have
been used instead of the rule for
a reflection in the *x*-axis;
$C(-1, 1) \rightarrow C'(1, 1)$,
$D(2, 3) \rightarrow D'(3, -2)$

26. The rule for a 270° rotation,
$(x, y) \rightarrow (y, -x)$, should have been used
instead of the rule for a reflection in the
line $y = x$; $C(-1, 1) \rightarrow C'(1, 1)$,
$D(2, 3) \rightarrow D'(3, -2)$

27.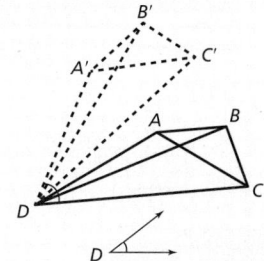

Mini-Assessment

1. Draw a 135° rotation of △ABC about point P.

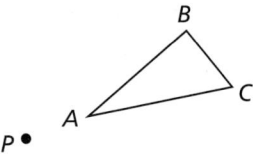

See Additional Answers.

2. $\overline{RS}$ has endpoints R(−2, 1) and S(1, 2). Graph $\overline{RS}$ and its image after the composition.
   Rotation: 90° about the origin
   Reflection: in the x-axis

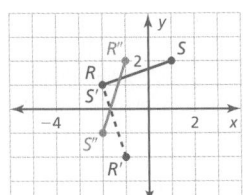

3. Does the figure have rotational symmetry? If so, describe any rotations that map the figure onto itself.

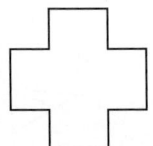

yes; 90°, 180°

31. **DRAWING CONCLUSIONS** A figure only has point symmetry. How many times can you rotate the figure before it is back where it started?

32. **ANALYZING RELATIONSHIPS** Is it possible for a figure to have 90° rotational symmetry but not 180° rotational symmetry? Explain your reasoning.

33. **ANALYZING RELATIONSHIPS** Is it possible for a figure to have 180° rotational symmetry but not 90° rotational symmetry? Explain your reasoning.

34. **THOUGHT PROVOKING** Can rotations of 90°, 180°, 270°, and 360° be written as the composition of two reflections? Justify your answer.

35. **USING AN EQUATION** Inside a kaleidoscope, two mirrors are placed next to each other to form a V. The angle between the mirrors determines the number of lines of symmetry in the image. Use the formula $n(m\angle 1) = 180°$ to find the measure of ∠1, the angle between the mirrors, for the number n of lines of symmetry.

a.

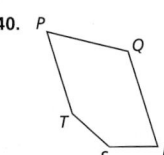

b.

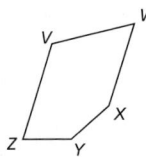

36. **REASONING** Use the coordinate rules for counterclockwise rotations about the origin to write coordinate rules for clockwise rotations of 90°, 180°, or 270° about the origin.

37. **USING STRUCTURE** △XYZ has vertices X(2, 5), Y(3, 1), and Z(0, 2). Rotate △XYZ 90° about the point P(−2, −1).

Maintaining Mathematical Proficiency
Reviewing what you learned in previous grades and lessons

The figures are congruent. Name the corresponding angles and the corresponding sides.
(Skills Review Handbook)

40.

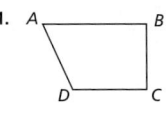

41.

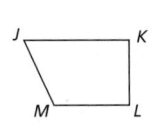

38. **HOW DO YOU SEE IT?** You are finishing the puzzle. The remaining two pieces both have rotational symmetry.

a. Describe the rotational symmetry of Piece 1 and of Piece 2.

b. You pick up Piece 1. How many different ways can it fit in the puzzle?

c. Before putting Piece 1 into the puzzle, you connect it to Piece 2. Now how many ways can it fit in the puzzle? Explain.

39. **USING STRUCTURE** A polar coordinate system locates a point in a plane by its distance from the origin O and by the measure of an angle with its vertex at the origin. For example, the point A(2, 30°) is 2 units from the origin and $m\angle XOA = 30°$. What are the polar coordinates of the image of point A after a 90° rotation? a 180° rotation? a 270° rotation? Explain.

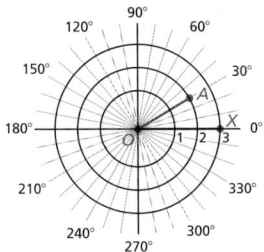

If students need help...

Resources by Chapter
- Practice A and Practice B
- Puzzle Time

Student Journal
- Practice

Differentiating the Lesson
Skills Review Handbook

If students got it...

Resources by Chapter
- Enrichment and Extension
- Cumulative Review

Start the *next* Section

Core Vocabulary

vector, *p. 174*	preimage, *p. 174*	line symmetry, *p. 185*
initial point, *p. 174*	translation, *p. 174*	line of symmetry, *p. 185*
terminal point, *p. 174*	rigid motion, *p. 176*	rotation, *p. 190*
horizontal component, *p. 174*	composition of transformations,	center of rotation, *p. 190*
vertical component, *p. 174*	*p. 176*	angle of rotation, *p. 190*
component form, *p. 174*	reflection, *p. 182*	rotational symmetry, *p. 193*
transformation, *p. 174*	line of reflection, *p. 182*	center of symmetry, *p. 193*
image, *p. 174*	glide reflection, *p. 184*	

Core Concepts

Section 4.1

Vectors, *p. 174*

Translations, *p. 174*

Postulate 4.1 Translation Postulate, *p. 176*

Theorem 4.1 Composition Theorem, *p. 176*

Section 4.2

Reflections, *p. 182*

Coordinate Rules for Reflections, *p. 183*

Postulate 4.2 Reflection Postulate, *p. 184*

Line Symmetry, *p. 185*

Section 4.3

Rotations, *p. 190*

Coordinate Rules for Rotations
about the Origin, *p. 191*

Postulate 4.3 Rotation Postulate, *p. 192*

Rotational Symmetry, *p. 193*

Mathematical Practices

1. How could you determine whether your results make sense in Exercise 26 on page 179?

2. State the meaning of the numbers and symbols you chose in Exercise 28 on page 187.

3. Describe the steps you would take to arrive at the answer to Exercise 29 part (a) on page 195.

- - - - - - - - Study Skills - - - - - - - -

Keeping a Positive Attitude

Ever feel frustrated or overwhelmed by math? You're not alone.
Just take a deep breath and assess the situation. Try to find a
productive study environment, review your notes and examples
in the textbook, and ask your teacher or peers for help.

197

Dynamic Teaching Tools

Dynamic Assessment & Progress Monitoring Tool

Interactive Whiteboard Lesson Library

Dynamic Classroom with Dynamic Investigations

ANSWERS

1. Recreate the chess board on a coordinate plane and substitute the coordinates into your rule to verify both the composition and the single translation yield the same result.

2. $x + 3$ means that the figure will slide 3 units to the right, and $y + 3$ means the figure will slide 3 units up.

3. Find two points on the line $y = 2x - 3$, their images after the rotation, and use the images to find the equation of the new line.

ANSWERS

1.

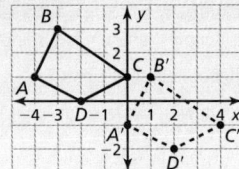

2.

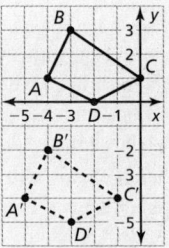

3.

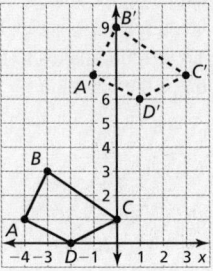

4.

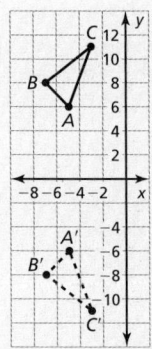

5.

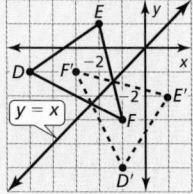

6.

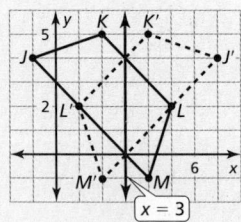

7–9. See Additional Answers.

10. 6

11. 0

12. 2

13. 1

Graph quadrilateral *ABCD* with vertices *A*(−4, 1), *B*(−3, 3), *C*(0, 1), and *D*(−2, 0) and its image after the translation. *(Section 4.1)*

1. $(x, y) \rightarrow (x + 4, y - 2)$ **2.** $(x, y) \rightarrow (x - 1, y - 5)$ **3.** $(x, y) \rightarrow (x + 3, y + 6)$

Graph the polygon with the given vertices and its image after a reflection in the given line. *(Section 4.2)*

4. *A*(−5, 6), *B*(−7, 8), *C*(−3, 11); *x*-axis

5. *D*(−5, −1), *E*(−2, 1), *F*(−1, −3); *y* = *x*

6. *J*(−1, 4), *K*(2, 5), *L*(5, 2), *M*(4, −1); *x* = 3

7. *P*(2, −4), *Q*(6, −1), *R*(9, −4), *S*(6, −6); *y* = −2

Graph △*ABC* with vertices *A*(2, −1), *B*(5, 2), and *C*(8, −2) and its image after the glide reflection. *(Section 4.2)*

8. **Translation:** $(x, y) \rightarrow (x, y + 6)$
Reflection: in the *y*-axis

9. **Translation:** $(x, y) \rightarrow (x - 9, y)$
Reflection: in the line *y* = 1

Determine the number of lines of symmetry for the figure. *(Section 4.2)*

10.  **11.** 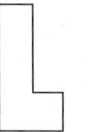 **12.**  **13.**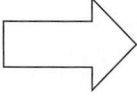

Graph the polygon and its image after a rotation of the given number of degrees about the origin. *(Section 4.3)*

14. 90° 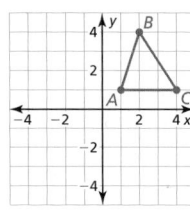 **15.** 270° 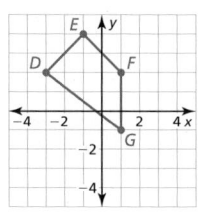 **16.** 180°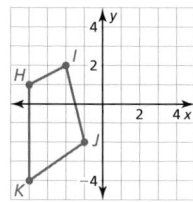

Graph △*LMN* with vertices *L*(−3, −2), *M*(−1, 1), and *N*(2, −3) and its image after the composition. *(Sections 4.1–4.3)*

17. **Translation:** $(x, y) \rightarrow (x - 4, y + 3)$
Rotation: 180° about the origin

18. **Rotation:** 90° about the origin
Reflection: in the *y*-axis

19. The figure shows a game in which the object is to create solid rows using the pieces given. Using only translations and rotations, describe the transformations for each piece at the top that will form two solid rows at the bottom. *(Section 4.1 and Section 4.3)*

14.

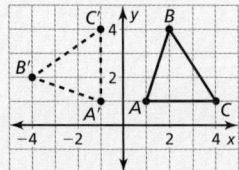

15.

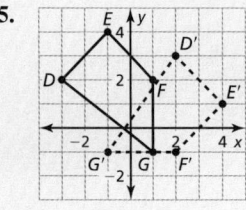

16.

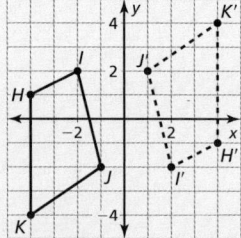

17–19. See Additional Answers.

Overview of Section 4.4

Introduction

- In grade 8, the concept of congruency was introduced. Students should understand that a two-dimensional figure is congruent to another when the second can be obtained from the first by a sequence of rotations, reflections, and translations.
- In this chapter, students have studied three rigid transformations, all congruence preserving in terms of length and angle measure. Students learned that a composition of rigid motions will also be a rigid motion. Two specific compositions are explored in this lesson: successive reflections in parallel lines and successive reflections in intersecting lines. The results are stated as theorems.

Resources

- **MP5 Use Appropriate Tools Strategically:** To enable students to see the results of two or more rigid transformations, use dynamic geometry software, tracing paper, transparencies, and reflecting devices. At home, students can use parchment paper or waxed paper.

Teaching Strategy

- The coordinate plane provides a calibrated environment, which aids students' visual skills when performing a rigid transformation on a figure. When using dynamic geometry software, transformations can be done on a coordinate grid or not.
- You can model both environments without software! Use an overhead projector and two layers of transparencies, one that has a coordinate grid on it and one that is clear.
- Draw the figures from Example 1 or 2 on the clear transparency and overlay on the coordinate grid. Have students identify the congruent figures and describe the transformations. Use tick marks to indicate lengths that are congruent. Slide the coordinate grid out from under the top transparency.

? "Are the figures congruent?" yes

Extensions

- Natural extensions to this lesson would be to perform more than two reflections (in parallel or intersecting lines) and look for patterns.

Pacing Suggestion

- In the explorations, the students explore the two theorems presented in the lesson. The discussion and examples in the formal lesson related to the theorems will require less time.

Common Core State Standards

HSG-CO.A.5 Given a geometric figure and a rotation, reflection, or translation, draw the transformed figure using, e.g., graph paper, … or geometry software. Specify a sequence of transformations that will carry a given figure onto another.

HSG-CO.B.6 Use geometric descriptions of rigid motions to transform figures and to predict the effect of a given rigid motion on a given figure; given two figures, use the definition of congruence in terms of rigid motions to decide if they are congruent.

Laurie's Notes

Exploration

Parallel fold lines

Perpendicular fold lines

Motivate

- Fold a piece of paper in half and in half again so that the fold lines are parallel, as shown. Use a handheld paper punch to punch one hole through all layers. Have students describe what the paper will look like when opened.

- Fold a piece of paper in half and in half again so that the fold lines are perpendicular, as shown. Use a handheld paper punch to punch one hole through all layers. Have students describe what the paper will look like when opened.

- Discuss the location of the lines of reflection on the opened paper. Explain to students that today they will be investigating reflections in lines.

Exploration Note

- Each exploration investigates a theorem presented in the formal lesson. It is possible to simply pose the conditions to students and let them explore.

Exploration 1

- The correspondence of sides is easier to see when a scalene triangle is used. Note that the coordinate grid is not necessary in this exploration.

- If you want students to discover the relationship, then I think it is best when students are not looking at a graphic of the finished construction. Just give brief instructions.

  - Say, "Construct a scalene triangle on the left side of the screen. Draw two parallel lines that you can reflect your triangle in. Reflect your triangle in the first line followed by the second line. I'm curious about the relationship between the original triangle and the final triangle."

- Depending on how far apart the parallel lines are, or how far the triangle is from the first line, the resulting construction can be more difficult for students to read and interpret. Fortunately, with the dynamic geometry software the position of the parallel lines can be changed easily.

- It is actually okay when the reflected triangles intersect either of the parallel lines. The conjecture you want students to make will not change.

- **? Probing Question:** If students need a little assistance, say, "Hide the middle triangle, the image of the first reflection. What do you notice?" At this point, students should recognize that the final image is a translation of the original triangle.

- **?** "What is the vector for this translation?" The vector is two times the distance between the parallel lines. If students do not observe the connection of the vector to the distance between the parallel lines, suggest that they click and drag on one of the parallel lines.

Exploration 2

- I prefer to have students explore without the benefit of a diagram.
  - To introduce the exploration, ask, "What if the lines in Exploration 1 were not parallel? Would there be a relationship between the original triangle and the final image?"

- Ask probing questions to assist students' discovery of the relationship being explored.

Communicate Your Answer

- **MP5:** If students are having difficulty with Question 4, suggest that they draw a sketch.

Connecting to Next Step

- The explorations students have explored will be presented in the formal lesson as theorems.

4.4 Congruence and Transformations

Essential Question
What conjectures can you make about a figure reflected in two lines?

EXPLORATION 1   Reflections in Parallel Lines

Work with a partner. Use dynamic geometry software to draw any scalene triangle and label it △ABC.

a. Draw any line $\overleftrightarrow{DE}$. Reflect △ABC in $\overleftrightarrow{DE}$ to form △A′B′C′.

b. Draw a line parallel to $\overleftrightarrow{DE}$. Reflect △A′B′C′ in the new line to form △A″B″C″.

c. Draw the line through point A that is perpendicular to $\overleftrightarrow{DE}$. What do you notice?

d. Find the distance between points A and A″. Find the distance between the two parallel lines. What do you notice?

e. Hide △A′B′C′. Is there a single transformation that maps △ABC to △A″B″C″? Explain.

f. Make conjectures based on your answers in parts (c)–(e). Test your conjectures by changing △ABC and the parallel lines.

Sample

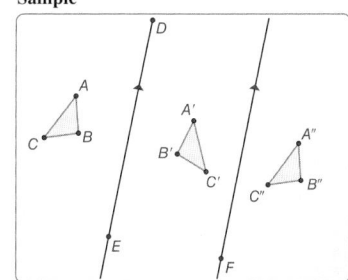

CONSTRUCTING VIABLE ARGUMENTS

To be proficient in math, you need to make conjectures and justify your conclusions.

EXPLORATION 2   Reflections in Intersecting Lines

Work with a partner. Use dynamic geometry software to draw any scalene triangle and label it △ABC.

a. Draw any line $\overrightarrow{DE}$. Reflect △ABC in $\overrightarrow{DE}$ to form △A′B′C′.

b. Draw any line $\overrightarrow{DF}$ so that angle EDF is less than or equal to 90°. Reflect △A′B′C′ in $\overrightarrow{DF}$ to form △A″B″C″.

c. Find the measure of ∠EDF. Rotate △ABC counterclockwise about point D using an angle twice the measure of ∠EDF.

d. Make a conjecture about a figure reflected in two intersecting lines. Test your conjecture by changing △ABC and the lines.

Sample

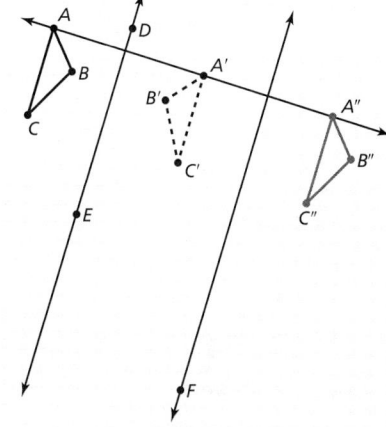

Communicate Your Answer

3. What conjectures can you make about a figure reflected in two lines?

4. Point Q is reflected in two parallel lines, $\overleftrightarrow{GH}$ and $\overleftrightarrow{JK}$, to form Q′ and Q″. The distance from $\overleftrightarrow{GH}$ to $\overleftrightarrow{JK}$ is 3.2 inches. What is the distance QQ″?

Section 4.4   Congruence and Transformations   **199**

Dynamic Teaching Tools

Dynamic Assessment & Progress Monitoring Tool

Lesson Planning Tool

Interactive Whiteboard Lesson Library

Dynamic Classroom with Dynamic Investigations

ANSWERS

1. a. Check student's work.

    b. Check student's work.

    c. *Sample answer:*

The line passes through A′ and A″.

    d. The distance between A and A″ is twice the distance between the parallel lines.

    e. yes; △A″B″C″ is a translation of △ABC.

    f. If two lines are parallel, and a preimage is reflected in the first line and then in the second, the final image is a translation of the preimage. The distance between each point in the preimage and its corresponding point in the final image is twice the distance between the parallel lines.

2. a. Check student's work.

    b. Check student's work.

    c. *Sample answer:* 50°

    d. The final image after the reflections is the same as a rotation about point D using an angle that is twice the measure of the angle of intersection.

3. The image of a figure reflected in two lines is congruent to the preimage. The image of a figure reflected in two parallel lines is a translation of the preimage. The image of a figure reflected in two lines that intersect at point D is a rotation about point D of the preimage.

4. 6.4 in.

Extra Example 1

Identify any congruent figures in the coordinate plane. Explain.

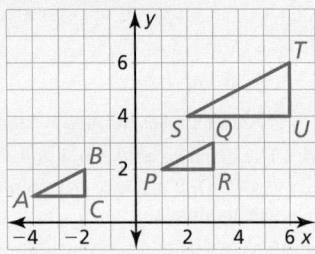

$\triangle ABC$ is congruent to $\triangle PQR$, because $\triangle PQR$ is a translation of $\triangle ABC$ 5 units right and 1 unit up.

MONITORING PROGRESS ANSWER

1. $\triangle DEF \cong \triangle ABC$, $\triangle KLM \cong \triangle STU$, $\square GHIJ \cong \square NPQR$; $\triangle DEF$ is a 90° rotation of $\triangle ABC$. $\triangle KLM$ is a reflection of $\triangle STU$ in the y-axis. $\square GHIJ$ is a translation 6 units up of $\square NPQR$.

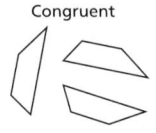

4.4 Lesson

Core Vocabulary

congruent figures, *p. 200*
congruence transformation, *p. 201*

What You Will Learn

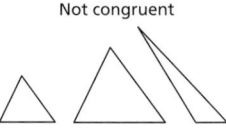

▶ Identify congruent figures.

▶ Describe congruence transformations.

▶ Use theorems about congruence transformations.

Identifying Congruent Figures

Two geometric figures are **congruent figures** if and only if there is a rigid motion or a composition of rigid motions that maps one of the figures onto the other. Congruent figures have the same size and shape.

Congruent   Not congruent

same size and shape   different sizes or shapes

You can identify congruent figures in the coordinate plane by identifying the rigid motion or composition of rigid motions that maps one of the figures onto the other. Recall from Postulates 4.1–4.3 and Theorem 4.1 that translations, reflections, rotations, and compositions of these transformations are rigid motions.

EXAMPLE 1   Identifying Congruent Figures

Identify any congruent figures in the coordinate plane. Explain.

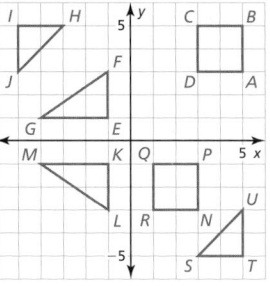

SOLUTION

Square *NPQR* is a translation of square *ABCD* 2 units left and 6 units down. So, square *ABCD* and square *NPQR* are congruent.

$\triangle KLM$ is a reflection of $\triangle EFG$ in the x-axis. So, $\triangle EFG$ and $\triangle KLM$ are congruent.

$\triangle STU$ is a 180° rotation of $\triangle HIJ$. So, $\triangle HIJ$ and $\triangle STU$ are congruent.

Monitoring Progress Help in English and Spanish at *BigIdeasMath.com*

1. Identify any congruent figures in the coordinate plane. Explain.

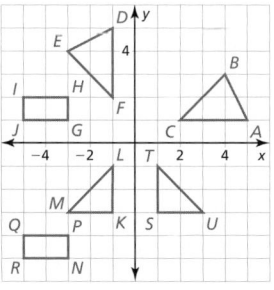

Laurie's Notes   Teacher Actions

? **"What does it mean for two figures to be congruent?"** Answers will vary, but it is likely that students will say things such as "same shape and same size," or "all the corresponding sides are congruent and all corresponding angles are congruent." These responses reflect an understanding of congruence from middle school.

• Define *congruent figures* in terms of a rigid motion. Note the "if and only if" language of the definition.

• **FYI:** $\triangle STU$ is also a reflection of $\triangle JIH$ in the line $y = x$.

• **MP3 Construct Viable Arguments and Critique the Reasoning of Others:** Have students *Turn and Talk* to answer the *Monitoring Progress* question. What evidence are partners offering? They should be stating a rigid motion that mapped one figure to another.

Congruence Transformations

Another name for a rigid motion or a combination of rigid motions is a **congruence transformation** because the preimage and image are congruent. The terms "rigid motion" and "congruence transformation" are interchangeable.

READING

You can read the notation ▭*ABCD* as "parallelogram *A, B, C, D.*"

EXAMPLE 2   Describing a Congruence Transformation

Describe a congruence transformation that maps ▭*ABCD* to ▭*EFGH*.

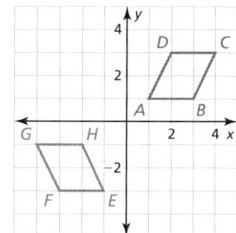

SOLUTION

The two vertical sides of ▭*ABCD* rise from left to right, and the two vertical sides of ▭*EFGH* fall from left to right. If you reflect ▭*ABCD* in the *y*-axis, as shown, then the image, ▭*A′B′C′D′*, will have the same orientation as ▭*EFGH*.

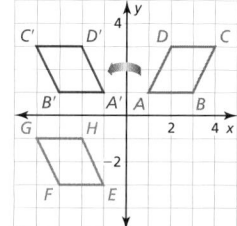

Then you can map ▭*A′B′C′D′* to ▭*EFGH* using a translation of 4 units down.

▶ So, a congruence transformation that maps ▭*ABCD* to ▭*EFGH* is a reflection in the *y*-axis followed by a translation of 4 units down.

Monitoring Progress Help in English and Spanish at *BigIdeasMath.com*

2. In Example 2, describe another congruence transformation that maps ▭*ABCD* to ▭*EFGH*.

3. Describe a congruence transformation that maps △*JKL* to △*MNP*.

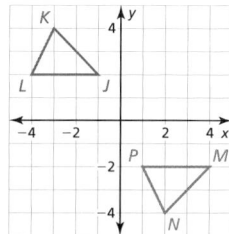

English Language Learners

Group Activity

Some students may struggle with the fact that the terms *congruence transformation* and *rigid motion* are interchangeable. Form small groups of English learners and English speakers. Have each group find five sets of interchangeable terms (mathematical or otherwise). Ask groups to share their findings. As needed, discuss the difference between interchangeable terms and a pair of terms where one describes a subset of the other (such as *square* and *quadrilateral*).

Extra Example 2

Describe a congruence transformation that maps quadrilateral *ABCD* to quadrilateral *PQRS*.

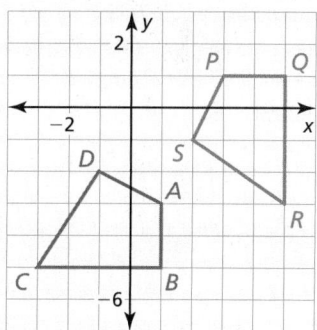

90° rotation about the origin

MONITORING PROGRESS ANSWERS

2. *Sample answer:* reflection in the *x*-axis followed by a translation 5 units left

3. *Sample answer:* reflection in the *x*-axis followed by a translation 5 units right

---

Laurie's Notes   Teacher Actions

- Define *congruence transformation*. The term *isometry* could also be used.
- Pose Example 2 as given. Check with a *Thumbs Up* that students understand the problem statement. Give time for partners to work together.
- **Popsicle Sticks:** Solicit a solution from the class. "Did everyone have that solution?" There are different compositions of rigid motions that will work.
- **Extension:** Have students explore whether a translation followed by a reflection is commutative, meaning does the order in which the rigid motions are performed matter?

Extra Example 3

In the diagram, a reflection in line a maps $\overline{PQ}$ to $\overline{P'Q'}$. A reflection in line b maps $\overline{P'Q'}$ to $\overline{P''Q''}$. Also, $PJ = 3$ and $LP'' = 8$.

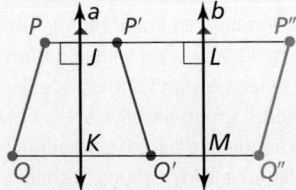

a. Name any segments congruent to each segment: $\overline{PQ}$, $\overline{PJ}$, and $\overline{QK}$.
$\overline{PQ} \cong \overline{P'Q'} \cong \overline{P''Q''}$; $\overline{PJ} \cong \overline{P'J}$; $\overline{QK} \cong \overline{Q'K}$

b. Does $JK = LM$? Explain. Yes, $JKML$ is a rectangle, and opposite sides of a rectangle are congruent.

c. What is the length of $\overline{PP''}$? 22 units

MONITORING PROGRESS ANSWERS

4. translation 3.2 cm right

5. They are perpendicular by Reflections in Parallel Lines (Thm. 4.2).

6. 3.2 cm

Using Theorems about Congruence Transformations

Compositions of two reflections result in either a translation or a rotation. A composition of two reflections in parallel lines results in a translation, as described in the following theorem.

Theorem

Theorem 4.2   Reflections in Parallel Lines Theorem

If lines k and m are parallel, then a reflection in line k followed by a reflection in line m is the same as a translation.

If A'' is the image of A, then

1. $\overline{AA''}$ is perpendicular to k and m, and
2. $AA'' = 2d$, where d is the distance between k and m.

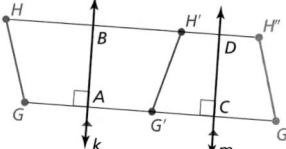

Proof Ex. 31, p. 206

EXAMPLE 3   Using the Reflections in Parallel Lines Theorem

In the diagram, a reflection in line k maps $\overline{GH}$ to $\overline{G'H'}$. A reflection in line m maps $\overline{G'H'}$ to $\overline{G''H''}$. Also, $HB = 9$ and $DH'' = 4$.

a. Name any segments congruent to each segment: $\overline{GH}$, $\overline{HB}$, and $\overline{GA}$.

b. Does $AC = BD$? Explain.

c. What is the length of $\overline{GG''}$?

SOLUTION

a. $\overline{GH} \cong \overline{G'H'}$, and $\overline{GH} \cong \overline{G''H''}$. $\overline{HB} \cong \overline{H'B}$. $\overline{GA} \cong \overline{G'A}$.

b. Yes, $AC = BD$ because $\overline{GG''}$ and $\overline{HH''}$ are perpendicular to both k and m. So, $\overline{BD}$ and $\overline{AC}$ are opposite sides of a rectangle.

c. By the properties of reflections, $H'B = 9$ and $H'D = 4$. The Reflections in Parallel Lines Theorem implies that $GG'' = HH'' = 2 \cdot BD$, so the length of $\overline{GG''}$ is $2(9 + 4) = 26$ units.

Monitoring Progress 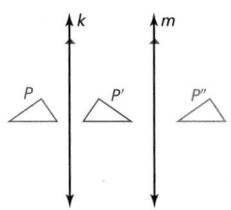 Help in English and Spanish at *BigIdeasMath.com*

Use the figure. The distance between line k and line m is 1.6 centimeters.

4. The preimage is reflected in line k, then in line m. Describe a single transformation that maps the blue figure to the green figure.

5. What is the relationship between $\overline{PP'}$ and line k? Explain.

6. What is the distance between P and P''?

Laurie's Notes   Teacher Actions

- The *Reflections in Parallel Lines Theorem* (Thm. 4.2) was explored in Exploration 1. Whether the exploration was done or not, use dynamic geometry software to demonstrate the result of composing two reflections in parallel lines. Click and drag the parallel lines, changing the distance d between them and hence the distance $2d$ between the preimage and image.

- **MP5:** Students need to have the opportunity to explore the *Reflections in Parallel Lines Theorem* (Thm. 4.2) with technology, reflectors, or compass and straightedge. Students should develop the habit of mind of verifying statements using appropriate tools.

- **Alternate Approach:** For Example 3, display the diagram. Give partners a whiteboard and ask them to record everything they know to be true from the diagram. They should be prepared to justify their statements.

A composition of two reflections in intersecting lines results in a rotation, as described in the following theorem.

↻ Theorem

Theorem 4.3 Reflections in Intersecting Lines Theorem

If lines k and m intersect at point P, then a reflection in line k followed by a reflection in line m is the same as a rotation about point P.

The angle of rotation is $2x°$, where $x°$ is the measure of the acute or right angle formed by lines k and m.

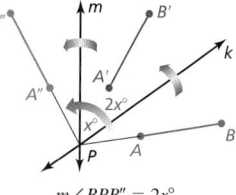

$m\angle BPB'' = 2x°$

Proof Ex. 31, p. 250

EXAMPLE 4 **Using the Reflections in Intersecting Lines Theorem**

In the diagram, the figure is reflected in line k. The image is then reflected in line m. Describe a single transformation that maps F to F''.

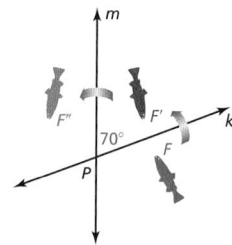

SOLUTION

By the Reflections in Intersecting Lines Theorem, a reflection in line k followed by a reflection in line m is the same as a rotation about point P. The measure of the acute angle formed between lines k and m is $70°$. So, by the Reflections in Intersecting Lines Theorem, the angle of rotation is $2(70°) = 140°$. A single transformation that maps F to F'' is a $140°$ rotation about point P.

▶ You can check that this is correct by tracing lines k and m and point F, then rotating the point $140°$.

Monitoring Progress 🔊 Help in English and Spanish at *BigIdeasMath.com*

7. In the diagram, the preimage is reflected in line k, then in line m. Describe a single transformation that maps the blue figure onto the green figure.

8. A rotation of $76°$ maps C to C'. To map C to C' using two reflections, what is the measure of the angle formed by the intersecting lines of reflection?

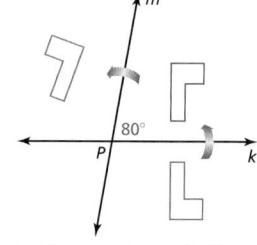

Section 4.4   Congruence and Transformations   **203**

Extra Example 4

In the diagram, the figure is reflected in line k. The image is then reflected in line m. Describe a single transformation that maps F to F''.

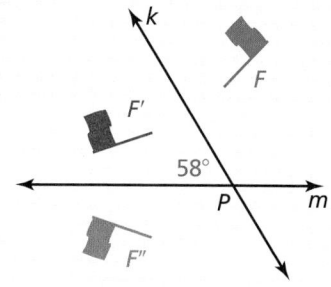

A rotation of $116°$ about point P

MONITORING PROGRESS ANSWERS

7. $160°$ rotation about point P

8. $38°$

Laurie's Notes   Teacher Actions

- The *Reflections in Intersecting Lines Theorem* (Thm. 4.3) is more difficult to see for most students than the previous theorem. Rotations in general are more difficult to visualize than translations.
- Use software to demonstrate the result of composing two reflections in intersecting lines. Click and drag either of the intersecting lines, changing $x°$, the acute or right angle formed by the intersecting lines, and hence, the angle of rotation $2x°$ between the preimage and image.
- **Note:** A reflection in the x-axis followed by a reflection in the y-axis is equivalent to a rotation of $180°$. This special case is one that should be familiar to students.

- **Teaching Tip:** Using a figure that is not a polygon, like Example 4, can help students view the orientation that changes when a figure is reflected.

Closure

- **Writing Prompt:** A congruence transformation is … a rigid motion where the preimage and image are congruent.
- **Writing Prompt:** The composition of two reflections is equivalent to … a translation when the lines are parallel and is equivalent to a rotation when the lines are intersecting.

Section 4.4   **203**

ANSWERS

1. congruent

2. The preimage and image are congruent in a rigid transformation.

3. $\triangle HJK \cong \triangle QRS$, $\square DEFG \cong \square LMNP$; $\triangle HJK$ is a 90° rotation of $\triangle QRS$. $\square DEFG$ is a translation 7 units right and 3 units down of $\square LMNP$.

4. $\triangle MNP \cong \triangle TUV$, $\triangle EFG \cong \triangle QRS$, $\square HJKL \cong \square ABCD$; $\triangle MNP$ is a 90° rotation of $\triangle TUV$. $\triangle EFG$ is a 180° rotation of $\triangle QRS$. $\square HJKL$ is a translation 4 units down and 7 units right of $\square ABCD$.

5. *Sample answer:* 180° rotation about the origin followed by a translation 5 units left and 1 unit down

6. *Sample answer:* 180° rotation about the origin

7. yes; $\triangle TUV$ is a translation 4 units right of $\triangle QRS$. So, $\triangle TUV \cong \triangle QRS$.

8. yes; $\square CDEF$ is a 90° rotation of $\square WXYZ$. So, $\square CDEF \cong \square WXYZ$.

9. no; M and N are translated 2 units right of their corresponding vertices, L and K, but P is translated only 1 unit right of its corresponding vertex, J. So, this is not a rigid motion.

10. yes; A congruence transformation that maps $\square ABCD$ to $\square GHEF$ is a translation 5 units down, followed by a reflection in the y-axis. So, $\square ABCD \cong \square GHEF$.

11. $\triangle A''B''C''$

12. line k and line m

13. 5.2 in.

14. yes; Because $\triangle A''B''C''$ is a reflection of $\triangle A'B'C'$ in line m, each vertex in the image is the same distance from the line of reflection as its preimage.

4.4 Exercises

Dynamic Solutions available at *BigIdeasMath.com*

Vocabulary and Core Concept Check

1. **COMPLETE THE SENTENCE** Two geometric figures are _____ if and only if there is a rigid motion or a composition of rigid motions that moves one of the figures onto the other.

2. **VOCABULARY** Why is the term *congruence transformation* used to refer to a rigid motion?

Monitoring Progress and Modeling with Mathematics

In Exercises 3 and 4, identify any congruent figures in the coordinate plane. Explain. *(See Example 1.)*

3.

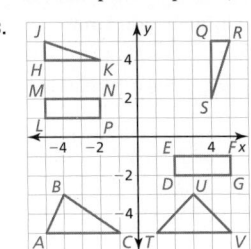

4.

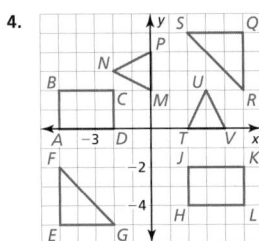

In Exercises 5 and 6, describe a congruence transformation that maps the blue preimage to the green image. *(See Example 2.)*

5.

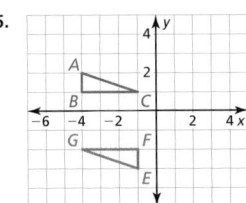

6.

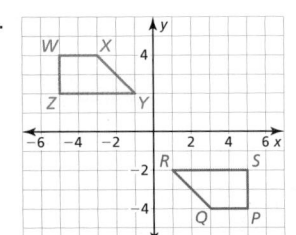

In Exercises 7–10, determine whether the polygons with the given vertices are congruent. Use transformations to explain your reasoning.

7. $Q(2, 4)$, $R(5, 4)$, $S(4, 1)$ and $T(6, 4)$, $U(9, 4)$, $V(8, 1)$

8. $W(-3, 1)$, $X(2, 1)$, $Y(4, -4)$, $Z(-5, -4)$ and $C(-1, -3)$, $D(-1, 2)$, $E(4, 4)$, $F(4, -5)$

9. $J(1, 1)$, $K(3, 2)$, $L(4, 1)$ and $M(6, 1)$, $N(5, 2)$, $P(2, 1)$

10. $A(0, 0)$, $B(1, 2)$, $C(4, 2)$, $D(3, 0)$ and $E(0, -5)$, $F(-1, -3)$, $G(-4, -3)$, $H(-3, -5)$

In Exercises 11–14, $k \parallel m$, $\triangle ABC$ is reflected in line k, and $\triangle A'B'C'$ is reflected in line m. *(See Example 3.)*

11. A translation maps $\triangle ABC$ onto which triangle?

12. Which lines are perpendicular to $\overline{AA''}$?

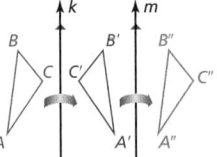

13. If the distance between k and m is 2.6 inches, what is the length of $\overline{CC''}$?

14. Is the distance from B' to m the same as the distance from B'' to m? Explain.

In Exercises 15 and 16, find the angle of rotation that maps A onto A". *(See Example 4.)*

15.

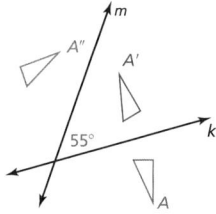

16.

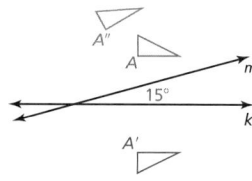

17. ERROR ANALYSIS Describe and correct the error in describing the congruence transformation.

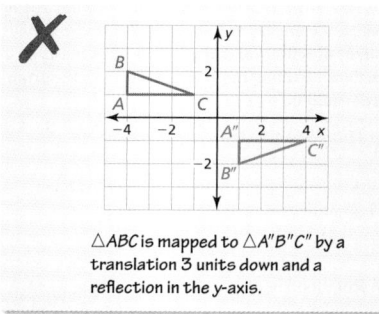

△ABC is mapped to △A"B"C" by a translation 3 units down and a reflection in the y-axis.

18. ERROR ANALYSIS Describe and correct the error in using the Reflections in Intersecting Lines Theorem (Theorem 4.3).

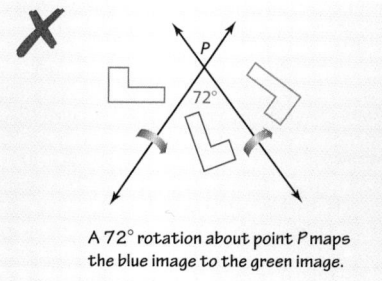

A 72° rotation about point P maps the blue image to the green image.

In Exercises 19–22, find the measure of the acute or right angle formed by intersecting lines so that C can be mapped to C' using two reflections.

19. A rotation of 84° maps C to C'.

20. A rotation of 24° maps C to C'.

21. The rotation $(x, y) \rightarrow (-x, -y)$ maps C to C'.

22. The rotation $(x, y) \rightarrow (y, -x)$ maps C to C'.

23. REASONING Use the Reflections in Parallel Lines Theorem (Theorem 4.2) to explain how you can make a glide reflection using three reflections. How are the lines of reflection related?

24. DRAWING CONCLUSIONS The pattern shown is called a *tessellation.*

    a. What transformations did the artist use when creating this tessellation?

    b. Are the individual figures in the tessellation congruent? Explain your reasoning.

CRITICAL THINKING In Exercises 25–28, tell whether the statement is *always*, *sometimes*, or *never* true. Explain your reasoning.

25. A congruence transformation changes the size of a figure.

26. If two figures are congruent, then there is a rigid motion or a composition of rigid motions that maps one figure onto the other.

27. The composition of two reflections results in the same image as a rotation.

28. A translation results in the same image as the composition of two reflections.

29. REASONING During a presentation, a marketing representative uses a projector so everyone in the auditorium can view the advertisement. Is this projection a congruence transformation? Explain your reasoning.

ANSWERS

15. 110°

16. 30°

17. A translation 5 units right and a reflection in the x-axis should have been used; △ABC is mapped to △A'B'C' by a translation 5 units right, followed by a reflection in the x-axis.

18. If $x°$ is the measure of the acute angle formed by the intersecting lines, an angle of $2x°$ should be used to describe the angle of rotation; A 144° rotation about point P maps the blue image to the green image.

19. 42°

20. 12°

21. 90°

22. 45°

23. Reflect the figure in two parallel lines instead of translating the figure; The third line of reflection is perpendicular to the parallel lines.

24. a. rotations and translations

    b. yes; All of the figures could be created using one or more rigid transformations of an original shape.

25. never; Congruence transformations are rigid motions.

26. always; Every figure can be mapped onto a congruent figure using transformations.

27. sometimes; Reflecting in $y = x$ then $y = x$ is not a rotation. Reflecting in the y-axis then x-axis is a rotation of 180°.

28. sometimes; It would depend on the translations.

29. no; The image on the screen is larger.

ANSWERS

30–43. See Additional Answers.

Mini-Assessment

1. Identify any congruent figures in the coordinate plane. Explain.

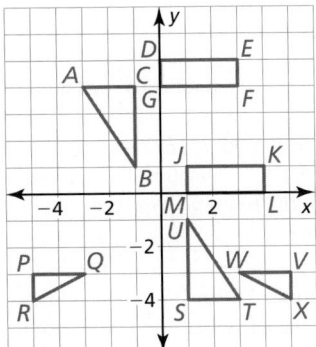

See Additional Answers.

2. Describe a congruence transformation that maps △JKL to △MNP.

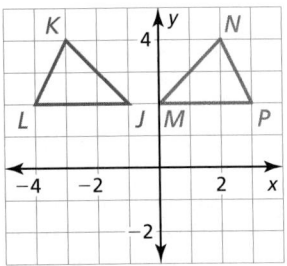

See Additional Answers.

3. △TUV is reflected over line k, and then that image is reflected over line m. The distance between lines k and m is 2.8 cm. What is the distance between T and T″?

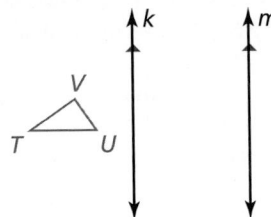

5.6 cm

4. Lines k and m intersect. Figure A is reflected over line k and then that image is reflected over line m to produce figure A″. A 24° rotation about the intersection of lines m and k maps A to A″. What is the measure of the acute angle formed by the lines? 12°

206   Chapter 4

---

30. **HOW DO YOU SEE IT?** What type of congruence transformation can be used to verify each statement about the stained glass window?

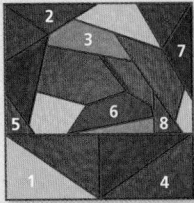

   a. Triangle 5 is congruent to Triangle 8.
   b. Triangle 1 is congruent to Triangle 4.
   c. Triangle 2 is congruent to Triangle 7.
   d. Pentagon 3 is congruent to Pentagon 6.

31. **PROVING A THEOREM** Prove the Reflections in Parallel Lines Theorem (Theorem 4.2).

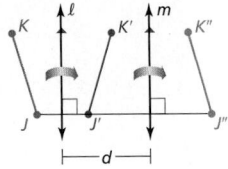

   Given A reflection in line ℓ maps $\overline{JK}$ to $\overline{J'K'}$, a reflection in line m maps $\overline{J'K'}$ to $\overline{J''K''}$, and $\ell \parallel m$.

   Prove a. $\overline{KK''}$ is perpendicular to ℓ and m.

   b. $KK'' = 2d$, where d is the distance between ℓ and m.

32. **THOUGHT PROVOKING** A *tessellation* is the covering of a plane with congruent figures so that there are no gaps or overlaps (see Exercise 24). Draw a tessellation that involves two or more types of transformations. Describe the transformations that are used to create the tessellation.

Maintaining Mathematical Proficiency
Reviewing what you learned in previous grades and lessons

Solve the equation. Check your solution. *(Skills Review Handbook)*

37. $5x + 16 = -3x$ 38. $12 + 6m = 2m$ 39. $4b + 8 = 6b - 4$

40. $7w - 9 = 13 - 4w$ 41. $7(2n + 11) = 4n$ 42. $-2(8 - y) = -6y$

43. Last year, the track team's yard sale earned $500. This year, the yard sale earned $625. What is the percent of increase? *(Skills Review Handbook)*

---

33. **MAKING AN ARGUMENT** $\overline{PQ}$, with endpoints $P(1, 3)$ and $Q(3, 2)$, is reflected in the y-axis. The image $\overline{P'Q'}$ is then reflected in the x-axis to produce the image $\overline{P''Q''}$. One classmate says that $\overline{PQ}$ is mapped to $\overline{P''Q''}$ by the translation $(x, y) \rightarrow (x - 4, y - 5)$. Another classmate says that $\overline{PQ}$ is mapped to $\overline{P''Q''}$ by a $(2 \cdot 90)°$, or 180°, rotation about the origin. Which classmate is correct? Explain your reasoning.

34. **CRITICAL THINKING** Does the order of reflections for a composition of two reflections in parallel lines matter? For example, is reflecting △XYZ in line ℓ and then its image in line m the same as reflecting △XYZ in line m and then its image in line ℓ?

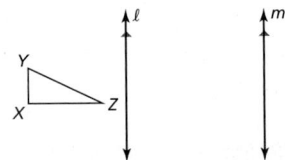

CONSTRUCTION In Exercises 35 and 36, copy the figure. Then use a compass and straightedge to construct two lines of reflection that produce a composition of reflections resulting in the same image as the given transformation.

35. **Translation:** △ABC → △A″B″C″

36. **Rotation about P:** △XYZ → △X″Y″Z″

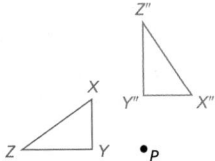

If students need help...	If students got it...
Resources by Chapter • Practice A and Practice B • Puzzle Time	Resources by Chapter • Enrichment and Extension • Cumulative Review
Student Journal • Practice	Start the *next* Section
Differentiating the Lesson Skills Review Handbook	

Dynamic Teaching Tools

Dynamic Assessment & Progress Monitoring Tool
Lesson Planning Tool
Interactive Whiteboard Lesson Library
Dynamic Classroom with Dynamic Investigations

Laurie's Notes

Overview of Section 4.5

Introduction

- Dilations were studied in grade 8 where students were expected to describe the effect of dilations on two-dimensional figures using coordinates. New in this lesson is that the centers of dilation do not need to be at the origin, and students are constructing dilations with a straightedge and a compass.
- The explorations provide an opportunity for students to explore different scale factors and centers of dilation. Encourage students to measure lengths and angles when they are using the dynamic geometry software.
- The scale factor of a dilation is the ratio of corresponding sides of the image and preimage. This ratio is used to solve real-life applications.

Resources

- A flashlight can be used to demonstrate the center of dilation. Darken the room. Use the flashlight to project the image of a figure onto a wall.

Formative Assessment Tips

- **Think-Alouds:** This technique is used when you want to hear how well partners comprehend a process involved with solving a problem. It is important to model the process first so that students have a sense of what is expected in *Think-Alouds*.
- *Think-Alouds* give students the opportunity to hear the metacognitive processes used by someone who is a proficient problem solver.
- **MP1 Make Sense of Problems and Persevere in Solving Them** and **MP6 Attend to Precision:** Hearing someone else describe a process using mathematical language will improve all students' problem-solving abilities; they can now apply the process with their partners to the problem being solved.
- Use this technique with a multi-step problem. Model using a starter sentence such as: "The problem is asking … ," "I can use the strategy of … ," "The steps I will use in solving this problem are … ," "This problem is similar to … ," and "I can check my answer by … ."
- Use this technique for a variety of problem types. Listen for comprehension of skills, concepts, and procedures as well as precision of language.

Applications

- Print and frame sizes for photographs are explored in Exercise 37 on page 213. Standard photographic sizes are: $2.5'' \times 3.5''$, $3.5'' \times 5''$, $4'' \times 6''$, $5'' \times 7''$, $8'' \times 10''$, $11'' \times 14''$, and $16'' \times 20''$. Ask students whether any of these could be a dilation of another.

Pacing Suggestion

- The formal lesson is long; however, experience with the explorations helps students develop essential understanding of dilations. You might consider having half the class do Exploration 1(a) and the other half do Exploration 1(b).

HSG-CO.A.2 Represent transformations in the plane using, e.g., . . . geometry software; . . . Compare transformations that preserve distance and angle to those that do not (e.g., translation versus horizontal stretch).

HSG-SRT.A.1a A dilation takes a line not passing through the center of the dilation to a parallel line, and leaves a line passing through the center unchanged.

HSG-SRT.A.1b The dilation of a line segment is longer or shorter in the ratio given by the scale factor.

Laurie's Notes

Exploration

Motivate

- Cut a rectangle out of heavier card stock. Use a flashlight to cast a shadow of the rectangle onto the wall.
- **?** "Do the angles still appear to be right angles?" yes; They should be unless the rectangle is not parallel to the surface it is reflected onto.
- Vary the distance between the bulb of the flashlight and the rectangle. Discuss how this changes the shadow.
- **?** "Is the shadow always similar to the original figure?" It should be when the figure is held parallel to the wall and the flashlight is perpendicular to the wall.

Exploration 1

- This first exploration serves to familiarize students with the *dilate* command in the dynamic geometry software. Students should also be comfortable with the exploration posed verbally so that they are not looking at the result of the dilation in the book.
- Students should be comfortable clicking and dragging to change the shape and location of $\triangle ABC$.
- **? Popsicle Sticks:** "What do you observe about the side lengths?" The sides of $\triangle A'B'C'$ are twice the length of the sides of $\triangle ABC$. "What do you observe about the angle measures?" The measures of corresponding angles are equal.
- In part (b), students should again try different locations and shapes for $\triangle ABC$ and make observations about the coordinates of $\triangle A'B'C'$.
- **Turn and Talk:** Discuss observations with partners when the center is (0, 0) and the scale factor is $\frac{1}{2}$.
- **? Extension:** "When the scale factor is 1, what will the image look like?" It will be congruent to the preimage.
- **Extension:** Usually there is at least one student who will enter a negative scale factor such as $-\frac{1}{2}$. If so, then the student should share his or her observations with the class. If time permits, have all students try a negative scale factor. Explain the effect of the negative sign.

Exploration 2

- You could pose this exploration to students verbally so that they are not looking at the result of the dilation in the book.
- Ask students to make a conjecture about what they think is going to happen when they dilate a line through the origin and a line not through the origin.
- When students dilate the line through the origin, they may say, "Nothing happened!" Do not give it away. Have them dilate a line not through the origin, which they will be able to see.
- **Big Idea:** A line through the origin has an equation $y = kx$ (direct variation). Multiplying (x, y) by a scale factor of 3 will result in ordered pairs that are on the same line. ($3y = 3kx$ simplifies to $y = kx$.) A line that does not pass through the origin has an equation $y = mx + b$, where $b \neq 0$. Multiplying (x, y) by a scale factor of 3 will result in ordered pairs that are on a line parallel to the original line.

Communicate Your Answer

- Ask different students to share their understanding of what it means to dilate a figure.

Connecting to Next Step

- Students have now been introduced to dilations. In the formal lesson, students will construct dilations with a compass and a straightedge and will construct dilations in the coordinate plane.

4.5 Dilations

Essential Question
What does it mean to dilate a figure?

EXPLORATION 1 — Dilating a Triangle in a Coordinate Plane

Work with a partner. Use dynamic geometry software to draw any triangle and label it $\triangle ABC$.

a. *Dilate* $\triangle ABC$ using a *scale factor* of 2 and a *center of dilation* at the origin to form $\triangle A'B'C'$. Compare the coordinates, side lengths, and angle measures of $\triangle ABC$ and $\triangle A'B'C'$.

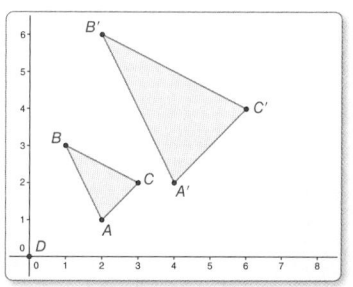

Sample

Points
$A(2, 1)$
$B(1, 3)$
$C(3, 2)$

Segments
$AB = 2.24$
$BC = 2.24$
$AC = 1.41$

Angles
$m\angle A = 71.57°$
$m\angle B = 36.87°$
$m\angle C = 71.57°$

> **LOOKING FOR STRUCTURE**
> To be proficient in math, you need to look closely to discern a pattern or structure.

b. Repeat part (a) using a *scale factor* of $\frac{1}{2}$.

c. What do the results of parts (a) and (b) suggest about the coordinates, side lengths, and angle measures of the image of $\triangle ABC$ after a dilation with a scale factor of k?

EXPLORATION 2 — Dilating Lines in a Coordinate Plane

Work with a partner. Use dynamic geometry software to draw $\overleftrightarrow{AB}$ that passes through the origin and $\overleftrightarrow{AC}$ that does not pass through the origin.

a. *Dilate* $\overleftrightarrow{AB}$ using a *scale factor* of 3 and a *center of dilation* at the origin. Describe the image.

b. *Dilate* $\overleftrightarrow{AC}$ using a *scale factor* of 3 and a *center of dilation* at the origin. Describe the image.

c. Repeat parts (a) and (b) using a scale factor of $\frac{1}{4}$.

d. What do you notice about dilations of lines passing through the center of dilation and dilations of lines not passing through the center of dilation?

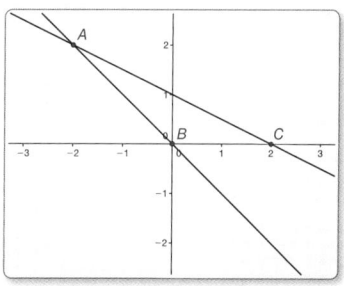

Sample

Points	Lines
$A(-2, 2)$	$x + y = 0$
$B(0, 0)$	$x + 2y = 2$
$C(2, 0)$	

Communicate Your Answer

3. What does it mean to dilate a figure?

4. Repeat Exploration 1 using a center of dilation at a point other than the origin.

---

2. a. The image is a line that coincides with $\overleftrightarrow{AB}$.

b. The image is a line that is parallel to $\overleftrightarrow{AC}$. The x- and y-intercepts of the image are each three times the x- and y-intercepts of $\overleftrightarrow{AC}$.

c. The image of $\overleftrightarrow{AB}$ is a line that coincides with $\overleftrightarrow{AB}$. The image of $\overleftrightarrow{AC}$ is a line that is parallel to $\overleftrightarrow{AC}$. The x- and y-intercepts of the image are each one-fourth of the x- and y-intercepts of $\overleftrightarrow{AC}$.

d. When you dilate an image that passes through the center of dilation, the image coincides with the preimage. When you dilate a line that does not pass through the center of dilation, the image is parallel to the preimage, and the image has intercepts that can be found by multiplying the intercepts of the preimage by the constant of dilation.

3. to reduce or enlarge a figure so that the image is proportional to the preimage

4. See Additional Answers.

ANSWERS

1. a. Check students' work. The x-value of each vertex of $\triangle A'B'C'$ is twice the x-value of its corresponding vertex of $\triangle ABC$, and the y-value of each vertex of $\triangle A'B'C'$ is twice the y-value of its corresponding vertex of $\triangle ABC$. Each side of $\triangle A'B'C'$ is twice as long as its corresponding side of $\triangle ABC$. Each angle of $\triangle A'B'C'$ is congruent to its corresponding angle of $\triangle ABC$.

b. *Sample answer:*

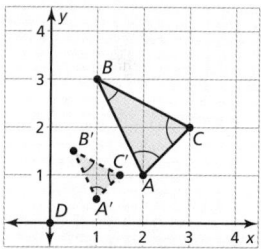

The x-value of each vertex of $\triangle A'B'C'$ is half of the x-value of its corresponding vertex of $\triangle ABC$, and the y-value of each vertex of $\triangle A'B'C'$ is half of the y-value of its corresponding vertex of $\triangle ABC$. Each side of $\triangle A'B'C'$ is half as long as its corresponding side of $\triangle ABC$. Each angle of $\triangle A'B'C'$ is congruent to its corresponding angle of $\triangle ABC$.

c. The x-value of each vertex of $\triangle A'B'C'$ is k times the x-value of its corresponding vertex of $\triangle ABC$, and the y-value of each vertex of $\triangle A'B'C'$ is k times the y-value of its corresponding vertex of $\triangle ABC$. Each side of $\triangle A'B'C'$ is k times as long as its corresponding side of $\triangle ABC$. Each angle of $\triangle A'B'C'$ is congruent to its corresponding angle of $\triangle ABC$.

Extra Example 1

Find the scale factor of the dilation. Then tell whether the dilation is a *reduction* or an *enlargement*.

a.

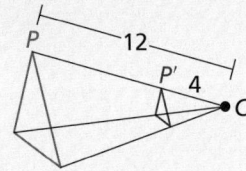

$k = \frac{1}{3}$; reduction

b.

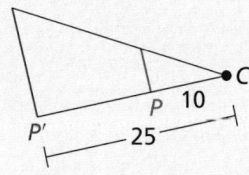

$k = \frac{5}{2}$; enlargement

MONITORING PROGRESS ANSWER

1. $k = \frac{1}{4}$; reduction

4.5 Lesson

Core Vocabulary

dilation, *p. 208*
center of dilation, *p. 208*
scale factor, *p. 208*
enlargement, *p. 208*
reduction, *p. 208*

What You Will Learn

▶ Identify and perform dilations.
▶ Solve real-life problems involving scale factors and dilations.

Identifying and Performing Dilations

Core Concept

Dilations

A **dilation** is a transformation in which a figure is enlarged or reduced with respect to a fixed point C called the **center of dilation** and a **scale factor** k, which is the ratio of the lengths of the corresponding sides of the image and the preimage.

A dilation with center of dilation C and scale factor k maps every point P in a figure to a point P' so that the following are true.

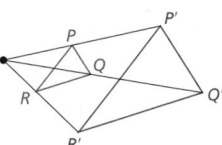

- If P is the center point C, then $P = P'$.
- If P is not the center point C, then the image point P' lies on $\overrightarrow{CP}$. The scale factor k is a positive number such that $k = \dfrac{CP'}{CP}$.
- Angle measures are preserved.

A dilation does not change any line that passes through the center of dilation. A dilation maps a line that does not pass through the center of dilation to a parallel line. In the figure above, $\overleftrightarrow{PR} \parallel \overleftrightarrow{P'R'}$, $\overleftrightarrow{PQ} \parallel \overleftrightarrow{P'Q'}$, and $\overleftrightarrow{QR} \parallel \overleftrightarrow{Q'R'}$.

When the scale factor $k > 1$, a dilation is an **enlargement**. When $0 < k < 1$, a dilation is a **reduction**.

EXAMPLE 1 Identifying Dilations

Find the scale factor of the dilation. Then tell whether the dilation is a *reduction* or an *enlargement*.

a.

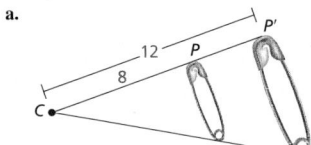

b.

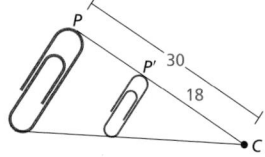

READING

The scale factor of a dilation can be written as a fraction, decimal, or percent.

SOLUTION

a. Because $\dfrac{CP'}{CP} = \dfrac{12}{8}$, the scale factor is $k = \dfrac{3}{2}$. So, the dilation is an enlargement.

b. Because $\dfrac{CP'}{CP} = \dfrac{18}{30}$, the scale factor is $k = \dfrac{3}{5}$. So, the dilation is a reduction.

Monitoring Progress Help in English and Spanish at *BigIdeasMath.com*

1. In a dilation, $CP' = 3$ and $CP = 12$. Find the scale factor. Then tell whether the dilation is a *reduction* or an *enlargement*.

Laurie's Notes | Teacher Actions

- Take time to fully discuss the definition of *dilation*. Connect to the explorations completed by students.
- ❓ "What will the *scale factor* k tell you about the dilation?" If students have done the explorations, they will know that when $k > 1$, the dilation will be an enlargement and when $0 < k < 1$, the dilation will be a reduction.
- Students may have tried a scale factor that was negative with the dynamic geometry software. This is discussed on page 210.
- **Turn and Talk:** Have students discuss how to find the scale factor for each dilation.

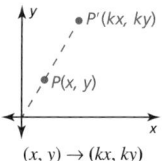 Core Concept

Coordinate Rule for Dilations

If $P(x, y)$ is the preimage of a point, then its image after a dilation centered at the origin $(0, 0)$ with scale factor k is the point $P'(kx, ky)$.

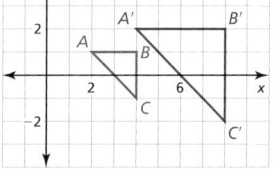

$$(x, y) \rightarrow (kx, ky)$$

EXAMPLE 2   Dilating a Figure in the Coordinate Plane

Graph $\triangle ABC$ with vertices $A(2, 1)$, $B(4, 1)$, and $C(4, -1)$ and its image after a dilation with a scale factor of 2.

SOLUTION

Use the coordinate rule for a dilation with $k = 2$ to find the coordinates of the vertices of the image. Then graph $\triangle ABC$ and its image.

$$(x, y) \rightarrow (2x, 2y)$$
$$A(2, 1) \rightarrow A'(4, 2)$$
$$B(4, 1) \rightarrow B'(8, 2)$$
$$C(4, -1) \rightarrow C'(8, -2)$$

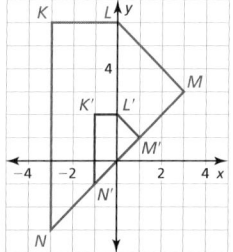

Notice the relationships between the lengths and slopes of the sides of the triangles in Example 2. Each side length of $\triangle A'B'C'$ is longer than its corresponding side by the scale factor. The corresponding sides are parallel because their slopes are the same.

EXAMPLE 3   Dilating a Figure in the Coordinate Plane

Graph quadrilateral $KLMN$ with vertices $K(-3, 6)$, $L(0, 6)$, $M(3, 3)$, and $N(-3, -3)$ and its image after a dilation with a scale factor of $\frac{1}{3}$.

SOLUTION

Use the coordinate rule for a dilation with $k = \frac{1}{3}$ to find the coordinates of the vertices of the image. Then graph quadrilateral $KLMN$ and its image.

$$(x, y) \rightarrow \left(\frac{1}{3}x, \frac{1}{3}y\right)$$
$$K(-3, 6) \rightarrow K'(-1, 2)$$
$$L(0, 6) \rightarrow L'(0, 2)$$
$$M(3, 3) \rightarrow M'(1, 1)$$
$$N(-3, -3) \rightarrow N'(-1, -1)$$

Monitoring Progress 🔊 Help in English and Spanish at *BigIdeasMath.com*

Graph $\triangle PQR$ and its image after a dilation with scale factor k.

2. $P(-2, -1)$, $Q(-1, 0)$, $R(0, -1)$; $k = 4$

3. $P(5, -5)$, $Q(10, -5)$, $R(10, 5)$; $k = 0.4$

READING DIAGRAMS

In this chapter, for all of the dilations in the coordinate plane, the center of dilation is the origin unless otherwise noted.

English Language Learners

Comprehension

Make sure students understand the relationship between the *scale factor* and the effects of a dilation. Use examples to guide students through a discussion developing the inequalities $0 < k < 1$ and $k < 0$ as guides for identifying whether a dilation with a scale factor k is a *reduction* or an *enlargement*.

Extra Example 2

Graph $\triangle PQR$ with vertices $P(0, 2)$, $Q(1, 0)$, and $R(2, 2)$ and its image after a dilation with scale factor 3.

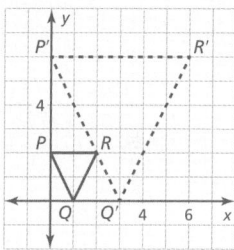

Extra Example 3

Graph $\triangle PQR$ with vertices $P(4, 6)$, $Q(-4, 2)$, and $R(2, -6)$ and its image after a dilation with scale factor 0.5.

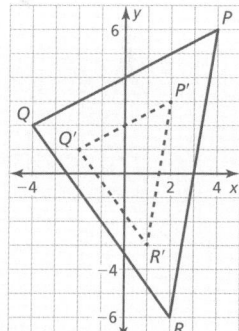

MONITORING PROGRESS ANSWERS

2.

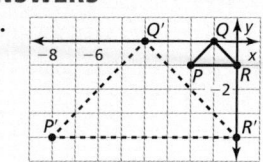

3. See Additional Answers.

Laurie's Notes   Teacher Actions

- Write the *Core Concept*.
- ❓ **Fact-First Question:** "If the preimage is in Quadrant III, then the image will be in Quadrant III. Explain why." The point P' is on $\overrightarrow{CP}$, where C is the center of dilation, so P' will still be in Quadrant III.
- **Think-Alouds:** Pose Example 2 and say, "To solve this example, I need to ... ." Ask partner A to think aloud for partner B to hear the problem-solving process. When students have finished the example, *Popsicle Sticks* a response.
- **Think-Alouds:** Pose Example 3 and say, "In this example, I predict ... ." Ask partner B to think aloud for partner A to hear the prediction. When students have finished the example, *Popsicle Sticks* a response.

Extra Example 4

Graph △*FGH* with vertices *F*(3, 6), *G*(3, −3), and *H*(6, 6) and its image after a dilation with a scale factor of $-\frac{1}{3}$.

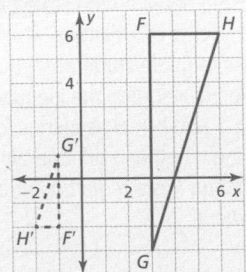

MONITORING PROGRESS ANSWERS

4.

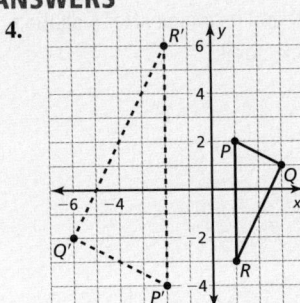

5. According to the Coordinate Rule for Dilations, if the origin *P*(0, 0) is the preimage of a point, then its image after a dilation centered at the origin with a scale factor *k* is the point *P*′(*k* • 0, *k* • 0), which is also the origin, or (0, 0).

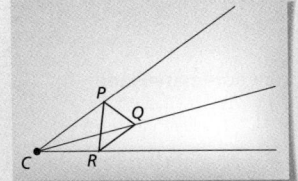 **Constructing a Dilation**

Use a compass and straightedge to construct a dilation of △*PQR* with a scale factor of 2. Use a point *C* outside the triangle as the center of dilation.

SOLUTION

Step 1	Step 2	Step 3

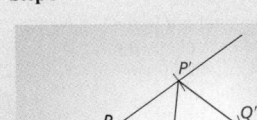

Draw a triangle Draw △*PQR* and choose the center of the dilation *C* outside the triangle. Draw rays from *C* through the vertices of the triangle.

Use a compass Use a compass to locate *P*′ on $\overrightarrow{CP}$ so that *CP*′ = 2(*CP*). Locate *Q*′ and *R*′ using the same method.

Connect points Connect points *P*′, *Q*′, and *R*′ to form △*P*′*Q*′*R*′.

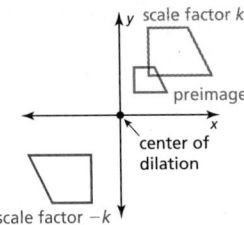

In the coordinate plane, you can have scale factors that are negative numbers. When this occurs, the figure rotates 180°. So, when *k* > 0, a dilation with a scale factor of −*k* is the same as the composition of a dilation with a scale factor of *k* followed by a rotation of 180° about the center of dilation. Using the coordinate rules for a dilation and a rotation of 180°, you can think of the notation as

$$(x, y) \rightarrow (kx, ky) \rightarrow (-kx, -ky).$$

EXAMPLE 4 **Using a Negative Scale Factor**

Graph △*FGH* with vertices *F*(−4, −2), *G*(−2, 4), and *H*(−2, −2) and its image after a dilation with a scale factor of $-\frac{1}{2}$.

SOLUTION

Use the coordinate rule for a dilation with $k = -\frac{1}{2}$ to find the coordinates of the vertices of the image. Then graph △*FGH* and its image.

$$(x, y) \rightarrow \left(-\frac{1}{2}x, -\frac{1}{2}y\right)$$

$$F(-4, -2) \rightarrow F'(2, 1)$$
$$G(-2, 4) \rightarrow G'(1, -2)$$
$$H(-2, -2) \rightarrow H'(1, 1)$$

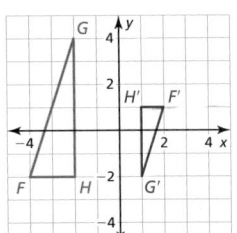

Monitoring Progress Help in English and Spanish at *BigIdeasMath.com*

4. Graph △*PQR* with vertices *P*(1, 2), *Q*(3, 1), and *R*(1, −3) and its image after a dilation with a scale factor of −2.

5. Suppose a figure containing the origin is dilated. Explain why the corresponding point in the image of the figure is also the origin.

Laurie's Notes | Teacher Actions

- The construction of a dilation with scale factor of 2 is shown. You could differentiate at this point and hand slips of paper to different groups stating the scale factor. Groups of students ready for a more demanding task could use scale factors of $\frac{5}{2}$, 3, $\frac{1}{2}$, or $\frac{2}{3}$.

- **MP5 Use Appropriate Tools Strategically:** Use dynamic geometry software to demonstrate negative scale factors, or search the Internet ("GCSE transformations videos") for a video. Using a scalene figure will help students see the rotation of 180°.

- **Connection:** Rotation of 180° about the origin maps (*x*, *y*) → (−*x*, −*y*). Dilation by scale factor of −*k* centered at the origin maps (*x*, *y*) → (−*kx*, −*ky*).

- **? Always-Sometimes-Never True:** "A dilation of −*k* results in an image in Quadrant III." sometimes true; When the preimage is in Quadrant I, the image will be in Quadrant III; otherwise it will be in a different quadrant.

- Circulate as students try Example 4 with their partners.

Solving Real-Life Problems

EXAMPLE 5 Finding a Scale Factor

You are making your own photo stickers. Your photo is 4 inches by 4 inches. The image on the stickers is 1.1 inches by 1.1 inches. What is the scale factor of this dilation?

4 in.

1.1 in.

READING

Scale factors are written so that the units in the numerator and denominator divide out.

SOLUTION

The scale factor is the ratio of a side length of the sticker image to a side length of the original photo, or $\frac{1.1 \text{ in.}}{4 \text{ in.}}$.

▶ So, in simplest form, the scale factor is $\frac{11}{40}$.

EXAMPLE 6 Finding the Length of an Image

You are using a magnifying glass that shows the image of an object that is six times the object's actual size. Determine the length of the image of the spider seen through the magnifying glass.

1.5 cm

SOLUTION

$$\frac{\text{image length}}{\text{actual length}} = k$$

$$\frac{x}{1.5} = 6$$

$$x = 9$$

▶ So, the image length through the magnifying glass is 9 centimeters.

Monitoring Progress Help in English and Spanish at *BigIdeasMath.com*

6. An optometrist dilates the pupils of a patient's eyes to get a better look at the back of the eyes. A pupil dilates from 4.5 millimeters to 8 millimeters. What is the scale factor of this dilation?

7. The image of a spider seen through the magnifying glass in Example 6 is shown at the left. Find the actual length of the spider.

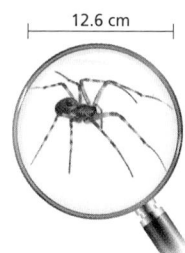
12.6 cm

When a transformation, such as a dilation, changes the shape or size of a figure, the transformation is *nonrigid*. In addition to dilations, there are many possible nonrigid transformations. Two examples are shown below. It is important to pay close attention to whether a nonrigid transformation preserves lengths and angle measures.

Horizontal Stretch

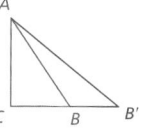

A
C   B   B'

Vertical Stretch

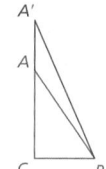

A'
A
C   B

Section 4.5   Dilations   **211**

---

212   Chapter 4

Assignment Guide and Homework Check

ASSIGNMENT

Basic: 1, 2, 3–35 odd, 38, 48, 52–57

Average: 1, 2, 4, 8, 14, 19, 24–34 even, 38–42, 48, 52–57

Advanced: 1, 2, 10, 16, 22–36 even, 38–49, 52–57

HOMEWORK CHECK

Basic: 5, 7, 21, 25, 31

Average: 14, 19, 24, 26, 39

Advanced: 22, 30, 39, 46, 47

ANSWERS

1. $P'(kx, ky)$

2. 60%; Because $0.6 < 1$, 60% is a scale factor for a reduction. The other three are scale factors for enlargements.

3. $\frac{3}{7}$; reduction

4. $\frac{8}{3}$; enlargement

5. $\frac{3}{5}$; reduction

6. $\frac{7}{2}$; enlargement

7–14. See Additional Answers.

15.
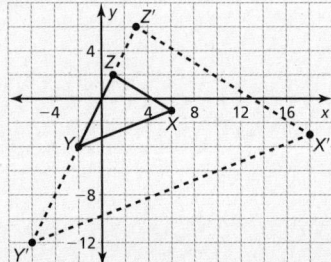

16.
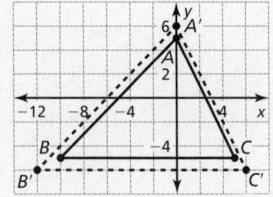

Vocabulary and Core Concept Check

1. **COMPLETE THE SENTENCE** If $P(x, y)$ is the preimage of a point, then its image after a dilation centered at the origin $(0, 0)$ with scale factor k is the point _____.

2. **WHICH ONE DOESN'T BELONG?** Which scale factor does *not* belong with the other three? Explain your reasoning.

| $\frac{5}{4}$ | 60% | 115% | 2 |

Monitoring Progress and Modeling with Mathematics

In Exercises 3–6, find the scale factor of the dilation. Then tell whether the dilation is a *reduction* or an *enlargement*. *(See Example 1.)*

3.
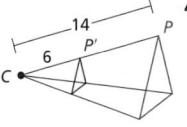

4.
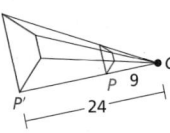

5.
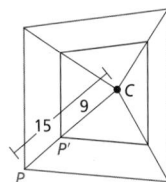

6.
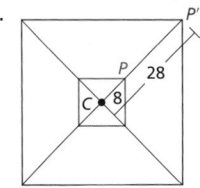

CONSTRUCTION In Exercises 7–10, copy the diagram. Then use a compass and straightedge to construct a dilation of $\triangle LMN$ with the given center and scale factor k.

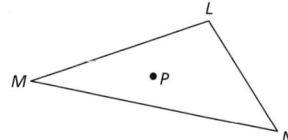

7. Center C, $k = 2$

8. Center P, $k = 3$

9. Center M, $k = \frac{1}{2}$

10. Center C, $k = 25\%$

212   Chapter 4   Transformations

CONSTRUCTION In Exercises 11–14, copy the diagram. Then use a compass and straightedge to construct a dilation of quadrilateral *RSTU* with the given center and scale factor k.

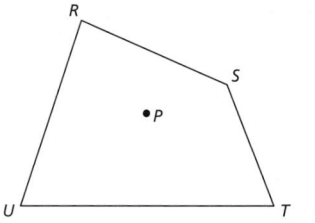

11. Center C, $k = 3$

12. Center P, $k = \frac{1}{3}$

13. Center R, $k = 0.25$

14. Center C, $k = 75\%$

In Exercises 15–18, graph the polygon and its image after a dilation with scale factor k. *(See Examples 2 and 3.)*

15. $X(6, -1)$, $Y(-2, -4)$, $Z(1, 2)$; $k = 3$

16. $A(0, 5)$, $B(-10, -5)$, $C(5, -5)$; $k = 120\%$

17. $T(9, -3)$, $U(6, 0)$, $V(3, 9)$, $W(0, 0)$; $k = \frac{2}{3}$

18. $J(4, 0)$, $K(-8, 4)$, $L(0, -4)$, $M(12, -8)$; $k = 0.25$

In Exercises 19–22, graph the polygon and its image after a dilation with scale factor k. *(See Example 4.)*

19. $B(-5, -10)$, $C(-10, 15)$, $D(0, 5)$; $k = -\frac{1}{5}$

20. $L(0, 0)$, $M(-4, 1)$, $N(-3, -6)$; $k = -3$

21. $R(-7, -1)$, $S(2, 5)$, $T(-2, -3)$, $U(-3, -3)$; $k = -4$

22. $W(8, -2)$, $X(6, 0)$, $Y(-6, 4)$, $Z(-2, 2)$; $k = -0.5$

17.
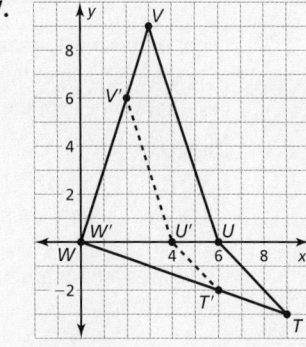

18.
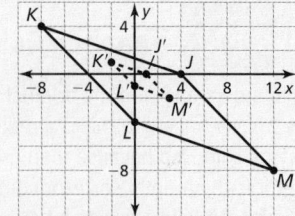

19–22. See Additional Answers.

ERROR ANALYSIS In Exercises 23 and 24, describe and correct the error in finding the scale factor of the dilation.

23.

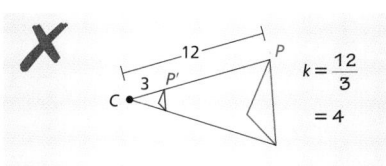

$$k = \frac{12}{3}$$
$$= 4$$

24.

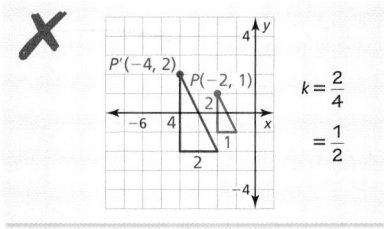

$$k = \frac{2}{4}$$
$$= \frac{1}{2}$$

In Exercises 25–28, the red figure is the image of the blue figure after a dilation with center *C*. Find the scale factor of the dilation. Then find the value of the variable.

25.

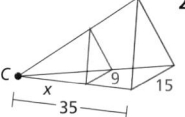

26.

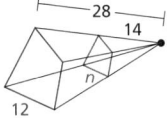

27.

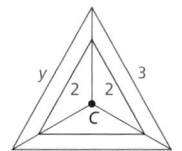

28.

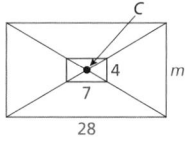

29. FINDING A SCALE FACTOR You receive wallet-sized photos of your school picture. The photo is 2.5 inches by 3.5 inches. You decide to dilate the photo to 5 inches by 7 inches at the store. What is the scale factor of this dilation? *(See Example 5.)*

30. FINDING A SCALE FACTOR Your visually impaired friend asked you to enlarge your notes from class so he can study. You took notes on 8.5-inch by 11-inch paper. The enlarged copy has a smaller side with a length of 10 inches. What is the scale factor of this dilation? *(See Example 5.)*

In Exercises 31–34, you are using a magnifying glass. Use the length of the insect and the magnification level to determine the length of the image seen through the magnifying glass. *(See Example 6.)*

31. emperor moth
Magnification: 5×

60 mm

32. ladybug
Magnification: 10×

4.5 mm

33. dragonfly
Magnification: 20×

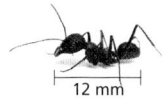

47 mm

34. carpenter ant
Magnification: 15×

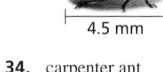

12 mm

35. ANALYZING RELATIONSHIPS Use the given actual and magnified lengths to determine which of the following insects were looked at using the same magnifying glass. Explain your reasoning.

grasshopper
Actual: 2 in.
Magnified: 15 in.

black beetle
Actual: 0.6 in.
Magnified: 4.2 in.

honeybee
Actual: $\frac{5}{8}$ in.
Magnified: $\frac{75}{16}$ in.

monarch butterfly
Actual: 3.9 in.
Magnified: 29.25 in.

36. THOUGHT PROVOKING Draw $\triangle ABC$ and $\triangle A'B'C'$ so that $\triangle A'B'C'$ is a dilation of $\triangle ABC$. Find the center of dilation and explain how you found it.

37. REASONING Your friend prints a 4-inch by 6-inch photo for you from the school dance. All you have is an 8-inch by 10-inch frame. Can you dilate the photo to fit the frame? Explain your reasoning.

Dynamic Teaching Tools

Dynamic Assessment & Progress Monitoring Tool

Interactive Whiteboard Lesson Library

Dynamic Classroom with Dynamic Investigations

ANSWERS

23. The scale factor should be calculated by finding $\frac{CP'}{CP}$, not $\frac{CP}{CP'}$; $k = \frac{3}{12} = \frac{1}{4}$

24. The scale factor should be calculated by finding the ratio of the length of a side of the image to the length of the corresponding side of the preimage; $k = \frac{4}{2} = 2$

25. $k = \frac{5}{3}; x = 21$

26. $k = 2; n = 6$

27. $k = \frac{2}{3}; y = 3$

28. $k = \frac{1}{4}; m = 16$

29. $k = 2$

30. $k = \frac{20}{17}$

31. 300 mm

32. 45 mm

33. 940 mm

34. 180 mm

35. grasshopper, honey bee, and monarch butterfly; The scale factor for these three is $k = \frac{15}{2}$. The scale factor for the black beetle is $k = 7$.

36. *Sample answer:*

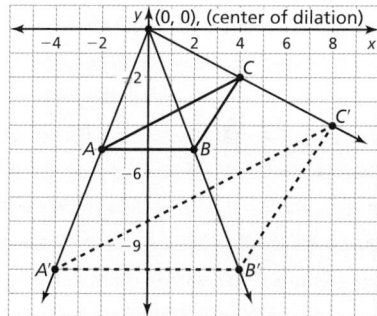

the origin (0,0); After drawing $\triangle ABC$ and its dilation, draw the lines connecting each vertex in the preimage with its corresponding vertex in the image. These three lines intersect at the center of dilation.

37. no; The scale factor for the shorter sides is $\frac{8}{4} = 2$, but the scale factor for the longer sides is $\frac{10}{6} = \frac{5}{3}$. The scale factor for both sides has to be the same or the picture will be distorted.

ANSWERS

38. larger star; smaller star; Because the scale factor is between 0 and 1, the dilation is a reduction.

39. $x = 5$, $y = 25$

40. A figure that is 200% larger than the preimage will be twice as large.

41. original

42. dilated

43. original

44. dilated

45–49. See Additional Answers.

50. The center of dilation must be on that page. So, this point will be in the same place for both the original figure and the dilated figure.

51. $A'(4, 4)$, $B'(4, 12)$, $C'(10, 4)$

52. $A'(2, -5)$, $B'(0, 0)$, $C'(-3, 1)$

53. $A'(1, 2)$, $B'(-1, 7)$, $C'(-4, 8)$

54. $A'(5, -2)$, $B'(3, 3)$, $C'(0, 4)$

55. $A'(0, -1)$, $B'(-2, 4)$, $C'(-5, 5)$

56. $A'(3, -3)$, $B'(1, 2)$, $C'(-2, 3)$

57. $A'(-1, 0)$, $B'(-3, 5)$, $C'(-6, 6)$

Mini-Assessment

1. Find the scale factor of the dilation. Then tell whether it is a *reduction* or an *enlargement*.

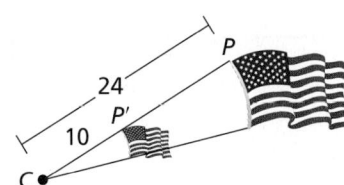

$k = \frac{5}{12}$, reduction

2. Graph $\triangle DEF$ with vertices $D(2, 6)$, $E(2, 2)$, and $F(4, 2)$ and its image after a dilation with scale factor $-\frac{1}{2}$.

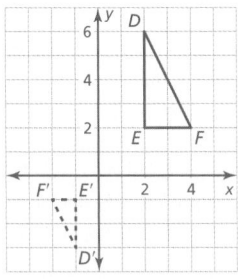

3. A photographer enlarges a 4 inch $\times$ 5 inch photo to an 8 inch $\times$ 10 inch photo. What is the scale factor of the dilation? 2

214   Chapter 4

---

38. HOW DO YOU SEE IT? Point C is the center of dilation of the images. The scale factor is $\frac{1}{3}$. Which figure is the original figure? Which figure is the dilated figure? Explain your reasoning.

39. MATHEMATICAL CONNECTIONS The larger triangle is a dilation of the smaller triangle. Find the values of x and y.

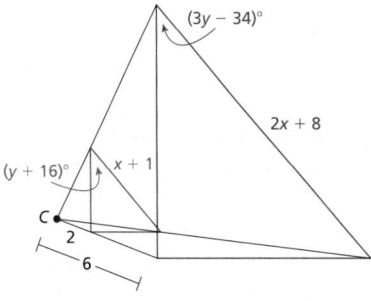

40. WRITING Explain why a scale factor of 2 is the same as 200%.

In Exercises 41–44, determine whether the dilated figure or the original figure is closer to the center of dilation. Use the given location of the center of dilation and scale factor k.

41. Center of dilation: inside the figure; $k = 3$

42. Center of dilation: inside the figure; $k = \frac{1}{2}$

43. Center of dilation: outside the figure; $k = 120\%$

44. Center of dilation: outside the figure; $k = 0.1$

---

45. ANALYZING RELATIONSHIPS Dilate the line through $O(0, 0)$ and $A(1, 2)$ using a scale factor of 2.

  a. What do you notice about the lengths of $\overline{O'A'}$ and $\overline{OA}$?

  b. What do you notice about $\overleftrightarrow{O'A'}$ and $\overleftrightarrow{OA}$?

46. ANALYZING RELATIONSHIPS Dilate the line through $A(0, 1)$ and $B(1, 2)$ using a scale factor of $\frac{1}{2}$.

  a. What do you notice about the lengths of $\overline{A'B'}$ and $\overline{AB}$?

  b. What do you notice about $\overleftrightarrow{A'B'}$ and $\overleftrightarrow{AB}$?

47. ATTENDING TO PRECISION You are making a blueprint of your house. You measure the lengths of the walls of your room to be 11 feet by 12 feet. When you draw your room on the blueprint, the lengths of the walls are 8.25 inches by 9 inches. What scale factor dilates your room to the blueprint?

48. MAKING AN ARGUMENT Your friend claims that dilating a figure by 1 is the same as dilating a figure by -1 because the original figure will not be enlarged or reduced. Is your friend correct? Explain your reasoning.

49. USING STRUCTURE Rectangle $WXYZ$ has vertices $W(-3, -1)$, $X(-3, 3)$, $Y(5, 3)$, and $Z(5, -1)$.

  a. Find the perimeter and area of the rectangle.

  b. Dilate the rectangle using a scale factor of 3. Find the perimeter and area of the dilated rectangle. Compare with the original rectangle. What do you notice?

  c. Repeat part (b) using a scale factor of $\frac{1}{4}$.

  d. Make a conjecture for how the perimeter and area change when a figure is dilated.

50. REASONING You put a reduction of a page on the original page. Explain why there is a point that is in the same place on both pages.

51. REASONING $\triangle ABC$ has vertices $A(4, 2)$, $B(4, 6)$, and $C(7, 2)$. Find the coordinates of the vertices of the image after a dilation with center $(4, 0)$ and a scale factor of 2.

Maintaining Mathematical Proficiency   Reviewing what you learned in previous grades and lessons

The vertices of $\triangle ABC$ are $A(2, -1)$, $B(0, 4)$, and $C(-3, 5)$. Find the coordinates of the vertices of the image after the translation. *(Section 4.1)*

52. $(x, y) \rightarrow (x, y - 4)$ **53.** $(x, y) \rightarrow (x - 1, y + 3)$ **54.** $(x, y) \rightarrow (x + 3, y - 1)$

55. $(x, y) \rightarrow (x - 2, y)$ **56.** $(x, y) \rightarrow (x + 1, y - 2)$ **57.** $(x, y) \rightarrow (x - 3, y + 1)$

214   Chapter 4   Transformations

If students need help...	If students got it...
Resources by Chapter • Practice A and Practice B • Puzzle Time	Resources by Chapter • Enrichment and Extension • Cumulative Review
Student Journal • Practice	Start the *next* Section
Differentiating the Lesson Skills Review Handbook	

Dynamic Teaching Tools

Dynamic Assessment & Progress Monitoring Tool

Lesson Planning Tool

Interactive Whiteboard Lesson Library

Dynamic Classroom with Dynamic Investigations

Overview of Section 4.6

Introduction

- In grade 8, similar figures were defined as figures that have the same shape but not necessarily the same size. Two figures are similar when corresponding side lengths are proportional and corresponding angles are congruent. Finally, perimeters and areas of similar figures and surface areas and volumes of similar solids were studied.
- In this section, similarity is defined in terms of similarity transformations. Students need to understand that a similarity transformation is a dilation or a composition of rigid motions and dilations. To decide (prove) whether two figures are similar, you need to map one figure onto the other by a single dilation or a composition of rigid motions and dilations. The composition of rigid motions and dilations may not be unique.
- **FYI:** Similarity is revisited in Chapter 8, where different conditions are presented to show that triangles are similar. The transformational approach is presented in this lesson.

Resources

- Use dynamic geometry software to demonstrate, or perform, a similarity transformation. Use the software to determine whether there is a similarity transformation that maps one figure onto another.

Formative Assessment Tips

- **3-2-1:** This formative assessment strategy is useful in giving students a structured way in which to reflect on their learning, particularly at the conclusion of a unit of study. Students are asked to respond to three writing prompts, giving three responses to the first prompt, two responses to the second prompt, and one response to the third prompt. All six responses relate to what students have learned during the unit of study—in this case, a chapter on transformations.
- Distribute a printed *3-2-1* reflection sheet and give time for students to reflect on their learning and to write.
  - 3 new things (concepts, skills, procedures, …) I learned in this chapter
  - 2 things (concepts, skills, procedures, …) I am still struggling with
  - 1 thing that will help me tomorrow
- Collect and review student reflections and plan instruction for tomorrow accordingly. For students, the reflection allows them to see what learning has occurred and where they should focus their attention.

Pacing Suggestion

- Once students have worked the explorations, continue with the formal lesson. Alternatively, simply use the software to perform the similarity transformations in the formal lesson.

Common Core State Standards

HSG-CO.A.5 Given a geometric figure and a rotation, reflection, or translation, draw the transformed figure using, e.g., graph paper, ... or geometry software. Specify a sequence of transformations that will carry a given figure onto another.

HSG-SRT.A.2 Given two figures, use the definition of similarity in terms of similarity transformations to decide if they are similar; explain using similarity transformations the meaning of similarity for triangles as the equality of all corresponding pairs of angles and the proportionality of all corresponding pairs of sides.

Laurie's Notes

Exploration

Motivate

- Draw a simple stick figure or other image on a stretchable surface, such as a balloon, physical therapy elastic, or play putty.
- ❓ Ask students what they think will happen to the figure when you pull the picture to the right. The image will be distorted. Pull one of the sides of the picture to confirm.
- Pull the top of the picture so that students see this result as the same.
- ❓ Ask students what they think will happen when the stretchable surface is pulled in both directions (right and up). The image will enlarge proportionally.
- **Alternate Approach:** If you can display a computer image to the class, you can drag a side to distort the image, or drag a corner to change the size of the image proportionally.

Discuss

- Similar figures can be congruent. Two congruent figures meet the definition of similarity: corresponding side lengths are proportional (1 : 1) and corresponding angles are congruent.
- Note that the definition of a dilation excludes a scale factor of 1. For that reason, the dilation is referred to as a nonrigid motion because the size changes.

Exploration 1

- Note that the center of dilation does not need to be the origin.
- ❓ **MP3 Construct Viable Arguments and Critique the Reasoning of Others:** "Are the triangles similar? How do you know?" Listen for the ratio of corresponding sides all equal 3, and the corresponding angles are congruent.
- **Extension:** Have students repeat the exploration (a) using one of the vertices as the center of dilation and (b) using a point inside the original triangle (but not the origin) as the center of dilation.
    - ❓ "When the center of dilation is a vertex of the original triangle, will the triangles be similar? Explain." yes; The ratio of corresponding sides all equal 3, and the corresponding angles are congruent.
    - ❓ "When the center of dilation is inside the original triangle, will the triangles be similar? Explain." yes; The ratio of corresponding sides all equal 3, and the corresponding angles are congruent.

Exploration 2

- In each construction, ask students how they know the preimage and the image are similar.
- **MP2 Reason Abstractly and Quantitatively** and **MP3:** What you hope is that students will say that translations, reflections, and rotations are isometries, congruence-preserving transformations. If two figures are congruent, then they are similar. They should not need to measure!
- ❓ **Always-Sometimes-Never True:** "If two figures are congruent, then they are similar." always true
- ❓ **Always-Sometimes-Never True:** "If two figures are similar, then they are congruent." sometimes true

Communicate Your Answer

- Listen for student understanding of rigid transformations producing congruent and, hence, similar images. Dilations are nonrigid, and the image is similar to the original figure.
- Question 4 prepares students for content in the formal lesson.

Connecting to Next Step

- The explorations should be a review of rigid and nonrigid transformations as well as the definition of similar figures. Quickly transition to the formal lesson.

4.6 Similarity and Transformations

Essential Question
When a figure is translated, reflected, rotated, or dilated in the plane, is the image always similar to the original figure?

Two figures are *similar figures* when they have the same shape but not necessarily the same size.

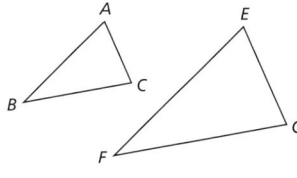

Similar Triangles

ATTENTING TO PRECISION
To be proficient in math, you need to use clear definitions in discussions with others and in your own reasoning.

EXPLORATION 1   Dilations and Similarity

Work with a partner.

a. Use dynamic geometry software to draw any triangle and label it △ABC.

b. Dilate the triangle using a scale factor of 3. Is the image similar to the original triangle? Justify your answer.

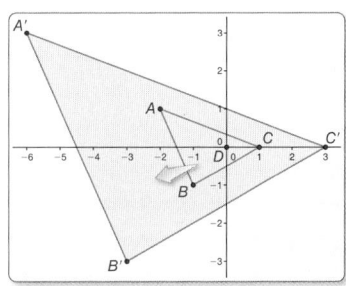

Sample
Points
$A(-2, 1)$
$B(-1, -1)$
$C(1, 0)$
$D(0, 0)$
Segments
$AB = 2.24$
$BC = 2.24$
$AC = 3.16$
Angles
$m\angle A = 45°$
$m\angle B = 90°$
$m\angle C = 45°$

EXPLORATION 2   Rigid Motions and Similarity

Work with a partner.

a. Use dynamic geometry software to draw any triangle.

b. Copy the triangle and translate it 3 units left and 4 units up. Is the image similar to the original triangle? Justify your answer.

c. Reflect the triangle in the *y*-axis. Is the image similar to the original triangle? Justify your answer.

d. Rotate the original triangle 90° counterclockwise about the origin. Is the image similar to the original triangle? Justify your answer.

Communicate Your Answer

3. When a figure is translated, reflected, rotated, or dilated in the plane, is the image always similar to the original figure? Explain your reasoning.

4. A figure undergoes a composition of transformations, which includes translations, reflections, rotations, and dilations. Is the image similar to the original figure? Explain your reasoning.

Section 4.6   Similarity and Transformations   **215**

---

4. yes; According to Composition Theorem (Thm. 4.1), the composition of two or more rigid motions is a rigid motion. Also, a dilation preserves angle measures and results in an image with lengths proportional to the preimage lengths. So, a composition of rigid motions or dilations will result in an image that has angle measures congruent to the corresponding angle measures of the original figure, and sides that are either congruent or proportional to the corresponding sides of the original figure.

Dynamic Teaching Tools
Dynamic Assessment & Progress Monitoring Tool
Lesson Planning Tool
Interactive Whiteboard Lesson Library
Dynamic Classroom with Dynamic Investigations

ANSWERS

1. **a.** Check students' work.
   b. Check students' work; yes; Each side of △A′B′C′ is three times as long as its corresponding side of △ABC. The corresponding angles are congruent. Because the corresponding sides are proportional and the corresponding angles are congruent, the image is similar to the original triangle.

2. **a.** *Sample answer:*

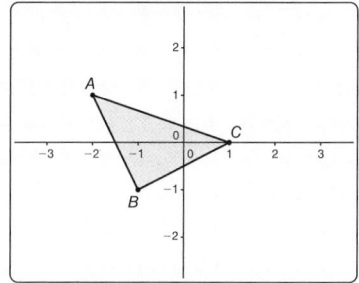

   b. *Sample answer:*

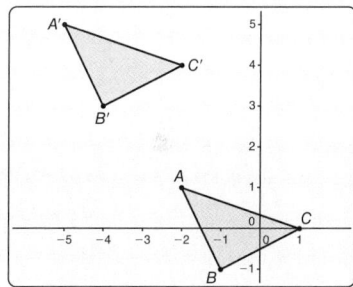

   yes; Because the corresponding sides are congruent and the corresponding angles are congruent, the image is similar to the original triangle.

2c–d. See Additional Answers.

3. yes; The corresponding sides are always congruent or proportional, and the corresponding angles are always congruent.

Extra Example 1

Graph $\overline{AB}$ with endpoints $A(12, -6)$ and $B(0, -3)$ and its image after the similarity transformation.

Reflection: in the y-axis

Dilation: $(x, y) \rightarrow \left(\frac{1}{3}x, \frac{1}{3}y\right)$

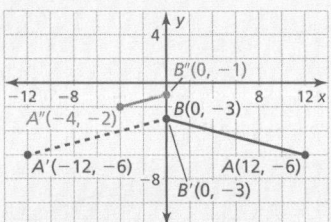

MONITORING PROGRESS ANSWERS

1.

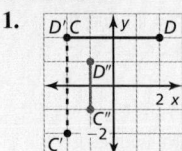

2.

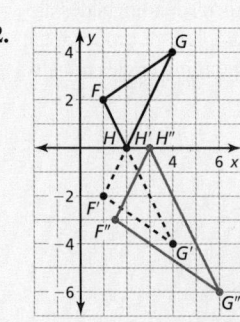

4.6 Lesson

Core Vocabulary

similarity transformation, *p. 216*
similar figures, *p. 216*

What You Will Learn

▶ Perform similarity transformations.
▶ Describe similarity transformations.
▶ Prove that figures are similar.

Performing Similarity Transformations

A dilation is a transformation that preserves shape but not size. So, a dilation is a nonrigid motion. A **similarity transformation** is a dilation or a composition of rigid motions and dilations. Two geometric figures are **similar figures** if and only if there is a similarity transformation that maps one of the figures onto the other. Similar figures have the same shape but not necessarily the same size.

Congruence transformations preserve length and angle measure. When the scale factor of the dilation(s) is not equal to 1 or -1, similarity transformations preserve angle measure only.

EXAMPLE 1   Performing a Similarity Transformation

Graph $\triangle ABC$ with vertices $A(-4, 1)$, $B(-2, 2)$, and $C(-2, 1)$ and its image after the similarity transformation.

> **Translation:** $(x, y) \rightarrow (x + 5, y + 1)$
> **Dilation:** $(x, y) \rightarrow (2x, 2y)$

SOLUTION

Step 1   Graph $\triangle ABC$.

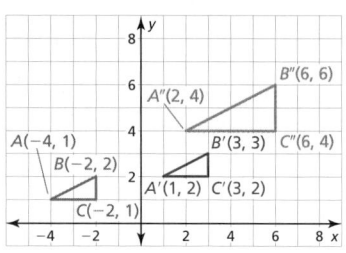

Step 2   Translate $\triangle ABC$ 5 units right and 1 unit up. $\triangle A'B'C'$ has vertices $A'(1, 2)$, $B'(3, 3)$, and $C'(3, 2)$.

Step 3   Dilate $\triangle A'B'C'$ using a scale factor of 2. $\triangle A''B''C''$ has vertices $A''(2, 4)$, $B''(6, 6)$, and $C''(6, 4)$.

Monitoring Progress 🔊 Help in English and Spanish at *BigIdeasMath.com*

1. Graph $\overline{CD}$ with endpoints $C(-2, 2)$ and $D(2, 2)$ and its image after the similarity transformation.

   Rotation: 90° about the origin

   Dilation: $(x, y) \rightarrow \left(\frac{1}{2}x, \frac{1}{2}y\right)$

2. Graph $\triangle FGH$ with vertices $F(1, 2)$, $G(4, 4)$, and $H(2, 0)$ and its image after the similarity transformation.

   Reflection: in the x-axis

   Dilation: $(x, y) \rightarrow (1.5x, 1.5y)$

Laurie's Notes   Teacher Actions

- Discuss dilations—they are nonrigid, meaning that the size will change and the scale factor k *does not equal* 1. Similar figures on the other hand can be congruent.
- Note that *similarity transformation* is defined and then used to determine whether two figures are similar. Again note the "if and only if" portion of the statement. To help demonstrate this, draw two similar trapezoids, rotating one 90°, on the board. The figures are similar *if there are* similarity transformations mapping one to the other, *and if the figures are similar*, then there are similarity transformations that would map one to the other.
- Pose Example 1 and ask for a *Thumbs Up* indication when partners are ready to begin the example.
- **Monitoring Progress:** Using whiteboards, have half the class do Question 1 and the other half do Question 2.

Describing Similarity Transformations

EXAMPLE 2 **Describing a Similarity Transformation**

Describe a similarity transformation that maps trapezoid *PQRS* to trapezoid *WXYZ*.

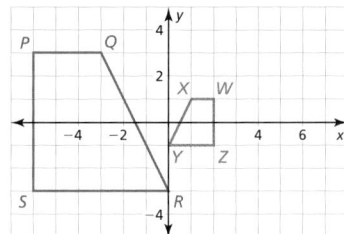

SOLUTION

$\overline{QR}$ falls from left to right, and $\overline{XY}$ rises from left to right. If you reflect trapezoid *PQRS* in the *y*-axis as shown, then the image, trapezoid *P′Q′R′S′*, will have the same orientation as trapezoid *WXYZ*.

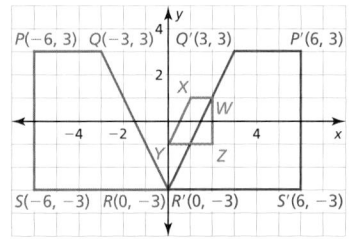

Trapezoid *WXYZ* appears to be about one-third as large as trapezoid *P′Q′R′S′*. Dilate trapezoid *P′Q′R′S′* using a scale factor of $\frac{1}{3}$.

$$(x, y) \rightarrow \left(\tfrac{1}{3}x, \tfrac{1}{3}y\right)$$

$P'(6, 3) \rightarrow P''(2, 1)$

$Q'(3, 3) \rightarrow Q''(1, 1)$

$R'(0, -3) \rightarrow R''(0, -1)$

$S'(6, -3) \rightarrow S''(2, -1)$

The vertices of trapezoid *P″Q″R″S″* match the vertices of trapezoid *WXYZ*.

 So, a similarity transformation that maps trapezoid *PQRS* to trapezoid *WXYZ* is a reflection in the *y*-axis followed by a dilation with a scale factor of $\frac{1}{3}$.

Monitoring Progress 🔊 Help in English and Spanish at *BigIdeasMath.com*

3. In Example 2, describe another similarity transformation that maps trapezoid *PQRS* to trapezoid *WXYZ*.

4. Describe a similarity transformation that maps quadrilateral *DEFG* to quadrilateral *STUV*.

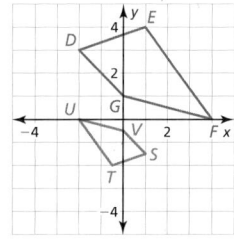

Extra Example 2

Describe a similarity transformation that maps trapezoid *WXYZ* to trapezoid *PQRS*.

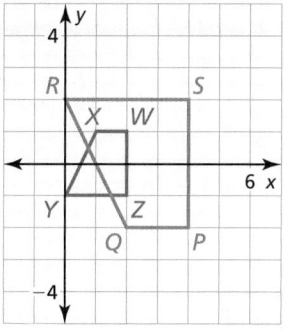

Sample answer: A reflection in the *x*-axis followed by a dilation with a scale factor of 2.

MONITORING PROGRESS ANSWERS

3. *Sample answer:* reflection in the *x*-axis followed by a dilation with a scale factor of $-\frac{1}{3}$

4. *Sample answer:* dilation with a scale factor of $\frac{1}{2}$ followed by a 180° rotation about the origin

---

Laurie's Notes   Teacher Actions

- Describing a similarity transformation is more challenging than performing a similarity transformation. Students are often uncertain where to begin.
- **Teaching Tip:** Have students focus on a pair of corresponding sides. What dilation about the origin will make them the same size? Does the orientation need to change (reflection)? Does the location need to change (translation)? Does the position need to change (rotation)?
- **Alternate Approach:** Have students use dynamic geometry software to answer the question.
- **Monitoring Progress:** Question 3 suggests that the solution (similarity transformation) is not unique! This is a *Big Idea* for students to explore.
- **MP5 Use Appropriate Tools Strategically:** If students are using dynamic geometry software, take time for them to generate a sample of different similarity transformations for Example 2.

Extra Example 3

Prove that square *ABCD* is similar to square *EFGH*.

Given Square *ABCD* with side length *s*, square *EFGH* with side length 2*s*, $\overline{AD} \parallel \overline{EH}$

Prove Square *ABCD* is similar to square *EFGH*.

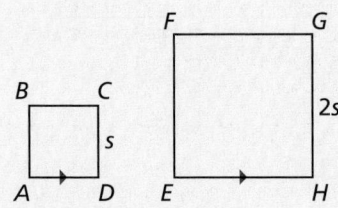

See Additional Answers.

MONITORING PROGRESS ANSWER

5. See Additional Answers.

Proving Figures Are Similar

To prove that two figures are similar, you must prove that a similarity transformation maps one of the figures onto the other.

EXAMPLE 3 **Proving That Two Squares Are Similar**

Prove that square *ABCD* is similar to square *EFGH*.

Given Square *ABCD* with side length *r*, square *EFGH* with side length *s*, $\overline{AD} \parallel \overline{EH}$

Prove Square *ABCD* is similar to square *EFGH*.

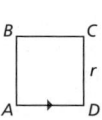 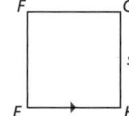

SOLUTION

Translate square *ABCD* so that point *A* maps to point *E*. Because translations map segments to parallel segments and $\overline{AD} \parallel \overline{EH}$, the image of $\overline{AD}$ lies on $\overline{EH}$.

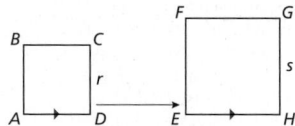 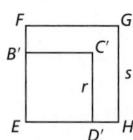

Because translations preserve length and angle measure, the image of *ABCD*, *EB'C'D'*, is a square with side length *r*. Because all the interior angles of a square are right angles, $\angle B'ED' \cong \angle FEH$. When $\overrightarrow{ED'}$ coincides with $\overrightarrow{EH}$, $\overrightarrow{EB'}$ coincides with $\overrightarrow{EF}$. So, $\overline{EB'}$ lies on $\overline{EF}$. Next, dilate square *EB'C'D'* using center of dilation *E*. Choose the scale factor to be the ratio of the side lengths of *EFGH* and *EB'C'D'*, which is $\frac{s}{r}$.

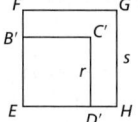 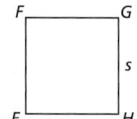

This dilation maps $\overline{ED'}$ to $\overline{EH}$ and $\overline{EB'}$ to $\overline{EF}$ because the images of $\overline{ED'}$ and $\overline{EB'}$ have side length $\frac{s}{r}(r) = s$ and the segments $\overline{ED'}$ and $\overline{EB'}$ lie on lines passing through the center of dilation. So, the dilation maps *B'* to *F* and *D'* to *H*. The image of *C'* lies $\frac{s}{r}(r) = s$ units to the right of the image of *B'* and $\frac{s}{r}(r) = s$ units above the image of *D'*. So, the image of *C'* is *G*.

▶ A similarity transformation maps square *ABCD* to square *EFGH*. So, square *ABCD* is similar to square *EFGH*.

Monitoring Progress 🔊 Help in English and Spanish at *BigIdeasMath.com*

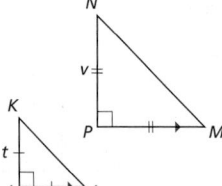

5. Prove that △*JKL* is similar to △*MNP*.

   Given Right isosceles △*JKL* with leg length *t*, right isosceles △*MNP* with leg length *v*, $\overline{LJ} \parallel \overline{PM}$

   Prove △*JKL* is similar to △*MNP*.

Laurie's Notes Teacher Actions

- Remind students of the definition of a square.
- ❓ "How can you prove that two squares are similar?" You have to show that there is a similarity transformation that maps one square onto the other square.
- The proof may seem unnecessarily long and wordy to students, but it models what it means to prove that two figures are similar. We need to show that there is a sequence of similarity transformations that map square *ABCD* onto square *EFGH*. Note that if $\overline{AD}$ and $\overline{EH}$ were not given to be parallel, then a rotation would have been necessary as well.

❓ Work through the proof as shown. Ask, "Is there another series of similarity transformations that map square *ABCD* onto square *EFGH*? Explain." yes; One possibility would be to dilate first and then translate.

Closure

- **3-2-1:** Hand out a *3-2-1* reflection sheet as described on page T-214.

Vocabulary and Core Concept Check

1. **VOCABULARY** What is the difference between *similar figures* and *congruent figures*?

2. **COMPLETE THE SENTENCE** A transformation that produces a similar figure, such as a dilation, is called a _____.

Monitoring Progress and Modeling with Mathematics

In Exercises 3–6, graph △*FGH* with vertices *F*(−2, 2), *G*(−2, −4), and *H*(−4, −4) and its image after the similarity transformation. *(See Example 1.)*

3. **Translation:** $(x, y) \to (x + 3, y + 1)$
   Dilation: $(x, y) \to (2x, 2y)$

4. **Dilation:** $(x, y) \to \left(\frac{1}{2}x, \frac{1}{2}y\right)$
   Reflection: in the *y*-axis

5. **Rotation:** 90° about the origin
   Dilation: $(x, y) \to (3x, 3y)$

6. **Dilation:** $(x, y) \to \left(\frac{3}{4}x, \frac{3}{4}y\right)$
   Reflection: in the *x*-axis

In Exercises 7 and 8, describe a similarity transformation that maps the blue preimage to the green image. *(See Example 2.)*

7.
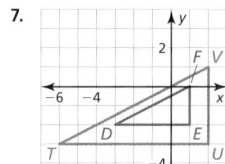

8.
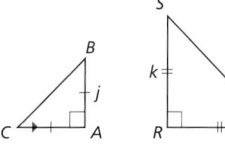

In Exercises 9–12, determine whether the polygons with the given vertices are similar. Use transformations to explain your reasoning.

9. *A*(6, 0), *B*(9, 6), *C*(12, 6) and *D*(0, 3), *E*(1, 5), *F*(2, 5)

10. *Q*(−1, 0), *R*(−2, 2), *S*(1, 3), *T*(2, 1) and *W*(0, 2), *X*(4, 4), *Y*(6, −2), *Z*(2, −4)

11. *G*(−2, 3), *H*(4, 3), *I*(4, 0) and *J*(1, 0), *K*(6, −2), *L*(1, −2)

12. *D*(−4, 3), *E*(−2, 3), *F*(−1, 1), *G*(−4, 1) and *L*(1, −1), *M*(3, −1), *N*(6, −3), *P*(1, −3)

In Exercises 13 and 14, prove that the figures are similar. *(See Example 3.)*

13. **Given** Right isosceles △*ABC* with leg length *j*, right isosceles △*RST* with leg length *k*, $\overline{CA} \parallel \overline{RT}$
    Prove △*ABC* is similar to △*RST*.

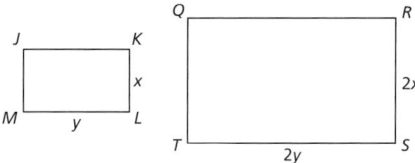

14. **Given** Rectangle *JKLM* with side lengths *x* and *y*, rectangle *QRST* with side lengths 2*x* and 2*y*
    Prove Rectangle *JKLM* is similar to rectangle *QRST*.

Assignment Guide and Homework Check

ASSIGNMENT

Basic: 1, 2, 3–15 odd, 16–18, 23–26

Average: 1, 2, 4–14 even, 16–18, 21–26

Advanced: 1, 2, 8, 12, 14–18, 20–26

HOMEWORK CHECK

Basic: 5, 7, 9, 18

Average: 8, 10, 14, 18

Advanced: 8, 14, 18, 20

ANSWERS

1. Congruent figures have the same size and shape. Similar figures have the same shape, but not necessarily the same size.

2. similarity transformation

3.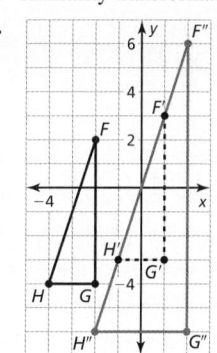

4.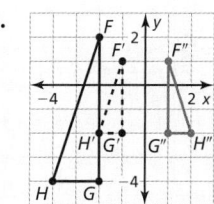

5.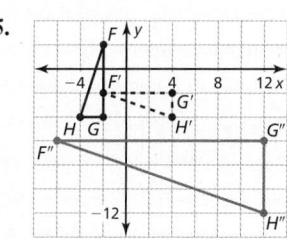

6.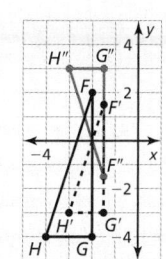

---

7. *Sample answer:* translation 1 unit down and 1 unit right followed by a dilation with center at *E*(2, −3) and a scale factor of 2

8. *Sample answer:* dilation with center at the origin and a scale factor of $\frac{1}{2}$ followed by a reflection in the *y*-axis

9. yes; △*ABC* can be mapped to △*DEF* by a dilation with center at the origin and a scale factor of $\frac{1}{3}$ followed by a translation of 2 units left and 3 units up.

10. yes; □*QRST* can be mapped to □*WXYZ* by a 270° rotation about the origin followed by a dilation with center at the origin and a scale factor of 2.

11. no; The scale factor from $\overline{HI}$ to $\overline{JL}$ is $\frac{2}{3}$, but the scale factor from $\overline{GH}$ to $\overline{KL}$ is $\frac{5}{6}$.

12. no; The scale factor from $\overline{DG}$ to $\overline{LP}$ is 1, but the scale factor from $\overline{FG}$ to $\overline{NP}$ is $\frac{5}{3}$.

13–14. See Additional Answers.

ANSWERS

15. yes; The stop sign sticker can be mapped to the regular-sized stop sign by translating the sticker to the left until the centers match, and then dilating the sticker with a scale factor of 3.15. Because there is a similarity transformation that maps one stop sign to the other, the sticker is similar to the regular-sized stop sign.

16. See Additional Answers.

17. no; The scale factor is 6 for both dimensions. So, the enlarged banner is proportional to the smaller one.

18–26. See Additional Answers.

Mini-Assessment

1. $\overline{AB}$ has endpoints $A(-8, 6)$ and $B(6, 0)$. Find the endpoints of its image after the similarity transformation.

Translation: $(x, y) \rightarrow (x, y - 6)$

Dilation: $(x, y) \rightarrow \left(\frac{1}{2}x, \frac{1}{2}y\right)$

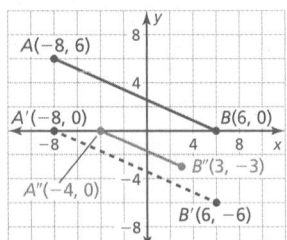

2. Describe a similarity transformation that maps quadrilateral *STUV* to quadrilateral *DEFG*.

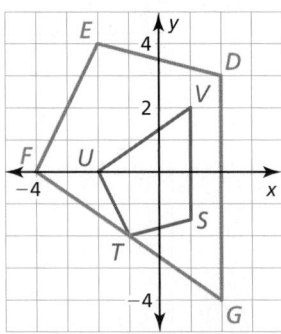

Sample answer: A reflection in the x-axis followed by a dilation with a scale factor of 2

---

15. **MODELING WITH MATHEMATICS** Determine whether the regular-sized stop sign and the stop sign sticker are similar. Use transformations to explain your reasoning.

12.6 in.   4 in.

16. **ERROR ANALYSIS** Describe and correct the error in comparing the figures.

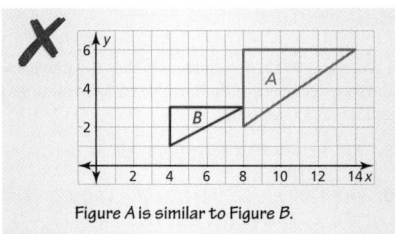

Figure A is similar to Figure B.

17. **MAKING AN ARGUMENT** A member of the homecoming decorating committee gives a printing company a banner that is 3 inches by 14 inches to enlarge. The committee member claims the banner she receives is distorted. Do you think the printing company distorted the image she gave it? Explain.

84 in.

18 in.

18. **HOW DO YOU SEE IT?** Determine whether each pair of figures is similar. Explain your reasoning.

a.   b.

19. **ANALYZING RELATIONSHIPS** Graph a polygon in a coordinate plane. Use a similarity transformation involving a dilation (where *k* is a whole number) and a translation to graph a second polygon. Then describe a similarity transformation that maps the second polygon onto the first.

20. **THOUGHT PROVOKING** Is the composition of a rotation and a dilation commutative? (In other words, do you obtain the same image regardless of the order in which you perform the transformations?) Justify your answer.

21. **MATHEMATICAL CONNECTIONS** Quadrilateral *JKLM* is mapped to quadrilateral *J′K′L′M′* using the dilation $(x, y) \rightarrow \left(\frac{3}{2}x, \frac{3}{2}y\right)$. Then quadrilateral *J′K′L′M′* is mapped to quadrilateral *J″K″L″M″* using the translation $(x, y) \rightarrow (x + 3, y - 4)$. The vertices of quadrilateral *J′K′L′M′* are $J(-12, 0)$, $K(-12, 18)$, $L(-6, 18)$, and $M(-6, 0)$. Find the coordinates of the vertices of quadrilateral *JKLM* and quadrilateral *J″K″L″M″*. Are quadrilateral *JKLM* and quadrilateral *J″K″L″M″* similar? Explain.

22. **REPEATED REASONING** Use the diagram.

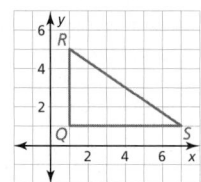

a. Connect the midpoints of the sides of △*QRS* to make another triangle. Is this triangle similar to △*QRS*? Use transformations to support your answer.

b. Repeat part (a) for two other triangles. What conjecture can you make?

Maintaining Mathematical Proficiency   Reviewing what you learned in previous grades and lessons

Classify the angle as *acute*, *obtuse*, *right*, or *straight*.   *(Section 1.5)*

23.   **24.**   **25.**   **26.**

113°   82°

If students need help...	If students got it...
Resources by Chapter • Practice A and Practice B • Puzzle Time	Resources by Chapter • Enrichment and Extension • Cumulative Review
Student Journal • Practice	Start the *next* Section
Differentiating the Lesson Skills Review Handbook	

4.4–4.6   What Did You Learn?

Core Vocabulary

congruent figures, *p. 200*
congruence transformation, *p. 201*
dilation, *p. 208*
center of dilation, *p. 208*
scale factor, *p. 208*

enlargement, *p. 208*
reduction, *p. 208*
similarity transformation, *p. 216*
similar figures, *p. 216*

Core Concepts

Section 4.4

Identifying Congruent Figures, *p. 200*
Describing a Congruence Transformation, *p. 201*
Theorem 4.2 Reflections in Parallel Lines Theorem, *p. 202*
Theorem 4.3 Reflections in Intersecting Lines Theorem, *p. 203*

Section 4.5

Dilations and Scale Factor, *p. 208*   Negative Scale Factors, *p. 210*
Coordinate Rule for Dilations, *p. 209*

Section 4.6

Similarity Transformations, *p. 216*

Mathematical Practices

1. Revisit Exercise 31 on page 206. Try to recall the process you used to reach the solution. Did you have to change course at all? If so, how did you approach the situation?

2. Describe a real-life situation that can be modeled by Exercise 28 on page 213.

ANSWERS

1. *Sample answer:* Draw a picture and label the given information. Then look at the results and try to figure out what needs to be proven in order to get there; yes; When unsure, look back at related definitions, postulates, and theorems to see which ones might be helpful. Points L and M must be identified, so use the Ruler Postulate (Post. 1.1) and Segment Addition Postulate (Post. 1.2). Then the rest will start falling into place.

2. *Sample answer:* This drawing could represent the reduction of a 16×28 painting into a 4×7 photograph or computer graphic.

Performance Task

The Magic of Optics

Look at yourself in a shiny spoon. What happened to your reflection? Can you describe this mathematically? Now turn the spoon over and look at your reflection on the back of the spoon. What happened? Why?

To explore the answers to these questions and more, go to *BigIdeasMath.com*.

221

1.
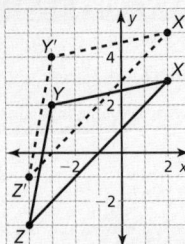

2.
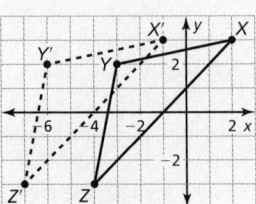

3.
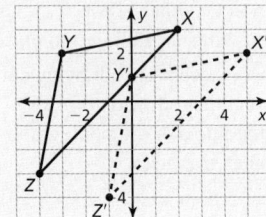

4.
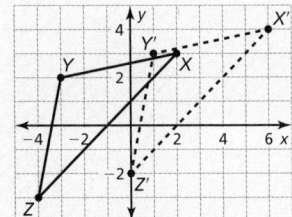

5.
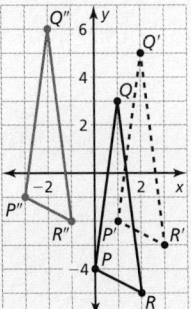

6.
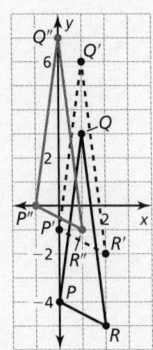

4 Chapter Review
Dynamic Solutions available at *BigIdeasMath.com*

4.1 Translations *(pp. 173–180)*

Graph quadrilateral *ABCD* with vertices *A*(1, −2), *B*(3, −1), *C*(0, 3), and *D*(−4, 1) and its image after the translation $(x, y) \to (x + 2, y − 2)$.

Graph quadrilateral *ABCD*. To find the coordinates of the vertices of the image, add 2 to the *x*-coordinates and subtract 2 from the *y*-coordinates of the vertices of the preimage. Then graph the image.

$(x, y) \to (x + 2, y − 2)$

$A(1, −2) \to A'(3, −4)$
$B(3, −1) \to B'(5, −3)$
$C(0, 3) \to C'(2, 1)$
$D(−4, 1) \to D'(−2, −1)$

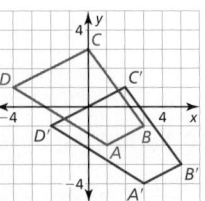

Graph △*XYZ* with vertices *X*(2, 3), *Y*(−3, 2), and *Z*(−4, −3) and its image after the translation.

1. $(x, y) \to (x, y + 2)$
2. $(x, y) \to (x − 3, y)$
3. $(x, y) \to (x + 3, y − 1)$
4. $(x, y) \to (x + 4, y + 1)$

Graph △*PQR* with vertices *P*(0, −4), *Q*(1, 3), and *R*(2, −5) and its image after the composition.

5. Translation: $(x, y) \to (x + 1, y + 2)$
   Translation: $(x, y) \to (x − 4, y + 1)$

6. Translation: $(x, y) \to (x, y + 3)$
   Translation: $(x, y) \to (x − 1, y + 1)$

4.2 Reflections *(pp. 181–188)*

Graph △*ABC* with vertices *A*(1, −1), *B*(3, 2), and *C*(4, −4) and its image after a reflection in the line *y* = *x*.

Graph △*ABC* and the line *y* = *x*. Then use the coordinate rule for reflecting in the line *y* = *x* to find the coordinates of the vertices of the image.

$(a, b) \to (b, a)$

$A(1, −1) \to A'(−1, 1)$
$B(3, 2) \to B'(2, 3)$
$C(4, −4) \to C'(−4, 4)$

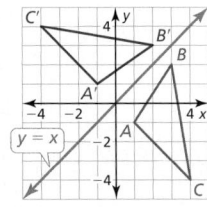

Graph the polygon and its image after a reflection in the given line.

7. $x = 4$
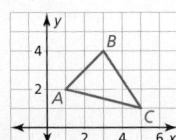

8. $y = 3$
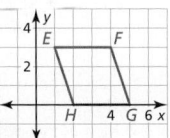

9. How many lines of symmetry does the figure have?
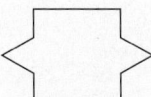

7.
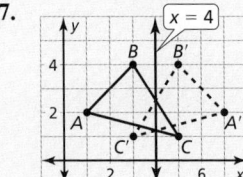

8.
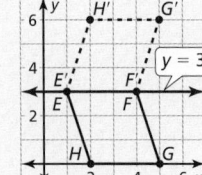

9. 2

4.3 Rotations *(pp. 189–196)*

Graph △LMN with vertices L(1, −1), M(2, 3), and N(4, 0) and its image after a 270° rotation about the origin.

Use the coordinate rule for a 270° rotation to find the coordinates of the vertices of the image. Then graph △LMN and its image.

$$(a, b) \rightarrow (b, -a)$$
$$L(1, -1) \rightarrow L'(-1, -1)$$
$$M(2, 3) \rightarrow M'(3, -2)$$
$$N(4, 0) \rightarrow N'(0, -4)$$

Graph the polygon with the given vertices and its image after a rotation of the given number of degrees about the origin.

10. *A*(−3, −1), *B*(2, 2), *C*(3, −3); 90°
11. *W*(−2, −1), *X*(−1, 3), *Y*(3, 3), *Z*(3, −3); 180°
12. Graph $\overline{XY}$ with endpoints *X*(5, −2) and *Y*(3, −3) and its image after a reflection in the *x*-axis and then a rotation of 270° about the origin.

Determine whether the figure has rotational symmetry. If so, describe any rotations that map the figure onto itself.

13.

14.

4.4 Congruence and Transformations *(pp. 199–206)*

Describe a congruence transformation that maps quadrilateral *ABCD* to quadrilateral *WXYZ*, as shown at the right.

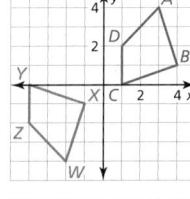

$\overline{AB}$ falls from left to right, and $\overline{WX}$ rises from left to right. If you reflect quadrilateral *ABCD* in the *x*-axis as shown at the bottom right, then the image, quadrilateral *A′B′C′D′*, will have the same orientation as quadrilateral *WXYZ*. Then you can map quadrilateral *A′B′C′D′* to quadrilateral *WXYZ* using a translation of 5 units left.

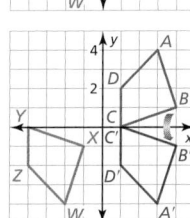

▶ So, a congruence transformation that maps quadrilateral *ABCD* to quadrilateral *WXYZ* is a reflection in the *x*-axis followed by a translation of 5 units left.

Describe a congruence transformation that maps △DEF to △JKL.

15. *D*(2, −1), *E*(4, 1), *F*(1, 2) and *J*(−2, −4), *K*(−4, −2), *L*(−1, −1)
16. *D*(−3, −4), *E*(−5, −1), *F*(−1, 1) and *J*(1, 4), *K*(−1, 1), *L*(3, −1)
17. Which transformation is the same as reflecting an object in two parallel lines? in two intersecting lines?

10.

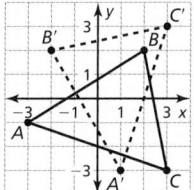

11.

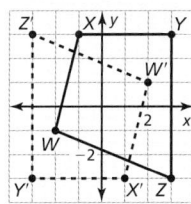

12.

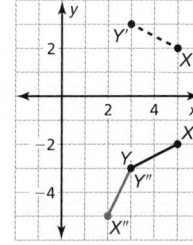

13. yes; Rotations of 60°, 120°, and 180° about the center map the figure onto itself.

14. yes; Rotations of 72° and 144° about the center map the figure onto itself.

15. *Sample answer:* reflection in the *y*-axis followed by a translation 3 units down

16. *Sample answer:* 180° rotation about the origin followed by a reflection in the line *x* = 2

17. translation; rotation

18.

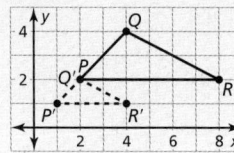

19.

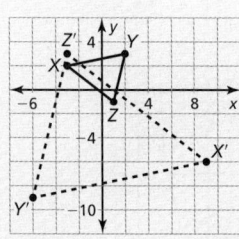

20. 1.9 cm

21. *Sample answer:* reflection in the line $x = -1$ followed by a dilation with center $(-3, 0)$ and $k = 3$

22. *Sample answer:* dilation with center at the origin and $k = \frac{1}{2}$, followed by a reflection in the line $y = x$

23. *Sample answer:* 270° rotation about the origin followed by a dilation with center at the origin and $k = 2$

4.5 **Dilations** *(pp. 207–214)*

Graph trapezoid *ABCD* with vertices $A(1, 1)$, $B(1, 3)$, $C(3, 2)$, and $D(3, 1)$ and its image after a dilation with a scale factor of 2.

Use the coordinate rule for a dilation with $k = 2$ to find the coordinates of the vertices of the image. Then graph trapezoid *ABCD* and its image.

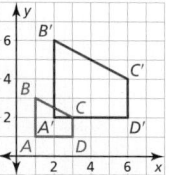

$$(x, y) \to (2x, 2y)$$
$$A(1, 1) \to A'(2, 2)$$
$$B(1, 3) \to B'(2, 6)$$
$$C(3, 2) \to C'(6, 4)$$
$$D(3, 1) \to D'(6, 2)$$

Graph the triangle and its image after a dilation with scale factor *k*.

18. $P(2, 2)$, $Q(4, 4)$, $R(8, 2)$; $k = \frac{1}{2}$

19. $X(-3, 2)$, $Y(2, 3)$, $Z(1, -1)$; $k = -3$

20. You are using a magnifying glass that shows the image of an object that is eight times the object's actual size. The image length is 15.2 centimeters. Find the actual length of the object.

4.6 **Similarity and Transformations** *(pp. 215–220)*

Describe a similarity transformation that maps △*FGH* to △*LMN*, as shown at the right.

$\overline{FG}$ is horizontal, and $\overline{LM}$ is vertical. If you rotate △*FGH* 90° about the origin as shown at the bottom right, then the image, △*F'G'H'*, will have the same orientation as △*LMN*. △*LMN* appears to be half as large as △*F'G'H'*. Dilate △*F'G'H'* using a scale factor of $\frac{1}{2}$.

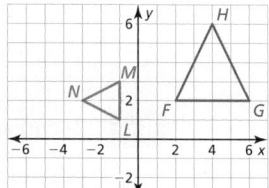

$$(x, y) \to \left(\tfrac{1}{2}x, \tfrac{1}{2}y\right)$$
$$F'(-2, 2) \to F''(-1, 1)$$
$$G'(-2, 6) \to G''(-1, 3)$$
$$H'(-6, 4) \to H''(-3, 2)$$

The vertices of △*F″G″H″* match the vertices of △*LMN*.

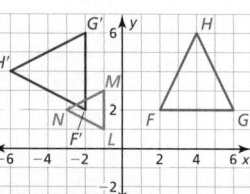

▶ So, a similarity transformation that maps △*FGH* to △*LMN* is a rotation of 90° about the origin followed by a dilation with a scale factor of $\frac{1}{2}$.

Describe a similarity transformation that maps △*ABC* to △*RST*.

21. $A(1, 0)$, $B(-2, -1)$, $C(-1, -2)$ and $R(-3, 0)$, $S(6, -3)$, $T(3, -6)$

22. $A(6, 4)$, $B(-2, 0)$, $C(-4, 2)$ and $R(2, 3)$, $S(0, -1)$, $T(1, -2)$

23. $A(3, -2)$, $B(0, 4)$, $C(-1, -3)$ and $R(-4, -6)$, $S(8, 0)$, $T(-6, 2)$

Graph △*RST* with vertices *R*(−4, 1), *S*(−2, 2), and *T*(3, −2) and its image after the translation.

1. $(x, y) \rightarrow (x - 4, y + 1)$

2. $(x, y) \rightarrow (x + 2, y - 2)$

Graph the polygon with the given vertices and its image after a rotation of the given number of degrees about the origin.

3. *D*(−1, −1), *E*(−3, 2), *F*(1, 4); 270°

4. *J*(−1, 1), *K*(3, 3), *L*(4, −3), *M*(0, −2); 90°

Determine whether the polygons with the given vertices are congruent or similar. Use transformations to explain your reasoning.

5. *Q*(2, 4), *R*(5, 4), *S*(6, 2), *T*(1, 2) and
W(6, −12), *X*(15, −12), *Y*(18, −6), *Z*(3, −6)

6. *A*(−6, 6), *B*(−6, 2), *C*(−2, −4) and
D(9, 7), *E*(5, 7), *F*(−1, 3)

Determine whether the object has line symmetry and whether it has rotational symmetry. Identify all lines of symmetry and angles of rotation that map the figure onto itself.

7.

8.

9.

10. Draw a diagram using a coordinate plane, two parallel lines, and a parallelogram that demonstrates the Reflections in Parallel Lines Theorem (Theorem 4.2).

11. A rectangle with vertices *W*(−2, 4), *X*(2, 4), *Y*(2, 2), and *Z*(−2, 2) is reflected in the *y*-axis. Your friend says that the image, rectangle *W'X'Y'Z'*, is exactly the same as the preimage. Is your friend correct? Explain your reasoning.

12. Write a composition of transformations that maps △*ABC* onto △*CDB* in the tessellation shown. Is the composition a congruence transformation? Explain your reasoning.

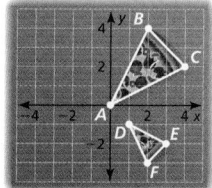

13. There is one slice of a large pizza and one slice of a small pizza in the box.

   a. Describe a similarity transformation that maps pizza slice *ABC* to pizza slice *DEF*.

   b. What is one possible scale factor for a medium slice of pizza? Explain your reasoning. (Use a dilation on the large slice of pizza.)

14. The original photograph shown is 4 inches by 6 inches.

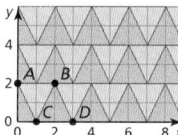

   a. What transformations can you use to produce the new photograph?

   b. You dilate the original photograph by a scale factor of $\frac{1}{2}$. What are the dimensions of the new photograph?

   c. You have a frame that holds photos that are 8.5 inches by 11 inches. Can you dilate the original photograph to fit the frame? Explain your reasoning.

If students need help...	If students got it...
Lesson Tutorials	Resources by Chapter • Enrichment and Extension • Cumulative Review
Skills Review Handbook	Performance Task
BigIdeasMath.com	Start the *next* Section

ANSWERS

1.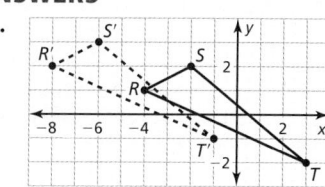

2.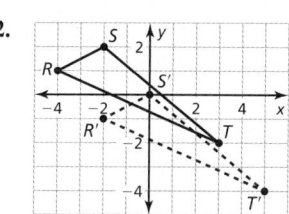

3.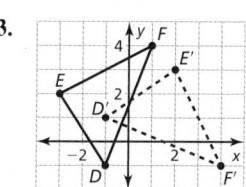

4.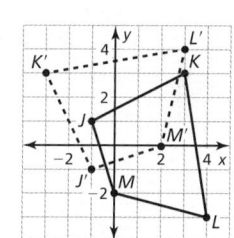

5. similar; Quadrilateral *QRST* can be mapped to quadrilateral *WXYZ* by a dilation with the center at the origin and *k* = 3, followed by a reflection in the *x*-axis. Because this composition has a rigid motion and a dilation, it is a similarity transformation.

6. congruent; △*ABC* can be mapped to △*DEF* by a 270° rotation about the origin followed by a translation 1 unit up and 3 units right. Because this is a composition of two rigid motions, the composition is rigid.

7. yes, yes; The lines of symmetry are vertically through the center of the ball and horizontally through the center of the ball; 180°

8. yes, no; The line of symmetry runs from the center of the base of the guitar, and through the sound hole to the center of the headstock of the guitar.

9. no, yes; 180°

10–14. See Additional Answers.

1. B

2. Step 1. Place the compass at *P*. Draw an arc that intersects line *m* in two different places. Label the points of intersection *A* and *B*.

   Step 2. With the compass at *A*, draw an arc below line *m* using a setting greater than $\frac{1}{2}$ *AB*. Using the same compass setting, draw an arc from *B* that intersects the previous arc. Label the intersection *Q*.

   Step 3. Use a straightedge to draw $\overline{PQ}$.

3. yes; She could find the side lengths and the bottom length by counting units, and then find the angled lengths using the Pythagorean Theorem.

1. Which composition of transformations maps △*ABC* to △*DEF*?

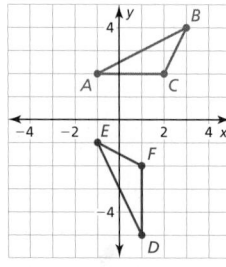

- Ⓐ **Rotation:** 90° counterclockwise about the origin
  Translation: $(x, y) \rightarrow (x + 4, y - 3)$
- Ⓑ **Translation:** $(x, y) \rightarrow (x - 4, y - 3)$
  Rotation: 90° counterclockwise about the origin
- Ⓒ **Translation:** $(x, y) \rightarrow (x + 4, y - 3)$
  Rotation: 90° counterclockwise about the origin
- Ⓓ **Rotation:** 90° counterclockwise about the origin
  Translation: $(x, y) \rightarrow (x - 4, y - 3)$

2. Use the diagrams to describe the steps you would take to construct a line perpendicular to line *m* through point *P*, which is not on line *m*.

Step 1 **Step 2** **Step 3**

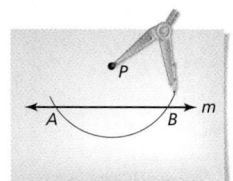 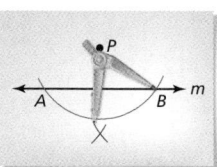 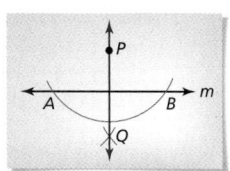

3. Your friend claims that she can find the perimeter of the school crossing sign without using the Distance Formula. Do you support your friend's claim? Explain your reasoning.

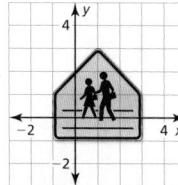

4. Graph the directed line segment ST with endpoints $S(-3, -2)$ and $T(4, 5)$. Then find the coordinates of point P along the directed line segment ST so that the ratio of SP to PT is 3 to 4.

5. The graph shows quadrilateral $WXYZ$ and quadrilateral $ABCD$.

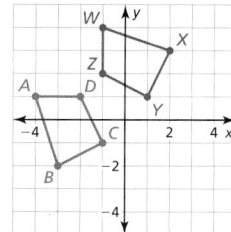

   a. Write a composition of transformations that maps quadrilateral $WXYZ$ to quadrilateral $ABCD$.

   b. Are the quadrilaterals congruent? Explain your reasoning.

6. Which equation represents the line passing through the point $(-6, 3)$ that is parallel to the line $y = -\frac{1}{3}x - 5$?

   Ⓐ $y = 3x + 21$

   Ⓑ $y = -\frac{1}{3}x - 5$

   Ⓒ $y = 3x - 15$

   Ⓓ $y = -\frac{1}{3}x + 1$

7. Which scale factor(s) would create a dilation of $\overline{AB}$ that is shorter than $\overline{AB}$? Select all that apply.

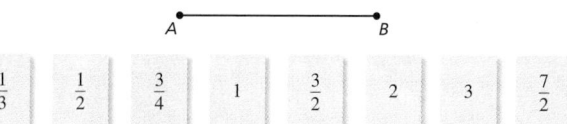

| $\frac{1}{3}$ | $\frac{1}{2}$ | $\frac{3}{4}$ | 1 | $\frac{3}{2}$ | 2 | 3 | $\frac{7}{2}$ |

8. List one possible set of coordinates of the vertices of quadrilateral $ABCD$ for each description.

   a. A reflection in the y-axis maps quadrilateral $ABCD$ onto itself.

   b. A reflection in the x-axis maps quadrilateral $ABCD$ onto itself.

   c. A rotation of $90°$ about the origin maps quadrilateral $ABCD$ onto itself.

   d. A rotation of $180°$ about the origin maps quadrilateral $ABCD$ onto itself.

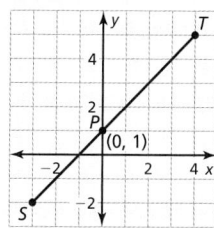

Chapter 5 Pacing Guide

Chapter Opener/ Mathematical Practices	0.5 Day
Section 1	1.5 Days
Section 2	1 Day
Section 3	1 Day
Section 4	2 Days
Quiz	0.5 Day
Section 5	1.5 Days
Section 6	2 Days
Section 7	1 Day
Section 8	2 Days
Chapter Review/ Chapter Tests	2 Days
Total Chapter 5	15 Days
Year-to-Date	63 Days

5 Congruent Triangles

SEE the Big Idea

Hang Glider (p. 278)

Lifeguard Tower (p. 255)

Barn (p. 248)

Home Decor (p. 241)

Painting (p. 235)

Chapter Summary

- In this chapter, students will work with a variety of proof formats as they investigate triangle congruence. Methods for establishing triangle congruence (SAS, SSS, ASA, and AAS) are established using rigid motions.
- The proof of each congruence criteria for triangles is done by composing transformations. This means a sequence of rigid motions maps one triangle onto another triangle.
- Other proof styles presented in this chapter include the two-column proof, the paragraph or narrative proof, and finally, in the last lesson, the coordinate proof.
- In addition to working with proofs, there are properties of equilateral and isosceles triangles that are proven.
- The use of dynamic geometry software for the explorations is highly encouraged. This tool provides students the opportunity to explore and make conjectures, mathematical practices we want to develop in all students.

Scaffolding in the Classroom

Graphic Organizers: Y-Chart

A Y-Chart can be used to compare two topics. Students list differences between the two topics in the branches of the Y and similarities in the base of the Y. A Y-Chart serves as a good tool for assessing students' knowledge of a pair of topics that have subtle but important differences. You can include blank Y-Charts on tests or quizzes for this purpose.

 ## COMMON CORE PROGRESSION

Middle School
- Understand that figures are congruent if they can be related by a sequence of translations, reflections, and rotations.
- Draw triangles with given conditions.
- Find the distance between points with the same x- or y-coordinate.
- Solve two-step equations.

Algebra 1
- Write equations in one variable.
- Solve linear equations that have variables on both sides.
- Graph points and lines in the coordinate plane.
- Use properties of radicals to simplify expressions.

Geometry
- Identify and use corresponding parts.
- Use theorems about the angles of a triangle.
- Use SAS, SSS, HL, ASA, and AAS to prove two triangles congruent.
- Prove constructions.
- Write coordinate proofs.

Standards Summary		
Section	**Common Core State Standards**	
5.1	Learning	HSG-CO.C.10, HSG-MG.A.1
5.2	Learning	HSG-CO.B.7
5.3	Learning	HSG-CO.B.8, HSG-MG.A.1
5.4	Learning	HSG-CO.C.10, HSG-CO.D.13, HSG-MG.A.1
5.5	Learning	HSG-CO.B.8, HSG-MG.A.1, HSG-MG.A.3
5.6	Learning	HSG-CO.B.8
5.7	Learning	HSG-SRT.B.5
5.8	Learning	HSG-GPE.B.4

Questioning in the Classroom

What I really want to know is ...
Have each student write a "pertinent" question on a 3 × 5 card. Collect the cards (check the cards before using them), and randomly select a question to ask the class. After class discussion, the last person to participate randomly selects another question to ask the class.

Laurie's Notes

Maintaining Mathematical Proficiency

Using the Midpoint and Distance Formulas

• Have students review the Midpoint Formula, page 22, and the Distance Formula, page 23.
COMMON ERROR Students may subtract instead of adding when using the Midpoint Formula. Point out that the coordinates of the midpoint of a segment are the means (averages) of the coordinates of the endpoints.

Solving Equations with Variable on Both Sides

• Remind students that the goal is to get the variable alone on one side of the equation.
COMMON ERROR Because students are undoing an equation, addition and subtraction should be undone before multiplication and division—the opposite of the Order of Operations.

Mathematical Practices (continued on page 230)

• The eight *Mathematical Practices* focus attention on how mathematics is learned—process versus content. Page 230 demonstrates the need for students to understand that definitions are biconditional statements. Although a definition may be stated with many fewer words, it can also be written as a biconditional statement.
• Use the *Mathematical Practices* page to help students develop mathematical habits of mind—how mathematics can be explored and how mathematics is thought about.

If students need help...		If students got it...
Student Journal • Maintaining Mathematical Proficiency		Game Closet at *BigIdeasMath.com*
Lesson Tutorials		Start the *next* Section
Skills Review Handbook		

Maintaining Mathematical Proficiency

Using the Midpoint and Distance Formulas

Example 1 The endpoints of $\overline{AB}$ are $A(-2, 3)$ and $B(4, 7)$. Find the coordinates of the midpoint M.

Use the Midpoint Formula.

$$M\left(\frac{-2 + 4}{2}, \frac{3 + 7}{2}\right) = M\left(\frac{2}{2}, \frac{10}{2}\right)$$

$$= M(1, 5)$$

▶ The coordinates of the midpoint M are $(1, 5)$.

Example 2 Find the distance between $C(0, -5)$ and $D(3, 2)$.

$$CD = \sqrt{(x_2 - x_1)^2 + (y_2 - y_1)^2} \quad \text{Distance Formula}$$

$$= \sqrt{(3 - 0)^2 + [2 - (-5)]^2} \quad \text{Substitute.}$$

$$= \sqrt{3^2 + 7^2} \quad \text{Subtract.}$$

$$= \sqrt{9 + 49} \quad \text{Evaluate powers.}$$

$$= \sqrt{58} \quad \text{Add.}$$

$$\approx 7.6 \quad \text{Use a calculator.}$$

▶ The distance between $C(0, -5)$ and $D(3, 2)$ is about 7.6.

Find the coordinates of the midpoint M of the segment with the given endpoints. Then find the distance between the two points.

1. $P(-4, 1)$ and $Q(0, 7)$ 2. $G(3, 6)$ and $H(9, -2)$ 3. $U(-1, -2)$ and $V(8, 0)$

Solving Equations with Variables on Both Sides

Example 3 Solve $2 - 5x = -3x$.

$$2 - 5x = -3x \quad \text{Write the equation.}$$

$$\underline{+5x \quad +5x} \quad \text{Add } 5x \text{ to each side.}$$

$$2 = 2x \quad \text{Simplify.}$$

$$\frac{2}{2} = \frac{2x}{2} \quad \text{Divide each side by 2.}$$

$$1 = x \quad \text{Simplify.}$$

▶ The solution is $x = 1$.

Solve the equation.

4. $7x + 12 = 3x$ 5. $14 - 6t = t$ 6. $5p + 10 = 8p + 1$

7. $w + 13 = 11w - 7$ 8. $4x + 1 = 3 - 2x$ 9. $z - 2 = 4 + 9z$

10. **ABSTRACT REASONING** Is it possible to find the length of a segment in a coordinate plane without using the Distance Formula? Explain your reasoning.

Dynamic Solutions available at *BigIdeasMath.com*

Common Core State Standards

8.G.B.8 … find the distance between two points in a coordinate system.

HSA-REI.B.3 Solve linear equations … in one variable, ….

ANSWERS

1. $M(-2, 4)$; about 7.2 units
2. $M(6, 2)$; 10 units
3. $M\left(\frac{7}{2}, -1\right)$; about 9.2 units
4. $x = -3$
5. $t = 2$
6. $p = 3$
7. $w = 2$
8. $x = \frac{1}{3}$
9. $z = -\frac{3}{4}$
10. yes; The length can be found using the Pythagorean Theorem.

Vocabulary Review

Have students make a Concept Circle for each of the following topics.

- Using the Midpoint Formula to find the midpoint of a segment
- Using the Distance Formula to find the length of a segment
- Solving a linear equation in one variable with the variable on both sides

Mathematical Practices

Mathematically proficient students understand and use given definitions.

Definitions, Postulates, and Theorems

Core Concept

Definitions and Biconditional Statements

A definition is always an "if and only if" statement. Here is an example.

Definition: Two geometric figures are *congruent figures* if and only if there is a rigid motion or a composition of rigid motions that maps one of the figures onto the other.

Because this is a definition, it is a biconditional statement. It implies the following two conditional statements.

1. If two geometric figures are congruent figures, then there is a rigid motion or a composition of rigid motions that maps one of the figures onto the other.

2. If there is a rigid motion or a composition of rigid motions that maps one geometric figure onto another, then the two geometric figures are congruent figures.

Definitions, postulates, and theorems are the building blocks of geometry. In two-column proofs, the statements in the *reason* column are almost always definitions, postulates, or theorems.

EXAMPLE 1 **Identifying Definitions, Postulates, and Theorems**

Classify each statement as a definition, a postulate, or a theorem.

a. If two lines are cut by a transversal so that alternate interior angles are congruent, then the lines are parallel.

b. If two coplanar lines have no point of intersection, then the lines are parallel.

c. If there is a line and a point not on the line, then there is exactly one line through the point parallel to the given line.

SOLUTION

a. This is a theorem. It is the Alternate Interior Angles Converse Theorem (Theorem 3.6) studied in Section 3.3.

b. This is the definition of parallel lines.

c. This is a postulate. It is the Parallel Postulate (Postulate 3.1) studied in Section 3.1. In Euclidean geometry, it is assumed, not proved, to be true.

Monitoring Progress

Classify each statement as a definition, a postulate, or a theorem. Explain your reasoning.

1. In a coordinate plane, two nonvertical lines are perpendicular if and only if the product of their slopes is -1.

2. If two lines intersect to form a linear pair of congruent angles, then the lines are perpendicular.

3. If two lines intersect to form a right angle, then the lines are perpendicular.

4. Through any two points, there exists exactly one line.

Laurie's Notes Mathematical Practices (continued from page T-229)

- Definitions, postulates, theorems, and algebraic properties are generally the justification for most of the statements one makes in writing a proof. It is important that students be able to recognize these building blocks of geometry, particularly when constructing an argument or writing a proof.
- Students should note that in the example all of the statements are written as if-then (conditional) statements.
- Give time for students to work through Questions 1–4, and then discuss as a class.

Overview of Section 5.1

Introduction

- Students should be familiar with both theorems presented in this lesson. There are many explorations students may have done in middle school to discover that the sum of the interior angles of a triangle is 180° and that the measure of an exterior angle of a triangle is equal to the sum of the two nonadjacent interior angles.
- The approach in this lesson is to reason deductively and write a formal proof of these angle relationships. The relationships are then used in problem solving.

Formative Assessment Tips

- We are approaching the middle portion of the book and the year. You should be comfortable with a variety of formative assessment techniques, and students should be comfortable with speaking aloud in class and with partners. The goal of your efforts is certainly to improve teaching and learning as result of the activities carried out during the instructional process. Although formative assessment is often described as a tool to identify certain student conceptions and misconceptions during the instructional phase, it is also a process by which your instruction is improved.
- Some formative assessment techniques are carried out over a period or unit of instruction. Throughout this chapter, you are encouraged to try a particular technique while still integrating and practicing previously learned techniques.
- **Response (Thinking) Logs:** This is a type of writing journal that will be used throughout this chapter after computations, during a conceptual activity, or as part of a problem-solving activity. Students will respond to a short writing prompt or sentence stem, reflecting on what they are learning. In the response log, students record the process they have gone through to learn something new, any questions they may need to have clarified, what they find challenging, or what information they need to have clarified. The response log allows students to make connections to what they have learned, set goals, and reflect on their learning process. The act of writing helps students become more aware of their own learning and what they can do to self-direct it.
- The *Response Log* is private. The purpose is to promote metacognition. If there are times when you want to collect the response logs, perhaps because you sense a need to redirect your instruction, students should be told this. If there is a possibility that the response log will not remain private, I let my students know this.
- Provide 4–6 pieces of lined paper stapled together or, alternatively, have students set aside a place in their spiral notebooks. On the left one-third of the paper, the writing stem or prompt is written. The right two-thirds of the paper is where the response is written. I have a large poster in my room with writing stems listed. Throughout the year, students suggest additions to the writing stems.
- I suggest writing stems throughout, though you should feel free to substitute or leave open for student selection any of the writing stems. For a beginning list of writing stems, see page T-238.

Pacing Suggestion

- Complete the explorations and discuss students' observations. Transition to the formal lesson.

Dynamic Teaching Tools
Dynamic Assessment & Progress Monitoring Tool
Lesson Planning Tool
Interactive Whiteboard Lesson Library
Dynamic Classroom with Dynamic Investigations

**Common Core
State Standards**

HSG-CO.C.10 Prove theorems about triangles.

HSG-MG.A.1 Use geometric shapes, their measures, and their properties to describe objects (e.g., modeling a tree trunk or a human torso as a cylinder).

Laurie's Notes

Exploration

Motivate
- Before students arrive, cut out large models of triangles. My set of seven triangles is laminated because I use them throughout the year for different discussions.
- Here's a sample of triangles to cut:

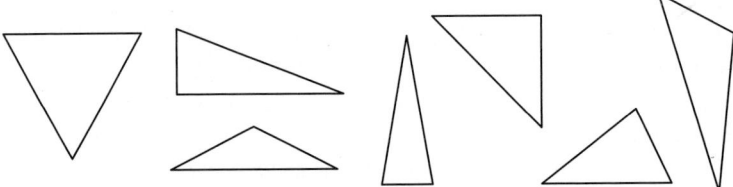

- Ask for seven volunteers. Hand each of them a triangle.
- Have students sort the triangles by angle measure and then by side length.
- **?** "What do they all have in common?" three sides; three angles; The interior angles sum to 180°.
- Explain that in today's lesson the vocabulary of triangles will be reviewed, and students will prove their conjecture about the sum of the interior angles of a triangle.

Exploration 1
- It is quite likely that students are aware that the interior angles of a triangle sum to 180°. The focus of the exploration, therefore, is on the process. Students are using a tool to investigate a relationship and as a result of inductive reasoning a conjecture is made.
- This process can be contrasted with the deductive approach in the lesson.
- Check that students are using the dynamic aspect of the software.

Exploration 2
- This exploration, as written, is direct in telling students what to measure. Therefore, students do not discover the relationship between an exterior angle and the two nonadjacent interior angles. If you wish students to have the opportunity for this discovery, then change the directions.
- **Another Way:**
  - Use dynamic geometry software to draw any △ABC and an exterior angle at any vertex.
  - **?** "How does the measure of the exterior angle compare to one or more of the interior angles?" *Sample conjectures*: The exterior angle is supplementary to the adjacent interior angle. The exterior angle can be acute, right, or obtuse. The exterior angle can be congruent to at most one interior angle.
  - Make your conjecture(s). Draw several triangles and test your conjecture(s).
- Regardless of approach, students are using inductive reasoning to make a conjecture.

Communicate Your Answer
- Have students share their reasoning for Question 4.

Connecting to Next Step
- The explorations provide an opportunity for students to make conjectures about angle relationships in a triangle. These conjectures will be proven deductively in the formal lesson.

5.1 Angles of Triangles

Essential Question How are the angle measures of a triangle related?

EXPLORATION 1 **Writing a Conjecture**

Work with a partner.

a. Use dynamic geometry software to draw any triangle and label it $\triangle ABC$.

b. Find the measures of the interior angles of the triangle.

c. Find the sum of the interior angle measures.

d. Repeat parts (a)–(c) with several other triangles. Then write a conjecture about the sum of the measures of the interior angles of a triangle.

CONSTRUCTING VIABLE ARGUMENTS

To be proficient in math, you need to reason inductively about data and write conjectures.

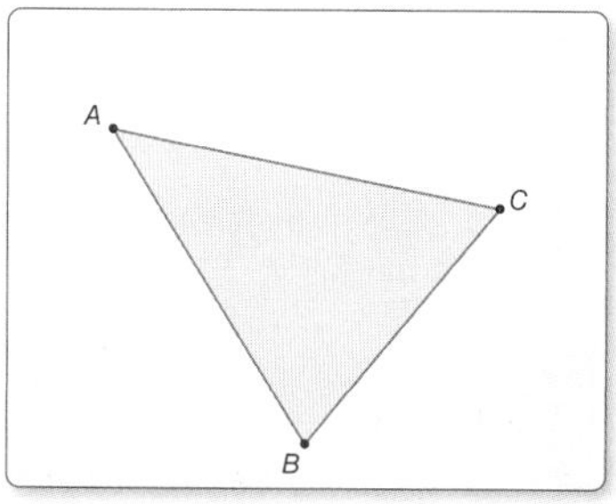

Sample

Angles

$m\angle A = 43.67°$

$m\angle B = 81.87°$

$m\angle C = 54.46°$

EXPLORATION 2 **Writing a Conjecture**

Work with a partner.

a. Use dynamic geometry software to draw any triangle and label it $\triangle ABC$.

b. Draw an exterior angle at any vertex and find its measure.

c. Find the measures of the two nonadjacent interior angles of the triangle.

d. Find the sum of the measures of the two nonadjacent interior angles. Compare this sum to the measure of the exterior angle.

e. Repeat parts (a)–(d) with several other triangles. Then write a conjecture that compares the measure of an exterior angle with the sum of the measures of the two nonadjacent interior angles.

Sample

Angles

$m\angle A = 43.67°$

$m\angle B = 81.87°$

$m\angle ACD = 125.54°$

Communicate Your Answer

3. How are the angle measures of a triangle related?

4. An exterior angle of a triangle measures 32°. What do you know about the measures of the interior angles? Explain your reasoning.

Dynamic Teaching Tools

- Dynamic Assessment & Progress Monitoring Tool
- Lesson Planning Tool
- Interactive Whiteboard Lesson Library
- Dynamic Classroom with Dynamic Investigations

ANSWERS

1. a. Check students' work.

b. Check students' work.

c. 180°

d. Check students' work; The sum of the measures of the interior angles of a triangle is 180°.

2. a. Check students' work.

b. Check students' work.

c. Check students' work.

d. Check students' work; The sum is equal to the measure of the exterior angle.

e. Check students' work; The measure of an exterior angle of a triangle is equal to the sum of the measures of the two nonadjacent interior angles.

3. The sum of the measures of the interior angles of a triangle is 180°, and the measure of an exterior angle of a triangle is equal to the sum of the measures of the two nonadjacent interior angles.

4. The sum of the measures of the two nonadjacent interior angles is 32°, and the measure of the adjacent interior angle is 148°; These are known because of the conjectures made in Explorations 1 and 2.

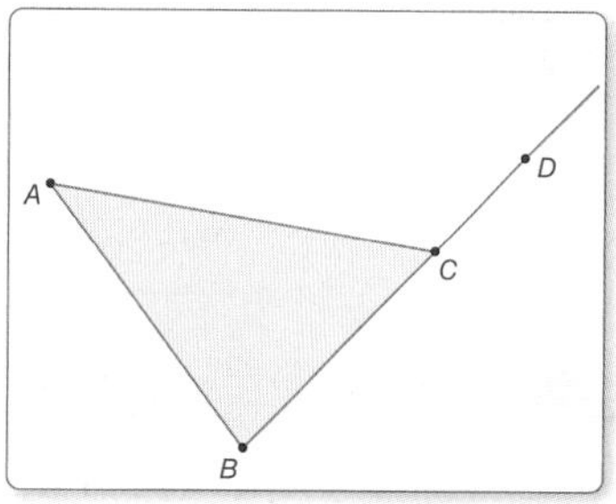

Extra Example 1

Classify the triangular shape of the support beams in the diagram by its sides and by measuring its angles.

scalene right triangle

MONITORING PROGRESS ANSWER

1. *Sample answer:*

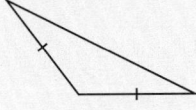 

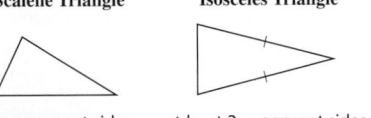

5.1 Lesson

Core Vocabulary

interior angles, *p. 233*
exterior angles, *p. 233*
corollary to a theorem, *p. 235*

Previous
triangle

What You Will Learn

▶ Classify triangles by sides and angles.

▶ Find interior and exterior angle measures of triangles.

Classifying Triangles by Sides and by Angles

Recall that a *triangle* is a polygon with three sides. You can classify triangles by sides and by angles, as shown below.

🔑 Core Concept

Classifying Triangles by Sides

Scalene Triangle	Isosceles Triangle	Equilateral Triangle
no congruent sides	at least 2 congruent sides	3 congruent sides

Classifying Triangles by Angles

Acute Triangle	Right Triangle	Obtuse Triangle	Equiangular Triangle
3 acute angles	1 right angle	1 obtuse angle	3 congruent angles

---

EXAMPLE 1   **Classifying Triangles by Sides and by Angles**

Classify the triangular shape of the support beams in the diagram by its sides and by measuring its angles.

SOLUTION

The triangle has a pair of congruent sides, so it is isosceles. By measuring, the angles are 55°, 55°, and 70°.

▶ So, it is an acute isosceles triangle.

Monitoring Progress Help in English and Spanish at *BigIdeasMath.com*

1. Draw an obtuse isosceles triangle and an acute scalene triangle.

Laurie's Notes   Teacher Actions

- **Whiteboarding:** State the name of each type of triangle, and have students draw a sketch. Students should mark enough information on the triangle to convey knowledge of the definition of the triangle.

- **Probing Question:** Have students sketch triangles that are specified by sides and angles, where not all are possible. *Examples*: acute isosceles; right scalene; obtuse equilateral (not possible); acute scalene

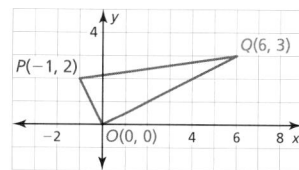

EXAMPLE 2 Classifying a Triangle in the Coordinate Plane

Classify $\triangle OPQ$ by its sides. Then determine whether it is a right triangle.

SOLUTION

Step 1 Use the Distance Formula to find the side lengths.

$$OP = \sqrt{(x_2 - x_1)^2 + (y_2 - y_1)^2} = \sqrt{(-1 - 0)^2 + (2 - 0)^2} = \sqrt{5} \approx 2.2$$

$$OQ = \sqrt{(x_2 - x_1)^2 + (y_2 - y_1)^2} = \sqrt{(6 - 0)^2 + (3 - 0)^2} = \sqrt{45} \approx 6.7$$

$$PQ = \sqrt{(x_2 - x_1)^2 + (y_2 - y_1)^2} = \sqrt{[6 - (-1)]^2 + (3 - 2)^2} = \sqrt{50} \approx 7.1$$

Because no sides are congruent, $\triangle OPQ$ is a scalene triangle.

Step 2 Check for right angles. The slope of $\overline{OP}$ is $\frac{2 - 0}{-1 - 0} = -2$. The slope of $\overline{OQ}$ is $\frac{3 - 0}{6 - 0} = \frac{1}{2}$. The product of the slopes is $-2\left(\frac{1}{2}\right) = -1$. So, $\overline{OP} \perp \overline{OQ}$ and $\angle POQ$ is a right angle.

▶ So, $\triangle OPQ$ is a right scalene triangle.

Monitoring Progress 🔊 Help in English and Spanish at *BigIdeasMath.com*

2. $\triangle ABC$ has vertices $A(0, 0)$, $B(3, 3)$, and $C(-3, 3)$. Classify the triangle by its sides. Then determine whether it is a right triangle.

Finding Angle Measures of Triangles

When the sides of a polygon are extended, other angles are formed. The original angles are the **interior angles**. The angles that form linear pairs with the interior angles are the **exterior angles**.

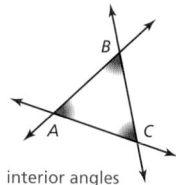

interior angles

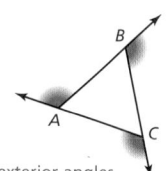

exterior angles

🔄 Theorem

Theorem 5.1 Triangle Sum Theorem

The sum of the measures of the interior angles of a triangle is 180°.

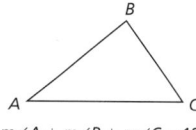

Proof p. 234; Ex. 53, p. 238

$$m\angle A + m\angle B + m\angle C = 180°$$

Differentiated Instruction

Kinesthetic
Have students draw a large triangle on a sheet of paper and cut it out. Then tear off the "corners." Arrange the torn pieces so that their vertices coincide and form three adjacent angles. Based on their arrangement, ask students what appears to be true about the sum of the measures of the three interior angles in a triangle.

Extra Example 2
Classify $\triangle ABC$ by its sides. Then determine whether it is a right triangle.

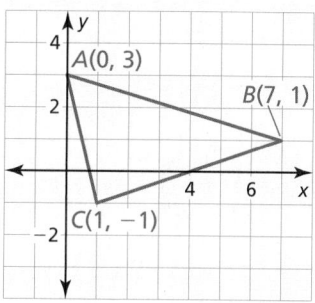

$\triangle ABC$ is a scalene acute triangle. It is not a right triangle.

MONITORING PROGRESS ANSWER

2. isosceles; right

Laurie's Notes | Teacher Actions

? State the coordinates of $\triangle OPQ$. "How can you classify the triangle by its sides and angles?" Use the Distance Formula to find the length of each side of the triangle. Find the slopes of the sides to see whether two sides are perpendicular.

- **MP3 Construct Viable Arguments and Critique the Reasoning of Others:** Some students will try to answer by simply graphing and using eyesight. Students must be able to provide a viable argument, and eyesight is not sufficient!
- **Common Misconception:** There are two exterior angles at each vertex, not just one.

Extra Example 3

Find $m\angle PQS$.

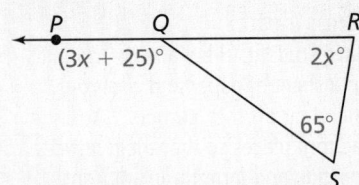

$m\angle PQS = 145°$

To prove certain theorems, you may need to add a line, a segment, or a ray to a given diagram. An *auxiliary* line is used in the proof of the Triangle Sum Theorem.

PROOF **Triangle Sum Theorem**

Given $\triangle ABC$

Prove $m\angle 1 + m\angle 2 + m\angle 3 = 180°$

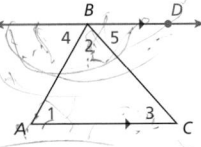

Plan for Proof
  a. Draw an auxiliary line through B that is parallel to $\overleftrightarrow{AC}$.
  b. Show that $m\angle 4 + m\angle 2 + m\angle 5 = 180°$, $\angle 1 \cong \angle 4$, and $\angle 3 \cong \angle 5$.
  c. By substitution, $m\angle 1 + m\angle 2 + m\angle 3 = 180°$.

Plan in Action	STATEMENTS	REASONS
a.	**1.** Draw $\overleftrightarrow{BD}$ parallel to $\overleftrightarrow{AC}$.	**1.** Parallel Postulate (Post. 3.1)
b.	**2.** $m\angle 4 + m\angle 2 + m\angle 5 = 180°$	**2.** Angle Addition Postulate (Post. 1.4) and definition of straight angle
	3. $\angle 1 \cong \angle 4, \angle 3 \cong \angle 5$	**3.** Alternate Interior Angles Theorem (Thm. 3.2)
	4. $m\angle 1 = m\angle 4, m\angle 3 = m\angle 5$	**4.** Definition of congruent angles
c.	**5.** $m\angle 1 + m\angle 2 + m\angle 3 = 180°$	**5.** Substitution Property of Equality

⑤ Theorem

Theorem 5.2 Exterior Angle Theorem

The measure of an exterior angle of a triangle is equal to the sum of the measures of the two nonadjacent interior angles.

Proof Ex. 42, p. 237

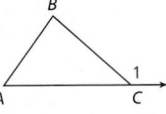

$m\angle 1 = m\angle A + m\angle B$

EXAMPLE 3 **Finding an Angle Measure**

Find $m\angle JKM$.

SOLUTION

Step 1 Write and solve an equation to find the value of x.

$(2x - 5)° = 70° + x°$ Apply the Exterior Angle Theorem.

$x = 75$ Solve for x.

Step 2 Substitute 75 for x in $2x - 5$ to find $m\angle JKM$.

$2x - 5 = 2 \cdot 75 - 5 = 145$

▶ So, the measure of $\angle JKM$ is $145°$.

Laurie's Notes Teacher Actions

- Draw $\triangle ABC$ and label $\angle 1$, $\angle 2$, and $\angle 3$. Draw and explain what an auxiliary line is.
- **Turn and Talk:** "How could you prove that the three angles sum to 180°?" Give partners time to talk and plan. Use *Popsicle Sticks* to solicit suggestions from students. Write a proof for this theorem.
- Repeat a similar process for *the Exterior Angle Theorem*, but do not write a proof if it is part of the homework assignment.
- **Response Logs:** "Right now I am thinking about …"

A **corollary to a theorem** is a statement that can be proved easily using the theorem. The corollary below follows from the Triangle Sum Theorem.

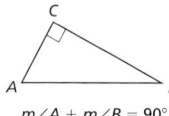 **Corollary**

Corollary 5.1 Corollary to the Triangle Sum Theorem

The acute angles of a right triangle are complementary.

$$m\angle A + m\angle B = 90°$$

Proof Ex. 41, p. 237

EXAMPLE 4 Modeling with Mathematics

In the painting, the red triangle is a right triangle. The measure of one acute angle in the triangle is twice the measure of the other. Find the measure of each acute angle.

SOLUTION

1. **Understand the Problem** You are given a right triangle and the relationship between the two acute angles in the triangle. You need to find the measure of each acute angle.

2. **Make a Plan** First, sketch a diagram of the situation. You can use the Corollary to the Triangle Sum Theorem and the given relationship between the two acute angles to write and solve an equation to find the measure of each acute angle.

3. **Solve the Problem** Let the measure of the smaller acute angle be $x°$. Then the measure of the larger acute angle is $2x°$. The Corollary to the Triangle Sum Theorem states that the acute angles of a right triangle are complementary.

   Use the corollary to set up and solve an equation.

   $$x° + 2x° = 90°$$ Corollary to the Triangle Sum Theorem
   $$x = 30$$ Solve for x.

   ▶ So, the measures of the acute angles are 30° and 2(30°) = 60°.

4. **Look Back** Add the two angles and check that their sum satisfies the Corollary to the Triangle Sum Theorem.

   $$30° + 60° = 90°\ ✓$$

Monitoring Progress ◀))) Help in English and Spanish at *BigIdeasMath.com*

3. Find the measure of $\angle 1$.

4. Find the measure of each acute angle.

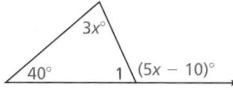

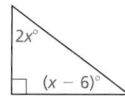

Extra Example 4
The measure of one acute angle of a right triangle is 1.5 times the measure of the other acute angle. Find the measure of each acute angle.
36° and 54°

MONITORING PROGRESS ANSWERS
3. 65°
4. 64°, 26°

| **Laurie's Notes** | **Teacher Actions** |

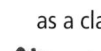

? Fact-First Questioning: "The acute angles of a right triangle are complementary. Explain why." Listen for valid reasoning.

- Explain what a corollary is, and write the Corollary to the Triangle Sum Theorem.
- **Think-Pair-Share:** Have students answer Questions 3 and 4, and then share and discuss as a class.

Closure

- **Response Logs:** "I figured out that …", or "What is confusing me the most is …."

ANSWERS

1. no; By the Corollary to the Triangle Sum Theorem (Cor. 5.1), the acute angles of a right triangle are complementary. Because their measures have to add up to 90°, neither angle could have a measure greater than 90°.

2. nonadjacent

3. right isosceles

4. equiangular equilateral

5. obtuse scalene

6. acute scalene

7. isosceles; right

8. isosceles; not right

9. scalene; not right

10. scalene; right

11. 71°; acute

12. 110°; obtuse

13. 52°; right

14. 60°; equiangular

15. 139°

16. 92°

17. 114°

18. 68°

19. 36°, 54°

20. 22°, 68°

21. 37°, 53°

22. 34°, 56°

Vocabulary and Core Concept Check

1. **WRITING** Can a right triangle also be obtuse? Explain your reasoning.

2. **COMPLETE THE SENTENCE** The measure of an exterior angle of a triangle is equal to the sum of the measures of the two _____ interior angles.

Monitoring Progress and Modeling with Mathematics

In Exercises 3–6, classify the triangle by its sides and by measuring its angles. *(See Example 1.)*

3.
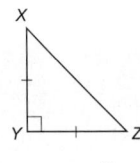

4.
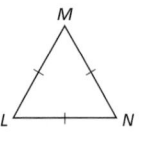

5.
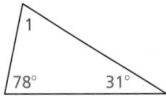

6.

In Exercises 7–10, classify △ABC by its sides. Then determine whether it is a right triangle. *(See Example 2.)*

7. $A(2, 3), B(6, 3), C(2, 7)$

8. $A(3, 3), B(6, 9), C(6, -3)$

9. $A(1, 9), B(4, 8), C(2, 5)$

10. $A(-2, 3), B(0, -3), C(3, -2)$

In Exercises 11–14, find $m\angle 1$. Then classify the triangle by its angles.

11.
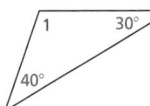

12.
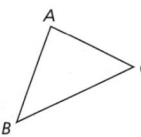

13.

14.

In Exercises 15–18, find the measure of the exterior angle. *(See Example 3.)*

15.
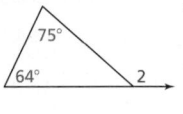

16.
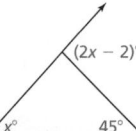

17.
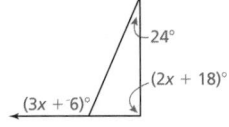

18.
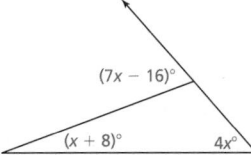

In Exercises 19–22, find the measure of each acute angle. *(See Example 4.)*

19.
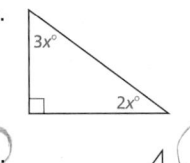

20.
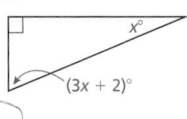

21.
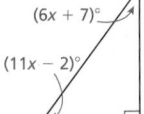

22.

In Exercises 23–26, find the measure of each acute angle in the right triangle. *(See Example 4.)*

23. The measure of one acute angle is 5 times the measure of the other acute angle.

24. The measure of one acute angle is 8 times the measure of the other acute angle.

25. The measure of one acute angle is 3 times the sum of the measure of the other acute angle and 8.

26. The measure of one acute angle is twice the difference of the measure of the other acute angle and 12.

ERROR ANALYSIS In Exercises 27 and 28, describe and correct the error in finding $m\angle 1$.

27.

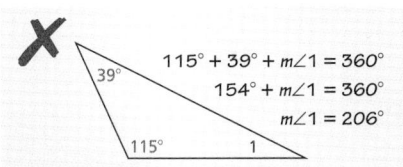

$$115° + 39° + m\angle 1 = 360°$$
$$154° + m\angle 1 = 360°$$
$$m\angle 1 = 206°$$

28.

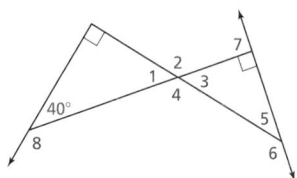

$$m\angle 1 + 80° + 50° = 180°$$
$$m\angle 1 + 130° = 180°$$
$$m\angle 1 = 50°$$

In Exercises 29–36, find the measure of the numbered angle.

29. $\angle 1$ **30.** $\angle 2$

31. $\angle 3$ **32.** $\angle 4$

33. $\angle 5$ **34.** $\angle 6$

35. $\angle 7$ **36.** $\angle 8$

---

37. USING TOOLS Three people are standing on a stage. The distances between the three people are shown in the diagram. Classify the triangle by its sides and by measuring its angles.

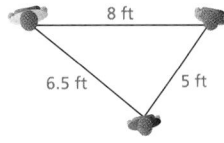

38. USING STRUCTURE Which of the following sets of angle measures could form a triangle? Select all that apply.

Ⓐ 100°, 50°, 40°   Ⓑ 96°, 74°, 10°

Ⓒ 165°, 113°, 82°   Ⓓ 101°, 41°, 38°

Ⓔ 90°, 45°, 45°   Ⓕ 84°, 62°, 34°

39. MODELING WITH MATHEMATICS You are bending a strip of metal into an isosceles triangle for a sculpture. The strip of metal is 20 inches long. The first bend is made 6 inches from one end. Describe two ways you could complete the triangle.

40. THOUGHT PROVOKING Find and draw an object (or part of an object) that can be modeled by a triangle and an exterior angle. Describe the relationship between the interior angles of the triangle and the exterior angle in terms of the object.

41. PROVING A COROLLARY Prove the Corollary to the Triangle Sum Theorem (Corollary 5.1).

Given $\triangle ABC$ is a right triangle.

Prove $\angle A$ and $\angle B$ are complementary.

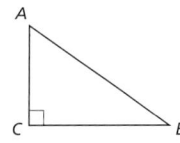

42. PROVING A THEOREM Prove the Exterior Angle Theorem (Theorem 5.2).

Given $\triangle ABC$, exterior $\angle BCD$

Prove $m\angle A + m\angle B = m\angle BCD$

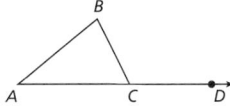

Section 5.1   Angles of Triangles   **237**

ANSWERS

23. 15°, 75°

24. 10°, 80°

25. 16.5°, 73.5°

26. 38°, 52°

27. The sum of the measures of the angles should be 180°;

$$115° + 39° + m\angle 1 = 180°$$
$$154° + m\angle 1 = 180°$$
$$m\angle 1 = 26°$$

28. The measure of the exterior angle should be equal to the sum of the measures of the two nonadjacent interior angles;

$$m\angle 1 = 80° + 50°$$
$$m\angle 1 = 130°$$

29. 50°

30. 130°

31. 50°

32. 130°

33. 40°

34. 140°

35. 90°

36. 140°

37. acute scalene

38. B, D, E, F

39. You could make another bend 6 inches from the first bend and leave the last side 8 inches long, or you could make another bend 7 inches from the first bend and then the last side will also be 7 inches long.

40. *Sample answer:*

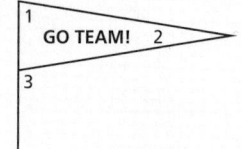

When a triangular pennant is on a stick, the two angles on the top edge of the pennant ($\angle 1$ and $\angle 2$) should have measures such that their sum is equal to the measure of the angle formed by the stick and the bottom edge of the pennant ($\angle 3$).

41–42. See Additional Answers.

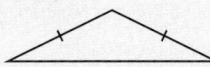
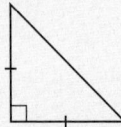
Mini-Assessment

1. Classify the triangle by its sides and by measuring its angles.

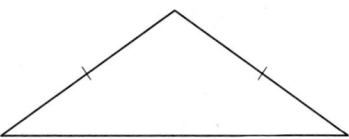

obtuse isosceles triangle

2. Find the measure of the exterior angle.

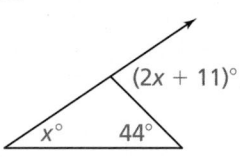

77°

3. The measure of one acute angle of a right triangle is 6 less than twice the measure of the other acute angle. Find the measure of each acute angle. 32° and 58°

4. △ABC has vertices $A(-6, 2)$, $B(5, -1)$, and $C(4, 4)$. Classify △ABC by its sides. Then determine whether it is a right triangle. scalene triangle; yes, it is a right triangle.

---

43. CRITICAL THINKING Is it possible to draw an obtuse isosceles triangle? obtuse equilateral triangle? If so, provide examples. If not, explain why it is not possible.

44. CRITICAL THINKING Is it possible to draw a right isosceles triangle? right equilateral triangle? If so, provide an example. If not, explain why it is not possible.

45. MATHEMATICAL CONNECTIONS △ABC is isosceles, $AB = x$, and $BC = 2x - 4$.

a. Find two possible values for x when the perimeter of △ABC is 32.

b. How many possible values are there for x when the perimeter of △ABC is 12?

46. HOW DO YOU SEE IT? Classify the triangles, in as many ways as possible, without finding any measurements.

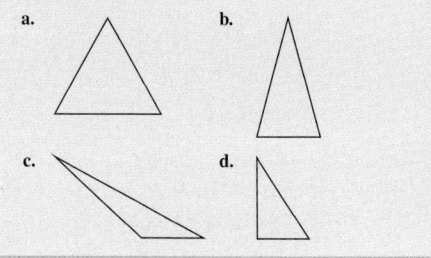

a.   **b.**

c.   **d.**

47. ANALYZING RELATIONSHIPS Which of the following could represent the measures of an exterior angle and two interior angles of a triangle? Select all that apply.

Ⓐ 100°, 62°, 38°   Ⓑ 81°, 57°, 24°

Ⓒ 119°, 68°, 49°   Ⓓ 95°, 85°, 28°

Ⓔ 92°, 78°, 68°   Ⓕ 149°, 101°, 48°

48. MAKING AN ARGUMENT Your friend claims the measure of an exterior angle will always be greater than the sum of the nonadjacent interior angle measures. Is your friend correct? Explain your reasoning.

MATHEMATICAL CONNECTIONS In Exercises 49–52, find the values of x and y.

49.

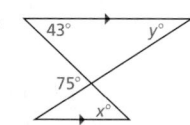

50.

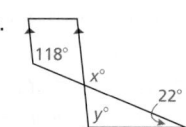

51.   **52.**

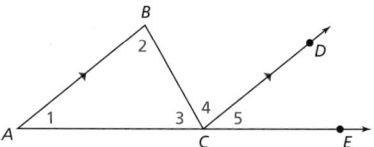

53. PROVING A THEOREM Use the diagram to write a proof of the Triangle Sum Theorem (Theorem 5.1). Your proof should be different from the proof of the Triangle Sum Theorem shown in this lesson.

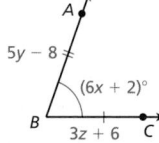

Maintaining Mathematical Proficiency   Reviewing what you learned in previous grades and lessons

Use the diagram to find the measure of the segment or angle. *(Section 1.2 and Section 1.5)*

54. $m\angle KHL$

55. $m\angle ABC$

56. GH

57. BC

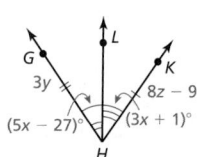

If students need help...

If students need help...	If students got it...
Resources by Chapter • Practice A and Practice B • Puzzle Time	Resources by Chapter • Enrichment and Extension • Cumulative Review
Student Journal • Practice	Start the *next* Section
Differentiating the Lesson Skills Review Handbook	

Overview of Section 5.2

Introduction

- Students have previously studied congruent angles and congruent segments. In this lesson, congruency is extended to polygons. Students will identify and use corresponding parts of congruent polygons to solve problems.
- A rigid motion is an isometry, so segment lengths and angle measures are preserved. This allows us to say that the corresponding parts of congruent figures are congruent.
- The properties of congruence—reflexive, symmetric, and transitive—are stated for triangles.
- The Third Angles Theorem (Thm. 5.4) is presented, with the proof left for the exercises.

Resources

- Tracing paper and dynamic geometry software are used in the explorations.

Common Misconceptions

- When naming congruent polygons that have more than three sides, you need to pay attention to how the vertices are listed. Given $ABCD \cong WXYZ$, it is not true that $ACDB \cong WYZX$ even though the same letters are still matched in each statement. The vertices must be in order when naming the polygon. $\overline{AC}$ is a diagonal, not a side.

Formative Assessment Tips

- Refer to page T-230 for a description of *Response Logs*. In this lesson and throughout this chapter, there will be sentence stems to prompt student writing. Use your judgment for placement in the lesson, amount of time to allow for writing, and the actual sentence stem given to students.
- Beginning list of writing stems:

A sticky part for me is …	At first I thought … but now I think …
I am feeling good about …	I didn't expect …
I feel confident about …	I feel like I made progress today …
I figured out that …	I figured these out because …
I got stuck …	I learned to …
I made progress with …	I need to rethink…
I was really surprised when …	I was successful in …
I will understand this better if I …	I wish I could …
I wish I had …	I'm not sure …
I'm still not sure about …	It helped me today when …
Right now I am thinking about …	Right now I know …
Right now I need to …	The hardest part right now is …
Tomorrow I need to find out …	What confused me the most was …
What is confusing me the most is …	What is puzzling me the most is …

Pacing Suggestion

- Complete the explorations and then start the formal lesson with a discussion of corresponding parts of congruent figures.

Dynamic Teaching Tools

Dynamic Assessment & Progress Monitoring Tool
Lesson Planning Tool
Interactive Whiteboard Lesson Library
Dynamic Classroom with Dynamic Investigations

Common Core State Standards

HSG-CO.B.7 Use the definition of congruence in terms of rigid motions to show that two triangles are congruent if and only if corresponding pairs of sides and corresponding pairs of angles are congruent.

Laurie's Notes

Exploration

Motivate

- **Story Time:** Tell students about an antique patchwork quilt that you purchased recently that needs a bit of repair. There are several triangular pieces, each different from the others, that are worn and need to be replaced.
- **?** "What would a quilt restorer need to measure in order to repair the quilt?" Students should recognize that there are three sides and three angles for each triangle and these six parts would need to be measured.

Exploration Note

- To show that two triangles are congruent using a transformational approach, you need to perform one or more rigid motions to map one triangle to the other. In Exploration 2, students explore what this would look like for a triangle that begins in Quadrant II and, after a composition of rigid motions, has its image in Quadrant IV.

Exploration 1

- This first exploration should be a fairly quick discussion between partners. Have students share their thinking.

Exploration 2

- This exploration can be challenging for students with weaker spatial skills.
- **Teaching Tip:** Use tracing paper and draw $\triangle ABC$. Students can manipulate the tracing paper to make a conjecture about the composition of rigid motions needed to map $\triangle ABC$ to $\triangle DEF$.
- Circulate to see that students are making a conjecture about the rigid motions that map $\triangle ABC$ to $\triangle DEF$ versus using trial and error with the dynamic software.
- **?** "What do you know about $\triangle ABC$ and $\triangle DEF$? Explain." They are congruent. Listen for valid reasoning.
- **Extension:** Have students explore the orientation, clockwise (CW) or counter-clockwise (CCW), of the letters labeling the vertices of the triangle. A reflection will change the orientation of the letters. For the original figure, $\triangle ABC$, the orientation of the letters is CCW. If the orientation of the letters in $\triangle DEF$ is CW, then an odd number of reflections have been performed. If the orientation of the letters in $\triangle DEF$ is CCW, then no reflection has occurred or an even number of reflections have been performed.

Communicate Your Answer

- Listen to student discussion. A composition of isometries results in the image being congruent to the original figure.

Connecting to Next Step

- The explorations use rigid motions taught in the previous chapter to introduce corresponding parts of congruent figures, which are presented in the formal lesson.

5.2 Congruent Polygons

Essential Question Given two congruent triangles, how can you use rigid motions to map one triangle to the other triangle?

Dynamic Teaching Tools

Dynamic Assessment & Progress Monitoring Tool

Lesson Planning Tool

Interactive Whiteboard Lesson Library

Dynamic Classroom with Dynamic Investigations

EXPLORATION 1 **Describing Rigid Motions**

Work with a partner. Of the four transformations you studied in Chapter 4, which are rigid motions? Under a rigid motion, why is the image of a triangle always congruent to the original triangle? Explain your reasoning.

LOOKING FOR STRUCTURE

To be proficient in math, you need to look closely to discern a pattern or structure.

Translation   Reflection   Rotation   Dilation

EXPLORATION 2 **Finding a Composition of Rigid Motions**

Work with a partner. Describe a composition of rigid motions that maps △ABC to △DEF. Use dynamic geometry software to verify your answer.

a. △ABC ≅ △DEF

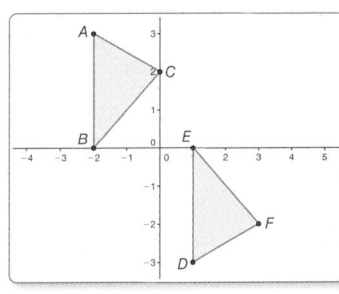

b. △ABC ≅ △DEF

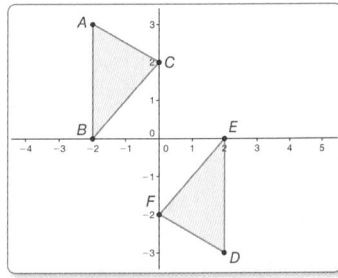

c. △ABC ≅ △DEF

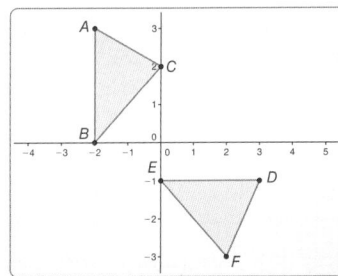

d. △ABC ≅ △DEF

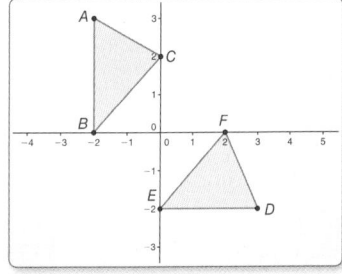

Communicate Your Answer

3. Given two congruent triangles, how can you use rigid motions to map one triangle to the other triangle?

4. The vertices of △ABC are $A(1, 1)$, $B(3, 2)$, and $C(4, 4)$. The vertices of △DEF are $D(2, -1)$, $E(0, 0)$, and $F(-1, 2)$. Describe a composition of rigid motions that maps △ABC to △DEF.

Section 5.2   Congruent Polygons   **239**

ANSWERS

1. translation, reflection, rotation; A rigid motion maps each part of a figure to a corresponding part of its image. Because rigid motions preserve length and angle measure, corresponding parts of a figure and its image are congruent. In triangles, this means that the corresponding sides and corresponding angles are congruent, which is sufficient to say that the triangles are congruent.

2. **a.** *Sample answer:* a translation 3 units right followed by a reflection in the *x*-axis

   b. *Sample answer:* a 180° rotation about the origin

   c. *Sample answer:* a 270° counterclockwise rotation about the origin followed by a translation 3 units down

   d. *Sample answer:* a 270° clockwise rotation about the origin followed by a reflection in the *y*-axis

3. Look at the orientation of the original triangle and decide which rigid motion or composition of rigid motions will result in the same orientation as the second triangle. Then, if necessary, use a translation to move the first triangle so that it coincides with the second.

4. *Sample answer:* a reflection in the *y*-axis followed by a translation 3 units right and 2 units down

Extra Example 1

Write a congruence statement for the triangles. Identify all pairs of congruent corresponding parts.

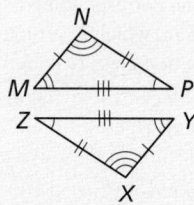

$\triangle MNP \cong \triangle YXZ$; $\angle N \cong \angle X$, $\angle P \cong \angle Z$, $\angle M \cong \angle Y$, $\overline{MN} \cong \overline{YX}$, $\overline{NP} \cong \overline{XZ}$, $\overline{PM} \cong \overline{ZY}$

5.2 Lesson

Core Vocabulary

corresponding parts, p. 240

Previous
congruent figures

STUDY TIP

Notice that both of the following statements are true.

1. If two triangles are congruent, then all their corresponding parts are congruent.

2. If all the corresponding parts of two triangles are congruent, then the triangles are congruent.

VISUAL REASONING

To help you identify corresponding parts, rotate $\triangle TSR$.

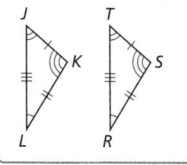

What You Will Learn

▶ Identify and use corresponding parts.

▶ Use the Third Angles Theorem.

Identifying and Using Corresponding Parts

Recall that two geometric figures are congruent if and only if a rigid motion or a composition of rigid motions maps one of the figures onto the other. A rigid motion maps each part of a figure to a **corresponding part** of its image. Because rigid motions preserve length and angle measure, corresponding parts of congruent figures are congruent. In congruent polygons, this means that the *corresponding sides* and the *corresponding angles* are congruent.

When $\triangle DEF$ is the image of $\triangle ABC$ after a rigid motion or a composition of rigid motions, you can write congruence statements for the corresponding angles and corresponding sides.

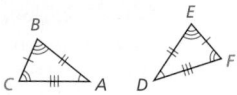

Corresponding angles	**Corresponding sides**
$\angle A \cong \angle D$, $\angle B \cong \angle E$, $\angle C \cong \angle F$	$\overline{AB} \cong \overline{DE}$, $\overline{BC} \cong \overline{EF}$, $\overline{AC} \cong \overline{DF}$

When you write a congruence statement for two polygons, always list the corresponding vertices in the same order. You can write congruence statements in more than one way. Two possible congruence statements for the triangles above are $\triangle ABC \cong \triangle DEF$ or $\triangle BCA \cong \triangle EFD$.

When all the corresponding parts of two triangles are congruent, you can show that the triangles are congruent. Using the triangles above, first translate $\triangle ABC$ so that point A maps to point D. This translation maps $\triangle ABC$ to $\triangle DB'C'$. Next, rotate $\triangle DB'C'$ counterclockwise through $\angle C'DF$ so that the image of $\overrightarrow{DC'}$ coincides with $\overrightarrow{DF}$. Because $\overline{DC'} \cong \overline{DF}$, the rotation maps point C' to point F. So, this rotation maps $\triangle DB'C'$ to $\triangle DB''F$.

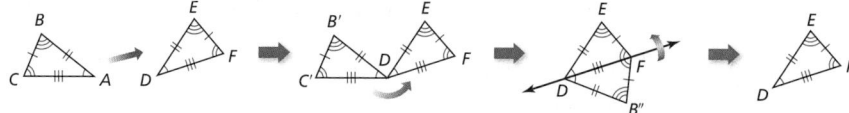

Now, reflect $\triangle DB''F$ in the line through points D and F. This reflection maps the sides and angles of $\triangle DB''F$ to the corresponding sides and corresponding angles of $\triangle DEF$, so $\triangle ABC \cong \triangle DEF$.

So, to show that two triangles are congruent, it is sufficient to show that their corresponding parts are congruent. In general, this is true for all polygons.

EXAMPLE 1   Identifying Corresponding Parts

Write a congruence statement for the triangles. Identify all pairs of congruent corresponding parts.

SOLUTION

The diagram indicates that $\triangle JKL \cong \triangle TSR$.

Corresponding angles	$\angle J \cong \angle T$, $\angle K \cong \angle S$, $\angle L \cong \angle R$
Corresponding sides	$\overline{JK} \cong \overline{TS}$, $\overline{KL} \cong \overline{SR}$, $\overline{LJ} \cong \overline{RT}$

Laurie's Notes   Teacher Actions

❓ Probing Questions: "What does it mean for two objects to be congruent?" Answers will vary. "What does it mean for two polygons to be congruent?" Answers will vary. Draw and label two congruent triangles. "What does it mean for two triangles to be congruent?" Students should make a list (i.e., corresponding parts) of what would be true.

• **MP3 Construct Viable Arguments and Critique the Reasoning of Others** and **Turn and Talk:** "How could rigid motions be used to show that two triangles are congruent?" Listen for valid reasoning. Discuss notation and marking diagrams of congruent polygons.

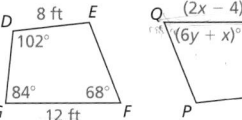 **EXAMPLE 2** **Using Properties of Congruent Figures**

In the diagram, $DEFG \cong SPQR$.

a. Find the value of x.

b. Find the value of y.

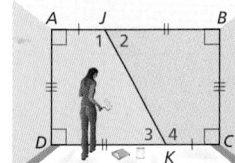

SOLUTION

a. You know that $\overline{FG} \cong \overline{QR}$.

$FG = QR$

$12 = 2x - 4$

$16 = 2x$

$8 = x$

b. You know that $\angle F \cong \angle Q$.

$m\angle F = m\angle Q$

$68° = (6y + x)°$

$68 = 6y + 8$

$10 = y$

EXAMPLE 3 **Showing That Figures Are Congruent**

You divide the wall into orange and blue sections along $\overline{JK}$. Will the sections of the wall be the same size and shape? Explain.

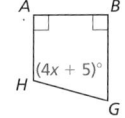

SOLUTION

From the diagram, $\angle A \cong \angle C$ and $\angle D \cong \angle B$ because all right angles are congruent. Also, by the Lines Perpendicular to a Transversal Theorem (Thm. 3.12), $\overline{AB} \parallel \overline{DC}$. Then $\angle 1 \cong \angle 4$ and $\angle 2 \cong \angle 3$ by the Alternate Interior Angles Theorem (Thm. 3.2). So, all pairs of corresponding angles are congruent. The diagram shows $\overline{AJ} \cong \overline{CK}$, $\overline{KD} \cong \overline{JB}$, and $\overline{DA} \cong \overline{BC}$. By the Reflexive Property of Congruence (Thm. 2.1), $\overline{JK} \cong \overline{KJ}$. So, all pairs of corresponding sides are congruent. Because all corresponding parts are congruent, $AJKD \cong CKJB$.

▶ Yes, the two sections will be the same size and shape.

Monitoring Progress 🔊 Help in English and Spanish at *BigIdeasMath.com*

In the diagram, $ABGH \cong CDEF$.

1. Identify all pairs of congruent corresponding parts.

2. Find the value of x.

3. In the diagram at the left, show that $\triangle PTS \cong \triangle RTQ$.

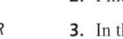

🔄 Theorem

STUDY TIP

The properties of congruence that are true for segments and angles are also true for triangles.

Theorem 5.3   Properties of Triangle Congruence

Triangle congruence is reflexive, symmetric, and transitive.

Reflexive   For any triangle $\triangle ABC$, $\triangle ABC \cong \triangle ABC$.

Symmetric   If $\triangle ABC \cong \triangle DEF$, then $\triangle DEF \cong \triangle ABC$.

Transitive   If $\triangle ABC \cong \triangle DEF$ and $\triangle DEF \cong \triangle JKL$, then $\triangle ABC \cong \triangle JKL$.

Proof BigIdeasMath.com

Section 5.2   Congruent Polygons   **241**

Extra Example 2

In the diagram, $DEFG \cong QMNP$.

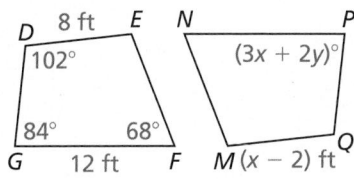

a. Find the value of x. 10

b. Find the value of y. 27

Extra Example 3

Show that $\triangle ABD \cong \triangle CDB$. Explain your reasoning.

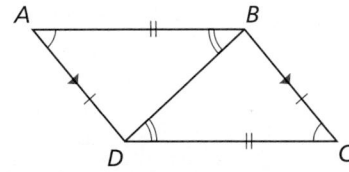

From the diagram, $\overline{AB} \cong \overline{CD}$ and $\overline{AD} \cong \overline{BC}$. By the Reflexive Property of Congruence (Thm. 2.1), $\overline{BD} \cong \overline{DB}$. So, all pairs of corresponding sides are congruent. From the diagram, $\angle A \cong \angle C$ and $\angle ABD \cong \angle CDB$. Because $\overline{AD} \parallel \overline{BC}$, $\angle ADB \cong \angle CBD$ by the Alternate Interior Angles Theorem (Thm. 3.2). So, all pairs of corresponding angles are congruent. Because all corresponding parts are congruent, $\triangle ABD \cong \triangle CDB$.

MONITORING PROGRESS ANSWERS

1. corresponding angles: $\angle A \cong \angle C$, $\angle B \cong \angle D$, $\angle G \cong \angle E$, $\angle H \cong \angle F$; corresponding sides: $\overline{AB} \cong \overline{CD}$, $\overline{BG} \cong \overline{DE}$, $\overline{GH} \cong \overline{EF}$, $\overline{AH} \cong \overline{CF}$

2. $x = 25$

3. From the diagram, $\overline{PS} \cong \overline{RQ}$, $\overline{PT} \cong \overline{RT}$, and $\overline{ST} \cong \overline{QT}$. Also, by the Vertical Angles Congruence Theorem (Thm. 2.6), $\angle PTS \cong \angle RTQ$. Fom the diagram, $\overline{PS} \parallel \overline{RQ}$, and $\angle P \cong \angle R$ and $\angle S \cong \angle Q$ by the Alternate Interior Angles Theorem (Thm. 3.2). Because all corresponding parts are congruent, $\triangle PTS \cong \triangle RTQ$.

Laurie's Notes Teacher Actions

? Extension: "Is there another way to write the congruence statement for $DEFG \cong SPQR$? Explain." yes; $EFGD \cong PQRS$, as long as the corresponding vertices are in the same order.

? Fact-First Questioning: "The Reflexive, Symmetric, and Transitive Properties can be applied to triangle congruence. Explain what this means and why it is true." Listen for correct statements and valid reasoning.

• Write the Properties of Triangle Congruence.

Extra Example 4

Find $m\angle P$.

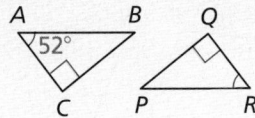

$38°$

Extra Example 5

Use the information in the figure to prove that $\triangle WXY \cong \triangle ZVY$.

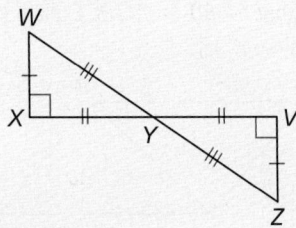

Statements (Reasons)

1. $\overline{WX} \cong \overline{ZV}, \overline{XY} \cong \overline{VY}, \overline{WY} \cong \overline{ZY}$ (Given)
2. $\angle X$ and $\angle V$ are right angles. (Given)
3. $\angle X \cong \angle V$ (All rt. $\angle s \cong$.)
4. $\angle WYX \cong \angle VYZ$
   (Vertical $\angle s \cong$ Thm. 2.6)
5. $\angle W \cong \angle Z$ (Third Angles Thm. 5.4)
6. $\triangle WXY \cong \triangle ZVY$ (All corr. parts $\cong$.)

MONITORING PROGRESS ANSWERS

4. $75°$
5. $\overline{CD} \cong \overline{RS}, \overline{DN} \cong \overline{SN}$

Using the Third Angles Theorem

🔄 Theorem

Theorem 5.4   Third Angles Theorem

If two angles of one triangle are congruent to two angles of another triangle, then the third angles are also congruent.

Proof Ex. 19, p. 244

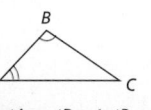 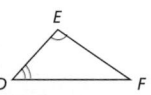

If $\angle A \cong \angle D$ and $\angle B \cong \angle E$, then $\angle C \cong \angle F$.

EXAMPLE 4   **Using the Third Angles Theorem**

Find $m\angle BDC$.

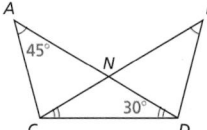

SOLUTION

$\angle A \cong \angle B$ and $\angle ADC \cong \angle BCD$, so by the Third Angles Theorem, $\angle ACD \cong \angle BDC$. By the Triangle Sum Theorem (Theorem 5.1), $m\angle ACD = 180° - 45° - 30° = 105°$.

▶ So, $m\angle BDC = m\angle ACD = 105°$ by the definition of congruent angles.

EXAMPLE 5   **Proving That Triangles Are Congruent**

Use the information in the figure to prove that $\triangle ACD \cong \triangle CAB$.

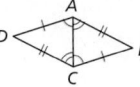

SOLUTION

Given $\overline{AD} \cong \overline{CB}, \overline{DC} \cong \overline{BA}, \angle ACD \cong \angle CAB, \angle CAD \cong \angle ACB$

Prove $\triangle ACD \cong \triangle CAB$

Plan for Proof
a. Use the Reflexive Property of Congruence (Thm. 2.1) to show that $\overline{AC} \cong \overline{CA}$.
b. Use the Third Angles Theorem to show that $\angle B \cong \angle D$.

Plan in Action	STATEMENTS	REASONS
	1. $\overline{AD} \cong \overline{CB}, \overline{DC} \cong \overline{BA}$	1. Given
a.	2. $\overline{AC} \cong \overline{CA}$	2. Reflexive Property of Congruence (Theorem 2.1)
	3. $\angle ACD \cong \angle CAB$, $\angle CAD \cong \angle ACB$	3. Given
b.	4. $\angle B \cong \angle D$	4. Third Angles Theorem
	5. $\triangle ACD \cong \triangle CAB$	5. All corresponding parts are congruent.

Monitoring Progress 🔊 Help in English and Spanish at *BigIdeasMath.com*

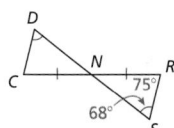

Use the diagram.

4. Find $m\angle DCN$.
5. What additional information is needed to conclude that $\triangle NDC \cong \triangle NSR$?

Laurie's Notes   Teacher Actions

- **MP3:** In Example 4, students may know that $m\angle BDC = 105°$, but can they explain why? Do not ignore the reasoning behind the answer.
- In Example 5, draw the diagram and pose the question.
- **Turn and Talk:** "How could you prove that the two triangles are congruent?" Give partners time to talk and plan. Use *Popsicle Sticks* to solicit suggestions from students. Ask a volunteer to write the proof.

Closure

- **Response Logs:** Select from "What is puzzling me the most is …" or "I was successful in …" or "I'm not sure …."

Vocabulary and Core Concept Check

1. **WRITING** Based on this lesson, what information do you need to prove that two triangles are congruent? Explain your reasoning.

2. **DIFFERENT WORDS, SAME QUESTION** Which is different? Find "both" answers.

Is △JKL ≅ △RST?   Is △KJL ≅ △SRT?

Is △JLK ≅ △STR?   Is △LKJ ≅ △TSR?

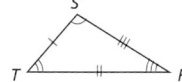

Monitoring Progress and Modeling with Mathematics

In Exercises 3 and 4, identify all pairs of congruent corresponding parts. Then write another congruence statement for the polygons. *(See Example 1.)*

3. △ABC ≅ △DEF

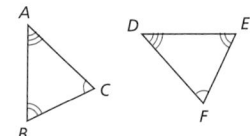

4. GHJK ≅ QRST

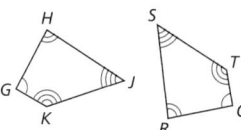

In Exercises 5–8, △XYZ ≅ △MNL. Copy and complete the statement.

5. m∠Y = _____

6. m∠M = _____

7. m∠Z = _____

8. XY = _____

In Exercises 9 and 10, find the values of x and y. *(See Example 2.)*

9. ABCD ≅ EFGH

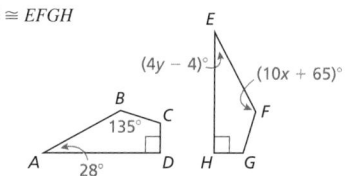

10. △MNP ≅ △TUS

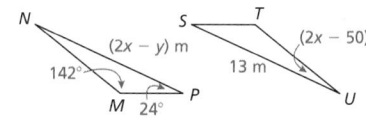

In Exercises 11 and 12, show that the polygons are congruent. Explain your reasoning. *(See Example 3.)*

11.

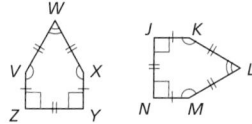

12.

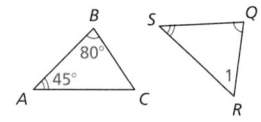

In Exercises 13 and 14, find m∠1. *(See Example 4.)*

13.

14.

Section 5.2   Congruent Polygons   **243**

ANSWERS

1. To show that two triangles are congruent, you need to show that all corresponding parts are congruent. If two triangles have the same side lengths and angle measures, then they must be the same size and shape.

2. Is △JLK ≅ △STR?; no; yes

3. corresponding angles: ∠A ≅ ∠D, ∠B ≅ ∠E, ∠C ≅ ∠F; corresponding sides: $\overline{AB} ≅ \overline{DE}$, $\overline{BC} ≅ \overline{EF}$, $\overline{AC} ≅ \overline{DF}$; *Sample answer:* △BCA ≅ △EFD

4. corresponding angles: ∠G ≅ ∠Q, ∠H ≅ ∠R, ∠J ≅ ∠S, ∠K ≅ ∠T; corresponding sides: $\overline{GH} ≅ \overline{QR}$, $\overline{HJ} ≅ \overline{RS}$, $\overline{JK} ≅ \overline{ST}$, $\overline{GK} ≅ \overline{QT}$; *Sample answer:* HJKG ≅ RSTQ

5. 124°   6. 33°

7. 23°   8. 8

9. x = 7, y = 8   10. x = 32; y = 51

11. From the diagram, $\overline{WX} ≅ \overline{LM}$, $\overline{XY} ≅ \overline{MN}$, $\overline{YZ} ≅ \overline{NJ}$, $\overline{VZ} ≅ \overline{KJ}$, and $\overline{WV} ≅ \overline{LK}$. Also from the diagram, ∠V ≅ ∠K, ∠W ≅ ∠L, ∠X ≅ ∠M, ∠Y ≅ ∠N, and ∠Z ≅ ∠J. Because all corresponding parts are congruent, VWXYZ ≅ KLMNJ.

12. From the diagram, $\overline{WX} ≅ \overline{YZ}$ and $\overline{XY} ≅ \overline{ZW}$. By the Reflexive Property of Congruence (Thm. 2.1), $\overline{WY} ≅ \overline{WY}$. Also from the diagram, ∠X ≅ ∠Z. Then, from the markings in the diagram, $\overline{XY} \parallel \overline{ZW}$ and $\overline{XW} \parallel \overline{ZY}$. You can conclude that ∠XYW ≅ ∠ZWY and ∠XWY ≅ ∠ZYW by the Alternate Interior Angles Theorem (Thm. 3.2). Because all corresponding parts are congruent, △WXY ≅ △YZW.

13. 20°

14. 55°

ANSWERS

15–16. See Additional Answers.

17. The congruence statement should be used to ensure that corresponding parts are matched up correctly; $\angle S \cong \angle Y$; $m\angle S = m\angle Y$; $m\angle S = 90° - 42° = 48°$

18. In order to conclude that triangles are congruent, the sides must also be congruent; $\triangle MNP$ is not congruent to $\triangle RSP$ because the corresponding sides are not congruent.

19–29. See Additional Answers.

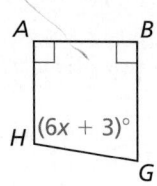 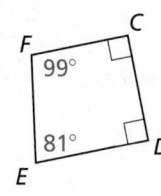
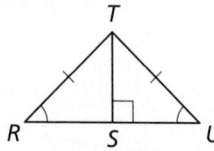
15. PROOF Triangular postage stamps, like the ones shown, are highly valued by stamp collectors. Prove that $\triangle AEB \cong \triangle CED$. (*See Example 5.*)

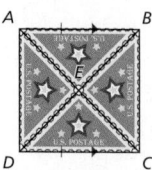

Given $\overline{AB} \parallel \overline{DC}, \overline{AB} \cong \overline{DC}$, E is the midpoint of $\overline{AC}$ and $\overline{BD}$.

Prove $\triangle AEB \cong \triangle CED$

16. PROOF Use the information in the figure to prove that $\triangle ABG \cong \triangle DCF$.

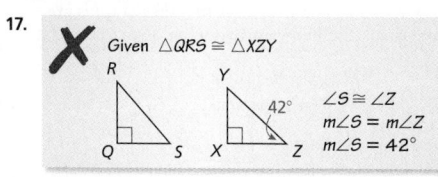

ERROR ANALYSIS In Exercises 17 and 18, describe and correct the error.

17.

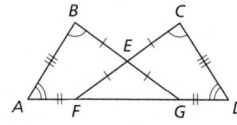

18.

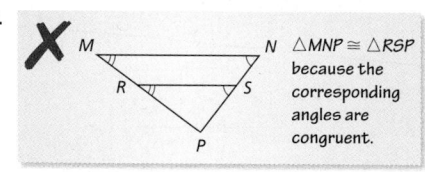

Maintaining Mathematical Proficiency
Reviewing what you learned in previous grades and lessons

What can you conclude from the diagram? (*Section 1.6*)

26. 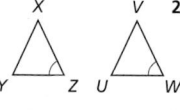   **27.** 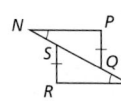   **28.**   **29.**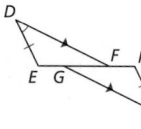

19. PROVING A THEOREM Prove the Third Angles Theorem (Theorem 5.4) by using the Triangle Sum Theorem (Theorem 5.1).

20. THOUGHT PROVOKING Draw a triangle. Copy the triangle multiple times to create a rug design made of congruent triangles. Which property guarantees that all the triangles are congruent?

21. REASONING $\triangle JKL$ is congruent to $\triangle XYZ$. Identify all pairs of congruent corresponding parts.

22. HOW DO YOU SEE IT? In the diagram, $ABEF \cong CDEF$.

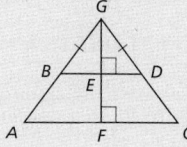

a. Explain how you know that $\overline{BE} \cong \overline{DE}$ and $\angle ABE \cong \angle CDE$.

b. Explain how you know that $\angle GBE \cong \angle GDE$.

c. Explain how you know that $\angle GEB \cong \angle GED$.

d. Do you have enough information to prove that $\triangle BEG \cong \triangle DEG$? Explain.

MATHEMATICAL CONNECTIONS In Exercises 23 and 24, use the given information to write and solve a system of linear equations to find the values of x and y.

23. $\triangle LMN \cong \triangle PQR$, $m\angle L = 40°$, $m\angle M = 90°$, $m\angle P = (17x - y)°$, $m\angle R = (2x + 4y)°$

24. $\triangle STU \cong \triangle XYZ$, $m\angle T = 28°$, $m\angle U = (4x + y)°$, $m\angle X = 130°$, $m\angle Y = (8x - 6y)°$

25. PROOF Prove that the criteria for congruent triangles in this lesson is equivalent to the definition of congruence in terms of rigid motions.

Overview of Section 5.3

Introduction

- The Side-Angle-Side (SAS) Congruence Theorem, the first of the triangle congruence theorems, is presented in this lesson. It is first investigated in the exploration and then proven in the formal lesson.
- Different approaches are used in the proof examples in the formal lesson: transformational, two-column, and paragraph.
- One additional construction is presented—how to copy a triangle using the SAS Congruence Theorem.

Resources

- Dynamic geometry software is used in the exploration, and a compass and straightedge are used in the lesson.

Formative Assessment Tips

- Refer to page T-230 for a description of *Response Logs*. In this lesson and throughout this chapter, there will be sentence stems to prompt student writing. Use your judgment for placement in the lesson, amount of time to allow for writing, and the actual sentence stem given to students.
- For a beginning list of writing stems, see page T-238.

Another Way

- The classic, traditional approach to introducing the SAS Congruence Theorem is to use objects such as coffee stirrers to represent two sides of a triangle and then fix an angle measure between them. Regardless of the orientation of the stirrers, the triangles formed will all be congruent.

Pacing Suggestion

- Take time for students to explore and discover the SAS congruence relationship using dynamic geometry software, and then transition to the formal lesson.

Dynamic Teaching Tools

Dynamic Assessment & Progress Monitoring Tool

Lesson Planning Tool

Interactive Whiteboard Lesson Library

Dynamic Classroom with Dynamic Investigations

**Common Core
State Standards**

HSG-CO.B.8 Explain how the criteria for triangle congruence (… SAS, …) follow from the definition of congruence in terms of rigid motions.

HSG-MG.A.1 Use geometric shapes, their measures, and their properties to describe objects (e.g., modeling a tree trunk or a human torso as a cylinder).

Laurie's Notes

Exploration

Motivate

- Pose the following problem to get students thinking about triangles.
- "Draw six segments of equal length to form a closed figure that contains eight equilateral triangles."
- Give students time to fool around with the problem.
- Here is one solution. The figure has six small equilateral triangles and two large equilateral triangles, for a total of eight equilateral triangles.

Exploration

- The last lesson established that to show two triangles are congruent it is necessary to show that all three pairs of corresponding angles are congruent and all three pairs of corresponding sides are congruent.
- The Side-Angle-Side (SAS) Congruence Theorem (Thm. 5.5) is the first of several theorems to show that less than six pieces of information are needed to prove that two triangles are congruent.
- This exploration may not be a familiar approach to verifying the SAS triangle congruence method, so become familiar with the construction steps and potential for extensions.

Exploration 1

- **MP5 Use Appropriate Tools Strategically:** Students should be familiar enough with the software to follow the construction described. The software will label points in the construction process that may differ from how the diagram and table are labeled. Tell students to make adjustments as needed.
- The ordered pairs for points *B* and *C* will differ for each student, but the length of the third side and the two missing angles will be the same.
- In constructing △*ABC*, students should try each orientation, clockwise and counterclockwise. Are the results the same?
- Have students discuss the results of their explorations and make conjectures.
- **Extension:** Repeat the construction for two circles of different radii or for a different angle.

Communicate Your Answer

- **MP3 Construct Viable Arguments and Critique the Reasoning of Others:** Students should conclude that when two pairs of sides and the included angle of two triangles are congruent, the triangles will be congruent.

Connecting to Next Step

- The exploration allows students to discover and make sense of the SAS congruence relationship that will be presented formally in the lesson.

Essential Question What can you conclude about two triangles when you know that two pairs of corresponding sides and the corresponding included angles are congruent?

EXPLORATION 1   **Drawing Triangles**

Work with a partner. Use dynamic geometry software.

a. Construct circles with radii of 2 units and 3 units centered at the origin. Construct a 40° angle with its vertex at the origin. Label the vertex *A*.

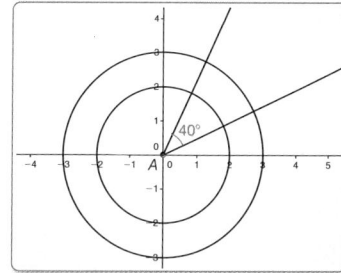

USING TOOLS STRATEGICALLY

To be proficient in math, you need to use technology to help visualize the results of varying assumptions, explore consequences, and compare predictions with data.

b. Locate the point where one ray of the angle intersects the smaller circle and label this point *B*. Locate the point where the other ray of the angle intersects the larger circle and label this point *C*. Then draw △*ABC*.

c. Find *BC*, *m*∠*B*, and *m*∠*C*.

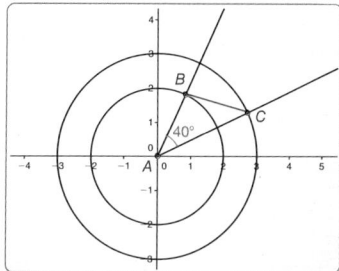

d. Repeat parts (a)–(c) several times, redrawing the angle in different positions. Keep track of your results by copying and completing the table below. What can you conclude?

	A	B	C	AB	AC	BC	m∠A	m∠B	m∠C
1.	(0, 0)			2	3		40°		
2.	(0, 0)			2	3		40°		
3.	(0, 0)			2	3		40°		
4.	(0, 0)			2	3		40°		
5.	(0, 0)			2	3		40°		

Communicate Your Answer

2. What can you conclude about two triangles when you know that two pairs of corresponding sides and the corresponding included angles are congruent?

3. How would you prove your conclusion in Exploration 1(d)?

ANSWERS

1. **a.** Check students' work
    b. Check students' work.
    c. $BC \approx 1.95$, $m\angle B \approx 98.79°$, $m\angle C \approx 41.21°$
    d. Check students' work; If two sides and the included angle of a triangle are congruent to two sides and the included angle of another triangle, then the triangles are congruent.

2. The triangles are congruent.

3. Start with two triangles so that two sides and the included angle of one triangle are congruent to two sides and the included angle of another triangle. Then show that one triangle can be translated until it coincides with the other triangle by a composition of rigid motions.

5.3 Lesson

Core Vocabulary

Previous
congruent figures
rigid motion

What You Will Learn

▶ Use the Side-Angle-Side (SAS) Congruence Theorem.

▶ Solve real-life problems.

Using the Side-Angle-Side Congruence Theorem

Theorem

Theorem 5.5   Side-Angle-Side (SAS) Congruence Theorem

If two sides and the included angle of one triangle are congruent to two sides and the included angle of a second triangle, then the two triangles are congruent.

If $\overline{AB} \cong \overline{DE}$, $\angle A \cong \angle D$, and $\overline{AC} \cong \overline{DF}$, then $\triangle ABC \cong \triangle DEF$.

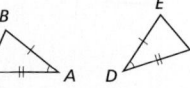

Proof p. 246

PROOF   Side-Angle-Side (SAS) Congruence Theorem

Given $\overline{AB} \cong \overline{DE}$, $\angle A \cong \angle D$, $\overline{AC} \cong \overline{DF}$

Prove $\triangle ABC \cong \triangle DEF$

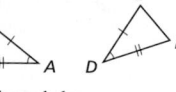

First, translate $\triangle ABC$ so that point A maps to point D, as shown below.

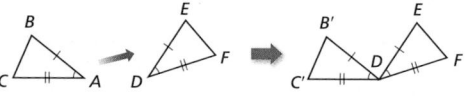

This translation maps $\triangle ABC$ to $\triangle DB'C'$. Next, rotate $\triangle DB'C'$ counterclockwise through $\angle C'DF$ so that the image of $\overrightarrow{DC'}$ coincides with $\overrightarrow{DF}$, as shown below.

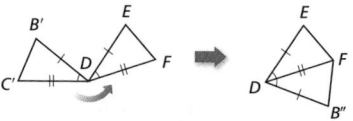

Because $\overline{DC'} \cong \overline{DF}$, the rotation maps point C' to point F. So, this rotation maps $\triangle DB'C'$ to $\triangle DB''F$. Now, reflect $\triangle DB''F$ in the line through points D and F, as shown below.

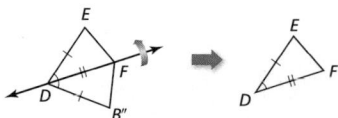

Because points D and F lie on $\overleftrightarrow{DF}$, this reflection maps them onto themselves. Because a reflection preserves angle measure and $\angle B''DF \cong \angle EDF$, the reflection maps $\overrightarrow{DB''}$ to $\overrightarrow{DE}$. Because $\overline{DB''} \cong \overline{DE}$, the reflection maps point B'' to point E. So, this reflection maps $\triangle DB''F$ to $\triangle DEF$.

Because you can map $\triangle ABC$ to $\triangle DEF$ using a composition of rigid motions, $\triangle ABC \cong \triangle DEF$.

Laurie's Notes | Teacher Actions

- The Side-Angle-Side (SAS) Congruence Theorem should make sense following the exploration. Draw the diagram of the two triangles as shown. Mark the triangles.
- **Turn and Talk:** "How could you use a composition of rigid motions to map $\triangle ABC$ to $\triangle DEF$?" After partners have discussed, solicit ideas. Students will likely suggest a translation, rotation, and then reflection.
- **MP5** and **Teaching Tip:** Construct a similar image using construction software. Perform the steps in the proof as students suggest them.

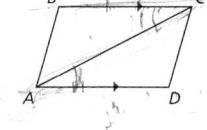 **EXAMPLE 1** **Using the SAS Congruence Theorem**

Write a proof.
Given $\overline{BC} \cong \overline{DA}, \overline{BC} \parallel \overline{AD}$
Prove $\triangle ABC \cong \triangle CDA$

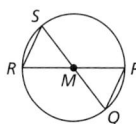

STUDY TIP

Make your proof easier to read by identifying the steps where you show congruent sides (S) and angles (A).

SOLUTION

STATEMENTS	REASONS
S 1. $\overline{BC} \cong \overline{DA}$	1. Given
2. $\overline{BC} \parallel \overline{AD}$	2. Given
A 3. $\angle BCA \cong \angle DAC$	3. Alternate Interior Angles Theorem (Thm. 3.2)
S 4. $\overline{AC} \cong \overline{CA}$	4. Reflexive Property of Congruence (Thm. 2.1)
5. $\triangle ABC \cong \triangle CDA$	5. SAS Congruence Theorem

EXAMPLE 2 **Using SAS and Properties of Shapes**

In the diagram, $\overline{QS}$ and $\overline{RP}$ pass through the center M of the circle. What can you conclude about $\triangle MRS$ and $\triangle MPQ$?

SOLUTION

Because they are vertical angles, $\angle PMQ \cong \angle RMS$. All points on a circle are the same distance from the center, so $\overline{MP}, \overline{MQ}, \overline{MR}$, and $\overline{MS}$ are all congruent.

▶ So, $\triangle MRS$ and $\triangle MPQ$ are congruent by the SAS Congruence Theorem.

Monitoring Progress 🔊 Help in English and Spanish at *BigIdeasMath.com*

In the diagram, *ABCD* is a square with four congruent sides and four right angles. *R, S, T,* and *U* are the midpoints of the sides of *ABCD*. Also, $\overline{RT} \perp \overline{SU}$ and $\overline{SV} \cong \overline{VU}$.

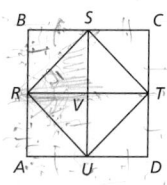

1. Prove that $\triangle SVR \cong \triangle UVR$.
2. Prove that $\triangle BSR \cong \triangle DUT$.

Extra Example 1
Write a proof.
Given B is the midpoint of $\overline{AD}$. $\angle ABC$ and $\angle DBC$ are right angles.
Prove $\triangle ABC \cong \triangle DBC$

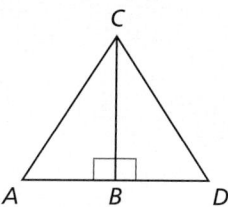

Statements (Reasons)
1. B is the midpoint of $\overline{AD}$. (Given)
2. $\overline{AB} \cong \overline{BD}$ (Def. of midpoint)
3. $\angle ABC$ and $\angle DBC$ are right angles. (Given)
4. $\angle ABC \cong \angle DBC$ (Right $\angle$s $\cong$ Thm. 2.3)
5. $\overline{BC} \cong \overline{BC}$ (Reflex. Prop. $\cong$ Thm. 2.1)
6. $\triangle ABC \cong \triangle DBC$ (SAS $\cong$ Thm. 5.5)

Extra Example 2
What can you conclude about $\triangle PTS$ and $\triangle RTQ$?

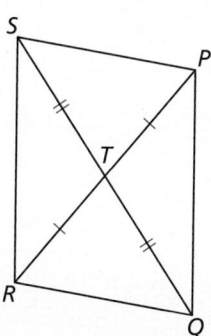

Because they are vertical angles, $\angle PTS \cong \angle RTQ$. So, $\triangle PTS \cong \triangle RTQ$ by the SAS Congruence Theorem (Thm. 5.5).

MONITORING PROGRESS ANSWERS
1–2. See Additional Answers.

Laurie's Notes   Teacher Actions

- Pose Example 1. Have students mark their diagrams with known information or information that can be concluded from given information.
- Work through the proof as shown. Compare and contrast this synthetic, two-column proof with the transformational proof on page 246.
- **MP3:** The solution in Example 2 is a paragraph style proof. Valid reasoning outlines how to show that the triangles are congruent.
- **Response Logs:** Select from "I made progress with …" or "I got stuck …."

Extra Example 3

The wings of a paper airplane have two congruent sides and two congruent angles. Use the SAS Congruence Theorem (Thm. 5.5) to show that $\triangle IPA \cong \triangle IPR$.

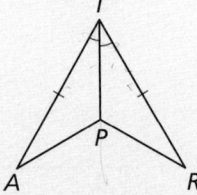

You are given that $\overline{AI} \cong \overline{RI}$ and $\angle PIA \cong \angle PIR$. By the Reflexive Property of Congruence (Thm. 2.1), $\overline{IP} \cong \overline{IP}$. So, two pairs of sides and their included angles are congruent. Therefore, $\triangle IPA \cong \triangle IPR$ by the SAS $\cong$ Theorem (Thm. 5.5).

MONITORING PROGRESS ANSWER

3. See Additional Answers.

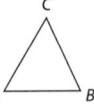

CONSTRUCTION **Copying a Triangle Using SAS**

Construct a triangle that is congruent to $\triangle ABC$ using the SAS Congruence Theorem. Use a compass and straightedge.

SOLUTION

Step 1	Step 2	Step 3	Step 4
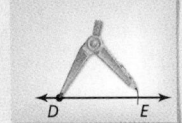	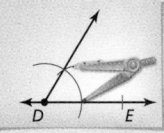	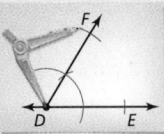	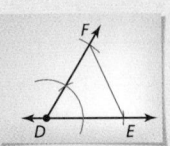
Construct a side Construct $\overline{DE}$ so that it is congruent to $\overline{AB}$.	**Construct an angle** Construct $\angle D$ with vertex D and side $\overline{DE}$ so that it is congruent to $\angle A$.	**Construct a side** Construct $\overline{DF}$ so that it is congruent to $\overline{AC}$.	**Draw a triangle** Draw $\triangle DEF$. By the SAS Congruence Theorem, $\triangle ABC \cong \triangle DEF$.

Solving Real-Life Problems

EXAMPLE 3 **Solving a Real-Life Problem**

You are making a canvas sign to hang on the triangular portion of the barn wall shown in the picture. You think you can use two identical triangular sheets of canvas. You know that $\overline{RP} \perp \overline{QS}$ and $\overline{PQ} \cong \overline{PS}$. Use the SAS Congruence Theorem to show that $\triangle PQR \cong \triangle PSR$.

SOLUTION

You are given that $\overline{PQ} \cong \overline{PS}$. By the Reflexive Property of Congruence (Theorem 2.1), $\overline{RP} \cong \overline{RP}$. By the definition of perpendicular lines, both $\angle RPQ$ and $\angle RPS$ are right angles, so they are congruent. So, two pairs of sides and their included angles are congruent.

▶ $\triangle PQR$ and $\triangle PSR$ are congruent by the SAS Congruence Theorem.

Monitoring Progress Help in English and Spanish at *BigIdeasMath.com*

3. You are designing the window shown in the photo. You want to make $\triangle DRA$ congruent to $\triangle DRG$. You design the window so that $\overline{DA} \cong \overline{DG}$ and $\angle ADR \cong \angle GDR$. Use the SAS Congruence Theorem to prove $\triangle DRA \cong \triangle DRG$.

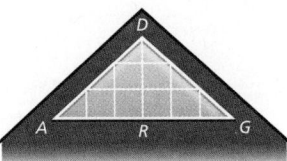

Laurie's Notes | Teacher Actions

- Have students draw different types of triangles and label them $\triangle ABC$. This construction involves copying an angle and copying two sides. Have students compare their work with one another.
- **Teaching Tip:** In Example 3, draw $\triangle QRS$ with perpendicular bisector $\overline{RP}$ without the photo behind it. Mark the diagram.

Closure

- **Response Logs:** Select from "I feel confident about …" or "At first I thought … but now I think …."

Vocabulary and Core Concept Check

1. **WRITING** What is an included angle?

2. **COMPLETE THE SENTENCE** If two sides and the included angle of one triangle are congruent to two sides and the included angle of a second triangle, then _____.

Monitoring Progress and Modeling with Mathematics

In Exercises 3–8, name the included angle between the pair of sides given.

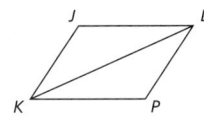

3. $\overline{JK}$ and $\overline{KL}$

4. $\overline{PK}$ and $\overline{LK}$

5. $\overline{LP}$ and $\overline{LK}$

6. $\overline{JL}$ and $\overline{JK}$

7. $\overline{KL}$ and $\overline{JL}$

8. $\overline{KP}$ and $\overline{PL}$

In Exercises 9–14, decide whether enough information is given to prove that the triangles are congruent using the SAS Congruence Theorem (Theorem 5.5). Explain.

9. $\triangle ABD$, $\triangle CDB$

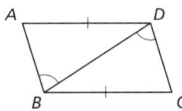

10. $\triangle LMN$, $\triangle NQP$

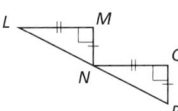

11. $\triangle YXZ$, $\triangle WXZ$

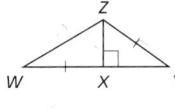

12. $\triangle QRV$, $\triangle TSU$

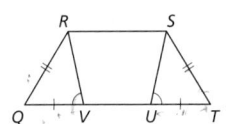

13. $\triangle EFH$, $\triangle GHF$

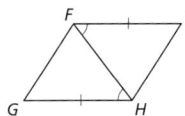

14. $\triangle KLM$, $\triangle MNK$

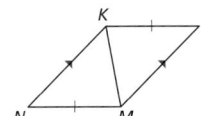

In Exercises 15–18, write a proof. *(See Example 1.)*

15. **Given** $\overline{PQ}$ bisects $\angle SPT$, $\overline{SP} \cong \overline{TP}$
    Prove $\triangle SPQ \cong \triangle TPQ$

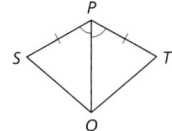

16. **Given** $\overline{AB} \cong \overline{CD}$, $\overline{AB} \parallel \overline{CD}$
    Prove $\triangle ABC \cong \triangle CDA$

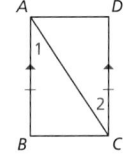

17. **Given** C is the midpoint of $\overline{AE}$ and $\overline{BD}$.
    Prove $\triangle ABC \cong \triangle EDC$

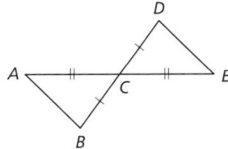

18. **Given** $\overline{PT} \cong \overline{RT}$, $\overline{QT} \cong \overline{ST}$
    Prove $\triangle PQT \cong \triangle RST$

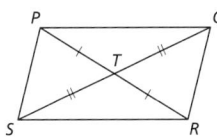

Assignment Guide and Homework Check

ASSIGNMENT

Basic: 1, 2, 3–15 odd, 19, 25, 26, 30, 32–35

Average: 1, 2, 8–24 even, 25, 26, 29, 30, 32–35

Advanced: 1, 2, 10–24 even, 25–35

HOMEWORK CHECK

Basic: 3, 9, 11, 15, 19

Average: 10, 16, 22, 24, 26

Advanced: 14, 16, 22, 26, 29

ANSWERS

1. an angle formed by two sides

2. the two triangles are congruent

3. $\angle JKL$

4. $\angle PKL$

5. $\angle KLP$

6. $\angle KJL$

7. $\angle JLK$

8. $\angle KPL$

9. no; The congruent angles are not the included angles.

10. yes; Two pairs of sides and the included angles are congruent.

11. no; One of the congruent angles is not the included angle.

12. no; The congruent angles are not the included angles.

13. yes; Two pairs of sides and the included angles are congruent.

14. no; $\angle NKM$ and $\angle KML$ are congruent by the Alternate Interior Angles Theorem (Thm. 3.2) but they are not the included angles.

15–18. See Additional Answers.

ANSWERS
19–35. See Additional Answers.

Mini-Assessment

1. Use the SAS Congruence Theorem to show that △WXZ ≅ △YZX.

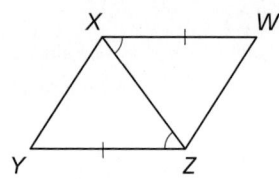

You are given $\overline{XW} \cong \overline{ZY}$ and $\angle WXZ \cong \angle YZX$. By the Reflexive Property of Congruence (Thm. 2.1), $\overline{XZ} \cong \overline{ZX}$. So, △WXZ ≅ △YZX by the SAS Congruence Theorem (Thm. 5.5).

2. The two triangles in the diagram represent congruent banners. You know that $\overline{AB} \cong \overline{DE}$ and $\overline{BC} \cong \overline{EF}$. What pair of angles must be congruent to show that △ABC ≅ △DEF by the SAS Congruence Theorem?

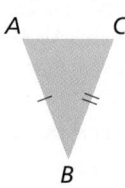
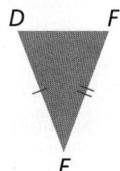

$\angle B \cong \angle E$

3. Write a proof.

Given $\overline{PQ}$ bisects $\angle SPT, \overline{PS} \cong \overline{PT}$

Prove △PQS ≅ △PQT

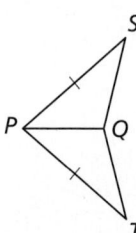

See Additional Answers.

250   Chapter 5

In Exercises 19–22, use the given information to name two triangles that are congruent. Explain your reasoning. *(See Example 2.)*

19. $\angle SRT \cong \angle URT$, and R is the center of the circle.

20. $ABCD$ is a square with four congruent sides and four congruent angles.

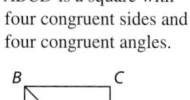

21. $RSTUV$ is a regular pentagon.

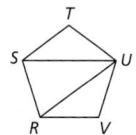

22. $\overline{MK} \perp \overline{MN}, \overline{KL} \perp \overline{NL}$, and M and L are centers of circles.

CONSTRUCTION In Exercises 23 and 24, construct a triangle that is congruent to △ABC using the SAS Congruence Theorem (Theorem 5.5).

23.

24.

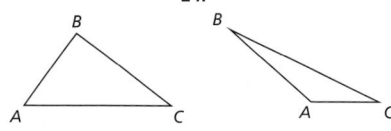

25. **ERROR ANALYSIS** Describe and correct the error in finding the value of x.

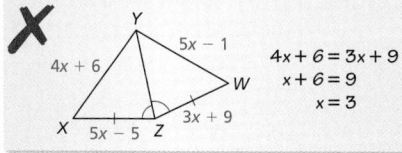

$4x + 6 = 3x + 9$
$x + 6 = 9$
$x = 3$

Maintaining Mathematical Proficiency Reviewing what you learned in previous grades and lessons

Classify the triangle by its sides and by measuring its angles. *(Section 5.1)*

32.   33.   34.   35.

250   Chapter 5   Congruent Triangles

---

26. **HOW DO YOU SEE IT?** What additional information do you need to prove that △ABC ≅ △DBC?

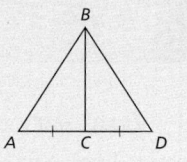

27. **PROOF** The Navajo rug is made of isosceles triangles. You know $\angle B \cong \angle D$. Use the SAS Congruence Theorem (Theorem 5.5) to show that △ABC ≅ △CDE. *(See Example 3.)*

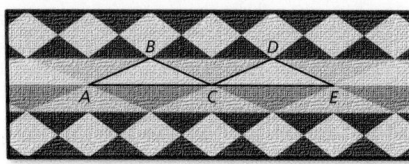

28. **THOUGHT PROVOKING** There are six possible subsets of three sides or angles of a triangle: SSS, SAS, SSA, AAA, ASA, and AAS. Which of these correspond to congruence theorems? For those that do not, give a counterexample.

29. **MATHEMATICAL CONNECTIONS** Prove that △ABC ≅ △DEC. Then find the values of x and y.

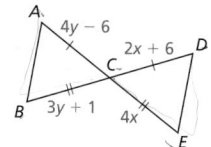

30. **MAKING AN ARGUMENT** Your friend claims it is possible to construct a triangle congruent to △ABC by first constructing $\overline{AB}$ and $\overline{AC}$, and then copying $\angle C$. Is your friend correct? Explain your reasoning.

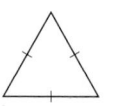

31. **PROVING A THEOREM** Prove the Reflections in Intersecting Lines Theorem (Theorem 4.3).

Overview of Section 5.4

Introduction
- In this lesson, there are two theorems, two corollaries, and a construction.
- The two theorems, investigated in the exploration, are converses of each other. Students think of an isosceles triangle as being symmetric, so having base angles congruent is not a surprise. The challenge for students in proving the theorem is that an auxiliary line is drawn.
- The two corollaries are converses of each other, and when combined as a biconditional, the statement says a triangle is equilateral if and only if it is equiangular.
- Students will construct an equilateral triangle.

Formative Assessment Tips
- Refer to page T-230 for a description of *Response Logs*. In this lesson and throughout this chapter, there will be sentence stems to prompt student writing. Use your judgment for placement in the lesson, amount of time to allow for writing, and the actual sentence stem given to students.
- For a beginning list of writing stems, see page T-238.

Pacing Suggestion
- Once students have discovered the relationship about the angles in an isosceles triangle using dynamic geometry software, transition to the formal lesson.

Dynamic Teaching Tools
Dynamic Assessment & Progress Monitoring Tool
Lesson Planning Tool
Interactive Whiteboard Lesson Library
Dynamic Classroom with Dynamic Investigations

**Common Core
State Standards**

HSG-CO.C.10 Prove theorems about triangles.

HSG-CO.D.13 Construct an equilateral triangle, …

HSG-MG.A.1 Use geometric shapes, their measures, and their properties to describe objects (e.g., modeling a tree trunk or a human torso as a cylinder).

Laurie's Notes

Exploration

Motivate
- Isosceles and equilateral triangles appear in many figures that students will study in art and architecture. Tell students that in this lesson they will learn properties of triangles that have two or more congruent sides or angles.

Exploration 1
- **MP5 Use Appropriate Tools Strategically:** Students should be familiar enough with the software to follow the construction described. The software will label points in the construction process that may differ from how the diagram and table are labeled. Tell students to make adjustments as needed.
- The ordered pairs for points B and C will differ for each student, as will the length of $\overline{BC}$.
- Have students discuss the results of their explorations and make conjectures.
- ❓ "How do you classify $\triangle ABC$ by its sides?" It is isosceles. "Could it be equilateral? Explain." yes. It is equilateral when $BC = 3$.
- ❓ "How do you classify $\triangle ABC$ by its angles?" It varies. It could be acute, right, or obtuse.
- ❓ **MP3 Construct Viable Arguments and Critique the Reasoning of Others** and **MP6 Attend to Precision:** "What conjecture can you write about the angle measures of an isosceles triangle?" Be sure that students refer to the angles opposite the two congruent sides as being congruent. It is not enough to say that two of the three angles in an isosceles triangle are congruent.
- Discuss the converse of their conjecture.

Communicate Your Answer
- **MP3:** Listen for valid student reasoning as they describe how they could prove their conjectures.

Connecting to Next Step
- Now that students have investigated a property of the base angles of an isosceles triangle, they should be prepared to write a proof in the formal lesson.

5.4 Equilateral and Isosceles Triangles

Essential Question What conjectures can you make about the side lengths and angle measures of an isosceles triangle?

EXPLORATION 1 Writing a Conjecture about Isosceles Triangles

Work with a partner. Use dynamic geometry software.

a. Construct a circle with a radius of 3 units centered at the origin.

b. Construct △*ABC* so that *B* and *C* are on the circle and *A* is at the origin.

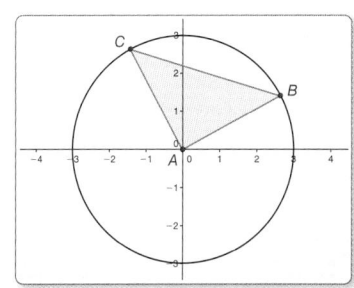

Sample

Points
A(0, 0)
B(2.64, 1.42)
C(−1.42, 2.64)
Segments
AB = 3
AC = 3
BC = 4.24
Angles
m∠A = 90°
m∠B = 45°
m∠C = 45°

> **CONSTRUCTING VIABLE ARGUMENTS**
>
> To be proficient in math, you need to make conjectures and build a logical progression of statements to explore the truth of your conjectures.

c. Recall that a triangle is *isosceles* if it has at least two congruent sides. Explain why △*ABC* is an isosceles triangle.

d. What do you observe about the angles of △*ABC*?

e. Repeat parts (a)–(d) with several other isosceles triangles using circles of different radii. Keep track of your observations by copying and completing the table below. Then write a conjecture about the angle measures of an isosceles triangle.

		A	**B**	**C**	**AB**	**AC**	**BC**	**m∠A**	**m∠B**	**m∠C**
Sample	**1.**	(0, 0)	(2.64, 1.42)	(−1.42, 2.64)	3	3	4.24	90°	45°	45°
	2.	(0, 0)								
	3.	(0, 0)								
	4.	(0, 0)								
	5.	(0, 0)								

f. Write the converse of the conjecture you wrote in part (e). Is the converse true?

Communicate Your Answer

2. What conjectures can you make about the side lengths and angle measures of an isosceles triangle?

3. How would you prove your conclusion in Exploration 1(e)? in Exploration 1(f)?

ANSWERS

1. a. Check students' work.

 b. Check students' work.

 c. Because all points on a circle are the same distance from the center, $\overline{AB} \cong \overline{AC}$.

 d. ∠*B* ≅ ∠*C*

 e. Check students' work; If two sides of a triangle are congruent, then the angles opposite them are congruent.

 f. If two angles of a triangle are congruent, then the sides opposite them are congruent; yes

2. In an isosceles triangle, two sides are congruent, and the angles opposite them are congruent.

3. Draw the angle bisector of the included angle between the congruent sides to divide the given isosceles triangle into two triangles. Use the SAS Congruence Theorem (Thm. 5.5) to show that these two triangles are congruent. Then, use properties of congruent triangles to show that the two angles opposite the shared sides are congruent.

For the converse, draw the angle bisector of the angle that is not congruent to the other two. This divides the given triangle into two triangles that have two pairs of corresponding congruent angles. The third pair of angles are congruent by the Third Angles Theorem (Thm. 5.4). Also, the angle bisector is congruent to itself by the Reflexive Property of Congruence (Thm. 2.1). So, the triangles are congruent, and the sides opposite the congruent angles in the original triangle are congruent.

5.4 Lesson

Core Vocabulary

legs, *p. 252*
vertex angle, *p. 252*
base, *p. 252*
base angles, *p. 252*

What You Will Learn

▶ Use the Base Angles Theorem.
▶ Use isosceles and equilateral triangles.

Using the Base Angles Theorem

A triangle is isosceles when it has at least two congruent sides. When an isosceles triangle has exactly two congruent sides, these two sides are the **legs**. The angle formed by the legs is the **vertex angle**. The third side is the **base** of the isosceles triangle. The two angles adjacent to the base are called **base angles**.

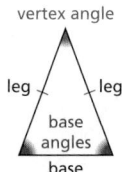

vertex angle
leg   leg
base angles
base

🔁 Theorems

Theorem 5.6   Base Angles Theorem

If two sides of a triangle are congruent, then the angles opposite them are congruent.

If $\overline{AB} \cong \overline{AC}$, then $\angle B \cong \angle C$.

Proof p. 252

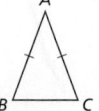

Theorem 5.7   Converse of the Base Angles Theorem

If two angles of a triangle are congruent, then the sides opposite them are congruent.

If $\angle B \cong \angle C$, then $\overline{AB} \cong \overline{AC}$.

Proof Ex. 27, p. 275

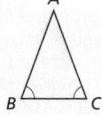

PROOF   Base Angles Theorem

Given $\overline{AB} \cong \overline{AC}$

Prove $\angle B \cong \angle C$

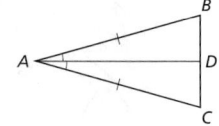

Plan for Proof
a. Draw $\overline{AD}$ so that it bisects $\angle CAB$.
b. Use the SAS Congruence Theorem to show that $\triangle ADB \cong \triangle ADC$.
c. Use properties of congruent triangles to show that $\angle B \cong \angle C$.

Plan in Action	STATEMENTS	REASONS
a.	1. Draw $\overline{AD}$, the angle bisector of $\angle CAB$.	1. Construction of angle bisector
	2. $\angle CAD \cong \angle BAD$	2. Definition of angle bisector
	3. $\overline{AB} \cong \overline{AC}$	3. Given
	4. $\overline{DA} \cong \overline{DA}$	4. Reflexive Property of Congruence (Thm. 2.1)
b.	5. $\triangle ADB \cong \triangle ADC$	5. SAS Congruence Theorem (Thm. 5.5)
c.	6. $\angle B \cong \angle C$	6. Corresponding parts of congruent triangles are congruent.

Laurie's Notes   Teacher Actions

• Discuss the definition and vocabulary associated with an isosceles triangle.
❓ Always-Sometimes-Never True: "An equilateral triangle is an isosceles triangle." always true
• Discuss a plan for proving the Base Angles Theorem. Give students time to try the proof on their own before discussing as a class. Discuss what the proof would look like if rigid motions were used.
• **Common Misconception:** Be sure students understand that there is more than one order in which the steps of a proof can be written.

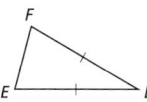 **EXAMPLE 1** **Using the Base Angles Theorem**

In △DEF, $\overline{DE} \cong \overline{DF}$. Name two congruent angles.

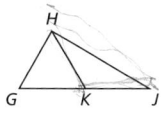

SOLUTION

▶ $\overline{DE} \cong \overline{DF}$, so by the Base Angles Theorem, $\angle E \cong \angle F$.

Monitoring Progress Help in English and Spanish at *BigIdeasMath.com*

Copy and complete the statement.

1. If $\overline{HG} \cong \overline{HK}$, then $\angle$____ $\cong \angle$____.

2. If $\angle KHJ \cong \angle KJH$, then ____ $\cong$ ____.

Recall that an equilateral triangle has three congruent sides.

Corollaries

READING

The corollaries state that a triangle is *equilateral* if and only if it is *equiangular*.

Corollary 5.2 Corollary to the Base Angles Theorem

If a triangle is equilateral, then it is equiangular.

Proof Ex. 37, p. 258; Ex. 10, p. 353

Corollary 5.3 Corollary to the Converse of the Base Angles Theorem

If a triangle is equiangular, then it is equilateral.

Proof Ex. 39, p. 258

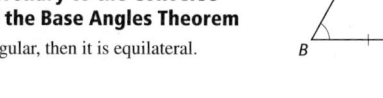

 **EXAMPLE 2** **Finding Measures in a Triangle**

Find the measures of $\angle P$, $\angle Q$, and $\angle R$.

SOLUTION

The diagram shows that △PQR is equilateral. So, by the Corollary to the Base Angles Theorem, △PQR is equiangular. So, $m\angle P = m\angle Q = m\angle R$.

$$3(m\angle P) = 180° \quad \text{Triangle Sum Theorem (Theorem 5.1)}$$
$$m\angle P = 60° \quad \text{Divide each side by 3.}$$

▶ The measures of $\angle P$, $\angle Q$, and $\angle R$ are all 60°.

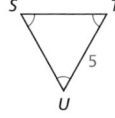

Monitoring Progress Help in English and Spanish at *BigIdeasMath.com*

3. Find the length of $\overline{ST}$ for the triangle at the left.

Section 5.4 Equilateral and Isosceles Triangles **253**

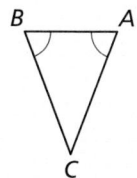

English Language Learners

Notebook Development
Have students record the theorems and corollaries on pages 252 and 253 in their notebooks. For each statement, include a sketch and an example.

Extra Example 1
In the figure, $\angle A \cong \angle B$. Name two congruent sides.

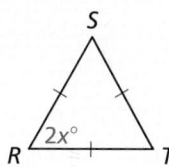

$\overline{AC} \cong \overline{BC}$

Extra Example 2
Find the value of *x*.

$x = 30$

MONITORING PROGRESS ANSWERS

1. *HGK, HKG*

2. $\overline{KH}, \overline{KJ}$

3. 5

Laurie's Notes **Teacher Actions**

• You could change Example 1. Have students draw an isosceles triangle. Mark the congruent angles. Have students name the congruent sides.

? "If a conditional statement is true, then is its converse true?" not always

• Write the two corollaries. Explain that they could be combined into one statement called a *biconditional*.

• **Response Logs:** "Right now I know …"

Section 5.4 **253**

Extra Example 3

Find the values of x and y.

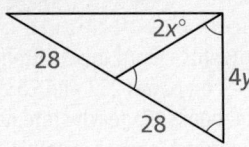

$x = 15, y = 7$

Using Isosceles and Equilateral Triangles

CONSTRUCTION   Constructing an Equilateral Triangle

Construct an equilateral triangle that has side lengths congruent to $\overline{AB}$. Use a compass and straightedge.

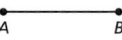

SOLUTION

Step 1	Step 2	Step 3	Step 4
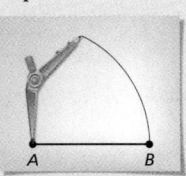		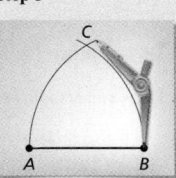	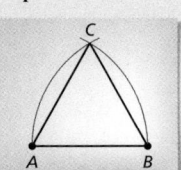

Copy a segment Copy $\overline{AB}$.

Draw an arc Draw an arc with center A and radius AB.

Draw an arc Draw an arc with center B and radius AB. Label the intersection of the arcs from Steps 2 and 3 as C.

Draw a triangle Draw $\triangle ABC$. Because $\overline{AB}$ and $\overline{AC}$ are radii of the same circle, $\overline{AB} \cong \overline{AC}$. Because $\overline{AB}$ and $\overline{BC}$ are radii of the same circle, $\overline{AB} \cong \overline{BC}$. By the Transitive Property of Congruence (Theorem 2.1), $\overline{AC} \cong \overline{BC}$. So, $\triangle ABC$ is equilateral.

EXAMPLE 3   Using Isosceles and Equilateral Triangles

Find the values of x and y in the diagram.

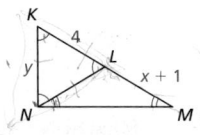

COMMON ERROR

You cannot use N to refer to $\angle LNM$ because three angles have N as their vertex.

SOLUTION

Step 1 Find the value of y. Because $\triangle KLN$ is equiangular, it is also equilateral and $\overline{KN} \cong \overline{KL}$. So, $y = 4$.

Step 2 Find the value of x. Because $\angle LNM \cong \angle LMN, \overline{LN} \cong \overline{LM}$, and $\triangle LMN$ is isosceles. You also know that $LN = 4$ because $\triangle KLN$ is equilateral.

$LN = LM$	Definition of congruent segments
$4 = x + 1$	Substitute 4 for LN and $x + 1$ for LM.
$3 = x$	Subtract 1 from each side.

Laurie's Notes   Teacher Actions

- Have students do the construction of the equilateral triangle. Ask, "How would you construct an isosceles triangle that is not equilateral?" Listen for correct reasoning. If time permits, have students construct equilateral and isosceles triangles using construction software.
- **Turn and Talk:** Pose the problem in Example 3. "How can you solve for x and y in this diagram?" Give partners time to work through the problem. Use *Popsicle Sticks* to solicit solutions.
- **MP3:** Have students critique the reasoning used by their peers.

EXAMPLE 4 Solving a Multi-Step Problem

In the lifeguard tower, $\overline{PS} \cong \overline{QR}$ and $\angle QPS \cong \angle PQR$.

a. Explain how to prove that $\triangle QPS \cong \triangle PQR$.
b. Explain why $\triangle PQT$ is isosceles.

COMMON ERROR

When you redraw the triangles so that they do not overlap, be careful to copy all given information and labels correctly.

SOLUTION

a. Draw and label $\triangle QPS$ and $\triangle PQR$ so that they do not overlap. You can see that $\overline{PQ} \cong \overline{QP}$, $\overline{PS} \cong \overline{QR}$, and $\angle QPS \cong \angle PQR$. So, by the SAS Congruence Theorem (Theorem 5.5), $\triangle QPS \cong \triangle PQR$.

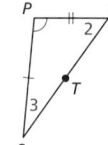 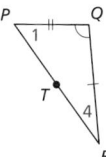

b. From part (a), you know that $\angle 1 \cong \angle 2$ because corresponding parts of congruent triangles are congruent. By the Converse of the Base Angles Theorem, $\overline{PT} \cong \overline{QT}$, and $\triangle PQT$ is isosceles.

Monitoring Progress 🔊 Help in English and Spanish at *BigIdeasMath.com*

4. Find the values of x and y in the diagram.

5. In Example 4, show that $\triangle PTS \cong \triangle QTR$.

Section 5.4   Equilateral and Isosceles Triangles   **255**

Extra Example 4

In the diagram, $\overline{PT} \cong \overline{ST}$ and $\overline{PQ} \cong \overline{SR}$.

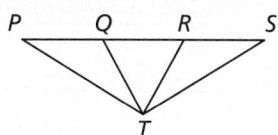

a. Explain how to prove that $\triangle PQT \cong \triangle SRT$.
   Given: $\overline{PQ} \cong \overline{SR}$. Because $\overline{PT} \cong \overline{ST}$, $\triangle PTS$ is an isosceles triangle. By the Base Angles Theorem (Thm. 5.6), $\angle P \cong \angle S$. So, $\triangle PQT \cong \triangle SRT$ by SAS $\cong$ Theorem (Thm. 5.5).

b. Explain why $\triangle QRT$ is isosceles.
   From part (a), $\overline{TQ} \cong \overline{TR}$ because corresponding parts of $\cong$ $\triangle$s are $\cong$. So $\triangle QRT$ is isosceles by definition.

MONITORING PROGRESS ANSWERS

4. $x = 60$, $y = 120$

5. From Example 4, you know that $\overline{PT} \cong \overline{QT}$ and $\angle 1 \cong \angle 2$. It is stated that $\overline{PS} \cong \overline{QR}$ and $\angle QPS \cong \angle PQR$. By the definition of congruent angles, $m\angle 1 = m\angle 2$ and $m\angle QPS = m\angle PQR$. Also, by the Angle Addition Postulate (Post. 1.4), $m\angle 1 + m\angle TPS = m\angle QPS$ and $m\angle 2 + m\angle TQR = m\angle PQR$. By substituting $m\angle 1$ for $m\angle 2$ and $m\angle QPS$ for $m\angle PQR$, you get $m\angle 1 + m\angle TQR = m\angle QPS$. Then, by the Transitive Property of Equality, $m\angle 1 + m\angle TPS = m\angle 1 + m\angle TQR$. So, by the Subtraction Property of Equality, $m\angle TPS = m\angle TQR$. Because $\angle TPS \cong \angle TQR$ by the definition of congruent angles, you can conclude that $\triangle PTS \cong \triangle QTR$ by the SAS Congruence Theorem (Thm. 5.5).

Laurie's Notes   Teacher Actions

- **Teaching Tip:** When triangles overlap in a diagram, it is helpful to make a new diagram with the triangles not overlapping. Referencing angles by numbers versus three letters is easier to see and say.
- Discuss the plan for the solution, and then have students work independently to write a solution.

Closure

- **Response Logs:** Select from "When I am writing a proof ..." or "Tomorrow I need to find out ..." or "I wish I could ...."

Section 5.4   **255**

ANSWERS

1. The vertex angle is the angle formed by the congruent sides, or legs, of an isosceles triangle.

2. The base angles of an isosceles triangle are opposite the congruent sides, and they are congruent by the Base Angles Theorem (Thm. 5.6).

3. *A, D;* Base Angles Theorem (Thm. 5.6)

4. *A, BEA;* Base Angles Theorem (Thm. 5.6)

5. $\overline{CD}, \overline{CE}$; Converse of the Base Angles Theorem (Thm. 5.7)

6. $\overline{EB}, \overline{EC}$; Converse of the Base Angles Theorem (Thm. 5.7)

7. $x = 12$

8. $x = 16$

9. $x = 60$

10. $x = 20$

11. $x = 79, y = 22$

12. *Sample answer:*

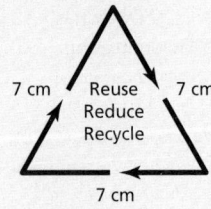

13. $x = 60, y = 60$

14. $x = 20, y = 70$

15. $x = 30, y = 5$

16. $x = 7, y = 4$

17.

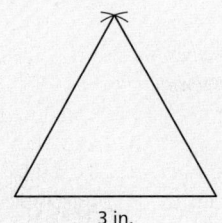

3 in.

18.

1.25 in.

19. When two angles of a triangle are congruent, the sides opposite the angles are congruent; Because $\angle A \cong \angle C, \overline{AB} \cong \overline{BC}$. So, $BC = 5$.

Vocabulary and Core Concept Check

1. **VOCABULARY** Describe how to identify the *vertex angle* of an isosceles triangle.

2. **WRITING** What is the relationship between the base angles of an isosceles triangle? Explain.

Monitoring Progress and Modeling with Mathematics

In Exercises 3–6, copy and complete the statement. State which theorem you used. *(See Example 1.)*

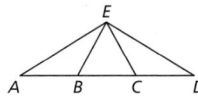

3. If $\overline{AE} \cong \overline{DE}$, then $\angle$___ $\cong \angle$___.

4. If $\overline{AB} \cong \overline{EB}$, then $\angle$___ $\cong \angle$___.

5. If $\angle D \cong \angle CED$, then ___ $\cong$ ___.

6. If $\angle EBC \cong \angle ECB$, then ___ $\cong$ ___.

In Exercises 7–10, find the value of *x*. *(See Example 2.)*

7.

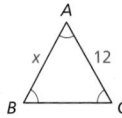

8.

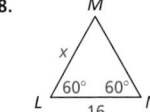

9.

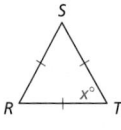

10.

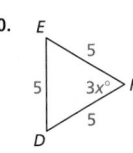

11. **MODELING WITH MATHEMATICS** The dimensions of a sports pennant are given in the diagram. Find the values of *x* and *y*.

12. **MODELING WITH MATHEMATICS** A logo in an advertisement is an equilateral triangle with a side length of 7 centimeters. Sketch the logo and give the measure of each side.

In Exercises 13–16, find the values of *x* and *y*. *(See Example 3.)*

13.

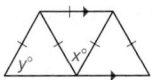

14.

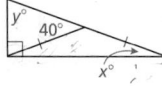

15.

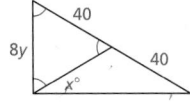

16.

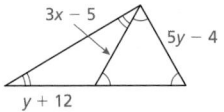

CONSTRUCTION In Exercises 17 and 18, construct an equilateral triangle whose sides are the given length.

17. 3 inches

18. 1.25 inches

19. **ERROR ANALYSIS** Describe and correct the error in finding the length of $\overline{BC}$.

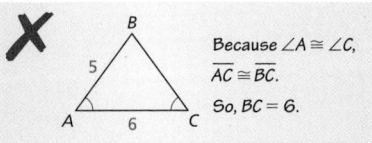

Because $\angle A \cong \angle C$, $\overline{AC} \cong \overline{BC}$.

So, $BC = 6$.

20. PROBLEM SOLVING

The diagram represents part of the exterior of the Bow Tower in Calgary, Alberta, Canada. In the diagram, △ABD and △CBD are congruent equilateral triangles. *(See Example 4.)*

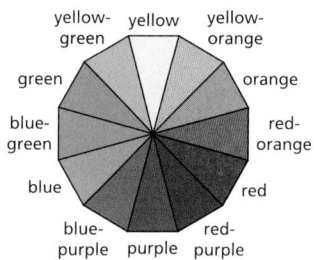

a. Explain why △ABC is isosceles.

b. Explain why ∠BAE ≅ ∠BCE.

c. Show that △ABE and △CBE are congruent.

d. Find the measure of ∠BAE.

21. FINDING A PATTERN In the pattern shown, each small triangle is an equilateral triangle with an area of 1 square unit.

a. Explain how you know that any triangle made out of equilateral triangles is equilateral.

b. Find the areas of the first four triangles in the pattern.

c. Describe any patterns in the areas. Predict the area of the seventh triangle in the pattern. Explain your reasoning.

Triangle	Area
△	1 square unit
▲	
▲	
▲	

22. REASONING The base of isosceles △XYZ is $\overline{YZ}$. What can you prove? Select all that apply.

Ⓐ $\overline{XY} \cong \overline{XZ}$ Ⓑ ∠X ≅ ∠Y

Ⓒ ∠Y ≅ ∠Z Ⓓ $\overline{YZ} \cong \overline{ZX}$

In Exercises 23 and 24, find the perimeter of the triangle.

23.
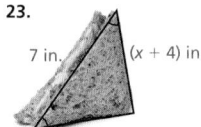
7 in. (x + 4) in.
(4x + 1) in.

24. (21 − x) in.
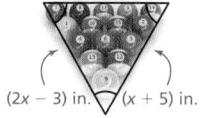
(2x − 3) in. (x + 5) in.

MODELING WITH MATHEMATICS In Exercises 25–28, use the diagram based on the color wheel. The 12 triangles in the diagram are isosceles triangles with congruent vertex angles.

yellow-green yellow yellow-orange
green   orange
blue-green   red-orange
blue   red
blue-purple purple red-purple

25. Complementary colors lie directly opposite each other on the color wheel. Explain how you know that the yellow triangle is congruent to the purple triangle.

26. The measure of the vertex angle of the yellow triangle is 30°. Find the measures of the base angles.

27. Trace the color wheel. Then form a triangle whose vertices are the midpoints of the bases of the red, yellow, and blue triangles. (These colors are the *primary colors*.) What type of triangle is this?

28. Other triangles can be formed on the color wheel that are congruent to the triangle in Exercise 27. The colors on the vertices of these triangles are called *triads*. What are the possible triads?

29. CRITICAL THINKING Are isosceles triangles always acute triangles? Explain your reasoning.

30. CRITICAL THINKING Is it possible for an equilateral triangle to have an angle measure other than 60°? Explain your reasoning.

31. MATHEMATICAL CONNECTIONS The lengths of the sides of a triangle are $3t$, $5t − 12$, and $t + 20$. Find the values of t that make the triangle isosceles. Explain your reasoning.

32. MATHEMATICAL CONNECTIONS The measure of an exterior angle of an isosceles triangle is $x°$. Write expressions representing the possible angle measures of the triangle in terms of x.

33. WRITING Explain why the measure of the vertex angle of an isosceles triangle must be an even number of degrees when the measures of all the angles of the triangle are whole numbers.

26. 75°

27.
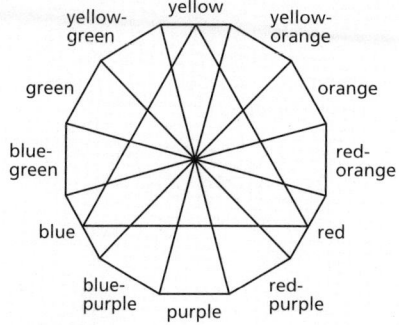
yellow-green yellow yellow-orange
green   orange
blue-green   red-orange
blue   red
blue-purple purple red-purple

equiangular equilateral

28. yellow-orange, red-purple, and blue-green; green, orange, and purple; red-orange, blue-purple, and yellow-green

29. no; The two sides that are congruent can form an obtuse angle or a right angle.

30. no; The sum of the angles of a triangle is always 180°. So, if all three angles are congruent, then they will always be $\frac{180°}{3} = 60°$.

31–33. See Additional Answers.

Dynamic Teaching Tools

Dynamic Assessment & Progress Monitoring Tool

Interactive Whiteboard Lesson Library

Dynamic Classroom with Dynamic Investigations

ANSWERS

20. a. Because △ABD and △CBD are congruent and equilateral, you know that $\overline{AB} \cong \overline{CB}$. So, △ABC is isosceles.

b. Because △ABC is isosceles, ∠BAE ≅ ∠BCE by the Base Angles Theorem (Thm. 5.6).

c. By the Reflexive Property of Congruence (Thm. 2.1), $\overline{BE} \cong \overline{BE}$. Because △ABD and △CBD are congruent and equilateral, and also equiangular by the Corollary to the Base Angles Theorem (Cor. 5.2), you can conclude that ∠ABE ≅ ∠CBE. Also, $\overline{AB} \cong \overline{CB}$ as explained in part (a). So, by the SAS Congruence Theorem (Thm. 5.5), △ABE ≅ △CBE.

d. 30°

21. a. Each edge is made out of the same number of sides of the original equilateral triangle.

b. 1 square unit, 4 square units, 9 square units, 16 square units

c. Triangle 1 has an area of $1^2 = 1$, Triangle 2 has an area of $2^2 = 4$, Triangle 3 has an area of $3^2 = 9$, and so on. So, by inductive reasoning, you can predict that Triangle n has an area of n^2; 49 square units; $n^2 = 7^2 = 49$

22. A, C   **23.** 17 in.

24. 39 in.

25. By the Reflexive Property of Congruence (Thm. 2.1), the yellow triangle and the yellow-orange triangle share a congruent side. Because the triangles are all isosceles, by the Transitive Property of Congruence (Thm. 2.1), the yellow-orange triangle and the orange triangle share a side that is congruent to the one shared by the yellow triangle and the yellow-orange triangle. This reasoning can be continued around the wheel, so the legs of the isosceles triangles are all congruent. Because you are given that the vertex angles are all congruent, you can conclude that the yellow triangle is congruent to the purple triangle by the SAS Congruence Theorem (Thm. 5.5).

ANSWERS

34. a. ∠XVY, ∠UXV; ∠WUX ≅ ∠XVY because they are both vertex angles of congruent isosceles triangles. Also, m∠UXV + m∠VXY = m∠UXY by the Angle Addition Postulate (Post. 1.4), and m∠UXY = m∠WUX + m∠UWX by the Exterior Angle Theorem (Thm. 5.2). So, by the Transitive Property of Equality, m∠UXV + m∠VXY = m∠WUX + m∠UWX. Also, m∠UWX = m∠VXY because they are base angles of congruent isosceles triangles. By substituting m∠UWX for m∠VXY, you get m∠UXV + m∠UWX = m∠WUX + m∠UWX. By the Subtraction Property of Equality, m∠UXV = m∠WUX, so ∠UXV ≅ ∠WUX.

b. 8 m

35–44. See Additional Answers.

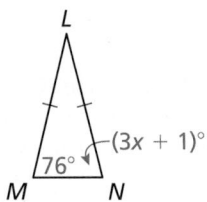
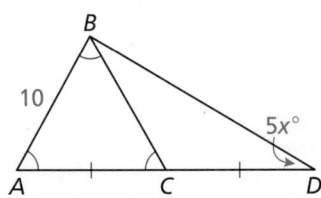
34. PROBLEM SOLVING The triangular faces of the peaks on a roof are congruent isosceles triangles with vertex angles U and V.

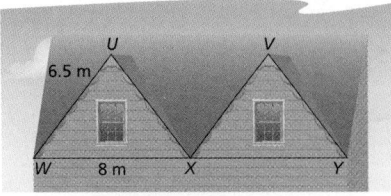

a. Name two angles congruent to ∠WUX. Explain your reasoning.

b. Find the distance between points U and V.

35. PROBLEM SOLVING A boat is traveling parallel to the shore along $\overrightarrow{RT}$. When the boat is at point R, the captain measures the angle to the lighthouse as 35°. After the boat has traveled 2.1 miles, the captain measures the angle to the lighthouse to be 70°.

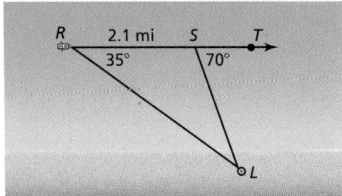

a. Find SL. Explain your reasoning.

b. Explain how to find the distance between the boat and the shoreline.

36. THOUGHT PROVOKING The postulates and theorems in this book represent Euclidean geometry. In spherical geometry, all points are points on the surface of a sphere. A line is a circle on the sphere whose diameter is equal to the diameter of the sphere. In spherical geometry, do all equiangular triangles have the same angle measures? Justify your answer.

37. PROVING A COROLLARY Prove that the Corollary to the Base Angles Theorem (Corollary 5.2) follows from the Base Angles Theorem (Theorem 5.6).

38. HOW DO YOU SEE IT? You are designing fabric purses to sell at the school fair.

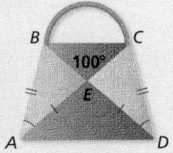

a. Explain why △ABE ≅ △DCE.

b. Name the isosceles triangles in the purse.

c. Name three angles that are congruent to ∠EAD.

39. PROVING A COROLLARY Prove that the Corollary to the Converse of the Base Angles Theorem (Corollary 5.3) follows from the Converse of the Base Angles Theorem (Theorem 5.7).

40. MAKING AN ARGUMENT The coordinates of two points are T(0, 6) and U(6, 0). Your friend claims that points T, U, and V will always be the vertices of an isosceles triangle when V is any point on the line y = x. Is your friend correct? Explain your reasoning.

41. PROOF Use the diagram to prove that △DEF is equilateral.

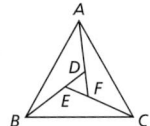

Given △ABC is equilateral.
∠CAD ≅ ∠ABE ≅ ∠BCF

Prove △DEF is equilateral.

Maintaining Mathematical Proficiency
Reviewing what you learned in previous grades and lessons

Use the given property to complete the statement. *(Section 2.5)*

42. Reflexive Property of Congruence (Theorem 2.1): _____ ≅ $\overline{SE}$

43. Symmetric Property of Congruence (Theorem 2.1): If _____ ≅ _____, then $\overline{RS}$ ≅ $\overline{JK}$.

44. Transitive Property of Congruence (Theorem 2.1): If $\overline{EF}$ ≅ $\overline{PQ}$, and $\overline{PQ}$ ≅ $\overline{UV}$, then _____ ≅ _____.

Core Vocabulary

interior angles, *p. 233*
exterior angles, *p. 233*
corollary to a theorem, *p. 235*
corresponding parts, *p. 240*

legs (of an isosceles triangle), *p. 252*
vertex angle (of an isosceles triangle), *p. 252*
base (of an isosceles triangle), *p. 252*
base angles (of an isosceles triangle), *p. 252*

Core Concepts

Classifying Triangles by Sides, *p. 232*
Classifying Triangles by Angles, *p. 232*
Theorem 5.1 Triangle Sum Theorem, *p. 233*
Theorem 5.2 Exterior Angle Theorem, *p. 234*
Corollary 5.1 Corollary to the Triangle Sum Theorem, *p. 235*
Identifying and Using Corresponding Parts, *p. 240*
Theorem 5.3 Properties of Triangle Congruence, *p. 241*
Theorem 5.4 Third Angles Theorem, *p. 242*

Theorem 5.5 Side-Angle-Side (SAS) Congruence Theorem, *p. 246*
Theorem 5.6 Base Angles Theorem, *p. 252*
Theorem 5.7 Converse of the Base Angles Theorem, *p. 252*
Corollary 5.2 Corollary to the Base Angles Theorem, *p. 253*
Corollary 5.3 Corollary to the Converse of the Base Angles Theorem, *p. 253*

Mathematical Practices

1. In Exercise 37 on page 237, what are you given? What relationships are present? What is your goal?

2. Explain the relationships present in Exercise 23 on page 244.

3. Describe at least three different patterns created using triangles for the picture in Exercise 20 on page 257.

- - - - - - - - - - - Study Skills - - - - - - - - - - -

Visual Learners

Draw a picture of a word problem.

- Draw a picture of a word problem before starting to solve the problem. You do not have to be an artist.

- When making a review card for a word problem, include a picture. This will help you recall the information while taking a test.

- Make sure your notes are visually neat for easy recall.

259

Dynamic Teaching Tools

Dynamic Assessment & Progress Monitoring Tool

Interactive Whiteboard Lesson Library

Dynamic Classroom with Dynamic Investigations

ANSWERS

1. You are given a diagram of the triangle made from the segments that connect each person to the other two, along with the length of each segment; The people are all standing on the same stage (plane), so the points are coplanar; You are asked to classify the triangle by its sides and by measuring its angles.

2. There is a pair of congruent triangles, so all pairs of corresponding sides and angles are congruent. By the Triangle Sum Theorem (Thm. 5.1), the three angles in $\triangle LMN$ have measures that add up to 180°. You are given two measures, so you can find the third using this theorem. The measure of $\angle P$ is equal to the measure of its corresponding angle, $\angle L$. The measure of $\angle R$ is equal to the measure of its corresponding angle, $\angle N$. Once you write this system of equations, you can solve for the values of the variables.

3. *Sample answer:* a large triangle made up of 9 small triangles, a hexagon, a parallelogram

ANSWERS

1. 110°

2. 138°

3. 139°

4. corresponding sides: $\overline{AB} \cong \overline{DE}$, $\overline{BC} \cong \overline{EF}$, $\overline{AC} \cong \overline{DF}$; corresponding Angles: $\angle A \cong \angle D$, $\angle B \cong \angle E$, $\angle C \cong \angle F$; Sample answer: $\triangle CAB \cong \triangle FDE$

5. corresponding sides: $\overline{QR} \cong \overline{WX}$, $\overline{RS} \cong \overline{XY}$, $\overline{ST} \cong \overline{YZ}$, $\overline{QT} \cong \overline{WZ}$; corresponding angles: $\angle Q \cong \angle W$, $\angle R \cong \angle X$, $\angle S \cong \angle Y$, $\angle T \cong \angle Z$; Sample answer: $RSTQ \cong XYZW$

6. no; The congruent angles are not the included angle.

7–8. See Additional Answers.

9. $\angle WVX$, $\angle WXV$; Base Angles Theorem (Thm. 5.6)

10. $\angle XZY$, $\angle XYZ$; Base Angles Theorem (Thm. 5.6)

11. $\overline{ZV}$, $\overline{ZX}$; Converse of the Base Angles Theorem (Thm. 5.7)

12. $\overline{ZX}$, $\overline{ZY}$; Converse of the Base Angles Theorem (Thm. 5.7)

13. $x = 13$, $y = 9$

14. $x = 5$, $y = 20$

15. 22°, 68°

16. a. right, obtuse, acute, equiangular

    b. equilateral, scalene, isosceles

    c. See Additional Answers.

5.1–5.4 Quiz

Find the measure of the exterior angle. *(Section 5.1)*

1.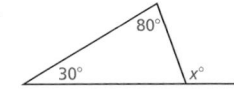

2.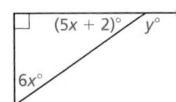

3.

Identify all pairs of congruent corresponding parts. Then write another congruence statement for the polygons. *(Section 5.2)*

4. $\triangle ABC \cong \triangle DEF$

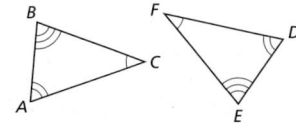

5. $QRST \cong WXYZ$

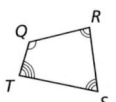 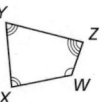

Decide whether enough information is given to prove that the triangles are congruent using the SAS Congruence Theorem (Thm. 5.5). If so, write a proof. If not, explain why. *(Section 5.3)*

6. $\triangle CAD$, $\triangle CBD$

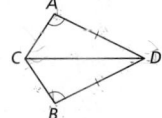

7. $\triangle GHF$, $\triangle KHJ$

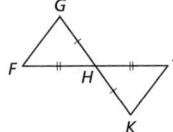

8. $\triangle LMP$, $\triangle NMP$

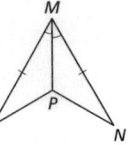

Copy and complete the statement. State which theorem you used. *(Section 5.4)*

9. If $VW \cong WX$, then $\angle$___ $\cong \angle$___.

10. If $XZ \cong XY$, then $\angle$___ $\cong \angle$___.

11. If $\angle ZVX \cong \angle ZXV$, then ___ $\cong$ ___.

12. If $\angle XYZ \cong \angle ZXY$, then ___ $\cong$ ___.

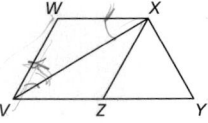

Find the values of x and y. *(Section 5.2 and Section 5.4)*

13. $\triangle DEF \cong \triangle QRS$

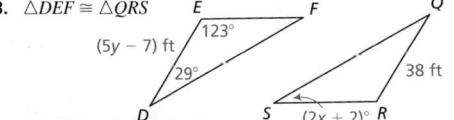

14.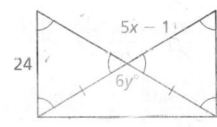

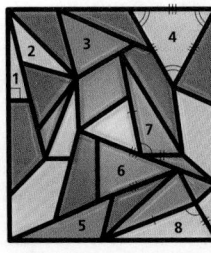

15. In a right triangle, the measure of one acute angle is 4 times the difference of the measure of the other acute angle and 5. Find the measure of each acute angle in the triangle. *(Section 5.1)*

16. The figure shows a stained glass window. *(Section 5.1 and Section 5.3)*

    a. Classify triangles 1–4 by their angles.

    b. Classify triangles 4–6 by their sides.

    c. Is there enough information given to prove that $\triangle 7 \cong \triangle 8$? If so, label the vertices and write a proof. If not, determine what additional information is needed.

Overview of Section 5.5

Introduction

- Side-Side-Side is usually the first method presented for proving two triangles congruent, and it is usually a postulate, with the remaining methods being presented and proven as theorems.
- The approach used in this chapter is to begin with the Side-Angle-Side (SAS) Congruence Theorem (Thm. 5.5). In this lesson, Side-Side-Side is presented as a theorem and proven using a transformational approach. A third method, Hypotenuse-Leg (HL), is presented as a theorem in this lesson.
- Different approaches are used in the proof examples in the formal lesson: transformational, two-column, and paragraph. Students should be comfortable with all three styles.
- A new construction is presented—how to copy a triangle using the Side-Side-Side (SSS) Congruence Theorem.

Formative Assessment Tips

- Refer to page T-230 for a description of *Response Logs*. In this lesson and throughout this chapter, there will be sentence stems to prompt student writing. Use your judgment for placement in the lesson, amount of time to allow for writing, and the actual sentence stem given to students.
- For a beginning list of writing stems, see page T-238.

Another Way

- The classic, traditional approach to introducing the SSS Congruence Theorem is to use objects such as coffee stirrers to represent the sides of a triangle. Using stirrers of lengths 4, 5, and 6 inches, there is only one triangle that can be made.

Pacing Suggestion

- Take time for students to explore and discover the SSS congruence relationship using dynamic geometry software, and then transition to the formal lesson.

Common Core
State Standards

HSG-CO.B.8 Explain how the criteria for triangle congruence (… SSS) follow from the definition of congruence in terms of rigid motions.

HSG-MG.A.1 Use geometric shapes, their measures, and their properties to describe objects (e.g., modeling a tree trunk or a human torso as a cylinder).

HSG-MG.A.3 Apply geometric methods to solve design problems (e.g., designing an object or structure to satisfy physical constraints or minimize cost; working with typographic grid systems based on ratios).

Laurie's Notes

Exploration

Motivate
- Ask students to consider the following statements and whether the two triangles would be congruent.
  - All equilateral triangles are congruent. no
  - All equiangular triangles are congruent. no
  - All isosceles triangles with a vertex angle of 40° are congruent. no
  - All isosceles triangles with legs of 4 inches and a vertex angle of 40° are congruent. yes
  - All scalene triangles with side lengths 3 inches, 4 inches, and 5 inches are congruent.
    Students may say "yes" to this one. Indeed it is "yes" and that will be proven in this lesson.

Exploration
- The Side-Side-Side (SSS) Congruence Theorem (Thm. 5.8) is the second of several theorems to show that less than six pieces of information are needed to prove that two triangles are congruent.
- This exploration may not be a familiar approach to verifying the SSS triangle congruence method, so become familiar with the construction steps and potential for extensions.

Exploration 1
- **MP5 Use Appropriate Tools Strategically:** Students should be familiar enough with the software to follow the construction described. The software will label points in the construction process that may differ from how the diagram and table are labeled. Tell students to make adjustments as needed.
- The ordered pairs for points B and C will differ for each student, but the lengths of the three sides are still 2, 3, and 4 units, and the three missing angles will be the same measure.
- In constructing $\triangle ABC$, students should try each orientation, clockwise and counterclockwise. Are the results the same?
- Have students discuss the results of their explorations and make conjectures.
- **Extension:** Repeat the construction for two circles of different radii or for a different length of $\overline{BC}$.

Communicate Your Answer
- **MP3 Construct Viable Arguments and Critique the Reasoning of Others:** Students should conclude that when three sides of one triangle are congruent to the three sides of another triangle, the triangles are congruent.

Connecting to Next Step
- The exploration allows students to discover and make sense of the SSS congruence relationship that will be presented formally in the lesson.

Proving Triangle Congruence by SSS

Essential Question

What can you conclude about two triangles when you know the corresponding sides are congruent?

EXPLORATION 1 Drawing Triangles

Work with a partner. Use dynamic geometry software.

a. Construct circles with radii of 2 units and 3 units centered at the origin. Label the origin A. Then draw $\overline{BC}$ of length 4 units.

b. Move $\overline{BC}$ so that B is on the smaller circle and C is on the larger circle. Then draw $\triangle ABC$.

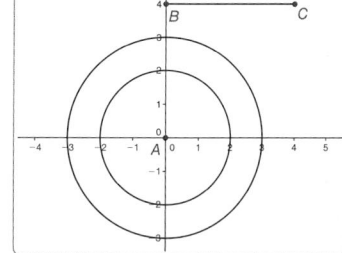

USING TOOLS STRATEGICALLY

To be proficient in math, you need to use technology to help visualize the results of varying assumptions, explore consequences, and compare predictions with data.

c. Explain why the side lengths of $\triangle ABC$ are 2, 3, and 4 units.

d. Find $m\angle A$, $m\angle B$, and $m\angle C$.

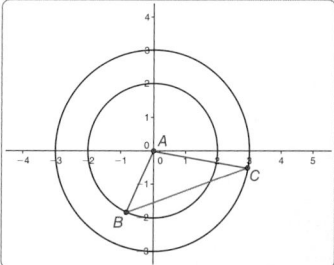

e. Repeat parts (b) and (d) several times, moving $\overline{BC}$ to different locations. Keep track of your results by copying and completing the table below. What can you conclude?

	A	B	C	AB	AC	BC	$m\angle A$	$m\angle B$	$m\angle C$
1.	(0, 0)			2	3	4			
2.	(0, 0)			2	3	4			
3.	(0, 0)			2	3	4			
4.	(0, 0)			2	3	4			
5.	(0, 0)			2	3	4			

Communicate Your Answer

2. What can you conclude about two triangles when you know the corresponding sides are congruent?

3. How would you prove your conclusion in Exploration 1(e)?

ANSWERS

1. a. Check students' work

  b. Check students' work.

  c. $AB = 2$ because $\overline{AB}$ has one endpoint at the origin and one endpoint on a circle with a radius of 2 units.
  $AC = 3$ because $\overline{AC}$ has one endpoint at the origin and one endpoint on a circle with a radius of 3 units. $BC = 4$ because it was created that way.

  d. $m\angle A = 104.43°$, $m\angle B = 46.61°$, $m\angle C = 28.96°$

  e. Check students' work; If two triangles have three pairs of congruent sides, then they will have three pairs of congruent angles.

2. The corresponding angles are also congruent and therefore, the triangles are congruent.

3. Use rigid transformations to map triangles.

Differentiated Instruction

Inclusion

Remind students that the sides of a triangle are segments. Segments can be *congruent* when their lengths are *equal*. Likewise, the angles in a triangle are *congruent* when their measures are *equal*. Point out that the SAS and SSS Congruence Theorems require that pairs of *congruent* corresponding parts be identified. This will help students when proving the congruence of two triangles.

What You Will Learn

▶ Use the Side-Side-Side (SSS) Congruence Theorem.
▶ Use the Hypotenuse-Leg (HL) Congruence Theorem.

Core Vocabulary

legs, *p. 264*
hypotenuse, *p. 264*

Previous
congruent figures
rigid motion

Using the Side-Side-Side Congruence Theorem

🅖 Theorem

Theorem 5.8   Side-Side-Side (SSS) Congruence Theorem

If three sides of one triangle are congruent to three sides of a second triangle, then the two triangles are congruent.

If $\overline{AB} \cong \overline{DE}$, $\overline{BC} \cong \overline{EF}$, and $\overline{AC} \cong \overline{DF}$, then $\triangle ABC \cong \triangle DEF$.

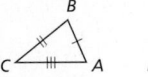 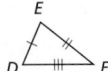

PROOF   Side-Side-Side (SSS) Congruence Theorem

Given $\overline{AB} \cong \overline{DE}$, $\overline{BC} \cong \overline{EF}$, $\overline{AC} \cong \overline{DF}$

Prove $\triangle ABC \cong \triangle DEF$

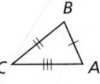 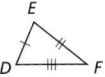

First, translate $\triangle ABC$ so that point A maps to point D, as shown below.

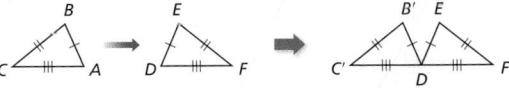

This translation maps $\triangle ABC$ to $\triangle DB'C'$. Next, rotate $\triangle DB'C'$ counterclockwise through $\angle C'DF$ so that the image of $\overrightarrow{DC'}$ coincides with $\overrightarrow{DF}$, as shown below.

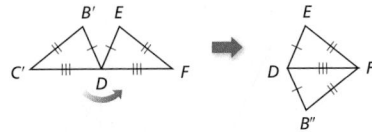

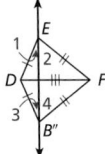

Because $\overline{DC'} \cong \overline{DF}$, the rotation maps point C' to point F. So, this rotation maps $\triangle DB'C'$ to $\triangle DB''F$. Draw an auxiliary line through points E and B''. This line creates $\angle 1$, $\angle 2$, $\angle 3$, and $\angle 4$, as shown at the left.

Because $\overline{DE} \cong \overline{DB''}$, $\triangle DEB''$ is an isosceles triangle. Because $\overline{FE} \cong \overline{FB''}$, $\triangle FEB''$ is an isosceles triangle. By the Base Angles Theorem (Thm. 5.6), $\angle 1 \cong \angle 3$ and $\angle 2 \cong \angle 4$. By the definition of congruence, $m\angle 1 = m\angle 3$ and $m\angle 2 = m\angle 4$. By construction, $m\angle DEF = m\angle 1 + m\angle 2$ and $m\angle DB''F = m\angle 3 + m\angle 4$. You can now use the Substitution Property of Equality to show $m\angle DEF = m\angle DB''F$.

$m\angle DEF = m\angle 1 + m\angle 2$	Angle Addition Postulate (Postulate 1.4)
$= m\angle 3 + m\angle 4$	Substitute $m\angle 3$ for $m\angle 1$ and $m\angle 4$ for $m\angle 2$.
$= m\angle DB''F$	Angle Addition Postulate (Postulate 1.4)

By the definition of congruence, $\angle DEF \cong \angle DB''F$. So, two pairs of sides and their included angles are congruent. By the SAS Congruence Theorem (Thm. 5.5), $\triangle DB''F \cong \triangle DEF$. So, a composition of rigid motions maps $\triangle DB''F$ to $\triangle DEF$. Because a composition of rigid motions maps $\triangle ABC$ to $\triangle DB''F$ and a composition of rigid motions maps $\triangle DB''F$ to $\triangle DEF$, a composition of rigid motions maps $\triangle ABC$ to $\triangle DEF$. So, $\triangle ABC \cong \triangle DEF$.

Laurie's Notes   Teacher Actions

• The Side-Side-Side (SSS) Congruence Theorem should make sense following the exploration. Discuss the first few steps in the proof.

COMMON ERROR Once $\triangle ABC$ has been translated and rotated, students want to reflect $\triangle DB''F$ onto $\triangle DEF$. Because no relationship is known about the angles yet, $\triangle DB''F$ would map onto $\triangle DEF$ only if SSS was a valid congruence method, but that is what we are proving and that would be circular reasoning. Work through the remaining steps of the proof as shown.

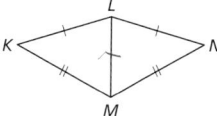 **EXAMPLE 1** Using the SSS Congruence Theorem

Write a proof.

Given $\overline{KL} \cong \overline{NL}, \overline{KM} \cong \overline{NM}$

Prove $\triangle KLM \cong \triangle NLM$

SOLUTION

STATEMENTS	REASONS
S 1. $\overline{KL} \cong \overline{NL}$	1. Given
S 2. $\overline{KM} \cong \overline{NM}$	2. Given
S 3. $\overline{LM} \cong \overline{LM}$	3. Reflexive Property of Congruence (Thm. 2.1)
4. $\triangle KLM \cong \triangle NLM$	4. SSS Congruence Theorem

Monitoring Progress 🔊 Help in English and Spanish at *BigIdeasMath.com*

Decide whether the congruence statement is true. Explain your reasoning.

1. $\triangle DFG \cong \triangle HJK$ 2. $\triangle ACB \cong \triangle CAD$ 3. $\triangle QPT \cong \triangle RST$

 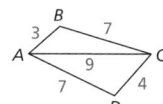 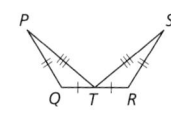

EXAMPLE 2 Solving a Real-Life Problem

Explain why the bench with the diagonal support is stable, while the one without the support can collapse.

SOLUTION

The bench with the diagonal support forms triangles with fixed side lengths. By the SSS Congruence Theorem, these triangles cannot change shape, so the bench is stable. The bench without the diagonal support is not stable because there are many possible quadrilaterals with the given side lengths.

Monitoring Progress 🔊 Help in English and Spanish at *BigIdeasMath.com*

Determine whether the figure is stable. Explain your reasoning.

4.    5.    6.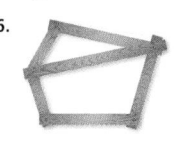

Laurie's Notes   Teacher Actions

- **Turn and Talk:** Pose Example 1. "What additional information is needed to prove the triangles congruent?"
- **Think-Pair-Share:** Have students answer Questions 1–3, and then share and discuss as a class.
- Ask students whether any of them have seen the cross brace that builders use when a wall has only the vertical two-by-four studs. The brace prevents the wall from leaning left or right. The application in Example 2 is similar.

Extra Example 1
Write a proof.
Given $\overline{PQ} \cong \overline{RQ}, \overline{PS} \cong \overline{RS}$
Prove $\triangle PQS \cong \triangle RQS$

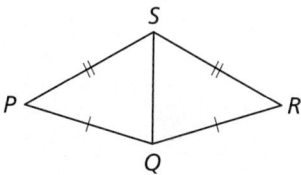

Statements (Reasons)
1. $\overline{PQ} \cong \overline{RQ}, \overline{PS} \cong \overline{RS}$ (Given)
2. $\overline{QS} \cong \overline{QS}$ (Reflex. Prop. $\cong$ Thm. 2.1)
3. $\triangle PQS \cong \triangle RQS$ (SSS $\cong$ Thm. 5.8)

Extra Example 2
Determine whether the hexagon is stable. Explain your reasoning.

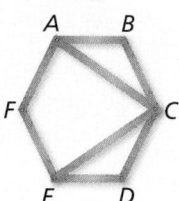

The diagonal supports form two triangles and a quadrilateral *ACEF*. The figure is not stable because there are many possible quadrilaterals with the given side lengths.

MONITORING PROGRESS ANSWERS
1. yes; From the diagram markings, $\overline{DF} \cong \overline{HJ}, \overline{FG} \cong \overline{JK}$, and $\overline{DG} \cong \overline{HK}$. So, $\triangle DFG \cong \triangle HJK$ by the SSS Congruence Theorem (Thm. 5.8).
2–6. See Additional Answers.

CONSTRUCTION Copying a Triangle Using SSS

Construct a triangle that is congruent to △*ABC* using the
SSS Congruence Theorem. Use a compass and straightedge.

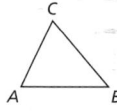

SOLUTION

Step 1	Step 2	Step 3	Step 4
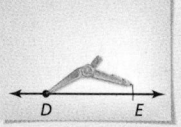	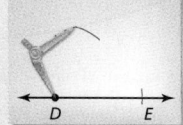	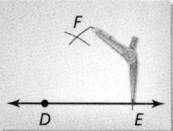	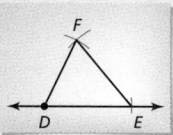
Construct a side Construct $\overline{DE}$ so that it is congruent to $\overline{AB}$.	**Draw an arc** Open your compass to the length *AC*. Use this length to draw an arc with center *D*.	**Draw an arc** Draw an arc with radius *BC* and center *E* that intersects the arc from Step 2. Label the intersection point *F*.	**Draw a triangle** Draw △*DEF*. By the SSS Congruence Theorem, △*ABC* ≅ △*DEF*.

Using the Hypotenuse-Leg Congruence Theorem

You know that SAS and SSS are valid methods for proving that triangles are
congruent. What about SSA?

In general, SSA is *not* a valid method for proving that triangles are congruent. In the
triangles below, two pairs of sides and a pair of angles not included between them are
congruent, but the triangles are not congruent.

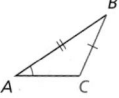 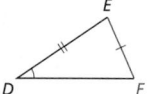

While SSA is not valid in general, there is a special case for right triangles.

In a right triangle, the sides adjacent to the right angle are called the **legs**. The side
opposite the right angle is called the **hypotenuse** of the right triangle.

⟲ Theorem

Theorem 5.9   Hypotenuse-Leg (HL) Congruence Theorem

If the hypotenuse and a leg of a right
triangle are congruent to the hypotenuse
and a leg of a second right triangle, then
the two triangles are congruent.

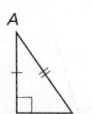 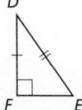

If $\overline{AB} \cong \overline{DE}$, $\overline{AC} \cong \overline{DF}$, and
$m\angle C = m\angle F = 90°$, then △*ABC* ≅ △*DEF*.

Proof Ex. 38, p. 470; *BigIdeasMath.com*

Laurie's Notes **Teacher Actions**

? "How could you construct a copy of a triangle using the SSS Congruence Theorem (Thm. 5.8)?"
Listen for steps shown in the construction.

? **Probing Question:** "You know that SAS and SSS are two methods for proving triangles
congruent. Do you think SSA is a valid method?" Answers will vary. Ask students to draw ∠*A*
measuring 40°. Construct side $\overline{AB}$ with length 4 inches. Now construct side $\overline{BC}$ with length
3 inches. Two possible triangles can be formed, meaning SSA is not a valid triangle congruence
method, except for right triangles.

• Discuss the Hypotenuse-Leg (HL) Congruence Theorem.

EXAMPLE 3 Using the Hypotenuse-Leg Congruence Theorem

Write a proof.

Given $\overline{WY} \cong \overline{XZ}$, $\overline{WZ} \perp \overline{ZY}$, $\overline{XY} \perp \overline{ZY}$

Prove $\triangle WYZ \cong \triangle XZY$

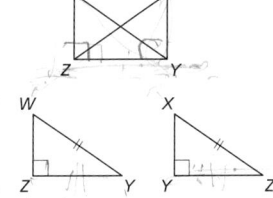

SOLUTION

Redraw the triangles so they are side by side with corresponding parts in the same position. Mark the given information in the diagram.

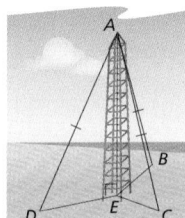

STATEMENTS	REASONS
H **1.** $\overline{WY} \cong \overline{XZ}$	1. Given
2. $\overline{WZ} \perp \overline{ZY}, \overline{XY} \perp \overline{ZY}$	2. Given
3. $\angle Z$ and $\angle Y$ are right angles.	3. Definition of $\perp$ lines
4. $\triangle WYZ$ and $\triangle XZY$ are right triangles.	4. Definition of a right triangle
L **5.** $\overline{ZY} \cong \overline{YZ}$	5. Reflexive Property of Congruence (Thm. 2.1)
6. $\triangle WYZ \cong \triangle XZY$	6. HL Congruence Theorem

EXAMPLE 4 Using the Hypotenuse-Leg Congruence Theorem

The television antenna is perpendicular to the plane containing points B, C, D, and E. Each of the cables running from the top of the antenna to B, C, and D has the same length. Prove that $\triangle AEB$, $\triangle AEC$, and $\triangle AED$ are congruent.

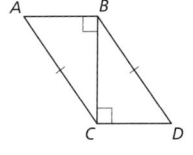

Given $\overline{AE} \perp \overline{EB}$, $\overline{AE} \perp \overline{EC}$, $\overline{AE} \perp \overline{ED}$, $\overline{AB} \cong \overline{AC} \cong \overline{AD}$

Prove $\triangle AEB \cong \triangle AEC \cong \triangle AED$

SOLUTION

You are given that $\overline{AE} \perp \overline{EB}$ and $\overline{AE} \perp \overline{EC}$. So, $\angle AEB$ and $\angle AEC$ are right angles by the definition of perpendicular lines. By definition, $\triangle AEB$ and $\triangle AEC$ are right triangles. You are given that the hypotenuses of these two triangles, $\overline{AB}$ and $\overline{AC}$, are congruent. Also, $\overline{AE}$ is a leg for both triangles, and $\overline{AE} \cong \overline{AE}$ by the Reflexive Property of Congruence (Thm. 2.1). So, by the Hypotenuse-Leg Congruence Theorem, $\triangle AEB \cong \triangle AEC$. You can use similar reasoning to prove that $\triangle AEC \cong \triangle AED$.

▶ So, by the Transitive Property of Triangle Congruence (Thm. 5.3), $\triangle AEB \cong \triangle AEC \cong \triangle AED$.

Monitoring Progress 🔊 Help in English and Spanish at *BigIdeasMath.com*

Use the diagram.

7. Redraw $\triangle ABC$ and $\triangle DCB$ side by side with corresponding parts in the same position.

8. Use the information in the diagram to prove that $\triangle ABC \cong \triangle DCB$.

Laurie's Notes   **Teacher Actions**

- **MP4 Model with Mathematics:** To complete the proof in Example 3, a useful technique is to redraw the diagram so that the triangles do not overlap.
- **MP3:** Note the sequence of steps in this proof. The perpendicular segments give you right angles and then you have right triangles.
- For Example 4, you might have students take the paragraph proof and rewrite it as a two-column proof.

Closure

- **Response Logs:** Select from "What confused me the most was …" or "I will understand this better if I …" or "I am feeling good about … ."

Extra Example 3

Write a proof.
Given $\overline{PQ} \cong \overline{RS}$, $\angle Q$ and $\angle S$ are right angles.
Prove $\triangle PQR \cong \triangle RSP$

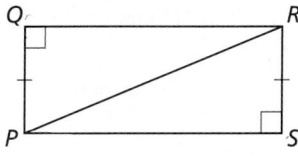

Statements (Reasons)
1. $\overline{PQ} \cong \overline{RS}$ (Given)
2. $\angle Q$ and $\angle S$ are right angles. (Given)
3. $\triangle PQR$ and $\triangle RSP$ are right triangles. (Def. of rt. $\triangle$)
4. $\overline{PR} \cong \overline{RP}$ (Reflex. Prop. of $\cong$ Thm. 2.1)
5. $\triangle PQR \cong \triangle RSP$ (HL $\cong$ Thm. 5.9)

Extra Example 4

Two windows in a building are right triangles, with $\overline{WX} \cong \overline{XY}$. Prove that the triangles are congruent.
Given $\triangle WXZ$ and $\triangle YXZ$ are right triangles, $\overline{WX} \cong \overline{XY}$.
Prove $\triangle WXZ \cong \triangle YXZ$

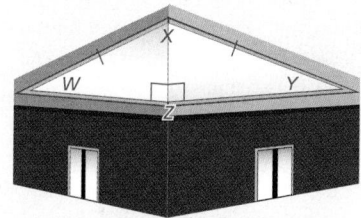

You are given that $\overline{WX} \cong \overline{XY}$ and that the triangles are right triangles. So, the hypotenuses of the triangles are congruent. By the Reflexive Property of $\cong$ (Thm. 2.1), $\overline{XZ} \cong \overline{XZ}$. So, by the HL $\cong$ Theorem (Thm. 5.9), $\triangle WXZ \cong \triangle YXZ$.

MONITORING PROGRESS ANSWERS

7.

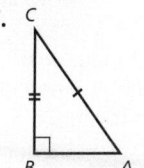 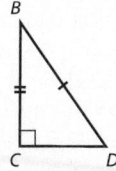

8. See Additional Answers.

ANSWERS

1. hypotenuse

2.

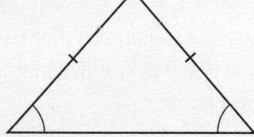

This is the only triangle with legs that are not the legs of a right triangle.

3. yes; $\overline{AB} \cong \overline{DB}, \overline{BC} \cong \overline{BE}, \overline{AC} \cong \overline{DE}$

4. no; You cannot tell for sure from the diagram whether or not $\overline{PS}$ and $\overline{RS}$ are congruent.

5. yes; $\angle B$ and $\angle E$ are right angles, $\overline{AB} \cong \overline{FE}, \overline{AC} \cong \overline{FD}$

6. no; The hypotenuses are not marked as congruent.

7. no; You are given that $\overline{RS} \cong \overline{PQ}$, $\overline{ST} \cong \overline{QT}$, and $\overline{RT} \cong \overline{PT}$. So, it should say $\triangle RST \cong \triangle PQT$ by the SSS Congruence Theorem (Thm. 5.8).

8. yes; You are given that $\overline{AB} \cong \overline{CD}$ and $\overline{AD} \cong \overline{CB}$. Also, $\overline{BD} \cong \overline{BD}$ by the Reflexive Property of Congruence (Thm. 2.1). So, $\triangle ABD \cong \triangle CDB$ by the SSS Congruence Theorem (Thm. 5.8).

9. yes; You are given that $\overline{EF} \cong \overline{GF}$ and $\overline{DE} \cong \overline{DG}$. Also, $\overline{DF} \cong \overline{DF}$ by the Reflexive Property of Congruence (Thm. 2.1). So, $\triangle DEF \cong \triangle DGF$ by the SSS Congruence Theorem (Thm. 5.8).

10. no; You are given that $\overline{JK} \cong \overline{KL} \cong \overline{LM} \cong \overline{MJ}$. Also, $\overline{JL} \cong \overline{JL}$ by the Reflexive Property of Congruence (Thm. 2.1). So, it should say $\triangle JKL \cong \triangle LMJ$ or $\triangle JKL \cong \triangle JML$ by the SSS Congruence Theorem (Thm. 5.8).

Vocabulary and Core Concept Check

1. **COMPLETE THE SENTENCE** The side opposite the right angle is called the _____ of the right triangle.

2. **WHICH ONE DOESN'T BELONG?** Which triangle's legs do *not* belong with the other three? Explain your reasoning.

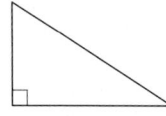 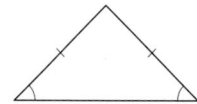 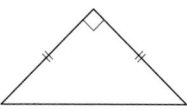 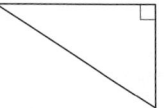

Monitoring Progress and Modeling with Mathematics

In Exercises 3 and 4, decide whether enough information is given to prove that the triangles are congruent using the SSS Congruence Theorem (Theorem 5.8). Explain.

3. $\triangle ABC, \triangle DBE$

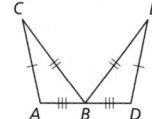

4. $\triangle PQS, \triangle RQS$

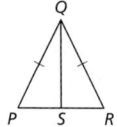

In Exercises 5 and 6, decide whether enough information is given to prove that the triangles are congruent using the HL Congruence Theorem (Theorem 5.9). Explain.

5. $\triangle ABC, \triangle FED$

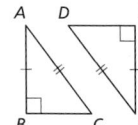

6. $\triangle PQT, \triangle SRT$

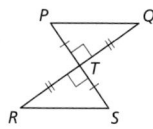

In Exercises 7–10, decide whether the congruence statement is true. Explain your reasoning. *(See Example 1.)*

7. $\triangle RST \cong \triangle TQP$

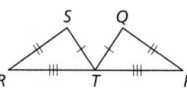

8. $\triangle ABD \cong \triangle CDB$

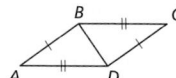

9. $\triangle DEF \cong \triangle DGF$

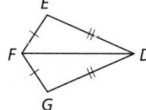

10. $\triangle JKL \cong \triangle LJM$

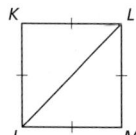

In Exercises 11 and 12, determine whether the figure is stable. Explain your reasoning. *(See Example 2.)*

11.

12.

In Exercises 13 and 14, redraw the triangles so they are side by side with corresponding parts in the same position. Then write a proof. *(See Example 3.)*

13. **Given** $\overline{AC} \cong \overline{BD}$, $\overline{AB} \perp \overline{AD}$, $\overline{CD} \perp \overline{AD}$

    Prove $\triangle BAD \cong \triangle CDA$

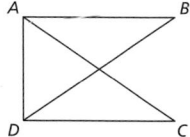

14. **Given** G is the midpoint of $\overline{EH}$, $\overline{FG} \cong \overline{GI}$, $\angle E$ and $\angle H$ are right angles.

    Prove $\triangle EFG \cong \triangle HIG$

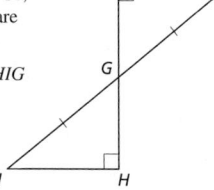

11. yes; The diagonal supports in this figure form triangles with fixed side lengths. By the SSS Congruence Theorem (Thm. 5.8), these triangles cannot change shape, so the figure is stable.

12. no; The support in this figure forms two quadrilaterals, which are not stable because there are many possible quadrilaterals with the given side lengths.

13–14. See Additional Answers.

In Exercises 15 and 16, write a proof.

15. Given $\overline{LM} \cong \overline{JK}, \overline{MJ} \cong \overline{KL}$

 Prove $\triangle LMJ \cong \triangle JKL$

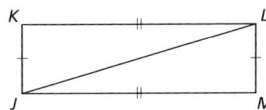

16. Given $\overline{WX} \cong \overline{VZ}, \overline{WY} \cong \overline{VY}, \overline{YZ} \cong \overline{YX}$

 Prove $\triangle VWX \cong \triangle WVZ$

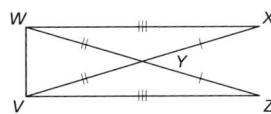

CONSTRUCTION In Exercises 17 and 18, construct a triangle that is congruent to $\triangle QRS$ using the SSS Congruence Theorem (Theorem 5.8).

17. **18.**

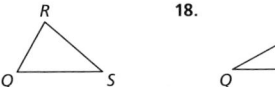

19. ERROR ANALYSIS Describe and correct the error in identifying congruent triangles.

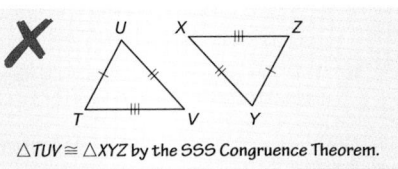

$\triangle TUV \cong \triangle XYZ$ by the SSS Congruence Theorem.

20. ERROR ANALYSIS Describe and correct the error in determining the value of x that makes the triangles congruent.

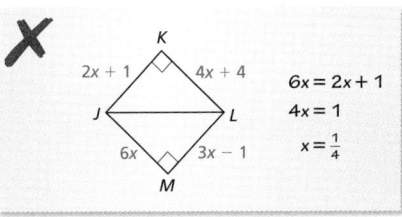

$6x = 2x + 1$
$4x = 1$
$x = \frac{1}{4}$

21. MAKING AN ARGUMENT Your friend claims that in order to use the SSS Congruence Theorem (Theorem 5.8) to prove that two triangles are congruent, both triangles must be equilateral triangles. Is your friend correct? Explain your reasoning.

22. MODELING WITH MATHEMATICS The distances between consecutive bases on a softball field are the same. The distance from home plate to second base is the same as the distance from first base to third base. The angles created at each base are 90°. Prove $\triangle HFS \cong \triangle FST \cong \triangle STH$. *(See Example 4.)*

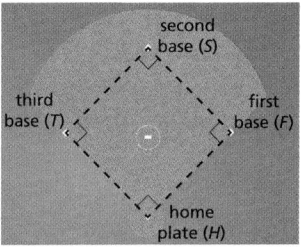

23. REASONING To support a tree, you attach wires from the trunk of the tree to stakes in the ground, as shown in the diagram.

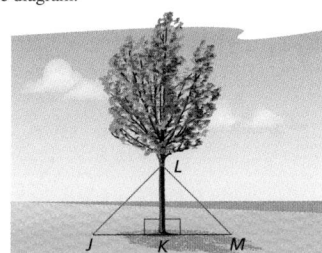

a. What additional information do you need to use the HL Congruence Theorem (Theorem 5.9) to prove that $\triangle JKL \cong \triangle MKL$?

b. Suppose K is the midpoint of JM. Name a theorem you could use to prove that $\triangle JKL \cong \triangle MKL$. Explain your reasoning.

24. REASONING Use the photo of the Navajo rug, where $\overline{BC} \cong \overline{DE}$ and $\overline{AC} \cong \overline{CE}$.

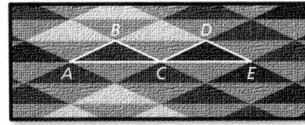

a. What additional information do you need to use the SSS Congruence Theorem (Theorem 5.8) to prove that $\triangle ABC \cong \triangle CDE$?

b. What additional information do you need to use the HL Congruence Theorem (Theorem 5.9) to prove that $\triangle ABC \cong \triangle CDE$?

Section 5.5 Proving Triangle Congruence by SSS **267**

Dynamic Teaching Tools

Dynamic Assessment & Progress Monitoring Tool

Interactive Whiteboard Lesson Library

Dynamic Classroom with Dynamic Investigations

ANSWERS

15–16. See Additional Answers.

17.

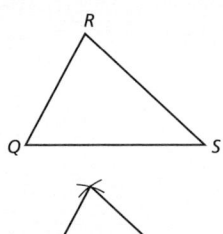

18.

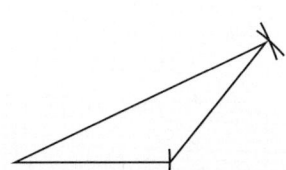

19. The order of the points in the congruence statement should reflect the corresponding sides and angles; $\triangle TUV \cong \triangle ZYX$ by the SSS Congruence Theorem (Thm. 5.8).

20. When you substitute $\frac{1}{4}$ for x, $\overline{KL} \neq \overline{LM}$; $6x = 4x + 4$ and $2x + 1 = 3x - 1$; $x = 2$.

21. no; The sides of a triangle do not have to be congruent to each other, but each side of one triangle must be congruent to the corresponding side of the other triangle.

22. See Additional Answers.

23. a. You need to know that the hypotenuses are congruent: $\overline{JL} \cong \overline{ML}$.

 b. SAS Congruence Theorem (Thm. 5.5); By definition of midpoint, $\overline{JK} \cong \overline{MK}$. Also, $\overline{LK} \cong \overline{LK}$, by the Reflexive Property of Congruence (Thm. 2.1), and $\angle JKL \cong \angle MKL$ by the Right Angles Congruence Theorem (Thm. 2.3).

24. a. $\overline{AB} \cong \overline{CD}$

 b. $\angle B$ and $\angle D$ are right angles.

ANSWERS

25. congruent
26. not congruent
27. congruent
28. not congruent
29. yes; Use the string to compare the lengths of the corresponding sides of the two triangles to determine whether SSS Congruence Theorem (Thm. 5.8) applies.
30–40. See Additional Answers.

Mini-Assessment

Decide whether the statement is true. Explain your reasoning.

1. $\triangle ABC \cong \triangle DEF$

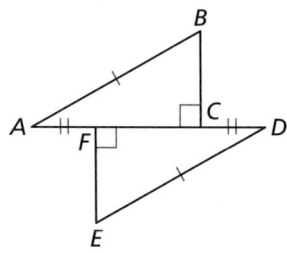

Yes, HL $\cong$ Theorem (Thm. 5.9)

2. $\triangle WXY \cong \triangle YZW$

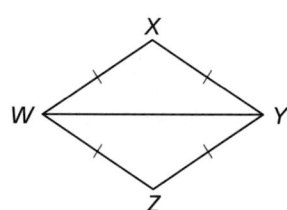

Yes, SSS $\cong$ Theorem (Thm. 5.8)

3. $\triangle ABC \cong \triangle FED$

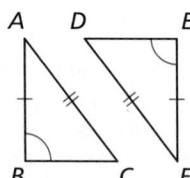

No, the HL $\cong$ Theorem (Thm. 5.9) applies only to right triangles, and the measures of $\angle B$ and $\angle E$ are not known.

In Exercises 25–28, use the given coordinates to determine whether $\triangle ABC \cong \triangle DEF$.

25. $A(-2, -2)$, $B(4, -2)$, $C(4, 6)$, $D(5, 7)$, $E(5, 1)$, $F(13, 1)$

26. $A(-2, 1)$, $B(3, -3)$, $C(7, 5)$, $D(3, 6)$, $E(8, 2)$, $F(10, 11)$

27. $A(0, 0)$, $B(6, 5)$, $C(9, 0)$, $D(0, -1)$, $E(6, -6)$, $F(9, -1)$

28. $A(-5, 7)$, $B(-5, 2)$, $C(0, 2)$, $D(0, 6)$, $E(0, 1)$, $F(4, 1)$

29. **CRITICAL THINKING** You notice two triangles in the tile floor of a hotel lobby. You want to determine whether the triangles are congruent, but you only have a piece of string. Can you determine whether the triangles are congruent? Explain.

30. **HOW DO YOU SEE IT?** There are several theorems you can use to show that the triangles in the "square" pattern are congruent. Name two of them.

31. **MAKING AN ARGUMENT** Your cousin says that $\triangle JKL$ is congruent to $\triangle LMJ$ by the SSS Congruence Theorem (Thm. 5.8). Your friend says that $\triangle JKL$ is congruent to $\triangle LMJ$ by the HL Congruence Theorem (Thm. 5.9). Who is correct? Explain your reasoning.

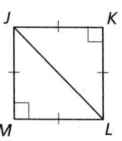

Maintaining Mathematical Proficiency   Reviewing what you learned in previous grades and lessons

Use the congruent triangles.   *(Section 5.2)*

37. Name the segment in $\triangle DEF$ that is congruent to $\overline{AC}$.

38. Name the segment in $\triangle ABC$ that is congruent to $\overline{EF}$.

39. Name the angle in $\triangle DEF$ that is congruent to $\angle B$.

40. Name the angle in $\triangle ABC$ that is congruent to $\angle F$.

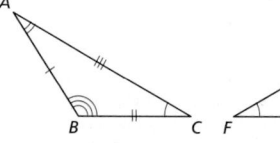

---

32. **THOUGHT PROVOKING** The postulates and theorems in this book represent Euclidean geometry. In spherical geometry, all points are points on the surface of a sphere. A line is a circle on the sphere whose diameter is equal to the diameter of the sphere. In spherical geometry, do you think that two triangles are congruent if their corresponding sides are congruent? Justify your answer.

USING TOOLS In Exercises 33 and 34, use the given information to sketch $\triangle LMN$ and $\triangle STU$. Mark the triangles with the given information.

33. $\overline{LM} \perp \overline{MN}$, $\overline{ST} \perp \overline{TU}$, $\overline{LM} \cong \overline{NM} \cong \overline{UT} \cong \overline{ST}$

34. $\overline{LM} \perp \overline{MN}$, $\overline{ST} \perp \overline{TU}$, $\overline{LM} \cong \overline{ST}$, $\overline{LN} \cong \overline{SU}$

35. **CRITICAL THINKING** The diagram shows the light created by two spotlights. Both spotlights are the same distance from the stage.

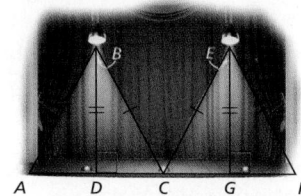

   a. Show that $\triangle ABD \cong \triangle CBD$. State which theorem or postulate you used and explain your reasoning.

   b. Are all four right triangles shown in the diagram congruent? Explain your reasoning.

36. **MATHEMATICAL CONNECTIONS** Find all values of x that make the triangles congruent. Explain.

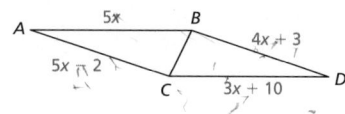

---

268   Chapter 5   Congruent Triangles

If students need help...	If students got it...
Resources by Chapter • Practice A and Practice B • Puzzle Time	**Resources by Chapter** • Enrichment and Extension • Cumulative Review
Student Journal • Practice	Start the *next* Section
Differentiating the Lesson **Skills Review Handbook**	

Overview of Section 5.6

Introduction

- Two additional triangle congruence theorems are introduced in this lesson, Angle-Side-Angle (ASA) and Angle-Angle-Side (AAS). Like the previous lessons, there is a blend of proof styles: transformations, two-column, and paragraph.
- The construction presented in this lesson is copying a triangle using the ASA Congruence Theorem.
- Additional examples with proving triangles congruent are presented, requiring students to recall previously proven theorems.

Formative Assessment Tips

- Refer to page T-230 for a description of *Response Logs*. In this lesson and throughout this chapter, there will be sentence stems to prompt student writing. Use your judgment for placement in the lesson, amount of time to allow for writing, and the actual sentence stem given to students.
- For a beginning list of writing stems, see page T-238.

Another Way

- A low-tech version of investigating the validity of different congruence theorems is to draw triangle "parts" on pieces of transparency. Make several copies of each of the parts so that two [possibly] congruent triangles can be made. The angles should be drawn with long enough rays so that points of intersection can be found. My collection of angle pieces includes angles of 40°, 60°, and 80°. My collection of side pieces includes lengths of 2 centimeters, 3 centimeters, 4 centimeters, and 5 centimeters.
- **FYI:** This collection of pieces is also used to show that sides of lengths 2, 3, and 5 do not form a triangle.

Pacing Suggestion

- Once students have worked the explorations, continue with the formal lesson.

Dynamic Teaching Tools

Dynamic Assessment & Progress Monitoring Tool

Lesson Planning Tool

Interactive Whiteboard Lesson Library

Dynamic Classroom with Dynamic Investigations

Laurie's Notes

Exploration

Motivate

- If possible, bring a wall mirror to class. Stand in front of the mirror and describe the amount of your reflection that you see in the mirror.
- **?** "If I move closer to or farther away from the mirror, will the amount of reflection I see change?" Answers will vary.
- Explain that in this lesson additional congruence theorems will be introduced, and in the exercises students will explore this question.

Exploration 1

- This exploration helps students understand why the Side-Side-Angle (SSA) method is not a valid triangle-congruence theorem. A note about this method was made on page 264, prior to introducing the HL Congruence Theorem (Thm. 5.9).
- **MP5 Use Appropriate Tools Strategically:** Students should be familiar enough with the software to follow the construction described. The software will label points in the construction process that may differ from how the diagram and table are labeled. Tell students to make adjustments as needed.
- **?** "What do you know about the sides and angles of $\triangle ABC$ and $\triangle ABD$?" $\overline{AB}$ is in both triangles, and $\overline{BC}$ in $\triangle ABC$ is congruent to $\overline{BD}$ in $\triangle ABD$; $\angle A$ is in both triangles.
- **?** "Is $\triangle ABC \cong \triangle ABD$? Explain." no; The third sides of the two triangles are not congruent: $\overline{AC} \not\cong \overline{AD}$.

Exploration 2

- Students have already concluded that SAS (Thm. 5.5) and SSS (Thm. 5.8) are valid triangle-congruence theorems and that SSA is not.
- **Alternate Method:** You might have other approaches such as compass and protractor that students could use to explore Angle-Angle-Side (AAS), Angle-Side-Angle (ASA), and Angle-Angle-Angle (AAA) methods.

Communicate Your Answer

- **MP3 Construct Viable Arguments and Critique the Reasoning of Others:** Students should conclude that having three pieces of information about two triangles is not always sufficient to conclude that the triangles are congruent.

Connecting to Next Step

- The exploration allows students to discover and make sense of why SSA is not a valid method and to see that there may be other methods besides SSS and SAS to investigate. These will be presented formally in the lesson.

5.6 Proving Triangle Congruence by ASA and AAS

Essential Question What information is sufficient to determine whether two triangles are congruent?

EXPLORATION 1   Determining Whether SSA Is Sufficient

Work with a partner.

a. Use dynamic geometry software to construct $\triangle ABC$. Construct the triangle so that vertex B is at the origin, $\overline{AB}$ has a length of 3 units, and $\overline{BC}$ has a length of 2 units.

b. Construct a circle with a radius of 2 units centered at the origin. Locate point D where the circle intersects $\overline{AC}$. Draw $\overline{BD}$.

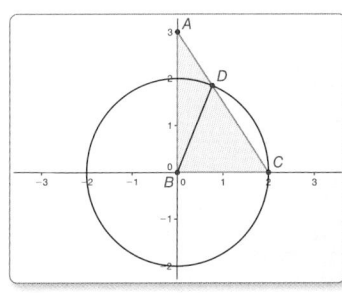

Sample

Points
$A(0, 3)$
$B(0, 0)$
$C(2, 0)$
$D(0.77, 1.85)$
Segments
$AB = 3$
$AC = 3.61$
$BC = 2$
$AD = 1.38$
Angle
$m\angle A = 33.69°$

c. $\triangle ABC$ and $\triangle ABD$ have two congruent sides and a nonincluded congruent angle. Name them.

d. Is $\triangle ABC \cong \triangle ABD$? Explain your reasoning.

e. Is SSA sufficient to determine whether two triangles are congruent? Explain your reasoning.

EXPLORATION 2   Determining Valid Congruence Theorems

Work with a partner. Use dynamic geometry software to determine which of the following are valid triangle congruence theorems. For those that are not valid, write a counterexample. Explain your reasoning.

CONSTRUCTING VIABLE ARGUMENTS

To be proficient in math, you need to recognize and use counterexamples.

Possible Congruence Theorem	Valid or not valid?
SSS	
SSA	
SAS	
AAS	
ASA	
AAA	

Communicate Your Answer

3. What information is sufficient to determine whether two triangles are congruent?

4. Is it possible to show that two triangles are congruent using more than one congruence theorem? If so, give an example.

Section 5.6   Proving Triangle Congruence by ASA and AAS   **269**

ANSWERS

1. a. Check students' work.

   b. Check students' work.

   c. $\overline{AB} \cong \overline{AB}$, $\overline{BD} \cong \overline{BC}$, and $\angle A \cong \angle A$

   d. no; The third pair of sides are not congruent.

   e. no; These two triangles provide a counterexample for SSA. They have two pairs of congruent sides and a pair of nonincluded congruent angles, but the triangles are not congruent.

2. See Additional Answers.

3. In order to determine that two triangles are congruent, one of the following must be true.

   All three pairs of corresponding sides are congruent (SSS).

   Two pairs of corresponding sides and the pair of included angles are congruent (SAS).

   Two pairs of corresponding angles and the pair of included sides are congruent (ASA).

   Two pairs of corresponding angles and one pair of nonincluded sides are congruent (AAS).

   The hypotenuses and one pair of corresponding legs of two right triangles are congruent (HL).

4. yes; *Sample answer:*

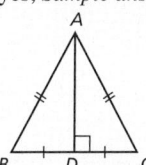

   In the diagram, $\triangle ABD \cong \triangle ACD$ by the HL Congruence Theorem (Thm. 5.9), the SSS Congruence Theorem (Thm. 5.8), and the SAS Congruence Theorem (Thm. 5.5).

5.6 Lesson

Core Vocabulary

Previous
congruent figures
rigid motion

What You Will Learn

▶ Use the ASA and AAS Congruence Theorems.

Using the ASA and AAS Congruence Theorems

🗘 Theorem

Theorem 5.10   Angle-Side-Angle (ASA) Congruence Theorem

If two angles and the included side of one triangle are congruent to two angles and the included side of a second triangle, then the two triangles are congruent.

If $\angle A \cong \angle D$, $\overline{AC} \cong \overline{DF}$, and $\angle C \cong \angle F$, then $\triangle ABC \cong \triangle DEF$.

Proof p. 270

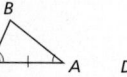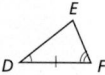

PROOF   Angle-Side-Angle (ASA) Congruence Theorem

Given $\angle A \cong \angle D$, $\overline{AC} \cong \overline{DF}$, $\angle C \cong \angle F$

Prove $\triangle ABC \cong \triangle DEF$

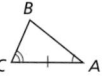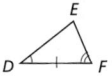

First, translate $\triangle ABC$ so that point A maps to point D, as shown below.

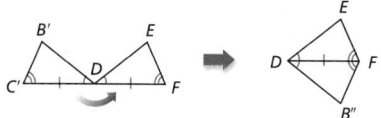

This translation maps $\triangle ABC$ to $\triangle DB'C'$. Next, rotate $\triangle DB'C'$ counterclockwise through $\angle C'DF$ so that the image of $\overrightarrow{DC'}$ coincides with $\overrightarrow{DF}$, as shown below.

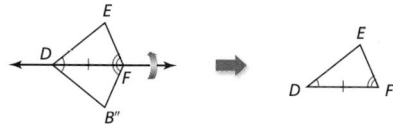

Because $\overline{DC'} \cong \overline{DF}$, the rotation maps point C' to point F. So, this rotation maps $\triangle DB'C'$ to $\triangle DB''F$. Now, reflect $\triangle DB''F$ in the line through points D and F, as shown below.

Because points D and F lie on $\overleftrightarrow{DF}$, this reflection maps them onto themselves. Because a reflection preserves angle measure and $\angle B''DF \cong \angle EDF$, the reflection maps $\overrightarrow{DB''}$ to $\overrightarrow{DE}$. Similarly, because $\angle B''FD \cong \angle EFD$, the reflection maps $\overrightarrow{FB''}$ to $\overrightarrow{FE}$. The image of B'' lies on $\overrightarrow{DE}$ and $\overrightarrow{FE}$. Because $\overrightarrow{DE}$ and $\overrightarrow{FE}$ only have point E in common, the image of B'' must be E. So, this reflection maps $\triangle DB''F$ to $\triangle DEF$.

Because you can map $\triangle ABC$ to $\triangle DEF$ using a composition of rigid motions, $\triangle ABC \cong \triangle DEF$.

Laurie's Notes   Teacher Actions

? Draw $\triangle ABC$ and $\triangle DEF$ and mark two pairs of angles congruent. "What pair of sides would need to be congruent if Angle-Side-Angle (ASA) is a valid triangle-congruence method?" the side between the angles

• **Turn and Talk:** "How could you prove ASA works using transformations?" Give partners time to discuss the steps needed. Be sure that students rotate C' to F, mapping the congruent sides onto one another.

 **Theorem**

Theorem 5.11   Angle-Angle-Side (AAS) Congruence Theorem

If two angles and a non-included side of one triangle are congruent to two angles and the corresponding non-included side of a second triangle, then the two triangles are congruent.

If $\angle A \cong \angle D$, $\angle C \cong \angle F$, and $\overline{BC} \cong \overline{EF}$, then $\triangle ABC \cong \triangle DEF$.

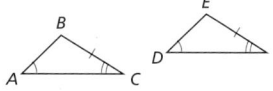

Proof p. 271

PROOF   Angle-Angle-Side (AAS) Congruence Theorem

Given $\angle A \cong \angle D$,
$\angle C \cong \angle F$,
$\overline{BC} \cong \overline{EF}$

Prove $\triangle ABC \cong \triangle DEF$

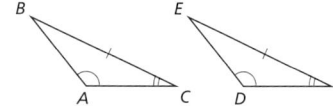

You are given $\angle A \cong \angle D$ and $\angle C \cong \angle F$. By the Third Angles Theorem (Theorem 5.4), $\angle B \cong \angle E$. You are given $\overline{BC} \cong \overline{EF}$. So, two pairs of angles and their included sides are congruent. By the ASA Congruence Theorem, $\triangle ABC \cong \triangle DEF$.

EXAMPLE 1   Identifying Congruent Triangles

Can the triangles be proven congruent with the information given in the diagram? If so, state the theorem you would use.

a.

b.
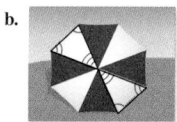

c.
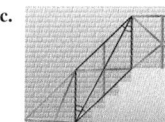

COMMON ERROR

You need at least one pair of congruent corresponding sides to prove two triangles are congruent.

SOLUTION

a. The vertical angles are congruent, so two pairs of angles and a pair of non-included sides are congruent. The triangles are congruent by the AAS Congruence Theorem.

b. There is not enough information to prove the triangles are congruent, because no sides are known to be congruent.

c. Two pairs of angles and their included sides are congruent. The triangles are congruent by the ASA Congruence Theorem.

Monitoring Progress   Help in English and Spanish at *BigIdeasMath.com*

1. Can the triangles be proven congruent with the information given in the diagram? If so, state the theorem you would use.

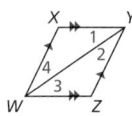

English Language Learners

Words and Abbreviations

Ask students to explain the importance of the order of the letters in the SAS, ASA, and AAS Congruence Theorems.

Extra Example 1

Can the triangles be proven congruent with the information given in the diagram? If so, state the theorem you would use.

a. $\triangle EFG$ and $\triangle HDG$

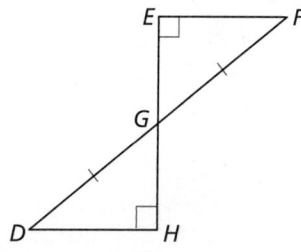

Yes, AAS $\cong$ Theorem (Thm. 5.11)

b. $\triangle PQM$ and $\triangle RQM$

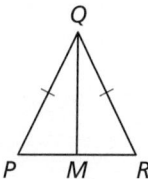

No

c. $\triangle LMP$ and $\triangle NMP$

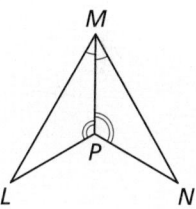

Yes, ASA $\cong$ Theorem (Thm. 5.10)

MONITORING PROGRESS ANSWER

1. yes; ASA Congruence Theorem (Thm. 5.10)

Laurie's Notes   Teacher Actions

❓ Draw $\triangle ABC$ and $\triangle DEF$ and mark two pairs of angles congruent. "What pair of sides would need to be congruent if Angle-Angle-Side (AAS) is a valid triangle-congruence method?" a side not between the angles Discuss the outline of the proof for the AAS Congruence Theorem.

• **Think-Pair-Share:** Have students try the three parts in Example 1 independently before discussing as a class.

• **Response Logs:** "Right now I need to …"

Extra Example 2

Write a proof.

Given $\overline{DH} \parallel \overline{FG}, \overline{DE} \cong \overline{EG}$

Prove $\triangle DEH \cong \triangle GEF$

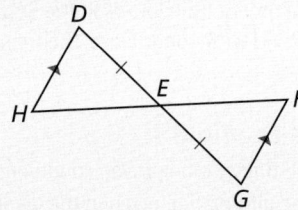

Sample answer:

Statements (Reasons)

1. $\overline{DH} \parallel \overline{FG}, \overline{DE} \cong \overline{EG}$ (Given)
2. $\angle DEH \cong \angle GEF$ (Vert. $\angle$s $\cong$ Thm. 2.6)
3. $\angle D \cong \angle G$ (Alt. Int. $\angle$s Thm. 3.2)
4. $\triangle DEH \cong \triangle GEF$ (ASA $\cong$ Thm. 5.10)

MONITORING PROGRESS ANSWER

2. See Additional Answers.

CONSTRUCTION Copying a Triangle Using ASA

Construct a triangle that is congruent to $\triangle ABC$ using the ASA Congruence Theorem. Use a compass and straightedge.

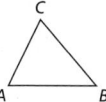

SOLUTION

Step 1	Step 2	Step 3	Step 4
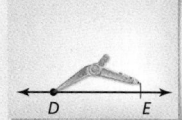	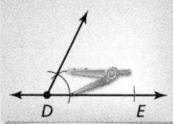	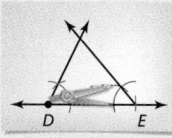	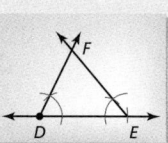
Construct a side Construct $\overline{DE}$ so that it is congruent to $\overline{AB}$.	**Construct an angle** Construct $\angle D$ with vertex D and side $\overrightarrow{DE}$ so that it is congruent to $\angle A$.	**Construct an angle** Construct $\angle E$ with vertex E and side $\overrightarrow{ED}$ so that it is congruent to $\angle B$.	**Label a point** Label the intersection of the sides of $\angle D$ and $\angle E$ that you constructed in Steps 2 and 3 as F. By the ASA Congruence Theorem, $\triangle ABC \cong \triangle DEF$.

EXAMPLE 2 Using the ASA Congruence Theorem

Write a proof.

Given $\overline{AD} \parallel \overline{EC}, \overline{BD} \cong \overline{BC}$

Prove $\triangle ABD \cong \triangle EBC$

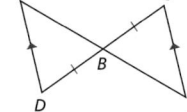

SOLUTION

STATEMENTS	REASONS
1. $\overline{AD} \parallel \overline{EC}$	1. Given
A **2.** $\angle D \cong \angle C$	2. Alternate Interior Angles Theorem (Thm. 3.2)
S **3.** $\overline{BD} \cong \overline{BC}$	3. Given
A **4.** $\angle ABD \cong \angle EBC$	4. Vertical Angles Congruence Theorem (Thm 2.6)
5. $\triangle ABD \cong \triangle EBC$	5. ASA Congruence Theorem

Monitoring Progress Help in English and Spanish at *BigIdeasMath.com*

2. In the diagram, $\overline{AB} \perp \overline{AD}, \overline{DE} \perp \overline{AD}$, and $\overline{AC} \cong \overline{DC}$. Prove $\triangle ABC \cong \triangle DEC$.

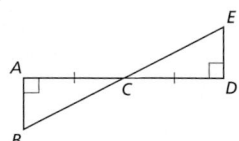

Laurie's Notes   Teacher Actions

- Constructing angles at each endpoint of the segment can be challenging for students, particularly when $\overline{DE}$ is short. Encourage students to begin with a reasonably sized triangle to copy using the ASA Congruence Theorem.
- **Whiteboarding:** Have students work with partners to write a proof for Example 2. Circulate to observe their approaches.
- **MP3:** Select several students to share their proofs, demonstrating that the order of the steps may vary and that there are two possible methods (ASA and AAS).

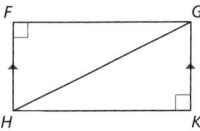

EXAMPLE 3 Using the AAS Congruence Theorem

Write a proof.

Given $\overline{HF} \parallel \overline{GK}$, $\angle F$ and $\angle K$ are right angles.

Prove $\triangle HFG \cong \triangle GKH$

SOLUTION

STATEMENTS	REASONS
1. $\overline{HF} \parallel \overline{GK}$	1. Given
A 2. $\angle GHF \cong \angle HGK$	2. Alternate Interior Angles Theorem (Theorem 3.2)
3. $\angle F$ and $\angle K$ are right angles.	3. Given
A 4. $\angle F \cong \angle K$	4. Right Angles Congruence Theorem (Theorem 2.3)
S 5. $\overline{HG} \cong \overline{GH}$	5. Reflexive Property of Congruence (Theorem 2.1)
6. $\triangle HFG \cong \triangle GKH$	6. AAS Congruence Theorem

Monitoring Progress Help in English and Spanish at *BigIdeasMath.com*

3. In the diagram, $\angle S \cong \angle U$ and $\overline{RS} \cong \overline{VU}$. Prove $\triangle RST \cong \triangle VUT$.

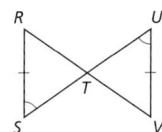

Concept Summary

Triangle Congruence Theorems

You have learned five methods for proving that triangles are congruent.

SAS	SSS	HL (right △ only)	ASA	AAS
Two sides and the included angle are congruent.	All three sides are congruent.	The hypotenuse and one of the legs are congruent.	Two angles and the included side are congruent.	Two angles and a non-included side are congruent.

In the Exercises, you will prove three additional theorems about the congruence of right triangles: **Hypotenuse-Angle, Leg-Leg,** and **Angle-Leg.**

Section 5.6 Proving Triangle Congruence by ASA and AAS **273**

Extra Example 3

Write a proof.

Use the diagram and the given information in Example 2. Prove $\triangle ABD \cong \triangle EBC$ using the AAS Congruence Theorem.

Sample answer:

Statements (Reasons)

1. $\overline{AD} \parallel \overline{EC}$ (Given)
2. $\angle A \cong \angle E$ (Alt. Int. $\angle$s Thm. 3.2)
3. $\angle D \cong \angle C$ (Alt. Int. $\angle$s Thm. 3.2)
4. $\overline{BD} \cong \overline{BC}$ (Given)
5. $\triangle ABD \cong \triangle EBC$ (AAS $\cong$ Thm. 5.11)

MONITORING PROGRESS ANSWER

3. See Additional Answers.

Laurie's Notes — Teacher Actions

COMMON ERROR In Example 3, students may try to state $\angle FGH \cong \angle KHG$. These are alternate interior angles for two sides not known to be parallel, $\overline{FG}$ and $\overline{HK}$.

• **Teaching Tip:** Use a color highlighter to extend the parallel sides $\overline{HF}$ and $\overline{GK}$. Transversal $\overline{HG}$ forms congruent alternate interior angles $\angle GHF$ and $\angle HGK$.

Closure

• **Response Logs:** Select from: "I feel like I made progress today …" or "I'm still not sure about …" or "A sticky part for me is …."

ANSWERS

1. Both theorems are used to prove that two triangles are congruent, and both require two pairs of corresponding angles to be congruent. In order to use the AAS Congruence Theorem (Thm. 5.11), one pair of corresponding nonincluded sides must also be congruent. In order to use the ASA Congruence Theorem (Thm. 5.10), the pair of corresponding included sides must be congruent.

2. You need to know that one pair of corresponding sides are congruent.

3. yes; AAS Congruence Theorem (Thm. 5.11)

4. yes; AAS Congruence Theorem (Thm 5.11)

5. no

6. yes; ASA Congruence Theorem (Thm. 5.10)

7. $\angle F$; $\angle L$

8. $\angle F$; $\angle L$

9. yes; $\triangle ABC \cong \triangle DEF$ by the ASA Congruence Theorem (Thm. 5.10)

10. no; The congruence statements follow the pattern SSA, which is not sufficient to conclude that the triangles are congruent.

11. no; $\overline{AC}$ and $\overline{DE}$ do not correspond.

12. yes; $\triangle ABC \cong \triangle DEF$ by the AAS Congruence Theorem (Thm. 5.11).

13.

14.

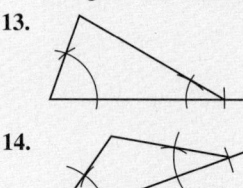

Vocabulary and Core Concept Check

1. **WRITING** How are the AAS Congruence Theorem (Theorem 5.11) and the ASA Congruence Theorem (Theorem 5.10) similar? How are they different?

2. **WRITING** You know that a pair of triangles has two pairs of congruent corresponding angles. What other information do you need to show that the triangles are congruent?

Monitoring Progress and Modeling with Mathematics

In Exercises 3–6, decide whether enough information is given to prove that the triangles are congruent. If so, state the theorem you would use. *(See Example 1.)*

3. $\triangle ABC$, $\triangle QRS$

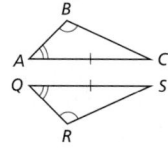

4. $\triangle ABC$, $\triangle DBC$

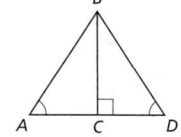

5. $\triangle XYZ$, $\triangle JKL$

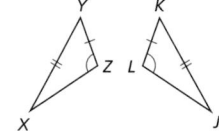

6. $\triangle RSV$, $\triangle UTV$

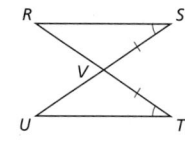

In Exercises 7 and 8, state the third congruence statement that is needed to prove that $\triangle FGH \cong \triangle LMN$ using the given theorem.

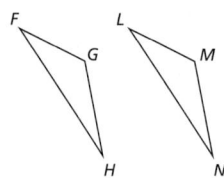

7. Given $\overline{GH} \cong \overline{MN}$, $\angle G \cong \angle M$, ___ $\cong$ ____

   Use the AAS Congruence Theorem (Thm. 5.11).

8. Given $\overline{FG} \cong \overline{LM}$, $\angle G \cong \angle M$, ___ $\cong$ ____

   Use the ASA Congruence Theorem (Thm. 5.10).

In Exercises 9–12, decide whether you can use the given information to prove that $\triangle ABC \cong \triangle DEF$. Explain your reasoning.

9. $\angle A \cong \angle D$, $\angle C \cong \angle F$, $\overline{AC} \cong \overline{DF}$

10. $\angle C \cong \angle F$, $\overline{AB} \cong \overline{DE}$, $\overline{BC} \cong \overline{EF}$

11. $\angle B \cong \angle E$, $\angle C \cong \angle F$, $\overline{AC} \cong \overline{DE}$

12. $\angle A \cong \angle D$, $\angle B \cong \angle E$, $\overline{BC} \cong \overline{EF}$

CONSTRUCTION In Exercises 13 and 14, construct a triangle that is congruent to the given triangle using the ASA Congruence Theorem (Theorem 5.10). Use a compass and straightedge.

13.

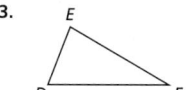

14.

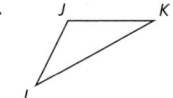

ERROR ANALYSIS In Exercises 15 and 16, describe and correct the error.

15.

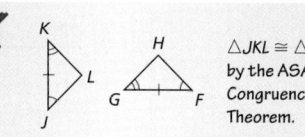

$\triangle JKL \cong \triangle FHG$ by the ASA Congruence Theorem.

16.

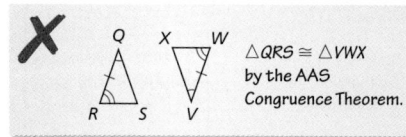

$\triangle QRS \cong \triangle VWX$ by the AAS Congruence Theorem.

---

15. In the congruence statement, the vertices should be in corresponding order; $\triangle JKL \cong \triangle FGH$ by the ASA Congruence Theorem (Thm. 5.10).

16. The included sides are congruent; $\triangle QRS \cong \triangle VUX$ by the ASA Congruence Theorem (Thm. 5.10).

PROOF In Exercises 17 and 18, prove that the triangles are congruent using the ASA Congruence Theorem (Theorem 5.10). *(See Example 2.)*

17. Given M is the midpoint of $\overline{NL}$.
$\overline{NL} \perp \overline{NQ}, \overline{NL} \perp \overline{MP}, \overline{QM} \parallel \overline{PL}$

Prove $\triangle NQM \cong \triangle MPL$

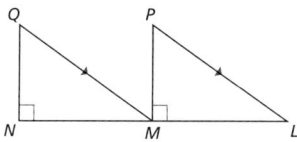

18. Given $\overline{AJ} \cong \overline{KC}, \angle BJK \cong \angle BKJ, \angle A \cong \angle C$

Prove $\triangle ABK \cong \triangle CBJ$

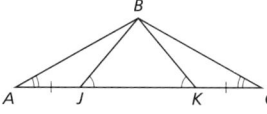

PROOF In Exercises 19 and 20, prove that the triangles are congruent using the AAS Congruence Theorem (Theorem 5.11). *(See Example 3.)*

19. Given $\overline{VW} \cong \overline{UW}, \angle X \cong \angle Z$

Prove $\triangle XWV \cong \triangle ZWU$

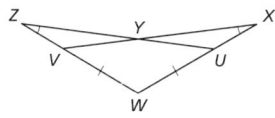

20. Given $\angle NKM \cong \angle LMK, \angle L \cong \angle N$

Prove $\triangle NMK \cong \triangle LKM$

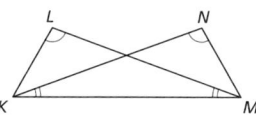

PROOF In Exercises 21–23, write a paragraph proof for the theorem about right triangles.

21. Hypotenuse-Angle (HA) Congruence Theorem If an angle and the hypotenuse of a right triangle are congruent to an angle and the hypotenuse of a second right triangle, then the triangles are congruent.

22. Leg-Leg (LL) Congruence Theorem If the legs of a right triangle are congruent to the legs of a second right triangle, then the triangles are congruent.

23. Angle-Leg (AL) Congruence Theorem If an angle and a leg of a right triangle are congruent to an angle and a leg of a second right triangle, then the triangles are congruent.

24. REASONING What additional information do you need to prove $\triangle JKL \cong \triangle MNL$ by the ASA Congruence Theorem (Theorem 5.10)?

Ⓐ $\overline{KM} \cong \overline{KJ}$

Ⓑ $\overline{KH} \cong \overline{NH}$

Ⓒ $\angle M \cong \angle J$

Ⓓ $\angle LKJ \cong \angle LNM$

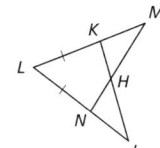

25. MATHEMATICAL CONNECTIONS This toy contains $\triangle ABC$ and $\triangle DBC$. Can you conclude that $\triangle ABC \cong \triangle DBC$ from the given angle measures? Explain.

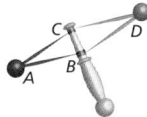

$m\angle ABC = (8x - 32)°$

$m\angle DBC = (4y - 24)°$

$m\angle BCA = (5x + 10)°$

$m\angle BCD = (3y + 2)°$

$m\angle CAB = (2x - 8)°$

$m\angle CDB = (y - 6)°$

26. REASONING Which of the following congruence statements are true? Select all that apply.

Ⓐ $\overline{TU} \cong \overline{UV}$

Ⓑ $\triangle STV \cong \triangle XVW$

Ⓒ $\triangle TVS \cong \triangle VWU$

Ⓓ $\triangle VST \cong \triangle VUW$

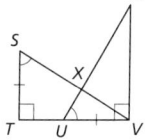

27. PROVING A THEOREM Prove the Converse of the Base Angles Theorem (Theorem 5.7). (*Hint:* Draw an auxiliary line inside the triangle.)

28. MAKING AN ARGUMENT Your friend claims to be able to rewrite any proof that uses the AAS Congruence Theorem (Thm. 5.11) as a proof that uses the ASA Congruence Theorem (Thm. 5.10). Is this possible? Explain your reasoning.

28. yes; When two triangles are congruent by the AAS Congruence Theorem (Thm. 5.11), their third angles are congruent by the Third Angles Theorem (Thm. 5.4), so the ASA Congruence Theorem (Thm. 5.10) will also apply.

ANSWERS

17–20. See Additional Answers.

21. You are given two right triangles, so the triangles have congruent right angles by the Right Angles Congruence Theorem (Thm. 2.3). Because another pair of angles and a pair of corresponding nonincluded sides (the hypotenuses) are congruent, the triangles are congruent by the AAS Congruence Theorem (Thm. 5.11).

22. You are given two right triangles, so the triangles have congruent right angles by the Right Angles Congruence Theorem (Thm. 2.3). Because both pairs of legs are congruent, and the congruent right angles are the included angles, the triangles are congruent by the SAS Congruence Theorem (Thm. 5.5)

23. You are given two right triangles, so the triangles have congruent right angles by the Right Angles Congruence Theorem (Thm. 2.3). There is also another pair of congruent corresponding angles and a pair of congruent corresponding sides. If the pair of congruent sides is the included side, then the triangles are congruent by the ASA Congruence Theorem (Thm. 5.10). If the pair of congruent sides is a nonincluded pair, then the triangles are congruent by the AAS Congruence Theorem (Thm. 5.11).

24. D

25. yes; When $x = 14$ and $y = 26$, $m\angle ABC = m\angle DBC = m\angle BCA = m\angle BCD = 80°$ and $m\angle CAB = m\angle CDB = 20°$. This satisfies the Triangle Sum Theorem (Thm. 5.1) for both triangles. Because $\overline{CB} \cong \overline{CB}$ by the Reflexive Property of Congruence (Thm. 2.1), you can conclude that $\triangle ABC \cong \triangle DBC$ by the ASA Congruence Theorem (Thm. 5.10) or the AAS Congruence Theorem (Thm. 5.11).

26. C

27. See Additional Answers.

ANSWERS

29–30. See Additional Answers.

31. *Sample answer:*

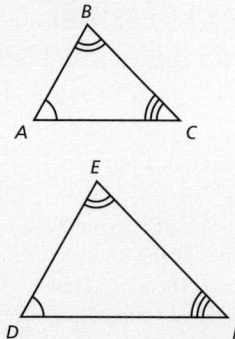

32. yes; Both triangles will always have 3 vertices. So, each vertex of one triangle can be mapped to one vertex of the other triangle so that each vertex is only used once, and adjacent vertices of one triangle must be adjacent in the other.

33–38. See Additional Answers.

Mini-Assessment

Can the triangles be proven congruent with the information given in the diagram? If so, state the theorem you would use.

1. △QPM ≅ △MNQ

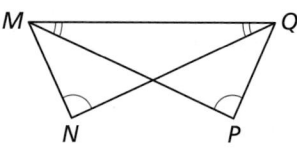

Yes, AAS ≅ Thm. 5.11 or
ASA ≅ Thm. 5.10

2. △DEF ≅ △QRS

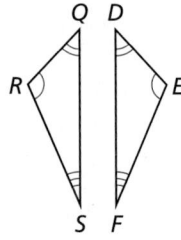

No

3. △ABC ≅ △FED

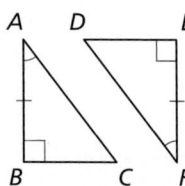

Yes, ASA ≅ Thm. 5.10 or
AAS ≅ Thm. 5.11

29. MODELING WITH MATHEMATICS When a light ray from an object meets a mirror, it is reflected back to your eye. For example, in the diagram, a light ray from point C is reflected at point D and travels back to point A. The *law of reflection* states that the angle of incidence, $\angle CDB$, is congruent to the angle of reflection, $\angle ADB$.

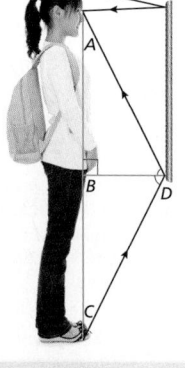

  a. Prove that $\triangle ABD$ is congruent to $\triangle CBD$.

    Given $\angle CDB \cong \angle ADB$,
          $\overline{DB} \perp \overline{AC}$

    Prove $\triangle ABD \cong \triangle CBD$

  b. Verify that $\triangle ACD$ is isosceles.

  c. Does moving away from the mirror have any effect on the amount of his or her reflection a person sees? Explain.

30. HOW DO YOU SEE IT? Name as many pairs of congruent triangles as you can from the diagram. Explain how you know that each pair of triangles is congruent.

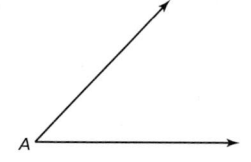

31. CONSTRUCTION Construct a triangle. Show that there is no AAA congruence rule by constructing a second triangle that has the same angle measures but is not congruent.

32. THOUGHT PROVOKING Graph theory is a branch of mathematics that studies vertices and the way they are connected. In graph theory, two polygons are *isomorphic* if there is a one-to-one mapping from one polygon's vertices to the other polygon's vertices that preserves adjacent vertices. In graph theory, are any two triangles isomorphic? Explain your reasoning.

33. MATHEMATICAL CONNECTIONS Six statements are given about △TUV and △XYZ.

$\overline{TU} \cong \overline{XY}$ $\overline{UV} \cong \overline{YZ}$ $\overline{TV} \cong \overline{XZ}$

$\angle T \cong \angle X$ $\angle U \cong \angle Y$ $\angle V \cong \angle Z$

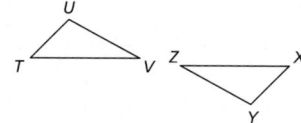

  a. List all combinations of three given statements that would provide enough information to prove that △TUV is congruent to △XYZ.

  b. You choose three statements at random. What is the probability that the statements you choose provide enough information to prove that the triangles are congruent?

Maintaining Mathematical Proficiency *Reviewing what you learned in previous grades and lessons*

Find the coordinates of the midpoint of the line segment with the given endpoints. *(Section 1.3)*

34. $C(1, 0)$ and $D(5, 4)$ **35.** $J(-2, 3)$ and $K(4, -1)$ **36.** $R(-5, -7)$ and $S(2, -4)$

Copy the angle using a compass and straightedge. *(Section 1.5)*

37.

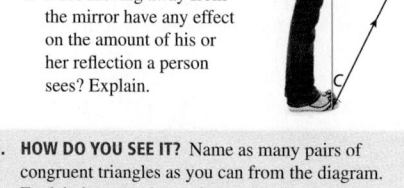

38.

If students need help...	If students got it...
Resources by Chapter • Practice A and Practice B • Puzzle Time	Resources by Chapter • Enrichment and Extension • Cumulative Review
Student Journal • Practice	Start the *next* Section
Differentiating the Lesson Skills Review Handbook	

Dynamic Teaching Tools

Dynamic Assessment & Progress Monitoring Tool

Lesson Planning Tool

Interactive Whiteboard Lesson Library

Dynamic Classroom with Dynamic Investigations

Overview of Section 5.7

Introduction

- This is a short lesson that extends students' understanding of congruent triangles. Once two triangles have been proven congruent using three corresponding parts in the two triangles, there are additional corresponding parts that can now be deduced to be congruent.
- In addition to using corresponding parts of congruent triangles, prior compass constructions will also be proven as valid methods.

Formative Assessment Tips

- Refer to page T-230 for a description of *Response Logs*. In this lesson and throughout this chapter, there will be sentence stems to prompt student writing. Use your judgment for placement in the lesson, amount of time to allow for writing, and the actual sentence stem given to students.
- For a beginning list of writing stems, see page T-238.

Pacing Suggestion

- If both explorations have been explored thoroughly, including the proofs, you may feel comfortable beginning the formal lesson with Example 3.

HSG-SRT.B.5 Use congruence ... criteria
for triangles to solve problems and to
prove relationships in geometric figures.

Laurie's Notes

Exploration

Motivate

- Ask students what they know about Napoleon Bonaparte.
- Here are a few facts that you might expect to hear:
  - military leader and first emperor of France
  - lived 1769–1821
  - considered one of the world's greatest military leaders
  - led reform within France (legal system, education, economy, and church)
- Explain to students that the second exploration is connected to Napoleon.

Discuss

- If you know your community of students and families, it is possible that someone has access to an electronic transit. If so, perhaps they would come to your class to demonstrate how the transit works and to do an indirect measurement of some object or distance near your school.
- You can also simulate the method in your classroom using rope or yarn. Even though you can reach all of the areas in your room, pretend there is a gorge that cannot be crossed but could be sited with the transit! You want to find the distance across the gorge. Use the method from Exploration 1 or 2.

Exploration 1

- Discuss with students what a transit is and what a surveyor does. Have partners study the picture.
- Ask at least two volunteers to share their proof at the board. Although the method will be the same (ASA), the order in which students write the steps may well vary.
- **MP3 Construct Viable Arguments and Critique the Reasoning of Others:** In examining peers' proofs, students should critique the logical progression of statements and whether the reasoning is correct.

Exploration 2

- This problem is similar to the first exploration and again uses corresponding parts of congruent triangles to determine a distance.
- You could replicate this method outside on a playing field or in the school's gymnasium.

Communicate Your Answer

- Have students share their descriptions of indirect measurement.

Connecting to Next Step

- The explorations give students time to explore in real-life problems how corresponding parts of congruent triangles can be used. Once explored, students will be better able to consider deductive proofs using congruent triangles.

5.7 Using Congruent Triangles

Essential Question
How can you use congruent triangles to make an indirect measurement?

EXPLORATION 1   Measuring the Width of a River

Work with a partner. The figure shows how a surveyor can measure the width of a river by making measurements on only one side of the river.

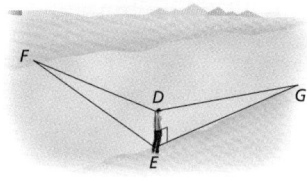

a. Study the figure. Then explain how the surveyor can find the width of the river.

b. Write a proof to verify that the method you described in part (a) is valid.

Given $\angle A$ is a right angle, $\angle D$ is a right angle, $\overline{AC} \cong \overline{CD}$

c. Exchange proofs with your partner and discuss the reasoning used.

EXPLORATION 2   Measuring the Width of a River

Work with a partner. It was reported that one of Napoleon's officers estimated the width of a river as follows. The officer stood on the bank of the river and lowered the visor on his cap until the farthest thing visible was the edge of the bank on the other side. He then turned and noted the point on his side that was in line with the tip of his visor and his eye. The officer then paced the distance to this point and concluded that distance was the width of the river.

a. Study the figure. Then explain how the officer concluded that the width of the river is *EG*.

b. Write a proof to verify that the conclusion the officer made is correct.

Given $\angle DEG$ is a right angle, $\angle DEF$ is a right angle, $\angle EDG \cong \angle EDF$

c. Exchange proofs with your partner and discuss the reasoning used.

Communicate Your Answer

3. How can you use congruent triangles to make an indirect measurement?

4. Why do you think the types of measurements described in Explorations 1 and 2 are called *indirect* measurements?

ANSWERS

1–2. See Additional Answers.

3. By creating a triangle that is congruent to a triangle with an unknown side length or angle measure, you can measure the created triangle and use it to find the unknown measure indirectly.

4. You do not actually measure the side length or angle measure you are trying to find. You measure the side length or angle measure of a triangle that is congruent to the one you are trying to find.

Visual

When working with overlapping triangles, students may find it helpful to redraw the figure as two separate figures, and then use colors to designate corresponding parts.

Extra Example 1

Use the diagram in Example 1. Explain how using this new given information would change the proof in Example 1.

Given $\angle QRT \cong \angle SRT$, $\angle RTQ \cong \angle RTS$

Prove $\overline{QT} \cong \overline{ST}$

Instead of the AAS $\cong$ Thm. (5.11), the proof would use the ASA $\cong$ Thm. (5.10) to prove the triangles congruent.

MONITORING PROGRESS ANSWER

1. All three pairs of sides are congruent. So, by the SSS Congruence Theorem (Thm. 5.8), $\triangle ABD \cong \triangle CBD$. Because corresponding parts of congruent triangles are congruent, $\angle A \cong \angle C$.

5.7 Lesson

Core Vocabulary

Previous
congruent figures
corresponding parts
construction

What You Will Learn

▸ Use congruent triangles.

▸ Prove constructions.

Using Congruent Triangles

Congruent triangles have congruent corresponding parts. So, if you can prove that two triangles are congruent, then you know that their corresponding parts must be congruent as well.

EXAMPLE 1   Using Congruent Triangles

Explain how you can use the given information to prove that the hang glider parts are congruent.

Given $\angle 1 \cong \angle 2$, $\angle RTQ \cong \angle RTS$
Prove $\overline{QT} \cong \overline{ST}$

SOLUTION

If you can show that $\triangle QRT \cong \triangle SRT$, then you will know that $\overline{QT} \cong \overline{ST}$. First, copy the diagram and mark the given information. Then mark the information that you can deduce. In this case, $\angle RQT$ and $\angle RST$ are supplementary to congruent angles, so $\angle RQT \cong \angle RST$. Also, $\overline{RT} \cong \overline{RT}$ by the Reflexive Property of Congruence (Theorem 2.1).

Mark given information.   Mark deduced information.

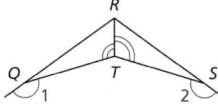   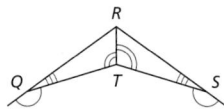

Two angle pairs and a non-included side are congruent, so by the AAS Congruence Theorem (Theorem 5.11), $\triangle QRT \cong \triangle SRT$.

▸ Because corresponding parts of congruent triangles are congruent, $\overline{QT} \cong \overline{ST}$.

Monitoring Progress Help in English and Spanish at *BigIdeasMath.com*

1. Explain how you can prove that $\angle A \cong \angle C$.

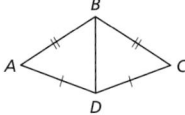

Laurie's Notes   Teacher Actions

- **Big Idea:** It takes three pieces of information to prove that two triangles are congruent (SAS, SSS, ASA, AAS, HL). Once proven congruent, there are three additional pieces of information that can be deduced to be true about the two triangles. Explain to students that in this lesson they will prove triangles congruent. Any corresponding parts that were not used in the proof can now be deduced to be congruent.
- Discuss Example 1. Have partners work together to write the proof.

EXAMPLE 2 **Using Congruent Triangles for Measurement**

MAKING SENSE OF PROBLEMS

When you cannot easily measure a length directly, you can make conclusions about the length *indirectly*, usually by calculations based on known lengths.

Use the following method to find the distance across a river, from point N to point P.

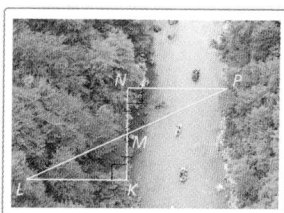

- Place a stake at K on the near side so that $\overline{NK} \perp \overline{NP}$.
- Find M, the midpoint of $\overline{NK}$.
- Locate the point L so that $\overline{NK} \perp \overline{KL}$ and L, P, and M are collinear.

Explain how this plan allows you to find the distance.

SOLUTION

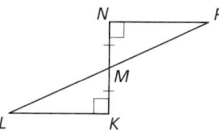

Because $\overline{NK} \perp \overline{NP}$ and $\overline{NK} \perp \overline{KL}$, $\angle N$ and $\angle K$ are congruent right angles. Because M is the midpoint of $\overline{NK}$, $\overline{NM} \cong \overline{KM}$. The vertical angles $\angle KML$ and $\angle NMP$ are congruent. So, $\triangle MLK \cong \triangle MPN$ by the ASA Congruence Theorem (Theorem 5.10). Then because corresponding parts of congruent triangles are congruent, $\overline{KL} \cong \overline{NP}$. So, you can find the distance NP across the river by measuring $\overline{KL}$.

EXAMPLE 3 **Planning a Proof Involving Pairs of Triangles**

Use the given information to write a plan for proof.

Given $\angle 1 \cong \angle 2$, $\angle 3 \cong \angle 4$

Prove $\triangle BCE \cong \triangle DCE$

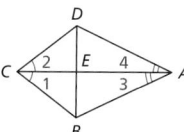

SOLUTION

In $\triangle BCE$ and $\triangle DCE$, you know that $\angle 1 \cong \angle 2$ and $\overline{CE} \cong \overline{CE}$. If you can show that $\overline{CB} \cong \overline{CD}$, then you can use the SAS Congruence Theorem (Theorem 5.5).

To prove that $\overline{CB} \cong \overline{CD}$, you can first prove that $\triangle CBA \cong \triangle CDA$. You are given $\angle 1 \cong \angle 2$ and $\angle 3 \cong \angle 4$. $\overline{CA} \cong \overline{CA}$ by the Reflexive Property of Congruence (Theorem 2.1). You can use the ASA Congruence Theorem (Theorem 5.10) to prove that $\triangle CBA \cong \triangle CDA$.

▶ **Plan for Proof** Use the ASA Congruence Theorem (Theorem 5.10) to prove that $\triangle CBA \cong \triangle CDA$. Then state that $\overline{CB} \cong \overline{CD}$. Use the SAS Congruence Theorem (Theorem 5.5) to prove that $\triangle BCE \cong \triangle DCE$.

Monitoring Progress 🔊 Help in English and Spanish at *BigIdeasMath.com*

2. In Example 2, does it matter how far from point N you place a stake at point K? Explain.

3. Write a plan to prove that $\triangle PTU \cong \triangle UQP$.

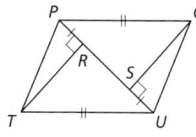

Section 5.7   Using Congruent Triangles   **279**

Extra Example 2

Explain how to use the measurements in the diagram to find the distance across the pond.

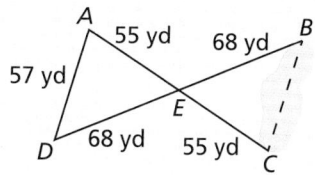

By Vertical $\angle$s $\cong$ Thm. (2.6), $\angle AED \cong \angle CEB$. Because $AE = 55$, $CE = 55$, $DE = 68$, and $BE = 68$, $\overline{AE} \cong \overline{CE}$ and $\overline{DE} \cong \overline{BE}$. By SAS $\cong$ Thm. (5.5), $\triangle AED \cong \triangle CEB$. So, $\overline{AD} \cong \overline{BC}$ by CPCTC, and the length of the pond is 57 yards.

Extra Example 3

Use the diagram in Example 3. Write a plan to prove that $\triangle ADE \cong \triangle ABE$.
Plan for Proof Use the ASA Congruence Theorem (Thm. 5.10) to prove that $\triangle ADC \cong \triangle ABC$. Then state that $\overline{AD} \cong \overline{AB}$. Use the SAS Congruence Theorem (Thm. 5.5) to prove that $\triangle ADE \cong \triangle ABE$.

MONITORING PROGRESS ANSWERS

2. no; As long as the rest of the steps are followed correctly, $\triangle LKM$ will still be congruent to $\triangle PNM$. So, the corresponding parts will still be congruent, and you will still be able to find NP by measuring $\overline{LK}$.

3. Use the HL Congruence Theorem (Thm. 5.9) to prove that $\triangle QSP \cong \triangle TRU$. Use the SAS Congruence Theorem (Thm. 5.5) to prove that $\triangle PRT \cong \triangle USQ$. Then state that $\overline{PT} \cong \overline{UQ}$. Use the SSS Congruence Theorem (Thm. 5.8) to prove that $\triangle PTU \cong \triangle UQP$.

Laurie's Notes **Teacher Actions**

- Have students sketch the diagram for Example 2. As you read the method for constructing the triangles, have students mark the diagram with the known information.
- ❓ "Is there additional information that you can deduce?" yes; Vertical angles are congruent.
- **MP1 Make Sense of Problems and Persevere in Solving Them:** Discuss the plan for the proof in Example 3. Have students self-assess with *Thumbs Up*. Have partners work together to write the proof.
- **Response Logs:** "It helped me today when ..."

Extra Example 4

Write a proof to verify that the construction of the midpoint of a segment is valid.

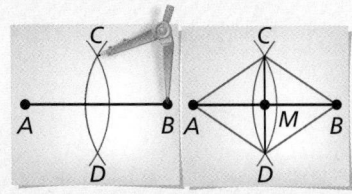

Given $\overline{AC} \cong \overline{AD} \cong \overline{BC} \cong \overline{BD}$
Prove M is the midpoint of $\overline{AB}$.

Statements (Reasons)

1. $\overline{AC} \cong \overline{AD} \cong \overline{BC} \cong \overline{BD}$ (Given)
2. $\overline{CD} \cong \overline{CD}$ (Refl. Prop. $\cong$ Thm. 2.1)
3. $\triangle ACD \cong \triangle BCD$ (SSS $\cong$ Thm. 5.8)
4. $\angle ACM \cong \angle BCM$ (CPCTC)
5. $\overline{CM} \cong \overline{CM}$ (Refl. Prop. $\cong$ Thm. 2.1)
6. $\triangle ACM \cong \triangle BCM$ (SAS $\cong$ Thm. 5.5)
7. $\overline{MA} \cong \overline{MB}$ (CPCTC)
8. M is the midpoint of $\overline{AB}$. (Def. of midpoint)

MONITORING PROGRESS ANSWER

4. $\overline{AB}$ and $\overline{AC}$

Proving Constructions

Recall that you can use a compass and a straightedge to copy an angle. The construction is shown below. You can use congruent triangles to prove that this construction is valid.

Step 1

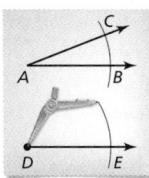

Draw a segment and arcs
To copy $\angle A$, draw a segment with initial point D. Draw an arc with center A. Using the same radius, draw an arc with center D. Label points B, C, and E.

Step 2

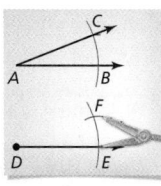

Draw an arc
Draw an arc with radius BC and center E. Label the intersection F.

Step 3

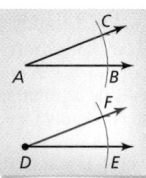

Draw a ray
Draw $\overrightarrow{DF}$. In Example 4, you will prove that $\angle D \cong \angle A$.

EXAMPLE 4 **Proving a Construction**

Write a proof to verify that the construction for copying an angle is valid.

SOLUTION

Add $\overline{BC}$ and $\overline{EF}$ to the diagram. In the construction, one compass setting determines $\overline{AB}$, $\overline{DE}$, $\overline{AC}$, and $\overline{DF}$, and another compass setting determines $\overline{BC}$ and $\overline{EF}$. So, you can assume the following as given statements.

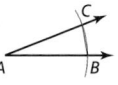

Given $\overline{AB} \cong \overline{DE}, \overline{AC} \cong \overline{DF}, \overline{BC} \cong \overline{EF}$
Prove $\angle D \cong \angle A$

Plan for Proof Show that $\triangle DEF \cong \triangle ABC$, so you can conclude that the corresponding parts $\angle D$ and $\angle A$ are congruent.

Plan in Action	STATEMENTS	REASONS
	1. $\overline{AB} \cong \overline{DE}, \overline{AC} \cong \overline{DF}, \overline{BC} \cong \overline{EF}$	**1.** Given
	2. $\triangle DEF \cong \triangle ABC$	**2.** SSS Congruence Theorem (Theorem 5.8)
	3. $\angle D \cong \angle A$	**3.** Corresponding parts of congruent triangles are congruent.

Monitoring Progress Help in English and Spanish at *BigIdeasMath.com*

4. Use the construction of an angle bisector on page 42. What segments can you assume are congruent?

Laurie's Notes   Teacher Actions

- Explain that the constructions students have done in this chapter can be proven valid by using one of the triangle-congruence theorems.
- Differentiate and have different groups of students prove one of the constructions presented in this chapter. Have each group present their proof to the class.

Closure

- **Response Logs:** Select from "I didn't expect …" or "I learned to …" or "The hardest part right now is …."

Vocabulary and Core Concept Check

1. **COMPLETE THE SENTENCE** _____ parts of congruent triangles are congruent.

2. **WRITING** Describe a situation in which you might choose to use indirect measurement with congruent triangles to find a measure rather than measuring directly.

Monitoring Progress and Modeling with Mathematics

In Exercises 3–8, explain how to prove that the statement is true. *(See Example 1.)*

3. $\angle A \cong \angle D$

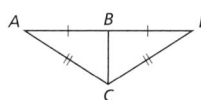

4. $\angle Q \cong \angle T$

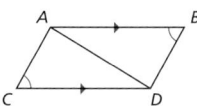

5. $\overline{JM} \cong \overline{LM}$

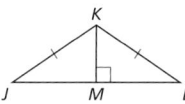

6. $\overline{AC} \cong \overline{DB}$

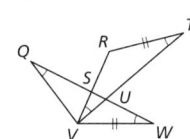

7. $\overline{GK} \cong \overline{HJ}$

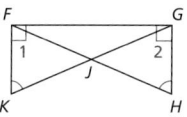

8. $\overline{QW} \cong \overline{VT}$

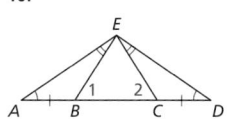

In Exercises 9–12, write a plan to prove that $\angle 1 \cong \angle 2$. *(See Example 3.)*

9.

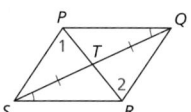

10.

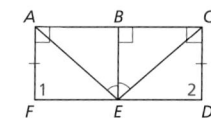

11.

12.

In Exercises 13 and 14, write a proof to verify that the construction is valid. *(See Example 4.)*

13. Line perpendicular to a line through a point not on the line

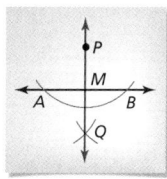

Plan for Proof Show that $\triangle APQ \cong \triangle BPQ$ by the SSS Congruence Theorem (Theorem 5.8). Then show that $\triangle APM \cong \triangle BPM$ using the SAS Congruence Theorem (Theorem 5.5). Use corresponding parts of congruent triangles to show that $\angle AMP$ and $\angle BMP$ are right angles.

14. Line perpendicular to a line through a point on the line

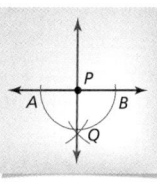

Plan for Proof Show that $\triangle APQ \cong \triangle BPQ$ by the SSS Congruence Theorem (Theorem 5.8). Use corresponding parts of congruent triangles to show that $\angle QPA$ and $\angle QPB$ are right angles.

In Exercises 15 and 16, use the information given in the diagram to write a proof.

15. Prove $\overline{FL} \cong \overline{HN}$

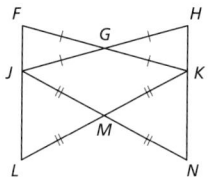

Assignment Guide and Homework Check

ASSIGNMENT

Basic: 1, 2, 3–17 odd, 18, 21, 24, 25

Average: 1, 2, 6–18 even, 21, 22, 24, 25

Advanced: 1, 2, 6–20 even, 21–25

HOMEWORK CHECK

Basic: 3, 11, 13, 15, 18

Average: 6, 10, 14, 16, 18

Advanced: 10, 14, 16, 18, 22

ANSWERS

1. Corresponding

2. *Sample answer:* You might use indirect measurement to find the height of a cave opening on the side of a cliff.

3. All three pairs of sides are congruent. So, by the SSS Congruence Theorem (Thm. 5.8), $\triangle ABC \cong \triangle DBC$. Because corresponding parts of congruent triangles are congruent, $\angle A \cong \angle D$.

4. Two pairs of sides and the pair of included angles are congruent. So, by the SAS Congruence Theorem (Thm. 5.5), $\triangle QPR \cong \triangle TPS$. Because corresponding parts of congruent triangles are congruent, $\angle Q \cong \angle T$.

5. The hypotenuses and one pair of legs of two right triangles are congruent. So, by the HL Congruence Theorem (Thm. 5.9), $\triangle JMK \cong \triangle LMK$. Because corresponding parts of congruent triangles are congruent, $\overline{JM} \cong \overline{LM}$.

6. $\angle BAD \cong \angle CDA$ by the Alternate Interior Angles Theorem (Thm. 3.2). From the diagram, $\angle B \cong \angle C$. $\overline{AD} \cong \overline{AD}$ by the Reflexive Property of Congruence (Thm. 2.1). So, by the AAS Congruence Theorem (Thm. 5.11), $\triangle ACD \cong \triangle DBA$. Because corresponding parts of congruent triangles are congruent, $\overline{AC} \cong \overline{DB}$.

7. From the diagram, $\angle JHN \cong \angle KGL$, $\angle N \cong \angle L$, and $\overline{JN} \cong \overline{KL}$. So, by the AAS Congruence Theorem (Thm. 5.11), $\triangle JNH \cong \triangle KLG$. Because corresponding parts of congruent triangles are congruent, $\overline{GK} \cong \overline{HJ}$.

8. From the diagram, $\angle Q \cong \angle W \cong \angle RVT \cong \angle T$ and $\overline{VW} \cong \overline{RT}$. So, by the AAS Congruence Theorem (Thm. 5.11), $\triangle QVW \cong \triangle VRT$. Because corresponding parts of congruent triangles are congruent, $\overline{QW} \cong \overline{VT}$.

9. Use the AAS Congruence Theorem (Thm. 5.11) to prove that $\triangle FHG \cong \triangle GKF$. Then, state that $\angle FGK \cong \angle GFH$. Use the Congruent Complements Theorem (Thm. 2.5) to prove that $\angle 1 \cong \angle 2$.

10. Use the AAS Congruence Theorem (Thm. 5.11) to prove that $\triangle ABE \cong \triangle DCE$. Then, state that $\overline{BE} \cong \overline{CE}$ because corresponding parts of congruent triangles are congruent. Use the Base Angles Theorem (Thm. 5.6) to prove that $\angle 1 \cong \angle 2$.

11. Use the ASA Congruence Theorem (Thm. 5.10) to prove that $\triangle STR \cong \triangle QTP$. Then, state that $\overline{PT} \cong \overline{RT}$ because corresponding parts of congruent triangles are congruent. Use the SAS Congruence Theorem (Thm. 5.5) to prove that $\triangle STP \cong \triangle QTR$. So, $\angle 1 \cong \angle 2$.

12–15. See Additional Answers.

ANSWERS

16–17. See Additional Answers.

18. a. the red triangle

    b. 4 times

19. See Additional Answers.

20. $MS \approx 1034$ mi, $SB \approx 956$ mi,
$MB \approx 1035$ mi, $P \approx 3025$ mi,
$A \approx 439{,}000$ mi^2; *Sample answer:*
A triangle with vertices at Topeka,
KS, Buffalo, NY, and Orlando, FL
is approximately congruent to the
Bermuda Triangle.

21–25. See Additional Answers.

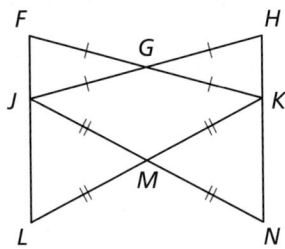
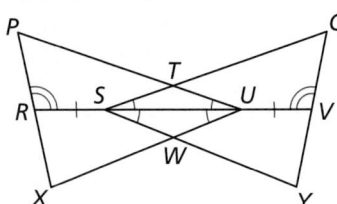
---

16. Prove $\triangle PUX \cong \triangle QSY$

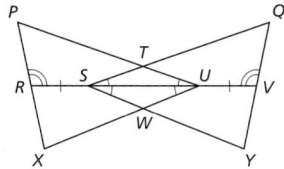

17. MODELING WITH MATHEMATICS Explain how to find
the distance across the canyon. *(See Example 2.)*

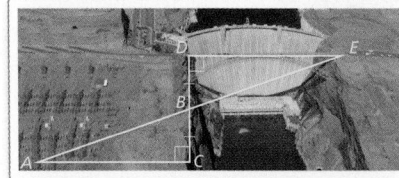

18. HOW DO YOU SEE IT?
Use the tangram puzzle.

  a. Which triangle(s)
have an area that is
twice the area of the
purple triangle?

  b. How many times greater is the area of the orange
triangle than the area of the purple triangle?

19. PROOF Prove that the green triangles in the Jamaican
flag are congruent if $\overline{AD} \parallel \overline{BC}$ and E is the midpoint
of $\overline{AC}$.

Maintaining Mathematical Proficiency
Reviewing what you learned in previous grades and lessons

Find the perimeter of the polygon with the given vertices. *(Section 1.4)*

24. $A(-1, 1)$, $B(4, 1)$, $C(4, -2)$, $D(-1, -2)$ **25.** $J(-5, 3)$, $K(-2, 1)$, $L(3, 4)$

---

20. THOUGHT PROVOKING The Bermuda Triangle is a
region in the Atlantic Ocean in which many ships and
planes have mysteriously disappeared. The vertices
are Miami, San Juan, and Bermuda. Use the Internet
or some other resource to find the side lengths, the
perimeter, and the area of this triangle (in miles).
Then create a congruent triangle on land using cities
as vertices.

21. MAKING AN ARGUMENT Your friend claims that
$\triangle WZY$ can be proven congruent to $\triangle YXW$ using
the HL Congruence
Theorem (Thm. 5.9).
Is your friend
correct? Explain
your reasoning.

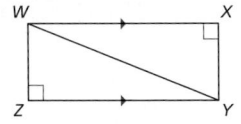

22. CRITICAL THINKING Determine whether each
conditional statement is true or false. If the statement
is false, rewrite it as a true statement using the
converse, inverse, or contrapositive.

  a. If two triangles have the same perimeter, then they
are congruent.

  b. If two triangles are congruent, then they have the
same area.

23. ATTENDING TO PRECISION Which triangles are
congruent to $\triangle ABC$? Select all that apply.

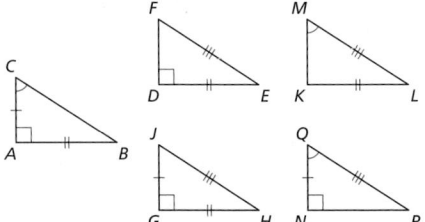

Dynamic Teaching Tools

Dynamic Assessment & Progress Monitoring Tool
Lesson Planning Tool
Interactive Whiteboard Lesson Library
Dynamic Classroom with Dynamic Investigations

Overview of Section 5.8

Introduction

- This lesson presents a new type of proof format, the coordinate proof.
- While students have used formulas to find distances, slopes, and midpoints, in this lesson the coordinates are replaced with variables. When a proof is done with variable coordinates, the results are true for all figures of that type.
- Students will recognize that the orientation of a figure in the coordinate plane can assist in making the computations easier.

Formative Assessment Tips

- Refer to page T-230 for a description of *Response Logs*. In this lesson and throughout this chapter, there will be sentence stems to prompt student writing. Use your judgment for placement in the lesson, amount of time to allow for writing, and the actual sentence stem given to students.
- For a beginning list of writing stems, see page T-238.

Another Way

- The two explorations could be done with pencil and graph paper because there is no need to make this a dynamic sketch.

Pacing Suggestion

- Once students have completed the explorations, continue with the formal lesson.

Common Core
State Standards

HSG-GPE.B.4 Use coordinates to prove simple geometric theorems algebraically.

Laurie's Notes

Exploration

Motivate
- Write on the board: $A(-3, 0)$, $B(2, -3)$, and $C(5, 2)$.
- Divide the class into three groups: $\overline{AB}$, $\overline{BC}$, and $\overline{AC}$. Have each group find the slope, length, and midpoint of their segment. $\overline{AB}$: $-\frac{3}{5}$, $\sqrt{34}$, $\left(-\frac{1}{2}, -\frac{3}{2}\right)$; $\overline{BC}$: $\frac{5}{3}$, $\sqrt{34}$, $\left(\frac{7}{2}, -\frac{1}{2}\right)$; $\overline{AC}$: $\frac{1}{4}$, $\sqrt{68}$, $(1, 1)$
- Have a volunteer from each group record the results of their work.
- **? Turn and Talk:** "What type of triangle is $\triangle ABC$? How do you know?" The triangle is a right isosceles triangle. Explanations will vary. Some may use slope to justify that there is a right angle. Others may use the Converse of the Pythagorean Theorem (grade 8). The Distance Formula shows that the triangle is isosceles.
- Explain to students that they are going to work with coordinate proofs in this lesson, and the formulas learned in prior math classes will be important.

Exploration
- These explorations as well as the examples in the formal lesson require that students recall the Distance Formula, Midpoint Formula, and slope formula.

Exploration 1
- **?** "You know the coordinates of points A, B, and C. What is necessary to prove that $\triangle ABC$ is isosceles?" You need at least two congruent sides.
- **?** "Without using the measurement tool, how can you show that there are at least two congruent sides?" Use the Distance Formula to find AB and BC.
- Confirm that students recall the Distance Formula.

Exploration 2
- **?** "What is necessary to prove that $\triangle ABC$ is a right isosceles triangle?" Show that two sides are congruent and that the angle between the congruent sides is a right angle.
- **?** "How do you show that the sides form a right angle?" Show that the sides are perpendicular by finding the slope of each line segment.
- Have partners work through the algebra to show that $\triangle ABC$ is a right isosceles triangle.
- Have different groups of students select a different point for C below the x-axis, such as $(3, -1)$, $(3, -2)$, $(3, -3)$, or $(3, -4)$.
- **MP3 Construct Viable Arguments and Critique the Reasoning of Others:** Have students summarize what they believe is true in this exploration. Listen for an understanding that as long as C is on the line $x = 3$, $\triangle ABC$ is isosceles. If C is $(3, 3)$ or $(3, -3)$, then the triangle is also a right triangle.
- **Extension:** Have students also explore when $\triangle ABC$ will be an obtuse isosceles triangle and when it will be an acute isosceles triangle.

Communicate Your Answer
- **MP1 Make Sense of Problems and Persevere in Solving Them** and **MP2 Reason Abstractly and Quantitatively:** Skills learned in an algebra class are essential in writing a coordinate proof. Using variables as the coordinates versus real numbers means that the proof is true for all figures of this type.

Connecting to Next Step
- The explorations give students the opportunity to recall and use the algebraic techniques that will be necessary in writing coordinate proofs in the formal lesson.

5.8 Coordinate Proofs

Essential Question
How can you use a coordinate plane to write a proof?

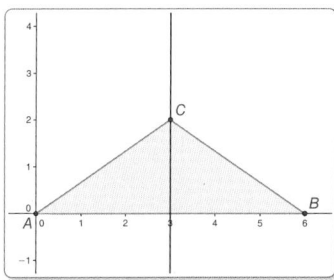

EXPLORATION 1   Writing a Coordinate Proof

Work with a partner.

a. Use dynamic geometry software to draw $\overline{AB}$ with endpoints $A(0, 0)$ and $B(6, 0)$.

b. Draw the vertical line $x = 3$.

c. Draw $\triangle ABC$ so that C lies on the line $x = 3$.

d. Use your drawing to prove that $\triangle ABC$ is an isosceles triangle.

Sample
Points
$A(0, 0)$
$B(6, 0)$
$C(3, y)$
Segments
$AB = 6$
Line
$x = 3$

EXPLORATION 2   Writing a Coordinate Proof

Work with a partner.

a. Use dynamic geometry software to draw $\overline{AB}$ with endpoints $A(0, 0)$ and $B(6, 0)$.

b. Draw the vertical line $x = 3$.

c. Plot the point $C(3, 3)$ and draw $\triangle ABC$. Then use your drawing to prove that $\triangle ABC$ is an isosceles right triangle.

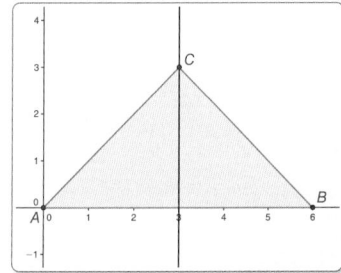

Sample
Points
$A(0, 0)$
$B(6, 0)$
$C(3, 3)$
Segments
$AB = 6$
$BC = 4.24$
$AC = 4.24$
Line
$x = 3$

CRITIQUING THE REASONING OF OTHERS

To be proficient in math, you need to understand and use stated assumptions, definitions, and previously established results.

d. Change the coordinates of C so that C lies below the x-axis and $\triangle ABC$ is an isosceles right triangle.

e. Write a coordinate proof to show that if C lies on the line $x = 3$ and $\triangle ABC$ is an isosceles right triangle, then C must be the point $(3, 3)$ or the point found in part (d).

Communicate Your Answer

3. How can you use a coordinate plane to write a proof?

4. Write a coordinate proof to prove that $\triangle ABC$ with vertices $A(0, 0)$, $B(6, 0)$, and $C(3, 3\sqrt{3})$ is an equilateral triangle.

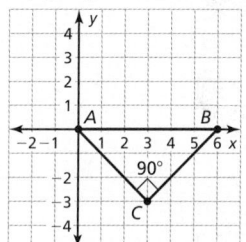

Section 5.8   Coordinate Proofs   **283**

ANSWERS

1.   a. Check students' work.

     b. Check students' work.

     c. Check students' work.

     d. Using the Distance Formula, $AC = \sqrt{9 + y^2}$ and $AB = \sqrt{9 + y^2}$. $\overline{AC} \cong \overline{BC}$, so $\triangle ABC$ is an isosceles triangle.

2.   a. Check students' work.

     b. Check students' work.

     c. Check students' work; $AC = 3\sqrt{2}$, $m_{\overline{AC}} = 1$, $BC = 3\sqrt{2}$, and $m_{\overline{BC}} = -1$. So, $AC \perp BC$ and $\triangle ABC$ is a right isosceles triangle.

     d. $C(3, -3)$

e. If C lies on the line $x = 3$, then the coordinates are $C(3, y)$. Because $\triangle ABC$ is an isosceles triangle,

$$m_{\overline{AC}} = \frac{y}{3}, \text{ and } m_{\overline{BC}} = \frac{y}{-3}.$$

$\triangle ABC$ is a right triangle, so it must have a right angle. Because $\overline{AC}$ and $\overline{BC}$ are the congruent legs of $\triangle ABC$, $\angle A$ and $\angle B$ are the congruent base angles by the Base Angles Theorem (Thm. 5.6). The vertex angle, $\angle C$, must be the right angle, which means that $\overline{AC} \perp \overline{BC}$ by the definition of perpendicular lines. By the Slopes of Perpendicular Lines Theorem (Thm. 3.14),

$$\frac{y}{3} \cdot \frac{y}{-3} = -1 \text{ and } y = \pm 3.$$

So, the coordinates of C must be $(3, 3)$ or $(3, -3)$.

3. You can position the figure in a coordinate plane and then use deductive reasoning to show that what you are trying to prove must be true based on the coordinates of the figure.

4. Using the Distance Formula, $AC = 6$, $AB = 6$, and $BC = 6$. $\overline{AC} \cong \overline{AB} \cong \overline{BC}$, so $\triangle ABC$ is an equilateral triangle.

Extra Example 1

Place each figure in a coordinate plane in a way that is convenient for finding side lengths. Assign coordinates to each vertex.

a. scalene right triangle

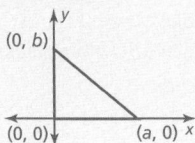

b. isosceles trapezoid

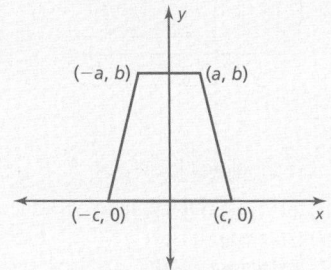

Extra Example 2

Use the information in Example 2. Write a plan for a proof that uses the SAS Congruence Theorem (Thm. 5.5).

Plan for Proof The *x*- and *y*-axes are perpendicular, so use definitions to show $\angle SOP \cong \angle SOR$. Use the Distance Formula to show $RO = PO$. Use the Reflexive Prop. $\cong$ (Thm. 2.1) to show $\overline{SO} \cong \overline{SO}$. Use SAS $\cong$ Thm. (5.5) to show that $\triangle POS \cong \triangle ROS$. Then use CPCTC to conclude that $\angle PSO \cong \angle RSO$, which implies $\overrightarrow{SO}$ bisects $\angle PSR$.

MONITORING PROGRESS ANSWERS

1. See Additional Answers.

2. (m, m)

5.8 Lesson

Core Vocabulary
coordinate proof, *p. 284*

What You Will Learn

▶ Place figures in a coordinate plane.

▶ Write coordinate proofs.

Placing Figures in a Coordinate Plane

A **coordinate proof** involves placing geometric figures in a coordinate plane. When you use variables to represent the coordinates of a figure in a coordinate proof, the results are true for all figures of that type.

EXAMPLE 1 Placing a Figure in a Coordinate Plane

Place each figure in a coordinate plane in a way that is convenient for finding side lengths. Assign coordinates to each vertex.

a. a rectangle   **b.** a scalene triangle

SOLUTION

It is easy to find lengths of horizontal and vertical segments and distances from (0, 0), so place one vertex at the origin and one or more sides on an axis.

a. Let *h* represent the length and *k* represent the width.

b. Notice that you need to use three different variables.

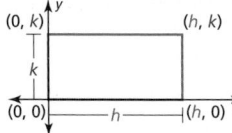 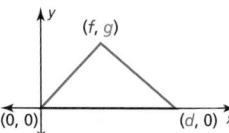

Monitoring Progress Help in English and Spanish at *BigIdeasMath.com*

1. Show another way to place the rectangle in Example 1 part (a) that is convenient for finding side lengths. Assign new coordinates.

2. A square has vertices (0, 0), (m, 0), and (0, m). Find the fourth vertex.

Once a figure is placed in a coordinate plane, you may be able to prove statements about the figure.

EXAMPLE 2 Writing a Plan for a Coordinate Proof

Write a plan to prove that $\overrightarrow{SO}$ bisects $\angle PSR$.

Given Coordinates of vertices of $\triangle POS$ and $\triangle ROS$.

Prove $\overrightarrow{SO}$ bisects $\angle PSR$.

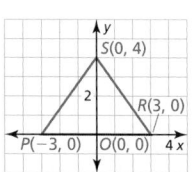

SOLUTION

Plan for Proof Use the Distance Formula to find the side lengths of $\triangle POS$ and $\triangle ROS$. Then use the SSS Congruence Theorem (Theorem 5.8) to show that $\triangle POS \cong \triangle ROS$. Finally, use the fact that corresponding parts of congruent triangles are congruent to conclude that $\angle PSO \cong \angle RSO$, which implies that $\overrightarrow{SO}$ bisects $\angle PSR$.

Laurie's Notes   Teacher Actions

- Explain the difference between performing a calculation using real numbers and using variables. Define a *coordinate proof*.
- Draw coordinate axes without scaling either axis. Locate a point at the origin, on the positive *x*-axis, and in the first quadrant.
- **?** "What coordinates do you know with certainty?" (0, 0) and the *y*-coordinate of the point on the positive *x*-axis
- **Turn and Talk:** "In Example 2, how could you show that $\overrightarrow{SO}$ bisects $\angle PSR$?" Students will see that the triangles can be proven congruent.

3. Write a plan for the proof.

    Given $\overrightarrow{GJ}$ bisects $\angle OGH$.

    Prove $\triangle GJO \cong \triangle GJH$

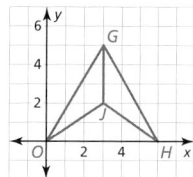

The coordinate proof in Example 2 applies to a specific triangle. When you want to prove a statement about a more general set of figures, it is helpful to use variables as coordinates.

For instance, you can use variable coordinates to duplicate the proof in Example 2. Once this is done, you can conclude that $\overrightarrow{SO}$ bisects $\angle PSR$ for any triangle whose coordinates fit the given pattern.

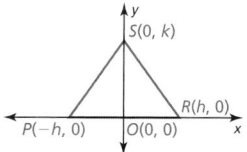

EXAMPLE 3   Applying Variable Coordinates

Place an isosceles right triangle in a coordinate plane. Then find the length of the hypotenuse and the coordinates of its midpoint M.

SOLUTION

Place $\triangle PQO$ with the right angle at the origin. Let the length of the legs be k. Then the vertices are located at $P(0, k)$, $Q(k, 0)$, and $O(0, 0)$.

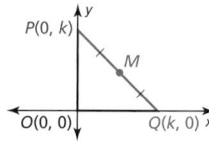

Use the Distance Formula to find PQ, the length of the hypotenuse.

$$PQ = \sqrt{(k-0)^2 + (0-k)^2} = \sqrt{k^2 + (-k)^2} = \sqrt{k^2 + k^2} = \sqrt{2k^2} = k\sqrt{2}$$

Use the Midpoint Formula to find the midpoint M of the hypotenuse.

$$M\left(\frac{0+k}{2}, \frac{k+0}{2}\right) = M\left(\frac{k}{2}, \frac{k}{2}\right)$$

▶ So, the length of the hypotenuse is $k\sqrt{2}$ and the midpoint of the hypotenuse is $\left(\frac{k}{2}, \frac{k}{2}\right)$.

4. Graph the points $O(0, 0)$, $H(m, n)$, and $J(m, 0)$. Is $\triangle OHJ$ a right triangle? Find the side lengths and the coordinates of the midpoint of each side.

FINDING AN ENTRY POINT

Another way to solve Example 3 is to place a triangle with point C at $(0, h)$ on the y-axis and hypotenuse $\overline{AB}$ on the x-axis. To make $\angle ACB$ a right angle, position A and B so that legs $\overline{CA}$ and $\overline{CB}$ have slopes of 1 and -1, respectively.

Slope is 1.   Slope is -1.

Length of hypotenuse = $2h$

$$M\left(\frac{-h+h}{2}, \frac{0+0}{2}\right) = M(0, 0)$$

Extra Example 3

Place an isosceles triangle on a coordinate plane with vertices $P(-2a, 0)$, $Q(0, a)$, and $R(2a, 0)$. Find the length of each side. Then find the coordinates of the midpoint of each side. $PQ = QR = a\sqrt{5}$, $PR = 4a$; the midpoint of $\overline{PQ}$ is $\left(-a, \frac{a}{2}\right)$, the midpoint of $\overline{QR}$ is $\left(a, \frac{a}{2}\right)$, and the midpoint of $\overline{PR}$ is $(0, 0)$.

MONITORING PROGRESS ANSWERS

3. Use the Distance Formula to find GO and GH in order to show that $\overline{GO} \cong \overline{GH}$. State that $\angle OGJ \cong \angle HGJ$ by the definition of angle bisector and $\overline{GJ} \cong \overline{GJ}$ by the Reflexive Property of Congruence (Thm. 2.1). Then use the SAS Congruence Theorem (Thm. 5.5) to show that $\triangle GJO \cong \triangle GJH$.

4.

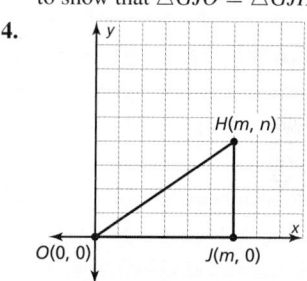

yes; $OJ = m$, $M_{\overline{OJ}}\left(\frac{m}{2}, 0\right)$,

$HJ = n$, $M_{\overline{HJ}}\left(m, \frac{n}{2}\right)$,

$OH = \sqrt{m^2 + n^2}$, $M_{\overline{OH}}\left(\frac{m}{2}, \frac{n}{2}\right)$

Laurie's Notes   Teacher Actions

? "In Example 2, how would the proof change if the coordinates of P and R were $(-a, 0)$ and $(a, 0)$?" The process and proof would be the same.

• Discuss elements of a coordinate proof. Positioning a polygon to make use of the origin and intercepts is common.

• **MP1:** Pose Example 3, noting that there are two suggested orientations. This problem is related to a later lesson when students will determine that the length of the hypotenuse of a right isosceles triangle is $\sqrt{2}$ times the length of the leg.

Extra Example 4

Write a coordinate proof.
Use the diagram and the given information in Example 4. Prove that $\angle TOU \cong \angle VUO$.
The slope of $\overline{TO}$ is $\dfrac{k-0}{m-0} = \dfrac{k}{m}$. The slope of $\overline{UV}$ is $\dfrac{k-0}{(m+h)-h} = \dfrac{k}{m}$. So, $\overline{TO} \parallel \overline{UV}$.
By the Alternate Interior Angles Theorem (Thm. 3.2), $\angle TOU \cong \angle VUO$.

Extra Example 5

As part of a graphic design, you draw a rectangle and then connect the midpoints of the sides. Prove that the quadrilateral *MNPQ* formed has four congruent sides.

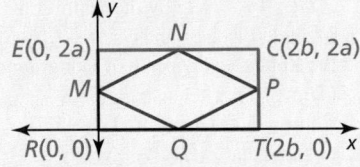

The coordinates of the midpoints are $M(0, a)$, $N(b, 2a)$, $P(2b, a)$, and $Q(b, 0)$. The lengths of $\overline{MN}$, $\overline{NP}$, $\overline{PQ}$, and $\overline{QM}$ are
$\sqrt{(b-0)^2 + (2a-a)^2}$,
$\sqrt{(2b-b)^2 + (a-2a)^2}$,
$\sqrt{(2b-b)^2 + (a-0)^2}$, and
$\sqrt{(b-0)^2 + (0-a)^2}$. Each expression simplifies to $\sqrt{b^2 + a^2}$, so the four segments are congruent.

MONITORING PROGRESS ANSWER

5. Using the Distance Formula, $PN = h\sqrt{2}$, $MN = h\sqrt{2}$, $PO = 2h$, and $MO = 2h$. So, $\overline{PN} \cong \overline{MN}$ and $\overline{PO} \cong \overline{MO}$, and by the Reflexive Property of Congruence (Thm. 2.1), $\overline{ON} \cong \overline{ON}$. So, you can apply the SSS Congruence Theorem (Thm. 5.8) to conclude that $\triangle NPO \cong \triangle NMO$.

Writing Coordinate Proofs

EXAMPLE 4 Writing a Coordinate Proof

Write a coordinate proof.

Given Coordinates of vertices of quadrilateral *OTUV*

Prove $\triangle OTU \cong \triangle UVO$

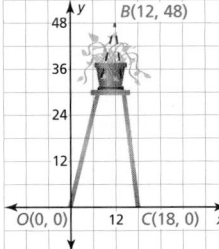

SOLUTION

Segments $\overline{OV}$ and $\overline{UT}$ have the same length.

$$OV = |h - 0| = h$$
$$UT = |(m+h) - m| = h$$

Horizontal segments $\overline{UT}$ and $\overline{OV}$ each have a slope of 0, which implies that they are parallel. Segment $\overline{OU}$ intersects $\overline{UT}$ and $\overline{OV}$ to form congruent alternate interior angles, $\angle TUO$ and $\angle VOU$. By the Reflexive Property of Congruence (Theorem 2.1), $\overline{OU} \cong \overline{OU}$.

▶ So, you can apply the SAS Congruence Theorem (Theorem 5.5) to conclude that $\triangle OTU \cong \triangle UVO$.

EXAMPLE 5 Writing a Coordinate Proof

You buy a tall, three-legged plant stand. When you place a plant on the stand, the stand appears to be unstable under the weight of the plant. The diagram at the right shows a coordinate plane superimposed on one pair of the plant stand's legs. The legs are extended to form $\triangle OBC$. Prove that $\triangle OBC$ is a scalene triangle. Explain why the plant stand may be unstable.

SOLUTION

First, find the side lengths of $\triangle OBC$.

$$OB = \sqrt{(48-0)^2 + (12-0)^2} = \sqrt{2448} \approx 49.5$$
$$BC = \sqrt{(18-12)^2 + (0-48)^2} = \sqrt{2340} \approx 48.4$$
$$OC = |18 - 0| = 18$$

▶ Because $\triangle OBC$ has no congruent sides, $\triangle OBC$ is a scalene triangle by definition. The plant stand may be unstable because $\overline{OB}$ is longer than $\overline{BC}$, so the plant stand is leaning to the right.

Monitoring Progress Help in English and Spanish at *BigIdeasMath.com*

5. Write a coordinate proof.

   Given Coordinates of vertices of $\triangle NPO$ and $\triangle NMO$

   Prove $\triangle NPO \cong \triangle NMO$

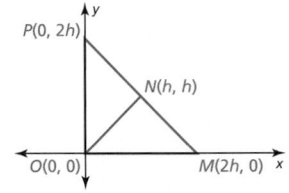

Laurie's Notes   Teacher Actions

- In Example 4, help students make sense of the coordinates for vertex *U*.
- **?** "How can you show that two segments are parallel?" Students may say they need alternate interior angles congruent or show that the line segments have the same slope.
- **Think-Pair-Share:** Have students try Example 5 independently before discussing as a class.

Closure

- **Response Logs:** Select from "I figured these out because …" or "I am feeling good about …" or "When I am writing a proof …."

Vocabulary and Core Concept Check

1. **VOCABULARY** How is a *coordinate proof* different from other types of proofs you have studied? How is it the same?

2. **WRITING** Explain why it is convenient to place a right triangle on the grid as shown when writing a coordinate proof.

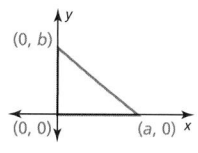

Monitoring Progress and Modeling with Mathematics

In Exercises 3–6, place the figure in a coordinate plane in a convenient way. Assign coordinates to each vertex. Explain the advantages of your placement. *(See Example 1.)*

3. a right triangle with leg lengths of 3 units and 2 units

4. a square with a side length of 3 units

5. an isosceles right triangle with leg length p

6. a scalene triangle with one side length of $2m$

In Exercises 7 and 8, write a plan for the proof. *(See Example 2.)*

7. **Given** Coordinates of vertices of $\triangle OPM$ and $\triangle ONM$
   Prove $\triangle OPM$ and $\triangle ONM$ are isosceles triangles.

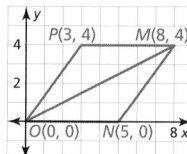

8. **Given** G is the midpoint of $\overline{HF}$.
   Prove $\triangle GHJ \cong \triangle GFO$

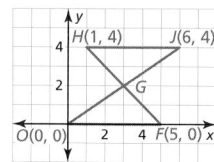

In Exercises 9–12, place the figure in a coordinate plane and find the indicated length.

9. a right triangle with leg lengths of 7 and 9 units; Find the length of the hypotenuse.

10. an isosceles triangle with a base length of 60 units and a height of 50 units; Find the length of one of the legs.

11. a rectangle with a length of 5 units and a width of 4 units; Find the length of the diagonal.

12. a square with side length n; Find the length of the diagonal.

In Exercises 13 and 14, graph the triangle with the given vertices. Find the length and the slope of each side of the triangle. Then find the coordinates of the midpoint of each side. Is the triangle a right triangle? isosceles? Explain. (Assume all variables are positive and $m \neq n$.) *(See Example 3.)*

13. $A(0, 0)$, $B(h, h)$, $C(2h, 0)$

14. $D(0, n)$, $E(m, n)$, $F(m, 0)$

In Exercises 15 and 16, find the coordinates of any unlabeled vertices. Then find the indicated length(s).

15. Find ON and MN.

16. Find OT.

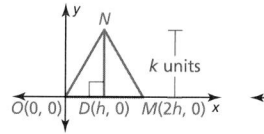

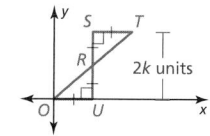

5. *Sample answer:*

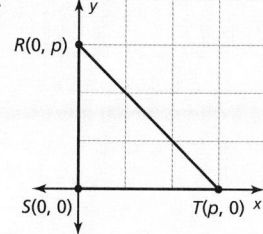

It is easy to find the lengths of horizontal and vertical segments and distances from the origin.

6. *Sample answer:*

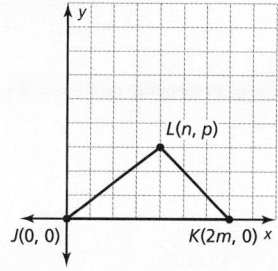

It is easy to find the lengths of horizontal segments and distances from the origin.

7–16. See Additional Answers.

Assignment Guide and Homework Check

ASSIGNMENT
Basic: 1, 2, 3–19 odd, 20, 26, 28, 29
Average: 1, 2, 6–22 even, 26, 28, 29
Advanced: 1, 2, 6, 12–20 even, 22–29

HOMEWORK CHECK
Basic: 5, 7, 13, 15, 17
Average: 6, 12, 14, 16, 18
Advanced: 6, 12, 14, 18, 22

ANSWERS

1. In a coordinate proof, you have to assign coordinates to vertices and write expressions for the side lengths and the slopes of segments in order to show how sides are related; As with other types of proofs, you still have to use deductive reasoning and justify every conclusion with theorems, proofs, and properties of mathematics.

2. When the triangle is positioned as shown, you are using zeros in your expressions, so the side lengths are often the same as one of the coordinates.

3. *Sample answer:*

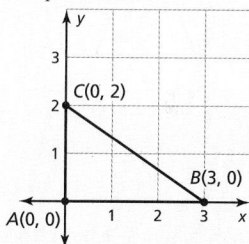

It is easy to find the lengths of horizontal and vertical segments and distances from the origin.

4. *Sample answer:*

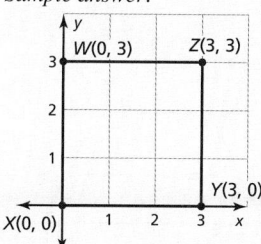

It is easy to find the lengths of horizontal and vertical segments and distances from the origin.

ANSWERS

17–21. See Additional Answers.

22. B   23. A

24–29. See Additional Answers.

Mini-Assessment

Supply the missing coordinates.

1. *POST* is a square.

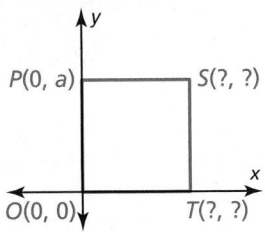

S(a, a), T(a, 0)

2. △*FOG* is isosceles.

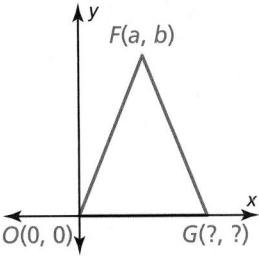

G(2a, 0)

3. Write a coordinate proof.

Given Coordinates of the vertices of isosceles trapezoid *HIJK*, *M* is the midpoint of $\overline{HK}$, *N* is the midpoint of $\overline{IJ}$.

Prove $MN = \frac{1}{2}(HI + KJ)$

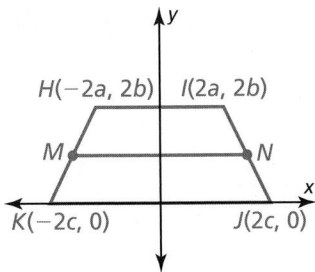

First, find the coordinates of *M* and *N*: *M*(−a − c, b), *N*(a + c, b). Then find that *MN* = 2a + 2c, *HI* = 4a, and *JK* = 4c. So, $\frac{1}{2}(HI + KJ) = $ 2a + 2c = *MN*.

288   Chapter 5

PROOF In Exercises 17 and 18, write a coordinate proof.
(See Example 4.)

17. **Given** Coordinates of vertices of △*DEC* and △*BOC*

Prove △*DEC* ≅ △*BOC*

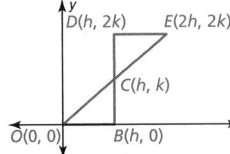

18. **Given** Coordinates of △*DEA*, *H* is the midpoint of $\overline{DA}$, *G* is the midpoint of $\overline{EA}$.

Prove $\overline{DG} \cong \overline{EH}$

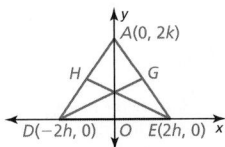

19. **MODELING WITH MATHEMATICS** You and your cousin are camping in the woods. You hike to a point that is 500 meters east and 1200 meters north of the campsite. Your cousin hikes to a point that is 1000 meters east of the campsite. Use a coordinate proof to prove that the triangle formed by your position, your cousin's position, and the campsite is isosceles. *(See Example 5.)*

20. **MAKING AN ARGUMENT** Two friends see a drawing of quadrilateral *PQRS* with vertices *P*(0, 2), *Q*(3, −4), *R*(1, −5), and *S*(−2, 1). One friend says the quadrilateral is a parallelogram but not a rectangle. The other friend says the quadrilateral is a rectangle. Which friend is correct? Use a coordinate proof to support your answer.

21. **MATHEMATICAL CONNECTIONS** Write an algebraic expression for the coordinates of each endpoint of a line segment whose midpoint is the origin.

Maintaining Mathematical Proficiency   Reviewing what you learned in previous grades and lessons

$\overrightarrow{YW}$ bisects $\angle XYZ$ such that $m\angle XYW = (3x − 7)°$ and $m\angle WYZ = (2x + 1)°$. *(Section 1.5)*

28. Find the value of *x*.   **29.** Find $m\angle XYZ$.

288   Chapter 5   Congruent Triangles

---

22. **REASONING** The vertices of a parallelogram are $(w, 0)$, $(0, v)$, $(−w, 0)$, and $(0, −v)$. What is the midpoint of the side in Quadrant III?

Ⓐ $\left(\frac{w}{2}, \frac{v}{2}\right)$ Ⓑ $\left(−\frac{w}{2}, −\frac{v}{2}\right)$

Ⓒ $\left(−\frac{w}{2}, \frac{v}{2}\right)$ Ⓓ $\left(\frac{w}{2}, −\frac{v}{2}\right)$

23. **REASONING** A rectangle with a length of $3h$ and a width of k has a vertex at $(−h, k)$. Which point cannot be a vertex of the rectangle?

Ⓐ (h, k) Ⓑ $(−h, 0)$

Ⓒ $(2h, 0)$ Ⓓ $(2h, k)$

24. **THOUGHT PROVOKING** Choose one of the theorems you have encountered up to this point that you think would be easier to prove with a coordinate proof than with another type of proof. Explain your reasoning. Then write a coordinate proof.

25. **CRITICAL THINKING** The coordinates of a triangle are $(5d, −5d)$, $(0, −5d)$, and $(5d, 0)$. How should the coordinates be changed to make a coordinate proof easier to complete?

26. **HOW DO YOU SEE IT?** Without performing any calculations, how do you know that the diagonals of square *TUVW* are perpendicular to each other? How can you use a similar diagram to show that the diagonals of any square are perpendicular to each other?

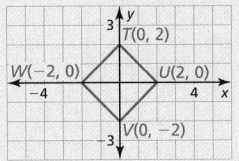

27. **PROOF** Write a coordinate proof for each statement.

a. The midpoint of the hypotenuse of a right triangle is the same distance from each vertex of the triangle.

b. Any two congruent right isosceles triangles can be combined to form a single isosceles triangle.

Core Vocabulary

legs (of a right triangle), *p. 264*
hypotenuse (of a right triangle), *p. 264*
coordinate proof, *p. 284*

Core Concepts

Theorem 5.8 Side-Side-Side (SSS) Congruence Theorem, *p. 262*
Theorem 5.9 Hypotenuse-Leg (HL) Congruence Theorem, *p. 264*
Theorem 5.10 Angle-Side-Angle (ASA) Congruence Theorem, *p. 270*
Theorem 5.11 Angle-Angle-Side (AAS) Congruence Theorem, *p. 271*
Using Congruent Triangles, *p. 278*
Proving Constructions, *p. 280*
Placing Figures in a Coordinate Plane, *p. 284*
Writing Coordinate Proofs, *p. 286*

Mathematical Practices

1. Write a simpler problem that is similar to Exercise 22 on page 267. Describe how to use the simpler problem to gain insight into the solution of the more complicated problem in Exercise 22.

2. Make a conjecture about the meaning of your solutions to Exercises 21–23 on page 275.

3. Identify at least two external resources that you could use to help you solve Exercise 20 on page 282.

- - - - - - - - - - **Performance Task** - - - - - - - -

Creating the Logo

Congruent triangles are often used to create company logos. Why are they used and what are the properties that make them attractive? Following the required constraints, create your new logo and justify how your shape contains the required properties.

To explore the answers to these questions and more, go to *BigIdeasMath.com*.

289

Dynamic Teaching Tools

Dynamic Assessment & Progress Monitoring Tool
Interactive Whiteboard Lesson Library
Dynamic Classroom with Dynamic Investigations

ANSWERS

1. Given square *ABCD* with diagonal $\overline{BD}$, prove $\triangle BAD \cong \triangle DCB$; In this problem, the square could represent the baseball "diamond," and then diagonal $\overline{BD}$ would represent the distance from home plate to second base. So, you could use this problem to prove the equivalent of $\triangle HFS \cong \triangle STH$. Then you could just redraw square *ABCD* with diagonal $\overline{AC}$ this time, so that $\triangle CBA$ is the equivalent of $\triangle FST$. It could easily be shown that the third triangle is congruent to the first two.

2. The theorems on page 275 correspond to other triangle congruence theorems given. HA corresponds to AAS, LL corresponds to SAS, and AL corresponds to ASA or AAS.

3. *Sample answer:* a distance website and a map website

5.1   Angles of Triangles   *(pp. 231–238)*

Classify the triangle by its sides and by measuring its angles.

The triangle does not have any congruent sides, so it is scalene. The measure of $\angle B$ is 117°, so the triangle is obtuse.

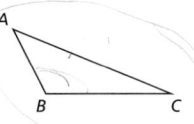

▶   The triangle is an obtuse scalene triangle.

1. Classify the triangle at the right by its sides and by measuring its angles.

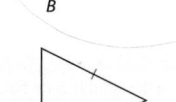

Find the measure of the exterior angle.

2.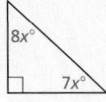

3.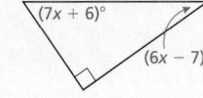

Find the measure of each acute angle.

4.

5.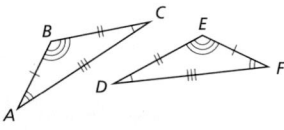

5.2   Congruent Polygons   *(pp. 239–244)*

Write a congruence statement for the triangles. Identify all pairs of congruent corresponding parts.

The diagram indicates that $\triangle ABC \cong \triangle FED$.

Corresponding angles $\angle A \cong \angle F$, $\angle B \cong \angle E$, $\angle C \cong \angle D$

Corresponding sides $\overline{AB} \cong \overline{FE}$, $\overline{BC} \cong \overline{ED}$, $\overline{AC} \cong \overline{FD}$

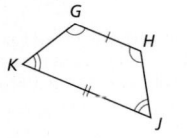

6. In the diagram, $GHJK \cong LMNP$. Identify all pairs of congruent corresponding parts. Then write another congruence statement for the quadrilaterals.

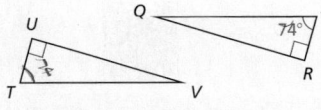

7. Find $m\angle V$.

5.3 Proving Triangle Congruence by SAS *(pp. 245–250)*

Write a proof.

Given $\overline{AC} \cong \overline{EC}, \overline{BC} \cong \overline{DC}$

Prove $\triangle ABC \cong \triangle EDC$

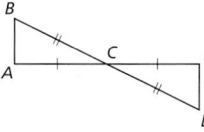

STATEMENTS	REASONS
1. $\overline{AC} \cong \overline{EC}$	**1.** Given
2. $\overline{BC} \cong \overline{DC}$	**2.** Given
3. $\angle ACB \cong \angle ECD$	**3.** Vertical Angles Congruence Theorem (Theorem 2.6)
4. $\triangle ABC \cong \triangle EDC$	**4.** SAS Congruence Theorem (Theorem 5.5)

Decide whether enough information is given to prove that $\triangle WXZ \cong \triangle YZX$ **using the SAS Congruence Theorem (Theorem 5.5). If so, write a proof. If not, explain why.**

8.
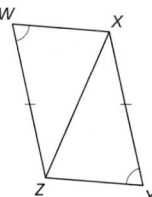

9.
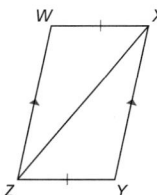

5.4 Equilateral and Isosceles Triangles *(pp. 251–258)*

In $\triangle LMN, \overline{LM} \cong \overline{LN}$. **Name two congruent angles.**

▶ $\overline{LM} \cong \overline{LN}$, so by the Base Angles Theorem (Theorem 5.6), $\angle M \cong \angle N$.

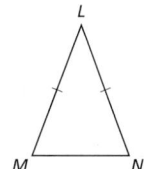

Copy and complete the statement.

10. If $\overline{QP} \cong \overline{QR}$, then $\angle \underline{\quad} \cong \angle \underline{\quad}$.

11. If $\angle TRV \cong \angle TVR$, then $\underline{\quad} \cong \underline{\quad}$.

12. If $\overline{RQ} \cong \overline{RS}$, then $\angle \underline{\quad} \cong \angle \underline{\quad}$.

13. If $\angle SRV \cong \angle SVR$, then $\underline{\quad} \cong \underline{\quad}$.

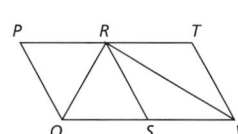

14. Find the values of x and y in the diagram.

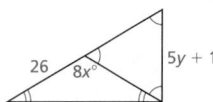

15. no; There is only enough information to conclude that two pairs of sides are congruent.

16. See Additional Answers.

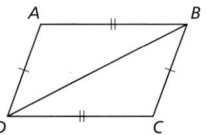

5.5 **Proving Triangle Congruence by SSS** (pp. 261–268)

Write a proof.

Given $\overline{AD} \cong \overline{CB}, \overline{AB} \cong \overline{CD}$

Prove $\triangle ABD \cong \triangle CDB$

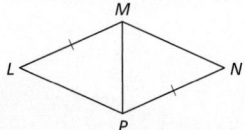

STATEMENTS	REASONS
1. $\overline{AD} \cong \overline{CB}$	**1.** Given
2. $\overline{AB} \cong \overline{CD}$	**2.** Given
3. $\overline{BD} \cong \overline{DB}$	**3.** Reflexive Property of Congruence (Theorem 2.1)
4. $\triangle ABD \cong \triangle CDB$	**4.** SSS Congruence Theorem (Theorem 5.8)

15. Decide whether enough information is given to prove that $\triangle LMP \cong \triangle NPM$ using the SSS Congruence Theorem (Thm. 5.8). If so, write a proof. If not, explain why.

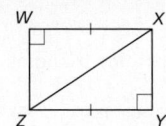

16. Decide whether enough information is given to prove that $\triangle WXZ \cong \triangle YZX$ using the HL Congruence Theorem (Thm. 5.9). If so, write a proof. If not, explain why.

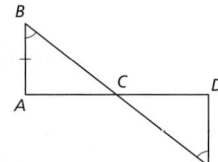

5.6 **Proving Triangle Congruence by ASA and AAS** (pp. 269–276)

Write a proof.

Given $\overline{AB} \cong \overline{DE}$, $\angle ABC \cong \angle DEC$

Prove $\triangle ABC \cong \triangle DEC$

STATEMENTS	REASONS
1. $\overline{AB} \cong \overline{DE}$	**1.** Given
2. $\angle ABC \cong \angle DEC$	**2.** Given
3. $\angle ACB \cong \angle DCE$	**3.** Vertical Angles Congruence Theorem (Thm. 2.6)
4. $\triangle ABC \cong \triangle DEC$	**4.** AAS Congruence Theorem (Thm. 5.11)

292 **Chapter 5** Congruent Triangles

Decide whether enough information is given to prove that the triangles are congruent using the AAS Congruence Theorem (Thm. 5.11). If so, write a proof. If not, explain why.

17. △EFG, △HJK

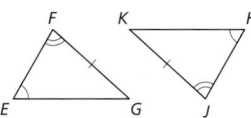

18. △TUV, △QRS

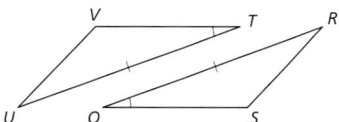

Decide whether enough information is given to prove that the triangles are congruent using the ASA Congruence Theorem (Thm. 5.10). If so, write a proof. If not, explain why.

19. △LPN, △LMN

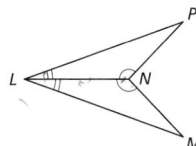

20. △WXZ, △YZX

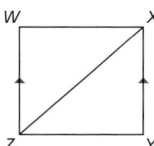

5.7 **Using Congruent Triangles** *(pp. 277–282)*

Explain how you can prove that ∠A ≅ ∠D.

If you can show that △ABC ≅ △DCB, then you will know that ∠A ≅ ∠D. You are given $\overline{AC} \cong \overline{DB}$ and ∠ACB ≅ ∠DBC. You know that $\overline{BC} \cong \overline{CB}$ by the Reflexive Property of Congruence (Thm. 2.1). Two pairs of sides and their included angles are congruent, so by the SAS Congruence Theorem (Thm. 5.5), △ABC ≅ △DCB.

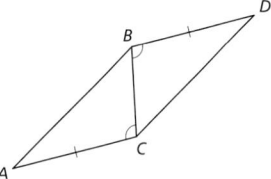

▶ Because corresponding parts of congruent triangles are congruent, ∠A ≅ ∠D.

21. Explain how to prove that ∠K ≅ ∠N.

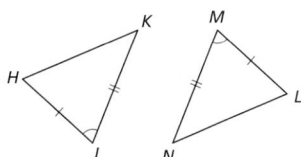

22. Write a plan to prove that ∠1 ≅ ∠2.

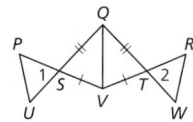

---

17. See Additional Answers.

18. no; There is only enough information to conclude that one pair of angles and one pair of sides are congruent.

19. See Additional Answers.

20. no; There is only enough information to conclude that one pair of angles and one pair of sides are congruent.

21. By the SAS Congruence Theorem (Thm. 5.5), △HJK ≅ △LMN. Because corresponding parts of congruent triangles are congruent, ∠K ≅ ∠N.

22. First, state that $\overline{QV} \cong \overline{QV}$. Then, use the SSS Congruence Theorem (Thm. 5.8) to prove that △QSV ≅ △QTV. Because corresponding parts of congruent triangles are congruent, ∠QSV ≅ ∠QTV. ∠QSV ≅ ∠1 and ∠QTV ≅ ∠2 by the Vertical Angles Congruence Theorem (Thm. 2.6). So, by the Transitive Property of Congruence (Thm. 2.2), ∠1 ≅ ∠2.

23. Using the Distance Formula,
$OP = \sqrt{h^2 + k^2}$, $QR = \sqrt{h^2 + k^2}$,
$OR = j$, and $QP = j$. So, $\overline{OP} \cong \overline{QR}$
and $\overline{OR} \cong \overline{QP}$. Also, by the Reflexive
Property of Congruence (Thm. 2.1),
$\overline{QO} \cong \overline{QO}$. So, you can apply the SSS
Congruence Theorem (Thm. 5.8) to
conclude that $\triangle OPQ \cong \triangle QRO$.

24.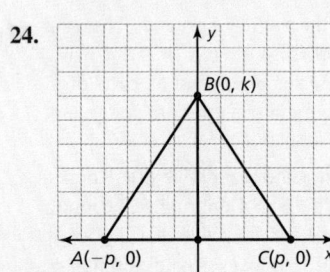

25. $(2k, k)$

Write a coordinate proof.

Given   Coordinates of vertices of $\triangle ODB$ and $\triangle BDC$

Prove $\triangle ODB \cong \triangle BDC$

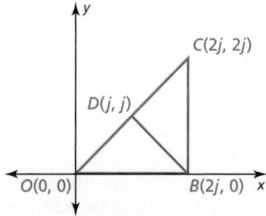

Segments $\overline{OD}$ and $\overline{BD}$ have the same length.

$$OD = \sqrt{(j - 0)^2 + (j - 0)^2} = \sqrt{j^2 + j^2} = \sqrt{2j^2} = j\sqrt{2}$$
$$BD = \sqrt{(j - 2j)^2 + (j - 0)^2} = \sqrt{(-j)^2 + j^2} = \sqrt{2j^2} = j\sqrt{2}$$

Segments $\overline{DB}$ and $\overline{DC}$ have the same length.

$$DB = BD = j\sqrt{2}$$
$$DC = \sqrt{(2j - j)^2 + (2j - j)^2} = \sqrt{j^2 + j^2} = \sqrt{2j^2} = j\sqrt{2}$$

Segments $\overline{OB}$ and $\overline{BC}$ have the same length.

$$OB = |2j - 0| = 2j$$
$$BC = |2j - 0| = 2j$$

▶ So, you can apply the SSS Congruence Theorem (Theorem 5.8) to conclude that $\triangle ODB \cong \triangle BDC$.

23. Write a coordinate proof.

     Given   Coordinates of vertices of quadrilateral $OPQR$

     Prove $\triangle OPQ \cong \triangle QRO$

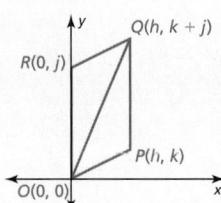

24. Place an isosceles triangle in a coordinate plane in a way that is convenient for finding side lengths. Assign coordinates to each vertex.

25. A rectangle has vertices $(0, 0)$, $(2k, 0)$, and $(0, k)$. Find the fourth vertex.

5 Chapter Test

Write a proof.

1. **Given** $\overline{CA} \cong \overline{CB} \cong \overline{CD} \cong \overline{CE}$
   Prove $\triangle ABC \cong \triangle EDC$

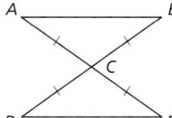

2. **Given** $\overline{JK} \parallel \overline{ML}, \overline{MJ} \parallel \overline{KL}$
   Prove $\triangle MJK \cong \triangle KLM$

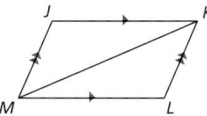

3. **Given** $\overline{QR} \cong \overline{RS}, \angle P \cong \angle T$
   Prove $\triangle SRP \cong \triangle QRT$

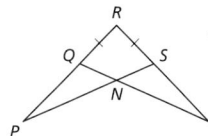

4. Find the measure of each acute angle in the figure at the right.

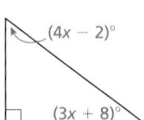

5. Is it possible to draw an equilateral triangle that is not equiangular? If so, provide an example. If not, explain why.

6. Can you use the Third Angles Theorem (Theorem 5.4) to prove that two triangles are congruent? Explain your reasoning.

Write a plan to prove that $\angle 1 \cong \angle 2$.

7.
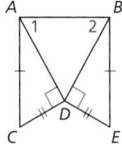

8.
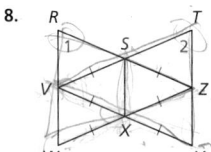

9. Is there more than one theorem that could be used to prove that $\triangle ABD \cong \triangle CDB$? If so, list all possible theorems.

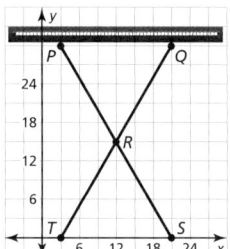

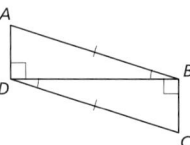

10. Write a coordinate proof to show that the triangles created by the keyboard stand are congruent.

11. The picture shows the Pyramid of Cestius, which is located in Rome, Italy. The measure of the base for the triangle shown is 100 Roman feet. The measures of the other two sides of the triangle are both 144 Roman feet.

   a. Classify the triangle shown by its sides.

   b. The measure of $\angle 3$ is 40°. What are the measures of $\angle 1$ and $\angle 2$? Explain your reasoning.

If students need help...	If students got it...
Lesson Tutorials	Resources by Chapter • Enrichment and Extension • Cumulative Review
Skills Review Handbook	Performance Task
BigIdeasMath.com	Start the *next* Section

ANSWERS

1–3. See Additional Answers.

4. 44°, 46°

5. no; By the Corollary to the Base Angles Theorem (Cor. 5.2), if a triangle is equilateral, then it is also equiangular.

6. no; The Third Angles Theorem (Thm. 5.4) can be used to prove that two triangles are equiangular, but AAA is not sufficient to prove that the triangles are congruent. You need to know that at least one pair of corresponding sides are congruent.

7. First, use the HL Congruence Theorem (Thm. 5.9) to prove that $\triangle ACD \cong \triangle BED$. Because corresponding parts of congruent triangles are congruent, $\overline{AD} \cong \overline{BD}$. Then, use the Base Angles Theorem (Thm. 5.6) to prove that $\angle 1 \cong \angle 2$.

8. Use the SSS Congruence Theorem (Thm. 5.8) to prove that $\triangle SVX \cong \triangle SZX$. Use the Vertical Angles Congruence Theorem (Thm. 2.6) and the SAS Congruence Theorem (Thm. 5.5) to prove that $\triangle VXW \cong \triangle ZXY$. Because corresponding parts of congruent triangles are congruent, $\angle SZX \cong \angle SVX$ and $\angle W \cong \angle Y$. Use the Segment Addition Postulate (Post. 1.2) to show that $\overline{VY} \cong \overline{ZW}$. Then, use the ASA Congruence Theorem (Thm. 5.10) to prove that $\triangle VYT \cong \triangle ZWR$. Because corresponding parts of congruent triangles are congruent, $\angle 1 \cong \angle 2$.

9. yes; HL Congruence Theorem (Thm. 5.9), ASA Congruence Theorem (Thm. 5.10), AAS Congruence Theorem (Thm. 5.11), SAS Congruence Theorem (Thm. 5.5)

10. Using the Distance Formula, $PQ = 18$ and $ST = 18$. So, $\overline{PQ} \cong \overline{ST}$. Also, the horizontal segments $\overline{PQ}$ and $\overline{ST}$ each have a slope of 0, which implies that they are parallel. So, $\overline{PS}$ intersects $\overline{PQ}$ and $\overline{ST}$ to form congruent alternate interior angles, $\angle P$ and $\angle S$. By the Vertical Angles Congruence Theorem (Thm. 2.6), $\angle PRQ \cong \angle SRT$. So, by the AAS Congruence Theorem (Thm. 5.11), $\triangle PQR \cong \triangle STR$.

11. See Additional Answers.

ANSWERS

1. no; The Exterior Angle Theorem (Thm. 5.2) follows from the Triangle Sum Theorem (Thm. 5.1). Also, the Triangle Sum Theorem (Thm. 5.1) is used to prove the Exterior Angle Theorem (Thm. 5.2), so you cannot use the Exterior Angle Theorem (Thm. 5.2) to prove the Triangle Sum Theorem (Thm. 5.1).

2. By step 1, a line through point P intersects line m in point Q. By steps 2 and 3, $\overline{QA} \cong \overline{QB} \cong \overline{PC} \cong \overline{PD}$ and $\overline{AB} \cong \overline{CD}$ because congruent segments were drawn with the same compass setting. So, in step 4, you see that if $\overline{AB}$ and $\overline{CD}$ were drawn, then $\triangle AQB$ and $\triangle CPD$ would be congruent by the SSS Congruence Theorem (Thm. 5.8). Because corresponding parts of congruent triangles are congruent, $\angle CBD \cong \angle AQB$, which means that $\overrightarrow{PD} \parallel m$ by the Corresponding Angles Converse (Thm. 3.5).

3. a. *Sample answer:* a reflection in the x-axis followed by a translation 4 units right
   b. yes; corresponding sides: $\overline{JK} \cong \overline{XY}$, $\overline{KL} \cong \overline{YZ}$, $\overline{JL} \cong \overline{XZ}$; corresponding angles: $\angle J \cong \angle X$, $\angle K \cong \angle Y$, $\angle L \cong \angle Z$

4. C

---

1. Your friend claims that the Exterior Angle Theorem (Theorem 5.2) can be used to prove the Triangle Sum Theorem (Theorem 5.1). Is your friend correct? Explain your reasoning.

2. Use the steps in the construction to explain how you know that the line through point P is parallel to line m.

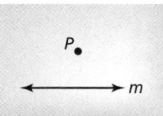

Step 1   Step 2   Step 3   Step 4

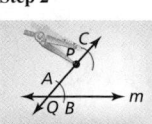 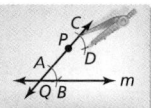 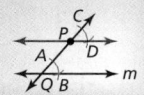

3. The coordinate plane shows $\triangle JKL$ and $\triangle XYZ$.

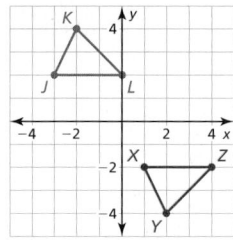

   a. Write a composition of transformations that maps $\triangle JKL$ to $\triangle XYZ$.

   b. Is the composition a congruence transformation? If so, identify all congruent corresponding parts.

4. The directed line segment RS is shown. Point Q is located along $\overline{RS}$ so that the ratio of RQ to QS is 2 to 3. What are the coordinates of point Q?

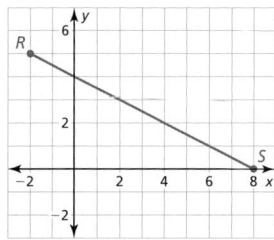

   Ⓐ $Q(1.2, 3)$ Ⓑ $Q(4, 2)$ Ⓒ $Q(2, 3)$ Ⓓ $Q(-6, 7)$

5. The coordinate plane shows △ABC and △DEF.

  a. Prove △ABC ≅ △DEF using the given information.

  b. Describe the composition of rigid motions that maps △ABC to △DEF.

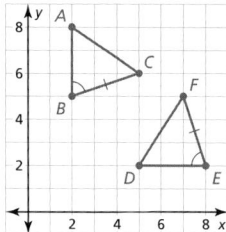

6. The vertices of a quadrilateral are $W(0, 0)$, $X(-1, 3)$, $Y(2, 7)$, and $Z(4, 2)$. Your friend claims that point W will not change after dilating quadrilateral $WXYZ$ by a scale factor of 2. Is your friend correct? Explain your reasoning.

7. Which figure(s) have rotational symmetry? Select all that apply.

Ⓐ    Ⓑ 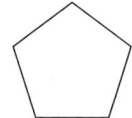   Ⓒ    Ⓓ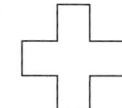

8. Write a coordinate proof.

  Given Coordinates of vertices of quadrilateral ABCD

  Prove Quadrilateral ABCD is a rectangle.

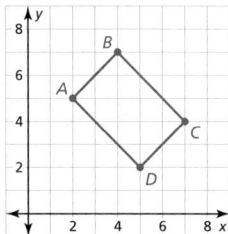

9. Write a proof to verify that the construction of the equilateral triangle shown below is valid.

Step 1   **Step 2**   **Step 3**   **Step 4**

 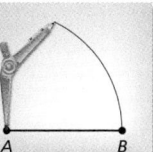 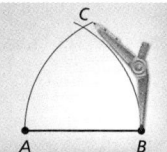 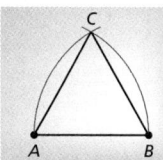

5. a. The segments $\overline{AB}$ and $\overline{DE}$ have the same measure ($AB = DE = 3$) and are therefore congruent. Also, from the markings in the diagram, $\angle B \cong \angle E$ and $\overline{BC} \cong \overline{EF}$. So, by the SAS Congruence Theorem (Thm. 5.5), △ABC ≅ △DEF.

  b. a 90° counterclockwise rotation about the origin followed by a translation 13 units right

6. yes; The coordinate rule for dilations is to multiply each coordinate of each point by the scale factor, which is 2 in this case. So, when you do this to the coordinates of point W, you get $(2 \cdot 0, 2 \cdot 0)$ which is still $(0, 0)$.

7. A, B, D

8. $AD = 3\sqrt{2}$, $m_{\overline{AD}} = -1$, $BC = 3\sqrt{2}$, $m_{\overline{BC}} = -1$, $AB = 2\sqrt{2}$, $m_{\overline{AB}} = 1$, $DC = 2\sqrt{2}$, $= m_{\overline{DC}} = 1$

  Sides $\overline{AD}$ and $\overline{BC}$ have the same measure and the same slope, as do $\overline{AB}$ and $\overline{DC}$. So, by the Slopes of Parallel Lines Theorem (Thm. 3.13), $\overline{AD} \parallel \overline{BC}$ and $\overline{AB} \parallel \overline{DC}$. Because the product of their slopes is -1, $\overline{AD} \perp \overline{AB}$, $\overline{AD} \perp \overline{DC}$, $\overline{BC} \perp \overline{AB}$, and $\overline{BC} \perp \overline{DC}$. So, ABCD is a rectangle.

9. Because the same compass settings were used, $\overline{AB} \cong \overline{AC} \cong \overline{BC}$. So, △ABC is equilateral.

6 Relationships Within Triangles

Biking (p. 346)

Montana (p. 341)

SEE the Big Idea

Roof Truss (p. 331)

Windmill (p. 318)

Bridge (p. 303)

Chapter Summary

- This chapter uses the deductive skills developed in the last chapter to explore special segments in a triangle. These segments include perpendicular bisectors, angle bisectors, medians, altitudes, and midsegments.
- Students are able to discover special properties of these segments by using dynamic geometry software. To prove these relationships, a variety of proof formats and approaches are used: transformational, synthetic, analytic, and paragraph.
- The last two lessons in the chapter are about inequalities within one triangle and in two triangles. The indirect proof is introduced and used to prove several of the theorems in these lessons.
- Triangles have been the geometric structure used to help students develop their deductive reasoning skills. In the next chapter, quadrilaterals and other polygons are studied.

 COMMON CORE PROGRESSION

Middle School
- Construct geometric figures with given conditions.
- Draw polygons in the coordinate plane given vertices and find lengths of sides.
- Establish facts about interior and exterior angles of triangles.
- Read, write, and evaluate algebraic expressions.

Algebra 1
- Write and solve linear equations in one variable.
- Use linear equations to solve real-life problems.
- Graph in the coordinate plane.
- Find the slope of a line.

Geometry
- Understand and use angle bisectors and perpendicular bisectors to find measures.
- Find and use the circumcenter, incenter, centroid, and orthocenter of a triangle.
- Use the Triangle Midsegment Theorem and the Triangle Inequality Theorem.
- Write indirect proofs.

Dynamic Teaching Tools

- Dynamic Assessment & Progress Monitoring Tool
- Lesson Planning Tool
- Interactive Whiteboard Lesson Library
- Dynamic Classroom with Dynamic Investigations
- Real-Life STEM Videos

Scaffolding in the Classroom

Graphic Organizers: Word Magnet

A Word Magnet can be used to organize information associated with a vocabulary word or term. Students write the word or term inside the magnet. Students write associated information on the blank lines that "radiate" from the magnet. Associated information can include, but is not limited to: other vocabulary words or terms, definitions, formulas, procedures, examples, and visuals. This type of organizer serves as a good summary tool because any information related to a topic can be included.

	Standards Summary	
Section	**Common Core State Standards**	
6.1	Learning	HSG-CO.C.9, HSG-MG.A.1
6.2	Learning	HSG-CO.D.12, HSG-C.A.3, HSG-MG.A.1, HSG-MG.A.3
6.3	Learning	HSG-CO.C.10
6.4	Learning	HSG-CO.C.10, HSG-MG.A.1
6.5	Learning	HSG-CO.C.10
6.6	Learning	HSG-CO.C.10

What do you think?

Allow students time to write their answers on individual whiteboards. After the allotted time, they can hold up their boards. The teacher can see what students are thinking and follow up with discussion.

Laurie's Notes

Maintaining Mathematical Proficiency

Writing an Equation of a Perpendicular Line

- Students should review Writing Equations of Parallel and Perpendicular Lines, page 158.

COMMON ERROR Students substitute incorrectly when finding the value of b. Have them write the slope-intercept form of an equation of a line, $y = mx + b$. Then remind students to substitute the first coordinate of the given point for x and the second coordinate for y.

Writing Compound Inequalities

- Be sure students understand the implications of the words *and* and *or*.
- Remind students that when a compound inequality uses the word *and*, the variable must satisfy both inequalities. When a compound inequality uses the word *or*, the variable needs to satisfy only one of the inequalities.

COMMON ERROR Students sometimes switch *and* and *or* when writing inequalities, which leads to confusion when they have to solve a compound inequality.

Mathematical Practices (continued on page 300)

- The eight *Mathematical Practices* focus attention on how mathematics is learned—process versus content. Page 300 demonstrates that by using technological tools, students can explore and discover geometric relationships. Although these relationships can be explored in other manners, dynamic geometry software can be very effective and efficient.
- Use the *Mathematical Practices* page to help students develop mathematical habits of mind—how mathematics can be explored and how mathematics is thought about.

If students need help...	If students got it...
Student Journal • Maintaining Mathematical Proficiency	Game Closet at *BigIdeasMath.com*
Lesson Tutorials	Start the *next* Section
Skills Review Handbook	

Maintaining Mathematical Proficiency

Writing an Equation of a Perpendicular Line

Example 1 Write the equation of a line passing through the point $(-2, 0)$ that is perpendicular to the line $y = 2x + 8$.

Step 1 Find the slope m of the perpendicular line. The line $y = 2x + 8$ has a slope of 2. Use the Slopes of Perpendicular Lines Theorem (Theorem 3.14).

$$2 \cdot m = -1 \qquad \text{The product of the slopes of } \perp \text{ lines is } -1.$$

$$m = -\frac{1}{2} \qquad \text{Divide each side by 2.}$$

Step 2 Find the y-intercept b by using $m = -\frac{1}{2}$ and $(x, y) = (-2, 0)$.

$$y = mx + b \qquad \text{Use the slope-intercept form.}$$

$$0 = -\frac{1}{2}(-2) + b \qquad \text{Substitute for } m, x, \text{ and } y.$$

$$-1 = b \qquad \text{Solve for } b.$$

▶ Because $m = -\frac{1}{2}$ and $b = -1$, an equation of the line is $y = -\frac{1}{2}x - 1$.

Write an equation of the line passing through point P that is perpendicular to the given line.

1. $P(3, 1), y = \frac{1}{3}x - 5$ **2.** $P(4, -3), y = -x - 5$ **3.** $P(-1, -2), y = -4x + 13$

Writing Compound Inequalities

Example 2 Write each sentence as an inequality.

a. A number x is greater than or equal to -1 and less than 6.

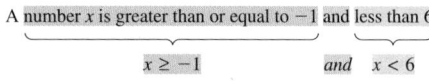

A number x is greater than or equal to -1 and less than 6.

$$x \geq -1 \qquad and \qquad x < 6$$

▶ An inequality is $-1 \leq x < 6$.

b. A number y is at most 4 or at least 9.

A number y is at most 4 or at least 9.

$$y \leq 4 \qquad or \qquad y \geq 9$$

▶ An inequality is $y \leq 4$ or $y \geq 9$.

Write the sentence as an inequality.

4. A number w is at least -3 and no more than 8.   **5.** A number m is more than 0 and less than 11.

6. A number s is less than or equal to 5 or greater than 2.   **7.** A number d is fewer than 12 or no less than -7.

8. ABSTRACT REASONING Is it possible for the solution of a compound inequality to be all real numbers? Explain your reasoning.

Dynamic Solutions available at *BigIdeasMath.com*

 Common Core State Standards

HSG-GPE.B.5 Prove the slope criteria for ... perpendicular lines and use them to solve geometric problems (e.g., find the equation of a line ... perpendicular to a given line that passes through a given point).

HSA-CED.A.1 Create ... inequalities in one variable and use them to solve problems.

ANSWERS

1. $y = -3x + 10$

2. $y = x - 7$

3. $y = \frac{1}{4}x - \frac{7}{4}$

4. $-3 \leq w \leq 8$

5. $0 < m < 11$

6. $s \leq 5$ *or* $s > 2$

7. $d < 12$ *or* $d \geq -7$

8. yes; As with Exercises 6 and 7, if the graphs of the two inequalities overlap going in opposite directions and the variable only has to make one or the other true, then every number on the number line makes the compound inequality true.

Vocabulary Review

Have students make a Summary Triangle to explain how to write an equation of a perpendicular line. Include the following terms.

- Slope
- Slope-intercept form
- y-intercept

Mathematical Practices

Mathematically proficient students use technological tools to explore concepts.

Lines, Rays, and Segments in Triangles

Core Concept

Lines, Rays, and Segments in Triangles

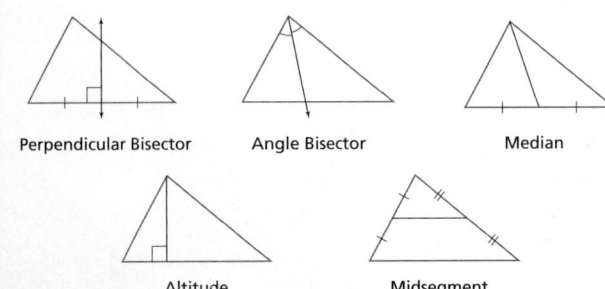

Perpendicular Bisector   Angle Bisector   Median

Altitude   Midsegment

EXAMPLE 1   **Drawing a Perpendicular Bisector**

Use dynamic geometry software to construct the perpendicular bisector of one of the sides of the triangle with vertices $A(-1, 2)$, $B(5, 4)$, and $C(4, -1)$. Find the lengths of the two segments of the bisected side.

SOLUTION

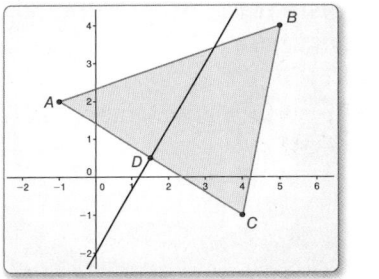

Sample
Points
$A(-1, 2)$
$B(5, 4)$
$C(4, -1)$
Line
$-5x + 3y = -6$
Segments
$AD = 2.92$
$CD = 2.92$

▶ The two segments of the bisected side have the same length, $AD = CD = 2.92$ units.

Monitoring Progress

Refer to the figures at the top of the page to describe each type of line, ray, or segment in a triangle.

1. perpendicular bisector   2. angle bisector   3. median

4. altitude   5. midsegment

Laurie's Notes   **Mathematical Practices** (continued from page T-299)

- There are many definitions that students will encounter in their study of geometry. Exploring with technology can help students discover the meaning of a word.
- Give time for students to work through the questions in the *Monitoring Progress*, and then discuss as a class.

Overview of Section 6.1

Introduction

- Segment bisectors, perpendicular bisectors, and angle bisectors were defined in an earlier chapter.
- In this lesson, properties of perpendicular bisectors and angle bisectors are presented.
- The Perpendicular Bisector Theorem and its converse (Thm. 6.1 and 6.2) and the Angle Bisector Theorem and its converse (Thm. 6.3 and 6.4) are stated. One of the four theorems is proven in the lesson, with the other three proofs left for the exercises.
- The lesson ends with a real-life application of the Angle Bisector Theorem and a problem integrating previously learned algebra skills.

Resources

- Tracing paper is helpful when the explorations are done by paper folding.

Teaching Strategy

- If you do not have access to dynamic geometry software, an alternate way to introduce this lesson would be through a paper-folding activity or a compass construction activity. It is powerful for students to explore and discover the properties of perpendicular bisectors and angle bisectors.
- Give directions similar to what is written in the explorations for students to paper fold (or construct) the perpendicular bisector (Exploration 1) and the angle bisector (Exploration 2). Distances can be measured using a compass or ruler. Although precision may be a problem, the focus is on the discovery. A deductive proof follows in the lesson.

Another Way

- The Perpendicular Bisector Theorem (Thm. 6.1) can be done as a coordinate proof. The explorations from Section 5.8 on page 283 involve a specific segment length. Begin with a segment where the coordinates of the endpoints contain variables. Proceed with the proof in a similar fashion.

Pacing Suggestion

- The explorations allow students to explore and discover two relationships that will be stated as theorems in the formal lesson. The constructions and investigation are not long and should be followed with the statement of the Perpendicular Bisector Theorem (Thm. 6.1) in the lesson.

**Common Core
State Standards**

HSG-CO.C.9 Prove theorems about lines and angles.

HSG-MG.A.1 Use geometric shapes, their measures, and their properties to describe objects (e.g., modeling a tree trunk or a human torso as a cylinder).

Laurie's Notes

Exploration

Motivate

- You will need four volunteers and some yarn or string.
- Have two students (A and B) position themselves on opposite sides of the classroom holding a piece of string between them. They represent the endpoints of a segment.
- Have the other two students (C and D) position themselves anywhere in the classroom as long as they are the same distance from A and B. If you wish, you could have additional students (E, F, G, and H) join in and use the same condition—they must be the same distance from A and B.
- ? "What do you notice about everyone except A and B?" Students will describe them as being in a line. "Do you notice anything special about the line?" It is the perpendicular bisector of $\overline{AB}$.
- Explain to students that they have just modeled one of the theorems they will work with in this lesson, the Converse of the Perpendicular Bisector Theorem (Thm. 6.2).

Exploration 1

- This is a quick construction using dynamic geometric software. It is not necessary for the coordinate axes to be visible.
- Students should click and drag on point C, moving it to both sides of $\overline{AB}$.
- **MP5 Use Appropriate Tools Strategically:** Students can quickly explore other segments by clicking and dragging on point A or point B.
- ? **MP3 Construct Viable Arguments and Critique the Reasoning of Others:** "What conjecture(s) can you make?" $\overline{CA}$ and $\overline{CB}$ are always the same length.
- Students may make other observations about what a perpendicular bisector is and may also mention that the base angles, $\angle A$ and $\angle B$, are congruent.

Exploration 2

- When constructing the perpendiculars from point D to the sides of the angle, lines will be drawn, not segments. You may want to show students how to construct the perpendiculars, draw the segments, and then hide the lines.
- Students should click and drag on point D, moving it closer and further away from the vertex, point A.
- **MP5:** Students can quickly explore other angles by clicking and dragging on point B or point C.
- ? **MP3:** "What conjecture(s) can you make?" $\overline{DE}$ and $\overline{DF}$ are always the same length.
- Students may make other observations about what an angle bisector is. They may also mention that the right triangles, $\triangle AED$ and $\triangle AFD$, are congruent.

Communicate Your Answer

- **MP3:** Students should state conjectures that are complete sentences and complete thoughts. Instead of saying, "They are congruent," students should say, "If point C is a point on the perpendicular bisector of $\overline{AB}$, then $\overline{CA}$ and $\overline{CB}$ are always congruent."

Connecting to Next Step

- The explorations are related to the theorems and converses presented in the lesson.

6.1 Perpendicular and Angle Bisectors

Essential Question

What conjectures can you make about a point on the perpendicular bisector of a segment and a point on the bisector of an angle?

Dynamic Teaching Tools

Dynamic Assessment & Progress Monitoring Tool

Lesson Planning Tool

Interactive Whiteboard Lesson Library

Dynamic Classroom with Dynamic Investigations

EXPLORATION 1 Points on a Perpendicular Bisector

Work with a partner. Use dynamic geometry software.

a. Draw any segment and label it $\overline{AB}$. Construct the perpendicular bisector of $\overline{AB}$.

b. Label a point C that is on the perpendicular bisector of $\overline{AB}$ but is not on $\overline{AB}$.

c. Draw $\overline{CA}$ and $\overline{CB}$ and find their

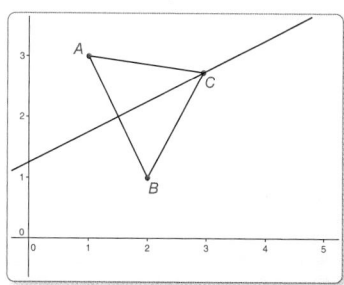

Sample
Points
$A(1, 3)$
$B(2, 1)$
$C(2.95, 2.73)$
Segments
$AB = 2.24$
$CA = ?$
$CB = ?$
Line
$-x + 2y = 2.5$

lengths. Then move point C to other locations on the perpendicular bisector and note the lengths of $\overline{CA}$ and $\overline{CB}$.

d. Repeat parts (a)–(c) with other segments. Describe any relationship(s) you notice.

EXPLORATION 2 Points on an Angle Bisector

Work with a partner. Use dynamic geometry software.

a. Draw two rays $\overrightarrow{AB}$ and $\overrightarrow{AC}$ to form $\angle BAC$. Construct the bisector of $\angle BAC$.

b. Label a point D on the bisector of $\angle BAC$.

c. Construct and find the lengths of the perpendicular segments from D to the sides of $\angle BAC$. Move point D along the angle bisector and note how the lengths change.

d. Repeat parts (a)–(c) with other angles. Describe any relationship(s) you notice.

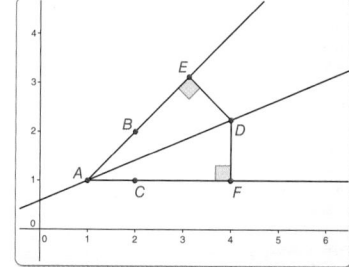

Sample
Points
$A(1, 1)$
$B(2, 2)$
$C(2, 1)$
$D(4, 2.24)$
Rays
$AB = -x + y = 0$
$AC = y = 1$
Line
$-0.38x + 0.92y = 0.54$

USING TOOLS STRATEGICALLY

To be proficient in math, you need to visualize the results of varying assumptions, explore consequences, and compare predictions with data.

Communicate Your Answer

3. What conjectures can you make about a point on the perpendicular bisector of a segment and a point on the bisector of an angle?

4. In Exploration 2, what is the distance from point D to $\overrightarrow{AB}$ when the distance from D to $\overrightarrow{AC}$ is 5 units? Justify your answer.

Section 6.1   Perpendicular and Angle Bisectors   **301**

ANSWERS

1. a. Check students' work.

   b. Check students' work.

   c. Check students' work (for sample in text, $CA \approx 1.97$, $CB \approx 1.97$); For all locations of C, $\overline{CA}$ and $\overline{CB}$ have the same measure.

   d. Every point on the perpendicular bisector of a segment is equidistant from the endpoints of the segment.

2. a. Check students' work.

   b. Check students' work.

   c. Check students' work (for sample in text, $DE \approx 1.24$, $DF \approx 1.24$); For all locations of D on the angle bisector, $\overline{ED}$ and $\overline{FD}$ have the same measure.

   d. Every point on an angle bisector is equidistant from both sides of the angle.

3. If a point is on the perpendicular bisector of a segment, then it is equidistant from the endpoints of the segment. Every point on the bisector of an angle is equidistant from the sides of the angle.

4. 5 units; Point D is on the angle bisector, so it is equidistant from either side of the angle.

6.1 Lesson

Core Vocabulary

equidistant, p. 302

Previous
perpendicular bisector
angle bisector

STUDY TIP

A perpendicular bisector can be a segment, a ray, a line, or a plane.

What You Will Learn

▶ Use perpendicular bisectors to find measures.
▶ Use angle bisectors to find measures and distance relationships.
▶ Write equations for perpendicular bisectors.

Using Perpendicular Bisectors

In Section 3.4, you learned that a *perpendicular bisector* of a line segment is the line that is perpendicular to the segment at its midpoint.

A point is **equidistant** from two figures when the point is the *same distance* from each figure.

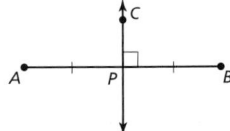

$\overleftrightarrow{CP}$ is a $\perp$ bisector of $\overline{AB}$.

🅖 Theorems

Theorem 6.1   Perpendicular Bisector Theorem

In a plane, if a point lies on the perpendicular bisector of a segment, then it is equidistant from the endpoints of the segment.

If $\overleftrightarrow{CP}$ is the $\perp$ bisector of $\overline{AB}$, then $CA = CB$.

Proof p. 302

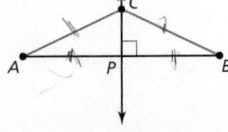

Theorem 6.2   Converse of the Perpendicular Bisector Theorem

In a plane, if a point is equidistant from the endpoints of a segment, then it lies on the perpendicular bisector of the segment.

If $DA = DB$, then point D lies on the $\perp$ bisector of $\overline{AB}$.

Proof Ex. 32, p. 308

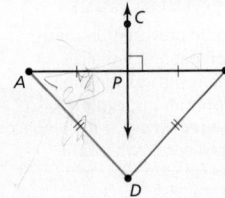

PROOF   **Perpendicular Bisector Theorem**

Given $\overleftrightarrow{CP}$ is the perpendicular bisector of $\overline{AB}$.

Prove $CA = CB$

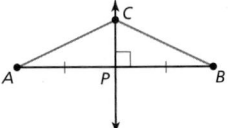

Paragraph Proof Because $\overleftrightarrow{CP}$ is the perpendicular bisector of $\overline{AB}$, $\overleftrightarrow{CP}$ is perpendicular to $\overline{AB}$ and point P is the midpoint of $\overline{AB}$. By the definition of midpoint, $AP = BP$, and by the definition of perpendicular lines, $m\angle CPA = m\angle CPB = 90°$. Then by the definition of segment congruence, $\overline{AP} \cong \overline{BP}$, and by the definition of angle congruence, $\angle CPA \cong \angle CPB$. By the Reflexive Property of Congruence (Theorem 2.1), $\overline{CP} \cong \overline{CP}$. So, $\triangle CPA \cong \triangle CPB$ by the SAS Congruence Theorem (Theorem 5.5), and $\overline{CA} \cong \overline{CB}$ because corresponding parts of congruent triangles are congruent. So, $CA = CB$ by the definition of segment congruence.

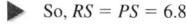 **EXAMPLE 1** **Using the Perpendicular Bisector Theorems**

Find each measure.

a. *RS*

From the figure, $\overleftrightarrow{SQ}$ is the perpendicular bisector of $\overline{PR}$. By the Perpendicular Bisector Theorem, $PS = RS$.

▶ So, $RS = PS = 6.8$.

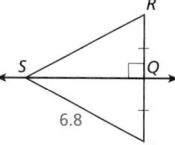

b. *EG*

Because $EH = GH$ and $\overleftrightarrow{HF} \perp \overline{EG}$, $\overleftrightarrow{HF}$ is the perpendicular bisector of $\overline{EG}$ by the Converse of the Perpendicular Bisector Theorem. By the definition of segment bisector, $EG = 2GF$.

▶ So, $EG = 2(9.5) = 19$.

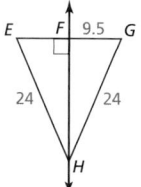

c. *AD*

From the figure, $\overleftrightarrow{BD}$ is the perpendicular bisector of $\overline{AC}$.

$AD = CD$	Perpendicular Bisector Theorem
$5x = 3x + 14$	Substitute.
$x = 7$	Solve for *x*.

▶ So, $AD = 5x = 5(7) = 35$.

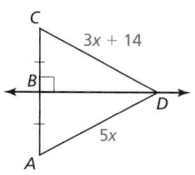

 **EXAMPLE 2** **Solving a Real-Life Problem**

Is there enough information in the diagram to conclude that point *N* lies on the perpendicular bisector of $\overline{KM}$?

SOLUTION

It is given that $\overline{KL} \cong \overline{ML}$. So, $\overline{LN}$ is a segment bisector of $\overline{KM}$. You do not know whether $\overline{LN}$ is perpendicular to $\overline{KM}$ because it is not indicated in the diagram.

▶ So, you cannot conclude that point *N* lies on the perpendicular bisector of $\overline{KM}$.

Monitoring Progress Help in English and Spanish at *BigIdeasMath.com*

Use the diagram and the given information to find the indicated measure.

1. $\overleftrightarrow{ZX}$ is the perpendicular bisector of $\overline{WY}$, and $YZ = 13.75$. Find *WZ*.

2. $\overleftrightarrow{ZX}$ is the perpendicular bisector of $\overline{WY}$, $WZ = 4n - 13$, and $YZ = n + 17$. Find *YZ*.

3. Find *WX* when $WZ = 20.5$, $WY = 14.8$, and $YZ = 20.5$.

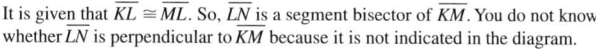

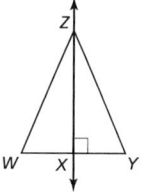

Section 6.1   Perpendicular and Angle Bisectors   **303**

Laurie's Notes **Teacher Actions**

- Example 1 problems are applications of the two previous theorems. Pose the problems and have students work independently to solve.

? "In Example 2, what information is needed to know that $\overline{LN}$ is perpendicular to $\overline{KM}$?"
Either the perpendicular symbol is present or $\overline{NK} \cong \overline{NM}$.

COMMON ERROR Example 2 highlights the common error of assuming that because a segment looks perpendicular, it must be.

- **Think-Pair-Share:** Have students answer Questions 1–3, and then share and discuss as a class.

Differentiated Instruction

Kinesthetic
Discuss the difference between a *perpendicular bisector* and an *angle bisector*. Have students draw a triangle in which the perpendicular bisector of each side is also an angle bisector. Have students draw a triangle in which no perpendicular bisector is also an angle bisector.

Extra Example 1
Find each measure.
a. *CD*

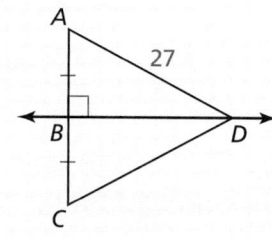

$CD = 27$

b. *PR*

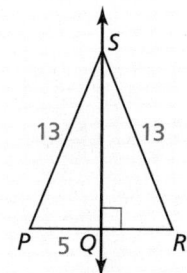

$PR = 10$

c. *GH*

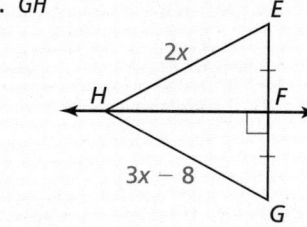

$GH = 16$

Extra Example 2
Is there enough information given in the diagram in Example 2 to conclude that point *L* lies on the perpendicular bisector of $\overline{KM}$? Yes. Because $LK = LM$, point *L* must lie on the perpendicular bisector of $\overline{KM}$ by the Converse of the Perpendicular Bisector Theorem (Thm. 6.2).

MONITORING PROGRESS ANSWERS
1–3. See Additional Answers.

Extra Example 3

Find each measure.

a. $m\angle ABC$

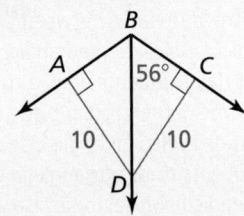

$m\angle ABC = 112°$

b. JM

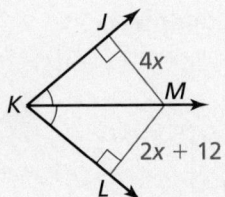

$JM = 24$

MONITORING PROGRESS ANSWERS

4. 6.9
5. 19
6. 78°

Using Angle Bisectors

In Section 1.5, you learned that an *angle bisector* is a ray that divides an angle into two congruent adjacent angles. You also know that the *distance from a point to a line* is the length of the perpendicular segment from the point to the line. So, in the figure, $\overrightarrow{AD}$ is the bisector of $\angle BAC$, and the distance from point D to $\overrightarrow{AB}$ is DB, where $\overline{DB} \perp \overrightarrow{AB}$.

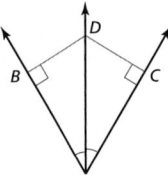

↻ Theorems

Theorem 6.3   Angle Bisector Theorem

If a point lies on the bisector of an angle, then it is equidistant from the two sides of the angle.

If $\overrightarrow{AD}$ bisects $\angle BAC$ and $\overline{DB} \perp \overrightarrow{AB}$ and $\overline{DC} \perp \overrightarrow{AC}$, then $DB = DC$.

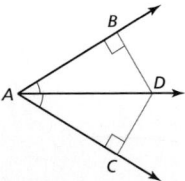

Proof Ex. 33(a), p. 308

Theorem 6.4   Converse of the Angle Bisector Theorem

If a point is in the interior of an angle and is equidistant from the two sides of the angle, then it lies on the bisector of the angle.

If $\overline{DB} \perp \overrightarrow{AB}$ and $\overline{DC} \perp \overrightarrow{AC}$ and $DB = DC$, then $\overrightarrow{AD}$ bisects $\angle BAC$.

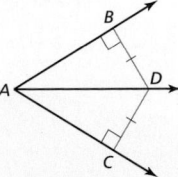

Proof Ex. 33(b), p. 308

EXAMPLE 3   Using the Angle Bisector Theorems

Find each measure.

a. $m\angle GFJ$

Because $\overline{JG} \perp \overrightarrow{FG}$ and $\overline{JH} \perp \overrightarrow{FH}$ and $JG = JH = 7$, $\overrightarrow{FJ}$ bisects $\angle GFH$ by the Converse of the Angle Bisector Theorem.

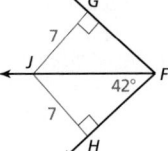

▶ So, $m\angle GFJ = m\angle HFJ = 42°$.

b. RS

$PS = RS$	Angle Bisector Theorem
$5x = 6x - 5$	Substitute.
$5 = x$	Solve for x.

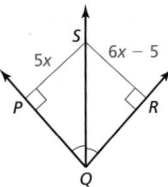

▶ So, $RS = 6x - 5 = 6(5) - 5 = 25$.

Monitoring Progress Help in English and Spanish at *BigIdeasMath.com*

Use the diagram and the given information to find the indicated measure.

4. $\overrightarrow{BD}$ bisects $\angle ABC$, and $DC = 6.9$. Find DA.

5. $\overrightarrow{BD}$ bisects $\angle ABC$, $AD = 3z + 7$, and $CD = 2z + 11$. Find CD.

6. Find $m\angle ABC$ when $AD = 3.2$, $CD = 3.2$, and $m\angle DBC = 39°$.

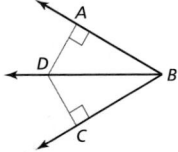

Laurie's Notes   Teacher Actions

- Ask how the altitude of an airplane is measured. It is a perpendicular distance from the plane to the ground. When students find the distance from a point on the angle bisector to the side of the angle, remind them that it needs to be a perpendicular segment.
- State the Angle Bisector Theorem and its converse. Take time to solicit ideas about an outline for the proof of each theorem.
- Example 3 problems are applications of the two previous theorems. Pose the problems and have students work independently to solve.

EXAMPLE 4 Solving a Real-Life Problem

A soccer goalie's position relative to the ball and goalposts forms congruent angles, as shown. Will the goalie have to move farther to block a shot toward the right goalpost R or the left goalpost L?

SOLUTION

The congruent angles tell you that the goalie is on the bisector of $\angle LBR$. By the Angle Bisector Theorem, the goalie is equidistant from $\overrightarrow{BR}$ and $\overrightarrow{BL}$.

▶ So, the goalie must move the same distance to block either shot.

Writing Equations for Perpendicular Bisectors

EXAMPLE 5 Writing an Equation for a Bisector

Write an equation of the perpendicular bisector of the segment with endpoints $P(-2, 3)$ and $Q(4, 1)$.

SOLUTION

Step 1 Graph $\overline{PQ}$. By definition, the perpendicular bisector of $\overline{PQ}$ is perpendicular to $\overline{PQ}$ at its midpoint.

Step 2 Find the midpoint M of $\overline{PQ}$.

$$M\left(\frac{-2+4}{2}, \frac{3+1}{2}\right) = M\left(\frac{2}{2}, \frac{4}{2}\right) = M(1, 2)$$

Step 3 Find the slope of the perpendicular bisector.

$$\text{slope of } \overline{PQ} = \frac{1-3}{4-(-2)} = \frac{-2}{6} = -\frac{1}{3}$$

Because the slopes of perpendicular lines are negative reciprocals, the slope of the perpendicular bisector is 3.

Step 4 Write an equation. The bisector of $\overline{PQ}$ has slope 3 and passes through $(1, 2)$.

$y = mx + b$	Use slope-intercept form.
$2 = 3(1) + b$	Substitute for m, x, and y.
$-1 = b$	Solve for b.

▶ So, an equation of the perpendicular bisector of $\overline{PQ}$ is $y = 3x - 1$.

Monitoring Progress 🔊 Help in English and Spanish at *BigIdeasMath.com*

7. Do you have enough information to conclude that $\overrightarrow{QS}$ bisects $\angle PQR$? Explain.

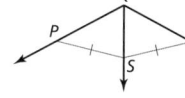

8. Write an equation of the perpendicular bisector of the segment with endpoints $(-1, -5)$ and $(3, -1)$.

Extra Example 4

A parachutist lands in a triangular field at point P, and then walks to a road. Will he have to walk further to Wells Road or to Turner Road?

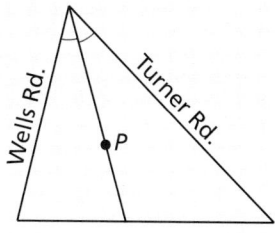

Neither. The distances to both roads are the same.

Extra Example 5

Write an equation of the perpendicular bisector of the segment with endpoints $D(5, -1)$ and $E(-11, 3)$. $y = 4x + 13$

MONITORING PROGRESS ANSWERS

7. no; In order to use the Converse of the Angle Bisector Theorem (Thm. 6.4), $\overline{PS}$ would have to be perpendicular to $\overrightarrow{QP}$, and $\overline{RS}$ would have to be perpendicular to $\overrightarrow{QR}$.

8. $y = -x - 2$

Laurie's Notes Teacher Actions

• Ask whether any student plays the goalie position in any sport. If so, he or she can explain why goalies position themselves on the angle bisector formed by the opponent and the goalposts. This can also be modeled using dynamic geometry software.

• Pose Example 5. Use whiteboards and have partners work to write the equation of the perpendicular bisector.

Closure

• **Writing Prompt:** The *Big Ideas* presented in today's lesson …

Assignment Guide and Homework Check

ASSIGNMENT

Basic: 1, 2, 3–25 odd, 31, 34, 39–44

Average: 1, 2, 6–30 even, 31, 32, 34, 39–44

Advanced: 1, 2, 6–26 even, 29–32, 34–44

HOMEWORK CHECK

Basic: 3, 7, 13, 19, 25

Average: 6, 14, 22, 26, 30

Advanced: 6, 14, 22, 26, 30

ANSWERS

1. bisector

2. Is point B collinear with X and Z?; no; yes

3. 4.6; Because $GK = KJ$ and $\overleftrightarrow{HK} \perp \overline{GJ}$, point H is on the perpendicular bisector of $\overline{GJ}$. So, by the Perpendicular Bisector Theorem (Thm. 6.1), $GH = HJ = 4.6$.

4. 1.3; Because point T is equidistant from Q and S, point T is on the perpendicular bisector of $\overline{QS}$ by the Converse of the Perpendicular Bisector Theorem (Thm. 6.2). So, by definition of segment bisector, $QR = RS = 1.3$.

5. 15; Because $\overleftrightarrow{DB} \perp \overleftrightarrow{AC}$ and point D is equidistant from A and C, point D is on the perpendicular bisector of $\overline{AC}$ by the Converse of the Perpendicular Bisector Theorem (Thm. 6.2). By definition of segment bisector, $AB = BC$. So, $5x = 4x + 3$, and the solution is $x = 3$. So, $AB = 5x = 5(3) = 15$.

6. 55; Because $\overline{VD} \cong \overline{WD}$ and $\overleftrightarrow{UX} \perp \overline{VW}$, point U is on the perpendicular bisector of $\overline{VW}$. So, by the Perpendicular Bisector Theorem (Thm. 6.1), $VU = WU$. So, $9x + 1 = 7x + 13$, and the solution is $x = 6$, which means that $UW = 7x + 13 = 7(6) + 13 = 55$.

7. yes; Because point N is equidistant from L and M, point N is on the perpendicular bisector of $\overline{LM}$ by the Converse of the Perpendicular Bisector Theorem (Thm. 6.2). Because only one line can be perpendicular to $\overline{LM}$ at point K, $\overleftrightarrow{NK}$ must be the perpendicular bisector of $\overline{LM}$, and P is on $\overleftrightarrow{NK}$.

6.1 Exercises

Dynamic Solutions available at *BigIdeasMath.com*

Vocabulary and Core Concept Check

1. **COMPLETE THE SENTENCE** Point C is in the interior of $\angle DEF$. If $\angle DEC$ and $\angle CEF$ are congruent, then $\overrightarrow{EC}$ is the _____ of $\angle DEF$.

2. **DIFFERENT WORDS, SAME QUESTION** Which is different? Find "both" answers.

   Is point B the same distance from both X and Z?

   Is point B equidistant from X and Z?

   Is point B collinear with X and Z?

   Is point B on the perpendicular bisector of $\overline{XZ}$?

   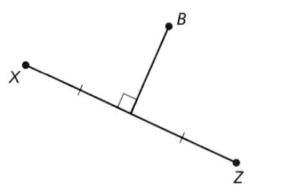

Monitoring Progress and Modeling with Mathematics

In Exercises 3–6, find the indicated measure. Explain your reasoning. *(See Example 1.)*

3. GH

   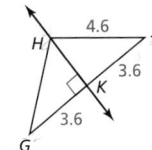

4. QR

   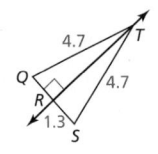

5. AB

   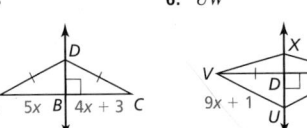

6. UW

   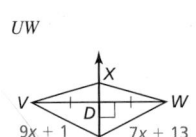

In Exercises 7–10, tell whether the information in the diagram allows you to conclude that point P lies on the perpendicular bisector of $\overline{LM}$. Explain your reasoning. *(See Example 2.)*

7.

   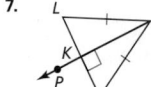

8.

   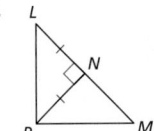

9.

   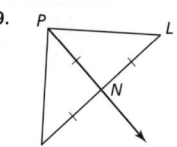

10.

   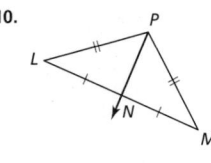

In Exercises 11–14, find the indicated measure. Explain your reasoning. *(See Example 3.)*

11. $m\angle ABD$

   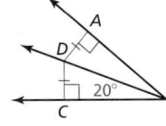

12. PS

   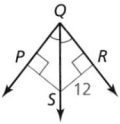

13. $m\angle KJL$

   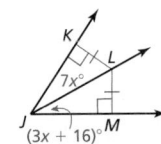

14. FG

   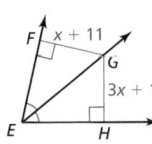

306   Chapter 6   Relationships Within Triangles

---

8. no; You would need to know that either $LN = MN$ or $LP = MP$.

9. no; You would need to know that $\overleftrightarrow{PN} \perp \overline{ML}$.

10. yes; Because point P is equidistant from L and M, point P is on the perpendicular bisector of $\overline{LM}$ by the Converse of the Perpendicular Bisector Theorem (Thm. 6.2). Also, $\overline{LN} \cong \overline{MN}$, so $\overleftrightarrow{PN}$ is a bisector of $\overline{LM}$. Because P can only be on one of the bisectors, $\overleftrightarrow{PN}$ is the perpendicular bisector of $\overline{LM}$.

11. 20°; Because D is equidistant from $\overrightarrow{BC}$ and $\overrightarrow{BA}$, $\overrightarrow{BD}$ bisects $\angle ABC$ by the Converse of the Angle Bisector Theorem (Thm. 6.4). So, $m\angle ABD = m\angle CBD = 20°$.

12. 12; $\overrightarrow{QS}$ is an angle bisector of $\angle PQR$, $\overline{PS} \perp \overline{QP}$, and $\overline{SR} \perp \overline{QR}$. So, by the Angle Bisector Theorem (Thm. 6.3), $PS = RS = 12$.

13. 28°; Because L is equidistant from $\overrightarrow{JK}$ and $\overrightarrow{JM}$, $\overrightarrow{JL}$ bisects $\angle KJM$ by the Angle Bisector Theorem (Thm. 6.3). This means that $7x = 3x + 16$, and the solution is $x = 4$. So, $m\angle KJL = 7x = 7(4) = 28°$.

14. See Additional Answers.

In Exercises 15 and 16, tell whether the information in the diagram allows you to conclude that $\overrightarrow{EH}$ bisects $\angle FEG$. Explain your reasoning. *(See Example 4.)*

15.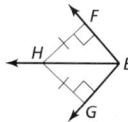

16.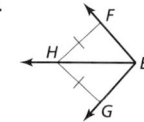

In Exercises 17 and 18, tell whether the information in the diagram allows you to conclude that $DB = DC$. Explain your reasoning.

17.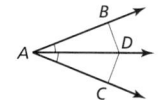

18.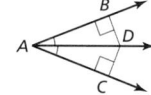

In Exercises 19–22, write an equation of the perpendicular bisector of the segment with the given endpoints. *(See Example 5.)*

19. $M(1, 5), N(7, -1)$

20. $Q(-2, 0), R(6, 12)$

21. $U(-3, 4), V(9, 8)$

22. $Y(10, -7), Z(-4, 1)$

ERROR ANALYSIS In Exercises 23 and 24, describe and correct the error in the student's reasoning.

23.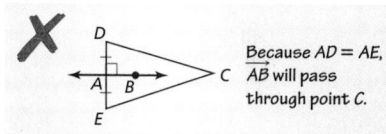

Because $AD = AE$, $\overleftrightarrow{AB}$ will pass through point C.

24.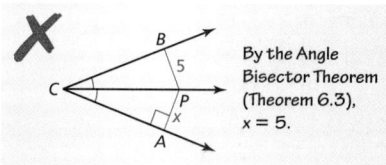

By the Angle Bisector Theorem (Theorem 6.3), $x = 5$.

25. **MODELING MATHEMATICS** In the photo, the road is perpendicular to the support beam and $\overline{AB} \cong \overline{CB}$. Which theorem allows you to conclude that $\overline{AD} \cong \overline{CD}$?

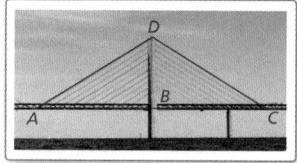

26. **MODELING WITH MATHEMATICS** The diagram shows the position of the goalie and the puck during a hockey game. The goalie is at point G, and the puck is at point P.

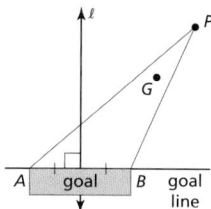

a. What should be the relationship between $\overrightarrow{PG}$ and $\angle APB$ to give the goalie equal distances to travel on each side of $\overrightarrow{PG}$?

b. How does $m\angle APB$ change as the puck gets closer to the goal? Does this change make it easier or more difficult for the goalie to defend the goal? Explain your reasoning.

27. **CONSTRUCTION** Use a compass and straightedge to construct a copy of $\overline{XY}$. Construct a perpendicular bisector and plot a point Z on the bisector so that the distance between point Z and $\overline{XY}$ is 3 centimeters. Measure $\overline{XZ}$ and $\overline{YZ}$. Which theorem does this construction demonstrate?

28. **WRITING** Explain how the Converse of the Perpendicular Bisector Theorem (Theorem 6.2) is related to the construction of a perpendicular bisector.

29. **REASONING** What is the value of x in the diagram?

Ⓐ 13

Ⓑ 18

Ⓒ 33

Ⓓ not enough information

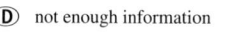

$(3x - 9)°$

30. **REASONING** Which point lies on the perpendicular bisector of the segment with endpoints $M(7, 5)$ and $N(-1, 5)$?

Ⓐ $(2, 0)$ Ⓑ $(3, 9)$

Ⓒ $(4, 1)$ Ⓓ $(1, 3)$

31. **MAKING AN ARGUMENT** Your friend says it is impossible for an angle bisector of a triangle to be the same line as the perpendicular bisector of the opposite side. Is your friend correct? Explain your reasoning.

ANSWERS

15. yes; Because H is equidistant from $\overrightarrow{EF}$ and $\overrightarrow{EG}$, $\overrightarrow{EH}$ bisects $\angle FEG$ by the Angle Bisector Theorem (Thm. 6.3).

16. no; Congruent segments connect H to both $\overrightarrow{EF}$ and $\overrightarrow{EG}$, but unless those segments are also perpendicular to $\overrightarrow{EF}$ and $\overrightarrow{EG}$, you cannot conclude that H is equidistant from $\overrightarrow{EF}$ and $\overrightarrow{EG}$.

17. no; Because neither $\overline{BD}$ nor $\overline{DC}$ are marked as perpendicular to $\overrightarrow{AB}$ or $\overrightarrow{AC}$ respectively, you cannot conclude that $DB = DC$.

18. yes; D is on the angle bisector of $\angle BAC, \overline{DB} \perp \overrightarrow{AB}$ and $\overline{CD} \perp \overrightarrow{AC}$. So, $DB = DC$ by the Angle Bisector Theorem (Thm. 6.3).

19. $y = x - 2$

20. $y = -\frac{2}{3}x + \frac{22}{3}$ *y = mx + b*

21. $y = -3x + 15$

22. $y = \frac{7}{4}x - \frac{33}{4}$

23. Because $\overline{DC}$ is not necessarily congruent to $\overline{EC}$, $\overleftrightarrow{AB}$ will not necessarily pass through point C; Because $AD = AE$, and $\overleftrightarrow{AB} \perp \overline{DE}$, $\overleftrightarrow{AB}$ is the perpendicular bisector of $\overline{DE}$.

24. Because $\overleftrightarrow{BP}$ is not necessarily perpendicular to $\overrightarrow{CB}$, you do not have sufficient evidence to say that $BP = AP$. By the Angle Bisector Theorem (Thm. 6.3), point P is equidistant from $\overrightarrow{CB}$ and $\overrightarrow{CA}$.

25. Perpendicular Bisector Theorem (Thm. 6.1)

26. a. $\overrightarrow{PG}$ should bisect $\angle APB$.

    b. $m\angle APB$ gets larger; more difficult; As the angle increases, the goalie is farther away from each side of the angle.

27.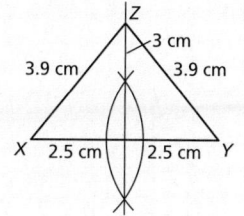

Perpendicular Bisector Theorem (Thm. 6.1)

28. Because every point on a compass arc is the same distance from one endpoint, and every point on the other compass arc with the same setting is the same distance from the other endpoint, the line connecting the points where these arcs intersect contains the points that are equidistant from both endpoints. You know from the Converse of the Perpendicular Bisector Theorem (Thm. 6.2) that the set of points that are equidistant from both endpoints make up the perpendicular bisector of the given segment.

29. B

30. B

31. no; If the triangle is an isosceles triangle, then the angle bisector of the vertex angle will also be the perpendicular bisector of the base.

32.

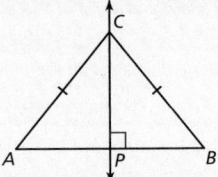

Given isosceles $\triangle ACB$, construct $\overrightarrow{CP}$ such that point P is on $\overline{AB}$ and $\overrightarrow{CP} \perp \overline{AB}$. So, $\angle CPB$ and $\angle CPA$ are right angles by the definition of perpendicular lines, and $\triangle CPB$ and $\triangle CPA$ are right triangles. Also, because $\overline{AC} \cong \overline{BC}$ and $\overline{CP} \cong \overline{CP}$ by the Reflexive Property of Congruence (Thm. 2.1), $\triangle CPB \cong \triangle CPA$ by the HL Congruence Theorem (Thm. 5.9). So, $\overline{AP} \cong \overline{BP}$ because corresponding parts of congruent triangles are congruent, which means that point P is the midpoint of $\overline{AB}$, and $\overrightarrow{CP}$ is the perpendicular bisector of $\overline{AB}$.

33–44. See Additional Answers.

Mini-Assessment

1. Write an equation of the perpendicular bisector of the segment with endpoints $A(-1, -1)$ and $B(5, 3)$. $y = -1.5x + 4$

2. Find AD.

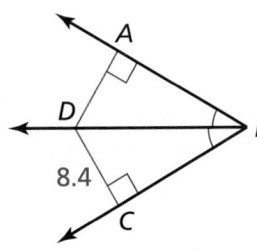

$AD = 8.4$

3. Find YZ.

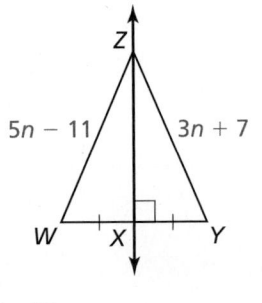

$YZ = 34$

---

32. PROVING A THEOREM Prove the Converse of the Perpendicular Bisector Theorem (Thm. 6.2). (*Hint:* Construct a line through point C perpendicular to $\overline{AB}$ at point P.)

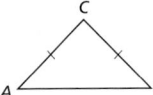

Given $CA = CB$

Prove Point C lies on the perpendicular bisector of $\overline{AB}$.

33. PROVING A THEOREM Use a congruence theorem to prove each theorem.

   a. Angle Bisector Theorem (Thm. 6.3)

   b. Converse of the Angle Bisector Theorem (Thm. 6.4)

34. HOW DO YOU SEE IT? The figure shows a map of a city. The city is arranged so each block north to south is the same length and each block east to west is the same length.

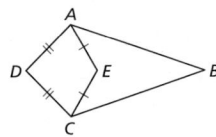

   a. Which school is approximately equidistant from both hospitals? Explain your reasoning.

   b. Is the museum approximately equidistant from Wilson School and Roosevelt School? Explain your reasoning.

Maintaining Mathematical Proficiency
Reviewing what you learned in previous grades and lessons

Classify the triangle by its sides. *(Section 5.1)*

39.

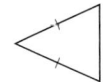

40.

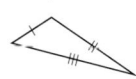

41.

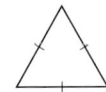

Classify the triangle by its angles. *(Section 5.1)*

42.

$55°$ $45°$ $80°$

43.

$65°$ $25°$

44.

$40°$ $20°$ $120°$

---

35. MATHEMATICAL CONNECTIONS Write an equation whose graph consists of all the points in the given quadrants that are equidistant from the x- and y-axes.

   a. I and III   **b.** II and IV   **c.** I and II

36. THOUGHT PROVOKING The postulates and theorems in this book represent Euclidean geometry. In spherical geometry, all points are on the surface of a sphere. A line is a circle on the sphere whose diameter is equal to the diameter of the sphere. In spherical geometry, is it possible for two lines to be perpendicular but not bisect each other? Explain your reasoning.

37. PROOF Use the information in the diagram to prove that $\overline{AB} \cong \overline{CB}$ if and only if points D, E, and B are collinear.

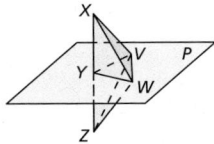

38. PROOF Prove the statements in parts (a)–(c).

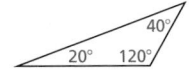

Given Plane P is a perpendicular bisector of $\overline{XZ}$ at point Y.

Prove **a.** $\overline{XW} \cong \overline{ZW}$

       b. $\overline{XV} \cong \overline{ZV}$

       c. $\angle VXW \cong \angle VZW$

Dynamic Teaching Tools

Dynamic Assessment & Progress Monitoring Tool

Lesson Planning Tool

Interactive Whiteboard Lesson Library

Dynamic Classroom with Dynamic Investigations

Overview of Section 6.2

Introduction

- In the last lesson, perpendicular bisectors and angle bisectors were reviewed and their properties explored.
- In this lesson, the three perpendicular bisectors in a triangle are constructed and the circumcenter, the *point of concurrency*, is found. The *circumcenter* is the point that is equidistant from all three vertices of the triangle.
- In the second part of the lesson, the three angle bisectors in a triangle are constructed and the incenter, the *point of concurrency*, is found. The *incenter* is the point that is equidistant from all three sides of the triangle.

Resources

- Tracing paper is helpful when the explorations are done by paper folding.

Teaching Strategy

- For either of the constructions in this lesson (circumcenter and incenter), consider using a local map that your students would be familiar with. Take a screen shot of the image and import it to your dynamic geometry software.
- In the example shown, I currently live at point *A*, I lived for many years at point *B*, and I work at point *C*.
- Think of the type of applications for the circumcenter and incenter, and select an image that will make sense.

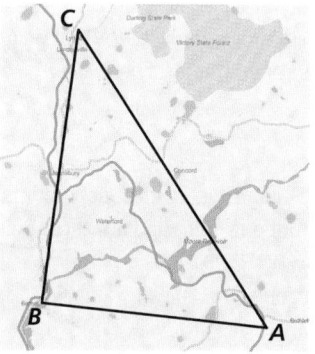

Pacing Suggestion

- The explorations allow students to explore and discover two relationships that will be stated as theorems in the formal lesson. The constructions and investigations are not long and should be followed with the statement of the Circumcenter Theorem (Thm. 6.5) in the lesson. You may choose to omit the two compass constructions in the lesson.

HSG-CO.D.12 Make formal geometric constructions with a variety of tools and methods (compass and straightedge, string, ... dynamic geometric software, etc.). ...

HSG-C.A.3 Construct the inscribed and circumscribed circles of a triangle, ...

HSG-MG.A.1 Use geometric shapes, their measures, and their properties to describe objects (e.g., modeling a tree trunk or a human torso as a cylinder).

HSG-MG.A.3 Apply geometric methods to solve design problems (e.g., designing an object or structure to satisfy physical constraints or minimize cost; working with typographic grid systems based on ratios).

Laurie's Notes

Exploration

Motivate

- There are three high schools located in different parts of the city. You want to open an after-school tutoring service for students from all of the schools. Where would you locate your service so that any student has the same distance to drive?
- Let students discuss the scenario.
- Explain to students that after this lesson they should be able to give an expert opinion about the location of the tutoring service.

Exploration 1

- This is a quick construction using dynamic geometric software. It is not necessary for the coordinate axes to be visible.
- Students observe that the three perpendicular bisectors appear to intersect at one point.
- **Turn and Talk:** "How could you show that the lines intersect at just one point and not at points that are simply very close together?" One way is to label the points of intersection of each pair of lines D, E, and F. If coordinates appear, students will note that D, E, and F are the same point. If the construction was not done in a coordinate plane, measure $\overline{DE}$, $\overline{DF}$, and $\overline{FE}$. All segments will have a length of 0, meaning D, E, and F are the same point.
- **❓ MP3 Construct Viable Arguments and Critique the Reasoning of Others:** Draw the circle. "What conjecture(s) can you make?" The circle goes through the three vertices of the triangle.
- **MP5 Use Appropriate Tools Strategically:** Students can quickly explore other triangles by clicking and dragging on any vertex of the triangle.
- Students may make other observations, for instance that point D is the same distance from all three vertices because D is the center of the circle.

Exploration 2

- This also is a quick construction.
- Students observe that the three angle bisectors appear to intersect at one point. Have students confirm that there is but one point and not three points that are simply close together.
- **❓ MP3:** Draw the circle. "What conjecture(s) can you make?" The circle touches each side of the triangle.
- **MP5:** Students can quickly explore other triangles by clicking and dragging on any vertex of the triangle.
- Students may make other observations—for instance, that the circle stays inside the sides of the triangle.

Communicate Your Answer

- Students should state that the three perpendicular bisectors of the sides of a triangle intersect at one point, and the three angle bisectors of a triangle intersect at one point.

Connecting to Next Step

- The explorations are related to the theorems presented in the lesson, helping students make sense of the theorems before proving them to be true.

6.2 Bisectors of Triangles

Essential Question
What conjectures can you make about the perpendicular bisectors and the angle bisectors of a triangle?

EXPLORATION 1 — Properties of the Perpendicular Bisectors of a Triangle

Work with a partner. Use dynamic geometry software. Draw any $\triangle ABC$.

a. Construct the perpendicular bisectors of all three sides of $\triangle ABC$. Then drag the vertices to change $\triangle ABC$. What do you notice about the perpendicular bisectors?

b. Label a point D at the intersection of the perpendicular bisectors.

c. Draw the circle with center D through vertex A of $\triangle ABC$. Then drag the vertices to change $\triangle ABC$. What do you notice?

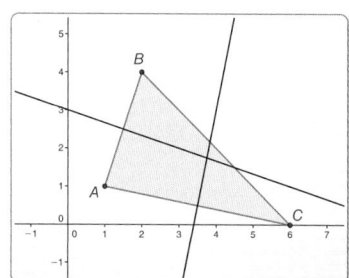

Sample

Points
$A(1, 1)$
$B(2, 4)$
$C(6, 0)$

Segments
$BC = 5.66$
$AC = 5.10$
$AB = 3.16$

Lines
$x + 3y = 9$
$-5x + y = -17$

EXPLORATION 2 — Properties of the Angle Bisectors of a Triangle

Work with a partner. Use dynamic geometry software. Draw any $\triangle ABC$.

a. Construct the angle bisectors of all three angles of $\triangle ABC$. Then drag the vertices to change $\triangle ABC$. What do you notice about the angle bisectors?

b. Label a point D at the intersection of the angle bisectors.

c. Find the distance between D and $\overline{AB}$. Draw the circle with center D and this distance as a radius. Then drag the vertices to change $\triangle ABC$. What do you notice?

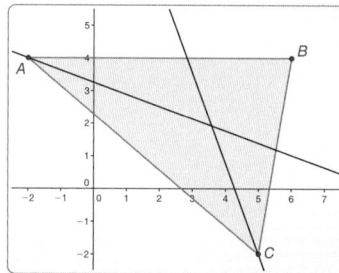

Sample

Points
$A(-2, 4)$
$B(6, 4)$
$C(5, -2)$

Segments
$BC = 6.08$
$AC = 9.22$
$AB = 8$

Lines
$0.35x + 0.94y = 3.06$
$-0.94x - 0.34y = -4.02$

LOOKING FOR STRUCTURE

To be proficient in math, you need to see complicated things as single objects or as being composed of several objects.

Communicate Your Answer

3. What conjectures can you make about the perpendicular bisectors and the angle bisectors of a triangle?

Section 6.2   Bisectors of Triangles   **309**

ANSWERS

1. a–c. *Sample answer:*

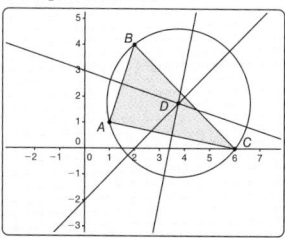

a. The perpendicular bisectors all intersect at one point.

c. The circle passes through all three vertices of $\triangle ABC$.

2. a–c. *Sample answer:*

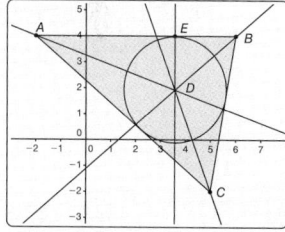

a. The angle bisectors all intersect at one point.

c. distance ≈ 2.06; The circle passes through exactly one point of each side of $\triangle ABC$.

3. The perpendicular bisectors of the sides of a triangle meet at a point that is the same distance from each vertex of the triangle. The angle bisectors of a triangle meet at a point that is the same distance from each side of the triangle.

6.2 Lesson

Core Vocabulary

concurrent, *p. 310*
point of concurrency, *p. 310*
circumcenter, *p. 310*
incenter, *p. 313*

Previous
perpendicular bisector
angle bisector

What You Will Learn

▶ Use and find the circumcenter of a triangle.
▶ Use and find the incenter of a triangle.

Using the Circumcenter of a Triangle

When three or more lines, rays, or segments intersect in the same point, they are called **concurrent** lines, rays, or segments. The point of intersection of the lines, rays, or segments is called the **point of concurrency**.

In a triangle, the three perpendicular bisectors are concurrent. The point of concurrency is the **circumcenter** of the triangle.

↻ Theorems

Theorem 6.5   Circumcenter Theorem

The circumcenter of a triangle is equidistant from the vertices of the triangle.

If $\overline{PD}, \overline{PE},$ and $\overline{PF}$ are perpendicular bisectors, then $PA = PB = PC$.

Proof p. 310

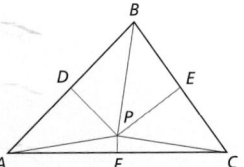

PROOF   **Circumcenter Theorem**

Given $\triangle ABC$; the perpendicular bisectors of $\overline{AB}, \overline{BC},$ and $\overline{AC}$

Prove   The perpendicular bisectors intersect in a point; that point is equidistant from A, B, and C.

Plan for Proof   Show that P, the point of intersection of the perpendicular bisectors of $\overline{AB}$ and $\overline{BC}$, also lies on the perpendicular bisector of $\overline{AC}$. Then show that point P is equidistant from the vertices of the triangle.

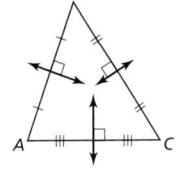

STUDY TIP

Use diagrams like the one below to help visualize your proof.

Plan in Action	STATEMENTS	REASONS
	1. $\triangle ABC$; the perpendicular bisectors of $\overline{AB}, \overline{BC},$ and $\overline{AC}$	1. Given
	2. The perpendicular bisectors of $\overline{AB}$ and $\overline{BC}$ intersect at some point P.	2. Because the sides of a triangle cannot be parallel, these perpendicular bisectors must intersect in some point. Call it P.
	3. Draw $\overline{PA}, \overline{PB},$ and $\overline{PC}$.	3. Two Point Postulate (Post. 2.1)
	4. $PA = PB, PB = PC$	4. Perpendicular Bisector Theorem (Thm. 6.1)
	5. $PA = PC$	5. Transitive Property of Equality
	6. P is on the perpendicular bisector of $\overline{AC}$.	6. Converse of the Perpendicular Bisector Theorem (Thm. 6.2)
	7. $PA = PB = PC$. So, P is equidistant from the vertices of the triangle.	7. From the results of Steps 4 and 5 and the definition of equidistant

Laurie's Notes   Teacher Actions

• Ask what the word *concurrent* means. Relate *point of concurrency* with the two explorations.
? Draw $\triangle ABC$ and sketch one perpendicular bisector. "What do you know about any point on this perpendicular bisector?"   It is equidistant from the two vertices of the bisected side.
? Repeat for a second perpendicular bisector. Where the two bisectors intersect ask, "What is true about this point?"   It is equidistant from all three vertices of the triangle.
• State the Circumcenter Theorem and discuss the proof.

EXAMPLE 1 Solving a Real-Life Problem

Three snack carts sell frozen yogurt from points A, B, and C outside a city. Each of the three carts is the same distance from the frozen yogurt distributor.

Find the location of the distributor.

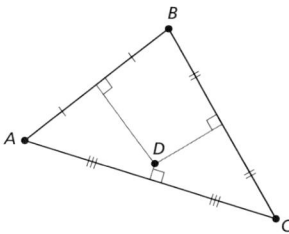

SOLUTION

The distributor is equidistant from the three snack carts. The Circumcenter Theorem shows that you can find a point equidistant from three points by using the perpendicular bisectors of the triangle formed by those points.

Copy the positions of points A, B, and C and connect the points to draw $\triangle ABC$. Then use a ruler and protractor to draw the three perpendicular bisectors of $\triangle ABC$. The circumcenter D is the location of the distributor.

Monitoring Progress 🔊 Help in English and Spanish at *BigIdeasMath.com*

1. Three snack carts sell hot pretzels from points A, B, and E. What is the location of the pretzel distributor if it is equidistant from the three carts? Sketch the triangle and show the location.

READING

The prefix *circum-* means "around" or "about," as in *circumference* (distance around a circle).

The circumcenter P is equidistant from the three vertices, so P is the center of a circle that passes through all three vertices. As shown below, the location of P depends on the type of triangle. The circle with center P is said to be *circumscribed* about the triangle.

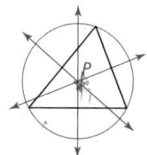

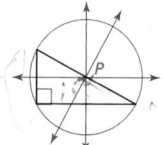

Acute triangle	Right triangle	Obtuse triangle
P is inside triangle.	P is on triangle.	P is outside triangle.

Section 6.2 Bisectors of Triangles **311**

Extra Example 1
A carnival operator wants to locate a food stand so that it is the same distance from the carousel (C), the Ferris wheel (F), and the bumper cars (B). Find the location of the food stand (S).

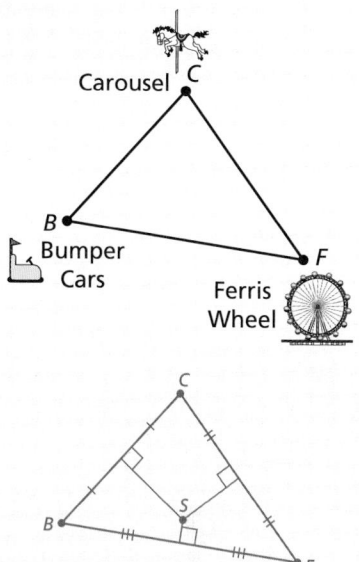

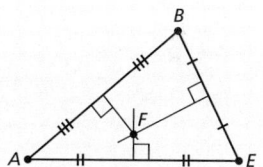

The circumcenter S of $\triangle BCF$ is the location of the food stand.

MONITORING PROGRESS ANSWER

1. The pretzel distributor is located at point F, which is the circumcenter of $\triangle ABE$.

Laurie's Notes | **Teacher Actions**

- **Extension:** To make Example 1 more interesting, print a street map of your area. Locate three points that are known to students and describe a plausible context. Locate the circumcenter for the triangle formed by the three fixed points.
- ❓ **Fact-First Questioning:** "The circumcenter could be located on the side of a triangle. What type of triangle would it be?" If students explored the circumcenter with dynamic geometry software, they likely know the triangle would be a right triangle. Note the summary at the bottom of the page.

312   Chapter 6

Differentiated Instruction

Auditory

Have students work in pairs. One student should read aloud the steps in circumscribing a circle about a triangle, while the other student carries out the construction. Then students should reverse roles.

Extra Example 2

Find the coordinates of the circumcenter of $\triangle DEF$ with vertices $D(6, 4)$, $E(-2, 4)$, and $F(-2, -2)$. $(2, 1)$

MONITORING PROGRESS ANSWERS

2. $(-4, 2)$

3. $(0, -1)$

CONSTRUCTION   **Circumscribing a Circle About a Triangle**

Use a compass and straightedge to construct a circle that is circumscribed about $\triangle ABC$.

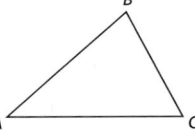

SOLUTION

Step 1	Step 2	Step 3
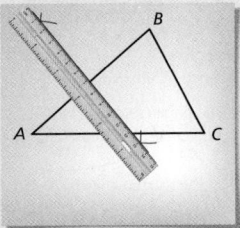	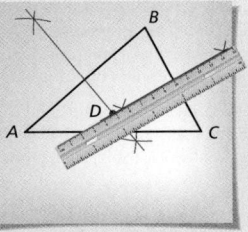	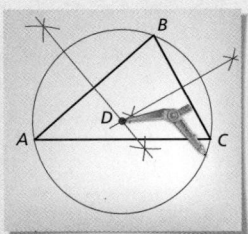
Draw a bisector Draw the perpendicular bisector of $\overline{AB}$.	**Draw a bisector** Draw the perpendicular bisector of $\overline{BC}$. Label the intersection of the bisectors D. This is the circumcenter.	**Draw a circle** Place the compass at D. Set the width by using any vertex of the triangle. This is the radius of the *circumcircle*. Draw the circle. It should pass through all three vertices A, B, and C.

STUDY TIP

Note that you only need to find the equations for *two* perpendicular bisectors. You can use the perpendicular bisector of the third side to verify your result.

MAKING SENSE OF PROBLEMS

Because $\triangle ABC$ is a right triangle, the circumcenter lies on the triangle.

EXAMPLE 2   **Finding the Circumcenter of a Triangle**

Find the coordinates of the circumcenter of $\triangle ABC$ with vertices $A(0, 3)$, $B(0, -1)$, and $C(6, -1)$.

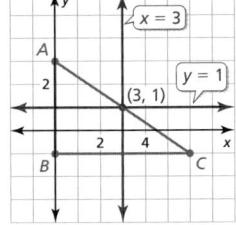

SOLUTION

Step 1 Graph $\triangle ABC$.

Step 2 Find equations for two perpendicular bisectors. Use the Slopes of Perpendicular Lines Theorem (Theorem 3.14), which states that horizontal lines are perpendicular to vertical lines.

The midpoint of $\overline{AB}$ is $(0, 1)$. The line through $(0, 1)$ that is perpendicular to $\overline{AB}$ is $y = 1$.

The midpoint of $\overline{BC}$ is $(3, -1)$. The line through $(3, -1)$ that is perpendicular to $\overline{BC}$ is $x = 3$.

Step 3 Find the point where $x = 3$ and $y = 1$ intersect. They intersect at $(3, 1)$.

▶ So, the coordinates of the circumcenter are $(3, 1)$.

Monitoring Progress Help in English and Spanish at *BigIdeasMath.com*

Find the coordinates of the circumcenter of the triangle with the given vertices.

2. $R(-2, 5)$, $S(-6, 5)$, $T(-2, -1)$ 3. $W(-1, 4)$, $X(1, 4)$, $Y(1, -6)$

Laurie's Notes   Teacher Actions

- Construct the circumcenter. Vary the type of triangle (right, obtuse, acute) used by students.
- You might choose to modify Example 2 so that the perpendicular bisectors are not vertical or horizontal. Students should have the prerequisite skills to find the point of intersection for a more challenging problem. Alternately, consider using dynamic geometry software with a map that has been imported. See the *Teaching Strategy* on page T-308.

Using the Incenter of a Triangle

Just as a triangle has three perpendicular bisectors, it also has three angle bisectors. The angle bisectors of a triangle are also concurrent. This point of concurrency is the **incenter** of the triangle. For any triangle, the incenter always lies inside the triangle.

↻ Theorem

Theorem 6.6 Incenter Theorem

The incenter of a triangle is equidistant from the sides of the triangle.

If $\overline{AP}$, $\overline{BP}$, and $\overline{CP}$ are angle bisectors of $\triangle ABC$, then $PD = PE = PF$.

Proof Ex. 38, p. 317

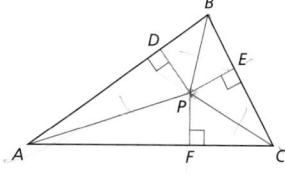

EXAMPLE 3 Using the Incenter of a Triangle

In the figure shown, $ND = 5x - 1$ and $NE = 2x + 11$.

a. Find NF.

b. Can NG be equal to 18? Explain your reasoning.

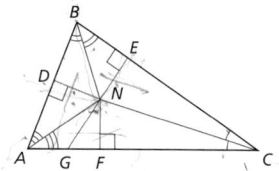

SOLUTION

a. N is the incenter of $\triangle ABC$ because it is the point of concurrency of the three angle bisectors. So, by the Incenter Theorem, $ND = NE = NF$.

Step 1 Solve for x.

$ND = NE$	Incenter Theorem
$5x - 1 = 2x + 11$	Substitute.
$x = 4$	Solve for x.

Step 2 Find ND (or NE).

$$ND = 5x - 1 = 5(4) - 1 = 19$$

▶ So, because $ND = NF$, $NF = 19$.

b. Recall that the shortest distance between a point and a line is a perpendicular segment. In this case, the perpendicular segment is $\overline{NF}$, which has a length of 19. Because $18 < 19$, NG cannot be equal to 18.

Monitoring Progress Help in English and Spanish at *BigIdeasMath.com*

4. In the figure shown, $QM = 3x + 8$ and $QN = 7x + 2$. Find QP.

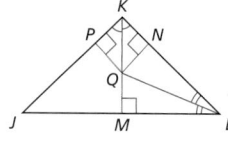

Extra Example 3

In the figure shown, $NE = 6x + 1$ and $NF = 4x + 15$.

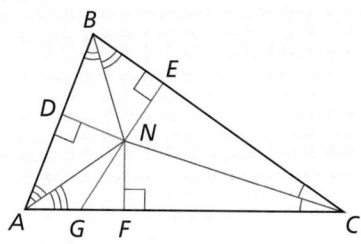

a. Find ND. 43

b. Can $NB = 40$? Explain your reasoning.
No. The shortest distance from a point to a line is the length of the perpendicular segment from the point to the line. In this case, the perpendicular segment is $\overline{ND}$, which has a length of 43. Because $40 < 43$, NB cannot equal 40.

MONITORING PROGRESS ANSWER

4. 12.5

Laurie's Notes   Teacher Actions

❓ MP3 and Fact-First Questioning: "The incenter of a triangle is always in the interior of the triangle. Explain why." Listen for correct reasoning involving the three angle bisectors intersecting at a point in the interior of all three angles.

- **Extension:** To make Example 3 more interesting, print a street map of your area. Locate three points that are known to students and describe a plausible context. Locate the incenter for the triangle formed by the three fixed points.

Extra Example 4

A school has fenced in an area in the shape of a scalene triangle to use for a new playground. The school wants to place a swing set where it will be the same distance from all three fences. Should the swing set be placed at the *circumcenter* or the *incenter* of the triangular playground? Explain. The incenter of a triangle is equidistant from the sides of the triangle, so the swing set should be at the incenter.

MONITORING PROGRESS ANSWER

5.

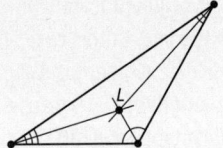

Because the incenter *P* is equidistant from the three sides of the triangle, a circle drawn using *P* as the center and the distance to one side of the triangle as the radius will just touch the other two sides of the triangle. The circle is said to be *inscribed* within the triangle.

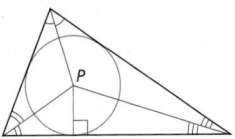

CONSTRUCTION   Inscribing a Circle Within a Triangle

Use a compass and straightedge to construct a circle that is inscribed within △*ABC*.

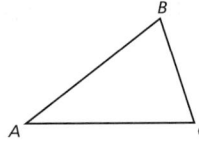

SOLUTION

Step 1
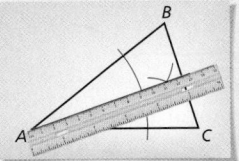
Draw a bisector Draw the angle bisector of ∠*A*.

Step 2
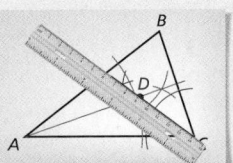
Draw a bisector Draw the angle bisector of ∠*C*. Label the intersection of the bisectors *D*. This is the incenter.

Step 3
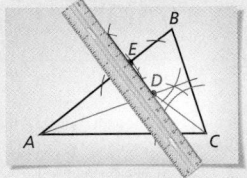
Draw a perpendicular line Draw the perpendicular line from *D* to $\overline{AB}$. Label the point where it intersects $\overline{AB}$ as *E*.

Step 4
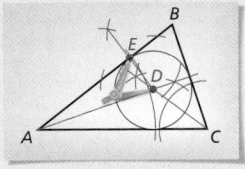
Draw a circle Place the compass at *D*. Set the width to *E*. This is the radius of the *incircle*. Draw the circle. It should touch each side of the triangle.

EXAMPLE 4   Solving a Real-Life Problem

A city wants to place a lamppost on the boulevard shown so that the lamppost is the same distance from all three streets. Should the location of the lamppost be at the *circumcenter* or *incenter* of the triangular boulevard? Explain.

ATTENTION TO PRECISION

Pay close attention to how a problem is stated. The city wants the lamppost to be the *same distance* from the three streets, not from where the streets intersect.

SOLUTION

Because the shape of the boulevard is an obtuse triangle, its circumcenter lies outside the triangle. So, the location of the lamppost cannot be at the circumcenter. The city wants the lamppost to be the same distance from all three streets. By the Incenter Theorem, the incenter of a triangle is equidistant from the sides of a triangle.

▶ So, the location of the lamppost should be at the incenter of the boulevard.

Monitoring Progress Help in English and Spanish at *BigIdeasMath.com*

5. Draw a sketch to show the location *L* of the lamppost in Example 4.

Laurie's Notes   Teacher Actions

- Construct the incenter. Vary the type of triangle (right, obtuse, acute) used by students.
- **MP6 Attend to Precision:** Note that Example 4 states that the lamppost is to be the same distance from the three streets, not from where they intersect.
- ❓ "Can you think of other contexts where knowing the incenter would be necessary?" Answers will vary.

Closure

- **Exit Ticket:** Explain what the circumcenter and incenter of a triangle are and how they can be found. The circumcenter of a triangle is equidistant from the vertices of the triangle. To find the circumcenter, find the intersection of the perpendicular bisectors of the sides of the triangle. The incenter of a triangle is equidistant from the sides of the triangle. To find the incenter, find the intersection of the angle bisectors of the interior angles of the triangle.

Vocabulary and Core Concept Check

1. **VOCABULARY** When three or more lines, rays, or segments intersect in the same point, they are called _____ lines, rays, or segments.

2. **WHICH ONE DOESN'T BELONG?** Which triangle does *not* belong with the other three? Explain your reasoning.

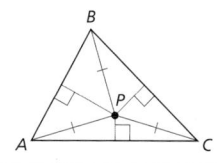 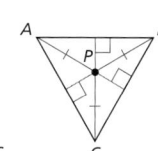 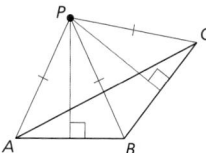 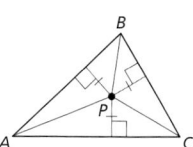

Monitoring Progress and Modeling with Mathematics

In Exercises 3 and 4, the perpendicular bisectors of △ABC intersect at point G and are shown in blue. Find the indicated measure.

3. Find *BG*.   4. Find *GA*.

 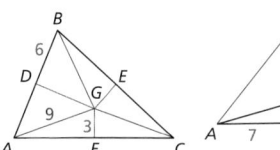

In Exercises 5 and 6, the angle bisectors of △XYZ intersect at point P and are shown in red. Find the indicated measure.

5. Find *PB*.   6. Find *HP*.

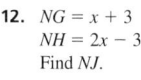

In Exercises 7–10, find the coordinates of the circumcenter of the triangle with the given vertices.
(See Example 2.)

7. $A(2, 6), B(8, 6), C(8, 10)$

8. $D(-7, -1), E(-1, -1), F(-7, -9)$

9. $H(-10, 7), J(-6, 3), K(-2, 3)$

10. $L(3, -6), M(5, -3), N(8, -6)$

In Exercises 11–14, N is the incenter of △ABC. Use the given information to find the indicated measure.
(See Example 3.)

11. $ND = 6x - 2$
    $NE = 3x + 7$
    Find *NF*.

12. $NG = x + 3$
    $NH = 2x - 3$
    Find *NJ*.

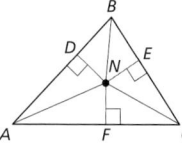 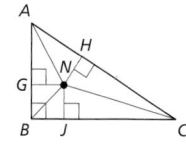

13. $NK = 2x - 2$
    $NL = -x + 10$
    Find *NM*.

14. $NQ = 2x$
    $NR = 3x - 2$
    Find *NS*.

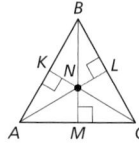 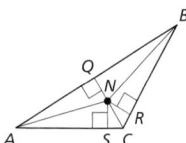

15. *P* is the circumcenter of △XYZ. Use the given information to find *PZ*.

$PX = 3x + 2$
$PY = 4x - 8$

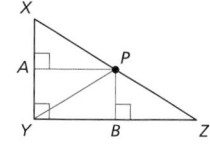

Assignment Guide and Homework Check

ASSIGNMENT

Basic: 1, 2, 3–27 odd, 28, 45, 46, 52–59

Average: 1, 2–28 even, 41–45 odd, 46, 52–59

Advanced: 1, 2–8 even, 14–42 even, 43–59

HOMEWORK CHECK

Basic: 3, 5, 7, 13, 28

Average: 4, 6, 8, 14, 18

Advanced: 6, 14, 18, 34, 43

ANSWERS

1. concurrent

2. the fourth triangle; This triangle shows the incenter of the triangle, but the other three show the circumcenter.

3. 9

4. 11

5. 9

6. 15

7. (5, 8)

8. (−4, −5)

9. (−4, 9)

10. (5.5, −5.5)

11. 16

12. 9

13. 6

14. 4

15. 32

ANSWERS

16. 31

17. *Sample answer:*

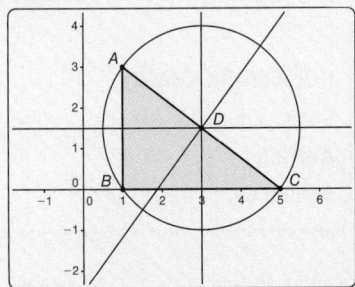

18. *Sample answer:*

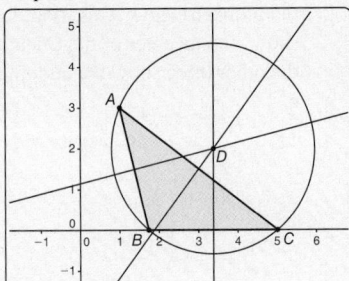

19. *Sample answer:*

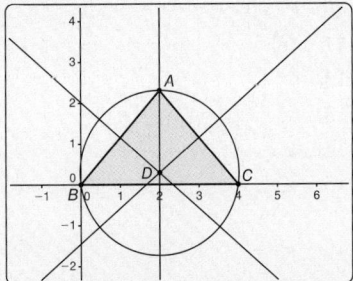

20. *Sample answer:*

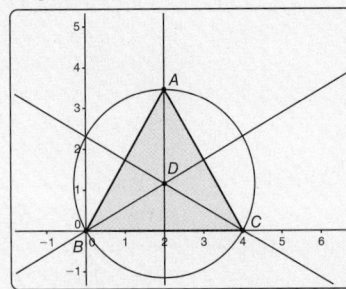

---

16. *P* is the circumcenter of △*XYZ*. Use the given information to find *PY*.

$PX = 4x + 3$
$PZ = 6x - 11$

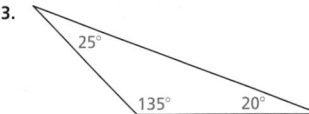

CONSTRUCTION In Exercises 17–20, draw a triangle of the given type. **Find the circumcenter. Then construct the circumscribed circle.**

17. right

18. obtuse

19. acute isosceles

20. equilateral

CONSTRUCTION In Exercises 21–24, copy the triangle with the given angle measures. **Find the incenter. Then construct the inscribed circle.**

21.

50°
40°

22.

85°
55°   40°

23.

25°
135°   20°

24.

60°
60°   60°

ERROR ANALYSIS In Exercises 25 and 26, describe and correct the error in identifying equal distances inside the triangle.

25.

$GD = GF$

26.

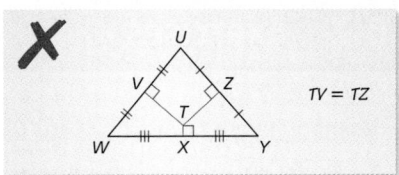

$TV = TZ$

27. MODELING WITH MATHEMATICS You and two friends plan to meet to walk your dogs together. You want the meeting place to be the same distance from each person's house. Explain how you can use the diagram to locate the meeting place. *(See Example 1.)*

your house   friend's house

friend's house

28. MODELING WITH MATHEMATICS You are placing a fountain in a triangular koi pond. You want the fountain to be the same distance from each edge of the pond. Where should you place the fountain? Explain your reasoning. Use a sketch to support your answer. *(See Example 4.)*

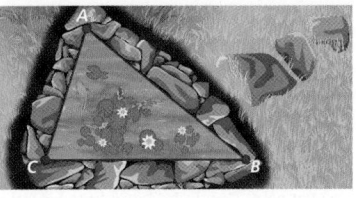

CRITICAL THINKING In Exercises 29–32, complete the statement with *always*, *sometimes*, or *never*. Explain your reasoning.

29. The circumcenter of a scalene triangle is _____ inside the triangle.

30. If the perpendicular bisector of one side of a triangle intersects the opposite vertex, then the triangle is _____ isosceles.

31. The perpendicular bisectors of a triangle intersect at a point that is _____ equidistant from the midpoints of the sides of the triangle.

32. The angle bisectors of a triangle intersect at a point that is _____ equidistant from the sides of the triangle.

---

21. *Sample answer:*

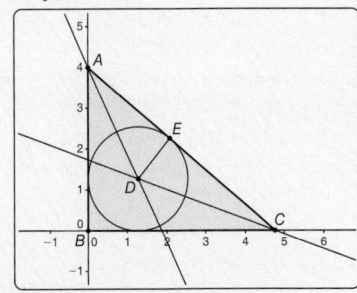

22. *Sample answer:*

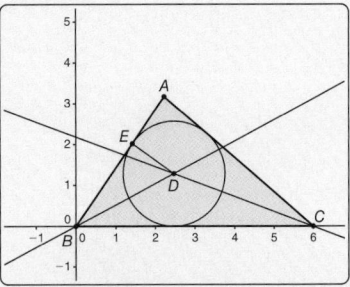

23–32. See Additional Answers.

CRITICAL THINKING In Exercises 33 and 34, find the coordinates of the circumcenter of the triangle with the given vertices.

33. $A(2, 5)$, $B(6, 6)$, $C(12, 3)$

34. $D(-9, -5)$, $E(-5, -9)$, $F(-2, -2)$

MATHEMATICAL CONNECTIONS In Exercises 35 and 36, find the value of x that makes N the incenter of the triangle.

35.

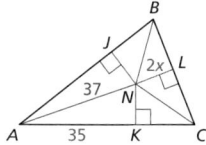

36.

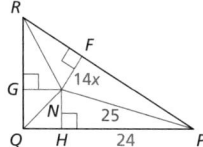

37. **PROOF** Where is the circumcenter located in any right triangle? Write a coordinate proof of this result.

38. **PROVING A THEOREM** Write a proof of the Incenter Theorem (Theorem 6.6).

Given $\triangle ABC$, $\overline{AD}$ bisects $\angle CAB$, $\overline{BD}$ bisects $\angle CBA$, $\overline{DE} \perp \overline{AB}$, $\overline{DF} \perp \overline{BC}$, and $\overline{DG} \perp \overline{CA}$.

Prove The angle bisectors intersect at D, which is equidistant from $\overline{AB}$, $\overline{BC}$, and $\overline{CA}$.

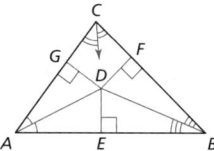

39. **WRITING** Explain the difference between the circumcenter and the incenter of a triangle.

40. **REASONING** Is the incenter of a triangle ever located outside the triangle? Explain your reasoning.

41. **MODELING WITH MATHEMATICS** You are installing a circular pool in the triangular courtyard shown. You want to have the largest pool possible on the site without extending into the walkway.

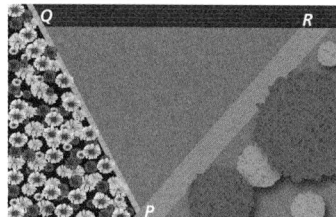

a. Copy the triangle and show how to install the pool so that it just touches each edge. Then explain how you can be sure that you could not fit a larger pool on the site.

b. You want to have the largest pool possible while leaving at least 1 foot of space around the pool. Would the center of the pool be in the same position as in part (a)? Justify your answer.

42. **MODELING WITH MATHEMATICS** Archaeologists find three stones. They believe that the stones were once part of a circle of stones with a community fire pit at its center. They mark the locations of stones A, B, and C on a graph, where distances are measured in feet.

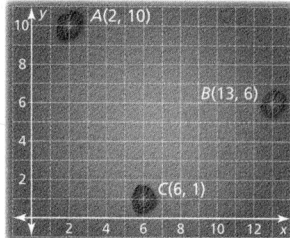

a. Explain how archaeologists can use a sketch to estimate the center of the circle of stones.

b. Copy the diagram and find the approximate coordinates of the point at which the archaeologists should look for the fire pit.

43. **REASONING** Point P is inside $\triangle ABC$ and is equidistant from points A and B. On which of the following segments must P be located?

Ⓐ $\overline{AB}$

Ⓑ the perpendicular bisector of $\overline{AB}$

Ⓒ $\overline{AC}$

Ⓓ the perpendicular bisector of $\overline{AC}$

Section 6.2   Bisectors of Triangles   **317**

41. a.

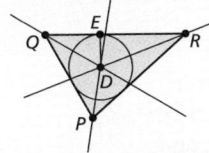

Because this circle is inscribed in the triangle, it is the largest circle that fits inside the triangle without extending into the boundaries.

b. yes; You would keep the center of the pool as the incenter of the triangle, but you would make the radius of the pool at least 1 foot shorter.

42. a. The archaeologists need to locate the circumcenter of the three stones, because that will be the center of the circle that contains all three stones. In order to locate the circumcenter, the archaeologists need to find the point of concurrency of the perpendicular bisectors of the sides of the triangle formed by the three stones.

42b–43. See Additional Answers.

44. no; When you find the circumcenter of three of the points and draw the circle that circumscribes those three points, it does not pass through the fourth point. An example of one circle is shown.

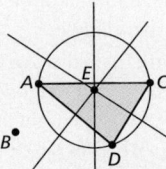

45. yes; In an equilateral triangle, each perpendicular bisector passes through the opposite vertex and divides the triangle into two congruent triangles. So, it is also an angle bisector.

46. incenter

47. a. equilateral; 3; In an equilateral triangle, each perpendicular bisector also bisects the opposite angle.

   b. scalene; 6; In a scalene triangle, none of the perpendicular bisectors will also bisect an angle.

48–59. See Additional Answers.

Mini-Assessment

1. Find the coordinates of the circumcenter of △*ABC* with vertices *A*(0, 5), *B*(4, 5), and *C*(4, −1). (2, 2)

2. In the figure shown, $QP = 2x + 9$ and $QM = 5x − 3$. Find *QN*.

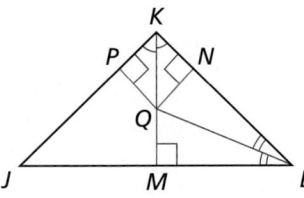

   $QN = 17$

3. In the figure shown, *P* is the circumcenter of △*XYZ*, $PY = 5x − 4$, and $PZ = 4x + 11$. Find *PX*.

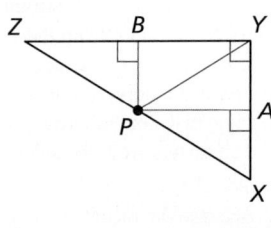

   $PX = 71$

---

44. CRITICAL THINKING A high school is being built for the four towns shown on the map. Each town agrees that the school should be an equal distance from each of the four towns. Is there a single point where they could agree to build the school? If so, find it. If not, explain why not. Justify your answer with a diagram.

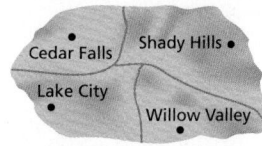

45. MAKING AN ARGUMENT Your friend says that the circumcenter of an equilateral triangle is also the incenter of the triangle. Is your friend correct? Explain your reasoning.

46. HOW DO YOU SEE IT? The arms of the windmill are the angle bisectors of the red triangle. What point of concurrency is the point that connects the three arms?

47. ABSTRACT REASONING You are asked to draw a triangle and all its perpendicular bisectors and angle bisectors.

   a. For which type of triangle would you need the fewest segments? What is the minimum number of segments you would need? Explain.

   b. For which type of triangle would you need the most segments? What is the maximum number of segments you would need? Explain.

Maintaining Mathematical Proficiency
Reviewing what you learned in previous grades and lessons

The endpoints of $\overline{AB}$ are given. Find the coordinates of the midpoint *M*. Then find *AB*. *(Section 1.3)*

52. $A(−3, 5), B(3, 5)$
53. $A(2, −1), B(10, 7)$
54. $A(−5, 1), B(4, −5)$
55. $A(−7, 5), B(5, 9)$

Write an equation of the line passing through point *P* that is perpendicular to the given line. Graph the equations of the lines to check that they are perpendicular. *(Section 3.5)*

56. $P(2, 8), y = 2x + 1$
57. $P(6, −3), y = −5$
58. $P(−8, −6), 2x + 3y = 18$
59. $P(−4, 1), y + 3 = −4(x + 3)$

---

48. THOUGHT PROVOKING The diagram shows an official hockey rink used by the National Hockey League. Create a triangle using hockey players as vertices in which the center circle is inscribed in the triangle. The center dot should be the incenter of your triangle. Sketch a drawing of the locations of your hockey players. Then label the actual lengths of the sides and the angle measures in your triangle.

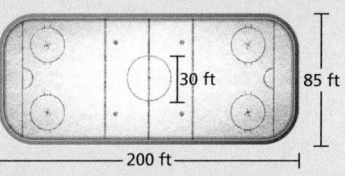

COMPARING METHODS In Exercises 49 and 50, state whether you would use *perpendicular bisectors* or *angle bisectors*. Then solve the problem.

49. You need to cut the largest circle possible from an isosceles triangle made of paper whose sides are 8 inches, 12 inches, and 12 inches. Find the radius of the circle.

50. On a map of a camp, you need to create a circular walking path that connects the pool at (10, 20), the nature center at (16, 2), and the tennis court at (2, 4). Find the coordinates of the center of the circle and the radius of the circle.

51. CRITICAL THINKING Point *D* is the incenter of △*ABC*. Write an expression for the length *x* in terms of the three side lengths *AB*, *AC*, and *BC*.

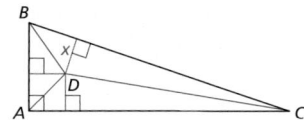

If students need help...	If students got it...
Resources by Chapter • Practice A and Practice B • Puzzle Time	Resources by Chapter • Enrichment and Extension • Cumulative Review
Student Journal • Practice	Start the *next* Section
Differentiating the Lesson Skills Review Handbook	

Overview of Section 6.3

Introduction

- In this lesson, the *medians of a triangle* are constructed and the centroid, the point of concurrency, is found. The *centroid* is the point that is $\frac{2}{3}$ the distance from the vertex to the midpoint of the opposite side.
- In the second part of the lesson, the three *altitudes of a triangle* are constructed and the *orthocenter*, the point of concurrency, is found.
- The lesson also integrates algebraic skills as students find the coordinates of the centroid and orthocenter.

Resources

- Tracing paper is helpful when the explorations are done by paper folding.

Teaching Strategy

- Like the last lesson, the points of concurrency in this lesson are quickly constructed using dynamic geometry software as shown in the explorations.
- If you do not have access to software, an alternate way to introduce this lesson would be through a paper-folding activity or a compass construction activity. It is powerful for students to explore and discover the properties of medians and altitudes.
- Give directions similar to what is written in the explorations for students to paper fold (or construct) the medians (Exploration 1) and the altitudes (Exploration 2). Distances can be measured using a compass or ruler. Although precision may be a problem, the focus is on the discovery.

Extensions

- There is a famous construction called the Nine-Point Circle for which you can find references in many places. When your students have finished this lesson, they will have the vocabulary necessary to perform this construction. It can be done with a compass and a straightedge or with dynamic geometry software.

Pacing Suggestion

- The explorations allow students to explore and discover two relationships that will be stated formally in the lesson. The constructions and investigations are not long and should be followed with the statement of the Centroid Theorem (Thm. 6.7) in the lesson. You may choose to omit the compass construction in the lesson.

Dynamic Teaching Tools

Dynamic Assessment & Progress Monitoring Tool
Lesson Planning Tool
Interactive Whiteboard Lesson Library
Dynamic Classroom with Dynamic Investigations

Laurie's Notes

Exploration

Motivate
- Before students arrive, cut a triangle out of heavier weight paper so that it remains rigid when held. You will also need a sharp pencil.
- When students arrive, ask them whether they think you could balance the triangle on the tip of your pencil.
- Explain to students that in this lesson they will learn about a special point in a triangle that is called the *centroid*, which is the balancing point of the triangle. (See Exercise 50.)

Exploration 1
- This is a quick and straightforward construction using dynamic geometric software. Students should be comfortable at this point knowing that the triangle will be manipulated so that various cases can be explored.
- Students observe that the three medians appear to intersect at one point.
- **Turn and Talk:** "How could you show that the segments intersect at just one point and not at points that are simply very close together?" One way is to label the points of intersection of each pair of segments *G*, *H*, and *I*. If coordinates appear, students will note that *G*, *H*, and *I* are the same point. If the construction was not done in a coordinate plane, measure $\overline{GH}$, $\overline{HI}$, and $\overline{IG}$. All segments will have a length of 0, meaning *G*, *H*, and *I* are the same point.
- **? MP3 Construct Viable Arguments and Critique the Reasoning of Others:** Measure the segments identified and compute the ratios. "What conjecture(s) can you make?" *Sample answer:* The ratio of the length of the longer segment to the length of the median is 2:3.
- **Extension:** If time permits, have students construct $\triangle DEF$, where *D*, *E*, and *F* are the midpoints of the three sides of $\triangle ABC$. Ask students to make observations about the central triangle, all four small triangles, and the original $\triangle ABC$.

Exploration 2
- When constructing the perpendicular line from a vertex to the opposite side of the triangle, a line will be drawn, not a segment. You may want to show students how to construct the perpendicular, draw the segment, and then hide the line.
- **MP3:** Students will observe that the lines containing the three altitudes are concurrent. They should also notice when they click and drag on the vertices that the point of concurrency is not always in the interior of the triangle.

Communicate Your Answer
- Students should state that the three medians of a triangle intersect at one point, and the lines containing the three altitudes of a triangle intersect at one point.

Connecting to Next Step
- The explorations are related to the theorem and properties presented in the lesson, helping students make sense of these before proving them to be true.

6.3 Medians and Altitudes of Triangles

Essential Question What conjectures can you make about the medians and altitudes of a triangle?

EXPLORATION 1 Finding Properties of the Medians of a Triangle

Work with a partner. Use dynamic geometry software. Draw any △ABC.

a. Plot the midpoint of $\overline{BC}$ and label it D. Draw $\overline{AD}$, which is a *median* of △ABC. Construct the medians to the other two sides of △ABC.

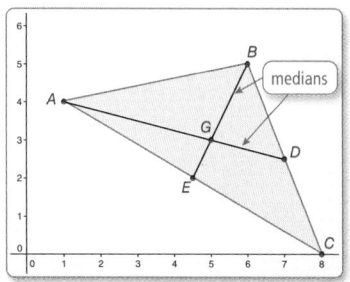

Sample
Points
A(1, 4)
B(6, 5)
C(8, 0)
D(7, 2.5)
E(4.5, 2)
G(5, 3)

b. What do you notice about the medians? Drag the vertices to change △ABC. Use your observations to write a conjecture about the medians of a triangle.

c. In the figure above, point G divides each median into a shorter segment and a longer segment. Find the ratio of the length of each longer segment to the length of the whole median. Is this ratio always the same? Justify your answer.

EXPLORATION 2 Finding Properties of the Altitudes of a Triangle

Work with a partner. Use dynamic geometry software. Draw any △ABC.

a. Construct the perpendicular segment from vertex A to $\overline{BC}$. Label the endpoint D. $\overline{AD}$ is an *altitude* of △ABC.

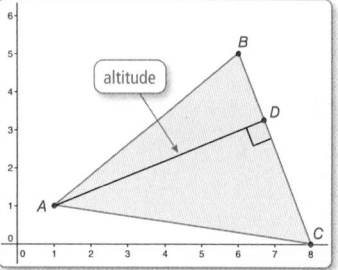

b. Construct the altitudes to the other two sides of △ABC. What do you notice?

c. Write a conjecture about the altitudes of a triangle. Test your conjecture by dragging the vertices to change △ABC.

LOOKING FOR STRUCTURE

To be proficient in math, you need to look closely to discern a pattern or structure.

Communicate Your Answer

3. What conjectures can you make about the medians and altitudes of a triangle?

4. The length of median $\overline{RU}$ in △RST is 3 inches. The point of concurrency of the three medians of △RST divides $\overline{RU}$ into two segments. What are the lengths of these two segments?

Dynamic Teaching Tools

Dynamic Assessment & Progress Monitoring Tool
Lesson Planning Tool
Interactive Whiteboard Lesson Library
Dynamic Classroom with Dynamic Investigations

ANSWERS

1. a. *Sample answer:*

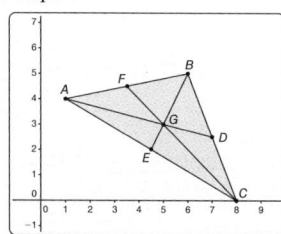

b. The medians of a triangle are concurrent at a point inside the triangle.

c. 2 : 3; yes; The ratio is the same for each median and does not change when you change the triangle.

2. a. Check students' work.

b. *Sample answer:*

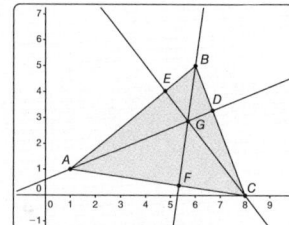

They meet at the same point.

c. The altitudes of a triangle meet at a point that may be inside, on, or outside of the triangle.

3. The medians meet at a point inside the triangle that divides each median into two segments whose lengths have the ratio 1 : 2. The altitudes meet at a point inside, on, or outside the triangle depending on whether the triangle is acute, right, or obtuse.

4. 1 in. and 2 in.

Extra Example 1

In $\triangle RST$, point Q is the centroid, and $VQ = 5$. Find RQ and RV.

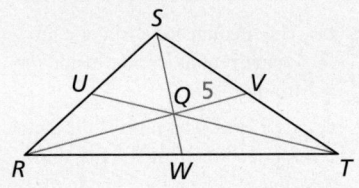

$RQ = 10, RV = 15$

6.3 Lesson

Core Vocabulary

median of a triangle, *p. 320*
centroid, *p. 320*
altitude of a triangle, *p. 321*
orthocenter, *p. 321*

Previous
midpoint
concurrent
point of concurrency

What You Will Learn

▶ Use medians and find the centroids of triangles.
▶ Use altitudes and find the orthocenters of triangles.

Using the Median of a Triangle

A **median of a triangle** is a segment from a vertex to the midpoint of the opposite side. The three medians of a triangle are concurrent. The point of concurrency, called the **centroid**, is inside the triangle.

🔄 Theorem

Theorem 6.7   Centroid Theorem

The centroid of a triangle is two-thirds of the distance from each vertex to the midpoint of the opposite side.

The medians of $\triangle ABC$ meet at point P, and $AP = \frac{2}{3}AE$, $BP = \frac{2}{3}BF$, and $CP = \frac{2}{3}CD$.

Proof   BigIdeasMath.com

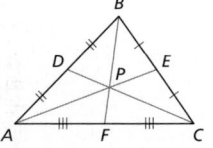

CONSTRUCTION   **Finding the Centroid of a Triangle**

Use a compass and straightedge to construct the medians of $\triangle ABC$.

SOLUTION

Step 1	Step 2	Step 3
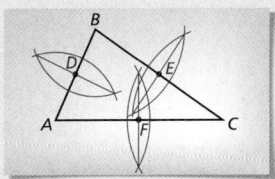	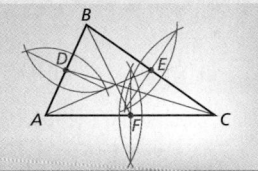	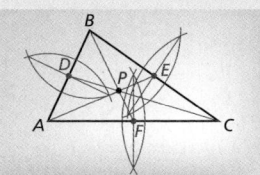
Find midpoints Draw $\triangle ABC$. Find the midpoints of $\overline{AB}, \overline{BC},$ and $\overline{AC}$. Label the midpoints of the sides D, E, and F, respectively.	**Draw medians** Draw $\overline{AE}, \overline{BF},$ and $\overline{CD}$. These are the three medians of $\triangle ABC$.	**Label a point** Label the point where $\overline{AE}, \overline{BF},$ and $\overline{CD}$ intersect as P. This is the centroid.

EXAMPLE 1   **Using the Centroid of a Triangle**

In $\triangle RST$, point Q is the centroid, and $SQ = 8$. Find QW and SW.

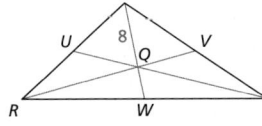

SOLUTION

$SQ = \frac{2}{3}SW$ — Centroid Theorem

$8 = \frac{2}{3}SW$ — Substitute 8 for SQ.

$12 = SW$ — Multiply each side by the reciprocal, $\frac{3}{2}$.

Then $QW = SW - SQ = 12 - 8 = 4$.

▶ So, $QW = 4$ and $SW = 12$.

Laurie's Notes   Teacher Actions

- The Centroid Theorem follows from the first exploration. The centroid divides the median into two pieces that are in the ratio of 1:2. This also means that the ratio of the longer segment to the median is 2:3.
- **Extension:** You can find lots of information about centroids, balancing points, and centers of gravity. The U.S. Census Bureau also defines a population centroid. Search the Internet for "population centroid."

FINDING AN
ENTRY POINT

The median $\overline{SV}$ is chosen
in Example 2 because it is
easier to find a distance
on a vertical segment.

EXAMPLE 2 Finding the Centroid of a Triangle

Find the coordinates of the centroid of △RST with vertices R(2, 1), S(5, 8), and T(8, 3).

SOLUTION

Step 1 Graph △RST.

Step 2 Use the Midpoint Formula to find the midpoint V of $\overline{RT}$ and sketch median $\overline{SV}$.

$$V\left(\frac{2+8}{2}, \frac{1+3}{2}\right) = (5, 2)$$

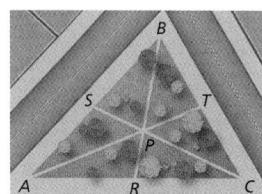

**JUSTIFYING
CONCLUSIONS**

You can check your result
by using a different median
to find the centroid.

Step 3 Find the centroid. It is two-thirds of the distance from each vertex to the midpoint of the opposite side.

The distance from vertex S(5, 8) to V(5, 2) is 8 − 2 = 6 units. So, the centroid is $\frac{2}{3}(6)$ = 4 units down from vertex S on $\overline{SV}$.

▶ So, the coordinates of the centroid P are (5, 8 − 4), or (5, 4).

Monitoring Progress Help in English and Spanish at *BigIdeasMath.com*

There are three paths through a triangular park. Each path goes from the midpoint of one edge to the opposite corner. The paths meet at point P.

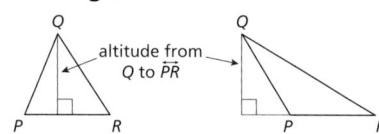

1. Find PS and PC when SC = 2100 feet.

2. Find TC and BC when BT = 1000 feet.

3. Find PA and TA when PT = 800 feet.

Find the coordinates of the centroid of the triangle with the given vertices.

4. F(2, 5), G(4, 9), H(6, 1)   5. X(−3, 3), Y(1, 5), Z(−1, −2)

READING

In the area formula for a
triangle, $A = \frac{1}{2}bh$, you can
use the length of any side
for the base b. The height h
is the length of the altitude
to that side from the
opposite vertex.

Using the Altitude of a Triangle

An **altitude of a triangle** is the perpendicular segment from a vertex to the opposite side or to the line that contains the opposite side.

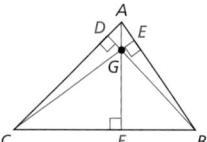

altitude from Q to $\overline{PR}$

Core Concept

Orthocenter

The lines containing the altitudes of a triangle are concurrent. This point of concurrency is the **orthocenter** of the triangle.

The lines containing $\overline{AF}$, $\overline{BD}$, and $\overline{CE}$ meet at the orthocenter G of △ABC.

Section 6.3   Medians and Altitudes of Triangles   **321**

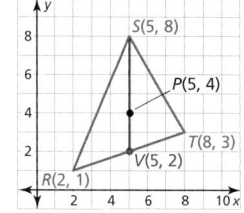

Extra Example 2
Find the coordinates of the centroid of △ABC with vertices A(0, 4), B(−4, −2), and C(7, 1). (1, 1)

**MONITORING PROGRESS
ANSWERS**

1. 700 ft, 1400 ft

2. 1000 ft, 2000 ft

3. 1600 ft, 2400 ft

4. (4, 5)

5. (−1, 2)

Laurie's Notes   Teacher Actions

• You might consider having different groups of students use different medians in Example 2 when finding the coordinates of the centroid.

• **Think-Pair-Share:** Have students answer Questions 1−5, and then share and discuss as a class.

• **Teaching Tip:** To sketch the three altitudes, students find it helpful to rotate their paper so that they are drawing a vertical line from the vertex, perpendicular to the opposite side. They rotate the triangle for each altitude sketched.

Extra Example 3
Find the coordinates of the orthocenter of △*DEF* with vertices *D*(0, 6), *E*(−4, −2), and *F*(4, 6). (−4, 10)

MONITORING PROGRESS ANSWERS

6. outside; (−1, −3)
7. on; (−3, 4)

As shown below, the location of the orthocenter *P* of a triangle depends on the type of triangle.

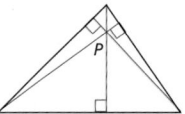
Acute triangle
P is inside triangle.

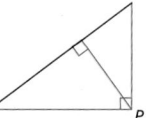
Right triangle
P is on triangle.

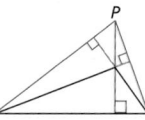
Obtuse triangle
P is outside triangle.

EXAMPLE 3 **Finding the Orthocenter of a Triangle**

Find the coordinates of the orthocenter of △*XYZ* with vertices *X*(−5, −1), *Y*(−2, 4), and *Z*(3, −1).

SOLUTION

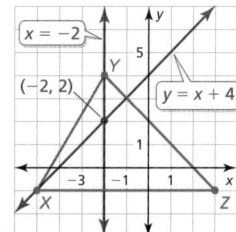

Step 1 Graph △*XYZ*.

Step 2 Find an equation of the line that contains the altitude from *Y* to $\overline{XZ}$. Because $\overline{XZ}$ is horizontal, the altitude is vertical. The line that contains the altitude passes through *Y*(−2, 4). So, the equation of the line is $x = -2$.

Step 3 Find an equation of the line that contains the altitude from *X* to $\overline{YZ}$.

$$\text{slope of } \overleftrightarrow{YZ} = \frac{-1 - 4}{3 - (-2)} = -1$$

Because the product of the slopes of two perpendicular lines is −1, the slope of a line perpendicular to $\overleftrightarrow{YZ}$ is 1. The line passes through *X*(−5, −1).

$y = mx + b$ Use slope-intercept form.

$-1 = 1(-5) + b$ Substitute −1 for *y*, 1 for *m*, and −5 for *x*.

$4 = b$ Solve for *b*.

So, the equation of the line is $y = x + 4$.

Step 4 Find the point of intersection of the graphs of the equations $x = -2$ and $y = x + 4$.

Substitute −2 for *x* in the equation $y = x + 4$. Then solve for *y*.

$y = x + 4$ Write equation.

$y = -2 + 4$ Substitute −2 for *x*.

$y = 2$ Solve for *y*.

▶ So, the coordinates of the orthocenter are (−2, 2).

Monitoring Progress Help in English and Spanish at *BigIdeasMath.com*

Tell whether the orthocenter of the triangle with the given vertices is *inside*, *on*, or *outside* the triangle. Then find the coordinates of the orthocenter.

6. *A*(0, 3), *B*(0, −2), *C*(6, −3)   7. *J*(−3, −4), *K*(−3, 4), *L*(5, 4)

Laurie's Notes   Teacher Actions

? "Is the orthocenter always located in the interior of the triangle?" no; It is in the interior for an acute triangle, at the vertex of the right angle for a right triangle, and in the exterior for an obtuse triangle.

• **Thumbs Up:** You might consider having different groups of students use different pairs of altitudes in Example 3 when finding the coordinates of the orthocenter. Ask students to give a *Thumbs Up* assessment of the process before they begin.

In an isosceles triangle, the perpendicular bisector, angle bisector, median, and altitude from the vertex angle to the base are all the same segment. In an equilateral triangle, this is true for any vertex.

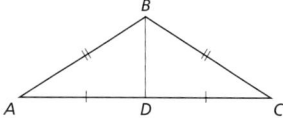 **EXAMPLE 4** Proving a Property of Isosceles Triangles

Prove that the median from the vertex angle to the base of an isosceles triangle is an altitude.

SOLUTION

Given $\triangle ABC$ is isosceles, with base $\overline{AC}$.
$\overline{BD}$ is the median to base $\overline{AC}$.

Prove $\overline{BD}$ is an altitude of $\triangle ABC$.

Paragraph Proof Legs $\overline{AB}$ and $\overline{BC}$ of isosceles $\triangle ABC$ are congruent. $\overline{CD} \cong \overline{AD}$ because $\overline{BD}$ is the median to $\overline{AC}$. Also, $\overline{BD} \cong \overline{BD}$ by the Reflexive Property of Congruence (Thm. 2.1). So, $\triangle ABD \cong \triangle CBD$ by the SSS Congruence Theorem (Thm. 5.8). $\angle ADB \cong \angle CDB$ because corresponding parts of congruent triangles are congruent. Also, $\angle ADB$ and $\angle CDB$ are a linear pair. $\overline{BD}$ and $\overline{AC}$ intersect to form a linear pair of congruent angles, so $\overline{BD} \perp \overline{AC}$ and $\overline{BD}$ is an altitude of $\triangle ABC$.

Monitoring Progress 🔊 Help in English and Spanish at *BigIdeasMath.com*

8. **WHAT IF?** In Example 4, you want to show that median $\overline{BD}$ is also an angle bisector. How would your proof be different?

Concept Summary

Segments, Lines, Rays, and Points in Triangles

	Example	Point of Concurrency	Property	Example
perpendicular bisector		circumcenter	The circumcenter P of a triangle is equidistant from the vertices of the triangle.	
angle bisector		incenter	The incenter I of a triangle is equidistant from the sides of the triangle.	
median		centroid	The centroid R of a triangle is two thirds of the distance from each vertex to the midpoint of the opposite side.	
altitude		orthocenter	The lines containing the altitudes of a triangle are concurrent at the orthocenter O.	

Section 6.3   323

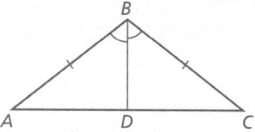 **Extra Example 4**

Prove that the bisector of the vertex angle of an isosceles triangle is an altitude.

Given $\triangle ABC$ is isosceles, $\overline{BD}$ bisects $\angle ABC$.

Prove $\overline{BD}$ is an altitude of $\triangle ABC$.

Paragraph Proof $\overline{AB} \cong \overline{BC}$ by definition of isosceles triangle. $\angle ABD \cong \angle CBD$ by definition of angle bisector. $\overline{BD} \cong \overline{BD}$ by the Reflex. Prop. $\cong$ (Thm. 2.1). So $\triangle ABD \cong \triangle CBD$ by SAS $\cong$ (Thm. 5.5). $\angle ADB \cong \angle CDB$ by CPCTC. Also, they are a linear pair. $\overline{BD}$ and $\overline{AC}$ intersect to form a linear pair of $\cong$ $\angle$s, so $\overline{BD} \perp \overline{AC}$, and $\overline{BD}$ is an altitude of $\triangle ABC$.

MONITORING PROGRESS ANSWER

8. Proving $\triangle ABD \cong \triangle CBD$ by the SSS Congruence Theorem (Thm. 5.8) at the beginning of the proof would be the same. But then you would state that $\angle ABD \cong \angle CBD$ because corresponding parts of congruent triangles are congruent. This means that $\overline{BD}$ is also an angle bisector by definition.

Laurie's Notes   Teacher Actions

- **Turn and Talk:** "Are the four points of concurrency distinct points in every triangle?" Listen for valid reasoning.
- **Whiteboarding:** Pose Example 4. Use whiteboards and have partners work on the proof. Compare and contrast proofs from different pairs of students.
- Students should find the *Concept Summary* helpful.

Closure

- **Exit Ticket:** Draw a right scalene triangle. Sketch the three medians. Draw an obtuse isosceles triangle. Sketch the three altitudes. Check students' work.

ANSWERS

1. circumcenter, incenter, centroid, orthocenter; perpendicular bisectors form the circumcenter, angle bisectors form the incenter, medians form the centroid, altitudes form the orthocenter

2. $\frac{2}{3}$

3. 6, 3

4. 14, 7

5. 20, 10

6. 28, 14

7. 10, 15

8. 22, 33

9. 18, 27

10. 30, 45

11. 12

12. 9

13. 10

14. 5

15. $\left(5, \frac{11}{3}\right)$

16. $\left(-\frac{7}{3}, 5\right)$

17. $(5, 1)$

18. $\left(\frac{10}{3}, 3\right)$

19. outside; $(0, -5)$

20. on; $(-3, 2)$

21. inside; $(-1, 2)$

22. inside; $\left(0, \frac{7}{3}\right)$

23.

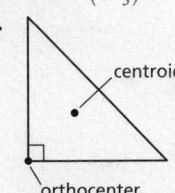

Vocabulary and Core Concept Check

1. **VOCABULARY** Name the four types of points of concurrency. Which lines intersect to form each of the points?

2. **COMPLETE THE SENTENCE** The length of a segment from a vertex to the centroid is _____ the length of the median from that vertex.

Monitoring Progress and Modeling with Mathematics

In Exercises 3–6, point P is the centroid of △LMN. Find *PN* and *QP*. (*See Example 1.*)

3. $QN = 9$

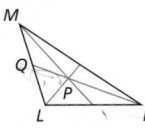

4. $QN = 21$

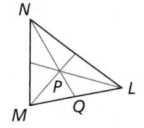

5. $QN = 30$

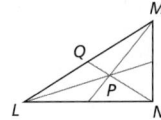

6. $QN = 42$

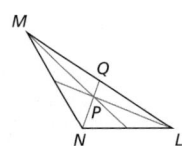

In Exercises 7–10, point D is the centroid of △ABC. Find *CD* and *CE*.

7. $DE = 5$

8. $DE = 11$

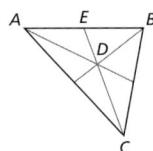

9. $DE = 9$

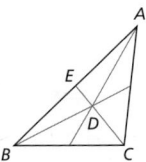

10. $DE = 15$

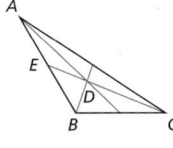

In Exercises 11–14, point G is the centroid of △ABC. $BG = 6$, $AF = 12$, and $AE = 15$. Find the length of the segment.

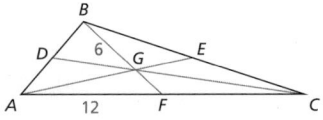

11. $\overline{FC}$

12. $\overline{BF}$

13. $\overline{AG}$

14. $\overline{GE}$

In Exercises 15–18, find the coordinates of the centroid of the triangle with the given vertices. (*See Example 2.*)

15. $A(2, 3)$, $B(8, 1)$, $C(5, 7)$

16. $F(1, 5)$, $G(-2, 7)$, $H(-6, 3)$

17. $S(5, 5)$, $T(11, -3)$, $U(-1, 1)$

18. $X(1, 4)$, $Y(7, 2)$, $Z(2, 3)$

In Exercises 19–22, tell whether the orthocenter is *inside*, *on*, or *outside* the triangle. Then find the coordinates of the orthocenter. (*See Example 3.*)

19. $L(0, 5)$, $M(3, 1)$, $N(8, 1)$

20. $X(-3, 2)$, $Y(5, 2)$, $Z(-3, 6)$

21. $A(-4, 0)$, $B(1, 0)$, $C(-1, 3)$

22. $T(-2, 1)$, $U(2, 1)$, $V(0, 4)$

CONSTRUCTION In Exercises 23–26, draw the indicated triangle and find its centroid and orthocenter.

23. isosceles right triangle   24. obtuse scalene triangle

25. right scalene triangle   26. acute isosceles triangle

---

24. *Sample answer:*

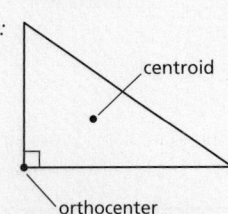

25. *Sample answer:*

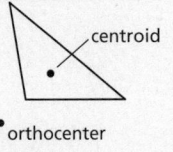

26. *Sample answer:*

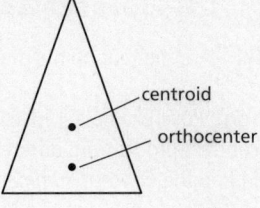

ERROR ANALYSIS In Exercises 27 and 28, describe and correct the error in finding *DE*. Point *D* is the centroid of △*ABC* .

27.

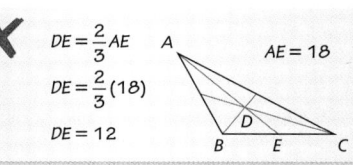

28.

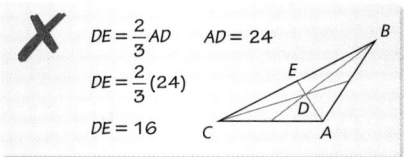

PROOF In Exercises 29 and 30, write a proof of the statement. *(See Example 4.)*

29. The angle bisector from the vertex angle to the base of an isosceles triangle is also a median.

30. The altitude from the vertex angle to the base of an isosceles triangle is also a perpendicular bisector.

CRITICAL THINKING In Exercises 31–36, complete the statement with *always*, *sometimes*, or *never*. **Explain your reasoning.**

31. The centroid is _____ on the triangle.

32. The orthocenter is _____ outside the triangle.

33. A median is _____ the same line segment as a perpendicular bisector.

34. An altitude is _____ the same line segment as an angle bisector.

35. The centroid and orthocenter are _____ the same point.

36. The centroid is _____ formed by the intersection of the three medians.

37. **WRITING** Compare an altitude of a triangle with a perpendicular bisector of a triangle.

38. **WRITING** Compare a median, an altitude, and an angle bisector of a triangle.

39. **MODELING WITH MATHEMATICS** Find the area of the triangular part of the paper airplane wing that is outlined in red. Which special segment of the triangle did you use?

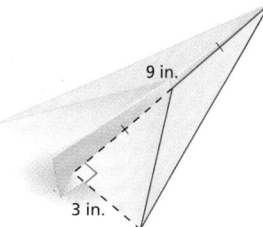

40. **ANALYZING RELATIONSHIPS** Copy and complete the statement for △*DEF* with centroid *K* and medians $\overline{DH}$, $\overline{EJ}$, and $\overline{FG}$.

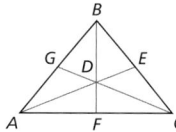

a. *EJ* = _____ *KJ*   b. *DK* = _____ *KH*

c. *FG* = _____ *KF*   d. *KG* = _____ *FG*

MATHEMATICAL CONNECTIONS In Exercises 41–44, point *D* is the centroid of △*ABC*. Use the given information to find the value of *x*.

41. *BD* = 4*x* + 5 and *BF* = 9*x*

42. *GD* = 2*x* − 8 and *GC* = 3*x* + 3

43. *AD* = 5*x* and *DE* = 3*x* − 2

44. *DF* = 4*x* − 1 and *BD* = 6*x* + 4

45. **MATHEMATICAL CONNECTIONS** Graph the lines on the same coordinate plane. Find the centroid of the triangle formed by their intersections.

$$y_1 = 3x - 4$$

$$y_2 = \tfrac{3}{4}x + 5$$

$$y_3 = -\tfrac{3}{2}x - 4$$

46. **CRITICAL THINKING** In what type(s) of triangles can a vertex be one of the points of concurrency of the triangle? Explain your reasoning.

ANSWERS

27. The length of $\overline{DE}$ should be $\tfrac{1}{3}$ of the length of $\overline{AE}$ because it is the shorter segment from the centroid to the side;

$DE = \tfrac{1}{3}AE$

$DE = \tfrac{1}{3}(18)$

$DE = 6$

28. The length of $\overline{DE}$ is $\tfrac{1}{2}$ of the length of $\overline{AD}$ because $DE = \tfrac{1}{3}AE$ and $AD = \tfrac{2}{3}AE$;

$DE = \tfrac{1}{2}AD$

$DE = \tfrac{1}{2}(24)$

$DE = 12$

29.

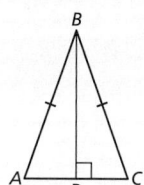

Legs $\overline{AB}$ and $\overline{BC}$ of isosceles △*ABC* are congruent. ∠*ABD* ≅ ∠*CBD* because $\overline{BD}$ is an angle bisector of vertex angle *ABC*. Also, $\overline{BD}$ ≅ $\overline{BD}$ by the Reflexive Property of Congruence (Thm. 2.1). So, △*ABD* ≅ △*CBD* by the SAS Congruence Theorem (Thm. 5.5). $\overline{AD}$ ≅ $\overline{CD}$ because corresponding parts of congruent triangles are congruent. So, $\overline{BD}$ is a median.

30.

Legs $\overline{AB}$ and $\overline{BC}$ of isosceles △*ABC* are congruent. ∠*ADB* and ∠*CDB* are right angles because $\overline{BD}$ is an altitude from vertex angle ∠*ABC* to base $\overline{AC}$ of △*ABC*. So, △*ABD* and △*CBD* are right triangles. Also, $\overline{BD}$ ≅ $\overline{BD}$ by the Reflexive Property of Congruence (Thm. 2.1). So, △*ABD* ≅ △*CBD* by the HL Congruence Theorem (Thm. 5.9). $\overline{AD}$ ≅ $\overline{CD}$ because corresponding parts of congruent triangles are congruent. So, $\overline{BD}$ is a perpendicular bisector.

31. never; Because medians are always inside a triangle, and the centroid is the point of concurrency of the medians, it will always be inside the triangle.

32. sometimes; An orthocenter can be inside, on, or outside the triangle depending on whether the triangle is acute, right, or obtuse.

33. sometimes; A median is the same line segment as the perpendicular bisector if the triangle is equilateral or if the segment is connecting the vertex angle to the base of an isosceles triangle. Otherwise, the median and the perpendicular bisectors are not the same segment.

34. sometimes; An altitude is the same line segment as the angle bisector if the triangle is equilateral or if the segment is connecting the vertex angle to the base of an isosceles triangle. Otherwise, the altitude and the angle bisector are not the same segment.

35. sometimes; The centroid and the orthocenter are not the same point unless the triangle is equilateral.

36–46. See Additional Answers.

ANSWERS

47. $PE = \frac{1}{3}AE$, $PE = \frac{1}{2}AP$,
    $PE = AE - AP$

48. **a.** median; centroid

    b. altitude; orthocenter

    c. $\triangle JKM$ and $\triangle KLM$ both have an area of $4.5h$; yes; The triangles formed by the median will always have the same area, because they will have the same base length and height.

49. yes; If the triangle is equilateral, then the perpendicular bisectors, angle bisectors, medians, and altitudes will all be the same three segments.

50. centroid; Because the triangles formed by the median of any triangle will always be congruent, the mass of the triangle on either side of the median is the same. So, the centroid is the point that has an equal distribution of mass on all sides.

51–58. See Additional Answers.

---

47. **WRITING EQUATIONS** Use the numbers and symbols to write three different equations for *PE*.

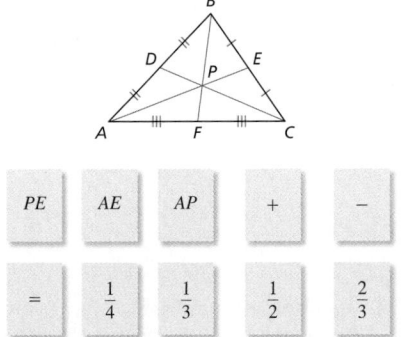

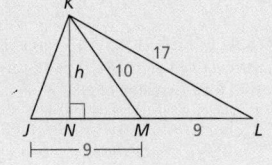

48. **HOW DO YOU SEE IT?** Use the figure.

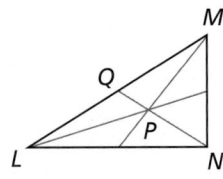

   a. What type of segment is $\overline{KM}$? Which point of concurrency lies on $\overline{KM}$?

   b. What type of segment is $\overline{KN}$? Which point of concurrency lies on $\overline{KN}$?

   c. Compare the areas of $\triangle JKM$ and $\triangle KLM$. Do you think the areas of the triangles formed by the median of any triangle will always compare this way? Explain your reasoning.

49. **MAKING AN ARGUMENT** Your friend claims that it is possible for the circumcenter, incenter, centroid, and orthocenter to all be the same point. Do you agree? Explain your reasoning.

50. **DRAWING CONCLUSIONS** The center of gravity of a triangle, the point where a triangle can balance on the tip of a pencil, is one of the four points of concurrency. Draw and cut out a large scalene triangle on a piece of cardboard. Which of the four points of concurrency is the center of gravity? Explain.

51. **PROOF** Prove that a median of an equilateral triangle is also an angle bisector, perpendicular bisector, and altitude.

52. **THOUGHT PROVOKING** Construct an acute scalene triangle. Find the orthocenter, centroid, and circumcenter. What can you conclude about the three points of concurrency?

53. **CONSTRUCTION** Follow the steps to construct a nine-point circle. Why is it called a nine-point circle?

   Step 1 Construct a large acute scalene triangle.

   Step 2 Find the orthocenter and circumcenter of the triangle.

   Step 3 Find the midpoint between the orthocenter and circumcenter.

   Step 4 Find the midpoint between each vertex and the orthocenter.

   Step 5 Construct a circle. Use the midpoint in Step 3 as the center of the circle, and the distance from the center to the midpoint of a side of the triangle as the radius.

54. **PROOF** Prove the statements in parts (a)−(c).

   Given $\overline{LP}$ and $\overline{MQ}$ are medians of scalene $\triangle LMN$. Point R is on $\overrightarrow{LP}$ such that $\overline{LP} \cong \overline{PR}$. Point S is on $\overrightarrow{MQ}$ such that $\overline{MQ} \cong \overline{QS}$.

   Prove **a.** $\overline{NS} \cong \overline{NR}$

   b. $\overline{NS}$ and $\overline{NR}$ are both parallel to $\overline{LM}$.

   c. R, N, and S are collinear.

Maintaining Mathematical Proficiency
Reviewing what you learned in previous grades and lessons

Determine whether $\overleftrightarrow{AB}$ is parallel to $\overleftrightarrow{CD}$. *(Section 3.5)*

55. $A(5, 6)$, $B(-1, 3)$, $C(-4, 9)$, $D(-16, 3)$

56. $A(-3, 6)$, $B(5, 4)$, $C(-14, -10)$, $D(-2, -7)$

57. $A(6, -3)$, $B(5, 2)$, $C(-4, -4)$, $D(-5, 2)$

58. $A(-5, 6)$, $B(-7, 2)$, $C(7, 1)$, $D(4, -5)$

Mini-Assessment

1. Find the coordinates of the centroid of $\triangle ABC$ with vertices $A(-1, 5)$, $B(-3, -2)$, and $C(1, 0)$. $(-1, 1)$

2. Point P is the centroid of $\triangle LMN$, and $QN = 12.6$. Find PN and QP.

   $PN = 8.4$, $QP = 4.2$

3. Find the coordinates of the orthocenter of $\triangle DEF$ with vertices $D(-1, -3)$, $E(-1, 5)$, and $F(5, -1)$. $(1, -1)$

If students need help...	If students got it...
Resources by Chapter • Practice A and Practice B • Puzzle Time	Resources by Chapter • Enrichment and Extension • Cumulative Review
Student Journal • Practice	Start the *next* Section
Differentiating the Lesson Skills Review Handbook	

Core Vocabulary

equidistant, *p. 302*

concurrent, *p. 310*

point of concurrency, *p. 310*

circumcenter, *p. 310*

incenter, *p. 313*

median of a triangle, *p. 320*

centroid, *p. 320*

altitude of a triangle, *p. 321*

orthocenter, *p. 321*

Core Concepts

Section 6.1

Theorem 6.1 Perpendicular Bisector Theorem, *p. 302*

Theorem 6.2 Converse of the Perpendicular Bisector Theorem, *p. 302*

Theorem 6.3 Angle Bisector Theorem, *p. 304*

Theorem 6.4 Converse of the Angle Bisector Theorem, *p. 304*

Section 6.2

Theorem 6.5 Circumcenter Theorem, *p. 310*

Theorem 6.6 Incenter Theorem, *p. 313*

Section 6.3

Theorem 6.7 Centroid Theorem, *p. 320*

Orthocenter, *p. 321*

Segments, Lines, Rays, and Points in Triangles, *p. 323*

Mathematical Practices

1. Did you make a plan before completing your proof in Exercise 37 on page 308? Describe your thought process.

2. What tools did you use to complete Exercises 17–20 on page 316? Describe how you could use technological tools to complete these exercises.

3. What conjecture did you make when answering Exercise 46 on page 325? What logical progression led you to determine whether your conjecture was true?

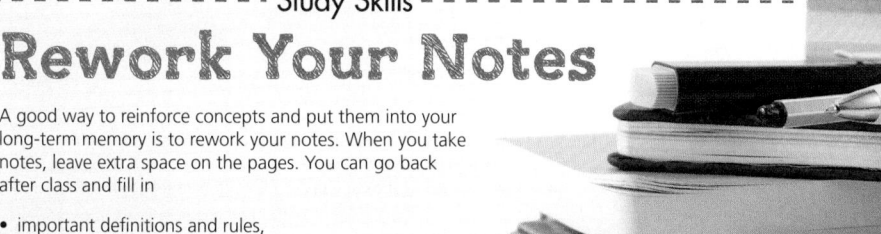

- - - - - - - - - - Study Skills - - - - - - - - - -

Rework Your Notes

A good way to reinforce concepts and put them into your long-term memory is to rework your notes. When you take notes, leave extra space on the pages. You can go back after class and fill in

- important definitions and rules,
- additional examples, and
- questions you have about the material.

327

ANSWERS

1. *Sample answer:* yes; You realize that if you construct the segment $\overline{AC}$, you have created two isosceles triangles that share vertices A and C, and a third triangle that shares the same vertices. Then, you look back at the Perpendicular Bisector Theorem (Thm. 6.1) and its converse to see that points D and E would have to be on the perpendicular bisector of $\overline{AC}$. Then, in the same way, in order for B to also be on the same perpendicular bisector, $\overline{AB}$ and $\overline{CB}$ would have to be congruent.

2. *Sample answer:* These can be constructed with a compass and a straightedge, or they can be constructed with geometry software; If you construct them with geometry software, you create a triangle that fits the description first. Then, use the software to draw the perpendicular bisectors of each side. Next, label the point where these three lines meet. Finally, draw a circle with its center at this point of intersection that passes through one vertex of the triangle. It will automatically pass through the other two vertices.

3. *Sample answer:* Right triangles are the only kind of triangles that have one of the points of intersection on the vertex of the triangle; While all segment types can be inside the triangle, only the perpendicular bisectors and altitudes can be on or outside the triangle.

ANSWERS

1. 15; Because $\overline{SW} \cong \overline{UW}$ and $\overrightarrow{VW} \perp \overline{SU}$, point V is on the perpendicular bisector of $\overline{SU}$. So, by the Perpendicular Bisector Theorem (Thm. 6.1), $SV = UV$. So, $2x + 11 = 8x - 1$, and the solution is $x = 2$, which means that $UV = 8x - 1 = 8(2) - 1 = 15$.

2. 18; $\overrightarrow{SQ}$ is an angle bisector of $\angle PSR$, $\overrightarrow{PQ} \perp \overrightarrow{SP}$, and $\overrightarrow{RQ} \perp \overrightarrow{SR}$. So, by the Angle Bisector Theorem (Thm. 6.3), $PQ = RQ$. So, $6x = 3x + 9$, and the solution is $x = 3$, which means that $QP = 6x = 6(3) = 18$.

3. 59°; Because J is equidistant from $\overrightarrow{GH}$ and $\overrightarrow{GK}$, $\overrightarrow{GJ}$ bisects $\angle HGK$ by the Angle Bisector Theorem (Thm. 6.3). This means that $5x - 4 = 4x + 3$, and the solution is $x = 7$. So, $m\angle JGK = 4x + 3 = 4(7) + 3 = 31°$. So, by the Triangle Sum Theorem (Thm. 5.1), $m\angle GJK = 180 - 90 - 31 = 59°$.

4. $(-2, -1)$

5. $(7, 5)$

6. 11

7. 15

8. 26

9. $(3, 2)$

10. $(-4, -4)$

11. inside; $(0, 4)$

12. on; $(7, -4)$

13. **a.** incenter; angle bisectors

   b. HL Congruence Theorem (Thm. 5.9)

   c. 3.9 cm; Because $\triangle BGF \cong \triangle BGE$ and corresponding parts of congruent triangles are congruent, $BE = BF = 3$ centimeters. So, $AE = 10 - 3 = 7$ centimeters. Then, you can use the Pythagorean Theorem for $\triangle AEG$ to find EG, which is the radius of the wheel.

14. **a.** centroid

   b. no; This point is not equidistant from the three cities. The circumcenter would be equidistant from the cities.

6.1–6.3   Quiz

Find the indicated measure. Explain your reasoning. *(Section 6.1)*

1. UV

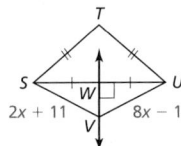

2. QP

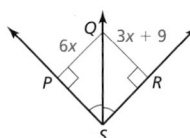

3. $m\angle GJK$

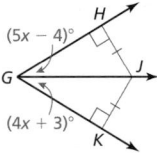

Find the coordinates of the circumcenter of the triangle with the given vertices. *(Section 6.2)*

4. $A(-4, 2), B(-4, -4), C(0, -4)$

5. $D(3, 5), E(7, 9), F(11, 5)$

The incenter of $\triangle ABC$ is point N. Use the given information to find the indicated measure. *(Section 6.2)*

6. $NQ = 2x + 1, NR = 4x - 9$
Find NS.

7. $NU = -3x + 6, NV = -5x$
Find NT.

8. $NZ = 4x - 10, NY = 3x - 1$
Find NW.

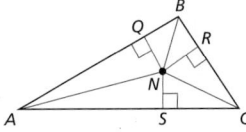 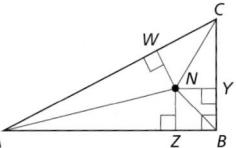 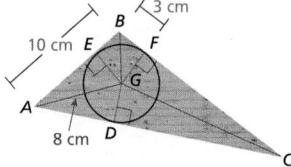

Find the coordinates of the centroid of the triangle with the given vertices. *(Section 6.3)*

9. $J(-1, 2), K(5, 6), L(5, -2)$

10. $M(-8, -6), N(-4, -2), P(0, -4)$

Tell whether the orthocenter is *inside*, *on*, or *outside* the triangle. Then find its coordinates. *(Section 6.3)*

11. $T(-2, 5), U(0, 1), V(2, 5)$

12. $X(-1, -4), Y(7, -4), Z(7, 4)$

13. A woodworker is cutting the largest wheel possible from a triangular scrap of wood. The wheel just touches each side of the triangle, as shown. *(Section 6.2)*

   a. Which point of concurrency is the center of the circle? What type of segments are $\overline{BG}$, $\overline{CG}$, and $\overline{AG}$?

   b. Which theorem can you use to prove that $\triangle BGF \cong \triangle BGE$?

   c. Find the radius of the wheel to the nearest tenth of a centimeter. Justify your answer.

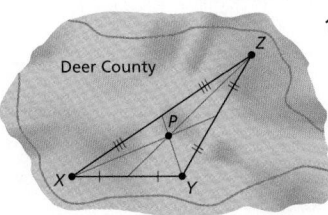

14. The Deer County Parks Committee plans to build a park at point P, equidistant from the three largest cities labeled X, Y, and Z. The map shown was created by the committee. *(Section 6.2 and Section 6.3)*

   a. Which point of concurrency did the committee use as the location of the park?

   b. Did the committee use the best point of concurrency for the location of the park? If not, which point would be better to use? Explain.

Deer County

Dynamic Teaching Tools

Dynamic Assessment & Progress Monitoring Tool
Lesson Planning Tool
Interactive Whiteboard Lesson Library
Dynamic Classroom with Dynamic Investigations

Overview of Section 6.4

Introduction

- This lesson presents the last special segment in a triangle, the midsegment. The *midsegment* connects the midpoints of two sides of a triangle. It is parallel to the third side and half its length.
- The Triangle Midsegment Theorem (Thm. 6.8) is proven with a coordinate proof, integrating algebraic skills.

Resources

- Tracing paper is helpful when the explorations are done by paper folding.

Teaching Strategy

- If you do not have access to software, an alternate way to introduce this lesson would be through a paper-folding activity or a compass construction activity. It is powerful for students to explore and discover the properties of a midsegment.
- Give directions similar to what is written in the explorations for students to paper fold (or construct) the midsegments. Once all three midsegments are folded (or constructed), the construction can be used for Exploration 2.
- **Extension:** Paper fold the three midsegments. Cut out the original triangle. The three outer triangles will fold up to make a pyramid.

Extensions

- Have students investigate the Sierpinski triangle. The images are related to the midsegments of a triangle. (See Exercise 25.)

Pacing Suggestion

- The explorations allow students to explore and discover two properties of a midsegment that will be stated as a theorem in the formal lesson. When students have finished the explorations, transition to the formal lesson.

**Common Core
State Standards**

HSG-CO.C.10 Prove theorems about triangles.

HSG-MG.A.1 Use geometric shapes, their measures, and their properties to describe objects (e.g., modeling a tree trunk or a human torso as a cylinder).

Exploration

Motivate

- Show a photo of a roof truss that contains a midsegment. More than likely, it will have two midsegments, as shown at the right in the Howe roof truss design.
- Trace lines over the midsegments and ask students whether they have any observations about the segments (not the lines).
- Explain to students that in this lesson they will explore properties of the midsegment.

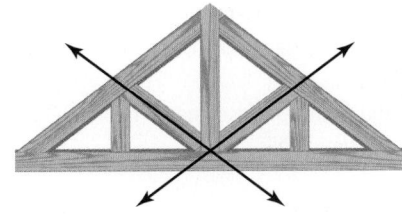

Exploration 1

- This is a straightforward construction using dynamic geometric software. Students should be comfortable at this point knowing that the triangle will be manipulated so that various cases can be explored.
- **?** "What conjecture can you make about midsegment $\overline{DE}$?" Students should mention that it is parallel to side $\overline{AC}$ and also half the length of side $\overline{AC}$.
- **Extension:** If time permits, have students construct the midsegment of $\triangle DBE$. Ask students whether their conjecture for midsegment $\overline{DE}$ is also valid for the new midsegment.

Exploration 2

- This exploration is an extension of the previous exploration.
- **MP3 Construct Viable Arguments and Critique the Reasoning of Others:** There are a number of conjectures that students will make about the triangles formed when all three midsegments are constructed. The conjectures are likely connected to the conjectures made for a single midsegment. In each case, ask students to consider how they might prove their conjectures.
- Students may state that the four smaller triangles formed are congruent, that the four triangles have the same areas, and they have the same perimeters. If students compare the small triangles to $\triangle ABC$, they may also say that the perimeter of each small triangle is $\frac{1}{2}$ the perimeter of $\triangle ABC$ and the area of each triangle is $\frac{1}{4}$ the area of $\triangle ABC$.
- Be sure that students click and drag on different vertices to see whether their conjectures hold true for various triangles.

Communicate Your Answer

- Students should state that the midsegment of a triangle is parallel to the third side of the triangle and half the length of the third side.

Connecting to Next Step

- The explorations are related to the theorem presented in the lesson, helping students make sense of the theorem before proving it to be true.

6.4 The Triangle Midsegment Theorem

Essential Question How are the midsegments of a triangle related to the sides of the triangle?

EXPLORATION 1 Midsegments of a Triangle

Work with a partner. Use dynamic geometry software. Draw any △ABC.

a. Plot midpoint D of $\overline{AB}$ and midpoint E of $\overline{BC}$. Draw $\overline{DE}$, which is a *midsegment* of △ABC.

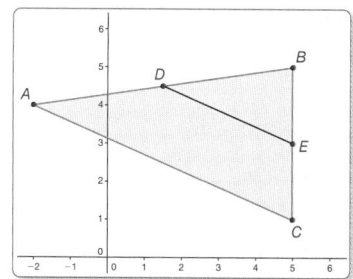

Sample

Points
A(−2, 4)
B(5, 5)
C(5, 1)
D(1.5, 4.5)
E(5, 3)

Segments
BC = 4
AC = 7.62
AB = 7.07
DE = ?

b. Compare the slope and length of $\overline{DE}$ with the slope and length of $\overline{AC}$.

c. Write a conjecture about the relationships between the midsegments and sides of a triangle. Test your conjecture by drawing the other midsegments of △ABC, dragging vertices to change △ABC, and noting whether the relationships hold.

CONSTRUCTING VIABLE ARGUMENTS

To be proficient in math, you need to make conjectures and build a logical progression of statements to explore the truth of your conjectures.

EXPLORATION 2 Midsegments of a Triangle

Work with a partner. Use dynamic geometry software. Draw any △ABC.

a. Draw all three midsegments of △ABC.

b. Use the drawing to write a conjecture about the triangle formed by the midsegments of the original triangle.

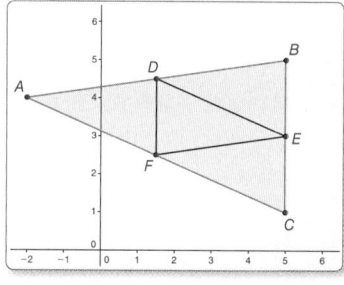

Sample

Points	Segments
A(−2, 4)	BC = 4
B(5, 5)	AC = 7.62
C(5, 1)	AB = 7.07
D(1.5, 4.5)	DE = ?
E(5, 3)	DF = ?
	EF = ?

Communicate Your Answer

3. How are the midsegments of a triangle related to the sides of the triangle?

4. In △RST, $\overline{UV}$ is the midsegment connecting the midpoints of $\overline{RS}$ and $\overline{ST}$. Given UV = 12, find RT.

Section 6.4 The Triangle Midsegment Theorem **329**

ANSWERS

1. a. Check students' work.

   b. *Sample answer:* The slopes are the same (−0.43). Because $3.81 = \frac{1}{2}(7.62)$, $DE = \frac{1}{2}AC$.

   c. The segment connecting the midpoints of two sides of a triangle is parallel to the third side and is half as long as that side.

2. a. Check students' work.

   b. The triangle formed by the midsegments of a triangle, △EFD, is similar to the original triangle, △ABC, and has a scale factor of $\frac{1}{2}$.

3. Each midsegment is parallel to a side of the triangle and is half as long as that side.

4. 24

Extra Example 1

In $\triangle RST$, show that midsegment $\overline{MN}$ is parallel to $\overline{RS}$ and that $MN = \frac{1}{2}RS$.

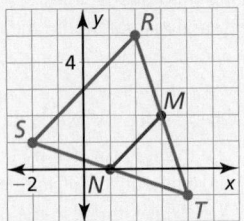

The vertices of the triangle are $R(2, 5)$, $S(-2, 1)$, and $T(4, -1)$.

Find the coordinates of midpoints M and N. $M = \left(\dfrac{2+4}{2}, \dfrac{5+(-1)}{2}\right) = (3, 2)$

and $N = \left(\dfrac{-2+4}{2}, \dfrac{1+(-1)}{2}\right) = (1, 0)$.

Compare the slopes of $\overline{MN}$ and $\overline{RS}$. The slope of $\overline{MN} = \dfrac{2-0}{3-1} = 1$.

The slope of $\overline{RS} = \dfrac{5-1}{2-(-2)} = 1$. Because the slopes are the same, $\overline{MN} \parallel \overline{RS}$.

Compare the lengths of $\overline{MN}$ and $\overline{RS}$.

$MN = \sqrt{(3-1)^2 + (2-0)^2} = \sqrt{8} = 2\sqrt{2}$

and $RS = \sqrt{(2-(-2))^2 + (5-1)^2}$

$= \sqrt{32} = 4\sqrt{2}$.

Because $2\sqrt{2} = \frac{1}{2}(4\sqrt{2})$, $MN = \frac{1}{2}RS$.

MONITORING PROGRESS ANSWERS

1. Because the slopes of $\overline{DE}$ and $\overline{AC}$ are the same $\left(\frac{3}{2}\right)$, $\overline{DE} \parallel \overline{AC}$.

   $DE = \sqrt{13}$ and $AC = 2\sqrt{13}$. Because $\sqrt{13} = \frac{1}{2}(2\sqrt{13})$, $DE = \frac{1}{2}AC$.

2. $E(2, 2)$, $F(3, -3)$; Because the slopes of $\overline{EF}$ and $\overline{AB}$ are the same (-5), $\overline{EF} \parallel \overline{AB}$. $EF = \sqrt{26}$ and $AB = 2\sqrt{26}$. Because $\sqrt{26} = \frac{1}{2}(2\sqrt{26})$, $EF = \frac{1}{2}AB$.

6.4 Lesson

Core Vocabulary

midsegment of a triangle, p. 330

Previous
midpoint
parallel
slope
coordinate proof

READING

In the figure for Example 1, midsegment $\overline{MN}$ can be called "the midsegment opposite $\overline{JL}$."

What You Will Learn

▶ Use midsegments of triangles in the coordinate plane.
▶ Use the Triangle Midsegment Theorem to find distances.

Using the Midsegment of a Triangle

A **midsegment of a triangle** is a segment that connects the midpoints of two sides of the triangle. Every triangle has three midsegments, which form the *midsegment triangle*.

The midsegments of $\triangle ABC$ at the right are $\overline{MP}$, $\overline{MN}$, and $\overline{NP}$. The *midsegment triangle* is $\triangle MNP$.

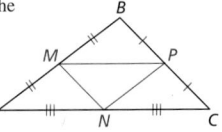

EXAMPLE 1   **Using Midsegments in the Coordinate Plane**

In $\triangle JKL$, show that midsegment $\overline{MN}$ is parallel to $\overline{JL}$ and that $MN = \frac{1}{2}JL$.

SOLUTION

Step 1   Find the coordinates of M and N by finding the midpoints of $\overline{JK}$ and $\overline{KL}$.

$$M\left(\frac{-6 + (-2)}{2}, \frac{1 + 5}{2}\right) = M\left(\frac{-8}{2}, \frac{6}{2}\right) = M(-4, 3)$$

$$N\left(\frac{-2 + 2}{2}, \frac{5 + (-1)}{2}\right) = N\left(\frac{0}{2}, \frac{4}{2}\right) = N(0, 2)$$

Step 2   Find and compare the slopes of $\overline{MN}$ and $\overline{JL}$.

$$\text{slope of } \overline{MN} = \frac{2 - 3}{0 - (-4)} = -\frac{1}{4} \qquad \text{slope of } \overline{JL} = \frac{-1 - 1}{2 - (-6)} = -\frac{2}{8} = -\frac{1}{4}$$

▶ Because the slopes are the same, $\overline{MN}$ is parallel to $\overline{JL}$.

Step 3   Find and compare the lengths of $\overline{MN}$ and $\overline{JL}$.

$$MN = \sqrt{[0 - (-4)]^2 + (2 - 3)^2} = \sqrt{16 + 1} = \sqrt{17}$$

$$JL = \sqrt{[2 - (-6)]^2 + (-1 - 1)^2} = \sqrt{64 + 4} = \sqrt{68} = 2\sqrt{17}$$

▶ Because $\sqrt{17} = \frac{1}{2}(2\sqrt{17})$, $MN = \frac{1}{2}JL$.

Monitoring Progress   Help in English and Spanish at *BigIdeasMath.com*

Use the graph of $\triangle ABC$.

1. In $\triangle ABC$, show that midsegment $\overline{DE}$ is parallel to $\overline{AC}$ and that $DE = \frac{1}{2}AC$.

2. Find the coordinates of the endpoints of midsegment $\overline{EF}$, which is opposite $\overline{AB}$. Show that $\overline{EF}$ is parallel to $\overline{AB}$ and that $EF = \frac{1}{2}AB$.

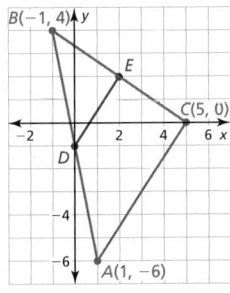

Laurie's Notes   Teacher Actions

- Students will be familiar with midsegments and the midsegment triangle from the explorations.
- **Thumbs Up:** Example 1 tests the conjectures made about a midsegment. Verify with *Thumbs Up* that students understand the problem. Give partners time to complete the example.
- Students may not recognize that $MN = \frac{1}{2}JL$ unless they simplify the radical $\sqrt{68}$. Review this skill if needed.

Using the Triangle Midsegment Theorem

🔄 Theorem

Theorem 6.8 Triangle Midsegment Theorem

The segment connecting the midpoints of two sides of a triangle is parallel to the third side and is half as long as that side.

$\overline{DE}$ is a midsegment of $\triangle ABC$, $\overline{DE} \parallel \overline{AC}$, and $DE = \frac{1}{2}AC$.

Proof Example 2, p. 331; Monitoring Progress Question 3, p. 331; Ex. 22, p. 334

EXAMPLE 2 Proving the Triangle Midsegment Theorem

Write a coordinate proof of the Triangle Midsegment Theorem for one midsegment.

Given $\overline{DE}$ is a midsegment of $\triangle OBC$.

Prove $\overline{DE} \parallel \overline{OC}$ and $DE = \frac{1}{2}OC$

SOLUTION

Step 1 Place $\triangle OBC$ in a coordinate plane and assign coordinates. Because you are finding midpoints, use 2p, 2q, and 2r. Then find the coordinates of D and E.

$$D\left(\frac{2q + 0}{2}, \frac{2r + 0}{2}\right) = D(q, r) \qquad E\left(\frac{2q + 2p}{2}, \frac{2r + 0}{2}\right) = E(q + p, r)$$

Step 2 Prove $\overline{DE} \parallel \overline{OC}$. The y-coordinates of D and E are the same, so $\overline{DE}$ has a slope of 0. $\overline{OC}$ is on the x-axis, so its slope is 0.

▶ Because their slopes are the same, $\overline{DE} \parallel \overline{OC}$.

Step 3 Prove $DE = \frac{1}{2}OC$. Use the Ruler Postulate (Post. 1.1) to find DE and OC.

$$DE = |(q + p) - q| = p \qquad OC = |2p - 0| = 2p$$

▶ Because $p = \frac{1}{2}(2p)$, $DE = \frac{1}{2}OC$.

Monitoring Progress 🔊 Help in English and Spanish at *BigIdeasMath.com*

3. In Example 2, find the coordinates of F, the midpoint of $\overline{OC}$. Show that $\overline{FE} \parallel \overline{OB}$ and $FE = \frac{1}{2}OB$.

EXAMPLE 3 Using the Triangle Midsegment Theorem

Triangles are used for strength in roof trusses. In the diagram, $\overline{UV}$ and $\overline{VW}$ are midsegments of $\triangle RST$. Find UV and RS.

SOLUTION

$$UV = \frac{1}{2} \cdot RT = \frac{1}{2}(90 \text{ in.}) = 45 \text{ in.}$$

$$RS = 2 \cdot VW = 2(57 \text{ in.}) = 114 \text{ in.}$$

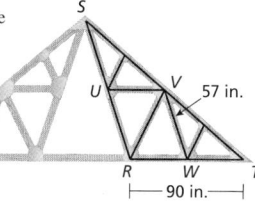

Section 6.4   The Triangle Midsegment Theorem   **331**

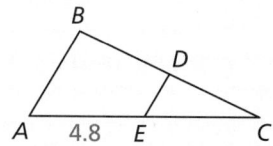

Laurie's Notes   **Teacher Actions**

- State the Triangle Midsegment Theorem. *Note:* This theorem is sometimes presented later in the course after similar triangles have been introduced. Logically, it fits with the other special segments in a triangle.
- Explain the *Study Tip* to students.
- **?** "How can you find the coordinates of points D and E?" Use the Midpoint Formula. "How will you show that the midsegment is parallel to $\overline{OC}$?" Find the slope of each segment. "How will you show $DE = \frac{1}{2}OC$?" Use the Distance Formula. Give partners time to complete the proof.

Extra Example 4

In the figure in Example 4, $CF = FB$ and $CD = DA$. Which segments must be parallel? $\overline{DF}$ and $\overline{AB}$

Extra Example 5

A walking path $\overline{BD}$ in a park intersects the sides of the park at their midpoints. You walk from park corner A to walking path $\overline{BD}$, over the path to the other side of the park, up to corner E, and then back down to your starting point. How many yards do you walk?

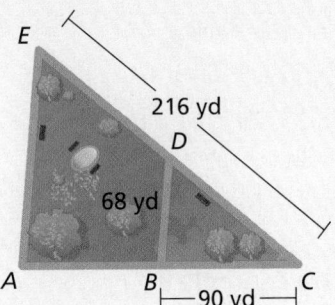

402 yards

MONITORING PROGRESS ANSWERS

4.

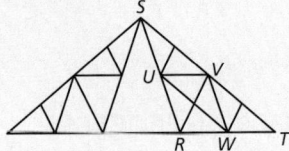

midsegment: $\overline{UW}$; 81 in.

5. $\overline{DF}$ is a midsegment, $\overline{DF} \parallel \overline{AB}$, $\overline{DF} = \frac{1}{2}AB$

6. yes; The distance along the new route is 6.775 miles.

EXAMPLE 4 **Using the Triangle Midsegment Theorem**

In the kaleidoscope image, $\overline{AE} \cong \overline{BE}$ and $\overline{AD} \cong \overline{CD}$. Show that $\overline{CB} \parallel \overline{DE}$.

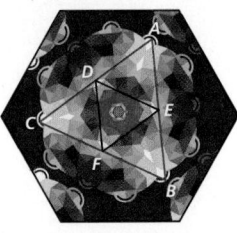

SOLUTION

Because $\overline{AE} \cong \overline{BE}$ and $\overline{AD} \cong \overline{CD}$, E is the midpoint of $\overline{AB}$ and D is the midpoint of $\overline{AC}$ by definition. Then $\overline{DE}$ is a midsegment of $\triangle ABC$ by definition and $\overline{CB} \parallel \overline{DE}$ by the Triangle Midsegment Theorem.

EXAMPLE 5 **Modeling with Mathematics**

Pear Street intersects Cherry Street and Peach Street at their midpoints. Your home is at point P. You leave your home and jog down Cherry Street to Plum Street, over Plum Street to Peach Street, up Peach Street to Pear Street, over Pear Street to Cherry Street, and then back home up Cherry Street. About how many miles do you jog?

SOLUTION

1. **Understand the Problem** You know the distances from your home to Plum Street along Peach Street, from Peach Street to Cherry Street along Plum Street, and from Pear Street to your home along Cherry Street. You need to find the other distances on your route, then find the total number of miles you jog.

2. **Make a Plan** By definition, you know that Pear Street is a midsegment of the triangle formed by the other three streets. Use the Triangle Midsegment Theorem to find the length of Pear Street and the definition of midsegment to find the length of Cherry Street. Then add the distances along your route.

3. **Solve the Problem**

   length of Pear Street $= \frac{1}{2} \cdot$ (length of Plum St.) $= \frac{1}{2}(1.4$ mi$) = 0.7$ mi

   length of Cherry Street $= 2 \cdot$ (length from P to Pear St.) $= 2(1.3$ mi$) = 2.6$ mi

   distance along your route: $2.6 + 1.4 + \frac{1}{2}(2.25) + 0.7 + 1.3 = 7.125$

   ▶ So, you jog about 7 miles.

4. **Look Back** Use compatible numbers to check that your answer is reasonable.

   total distance:

   $$2.6 + 1.4 + \tfrac{1}{2}(2.25) + 0.7 + 1.3 \approx 2.5 + 1.5 + 1 + 0.5 + 1.5 = 7 \checkmark$$

Monitoring Progress 🔊 Help in English and Spanish at *BigIdeasMath.com*

4. Copy the diagram in Example 3. Draw and name the third midsegment. Then find the length of $\overline{VS}$ when the length of the third midsegment is 81 inches.

5. In Example 4, if F is the midpoint of $\overline{CB}$, what do you know about $\overline{DF}$?

6. **WHAT IF?** In Example 5, you jog down Peach Street to Plum Street, over Plum Street to Cherry Street, up Cherry Street to Pear Street, over Pear Street to Peach Street, and then back home up Peach Street. Do you jog more miles in Example 5? Explain.

Laurie's Notes   Teacher Actions

- If you have a kaleidoscope, bring it to class for students to view. Traditional kaleidoscopes will have several midsegments visible.
- **Think-Pair-Share:** Have students work independently to answer Example 5. When students have finished, discuss the answers.
- ❓**Probing Question:** "If you found the segment midway between Pear Street and Plum Street and parallel to both, what would its length be?" 1.05 miles

Closure

- A midsegment triangle has side lengths of 3 inches, 4 inches, and 5 inches. Sketch the original triangle. What are the lengths of its sides? Check students' work. The triangle will have side lengths of 6 inches, 8 inches, and 10 inches.

Vocabulary and Core Concept Check

1. **VOCABULARY** The _____ of a triangle is a segment that connects the midpoints of two sides of the triangle.

2. **COMPLETE THE SENTENCE** If $\overline{DE}$ is the midsegment opposite $\overline{AC}$ in $\triangle ABC$, then $\overline{DE} \parallel \overline{AC}$ and $DE =$ ___AC by the Triangle Midsegment Theorem (Theorem 6.8).

Monitoring Progress and Modeling with Mathematics

In Exercises 3–6, use the graph of $\triangle ABC$ with midsegments $\overline{DE}, \overline{EF}$, and $\overline{DF}$. *(See Example 1.)*

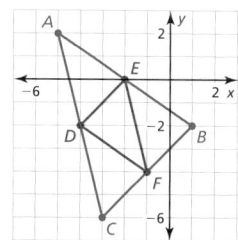

3. Find the coordinates of points D, E, and F.

4. Show that $\overline{DE}$ is parallel to $\overline{CB}$ and that $DE = \frac{1}{2}CB$.

5. Show that $\overline{EF}$ is parallel to $\overline{AC}$ and that $EF = \frac{1}{2}AC$.

6. Show that $\overline{DF}$ is parallel to $\overline{AB}$ and that $DF = \frac{1}{2}AB$.

In Exercises 7–10, $\overline{DE}$ is a midsegment of $\triangle ABC$. Find the value of x. *(See Example 3.)*

7.
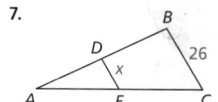

8.
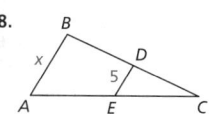

9.
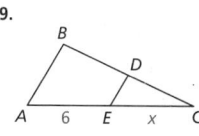

10.
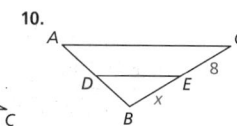

In Exercises 11–16, $\overline{XJ} \cong \overline{JY}, \overline{YL} \cong \overline{LZ}$, and $\overline{XK} \cong \overline{KZ}$. Copy and complete the statement. *(See Example 4.)*

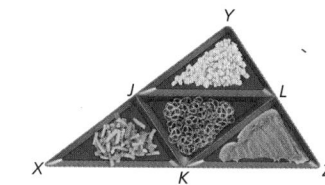

11. $\overline{JK} \parallel$ ___

12. $\overline{JL} \parallel$ ___

13. $\overline{XY} \parallel$ ___

14. $\overline{JY} \cong$ ___ $\cong$ ___

15. $\overline{JL} \cong$ ___ $\cong$ ___

16. $\overline{JK} \cong$ ___ $\cong$ ___

MATHEMATICAL CONNECTIONS In Exercises 17–19, use $\triangle GHJ$, where A, B, and C are midpoints of the sides.

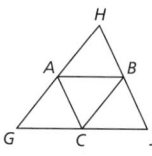

17. When $AB = 3x + 8$ and $GJ = 2x + 24$, what is AB?

18. When $AC = 3y - 5$ and $HJ = 4y + 2$, what is HB?

19. When $GH = 7z - 1$ and $CB = 4z - 3$, what is GA?

20. **ERROR ANALYSIS** Describe and correct the error.

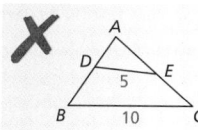

$DE = \frac{1}{2}BC$, so by the Triangle Midsegment Theorem (Thm. 6.8), $\overline{AD} \cong \overline{DB}$ and $\overline{AE} \cong \overline{EC}$.

ANSWERS

1. midsegment

2. $\frac{1}{2}$

3. $D(-4, -2)$, $E(-2, 0)$, $F(-1, -4)$

4. Because the slopes of $\overline{DE}$ and $\overline{CB}$ are the same (1), $\overline{DE} \parallel \overline{CB}$. $DE = 2\sqrt{2}$ and $CB = 4\sqrt{2}$. Because $2\sqrt{2} = \frac{1}{2}(4\sqrt{2})$, $DE = \frac{1}{2}CB$.

5. Because the slopes of $\overline{EF}$ and $\overline{AC}$ are the same (-4), $\overline{EF} \parallel \overline{AC}$. $EF = \sqrt{17}$ and $AC = 2\sqrt{17}$. Because $\sqrt{17} = \frac{1}{2}(2\sqrt{17})$, $EF = \frac{1}{2}AC$.

6. Because the slopes of $\overline{DF}$ and $\overline{AB}$ are the same $\left(-\frac{2}{3}\right)$, $\overline{DF} \parallel \overline{AB}$. $DF = \sqrt{13}$ and $AB = 2\sqrt{13}$. Because $\sqrt{13} = \frac{1}{2}(2\sqrt{13})$, $DF = \frac{1}{2}AB$.

7. $x = 13$

8. $x = 10$

9. $x = 6$

10. $x = 8$

11. $\overline{JK} \parallel \overline{YZ}$

12. $\overline{JL} \parallel \overline{XZ}$

13. $\overline{XY} \parallel \overline{KL}$

14. $\overline{JY} \cong \overline{JX} \cong \overline{KL}$

15. $\overline{JL} \cong \overline{XK} \cong \overline{KZ}$

16. $\overline{JK} \cong \overline{YL} \cong \overline{LZ}$

17. 14

18. 13

19. 17

20. $\overline{DE}$ is not parallel to $\overline{BC}$. So, $\overline{DE}$ is not a midsegment. So, according to the contrapositive of the Triangle Midsegment Theorem (Thm. 6.8), $\overline{DE}$ does not connect the midpoints of $\overline{AC}$ and $\overline{AB}$.

ANSWERS

21. 45 ft

22–29. See Additional Answers.

Mini-Assessment

1. *A*, *B*, and *C* are the midpoints of the sides of △*GHJ*. *AB* = 3.4, *BC* = 4.2, and *AC* = 3.8. Find the perimeter of △*GHJ*.

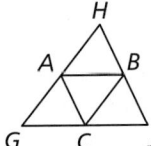

22.8

2. In △*RST*, show that midsegment $\overline{MN}$ is parallel to $\overline{ST}$.

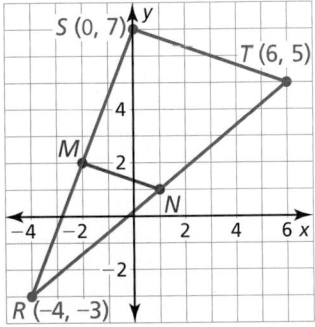

The coordinates of midpoints *M* and *N* are *M*(−2, 2) and *N*(1, 1). The slopes of both $\overline{MN}$ and $\overline{ST}$ = $-\frac{1}{3}$.

Because the slopes are the same, $\overline{MN}$ and $\overline{ST}$ are parallel.

3. $\overline{DE}$ is a midsegment of △*ABC*. $\overline{FG}$ is a midsegment of △*EDC*. *AE* = 22. Find *FC*.

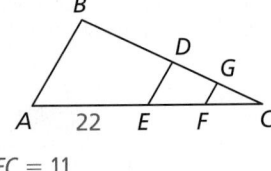

FC = 11

334   Chapter 6

---

21. MODELING WITH MATHEMATICS The distance between consecutive bases on a baseball field is 90 feet. A second baseman stands halfway between first base and second base, a shortstop stands halfway between second base and third base, and a pitcher stands halfway between first base and third base. Find the distance between the shortstop and the pitcher. *(See Example 5.)*

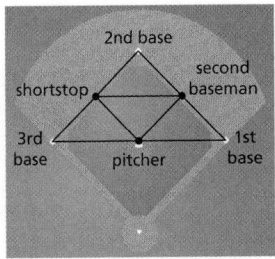

22. PROVING A THEOREM Use the figure from Example 2 to prove the Triangle Midsegment Theorem (Theorem 6.8) for midsegment $\overline{DF}$, where *F* is the midpoint of $\overline{OC}$. *(See Example 2.)*

23. CRITICAL THINKING $\overline{XY}$ is a midsegment of △*LMN*. Suppose $\overline{DE}$ is called a "quarter segment" of △*LMN*. What do you think an "eighth segment" would be? Make conjectures about the properties of a quarter segment and an eighth segment. Use variable coordinates to verify your conjectures.

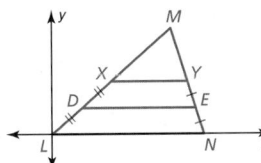

24. THOUGHT PROVOKING Find a real-life object that uses midsegments as part of its structure. Print a photograph of the object and identify the midsegments of one of the triangles in the structure.

---

25. ABSTRACT REASONING To create the design shown, shade the triangle formed by the three midsegments of the triangle. Then repeat the process for each unshaded triangle.

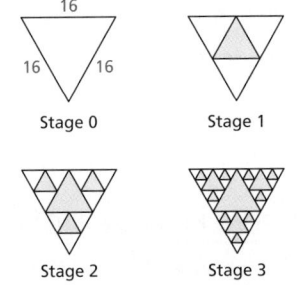

a. What is the perimeter of the shaded triangle in Stage 1?

b. What is the total perimeter of all the shaded triangles in Stage 2?

c. What is the total perimeter of all the shaded triangles in Stage 3?

26. HOW DO YOU SEE IT? Explain how you know that the yellow triangle is the midsegment triangle of the red triangle in the pattern of floor tiles shown.

27. ATTENDING TO PRECISION The points *P*(2, 1), *Q*(4, 5), and *R*(7, 4) are the midpoints of the sides of a triangle. Graph the three midsegments. Then show how to use your graph and the properties of midsegments to draw the original triangle. Give the coordinates of each vertex.

Maintaining Mathematical Proficiency Reviewing what you learned in previous grades and lessons

Find a counterexample to show that the conjecture is false. *(Section 2.2)*

28. The difference of two numbers is always less than the greater number.

29. An isosceles triangle is always equilateral.

If students need help...	If students got it...
Resources by Chapter • Practice A and Practice B • Puzzle Time	Resources by Chapter • Enrichment and Extension • Cumulative Review
Student Journal • Practice	Start the *next* Section
Differentiating the Lesson Skills Review Handbook	

Overview of Section 6.5

Introduction

- This lesson presents two theorems that relate the side lengths and angle measures of a triangle. This relationship is first discovered in the explorations and then proven in the lesson using an indirect proof.
- The indirect proof method can be challenging for students to understand and grasp. It feels unnatural to assume something is true that is the negation of what you were first trying to prove true.
- The Triangle Inequality Theorem (Thm. 6.11) is introduced, and students use the theorem to find possible lengths for the third side of a triangle when two side lengths are known.

Formative Assessment Tips

- **Muddiest Point:** This technique is the opposite of *Point of Most Significance* (Section 3.4). Students are asked to reflect on the most difficult or confusing point in the lesson. Their written comments are collected at the end of the lesson so that the following day's instruction can address the confusion.
- This technique can be used at any time during instruction.
- It is important for teachers to know whether there was a point in the lesson that was confusing for students so that the lesson can be modified. Share with students what you learned from their reflections. Students will take the reflections more seriously when they are valued and used.

Applications

- When discussing the Triangle Inequality Theorem (Thm. 6.11), ask students how many have cut across lawns or parking lots instead of following sidewalks. It is likely that all students have. Long before giving a name to the theorem, students know that cutting across a diagonal is faster (shorter distance) than sticking to the sidewalks.

Pacing Suggestion

- The explorations allow students to explore and discover relationships between angle measures and side lengths of a triangle that will be stated as theorems in the formal lesson. When students have finished the explorations, transition to the formal lesson.

Exploration

Motivate
- Give each student three straws of various lengths, some of which form triangles and some of which do not. Have students investigate when three straws can form a triangle and when they cannot. Tell students that they will describe and examine this property in the lesson.

Exploration 1
- Students will be able to quickly measure the sides and angles of scalene $\triangle ABC$.
- Students may not observe a connection between the angle measures and side lengths. When students order the side lengths, have them write the name of the side, not simply the measure. When they order the angle measures, have them write the name of the angle, not simply the measure.
- If students do not observe any relationship, suggest that they complete part (c).
- **? Probing Question:** "If $\angle A$ has the greatest measure, what side would you expect to be the longest?" This may result in students observing the relationship between angle measures and side lengths in a triangle.

Exploration 2
- **MP6 Attend to Precision:** When asked to compare each side length with the sum of the lengths of the other two sides, students should be thinking about less than ($<$) and greater than ($>$). This is not always obvious to students who try to make more out of "compare" than it is.
- When you click and drag a vertex toward the opposite side so that the triangle begins to collapse, the sum of the two side lengths gets very close to the length of the third side.

Communicate Your Answer
- Students should state that the longest side of a triangle is opposite the largest angle and the shortest side is opposite the smallest angle.

Connecting to Next Step
- The explorations are related to the theorems presented in the lesson, one of which will be proven using an indirect proof.

6.5 Indirect Proof and Inequalities in One Triangle

Essential Question How are the sides related to the angles of a triangle? How are any two sides of a triangle related to the third side?

EXPLORATION 1 Comparing Angle Measures and Side Lengths

Work with a partner. Use dynamic geometry software. Draw any scalene △*ABC*.

a. Find the side lengths and angle measures of the triangle.

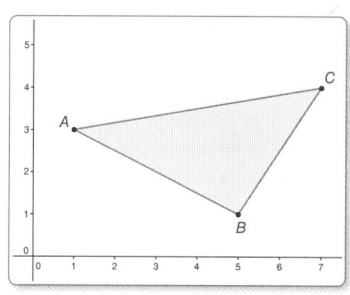

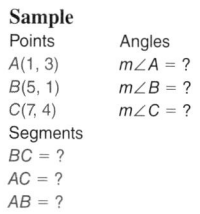

Sample

Points	Angles
$A(1, 3)$	$m\angle A = ?$
$B(5, 1)$	$m\angle B = ?$
$C(7, 4)$	$m\angle C = ?$

Segments
$BC = ?$
$AC = ?$
$AB = ?$

b. Order the side lengths. Order the angle measures. What do you observe?

c. Drag the vertices of △*ABC* to form new triangles. Record the side lengths and angle measures in a table. Write a conjecture about your findings.

EXPLORATION 2 A Relationship of the Side Lengths of a Triangle

Work with a partner. Use dynamic geometry software. Draw any △*ABC*.

a. Find the side lengths of the triangle.

b. Compare each side length with the sum of the other two side lengths.

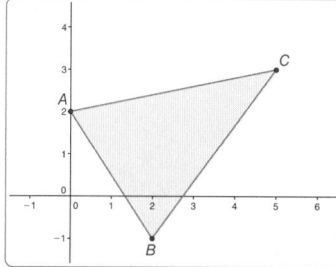

Sample

Points
$A(0, 2)$
$B(2, -1)$
$C(5, 3)$

Segments
$BC = ?$
$AC = ?$
$AB = ?$

c. Drag the vertices of △*ABC* to form new triangles and repeat parts (a) and (b). Organize your results in a table. Write a conjecture about your findings.

Communicate Your Answer

3. How are the sides related to the angles of a triangle? How are any two sides of a triangle related to the third side?

4. Is it possible for a triangle to have side lengths of 3, 4, and 10? Explain.

Section 6.5 Indirect Proof and Inequalities in One Triangle **335**

ATTENDING TO PRECISION

To be proficient in math, you need to express numerical answers with a degree of precision appropriate for the content.

Dynamic Teaching Tools

Dynamic Assessment & Progress Monitoring Tool

Lesson Planning Tool

Interactive Whiteboard Lesson Library

Dynamic Classroom with Dynamic Investigations

ANSWERS

1. a. Check students' work. (For sample in text, $AB \approx 4.47$, $AC \approx 6.08$, $BC \approx 3.61$, $m\angle A \approx 36.03°$, $m\angle B \approx 97.13°$, and $m\angle C \approx 46.85°$.)

b. Check students' work. (For sample in text, $BC < AB < AC$ and $m\angle A < m\angle C < m\angle B$.); The shortest side is across from the smallest angle, and the longest side is across from the largest angle.

c. See Additional Answers.

2. a. Check students' work. (For sample in text, $AB \approx 3.61$, $AC \approx 5.10$, and $BC = 5$.)

b. For the sample in the text, $BC = 5 < 8.71 = AC + AB$, $AC = 5.10 < 8.61 = BC + AB$, and $AB = 3.61 < 10.10 = BC + AC$.

c. See Additional Answers.

3. The largest angle is opposite the longest side, and the smallest angle is opposite the shortest side; The sum of any two side lengths is greater than the third side length.

4. no; The sum $3 + 4$ is not greater than 10, and it is not possible to form a triangle when the sum of the lengths of the two sides is less than the length of the third side.

Extra Example 1

Write an indirect proof.

Given Line ℓ is not parallel to line k.

Prove $\angle 3$ and $\angle 5$ are not supplementary.

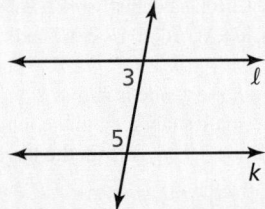

Assume temporarily that $\angle 3$ and $\angle 5$ are supplementary. By the Converse of the Consecutive Interior Angles Theorem (Thm. 3.8), line ℓ is parallel to line k. This contradicts the given information. So, the assumption must be false, which proves that $\angle 3$ and $\angle 5$ are not supplementary.

MONITORING PROGRESS ANSWER

1. Assume temporarily that $\triangle ABC$ is a scalene triangle with $\angle A \cong \angle B$. By the Converse of Base Angles Theorem (Thm. 5.7), if $\angle A \cong \angle B$, then the opposite sides are congruent: $\overline{RC} \cong \overline{AC}$. A scalene triangle cannot have two congruent sides. So, this contradicts the given information. So, the assumption that $\triangle ABC$ is a scalene triangle with two congruent angles must be false, which proves that a scalene triangle cannot have two congruent angles.

6.5 Lesson

Core Vocabulary

indirect proof, *p. 336*

Previous
proof
inequality

What You Will Learn

▶ Write indirect proofs.

▶ List sides and angles of a triangle in order by size.

▶ Use the Triangle Inequality Theorem to find possible side lengths of triangles.

Writing an Indirect Proof

Suppose a student looks around the cafeteria, concludes that hamburgers are not being served, and explains as follows.

> *At first, I assumed that we are having hamburgers because today is Tuesday, and Tuesday is usually hamburger day.*
>
> *There is always ketchup on the table when we have hamburgers, so I looked for the ketchup, but I didn't see any.*
>
> *So, my assumption that we are having hamburgers must be false.*

The student uses *indirect* reasoning. In an **indirect proof**, you start by making the temporary assumption that the desired conclusion is false. By then showing that this assumption leads to a logical impossibility, you prove the original statement true *by contradiction*.

🔄 Core Concept

How to Write an Indirect Proof (Proof by Contradiction)

Step 1 Identify the statement you want to prove. Assume temporarily that this statement is false by assuming that its opposite is true.

Step 2 Reason logically until you reach a contradiction.

Step 3 Point out that the desired conclusion must be true because the contradiction proves the temporary assumption false.

EXAMPLE 1 Writing an Indirect Proof

Write an indirect proof that in a given triangle, there can be at most one right angle.

Given $\triangle ABC$

Prove $\triangle ABC$ can have at most one right angle.

SOLUTION

Step 1 Assume temporarily that $\triangle ABC$ has two right angles. Then assume $\angle A$ and $\angle B$ are right angles.

Step 2 By the definition of right angle, $m\angle A = m\angle B = 90°$. By the Triangle Sum Theorem (Theorem 5.1), $m\angle A + m\angle B + m\angle C = 180°$. Using the Substitution Property of Equality, $90° + 90° + m\angle C = 180°$. So, $m\angle C = 0°$ by the Subtraction Property of Equality. A triangle cannot have an angle measure of $0°$. So, this contradicts the given information.

Step 3 So, the assumption that $\triangle ABC$ has two right angles must be false, which proves that $\triangle ABC$ can have at most one right angle.

READING

You have reached a *contradiction* when you have two statements that cannot both be true at the same time.

Monitoring Progress Help in English and Spanish at *BigIdeasMath.com*

1. Write an indirect proof that a scalene triangle cannot have two congruent angles.

Laurie's Notes | Teacher Actions

- A scenario is suggested as a way of introducing indirect reasoning. You may have your own favorite example. It is helpful to have a contextual, non-geometric example to discuss before explaining the steps of an indirect proof.

- **MP2 Reason Abstractly and Quantitatively:** Say, "Either a triangle has at most one right angle or more than one right angle. Both of these statements cannot be true. By showing that the latter leads to a contradiction, the former must be true." Work through Example 1, identifying the steps of an indirect proof.

Relating Sides and Angles of a Triangle

EXAMPLE 2   Relating Side Length and Angle Measure

Draw an obtuse scalene triangle. Find the largest angle and longest side and mark them in red. Find the smallest angle and shortest side and mark them in blue. What do you notice?

SOLUTION

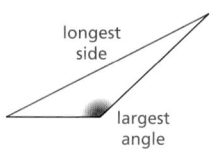
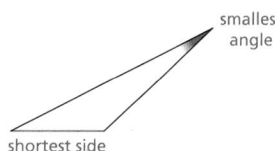

The longest side and largest angle are opposite each other.

The shortest side and smallest angle are opposite each other.

The relationships in Example 2 are true for all triangles, as stated in the two theorems below. These relationships can help you decide whether a particular arrangement of side lengths and angle measures in a triangle may be possible.

COMMON ERROR

Be careful not to confuse the symbol ∠ meaning *angle* with the symbol < meaning *is less than*. Notice that the bottom edge of the angle symbol is horizontal.

🌀 Theorems

Theorem 6.9   **Triangle Longer Side Theorem**

If one side of a triangle is longer than another side, then the angle opposite the longer side is larger than the angle opposite the shorter side.

Proof Ex. 43, p. 342

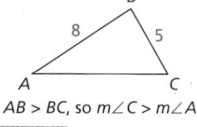

$AB > BC$, so $m\angle C > m\angle A$.

Theorem 6.10   **Triangle Larger Angle Theorem**

If one angle of a triangle is larger than another angle, then the side opposite the larger angle is longer than the side opposite the smaller angle.

Proof p. 337

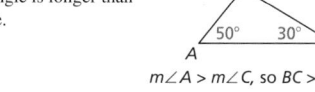

$m\angle A > m\angle C$, so $BC > AB$.

PROOF   **Triangle Larger Angle Theorem**

COMMON ERROR

Be sure to consider all cases when assuming the opposite is true.

Given $m\angle A > m\angle C$

Prove $BC > AB$

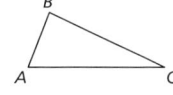

Indirect Proof

Step 1   Assume temporarily that $BC \not> AB$. Then it follows that either $BC < AB$ or $BC = AB$.

Step 2   If $BC < AB$, then $m\angle A < m\angle C$ by the Triangle Longer Side Theorem. If $BC = AB$, then $m\angle A = m\angle C$ by the Base Angles Theorem (Thm. 5.6).

Step 3   Both conclusions contradict the given statement that $m\angle A > m\angle C$. So, the temporary assumption that $BC \not> AB$ cannot be true. This proves that $BC > AB$.

Section 6.5   Indirect Proof and Inequalities in One Triangle   **337**

Differentiated Instruction

Inclusion

Have students describe how they use indirect reasoning in everyday life.

Extra Example 2

Draw an obtuse isosceles triangle. Find the largest angle and the longest side and mark them in red. Find the smallest angle and shortest side and mark them in blue. What do you notice?

Check students' drawings. *Sample drawing of an obtuse isosceles triangle:*

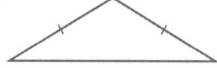

The longest side is opposite the largest angle, which is the obtuse angle. There are two congruent smallest angles. They are the base angles of the isosceles triangle, because the two sides are congruent. The two congruent sides are the smallest sides.

Laurie's Notes   Teacher Actions

- If students have worked through the explorations, the example and theorems will make sense.
- **?** "What would it sound like if you combined both theorems into one statement?" Answers will vary. Listen for something like "when you put the sides in order from longest to shortest, the angles opposite them will be in order from largest to smallest."

COMMON ERROR "If $BC \not> AB$, what do you know?" Either $BC = AB$ or $BC < AB$. Students often forget the case $BC = AB$.

Extra Example 3

List the angles of $\triangle ABC$ in order from smallest to largest.

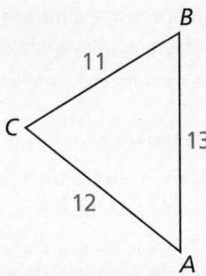

$\angle A, \angle B, \angle C$

Extra Example 4

List the sides of $\triangle ABC$ in order from shortest to longest.

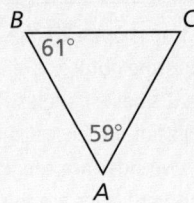

$\overline{BC}, \overline{AB}, \overline{AC}$

MONITORING PROGRESS ANSWERS

2. $\angle Q, \angle P, \angle R$
3. $\overline{ST}, \overline{RS}, \overline{RT}$

Ordering Angle Measures of a Triangle

You are constructing a stage prop that shows a large triangular mountain. The bottom edge of the mountain is about 32 feet long, the left slope is about 24 feet long, and the right slope is about 26 feet long. List the angles of $\triangle JKL$ in order from smallest to largest.

SOLUTION

Draw the triangle that represents the mountain. Label the side lengths.

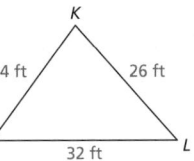

The sides from shortest to longest are $\overline{JK}$, $\overline{KL}$, and $\overline{JL}$. The angles opposite these sides are $\angle L$, $\angle J$, and $\angle K$, respectively.

▶ So, by the Triangle Longer Side Theorem, the angles from smallest to largest are $\angle L$, $\angle J$, and $\angle K$.

EXAMPLE 4 **Ordering Side Lengths of a Triangle**

List the sides of $\triangle DEF$ in order from shortest to longest.

SOLUTION

First, find $m\angle F$ using the Triangle Sum Theorem (Theorem 5.1).

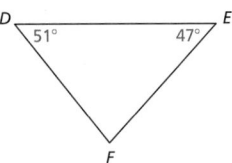

$$m\angle D + m\angle E + m\angle F = 180°$$
$$51° + 47° + m\angle F = 180°$$
$$m\angle F = 82°$$

The angles from smallest to largest are $\angle E$, $\angle D$, and $\angle F$. The sides opposite these angles are $\overline{DF}$, $\overline{EF}$, and $\overline{DE}$, respectively.

▶ So, by the Triangle Larger Angle Theorem, the sides from shortest to longest are $\overline{DF}$, $\overline{EF}$, and $\overline{DE}$.

Monitoring Progress ◄)) Help in English and Spanish at *BigIdeasMath.com*

2. List the angles of $\triangle PQR$ in order from smallest to largest.

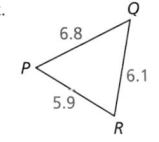

3. List the sides of $\triangle RST$ in order from shortest to longest.

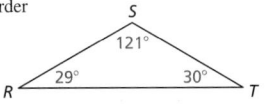

Laurie's Notes Teacher Actions

- **Popsicle Sticks:** Pose Example 3 and have students work with their partners to solve. Use *Popsicle Sticks* for students to share their results.
- ❓ **MP2** and **MP3 Construct Viable Arguments and Critique the Reasoning of Others:** "In Example 4, the diagram may not be drawn to scale. How do you know $\angle F$ is the largest angle without computing its measure?" All angles are 60° in an equiangular triangle. Because $\angle D$ and $\angle E$ are each less than 60°, $\angle F$ has to be greater than 60°.
- **Think-Pair-Share:** Have students answer Questions 2 and 3, and then share and discuss as a class.

Using the Triangle Inequality Theorem

Not every group of three segments can be used to form a triangle. The lengths of the segments must fit a certain relationship. For example, three attempted triangle constructions using segments with given lengths are shown below. Only the first group of segments forms a triangle.

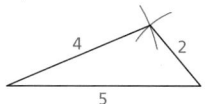 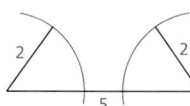 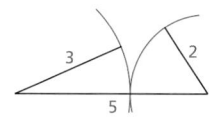

When you start with the longest side and attach the other two sides at its endpoints, you can see that the other two sides are not long enough to form a triangle in the second and third figures. This leads to the *Triangle Inequality Theorem*.

↻ Theorem

Theorem 6.11 Triangle Inequality Theorem

The sum of the lengths of any two sides of a triangle is greater than the length of the third side.

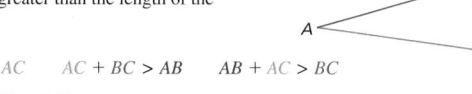

$$AB + BC > AC \qquad AC + BC > AB \qquad AB + AC > BC$$

Proof Ex. 47, p. 342

EXAMPLE 5   Finding Possible Side Lengths

A triangle has one side of length 14 and another side of length 9. Describe the possible lengths of the third side.

SOLUTION

Let x represent the length of the third side. Draw diagrams to help visualize the small and large values of x. Then use the Triangle Inequality Theorem to write and solve inequalities.

READING

You can combine the two inequalities, $x > 5$ and $x < 23$, to write the compound inequality $5 < x < 23$. This can be read as *x is between 5 and 23*.

Small values of x	Large values of x

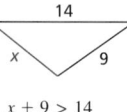 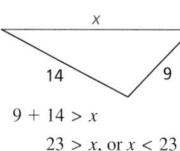

$$x + 9 > 14 \qquad\qquad 9 + 14 > x$$
$$x > 5 \qquad\qquad 23 > x, \text{ or } x < 23$$

▶ The length of the third side must be greater than 5 and less than 23.

Monitoring Progress 🔊 Help in English and Spanish at *BigIdeasMath.com*

4. A triangle has one side of length 12 inches and another side of length 20 inches. Describe the possible lengths of the third side.

Decide whether it is possible to construct a triangle with the given side lengths. Explain your reasoning.

5. 4 ft, 9 ft, 10 ft   6. 8 m, 9 m, 18 m   7. 5 cm, 7 cm, 12 cm

---

Extra Example 5

A triangle has one side of length 6 and another side of length 15. Describe the possible lengths of the third side. The length of the third side must be greater than 9 and less than 21.

MONITORING PROGRESS ANSWERS

4. 8 in. $< x <$ 32 in.

5. Yes; The sum of any two side lengths is greater than the length of the third side.

6. No; The sum $8 + 9$ is not greater than 18.

7. No; The sum $5 + 7$ is not greater than 12.

Laurie's Notes   Teacher Actions

- **MP5 Use Appropriate Tools Strategically:** The Triangle Inequality Theorem is easy to demonstrate using dynamic geometry software. Also see the *Motivate* on page T-335.

? Pose Example 5 and give students time to work with their partners. "What is the smallest integer value for the third side?" 6 "What is the largest integer value for the third side?" 22

Closure

- **Muddiest Point:** Ask students to identify, aloud or on a paper to be collected, the muddiest point(s) about the lesson. What was difficult to understand?

ASSIGNMENT

Basic: 1, 2, 3–29 odd, 35, 42, 45, 50–53

Average: 1, 2, 8–30 even, 36–42 even, 45, 50–53

Advanced: 1, 2, 8, 16–32 even, 37–40, 42, 45–48, 50–53

HOMEWORK CHECK

Basic: 3, 7, 11, 13, 17

Average: 8, 12, 14, 22, 40

Advanced: 8, 22, 37, 40, 47

ANSWERS

1. In an indirect proof, rather than proving a statement directly, you show that when the statement is false, it leads to a contradiction.

2. The longest side is opposite the largest angle, and the shortest side is opposite the smallest angle.

3. Assume temporarily that $WV = 7$ inches.

4. Assume temporarily that xy is even.

5. Assume temporarily that $\angle B$ is a right angle.

6. Assume temporarily that $\overline{JM}$ is not a median.

7. A and C; The angles of an equilateral triangle are always 60°. So, an equilateral triangle cannot have a 90° angle, and cannot be a right triangle.

8. B and C; If both $\angle X$ and $\angle Y$ have measures less than 30°, then their total is less than 60°. So, the sum of their measures cannot be 62°.

9.

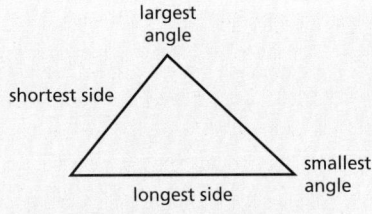

The longest side is across from the largest angle, and the shortest side is across from the smallest angle.

10.

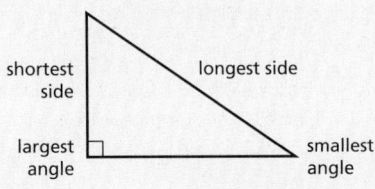

6.5   Exercises

Dynamic Solutions available at *BigIdeasMath.com*

Vocabulary and Core Concept Check

1. **VOCABULARY** Why is an indirect proof also called a *proof by contradiction*?

2. **WRITING** How can you tell which side of a triangle is the longest from the angle measures of the triangle? How can you tell which side is the shortest?

Monitoring Progress and Modeling with Mathematics

In Exercises 3–6, write the first step in an indirect proof of the statement. *(See Example 1.)*

3. If $WV + VU \neq 12$ inches and $VU = 5$ inches, then $WV \neq 7$ inches.

4. If x and y are odd integers, then xy is odd.

5. In $\triangle ABC$, if $m\angle A = 100°$, then $\angle B$ is not a right angle.

6. In $\triangle JKL$, if M is the midpoint of $\overline{KL}$, then $\overline{JM}$ is a median.

In Exercises 7 and 8, determine which two statements contradict each other. Explain your reasoning.

7. Ⓐ $\triangle LMN$ is a right triangle.
   Ⓑ $\angle L \cong \angle N$
   Ⓒ $\triangle LMN$ is equilateral.

8. Ⓐ Both $\angle X$ and $\angle Y$ have measures greater than 20°.
   Ⓑ Both $\angle X$ and $\angle Y$ have measures less than 30°.
   Ⓒ $m\angle X + m\angle Y = 62°$

In Exercises 9 and 10, use a ruler and protractor to draw the given type of triangle. Mark the largest angle and longest side in red and the smallest angle and shortest side in blue. What do you notice? *(See Example 2.)*

9. acute scalene

10. right scalene

In Exercises 11 and 12, list the angles of the given triangle from smallest to largest. *(See Example 3.)*

11.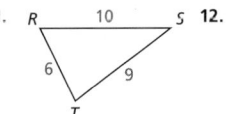

12.

In Exercises 13–16, list the sides of the given triangle from shortest to longest. *(See Example 4.)*

13.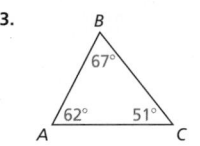

14.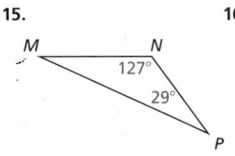

15.

16.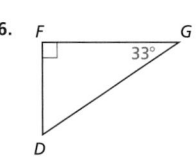

In Exercises 17–20, describe the possible lengths of the third side of the triangle given the lengths of the other two sides. *(See Example 5.)*

17. 5 inches, 12 inches

18. 12 feet, 18 feet

19. 2 feet, 40 inches

20. 25 meters, 25 meters

In Exercises 21–24, is it possible to construct a triangle with the given side lengths? If not, explain why not.

21. 6, 7, 11

22. 3, 6, 9

23. 28, 17, 46

24. 35, 120, 125

25. **ERROR ANALYSIS** Describe and correct the error in writing the first step of an indirect proof.

Show that $\angle A$ is obtuse.
Step 1   Assume temporarily that $\angle A$ is acute.

The longest side is the hypotenuse, and it is across from the right angle, which is the largest angle. The shortest side is across from the smallest angle.

11. $\angle S, \angle R, \angle T$

12. $\angle J, \angle K, \angle L$

13. $\overline{AB}, \overline{BC}, \overline{AC}$

14. $\overline{XY}, \overline{YZ}, \overline{XZ}$

15. $\overline{NP}, \overline{MN}, \overline{MP}$

16. $\overline{FD}, \overline{FG}, \overline{DG}$

17. 7 in. $< x <$ 17 in.

18. 6 ft $< x <$ 30 ft

19. 16 in. $< x <$ 64 in.

20. 0 m $< x <$ 50 m

21. yes

22. no; $3 + 6 \not> 9$

23. no; $28 + 17 \not> 46$

24. yes

25. An angle that is not obtuse could be acute or right; Assume temporarily that $\angle A$ is not obtuse.

26. ERROR ANALYSIS Describe and correct the error in labeling the side lengths 1, 2, and $\sqrt{3}$ on the triangle.

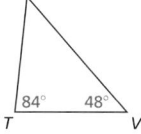

27. REASONING You are a lawyer representing a client who has been accused of a crime. The crime took place in Los Angeles, California. Security footage shows your client in New York at the time of the crime. Explain how to use indirect reasoning to prove your client is innocent.

28. REASONING Your class has fewer than 30 students. The teacher divides your class into two groups. The first group has 15 students. Use indirect reasoning to show that the second group must have fewer than 15 students.

29. PROBLEM SOLVING Which statement about $\triangle TUV$ is false?

Ⓐ $UV > TU$

Ⓑ $UV + TV > TU$

Ⓒ $UV < TV$

Ⓓ $\triangle TUV$ is isosceles.

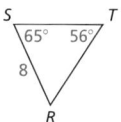

30. PROBLEM SOLVING In $\triangle RST$, which is a possible side length for ST? Select all that apply.

Ⓐ 7

Ⓑ 8

Ⓒ 9

Ⓓ 10

31. PROOF Write an indirect proof that an odd number is not divisible by 4.

32. PROOF Write an indirect proof of the statement "In $\triangle QRS$, if $m\angle Q + m\angle R = 90°$, then $m\angle S = 90°$."

33. WRITING Explain why the hypotenuse of a right triangle must always be longer than either leg.

34. CRITICAL THINKING Is it possible to decide if three side lengths form a triangle without checking all three inequalities shown in the Triangle Inequality Theorem (Theorem 6.11)? Explain your reasoning.

35. MODELING WITH MATHEMATICS You can estimate the width of the river from point A to the tree at point B by measuring the angle to the tree at several locations along the riverbank. The diagram shows the results for locations C and D.

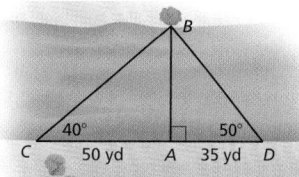

a. Using $\triangle BCA$ and $\triangle BDA$, determine the possible widths of the river. Explain your reasoning.

b. What could you do if you wanted a closer estimate?

36. MODELING WITH MATHEMATICS You travel from Fort Peck Lake to Glacier National Park and from Glacier National Park to Granite Peak.

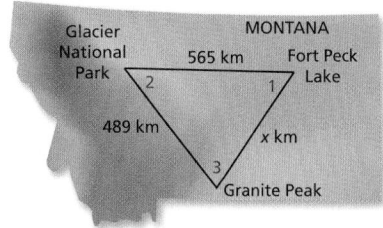

a. Write two inequalities to represent the possible distances from Granite Peak back to Fort Peck Lake.

b. How is your answer to part (a) affected if you know that $m\angle 2 < m\angle 1$ and $m\angle 2 < m\angle 3$?

37. REASONING In the figure, $\overrightarrow{XY}$ bisects $\angle WYZ$. List all six angles of $\triangle XYZ$ and $\triangle WXY$ in order from smallest to largest. Explain your reasoning.

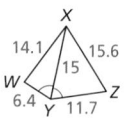

38. MATHEMATICAL CONNECTIONS In $\triangle DEF$, $m\angle D = (x + 25)°$, $m\angle E = (2x - 4)°$, and $m\angle F = 63°$. List the side lengths and angle measures of the triangle in order from least to greatest.

---

33. The right angle of a right triangle must always be the largest angle because the other two will have a sum of 90°. So, according to the Triangle Longer Angle Theorem (Thm. 6.10), because the right angle is larger than either of the other angles, the side opposite the right angle, which is the hypotenuse, will always have to be longer than either of the legs.

34. yes; If the sum of the lengths of the two shortest sides is greater than the length of the longest side, then the other two inequalities will also be true.

35. a. The width of the river must be greater than 35 yards and less than 50 yards. In $\triangle BCA$, the width of the river, $\overline{BA}$, must be less than the length of $\overline{CA}$, which is 50 yards, because the measure of the angle opposite $\overline{BA}$ is less than the measure of the angle opposite $\overline{CA}$, which must be 50°. In $\triangle BDA$, the width of the river, $\overline{BA}$, must be greater than the length of $\overline{DA}$, which is 35 yards, because the measure of the angle opposite $\overline{BA}$ is greater than the measure of the angle opposite $\overline{DA}$, which must be 40°.

35b–38. See Additional Answers.

ANSWERS

26. Because $30° < 60° < 90°$ and $1 < \sqrt{3} < 2$, the longest side, which is 2 units long, should be across from the largest angle, which is the right angle.

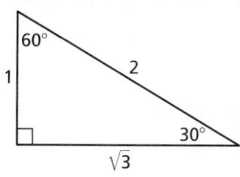

27. Assume temporarily that the client is guilty. Then the client would have been in Los Angeles, California at the time of the crime. Because the client was in New York at the time of the crime, the assumption must be false, and the client must be innocent.

28. Assume temporarily that the second group has 15 or more students. Because the first group has 15 students, the total number of students in the class would be 30 students or more. Because the class has fewer than 30 students, the assumption must be false, and the second group must have fewer than 15 students.

29. C

30. C, D

31. Assume temporarily that an odd number is divisible by 4. Let the odd number be represented by $2y + 1$ where y is a positive integer. Then, there must be a positive integer x such that $4x = 2y + 1$. However, when you divide each side of the equation by 4, you get $x = \frac{1}{2}y + \frac{1}{4}$, which is not an integer. So, the assumption must be false, and an odd number is not divisible by 4.

32. Assume temporarily that in $\triangle QRS$, $m\angle Q + m\angle R = 90°$ and $m\angle S \neq 90°$. By the Triangle Sum Theorem (Thm. 5.1), $m\angle Q + m\angle R + m\angle S = 180°$. Using the Substitution Property of Equality, $90° + m\angle S = 180°$. So, $m\angle S = 90°$ by the Subtraction Property of Equality, but this contradicts the given information. So, the assumption must be false, which proves that in $\triangle QRS$, if $m\angle Q + m\angle R = 90°$, then $m\angle S = 90°$.

39. By the Exterior Angle Theorem (Thm. 5.2), $m\angle 1 = m\angle A + m\angle B$. Then by the Subtraction Property of Equality, $m\angle 1 - m\angle B = m\angle A$. If you assume temporarily that $m\angle 1 \leq m\angle B$, then $m\angle A \leq 0$. Because the measure of any angle in a triangle must be a positive number, the assumption must be false. So, $m\angle 1 > m\angle B$. Similarly, by the Subtraction Property of Equality, $m\angle 1 - m\angle A = m\angle B$. If you assume temporarily that $m\angle 1 \leq m\angle A$, then $m\angle B \leq 0$. Because the measure of any angle in a triangle must be a positive number, the assumption must be false. So, $m\angle 1 > m\angle A$.

40. $2 < x < 15$

41. $2\frac{1}{7} < x < 13$

42–53. See Additional Answers.

Mini-Assessment

1. A triangle has one side of length 46 and another side of length 49. Describe the possible lengths of the third side. The length of the third side must be greater than 3 and less than 95.

2. Write the first step in an indirect proof of the following statement: If $AM > MB$, then M is not the midpoint of $\overline{AB}$.
   Assume temporarily that M is the midpoint of $\overline{AB}$.

3. List the sides of $\triangle DFG$ in order from shortest to longest.

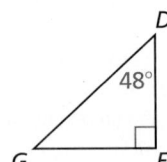

$\overline{DF}, \overline{FG}, \overline{DG}$

4. List the angles of the triangle in order from largest to smallest.

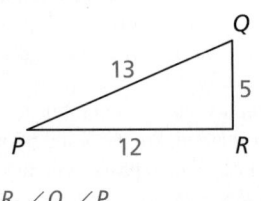

$\angle R, \angle Q, \angle P$

---

39. **ANALYZING RELATIONSHIPS** Another triangle inequality relationship is given by the Exterior Angle Inequality Theorem. It states:

    The measure of an exterior angle of a triangle is greater than the measure of either of the nonadjacent interior angles.

    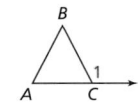

    Explain how you know that $m\angle 1 > m\angle A$ and $m\angle 1 > m\angle B$ in $\triangle ABC$ with exterior angle $\angle 1$.

MATHEMATICAL CONNECTIONS In Exercises 40 and 41, describe the possible values of x.

40.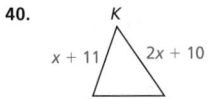

41.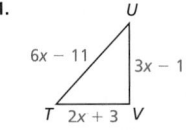

42. **HOW DO YOU SEE IT?** Your house is on the corner of Hill Street and Eighth Street. The library is on the corner of View Street and Seventh Street. What is the shortest route to get from your house to the library? Explain your reasoning.

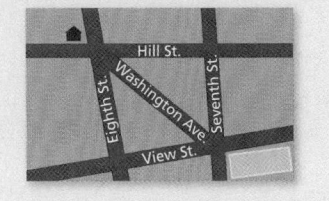

43. **PROVING A THEOREM** Use the diagram to prove the Triangle Longer Side Theorem (Theorem 6.9).

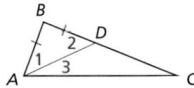

Given $BC > AB, BD = BA$

Prove $m\angle BAC > m\angle C$

Maintaining Mathematical Proficiency
Reviewing what you learned in previous grades and lessons

Name the included angle between the pair of sides given. *(Section 5.3)*

50. $\overline{AE}$ and $\overline{BE}$

51. $\overline{AC}$ and $\overline{DC}$

52. $\overline{AD}$ and $\overline{DC}$

53. $\overline{CE}$ and $\overline{BE}$

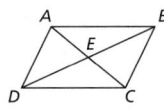

---

44. **USING STRUCTURE** The length of the base of an isosceles triangle is ℓ. Describe the possible lengths for each leg. Explain your reasoning.

45. **MAKING AN ARGUMENT** Your classmate claims to have drawn a triangle with one side length of 13 inches and a perimeter of 2 feet. Is this possible? Explain your reasoning.

46. **THOUGHT PROVOKING** Cut two pieces of string that are each 24 centimeters long. Construct an isosceles triangle out of one string and a scalene triangle out of the other. Measure and record the side lengths. Then classify each triangle by its angles.

47. **PROVING A THEOREM** Prove the Triangle Inequality Theorem (Theorem 6.11).

    Given $\triangle ABC$

    Prove $AB + BC > AC, AC + BC > AB$, and $AB + AC > BC$

48. **ATTENDING TO PRECISION** The perimeter of $\triangle HGF$ must be between what two integers? Explain your reasoning.

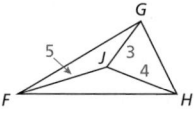

49. **PROOF** Write an indirect proof that a perpendicular segment is the shortest segment from a point to a plane.

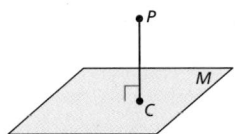

Given $\overline{PC} \perp$ plane M

Prove $\overline{PC}$ is the shortest segment from P to plane M.

Dynamic Teaching Tools

Dynamic Assessment & Progress Monitoring Tool
Lesson Planning Tool
Interactive Whiteboard Lesson Library
Dynamic Classroom with Dynamic Investigations

Laurie's Notes

Overview of Section 6.6

Introduction

- The last lesson looked at inequalities within one triangle. How are sides and angles related when the side lengths are not the same measure?
- In this lesson, inequalities in two triangles are explored. When two sides of one triangle are congruent to two sides in another triangle, what is the relationship between the third sides and the angles opposite them?
- Indirect proof and paragraph proof are each used in this lesson.

Formative Assessment Tips

- **Look Back:** This technique is used when you want students to look back over a period of instruction and summarize their learning. What do they understand now that they did not before? It is helpful for students to articulate what helped them to learn a concept or skill.
- You may want students to focus on just the last two lessons, inequalities in one or two triangles. How are the side and angle relationships the same? How were indirect proofs used in the lessons? Having students summarize what they understand about indirect proofs and what helped them learn it will enable you to make instruction more effective for your students in the future.
- If this is the first time you have used this technique, allow 6–8 minutes of class time to model what it looks like. Say, "Over the last two lessons, we have studied inequalities in one or two triangles and indirect proof. Take a piece of paper and draw a vertical line down the middle. I'm going to give you 5 minutes. On the left side, make a list of the things you learned that you did not know or understand before we began. On the right side, describe how you learned these things. What technique(s) were effective in helping you learn?"
- Evaluate what worked for your students: particular examples, talking with partners, making tables, using a model, exploring relationships with dynamic geometry software, discussion of a particular problem, and so on.

Pacing Suggestion

- The exploration will enable students to make sense of the Hinge Theorem and its converse (Thm. 6.12 and 6.13), which are presented in the formal lesson. When students have finished the exploration, transition to the formal lesson.

Laurie's Notes

Exploration

Motivate
- If you have two door hinges or similar objects, bring them to class. Students know how a hinge operates. I tie a rubber band on the outer edges of each hinge to simulate the third side of each triangle.
- **?** Have two students hold the hinges so that the angle of the opened hinges is the same. "What do you observe about the third side (rubber bands)?" The third sides are the same length.
- **?** Have one student open his or her hinge wider. "What is true about the angle of the hinges now?" One hinge angle is greater than the other hinge angle. "What do you observe about the third side of the hinge that is opened wider?" The third side is longer.
- Explain to students that in the exploration and in the lesson they will make conjectures about sides and angles of two triangles.

Exploration 1
- It will be helpful if students use the same lettering as the diagram so that when they collect data in the table, the column headings will not need to be changed.
- **?** Once the basic construction is completed ask, "What is true about the sides of $\triangle ACB$ and $\triangle DCB$?" The two triangles have two pairs of sides that are congruent. $\overline{AC} \cong \overline{DC}$ because they are radii of the same circle, and $\overline{BC} \cong \overline{BC}$ because of the Reflexive Property.
- **?** "Could the third sides of the two triangles be congruent?" yes "Do they have to be?" no
- Have students gather data by dragging point D to different positions.
- **MP3 Construct Viable Arguments and Critique the Reasoning of Others:** Ask students to make a conjecture after looking for patterns in the table. The organization of the columns in the table should help students observe patterns.
- In addition to recognizing the pattern known as the Hinge Theorem (Thm. 6.12), students might also observe other relationships, such as when side $\overline{AB}$ increases, $\angle ACB$ also increases.

Communicate Your Answer
- You should hear a number of observations from students about the third sides of the two triangles: they may be congruent or not; when they are congruent, the angle opposite each is congruent; when they are not congruent, the angles opposite are not congruent and the largest angle will be opposite the longest side.

Connecting to Next Step
- The exploration is related to the theorem and its converse presented in the lesson, helping students make sense of the theorems before proving them to be true.

6.6 Inequalities in Two Triangles

Essential Question If two sides of one triangle are congruent to two sides of another triangle, what can you say about the third sides of the triangles?

EXPLORATION 1 Comparing Measures in Triangles

Work with a partner. Use dynamic geometry software.

a. Draw $\triangle ABC$, as shown below.

b. Draw the circle with center $C(3, 3)$ through the point $A(1, 3)$.

c. Draw $\triangle DBC$ so that D is a point on the circle.

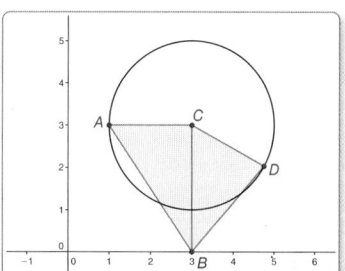

Sample
Points
$A(1, 3)$
$B(3, 0)$
$C(3, 3)$
$D(4.75, 2.03)$
Segments
$BC = 3$
$AC = 2$
$DC = 2$
$AB = 3.61$
$DB = 2.68$

d. Which two sides of $\triangle ABC$ are congruent to two sides of $\triangle DBC$? Justify your answer.

e. Compare the lengths of $\overline{AB}$ and $\overline{DB}$. Then compare the measures of $\angle ACB$ and $\angle DCB$. Are the results what you expected? Explain.

f. Drag point D to several locations on the circle. At each location, repeat part (e). Copy and record your results in the table below.

CONSTRUCTING VIABLE ARGUMENTS

To be proficient in math, you need to make conjectures and build a logical progression of statements to explore the truth of your conjectures.

	D	AC	BC	AB	BD	$m\angle ACB$	$m\angle BCD$
1.	(4.75, 2.03)	2	3				
2.		2	3				
3.		2	3				
4.		2	3				
5.		2	3				

g. Look for a pattern of the measures in your table. Then write a conjecture that summarizes your observations.

Communicate Your Answer

2. If two sides of one triangle are congruent to two sides of another triangle, what can you say about the third sides of the triangles?

3. Explain how you can use the hinge shown at the left to model the concept described in Question 2.

Section 6.6 Inequalities in Two Triangles **343**

ANSWERS

1. a. Check students' work.

   b. Check students' work.

   c. Check students' work.

   d. $\overline{AC} \cong \overline{DC}$, because all points on a circle are equidistant from the center; $\overline{BC} \cong \overline{BC}$ by the Reflexive Property of Congruence (Thm. 2.1).

   e. $AB > DB$; $m\angle ACB > m\angle DCB$; yes; The triangle with the longer third side has the larger angle opposite the third side.

   f. See Additional Answers.

   g. If two sides of one triangle are congruent to two sides of another triangle, and the included angle of the first is larger than the included angle of the second, then the third side of the first is longer than the third side of the second.

2. If the included angle of one is larger than the included angle of the other, then the third side of the first is longer than the third side of the second. If the included angles are congruent, then you already know that the triangles are congruent by the SAS Congruence Theorem (Thm. 5.5). Therefore the third sides are congruent because corresponding parts of congruent triangles are congruent.

3. Because the sides of the hinge do not change in length, the angle of the hinge can model the included angle and the distance between the opposite ends of the hinge can model the third side. When the hinge is open wider, the angle is larger and the ends of the hinge are farther apart. If the hinge is open less, the ends are closer together.

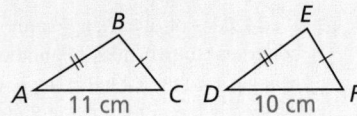
6.6 Lesson

What You Will Learn

▶ Compare measures in triangles.
▶ Solve real-life problems using the Hinge Theorem.

Comparing Measures in Triangles

Imagine a gate between fence posts A and B that has hinges at A and swings open at B.

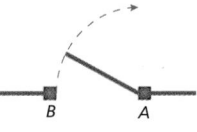

As the gate swings open, you can think of $\triangle ABC$, with side $\overline{AC}$ formed by the gate itself, side $\overline{AB}$ representing the distance between the fence posts, and side $\overline{BC}$ representing the opening between post B and the outer edge of the gate.

 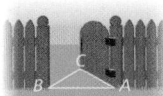 

Notice that as the gate opens wider, both the measure of $\angle A$ and the distance BC increase. This suggests the *Hinge Theorem*.

🔄 Theorems

Theorem 6.12   Hinge Theorem

If two sides of one triangle are congruent to two sides of another triangle, and the included angle of the first is larger than the included angle of the second, then the third side of the first is longer than the third side of the second.

Proof BigIdeasMath.com

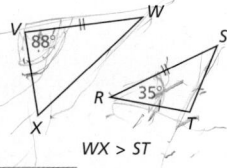

$WX > ST$

Theorem 6.13   Converse of the Hinge Theorem

If two sides of one triangle are congruent to two sides of another triangle, and the third side of the first is longer than the third side of the second, then the included angle of the first is larger than the included angle of the second.

Proof Example 3, p. 345

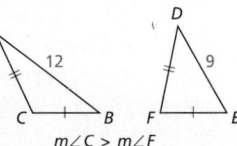

$m\angle C > m\angle F$

EXAMPLE 1   Using the Converse of the Hinge Theorem

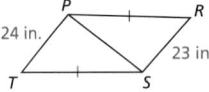

Given that $\overline{ST} \cong \overline{PR}$, how does $m\angle PST$ compare to $m\angle SPR$?

SOLUTION

You are given that $\overline{ST} \cong \overline{PR}$, and you know that $\overline{PS} \cong \overline{PS}$ by the Reflexive Property of Congruence (Theorem 2.1). Because 24 inches > 23 inches, $PT > SR$. So, two sides of $\triangle STP$ are congruent to two sides of $\triangle PRS$ and the third side of $\triangle STP$ is longer.

▶ By the Converse of the Hinge Theorem, $m\angle PST > m\angle SPR$.

EXAMPLE 2 Using the Hinge Theorem

Given that $\overline{JK} \cong \overline{LK}$, how does JM compare to LM?

SOLUTION

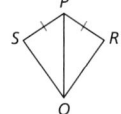

You are given that $\overline{JK} \cong \overline{LK}$, and you know that $\overline{KM} \cong \overline{KM}$ by the Reflexive Property of Congruence (Theorem 2.1). Because $64° > 61°$, $m\angle JKM > m\angle LKM$. So, two sides of $\triangle JKM$ are congruent to two sides of $\triangle LKM$, and the included angle in $\triangle JKM$ is larger.

▶ By the Hinge Theorem, $JM > LM$.

Monitoring Progress 🔊 Help in English and Spanish at *BigIdeasMath.com*

Use the diagram.

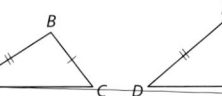

1. If $PR = PS$ and $m\angle QPR > m\angle QPS$, which is longer, $\overline{SQ}$ or $\overline{RQ}$?

2. If $PR = PS$ and $RQ < SQ$, which is larger, $\angle RPQ$ or $\angle SPQ$?

EXAMPLE 3 Proving the Converse of the Hinge Theorem

Write an indirect proof of the Converse of the Hinge Theorem.

Given $\overline{AB} \cong \overline{DE}, \overline{BC} \cong \overline{EF}, AC > DF$

Prove $m\angle B > m\angle E$

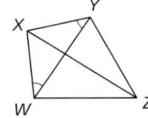

Indirect Proof

Step 1 Assume temporarily that $m\angle B \not> m\angle E$. Then it follows that either $m\angle B < m\angle E$ or $m\angle B = m\angle E$.

Step 2 If $m\angle B < m\angle E$, then $AC < DF$ by the Hinge Theorem.

If $m\angle B = m\angle E$, then $\angle B \cong \angle E$. So, $\triangle ABC \cong \triangle DEF$ by the SAS Congruence Theorem (Theorem 5.5) and $AC = DF$.

Step 3 Both conclusions contradict the given statement that $AC > DF$. So, the temporary assumption that $m\angle B \not> m\angle E$ cannot be true. This proves that $m\angle B > m\angle E$.

EXAMPLE 4 Proving Triangle Relationships

Write a paragraph proof.

Given $\angle XWY \cong \angle XYW, WZ > YZ$

Prove $m\angle WXZ > m\angle YXZ$

Paragraph Proof Because $\angle XWY \cong \angle XYW$, $\overline{XY} \cong \overline{XW}$ by the Converse of the Base Angles Theorem (Theorem 5.7). By the Reflexive Property of Congruence (Theorem 2.1), $\overline{XZ} \cong \overline{XZ}$. Because $WZ > YZ$, $m\angle WXZ > m\angle YXZ$ by the Converse of the Hinge Theorem.

Monitoring Progress 🔊 Help in English and Spanish at *BigIdeasMath.com*

3. Write a temporary assumption you can make to prove the Hinge Theorem indirectly. What two cases does that assumption lead to?

Section 6.6   Inequalities in Two Triangles   **345**

Extra Example 2

Given that $\overline{AB} \cong \overline{DE}$ and $\overline{BC} \cong \overline{EC}$, how does AC compare to DC?

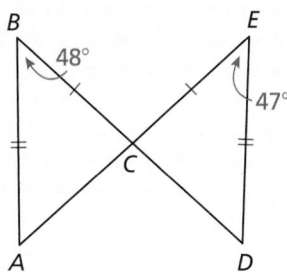

$AC > DC$

Extra Example 3

What can you conclude about the measures of $\angle A$ and $\angle Q$ in this figure? Explain.

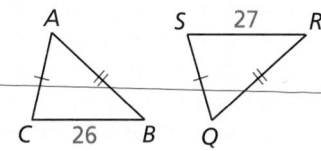

$m\angle A < m\angle Q$, by the Converse of the Hinge Theorem (Thm. 6.13) because $BC < RS$.

Extra Example 4

Write a paragraph proof.
Given $\overline{AB} \cong \overline{BC}, AD > CD$
Prove $m\angle ABD > m\angle CBD$

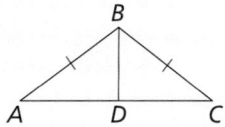

It is given that $\overline{AB} \cong \overline{BC}$. By the Reflexive Property of Congruence (Thm. 2.1), $\overline{BD} \cong \overline{BD}$. Because $AD > CD$, $m\angle ABD > m\angle CBD$ by the Converse of the Hinge Theorem (Thm. 6.13).

MONITORING PROGRESS ANSWERS

1. $\overline{RQ}$

2. $\angle SPQ$

3. Assume temporarily that the third side of the first triangle is not longer than the third side of the second triangle. The third side of the first triangle is either equal to the third side of the second triangle or less than the third side of the second triangle.

Laurie's Notes   Teacher Actions

• In proving the Converse of the Hinge Theorem (Example 3), state the given information. The congruent sides are marked on the diagram, but the given information that $AC > DF$ is not. It is important that this is written. The contradiction relates back to this piece of given information.

• **MP3** and **MP6 Attend to Precision:** Have partners work collaboratively on Example 4. Have several pairs share their proofs. Critique the reasoning used in each proof and the clarity and precision of the language used.

Extra Example 5

In Example 5, Group D leaves camp and travels 2 miles due south, then turns 25° toward east and travels 1.2 miles. Is Group D farther from camp than Group A, Group B, both groups, or neither group? Explain your reasoning. **Both groups. The included angle for Group D is 155°, which is greater than the included angle for Group A and for Group B. So, Group D is farthest from camp.**

MONITORING PROGRESS ANSWER

4. Group B is the farthest from camp, Group C is next, and Group A is the closest to camp.

Solving Real-Life Problems

EXAMPLE 5 Solving a Real-Life Problem

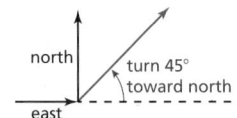

Two groups of bikers leave the same camp heading in opposite directions. Each group travels 2 miles, then changes direction and travels 1.2 miles. Group A starts due east and then turns 45° toward north. Group B starts due west and then turns 30° toward south. Which group is farther from camp? Explain your reasoning.

SOLUTION

1. **Understand the Problem** You know the distances and directions that the groups of bikers travel. You need to determine which group is farther from camp. You can interpret a turn of 45° toward north, as shown.

2. **Make a Plan** Draw a diagram that represents the situation and mark the given measures. The distances that the groups bike and the distances back to camp form two triangles. The triangles have two congruent side lengths of 2 miles and 1.2 miles. Include the third side of each triangle in the diagram.

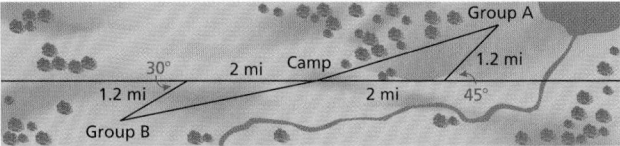

3. **Solve the Problem** Use linear pairs to find the included angles for the paths that the groups take.

   Group A: $180° - 45° = 135°$ **Group B:** $180° - 30° = 150°$

   The included angles are 135° and 150°.

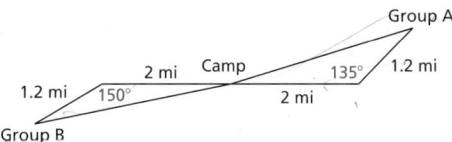

   Because $150° > 135°$, the distance Group B is from camp is greater than the distance Group A is from camp by the Hinge Theorem.

   ▶ So, Group B is farther from camp.

4. **Look Back** Because the included angle for Group A is 15° less than the included angle for Group B, you can reason that Group A would be closer to camp than Group B. So, Group B is farther from camp.

Monitoring Progress ◄)) Help in English and Spanish at *BigIdeasMath.com*

4. **WHAT IF?** In Example 5, Group C leaves camp and travels 2 miles due north, then turns 40° toward east and travels 1.2 miles. Compare the distances from camp for all three groups.

Laurie's Notes | Teacher Actions

- **MP4 Model with Mathematics:** Read Example 5 and ask students to make a diagram of the problem. Have students compare their diagrams and modify as needed. Once a diagram has been drawn, ask partners to write an explanation of which group is farther from the camp.
- **Think-Pair-Share:** Have students answer Question 4, and then share and discuss as a class.

Closure

- **Look Back:** Have students *Look Back* over Sections 6.5 and 6.6. Have them summarize what they understand about inequalities in one triangle and inequalities in two triangles, as well as what helped them learn it.

Vocabulary and Core Concept Check

1. **WRITING** Explain why Theorem 6.12 is named the "Hinge Theorem."

2. **COMPLETE THE SENTENCE** In △ABC and △DEF, $\overline{AB} \cong \overline{DE}$, $\overline{BC} \cong \overline{EF}$, and $AC < DF$.
So $m\angle\_\_\_\_ > m\angle\_\_\_\_$ by the Converse of the Hinge Theorem (Theorem 6.13).

Monitoring Progress and Modeling with Mathematics

In Exercises 3–6, copy and complete the statement with <, >, or =. Explain your reasoning. *(See Example 1.)*

3. $m\angle1 \_\_\_\_ m\angle2$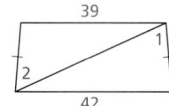

4. $m\angle1 \_\_\_\_ m\angle2$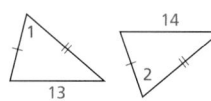

5. $m\angle1 \_\_\_\_ m\angle2$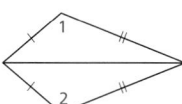

6. $m\angle1 \_\_\_\_ m\angle2$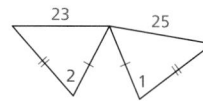

In Exercises 7–10, copy and complete the statement with <, >, or =. Explain your reasoning. *(See Example 2.)*

7. $AD \_\_\_\_ CD$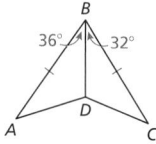

8. $MN \_\_\_\_ LK$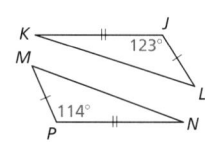

9. $TR \_\_\_\_ UR$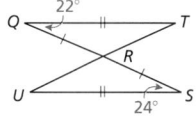

10. $AC \_\_\_\_ DC$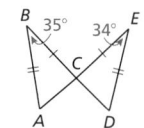

PROOF In Exercises 11 and 12, write a proof. *(See Example 4.)*

11. **Given** $\overline{XY} \cong \overline{YZ}$, $m\angle WYZ > m\angle WYX$
Prove $WZ > WX$

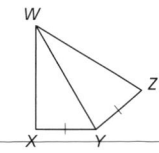

12. **Given** $\overline{BC} \cong \overline{DA}$, $DC < AB$
Prove $m\angle BCA > m\angle DAC$

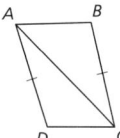

In Exercises 13 and 14, you and your friend leave on different flights from the same airport. Determine which flight is farther from the airport. Explain your reasoning. *(See Example 5.)*

13. **Your flight:** Flies 100 miles due west, then turns 20° toward north and flies 50 miles.

Friend's flight: Flies 100 miles due north, then turns 30° toward east and flies 50 miles.

14. **Your flight:** Flies 210 miles due south, then turns 70° toward west and flies 80 miles.

Friend's flight: Flies 80 miles due north, then turns 50° toward east and flies 210 miles.

Section 6.6   Inequalities in Two Triangles   **347**

ANSWERS

1. Theorem 6.12 refers to two angles with two pairs of sides that have the same measure, just like two hinges whose sides are the same length. Then, the angle whose measure is greater is opposite a longer side, just like the ends of a hinge are farther apart when the hinge is open wider.

2. $m\angle E > m\angle B$

3. $m\angle1 > m\angle2$; By the Converse of the Hinge Theorem (Thm. 6.13), because $\angle1$ is the included angle in the triangle with the longer third side, its measure is greater than that of $\angle2$.

4. $m\angle1 < m\angle2$; By the Converse of the Hinge Theorem (Thm. 6.13), because $\angle1$ is the included angle in the triangle with the shorter third side, its measure is less than that of $\angle2$.

5. $m\angle1 = m\angle2$; The triangles are congruent by the SSS Congruence Theorem (Thm. 5.8). So, $\angle1 \cong \angle2$ because corresponding parts of congruent triangles are congruent.

6. $m\angle1 > m\angle2$; By the Converse of the Hinge Theorem (Thm. 6.12), because $\angle1$ is the included angle in the triangle with the longer third side, its measure is greater than that of $\angle2$.

7. $AD > CD$; By the Hinge Theorem (Thm. 6.12), because $\overline{AD}$ is the third side of the triangle with the larger included angle, it is longer than $\overline{CD}$.

8. $MN < LK$; By the Hinge Theorem (Thm. 6.12), because $\overline{MN}$ is the third side of the triangle with the smaller included angle, it is shorter than $\overline{LK}$.

9. $TR < UR$; By the Hinge Theorem (Thm. 6.12), because $\overline{TR}$ is the third side of the triangle with the smaller included angle, it is shorter than $\overline{UR}$.

10. $AC > DC$; By the Hinge Theorem (Thm. 6.12), because $\overline{AC}$ is the third side of the triangle with the larger included angle, it is longer than $\overline{DC}$.

11. $\overline{XY} \cong \overline{YZ}$ and $m\angle WYZ > m\angle WYX$ are given. By the Reflexive Property of Congruence (Thm. 2.1), $\overline{WY} \cong \overline{WY}$. So, by the Hinge Theorem (Thm. 6.12), $WZ > WX$.

12. $\overline{BC} \cong \overline{DA}$ and $DC < AB$ are given. By the Reflexive Property of Congruence (Thm. 2.1), $\overline{AC} \cong \overline{AC}$. So, by the Converse of the Hinge Theorem (Thm. 6.13), $m\angle BCA > m\angle DAC$.

13. your flight; Because $160° > 150°$, the distance you flew is a greater distance than the distance your friend flew by the Hinge Theorem (Thm. 6.12).

14. friend's flight; Because $130° > 110°$, the distance your friend flew is a greater distance than the distance you flew by the Hinge Theorem (Thm. 6.12).

ANSWERS

15. The measure of the included angle in $\triangle PSQ$ is greater than the measure of the included angle in $\triangle SQR$; By the Hinge Theorem (Thm. 6.12), $PQ > SR$.

16. A, B

17. $m\angle EGF > m\angle DGE$ by the Hinge Theorem (Thm. 6.12).

18–24. See Additional Answers.

25. $x = 38$

26. $x = 72$

27. $x = 60$

28. $x = 108$

Mini-Assessment

Use the figure.

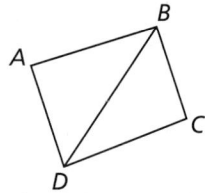

1. **Given** $AB = DC$, $m\angle ABD = 35°$, and $m\angle BDC = 25°$. How does AD compare to BC? $AD > BC$

2. **Given** $AB = DC$, $AD = 14$, and $BC = 15$. How does $m\angle ABD$ compare to $m\angle BDC$?
$m\angle ABD < m\angle BDC$

3. Complete the statement with <, >, or =.

$m\angle P$ ___ $m\angle R$

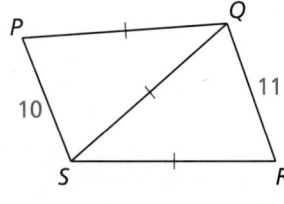

$m\angle P > m\angle R$

---

15. **ERROR ANALYSIS** Describe and correct the error in using the Hinge Theorem (Theorem 6.12).

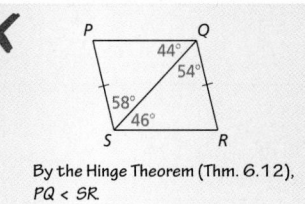

By the Hinge Theorem (Thm. 6.12), PQ < SR

16. **REPEATED REASONING** Which is a possible measure for $\angle JKM$? Select all that apply.

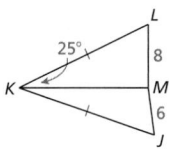

Ⓐ 15°   Ⓑ 22°   Ⓒ 25°   Ⓓ 35°

17. **DRAWING CONCLUSIONS** The path from E to F is longer than the path from E to D. The path from G to D is the same length as the path from G to F. What can you conclude about the angles of the paths? Explain your reasoning.

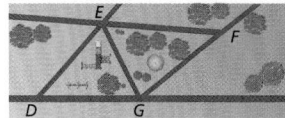

18. **ABSTRACT REASONING** In $\triangle EFG$, the bisector of $\angle F$ intersects the bisector of $\angle G$ at point H. Explain why $\overline{FG}$ must be longer than $\overline{FH}$ or $\overline{HG}$.

19. **ABSTRACT REASONING** $\overline{NR}$ is a median of $\triangle NPQ$, and $NQ > NP$. Explain why $\angle NRQ$ is obtuse.

MATHEMATICAL CONNECTIONS In Exercises 20 and 21, write and solve an inequality for the possible values of x.

20.
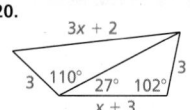

21.

22. **HOW DO YOU SEE IT?** In the diagram, triangles are formed by the locations of the players on the basketball court. The dashed lines represent the possible paths of the basketball as the players pass. How does $m\angle ACB$ compare with $m\angle ACD$?

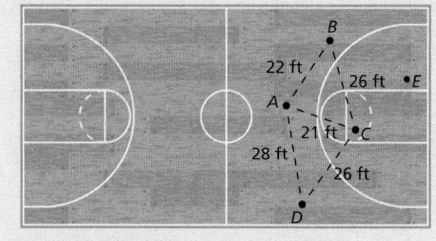

23. **CRITICAL THINKING** In $\triangle ABC$, the altitudes from B and C meet at point D, and $m\angle BAC > m\angle BDC$. What is true about $\triangle ABC$? Justify your answer.

24. **THOUGHT PROVOKING** The postulates and theorems in this book represent Euclidean geometry. In spherical geometry, all points are on the surface of a sphere. A line is a circle on the sphere whose diameter is equal to the diameter of the sphere. In spherical geometry, state an inequality involving the sum of the angles of a triangle. Find a formula for the area of a triangle in spherical geometry.

Maintaining Mathematical Proficiency
Reviewing what you learned in previous grades and lessons

Find the value of x.   *(Section 5.1 and Section 5.4)*

25.

26.

27.

28.

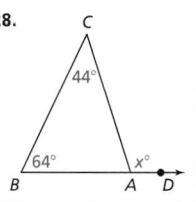

If students need help...	If students got it...
Resources by Chapter • Practice A and Practice B • Puzzle Time	**Resources by Chapter** • Enrichment and Extension • Cumulative Review
Student Journal • Practice	Start the *next* Section
Differentiating the Lesson Skills Review Handbook	

Core Vocabulary

midsegment of a triangle, *p. 330*
indirect proof, *p. 336*

Core Concepts

Section 6.4

Using the Midsegment of a Triangle, *p. 330*
Theorem 6.8 Triangle Midsegment Theorem, *p. 331*

Section 6.5

How to Write an Indirect Proof (Proof by Contradiction), *p. 336*
Theorem 6.9 Triangle Longer Side Theorem, *p. 337*
Theorem 6.10 Triangle Larger Angle Theorem, *p. 337*
Theorem 6.11 Triangle Inequality Theorem, *p. 339*

Section 6.6

Theorem 6.12 Hinge Theorem, *p. 344*
Theorem 6.13 Converse of the Hinge Theorem, *p. 344*

Mathematical Practices

1. In Exercise 25 on page 334, analyze the relationship between the stage and the total perimeter of all the shaded triangles at that stage. Then predict the total perimeter of all the shaded triangles in Stage 4.

2. In Exercise 17 on page 340, write all three inequalities using the Triangle Inequality Theorem (Theorem 6.11). Determine the reasonableness of each one. Why do you only need to use two of the three inequalities?

3. In Exercise 23 on page 348, try all three cases of triangles (acute, right, obtuse) to gain insight into the solution.

- - - - - - - **Performance Task** - - -

Bicycle Renting Stations

The city planners for a large town want to add bicycle renting stations around downtown. How will you decide the best locations? Where will you place the rental stations based on the ideas of the city planners?

To explore the answers to these questions and more, go to
BigIdeasMath.com.

349

ANSWERS

1. Let n be the stage, then the side length of the new triangles in each stage is 2^{4-n}. So, the perimeter of each new triangle is $(3 \cdot 2^{4-n})$. The number of new triangles is given by (3^{n-1}). So, to find the perimeter of all the shaded triangles in each stage, start with the total from the previous stage and add $(3 \cdot 2^{4-n})(3^{n-1})$. The perimeter of the new triangles in stage 4 will be $(3 \cdot 2^{4-4})(3^{4-1}) = 81$. The total perimeter of the new triangles and old triangles is $81 + 114 = 195$ units.

2. $x + 5 > 12$, $x + 12 > 5$, $5 + 12 > x$; Because the length of the third side has to be a positive value, the inequality $x + 12 > 5$ will always be true. So, you do not have to consider this inequality in determining the possible values of x. Solve the other two inequalities to find that the length of the third side must be greater than 7 and less than 19.

3. If $m\angle BAC < m\angle BDC$, then the orthocenter D is inside the triangle, and $\triangle ABC$ is an acute triangle. If $m\angle BAC = m\angle BDC$, then the orthocenter D is on vertex A, and $\triangle ABC$ is a right triangle, with $\angle A$ being the right angle. If $m\angle BAC > m\angle BDC$, then the orthocenter D is outside the triangle, and $\triangle ABC$ is an obtuse triangle, with $\angle A$ being the obtuse angle.

1. 20; Point B is equidistant from A and C, and $\overleftrightarrow{BD} \perp \overleftrightarrow{AC}$. So, by the Converse of the Perpendicular Bisector Theorem (Thm. 6.2), $DC = AD = 20$.

2. 23; $\angle PQS \cong \angle RQS$, $\overline{SR} \perp \overrightarrow{QR}$, and $\overline{SP} \perp \overrightarrow{QP}$. So, by the Angle Bisector Theorem (Thm. 6.3), $SR = SP$. This means that $6x + 5 = 9x - 4$, and the solution is $x = 3$. So, $RS = 9(3) - 4 = 23$.

3. 47°; Point J is equidistant from $\overrightarrow{FG}$ and $\overrightarrow{FH}$. So, by the Converse of the Angle Bisector Theorem (Thm. 6.4), $m\angle JFH = m\angle JFG = 47°$.

4. $(-3, -3)$

5. $(4, 3)$

6. $x = 5$

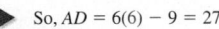

6.1 **Perpendicular and Angle Bisectors** *(pp. 301–308)*

Find AD.

From the figure, $\overleftrightarrow{AC}$ is the perpendicular bisector of $\overline{BD}$.

$\quad AB = AD$ Perpendicular Bisector Theorem (Theorem 6.1)

$4x + 3 = 6x - 9$ Substitute.

$\quad\quad x = 6$ Solve for x.

▶ So, $AD = 6(6) - 9 = 27$.

Find the indicated measure. Explain your reasoning.

1. DC

2. RS

3. $m\angle JFH$

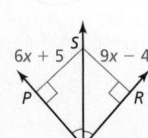

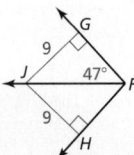

6.2 **Bisectors of Triangles** *(pp. 309–318)*

Find the coordinates of the circumcenter of $\triangle QRS$ with vertices $Q(3, 3)$, $R(5, 7)$, and $S(9, 3)$.

Step 1 Graph $\triangle QRS$.

Step 2 Find equations for two perpendicular bisectors.

The midpoint of $\overline{QS}$ is $(6, 3)$. The line through $(6, 3)$ that is perpendicular to $\overline{QS}$ is $x = 6$.

The midpoint of $\overline{QR}$ is $(4, 5)$. The line through $(4, 5)$ that is perpendicular to $\overline{QR}$ is $y = -\frac{1}{2}x + 7$.

Step 3 Find the point where $x = 6$ and $y = -\frac{1}{2}x + 7$ intersect. They intersect at $(6, 4)$.

▶ So, the coordinates of the circumcenter are $(6, 4)$.

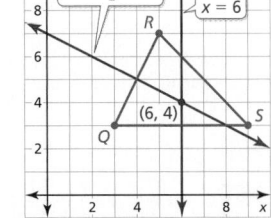

Find the coordinates of the circumcenter of the triangle with the given vertices.

4. $T(-6, -5)$, $U(0, -1)$, $V(0, -5)$

5. $X(-2, 1)$, $Y(2, -3)$, $Z(6, -3)$

6. Point D is the incenter of $\triangle LMN$. Find the value of x.

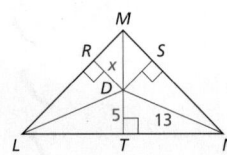

7. $(-6, 3)$

8. $(4, -4)$

9. inside; $(3, 5.2)$

10. outside; $(-6, -1)$

11. $(-6, 6), (-3, 6), (-3, 4)$

12. $(0, 3), (2, 0), (-1, -2)$

6.3   Medians and Altitudes of Triangles   (pp. 319–326)

Find the coordinates of the centroid of △TUV with vertices T(1, −8), U(4, −1), and V(7, −6).

Step 1   Graph △TUV.

Step 2   Use the Midpoint Formula to find the midpoint W of $\overline{TV}$. Sketch median $\overline{UW}$.

$$W\left(\frac{1+7}{2}, \frac{-8+(-6)}{2}\right) = (4, -7)$$

Step 3   Find the centroid. It is two-thirds of the distance from each vertex to the midpoint of the opposite side.

The distance from vertex U(4, −1) to W(4, −7) is −1 − (−7) = 6 units.

So, the centroid is $\frac{2}{3}(6) = 4$ units down from vertex U on $\overline{UW}$.

▶   So, the coordinates of the centroid P are (4, −1 − 4), or (4, −5).

Find the coordinates of the centroid of the triangle with the given vertices.

7. A(−10, 3), B(−4, 5), C(−4, 1)   **8.** D(2, −8), E(2, −2), F(8, −2)

Tell whether the orthocenter of the triangle with the given vertices is *inside*, *on*, or *outside* the triangle. Then find the coordinates of the orthocenter.

9. G(1, 6), H(5, 6), J(3, 1)   **10.** K(−8, 5), L(−6, 3), M(0, 5)

6.4   The Triangle Midsegment Theorem   (pp. 329–334)

In △JKL, show that midsegment $\overline{MN}$ is parallel to $\overline{JL}$ and that $MN = \frac{1}{2}JL$.

Step 1   Find the coordinates of M and N by finding the midpoints of $\overline{JK}$ and $\overline{KL}$.

$$M\left(\frac{-8+(-4)}{2}, \frac{1+7}{2}\right) = M\left(\frac{-12}{2}, \frac{8}{2}\right) = M(-6, 4)$$

$$N\left(\frac{-4+(-2)}{2}, \frac{7+3}{2}\right) = N\left(\frac{-6}{2}, \frac{10}{2}\right) = N(-3, 5)$$

Step 2   Find and compare the slopes of $\overline{MN}$ and $\overline{JL}$.

slope of $\overline{MN} = \frac{5-4}{-3-(-6)} = \frac{1}{3}$

slope of $\overline{JL} = \frac{3-1}{-2-(-8)} = \frac{2}{6} = \frac{1}{3}$

▶   Because the slopes are the same, $\overline{MN}$ is parallel to $\overline{JL}$.

Step 3   Find and compare the lengths of $\overline{MN}$ and $\overline{JL}$.

$MN = \sqrt{[-3-(-6)]^2 + (5-4)^2} = \sqrt{9+1} = \sqrt{10}$

$JL = \sqrt{[-2-(-8)]^2 + (3-1)^2} = \sqrt{36+4} = \sqrt{40} = 2\sqrt{10}$

▶   Because $\sqrt{10} = \frac{1}{2}(2\sqrt{10})$, $MN = \frac{1}{2}JL$.

Find the coordinates of the vertices of the midsegment triangle for the triangle with the given vertices.

11. A(−6, 8), B(−6, 4), C(0, 4)   **12.** D(−3, 1), E(3, 5), F(1, −5)

Chapter 6   Chapter Review   **351**

13. 4 in. < x < 12 in.

14. 3 m < x < 15 m

15. 7 ft < x < 29 ft

16. Assume temporarily that YZ ≯ 4. Then, it follows that either YZ < 4 or YZ = 4. If YZ < 4, then XY + YZ < XZ because 4 + YZ < 8 when YZ < 4. If YZ = 4, then XY + YZ = XZ because 4 + 4 = 8. Both conclusions contradict the Triangle Inequality Theorem (Thm. 6.11), which says that XY + YZ > XZ. So, the temporary assumption that YZ ≯ 4 cannot be true. This proves that in △XYZ, if XY = 4 and XZ = 8, then YZ > 4.

17. QT > ST

18. m∠QRT > m∠SRT

6.5 **Indirect Proof and Inequalities in One Triangle** *(pp. 335–342)*

a. List the sides of △ABC in order from shortest to longest.

First, find m∠C using the Triangle Sum Theorem (Thm. 5.1).

$$m\angle A + m\angle B + m\angle C = 180°$$
$$35° + 95° + m\angle C = 180°$$
$$m\angle C = 50°$$

The angles from smallest to largest are ∠A, ∠C, and ∠B. The sides opposite these angles are $\overline{BC}$, $\overline{AB}$, and $\overline{AC}$, respectively.

▶ So, by the Triangle Larger Angle Theorem (Theorem 6.10), the sides from shortest to longest are $\overline{BC}$, $\overline{AB}$, and $\overline{AC}$.

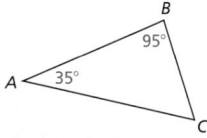

b. List the angles of △DEF in order from smallest to largest.

The sides from shortest to longest are $\overline{DF}$, $\overline{EF}$, and $\overline{DE}$. The angles opposite these sides are ∠E, ∠D, and ∠F, respectively.

▶ So, by the Triangle Longer Side Theorem (Theorem 6.9), the angles from smallest to largest are ∠E, ∠D, and ∠F.

Describe the possible lengths of the third side of the triangle given the lengths of the other two sides.

13. 4 inches, 8 inches   14. 6 meters, 9 meters   15. 11 feet, 18 feet

16. Write an indirect proof of the statement "In △XYZ, if XY = 4 and XZ = 8, then YZ > 4."

6.6 **Inequalities in Two Triangles** *(pp. 343–348)*

Given that $\overline{WZ} \cong \overline{YZ}$, how does XY compare to XW?

You are given that $\overline{WZ} \cong \overline{YZ}$, and you know that $\overline{XZ} \cong \overline{XZ}$ by the Reflexive Property of Congruence (Theorem 2.1).

Because 90° > 80°, m∠XZY > m∠XZW. So, two sides of △XZY are congruent to two sides of △XZW and the included angle in △XZY is larger.

▶ By the Hinge Theorem (Theorem 6.12), XY > XW.

Use the diagram.

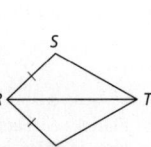

17. If RQ = RS and m∠QRT > m∠SRT, then how does $\overline{QT}$ compare to $\overline{ST}$?

18. If RQ = RS and QT > ST, then how does ∠QRT compare to ∠SRT?

6 Chapter Test

In Exercises 1 and 2, $\overline{MN}$ is a midsegment of $\triangle JKL$. Find the value of x.

1.

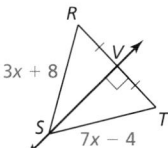

2.

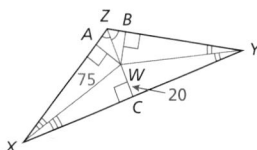

Find the indicated measure. Identify the theorem you use.

3. ST

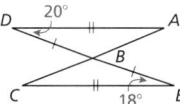

4. WY

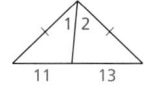

5. BW

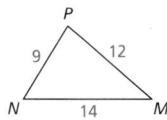

Copy and complete the statement with <, >, or =.

6. AB ___ CB

7. $m\angle 1$ ___ $m\angle 2$

8. $m\angle MNP$ ___ $m\angle NPM$

9. Find the coordinates of the circumcenter, orthocenter, and centroid of the triangle with vertices $A(0, -2)$, $B(4, -2)$, and $C(0, 6)$.

10. Write an indirect proof of the Corollary to the Base Angles Theorem (Corollary 5.2): If $\triangle PQR$ is equilateral, then it is equiangular.

11. $\triangle DEF$ is a right triangle with area A. Use the area for $\triangle DEF$ to write an expression for the area of $\triangle GEH$. Justify your answer.

12. Two hikers start at a visitor center. The first hikes 4 miles due west, then turns 40° toward south and hikes 1.8 miles. The second hikes 4 miles due east, then turns 52° toward north and hikes 1.8 miles. Which hiker is farther from the visitor center? Explain how you know.

In Exercises 13–15, use the map.

13. Describe the possible lengths of Pine Avenue.

14. You ride your bike along a trail that represents the shortest distance from the beach to Main Street. You end up exactly halfway between your house and the movie theatre. How long is Pine Avenue? Explain.

15. A market is the same distance from your house, the movie theater, and the beach. Copy the map and locate the market.

ANSWERS

1. $x = 6$

2. $x = 9$

3. $ST = 17$; Perpendicular Bisector Theorem (Thm. 6.1)

4. $WY = 32$; Angle Bisector Theorem (Thm. 6.3)

5. $BW = 20$; Incenter Theorem (Thm. 6.6)

6. $AB > CB$

7. $m\angle 1 < m\angle 2$

8. $m\angle MNP < m\angle NPM$

9. $(2, 2)$; $(0, -2)$; $\left(\frac{4}{3}, \frac{2}{3}\right)$

10. Assume temporarily that $\triangle PQR$ is equilateral and equiangular. Then it follows that $m\angle P \neq m\angle Q$, $m\angle Q \neq m\angle R$, or $m\angle P \neq m\angle R$. By the contrapositive of the Base Angles Theorem (Thm. 5.6), if $m\angle P \neq m\angle Q$, then $PR \neq QR$, if $m\angle Q \neq m\angle R$, then $QP \neq RP$, and if $m\angle P \neq m\angle R$, then $PQ \neq RQ$. All three conclusions contradict the fact that $\triangle PQR$ is equilateral. So, the temporary conclusion must be false. This proves that if $\triangle PQR$ is equilateral, it must also be equiangular.

11. area of $\triangle GEH = \frac{1}{4}A$; By the Triangle Midsegment Theorem (Thm. 6.8), $GH = \frac{1}{2}FD$. By the markings $EG = GD$. By the Segment Addition Postulate (Post. 1.2), $EG + GD = ED$. So, when you substitute EG for GD, you get $EG + EG = ED$, or $2(EG) = ED$, which means that $EG = \frac{1}{2}ED$. So, the area of

$$\triangle GEH = \frac{1}{2}bh$$
$$= \frac{1}{2}(EG)(GH)$$
$$= \frac{1}{2}\left(\frac{1}{2}ED\right)\left(\frac{1}{2}FD\right)$$
$$= \frac{1}{8}(ED)(FD).$$

Note that the area of $\triangle DEF = \frac{1}{2}bh = \frac{1}{2}(ED)(FD)$. So, the area of $\triangle GEH = \frac{1}{8}(ED)(FD) = \frac{1}{4}\left[\frac{1}{2}(ED)(FD)\right] = \frac{1}{4}A$.

12. the first hiker; Because $140° > 128°$, the first hiker is a farther distance, because the longer side is opposite the larger angle.

13. Pine Avenue must be longer than 2 miles and shorter than 16 miles.

14–15. See Additional Answers.

If students need help...	If students got it...
Lesson Tutorials	Resources by Chapter • Enrichment and Extension • Cumulative Review
Skills Review Handbook	Performance Task
BigIdeasMath.com	Start the *next* Section

ANSWERS

1. definition of perpendicular bisector, definition of segment congruence

2. See Additional Answers.

3. B

4. In step 1, the constructed line connects two points that are each equidistant from both A and B. So, it is the perpendicular bisector of $\overline{AB}$, and therefore every point on the line is equidistant from A and B. In step 2, the constructed line connects two points that are each equidistant from both B and C. So, it is the perpendicular bisector of $\overline{BC}$, and therefore every point on the line is equidistant from B and C. So, the point where these two lines intersect is equidistant from all three points. So, the circle with this point as the center that passes through one of the points will also pass through the other two.

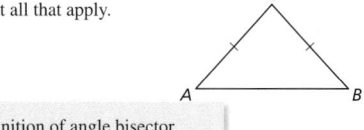

6 Cumulative Assessment

1. Which definition(s) and/or theorem(s) do you need to use to prove the Converse of the Perpendicular Bisector Theorem (Theorem 6.2)? Select all that apply.

   Given $CA = CB$

   Prove Point C lies on the perpendicular bisector of $\overline{AB}$.

   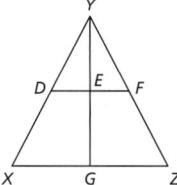

definition of perpendicular bisector	definition of angle bisector
definition of segment congruence	definition of angle congruence
Base Angles Theorem (Theorem 5.6)	Converse of the Base Angles Theorem (Theorem 5.7)
ASA Congruence Theorem (Theorem 5.10)	AAS Congruence Theorem (Theorem 5.11)

2. Use the given information to write a two-column proof.

   Given $\overline{YG}$ is the perpendicular bisector of $\overline{DF}$.

   Prove $\triangle DEY \cong \triangle FEY$

   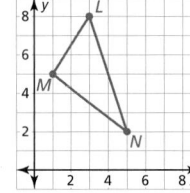

3. What are the coordinates of the centroid of $\triangle LMN$?

   (A) $(2, 5)$

   (B) $(3, 5)$

   (C) $(4, 5)$

   (D) $(5, 5)$

4. Use the steps in the construction to explain how you know that the circle is circumscribed about $\triangle ABC$.

   Step 1

   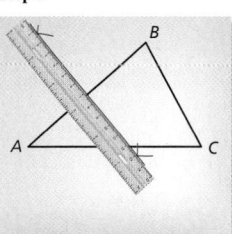

   Step 2

   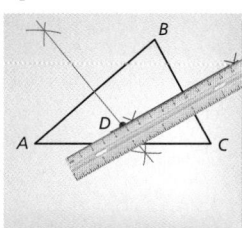

   Step 3

   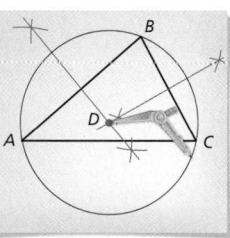

5. Enter the missing reasons in the proof of the Base Angles Theorem (Theorem 5.6).

Given $\overline{AB} \cong \overline{AC}$

Prove $\angle B \cong \angle C$

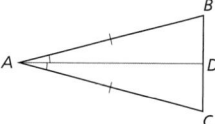

STATEMENTS	REASONS
1. Draw $\overline{AD}$, the angle bisector of $\angle CAB$.	**1.** Construction of angle bisector
2. $\angle CAD \cong \angle BAD$	**2.** _____
3. $\overline{AB} \cong \overline{AC}$	**3.** _____
4. $\overline{DA} \cong \overline{DA}$	**4.** _____
5. $\triangle ADB \cong \triangle ADC$	**5.** _____
6. $\angle B \cong \angle C$	**6.** _____

6. Use the graph of $\triangle QRS$.

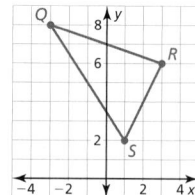

a. Find the coordinates of the vertices of the midsegment triangle. Label the vertices T, U, and V.

b. Show that each midsegment joining the midpoints of two sides is parallel to the third side and is equal to half the length of the third side.

7. A triangle has vertices $X(-2, 2)$, $Y(1, 4)$, and $Z(2, -2)$. Your friend claims that a translation of $(x, y) \rightarrow (x + 2, y - 3)$ and a dilation by a scale factor of 3 will produce a similarity transformation. Do you support your friend's claim? Explain your reasoning.

8. The graph shows a dilation of quadrilateral $ABCD$ by a scale factor of 2. Show that the line containing points B and D is parallel to the line containing points B' and D'.

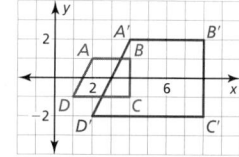

5. definition of angle bisector; given; Reflexive Property of Congruence (Thm. 2.1); SAS Congruence Theorem (Thm. 5.5); Corresponding parts of congruent triangles are congruent.

6. a. $T(0, 7)$, $U(2, 4)$, $V(-1, 5)$

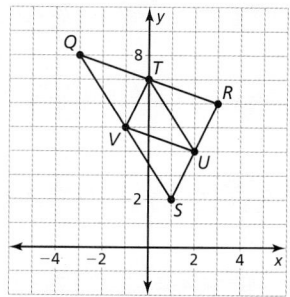

b. slope of $\overline{TV} = 2$, slope of $\overline{SR} = 2$,
Because the slopes are the same, $\overline{TV} \parallel \overline{RS}$.
slope of $\overline{TU} = -\frac{3}{2}$, slope of $\overline{QS} = -\frac{3}{2}$,
Because the slopes are the same, $\overline{TU} \parallel \overline{QS}$.
slope of $\overline{VU} = -\frac{1}{3}$, slope of $\overline{QR} = -\frac{1}{3}$
Because the slopes are the same, $\overline{VU} \parallel \overline{QR}$.
$TV = \sqrt{5}$, $SR = 2\sqrt{5}$,
Because $\sqrt{5} = \frac{1}{2}(2\sqrt{5})$,
$TV = \frac{1}{2}SR$.
$TU = \sqrt{13}$, $QS = 2\sqrt{13}$,
Because $\sqrt{13} = \frac{1}{2}(2\sqrt{13})$,
$TU = \frac{1}{2}QS$.
$VU = \sqrt{10}$, $QR = 2\sqrt{10}$,
Because $\sqrt{10} = \frac{1}{2}(2\sqrt{10})$,
$VU = \frac{1}{2}QR$.

7. yes; Because translations are rigid motions, the image will be congruent to the original triangle after the translation. Then, because dilations are similarity motions, the image after the dilation will be similar to the previous image and the original triangle.

8. slope of $\overleftrightarrow{BD} = \frac{2}{3}$, slope of $\overleftrightarrow{B'D'} = \frac{2}{3}$
Because the slopes are the same, $\overleftrightarrow{BD} \parallel \overleftrightarrow{B'D'}$.

Chapter 7 Pacing Guide	
Chapter Opener/ Mathematical Practices	0.5 Day
Section 1	1.5 Days
Section 2	2 Days
Section 3	2 Days
Quiz	0.5 Day
Section 4	1.5 Days
Section 5	2 Days
Chapter Review/ Chapter Tests	2 Days
Total Chapter 7	12 Days
Year-to-Date	88 Days

7 Quadrilaterals and Other Polygons

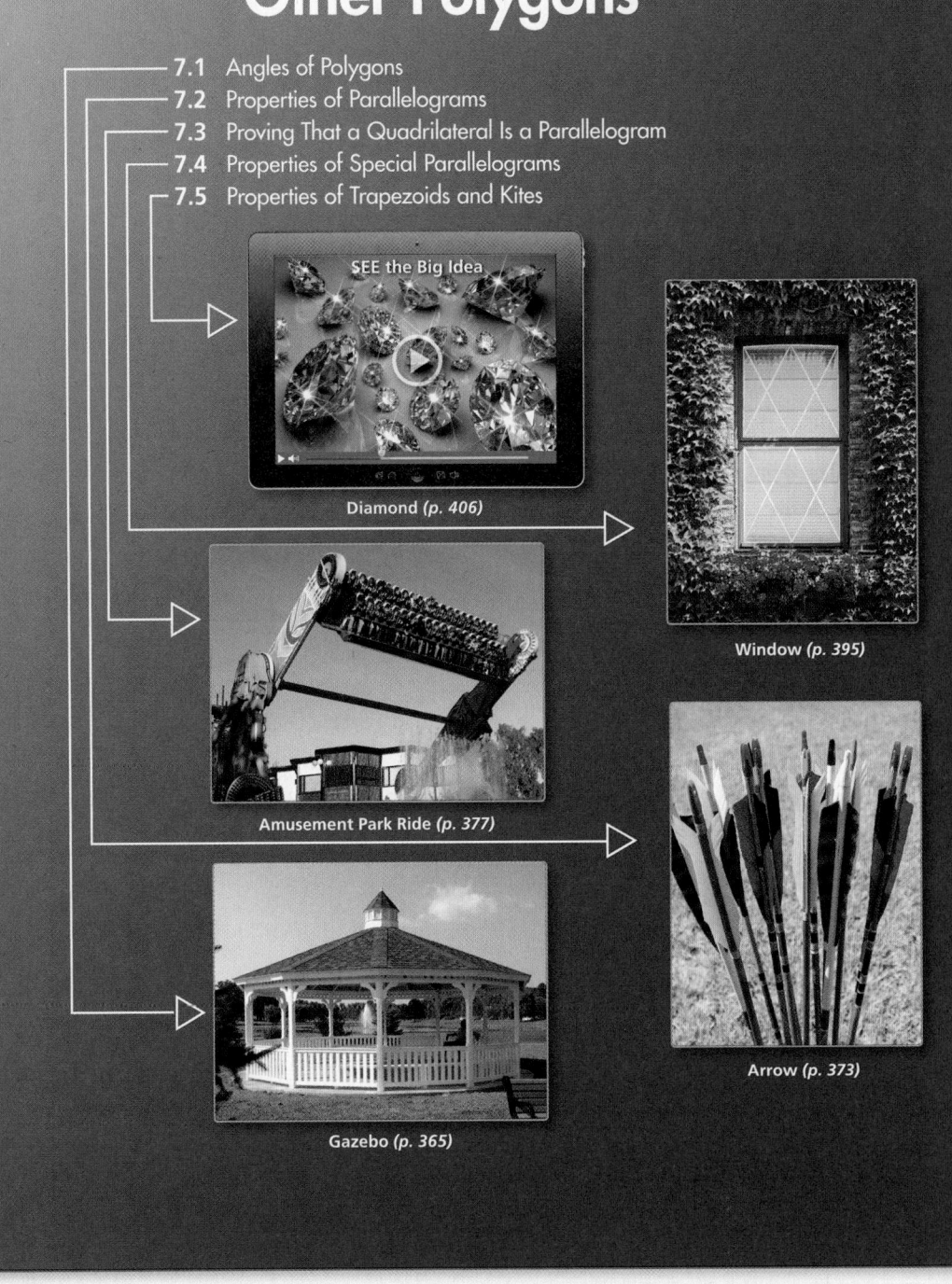

SEE the Big Idea

Diamond (p. 406)

Window (p. 395)

Amusement Park Ride (p. 377)

Arrow (p. 373)

Gazebo (p. 365)

Chapter Summary

- Students have studied the special quadrilaterals in middle school and should be familiar with their definitions and some of their properties. Special quadrilaterals include parallelograms, rectangles, rhombuses, squares, trapezoids, isosceles trapezoids, and kites. Students would have investigated the properties of these special quadrilaterals using inductive reasoning.
- In this chapter, students are able to investigate the properties of special quadrilaterals by using dynamic geometry software. The properties are then proven using a variety of proof formats: transformational, synthetic, analytic, and paragraph.
- The first lesson in the chapter is about the angle measures in a polygon. First, students derive a formula for the sum of the interior angles and then a formula for the sum of the exterior angles.
- The last four lessons are about the special quadrilaterals.
- In Chapter 5, students proved triangles congruent given different hypotheses. The reasoning used in that chapter is applied to proofs involving quadrilaterals in this chapter.

Scaffolding in the Classroom

Graphic Organizers: Summary Triangle
A Summary Triangle can be used to explain a concept. Typically, the Summary Triangle is divided into 3 or 4 parts. In the top part, students write the concept being explained. In the middle part(s), students write any procedure, explanation, description, definition, theorem, and/or formula(s). In the bottom part, students write an example to illustrate the concept. A Summary Triangle can be used as an assessment tool, in which blanks are left for students to complete. Also, students can place their Summary Triangles on note cards to use as quick study references.

 COMMON CORE PROGRESSION

Middle School
- Solve real-world problems involving angle measure.
- Solve linear equations with rational number coefficients.
- Draw polygons in the coordinate plane given vertices and find lengths of sides.

Algebra 1
- Create equations in one variable.
- Solve linear equations in one variable.
- Graph points in the coordinate plane.
- Identify and write equations of parallel and perpendicular lines.

Geometry
- Find and use the interior and exterior angle measures of polygons.
- Use properties of parallelograms and special parallelograms.
- Prove that a quadrilateral is a parallelogram.
- Identify and use properties of trapezoids and kites.

	Standards Summary	
Section	**Common Core State Standards**	
7.1	Preparing	HSG-CO.C.11
7.2	Learning	HSG-CO.C.11, HSG-SRT.B.5
7.3	Learning	HSG-CO.C.11, HSG-SRT.B.5, HSG-MG.A.1
7.4	Learning	HSG-CO.C.11, HSG-SRT.B.5, HSG-MG.A.1, HSG-MG.A.3
7.5	Learning	HSG-SRT.B.5, HSG-MG.A.1

Questioning in the Classroom
How will this work?
Look for examples, exercises, problems, and questions that do not have a specific solution or answer. Ask students to explain how to solve the problem.

Laurie's Notes

Maintaining Mathematical Proficiency

Using Structure to Solve a Multi-Step Equation

- Some students may find it easier to substitute z for the expression in parentheses, solve the equation for z, and then use the value of z to find the value of x.

COMMON ERROR Students may have trouble understanding the meaning of the direction line and use the Distributive Property as the first step. Explain that the method shown does *not* involve distributing the factor 3 but instead performs inverse operations on the expression $(2 + x)$.

Identifying Parallel and Perpendicular Lines

- Review the relationships between slopes of parallel lines and slopes of perpendicular lines in Section 3.5.

COMMON ERROR Some students may forget the slope formula. Remind students that they can also use the expression $\frac{\text{rise}}{\text{run}}$ to find the slope.

Mathematical Practices (continued on page 358)

- The eight *Mathematical Practices* focus attention on how mathematics is learned—process versus content. Page 358 demonstrates how a model such as a Venn diagram can help students see the relationship between different types of quadrilaterals. There are other types of models, such as flowcharts, that also help students see relationships between the different types of quadrilaterals.
- Use the *Mathematical Practices* page to help students develop mathematical habits of mind—how mathematics can be explored and how mathematics is thought about.

If students need help...	If students got it...
Student Journal • Maintaining Mathematical Proficiency	Game Closet at *BigIdeasMath.com*
Lesson Tutorials	Start the *next* Section
Skills Review Handbook	

Maintaining Mathematical Proficiency

Using Structure to Solve a Multi-Step Equation

Example 1 Solve $3(2 + x) = -9$ by interpreting the expression $2 + x$ as a single quantity.

$$3(2 + x) = -9$$ Write the equation.

$$\frac{3(2 + x)}{3} = \frac{-9}{3}$$ Divide each side by 3.

$$2 + x = -3$$ Simplify.

$$\underline{-2 \qquad -2}$$ Subtract 2 from each side.

$$x = -5$$ Simplify.

Solve the equation by interpreting the expression in parentheses as a single quantity.

1. $4(7 - x) = 16$ **2.** $7(1 - x) + 2 = -19$ **3.** $3(x - 5) + 8(x - 5) = 22$

Identifying Parallel and Perpendicular Lines

Example 2 Determine which of the lines are parallel and which are perpendicular.

Find the slope of each line.

Line a: $m = \dfrac{3 - (-3)}{-4 - (-2)} = -3$

Line b: $m = \dfrac{-1 - (-4)}{1 - 2} = -3$

Line c: $m = \dfrac{2 - (-2)}{3 - 4} = -4$

Line d: $m = \dfrac{2 - 0}{2 - (-4)} = \dfrac{1}{3}$

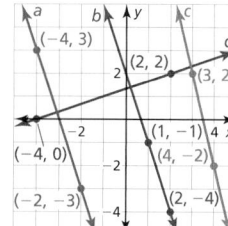

Because lines a and b have the same slope, lines a and b are parallel. Because $\frac{1}{3}(-3) = -1$, lines a and d are perpendicular and lines b and d are perpendicular.

Determine which lines are parallel and which are perpendicular.

4. 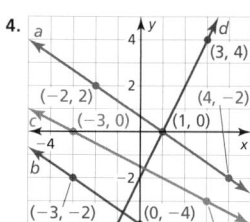   **5.** 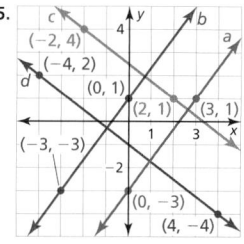   **6.**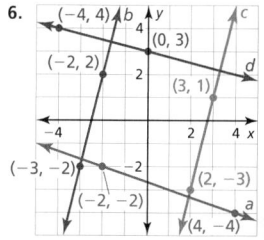

7. ABSTRACT REASONING Explain why interpreting an expression as a single quantity does not contradict the order of operations.

Common Core State Standards

HSA-REI.B.3 Solve linear equations … in one variable….

HSA-SSE.A.1b Interpret complicated expressions by viewing one or more of their parts as a single entity.

HSG-GPE.B.5 Prove the slope criteria for parallel and perpendicular lines and use them to solve geometric problems (e.g., find the equation of a line parallel or perpendicular to a given line that passes through a given point.)

ANSWERS

1. $x = 3$

2. $x = 4$

3. $x = 7$

4. $a \parallel b, c \perp d$

5. $a \parallel b, c \parallel d, a \perp c, a \perp d, b \perp c, b \perp d$

6. $b \parallel c, b \perp d, c \perp d$

7. You can follow the order of operations with all of the other operations in the equation and treat the operations in the expression separately.

Vocabulary Review

Have students make a Comparison Chart for parallel and perpendicular lines in the coordinate plane. Include the following terms.

- Slope
- Parallel
- Perpendicular

1. false; There is no overlap between the set of trapezoids and the set of kites.

2. true; There is no overlap between the set of kites and the set of parallelograms.

3. false; There is area inside the parallelogram circle for rhombuses and other parallelograms that do not fall inside the circle for rectangles.

4. true; All squares are inside the category of quadrilaterals.

5. *Sample answer:* All kites are quadrilaterals. No trapezoids are kites. All squares are parallelograms. All squares are rectangles. Some rectangles are squares. No rhombuses are trapezoids.

6. See Additional Answers.

Mathematical Practices

Mathematically proficient students use diagrams to show relationships.

Mapping Relationships

⑤ Core Concept

Classifications of Quadrilaterals

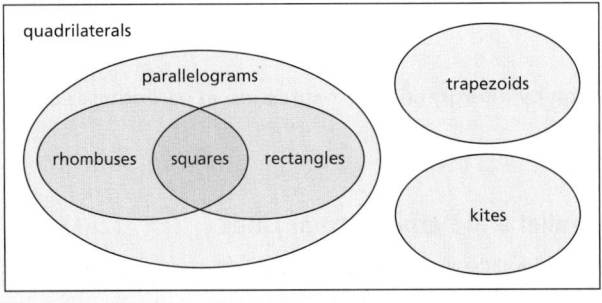

EXAMPLE 1 Writing Statements about Quadrilaterals

Use the Venn diagram above to write three true statements about different types of quadrilaterals.

SOLUTION

Here are three true statements that can be made about the relationships shown in the Venn diagram.

- All rhombuses are parallelograms.
- Some rhombuses are rectangles.
- No trapezoids are parallelograms.

Monitoring Progress

Use the Venn diagram above to decide whether each statement is true or false. Explain your reasoning.

1. Some trapezoids are kites.

2. No kites are parallelograms.

3. All parallelograms are rectangles.

4. Some quadrilaterals are squares.

5. Example 1 lists three true statements based on the Venn diagram above. Write six more true statements based on the Venn diagram.

6. A cyclic quadrilateral is a quadrilateral that can be circumscribed by a circle so that the circle touches each vertex. Redraw the Venn diagram so that it includes cyclic quadrilaterals.

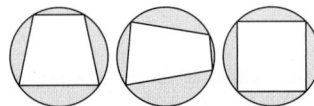

Laurie's Notes — Mathematical Practices (continued from page T-357)

- Students should be familiar with how to read a Venn diagram.
- Complete Example 1 together.
- Give time for students to work through the questions in the *Monitoring Progress*, and then discuss as a class.
- **Extension:** There is a different, less common definition for *trapezoid*. It says that a trapezoid has at least one pair of parallel sides. If this were the accepted definition, the Venn diagram would be different. Have students redraw the Venn diagram and make statements about the relationships shown based on this definition.

Overview of Section 7.1

Introduction

- Students should be familiar with the content in this lesson from middle school mathematics, specifically grade 8.
- The lesson presents theorems for the sum of the interior angles and the sum of the exterior angles of a polygon. Interior and exterior angles of regular polygons are also discussed.

Teaching Strategy

- The explorations focus on discovering the relationship between the number of sides in a polygon and the sum of the interior angles.
- There are several ways in which the sum of the exterior angles can be explored.
- The low-tech version is to draw a polygon and then extend each side to form an exterior angle at each vertex. Be sure to extend in the same direction (clockwise or counterclockwise) at each vertex. Place a pencil or pointer along one side of the polygon. Simulate what happens when the pencil travels along each side of the polygon without being lifted. The pencil turns at the vertices, rotating through each exterior angle. When the pencil returns to the starting position, it has rotated through a total of 360°.
- A second way to investigate exterior angles is to use a slider and create dilations of the polygon. Place the point of dilation at the center of the polygon and draw smaller and smaller images. The polygon collapses to the point of dilation. The result is a very visual demonstration that the sum of the exterior angles is 360°.

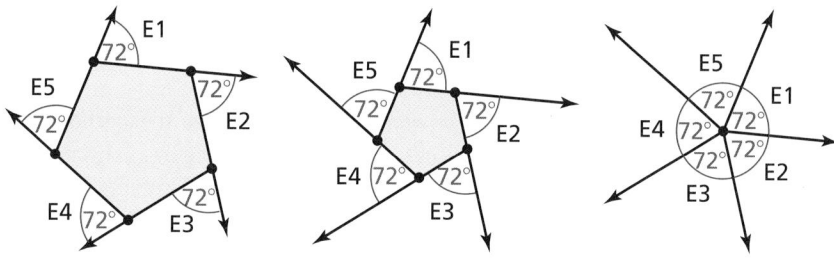

- You can find simulations of these methods online by searching for "simulation sum of exterior angles of a polygon."

Pacing Suggestion

- Exploration 1 is long when done in its entirety. You could assign Exploration 2 for homework. If students work through Exploration 1 and they have familiarity with the content from middle school, then you might be selective with the number of examples modeled.

**Common Core
State Standards**

HSG-CO.C.11 Prove theorems about
parallelograms.

Laurie's Notes

Exploration

Motivate

- Capture and display images from the Internet of common objects that are shaped like various polygons.
- *Examples:* pentagon: top of fire hydrant; hexagon: honeycomb; octagon: stop sign or tiles; decagon: concave five-pointed star
- Explain to students that in this lesson they will be investigating properties of polygons.

Exploration Note

- Depending on the software and preference settings, you may have reflex angles (angles with measures greater than 180°) that result when students click and drag on a vertex. Students should include observations about concave polygons.
- Depending on the software, spreadsheet functionality may be built in. If not, students should use a spreadsheet to work with the data analytically.

Exploration 1

- The summing process should be set up dynamically so that students can click and drag on a vertex and observe that, although the angle measures change, the sum remains a constant. This is true even for concave polygons.
- This is a longer exploration, but it is important for students to experience the dynamic features of this investigation. For instance, what changes and what stays the same when you drag on one vertex of a polygon?
- **?** "What is the independent variable, and what is the dependent variable?" The independent variable is the number of sides of the polygon, and the dependent variable is the sum of the angle measures.
- Students should not need to perform a regression to write the function. The function they write will likely be $S = 180n - 360$. The focus is on the sum increasing by a constant rate (slope) of 180 each time another side is added to the polygon. So it makes sense that their equation would be in slope-intercept form.
- If this exploration had used the approach of drawing in all the diagonals from one vertex to form triangular regions inside the polygon, the equation the students write would have been $S = 180(n - 2)$. The $(n - 2)$ represents the number of triangles formed inside an n-gon when all the diagonals from one vertex are drawn.
- Make sure students see the connection between the two forms of the equation.

Exploration 2

- **?** "What is a regular polygon?" a polygon whose sides are all congruent and whose angles are all congruent
- If the data from the first exploration have been entered into a spreadsheet, students can add an additional column that divides the sum by the number of the sides, which is also the number of angles.

Communicate Your Answer

- If students have written an equation for the sum of the interior angles of a polygon, they only need to evaluate the equation for $n = 12$.

Connecting to Next Step

- If students have worked through the first exploration completely, they could do the first four examples in the lesson independently and quickly.

7.1 Angles of Polygons

Essential Question What is the sum of the measures of the interior angles of a polygon?

EXPLORATION 1 The Sum of the Angle Measures of a Polygon

Work with a partner. Use dynamic geometry software.

a. Draw a quadrilateral and a pentagon. Find the sum of the measures of the interior angles of each polygon.

Sample

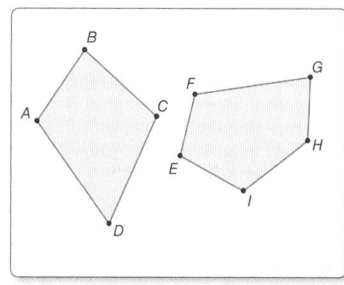

b. Draw other polygons and find the sums of the measures of their interior angles. Record your results in the table below.

CONSTRUCTING VIABLE ARGUMENTS

To be proficient in math, you need to reason inductively about data.

Number of sides, n	3	4	5	6	7	8	9
Sum of angle measures, S							

c. Plot the data from your table in a coordinate plane.

d. Write a function that fits the data. Explain what the function represents.

EXPLORATION 2 Measure of One Angle in a Regular Polygon

Work with a partner.

a. Use the function you found in Exploration 1 to write a new function that gives the measure of one interior angle in a regular polygon with n sides.

b. Use the function in part (a) to find the measure of one interior angle of a regular pentagon. Use dynamic geometry software to check your result by constructing a regular pentagon and finding the measure of one of its interior angles.

c. Copy your table from Exploration 1 and add a row for the measure of one interior angle in a regular polygon with n sides. Complete the table. Use dynamic geometry software to check your results.

Communicate Your Answer

3. What is the sum of the measures of the interior angles of a polygon?

4. Find the measure of one interior angle in a regular dodecagon (a polygon with 12 sides).

Dynamic Teaching Tools

Dynamic Assessment & Progress Monitoring Tool

Lesson Planning Tool

Interactive Whiteboard Lesson Library

Dynamic Classroom with Dynamic Investigations

ANSWERS

1. a. 360°, 540°

   b. 180°, 360°, 540°, 720°, 900°, 1080°, 1260°

   c.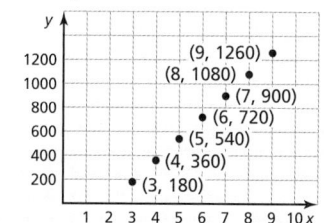

   d. $S = (n - 2) \cdot 180$; Let $n =$ the number of sides of the polygon. If you subtract 2 and multiply the difference by 180°, then you get the sum of the measures of the interior angles of a polygon.

2. a. $S = \dfrac{(n - 2) \cdot 180}{n}$

   b. 108°

   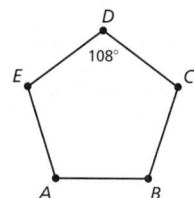

   c.

Number of Sides, n	3	4	5	6
Sum of Angle Measures, S	180°	360°	540°	720°
Interior Angle	60°	90°	108°	120°

Number of Sides, n	7	8	9
Sum of Angle Measures, S	900°	1080°	1260°
Interior Angle	128.57°	135°	140°

3. The sum S of the measures of the interior angles of a polygon with n sides is given by $S = (n - 2)180$.

4. 150°

Extra Example 1

Find the sum of the measures of the interior angles of the figure.

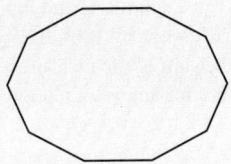

1440°

MONITORING PROGRESS ANSWER

1. 1620°

7.1 Lesson

What You Will Learn

▶ Use the interior angle measures of polygons.

▶ Use the exterior angle measures of polygons.

Core Vocabulary

diagonal, *p. 360*
equilateral polygon, *p. 361*
equiangular polygon, *p. 361*
regular polygon, *p. 361*

Previous
polygon
convex
interior angles
exterior angles

Using Interior Angle Measures of Polygons

In a polygon, two vertices that are endpoints of the same side are called *consecutive vertices*. A **diagonal** of a polygon is a segment that joins two nonconsecutive vertices.

As you can see, the diagonals from one vertex divide a polygon into triangles. Dividing a polygon with n sides into $(n - 2)$ triangles shows that the sum of the measures of the interior angles of a polygon is a multiple of 180°.

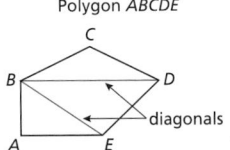

Polygon *ABCDE*

A and B are consecutive vertices.
Vertex B has two diagonals, $\overline{BD}$ and $\overline{BE}$.

> **REMEMBER**
>
> A polygon is *convex* when no line that contains a side of the polygon contains a point in the interior of the polygon.

🔄 Theorem

Theorem 7.1 Polygon Interior Angles Theorem

The sum of the measures of the interior angles of a convex n-gon is $(n - 2) \cdot 180°$.

$$m\angle 1 + m\angle 2 + \cdots + m\angle n = (n - 2) \cdot 180°$$

Proof Ex. 42 (for pentagons), p. 365

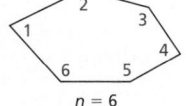

$n = 6$

EXAMPLE 1   Finding the Sum of Angle Measures in a Polygon

Find the sum of the measures of the interior angles of the figure.

SOLUTION

The figure is a convex octagon. It has 8 sides. Use the Polygon Interior Angles Theorem.

$(n - 2) \cdot 180° = (8 - 2) \cdot 180°$	Substitute 8 for n.
$= 6 \cdot 180°$	Subtract.
$= 1080°$	Multiply.

▶ The sum of the measures of the interior angles of the figure is 1080°.

Monitoring Progress 🔊 Help in English and Spanish at *BigIdeasMath.com*

1. The coin shown is in the shape of an 11-gon. Find the sum of the measures of the interior angles.

Laurie's Notes   Teacher Actions

- Theorem 7.1 is a statement of the results found by students in the first exploration. Note that it is written in the factored form. Connect this to the number of triangles formed when the diagonals from one vertex are drawn.
- Note that the theorem is stated for convex n-gons. While the formula is valid for concave polygons, reflex angles have not been defined.
- **Think-Pair-Share:** Have students work independently on Example 1 and then compare with partners.

EXAMPLE 2   **Finding the Number of Sides of a Polygon**

The sum of the measures of the interior angles of a convex polygon is 900°. Classify the polygon by the number of sides.

SOLUTION

Use the Polygon Interior Angles Theorem to write an equation involving the number of sides n. Then solve the equation to find the number of sides.

$(n-2) \cdot 180° = 900°$	Polygon Interior Angles Theorem
$n - 2 = 5$	Divide each side by 180°.
$n = 7$	Add 2 to each side.

▶   The polygon has 7 sides. It is a heptagon.

⟳ Corollary

Corollary 7.1   Corollary to the Polygon Interior Angles Theorem

The sum of the measures of the interior angles of a quadrilateral is 360°.

Proof Ex. 43, p. 366

EXAMPLE 3   **Finding an Unknown Interior Angle Measure**

Find the value of x in the diagram.

SOLUTION

The polygon is a quadrilateral. Use the Corollary to the Polygon Interior Angles Theorem to write an equation involving x. Then solve the equation.

$x° + 108° + 121° + 59° = 360°$	Corollary to the Polygon Interior Angles Theorem
$x + 288 = 360$	Combine like terms.
$x = 72$	Subtract 288 from each side.

▶   The value of x is 72.

Monitoring Progress 🔊 Help in English and Spanish at *BigIdeasMath.com*

2. The sum of the measures of the interior angles of a convex polygon is 1440°. Classify the polygon by the number of sides.

3. The measures of the interior angles of a quadrilateral are $x°$, $3x°$, $5x°$, and $7x°$. Find the measures of all the interior angles.

In an **equilateral polygon**, all sides are congruent.

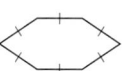

In an **equiangular polygon**, all angles in the interior of the polygon are congruent.

A **regular polygon** is a convex polygon that is both equilateral and equiangular.

Section 7.1   Angles of Polygons   **361**

Extra Example 2

The sum of the measures of the interior angles of a convex polygon is 1800°. Classify the polygon by the number of sides.   12 sides; It is a dodecagon.

Extra Example 3

Find the value of x in the diagram.

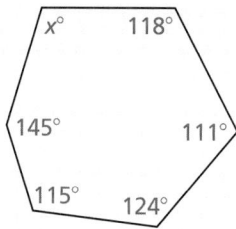

$x = 107$

MONITORING PROGRESS ANSWERS

 2. decagon

 3. 22.5°, 67.5°, 112.5°, 157.5°

Laurie's Notes   Teacher Actions

- Students become adept at remembering the list of polygon sums and may recall the number of sides in the polygon without solving.

❓ **"What is a corollary?"** It is a statement that follows directly from a theorem. Because quadrilaterals are studied in the remainder of the chapter, this corollary is stated for use in future problems.

- **Turn and Talk:** "Is it possible for a polygon to be equilateral and not equiangular? Equiangular and not equilateral? Both? Neither?"

Extra Example 4

A polygon is shown.

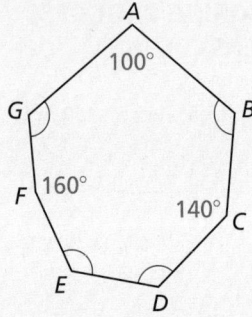

a. Is the polygon regular? Explain your reasoning.

The polygon is not equiangular, so it is not regular.

b. Find the measures of ∠*B*, ∠*D*, ∠*E*, and ∠*G*.

$m\angle B = m\angle D = m\angle E = m\angle G = 125°$

MONITORING PROGRESS ANSWERS

4. $m\angle S = m\angle T = 103°$

5.

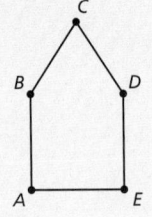

EXAMPLE 4   **Finding Angle Measures in Polygons**

A home plate for a baseball field is shown.

a. Is the polygon regular? Explain your reasoning.

b. Find the measures of ∠*C* and ∠*E*.

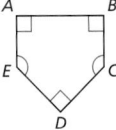

SOLUTION

a. The polygon is not equilateral or equiangular. So, the polygon is not regular.

b. Find the sum of the measures of the interior angles.

$(n - 2) \cdot 180° = (5 - 2) \cdot 180° = 540°$ Polygon Interior Angles Theorem

Then write an equation involving *x* and solve the equation.

$$x° + x° + 90° + 90° + 90° = 540°$$ Write an equation.

$$2x + 270 = 540$$ Combine like terms.

$$x = 135$$ Solve for *x*.

▶ So, $m\angle C = m\angle E = 135°$.

Monitoring Progress  Help in English and Spanish at *BigIdeasMath.com*

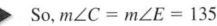

4. Find $m\angle S$ and $m\angle T$ in the diagram.

5. Sketch a pentagon that is equilateral but not equiangular.

Using Exterior Angle Measures of Polygons

Unlike the sum of the interior angle measures of a convex polygon, the sum of the exterior angle measures does *not* depend on the number of sides of the polygon. The diagrams suggest that the sum of the measures of the exterior angles, one angle at each vertex, of a pentagon is 360°. In general, this sum is 360° for any convex polygon.

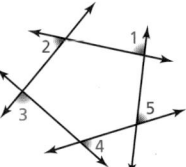

JUSTIFYING STEPS

To help justify this conclusion, you can visualize a circle containing two straight angles. So, there are 180° + 180°, or 360°, in a circle.

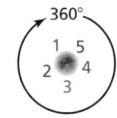

Step 1 Shade one exterior angle at each vertex.

Step 2 Cut out the exterior angles.

Step 3 Arrange the exterior angles to form 360°.

🌀 Theorem

Theorem 7.2   Polygon Exterior Angles Theorem

The sum of the measures of the exterior angles of a convex polygon, one angle at each vertex, is 360°.

$$m\angle 1 + m\angle 2 + \cdots + m\angle n = 360°$$

Proof Ex. 51, p. 366

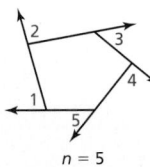

$n = 5$

Laurie's Notes   Teacher Actions

❓ **MP3 Construct Viable Arguments and Critique the Reasoning of Others:** After Example 4 ask, "Is it possible for a pentagon to have four right angles? Explain." Answers will vary. Listen for knowledge that the answer is no. Students may reference that the last angle would be 180° or that it is also impossible to construct.

• Students can discover that the measures of the exterior angles of a polygon sum to 360° using the method shown. Alternate approaches are suggested in the *Teaching Strategy* on page T-358. Write Theorem 7.2.

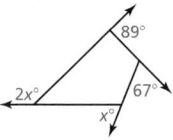 **EXAMPLE 5** Finding an Unknown Exterior Angle Measure

Find the value of *x* in the diagram.

SOLUTION

Use the Polygon Exterior Angles Theorem to write and solve an equation.

$x° + 2x° + 89° + 67° = 360°$ Polygon Exterior Angles Theorem

$3x + 156 = 360$ Combine like terms.

$x = 68$ Solve for *x*.

▶ The value of *x* is 68.

REMEMBER

A *dodecagon* is a polygon with 12 sides and 12 vertices.

EXAMPLE 6 Finding Angle Measures in Regular Polygons

The trampoline shown is shaped like a regular dodecagon.

a. Find the measure of each interior angle.

b. Find the measure of each exterior angle.

SOLUTION

a. Use the Polygon Interior Angles Theorem to find the sum of the measures of the interior angles.

$$(n - 2) \cdot 180° = (12 - 2) \cdot 180°$$
$$= 1800°$$

Then find the measure of one interior angle. A regular dodecagon has 12 congruent interior angles. Divide 1800° by 12.

$$\frac{1800°}{12} = 150°$$

▶ The measure of each interior angle in the dodecagon is 150°.

b. By the Polygon Exterior Angles Theorem, the sum of the measures of the exterior angles, one angle at each vertex, is 360°. Divide 360° by 12 to find the measure of one of the 12 congruent exterior angles.

$$\frac{360°}{12} = 30°$$

▶ The measure of each exterior angle in the dodecagon is 30°.

Monitoring Progress 🔊 Help in English and Spanish at *BigIdeasMath.com*

6. A convex hexagon has exterior angles with measures 34°, 49°, 58°, 67°, and 75°. What is the measure of an exterior angle at the sixth vertex?

7. An interior angle and an adjacent exterior angle of a polygon form a linear pair. How can you use this fact as another method to find the measure of each exterior angle in Example 6?

Extra Example 5

Find the value of *x* in the diagram.

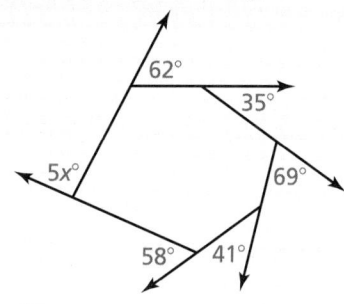

$x = 19$

Extra Example 6

Each face of the dodecahedron is shaped like a regular pentagon.

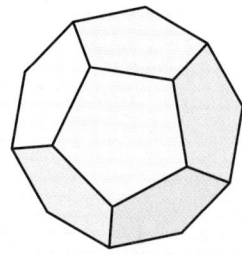

a. Find the measure of each interior angle of a regular pentagon. 108°

b. Find the measure of each exterior angle of a regular pentagon. 72°

MONITORING PROGRESS ANSWERS

6. 77°

7. You can find the measure of each exterior angle by subtracting the measure of the interior angle from 180°. In Example 6, the measure of each exterior angle is $180° - 150° = 30°$.

Laurie's Notes   **Teacher Actions**

• **Think-Pair-Share:** Have students work independently on Example 5 and then compare with partners.

• **Turn and Talk:** "How can you find the measure of each interior angle of a regular polygon? Each exterior angle?"

? **Probing Question:** "If you know that the measure of an interior angle of a regular decagon is 144°, how can you find the exterior angle measure?" The interior and exterior angles are supplementary, so the exterior angle would be 36°.

Closure

• **Writing Prompt:** To find the sum of the measures of the interior angles of an *n*-gon …

ANSWERS

1. A segment connecting consecutive vertices is a side of the polygon, not a diagonal.
2. the sum of the measures of the interior angles of a pentagon; This sum is 540°, but the other sums are 360°.
3. 1260°
4. 2160°
5. 2520°
6. 3240°
7. hexagon
8. octagon
9. 16-gon
10. 20-gon
11. $x = 64$
12. $x = 66$
13. $x = 89$
14. $x = 99$
15. $x = 70$
16. $x = 117$
17. $x = 150$
18. $x = 88\frac{1}{3}$
19. $m\angle X = m\angle Y = 92°$
20. $m\angle X = m\angle Y = 142°$
21. $m\angle X = m\angle Y = 100.5°$
22. $m\angle X = m\angle Y = 135°$

7.1 Exercises

Dynamic Solutions available at *BigIdeasMath.com*

Vocabulary and Core Concept Check

1. **VOCABULARY** Why do vertices connected by a diagonal of a polygon have to be nonconsecutive?

2. **WHICH ONE DOESN'T BELONG?** Which sum does *not* belong with the other three? Explain your reasoning.

the sum of the measures of the interior angles of a quadrilateral	the sum of the measures of the exterior angles of a quadrilateral
the sum of the measures of the interior angles of a pentagon	the sum of the measures of the exterior angles of a pentagon

Monitoring Progress and Modeling with Mathematics

In Exercises 3–6, find the sum of the measures of the interior angles of the indicated convex polygon. *(See Example 1.)*

3. nonagon
4. 14-gon
5. 16-gon
6. 20-gon

In Exercises 7–10, the sum of the measures of the interior angles of a convex polygon is given. Classify the polygon by the number of sides. *(See Example 2.)*

7. 720°
8. 1080°
9. 2520°
10. 3240°

In Exercises 11–14, find the value of *x*. *(See Example 3.)*

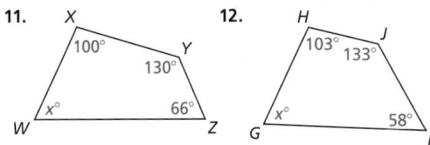

11.
12.

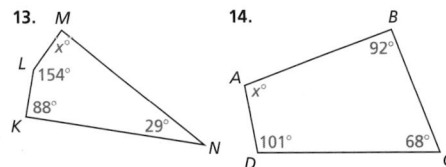

13.
14.

In Exercises 15–18, find the value of *x*.

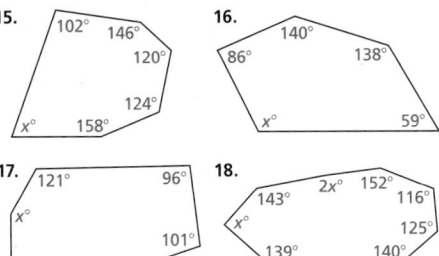

15.
16.

17.
18.

In Exercises 19–22, find the measures of $\angle X$ and $\angle Y$. *(See Example 4.)*

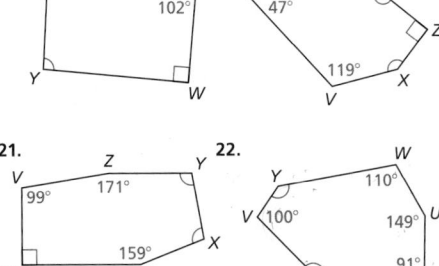

19.
20.

21.
22.

364   Chapter 7   Quadrilaterals and Other Polygons

In Exercises 23–26, find the value of x. (See Example 5.)

23.
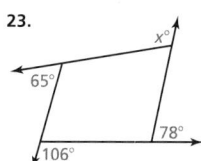

24.
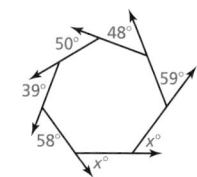

25.
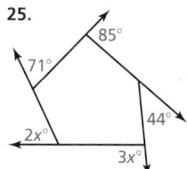

26.
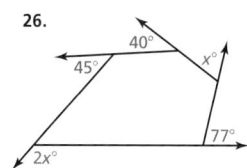

In Exercises 27–30, find the measure of each interior angle and each exterior angle of the indicated regular polygon. (See Example 6.)

27. pentagon

28. 18-gon

29. 45-gon

30. 90-gon

ERROR ANALYSIS In Exercises 31 and 32, describe and correct the error in finding the measure of one exterior angle of a regular pentagon.

31.

$(n - 2) \cdot 180° = (5 - 2) \cdot 180°$
$= 3 \cdot 180°$
$= 540°$

The sum of the measures of the angles is 540°. There are five angles, so the measure of one exterior angle is $\frac{540°}{5} = 108°$.

32.

There are a total of 10 exterior angles, two at each vertex, so the measure of one exterior angle is $\frac{360°}{10} = 36°$.

33. **MODELING WITH MATHEMATICS** The base of a jewelry box is shaped like a regular hexagon. What is the measure of each interior angle of the jewelry box base?

34. **MODELING WITH MATHEMATICS** The floor of the gazebo shown is shaped like a regular decagon. Find the measure of each interior angle of the regular decagon. Then find the measure of each exterior angle.

35. **WRITING A FORMULA** Write a formula to find the number of sides n in a regular polygon given that the measure of one interior angle is x°.

36. **WRITING A FORMULA** Write a formula to find the number of sides n in a regular polygon given that the measure of one exterior angle is x°.

REASONING In Exercises 37–40, find the number of sides for the regular polygon described.

37. Each interior angle has a measure of 156°.

38. Each interior angle has a measure of 165°.

39. Each exterior angle has a measure of 9°.

40. Each exterior angle has a measure of 6°.

41. **DRAWING CONCLUSIONS** Which of the following angle measures are possible interior angle measures of a regular polygon? Explain your reasoning. Select all that apply.

Ⓐ 162°   Ⓑ 171°   Ⓒ 75°   Ⓓ 40°

42. **PROVING A THEOREM** The Polygon Interior Angles Theorem (Theorem 7.1) states that the sum of the measures of the interior angles of a convex n-gon is $(n - 2) \cdot 180°$. Write a paragraph proof of this theorem for the case when n = 5.

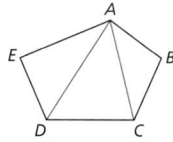

ANSWERS

23. x = 111

24. x = 53

25. x = 32

26. x = 66

27. 108°, 72°

28. 160°, 20°

29. 172°, 8°

30. 176°, 4°

31. The measure of one interior angle of a regular pentagon was found, but the exterior angle should be found by dividing 360° by the number of angles; $\frac{360°}{5} = 72°$

32. There is one exterior angle at each vertex, so the measure of one exterior angle is found by dividing 360° by the number of vertices; $\frac{360°}{5} = 72°$

33. 120°

34. 144°; 36°

35. $n = \frac{360}{180 - x}$

36. $n = \frac{360}{x}$

37. 15

38. 24

39. 40

40. 60

41. A, B; Solving the equation found in Exercise 35 for n yields a positive integer greater than or equal to 3 for A and B, but not for C and D.

42. In a pentagon, when all the diagonals from one vertex are drawn, the polygon is divided into three triangles. Because the sum of the measures of the interior angles of each triangle is 180°, the sum of the measures of the interior angles of the pentagon is $(5 - 2) \cdot 180° = 3 \cdot 180° = 540°$.

43. In a quadrilateral, when all the diagonals from one vertex are drawn, the polygon is divided into two triangles. Because the sum of the measures of the interior angles of each triangle is 180°, the sum of the measures of the interior angles of the quadrilateral is 2 • 180° = 360°.

44. yes; Because an interior angle and an adjacent exterior angle of a polygon form a linear pair, you can use the Polygon Exterior Angles Theorem (Thm. 7.2) to find the measure of the exterior angles, and then you can subtract this value from 180° to find the interior angle measures of a regular polygon.

45. 21°, 21°, 21°, 21°, 138°, 138°

46. yes; The measure of the angle where the polygon caves in is greater than 180° but less than 360°.

47–56. See Additional Answers.

Mini-Assessment

1. A bumper pool table is shaped like a regular octagon.

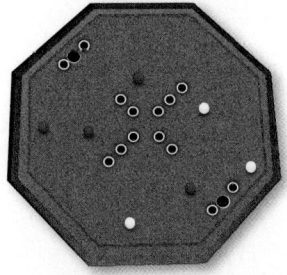

  a. Find the measure of each interior angle. **135°**

  b. Find the measure of each exterior angle. **45°**

2. The sum of the measures of the interior angles of a convex polygon is 2700°. Classify the polygon by the number of sides. **The polygon has 17 sides, so it is a 17-gon.**

3. The measures of three of the exterior angles of a convex quadrilateral are 90°, 76°, and 110°. What is the measure of the exterior angle at the fourth vertex? **84°**

---

43. **PROVING A COROLLARY** Write a paragraph proof of the Corollary to the Polygon Interior Angles Theorem (Corollary 7.1).

44. **MAKING AN ARGUMENT** Your friend claims that to find the interior angle measures of a regular polygon, you do not have to use the Polygon Interior Angles Theorem (Theorem 7.1). You instead can use the Polygon Exterior Angles Theorem (Theorem 7.2) and then the Linear Pair Postulate (Postulate 2.8). Is your friend correct? Explain your reasoning.

45. **MATHEMATICAL CONNECTIONS** In an equilateral hexagon, four of the exterior angles each have a measure of $x°$. The other two exterior angles each have a measure of twice the sum of x and 48. Find the measure of each exterior angle.

46. **THOUGHT PROVOKING** For a concave polygon, is it true that at least one of the interior angle measures must be greater than 180°? If not, give an example. If so, explain your reasoning.

47. **WRITING EXPRESSIONS** Write an expression to find the sum of the measures of the interior angles for a concave polygon. Explain your reasoning.

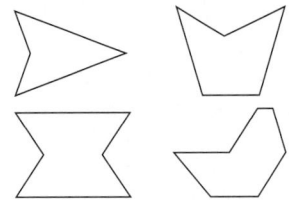

48. **ANALYZING RELATIONSHIPS** Polygon $ABCDEFGH$ is a regular octagon. Suppose sides $\overline{AB}$ and $\overline{CD}$ are extended to meet at a point P. Find $m\angle BPC$. Explain your reasoning. Include a diagram with your answer.

49. **MULTIPLE REPRESENTATIONS** The formula for the measure of each interior angle in a regular polygon can be written in function notation.

  a. Write a function $h(n)$, where n is the number of sides in a regular polygon and $h(n)$ is the measure of any interior angle in the regular polygon.

  b. Use the function to find $h(9)$.

  c. Use the function to find n when $h(n) = 150°$.

  d. Plot the points for $n = 3, 4, 5, 6, 7,$ and 8. What happens to the value of $h(n)$ as n gets larger?

50. **HOW DO YOU SEE IT?** Is the hexagon a regular hexagon? Explain your reasoning.

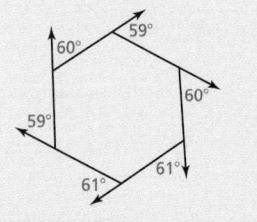

51. **PROVING A THEOREM** Write a paragraph proof of the Polygon Exterior Angles Theorem (Theorem 7.2). (*Hint:* In a convex n-gon, the sum of the measures of an interior angle and an adjacent exterior angle at any vertex is 180°.)

52. **ABSTRACT REASONING** You are given a convex polygon. You are asked to draw a new polygon by increasing the sum of the interior angle measures by 540°. How many more sides does your new polygon have? Explain your reasoning.

Maintaining Mathematical Proficiency   Reviewing what you learned in previous grades and lessons

Find the value of x. *(Section 3.2)*

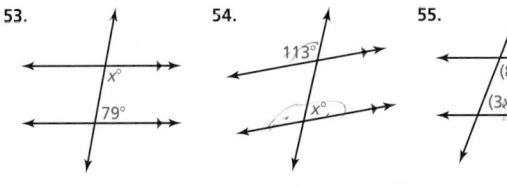

53.   **54.**   **55.**   **56.**

If students need help...	If students got it...
Resources by Chapter • Practice A and Practice B • Puzzle Time	Resources by Chapter • Enrichment and Extension • Cumulative Review
Student Journal • Practice	Start the *next* Section
Differentiating the Lesson Skills Review Handbook	

Laurie's Notes

Overview of Section 7.2

Introduction

- This lesson is about the properties of a parallelogram. The properties are investigated in the explorations.
- Thinking about the hierarchy of quadrilaterals, the parallelogram is just one type of quadrilateral. Other quadrilaterals that are not parallelograms are presented in Section 7.5.

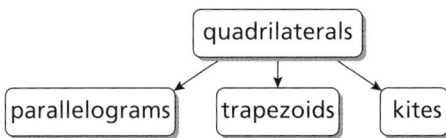

- Synthetic, transformational, and analytic proofs could be used for different theorems in this lesson.

Teaching Strategy

- **Transformational Proof:** Here is a proof using transformations of Theorem 7.3, which states that the opposite sides of a parallelogram are congruent.

  Given $ABCD$ is a parallelogram.
  Prove $\overline{AB} \cong \overline{DC}$, $\overline{BC} \cong \overline{AD}$

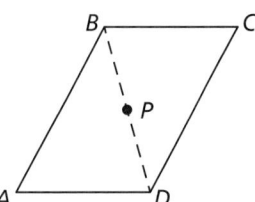

  - Draw diagonal $\overline{BD}$ and let P be the midpoint of $\overline{BD}$.
  - Rotate the figure $180°$ about point P.
  - $\overline{BD}$ rotates to itself.
  - Because P is the midpoint of $\overline{BD}$, $\overline{PB} \cong \overline{PD}$ and B and D rotate to each other.
  - By definition of a parallelogram, $\overline{AB} \parallel \overline{DC}$ and $\overline{BC} \parallel \overline{AD}$, so $\angle ABD \cong \angle CDB$ and $\angle ADB \cong \angle CBD$ by the Alternate Interior Angles Theorem (Thm. 3.2). Therefore, the two pairs of angles, $\angle ABD$ and $\angle CDB$, and $\angle ADB$ and $\angle CBD$, rotate to each other.
  - Because $\angle ABD$ and $\angle CDB$ coincide, $\overrightarrow{BA}$ and $\overrightarrow{DC}$ coincide. Because $\angle ADB$ and $\angle CBD$ coincide, $\overrightarrow{DA}$ and $\overrightarrow{BC}$ coincide.
  - Because two lines intersect in only one point, the intersection of $\overline{BA}$ and $\overline{DA}$, point A, rotates to the intersection of $\overline{DC}$ and $\overline{BC}$, point C, and vice versa.
  - Therefore, the image of parallelogram $ABCD$ is parallelogram $CDAB$.
  - Based on what coincides, $\overline{AB} \cong \overline{DC}$ and $\overline{BC} \cong \overline{AD}$.

Pacing Suggestion

- The explorations provide an opportunity for students to discover the properties of a parallelogram. Transition to the formal lesson as soon as students have discussed each exploration.

Exploration

Motivate

- Capture and display images from the Internet of parallelograms used in structural and artistic designs. Refer back to these images at the end of the lesson, and identify the properties of parallelograms.

Exploration Note

- **MP8 Look For and Express Regularity in Repeated Reasoning:** Mathematically proficient students do not base a conjecture on one construction. The construction must be repeated several times, each time with the hypothesis being satisfied. Each time, look for patterns.

Exploration 1

- There is a difference between constructing a quadrilateral that looks like a parallelogram and constructing a parallelogram. When it only looks like a parallelogram, it will certainly change when you drag on a vertex!
- The construction will show lines versus segments. Students do not need to hide the rays that extend beyond the vertices of the parallelogram. Time is not well spent doing this.
- ❓ "What observations do you have about the angles of a parallelogram?" Opposite angles are congruent. Adjacent angles are supplementary.
- ❓ "What observations do you have about the sides of a parallelogram?" Opposite sides are congruent.

Exploration 2

- In this exploration, you could have students construct the diagonals and make observations versus telling students to measure particular segments.
- ❓ "What observations do you have about the diagonals of a parallelogram?" The diagonals bisect each other.
- ❓ "Are the diagonals perpendicular?" sometimes "Are the diagonals congruent?" sometimes

Communicate Your Answer

- There are many properties of parallelograms that students may mention. Make a list of the properties suggested by students.

Connecting to Next Step

- The properties discovered by students will be stated and proven as theorems in the formal lesson.

7.2 Properties of Parallelograms

Essential Question What are the properties of parallelograms?

EXPLORATION 1 Discovering Properties of Parallelograms

Work with a partner. Use dynamic geometry software.

a. Construct any parallelogram and label it *ABCD*. Explain your process.

Sample

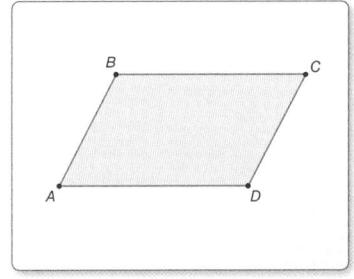

b. Find the angle measures of the parallelogram. What do you observe?

c. Find the side lengths of the parallelogram. What do you observe?

d. Repeat parts (a)–(c) for several other parallelograms. Use your results to write conjectures about the angle measures and side lengths of a parallelogram.

EXPLORATION 2 Discovering a Property of Parallelograms

Work with a partner. Use dynamic geometry software.

a. Construct any parallelogram and label it *ABCD*.

b. Draw the two diagonals of the parallelogram. Label the point of intersection *E*.

Sample

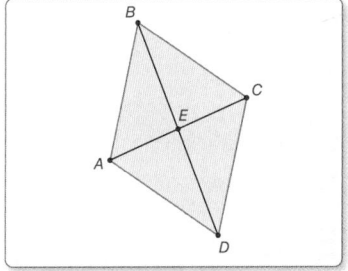

MAKING SENSE OF PROBLEMS

To be proficient in math, you need to analyze givens, constraints, relationships, and goals.

c. Find the segment lengths *AE*, *BE*, *CE*, and *DE*. What do you observe?

d. Repeat parts (a)–(c) for several other parallelograms. Use your results to write a conjecture about the diagonals of a parallelogram.

Communicate Your Answer

3. What are the properties of parallelograms?

Dynamic Teaching Tools

Dynamic Assessment & Progress Monitoring Tool

Lesson Planning Tool

Interactive Whiteboard Lesson Library

Dynamic Classroom with Dynamic Investigations

ANSWERS

1. **a.** Check students' work; Construct $\overleftrightarrow{AB}$ and a line parallel to $\overleftrightarrow{AB}$ through point *C*. Construct $\overleftrightarrow{BC}$ and a line parallel to $\overleftrightarrow{BC}$ through point *A*. Construct a point *D* at the intersection of the line drawn parallel to $\overleftrightarrow{AB}$ and the line drawn parallel to $\overleftrightarrow{BC}$. Finally, construct $\overline{AB}$, $\overline{BC}$, $\overline{CD}$, and $\overline{DA}$ by removing the rest of the parallel lines drawn.

   b. Check students' work. (For sample in text, $m\angle A = m\angle C = 63.43°$ and $m\angle B = m\angle D = 116.57°$.); Opposite angles are congruent, and consecutive angles are supplementary.

   c. Check students' work. (For sample in text, $AB = CD = 2.24$ and $BC = AD = 4$.); Opposite sides are congruent.

   d. Check students' work; Opposite angles of a parallelogram are congruent. Consecutive angles of a parallelogram are supplementary. Opposite sides of a parallelogram are congruent.

2. **a.** Check students' work.

   b. Check students' work.

   c. Check student's work. (For sample in text, $AE = CE = 1.58$ and $BE = DE = 2.55$.); Point *E* bisects $\overline{AC}$ and $\overline{BD}$.

   d. The diagonals of a parallelogram bisect each other.

3. A parallelogram is a quadrilateral where both pairs of opposite sides are congruent and parallel, opposite angles are congruent, consecutive angles are supplementary, and the diagonals bisect each other.

7.2 Lesson

Core Vocabulary

parallelogram, *p. 368*

Previous
quadrilateral
diagonal
interior angles
segment bisector

What You Will Learn

▶ Use properties to find side lengths and angles of parallelograms.

▶ Use parallelograms in the coordinate plane.

Using Properties of Parallelograms

A **parallelogram** is a quadrilateral with both pairs of opposite sides parallel. In □*PQRS*, $\overline{PQ} \parallel \overline{RS}$ and $\overline{QR} \parallel \overline{PS}$ by definition. The theorems below describe other properties of parallelograms.

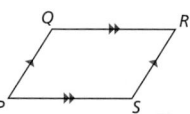

🔁 Theorems

Theorem 7.3   Parallelogram Opposite Sides Theorem

If a quadrilateral is a parallelogram, then its opposite sides are congruent.

If *PQRS* is a parallelogram, then $\overline{PQ} \cong \overline{RS}$ and $\overline{QR} \cong \overline{SP}$.

Proof p. 368

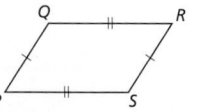

Theorem 7.4   Parallelogram Opposite Angles Theorem

If a quadrilateral is a parallelogram, then its opposite angles are congruent.

If *PQRS* is a parallelogram, then $\angle P \cong \angle R$ and $\angle Q \cong \angle S$.

Proof Ex. 37, p. 373

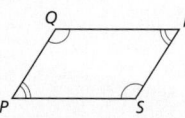

PROOF   Parallelogram Opposite Sides Theorem

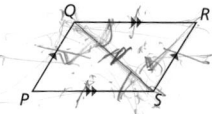

Given   *PQRS* is a parallelogram.
Prove $\overline{PQ} \cong \overline{RS}, \overline{QR} \cong \overline{SP}$

Plan for Proof
a. Draw diagonal $\overline{QS}$ to form △*PQS* and △*RSQ*.
b. Use the ASA Congruence Theorem (Thm. 5.10) to show that △*PQS* ≅ △*RSQ*.
c. Use congruent triangles to show that $\overline{PQ} \cong \overline{RS}$ and $\overline{QR} \cong \overline{SP}$.

Plan in Action	STATEMENTS	REASONS
	1. *PQRS* is a parallelogram.	1. Given
a.	2. Draw $\overline{QS}$.	2. Through any two points, there exists exactly one line.
	3. $\overline{PQ} \parallel \overline{RS}, \overline{QR} \parallel \overline{PS}$	3. Definition of parallelogram
b.	4. $\angle PQS \cong \angle RSQ$, $\angle PSQ \cong \angle RQS$	4. Alternate Interior Angles Theorem (Thm. 3.2)
	5. $\overline{QS} \cong \overline{SQ}$	5. Reflexive Property of Congruence (Thm. 2.1)
	6. △*PQS* ≅ △*RSQ*	6. ASA Congruence Theorem (Thm. 5.10)
c.	7. $\overline{PQ} \cong \overline{RS}, \overline{QR} \cong \overline{SP}$	7. Corresponding parts of congruent triangles are congruent.

Laurie's Notes   Teacher Actions

- **MP6 Attend to Precision:** Urge students to be careful with the definition of *parallelogram*. "A quadrilateral with parallel sides" is not the same as saying "a quadrilateral with both pairs of opposite sides parallel." The first phrase could mean it is sufficient for only one pair of sides to be parallel.
- **Whiteboarding:** Discuss the first theorem. Have partners write a proof.
- **MP3 Construct Viable Arguments and Critique the Reasoning of Others:** Compare and critique the proofs offered by several volunteers.
- **Extension:** You might also write a transformational proof of Theorem 7.3. See the *Teaching Strategy* on page T-366 for a sample proof.

EXAMPLE 1 **Using Properties of Parallelograms**

Find the values of x and y.

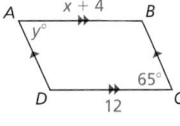

SOLUTION

$ABCD$ is a parallelogram by the definition of a parallelogram. Use the Parallelogram Opposite Sides Theorem to find the value of x.

$AB = CD$	Opposite sides of a parallelogram are congruent.
$x + 4 = 12$	Substitute $x + 4$ for AB and 12 for CD.
$x = 8$	Subtract 4 from each side.

By the Parallelogram Opposite Angles Theorem, $\angle A \cong \angle C$, or $m\angle A = m\angle C$. So, $y° = 65°$.

▶ In $\square ABCD$, $x = 8$ and $y = 65$.

Monitoring Progress Help in English and Spanish at *BigIdeasMath.com*

1. Find FG and $m\angle G$.

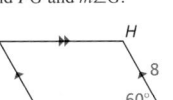

2. Find the values of x and y.

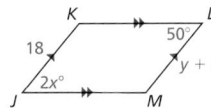

The Consecutive Interior Angles Theorem (Theorem 3.4) states that if two parallel lines are cut by a transversal, then the pairs of consecutive interior angles formed are supplementary.

A pair of consecutive angles in a parallelogram is like a pair of consecutive interior angles between parallel lines. This similarity suggests the Parallelogram Consecutive Angles Theorem.

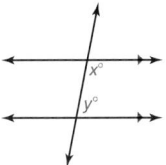

Theorems

Theorem 7.5 Parallelogram Consecutive Angles Theorem

If a quadrilateral is a parallelogram, then its consecutive angles are supplementary.

If $PQRS$ is a parallelogram, then $x° + y° = 180°$.

Proof Ex. 38, p. 373

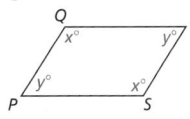

Theorem 7.6 Parallelogram Diagonals Theorem

If a quadrilateral is a parallelogram, then its diagonals bisect each other.

If $PQRS$ is a parallelogram, then $\overline{QM} \cong \overline{SM}$ and $\overline{PM} \cong \overline{RM}$.

Proof p. 370

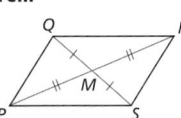

Section 7.2   Properties of Parallelograms   **369**

Extra Example 1

Find the values of x and y.

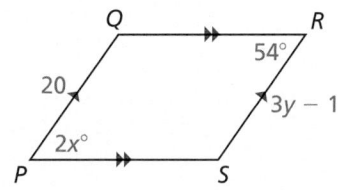

$x = 27, y = 7$

MONITORING PROGRESS ANSWERS

1. $FG = 8, m\angle G = 60°$
2. $x = 25, y = 15$

Laurie's Notes   Teacher Actions

- **Think-Pair-Share:** Have students work independently on Example 1 and then compare with partners.
- **?** "If you know the measure of one angle of a parallelogram, how can you find the measure of the two adjacent angles?" The adjacent angles will be supplementary to the known angle, because the consecutive interior angles formed by parallel lines cut by a transversal are supplementary.
- **?** "What do you know about the diagonals of a parallelogram?" They bisect each other.

Extra Example 2

In parallelogram *PQRS*, *m*∠*P* is four times *m*∠*Q*. Find *m*∠*P*. 144°

Extra Example 3

Use the figure in Example 3. Write a two-column proof.

Given *ABCD* and *GDEF* are parallelograms.

Prove ∠*C* ≅ ∠*G*

Statements (Reasons)

1. *ABCD* and *GDEF* are parallelograms. (Given)
2. ∠*C* and ∠*CDA* are supplementary, ∠*G* and ∠*EDG* are supplementary. (Parallelogram Consec. ∠s Thm. 7.5)
3. ∠*CDA* ≅ ∠*EDG* (Vert. ∠s ≅ Thm. 2.6)
4. ∠*C* ≅ ∠*G* (≅ Supplements Thm. 2.4)

MONITORING PROGRESS ANSWERS

3. 60°

4. See Additional Answers.

Given *PQRS* is a parallelogram. Diagonals $\overline{PR}$ and $\overline{QS}$ intersect at point *M*.

Prove *M* bisects $\overline{QS}$ and $\overline{PR}$.

STATEMENTS	REASONS
1. *PQRS* is a parallelogram.	1. Given
2. $\overline{PQ} \parallel \overline{RS}$	2. Definition of a parallelogram
3. ∠*QPR* ≅ ∠*SRP*, ∠*PQS* ≅ ∠*RSQ*	3. Alternate Interior Angles Theorem (Thm. 3.2)
4. $\overline{PQ} \cong \overline{RS}$	4. Parallelogram Opposite Sides Theorem
5. △*PMQ* ≅ △*RMS*	5. ASA Congruence Theorem (Thm. 5.10)
6. $\overline{QM} \cong \overline{SM}$, $\overline{PM} \cong \overline{RM}$	6. Corresponding parts of congruent triangles are congruent.
7. *M* bisects $\overline{QS}$ and $\overline{PR}$.	7. Definition of segment bisector

EXAMPLE 2 **Using Properties of a Parallelogram**

As shown, part of the extending arm of a desk lamp is a parallelogram. The angles of the parallelogram change as the lamp is raised and lowered. Find *m*∠*BCD* when *m*∠*ADC* = 110°.

SOLUTION

By the Parallelogram Consecutive Angles Theorem, the consecutive angle pairs in □*ABCD* are supplementary. So, *m*∠*ADC* + *m*∠*BCD* = 180°. Because *m*∠*ADC* = 110°, *m*∠*BCD* = 180° − 110° = 70°.

EXAMPLE 3 **Writing a Two-Column Proof**

Write a two-column proof.

Given *ABCD* and *GDEF* are parallelograms.

Prove ∠*B* ≅ ∠*F*

STATEMENTS	REASONS
1. *ABCD* and *GDEF* are parallelograms.	1. Given
2. ∠*CDA* ≅ ∠*B*, ∠*EDG* ≅ ∠*F*	2. If a quadrilateral is a parallelogram, then its opposite angles are congruent.
3. ∠*CDA* ≅ ∠*EDG*	3. Vertical Angles Congruence Theorem (Thm. 2.6)
4. ∠*B* ≅ ∠*F*	4. Transitive Property of Congruence (Thm. 2.2)

Monitoring Progress 🔊 Help in English and Spanish at *BigIdeasMath.com*

3. **WHAT IF?** In Example 2, find *m*∠*BCD* when *m*∠*ADC* is twice the measure of ∠*BCD*.

4. Using the figure and the given statement in Example 3, prove that ∠*C* and ∠*F* are supplementary angles.

Laurie's Notes   Teacher Actions

❓ "What is the given information in the proof of the Parallelogram Diagonals Theorem and what do we need to prove?" We have a parallelogram and we want to prove that the diagonals bisect each other.

- There are four pairs of non-overlapping triangles that could be proven congruent. Have students discuss what pairs might be helpful, meaning corresponding parts that yield $\overline{QM} \cong \overline{SM}$ and $\overline{PM} \cong \overline{RM}$. Have partners work on a proof of one pair of triangles.

❓ In Example 2 ask, "Does the measure of ∠*ADC* always equal 110°?" No, it changes when the lamp is repositioned.

Using Parallelograms in the Coordinate Plane

Section 7.2 371

Find the coordinates of the intersection of the diagonals of $\square ABCD$ with vertices $A(1, 0)$, $B(6, 0)$, $C(5, 3)$, and $D(0, 3)$. $\left(3, \frac{3}{2}\right)$

Extra Example 5

Three vertices of $\square DEFG$ are $D(-1, 4)$, $E(2, 3)$, and $F(4, -2)$. Find the coordinates of vertex G. $(1, -1)$

MONITORING PROGRESS ANSWERS

5. $(2, 3)$
6. $D(0, 1)$

JUSTIFYING STEPS

In Example 4, you can use either diagonal to find the coordinates of the intersection. Using diagonal $\overline{OM}$ helps simplify the calculation because one endpoint is $(0, 0)$.

EXAMPLE 4   Using Parallelograms in the Coordinate Plane

Find the coordinates of the intersection of the diagonals of $\square LMNO$ with vertices $L(1, 4)$, $M(7, 4)$, $N(6, 0)$, and $O(0, 0)$.

SOLUTION

By the Parallelogram Diagonals Theorem, the diagonals of a parallelogram bisect each other. So, the coordinates of the intersection are the midpoints of diagonals $\overline{LN}$ and $\overline{OM}$.

coordinates of midpoint of $\overline{OM} = \left(\dfrac{7 + 0}{2}, \dfrac{4 + 0}{2}\right) = \left(\dfrac{7}{2}, 2\right)$ Midpoint Formula

▶ The coordinates of the intersection of the diagonals are $\left(\dfrac{7}{2}, 2\right)$. You can check your answer by graphing $\square LMNO$ and drawing the diagonals. The point of intersection appears to be correct.

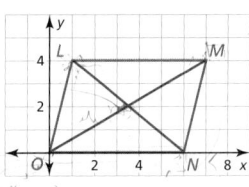

REMEMBER

When graphing a polygon in the coordinate plane, the name of the polygon gives the order of the vertices.

EXAMPLE 5   Using Parallelograms in the Coordinate Plane

Three vertices of $\square WXYZ$ are $W(-1, -3)$, $X(-3, 2)$, and $Z(4, -4)$. Find the coordinates of vertex Y.

SOLUTION

Step 1   Graph the vertices W, X, and Z.

Step 2   Find the slope of $\overline{WX}$.

slope of $\overline{WX} = \dfrac{2 - (-3)}{-3 - (-1)} = \dfrac{5}{-2} = -\dfrac{5}{2}$

Step 3   Start at $Z(4, -4)$. Use the rise and run from Step 2 to find vertex Y.

A rise of 5 represents a change of 5 units up. A run of -2 represents a change of 2 units left.

So, plot the point that is 5 units up and 2 units left from $Z(4, -4)$. The point is $(2, 1)$. Label it as vertex Y.

Step 4   Find the slopes of $\overline{XY}$ and $\overline{WZ}$ to verify that they are parallel.

slope of $\overline{XY} = \dfrac{1 - 2}{2 - (-3)} = \dfrac{-1}{5} = -\dfrac{1}{5}$ slope of $\overline{WZ} = \dfrac{-4 - (-3)}{4 - (-1)} = \dfrac{-1}{5} = -\dfrac{1}{5}$

▶ So, the coordinates of vertex Y are $(2, 1)$.

Monitoring Progress Help in English and Spanish at *BigIdeasMath.com*

5. Find the coordinates of the intersection of the diagonals of $\square STUV$ with vertices $S(-2, 3)$, $T(1, 5)$, $U(6, 3)$, and $V(3, 1)$.

6. Three vertices of $\square ABCD$ are $A(2, 4)$, $B(5, 2)$, and $C(3, -1)$. Find the coordinates of vertex D.

Section 7.2   Properties of Parallelograms   **371**

Laurie's Notes   Teacher Actions

- **Extension:** The Midpoint Formula is used in Example 4. Alternately, determine the equations of the diagonals and find the point of intersection.
- **?** In Example 5, the name of the parallelogram is given, which determines the order of the vertices. Ask, "In general, given three coordinates of a parallelogram, is there more than one possible location for the fourth vertex? Explain." yes; $(6, -9)$ also works.

Closure

- **Exit Ticket:** Draw parallelogram $ABCD$ with $m\angle A = 72°$ and $BC = 8.2$ centimeters. Find $m\angle B$ and the length of $\overline{AD}$. $108°$; 8.2 centimeters

Assignment Guide and Homework Check

ASSIGNMENT

Basic: 1, 2, 3–29 odd, 33, 42, 48–50

Average: 1, 2, 6–32 even, 33, 36, 39–42, 45, 48–50

Advanced: 1, 2, 6–26 even, 30–34, 40–50

HOMEWORK CHECK

Basic: 5, 9, 19, 25, 27

Average: 6, 10, 20, 24, 26

Advanced: 10, 20, 26, 45, 47

ANSWERS

1. In order to be a quadrilateral, a polygon must have 4 sides, and parallelograms always have 4 sides. In order to be a parallelogram, a polygon must have 4 sides with opposite sides parallel. Quadrilaterals always have 4 sides, but do not always have opposite sides parallel.

2. The two angles that are consecutive to the given angle are supplementary to it. So, you can find each of their measures by subtracting the measure of the given angle from 180°. The angle opposite the given angle is congruent and therefore has the same measure.

3. $x = 9$, $y = 15$

4. $m = 5$, $n = 12$

5. $d = 126$, $z = 28$

6. $g = 61$, $h = 9$

7. 129°

8. 85°

9. 13; By the Parallelogram Opposite Sides Theorem (Thm. 7.3), $LM = QN$.

10. 7; By the Parallelogram Diagonals Theorem (Thm. 7.6), $LP = PN$.

11. 8; By the Parallelogram Opposite Sides Theorem (Thm. 7.3), $LQ = MN$.

12. 16.4; By the Parallelogram Diagonals Theorem (Thm. 7.6), $MP = PQ$. So, $MQ = 2 \cdot 8.2$.

13. 80°; By the Parallelogram Consecutive Angles Theorem (Thm. 7.5), $\angle QLM$ and $\angle LMN$ are supplementary. So, $m\angle LMN = 180° - 100°$.

Vocabulary and Core Concept Check

1. **VOCABULARY** Why is a parallelogram always a quadrilateral, but a quadrilateral is only sometimes a parallelogram?

2. **WRITING** You are given one angle measure of a parallelogram. Explain how you can find the other angle measures of the parallelogram.

Monitoring Progress and Modeling with Mathematics

In Exercises 3–6, find the value of each variable in the parallelogram. *(See Example 1.)*

3.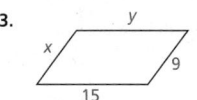

4.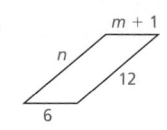

5.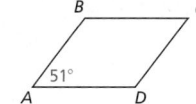

6.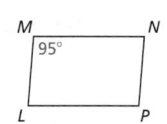

In Exercises 7 and 8, find the measure of the indicated angle in the parallelogram. *(See Example 2.)*

7. Find $m\angle B$.

8. Find $m\angle N$.

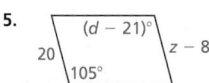

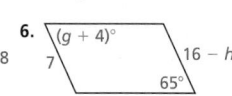

In Exercises 9–16, find the indicated measure in □*LMNQ*. Explain your reasoning.

9. LM

10. LP

11. LQ

12. MQ

13. $m\angle LMN$

14. $m\angle NQL$

15. $m\angle MNQ$

16. $m\angle LMQ$

In Exercises 17–20, find the value of each variable in the parallelogram.

17.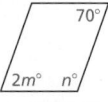

18.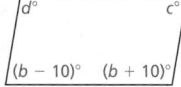

19.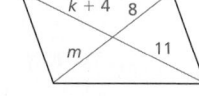

20.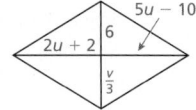

ERROR ANALYSIS In Exercises 21 and 22, describe and correct the error in using properties of parallelograms.

21.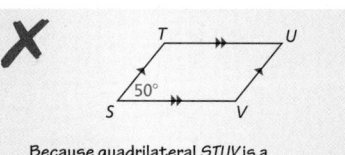

Because quadrilateral *STUV* is a parallelogram, $\angle S \cong \angle V$. So, $m\angle V = 50°$.

22.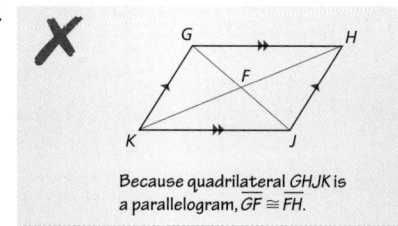

Because quadrilateral *GHJK* is a parallelogram, $\overline{GF} \cong \overline{FH}$.

---

14. 80°; By the Parallelogram Consecutive Angles Theorem (Thm. 7.5), $\angle QLM$ and $\angle NQL$ are supplementary. So, $m\angle NQL = 180° - 100°$.

15. 100°; By the Parallelogram Opposite Angles Theorem (Thm. 7.4), $m\angle QLM = m\angle MNQ$.

16. 29°; By the Alternate Interior Angles Theorem (Thm. 3.2), $m\angle LMQ = m\angle MQN$.

17. $m = 35$, $n = 110$

18. $b = 90$, $c = 80$, $d = 100$

19. $k = 7$, $m = 8$

20. $u = 4$, $v = 18$

21. In a parallelogram, consecutive angles are supplementary; Because quadrilateral *STUV* is a parallelogram, $\angle S$ and $\angle V$ are supplementary. So, $m\angle V = 180° - 50° = 130°$.

22. In a parallelogram, the diagonals bisect each other. So the two parts of $\overline{GJ}$ are congruent to each other; Because quadrilateral *GHJK* is a parallelogram, $\overline{GF} \cong \overline{FJ}$.

PROOF In Exercises 23 and 24, write a two-column proof. *(See Example 3.)*

23. Given *ABCD* and *CEFD* are parallelograms.

    Prove $\overline{AB} \cong \overline{FE}$

    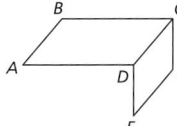

24. Given *ABCD*, *EBGF*, and *HJKD* are parallelograms.

    Prove $\angle 2 \cong \angle 3$

    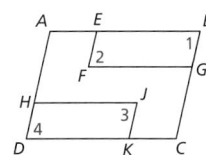

In Exercises 25 and 26, find the coordinates of the intersection of the diagonals of the parallelogram with the given vertices. *(See Example 4.)*

25. *W*(−2, 5), *X*(2, 5), *Y*(4, 0), *Z*(0, 0)

26. *Q*(−1, 3), *R*(5, 2), *S*(1, −2), *T*(−5, −1)

In Exercises 27–30, three vertices of □*DEFG* are given. Find the coordinates of the remaining vertex. *(See Example 5.)*

27. *D*(0, 2), *E*(−1, 5), *G*(4, 0)

28. *D*(−2, −4), *F*(0, 7), *G*(1, 0)

29. *D*(−4, −2), *E*(−3, 1), *F*(3, 3)

30. *E*(−1, 4), *F*(5, 6), *G*(8, 0)

MATHEMATICAL CONNECTIONS In Exercises 31 and 32, find the measure of each angle.

31. The measure of one interior angle of a parallelogram is 0.25 times the measure of another angle.

32. The measure of one interior angle of a parallelogram is 50 degrees more than 4 times the measure of another angle.

33. **MAKING AN ARGUMENT** In quadrilateral *ABCD*, $m\angle B = 124°$, $m\angle A = 56°$, and $m\angle C = 124°$. Your friend claims quadrilateral *ABCD* could be a parallelogram. Is your friend correct? Explain your reasoning.

34. **ATTENDING TO PRECISION** $\angle J$ and $\angle K$ are consecutive angles in a parallelogram, $m\angle J = (3x + 7)°$, and $m\angle K = (5x −11)°$. Find the measure of each angle.

35. **CONSTRUCTION** Construct any parallelogram and label it *ABCD*. Draw diagonals $\overline{AC}$ and $\overline{BD}$. Explain how to use paper folding to verify the Parallelogram Diagonals Theorem (Theorem 7.6) for □*ABCD*.

36. **MODELING WITH MATHEMATICS** The feathers on an arrow form two congruent parallelograms. The parallelograms are reflections of each other over the line that contains their shared side. Show that $m\angle 2 = 2m\angle 1$.

    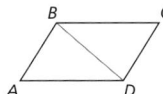

37. **PROVING A THEOREM** Use the diagram to write a two-column proof of the Parallelogram Opposite Angles Theorem (Theorem 7.4).

    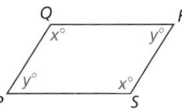

    Given *ABCD* is a parallelogram.

    Prove $\angle A \cong \angle C$, $\angle B \cong \angle D$

38. **PROVING A THEOREM** Use the diagram to write a two-column proof of the Parallelogram Consecutive Angles Theorem (Theorem 7.5).

    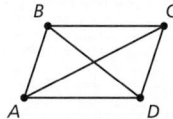

    Given *PQRS* is a parallelogram.

    Prove $x° + y° = 180°$

39. **PROBLEM SOLVING** The sides of □*MNPQ* are represented by the expressions below. Sketch □*MNPQ* and find its perimeter.

    $MQ = -2x + 37$ $QP = y + 14$

    $NP = x - 5$ $MN = 4y + 5$

40. **PROBLEM SOLVING** In □*LMNP*, the ratio of *LM* to *MN* is 4 : 3. Find *LM* when the perimeter of □*LMNP* is 28.

ANSWERS

23– 24. See Additional Answers.

25. (1, 2.5)

26. (0, 0.5)

27. *F*(3, 3)

28. *E*(−3, 3)

29. *G*(2, 0)

30. *D*(2, −2)

31. 36°, 144°

32. 26°, 154°

33. no; *Sample answer:* $\angle A$ and $\angle C$ are opposite angles, but $m\angle A \neq m\angle C$.

34. 76°, 104°

35. *Sample Answer:*

When you fold the parallelogram so that vertex *A* is on vertex *C*, the fold will pass through the point where the diagonals intersect, which demonstrates that this point of intersection is also the midpoint of $\overline{AC}$. Similarly, when you fold the parallelogram so that vertex *B* is on vertex *D*, the fold will pass through the point where the diagonals intersect, which demonstrates that this point of intersection is also the midpoint of $\overline{BD}$.

36–39. See Additional Answers.

40. 8

41. **ABSTRACT REASONING** Can you prove that two parallelograms are congruent by proving that all their corresponding sides are congruent? Explain your reasoning.

42. **HOW DO YOU SEE IT?** The mirror shown is attached to the wall by an arm that can extend away from the wall. In the figure, points P, Q, R, and S are the vertices of a parallelogram. This parallelogram is one of several that change shape as the mirror is extended.

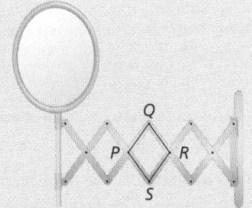

   a. What happens to $m\angle P$ as $m\angle Q$ increases? Explain.

   b. What happens to QS as $m\angle Q$ decreases? Explain.

   c. What happens to the overall distance between the mirror and the wall when $m\angle Q$ decreases? Explain.

43. **MATHEMATICAL CONNECTIONS** In $\square STUV$, $m\angle TSU = 32°$, $m\angle USV = (x^2)°$, $m\angle TUV = 12x°$, and $\angle TUV$ is an acute angle. Find $m\angle USV$.

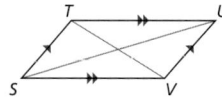

44. **THOUGHT PROVOKING** Is it possible that any triangle can be partitioned into four congruent triangles that can be rearranged to form a parallelogram? Explain your reasoning.

45. **CRITICAL THINKING** Points $W(1, 2)$, $X(3, 6)$, and $Y(6, 4)$ are three vertices of a parallelogram. How many parallelograms can be created using these three vertices? Find the coordinates of each point that could be the fourth vertex.

46. **PROOF** In the diagram, $\overline{EK}$ bisects $\angle FEH$, and $\overline{FJ}$ bisects $\angle EFG$. Prove that $\overrightarrow{EK} \perp \overrightarrow{FJ}$. (*Hint*: Write equations using the angle measures of the triangles and quadrilaterals formed.)

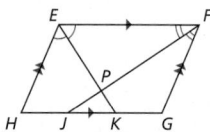

47. **PROOF** Prove the *Congruent Parts of Parallel Lines Corollary*: If three or more parallel lines cut off congruent segments on one transversal, then they cut off congruent segments on every transversal.

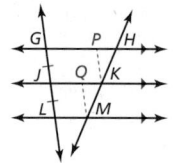

   Given $\overleftrightarrow{GH} \parallel \overleftrightarrow{JK} \parallel \overleftrightarrow{LM}, \overline{GJ} \cong \overline{JL}$

   Prove $\overline{HK} \cong \overline{KM}$

   (*Hint*: Draw $\overline{KP}$ and $\overline{MQ}$ such that quadrilateral $GPKJ$ and quadrilateral $JQML$ are parallelograms.)

Maintaining Mathematical Proficiency *Reviewing what you learned in previous grades and lessons*

Determine whether lines ℓ and m are parallel. Explain your reasoning. *(Section 3.3)*

48.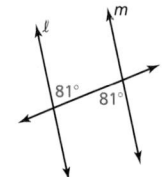

49.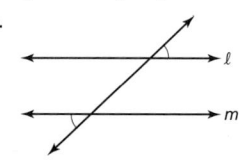

50.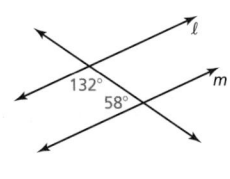

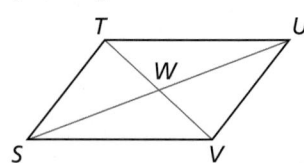
If students need help...	If students got it...
Resources by Chapter • Practice A and Practice B • Puzzle Time	Resources by Chapter • Enrichment and Extension • Cumulative Review
Student Journal • Practice	Start the *next* Section
Differentiating the Lesson Skills Review Handbook	

Overview of Section 7.3

Introduction
- There are four theorems presented in this lesson, three of which are converses of theorems in the last lesson. Students should recall that although a statement is true, its converse may not be.
- Each of the four theorems can be used to show that a quadrilateral is a parallelogram.

Teaching Strategy
- All the theorems in this lesson can be introduced in a very low-tech fashion that will give students a chance to visualize and think about the given conditions (the hypotheses) that can be used to show that a quadrilateral is a parallelogram.
- Make a collection of pieces that can be used to make a quadrilateral. The pieces are used to make the sides, angles, and diagonals of the quadrilateral.
- My collection is made on transparencies using a permanent marker. Make pairs of segments in various lengths (2, 3, 4, 5, and 6 inches) and pairs of angles of various measures (30°, 60°, 120°, and 150°).
- Give students the parts (i.e., opposite sides congruent), and have them place the pieces on the overhead to make a quadrilateral. Does the quadrilateral appear to be a parallelogram? How might you prove it?
- This same approach can be done using an interactive whiteboard where the pieces can be manipulated.

Pacing Suggestion
- The explorations provide an opportunity for students to consider how they can prove they have a parallelogram. Transition to the formal lesson as soon as students have discussed each exploration.

Dynamic Teaching Tools

Dynamic Assessment & Progress Monitoring Tool

Lesson Planning Tool

Interactive Whiteboard Lesson Library

Dynamic Classroom with Dynamic Investigations

**Common Core
State Standards**

HSG-CO.C.11 Prove theorems about parallelograms.

HSG-SRT.B.5 Use congruence … criteria for triangles to solve problems and to prove relationships in geometric figures.

HSG-MG.A.1 Use geometric shapes, their measures, and their properties to describe objects (e.g., modeling a tree trunk or a human torso as a cylinder).

Laurie's Notes

Exploration

Motivate
- Ask for a volunteer. Hand the student two 5-inch straws and two 3-inch straws. Ask him or her to arrange the straws to make a quadrilateral.
- There are three possibilities. The student will make a quadrilateral that appears to be parallelogram, a convex kite, or a concave kite.
- Focus on the quadrilateral with opposite sides congruent, and ask students whether it could be proven that this is a parallelogram. Give time for discussion.
- Explain to students that in the lesson they will complete the proof!

Exploration Note
- **MP8 Look For and Express Regularity in Repeated Reasoning:** Mathematically proficient students do not base a conjecture on one construction. The construction must be repeated several times, each time with the hypothesis being satisfied. Each time, look for patterns.

Exploration 1
- There are different ways in which students could construct the quadrilateral and satisfy the hypothesis. Knowing the features of the software that your students work with is important. An alternate approach with the focus on angles is explained in Exploration 2.
- The software I use allows me to create four consecutive segments using five points, with $AB = CD$ and $BC = DE$. I then wrap the segment around until points E and A coincide.
- **? MP3 Construct Viable Arguments and Critique the Reasoning of Others:** "How did you decide whether the quadrilateral was a parallelogram?" Listen for valid reasoning. Most students measure the angles and determine that opposite sides are parallel because interior angles on the same side of the transversal are supplementary. They also could find the slopes of opposite sides.
- Suggest to students that they begin with a quadrilateral having sides parallel to the x- or y-axis.
- Students should conclude that when a quadrilateral has opposite sides congruent, the quadrilateral is a parallelogram.

Exploration 2
- The second construction can be done by rotating a triangle 180° about the midpoint of one side.
- **? MP3:** "How did you decide whether the quadrilateral was a parallelogram?" Listen for valid reasoning similar to that in Exploration 1.
- Students should conclude that when the opposite angles of a quadrilateral are congruent, the quadrilateral is a parallelogram.

Communicate Your Answer
- Listen for valid reasoning from students. They may already sense that this lesson is very much connected to the properties studied in the last lesson.

Connecting to Next Step
- The conjectures made by students will be stated and proven as theorems in the formal lesson.

7.3 Proving That a Quadrilateral Is a Parallelogram

Essential Question How can you prove that a quadrilateral is a parallelogram?

EXPLORATION 1 Proving That a Quadrilateral Is a Parallelogram

Work with a partner. Use dynamic geometry software.

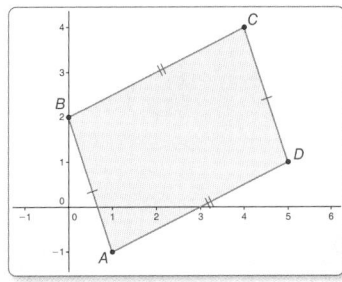

Sample

Points
$A(1, -1)$
$B(0, 2)$
$C(4, 4)$
$D(5, 1)$

Segments
$AB = 3.16$
$BC = 4.47$
$CD = 3.16$
$DA = 4.47$

REASONING ABSTRACTLY

To be proficient in math, you need to know and flexibly use different properties of objects.

a. Construct any quadrilateral *ABCD* whose opposite sides are congruent.

b. Is the quadrilateral a parallelogram? Justify your answer.

c. Repeat parts (a) and (b) for several other quadrilaterals. Then write a conjecture based on your results.

d. Write the converse of your conjecture. Is the converse true? Explain.

EXPLORATION 2 Proving That a Quadrilateral Is a Parallelogram

Work with a partner. Use dynamic geometry software.

a. Construct any quadrilateral *ABCD* whose opposite angles are congruent.

b. Is the quadrilateral a parallelogram? Justify your answer.

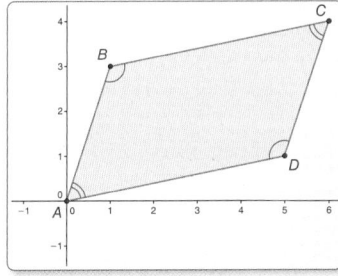

Sample

Points
$A(0, 0)$
$B(1, 3)$
$C(6, 4)$
$D(5, 1)$

Angles
$\angle A = 60.26°$
$\angle B = 119.74°$
$\angle C = 60.26°$
$\angle D = 119.74°$

c. Repeat parts (a) and (b) for several other quadrilaterals. Then write a conjecture based on your results.

d. Write the converse of your conjecture. Is the converse true? Explain.

Communicate Your Answer

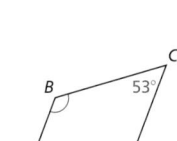

3. How can you prove that a quadrilateral is a parallelogram?

4. Is the quadrilateral at the left a parallelogram? Explain your reasoning.

Section 7.3   Proving That a Quadrilateral Is a Parallelogram   375

ANSWERS

1. a. Check students' work.

   b. yes; Because they have the same slope, opposite sides are parallel.

   c. Check students' work. If the opposite sides of a quadrilateral are congruent, then the quadrilateral is a parallelogram.

   d. If a quadrilateral is a parallelogram, then its opposite sides are congruent; yes; This is the Parallelogram Opposite Sides Theorem (Thm. 7.3).

2. a. Check students' work.

   b. yes; Because they have the same slope, opposite sides are parallel.

   c. Check students' work. If the opposite angles of a quadrilateral are congruent, then the quadrilateral is a parallelogram.

   d. If a quadrilateral is a parallelogram, then its opposite angles are congruent; yes; This is the Parallelogram Opposite Angles Theorem (Thm. 7.4).

3. Show that the opposite sides or opposite angles are congruent.

4. yes; The opposite angles are congruent.

7.3 Lesson

Core Vocabulary

Previous
diagonal
parallelogram

What You Will Learn

▶ Identify and verify parallelograms.

▶ Show that a quadrilateral is a parallelogram in the coordinate plane.

Identifying and Verifying Parallelograms

Given a parallelogram, you can use the Parallelogram Opposite Sides Theorem (Theorem 7.3) and the Parallelogram Opposite Angles Theorem (Theorem 7.4) to prove statements about the sides and angles of the parallelogram. The converses of the theorems are stated below. You can use these and other theorems in this lesson to prove that a quadrilateral with certain properties is a parallelogram.

🗘 Theorems

Theorem 7.7   Parallelogram Opposite Sides Converse

If both pairs of opposite sides of a quadrilateral are congruent, then the quadrilateral is a parallelogram.

If $\overline{AB} \cong \overline{CD}$ and $\overline{BC} \cong \overline{DA}$, then $ABCD$ is a parallelogram.

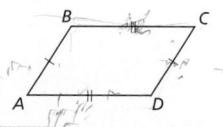

Theorem 7.8   Parallelogram Opposite Angles Converse

If both pairs of opposite angles of a quadrilateral are congruent, then the quadrilateral is a parallelogram.

If $\angle A \cong \angle C$ and $\angle B \cong \angle D$, then $ABCD$ is a parallelogram.

Proof Ex. 39, p. 383

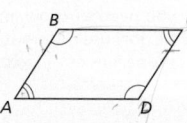

PROOF   Parallelogram Opposite Sides Converse

Given $\overline{AB} \cong \overline{CD}, \overline{BC} \cong \overline{DA}$

Prove $ABCD$ is a parallelogram.

Plan for Proof
a. Draw diagonal $\overline{AC}$ to form $\triangle ABC$ and $\triangle CDA$.
b. Use the SSS Congruence Theorem (Thm. 5.8) to show that $\triangle ABC \cong \triangle CDA$.
c. Use the Alternate Interior Angles Converse (Thm. 3.6) to show that opposite sides are parallel.

Plan in Action	STATEMENTS	REASONS
a.	1. $\overline{AB} \cong \overline{CD}, \overline{BC} \cong \overline{DA}$	1. Given
	2. Draw $\overline{AC}$.	2. Through any two points, there exists exactly one line.
	3. $\overline{AC} \cong \overline{CA}$	3. Reflexive Property of Congruence (Thm. 2.1)
b.	4. $\triangle ABC \cong \triangle CDA$	4. SSS Congruence Theorem (Thm. 5.8)
c.	5. $\angle BAC \cong \angle DCA,$ $\angle BCA \cong \angle DAC$	5. Corresponding parts of congruent triangles are congruent.
	6. $\overline{AB} \parallel \overline{CD}, \overline{BC} \parallel \overline{DA}$	6. Alternate Interior Angles Converse (Thm. 3.6)
	7. $ABCD$ is a parallelogram.	7. Definition of parallelogram

Laurie's Notes   Teacher Actions

? Sketch quadrilateral $ABCD$ that appears to be a parallelogram. "What information would you need in order to know that $ABCD$ is a parallelogram?" The opposite sides are parallel. If students start to list additional properties, remind them of the definition.

• Explain to students that in this lesson they will look back at the theorems of the last lesson to see whether the converse of each is true.

• **Whiteboarding:** Discuss Theorem 7.7. Have partners write a proof.

• **MP3:** Compare and critique the proofs offered by several volunteers.

EXAMPLE 1   Identifying a Parallelogram

An amusement park ride has a moving platform attached to four swinging arms. The platform swings back and forth, higher and higher, until it goes over the top and around in a circular motion. In the diagram below, $\overline{AD}$ and $\overline{BC}$ represent two of the swinging arms, and $\overline{DC}$ is parallel to the ground (line ℓ). Explain why the moving platform $\overline{AB}$ is always parallel to the ground.

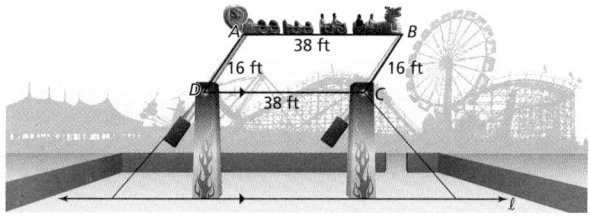

SOLUTION

The shape of quadrilateral $ABCD$ changes as the moving platform swings around, but its side lengths do not change. Both pairs of opposite sides are congruent, so $ABCD$ is a parallelogram by the Parallelogram Opposite Sides Converse.

By the definition of a parallelogram, $\overline{AB} \parallel \overline{DC}$. Because $\overline{DC}$ is parallel to line ℓ, $\overline{AB}$ is also parallel to line ℓ by the Transitive Property of Parallel Lines (Theorem 3.9). So, the moving platform is parallel to the ground.

Monitoring Progress Help in English and Spanish at *BigIdeasMath.com*

1. In quadrilateral $WXYZ$, $m\angle W = 42°$, $m\angle X = 138°$, and $m\angle Y = 42°$. Find $m\angle Z$. Is $WXYZ$ a parallelogram? Explain your reasoning.

EXAMPLE 2   Finding Side Lengths of a Parallelogram

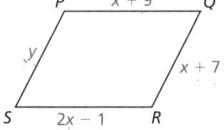

For what values of x and y is quadrilateral $PQRS$ a parallelogram?

SOLUTION

By the Parallelogram Opposite Sides Converse, if both pairs of opposite sides of a quadrilateral are congruent, then the quadrilateral is a parallelogram. Find x so that $\overline{PQ} \cong \overline{SR}$.

$PQ = SR$	Set the segment lengths equal.
$x + 9 = 2x - 1$	Substitute $x + 9$ for PQ and $2x - 1$ for SR.
$10 = x$	Solve for x.

When $x = 10$, $PQ = 10 + 9 = 19$ and $SR = 2(10) - 1 = 19$. Find y so that $\overline{PS} \cong \overline{QR}$.

$PS = QR$	Set the segment lengths equal.
$y = x + 7$	Substitute y for PS and $x + 7$ for QR.
$y = 10 + 7$	Substitute 10 for x.
$y = 17$	Add.

When $x = 10$ and $y = 17$, $PS = 17$ and $QR = 10 + 7 = 17$.

▶ Quadrilateral $PQRS$ is a parallelogram when $x = 10$ and $y = 17$.

Section 7.3   Proving That a Quadrilateral Is a Parallelogram   **377**

Extra Example 1
In quadrilateral $ABCD$, $AB = BC$ and $CD = AD$. Is $ABCD$ a parallelogram? Explain your reasoning. You cannot tell. Two pairs of opposite sides must be congruent, not two pairs of adjacent sides.

Extra Example 2
For what values of x and y is quadrilateral $STUV$ a parallelogram?

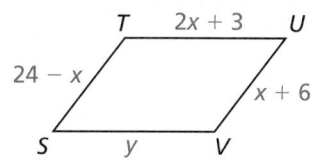

$x = 9$, $y = 21$

MONITORING PROGRESS ANSWER

1. 138°; yes; Because opposite angles are congruent, quadrilateral $WXYZ$ is a parallelogram.

Laurie's Notes   Teacher Actions

- Discuss the amusement park ride to be sure students know how it operates. Listen for student justification of why $\overline{AB}$ is parallel to the ground.
- **Extension:** There may be students who want to construct a model of this ride using dynamic geometry software.

COMMON ERROR In Example 2, students may try to work with all four expressions simultaneously. They need to work with the pair involving only x first, and then move to the other pair of expressions.

Extra Example 3

Use the photograph in Example 3. Explain how you know that $\angle S \cong \angle U$. By the Opposite Sides Parallel and Congruent Theorem (Thm. 7.9), quadrilateral *STUV* is a parallelogram. By the Parallelogram Opposite Angles Theorem (Thm 7.4), the opposite angles of a parallelogram are congruent. So, $\angle S \cong \angle U$.

Extra Example 4

For what value of *x* is quadrilateral *CDEF* a parallelogram?

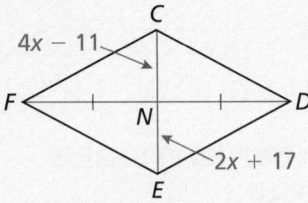

$x = 14$

🔄 Theorems

Theorem 7.9 Opposite Sides Parallel and Congruent Theorem

If one pair of opposite sides of a quadrilateral are congruent and parallel, then the quadrilateral is a parallelogram.

If $\overline{BC} \parallel \overline{AD}$ and $\overline{BC} \cong \overline{AD}$, then *ABCD* is a parallelogram.

Proof Ex. 40, p. 383

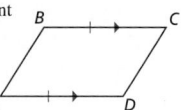

Theorem 7.10 Parallelogram Diagonals Converse

If the diagonals of a quadrilateral bisect each other, then the quadrilateral is a parallelogram.

If $\overline{BD}$ and $\overline{AC}$ bisect each other, then *ABCD* is a parallelogram.

Proof Ex. 41, p. 383

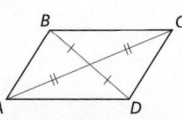

EXAMPLE 3 Identifying a Parallelogram

The doorway shown is part of a building in England. Over time, the building has leaned sideways. Explain how you know that $SV = TU$.

SOLUTION

In the photograph, $\overline{ST} \parallel \overline{UV}$ and $\overline{ST} \cong \overline{UV}$. By the Opposite Sides Parallel and Congruent Theorem, quadrilateral *STUV* is a parallelogram. By the Parallelogram Opposite Sides Theorem (Theorem 7.3), you know that opposite sides of a parallelogram are congruent. So, $SV = TU$.

EXAMPLE 4 Finding Diagonal Lengths of a Parallelogram

For what value of *x* is quadrilateral *CDEF* a parallelogram?

SOLUTION

By the Parallelogram Diagonals Converse, if the diagonals of *CDEF* bisect each other, then it is a parallelogram. You are given that $\overline{CN} \cong \overline{EN}$. Find *x* so that $\overline{FN} \cong \overline{DN}$.

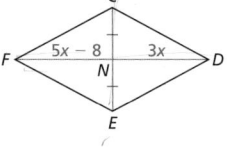

$FN = DN$	Set the segment lengths equal.
$5x - 8 = 3x$	Substitute $5x - 8$ for *FN* and $3x$ for *DN*.
$2x - 8 = 0$	Subtract $3x$ from each side.
$2x = 8$	Add 8 to each side.
$x = 4$	Divide each side by 2.

When $x = 4$, $FN = 5(4) - 8 = 12$ and $DN = 3(4) = 12$.

▶ Quadrilateral *CDEF* is a parallelogram when $x = 4$.

Laurie's Notes Teacher Actions

- Theorem 7.9 is not a converse of an earlier theorem. This hypothesis can easily be demonstrated using dynamic geometry software. As long as two segments remain congruent and parallel, the quadrilateral formed when joining adjacent endpoints will be a parallelogram.

COMMON ERROR Students sometimes use faulty reasoning in a problem like Example 3. They say *STUV* is a parallelogram because both pairs of opposite sides are parallel, and they say $SV = TU$ because opposite sides of a parallelogram are congruent.

Monitoring Progress Help in English and Spanish at *BigIdeasMath.com*

2. For what values of x and y is quadrilateral $ABCD$ a parallelogram? Explain your reasoning.

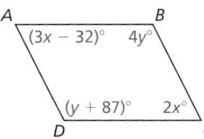

State the theorem you can use to show that the quadrilateral is a parallelogram.

3.

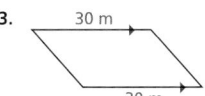

30 m
30 m

4.

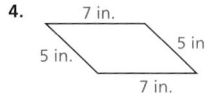

7 in.
5 in.   5 in.
7 in.

5.

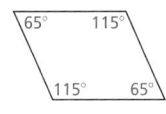

65°   115°
115°   65°

6. For what value of x is quadrilateral $MNPQ$ a parallelogram? Explain your reasoning.

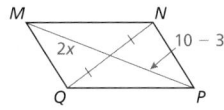

Concept Summary

Ways to Prove a Quadrilateral Is a Parallelogram

1. Show that both pairs of opposite sides are parallel. *(Definition)*	
2. Show that both pairs of opposite sides are congruent. *(Parallelogram Opposite Sides Converse)*	
3. Show that both pairs of opposite angles are congruent. *(Parallelogram Opposite Angles Converse)*	
4. Show that one pair of opposite sides are congruent and parallel. *(Opposite Sides Parallel and Congruent Theorem)*	
5. Show that the diagonals bisect each other. *(Parallelogram Diagonals Converse)*	

Differentiated Instruction

Organization
Have students copy the Ways to Prove a Quadrilateral Is a Parallelogram table into their notebooks. Ask students to explain which methods might be best suited and least suited to use in a coordinate proof.

MONITORING PROGRESS ANSWERS

2. $x = 32$, $y = 29$; By the Parallelogram Opposite Angles Converse (Thm. 7.8), if both pairs of opposite angles of a quadrilateral are congruent, then the quadrilateral is a parallelogram. So, solve $3x - 32 = 2x$ for x, and $4y = y + 87$ for y.

3. Opposite Sides Parallel and Congruent Theorem (Thm. 7.9)

4. Parallelogram Opposite Sides Converse (Thm. 7.7)

5. Parallelogram Opposite Angles Converse (Thm. 7.8)

6. $x = 2$; By the Parallelogram Diagonals Converse (Thm. 7.10), if the diagonals of a quadrilateral bisect each other, then the quadrilateral is a parallelogram. So, solve $2x = 10 - 3x$ for x.

Laurie's Notes   Teacher Actions

- **Think-Pair-Share:** Have students answer Questions 2–6, and then share and discuss as a class.
- Have students list a summary of different ways to prove that a quadrilateral is a parallelogram.
- **?** "How might you know that the opposite sides are parallel?" Listen for suggestions such as knowing something about their slopes or knowing the measures of interior angles.

Extra Example 5

Show that quadrilateral *ABCD* is a parallelogram.

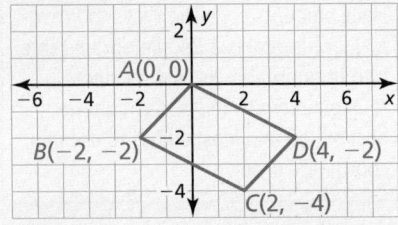

Sample answer: Show that the diagonals $\overline{AC}$ and $\overline{BD}$ bisect each other. Midpoint of $\overline{AC}$ is $\left(\dfrac{0+2}{2}, \dfrac{0+(-4)}{2}\right) = (1, -2)$.

Midpoint of $\overline{BD}$ is $\left(\dfrac{-2+4}{2}, \dfrac{-2+(-2)}{2}\right)$ $= (1, -2)$. The diagonals have the same midpoint, so they bisect each other. So, by the Parallelogram Diagonals Converse Theorem (Thm. 7.10), quadrilateral *ABCD* is a parallelogram.

MONITORING PROGRESS ANSWERS

7. *Sample answer (using Method 1):* Because $JK = LM = \sqrt{37}, \overline{JK} \cong \overline{LM}$. Because the slopes of $\overline{JK}$ and $\overline{LM}$ are both -6, they are parallel. So, $\overline{JK}$ and $\overline{LM}$ are congruent and parallel, which means that *JKLM* is a parallelogram by the Opposite Sides Parallel and Congruent Theorem (Thm. 7.9).

8. *Sample answer:* Find the slopes of all four sides and show that opposite sides are parallel. Another way is to find the point of intersection of the diagonals and show that the diagonals bisect each other.

Using Coordinate Geometry

EXAMPLE 5   Identifying a Parallelogram in the Coordinate Plane

Show that quadrilateral *ABCD* is a parallelogram.

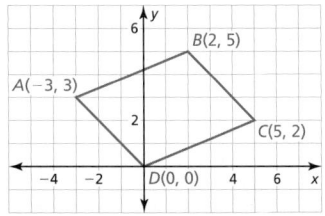

SOLUTION

Method 1   Show that a pair of sides are congruent and parallel. Then apply the Opposite Sides Parallel and Congruent Theorem.

First, use the Distance Formula to show that $\overline{AB}$ and $\overline{CD}$ are congruent.

$$AB = \sqrt{[2 - (-3)]^2 + (5 - 3)^2} = \sqrt{29}$$
$$CD = \sqrt{(5 - 0)^2 + (2 - 0)^2} = \sqrt{29}$$

Because $AB = CD = \sqrt{29}, \overline{AB} \cong \overline{CD}$.

Then, use the slope formula to show that $\overline{AB} \parallel \overline{CD}$.

$$\text{slope of } \overline{AB} = \frac{5 - 3}{2 - (-3)} = \frac{2}{5}$$

$$\text{slope of } \overline{CD} = \frac{2 - 0}{5 - 0} = \frac{2}{5}$$

Because $\overline{AB}$ and $\overline{CD}$ have the same slope, they are parallel.

▶ $\overline{AB}$ and $\overline{CD}$ are congruent and parallel. So, *ABCD* is a parallelogram by the Opposite Sides Parallel and Congruent Theorem.

Method 2   Show that opposite sides are congruent. Then apply the Parallelogram Opposite Sides Converse. In Method 1, you already have shown that because $AB = CD = \sqrt{29}, \overline{AB} \cong \overline{CD}$. Now find *AD* and *BC*.

$$AD = \sqrt{(-3 - 0)^2 + (3 - 0)^2} = 3\sqrt{2}$$
$$BC = \sqrt{(2 - 5)^2 + (5 - 2)^2} = 3\sqrt{2}$$

Because $AD = BC = 3\sqrt{2}, \overline{AD} \cong \overline{BC}$.

▶ $\overline{AB} \cong \overline{CD}$ and $\overline{AD} \cong \overline{BC}$. So, *ABCD* is a parallelogram by the Parallelogram Opposite Sides Converse.

Monitoring Progress Help in English and Spanish at *BigIdeasMath.com*

7. Show that quadrilateral *JKLM* is a parallelogram.

8. Refer to the Concept Summary on page 379. Explain two other methods you can use to show that quadrilateral *ABCD* in Example 5 is a parallelogram.

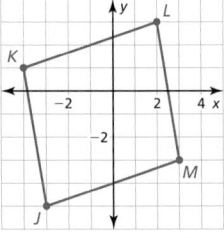

Laurie's Notes   Teacher Actions

- Pose Example 5, and then give partners time to work on the problem.
- **MP1 Make Sense of Problems and Persevere in Solving Them:** Do not rush in to solve this for them. Students know how to determine distances, find a slope, and compute the midpoint.
- **Selective Responses:** This is a problem in which students may use different strategies to prove *ABCD* is a parallelogram. Allow ample work time before asking selected students to share.

Closure

- **Point of Most Significance:** Ask students to identify, aloud or on a paper to be collected, the most significant point (or part) in the lesson that aided their learning.

Vocabulary and Core Concept Check

1. **WRITING** A quadrilateral has four congruent sides. Is the quadrilateral a parallelogram? Justify your answer.

2. **DIFFERENT WORDS, SAME QUESTION** Which is different? Find "both" answers.

Construct a quadrilateral with opposite sides congruent.	Construct a quadrilateral with one pair of parallel sides.
Construct a quadrilateral with opposite angles congruent.	Construct a quadrilateral with one pair of opposite sides congruent and parallel.

Monitoring Progress and Modeling with Mathematics

In Exercises 3–8, state which theorem you can use to show that the quadrilateral is a parallelogram. *(See Examples 1 and 3.)*

3.

4.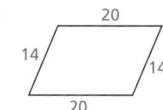

5.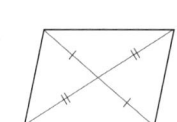

6.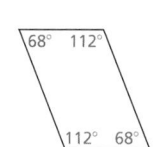

7.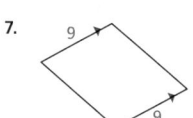

8.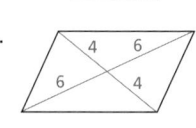

In Exercises 9–12, find the values of x and y that make the quadrilateral a parallelogram. *(See Example 2.)*

9.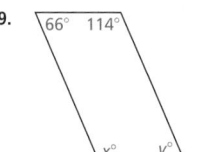

10.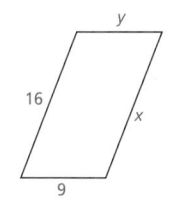

11.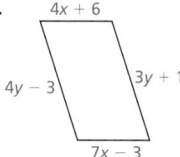

12.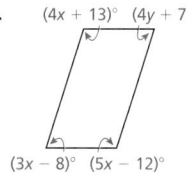

In Exercises 13–16, find the value of x that makes the quadrilateral a parallelogram. *(See Example 4.)*

13.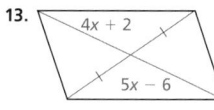

14.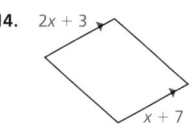

15.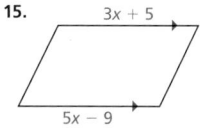

16.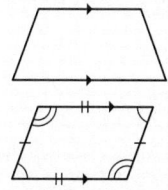

In Exercises 17–20, graph the quadrilateral with the given vertices in a coordinate plane. Then show that the quadrilateral is a parallelogram. *(See Example 5.)*

17. $A(0, 1)$, $B(4, 4)$, $C(12, 4)$, $D(8, 1)$

18. $E(-3, 0)$, $F(-3, 4)$, $G(3, -1)$, $H(3, -5)$

19. $J(-2, 3)$, $K(-5, 7)$, $L(3, 6)$, $M(6, 2)$

20. $N(-5, 0)$, $P(0, 4)$, $Q(3, 0)$, $R(-2, -4)$

Assignment Guide and Homework Check

ASSIGNMENT
Basic: 1, 2, 3–21 odd, 24, 28–34 even, 44, 51–54

Average: 1, 2, 8–38 even, 43, 44, 51–54

Advanced: 1, 2, 8–42 even, 43–47, 49, 51–54

HOMEWORK CHECK
Basic: 3, 7, 11, 13, 17

Average: 8, 12, 18, 32, 43

Advanced: 12, 20, 36, 40, 47

ANSWERS

1. yes; If all four sides are congruent, then both pairs of opposite sides are congruent. So, the quadrilateral is a parallelogram by the Parallelogram Opposite Sides Converse (Thm. 7.7).

2. Construct a quadrilateral with one pair of parallel sides;

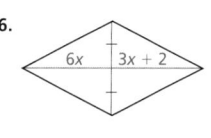

3. Parallelogram Opposite Angles Converse (Thm. 7.8)

4. Parallelogram Opposite Sides Converse (Thm. 7.7)

5. Parallelogram Diagonals Converse (Thm. 7.10)

6. Parallelogram Opposite Angles Converse (Thm. 7.8)

7. Opposite Sides Parallel and Congruent Theorem (Thm. 7.9)

8. Parallelogram Diagonals Converse (Thm. 7.10)

9. $x = 114$, $y = 66$

10. $x = 16$, $y = 9$

11. $x = 3$, $y = 4$

12. $x = 25$, $y = 15$

13. $x = 8$

14. $x = 4$

15. $x = 7$

16. $x = \frac{2}{3}$

17.

the Opposite Sides Parallel and Congruent Theorem (Thm. 7.9).

18–20. See Additional Answers.

Because $BC = AD = 8$, $\overline{BC} \cong \overline{AD}$. Because both $\overline{BC}$ and $\overline{AD}$ are horizontal lines, their slope is 0, and they are parallel. $\overline{BC}$ and $\overline{AD}$ are opposite sides that are both congruent and parallel. So, $ABCD$ is a parallelogram by

ANSWERS

21. In order to be a parallelogram, the quadrilateral must have two pairs of opposite sides that are congruent, not consecutive sides; *DEFG* is not a parallelogram.

22. In order to determine that *JKLM* is a parallelogram using the Opposite Sides Parallel and Congruent Theorem (Thm. 7.9), you would need to know that $\overline{JM} \parallel \overline{KL}$; There is not enough information provided to determine whether *JKLM* is a parallelogram.

23. $x = 5$; The diagonals must bisect each other so you could solve for x using either $2x + 1 = x + 6$ or $4x - 2 = 3x + 3$. Also, the opposite sides must be congruent, so you could solve for x using either $3x + 1 = 4x - 4$ or $3x + 10 = 5x$.

24. yes; By the Consecutive Interior Angles Converse (Thm. 3.8), $\overline{WX} \parallel \overline{ZY}$. Because $\overline{WX}$ and $\overline{ZY}$ are also congruent, *WXYZ* is a parallelogram by the Opposite Sides Parallel and Congruent Theorem (Thm. 7.9).

25. A quadrilateral is a parallelogram if and only if both pairs of opposite sides are congruent.

26. A quadrilateral is a parallelogram if and only if both pairs of opposite angles are congruent.

27. A quadrilateral is a parallelogram if and only if the diagonals bisect each other.

28. *Sample answer:* Draw two horizontal segments that are the same length and connect the endpoints.

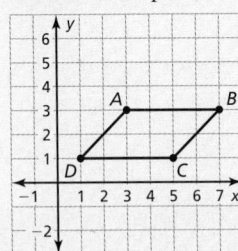

29. Check students' work; Because the diagonals bisect each other, this quadrilateral is a parallelogram by the Parallelogram Diagonals Converse (Thm. 7.10).

ERROR ANALYSIS In Exercises 21 and 22, describe and correct the error in identifying a parallelogram.

21.

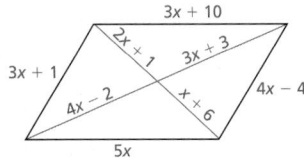

DEFG is a parallelogram by the Parallelogram Opposite Sides Converse (Theorem 7.7).

22.

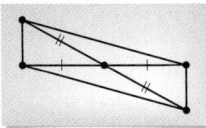

JKLM is a parallelogram by the Opposite Sides Parallel and Congruent Theorem (Theorem 7.9).

23. **MATHEMATICAL CONNECTIONS** What value of x makes the quadrilateral a parallelogram? Explain how you found your answer.

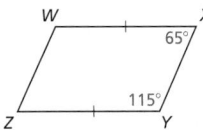

24. **MAKING AN ARGUMENT** Your friend says you can show that quadrilateral *WXYZ* is a parallelogram by using the Consecutive Interior Angles Converse (Theorem 3.8) and the Opposite Sides Parallel and Congruent Theorem (Theorem 7.9). Is your friend correct? Explain your reasoning.

ANALYZING RELATIONSHIPS In Exercises 25–27, write the indicated theorems as a biconditional statement.

25. Parallelogram Opposite Sides Theorem (Theorem 7.3) and Parallelogram Opposite Sides Converse (Theorem 7.7)

26. Parallelogram Opposite Angles Theorem (Theorem 7.4) and Parallelogram Opposite Angles Converse (Theorem 7.8)

---

27. Parallelogram Diagonals Theorem (Theorem 7.6) and Parallelogram Diagonals Converse (Theorem 7.10)

28. **CONSTRUCTION** Describe a method that uses the Opposite Sides Parallel and Congruent Theorem (Theorem 7.9) to construct a parallelogram. Then construct a parallelogram using your method.

29. **REASONING** Follow the steps below to construct a parallelogram. Explain why this method works. State a theorem to support your answer.

Step 1 Use a ruler to draw two segments that intersect at their midpoints.

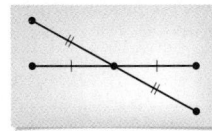

Step 2 Connect the endpoints of the segments to form a parallelogram.

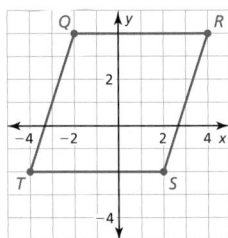

30. **MAKING AN ARGUMENT** Your brother says to show that quadrilateral *QRST* is a parallelogram, you must show that $\overline{QR} \parallel \overline{TS}$ and $\overline{QT} \parallel \overline{RS}$. Your sister says that you must show that $\overline{QR} \cong \overline{TS}$ and $\overline{QT} \cong \overline{RS}$. Who is correct? Explain your reasoning.

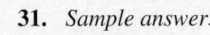

REASONING In Exercises 31 and 32, your classmate incorrectly claims that the marked information can be used to show that the figure is a parallelogram. Draw a quadrilateral with the same marked properties that is clearly *not* a parallelogram.

31.

32.

---

30. both; If you show that $\overline{QR} \parallel \overline{TS}$ and $\overline{QT} \parallel \overline{RS}$, then *QRST* is a parallelogram by definition. If you show that $\overline{QR} \cong \overline{TS}$ and $\overline{QT} \cong \overline{RS}$, then *QRST* is a parallelogram by the Parallelogram Opposite Sides Converse (Thm. 7.7).

31. *Sample answer:*

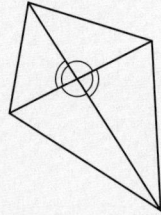

32. *Sample answer:*

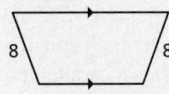

33. MODELING WITH MATHEMATICS You shoot a pool ball, and it rolls back to where it started, as shown in the diagram. The ball bounces off each wall at the same angle at which it hits the wall.

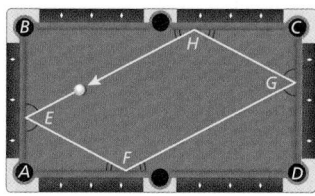

a. The ball hits the first wall at an angle of 63°. So $m\angle AEF = m\angle BEH = 63°$. What is $m\angle AFE$? Explain your reasoning.

b. Explain why $m\angle FGD = 63°$.

c. What is $m\angle GHC$? $m\angle EHB$?

d. Is quadrilateral *EFGH* a parallelogram? Explain your reasoning.

34. MODELING WITH MATHEMATICS In the diagram of the parking lot shown, $m\angle JKL = 60°$, $JK = LM = 21$ feet, and $KL = JM = 9$ feet.

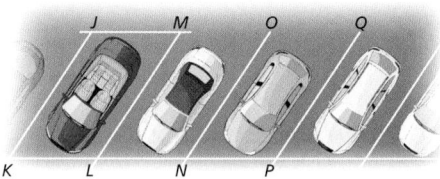

a. Explain how to show that parking space *JKLM* is a parallelogram.

b. Find $m\angle JML$, $m\angle KJM$, and $m\angle KLM$.

c. $\overline{LM} \parallel \overline{NO}$ and $\overline{NO} \parallel \overline{PQ}$. Which theorem could you use to show that $\overline{JK} \parallel \overline{PQ}$?

REASONING In Exercises 35–37, describe how to prove that *ABCD* is a parallelogram.

35.

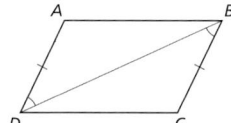

36.

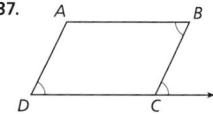

37.

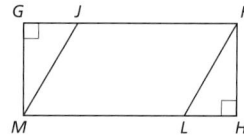

38. REASONING Quadrilateral *JKLM* is a parallelogram. Describe how to prove that $\triangle MGJ \cong \triangle KHL$.

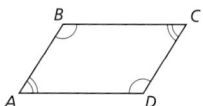

39. PROVING A THEOREM Prove the Parallelogram Opposite Angles Converse (Theorem 7.8). (*Hint:* Let $x°$ represent $m\angle A$ and $m\angle C$. Let $y°$ represent $m\angle B$ and $m\angle D$. Write and simplify an equation involving x and y.)

Given $\angle A \cong \angle C$, $\angle B \cong \angle D$

Prove *ABCD* is a parallelogram.

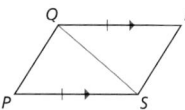

40. PROVING A THEOREM Use the diagram of *PQRS* with the auxiliary line segment drawn to prove the Opposite Sides Parallel and Congruent Theorem (Theorem 7.9).

Given $\overline{QR} \parallel \overline{PS}$, $\overline{QR} \cong \overline{PS}$

Prove *PQRS* is a parallelogram.

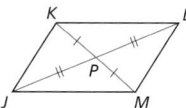

41. PROVING A THEOREM Prove the Parallelogram Diagonals Converse (Theorem 7.10).

Given Diagonals $\overline{JL}$ and $\overline{KM}$ bisect each other.

Prove *JKLM* is a parallelogram.

Section 7.3   Proving That a Quadrilateral Is a Parallelogram   **383**

ANSWERS

33. a. 27°; Because $\angle EAF$ is a right angle, the other two angles of $\triangle EAF$ must be complementary. So, $m\angle AFE = 90° - 63° = 27°$.

b. Because $\angle GDF$ is a right angle, the other two angles of $\triangle GDF$ must be complementary. So, $m\angle FGD = 90° - 27° = 63°$.

c. 27°; 27°

d. yes; $\angle HEF \cong \angle HGF$ because they both are adjacent to two congruent angles that together add up to 180°, and $\angle EHG \cong \angle GFE$ for the same reason. So, *EFGH* is a parallelogram by the Parallelogram Opposite Angles Converse (Thm. 7.8).

34. a. Because $\overline{JK} \cong \overline{LM}$ and $\overline{KL} \cong \overline{JM}$, *JKLM* is a parallelogram by the Parallelogram Opposite Sides Converse (Thm. 7.7).

b. 60°, 120°, 120°

c. Transitive Property of Parallel Lines (Thm. 3.9)

35. You can use the Alternate Interior Angles Converse (Thm. 3.6) to show that $\overline{AD} \parallel \overline{BC}$. Then, $\overline{AD}$ and $\overline{BC}$ are both congruent and parallel. So, *ABCD* is a parallelogram by the Opposite Sides Parallel and Congruent Theorem (Thm 7.9).

36. You can use the Alternate Interior Angles Converse (Thm. 3.6) to show that $\overline{AB} \parallel \overline{DC}$ and $\overline{AD} \parallel \overline{BC}$. Because both pairs of opposite sides are parallel, *ABCD* is a parallelogram by definition.

37. First, you can use the Linear Pair Postulate (Post. 2.8) and the Congruent Supplements Theorem (Thm. 2.4) to show that $\angle ABC$ and $\angle DCB$ are supplementary. Then, you can use the Consecutive Interior Angles Converse (Thm. 3.8) to show that $\overline{AB} \parallel \overline{DC}$ and $\overline{AD} \parallel \overline{BC}$. So, *ABCD* is a parallelogram by definition.

38. By the Parallelogram Opposite Sides Theorem (Thm 7.3), $\overline{JM} \cong \overline{LK}$. Also, you can use the Linear Pair Postulate (Thm. 2.8) and the Congruent Supplements Theorem (Thm. 2.4) to show that $\angle GJM \cong \angle HLK$. Because $\angle JGM$ and $\angle LHK$ are congruent right angles, you can now state that $\triangle MGJ \cong \triangle KHL$ by the AAS Congruence Theorem (Thm. 5.11).

39–41. See Additional Answers.

ANSWERS

42. See Additional Answers.

43. no; The fourth angle will be 113° because of the Corollary to the Polygon Interior Angles Theorem (Cor. 7.1), but these could also be the angle measures of an isosceles trapezoid with base angles that are each 67°.

44. $\overline{AE} \parallel \overline{DF}, \overline{EB} \parallel \overline{FC}, \overline{AD} \parallel \overline{EF} \parallel \overline{BC}$

45–54. See Additional Answers.

Mini-Assessment

1. Show that quadrilateral *ABCD* is a parallelogram.

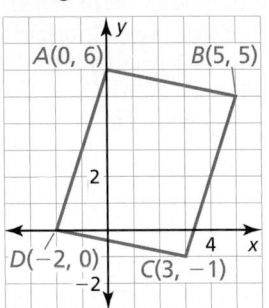

Sample answer: Use slope to show that both pairs of opposite sides are parallel.
Slope of $\overline{AB}$ = slope of $\overline{DC}$ = -0.2
Slope of $\overline{BC}$ = slope of $\overline{AD}$ = 3
Both pairs of opposite sides of *ABCD* are parallel. So, *ABCD* is a parallelogram by definition.

Is the given information sufficient to prove that quadrilateral *JKLM* is a parallelogram? Explain your reasoning.

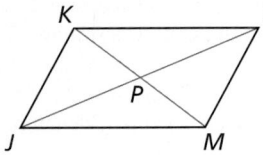

2. $JK = LM$ and $KL = JM$ Yes; Parallelogram Opposite Sides Converse Thm. (7.7)

3. $JK = LM$ and $\overline{KL} \parallel \overline{JM}$ No; by Opp. Sides $\parallel$ and $\cong$ Thm. (7.9), the congruent sides must also be parallel.

4. $JP = LP$ and $KP = MP$ Yes; Parallelogram Diagonals Converse Thm. (7.10)

384　　**Chapter 7**

---

42. PROOF Write a proof.

Given *DEBF* is a parallelogram.
　　　$AE = CF$

Prove *ABCD* is a parallelogram.

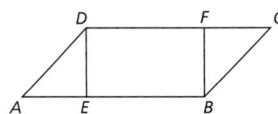

43. REASONING Three interior angle measures of a quadrilateral are 67°, 67°, and 113°. Is this enough information to conclude that the quadrilateral is a parallelogram? Explain your reasoning.

44. HOW DO YOU SEE IT? A music stand can be folded up, as shown. In the diagrams, *AEFD* and *EBCF* are parallelograms. Which labeled segments remain parallel as the stand is folded?

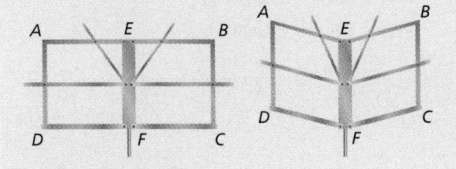

45. CRITICAL THINKING In the diagram, *ABCD* is a parallelogram, $BF = DE = 12$, and $CF = 8$. Find *AE*. Explain your reasoning.

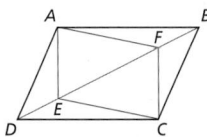

46. THOUGHT PROVOKING Create a regular hexagon using congruent parallelograms.

Maintaining Mathematical Proficiency　*Reviewing what you learned in previous grades and lessons*

Classify the quadrilateral. *(Skills Review Handbook)*

| **51.** | **52.** | **53.** | **54.** |

---

47. WRITING The Parallelogram Consecutive Angles Theorem (Theorem 7.5) says that if a quadrilateral is a parallelogram, then its consecutive angles are supplementary. Write the converse of this theorem. Then write a plan for proving the converse. Include a diagram.

48. PROOF Write a proof.

Given *ABCD* is a parallelogram.
　　　∠*A* is a right angle.

Prove ∠*B*, ∠*C*, and ∠*D* are right angles.

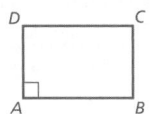

49. ABSTRACT REASONING The midpoints of the sides of a quadrilateral have been joined to form what looks like a parallelogram. Show that a quadrilateral formed by connecting the midpoints of the sides of any quadrilateral is always a parallelogram. (*Hint:* Draw a diagram. Include a diagonal of the larger quadrilateral. Show how two sides of the smaller quadrilateral relate to the diagonal.)

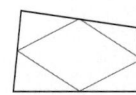

50. CRITICAL THINKING Show that if *ABCD* is a parallelogram with its diagonals intersecting at *E*, then you can connect the midpoints *F*, *G*, *H*, and *J* of $\overline{AE}, \overline{BE}, \overline{CE}$, and $\overline{DE}$, respectively, to form another parallelogram, *FGHJ*.

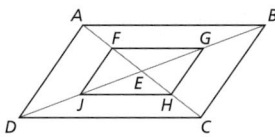

384　　**Chapter 7**　　Quadrilaterals and Other Polygons

If students need help...	If students got it...
Resources by Chapter • Practice A and Practice B • Puzzle Time	Resources by Chapter • Enrichment and Extension • Cumulative Review
Student Journal • Practice	Start the *next* Section
Differentiating the Lesson Skills Review Handbook	

Core Vocabulary

diagonal, *p. 360*   equiangular polygon, *p. 361*   parallelogram, *p. 368*
equilateral polygon, *p. 361*   regular polygon, *p. 361*

Core Concepts

Section 7.1

Theorem 7.1 Polygon Interior Angles Theorem, *p. 360*
Corollary 7.1 Corollary to the Polygon Interior Angles Theorem, *p. 361*
Theorem 7.2 Polygon Exterior Angles Theorem, *p. 362*

Section 7.2

Theorem 7.3 Parallelogram Opposite Sides Theorem, *p. 368*
Theorem 7.4 Parallelogram Opposite Angles Theorem, *p. 368*
Theorem 7.5 Parallelogram Consecutive Angles Theorem, *p. 369*
Theorem 7.6 Parallelogram Diagonals Theorem, *p. 369*
Using Parallelograms in the Coordinate Plane, *p. 371*

Section 7.3

Theorem 7.7 Parallelogram Opposite Sides Converse, *p. 376*
Theorem 7.8 Parallelogram Opposite Angles Converse, *p. 376*
Theorem 7.9 Opposite Sides Parallel and Congruent Theorem, *p. 378*
Theorem 7.10 Parallelogram Diagonals Converse, *p. 378*
Ways to Prove a Quadrilateral is a Parallelogram, *p. 379*
Showing That a Quadrilateral Is a Parallelogram in the Coordinate Plane, *p. 380*

Mathematical Practices

1. In Exercise 52 on page 366, what is the relationship between the 540° increase and the answer?

2. Explain why the process you used works every time in Exercise 25 on page 373. Is there another way to do it?

3. In Exercise 23 on page 382, explain how you started the problem. Why did you start that way? Could you have started another way? Explain.

- - - - - - - - - - Study Skills - - - - - - - - - -
Keeping Your Mind Focused during Class

- When you sit down at your desk, get all other issues out of your mind by reviewing your notes from the last class and focusing on just math.

- Repeat in your mind what you are writing in your notes.

- When the math is particularly difficult, ask your teacher for another example.

385

ANSWERS

1. $\dfrac{540°}{180°} = 3$

2. By the Parallelogram Diagonals Theorem (Thm. 7.6), the diagonals of a parallelogram bisect each other. So, the diagonals will have the same midpoint, and it will also be the point where the diagonals intersect. Therefore, with any parallelogram, you can find the midpoint of either diagonal, and it will be the coordinates of the intersection of the diagonals; Instead of this method, you could also find the equations of the lines that define each diagonal, set them equal to each other and solve for the values of the coordinates where the lines intersect.

3. *Sample answer:* Solve $5x = 3x + 10$; opposite sides of a parallelogram are congruent; yes; You could start by setting the two parts of either diagonal equal to each other by the Parallelogram Diagonals Theorem (Thm. 7.6).

ANSWERS

1. $x = 80$
2. $x = 135$
3. $x = 97$
4. $144°$, $36°$
5. $156°$, $24°$
6. $165°$, $15°$
7. $174°$, $6°$
8. 16; By the Parallelogram Opposite Sides Theorem (Thm. 7.3), $AB = CD$.
9. 7; By the Parallelogram Opposite Sides Theorem (Thm. 7.3), $AD = BC$.
10. 7; By the Parallelogram Diagonals Theorem (Thm. 7.6), $AE = EC$.
11. 20.4; By the Parallelogram Diagonals Theorem (Thm. 7.6), $BE = ED$. So, $BD = 2 \cdot 10.2$.
12. $120°$; By the Parallelogram Opposite Angles Theorem (Thm. 7.4), $m\angle DAB = m\angle BCD$.
13. $60°$; By the Parallelogram Consecutive Angles Theorem (Thm. 7.5), $\angle DAB$ and $\angle ABC$ are supplementary. So, $m\angle ABC = 180° - 120°$.
14. $60°$; By the Parallelogram Consecutive Angles Theorem (Thm. 7.5), $\angle DAB$ and $\angle ADC$ are supplementary. So, $m\angle ADC = 180° - 120°$.
15. $43°$; By the Alternate Interior Angles Theorem (Thm. 3.2), $m\angle DBC = m\angle ADB$.
16. Opposite Sides Parallel and Congruent Theorem (Thm. 7.9)
17. Parallelogram Diagonals Converse (Thm. 7.10)
18. Parallelogram Opposite Angles Converse (Thm 7.8)
19.

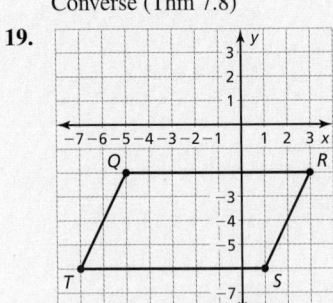

Because $QR = ST = 8$, $\overline{QR} \cong \overline{ST}$. Because both $\overline{QR}$ and $\overline{ST}$ are horizontal lines, their slope is 0, and they are parallel. $\overline{QR}$ and $\overline{ST}$ are opposite sides that are both congruent and parallel. So, $QRST$ is a parallelogram by the Opposite Sides Parallel and Congruent Theorem (Thm. 7.9).

386   Chapter 7

Find the value of x. *(Section 7.1)*

1.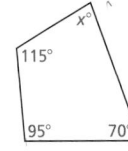

2.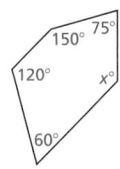

3.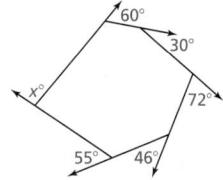

Find the measure of each interior angle and each exterior angle of the indicated regular polygon. *(Section 7.1)*

4. decagon   5. 15-gon   6. 24-gon   7. 60-gon

Find the indicated measure in ▱ABCD. Explain your reasoning. *(Section 7.2)*

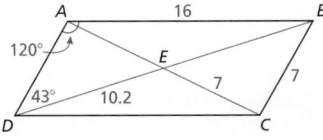

8. CD
9. AD
10. AE
11. BD
12. $m\angle BCD$
13. $m\angle ABC$
14. $m\angle ADC$
15. $m\angle DBC$

State which theorem you can use to show that the quadrilateral is a parallelogram. *(Section 7.3)*

16.

17.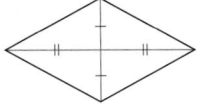

18.

Graph the quadrilateral with the given vertices in a coordinate plane. Then show that the quadrilateral is a parallelogram. *(Section 7.3)*

19. $Q(-5, -2)$, $R(3, -2)$, $S(1, -6)$, $T(-7, -6)$
20. $W(-3, 7)$, $X(3, 3)$, $Y(1, -3)$, $Z(-5, 1)$

21. A stop sign is a regular polygon. *(Section 7.1)*
   a. Classify the stop sign by its number of sides.
   b. Find the measure of each interior angle and each exterior angle of the stop sign.

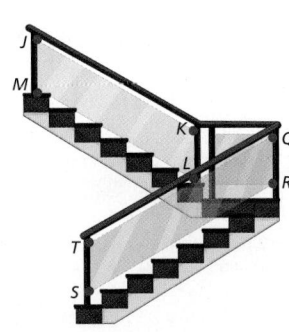

22. In the diagram of the staircase shown, $JKLM$ is a parallelogram, $\overline{QT} \parallel \overline{RS}$, $QT = RS = 9$ feet, $QR = 3$ feet, and $m\angle QRS = 123°$. *(Section 7.2 and Section 7.3)*
   a. List all congruent sides and angles in ▱$JKLM$. Explain your reasoning.
   b. Which theorem could you use to show that $QRST$ is a parallelogram?
   c. Find ST, $m\angle QTS$, $m\angle TQR$, and $m\angle TSR$. Explain your reasoning.

20.

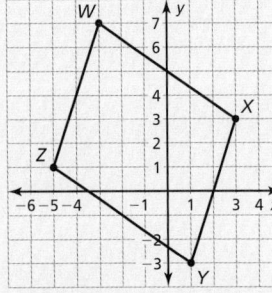

Because the slopes of $\overline{WX}$ and $\overline{YZ}$ are both $-\frac{2}{3}$, they are parallel. Because the slopes of $\overline{XY}$ and $\overline{WZ}$ are both 3, they are parallel. Because both pairs of opposite sides are parallel, $WXYZ$ is a parallelogram by definition.

21. a. octagon
    b. $135°$, $45°$
22. See Additional Answers.

Overview of Section 7.4

Introduction

- This lesson is about special parallelograms: rectangles, rhombuses, and squares.
- Properties about the diagonals and opposite angles are presented as biconditional statements.

Resources

- Use bendable straws to make models of a rectangle and a rhombus. Use elastic thread (available where sewing notions are sold) tied at the vertices to represent the diagonals.
- By flexing the straws, it is possible to show how the diagonals of a parallelogram become congruent as the parallelogram is straightened to become a rectangle.
- For the model of the rhombus, the diagonals become perpendicular as the parallelogram is resized to become a rhombus.

Teaching Strategy

- **Draw a Diagram:** One way to show the relationships between quadrilaterals is to draw a Venn diagram. A flowchart is another strategy to show the hierarchical relationships of these quadrilaterals.
- Because rectangles, rhombuses, and squares are special parallelograms, they have all of the properties of parallelograms.
- The definition of each of the new quadrilaterals begins with, "A ___ is a parallelogram with …." Without having to repeat the definition or list any properties, these attributes are already known.
- You can discuss the properties of the diagonals of each quadrilateral in the flowchart.

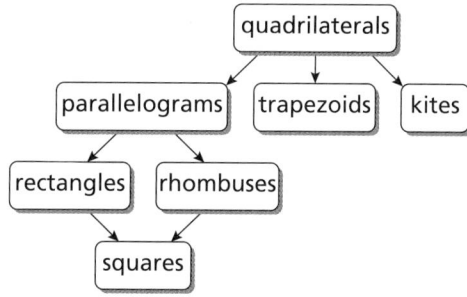

Pacing Suggestion

- The explorations provide an opportunity for students to consider how they can prove they have a rectangle or a rhombus. Transition to the formal lesson as soon as students have discussed each exploration.

Dynamic Teaching Tools

Dynamic Assessment & Progress Monitoring Tool
Lesson Planning Tool
Interactive Whiteboard Lesson Library
Dynamic Classroom with Dynamic Investigations

HSG-CO.C.11 Prove theorems about parallelograms.

HSG-SRT.B.5 Use congruence … criteria for triangles to solve problems and to prove relationships in geometric figures.

HSG-MG.A.1 Use geometric shapes, their measures, and their properties to describe objects (e.g., modeling a tree trunk or a human torso as a cylinder).

HSG-MG.A.3 Apply geometric methods to solve design problems (e.g., designing an object or structure to satisfy physical constraints or minimize cost; working with typographic grid systems based on ratios).

Laurie's Notes

Exploration

Motivate
- Draw and cut out a large copy of a rhombus. It should not be a square.
- **MP6 Attend to Precision:** Ask students to describe the symmetry of the rhombus, both rotational and line.
- The rhombus has 180° rotational symmetry and line symmetries through the opposite vertices.
- Fold and crease the rhombus on both lines of symmetry. If possible, display it under a document camera.
- **Turn and Talk:** "What does the symmetry tell you about the diagonals of a rhombus? About the opposite angles of a rhombus?"

Exploration Note
- **MP8 Look For and Express Regularity in Repeated Reasoning:** Mathematically proficient students do not base a conjecture on one construction. The construction must be repeated several times, each time with the hypothesis being satisfied. Each time, look for patterns.

Exploration 1
- Students are familiar with the definitions of *rhombus*, *rectangle*, and *square* from middle school.
- **?** It is important for students to recognize what the hypothesis is. "What is true about the quadrilateral you are investigating in this exploration?" The diagonals of the quadrilateral are congruent.
- **?** **MP3 Construct Viable Arguments and Critique the Reasoning of Others:** "How do you know the quadrilateral is a parallelogram?" The diagonals are bisected, so the quadrilateral must be a parallelogram.
- Students should observe that the parallelograms in this exploration are always rectangles, and in some cases they are squares.
- **?** **MP3:** "How did you determine that the parallelogram was a rectangle or a square?" Answers will vary.

Exploration 2
- **?** It is important for students to recognize what the hypothesis is. "What is true about the quadrilateral you are investigating in this exploration?" The diagonals of the quadrilateral are perpendicular bisectors of each other.
- **?** **MP3:** "How do you know the quadrilateral is a parallelogram?" The diagonals are bisected, so the quadrilateral must be a parallelogram.
- Students should observe that the parallelograms in this investigation are always rhombuses, and in some cases they are squares.
- **?** **MP3:** "How did you determine that the parallelogram was a rhombus or a square?" Answers will vary.

Communicate Your Answer
- Listen carefully as students distinguish between the various parallelograms.
  - If the diagonals of a parallelogram are congruent, then it is a rectangle.
  - If the diagonals of a parallelogram are perpendicular, then it is a rhombus.
  - If the diagonals of a parallelogram are congruent and perpendicular, then it is a square.

Connecting to Next Step
- The conjectures made by students will be stated and proven as theorems in the formal lesson.

7.4 Properties of Special Parallelograms

Essential Question
What are the properties of the diagonals of rectangles, rhombuses, and squares?

Recall the three types of parallelograms shown below.

 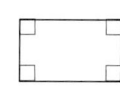

Rhombus   Rectangle   Square

EXPLORATION 1 Identifying Special Quadrilaterals

Work with a partner. Use dynamic geometry software.

a. Draw a circle with center A.

b. Draw two diameters of the circle. Label the endpoints B, C, D, and E.

c. Draw quadrilateral $BDCE$.

d. Is $BDCE$ a parallelogram? rectangle? rhombus? square? Explain your reasoning.

e. Repeat parts (a)–(d) for several other circles. Write a conjecture based on your results.

Sample

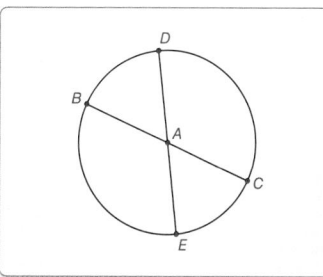

EXPLORATION 2 Identifying Special Quadrilaterals

Work with a partner. Use dynamic geometry software.

a. Construct two segments that are perpendicular bisectors of each other. Label the endpoints A, B, D, and E. Label the intersection C.

b. Draw quadrilateral $AEBD$.

c. Is $AEBD$ a parallelogram? rectangle? rhombus? square? Explain your reasoning.

d. Repeat parts (a)–(c) for several other segments. Write a conjecture based on your results.

Sample

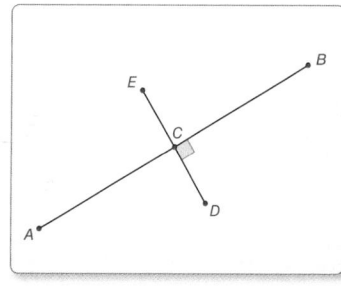

CONSTRUCTING VIABLE ARGUMENTS

To be proficient in math, you need to make conjectures and build a logical progression of statements to explore the truth of your conjectures.

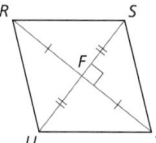

Communicate Your Answer

3. What are the properties of the diagonals of rectangles, rhombuses, and squares?

4. Is $RSTU$ a parallelogram? rectangle? rhombus? square? Explain your reasoning.

5. What type of quadrilateral has congruent diagonals that bisect each other?

ANSWERS

1. a. Check students' work.

   b. Check students' work.

   c.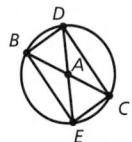

   d. yes; yes; no; no; Because all points on a circle are the same distance from the center, $\overline{AB} \cong \overline{AE} \cong \overline{AC} \cong \overline{AD}$. So, the diagonals of quadrilateral $BDCE$ bisect each other, which means it is a parallelogram by the Parallelogram Diagonals Converse (Thm. 7.10). Because all 4 angles of $BDCE$ are right angles, it is a rectangle. $BDCE$ is neither a rhombus nor a square because $\overline{BD}$ and $\overline{EC}$ are not necessarily the same length as $\overline{BE}$ and $\overline{DC}$.

   e. Check students' work; The quadrilateral formed by the endpoints of two diameters is a rectangle (and a parallelogram). In other words, a quadrilateral is a rectangle if and only if its diagonals are congruent and bisect each other.

2. a. Check students' work.

   b.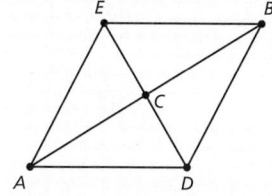

   c. yes; no; yes; no; Because the diagonals bisect each other, $AEBD$ is a parallelogram by the Parallelogram Diagonals Converse (Thm. 7.10). Because $EB = BD = AD = AE$, $AEBD$ is a rhombus. $AEBD$ is neither a rectangle nor a square because its angles are not necessarily right angles.

---

2. d. Check students' work; A quadrilateral is a rhombus if and only if the diagonals are perpendicular bisectors of each other.

3. Because rectangles, rhombuses, and squares are all parallelograms, their diagonals bisect each other by the Parallelogram Diagonals Theorem (Thm. 7.6). The diagonals of a rectangle are congruent. The diagonals of a rhombus are perpendicular. The diagonals of a square are congruent and perpendicular.

4. yes; no; yes; no; $RSTU$ is a parallelogram because the diagonals bisect each other. $RSTU$ is not a rectangle because the diagonals are not congruent. $RSTU$ is a rhombus because the diagonals are perpendicular. $RSTU$ is not a square because the diagonals are not congruent.

5. rectangle

7.4 Lesson

Core Vocabulary
rhombus, *p. 388*
rectangle, *p. 388*
square, *p. 388*

Previous
quadrilateral
parallelogram
diagonal

What You Will Learn

▶ Use properties of special parallelograms.
▶ Use properties of diagonals of special parallelograms.
▶ Use coordinate geometry to identify special types of parallelograms.

Using Properties of Special Parallelograms

In this lesson, you will learn about three special types of parallelograms: *rhombuses*, *rectangles*, and *squares*.

🄖 Core Concept

Rhombuses, Rectangles, and Squares

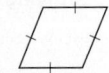 

A **rhombus** is a parallelogram with four congruent sides.

A **rectangle** is a parallelogram with four right angles.

A **square** is a parallelogram with four congruent sides and four right angles.

You can use the corollaries below to prove that a quadrilateral is a rhombus, rectangle, or square, without first proving that the quadrilateral is a parallelogram.

🄖 Corollaries

Corollary 7.2   Rhombus Corollary

A quadrilateral is a rhombus if and only if it has four congruent sides.

ABCD is a rhombus if and only if $\overline{AB} \cong \overline{BC} \cong \overline{CD} \cong \overline{AD}$.

Proof Ex. 81, p. 396

Corollary 7.3   Rectangle Corollary

A quadrilateral is a rectangle if and only if it has four right angles.

ABCD is a rectangle if and only if $\angle A$, $\angle B$, $\angle C$, and $\angle D$ are right angles.

Proof Ex. 82, p. 396

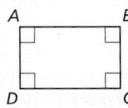

Corollary 7.4   Square Corollary

A quadrilateral is a square if and only if it is a rhombus and a rectangle.

ABCD is a square if and only if $\overline{AB} \cong \overline{BC} \cong \overline{CD} \cong \overline{AD}$ and $\angle A$, $\angle B$, $\angle C$, and $\angle D$ are right angles.

Proof Ex. 83, p. 396

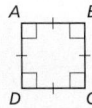

Laurie's Notes   Teacher Actions

- **Common Misconception:** Students often think that they should include everything they know about a polygon in its definition. While definitions may differ in language, it is generally agreed that good definitions are precise and without extraneous information.
- **MP2 Reason Abstractly and Quantitatively:** Be sure students understand how corollaries will be used.
- **Turn and Talk:** Have partners select a corollary and discuss how to prove it.
- **Selective Responses:** Students may use different strategies. Allow ample work time before asking selected students to share their proofs.

The Venn diagram below illustrates some important relationships among parallelograms, rhombuses, rectangles, and squares. For example, you can see that a square is a rhombus because it is a parallelogram with four congruent sides. Because it has four right angles, a square is also a rectangle.

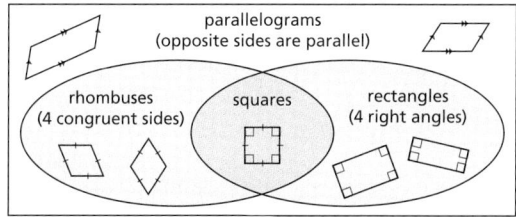

EXAMPLE 1 Using Properties of Special Quadrilaterals

For any rhombus *QRST*, decide whether the statement is *always* or *sometimes* true. Draw a diagram and explain your reasoning.

a. ∠*Q* ≅ ∠*S*   **b.** ∠*Q* ≅ ∠*R*

SOLUTION

a. By definition, a rhombus is a parallelogram with four congruent sides. By the Parallelogram Opposite Angles Theorem (Theorem 7.4), opposite angles of a parallelogram are congruent. So, ∠*Q* ≅ ∠*S*. The statement is *always* true.

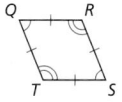

b. If rhombus *QRST* is a square, then all four angles are congruent right angles. So, ∠*Q* ≅ ∠*R* when *QRST* is a square. Because not all rhombuses are also squares, the statement is *sometimes* true.

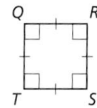

EXAMPLE 2 Classifying Special Quadrilaterals

Classify the special quadrilateral. Explain your reasoning.

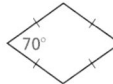

SOLUTION

The quadrilateral has four congruent sides. By the Rhombus Corollary, the quadrilateral is a rhombus. Because one of the angles is not a right angle, the rhombus cannot be a square.

Monitoring Progress   Help in English and Spanish at *BigIdeasMath.com*

1. For any square *JKLM*, is it *always* or *sometimes* true that $\overline{JK} \perp \overline{KL}$? Explain your reasoning.

2. For any rectangle *EFGH*, is it *always* or *sometimes* true that $\overline{FG} \cong \overline{GH}$? Explain your reasoning.

3. A quadrilateral has four congruent sides and four congruent angles. Sketch the quadrilateral and classify it.

Section 7.4   Properties of Special Parallelograms   **389**

Extra Example 1

For any rectangle *ABCD*, decide whether the statement is *always* or *sometimes* true. Explain your reasoning.

a. *AB* = *BC*

If rectangle *ABCD* is a square, then all four sides are congruent. So, *AB* = *BC* when *ABCD* is a square. Because not all rectangles are also squares, the statement is *sometimes* true.

b. *AB* = *CD*

By definition, a rectangle is a parallelogram. By the Parallelogram Opposite Sides Theorem (Thm. 7.3), opposite sides of a parallelogram are congruent. So, *AB* = *CD* is *always* true.

Extra Example 2

Classify the special quadrilateral. Explain your reasoning.

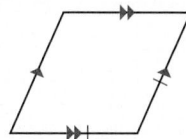

The figure is a rhombus. Two pairs of opposite sides are parallel. So, by definition, the figure is a parallelogram. In a parallelogram, opposite sides are congruent. The figure has two adjacent sides that are congruent. So, by the Transitive Property of Congruence (Thm. 2.1), all four sides are congruent.

MONITORING PROGRESS ANSWERS

1. always; By definition, a square has four right angles.

2. sometimes; Some rectangles are squares.

3.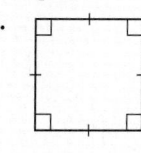

   square

Using Properties of Diagonals

Theorems

Theorem 7.11   Rhombus Diagonals Theorem

A parallelogram is a rhombus if and only if its diagonals are perpendicular.

$\square ABCD$ is a rhombus if and only if $\overline{AC} \perp \overline{BD}$.

Proof p. 390; Ex. 72, p. 395

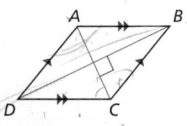

Theorem 7.12   Rhombus Opposite Angles Theorem

A parallelogram is a rhombus if and only if each diagonal bisects a pair of opposite angles.

$\square ABCD$ is a rhombus if and only if $\overline{AC}$ bisects $\angle BCD$ and $\angle BAD$, and $\overline{BD}$ bisects $\angle ABC$ and $\angle ADC$.

Proof Exs. 73 and 74, p. 395

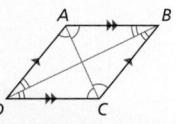

READING

Recall that biconditionals, such as the Rhombus Diagonals Theorem, can be rewritten as two parts. To prove a biconditional, you must prove both parts.

PROOF   **Part of Rhombus Diagonals Theorem**

Given $ABCD$ is a rhombus.

Prove $\overline{AC} \perp \overline{BD}$

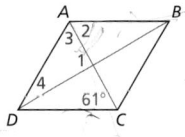

$ABCD$ is a rhombus. By the definition of a rhombus, $\overline{AB} \cong \overline{BC}$. Because a rhombus is a parallelogram and the diagonals of a parallelogram bisect each other, $\overline{BD}$ bisects $\overline{AC}$ at E. So, $\overline{AE} \cong \overline{EC}$. $\overline{BE} \cong \overline{BE}$ by the Reflexive Property of Congruence (Theorem 2.1). So, $\triangle AEB \cong \triangle CEB$ by the SSS Congruence Theorem (Theorem 5.8). $\angle AEB \cong \angle CEB$ because corresponding parts of congruent triangles are congruent. Then by the Linear Pair Postulate (Postulate 2.8), $\angle AEB$ and $\angle CEB$ are supplementary. Two congruent angles that form a linear pair are right angles, so $m\angle AEB = m\angle CEB = 90°$ by the definition of a right angle. So, $\overline{AC} \perp \overline{BD}$ by the definition of perpendicular lines.

EXAMPLE 3   **Finding Angle Measures in a Rhombus**

Find the measures of the numbered angles in rhombus $ABCD$.

SOLUTION

Use the Rhombus Diagonals Theorem and the Rhombus Opposite Angles Theorem to find the angle measures.

$m\angle 1 = 90°$	The diagonals of a rhombus are perpendicular.
$m\angle 2 = 61°$	Alternate Interior Angles Theorem (Theorem 3.2)
$m\angle 3 = 61°$	Each diagonal of a rhombus bisects a pair of opposite angles, and $m\angle 2 = 61°$.
$m\angle 1 + m\angle 3 + m\angle 4 = 180°$	Triangle Sum Theorem (Theorem 5.1)
$90° + 61° + m\angle 4 = 180°$	Substitute 90° for $m\angle 1$ and 61° for $m\angle 3$.
$m\angle 4 = 29°$	Solve for $m\angle 4$.

▶ So, $m\angle 1 = 90°$, $m\angle 2 = 61°$, $m\angle 3 = 61°$, and $m\angle 4 = 29°$.

Laurie's Notes   **Teacher Actions**

? "What do you know about the diagonals of a rhombus from the exploration?" When diagonals are perpendicular bisectors of each other, the quadrilateral is a rhombus.

• Review the language of a biconditional statement. To prove a biconditional, both parts must be proven.

• **Think-Alouds:** Write Theorem 7.11 and say, "To prove one part of this theorem, I would …." Ask partner A to think aloud for partner B to hear the reasoning process. Reverse roles for proving the second part. When students have finished the problem, use *Popsicle Sticks* to solicit responses.

Monitoring Progress Help in English and Spanish at *BigIdeasMath.com*

4. In Example 3, what is $m\angle ADC$ and $m\angle BCD$?

5. Find the measures of the numbered angles in rhombus *DEFG*.

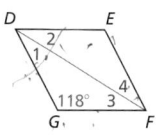

Theorem

Theorem 7.13 Rectangle Diagonals Theorem

A parallelogram is a rectangle if and only if its diagonals are congruent.

☐*ABCD* is a rectangle if and only if $\overline{AC} \cong \overline{BD}$.

Proof Exs. 87 and 88, p. 396

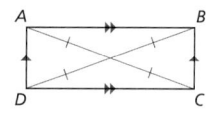

EXAMPLE 4 Identifying a Rectangle

You are building a frame for a window. The window will be installed in the opening shown in the diagram.

a. The opening must be a rectangle. Given the measurements in the diagram, can you assume that it is? Explain.

b. You measure the diagonals of the opening. The diagonals are 54.8 inches and 55.3 inches. What can you conclude about the shape of the opening?

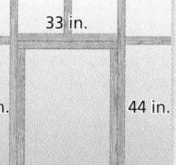

SOLUTION

a. No, you cannot. The boards on opposite sides are the same length, so they form a parallelogram. But you do not know whether the angles are right angles.

b. By the Rectangle Diagonals Theorem, the diagonals of a rectangle are congruent. The diagonals of the quadrilateral formed by the boards are not congruent, so the boards do not form a rectangle.

EXAMPLE 5 Finding Diagonal Lengths in a Rectangle

In rectangle *QRST*, $QS = 5x - 31$ and $RT = 2x + 11$. Find the lengths of the diagonals of *QRST*.

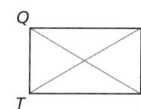

SOLUTION

By the Rectangle Diagonals Theorem, the diagonals of a rectangle are congruent. Find x so that $\overline{QS} \cong \overline{RT}$.

$QS = RT$	Set the diagonal lengths equal.
$5x - 31 = 2x + 11$	Substitute $5x - 31$ for QS and $2x + 11$ for RT.
$3x - 31 = 11$	Subtract $2x$ from each side.
$3x = 42$	Add 31 to each side.
$x = 14$	Divide each side by 3.

When $x = 14$, $QS = 5(14) - 31 = 39$ and $RT = 2(14) + 11 = 39$.

▶ Each diagonal has a length of 39 units.

Section 7.4   Properties of Special Parallelograms   **391**

Extra Example 4

Use the diagram in Example 4. Suppose you measure one angle of the window opening and its measure is 90°. Can you conclude that the shape of the opening is a rectangle? Explain.

Yes. Both pairs of opposite sides are congruent, so the quadrilateral is a parallelogram (Thm. 7.7). Opposite angles of a parallelogram are congruent (Thm. 7.4), so the parallelogram has two right angles. Consecutive angles of a parallelogram are supplementary (Thm. 7.5), so the other two angles of the parallelogram are also right angles. A parallelogram with four right angles is a rectangle by definition.

Extra Example 5

In rectangle *ABCD*, $AC = 7x - 15$ and $BD = 2x + 25$. Find the lengths of the diagonals of *ABCD*.

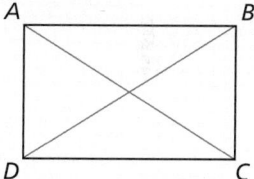

41 units

MONITORING PROGRESS ANSWERS

4. 58°; 122°

5. $m\angle 1 = 31°$; $m\angle 2 = 31°$; $m\angle 3 = 31°$; $m\angle 4 = 31°$

Laurie's Notes   Teacher Actions

? "Are the diagonals of a rectangle (that is not a square) perpendicular?" no "Do they bisect one another?" yes

• Write Theorem 7.13, and have partners discuss an outline of the proof.

• **Common Misconception:** In Example 4, the opposite sides are congruent and the shape appears to be a rectangle. Discuss that this is not a rigid shape and can sway to one side.

? "If the diagonals of another window frame were congruent and you didn't measure the sides of the frame would you be able to say the frame is a rectangle? Explain your reasoning." no; The Rectangle Diagonals Theorem requires that the quadrilateral be a parallelogram and you do not know if opposite sides are congruent.

Extra Example 6

Decide whether ▱*ABCD* with vertices *A*(−2, 3), *B*(2, 2), *C*(1, −2), and *D*(−3, −1) is a *rectangle*, a *rhombus*, or a *square*. Give all names that apply. **a rectangle, a rhombus, and a square**

MONITORING PROGRESS ANSWERS

6. no; The quadrilateral might not be a parallelogram.

7. 77

8. rectangle, rhombus, square

6. Suppose you measure only the diagonals of the window opening in Example 4 and they have the same measure. Can you conclude that the opening is a rectangle? Explain.

7. **WHAT IF?** In Example 5, $QS = 4x − 15$ and $RT = 3x + 8$. Find the lengths of the diagonals of *QRST*.

Using Coordinate Geometry

EXAMPLE 6   Identifying a Parallelogram in the Coordinate Plane

Decide whether ▱*ABCD* with vertices $A(−2, 6)$, $B(6, 8)$, $C(4, 0)$, and $D(−4, −2)$ is a *rectangle*, a *rhombus*, or a *square*. Give all names that apply.

SOLUTION

1. **Understand the Problem** You know the vertices of ▱*ABCD*. You need to identify the type of parallelogram.

2. **Make a Plan** Begin by graphing the vertices. From the graph, it appears that all four sides are congruent and there are no right angles.

   Check the lengths and slopes of the diagonals of ▱*ABCD*. If the diagonals are congruent, then ▱*ABCD* is a rectangle. If the diagonals are perpendicular, then ▱*ABCD* is a rhombus. If they are both congruent and perpendicular, then ▱*ABCD* is a rectangle, a rhombus, and a square.

3. **Solve the Problem** Use the Distance Formula to find *AC* and *BD*.

$$AC = \sqrt{(−2 − 4)^2 + (6 − 0)^2} = \sqrt{72} = 6\sqrt{2}$$

$$BD = \sqrt{[6 − (−4)]^2 + [8 − (−2)]^2} = \sqrt{200} = 10\sqrt{2}$$

Because $6\sqrt{2} \neq 10\sqrt{2}$, the diagonals are not congruent. So, ▱*ABCD* is not a rectangle. Because it is not a rectangle, it also cannot be a square.

Use the slope formula to find the slopes of the diagonals $\overline{AC}$ and $\overline{BD}$.

$$\text{slope of } \overline{AC} = \frac{6 − 0}{−2 − 4} = \frac{6}{−6} = −1 \qquad \text{slope of } \overline{BD} = \frac{8 − (−2)}{6 − (−4)} = \frac{10}{10} = 1$$

Because the product of the slopes of the diagonals is −1, the diagonals are perpendicular.

▶ So, ▱*ABCD* is a rhombus.

4. **Look Back** Check the side lengths of ▱*ABCD*. Each side has a length of $2\sqrt{17}$ units, so ▱*ABCD* is a rhombus. Check the slopes of two consecutive sides.

$$\text{slope of } \overline{AB} = \frac{8 − 6}{6 − (−2)} = \frac{2}{8} = \frac{1}{4} \qquad \text{slope of } \overline{BC} = \frac{8 − 0}{6 − 4} = \frac{8}{2} = 4$$

Because the product of these slopes is not −1, $\overline{AB}$ is not perpendicular to $\overline{BC}$.

So, ∠*ABC* is not a right angle, and ▱*ABCD* cannot be a rectangle or a square. ✓

8. Decide whether ▱*PQRS* with vertices $P(−5, 2)$, $Q(0, 4)$, $R(2, −1)$, and $S(−3, −3)$ is a *rectangle*, a *rhombus*, or a *square*. Give all names that apply.

Laurie's Notes   Teacher Actions

- **MP1 Make Sense of Problems and Persevere in Solving Them:** Give partners sufficient *Wait Time* to work on the example. When students do a quick plot, they may assume it is a rhombus. Let students decide what they need to calculate to determine that it is a rhombus.
- **Selective Responses:** This is a problem in which students may use different strategies. Allow ample work time before asking selected students to share.

Closure

- **Exit Ticket:** List different ways in which you can prove a quadrilateral is a rectangle, a rhombus, and a square.

Vocabulary and Core Concept Check

1. **VOCABULARY** What is another name for an equilateral rectangle?

2. **WRITING** What should you look for in a parallelogram to know if the parallelogram is also a rhombus?

Monitoring Progress and Modeling with Mathematics

In Exercises 3–8, for any rhombus *JKLM*, decide whether the statement is *always* or *sometimes* true. Draw a diagram and explain your reasoning. *(See Example 1.)*

3. $\angle L \cong \angle M$ 4. $\angle K \cong \angle M$

5. $\overline{JM} \cong \overline{KL}$ 6. $\overline{JK} \cong \overline{KL}$

7. $\overline{JL} \cong \overline{KM}$ 8. $\angle JKM \cong \angle LKM$

In Exercises 9–12, classify the quadrilateral. Explain your reasoning. *(See Example 2.)*

9.    10.

11.    12.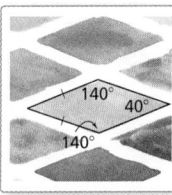

In Exercises 13–16, find the measures of the numbered angles in rhombus *DEFG*. *(See Example 3.)*

13. 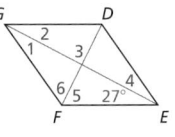   14.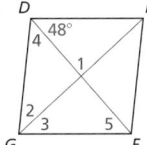

15. 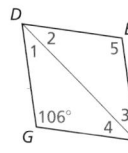   16.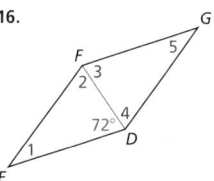

In Exercises 17–22, for any rectangle *WXYZ*, decide whether the statement is *always* or *sometimes* true. Draw a diagram and explain your reasoning.

17. $\angle W \cong \angle X$ 18. $\overline{WX} \cong \overline{YZ}$

19. $\overline{WX} \cong \overline{XY}$ 20. $\overline{WY} \cong \overline{XZ}$

21. $\overline{WY} \perp \overline{XZ}$ 22. $\angle WXZ \cong \angle YXZ$

In Exercises 23 and 24, determine whether the quadrilateral is a rectangle. *(See Example 4.)*

23.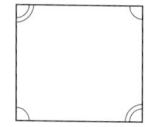

24.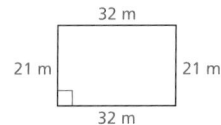

In Exercises 25–28, find the lengths of the diagonals of rectangle *WXYZ*. *(See Example 5.)*

25. $WY = 6x - 7$
    $XZ = 3x + 2$

26. $WY = 14x + 10$
    $XZ = 11x + 22$

27. $WY = 24x - 8$
    $XZ = -18x + 13$

28. $WY = 16x + 2$
    $XZ = 36x - 6$

Assignment Guide and Homework Check

ASSIGNMENT

Basic: 1, 2, 3–55 odd, 63–69 odd, 78, 84, 89–91

Average: 1, 2, 6–58 even, 64–78 even, 84, 89–91

Advanced: 1, 2, 8–70 even, 74–84, 88–91

HOMEWORK CHECK

Basic: 3, 11, 15, 25, 55

Average: 10, 16, 28, 50, 56

Advanced: 36, 60, 62, 78, 80

ANSWERS

1. square

2. two consecutive sides that are congruent

3. sometimes; Some rhombuses are squares.
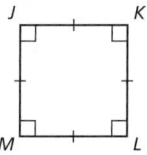

4. always; A rhombus is a parallelogram, and the opposite angles of a parallelogram are congruent.
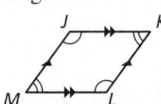

5. always; By definition, a rhombus is a parallelogram, and opposite sides of a parallelogram are congruent.
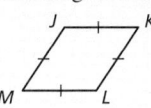

6. always; By definition, a rhombus is a parallelogram with four congruent sides.
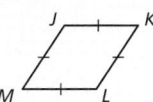

7. sometimes; Some rhombuses are squares.
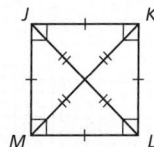

8. always; Each diagonal of a rhombus bisects a pair of opposite angles.
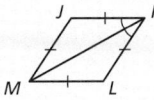

9. square; All of the sides are congruent, and all of the angles are congruent.

10. rectangle; Opposite sides are congruent and the angles are 90°.

11. rectangle; Opposite sides are parallel and the angles are 90°.

12. rhombus; Opposite angles are congruent and adjacent sides are congruent.

13. $m\angle 1 = m\angle 2 = m\angle 4 = 27°$, $m\angle 3 = 90°$; $m\angle 5 = m\angle 6 = 63°$

14. $m\angle 1 = 90°$; $m\angle 2 = m\angle 3 = 42°$; $m\angle 4 = m\angle 5 = 48°$

15. $m\angle 1 = m\angle 2 = m\angle 3 = m\angle 4 = 37°$; $m\angle 5 = 106°$

16. $m\angle 1 = m\angle 5 = 36°$; $m\angle 2 = m\angle 3 = m\angle 4 = 72°$

17–28. See Additional Answers.

ANSWERS

29. rectangle, square

30. square

31. rhombus, square

32. parallelogram, rectangle, rhombus, square

33. parallelogram, rectangle, rhombus, square

34. rhombus, square

35. Diagonals do not necessarily bisect opposite angles of a rectangle;

   $m\angle QSR = 90° - m\angle QSP$

   $x = 32$

36. $\angle QSP$ and $\angle RQS$ should be complementary because they are the two acute angles of a right triangle;

   $m\angle QSP = 90° - m\angle RQS$

   $x = 53$

37. 53°

38. 90°

39. 74°

40. 16

41. 6

42. 12

43. 56°

44. 34°

45. 56°

46. 5

47. 10

48. 5

49. 90°

50. 45°

51. 45°

52. 1

53. 2

54. 2

55. rectangle, rhombus, square; The diagonals are congruent and perpendicular.

56. rhombus; The diagonals are perpendicular and not congruent.

57. rectangle; The sides are perpendicular and not congruent.

58. rectangle; The diagonals are congruent and not perpendicular.

59. rhombus; The diagonals are perpendicular and not congruent.

60. rectangle, rhombus, square; The diagonals are perpendicular and congruent.

In Exercises 29–34, name each quadrilateral— *parallelogram, rectangle, rhombus,* **or** *square***—for which the statement is always true.**

29. It is equiangular.

30. It is equiangular and equilateral.

31. The diagonals are perpendicular.

32. Opposite sides are congruent.

33. The diagonals bisect each other.

34. The diagonals bisect opposite angles.

35. **ERROR ANALYSIS** Quadrilateral *PQRS* is a rectangle. Describe and correct the error in finding the value of *x*.

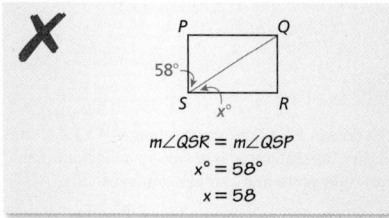

$$m\angle QSR = m\angle QSP$$
$$x° = 58°$$
$$x = 58$$

36. **ERROR ANALYSIS** Quadrilateral *PQRS* is a rhombus. Describe and correct the error in finding the value of *x*.

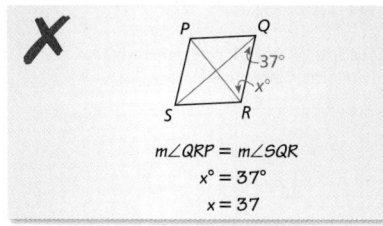

$$m\angle QRP = m\angle SQR$$
$$x° = 37°$$
$$x = 37$$

In Exercises 37–42, the diagonals of rhombus *ABCD* intersect at *E*. Given that $m\angle BAC = 53°$, $DE = 8$, and $EC = 6$, find the indicated measure.

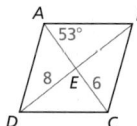

37. $m\angle DAC$ 38. $m\angle AED$

39. $m\angle ADC$ 40. DB

41. AE 42. AC

394   Chapter 7   Quadrilaterals and Other Polygons

In Exercises 43–48, the diagonals of rectangle *QRST* intersect at *P*. Given that $m\angle PTS = 34°$ and $QS = 10$, find the indicated measure.

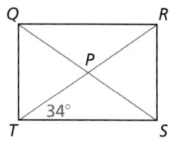

43. $m\angle QTR$ 44. $m\angle QRT$

45. $m\angle SRT$ 46. QP

47. RT 48. RP

In Exercises 49–54, the diagonals of square *LMNP* intersect at *K*. Given that $LK = 1$, find the indicated measure.

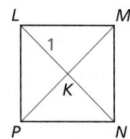

49. $m\angle MKN$ 50. $m\angle LMK$

51. $m\angle LPK$ 52. KN

53. LN 54. MP

In Exercises 55–60, decide whether □*JKLM* is a rectangle, a rhombus, or a square. Give all names that apply. Explain your reasoning. *(See Example 6.)*

55. $J(-4, 2), K(0, 3), L(1, -1), M(-3, -2)$

56. $J(-2, 7), K(7, 2), L(-2, -3), M(-11, 2)$

57. $J(3, 1), K(3, -3), L(-2, -3), M(-2, 1)$

58. $J(-1, 4), K(-3, 2), L(2, -3), M(4, -1)$

59. $J(5, 2), K(1, 9), L(-3, 2), M(1, -5)$

60. $J(5, 2), K(2, 5), L(-1, 2), M(2, -1)$

MATHEMATICAL CONNECTIONS In Exercises 61 and 62, classify the quadrilateral. Explain your reasoning. Then find the values of *x* and *y*.

61.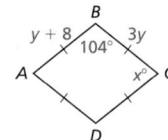

62.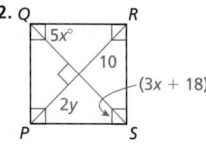

61. rhombus; The sides are congruent; $x = 76$; $y = 4$

62. square; Because all four angles are 90° and the diagonals are perpendicular; $x = 9$; $y = 5$

63. DRAWING CONCLUSIONS In the window, $\overline{BD} \cong \overline{DF} \cong \overline{BH} \cong \overline{HF}$. Also, ∠HAB, ∠BCD, ∠DEF, and ∠FGH are right angles.

a. Classify *HBDF* and *ACEG*. Explain your reasoning.

b. What can you conclude about the lengths of the diagonals $\overline{AE}$ and $\overline{GC}$? Given that these diagonals intersect at *J*, what can you conclude about the lengths of $\overline{AJ}, \overline{JE}, \overline{CJ}$, and $\overline{JG}$? Explain.

64. ABSTRACT REASONING Order the terms in a diagram so that each term builds off the previous term(s). Explain why each figure is in the location you chose.

quadrilateral	square
rectangle	rhombus
parallelogram	

CRITICAL THINKING In Exercises 65–70, complete each statement with *always*, *sometimes*, or *never*. Explain your reasoning.

65. A square is _____ a rhombus.

66. A rectangle is _____ a square.

67. A rectangle _____ has congruent diagonals.

68. The diagonals of a square _____ bisect its angles.

69. A rhombus _____ has four congruent angles.

70. A rectangle _____ has perpendicular diagonals.

71. USING TOOLS You want to mark off a square region for a garden at school. You use a tape measure to mark off a quadrilateral on the ground. Each side of the quadrilateral is 2.5 meters long. Explain how you can use the tape measure to make sure that the quadrilateral is a square.

72. PROVING A THEOREM Use the plan for proof below to write a paragraph proof for one part of the Rhombus Diagonals Theorem (Theorem 7.11).

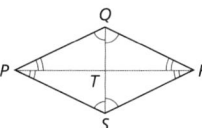

Given *ABCD* is a parallelogram.
$\overline{AC} \perp \overline{BD}$

Prove *ABCD* is a rhombus.

Plan for Proof Because *ABCD* is a parallelogram, its diagonals bisect each other at *X*. Use $\overline{AC} \perp \overline{BD}$ to show that △BXC ≅ △DXC. Then show that $\overline{BC} \cong \overline{DC}$. Use the properties of a parallelogram to show that *ABCD* is a rhombus.

PROVING A THEOREM In Exercises 73 and 74, write a proof for part of the Rhombus Opposite Angles Theorem (Theorem 7.12).

73. Given *PQRS* is a parallelogram.
$\overline{PR}$ bisects ∠SPQ and ∠QRS.
$\overline{SQ}$ bisects ∠PSR and ∠RQP.

Prove *PQRS* is a rhombus.

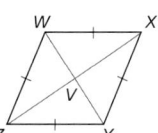

74. Given *WXYZ* is a rhombus.

Prove $\overline{WY}$ bisects ∠ZWX and ∠XYZ.
$\overline{ZX}$ bisects ∠WZY and ∠YXW.

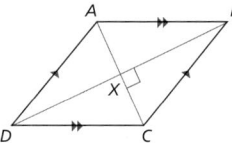

ANSWERS

63. a. rhombus; rectangle; *HBDF* has four congruent sides; *ACEG* has four right angles.

b. *AE* = *GC*; *AJ* = *JE* = *CJ* = *JG*; The diagonals of a rectangle are congruent and bisect each other.

64.

> quadrilateral
>
> parallelogram
>
> rectangle   rhombus
>
> square

All of the shapes have 4 sides. So, quadrilateral is at the top of the diagram. Because the rest all have two pairs of parallel sides, they are all parallelograms. Then, parallelograms with four right angles make one category (rectangle), while those with four congruent sides make another (rhombus), and if a parallelogram is both a rhombus and a rectangle, then it is a square.

65. always; By the Square Corollary (Cor. 7.4), a square is a rhombus.

66. sometimes; Some rectangles are squares.

67. always; The diagonals of a rectangle are congruent by the Rectangle Diagonals Theorem (Thm. 7.13).

68. always; A square is a rhombus.

69. sometimes; Some rhombuses are squares.

70. sometimes; Some rectangles are rhombuses.

71. Measure the diagonals to see if they are congruent.

72. Because *ABCD* is a parallelogram, its diagonals bisect each other by the Parallelogram Diagonals Theorem (Thm. 7.6). So, $\overline{BX} \cong \overline{DX}$ by definition of segment bisector. Because $\overline{AC} \perp \overline{BD}$, ∠DXC ≅ ∠BXC. By the Reflexive Property of Congruence (Thm. 2.1), $\overline{XC} \cong \overline{XC}$. So, △BXC ≅ △DXC by the SAS Congruence Theorem (Thm. 5.5). So, $\overline{BC} \cong \overline{DC}$ because corresponding parts of congruent triangles are congruent. Also, $\overline{AD} \cong \overline{BC}$ and $\overline{DC} \cong \overline{AB}$ because opposite sides of a parallelogram are congruent. So, by the Transitive Property of Congruence (Thm. 2.1), $\overline{AB} \cong \overline{BC} \cong \overline{DC} \cong \overline{AD}$, which means that by the Rhombus Corollary (Cor. 7.2), *ABCD* is a rhombus.

73–74. See Additional Answers.

ANSWERS

75. no; The diagonals of a square always create two right triangles.

76. yes; If the angles of a rhombus are 60°, 120°, 60°, and 120°, the diagonal that bisects the opposite 120° angles will divide the rhombus into two equilateral triangles.

77. square; A square has four congruent sides and four congruent angles.

78. *Sample answer:* You need to know whether the figure is a parallelogram.

79. no; yes; Corresponding angles of two rhombuses might not be congruent; Corresponding angles of two squares are congruent.

80. Because the line connecting a point with its preimage in a reflection is always perpendicular to the line of reflection, when a diagonal connecting two vertices is perpendicular to the other diagonal, both can be a line of symmetry.

81–83. See Additional Answers.

84. no; If a rhombus is a square, then it is also a rectangle.

85–88. See Additional Answers.

89. $x = 10, y = 8$

90. $x = 14, y = 6$

91. $x = 9, y = 26$

Mini-Assessment

1. Decide whether □ABCD with vertices $A(-3, 4)$, $B(3, 2)$, $C(2, -1)$, and $D(-4, 1)$ is a *rectangle*, a *rhombus*, or a *square*. Give all names that apply.
a rectangle

WXYZ is a rhombus.

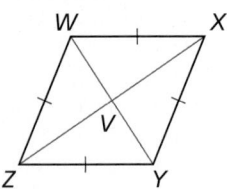

2. Find $m\angle WVX$. 90°

3. $m\angle ZYX = 128°$. Find $m\angle XYW$ and $m\angle ZXY$. $m\angle XYW = 64°$, $m\angle ZXY = 26°$

4. What can you conclude about a rhombus with congruent diagonals? It is also a rectangle and a square.

75. ABSTRACT REASONING Will a diagonal of a square ever divide the square into two equilateral triangles? Explain your reasoning.

76. ABSTRACT REASONING Will a diagonal of a rhombus ever divide the rhombus into two equilateral triangles? Explain your reasoning.

77. CRITICAL THINKING Which quadrilateral could be called a regular quadrilateral? Explain your reasoning.

78. HOW DO YOU SEE IT? What other information do you need to determine whether the figure is a rectangle?

79. REASONING Are all rhombuses similar? Are all squares similar? Explain your reasoning.

80. THOUGHT PROVOKING Use the Rhombus Diagonals Theorem (Theorem 7.11) to explain why every rhombus has at least two lines of symmetry.

PROVING A COROLLARY In Exercises 81–83, write the corollary as a conditional statement and its converse. Then explain why each statement is true.

81. Rhombus Corollary (Corollary 7.2)

82. Rectangle Corollary (Corollary 7.3)

83. Square Corollary (Corollary 7.4)

84. MAKING AN ARGUMENT Your friend claims a rhombus will never have congruent diagonals because it would have to be a rectangle. Is your friend correct? Explain your reasoning.

85. PROOF Write a proof in the style of your choice.

Given $\triangle XYZ \cong \triangle XWZ, \angle XYW \cong \angle ZWY$

Prove *WXYZ* is a rhombus.

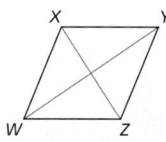

86. PROOF Write a proof in the style of your choice.

Given $\overline{BC} \cong \overline{AD}, \overline{BC} \perp \overline{DC}, \overline{AD} \perp \overline{DC}$

Prove *ABCD* is a rectangle.

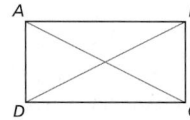

PROVING A THEOREM In Exercises 87 and 88, write a proof for part of the Rectangle Diagonals Theorem (Theorem 7.13).

87. Given *PQRS* is a rectangle.

Prove $\overline{PR} \cong \overline{SQ}$

88. Given *PQRS* is a parallelogram. $\overline{PR} \cong \overline{SQ}$

Prove *PQRS* is a rectangle.

Maintaining Mathematical Proficiency
Reviewing what you learned in previous grades and lessons

$\overline{DE}$ is a midsegment of $\triangle ABC$. Find the values of *x* and *y*. *(Section 6.4)*

89.

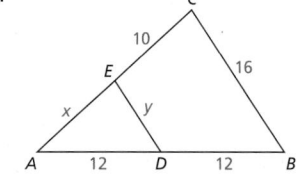

90.

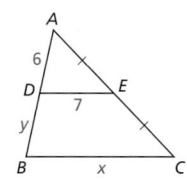

91.

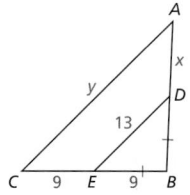

If students need help...	If students got it...
Resources by Chapter • Practice A and Practice B • Puzzle Time	Resources by Chapter • Enrichment and Extension • Cumulative Review
Student Journal • Practice	Start the *next* Section
Differentiating the Lesson Skills Review Handbook	

396 Chapter 7 Quadrilaterals and Other Polygons

Overview of Section 7.5

Introduction

- This lesson is about two additional special quadrilaterals: trapezoids and kites.
- Properties about the diagonals and angles of these special quadrilaterals are presented, with some proven in the lesson and the remainder in the exercises.
- The midsegment of a trapezoid is defined. Students will see the connection to the midsegment of a triangle.
- The lesson ends with a flowchart summary of all of the special quadrilaterals presented in this chapter.

Teaching Strategy

- There are common ways in which a trapezoid is often drawn, leading students to believe that all trapezoids look like the one shown on the left. Be sure to draw trapezoids in different orientations and not all isosceles.

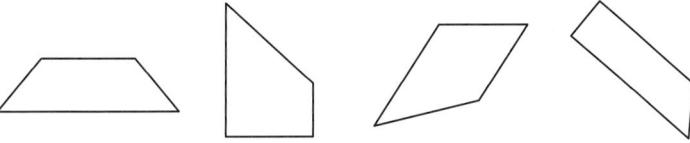

- A kite is defined in this lesson as a quadrilateral with two pairs of consecutive congruent sides, but opposite sides are not congruent. Here are two alternate definitions. Have students discuss each and decide what information is known about a kite from its definition.
  - A kite is a quadrilateral with two distinct pairs of adjacent sides that are congruent.
  - A kite is quadrilateral with perpendicular diagonals and exactly one line of symmetry.

Pacing Suggestion

- The explorations provide an opportunity for students to consider how they can prove they have a trapezoid or a kite. Transition to the formal lesson as soon as students have discussed each exploration.

Common Core State Standards

HSG-SRT.B.5 Use congruence … criteria for triangles to solve problems and to prove relationships in geometric figures.

HSG-MG.A.1 Use geometric shapes, their measures, and their properties to describe objects (e.g., modeling a tree trunk or a human torso as a cylinder).

Laurie's Notes

Exploration

Motivate

- Ask students to sketch quadrilaterals with different numbers of lines of symmetry: 0, 1, 2, 3, and 4.
- **Popsicle Sticks:** Use *Popsicle Sticks* to solicit responses for each. A square is the only quadrilateral with 4 lines of symmetry. No quadrilateral has 3 lines of symmetry. Rectangles and rhombuses have 2 lines of symmetry. Isosceles trapezoids and kites have 1 line of symmetry. Parallelograms and non-isosceles trapezoids have 0 lines of symmetry.
- Explain that today's lesson is about trapezoids and kites.

Exploration 1

- There are many different ways in which students could construct a trapezoid with base angles congruent.
- One method is to draw a line, $\overleftrightarrow{AB}$, and construct a line parallel to this line through a point C not on the line. Construct the perpendicular bisector of $\overline{AB}$ and reflect point C in the perpendicular bisector. Quadrilateral $ABC'C$ has congruent base angles and is an isosceles trapezoid.

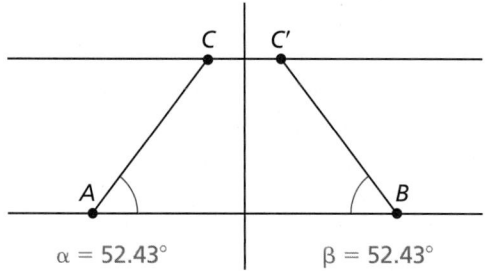

$$\alpha = 52.43° \qquad \beta = 52.43°$$

- **MP3 Construct Viable Arguments and Critique the Reasoning of Others:** Ask students to share methods used to construct a trapezoid with congruent base angles.
- Measuring the legs reveals that the trapezoid is isosceles.

Exploration 2

- Students should not have difficulty constructing a kite. Kites have exactly one line of symmetry. Begin with a scalene triangle and reflect the triangle in one side.

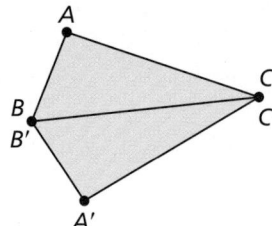

- If students use a reflection to construct the kite, they will easily recognize that one pair of opposite angles are congruent and the other pair of opposite angles are bisected by a diagonal.

Communicate Your Answer

- Listen for students to share the properties of trapezoids, isosceles trapezoids, and kites. Although the explorations did not explore diagonals, students may have conjectures.

Connecting to Next Step

- The conjectures made by students will be stated and proven as theorems in the formal lesson.

7.5 Properties of Trapezoids and Kites

Essential Question
What are some properties of trapezoids and kites?

Recall the types of quadrilaterals shown below.

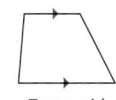 

Trapezoid   Isosceles Trapezoid   Kite

PERSEVERE IN SOLVING PROBLEMS

To be proficient in math, you need to draw diagrams of important features and relationships, and search for regularity or trends.

EXPLORATION 1   Making a Conjecture about Trapezoids

Work with a partner. Use dynamic geometry software.

a. Construct a trapezoid whose base angles are congruent. Explain your process.

b. Is the trapezoid isosceles? Justify your answer.

c. Repeat parts (a) and (b) for several other trapezoids. Write a conjecture based on your results.

Sample

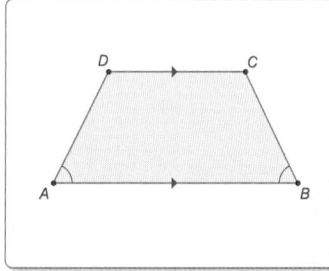

EXPLORATION 2   Discovering a Property of Kites

Work with a partner. Use dynamic geometry software.

a. Construct a kite. Explain your process.

b. Measure the angles of the kite. What do you observe?

c. Repeat parts (a) and (b) for several other kites. Write a conjecture based on your results.

Sample

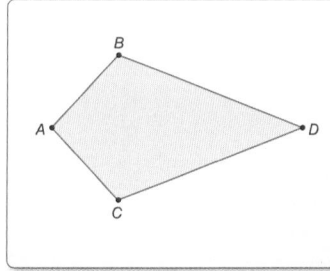

Communicate Your Answer

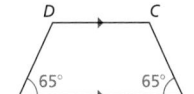

3. What are some properties of trapezoids and kites?

4. Is the trapezoid at the left isosceles? Explain.

5. A quadrilateral has angle measures of 70°, 70°, 110°, and 110°. Is the quadrilateral a kite? Explain.

Section 7.5   Properties of Trapezoids and Kites   **397**

ANSWERS

1. a. Check students' work.

   b. yes; $AD = BC$

   c. If the base angles of a trapezoid are congruent, then the trapezoid is isosceles.

2. a. Check students' work.

   b. $\angle B \cong \angle C$

   c. If a quadrilateral is a kite, then it has exactly one pair of congruent opposite angles.

3. A trapezoid is a quadrilateral with exactly one pair of parallel sides; A trapezoid that has congruent base angles is isosceles; A kite has exactly one pair of congruent opposite angles.

4. yes; When the base angles are congruent, the opposite sides are also congruent.

5. no; In a kite, only one pair of opposite angles is congruent.

Extra Example 1

Show that *ABCD* is a trapezoid and decide whether it is isosceles.

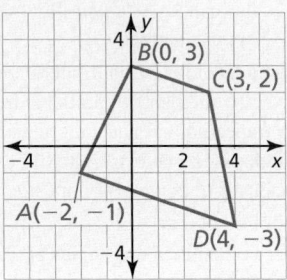

The slope of $\overline{BC}$ = slope of $\overline{AD} = -\frac{1}{3}$, so $\overline{BC} \parallel \overline{AD}$. The slope of $\overline{AB} = 2$ and the slope of $\overline{CD} = -5$, so $\overline{AB}$ is not parallel to $\overline{CD}$. With exactly one pair of parallel sides, *ABCD* is a trapezoid. The length of leg $\overline{AB}$ is $\sqrt{20}$, and the length of leg $\overline{CD}$ is $\sqrt{26}$. So, the legs are not congruent, and *ABCD* is not an isosceles trapezoid.

MONITORING PROGRESS ANSWER

1. slope of $\overline{AB}$ = slope of $\overline{DC}$ and slope of $\overline{AD} \neq$ slope of $\overline{BC}$. $AD = BC$, so *ABCD* is an isosceles trapezoid.

7.5 Lesson

Core Vocabulary

trapezoid, *p. 398*
bases, *p. 398*
base angles, *p. 398*
legs, *p. 398*
isosceles trapezoid, *p. 398*
midsegment of a trapezoid, *p. 400*
kite, *p. 401*

Previous
diagonal
parallelogram

What You Will Learn

▶ Use properties of trapezoids.
▶ Use the Trapezoid Midsegment Theorem to find distances.
▶ Use properties of kites.
▶ Identify quadrilaterals.

Using Properties of Trapezoids

A **trapezoid** is a quadrilateral with exactly one pair of parallel sides. The parallel sides are the **bases**.

Base angles of a trapezoid are two consecutive angles whose common side is a base. A trapezoid has two pairs of base angles. For example, in trapezoid *ABCD*, ∠*A* and ∠*D* are one pair of base angles, and ∠*B* and ∠*C* are the second pair. The nonparallel sides are the **legs** of the trapezoid.

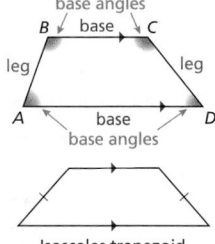

If the legs of a trapezoid are congruent, then the trapezoid is an **isosceles trapezoid**.

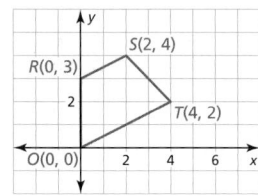

Isosceles trapezoid

EXAMPLE 1   **Identifying a Trapezoid in the Coordinate Plane**

Show that *ORST* is a trapezoid. Then decide whether it is isosceles.

SOLUTION

Step 1   Compare the slopes of opposite sides.

$$\text{slope of } \overline{RS} = \frac{4-3}{2-0} = \frac{1}{2}$$

$$\text{slope of } \overline{OT} = \frac{2-0}{4-0} = \frac{2}{4} = \frac{1}{2}$$

The slopes of $\overline{RS}$ and $\overline{OT}$ are the same, so $\overline{RS} \parallel \overline{OT}$.

$$\text{slope of } \overline{ST} = \frac{2-4}{4-2} = \frac{-2}{2} = -1 \qquad \text{slope of } \overline{RO} = \frac{3-0}{0-0} = \frac{3}{0} \quad \text{Undefined}$$

The slopes of $\overline{ST}$ and $\overline{RO}$ are not the same, so $\overline{ST}$ is not parallel to $\overline{OR}$.

▶ Because *ORST* has exactly one pair of parallel sides, it is a trapezoid.

Step 2   Compare the lengths of legs $\overline{RO}$ and $\overline{ST}$.

$$RO = |3-0| = 3 \qquad ST = \sqrt{(2-4)^2 + (4-2)^2} = \sqrt{8} = 2\sqrt{2}$$

Because $RO \neq ST$, legs $\overline{RO}$ and $\overline{ST}$ are *not* congruent.

▶ So, *ORST* is not an isosceles trapezoid.

Monitoring Progress Help in English and Spanish at *BigIdeasMath.com*

1. The points $A(-5, 6)$, $B(4, 9)$, $C(4, 4)$, and $D(-2, 2)$ form the vertices of a quadrilateral. Show that *ABCD* is a trapezoid. Then decide whether it is isosceles.

Laurie's Notes   Teacher Actions

- **Turn and Talk:** "What is a trapezoid and what properties does a trapezoid have?" From this assessing question, you'll find that students have prior knowledge about trapezoids. The theorems about trapezoids will make sense to students.

  COMMON ERROR In Example 1, students will find that the slopes of $\overline{RS}$ and $\overline{OT}$ are equal and conclude that *ORST* is a trapezoid. Remind students that they must also show that the other pair of opposite sides, $\overline{ST}$ and $\overline{OR}$, are not parallel.

⟲ Theorems

Theorem 7.14 Isosceles Trapezoid Base Angles Theorem

If a trapezoid is isosceles, then each pair of base angles is congruent.

If trapezoid $ABCD$ is isosceles, then $\angle A \cong \angle D$
and $\angle B \cong \angle C$.

Proof Ex. 39, p. 405

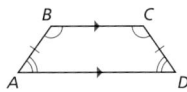

Theorem 7.15 Isosceles Trapezoid Base Angles Converse

If a trapezoid has a pair of congruent base angles, then it is an isosceles trapezoid.

If $\angle A \cong \angle D$ (or if $\angle B \cong \angle C$), then trapezoid
$ABCD$ is isosceles.

Proof Ex. 40, p. 405

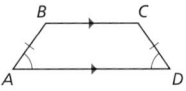

Theorem 7.16 Isosceles Trapezoid Diagonals Theorem

A trapezoid is isosceles if and only if its diagonals are congruent.

Trapezoid $ABCD$ is isosceles if and only
if $\overline{AC} \cong \overline{BD}$.

Proof Ex. 51, p. 406

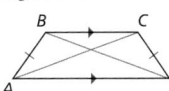

EXAMPLE 2   **Using Properties of Isosceles Trapezoids**

The stone above the arch in the diagram is an
isosceles trapezoid. Find $m\angle K$, $m\angle M$, and $m\angle J$.

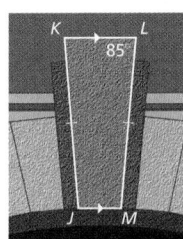

SOLUTION

Step 1 Find $m\angle K$. $JKLM$ is an isosceles trapezoid.
So, $\angle K$ and $\angle L$ are congruent base angles,
and $m\angle K = m\angle L = 85°$.

Step 2 Find $m\angle M$. Because $\angle L$ and $\angle M$ are
consecutive interior angles formed
by $\overleftrightarrow{LM}$ intersecting two parallel lines,
they are supplementary. So,
$m\angle M = 180° - 85° = 95°$.

Step 3 Find $m\angle J$. Because $\angle J$ and $\angle M$ are
a pair of base angles, they are congruent,
and $m\angle J = m\angle M = 95°$.

▶ So, $m\angle K = 85°$, $m\angle M = 95°$, and $m\angle J = 95°$.

Monitoring Progress Help in English and Spanish at *BigIdeasMath.com*

In Exercises 2 and 3, use trapezoid $EFGH$.

2. If $EG = FH$, is trapezoid $EFGH$ isosceles?
   Explain.

3. If $m\angle HEF = 70°$ and $m\angle FGH = 110°$,
   is trapezoid $EFGH$ isosceles? Explain.

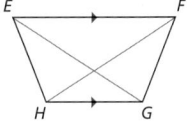

$ABCD$ is an isosceles trapezoid, and
$m\angle A = 42°$. Find $m\angle B$, $m\angle C$, and $m\angle D$.

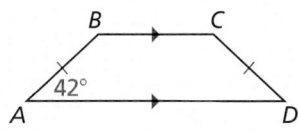

$m\angle B = 138°$, $m\angle C = 138°$,
$m\angle D = 42°$

MONITORING PROGRESS ANSWERS

2. yes, by the Isosceles Trapezoid
   Diagonals Theorem (Thm. 7.16)

3. yes; $m\angle GFE = 70°$,
   $\angle HEF \cong \angle GFE$

Laurie's Notes   Teacher Actions

- **MP2 Reason Abstractly and Quantitatively:** Discuss each theorem and have students label the diagrams.
- **Turn and Talk** and **Selective Responses:** Have partners select a theorem and discuss how to prove it. Students may use different strategies. Allow ample work time before asking selected students to share their proofs.
- **?** "What is known in this example?" You have an isosceles trapezoid and the measure of one base angle.
- **MP2:** For each angle, students should give reasoning for how they know the angle measure. Can they use the language of the theorems correctly?

Extra Example 3

In the diagram, $\overline{MN}$ is the midsegment of trapezoid PQRS. Find MN.

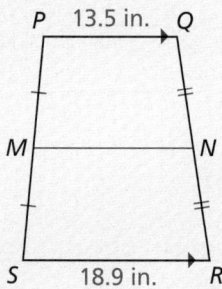

16.2 inches

Extra Example 4

Find the length of midsegment $\overline{YZ}$ in trapezoid PQRS.

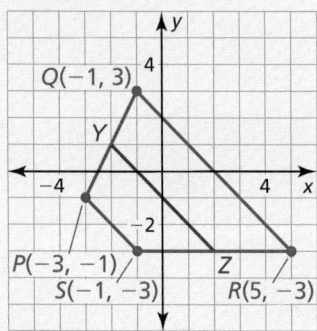

$4\sqrt{2}$ units

MONITORING PROGRESS ANSWERS

4.

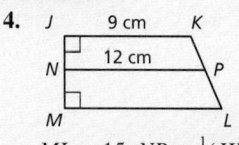

$ML = 15$; $NP = \frac{1}{2}(JK + ML)$

5. *Sample answer:* Find the coordinates of Y and Z and calculate the distance between the points.

Using the Trapezoid Midsegment Theorem

Recall that a midsegment of a triangle is a segment that connects the midpoints of two sides of the triangle. The **midsegment of a trapezoid** is the segment that connects the midpoints of its legs. The theorem below is similar to the Triangle Midsegment Theorem (Thm. 6.8).

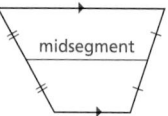

READING

The midsegment of a trapezoid is sometimes called the *median* of the trapezoid.

🔄 Theorem

Theorem 7.17   Trapezoid Midsegment Theorem

The midsegment of a trapezoid is parallel to each base, and its length is one-half the sum of the lengths of the bases.

If $\overline{MN}$ is the midsegment of trapezoid ABCD, then $\overline{MN} \parallel \overline{AB}$, $\overline{MN} \parallel \overline{DC}$, and $MN = \frac{1}{2}(AB + CD)$.

Proof Ex. 49, p. 406

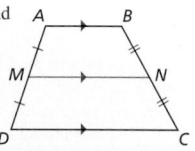

EXAMPLE 3   Using the Midsegment of a Trapezoid

In the diagram, $\overline{MN}$ is the midsegment of trapezoid PQRS. Find MN.

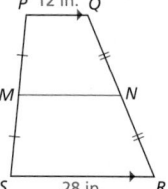

SOLUTION

$MN = \frac{1}{2}(PQ + SR)$ Trapezoid Midsegment Theorem

$\quad = \frac{1}{2}(12 + 28)$ Substitute 12 for PQ and 28 for SR.

$\quad = 20$ Simplify.

▶ The length of $\overline{MN}$ is 20 inches.

EXAMPLE 4   Using a Midsegment in the Coordinate Plane

Find the length of midsegment $\overline{YZ}$ in trapezoid STUV.

SOLUTION

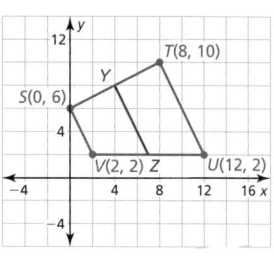

Step 1 Find the lengths of $\overline{SV}$ and $\overline{TU}$.

$SV = \sqrt{(0-2)^2 + (6-2)^2} = \sqrt{20} = 2\sqrt{5}$

$TU = \sqrt{(8-12)^2 + (10-2)^2} = \sqrt{80} = 4\sqrt{5}$

Step 2 Multiply the sum of SV and TU by $\frac{1}{2}$.

$YZ = \frac{1}{2}(2\sqrt{5} + 4\sqrt{5}) = \frac{1}{2}(6\sqrt{5}) = 3\sqrt{5}$

▶ So, the length of $\overline{YZ}$ is $3\sqrt{5}$ units.

Monitoring Progress 🔊 Help in English and Spanish at *BigIdeasMath.com*

4. In trapezoid JKLM, $\angle J$ and $\angle M$ are right angles, and $JK = 9$ centimeters. The length of midsegment $\overline{NP}$ of trapezoid JKLM is 12 centimeters. Sketch trapezoid JKLM and its midsegment. Find ML. Explain your reasoning.

5. Explain another method you can use to find the length of $\overline{YZ}$ in Example 4.

Laurie's Notes   Teacher Actions

- Use dynamic geometry software to investigate the midsegment of a trapezoid. If you click and drag on a vertex to decrease the length of a parallel base, the trapezoid begins to look like a triangle. Connect this to the Triangle Midsegment Theorem.

COMMON ERROR If students correctly find the length of each base in Example 4 and do not simplify the radicals, they may incorrectly say that the length of the midsegment is $\sqrt{50}$, reasoning that it is halfway between $\sqrt{20}$ and $\sqrt{80}$.

Using Properties of Kites

A **kite** is a quadrilateral that has two pairs of consecutive congruent sides, but opposite sides are not congruent.

⟲ Theorems

Theorem 7.18 Kite Diagonals Theorem

If a quadrilateral is a kite, then its diagonals are perpendicular.

If quadrilateral $ABCD$ is a kite, then $\overline{AC} \perp \overline{BD}$.

Proof p. 401

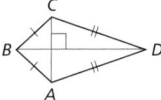

Theorem 7.19 Kite Opposite Angles Theorem

If a quadrilateral is a kite, then exactly one pair of opposite angles are congruent.

If quadrilateral $ABCD$ is a kite and $\overline{BC} \cong \overline{BA}$, then $\angle A \cong \angle C$ and $\angle B \not\cong \angle D$.

Proof Ex. 47, p. 406

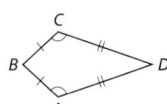

STUDY TIP

The congruent angles of a kite are formed by the noncongruent adjacent sides.

PROOF Kite Diagonals Theorem

Given $ABCD$ is a kite, $\overline{BC} \cong \overline{BA}$, and $\overline{DC} \cong \overline{DA}$.
Prove $\overline{AC} \perp \overline{BD}$

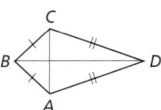

STATEMENTS	REASONS
1. $ABCD$ is a kite with $\overline{BC} \cong \overline{BA}$ and $\overline{DC} \cong \overline{DA}$.	1. Given
2. B and D lie on the $\perp$ bisector of $\overline{AC}$.	2. Converse of the $\perp$ Bisector Theorem (Theorem 6.2)
3. $\overline{BD}$ is the $\perp$ bisector of $\overline{AC}$.	3. Through any two points, there exists exactly one line.
4. $\overline{AC} \perp \overline{BD}$	4. Definition of $\perp$ bisector

EXAMPLE 5 Finding Angle Measures in a Kite

Find $m\angle D$ in the kite shown.

SOLUTION

By the Kite Opposite Angles Theorem, $DEFG$ has exactly one pair of congruent opposite angles. Because $\angle E \not\cong \angle G$, $\angle D$ and $\angle F$ must be congruent. So, $m\angle D = m\angle F$. Write and solve an equation to find $m\angle D$.

$$m\angle D + m\angle F + 115° + 73° = 360° \qquad \text{Corollary to the Polygon Interior Angles Theorem (Corollary 7.1)}$$

$$m\angle D + m\angle D + 115° + 73° = 360° \qquad \text{Substitute } m\angle D \text{ for } m\angle F.$$

$$2m\angle D + 188° = 360° \qquad \text{Combine like terms.}$$

$$m\angle D = 86° \qquad \text{Solve for } m\angle D.$$

Differentiated Instruction

Kinesthetic

Have students use a compass and straightedge (or dynamic software application) and draw two intersecting circles of unequal radii. Draw the radii (sides) and the diagonals as shown. Measure the angles at the intersection of the diagonals. Ask students to write a conjecture based on their result.

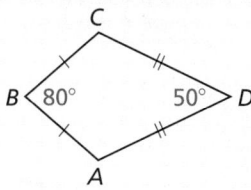

Extra Example 5

Find $m\angle C$ in the kite shown.

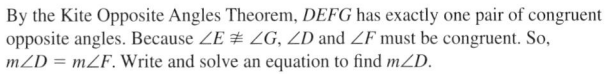

$m\angle C = 115°$

Laurie's Notes   Teacher Actions

- Kites may be convex or concave. The theorems hold true for each type. Only convex kites are considered in this lesson.
- **Turn and Talk:** "How could you prove that the diagonals of a kite are perpendicular?" Students often prove pairs of triangles congruent, and it is a much longer proof than the one shown. If time permits, have students share alternate methods.
- **Think-Pair-Share:** Have students work on Example 5, and then share and discuss as a class.

Extra Example 6

What is the most specific name for quadrilateral *JKLM*?

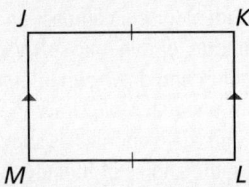

$\overline{JM} \parallel \overline{KL}$ and $JK = ML$. You do not know that the parallel sides are congruent or that the congruent sides are parallel. So, the most specific name for *JKLM* is a quadrilateral.

MONITORING PROGRESS ANSWERS

6. $x = 25; 75°$

7. parallelogram, rectangle, rhombus, square, and isosceles trapezoid

8. kite; Two pairs of consecutive sides are congruent and opposite sides are not congruent.

9. trapezoid; Two sides are parallel and the diagonals do not bisect each other.

10. quadrilateral; The markings are not sufficient to give it a more specific name.

Monitoring Progress Help in English and Spanish at *BigIdeasMath.com*

6. In a kite, the measures of the angles are $3x°$, $75°$, $90°$, and $120°$. Find the value of *x*. What are the measures of the angles that are congruent?

Identifying Special Quadrilaterals

The diagram shows relationships among the special quadrilaterals you have studied in this chapter. Each shape in the diagram has the properties of the shapes linked above it. For example, a rhombus has the properties of a parallelogram and a quadrilateral.

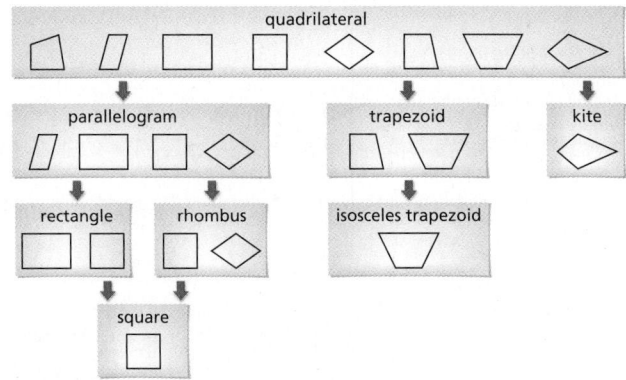

READING DIAGRAMS

In Example 6, *ABCD* looks like a square. But you must rely only on marked information when you interpret a diagram.

EXAMPLE 6 Identifying a Quadrilateral

What is the most specific name for quadrilateral *ABCD*?

SOLUTION

The diagram shows $\overline{AE} \cong \overline{CE}$ and $\overline{BE} \cong \overline{DE}$. So, the diagonals bisect each other. By the Parallelogram Diagonals Converse (Theorem 7.10), *ABCD* is a parallelogram.

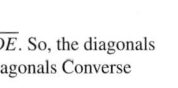

Rectangles, rhombuses, and squares are also parallelograms. However, there is no information given about the side lengths or angle measures of *ABCD*. So, you cannot determine whether it is a rectangle, a rhombus, or a square.

▶ So, the most specific name for *ABCD* is a parallelogram.

Monitoring Progress Help in English and Spanish at *BigIdeasMath.com*

7. Quadrilateral *DEFG* has at least one pair of opposite sides congruent. What types of quadrilaterals meet this condition?

Give the most specific name for the quadrilateral. Explain your reasoning.

8.

```
        S
   50      50
 R           T
   51      51
        U
```

9.

```
  V  ───▶  W
   64    62
   75    80
  Y  ───▶  X
```

10.

```
  D         E
              9
      G
  C         F
```

Laurie's Notes   Teacher Actions

- The flowchart shows how the special quadrilaterals are related. Any quadrilateral takes the properties and attributes of the quadrilateral above it and adds an additional property. It also shows that special quadrilaterals are parallelograms, trapezoids, or kites.
- Discuss the note in the side column. Students often assume from eyesight versus from reasoning.

Closure

- *3-2-1:* Hand out a *3-2-1* reflection sheet as described on page T-214.

Vocabulary and Core Concept Check

1. **WRITING** Describe the differences between a trapezoid and a kite.

2. **DIFFERENT WORDS, SAME QUESTION** Which is different? Find "both" answers.

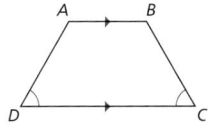

> Is there enough information to prove that trapezoid *ABCD* is isosceles?

> Is there enough information to prove that $\overline{AB} \cong \overline{DC}$?

> Is there enough information to prove that the non-parallel sides of trapezoid *ABCD* are congruent?

> Is there enough information to prove that the legs of trapezoid *ABCD* are congruent?

Monitoring Progress and Modeling with Mathematics

In Exercises 3–6, show that the quadrilateral with the given vertices is a trapezoid. Then decide whether it is isosceles. *(See Example 1.)*

3. $W(1, 4), X(1, 8), Y(-3, 9), Z(-3, 3)$

4. $D(-3, 3), E(-1, 1), F(1, -4), G(-3, 0)$

5. $M(-2, 0), N(0, 4), P(5, 4), Q(8, 0)$

6. $H(1, 9), J(4, 2), K(5, 2), L(8, 9)$

In Exercises 7 and 8, find the measure of each angle in the isosceles trapezoid. *(See Example 2.)*

7.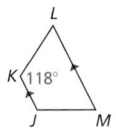

8.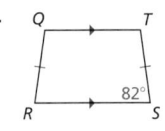

In Exercises 9 and 10, find the length of the midsegment of the trapezoid. *(See Example 3.)*

9.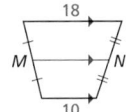

10.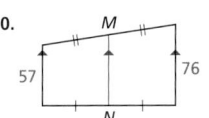

In Exercises 11 and 12, find *AB*.

11.   12.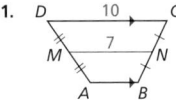

In Exercises 13 and 14, find the length of the midsegment of the trapezoid with the given vertices. *(See Example 4.)*

13. $A(2, 0), B(8, -4), C(12, 2), D(0, 10)$

14. $S(-2, 4), T(-2, -4), U(3, -2), V(13, 10)$

In Exercises 15–18, find $m\angle G$. *(See Example 5.)*

15.   16.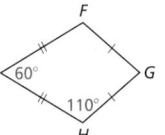

17.   18.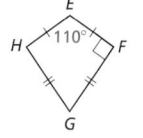

Section 7.5   Properties of Trapezoids and Kites   **403**

ANSWERS

1. A trapezoid has exactly one pair of parallel sides, and a kite has two pairs of consecutive congruent sides.

2. Is there enough information to prove that $\overline{AB} \cong \overline{DC}$?; no; yes

3. slope of $\overline{YZ}$ = slope of $\overline{XW}$ and slope of $\overline{XY} \neq$ slope of $\overline{WZ}$; $XY = WZ$, so $WXYZ$ is isosceles.

4. slope of $\overline{DE}$ = slope of $\overline{FG}$ and slope of $\overline{EF} \neq$ slope of $\overline{DG}$; $EF \neq DG$, so $DEFG$ is not isosceles.

5. slope of $\overline{MQ}$ = slope of $\overline{NP}$ and slope of $\overline{MN} \neq$ slope of $\overline{PQ}$; $MN \neq PQ$, so $MNPQ$ is not isosceles.

6. slope of $\overline{HL}$ = slope of $\overline{JK}$ and slope of $\overline{HJ} \neq$ slope of $\overline{LK}$; $HJ = LK$, so $HJKL$ is isosceles.

7. $m\angle L = m\angle M = 62°$, $m\angle K = m\angle J = 118°$

8. $m\angle Q = m\angle T = 98°$, $m\angle R = m\angle S = 82°$

9. 14

10. 66.5

11. 4

12. 25.9

13. $3\sqrt{13}$

14. $2\sqrt{29}$

15. 110°

16. 60°

17. 80°

18. 70°

ANSWERS

19. Because $MN = \frac{1}{2}(AB + DC)$, when you solve for DC, you should get $DC = 2(MN) - AB$; $DC = 2(8) - 14 = 2$.

20. In the kite shown, $\angle B \cong \angle D$. Find $m\angle A$ by subtracting the measures of the other three angles from $360°$, $m\angle A = 360° - 50° - 2(120°) = 70°$.

21. rectangle; $JKLM$ is a quadrilateral with 4 right angles.

22. trapezoid; $\overline{PS} \parallel \overline{QR}$ and $\angle QPS$ and $\angle PSR$ are not supplementary.

23. square; All four sides are congruent and the angles are 90°.

24. kite; $WXYZ$ has two pairs of consecutive congruent sides and opposite sides are not congruent.

25. no; It could be a kite.

26. no; It could be a rectangle.

27. 3

28. 6

29. 26 in.

30. 18 in., 29 in.; Consecutive sides are congruent.

31. $\angle A \cong \angle D$, or $\angle B \cong \angle C$; $\overline{AB} \parallel \overline{CD}$, so base angles need to be congruent.

32. *Sample answer:* $\overline{BC} \cong \overline{DC}$; Then $\triangle ABC \cong \triangle ADC$ and $ABCD$ has two pairs of consecutive congruent sides.

33. *Sample answer:* $\overline{BE} \cong \overline{DE}$; Then the diagonals bisect each other.

34. *Sample answer:* $\overline{AB} \cong \overline{BC}$; A rectangle with a pair of congruent adjacent sides is a square.

---

19. **ERROR ANALYSIS** Describe and correct the error in finding DC.

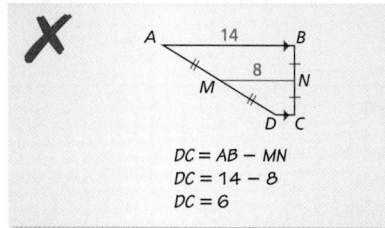

$$DC = AB - MN$$
$$DC = 14 - 8$$
$$DC = 6$$

20. **ERROR ANALYSIS** Describe and correct the error in finding $m\angle A$.

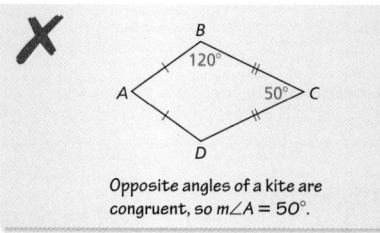

Opposite angles of a kite are congruent, so $m\angle A = 50°$.

In Exercises 21–24, give the most specific name for the quadrilateral. Explain your reasoning. *(See Example 6.)*

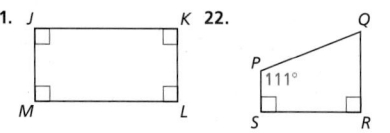

21.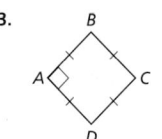

22.

23.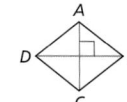

24.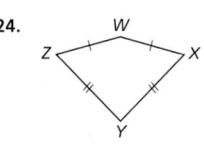

REASONING In Exercises 25 and 26, tell whether enough information is given in the diagram to classify the quadrilateral by the indicated name. Explain.

25. rhombus

26. square

MATHEMATICAL CONNECTIONS In Exercises 27 and 28, find the value of x.

27.

28.

29. **MODELING WITH MATHEMATICS** In the diagram, $NP = 8$ inches, and $LR = 20$ inches. What is the diameter of the bottom layer of the cake?

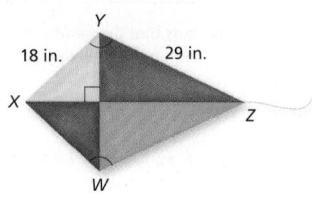

30. **PROBLEM SOLVING** You and a friend are building a kite. You need a stick to place from X to W and a stick to place from W to Z to finish constructing the frame. You want the kite to have the geometric shape of a kite. How long does each stick need to be? Explain your reasoning.

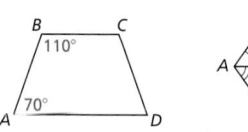

18 in.   29 in.

REASONING In Exercises 31–34, determine which pairs of segments or angles must be congruent so that you can prove that $ABCD$ is the indicated quadrilateral. Explain your reasoning. (There may be more than one right answer.)

31. isosceles trapezoid

32. kite

33. parallelogram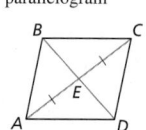

34. square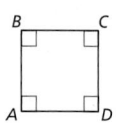

35. PROOF Write a proof.

Given $\overline{JL} \cong \overline{LN}$, $\overline{KM}$ is a midsegment of $\triangle JLN$.

Prove Quadrilateral $JKMN$ is an isosceles trapezoid.

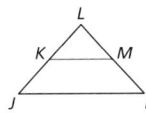

36. PROOF Write a proof.

Given $ABCD$ is a kite.
$\overline{AB} \cong \overline{CB}$, $\overline{AD} \cong \overline{CD}$

Prove $\overline{CE} \cong \overline{AE}$

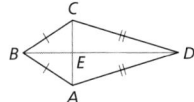

37. ABSTRACT REASONING Point U lies on the perpendicular bisector of $\overline{RT}$. Describe the set of points S for which $RSTU$ is a kite.

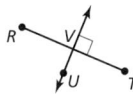

38. REASONING Determine whether the points $A(4, 5)$, $B(-3, 3)$, $C(-6, -13)$, and $D(6, -2)$ are the vertices of a kite. Explain your reasoning.

PROVING A THEOREM In Exercises 39 and 40, use the diagram to prove the given theorem. In the diagram, $\overline{EC}$ is drawn parallel to $\overline{AB}$.

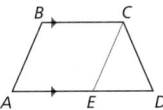

39. Isosceles Trapezoid Base Angles Theorem (Theorem 7.14)

Given $ABCD$ is an isosceles trapezoid.
$\overline{BC} \parallel \overline{AD}$

Prove $\angle A \cong \angle D$, $\angle B \cong \angle BCD$

40. Isosceles Trapezoid Base Angles Converse (Theorem 7.15)

Given $ABCD$ is a trapezoid.
$\angle A \cong \angle D$, $\overline{BC} \parallel \overline{AD}$

Prove $ABCD$ is an isosceles trapezoid.

41. MAKING AN ARGUMENT Your cousin claims there is enough information to prove that $JKLM$ is an isosceles trapezoid. Is your cousin correct? Explain.

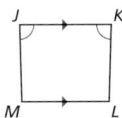

42. MATHEMATICAL CONNECTIONS The bases of a trapezoid lie on the lines $y = 2x + 7$ and $y = 2x - 5$. Write the equation of the line that contains the midsegment of the trapezoid.

43. CONSTRUCTION $\overline{AC}$ and $\overline{BD}$ bisect each other.

a. Construct quadrilateral $ABCD$ so that $\overline{AC}$ and $\overline{BD}$ are congruent, but not perpendicular. Classify the quadrilateral. Justify your answer.

b. Construct quadrilateral $ABCD$ so that $\overline{AC}$ and $\overline{BD}$ are perpendicular, but not congruent. Classify the quadrilateral. Justify your answer.

44. PROOF Write a proof.

Given $QRST$ is an isosceles trapezoid.

Prove $\angle TQS \cong \angle SRT$

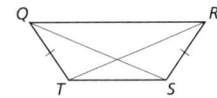

45. MODELING WITH MATHEMATICS A plastic spiderweb is made in the shape of a regular dodecagon (12-sided polygon). $\overline{AB} \parallel \overline{PQ}$, and X is equidistant from the vertices of the dodecagon.

a. Are you given enough information to prove that $ABPQ$ is an isosceles trapezoid?

b. What is the measure of each interior angle of $ABPQ$?

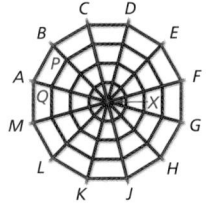

46. ATTENDING TO PRECISION In trapezoid $PQRS$, $\overline{PQ} \parallel \overline{RS}$ and $\overline{MN}$ is the midsegment of $PQRS$. If $RS = 5 \cdot PQ$, what is the ratio of MN to RS?

(A) $3:5$

(B) $5:3$

(C) $1:2$

(D) $3:1$

ANSWERS

35–36. See Additional Answers.

37. any point on $\overleftrightarrow{UV}$ such that $UV \neq SV$

38. yes; $AB = AD = \sqrt{53}$ and $BC = DC = \sqrt{265}$

39. Given isosceles trapezoid $ABCD$ with $\overline{BC} \parallel \overline{AD}$, construct $\overline{CE}$ parallel to $\overline{BA}$. Then, $ABCE$ is a parallelogram by definition, so $\overline{AB} \cong \overline{EC}$. Because $\overline{AB} \cong \overline{CD}$ by the definition of an isosceles trapezoid, $\overline{CE} \cong \overline{CD}$ by the Transitive Property of Congruence (Thm. 2.1). So, $\angle CED \cong \angle D$ by the Base Angles Theorem (Thm. 5.6) and $\angle A \cong \angle CED$ by the Corresponding Angles Theorem (Thm. 3.1). So, $\angle A \cong \angle D$ by the Transitive Property of Congruence (Thm. 2.2). Next, by the Consecutive Interior Angles Theorem (Thm. 3.4), $\angle B$ and $\angle A$ are supplementary and so are $\angle BCD$ and $\angle D$. So, $\angle B \cong \angle BCD$ by the Congruent Supplements Theorem (Thm. 2.4).

40. Given trapezoid $ABCD$ with $\angle A \cong \angle D$ and $\overline{BC} \parallel \overline{AD}$, construct $\overline{CE}$ parallel to $\overline{BA}$. Then, $ABCE$ is a parallelogram by definition, so $\overline{AB} \cong \overline{EC}$. $\angle A \cong \angle CED$ by the Corresponding Angles Theorem (Thm. 3.1), so $\angle CED \cong \angle D$ by the Transitive Property of Congruence (Thm. 2.2). Then by the Converse of the Base Angles Theorem (Thm. 5.7), $\overline{EC} \cong \overline{DC}$. So, $\overline{AB} \cong \overline{DC}$ by the Transitive Property of Congruence (Thm. 2.1), and trapezoid $ABCD$ is isosceles.

41. no; It could be a square.

42. $y = 2x + 1$

43. a.

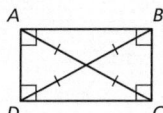

rectangle; The diagonals are congruent, but not perpendicular.

b.

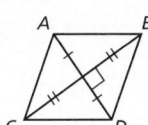

rhombus; The diagonals are perpendicular, but not congruent.

44. See Additional Answers.

45. a. yes

b. $75°$, $75°$, $105°$, $105°$

46. A

ANSWERS

47. See Additional Answers.
48. a. trapezoid
    b. isosceles trapezoid
49. By the Triangle Midsegment Theorem (Thm. 6.8), $\overline{BG} \parallel \overline{CD}$, $BG = \frac{1}{2}CD$, $\overline{GE} \parallel \overline{AF}$, and $GE = \frac{1}{2}AF$. By the Transitive Property of Parallel Lines (Thm. 3.9), $\overline{CD} \parallel \overline{BE} \parallel \overline{AF}$. Also, by the Segment Addition Postulate (Post. 1.2), $BE = BG + GE$. So, by the Substitution Property of Equality, $BE = \frac{1}{2}CD + \frac{1}{2}AF = \frac{1}{2}(CD + AF)$.

50–54. See Additional Answers.

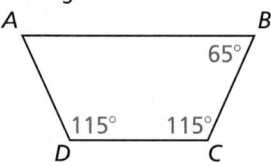
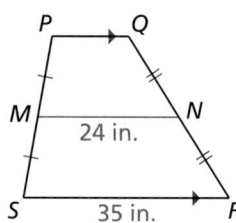
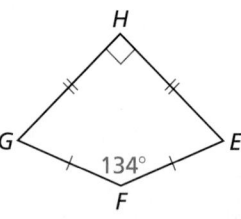
---

47. **PROVING A THEOREM** Use the plan for proof below to write a paragraph proof of the Kite Opposite Angles Theorem (Theorem 7.19).

    Given *EFGH* is a kite.
    $\overline{EF} \cong \overline{FG}, \overline{EH} \cong \overline{GH}$

    Prove ∠*E* ≅ ∠*G*, ∠*F* ≇ ∠*H*

    Plan for Proof First show that ∠*E* ≅ ∠*G*. Then use an indirect argument to show that ∠*F* ≇ ∠*H*.

48. **HOW DO YOU SEE IT?** One of the earliest shapes used for cut diamonds is called the *table cut*, as shown in the figure. Each face of a cut gem is called a *facet*.

    a. $\overline{BC} \parallel \overline{AD}$, and $\overline{AB}$ and $\overline{DC}$ are not parallel. What shape is the facet labeled *ABCD*?

    b. $\overline{DE} \parallel \overline{GF}$, and $\overline{DG}$ and $\overline{EF}$ are congruent but not parallel. What shape is the facet labeled *DEFG*?

    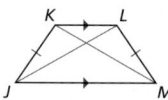

49. **PROVING A THEOREM** In the diagram below, $\overline{BG}$ is the midsegment of △*ACD*, and $\overline{GE}$ is the midsegment of △*ADF*. Use the diagram to prove the Trapezoid Midsegment Theorem (Theorem 7.17).

    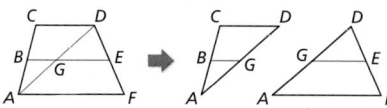

50. **THOUGHT PROVOKING** Is SSASS a valid congruence theorem for kites? Justify your answer.

51. **PROVING A THEOREM** To prove the biconditional statement in the Isosceles Trapezoid Diagonals Theorem (Theorem 7.16), you must prove both parts separately.

    a. Prove part of the Isosceles Trapezoid Diagonals Theorem (Theorem 7.16).

       Given *JKLM* is an isosceles trapezoid.
       $\overline{KL} \parallel \overline{JM}, \overline{JK} \cong \overline{LM}$

       Prove $\overline{JL} \cong \overline{KM}$

       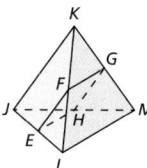

    b. Write the other part of the Isosceles Trapezoid Diagonals Theorem (Theorem 7.16) as a conditional. Then prove the statement is true.

52. **PROOF** What special type of quadrilateral is *EFGH*? Write a proof to show that your answer is correct.

    Given In the three-dimensional figure, $\overline{JK} \cong \overline{LM}$. *E*, *F*, *G*, and *H* are the midpoints of $\overline{JL}$, $\overline{KL}$, $\overline{KM}$, and $\overline{JM}$, respectively.

    Prove *EFGH* is a _____.

    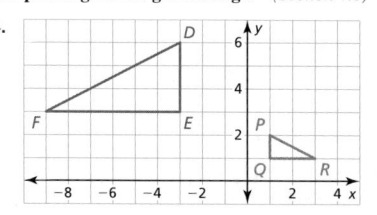

Maintaining Mathematical Proficiency   <small>Reviewing what you learned in previous grades and lessons</small>

Describe a similarity transformation that maps the blue preimage to the green image.   *(Section 4.6)*

53.

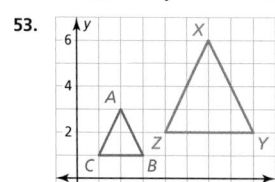

54.

Core Vocabulary

rhombus, *p. 388*
rectangle, *p. 388*
square, *p. 388*
trapezoid, *p. 398*
bases (of a trapezoid), *p. 398*

base angles (of a trapezoid), *p. 398*
legs (of a trapezoid), *p. 398*
isosceles trapezoid, *p. 398*
midsegment of a trapezoid, *p. 400*
kite, *p. 401*

ANSWERS

1. They are congruent base angles of congruent isosceles triangles, $\triangle DEF$ and $\triangle DGF$.

2. If one type of quadrilateral is under another in the diagram, then a quadrilateral from the lower category will always fit into the category above it.

3. Find the difference between the length of the midsegment and the length of the given base, and then either add or subtract that amount to the midsegment to find the other base.

Core Concepts

Section 7.4

Corollary 7.2 Rhombus Corollary, *p. 388*
Corollary 7.3 Rectangle Corollary, *p. 388*
Corollary 7.4 Square Corollary, *p. 388*
Relationships between Special Parallelograms, *p. 389*
Theorem 7.11 Rhombus Diagonals Theorem, *p. 390*

Theorem 7.12 Rhombus Opposite Angles Theorem, *p. 390*
Theorem 7.13 Rectangle Diagonals Theorem, *p. 391*
Identifying Special Parallelograms in the Coordinate Plane, *p. 392*

Section 7.5

Showing That a Quadrilateral Is a Trapezoid in the Coordinate Plane, *p. 398*
Theorem 7.14 Isosceles Trapezoid Base Angles Theorem, *p. 399*
Theorem 7.15 Isosceles Trapezoid Base Angles Converse, *p. 399*

Theorem 7.16 Isosceles Trapezoid Diagonals Theorem, *p. 399*
Theorem 7.17 Trapezoid Midsegment Theorem, *p. 400*
Theorem 7.18 Kite Diagonals Theorem, *p. 401*
Theorem 7.19 Kite Opposite Angles Theorem, *p. 401*
Identifying Special Quadrilaterals, *p. 402*

Mathematical Practices

1. In Exercise 14 on page 393, one reason $m\angle 4$, $m\angle 5$, and $m\angle DFE$ are all 48° is because diagonals of a rhombus bisect each other. What is another reason they are equal?

2. Explain how the diagram you created in Exercise 64 on page 395 can help you answer questions like Exercises 65–70.

3. In Exercise 29 on page 404, describe a pattern you can use to find the measure of a base of a trapezoid when given the length of the midsegment and the other base.

Performance Task

Scissor Lifts

A scissor lift is a work platform with an adjustable height that is stable and convenient. The platform is supported by crisscrossing beams that raise and lower the platform. What quadrilaterals do you see in the scissor lift design? What properties of those quadrilaterals play a key role in the successful operation of the lift?

To explore the answers to this question and more, go to *BigIdeasMath.com*.

ANSWERS

1. 5040°; 168°; 12°
2. 133
3. 82
4. 15
5. $a = 79, b = 101$
6. $a = 28, b = 87$
7. $c = 6, d = 10$
8. $(-2, -1)$
9. $M(2, -2)$

7.1   Angles of Polygons   *(pp. 359–366)*

Find the sum of the measures of the interior angles of the figure.

The figure is a convex hexagon. It has 6 sides. Use the Polygon Interior Angles Theorem (Theorem 7.1).

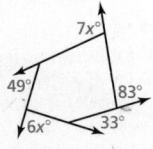

$$(n - 2) \cdot 180° = (6 - 2) \cdot 180° \qquad \text{Substitute 6 for } n.$$
$$= 4 \cdot 180° \qquad \text{Subtract.}$$
$$= 720° \qquad \text{Multiply.}$$

▶ The sum of the measures of the interior angles of the figure is 720°.

1. Find the sum of the measures of the interior angles of a regular 30-gon. Then find the measure of each interior angle and each exterior angle.

Find the value of x.

2.   3.   4.

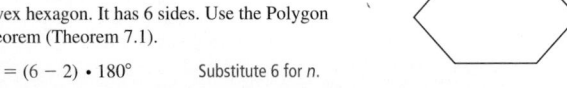

7.2   Properties of Parallelograms   *(pp. 367–374)*

Find the values of x and y.

ABCD is a parallelogram by the definition of a parallelogram. Use the Parallelogram Opposite Sides Theorem (Thm. 7.3) to find the value of *x*.

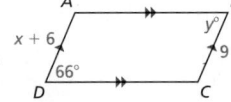

$$AD = BC \qquad \text{Opposite sides of a parallelogram are congruent.}$$
$$x + 6 = 9 \qquad \text{Substitute } x + 6 \text{ for } AD \text{ and 9 for } BC.$$
$$x = 3 \qquad \text{Subtract 6 from each side.}$$

By the Parallelogram Opposite Angles Theorem (Thm. 7.4), $\angle D \cong \angle B$, or $m\angle D = m\angle B$. So, $y° = 66°$.

▶ In $\square ABCD$, $x = 3$ and $y = 66$.

Find the value of each variable in the parallelogram.

5.   6.   7.

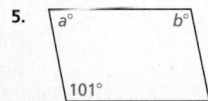 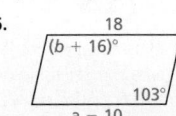 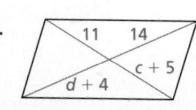

8. Find the coordinates of the intersection of the diagonals of $\square QRST$ with vertices $Q(-8, 1)$, $R(2, 1)$, $S(4, -3)$, and $T(-6, -3)$.

9. Three vertices of $\square JKLM$ are $J(1, 4)$, $K(5, 3)$, and $L(6, -3)$. Find the coordinates of vertex M.

7.3 Proving That a Quadrilateral Is a Parallelogram (pp. 375–384)

For what value of x is quadrilateral $DEFG$ a parallelogram?

By the Opposite Sides Parallel and Congruent Theorem (Thm. 7.9), if one pair of opposite sides are congruent and parallel, then $DEFG$ is a parallelogram. You are given that $\overline{DE} \parallel \overline{FG}$. Find x so that $\overline{DE} \cong \overline{FG}$.

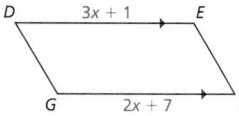

$DE = FG$	Set the segment lengths equal.
$3x + 1 = 2x + 7$	Substitute $3x + 1$ for DE and $2x + 7$ for FG.
$x + 1 = 7$	Subtract $2x$ from each side.
$x = 6$	Subtract 1 from each side.

When $x = 6$, $DE = 3(6) + 1 = 19$ and $FG = 2(6) + 7 = 19$.

▶ Quadrilateral $DEFG$ is a parallelogram when $x = 6$.

State which theorem you can use to show that the quadrilateral is a parallelogram.

10.

11.

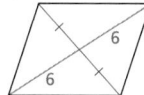

12.

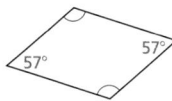

13. Find the values of x and y that make the quadrilateral a parallelogram.

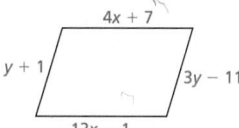

14. Find the value of x that makes the quadrilateral a parallelogram.

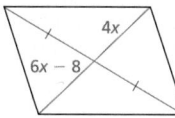

15. Show that quadrilateral $WXYZ$ with vertices $W(-1, 6)$, $X(2, 8)$, $Y(1, 0)$, and $Z(-2, -2)$ is a parallelogram.

7.4 Properties of Special Parallelograms (pp. 387–396)

Classify the special quadrilateral. Explain your reasoning.

The quadrilateral has four right angles. By the Rectangle Corollary (Corollary 7.3), the quadrilateral is a rectangle. Because the four sides are not marked as congruent, you cannot conclude that the rectangle is a square.

Classify the special quadrilateral. Explain your reasoning.

16.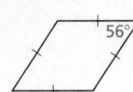

17.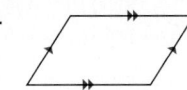

18.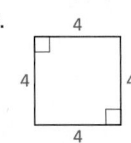

19. Find the lengths of the diagonals of rectangle *WXYZ* where $WY = -2x + 34$ and $XZ = 3x - 26$.

20. Decide whether ▱*JKLM* with vertices $J(5, 8)$, $K(9, 6)$, $L(7, 2)$, and $M(3, 4)$ is a rectangle, a rhombus, or a square. Give all names that apply. Explain.

7.5   Properties of Trapezoids and Kites *(pp. 397–406)*

Find the length of midsegment $\overline{EF}$ in trapezoid *ABCD*.

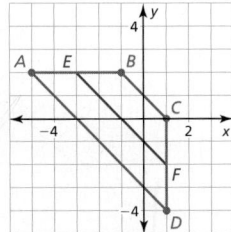

Step 1   Find the lengths of $\overline{AD}$ and $\overline{BC}$.

$$AD = \sqrt{[1 - (-5)]^2 + (-4 - 2)^2}$$
$$= \sqrt{72} = 6\sqrt{2}$$
$$BC = \sqrt{[1 - (-1)]^2 + (0 - 2)^2}$$
$$= \sqrt{8} = 2\sqrt{2}$$

Step 2   Multiply the sum of *AD* and *BC* by $\frac{1}{2}$.

$$EF = \tfrac{1}{2}(6\sqrt{2} + 2\sqrt{2}) = \tfrac{1}{2}(8\sqrt{2}) = 4\sqrt{2}$$

▶ So, the length of $\overline{EF}$ is $4\sqrt{2}$ units.

21. Find the measure of each angle in the isosceles trapezoid *WXYZ*.

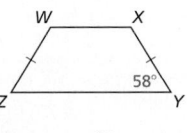

22. Find the length of the midsegment of trapezoid *ABCD*.

23. Find the length of the midsegment of trapezoid *JKLM* with vertices $J(6, 10)$, $K(10, 6)$, $L(8, 2)$, and $M(2, 2)$.

24. A kite has angle measures of $7x°$, 65°, 85°, and 105°. Find the value of *x*. What are the measures of the angles that are congruent?

25. Quadrilateral *WXYZ* is a trapezoid with one pair of congruent base angles. Is *WXYZ* an isosceles trapezoid? Explain your reasoning.

Give the most specific name for the quadrilateral. Explain your reasoning.

26.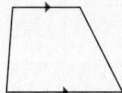

27.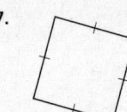

28.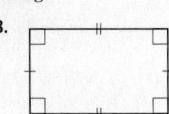

Find the value of each variable in the parallelogram.

1.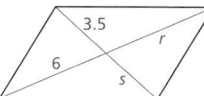

2.

3.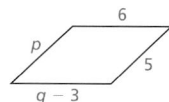

Give the most specific name for the quadrilateral. Explain your reasoning.

4.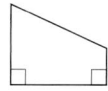

5.

6.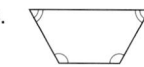

7. In a convex octagon, three of the exterior angles each have a measure of $x°$. The other five exterior angles each have a measure of $(2x + 7)°$. Find the measure of each exterior angle.

8. Quadrilateral $PQRS$ has vertices $P(5, 1)$, $Q(9, 6)$, $R(5, 11)$, and $S(1, 6)$. Classify quadrilateral $PQRS$ using the most specific name.

Determine whether enough information is given to show that the quadrilateral is a parallelogram. Explain your reasoning.

9.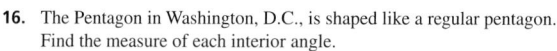

10.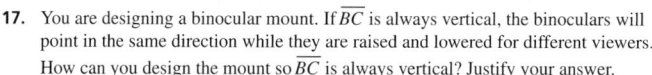

11.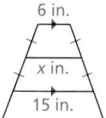

12. Explain why a parallelogram with one right angle must be a rectangle.

13. Summarize the ways you can prove that a quadrilateral is a square.

14. Three vertices of ▱$JKLM$ are $J(-2, -1)$, $K(0, 2)$, and $L(4, 3)$.

   a. Find the coordinates of vertex M.

   b. Find the coordinates of the intersection of the diagonals of ▱$JKLM$.

15. You are building a plant stand with three equally-spaced circular shelves. The diagram shows a vertical cross section of the plant stand. What is the diameter of the middle shelf?

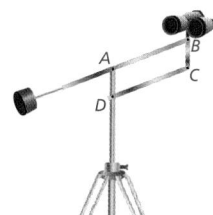

16. The Pentagon in Washington, D.C., is shaped like a regular pentagon. Find the measure of each interior angle.

17. You are designing a binocular mount. If $\overline{BC}$ is always vertical, the binoculars will point in the same direction while they are raised and lowered for different viewers. How can you design the mount so $\overline{BC}$ is always vertical? Justify your answer.

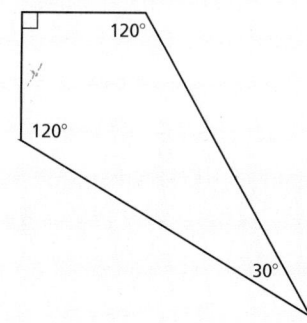

18. The measure of one angle of a kite is 90°. The measure of another angle in the kite is 30°. Sketch a kite that matches this description.

ANSWERS

1. $r = 6$, $s = 3.5$
2. $a = 79$, $b = 101$
3. $p = 5$, $q = 9$
4. trapezoid; There is one pair of parallel sides.
5. kite; There are two pairs of consecutive congruent sides but opposite sides are not congruent.
6. isosceles trapezoid; Base angles are congruent
7. 25°, 25°, 25°, 57°, 57°, 57°, 57°, 57°
8. rhombus
9. yes; The diagonals bisect each other.
10. no; $\overline{JK}$ and $\overline{ML}$ might not be parallel.
11. yes; Opposite angles are congruent.
12. Consecutive angles are supplementary.
13. Show that a quadrilateral is a parallelogram with four congruent sides and four right angles, or show that a quadrilateral is both a rectangle and a rhombus.
14. **a.** $M(2, 0)$
   b. $(1, 1)$
15. 10.5 in.
16. 108°
17. Design $AB = DC$ and $AD = BC$, then $ABCD$ is a parallelogram.
18. *Sample answer:*

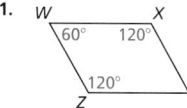

If students need help...	If students got it...
Lesson Tutorials	Resources by Chapter • Enrichment and Extension • Cumulative Review
Skills Review Handbook	Performance Task
BigIdeasMath.com	Start the *next* Section

ANSWERS

1. Definition of parallelogram; Alternate Interior Angles Theorem (Thm. 3.2); Reflexive Property of Congruence (Thm. 2.1); Definition of congruent angles; Angle Addition Postulate (Post. 1.4); Transitive Property of Equality; Definition of congruent angles; ASA Congruence Theorem (Thm. 5.10); Corresponding parts of congruent triangles are congruent

2. Point D is the incenter of the triangle and ED is the radius.

3. no; You cannot use a theorem to prove itself.

4. $6\sqrt{10}$; yes; no; no; The polygon is equilateral because each side has a length of $\sqrt{10}$ units. The polygon is not equiangular because the measure of each angle in an equiangular hexagon is 120° and $m\angle Q = 90°$. Because the polygon is not equiangular, it is not regular.

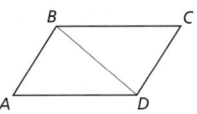

7 Cumulative Assessment

1. Copy and complete the flowchart proof of the Parallelogram Opposite Angles Theorem (Thm. 7.4).

   Given *ABCD* is a parallelogram.

   Prove $\angle A \cong \angle C$, $\angle B \cong \angle D$

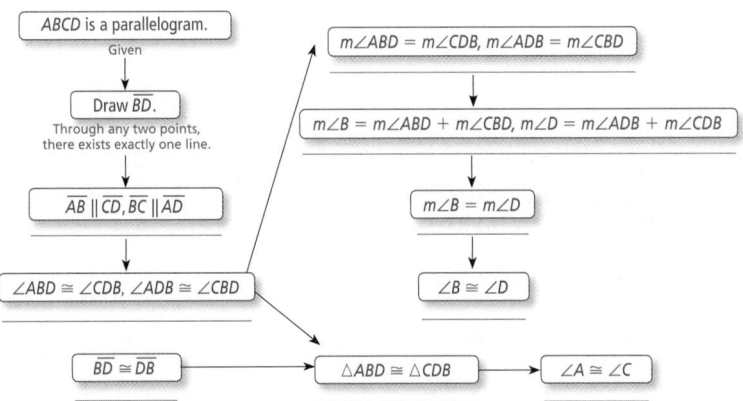

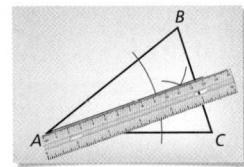
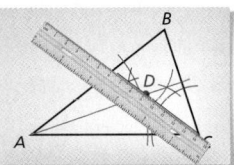
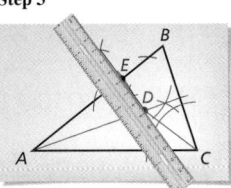
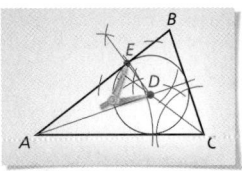

2. Use the steps in the construction to explain how you know that the circle is inscribed within $\triangle ABC$.

   Step 1

   Step 2

   Step 3

   Step 4

3. Your friend claims that he can prove the Parallelogram Opposite Sides Theorem (Thm. 7.3) using the SSS Congruence Theorem (Thm. 5.8) and the Parallelogram Opposite Sides Theorem (Thm. 7.3). Is your friend correct? Explain your reasoning.

4. Find the perimeter of polygon *QRSTUV*. Is the polygon equilateral? equiangular? regular? Explain your reasoning.

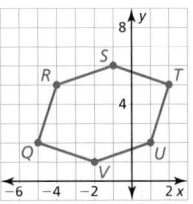

412   Chapter 7   Quadrilaterals and Other Polygons

412   Chapter 7

5. Choose the correct symbols to complete the proof of the Converse of the Hinge Theorem (Theorem 6.13).

Given $\overline{AB} \cong \overline{DE}, \overline{BC} \cong \overline{EF}, AC > DF$

Prove $m\angle B > m\angle E$

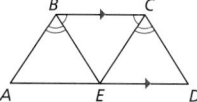

Indirect Proof

Step 1 Assume temporarily that $m\angle B \not> m\angle E$. Then it follows that either $m\angle B$ ___ $m\angle E$ or $m\angle B$ ___ $m\angle E$.

Step 2 If $m\angle B$ ___ $m\angle E$, then AC ___ DF by the Hinge Theorem (Theorem 6.12).
If $m\angle B$ ___ $m\angle E$, then $\angle B$ ___ $\angle E$. So, $\triangle ABC$ ___ $\triangle DEF$ by the SAS Congruence Theorem (Theorem 5.5) and AC ___ DF.

Step 3 Both conclusions contradict the given statement that AC ___ DF. So, the temporary assumption that $m\angle B \not> m\angle E$ cannot be true. This proves that $m\angle B$ ___ $m\angle E$.

>	<	=	≠	≅

6. Use the Isosceles Trapezoid Base Angles Converse (Thm. 7.15) to prove that $ABCD$ is an isosceles trapezoid.

Given $\overline{BC} \parallel \overline{AD}, \angle EBC \cong \angle ECB, \angle ABE \cong \angle DCE$

Prove $ABCD$ is an isosceles trapezoid.

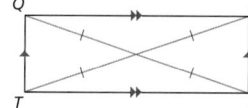

7. One part of the Rectangle Diagonals Theorem (Thm. 7.13) says, "If the diagonals of a parallelogram are congruent, then it is a rectangle." Using the reasons given, there are multiple ways to prove this part of the theorem. Provide a statement for each reason to form one possible proof of this part of the theorem.

Given $QRST$ is a parallelogram.
$\overline{QS} \cong \overline{RT}$

Prove $QRST$ is a rectangle.

STATEMENTS	REASONS
1. $\overline{QS} \cong \overline{RT}$	**1.** Given
2. _____	**2.** Parallelogram Opposite Sides Theorem (Thm. 7.3)
3. _____	**3.** SSS Congruence Theorem (Thm. 5.8)
4. _____	**4.** Corresponding parts of congruent triangles are congruent.
5. _____	**5.** Parallelogram Consecutive Angles Theorem (Thm. 7.5)
6. _____	**6.** Congruent supplementary angles have the same measure.
7. _____	**7.** Parallelogram Consecutive Angles Theorem (Thm. 7.5)
8. _____	**8.** Subtraction Property of Equality
9. _____	**9.** Definition of a right angle
10. _____	**10.** Definition of a rectangle

5. $<; =; <; <; =; \cong; \cong; =; >; >$

6. See Additional Answers.

7. *Sample answer:*

2. $\overline{QT} \cong \overline{RS}, \overline{QR} \cong \overline{TS}$

3. $\triangle QRS \cong \triangle RQT$

4. $\angle QRS \cong \angle RQT$

5. $m\angle QRS + m\angle RQT = 180°$

6. $m\angle QRS = m\angle RQT = 90°$

7. $m\angle TSR + 90° = 180°, m\angle STQ + 90° = 180°$

8. $m\angle TSR = 90°, m\angle STQ = 90°$

9. $\angle RQT, \angle QRS, \angle TSR$, and $\angle STQ$ are right angles.

10. $QRST$ is a rectangle.

8 Similarity

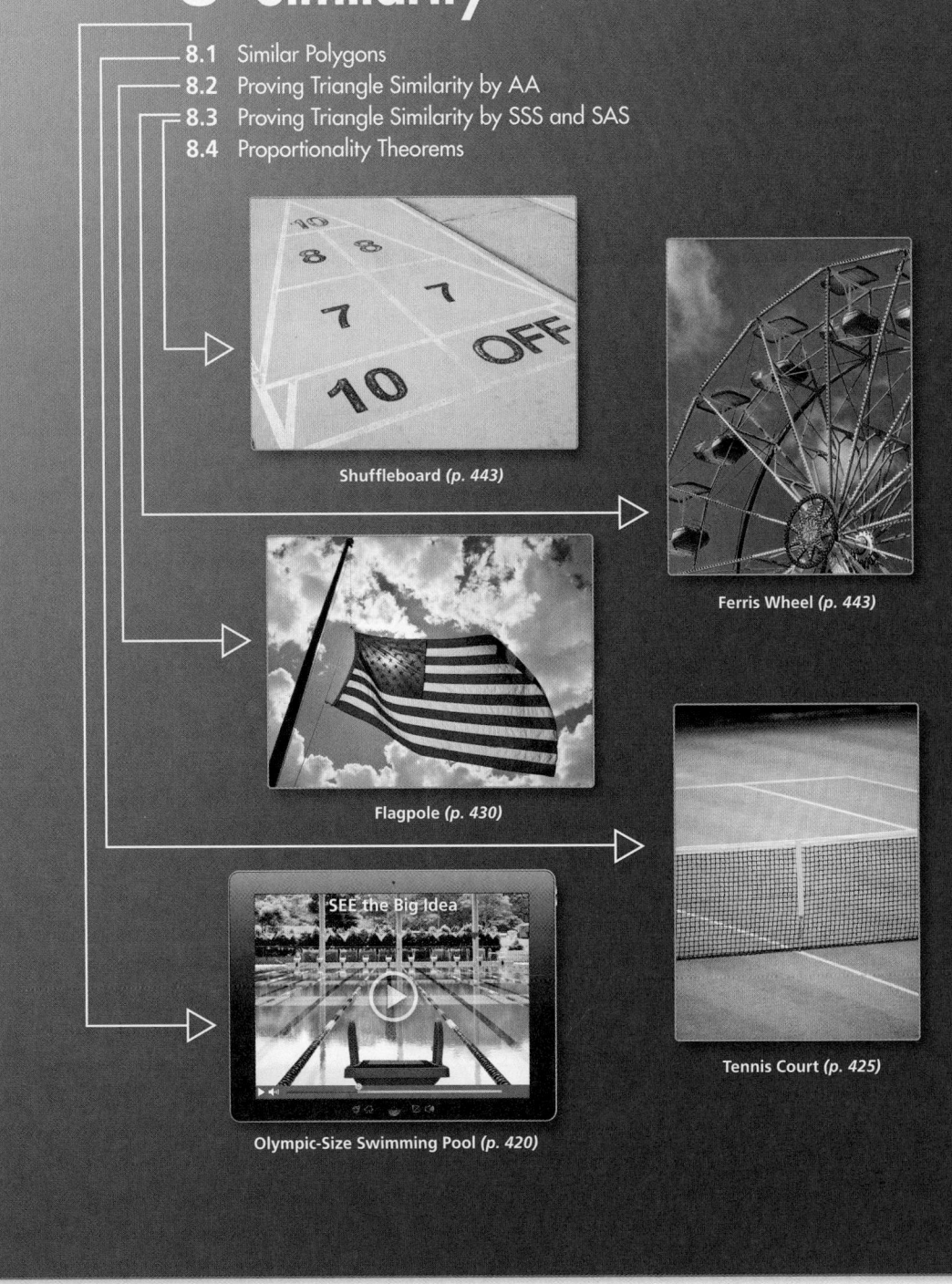

Shuffleboard (p. 443)

Ferris Wheel (p. 443)

Flagpole (p. 430)

SEE the Big Idea

Tennis Court (p. 425)

Olympic-Size Swimming Pool (p. 420)

Chapter Summary

- This is a short chapter that revisits similarity, a concept first introduced in Chapter 4.
- The first lesson introduces what it means for two polygons to be similar: corresponding sides are proportional and corresponding angles are congruent.
- The next two lessons present methods for proving two triangles are similar. One of the methods involves only angles (AA), with the other two methods involving only sides (SSS) or sides and the included angle (SAS). Unlike congruency methods, the corresponding sides must be proportional versus congruent.
- The last lesson presents several proportionality theorems, mostly connected to triangles.
- Properties of similar triangles will be needed in the next chapter when trigonometric ratios are defined.

 COMMON CORE PROGRESSION

Middle School
- Understand ratios and describe ratio relationships.
- Decide whether two quantities are proportional (ratio tables, graphs).
- Represent proportional relationships with equations.
- Understand that two figures are similar if they can be related by a sequence of transformations that includes dilations.
- Understand the angle-angle criterion for similarity of triangles.

Algebra 1
- Write and solve linear equations in one variable.
- Use linear equations to solve real-life problems.
- Find the slope of a line.
- Identify and use parallel and perpendicular lines in real-life problems.

Geometry
- Use the AA, SSS, and SAS Similarity Theorems to prove triangles are similar.
- Decide whether polygons are similar.
- Use similarity criteria to solve problems about lengths, perimeters, and areas.
- Prove the slope criteria using similar triangles.
- Use the Triangle Proportionality Theorem and other proportionality theorems.

Scaffolding in the Classroom

Graphic Organizers: Example and Non-Example Chart

An Example and Non-Example Chart can be used to list examples and non-examples of a vocabulary word or term. Students write examples of the word or term in the left column and non-examples in the right column. This type of organizer serves as a good tool for assessing students' knowledge of pairs of topics that have subtle but important differences, such as complementary and supplementary angles. Blank Example and Non-Example Charts can be included on tests or quizzes for this purpose.

Standards Summary

Section		Common Core State Standards
8.1	Learning	HSG-SRT.A.2, HSG-MG.A.3
8.2	Learning	HSG-SRT.A.3, HSG-SRT.B.5
8.3	Learning	HSG-SRT.B.4, HSG-SRT.B.5, HSG-GPE.B.5, HSG-MG.A.1
8.4	Learning	HSG-SRT.B.4, HSG-SRT.B.5, HSG-GPE.B.6

How would you begin?

Before beginning the homework, select one challenging problem from the exercise set. Have students work in pairs or small groups to discuss how they would begin the problem. Students share their ideas before actually solving the problems, discussing the pros and cons of different methods.

Laurie's Notes

Maintaining Mathematical Proficiency

Determining Whether Ratios Form a Proportion

- Another way to check whether ratios form a proportion is to check their cross products: $\frac{a}{b} = \frac{c}{d}$ ($b \neq 0, d \neq 0$) if and only if $ad = bc$. Demonstrate this with Example 1.

COMMON ERROR Students often confuse *ratio* with *rate*. Remind them that a ratio is the relationship between two numbers, often written without units, such as 3 to 5. A rate is a ratio that compares two quantities with different units, such as 35 miles per hour.

Finding a Scale Factor

- Students may benefit from a review of dilations in Section 4.5.
- Remind students that the scale factor in a transformation is the ratio of the length of a side in the image to the corresponding side length of the preimage.

COMMON ERROR Students may put the side length of the preimage first in the ratio for scale factor. Make sure they understand that the scale factor shows how long the *image* is compared to the *preimage*.

Mathematical Practices (continued on page 416)

- The eight *Mathematical Practices* focus attention on how mathematics is learned—process versus content. Page 416 demonstrates how a mathematically proficient student uses structure to recognize a pattern in data. When perimeters and areas of similar polygons are explored, a pattern can be discerned.
- Use the *Mathematical Practices* page to help students develop mathematical habits of mind—how mathematics can be explored and how mathematics is thought about.

If students need help...	If students got it...
Student Journal • Maintaining Mathematical Proficiency	Game Closet at *BigIdeasMath.com*
Lesson Tutorials	Start the *next* Section
Skills Review Handbook	

Maintaining Mathematical Proficiency

Determining Whether Ratios Form a Proportion

Example 1 Tell whether $\frac{2}{8}$ and $\frac{3}{12}$ form a proportion.

Compare the ratios in simplest form.

$$\frac{2}{8} = \frac{2 \div 2}{8 \div 2} = \frac{1}{4}$$

$$\frac{3}{12} = \frac{3 \div 3}{12 \div 3} = \frac{1}{4}$$

The ratios are equivalent.

▶ So, $\frac{2}{8}$ and $\frac{3}{12}$ form a proportion.

Tell whether the ratios form a proportion.

1. $\frac{5}{3}, \frac{35}{21}$ **2.** $\frac{9}{24}, \frac{24}{64}$ **3.** $\frac{8}{56}, \frac{6}{28}$

4. $\frac{18}{4}, \frac{27}{9}$ **5.** $\frac{15}{21}, \frac{55}{77}$ **6.** $\frac{26}{8}, \frac{39}{12}$

Finding a Scale Factor

Example 2 Find the scale factor of each dilation.

a.
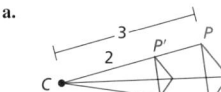

▶ Because $\frac{CP'}{CP} = \frac{2}{3}$, the scale factor is $k = \frac{2}{3}$.

b.
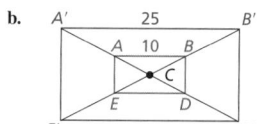

▶ Because $\frac{A'B'}{AB} = \frac{25}{10}$, the scale factor is $k = \frac{25}{10} = \frac{5}{2}$.

Find the scale factor of the dilation.

7.
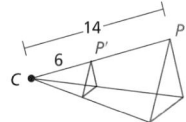

8.
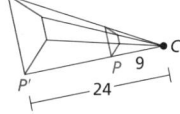

9.
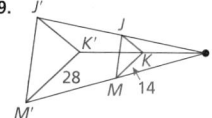

10. ABSTRACT REASONING If ratio X and ratio Y form a proportion and ratio Y and ratio Z form a proportion, do ratio X and ratio Z form a proportion? Explain your reasoning.

Dynamic Solutions available at *BigIdeasMath.com*

Common Core State Standards

7.RP.A.2a Decide whether two quantities are in a proportional relationship, e.g., by testing for equivalent ratios. …

HSG-SRT.A.1b The dilation of a line segment is longer or shorter in the ratio given by the scale factor.

ANSWERS

1. yes
2. yes
3. no
4. no
5. yes
6. yes
7. $k = \frac{3}{7}$
8. $k = \frac{8}{3}$
9. $k = 2$
10. yes; All of the ratios are equivalent by the Transitive Property of Equality.

Vocabulary Review

Have students make an Idea and Examples Chart for each of the following terms.

- Proportion
- Dilation

Mathematical Practices

Mathematically proficient students look for and make use of a pattern or structure.

Discerning a Pattern or Structure

🔄 Core Concept

Dilations, Perimeter, Area, and Volume

Consider a figure that is dilated by a scale factor of k.

1. The perimeter of the image is k times the perimeter of the original figure.
2. The area of the image is k^2 times the area of the original figure.
3. If the original figure is three dimensional, then the volume of the image is k^3 times the volume of the original figure.

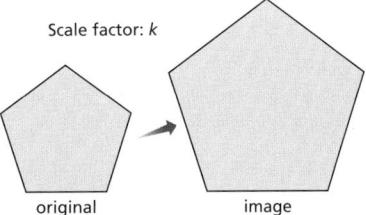

Scale factor: k

original   image

EXAMPLE 1 **Finding Perimeter and Area after a Dilation**

The triangle shown has side lengths of 3 inches, 4 inches, and 5 inches. Find the perimeter and area of the image when the triangle is dilated by a scale factor of (a) 2, (b) 3, and (c) 4.

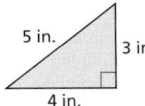

5 in. 3 in.
4 in.

SOLUTION

Perimeter: $P = 5 + 3 + 4 = 12$ in.   Area: $A = \frac{1}{2}(4)(3) = 6$ in.²

	Scale factor: k	Perimeter: kP	Area: k^2A
a.	2	$2(12) = 24$ in.	$(2^2)(6) = 24$ in.²
b.	3	$3(12) = 36$ in.	$(3^2)(6) = 54$ in.²
c.	4	$4(12) = 48$ in.	$(4^2)(6) = 96$ in.²

Monitoring Progress

1. Find the perimeter and area of the image when the trapezoid is dilated by a scale factor of (a) 2, (b) 3, and (c) 4.

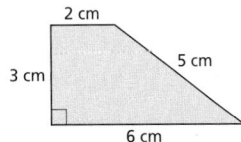

2 cm
3 cm   5 cm
6 cm

2. Find the perimeter and area of the image when the parallelogram is dilated by a scale factor of (a) 2, (b) 3, and (c) $\frac{1}{2}$.

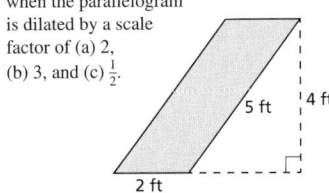

5 ft   4 ft
2 ft

3. A rectangular prism is 3 inches wide, 4 inches long, and 5 inches tall. Find the surface area and volume of the image of the prism when it is dilated by a scale factor of (a) 2, (b) 3, and (c) 4.

Laurie's Notes   **Mathematical Practices** (continued from page T-415)

*   The *Core Concept* states three relationships that students should be familiar with from middle school.
*   Pose Example 1. Students may be tempted to write the dimensions of each similar triangle. They should not need to do this in order to find the related perimeters and areas.
*   **Extension:** Use a scale factor that results in a reduction, $0 < k < 1$. Have students compute several perimeters and areas.
*   Give time for students to work through the *Monitoring Progress* questions, and then discuss as a class.

Overview of Section 8.1

Introduction
- Students should have recall of relationships between similar polygons from middle school and Chapter 4 of this book.
- In this lesson, corresponding parts of similar triangles are defined by a similarity transformation. Corresponding side lengths are proportional, and corresponding angles are congruent.
- Perimeters and areas of similar polygons are calculated and used to solve real-life problems.

Resources
- Dynamic geometry software is helpful in demonstrating the connections between dilations and similar polygons. It is also helpful in developing spatial skills.

Formative Assessment Tips
- **Agree-Disagree Statement:** This technique has two parts. First, students are given a statement with which they may agree or disagree, or they could indicate that they need additional information in order to decide. They are then asked to explain why they agree or disagree, or why they might need additional information. The second part of the technique involves students describing how they could investigate, figure out, or test their thinking.
- This technique gives students the opportunity to think about their own understanding of a concept or process. Further, it helps students practice the skill of actively investigating their own thinking. In listening to their own words, and in listening to the thinking of others, students can solidify or modify their own beliefs.
- This technique can be used at the beginning of a class or unit of study to assess students' understanding of a concept. Student responses will help inform your instruction by knowing what experiences students need to help guide their learning.
- *Note*: The statements made are not low cognitive demand questions, such as true-false or yes-no questions. The goal is to uncover student conception about bigger ideas, such as whether all functions have an inverse or whether multiplying positive numbers gives a product greater than either factor.

Pacing Suggestion
- As students work through the explorations, listen and probe recall of prior knowledge, and then continue with the formal lesson. Be selective in the examples done based on students' recall of similar polygons.

Dynamic Teaching Tools
Dynamic Assessment & Progress Monitoring Tool
Lesson Planning Tool
Interactive Whiteboard Lesson Library
Dynamic Classroom with Dynamic Investigations

HSG-SRT.A.2 Given two figures, use the definition of similarity in terms of similarity transformations to decide if they are similar; explain using similarity transformations the meaning of similarity for triangles as the equality of all corresponding pairs of angles and the proportionality of all corresponding pairs of sides.

HSG-MG.A.3 Apply geometric methods to solve design problems (e.g., designing an object or structure to satisfy physical constraints or minimize cost; working with typographic grid systems based on ratios).

Laurie's Notes

Exploration

Motivate
- Display an image of a Major League baseball diamond and a Little League baseball diamond.
- ? "Are these polygons similar? Explain." Students should be comfortable in knowing that all squares are similar.
- ? "How are the ratios of the perimeter of the base path to the distance from home plate to second base related?" The ratios are the same.
- ? "How is the the ratio of infield areas related to the ratio of the perimeters?" The ratio of the infield areas is the square of the ratio of the perimeters.
- Explain to students that in this lesson they will be working with relationships found in similar polygons.

For Your Information
- To save time, you might combine both explorations into one because the direction lines are the same.

Exploration 1
- Students should be very familiar with the functionality of dynamic geometry software. Note that the direction states that any scale factor and any center of dilation may be used.
- ? "What do you observe about the corresponding angles of similar triangles?" They are congruent.
- ? "What do you observe about the ratios of corresponding sides of similar triangles?" The ratios are all equal and the same as the scale factor.
- While the observations should not be new to students, this exploration helps students to review relationships found in similar triangles.

Exploration 2
- This exploration reviews the relationships about the perimeters and areas of similar triangles.
- **Extension:** You could have students begin with a quadrilateral versus a triangle.

Communicate Your Answer
- **MP6 Attend to Precision:** There are many relationships students should mention about similar polygons. Students should not say, "Similar polygons are the same shape but not necessarily the same size."

Connecting to Next Step
- The explorations should be a review of relationships found in similar polygons. Quickly transition to the formal lesson.

8.1 Similar Polygons

Essential Question How are similar polygons related?

EXPLORATION 1 Comparing Triangles after a Dilation

Work with a partner. Use dynamic geometry software to draw any $\triangle ABC$. Dilate $\triangle ABC$ to form a similar $\triangle A'B'C'$ using any scale factor k and any center of dilation.

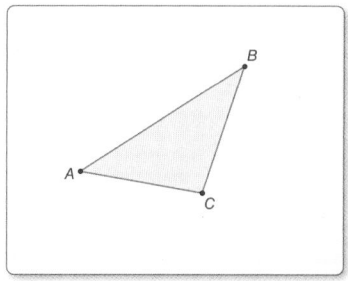

a. Compare the corresponding angles of $\triangle A'B'C'$ and $\triangle ABC$.

b. Find the ratios of the lengths of the sides of $\triangle A'B'C'$ to the lengths of the corresponding sides of $\triangle ABC$. What do you observe?

c. Repeat parts (a) and (b) for several other triangles, scale factors, and centers of dilation. Do you obtain similar results?

EXPLORATION 2 Comparing Triangles after a Dilation

Work with a partner. Use dynamic geometry software to draw any $\triangle ABC$. Dilate $\triangle ABC$ to form a similar $\triangle A'B'C'$ using any scale factor k and any center of dilation.

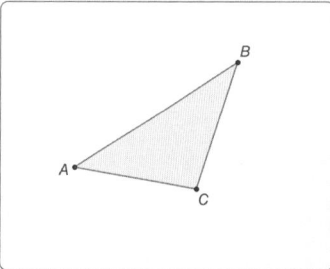

LOOKING FOR STRUCTURE

To be proficient in math, you need to look closely to discern a pattern or structure.

a. Compare the perimeters of $\triangle A'B'C'$ and $\triangle ABC$. What do you observe?

b. Compare the areas of $\triangle A'B'C'$ and $\triangle ABC$. What do you observe?

c. Repeat parts (a) and (b) for several other triangles, scale factors, and centers of dilation. Do you obtain similar results?

Communicate Your Answer

3. How are similar polygons related?

4. A $\triangle RST$ is dilated by a scale factor of 3 to form $\triangle R'S'T'$. The area of $\triangle RST$ is 1 square inch. What is the area of $\triangle R'S'T'$?

Section 8.1   Similar Polygons   **417**

Dynamic Teaching Tools

Dynamic Assessment & Progress Monitoring Tool

Lesson Planning Tool

Interactive Whiteboard Lesson Library

Dynamic Classroom with Dynamic Investigations

ANSWERS

1. a. The corresponding angles are congruent.
   b. The ratios are equal to the scale factor.
   c. yes

2. a. The perimeter of $\triangle A'B'C'$ is equal to k times the perimeter of $\triangle ABC$.
   b. The area of $\triangle A'B'C'$ is equal to k^2 times the area of $\triangle ABC$.
   c. yes

3. Corresponding angles are congruent, and corresponding side lengths are proportional.

4. 9 in.^{2}

Extra Example 1

In the diagram, $\triangle ABC \sim \triangle JKL$.

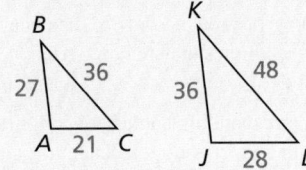

a. Find the scale factor from $\triangle ABC$ to $\triangle JKL$. $\frac{4}{3}$

b. List all pairs of congruent angles.
$\angle A \cong \angle J$, $\angle B \cong \angle K$, $\angle C \cong \angle L$

c. Write the ratios of the corresponding side lengths in a *statement of proportionality*.
Sample answer: $\dfrac{JK}{AB} = \dfrac{KL}{BC} = \dfrac{LJ}{CA}$

MONITORING PROGRESS ANSWER

1. $\dfrac{3}{2}$; $\angle J \cong \angle P$, $\angle K \cong \angle Q$, $\angle L \cong \angle R$; $\dfrac{PQ}{JK} = \dfrac{QR}{KL} = \dfrac{PR}{JL}$

8.1 Lesson

Core Vocabulary

Previous
similar figures
similarity transformation
corresponding parts

LOOKING FOR STRUCTURE

Notice that any two congruent figures are also similar. In $\triangle LMN$ and $\triangle WXY$ below, the scale factor is $\frac{5}{5} = \frac{6}{6} = \frac{7}{7} = 1$. So, you can write $\triangle LMN \sim \triangle WXY$ and $\triangle LMN \cong \triangle WXY$.

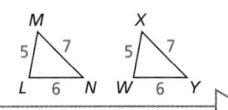

READING

In a *statement of proportionality*, any pair of ratios forms a true proportion.

What You Will Learn

▶ Use similarity statements.
▶ Find corresponding lengths in similar polygons.
▶ Find perimeters and areas of similar polygons.
▶ Decide whether polygons are similar.

Using Similarity Statements

Recall from Section 4.6 that two geometric figures are similar figures if and only if there is a similarity transformation that maps one figure onto the other.

🌀 Core Concept

Corresponding Parts of Similar Polygons

In the diagram below, $\triangle ABC$ is similar to $\triangle DEF$. You can write "$\triangle ABC$ is similar to $\triangle DEF$" as $\triangle ABC \sim \triangle DEF$. A similarity transformation preserves angle measure. So, corresponding angles are congruent. A similarity transformation also enlarges or reduces side lengths by a scale factor k. So, corresponding side lengths are proportional.

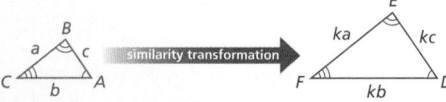

Corresponding angles

$\angle A \cong \angle D$, $\angle B \cong \angle E$, $\angle C \cong \angle F$

Ratios of corresponding side lengths

$\dfrac{DE}{AB} = \dfrac{EF}{BC} = \dfrac{FD}{CA} = k$

EXAMPLE 1 Using Similarity Statements

In the diagram, $\triangle RST \sim \triangle XYZ$.

a. Find the scale factor from $\triangle RST$ to $\triangle XYZ$.

b. List all pairs of congruent angles.

c. Write the ratios of the corresponding side lengths in a *statement of proportionality*.

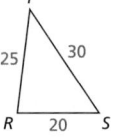
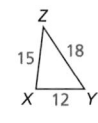

SOLUTION

a. $\dfrac{XY}{RS} = \dfrac{12}{20} = \dfrac{3}{5}$ $\dfrac{YZ}{ST} = \dfrac{18}{30} = \dfrac{3}{5}$ $\dfrac{ZX}{TR} = \dfrac{15}{25} = \dfrac{3}{5}$

So, the scale factor is $\dfrac{3}{5}$.

b. $\angle R \cong \angle X$, $\angle S \cong \angle Y$, and $\angle T \cong \angle Z$.

c. Because the ratios in part (a) are equal, $\dfrac{XY}{RS} = \dfrac{YZ}{ST} = \dfrac{ZX}{TR}$.

Monitoring Progress 🔊 Help in English and Spanish at *BigIdeasMath.com*

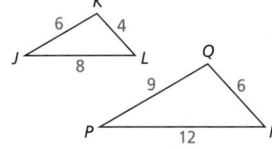

1. In the diagram, $\triangle JKL \sim \triangle PQR$. Find the scale factor from $\triangle JKL$ to $\triangle PQR$. Then list all pairs of congruent angles and write the ratios of the corresponding side lengths in a statement of proportionality.

418   Chapter 8   Similarity

Laurie's Notes   Teacher Actions

• Write the *Core Concept*, noting the language.
• **Turn and Talk:** "Compare a congruency transformation (isometry) and a *similarity transformation*." After comparisons are discussed, ask, "Are congruent figures similar? Explain." Listen for correct reasoning.
• **Whiteboarding:** Have partners work independently on Example 1. Have partners share solutions. Circulate and listen to students' conversations.
• The *statement of proportionality* may be unfamiliar language.

Finding Corresponding Lengths in Similar Polygons

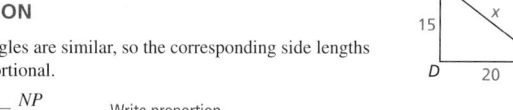

Core Concept

Corresponding Lengths in Similar Polygons

If two polygons are similar, then the ratio of any two corresponding lengths in the polygons is equal to the scale factor of the similar polygons.

> **READING**
> Corresponding lengths in similar triangles include side lengths, altitudes, medians, and midsegments.

 **Finding a Corresponding Length**

In the diagram, $\triangle DEF \sim \triangle MNP$. Find the value of x.

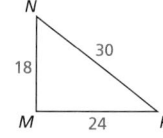

SOLUTION

The triangles are similar, so the corresponding side lengths are proportional.

$$\frac{MN}{DE} = \frac{NP}{EF} \qquad \text{Write proportion.}$$

$$\frac{18}{15} = \frac{30}{x} \qquad \text{Substitute.}$$

$$18x = 450 \qquad \text{Cross Products Property}$$

$$x = 25 \qquad \text{Solve for } x.$$

▶ The value of x is 25.

> **FINDING AN ENTRY POINT**
> There are several ways to write the proportion. For example, you could write $\dfrac{DF}{MP} = \dfrac{EF}{NP}$.

EXAMPLE 3 **Finding a Corresponding Length**

In the diagram, $\triangle TPR \sim \triangle XPZ$. Find the length of the altitude $\overline{PS}$.

SOLUTION

First, find the scale factor from $\triangle XPZ$ to $\triangle TPR$.

$$\frac{TR}{XZ} = \frac{6+6}{8+8} = \frac{12}{16} = \frac{3}{4}$$

Because the ratio of the lengths of the altitudes in similar triangles is equal to the scale factor, you can write the following proportion.

$$\frac{PS}{PY} = \frac{3}{4} \qquad \text{Write proportion.}$$

$$\frac{PS}{20} = \frac{3}{4} \qquad \text{Substitute 20 for } PY.$$

$$PS = 15 \qquad \text{Multiply each side by 20 and simplify.}$$

▶ The length of the altitude $\overline{PS}$ is 15.

Monitoring Progress ◀)) Help in English and Spanish at *BigIdeasMath.com*

2. Find the value of x.

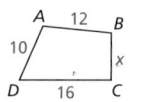

$ABCD \sim QRST$

3. Find KM.

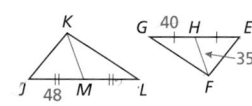

$\triangle JKL \sim \triangle EFG$

Section 8.1   Similar Polygons   **419**

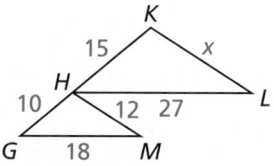

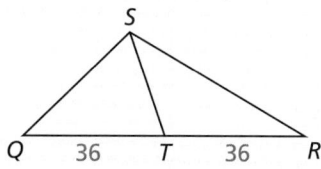

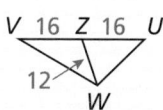

Differentiated Instruction

Inclusion

In Example 2, point out that there are many ways to write a proportion correctly. Ask students to identify other correct proportions in $\triangle DEF$ and $\triangle MNP$. Have them write these proportions on the board.

Extra Example 2

In the diagram, $\triangle GHM \sim \triangle HKL$. Find the value of x.

The value of x is 18.

Extra Example 3

In the diagram, $\triangle UVW \sim \triangle QRS$. Find the length of the median $\overline{ST}$.

The length of the median $\overline{ST}$ is 27.

MONITORING PROGRESS ANSWERS

2. $x = 8$

3. $KM = 42$

Laurie's Notes   Teacher Actions

- **Common Misconception:** The *Core Concept* refers to corresponding lengths in similar polygons. Lengths are not restricted to only side lengths. Corresponding lengths also refer to special segments, such as altitudes, medians, and so on, as well as corresponding diagonals.
- Have partners work independently on Examples 2 and 3 and then compare how the proportions were set up.
- **MP3 Construct Viable Arguments and Critique the Reasoning of Others:** As students share their results, they should justify why they wrote their proportions as they did.

Extra Example 4

Your neighbor has decided to enlarge his garden. The garden is rectangular with width 6 feet and length 15 feet. The new garden will be similar to the original one, but will have a length of 35 feet. Find the perimeter of the original garden and the enlarged garden. *The perimeter of the original garden is 42 feet. The perimeter of the enlarged garden is 98 feet.*

MONITORING PROGRESS ANSWER

4. 46 m

Finding Perimeters and Areas of Similar Polygons

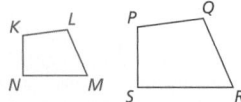 Theorem

Theorem 8.1 Perimeters of Similar Polygons

If two polygons are similar, then the ratio of their perimeters is equal to the ratios of their corresponding side lengths.

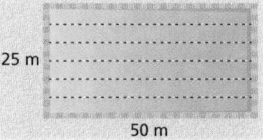

If $KLMN \sim PQRS$, then $\dfrac{PQ + QR + RS + SP}{KL + LM + MN + NK} = \dfrac{PQ}{KL} = \dfrac{QR}{LM} = \dfrac{RS}{MN} = \dfrac{SP}{NK}$.

Proof Ex. 52, p. 426; *BigIdeasMath.com*

ANALYZING RELATIONSHIPS

When two similar polygons have a scale factor of k, the ratio of their perimeters is equal to k.

EXAMPLE 4 **Modeling with Mathematics**

A town plans to build a new swimming pool. An Olympic pool is rectangular with a length of 50 meters and a width of 25 meters. The new pool will be similar in shape to an Olympic pool but will have a length of 40 meters. Find the perimeters of an Olympic pool and the new pool.

25 m

50 m

SOLUTION

1. **Understand the Problem** You are given the length and width of a rectangle and the length of a similar rectangle. You need to find the perimeters of both rectangles.

2. **Make a Plan** Find the scale factor of the similar rectangles and find the perimeter of an Olympic pool. Then use the Perimeters of Similar Polygons Theorem to write and solve a proportion to find the perimeter of the new pool.

3. **Solve the Problem** Because the new pool will be similar to an Olympic pool, the scale factor is the ratio of the lengths, $\frac{40}{50} = \frac{4}{5}$. The perimeter of an Olympic pool is $2(50) + 2(25) = 150$ meters. Write and solve a proportion to find the perimeter x of the new pool.

$$\frac{x}{150} = \frac{4}{5} \qquad \text{Perimeters of Similar Polygons Theorem}$$

$$x = 120 \qquad \text{Multiply each side by 150 and simplify.}$$

▶ So, the perimeter of an Olympic pool is 150 meters, and the perimeter of the new pool is 120 meters.

4. **Look Back** Check that the ratio of the perimeters is equal to the scale factor.

$$\frac{120}{150} = \frac{4}{5} \checkmark$$

STUDY TIP

You can also write the scale factor as a decimal. In Example 4, you can write the scale factor as 0.8 and multiply by 150 to get $x = 0.8(150) = 120$.

Monitoring Progress 🔊 Help in English and Spanish at *BigIdeasMath.com*

4. The two gazebos shown are similar pentagons. Find the perimeter of Gazebo A.

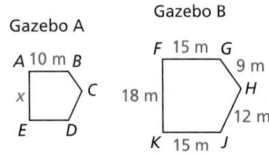

Laurie's Notes   Teacher Actions

? Write the Perimeters of Similar Polygons Theorem. "What other name could you give for the ratio of corresponding side lengths?" scale factor

? "Do you need to find the width of the new pool in order to find the perimeter? Explain." no; Because you can determine the perimeter of the Olympic-sized pool and the scale factor of the similar rectangles, you can find the perimeter of the new pool.

• Note that the *Study Tip* in the side margin suggests another way to solve the problem.

Theorem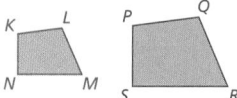

Theorem 8.2 Areas of Similar Polygons

If two polygons are similar, then the ratio of
their areas is equal to the squares of the ratios
of their corresponding side lengths.

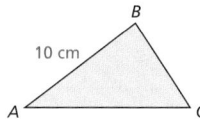 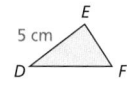

If $KLMN \sim PQRS$, then $\dfrac{\text{Area of } PQRS}{\text{Area of } KLMN} = \left(\dfrac{PQ}{KL}\right)^2 = \left(\dfrac{QR}{LM}\right)^2 = \left(\dfrac{RS}{MN}\right)^2 = \left(\dfrac{SP}{NK}\right)^2.$

Proof Ex. 53, p. 426; *BigIdeasMath.com*

ANALYZING RELATIONSHIPS

When two similar polygons have a scale factor of k, the ratio of their areas is equal to k^2.

EXAMPLE 5 Finding Areas of Similar Polygons

In the diagram, $\triangle ABC \sim \triangle DEF$. Find the area of $\triangle DEF$.

Area of $\triangle ABC = 36$ cm^2

SOLUTION

Because the triangles are similar, the ratio of the area of $\triangle ABC$ to the area of $\triangle DEF$ is equal to the square of the ratio of AB to DE. Write and solve a proportion to find the area of $\triangle DEF$. Let A represent the area of $\triangle DEF$.

$\dfrac{\text{Area of } \triangle ABC}{\text{Area of } \triangle DEF} = \left(\dfrac{AB}{DE}\right)^2$ Areas of Similar Polygons Theorem

$\dfrac{36}{A} = \left(\dfrac{10}{5}\right)^2$ Substitute.

$\dfrac{36}{A} = \dfrac{100}{25}$ Square the right side of the equation.

$36 \cdot 25 = 100 \cdot A$ Cross Products Property

$900 = 100A$ Simplify.

$9 = A$ Solve for A.

▶ The area of $\triangle DEF$ is 9 square centimeters.

Monitoring Progress 🔊 Help in English and Spanish at *BigIdeasMath.com*

5. In the diagram, $GHJK \sim LMNP$. Find the area of $LMNP$.

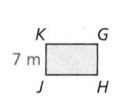 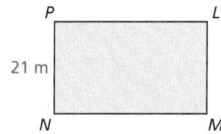

Area of $GHJK = 84$ m^2

Section 8.1   Similar Polygons   **421**

Extra Example 5

In the diagram, $\triangle PQT \sim \triangle RST$, and the area of $\triangle RST$ is 75 square meters. Find the area of $\triangle PQT$.

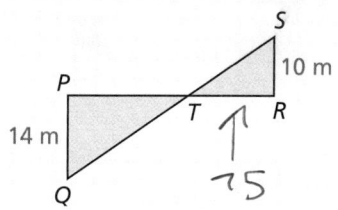

The area of $\triangle PQT$ is 147 square meters.

MONITORING PROGRESS ANSWER

5. 756 m^2

Laurie's Notes Teacher Actions

- Although the relationship between the areas of similar polygons was explored in middle school, students find it challenging to apply, particularly for non-integer scale factors.
- **Common Misconception:** Students are uncertain whether they can simplify a ratio written in a proportion. In Example 5, the ratio $\frac{10}{5}$ can be simplified to $\frac{2}{1}$. Have students work the example with and without simplifying the ratio to clarify the misconception.

Section 8.1   **421**

Extra Example 6

Decide whether *GNMH* and *MLKH* are similar. Explain your reasoning.

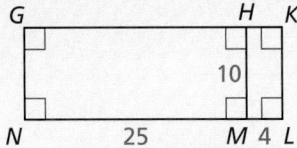

yes; Both quadrilaterals *GNMH* and *MLKH* are rectangles because each has four right angles. So, the corresponding angles are congruent. Sides *GN* = *HM* = *KL* = 10 because opposite sides in a rectangle are congruent. In rectangle *GNMH*, $\frac{GN}{NM} = \frac{10}{25} = \frac{2}{5}$, and in rectangle *MLKH*, $\frac{ML}{LK} = \frac{4}{10} = \frac{2}{5}$.

The lengths of the corresponding sides are in proportion. So, *GNMH* and *MLKH* are similar.

MONITORING PROGRESS ANSWERS

6. no; The blue hexagon is not regular, so corresponding side lengths are not proportional.

7. yes; Both hexagons are regular, so corresponding angles are congruent and corresponding side lengths are proportional.

Deciding Whether Polygons Are Similar

EXAMPLE 6 **Deciding Whether Polygons Are Similar**

Decide whether *ABCDE* and *KLQRP* are similar. Explain your reasoning.

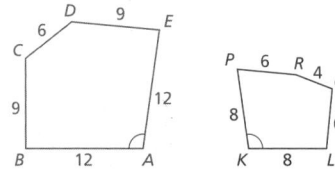

SOLUTION

Corresponding sides of the pentagons are proportional with a scale factor of $\frac{2}{3}$. However, this does not necessarily mean the pentagons are similar. A dilation with center *A* and scale factor $\frac{2}{3}$ moves *ABCDE* onto *AFGHJ*. Then a reflection moves *AFGHJ* onto *KLMNP*.

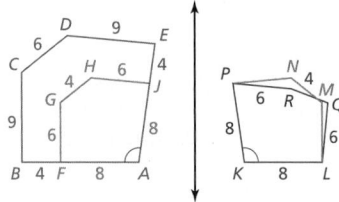

KLMNP does not exactly coincide with *KLQRP*, because not all the corresponding angles are congruent. (Only ∠*A* and ∠*K* are congruent.)

 Because angle measure is not preserved, the two pentagons are not similar.

Monitoring Progress ◉) Help in English and Spanish at *BigIdeasMath.com*

Refer to the floor tile designs below. In each design, the red shape is a regular hexagon.

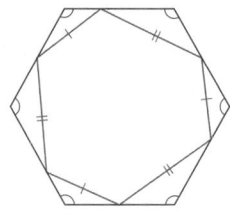

Tile Design 1

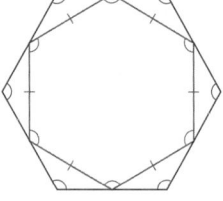

Tile Design 2

6. Decide whether the hexagons in Tile Design 1 are similar. Explain.

7. Decide whether the hexagons in Tile Design 2 are similar. Explain.

Laurie's Notes   Teacher Actions

? **Agree-Disagree Statement:** "The corresponding sides of two polygons are proportional, so the polygons are similar. Agree/Disagree. Explain." Students should discuss their understanding of similar figures. What students often forget is that corresponding angles must also be congruent.

• Now pose Example 6 for students to consider.

Closure

• **Writing Prompt:** If two polygons are similar, then …

Vocabulary and Core Concept Check

1. **COMPLETE THE SENTENCE** For two figures to be similar, the corresponding angles must be _____, and the corresponding side lengths must be _____.

2. **DIFFERENT WORDS, SAME QUESTION** Which is different? Find "both" answers.

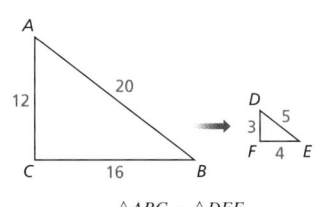

△ABC ~ △DEF

| What is the scale factor? |

| What is the ratio of their areas? |

| What is the ratio of their corresponding side lengths? |

| What is the ratio of their perimeters? |

Monitoring Progress and Modeling with Mathematics

In Exercises 3 and 4, find the scale factor. Then list all pairs of congruent angles and write the ratios of the corresponding side lengths in a statement of proportionality. *(See Example 1.)*

3. △ABC ~ △LMN

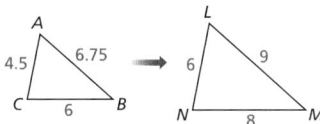

4. DEFG ~ PQRS

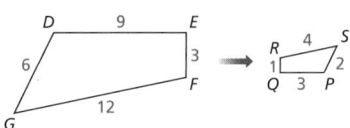

In Exercises 5–8, the polygons are similar. Find the value of x. *(See Example 2.)*

5.

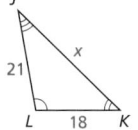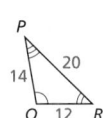

6.

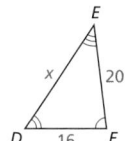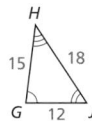

7.

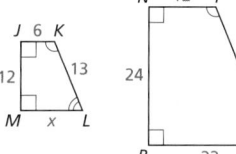

8.

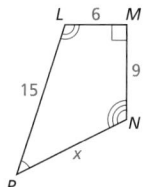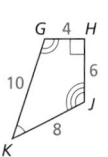

Assignment Guide and Homework Check

ASSIGNMENT

Basic: 1, 2, 3–25 odd, 29, 49, 50, 57–60

Average: 1, 2–38 even, 44, 49, 50, 57–60

Advanced: 1, 2, 4, 8, 10, 24–34 even, 38, 42, 48–60

HOMEWORK CHECK

Basic: 5, 9, 17, 21, 50

Average: 6, 10, 18, 26, 50

Advanced: 8, 10, 26, 38, 50

ANSWERS

1. congruent; proportional

2. What is the ratio of their areas?; $\frac{1}{16}$; $\frac{1}{4}$

3. $\frac{4}{3}$; $\angle A \cong \angle L$, $\angle B \cong \angle M$, $\angle C \cong \angle N$; $\frac{LM}{AB} = \frac{MN}{BC} = \frac{NL}{CA}$

4. $\frac{1}{3}$; $\angle D \cong \angle P$, $\angle E \cong \angle Q$, $\angle F \cong \angle R$, $\angle G \cong \angle S$;

   $\frac{PQ}{DE} = \frac{QR}{EF} = \frac{RS}{FG} = \frac{SP}{GD}$

5. $x = 30$

6. $x = 24$

7. $x = 11$

8. $x = 12$

ANSWERS

9. altitude; 24

10. median; 9

11. 2 : 3

12. 4 : 3

13. 72 cm

14. 88 ft

15. 20 yd

16. 34 m

17. 288 ft, 259.2 ft

18. 130 ft, 52 ft

19. 108 ft²

20. 90 cm²

21. 4 in.²

22. 6 cm²

23. Because the first ratio has a side length of B over a side length of A, the second ratio should have the perimeter of B over the perimeter of A;

$$\frac{5}{10} = \frac{x}{28}$$

$$x = 14$$

24. The square of the ratio of their corresponding side lengths should be set equal to the ratio of their areas;

$$\left(\frac{6}{18}\right)^2 = \frac{24}{x}$$

$$x = 216$$

In Exercises 9 and 10, the black triangles are similar. Identify the type of segment shown in blue and find the value of the variable. *(See Example 3.)*

9.

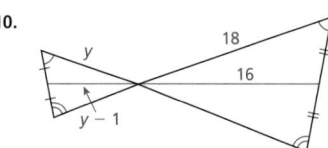

10.

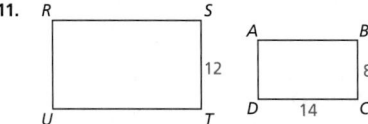

In Exercises 11 and 12, *RSTU ~ ABCD*. Find the ratio of their perimeters.

11.

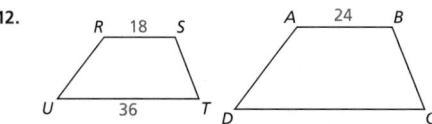

12.

In Exercises 13–16, two polygons are similar. The perimeter of one polygon and the ratio of the corresponding side lengths are given. Find the perimeter of the other polygon.

13. perimeter of smaller polygon: 48 cm; ratio: $\frac{2}{3}$

14. perimeter of smaller polygon: 66 ft; ratio: $\frac{3}{4}$

15. perimeter of larger polygon: 120 yd; ratio: $\frac{1}{6}$

16. perimeter of larger polygon: 85 m; ratio: $\frac{2}{5}$

17. **MODELING WITH MATHEMATICS** A school gymnasium is being remodeled. The basketball court will be similar to an NCAA basketball court, which has a length of 94 feet and a width of 50 feet. The school plans to make the width of the new court 45 feet. Find the perimeters of an NCAA court and of the new court in the school. *(See Example 4.)*

---

18. **MODELING WITH MATHEMATICS** Your family has decided to put a rectangular patio in your backyard, similar to the shape of your backyard. Your backyard has a length of 45 feet and a width of 20 feet. The length of your new patio is 18 feet. Find the perimeters of your backyard and of the patio.

In Exercises 19–22, the polygons are similar. The area of one polygon is given. Find the area of the other polygon. *(See Example 5.)*

19.

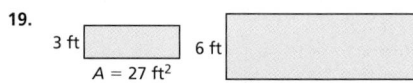

20.

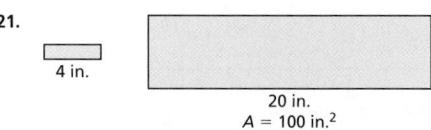

21.

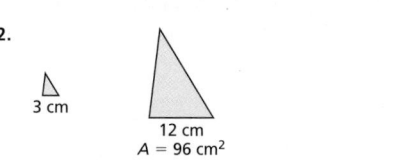

22.

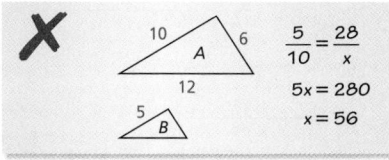

23. **ERROR ANALYSIS** Describe and correct the error in finding the perimeter of triangle B. The triangles are similar.

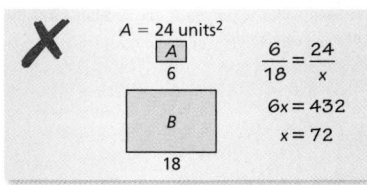

24. **ERROR ANALYSIS** Describe and correct the error in finding the area of rectangle B. The rectangles are similar.

In Exercises 25 and 26, decide whether the red and blue polygons are similar. *(See Example 6.)*

25.

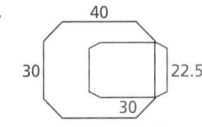

26.

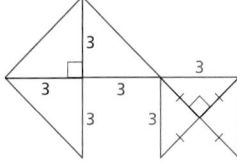

27. REASONING Triangles *ABC* and *DEF* are similar. Which statement is correct? Select all that apply.

Ⓐ $\dfrac{BC}{EF} = \dfrac{AC}{DF}$ Ⓑ $\dfrac{AB}{DE} = \dfrac{CA}{FE}$

Ⓒ $\dfrac{AB}{EF} = \dfrac{BC}{DE}$ Ⓓ $\dfrac{CA}{FD} = \dfrac{BC}{EF}$

ANALYZING RELATIONSHIPS In Exercises 28–34, *JKLM* ~ *EFGH*.

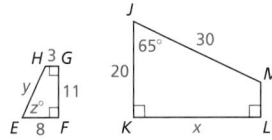

28. Find the scale factor of *JKLM* to *EFGH*.

29. Find the scale factor of *EFGH* to *JKLM*.

30. Find the values of *x*, *y*, and *z*.

31. Find the perimeter of each polygon.

32. Find the ratio of the perimeters of *JKLM* to *EFGH*.

33. Find the area of each polygon.

34. Find the ratio of the areas of *JKLM* to *EFGH*.

35. USING STRUCTURE Rectangle A is similar to rectangle B. Rectangle A has side lengths of 6 and 12. Rectangle B has a side length of 18. What are the possible values for the length of the other side of rectangle B? Select all that apply.

Ⓐ 6   Ⓑ 9   Ⓒ 24   Ⓓ 36

36. DRAWING CONCLUSIONS In table tennis, the table is a rectangle 9 feet long and 5 feet wide. A tennis court is a rectangle 78 feet long and 36 feet wide. Are the two surfaces similar? Explain. If so, find the scale factor of the tennis court to the table.

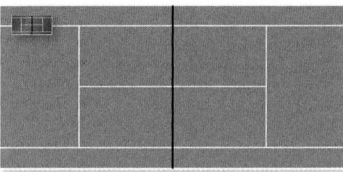

MATHEMATICAL CONNECTIONS In Exercises 37 and 38, the two polygons are similar. Find the values of *x* and *y*.

37.

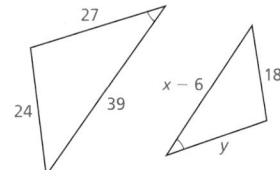

38.

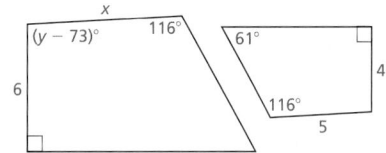

ATTENDING TO PRECISION In Exercises 39–42, the figures are similar. Find the missing corresponding side length.

39. Figure A has a perimeter of 72 meters and one of the side lengths is 18 meters. Figure B has a perimeter of 120 meters.

40. Figure A has a perimeter of 24 inches. Figure B has a perimeter of 36 inches and one of the side lengths is 12 inches.

41. Figure A has an area of 48 square feet and one of the side lengths is 6 feet. Figure B has an area of 75 square feet.

42. Figure A has an area of 18 square feet. Figure B has an area of 98 square feet and one of the side lengths is 14 feet.

ANSWERS

25. no; Corresponding angles are not congruent.

26. yes; Corresponding side lengths are proportional and corresponding angles are congruent.

27. A, D

28. $\dfrac{2}{5}$

29. $\dfrac{5}{2}$

30. $x = 27.5$, $y = 12$, $z = 65$

31. 34, 85

32. 5 : 2

33. 60.5, 378.125

34. 25 : 4

35. B, D

36. no; Corresponding side lengths are not proportional.

37. $x = 35.25$, $y = 20.25$

38. $x = 7.5$, $y = 166$

39. 30 m

40. 8 in.

41. 7.5 ft

42. 6 ft

Mini-Assessment

1. In the diagram, $\triangle ABE \sim \triangle DBC$. Find the value of x.

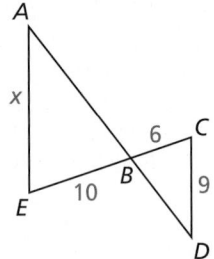

$x = 15$

2. In the diagram, $\triangle NOW \sim \triangle PQR$. Identify the type of segment shown in blue and find the value of x.

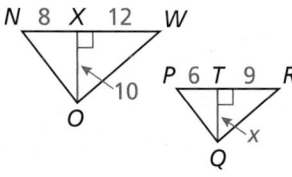

$\overline{OX}$ and $\overline{QT}$ are altitudes; $x = 7.5$

3. The two rectangles are similar. The area of the smaller rectangle is 7.5 square inches. Find the area of the larger rectangle.

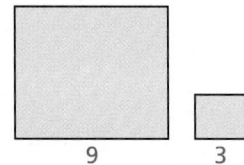

67.5 square inches

4. True or false? All squares are similar. Explain your reasoning.
   True. A square has four right angles. So, the corresponding angles in all squares are congruent. A square has four congruent sides. If each side of one square has length s, and each side of a second square has length ks, then k is the scale factor, and the ratio between any two pairs of corresponding sides is $\frac{ks}{s} = k$. The squares are similar by definition.

426   Chapter 8

CRITICAL THINKING In Exercises 43–48, tell whether the polygons are *always*, *sometimes*, or *never* similar.

43. two isosceles triangles
44. two isosceles trapezoids
45. two rhombuses
46. two squares
47. two regular polygons
48. a right triangle and an equilateral triangle

49. **MAKING AN ARGUMENT** Your sister claims that when the side lengths of two rectangles are proportional, the two rectangles must be similar. Is she correct? Explain your reasoning.

50. **HOW DO YOU SEE IT?** You shine a flashlight directly on an object to project its image onto a parallel screen. Will the object and the image be similar? Explain your reasoning.

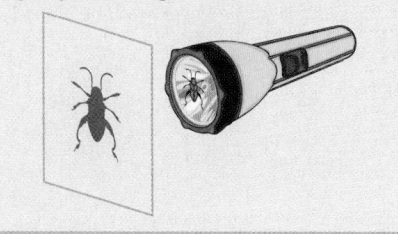

51. **MODELING WITH MATHEMATICS** During a total eclipse of the Sun, the moon is directly in line with the Sun and blocks the Sun's rays. The distance *DA* between Earth and the Sun is 93,000,000 miles, the distance *DE* between Earth and the moon is 240,000 miles, and the radius *AB* of the Sun is 432,500 miles. Use the diagram and the given measurements to estimate the radius *EC* of the moon.

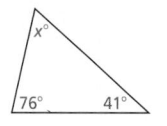
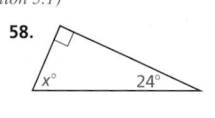
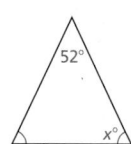

$\triangle DEC \sim \triangle DAB$ Not drawn to scale

52. **PROVING A THEOREM** Prove the Perimeters of Similar Polygons Theorem (Theorem 8.1) for similar rectangles. Include a diagram in your proof.

53. **PROVING A THEOREM** Prove the Areas of Similar Polygons Theorem (Theorem 8.2) for similar rectangles. Include a diagram in your proof.

54. **THOUGHT PROVOKING** The postulates and theorems in this book represent Euclidean geometry. In spherical geometry, all points are points on the surface of a sphere. A line is a circle on the sphere whose diameter is equal to the diameter of the sphere. A plane is the surface of the sphere. In spherical geometry, is it possible that two triangles are similar but not congruent? Explain your reasoning.

55. **CRITICAL THINKING** In the diagram, *PQRS* is a square, and $PLMS \sim LMRQ$. Find the exact value of x. This value is called the *golden ratio*. Golden rectangles have their length and width in this ratio. Show that the similar rectangles in the diagram are golden rectangles.

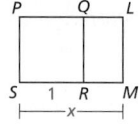

56. **MATHEMATICAL CONNECTIONS** The equations of the lines shown are $y = \frac{4}{3}x + 4$ and $y = \frac{4}{3}x - 8$. Show that $\triangle AOB \sim \triangle COD$.

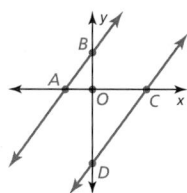

Maintaining Mathematical Proficiency   *Reviewing what you learned in previous grades and lessons*

Find the value of x.   *(Section 5.1)*

57.
58.
59.
60.

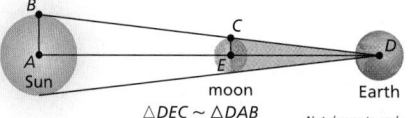

If students need help...	If students got it...
Resources by Chapter • Practice A and Practice B • Puzzle Time	Resources by Chapter • Enrichment and Extension • Cumulative Review
Student Journal • Practice	Start the *next* Section
Differentiating the Lesson Skills Review Handbook	

Overview of Section 8.2

Introduction
- In Chapter 5, students learned several ways to prove that two triangles are congruent. If two triangles are congruent, then they are similar. The converse is not true.
- This is a short lesson that introduces the first method for proving two triangles similar: Angle-Angle Similarity Theorem.
- Students will use AA to prove that triangles are similar. They will also apply the theorem in a real-life application to find the height of an object using indirect measure.

Resources
- Students will need a small mirror or a sunny day in order to find the height of an object using the strategy described below. A tape measure is needed for either method.

Teaching Strategy
- Students will enjoy being outside to find the height of an object using indirect measure. There are two common methods that use the Angle-Angle Similarity Theorem introduced in this lesson.
- On a sunny day, measure the shadows cast by the object and the student. Measure the student's height.
- **?** "Why are the two triangles similar?" Each triangle has a right angle, and the angle of elevation to the sun is the same for both triangles.

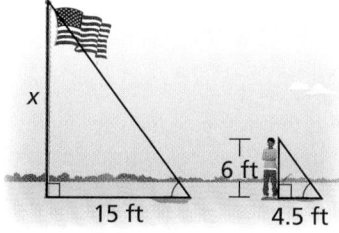

- A second method is to place a mirror on the ground between the person and the object. The student should position himself or herself so that he or she can see the top of the object in the middle of the mirror.
- **?** "Why are the two triangles similar?" Each triangle has a right angle, and the angle of incidence and the angle of reflection are the same for both triangles.

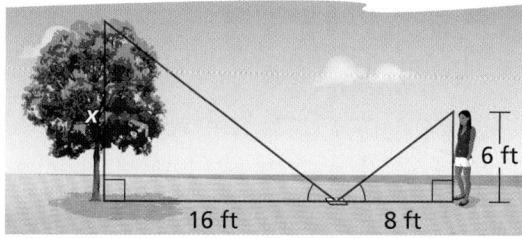

Pacing Suggestion
- Once students have worked the exploration, continue with the formal lesson.

**Common Core
State Standards**

HSG-SRT.A.3 Use the properties of similarity transformations to establish the AA criterion for two triangles to be similar.

HSG-SRT.B.5 Use … similarity criteria for triangles to solve problems and to prove relationships in geometric figures.

Exploration

Motivate
- Refer to an object outside your school building, such as a flagpole, tree, or building.
- **?** "How tall do you think the object is?"   Answers will vary.
- Explain to students that in today's lesson they will learn a technique for measuring the height of an object using a method that uses *indirect measure.*

Exploration Note
- In an earlier lesson, students proved that if two angles of one triangle are congruent to two angles of a second triangle, then the third angles are congruent. In this exploration, they take it one step further and investigate the side lengths of the two triangles.

Exploration 1
- Constructing a pair of triangles with the specified angle measures should not take students very long.
- If the labels for the vertices of their triangles are not the same as what is shown in the table, either rename the labels on their construction or rename angles and segments in the table.
- Be sure that students do not omit part (e) of the exploration.
- When students have had sufficient time to gather data, solicit conjectures and justifications.

Communicate Your Answer
- Expect students to offer conclusions similar to the conjectures made at the end of the exploration.

Connecting to Next Step
- The exploration allows students to investigate the side lengths of two triangles that share two pairs of congruent angles. The Angle-Angle Similarity Theorem is stated in the formal lesson.

8.2 Proving Triangle Similarity by AA

Essential Question What can you conclude about two triangles
when you know that two pairs of corresponding angles are congruent?

EXPLORATION 1 **Comparing Triangles**

Work with a partner. Use dynamic geometry software.

a. Construct △ABC and △DEF
so that $m\angle A = m\angle D = 106°$,
$m\angle B = m\angle E = 31°$, and
△DEF is not congruent
to △ABC.

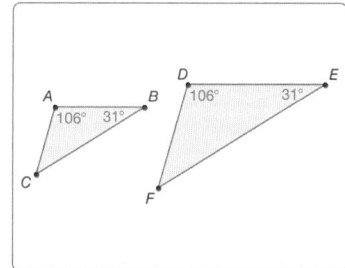

b. Find the third angle measure and the side lengths of each triangle. Copy the table
below and record your results in column 1.

	1.	2.	3.	4.	5.	6.
$m\angle A$, $m\angle D$	106°	88°	40°			
$m\angle B$, $m\angle E$	31°	42°	65°			
$m\angle C$						
$m\angle F$						
AB						
DE						
BC						
EF						
AC						
DF						

**CONSTRUCTING
VIABLE ARGUMENTS**

To be proficient in math,
you need to understand
and use stated assumptions,
definitions, and previously
established results in
constructing arguments.

c. Are the two triangles similar? Explain.

d. Repeat parts (a)–(c) to complete columns 2 and 3 of the table for the given
angle measures.

e. Complete each remaining column of the table using your own choice of two pairs
of equal corresponding angle measures. Can you construct two triangles in this way
that are *not* similar?

f. Make a conjecture about any two triangles with two pairs of congruent
corresponding angles.

Communicate Your Answer

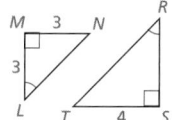

2. What can you conclude about two triangles when you know that two pairs of
corresponding angles are congruent?

3. Find *RS* in the figure at the left.

ANSWERS
1. See Additional Answers.
2. They are similar.
3. $RS = 4$

8.2 Lesson

Core Vocabulary

Previous
similar figures
similarity transformation

What You Will Learn

▶ Use the Angle-Angle Similarity Theorem.
▶ Solve real-life problems.

Using the Angle-Angle Similarity Theorem

Theorem

Theorem 8.3   Angle-Angle (AA) Similarity Theorem

If two angles of one triangle are congruent to two angles of another triangle, then the two triangles are similar.

If $\angle A \cong \angle D$ and $\angle B \cong \angle E$, then $\triangle ABC \sim \triangle DEF$.

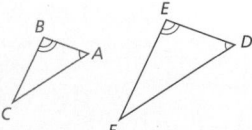

Proof p. 428

PROOF   **Angle-Angle (AA) Similarity Theorem**

Given $\angle A \cong \angle D$, $\angle B \cong \angle E$

Prove $\triangle ABC \sim \triangle DEF$

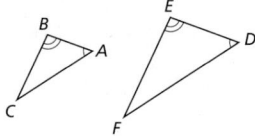

Dilate $\triangle ABC$ using a scale factor of $k = \dfrac{DE}{AB}$ and center A. The image of $\triangle ABC$ is $\triangle AB'C'$.

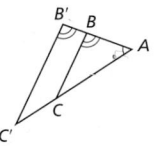

Because a dilation is a similarity transformation, $\triangle ABC \sim \triangle AB'C'$. Because the ratio of corresponding lengths of similar polygons equals the scale factor, $\dfrac{AB'}{AB} = \dfrac{DE}{AB}$. Multiplying each side by AB yields $AB' = DE$. By the definition of congruent segments, $\overline{AB'} \cong \overline{DE}$.

By the Reflexive Property of Congruence (Theorem 2.2), $\angle A \cong \angle A$. Because corresponding angles of similar polygons are congruent, $\angle B' \cong \angle B$. Because $\angle B' \cong \angle B$ and $\angle B \cong \angle E$, $\angle B' \cong \angle E$ by the Transitive Property of Congruence (Theorem 2.2).

Because $\angle A \cong \angle D$, $\angle B' \cong \angle E$, and $\overline{AB'} \cong \overline{DE}$, $\triangle AB'C' \cong \triangle DEF$ by the ASA Congruence Theorem (Theorem 5.10). So, a composition of rigid motions maps $\triangle AB'C'$ to $\triangle DEF$.

Because a dilation followed by a composition of rigid motions maps $\triangle ABC$ to $\triangle DEF$, $\triangle ABC \sim \triangle DEF$.

Laurie's Notes   Teacher Actions

- State the Angle-Angle Similarity Theorem.
- **Turn and Talk:** "How can you prove this theorem?" Students will know that the third angles are congruent, and hopefully they will think about transformations as a way to prove the theorem.
- **MP3 Construct Viable Arguments and Critique the Reasoning of Others:** Give time for partners to sketch out a proof. Have a class discussion, and listen for correct reasoning.
- This is the first method for proving two triangles similar that are not necessarily congruent.

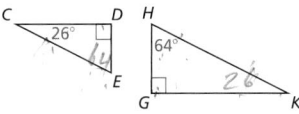 **Using the AA Similarity Theorem**

Determine whether the triangles are similar. If they are, write a similarity statement. Explain your reasoning.

SOLUTION

Because they are both right angles, $\angle D$ and $\angle G$ are congruent.

By the Triangle Sum Theorem (Theorem 5.1), $26° + 90° + m\angle E = 180°$, so $m\angle E = 64°$. So, $\angle E$ and $\angle H$ are congruent.

▶ So, $\triangle CDE \sim \triangle KGH$ by the AA Similarity Theorem.

EXAMPLE 2 **Using the AA Similarity Theorem**

Show that the two triangles are similar.

a. $\triangle ABE \sim \triangle ACD$ **b.** $\triangle SVR \sim \triangle UVT$

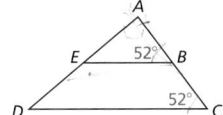   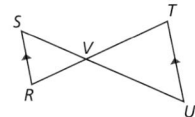

SOLUTION

a. Because $m\angle ABE$ and $m\angle C$ both equal $52°$, $\angle ABE \cong \angle C$. By the Reflexive Property of Congruence (Theorem 2.2), $\angle A \cong \angle A$.

▶ So, $\triangle ABE \sim \triangle ACD$ by the AA Similarity Theorem.

b. You know $\angle SVR \cong \angle UVT$ by the Vertical Angles Congruence Theorem (Theorem 2.6). The diagram shows $\overline{RS} \parallel \overline{UT}$, so $\angle S \cong \angle U$ by the Alternate Interior Angles Theorem (Theorem 3.2).

▶ So, $\triangle SVR \sim \triangle UVT$ by the AA Similarity Theorem.

Monitoring Progress 🔊 Help in English and Spanish at *BigIdeasMath.com*

Show that the triangles are similar. Write a similarity statement.

1. $\triangle FGH$ and $\triangle RQS$ **2.** $\triangle CDF$ and $\triangle DEF$

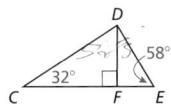

3. WHAT IF? Suppose that $\overline{SR} \not\parallel \overline{TU}$ in Example 2 part (b). Could the triangles still be similar? Explain.

Section 8.2   Proving Triangle Similarity by AA   **429**

VISUAL REASONING

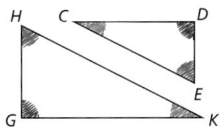

Use colored pencils to show congruent angles. This will help you write similarity statements.

VISUAL REASONING

You may find it helpful to redraw the triangles separately.

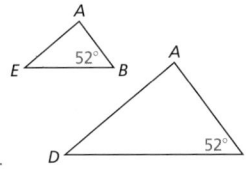

Extra Example 1

Determine whether the triangles are similar. If they are, write a similarity statement. Explain your reasoning.

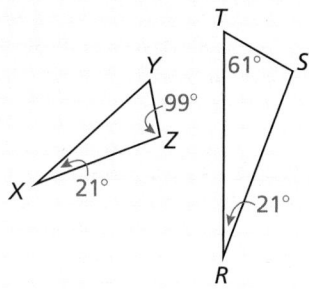

Sample answer: Given that $m\angle X = m\angle R = 21°$, so $\angle X \cong \angle R$. By the Triangle Sum Theorem (Thm. 5.1), $m\angle Y + 21° + 99° = 180°$ and $m\angle S + 21° + 61° = 180°$. So, $m\angle Y = 60°$ and $m\angle S = 98°$. That means only one pair of angles in the two triangles is congruent. By the definition of similar triangles, $\triangle XYZ$ and $\triangle RTS$ are not similar.

Extra Example 2

Show that $\triangle QPR \sim \triangle QTP$.

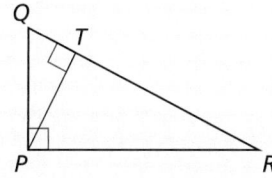

Sample answer: $\angle Q \cong \angle Q$ by the Reflexive Prop. of Angle Congruence (Thm. 2.2). $\angle QPR \cong \angle QTP$ by the Right Angles Congruence Theorem (Thm. 2.3). So, $\triangle QPR \sim \triangle QTP$ by the AA Similarity Theorem (Thm. 8.3).

MONITORING PROGRESS ANSWERS

1. $\angle F \cong \angle R$ and $\angle G \cong \angle Q$, so $\triangle FGH \sim \triangle RQS$.

2. $m\angle CDF = 58°$ and $m\angle DFE = 90°$, so $\angle CDF \cong \angle DEF$ and $\angle CFD \cong \angle DFE$, So, $\triangle CDF \sim \triangle DEF$.

3. yes; If $\angle S \cong \angle T$, then $\triangle SVR \sim \triangle TVU$.

Laurie's Notes   **Teacher Actions**

• Pose Example 1, and have partners solve independently.

❓ "Will all similarity statements be the same? Explain." no; There are different but equivalent ways in which the similarity statements can be written.

• **Think-Alouds:** Model Example 2(a), and then do a *Think-Aloud* as partner A shows partner B how the two triangles are similar. "I know the triangles are similar because …." Partners now reverse roles as partner B explains when the triangles in part (b) are similar.

Section 8.2   **429**

Extra Example 3

A school flagpole casts a shadow that is 45 feet long. At the same time, a boy who is five feet eight inches tall casts a shadow that is 51 inches long. How tall is the flagpole to the nearest foot? **The flagpole is 60 feet tall.**

MONITORING PROGRESS ANSWERS

4. $36\frac{1}{4}$ in.

5. $\dfrac{\dfrac{\text{your height}}{\text{length of your shadow}}}{\dfrac{x}{\text{length of tree's shadow}}} =$

Solving Real-Life Problems

Previously, you learned a way to use congruent triangles to find measurements indirectly. Another useful way to find measurements indirectly is by using similar triangles.

EXAMPLE 3 **Modeling with Mathematics**

A flagpole casts a shadow that is 50 feet long. At the same time, a woman standing nearby who is 5 feet 4 inches tall casts a shadow that is 40 inches long. How tall is the flagpole to the nearest foot?

Not drawn to scale

SOLUTION

1. **Understand the Problem** You are given the length of a flagpole's shadow, the height of a woman, and the length of the woman's shadow. You need to find the height of the flagpole.

2. **Make a Plan** Use similar triangles to write a proportion and solve for the height of the flagpole.

3. **Solve the Problem** The flagpole and the woman form sides of two right triangles with the ground. The Sun's rays hit the flagpole and the woman at the same angle. You have two pairs of congruent angles, so the triangles are similar by the AA Similarity Theorem.

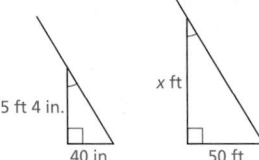

You can use a proportion to find the height x. Write 5 feet 4 inches as 64 inches so that you can form two ratios of feet to inches.

$$\frac{x \text{ ft}}{64 \text{ in.}} = \frac{50 \text{ ft}}{40 \text{ in.}} \qquad \text{Write proportion of side lengths.}$$

$$40x = 3200 \qquad \text{Cross Products Property}$$

$$x = 80 \qquad \text{Solve for } x.$$

 The flagpole is 80 feet tall.

4. **Look Back** Attend to precision by checking that your answer has the correct units. The problem asks for the height of the flagpole to the nearest *foot*. Because your answer is 80 feet, the units match.

Also, check that your answer is reasonable in the context of the problem. A height of 80 feet makes sense for a flagpole. You can estimate that an eight-story building would be about 8(10 feet) = 80 feet, so it is reasonable that a flagpole could be that tall.

Monitoring Progress ◀)) Help in English and Spanish at *BigIdeasMath.com*

4. **WHAT IF?** A child who is 58 inches tall is standing next to the woman in Example 3. How long is the child's shadow?

5. You are standing outside, and you measure the lengths of the shadows cast by both you and a tree. Write a proportion showing how you could find the height of the tree.

Laurie's Notes Teacher Actions

- Say, "Recall that we used indirect measure in working with congruent triangles. We were able to find distances indirectly because we had congruent triangles. A similar approach can be used with similar triangles." Work through the example as shown.
- **MP4 Model with Mathematics:** This example can be modeled on a sunny day or by using a mirror. See the *Teaching Strategy* on page T-426.

Closure

- **Exit Ticket:** One triangle has angles of 18° and 96°, and a second triangle has angles of 56° and 96°. Are the triangles similar? Explain. no; The first triangle has angles of 18°, 66°, and 96°. The second triangle has angles of 28°, 56°, and 96°. The triangles have only one pair of angles that are congruent.

Vocabulary and Core Concept Check

1. **COMPLETE THE SENTENCE** If two angles of one triangle are congruent to two angles of another triangle, then the triangles are _____.

2. **WRITING** Can you assume that corresponding sides and corresponding angles of any two similar triangles are congruent? Explain.

Monitoring Progress and Modeling with Mathematics

In Exercises 3–6, determine whether the triangles are similar. If they are, write a similarity statement. Explain your reasoning. *(See Example 1.)*

3.   4.

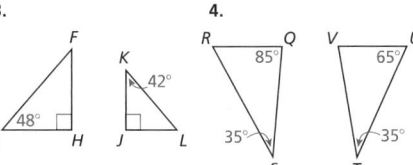

5.   6.

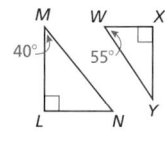
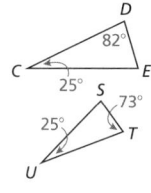

In Exercises 7–10, show that the two triangles are similar. *(See Example 2.)*

7.   8.

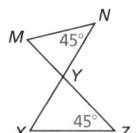
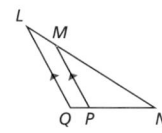

9.   10.

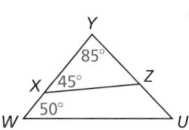
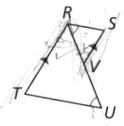

In Exercises 11–18, use the diagram to copy and complete the statement.

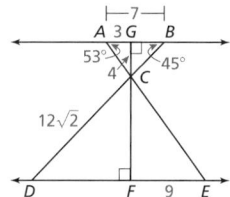

11. $\triangle CAG \sim$ ▨   12. $\triangle DCF \sim$ ▨

13. $\triangle ACB \sim$ ▨   14. $m\angle ECF =$ ▨

15. $m\angle ECD =$ ▨   16. $CF =$ ▨

17. $BC =$ ▨   18. $DE =$ ▨

19. **ERROR ANALYSIS** Describe and correct the error in using the AA Similarity Theorem (Theorem 8.3).

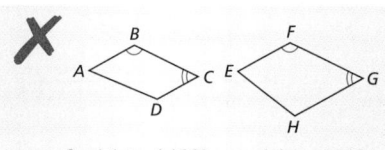

Quadrilateral *ABCD* ~ quadrilateral *EFGH* by the AA Similarity Theorem.

20. **ERROR ANALYSIS** Describe and correct the error in finding the value of *x*.

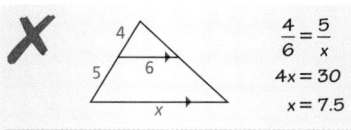

$$\frac{4}{6} = \frac{5}{x}$$
$$4x = 30$$
$$x = 7.5$$

ANSWERS

1. similar

2. no; Corresponding side lengths are proportional and not necessarily congruent.

3. yes; $\angle H \cong \angle J$ and $\angle F \cong \angle K$, so $\triangle FGH \sim \triangle KLJ$.

4. no; $m\angle R = 60°$

5. no; $m\angle N = 50°$

6. yes; $\angle C \cong \angle U$ and $\angle E \cong \angle T$, so $\triangle CDE \sim \triangle UST$.

7. $\angle N \cong \angle Z$ and $\angle MYN \cong \angle XYZ$, so $\triangle MYN \sim \triangle XYZ$.

8. $\angle Q \cong \angle MPN$ and $\angle N \cong \angle N$, so $\triangle LNQ \sim \triangle MNP$.

9. $\angle Y \cong \angle Y$ and $\angle YZX \cong \angle W$, so $\triangle XYZ \sim \triangle UYW$.

10. $\angle VRS \cong \angle RUT$ and $\angle SVR \cong \angle TRU$, so $\triangle SVR \sim \triangle TRU$.

11. $\triangle CAG \sim \triangle CEF$

12. $\triangle DCF \sim \triangle BCG$

13. $\triangle ACB \sim \triangle ECD$

14. $m\angle ECF = 37°$

15. $m\angle ECD = 82°$

16. $CF = 12$

17. $BC = 4\sqrt{2}$

18. $DE = 21$

19. The AA Similarity Theorem (Thm. 8.3) does not apply to quadrilaterals. There is not enough information to determine whether or not quadrilaterals *ABCD* and *EFGH* are similar.

20. The side of the larger triangle has a length of 9, not 5.

$$\frac{4}{6} = \frac{9}{x}$$

$$x = 13.5$$

Assignment Guide and Homework Check

ASSIGNMENT

Basic: 1, 2, 3–21 odd, 22, 23, 28, 34–36

Average: 1, 2–20 even, 21, 22–28 even, 29, 33–36

Advanced: 1, 2, 6, 10, 12–26 even, 27–36

HOMEWORK CHECK

Basic: 5, 7, 15, 21, 28

Average: 6, 8, 16, 21, 28

Advanced: 6, 10, 18, 26, 33

ANSWERS

21. 78 m; Corresponding angles are congruent, so the triangles are similar.

22–36. See Additional Answers.

Mini-Assessment

1. Determine whether the triangles are similar. If they are, write a similarity statement. Explain your reasoning.

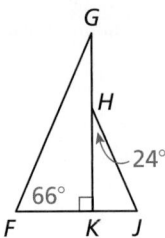

Sample answer: ∠GKF ≅ ∠HKJ by the Right ∠s ≅ Thm. (2.3). By the Triangle Sum Thm. (5.1), 66° + 90° + m∠G = 180°, so m∠G = 24°. So, ∠G ≅ ∠JHK. By the AA ~ Thm. (8.3), △FGK ~ △JHK.

2. Show that △LMN ~ △QPN without using vertical angles.

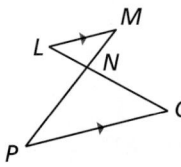

Sample answer: $\overline{LM} \parallel \overline{QP}$, so ∠L ≅ ∠Q and ∠M ≅ ∠P by the Alt. Int. ∠s Thm. (3.2). So, by the AA ~ Thm. (8.3), △LMN ~ △QPN.

3. The diagram shows a triangular ramp leading up to the entrance of a building. How long in feet is the vertical support shown in blue?

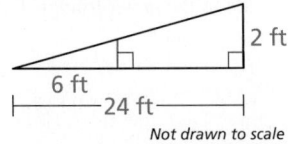

Not drawn to scale

The ramp support is 0.5 foot.

21. MODELING WITH MATHEMATICS You can measure the width of the lake using a surveying technique, as shown in the diagram. Find the width of the lake, *WX*. Justify your answer.

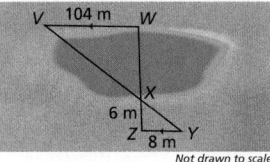

Not drawn to scale

22. MAKING AN ARGUMENT You and your cousin are trying to determine the height of a telephone pole. Your cousin tells you to stand in the pole's shadow so that the tip of your shadow coincides with the tip of the pole's shadow. Your cousin claims to be able to use the distance between the tips of the shadows and you, the distance between you and the pole, and your height to estimate the height of the telephone pole. Is this possible? Explain. Include a diagram in your answer.

REASONING In Exercises 23–26, is it possible for △JKL and △XYZ to be similar? Explain your reasoning.

23. m∠J = 71°, m∠K = 52°, m∠X = 71°, and m∠Z = 57°

24. △JKL is a right triangle and m∠X + m∠Y = 150°.

25. m∠L = 87° and m∠Y = 94°

26. m∠J + m∠K = 85° and m∠Y + m∠Z = 80°

27. MATHEMATICAL CONNECTIONS Explain how you can use similar triangles to show that any two points on a line can be used to find its slope.

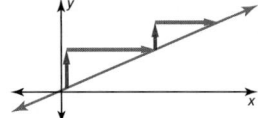

28. HOW DO YOU SEE IT? In the diagram, which triangles would you use to find the distance *x* between the shoreline and the buoy? Explain your reasoning.

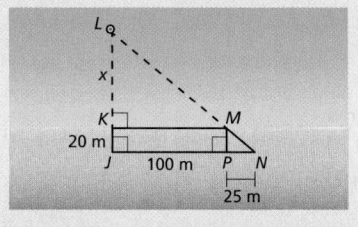

29. WRITING Explain why all equilateral triangles are similar.

30. THOUGHT PROVOKING Decide whether each is a valid method of showing that two quadrilaterals are similar. Justify your answer.

    a. AAA   **b.** AAAA

31. PROOF Without using corresponding lengths in similar polygons, prove that the ratio of two corresponding angle bisectors in similar triangles is equal to the scale factor.

32. PROOF Prove that if the lengths of two sides of a triangle are *a* and *b*, respectively, then the lengths of the corresponding altitudes to those sides are in the ratio $\frac{b}{a}$.

33. MODELING WITH MATHEMATICS A portion of an amusement park ride is shown. Find *EF*. Justify your answer.

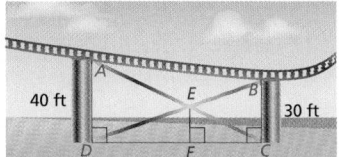

Maintaining Mathematical Proficiency
Reviewing what you learned in previous grades and lessons

Determine whether there is enough information to prove that the triangles are congruent. Explain your reasoning. *(Section 5.3, Section 5.5, and Section 5.6)*

34.

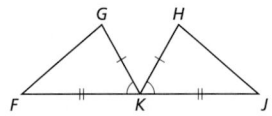

35.

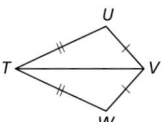

36.

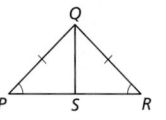

If students need help...	If students got it...
Resources by Chapter • Practice A and Practice B • Puzzle Time	Resources by Chapter • Enrichment and Extension • Cumulative Review
Student Journal • Practice	Start the *next* Section
Differentiating the Lesson Skills Review Handbook	

Core Concepts

Section 8.1

Corresponding Parts of Similar Polygons, *p. 418*
Corresponding Lengths in Similar Polygons, *p. 419*
Theorem 8.1 Perimeters of Similar Polygons, *p. 420*
Theorem 8.2 Areas of Similar Polygons, *p. 421*

Section 8.2

Theorem 8.3 Angle-Angle (AA) Similarity Theorem, *p. 428*

Mathematical Practices

1. In Exercise 35 on page 425, why is there more than one correct answer for the length of the other side?

2. In Exercise 50 on page 426, how could you find the scale factor of the similar figures? Describe any tools that might be helpful.

3. In Exercise 21 on page 432, explain why the surveyor needs *V*, *X*, and *Y* to be collinear and *Z*, *X*, and *W* to be collinear.

- - - - - - - Study Skills - - - - - - -

Take Control of Your Class Time

- Sit where you can easily see and hear the teacher, and the teacher can see you. The teacher may be able to tell when you are confused just by the look on your face and may adjust the lesson accordingly. In addition, sitting in this strategic place will keep your mind from wandering.

- Pay attention to what the teacher says about the math, not just what is written on the board. Write problems on the left side of your notes and what the teacher says about the problems on the right side.

- If the teacher is moving through the material too fast, ask a question. Questions help slow the pace for a few minutes and also clarify what is confusing to you.

- Try to memorize new information while learning it. Repeat in your head what you are writing in your notes. That way you are reviewing the information twice.

433

Dynamic Teaching Tools

Dynamic Assessment & Progress Monitoring Tool
Interactive Whiteboard Lesson Library
Dynamic Classroom with Dynamic Investigations

ANSWERS

1. The side with length 18 could correspond to either side of Rectangle A.

2. Measure the object and the image with a tape measure.

3. so that vertical angles are formed at *X*

ANSWERS

1. $\angle B \cong \angle M$, $\angle D \cong \angle P$,
   $\angle G \cong \angle Q$; $\dfrac{BD}{MP} = \dfrac{DG}{PQ} = \dfrac{GB}{QM}$

2. $\angle D \cong \angle H$, $\angle E \cong \angle J$,
   $\angle F \cong \angle K$, $\angle G \cong \angle L$;
   $\dfrac{DE}{HJ} = \dfrac{EF}{JK} = \dfrac{FG}{KL} = \dfrac{GD}{LH}$

3. $x = 18$

4. $x = 5$

5. no; Corresponding angles are not congruent.

6. no; $m\angle L = 40°$

7. yes; $\triangle ABC \sim \triangle DEF$; $m\angle C = 45°$

8. $\angle CBD \cong \angle A$ and $\angle C \cong \angle C$, so $\triangle ACE \sim \triangle BCD$.

9. $\angle G \cong \angle K$ and $\angle FHG \cong \angle JHK$, so $\triangle FGH \sim \triangle JKH$.

10. $\angle GEF \cong \angle HDF$ and $\angle F \cong \angle F$, so $\triangle DHF \sim \triangle EGF$.

11. **a.** yes
    b. $\dfrac{25}{1}$; $\dfrac{625}{1}$

12. yes; Corresponding angles are congruent.

List all pairs of congruent angles. Then write the ratios of the corresponding side lengths in a statement of proportionality. *(Section 8.1)*

1. $\triangle BDG \sim \triangle MPQ$

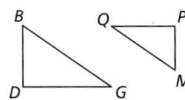

2. $DEFG \sim HJKL$

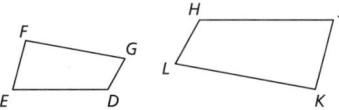

The polygons are similar. Find the value of x. *(Section 8.1)*

3.

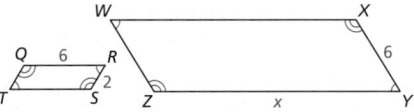

4.

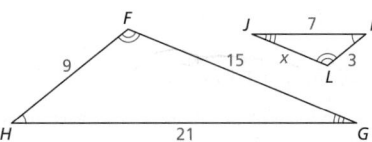

Determine whether the polygons are similar. If they are, write a similarity statement. Explain your reasoning. *(Section 8.1 and Section 8.2)*

5.

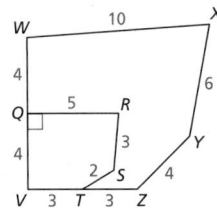

6.

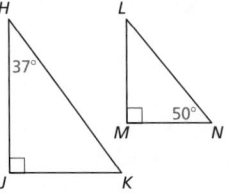

7.

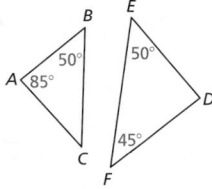

Show that the two triangles are similar. *(Section 8.2)*

8.

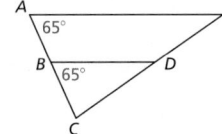

9.

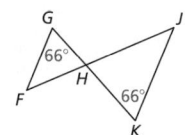

10.

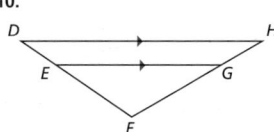

11. The dimensions of an official hockey rink used by the National Hockey League (NHL) are 200 feet by 85 feet. The dimensions of an air hockey table are 96 inches by 40.8 inches. Assume corresponding angles are congruent. *(Section 8.1)*

    a. Determine whether the two surfaces are similar.

    b. If the surfaces are similar, find the ratio of their perimeters and the ratio of their areas. If not, find the dimensions of an air hockey table that are similar to an NHL hockey rink.

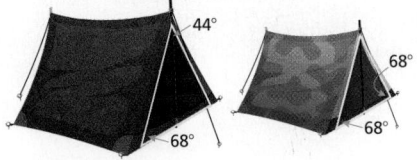

12. You and a friend buy camping tents made by the same company but in different sizes and colors. Use the information given in the diagram to decide whether the triangular faces of the tents are similar. Explain your reasoning. *(Section 8.2)*

Overview of Section 8.3

Introduction

- Students have proven triangles similar by using the definition of similarity and by using the Angle-Angle Similarity Theorem.
- In this lesson, two additional methods are explored and then stated as valid methods: the Side-Side-Side Similarity Theorem and the Side-Angle-Side Similarity Theorem.
- The last part of the lesson revisits two earlier theorems about slopes of parallel and perpendicular lines. These theorems are first stated in algebra.
- These slope criterion theorems can be proven using similar triangles. The purpose is not that students learn to write a lengthy proof. Students should, however, be able to read, understand, and appreciate the reasoning used in the proofs of these theorems.

Formative Assessment Tips

- **Three-Minute Pause:** This technique is used when a lesson involves a particularly large amount of information or a lengthy process. The teacher takes a three-minute break after a period of instruction, and students work with partners or in small groups to process the information they have just learned. They might ask one another questions or clarify what their understanding is relative to the activity or instruction they have just experienced.
- The break in instruction allows students to resolve questions and ask for feedback from peers. Once the three minutes are up, the instruction continues until the next *Three-Minute Pause*.
- After the final *Three-Minute Pause*, any lingering questions can be written down and used by the teacher to clarify concepts taught in the lesson.

Pacing Suggestion

- In the explorations, students will investigate two new ways to establish that triangles are similar. After students have discussed the explorations, transition to the formal lesson.

Dynamic Teaching Tools

Dynamic Assessment & Progress Monitoring Tool

Lesson Planning Tool

Interactive Whiteboard Lesson Library

Dynamic Classroom with Dynamic Investigations

Common Core
State Standards

HSG-SRT.B.4 Prove theorems about triangles.

HSG-SRT.B.5 Use ... similarity criteria for triangles to solve problems and to prove relationships in geometric figures.

HSG-GPE.B.5 Prove the slope criteria for parallel and perpendicular lines. ...

HSG-MG.A.1 Use geometric shapes, their measures, and their properties to describe objects (e.g., modeling a tree trunk or a human torso as a cylinder).

Laurie's Notes

Exploration

Motivate
- Gather pictures of quilts that contain what appear to be similar triangles and likely congruent triangles as well. Make a slide show of the quilts.
- Have students identify triangles that appear to be similar.
- Explain to students that in this lesson they will learn additional ways to prove triangles are similar besides the Angle-Angle Similarity Theorem.

Exploration Note
- Students may need guidance in constructing the triangles in both of the explorations, depending on the software being used and what functionality the software has.
- Before students begin, you could discuss techniques with students.

Exploration 1
- You may consider having different groups of students construct a subset of the problems and then share results with the whole class. For each pair of triangles, students not only construct the triangles from the given side lengths, they must also measure all six angles.
- **?** "What do you observe about the corresponding angles when the corresponding sides are proportional?" They are congruent. "Are the triangles similar? Explain." Yes; by the definition of similar triangles, they are similar.
- **?** "What do you observe about the corresponding angles when the corresponding sides are not proportional?" The angles are not congruent.

Exploration 2
- In constructing the triangles, students should be careful to make sure that the given angle is between the two given sides.
- Students should try values of k that result in enlargements and reductions.
- In deciding whether the triangles are similar, students could use the Angle-Angle Similarity Theorem from the last lesson.
- Students should conclude that the triangles are similar.

Communicate Your Answer
- **MP3 Construct Viable Arguments and Critique the Reasoning of Others:** In describing the results of the explorations, be sure that students do not confuse SSS and SAS congruency theorems with proportional side relationships in these explorations.

Connecting to Next Step
- The explorations help students develop an understanding of the theorems that will be stated in the formal lesson.

Proving Triangle Similarity by SSS and SAS

Dynamic Teaching Tools

Dynamic Assessment & Progress Monitoring Tool

Lesson Planning Tool

Interactive Whiteboard Lesson Library

Dynamic Classroom with Dynamic Investigations

Essential Question What are two ways to use corresponding sides of two triangles to determine that the triangles are similar?

EXPLORATION 1   Deciding Whether Triangles Are Similar

Work with a partner. Use dynamic geometry software.

a. Construct △ABC and △DEF with the side lengths given in column 1 of the table below.

	1.	2.	3.	4.	5.	6.	7.
AB	5	5	6	15	9	24	
BC	8	8	8	20	12	18	
AC	10	10	10	10	8	16	
DE	10	15	9	12	12	8	
EF	16	24	12	16	15	6	
DF	20	30	15	8	10	8	
m∠A							
m∠B							
m∠C							
m∠D							
m∠E							
m∠F							

b. Copy the table and complete column 1.

c. Are the triangles similar? Explain your reasoning.

d. Repeat parts (a)–(c) for columns 2–6 in the table.

e. How are the corresponding side lengths related in each pair of triangles that are similar? Is this true for each pair of triangles that are not similar?

f. Make a conjecture about the similarity of two triangles based on their corresponding side lengths.

g. Use your conjecture to write another set of side lengths of two similar triangles. Use the side lengths to complete column 7 of the table.

EXPLORATION 2   Deciding Whether Triangles Are Similar

Work with a partner. Use dynamic geometry software. Construct any △ABC.

a. Find AB, AC, and m∠A. Choose any positive rational number k and construct △DEF so that DE = k • AB, DF = k • AC, and m∠D = m∠A.

b. Is △DEF similar to △ABC? Explain your reasoning.

c. Repeat parts (a) and (b) several times by changing △ABC and k. Describe your results.

Communicate Your Answer

3. What are two ways to use corresponding sides of two triangles to determine that the triangles are similar?

Section 8.3   Proving Triangle Similarity by SSS and SAS   **435**

> **CONSTRUCTING VIABLE ARGUMENTS**
>
> To be proficient in math, you need to analyze situations by breaking them into cases and recognize and use counterexamples.

ANSWERS

1. a.

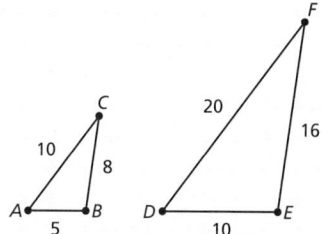

   b. See Additional Answers.

   c. yes; Corresponding angles are congruent.

   d. See Additional Answers for table. The triangles are similar in columns 2–4 because corresponding angles are congruent. The triangles are not similar in columns 5 and 6 because corresponding angles are not congruent.

   e. They are proportional; no

   f. If the corresponding side lengths of two triangles are proportional, then the triangles are similar.

   g. See Additional Answers.

2. a. *Sample answer:*

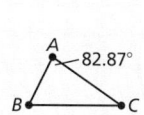 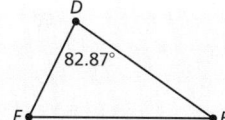

   b. yes; Corresponding angles are congruent.

   c. The triangles are similar in each case.

3. If all three pairs of corresponding side lengths of two triangles are proportional, then the triangles are similar. If an angle of one triangle is congruent to an angle of a second triangle and the lengths of the sides including these angles are proportional, then the triangles are similar.

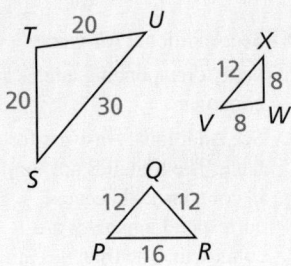
8.3 Lesson

Core Vocabulary

Previous
similar figures
corresponding parts
slope
parallel lines
perpendicular lines

What You Will Learn

▶ Use the Side-Side-Side Similarity Theorem.
▶ Use the Side-Angle-Side Similarity Theorem.
▶ Prove slope criteria using similar triangles.

Using the Side-Side-Side Similarity Theorem

In addition to using congruent corresponding angles to show that two triangles are similar, you can use proportional corresponding side lengths.

🔄 Theorem

Theorem 8.4 Side-Side-Side (SSS) Similarity Theorem

If the corresponding side lengths of two triangles are proportional, then the triangles are similar.

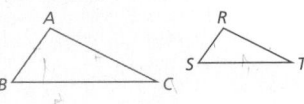

If $\dfrac{AB}{RS} = \dfrac{BC}{ST} = \dfrac{CA}{TR}$, then $\triangle ABC \sim \triangle RST$.

Proof p. 437

EXAMPLE 1 **Using the SSS Similarity Theorem**

Is either $\triangle DEF$ or $\triangle GHJ$ similar to $\triangle ABC$?

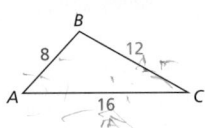 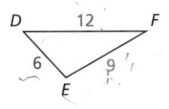 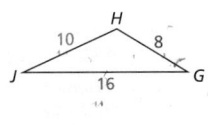

FINDING AN ENTRY POINT

When using the SSS Similarity Theorem, compare the shortest sides, the longest sides, and then the remaining sides.

SOLUTION

Compare $\triangle ABC$ and $\triangle DEF$ by finding ratios of corresponding side lengths.

Shortest sides	Longest sides	Remaining sides
$\dfrac{AB}{DE} = \dfrac{8}{6}$	$\dfrac{CA}{FD} = \dfrac{16}{12}$	$\dfrac{BC}{EF} = \dfrac{12}{9}$
$= \dfrac{4}{3}$	$= \dfrac{4}{3}$	$= \dfrac{4}{3}$

▶ All the ratios are equal, so $\triangle ABC \sim \triangle DEF$.

Compare $\triangle ABC$ and $\triangle GHJ$ by finding ratios of corresponding side lengths.

Shortest sides	Longest sides	Remaining sides
$\dfrac{AB}{GH} = \dfrac{8}{8}$	$\dfrac{CA}{JG} = \dfrac{16}{16}$	$\dfrac{BC}{HJ} = \dfrac{12}{10}$
$= 1$	$= 1$	$= \dfrac{6}{5}$

▶ The ratios are not all equal, so $\triangle ABC$ and $\triangle GHJ$ are not similar.

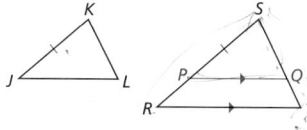 **SSS Similarity Theorem**

Given $\dfrac{RS}{JK} = \dfrac{ST}{KL} = \dfrac{TR}{LJ}$

Prove $\triangle RST \sim \triangle JKL$

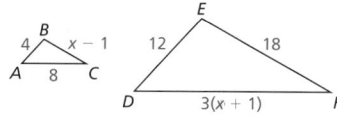

JUSTIFYING STEPS

The Parallel Postulate (Postulate 3.1) allows you to draw an auxiliary line $\overleftrightarrow{PQ}$ in $\triangle RST$. There is only one line through point P parallel to $\overleftrightarrow{RT}$, so you are able to draw it.

Locate P on $\overline{RS}$ so that $PS = JK$. Draw $\overline{PQ}$ so that $\overline{PQ} \parallel \overline{RT}$. Then $\triangle RST \sim \triangle PSQ$ by the AA Similarity Theorem (Theorem 8.3), and $\dfrac{RS}{PS} = \dfrac{ST}{SQ} = \dfrac{TR}{QP}$. You can use the given proportion and the fact that $PS = JK$ to deduce that $SQ = KL$ and $QP = LJ$. By the SSS Congruence Theorem (Theorem 5.8), it follows that $\triangle PSQ \cong \triangle JKL$. Finally, use the definition of congruent triangles and the AA Similarity Theorem (Theorem 8.3) to conclude that $\triangle RST \sim \triangle JKL$.

EXAMPLE 2 **Using the SSS Similarity Theorem**

Find the value of x that makes $\triangle ABC \sim \triangle DEF$.

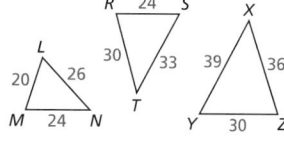

FINDING AN ENTRY POINT

You can use either $\dfrac{AB}{DE} = \dfrac{BC}{EF}$ or $\dfrac{AB}{DE} = \dfrac{AC}{DF}$ in Step 1.

SOLUTION

Step 1 Find the value of x that makes corresponding side lengths proportional.

$$\dfrac{AB}{DE} = \dfrac{BC}{EF} \qquad \text{Write proportion.}$$

$$\dfrac{4}{12} = \dfrac{x-1}{18} \qquad \text{Substitute.}$$

$$4 \cdot 18 = 12(x-1) \qquad \text{Cross Products Property}$$

$$72 = 12x - 12 \qquad \text{Simplify.}$$

$$7 = x \qquad \text{Solve for } x.$$

Step 2 Check that the side lengths are proportional when $x = 7$.

$$BC = x - 1 = 6 \qquad\qquad DF = 3(x+1) = 24$$

$$\dfrac{AB}{DE} \overset{?}{=} \dfrac{BC}{EF} \Rightarrow \dfrac{4}{12} = \dfrac{6}{18} \checkmark \qquad \dfrac{AB}{DE} \overset{?}{=} \dfrac{AC}{DF} \Rightarrow \dfrac{4}{12} = \dfrac{8}{24} \checkmark$$

▶ When $x = 7$, the triangles are similar by the SSS Similarity Theorem.

Monitoring Progress 🔊 Help in English and Spanish at *BigIdeasMath.com*

Use the diagram.

1. Which of the three triangles are similar? Write a similarity statement.

2. The shortest side of a triangle similar to $\triangle RST$ is 12 units long. Find the other side lengths of the triangle.

Extra Example 2
Find the value of x that makes $\triangle XYZ \sim \triangle HJK$.

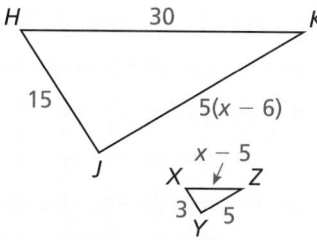

When $x = 11$, the triangles are similar by the SSS Similarity Theorem (Thm. 8.4).

MONITORING PROGRESS ANSWERS
1. $\triangle LMN \sim \triangle YZX$
2. 15, 16.5

Laurie's Notes **Teacher Actions**

- **Turn and Talk:** Have partners read the proof of the SSS Similarity Theorem. "What are the key steps in the proof narrative presented?" Listen for: drawing the auxiliary line so that the overlapping triangles are similar, showing smaller triangles are congruent, and using corresponding parts and the AA Similarity Theorem to show given triangles are similar.
- In Example 2, students may use the orientation of the triangles to set up the proportions. They should confirm with the triangle similarity statement.

Extra Example 3

The diagram is a scale drawing of a triangular roof truss. The lengths of the two upper sides of the actual truss are 18 feet and 40 feet. The actual truss and the scale drawing both have an included angle of 110°. Is the scale drawing of the truss similar to the actual truss? Explain.

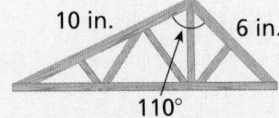

No, the drawing is not similar to the actual truss. Although the measure of the included angles between the sides is 110°, the lengths of the corresponding sides are not proportional: $\frac{10}{40} = \frac{1}{4}$ and $\frac{6}{18} = \frac{1}{3}$.

MONITORING PROGRESS ANSWERS

3. $\angle R \cong \angle N$ and $\frac{SR}{PN} = \frac{RT}{NQ} = \frac{4}{3}$, so $\triangle RST \sim \triangle NPQ$.

4. *Sample answer:* Corresponding side lengths are proportional, so $\triangle XYZ \sim \triangle WXZ$.

Using the Side-Angle-Side Similarity Theorem

 Theorem

Theorem 8.5   Side-Angle-Side (SAS) Similarity Theorem

If an angle of one triangle is congruent to an angle of a second triangle and the lengths of the sides including these angles are proportional, then the triangles are similar.

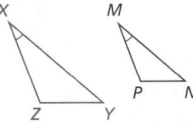

If $\angle X \cong \angle M$ and $\frac{ZX}{PM} = \frac{XY}{MN}$, then $\triangle XYZ \sim \triangle MNP$.

Proof Ex. 33, p. 443

EXAMPLE 3   **Using the SAS Similarity Theorem**

You are building a lean-to shelter starting from a tree branch, as shown. Can you construct the right end so it is similar to the left end using the angle measure and lengths shown?

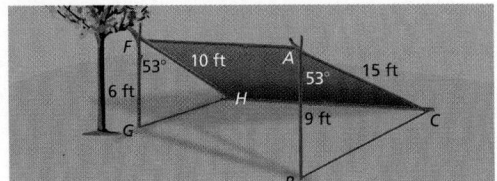

SOLUTION

Both $m\angle A$ and $m\angle F$ equal 53°, so $\angle A \cong \angle F$. Next, compare the ratios of the lengths of the sides that include $\angle A$ and $\angle F$.

Shorter sides

$$\frac{AB}{FG} = \frac{9}{6}$$
$$= \frac{3}{2}$$

Longer sides

$$\frac{AC}{FH} = \frac{15}{10}$$
$$= \frac{3}{2}$$

The lengths of the sides that include $\angle A$ and $\angle F$ are proportional. So, by the SAS Similarity Theorem, $\triangle ABC \sim \triangle FGH$.

▶ Yes, you can make the right end similar to the left end of the shelter.

Monitoring Progress Help in English and Spanish at *BigIdeasMath.com*

Explain how to show that the indicated triangles are similar.

3. $\triangle SRT \sim \triangle PNQ$

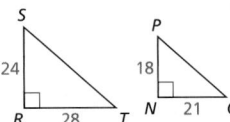

4. $\triangle XZW \sim \triangle YZX$

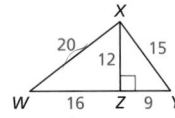

Laurie's Notes   Teacher Actions

- State the SAS Similarity Theorem. Distinguish the differences from the SAS Congruence Theorem.
- **Whiteboarding:** "Sketch a picture to show why there is no SAS Similarity Theorem for quadrilaterals." Use whiteboards to share sketches.
- **Popsicle Sticks:** Pose Example 3, and have partners independently solve the problem. Use *Popsicle Sticks* for steps in the solution.
- **Think-Pair-Share:** Have students answer Questions 3 and 4, and then share and discuss as a class.

Concept Summary

Triangle Similarity Theorems

AA Similarity Theorem

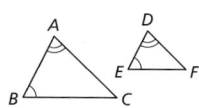

If $\angle A \cong \angle D$ and $\angle B \cong \angle E$, then $\triangle ABC \sim \triangle DEF$.

SSS Similarity Theorem

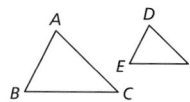

If $\dfrac{AB}{DE} = \dfrac{BC}{EF} = \dfrac{AC}{DF}$, then $\triangle ABC \sim \triangle DEF$.

SAS Similarity Theorem

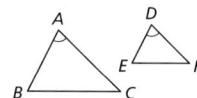

If $\angle A \cong \angle D$ and $\dfrac{AB}{DE} = \dfrac{AC}{DF}$, then $\triangle ABC \sim \triangle DEF$.

Proving Slope Criteria Using Similar Triangles

You can use similar triangles to prove the Slopes of Parallel Lines Theorem (Theorem 3.13). Because the theorem is biconditional, you must prove both parts.

1. If two nonvertical lines are parallel, then they have the same slope.

2. If two nonvertical lines have the same slope, then they are parallel.

The first part is proved below. The second part is proved in the exercises.

PROOF   Part of Slopes of Parallel Lines Theorem (Theorem 3.13)

Given $\ell \parallel n$, ℓ and n are nonvertical.

Prove $m_\ell = m_n$

First, consider the case where ℓ and n are horizontal. Because all horizontal lines are parallel and have a slope of 0, the statement is true for horizontal lines.

For the case of nonhorizontal, nonvertical lines, draw two such parallel lines, ℓ and n, and label their x-intercepts A and D, respectively. Draw a vertical segment $\overline{BC}$ parallel to the y-axis from point B on line ℓ to point C on the x-axis. Draw a vertical segment $\overline{EF}$ parallel to the y-axis from point E on line n to point F on the x-axis. Because vertical and horizontal lines are perpendicular, $\angle BCA$ and $\angle EFD$ are right angles.

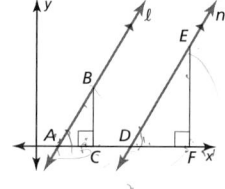

STATEMENTS	REASONS
1. $\ell \parallel n$	1. Given
2. $\angle BAC \cong \angle EDF$	2. Corresponding Angles Theorem (Thm. 3.1)
3. $\angle BCA \cong \angle EFD$	3. Right Angles Congruence Theorem (Thm. 2.3)
4. $\triangle ABC \sim \triangle DEF$	4. AA Similarity Theorem (Thm. 8.3)
5. $\dfrac{BC}{EF} = \dfrac{AC}{DF}$	5. Corresponding sides of similar figures are proportional.
6. $\dfrac{BC}{AC} = \dfrac{EF}{DF}$	6. Rewrite proportion.
7. $m_\ell = \dfrac{BC}{AC}, m_n = \dfrac{EF}{DF}$	7. Definition of slope
8. $m_n = \dfrac{BC}{AC}$	8. Substitution Property of Equality
9. $m_\ell = m_n$	9. Transitive Property of Equality

Laurie's Notes   Teacher Actions

- **Turn and Talk:** Summarize the ways in which you can prove two triangles are similar.
- In Chapter 3, the Slopes of Parallel Lines Theorem (3.13) was stated. One part of the proof is shown here. Students are not expected to replicate the proof, though they should be able to read, understand, and appreciate the reasoning utilized. Ask what remains to be proven.
- **Teaching Tip:** Discuss the construction and provide the statements. Have partners work together to provide the reasons.

To prove the Slopes of Perpendicular Lines Theorem (Theorem 3.14), you must prove both parts.

1. If two nonvertical lines are perpendicular, then the product of their slopes is -1.

2. If the product of the slopes of two nonvertical lines is -1, then the lines are perpendicular.

The first part is proved below. The second part is proved in the exercises.

PROOF **Part of Slopes of Perpendicular Lines Theorem (Theorem 3.14)**

Given $\ell \perp n$, ℓ and n are nonvertical.

Prove $m_\ell m_n = -1$

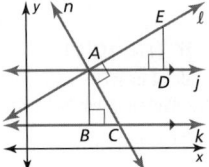

Draw two nonvertical, perpendicular lines, ℓ and n, that intersect at point A. Draw a horizontal line j parallel to the x-axis through point A. Draw a horizontal line k parallel to the x-axis through point C on line n. Because horizontal lines are parallel, $j \parallel k$. Draw a vertical segment $\overline{AB}$ parallel to the y-axis from point A to point B on line k. Draw a vertical segment $\overline{ED}$ parallel to the y-axis from point E on line ℓ to point D on line j. Because horizontal and vertical lines are perpendicular, $\angle ABC$ and $\angle ADE$ are right angles.

STATEMENTS	REASONS
1. $\ell \perp n$	1. Given
2. $m\angle CAE = 90°$	2. $\ell \perp n$
3. $m\angle CAE = m\angle DAE + m\angle CAD$	3. Angle Addition Postulate (Post. 1.4)
4. $m\angle DAE + m\angle CAD = 90°$	4. Transitive Property of Equality
5. $\angle BCA \cong \angle CAD$	5. Alternate Interior Angles Theorem (Thm. 3.2)
6. $m\angle BCA = m\angle CAD$	6. Definition of congruent angles
7. $m\angle DAE + m\angle BCA = 90°$	7. Substitution Property of Equality
8. $m\angle DAE = 90° - m\angle BCA$	8. Solve statement 7 for $m\angle DAE$.
9. $m\angle BCA + m\angle BAC + 90° = 180°$	9. Triangle Sum Theorem (Thm. 5.1)
10. $m\angle BAC = 90° - m\angle BCA$	10. Solve statement 9 for $m\angle BAC$.
11. $m\angle DAE = m\angle BAC$	11. Transitive Property of Equality
12. $\angle DAE \cong \angle BAC$	12. Definition of congruent angles
13. $\angle ABC \cong \angle ADE$	13. Right Angles Congruence Theorem (Thm. 2.3)
14. $\triangle ABC \sim \triangle ADE$	14. AA Similarity Theorem (Thm. 8.3)
15. $\dfrac{AD}{AB} = \dfrac{DE}{BC}$	15. Corresponding sides of similar figures are proportional.
16. $\dfrac{AD}{DE} = \dfrac{AB}{BC}$	16. Rewrite proportion.
17. $m_\ell = \dfrac{DE}{AD}, m_n = -\dfrac{AB}{BC}$	17. Definition of slope
18. $m_\ell m_n = \dfrac{DE}{AD} \cdot \left(-\dfrac{AB}{BC}\right)$	18. Substitution Property of Equality
19. $m_\ell m_n = \dfrac{DE}{AD} \cdot \left(-\dfrac{AD}{DE}\right)$	19. Substitution Property of Equality
20. $m_\ell m_n = -1$	20. Simplify.

Laurie's Notes   Teacher Actions

- Use a similar procedure with this proof as the previous proof on page 439. Discuss the construction and provide the statements. Partners provide the reasons.
- **Three-Minute Pause:** Pause three minutes for students to confer with partners or in small groups. Have them discuss the last two proofs. Why were they constructed in the coordinate plane? How were auxiliary lines used? Was the order of the steps in the proofs unique?

Closure

- **Exit Ticket:** Draw a triangle with sides of 7 centimeters and 10 centimeters and an included angle of 42°. Draw and label a similar triangle with a side of 15 centimeters. Answers will vary. Check students' work.

Vocabulary and Core Concept Check

1. **COMPLETE THE SENTENCE** You plan to show that $\triangle QRS$ is similar to $\triangle XYZ$ by the SSS Similarity Theorem (Theorem 8.4). Copy and complete the proportion that you will use: $\dfrac{QR}{\boxed{}} = \dfrac{\boxed{}}{YZ} = \dfrac{QS}{\boxed{}}$.

2. **WHICH ONE DOESN'T BELONG?** Which triangle does *not* belong with the other three? Explain your reasoning.

 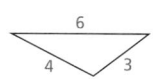  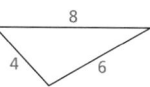

Monitoring Progress and Modeling with Mathematics

In Exercises 3 and 4, determine whether $\triangle JKL$ or $\triangle RST$ is similar to $\triangle ABC$. *(See Example 1.)*

3.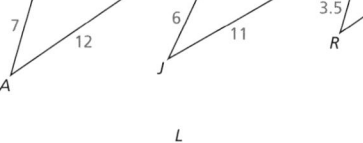

4.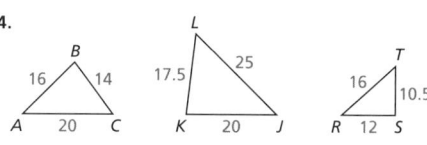

In Exercises 5 and 6, find the value of x that makes $\triangle DEF \sim \triangle XYZ$. *(See Example 2.)*

5.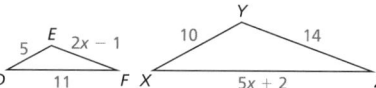

6.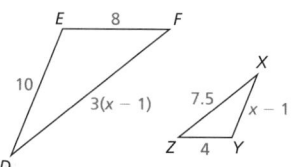

In Exercises 7 and 8, verify that $\triangle ABC \sim \triangle DEF$. Find the scale factor of $\triangle ABC$ to $\triangle DEF$.

7. $\triangle ABC$: $BC = 18$, $AB = 15$, $AC = 12$
   $\triangle DEF$: $EF = 12$, $DE = 10$, $DF = 8$

8. $\triangle ABC$: $AB = 10$, $BC = 16$, $CA = 20$
   $\triangle DEF$: $DE = 25$, $EF = 40$, $FD = 50$

In Exercises 9 and 10, determine whether the two triangles are similar. If they are similar, write a similarity statement and find the scale factor of triangle B to triangle A. *(See Example 3.)*

9.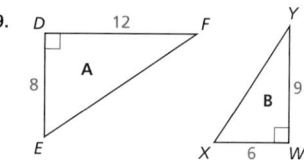

10.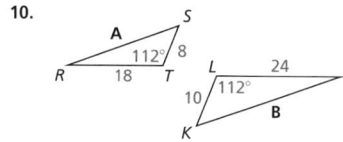

In Exercises 11 and 12, sketch the triangles using the given description. Then determine whether the two triangles can be similar.

11. In $\triangle RST$, $RS = 20$, $ST = 32$, and $m\angle S = 16°$. In $\triangle FGH$, $GH = 30$, $HF = 48$, and $m\angle H = 24°$.

12. The side lengths of $\triangle ABC$ are 24, $8x$, and 48, and the side lengths of $\triangle DEF$ are 15, 25, and $6x$.

Section 8.3   Proving Triangle Similarity by SSS and SAS   **441**

Assignment Guide and Homework Check

ASSIGNMENT

Basic: 1, 2, 3–19 odd, 27, 36, 43–45

Average: 1, 2–18 even, 19, 22–26 even, 27, 28, 30, 36, 40, 43–45

Advanced: 1, 2–18 even, 19, 20–26 even, 27, 29, 32–38 even, 42–45

HOMEWORK CHECK

Basic: 3, 5, 9, 15, 36

Average: 6, 10, 14, 18, 36

Advanced: 6, 12, 19, 20, 36

ANSWERS

1. $\dfrac{QR}{XY} = \dfrac{RS}{YZ} = \dfrac{QS}{XZ}$

2. The triangle with side lengths 4, 6, and 8 does not belong because the other three are similar by the SSS Similarity Theorem (Thm. 8.4).

3. $\triangle RST$

4. $\triangle JKL$

5. $x = 4$

6. $x = 6$

7. $\dfrac{12}{18} = \dfrac{10}{15} = \dfrac{8}{12} = \dfrac{2}{3}$

8. $\dfrac{25}{10} = \dfrac{40}{16} = \dfrac{50}{20} = \dfrac{5}{2}$

9. similar; $\triangle DEF \sim \triangle WXY$; $\dfrac{4}{3}$

10. not similar

11.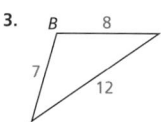

no

12.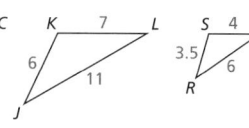

yes

ANSWERS

13. $\dfrac{HG}{HF} = \dfrac{HJ}{HK} = \dfrac{GJ}{FK}$, so $\triangle GHJ \sim \triangle FHK$.

14. $\angle ACB \cong \angle DCE$ and $\dfrac{CE}{CB} = \dfrac{DC}{AC}$, so $\triangle ABC \sim \triangle DEC$.

15. $\angle X \cong \angle D$ and $\dfrac{XY}{DJ} = \dfrac{XZ}{DG}$, so $\triangle XYZ \sim \triangle DJG$.

16. $\dfrac{RS}{UV} = \dfrac{RQ}{UT} = \dfrac{QS}{TV}$, so $\triangle QRS \sim \triangle TUV$.

17. 24, 26

18. 30, 36

19. Because $\overline{AB}$ corresponds to $\overline{RQ}$ and $\overline{BC}$ corresponds to $\overline{QP}$, the proportionality statement should be $\triangle ABC \sim \triangle RQP$.

20. $n = 3$

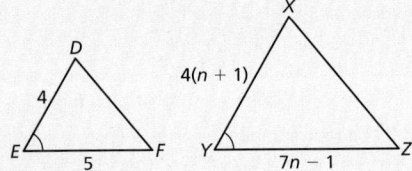

21. 61°

22. 89°

23. 30°

24. 7

25. 91°

26. 44.5°

27. no; The included angles are not congruent.

28. the pieces with side lengths of 5.25 inches and 7 inches

29. D; $\angle M \cong \angle M$, so $\triangle MNP \sim \triangle MRQ$ by the SAS Similarity Theorem (Thm. 8.5).

30. not necessarily; The acute angles might not be congruent.

In Exercises 13–16, show that the triangles are similar and write a similarity statement. Explain your reasoning.

13.
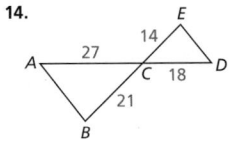

14.
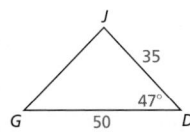

15.
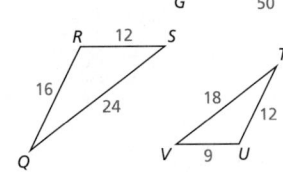

16.
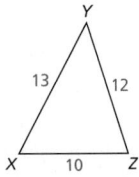

In Exercises 17 and 18, use $\triangle XYZ$.

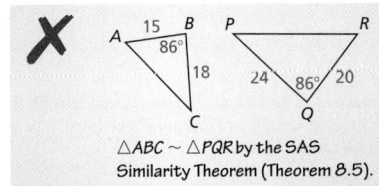

17. The shortest side of a triangle similar to $\triangle XYZ$ is 20 units long. Find the other side lengths of the triangle.

18. The longest side of a triangle similar to $\triangle XYZ$ is 39 units long. Find the other side lengths of the triangle.

19. **ERROR ANALYSIS** Describe and correct the error in writing a similarity statement.

> $\triangle ABC \sim \triangle PQR$ by the SAS Similarity Theorem (Theorem 8.5).

20. **MATHEMATICAL CONNECTIONS** Find the value of n that makes $\triangle DEF \sim \triangle XYZ$ when $DE = 4$, $EF = 5$, $XY = 4(n + 1)$, $YZ = 7n - 1$, and $\angle E \cong \angle Y$. Include a sketch.

ATTENDING TO PRECISION In Exercises 21–26, use the diagram to copy and complete the statement.

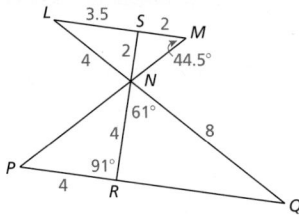

21. $m\angle LNS = $ ▭   22. $m\angle NRQ = $ ▭

23. $m\angle NQR = $ ▭   24. $RQ = $ ▭

25. $m\angle NSM = $ ▭   26. $m\angle NPR = $ ▭

27. **MAKING AN ARGUMENT** Your friend claims that $\triangle JKL \sim \triangle MNO$ by the SAS Similarity Theorem (Theorem 8.5) when $JK = 18$, $m\angle K = 130°$, $KL = 16$, $MN = 9$, $m\angle N = 65°$, and $NO = 8$. Do you support your friend's claim? Explain your reasoning.

28. **ANALYZING RELATIONSHIPS** Certain sections of stained glass are sold in triangular, beveled pieces. Which of the three beveled pieces, if any, are similar?

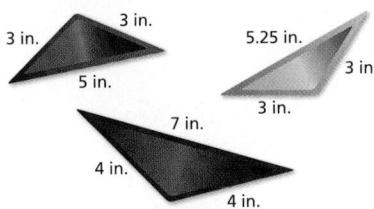

29. **ATTENDING TO PRECISION** In the diagram, $\dfrac{MN}{MR} = \dfrac{MP}{MQ}$. Which of the statements must be true? Select all that apply. Explain your reasoning.

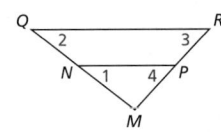

(A) $\angle 1 \cong \angle 2$ (B) $\overline{QR} \parallel \overline{NP}$

(C) $\angle 1 \cong \angle 4$ (D) $\triangle MNP \sim \triangle MRQ$

30. **WRITING** Are any two right triangles similar? Explain.

31. MODELING WITH MATHEMATICS In the portion of the shuffleboard court shown, $\dfrac{BC}{AC} = \dfrac{BD}{AE}$.

a. What additional information do you need to show that $\triangle BCD \sim \triangle ACE$ using the SSS Similarity Theorem (Theorem 8.4)?

b. What additional information do you need to show that $\triangle BCD \sim \triangle ACE$ using the SAS Similarity Theorem (Theorem 8.5)?

32. PROOF Given that $\triangle BAC$ is a right triangle and D, E, and F are midpoints, prove that $m\angle DEF = 90°$.

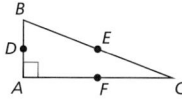

33. PROVING A THEOREM Write a two-column proof of the SAS Similarity Theorem (Theorem 8.5).

Given $\angle A \cong \angle D$, $\dfrac{AB}{DE} = \dfrac{AC}{DF}$

Prove $\triangle ABC \sim \triangle DEF$

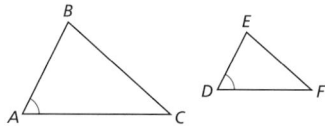

34. CRITICAL THINKING You are given two right triangles with one pair of corresponding legs and the pair of hypotenuses having the same length ratios.

a. The lengths of the given pair of corresponding legs are 6 and 18, and the lengths of the hypotenuses are 10 and 30. Use the Pythagorean Theorem to find the lengths of the other pair of corresponding legs. Draw a diagram.

b. Write the ratio of the lengths of the second pair of corresponding legs.

c. Are these triangles similar? Does this suggest a Hypotenuse-Leg Similarity Theorem for right triangles? Explain.

35. WRITING Can two triangles have all three ratios of corresponding angle measures equal to a value greater than 1? less than 1? Explain.

36. HOW DO YOU SEE IT? Which theorem could you use to show that $\triangle OPQ \sim \triangle OMN$ in the portion of the Ferris wheel shown when $PM = QN = 5$ feet and $MO = NO = 10$ feet?

37. DRAWING CONCLUSIONS Explain why it is not necessary to have an Angle-Side-Angle Similarity Theorem.

38. THOUGHT PROVOKING Decide whether each is a valid method of showing that two quadrilaterals are similar. Justify your answer.

a. SASA   b. SASAS   c. SSSS   d. SASSS

39. MULTIPLE REPRESENTATIONS Use a diagram to show why there is no Side-Side-Angle Similarity Theorem.

40. MODELING WITH MATHEMATICS The dimensions of an actual swing set are shown. You want to create a scale model of the swing set for a dollhouse using similar triangles. Sketch a drawing of your swing set and label each side length. Write a similarity statement for each pair of similar triangles. State the scale factor you used to create the scale model.

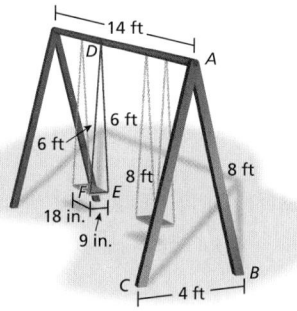

ANSWERS

31. a. $\dfrac{CD}{CE} = \dfrac{BC}{AC}$

b. $\angle CBD \cong \angle CAE$

32. $EF = \dfrac{1}{2}BA$, $DE = \dfrac{1}{2}AC$, and $DF = \dfrac{1}{2}BC$ by the Triangle Midsegment Theorem (Thm. 6.8). So, $\dfrac{EF}{BA} = \dfrac{DE}{AC} = \dfrac{DF}{BC} = \dfrac{1}{2}$, and $\triangle DEF \sim \triangle CAB$. Because corresponding angles of similar figures are congruent, $m\angle CAB = m\angle DEF = 90°$.

33. See Additional Answers.

34. a. 8, 24

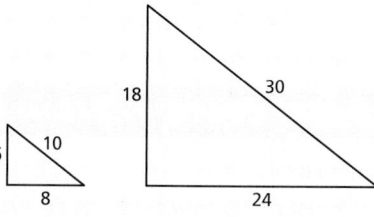

b. $\dfrac{1}{3}$

c. yes; yes; The other legs will also be proportional by the Pythagorean Theorem.

35. no; no; The sum of the angle measures would not be 180°.

36. SAS Similarity Theorem (Thm. 8.5)

37. If two angles are congruent, then the triangles are similar by the AA Similarity Theorem (Thm. 8.3).

38. a. no; Two right trapezoids can have proportional heights and lengths of one base and not be similar.

b. yes; The fourth pair of sides must be proportional, and the angles must be congruent.

c. no; The angles might not be congruent.

d. no; Two kites can have proportional sides and one pair of congruent angles but not be similar.

39–40. See Additional Answers.

41. the Substitution Property of Equality; $\dfrac{BC}{EF} = \dfrac{AC}{DF}$;

$\angle ACB \cong \angle DFE$; SAS Similarity Theorem (Thm. 8.5); Corresponding Angles Converse (Thm. 3.5)

42. See Additional Answers.

43. $P(0, 3)$

44. $P(0, -4)$

45. $P(5, 6)$

Mini-Assessment

1. Determine whether $\triangle FGH$ or $\triangle JKL$ is similar to $\triangle CDE$.

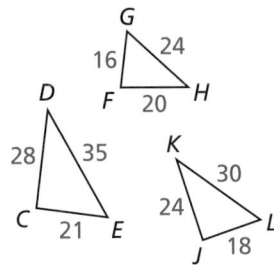

$\triangle JKL \sim \triangle CDE$; $\triangle FGH$ is not similar to $\triangle CDE$.

2. Find the value of x that makes $\triangle MNP \sim \triangle QRS$.

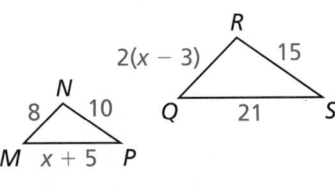

$x = 9$

3. Determine whether the triangles are similar. If they are, find the scale factor of $\triangle GHJ$ to $\triangle KLM$.

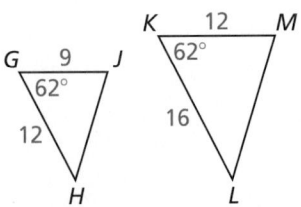

The triangles are similar by the SAS Similarity Theorem (Thm. 8.5); the scale factor is $\dfrac{3}{4}$.

---

41. PROVING A THEOREM Copy and complete the paragraph proof of the second part of the Slopes of Parallel Lines Theorem (Theorem 3.13) from page 439.

Given $m_\ell = m_n$, ℓ and n are nonvertical.

Prove $\ell \parallel n$

You are given that $m_\ell = m_n$. By the definition of slope, $m_\ell = \dfrac{BC}{AC}$ and $m_n = \dfrac{EF}{DF}$. By _____, $\dfrac{BC}{AC} = \dfrac{EF}{DF}$. Rewriting this proportion yields _____. By the Right Angles Congruence Theorem (Thm. 2.3), _____. So, $\triangle ABC \sim \triangle DEF$ by _____. Because corresponding angles of similar triangles are congruent, $\angle BAC \cong \angle EDF$. By _____, $\ell \parallel n$.

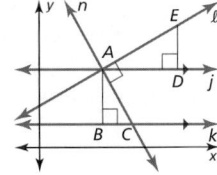

42. PROVING A THEOREM Copy and complete the two-column proof of the second part of the Slopes of Perpendicular Lines Theorem (Theorem 3.14) from page 440.

Given $m_\ell m_n = -1$, ℓ and n are nonvertical.

Prove $\ell \perp n$

STATEMENTS	REASONS
1. $m_\ell m_n = -1$	**1.** Given
2. $m_\ell = \dfrac{DE}{AD}, m_n = -\dfrac{AB}{BC}$	**2.** Definition of slope
3. $\dfrac{DE}{AD} \cdot -\dfrac{AB}{BC} = -1$	**3.** _____
4. $\dfrac{DE}{AD} = \dfrac{BC}{AB}$	**4.** Multiply each side of statement 3 by $-\dfrac{BC}{AB}$.
5. $\dfrac{DE}{BC} = $ ___	**5.** Rewrite proportion.
6. _____	**6.** Right Angles Congruence Theorem (Thm. 2.3)
7. $\triangle ABC \sim \triangle ADE$	**7.** _____
8. $\angle BAC \cong \angle DAE$	**8.** Corresponding angles of similar figures are congruent.
9. $\angle BCA \cong \angle CAD$	**9.** Alternate Interior Angles Theorem (Thm. 3.2)
10. $m\angle BAC = m\angle DAE, m\angle BCA = m\angle CAD$	**10.** _____
11. $m\angle BAC + m\angle BCA + 90° = 180°$	**11.** _____
12. _____	**12.** Subtraction Property of Equality
13. $m\angle CAD + m\angle DAE = 90°$	**13.** Substitution Property of Equality
14. $m\angle CAE = m\angle DAE + m\angle CAD$	**14.** Angle Addition Postulate (Post. 1.4)
15. $m\angle CAE = 90°$	**15.** _____
16. _____	**16.** Definition of perpendicular lines

Maintaining Mathematical Proficiency
Reviewing what you learned in previous grades and lessons

Find the coordinates of point P along the directed line segment AB so that AP to PB is the given ratio.
(Section 3.5)

43. $A(-3, 6), B(2, 1)$; 3 to 2 **44.** $A(-3, -5), B(9, -1)$; 1 to 3 **45.** $A(1, -2), B(8, 12)$; 4 to 3

If students need help...	If students got it...
Resources by Chapter • Practice A and Practice B • Puzzle Time	Resources by Chapter • Enrichment and Extension • Cumulative Review
Student Journal • Practice	Start the *next* Section
Differentiating the Lesson Skills Review Handbook	

Overview of Section 8.4

Introduction
- Students will use their knowledge of solving proportions in this lesson.
- Four theorems are presented in this lesson, all involving proportions. The Triangle Proportionality Theorem and its converse involve a segment parallel to a side of a triangle. As noted in the *Teaching Strategy* below, there are different but equivalent ways in which the proportions can be written.
- Two additional proportionality theorems are also presented and used to solve problems.

Teaching Strategy
- **Proportional Triangles:** Given a proportion, students should be familiar with different but equivalent ways in which the proportion can be written.
- Use the sketch from the Triangle Proportionality Theorem. The conclusion of the theorem states that $\dfrac{RT}{TQ} = \dfrac{RU}{US}$.

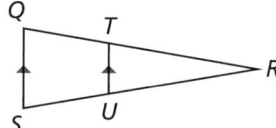

- Discuss with students additional and equivalent proportions.

$$\frac{RT}{TQ} = \frac{RU}{US} \rightarrow \frac{RT}{RU} = \frac{TQ}{US} \rightarrow \frac{RT}{RQ} = \frac{RU}{RS}$$

- Being comfortable with multiple ways in which a proportion can be correctly written to represent a situation will help students get started in solving the problem.

Pacing Suggestion
- The explorations provide an opportunity for students to investigate and make sense of two theorems in the formal lesson. Transition to the formal lesson as soon as students have discussed the explorations.

Laurie's Notes

Exploration

Motivate

- Display a street map, as shown, with parallel city streets that are intersected by nonparallel streets.

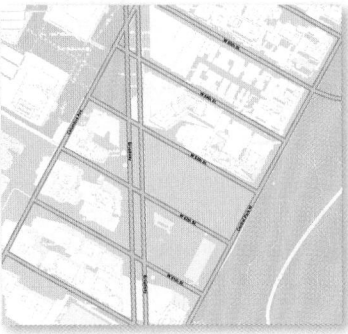

- Have students describe the orientations of the various streets. Explain to students that in this lesson they will look at proportional segments found in triangles.

Exploration 1

- This exploration can be constructed quickly using dynamic geometry software. It can then be explored dynamically, providing numerous cases to compare.
- Be sure that students explore multiple locations of the parallel segment within one triangle, followed by trials with different triangles. Students should not shy away from special cases such as right, equilateral, and obtuse triangles.
- **?** "What do you observe when you construct a segment parallel to one side of a triangle that intersects the other two sides?" The segment divides the other two sides proportionally.

Exploration 2

- Again, the results of this construction can be explored on multiple triangles utilizing the dynamic nature of the software. Be sure that students try special triangles such as right, equilateral, and obtuse triangles.
- **?** "What do you observe when you construct the angle bisector of one angle of a triangle and it intersects the opposite side of the triangle?" The angle bisector divides the opposite side into two segments whose lengths are proportional to the lengths of the other two sides.

Communicate Your Answer

- **Turn and Talk:** Have partners discuss the questions together before sharing as a class.

Connecting to Next Step

- Two of the four theorems in this lesson are investigated in these explorations. Refer to the explorations when stating the theorems.

8.4 Proportionality Theorems

Essential Question What proportionality relationships exist in a triangle intersected by an angle bisector or by a line parallel to one of the sides?

EXPLORATION 1 Discovering a Proportionality Relationship

Work with a partner. Use dynamic geometry software to draw any $\triangle ABC$.

a. Construct $\overline{DE}$ parallel to $\overline{BC}$ with endpoints on $\overline{AB}$ and $\overline{AC}$, respectively.

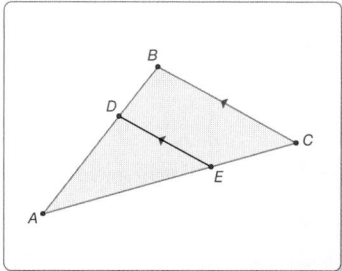

LOOKING FOR STRUCTURE

To be proficient in math, you need to look closely to discern a pattern or structure.

b. Compare the ratios of AD to BD and AE to CE.

c. Move $\overline{DE}$ to other locations parallel to $\overline{BC}$ with endpoints on $\overline{AB}$ and $\overline{AC}$, and repeat part (b).

d. Change $\triangle ABC$ and repeat parts (a)–(c) several times. Write a conjecture that summarizes your results.

EXPLORATION 2 Discovering a Proportionality Relationship

Work with a partner. Use dynamic geometry software to draw any $\triangle ABC$.

a. Bisect $\angle B$ and plot point D at the intersection of the angle bisector and $\overline{AC}$.

b. Compare the ratios of AD to DC and BA to BC.

c. Change $\triangle ABC$ and repeat parts (a) and (b) several times. Write a conjecture that summarizes your results.

Communicate Your Answer

3. What proportionality relationships exist in a triangle intersected by an angle bisector or by a line parallel to one of the sides?

4. Use the figure at the right to write a proportion.

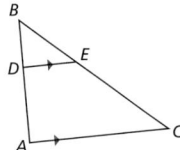

ANSWERS

1. a. Check students' work.

   b. $\dfrac{AD}{BD} = \dfrac{AE}{CE}$

   c. Check students' work; $\dfrac{AD}{BD} = \dfrac{AE}{CE}$

   d. Check students' work; If $\overline{DE} \parallel \overline{AC}$ in $\triangle ABC$, then $\dfrac{AD}{BD} = \dfrac{AE}{CE}$.

2. a. Check students' work.

   b. $\dfrac{AD}{DC} = \dfrac{BA}{BC}$

   c. Check students' work; If $\overline{BD}$ bisects $\angle B$ in $\triangle ABC$, $\dfrac{AD}{DC} = \dfrac{BA}{BC}$.

3. If a ray bisects an angle of a triangle, then the opposite segments are proportional to the lengths of the other two sides. If a line parallel to one side of a triangle intersects the other two sides, then it divides the two sides proportionally.

4. $\dfrac{BD}{DA} = \dfrac{BE}{EC}$

Extra Example 1

In the diagram, $\overline{WZ} \parallel \overline{XY}$, $WX = 12$, $VZ = 10$, and $ZY = 8$. What is the length of $\overline{VW}$?

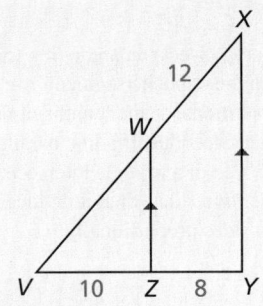

The length of $\overline{VW}$ is 15 units.

MONITORING PROGRESS ANSWER

1. $\frac{315}{11}$

Core Vocabulary

Previous
corresponding angles
ratio
proportion

What You Will Learn

▶ Use the Triangle Proportionality Theorem and its converse.
▶ Use other proportionality theorems.

Using the Triangle Proportionality Theorem

🔄 Theorems

Theorem 8.6   Triangle Proportionality Theorem

If a line parallel to one side of a triangle intersects the other two sides, then it divides the two sides proportionally.

Proof Ex. 27, p. 451

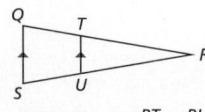

If $\overline{TU} \parallel \overline{QS}$, then $\frac{RT}{TQ} = \frac{RU}{US}$.

Theorem 8.7   Converse of the Triangle Proportionality Theorem

If a line divides two sides of a triangle proportionally, then it is parallel to the third side.

Proof Ex. 28, p. 451

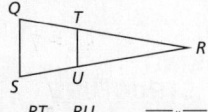

If $\frac{RT}{TQ} = \frac{RU}{US}$, then $\overline{TU} \parallel \overline{QS}$.

EXAMPLE 1   Finding the Length of a Segment

In the diagram, $\overline{QS} \parallel \overline{UT}$, $RS = 4$, $ST = 6$, and $QU = 9$. What is the length of $\overline{RQ}$?

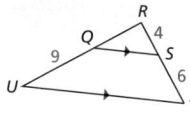

SOLUTION

$\dfrac{RQ}{QU} = \dfrac{RS}{ST}$ Triangle Proportionality Theorem

$\dfrac{RQ}{9} = \dfrac{4}{6}$ Substitute.

$RQ = 6$ Multiply each side by 9 and simplify.

▶ The length of $\overline{RQ}$ is 6 units.

Monitoring Progress Help in English and Spanish at *BigIdeasMath.com*

1. Find the length of $\overline{YZ}$.

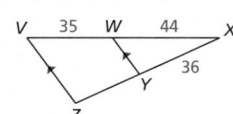

Laurie's Notes   Teacher Actions

- State the Triangle Proportionality Theorem and its converse.
- **Turn and Talk:** "How would you prove these theorems?" Give *Wait Time* and then solicit thoughts from students. They should be gaining confidence in their ability to prove statements.
- Pose Example 1. Have partners work to solve. Share not only the solution, but also the original proportion.
- **MP3 Construct Viable Arguments and Critique the Reasoning of Others:** Discuss the equivalent proportions that students likely used. See the *Teaching Strategy* on page T-444.

The theorems on the previous page also imply the following:

Contrapositive of the Triangle Proportionality Theorem

If $\dfrac{RT}{TQ} \neq \dfrac{RU}{US}$, then $\overline{TU} \nparallel \overline{QS}$.

Inverse of the Triangle Proportionality Theorem

If $\overline{TU} \nparallel \overline{QS}$, then $\dfrac{RT}{TQ} \neq \dfrac{RU}{US}$.

EXAMPLE 2 Solving a Real-Life Problem

On the shoe rack shown, $BA = 33$ centimeters, $CB = 27$ centimeters, $CD = 44$ centimeters, and $DE = 25$ centimeters. Explain why the shelf is not parallel to the floor.

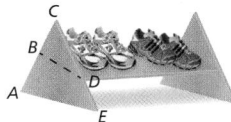

SOLUTION

Find and simplify the ratios of the lengths.

$$\frac{CD}{DE} = \frac{44}{25} \qquad \frac{CB}{BA} = \frac{27}{33} = \frac{9}{11}$$

▶ Because $\dfrac{44}{25} \neq \dfrac{9}{11}$, $\overline{BD}$ is not parallel to $\overline{AE}$. So, the shelf is not parallel to the floor.

Monitoring Progress Help in English and Spanish at *BigIdeasMath.com*

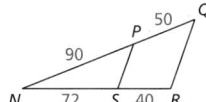

2. Determine whether $\overline{PS} \parallel \overline{QR}$.

Recall that you partitioned a directed line segment in the coordinate plane in Section 3.5. You can apply the Triangle Proportionality Theorem to construct a point along a directed line segment that partitions the segment in a given ratio.

CONSTRUCTION Constructing a Point along a Directed Line Segment

Construct the point L on $\overline{AB}$ so that the ratio of AL to LB is 3 to 1.

SOLUTION

Step 1

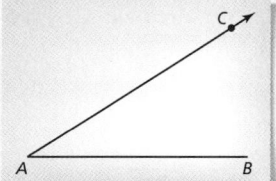

Draw a segment and a ray
Draw $\overline{AB}$ of any length. Choose any point C not on $\overline{AB}$. Draw $\overrightarrow{AC}$.

Step 2

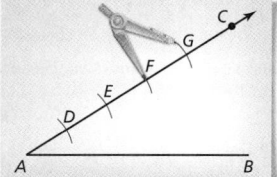

Draw arcs Place the point of a compass at A and make an arc of any radius intersecting $\overrightarrow{AC}$. Label the point of intersection D. Using the same compass setting, make three more arcs on $\overrightarrow{AC}$, as shown. Label the points of intersection E, F, and G and note that $AD = DE = EF = FG$.

Step 3

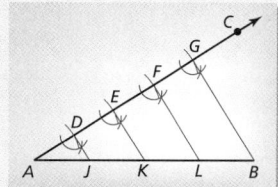

Draw a segment Draw $\overline{GB}$. Copy $\angle AGB$ and construct congruent angles at D, E, and F with sides that intersect $\overline{AB}$ at J, K, and L. Sides $\overline{DJ}$, $\overline{EK}$, and $\overline{FL}$ are all parallel, and they divide $\overline{AB}$ equally. So, $AJ = JK = KL = LB$. Point L divides directed line segment AB in the ratio 3 to 1.

Extra Example 2
Use the diagram in Example 2.
$BA = 35$ centimeters,
$CB = 25$ centimeters,
$CD = 20$ centimeters, and
$DE = 28$ centimeters. Explain why the shelf is parallel to the floor.

The ratios of the corresponding lengths are $\dfrac{CD}{DE} = \dfrac{20}{28} = \dfrac{5}{7}$ and $\dfrac{CB}{BA} = \dfrac{25}{35} = \dfrac{5}{7}$.

Because $\dfrac{5}{7} = \dfrac{5}{7}$, $\overline{BD} \parallel \overline{AE}$ by the Converse of the Triangle Proportionality Theorem (Thm. 8.7). So, the shelf is parallel to the floor.

MONITORING PROGRESS ANSWER

2. yes

Laurie's Notes **Teacher Actions**

• State the contrapositive of each theorem, and have students discuss with their partners whether these statements are valid.
• **Common Misconception:** Note that the ratio $\frac{27}{33}$ is simplified before being used in the proportion, which is mathematically correct.
? Have students perform the construction as shown. "Why are $\overline{DJ}$, $\overline{EK}$, and $\overline{FL}$ parallel?"
  Corresponding angles are congruent, so the lines are parallel.
? "Are there other methods you could use to construct a series of parallel segments?" Answers will vary.

Differentiated Instruction

Visual

Have students color-code their diagrams when solving problems involving proportions. In Example 3, for instance, students can color the line segments and use the same colors when setting up a proportion involving the lengths of the colored segments.

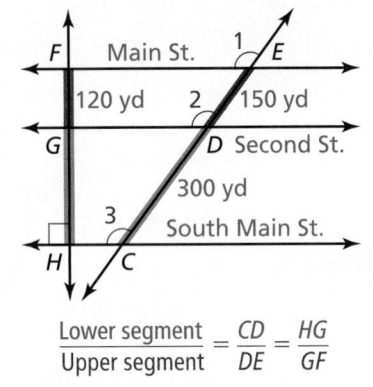

$$\frac{\text{Lower segment}}{\text{Upper segment}} = \frac{CD}{DE} = \frac{HG}{GF}$$

Extra Example 3

In the diagram, $\angle ADE$, $\angle BEF$, and $\angle CFG$ are all congruent. $AB = 30$, $BC = 12$, and $DE = 35$. Find DF.

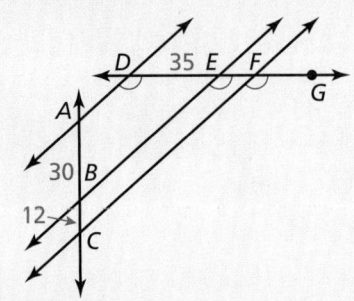

$DF = 49$ units

(handwritten work)

$\frac{120}{X}$ $\frac{150}{300}$

$X \times 300$
$120 \quad 150$

$36000 = 150x$
$\overline{150} \qquad \overline{150}$

$\boxed{240 = X}$

Using Other Proportionality Theorems

Theorem

Theorem 8.8   Three Parallel Lines Theorem

If three parallel lines intersect two transversals, then they divide the transversals proportionally.

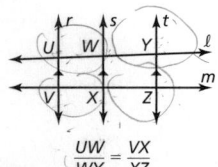

Proof Ex. 32, p. 451

$$\frac{UW}{WY} = \frac{VX}{XZ}$$

EXAMPLE 3   Using the Three Parallel Lines Theorem

In the diagram, $\angle 1$, $\angle 2$, and $\angle 3$ are all congruent, $GF = 120$ yards, $DE = 150$ yards, and $CD = 300$ yards. Find the distance HF between Main Street and South Main Street.

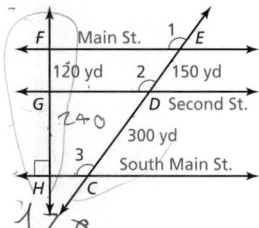

SOLUTION

Corresponding angles are congruent, so $\overleftrightarrow{FE}$, $\overleftrightarrow{GD}$, and $\overleftrightarrow{HC}$ are parallel. There are different ways you can write a proportion to find HG.

Method 1   Use the Three Parallel Lines Theorem to set up a proportion.

$$\frac{HG}{GF} = \frac{CD}{DE} \qquad \text{Three Parallel Lines Theorem}$$

$$\frac{HG}{120} = \frac{300}{150} \qquad \text{Substitute.}$$

$$HG = 240 \qquad \text{Multiply each side by 120 and simplify.}$$

By the Segment Addition Postulate (Postulate 1.2), $HF = HG + GF = 240 + 120 = 360$.

▶ The distance between Main Street and South Main Street is 360 yards.

Method 2   Set up a proportion involving total and partial distances.

Step 1   Make a table to compare the distances.

	$\overleftrightarrow{CE}$	$\overleftrightarrow{HF}$
Total distance	$CE = 300 + 150 = 450$	HF
Partial distance	$DE = 150$	$GF = 120$

Step 2   Write and solve a proportion.

$$\frac{450}{150} = \frac{HF}{120} \qquad \text{Write proportion.}$$

$$360 = HF \qquad \text{Multiply each side by 120 and simplify.}$$

▶ The distance between Main Street and South Main Street is 360 yards.

Laurie's Notes   Teacher Actions

- **Teaching Tip:** Using lined paper, have students trace any three of the lines on the paper. Use a straightedge to draw two lines that intersect the three parallel lines. Use this model to discuss the Three Parallel Lines Theorem.
- Pose Example 3. Use whiteboards and give partners time to solve the problem. Circulate and observe methods of solution. Solicit solutions from multiple students, assuring that more than one method will be demonstrated. Discuss.

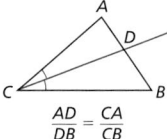 Theorem

Theorem 8.9 Triangle Angle Bisector Theorem

If a ray bisects an angle of a triangle, then it divides the opposite side into segments whose lengths are proportional to the lengths of the other two sides.

Proof Ex. 35, p. 452

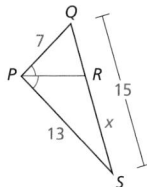

$$\frac{AD}{DB} = \frac{CA}{CB}$$

EXAMPLE 4 **Using the Triangle Angle Bisector Theorem**

In the diagram, $\angle QPR \cong \angle RPS$. Use the given side lengths to find the length of $\overline{RS}$.

SOLUTION

Because $\overrightarrow{PR}$ is an angle bisector of $\angle QPS$, you can apply the Triangle Angle Bisector Theorem. Let $RS = x$. Then $RQ = 15 - x$.

$\dfrac{RQ}{RS} = \dfrac{PQ}{PS}$	Triangle Angle Bisector Theorem
$\dfrac{15 - x}{x} = \dfrac{7}{13}$	Substitute.
$195 - 13x = 7x$	Cross Products Property
$9.75 = x$	Solve for x.

▶ The length of $\overline{RS}$ is 9.75 units.

Monitoring Progress Help in English and Spanish at *BigIdeasMath.com*

Find the length of the given line segment.

3. $\overline{BD}$

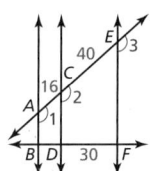

4. $\overline{JM}$

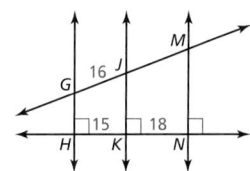

Find the value of the variable.

5.

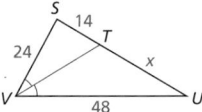

6.

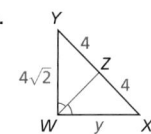

In the diagram, $\angle BAC \cong \angle CAD$. Use the given lengths to find the length of $\overline{CD}$.

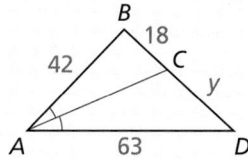

The length of $\overline{CD}$ is 27 units.

MONITORING PROGRESS ANSWERS

3. 12

4. 19.2

5. 28

6. $4\sqrt{2}$

Laurie's Notes   Teacher Actions

- Refer to Exploration 2 on page 445, and then state the Triangle Angle Bisector Theorem.

? "What is an equivalent proportion that results from this construction?" $\dfrac{AD}{CA} = \dfrac{DB}{CB}$

? "In Example 4, how can you represent the length of $\overline{RQ}$?" $15 - x$ Continue to work through the example as shown.

Closure

- **3-2-1:** Hand out a *3-2-1* reflection sheet as described on page T-214.

ANSWERS

1. parallel, Converse of the Triangle Proportionality Theorem (Thm. 8.7)

2. $\dfrac{BR}{RC} = \dfrac{AB}{AC}$

3. 9

4. 21

5. yes

6. yes

7. no

8. no

9.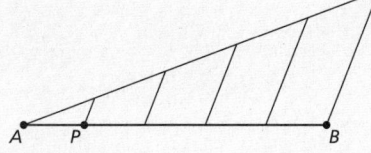

10.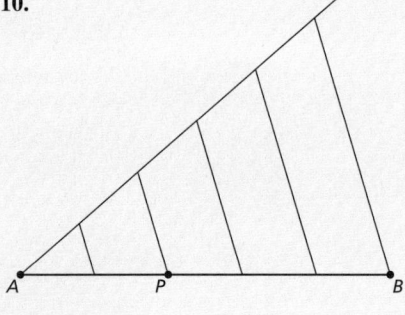

11.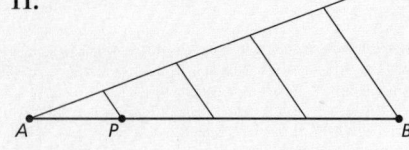

8.4 Exercises

<Dynamic>Dynamic Solutions available at BigIdeasMath.com</Dynamic>

Vocabulary and Core Concept Check

1. **COMPLETE THE STATEMENT** If a line divides two sides of a triangle proportionally, then it is _____ to the third side. This theorem is known as the _____.

2. **VOCABULARY** In $\triangle ABC$, point R lies on $\overline{BC}$ and $\overrightarrow{AR}$ bisects $\angle CAB$. Write the proportionality statement for the triangle that is based on the Triangle Angle Bisector Theorem (Theorem 8.9).

Monitoring Progress and Modeling with Mathematics

In Exercises 3 and 4, find the length of $\overline{AB}$.
(See Example 1.)

3.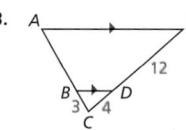

4.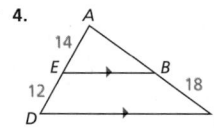

In Exercises 5–8, determine whether $\overline{KM} \parallel \overline{JN}$.
(See Example 2.)

5.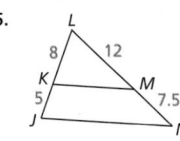

6.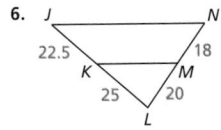

7.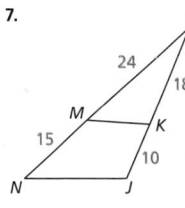

8.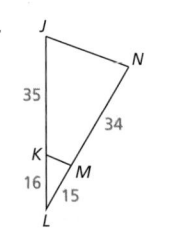

CONSTRUCTION In Exercises 9–12, draw a segment with the given length. Construct the point that divides the segment in the given ratio.

9. 3 in.; 1 to 4

10. 2 in.; 2 to 3

11. 12 cm; 1 to 3

12. 9 cm; 2 to 5

In Exercises 13–16, use the diagram to complete the proportion.

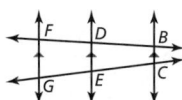

13. $\dfrac{BD}{BF} = \dfrac{}{CG}$

14. $\dfrac{CG}{} = \dfrac{BF}{DF}$

15. $\dfrac{EG}{CE} = \dfrac{DF}{}$

16. $\dfrac{}{BD} = \dfrac{CG}{CE}$

In Exercises 17 and 18, find the length of the indicated line segment. *(See Example 3.)*

17. $\overline{VX}$

18. $\overline{SU}$

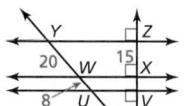
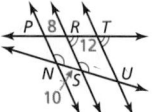

In Exercises 19–22, find the value of the variable. *(See Example 4.)*

19.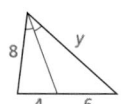

20.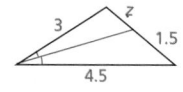

21.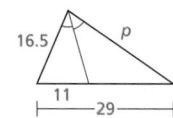

22.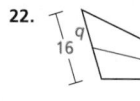

12.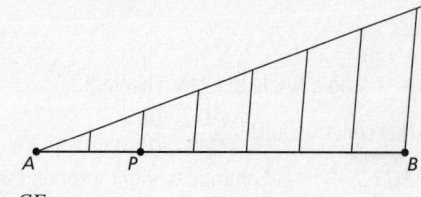

13. CE

14. EG

15. BD

16. BF

17. 6

18. 15

19. 12

20. 1

21. 27

22. 9

23. ERROR ANALYSIS Describe and correct the error in solving for x.

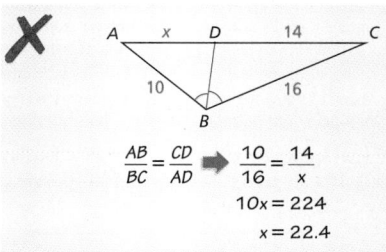

$$\frac{AB}{BC} = \frac{CD}{AD} \implies \frac{10}{16} = \frac{14}{x}$$
$$10x = 224$$
$$x = 22.4$$

24. ERROR ANALYSIS Describe and correct the error in the student's reasoning.

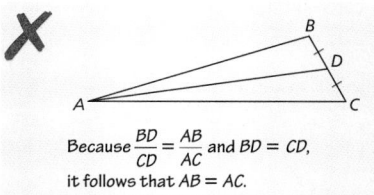

Because $\dfrac{BD}{CD} = \dfrac{AB}{AC}$ and $BD = CD$, it follows that $AB = AC$.

MATHEMATICAL CONNECTIONS In Exercises 25 and 26, find the value of x for which $\overline{PQ} \parallel \overline{RS}$.

25.
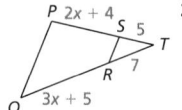

26.
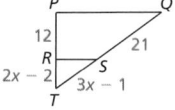

27. PROVING A THEOREM Prove the Triangle Proportionality Theorem (Theorem 8.6).

Given $\overline{QS} \parallel \overline{TU}$

Prove $\dfrac{QT}{TR} = \dfrac{SU}{UR}$

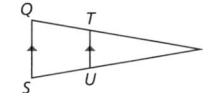

28. PROVING A THEOREM Prove the Converse of the Triangle Proportionality Theorem (Theorem 8.7).

Given $\dfrac{ZY}{YW} = \dfrac{ZX}{XV}$

Prove $\overline{YX} \parallel \overline{WV}$

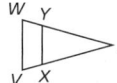

29. MODELING WITH MATHEMATICS The real estate term *lake frontage* refers to the distance along the edge of a piece of property that touches a lake.

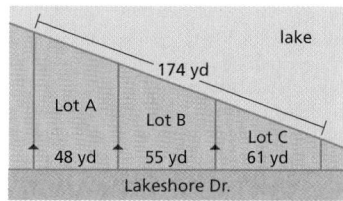

a. Find the lake frontage (to the nearest tenth) of each lot shown.

b. In general, the more lake frontage a lot has, the higher its selling price. Which lot(s) should be listed for the highest price?

c. Suppose that lot prices are in the same ratio as lake frontages. If the least expensive lot is $250,000, what are the prices of the other lots? Explain your reasoning.

30. USING STRUCTURE Use the diagram to find the values of x and y.

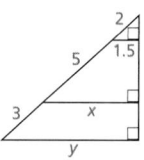

31. REASONING In the construction on page 447, explain why you can apply the Triangle Proportionality Theorem (Theorem 8.6) in Step 3.

32. PROVING A THEOREM Use the diagram with the auxiliary line drawn to write a paragraph proof of the Three Parallel Lines Theorem (Theorem 8.8).

Given $k_1 \parallel k_2 \parallel k_3$

Prove $\dfrac{CB}{BA} = \dfrac{DE}{EF}$

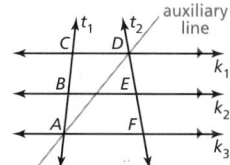

ANSWERS

23. The proportion should show that AD corresponds with DC and BA corresponds with BC;

$$\frac{AD}{DC} = \frac{BA}{BC}$$

$$\frac{x}{14} = \frac{10}{16}$$

$$x = 8.75$$

24. $\overline{AD}$ is a median, not an angle bisector.

25. $x = 3$

26. $x = 5$

27–28. See Additional Answers.

29. a. about 50.9 yd, about 58.4 yd, about 64.7 yd

b. Lot C

c. about $287,000, about $318,000; $\dfrac{50.9}{250,000} \approx \dfrac{58.4}{287,000}$

and $\dfrac{50.9}{250,000} \approx \dfrac{64.7}{318,000}$

30. $x = 5.25$, $y = 7.5$

31. Because $\overrightarrow{DJ}, \overrightarrow{EK}, \overrightarrow{FL}$, and $\overrightarrow{GB}$ are cut by a transversal $\overrightarrow{AC}$, and $\angle ADJ \cong \angle DEK \cong \angle EFL \cong \angle FGB$ by construction, $\overrightarrow{DJ} \parallel \overrightarrow{EK} \parallel \overrightarrow{FL} \parallel \overrightarrow{GB}$ by the Corresponding Angles Converse (Thm. 3.5).

32. Let G be the point of intersection of $\overleftrightarrow{AD}$ and k_2. Because $k_2 \parallel k_3$, and $k_2 \parallel k_1$, $\dfrac{DG}{GA} = \dfrac{DE}{EF}$ and $\dfrac{CB}{BA} = \dfrac{DG}{GA}$ by the Triangle Proportionality Theorem (Thm. 8.6). So, by the Transitive Property of Equality, $\dfrac{CB}{BA} = \dfrac{DE}{EF}$.

ANSWERS

Mini-Assessment

1. In the diagram, $\overline{QT} \parallel \overline{RS}$, $PQ = 6$, $QR = 1.5$, and $PT = 12$. Find ST.

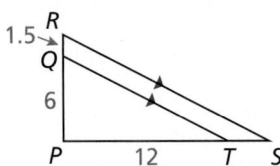

$ST = 3$ units

2. Determine whether $\overline{BE} \parallel \overline{CD}$. Explain your reasoning.

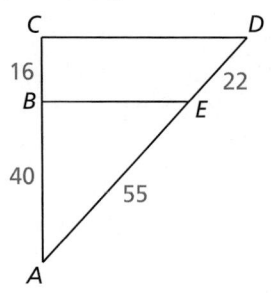

Yes, $\overline{BE} \parallel \overline{CD}$, because the sides are divided proportionally:

$\dfrac{CB}{BA} = \dfrac{16}{40} = \dfrac{2}{5}$ and $\dfrac{DE}{EA} = \dfrac{22}{55} = \dfrac{2}{5}$.

3. Find AC.

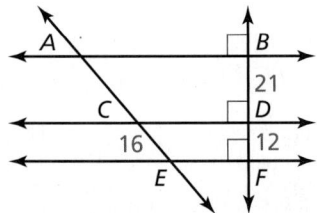

$AC = 28$ units

4. In the diagram, $\angle XWY \cong \angle ZWY$. Find XY.

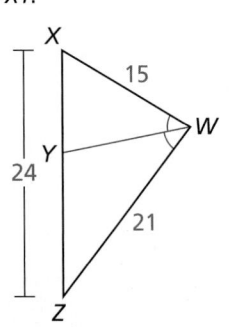

$XY = 10$ units

---

33. **CRITICAL THINKING** In $\triangle LMN$, the angle bisector of $\angle M$ also bisects $\overline{LN}$. Classify $\triangle LMN$ as specifically as possible. Justify your answer.

34. **HOW DO YOU SEE IT?** During a football game, the quarterback throws the ball to the receiver. The receiver is between two defensive players, as shown. If Player 1 is closer to the quarterback when the ball is thrown and both defensive players move at the same speed, which player will reach the receiver first? Explain your reasoning.

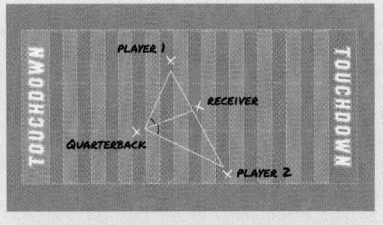

35. **PROVING A THEOREM** Use the diagram with the auxiliary lines drawn to write a paragraph proof of the Triangle Angle Bisector Theorem (Theorem 8.9).

Given $\angle YXW \cong \angle WXZ$

Prove $\dfrac{YW}{WZ} = \dfrac{XY}{XZ}$

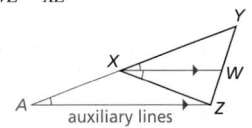

auxiliary lines

36. **THOUGHT PROVOKING** Write the converse of the Triangle Angle Bisector Theorem (Theorem 8.9). Is the converse true? Justify your answer.

37. **REASONING** How is the Triangle Midsegment Theorem (Theorem 6.8) related to the Triangle Proportionality Theorem (Theorem 8.6)? Explain your reasoning.

38. **MAKING AN ARGUMENT** Two people leave points A and B at the same time. They intend to meet at point C at the same time. The person who leaves point A walks at a speed of 3 miles per hour. You and a friend are trying to determine how fast the person who leaves point B must walk. Your friend claims you need to know the length of $\overline{AC}$. Is your friend correct? Explain your reasoning.

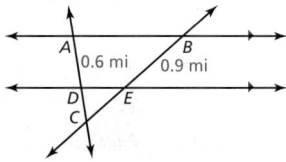

39. **CONSTRUCTION** Given segments with lengths r, s, and t, construct a segment of length x, such that $\dfrac{r}{s} = \dfrac{t}{x}$.

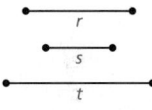

40. **PROOF** Prove *Ceva's Theorem*: If P is any point inside $\triangle ABC$, then $\dfrac{AY}{YC} \cdot \dfrac{CX}{XB} \cdot \dfrac{BZ}{ZA} = 1$.

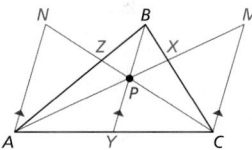

(*Hint*: Draw segments parallel to $\overline{BY}$ through A and C, as shown. Apply the Triangle Proportionality Theorem (Theorem 8.6) to $\triangle ACM$. Show that $\triangle APN \sim \triangle MPC$, $\triangle CXM \sim \triangle BXP$, and $\triangle BZP \sim \triangle AZN$.)

Maintaining Mathematical Proficiency
Reviewing what you learned in previous grades and lessons

Use the triangle. *(Section 5.5)*

41. Which sides are the legs?

42. Which side is the hypotenuse?

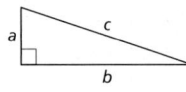

Solve the equation. *(Skills Review Handbook)*

43. $x^2 = 121$

44. $x^2 + 16 = 25$

45. $36 + x^2 = 85$

If students need help...	If students got it...
Resources by Chapter • Practice A and Practice B • Puzzle Time	Resources by Chapter • Enrichment and Extension • Cumulative Review
Student Journal • Practice	Start the *next* Section
Differentiating the Lesson Skills Review Handbook	

Core Concepts

Section 8.3

Theorem 8.4 Side-Side-Side (SSS) Similarity Theorem, *p. 436*
Theorem 8.5 Side-Angle-Side (SAS) Similarity Theorem, *p. 438*
Proving Slope Criteria Using Similar Triangles, *p. 439*

Section 8.4

Theorem 8.6 Triangle Proportionality Theorem, *p. 446*
Theorem 8.7 Converse of the Triangle Proportionality Theorem, *p. 446*
Theorem 8.8 Three Parallel Lines Theorem, *p. 448*
Theorem 8.9 Triangle Angle Bisector Theorem, *p. 449*

Mathematical Practices

1. In Exercise 17 on page 442, why must you be told which side is 20 units long?

2. In Exercise 42 on page 444, analyze the given statement. Describe the relationship between the slopes of the lines.

3. In Exercise 4 on page 450, is it better to use $\frac{7}{6}$ or 1.17 as your ratio of the lengths when finding the length of $\overline{AB}$? Explain your reasoning.

---- **Performance Task** ----

Judging the Math Fair

You have been selected to be one of the judges for the Middle School Math Fair. In one competition, seventh-grade students were asked to create scale drawings or scale models of real-life objects. As a judge, you need to verify that the objects are scaled correctly in at least two different ways. How will you verify that the entries are scaled correctly?

To explore the answers to this question and more, go to *BigIdeasMath.com*.

453

ANSWERS

1. You have to know which side it corresponds with in order to set up the proportion correctly.

2. They are negative reciprocals of each other.

3. $\frac{7}{6}$; $\frac{7}{6}$ is an exact value.

8 Chapter Review

Dynamic Solutions available at BigIdeasMath.com

8.1 Similar Polygons *(pp. 417–426)*

In the diagram, *EHGF ~ KLMN*. Find the scale factor from *EHGF* to *KLMN*. Then list all pairs of congruent angles and write the ratios of the corresponding side lengths in a statement of proportionality.

From the diagram, you can see that $\overline{EH}$ and $\overline{KL}$ are corresponding sides. So, the scale factor of

EHGF to *KLMN* is $\dfrac{KL}{EH} = \dfrac{18}{12} = \dfrac{3}{2}$.

$\angle E \cong \angle K$, $\angle H \cong \angle L$, $\angle G \cong \angle M$, and $\angle F \cong \angle N$.

$\dfrac{KL}{EH} = \dfrac{LM}{HG} = \dfrac{MN}{GF} = \dfrac{NK}{FE}$

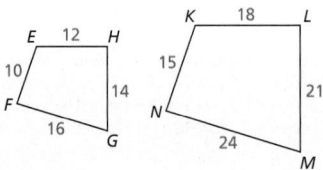

Find the scale factor. Then list all pairs of congruent angles and write the ratios of the corresponding side lengths in a statement of proportionality.

1. *ABCD ~ EFGH*

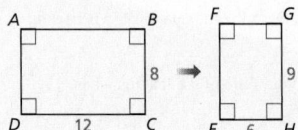

2. $\triangle XYZ \sim \triangle RPQ$

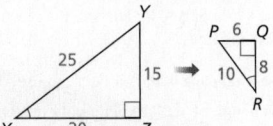

3. Two similar triangles have a scale factor of 3 : 5. The altitude of the larger triangle is 24 inches. What is the altitude of the smaller triangle?

4. Two similar triangles have a pair of corresponding sides of length 12 meters and 8 meters. The larger triangle has a perimeter of 48 meters and an area of 180 square meters. Find the perimeter and area of the smaller triangle.

8.2 Proving Triangle Similarity by AA *(pp. 427–432)*

Determine whether the triangles are similar. If they are, write a similarity statement. Explain your reasoning.

Because they are both right angles, $\angle F$ and $\angle B$ are congruent.
By the Triangle Sum Theorem (Theorem 5.1), $61° + 90° + m\angle E = 180°$, so $m\angle E = 29°$. So, $\angle E$ and $\angle A$ are congruent. So, $\triangle DFE \sim \triangle CBA$ by the AA Similarity Theorem (Theorem 8.3).

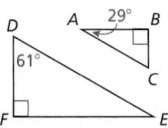

Show that the triangles are similar. Write a similarity statement.

5.

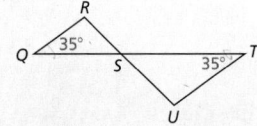

6.

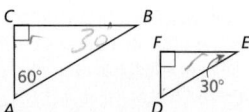

7. A cellular telephone tower casts a shadow that is 72 feet long, while a nearby tree that is 27 feet tall casts a shadow that is 6 feet long. How tall is the tower?

8. $\angle C \cong \angle C$ and $\dfrac{CD}{CE} = \dfrac{CB}{CA}$, so $\triangle CBD \sim \triangle CAE$.

9. $\dfrac{QU}{QT} = \dfrac{QR}{QS} = \dfrac{UR}{TS}$, so $\triangle QUR \sim \triangle QTS$.

10. $x = 4$

8.3 Proving Triangle Similarity by SSS and SAS *(pp. 435–444)*

Show that the triangles are similar.

a.
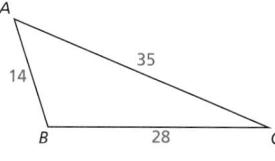

Compare $\triangle ABC$ and $\triangle DEF$ by finding ratios of corresponding side lengths.

Shortest sides	Longest sides	Remaining sides
$\dfrac{AB}{DE} = \dfrac{14}{6} = \dfrac{7}{3}$	$\dfrac{AC}{DF} = \dfrac{35}{15} = \dfrac{7}{3}$	$\dfrac{BC}{EF} = \dfrac{28}{12} = \dfrac{7}{3}$

All the ratios are equal, so $\triangle ABC \sim \triangle DEF$ by the SSS Similarity Theorem (Theorem 8.4).

b.
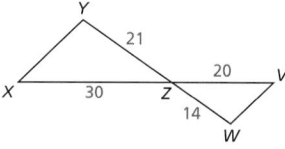

$\angle YZX \cong \angle WZV$ by the Vertical Angles Congruence Theorem (Theorem 2.6). Next, compare the ratios of the corresponding side lengths of $\triangle YZX$ and $\triangle WZV$.

$$\frac{WZ}{YZ} = \frac{14}{21} = \frac{2}{3} \qquad \frac{VZ}{XZ} = \frac{20}{30} = \frac{2}{3}$$

▶ So, by the SAS Similarity Theorem (Theorem 8.5), $\triangle YZX \sim \triangle WZV$.

Use the SSS Similarity Theorem (Theorem 8.4) or the SAS Similarity Theorem (Theorem 8.5) to show that the triangles are similar.

8.
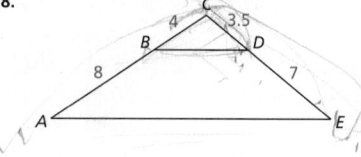

9.
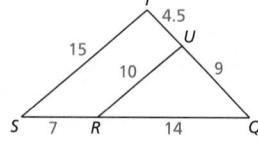

10. Find the value of x that makes $\triangle ABC \sim \triangle DEF$.

 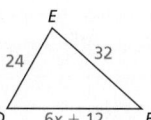

8.4 Proportionality Theorems *(pp. 445–452)*

a. Determine whether $\overline{MP} \parallel \overline{LQ}$.

Begin by finding and simplifying ratios of lengths determined by $\overline{MP}$.

$$\frac{NM}{ML} = \frac{8}{4} = \frac{2}{1} = 2$$

$$\frac{NP}{PQ} = \frac{24}{12} = \frac{2}{1} = 2$$

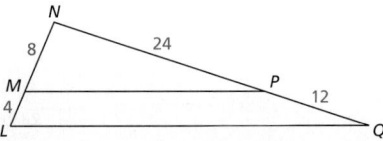

Because $\frac{NM}{ML} = \frac{NP}{PQ}$, $\overline{MP}$ is parallel to $\overline{LQ}$ by the Converse of the Triangle Proportionality Theorem (Theorem 8.7).

b. In the diagram, $\overline{AD}$ bisects $\angle CAB$. Find the length of $\overline{DB}$.

Because $\overline{AD}$ is an angle bisector of $\angle CAB$, you can apply the Triangle Angle Bisector Theorem (Theorem 8.9).

$$\frac{DB}{DC} = \frac{AB}{AC} \qquad \text{Triangle Angle Bisector Theorem}$$

$$\frac{x}{5} = \frac{15}{8} \qquad \text{Substitute.}$$

$$8x = 75 \qquad \text{Cross Products Property}$$

$$9.375 = x \qquad \text{Solve for } x.$$

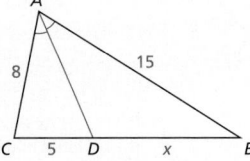

▶ The length of $\overline{DB}$ is 9.375 units.

Determine whether $\overline{AB} \parallel \overline{CD}$.

11.

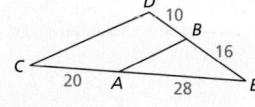

12.

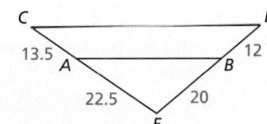

13. Find the length of $\overline{YB}$.

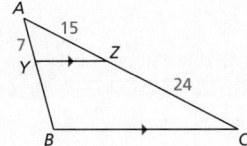

Find the length of $\overline{AB}$.

14.

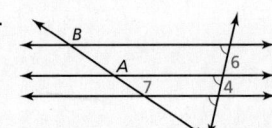

15.

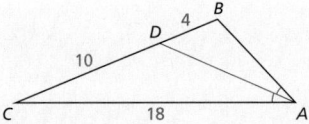

Determine whether the triangles are similar. If they are, write a similarity statement. Explain your reasoning.

1.
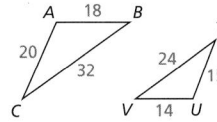

2.
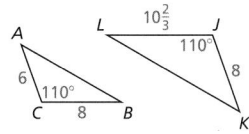

3.
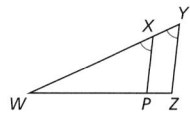

Find the value of the variable.

4.
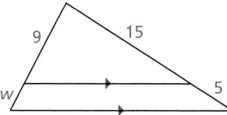

5.
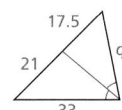

6.
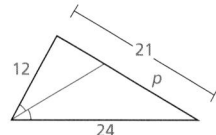

7. Given $\triangle QRS \sim \triangle MNP$, list all pairs of congruent angles. Then write the ratios of the corresponding side lengths in a statement of proportionality.

Use the diagram.

8. Find the length of $\overline{EF}$.

9. Find the length of $\overline{FG}$.

10. Is quadrilateral $FECB$ similar to quadrilateral $GFBA$? If so, what is the scale factor of the dilation that maps quadrilateral $FECB$ to quadrilateral $GFBA$?

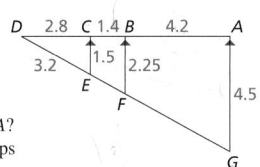
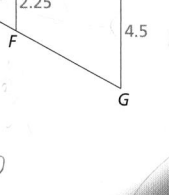

11. You are visiting the Unisphere at Flushing Meadows Corona Park in New York. To estimate the height of the stainless steel model of Earth, you place a mirror on the ground and stand where you can see the top of the model in the mirror. Use the diagram to estimate the height of the model. Explain why this method works.

12. You are making a scale model of a rectangular park for a school project. Your model has a length of 2 feet and a width of 1.4 feet. The actual park is 800 yards long. What are the perimeter and area of the actual park?

13. In a *perspective drawing*, lines that are parallel in real life must meet at a vanishing point on the horizon. To make the train cars in the drawing appear equal in length, they are drawn so that the lines connecting the opposite corners of each car are parallel. Use the dimensions given and the yellow parallel lines to find the length of the bottom edge of the drawing of Car 2.

ANSWERS

1. no; Corresponding side lengths are not proportional.

2. yes; $\triangle ABC \sim \triangle KLJ$; $\dfrac{AC}{KJ} = \dfrac{BC}{LJ}$ and $\angle C \cong \angle J$.

3. yes; $\triangle WXP \sim \triangle WYZ$; $\angle X \cong \angle Y$ and $\angle W \cong \angle W$

4. $w = 3$

5. $q = 27.5$

6. $p = 14$

7. $\angle Q \cong \angle M$, $\angle R \cong \angle N$, $\angle S \cong \angle P$; $\dfrac{QR}{MN} = \dfrac{RS}{NP} = \dfrac{QS}{MP}$

8. 1.6

9. 4.8

10. no

11. 140 ft; The triangles are similar.

12. $P = 2720$ yd; $A = 448{,}000$ yd^2

13. about 4.3 cm

If students need help...	If students got it...
Lesson Tutorials	Resources by Chapter • Enrichment and Extension • Cumulative Review
Skills Review Handbook	Performance Task
BigIdeasMath.com	Start the *next* Section

Chapter 8   457

ANSWERS

1. **a.** A 270° rotation about the origin followed by a dilation with the center at the origin and a scale factor of $k = \frac{1}{2}$.

   b. yes; The angles are congruent and the sides are proportional.

2. SAS Congruence Theorem (Thm. 5.5), SSS Congruence Theorem (Thm. 5.8), ASA Congruence Theorem (Thm. 5.10), AAS Congruence Theorem (Thm. 5.11)

3. *Sample answer:* 5 and 7.5; 6 and 9; 8 and 12

4. B

---

8 Cumulative Assessment

1. Use the graph of quadrilaterals *ABCD* and *QRST*.

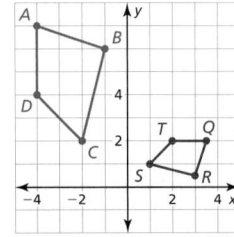

   a. Write a composition of transformations that maps quadrilateral *ABCD* to quadrilateral *QRST*.

   b. Are the quadrilaterals similar? Explain your reasoning.

2. In the diagram, *ABCD* is a parallelogram. Which congruence theorem(s) could you use to show that $\triangle AED \cong \triangle CEB$? Select all that apply.

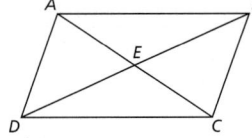

   | SAS Congruence Theorem (Theorem 5.5) |
   | SSS Congruence Theorem (Theorem 5.8) |
   | HL Congruence Theorem (Theorem 5.9) |
   | ASA Congruence Theorem (Theorem 5.10) |
   | AAS Congruence Theorem (Theorem 5.11) |

3. By the Triangle Proportionality Theorem (Theorem 8.6), $\frac{VW}{WY} = \frac{VX}{XZ}$. In the diagram, $VX > VW$ and $XZ > WY$. List three possible values for *VX* and *XZ*.

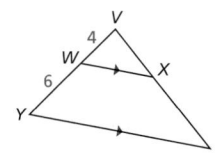

4. The slope of line ℓ is $-\frac{3}{4}$. The slope of line *n* is $\frac{4}{3}$. What must be true about lines ℓ and *n*?

   (A) Lines ℓ and *n* are parallel. (B) Lines ℓ and *n* are perpendicular.

   (C) Lines ℓ and *n* are skew. (D) Lines ℓ and *n* are the same line.

458   Chapter 8   Similarity

---

458   **Chapter 8**

5. Enter a statement or reason in each blank to complete the two-column proof.

Given $\dfrac{KJ}{KL} = \dfrac{KH}{KM}$

Prove $\angle LMN \cong \angle JHG$

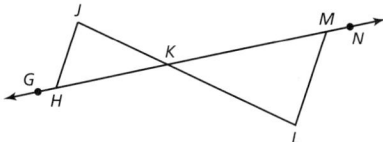

STATEMENTS	REASONS
1. $\dfrac{KJ}{KL} = \dfrac{KH}{KM}$	1. Given
2. $\angle JKH \cong \angle LKM$	2. _____
3. $\triangle JKH \sim \triangle LKM$	3. _____
4. $\angle KHJ \cong \angle KML$	4. _____
5. _____	5. Definition of congruent angles
6. $m\angle KHJ + m\angle JHG = 180°$	6. Linear Pair Postulate (Post. 2.8)
7. $m\angle JHG = 180° - m\angle KHJ$	7. _____
8. $m\angle KML + m\angle LMN = 180°$	8. _____
9. _____	9. Subtraction Property of Equality
10. $m\angle LMN = 180° - m\angle KHJ$	10. _____
11. _____	11. Transitive Property of Equality
12. $\angle LMN \cong \angle JHG$	12. _____

6. The coordinates of the vertices of $\triangle DEF$ are $D(-8, 5)$, $E(-5, 8)$, and $F(-1, 4)$. The coordinates of the vertices of $\triangle JKL$ are $J(16, -10)$, $K(10, -16)$, and $L(2, -8)$. $\angle D \cong \angle J$. Can you show that $\triangle DEF \sim \triangle JKL$ by using the AA Similarity Theorem (Theorem 8.3)? If so, do so by listing the congruent corresponding angles and writing a similarity transformation that maps $\triangle DEF$ to $\triangle JKL$. If not, explain why not.

7. Classify the quadrilateral using the most specific name.

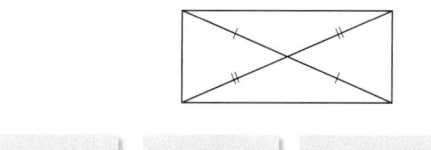

rectangle	square	parallelogram	rhombus

8. Your friend makes the statement "Quadrilateral $PQRS$ is similar to quadrilateral $WXYZ$." Describe the relationships between corresponding angles and between corresponding sides that make this statement true.

5. Vertical Angles Congruence Theorem (Thm. 2.6); SAS Similarity Theorem (Thm. 8.5); Corresponding angles of similar figures are congruent; $m\angle KHJ = m\angle KML$; Subtraction Property of Equality; Linear Pair Postulate (Post. 2.8); $m\angle LMN = 180° - m\angle KML$; Substitution Property of Equality; $m\angle LMN = m\angle JHG$; Definition of congruent angles

6. yes; $\angle D \cong \angle J$ and $\angle E \cong \angle K$; a 180° rotation about the origin followed by a dilation with center at the origin and a scale factor of $k = 2$.

7. parallelogram

8. Corresponding angles are congruent, and corresponding side lengths are proportional.

Chapter 9 Pacing Guide

Chapter Opener/ Mathematical Practices	0.5 Day
Section 1	1.5 Days
Section 2	1 Day
Section 3	2 Days
Quiz	0.5 Day
Section 4	1.5 Days
Section 5	2 Days
Section 6	2 Days
Section 7	2 Days
Chapter Review/ Chapter Tests	2 Days
Total Chapter 9	15 Days
Year-to-Date	113 Days

9 Right Triangles and Trigonometry

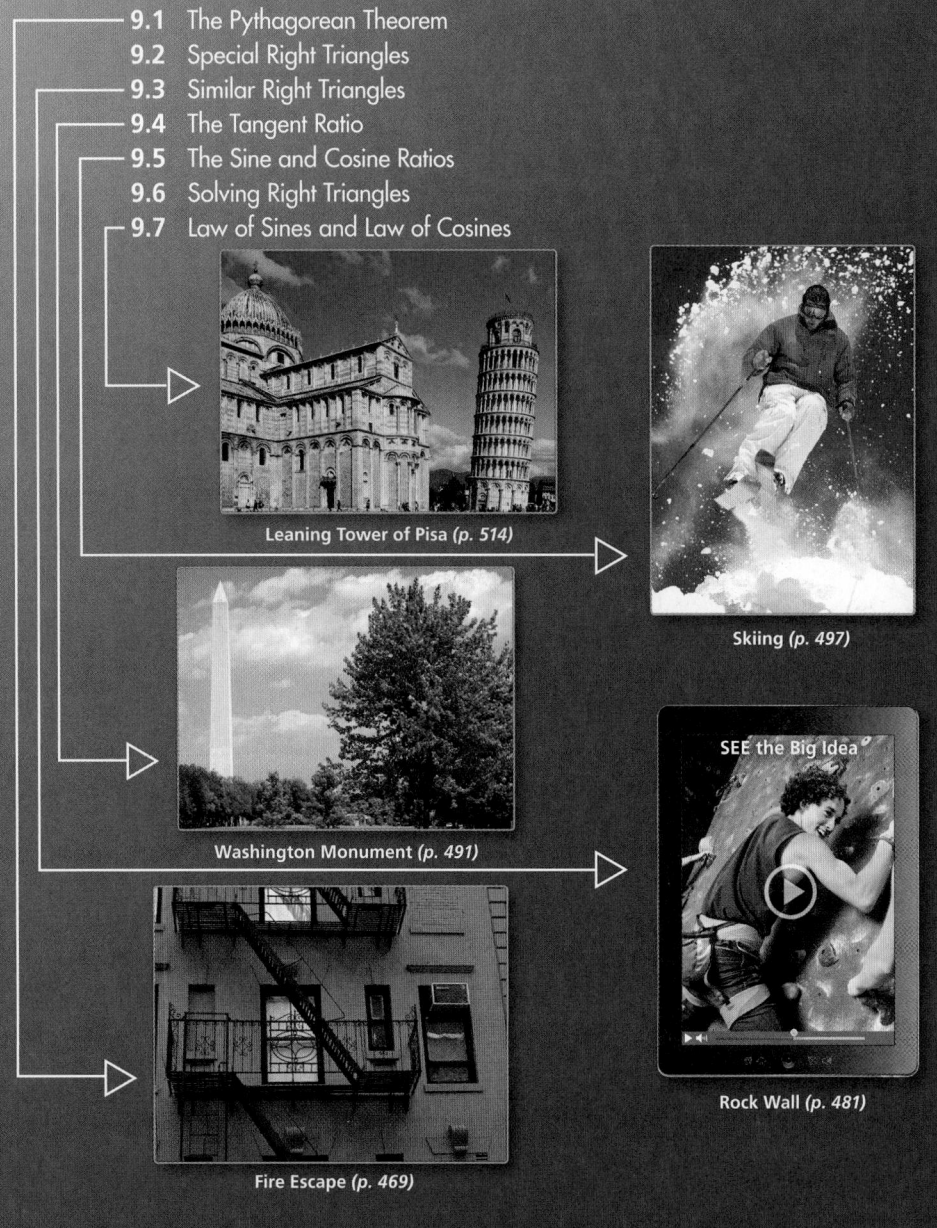

Leaning Tower of Pisa (p. 514)

Skiing (p. 497)

Washington Monument (p. 491)

SEE the Big Idea

Rock Wall (p. 481)

Fire Escape (p. 469)

Chapter Summary

- This is a fairly long chapter that introduces students to right triangle trigonometry. Students will encounter a more in-depth study of trigonometry in Algebra 2.
- The first lesson on the Pythagorean Theorem will not be completely new to students who will have familiarity with this theorem from middle school.
- The next two lessons use knowledge of similar triangles to investigate relationships in special right triangles (30°-60°-90° and 45°-45°-90°) as well as similar triangles that are formed when the altitude to the hypotenuse is drawn in a right triangle. Being familiar with these relationships and solving for segment lengths in triangles will be helpful in subsequent lessons.
- The next three lessons present the tangent, sine, and cosine ratios. The focus of these lessons is to solve for parts of a right triangle. Many real-life applications are presented.
- The last lesson of the chapter introduces the Law of Sines and the Law of Cosines so that non-right triangles can be solved.

 COMMON CORE PROGRESSION

Middle School
- Understand ratios and describe ratio relationships.
- Use proportionality to solve ratio and real-life problems.
- Find the areas of right triangles and other triangles.
- Solve real-life and mathematical problems involving area and angle measure.
- Use the Pythagorean Theorem to find missing measures in two dimensions and find the distance between two points in the coordinate plane.

Algebra 1
- Write equations in one variable.
- Solve linear equations in one variable.
- Use multi-step equations to solve real-life problems.
- Rewrite and use area formulas and other common formulas.

Geometry
- Use the Pythagorean Theorem and the Converse of the Pythagorean Theorem.
- Use geometric means.
- Find side lengths and solve real-life problems involving special right triangles.
- Find the tangent, sine, and cosine ratios and use them to solve real-life problems.
- Use the Law of Sines and Law of Cosines to solve triangles.

Dynamic Teaching Tools
Dynamic Assessment & Progress Monitoring Tool
Lesson Planning Tool
Interactive Whiteboard Lesson Library
Dynamic Classroom with Dynamic Investigations
Real-Life STEM Videos

Scaffolding in the Classroom
Build on prior knowledge.
Instead of reteaching a topic, use review. Begin with the statement, "Remember when we did _____?" This lets the students know that you know they have previously learned the concept or process. Use a problem to review. Then say, "Today we will use this idea to _____."

Standards Summary		
Section	**Common Core State Standards**	
9.1	Learning	HSG-SRT.B.4, HSG-SRT.C.8
9.2	Preparing	HSG-SRT.C.8, HSG-MG.A.1
9.3	Learning	HSG-SRT.B.5
9.4	Learning	HSG-SRT.C.6, HSG-SRT.C.8
9.5	Learning	HSG-SRT.C.6, HSG-SRT.C.7, HSG-SRT.C.8
9.6	Learning	HSG-SRT.C.8, HSG-MG.A.1, HSG-MG.A.3
9.7	Learning	HSG-SRT.D.9, HSG-SRT.D.10, HSG-SRT.D.11, HSG-MG.A.3

Laurie's Notes

Maintaining Mathematical Proficiency

Using Properties of Radicals

• Review the Product Property of Square Roots: For all real numbers $a \geq 0$ and $b \geq 0$, $\sqrt{ab} = \sqrt{a}\sqrt{b}$.

• Remind students that they need to find all perfect-square factors of the radicand. Then they can rewrite the radicand as a product of perfect-square factors and the remaining factors.

• For Example 2, point out that when students multiply by $\dfrac{\sqrt{5}}{\sqrt{5}}$, they are multiplying by 1, which does not change the value of the expression.

COMMON ERROR When rationalizing the denominator of a radical expression, students may forget to multiply *both* the numerator and denominator by the same number.

Solving Proportions

• Review the Cross Products Property: If $\dfrac{a}{b} = \dfrac{c}{d}$, then $ad = bc$ ($b \neq 0$, $d \neq 0$).

• Ask students how to solve the proportion in Example 3 by using the Multiplication Property of Equality instead of the Cross Products Property.

COMMON ERROR Some students may try to solve a proportion by multiplying the numerators together and the denominators together, and then setting these products equal. Encourage these students to use the Multiplication Property of Equality, instead of the Cross Products Property, to solve a proportion.

Mathematical Practices (continued on page 462)

• The eight *Mathematical Practices* focus attention on how mathematics is learned—process versus content. Page 462 demonstrates that mathematically proficient students understand the importance of precise definitions. They also understand the difference between precise and approximate measures, and they know from the context of a problem what type of measurement is called for.

• Use the *Mathematical Practices* page to help students develop mathematical habits of mind—how mathematics can be explored and how mathematics is thought about.

• Students will be working with unit circle trigonometry on this page and therefore need to be familiar with the definition of a right triangle in *standard position*. In the *Core Concept*, the three necessary conditions for the standard position of a right triangle are described.

If students need help...	If students got it...
Student Journal • Maintaining Mathematical Proficiency	Game Closet at *BigIdeasMath.com*
Lesson Tutorials	Start the *next* Section
Skills Review Handbook	

Maintaining Mathematical Proficiency

Using Properties of Radicals

Example 1 Simplify $\sqrt{128}$.

$$\sqrt{128} = \sqrt{64 \cdot 2}$$ Factor using the greatest perfect square factor.

$$= \sqrt{64} \cdot \sqrt{2}$$ Product Property of Square Roots

$$= 8\sqrt{2}$$ Simplify.

Example 2 Simplify $\dfrac{4}{\sqrt{5}}$.

$$\dfrac{4}{\sqrt{5}} = \dfrac{4}{\sqrt{5}} \cdot \dfrac{\sqrt{5}}{\sqrt{5}}$$ Multiply by $\dfrac{\sqrt{5}}{\sqrt{5}}$.

$$= \dfrac{4\sqrt{5}}{\sqrt{25}}$$ Product Property of Square Roots

$$= \dfrac{4\sqrt{5}}{5}$$ Simplify.

Simplify the expression.

1. $\sqrt{75}$

2. $\sqrt{270}$

3. $\sqrt{135}$

4. $\dfrac{2}{\sqrt{7}}$

5. $\dfrac{5}{\sqrt{2}}$

6. $\dfrac{12}{\sqrt{6}}$

Solving Proportions

Example 3 Solve $\dfrac{x}{10} = \dfrac{3}{2}$.

$$\dfrac{x}{10} = \dfrac{3}{2}$$ Write the proportion.

$$x \cdot 2 = 10 \cdot 3$$ Cross Products Property

$$2x = 30$$ Multiply.

$$\dfrac{2x}{2} = \dfrac{30}{2}$$ Divide each side by 2.

$$x = 15$$ Simplify.

Solve the proportion.

7. $\dfrac{x}{12} = \dfrac{3}{4}$

8. $\dfrac{x}{3} = \dfrac{5}{2}$

9. $\dfrac{4}{x} = \dfrac{7}{56}$

10. $\dfrac{10}{23} = \dfrac{4}{x}$

11. $\dfrac{x+1}{2} = \dfrac{21}{14}$

12. $\dfrac{9}{3x-15} = \dfrac{3}{12}$

13. **ABSTRACT REASONING** The Product Property of Square Roots allows you to simplify the square root of a product. Are you able to simplify the square root of a sum? of a difference? Explain.

Dynamic Solutions available at *BigIdeasMath.com*

Common Core State Standards

HSN-RN.A.2 Rewrite expressions involving radicals ... using the properties of exponents.

7.RP.A.2b Identify ... proportionality ... in ... equations ....

ANSWERS

1. $5\sqrt{3}$
2. $3\sqrt{30}$
3. $3\sqrt{15}$
4. $\dfrac{2\sqrt{7}}{7}$
5. $\dfrac{5\sqrt{2}}{2}$
6. $2\sqrt{6}$
7. $x = 9$
8. $x = 7.5$
9. $x = 32$
10. $x = 9.2$
11. $x = 2$
12. $x = 17$
13. no; no; Because square roots have to do with factors, the rule allows you to simplify with products, not sums and differences.

Vocabulary Review

Have students make an Information Wheel for each of the following properties.

- Product Property of Square Roots
- Cross Products Property

1. *Sample answer:*

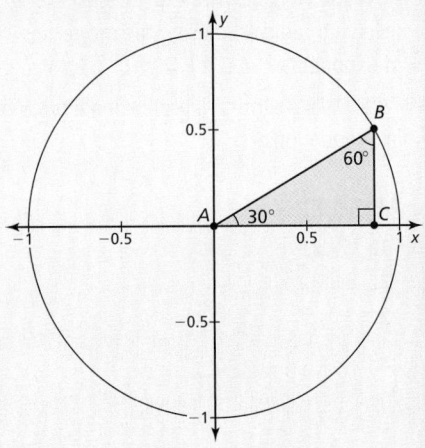

$$A(0, 0), B\left(\frac{\sqrt{3}}{2}, \frac{1}{2}\right), C\left(\frac{\sqrt{3}}{2}, 0\right)$$

2. *Sample answer:*

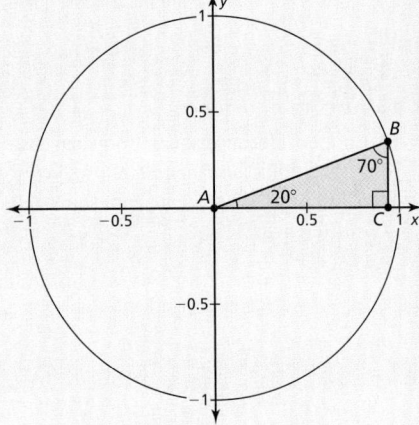

$A(0, 0), B(0.94, 0.34), C(0.94, 0)$

Mathematical Practices

Mathematically proficient students express numerical answers precisely.

Attending to Precision

Core Concept

Standard Position for a Right Triangle

In *unit circle trigonometry*, a right triangle is in **standard position** when:

1. The hypotenuse is a radius of the circle of radius 1 with center at the origin.

2. One leg of the right triangle lies on the *x*-axis.

3. The other leg of the right triangle is perpendicular to the *x*-axis.

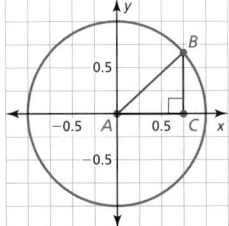

EXAMPLE 1   **Drawing an Isosceles Right Triangle in Standard Position**

Use dynamic geometry software to construct an isosceles right triangle in standard position. What are the exact coordinates of its vertices?

SOLUTION

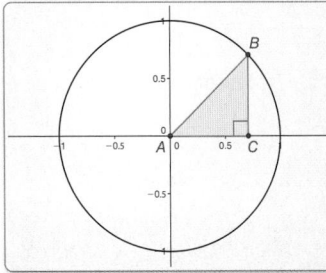

Sample

Points
A(0, 0)
B(0.71, 0.71)
C(0.71, 0)
Segments
AB = 1
BC = 0.71
AC = 0.71
Angle
m∠A = 45°

To determine the exact coordinates of the vertices, label the length of each leg *x*. By the Pythagorean Theorem, which you will study in Section 9.1, $x^2 + x^2 = 1$. Solving this equation yields

$$x = \frac{1}{\sqrt{2}}, \text{ or } \frac{\sqrt{2}}{2}.$$

▶ So, the exact coordinates of the vertices are $A(0, 0)$, $B\left(\frac{\sqrt{2}}{2}, \frac{\sqrt{2}}{2}\right)$, and $C\left(\frac{\sqrt{2}}{2}, 0\right)$.

Monitoring Progress

1. Use dynamic geometry software to construct a right triangle with acute angle measures of 30° and 60° in standard position. What are the exact coordinates of its vertices?

2. Use dynamic geometry software to construct a right triangle with acute angle measures of 20° and 70° in standard position. What are the approximate coordinates of its vertices?

Laurie's Notes   Mathematical Practices (continued from page T-461)

- Example 1 shows the construction of a right isosceles triangle in standard position. The approximate coordinates can be found using a function of the software. To find the exact coordinate, the Pythagorean Theorem is needed. This theorem is formally presented in the first lesson of this chapter. However, students should be familiar with the theorem from middle school.

- Work through the steps in solving for the exact coordinates.

- Give time for students to work through the *Monitoring Progress* questions, and then discuss as a class.

Overview of Section 9.1

Introduction

- Students should certainly be familiar with the Pythagorean Theorem from middle school. In this lesson, the theorem and its converse are presented. Two proofs of the theorem are investigated in the explorations.
- Also in this lesson, students will use the Pythagorean Inequalities Theorem to classify triangles as right, acute, or obtuse when the side lengths are given. This theorem can easily be explored using dynamic geometry software.

Resources

- There are many online resources related to the Pythagorean Theorem. Some resources are applets that present a dynamic proof of the theorem. Others allow the user to input three side lengths, and the output is the type of triangle formed, classified by its angles.

Formative Assessment Tips

- **Paired Verbal Fluency (PVF):** This technique is used between two partners where each person takes a turn speaking, uninterrupted, for a specified period of time. The roles reverse and the listener then speaks, uninterrupted, for the same amount of time.
- The technique can be used at the beginning, middle, or end of instruction. Used at the beginning of instruction, students share their prior knowledge about a particular topic, skill, or concept. Used in the middle of instruction, students can share their understanding of a particular problem. Used at the end of instruction, students reflect on learning that occurred during the lesson or at the end of a connected group of lessons.
- Verbalizing their understanding and being an attentive listener will activate student thinking and should help identify areas of difficulty or uncertainty.
- In this lesson, students will be asked to reflect on their knowledge of the Pythagorean Theorem from prior mathematics courses.

Pacing Suggestion

- Students should be familiar with at least one proof of the Pythagorean Theorem. The explorations provide two proofs within the reach of geometry students. Complete the explorations and transition to the formal lesson.

Common Core State Standards

HSG-SRT.B.4 Prove theorems about triangles.

HSG-SRT.C.8 Use trigonometric ratios and the Pythagorean Theorem to solve right triangles in applied problems.

Laurie's Notes

Exploration

Motivate
- Share information about Pythagoras, who was born in Greece in 569 B.C.
  - He is known as the Father of Numbers.
  - He traveled extensively in Egypt, learning math, astronomy, and music.
  - Pythagoras undertook a reform of the cultural life of Cretona, urging the citizens to follow his religious, political, and philosophical goals.
  - He created a school where his followers, known as Pythagoreans, lived and worked. They observed a rule of silence called echemythia, the breaking of which was punishable by death. One had to remain silent for five years before being allowed to contribute to the group.
  - Over the years, many mathematicians and non-mathematicians have given various proofs of the Pythagorean Theorem. One of our former presidents, President James Garfield, is credited with a proof.

Exploration Note
- The explorations on this page are two of the many ways in which the Pythagorean Theorem can be proven to be true. Consider having some students work on Exploration 1 while others work on Exploration 2. Students then present their results to the other group.
- To help facilitate the first exploration, make a template for students to work with for part of the exploration. Draw the large square with sides subdivided into segments a and b, as shown. From this template students can quickly create the four triangles and the small square.
- I have found that students are not always accurate enough in making copies of the right triangle to have this exploration work well, hence the initial template.

Exploration 1
- Distribute the template, a straightedge, and a pair of scissors to students so that the exploration can be completed efficiently.
- Students should be able to write equations for the areas of each of the polygons.
- **?** "What is the area of the large square in terms of the area of the four triangles and the small square?" Answers will vary but should be equivalent to $4\left(\frac{1}{2}ab\right) + c^2 = 2ab + c^2$.
- **?** "What is the area of the large square in terms of the area of the two rectangles and two smaller squares?" Answers will vary but should be equivalent to $2ab + a^2 + b^2$.
- **MP3 Construct Viable Arguments and Critique the Reasoning of Others:** Ask a volunteer to explain how this work is related to the Pythagorean Theorem.

Exploration 2
- Students must first determine why the three triangles are similar. If they need a hint, refer them to Section 8.2.
- Students should begin by writing proportional relationships that they are confident of. Substitute side names with a, b, and c whenever possible.

Communicate Your Answer
- Question 4 could be used as an extra credit problem.

Connecting to Next Step
- Students are familiar with the Pythagorean Theorem from middle school, but they would not have proven the theorem. Students should now be ready to work with the theorem in the formal lesson.

9.1   The Pythagorean Theorem

Essential Question How can you prove the Pythagorean Theorem?

EXPLORATION 1 **Proving the Pythagorean Theorem without Words**

Work with a partner.

a. Draw and cut out a right triangle with legs a and b, and hypotenuse c.

b. Make three copies of your right triangle. Arrange all four triangles to form a large square, as shown.

c. Find the area of the large square in terms of a, b, and c by summing the areas of the triangles and the small square.

d. Copy the large square. Divide it into two smaller squares and two equally-sized rectangles, as shown.

e. Find the area of the large square in terms of a and b by summing the areas of the rectangles and the smaller squares.

f. Compare your answers to parts (c) and (e). Explain how this proves the Pythagorean Theorem.

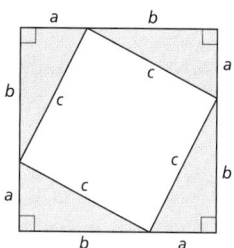

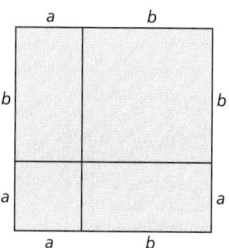

EXPLORATION 2 **Proving the Pythagorean Theorem**

Work with a partner.

a. Draw a right triangle with legs a and b, and hypotenuse c, as shown. Draw the altitude from C to $\overline{AB}$. Label the lengths, as shown.

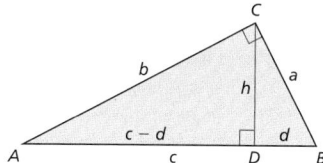

REASONING ABSTRACTLY

To be proficient in math, you need to know and flexibly use different properties of operations and objects.

b. Explain why $\triangle ABC$, $\triangle ACD$, and $\triangle CBD$ are similar.

c. Write a two-column proof using the similar triangles in part (b) to prove that $a^2 + b^2 = c^2$.

Communicate Your Answer

3. How can you prove the Pythagorean Theorem?

4. Use the Internet or some other resource to find a way to prove the Pythagorean Theorem that is different from Explorations 1 and 2.

4. *Sample answer:* Arrange the same triangles from method 1 as shown at the right. The area of the large square is c^2. The area of the small square is $(b - a)^2 = b^2 - 2ab + a^2$, or it can be written as the area of the large square minus the area of the triangles: $c^2 - 4\left(\frac{1}{2}ab\right) = c^2 - 2ab$. Set these two expressions equal to each other to get $b^2 - 2ab + a^2 = c^2 - 2ab$, which becomes $a^2 + b^2 = c^2$, when $2ab$ is added to each side.

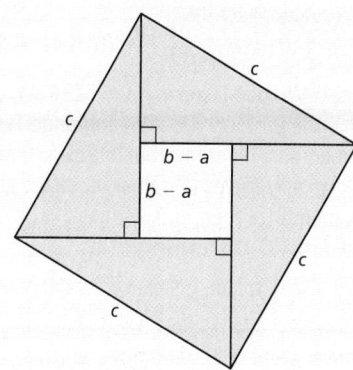

Vocabulary

Some students may confuse the legs of an isosceles triangle with the legs of a right triangle. Have students practice classifying triangles and identifying the legs, base, and hypotenuse when present. Discuss the properties of each type of *leg* and ask students if it is possible for a single triangle to contain both types of legs.

Extra Example 1

Find the value of *x*. Then tell whether the side lengths form a Pythagorean triple.

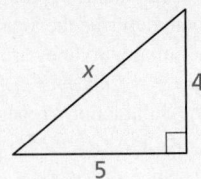

$x = \sqrt{41}$; $\sqrt{41}$ is not an integer, so the side lengths do not form a Pythagorean triple.

9.1 Lesson

Core Vocabulary

Pythagorean triple, *p. 464*

Previous
right triangle
legs of a right triangle
hypotenuse

What You Will Learn

▶ Use the Pythagorean Theorem.
▶ Use the Converse of the Pythagorean Theorem.
▶ Classify triangles.

Using the Pythagorean Theorem

One of the most famous theorems in mathematics is the Pythagorean Theorem, named for the ancient Greek mathematician Pythagoras. This theorem describes the relationship between the side lengths of a right triangle.

⟳ Theorem

Theorem 9.1 Pythagorean Theorem

In a right triangle, the square of the length of the hypotenuse is equal to the sum of the squares of the lengths of the legs.

Proof Explorations 1 and 2, p. 463; Ex. 39, p. 484

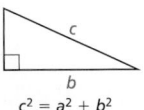

$$c^2 = a^2 + b^2$$

A **Pythagorean triple** is a set of three positive integers a, b, and c that satisfy the equation $c^2 = a^2 + b^2$.

⟳ Core Concept

Common Pythagorean Triples and Some of Their Multiples

3, 4, 5	**5, 12, 13**	**8, 15, 17**	**7, 24, 25**
6, 8, 10	10, 24, 26	16, 30, 34	14, 48, 50
9, 12, 15	15, 36, 39	24, 45, 51	21, 72, 75
$3x, 4x, 5x$	$5x, 12x, 13x$	$8x, 15x, 17x$	$7x, 24x, 25x$

The most common Pythagorean triples are in bold. The other triples are the result of multiplying each integer in a bold-faced triple by the same factor.

STUDY TIP

You may find it helpful to memorize the basic Pythagorean triples, shown in **bold**, for standardized tests.

EXAMPLE 1 Using the Pythagorean Theorem

Find the value of x. Then tell whether the side lengths form a Pythagorean triple.

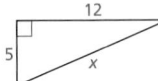

SOLUTION

$c^2 = a^2 + b^2$	Pythagorean Theorem
$x^2 = 5^2 + 12^2$	Substitute.
$x^2 = 25 + 144$	Multiply.
$x^2 = 169$	Add.
$x = 13$	Find the positive square root.

▶ The value of x is 13. Because the side lengths 5, 12, and 13 are integers that satisfy the equation $c^2 = a^2 + b^2$, they form a Pythagorean triple.

Laurie's Notes   Teacher Actions

- **Paired Verbal Fluency** and **MP6 Attend to Precision:** Have students pair up and follow the protocol described on page T-462. Ask students to share what they recall about the Pythagorean Theorem from middle school. Students should be precise in their summaries.
- *Pythagorean triples* and their multiples are a handy list to remember. Suggest to students that they memorize the four key triples in bold.
- ❓ **Fact-First Questioning:** Say, "If p, q, and r satisfy the Pythagorean Theorem, then $\frac{p}{2}$, $\frac{q}{2}$, and $\frac{r}{2}$ will also. Explain." Listen for valid reasoning.

EXAMPLE 2 Using the Pythagorean Theorem

Find the value of x. Then tell whether the side lengths form a Pythagorean triple.

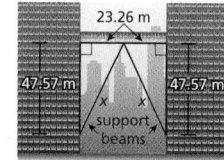

SOLUTION

$c^2 = a^2 + b^2$	Pythagorean Theorem
$14^2 = 7^2 + x^2$	Substitute.
$196 = 49 + x^2$	Multiply.
$147 = x^2$	Subtract 49 from each side.
$\sqrt{147} = x$	Find the positive square root.
$\sqrt{49} \cdot \sqrt{3} = x$	Product Property of Square Roots
$7\sqrt{3} = x$	Simplify.

▶ The value of x is $7\sqrt{3}$. Because $7\sqrt{3}$ is not an integer, the side lengths do not form a Pythagorean triple.

EXAMPLE 3 Solving a Real-Life Problem

The skyscrapers shown are connected by a skywalk with support beams. Use the Pythagorean Theorem to approximate the length of each support beam.

SOLUTION

Each support beam forms the hypotenuse of a right triangle. The right triangles are congruent, so the support beams are the same length.

$x^2 = (23.26)^2 + (47.57)^2$	Pythagorean Theorem
$x = \sqrt{(23.26)^2 + (47.57)^2}$	Find the positive square root.
$x \approx 52.95$	Use a calculator to approximate.

▶ The length of each support beam is about 52.95 meters.

Monitoring Progress 🔊 Help in English and Spanish at *BigIdeasMath.com*

Find the value of x. Then tell whether the side lengths form a Pythagorean triple.

1.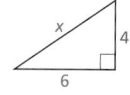

2.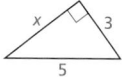

3. An anemometer is a device used to measure wind speed. The anemometer shown is attached to the top of a pole. Support wires are attached to the pole 5 feet above the ground. Each support wire is 6 feet long. How far from the base of the pole is each wire attached to the ground?

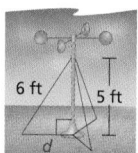

Section 9.1   The Pythagorean Theorem   **465**

Extra Example 2
Find the value of x. Then tell whether the side lengths form a Pythagorean triple.

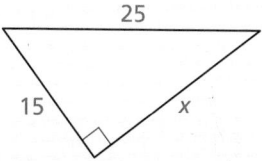

$x = 20$; Because the side lengths 15, 20, and 25 are integers that satisfy the equation $a^2 + b^2 = c^2$, they form a Pythagorean triple.

Extra Example 3
The flagpole shown is supported by two wires. Use the Pythagorean Theorem to approximate the length of each wire.

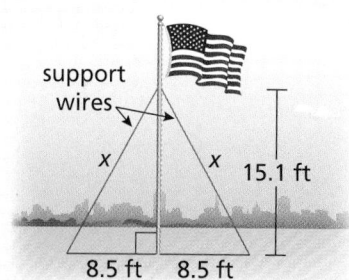

The length of each wire is about 17.3 feet.

MONITORING PROGRESS ANSWERS

1. $x = 2\sqrt{13} \approx 7.2$; no
2. $x = 4$; yes
3. about 3.32 ft

Laurie's Notes   Teacher Actions

- **Think-Pair-Share:** Pose Example 2, and have students work independently to solve.
- **MP5 Use Appropriate Tools Strategically:** Calculators are useful tools for this chapter.
- **MP6:** In Example 3, students are asked to approximate the length of each support beam. While a calculator could give a decimal answer with many place values, students should understand why a rounded answer is sufficient for the context.
- **Think-Pair-Share:** Have students answer Questions 1–3, and then share and discuss as a class.

Extra Example 4

Tell whether each triangle is a right triangle.

a.

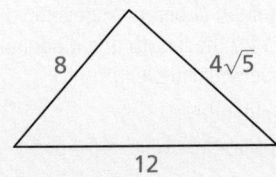

yes

b.

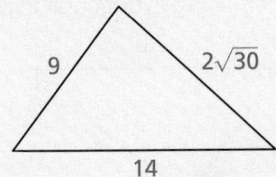

no

MONITORING PROGRESS ANSWERS

4. yes
5. no

Using the Converse of the Pythagorean Theorem

The converse of the Pythagorean Theorem is also true. You can use it to determine whether a triangle with given side lengths is a right triangle.

 Theorem

Theorem 9.2 Converse of the Pythagorean Theorem

If the square of the length of the longest side of a triangle is equal to the sum of the squares of the lengths of the other two sides, then the triangle is a right triangle.

If $c^2 = a^2 + b^2$, then $\triangle ABC$ is a right triangle.

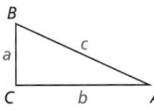

Proof Ex. 39, p. 470

EXAMPLE 4 **Verifying Right Triangles**

Tell whether each triangle is a right triangle.

a.

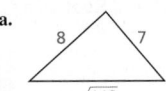

b.

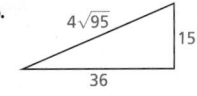

USING TOOLS STRATEGICALLY

Use a calculator to determine that $\sqrt{113} \approx 10.630$ is the length of the longest side in part (a).

SOLUTION

Let c represent the length of the longest side of the triangle. Check to see whether the side lengths satisfy the equation $c^2 = a^2 + b^2$.

a. $(\sqrt{113})^2 \stackrel{?}{=} 7^2 + 8^2$

$113 \stackrel{?}{=} 49 + 64$

$113 = 113$ ✔

▶ The triangle is a right triangle.

b. $(4\sqrt{95})^2 \stackrel{?}{=} 15^2 + 36^2$

$4^2 \cdot (\sqrt{95})^2 \stackrel{?}{=} 15^2 + 36^2$

$16 \cdot 95 \stackrel{?}{=} 225 + 1296$

$1520 \neq 1521$ ✗

▶ The triangle is *not* a right triangle.

Monitoring Progress 🔊 Help in English and Spanish at *BigIdeasMath.com*

Tell whether the triangle is a right triangle.

4.

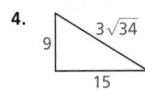

5.

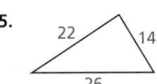

Laurie's Notes   Teacher Actions

❓ "Is the converse of every true statement also true?" no

❓ "What is the converse of the Pythagorean Theorem?" If the sum of the squares of the lengths of the two shorter sides of a triangle equals the square of the length of the longest side, then the triangle is a right triangle. Say, "The converse is true."

• **Think-Alouds:** In Example 4, have partner A *Think-Aloud* as he or she decides whether the triangle in part (a) is a right triangle. "If the triangle is a right triangle, then …." Partners now reverse roles as partner B decides whether the triangle in part (b) is a right triangle.

Classifying Triangles

The Converse of the Pythagorean Theorem is used to determine whether a triangle is a right triangle. You can use the theorem below to determine whether a triangle is acute or obtuse.

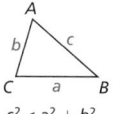 **Theorem**

Theorem 9.3 Pythagorean Inequalities Theorem

For any $\triangle ABC$, where c is the length of the longest side, the following statements are true.

If $c^2 < a^2 + b^2$, then $\triangle ABC$ is acute.   If $c^2 > a^2 + b^2$, then $\triangle ABC$ is obtuse.

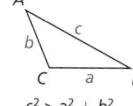

$$c^2 < a^2 + b^2$$ $$c^2 > a^2 + b^2$$

Proof Exs. 42 and 43, p. 470

REMEMBER

The Triangle Inequality Theorem (Theorem 6.11) on page 339 states that the sum of the lengths of any two sides of a triangle is greater than the length of the third side.

EXAMPLE 5 **Classifying Triangles**

Verify that segments with lengths of 4.3 feet, 5.2 feet, and 6.1 feet form a triangle. Is the triangle *acute*, *right*, or *obtuse*?

SOLUTION

Step 1 Use the Triangle Inequality Theorem (Theorem 6.11) to verify that the segments form a triangle.

$$4.3 + 5.2 \overset{?}{>} 6.1 \qquad 4.3 + 6.1 \overset{?}{>} 5.2 \qquad 5.2 + 6.1 \overset{?}{>} 4.3$$

$$9.5 > 6.1 \checkmark \qquad 10.4 > 5.2 \checkmark \qquad 11.3 > 4.3 \checkmark$$

▶ The segments with lengths of 4.3 feet, 5.2 feet, and 6.1 feet form a triangle.

Step 2 Classify the triangle by comparing the square of the length of the longest side with the sum of the squares of the lengths of the other two sides.

c^2 ▨ $a^2 + b^2$		Compare c^2 with $a^2 + b^2$.
6.1^2 ▨ $4.3^2 + 5.2^2$		Substitute.
37.21 ▨ $18.49 + 27.04$		Simplify.
$37.21 < 45.53$		c^2 is less than $a^2 + b^2$.

▶ The segments with lengths of 4.3 feet, 5.2 feet, and 6.1 feet form an acute triangle.

Monitoring Progress Help in English and Spanish at *BigIdeasMath.com*

6. Verify that segments with lengths of 3, 4, and 6 form a triangle. Is the triangle *acute*, *right*, or *obtuse*?

7. Verify that segments with lengths of 2.1, 2.8, and 3.5 form a triangle. Is the triangle *acute*, *right*, or *obtuse*?

Extra Example 5

Verify that segments with lengths of 14 meters, 15 meters, and 11 meters form a triangle. Is the triangle *acute*, *right*, or *obtuse*?

The segments form a triangle, because $14 + 15 > 11$, $15 + 11 > 14$, and $14 + 11 > 15$. Because $15^2 < 14^2 + 11^2$, the triangle is acute.

MONITORING PROGRESS ANSWERS

6. yes; obtuse

7. yes; right

Laurie's Notes   Teacher Actions

- **MP5:** Use dynamic geometry software to demonstrate the relationships stated in the Pythagorean Inequalities Theorem.
- In working independently on Example 5, students must reason about how to write the initial statement (equality or inequality). The sum of the squares of the lengths of the two shorter sides is compared to the square of the length of the longest side.

Closure

- **Exit Ticket:** Classify the triangles as acute, right, or obtuse. (a) sides 7, 9, and 11; (b) sides 6, 8, and 10 (a) acute triangle; (b) right triangle

ANSWERS

1. A Pythagorean triple is a set of three positive integers a, b, and c that satisfy the equation $c^2 = a^2 + b^2$.

2. Find the length of the longest leg; 4; 5

3. $x = \sqrt{170} \approx 13.0$; no

4. $x = 34$; yes

5. $x = 41$; yes

6. $x = 2\sqrt{13} \approx 7.2$; no

7. $x = 15$; yes

8. $x = 3\sqrt{55} \approx 22.2$; no

9. $x = 14$; yes

10. $x = 4\sqrt{2} \approx 5.7$; no

11. Exponents cannot be distributed as shown in the third line;
$c^2 = a^2 + b^2$; $x^2 = 7^2 + 24^2$;
$x^2 = 49 + 576$; $x^2 = 625$;
$x = 25$

12. Because 26 is the length of the hypotenuse, it should be substituted for c; $c^2 = a^2 + b^2$; $26^2 = 10^2 + x^2$; $676 = 100 + x^2$; $576 = x^2$; $24 = x$

Vocabulary and Core Concept Check

1. **VOCABULARY** What is a Pythagorean triple?

2. **DIFFERENT WORDS, SAME QUESTION** Which is different? Find "both" answers.

Find the length of the longest side.

Find the length of the hypotenuse.

Find the length of the longest leg.

Find the length of the side opposite the right angle.

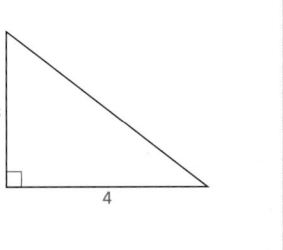

Monitoring Progress and Modeling with Mathematics

In Exercises 3–6, find the value of x. Then tell whether the side lengths form a Pythagorean triple. *(See Example 1.)*

3.
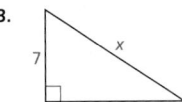

4.
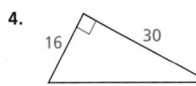

5.
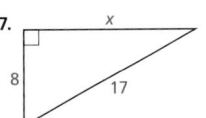

6.
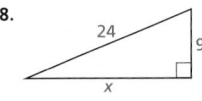

9.
10.
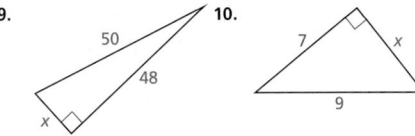

In Exercises 7–10, find the value of x. Then tell whether the side lengths form a Pythagorean triple. *(See Example 2.)*

7.
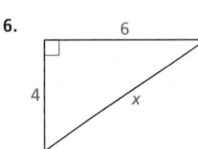

8.

ERROR ANALYSIS In Exercises 11 and 12, describe and correct the error in using the Pythagorean Theorem (Theorem 9.1).

11.
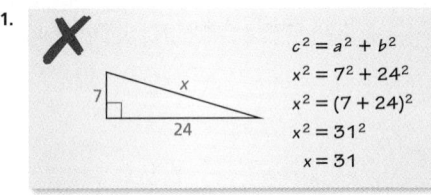

12.
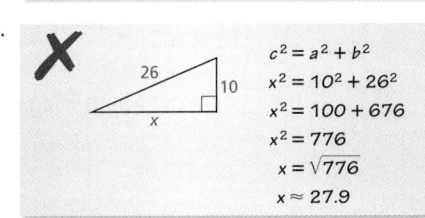

13. MODELING WITH MATHEMATICS The fire escape forms a right triangle, as shown. Use the Pythagorean Theorem (Theorem 9.1) to approximate the distance between the two platforms. *(See Example 3.)*

14. MODELING WITH MATHEMATICS The backboard of the basketball hoop forms a right triangle with the supporting rods, as shown. Use the Pythagorean Theorem (Theorem 9.1) to approximate the distance between the rods where they meet the backboard.

In Exercises 15–20, tell whether the triangle is a right triangle. *(See Example 4.)*

15.

16.
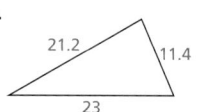

17.
 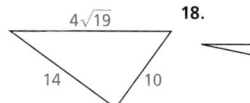

18.
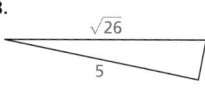

19.

20.
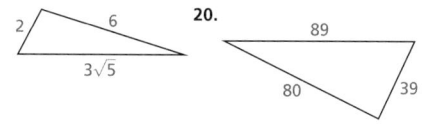

In Exercises 21–28, verify that the segment lengths form a triangle. Is the triangle *acute*, *right*, or *obtuse*? *(See Example 5.)*

21. 10, 11, and 14

22. 6, 8, and 10

23. 12, 16, and 20

24. 15, 20, and 36

25. 5.3, 6.7, and 7.8

26. 4.1, 8.2, and 12.2

27. 24, 30, and $6\sqrt{43}$

28. 10, 15, and $5\sqrt{13}$

29. MODELING WITH MATHEMATICS In baseball, the lengths of the paths between consecutive bases are 90 feet, and the paths form right angles. The player on first base tries to steal second base. How far does the ball need to travel from home plate to second base to get the player out?

30. REASONING You are making a canvas frame for a painting using stretcher bars. The rectangular painting will be 10 inches long and 8 inches wide. Using a ruler, how can you be certain that the corners of the frame are 90°?

In Exercises 31–34, find the area of the isosceles triangle.

31.
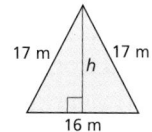

32.
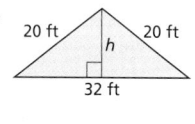

33.
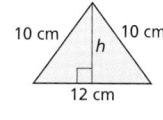

34.
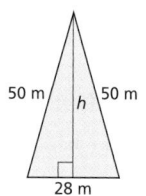

ANSWERS

13. about 14.1 ft
14. about 9.14 in.
15. yes
16. no
17. no
18. yes
19. no
20. yes
21. yes; acute
22. yes; right
23. yes; right
24. no
25. yes; acute
26. yes; obtuse
27. yes; obtuse
28. yes; right
29. about 127.3 ft
30. Each diagonal should form a right triangle with $c^2 = 8^2 + 10^2$, so each diagonal should be about 12.8 inches long.
31. 120 m²
32. 192 ft²
33. 48 cm²
34. 672 m²

ANSWERS

35. The horizontal distance between any two points is given by $(x_2 - x_1)$, and the vertical distance is given by $(y_2 - y_1)$. The horizontal and vertical segments that represent these distances form a right angle, with the segment between the two points being the hypotenuse. So, you can use the Pythagorean Theorem (Thm. 9.1) to say $d^2 = (x_2 - x_1)^2 + (y_2 - y_1)^2$, and when you solve for d, you get the distance formula: $d = \sqrt{(x_2 - x_1)^2 + (y_2 - y_1)^2}$.

36. Because $10^2 = 6^2 + 8^2$, by the Converse of the Pythagorean Theorem (Thm. 9.2), $\triangle ABC$ is a right triangle.

37. 2 packages

38–47. See Additional Answers.

Mini-Assessment

1. Tell whether a triangle with side lengths 8, $2\sqrt{65}$, and 14 is a right triangle. **yes**

2. Do segments with lengths 11 feet, 12 feet, and 20 feet form a triangle? If so, classify the triangle as *acute*, *right*, or *obtuse*. **Yes, the segments form a triangle because $11 + 12 > 20$, $11 + 20 > 12$, and $12 + 20 > 11$. Because $20^2 > 11^2 + 12^2$, the triangle is obtuse.**

3. A boat travels 1 mile east and then turns and travels 2.4 miles north. How far is the boat from its starting point? **2.6 miles**

4. The sides of a triangle have lengths 5, 7 and x.
   a. For what values of x is the triangle a right triangle? **$2\sqrt{6}$ and $\sqrt{74}$**
   b. Tell whether the side lengths form a Pythagorean triple. **no; The values of x are not integers.**

470   Chapter 9

---

35. ANALYZING RELATIONSHIPS Justify the Distance Formula using the Pythagorean Theorem (Thm. 9.1).

36. HOW DO YOU SEE IT? How do you know $\angle C$ is a right angle without using the Pythagorean Theorem (Theorem 9.1)?

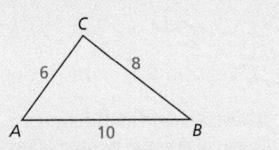

37. PROBLEM SOLVING You are making a kite and need to figure out how much binding to buy. You need the binding for the perimeter of the kite. The binding comes in packages of two yards. How many packages should you buy?

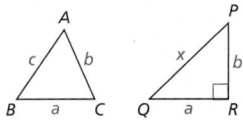

15 in.
12 in.
12 in.
20 in.

38. PROVING A THEOREM Use the Pythagorean Theorem (Theorem 9.1) to prove the Hypotenuse-Leg (HL) Congruence Theorem (Theorem 5.9).

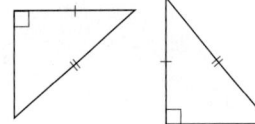

39. PROVING A THEOREM Prove the Converse of the Pythagorean Theorem (Theorem 9.2). (*Hint*: Draw $\triangle ABC$ with side lengths a, b, and c, where c is the length of the longest side. Then draw a right triangle with side lengths a, b, and x, where x is the length of the hypotenuse. Compare lengths c and x.)

40. THOUGHT PROVOKING Consider two integers m and n, where $m > n$. Do the following expressions produce a Pythagorean triple? If yes, prove your answer. If no, give a counterexample.

$$2mn, \quad m^2 - n^2, \quad m^2 + n^2$$

41. MAKING AN ARGUMENT Your friend claims 72 and 75 cannot be part of a Pythagorean triple because $72^2 + 75^2$ does not equal a positive integer squared. Is your friend correct? Explain your reasoning.

42. PROVING A THEOREM Copy and complete the proof of the Pythagorean Inequalities Theorem (Theorem 9.3) when $c^2 < a^2 + b^2$.

Given In $\triangle ABC$, $c^2 < a^2 + b^2$, where c is the length of the longest side. $\triangle PQR$ has side lengths a, b, and x, where x is the length of the hypotenuse, and $\angle R$ is a right angle.

Prove $\triangle ABC$ is an acute triangle.

STATEMENTS	REASONS
1. In $\triangle ABC$, $c^2 < a^2 + b^2$, where c is the length of the longest side. $\triangle PQR$ has side lengths a, b, and x, where x is the length of the hypotenuse, and $\angle R$ is a right angle.	1. _____
2. $a^2 + b^2 = x^2$	2. _____
3. $c^2 < x^2$	3. _____
4. $c < x$	4. Take the positive square root of each side.
5. $m\angle R = 90°$	5. _____
6. $m\angle C < m\angle R$	6. Converse of the Hinge Theorem (Theorem 6.13)
7. $m\angle C < 90°$	7. _____
8. $\angle C$ is an acute angle.	8. _____
9. $\triangle ABC$ is an acute triangle.	9. _____

43. PROVING A THEOREM Prove the Pythagorean Inequalities Theorem (Theorem 9.3) when $c^2 > a^2 + b^2$. (*Hint*: Look back at Exercise 42.)

Maintaining Mathematical Proficiency   Reviewing what you learned in previous grades and lessons

Simplify the expression by rationalizing the denominator. (*Skills Review Handbook*)

44. $\dfrac{7}{\sqrt{2}}$ **45.** $\dfrac{14}{\sqrt{3}}$ **46.** $\dfrac{8}{\sqrt{2}}$ **47.** $\dfrac{12}{\sqrt{3}}$

470   Chapter 9   Right Triangles and Trigonometry

If students need help...	If students got it...
Resources by Chapter • Practice A and Practice B • Puzzle Time	Resources by Chapter • Enrichment and Extension • Cumulative Review
Student Journal • Practice	Start the *next* Section
Differentiating the Lesson Skills Review Handbook	

Dynamic Teaching Tools

Dynamic Assessment & Progress Monitoring Tool

Lesson Planning Tool

Interactive Whiteboard Lesson Library

Dynamic Classroom with Dynamic Investigations

Overview of Section 9.2

Introduction

- In this lesson, students will use their knowledge of similar triangles and the Pythagorean Theorem to deduce relationships about special right triangles.
- The two special triangles are the 45°-45°-90° and 30°-60°-90° triangles. The ratio of any two sides of a right isosceles triangle (i.e., hypotenuse to leg) will be the same regardless of the size of the right isosceles triangle. These relationships are stated as theorems.
- The lesson ends with using the side length relationships of special right triangles to solve real-life problems.

Teaching Strategy

- I have found that it is important for students to do some sort of investigation to appreciate and make sense of the relationship between the legs and the hypotenuse in a right isosceles triangle. A technological approach is presented in the first exploration. Alternately, the investigation can be done with paper folding.
- Begin with a 6-inch square piece of paper. Fold the square on its diagonal to form two isosceles right triangles. Measure and record the lengths of a leg and the hypotenuse in a table.
- Continue folding the paper into smaller isosceles right triangles and filling in the table.

Number of Folds	Leg Length	Hypotenuse	Hypotenuse / Leg Length
1			
2			
3			
4			
5			

- Use a calculator to find the ratios of hypotenuse to leg length. Depending upon the accuracy of students' measurements, the ratios should always be close to 1.41, the approximation of $\sqrt{2}$.
- Write $\dfrac{\text{hypotenuse}}{\text{leg}} = \sqrt{2}$. Solving for the length of the hypotenuse, hypotenuse $= \text{leg} \cdot \sqrt{2}$.

Pacing Suggestion

- Take time for students to explore and discover the relationships between the side lengths in special right triangles, and then transition to the formal lesson.

Common Core
State Standards

HSG-SRT.C.8 Use trigonometric ratios and the Pythagorean Theorem to solve right triangles in applied problems.

HSG-MG.A.1 Use geometric shapes, their measures, and their properties to describe objects (e.g., modeling a tree trunk or a human torso as a cylinder).

Laurie's Notes

Exploration

Motivate

- Pose a baseball problem for students. If you are located near a major league team, you could display the team's logo!
- "The distance between bases is 90 feet. What is the *exact* distance from home plate to second base?" Students should note the use of the word *exact*, and they should also realize that the problem involves finding the length of a diagonal of a square where the side lengths are known.
- This problem allows you to review simplifying expressions involving radicals, a technique that is needed in this lesson.
- The exact distance is $90\sqrt{2}$ feet.

Exploration Note

- There are different techniques students can use to construct the special triangles in the two explorations.
- One way is certainly to look at the coordinates in the diagram. Students should be able to reason why (0, 0), (4, 0), and (0, 4) are the coordinates of a right isosceles triangle.
- This technique is not possible for the 30°-60°-90° triangle because the *y*-coordinate of vertex *A* is not obvious. One way my students have efficiently constructed a 30°-60°-90° triangle is to construct an equilateral triangle and then construct one of the angle bisectors.
- Whatever method(s) students use, they should note that the construction and subsequent measurements are going to be repeated several times. Students might want to consider how to perform the construction so that the construction and measurements are dynamic.

Exploration 1

- Circulate as students construct the right isosceles triangle so that you know the various methods used by your students.
- The lengths of the sides are measured, and three ratios are calculated.
- **?** "What did you observe about the computed ratios? Explain why this occurred." The triangles are all similar by AA. The ratio of any two sides is going to stay the same as the triangle is enlarged or reduced proportionally.
- **MP6 Attend to Precision:** Ask students to explain how to find the exact ratio versus an approximation. This will take some students longer to reason through. Give *Wait Time* for partners to discuss this. The Pythagorean Theorem should come to mind! Using one of the triangles where the legs are integer values will allow students to find the hypotenuse exactly.

Exploration 2

- Have students work through this exploration in a manner similar to the first. The difference being that to find the exact values, it will be the shorter leg and the hypotenuse that will be integer values.

Communicate Your Answer

- Listen for students to describe the relationships found while working through the explorations.

Connecting to Next Step

- Students have discovered the special relationships between the side lengths in 45°-45°-90° and 30°-60°-90° triangles. These will be stated as theorems in the formal lesson.

9.2 Special Right Triangles

Essential Question
What is the relationship among the side lengths of 45°-45°-90° triangles? 30°-60°-90° triangles?

EXPLORATION 1   Side Ratios of an Isosceles Right Triangle

Work with a partner.

a. Use dynamic geometry software to construct an isosceles right triangle with a leg length of 4 units.

b. Find the acute angle measures. Explain why this triangle is called a 45°-45°-90° triangle.

> **ATTENDING TO PRECISION**
> To be proficient in math, you need to express numerical answers with a degree of precision appropriate for the problem context.

c. Find the exact ratios of the side lengths (using square roots).

$$\frac{AB}{AC} = $$

$$\frac{AB}{BC} = $$

$$\frac{AC}{BC} = $$

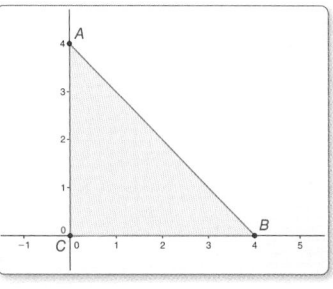

Sample

Points
$A(0, 4)$
$B(4, 0)$
$C(0, 0)$
Segments
$AB = 5.66$
$BC = 4$
$AC = 4$
Angles
$m\angle A = 45°$
$m\angle B = 45°$

d. Repeat parts (a) and (c) for several other isosceles right triangles. Use your results to write a conjecture about the ratios of the side lengths of an isosceles right triangle.

EXPLORATION 2   Side Ratios of a 30°-60°-90° Triangle

Work with a partner.

a. Use dynamic geometry software to construct a right triangle with acute angle measures of 30° and 60° (a 30°-60°-90° triangle), where the shorter leg length is 3 units.

b. Find the exact ratios of the side lengths (using square roots).

$$\frac{AB}{AC} = $$

$$\frac{AB}{BC} = $$

$$\frac{AC}{BC} = $$

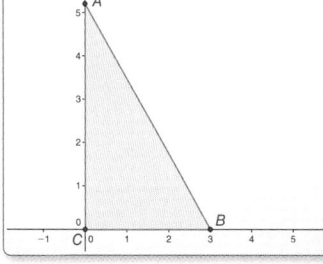

Sample

Points
$A(0, 5.20)$
$B(3, 0)$
$C(0, 0)$
Segments
$AB = 6$
$BC = 3$
$AC = 5.20$
Angles
$m\angle A = 30°$
$m\angle B = 60°$

c. Repeat parts (a) and (b) for several other 30°-60°-90° triangles. Use your results to write a conjecture about the ratios of the side lengths of a 30°-60°-90° triangle.

Communicate Your Answer

3. What is the relationship among the side lengths of 45°-45°-90° triangles? 30°-60°-90° triangles?

Section 9.2   Special Right Triangles   **471**

Dynamic Teaching Tools

Dynamic Assessment & Progress Monitoring Tool

Lesson Planning Tool

Interactive Whiteboard Lesson Library

Dynamic Classroom with Dynamic Investigations

ANSWERS

1. a. Check students' work.

b. 45° and 45°; 45°-45°-90° describes the angle measures.

c. $\sqrt{2}$; $\sqrt{2}$; 1

d. Check students' work. The ratio of the length of each leg to the length of the hypotenuse is $\sqrt{2}$. The ratio of the length of one leg to the other is 1.

2. a. Check students' work.

b. $\dfrac{2}{\sqrt{3}}$; 2; $\sqrt{3}$

c. Check students' work. The ratio of the length of the hypotenuse to the length of the longer leg is $\dfrac{2}{\sqrt{3}}$. The ratio of the length of the hypotenuse to the length of the shorter leg is 2. The ratio of the length of the longer leg to the length of the shorter leg is $\sqrt{3}$.

3. In a 45°-45°-90° triangle, the legs are the same length, and the length of the hypotenuse is $\sqrt{2}$ times as long as each leg. In a 30°-60°-90° triangle, the hypotenuse is twice as long as the shorter leg, and the longer leg is $\sqrt{3}$ times as long as the shorter leg.

Extra Example 1

Find the value of *x*. Write your answer in simplest form.

a.

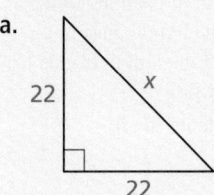

22
x
22

$22\sqrt{2}$

b.

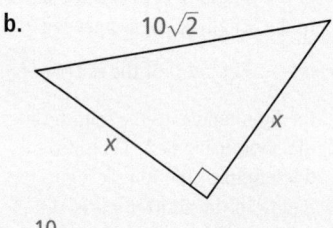

$10\sqrt{2}$
x
x
10

9.2 Lesson

Core Vocabulary

Previous
isosceles triangle

What You Will Learn

▶ Find side lengths in special right triangles.
▶ Solve real-life problems involving special right triangles.

Finding Side Lengths in Special Right Triangles

A 45°-45°-90° triangle is an *isosceles right triangle* that can be formed by cutting a square in half diagonally.

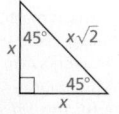

🌀 Theorem

Theorem 9.4   45°-45°-90° Triangle Theorem

In a 45°-45°-90° triangle, the hypotenuse is $\sqrt{2}$ times as long as each leg.

x
45°
$x\sqrt{2}$
45°
x

$\text{hypotenuse} = \text{leg} \cdot \sqrt{2}$

Proof Ex. 19, p. 476

EXAMPLE 1   **Finding Side Lengths in 45°-45°-90° Triangles**

Find the value of *x*. Write your answer in simplest form.

a.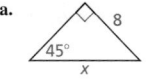

45°
8
x

b.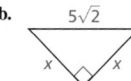

$5\sqrt{2}$
x
x

SOLUTION

a. By the Triangle Sum Theorem (Theorem 5.1), the measure of the third angle must be 45°, so the triangle is a 45°-45°-90° triangle.

$\text{hypotenuse} = \text{leg} \cdot \sqrt{2}$ 45°-45°-90° Triangle Theorem

$x = 8 \cdot \sqrt{2}$ Substitute.

$x = 8\sqrt{2}$ Simplify.

▶ The value of *x* is $8\sqrt{2}$.

b. By the Base Angles Theorem (Theorem 5.6) and the Corollary to the Triangle Sum Theorem (Corollary 5.1), the triangle is a 45°-45°-90° triangle.

$\text{hypotenuse} = \text{leg} \cdot \sqrt{2}$ 45°-45°-90° Triangle Theorem

$5\sqrt{2} = x \cdot \sqrt{2}$ Substitute.

$\dfrac{5\sqrt{2}}{\sqrt{2}} = \dfrac{x\sqrt{2}}{\sqrt{2}}$ Divide each side by $\sqrt{2}$.

$5 = x$ Simplify.

▶ The value of *x* is 5.

Laurie's Notes   Teacher Actions

- State the theorem and connect to Exploration 1 done by students. See the *Teaching Strategy* on page T-470.
- In answering problems, such as Example 1, students will often start to use the Pythagorean Theorem to solve for the missing side length versus applying Theorem 9.4.
- **MP2 Reason Abstractly and Quantitatively:** Mathematically proficient students understand that all right isosceles triangles possess the relationship stated in the theorem. They use the theorem versus performing a computation each time.

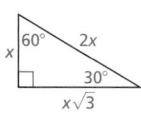 **Theorem**

Theorem 9.5 30°-60°-90° Triangle Theorem

In a 30°-60°-90° triangle, the hypotenuse is twice as long as the shorter leg, and the longer leg is $\sqrt{3}$ times as long as the shorter leg.

hypotenuse = shorter leg · 2
longer leg = shorter leg · $\sqrt{3}$

Proof Ex. 21, p. 476

EXAMPLE 2 Finding Side Lengths in a 30°-60°-90° Triangle

Find the values of x and y. Write your answer in simplest form.

SOLUTION

Step 1 Find the value of x.

longer leg = shorter leg · $\sqrt{3}$	30°-60°-90° Triangle Theorem
$9 = x \cdot \sqrt{3}$	Substitute.
$\dfrac{9}{\sqrt{3}} = x$	Divide each side by $\sqrt{3}$.
$\dfrac{9}{\sqrt{3}} \cdot \dfrac{\sqrt{3}}{\sqrt{3}} = x$	Multiply by $\dfrac{\sqrt{3}}{\sqrt{3}}$.
$\dfrac{9\sqrt{3}}{3} = x$	Multiply fractions.
$3\sqrt{3} = x$	Simplify.

▶ The value of x is $3\sqrt{3}$.

Step 2 Find the value of y.

hypotenuse = shorter leg · 2	30°-60°-90° Triangle Theorem
$y = 3\sqrt{3} \cdot 2$	Substitute.
$y = 6\sqrt{3}$	Simplify.

▶ The value of y is $6\sqrt{3}$.

Monitoring Progress ◀)) Help in English and Spanish at *BigIdeasMath.com*

Find the value of the variable. Write your answer in simplest form.

1.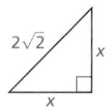

2.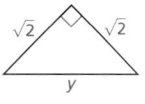

3.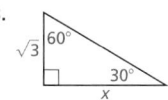

4.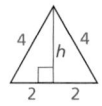

REMEMBER

Because the angle opposite 9 is larger than the angle opposite x, the leg with length 9 is longer than the leg with length x by the Triangle Larger Angle Theorem (Theorem 6.10).

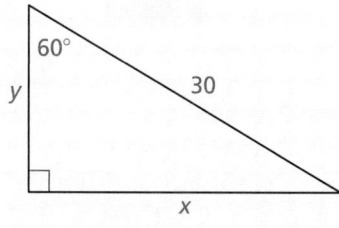

Differentiated Instruction

Inclusion

Work with advanced students to develop the formula for the area A of a 30°-60°-90° triangle with hypotenuse of length s. Check to see whether they wrote $A = \dfrac{s^2\sqrt{3}}{8}$.

Extra Example 2

Find the values of x and y. Write your answer in simplest form.

$x = 15\sqrt{3}$, $y = 15$

MONITORING PROGRESS ANSWERS

1. $x = 2$
2. $y = 2$
3. $x = 3$
4. $h = 2\sqrt{3}$

Laurie's Notes   Teacher Actions

- State the theorem and connect to Exploration 2 done by students. Stress that there are two relationships stated in this theorem.
- Discuss with students that the shorter leg is also referred to as the side opposite 30° and the longer leg is the side opposite 60°.
- **?** "How do you simplify an expression that has a radical in the denominator?" Multiply by a factor of 1 — the radical divided by itself.
- **Think-Pair-Share:** Have students answer Questions 1–4, and then share and discuss as a class.

Extra Example 3

A warning sticker is shaped like an equilateral triangle with side length of 4 inches. Estimate the area of the sticker by finding the area of the equilateral triangle to the nearest tenth of an inch.

The area of the sign is about 6.9 square inches.

Extra Example 4

Use the diagram in Example 4. How high is the end of a 54-foot ramp when the tipping angle is 30°? **27 feet**

MONITORING PROGRESS ANSWERS

5. about 15.59 cm²

6. about 12 ft

Solving Real-Life Problems

EXAMPLE 3   **Modeling with Mathematics**

The road sign is shaped like an equilateral triangle. Estimate the area of the sign by finding the area of the equilateral triangle.

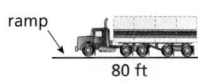

SOLUTION

First find the height h of the triangle by dividing it into two 30°-60°-90° triangles. The length of the longer leg of one of these triangles is h. The length of the shorter leg is 18 inches.

$$h = 18 \cdot \sqrt{3} = 18\sqrt{3} \qquad \text{30°-60°-90° Triangle Theorem}$$

Use $h = 18\sqrt{3}$ to find the area of the equilateral triangle.

$$\text{Area} = \tfrac{1}{2}bh = \tfrac{1}{2}(36)(18\sqrt{3}) \approx 561.18$$

▶ The area of the sign is about 561 square inches.

EXAMPLE 4   **Finding the Height of a Ramp**

A tipping platform is a ramp used to unload trucks. How high is the end of an 80-foot ramp when the tipping angle is 30°? 45°?

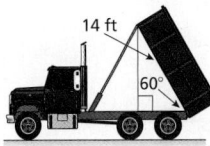

SOLUTION

When the tipping angle is 30°, the height h of the ramp is the length of the shorter leg of a 30°-60°-90° triangle. The length of the hypotenuse is 80 feet.

$$80 = 2h \qquad \text{30°-60°-90° Triangle Theorem}$$

$$40 = h \qquad \text{Divide each side by 2.}$$

When the tipping angle is 45°, the height h of the ramp is the length of a leg of a 45°-45°-90° triangle. The length of the hypotenuse is 80 feet.

$$80 = h \cdot \sqrt{2} \qquad \text{45°-45°-90° Triangle Theorem}$$

$$\frac{80}{\sqrt{2}} = h \qquad \text{Divide each side by } \sqrt{2}.$$

$$56.6 \approx h \qquad \text{Use a calculator.}$$

▶ When the tipping angle is 30°, the ramp height is 40 feet. When the tipping angle is 45°, the ramp height is about 56 feet 7 inches.

Monitoring Progress Help in English and Spanish at *BigIdeasMath.com*

5. The logo on a recycling bin resembles an equilateral triangle with side lengths of 6 centimeters. Approximate the area of the logo.

6. The body of a dump truck is raised to empty a load of sand. How high is the 14-foot-long body from the frame when it is tipped upward by a 60° angle?

Laurie's Notes   Teacher Actions

? "In Example 3, why is the answer not left in exact form?" An estimate was asked for, and in using the answer for a contextual purpose, an approximation may be more helpful.

? "In Example 4, as the tipping angle increases, what happens to the height of the front of the truck?" It increases.

Closure

- **Exit Ticket:** (a) The hypotenuse of a right isosceles triangle is 12. Find the length of the legs. $6\sqrt{2}$ (b) The hypotenuse of a 30°-60°-90° triangle is 12. Find the lengths of the legs. 6 and $6\sqrt{3}$

9.2 Exercises

Dynamic Solutions available at *BigIdeasMath.com*

Vocabulary and Core Concept Check

1. **VOCABULARY** Name two special right triangles by their angle measures.

2. **WRITING** Explain why the acute angles in an isosceles right triangle always measure 45°.

Monitoring Progress and Modeling with Mathematics

In Exercises 3–6, find the value of x. Write your answer in simplest form. *(See Example 1.)*

3.
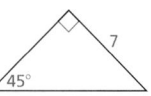

4.
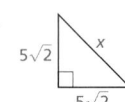

5.

6.
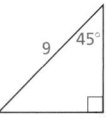

In Exercises 7–10, find the values of x and y. Write your answers in simplest form. *(See Example 2.)*

7.
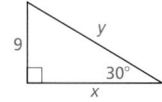

8.
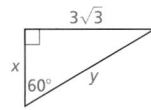

9.
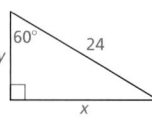

10.
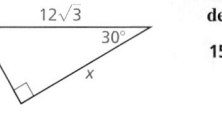

ERROR ANALYSIS In Exercises 11 and 12, describe and correct the error in finding the length of the hypotenuse.

11.

By the Triangle Sum Theorem (Theorem 5.1), the measure of the third angle must be 60°. So, the triangle is a 30°-60°-90° triangle.

hypotenuse = shorter leg • $\sqrt{3}$ = $7\sqrt{3}$

So, the length of the hypotenuse is $7\sqrt{3}$ units.

12.
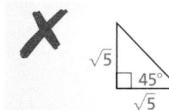

By the Triangle Sum Theorem (Theorem 5.1), the measure of the third angle must be 45°. So, the triangle is a 45°-45°-90° triangle.

hypotenuse = leg • leg • $\sqrt{2}$ = $5\sqrt{2}$

So, the length of the hypotenuse is $5\sqrt{2}$ units.

In Exercises 13 and 14, sketch the figure that is described. Find the indicated length. Round decimal answers to the nearest tenth.

13. The side length of an equilateral triangle is 5 centimeters. Find the length of an altitude.

14. The perimeter of a square is 36 inches. Find the length of a diagonal.

In Exercises 15 and 16, find the area of the figure. Round decimal answers to the nearest tenth. *(See Example 3.)*

15.
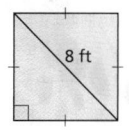

16.
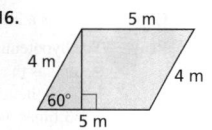

17. **PROBLEM SOLVING** Each half of the drawbridge is about 284 feet long. How high does the drawbridge rise when x is 30°? 45°? 60°? *(See Example 4.)*

Section 9.2   Special Right Triangles   **475**

Assignment Guide and Homework Check

ASSIGNMENT

Basic: 1, 2, 3–17 odd, 20, 24, 26, 27

Average: 1, 2, 6–20 even, 21, 24, 26, 27

Advanced: 1, 2, 6–18 even, 19–27

HOMEWORK CHECK

Basic: 5, 9, 13, 15, 20

Average: 6, 10, 14, 16, 21

Advanced: 6, 10, 14, 16, 22

ANSWERS

1. 45°-45°-90°, 30°-60°-90°

2. Because the acute angles of a right isosceles triangle must be congruent by the Base Angles Theorem (Thm. 5.6), and complementary, the measures must be $\frac{90°}{2} = 45°$.

3. $x = 7\sqrt{2}$

4. $x = 10$

5. $x = 3$

6. $x = \dfrac{9\sqrt{2}}{2}$

7. $x = 9\sqrt{3}$, $y = 18$

8. $x = 3$, $y = 6$

9. $x = 12\sqrt{3}$, $y = 12$

10. $x = 18$; $y = 6\sqrt{3}$

11. The hypotenuse of a 30°-60°-90° triangle is equal to the shorter leg times 2; hypotenuse = shorter leg • 2 = 7 • 2 = 14; So, the length of the hypotenuse is 14 units.

12. The hypotenuse of a 45°-45°-90° triangle is equal to a leg times $\sqrt{2}$; hypotenuse = leg • $\sqrt{2}$ = $\sqrt{5}$ • $\sqrt{2}$ = $\sqrt{10}$; So, the length of the hypotenuse is $\sqrt{10}$ units.

13.

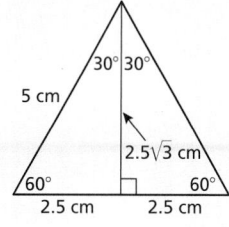

about 4.3 cm

14.
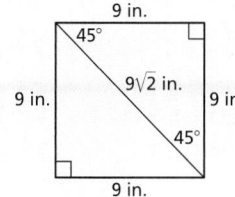

about 12.7 in.

15. 32 ft²

16. about 17.3 m²

17. 142 ft; about 200.82 ft; about 245.95 ft

ANSWERS

18. $x = \sqrt{3}$ cm

19. Because $\triangle DEF$ is a 45°-45°-90° triangle, by the Converse of the Base Angles Theorem (Thm. 5.7), $\overline{DF} \cong \overline{FE}$. So, let $x = DF = FE$. By the Pythagorean Theorem (Thm. 9.1), $x^2 + x^2 = c^2$, where c is the length of the hypotenuse. So, $2x^2 = c^2$ by the Distributive Property. Take the positive square root of each side to get $x\sqrt{2} = c$. So, the hypotenuse is $\sqrt{2}$ times as long as each leg.

20–25. See Additional Answers.

26. $x = 18$

27. $x = 2$

Mini-Assessment

1. This quilt is made up of cloth pieces shaped like isosceles right triangles. The hypotenuse of each triangle is 16 centimeters long. Find the area of one cloth triangle.

64 square centimeters

2. Use the diagram in Example 4. How high is the end of a 38-foot ramp when the tipping angle is 30°?
19 feet

3. Find the values of x and y.

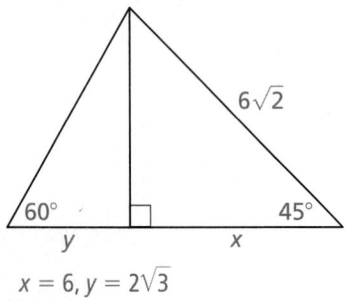

$x = 6$, $y = 2\sqrt{3}$

---

18. MODELING WITH MATHEMATICS A nut is shaped like a regular hexagon with side lengths of 1 centimeter. Find the value of x. (*Hint:* A regular hexagon can be divided into six congruent triangles.)

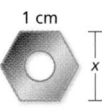

19. PROVING A THEOREM Write a paragraph proof of the 45°-45°-90° Triangle Theorem (Theorem 9.4).

Given $\triangle DEF$ is a 45°-45°-90° triangle.

Prove The hypotenuse is $\sqrt{2}$ times as long as each leg.

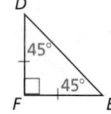

20. HOW DO YOU SEE IT? The diagram shows part of the *Wheel of Theodorus*.

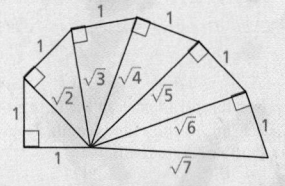

  a. Which triangles, if any, are 45°-45°-90° triangles?

  b. Which triangles, if any, are 30°-60°-90° triangles?

21. PROVING A THEOREM Write a paragraph proof of the 30°-60°-90° Triangle Theorem (Theorem 9.5). (*Hint:* Construct $\triangle JML$ congruent to $\triangle JKL$.)

Given $\triangle JKL$ is a 30°-60°-90° triangle.

Prove The hypotenuse is twice as long as the shorter leg, and the longer leg is $\sqrt{3}$ times as long as the shorter leg.

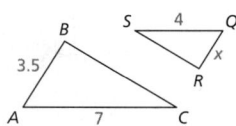

Maintaining Mathematical Proficiency
Reviewing what you learned in previous grades and lessons

Find the value of x. (*Section 8.1*)

26. $\triangle DEF \sim \triangle LMN$

27. $\triangle ABC \sim \triangle QRS$

---

22. THOUGHT PROVOKING A special right triangle is a right triangle that has rational angle measures and each side length contains at most one square root. There are only three special right triangles. The diagram below is called the *Ailles rectangle*. Label the sides and angles in the diagram. Describe all three special right triangles.

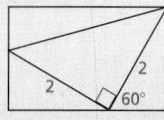

23. WRITING Describe two ways to show that all isosceles right triangles are similar to each other.

24. MAKING AN ARGUMENT Each triangle in the diagram is a 45°-45°-90° triangle. At Stage 0, the legs of the triangle are each 1 unit long. Your brother claims the lengths of the legs of the triangles added are halved at each stage. So, the length of a leg of a triangle added in Stage 8 will be $\frac{1}{256}$ unit. Is your brother correct? Explain your reasoning.

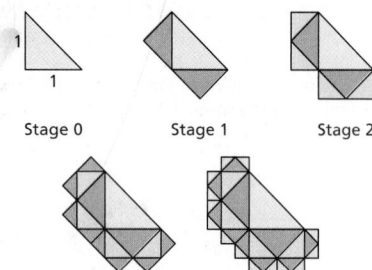

25. USING STRUCTURE $\triangle TUV$ is a 30°-60°-90° triangle, where two vertices are $U(3, -1)$ and $V(-3, -1)$, $\overline{UV}$ is the hypotenuse, and point T is in Quadrant I. Find the coordinates of T.

Overview of Section 9.3

Introduction

- This lesson applies students' understanding of similar triangles to the triangles formed when the altitude to the hypotenuse in a right triangle is drawn.
- The theorems that follow reference certain segments as being the *geometric mean* of two other segments.
- The geometric mean is used to solve real-life problems.

Teaching Strategy

- The challenge many students have with the Right Triangle Similarity Theorem is in correctly naming the pairs of triangles that are similar. One reason for the difficulty is that the triangles are in different orientations.
- It is helpful to actually have physical copies of the three triangles or to create them using dynamic geometry software or an interactive whiteboard.
- To make physical copies to manipulate, cut two congruent right scalene triangles. Draw the altitude to the hypotenuse in one of the right triangles. Cut along the altitude, making two smaller triangles.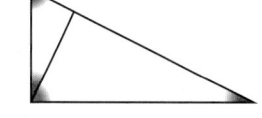
- You can overlay the triangles to see the congruent angles. In doing so, it becomes obvious that the smaller triangles must be reflected in order to overlay the original triangle. It is this spatial manipulation that makes it difficult for students to write the similarity statements for these triangles.

Pacing Suggestion

- The two explorations provide an introduction to geometric means and the similar triangles found when the altitude to the hypotenuse is drawn in a right triangle. Transition to the formal lesson after the second exploration has been discussed.

Common Core State Standards

HSG-SRT.B.5 Use … similarity criteria for triangles to solve problems and to prove relationships in geometric figures.

Exploration

Motivate
- Pose the following problem: You invest $1000. The first year your money earns 10%, and the second year your money earns 20%. What is your average rate of return over the two years?
- Students may incorrectly say 15%. Perform the computation: $1000 × 1.1 = $1100 at the end of year one. $1100 × 1.2 = $1320 at the end of year two.
- The geometric mean of 1.1 (110%) and 1.2 (120%) is approximately 1.1489, which is the average rate of return over two years.
- Today's lesson involves finding geometric means.

Exploration 1
- The construction of the right triangle and altitude are straightforward. Students will need to read and understand the definition of a *geometric mean*, which is not difficult.
- A similarity statement is given for the two smaller triangles: $\triangle CBD \sim \triangle ACD$. Ask students how they could prove that the triangles are similar.
- In part (c), finding *CD* is done by setting up the proportion. The measure can be verified using the software.
- Some students may want to repeat the construction for several right triangles to ensure that they understand the relationship between the altitude and the segments formed on the hypotenuse. The generalization follows from the smaller triangles being similar.

Exploration 2
- This exploration can be done using a spreadsheet or lists in the graphing calculator.
- **Extension:** Students should be aware that there is a third type of (Pythagorean) mean—the harmonic mean. The harmonic mean for two positive numbers a and b is $\dfrac{2}{\frac{1}{a} + \frac{1}{b}}$. When compared to the arithmetic mean and the geometric mean, given two positive numbers, the following relationship is true: arithmetic mean ≥ geometric mean ≥ harmonic mean.

Communicate Your Answer
- Have students share their thinking about the relationship between altitudes and geometric means of right triangles.

Connecting to Next Step
- Students have now explored the altitude to the hypotenuse in a right triangle. The relationship between the altitude and the segments formed on the hypotenuse will be stated at the beginning of the formal lesson.

9.3 Similar Right Triangles

Essential Question
How are altitudes and geometric means of right triangles related?

EXPLORATION 1   Writing a Conjecture

Work with a partner.

a. Use dynamic geometry software to construct right △ABC, as shown. Draw $\overline{CD}$ so that it is an altitude from the right angle to the hypotenuse of △ABC.

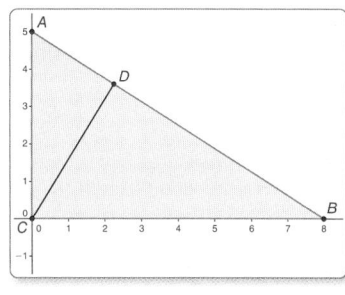

Points
A(0, 5)
B(8, 0)
C(0, 0)
D(2.25, 3.6)
Segments
AB = 9.43
BC = 8
AC = 5

CONSTRUCTING VIABLE ARGUMENTS

To be proficient in math, you need to understand and use stated assumptions, definitions, and previously established results in constructing arguments.

b. The **geometric mean** of two positive numbers a and b is the positive number x that satisfies

$$\frac{a}{x} = \frac{x}{b}.$$ x is the geometric mean of a and b.

Write a proportion involving the side lengths of △CBD and △ACD so that CD is the geometric mean of two of the other side lengths. Use similar triangles to justify your steps.

c. Use the proportion you wrote in part (b) to find CD.

d. Generalize the proportion you wrote in part (b). Then write a conjecture about how the geometric mean is related to the altitude from the right angle to the hypotenuse of a right triangle.

EXPLORATION 2   Comparing Geometric and Arithmetic Means

Work with a partner. Use a spreadsheet to find the arithmetic mean and the geometric mean of several pairs of positive numbers. Compare the two means. What do you notice?

	A	B	C	D
1	a	b	Arithmetic Mean	Geometric Mean
2	3	4	3.5	3.464
3	4	5		
4	6	7		
5	0.5	0.5		
6	0.4	0.8		
7	2	5		
8	1	4		
9	9	16		
10	10	100		
11				

Communicate Your Answer

3. How are altitudes and geometric means of right triangles related?

3. In a right triangle, the altitude from the right angle to the hypotenuse divides the hypotenuse into two segments. The length of the altitude is the geometric mean of the lengths of the two segments of the hypotenuse.

Dynamic Teaching Tools

Dynamic Assessment & Progress Monitoring Tool

Lesson Planning Tool

Interactive Whiteboard Lesson Library

Dynamic Classroom with Dynamic Investigations

ANSWERS

1. a. Check students' work.

   b. $\frac{AD}{CD} = \frac{CD}{BD}$; By the Corollary to the Triangle Sum Theorem (Cor. 5.1), two pairs of angles are complementary, ∠A and ∠ACD as well as ∠B and ∠BCD. Also, because adjacent angles ∠ACD and ∠BCD form a right angle, they are complementary. Then, by the Congruent Complements Theorem (Thm. 2.5), ∠A ≅ ∠BCD and ∠B ≅ ∠ACD. So, △ACD ~ △BCD by the AA Similarity Theorem (Thm. 8.3). Then, because corresponding sides of similar figures are proportional, $\frac{AD}{CD} = \frac{CD}{BD}$.

   c. about 4.24 units

   d. In a right triangle, △ABC, where $\overline{AB}$ is the hypotenuse, the altitude, $\overline{CD}$, from the right angle to the hypotenuse, divides the hypotenuse into two segments, $\overline{AD}$ and $\overline{BD}$. The length of the altitude is the geometric mean of the lengths of the two segments of the hypotenuse: $\frac{AD}{CD} = \frac{CD}{BD}$.

2.

	A	B	C	D
1	a	b	Arithmetic Mean	Geometric Mean
2	3	4	3.5	3.464
3	4	5	4.5	4.472
4	6	7	6.5	6.481
5	0.5	0.5	0.5	0.5
6	0.4	0.8	0.6	0.566
7	2	5	3.5	3.162
8	1	4	2.5	2
9	9	16	12.5	12
10	10	100	55	31.623

Sample answer: The geometric mean is always less than or equal to the arithmetic mean. If the pair of positive numbers are closer together, so are the two means. If the pair of positive numbers are equal, they are also equal to each mean.

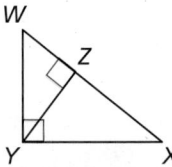
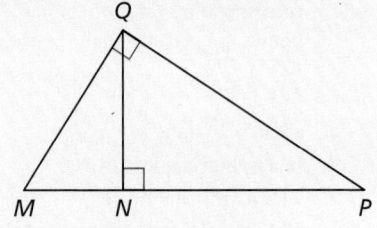
9.3 Lesson

Core Vocabulary

geometric mean, *p. 480*

Previous
altitude of a triangle
similar figures

What You Will Learn

▶ Identify similar triangles.
▶ Solve real-life problems involving similar triangles.
▶ Use geometric means.

Identifying Similar Triangles

When the altitude is drawn to the hypotenuse of a right triangle, the two smaller triangles are similar to the original triangle and to each other.

ⓢ Theorem

Theorem 9.6   Right Triangle Similarity Theorem

If the altitude is drawn to the hypotenuse of a right triangle, then the two triangles formed are similar to the original triangle and to each other.

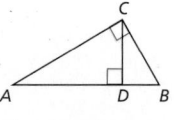

$\triangle CBD \sim \triangle ABC$, $\triangle ACD \sim \triangle ABC$, and $\triangle CBD \sim \triangle ACD$.

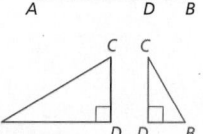

Proof Ex. 45, p. 484

EXAMPLE 1   **Identifying Similar Triangles**

Identify the similar triangles in the diagram.

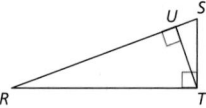

SOLUTION

Sketch the three similar right triangles so that the corresponding angles and sides have the same orientation.

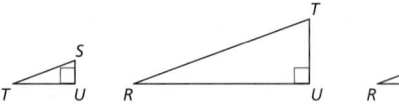

▶ $\triangle TSU \sim \triangle RTU \sim \triangle RST$

Monitoring Progress 🔊 Help in English and Spanish at *BigIdeasMath.com*

Identify the similar triangles.

1.

2.
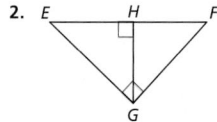

Solving Real-Life Problems

EXAMPLE 2   **Modeling with Mathematics**

A roof has a cross section that is a right triangle. The diagram shows the approximate dimensions of this cross section. Find the height h of the roof.

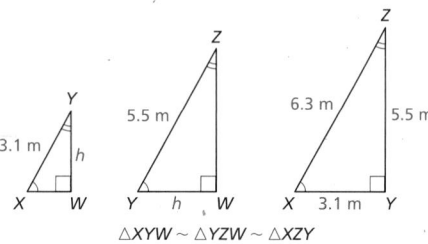

SOLUTION

1. **Understand the Problem** You are given the side lengths of a right triangle. You need to find the height of the roof, which is the altitude drawn to the hypotenuse.

2. **Make a Plan** Identify any similar triangles. Then use the similar triangles to write a proportion involving the height and solve for h.

3. **Solve the Problem** Identify the similar triangles and sketch them.

$$\triangle XYW \sim \triangle YZW \sim \triangle XZY$$

COMMON ERROR

Notice that if you tried to write a proportion using $\triangle XYW$ and $\triangle YZW$, then there would be two unknowns, so you would not be able to solve for h.

Because $\triangle XYW \sim \triangle XZY$, you can write a proportion.

$$\frac{YW}{ZY} = \frac{XY}{XZ}$$ Corresponding side lengths of similar triangles are proportional.

$$\frac{h}{5.5} = \frac{3.1}{6.3}$$ Substitute.

$$h \approx 2.7$$ Multiply each side by 5.5.

▶ The height of the roof is about 2.7 meters.

4. **Look Back** Because the height of the roof is a leg of right $\triangle YZW$ and right $\triangle XYW$, it should be shorter than each of their hypotenuses. The lengths of the two hypotenuses are $YZ = 5.5$ and $XY = 3.1$. Because $2.7 < 3.1$, the answer seems reasonable.

Monitoring Progress 🔊 Help in English and Spanish at *BigIdeasMath.com*

Find the value of x.

3.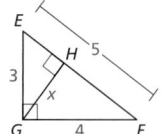

4.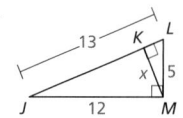

Extra Example 2

A roof has a cross section that is a right triangle. The diagram shows the approximate dimensions of this cross section. Find the height h of the roof.

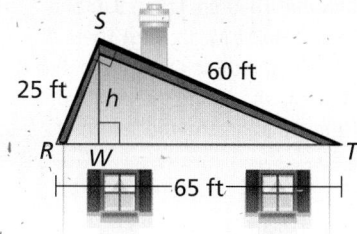

The height is about 23.1 feet.

MONITORING PROGRESS ANSWERS

3. $x = \frac{12}{5} = 2.4$

4. $x = \frac{60}{13} \approx 4.62$

Laurie's Notes   Teacher Actions

- Pose Example 2. Have students work with their partners to draw and label the three similar triangles.
- An alternative to writing three separate similarity statements for each pair of triangles is to write one statement showing the relationship between all three. In other words, instead of writing $\triangle 1 \sim \triangle 2$, $\triangle 2 \sim \triangle 3$, and $\triangle 1 \sim \triangle 3$, simply write $\triangle 1 \sim \triangle 2 \sim \triangle 3$.
- Labeling the known dimensions on each triangle will help students see how to use corresponding sides to write a solvable proportion.

Using a Geometric Mean

Core Concept

Geometric Mean

The **geometric mean** of two positive numbers a and b is the positive number x that satisfies $\frac{a}{x} = \frac{x}{b}$. So, $x^2 = ab$ and $x = \sqrt{ab}$.

EXAMPLE 3 Finding a Geometric Mean

Find the geometric mean of 24 and 48.

SOLUTION

$x^2 = ab$	Definition of geometric mean
$x^2 = 24 \cdot 48$	Substitute 24 for a and 48 for b.
$x = \sqrt{24 \cdot 48}$	Take the positive square root of each side.
$x = \sqrt{24 \cdot 24 \cdot 2}$	Factor.
$x = 24\sqrt{2}$	Simplify.

▶ The geometric mean of 24 and 48 is $24\sqrt{2} \approx 33.9$.

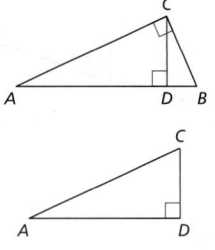

In right $\triangle ABC$, altitude $\overline{CD}$ is drawn to the hypotenuse, forming two smaller right triangles that are similar to $\triangle ABC$. From the Right Triangle Similarity Theorem, you know that $\triangle CBD \sim \triangle ACD \sim \triangle ABC$. Because the triangles are similar, you can write and simplify the following proportions involving geometric means.

$$\frac{CD}{AD} = \frac{BD}{CD} \qquad \frac{CB}{DB} = \frac{AB}{CB} \qquad \frac{AC}{AD} = \frac{AB}{AC}$$

$$CD^2 = AD \cdot BD \qquad CB^2 = DB \cdot AB \qquad AC^2 = AD \cdot AB$$

Theorems

Theorem 9.7   Geometric Mean (Altitude) Theorem

In a right triangle, the altitude from the right angle to the hypotenuse divides the hypotenuse into two segments.

The length of the altitude is the geometric mean of the lengths of the two segments of the hypotenuse.

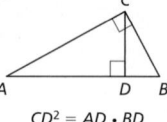

$CD^2 = AD \cdot BD$

Proof Ex. 41, p. 484

Theorem 9.8   Geometric Mean (Leg) Theorem

In a right triangle, the altitude from the right angle to the hypotenuse divides the hypotenuse into two segments.

The length of each leg of the right triangle is the geometric mean of the lengths of the hypotenuse and the segment of the hypotenuse that is adjacent to the leg.

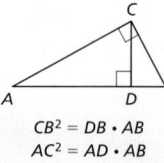

$CB^2 = DB \cdot AB$
$AC^2 = AD \cdot AB$

Proof Ex. 42, p. 484

480   Chapter 9   Right Triangles and Trigonometry

English Language Learners

Graphic Organizer

Have students make a Summary Triangle for the Geometric Mean (Altitude) Theorem (Thm. 9.7) and the Geometric Mean (Leg) Theorem, (Thm. 9.8). Include examples of using the theorems to find the length of an altitude and finding the length of a leg.

Extra Example 3

Find the geometric mean of 8 and 10.
$4\sqrt{5} \approx 8.9$

Laurie's Notes   Teacher Actions

- **MP6 Attend to Precision:** Write the *Core Concept*. Students should note that the *geometric mean* is the positive square root of the product ab.
- **Teaching Tip:** Students can get lost in the notation and words of these theorems. In Theorem 9.8, help students see that the shortest side of the original right triangle is also the hypotenuse of the smallest right triangle, so that side is written twice in the proportion. Similarly, the altitude of the original triangle is the longer leg of the smallest triangle, which leads to the relationship given in Theorem 9.7.

480   Chapter 9

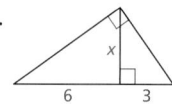 **EXAMPLE 4** **Using a Geometric Mean**

Find the value of each variable.

COMMON ERROR

In Example 4(b), the Geometric Mean (Leg) Theorem gives $y^2 = 2 \cdot (5 + 2)$, not $y^2 = 5 \cdot (5 + 2)$, because the side with length y is adjacent to the segment with length 2.

a.
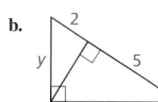

b.

SOLUTION

a. Apply the Geometric Mean (Altitude) Theorem.

$$x^2 = 6 \cdot 3$$
$$x^2 = 18$$
$$x = \sqrt{18}$$
$$x = \sqrt{9} \cdot \sqrt{2}$$
$$x = 3\sqrt{2}$$

▶ The value of x is $3\sqrt{2}$.

b. Apply the Geometric Mean (Leg) Theorem.

$$y^2 = 2 \cdot (5 + 2)$$
$$y^2 = 2 \cdot 7$$
$$y^2 = 14$$
$$y = \sqrt{14}$$

▶ The value of y is $\sqrt{14}$.

EXAMPLE 5 **Using Indirect Measurement**

To find the cost of installing a rock wall in your school gymnasium, you need to find the height of the gym wall. You use a cardboard square to line up the top and bottom of the gym wall. Your friend measures the vertical distance from the ground to your eye and the horizontal distance from you to the gym wall. Approximate the height of the gym wall.

SOLUTION

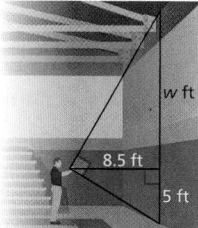

By the Geometric Mean (Altitude) Theorem, you know that 8.5 is the geometric mean of w and 5.

$$8.5^2 = w \cdot 5 \qquad \text{Geometric Mean (Altitude) Theorem}$$
$$72.25 = 5w \qquad \text{Square 8.5.}$$
$$14.45 = w \qquad \text{Divide each side by 5.}$$

▶ The height of the wall is $5 + w = 5 + 14.45 = 19.45$ feet.

Monitoring Progress Help in English and Spanish at *BigIdeasMath.com*

Find the geometric mean of the two numbers.

5. 12 and 27   **6.** 18 and 54   **7.** 16 and 18

8. Find the value of x in the triangle at the left.

9. WHAT IF? In Example 5, the vertical distance from the ground to your eye is 5.5 feet and the distance from you to the gym wall is 9 feet. Approximate the height of the gym wall.

Extra Example 4
Find the value of each variable.

a.
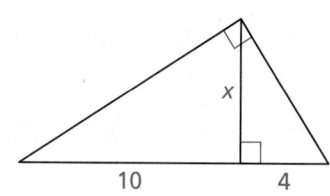

$$x = 2\sqrt{10}$$

b.
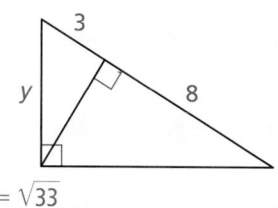

$$y = \sqrt{33}$$

Extra Example 5
Use the diagram and information in Example 5. The vertical distance from the ground to your eye is 5.4 feet and the distance from you to the gym wall is 8.1 feet. Approximate the height of the gym wall. 17.55 feet

MONITORING PROGRESS ANSWERS

5. 18
6. $18\sqrt{3} \approx 31.2$
7. $12\sqrt{2} \approx 17.0$
8. $x = 6$
9. about 20.2 ft

Laurie's Notes **Teacher Actions**

- **Think-Alouds:** In Example 4, have partner A *Think Aloud* as he or she finds the value of the variable. "Because x is the altitude of the right triangle, then … ." Partners now reverse roles as partner B finds the value of y in part (b). Have students self-assess with *Thumbs Up*.
- **MP6:** Model Example 5 in the school gym or another similar area in the building.

Closure

- **Point of Most Significance:** Ask students to identify, aloud or on a paper, the most significant point (or part) in the lesson that aided their learning.

ANSWERS

1. each other

2. *Sample answer:* Geometric mean is a measure of center between two values. The ratio of the smaller of two values to the geometric mean is equal to the ratio of the geometric mean to the larger of two values.

3. $\triangle HFE \sim \triangle GHE \sim \triangle GFH$

4. $\triangle MKN \sim \triangle LMN \sim \triangle LKM$

5. $x = \frac{168}{25} = 6.72$

6. $x = \frac{48}{5} = 9.6$

7. $x = \frac{180}{13} \approx 13.8$

8. $x = \frac{240}{17} \approx 14.1$

9. about 11.2 ft

10. about 2.8 ft

11. 16

12. 12

13. $2\sqrt{70} \approx 16.7$

14. $5\sqrt{35} \approx 29.6$

15. 20

16. $4\sqrt{14} \approx 15.0$

17. $6\sqrt{17} \approx 24.7$

18. $6\sqrt{30} \approx 32.9$

19. $x = 8$

20. $y = 2\sqrt{10} \approx 6.3$

21. $y = 27$

22. $x = 4$

23. $x = 3\sqrt{5} \approx 6.7$

24. $b = 4\sqrt{22} \approx 18.8$

25. $z = \frac{729}{16} \approx 45.6$

26. $x = 4\sqrt{3} \approx 6.9$

9.3 Exercises

Dynamic Solutions available at *BigIdeasMath.com*

Vocabulary and Core Concept Check

1. **COMPLETE THE SENTENCE** If the altitude is drawn to the hypotenuse of a right triangle, then the two triangles formed are similar to the original triangle and _____.

2. **WRITING** In your own words, explain *geometric mean*.

Monitoring Progress and Modeling with Mathematics

In Exercises 3 and 4, identify the similar triangles.
(See Example 1.)

3.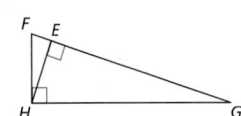

4.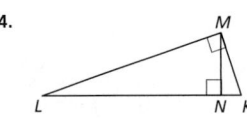

In Exercises 5–10, find the value of *x*. *(See Example 2.)*

5.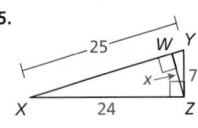

6.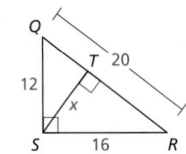

7.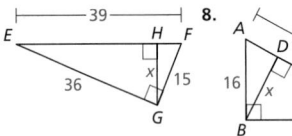

8.

9.

10.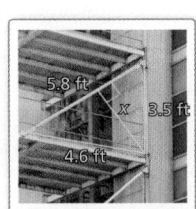

In Exercises 11–18, find the geometric mean of the two numbers. *(See Example 3.)*

11. 8 and 32

12. 9 and 16

13. 14 and 20

14. 25 and 35

15. 16 and 25

16. 8 and 28

17. 17 and 36

18. 24 and 45

In Exercises 19–26, find the value of the variable.
(See Example 4.)

19.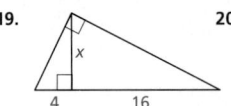

20.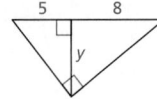

21.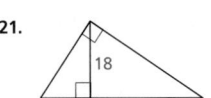

22.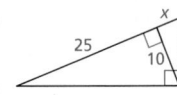

23.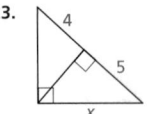

24.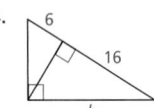

25.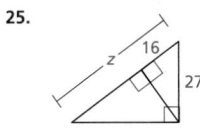

26.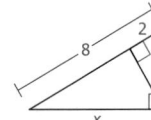

ERROR ANALYSIS In Exercises 27 and 28, describe and correct the error in writing an equation for the given diagram.

27.

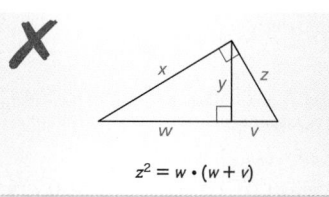

$$z^2 = w \cdot (w + v)$$

28.

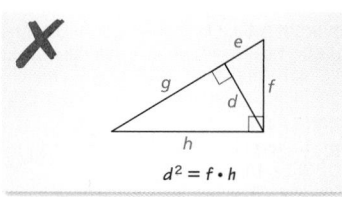

$$d^2 = f \cdot h$$

MODELING WITH MATHEMATICS In Exercises 29 and 30, use the diagram. *(See Example 5.)*

Ex. 29   Ex. 30

29. You want to determine the height of a monument at a local park. You use a cardboard square to line up the top and bottom of the monument, as shown at the above left. Your friend measures the vertical distance from the ground to your eye and the horizontal distance from you to the monument. Approximate the height of the monument.

30. Your classmate is standing on the other side of the monument. She has a piece of rope staked at the base of the monument. She extends the rope to the cardboard square she is holding lined up to the top and bottom of the monument. Use the information in the diagram above to approximate the height of the monument. Do you get the same answer as in Exercise 29? Explain your reasoning.

MATHEMATICAL CONNECTIONS In Exercises 31–34, find the value(s) of the variable(s).

31.

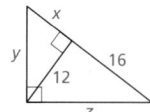

32.

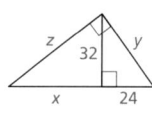

33.

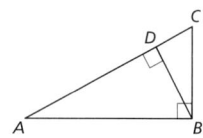

34.

35. REASONING Use the diagram. Decide which proportions are true. Select all that apply.

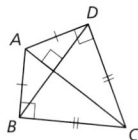

Ⓐ $\dfrac{DB}{DC} = \dfrac{DA}{DB}$ Ⓑ $\dfrac{BA}{CB} = \dfrac{CB}{BD}$

Ⓒ $\dfrac{CA}{BA} = \dfrac{BA}{CA}$ Ⓓ $\dfrac{DB}{BC} = \dfrac{DA}{BA}$

36. ANALYZING RELATIONSHIPS You are designing a diamond-shaped kite. You know that $AD = 44.8$ centimeters, $DC = 72$ centimeters, and $AC = 84.8$ centimeters. You want to use a straight crossbar $\overline{BD}$. About how long should it be? Explain your reasoning.

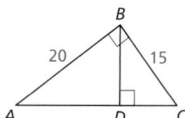

37. ANALYZING RELATIONSHIPS Use the Geometric Mean Theorems (Theorems 9.7 and 9.8) to find AC and BD.

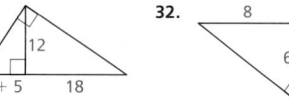

ANSWERS

27. The length of leg z should be the geometric mean of the length of the hypotenuse, $(w + v)$, and the segment of the hypotenuse that is adjacent to z, which is v, not w; $z^2 = v \cdot (w + v)$

28. The length of altitude d should be the geometric mean of the lengths of the two segments of the hypotenuse, e and g, not the legs f and h; $d^2 = e \cdot g$

29. about 14.9 ft

30. about 15.0 ft; yes; Both answers give an approximate height of about 15 feet. Because the values that were used to calculate the answer were only measured to 2 digits of accuracy, only two digits of the answer are reasonably accurate, which is 15 feet for both of these methods.

31. $a = 3$

32. $b = \dfrac{3}{2} = 1.5$

33. $x = 9$, $y = 15$, $z = 20$

34. $x = \dfrac{128}{3} \approx 42.7$, $y = 40$, $z = \dfrac{160}{3} \approx 53.3$

35. A, D

36. about 76.1 cm; Use the Geometric Mean (Leg) Theorem (Thm. 9.8) to find the length of the short segment of $\overline{AC}$. Then, use the Pythagorean Theorem (Thm. 9.1) to find $\dfrac{1}{2}$ of BD, and double your answer.

37. $AC = 25$, $BD = 12$

38. B

39. given; Geometric Mean (Leg) Theorem (Thm. 9.8); a^2; Substitution Property of Equality; Distributive Property; c; Substitution Property of Equality

40. no; The geometric mean of 4 and 9 is 6, but the labels are incorrect on the triangle. The altitude could be 6, and would be the geometric mean of the two segments that make up the hypotenuse. Or, a leg could be 6, and would be the geometric mean of the length of the hypotenuse and the segment of the hypotenuse that is adjacent to the leg.

41–43. See Additional Answers.

44. $\dfrac{x+y}{2} \geq \sqrt{xy}$; They are only equal if $x = y$. Otherwise, the arithmetic mean is always greater than or equal to the geometric mean.

45–49. See Additional Answers.

Mini-Assessment

1. Find the values of x, y, and z.

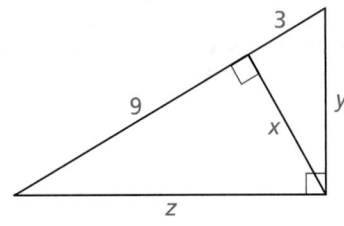

$x = 3\sqrt{3}$, $y = 6$, $z = 6\sqrt{3}$

2. Use the diagram and information in Example 5. The vertical distance from the ground to your eye is 5 feet and the distance from you to the gym wall is 9.5 feet. Approximate the height of the gym wall. 23.05 feet

3. Identify the similar triangles.

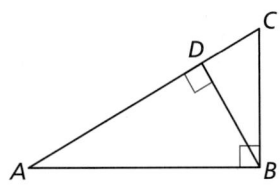

$\triangle ABC \sim \triangle BDC \sim \triangle ADB$

4. Find the geometric mean of $6\sqrt{3}$ and $2\sqrt{3}$. 6

---

38. **HOW DO YOU SEE IT?** In which of the following triangles does the Geometric Mean (Altitude) Theorem (Theorem 9.7) apply?

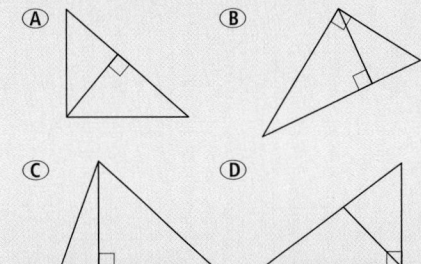

Ⓐ   Ⓑ

Ⓒ   Ⓓ

39. **PROVING A THEOREM** Use the diagram of $\triangle ABC$. Copy and complete the proof of the Pythagorean Theorem (Theorem 9.1).

Given In $\triangle ABC$, $\angle BCA$ is a right angle.

Prove $c^2 = a^2 + b^2$

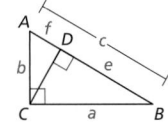

STATEMENTS	REASONS
1. In $\triangle ABC$, $\angle BCA$ is a right angle.	**1.** _____
2. Draw a perpendicular segment (altitude) from C to $\overline{AB}$.	**2.** Perpendicular Postulate (Postulate 3.2)
3. $ce = a^2$ and $cf = b^2$	**3.** _____
4. $ce + b^2 = $ ___ $+ b^2$	**4.** Addition Property of Equality
5. $ce + cf = a^2 + b^2$	**5.** _____
6. $c(e + f) = a^2 + b^2$	**6.** _____
7. $e + f = $ ___	**7.** Segment Addition Postulate (Postulate 1.2)
8. $c \cdot c = a^2 + b^2$	**8.** _____
9. $c^2 = a^2 + b^2$	**9.** Simplify.

Maintaining Mathematical Proficiency
Reviewing what you learned in previous grades and lessons

Solve the equation for x. *(Skills Review Handbook)*

46. $13 = \dfrac{x}{5}$ **47.** $29 = \dfrac{x}{4}$ **48.** $9 = \dfrac{78}{x}$ **49.** $30 = \dfrac{115}{x}$

---

40. **MAKING AN ARGUMENT** Your friend claims the geometric mean of 4 and 9 is 6, and then labels the triangle, as shown. Is your friend correct? Explain your reasoning.

In Exercises 41 and 42, use the given statements to prove the theorem.

Given $\triangle ABC$ is a right triangle.
       Altitude $\overline{CD}$ is drawn to hypotenuse $\overline{AB}$.

41. **PROVING A THEOREM** Prove the Geometric Mean (Altitude) Theorem (Theorem 9.7) by showing that $CD^2 = AD \cdot BD$.

42. **PROVING A THEOREM** Prove the Geometric Mean (Leg) Theorem (Theorem 9.8) by showing that $CB^2 = DB \cdot AB$ and $AC^2 = AD \cdot AB$.

43. **CRITICAL THINKING** Draw a right isosceles triangle and label the two leg lengths x. Then draw the altitude to the hypotenuse and label its length y. Now, use the Right Triangle Similarity Theorem (Theorem 9.6) to draw the three similar triangles from the image and label any side length that is equal to either x or y. What can you conclude about the relationship between the two smaller triangles? Explain your reasoning.

44. **THOUGHT PROVOKING** The arithmetic mean and geometric mean of two nonnegative numbers x and y are shown.

arithmetic mean $= \dfrac{x+y}{2}$

geometric mean $= \sqrt{xy}$

Write an inequality that relates these two means. Justify your answer.

45. **PROVING A THEOREM** Prove the Right Triangle Similarity Theorem (Theorem 9.6) by proving three similarity statements.

Given $\triangle ABC$ is a right triangle.
       Altitude $\overline{CD}$ is drawn to hypotenuse $\overline{AB}$.

Prove $\triangle CBD \sim \triangle ABC$, $\triangle ACD \sim \triangle ABC$, $\triangle CBD \sim \triangle ACD$

If students need help...	If students got it...
Resources by Chapter • Practice A and Practice B • Puzzle Time	**Resources by Chapter** • Enrichment and Extension • Cumulative Review
Student Journal • Practice	Start the *next* Section
Differentiating the Lesson Skills Review Handbook	

Core Vocabulary

Pythagorean triple, *p. 464*　　　　　　geometric mean, *p. 480*

Core Concepts

Section 9.1
Theorem 9.1 Pythagorean Theorem, *p. 464*
Common Pythagorean Triples and Some of Their Multiples, *p. 464*
Theorem 9.2 Converse of the Pythagorean Theorem, *p. 466*
Theorem 9.3 Pythagorean Inequalities Theorem, *p. 467*

Section 9.2
Theorem 9.4 45°-45°-90° Triangle Theorem, *p. 472*
Theorem 9.5 30°-60°-90° Triangle Theorem, *p. 473*

Section 9.3
Theorem 9.6 Right Triangle Similarity Theorem, *p. 478*
Theorem 9.7 Geometric Mean (Altitude) Theorem, *p. 480*
Theorem 9.8 Geometric Mean (Leg) Theorem, *p. 480*

Mathematical Practices

1. In Exercise 31 on page 469, describe the steps you took to find the area of the triangle.

2. In Exercise 23 on page 476, can one of the ways be used to show that all 30°-60°-90° triangles are similar? Explain.

3. Explain why the Geometric Mean (Altitude) Theorem (Theorem 9.7) does not apply to three of the triangles in Exercise 38 on page 484.

- - - - - - - - - - - - - Study Skills - - - - - - - - - - - - -

Form a Weekly Study Group, Set Up Rules

Consider using the following rules.

- Members must attend regularly, be on time, and participate.
- The sessions will focus on the key math concepts, not on the needs of one student.
- Students who skip classes will not be allowed to participate in the study group.
- Students who keep the group from being productive will be asked to leave the group.

485

ANSWERS

1. The altitude, h, divides the original triangle into two congruent smaller triangles by the HL Congruence Theorem (Thm. 5.9). So, each of these smaller triangles has a side length of $\frac{16}{2} = 8$ meters. Use the Pythagorean Theorem (Thm. 9.1), $h^2 + 8^2 = 17^2$, to solve for the height, $h = 15$ meters. The area of the original triangle is $A = \frac{1}{2}bh = \frac{1}{2}(16)(15) = 120$ square meters.

2. yes; You can also use the AA Similarity Theorem (Thm. 8.3) to conclude that all 30°-60°-90° triangles are similar because they have congruent corresponding angles.

3. The Geometric Mean (Altitude) Theorem (Thm. 9.7) applies when the triangle is a right triangle, and the altitude from the right angle to the hypotenuse divides the hypotenuse into two segments. Triangles A and C have altitudes drawn, but the original triangles are not right triangles. Triangle D is a right triangle, but the segment drawn from the right angle is not an altitude.

ANSWERS

1. $x = 15$; yes
2. $x = \sqrt{113} \approx 10.6$; no
3. $x = 4\sqrt{3} \approx 6.9$; no
4. yes; right
5. yes; obtuse
6. yes; acute
7. $x = 6, y = 6\sqrt{2}$
8. $x = 16, y = 8\sqrt{3}$
9. $x = 5\sqrt{2}, y = 5\sqrt{6}$
10. $6\sqrt{2} \approx 8.5$
11. $10\sqrt{3} \approx 17.3$
12. $6\sqrt{13} \approx 21.6$
13. $\triangle ABC \sim \triangle BDC \sim \triangle ADB$;
    $x = 4\sqrt{2} \approx 5.7$
14. $\triangle EFG \sim \triangle FHG \sim \triangle EHF$;
    $y = 3\sqrt{15} \approx 11.6$
15. $\triangle JKL \sim \triangle KML \sim \triangle JMK$; $z = 27$
16. yes; The diagonal of the television shown is about 41.3 inches.
17. a. yes; Triangles A and C are 45°-45°-90° triangles, because the ratio of their sides is $x : x : x\sqrt{2}$. Triangles B and E are 30°-60°-90° triangles because the ratio of their side lengths is $x : x\sqrt{3} : 2x$.
    b. $\triangle A \sim \triangle C, \triangle B \sim \triangle E$
    c. $\dfrac{3\sqrt{3}}{2} \approx 2.6, 3\sqrt{2} \approx 4.2$

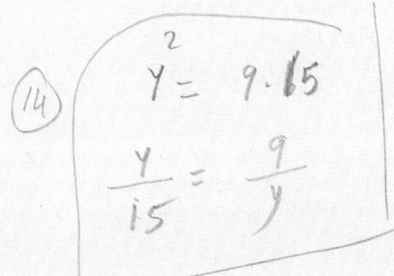

Find the value of x. Tell whether the side lengths form a Pythagorean triple.
(Section 9.1)

1.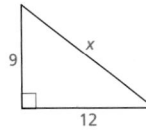
2.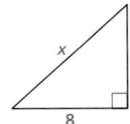
3.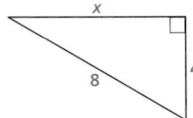

Verify that the segment lengths form a triangle. Is the triangle *acute*, *right*, or *obtuse*?
(Section 9.1)

4. 24, 32, and 40
5. 7, 9, and 13
6. 12, 15, and $10\sqrt{3}$

Find the values of x and y. Write your answers in simplest form. *(Section 9.2)*

7.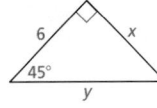
8.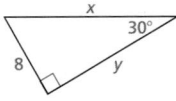
9.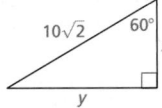

Find the geometric mean of the two numbers. *(Section 9.3)*

10. 6 and 12
11. 15 and 20
12. 18 and 26

Identify the similar right triangles. Then find the value of the variable. *(Section 9.3)*

13.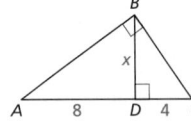
14.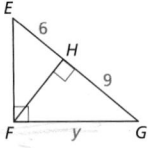
15.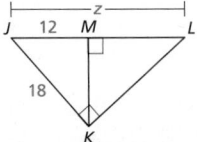

16. Television sizes are measured by the length of their diagonal. You want to purchase a television that is at least 40 inches. Should you purchase the television shown? Explain your reasoning. *(Section 9.1)*

17. Each triangle shown below is a right triangle. *(Sections 9.1–9.3)*
    a. Are any of the triangles special right triangles? Explain your reasoning.
    b. List all similar triangles, if any.
    c. Find the lengths of the altitudes of triangles B and C.

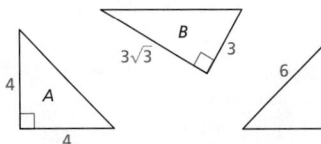

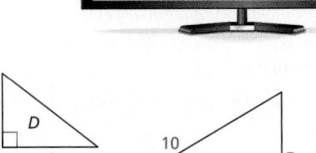

36 in.

20.25 in.

Overview of Section 9.4

Introduction

- The tangent of an angle, the first of three trigonometric ratios studied in geometry, is defined and used in this lesson to solve application problems.

Resources

- Make clinometers that students can use to measure the angle of elevation (inclination) of an object so they can use a tangent ratio to determine its height.

Common Misconceptions

- Students can become sloppy and simply write $\tan = \dfrac{\text{opposite side}}{\text{adjacent side}}$, forgetting to specify the angle. Tangent is the name of the function, and the angle measure is the independent variable. Forgetting to write the angle measure is like writing $\sqrt[\square]{\square} = 4$, which does not give enough information to find either the radicand or the index of the radical.

Formative Assessment Tips

- **Which One Doesn't Belong?:** This technique is one that you should be quite familiar with because it is often used in the *Vocabulary and Core Concept Check* at the beginning of exercise sets! Students are presented with four expressions, quantities, images, or words and asked which one does not belong with the other three. They are also expected to give a reason for their choice.
- This technique gives students the opportunity to analyze and compare items in a set and determine what is alike in three of the four cases. This technique challenges students' reasoning and understanding of some aspect of the lesson they have just learned or what knowledge and conceptions they have about content to be learned.
- Used at the end of instruction, this technique informs you as to how students have conceptualized and made connections in their learning. The reasoning or justification for their choice can be quite informative. Used at the beginning of a lesson, this technique can inform you about what knowledge students already have about the topic.
- Select four items where it is not immediately obvious which one does not belong. You want to encourage deeper thinking.

Pacing Suggestion

- Take time for students to explore and discover the tangent ratio for acute angles, and then transition to the formal lesson.

Common Core State Standards

HSG-SRT.C.6 Understand that by similarity, side ratios in right triangles are properties of the angles in the triangle, leading to definitions of trigonometric ratios for acute angles.

HSG-SRT.C.8 Use trigonometric ratios and the Pythagorean Theorem to solve right triangles in applied problems.

Exploration

Motivate

- Draw a right triangle and label the sides a, b, and c.
- **?** "How many different ratios can be written using the sides a, b, and c? Explain." six: $a : b$, $a : c, b : a, b : c, c : a, c : b$
- Explain to students that today they will learn about the tangent of an angle, one of the six trigonometric ratios. Share a bit of the history of trigonometry if time permits.

Exploration 1

- The first exploration will take a little time for students to set up. To save a bit of time, you could create the template so that students spend their time with the measurements. *Note:* The template could also be used in the next lesson.
- Alternately, different groups of students could work with different angle measures for $\angle BAC$, noting that Exploration 2 would then need to be adjusted.
- This is a powerful exploration for students to experience. It is essential for students to recognize the similar triangles that have been constructed.
- **?** "How can you show $\triangle AQJ \sim \triangle API$?" Use AA. Each triangle contains $\angle A$ and a right angle.
- The second relationship for students to understand is that instead of comparing corresponding sides in similar triangles, the tangent ratios compare two sides in one triangle, the legs opposite and adjacent to a given angle.

Exploration 2

- **FYI:** Students' calculators need to be in degree mode, not radian mode.
- If other angle measures have been used in Exploration 1, make the appropriate adjustment.

Communicate Your Answer

- **Think-Pair-Share:** Have students work with their partners to answer Questions 3 and 4. Discuss as a class.

Connecting to Next Step

- The tangent ratio in a right triangle is defined in the formal lesson.

9.4 The Tangent Ratio

Essential Question

How is a right triangle used to find the tangent of an acute angle? Is there a unique right triangle that must be used?

Let $\triangle ABC$ be a right triangle with acute $\angle A$. The *tangent* of $\angle A$ (written as tan A) is defined as follows.

$$\tan A = \frac{\text{length of leg opposite } \angle A}{\text{length of leg adjacent to } \angle A} = \frac{BC}{AC}$$

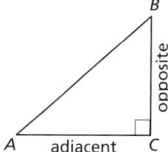

EXPLORATION 1   Calculating a Tangent Ratio

Work with a partner. Use dynamic geometry software.

a. Construct $\triangle ABC$, as shown. Construct segments perpendicular to $\overline{AC}$ to form right triangles that share vertex A and are similar to $\triangle ABC$ with vertices, as shown.

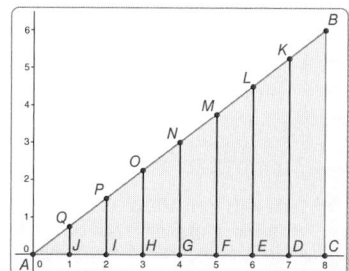

Sample
Points
$A(0, 0)$
$B(8, 6)$
$C(8, 0)$
Angle
$m\angle BAC = 36.87°$

b. Calculate each given ratio to complete the table for the decimal value of tan A for each right triangle. What can you conclude?

Ratio	$\dfrac{BC}{AC}$	$\dfrac{KD}{AD}$	$\dfrac{LE}{AE}$	$\dfrac{MF}{AF}$	$\dfrac{NG}{AG}$	$\dfrac{OH}{AH}$	$\dfrac{PI}{AI}$	$\dfrac{QJ}{AJ}$
tan A								

EXPLORATION 2   Using a Calculator

Work with a partner. Use a calculator that has a tangent key to calculate the tangent of 36.87°. Do you get the same result as in Exploration 1? Explain.

Communicate Your Answer

3. Repeat Exploration 1 for $\triangle ABC$ with vertices $A(0, 0)$, $B(8, 5)$, and $C(8, 0)$. Construct the seven perpendicular segments so that not all of them intersect $\overline{AC}$ at integer values of x. Discuss your results.

4. How is a right triangle used to find the tangent of an acute angle? Is there a unique right triangle that must be used?

> **ATTENDING TO PRECISION**
> To be proficient in math, you need to express numerical answers with a degree of precision appropriate for the problem context.

Dynamic Teaching Tools

Dynamic Assessment & Progress Monitoring Tool

Lesson Planning Tool

Interactive Whiteboard Lesson Library

Dynamic Classroom with Dynamic Investigations

ANSWERS

1. a. Check students' work.

   b. 0.75, 0.75, 0.75, 0.75, 0.75, 0.75, 0.75, 0.75; In all of the similar triangles for which $m\angle A = 36.87°$, tan $A = 0.75$.

2. tan $A \approx 0.7500027913$; Because the angle measure used was rounded to 2 decimal places, the answer did not come out to 0.75 exactly, but when you consider the level of accuracy of the angle measure, they are essentially equivalent.

3. *Sample answer:*

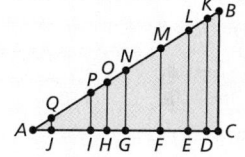

Ratio	$\dfrac{BC}{AC}$	$\dfrac{KD}{AD}$	$\dfrac{LE}{AE}$	$\dfrac{MF}{AF}$
Tan A	0.625	0.6253	0.6254	0.6255

Ratio	$\dfrac{NG}{AG}$	$\dfrac{OH}{AH}$	$\dfrac{PI}{AI}$	$\dfrac{QJ}{AJ}$
Tan A	0.625	0.625	0.624	0.625

When the side lengths used are approximate decimal values, the calculated ratios are approximate as well. In this case, all the ratios are equivalent to about 0.625.

4. You can use a right triangle to find the tangent of an acute angle by calculating the ratio of the length of the opposite leg to the length of the adjacent leg; no

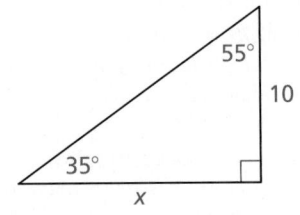
Extra Example 1

Find $\tan A$ and $\tan B$. Write each answer as a fraction and as a decimal rounded to four places.

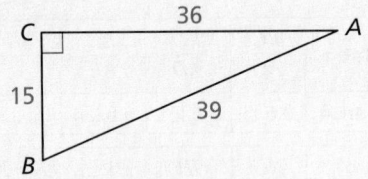

$\tan A = \dfrac{15}{36} = \dfrac{5}{12} \approx 0.4167$,

$\tan B = \dfrac{36}{15} = \dfrac{12}{5} = 2.4000$

MONITORING PROGRESS ANSWERS

1. $\dfrac{3}{4} = 0.7500$, $\dfrac{4}{3} \approx 1.3333$
2. $\dfrac{8}{15} \approx 0.5333$, $\dfrac{15}{8} = 1.8750$

9.4 Lesson

Core Vocabulary

trigonometric ratio, p. 488
tangent, p. 488
angle of elevation, p. 490

What You Will Learn

▶ Use the tangent ratio.
▶ Solve real-life problems involving the tangent ratio.

Using the Tangent Ratio

A **trigonometric ratio** is a ratio of the lengths of two sides in a right triangle. All right triangles with a given acute angle are similar by the AA Similarity Theorem (Theorem 8.3). So, $\triangle JKL \sim \triangle XYZ$, and you can write $\dfrac{KL}{YZ} = \dfrac{JL}{XZ}$. This can be rewritten as $\dfrac{KL}{JL} = \dfrac{YZ}{XZ}$, which is a trigonometric ratio. So, trigonometric ratios are constant for a given angle measure.

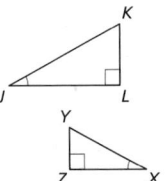

The **tangent** ratio is a trigonometric ratio for acute angles that involves the lengths of the legs of a right triangle.

🔁 Core Concept

Tangent Ratio

Let $\triangle ABC$ be a right triangle with acute $\angle A$.

The tangent of $\angle A$ (written as $\tan A$) is defined as follows.

$$\tan A = \frac{\text{length of leg opposite } \angle A}{\text{length of leg adjacent to } \angle A} = \frac{BC}{AC}$$

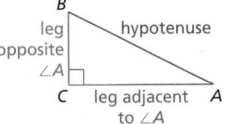

In the right triangle above, $\angle A$ and $\angle B$ are complementary. So, $\angle B$ is acute. You can use the same diagram to find the tangent of $\angle B$. Notice that the leg adjacent to $\angle A$ is the leg *opposite* $\angle B$ and the leg opposite $\angle A$ is the leg *adjacent* to $\angle B$.

EXAMPLE 1 Finding Tangent Ratios

Find $\tan S$ and $\tan R$. Write each answer as a fraction and as a decimal rounded to four places.

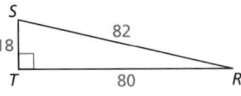

SOLUTION

$$\tan S = \frac{\text{opp. } \angle S}{\text{adj. to } \angle S} = \frac{RT}{ST} = \frac{80}{18} = \frac{40}{9} \approx 4.4444$$

$$\tan R = \frac{\text{opp. } \angle R}{\text{adj. to } \angle R} = \frac{ST}{RT} = \frac{18}{80} = \frac{9}{40} = 0.2250$$

Monitoring Progress Help in English and Spanish at *BigIdeasMath.com*

Find $\tan J$ and $\tan K$. Write each answer as a fraction and as a decimal rounded to four places.

1.

2.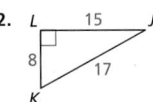

Laurie's Notes Teacher Actions

- Discuss the introduction to the *tangent ratio*. All 10°-80°-90° triangles are similar, so the ratio of the sides opposite and adjacent to the 10° angle will be constant.
- Introduce the abbreviations for opposite, adjacent, and hypotenuse.
- **Common Misconception:** While the hypotenuse is adjacent to each acute angle, it is only referred to as the hypotenuse.
- **MP6 Attend to Precision:** Reference the *Attending to Precision* note so that students will know how precise their measures need to be.

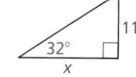

EXAMPLE 2 Finding a Leg Length

Find the value of x. Round your answer to the nearest tenth.

SOLUTION

Use the tangent of an acute angle to find a leg length.

$\tan 32° = \dfrac{\text{opp.}}{\text{adj.}}$	Write ratio for tangent of 32°.
$\tan 32° = \dfrac{11}{x}$	Substitute.
$x \cdot \tan 32° = 11$	Multiply each side by x.
$x = \dfrac{11}{\tan 32°}$	Divide each side by tan 32°.
$x \approx 17.6$	Use a calculator.

▶ The value of x is about 17.6.

USING TOOLS STRATEGICALLY

You can also use the Table of Trigonometric Ratios available at *BigIdeasMath.com* to find the decimal approximations of trigonometric ratios.

You can find the tangent of an acute angle measuring 30°, 45°, or 60° by applying what you know about special right triangles.

EXAMPLE 3 Using a Special Right Triangle to Find a Tangent

Use a special right triangle to find the tangent of a 60° angle.

SOLUTION

STUDY TIP

The tangents of all 60° angles are the same constant ratio. Any right triangle with a 60° angle can be used to determine this value.

Step 1 Because all 30°-60°-90° triangles are similar, you can simplify your calculations by choosing 1 as the length of the shorter leg. Use the 30°-60°-90° Triangle Theorem (Theorem 9.5) to find the length of the longer leg.

longer leg = shorter leg $\cdot \sqrt{3}$	30°-60°-90° Triangle Theorem
$= 1 \cdot \sqrt{3}$	Substitute.
$= \sqrt{3}$	Simplify.

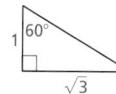

Step 2 Find tan 60°.

$\tan 60° = \dfrac{\text{opp.}}{\text{adj.}}$	Write ratio for tangent of 60°.
$\tan 60° = \dfrac{\sqrt{3}}{1}$	Substitute.
$\tan 60° = \sqrt{3}$	Simplify.

▶ The tangent of any 60° angle is $\sqrt{3} \approx 1.7321$.

Monitoring Progress Help in English and Spanish at *BigIdeasMath.com*

Find the value of x. Round your answer to the nearest tenth.

3.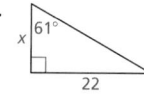

4.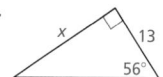

5. **WHAT IF?** In Example 3, the length of the shorter leg is 5 instead of 1. Show that the tangent of 60° is still equal to $\sqrt{3}$.

Extra Example 2

Find the value of x. Round your answer to the nearest tenth.

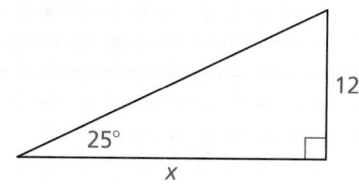

$x \approx 25.7$

Extra Example 3

Use a special right triangle to find the tangent of a 30° angle.

The tangent of any 30° angle is

$\dfrac{1}{\sqrt{3}} = \dfrac{\sqrt{3}}{3} \approx 0.5773$.

MONITORING PROGRESS ANSWERS

3. $x \approx 12.2$
4. $x \approx 19.3$
5. longer leg = shorter leg $\cdot \sqrt{3} = 5\sqrt{3}$,
   $\tan 60° = \dfrac{5\sqrt{3}}{5} = \dfrac{\sqrt{3}}{1} = \sqrt{3}$

Laurie's Notes **Teacher Actions**

COMMON ERROR Solving the ratio $\tan 32° = \dfrac{11}{x}$, students incorrectly divide both sides by 11.

Explain that this would still leave $11 \tan 32° = \dfrac{1}{x}$. This is the same error students will make in solving Question 3.

❓ Which One Doesn't Belong: Draw a 30°-60°-90° triangle and correctly label the sides 2, $2\sqrt{3}$, and 4. Write: $\tan 30° = \dfrac{\sqrt{3}}{3}$, $2\sqrt{3} \cdot \tan 60° = 2$, $2 \cdot \tan 60° = 2\sqrt{3}$, and $\sqrt{3} \cdot \tan 30° = 1$. Ask, "Which one doesn't belong? Explain." $2\sqrt{3} \cdot \tan 60° = 2$ is not a correct ratio. The rest are correct.

Extra Example 4

You are measuring the height of a tree. You stand 40 feet from the base of the tree. The angle of elevation to the top of the tree is 65°. Find the height of the tree to the nearest foot. about 86 feet

MONITORING PROGRESS ANSWER

6. about 110 in.

Solving Real-Life Problems

The angle that an upward line of sight makes with a horizontal line is called the **angle of elevation**.

EXAMPLE 4 **Modeling with Mathematics**

You are measuring the height of a spruce tree. You stand 45 feet from the base of the tree. You measure the angle of elevation from the ground to the top of the tree to be 59°. Find the height h of the tree to the nearest foot.

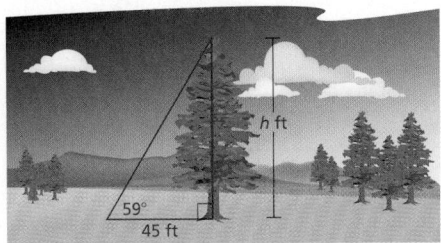

SOLUTION

1. **Understand the Problem** You are given the angle of elevation and the distance from the tree. You need to find the height of the tree to the nearest foot.

2. **Make a Plan** Write a trigonometric ratio for the tangent of the angle of elevation involving the height h. Then solve for h.

3. **Solve the Problem**

   $$\tan 59° = \frac{\text{opp.}}{\text{adj.}} \qquad \text{Write ratio for tangent of 59°.}$$

   $$\tan 59° = \frac{h}{45} \qquad \text{Substitute.}$$

   $$45 \cdot \tan 59° = h \qquad \text{Multiply each side by 45.}$$

   $$74.9 \approx h \qquad \text{Use a calculator.}$$

   ▶ The tree is about 75 feet tall.

4. **Look Back** Check your answer. Because 59° is close to 60°, the value of h should be close to the length of the longer leg of a 30°-60°-90° triangle, where the length of the shorter leg is 45 feet.

   $$\text{longer leg} = \text{shorter leg} \cdot \sqrt{3} \qquad \text{30°-60°-90° Triangle Theorem}$$

   $$= 45 \cdot \sqrt{3} \qquad \text{Substitute.}$$

   $$\approx 77.9 \qquad \text{Use a calculator.}$$

   The value of 77.9 feet is close to the value of h. ✔

Monitoring Progress 🔊 Help in English and Spanish at *BigIdeasMath.com*

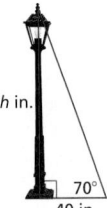

6. You are measuring the height of a lamppost. You stand 40 inches from the base of the lamppost. You measure the angle of elevation from the ground to the top of the lamppost to be 70°. Find the height h of the lamppost to the nearest inch.

Laurie's Notes Teacher Actions

- Explain angle of elevation.
- **Wait Time:** Have partners work together to solve Example 4. Give sufficient *Wait Time*, and do not rush in to solve for students.
- **MP6:** Be sure that students label the answer with the correct units.
- **Connection:** Have students compare this method to what was done in the previous chapter in finding the height of a flagpole. If time permits, use this method outside to determine the height of an object.

Closure

- **Writing Prompt:** The tangent ratio is constant for an acute $\angle A$ because …

Vocabulary and Core Concept Check

1. **COMPLETE THE SENTENCE** The tangent ratio compares the length of _____ to the length of _____.

2. **WRITING** Explain how you know the tangent ratio is constant for a given angle measure.

Monitoring Progress and Modeling with Mathematics

In Exercises 3–6, find the tangents of the acute angles in the right triangle. Write each answer as a fraction and as a decimal rounded to four decimal places. *(See Example 1.)*

3.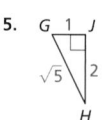

4.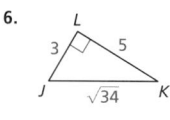

5.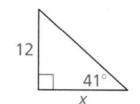

6.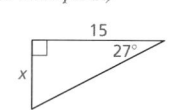

In Exercises 7–10, find the value of *x*. Round your answer to the nearest tenth. *(See Example 2.)*

7.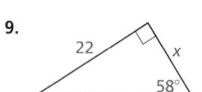

8.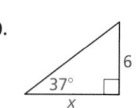

9.

10.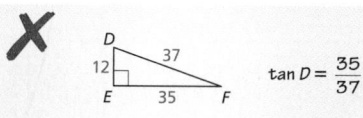

ERROR ANALYSIS In Exercises 11 and 12, describe the error in the statement of the tangent ratio. Correct the error if possible. Otherwise, write not possible.

11.

$$\tan D = \frac{35}{37}$$

12.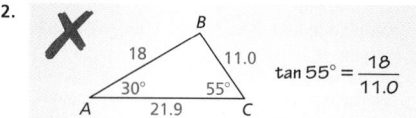

$$\tan 55° = \frac{18}{11.0}$$

In Exercises 13 and 14, use a special right triangle to find the tangent of the given angle measure. *(See Example 3.)*

13. 45°

14. 30°

15. **MODELING WITH MATHEMATICS** A surveyor is standing 118 feet from the base of the Washington Monument. The surveyor measures the angle of elevation from the ground to the top of the monument to be 78°. Find the height *h* of the Washington Monument to the nearest foot. *(See Example 4.)*

16. **MODELING WITH MATHEMATICS** Scientists can measure the depths of craters on the moon by looking at photos of shadows. The length of the shadow cast by the edge of a crater is 500 meters. The angle of elevation of the rays of the Sun is 55°. Estimate the depth *d* of the crater.

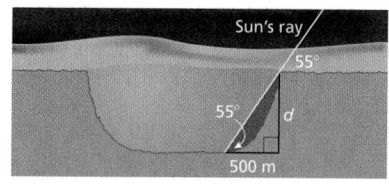

17. **USING STRUCTURE** Find the tangent of the smaller acute angle in a right triangle with side lengths 5, 12, and 13.

Assignment Guide and Homework Check

ASSIGNMENT

Basic: 1, 2, 3–15 odd, 21, 22, 27–29

Average: 1, 2, 6–20 even, 21–23, 27–29

Advanced: 1, 2, 6–20 even, 21–29

HOMEWORK CHECK

Basic: 3, 9, 11, 15, 22

Average: 6, 10, 12, 16, 20

Advanced: 6, 10, 16, 20, 24

ANSWERS

1. the opposite leg, the adjacent leg

2. All right triangles with the given angle measure will be similar by the AA Similarity Theorem (Thm. 8.3). So, the corresponding sides lengths will be proportional and the ratio will be constant.

3. $\tan R = \frac{45}{28} \approx 1.6071$, $\tan S = \frac{28}{45} \approx 0.6222$

4. $\tan D = \frac{7}{24} \approx 0.2917$, $\tan F = \frac{24}{7} \approx 3.4286$

5. $\tan G = \frac{2}{1} = 2.0000$, $\tan H = \frac{1}{2} = 0.5000$

6. $\tan J = \frac{5}{3} \approx 1.6667$, $\tan K = \frac{3}{5} = 0.6000$

7. $x \approx 13.8$

8. $x \approx 7.6$

9. $x \approx 13.7$

10. $x \approx 8.0$

11. The tangent ratio should be the length of the leg opposite $\angle D$ to the length of the leg adjacent to $\angle D$, not the length of the hypotenuse; $\tan D = \frac{35}{12}$

12. Because $\triangle ABC$ is not a right triangle, the tangent ratio cannot be used; not possible

13. 1

14. $\frac{\sqrt{3}}{3} \approx 0.5774$

15. about 555 ft

16. about 714.1 m

17. $\frac{5}{12} \approx 0.4167$

ANSWERS

18. $\frac{4}{3} \approx 1.3333$

19. it increases; The opposite side gets longer.

20–25. See Additional Answers.

26. about 128.0 units

27. $x = 2\sqrt{3} \approx 3.5$

28. $x = \frac{7\sqrt{3}}{3} \approx 4.0$

29. $x = 5\sqrt{2} \approx 7.1$

Mini-Assessment

1. You are measuring the height of a tree. You stand 50 feet from the base of the tree. The angle of elevation to the top of the tree is 47°. Find the height of the tree to the nearest foot. about 54 feet

2. Find tan D and tan E. Write each answer as a fraction and as a decimal rounded to four places.

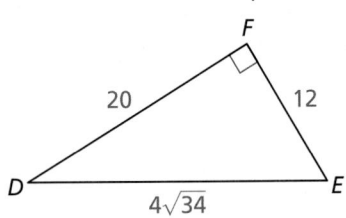

$\tan D = \frac{3}{5} = 0.6000,$

$\tan E = \frac{5}{3} \approx 1.6667$

3. Find the value of x. Round your answer to the nearest tenth.

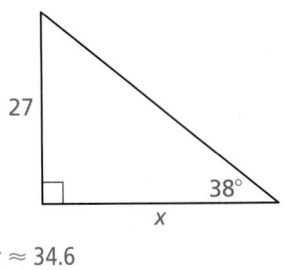

$x \approx 34.6$

---

18. **USING STRUCTURE** Find the tangent of the larger acute angle in a right triangle with side lengths 3, 4, and 5.

19. **REASONING** How does the tangent of an acute angle in a right triangle change as the angle measure increases? Justify your answer.

20. **CRITICAL THINKING** For what angle measure(s) is the tangent of an acute angle in a right triangle equal to 1? greater than 1? less than 1? Justify your answer.

21. **MAKING AN ARGUMENT** Your family room has a sliding-glass door. You want to buy an awning for the door that will be just long enough to keep the Sun out when it is at its highest point in the sky. The angle of elevation of the rays of the Sun at this point is 70°, and the height of the door is 8 feet. Your sister claims you can determine how far the overhang should extend by multiplying 8 by tan 70°. Is your sister correct? Explain.

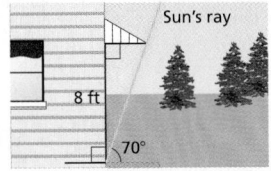

22. **HOW DO YOU SEE IT?** Write expressions for the tangent of each acute angle in the right triangle. Explain how the tangent of one acute angle is related to the tangent of the other acute angle. What kind of angle pair is ∠A and ∠B?

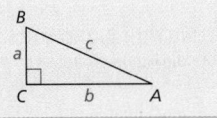

23. **REASONING** Explain why it is not possible to find the tangent of a right angle or an obtuse angle.

24. **THOUGHT PROVOKING** To create the diagram below, you begin with an isosceles right triangle with legs 1 unit long. Then the hypotenuse of the first triangle becomes the leg of a second triangle, whose remaining leg is 1 unit long. Continue the diagram until you have constructed an angle whose tangent is $\frac{1}{\sqrt{6}}$. Approximate the measure of this angle.

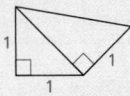

25. **PROBLEM SOLVING** Your class is having a class picture taken on the lawn. The photographer is positioned 14 feet away from the center of the class. The photographer turns 50° to look at either end of the class.

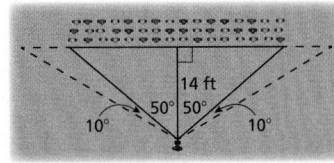

a. What is the distance between the ends of the class?

b. The photographer turns another 10° either way to see the end of the camera range. If each student needs 2 feet of space, about how many more students can fit at the end of each row? Explain.

26. **PROBLEM SOLVING** Find the perimeter of the figure, where $AC = 26$, $AD = BF$, and D is the midpoint of $\overline{AC}$.

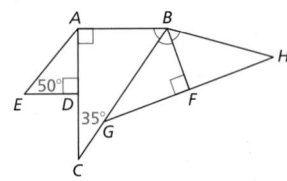

Maintaining Mathematical Proficiency   Reviewing what you learned in previous grades and lessons

Find the value of x. *(Section 9.2)*

27.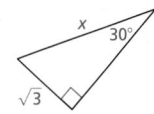

28.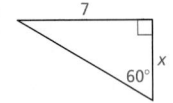

29.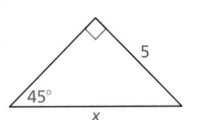

If students need help...	If students got it...
Resources by Chapter • Practice A and Practice B • Puzzle Time	Resources by Chapter • Enrichment and Extension • Cumulative Review
Student Journal • Practice	Start the *next* Section
Differentiating the Lesson Skills Review Handbook	

Overview of Section 9.5

Introduction

- The sine and cosine ratios are defined and used in this lesson to determine the lengths of missing sides of a right triangle.
- Connections are made to a previous lesson as students find the sine and cosine of angle measures in special right triangles.
- The lesson ends with students using the ratios to solve a real-life application.

Formative Assessment Tips

- **Give Me Five:** In Chapter 5, students wrote a great deal of private reflections. Since then they have had additional opportunities to be reflective about their learning. This technique is public. Students are given a prompt and asked to think and write privately for a couple of minutes. You then ask five (or fewer) students to share aloud their reflection. In doing so, you are (a) continuing to encourage students to be reflective about their learning and (b) letting students know that you value their thoughts and insights.
- The feedback you receive will help guide subsequent instruction. If used at the end of the period, you will have insightful knowledge of students' learning that day and what subsequent instruction may be needed tomorrow. If used during the middle of the class after a critical point, be prepared to make course corrections to address what students have shared.
- As students share, you might have other students with similar thoughts indicate so by a show of hands. If many of the reflections are quite similar, it will not be necessary to have five students share.
- Sample prompts:
  - How did today's lesson help you better understand finding a trigonometric function of an acute angle?
  - How well do you feel you understand how to find the side lengths of a right triangle?
  - As we have worked on trigonometric functions and special right triangles this week, what has helped you the most in making sense of this topic?
  - How are similar triangles related to trigonometric functions?

Pacing Suggestion

- Take time for students to explore and discover the sine and cosine ratios for acute angles, and then transition to the formal lesson.

Dynamic Teaching Tools

Dynamic Assessment & Progress Monitoring Tool

Lesson Planning Tool

Interactive Whiteboard Lesson Library

Dynamic Classroom with Dynamic Investigations

HSG-SRT.C.6 Understand that by similarity, side ratios in right triangles are properties of the angles in the triangle, leading to definitions of trigonometric ratios for acute angles.

HSG-SRT.C.7 Explain and use the relationship between the sine and cosine of complementary angles.

HSG-SRT.C.8 Use trigonometric ratios and the Pythagorean Theorem to solve right triangles in applied problems.

Laurie's Notes

Exploration

Motivate

- **Story Time:** Share information with your students about a spring ski trip you (or your friends) are planning to Tuckerman Ravine, on the east side of Mt. Washington in the White Mountain National Forest of New Hampshire. Tuckerman Ravine is famous for its spectacular scenery, deep snow, and challenging terrain. Thousands of motivated skiers make the six-mile round trip to the floor of Tuckerman Ravine every year.
- There are no ski lifts—you hike in and hike out, thus you need to be motivated! To decide whether the hike is worth it, skiers want to know the length of the trail.
- Explain to students that in this lesson they will find a way to determine the length of a ski trail.

Exploration 1

- This exploration has the same setup as the exploration in the previous lesson, so students should be familiar with the setup and directions.
- If different groups of students worked with a different angle measure for $\angle BAC$ in the last lesson, you might consider having groups of students do the same for this lesson.
- Like the last lesson, this is an important exploration for students to investigate. The ratio of the length of the opposite side to the length of the hypotenuse is the same for $\angle A$ in every triangle in this exploration.

Communicate Your Answer

- **Think-Pair-Share:** Have students work with their partners to answer Questions 2 and 3. Discuss as a class.

Connecting to Next Step

- The sine and cosine ratios in a right triangle are defined in the formal lesson.

9.5 The Sine and Cosine Ratios

Essential Question
How is a right triangle used to find the sine and cosine of an acute angle? Is there a unique right triangle that must be used?

Let $\triangle ABC$ be a right triangle with acute $\angle A$. The *sine* of $\angle A$ and *cosine* of $\angle A$ (written as sin A and cos A, respectively) are defined as follows.

$$\sin A = \frac{\text{length of leg opposite } \angle A}{\text{length of hypotenuse}} = \frac{BC}{AB}$$

$$\cos A = \frac{\text{length of leg adjacent to } \angle A}{\text{length of hypotenuse}} = \frac{AC}{AB}$$

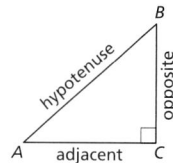

EXPLORATION 1 **Calculating Sine and Cosine Ratios**

Work with a partner. Use dynamic geometry software.

a. Construct $\triangle ABC$, as shown. Construct segments perpendicular to $\overline{AC}$ to form right triangles that share vertex A and are similar to $\triangle ABC$ with vertices, as shown.

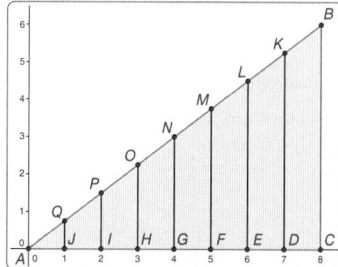

Sample
Points
$A(0, 0)$
$B(8, 6)$
$C(8, 0)$
Angle
$m\angle BAC = 36.87°$

b. Calculate each given ratio to complete the table for the decimal values of sin A and cos A for each right triangle. What can you conclude?

Sine ratio	$\frac{BC}{AB}$	$\frac{KD}{AK}$	$\frac{LE}{AL}$	$\frac{MF}{AM}$	$\frac{NG}{AN}$	$\frac{OH}{AO}$	$\frac{PI}{AP}$	$\frac{QJ}{AQ}$
sin A								
Cosine ratio	$\frac{AC}{AB}$	$\frac{AD}{AK}$	$\frac{AE}{AL}$	$\frac{AF}{AM}$	$\frac{AG}{AN}$	$\frac{AH}{AO}$	$\frac{AI}{AP}$	$\frac{AJ}{AQ}$
cos A								

Communicate Your Answer

LOOKING FOR STRUCTURE
To be proficient in math, you need to look closely to discern a pattern or structure.

2. How is a right triangle used to find the sine and cosine of an acute angle? Is there a unique right triangle that must be used?

3. In Exploration 1, what is the relationship between $\angle A$ and $\angle B$ in terms of their measures? Find sin B and cos B. How are these two values related to sin A and cos A? Explain why these relationships exist.

Section 9.5   The Sine and Cosine Ratios   **493**

ANSWERS

1. a. Check students' work.

 b. sin A: 0.6, 0.6, 0.6, 0.6, 0.6, 0.6, 0.6, 0.6; cos A: 0.8, 0.8, 0.8, 0.8, 0.8, 0.8, 0.8, 0.8; In all of the similar right triangles for which $m\angle A = 36.87°$, sin $A = 0.6$ and cos $A = 0.8$.

2. You use a right triangle to find the sine of an acute angle by calculating the ratio of the length of the opposite leg to the length of the hypotenuse. You use a right triangle to find the cosine of an acute angle by calculating the ratio of the the length of the adjacent leg to the length of the hypotenuse; no

3. $\angle A$ and $\angle B$ are complementary; sin $B = 0.8$, cos $B = 0.6$; sin $A = $ cos B, cos $A = $ sin B; The leg that is opposite $\angle A$ is the same leg that is adjacent to $\angle B$ and vice versa, but the length of the hypotenuse stays the same. So, the sine of one angle is equal to the cosine of its complementary angle.

Extra Example 1

Find sin A, sin B, cos A, and cos B. Write each answer as a fraction and as a decimal rounded to four places.

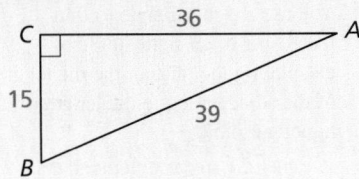

$\sin A = \cos B = \dfrac{15}{39} = \dfrac{5}{13} \approx 0.3846$,

$\sin B = \cos A = \dfrac{36}{39} = \dfrac{12}{13} \approx 0.9231$

9.5 Lesson

Core Vocabulary

sine, *p. 494*
cosine, *p. 494*
angle of depression, *p. 497*

> **READING**
>
> Remember the following abbreviations.
>
> sine → sin
> cosine → cos
> hypotenuse → hyp.

What You Will Learn

▶ Use the sine and cosine ratios.
▶ Find the sine and cosine of angle measures in special right triangles.
▶ Solve real-life problems involving sine and cosine ratios.

Using the Sine and Cosine Ratios

The **sine** and **cosine** ratios are trigonometric ratios for acute angles that involve the lengths of a leg and the hypotenuse of a right triangle.

◑ Core Concept

Sine and Cosine Ratios

Let $\triangle ABC$ be a right triangle with acute $\angle A$. The sine of $\angle A$ and cosine of $\angle A$ (written as sin A and cos A) are defined as follows.

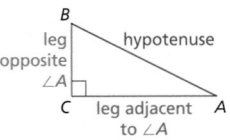

$$\sin A = \frac{\text{length of leg opposite } \angle A}{\text{length of hypotenuse}} = \frac{BC}{AB}$$

$$\cos A = \frac{\text{length of leg adjacent to } \angle A}{\text{length of hypotenuse}} = \frac{AC}{AB}$$

EXAMPLE 1   Finding Sine and Cosine Ratios

Find sin S, sin R, cos S, and cos R. Write each answer as a fraction and as a decimal rounded to four places.

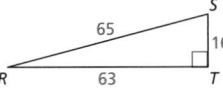

SOLUTION

$\sin S = \dfrac{\text{opp. } \angle S}{\text{hyp.}} = \dfrac{RT}{SR} = \dfrac{63}{65} \approx 0.9692$ $\sin R = \dfrac{\text{opp. } \angle R}{\text{hyp.}} = \dfrac{ST}{SR} = \dfrac{16}{65} \approx 0.2462$

$\cos S = \dfrac{\text{adj. to } \angle S}{\text{hyp.}} = \dfrac{ST}{SR} = \dfrac{16}{65} \approx 0.2462$ $\cos R = \dfrac{\text{adj. to } \angle R}{\text{hyp.}} = \dfrac{RT}{SR} = \dfrac{63}{65} \approx 0.9692$

In Example 1, notice that sin S = cos R and sin R = cos S. This is true because the side opposite $\angle S$ is adjacent to $\angle R$ and the side opposite $\angle R$ is adjacent to $\angle S$. The relationship between the sine and cosine of $\angle S$ and $\angle R$ is true for all complementary angles.

◑ Core Concept

Sine and Cosine of Complementary Angles

The sine of an acute angle is equal to the cosine of its complement. The cosine of an acute angle is equal to the sine of its complement.

Let A and B be complementary angles. Then the following statements are true.

$\sin A = \cos(90° - A) = \cos B$ $\sin B = \cos(90° - B) = \cos A$

$\cos A = \sin(90° - A) = \sin B$ $\cos B = \sin(90° - B) = \sin A$

Laurie's Notes   Teacher Actions

- Write the *Core Concept*, being sure to note the abbreviations and the need to specify the angle.
- **?** "What is the same about the sine and cosine ratios?" They have the same denominator, the length of the hypotenuse.
- **?** "If the sine and cosine ratios compare the length of a leg to the length of the hypotenuse, then what do you know about the ratios for acute angles?" The ratios are less than 1.
- **MP2 Reason Abstractly and Quantitatively** and **Turn and Talk:** "If A and B are complementary angles, then why does sin A = cos B?" Listen for correct reasoning.

EXAMPLE 2 Rewriting Trigonometric Expressions

Write sin 56° in terms of cosine.

SOLUTION

Use the fact that the sine of an acute angle is equal to the cosine of its complement.

$$\sin 56° = \cos(90° - 56°) = \cos 34°$$

▶ The sine of 56° is the same as the cosine of 34°.

You can use the sine and cosine ratios to find unknown measures in right triangles.

EXAMPLE 3 Finding Leg Lengths

Find the values of x and y using sine and cosine.
Round your answers to the nearest tenth.

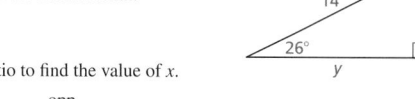

SOLUTION

Step 1 Use a sine ratio to find the value of x.

$\sin 26° = \dfrac{\text{opp.}}{\text{hyp.}}$	Write ratio for sine of 26°.
$\sin 26° = \dfrac{x}{14}$	Substitute.
$14 \cdot \sin 26° = x$	Multiply each side by 14.
$6.1 \approx x$	Use a calculator.

▶ The value of x is about 6.1.

Step 2 Use a cosine ratio to find the value of y.

$\cos 26° = \dfrac{\text{adj.}}{\text{hyp.}}$	Write ratio for cosine of 26°.
$\cos 26° = \dfrac{y}{14}$	Substitute.
$14 \cdot \cos 26° = y$	Multiply each side by 14.
$12.6 \approx y$	Use a calculator.

▶ The value of y is about 12.6.

Monitoring Progress ◀)) Help in English and Spanish at *BigIdeasMath.com*

1. Find sin D, sin F, cos D, and cos F. Write each answer as a fraction and as a decimal rounded to four places.

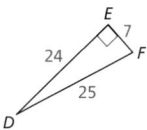

2. Write cos 23° in terms of sine.

3. Find the values of u and t using sine and cosine. Round your answers to the nearest tenth.

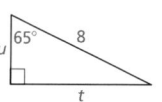

English Language Learners

Words and Abbreviations

This lesson uses many abbreviations for trigonometric ratios and parts of triangles. Encourage English learners to make a table in their notebooks showing the full word and the abbreviation.

Word	Abbreviation
sine	sin
cosine	cos
tangent	tan
adjacent	adj.
opposite	opp.
hypotenuse	hyp.

Extra Example 2

Write cos 69° in terms of sine.
sin 21°

Extra Example 3

Find the values of x and y using sine and cosine. Round your answers to the nearest tenth.

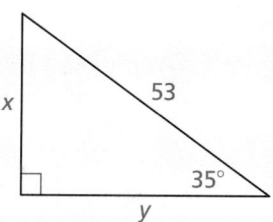

$x \approx 30.4$, $y \approx 43.4$

MONITORING PROGRESS ANSWERS

1. $\sin D = \dfrac{7}{25} = 0.2800$,
   $\sin F = \dfrac{24}{25} = 0.9600$,
   $\cos D = \dfrac{24}{25} = 0.9600$,
   $\cos F = \dfrac{7}{25} = 0.2800$

2. sin 67°

3. $u \approx 3.4$, $t \approx 7.3$

Laurie's Notes **Teacher Actions**

❓ "In Example 3, what are the angle measures of the triangle?" 26°, 64°, and 90°

❓ "What trigonometric equation can you write to solve for x?" $\sin 26° = \dfrac{x}{14}$ or $\cos 64° = \dfrac{x}{14}$
Ask a similar question in solving for y.

❓ **Extension:** After solving for x and y, ask, "How can you check to see whether your answers are reasonable?" Use the Pythagorean Theorem: $x^2 + y^2 = 14^2$. Accounting for rounding, the values for x and y should work in this equation.

Extra Example 4

Which ratios are equal to $\dfrac{\sqrt{2}}{2}$? Select all that apply.

- sin A
- cos A
- tan A
- sin B
- cos B
- tan B

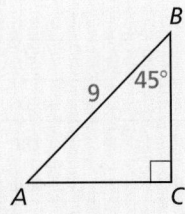

sin A, cos A, sin B, cos B

Extra Example 5

Which ratios are equal to $\dfrac{\sqrt{3}}{2}$? Select all that apply.

- sin M
- sin P
- cos M
- cos P

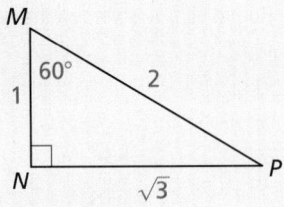

sin M, cos P

MONITORING PROGRESS ANSWER

4. $\sin 60° = \dfrac{\sqrt{3}}{2} \approx 0.8660,$

$\cos 60° = \dfrac{1}{2} = 0.5000$

Finding Sine and Cosine in Special Right Triangles

EXAMPLE 4   Finding the Sine and Cosine of 45°

Find the sine and cosine of a 45° angle.

SOLUTION

Begin by sketching a 45°-45°-90° triangle. Because all such triangles are similar, you can simplify your calculations by choosing 1 as the length of each leg. Using the 45°-45°-90° Triangle Theorem (Theorem 9.4), the length of the hypotenuse is $\sqrt{2}$.

STUDY TIP

Notice that

$\sin 45° = \cos(90 - 45)°$

$= \cos 45°.$

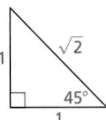

$$\sin 45° = \dfrac{\text{opp.}}{\text{hyp.}} \qquad\qquad \cos 45° = \dfrac{\text{adj.}}{\text{hyp.}}$$

$$= \dfrac{1}{\sqrt{2}} \qquad\qquad\qquad = \dfrac{1}{\sqrt{2}}$$

$$= \dfrac{\sqrt{2}}{2} \qquad\qquad\qquad = \dfrac{\sqrt{2}}{2}$$

$$\approx 0.7071 \qquad\qquad\qquad \approx 0.7071$$

EXAMPLE 5   Finding the Sine and Cosine of 30°

Find the sine and cosine of a 30° angle.

SOLUTION

Begin by sketching a 30°-60°-90° triangle. Because all such triangles are similar, you can simplify your calculations by choosing 1 as the length of the shorter leg. Using the 30°-60°-90° Triangle Theorem (Theorem 9.5), the length of the longer leg is $\sqrt{3}$ and the length of the hypotenuse is 2.

$$\sin 30° = \dfrac{\text{opp.}}{\text{hyp.}} \qquad\qquad \cos 30° = \dfrac{\text{adj.}}{\text{hyp.}}$$

$$= \dfrac{1}{2} \qquad\qquad\qquad = \dfrac{\sqrt{3}}{2}$$

$$= 0.5000 \qquad\qquad\qquad \approx 0.8660$$

Monitoring Progress 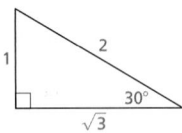 Help in English and Spanish at *BigIdeasMath.com*

4. Find the sine and cosine of a 60° angle.

Laurie's Notes   Teacher Actions

- Have students work in groups of two to four students.
- Say, "You have learned about special right triangles in an earlier lesson. Today, you have learned about the sine and cosine ratios. Work with your partners to find the exact and approximate values of the sine and cosine of 30°, 45°, and 60°."
- Let students work with one another as you circulate. Do not rush in to rescue! Trust that students have the necessary knowledge to answer the question. Solicit answers and summarize in a table. Look for patterns (i.e., $\sin \theta$ is an increasing function).

Solving Real-Life Problems

Recall from the previous lesson that the angle an upward line of sight makes with a horizontal line is called the *angle of elevation*. The angle that a downward line of sight makes with a horizontal line is called the **angle of depression**.

EXAMPLE 6   **Modeling with Mathematics**

You are skiing on a mountain with an altitude of 1200 feet. The angle of depression is 21°. Find the distance x you ski down the mountain to the nearest foot.

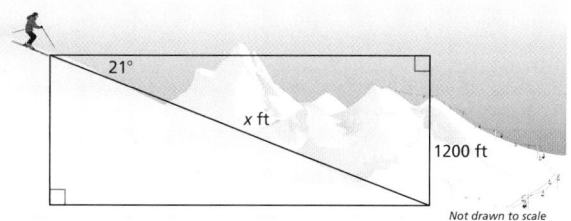

21°

x ft

1200 ft

Not drawn to scale

SOLUTION

1. **Understand the Problem** You are given the angle of depression and the altitude of the mountain. You need to find the distance that you ski down the mountain.

2. **Make a Plan** Write a trigonometric ratio for the sine of the angle of depression involving the distance x. Then solve for x.

3. **Solve the Problem**

$$\sin 21° = \frac{\text{opp.}}{\text{hyp.}} \qquad \text{Write ratio for sine of 21°.}$$

$$\sin 21° = \frac{1200}{x} \qquad \text{Substitute.}$$

$$x \cdot \sin 21° = 1200 \qquad \text{Multiply each side by } x.$$

$$x = \frac{1200}{\sin 21°} \qquad \text{Divide each side by sin 21°.}$$

$$x \approx 3348.5 \qquad \text{Use a calculator.}$$

▶ You ski about 3349 feet down the mountain.

4. **Look Back** Check your answer. The value of sin 21° is about 0.3584. Substitute for x in the sine ratio and compare the values.

$$\frac{1200}{x} \approx \frac{1200}{3348.5}$$

$$\approx 0.3584$$

This value is approximately the same as the value of sin 21°.

Monitoring Progress   ◀)) Help in English and Spanish at *BigIdeasMath.com*

5. **WHAT IF?** In Example 6, the angle of depression is 28°. Find the distance x you ski down the mountain to the nearest foot.

Section 9.5   497

Extra Example 6

You are skiing down a hill with an altitude of 800 feet. The angle of depression is 15°. Find the distance x you ski down the hill to the nearest foot.   about 3091 feet

MONITORING PROGRESS ANSWER

5. about 2556 ft

Laurie's Notes   Teacher Actions

- In the last lesson on the tangent ratio, only the leg lengths were used. Discuss with students that now problems also involve the hypotenuse.
- **Turn and Talk:** Pose Example 6. "How can you find the distance the skier skis?"
- **MP1 Make Sense of Problems and Persevere in Solving Them** and **MP4 Model with Mathematics:** Drawing a sketch is helpful in making sense of the problem. Note that students could use sine or cosine to solve.

Closure

- **Give Me Five:** Select one or more of the prompts on page T-492 for students to reflect on.

Assignment Guide and Homework Check

ASSIGNMENT

Basic: 1, 2, 3–27 odd, 31, 36, 41–44

Average: 1, 2, 8–20 even, 23–25, 28–31, 36, 41–44

Advanced: 1, 2, 8–22 even, 23–31, 34–40 even, 41–44

HOMEWORK CHECK

Basic: 7, 9, 13, 21, 27

Average: 8, 12, 20, 23, 30

Advanced: 8, 16, 22, 30, 40

ANSWERS

1. the opposite leg, the hypotenuse

2. $\tan B$; The other three are all equal to $\dfrac{AC}{BC}$, but $\tan B = \dfrac{AC}{AB}$.

3. $\sin D = \dfrac{4}{5} = 0.8000$,
   $\sin E = \dfrac{3}{5} = 0.6000$,
   $\cos D = \dfrac{3}{5} = 0.6000$,
   $\cos E = \dfrac{4}{5} = 0.8000$

4. $\sin D = \dfrac{35}{37} \approx 0.9459$,
   $\sin E = \dfrac{12}{37} \approx 0.3243$,
   $\cos D = \dfrac{12}{37} \approx 0.3243$,
   $\cos E = \dfrac{35}{37} \approx 0.9459$

5. $\sin D = \dfrac{28}{53} \approx 0.5283$,
   $\sin E = \dfrac{45}{53} \approx 0.8491$,
   $\cos D = \dfrac{45}{53} \approx 0.8491$,
   $\cos E = \dfrac{28}{53} \approx 0.5283$

6. $\sin D = \dfrac{4}{5} = 0.8000$,
   $\sin E = \dfrac{3}{5} = 0.6000$,
   $\cos D = \dfrac{3}{5} = 0.6000$,
   $\cos E = \dfrac{4}{5} = 0.8000$

7. $\sin D = \dfrac{\sqrt{3}}{2} \approx 0.8660$,
   $\sin E = \dfrac{1}{2} = 0.5000$,
   $\cos D = \dfrac{1}{2} = 0.5000$,
   $\cos E = \dfrac{\sqrt{3}}{2} \approx 0.8660$

8. $\sin D = \dfrac{8}{17} \approx 0.4706$,
   $\sin E = \dfrac{15}{17} \approx 0.8824$,
   $\cos D = \dfrac{15}{17} \approx 0.8824$,
   $\cos E = \dfrac{8}{17} \approx 0.4706$

9. $\cos 53°$

10. $\cos 9°$

11. $\cos 61°$

498   Chapter 9

9.5   Exercises

Dynamic Solutions available at *BigIdeasMath.com*

Vocabulary and Core Concept Check

1. **VOCABULARY** The sine ratio compares the length of _____ to the length of _____.

2. **WHICH ONE DOESN'T BELONG?** Which ratio does *not* belong with the other three? Explain your reasoning.

   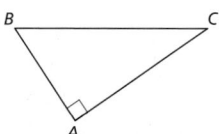

Monitoring Progress and Modeling with Mathematics

In Exercises 3–8, find $\sin D$, $\sin E$, $\cos D$, and $\cos E$. Write each answer as a fraction and as a decimal rounded to four places. *(See Example 1.)*

3. 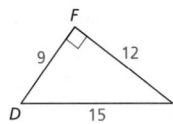   4.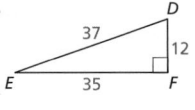

5. 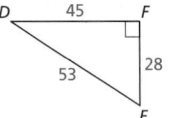   6.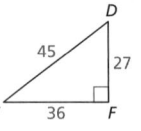

7. 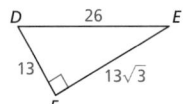   8.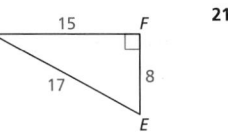

In Exercises 9–12, write the expression in terms of cosine. *(See Example 2.)*

9. $\sin 37°$ 10. $\sin 81°$

11. $\sin 29°$ 12. $\sin 64°$

In Exercises 13–16, write the expression in terms of sine.

13. $\cos 59°$ 14. $\cos 42°$

15. $\cos 73°$ 16. $\cos 18°$

In Exercises 17–22, find the value of each variable using sine and cosine. Round your answers to the nearest tenth. *(See Example 3.)*

17. 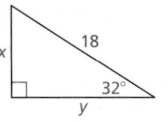   18.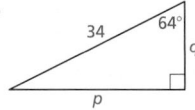

19. 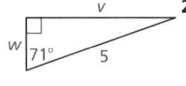   20.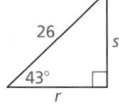

21. 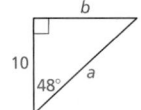   22.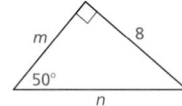

23. **REASONING** Which ratios are equal? Select all that apply. *(See Example 4.)*

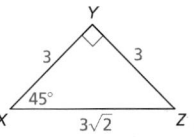

  $\sin X$ $\cos X$ $\sin Z$ $\cos Z$

498   Chapter 9   Right Triangles and Trigonometry

---

12. $\cos 26°$

13. $\sin 31°$

14. $\sin 48°$

15. $\sin 17°$

16. $\sin 72°$

17. $x \approx 9.5$, $y \approx 15.3$

18. $p \approx 30.6$, $q \approx 14.9$

19. $v \approx 4.7$, $w \approx 1.6$

20. $r \approx 19.0$, $s \approx 17.7$

21. $a \approx 14.9$, $b \approx 11.1$

22. $m \approx 6.7$, $n \approx 10.4$

23. $\sin X = \cos X = \sin Z = \cos Z$

24. REASONING Which ratios are equal to $\frac{1}{2}$? Select all that apply. *(See Example 5.)*

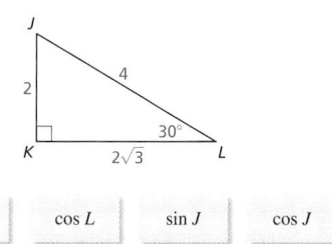

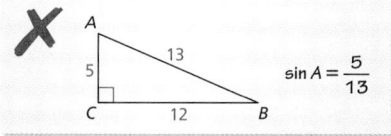

25. ERROR ANALYSIS Describe and correct the error in finding sin A.

26. WRITING Explain how to tell which side of a right triangle is adjacent to an angle and which side is the hypotenuse.

27. MODELING WITH MATHEMATICS The top of the slide is 12 feet from the ground and has an angle of depression of 53°. What is the length of the slide? *(See Example 6.)*

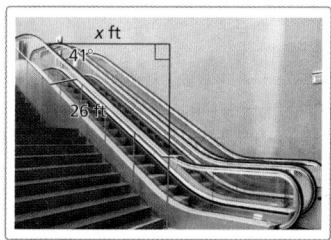

28. MODELING WITH MATHEMATICS Find the horizontal distance x the escalator covers.

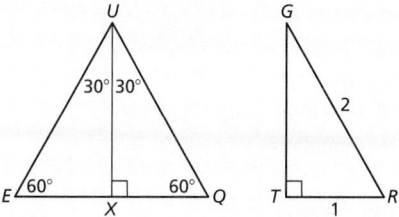

29. PROBLEM SOLVING You are flying a kite with 20 feet of string extended. The angle of elevation from the spool of string to the kite is 67°.

a. Draw and label a diagram that represents the situation.

b. How far off the ground is the kite if you hold the spool 5 feet off the ground? Describe how the height where you hold the spool affects the height of the kite.

30. MODELING WITH MATHEMATICS Planes that fly at high speeds and low elevations have radar systems that can determine the range of an obstacle and the angle of elevation to the top of the obstacle. The radar of a plane flying at an altitude of 20,000 feet detects a tower that is 25,000 feet away, with an angle of elevation of 1°.

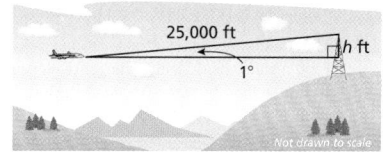

a. How many feet must the plane rise to pass over the tower?

b. Planes cannot come closer than 1000 feet vertically to any object. At what altitude must the plane fly in order to pass over the tower?

31. MAKING AN ARGUMENT Your friend uses the equation $\sin 49° = \frac{x}{16}$ to find BC. Your cousin uses the equation $\cos 41° = \frac{x}{16}$ to find BC. Who is correct? Explain your reasoning.

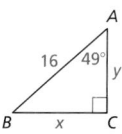

32. WRITING Describe what you must know about a triangle in order to use the sine ratio and what you must know about a triangle in order to use the cosine ratio.

33. MATHEMATICAL CONNECTIONS If $\triangle EQU$ is equilateral and $\triangle RGT$ is a right triangle with $RG = 2$, $RT = 1$, and $m\angle T = 90°$, show that $\sin E = \cos G$.

ANSWERS

24. sin L, cos J

25. The sine of $\angle A$ should be equal to the ratio of the length of the leg opposite the angle, to the length of the hypotenuse; $\sin A = \frac{12}{13}$

26. Any given acute angle in a right triangle is formed by one leg and the hypotenuse. The hypotenuse is across from the right angle, and the leg is called the adjacent leg.

27. about 15 ft

28. about 19.6 ft

29. a.

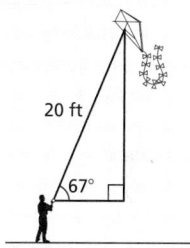

b. about 23.4 ft; The higher you hold the spool, the farther the kite is from the ground.

30. a. at least 437 ft

b. at least 21,437 ft

31. both; The sine of an acute angle is equal to the cosine of its complement, so these two equations are equivalent.

32. The sine function involves the measure of an acute angle, the length of the leg opposite that angle, and the length of the hypotenuse. You must know two out of three of those values to solve for the third (although you have not yet learned how to solve for the measure of the angle). The cosine function is the same, except it involves the measure of the leg adjacent to the acute angle.

33.

Because $\triangle EQU$ is an equilateral triangle, all three angles have a measure of 60°. When an altitude, $\overline{UX}$, is drawn from U to $\overline{EQ}$ as shown, two congruent 30°-60°-90° triangles are formed, where $m\angle E = 60°$. So,

$\sin E = \sin 60° = \frac{\sqrt{3}}{2}$. Also, in $\triangle RGT$, because the hypotenuse is twice as long as one of the legs, it is also a 30°-60°-90° triangle. Because $\angle G$ is across from the shorter leg, it must have a measure of 30°, which means that $\cos G = \cos 30° = \frac{\sqrt{3}}{2}$.

So, $\sin E = \cos G$.

Mini-Assessment

1. Find the values of x and y using sine and cosine. Round your answers to the nearest tenth.

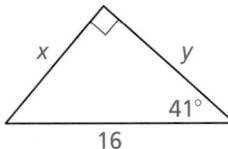

$x \approx 10.5$, $y \approx 12.1$

2. Write $\cos 81°$ in terms of sine.
   $\sin 9°$

3. Is $\cos 45°$ greater than or less than $\cos 60°$? Explain why. greater than;
   $$\cos 45° = \frac{\sqrt{2}}{2} \approx 0.7071,$$
   $$\cos 60° = \frac{1}{2} = 0.5000$$

4. The angle of elevation of a ladder leaning against a wall is 70°. The base of the ladder is 1.4 meters from the base of the wall. Find the length of the ladder to the nearest tenth of a meter.

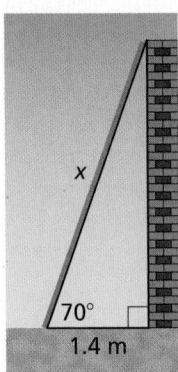

about 4.1 meters

500   **Chapter 9**

---

34. **MODELING WITH MATHEMATICS** Submarines use sonar systems, which are similar to radar systems, to detect obstacles. Sonar systems use sound to detect objects under water.

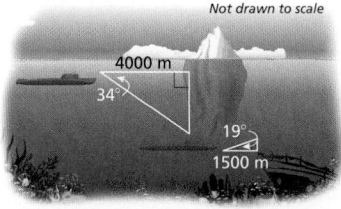

Not drawn to scale

4000 m
34°
19°
1500 m

a. You are traveling underwater in a submarine. The sonar system detects an iceberg 4000 meters ahead, with an angle of depression of 34° to the bottom of the iceberg. How many meters must the submarine lower to pass under the iceberg?

b. The sonar system then detects a sunken ship 1500 meters ahead, with an angle of elevation of 19° to the highest part of the sunken ship. How many meters must the submarine rise to pass over the sunken ship?

35. **ABSTRACT REASONING** Make a conjecture about how you could use trigonometric ratios to find angle measures in a triangle.

36. **HOW DO YOU SEE IT?** Using only the given information, would you use a sine ratio or a cosine ratio to find the length of the hypotenuse? Explain your reasoning.

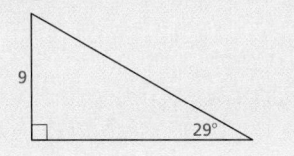

9
29°

37. **MULTIPLE REPRESENTATIONS** You are standing on a cliff above an ocean. You see a sailboat from your vantage point 30 feet above the ocean.

a. Draw and label a diagram of the situation.

b. Make a table showing the angle of depression and the length of your line of sight. Use the angles 40°, 50°, 60°, 70°, and 80°.

c. Graph the values you found in part (b), with the angle measures on the x-axis.

d. Predict the length of the line of sight when the angle of depression is 30°.

38. **THOUGHT PROVOKING** One of the following infinite series represents $\sin x$ and the other one represents $\cos x$ (where x is measured in radians). Which is which? Justify your answer. Then use each series to approximate the sine and cosine of $\frac{\pi}{6}$. (*Hints*: $\pi = 180°$; $5! = 5 \cdot 4 \cdot 3 \cdot 2 \cdot 1$; Find the values that the sine and cosine ratios approach as the angle measure approaches zero.)

a. $x - \dfrac{x^3}{3!} + \dfrac{x^5}{5!} - \dfrac{x^7}{7!} + \cdots$

b. $1 - \dfrac{x^2}{2!} + \dfrac{x^4}{4!} - \dfrac{x^6}{6!} + \cdots$

39. **CRITICAL THINKING** Let A be any acute angle of a right triangle. Show that (a) $\tan A = \dfrac{\sin A}{\cos A}$ and (b) $(\sin A)^2 + (\cos A)^2 = 1$.

40. **CRITICAL THINKING** Explain why the area of $\triangle ABC$ in the diagram can be found using the formula Area $= \frac{1}{2}ab \sin C$. Then calculate the area when $a = 4$, $b = 7$, and $m\angle C = 40°$.

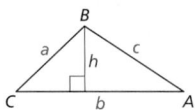
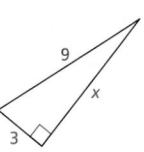

B
a   h   c
C   b   A

Maintaining Mathematical Proficiency   Reviewing what you learned in previous grades and lessons

Find the value of x. Tell whether the side lengths form a Pythagorean triple. (*Section 9.1*)

41.
6
10
x

42.
12   12
x

43.
x
27   36

44.
9
x
3

If students need help...	If students got it...
Resources by Chapter • Practice A and Practice B • Puzzle Time	**Resources by Chapter** • Enrichment and Extension • Cumulative Review
Student Journal • Practice	Start the *next* Section
Differentiating the Lesson Skills Review Handbook	

Overview of Section 9.6

Introduction

- Students are familiar with sine, cosine, and tangent ratios and have used these ratios to solve for missing sides of a right triangle.
- In this lesson, the inverse trigonometric ratios are presented, allowing students to now solve for the missing angles of a right triangle.
- Given sufficient starting information, students solve a right triangle completely—meaning they are able to find all three angle measures and all three side lengths.

Teaching Strategy

- Students enjoy the opportunity to apply their learning to a familiar context. There are many ways in which students can practice using trigonometric ratios and inverse trigonometric ratios around school.
- Any context that can be represented as a right triangle can be investigated. In my own setting, I have students investigate the angle of the main staircase. My school is located in an 1860 Victorian house, built long before building codes were in effect. Students know the stairs are steeper than those in their own homes, and they investigate the angle of the stairway. Ramps for people with disabilities represent another opportunity for investigation.
- Measuring inaccessible heights (in the gymnasium, of a flagpole or a roofline) is possible if you use a clinometer (mentioned on page T-486).
- Consider asking students to look around school for scenarios where a right triangle could represent the situation. What information is known, and what information can be solved for?

Pacing Suggestion

- The two explorations provide an introduction to inverse trigonometric ratios. Transition to the formal lesson after discussion of Questions 3 and 4.

Dynamic Teaching Tools

Dynamic Assessment & Progress Monitoring Tool

Lesson Planning Tool

Interactive Whiteboard Lesson Library

Dynamic Classroom with Dynamic Investigations

HSG-SRT.C.8 Use trigonometric ratios and the Pythagorean Theorem to solve right triangles in applied problems.

HSG-MG.A.1 Use geometric shapes, their measures, and their properties to describe objects (e.g., modeling a tree trunk or a human torso as a cylinder).

HSG-MG.A.3 Apply geometric methods to solve design problems (e.g., designing an object or structure to satisfy physical constraints or minimize cost; working with typographic grid systems based on ratios).

Laurie's Notes

Exploration

Motivate

- Show the Table of Trigonometric Ratios available at *BigIdeasMath.com.* Explain that before scientific calculators were readily available, tables such as these were included in textbooks. Also printed in textbooks were tables of square roots and cube roots!

Exploration 1

- In this first exploration, students are constructing triangles using information from the diagrams.
- In part (a), the coordinates of the triangle can be determined: (0, 0), (4, 0), and (4, 4). Students should recognize this as a right isosceles triangle.
- In part (b), the first step is to construct a circle of radius 4 centered at (0, 2). The coordinates of point *B* in the diagram correspond to the intersection of the circle and the *x*-axis.
- Measuring the lengths of the sides, the sine and cosine ratios can be found. The values should sound familiar to students, who can then verify the angles by measuring.
- **Extension:** Construct another triangle, *EDC,* similar to triangle *ABC* in part (b). Students should recognize that the sine and cosine ratios will be the same. Moreover, the measures of the corresponding angles will be congruent.

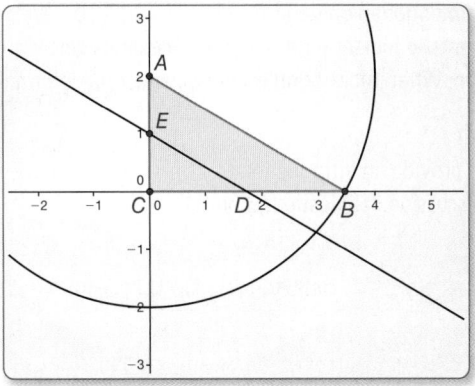

Exploration 2

- The triangles in this exploration have leg lengths that make finding the tangent ratio very easy.
- Students can compute the length of the hypotenuse using the software.
- Be sure that students have their calculators set for degree mode rather than radian mode.
- **MP6 Attend to Precision:** Tell students that $\sin^{-1}$ is read "inverse sine" and not "sine to the negative one."

Communicate Your Answer

- There are many online applets that simulate the leaning ladder problem. Although this problem specifies one exact location, it is an interesting problem for students to consider.

Connecting to Next Step

- Students have now been introduced to the inverse trigonometric ratios. In the formal lesson, these ratios will be defined formally and used to solve problems.

9.6 Solving Right Triangles

Essential Question
When you know the lengths of the sides of a right triangle, how can you find the measures of the two acute angles?

EXPLORATION 1 — Solving Special Right Triangles

Work with a partner. Use the figures to find the values of the sine and cosine of $\angle A$ and $\angle B$. Use these values to find the measures of $\angle A$ and $\angle B$. Use dynamic geometry software to verify your answers.

a.

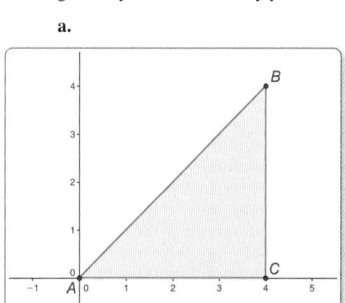

b.

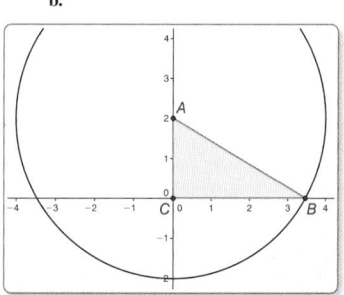

ATTENDING TO PRECISION

To be proficient in math, you need to calculate accurately and efficiently, expressing numerical answers with a degree of precision appropriate for the problem context.

EXPLORATION 2 — Solving Right Triangles

Work with a partner. You can use a calculator to find the measure of an angle when you know the value of the sine, cosine, or tangent of the angle. Use the inverse sine, inverse cosine, or inverse tangent feature of your calculator to approximate the measures of $\angle A$ and $\angle B$ to the nearest tenth of a degree. Then use dynamic geometry software to verify your answers.

a.

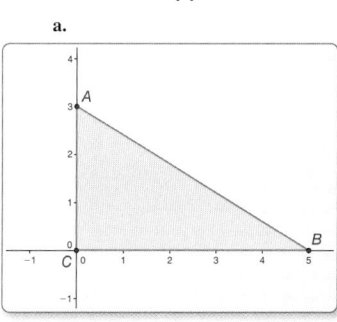

b.

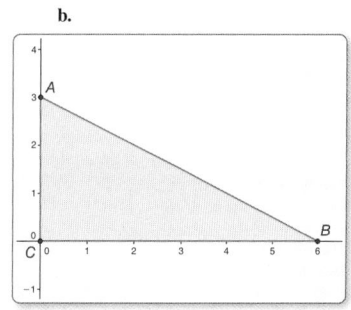

Communicate Your Answer

3. When you know the lengths of the sides of a right triangle, how can you find the measures of the two acute angles?

4. A ladder leaning against a building forms a right triangle with the building and the ground. The legs of the right triangle (in meters) form a 5-12-13 Pythagorean triple. Find the measures of the two acute angles to the nearest tenth of a degree.

Section 9.6   Solving Right Triangles   **501**

ANSWERS

1. **a.** $\sin A = \cos A = \sin B = \cos B = \dfrac{\sqrt{2}}{2}$; $m\angle A = m\angle B = 45°$

    b. $\sin A = \cos B = \dfrac{\sqrt{3}}{2}$, $\cos A = \sin B = \dfrac{1}{2}$; $m\angle A = 60°, m\angle B = 30°$

2. **a.** $m\angle A \approx 59.0°, m\angle B \approx 31.0°$

    b. $m\angle A \approx 63.4°, m\angle B \approx 26.6°$

3. You can find the ratio of two side lengths that gives the value of the sine, cosine, or tangent of an angle. If you recognize the ratio from a special right triangle, then you can find the measure of the angle that way. Otherwise, you can use the inverse sine, cosine, or tangent feature of your calculator to approximate the measure of the angle.

4. about 67.4°, about 22.6°

Extra Example 1

Determine which of the two acute angles has a sine of 0.4.

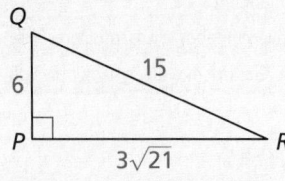

The acute angle that has a sine of 0.4 is $\angle R$.

Extra Example 2

Let $\angle A$, $\angle B$, and $\angle C$ be acute angles. Use a calculator to approximate the measures of $\angle A$, $\angle B$, and $\angle C$ to the nearest tenth of a degree.

a. $\tan A = 3.29$ $m\angle A \approx 73.1°$

b. $\sin B = 0.55$ $m\angle B \approx 33.4°$

c. $\cos C = 0.87$ $m\angle C \approx 29.5°$

MONITORING PROGRESS ANSWERS

1. $\angle E$

2. $\angle F$

Core Vocabulary

inverse tangent, *p. 502*
inverse sine, *p. 502*
inverse cosine, *p.502*
solve a right triangle, *p. 503*

What You Will Learn

▶ Use inverse trigonometric ratios.

▶ Solve right triangles.

Using Inverse Trigonometric Ratios

EXAMPLE 1   Identifying Angles from Trigonometric Ratios

Determine which of the two acute angles has a cosine of 0.5.

SOLUTION

Find the cosine of each acute angle.

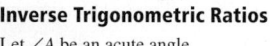
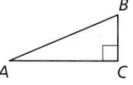

$$\cos A = \frac{\text{adj. to } \angle A}{\text{hyp.}} = \frac{\sqrt{3}}{2} \approx 0.8660 \qquad \cos B = \frac{\text{adj. to } \angle B}{\text{hyp.}} = \frac{1}{2} = 0.5$$

▶ The acute angle that has a cosine of 0.5 is $\angle B$.

If the measure of an acute angle is 60°, then its cosine is 0.5. The converse is also true. If the cosine of an acute angle is 0.5, then the measure of the angle is 60°. So, in Example 1, the measure of $\angle B$ must be 60° because its cosine is 0.5.

Core Concept

READING

The expression "$\tan^{-1} x$" is read as "the inverse tangent of x."

Inverse Trigonometric Ratios

Let $\angle A$ be an acute angle.

Inverse Tangent If $\tan A = x$, then $\tan^{-1} x = m\angle A$. $\tan^{-1} \dfrac{BC}{AC} = m\angle A$

Inverse Sine If $\sin A = y$, then $\sin^{-1} y = m\angle A$. $\sin^{-1} \dfrac{BC}{AB} = m\angle A$

Inverse Cosine If $\cos A = z$, then $\cos^{-1} z = m\angle A$. $\cos^{-1} \dfrac{AC}{AB} = m\angle A$

ANOTHER WAY

You can use the Table of Trigonometric Ratios available at *BigIdeasMath.com* to approximate $\tan^{-1} 0.75$ to the nearest degree. Find the number closest to 0.75 in the tangent column and read the angle measure at the left.

EXAMPLE 2   Finding Angle Measures

Let $\angle A$, $\angle B$, and $\angle C$ be acute angles. Use a calculator to approximate the measures of $\angle A$, $\angle B$, and $\angle C$ to the nearest tenth of a degree.

a. $\tan A = 0.75$ **b.** $\sin B = 0.87$ **c.** $\cos C = 0.15$

SOLUTION

a. $m\angle A = \tan^{-1} 0.75 \approx 36.9°$

b. $m\angle B = \sin^{-1} 0.87 \approx 60.5°$

c. $m\angle C = \cos^{-1} 0.15 \approx 81.4°$

Monitoring Progress 🔊 Help in English and Spanish at *BigIdeasMath.com*

Determine which of the two acute angles has the given trigonometric ratio.

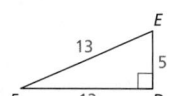

1. The sine of the angle is $\frac{12}{13}$.   2. The tangent of the angle is $\frac{5}{12}$.

Laurie's Notes   Teacher Actions

- Sketch the triangle shown in Example 1. Ask students to find the sine and cosine of angles A and B as well as the measure of each angle.
- State the *Core Concept*. Students find it helpful when you say, "$\tan^{-1}(1) = x$ means you want to find the angle whose tangent is 1." Another way of asking this question would be to write $\tan x = 1$.
- **Thumbs Up:** Have students work with partners to answer all parts of Example 2. Use *Thumbs Up* to assess students' understanding.

Monitoring Progress Help in English and Spanish at *BigIdeasMath.com*

Let ∠G, ∠H, and ∠K be acute angles. Use a calculator to approximate the measures of ∠G, ∠H, and ∠K to the nearest tenth of a degree.

3. tan G = 0.43   **4.** sin H = 0.68   **5.** cos K = 0.94

Solving Right Triangles

Core Concept

Solving a Right Triangle

To **solve a right triangle** means to find all unknown side lengths and angle measures. You can solve a right triangle when you know either of the following.

- two side lengths
- one side length and the measure of one acute angle

EXAMPLE 3   Solving a Right Triangle

Solve the right triangle. Round decimal answers to the nearest tenth.

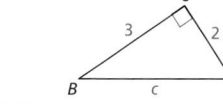

SOLUTION

Step 1   Use the Pythagorean Theorem (Theorem 9.1) to find the length of the hypotenuse.

$c^2 = a^2 + b^2$	Pythagorean Theorem
$c^2 = 3^2 + 2^2$	Substitute.
$c^2 = 13$	Simplify.
$c = \sqrt{13}$	Find the positive square root.
$c \approx 3.6$	Use a calculator.

ANOTHER WAY

You could also have found $m\angle A$ first by finding $\tan^{-1}\frac{3}{2} \approx 56.3°$.

Step 2   Find $m\angle B$.

$m\angle B = \tan^{-1}\frac{2}{3} \approx 33.7°$ Use a calculator.

Step 3   Find $m\angle A$.

Because ∠A and ∠B are complements, you can write

$m\angle A = 90° - m\angle B$

$\approx 90° - 33.7°$

$= 56.3°.$

▶ In △ABC, $c \approx 3.6$, $m\angle B \approx 33.7°$, and $m\angle A \approx 56.3°$.

Monitoring Progress Help in English and Spanish at *BigIdeasMath.com*

Solve the right triangle. Round decimal answers to the nearest tenth.

6. 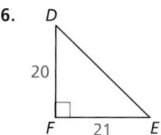   **7.**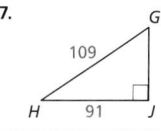

Extra Example 3

Solve the right triangle. Round decimal answers to the nearest tenth.

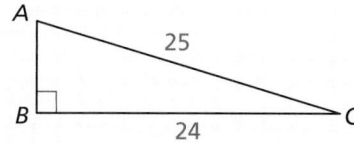

$AB = 7$, $m\angle A \approx 73.7°$, $m\angle C \approx 16.3°$

MONITORING PROGRESS ANSWERS

3. $m\angle G \approx 23.3°$

4. $m\angle H \approx 42.8°$

5. $m\angle K \approx 19.9°$

6. $DE = 29$, $m\angle D \approx 46.4°$, $m\angle E \approx 43.6°$

7. $GJ = 60$, $m\angle G \approx 56.6°$, $m\angle H \approx 33.4°$

Laurie's Notes   Teacher Actions

- Previously, students have used trigonometric ratios to find side lengths. Explain to students that now they will be able to find angle measures.
- **? Fact-First Questioning:** "If you know the lengths of two sides of a right triangle, then you can determine the third side and the two acute angle measures. How is this done?" Give partners time to discuss. Use *Popsicle Sticks* to solicit methods for solving a right triangle completely. *Sample answer:* Use the Pythagorean Theorem to find the length of the third side. Then use inverse trigonometric ratios to find the measures of the acute angles.
- **Think-Pair-Share:** Have partners work independently on Example 3, using the method(s) just described by peers.

Extra Example 4

Solve the right triangle. Round decimal answers to the nearest tenth.

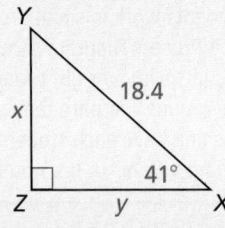

$x \approx 12.1$, $y \approx 13.9$, $m\angle Y = 49°$

Extra Example 5

Use the information in Example 5. Another raked stage is 25 feet long from front to back with a total rise of 1.5 feet. You want the rake to be 5° or less. Is the raked stage within your desired range? Explain. Yes; the rake is about 3.4°, so it is within the desired range.

MONITORING PROGRESS ANSWERS

8. $XY \approx 13.8$, $YZ \approx 10.9$, $m\angle Y = 38°$
9. no

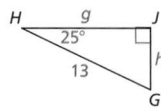 **Solving a Right Triangle**

Solve the right triangle. Round decimal answers to the nearest tenth.

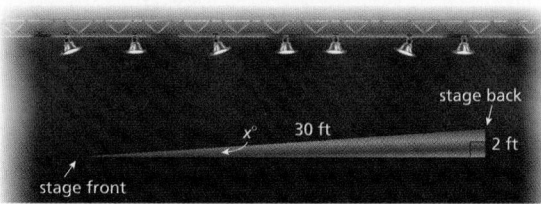

SOLUTION

Use trigonometric ratios to find the values of g and h.

$$\sin H = \frac{\text{opp.}}{\text{hyp.}} \qquad\qquad \cos H = \frac{\text{adj.}}{\text{hyp.}}$$

$$\sin 25° = \frac{h}{13} \qquad\qquad \cos 25° = \frac{g}{13}$$

$$13 \cdot \sin 25° = h \qquad\qquad 13 \cdot \cos 25° = g$$

$$5.5 \approx h \qquad\qquad\qquad 11.8 \approx g$$

Because $\angle H$ and $\angle G$ are complements, you can write

$$m\angle G = 90° - m\angle H = 90° - 25° = 65°.$$

▶ In $\triangle GHJ$, $h \approx 5.5$, $g \approx 11.8$, and $m\angle G = 65°$.

READING

A *raked stage* slants upward from front to back to give the audience a better view.

EXAMPLE 5 **Solving a Real-Life Problem**

Your school is building a *raked stage*. The stage will be 30 feet long from front to back, with a total rise of 2 feet. You want the rake (angle of elevation) to be 5° or less for safety. Is the raked stage within your desired range?

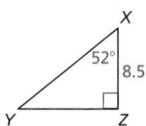

SOLUTION

Use the inverse sine ratio to find the degree measure x of the rake.

$$x \approx \sin^{-1} \frac{2}{30} \approx 3.8$$

▶ The rake is about 3.8°, so it is within your desired range of 5° or less.

Monitoring Progress ◀)) Help in English and Spanish at *BigIdeasMath.com*

8. Solve the right triangle. Round decimal answers to the nearest tenth.

9. **WHAT IF?** In Example 5, suppose another raked stage is 20 feet long from front to back with a total rise of 2 feet. Is the raked stage within your desired range?

Laurie's Notes   Teacher Actions

? "After solving a right triangle completely, how can you check your answers?" Answers will vary. Students may mention using the Pythagorean Theorem, or that the angles should still sum to 180°, or that the shortest side is opposite the least angle measure.

• **MP4 Model with Mathematics:** After working Example 5, consider any ramps on school property. See the *Teaching Strategy* on page T-500.

Closure

• **Exit Ticket:** A right triangle has legs of 8 centimeters and 13 centimeters. Solve the triangle completely. hypotenuse $= \sqrt{233}$ cm or ≈ 15.3 cm; angle measures $\approx 31.6°$, $\approx 58.4°$, 90°

Vocabulary and Core Concept Check

1. **COMPLETE THE SENTENCE** To solve a right triangle means to find the measures of all its _____ and _____.

2. **WRITING** Explain when you can use a trigonometric ratio to find a side length of a right triangle and when you can use the Pythagorean Theorem (Theorem 9.1).

Monitoring Progress and Modeling with Mathematics

In Exercises 3–6, determine which of the two acute angles has the given trigonometric ratio. *(See Example 1.)*

3. The cosine of the angle is $\frac{4}{5}$.

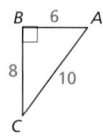

4. The sine of the angle is $\frac{5}{11}$.

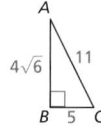

5. The sine of the angle is 0.96.

6. The tangent of the angle is 1.5.

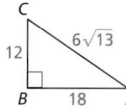

In Exercises 7–12, let $\angle D$ be an acute angle. Use a calculator to approximate the measure of $\angle D$ to the nearest tenth of a degree. *(See Example 2.)*

7. $\sin D = 0.75$

8. $\sin D = 0.19$

9. $\cos D = 0.33$

10. $\cos D = 0.64$

11. $\tan D = 0.28$

12. $\tan D = 0.72$

In Exercises 13–18, solve the right triangle. Round decimal answers to the nearest tenth. *(See Examples 3 and 4.)*

13.

14.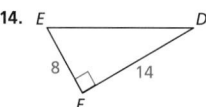

15.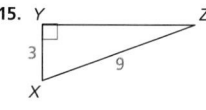

16.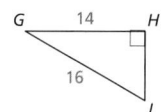

17.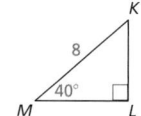

18.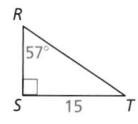

19. **ERROR ANALYSIS** Describe and correct the error in using an inverse trigonometric ratio.

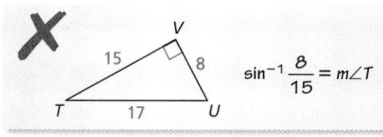

20. **PROBLEM SOLVING** In order to unload clay easily, the body of a dump truck must be elevated to at least 45°. The body of a dump truck that is 14 feet long has been raised 8 feet. Will the clay pour out easily? Explain your reasoning. *(See Example 5.)*

21. **PROBLEM SOLVING** You are standing on a footbridge that is 12 feet above a lake. You look down and see a duck in the water. The duck is 7 feet away from the footbridge. What is the angle of elevation from the duck to you?

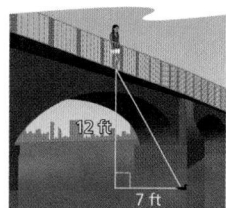

Section 9.6   Solving Right Triangles   **505**

Assignment Guide and Homework Check

ASSIGNMENT

Basic: 1, 2, 3–21 odd, 22, 26, 33–36

Average: 1, 2, 6–18 even, 19–23, 26–28, 33–36

Advanced: 1, 2, 6, 10, 16, 18–24, 26–31, 33–36

HOMEWORK CHECK

Basic: 5, 13, 15, 21, 26

Average: 6, 18, 20, 26, 28

Advanced: 6, 16, 20, 26, 30

ANSWERS

1. sides, angles

2. You can use a trigonometric ratio to find a side length of a right triangle when you know one of the acute angle measures and one of the other side lengths. You can use the Pythagorean Theorem (Thm. 9.1) when you know the other two side lengths.

3. $\angle C$

4. $\angle A$

5. $\angle A$

6. $\angle C$

7. about 48.6°

8. about 11.0°

9. about 70.7°

10. about 50.2°

11. about 15.6°

12. about 35.8°

13. $AB = 15$, $m\angle A \approx 53.1°$, $m\angle B \approx 36.9°$

14. $DE \approx 16.1$, $m\angle E \approx 60.3°$, $m\angle D \approx 29.7°$

15. $YZ \approx 8.5$, $m\angle X \approx 70.5°$, $m\angle Z \approx 19.5°$

16. $HJ \approx 7.7$, $m\angle G \approx 29.0°$, $m\angle J \approx 61.0°$

17. $KL \approx 5.1$, $ML \approx 6.1$, $m\angle K = 50°$

18. $RS \approx 9.7$, $RT \approx 17.9$, $m\angle T = 33°$

19. The sine ratio should be the length of the opposite side to the length of the hypotenuse, not the adjacent side; $\sin^{-1} \frac{8}{17} = m\angle T$

20. no; The body of the dump truck has only been elevated to about 34.8°, which is less than the recommended minimum angle of 45°.

21. about 59.7°

ANSWERS

22. $\tan^{-1}\dfrac{15}{22}$, $\sin^{-1}\dfrac{15}{26.6}$, $\cos^{-1}\dfrac{22}{26.6}$;

Sample answer: the expression with the inverse tangent; The other two expressions use the hypotenuse, which had to be calculated and rounded. You should use the given values whenever possible, in case there was an error in obtaining the calculated value. Also, you should use exact values over rounded or approximate values whenever possible, so that your answer is more accurate.

23–36. See Additional Answers.

 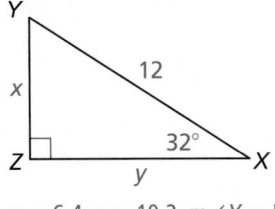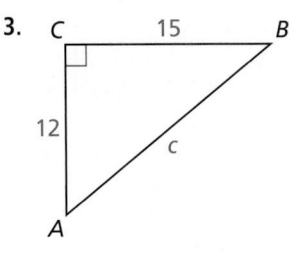
22. HOW DO YOU SEE IT? Write three expressions that can be used to approximate the measure of $\angle A$. Which expression would you choose? Explain your choice.

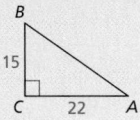

23. MODELING WITH MATHEMATICS The Uniform Federal Accessibility Standards specify that a wheelchair ramp may not have an incline greater than $4.76°$. You want to build a ramp with a vertical rise of 8 inches. You want to minimize the horizontal distance taken up by the ramp. Draw a diagram showing the approximate dimensions of your ramp.

24. MODELING WITH MATHEMATICS The horizontal part of a step is called the *tread*. The vertical part is called the *riser*. The recommended riser-to-tread ratio is 7 inches : 11 inches.

  a. Find the value of x for stairs built using the recommended riser-to-tread ratio.

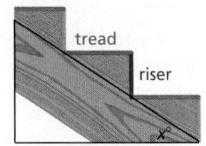

  b. You want to build stairs that are less steep than the stairs in part (a). Give an example of a riser-to-tread ratio that you could use. Find the value of x for your stairs.

25. USING TOOLS Find the measure of $\angle R$ without using a protractor. Justify your technique.

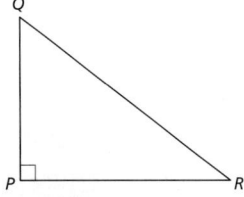

Maintaining Mathematical Proficiency   *Reviewing what you learned in previous grades and lessons*

Solve the equation. *(Skills Review Handbook)*

33. $\dfrac{12}{x} = \dfrac{3}{2}$ **34.** $\dfrac{13}{9} = \dfrac{x}{18}$ **35.** $\dfrac{x}{2.1} = \dfrac{4.1}{3.5}$ **36.** $\dfrac{5.6}{12.7} = \dfrac{4.9}{x}$

506   **Chapter 9**   Right Triangles and Trigonometry

26. MAKING AN ARGUMENT Your friend claims that $\tan^{-1} x = \dfrac{1}{\tan x}$. Is your friend correct? Explain your reasoning.

USING STRUCTURE In Exercises 27 and 28, solve each triangle.

27. $\triangle JKM$ and $\triangle LKM$

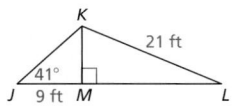

28. $\triangle TUS$ and $\triangle VTW$

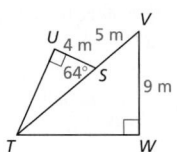

29. MATHEMATICAL CONNECTIONS Write an expression that can be used to find the measure of the acute angle formed by each line and the x-axis. Then approximate the angle measure to the nearest tenth of a degree.

  a. $y = 3x$

  b. $y = \dfrac{4}{3}x + 4$

30. THOUGHT PROVOKING Simplify each expression. Justify your answer.

  a. $\sin^{-1}(\sin x)$

  b. $\tan(\tan^{-1} y)$

  c. $\cos(\cos^{-1} z)$

31. REASONING Explain why the expression $\sin^{-1}(1.2)$ does not make sense.

32. USING STRUCTURE The perimeter of rectangle $ABCD$ is 16 centimeters, and the ratio of its width to its length is 1 : 3. Segment BD divides the rectangle into two congruent triangles. Find the side lengths and angle measures of these two triangles.

Overview of Section 9.7

Introduction

- This lesson presents two additional ways to solve a triangle. In prior lessons, the Pythagorean Theorem and trigonometric ratios were used to solve for parts of a right triangle.
- In this lesson, non-right triangles are solved using the Law of Sines and the Law of Cosines. Working with obtuse angle measures will be new for students and must be explained. Students must be careful with their calculations.
- Also introduced in this chapter are formulas for finding the area of a triangle.

Formative Assessment Tips

- **Partner Speaks:** This strategy provides a student the opportunity to share his or her thinking about a problem or concept with a partner. The partner then shares this thinking with the whole class.
- Thinking through a problem with a partner is less intimidating for many students than sharing it with an entire class. For the listener, he or she needs to pay attention to the thoughts of the speaker and set aside his or her own thinking about the problem. As students are engaged in this dialogue, circulate to hear the discussion and to gain an understanding of how students are thinking about the problem or concept. You will be able to judge appropriate next steps.
- The opportunity to speak to a partner and then have him or her share the student's thinking should not be used for simple, less challenging problems. It should be used as a way to pair students differently from the usual pairing of a student having a conversation with the person to his or her right.

Pacing Suggestion

- The formal lesson is quite long. Suggestions are made for combining parts of the two explorations, which are still important for students to experience prior to the formal lesson.

Dynamic Teaching Tools
Dynamic Assessment & Progress Monitoring Tool
Lesson Planning Tool
Interactive Whiteboard Lesson Library
Dynamic Classroom with Dynamic Investigations

HSG-SRT.D.9 Derive the formula $A = 1/2\, ab\, \sin(C)$ for the area of a triangle by drawing an auxiliary line from a vertex perpendicular to the opposite side.

HSG-SRT.D.10 Prove the Laws of Sines and Cosines and use them to solve problems.

HSG-SRT.D.11 Understand and apply the Law of Sines and the Law of Cosines to find unknown measurements in right and non-right triangles (e.g., surveying problems, resultant forces).

HSG-MG.A.3 Apply geometric methods to solve design problems (e.g., designing an object or structure to satisfy physical constraints or minimize cost; working with typographic grid systems based on ratios).

Laurie's Notes

Exploration

Motivate

- Prior to students arriving, draw a non-right triangle on the board with the sides labeled 6, 8, and 12 units.
- **?** "What do you need to know to find the area of this triangle?" You need to know the altitude to one of the sides.
- Write Heron's (or Hero's) formula: Area $= \sqrt{p(p-a)(p-b)(p-c)}$, where $p = \dfrac{a+b+c}{2}$. p is also known as the semi-perimeter.
- Have students use Heron's formula to find the area of this triangle. ≈ 21.3 square units
- Explain to students that in this lesson they will find that there is yet another way to find the area of a triangle without knowing the altitude to a side of the triangle.

Exploration 1

- Both explorations use the same construction. From the diagram, students can read the coordinates of the triangle: (0, 2), (5, 1), and (6, 4). Some of the measures used in this first exploration are also used in the second.
- The directions are clear and simple for students to follow.
- Students are generally surprised when they see that $\dfrac{\sin A}{a} = \dfrac{\sin B}{b} = \dfrac{\sin C}{c}$.
- Before making the construction dynamic, students should take the measurements needed for the second exploration.
- **?** "What observations can you make about this exploration?" Answers will vary. However, in addition to commenting on the ratio relationship, students should note that they are no longer working with just right triangles!

Exploration 2

- Again, the directions are clear and simple for students to follow.
- The computations will seem obscure, and in fact, students often wonder who thought up the relationship! In the formal lesson, students will recognize that depending upon the information known about the triangle, either the Law of Sines or the Law of Cosines will be used.
- Like the first exploration, students should note that this relationship is not restricted to right triangles.

Communicate Your Answer

- **MP3 Construct Viable Arguments and Critique the Reasoning of Others:** Students should describe the relationships observed in the two explorations.

Connecting to Next Step

- Students have now been introduced to the Law of Sines and the Law of Cosines. In the formal lesson, these relationships will be stated formally, along with a formula for finding the area of a triangle.

Essential Question What are the Law of Sines and the Law of Cosines?

EXPLORATION 1 **Discovering the Law of Sines**

Work with a partner.

a. Copy and complete the table for the triangle shown. What can you conclude?

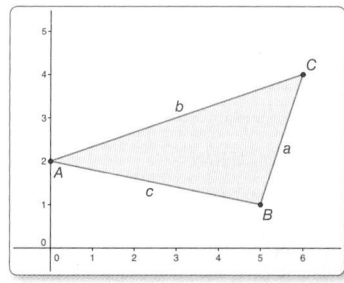

Sample
Segments
$a = 3.16$
$b = 6.32$
$c = 5.10$
Angles
$m\angle A = 29.74°$
$m\angle B = 97.13°$
$m\angle C = 53.13°$

USING TOOLS STRATEGICALLY

To be proficient in math, you need to use technology to compare predictions with data.

$m\angle A$	a	$\dfrac{\sin A}{a}$	$m\angle B$	b	$\dfrac{\sin B}{b}$	$m\angle C$	c	$\dfrac{\sin C}{c}$

b. Use dynamic geometry software to draw two other triangles. Copy and complete the table in part (a) for each triangle. Use your results to write a conjecture about the relationship between the sines of the angles and the lengths of the sides of a triangle.

EXPLORATION 2 **Discovering the Law of Cosines**

Work with a partner.

a. Copy and complete the table for the triangle in Exploration 1(a). What can you conclude?

c	c^2	a	a^2	b	b^2	$m\angle C$	$a^2 + b^2 - 2ab \cos C$

b. Use dynamic geometry software to draw two other triangles. Copy and complete the table in part (a) for each triangle. Use your results to write a conjecture about what you observe in the completed tables.

Communicate Your Answer

3. What are the Law of Sines and the Law of Cosines?

4. When would you use the Law of Sines to solve a triangle? When would you use the Law of Cosines to solve a triangle?

Section 9.7   Law of Sines and Law of Cosines   **507**

ANSWERS

1. a. 29.74°, 3.16, 0.157, 97.13°, 6.32, 0.157, 53.13°, 5.1, 0.157;

$$\frac{\sin A}{a} = \frac{\sin B}{b} = \frac{\sin C}{c}$$

  b. Check students' work. In any given triangle, the ratio of the sine of an angle measure to the length of the opposite side is the same as the ratio of the sine of any other angle measure to the length of its opposite side.

2. a. 5.1, 26.0, 3.16, 9.99, 6.32, 39.94, 53.13°, 26.0;
$a^2 + b^2 - 2ab \cos C = c^2$

  b. Check students' work. In any given triangle, the length of one side squared, c^2, equals $a^2 + b^2 - 2ab \cos C$, where a and b are the lengths of the other two sides, and $\angle C$ is the angle opposite side c.

3. For any triangle with sides of length a, b, and c, where the angles opposite each of the respective sides are $\angle A$, $\angle B$, and $\angle C$, the Law of Sines (Thm. 9.9) is $\dfrac{\sin A}{a} = \dfrac{\sin B}{b} = \dfrac{\sin C}{c}$, and the Law of Cosines (Thm. 9.10) is $c^2 = a^2 + b^2 - 2ab \cos C$. Both of these equations can be manipulated to solve for different values.

4. Use the Law of Sines (Thm. 9.9) to solve a triangle when you know the measures of two angles and any side, or when you know two sides and one nonincluded angle. Use the Law of Cosines (Thm. 9.10) when you know the measures of two sides and their included angle, or when you know the measures of all three sides.

508   Chapter 9

Differentiated Instruction

Organization

Have students copy the table (without the answers) in their notebooks. Tell students they will fill in the table as they work through the lesson and answer the questions, "When can you apply the Law of Sines to a triangle?" and "When can you apply the Law of Cosines to a triangle?" By the end of the lesson, students should have a complete table.

Known Values	Law of Sines	Law of Cosines
SSS	No	Yes
SAS	No	Yes
ASA	Yes	No
SSA	Yes	No
AAS	Yes	No

Extra Example 1

Use a calculator to find each trigonometric ratio. Round your answer to four decimal places.
a. tan 92° -28.6363
b. sin 175° 0.0872
c. cos 149° -0.8572

Extra Example 2

Find the area of the triangle. Round your answer to the nearest tenth.

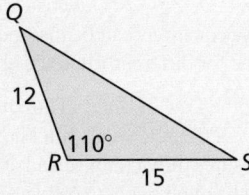

about 84.6 square units

MONITORING PROGRESS ANSWERS

1. about -2.7475
2. about 0.9925
3. about -0.9659
4. about 115.2 square units
5. about 285.6 square units

9.7 Lesson

Core Vocabulary

Law of Sines, *p. 509*
Law of Cosines, *p. 511*

What You Will Learn

▶ Find areas of triangles.
▶ Use the Law of Sines to solve triangles.
▶ Use the Law of Cosines to solve triangles.

Finding Areas of Triangles

So far, you have used trigonometric ratios to solve right triangles. In this lesson, you will learn how to solve any triangle. When the triangle is obtuse, you may need to find a trigonometric ratio for an obtuse angle.

EXAMPLE 1   Finding Trigonometric Ratios for Obtuse Angles

Use a calculator to find each trigonometric ratio. Round your answer to four decimal places.

a. tan 150°   b. sin 120°   c. cos 95°

SOLUTION

a. tan 150° ≈ -0.5774 b. sin 120° ≈ 0.8660   c. cos 95° ≈ -0.0872

Monitoring Progress Help in English and Spanish at *BigIdeasMath.com*

Use a calculator to find the trigonometric ratio. Round your answer to four decimal places.

1. tan 110°   2. sin 97°   3. cos 165°

Core Concept

Area of a Triangle

The area of any triangle is given by one-half the product of the lengths of two sides times the sine of their included angle. For $\triangle ABC$ shown, there are three ways to calculate the area.

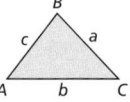

$$\text{Area} = \tfrac{1}{2}bc \sin A \qquad \text{Area} = \tfrac{1}{2}ac \sin B \qquad \text{Area} = \tfrac{1}{2}ab \sin C$$

EXAMPLE 2   Finding the Area of a Triangle

Find the area of the triangle. Round your answer to the nearest tenth.

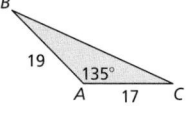

SOLUTION

$$\text{Area} = \tfrac{1}{2}bc \sin A = \tfrac{1}{2}(17)(19) \sin 135° ≈ 114.2$$

▶ The area of the triangle is about 114.2 square units.

Monitoring Progress Help in English and Spanish at *BigIdeasMath.com*

Find the area of $\triangle ABC$ with the given side lengths and included angle. Round your answer to the nearest tenth.

4. $m\angle B = 60°$, $a = 19$, $c = 14$ 5. $m\angle C = 29°$, $a = 38$, $b = 31$

Laurie's Notes   Teacher Actions

? "What does it mean to solve a right triangle?" You need to find any missing angle measures and side lengths.

• Explain to students that in this lesson they will continue to solve triangles, and not only right triangles. They will also find the trigonometric ratios for an obtuse angle.
• Write the *Core Concept*. Give students time to prove why these relationships are true.
• If needed, offer the starting point of drawing an altitude to any of the three sides and labeling the altitude *h*. Students should be able to see why the formula works.

Using the Law of Sines

The trigonometric ratios in the previous sections can only be used to solve right triangles. You will learn two laws that can be used to solve any triangle.

You can use the **Law of Sines** to solve triangles when two angles and the length of any side are known (AAS or ASA cases), or when the lengths of two sides and an angle opposite one of the two sides are known (SSA case).

 Theorem

Theorem 9.9   Law of Sines

The Law of Sines can be written in either of the following forms for $\triangle ABC$ with sides of length a, b, and c.

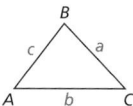

$$\frac{\sin A}{a} = \frac{\sin B}{b} = \frac{\sin C}{c} \qquad \frac{a}{\sin A} = \frac{b}{\sin B} = \frac{c}{\sin C}$$

Proof Ex. 51, p. 516

EXAMPLE 3   Using the Law of Sines (SSA Case)

Solve the triangle. Round decimal answers to the nearest tenth.

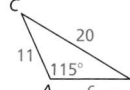

SOLUTION

Use the Law of Sines to find $m\angle B$.

$$\frac{\sin B}{b} = \frac{\sin A}{a} \qquad \text{Law of Sines}$$

$$\frac{\sin B}{11} = \frac{\sin 115°}{20} \qquad \text{Substitute.}$$

$$\sin B = \frac{11 \sin 115°}{20} \qquad \text{Multiply each side by 11.}$$

$$m\angle B \approx 29.9° \qquad \text{Use a calculator.}$$

By the Triangle Sum Theorem (Theorem 5.1), $m\angle C \approx 180° - 115° - 29.9° = 35.1°$.

Use the Law of Sines again to find the remaining side length c of the triangle.

$$\frac{c}{\sin C} = \frac{a}{\sin A} \qquad \text{Law of Sines}$$

$$\frac{c}{\sin 35.1°} = \frac{20}{\sin 115°} \qquad \text{Substitute.}$$

$$c = \frac{20 \sin 35.1°}{\sin 115°} \qquad \text{Multiply each side by } \sin 35.1°.$$

$$c \approx 12.7 \qquad \text{Use a calculator.}$$

▶ In $\triangle ABC$, $m\angle B \approx 29.9°$, $m\angle C \approx 35.1°$, and $c \approx 12.7$.

Monitoring Progress ◀)) Help in English and Spanish at *BigIdeasMath.com*

Solve the triangle. Round decimal answers to the nearest tenth.

6.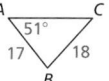

7.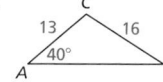

Extra Example 3

Solve the triangle. Round decimal answers to the nearest tenth.

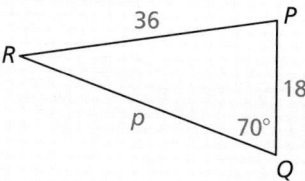

$m\angle R \approx 28.0°$, $m\angle P \approx 82.0°$, $p \approx 37.9$

MONITORING PROGRESS ANSWERS

6. $m\angle B \approx 81.8°$, $m\angle C \approx 47.2°$, $b \approx 22.9$

7. $m\angle B \approx 31.5°$, $m\angle C \approx 108.5°$, $c \approx 23.6$

Laurie's Notes   Teacher Actions

- Discuss solving non-right triangles and state the Law of Sines, which students investigated in the explorations.
- **MP3** and **Turn and Talk:** "If $\frac{\sin A}{a} = \frac{\sin B}{b} = \frac{\sin C}{c}$, then why is $\frac{a}{\sin A} = \frac{b}{\sin B} = \frac{c}{\sin C}$ also true?" Answers will vary. Listen for correct reasoning.
- **?** Pose Example 3. "What information is known?" measures of $\angle A$, side a (side opposite $\angle A$), and side b (side opposite $\angle B$) "What part of the triangle can you solve for?" measure of $\angle B$
- Continue to solve the example as shown. Note that $\angle A$ is used in solving for side c versus $\angle B$, which has been approximated.

Extra Example 4

Solve the triangle. Round decimal answers to the nearest tenth.

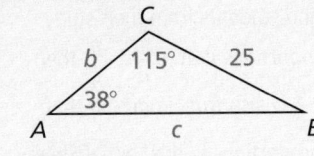

$m\angle B = 27°, b \approx 18.4, c \approx 36.8$

Extra Example 5

A surveyor makes the measurements shown to determine the length f of a walking bridge to be built across a pond in a city park. Find the length of the bridge $\overline{DE}$ to the nearest tenth.

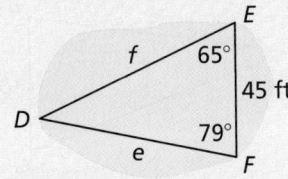

about 75.2 feet

MONITORING PROGRESS ANSWERS

8. $m\angle C = 66°, a \approx 4.4, c \approx 8.3$

9. $m\angle A = 29°, b \approx 19.4, c \approx 20.4$

10. about 187.9 m

EXAMPLE 4 **Using the Law of Sines (AAS Case)**

Solve the triangle. Round decimal answers to the nearest tenth.

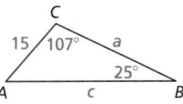

SOLUTION

By the Triangle Sum Theorem (Theorem 5.1), $m\angle A = 180° - 107° - 25° = 48°$.

By the Law of Sines, you can write $\dfrac{a}{\sin 48°} = \dfrac{15}{\sin 25°} = \dfrac{c}{\sin 107°}$.

$\dfrac{a}{\sin 48°} = \dfrac{15}{\sin 25°}$	Write two equations, each with one variable.	$\dfrac{c}{\sin 107°} = \dfrac{15}{\sin 25°}$
$a = \dfrac{15 \sin 48°}{\sin 25°}$	Solve for each variable.	$c = \dfrac{15 \sin 107°}{\sin 25°}$
$a \approx 26.4$	Use a calculator.	$c \approx 33.9$

▶ In $\triangle ABC$, $m\angle A = 48°$, $a \approx 26.4$, and $c \approx 33.9$.

EXAMPLE 5 **Using the Law of Sines (ASA Case)**

A surveyor makes the measurements shown to determine the length of a bridge to be built across a small lake from the North Picnic Area to the South Picnic Area. Find the length of the bridge.

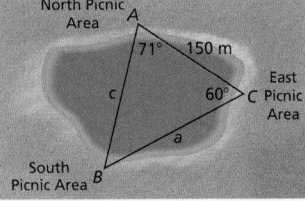

SOLUTION

In the diagram, c represents the distance from the North Picnic Area to the South Picnic Area, so c represents the length of the bridge.

By the Triangle Sum Theorem (Theorem 5.1), $m\angle B = 180° - 71° - 60° = 49°$.

By the Law of Sines, you can write $\dfrac{a}{\sin 71°} = \dfrac{150}{\sin 49°} = \dfrac{c}{\sin 60°}$.

$\dfrac{c}{\sin 60°} = \dfrac{150}{\sin 49°}$	Write an equation involving c.
$c = \dfrac{150 \sin 60°}{\sin 49°}$	Multiply each side by $\sin 60°$.
$c \approx 172.1$	Use a calculator.

▶ The length of the bridge will be about 172.1 meters.

Monitoring Progress Help in English and Spanish at *BigIdeasMath.com*

Solve the triangle. Round decimal answers to the nearest tenth.

8.

9.

10. **WHAT IF?** In Example 5, what would be the length of a bridge from the South Picnic Area to the East Picnic Area?

Laurie's Notes   Teacher Actions

- Examples 4 and 5 use prior skills and knowledge that students have.
- Pose Example 4 and say, "Work independently to solve this triangle. Then you will have time to share your thinking with partners."
- **Partner Speaks:** After students have had sufficient time, pair students. Only one person speaks. The listener asks for clarification or gives feedback. Ask the listener to describe to the whole class the solution method used by his or her partner.
- Pose Example 5. Roles will be reversed when it is time to share.

Using the Law of Cosines

You can use the **Law of Cosines** to solve triangles when two sides and the included angle are known (SAS case), or when all three sides are known (SSS case).

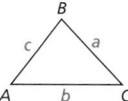 **Theorem**

Theorem 9.10   Law of Cosines

If $\triangle ABC$ has sides of length a, b, and c, as shown, then the following are true.

$$a^2 = b^2 + c^2 - 2bc \cos A$$

$$b^2 = a^2 + c^2 - 2ac \cos B$$

$$c^2 = a^2 + b^2 - 2ab \cos C$$

Proof Ex. 52, p. 516

EXAMPLE 6   Using the Law of Cosines (SAS Case)

Solve the triangle. Round decimal answers to the nearest tenth.

SOLUTION

Use the Law of Cosines to find side length b.

$b^2 = a^2 + c^2 - 2ac \cos B$	Law of Cosines
$b^2 = 11^2 + 14^2 - 2(11)(14) \cos 34°$	Substitute.
$b^2 = 317 - 308 \cos 34°$	Simplify.
$b = \sqrt{317 - 308 \cos 34°}$	Find the positive square root.
$b \approx 7.9$	Use a calculator.

ANOTHER WAY

When you know all three sides and one angle, you can use the Law of Cosines or the Law of Sines to find the measure of a second angle.

Use the Law of Sines to find $m\angle A$.

$\dfrac{\sin A}{a} = \dfrac{\sin B}{b}$	Law of Sines
$\dfrac{\sin A}{11} = \dfrac{\sin 34°}{\sqrt{317 - 308 \cos 34°}}$	Substitute.
$\sin A = \dfrac{11 \sin 34°}{\sqrt{317 - 308 \cos 34°}}$	Multiply each side by 11.
$m\angle A \approx 51.6°$	Use a calculator.

By the Triangle Sum Theorem (Theorem 5.1), $m\angle C \approx 180° - 34° - 51.6° = 94.4°$.

▶ In $\triangle ABC$, $b \approx 7.9$, $m\angle A \approx 51.6°$, and $m\angle C \approx 94.4°$.

COMMON ERROR

In Example 6, the smaller remaining angle is found first because the inverse sine feature of a calculator only gives angle measures from 0° to 90°. So, when an angle is obtuse, like $\angle C$ because $14^2 > (7.85)^2 + 11^2$, you will not get the obtuse measure.

Monitoring Progress 🔊 Help in English and Spanish at *BigIdeasMath.com*

Solve the triangle. Round decimal answers to the nearest tenth.

11.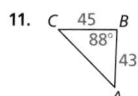

12.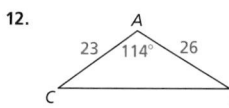

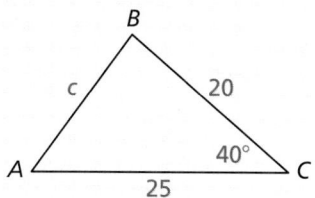

Extra Example 7

Solve the triangle. Round decimal answers to the nearest tenth.

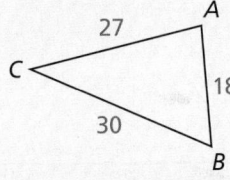

$m\angle A \approx 80.9°$, $m\angle B \approx 62.7°$,
$m\angle C \approx 36.4°$

Extra Example 8

Use the information in Example 8. Another dinosaur's footprints showed that the distance from C to B is 1.5 meters, the distance from B to A is 2 meters, and the distance from C to A is 3.2 meters. Find the step angle B to the nearest tenth of a degree. about 131.7°

MONITORING PROGRESS ANSWERS

13. $m\angle A \approx 41.4°$, $m\angle B \approx 82.8°$,
    $m\angle C \approx 55.8°$
14. $m\angle A \approx 58.1°$, $m\angle B \approx 85.6°$,
    $m\angle C \approx 36.3°$

EXAMPLE 7 Using the Law of Cosines (SSS Case)

Solve the triangle. Round decimal answers to the nearest tenth.

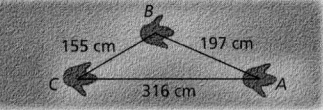

SOLUTION

First, find the angle opposite the longest side, $\overline{AC}$. Use the Law of Cosines to find $m\angle B$.

$$b^2 = a^2 + c^2 - 2ac \cos B \qquad \text{Law of Cosines}$$
$$27^2 = 12^2 + 20^2 - 2(12)(20) \cos B \qquad \text{Substitute.}$$
$$\frac{27^2 - 12^2 - 20^2}{-2(12)(20)} = \cos B \qquad \text{Solve for cos } B.$$
$$m\angle B \approx 112.7° \qquad \text{Use a calculator.}$$

Now, use the Law of Sines to find $m\angle A$.

$$\frac{\sin A}{a} = \frac{\sin B}{b} \qquad \text{Law of Sines}$$
$$\frac{\sin A}{12} = \frac{\sin 112.7°}{27} \qquad \text{Substitute for } a, b, \text{ and } B.$$
$$\sin A = \frac{12 \sin 112.7°}{27} \qquad \text{Multiply each side by 12.}$$
$$m\angle A \approx 24.2° \qquad \text{Use a calculator.}$$

By the Triangle Sum Theorem (Theorem 5.1), $m\angle C \approx 180° - 24.2° - 112.7° = 43.1°$.

▶ In $\triangle ABC$, $m\angle A \approx 24.2°$, $m\angle B \approx 112.7°$, and $m\angle C \approx 43.1°$.

EXAMPLE 8 Solving a Real-Life Problem

An organism's step angle is a measure of walking efficiency. The closer the step angle is to 180°, the more efficiently the organism walked. The diagram shows a set of footprints for a dinosaur. Find the step angle B.

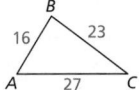

SOLUTION

$$b^2 = a^2 + c^2 - 2ac \cos B \qquad \text{Law of Cosines}$$
$$316^2 = 155^2 + 197^2 - 2(155)(197) \cos B \qquad \text{Substitute.}$$
$$\frac{316^2 - 155^2 - 197^2}{-2(155)(197)} = \cos B \qquad \text{Solve for cos } B.$$
$$127.3° \approx m\angle B \qquad \text{Use a calculator.}$$

▶ The step angle B is about 127.3°.

Monitoring Progress ◀)) Help in English and Spanish at *BigIdeasMath.com*

Solve the triangle. Round decimal answers to the nearest tenth.

13.

14.

> **COMMON ERROR**
>
> In Example 7, the largest angle is found first to make sure that the other two angles are acute. This way, when you use the Law of Sines to find another angle measure, you will know that it is between 0° and 90°.

Laurie's Notes   Teacher Actions

- Discuss the need to find the largest angle first. To help students understand, they can use their calculators to see that sin 30° = sin 150°.
- In Example 7, any of the angles could be found using the Law of Cosines. Finding the largest angle first allows the Law of Sines to be used for the remaining parts, a process requiring fewer computations.

Closure

- **3-2-1:** Hand out a 3-2-1 reflection sheet as described on page T-214.

Vocabulary and Core Concept Check

1. **WRITING** What type of triangle would you use the Law of Sines or the Law of Cosines to solve?

2. **VOCABULARY** What information do you need to use the Law of Sines?

Monitoring Progress and Modeling with Mathematics

In Exercises 3–8, use a calculator to find the trigonometric ratio. Round your answer to four decimal places. *(See Example 1.)*

3. sin 127°

4. sin 98°

5. cos 139°

6. cos 108°

7. tan 165°

8. tan 116°

In Exercises 9–12, find the area of the triangle. Round your answer to the nearest tenth. *(See Example 2.)*

9.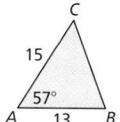

10.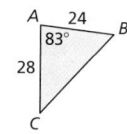

11.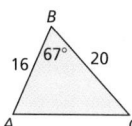

12.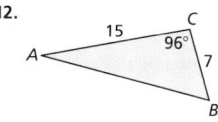

In Exercises 13–18, solve the triangle. Round decimal answers to the nearest tenth. *(See Examples 3, 4, and 5.)*

13.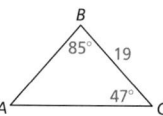

14.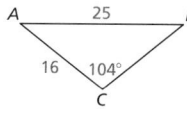

15.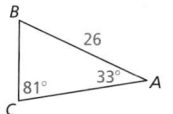

16.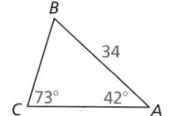

17.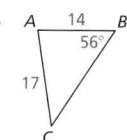

18.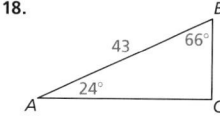

In Exercises 19–24, solve the triangle. Round decimal answers to the nearest tenth. *(See Examples 6 and 7.)*

19.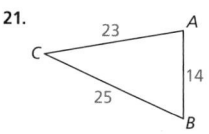

20.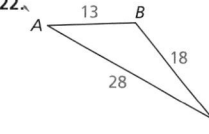

21.

22.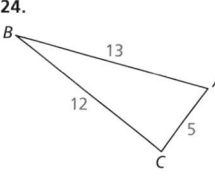

23.

24.

25. **ERROR ANALYSIS** Describe and correct the error in finding $m\angle C$.

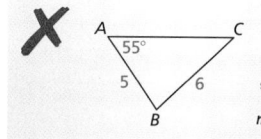

ANSWERS

1. Both the Law of Sines (Thm. 9.9) and the Law of Cosines (Thm. 9.10) can be used to solve any triangle.

2. The Law of Sines (Thm. 9.9) can be used to solve a triangle when you know the measures of two angles and the length of any side (AAS or ASA cases), or when you know the lengths of two sides and the measure of an angle opposite one of the two sides (SSA case).

3. about 0.7986

4. about 0.9903

5. about −0.7547

6. about −0.3090

7. about −0.2679

8. about −2.0503

9. about 81.8 square units

10. about 333.5 square units

11. about 147.3 square units

12. about 52.2 square units

13. $m\angle A = 48°$, $b \approx 25.5$, $c \approx 18.7$

14. $m\angle A \approx 37.6°$, $m\angle B \approx 38.4°$, $a \approx 15.7$

15. $m\angle B = 66°$, $a \approx 14.3$, $b \approx 24.0$

16. $m\angle B = 65°$, $a \approx 23.8$, $b \approx 32.2$

17. $m\angle A \approx 80.9°$, $m\angle C \approx 43.1°$, $a \approx 20.2$

18. $m\angle C = 90°$, $a \approx 17.5$, $b \approx 39.3$

19. $a \approx 5.2$, $m\angle B \approx 50.5°$, $m\angle C \approx 94.5°$

20. $b \approx 30.0$, $m\angle A \approx 26.5°$, $m\angle C \approx 15.5°$

21. $m\angle A \approx 81.1°$, $m\angle B \approx 65.3°$, $m\angle C \approx 33.6°$

22. $m\angle A \approx 30.3°$, $m\angle B \approx 128.4°$, $m\angle C \approx 21.3°$

23. $b \approx 35.8$, $m\angle A \approx 46.2°$, $m\angle C \approx 70.8°$

24. $m\angle A \approx 67.4°$, $m\angle B \approx 22.6°$, $m\angle C = 90°$

25. According to the Law of Sines (Thm. 9.9), the ratio of the sine of an angle's measure to the length of its opposite side should be equal to the ratio of the sine of another angle measure to the length of its opposite side; $\frac{\sin C}{5} = \frac{\sin 55°}{6}$, $\sin C = \frac{5 \sin 55°}{6}$, $m\angle C \approx 43.0°$

ANSWERS

26. The denominator of the fraction should be $-2bc$, not $-2ab$;

$$\cos A = \frac{19^2 - 21^2 - 11^2}{-2(21)(11)},$$

$m\angle A \approx 64.2°$

27. Law of Sines (Thm. 9.9); given two angle measures and the length of a side; $m\angle C = 64°$, $a \approx 19.2$, $c \approx 18.1$

28. Law of Sines (Thm. 9.9); given two angle measures and the length of a side; $m\angle A = 45°$, $b \approx 25.2$, $c \approx 15.3$

29. Law of Cosines (Thm. 9.10); given the lengths of two sides and the measure of the included angle; $c \approx 19.3$, $m\angle A \approx 34.3°$, $m\angle B \approx 80.7°$

30. Pythagorean Theorem (Thm. 9.1) and trigonometric ratios; given the length of the legs of a right triangle; $b \approx 16.2$, $m\angle A \approx 68.2°$, $m\angle C \approx 21.8°$

31. Law of Sines (Thm. 9.9); given the lengths of two sides and the measure of a nonincluded angle; $m\angle A \approx 111.2°$, $m\angle B \approx 28.8°$, $a \approx 52.2$

32. Law of Cosines (Thm. 9.10); given the lengths of all three sides; $m\angle A \approx 93.7°$, $m\angle B \approx 33.9°$, $m\angle C \approx 52.4°$

33. about 10.7 ft

34. about 92.5 ft

35. about 5.1 mi

36. about 12.8 ft

37. cousin; You are given the lengths of two sides and the measure of their included angle.

38. a. yes; You are given the measure of two angles and the length of a side.

   b. yes; You can also use the Pythagorean Theorem (Thm. 9.1) and trigonometric ratios to solve the triangle, because $\triangle XYZ$ is a right triangle.

---

26. ERROR ANALYSIS Describe and correct the error in finding $m\angle A$ in $\triangle ABC$ when $a = 19$, $b = 21$, and $c = 11$.

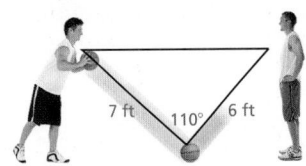

$$\cos A = \frac{19^2 - 21^2 - 11^2}{-2(19)(21)}$$

$$m\angle A \approx 75.4°$$

COMPARING METHODS In Exercises 27–32, tell whether you would use the Law of Sines, the Law of Cosines, or the Pythagorean Theorem (Theorem 9.1) and trigonometric ratios to solve the triangle with the given information. Explain your reasoning. Then solve the triangle.

27. $m\angle A = 72°$, $m\angle B = 44°$, $b = 14$

28. $m\angle B = 98°$, $m\angle C = 37°$, $a = 18$

29. $m\angle C = 65°$, $a = 12$, $b = 21$

30. $m\angle B = 90°$, $a = 15$, $c = 6$

31. $m\angle C = 40°$, $b = 27$, $c = 36$

32. $a = 34$, $b = 19$, $c = 27$

33. MODELING WITH MATHEMATICS You and your friend are standing on the baseline of a basketball court. You bounce a basketball to your friend, as shown in the diagram. What is the distance between you and your friend? *(See Example 8.)*

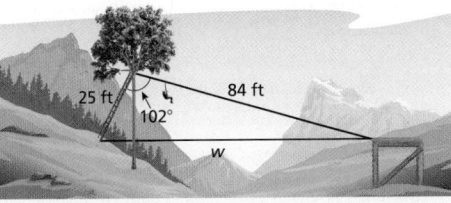

7 ft 110° 6 ft

34. MODELING WITH MATHEMATICS A zip line is constructed across a valley, as shown in the diagram. What is the width w of the valley?

25 ft 102° 84 ft w

35. MODELING WITH MATHEMATICS You are on the observation deck of the Empire State Building looking at the Chrysler Building. When you turn 145° clockwise, you see the Statue of Liberty. You know that the Chrysler Building and the Empire State Building are about 0.6 mile apart and that the Chrysler Building and the Statue of Liberty are about 5.6 miles apart. Estimate the distance between the Empire State Building and the Statue of Liberty.

36. MODELING WITH MATHEMATICS The Leaning Tower of Pisa in Italy has a height of 183 feet and is 4° off vertical. Find the horizontal distance d that the top of the tower is off vertical.

183 ft   4°

37. MAKING AN ARGUMENT Your friend says that the Law of Sines can be used to find JK. Your cousin says that the Law of Cosines can be used to find JK. Who is correct? Explain your reasoning.

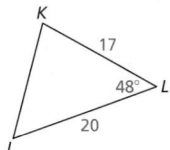

K 17 48° L 20 J

38. REASONING Use $\triangle XYZ$.

Z 17 64° X Y

a. Can you use the Law of Sines to solve $\triangle XYZ$? Explain your reasoning.

b. Can you use another method to solve $\triangle XYZ$? Explain your reasoning.

39. MAKING AN ARGUMENT Your friend calculates the area of the triangle using the formula $A = \frac{1}{2}qr \sin S$ and says that the area is approximately 208.6 square units. Is your friend correct? Explain your reasoning.

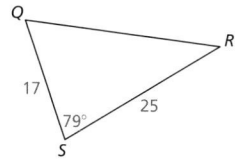

40. MODELING WITH MATHEMATICS You are fertilizing a triangular garden. One side of the garden is 62 feet long, and another side is 54 feet long. The angle opposite the 62-foot side is 58°.

   a. Draw a diagram to represent this situation.

   b. Use the Law of Sines to solve the triangle from part (a).

   c. One bag of fertilizer covers an area of 200 square feet. How many bags of fertilizer will you need to cover the entire garden?

41. MODELING WITH MATHEMATICS A golfer hits a drive 260 yards on a hole that is 400 yards long. The shot is 15° off target.

Not drawn to scale

   a. What is the distance x from the golfer's ball to the hole?

   b. Assume the golfer is able to hit the ball precisely the distance found in part (a). What is the maximum angle θ (theta) by which the ball can be off target in order to land no more than 10 yards from the hole?

42. COMPARING METHODS A building is constructed on top of a cliff that is 300 meters high. A person standing on level ground below the cliff observes that the angle of elevation to the top of the building is 72° and the angle of elevation to the top of the cliff is 63°.

   a. How far away is the person from the base of the cliff?

   b. Describe two different methods you can use to find the height of the building. Use one of these methods to find the building's height.

43. MATHEMATICAL CONNECTIONS Find the values of x and y.

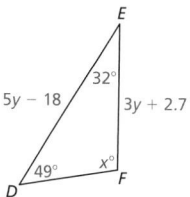

44. HOW DO YOU SEE IT? Would you use the Law of Sines or the Law of Cosines to solve the triangle?

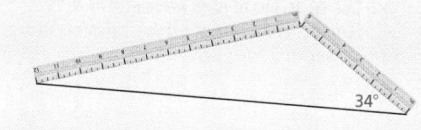

45. REWRITING A FORMULA Simplify the Law of Cosines for when the given angle is a right angle.

46. THOUGHT PROVOKING Consider any triangle with side lengths of a, b, and c. Calculate the value of s, which is half the perimeter of the triangle. What measurement of the triangle is represented by $\sqrt{s(s-a)(s-b)(s-c)}$?

47. ANALYZING RELATIONSHIPS The *ambiguous case* of the Law of Sines occurs when you are given the measure of one acute angle, the length of one adjacent side, and the length of the side opposite that angle, which is less than the length of the adjacent side. This results in two possible triangles. Using the given information, find two possible solutions for $\triangle ABC$. Draw a diagram for each triangle. (*Hint:* The inverse sine function gives only acute angle measures, so consider the acute angle and its supplement for $\angle B$.)

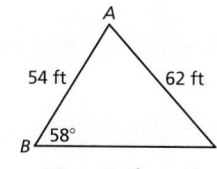

   a. $m\angle A = 40°$, $a = 13$, $b = 16$

   b. $m\angle A = 21°$, $a = 17$, $b = 32$

48. ABSTRACT REASONING Use the Law of Cosines to show that the measure of each angle of an equilateral triangle is 60°. Explain your reasoning.

49. CRITICAL THINKING An airplane flies 55° east of north from City A to City B, a distance of 470 miles. Another airplane flies 7° north of east from City A to City C, a distance of 890 miles. What is the distance between Cities B and C?

---

39. yes; The area of any triangle is given by one-half the product of the lengths of two sides times the sine of their included angle. For $\triangle QRS$,
$A = \frac{1}{2}qr \sin S = \frac{1}{2}(25)(17)\sin 79° \approx$ 208.6 square units.

40. a.

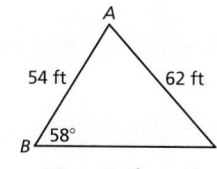

   b. $m\angle C \approx 47.6°$, $m\angle A \approx 74.4°$, $a \approx 70.4$ ft

   c. 9 bags

41. a. about 163.4 yd

   b. about 3.5°

42. a. about 152.9 m

   b. Use the tangent function to find the distance from the ground to the top of the building, and then subtract the height of the cliff from this distance. Or, use the Pythagorean Theorem (Thm 9.1) to find the hypotenuse of the triangle used in part (a). Then, subtract 63° from 72° to find the measure of the angle between the two lines of sight. Find the angle of this triangle opposite of the hypotenuse using the rules of supplementary angles, and use the Law of Sines (Thm. 9.9) to solve the triangle formed by the building and the two lines of sight; about 170.4 ft

43. $x = 99$, $y \approx 20.1$

44. Law of Sines (Thm. 9.9)

45. $c^2 = a^2 + b^2$

46. area

47. a. $m\angle B \approx 52.3°$, $m\angle C \approx 87.7°$, $c \approx 20.2$;
$m\angle B \approx 127.7°$, $m\angle C \approx 12.3°$, $c \approx 4.3$

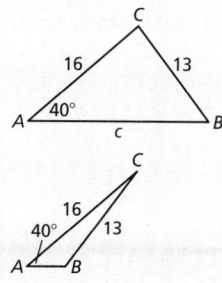

---

47. b. $m\angle B \approx 42.4°$, $m\angle C \approx 116.6°$, $c \approx 42.4$;
$m\angle B \approx 137.6°$, $m\angle C \approx 21.4°$, $c \approx 17.3$

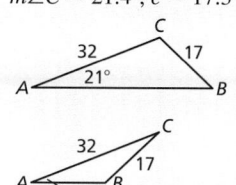

48. Because the triangle is equilateral, we can say $a = b = c = x$. So, the Law of Cosines (Thm. 9.10) is $x^2 = x^2 + x^2 - 2(x)(x)\cos X$ for all of the angles. By the Subtraction Property of Equality, $0 = x^2 - 2x^2 \cos X$. Then, by the Addition Property of Equality, $2x^2 \cos X = x^2$. By the Division Property of Equality, $2 \cos X = 1$, or $\cos X = \frac{1}{2}$. So, $X = \cos^{-1} \frac{1}{2} = 60°$. So, the measure of each angle of an equilateral triangle is 60°.

49. about 523.8 mi

ANSWERS

50. a.

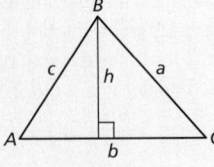

$$\text{Area} = \frac{1}{2}bh$$

b. $\sin C = \dfrac{h}{a}$

c. $\text{Area} = \dfrac{1}{2}ab \sin C$

51–56. See Additional Answers.

Mini-Assessment

1. Solve the triangle. Round decimal answers to the nearest tenth.

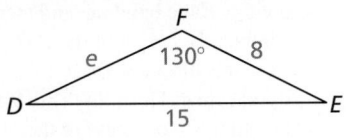

$m\angle D \approx 24.1°$, $m\angle E \approx 25.9°$, $e \approx 8.6$

2. In $\triangle ABC$, $AB = 16$, $BC = 32$, and $AC = 34$. Find the measure of $\angle A$ to the nearest tenth of a degree. $m\angle A \approx 69.1°$

3. In $\triangle DEF$, $m\angle D = 115°$, $DE = 23$, and $DF = 27$. Find the area of $\triangle DEF$. Round your answer to the nearest tenth.
about 281.4 square units

4. A lighthouse is 110 kilometers from one boat and 95 kilometers from another boat. The included angle of the sightlines from the lighthouse to the two boats is 52°. Approximate the distance between the two boats to the nearest tenth.

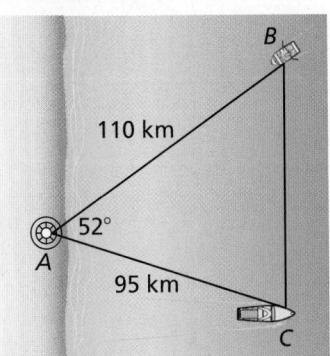

about 90.9 kilometers

---

50. REWRITING A FORMULA Follow the steps to derive the formula for the area of a triangle, $\text{Area} = \frac{1}{2}ab \sin C$.

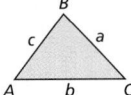

a. Draw the altitude from vertex B to $\overline{AC}$. Label the altitude as h. Write a formula for the area of the triangle using h.

b. Write an equation for $\sin C$.

c. Use the results of parts (a) and (b) to write a formula for the area of a triangle that does not include h.

52. PROVING A THEOREM Use the given information to complete the two-column proof of the Law of Cosines (Theorem 9.10).

Given $\overline{BD}$ is an altitude of $\triangle ABC$.

Prove $a^2 = b^2 + c^2 - 2bc \cos A$

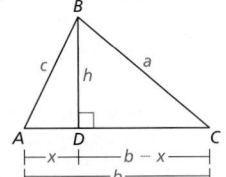

STATEMENTS	REASONS
1. $\overline{BD}$ is an altitude of $\triangle ABC$.	1. Given
2. $\triangle ADB$ and $\triangle CDB$ are right triangles.	2. _____
3. $a^2 = (b - x)^2 + h^2$	3. _____
4. _____	4. Expand binomial.
5. $x^2 + h^2 = c^2$	5. _____
6. _____	6. Substitution Property of Equality
7. $\cos A = \dfrac{x}{c}$	7. _____
8. $x = c \cos A$	8. _____
9. $a^2 = b^2 + c^2 - 2bc \cos A$	9. _____

51. PROVING A THEOREM Follow the steps to use the formula for the area of a triangle to prove the Law of Sines (Theorem 9.9).

a. Use the derivation in Exercise 50 to explain how to derive the three related formulas for the area of a triangle.

$$\text{Area} = \frac{1}{2}bc \sin A,$$
$$\text{Area} = \frac{1}{2}ac \sin B,$$
$$\text{Area} = \frac{1}{2}ab \sin C$$

b. Why can you use the formulas in part (a) to write the following statement?

$$\frac{1}{2}bc \sin A = \frac{1}{2}ac \sin B = \frac{1}{2}ab \sin C$$

c. Show how to rewrite the statement in part (b) to prove the Law of Sines. Justify each step.

Maintaining Mathematical Proficiency   Reviewing what you learned in previous grades and lessons

Find the radius and diameter of the circle.   *(Skills Review Handbook)*

53.
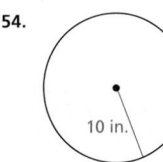
8 ft

54.

10 in.

55.
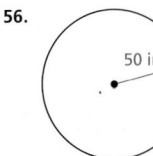
2 ft

56.
50 in.

If students need help...	If students got it...
Resources by Chapter • Practice A and Practice B • Puzzle Time	**Resources by Chapter** • Enrichment and Extension • Cumulative Review
Student Journal • Practice	Start the *next* Section
Differentiating the Lesson Skills Review Handbook	

Core Vocabulary

trigonometric ratio, *p. 488*
tangent, *p. 488*
angle of elevation, *p. 490*
sine, *p. 494*

cosine, *p. 494*
angle of depression, *p. 497*
inverse tangent, *p. 502*
inverse sine, *p. 502*

inverse cosine, *p. 502*
solve a right triangle, *p. 503*
Law of Sines, *p. 509*
Law of Cosines, *p. 511*

Core Concepts

Section 9.4

Tangent Ratio, *p. 488*

Section 9.5

Sine and Cosine Ratios, *p. 494*
Sine and Cosine of Complementary Angles, *p. 494*

Section 9.6

Inverse Trigonometric Ratios, *p. 502*
Solving a Right Triangle, *p. 503*

Section 9.7

Area of a Triangle, *p. 508*
Theorem 9.9 Law of Sines, *p. 509*
Theorem 9.10 Law of Cosines, *p. 511*

Mathematical Practices

1. In Exercise 21 on page 492, your brother claims that you could determine how far the overhang should extend by dividing 8 by tan 70°. Justify his conclusion and explain why it works.

2. In Exercise 29 on page 499, explain the flaw in the argument that the kite is 18.4 feet high.

3. In Exercise 31 on page 506, for what values does the inverse sine make sense?

- - - - - - - - - - - - - - - **Performance Task** - - - - - - - -

Triathlon

There is a big triathlon in town, and you are trying to take pictures of your friends at multiple locations during the event. How far would you need to walk to move between the photography locations?

To explore the answers to this question and more, go to *BigIdeasMath.com*.

517

ANSWERS

1. The Sun's ray and the awning form an angle congruent to the 70° shown. A triangle is created where the side opposite this angle is 8 feet, and the adjacent side to this angle is part of the porch, which can be labeled x. So, by the definition of the tangent ratio, $\tan 70° = \frac{8}{x}$, and $x = \frac{8}{\tan 70°}$.

2. The kite is 18.4 feet above the height of the spool, but you have to consider how high the spool is off the ground in order to the find how high the kite is off the ground.

3. all values between -1 and 1.

ANSWERS

1. $x = 2\sqrt{34} \approx 11.7$; no
2. $x = 12$; yes
3. $x = 2\sqrt{30} \approx 11.0$; no
4. yes; acute
5. yes; right
6. yes; obtuse
7. $x = 6\sqrt{2}$
8. $x = 7$
9. $x = 16\sqrt{3}$

9.1 The Pythagorean Theorem (pp. 463–470)

Find the value of x. Then tell whether the side lengths form a Pythagorean triple.

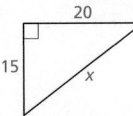

$c^2 = a^2 + b^2$ Pythagorean Theorem (Theorem 9.1)

$x^2 = 15^2 + 20^2$ Substitute.

$x^2 = 225 + 400$ Multiply.

$x^2 = 625$ Add.

$x = 25$ Find the positive square root.

▶ The value of x is 25. Because the side lengths 15, 20, and 25 are integers that satisfy the equation $c^2 = a^2 + b^2$, they form a Pythagorean triple.

Find the value of x. Then tell whether the side lengths form a Pythagorean triple.

1.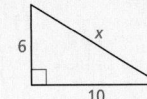
2.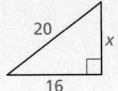
3.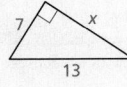

Verify that the segment lengths form a triangle. Is the triangle *acute*, *right*, or *obtuse*?

4. 6, 8, and 9   5. 10, $2\sqrt{2}$, and $6\sqrt{3}$ 6. 13, 18, and $3\sqrt{55}$

9.2 Special Right Triangles (pp. 471–476)

Find the value of x. Write your answer in simplest form.

By the Triangle Sum Theorem (Theorem 5.1), the measure of the third angle must be 45°, so the triangle is a 45°-45°-90° triangle.

hypotenuse = leg • $\sqrt{2}$ 45°-45°-90° Triangle Theorem (Theorem 9.4)

$x = 10 \cdot \sqrt{2}$ Substitute.

$x = 10\sqrt{2}$ Simplify.

▶ The value of x is $10\sqrt{2}$.

Find the value of x. Write your answer in simplest form.

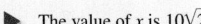

7.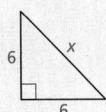
8.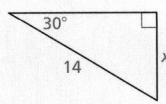
9.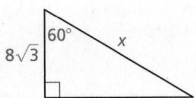

9.3 **Similar Right Triangles** *(pp. 477–484)*

Identify the similar triangles. Then find the value of *x*.

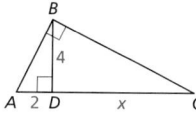

Sketch the three similar right triangles so that the corresponding angles and sides have the same orientation.

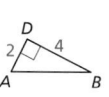 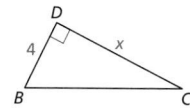 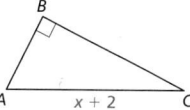

▶ △*DBA* ~ △*DCB* ~ △*BCA*

By the Geometric Mean (Altitude) Theorem (Theorem 9.7), you know that 4 is the geometric mean of 2 and *x*.

$4^2 = 2 \cdot x$ Geometric Mean (Altitude) Theorem

$16 = 2x$ Square 4.

$8 = x$ Divide each side by 2.

▶ The value of *x* is 8.

Identify the similar triangles. Then find the value of *x*.

10.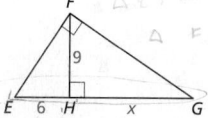

11.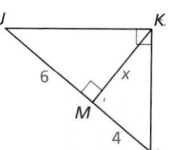

12.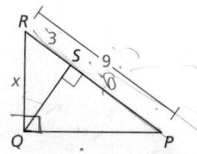

13.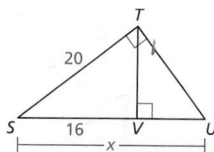

Find the geometric mean of the two numbers.

14. 9 and 25   **15.** 36 and 48   **16.** 12 and 42

10. △*GFH* ~ △*FEH* ~ △*GEF*; $x = 13.5$

11. △*KLM* ~ △*JKM* ~ △*JLK*; $x = 2\sqrt{6} \approx 4.9$

12. △*QRS* ~ △*PQS* ~ △*PRQ*; $x = 3\sqrt{3} \approx 5.2$

13. △*TUV* ~ △*STV* ~ △*SUT*; $x = 25$

14. 15

15. $24\sqrt{3} \approx 41.6$

16. $6\sqrt{14} \approx 22.4$

17. $\tan J = \frac{11}{60} \approx 0.1833$,

$\tan L = \frac{60}{11} \approx 5.4545$

18. $\tan N = \frac{12}{35} \approx 0.3429$,

$\tan P = \frac{35}{12} \approx 2.9167$

19. $\tan A = \frac{7\sqrt{2}}{8} \approx 1.2374$,

$\tan B = \frac{4\sqrt{2}}{7} \approx 0.8081$

20. $x \approx 44.0$

21. $x \approx 9.3$

22. $x \approx 12.8$

23. about 15 ft

9.4 **The Tangent Ratio** *(pp. 487–492)*

Find tan *M* and tan *N*. Write each answer as a fraction
and as a decimal rounded to four places.

$\tan M = \dfrac{\text{opp. } \angle M}{\text{adj. to } \angle M} = \dfrac{LN}{LM} = \dfrac{6}{8} = \dfrac{3}{4} = 0.7500$

$\tan N = \dfrac{\text{opp. } \angle N}{\text{adj. to } \angle N} = \dfrac{LM}{LN} = \dfrac{8}{6} = \dfrac{4}{3} \approx 1.3333$

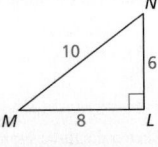

Find the tangents of the acute angles in the right triangle. Write each answer as a
fraction and as a decimal rounded to four decimal places.

17. 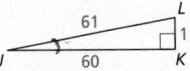   **18.** 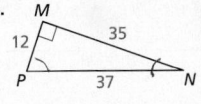   **19.**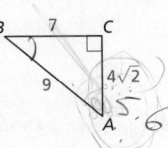

Find the value of *x*. Round your answer to the nearest tenth.

20. 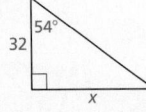   **21.** 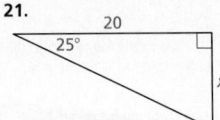   **22.**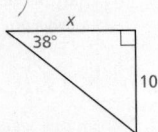

23. The angle between the bottom of a fence and the top of a
tree is 75°. The tree is 4 feet from the fence. How tall is the
tree? Round your answer to the nearest foot.

9.5 **The Sine and Cosine Ratios** *(pp. 493–500)*

Find sin *A*, sin *B*, cos *A*, and cos *B*. Write each answer
as a fraction and as a decimal rounded to four places.

$\sin A = \dfrac{\text{opp. } \angle A}{\text{hyp.}} = \dfrac{BC}{AB} = \dfrac{30}{34} = \dfrac{15}{17} \approx 0.8824$

$\sin B = \dfrac{\text{opp. } \angle B}{\text{hyp.}} = \dfrac{AC}{AB} = \dfrac{16}{34} = \dfrac{8}{17} \approx 0.4706$

$\cos A = \dfrac{\text{adj. to } \angle A}{\text{hyp.}} = \dfrac{AC}{AB} = \dfrac{16}{34} = \dfrac{8}{17} \approx 0.4706$

$\cos B = \dfrac{\text{adj. to } \angle B}{\text{hyp.}} = \dfrac{BC}{AB} = \dfrac{30}{34} = \dfrac{15}{17} \approx 0.8824$

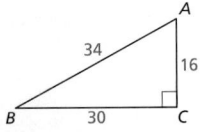

Find sin X, sin Z, cos X, and cos Z. Write each answer as a fraction and as a decimal rounded to four decimal places.

24.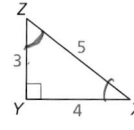

25.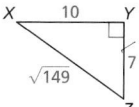

26.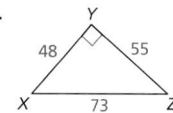

Find the value of each variable using sine and cosine. Round your answers to the nearest tenth.

27.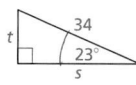

28.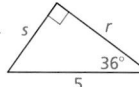

29.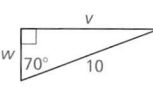

30. Write sin 72° in terms of cosine.

31. Write cos 29° in terms of sine.

9.6 **Solving Right Triangles** *(pp. 501–506)*

Solve the right triangle. Round decimal answers to the nearest tenth.

Step 1 Use the Pythagorean Theorem (Theorem 9.1) to find the length of the hypotenuse.

$c^2 = a^2 + b^2$	Pythagorean Theorem
$c^2 = 19^2 + 12^2$	Substitute.
$c^2 = 505$	Simplify.
$c = \sqrt{505}$	Find the positive square root.
$c \approx 22.5$	Use a calculator.

Step 2 Find $m\angle B$.

$$m\angle B = \tan^{-1}\frac{12}{19} \approx 32.3° \qquad \text{Use a calculator.}$$

Step 3 Find $m\angle A$.

Because $\angle A$ and $\angle B$ are complements, you can write $m\angle A = 90° - m\angle B \approx 90° - 32.3° = 57.7°$.

▶ In $\triangle ABC$, $c \approx 22.5$, $m\angle B \approx 32.3°$, and $m\angle A \approx 57.7°$.

Let $\angle Q$ be an acute angle. Use a calculator to approximate the measure of $\angle Q$ to the nearest tenth of a degree.

32. $\cos Q = 0.32$

33. $\sin Q = 0.91$

34. $\tan Q = 0.04$

Solve the right triangle. Round decimal answers to the nearest tenth.

35.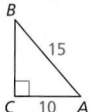

36.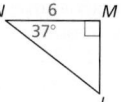

37.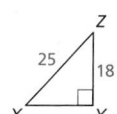

ANSWERS

24. $\sin X = \frac{3}{5} = 0.600,$
$\sin Z = \frac{4}{5} = 0.8000,$
$\cos X = \frac{4}{5} = 0.8000,$
$\cos Z = \frac{3}{5} = 0.6000$

25. $\sin X = \frac{7\sqrt{149}}{149} \approx 0.5735,$
$\sin Z = \frac{10\sqrt{149}}{149} \approx 0.8192,$
$\cos X = \frac{10\sqrt{149}}{149} \approx 0.8192,$
$\cos Z = \frac{7\sqrt{149}}{149} \approx 0.5735$

26. $\sin X = \frac{55}{73} \approx 0.7534,$
$\sin Z = \frac{48}{73} \approx 0.6575,$
$\cos X = \frac{48}{73} \approx 0.6575,$
$\cos Z = \frac{55}{73} \approx 0.7534$

27. $s \approx 31.3, t \approx 13.3$

28. $r \approx 4.0, s \approx 2.9$

29. $v \approx 9.4, w \approx 3.4$

30. $\cos 18°$

31. $\sin 61°$

32. $m\angle Q \approx 71.3°$

33. $m\angle Q \approx 65.5°$

34. $m\angle Q \approx 2.3°$

35. $m\angle A \approx 48.2°, m\angle B \approx 41.8°,$
$BC \approx 11.2$

36. $m\angle L = 53°, ML \approx 4.5, NL \approx 7.5$

37. $m\angle X \approx 46.1°, m\angle Z \approx 43.9°,$
$XY \approx 17.3$

38. about 41.0 square units

39. about 42.2 square units

40. about 208.6 square units

41. $m\angle B \approx 24.3°, m\angle C \approx 43.7°, c \approx 6.7$

42. $m\angle C = 88°, a \approx 25.8, b \approx 49.5$

43. $m\angle A \approx 99.9°, m\angle B \approx 32.1°,$
$a \approx 37.1$

44. $b \approx 5.4, m\angle A \approx 141.4°,$
$m\angle C \approx 13.6°$

45. $m\angle A = 35°, a \approx 12.3, c \approx 14.6$

46. $m\angle A \approx 42.6°, m\angle B \approx 11.7°,$
$m\angle C \approx 125.7°$

9.7 Law of Sines and Law of Cosines *(pp. 507–516)*

Solve the triangle. Round decimal answers to the nearest tenth.

a.

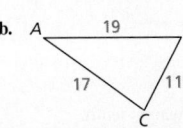

By the Triangle Sum Theorem (Theorem 5.1),
$m\angle B = 180° - 40° - 75° = 65°.$

By the Law of Sines, you can write $\dfrac{a}{\sin 40°} = \dfrac{b}{\sin 65°} = \dfrac{20}{\sin 75°}.$

$\dfrac{a}{\sin 40°} = \dfrac{20}{\sin 75°}$	Write two equations, each with one variable.	$\dfrac{b}{\sin 65°} = \dfrac{20}{\sin 75°}$
$a = \dfrac{20 \sin 40°}{\sin 75°}$	Solve for each variable.	$b = \dfrac{20 \sin 65°}{\sin 75°}$
$a \approx 13.3$	Use a calculator.	$b \approx 18.8$

▶ In $\triangle ABC, m\angle B = 65°, a \approx 13.3,$ and $b \approx 18.8.$

b.

First, find the angle opposite the longest side, $\overline{AB}$. Use the Law of Cosines to find $m\angle C$.

$$19^2 = 11^2 + 17^2 - 2(11)(17)\cos C \qquad \text{Law of Cosines}$$

$$\frac{19^2 - 11^2 - 17^2}{-2(11)(17)} = \cos C \qquad \text{Solve for cos C.}$$

$$m\angle C \approx 82.5° \qquad \text{Use a calculator.}$$

Now, use the Law of Sines to find $m\angle A$.

$$\frac{\sin A}{a} = \frac{\sin C}{c} \qquad \text{Law of Sines}$$

$$\frac{\sin A}{11} = \frac{\sin 82.5°}{19} \qquad \text{Substitute.}$$

$$\sin A = \frac{11 \sin 82.5°}{19} \qquad \text{Multiply each side by 11.}$$

$$m\angle A \approx 35.0° \qquad \text{Use a calculator.}$$

By the Triangle Sum Theorem (Theorem 5.1), $m\angle B \approx 180° - 35.0° - 82.5° = 62.5°.$

▶ In $\triangle ABC, m\angle A \approx 35.0°, m\angle B \approx 62.5°,$ and $m\angle C \approx 82.5°.$

Find the area of $\triangle ABC$ with the given side lengths and included angle.

38. $m\angle B = 124°, a = 9, c = 11$ **39.** $m\angle A = 68°, b = 13, c = 7$ **40.** $m\angle C = 79°, a = 25, b = 17$

Solve $\triangle ABC$. Round decimal answers to the nearest tenth.

41. $m\angle A = 112°, a = 9, b = 4$ **42.** $m\angle A = 28°, m\angle B = 64°, c = 55$

43. $m\angle C = 48°, b = 20, c = 28$ **44.** $m\angle B = 25°, a = 8, c = 3$

45. $m\angle B = 102°, m\angle C = 43°, b = 21$ **46.** $a = 10, b = 3, c = 12$

Find the value of each variable. Round your answers to the nearest tenth.

1.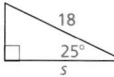

2.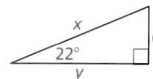

3.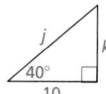

Verify that the segment lengths form a triangle. Is the triangle *acute*, *right*, or *obtuse*?

4. 16, 30, and 34

5. 4, $\sqrt{67}$, and 9

6. $\sqrt{5}$, 5, and 5.5

Solve $\triangle ABC$. Round decimal answers to the nearest tenth.

7.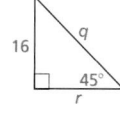

8.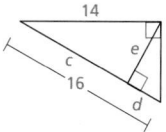

9.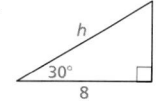

10. $m\angle A = 103°$, $b = 12$, $c = 24$

11. $m\angle A = 26°$, $m\angle C = 35°$, $b = 13$

12. $a = 38$, $b = 31$, $c = 35$

13. Write $\cos 53°$ in terms of sine.

Find the value of each variable. Write your answers in simplest form.

14.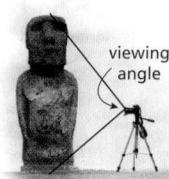

15.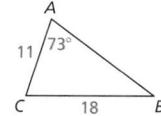

16.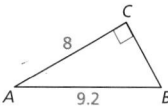

17. In $\triangle QRS$, $m\angle R = 57°$, $q = 9$, and $s = 5$. Find the area of $\triangle QRS$.

18. You are given the measures of both acute angles of a right triangle. Can you determine the side lengths? Explain.

19. You are at a parade looking up at a large balloon floating directly above the street. You are 60 feet from a point on the street directly beneath the balloon. To see the top of the balloon, you look up at an angle of 53°. To see the bottom of the balloon, you look up at an angle of 29°. Estimate the height h of the balloon.

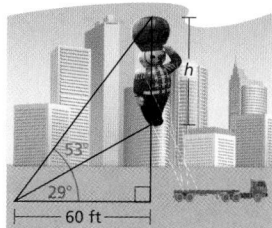

20. You want to take a picture of a statue on Easter Island, called a *moai*. The moai is about 13 feet tall. Your camera is on a tripod that is 5 feet tall. The vertical viewing angle of your camera is set at 90°. How far from the moai should you stand so that the entire height of the moai is perfectly framed in the photo?

viewing angle

ANSWERS

1. $s \approx 16.3$, $t \approx 7.6$

2. $x \approx 16.0$, $y \approx 14.9$

3. $j \approx 13.1$, $k \approx 8.4$

4. yes; right

5. yes; acute

6. yes; obtuse

7. $m\angle A \approx 24.4°$, $m\angle C \approx 65.6°$, $b \approx 12.1$

8. $m\angle B \approx 35.8°$, $m\angle C \approx 71.2°$, $c \approx 17.8$

9. $m\angle A \approx 29.6°$, $m\angle B \approx 60.4°$, $a \approx 4.5$

10. $a \approx 29.1$, $m\angle B \approx 23.7°$, $m\angle C \approx 53.3°$

11. $m\angle B = 119°$, $a \approx 6.5$, $c \approx 8.5$

12. $m\angle A \approx 70.0°$, $m\angle B \approx 50.0°$, $m\angle C \approx 60°$

13. $\sin 37°$

14. $q = 16\sqrt{2}$, $r = 16$

15. $c = 12\frac{1}{4}$, $d = 3\frac{3}{4}$, $e = \frac{7\sqrt{15}}{44}$

16. $f = \frac{8\sqrt{3}}{3}$, $h = \frac{16\sqrt{3}}{3}$

17. about 18.9 square units

18. no; There are infinitely many right triangles that can be created using the same acute angle measures. They are all similar by the AA Similarity Theorem (Thm. 8.3), and their corresponding sides are proportional, but not congruent.

19. about 46.4 ft

20. about 6.3 ft

If students need help...	If students got it...
Lesson Tutorials	Resources by Chapter • Enrichment and Extension • Cumulative Review
Skills Review Handbook	Performance Task
BigIdeasMath.com	Start the *next* Section

1. The size of a laptop screen is measured by the length of its diagonal. You want to purchase a laptop with the largest screen possible. Which laptop should you buy?

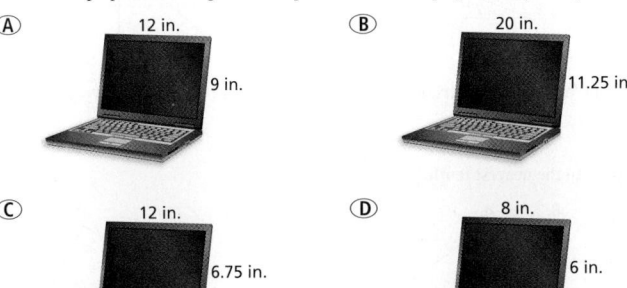

Ⓐ 12 in. 9 in.

Ⓑ 20 in. 11.25 in.

Ⓒ 12 in. 6.75 in.

Ⓓ 8 in. 6 in.

2. In $\triangle PQR$ and $\triangle SQT$, S is between P and Q, T is between R and Q, and $\dfrac{QS}{SP} = \dfrac{QT}{TR}$. What must be true about $\overline{ST}$ and $\overline{PR}$? Select all that apply.

| $\overline{ST} \perp \overline{PR}$ | $\overline{ST} \parallel \overline{PR}$ | $ST = PR$ | $ST = \dfrac{1}{2} PR$ |

3. In the diagram, $\triangle JKL \sim \triangle QRS$. Choose the symbol that makes each statement true.

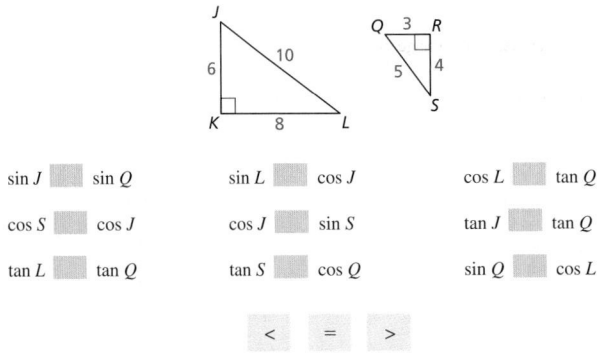

$\sin J$ ▨ $\sin Q$ $\sin L$ ▨ $\cos J$ $\cos L$ ▨ $\tan Q$

$\cos S$ ▨ $\cos J$ $\cos J$ ▨ $\sin S$ $\tan J$ ▨ $\tan Q$

$\tan L$ ▨ $\tan Q$ $\tan S$ ▨ $\cos Q$ $\sin Q$ ▨ $\cos L$

| < | = | > |

4. A surveyor makes the measurements shown. What is the width of the river?

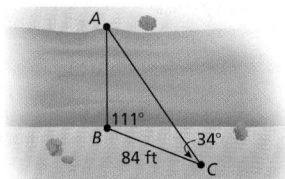

5. Create as many true equations as possible.

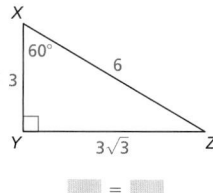

| sin X | cos X | tan X | $\dfrac{XY}{XZ}$ | $\dfrac{YZ}{XZ}$ |

| sin Z | cos Z | tan Z | $\dfrac{XY}{YZ}$ | $\dfrac{YZ}{XY}$ |

6. Prove that quadrilateral *DEFG* is a kite.

Given $\overline{HE} \cong \overline{HG}, \overline{EG} \perp \overline{DF}$

Prove $\overline{FE} \cong \overline{FG}, \overline{DE} \cong \overline{DG}$

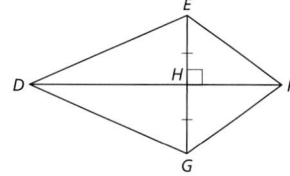

7. What are the coordinates of the vertices of the image of △*QRS* after the composition of transformations shown?

Translation: $(x, y) \rightarrow (x + 2, y + 3)$
Rotation: 180° about the origin

Ⓐ $Q'(1, 2), R'(5, 4), S'(4, -1)$

Ⓑ $Q'(-1, -2), R'(-5, -4), S'(-4, 1)$

Ⓒ $Q'(3, -2), R'(-1, -4), S'(0, 1)$

Ⓓ $Q'(-2, 1), R'(-4, 5), S'(1, 4)$

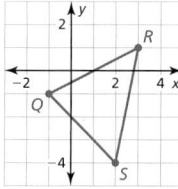

8. The Red Pyramid in Egypt has a square base. Each side of the base measures 722 feet. The height of the pyramid is 343 feet.

a. Use the side length of the base, the height of the pyramid, and the Pythagorean Theorem to find the *slant height*, *AB*, of the pyramid.

b. Find *AC*.

c. Name three possible ways of finding *m*∠1. Then, find *m*∠1.

5. $\sin X = \dfrac{YZ}{XZ}, \cos X = \dfrac{XY}{XZ},$

$\tan X = \dfrac{YZ}{XY}, \sin Z = \dfrac{XY}{XZ},$

$\cos Z = \dfrac{YZ}{XZ}, \tan Z = \dfrac{XY}{YZ},$

$\sin X = \cos Z, \cos X = \sin Z$

6. See Additional Answers.

7. B

8. a. about 498.0 ft

b. about 615.1 ft

c. Use any of the three trigonometric functions, sine, cosine, or tangent; about 35.9°

10 Circles

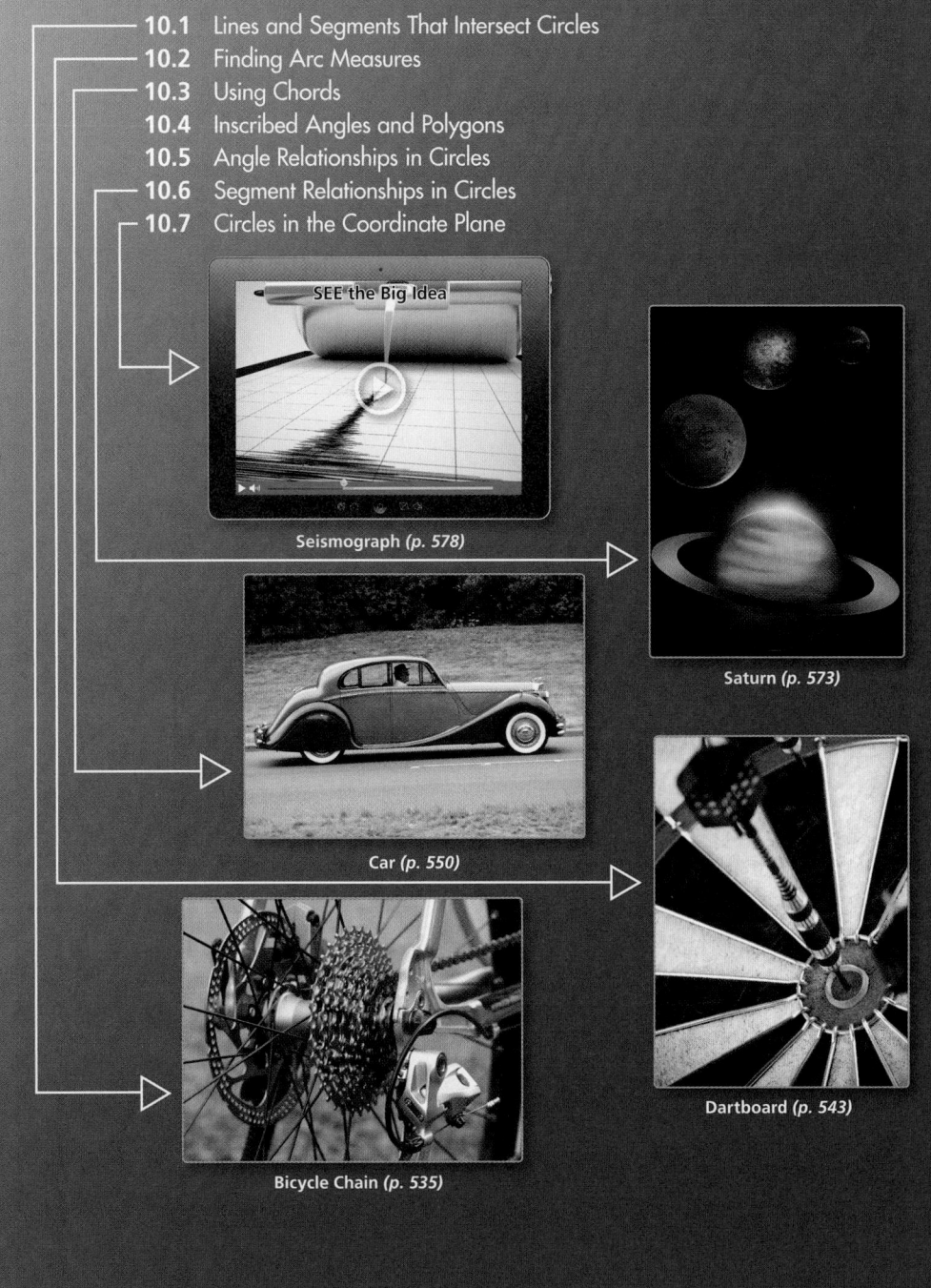

SEE the Big Idea

Seismograph (p. 578)

Saturn (p. 573)

Car (p. 550)

Dartboard (p. 543)

Bicycle Chain (p. 535)

Chapter Summary

- This chapter is all about circles. Many of the theorems will be investigated using dynamic geometry software.
- The first three lessons introduce the vocabulary and symbols related to circles.
- They are followed by a lesson looking at circular arcs that are intercepted by chords.
- The next lesson introduces all of the angle relationships that occur when two chords, secants, or tangents intersect a circle.
- An investigation of segment relationships that occur when two chords, secants, or tangents intersect a circle is the focus of the next lesson.
- In the last lesson, the circle is presented in the coordinate plane where the standard form of the equation is derived.
- Much of the earlier book has been devoted to lines, triangles, and polygons. Circles are presented here so that measured attributes (arc length, area of a sector, circumference of a circle, and area of a circle) can be studied in the next chapter.
- **Additional Topic:** The Additional Topic, *Focus of a Parabola*, may be taught after Section 10.7. This lesson starts on page T-720.
  - Common Core State Standards covered in this lesson are HSF-IF.B.4, HSF-IF.C.7c, and HSG-GPE.A.2.
  - Suggested pacing for this lesson is 2 days.
  - See Algebra 2, Section 2.3 for the additional resources that are available for *Focus of a Parabola*.

Scaffolding in the Classroom

Graphic Organizers: Four Square

A Four Square can be used to organize information about a topic. Students write the topic in the "bubble" in the middle of the Four Square. Then students write concepts related to the topic in the four squares surrounding the bubble. Any concept related to the topic can be used. Encourage students to include concepts that will help them learn the topic. Students can place their Four Squares on note cards to use as a quick study reference.

COMMON CORE PROGRESSION

Middle School
- Solve two-step equations.
- Use the Pythagorean Theorem to find the distance between two points in the coordinate plane.
- Solve real-world problems involving the area and circumference of a circle.
- Understand that figures are similar if they can be related by a sequence of transformations, including dilations.

Algebra 1
- Solve linear equations in one variable.
- Multiply binomials.
- Solve quadratic equations using square roots and by completing the square.
- Graph points and functions in the coordinate plane.

Geometry
- Identify chords, diameters, radii, secants, and tangents of circles.
- Find angle and arc measures.
- Use inscribed angles and polygons and circumscribed angles.
- Use properties of chords, tangents, and secants to solve problems.
- Write and graph equations of circles.

Standards Summary		
Section	**Common Core State Standards**	
10.1	Learning	HSG-CO.A.1, HSG-C.A.2, HSG-C.A.4
10.2	Learning	HSG-C.A.1, HSG-C.A.2
10.3	Learning	HSG-C.A.2, HSG-MG.A.3
10.4	Learning	HSG-CO.D.13, HSG-C.A.2, HSG-C.A.3
10.5	Learning	HSG-C.A.2
10.6	Learning	HSG-C.A.2, HSG-MG.A.1
10.7	Learning	HSG-GPE.A.1, HSG-GPE.B.4

Questioning in the Classroom
But why?
Ask questions that require critical thinking
so that follow-up questions may be asked.
Avoid questions having *yes* or *no* answers.
If this cannot be avoided, always follow
with *why*?

Laurie's Notes

Maintaining Mathematical Proficiency

Multiplying Binomials

- Remind students that when multiplying binomials, each term in the first binomial is distributed over the terms in the second binomial, resulting in the sum of four products.
- Explain that after finding the four products, students can combine like terms to simplify the expression.

COMMON ERROR Students may forget to include negative signs when distributing or students may combine like terms incorrectly.

Solving Quadratic Equations by Completing the Square

- Remind students that the goal in completing the square is to rewrite the equation in the form $(x + a)^2 = c$.
- Work through the example with students, emphasizing that the constant added to each side of the equation is the square of half of the coefficient of the linear term.
- Remind students to include both the positive and negative square roots when they take the square root of each side of the equation.

COMMON ERROR Students may add a constant to only one side of the equation or students may find half of the linear term's coefficient but forget to square it.

Mathematical Practices (continued on page 528)

- The eight *Mathematical Practices* focus attention on how mathematics is learned—process versus content. Page 528 demonstrates that mathematically proficient students understand the importance of precise definitions. They also are able to use definitions to make sense of a stated problem in order to seek a solution.
- Use the *Mathematical Practices* page to help students develop mathematical habits of mind—how mathematics can be explored and how mathematics is thought about.
- Students will be working with circles throughout the chapter, learning theorems related to circles, and applying previously learned concepts to circles. In the *Core Concept*, definitions of a circle and tangent circles are given. Students should note the references to "points in a plane" or "coplanar circles" in each definition. This will be a consistent reference throughout the chapter.

If students need help...	If students got it...
Student Journal • Maintaining Mathematical Proficiency	Game Closet at *BigIdeasMath.com*
Lesson Tutorials	Start the *next* Section
Skills Review Handbook	

Maintaining Mathematical Proficiency

Multiplying Binomials

Example 1 Find the product $(x + 3)(2x - 1)$.

$$\begin{aligned}
&\qquad\qquad\qquad \text{First} \quad \text{Outer} \quad \text{Inner} \quad \text{Last} \\
(x + 3)(2x - 1) &= x(2x) + x(-1) + 3(2x) + (3)(-1) \qquad \text{FOIL Method} \\
&= 2x^2 + (-x) + 6x + (-3) \qquad\qquad\qquad \text{Multiply.} \\
&= 2x^2 + 5x - 3 \qquad\qquad\qquad\qquad\quad \text{Simplify.}
\end{aligned}$$

▶ The product is $2x^2 + 5x - 3$.

Find the product.

1. $(x + 7)(x + 4)$
2. $(a + 1)(a - 5)$
3. $(q - 9)(3q - 4)$
4. $(2v - 7)(5v + 1)$
5. $(4h + 3)(2 + h)$
6. $(8 - 6b)(5 - 3b)$

Solving Quadratic Equations by Completing the Square

Example 2 Solve $x^2 + 8x - 3 = 0$ by completing the square.

$$\begin{aligned}
x^2 + 8x - 3 &= 0 \qquad\qquad \text{Write original equation.} \\
x^2 + 8x &= 3 \qquad\qquad \text{Add 3 to each side.} \\
x^2 + 8x + 4^2 &= 3 + 4^2 \qquad \text{Complete the square by adding } \left(\tfrac{8}{2}\right)^2, \text{ or } 4^2, \text{ to each side.} \\
(x + 4)^2 &= 19 \qquad\qquad \text{Write the left side as a square of a binomial.} \\
x + 4 &= \pm\sqrt{19} \qquad \text{Take the square root of each side.} \\
x &= -4 \pm\sqrt{19} \qquad \text{Subtract 4 from each side.}
\end{aligned}$$

▶ The solutions are $x = -4 + \sqrt{19} \approx 0.36$ and $x = -4 - \sqrt{19} \approx -8.36$.

Solve the equation by completing the square. Round your answer to the nearest hundredth, if necessary.

7. $x^2 - 2x = 5$
8. $r^2 + 10r = -7$
9. $w^2 - 8w = 9$
10. $p^2 + 10p - 4 = 0$
11. $k^2 - 4k - 7 = 0$
12. $-z^2 + 2z = 1$

13. **ABSTRACT REASONING** Write an expression that represents the product of two consecutive positive odd integers. Explain your reasoning.

Common Core State Standards

HSA-APR.A.1 … add, subtract, and multiply polynomials.

HSA-SSE.B.3b Complete the square in a quadratic expression …

ANSWERS

1. $x^2 + 11x + 28$
2. $a^2 - 4a - 5$
3. $3q^2 - 31q + 36$
4. $10v^2 - 33v - 7$
5. $4h^2 + 11h + 6$
6. $18b^2 - 54b + 40$
7. $x \approx -1.45; x \approx 3.45$
8. $r \approx -9.24; r \approx -0.76$
9. $w = -1, w = 9$
10. $p \approx -10.39; p \approx 0.39$
11. $k \approx -1.32; k \approx 5.32$
12. $z = 1$
13. *Sample answer:* $(2n + 1)(2n + 3)$; $2n + 1$ is positive and odd when n is a nonnegative integer. The next positive, odd integer is $2n + 3$.

Vocabulary Review

Have students make Process Diagrams for the following procedures.

- Multiplying binomials
- Completing the square

MONITORING PROGRESS
ANSWERS

1.

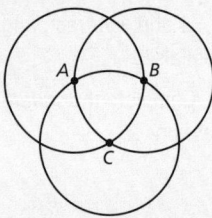

C must be 3 units from A and B, so C must lie on an intersection of circles A and B.

2.

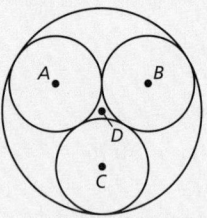

greater than; The radius of $\odot D$ is greater than the diameter of $\odot A$.

Mathematical Practices

Mathematically proficient students make sense of problems and do not give up when faced with challenges.

Analyzing Relationships of Circles

🔄 Core Concept

Circles and Tangent Circles

A **circle** is the set of all points in a plane that are equidistant from a given point called the **center** of the circle. A circle with center D is called "circle D" and can be written as $\odot D$.

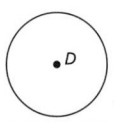

circle D, or $\odot D$

Coplanar circles that intersect in one point are called **tangent circles**.

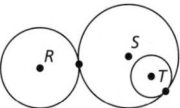

$\odot R$ and $\odot S$ are tangent circles.
$\odot S$ and $\odot T$ are tangent circles.

EXAMPLE 1 **Relationships of Circles and Tangent Circles**

a. Each circle at the right consists of points that are 3 units from the center. What is the greatest distance from any point on $\odot A$ to any point on $\odot B$?

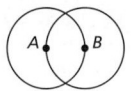

b. Three circles, $\odot C$, $\odot D$, and $\odot E$, consist of points that are 3 units from their centers. The centers C, D, and E of the circles are collinear, $\odot C$ is tangent to $\odot D$, and $\odot D$ is tangent to $\odot E$. What is the distance from $\odot C$ to $\odot E$?

SOLUTION

a. Because the points on each circle are 3 units from the center, the greatest distance from any point on $\odot A$ to any point on $\odot B$ is $3 + 3 + 3 = 9$ units.

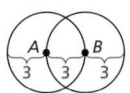

b. Because C, D, and E are collinear, $\odot C$ is tangent to $\odot D$, and $\odot D$ is tangent to $\odot E$, the circles are as shown. So, the distance from $\odot C$ to $\odot E$ is $3 + 3 = 6$ units.

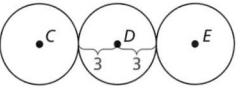

Monitoring Progress

Let $\odot A$, $\odot B$, and $\odot C$ consist of points that are 3 units from the centers.

1. Draw $\odot C$ so that it passes through points A and B in the figure at the right. Explain your reasoning.

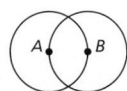

2. Draw $\odot A$, $\odot B$, and $\odot C$ so that each is tangent to the other two. Draw a larger circle, $\odot D$, that is tangent to each of the other three circles. Is the distance from point D to a point on $\odot D$ *less than*, *greater than*, or *equal to* 6? Explain.

Laurie's Notes Mathematical Practices (continued from page T-527)

- Example 1 applies the definitions of a circle and tangent circles in solving each problem. In solving the problems, it is helpful to be able to visualize the problem and draw a sketch.
- Work through each problem as shown.
- Give time for students to work through the *Monitoring Progress* questions. Students may find that a compass is a helpful tool. Discuss as a class.

Dynamic Teaching Tools
Dynamic Assessment & Progress Monitoring Tool
Lesson Planning Tool
Interactive Whiteboard Lesson Library
Dynamic Classroom with Dynamic Investigations

Overview of Section 10.1

Introduction
- This introductory lesson on circles presents the line and segment vocabulary associated with circles. Some of the vocabulary should be quite familiar to students.
- Internal and external lines and segments are drawn and identified.
- The second part of the lesson presents the properties of tangents, stated as theorems. The problems that follow integrate prior skills and content such as the Pythagorean Theorem and symbolic manipulation.

Teaching Strategy
- This lesson contains two theorems relating to tangents of a circle. Each theorem can be investigated using dynamic geometry software. This approach allows student discovery and extensions to problems.
- The External Tangent Congruence Theorem (Thm. 10.2) is easily constructed using most dynamic software. Clicking and dragging on the external point effectively demonstrates that the external tangent segments are always congruent regardless of the location of the external point.

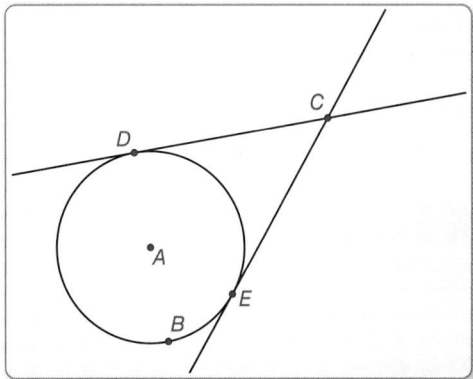

- Students in my class were curious about having two noncongruent tangent circles. Students wanted to select a point in the exterior of both circles and measure the tangent circles. In order to construct the tangent circles, they needed to use the first theorem in the lesson!

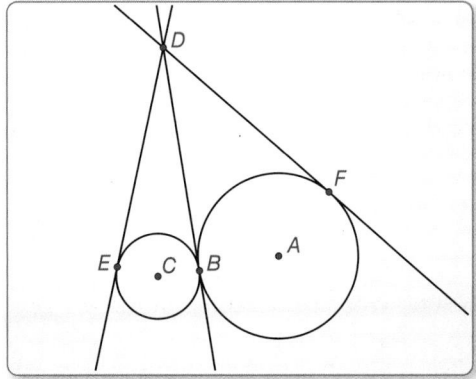

- Whenever possible, have students use dynamic geometry software to investigate and discover theorems.

Pacing Suggestion
- The explorations are a quick and engaging way for students to work with the vocabulary of a circle. Students should be ready to begin with Example 1 in the formal lesson.

HSG-CO.A.1 Know precise definitions of … circle, … based on the undefined notions of point, … and distance around a circular arc.

HSG-C.A.2 Identify and describe relationships among … radii, and chords.

HSG-C.A.4 Construct a tangent line from a point outside a given circle to the circle.

Laurie's Notes

Exploration

Motivate
- The circle is a common shape and hence a very common image when you look around. I like to begin this chapter by asking students to make a list of the places where a circular shape is seen.
- Have each student share one or two examples from his or her list.
- Share a short photo album of images such as bicycle gears, a round stained-glass window, and manhole covers. These are images you can refer back to throughout the chapter.

Exploration 1
- **MP6 Attend to Precision:** This exploration gives students the opportunity to practice writing a definition based upon an observation (i.e., looking at a sketch). Remind students that a definition needs to be precise so that it leads to only one possible object.
- **MP3 Construct Viable Arguments and Critique the Reasoning of Others:** Have students compare and contrast definitions. In critiquing the definitions of others, students learn to be analytic and to apply reasoning skills.

Exploration 2
- This is a quick, kinesthetic exploration that reinforces the definition of a circle.
- **Teaching Tip:** Another way to draw an accurate circle is to use a paper clip. Anchor the paper clip at one end with a pencil. Use a second pencil at the other end of the paper clip to draw the circle. Although different lengths of paper clips are available, the radius is still rather limited.

Communicate Your Answer
- **MP2 Reason Abstractly and Quantitatively:** Question 4 helps focus attention on the relationships between the various segments and lines associated with a circle.

Connecting to Next Step
- If accurate definitions result from the first exploration, begin the formal lesson with Example 1.

Essential Question
What are the definitions of the lines and segments that intersect a circle?

Lines and Line Segments That Intersect Circles

Work with a partner. The drawing at the right shows five lines or segments that intersect a circle. Use the relationships shown to write a definition for each type of line or segment. Then use the Internet or some other resource to verify your definitions.

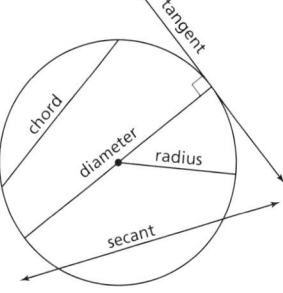

Chord:

Secant:

Tangent:

Radius:

Diameter:

EXPLORATION 2   **Using String to Draw a Circle**

Work with a partner. Use two pencils, a piece of string, and a piece of paper.

a. Tie the two ends of the piece of string loosely around the two pencils.

b. Anchor one pencil on the paper at the center of the circle. Use the other pencil to draw a circle around the anchor point while using slight pressure to keep the string taut. Do not let the string wind around either pencil.

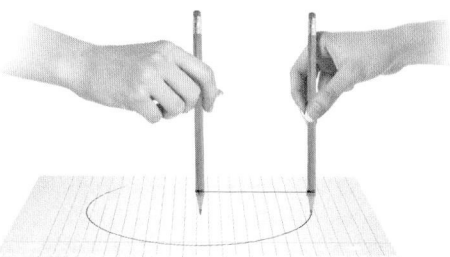

REASONING ABSTRACTLY

To be proficient in math, you need to know and flexibly use different properties of operations and objects.

c. Explain how the distance between the two pencil points as you draw the circle is related to two of the lines or line segments you defined in Exploration 1.

Communicate Your Answer

3. What are the definitions of the lines and segments that intersect a circle?

4. Of the five types of lines and segments in Exploration 1, which one is a subset of another? Explain.

5. Explain how to draw a circle with a diameter of 8 inches.

Section 10.1   Lines and Segments That Intersect Circles   **529**

ANSWERS

1. segment with endpoints on the circle; line that intersects a circle at two points; line in the plane of a circle that intersects the circle at exactly one point; segment whose endpoints are the center and any point on a circle; chord that contains the center of the circle

2. a. and b. Check students' work.

   c. The distance is the radius and half the diameter.

3. A chord is a segment with endpoints that lie on a circle. A diameter is a chord that passes through the center of a circle. A radius is a segment with one endpoint on the center of a circle and one endpoint on the circle. A secant line is a line that passes through two points on a circle. A tangent line is a line that passes through only one point on a circle.

4. diameters; A diameter is a chord that passes through the center of a circle.

5. Use two pencils tied together with a string that is 4 inches long.

Extra Example 1

Tell whether the line, ray, or segment is best described as a *radius*, *chord*, *diameter*, *secant*, or *tangent* of $\odot O$.

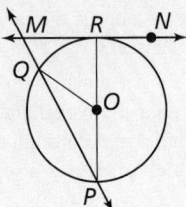

a. $\overline{PR}$ diameter

b. $\overleftrightarrow{MN}$ tangent

c. $\overrightarrow{PQ}$ secant

d. $\overline{QO}$ radius

MONITORING PROGRESS ANSWERS

1. chord; radius

2. *Sample answer:* $\overrightarrow{DE}, \overline{DB}$ or $\overline{DE}$

10.1 Lesson

Core Vocabulary

circle, *p. 530*
center, *p. 530*
radius, *p. 530*
chord, *p. 530*
diameter, *p. 530*
secant, *p. 530*
tangent, *p. 530*
point of tangency, *p. 530*
tangent circles, *p. 531*
concentric circles, *p. 531*
common tangent, *p. 531*

READING

The words "radius" and "diameter" refer to lengths as well as segments. For a given circle, think of *a* radius and *a* diameter as segments and *the* radius and *the* diameter as lengths.

STUDY TIP

In this book, assume that all segments, rays, or lines that appear to be tangent to a circle are tangents.

What You Will Learn

▶ Identify special segments and lines.

▶ Draw and identify common tangents.

▶ Use properties of tangents.

Identifying Special Segments and Lines

A **circle** is the set of all points in a plane that are equidistant from a given point called the **center** of the circle. A circle with center P is called "circle P" and can be written as $\odot P$.

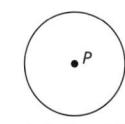

circle P, or $\odot P$

Core Concept

Lines and Segments That Intersect Circles

A segment whose endpoints are the center and any point on a circle is a **radius**.

A **chord** is a segment whose endpoints are on a circle. A **diameter** is a chord that contains the center of the circle.

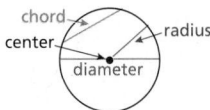

A **secant** is a line that intersects a circle in two points.

A **tangent** is a line in the plane of a circle that intersects the circle in exactly one point, the **point of tangency**. The *tangent ray* $\overrightarrow{AB}$ and the *tangent segment* $\overline{AB}$ are also called tangents.

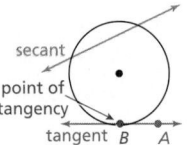

EXAMPLE 1 Identifying Special Segments and Lines

Tell whether the line, ray, or segment is best described as a *radius*, *chord*, *diameter*, *secant*, or *tangent* of $\odot C$.

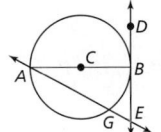

a. $\overline{AC}$

b. $\overline{AB}$

c. $\overrightarrow{DE}$

d. $\overleftrightarrow{AE}$

SOLUTION

a. $\overline{AC}$ is a radius because C is the center and A is a point on the circle.

b. $\overline{AB}$ is a diameter because it is a chord that contains the center C.

c. $\overrightarrow{DE}$ is a tangent ray because it is contained in a line that intersects the circle in exactly one point.

d. $\overleftrightarrow{AE}$ is a secant because it is a line that intersects the circle in two points.

Monitoring Progress Help in English and Spanish at *BigIdeasMath.com*

1. In Example 1, what word best describes $\overline{AG}$? $\overline{CB}$?

2. In Example 1, name a tangent and a tangent segment.

Laurie's Notes   Teacher Actions

- **Turn and Talk:** "What vocabulary of circles are you familiar with and what does it mean?" Circulate and listen. Solicit answers.

- ❓ "Are all chords diameters? Are all diameters chords?" All diameters are chords, but not all chords are diameters.

- ❓ **MP2:** "Why is it necessary to state that a tangent is in the same plane as a circle?" Answers will vary. Model what it would look like if that language were removed from the definition.

Drawing and Identifying Common Tangents

⑤ Core Concept

Coplanar Circles and Common Tangents

In a plane, two circles can intersect in two points, one point, or no points. Coplanar circles that intersect in one point are called **tangent circles**. Coplanar circles that have a common center are called **concentric circles**.

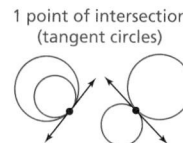
2 points of intersection

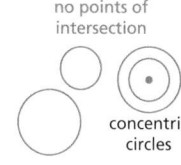
1 point of intersection (tangent circles)

no points of intersection

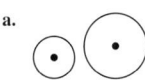
concentric circles

A line or segment that is tangent to two coplanar circles is called a **common tangent**. A *common internal tangent* intersects the segment that joins the centers of the two circles. A *common external tangent* does not intersect the segment that joins the centers of the two circles.

EXAMPLE 2 Drawing and Identifying Common Tangents

Tell how many common tangents the circles have and draw them. Use blue to indicate common external tangents and red to indicate common internal tangents.

a. 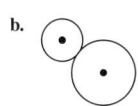   b. 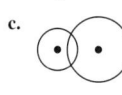   c.

SOLUTION

Draw the segment that joins the centers of the two circles. Then draw the common tangents. Use blue to indicate lines that do not intersect the segment joining the centers and red to indicate lines that intersect the segment joining the centers.

a. 4 common tangents   b. 3 common tangents   c. 2 common tangents

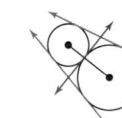   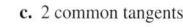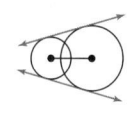

Monitoring Progress 🔊 Help in English and Spanish at *BigIdeasMath.com*

Tell how many common tangents the circles have and draw them. State whether the tangents are external tangents or internal tangents.

3.   4.   5.

Laurie's Notes **Teacher Actions**

❓ Whiteboarding: "What are the intersection possibilities for two circles—meaning what could they look like?" Use whiteboards for partners to consider the question. Follow their responses with the vocabulary in the *Core Concept*. Again, note the reference to coplanar circles.

• **Thumbs Up:** Have students use whiteboards to sketch their solutions for Example 2. Ask students to self-assess with *Thumbs Up*.

• Omit *Monitoring Progress* questions if you sense students are secure in their understanding of internal and external tangents.

Extra Example 2
Tell how many common tangents the circles have and draw them.

a.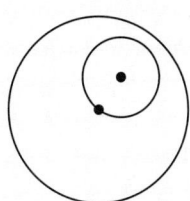

0 common tangents

b.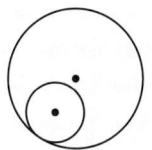

1 common external tangent

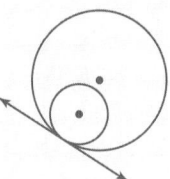

c.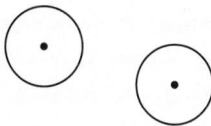

4 common tangents: 2 internal, 2 external

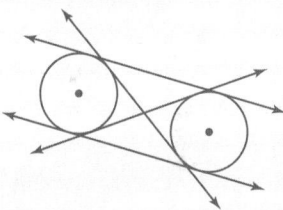

MONITORING PROGRESS ANSWERS

3. 2 internal, 2 external

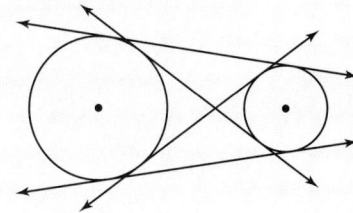

4. 1 external

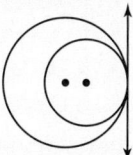

5. See Additional Answers.

Section 10.1   **531**

Extra Example 3

Is $\overline{ST}$ tangent to $\odot P$?

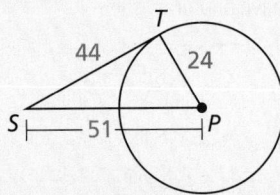

No, $\overline{ST}$ is not tangent to $\odot P$.

Extra Example 4

In the diagram, point P is a point of tangency. Find the radius r of $\odot O$.

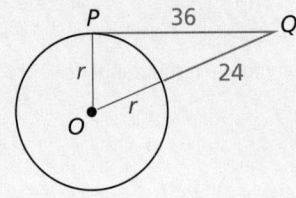

$r = 15$

Using Properties of Tangents

⚙ Theorems

Theorem 10.1   Tangent Line to Circle Theorem

In a plane, a line is tangent to a circle if and only if the line is perpendicular to a radius of the circle at its endpoint on the circle.

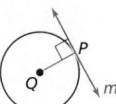

Line m is tangent to $\odot Q$ if and only if $m \perp \overline{QP}$.

Proof Ex. 47, p. 536

Theorem 10.2   External Tangent Congruence Theorem

Tangent segments from a common external point are congruent.

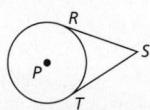

If $\overline{SR}$ and $\overline{ST}$ are tangent segments, then $\overline{SR} \cong \overline{ST}$.

Proof Ex. 46, p. 536

EXAMPLE 3   Verifying a Tangent to a Circle

Is $\overline{ST}$ tangent to $\odot P$?

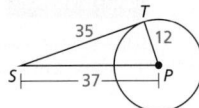

SOLUTION

Use the Converse of the Pythagorean Theorem (Theorem 9.2). Because $12^2 + 35^2 = 37^2$, $\triangle PTS$ is a right triangle and $\overline{ST} \perp \overline{PT}$. So, $\overline{ST}$ is perpendicular to a radius of $\odot P$ at its endpoint on $\odot P$.

▶ By the Tangent Line to Circle Theorem, $\overline{ST}$ is tangent to $\odot P$.

EXAMPLE 4   Finding the Radius of a Circle

In the diagram, point B is a point of tangency. Find the radius r of $\odot C$.

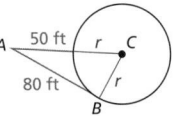

SOLUTION

You know from the Tangent Line to Circle Theorem that $\overline{AB} \perp \overline{BC}$, so $\triangle ABC$ is a right triangle. You can use the Pythagorean Theorem (Theorem 9.1).

$$AC^2 = BC^2 + AB^2 \qquad \text{Pythagorean Theorem}$$
$$(r + 50)^2 = r^2 + 80^2 \qquad \text{Substitute.}$$
$$r^2 + 100r + 2500 = r^2 + 6400 \qquad \text{Multiply.}$$
$$100r = 3900 \qquad \text{Subtract } r^2 \text{ and } 2500 \text{ from each side.}$$
$$r = 39 \qquad \text{Divide each side by 100.}$$

▶ The radius is 39 feet.

Laurie's Notes   Teacher Actions

- The theorems relating to tangents can be investigated using dynamic geometry software. See the *Teaching Strategy* on page T-528.
- Have partners discuss strategies for proving each theorem and then share as a class.
- **Wait Time:** Pose Example 4, and give partners sufficient *Wait Time* to work on the problem. Students should recall how to square a binomial and perform the symbolic manipulations.
- ❓ "Does B have to be a point of tangency to solve this problem in this manner?"   yes

CONSTRUCTION   **Constructing a Tangent to a Circle**

Given ⊙C and point A, construct a line tangent to ⊙C that passes through A. Use a compass and straightedge.

SOLUTION

Step 1

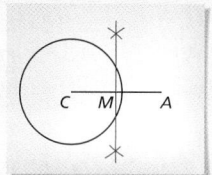

Find a midpoint
Draw $\overline{AC}$. Construct the bisector of the segment and label the midpoint M.

Step 2

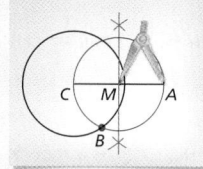

Draw a circle
Construct ⊙M with radius MA. Label one of the points where ⊙M intersects ⊙C as point B.

Step 3

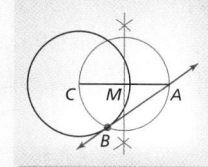

Construct a tangent line
Draw $\overleftrightarrow{AB}$. It is a tangent to ⊙C that passes through A.

EXAMPLE 5   **Using Properties of Tangents**

$\overline{RS}$ is tangent to ⊙C at S, and $\overline{RT}$ is tangent to ⊙C at T. Find the value of x.

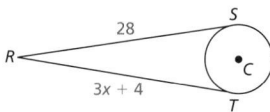

SOLUTION

$RS = RT$	External Tangent Congruence Theorem
$28 = 3x + 4$	Substitute.
$8 = x$	Solve for x.

▶ The value of x is 8.

Monitoring Progress 🔊 Help in English and Spanish at *BigIdeasMath.com*

6. Is $\overline{DE}$ tangent to ⊙C?

7. $\overline{ST}$ is tangent to ⊙Q. Find the radius of ⊙Q.

8. Points M and N are points of tangency. Find the value(s) of x.

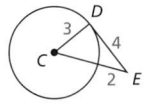
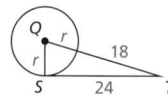
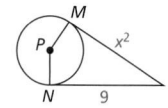

Extra Example 5
$\overleftrightarrow{JH}$ is tangent to ⊙L at H, and $\overleftrightarrow{JK}$ is tangent to ⊙L at K. Find the value of x.

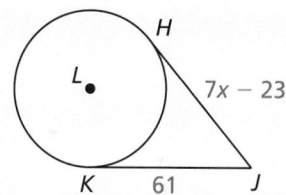

$x = 12$

MONITORING PROGRESS ANSWERS

6. yes

7. 7

8. ±3

Laurie's Notes   **Teacher Actions**

- **FYI:** The construction of a tangent from an external point is presented here with many of the properties of a tangent. The proof of why this is a valid construction requires the Measure of an Inscribed Angle Theorem (Thm. 10.10) in a later section. $\overline{CA}$ is a diameter and because the measure of inscribed ∠CBA is $\frac{1}{2}$ the measure of the 180° intercepted arc, $\overleftrightarrow{AB} \perp \overline{CB}$.

- **Think-Pair-Share:** Have students answer Questions 6–8, and then share and discuss as a class.

Closure

- **Exit Ticket:** Draw a figure like the one in Example 4. When $CB = 8$ centimeters and $AB = 12$ centimeters, what is AC? $4\sqrt{13} \approx 14.4$ centimeters

ANSWERS

1. They both intersect the circle in two points; Chords are segments and secants are lines.

2. When the context is measure, it refers to length.

3. concentric circles

4. tangent; It is outside the circle.

5. $\odot C$

6. $\overline{AC}, \overline{CD}$

7. $\overline{BH}, \overline{AD}$

8. $\overline{AD}$

9. $\overleftrightarrow{KG}$

10. $\overrightarrow{GE}$, F

11. 4

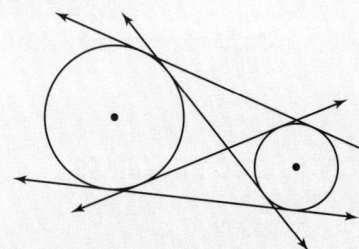

12. 0

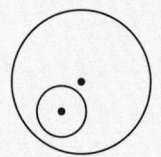

13. 2

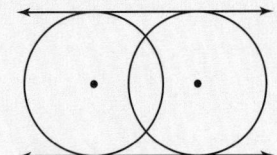

Vocabulary and Core Concept Check

1. **WRITING** How are chords and secants alike? How are they different?

2. **WRITING** Explain how you can determine from the context whether the words *radius* and *diameter* are referring to segments or lengths.

3. **COMPLETE THE SENTENCE** Coplanar circles that have a common center are called _____.

4. **WHICH ONE DOESN'T BELONG?** Which segment does *not* belong with the other three? Explain your reasoning.

| chord | radius | tangent | diameter |

Monitoring Progress and Modeling with Mathematics

In Exercises 5–10, use the diagram. *(See Example 1.)*

5. Name the circle.

6. Name two radii.

7. Name two chords.

8. Name a diameter.

9. Name a secant.

10. Name a tangent and a point of tangency.

In Exercises 11–14, copy the diagram. Tell how many common tangents the circles have and draw them. *(See Example 2.)*

11.

12.

13.

14.

In Exercises 15–18, tell whether the common tangent is *internal* or *external*.

15.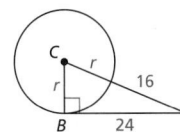

16.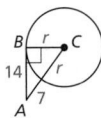

17.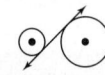

18.

In Exercises 19–22, tell whether $\overline{AB}$ is tangent to $\odot C$. Explain your reasoning. *(See Example 3.)*

19.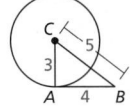

20.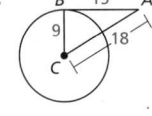

21.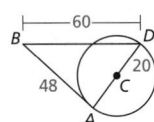

22.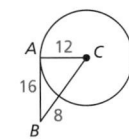

In Exercises 23–26, point B is a point of tangency. Find the radius r of $\odot C$. *(See Example 4.)*

23.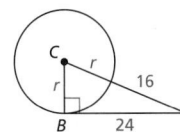

24.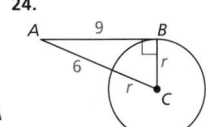

25.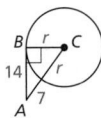

26.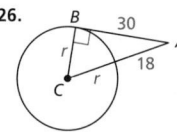

---

14. 1

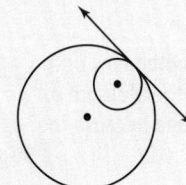

15. external

16. internal

17. internal

18. external

19. yes; $\triangle ABC$ is a right triangle.

20. no; $\triangle ABC$ is not a right triangle.

21. no; $\triangle ABD$ is not a right triangle.

22. yes; $\triangle ABC$ is a right triangle.

23. 10

24. 3.75

25. 10.5

26. 16

CONSTRUCTION In Exercises 27 and 28, construct ⊙*C* with the given radius and point *A* outside of ⊙*C*. Then construct a line tangent to ⊙*C* that passes through *A*.

27. *r* = 2 in.   **28.** *r* = 4.5 cm

In Exercises 29–32, points *B* and *D* are points of tangency. Find the value(s) of *x*. *(See Example 5.)*

29.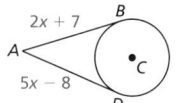
30.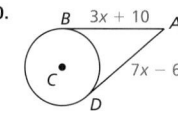

31.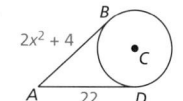
32.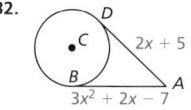

33. ERROR ANALYSIS Describe and correct the error in determining whether $\overline{XY}$ is tangent to ⊙*Z*.

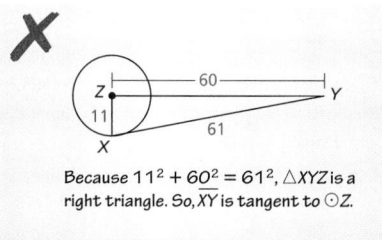

Because $11^2 + 60^2 = 61^2$, △*XYZ* is a right triangle. So, $\overline{XY}$ is tangent to ⊙*Z*.

34. ERROR ANALYSIS Describe and correct the error in finding the radius of ⊙*T*.

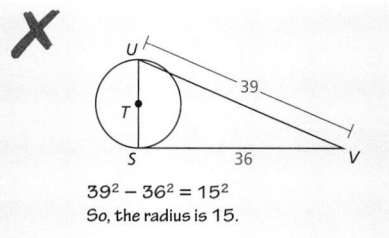

$39^2 - 36^2 = 15^2$
So, the radius is 15.

35. ABSTRACT REASONING For a point outside of a circle, how many lines exist tangent to the circle that pass through the point? How many such lines exist for a point on the circle? inside the circle? Explain your reasoning.

36. CRITICAL THINKING When will two lines tangent to the same circle not intersect? Justify your answer.

37. USING STRUCTURE Each side of quadrilateral *TVWX* is tangent to ⊙*Y*. Find the perimeter of the quadrilateral.

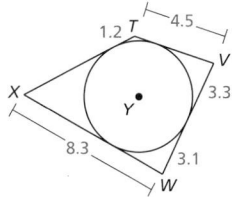

38. LOGIC In ⊙*C*, radii $\overline{CA}$ and $\overline{CB}$ are perpendicular. $\overrightarrow{BD}$ and $\overrightarrow{AD}$ are tangent to ⊙*C*.

    a. Sketch ⊙*C*, $\overline{CA}$, $\overline{CB}$, $\overrightarrow{BD}$, and $\overrightarrow{AD}$.

    b. What type of quadrilateral is *CADB*? Explain your reasoning.

39. MAKING AN ARGUMENT Two bike paths are tangent to an approximately circular pond. Your class is building a nature trail that begins at the intersection *B* of the bike paths and runs between the bike paths and over a bridge through the center *P* of the pond. Your classmate uses the Converse of the Angle Bisector Theorem (Theorem 6.4) to conclude that the trail must bisect the angle formed by the bike paths. Is your classmate correct? Explain your reasoning.

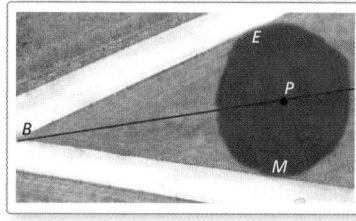

40. MODELING WITH MATHEMATICS A bicycle chain is pulled tightly so that $\overline{MN}$ is a common tangent of the gears. Find the distance between the centers of the gears.

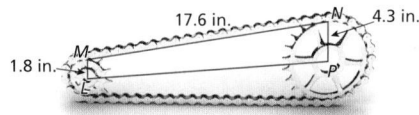

41. WRITING Explain why the diameter of a circle is the longest chord of the circle.

ANSWERS

27. *Sample answer:*

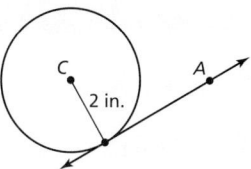

28. *Sample answer:*

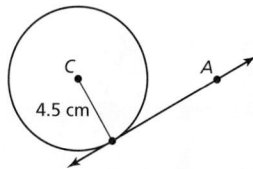

29. 5

30. 4

31. ±3

32. ±2

33. ∠*Z* is a right angle, not ∠*YXZ*; $\overline{XY}$ is not tangent to ⊙*Z*.

34. The diameter is 15; The radius is 7.5.

35. 2; 1; 0; *Sample answer:* There are two possible points of tangency from a point outside the circle, one from a point on the circle, and none from a point inside the circle.

36. when they are parallel; *Sample answer:* Two tangents perpendicular to the same diameter are parallel.

37. 25.6 units

38. a.

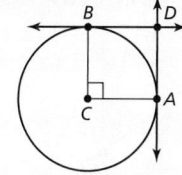

    b. square; $\overline{CA} \cong \overline{CB}$, $\overline{BD} \cong \overline{DA}$, $m\angle C = 90° = m\angle B = m\angle A$

39. yes; $\overline{PE}$ and $\overline{PM}$ are radii, so $\overline{PE} \cong \overline{PM}$.

40. about 17.78 in.

41. *Sample answer:* Every point is the same distance from the center, so the farthest two points can be from each other is opposite sides of the center.

ANSWERS

42–50. See Additional Answers.

Mini-Assessment

1. Tell whether the line, ray, or segment is best described as a *radius*, *chord*, *diameter*, *secant*, or *tangent* of ⊙P.

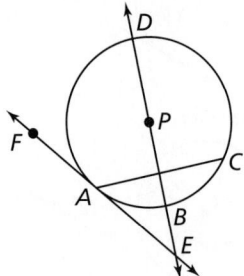

a. $\overline{AE}$ tangent segment

b. $\overline{BD}$ diameter

c. $\overleftrightarrow{BD}$ secant

d. $\overline{AC}$ chord

2. How many common external tangents do the circles have? How many common internal tangents?

2 external; 0 internal

3. In the diagram, point S is a point of tangency. Find the radius r of ⊙Q.

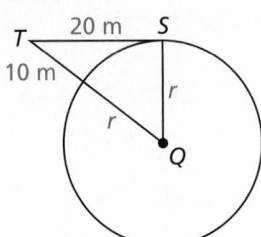

15 meters

4. $\overline{RS}$ is tangent to ⊙C at S, and $\overline{RT}$ is tangent to ⊙C at T. Find the value of x.

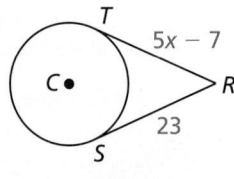

x = 6

536   Chapter 10

---

42. **HOW DO YOU SEE IT?** In the figure, $\overrightarrow{PA}$ is tangent to the dime, $\overrightarrow{PC}$ is tangent to the quarter, and $\overrightarrow{PB}$ is a common internal tangent. How do you know that $\overline{PA} \cong \overline{PB} \cong \overline{PC}$?

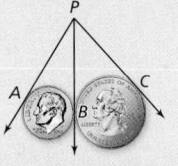

43. **PROOF** In the diagram, $\overline{RS}$ is a common internal tangent to ⊙A and ⊙B. Prove that $\dfrac{AC}{BC} = \dfrac{RC}{SC}$.

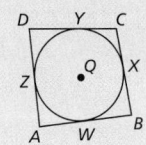

44. **THOUGHT PROVOKING** A polygon is *circumscribed* about a circle when every side of the polygon is tangent to the circle. In the diagram, quadrilateral *ABCD* is circumscribed about ⊙Q. Is it always true that AB + CD = AD + BC? Justify your answer.

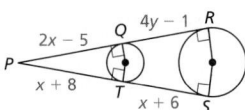

45. **MATHEMATICAL CONNECTIONS** Find the values of x and y. Justify your answer.

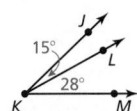

Maintaining Mathematical Proficiency   Reviewing what you learned in previous grades and lessons

Find the indicated measure. (*Section 1.2 and Section 1.5*)

49. m∠JKM

50. AB

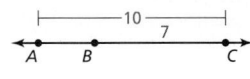

536   Chapter 10   Circles

---

46. **PROVING A THEOREM** Prove the External Tangent Congruence Theorem (Theorem 10.2).

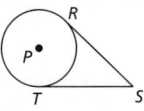

Given $\overline{SR}$ and $\overline{ST}$ are tangent to ⊙P.
Prove $\overline{SR} \cong \overline{ST}$

47. **PROVING A THEOREM** Use the diagram to prove each part of the biconditional in the Tangent Line to Circle Theorem (Theorem 10.1).

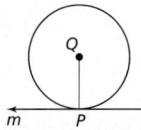

a. Prove indirectly that if a line is tangent to a circle, then it is perpendicular to a radius. (*Hint:* If you assume line *m* is not perpendicular to $\overline{QP}$, then the perpendicular segment from point *Q* to line *m* must intersect line *m* at some other point *R*.)

Given Line *m* is tangent to ⊙Q at point P.
Prove $m \perp \overline{QP}$

b. Prove indirectly that if a line is perpendicular to a radius at its endpoint, then the line is tangent to the circle.

Given $m \perp \overline{QP}$
Prove Line *m* is tangent to ⊙Q.

48. **REASONING** In the diagram, AB = AC = 12, BC = 8, and all three segments are tangent to ⊙P. What is the radius of ⊙P? Justify your answer.

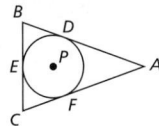

If students need help...	If students got it...
Resources by Chapter • Practice A and Practice B • Puzzle Time	Resources by Chapter • Enrichment and Extension • Cumulative Review
Student Journal • Practice	Start the *next* Section
Differentiating the Lesson Skills Review Handbook	

Overview of Section 10.2

Introduction

- This is a short lesson on how to name and measure minor and major arcs in a circle. The definitions of congruent circles and congruent arcs then allow students to identify congruent arcs from given information.
- The lesson ends with proving that all circles are similar.

Formative Assessment Tips

- **Agreement Circles:** Students should be expected to defend and give rationale for their beliefs or ideas. This technique is a kinesthetic way to engage students in defending their beliefs about a statement made by the teacher.
- Ask students to stand in a large circle. Make a statement to the class about a geometric concept or relationship. If students agree with the statement, they take a few steps forward. If they disagree with the statement, they do nothing. Depending upon the number in each group, divide the students into smaller discussion groups so that each group has a mix of agree and disagree members. The expectation is that students will explain and defend why they have their particular belief.
- The technique can be used before formal instruction is given to assess students' conceptions about the content to be studied. It can also be used during the instruction to help students solidify their understanding of the content.
- Students are making public their belief when they need to step forward or remain still. The dialogue that goes on between the two sides is also important. Students can revise and adjust their thinking based upon new ideas that are shared by peers.
- Sample statements to make in this lesson.
  - Arcs that have the same measure are congruent.
  - Circles with the same radius are congruent.
  - All circles are congruent.
  - If two circles are congruent, then they are similar.
  - All circles are similar.
  - If two arcs are similar, then they are congruent.

Pacing Suggestion

- Once students have worked the exploration, continue with the formal lesson.

Dynamic Teaching Tools

Dynamic Assessment & Progress Monitoring Tool
Lesson Planning Tool
Interactive Whiteboard Lesson Library
Dynamic Classroom with Dynamic Investigations

Common Core
State Standards

HSG-C.A.1 Prove that all circles are similar.

HSG-C.A.2 Identify and describe relationships among ... angles, radii, and chords.

Laurie's Notes

Exploration

Motivate

- Have students write on scrap paper to answer. Say, "List three things that are circular." Give students 15 seconds and then ask, "How many of you have pizza on your list?" It is fairly likely that all students in the room will have pizza on their lists!
- **?** "How many pieces are pizzas often cut into?" 6, 8, or 10
- **?** "What is the measure of each angle at the tip of each slice when the pizza is cut into 6 equal slices?" 60° "8 equal slices?" 45° "10 equal slices?" 36°
- Explain to students that in this lesson they will work with the central angle of a circle (the tip of the pizza slice) and also with the circular arc (the crust).

Exploration Note

- The exploration begins with a definition of a central angle and the measure of a circular arc. Check students' understanding of the definitions and notation.
- If dynamic geometry software is not available, students could still perform the construction with a protractor and straightedge. Gathering results from classmates may be sufficient to make a conjecture about the problem posed.

Exploration 1

- This exploration is a nice review of trigonometric ratios.
- Students must first construct each sketch. To find the measure of each circular arc, they need to measure the central angle.
- **?** "How did you verify your answer using trigonometry?" One way is to set up a tangent ratio, because you know the opposite and adjacent sides of an angle in a right triangle. For example, using the figure below, $\tan DAC = \dfrac{CD}{AD}$.

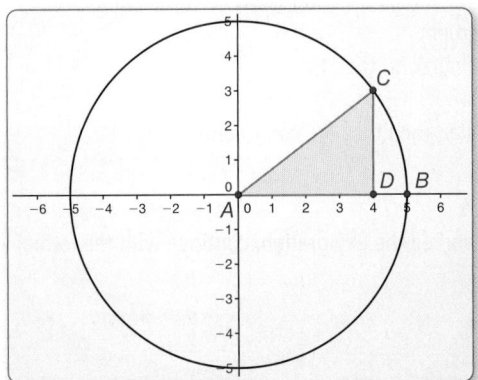

- **MP2 Reason Abstractly and Quantitatively:** In parts (c) and (d), students should offer other strategies for finding the measure of $\overset{\frown}{BC}$. For instance, in part (c) they may reason that the circular arc is the difference of the two circular arcs found in parts (a) and (b).

Communicate Your Answer

- For Question 3 there are different strategies that students could use to draw the circular arcs. Have students share and discuss the various methods.

Connecting to Next Step

- The exploration will help students make the connection between the measure of the central angle and the associated circular arc, which is the introduction to the formal lesson.

Essential Question How are circular arcs measured?

A **central angle** of a circle is an angle whose vertex is the center of the circle. A *circular arc* is a portion of a circle, as shown below. The measure of a circular arc is the measure of its central angle.

If $m\angle AOB < 180°$, then the circular arc is called a **minor arc** and is denoted by $\overset{\frown}{AB}$.

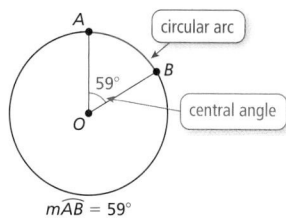

$m\overset{\frown}{AB} = 59°$

EXPLORATION 1   Measuring Circular Arcs

Work with a partner. Use dynamic geometry software to find the measure of $\overset{\frown}{BC}$. Verify your answers using trigonometry.

a.

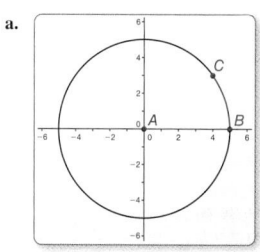

Points
A(0, 0)
B(5, 0)
C(4, 3)

b.

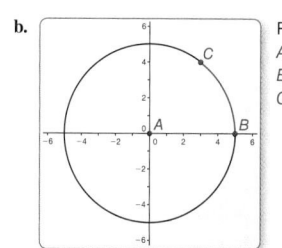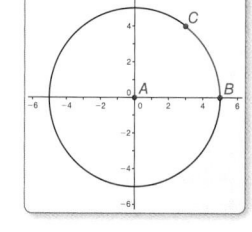

Points
A(0, 0)
B(5, 0)
C(3, 4)

c.

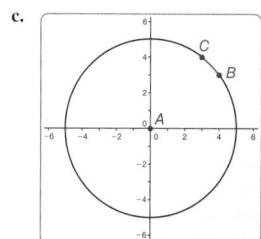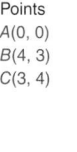

Points
A(0, 0)
B(4, 3)
C(3, 4)

d.

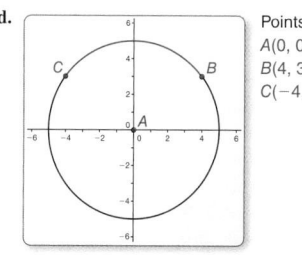

Points
A(0, 0)
B(4, 3)
C(−4, 3)

USING TOOLS STRATEGICALLY

To be proficient in math, you need to use technological tools to explore and deepen your understanding of concepts.

Communicate Your Answer

2. How are circular arcs measured?

3. Use dynamic geometry software to draw a circular arc with the given measure.

   a. 30°   **b.** 45°

   c. 60°   **d.** 90°

ANSWERS

1. a. 36.87°
   b. 53.13°
   c. 16.26°
   d. 106.26°

2. by their central angles

3. a.

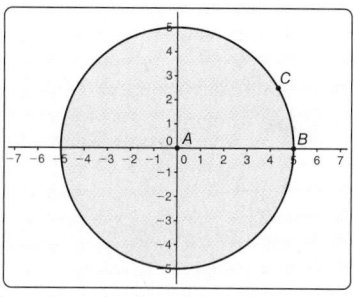

b.

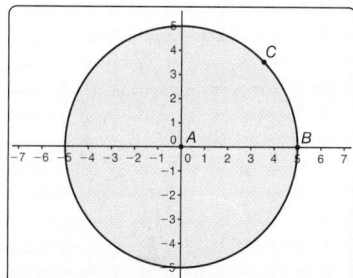

c.

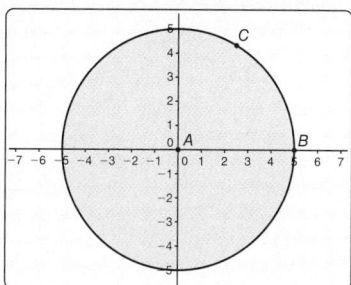

d.

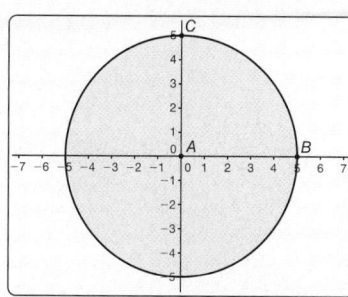

Extra Example 1

Find the measure of each arc of $\odot C$, where $\overline{AB}$ is a diameter.

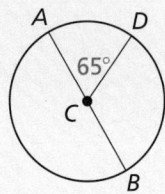

a. $\widehat{AD}$ 65°

b. $\widehat{DAB}$ 245°

c. $\widehat{BDA}$ 180°

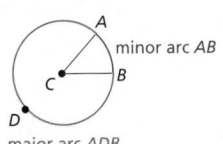

10.2 Lesson

Core Vocabulary

central angle, *p. 538*
minor arc, *p. 538*
major arc, *p. 538*
semicircle, *p. 538*
measure of a minor arc, *p. 538*
measure of a major arc, *p. 538*
adjacent arcs, *p. 539*
congruent circles, *p. 540*
congruent arcs, *p. 540*
similar arcs, *p. 541*

STUDY TIP

The measure of a minor arc is less than 180°. The measure of a major arc is greater than 180°.

What You Will Learn

▶ Find arc measures.

▶ Identify congruent arcs.

▶ Prove circles are similar.

Finding Arc Measures

A **central angle** of a circle is an angle whose vertex is the center of the circle. In the diagram, $\angle ACB$ is a central angle of $\odot C$.

If $m\angle ACB$ is less than 180°, then the points on $\odot C$ that lie in the interior of $\angle ACB$ form a **minor arc** with endpoints A and B. The points on $\odot C$ that do not lie on the minor arc AB form a **major arc** with endpoints A and B. A **semicircle** is an arc with endpoints that are the endpoints of a diameter.

minor arc AB

major arc ADB

Minor arcs are named by their endpoints. The minor arc associated with $\angle ACB$ is named $\widehat{AB}$. Major arcs and semicircles are named by their endpoints and a point on the arc. The major arc associated with $\angle ACB$ can be named $\widehat{ADB}$.

🔁 Core Concept

Measuring Arcs

The **measure of a minor arc** is the measure of its central angle. The expression $m\widehat{AB}$ is read as "the measure of arc AB."

The measure of the entire circle is 360°. The **measure of a major arc** is the difference of 360° and the measure of the related minor arc. The measure of a semicircle is 180°.

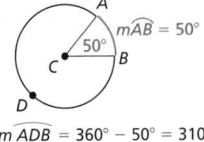

$m\widehat{AB} = 50°$

$m\widehat{ADB} = 360° - 50° = 310°$

EXAMPLE 1 Finding Measures of Arcs

Find the measure of each arc of $\odot P$, where $\overline{RT}$ is a diameter.

a. $\widehat{RS}$

b. $\widehat{RTS}$

c. $\widehat{RST}$

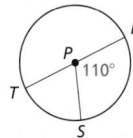

SOLUTION

a. $\widehat{RS}$ is a minor arc, so $m\widehat{RS} = m\angle RPS = 110°$.

b. $\widehat{RTS}$ is a major arc, so $m\widehat{RTS} = 360° - 110° = 250°$.

c. $\overline{RT}$ is a diameter, so $\widehat{RST}$ is a semicircle, and $m\widehat{RST} = 180°$.

538   Chapter 10   Circles

Laurie's Notes   Teacher Actions

- Discuss vocabulary: *minor arc*, *major arc*, and *semicircle*.
- ❓ **Turn and Talk:** "Why does a major arc require three letters to name?" With only two letters, it would be unclear whether the arc was a minor arc or a major arc.
- Write the *Core Concept*.
- **Think-Pair-Share:** Pose Example 1. Students should have little difficulty with these examples.
- ❓ "In any circle, is $m\widehat{ABC} = m\widehat{CBA}$? Explain." yes; It does not matter whether the major arc is named in a clockwise or counterclockwise direction.

Two arcs of the same circle are **adjacent arcs** when they intersect at exactly one point. You can add the measures of two adjacent arcs.

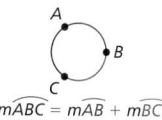 **Postulate**

Postulate 10.1 Arc Addition Postulate

The measure of an arc formed by two adjacent arcs is the sum of the measures of the two arcs.

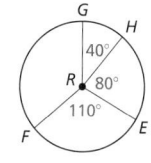

$$m\widehat{ABC} = m\widehat{AB} + m\widehat{BC}$$

EXAMPLE 2 Using the Arc Addition Postulate

Find the measure of each arc.

a. $\widehat{GE}$ b. $\widehat{GEF}$ c. $\widehat{GF}$

SOLUTION

a. $m\widehat{GE} = m\widehat{GH} + m\widehat{HE} = 40° + 80° = 120°$

b. $m\widehat{GEF} = m\widehat{GE} + m\widehat{EF} = 120° + 110° = 230°$

c. $m\widehat{GF} = 360° - m\widehat{GEF} = 360° - 230° = 130°$

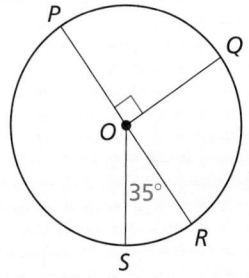

EXAMPLE 3 Finding Measures of Arcs

A recent survey asked teenagers whether they would rather meet a famous musician, athlete, actor, inventor, or other person. The circle graph shows the results. Find the indicated arc measures.

a. $m\widehat{AC}$ b. $m\widehat{ACD}$

c. $m\widehat{ADC}$ d. $m\widehat{EBD}$

Whom Would You Rather Meet?

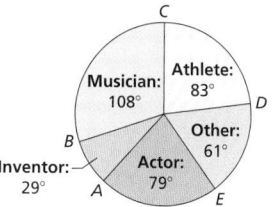

Musician: 108° Athlete: 83° Other: 61° Actor: 79° Inventor: 29°

SOLUTION

a. $m\widehat{AC} = m\widehat{AB} + m\widehat{BC}$
   $= 29° + 108°$
   $= 137°$

b. $m\widehat{ACD} = m\widehat{AC} + m\widehat{CD}$
   $= 137° + 83°$
   $= 220°$

c. $m\widehat{ADC} = 360° - m\widehat{AC}$
   $= 360° - 137°$
   $= 223°$

d. $m\widehat{EBD} = 360° - m\widehat{ED}$
   $= 360° - 61°$
   $= 299°$

Monitoring Progress Help in English and Spanish at *BigIdeasMath.com*

Identify the given arc as a *major arc*, *minor arc*, or *semicircle*. Then find the measure of the arc.

1. $\widehat{TQ}$ 2. $\widehat{QRT}$ 3. $\widehat{TQR}$

4. $\widehat{QS}$ 5. $\widehat{TS}$ 6. $\widehat{RST}$

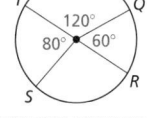

Section 10.2   Finding Arc Measures   **539**

Extra Example 2

Find the measure of each arc.

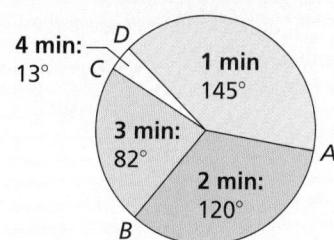

a. $\widehat{SQ}$ 125°

b. $\widehat{RPQ}$ 270°

c. $\widehat{PRS}$ 215°

Extra Example 3

A survey asked people how many minutes they spend brushing their teeth each morning. The circle graph shows the results. Find the indicated arc measures.

For How Long Did You Brush Your Teeth?

4 min: 13°   1 min: 145°   3 min: 82°   2 min: 120°

a. $m\widehat{ABC}$ 202°

b. $m\widehat{ACB}$ 240°

c. $m\widehat{BD}$ 95°

d. $m\widehat{CBD}$ 347°

MONITORING PROGRESS ANSWERS

1. minor arc; 120°
2. major arc; 240°
3. semicircle; 180°
4. minor arc; 160°
5. minor arc; 80°
6. semicircle; 180°

Laurie's Notes Teacher Actions

- **Connection:** The Arc Addition Postulate (Post. 10.1) is based on the Angle Addition Postulate (Post. 1.4) and how circular arcs are measured.
- It can be confusing for students when many points appear on a circle and naming an arc such as $\widehat{GE}$ in Example 2 does not include H. Explain that $\widehat{GE}$ and $\widehat{GHE}$ are the same arc. For simplicity and clarity, we use only the two letters in naming minor arc $\widehat{GE}$.
- Have partners work independently to solve Example 3, and then discuss as a class.

Extra Example 4

Tell whether the red arcs are congruent. Explain why or why not.

a.

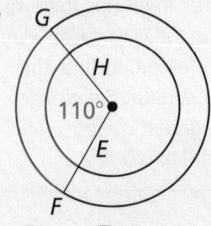

$\overarc{FG}$ and $\overarc{EH}$ are not congruent. They have the same measure, but they are arcs of circles that are not congruent.

b.

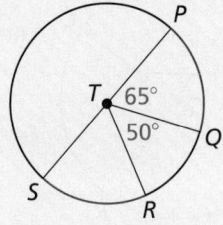

$\overarc{PQ} \cong \overarc{RS}$ by the Congruent Central Angles Theorem because they are arcs of the same circle and they have congruent central angles, $\angle PTQ \cong \angle RTS$.

c.

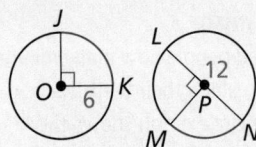

$\overarc{JK} \cong \overarc{MN}$ by the Congruent Central Angle Theorem because the arcs have congruent central angles of 90°. The circles are congruent because they both have radius 6.

Identifying Congruent Arcs

Two circles are **congruent circles** if and only if a rigid motion or a composition of rigid motions maps one circle onto the other. This statement is equivalent to the Congruent Circles Theorem below.

⟳ Theorem

Theorem 10.3   Congruent Circles Theorem

Two circles are congruent circles if and only if they have the same radius.

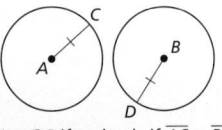

Proof Ex. 35, p. 544

$\odot A \cong \odot B$ if and only if $\overline{AC} \cong \overline{BD}$.

Two arcs are **congruent arcs** if and only if they have the same measure and they are arcs of the same circle or of congruent circles.

⟳ Theorem

Theorem 10.4   Congruent Central Angles Theorem

In the same circle, or in congruent circles, two minor arcs are congruent if and only if their corresponding central angles are congruent.

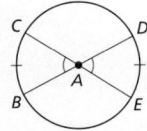

Proof Ex. 37, p. 544

$\overarc{BC} \cong \overarc{DE}$ if and only if $\angle BAC \cong \angle DAE$.

EXAMPLE 4   **Identifying Congruent Arcs**

Tell whether the red arcs are congruent. Explain why or why not.

a.

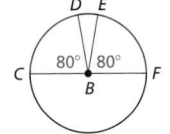

b.

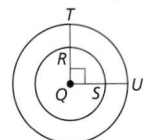

c.

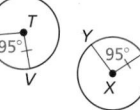

STUDY TIP

The two circles in part (c) are congruent by the Congruent Circles Theorem because they have the same radius.

SOLUTION

a. $\overarc{CD} \cong \overarc{EF}$ by the Congruent Central Angles Theorem because they are arcs of the same circle and they have congruent central angles, $\angle CBD \cong \angle FBE$.

b. $\overarc{RS}$ and $\overarc{TU}$ have the same measure, but are not congruent because they are arcs of circles that are not congruent.

c. $\overarc{UV} \cong \overarc{YZ}$ by the Congruent Central Angles Theorem because they are arcs of congruent circles and they have congruent central angles, $\angle UTV \cong \angle YXZ$.

Laurie's Notes   Teacher Actions

? "How would you define congruent arcs?"   Students will likely say that two arcs are congruent if their central angles are congruent.   They do not consider the size of the circle!

- An arc of 45° on noncongruent circles will have the same arc measure but not the same length. This naturally leads to the next question.

? "How would you define congruent circles?"   Congruent circles have the same radius.

- Remind students that congruence could also be defined in terms of rigid motions. An alternate approach is described in the *Teaching Strategy* on page T-568.

Monitoring Progress Help in English and Spanish at *BigIdeasMath.com*

Tell whether the red arcs are congruent. Explain why or why not.

7.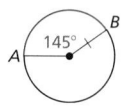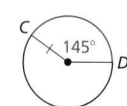

8.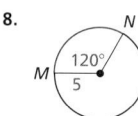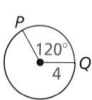

MONITORING PROGRESS ANSWERS

7. congruent; The circles are congruent and $m\widehat{AB} = m\widehat{CD}$.

8. not congruent; The circles are not congruent.

Proving Circles Are Similar

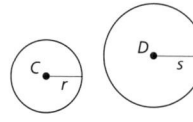 Theorem

> **Theorem 10.5   Similar Circles Theorem**
> All circles are similar.
> *Proof* p. 541; Ex. 33, p. 544

PROOF   **Similar Circles Theorem**

All circles are similar.

Given $\odot C$ with center C and radius r,
$\odot D$ with center D and radius s

Prove $\odot C \sim \odot D$

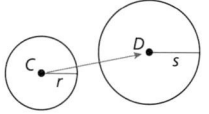 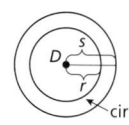

First, translate $\odot C$ so that point C maps to point D. The image of $\odot C$ is $\odot C'$ with center D. So, $\odot C'$ and $\odot D$ are concentric circles.

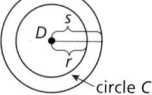 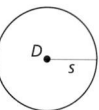

$\odot C'$ is the set of all points that are r units from point D. Dilate $\odot C'$ using center of dilation D and scale factor $\frac{s}{r}$.

This dilation maps the set of all the points that are r units from point D to the set of all points that are $\frac{s}{r}(r) = s$ units from point D. $\odot D$ is the set of all points that are s units from point D. So, this dilation maps $\odot C'$ to $\odot D$.

Because a similarity transformation maps $\odot C$ to $\odot D$, $\odot C \sim \odot D$.

Two arcs are **similar arcs** if and only if they have the same measure. All congruent arcs are similar, but not all similar arcs are congruent. For instance, in Example 4, the pairs of arcs in parts (a), (b), and (c) are similar but only the pairs of arcs in parts (a) and (c) are congruent.

Laurie's Notes   Teacher Actions

- Be sure students are comfortable with how congruent arcs and congruent radii are marked on a circle with a hash mark.
- **?** "How would you define similar circles?"   Students will pause on this question. Unlike polygons, there are no proportional sides and corresponding congruent angles.
- Work through the proof that all circles are similar. Discuss similar arcs.

Closure

- **Exit Ticket:** Phone a friend who was absent today and describe three key ideas from today's lesson.

Assignment Guide and Homework Check

ASSIGNMENT

Basic: 1, 2, 3–25 odd, 26, 27, 31, 36, 39–42

Average: 1, 2, 6–16 even, 17, 20–24 even, 25–27, 31, 32, 36, 39–42

Advanced: 1, 2, 6–18 even, 19–27, 30, 31, 34–42

HOMEWORK CHECK

Basic: 3, 13, 15, 17, 23

Average: 16, 17, 22, 24, 31

Advanced: 18, 22, 23, 35, 38

ANSWERS

1. congruent arcs
2. the one with diameter 6 in.; the others have diameter 12 in.
3. $\overarc{AB}$, 135°; $\overarc{ADB}$, 225°
4. $\overarc{EF}$, 68°; $\overarc{EGF}$, 292°
5. $\overarc{JL}$, 120°; $\overarc{JKL}$, 240°
6. $\overarc{MN}$, 170°; $\overarc{MPN}$, 190°
7. minor arc; 70°
8. minor arc; 65°
9. minor arc; 45°
10. minor arc; 70°
11. semicircle; 180°
12. semicircle; 180°
13. major arc; 290°
14. major arc; 315°
15. a. 132°
    b. 147°
    c. 200°
    d. 160°
16. a. 138°
    b. 180°
    c. 222°
    d. 138°
17. a. 103°
    b. 257°
    c. 196°
    d. 305°
    e. 79°
    f. 281°

Vocabulary and Core Concept Check

1. **VOCABULARY** Copy and complete: If ∠ACB and ∠DCE are congruent central angles of ⊙C, then $\overarc{AB}$ and $\overarc{DE}$ are _____.

2. **WHICH ONE DOESN'T BELONG?** Which circle does *not* belong with the other three? Explain your reasoning.

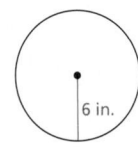 6 in. 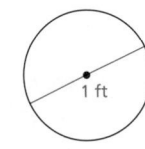 1 ft  12 in. 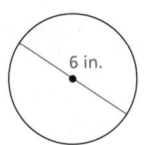 6 in.

Monitoring Progress and Modeling with Mathematics

In Exercises 3–6, name the red minor arc and find its measure. Then name the blue major arc and find its measure.

3.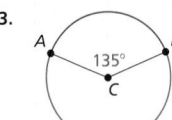

4.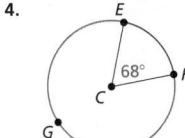

5.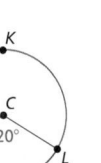

6.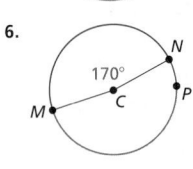

In Exercises 7–14, identify the given arc as a *major arc*, *minor arc*, or *semicircle*. Then find the measure of the arc. *(See Example 1.)*

7. $\overarc{BC}$ 8. $\overarc{DC}$

9. $\overarc{ED}$ 10. $\overarc{AE}$

11. $\overarc{EAB}$

12. $\overarc{ABC}$

13. $\overarc{BAC}$

14. $\overarc{EBD}$

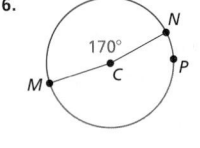

In Exercises 15 and 16, find the measure of each arc. *(See Example 2.)*

15. a. $\overarc{JL}$
    b. $\overarc{KM}$
    c. $\overarc{JLM}$
    d. $\overarc{JM}$

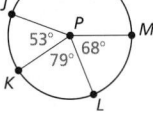

16. a. $\overarc{RS}$
    b. $\overarc{QRS}$
    c. $\overarc{QST}$
    d. $\overarc{QT}$

17. **MODELING WITH MATHEMATICS** A recent survey asked high school students their favorite type of music. The results are shown in the circle graph. Find each indicated arc measure. *(See Example 3.)*

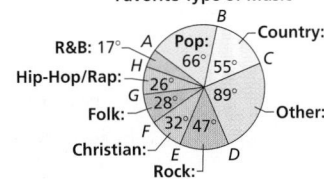

Favorite Type of Music

a. $m\overarc{AE}$ b. $m\overarc{ACE}$ c. $m\overarc{GDC}$

d. $m\overarc{BHC}$ e. $m\overarc{FD}$ f. $m\overarc{FBD}$

18. **ABSTRACT REASONING** The circle graph shows the percentages of students enrolled in fall sports at a high school. Is it possible to find the measure of each minor arc? If so, find the measure of the arc for each category shown. If not, explain why it is not possible.

High School Fall Sports

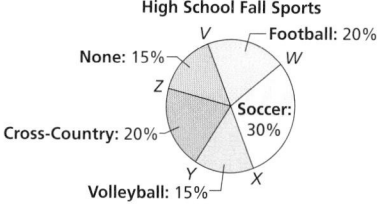

In Exercises 19–22, tell whether the red arcs are congruent. Explain why or why not. *(See Example 4.)*

19.
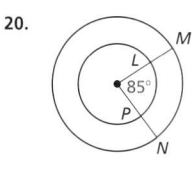

20.

21.
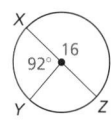

22.
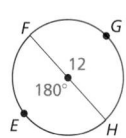

MATHEMATICAL CONNECTIONS In Exercises 23 and 24, find the value of *x*. Then find the measure of the red arc.

23.
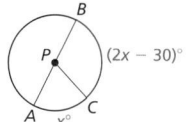

24.

25. **MAKING AN ARGUMENT** Your friend claims that any two arcs with the same measure are similar. Your cousin claims that any two arcs with the same measure are congruent. Who is correct? Explain.

26. **MAKING AN ARGUMENT** Your friend claims that there is not enough information given to find the value of *x*. Is your friend correct? Explain your reasoning.

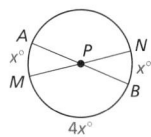

27. **ERROR ANALYSIS** Describe and correct the error in naming the red arc.

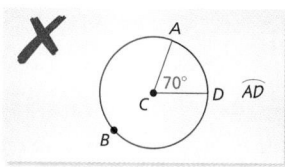

28. **ERROR ANALYSIS** Describe and correct the error in naming congruent arcs.

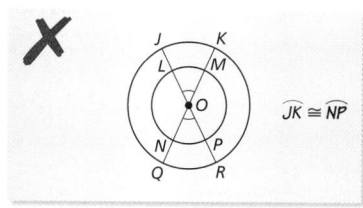

29. **ATTENDING TO PRECISION** Two diameters of ⊙*P* are $\overline{AB}$ and $\overline{CD}$. Find $m\widehat{ACD}$ and $m\widehat{AC}$ when $m\widehat{AD} = 20°$.

30. **REASONING** In ⊙*R*, $m\widehat{AB} = 60°$, $m\widehat{BC} = 25°$, $m\widehat{CD} = 70°$, and $m\widehat{DE} = 20°$. Find two possible measures of $\widehat{AE}$.

31. **MODELING WITH MATHEMATICS** On a regulation dartboard, the outermost circle is divided into twenty congruent sections. What is the measure of each arc in this circle?

ANSWERS

18. yes; $\widehat{WX} = 108°$, $\widehat{XY} = 54°$, $\widehat{YZ} = 72°$, $\widehat{ZV} = 54°$, $\widehat{VW} = 72°$

19. congruent; They are in the same circle and $m\widehat{AB} = m\widehat{CD}$.

20. not congruent; The circles are not congruent.

21. congruent; The circles are congruent and $m\widehat{VW} = m\widehat{XY}$.

22. not congruent; The circles are not congruent.

23. 70; 110°

24. 15; 195°

25. your friend; The arcs must be in the same circle or congruent circles.

26. no; $\widehat{AMB}$ is a semicircle, so $x + 4x = 180$.

27. $\widehat{AD}$ is the minor arc; $\widehat{ABD}$

28. $\widehat{JK}$ and $\widehat{NP}$ are not in the same circle; $\widehat{JK} \cong \widehat{RQ}$ or $\widehat{LM} \cong \widehat{NP}$

29. 340°; 160°

30. *Sample answer:* 175°, 135°

31. 18°

32. **a.** 15°

  b. 90°

  c. 3 A.M.

33. Translate ⊙A left a units so that point A maps to point O. The image of ⊙A is ⊙A' with center O, so ⊙A' and ⊙O are concentric circles. Dilate ⊙A' using center of dilation O and scale factor $\frac{r}{s}$, which maps the points s units from point O to the points $\frac{r}{s}(s) = r$ units from point O. So, this dilation maps ⊙A' to ⊙O. Because a similarity transformation maps ⊙A to ⊙O, ⊙$O \sim$ ⊙A.

34. yes; Both radii are $\overline{CD}$.

35–38. See Additional Answers.

39. 15; yes

40. about 18.38; no

41. about 13.04; no

42. about 9.80; no

Mini-Assessment

Use ⊙O, where $\overline{AD}$ is a diameter.

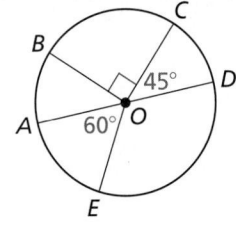

1. Name a semicircle. *Sample answer:* $\overarc{ABD}$, $\overarc{ACD}$ or $\overarc{AED}$

2. Find $m\overarc{AC}$. 135°

3. Find $m\overarc{DAE}$. 240°

4. Tell whether $\overarc{DB}$ and $\overarc{ED}$ are congruent. Explain why or why not. $\overarc{DB}$ and $\overarc{ED}$ are not congruent. They are arcs of the same circle, but $m\angle DOB = 45° + 90° = 135°$ and $m\angle EOD = 180° - 60° = 120°$. So, the corresponding central angles are not congruent.

5. Tell whether $\overarc{AB}$ and $\overarc{CD}$ are congruent. Explain why or why not. $\overarc{AB} \cong \overarc{CD}$ because they are arcs of the same circle with congruent central angles, $\angle AOB \cong \angle COD$.

---

32. **MODELING WITH MATHEMATICS** You can use the time zone wheel to find the time in different locations across the world. For example, to find the time in Tokyo when it is 4 P.M. in San Francisco, rotate the small wheel until 4 P.M. and San Francisco line up, as shown. Then look at Tokyo to see that it is 9 A.M. there.

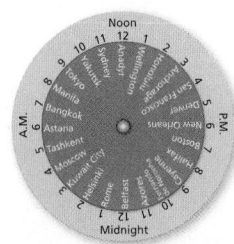

  a. What is the arc measure between each time zone on the wheel?

  b. What is the measure of the minor arc from the Tokyo zone to the Anchorage zone?

  c. If two locations differ by 180° on the wheel, then it is 3 P.M. at one location when it is _____ at the other location.

33. **PROVING A THEOREM** Write a coordinate proof of the Similar Circles Theorem (Theorem 10.5).

  Given ⊙O with center $O(0, 0)$ and radius r,
  ⊙A with center $A(a, 0)$ and radius s

  Prove ⊙$O \sim$ ⊙A

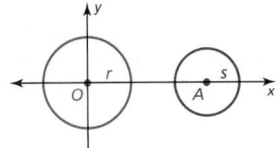

Maintaining Mathematical Proficiency
Reviewing what you learned in previous grades and lessons

Find the value of x. Tell whether the side lengths form a Pythagorean triple. *(Section 9.1)*

39.
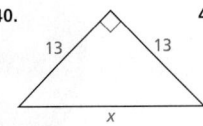

40.
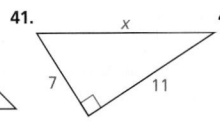

41.
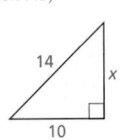

42.

34. **ABSTRACT REASONING** Is there enough information to tell whether ⊙$C \cong$ ⊙D? Explain your reasoning.

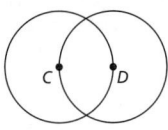

35. **PROVING A THEOREM** Use the diagram on page 540 to prove each part of the biconditional in the Congruent Circles Theorem (Theorem 10.3).

  a. **Given** $\overline{AC} \cong \overline{BD}$
  Prove ⊙$A \cong$ ⊙B

  b. **Given** ⊙$A \cong$ ⊙B
  Prove $\overline{AC} \cong \overline{BD}$

36. **HOW DO YOU SEE IT?** Are the circles on the target *similar* or *congruent*? Explain your reasoning.

37. **PROVING A THEOREM** Use the diagram to prove each part of the biconditional in the Congruent Central Angles Theorem (Theorem 10.4).

  a. **Given** $\angle BAC \cong \angle DAE$
  Prove $\overarc{BC} \cong \overarc{DE}$

  b. **Given** $\overarc{BC} \cong \overarc{DE}$
  Prove $\angle BAC \cong \angle DAE$

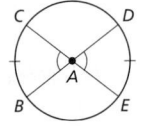

38. **THOUGHT PROVOKING** Write a formula for the length of a circular arc. Justify your answer.

If students need help...	If students got it...
Resources by Chapter • Practice A and Practice B • Puzzle Time	Resources by Chapter • Enrichment and Extension • Cumulative Review
Student Journal • Practice	Start the *next* Section
Differentiating the Lesson Skills Review Handbook	

Overview of Section 10.3

Introduction

- This lesson builds upon the language and circle concepts from the beginning of the chapter, and it also integrates prior skills such as working with perpendicular bisectors and the Pythagorean Theorem.
- The goal of the lesson is to determine whether two chords in a circle are congruent. If the chords are congruent, then there are other relationships that will be true.

Teaching Strategy

- Use the *Motivate* to launch the lesson. It is a classic application of the theorems in this lesson.
- Archeologists, forensic scientists, and tradesmen who have a portion of a circular object use the theorems in this lesson to determine something about the original size of the object.
- Make a handout with a sketch of the broken plate on it. As the closure for today's lesson, have students perform constructs to locate the center of the circle. Measure to determine the diameter of the circle.

Applications

- Finding a point that is equidistant from three (noncollinear) fixed points is fairly common. Where does a business locate a warehouse when it wants to be equidistant from its three stores? Where should three friends meet when you want everyone to travel the same distance from their house? Where do you locate a cell tower when you want to provide service to three locations?

Pacing Suggestion

- The formal lesson is fairly short. Through the explorations, students discover the relationship between the diameter of a circle and chords that intersect a diameter. The Perpendicular Chord Bisector Theorem (Thm. 10.7) and the Perpendicular Chord Bisector Converse (Thm. 10.8) will make sense to students.

Dynamic Teaching Tools

Dynamic Assessment & Progress Monitoring Tool
Lesson Planning Tool
Interactive Whiteboard Lesson Library
Dynamic Classroom with Dynamic Investigations

Common Core State Standards

HSG-C.A.2 Identify and describe relationships among inscribed angles, radii, and chords.

HSG-MG.A.3 Apply geometric methods to solve design problems (e.g., designing an object or structure to satisfy physical constraints or minimize cost; working with typographic grid systems based on ratios).

Laurie's Notes

Exploration

Motivate

- If possible, bring a piece of a broken dinner plate that has a portion of the edge remaining. If you have never broken a plate and saved a shattered piece, then you could instead tear a paper plate and make believe!
- If you are a storyteller, give details of the event that led up to the breaking of the plate. My (fictional) story was a dinner party at the new neighbor's house. I offered to help clear the table, and my heel caught on the carpet. The hostess's dress was hit with flying leftovers, and the plate that I was carrying broke. After apologizing profusely, I asked whether I could take part of the plate home. Then I display the broken piece of china.
- **?** "What was the diameter of the plate?" Give time for students to stop laughing and to consider the question. Students generally have a few ideas for estimating the diameter.
- Explain to students that in this lesson they will discover a method for locating the center of a circle.

Exploration Note

- **?** You might begin these explorations by asking something such as, "Is every chord a diameter?" no "Is every diameter a chord?" yes
- If dynamic geometry software is not available, students could still perform the constructions with a protractor and straightedge. Gathering results from classmates may be sufficient to make a conjecture about the problem posed.

Exploration 1

- This exploration serves to remind students that the diameter passes through the center of the circle—in this case, the origin.

Exploration 2

- **MP3 Construct Viable Arguments and Critique the Reasoning of Others:** Students need to use more than eyesight to state that the chord on the perpendicular bisector of chord $\overline{BC}$ passes through the center of the circle and therefore is a diameter.
- **?** "How do you know the perpendicular bisector of chord $\overline{BC}$ passes through A, besides the fact that it looks like it does?" One way students might prove the perpendicular bisector of chord $\overline{BC}$ passes through A is to construct a perpendicular through A to the chord. Are the two lines the same? On most software, the equations of these lines are displayed and the equations will be the same.
- **MP3:** Have students state their conjectures and explain their reasoning. Discuss.

Exploration 3

- Be sure that students investigate for different length chords.
- Students should discover that if a diameter of a circle is perpendicular to a chord of the circle, then the diameter bisects the chord.
- **MP3:** Have students state their conjectures and explain their reasoning. Discuss.

Communicate Your Answer

- The conjectures made by students are two ways to show that a chord is a diameter of a circle.

Connecting to Next Step

- The explorations allow students to discover two of the theorems in today's lesson.

Essential Question

What are two ways to determine when a chord is a diameter of a circle?

EXPLORATION 1 Drawing Diameters

Work with a partner. Use dynamic geometry software to construct a circle of radius 5 with center at the origin. Draw a diameter that has the given point as an endpoint. Explain how you know that the chord you drew is a diameter.

a. $(4, 3)$ b. $(0, 5)$ c. $(-3, 4)$ d. $(-5, 0)$

LOOKING FOR STRUCTURE

To be proficient in math, you need to look closely to discern a pattern or structure.

EXPLORATION 2 Writing a Conjecture about Chords

Work with a partner. Use dynamic geometry software to construct a chord $\overline{BC}$ of a circle A. Construct a chord on the perpendicular bisector of $\overline{BC}$. What do you notice? Change the original chord and the circle several times. Are your results always the same? Use your results to write a conjecture.

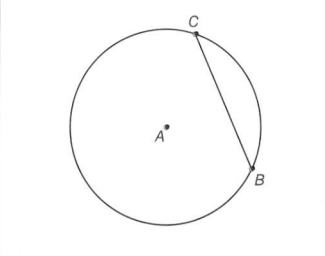

EXPLORATION 3 A Chord Perpendicular to a Diameter

Work with a partner. Use dynamic geometry software to construct a diameter $\overline{BC}$ of a circle A. Then construct a chord $\overline{DE}$ perpendicular to $\overline{BC}$ at point F. Find the lengths DF and EF. What do you notice? Change the chord perpendicular to $\overline{BC}$ and the circle several times. Do you always get the same results? Write a conjecture about a chord that is perpendicular to a diameter of a circle.

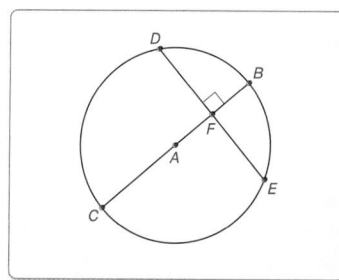

Communicate Your Answer

4. What are two ways to determine when a chord is a diameter of a circle?

Section 10.3 Using Chords **545**

ANSWERS

1. **a.**

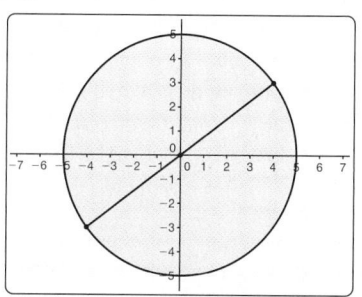

It passes through the center.

b.

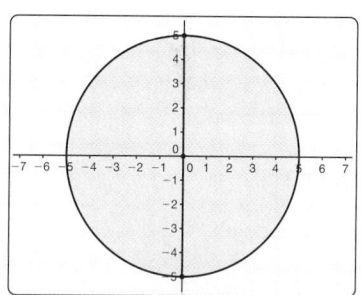

It passes through the center.

c.

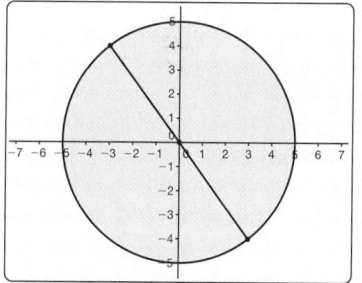

It passes through the center.

d.

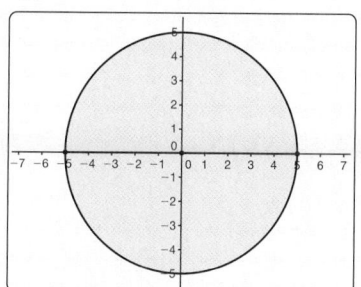

It passes through the center.

2. Check students' work; The perpendicular bisector is a diameter; yes; A perpendicular bisector of a chord is a diameter of the circle.

3. Check students' work; $DF = EF$; yes; If a chord is perpendicular to a diameter of a circle, then the diameter is a perpendicular bisector of the chord.

4. when it is a perpendicular bisector of a chord or passes through the center of the circle

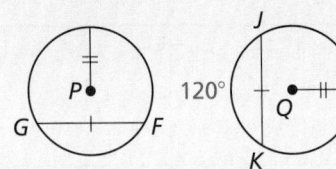
10.3 Lesson

What You Will Learn

▶ Use chords of circles to find lengths and arc measures.

Core Vocabulary

Previous
chord
arc
diameter

Using Chords of Circles

Recall that a *chord* is a segment with endpoints on a circle. Because its endpoints lie on the circle, any chord divides the circle into two arcs. A diameter divides a circle into two semicircles. Any other chord divides a circle into a minor arc and a major arc.

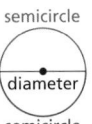

READING

If $\overset{\frown}{GD} \cong \overset{\frown}{GF}$, then the point G, and any line, segment, or ray that contains G, *bisects* $\overline{FD}$.

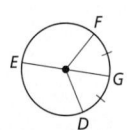

$\overline{EG}$ bisects $\overline{FD}$.

Theorems

Theorem 10.6   Congruent Corresponding Chords Theorem

In the same circle, or in congruent circles, two minor arcs are congruent if and only if their corresponding chords are congruent.

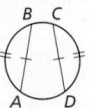

Proof Ex. 19, p. 550

$\overset{\frown}{AB} \cong \overset{\frown}{CD}$ if and only if $\overline{AB} \cong \overline{CD}$.

Theorem 10.7   Perpendicular Chord Bisector Theorem

If a diameter of a circle is perpendicular to a chord, then the diameter bisects the chord and its arc.

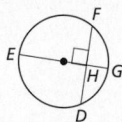

Proof Ex. 22, p. 550

If $\overline{EG}$ is a diameter and $\overline{EG} \perp \overline{DF}$, then $\overline{HD} \cong \overline{HF}$ and $\overset{\frown}{GD} \cong \overset{\frown}{GF}$.

Theorem 10.8   Perpendicular Chord Bisector Converse

If one chord of a circle is a perpendicular bisector of another chord, then the first chord is a diameter.

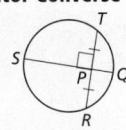

Proof Ex. 23, p. 550

If $\overline{QS}$ is a perpendicular bisector of $\overline{TR}$, then $\overline{QS}$ is a diameter of the circle.

EXAMPLE 1   Using Congruent Chords to Find an Arc Measure

In the diagram, $\odot P \cong \odot Q$, $\overline{FG} \cong \overline{JK}$, and $m\overset{\frown}{JK} = 80°$. Find $m\overset{\frown}{FG}$.

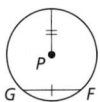
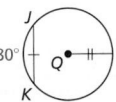

SOLUTION

Because $\overline{FG}$ and $\overline{JK}$ are congruent chords in congruent circles, the corresponding minor arcs $\overset{\frown}{FG}$ and $\overset{\frown}{JK}$ are congruent by the Congruent Corresponding Chords Theorem.

▶ So, $m\overset{\frown}{FG} = m\overset{\frown}{JK} = 80°$.

EXAMPLE 2 **Using a Diameter**

a. Find *HK*.   b. Find $m\widehat{HK}$.

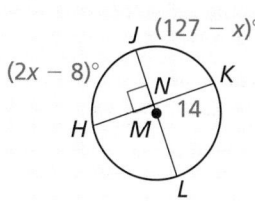

SOLUTION

a. Diameter $\overline{JL}$ is perpendicular to $\overline{HK}$. So, by the Perpendicular Chord Bisector Theorem, $\overline{JL}$ bisects $\overline{HK}$, and *HN = NK*.

▶ So, *HK* = 2(*NK*) = 2(7) = 14.

b. Diameter $\overline{JL}$ is perpendicular to $\overline{HK}$. So, by the Perpendicular Chord Bisector Theorem, $\overline{JL}$ bisects $\widehat{HK}$, and $m\widehat{HJ} = m\widehat{JK}$.

$m\widehat{HJ} = m\widehat{JK}$	Perpendicular Chord Bisector Theorem
$11x° = (70 + x)°$	Substitute.
$10x = 70$	Subtract *x* from each side.
$x = 7$	Divide each side by 10.

▶ So, $m\widehat{HJ} = m\widehat{JK} = (70 + x)° = (70 + 7)° = 77°$, and $m\widehat{HK} = 2(m\widehat{HJ}) = 2(77°) = 154°$.

EXAMPLE 3 **Using Perpendicular Bisectors**

Three bushes are arranged in a garden, as shown. Where should you place a sprinkler so that it is the same distance from each bush?

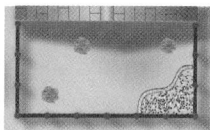

SOLUTION

Step 1   **Step 2**   **Step 3**

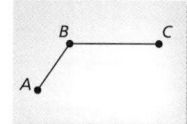   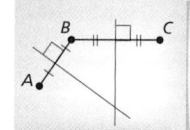   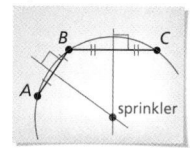

Label the bushes *A*, *B*, and *C*, as shown. Draw segments $\overline{AB}$ and $\overline{BC}$.

Draw the perpendicular bisectors of $\overline{AB}$ and $\overline{BC}$. By the Perpendicular Chord Bisector Converse, these lie on diameters of the circle containing *A*, *B*, and *C*.

Find the point where the perpendicular bisectors intersect. This is the center of the circle, which is equidistant from points *A*, *B*, and *C*.

Monitoring Progress 🔊 Help in English and Spanish at *BigIdeasMath.com*

In Exercises 1 and 2, use the diagram of ⊙*D*.

1. If $m\widehat{AB} = 110°$, find $m\widehat{BC}$.

2. If $m\widehat{AC} = 150°$, find $m\widehat{AB}$.

In Exercises 3 and 4, find the indicated length or arc measure.

3. *CE*

4. $m\widehat{CE}$

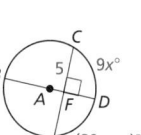

Extra Example 2

a. Find *KH*. 28

b. Find $m\widehat{HLK}$. 196°

Extra Example 3

A telephone company plans to install a cell tower that is the same distance from the centers of three towns, labeled *P*, *Q*, and *R*. Where should the cell tower be placed?

Q
P
R

The tower should be placed at point *T*, where the perpendicular bisectors of $\overline{PQ}$ and $\overline{QR}$ intersect.

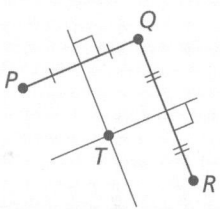

MONITORING PROGRESS ANSWERS

1. 110°

2. 105°

3. 10

4. 144°

Laurie's Notes   Teacher Actions

- **Think-Pair-Share:** Pose Example 2. Students should have little difficulty with either question.
- **Turn and Talk:** Sketch the garden and bushes in Example 3. "There are three bushes in the garden. Where should you place the sprinkler so that it is equidistant to all three bushes?"
- **Wait Time:** Solicit ideas from different partners.
- ❓ **MP4 Model with Mathematics:** "Can you think of other real-life applications similar to Example 3?" See the *Applications* on page T-544.

Extra Example 4

In the diagram, $EP = EQ = 12$, $CD = 5x + 7$, and $AB = 7x - 3$. Find the radius of $\odot E$.

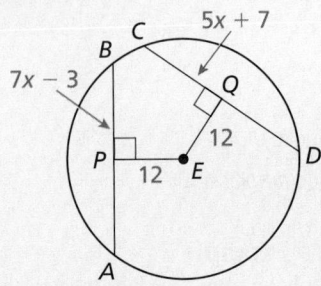

The radius is 20 units.

MONITORING PROGRESS ANSWER

5. 15

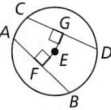
Theorem 10.9 Equidistant Chords Theorem

In the same circle, or in congruent circles, two chords are congruent if and only if they are equidistant from the center.

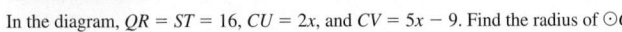

Proof Ex. 25, p. 550

$\overline{AB} \cong \overline{CD}$ if and only if $EF = EG$.

EXAMPLE 4   **Using Congruent Chords to Find a Circle's Radius**

In the diagram, $QR = ST = 16$, $CU = 2x$, and $CV = 5x - 9$. Find the radius of $\odot C$.

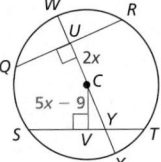

SOLUTION

Because $\overline{CQ}$ is a segment whose endpoints are the center and a point on the circle, it is a radius of $\odot C$. Because $\overline{CU} \perp \overline{QR}$, $\triangle QUC$ is a right triangle. Apply properties of chords to find the lengths of the legs of $\triangle QUC$.

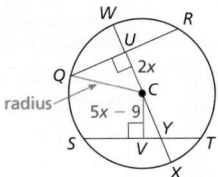

Step 1 Find CU.

Because $\overline{QR}$ and $\overline{ST}$ are congruent chords, $\overline{QR}$ and $\overline{ST}$ are equidistant from C by the Equidistant Chords Theorem. So, $CU = CV$.

$CU = CV$	Equidistant Chords Theorem
$2x = 5x - 9$	Substitute.
$x = 3$	Solve for x.

So, $CU = 2x = 2(3) = 6$.

Step 2 Find QU.

Because diameter $\overline{WX} \perp \overline{QR}$, $\overline{WX}$ bisects $\overline{QR}$ by the Perpendicular Chord Bisector Theorem.

So, $QU = \frac{1}{2}(16) = 8$.

Step 3 Find CQ.

Because the lengths of the legs are $CU = 6$ and $QU = 8$, $\triangle QUC$ is a right triangle with the Pythagorean triple 6, 8, 10. So, $CQ = 10$.

▶ So, the radius of $\odot C$ is 10 units.

Monitoring Progress 🔊 Help in English and Spanish at *BigIdeasMath.com*

5. In the diagram, $JK = LM = 24$, $NP = 3x$, and $NQ = 7x - 12$. Find the radius of $\odot N$.

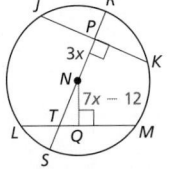

Laurie's Notes   Teacher Actions

- State the Equidistant Chords Theorem (Thm. 10.9), and ask students to compare and contrast it with the Congruent Corresponding Chords Theorem (Thm. 10.6). Both theorems are about congruent chords. One involves the intercepted minor arcs, while the other looks at distances to the center of a circle.

COMMON ERROR In Example 4, students often stop after they have solved for *x*. They need to finish the problem by finding the radius of the circle.

Closure

- Have students determine the diameter of the broken plate from the *Motivate*. See the *Teaching Strategy* on page T-544.

Vocabulary and Core Concept Check

1. **WRITING** Describe what it means to bisect a chord.

2. **WRITING** Two chords of a circle are perpendicular and congruent. Does one of them have to be a diameter? Explain your reasoning.

Monitoring Progress and Modeling with Mathematics

In Exercises 3–6, find the measure of the red arc or chord in ⊙C. *(See Example 1.)*

3.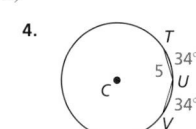

4.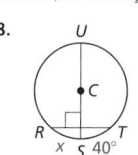

5.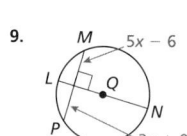

6.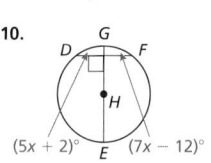

In Exercises 7–10, find the value of *x*. *(See Example 2.)*

7. 8.

9. 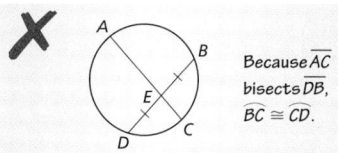 10.

11. **ERROR ANALYSIS** Describe and correct the error in reasoning.

> ✗ Because $\overline{AC}$ bisects $\overline{DB}$, $\overset{\frown}{BC} \cong \overset{\frown}{CD}$.

12. **PROBLEM SOLVING** In the cross section of the submarine shown, the control panels are parallel and the same length. Describe a method you can use to find the center of the cross section. Justify your method. *(See Example 3.)*

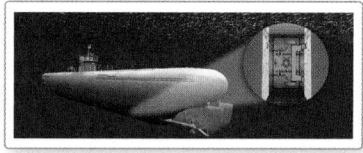

In Exercises 13 and 14, determine whether $\overline{AB}$ is a diameter of the circle. Explain your reasoning.

13. 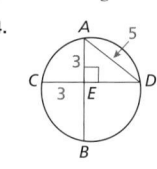 14.

In Exercises 15 and 16, find the radius of ⊙Q. *(See Example 4.)*

15. 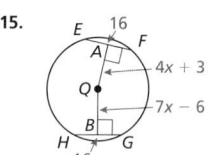 16.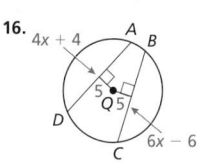

17. **PROBLEM SOLVING** An archaeologist finds part of a circular plate. What was the diameter of the plate to the nearest tenth of an inch? Justify your answer.

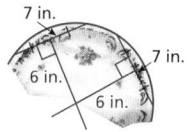

Section 10.3   Using Chords   **549**

ASSIGNMENT

Basic: 1, 2, 3–17 odd, 18, 26–28

Average: 1, 2, 6–10 even, 11, 12–22 even, 26–28

Advanced: 1, 2, 6, 10–22, 24, 26–28

HOMEWORK CHECK

Basic: 3, 7, 13, 15, 18

Average: 10, 14, 16, 18, 22

Advanced: 14, 16, 18, 22, 24

ANSWERS

1. Split the chord into two segments of equal length.

2. no; One chord does not necessarily bisect the other.

3. 75°

4. 5

5. 170°

6. 11

7. 8

8. 40°

9. 5

10. 7

11. $\overline{AC}$ and $\overline{DB}$ are not perpendicular; $\overset{\frown}{BC}$ is not congruent to $\overset{\frown}{CD}$.

12. *Sample answer:* Draw the perpendicular bisector of the control panels and find the midpoint; Because the control panels are parallel and congruent chords of the cross section, they are equal distances from the center, and their perpendicular bisectors form a diameter.

13. yes; The triangles are congruent, so $\overline{AB}$ is a perpendicular bisector of $\overline{CD}$.

14. no; $CE \neq ED$

15. 17

16. 13

17. about 13.9 in.; The perpendicular bisectors intersect at the center, so the right triangle with legs of 6 inches and 3.5 inches have a hypotenuse equal to the length of the radius.

Dynamic Teaching Tools

Dynamic Assessment & Progress Monitoring Tool

Interactive Whiteboard Lesson Library

Dynamic Classroom with Dynamic Investigations

ANSWERS

18–25. See Additional Answers.

26. yes; The diameter of the tire that is perpendicular to the ground is also perpendicular to $\overline{AB}$, so it bisects $\overarc{AB}$.

27. 259°

28. 122°

Mini-Assessment

The circle has center P.

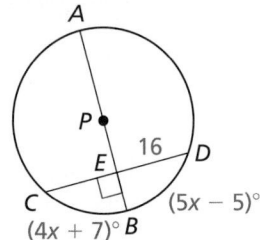

1. Find the value of x. **12**

2. Find CD. **32**

3. The circle has center O. Find AB.

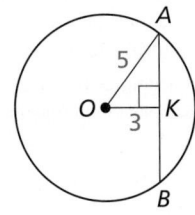

$AB = 8$

4. Q is the center of the circle. $CD = AB = 24$, $QM = x + 3$, and $QN = 2x + 1$. Find the radius of $\odot Q$.

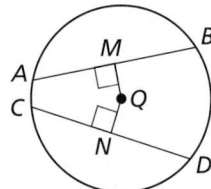

13 units

550 **Chapter 10**

---

18. **HOW DO YOU SEE IT?** What can you conclude from each diagram? Name a theorem that justifies your answer.

a.
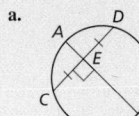

b.
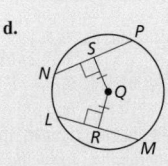

c. & d.
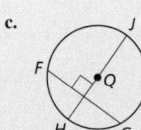

19. **PROVING A THEOREM** Use the diagram to prove each part of the biconditional in the Congruent Corresponding Chords Theorem (Theorem 10.6).

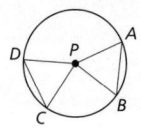

a. **Given** $\overline{AB}$ and $\overline{CD}$ are congruent chords.
   Prove $\overarc{AB} \cong \overarc{CD}$

b. **Given** $\overarc{AB} \cong \overarc{CD}$
   Prove $\overline{AB} \cong \overline{CD}$

20. **MATHEMATICAL CONNECTIONS** In $\odot P$, all the arcs shown have integer measures. Show that x must be even.

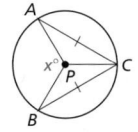

21. **REASONING** In $\odot P$, the lengths of the parallel chords are 20, 16, and 12. Find $m\overarc{AB}$. Explain your reasoning.

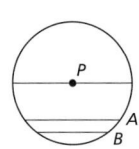

---

22. **PROVING A THEOREM** Use congruent triangles to prove the Perpendicular Chord Bisector Theorem (Theorem 10.7).

Given $\overline{EG}$ is a diameter of $\odot L$. $\overline{EG} \perp \overline{DF}$

Prove $\overline{DC} \cong \overline{FC}$, $\overarc{DG} \cong \overarc{FG}$

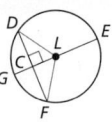

23. **PROVING A THEOREM** Write a proof of the Perpendicular Chord Bisector Converse (Theorem 10.8).

Given $\overline{QS}$ is a perpendicular bisector of $\overline{RT}$.

Prove $\overline{QS}$ is a diameter of the circle L.

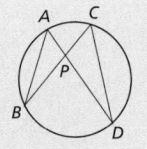

(*Hint*: Plot the center L and draw $\triangle LPT$ and $\triangle LPR$.)

24. **THOUGHT PROVOKING** Consider two chords that intersect at point P. Do you think that $\dfrac{AP}{BP} = \dfrac{CP}{DP}$? Justify your answer.

25. **PROVING A THEOREM** Use the diagram with the Equidistant Chords Theorem (Theorem 10.9) on page 548 to prove both parts of the biconditional of this theorem.

26. **MAKING AN ARGUMENT** A car is designed so that the rear wheel is only partially visible below the body of the car. The bottom edge of the panel is parallel to the ground. Your friend claims that the point where the tire touches the ground bisects $\overarc{AB}$. Is your friend correct? Explain your reasoning.

Maintaining Mathematical Proficiency

Reviewing what you learned in previous grades and lessons

Find the missing interior angle measure. (*Section 7.1*)

27. Quadrilateral $JKLM$ has angle measures $m\angle J = 32°$, $m\angle K = 25°$, and $m\angle L = 44°$. Find $m\angle M$.

28. Pentagon $PQRST$ has angle measures $m\angle P = 85°$, $m\angle Q = 134°$, $m\angle R = 97°$, and $m\angle S = 102°$. Find $m\angle T$.

550 **Chapter 10** Circles

If students need help...	If students got it...
Resources by Chapter • Practice A and Practice B • Puzzle Time	Resources by Chapter • Enrichment and Extension • Cumulative Review
Student Journal • Practice	Start the *next* Section
Differentiating the Lesson Skills Review Handbook	

Core Vocabulary

circle, *p. 530*
center, *p. 530*
radius, *p. 530*
chord, *p. 530*
diameter, *p. 530*
secant, *p. 530*
tangent, *p. 530*

point of tangency, *p. 530*
tangent circles, *p. 531*
concentric circles, *p. 531*
common tangent, *p. 531*
central angle, *p. 538*
minor arc, *p. 538*
major arc, *p. 538*

semicircle, *p. 538*
measure of a minor arc, *p. 538*
measure of a major arc, *p. 538*
adjacent arcs, *p. 539*
congruent circles, *p. 540*
congruent arcs, *p. 540*
similar arcs, *p. 541*

Core Concepts

Section 10.1

Lines and Segments That Intersect Circles, *p. 530*
Coplanar Circles and Common Tangents, *p. 531*
Theorem 10.1 Tangent Line to Circle Theorem, *p. 532*

Theorem 10.2 External Tangent Congruence Theorem,
 p. 532

Section 10.2

Measuring Arcs, *p. 538*
Postulate 10.1 Arc Addition Postulate, *p. 539*
Theorem 10.3 Congruent Circles Theorem, *p. 540*

Theorem 10.4 Congruent Central Angles Theorem,
 p. 540
Theorem 10.5 Similar Circles Theorem, *p. 541*

Section 10.3

Theorem 10.6 Congruent Corresponding Chords
 Theorem, *p. 546*
Theorem 10.7 Perpendicular Chord Bisector
 Theorem, *p. 546*

Theorem 10.8 Perpendicular Chord Bisector Converse,
 p. 546
Theorem 10.9 Equidistant Chords Theorem, *p. 548*

Mathematical Practices

1. Explain how separating quadrilateral *TVWX* into several segments helped you solve
   Exercise 37 on page 535.

2. In Exercise 30 on page 543, what two cases did you consider to reach your answers?
   Are there any other cases? Explain your reasoning.

3. Explain how you used inductive reasoning to solve Exercise 24 on page 550.

551

ANSWERS

1. *Sample answer:* The External
   Tangent Congruency Theorem
   (Thm. 10.2) could be used.

2. None of the arcs overlapped at more
   than one point, and point *E* was on
   $\overparen{CD}$; yes; *Sample answer:* Point *C*
   could be on $\overparen{AB}$.

3. A general conclusion was reached
   from several specific cases.

ANSWERS

1. ⊙P
2. *Sample answer:* $\overline{PK}$
3. $\overrightarrow{NK}$
4. *Sample answer:* $\overline{JL}$
5. $\overleftrightarrow{QS}$
6. $\overleftrightarrow{QM}$
7. 8
8. 7
9. minor arc; 144°
10. minor arc; 43°
11. minor arc; 110°
12. semicircle; 180°
13. major arc; 216°
14. major arc; 317°
15. congruent; They are in the same circle and $m\widehat{JM} = m\widehat{KL}$.
16. not congruent; The circles are not congruent.
17. 100°
18. 17
19. **a.** 30°
    b. 150°
    c. *Sample answer:* 5:00

10.1–10.3   Quiz

In Exercises 1–6, use the diagram. *(Section 10.1)*

1. Name the circle.
2. Name a radius.
3. Name a diameter.
4. Name a chord.
5. Name a secant.
6. Name a tangent.

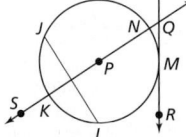

Find the value of *x*. *(Section 10.1)*

7.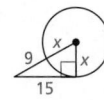
8.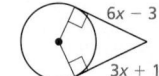

Identify the given arc as a *major arc*, *minor arc*, or *semicircle*. Then find the measure of the arc. *(Section 10.2)*

9. $\widehat{AE}$
10. $\widehat{BC}$
11. $\widehat{AC}$
12. $\widehat{ACD}$
13. $\widehat{ACE}$
14. $\widehat{BEC}$

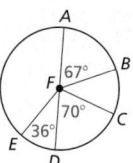

Tell whether the red arcs are congruent. Explain why or why not. *(Section 10.2)*

15.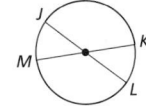
16.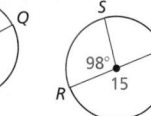

17. Find the measure of the red arc in ⊙Q. *(Section 10.3)*

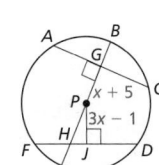

18. In the diagram, $AC = FD = 30$, $PG = x + 5$, and $PJ = 3x - 1$. Find the radius of ⊙P. *(Section 10.3)*

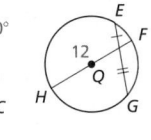

19. A circular clock can be divided into 12 congruent sections. *(Section 10.2)*
    a. Find the measure of each arc in this circle.
    b. Find the measure of the minor arc formed by the hour and minute hands when the time is 7:00.
    c. Find a time at which the hour and minute hands form an arc that is congruent to the arc in part (b).

552   Chapter 10   Circles

552   Chapter 10

Overview of Section 10.4

Introduction
- This lesson introduces the language and properties of inscribed angles. The key relationship is that the measure of an inscribed angle is half the measure of the intercepted arc.
- This relationship is extended to inscribed angles that intercept the same arc and to inscribed angles that intercept a diameter of the circle.
- The lesson ends by looking at inscribed polygons and constructing a square in a circle.

Formative Assessment Tips
- **Predict, Explain, Observe (P-E-O Probe):** This technique provides students the opportunity to make a prediction or to select a prediction from a set of options. Students explain why their prediction makes sense, and then they test their prediction. Finally, they analyze the results against their prediction and make adjustments to their thinking.
- This technique gives students the opportunity to reason about a problem, situation, or concept that is being probed, and students are asked to make a prediction related to the probe. Explaining the reason for their prediction is an important step. Curiosity piqued, students think of how to investigate their prediction. Students carry out their investigation and analyze the results. If their prediction is correct and it was based on valid reasoning (versus an educated guess), then their reasoning has been confirmed. If the results are not exactly what they had predicted, then the cognitive dissonance created should lead to more discussion, rethinking, and a new prediction.
- This technique is best used when you want to probe students' ideas. This technique does not need to be done only with individuals. Partners or small groups can make predictions, discussing their reasoning and rethinking their prediction after an investigation.

Another Way
- There is a quick demonstration that you can do to help students visualize and understand the theorem about inscribed angles. The demonstration can be done on an interactive board, under a document camera, or on an overhead projector.
- Use or reproduce a 360° protractor. Draw an angle with sufficiently long rays. Place the angle with its vertex at the center of the protractor. Ask students to note the measure of the angle and the measure of the intercepted arc.
- As the angle is translated away from the center of the protractor, observe what happens to the measure of the intercepted arc.

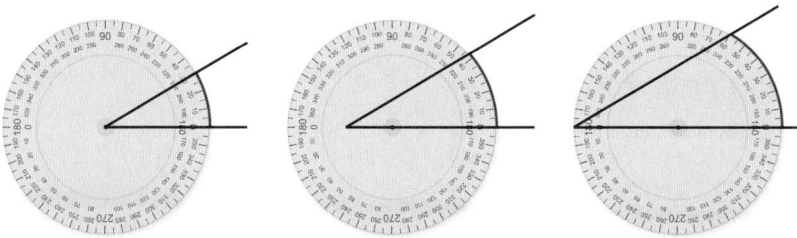

- As the angle is translated left in the image above, the angle measure remains the same and the measure of the intercepted arc is increasing.
- This same technique can be used in the next lesson to demonstrate other angle relationships in a circle.

Pacing Suggestion
- The explorations allow students to discover a relationship about inscribed angles and intercepted arcs, and the angles of an inscribed quadrilateral. Examples related to the theorems in the formal lesson should go quickly.

Dynamic Teaching Tools

Dynamic Assessment & Progress Monitoring Tool
Lesson Planning Tool
Interactive Whiteboard Lesson Library
Dynamic Classroom with Dynamic Investigations

**Common Core
State Standards**

HSG-CO.D.13 Construct an equilateral triangle, a square, and a regular hexagon inscribed in a circle.

HSG-C.A.2 Identify and describe relationships among inscribed angles, radii, and chords.

HSG-C.A.3 Construct the … circumscribed circles of a triangle, and prove properties of angles for a quadrilateral inscribed in a circle.

Laurie's Notes

Exploration

Motivate

- Show students a diagram of several soccer players standing on a circle that contains the posts of the goal. Discuss with them whether any player has the greatest "kicking angle" for the goal. Tell students that in this lesson they will see why each player has the same "kicking angle."

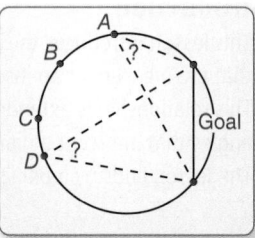

Discuss

- Discuss the vocabulary: inscribed angle, intercepted arc, and inscribed polygon.
- If dynamic geometry software is not available, students could still perform the construction with a protractor and straightedge. Gathering results from classmates may be sufficient to make a conjecture about the problem posed.

Exploration 1

- Have students work with their partners to investigate inscribed angles. Be sure that students try different conditions such as those shown.

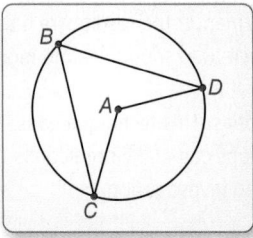 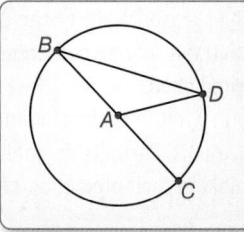 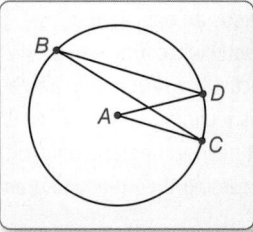

- As students make repeated trials, data should be recorded in a table.
- **MP3 Construct Viable Arguments and Critique the Reasoning of Others:** Have students state their conjectures and explain their reasoning. Discuss.

Exploration 2

? Before students begin, ask, "What is the sum of the angles of a quadrilateral?" 360°
"Do you think this relationship will change if you inscribe the quadrilateral in a circle?"
Hopefully, students will say *no*.

- With the vertices of the quadrilateral moving dynamically, students should recognize that the sum of the angles is still 360° and that opposite angles are supplementary.

Communicate Your Answer

- Students should summarize the conjectures made in each of the explorations.

Connecting to Next Step

- Each exploration is related to a theorem in today's lesson. Students will have a good sense of the theorem and perhaps how it might be proven.

Essential Question
How are inscribed angles related to their intercepted arcs? How are the angles of an inscribed quadrilateral related to each other?

An **inscribed angle** is an angle whose vertex is on a circle and whose sides contain chords of the circle. An arc that lies between two lines, rays, or segments is called an **intercepted arc**. A polygon is an **inscribed polygon** when all its vertices lie on a circle.

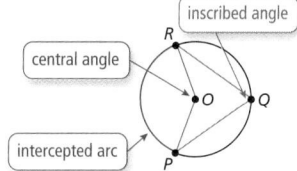

EXPLORATION 1   Inscribed Angles and Central Angles

Work with a partner. Use dynamic geometry software.

a. Construct an inscribed angle in a circle. Then construct the corresponding central angle.

b. Measure both angles. How is the inscribed angle related to its intercepted arc?

c. Repeat parts (a) and (b) several times. Record your results in a table. Write a conjecture about how an inscribed angle is related to its intercepted arc.

ATTENDING TO PRECISION

To be proficient in math, you need to communicate precisely with others.

Sample

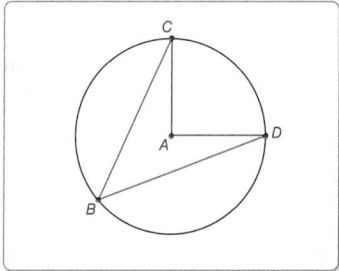

EXPLORATION 2   A Quadrilateral with Inscribed Angles

Work with a partner. Use dynamic geometry software.

a. Construct a quadrilateral with each vertex on a circle.

b. Measure all four angles. What relationships do you notice?

c. Repeat parts (a) and (b) several times. Record your results in a table. Then write a conjecture that summarizes the data.

Sample

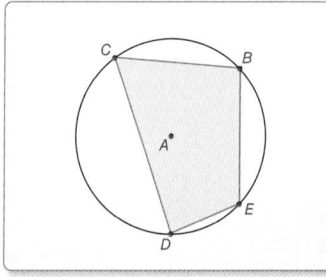

Communicate Your Answer

3. How are inscribed angles related to their intercepted arcs? How are the angles of an inscribed quadrilateral related to each other?

4. Quadrilateral *EFGH* is inscribed in $\odot C$, and $m\angle E = 80°$. What is $m\angle G$? Explain.

Section 10.4   Inscribed Angles and Polygons   **553**

ANSWERS

1. **a.** Check students' work.
   b. The inscribed angle is half of the intercepted arc.
   c. Check students' work; The measure of an inscribed angle is equal to half the measure of the intercepted arc.

2. **a.** Check students' work.
   b. *Sample answer:* The angles sum to 360°; Opposite angles sum to 180°.
   c. Check students' work; Opposite angles of an inscribed quadrilateral sum to 180°.

3. Inscribed angles are half of the intercepted arc; Opposite angles of an inscribed quadrilateral are supplementary.

4. 100°; $\angle E$ and $\angle G$ are supplementary.

Extra Example 1

Find the indicated measure.

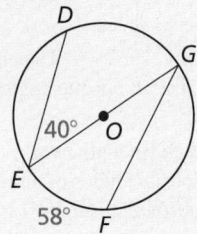

a. $m\widehat{DG}$ 80°

b. $m\angle G$ 29°

10.4 Lesson

Core Vocabulary

inscribed angle, *p. 554*
intercepted arc, *p. 554*
subtend, *p. 554*
inscribed polygon, *p. 556*
circumscribed circle, *p. 556*

What You Will Learn

▶ Use inscribed angles.

▶ Use inscribed polygons.

Using Inscribed Angles

🔄 Core Concept

Inscribed Angle and Intercepted Arc

An **inscribed angle** is an angle whose vertex is on a circle and whose sides contain chords of the circle. An arc that lies between two lines, rays, or segments is called an **intercepted arc**. If the endpoints of a chord or arc lie on the sides of an inscribed angle, then the chord or arc is said to **subtend** the angle.

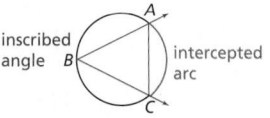

∠B intercepts $\widehat{AC}$.
$\widehat{AC}$ subtends ∠B.
$\overline{AC}$ subtends ∠B.

🔄 Theorem

Theorem 10.10   Measure of an Inscribed Angle Theorem

The measure of an inscribed angle is one-half the measure of its intercepted arc.

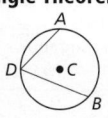

$m\angle ADB = \frac{1}{2}m\widehat{AB}$

Proof Ex. 37, p. 560

The proof of the Measure of an Inscribed Angle Theorem involves three cases.

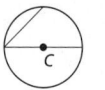 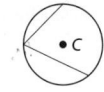

Case 1 Center *C* is on a side of the inscribed angle.

Case 2 Center *C* is inside the inscribed angle.

Case 3 Center *C* is outside the inscribed angle.

EXAMPLE 1   **Using Inscribed Angles**

Find the indicated measure.

a. $m\angle T$

b. $m\widehat{QR}$

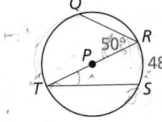

SOLUTION

a. $m\angle T = \frac{1}{2}m\widehat{RS} = \frac{1}{2}(48°) = 24°$

b. $m\widehat{TQ} = 2m\angle R = 2 \cdot 50° = 100°$
   Because $\widehat{TQR}$ is a semicircle, $m\widehat{QR} = 180° - m\widehat{TQ} = 180° - 100° = 80°$.

Laurie's Notes   Teacher Actions

- Write the *Core Concept*, which should be familiar from the explorations.
- Introduce the Measure of an Inscribed Angle Theorem (Thm. 10.10). It is helpful that students have explored this theorem dynamically with software. Even if students have explored this theorem with software, a quick visual demonstration resonates with them. See *Another Way* on page T-552.
- Have partners work independently to solve Example 1, and then discuss as a class.

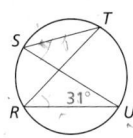

EXAMPLE 2 Finding the Measure of an Intercepted Arc

Find $m\overset{\frown}{RS}$ and $m\angle STR$. What do you notice about $\angle STR$ and $\angle RUS$?

SOLUTION

From the Measure of an Inscribed Angle Theorem, you know that $m\overset{\frown}{RS} = 2m\angle RUS = 2(31°) = 62°$.

Also, $m\angle STR = \frac{1}{2}m\overset{\frown}{RS} = \frac{1}{2}(62°) = 31°$.

▶ So, $\angle STR \cong \angle RUS$.

Example 2 suggests the Inscribed Angles of a Circle Theorem.

🔄 Theorem

Theorem 10.11 Inscribed Angles of a Circle Theorem

If two inscribed angles of a circle intercept the same arc, then the angles are congruent.

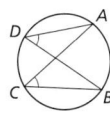

Proof Ex. 38, p. 560 $\angle ADB \cong \angle ACB$

EXAMPLE 3 Finding the Measure of an Angle

Given $m\angle E = 75°$, find $m\angle F$.

SOLUTION

Both $\angle E$ and $\angle F$ intercept $\overset{\frown}{GH}$. So, $\angle E \cong \angle F$ by the Inscribed Angles of a Circle Theorem.

▶ So, $m\angle F = m\angle E = 75°$.

Monitoring Progress 🔊 Help in English and Spanish at *BigIdeasMath.com*

Find the measure of the red arc or angle.

1.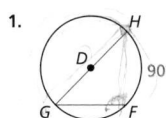

2.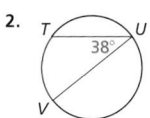

3.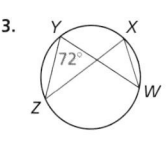

Extra Example 2

Find $m\overset{\frown}{HML}$ and $m\angle HJL$. What do you notice about $\angle HJL$ and $\angle LKH$?

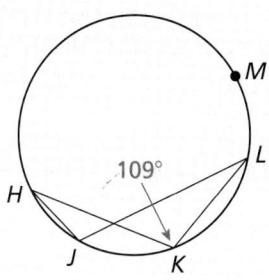

$m\overset{\frown}{HML} = 218°$ and $m\angle HJL = 109°$. So, $\angle HJL \cong \angle LKH$.

Extra Example 3

Given $m\angle C = 68°$, find $m\angle B$.

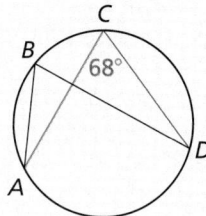

$m\angle B = 68°$

MONITORING PROGRESS ANSWERS

1. 45°
2. 76°
3. 72°

Laurie's Notes   Teacher Actions

- **Teaching Tip:** Sometimes it is helpful to extend the rays forming the inscribed angle to help students visualize the angle.
- **MP3:** Write the Inscribed Angles of a Circle Theorem (Thm. 10.11).
- **Turn and Talk:** "How could you prove this theorem?" Give sufficient *Wait Time*, and then solicit outlines for a proof.
- **Think-Pair-Share:** Have students answer Questions 1–3, and then share and discuss as a class.

Extra Example 4

Find the value of each variable.

a.

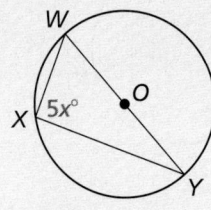

$x = 18$

b.

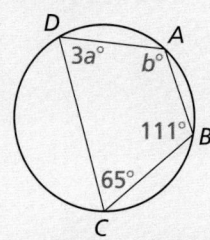

$a = 23, b = 115$

Using Inscribed Polygons

Core Concept

Inscribed Polygon

A polygon is an **inscribed polygon** when all its vertices lie on a circle. The circle that contains the vertices is a **circumscribed circle**.

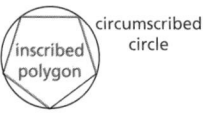

Theorems

Theorem 10.12 Inscribed Right Triangle Theorem

If a right triangle is inscribed in a circle, then the hypotenuse is a diameter of the circle. Conversely, if one side of an inscribed triangle is a diameter of the circle, then the triangle is a right triangle and the angle opposite the diameter is the right angle.

Proof Ex. 39, p. 560

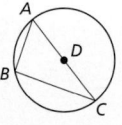

$m\angle ABC = 90°$ if and only if $\overline{AC}$ is a diameter of the circle.

Theorem 10.13 Inscribed Quadrilateral Theorem

A quadrilateral can be inscribed in a circle if and only if its opposite angles are supplementary.

Proof Ex. 40, p. 560;
BigIdeasMath.com

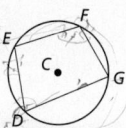

D, E, F, and G lie on $\odot C$ if and only if $m\angle D + m\angle F = m\angle E + m\angle G = 180°$.

EXAMPLE 4 **Using Inscribed Polygons**

Find the value of each variable.

a.

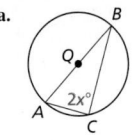

b.

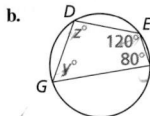

SOLUTION

a. $\overline{AB}$ is a diameter. So, $\angle C$ is a right angle, and $m\angle C = 90°$ by the Inscribed Right Triangle Theorem.

$$2x° = 90°$$
$$x = 45$$

▶ The value of x is 45.

b. *DEFG* is inscribed in a circle, so opposite angles are supplementary by the Inscribed Quadrilateral Theorem.

$$m\angle D + m\angle F = 180° \qquad m\angle E + m\angle G = 180°$$
$$z + 80 = 180 \qquad\qquad 120 + y = 180$$
$$z = 100 \qquad\qquad\qquad y = 60$$

▶ The value of z is 100 and the value of y is 60.

Laurie's Notes Teacher Actions

- Introduce the language of inscribed polygon and circumscribed circle.
- **? Always-Sometimes-Never True:** "Every triangle can be circumscribed. Explain." always true Students may recall the water sprinkler problem from Section 10.3.
- **Predict, Explain, Observe:** "Every quadrilateral can be circumscribed." Give groups time to investigate using dynamic geometry software. If they have completed Exploration 2 on page 553, they will already have a sense about this probe.

CONSTRUCTION **Constructing a Square Inscribed in a Circle**

Given ⊙C, construct a square inscribed in a circle.

SOLUTION

Step 1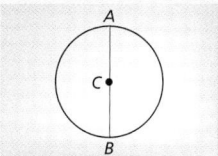

Draw a diameter
Draw any diameter. Label the endpoints A and B.

Step 2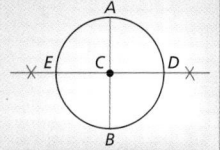

Construct a perpendicular bisector
Construct the perpendicular bisector of the diameter. Label the points where it intersects ⊙C as points D and E.

Step 3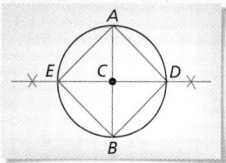

Form a square
Connect points A, D, B, and E to form a square.

EXAMPLE 5 **Using a Circumscribed Circle**

Your camera has a 90° field of vision, and you want to photograph the front of a statue. You stand at a location in which the front of the statue is all that appears in your camera's field of vision, as shown. You want to change your location. Where else can you stand so that the front of the statue is all that appears in your camera's field of vision?

SOLUTION

From the Inscribed Right Triangle Theorem, you know that if a right triangle is inscribed in a circle, then the hypotenuse of the triangle is a diameter of the circle. So, draw the circle that has the front of the statue as a diameter.

▶ The statue fits perfectly within your camera's 90° field of vision from any point on the semicircle in front of the statue.

Monitoring Progress Help in English and Spanish at *BigIdeasMath.com*

Find the value of each variable.

4.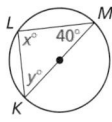

5.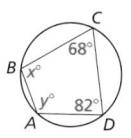

6.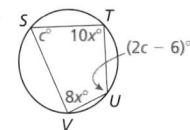

7. In Example 5, explain how to find locations where the left side of the statue is all that appears in your camera's field of vision.

Laurie's Notes **Teacher Actions**

❓**No-Hands Questioning:** "Given a circle of a particular radius, how could you construct a square inscribed in the circle?" After sufficient *Wait Time*, ask students to give a *Thumbs Up* signal when they are confident in how to proceed with the construction. Respond as needed.
• Have partners work independently to solve Example 5, and then discuss as a class.
• Discuss related applications.

Closure
• **Exit Ticket:** Quadrilateral *ABCD* is inscribed in a circle. Let $m\angle A = 72°$ and $m\angle B = 113°$. Find $m\angle C$ and $m\angle D$. $m\angle C = 108°$, $m\angle D = 67°$

Vocabulary and Core Concept Check

1. **VOCABULARY** If a circle is circumscribed about a polygon, then the polygon is an _____.

2. **DIFFERENT WORDS, SAME QUESTION** Which is different? Find "both" answers.

   Find $m\angle ABC$.   Find $m\angle AGC$.

   Find $m\angle AEC$.   Find $m\angle ADC$.

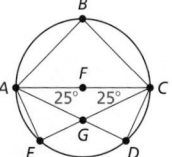

Monitoring Progress and Modeling with Mathematics

In Exercises 3–8, find the indicated measure. *(See Examples 1 and 2.)*

3. $m\angle A$

4. $m\angle G$

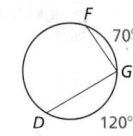

5. $m\angle N$

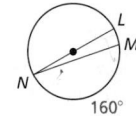

6. $m\widehat{RS}$

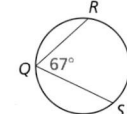

7. $m\widehat{VU}$

8. $m\widehat{WX}$

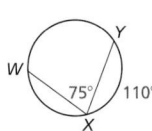

In Exercises 9 and 10, name two pairs of congruent angles.

9.

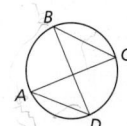

10.

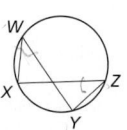

In Exercises 11 and 12, find the measure of the red arc or angle. *(See Example 3.)*

11.

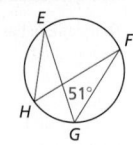

12.

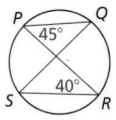

In Exercises 13–16, find the value of each variable. *(See Example 4.)*

13.

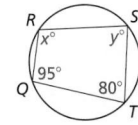

14.

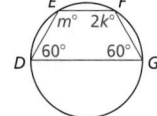

15.

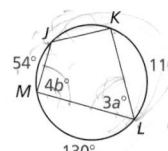

16.

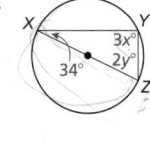

17. **ERROR ANALYSIS** Describe and correct the error in finding $m\widehat{BC}$.

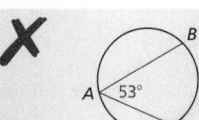

$m\widehat{BC} = 53°$

18. **MODELING WITH MATHEMATICS** A *carpenter's square* is an L-shaped tool used to draw right angles. You need to cut a circular piece of wood into two semicircles. How can you use the carpenter's square to draw a diameter on the circular piece of wood? *(See Example 5.)*

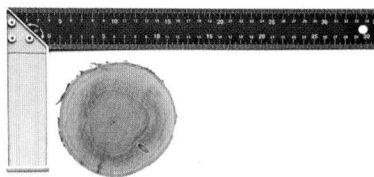

MATHEMATICAL CONNECTIONS In Exercises 19–21, find the values of *x* and *y*. Then find the measures of the interior angles of the polygon.

19. 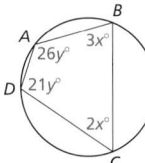 20.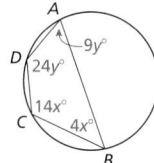

21.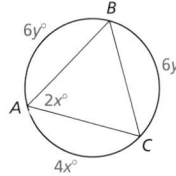

22. **MAKING AN ARGUMENT** Your friend claims that $\angle PTQ \cong \angle PSQ \cong \angle PRQ$. Is your friend correct? Explain your reasoning.

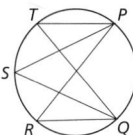

23. **CONSTRUCTION** Construct an equilateral triangle inscribed in a circle.

24. **CONSTRUCTION** The side length of an inscribed regular hexagon is equal to the radius of the circumscribed circle. Use this fact to construct a regular hexagon inscribed in a circle.

REASONING In Exercises 25–30, determine whether a quadrilateral of the given type can always be inscribed inside a circle. Explain your reasoning.

25. square   26. rectangle

27. parallelogram   28. kite

29. rhombus   30. isosceles trapezoid

31. **MODELING WITH MATHEMATICS** Three moons, A, B, and C, are in the same circular orbit 100,000 kilometers above the surface of a planet. The planet is 20,000 kilometers in diameter and $m\angle ABC = 90°$. Draw a diagram of the situation. How far is moon A from moon C?

32. **MODELING WITH MATHEMATICS** At the movie theater, you want to choose a seat that has the best *viewing angle*, so that you can be close to the screen and still see the whole screen without moving your eyes. You previously decided that seat F7 has the best viewing angle, but this time someone else is already sitting there. Where else can you sit so that your seat has the same viewing angle as seat F7? Explain.

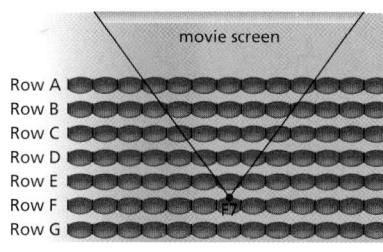

33. **WRITING** A right triangle is inscribed in a circle, and the radius of the circle is given. Explain how to find the length of the hypotenuse.

34. **HOW DO YOU SEE IT?** Let point *Y* represent your location on the soccer field below. What type of angle is $\angle AYB$ if you stand anywhere on the circle except at point *A* or point *B*?

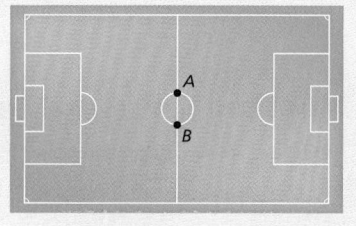

ANSWERS

18. Place the right angle of the carpenter's square on the edge of the circle and connect the points where the sides intersect the edge of the circle.

19. $x = 25$, $y = 5$; 130°, 75°, 50°, 105°

20. $x = 9$, $y = 6$; 54°, 36°, 126°, 144°

21. $x = 30$, $y = 20$; 60°, 60°, 60°

22. yes; The angles intercept the same arc.

23.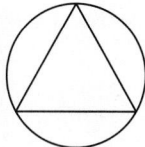

24.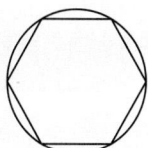

25. yes; Opposite angles are always supplementary.

26. yes; Opposite angles are always supplementary.

27. no; Opposite angles are not always supplementary.

28. no; Opposite angles are not always supplementary.

29. no; Opposite angles are not always supplementary.

30. yes; Opposite angles are always supplementary.

31.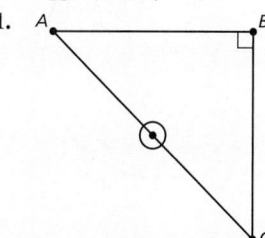

220,000 km

32. any point on the circle circumscribed about the triangle that seat F7 makes with the movie screen; The angle intercepts the same arc.

33. double the radius

34. right angle

ANSWERS

35. Each diagonal splits the rectangle into two right triangles.

36. yes; Every triangle has a circumcenter.

37–40. See Additional Answers.

41. 2.4 units

42. a. $\dfrac{JH}{GJ} = \dfrac{GJ}{FJ}$; Geometric Mean (Altitude) Theorem (Thm. 9.7)

    b. 6 in.; 2 in.; $2\sqrt{3}$ in.; $4\sqrt{3}$ in.

43. $x = \dfrac{145}{3}$

44. $x = 126$

45. $x = 120$

46. $x = 180$

Mini-Assessment

1. Find $m\widehat{DF}$ and $m\widehat{ED}$.

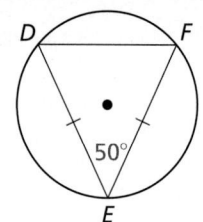

$m\widehat{DF} = 100°, m\widehat{ED} = 130°$

2. Find $m\widehat{CD}$.

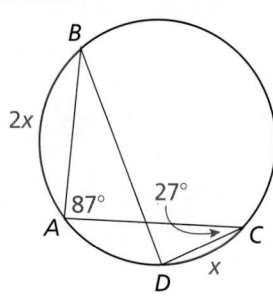

$m\widehat{CD} = 44°$

3. Find the value of each variable.

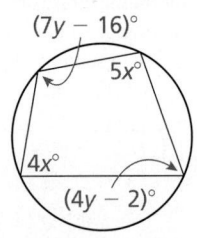

$x = 20, y = 18$

560   **Chapter 10**

---

35. WRITING Explain why the diagonals of a rectangle inscribed in a circle are diameters of the circle.

36. THOUGHT PROVOKING The figure shows a circle that is circumscribed about $\triangle ABC$. Is it possible to circumscribe a circle about any triangle? Justify your answer.

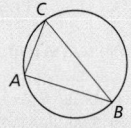

37. PROVING A THEOREM If an angle is inscribed in $\odot Q$, the center Q can be on a side of the inscribed angle, inside the inscribed angle, or outside the inscribed angle. Prove each case of the Measure of an Inscribed Angle Theorem (Theorem 10.10).

    a. Case 1

    Given $\angle ABC$ is inscribed in $\odot Q$.
    Let $m\angle B = x°$.
    Center Q lies on $\overline{BC}$.

    Prove $m\angle ABC = \frac{1}{2}m\widehat{AC}$

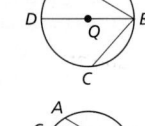

    (*Hint*: Show that $\triangle AQB$ is isosceles. Then write $m\widehat{AC}$ in terms of x.)

    b. Case 2 Use the diagram and auxiliary line to write **Given** and **Prove** statements for Case 2. Then write a proof.

    c. Case 3 Use the diagram and auxiliary line to write **Given** and **Prove** statements for Case 3. Then write a proof.

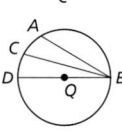

38. PROVING A THEOREM Write a paragraph proof of the Inscribed Angles of a Circle Theorem (Theorem 10.11). First, draw a diagram and write **Given** and **Prove** statements.

39. PROVING A THEOREM The Inscribed Right Triangle Theorem (Theorem 10.12) is written as a conditional statement and its converse. Write a plan for proof for each statement.

40. PROVING A THEOREM Copy and complete the paragraph proof for one part of the Inscribed Quadrilateral Theorem (Theorem 10.13).

    Given $\odot C$ with inscribed quadrilateral $DEFG$

    Prove $m\angle D + m\angle F = 180°$, $m\angle E + m\angle G = 180°$

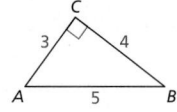

By the Arc Addition Postulate (Postulate 10.1), $m\widehat{EFG} + \_\_\_\_ = 360°$ and $m\widehat{FGD} + m\widehat{DEF} = 360°$. Using the _____ Theorem, $m\widehat{EDG} = 2m\angle F$, $m\widehat{EFG} = 2m\angle D$, $m\widehat{DEF} = 2m\angle G$, and $m\widehat{FGD} = 2m\angle E$. By the Substitution Property of Equality, $2m\angle D + \_\_\_ = 360°$, so ___. Similarly, ___.

41. CRITICAL THINKING In the diagram, $\angle C$ is a right angle. If you draw the smallest possible circle through C tangent to $\overline{AB}$, the circle will intersect $\overline{AC}$ at J and $\overline{BC}$ at K. Find the exact length of $\overline{JK}$.

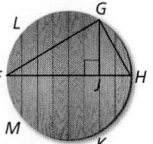

42. CRITICAL THINKING You are making a circular cutting board. To begin, you glue eight 1-inch boards together, as shown. Then you draw and cut a circle with an 8-inch diameter from the boards.

    a. $\overline{FH}$ is a diameter of the circular cutting board. Write a proportion relating GJ and JH. State a theorem to justify your answer.

    b. Find FJ, JH, and GJ. What is the length of the cutting board seam labeled $\overline{GK}$?

Maintaining Mathematical Proficiency
Reviewing what you learned in previous grades and lessons

Solve the equation. Check your solution. *(Skills Review Handbook)*

43. $3x = 145$

44. $\frac{1}{2}x = 63$

45. $240 = 2x$

46. $75 = \frac{1}{2}(x - 30)$

560   **Chapter 10**   Circles

If students need help...	If students got it...
Resources by Chapter • Practice A and Practice B • Puzzle Time	Resources by Chapter • Enrichment and Extension • Cumulative Review
Student Journal • Practice	Start the *next* Section
Differentiating the Lesson Skills Review Handbook	

Overview of Section 10.5

Introduction
- This lesson extends the relationships found in the last lesson about angles and intercepted arcs of a circle. There are four additional theorems about angle relationships in a circle.
- The lesson ends with a real-life application about the northern lights, a topic used as the *Motivate* for the lesson.

Teaching Strategy
- On page T-552, another way was suggested for investigating angle relationships in a circle—in particular, when two lines intersect on a circle forming an inscribed angle. In this lesson, the two lines might intersect in the interior or the exterior of the circle.
- Students can become overwhelmed, believing that there are a lot of theorems (formulas) to remember. To help students organize and summarize their thinking, have them consider the three intersection possibilities described in the *Core Concept* on page 562.
- **Turn and Talk:** Have students note similarities and differences in the theorems relating to these three cases. Students should recognize the following:
  - When the lines intersect the circle, arcs are intercepted.
  - All of the formulas involve taking $\frac{1}{2}$ of a measure.
  - When the lines intersect inside the circle, you add arc measures.
  - When the lines intersect outside the circle, you subtract arc measures.
  - When the lines intersect on the circle, there is only one arc to consider.

Pacing Suggestion
- The explorations allow students to discover additional relationships about angles formed when two lines intersect with a circle. Examples related to the theorems in the formal lesson should go quickly.

**Common Core
State Standards**

HSG-C.A.2 Identify and describe
relationships among inscribed angles,
radii, and chords.

Laurie's Notes

Exploration

Motivate
- Ask whether anyone can speak about aurora borealis, commonly known as the northern lights. Let students share what they know.
- **FYI:** Polar lights (aurora polaris) are a natural phenomenon found in both the northern and southern hemispheres. The polar lights are a natural light display in the sky, particularly in the high-latitude (Arctic and Antarctic) regions, caused by the collision of energetic charged particles with atoms in the high-altitude atmosphere.
- In this lesson, the connection to high altitudes is made.

Exploration Note
- If dynamic geometry software is not available, students could still perform the construction with a protractor and straightedge. Gathering results from classmates may be sufficient to make a conjecture about the problem posed.

Exploration 1
- Have students work with partners to explore the problem posed.
- Given the dynamic nature of the construction, students should click and drag on point C to observe any patterns.
- As students make repeated trials, data should be recorded in a table.
- **MP3 Construct Viable Arguments and Critique the Reasoning of Others:** Have students state their conjectures and explain their reasoning. Discuss.

Exploration 2
- This exploration is similar to the first.
- Students will likely ask which pair of vertical angles to measure, the obtuse pair or the acute pair—to which I generally respond, "Yes."
- As students make repeated trials, data should be recorded in a table.

Communicate Your Answer
- Listen for both conjectures made by students as a result of the two explorations.

Connecting to Next Step
- This lesson contains four theorems, two of which students have now explored using dynamic geometry software.

Essential Question
When a chord intersects a tangent line or another chord, what relationships exist among the angles and arcs formed?

EXPLORATION 1 **Angles Formed by a Chord and Tangent Line**

Work with a partner. Use dynamic geometry software.

a. Construct a chord in a circle. At one of the endpoints of the chord, construct a tangent line to the circle.

b. Find the measures of the two angles formed by the chord and the tangent line.

c. Find the measures of the two circular arcs determined by the chord.

d. Repeat parts (a)–(c) several times. Record your results in a table. Then write a conjecture that summarizes the data.

Sample

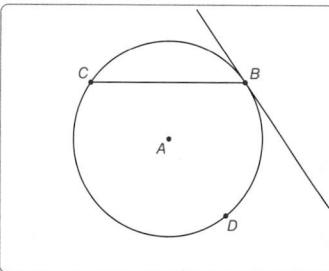

EXPLORATION 2 **Angles Formed by Intersecting Chords**

Work with a partner. Use dynamic geometry software.

a. Construct two chords that intersect inside a circle.

b. Find the measure of one of the angles formed by the intersecting chords.

c. Find the measures of the arcs intercepted by the angle in part (b) and its vertical angle. What do you observe?

d. Repeat parts (a)–(c) several times. Record your results in a table. Then write a conjecture that summarizes the data.

Sample

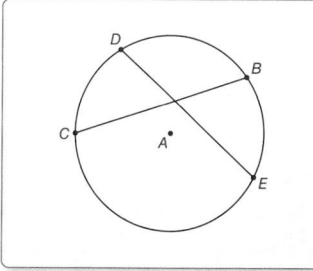

CONSTRUCTING VIABLE ARGUMENTS

To be proficient in math, you need to understand and use stated assumptions, definitions, and previously established results.

Communicate Your Answer

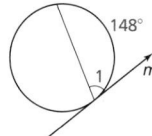

3. When a chord intersects a tangent line or another chord, what relationships exist among the angles and arcs formed?

4. Line *m* is tangent to the circle in the figure at the left. Find the measure of ∠1.

5. Two chords intersect inside a circle to form a pair of vertical angles with measures of 55°. Find the sum of the measures of the arcs intercepted by the two angles.

ANSWERS

1. a. Check students' work.
   b. *Sample answer:* 50°, 130°
   c. *Sample answer:* 100°, 260°
   d. Check students' work; The measure of each angle between a chord and a tangent is half of its intercepted arc.

2. a. Check students' work.
   b. *Sample answer:* 60°
   c. *Sample answer:* 40°, 80°; The angle measure is half of the sum of the measures of the intercepted arcs.
   d. Check students' work; The measure of an angle between two chords is half of the sum of the measure of the arcs intercepted by the angle and its vertical angle.

3. When a chord intersects a tangent line, the angle formed is half of the measure of the intercepted arc. When a chord intersects another chord, the measure of the angle is half of the sum of the measures of the arcs intercepted by the angle and its vertical angle.

4. 74°

5. 110°

Extra Example 1
Line *m* is tangent to the circle. Find the measure of the red angle or arc.

a.

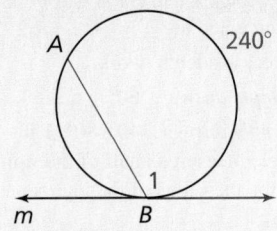

$m\angle 1 = 120°$

b.

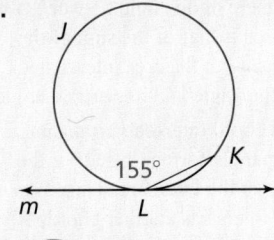

$m\widehat{KJL} = 310°$

MONITORING PROGRESS ANSWERS
1. 105°
2. 196°
3. 160°

10.5 Lesson

Core Vocabulary
circumscribed angle, *p. 564*

Previous
tangent
chord
secant

What You Will Learn
▶ Find angle and arc measures.
▶ Use circumscribed angles.

Finding Angle and Arc Measures

Theorem

Theorem 10.14 Tangent and Intersected Chord Theorem

If a tangent and a chord intersect at a point on a circle, then the measure of each angle formed is one-half the measure of its intercepted arc.

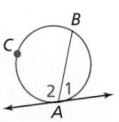

Proof Ex. 33, p. 568

$m\angle 1 = \frac{1}{2}m\widehat{AB} \quad m\angle 2 = \frac{1}{2}m\widehat{BCA}$

EXAMPLE 1 Finding Angle and Arc Measures

Line *m* is tangent to the circle. Find the measure of the red angle or arc.

a.

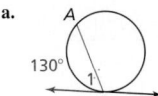

b.

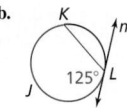

SOLUTION

a. $m\angle 1 = \frac{1}{2}(130°) = 65°$

b. $m\widehat{KJL} = 2(125°) = 250°$

Monitoring Progress ◀)) Help in English and Spanish at *BigIdeasMath.com*

Line *m* is tangent to the circle. Find the indicated measure.

1. $m\angle 1$

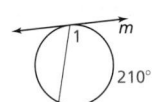

2. $m\widehat{RST}$

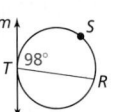

3. $m\widehat{XY}$

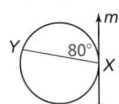

Core Concept

Intersecting Lines and Circles

If two nonparallel lines intersect a circle, there are three places where the lines can intersect.

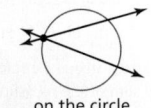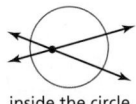

on the circle   inside the circle   outside the circle

562   Chapter 10   Circles

Laurie's Notes   Teacher Actions
- The first theorem in the lesson was explored on the previous page.
- ❓ "If $\overline{AB}$ is a diameter, what is $m\angle 1$ and $m\angle 2$ in the diagram?" They are each 90°.
- If $\overline{AB}$ is not a diameter, one of the intercepted arcs will be greater than 180° and one will be less than 180°.
- Have partners work independently to solve Example 1 and Questions 1–3. Discuss as a class.
- The *Core Concept* summarizes the three cases of intersecting lines and circles. See the *Teaching Strategy* on page T-560.

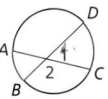
Theorems

Theorem 10.15   Angles Inside the Circle Theorem

If two chords intersect *inside* a circle, then the measure of each angle is one-half the *sum* of the measures of the arcs intercepted by the angle and its vertical angle.

$m\angle 1 = \frac{1}{2}(m\widehat{DC} + m\widehat{AB})$,

$m\angle 2 = \frac{1}{2}(m\widehat{AD} + m\widehat{BC})$

Proof Ex. 35, p. 568

Theorem 10.16   Angles Outside the Circle Theorem

If a tangent and a secant, two tangents, or two secants intersect *outside* a circle, then the measure of the angle formed is one-half the *difference* of the measures of the intercepted arcs.

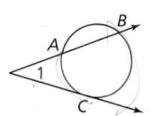 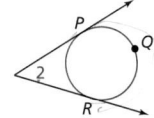 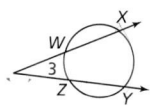

$m\angle 1 = \frac{1}{2}(m\widehat{BC} - m\widehat{AC})$ $m\angle 2 = \frac{1}{2}(m\widehat{PQR} - m\widehat{PR})$ $m\angle 3 = \frac{1}{2}(m\widehat{XY} - m\widehat{WZ})$

Proof Ex. 37, p. 568

EXAMPLE 2   Finding an Angle Measure

Find the value of *x*.

a.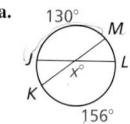

b.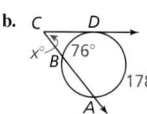

SOLUTION

a. The chords $\overline{JL}$ and $\overline{KM}$ intersect inside the circle. Use the Angles Inside the Circle Theorem.

$x° = \frac{1}{2}(m\widehat{JM} + m\widehat{LK})$

$x° = \frac{1}{2}(130° + 156°)$

$x = 143$

▶ So, the value of *x* is 143.

b. The tangent $\overrightarrow{CD}$ and the secant $\overrightarrow{CB}$ intersect outside the circle. Use the Angles Outside the Circle Theorem.

$m\angle BCD = \frac{1}{2}(m\widehat{AD} - m\widehat{BD})$

$x° = \frac{1}{2}(178° - 76°)$

$x = 51$

▶ So, the value of *x* is 51.

Monitoring Progress Help in English and Spanish at *BigIdeasMath.com*

Find the value of the variable.

4.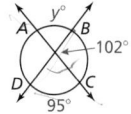

5.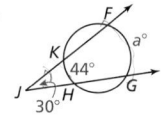

Visual

To help students see that the three cases of Theorem 10.16 are related, use a chalkboard compass or two yardsticks and a large circle drawn on the board. Use the sides of the compass to represent the sides of an angle whose vertex is outside the circle. Open and close the compass so the sides represent two tangents, then two secants, and then a tangent and a secant.

Extra Example 2
Find the value of *x*.

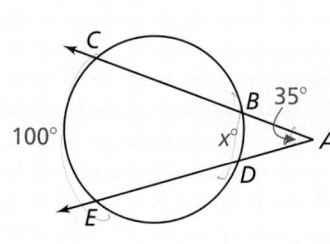

a.

$x = 92$

b.

$x = 30$

MONITORING PROGRESS ANSWERS

4. 61

5. 104

Laurie's Notes   Teacher Actions

- The first theorem on this page was explored on page 561. If time permits, have students explore the three cases of the theorem. An alternative is to demonstrate the theorem dynamically. An online search will reveal ready-made demonstrations.
- **Turn and Talk:** "How do you summarize the three cases for finding the angle measure of the angle formed by two intersecting lines and a circle?" See the *Teaching Strategy* on page T-560.

Extra Example 3

Find the value of x.

a.

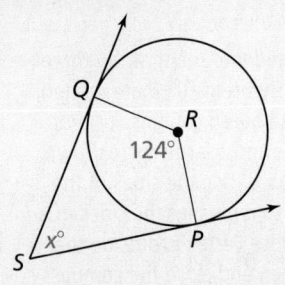

$x = 56$

b.

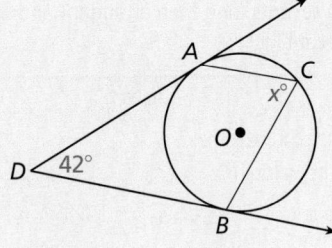

$x = 69$

Using Circumscribed Angles

Core Concept

Circumscribed Angle

A **circumscribed angle** is an angle whose sides are tangent to a circle.

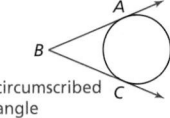

circumscribed angle

Theorem

Theorem 10.17   Circumscribed Angle Theorem

The measure of a circumscribed angle is equal to 180° minus the measure of the central angle that intercepts the same arc.

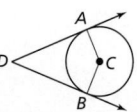

Proof Ex. 38, p. 568

$m\angle ADB = 180° - m\angle ACB$

EXAMPLE 3   **Finding Angle Measures**

Find the value of x.

a.

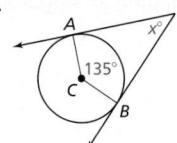

b.

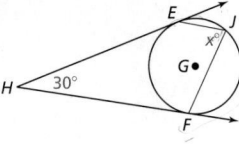

SOLUTION

a. Use the Circumscribed Angle Theorem to find $m\angle ADB$.

$m\angle ADB = 180° - m\angle ACB$	Circumscribed Angle Theorem
$x° = 180° - 135°$	Substitute.
$x = 45$	Subtract.

▶ So, the value of x is 45.

b. Use the Measure of an Inscribed Angle Theorem (Theorem 10.10) and the Circumscribed Angle Theorem to find $m\angle EJF$.

$m\angle EJF = \frac{1}{2}m\widehat{EF}$	Measure of an Inscribed Angle Theorem
$m\angle EJF = \frac{1}{2}m\angle EGF$	Definition of minor arc
$m\angle EJF = \frac{1}{2}(180° - m\angle EHF)$	Circumscribed Angle Theorem
$m\angle EJF = \frac{1}{2}(180° - 30°)$	Substitute.
$x = \frac{1}{2}(180 - 30)$	Substitute.
$x = 75$	Simplify.

▶ So, the value of x is 75.

Laurie's Notes   Teacher Actions

- Write the *Core Concept* and provide a sketch.
- State the Circumscribed Angle Theorem (Thm. 10.17). Ask, "How might you prove this theorem?" Give *Wait Time*, and then solicit ideas from students. Write a brief outline of the proof.
- **Think-Alouds:** Pose Example 3 and say, "To solve part (a), I need to ...." Ask partner A to think aloud for partner B to hear the problem-solving process. When students have finished the problem, reverse roles for part (b). Discuss solutions as a class.

EXAMPLE 4 Modeling with Mathematics

The northern lights are bright flashes of colored light between 50 and 200 miles above Earth. A flash occurs 150 miles above Earth at point C. What is the measure of $\overarc{BD}$, the portion of Earth from which the flash is visible? (Earth's radius is approximately 4000 miles.)

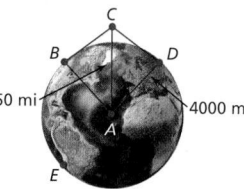

Not drawn to scale

SOLUTION

1. **Understand the Problem** You are given the approximate radius of Earth and the distance above Earth that the flash occurs. You need to find the measure of the arc that represents the portion of Earth from which the flash is visible.

2. **Make a Plan** Use properties of tangents, triangle congruence, and angles outside a circle to find the arc measure.

3. **Solve the Problem** Because $\overline{CB}$ and $\overline{CD}$ are tangents, $\overline{CB} \perp \overline{AB}$ and $\overline{CD} \perp \overline{AD}$ by the Tangent Line to Circle Theorem (Theorem 10.1). Also, $\overline{BC} \cong \overline{DC}$ by the External Tangent Congruence Theorem (Theorem 10.2), and $\overline{CA} \cong \overline{CA}$ by the Reflexive Property of Congruence (Theorem 2.1). So, $\triangle ABC \cong \triangle ADC$ by the Hypotenuse-Leg Congruence Theorem (Theorem 5.9). Because corresponding parts of congruent triangles are congruent, $\angle BCA \cong \angle DCA$. Solve right $\triangle CBA$ to find that $m\angle BCA \approx 74.5°$. So, $m\angle BCD \approx 2(74.5°) = 149°$.

COMMON ERROR

Because the value for $m\angle BCD$ is an approximation, use the symbol $\approx$ instead of $=$.

$m\angle BCD = 180° - m\angle BAD$	Circumscribed Angle Theorem
$m\angle BCD = 180° - m\overarc{BD}$	Definition of minor arc
$149° \approx 180° - m\overarc{BD}$	Substitute.
$31° \approx m\overarc{BD}$	Solve for $m\overarc{BD}$.

▶ The measure of the arc from which the flash is visible is about 31°.

4. **Look Back** You can use inverse trigonometric ratios to find $m\angle BAC$ and $m\angle DAC$.

$$m\angle BAC = \cos^{-1}\left(\frac{4000}{4150}\right) \approx 15.5°$$

$$m\angle DAC = \cos^{-1}\left(\frac{4000}{4150}\right) \approx 15.5°$$

So, $m\angle BAD \approx 15.5° + 15.5° = 31°$, and therefore $m\overarc{BD} \approx 31°$.

Monitoring Progress 🔊 Help in English and Spanish at *BigIdeasMath.com*

Find the value of x.

6.
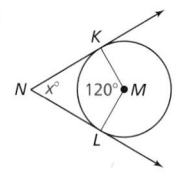

7.
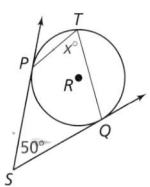

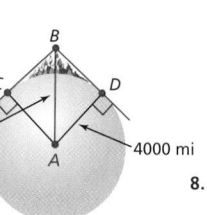

4002.73 mi — 4000 mi

Not drawn to scale

8. You are on top of Mount Rainier on a clear day. You are about 2.73 miles above sea level at point B. Find $m\overarc{CD}$, which represents the part of Earth that you can see.

Section 10.5   Angle Relationships in Circles   **565**

Extra Example 4

Use the information in Example 4. A flash occurs 100 miles above Earth at point C. Find the measure of $\overarc{BD}$, the portion of Earth from which the flash is visible.

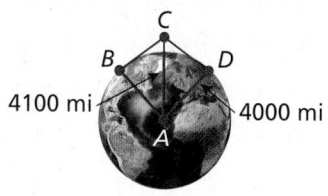

Not drawn to scale

about 25°

MONITORING PROGRESS ANSWERS

6. 60

7. 65

8. about 4°

Laurie's Notes   **Teacher Actions**

- **MP2 Reason Abstractly and Quantitatively** and **Paired Verbal Fluency:** Have students pair up and follow the protocol described on page T-462. Ask partner B to explain what he or she knows about the problem and a strategy for solving. When it is partner A's turn, he or she should build on the reasoning of partner B or explain why partner B's strategy is faulty. Discuss solutions as a class when students have finished.

Closure

- **Point of Most Significance:** Ask students to identify, aloud or on paper, the most significant point (or part) in the lesson that aided their learning.

Assignment Guide and Homework Check

ASSIGNMENT

Basic: 1, 2, 3–23 odd, 30, 34, 41–43

Average: 1, 2, 6–34 even, 41–43

Advanced: 1, 2, 6–40 even, 41–43

HOMEWORK CHECK

Basic: 3, 7, 9, 11, 23

Average: 6, 10, 12, 24, 32

Advanced: 10, 12, 24, 32, 40

ANSWERS

1. outside

2. Find the measure of the central angle that intercepts the same arc and subtract it from 180°.

3. 130°

4. 234°

5. 130°

6. 110°

7. 115

8. 90

9. 56

10. 38

11. 40

12. 11

13. 34

14. 15

15. $\angle SUT$ is not a central angle; $m\angle SUT = \frac{1}{2}\left(m\widehat{QR} + m\widehat{ST}\right) = 41.5°$

16. The $\frac{1}{2}$ was left out of the equation; $m\angle 1 = \frac{1}{2}(122 - 70) = 26°$

17. 60°; Because the sum of the angles of a triangle always equals 180°, solve the equation $90 + 30 + x = 180$.

18. 60°; When a chord intersects a tangent line, the angle formed is half of the measure of the intercepted arc, which in this case is 120°.

19. 30°; Because the sum of the angles of a triangle always equals 180°, solve the equation $60 + 90 + x = 180$.

20. 90°; Because $\angle 2$ and $\angle 5$ sum to 90° and form a straight line with $\angle 4$, the angles are supplementary.

21. 30°; This angle is complementary to $\angle 2$, which is 60°.

22. 60°; This angle is congruent to $\angle 1$.

Vocabulary and Core Concept Check

1. **COMPLETE THE SENTENCE** Points A, B, C, and D are on a circle, and $\overleftrightarrow{AB}$ intersects $\overleftrightarrow{CD}$ at point P. If $m\angle APC = \frac{1}{2}(m\widehat{BD} - m\widehat{AC})$, then point P is _____ the circle.

2. **WRITING** Explain how to find the measure of a circumscribed angle.

Monitoring Progress and Modeling with Mathematics

In Exercises 3–6, line t is tangent to the circle. Find the indicated measure. *(See Example 1.)*

3. $m\widehat{AB}$

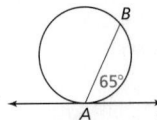

4. $m\widehat{DEF}$

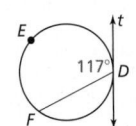

5. $m\angle 1$

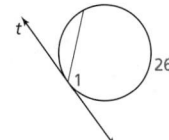

6. $m\angle 3$

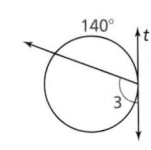

In Exercises 7–14, find the value of x. *(See Examples 2 and 3.)*

7.

8.

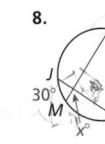

9.

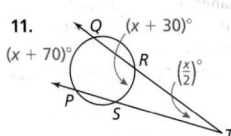

10.

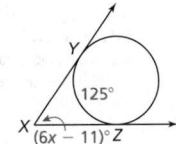

11.

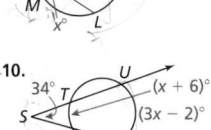

12.

13.

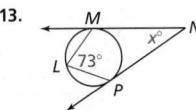

14.

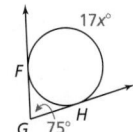

ERROR ANALYSIS In Exercises 15 and 16, describe and correct the error in finding the angle measure.

15.

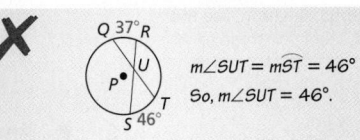

16.

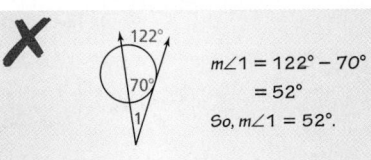

In Exercises 17–22, find the indicated angle measure. Justify your answer.

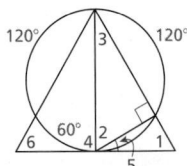

17. $m\angle 1$

18. $m\angle 2$

19. $m\angle 3$

20. $m\angle 4$

21. $m\angle 5$

22. $m\angle 6$

23. PROBLEM SOLVING You are flying in a hot air balloon about 1.2 miles above the ground. Find the measure of the arc that represents the part of Earth you can see. The radius of Earth is about 4000 miles. *(See Example 4.)*

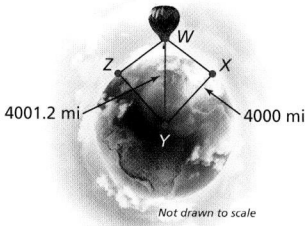

Not drawn to scale

24. PROBLEM SOLVING You are watching fireworks over San Diego Bay S as you sail away in a boat. The highest point the fireworks reach F is about 0.2 mile above the bay. Your eyes E are about 0.01 mile above the water. At point B you can no longer see the fireworks because of the curvature of Earth. The radius of Earth is about 4000 miles, and $\overline{FE}$ is tangent to Earth at point T. Find $m\widehat{SB}$. Round your answer to the nearest tenth.

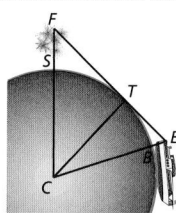

Not drawn to scale

25. MATHEMATICAL CONNECTIONS In the diagram, $\overrightarrow{BA}$ is tangent to $\odot E$. Write an algebraic expression for $m\widehat{CD}$ in terms of x. Then find $m\widehat{CD}$.

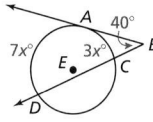

26. MATHEMATICAL CONNECTIONS The circles in the diagram are concentric. Write an algebraic expression for c in terms of a and b.

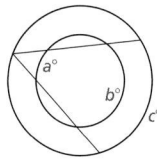

27. ABSTRACT REASONING In the diagram, $\overrightarrow{PL}$ is tangent to the circle, and $\overline{KJ}$ is a diameter. What is the range of possible angle measures of $\angle LPJ$? Explain your reasoning.

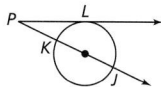

28. ABSTRACT REASONING In the diagram, $\overline{AB}$ is any chord that is not a diameter of the circle. Line m is tangent to the circle at point A. What is the range of possible values of x? Explain your reasoning. (The diagram is not drawn to scale.)

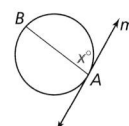

29. PROOF In the diagram, $\overrightarrow{JL}$ and $\overrightarrow{NL}$ are secant lines that intersect at point L. Prove that $m\angle JPN > m\angle JLN$.

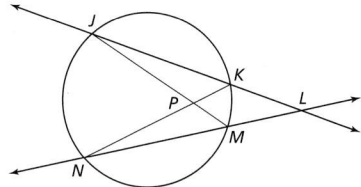

30. MAKING AN ARGUMENT Your friend claims that it is possible for a circumscribed angle to have the same measure as its intercepted arc. Is your friend correct? Explain your reasoning.

31. REASONING Points A and B are on a circle, and t is a tangent line containing A and another point C.

   a. Draw two diagrams that illustrate this situation.

   b. Write an equation for $m\widehat{AB}$ in terms of $m\angle BAC$ for each diagram.

   c. For what measure of $\angle BAC$ can you use either equation to find $m\widehat{AB}$? Explain.

32. REASONING $\triangle XYZ$ is an equilateral triangle inscribed in $\odot P$. $\overline{AB}$ is tangent to $\odot P$ at point X, $\overline{BC}$ is tangent to $\odot P$ at point Y, and $\overline{AC}$ is tangent to $\odot P$ at point Z. Draw a diagram that illustrates this situation. Then classify $\triangle ABC$ by its angles and sides. Justify your answer.

Section 10.5   Angle Relationships in Circles   **567**

ANSWERS

23. about 2.8°

24. about 0.7°

25. $360 - 10x$; 160°

26. $c = b - a$

27. $m\angle LPJ < 90$; The difference of $m\widehat{JL}$ and $m\widehat{LK}$ must be less than 180°, so $m\angle LPJ < 90$.

28. $x < 180$ and $x \neq 90$; $m\widehat{AB} \neq 180$; $\overline{AB}$ is not a diameter.

29. By the Angles Inside a Circle Theorem (Thm. 10.15), $m\angle JPN = \frac{1}{2}(m\widehat{JN} + m\widehat{KM})$. By the Angles Outside the Circle Theorem (Thm. 10.16), $m\angle JLN = \frac{1}{2}(m\widehat{JN} - m\widehat{KM})$. Because the angle measures are positive, $\frac{1}{2}(m\widehat{JN} + m\widehat{KM}) > \frac{1}{2}m\widehat{JN} > \frac{1}{2}(m\widehat{JN} - m\widehat{KM})$, so, $m\angle JPN > m\angle JLN$.

30. yes; When the circumscribed angle is 90°, the central angle is 90°.

31. a.

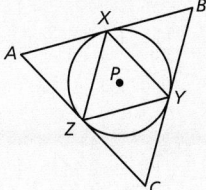

   b. $m\widehat{AB} = 2m\angle BAC$, $m\widehat{AB} = 360° - 2m\angle BAC$

   c. 90°; $2m\angle BAC = 360° - 2m\angle BAC$ when $m\angle BAC = 90°$.

32.

equilateral, equiangular; $m\widehat{XY}$, $m\widehat{YZ}$, and $m\widehat{XZ}$ are 120°.

ANSWERS

33–39. See Additional Answers.

40. $m\widehat{AB} = 85°$, $m\widehat{ED} = 75°$;
 Sample answer: $m\angle DHC = 65°$,
 $m\widehat{AE} = 45°$, $m\widehat{AF} = 25°$, $m\angle J = 30°$, so $m\widehat{AB} = 85°$; $m\angle FGD = 90°$,
 $m\widehat{FD} = 95°$, and $m\widehat{ED} = 75°$.

41. $x = -4$, $x = 3$

42. $x = 6 \pm \sqrt{71}$

43. $x = -3$, $x = -1$

Mini-Assessment

1. $\overleftrightarrow{WX}$ is tangent to the circle.
Find $m\widehat{XYZ}$.

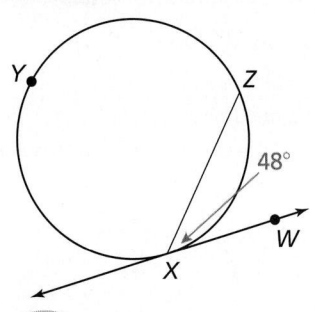

$m\widehat{XYZ} = 264°$

2. Find the value of x.

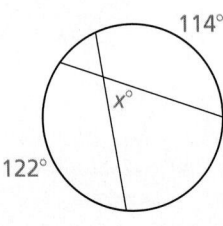

$x = 62$

3. Find the values of the variables.

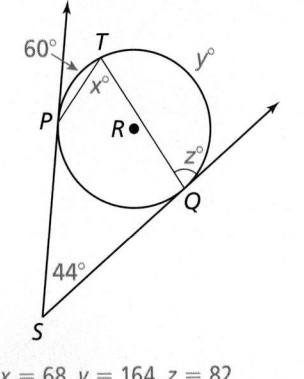

$x = 68$, $y = 164$, $z = 82$

568 Chapter 10

33. **PROVING A THEOREM** To prove the Tangent and Intersected Chord Theorem (Theorem 10.14), you must prove three cases.

 a. The diagram shows the case where $\overline{AB}$ contains the center of the circle. Use the Tangent Line to Circle Theorem (Theorem 10.1) to write a paragraph proof for this case.

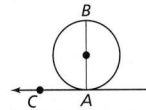

 b. Draw a diagram and write a proof for the case where the center of the circle is in the interior of $\angle CAB$.

 c. Draw a diagram and write a proof for the case where the center of the circle is in the exterior of $\angle CAB$.

34. **HOW DO YOU SEE IT?** In the diagram, television cameras are positioned at A and B to record what happens on stage. The stage is an arc of $\odot A$. You would like the camera at B to have a 30° view of the stage. Should you move the camera closer or farther away? Explain your reasoning.

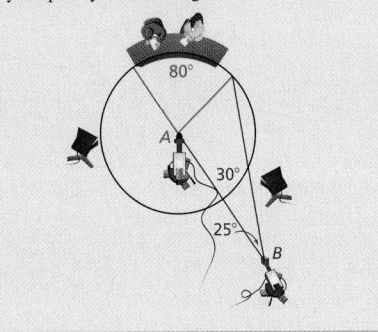

35. **PROVING A THEOREM** Write a proof of the Angles Inside the Circle Theorem (Theorem 10.15).

 Given Chords $\overline{AC}$ and $\overline{BD}$ intersect inside a circle.

 Prove $m\angle 1 = \frac{1}{2}(m\widehat{DC} + m\widehat{AB})$

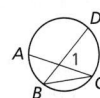

Maintaining Mathematical Proficiency
Reviewing what you learned in previous grades and lessons

Solve the equation. *(Skills Review Handbook)*

41. $x^2 + x = 12$ 42. $x^2 = 12x + 35$ 43. $-3 = x^2 + 4x$

568 Chapter 10 Circles

36. **THOUGHT PROVOKING** In the figure, $\overrightarrow{BP}$ and $\overrightarrow{CP}$ are tangent to the circle. Point A is any point on the major arc formed by the endpoints of the chord $\overline{BC}$. Label all congruent angles in the figure. Justify your reasoning.

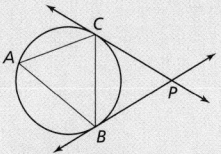

37. **PROVING A THEOREM** Use the diagram below to prove the Angles Outside the Circle Theorem (Theorem 10.16) for the case of a tangent and a secant. Then copy the diagrams for the other two cases on page 563 and draw appropriate auxiliary segments. Use your diagrams to prove each case.

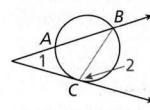

38. **PROVING A THEOREM** Prove that the Circumscribed Angle Theorem (Theorem 10.17) follows from the Angles Outside the Circle Theorem (Theorem 10.16).

In Exercises 39 and 40, find the indicated measure(s). Justify your answer.

39. Find $m\angle P$ when $m\widehat{WZY} = 200°$.

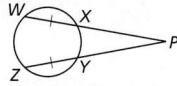

40. Find $m\widehat{AB}$ and $m\widehat{ED}$.

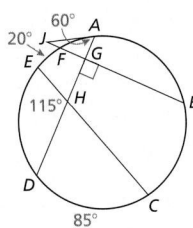

If students need help...	If students got it...
Resources by Chapter • Practice A and Practice B • Puzzle Time	**Resources by Chapter** • Enrichment and Extension • Cumulative Review
Student Journal • Practice	Start the *next* Section
Differentiating the Lesson Skills Review Handbook	

Overview of Section 10.6

Introduction

- This lesson is about segment lengths in a circle when chords, secants, and tangents intersect a circle. Students may find the lesson difficult, in part because of the language involved in trying to describe the segments. Help students to focus on what the theorems state about the product of different segments.

Teaching Strategy

- This lesson is a good time to return to transformations and look at the proofs from a transformational approach versus synthetically.
- To model this, consider the Segments of Chords Theorem (Thm. 10.18). It is possible to use transformations to show that the triangles are similar and therefore corresponding sides are proportional.
- Begin by constructing two chords and then drawing segments to form $\triangle DCF$ and $\triangle BEF$ (See Figure 1.)
- Construct the bisector of $\angle CFE$. (See Figure 2.)
- Reflect $\triangle DCF$ in the angle bisector. (See Figure 3.) At this point, students can dilate to map $\triangle DC'F'$ onto $\triangle BEF$.

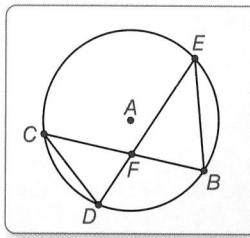 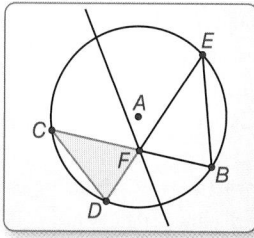 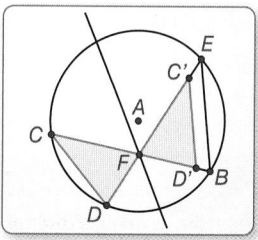

| Figure 1 | Figure 2 | Figure 3 |

- You want students to give explanations of the constructions along the way. A common error is that students try to rotate $\triangle DCF$ about point F, and this approach does not work.

Pacing Suggestion

- The explorations allow students to make conjectures about segments that are formed when two chords intersect or two secants intersect. In the formal lesson, the discussion of the theorems should not take long.

Dynamic Teaching Tools
Dynamic Assessment & Progress Monitoring Tool
Lesson Planning Tool
Interactive Whiteboard Lesson Library
Dynamic Classroom with Dynamic Investigations

**Common Core
State Standards**

HSG-C.A.2 Identify and describe relationships among inscribed angles, radii, and chords.

HSG-MG.A.1 Use geometric shapes, their measures, and their properties to describe objects (e.g., modeling a tree trunk or a human torso as a cylinder).

Laurie's Notes

Exploration

Motivate
- Pose the following problem: You are parasailing above the ocean and looking out at the horizon. If you know your height above the water and the radius of Earth, do you think you can calculate how far you can see?
- Students should recognize this as an application of the Pythagorean Theorem.
- Explain to students that they will look at an alternate way to solve this problem using a new theorem in this lesson.

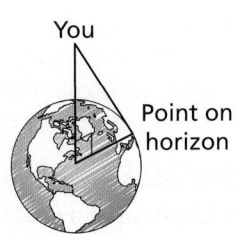

You

Point on horizon

Exploration Note
- The two explorations about segment lengths in a circle are more directed than other explorations in this chapter. It is less likely that students would discover the relationship without a bit of guidance.
- Unlike other explorations, measurement with a ruler may not be accurate enough for students to observe a pattern and make a conjecture. Dynamic geometry software is recommended.

Exploration 1
- Have partners perform the construction and take the measurements as directed.
- Given the dynamic nature of the software, students should be able to click and drag on one of the points of the circle to investigate many cases.
- **?** "What do you notice about the products of the segments of the chords?" The products are the same.
- **MP3 Construct Viable Arguments and Critique the Reasoning of Others:** Have students state their conjectures and explain their reasoning. Discuss.
- **?** "Is your conjecture still true if one or both of the chords is a diameter?" yes
- **?** "Do you have an idea as to how you could prove your conjecture?" Answers will vary.

Exploration 2
- Have partners perform the construction and take the measurements as directed.
- Given the dynamic nature of the software, students should be able to click and drag on one of the points of the circle to investigate many cases.
- **?** "What do you notice about the products of the segments of the secants?" The products are the same.
- **MP3:** Have students state their conjectures and explain their reasoning. Discuss.
- **?** "Is your conjecture still true if one of the secants passes through the center of the circle?" yes
- **?** "Do you have an idea as to how you could prove your conjecture?" Answers will vary.

Communicate Your Answer
- Listen for both conjectures made by students as a result of the two explorations.

Connecting to Next Step
- This lesson contains three theorems, two of which students have now explored using dynamic geometry software.

10.6 Segment Relationships in Circles

Essential Question
What relationships exist among the segments formed by two intersecting chords or among segments of two secants that intersect outside a circle?

EXPLORATION 1 — Segments Formed by Two Intersecting Chords

Work with a partner. Use dynamic geometry software.

a. Construct two chords $\overline{BC}$ and $\overline{DE}$ that intersect in the interior of a circle at a point F.

b. Find the segment lengths BF, CF, DF, and EF and complete the table. What do you observe?

BF	CF	BF · CF

DF	EF	DF · EF

Sample

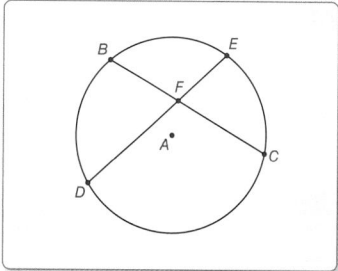

REASONING ABSTRACTLY

To be proficient in math, you need to make sense of quantities and their relationships in problem situations.

c. Repeat parts (a) and (b) several times. Write a conjecture about your results.

EXPLORATION 2 — Secants Intersecting Outside a Circle

Work with a partner. Use dynamic geometry software.

a. Construct two secants $\overleftrightarrow{BC}$ and $\overleftrightarrow{BD}$ that intersect at a point B outside a circle, as shown.

b. Find the segment lengths BE, BC, BF, and BD, and complete the table. What do you observe?

BE	BC	BE · BC

BF	BD	BF · BD

Sample

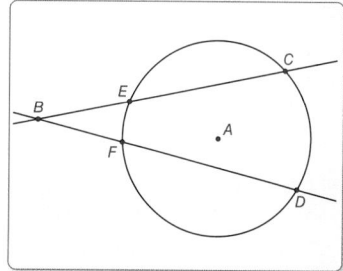

c. Repeat parts (a) and (b) several times. Write a conjecture about your results.

Communicate Your Answer

3. What relationships exist among the segments formed by two intersecting chords or among segments of two secants that intersect outside a circle?

4. Find the segment length AF in the figure at the left.

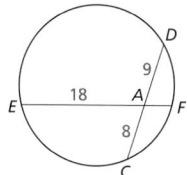

Section 10.6 Segment Relationships in Circles **569**

ANSWERS

1. **a.** Check students' work.

   b. *Sample answer:*

BF	CF	BF · CF
7.5	13.2	99

DF	EF	DF · EF
6.6	15	99

   The products are equal.

   c. If two chords intersect inside a circle, then the product of the lengths of the segments of one chord is equal to the product of the lengths of the segments of the other chord.

2. **a.** Check students' work.

   b. *Sample answer:*

BE	BC	BE · BC
17.6	35.9	631.84

BF	BD	BF · BD
22	28.72	631.84

   The products are equal.

   c. If two secants intersect outside a circle with a common endpoint, then the product of the lengths of the segments of one secant is equal to the product of the lengths of the segments of the other secant.

3. The products of the lengths of the segments of one chord or secant is equal to the product of the lengths of the other chord or secant.

4. 4

Extra Example 1
Find AB and PQ.

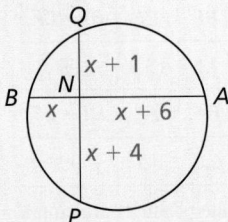

$AB = 14$, $PQ = 13$

MONITORING PROGRESS ANSWERS
1. 8
2. 5

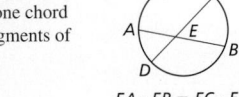

10.6 Lesson

What You Will Learn
▶ Use segments of chords, tangents, and secants.

Core Vocabulary
segments of a chord, *p. 570*
tangent segment, *p. 571*
secant segment, *p. 571*
external segment, *p. 571*

Using Segments of Chords, Tangents, and Secants
When two chords intersect in the interior of a circle, each chord is divided into two segments that are called **segments of the chord.**

↻ Theorem

Theorem 10.18   Segments of Chords Theorem
If two chords intersect in the interior of a circle, then the product of the lengths of the segments of one chord is equal to the product of the lengths of the segments of the other chord.

Proof Ex. 19, p. 574

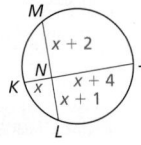

$EA \cdot EB = EC \cdot ED$

EXAMPLE 1   **Using Segments of Chords**

Find ML and JK.

SOLUTION

$$NK \cdot NJ = NL \cdot NM \qquad \text{Segments of Chords Theorem}$$
$$x \cdot (x + 4) = (x + 1) \cdot (x + 2) \qquad \text{Substitute.}$$
$$x^2 + 4x = x^2 + 3x + 2 \qquad \text{Simplify.}$$
$$4x = 3x + 2 \qquad \text{Subtract } x^2 \text{ from each side.}$$
$$x = 2 \qquad \text{Subtract } 3x \text{ from each side.}$$

Find ML and JK by substitution.

$$ML = (x + 2) + (x + 1) \qquad\qquad JK = x + (x + 4)$$
$$= 2 + 2 + 2 + 1 \qquad\qquad\qquad = 2 + 2 + 4$$
$$= 7 \qquad\qquad\qquad\qquad\qquad = 8$$

▶ So, $ML = 7$ and $JK = 8$.

Monitoring Progress 🔊 Help in English and Spanish at *BigIdeasMath.com*

Find the value of *x*.

1.
2.

Laurie's Notes   Teacher Actions

- **MP1 Make Sense of Problems and Persevere in Solving Them:** The first theorem in the lesson was explored on the previous page.
  ❓ State the theorem. "Do you have an idea as to how you could prove the theorem?" Answers will vary.
  - If there are no references to similar triangles, draw $\overline{AD}$ and $\overline{CB}$ and repeat the question. Give *Wait Time* for students to discuss the proof with their partners. They will recognize that the triangles are similar by the Angle-Angle Similarity Theorem (Thm. 8.3).
- **Popsicle Sticks:** Example 1 is an opportunity for students to review equation-solving skills. Use *Popsicle Sticks* to solicit a solution.

Core Concept

Tangent Segment and Secant Segment

A **tangent segment** is a segment that is tangent to a circle at an endpoint. A **secant segment** is a segment that contains a chord of a circle and has exactly one endpoint outside the circle. The part of a secant segment that is outside the circle is called an **external segment**.

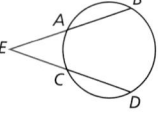

$\overline{PS}$ is a tangent segment.
$\overline{PR}$ is a secant segment.
$\overline{PQ}$ is the external segment of $\overline{PR}$.

Theorem

Theorem 10.19 Segments of Secants Theorem

If two secant segments share the same endpoint outside a circle, then the product of the lengths of one secant segment and its external segment equals the product of the lengths of the other secant segment and its external segment.

Proof Ex. 20, p. 574

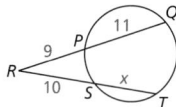

$EA \cdot EB = EC \cdot ED$

EXAMPLE 2   **Using Segments of Secants**

Find the value of x.

SOLUTION

$RP \cdot RQ = RS \cdot RT$	Segments of Secants Theorem
$9 \cdot (11 + 9) = 10 \cdot (x + 10)$	Substitute.
$180 = 10x + 100$	Simplify.
$80 = 10x$	Subtract 100 from each side.
$8 = x$	Divide each side by 10.

▶ The value of x is 8.

Monitoring Progress 🔊 Help in English and Spanish at *BigIdeasMath.com*

Find the value of x.

3.
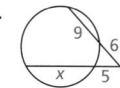

4.
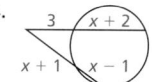

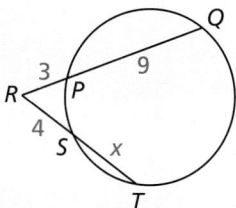
MONITORING PROGRESS ANSWERS

3. 13
4. 3

Laurie's Notes   Teacher Actions

- Write the *Core Concept*. Color-coding the various segments is helpful for some students.
- State the theorem and ask, "Do you have an idea as to how you could prove the theorem?" Students will likely suspect similar triangles are involved. Give partners time to discuss how the theorem might be proven.
- **Thumbs Up:** Have students work independently to solve Example 2. Ask students to self-assess with *Thumbs Up*.

Extra Example 3

Find WX.

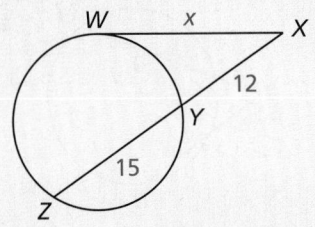

$WX = 18$

Extra Example 4

Find the radius of the circle.

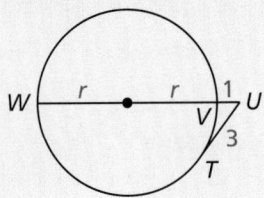

$r = 4$

MONITORING PROGRESS ANSWERS

5. 2
6. 4.8
7. 8
8. 36.75 ft

Theorem 10.20 **Segments of Secants and Tangents Theorem**

If a secant segment and a tangent segment share an endpoint outside a circle, then the product of the lengths of the secant segment and its external segment equals the square of the length of the tangent segment.

Proof Exs. 21 and 22, p. 574

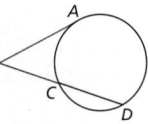

$EA^2 = EC \cdot ED$

EXAMPLE 3 **Using Segments of Secants and Tangents**

Find RS.

SOLUTION

$RQ^2 = RS \cdot RT$	Segments of Secants and Tangents Theorem
$16^2 = x \cdot (x + 8)$	Substitute.
$256 = x^2 + 8x$	Simplify.
$0 = x^2 + 8x - 256$	Write in standard form.
$x = \dfrac{-8 \pm \sqrt{8^2 - 4(1)(-256)}}{2(1)}$	Use Quadratic Formula.
$x = -4 \pm 4\sqrt{17}$	Simplify.

Use the positive solution because lengths cannot be negative.

▶ So, $x = -4 + 4\sqrt{17} \approx 12.49$, and $RS \approx 12.49$.

ANOTHER WAY

In Example 3, you can draw segments $\overline{QS}$ and $\overline{QT}$.

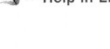

Because $\angle RQS$ and $\angle RTQ$ intercept the same arc, they are congruent. By the Reflexive Property of Congruence (Theorem 2.2), $\angle QRS \cong \angle TRQ$. So, $\triangle RSQ \sim \triangle RQT$ by the AA Similarity Theorem (Theorem 8.3). You can use this fact to write and solve a proportion to find x.

EXAMPLE 4 **Finding the Radius of a Circle**

Find the radius of the aquarium tank.

SOLUTION

$CB^2 = CE \cdot CD$	Segments of Secants and Tangents Theorem
$20^2 = 8 \cdot (2r + 8)$	Substitute.
$400 = 16r + 64$	Simplify.
$336 = 16r$	Subtract 64 from each side.
$21 = r$	Divide each side by 16.

▶ So, the radius of the tank is 21 feet.

Monitoring Progress 🔊 Help in English and Spanish at *BigIdeasMath.com*

Find the value of x.

5.

6.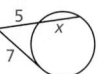

7.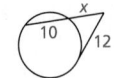

8. **WHAT IF?** In Example 4, $CB = 35$ feet and $CE = 14$ feet. Find the radius of the tank.

Laurie's Notes | Teacher Actions

- Write the theorem and again have a brief discussion of the proof. Similar triangles are again involved.
- Work through Example 3 as shown. In addition, help students set up the alternate solution method shown in the margin.
- If time permits, have students return to the problem posed in the *Motivate*. Suggest that you are parasailing 100 feet in the air.

Closure

- **Muddiest Point:** Ask students to identify, aloud or on paper, the muddiest point(s) about the lesson. What was difficult to understand?

Vocabulary and Core Concept Check

1. **VOCABULARY** The part of the secant segment that is outside the circle is called a(n) _____.

2. **WRITING** Explain the difference between a tangent segment and a secant segment.

Monitoring Progress and Modeling with Mathematics

In Exercises 3–6, find the value of *x*. *(See Example 1.)*

3.
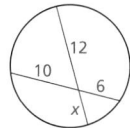

4.
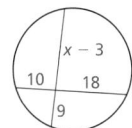

5.
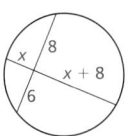

6.
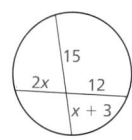

In Exercises 7–10, find the value of *x*. *(See Example 2.)*

7.
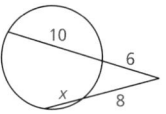

8.
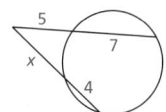

9.
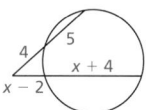

10.
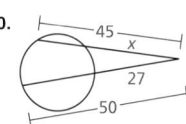

In Exercises 11–14, find the value of *x*. *(See Example 3.)*

11.
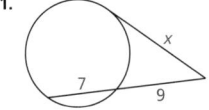

12.
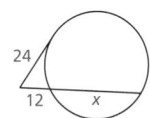

13.
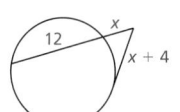

14.
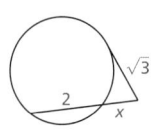

15. **ERROR ANALYSIS** Describe and correct the error in finding *CD*.

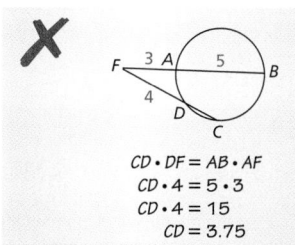

$$CD \cdot DF = AB \cdot AF$$
$$CD \cdot 4 = 5 \cdot 3$$
$$CD \cdot 4 = 15$$
$$CD = 3.75$$

16. **MODELING WITH MATHEMATICS** The Cassini spacecraft is on a mission in orbit around Saturn until September 2017. Three of Saturn's moons, Tethys, Calypso, and Telesto, have nearly circular orbits of radius 295,000 kilometers. The diagram shows the positions of the moons and the spacecraft on one of Cassini's missions. Find the distance *DB* from Cassini to Tethys when $\overline{AD}$ is tangent to the circular orbit. *(See Example 4.)*

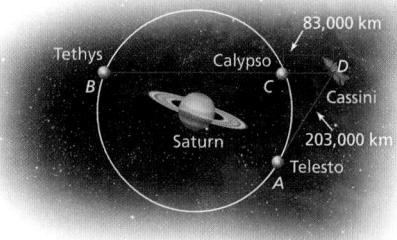

ANSWERS

1. external segment
2. A tangent intersects a circle at one point and a secant segment intersects a circle at two points.
3. 5
4. 23
5. 4
6. 5
7. 4
8. 6
9. 5
10. 30
11. 12
12. 36
13. 4
14. 1
15. The chords were used instead of the secant segments; $CF \cdot DF = BF \cdot AF$; $CD = 2$
16. about 496,494 km

ANSWERS

17. about 124.5 ft

18. 4 cm/sec; See Additional Answers.

19–30. See Additional Answers.

Mini-Assessment

1. Find the value of x.

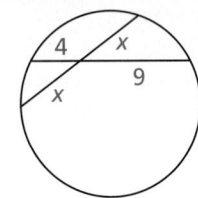

$x = 6$

2. Find the value of x.

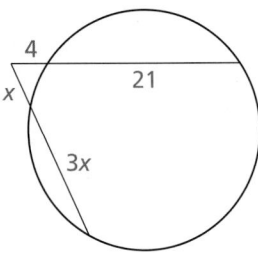

$x = 5$

3. Find BC and DC.

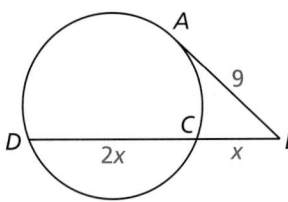

$BC = 3\sqrt{3} \approx 5.2$;
$DC = 6\sqrt{3} \approx 10.4$

4. The circle shows the cross-section of a pipe. Find the radius of the pipe.

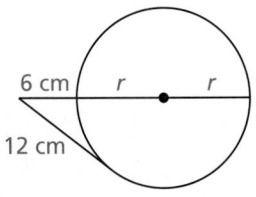

9 centimeters

17. MODELING WITH MATHEMATICS The circular stone mound in Ireland called Newgrange has a diameter of 250 feet. A passage 62 feet long leads toward the center of the mound. Find the perpendicular distance x from the end of the passage to either side of the mound.

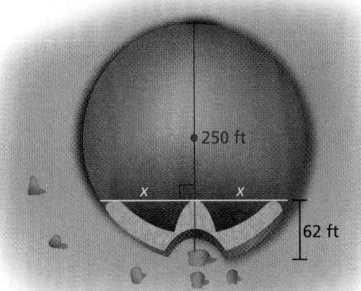

18. MODELING WITH MATHEMATICS You are designing an animated logo for your website. Sparkles leave point C and move to the outer circle along the segments shown so that all of the sparkles reach the outer circle at the same time. Sparkles travel from point C to point D at 2 centimeters per second. How fast should sparkles move from point C to point N? Explain.

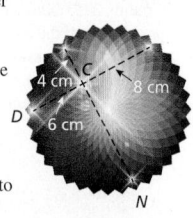

19. PROVING A THEOREM Write a two-column proof of the Segments of Chords Theorem (Theorem 10.18).

Plan for Proof Use the diagram from page 570. Draw $\overline{AC}$ and $\overline{DB}$. Show that $\triangle EAC$ and $\triangle EDB$ are similar. Use the fact that corresponding side lengths in similar triangles are proportional.

20. PROVING A THEOREM Prove the Segments of Secants Theorem (Theorem 10.19). (*Hint*: Draw a diagram and add auxiliary line segments to form similar triangles.)

21. PROVING A THEOREM Use the Tangent Line to Circle Theorem (Theorem 10.1) to prove the Segments of Secants and Tangents Theorem (Theorem 10.20) for the special case when the secant segment contains the center of the circle.

22. PROVING A THEOREM Prove the Segments of Secants and Tangents Theorem (Theorem 10.20). (*Hint*: Draw a diagram and add auxiliary line segments to form similar triangles.)

23. WRITING EQUATIONS In the diagram of the water well, AB, AD, and DE are known. Write an equation for BC using these three measurements.

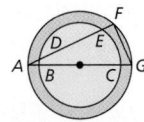

24. HOW DO YOU SEE IT? Which two theorems would you need to use to find PQ? Explain your reasoning.

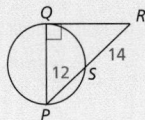

25. CRITICAL THINKING In the figure, $AB = 12$, $BC = 8$, $DE = 6$, $PD = 4$, and A is a point of tangency. Find the radius of $\odot P$.

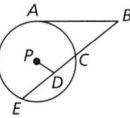

26. THOUGHT PROVOKING Circumscribe a triangle about a circle. Then, using the points of tangency, inscribe a triangle in the circle. Must it be true that the two triangles are similar? Explain your reasoning.

Maintaining Mathematical Proficiency
Reviewing what you learned in previous grades and lessons

Solve the equation by completing the square. (*Skills Review Handbook*)

27. $x^2 + 4x = 45$

28. $x^2 - 2x - 1 = 8$

29. $2x^2 + 12x + 20 = 34$

30. $-4x^2 + 8x + 44 = 16$

If students need help...	If students got it...
Resources by Chapter • Practice A and Practice B • Puzzle Time	**Resources by Chapter** • Enrichment and Extension • Cumulative Review
Student Journal • Practice	Start the *next* Section
Differentiating the Lesson Skills Review Handbook	

Dynamic Teaching Tools

Dynamic Assessment & Progress Monitoring Tool

Lesson Planning Tool

Interactive Whiteboard Lesson Library

Dynamic Classroom with Dynamic Investigations

Overview of Section 10.7

Introduction

- This last section of the chapter is about the standard equation of a circle. Students derive the equation in the exploration and then use the equation in the formal lesson. In addition to writing the equation, students will graph circles.
- The lesson ends with a real-life application involving seismographs.

Teaching Strategy

- Students are always curious about how to graph a circle on the graphing calculator. Because the equation of a circle is not a function, the equation has to be written as a split rule function.
- For Example 5 in the lesson, there are three circles to graph. The first circle has center $(-2, 2.5)$ and radius 7. The equation is $(x + 2)^2 + (y - 2.5)^2 = 7^2$. Solve this equation for y.

$$(x + 2)^2 + (y - 2.5)^2 = 7^2$$
$$(y - 2.5)^2 = 49 - (x + 2)^2$$
$$y - 2.5 = \pm \sqrt{49 - (x + 2)^2}$$
$$y = \pm \sqrt{49 - (x + 2)^2} + 2.5$$

- Graph the two cases in Y1 and Y2. Use a square viewing window to make the graph circular.

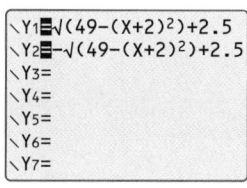
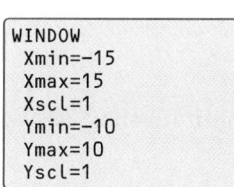
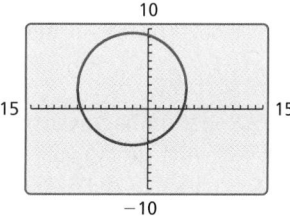

Pacing Suggestion

- Have students work through all three explorations and the questions that follow. You should be able to omit the *Core Concept* and Example 1.

HSG-GPE.A.1 Derive the equation of
a circle of given center and radius using
the Pythagorean Theorem; complete the
square to find the center and radius of a
circle given by an equation.

HSG-GPE.B.4 Use coordinates to prove
simple geometric theorems algebraically.

Laurie's Notes

Exploration

Motivate
? "What is a seismograph and what does it do?" Answers will vary.
- **FYI:** A rock thrown into a pond sends waves rippling out in all directions from the point of impact. Just as this impact sets waves in motion, an earthquake generates seismic waves that radiate out through the earth.
- Seismographs are instruments that detect and measure vibrations within the earth. Seismograph recordings are known as seismograms. The prefix *seismos* comes from the Greek, meaning "shock" or "earthquake." The devices are best known for studying earthquakes, although some types are used for underground surveying.

Exploration Note
- The approach in the first two explorations is to use the equation generated by the software to make a conjecture about the equation of a circle in standard form. In the third exploration, students derive the equation using the distance formula.

Exploration 1
- This first exploration will not take long to complete. Constructing concentric circles and examining the equations should be quick and easy for students at this point.
? **MP8 Look For and Express Regularity in Repeated Reasoning:** "What did you observe about the equations of the circles?" The equations were of the form $x^2 + y^2 = r^2$.
? "What would be the equation of a circle with center (0, 0) and radius 10?" $x^2 + y^2 = 100$

Exploration 2
- **MP2 Reason Abstractly and Quantitatively:** Students should recognize that in trying to see a pattern, they might want to use lattice points for the centers of the circle. Once they have a conjecture, they might want to test it with a random point.
- As you circulate, you might probe students about centers in all four quadrants if they have not constructed circles with centers in different quadrants or on either axis.
? **MP8:** "What did you observe about the equations of the circles?" The equations were of the form $(x - h)^2 + (y - k)^2 = 4$.
? "What would be the equation of a circle with center (5, −2) and radius 2?"
$(x - 5)^2 + (y + 2)^2 = 4$

Exploration 3
- **MP3 Construct Viable Arguments and Critique the Reasoning of Others:** This exploration is a great way to give evidence for the conjecture made in the last exploration, and it is nice to revisit an earlier skill.

Communicate Your Answer
- Listen for precise language as students state the equation of a circle with center (h, k) and radius r.

Connecting to Next Step
- Students should be ready to write an equation of a circle when given the radius and center.

10.7 Circles in the Coordinate Plane

Essential Question
What is the equation of a circle with center (h, k) and radius r in the coordinate plane?

Dynamic Teaching Tools

Dynamic Assessment & Progress Monitoring Tool

Lesson Planning Tool

Interactive Whiteboard Lesson Library

Dynamic Classroom with Dynamic Investigations

EXPLORATION 1 — The Equation of a Circle with Center at the Origin

Work with a partner. Use dynamic geometry software to construct and determine the equations of circles centered at $(0, 0)$ in the coordinate plane, as described below.

Radius	Equation of circle
1	
2	

a. Complete the first two rows of the table for circles with the given radii. Complete the other rows for circles with radii of your choice.

b. Write an equation of a circle with center $(0, 0)$ and radius r.

EXPLORATION 2 — The Equation of a Circle with Center (h, k)

Work with a partner. Use dynamic geometry software to construct and determine the equations of circles of radius 2 in the coordinate plane, as described below.

Center	Equation of circle
$(0, 0)$	
$(2, 0)$	

a. Complete the first two rows of the table for circles with the given centers. Complete the other rows for circles with centers of your choice.

b. Write an equation of a circle with center (h, k) and radius 2.

c. Write an equation of a circle with center (h, k) and radius r.

EXPLORATION 3 — Deriving the Standard Equation of a Circle

MAKING SENSE OF PROBLEMS

To be proficient in math, you need to explain correspondences between equations and graphs.

Work with a partner. Consider a circle with radius r and center (h, k).

Write the Distance Formula to represent the distance d between a point (x, y) on the circle and the center (h, k) of the circle. Then square each side of the Distance Formula equation.

How does your result compare with the equation you wrote in part (c) of Exploration 2?

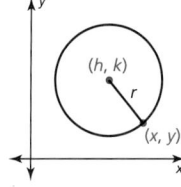

Communicate Your Answer

4. What is the equation of a circle with center (h, k) and radius r in the coordinate plane?

5. Write an equation of the circle with center $(4, -1)$ and radius 3.

Section 10.7   Circles in the Coordinate Plane   **575**

ANSWERS

1. a. *Sample answer:*

Radius	Equation of Circle
1	$x^2 + y^2 = 1$
2	$x^2 + y^2 = 4$
3	$x^2 + y^2 = 9$
5	$x^2 + y^2 = 25$
6	$x^2 + y^2 = 36$
9	$x^2 + y^2 = 81$

   b. $x^2 + y^2 = r^2$

2. a. *Sample answer:*

Center	Equation of Circle
$(0, 0)$	$x^2 + y^2 = 4$
$(2, 0)$	$(x - 2)^2 + y^2 = 4$
$(0, 3)$	$x^2 + (y - 3)^2 = 4$
$(2, -3)$	$(x - 2)^2 + (y + 3)^2 = 4$
$(-1, 4)$	$(x + 1)^2 + (y - 4)^2 = 4$
$(-3, -6)$	$(x + 3)^2 + (y + 6)^2 = 4$

   b. $(x - h)^2 + (y - k)^2 = 4$

   c. $(x - h)^2 + (y - k)^2 = r^2$

3. $\sqrt{(x - h)^2 + (y - k)^2} = d$;
   $(x - h)^2 + (y - k)^2 = d^2$;
   If $d = r$, then the equations are the same.

4. $(x - h)^2 + (y - k)^2 = r^2$

5. $(x - 4)^2 + (y + 1)^2 = 9$

Extra Example 1

Write the standard equation of each circle.

a.

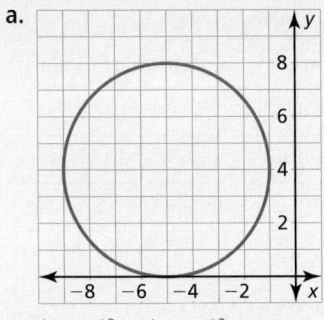

$(x + 5)^2 + (y - 4)^2 = 16$

b. a circle with center at the origin and radius 3.5 $x^2 + y^2 = 12.25$

MONITORING PROGRESS ANSWERS

1. $x^2 + y^2 = 6.25$
2. $(x + 2)^2 + (y - 5)^2 = 49$

10.7 Lesson

What You Will Learn

▶ Write and graph equations of circles.

▶ Write coordinate proofs involving circles.

▶ Solve real-life problems using graphs of circles.

Writing and Graphing Equations of Circles

Let (x, y) represent any point on a circle with center at the origin and radius r. By the Pythagorean Theorem (Theorem 9.1),

$$x^2 + y^2 = r^2.$$

This is the equation of a circle with center at the origin and radius r.

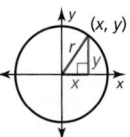

🔄 Core Concept

Standard Equation of a Circle

Let (x, y) represent any point on a circle with center (h, k) and radius r. By the Pythagorean Theorem (Theorem 9.1),

$$(x - h)^2 + (y - k)^2 = r^2.$$

This is the **standard equation of a circle** with center (h, k) and radius r.

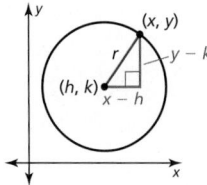

EXAMPLE 1 **Writing the Standard Equation of a Circle**

Write the standard equation of each circle.

a. the circle shown at the left

b. a circle with center $(0, -9)$ and radius 4.2

SOLUTION

a. The radius is 3, and the center is at the origin.

$$(x - h)^2 + (y - k)^2 = r^2 \quad \text{Standard equation of a circle}$$

$$(x - 0)^2 + (y - 0)^2 = 3^2 \quad \text{Substitute.}$$

$$x^2 + y^2 = 9 \quad \text{Simplify.}$$

▶ The standard equation of the circle is $x^2 + y^2 = 9$.

b. The radius is 4.2, and the center is at $(0, -9)$.

$$(x - h)^2 + (y - k)^2 = r^2$$

$$(x - 0)^2 + [y - (-9)]^2 = 4.2^2$$

$$x^2 + (y + 9)^2 = 17.64$$

▶ The standard equation of the circle is $x^2 + (y + 9)^2 = 17.64$.

Monitoring Progress 🔊 Help in English and Spanish at *BigIdeasMath.com*

Write the standard equation of the circle with the given center and radius.

1. center: $(0, 0)$, radius: 2.5

2. center: $(-2, 5)$, radius: 7

Laurie's Notes — Teacher Actions

• Write the *Core Concept*, the standard equation of a circle. Explain to students that it is desirable to leave the equation in this form versus squaring each binomial. Information about the graph is easy to see when it is left in standard form.

COMMON ERROR Students may use the incorrect sign. The equation is in the form of $(x - h)$. When h (or k) is a negative number and the subtraction is performed, it is written $(x + |h|)$.

 **EXAMPLE 2** **Writing the Standard Equation of a Circle**

The point $(-5, 6)$ is on a circle with center $(-1, 3)$. Write the standard equation of the circle.

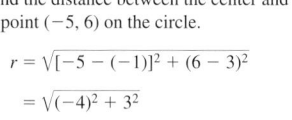

SOLUTION

To write the standard equation, you need to know the values of h, k, and r. To find r, find the distance between the center and the point $(-5, 6)$ on the circle.

$$r = \sqrt{[-5 - (-1)]^2 + (6 - 3)^2}$$ Distance Formula

$$= \sqrt{(-4)^2 + 3^2}$$ Simplify.

$$= 5$$ Simplify.

Substitute the values for the center and the radius into the standard equation of a circle.

$$(x - h)^2 + (y - k)^2 = r^2$$ Standard equation of a circle

$$[x - (-1)]^2 + (y - 3)^2 = 5^2$$ Substitute $(h, k) = (-1, 3)$ and $r = 5$.

$$(x + 1)^2 + (y - 3)^2 = 25$$ Simplify.

▶ The standard equation of the circle is $(x + 1)^2 + (y - 3)^2 = 25$.

REMEMBER

To complete the square for the expression $x^2 + bx$, add the square of half the coefficient of the term bx.

$$x^2 + bx + \left(\frac{b}{2}\right)^2 = \left(x + \frac{b}{2}\right)^2$$

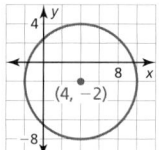

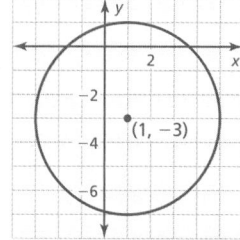

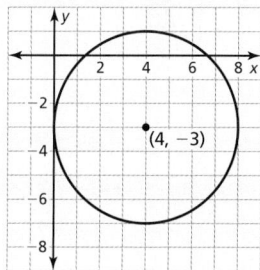

EXAMPLE 3 **Graphing a Circle**

The equation of a circle is $x^2 + y^2 - 8x + 4y - 16 = 0$. Find the center and the radius of the circle. Then graph the circle.

SOLUTION

You can write the equation in standard form by completing the square on the x-terms and the y-terms.

$$x^2 + y^2 - 8x + 4y - 16 = 0$$ Equation of circle

$$x^2 - 8x + y^2 + 4y = 16$$ Isolate constant. Group terms.

$$x^2 - 8x + 16 + y^2 + 4y + 4 = 16 + 16 + 4$$ Complete the square twice.

$$(x - 4)^2 + (y + 2)^2 = 36$$ Factor left side. Simplify right side.

$$(x - 4)^2 + [y - (-2)]^2 = 6^2$$ Rewrite the equation to find the center and the radius.

▶ The center is $(4, -2)$, and the radius is 6. Use a compass to graph the circle.

Monitoring Progress 🔊 Help in English and Spanish at *BigIdeasMath.com*

3. The point $(3, 4)$ is on a circle with center $(1, 4)$. Write the standard equation of the circle.

4. The equation of a circle is $x^2 + y^2 - 8x + 6y + 9 = 0$. Find the center and the radius of the circle. Then graph the circle.

Extra Example 2
The point $(4, 1)$ is on a circle with center $(1, 4)$. Write the standard equation of the circle. $(x - 1)^2 + (y - 4)^2 = 18$

Extra Example 3
The equation of a circle is $x^2 + y^2 - 2x + 6y - 6 = 0$. Find the center and the radius of the circle. Then graph the circle.   center $(1, -3)$; radius 4

MONITORING PROGRESS ANSWERS

3. $(x - 1)^2 + (y - 4)^2 = 4$

4. center: $(4, -3)$, radius: 4

Laurie's Notes **Teacher Actions**

❓ Pose Example 2. "Will using any point on the circle result in the same standard equation for the circle?" yes

❓ "What is the first step in solving this problem?" finding the radius of the circle

• Have students work with their partners to finish the example.

• Example 3 requires the technique of completing the square, twice.

• **Teaching Tip:** Write $(x^2 - 8x + \underline{?}) + (y^2 + 4y + \underline{?}) = 16$. "What needs to be in the blanks to make the quantity within each set of parentheses a perfect square trinomial?" 16 and 4

• The *Teaching Strategy* on page T-574 shows how to graph a circle in standard form on a graphing calculator.

Extra Example 4

Prove or disprove that the point $(3, \sqrt{7})$ lies on the circle centered at the origin and containing the point $(1, 4)$. The radius of the circle is $\sqrt{17} \approx 4.12$. The distance from $(3, \sqrt{7})$ to the origin is $\sqrt{16} = 4$. So, the point $(3, \sqrt{7})$ does not lie on the circle.

Extra Example 5

The epicenter of an earthquake is 10 miles away from $(-1, -3)$, 2 miles away from $(5, 3)$, and 5 miles away from $(2, 9)$. Find the coordinates of the epicenter.
about $(5, 5)$

MONITORING PROGRESS ANSWERS

5. The radius of the circle is 1.
$$\sqrt{(1-0)^2 + (\sqrt{5}-0)^2} = \sqrt{6},$$
so $(1, \sqrt{5})$ does not lie on the circle.

6. Two circles can intersect at more than one point.

Writing Coordinate Proofs Involving Circles

EXAMPLE 4   Writing a Coordinate Proof Involving a Circle

Prove or disprove that the point $(\sqrt{2}, \sqrt{2})$ lies on the circle centered at the origin and containing the point $(2, 0)$.

SOLUTION

The circle centered at the origin and containing the point $(2, 0)$ has the following radius.
$$r = \sqrt{(x-h)^2 + (y-k)^2} = \sqrt{(2-0)^2 + (0-0)^2} = 2$$

So, a point lies on the circle if and only if the distance from that point to the origin is 2. The distance from $(\sqrt{2}, \sqrt{2})$ to $(0, 0)$ is
$$d = \sqrt{(\sqrt{2}-0)^2 + (\sqrt{2}-0)^2} = 2.$$

▶ So, the point $(\sqrt{2}, \sqrt{2})$ lies on the circle centered at the origin and containing the point $(2, 0)$.

Monitoring Progress Help in English and Spanish at *BigIdeasMath.com*

5. Prove or disprove that the point $(1, \sqrt{5})$ lies on the circle centered at the origin and containing the point $(0, 1)$.

Solving Real-Life Problems

EXAMPLE 5   Using Graphs of Circles

The epicenter of an earthquake is the point on Earth's surface directly above the earthquake's origin. A seismograph can be used to determine the distance to the epicenter of an earthquake. Seismographs are needed in three different places to locate an earthquake's epicenter.

Use the seismograph readings from locations A, B, and C to find the epicenter of an earthquake.

- The epicenter is 7 miles away from $A(-2, 2.5)$.
- The epicenter is 4 miles away from $B(4, 6)$.
- The epicenter is 5 miles away from $C(3, -2.5)$.

SOLUTION

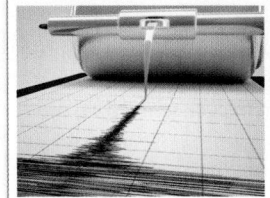

The set of all points equidistant from a given point is a circle, so the epicenter is located on each of the following circles.

⊙A with center $(-2, 2.5)$ and radius 7
⊙B with center $(4, 6)$ and radius 4
⊙C with center $(3, -2.5)$ and radius 5

To find the epicenter, graph the circles on a coordinate plane where each unit corresponds to one mile. Find the point of intersection of the three circles.

▶ The epicenter is at about $(5, 2)$.

Monitoring Progress Help in English and Spanish at *BigIdeasMath.com*

6. Why are three seismographs needed to locate an earthquake's epicenter?

Laurie's Notes   Teacher Actions

? Work through Example 4. "How else could you prove or disprove that $(\sqrt{2}, \sqrt{2})$ is on the circle?" See whether the coordinates satisfy the equation of the circle.

- **MP5 Use Appropriate Tools Strategically:** In Example 5, have students use a compass to construct the three circles on graph paper. Alternately, they can graph them using dynamic geometry software or a graphing calculator. The calculator technique is described in the *Teaching Strategy* on page T-574.

Closure

- **Exit Ticket:** Write the equation of a circle with center $(-1, 3)$ and radius 5. Graph the equation. $(x + 1)^2 + (y - 3)^2 = 25$; Check students' graphs.

Vocabulary and Core Concept Check

1. **VOCABULARY** What is the standard equation of a circle?

2. **WRITING** Explain why knowing the location of the center and one point on a circle is enough to graph the circle.

Monitoring Progress and Modeling with Mathematics

In Exercises 3–8, write the standard equation of the circle. *(See Example 1.)*

3.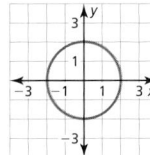

4.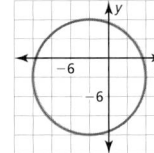

5. a circle with center $(0, 0)$ and radius 7

6. a circle with center $(4, 1)$ and radius 5

7. a circle with center $(-3, 4)$ and radius 1

8. a circle with center $(3, -5)$ and radius 7

In Exercises 9–11, use the given information to write the standard equation of the circle. *(See Example 2.)*

9. The center is $(0, 0)$, and a point on the circle is $(0, 6)$.

10. The center is $(1, 2)$, and a point on the circle is $(4, 2)$.

11. The center is $(0, 0)$, and a point on the circle is $(3, -7)$.

12. **ERROR ANALYSIS** Describe and correct the error in writing the standard equation of a circle.

> The standard equation of a circle with center $(-3, -5)$ and radius 3 is $(x - 3)^2 + (y - 5)^2 = 9$.

In Exercises 13–18, find the center and radius of the circle. Then graph the circle. *(See Example 3.)*

13. $x^2 + y^2 = 49$

14. $(x + 5)^2 + (y - 3)^2 = 9$

15. $x^2 + y^2 - 6x = 7$

16. $x^2 + y^2 + 4y = 32$

17. $x^2 + y^2 - 8x - 2y = -16$

18. $x^2 + y^2 + 4x + 12y = -15$

In Exercises 19–22, prove or disprove the statement. *(See Example 4.)*

19. The point $(2, 3)$ lies on the circle centered at the origin with radius 8.

20. The point $(4, \sqrt{5})$ lies on the circle centered at the origin with radius 3.

21. The point $(\sqrt{6}, 2)$ lies on the circle centered at the origin and containing the point $(3, -1)$.

22. The point $(\sqrt{7}, 5)$ lies on the circle centered at the origin and containing the point $(5, 2)$.

23. **MODELING WITH MATHEMATICS** A city's commuter system has three zones. Zone 1 serves people living within 3 miles of the city's center. Zone 2 serves those between 3 and 7 miles from the center. Zone 3 serves those over 7 miles from the center. *(See Example 5.)*

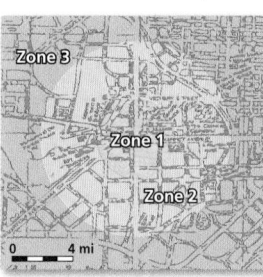

a. Graph this situation on a coordinate plane where each unit corresponds to 1 mile. Locate the city's center at the origin.

b. Determine which zone serves people whose homes are represented by the points $(3, 4)$, $(6, 5)$, $(1, 2)$, $(0, 3)$, and $(1, 6)$.

Assignment Guide and Homework Check

ASSIGNMENT

Basic: 1, 2, 3–11 odd, 12, 13–23 odd, 26, 33, 35–40

Average: 1, 2, 6–26 even, 33, 35–40

Advanced: 1, 2, 8–26 even, 28–40

HOMEWORK CHECK

Basic: 7, 11, 17, 19, 26

Average: 8, 10, 18, 22, 26

Advanced: 10, 18, 26, 28, 29

ANSWERS

1. $(x - h)^2 + (y - k)^2 = r^2$

2. The distance from the center to the point is the radius.

3. $x^2 + y^2 = 4$

4. $(x + 3)^2 + (y + 3)^2 = 81$

5. $x^2 + y^2 = 49$

6. $(x - 4)^2 + (y - 1)^2 = 25$

7. $(x + 3)^2 + (y - 4)^2 = 1$

8. $(x - 3)^2 + (y + 5)^2 = 49$

9. $x^2 + y^2 = 36$

10. $(x - 1)^2 + (y - 2)^2 = 9$

11. $x^2 + y^2 = 58$

12. The coordinates of the center should be subtracted; $[x - (-3)]^2 + [y - (-5)]^2 = (x + 3)^2 + (y + 5)^2 = 9$

13. center: $(0, 0)$, radius: 7

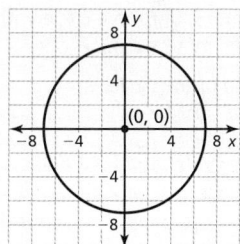

14. center: $(-5, 3)$, radius: 3

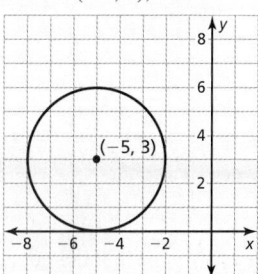

15. center: $(3, 0)$, radius: 4

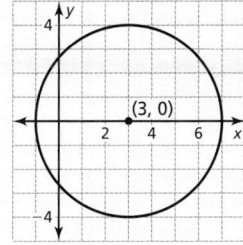

16. center: $(0, -2)$, radius: 6

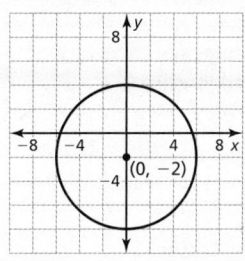

17–23. See Additional Answers.

ANSWERS

24. a.

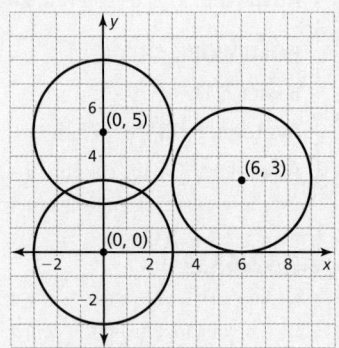

yes; Two circles overlap.

b. City B; Parts of City A do not have coverage.

25–40. See Additional Answers.

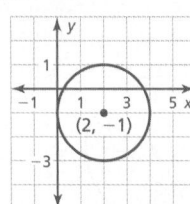
580   Chapter 10

---

24. **MODELING WITH MATHEMATICS** Telecommunication towers can be used to transmit cellular phone calls. A graph with units measured in kilometers shows towers at points $(0, 0)$, $(0, 5)$, and $(6, 3)$. These towers have a range of about 3 kilometers.

   a. Sketch a graph and locate the towers. Are there any locations that may receive calls from more than one tower? Explain your reasoning.

   b. The center of City A is located at $(-2, 2.5)$, and the center of City B is located at $(5, 4)$. Each city has a radius of 1.5 kilometers. Which city seems to have better cell phone coverage? Explain your reasoning.

25. **REASONING** Sketch the graph of the circle whose equation is $x^2 + y^2 = 16$. Then sketch the graph of the circle after the translation $(x, y) \rightarrow (x - 2, y - 4)$. What is the equation of the image? Make a conjecture about the equation of the image of a circle centered at the origin after a translation m units to the left and n units down.

26. **HOW DO YOU SEE IT?** Match each graph with its equation.

   a. 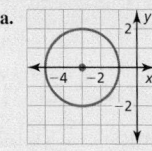   b.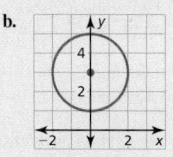

   c. 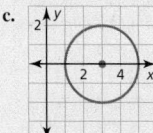   d.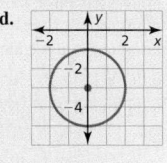

   A. $x^2 + (y + 3)^2 = 4$ B. $(x - 3)^2 + y^2 = 4$

   C. $(x + 3)^2 + y^2 = 4$ D. $x^2 + (y - 3)^2 = 4$

27. **USING STRUCTURE** The vertices of $\triangle XYZ$ are $X(4, 5)$, $Y(4, 13)$, and $Z(8, 9)$. Find the equation of the circle circumscribed about $\triangle XYZ$. Justify your answer.

28. **THOUGHT PROVOKING** A circle has center (h, k) and contains point (a, b). Write the equation of the line tangent to the circle at point (a, b).

MATHEMATICAL CONNECTIONS In Exercises 29–32, use the equations to determine whether the line is *a tangent*, *a secant*, *a secant that contains the diameter*, or *none of these*. Explain your reasoning.

29. Circle: $(x - 4)^2 + (y - 3)^2 = 9$
    Line: $y = 6$

30. Circle: $(x + 2)^2 + (y - 2)^2 = 16$
    Line: $y = 2x - 4$

31. Circle: $(x - 5)^2 + (y + 1)^2 = 4$
    Line: $y = \frac{1}{5}x - 3$

32. Circle: $(x + 3)^2 + (y - 6)^2 = 25$
    Line: $y = -\frac{4}{3}x + 2$

33. **MAKING AN ARGUMENT** Your friend claims that the equation of a circle passing through the points $(-1, 0)$ and $(1, 0)$ is $x^2 - 2yk + y^2 = 1$ with center $(0, k)$. Is your friend correct? Explain your reasoning.

34. **REASONING** Four tangent circles are centered on the x-axis. The radius of $\odot A$ is twice the radius of $\odot O$. The radius of $\odot B$ is three times the radius of $\odot O$. The radius of $\odot C$ is four times the radius of $\odot O$. All circles have integer radii, and the point $(63, 16)$ is on $\odot C$. What is the equation of $\odot A$? Explain your reasoning.

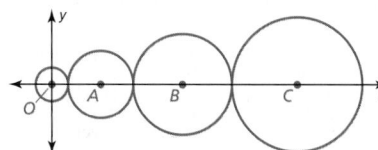

Maintaining Mathematical Proficiency

Reviewing what you learned in previous grades and lessons

Identify the arc as a *major arc*, *minor arc*, or *semicircle*. Then find the measure of the arc. *(Section 10.2)*

35. $\overset{\frown}{RS}$ 36. $\overset{\frown}{PR}$

37. $\overset{\frown}{PRT}$ 38. $\overset{\frown}{ST}$

39. $\overset{\frown}{RST}$ 40. $\overset{\frown}{QS}$

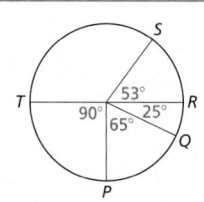

Core Vocabulary

inscribed angle, *p. 554*
intercepted arc, *p. 554*
subtend, *p. 554*
inscribed polygon, *p. 556*

circumscribed circle, *p. 556*
circumscribed angle, *p. 564*
segments of a chord, *p. 570*
tangent segment, *p. 571*

secant segment, *p. 571*
external segment, *p. 571*
standard equation of a circle, *p. 576*

ANSWERS
1. *Sample answer:* a compass and straightedge
2. $\angle BAC$ could be acute or obtuse.

Core Concepts

Section 10.4

Inscribed Angle and Intercepted Arc, *p. 554*
Theorem 10.10 Measure of an Inscribed Angle Theorem, *p. 554*
Theorem 10.11 Inscribed Angles of a Circle Theorem, *p. 555*

Inscribed Polygon, *p. 556*
Theorem 10.12 Inscribed Right Triangle Theorem, *p. 556*
Theorem 10.13 Inscribed Quadrilateral Theorem, *p. 556*

Section 10.5

Theorem 10.14 Tangent and Intersected Chord Theorem, *p. 562*
Intersecting Lines and Circles, *p. 562*
Theorem 10.15 Angles Inside the Circle Theorem, *p. 563*

Theorem 10.16 Angles Outside the Circle Theorem, *p. 563*
Circumscribed Angle, *p. 564*
Theorem 10.17 Circumscribed Angle Theorem, *p. 564*

Section 10.6

Theorem 10.18 Segments of Chords Theorem, *p. 570*
Tangent Segment and Secant Segment, *p. 571*
Theorem 10.19 Segments of Secants Theorem, *p. 571*

Theorem 10.20 Segments of Secants and Tangents Theorem, *p. 572*

Section 10.7

Standard Equation of a Circle, *p. 576*

Writing Coordinate Proofs Involving Circles, *p. 578*

Mathematical Practices

1. What other tools could you use to complete the task in Exercise 18 on page 559?

2. You have a classmate who is confused about why two diagrams are needed in part (a) of Exercise 31 on page 567. Explain to your classmate why two diagrams are needed.

- - - - - - - - - - - **Performance Task** - - -
Circular Motion

What do the properties of tangents tell us about the forces acting on a satellite orbiting around Earth? How would the path of the satellite change if the force of gravity were removed?

To explore the answers to this question and more, go to *BigIdeasMath.com*.

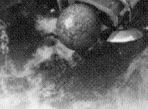

581

10.1 **Lines and Segments That Intersect Circles** *(pp. 529–536)*

In the diagram, $\overline{AB}$ is tangent to $\odot C$ at B and $\overline{AD}$ is tangent to $\odot C$ at D. Find the value of x.

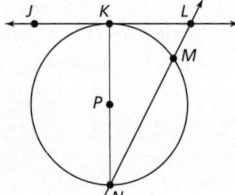

$AB = AD$	External Tangent Congruence Theorem (Theorem 10.2)
$2x + 5 = 33$	Substitute.
$x = 14$	Solve for x.

▶ The value of x is 14.

Tell whether the line, ray, or segment is best described as a *radius*, *chord*, *diameter*, *secant*, or *tangent* of $\odot P$.

1. $\overline{PK}$ 2. $\overline{NM}$

3. $\overrightarrow{JL}$ 4. $\overline{KN}$

5. $\overleftrightarrow{NL}$ 6. $\overline{PN}$

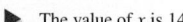

Tell whether the common tangent is *internal* or *external*.

7.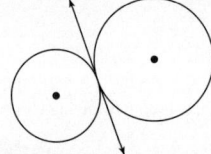

8.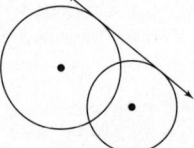

Points Y and Z are points of tangency. Find the value of the variable.

9.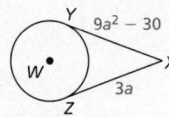

10.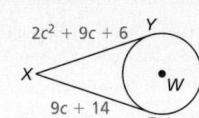

11.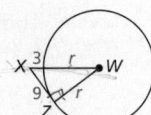

12. Tell whether $\overline{AB}$ is tangent to $\odot C$. Explain.

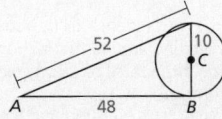

13. 100°
14. 60°
15. 160°
16. 80°
17. not congruent; The circles are not congruent.
18. congruent; The circles are congruent and $m\widehat{AB} = m\widehat{EF}$.
19. 61°
20. 65°
21. 91°
22. 26

10.2 **Finding Arc Measures** *(pp. 537–544)*

Find the measure of each arc of ⊙P, where $\overline{LN}$ is a diameter.

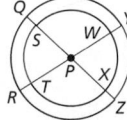

a. $\widehat{MN}$

▶ $\widehat{MN}$ is a minor arc, so $m\widehat{MN} = m\angle MPN = 120°$.

b. $\widehat{NLM}$

▶ $\widehat{NLM}$ is a major arc, so $m\widehat{NLM} = 360° - 120° = 240°$.

c. $\widehat{NML}$

▶ $\overline{NL}$ is a diameter, so $\widehat{NML}$ is a semicircle, and $m\widehat{NML} = 180°$.

Use the diagram above to find the measure of the indicated arc.

13. $\widehat{KL}$ 14. $\widehat{LM}$ 15. $\widehat{KM}$ 16. $\widehat{KN}$

Tell whether the red arcs are congruent. Explain why or why not.

17. 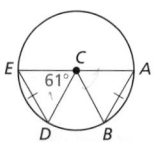   18.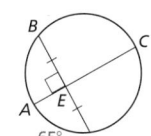

10.3 **Using Chords** *(pp. 545–550)*

In the diagram, ⊙$A \cong$ ⊙B, $\overline{CD} \cong \overline{FE}$, and $m\widehat{FE} = 75°$. Find $m\widehat{CD}$.

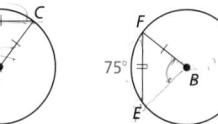

Because $\overline{CD}$ and $\overline{FE}$ are congruent chords in congruent circles, the corresponding minor arcs $\widehat{CD}$ and $\widehat{FE}$ are congruent by the Congruent Corresponding Chords Theorem (Theorem 10.6).

▶ So, $m\widehat{CD} = m\widehat{FE} = 75°$.

Find the measure of $\widehat{AB}$.

19. 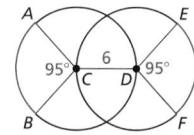   20.   21.

22. In the diagram, $QN = QP = 10$, $JK = 4x$, and $LM = 6x - 24$. Find the radius of ⊙Q.

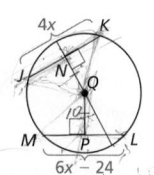

23. 80
24. $q = 100, r = 20$
25. 5
26. $y = 30, z = 10$
27. $m = 44, n = 39$
28. 28

10.4 **Inscribed Angles and Polygons** *(pp. 553–560)*

Find the value of each variable.

$LMNP$ is inscribed in a circle, so opposite angles are supplementary by the Inscribed Quadrilateral Theorem (Theorem 10.13).

$$m\angle L + m\angle N = 180° \qquad m\angle P + m\angle M = 180°$$
$$3a° + 3a° = 180° \qquad b° + 50° = 180°$$
$$6a = 180 \qquad b = 130$$
$$a = 30$$

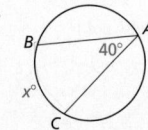

▶ The value of a is 30, and the value of b is 130.

Find the value(s) of the variable(s).

23.

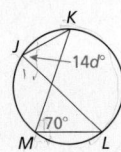

24.

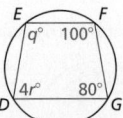

25.

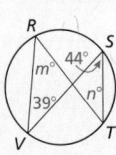

26.

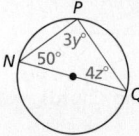

27.

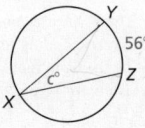

28.

10.5 **Angle Relationships in Circles** *(pp. 561–568)*

Find the value of y.

The tangent $\overrightarrow{RQ}$ and secant $\overrightarrow{RT}$ intersect outside the circle, so you can use the Angles Outside the Circle Theorem (Theorem 10.16).

$$y° = \tfrac{1}{2}(m\widehat{QT} - m\widehat{SQ}) \qquad \text{Angles Outside the Circle Theorem}$$
$$y° = \tfrac{1}{2}(190° - 60°) \qquad \text{Substitute.}$$
$$y = 65 \qquad \text{Simplify.}$$

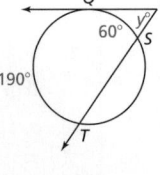

▶ The value of y is 65.

29. 70

30. 106

31. 16

32. 240°

33. 5

34. 3

35. 10

36. about 10.7 ft

Find the value of x.

29.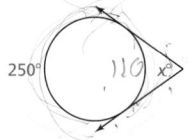

30.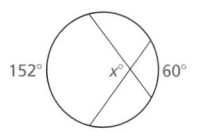

31.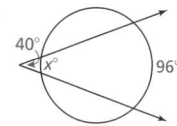

32. Line ℓ is tangent to the circle. Find $m\widehat{XYZ}$.

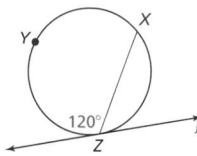

10.6 **Segment Relationships in Circles** *(pp. 569–574)*

Find the value of x.

The chords $\overline{EG}$ and $\overline{FH}$ intersect inside the circle, so you can use the Segments of Chords Theorem (Theorem 10.18).

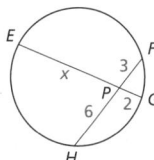

$EP \cdot PG = FP \cdot PH$ Segments of Chords Theorem

$x \cdot 2 = 3 \cdot 6$ Substitute.

$x = 9$ Simplify.

▶ The value of x is 9.

Find the value of x.

33.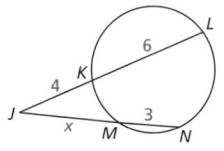

34.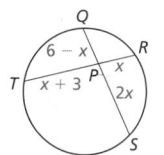

35.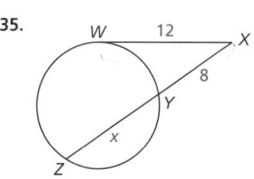

36. A local park has a circular ice skating rink. You are standing at point A, about 12 feet from the edge of the rink. The distance from you to a point of tangency on the rink is about 20 feet. Estimate the radius of the rink.

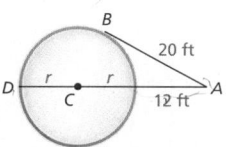

Chapter 10   Chapter Review   **585**

37. $(x - 4)^2 + (y + 1)^2 = 9$
38. $(x - 8)^2 + (y - 6)^2 = 36$
39. $x^2 + y^2 = 16$
40. $x^2 + y^2 = 81$
41. $(x + 5)^2 + (y - 2)^2 = 1.69$
42. $(x - 6)^2 + (y - 21)^2 = 16$
43. $(x + 3)^2 + (y - 2)^2 = 256$
44. $(x - 10)^2 + (y - 7)^2 = 12.25$
45. $x^2 + y^2 = 27.04$
46. $(x + 7)^2 + (y - 6)^2 = 25$
47. center: $(6, -4)$, radius: 2

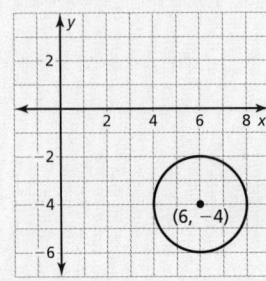

48. The radius of the circle is 5.
$d = \sqrt{(0 - 4)^2 + (0 + 3)^2} = 5$,
so $(4, -3)$ is on the circle.

10.7 **Circles in the Coordinate Plane** *(pp. 575–580)*

Write the standard equation of the circle shown.

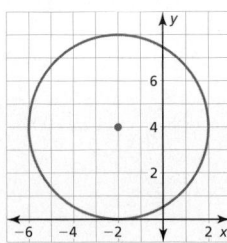

The radius is 4, and the center is $(-2, 4)$.

$(x - h)^2 + (y - k)^2 = r^2$ Standard equation of a circle

$[x - (-2)]^2 + (y - 4)^2 = 4^2$ Substitute.

$(x + 2)^2 + (y - 4)^2 = 16$ Simplify.

▶ The standard equation of the circle is $(x + 2)^2 + (y - 4)^2 = 16$.

Write the standard equation of the circle shown.

37.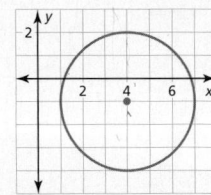

38.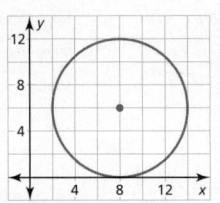

39.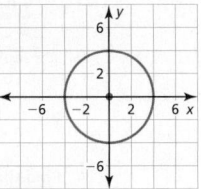

Write the standard equation of the circle with the given center and radius.

40. center: $(0, 0)$, radius: 9

41. center: $(-5, 2)$, radius: 1.3

42. center: $(6, 21)$, radius: 4

43. center: $(-3, 2)$, radius: 16

44. center: $(10, 7)$, radius: 3.5

45. center: $(0, 0)$, radius: 5.2

46. The point $(-7, 1)$ is on a circle with center $(-7, 6)$. Write the standard equation of the circle.

47. The equation of a circle is $x^2 + y^2 - 12x + 8y + 48 = 0$. Find the center and the radius of the circle. Then graph the circle.

48. Prove or disprove that the point $(4, -3)$ lies on the circle centered at the origin and containing the point $(-5, 0)$.

10 Chapter Test

Find the measure of each numbered angle in ⊙P. Justify your answer.

1.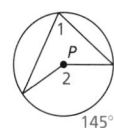

2.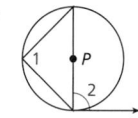

3.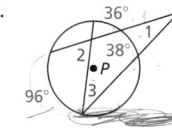

4.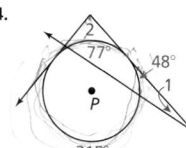

Use the diagram.

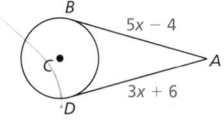

5. $AG = 2$, $GD = 9$, and $BG = 3$. Find GF.

6. $CF = 12$, $CB = 3$, and $CD = 9$. Find CE.

7. $BF = 9$ and $CB = 3$. Find CA.

8. Sketch a pentagon inscribed in a circle. Label the pentagon $ABCDE$. Describe the relationship between each pair of angles. Explain your reasoning.

    a. $\angle CDE$ and $\angle CAE$ **b.** $\angle CBE$ and $\angle CAE$

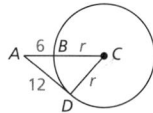

Find the value of the variable. Justify your answer.

9.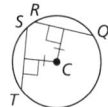

10.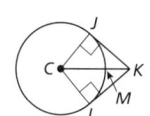

11. Prove or disprove that the point $\left(2\sqrt{2},\ -1\right)$ lies on the circle centered at $(0, 2)$ and containing the point $(-1, 4)$.

Prove the given statement.

12. $\overset{\frown}{ST} \cong \overset{\frown}{RQ}$
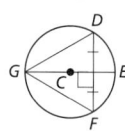

13. $\overset{\frown}{JM} \cong \overset{\frown}{LM}$

14. $\overset{\frown}{DG} \cong \overset{\frown}{FG}$

15. A bank of lighting hangs over a stage. Each light illuminates a circular region on the stage. A coordinate plane is used to arrange the lights, using a corner of the stage as the origin. The equation $(x - 13)^2 + (y - 4)^2 = 16$ represents the boundary of the region illuminated by one of the lights. Three actors stand at the points $A(11, 4)$, $B(8, 5)$, and $C(15, 5)$. Graph the given equation. Then determine which actors are illuminated by the light.

16. If a car goes around a turn too quickly, it can leave tracks that form an arc of a circle. By finding the radius of the circle, accident investigators can estimate the speed of the car.

    a. To find the radius, accident investigators choose points A and B on the tire marks. Then the investigators find the midpoint C of $\overline{AB}$. Use the diagram to find the radius r of the circle. Explain why this method works.

    b. The formula $S = 3.87\sqrt{fr}$ can be used to estimate a car's speed in miles per hour, where f is the *coefficient of friction* and r is the radius of the circle in feet. If $f = 0.7$, estimate the car's speed in part (a).

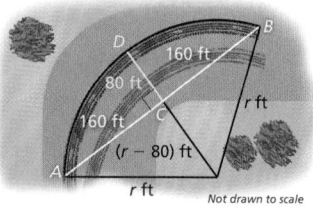

If students need help...	If students got it...

Lesson Tutorials	Resources by Chapter
	  • Enrichment and Extension
	  • Cumulative Review

Skills Review Handbook	Performance Task
BigIdeasMath.com	Start the *next* Section

ANSWERS

1. $m\angle 1 = 72.5°$, $m\angle 2 = 145°$; $\angle 1$ is an inscribed angle and $\angle 2$ is a central angle.

2. $m\angle 1 = 90°$, $m\angle 2 = 90°$; $\angle 1$ and $\angle 2$ intercept a semicircle.

3. $m\angle 1 = 29°$, $m\angle 2 = 66°$, $m\angle 3 = 37°$; $\angle 1$ is outside the circle, $\angle 2$ is inside the circle, and $\angle 3$ is an inscribed angle.

4. $m\angle 1 = 14.5°$, $m\angle 2 = 83°$; $\angle 1$ and $\angle 2$ are outside the circle.

5. 6   **6.** 4

7. 6

8. *Sample answer:*

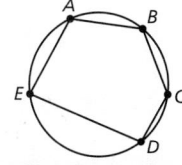

    a. They are supplementary; The arc measures sum to 360°.

    b. They are congruent; They intercept the same arc.

9. 5; $5x - 4 = 3x + 6$

10. 9; $m\angle D = 90°$, so $r^2 + 12^2 = (r + 6)^2$.

11. The radius of the circle is $\sqrt{5}$. $d = \sqrt{\left(2\sqrt{2} - 0\right)^2 + (-1 - 2)^2}$ $= \sqrt{17}$, so $\left(2\sqrt{2}, -1\right)$ does not lie on the circle.

12. By the Equidistant Chords Theorem (Thm. 10.19), $\overline{ST} \cong \overline{RQ}$. By the Congruent Corresponding Chords Theorem (Thm. 10.6), $\overset{\frown}{ST} \cong \overset{\frown}{RQ}$.

13. $\overline{CJ} \cong \overline{CL}$ and $\overline{CK} \cong \overline{CK}$, so $\triangle CKJ \cong \triangle CKL$ by the HL Congruence Theorem (Thm. 5.9). Then $\angle LCK \cong \angle JCK$, and by the Congruent Central Angles Theorem (Thm. 10.4), $\overset{\frown}{JM} \cong \overset{\frown}{LM}$.

14. $\overline{GE}$ is a perpendicular bisector of $\overline{DF}$, so $DG = FG$ by the Perpendicular Bisector Theorem (Thm. 6.1). By the Congruent Corresponding Chords Theorem (Thm. 10.6), $\overset{\frown}{DG} \cong \overset{\frown}{FG}$.

15.

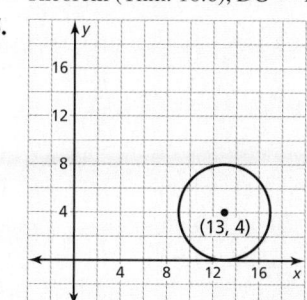

    A, C

16. **a.** 200 ft; $\overline{DC}$ lies on the diameter, so $160^2 + (r - 80)^2 = r^2$.

    b. about 46 mi/h

1. Classify each segment as specifically as possible.

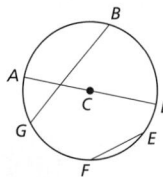

   a. $\overline{BG}$ **b.** $\overline{CD}$ **c.** $\overline{AD}$ **d.** $\overline{FE}$

2. Copy and complete the paragraph proof.

   Given Circle C with center $(2, 1)$ and radius 1, Circle D with center $(0, 3)$ and radius 4

   Prove Circle C is similar to Circle D.

   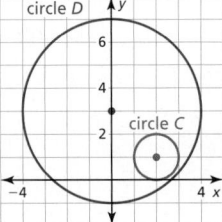

   Map Circle C to Circle C' by using the _____ $(x, y) \rightarrow$ _____ so that Circle C' and Circle D have the same center at $(\_, \_)$. Dilate Circle C' using a center of dilation $(\_, \_)$ and a scale factor of $\_\_$. Because there is a _____ transformation that maps Circle C to Circle D, Circle C is _____ Circle D.

3. Use the diagram to write a proof.

   Given $\triangle JPL \cong \triangle NPL$

   $\overline{PK}$ is an altitude of $\triangle JPL$.

   $\overline{PM}$ is an altitude of $\triangle NPL$.

   Prove $\triangle PKL \sim \triangle NMP$

   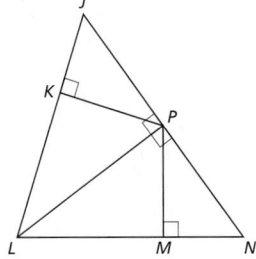

4. The equation of a circle is $x^2 + y^2 + 14x - 16y + 77 = 0$. What are the center and radius of the circle?

   Ⓐ center: $(14, -16)$, radius: 8.8

   Ⓑ center: $(-7, 8)$, radius: 6

   Ⓒ center: $(-14, 16)$, radius: 8.8

   Ⓓ center: $(7, -8)$, radius: 5.2

5. The coordinates of the vertices of a quadrilateral are $W(-7, -6)$, $X(1, -2)$, $Y(3, -6)$, and $Z(-5, -10)$. Prove that quadrilateral $WXYZ$ is a rectangle.

6. Which angles have the same measure as $\angle ACB$? Select all that apply.

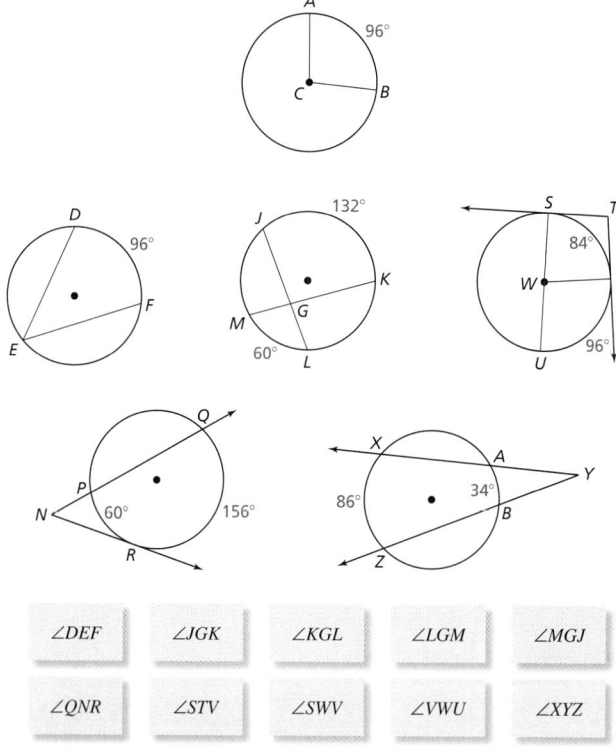

| $\angle DEF$ | $\angle JGK$ | $\angle KGL$ | $\angle LGM$ | $\angle MGJ$ |
| $\angle QNR$ | $\angle STV$ | $\angle SWV$ | $\angle VWU$ | $\angle XYZ$ |

7. Classify each related conditional statement based on the conditional statement "If you are a soccer player, then you are an athlete."

   a. If you are not a soccer player, then you are not an athlete.

   b. If you are an athlete, then you are a soccer player.

   c. You are a soccer player if and only if you are an athlete.

   d. If you are not an athlete, then you are not a soccer player.

8. Your friend claims that the quadrilateral shown can be inscribed in a circle. Is your friend correct? Explain your reasoning.

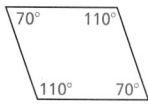

5. $WY = \sqrt{(-7-3)^2 + (-6-(-6))^2}$
   $= 10$
   $XZ = \sqrt{(1-(-5))^2 + (-2-(-10))^2}$
   $= 10$

   By the Rectangles Diagonals Theorem (Thm. 7.13), $WXYZ$ is a rectangle.

6. $\angle JGK$, $\angle LGM$, $\angle STV$, $\angle VWU$

7. a. inverse

   b. converse

   c. biconditional

   d. contrapositive

8. no; Opposite angles are not supplementary.

11 Circumference, Area, and Volume

Khafre's Pyramid (p. 637)

Gold Density (p. 628)

Basaltic Columns (p. 615)

SEE the Big Idea

Population Density (p. 603)

London Eye (p. 599)

Chapter Summary

- This chapter on circumference, area, and volume finishes the study of measurement of solids that began in middle school.
- Students will come to this chapter with knowledge of many formulas for surface area and volume. These will be reviewed and a few new formulas added to the list.
- Different from middle school is that students now have a greater ability to solve equations. They also know the Pythagorean Theorem and trigonometry, so they are able to solve for measures that previously had to be told to them.
- In this chapter, students will do additional work with circles involving arc length and area of sectors. Students will also find the area of regular polygons.

Scaffolding in the Classroom

Use vocabulary as a connector.
When introducing vocabulary, ask students whether they are familiar with the word and what they think it means. Have them explain how they think the word relates to math. Students then find the definition and compare their original ideas to the actual meaning.

 COMMON CORE PROGRESSION

Middle School
- Find the area and circumference of a circle.
- Find the areas of triangles, special quadrilaterals, and polygons.
- Describe the two-dimensional figures that result from slicing three-dimensional figures.
- Apply the formulas for the volumes of rectangular prisms, cones, cylinders, and spheres.
- Solve real-life problems involving area, volume, and surface area of composite figures and objects

Algebra 1
- Rewrite and use literal equations and formulas for area.
- Write and solve linear equations in one variable.
- Use multi-step linear equations to solve real-life problems.
- Use unit analysis to model real-life problems.
- Solve quadratic equations in one variable.

Geometry
- Measure angles in radians.
- Find arc lengths and areas of sectors of circles.
- Find areas of rhombuses, kites, and regular polygons.
- Find and use volumes of prisms, cylinders, pyramids, cones, and spheres.
- Describe cross-sections and solids of revolution.

Standards Summary		
Section	**Common Core State Standards**	
11.1	Learning	HSG-GMD.A.1, HSG-C.B.5, HSG-CO.A.1
11.2	Learning	HSG-GMD.A.1, HSG-MG.A.2, HSG-C.B.5
11.3	Preparing	HSG-GMD.A.3
11.4	Learning	HSG-GMD.B.4
11.5	Learning	HSG-GMD.A.1, HSG-GMD.A.2, HSG-GMD.A.3, HSG-MG.A.1, HSG-MG.A.2, HSG-MG.A.3
11.6	Learning	HSG-GMD.A.1, HSG-GMD.A.3, HSG-MG.A.1
11.7	Learning	HSG-GMD.A.1, HSG-GMD.A.3
11.8	Learning	HSG-GMD.A.2, HSG-GMD.A.3, HSG-MG.A.1

Questioning in the Classroom

Wait Time

Students need the opportunity to process the question before formulating an answer. Although the silence is difficult, make certain to give sufficient time before calling on someone or answering yourself.

Laurie's Notes

Maintaining Mathematical Proficiency

Finding Surface Area

• Remind students that the surface area of a prism is the sum of the areas of *all* the faces.

• Point out that the formula for the area A of a triangle with base b and corresponding height h is $A = \frac{1}{2}bh$.

COMMON ERROR Students may confuse lateral area and surface area. Referring to *total surface area* instead of *surface area* can help.

Finding a Missing Dimension

• Point out that the formula for the perimeter P of a rectangle $P = 2\ell + 2w$ can also be written as $P = 2(\ell + w)$.

• Remind students that after they substitute the known dimensions into the formula, they should solve using inverse operations, as they have done with other algebraic equations.

COMMON ERROR Students may confuse perimeter and area. Remind them that perimeter is measured in linear units and area is measured in square units.

Mathematical Practices (continued on page 592)

• The eight *Mathematical Practices* focus attention on how mathematics is learned—process versus content. Page 592 demonstrates that a mathematically proficient student can create a coherent representation of a problem. The representation helps to make sense of the problem and/or aids in the solution of the problem.

• Use the *Mathematical Practices* page to help students develop mathematical habits of mind—how mathematics can be explored and how mathematics is thought about.

If students need help...	If students got it...
Student Journal • Maintaining Mathematical Proficiency	Game Closet at *BigIdeasMath.com*
Lesson Tutorials	Start the *next* Section
Skills Review Handbook	

Maintaining Mathematical Proficiency

Finding Surface Area

Example 1 Find the surface area of the prism.

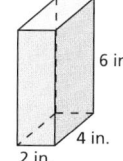
6 in.
4 in.
2 in.

$S = 2\ell w + 2\ell h + 2wh$ Write formula for surface area of a rectangular prism.

$= 2(2)(4) + 2(2)(6) + 2(4)(6)$ Substitute 2 for ℓ, 4 for w, and 6 for h.

$= 16 + 24 + 48$ Multiply.

$= 88$ Add.

▶ The surface area is 88 square inches.

Find the surface area of the prism.

1.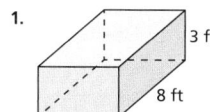
3 ft
8 ft
5 ft

2.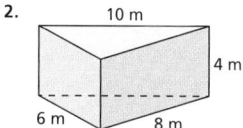
10 m
4 m
6 m
8 m

3.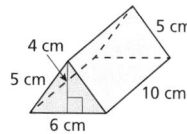
5 cm
4 cm
5 cm
10 cm
6 cm

Finding a Missing Dimension

Example 2 A rectangle has a perimeter of 10 meters and a length of 3 meters. What is the width of the rectangle?

$P = 2\ell + 2w$ Write formula for perimeter of a rectangle.

$10 = 2(3) + 2w$ Substitute 10 for P and 3 for ℓ.

$10 = 6 + 2w$ Multiply 2 and 3.

$4 = 2w$ Subtract 6 from each side.

$2 = w$ Divide each side by 2.

▶ The width is 2 meters.

Find the missing dimension.

4. A rectangle has a perimeter of 28 inches and a width of 5 inches. What is the length of the rectangle?

5. A triangle has an area of 12 square centimeters and a height of 12 centimeters. What is the base of the triangle?

6. A rectangle has an area of 84 square feet and a width of 7 feet. What is the length of the rectangle?

7. **ABSTRACT REASONING** Write an equation for the surface area of a prism with a length, width, and height of x inches. What solid figure does the prism represent?

Dynamic Solutions available at *BigIdeasMath.com*

591

 Common Core State Standards

7.G.B.6 Solve real-world and mathematical problems involving area … and surface area of two- and three-dimensional objects composed of triangles, quadrilaterals, polygons, cubes, and right prisms.

HSA-REI.B.3 Solve linear equations … in one variable, including equations with coefficients represented by letters.

ANSWERS

1. 158 ft^2
2. 144 m^2
3. 184 cm^2
4. 9 in.
5. 2 cm
6. 12 ft
7. $S = 6x^2$; cube

Vocabulary Review

Have students make Information Wheels for the following words.

- Surface area
- Area
- Perimeter

MONITORING PROGRESS ANSWERS

1.
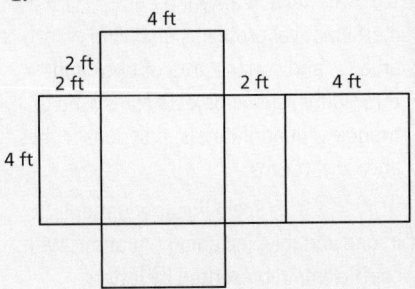

2.
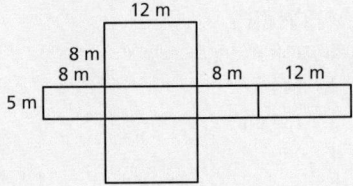

3.
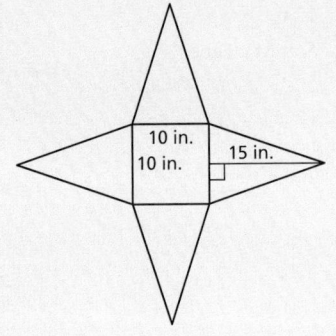

Mathematical Practices

Mathematically proficient students create valid representations of problems.

Creating a Valid Representation

🔁 Core Concept

Nets for Three-Dimensional Figures

A **net** for a three-dimensional figure is a two-dimensional pattern that can be folded to form the three-dimensional figure.

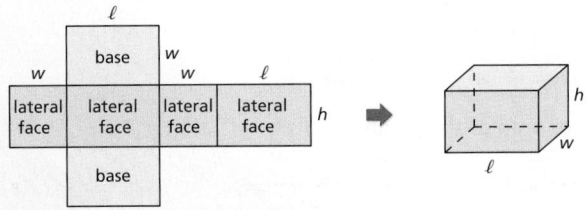

EXAMPLE 1   Drawing a Net for a Pyramid

Draw a net of the pyramid.

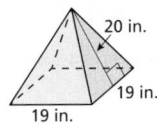

SOLUTION

The pyramid has a square base. Its four lateral faces are congruent isosceles triangles.

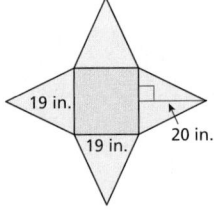

Monitoring Progress

Draw a net of the three-dimensional figure. Label the dimensions.

1.
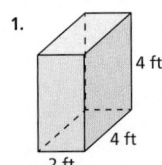

2.
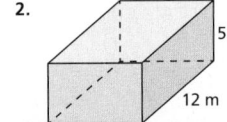

3.
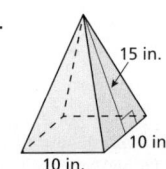

Laurie's Notes   Mathematical Practices (continued from page T-591)

- Students will be working with nets in this chapter, helping them make sense of how to find the surface area of three-dimensional figures. In the *Core Concept*, the net for a rectangular prism is shown. Students should be familiar with nets from middle school.
- Example 1 demonstrates how a net is drawn for a square pyramid. While there are other versions of a net that would fold to make the square pyramid, the one shown is easy to visualize folding into the pyramid.
- Give time for students to work through the *Monitoring Progress* questions. Be sure that students label the dimensions. Share nets with the whole class.

Overview of Section 11.1

Introduction

- This lesson reintroduces the formula for the circumference of a circle. In the last chapter, students worked with measures of circular arcs. Now they will work with the length of a circular arc.
- The lesson ends with an introduction to radian measure.

Teaching Strategy

- The *Core Concept* on page 595 presents two methods for finding arc length.
- Reading the proportion, "In a circle, the ratio of the length of a given arc to the circumference is equal to the ratio of the measure of the arc to 360°." Note that the ratio on the left side is in linear units, while the ratio on the right side is in degrees.

$$\frac{\text{Arc length of } \overset{\frown}{AB}}{2\pi r} = \frac{m\overset{\frown}{AB}}{360°} \qquad \textit{Note:} \; \frac{\text{linear units}}{\text{linear units}} = \frac{\text{degrees}}{\text{degrees}}$$

- Reading the equation that follows, "The length of a given arc is equal to a fractional amount of the circumference."

$$\text{Arc length of } \overset{\frown}{AB} = \frac{m\overset{\frown}{AB}}{360°} \cdot 2\pi r$$

- Structurally, the proportion and the equation are the same, which can be shown by multiplying both sides of the proportion by $2\pi r$. How students think about them is not the same! Students are thinking and reasoning proportionally with the former and thinking of a percentage or portion of a whole for the latter.
- Helping students understand each of these approaches is necessary.

Extensions

- The introduction to circumference can be investigated using dynamic geometry software. Inscribe a regular n-gon in a circle and find the perimeter. As n increases, the perimeter gets closer to the circumference.

Pacing Suggestion

- The explorations provide a brief introduction to arc length. When students have finished, transition to the formal lesson.

Dynamic Teaching Tools

Dynamic Assessment & Progress Monitoring Tool
Lesson Planning Tool
Interactive Whiteboard Lesson Library
Dynamic Classroom with Dynamic Investigations

**Common Core
State Standards**

HSG-GMD.A.1 Give an informal argument for the formulas for the circumference of a circle, area of a circle, ...

HSG-C.B.5 Derive using similarity the fact that the length of the arc intercepted by an angle is proportional to the radius, and define the radian measure of the angle as the constant of proportionality; ....

HSG-CO.A.1 Know precise definitions of angle, circle, ... based on the undefined notions of point, line, distance along a line, and distance around a circular arc.

Laurie's Notes

Exploration

Motivate
- A winter sport near where I live that is growing exponentially is fat-tire biking. Given the abundance of mountain bike, cross country, and snowmobile trails and a growing group of summer mountain bike enthusiasts, fat-tire biking is a natural evolution.
- The tires average 4 inches wide versus 2 inches on a mountain bike or 1 inch on a road bike. The diameter of the tires varies.
- Explain to students that in this lesson they will solve problems about tires.

Exploration Note
- Students should be familiar with the formula for the circumference of a circle from middle school.

Exploration 1
- The fractional amount of the circumference is stated, so a simple calculation is needed.
- **?** "How did you calculate the length of each arc?" Multiply the fractional part of the circle by $2\pi r$. Some students may also say πd for the circumference. It is also possible that some students will have set up a proportion to solve.
- **?** "What type of unit is used to label your answer?" a linear unit
- **? MP6 Attend to Precision:** "What is the exact answer for part (a)?" 8π units "What is an approximate answer for part (a)?" about 25.13 units

Exploration 2
- Students should recognize that this exploration is just an application of the problems found in the first exploration. The diameter is 25 inches.
- **?** "What fractional part of the whole circumference do you need to find?" $\frac{1}{2}$ of the circumference
- **? MP6:** "Should you leave your answer in terms of π? Explain." no; You need a decimal approximation to compare to the width of the rectangular box.

Communicate Your Answer
- Students will likely describe finding a fractional part of the circumference, or they will describe setting up a proportion. In either case, listen for the distinction between arc measure and arc length.

Connecting to Next Step
- Students have now found circumference and arc lengths. Today's lesson also includes applications and using arc length to find measures.

11.1 Circumference and Arc Length

Essential Question How can you find the length of a circular arc?

EXPLORATION 1 Finding the Length of a Circular Arc

Work with a partner. Find the length of each red circular arc.

a. entire circle

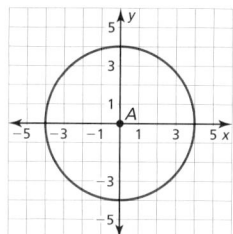

b. one-fourth of a circle

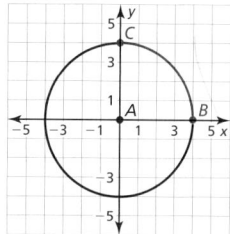

c. one-third of a circle

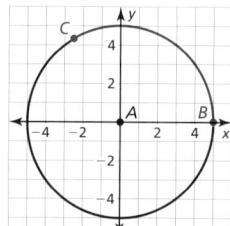

d. five-eighths of a circle

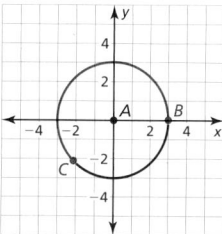

EXPLORATION 2 Using Arc Length

Work with a partner. The rider is attempting to stop with the front tire of the motorcycle in the painted rectangular box for a skills test. The front tire makes exactly one-half additional revolution before stopping. The diameter of the tire is 25 inches. Is the front tire still in contact with the painted box? Explain.

├── 3 ft ──┤

LOOKING FOR REGULARITY IN REPEATED REASONING

To be proficient in math, you need to notice if calculations are repeated and look both for general methods and for shortcuts.

Communicate Your Answer

3. How can you find the length of a circular arc?

4. A motorcycle tire has a diameter of 24 inches. Approximately how many inches does the motorcycle travel when its front tire makes three-fourths of a revolution?

ANSWERS

1. **a.** $8\pi \approx 25.13$ units

   b. $2\pi \approx 6.28$ units

   c. $\frac{10}{3}\pi \approx 10.47$ units

   d. $\frac{15}{4}\pi \approx 11.78$ units

2. no; *Sample answer:* One-half revolution of the tire is about 3.27 feet.

3. Multiply the fraction of the circle the arc represents by the circumference of the circle.

4. about 56.55 in.

Extra Example 1

Find each indicated measure.

a. circumference of a circle with a radius of 11 inches

The circumference is about 69.12 inches.

b. radius of a circle with a circumference of 4 millimeters

The radius is about 0.64 millimeters.

MONITORING PROGRESS ANSWERS

1. about 15.71 in.
2. about 5.41 ft

11.1 Lesson

Core Vocabulary

circumference, *p. 594*
arc length, *p. 595*
radian, *p. 597*

Previous
circle
diameter
radius

What You Will Learn

▶ Use the formula for circumference.
▶ Use arc lengths to find measures.
▶ Solve real-life problems.
▶ Measure angles in radians.

Using the Formula for Circumference

The **circumference** of a circle is the distance around the circle. Consider a regular polygon inscribed in a circle. As the number of sides increases, the polygon approximates the circle and the ratio of the perimeter of the polygon to the diameter of the circle approaches $\pi \approx 3.14159\ldots$

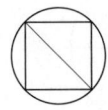 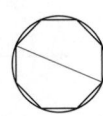 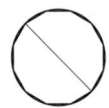

For all circles, the ratio of the circumference C to the diameter d is the same. This ratio is $\frac{C}{d} = \pi$. Solving for C yields the formula for the circumference of a circle, $C = \pi d$. Because $d = 2r$, you can also write the formula as $C = \pi(2r) = 2\pi r$.

🔁 Core Concept

Circumference of a Circle

The circumference C of a circle is $C = \pi d$ or $C = 2\pi r$, where d is the diameter of the circle and r is the radius of the circle.

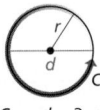

$C = \pi d = 2\pi r$

EXAMPLE 1   Using the Formula for Circumference

Find each indicated measure.

a. circumference of a circle with a radius of 9 centimeters

b. radius of a circle with a circumference of 26 meters

SOLUTION

ATTENTING TO PRECISION

You have sometimes used 3.14 to approximate the value of π. Throughout this chapter, you should use the π key on a calculator, then round to the hundredths place unless instructed otherwise.

a. $C = 2\pi r$
   $= 2 \cdot \pi \cdot 9$
   $= 18\pi$
   ≈ 56.55

   ▶ The circumference is about 56.55 centimeters.

b. $C = 2\pi r$
   $26 = 2\pi r$
   $\dfrac{26}{2\pi} = r$
   $4.14 \approx r$

   ▶ The radius is about 4.14 meters.

Monitoring Progress Help in English and Spanish at *BigIdeasMath.com*

1. Find the circumference of a circle with a diameter of 5 inches.

2. Find the diameter of a circle with a circumference of 17 feet.

Laurie's Notes   Teacher Actions

- Students should be very comfortable using different forms of the circumference formula.
- ❓ "What type of number is π?" irrational
- ❓ "What does *irrational* mean?" It is a non-repeating, non-terminating decimal.
- Pose Example 1, and have partners work to solve each part. Discuss the margin note.
- Omit Questions 1 and 2 if you believe students are secure in working with the formula for circumference.

Using Arc Lengths to Find Measures

An **arc length** is a portion of the circumference of a circle. You can use the measure of the arc (in degrees) to find its length (in linear units).

 **Core Concept**

Arc Length

In a circle, the ratio of the length of a given arc to the circumference is equal to the ratio of the measure of the arc to 360°.

$$\frac{\text{Arc length of } \overset{\frown}{AB}}{2\pi r} = \frac{m\overset{\frown}{AB}}{360°}, \text{ or}$$

$$\text{Arc length of } \overset{\frown}{AB} = \frac{m\overset{\frown}{AB}}{360°} \cdot 2\pi r$$

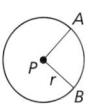

EXAMPLE 2 **Using Arc Lengths to Find Measures**

Find each indicated measure.

a. arc length of $\overset{\frown}{AB}$　　**b.** circumference of $\odot Z$　　**c.** $m\overset{\frown}{RS}$

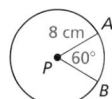　　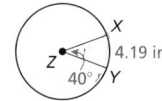　　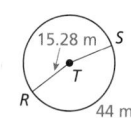

SOLUTION

a. Arc length of $\overset{\frown}{AB} = \dfrac{60°}{360°} \cdot 2\pi(8)$

≈ 8.38 cm

b. $\dfrac{\text{Arc length of } \overset{\frown}{XY}}{C} = \dfrac{m\overset{\frown}{XY}}{360°}$

$\dfrac{4.19}{C} = \dfrac{40°}{360°}$

$\dfrac{4.19}{C} = \dfrac{1}{9}$

37.71 in. $= C$

c. $\dfrac{\text{Arc length of } \overset{\frown}{RS}}{2\pi r} = \dfrac{m\overset{\frown}{RS}}{360°}$

$\dfrac{44}{2\pi(15.28)} = \dfrac{m\overset{\frown}{RS}}{360°}$

$360° \cdot \dfrac{44}{2\pi(15.28)} = m\overset{\frown}{RS}$

$165° \approx m\overset{\frown}{RS}$

Monitoring Progress Help in English and Spanish at *BigIdeasMath.com*

Find the indicated measure.

3. arc length of $\overset{\frown}{PQ}$　　**4.** circumference of $\odot N$　　**5.** radius of $\odot G$

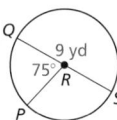　　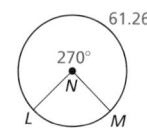　　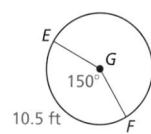

Extra Example 2

Find each indicated measure.

a. arc length of $\overset{\frown}{PR}$

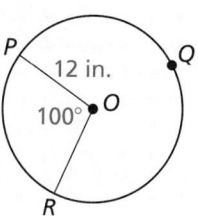

arc length of $\overset{\frown}{PR} \approx 20.94$ inches

b. circumference of $\odot P$

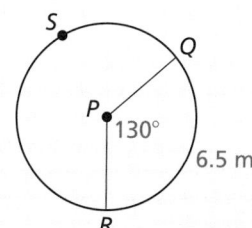

$C = 18$ meters

c. $m\overset{\frown}{JK}$

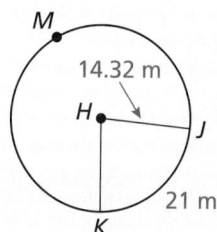

$m\overset{\frown}{JK} \approx 84°$

MONITORING PROGRESS ANSWERS

3. about 5.89 yd

4. 81.68 m

5. about 4.01 ft

Laurie's Notes　Teacher Actions

- **MP6:** Explain the difference between the length of an arc (linear units) and the measure of the arc (degrees).
- **MP7 Look For and Make Use of Structure:** To find arc length, set up a proportion (note the units) or find a fractional part of the circumference. Structurally, the proportion and the equation are the same—multiply both sides of the proportion by $2\pi r$ and you have the equation. Example 2 demonstrates these two approaches.
- **MP1 Make Sense of Problems and Persevere in Solving Them:** Students need to focus on what information is known, what they are solving for, and the approach they will use.

Differentiated Instruction

Kinesthetic

Demonstrate the relationship between the circumference of a wheel and the distance it travels in one revolution. Wrap a string once around a small wheel or tire and lay the string flat on a table. Have a student mark a point on the edge of the wheel and line up the mark so it is directly above one end of the string. Keep the string taut and roll the wheel along the string until the mark lies directly above the other end of the string. The distance the wheel traveled in one revolution is the length of the string—the circumference of the wheel.

Extra Example 3

The radius of a wheel on a toy truck is 4 inches. To the nearest foot, how far does the wheel travel when it makes 7 revolutions? The wheel travels approximately 15 feet.

Extra Example 4

A path is built around four congruent circular fields. The radius of each field is 100 feet. How long is the path? Round to the nearest hundred feet.

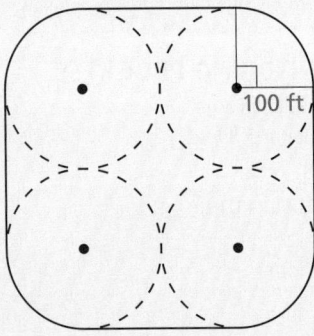

The path is about 1400 feet long.

MONITORING PROGRESS ANSWERS

6. about 68
7. about 445.4 m

Solving Real-Life Problems

EXAMPLE 3 **Using Circumference to Find Distance Traveled**

The dimensions of a car tire are shown. To the nearest foot, how far does the tire travel when it makes 15 revolutions?

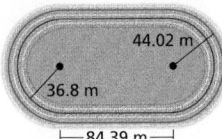

5.5 in.
15 in.
5.5 in.

SOLUTION

Step 1   Find the diameter of the tire.

$$d = 15 + 2(5.5) = 26 \text{ in.}$$

Step 2   Find the circumference of the tire.

$$C = \pi d = \pi \cdot 26 = 26\pi \text{ in.}$$

Step 3   Find the distance the tire travels in 15 revolutions. In one revolution, the tire travels a distance equal to its circumference. In 15 revolutions, the tire travels a distance equal to 15 times its circumference.

Distance traveled	=	Number of revolutions	•	Circumference

$$= 15 \cdot 26\pi \approx 1225.2 \text{ in.}$$

> **COMMON ERROR**
>
> Always pay attention to units. In Example 3, you need to convert units to get a correct answer.

Step 4   Use unit analysis. Change 1225.2 inches to feet.

$$1225.2 \text{ in.} \cdot \frac{1 \text{ ft}}{12 \text{ in.}} = 102.1 \text{ ft}$$

▶ The tire travels approximately 102 feet.

EXAMPLE 4 **Using Arc Length to Find Distances**

The curves at the ends of the track shown are 180° arcs of circles. The radius of the arc for a runner on the red path shown is 36.8 meters. About how far does this runner travel to go once around the track? Round to the nearest tenth of a meter.

44.02 m
36.8 m
84.39 m

SOLUTION

The path of the runner on the red path is made of two straight sections and two semicircles. To find the total distance, find the sum of the lengths of each part.

Distance	=	2 • Length of each straight section	+	2 • Length of each semicircle

$$= 2(84.39) + 2\left(\frac{1}{2} \cdot 2\pi \cdot 36.8\right)$$

$$\approx 400.0$$

▶ The runner on the red path travels about 400.0 meters.

Monitoring Progress 🔊 Help in English and Spanish at *BigIdeasMath.com*

6. A car tire has a diameter of 28 inches. How many revolutions does the tire make while traveling 500 feet?

7. In Example 4, the radius of the arc for a runner on the blue path is 44.02 meters, as shown in the diagram. About how far does this runner travel to go once around the track? Round to the nearest tenth of a meter.

Laurie's Notes | Teacher Actions

- **Whiteboarding:** For the problems on this page, whiteboards are helpful to quickly share work.
- Students will recognize that Example 3 involves the circumference of the tire.
- Students need to pay attention to units.
- Have partners work independently to solve the problem as you circulate.
- **?** "In Example 4, how do you find the distance around the track?" The two circular arcs equal a circumference. Then add the two lengths of the straight section.
- **?** "Is the length of the circular arc the same for all runners?" no
- **?** "Is the length of the straight section the same for all runners?" yes

Measuring Angles in Radians

Recall that in a circle, the ratio of the length of a given arc to the circumference is equal to the ratio of the measure of the arc to 360°. To see why, consider the diagram.

A circle of radius 1 has circumference 2π, so the arc length of $\overset{\frown}{CD}$ is $\dfrac{m\overset{\frown}{CD}}{360°} \cdot 2\pi$.

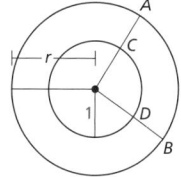

Recall that all circles are similar and corresponding lengths of similar figures are proportional. Because $m\overset{\frown}{AB} = m\overset{\frown}{CD}$, $\overset{\frown}{AB}$ and $\overset{\frown}{CD}$ are corresponding arcs. So, you can write the following proportion.

$$\frac{\text{Arc length of } \overset{\frown}{AB}}{\text{Arc length of } \overset{\frown}{CD}} = \frac{r}{1}$$

$$\text{Arc length of } \overset{\frown}{AB} = r \cdot \text{Arc length of } \overset{\frown}{CD}$$

$$\text{Arc length of } \overset{\frown}{AB} = r \cdot \frac{m\overset{\frown}{CD}}{360°} \cdot 2\pi$$

This form of the equation shows that the arc length associated with a central angle is *proportional to the radius* of the circle. The constant of proportionality, $\dfrac{m\overset{\frown}{CD}}{360°} \cdot 2\pi$, is defined to be the **radian** measure of the central angle associated with the arc.

In a circle of radius 1, the radian measure of a given central angle can be thought of as the length of the arc associated with the angle. The radian measure of a complete circle (360°) is exactly 2π radians, because the circumference of a circle of radius 1 is exactly 2π. You can use this fact to convert from degree measure to radian measure and vice versa.

Core Concept

Converting between Degrees and Radians

Degrees to radians

Multiply degree measure by

$$\frac{2\pi \text{ radians}}{360°}, \text{ or } \frac{\pi \text{ radians}}{180°}.$$

Radians to degrees

Multiply radian measure by

$$\frac{360°}{2\pi \text{ radians}}, \text{ or } \frac{180°}{\pi \text{ radians}}.$$

EXAMPLE 5 Converting between Degree and Radian Measure

a. Convert 45° to radians.

b. Convert $\dfrac{3\pi}{2}$ radians to degrees.

SOLUTION

a. $45° \cdot \dfrac{\pi \text{ radians}}{180°} = \dfrac{\pi}{4}$ radian

▶ So, $45° = \dfrac{\pi}{4}$ radian.

b. $\dfrac{3\pi}{2}$ radians $\cdot \dfrac{180°}{\pi \text{ radians}} = 270°$

▶ So, $\dfrac{3\pi}{2}$ radians $= 270°$.

Monitoring Progress Help in English and Spanish at BigIdeasMath.com

8. Convert 15° to radians.

9. Convert $\dfrac{4\pi}{3}$ radians to degrees.

Laurie's Notes   Teacher Actions

- Work slowly through the development of radian measure, being careful with language and symbols.
- Explain that the *radian* measure of a given central angle can be thought of as the length of the associated arc.
- Write the *Core Concept*, which states the conversion factors.
- Work through Example 5. It is helpful to finish with a circular model showing the angle and arc length marked for each problem.

Closure

- **Writing Prompt:** Explain how the radius, central angles, arc lengths, and circumference of a circle are related.

11.1 Exercises
Dynamic Solutions available at *BigIdeasMath.com*

ANSWERS

1. πd

2. Arc measure refers to the angle and arc length refers to the length.

3. about 37.70 in.

4. about 20.05 ft

5. 14 units

6. 5π in.

7. about 3.14 ft

8. about 50.02°

9. about 35.53 m

10. about 8.58 cm

11. The diameter was used as the radius; $C = \pi d = 9\pi$ in.

12. The arc measure should be divided by 360°; Arc length of
    $$\widehat{GH} = \frac{m\widehat{GH}}{360°} \cdot 2\pi r = \frac{25}{12}\pi \text{ cm}$$

13. 182 ft

14. 19

15. about 44.85 units

16. about 21.42 units

11.1 Exercises

Dynamic Solutions available at *BigIdeasMath.com*

Vocabulary and Core Concept Check

1. **COMPLETE THE SENTENCE** The circumference of a circle with diameter d is $C =$ _____.

2. **WRITING** Describe the difference between an arc measure and an arc length.

Monitoring Progress and Modeling with Mathematics

In Exercises 3–10, find the indicated measure. *(See Examples 1 and 2.)*

3. circumference of a circle with a radius of 6 inches

4. diameter of a circle with a circumference of 63 feet

5. radius of a circle with a circumference of 28π

6. exact circumference of a circle with a diameter of 5 inches

7. arc length of $\widehat{AB}$

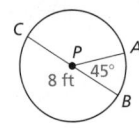

8. $m\widehat{DE}$

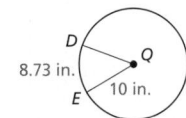

9. circumference of $\odot C$

10. radius of $\odot R$

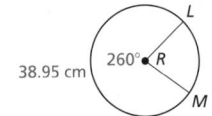

11. **ERROR ANALYSIS** Describe and correct the error in finding the circumference of $\odot C$.

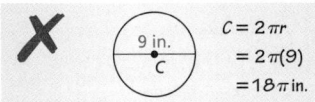

12. **ERROR ANALYSIS** Describe and correct the error in finding the length of $\widehat{GH}$.

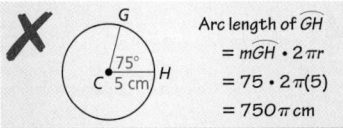

13. **PROBLEM SOLVING** A measuring wheel is used to calculate the length of a path. The diameter of the wheel is 8 inches. The wheel makes 87 complete revolutions along the length of the path. To the nearest foot, how long is the path? *(See Example 3.)*

14. **PROBLEM SOLVING** You ride your bicycle 40 meters. How many complete revolutions does the front wheel make?

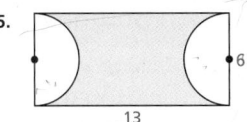

In Exercises 15–18, find the perimeter of the shaded region. *(See Example 4.)*

15.

16.

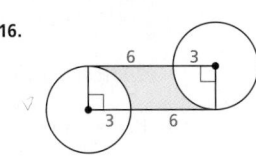

17.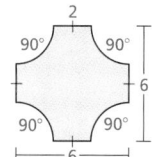

18.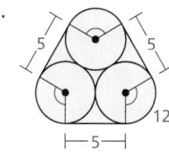

In Exercises 19–22, convert the angle measure.
(See Example 5.)

19. Convert 70° to radians.

20. Convert 300° to radians.

21. Convert $\frac{11\pi}{12}$ radians to degrees.

22. Convert $\frac{\pi}{8}$ radian to degrees.

23. PROBLEM SOLVING The London Eye is a Ferris wheel in London, England, that travels at a speed of 0.26 meter per second. How many minutes does it take the London Eye to complete one full revolution?

67.5 m

24. PROBLEM SOLVING You are planning to plant a circular garden adjacent to one of the corners of a building, as shown. You can use up to 38 feet of fence to make a border around the garden. What radius (in feet) can the garden have? Choose all that apply. Explain your reasoning.

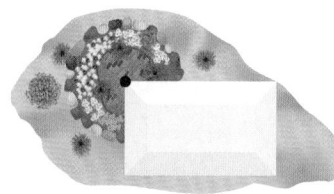

(A) 7   (B) 8   (C) 9   (D) 10

In Exercises 25 and 26, find the circumference of the circle with the given equation. Write the circumference in terms of π.

25. $x^2 + y^2 = 16$

26. $(x + 2)^2 + (y - 3)^2 = 9$

27. USING STRUCTURE A semicircle has endpoints $(-2, 5)$ and $(2, 8)$. Find the arc length of the semicircle.

28. REASONING $\overset{\frown}{EF}$ is an arc on a circle with radius r. Let $x°$ be the measure of $\overset{\frown}{EF}$. Describe the effect on the length of $\overset{\frown}{EF}$ if you (a) double the radius of the circle, and (b) double the measure of $\overset{\frown}{EF}$.

29. MAKING AN ARGUMENT Your friend claims that it is possible for two arcs with the same measure to have different arc lengths. Is your friend correct? Explain your reasoning.

30. PROBLEM SOLVING Over 2000 years ago, the Greek scholar Eratosthenes estimated Earth's circumference by assuming that the Sun's rays were parallel. He chose a day when the Sun shone straight down into a well in the city of Syene. At noon, he measured the angle the Sun's rays made with a vertical stick in the city of Alexandria. Eratosthenes assumed that the distance from Syene to Alexandria was equal to about 575 miles. Explain how Eratosthenes was able to use this information to estimate Earth's circumference. Then estimate Earth's circumference.

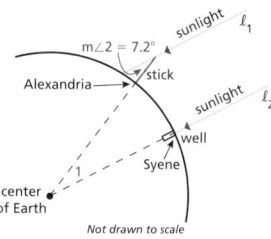

Not drawn to scale

31. ANALYZING RELATIONSHIPS In $\odot C$, the ratio of the length of $\overset{\frown}{PQ}$ to the length of $\overset{\frown}{RS}$ is 2 to 1. What is the ratio of $m\angle PCQ$ to $m\angle RCS$?

(A) 4 to 1   (B) 2 to 1

(C) 1 to 4   (D) 1 to 2

32. ANALYZING RELATIONSHIPS A 45° arc in $\odot C$ and a 30° arc in $\odot P$ have the same length. What is the ratio of the radius r_1 of $\odot C$ to the radius r_2 of $\odot P$? Explain your reasoning.

ANSWERS

17. about 20.57 units

18. about 30.71 units

19. $\frac{7\pi}{18}$ radian

20. $\frac{5\pi}{3}$ radians

21. 165°

22. 22.5°

23. about 27.19 min

24. A, B; *Sample answer:* The maximum radius is about 8.06 feet.

25. 8π units

26. 6π units

27. about 7.85 units

28. **a.** The length doubles.
   b. The length doubles.

29. yes; *Sample answer:* The arc length also depends on the radius.

30. *Sample answer:* Angles 1 and 2 are alternate interior angles, so the arc measure is 7.2°; 28,750 mi

31. B

32. 2 to 3; *Sample answer:* $\frac{1}{4}\pi r_1 = \frac{1}{6}\pi r_2$ implies $\frac{r_1}{r_2} = \frac{2}{3}$.

33. $2\frac{1}{3}$

34. a. about 62.83 in.

    b. about 26.66 cm

    c. about 16.32 in.

35. arc length of $\overarc{AB} = r\theta$; about 9.42 in.

36. They are the same; *Sample answer:* The radius of $\odot C$ is the same as the diameter of $\odot P$.

37. yes; *Sample answer:* The circumference of the red circle can be found using $2 = \frac{30°}{360°}C$. The circumference of the blue circle is double the circumference of the red circle.

38. a. $\frac{3\pi}{4}$ radian; *Sample answer:* The hour hand is halfway between 1 and 2, and the minute hand is on 6.

    b. $\frac{\pi}{24}$ radian; *Sample answer:* The hour hand is one-quarter way between 3 and 4, and the minute hand is on 3.

39. 28 units

40–44. See Additional Answers.

Mini-Assessment

Use the diagram.

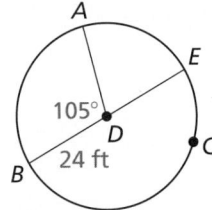

1. What is the circumference of $\odot D$? about 150.80 feet

2. What is the arc length of $\overarc{AB}$? about 43.98 feet

3. Children's bicycles are sized according to the diameter of their wheels. A bicycle recommended for six-year-olds has wheels whose diameters are 18 inches. How many revolutions does the wheel make when traveling 42 feet? about 9 revolutions

4. Convert 210° to radians. $\frac{7\pi}{6}$ radians

5. Convert $\frac{5\pi}{12}$ radians to degrees. 75°

---

33. **PROBLEM SOLVING** How many revolutions does the smaller gear complete during a single revolution of the larger gear?

34. **USING STRUCTURE** Find the circumference of each circle.

    a. a circle circumscribed about a right triangle whose legs are 12 inches and 16 inches long

    b. a circle circumscribed about a square with a side length of 6 centimeters

    c. a circle inscribed in an equilateral triangle with a side length of 9 inches

35. **REWRITING A FORMULA** Write a formula in terms of the measure θ (theta) of the central angle (in radians) that can be used to find the length of an arc of a circle. Then use this formula to find the length of an arc of a circle with a radius of 4 inches and a central angle of $\frac{3\pi}{4}$ radians.

36. **HOW DO YOU SEE IT?**
    Compare the circumference of $\odot P$ to the length of $\overarc{DE}$. Explain your reasoning.

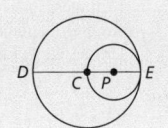

37. **MAKING AN ARGUMENT** In the diagram, the measure of the red shaded angle is 30°. The arc length a is 2. Your classmate claims that it is possible to find the circumference of the blue circle without finding the radius of either circle. Is your classmate correct? Explain your reasoning.

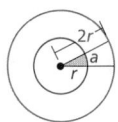

---

38. **MODELING WITH MATHEMATICS** What is the measure (in radians) of the angle formed by the hands of a clock at each time? Explain your reasoning.

    a. 1:30 P.M.   b. 3:15 P.M.

39. **MATHEMATICAL CONNECTIONS** The sum of the circumferences of circles A, B, and C is 63π. Find AC.

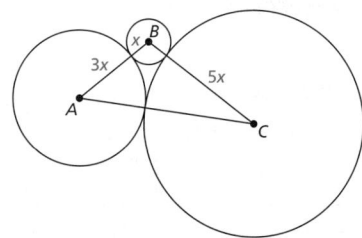

40. **THOUGHT PROVOKING** Is π a rational number? Compare the rational number $\frac{355}{113}$ to π. Find a different rational number that is even closer to π.

41. **PROOF** The circles in the diagram are concentric and $\overline{FG} \cong \overline{GH}$. Prove that $\overarc{JK}$ and $\overarc{NG}$ have the same length.

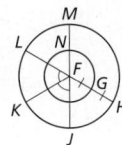

42. **REPEATED REASONING** $\overline{AB}$ is divided into four congruent segments, and semicircles with radius r are drawn.

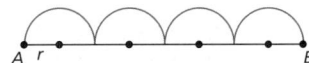

    a. What is the sum of the four arc lengths?

    b. What would the sum of the arc lengths be if $\overline{AB}$ was divided into 8 congruent segments? 16 congruent segments? n congruent segments? Explain your reasoning.

Maintaining Mathematical Proficiency   Reviewing what you learned in previous grades and lessons

Find the area of the polygon with the given vertices.   *(Section 1.4)*

43. $X(2, 4)$, $Y(8, -1)$, $Z(2, -1)$

44. $L(-3, 1)$, $M(4, 1)$, $N(4, -5)$, $P(-3, -5)$

If students need help...	If students got it...
Resources by Chapter • Practice A and Practice B • Puzzle Time	Resources by Chapter • Enrichment and Extension • Cumulative Review
Student Journal • Practice	Start the *next* Section
Differentiating the Lesson Skills Review Handbook	

Overview of Section 11.2

Introduction
- This lesson reintroduces the formula for the area of a circle.
- In this lesson, students will find the area of a *sector of a circle*.
- The lesson includes the definition of *population density*.

Formative Assessment Tips
- **Pass the Problem:** This technique provides students the opportunity to work with others on the solution of a problem or a proof that requires more than a few steps. Seeing how others approach and work the problem helps students to reflect on their own process.
- There are different ways, or configurations, to using this technique. Begin by posing a problem that individuals or pairs begin to work on. After a fixed amount of time, the problem is swapped with partners or another pair of students. The recipients finish solving the problem or make modifications or corrections to the problem. If changes are made, they must explain why there was an error or why the strategy that was begun is not going to be followed.
- This technique gives all students the opportunity to participate in the lesson. All students receive feedback on their work, not just one student that the teacher might have called on. If the work passed to another is not clear because steps are missing, students receive this feedback from peers, not just the teacher. If students or partners were unable to get started on a problem, they will hopefully be exchanging with others who can help them make sense of the problem.
- When students have finished the problem, the two or four people involved in swapping problems will confer with one another to discuss the problem and offer additional feedback. One thing you hope to hear is positive feedback on the clarity of thinking that was recorded, allowing the recipients to make sense of the work.

Extensions
- Exercise 24 on page 607 has a nice extension. Ask students to find the percent of the square that is shaded. Now imagine having 9 tangent circles drawn inside the same square. What percent of the square is shaded? Repeat for 16 and 25 tangent circles. Have students make observations.

Pacing Suggestion
- The explorations provide a brief introduction to areas of sectors. When students have finished, transition to the formal lesson. You might omit Example 1.

Common Core
State Standards

HSG-GMD.A.1 Give an informal argument for the formulas for the circumference of a circle, area of a circle, ….

HSG-MG.A.2 Apply concepts of density based on area … in modeling situations (e.g., persons per square mile, …).

HSG-C.B.5 Derive … the formula for the area of a sector.

Laurie's Notes

Exploration

Motivate
- **Story Time:** When students enter, display this iconic symbol and ask students whether they are familiar with it. Tell them that you were such a fan of this video game that, in college, you had a rug in this shape in your dorm room. Everyone envied you!
- "How big was this rug you ask? I'll tell you at the end of class!"

Exploration Note
- Students should be familiar with the formula for the area of a circle from middle school.

Exploration 1
- The fractional amount of the area is stated, so a simple calculation is needed.
- **?** "How did you calculate the area of each sector?" Multiply the fractional part of the circle by πr^2. It is also possible that students set up a proportion to solve.
- **?** "What type of unit is used to label your answer?" a square unit
- **? MP6 Attend to Precision:** "What is the exact answer for part (a)?" 36π square units
  "What is an approximate answer for part (a)?" about 113.10 square units

Exploration 2
- Students should recognize that this exploration is just an application of the problems found in the first exploration. The radius is 400 meters.
- **?** "What fractional part of the whole area do you need to find?" $\frac{1}{3}$ of the area
- **? MP6:** "Should you leave your answer in terms of π? Explain." no; You should use a decimal approximation.

Communicate Your Answer
- Students will likely describe finding a fractional part of the area, or they will describe setting up a proportion. In either case, listen for correct language.

Connecting to Next Step
- Students have now found the area of a circle and the areas of sectors. Applications of areas of sectors will be found in today's lesson.

11.2 Areas of Circles and Sectors

Essential Question
How can you find the area of a sector of a circle?

EXPLORATION 1   Finding the Area of a Sector of a Circle

Work with a partner. A **sector of a circle** is the region bounded by two radii of the circle and their intercepted arc. Find the area of each shaded circle or sector of a circle.

a. entire circle

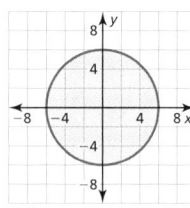

b. one-fourth of a circle

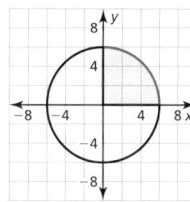

c. seven-eighths of a circle

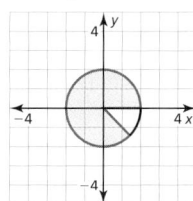

d. two-thirds of a circle

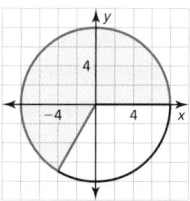

REASONING ABSTRACTLY

To be proficient in math, you need to explain to yourself the meaning of a problem and look for entry points to its solution.

EXPLORATION 2   Finding the Area of a Circular Sector

Work with a partner. A center pivot irrigation system consists of 400 meters of sprinkler equipment that rotates around a central pivot point at a rate of once every 3 days to irrigate a circular region with a diameter of 800 meters. Find the area of the sector that is irrigated by this system in one day.

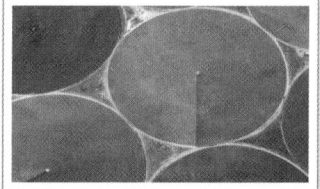

Communicate Your Answer

3. How can you find the area of a sector of a circle?

4. In Exploration 2, find the area of the sector that is irrigated in 2 hours.

Section 11.2   Areas of Circles and Sectors   **601**

Dynamic Teaching Tools

Dynamic Assessment & Progress Monitoring Tool

Lesson Planning Tool

Interactive Whiteboard Lesson Library

Dynamic Classroom with Dynamic Investigations

ANSWERS

1.   a.   about 113.10 square units
      b.   about 28.27 square units
      c.   about 11.00 square units
      d.   about 134.04 square units
2. about 167,552 m^2
3. Multiply the fraction of the circle the sector represents by the area of the circle.
4. about 13,963 m^2

English Language Learners

Group Activity

Organize the students into small groups of English learners and English speakers. Give each group a problem similar to Example 1 and have each group solve it together. When finished, have students share their work at the board.

Extra Example 1

Find each indicated measure.

a. area of a circle with a radius of 8.5 inches The area of the circle is about 226.98 square inches.

b. diameter of a circle with an area of 153.94 square feet The radius is about 7 feet, so the diameter is about 14 feet.

MONITORING PROGRESS ANSWERS

1. about 63.62 m^2
2. about 7.50 ft

11.2 Lesson

Core Vocabulary
population density, *p. 603*
sector of a circle, *p. 604*

Previous
circle
radius
diameter
intercepted arc

What You Will Learn

▶ Use the formula for the area of a circle.
▶ Use the formula for population density.
▶ Find areas of sectors.
▶ Use areas of sectors.

Using the Formula for the Area of a Circle

You can divide a circle into congruent sections and rearrange the sections to form a figure that approximates a parallelogram. Increasing the number of congruent sections increases the figure's resemblance to a parallelogram.

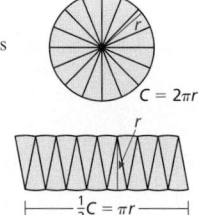

The base of the parallelogram that the figure approaches is half of the circumference, so $b = \frac{1}{2}C = \frac{1}{2}(2\pi r) = \pi r$. The height is the radius, so $h = r$. So, the area of the parallelogram is $A = bh = (\pi r)(r) = \pi r^2$.

Core Concept

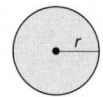

Area of a Circle

The area of a circle is

$$A = \pi r^2$$

where r is the radius of the circle.

EXAMPLE 1 Using the Formula for the Area of a Circle

Find each indicated measure.

a. area of a circle with a radius of 2.5 centimeters

b. diameter of a circle with an area of 113.1 square centimeters

SOLUTION

a. $A = \pi r^2$ Formula for area of a circle
    $= \pi \cdot (2.5)^2$ Substitute 2.5 for r.
    $= 6.25\pi$ Simplify.
    ≈ 19.63 Use a calculator.

▶ The area of the circle is about 19.63 square centimeters.

b. $A = \pi r^2$ Formula for area of a circle
   $113.1 = \pi r^2$ Substitute 113.1 for A.
   $\dfrac{113.1}{\pi} = r^2$ Divide each side by π.
      $6 \approx r$ Find the positive square root of each side.

▶ The radius is about 6 centimeters, so the diameter is about 12 centimeters.

Monitoring Progress 🔊 Help in English and Spanish at *BigIdeasMath.com*

1. Find the area of a circle with a radius of 4.5 meters.
2. Find the radius of a circle with an area of 176.7 square feet.

602   **Chapter 11**   Circumference, Area, and Volume

Laurie's Notes | Teacher Actions

- Although students may be familiar with the area formula, they may not have seen its derivation. The model shown can be easily made out of heavyweight paper and used each year. There are also online simulations and applets that model this approach.
- Write the *Core Concept*.
- **?** "What type of unit is used to measure area?" a square unit
- **Think-Pair-Share:** Have students work independently to answer Example 1. Discuss as a class. You might omit Questions 1 and 2.

Using the Formula for Population Density

The **population density** of a city, county, or state is a measure of how many people live within a given area.

$$\text{Population density} = \frac{\text{number of people}}{\text{area of land}}$$

Population density is usually given in terms of square miles but can be expressed using other units, such as city blocks.

EXAMPLE 2 Using the Formula for Population Density

a. About 430,000 people live in a 5-mile radius of a city's town hall. Find the population density in people per square mile.

b. A region with a 3-mile radius has a population density of about 6195 people per square mile. Find the number of people who live in the region.

SOLUTION

a. **Step 1** Find the area of the region.

$$A = \pi r^2 = \pi \cdot 5^2 = 25\pi$$

The area of the region is $25\pi \approx 78.54$ square miles.

Step 2 Find the population density.

$$\text{Population density} = \frac{\text{number of people}}{\text{area of land}} \qquad \text{Formula for population density}$$

$$= \frac{430{,}000}{25\pi} \qquad \text{Substitute.}$$

$$\approx 5475 \qquad \text{Use a calculator.}$$

▶ The population density is about 5475 people per square mile.

b. **Step 1** Find the area of the region.

$$A = \pi r^2 = \pi \cdot 3^2 = 9\pi$$

The area of the region is $9\pi \approx 28.27$ square miles.

Step 2 Let x represent the number of people who live in the region. Find the value of x.

$$\text{Population density} = \frac{\text{number of people}}{\text{area of land}} \qquad \text{Formula for population density}$$

$$6195 \approx \frac{x}{9\pi} \qquad \text{Substitute.}$$

$$175{,}159 \approx x \qquad \text{Multiply and use a calculator.}$$

▶ The number of people who live in the region is about 175,159.

Monitoring Progress 🔊 Help in English and Spanish at *BigIdeasMath.com*

3. About 58,000 people live in a region with a 2-mile radius. Find the population density in people per square mile.

4. A region with a 3-mile radius has a population density of about 1000 people per square mile. Find the number of people who live in the region.

Extra Example 2

a. About 124,000 people live in a 2-mile radius of a city's post office. Find the population density in people per square mile.
   The population density is about 9868 people per square mile.

b. A region with a 10-mile radius has a population density of about 869 people per square mile. Find the number of people who live in the region.
   The number of people who live in the region is about 273,004.

MONITORING PROGRESS ANSWERS

3. about 4615 people per mi^2
4. about 28,274 people

Laurie's Notes   Teacher Actions

- Define *population density*. If possible, state the population density for your town, county, and/or state.
- **Pass the Problem:** Explain this technique. Pose Example 2, and say that each part of the problem is to be solved. Give partners 1 to 2 minutes to discuss and begin a solution. Call "swap" and have partners continue to solve. Both groups debrief. Ask students to give a *Thumbs Up* self-assessment.

Extra Example 3

Find the areas of the sectors formed by $\angle PSQ$.

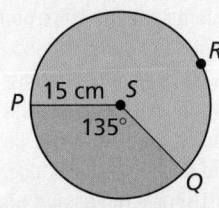

The area of the small sector is about 265.07 square centimeters. The area of the large sector is about 441.79 square centimeters.

MONITORING PROGRESS ANSWERS

5. about 205.25 ft^2
6. about 410.50 ft^2

Finding Areas of Sectors

A **sector of a circle** is the region bounded by two radii of the circle and their intercepted arc. In the diagram below, sector APB is bounded by $\overline{AP}$, $\overline{BP}$, and $\overarc{AB}$.

ANALYZING RELATIONSHIPS

The area of a sector is a fractional part of the area of a circle. The area of a sector formed by a 45° arc is $\frac{45°}{360°}$, or $\frac{1}{8}$ of the area of the circle.

Core Concept

Area of a Sector

The ratio of the area of a sector of a circle to the area of the whole circle (πr^2) is equal to the ratio of the measure of the intercepted arc to 360°.

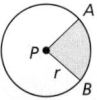

$$\frac{\text{Area of sector } APB}{\pi r^2} = \frac{m\overarc{AB}}{360°}, \text{ or}$$

$$\text{Area of sector } APB = \frac{m\overarc{AB}}{360°} \cdot \pi r^2$$

EXAMPLE 3 Finding Areas of Sectors

Find the areas of the sectors formed by $\angle UTV$.

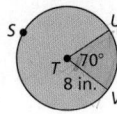

SOLUTION

Step 1 Find the measures of the minor and major arcs.

Because $m\angle UTV = 70°$, $m\overarc{UV} = 70°$ and $m\overarc{USV} = 360° - 70° = 290°$.

Step 2 Find the areas of the small and large sectors.

Area of small sector $= \dfrac{m\overarc{UV}}{360°} \cdot \pi r^2$		Formula for area of a sector
$= \dfrac{70°}{360°} \cdot \pi \cdot 8^2$		Substitute.
≈ 39.10		Use a calculator.
Area of large sector $= \dfrac{m\overarc{USV}}{360°} \cdot \pi r^2$		Formula for area of a sector
$= \dfrac{290°}{360°} \cdot \pi \cdot 8^2$		Substitute.
≈ 161.97		Use a calculator.

▶ The areas of the small and large sectors are about 39.10 square inches and about 161.97 square inches, respectively.

Monitoring Progress 🔊 Help in English and Spanish at *BigIdeasMath.com*

Find the indicated measure.

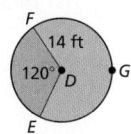

5. area of red sector
6. area of blue sector

Laurie's Notes   Teacher Actions

- **Connection:** Define *sector of a circle*. Explain that the area of the sector can be found using techniques similar to what was done in finding arc length.
- **MP7 Look For and Make Use of Structure:** Write the *Core Concept*. Structurally, the proportion and the equation are the same—multiply both sides of the proportion by πr^2 and you have the equation.
- Have students solve Example 3.
- ❓ "How could you check your two answers?" They should sum to the area of the circle.

Using Areas of Sectors

EXAMPLE 4 Using the Area of a Sector

Find the area of ⊙V.

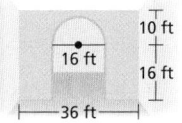

SOLUTION

$$\text{Area of sector } TVU = \frac{m\widehat{TU}}{360°} \cdot \text{Area of } \odot V \qquad \text{Formula for area of a sector}$$

$$35 = \frac{40°}{360°} \cdot \text{Area of } \odot V \qquad \text{Substitute.}$$

$$315 = \text{Area of } \odot V \qquad \text{Solve for area of } \odot V.$$

▶ The area of ⊙V is 315 square meters.

EXAMPLE 5 Finding the Area of a Region

A rectangular wall has an entrance cut into it. You want to paint the wall. To the nearest square foot, what is the area of the region you need to paint?

SOLUTION

The area you need to paint is the area of the rectangle minus the area of the entrance. The entrance can be divided into a semicircle and a square.

Area of wall = Area of rectangle − (Area of semicircle + Area of square)

$$= 36(26) - \left[\frac{180°}{360°} \cdot (\pi \cdot 8^2) + 16^2 \right]$$

$$= 936 - (32\pi + 256)$$

$$\approx 579.47$$

▶ The area you need to paint is about 579 square feet.

COMMON ERROR

Use the radius (8 feet), not the diameter (16 feet), when you calculate the area of the semicircle.

Monitoring Progress 🔊 Help in English and Spanish at *BigIdeasMath.com*

7. Find the area of ⊙H.

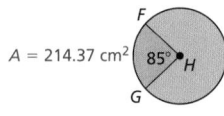

8. Find the area of the figure.

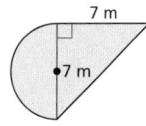

9. If you know the area and radius of a sector of a circle, can you find the measure of the intercepted arc? Explain.

Extra Example 4

Find the area of ⊙S.

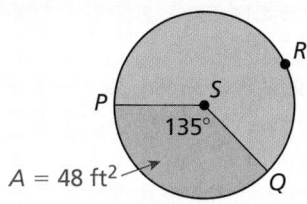

The area of ⊙S is 128 square feet.

Extra Example 5

A farmer has a field with the shape shown. Find the area of the shaded region to the nearest square meter.

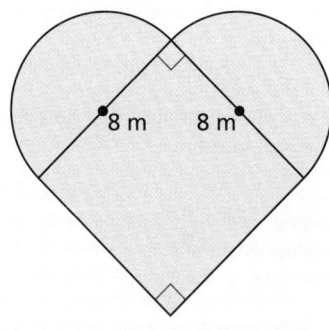

The area is about 114 square meters.

MONITORING PROGRESS ANSWERS

7. 907.92 cm²

8. about 43.74 m²

9. yes; Solve the formula for the measure of the intercepted arc.

Laurie's Notes Teacher Actions

? "In Example 4, what portion of the circle has an area of 35 square meters?" $\frac{40°}{360°} = \frac{1}{9}$

• Have students solve Example 4, being sure to label their answer.

• **Think-Alouds:** Pose Example 5 and say, "To solve this problem I need to …." Ask partner A to think aloud for partner B to hear the problem-solving process. When students have finished the problem, use *Popsicle Sticks* to solicit a response.

Closure

• **Exit Ticket:** Find the area of your teacher's college dorm room rug. The rug had a 6-foot diameter with a 60° sector removed. $\frac{15\pi}{2}$ or about 23.6 square feet

606   Chapter 11

Assignment Guide and Homework Check

ASSIGNMENT

Basic: 1, 2, 3–27 odd, 30, 36, 42–45

Average: 1, 2, 8–32 even, 34–36, 42–45

Advanced: 1, 2, 4, 10, 14, 18–40 even, 42–45

HOMEWORK CHECK

Basic: 5, 13, 17, 21, 27

Average: 8, 12, 16, 22, 26

Advanced: 10, 14, 18, 28, 30

ANSWERS

1. sector

2. yes; The sector area is proportional to the arc measure.

3. about 0.50 cm^2

4. about 314.16 in.^2

5. about 78.54 in.^2

6. about 201.06 ft^2

7. about 5.32 ft

8. about 11.00 in.

9. about 4.00 in.

10. 52 cm

11. about 464 people per mi^2

12. about 5747 people per mi^2

13. about 319,990 people

14. about 7 mi

15. about 52.36 in.^2; about 261.80 in.^2

16. about 177.88 cm^2; about 437.87 cm^2

17. about 937.31 m^2; about 1525.70 m^2

18. about 10.47 ft^2; about 39.79 ft^2

19. The diameter was substituted in the formula for area as the radius;
$A = \pi(6)^2 \approx 113.10 \text{ ft}^2$

20. The angle measures should be on the same side of the proportion;
$\dfrac{115}{360} = \dfrac{n}{255}$; $n \approx 81.46 \text{ ft}^2$

Vocabulary and Core Concept Check

1. **VOCABULARY** A(n) _____ of a circle is the region bounded by two radii of the circle and their intercepted arc.

2. **WRITING** The arc measure of a sector in a given circle is doubled. Will the area of the sector also be doubled? Explain your reasoning.

Monitoring Progress and Modeling with Mathematics

In Exercises 3–10, find the indicated measure. *(See Example 1.)*

3. area of $\odot C$

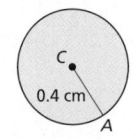

4. area of $\odot C$

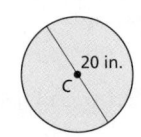

5. area of a circle with a radius of 5 inches

6. area of a circle with a diameter of 16 feet

7. radius of a circle with an area of 89 square feet

8. radius of a circle with an area of 380 square inches

9. diameter of a circle with an area of 12.6 square inches

10. diameter of a circle with an area of 676π square centimeters

In Exercises 11–14, find the indicated measure. *(See Example 2.)*

11. About 210,000 people live in a region with a 12-mile radius. Find the population density in people per square mile.

12. About 650,000 people live in a region with a 6-mile radius. Find the population density in people per square mile.

13. A region with a 4-mile radius has a population density of about 6366 people per square mile. Find the number of people who live in the region.

14. About 79,000 people live in a circular region with a population density of about 513 people per square mile. Find the radius of the region.

In Exercises 15–18, find the areas of the sectors formed by $\angle DFE$. *(See Example 3.)*

15.

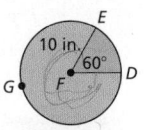

16.

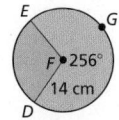

17.

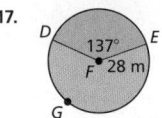

18.

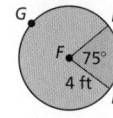

19. **ERROR ANALYSIS** Describe and correct the error in finding the area of the circle.

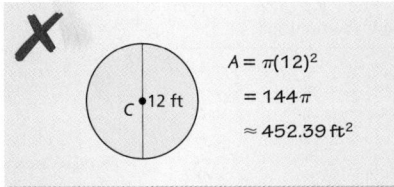

20. **ERROR ANALYSIS** Describe and correct the error in finding the area of sector *XZY* when the area of $\odot Z$ is 255 square feet.

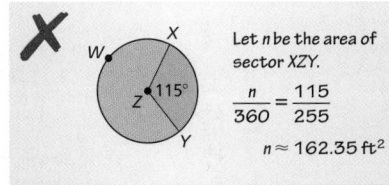

In Exercises 21 and 22, the area of the shaded sector is shown. Find the indicated measure. *(See Example 4.)*

21. area of ⊙M

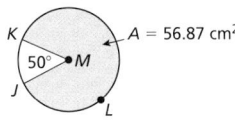

22. radius of ⊙M

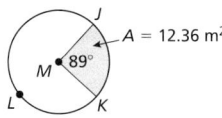

In Exercises 23–28, find the area of the shaded region. *(See Example 5.)*

23.

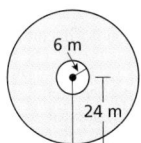

24.

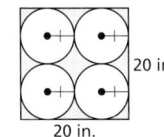

25.

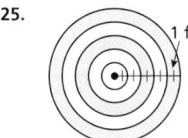

26.

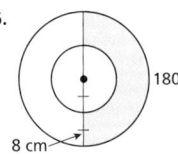

27.

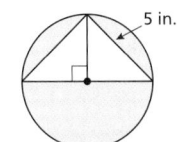

28.

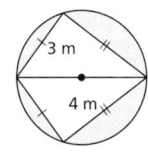

29. PROBLEM SOLVING The diagram shows the shape of a putting green at a miniature golf course. One part of the green is a sector of a circle. Find the area of the putting green.

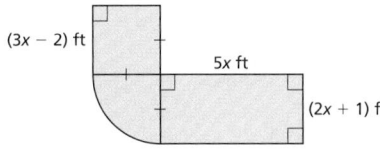

30. MAKING AN ARGUMENT Your friend claims that if the radius of a circle is doubled, then its area doubles. Is your friend correct? Explain your reasoning.

31. MODELING WITH MATHEMATICS The diagram shows the area of a lawn covered by a water sprinkler.

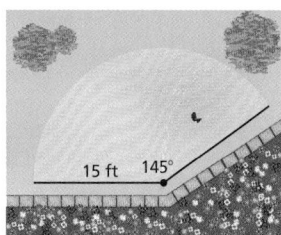

 a. What is the area of the lawn that is covered by the sprinkler?

 b. The water pressure is weakened so that the radius is 12 feet. What is the area of the lawn that will be covered?

32. MODELING WITH MATHEMATICS The diagram shows a projected beam of light from a lighthouse.

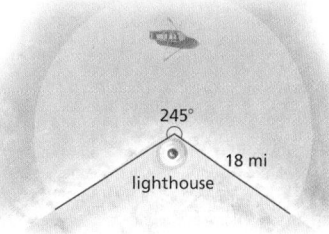

 a. What is the area of water that can be covered by the light from the lighthouse?

 b. What is the area of land that can be covered by the light from the lighthouse?

33. ANALYZING RELATIONSHIPS Look back at the Perimeters of Similar Polygons Theorem (Theorem 8.1) and the Areas of Similar Polygons Theorem (Theorem 8.2) in Section 8.1. How would you rewrite these theorems to apply to circles? Explain your reasoning.

34. ANALYZING RELATIONSHIPS A square is inscribed in a circle. The same square is also circumscribed about a smaller circle. Draw a diagram that represents this situation. Then find the ratio of the area of the larger circle to the area of the smaller circle.

ANSWERS

21. about 66.04 cm^2

22. about 3.99 m

23. about 1696.46 m^2

24. about 85.84 in.^{2}

25. about 43.98 ft^2

26. about 301.59 cm^2

27. about 26.77 in.^{2}

28. about 7.63 m^2

29. about 192.48 ft^2

30. no; *Sample answer:* The area is proportional to the square of the radius.

31. a. about 285 ft^2

 b. about 182 ft^2

32. a. about 693 mi^2

 b. about 325 mi^2

33. *Sample answer:* change side lengths to radii and perimeter to circumference; Different terms need to be used because a circle is not a polygon.

34.

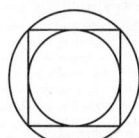

2 to 1

Mini-Assessment

1. Find the area of a circle with radius 12 feet. about 452.39 square feet

2. About 414,000 people live in a region with a 15-mile radius. Find the population density in people per square mile. about 586 people per square mile

3. Find the areas of the sectors formed by ∠LMN.

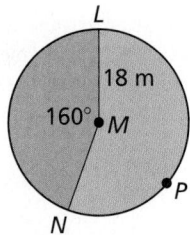

small sector: about 452.39 square meters; large sector: about 565.49 square meters

4. Find the area of ⊙E.

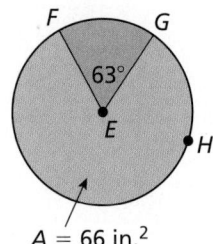

80 square inches

5. Find the area of the shaded region.

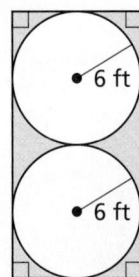

about 61.81 square feet

---

35. **CONSTRUCTION** The table shows how students get to school.

Method	Percent of students
bus	65%
walk	25%
other	10%

   a. Explain why a circle graph is appropriate for the data.

   b. You will represent each method by a sector of a circle graph. Find the central angle to use for each sector. Then construct the graph using a radius of 2 inches.

   c. Find the area of each sector in your graph.

36. **HOW DO YOU SEE IT?** The outermost edges of the pattern shown form a square. If you know the dimensions of the outer square, is it possible to compute the total colored area? Explain.

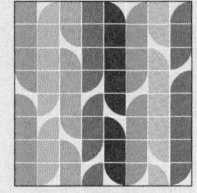

37. **ABSTRACT REASONING** A circular pizza with a 12-inch diameter is enough for you and 2 friends. You want to buy pizzas for yourself and 7 friends. A 10-inch diameter pizza with one topping costs $6.99 and a 14-inch diameter pizza with one topping costs $12.99. How many 10-inch and 14-inch pizzas should you buy in each situation? Explain.

   a. You want to spend as little money as possible.

   b. You want to have three pizzas, each with a different topping, and spend as little money as possible.

   c. You want to have as much of the thick outer crust as possible.

Maintaining Mathematical Proficiency   *Reviewing what you learned in previous grades and lessons*

Find the area of the figure. *(Skills Review Handbook)*

42.

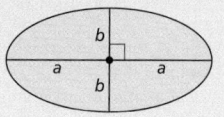

43.

44.

45.

---

38. **THOUGHT PROVOKING** You know that the area of a circle is πr^2. Find the formula for the area of an *ellipse*, shown below.

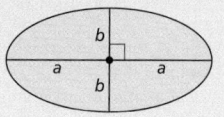

39. **MULTIPLE REPRESENTATIONS** Consider a circle with a radius of 3 inches.

   a. Complete the table, where x is the measure of the arc and y is the area of the corresponding sector. Round your answers to the nearest tenth.

x	30°	60°	90°	120°	150°	180°
y						

   b. Graph the data in the table.

   c. Is the relationship between x and y linear? Explain.

   d. If parts (a)–(c) were repeated using a circle with a radius of 5 inches, would the areas in the table change? Would your answer to part (c) change? Explain your reasoning.

40. **CRITICAL THINKING** Find the area between the three congruent tangent circles. The radius of each circle is 6 inches.

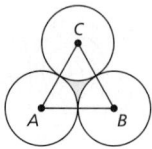

41. **PROOF** Semicircles with diameters equal to three sides of a right triangle are drawn, as shown. Prove that the sum of the areas of the two shaded crescents equals the area of the triangle.

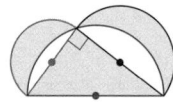

If students need help...	If students got it...
Resources by Chapter • Practice A and Practice B • Puzzle Time	Resources by Chapter • Enrichment and Extension • Cumulative Review
Student Journal • Practice	Start the *next* Section
Differentiating the Lesson Skills Review Handbook	

Overview of Section 11.3

Introduction

- Earlier in the book, students found the areas of triangles and special quadrilaterals. This lesson builds upon that knowledge and includes the area of kites, rhombuses, and regular polygons.
- To find the area of regular polygons, it is necessary to be able to find certain angle measures in the regular polygon along with the length of the apothem. Trigonometric ratios are used to find certain segment lengths that enable the area of the regular polygon to be found.

Teaching Strategy

- The explorations for this lesson help students to develop a strategy and understanding of how to find the area of any regular polygon. In the formal lesson, students will learn to find the length of the apothem using trigonometric ratios.
- If time permits, you could have students write a script or program for the dynamic geometry software they are familiar with that computes the area of regular polygons. Students should use a slider for the length of the side of the regular polygon and a second slider for the number of sides in the regular polygon.
- A quick online search will reveal that such work has already been done by others. Having students create the script deepens their understanding of the mathematics involved.

Pacing Suggestion

- The first exploration provides an opportunity for students to develop a conceptual understanding of how to find the area of a regular polygon. Transition to the formal lesson as soon as students have discussed the second exploration.

**Common Core
State Standards**

HSG-GMD.A.3 Use volume formulas for cylinders, pyramids, cones, and spheres to solve problems.

Laurie's Notes

Exploration

Motivate

- When students enter the room, have the stop sign displayed. You could tell them a story about a colleague who failed to notice this sign last week, or you could simply ask them what information they would need in order to find the area of the sign.
- Explain to students that in this lesson they will learn how to find the area of a regular polygon.

Exploration Note

- It is important in this exploration that students not use the functionality of the software to find the area of the regular polygon. The intent is for students to develop a strategy for finding the area of each regular polygon, which will likely be similar to the formula presented in this lesson.

Exploration 1

- The definition of the apothem is given. Finding the length of the apothem for each regular polygon is something students will need to figure out. Circulate and ask probing questions without telling students how to do it.
- **MP2 Reason Abstractly and Quantitatively:** Have students describe their method for finding the length of the apothem. Expected approaches include the following:
  - Find the midpoint of the segment between (0, 0) and the midpoint of the top side when the number of sides is even.
  - Find the point of intersection of the angle bisectors.
  - Find the intersection point of the perpendicular bisectors of the sides.
  - Find the intersection point of the diagonals between opposite vertices when the number of sides is even.
- **MP3 Construct Viable Arguments and Critique the Reasoning of Others:** Have students describe their method for finding the area of the polygon. Peers should listen carefully to ensure that the method is valid.

Exploration 2

- Explain that it is okay to simply let the length of the apothem be denoted by the variable a. The way in which students represent or write the formula will likely vary.
- **?** "Does your formula work for all polygons regardless of whether the number of sides is odd or even?" yes

Communicate Your Answer

- Verify that all students have the same area for Question 4, regardless of how the formula was written.

Connecting to Next Step

- Students should now have a good conceptual understanding of how to find the area of a regular polygon, one of the skills presented in this lesson.

11.3   Areas of Polygons

Essential Question   How can you find the area of a regular polygon?

The **center of a regular polygon** is the center of its circumscribed circle.

The distance from the center to any side of a regular polygon is called the **apothem of a regular polygon**.

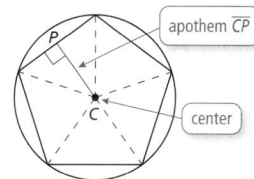

EXPLORATION 1   Finding the Area of a Regular Polygon

Work with a partner. Use dynamic geometry software to construct each regular polygon with side lengths of 4, as shown. Find the apothem and use it to find the area of the polygon. Describe the steps that you used.

a.
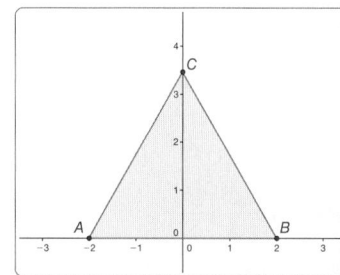

b.
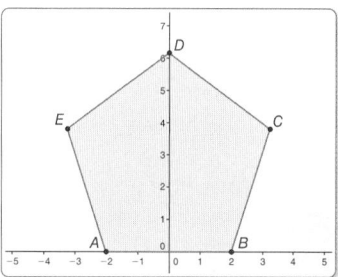

c.
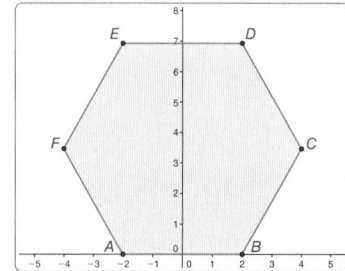

d.
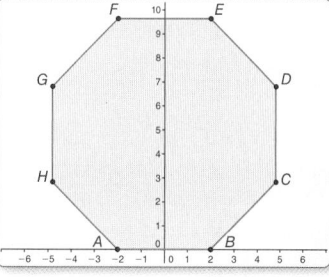

EXPLORATION 2   Writing a Formula for Area

Work with a partner. Generalize the steps you used in Exploration 1 to develop a formula for the area of a regular polygon.

> **REASONING ABSTRACTLY**
>
> To be proficient in math, you need to know and flexibly use different properties of operations and objects.

Communicate Your Answer

3. How can you find the area of a regular polygon?

4. Regular pentagon *ABCDE* has side lengths of 6 meters and an apothem of approximately 4.13 meters. Find the area of *ABCDE*.

Dynamic Teaching Tools

Dynamic Assessment & Progress Monitoring Tool

Lesson Planning Tool

Interactive Whiteboard Lesson Library

Dynamic Classroom with Dynamic Investigations

ANSWERS

1. **a.** 1.15 units; 6.9 square units
   b. 2.75 units; 27.5 square units
   c. 3.46 units; 41.52 square units
   d. 4.83 units; 77.28 square units

   Sample answer: Find the center of the regular *n*-gon by finding the center of its circumscribed circle. Then find the apothem. Use the center to divide the *n*-gon into *n* congruent triangles, each with a base that is a side of the *n*-gon and a height that is the apothem. Find the area of one triangle and multiply by *n* to find the area of the regular *n*-gon.

2. $A = \frac{1}{2}aP$, where *a* is the apothem and *P* is the perimeter

3. *Sample answer:* Find the perimeter and apothem and substitute the values in the formula $A = \frac{1}{2}aP$.

4. 61.95 m²

Extra Example 1

Find the area of each rhombus or kite.

a.

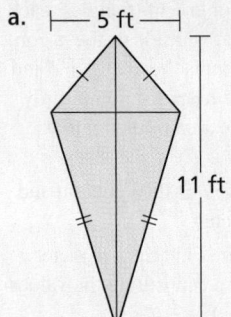

5 ft
11 ft

The area is 27.5 square feet.

b.

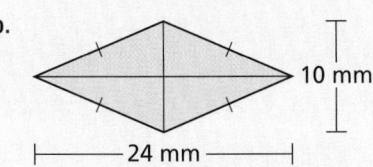

10 mm
24 mm

The area is 120 square millimeters.

MONITORING PROGRESS ANSWERS

1. 10 ft^2
2. 54 in.^2

11.3 Lesson

Core Vocabulary

center of a regular polygon, *p. 611*
radius of a regular polygon, *p. 611*
apothem of a regular polygon, *p. 611*
central angle of a regular polygon, *p. 611*

Previous
rhombus
kite

What You Will Learn

▶ Find areas of rhombuses and kites.
▶ Find angle measures in regular polygons.
▶ Find areas of regular polygons.

Finding Areas of Rhombuses and Kites

You can divide a rhombus or kite with diagonals d_1 and d_2 into two congruent triangles with base d_1, height $\frac{1}{2}d_2$, and area $\frac{1}{2}d_1\left(\frac{1}{2}d_2\right) = \frac{1}{4}d_1d_2$. So, the area of a rhombus or kite is $2\left(\frac{1}{4}d_1d_2\right) = \frac{1}{2}d_1d_2$.

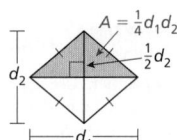
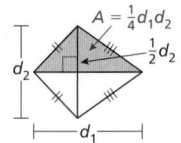

Core Concept

Area of a Rhombus or Kite

The area of a rhombus or kite with diagonals d_1 and d_2 is $\frac{1}{2}d_1d_2$.

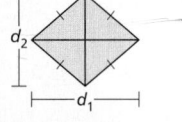
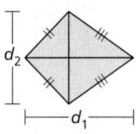

EXAMPLE 1 Finding the Area of a Rhombus or Kite

Find the area of each rhombus or kite.

a.

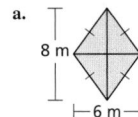

8 m
6 m

b.

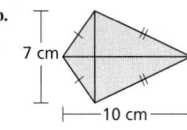

7 cm
10 cm

SOLUTION

a. $A = \frac{1}{2}d_1d_2$

$= \frac{1}{2}(6)(8)$

$= 24$

▶ So, the area is 24 square meters.

b. $A = \frac{1}{2}d_1d_2$

$= \frac{1}{2}(10)(7)$

$= 35$

▶ So, the area is 35 square centimeters.

Monitoring Progress Help in English and Spanish at *BigIdeasMath.com*

1. Find the area of a rhombus with diagonals $d_1 = 4$ feet and $d_2 = 5$ feet.
2. Find the area of a kite with diagonals $d_1 = 12$ inches and $d_2 = 9$ inches.

Laurie's Notes   Teacher Actions

? MP1 Make Sense of Problems and Persevere in Solving Them: "What are the attributes of the diagonals of a rhombus? A kite?" Diagonals of a rhombus are perpendicular bisectors of one another. Diagonals of a kite are perpendicular.

• Sketch the two quadrilaterals.
• "Develop a formula for the area of each that involves the diagonals." Given time and the suggestion that the formula involves the diagonals, many students can derive the formula.
• Have students work Example 1 with their partners. Discuss as a class.

Finding Angle Measures in Regular Polygons

The diagram shows a regular polygon inscribed in a circle. The **center of a regular polygon** and the **radius of a regular polygon** are the center and the radius of its circumscribed circle.

The distance from the center to any side of a regular polygon is called the **apothem of a regular polygon**. The apothem is the height to the base of an isosceles triangle that has two radii as legs. The word "apothem" refers to a segment as well as a length. For a given regular polygon, think of *an* apothem as a segment and *the* apothem as a length.

A **central angle of a regular polygon** is an angle formed by two radii drawn to consecutive vertices of the polygon. To find the measure of each central angle, divide 360° by the number of sides.

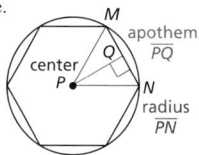

$\angle MPN$ is a central angle.

EXAMPLE 2   **Finding Angle Measures in a Regular Polygon**

In the diagram, *ABCDE* is a regular pentagon inscribed in $\odot F$. Find each angle measure.

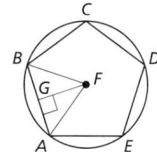

a. $m\angle AFB$ **b.** $m\angle AFG$ **c.** $m\angle GAF$

SOLUTION

a. $\angle AFB$ is a central angle, so $m\angle AFB = \dfrac{360°}{5} = 72°$.

b. $\overline{FG}$ is an apothem, which makes it an altitude of isosceles $\triangle AFB$.

So, $\overline{FG}$ bisects $\angle AFB$ and $m\angle AFG = \dfrac{1}{2}m\angle AFB = 36°$.

c. By the Triangle Sum Theorem (Theorem 5.1), the sum of the angle measures of right $\triangle GAF$ is 180°.

$$m\angle GAF = 180° - 90° - 36°$$
$$= 54°$$

So, $m\angle GAF = 54°$.

> **ANALYZING RELATIONSHIPS**
>
> $\overline{FG}$ is an altitude of an isosceles triangle, so it is also a median and angle bisector of the isosceles triangle.

Monitoring Progress 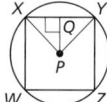 Help in English and Spanish at *BigIdeasMath.com*

In the diagram, *WXYZ* is a square inscribed in $\odot P$.

3. Identify the center, a radius, an apothem, and a central angle of the polygon.

4. Find $m\angle XPY$, $m\angle XPQ$, and $m\angle PXQ$.

English Language Learners

Build on Past Knowledge
Point out that the center, radius, and central angle of a regular polygon are the same as the center, radius, and central angle of its circumscribed circle. The only new term on this page is *apothem*.

Extra Example 2

In the diagram, polygon *ABCDEFGHJK* is a regular decagon inscribed in $\odot P$. Find each angle measure.

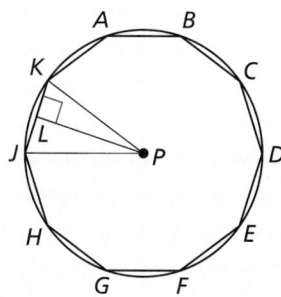

a. $m\angle KPJ$ 36°

b. $m\angle LPK$ 18°

c. $m\angle LJP$ 72°

MONITORING PROGRESS ANSWERS

3. center: *P*, radius: $\overline{PX}$ or $\overline{PY}$, apothem: $\overline{PQ}$, central angle: $\angle XPY$

4. $m\angle XPY = 90°$; $m\angle XPQ = 45°$; $m\angle PXQ = 45°$

Laurie's Notes   Teacher Actions

- **Paired Verbal Fluency:** Have students pair up and follow the protocol described on page T-462. Ask students to share what they recall about polygons and regular polygons. If students completed the explorations, they should mention area and the apothem.

- **Whiteboarding:** Have partners work on Example 2 and display their results on whiteboards. Circulate and give sufficient *Wait Time*. Have students share their solutions.

- **?** "Could the strategies you used for Example 2 be used to find the corresponding angles in any regular *n*-gon?" yes

Extra Example 3

A regular hexagon is inscribed in a circle with a diameter of 32 units. Find the area of the hexagon.

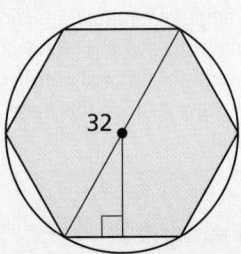

$A = \frac{1}{2}aP = \frac{1}{2}(8\sqrt{3})(6 \cdot 16)$, or about 665.11 square units

Finding Areas of Regular Polygons

You can find the area of any regular n-gon by dividing it into congruent triangles.

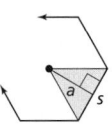

A = Area of one triangle • Number of triangles

$= \left(\frac{1}{2} \cdot s \cdot a\right) \cdot n$ Base of triangle is s and height of triangle is a. Number of triangles is n.

$= \frac{1}{2} \cdot a \cdot (n \cdot s)$ Commutative and Associative Properties of Multiplication

$= \frac{1}{2}a \cdot P$ There are n congruent sides of length s, so perimeter P is $n \cdot s$.

> **READING DIAGRAMS**
>
> In this book, a point shown inside a regular polygon marks the center of the circle that can be circumscribed about the polygon.

🌀 Core Concept

Area of a Regular Polygon

The area of a regular n-gon with side length s is one-half the product of the apothem a and the perimeter P.

$$A = \frac{1}{2}aP, \text{ or } A = \frac{1}{2}a \cdot ns$$

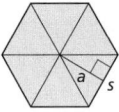

EXAMPLE 3   Finding the Area of a Regular Polygon

A regular nonagon is inscribed in a circle with a radius of 4 units. Find the area of the nonagon.

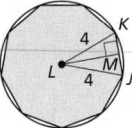

SOLUTION

The measure of central $\angle JLK$ is $\frac{360°}{9}$, or 40°. Apothem $\overline{LM}$ bisects the central angle, so $m\angle KLM$ is 20°. To find the lengths of the legs, use trigonometric ratios for right $\triangle KLM$.

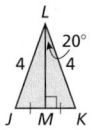

$\sin 20° = \dfrac{MK}{LK}$ $\cos 20° = \dfrac{LM}{LK}$

$\sin 20° = \dfrac{MK}{4}$ $\cos 20° = \dfrac{LM}{4}$

$4 \sin 20° = MK$ $4 \cos 20° = LM$

The regular nonagon has side length $s = 2(MK) = 2(4 \sin 20°) = 8 \sin 20°$, and apothem $a = LM = 4 \cos 20°$.

▶ So, the area is $A = \frac{1}{2}a \cdot ns = \frac{1}{2}(4 \cos 20°) \cdot (9)(8 \sin 20°) \approx 46.3$ square units.

612   **Chapter 11**   Circumference, Area, and Volume

Laurie's Notes | Teacher Actions

- Sketch a portion of a regular n-gon.
- Derive the formula for the area of a regular polygon. The first step should be similar to what students wrote for Exploration 2 on page 609.
- Write both forms of the formula. Many students prefer $A = \frac{1}{2}ans$ because *ans* triggers "answer."
- **?** Pose Example 3. "What is needed to find the area?" the length of the apothem and the side length of the regular nonagon
- **Teaching Tip:** Sketch one isosceles triangle and label the given information. Hopefully students will think about trigonometric ratios!

612   **Chapter 11**

EXAMPLE 4   Finding the Area of a Regular Polygon

You are decorating the top of a table by covering it with small ceramic tiles. The tabletop is a regular octagon with 15-inch sides and a radius of about 19.6 inches. What is the area you are covering?

 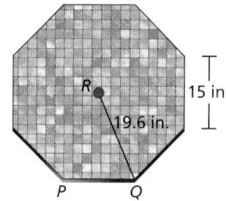

SOLUTION

Step 1 Find the perimeter P of the tabletop.
An octagon has 8 sides, so $P = 8(15) = 120$ inches.

Step 2 Find the apothem a. The apothem is height RS of $\triangle PQR$.

Because $\triangle PQR$ is isosceles, altitude $\overline{RS}$ bisects $\overline{QP}$.

So, $QS = \frac{1}{2}(QP) = \frac{1}{2}(15) = 7.5$ inches.

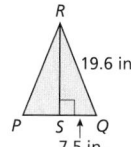

To find RS, use the Pythagorean Theorem (Theorem 9.1) for $\triangle RQS$.

$$a = RS = \sqrt{19.6^2 - 7.5^2} = \sqrt{327.91} \approx 18.108$$

Step 3 Find the area A of the tabletop.

$$A = \frac{1}{2}aP \qquad \text{Formula for area of a regular polygon}$$

$$= \frac{1}{2}(\sqrt{327.91})(120) \qquad \text{Substitute.}$$

$$\approx 1086.5 \qquad \text{Simplify.}$$

▶ The area you are covering with tiles is about 1086.5 square inches.

Monitoring Progress   Help in English and Spanish at *BigIdeasMath.com*

Find the area of the regular polygon.

5.
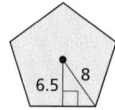

6.

Extra Example 4
A mirror is in the shape of a regular nonagon with 6-inch sides. What is the area of the mirror?

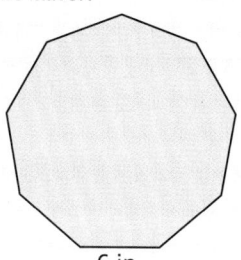

6 in.

$A = \dfrac{1}{2}aP = \dfrac{1}{2}\left(\dfrac{3}{\tan 20°}\right)(9 \cdot 6)$, or about 222.5 square inches

MONITORING PROGRESS ANSWERS
5. about 151.57 square units
6. about 377.02 square units

Laurie's Notes   Teacher Actions

- **Pass the Problem:** Explain this technique and pose Example 4. Give partners 1 to 2 minutes to discuss and begin a solution. Call "swap" and have partners continue to solve. Both groups debrief. Ask students what part of the problem was challenging. Was there a spot where they got stuck? What helped them make progress with the problem?

Closure

- **Exit Ticket:** Find the area of a stop sign when the side length is 10 inches.
  about 482.8 square inches

Assignment Guide and Homework Check

ASSIGNMENT

Basic: 1, 2, 3–21 odd, 25–29 odd, 40, 42, 44, 53–56

Average: 1, 2, 4–22 even, 26–36 even, 42, 44, 53–56

Advanced: 1, 2, 4, 12, 16, 20, 24–32 even, 33–44, 50–56

HOMEWORK CHECK

Basic: 3, 15, 19, 27, 40

Average: 4, 16, 20, 28, 36

Advanced: 12, 20, 28, 34, 37

ANSWERS

1. Divide 360° by the number of sides.
2. Find the apothem of regular polygon *ABCDE*; 5.5; 6.8
3. 361 square units
4. 72 square units
5. 70 square units
6. 24 square units
7. *P*
8. *Sample answer:* $\angle MPN$
9. 5 units
10. 4.05 units
11. 36°
12. 20°
13. 15°
14. 51.4°
15. 45°
16. 22.5°
17. 67.5°
18. 135°
19. about 62.35 square units
20. about 289.24 square units
21. about 20.87 square units
22. about 127.31 square units
23. about 342.24 square units
24. about 90.82 square units
25. The side lengths were used instead of the diagonals; $A = \frac{1}{2}(8)(4) = 16$

11.3 Exercises

Dynamic Solutions available at *BigIdeasMath.com*

Vocabulary and Core Concept Check

1. **WRITING** Explain how to find the measure of a central angle of a regular polygon.

2. **DIFFERENT WORDS, SAME QUESTION** Which is different? Find "both" answers.

Find the radius of $\odot F$.	Find the apothem of polygon *ABCDE*.
Find *AF*.	Find the radius of polygon *ABCDE*.

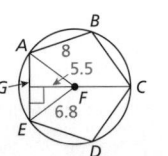

Monitoring Progress and Modeling with Mathematics

In Exercises 3–6, find the area of the kite or rhombus. *(See Example 1.)*

3.

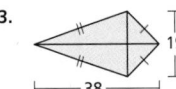

4.

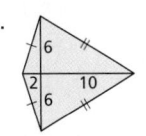

5.

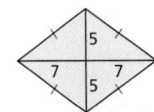

6.

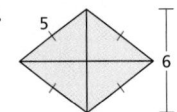

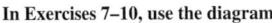

In Exercises 7–10, use the diagram.

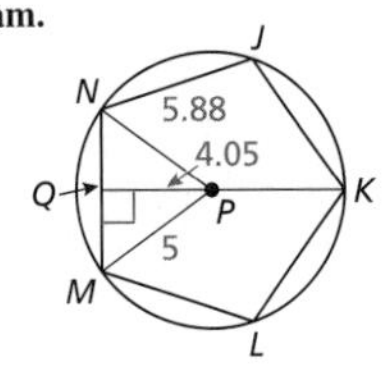

7. Identify the center of polygon *JKLMN*.

8. Identify a central angle of polygon *JKLMN*.

9. What is the radius of polygon *JKLMN*?

10. What is the apothem of polygon *JKLMN*?

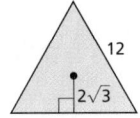

In Exercises 11–14, find the measure of a central angle of a regular polygon with the given number of sides. Round answers to the nearest tenth of a degree, if necessary.

11. 10 sides
12. 18 sides
13. 24 sides
14. 7 sides

In Exercises 15–18, find the given angle measure for regular octagon *ABCDEFGH*. *(See Example 2.)*

15. $m\angle GJH$
16. $m\angle GJK$
17. $m\angle KGJ$
18. $m\angle EJH$

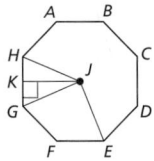

In Exercises 19–24, find the area of the regular polygon. *(See Examples 3 and 4.)*

19.

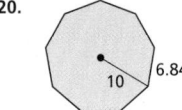

20.

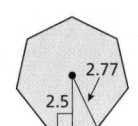

21.

22.

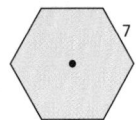

23. an octagon with a radius of 11 units

24. a pentagon with an apothem of 5 units

25. **ERROR ANALYSIS** Describe and correct the error in finding the area of the kite.

$A = \frac{1}{2}(3.6)(5.4)$
$= 9.72$

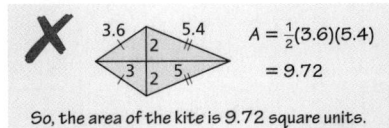

So, the area of the kite is 9.72 square units.

26. ERROR ANALYSIS Describe and correct the error in finding the area of the regular hexagon.

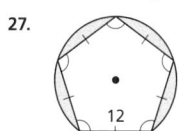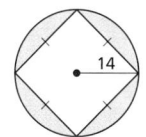

$$s = \sqrt{15^2 - 13^2} \approx 7.5$$
$$A = \frac{1}{2}a \cdot ns$$
$$\approx \frac{1}{2}(13)(6)(7.5)$$
$$= 292.5$$

So, the area of the hexagon is about 292.5 square units.

In Exercises 27–30, find the area of the shaded region.

27.

12

28.
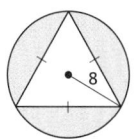
14

29.
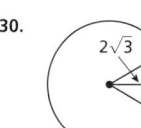
8

30.
$2\sqrt{3}$
60°

31. MODELING WITH MATHEMATICS Basaltic columns are geological formations that result from rapidly cooling lava. Giant's Causeway in Ireland contains many hexagonal basaltic columns. Suppose the top of one of the columns is in the shape of a regular hexagon with a radius of 8 inches. Find the area of the top of the column to the nearest square inch.

32. MODELING WITH MATHEMATICS A watch has a circular surface on a background that is a regular octagon. Find the area of the octagon. Then find the area of the silver border around the circular face.

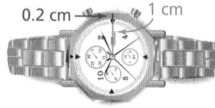
0.2 cm   1 cm

CRITICAL THINKING In Exercises 33–35, tell whether the statement is *true* or *false*. Explain your reasoning.

33. The area of a regular n-gon of a fixed radius r increases as n increases.

34. The apothem of a regular polygon is always less than the radius.

35. The radius of a regular polygon is always less than the side length.

36. REASONING Predict which figure has the greatest area and which has the least area. Explain your reasoning. Check by finding the area of each figure.

Ⓐ
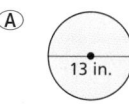
13 in.

Ⓑ
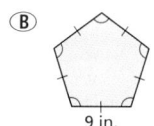
9 in.

Ⓒ
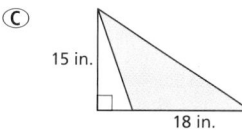
15 in.
18 in.

37. USING EQUATIONS Find the area of a regular pentagon inscribed in a circle whose equation is given by $(x - 4)^2 + (y + 2)^2 = 25$.

38. REASONING What happens to the area of a kite if you double the length of one of the diagonals? if you double the length of both diagonals? Justify your answer.

MATHEMATICAL CONNECTIONS In Exercises 39 and 40, write and solve an equation to find the indicated lengths. Round decimal answers to the nearest tenth.

39. The area of a kite is 324 square inches. One diagonal is twice as long as the other diagonal. Find the length of each diagonal.

40. One diagonal of a rhombus is four times the length of the other diagonal. The area of the rhombus is 98 square feet. Find the length of each diagonal.

41. REASONING The perimeter of a regular nonagon, or 9-gon, is 18 inches. Is this enough information to find the area? If so, find the area and explain your reasoning. If not, explain why not.

Dynamic Teaching Tools

Dynamic Assessment & Progress Monitoring Tool

Interactive Whiteboard Lesson Library

Dynamic Classroom with Dynamic Investigations

ANSWERS

26. Because 13 is the apothem, 7.5 is half the side length, not the entire side length; $s = 2\sqrt{15^2 - 13^2} \approx 15$; $A \approx 585$

27. about 79.60 square units

28. about 223.75 square units

29. about 117.92 square units

30. about 1.45 square units

31. about 166 in.^{2}

32. about 4.8 cm^2; about 1.6 cm^2

33. true; *Sample answer:* As the number of sides increases, the polygon fills more of the circle.

34. true; *Sample answer:* The radius is the hypotenuse of each triangle.

35. false; *Sample answer:* The radius can be less than or greater than the side length.

36. *Sample answer:* B; C; B appears largest and C appears smallest; A: about 132.73 in.^{2}, B: about 139.36 in.^{2}, C: 135 in.^{2}

37. about 59.44 square units

38. It doubles; It is 4 times greater; *Sample answer:* The area of a kite is the product of the lengths of the diagonals.

39. $x^2 = 324$; 18 in.; 36 in.

40. $2x^2 = 98$; 7 ft; 28 ft

41. yes; about 24.73 in.^{2}; *Sample answer:* Each side length is 2 inches, and the central angle is 40°.

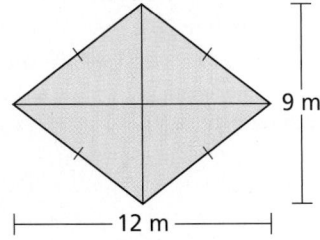
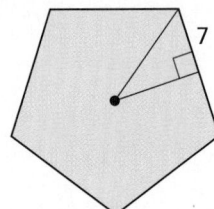
42. MAKING AN ARGUMENT Your friend claims that it is possible to find the area of any rhombus if you only know the perimeter of the rhombus. Is your friend correct? Explain your reasoning.

43. PROOF Prove that the area of any quadrilateral with perpendicular diagonals is $A = \frac{1}{2}d_1d_2$, where d_1 and d_2 are the lengths of the diagonals.

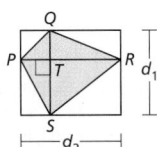

44. HOW DO YOU SEE IT? Explain how to find the area of the regular hexagon by dividing the hexagon into equilateral triangles.

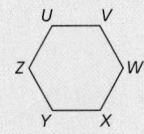

45. REWRITING A FORMULA Rewrite the formula for the area of a rhombus for the special case of a square with side length s. Show that this is the same as the formula for the area of a square, $A = s^2$.

46. REWRITING A FORMULA Use the formula for the area of a regular polygon to show that the area of an equilateral triangle can be found by using the formula $A = \frac{1}{4}s^2\sqrt{3}$, where s is the side length.

47. CRITICAL THINKING The area of a regular pentagon is 72 square centimeters. Find the length of one side.

48. CRITICAL THINKING The area of a dodecagon, or 12-gon, is 140 square inches. Find the apothem of the polygon.

49. USING STRUCTURE In the figure, an equilateral triangle lies inside a square inside a regular pentagon inside a regular hexagon. Find the approximate area of the entire shaded region to the nearest whole number.

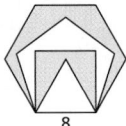

8

50. THOUGHT PROVOKING The area of a regular n-gon is given by $A = \frac{1}{2}aP$. As n approaches infinity, what does the n-gon approach? What does P approach? What does a approach? What can you conclude from your three answers? Explain your reasoning.

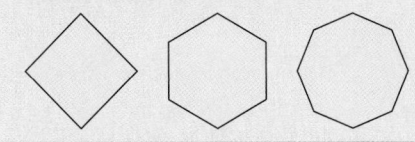

51. COMPARING METHODS Find the area of regular pentagon $ABCDE$ by using the formula $A = \frac{1}{2}aP$, or $A = \frac{1}{2}a \cdot ns$. Then find the area by adding the areas of smaller polygons. Check that both methods yield the same area. Which method do you prefer? Explain your reasoning.

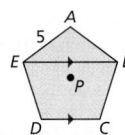

5

52. USING STRUCTURE Two regular polygons both have n sides. One of the polygons is inscribed in, and the other is circumscribed about, a circle of radius r. Find the area between the two polygons in terms of n and r.

Maintaining Mathematical Proficiency   *Reviewing what you learned in previous grades and lessons*

Determine whether the figure has *line symmetry*, *rotational symmetry*, *both*, or *neither*. If the figure has line symmetry, determine the number of lines of symmetry. If the figure has rotational symmetry, describe any rotations that map the figure onto itself. *(Section 4.2 and Section 4.3)*

53. 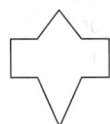   **54.**    **55.**    **56.**

If students need help...	If students got it...
Resources by Chapter • Practice A and Practice B • Puzzle Time	Resources by Chapter • Enrichment and Extension • Cumulative Review
Student Journal • Practice	Start the *next* Section
Differentiating the Lesson Skills Review Handbook	

Overview of Section 11.4

Introduction

- In this lesson, students will review the vocabulary of three-dimensional solids and be able to classify them by type.
- Two new skills introduced in this lesson are describing the cross sections of solids and sketching and describing solids of revolution.

Resources

- It is most helpful when you have a collection of interesting solids that can be displayed around the room. It is important for students to see and hold three-dimensional solids instead of only seeing them printed on paper.
- I keep a large tote bag filled with solids, many nested inside one another, so that there is always a sample of the solid for students to hold.
- Do not overlook having nets as well, meaning the flattened version of a (donut) box or cone (party hat).

Formative Assessment Tips

- **Example/Non-Example (teacher generated):** This technique enables students to develop their own definition of a concept by looking at examples and non-examples of a concept. When students compare and contrast the attributes, characteristics, and features of the examples and non-examples, they develop a deeper understanding of what the defining characteristics of the concepts are.
- After examining the examples and non-examples, students are asked to write a definition of the concept presented. This requires very different cognitive skills than simply memorizing a definition given to them. Once the definition is written, students can be asked to generate additional examples supported by their definition.
- In generating the examples, students can also be asked why their example is correct— meaning they provide justification. Listen carefully to students' language as they provide the justification.
- Note that this is an instructional technique used by teachers to introduce concepts, such as making a list of expressions that are monomials and those that are not monomials. It can also be used after instruction to assess or gauge how well students have learned a particular concept.
- This technique can be used by individuals, partners, or small groups.
- Be sure to allow sufficient time so that students receive feedback from others and/or you about their definition(s) and examples.

Pacing Suggestion

- As students work through the exploration, listen and probe for recall of prior concepts and vocabulary. This will inform where you need to start in the formal lesson.

Common Core State Standards

HSG-GMD.B.4 Identify the shapes of two-dimensional cross-sections of three-dimensional objects, and identify three-dimensional objects generated by rotations of two-dimensional objects.

Exploration

Motivate

- Hold a cube in your hand. A clear plastic one is best. Use a rubber band stretched around the center of the cube.
- **?** "If I sliced right through the cube where the rubber band is, what would the new exposed surface look like—meaning, what is the cross section?" a square
- **?** "How many cross-sectional shapes can be made when you slice through a cube?" Answers will vary.
- Tell students that you are not looking for the answer now, but you will return to this question at the end of the class.

Exploration 1

- The exploration should not take long for students to complete. The names of the Platonic solids may not all be familiar, but the language of vertices, faces, and edges should be.
- If possible, have examples of these solids for students to hold and rotate as they do their counting. This is particularly true for the dodecahedron and icosahedron.
- **MP2 Reason Abstractly and Quantitatively:** Students may reason about a strategy that allows them to count the vertices, faces, or edges in groups versus individually. For example, the icosahedron as pictured can be thought to have a top and bottom "hat" and then a band of triangles around the middle section. Whatever attributes the top portion has are repeated for the bottom portion.

Communicate Your Answer

- Students may come up with relationships that are true for some of the polyhedra but not all of them. Have students share their conjectures with the class so that students can test the conjecture on polyhedra that they have drawn in Question 3.

Connecting to Next Step

- Students have now reminded themselves of attributes of polyhedra that they had studied in middle school. In the formal lesson, they will also look at cross sections of polyhedra.

11.4 Three-Dimensional Figures

Essential Question What is the relationship between the numbers of vertices V, edges E, and faces F of a polyhedron?

A **polyhedron** is a solid that is bounded by polygons, called **faces**.

- Each *vertex* is a point.
- Each *edge* is a segment of a line.
- Each *face* is a portion of a plane.

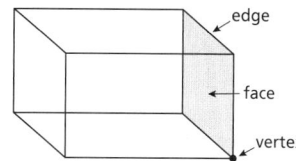

EXPLORATION 1 **Analyzing a Property of Polyhedra**

Work with a partner. The five *Platonic solids* are shown below. Each of these solids has congruent regular polygons as faces. Complete the table by listing the numbers of vertices, edges, and faces of each Platonic solid.

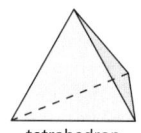
tetrahedron

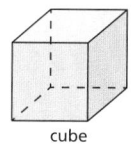
cube

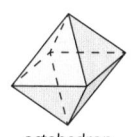
octahedron

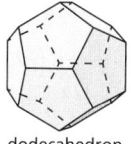
dodecahedron

icosahedron

Solid	Vertices, V	Edges, E	Faces, F
tetrahedron			
cube			
octahedron			
dodecahedron			
icosahedron			

CONSTRUCTING VIABLE ARGUMENTS

To be proficient in math, you need to reason inductively about data.

Communicate Your Answer

2. What is the relationship between the numbers of vertices V, edges E, and faces F of a polyhedron? (*Note:* Swiss mathematician Leonhard Euler (1707–1783) discovered a formula that relates these quantities.)

3. Draw three polyhedra that are different from the Platonic solids given in Exploration 1. Count the numbers of vertices, edges, and faces of each polyhedron. Then verify that the relationship you found in Question 2 is valid for each polyhedron.

Section 11.4 Three-Dimensional Figures **617**

ANSWERS

1. 4, 6, 4; 8, 12, 6; 6, 12, 8; 20, 30, 12; 12, 30, 20

2. $V - E + F = 2$

3. *Sample answer:*

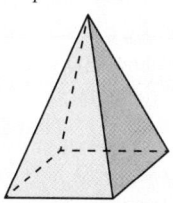

5 vertices, 8 edges, 5 faces;
$5 - 8 + 5 = 2$

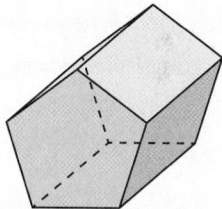

10 vertices, 15 edges, 7 faces;
$10 - 15 + 7 = 2$

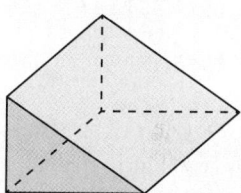

6 vertices, 9 edges, 5 faces;
$6 - 9 + 5 = 2$

Extra Example 1
Tell whether each solid is a polyhedron. If it is, name the polyhedron.

a.

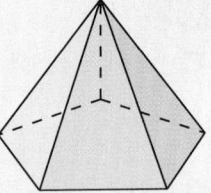

polyhedron; a pentagonal pyramid

b.

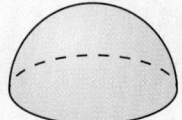

not a polyhedron

c.

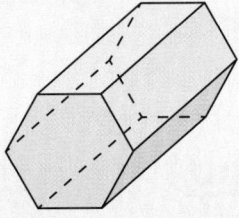

polyhedron; a hexagonal prism

11.4 Lesson

Core Vocabulary
polyhedron, *p. 618*
face, *p. 618*
edge, *p. 618*
vertex, *p. 618*
cross section, *p. 619*
solid of revolution, *p. 620*
axis of revolution, *p. 620*

Previous
solid
prism
pyramid
cylinder
cone
sphere
base

What You Will Learn
▶ Classify solids.
▶ Describe cross sections.
▶ Sketch and describe solids of revolution.

Classifying Solids
A three-dimensional figure, or solid, is bounded by flat or curved surfaces that enclose a single region of space. A **polyhedron** is a solid that is bounded by polygons, called **faces**. An **edge** of a polyhedron is a line segment formed by the intersection of two faces. A **vertex** of a polyhedron is a point where three or more edges meet. The plural of polyhedron is *polyhedra* or *polyhedrons*.

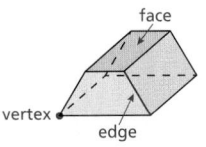

Core Concept
Types of Solids

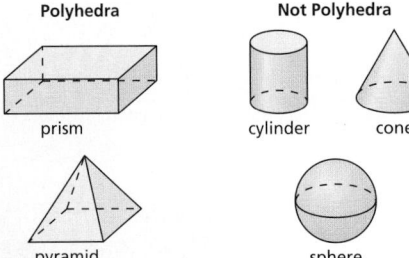

Pentagonal prism

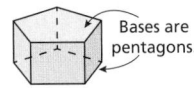

Bases are pentagons.

Triangular pyramid

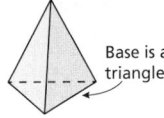

Base is a triangle.

To name a prism or a pyramid, use the shape of the *base*. The two bases of a prism are congruent polygons in parallel planes. For example, the bases of a pentagonal prism are pentagons. The base of a pyramid is a polygon. For example, the base of a triangular pyramid is a triangle.

EXAMPLE 1   Classifying Solids

Tell whether each solid is a polyhedron. If it is, name the polyhedron.

a.   b.   c.

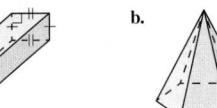  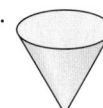

SOLUTION

a. The solid is formed by polygons, so it is a polyhedron. The two bases are congruent rectangles, so it is a rectangular prism.

b. The solid is formed by polygons, so it is a polyhedron. The base is a hexagon, so it is a hexagonal pyramid.

c. The cone has a curved surface, so it is not a polyhedron.

Laurie's Notes   Teacher Actions

- **Example/Non-Example:** Make two lists: polyhedra and not polyhedra. Give partners time to write a definition for polyhedra. Ask partners to sketch other examples of polyhedra or name objects in the room or other common objects that are examples. Use whiteboards to share and discuss results.
- Students should be familiar with certain vocabulary: vertex, face, edge, prism, pyramid, cylinder, cone, and sphere.
- **?** "How do you name prisms and pyramids?"   You name them by the base, such as pentagonal prism or triangular pyramid.

Monitoring Progress Help in English and Spanish at *BigIdeasMath.com*

Tell whether the solid is a polyhedron. If it is, name the polyhedron.

1. 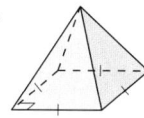   2. 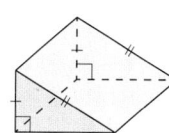   3.

Describing Cross Sections

Imagine a plane slicing through a solid. The intersection of the plane and the solid is called a **cross section**. For example, three different cross sections of a cube are shown below.

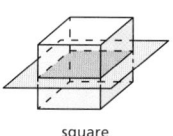   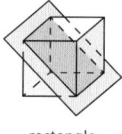   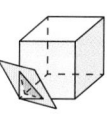

square   rectangle   triangle

EXAMPLE 2   Describing Cross Sections

Describe the shape formed by the intersection of the plane and the solid.

a. 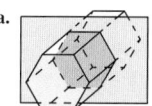   b. 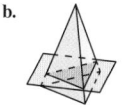   c.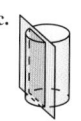

d. 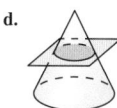   e. 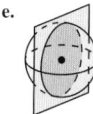   f.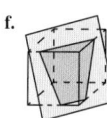

SOLUTION

a. The cross section is a hexagon.   **b.** The cross section is a triangle.

c. The cross section is a rectangle.   **d.** The cross section is a circle.

e. The cross section is a circle.   **f.** The cross section is a trapezoid.

Monitoring Progress Help in English and Spanish at *BigIdeasMath.com*

Describe the shape formed by the intersection of the plane and the solid.

4. 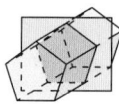   5. 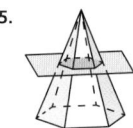   6.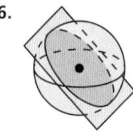

Extra Example 2

Describe the shape formed by the intersection of the plane and the solid.

a.

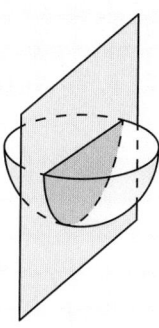

The cross-section is a semicircle.

b.

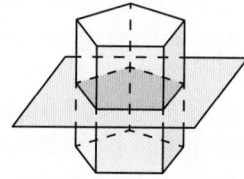

The cross-section is a pentagon.

MONITORING PROGRESS ANSWERS

1. yes; square pyramid
2. no
3. yes; triangular prism
4. pentagon
5. hexagon
6. circle

Laurie's Notes | Teacher Actions

- **Teaching Tip:** To help students understand what a cross section is, tell them to think of the solid being made of cheese. If you sliced through the solid in one motion (a plane), what would the exposed surface look like?
- **Common Misconception:** A solid can have multiple cross sections, not just one; the plane that slices through the solid can tilt.
- The shading of the cross section certainly helps in Example 2. Hold a solid in your hand and ask about cross section possibilities.

Extra Example 3

Sketch the solid produced by rotating the figure around the given axis. Then identify and describe the solid.

a.

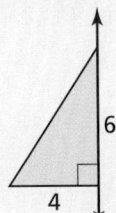

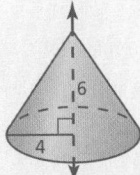

The solid is a cone with a height of 6 and a base radius of 4.

b.

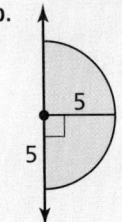

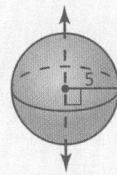

The solid is a sphere with radius 5.

MONITORING PROGRESS ANSWERS

7.

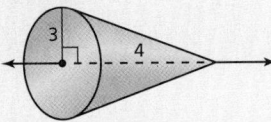

cone with height 4 and base radius 3

8.

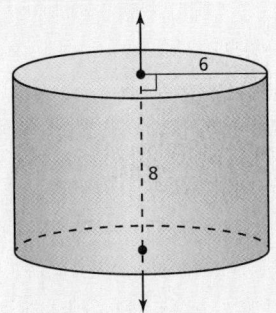

cylinder with height 8 and base radius 6

9. See Additional Answers.

Sketching and Describing Solids of Revolution

A **solid of revolution** is a three-dimensional figure that is formed by rotating a two-dimensional shape around an axis. The line around which the shape is rotated is called the **axis of revolution**.

For example, when you rotate a rectangle around a line that contains one of its sides, the solid of revolution that is produced is a cylinder.

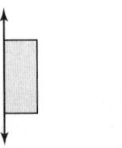 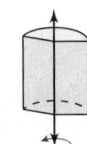 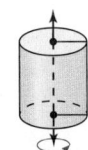

EXAMPLE 3 Sketching and Describing Solids of Revolution

Sketch the solid produced by rotating the figure around the given axis. Then identify and describe the solid.

a.

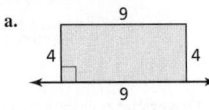

b.

SOLUTION

a.

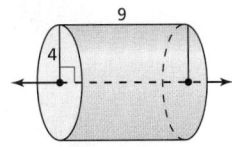

▶ The solid is a cylinder with a height of 9 and a base radius of 4.

b.

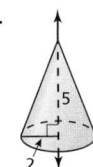

▶ The solid is a cone with a height of 5 and a base radius of 2.

Monitoring Progress Help in English and Spanish at *BigIdeasMath.com*

Sketch the solid produced by rotating the figure around the given axis. Then identify and describe the solid.

7.

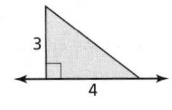

8.

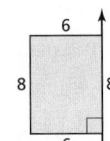

9.

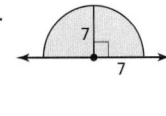

Laurie's Notes | Teacher Actions

- **Teaching Tip:** Use a wooden skewer or pencil and tape a cross section to it. Rotate it between your hands to help students visualize.
- **?** "If you rotate the rectangle in Example 3 about the side edge of 4, will the resulting cylinder be different?" yes
- **Think-Pair-Share:** Have students answer Questions 7–9, and then share and discuss as a class.

Closure

- **Exit Ticket:** Sketch and name the different cross sections of a cube. Check students' sketches; square, rectangle, hexagon, triangle

Vocabulary and Core Concept Check

1. **VOCABULARY** A(n) _____ is a solid that is bounded by polygons.

2. **WHICH ONE DOESN'T BELONG?** Which solid does *not* belong with the other three? Explain your reasoning.

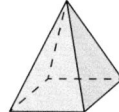 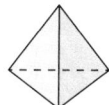  

Monitoring Progress and Modeling with Mathematics

In Exercises 3–6, match the polyhedron with its name.

3.
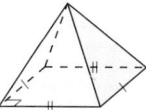

4.
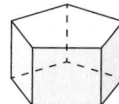

5.
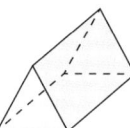

6.
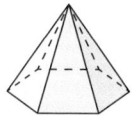

A. triangular prism   B. rectangular pyramid

C. hexagonal pyramid   D. pentagonal prism

In Exercises 7–10, tell whether the solid is a polyhedron. If it is, name the polyhedron. *(See Example 1.)*

7.
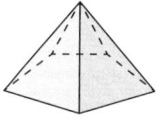

8.
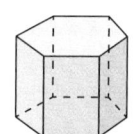

9.
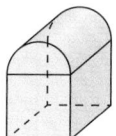

10.
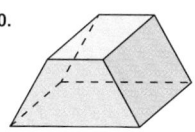

In Exercises 11–14, describe the cross section formed by the intersection of the plane and the solid.
(See Example 2.)

11.
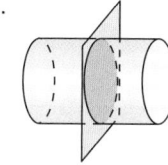

12.
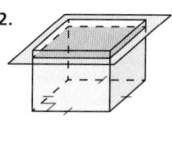

13.
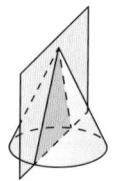

14.
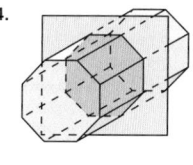

In Exercises 15–18, sketch the solid produced by rotating the figure around the given axis. Then identify and describe the solid. *(See Example 3.)*

15.
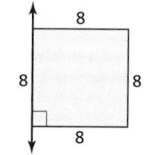

16.
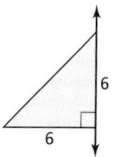

17.
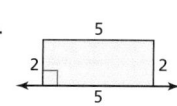

18.

17.
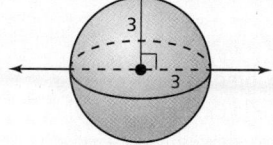
sphere with radius 3

18.
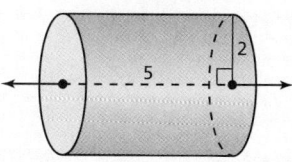
cylinder with height 5 and base radius 2

Assignment Guide and Homework Check

ASSIGNMENT

Basic: 1, 2, 3–19 odd, 20, 27, 37–39

Average: 1, 2–18 even, 19, 20, 25–30, 37–39

Advanced: 1–6, 10–18 even, 19, 20, 24, 27, 28–34 even, 35–39

HOMEWORK CHECK

Basic: 5, 9, 13, 15, 20

Average: 10, 14, 18, 20

Advanced: 14, 18, 24, 28, 32

ANSWERS

1. polyhedron
2. the cone; The others are pyramids.
3. B
4. D
5. A
6. C
7. yes; pentagonal pyramid
8. yes; hexagonal prism
9. no
10. yes; trapezoidal prism
11. circle
12. square
13. triangle
14. octagon
15.

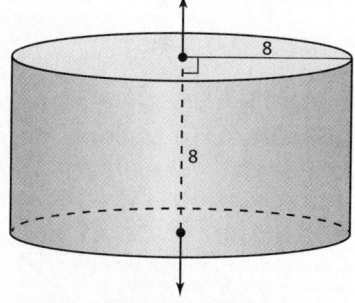

cylinder with height 8 and base radius 8

16.

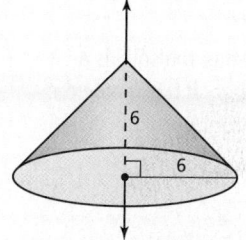

cone with height 6 and base radius 6

ANSWERS

19. There are two parallel, congruent bases, so it is a prism, not a pyramid; The solid is a triangular prism.

20. yes; octagonal prism

21–26. See Additional Answers.

27. your cousin; The sides come together at a point.

28–39. See Additional Answers.

Mini-Assessment

1. Sketch the solid produced by rotating the figure around the given axis. Then identify and describe the solid.

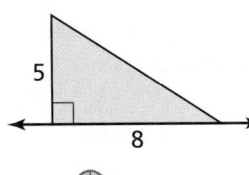

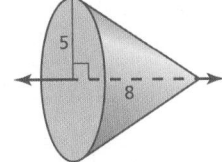

a cone with a height of 8 and a base radius of 5

2. Describe the cross section.

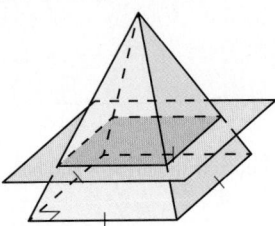

a square

3. Tell whether the solid is a polyhedron. If it is, name the polyhedron.

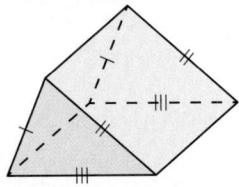

polyhedron; a triangular prism

622   Chapter 11

19. ERROR ANALYSIS Describe and correct the error in identifying the solid.

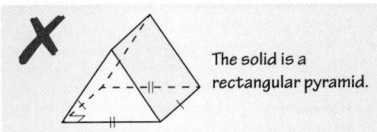
The solid is a rectangular pyramid.

20. HOW DO YOU SEE IT? Is the swimming pool shown a polyhedron? If it is, name the polyhedron. If not, explain why not.

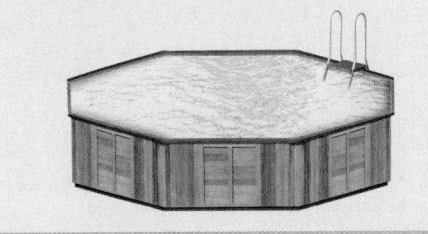

In Exercises 21–26, sketch the polyhedron.

21. triangular prism   **22.** rectangular prism

23. pentagonal prism   **24.** hexagonal prism

25. square pyramid   **26.** pentagonal pyramid

27. MAKING AN ARGUMENT Your friend says that the polyhedron shown is a triangular prism. Your cousin says that it is a triangular pyramid. Who is correct? Explain your reasoning.

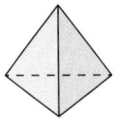

28. ATTENDING TO PRECISION The figure shows a plane intersecting a cube through four of its vertices. The edge length of the cube is 6 inches.

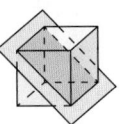

a. Describe the shape of the cross section.

b. What is the perimeter of the cross section?

c. What is the area of the cross section?

REASONING In Exercises 29–34, tell whether it is possible for a cross section of a cube to have the given shape. If it is, describe or sketch how the plane could intersect the cube.

29. circle   **30.** pentagon

31. rhombus   **32.** isosceles triangle

33. hexagon   **34.** scalene triangle

35. REASONING Sketch the composite solid produced by rotating the figure around the given axis. Then identify and describe the composite solid.

a.

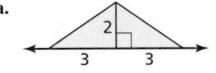

b.

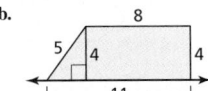

36. THOUGHT PROVOKING Describe how Plato might have argued that there are precisely five *Platonic Solids* (see page 617). (*Hint*: Consider the angles that meet at a vertex.)

Maintaining Mathematical Proficiency
Reviewing what you learned in previous grades and lessons

Decide whether enough information is given to prove that the triangles are congruent. If so, state the theorem you would use. (*Sections 5.3, 5.5, and 5.6*)

37. △ABD, △CDB

38. △JLK, △JLM

39. △RQP, △RTS

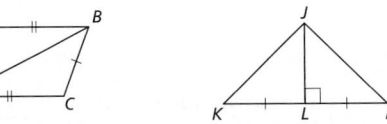

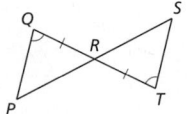

If students need help...	If students got it...
Resources by Chapter • Practice A and Practice B • Puzzle Time	Resources by Chapter • Enrichment and Extension • Cumulative Review
Student Journal • Practice	Start the *next* Section
Differentiating the Lesson Skills Review Handbook	

Core Vocabulary

circumference, *p. 594*
arc length, *p. 595*
radian, *p. 597*
population density, *p. 603*
sector of a circle, *p. 604*
center of a regular polygon, *p. 611*

radius of a regular polygon, *p. 611*
apothem of a regular polygon, *p. 611*
central angle of a regular polygon, *p. 611*
polyhedron, *p. 618*

face, *p. 618*
edge, *p. 618*
vertex, *p. 618*
cross section, *p. 619*
solid of revolution, *p. 620*
axis of revolution, *p. 620*

Core Concepts

Section 11.1

Circumference of a Circle, *p. 594*   Arc Length, *p. 595*   Converting between Degrees and Radians, *p. 597*

Section 11.2

Area of a Circle, *p. 602*   Population Density, *p. 603*   Area of a Sector, *p. 604*

Section 11.3

Area of a Rhombus or Kite, *p. 610*   Area of a Regular Polygon, *p. 612*

Section 11.4

Types of Solids, *p. 618*   Cross Section of a Solid, *p. 619*   Solids of Revolution, *p. 620*

Mathematical Practices

1. In Exercise 13 on page 598, why does it matter how many revolutions the wheel makes?

2. Your friend is confused with Exercise 19 on page 606. What question(s) could you ask your friend to help them figure it out?

3. In Exercise 38 on page 615, write a proof to support your answer.

- - - - - - - - - Study Skills - - - - - - - - -

Kinesthetic Learners

Incorporate physical activity.

- Act out a word problem as much as possible. Use props when you can.
- Solve a word problem on a large whiteboard. The physical action of writing is more kinesthetic when the writing is larger and you can move around while doing it.
- Make a review card.

623

ANSWERS

1. *Sample answer:* Each rotation of the wheel increases the total distance measured.

2. *Sample answer:* Is 12 the radius of the circle?

3. *Sample answer:* The original area is $A = \frac{1}{2}d_1 d_2$. Doubling the length of one diagonal produces $\frac{1}{2}(2d_1)d_2 = 2\left(\frac{1}{2}d_1 d_2\right) = 2A$, and doubling the lengths of both diagonals produces $\frac{1}{2}(2d_1)(2d_2) = 4\left(\frac{1}{2}d_1 d_2\right) = 4A$.

ANSWERS

1. about 124.14°
2. about 5.79 cm
3. 60 in.
4. $\frac{13\pi}{90}$ radian; 100°
5. about 125.66 yd²
6. about 326.73 yd²
7. center C; radius $\overline{CY}$ or $\overline{CR}$; apothem $\overline{CZ}$; central angle $\angle YCR$
8. $m\angle RCY = 45°$; $m\angle RCZ = 22.5°$; $m\angle ZRC = 67.5°$
9. about 181 square units
10. no
11. yes; octagonal pyramid
12. yes; pentagonal prism
13.

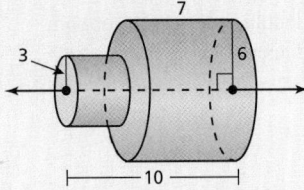

two cylinders, one with height 3 and base radius 3 and the other with height 7 and base radius 6
14. about 56.55 m²
15. 89.49 mm²; 55.5 mm²; 4029.18 mm²

Find the indicated measure. *(Section 11.1)*

1. $m\widehat{EF}$

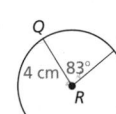

2. arc length of $\widehat{QS}$

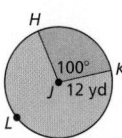

3. circumference of $\odot N$

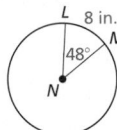

4. Convert 26° to radians and $\frac{5\pi}{9}$ radians to degrees. *(Section 11.1)*

Use the figure to find the indicated measure. *(Section 11.2)*

5. area of red sector

6. area of blue sector

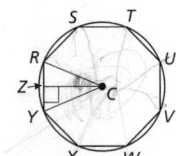

In the diagram, *RSTUVWXY* is a regular octagon inscribed in $\odot C$. *(Section 11.3)*

7. Identify the center, a radius, an apothem, and a central angle of the polygon.

8. Find $m\angle RCY$, $m\angle RCZ$, and $m\angle ZRC$.

9. The radius of the circle is 8 units. Find the area of the octagon.

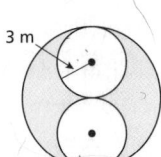

Tell whether the solid is a polyhedron. If it is, name the polyhedron. *(Section 11.4)*

10.

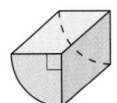

11.

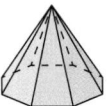

12.

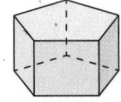

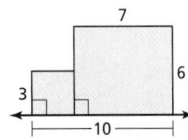

13. Sketch the composite solid produced by rotating the figure around the given axis. Then identify and describe the composite solid. *(Section 11.4)*

14. The two white congruent circles just fit into the blue circle. What is the area of the blue region? *(Section 11.2)*

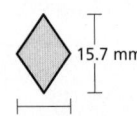

15. Find the area of each rhombus tile. Then find the area of the pattern. *(Section 11.3)*

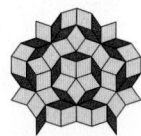

Overview of Section 11.5

Introduction

- This is the first of four lessons on the volumes of solids. In this lesson, students will find the volumes of prisms and cylinders, solids that structurally are the same. Also reviewed are the volumes of similar solids.
- The formulas for prisms and cylinders were taught in middle school, and the only new content is Cavalieri's Principle.
- Students will also work with the density formula of a solid.

Resources

- If you have a slinky, or a collection of interestingly shaped slinkies, use them to demonstrate Cavalieri's Principle.

Formative Assessment Tips

- **Example/Non-Example (student generated):** This technique asks students to generate examples and non-examples to demonstrate their understanding of a concept. To generate the examples and non-examples, students must have a deeper understanding of the concept than just memorization would yield.
- In generating the examples, students can also be asked why—meaning they should provide justification. Listen carefully to students' language as they provide the justification.
- Note that this technique is an instructional technique used by teachers to introduce concepts, such as making a list of expressions that are monomials and those that are not monomials. The difference here is that students are using their cognitive skills to generate the examples and non-examples.
- This technique can be used by individuals, partners, or small groups.
- Be sure to allow sufficient time so that students receive feedback from others and/or you about their examples and non-examples.

Applications

- **Note:** The *Exit Ticket* at the end of the lesson refers to the Leaning Tower of Pisa as a cylinder. There is actually a main cylinder and an upper cylinder (bell tower). Also, the interior and exterior diameters are not the same.

Pacing Suggestion

- Students will review some volume formulas in the explorations. You might be selective in the examples you do in the formal lesson.

Dynamic Teaching Tools

Dynamic Assessment & Progress Monitoring Tool
Lesson Planning Tool
Interactive Whiteboard Lesson Library
Dynamic Classroom with Dynamic Investigations

HSG-GMD.A.1 Give an informal argument for the formulas for the ... volume of a cylinder, ...

HSG-GMD.A.2 Give an informal argument using Cavalieri's principle for the formulas for the volume of a sphere and other solid figures.

HSG-GMD.A.3 Use volume formulas for cylinders, ... to solve problems.

HSG-MG.A.1 Use geometric shapes, their measures, and their properties to describe objects (e.g., modeling a tree trunk or a human torso as a cylinder).

HSG-MG.A.2 Apply concepts of density based on ... volume in modeling situations (e.g., ... BTUs per cubic foot).

HSG-MG.A.3 Apply geometric methods to solve design problems (e.g., designing an object or structure to satisfy physical constraints or minimize cost; working with typographic grid systems based on ratios).

Laurie's Notes

Exploration

Motivate
? "What do you think the capacity is of one of the largest farm grain silos in the country?"
Answers will vary.
- Share information about a silo located in Berks County, Pennsylvania.
  - It is equipped with an elevated floor that has a 12-foot clearance so that a feed truck can drive through and be quickly loaded.
  - It is equipped with an unloader, making the system capable of loading 50-plus tons of grain per hour and unloading 800 to 1200 pounds of grain per minute.
  - The silo has more than 94,000 cubic feet of storage capacity and should hold more than 4000 tons of corn silage.
- Share a picture of the silo, which you can find with an online search for "largest farm silo."
- Explain to students that in this lesson they will be finding volumes of prisms and cylinders.

Exploration Note
- **MP4 Model with Mathematics:** Students will benefit from having a model available; something as simple as a deck of cards will do.

Exploration 1
- **Common Misconception:** Not all students will be convinced that the volumes are the same for both stacks of paper. Let peers try to explain why the volumes remain the same. They will likely say something like, "The number of pieces of paper has not changed. None were added and none were taken away."
- **MP6 Attend to Precision** and **MP3 Construct Viable Arguments and Critique the Reasoning of Others:** Describing why the stacks have the same volume can be challenging for students. Push students to describe attributes of the stacks that go beyond referencing the fact that the stacks have the same number of pieces of paper.
- **? Probing Question:** "Did the height of the stack change when it was twisted, and how do you know?" no; Both stacks have the same number of layers. "What do you know about each layer?" They each have the same area.
- **MP3:** Students should listen to one another's conjecture to see whether the reasoning is valid or not.

Exploration 2
? "How do you find the volume of a cylinder?" Multiply the area of the base times the height of the cylinder.
- Be prepared. Some students may still be uncertain that the volumes remained the same. In these two problems, the layers are not visible, but they are all circles!

Communicate Your Answer
- Question 4 may cause some students to change their mind about the volume remaining the same when the stack of paper is twisted.

Connecting to Next Step
- This exploration is an introduction to Cavalieri's Principle, which is introduced in this lesson.

11.5 Volumes of Prisms and Cylinders

Essential Question
How can you find the volume of a prism or cylinder that is not a right prism or right cylinder?

Recall that the volume V of a right prism or a right cylinder is equal to the product of the area of a base B and the height h.

$$V = Bh$$

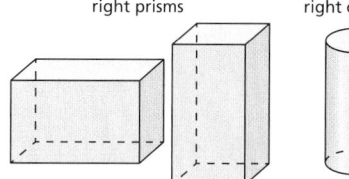

right prisms   right cylinder

Dynamic Teaching Tools

Dynamic Assessment & Progress Monitoring Tool

Lesson Planning Tool

Interactive Whiteboard Lesson Library

Dynamic Classroom with Dynamic Investigations

EXPLORATION 1 Finding Volume

Work with a partner. Consider a stack of square papers that is in the form of a right prism.

a. What is the volume of the prism?

b. When you twist the stack of papers, as shown at the right, do you change the volume? Explain your reasoning.

c. Write a carefully worded conjecture that describes the conclusion you reached in part (b).

d. Use your conjecture to find the volume of the twisted stack of papers.

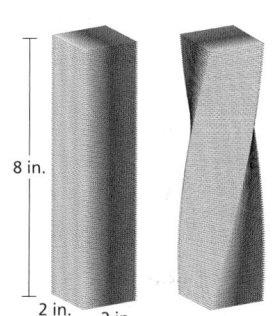

8 in.

2 in.   2 in.

ATTENDING TO PRECISION

To be proficient in math, you need to communicate precisely to others.

EXPLORATION 2 Finding Volume

Work with a partner. Use the conjecture you wrote in Exploration 1 to find the volume of the cylinder.

a.
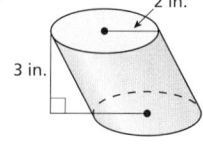
2 in.
3 in.

b.
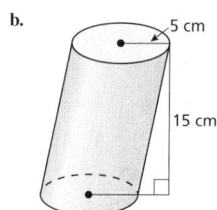
5 cm
15 cm

Communicate Your Answer

3. How can you find the volume of a prism or cylinder that is not a right prism or right cylinder?

4. In Exploration 1, would the conjecture you wrote change if the papers in each stack were not squares? Explain your reasoning.

ANSWERS

1. a. 32 in.^{3}

   b. no; *Sample answer:* The amount of paper is the same.

   c. *Sample answer:* If two solids have the same height and the same cross-sectional area at every level, then they have the same volume.

   d. 32 in.^{3}

2. a. about 37.70 in.^{3}

   b. about 1178.10 cm^3

3. *Sample answer:* Multiply the area of a base by the vertical height.

4. no; *Sample answer:* Each piece of paper would still have the same area.

Extra Example 1
Find the volume of each prism.

a.

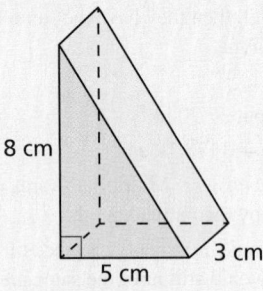

8 cm

5 cm   3 cm

60 cubic centimeters

b.

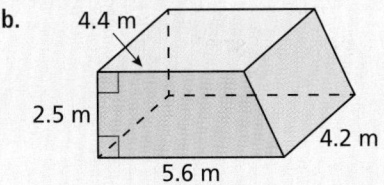

4.4 m

2.5 m

5.6 m   4.2 m

52.5 cubic meters

11.5 Lesson

Core Vocabulary
volume, *p. 626*
Cavalieri's Principle, *p. 626*
density, *p. 628*
similar solids, *p. 630*

Previous
prism
cylinder
composite solid

What You Will Learn

▶ Find volumes of prisms and cylinders.
▶ Use the formula for density.
▶ Use volumes of prisms and cylinders.

Finding Volumes of Prisms and Cylinders

The **volume** of a solid is the number of cubic units contained in its interior. Volume is measured in cubic units, such as cubic centimeters (cm^3). **Cavalieri's Principle**, named after Bonaventura Cavalieri (1598–1647), states that if two solids have the same height and the same cross-sectional area at every level, then they have the same volume. The prisms below have equal heights h and equal cross-sectional areas B at every level. By Cavalieri's Principle, the prisms have the same volume.

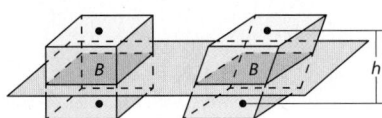

🔄 Core Concept

Volume of a Prism
The volume V of a prism is

$$V = Bh$$

where B is the area of a base and h is the height.

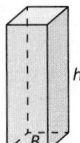
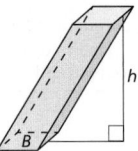

EXAMPLE 1   Finding Volumes of Prisms

Find the volume of each prism.

a.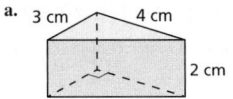
3 cm   4 cm
2 cm

b.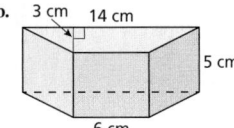
3 cm   14 cm
5 cm
6 cm

SOLUTION

a. The area of a base is $B = \frac{1}{2}(3)(4) = 6$ cm² and the height is $h = 2$ cm.

$$
\begin{aligned}
V &= Bh &&\text{Formula for volume of a prism} \\
&= 6(2) &&\text{Substitute.} \\
&= 12 &&\text{Simplify.}
\end{aligned}
$$

▶ The volume is 12 cubic centimeters.

b. The area of a base is $B = \frac{1}{2}(3)(6 + 14) = 30$ cm² and the height is $h = 5$ cm.

$$
\begin{aligned}
V &= Bh &&\text{Formula for volume of a prism} \\
&= 30(5) &&\text{Substitute.} \\
&= 150 &&\text{Simplify.}
\end{aligned}
$$

▶ The volume is 150 cubic centimeters.

Laurie's Notes   Teacher Actions

- **Example/Non-Example:** Make groups of four students. To gain a sense of how students think about the concept of volume, ask them to make two lists: one that contains a contextual question about volume and one that does not. *Example:* How much gas does my car hold? *Non-Example:* How much wrapping paper do I need for that present? After sufficient time, have groups share. Give feedback as needed.
- Discuss Cavalieri's Principle and write the *Core Concept*. Omit Example 1 if you believe students are secure with finding the volume.

Consider a cylinder with height h and base radius r and a rectangular prism with the same height that has a square base with sides of length $r\sqrt{\pi}$.

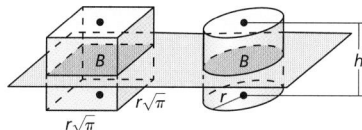

The cylinder and the prism have the same cross-sectional area, πr^2, at every level and the same height. By Cavalieri's Principle, the prism and the cylinder have the same volume. The volume of the prism is $V = Bh = \pi r^2 h$, so the volume of the cylinder is also $V = Bh = \pi r^2 h$.

Core Concept

Volume of a Cylinder

The volume V of a cylinder is

$$V = Bh = \pi r^2 h$$

where B is the area of a base, h is the height, and r is the radius of a base.

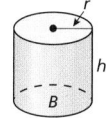
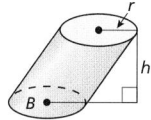

EXAMPLE 2 Finding Volumes of Cylinders

Find the volume of each cylinder.

a.
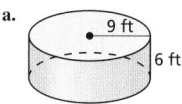

b.
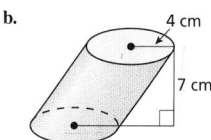

SOLUTION

a. The dimensions of the cylinder are $r = 9$ ft and $h = 6$ ft.

$$V = \pi r^2 h = \pi(9)^2(6) = 486\pi \approx 1526.81$$

▶ The volume is 486π, or about 1526.81 cubic feet.

b. The dimensions of the cylinder are $r = 4$ cm and $h = 7$ cm.

$$V = \pi r^2 h = \pi(4)^2(7) = 112\pi \approx 351.86$$

▶ The volume is 112π, or about 351.86 cubic centimeters.

Monitoring Progress 🔊 Help in English and Spanish at *BigIdeasMath.com*

Find the volume of the solid.

1.
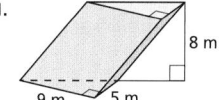

2.
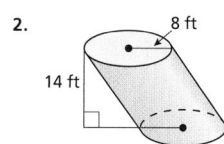

Section 11.5   Volumes of Prisms and Cylinders   **627**

Extra Example 2
Find the volume of each cylinder.

a.
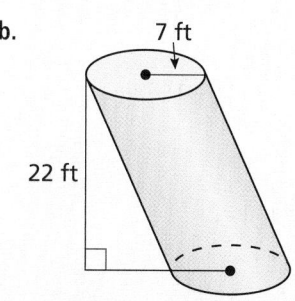

227.5π, or about 714.71 cubic meters

b.

7 ft

22 ft

1078π, or about 3386.64 cubic feet

MONITORING PROGRESS ANSWERS
1. 180 m^3
2. about 2814.87 ft^3

Laurie's Notes   **Teacher Actions**

- Explain that Cavalieri's Principle does not apply to just rectangular prisms. Note the volume comparison of a prism and a cylinder.
- **Think-Alouds:** Pose Example 2(a) and say, "To solve this problem I need to …." Ask partner A to think aloud for partner B to hear the problem-solving process. Switch roles and have partner B think aloud in solving part (b).
- Did students label the answers with correct units?
- **Think-Pair-Share:** Have students answer Questions 1 and 2, and then share and discuss as a class.

Extra Example 3

The density of water is 1000 kilograms per cubic meter. Find the mass of 1 cubic foot of water. Use the fact that 1 foot = 0.3048 meters. The mass of 1 cubic foot of water is about 28.32 kilograms.

MONITORING PROGRESS ANSWER

3. about 2,182,485 g

Using the Formula for Density

Density is the amount of matter that an object has in a given unit of volume. The density of an object is calculated by dividing its mass by its volume.

$$\text{Density} = \frac{\text{Mass}}{\text{Volume}}$$

Different materials have different densities, so density can be used to distinguish between materials that look similar. For example, table salt and sugar look alike. However, table salt has a density of 2.16 grams per cubic centimeter, while sugar has a density of 1.58 grams per cubic centimeter.

EXAMPLE 3 Using the Formula for Density

The diagram shows the dimensions of a standard gold bar at Fort Knox. Gold has a density of 19.3 grams per cubic centimeter. Find the mass of a standard gold bar to the nearest gram.

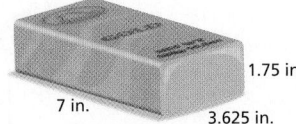

1.75 in.
7 in.
3.625 in.

SOLUTION

Step 1 Convert the dimensions to centimeters using 1 inch = 2.54 centimeters.

Length $7 \text{ in.} \cdot \dfrac{2.54 \text{ cm}}{1 \text{ in.}} = 17.78 \text{ cm}$

Width $3.625 \text{ in.} \cdot \dfrac{2.54 \text{ cm}}{1 \text{ in.}} = 9.2075 \text{ cm}$

Height $1.75 \text{ in.} \cdot \dfrac{2.54 \text{ cm}}{1 \text{ in.}} = 4.445 \text{ cm}$

Step 2 Find the volume.

The area of a base is $B = 17.78(9.2075) = 163.70935 \text{ cm}^2$ and the height is $h = 4.445$ cm.

$$V = Bh = 163.70935(4.445) \approx 727.69 \text{ cm}^3$$

Step 3 Let x represent the mass in grams. Substitute the values for the volume and the density in the formula for density and solve for x.

$$\text{Density} = \frac{\text{Mass}}{\text{Volume}} \qquad \text{Formula for density}$$

$$19.3 \approx \frac{x}{727.69} \qquad \text{Substitute.}$$

$$14{,}044 \approx x \qquad \text{Multiply each side by 727.69.}$$

▶ The mass of a standard gold bar is about 14,044 grams.

Monitoring Progress Help in English and Spanish at *BigIdeasMath.com*

3. The diagram shows the dimensions of a concrete cylinder. Concrete has a density of 2.3 grams per cubic centimeter. Find the mass of the concrete cylinder to the nearest gram.

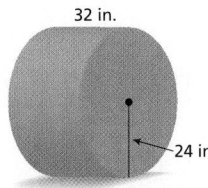

32 in.

24 in.

According to the U.S. Mint, Fort Knox houses about 9.2 million pounds of gold.

Laurie's Notes   Teacher Actions

- Students will be familiar with the formula for density from science class.
- **MP5 Use Appropriate Tools Strategically:** The density of gold is given in grams per cubic centimeter, and the dimensions of the gold bar are in inches.
- **Turn and Talk:** "How will you find the mass of the gold bar?" Once students have a problem-solving plan, they should begin.
- **? Extension:** "What is the value of the gold at Fort Knox if gold is $1300 per ounce?" about $191,360,000,000

Using Volumes of Prisms and Cylinders

EXAMPLE 4   Modeling with Mathematics

You are building a rectangular chest. You want the length to be 6 feet, the width to be 4 feet, and the volume to be 72 cubic feet. What should the height be?

$V = 72 \text{ ft}^3$

h

6 ft   4 ft

SOLUTION

1. **Understand the Problem** You know the dimensions of the base of a rectangular prism and the volume. You are asked to find the height.

2. **Make a Plan** Write the formula for the volume of a rectangular prism, substitute known values, and solve for the height h.

3. **Solve the Problem** The area of a base is $B = 6(4) = 24 \text{ ft}^2$ and the volume is $V = 72 \text{ ft}^3$.

$V = Bh$	Formula for volume of a prism
$72 = 24h$	Substitute.
$3 = h$	Divide each side by 24.

▶ The height of the chest should be 3 feet.

4. **Look Back** Check your answer.

$V = Bh = 24(3) = 72$ ✓

EXAMPLE 5   Solving a Real-Life Problem

You are building a 6-foot-tall dresser. You want the volume to be 36 cubic feet. What should the area of the base be? Give a possible length and width.

6 ft

$V = 36 \text{ ft}^3$

SOLUTION

$V = Bh$	Formula for volume of a prism
$36 = B \cdot 6$	Substitute.
$6 = B$	Divide each side by 6.

▶ The area of the base should be 6 square feet. The length could be 3 feet and the width could be 2 feet.

Monitoring Progress ◀ᴗ)) Help in English and Spanish at *BigIdeasMath.com*

4. **WHAT IF?** In Example 4, you want the length to be 5 meters, the width to be 3 meters, and the volume to be 60 cubic meters. What should the height be?

5. **WHAT IF?** In Example 5, you want the height to be 5 meters and the volume to be 75 cubic meters. What should the area of the base be? Give a possible length and width.

Section 11.5   Volumes of Prisms and Cylinders   **629**

Extra Example 4

You are building a cylindrical packing tube. You want the length of the tube to be 30 inches and the volume to be 589 cubic inches. What should the radius of the base be? about 2.50 inches

Extra Example 5

You are building a 3-foot tall dresser. You want the volume to be 42 cubic feet. What should the area of the base be? Give a possible length and width. The area of the base should be 14 square feet. The width could be 2 feet and the length could be 7 feet.

MONITORING PROGRESS ANSWERS

4. 4 m

5. 15 m²; *Sample answer:* length: 5 m, width: 3 m

English Language Learners

Build on Past Knowledge
Remind students of their study of similar polygons. Have students describe the characteristics of two similar triangles. Then connect students' understanding of similar polygons to the new concept of similar solids. Describe the characteristics of similar solids.

Extra Example 6
Square prism A and square prism B are similar. Each base edge of prism A is 4 inches, and each base edge of prism B is 6 inches. The volume of prism B is 135 cubic inches. Find the volume of prism A. *The volume of prism A is 40 cubic inches.*

Extra Example 7
Find the volume of the composite solid.

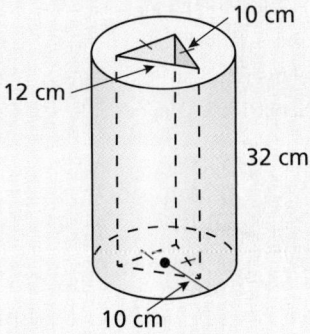

The volume is $3200\pi - 1536$, or about 8517.10 cubic centimeters.

MONITORING PROGRESS ANSWERS
6. 24 m^3
7. about 205.81 ft^3

Core Concept

Similar Solids

Two solids of the same type with equal ratios of corresponding linear measures, such as heights or radii, are called **similar solids**. The ratio of the corresponding linear measures of two similar solids is called the *scale factor*. If two similar solids have a scale factor of k, then the ratio of their volumes is equal to k^3.

EXAMPLE 6   Finding the Volume of a Similar Solid

Cylinder A and cylinder B are similar. Find the volume of cylinder B.

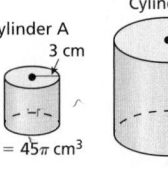

Cylinder A — 3 cm

Cylinder B — 6 cm

$V = 45\pi \text{ cm}^3$

SOLUTION

The scale factor is $k = \dfrac{\text{Radius of cylinder B}}{\text{Radius of cylinder A}}$

$= \dfrac{6}{3} = 2$.

Use the scale factor to find the volume of cylinder B.

$\dfrac{\text{Volume of cylinder B}}{\text{Volume of cylinder A}} = k^3$ The ratio of the volumes is k^3.

$\dfrac{\text{Volume of cylinder B}}{45\pi} = 2^3$ Substitute.

Volume of cylinder B $= 360\pi$ Solve for volume of cylinder B.

▶ The volume of cylinder B is 360π cubic centimeters.

Monitoring Progress 🔊 Help in English and Spanish at *BigIdeasMath.com*

6. Prism C and prism D are similar. Find the volume of prism D.

EXAMPLE 7   Finding the Volume of a Composite Solid

Find the volume of the concrete block.

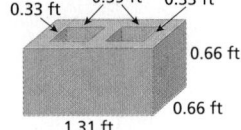

0.33 ft   0.39 ft   0.33 ft
0.66 ft
0.66 ft
1.31 ft

SOLUTION

To find the area of the base, subtract two times the area of the small rectangle from the large rectangle.

$B = \boxed{\text{Area of large rectangle}} - 2 \cdot \boxed{\text{Area of small rectangle}}$

$= 1.31(0.66) - 2(0.33)(0.39)$

$= 0.6072$

Using the formula for the volume of a prism, the volume is

$V = Bh = 0.6072(0.66) \approx 0.40$.

▶ The volume is about 0.40 cubic foot.

Monitoring Progress 🔊 Help in English and Spanish at *BigIdeasMath.com*

7. Find the volume of the composite solid.

COMMON ERROR
Be sure to write the ratio of the volumes in the same order you wrote the ratio of the radii.

Prism C

$V = 1536 \text{ m}^3$
12 m

Prism D

3 m

3 ft
6 ft
10 ft

Laurie's Notes   Teacher Actions

- Write the *Core Concept*, which students may recall from middle school.
- ❓ Pose Example 6. "What is the ratio of their linear measurements?" The radii are in the ratio of 2:1. "What is the ratio of their volumes?" The volumes are in the ratio of $2^3:1^3$ or 8:1.
- **Think-Pair-Share:** Have students answer Example 7, and then share and discuss as a class.

Closure
- **Exit Ticket:** Assume the Leaning Tower of Pisa is approximately a cylinder of height 55.9 meters and diameter of 15.5 meters. Find its volume. about 10,547.9 cubic meters

Dynamic Solutions available at *BigIdeasMath.com*

Vocabulary and Core Concept Check

1. **VOCABULARY** In what type of units is the volume of a solid measured?

2. **COMPLETE THE SENTENCE** Density is the amount of _____ that an object has in a given unit of _____.

Monitoring Progress and Modeling with Mathematics

In Exercises 3–6, find the volume of the prism.
(See Example 1.)

3.
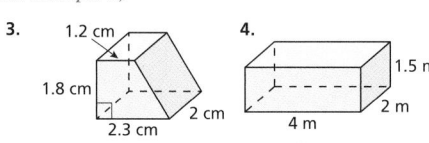

4.
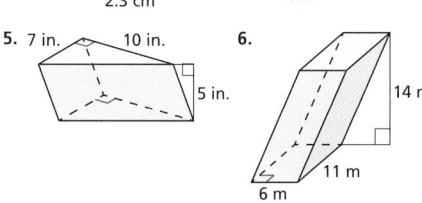

5.
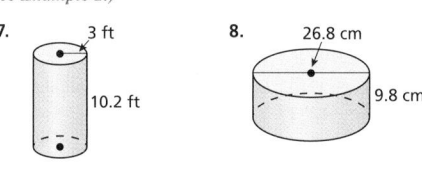

6.
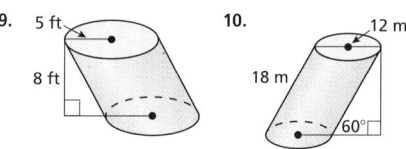

In Exercises 7–10, find the volume of the cylinder.
(See Example 2.)

7.   3 ft

10.2 ft

8.   26.8 cm

9.8 cm

9.   5 ft

8 ft

10.   12 m

18 m

60°

In Exercises 11 and 12, make a sketch of the solid and find its volume. Round your answer to the nearest hundredth.

11. A prism has a height of 11.2 centimeters and an equilateral triangle for a base, where each base edge is 8 centimeters.

12. A pentagonal prism has a height of 9 feet and each base edge is 3 feet.

13. **PROBLEM SOLVING** A piece of copper with a volume of 8.25 cubic centimeters has a mass of 73.92 grams. A piece of iron with a volume of 5 cubic centimeters has a mass of 39.35 grams. Which metal has the greater density?

copper

iron

14. **PROBLEM SOLVING** The United States has minted one-dollar silver coins called the American Eagle Silver Bullion Coin since 1986. Each coin has a diameter of 40.6 millimeters and is 2.98 millimeters thick. The density of silver is 10.5 grams per cubic centimeter. What is the mass of an American Eagle Silver Bullion Coin to the nearest gram? *(See Example 3.)*

15. **ERROR ANALYSIS** Describe and correct the error in finding the volume of the cylinder.

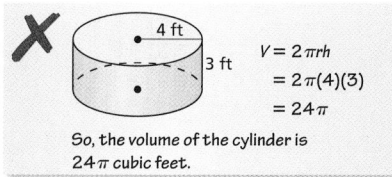

4 ft

3 ft

$V = 2\pi rh$
  $= 2\pi(4)(3)$
  $= 24\pi$

So, the volume of the cylinder is 24π cubic feet.

Section 11.5   Volumes of Prisms and Cylinders   **631**

Assignment Guide and Homework Check

ASSIGNMENT

Basic: 1, 2, 3–31 odd, 40, 51, 55–57

Average: 1, 2, 6–32 even, 38–44 even, 47–51 odd, 54–57

Advanced: 1, 2, 6, 10, 14–50 even, 51–57

HOMEWORK CHECK

Basic: 5, 9, 19, 25, 29

Average: 10, 14, 18, 26, 30

Advanced: 14, 18, 28, 32, 38

ANSWERS

1. cubic units
2. mass; volume
3. 6.3 cm^3
4. 12 m^3
5. 175 in.^{3}
6. 924 m^3
7. about 288.40 ft^3
8. about 5528.22 cm^3
9. about 628.32 ft^3
10. about 1763.01 m^3
11.

8 cm

11.2 cm

310.38 cm^3

12.   3 ft

9 ft

139.36 ft^3

13. copper
14. 41 g
15. The base circumference was used instead of the base area; $V = \pi r^2 h = 48\pi$ ft^3

ANSWERS

16. Density is $\dfrac{\text{mass}}{\text{volume}}$ not $\dfrac{\text{volume}}{\text{mass}}$;

    density $= \dfrac{24}{28.3} \approx 0.85$ g/cm^3

17. 10 ft

18. 15 yd

19. 4 cm

20. about 6.99 in.

21. about 11.04 ft

22. about 6.00 m

23. 14 in.^{2}; *Sample answer:* length: 7 in., width: 2 in.

24. 9 m^2; *Sample answer:* length: 3 m, width: 3 m

25. 99 cm^3

26. 9000π in.^{3}

27. 2 cm

28. 10 ft

29. 150 ft^3

30. about 89.13 in.^{3}

31. about 1900.66 in.^{3}

32. 35 ft^3

---

16. **ERROR ANALYSIS** Describe and correct the error in finding the density of an object that has a mass of 24 grams and a volume of 28.3 cubic centimeters.

density $= \dfrac{28.3}{24} \approx 1.18$

So, the density is about 1.18 cubic centimeters per gram.

In Exercises 17–22, find the missing dimension of the prism or cylinder. *(See Example 4.)*

17. Volume $= 560$ ft^3

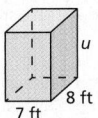

8 ft
7 ft

18. Volume $= 2700$ yd^3

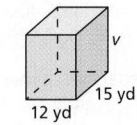

15 yd
12 yd

19. Volume $= 80$ cm^3

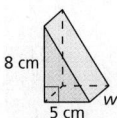

8 cm
5 cm
w

20. Volume $= 72.66$ in.^{3}

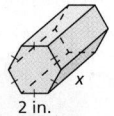

x
2 in.

21. Volume $= 3000$ ft^3

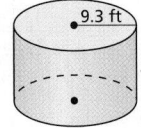

9.3 ft
y

22. Volume $= 1696.5$ m^3

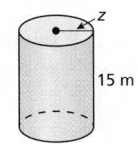

z
15 m

In Exercises 23 and 24, find the area of the base of the rectangular prism with the given volume and height. Then give a possible length and width. *(See Example 5.)*

23. $V = 154$ in.^{3}, $h = 11$ in.

24. $V = 27$ m^3, $h = 3$ m

In Exercises 25 and 26, the solids are similar. Find the volume of solid B. *(See Example 6.)*

25.

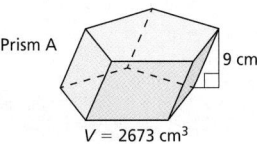

Prism A
9 cm
$V = 2673$ cm^3

Prism B 3 cm

26.

Cylinder A   Cylinder B

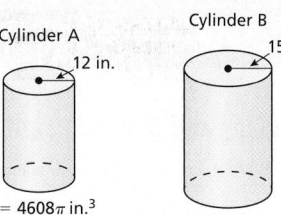

12 in.   15 in.

$V = 4608\pi$ in.^{3}

In Exercises 27 and 28, the solids are similar. Find the indicated measure.

27. height x of the base of prism A

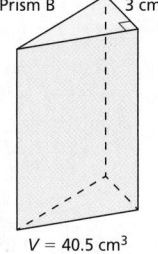

Prism A   Prism B   3 cm
x
$V = 12$ cm^3
$V = 40.5$ cm^3

28. height h of cylinder B

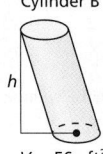

Cylinder A   Cylinder B
5 ft h
$V = 7\pi$ ft^3 $V = 56\pi$ ft^3

In Exercises 29–32, find the volume of the composite solid. *(See Example 7.)*

29.

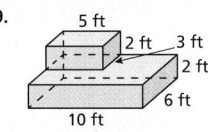

5 ft
2 ft   3 ft
2 ft
6 ft
10 ft

30.

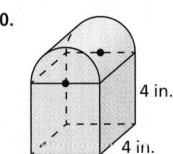

4 in.
4 in.
4 in.

31.

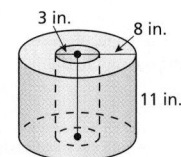

3 in.   8 in.
11 in.

32.

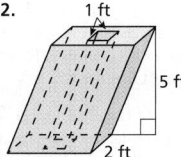

1 ft
5 ft
2 ft
4 ft

33. MODELING WITH MATHEMATICS The Great Blue Hole is a cylindrical trench located off the coast of Belize. It is approximately 1000 feet wide and 400 feet deep. About how many gallons of water does the Great Blue Hole contain? (1 ft³ ≈ 7.48 gallons)

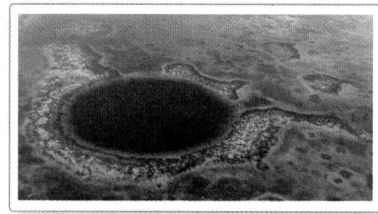

34. COMPARING METHODS The *Volume Addition Postulate* states that the volume of a solid is the sum of the volumes of all its nonoverlapping parts. Use this postulate to find the volume of the block of concrete in Example 7 by subtracting the volume of each hole from the volume of the large rectangular prism. Which method do you prefer? Explain your reasoning.

REASONING In Exercises 35 and 36, you are melting a rectangular block of wax to make candles. How many candles of the given shape can be made using a block that measures 10 centimeters by 9 centimeters by 20 centimeters?

35.

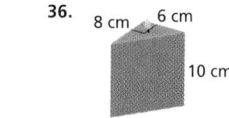

12 cm
├─9 cm─┤

36. 8 cm ← 6 cm

10 cm

37. PROBLEM SOLVING An aquarium shaped like a rectangular prism has a length of 30 inches, a width of 10 inches, and a height of 20 inches. You fill the aquarium $\frac{3}{4}$ full with water. When you submerge a rock in the aquarium, the water level rises 0.25 inch.

a. Find the volume of the rock.

b. How many rocks of this size can you place in the aquarium before water spills out?

38. PROBLEM SOLVING You drop an irregular piece of metal into a container partially filled with water and measure that the water level rises 4.8 centimeters. The square base of the container has a side length of 8 centimeters. You measure the mass of the metal to be 450 grams. What is the density of the metal?

39. WRITING Both of the figures shown are made up of the same number of congruent rectangles. Explain how Cavalieri's Principle can be adapted to compare the areas of these figures.

40. HOW DO YOU SEE IT? Each stack of memo papers contains 500 equally-sized sheets of paper. Compare their volumes. Explain your reasoning.

41. USING STRUCTURE Sketch the solid formed by the net. Then find the volume of the solid.

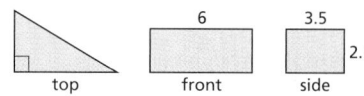

42. USING STRUCTURE Sketch the solid with the given views. Then find the volume of the solid.

top   front   side

43. OPEN-ENDED Sketch two rectangular prisms that have volumes of 100 cubic inches but different surface areas. Include dimensions in your sketches.

44. MODELING WITH MATHEMATICS Which box gives you more cereal for your money? Explain.

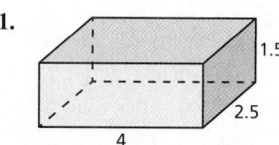

ANSWERS

33. about 2,350,000,000 gal

34. about 0.40 ft³; *Sample answer:* subtracting the volumes; Using the formula for the volume of a prism is simpler.

35. 2

36. 7

37. a. 75 in.³

   b. 20

38. about 1.46 g/cm³

39. *Sample answer:* The stacks have the same height and the rectangles have the same lengths, so the stacks have the same area.

40. They are the same; *Sample answer:* The stacks have the same height and cross-sectional area.

41.

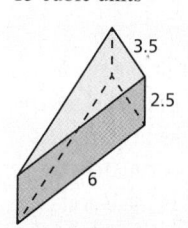

15 cubic units

42.

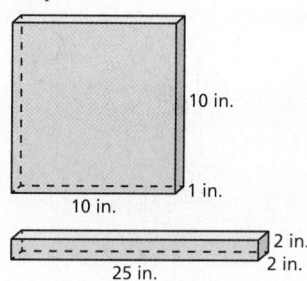

26.25 cubic units

43. *Sample answer:*

10 in.

10 in.   1 in.

2 in.
25 in.   2 in.

44. the $6 box; *Sample answer:* The unit cost is lesser.

45. the solid produced by rotating around the vertical line; *Sample answer:* The solid produced by rotating around the horizontal line has a volume of 45π cubic inches and the solid produced by rotating around the vertical line has a volume of 75π cubic inches.

46–57. See Additional Answers.

Mini-Assessment

1. A cylinder has base radius 4 feet and height 8.5 feet. Find its volume. 136π, or about 427.26 cubic feet

2. The base of a triangular prism is an equilateral triangle with sides 20 inches long. The height of the prism is 8 inches. Find the volume of the prism. $800\sqrt{3}$, or about 1385.64 cubic inches

3. A bar of lead is in the shape of a rectangular prism 2 cm by 3 cm by 4 cm. The density of lead is 11.34 grams per cubic centimeter. Find the mass of the bar of lead. 272.16 grams

4. A cylindrical hole is drilled through a wooden block that is in the shape of a rectangular prism. Find the volume of the resulting solid.

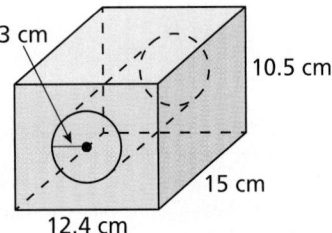

about 1528.88 cubic centimeters

5. The volume of the triangular prism is 1008 cubic centimeters. Find the base height.

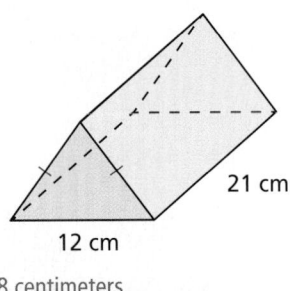

8 centimeters

---

45. **CRITICAL THINKING** A 3-inch by 5-inch index card is rotated around a horizontal line and a vertical line to produce two different solids. Which solid has a greater volume? Explain your reasoning.

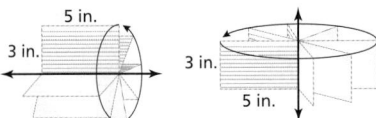

46. **CRITICAL THINKING** The height of cylinder X is twice the height of cylinder Y. The radius of cylinder X is half the radius of cylinder Y. Compare the volumes of cylinder X and cylinder Y. Justify your answer.

47. **USING STRUCTURE** Find the volume of the solid shown. The bases of the solid are sectors of circles.

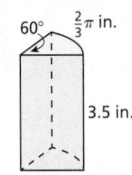

48. **MATHEMATICAL CONNECTIONS** You drill a circular hole of radius r through the base of a cylinder of radius R. Assume the hole is drilled completely through to the other base. You want the volume of the hole to be half the volume of the cylinder. Express r as a function of R.

49. **ANALYZING RELATIONSHIPS** How can you change the height of a cylinder so that the volume is increased by 25% but the radius remains the same?

50. **ANALYZING RELATIONSHIPS** How can you change the edge length of a cube so that the volume is reduced by 40%?

51. **MAKING AN ARGUMENT** You have two objects of equal volume. Your friend says you can compare the densities of the objects by comparing their mass, because the heavier object will have a greater density. Is your friend correct? Explain your reasoning.

52. **THOUGHT PROVOKING** Cavalieri's Principle states that the two solids shown below have the same volume. Do they also have the same surface area? Explain your reasoning.

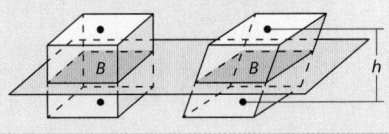

53. **PROBLEM SOLVING** A barn is in the shape of a pentagonal prism with the dimensions shown. The volume of the barn is 9072 cubic feet. Find the dimensions of each half of the roof.

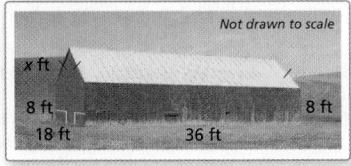

54. **PROBLEM SOLVING** A wooden box is in the shape of a regular pentagonal prism. The sides, top, and bottom of the box are 1 centimeter thick. Approximate the volume of wood used to construct the box. Round your answer to the nearest tenth.

Maintaining Mathematical Proficiency

Reviewing what you learned in previous grades and lessons

Find the surface area of the regular pyramid. *(Skills Review Handbook)*

55.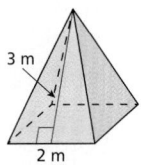

56.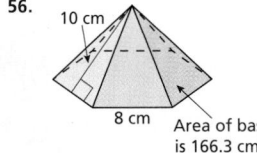

57.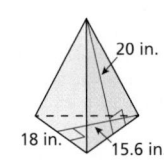

If students need help...	If students got it...
Resources by Chapter • Practice A and Practice B • Puzzle Time	Resources by Chapter • Enrichment and Extension • Cumulative Review
Student Journal • Practice	Start the *next* Section
Differentiating the Lesson Skills Review Handbook	

Dynamic Teaching Tools
Dynamic Assessment & Progress Monitoring Tool
Lesson Planning Tool
Interactive Whiteboard Lesson Library
Dynamic Classroom with Dynamic Investigations

Overview of Section 11.6

Introduction
- This is the second of four lessons on the volumes of solids. In this lesson, students will find the volumes of pyramids.
- Also reviewed are volumes of similar solids.

Formative Assessment Tips
- **Visitor Explanation:** This technique simulates what it would look like if a visitor were to enter your classroom during the middle of an exploration or activity. Could your students explain what they are doing and why they are doing it?
- This technique lets you know whether students understand the goal, or the essential question related to the exploration. Are students simply following directions or are they aware of the goal for today's exploration? Students are more engaged and their learning improves when the learning objective or purpose of the exploration is understood.
- This technique is best used when students are actively engaged in an exploration. This technique can be done as a *Think-Pair-Share* or as a *Writing Prompt*.
- The learning objective or essential question should have been made known to the students at the outset. This technique is not used to see whether students figured out the goal of the exploration or activity.

Pacing Suggestion
- Now that students have reviewed the formula for the volume of a pyramid, you might begin the formal lesson with Example 2.

HSG-GMD.A.1 Give an informal
argument for the formulas for the …
volume of a … pyramid, ….

HSG-GMD.A.3 Use volume formulas
for … pyramids, … to solve problems.

HSG-MG.A.1 Use geometric shapes, their
measures, and their properties to describe
objects (e.g., modeling a tree trunk or a
human torso as a cylinder).

Laurie's Notes

Exploration

Motivate
- Ask whether anyone has visited the famed Louvre Museum in Paris.
- The Louvre Pyramid is a large glass and metal pyramid, surrounded by three smaller pyramids, in the main courtyard. The large pyramid serves as the main entrance to the Louvre Museum.
- The Louvre Pyramid was designed by I. M. Pei, who also designed the Rock and Roll Hall of Fame in Cleveland, Ohio.
- Students will find the volume of the glass pyramid at the end of the lesson.

Exploration Note
- Students may recall the formula for the volume of a pyramid from middle school.

Exploration 1
- If you have a set of clear plastic solids to demonstrate this relationship, it would be more engaging than a static picture. Alternately, an online search will result in videos that demonstrate this relationship.
- **?** "What do the images suggest in order to find the volume of a pyramid?" Multiply $\frac{1}{3}$ times the area of the base times the height.

Exploration 2
- This exploration is a good review of Section 11.3, where students found the areas of regular polygons.
- Circulate and listen to students' strategies for computing the volume.
- Ask for a volunteer to share his or her work.

Communicate Your Answer
- Students will likely guess that the relationship between cones and cylinders is the same as the relationship between pyramids and prisms.

Connecting to Next Step
- Students have discovered, or perhaps recalled, the formula for the volume of a pyramid. In the lesson, they will also solve problems about the volumes of similar pyramids.

11.6 Volumes of Pyramids

Essential Question   How can you find the volume of a pyramid?

EXPLORATION 1   Finding the Volume of a Pyramid

Work with a partner. The pyramid and the prism have the same height and the same square base.

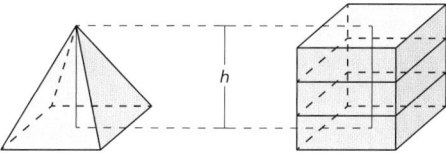

When the pyramid is filled with sand and poured into the prism, it takes three pyramids to fill the prism.

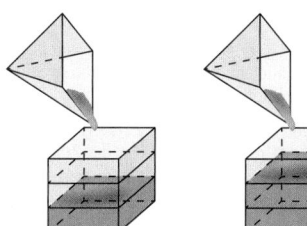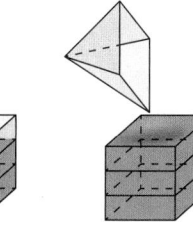

LOOKING FOR STRUCTURE

To be proficient in math, you need to look closely to discern a pattern or structure.

Use this information to write a formula for the volume *V* of a pyramid.

EXPLORATION 2   Finding the Volume of a Pyramid

Work with a partner. Use the formula you wrote in Exploration 1 to find the volume of the hexagonal pyramid.

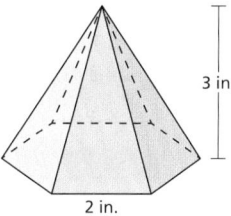

3 in.

2 in.

Communicate Your Answer

3. How can you find the volume of a pyramid?

4. In Section 11.7, you will study volumes of cones. How do you think you could use a method similar to the one presented in Exploration 1 to write a formula for the volume of a cone? Explain your reasoning.

Section 11.6   Volumes of Pyramids   **635**

ANSWERS

1. $V = \frac{1}{3}Bh$

2. about 10.39 in.^{3}

3. Use the formula $V = \frac{1}{3}Bh$.

4. *Sample answer:* Use a cone and cylinder with the same height and circular base and determine how many cones of sand are needed to fill the cylinder.

Extra Example 1

Find the volume of the pyramid.

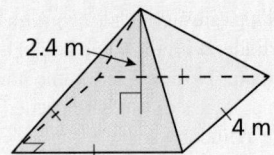

The volume is 12.8 cubic meters.

11.6 Lesson

Core Vocabulary

Previous
pyramid
composite solid

What You Will Learn

▶ Find volumes of pyramids.

▶ Use volumes of pyramids.

Finding Volumes of Pyramids

Consider a triangular prism with parallel, congruent bases △*JKL* and △*MNP*. You can divide this triangular prism into three triangular pyramids.

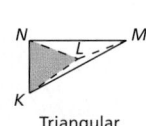
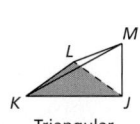
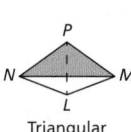

Triangular prism — Triangular pyramid 1 — Triangular pyramid 2 — Triangular pyramid 3

You can combine triangular pyramids 1 and 2 to form a pyramid with a base that is a parallelogram, as shown at the left. Name this pyramid *Q*. Similarly, you can combine triangular pyramids 1 and 3 to form pyramid *R* with a base that is a parallelogram.

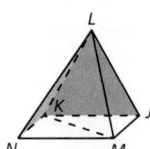

Pyramid Q

In pyramid *Q*, diagonal $\overline{KM}$ divides ▱*JKNM* into two congruent triangles, so the bases of triangular pyramids 1 and 2 are congruent. Similarly, you can divide any cross section parallel to ▱*JKNM* into two congruent triangles that are the cross sections of triangular pyramids 1 and 2.

By Cavalieri's Principle, triangular pyramids 1 and 2 have the same volume. Similarly, using pyramid *R*, you can show that triangular pyramids 1 and 3 have the same volume. By the Transitive Property of Equality, triangular pyramids 2 and 3 have the same volume.

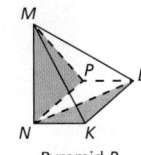

Pyramid R

The volume of each pyramid must be one-third the volume of the prism, or $V = \frac{1}{3}Bh$. You can generalize this formula to say that the volume of any pyramid with any base is equal to $\frac{1}{3}$ the volume of a prism with the same base and height because you can divide any polygon into triangles and any pyramid into triangular pyramids.

🟢 Core Concept

Volume of a Pyramid

The volume *V* of a pyramid is

$$V = \frac{1}{3}Bh$$

where *B* is the area of the base and *h* is the height.

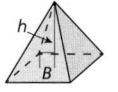
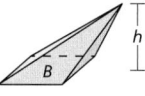

EXAMPLE 1   Finding the Volume of a Pyramid

Find the volume of the pyramid.

SOLUTION

$V = \frac{1}{3}Bh$ Formula for volume of a pyramid

$= \frac{1}{3}\left(\frac{1}{2} \cdot 4 \cdot 6\right)(9)$ Substitute.

$= 36$ Simplify.

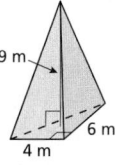

▶ The volume is 36 cubic meters.

Laurie's Notes   Teacher Actions

• The volume of pyramids was studied in middle school.

• The models described on this page can actually be constructed. The model, composed of three congruent pyramids that can be rearranged to make a prism, helps students make the connection to the $\frac{1}{3}$ in the formula.

❓ Write the *Core Concept*. "How do you find the area of the base of the pyramid?" It depends on what polygon it is!

• In Example 1, the height of the pyramid is 9 meters. The slant height is not 9 meters.

Find the volume of the pyramid.

1.
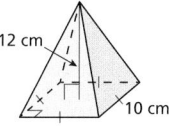
12 cm
10 cm

2.
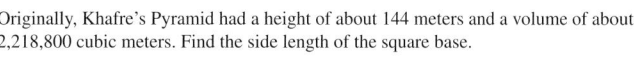
20 cm
12 cm

Differentiated Instruction

Auditory
Remind students that the base of a pyramid must be a polygon. Review the formulas for the areas of triangles and rectangles.

Using Volumes of Pyramids

EXAMPLE 2   **Using the Volume of a Pyramid**

Originally, Khafre's Pyramid had a height of about 144 meters and a volume of about 2,218,800 cubic meters. Find the side length of the square base.

SOLUTION

Khafre's Pyramid, Egypt

$$V = \frac{1}{3}Bh$$ Formula for volume of a pyramid

$$2{,}218{,}800 \approx \frac{1}{3}x^2(144)$$ Substitute.

$$6{,}656{,}400 \approx 144x^2$$ Multiply each side by 3.

$$46{,}225 \approx x^2$$ Divide each side by 144.

$$215 \approx x$$ Find the positive square root.

▶   Originally, the side length of the square base was about 215 meters.

EXAMPLE 3   **Using the Volume of a Pyramid**

Find the height of the triangular pyramid.

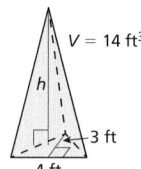
$V = 14$ ft³
h
3 ft
4 ft

SOLUTION

The area of the base is $B = \frac{1}{2}(3)(4) = 6$ ft² and the volume is $V = 14$ ft³.

$$V = \frac{1}{3}Bh$$ Formula for volume of a pyramid

$$14 = \frac{1}{3}(6)h$$ Substitute.

$$7 = h$$ Solve for h.

▶   The height is 7 feet.

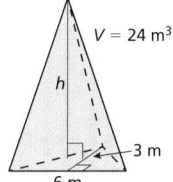
$V = 24$ m³
h
3 m
6 m

3. The volume of a square pyramid is 75 cubic meters and the height is 9 meters. Find the side length of the square base.

4. Find the height of the triangular pyramid at the left.

Section 11.6   Volumes of Pyramids   **637**

Extra Example 2
A square pyramid has a height of 12 centimeters and a volume of 64 cubic centimeters. Find the side length of the square base. **4 centimeters**

Extra Example 3
Find the height of the triangular pyramid.

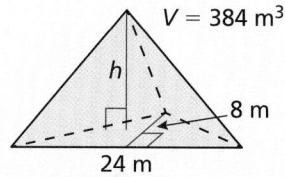
$V = 384$ m³
h
8 m
24 m

The height is 12 meters.

MONITORING PROGRESS ANSWERS

1. 400 cm³

2. about 2494.15 cm³

3. 5 m

4. 8 m

Laurie's Notes   Teacher Actions

- Question 2 will be more challenging due to the hexagonal base.
- **❓ MP2 Reason Abstractly and Quantitatively:** "What is known in Example 2?" You know the volume of the square pyramid and its height. "What are you trying to find?" the length of an edge on the square base Have students work independently to solve. Multiplying both sides by 3 clears the fraction.
- **Think-Pair-Share:** Have students answer Example 3, and then share and discuss as a class.

Extra Example 4

Square pyramid A and square pyramid B are similar. The height of pyramid A is 6 inches and the height of pyramid B is 15 inches. The volume of pyramid B is 312.5 cubic inches. Find the volume of pyramid A. The volume of pyramid A is 20 cubic inches.

Extra Example 5

Find the volume of the composite solid.

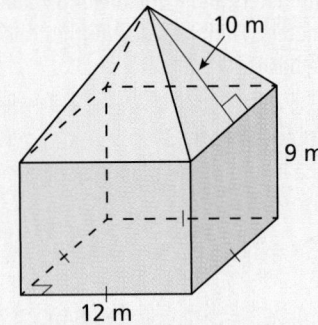

The volume is 1680 cubic meters.

MONITORING PROGRESS ANSWERS

5. 12 m^3
6. 96 ft^3

EXAMPLE 4   Finding the Volume of a Similar Solid

Pyramid A and pyramid B are similar. Find the volume of pyramid B.

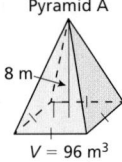
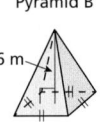

Pyramid A   Pyramid B

$V = 96 \text{ m}^3$

SOLUTION

The scale factor is $k = \dfrac{\text{Height of pyramid B}}{\text{Height of pyramid A}} = \dfrac{6}{8} = \dfrac{3}{4}$.

Use the scale factor to find the volume of pyramid B.

$\dfrac{\text{Volume of pyramid B}}{\text{Volume of pyramid A}} = k^3$ The ratio of the volumes is k^3.

$\dfrac{\text{Volume of pyramid B}}{96} = \left(\dfrac{3}{4}\right)^3$ Substitute.

$\text{Volume of pyramid B} = 40.5$ Solve for volume of pyramid B.

▶ The volume of pyramid B is 40.5 cubic meters.

Monitoring Progress 🔊 Help in English and Spanish at *BigIdeasMath.com*

5. Pyramid C and pyramid D are similar. Find the volume of pyramid D.

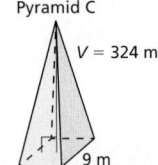

Pyramid C   Pyramid D

$V = 324 \text{ m}^3$

9 m   3 m

EXAMPLE 5   Finding the Volume of a Composite Solid

Find the volume of the composite solid.

SOLUTION

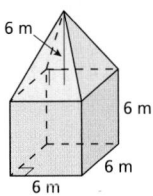

6 m

6 m

6 m

6 m

Volume of solid	=	Volume of cube	+	Volume of pyramid	

$= s^3 + \dfrac{1}{3}Bh$ Write formulas.

$= 6^3 + \dfrac{1}{3}(6)^2 \cdot 6$ Substitute.

$= 216 + 72$ Simplify.

$= 288$ Add.

▶ The volume is 288 cubic meters.

Monitoring Progress 🔊 Help in English and Spanish at *BigIdeasMath.com*

6. Find the volume of the composite solid.

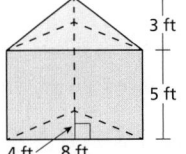

3 ft

5 ft

4 ft   8 ft

Laurie's Notes   Teacher Actions

• **Visitor Explanation:** Finish Example 4 and ask, "If a visitor entered the room right now, how would you explain what you are doing and why you are doing it?" Students should practice explanations with partners. Solicit oral responses or do a one-minute write.

COMMON ERROR When computing the area of the base in Example 5, the $\frac{1}{3}$ is not squared; only the 6 is squared.

Closure

• **Exit Ticket:** Find the volume of the Louvre Pyramid. It reaches a height of about 72 feet, and the square base has side length of about 116 feet. about 322,944 cubic feet

---

11.6 Exercises

Dynamic Solutions available at *BigIdeasMath.com*

Vocabulary and Core Concept Check

1. **VOCABULARY** Explain the difference between a triangular prism and a triangular pyramid.

2. **REASONING** A square pyramid and a cube have the same base and height. Compare the volume of the square pyramid to the volume of the cube.

Monitoring Progress and Modeling with Mathematics

In Exercises 3 and 4, find the volume of the pyramid.
(See Example 1.)

3.
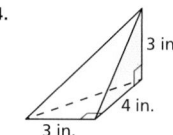
7 m, 16 m, 12 m

4.
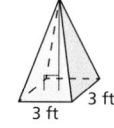
3 in., 4 in., 3 in.

In Exercises 5–8, find the indicated measure.
(See Example 2.)

5. A pyramid with a square base has a volume of 120 cubic meters and a height of 10 meters. Find the side length of the square base.

6. A pyramid with a square base has a volume of 912 cubic feet and a height of 19 feet. Find the side length of the square base.

7. A pyramid with a rectangular base has a volume of 480 cubic inches and a height of 10 inches. The width of the rectangular base is 9 inches. Find the length of the rectangular base.

8. A pyramid with a rectangular base has a volume of 105 cubic centimeters and a height of 15 centimeters. The length of the rectangular base is 7 centimeters. Find the width of the rectangular base.

9. **ERROR ANALYSIS** Describe and correct the error in finding the volume of the pyramid.

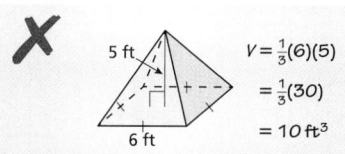
5 ft, 6 ft

$$V = \frac{1}{3}(6)(5)$$
$$= \frac{1}{3}(30)$$
$$= 10 \text{ ft}^3$$

10. **OPEN-ENDED** Give an example of a pyramid and a prism that have the same base and the same volume. Explain your reasoning.

In Exercises 11–14, find the height of the pyramid.
(See Example 3.)

11. Volume = 15 ft³
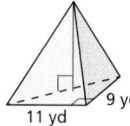
3 ft, 3 ft

12. Volume = 224 in.³

12 in., 8 in.

13. Volume = 198 yd³
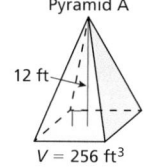
9 yd, 11 yd

14. Volume = 392 cm³

14 cm, 7 cm

In Exercises 15 and 16, the pyramids are similar. Find the volume of pyramid B. *(See Example 4.)*

15.   Pyramid A   Pyramid B
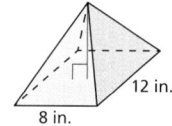
12 ft   3 ft
$V = 256 \text{ ft}^3$

16.   Pyramid A   Pyramid B

3 in.   6 in.
$V = 10 \text{ in.}^3$

Section 11.6   Volumes of Pyramids   **639**

Assignment Guide and Homework Check

ASSIGNMENT

Basic: 1, 2, 3–19 odd, 22, 26–29

Average: 1, 2, 4, 6, 9, 10–20 even, 21, 22, 25–29

Advanced: 1, 2, 9–29

HOMEWORK CHECK

Basic: 3, 5, 7, 11, 17

Average: 6, 12, 16, 20, 21

Advanced: 12, 20, 21, 23, 24

ANSWERS

1. *Sample answer:* A triangular prism has two parallel bases that are triangles. A triangular pyramid has one base that is a triangle, and the other faces all intersect at a single point.

2. The volume of the square pyramid is $\frac{1}{3}$ of the volume of the cube.

3. 448 m³

4. 6 in.³

5. 6 m

6. 12 ft

7. 16 in.

8. 3 cm

9. One side length was used in the formula as the base area;
   $V = \frac{1}{3}(6^2)(5) = 60 \text{ ft}^3$

10. *Sample answer:* A rectangular pyramid with a base area of 5 square meters and a height of 6 meters, and a rectangular prism with a base area of 5 square meters and a height of 2 meters; Both volumes are 10 cubic meters.

11. 5 ft

12. 7 in.

13. 12 yd

14. 24 cm

15. 4 ft³

16. 80 in.³

ANSWERS

17. 72 in.^{3}

18. 666 cm^3

19. about 213.33 cm^3

20. 1440 in.^{3}

21. **a.** The volume doubles.

    b. The volume is 4 times greater.

    c. yes; *Sample answer:*

    Square Pyramid: $V = \frac{1}{3}s^2h$

    double height:

    $V = \frac{1}{3}s^2(2h) = 2\left(\frac{1}{3}s^2h\right)$

    double side length of base:

    $V = \frac{1}{3}(2s)^2h = 4\left(\frac{1}{3}s^2h\right)$

22. *Sample answer:* The three pyramids have the same base and height as the prism, and the same volumes as each other, so each is $\frac{1}{3}$ the volume of the prism.

23. about 9.22 ft^3

24. $V = \frac{1}{3}(a^2 + ab + b^2)h$

25. about 78 in.^{3}

26–29. See Additional Answers.

Mini-Assessment

1. Two similar pyramids have heights 8 feet and 5 feet. What is the ratio of their volumes? **512:125**

2. A square pyramid has height 13 cm. Each base edge is 6 cm long. Find the volume.
156 cubic centimeters

3. The volume of the pyramid is 168 cubic inches. Find the length of the rectangular base.

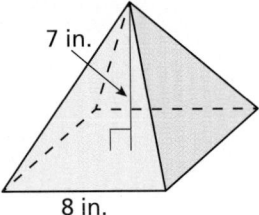

9 inches

4. The volume of a triangular pyramid with a right triangle base is 100 cubic feet. One leg of the base triangle is 4 feet. The height of the pyramid is 27 feet. Find the height of the base triangle.
about 5.56 feet

640   Chapter 11

In Exercises 17–20, find the volume of the composite solid. *(See Example 5.)*

17.

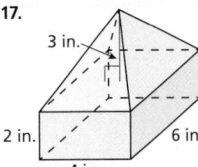

18.

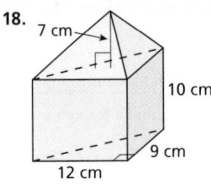

19.

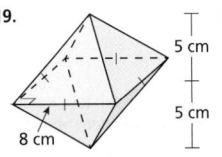

20.

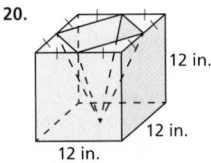

21. **ABSTRACT REASONING** A pyramid has a height of 8 feet and a square base with a side length of 6 feet.

    a. How does the volume of the pyramid change when the base stays the same and the height is doubled?

    b. How does the volume of the pyramid change when the height stays the same and the side length of the base is doubled?

    c. Are your answers to parts (a) and (b) true for any square pyramid? Explain your reasoning.

22. **HOW DO YOU SEE IT?** The cube shown is formed by three pyramids, each with the same square base and the same height. How could you use this to verify the formula for the volume of a pyramid?

Maintaining Mathematical Proficiency Reviewing what you learned in previous grades and lessons

Find the value of x. Round your answer to the nearest tenth. *(Section 9.4 and Section 9.5)*

26.

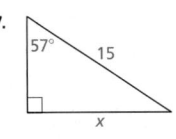

27.

28.

29.

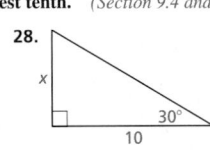

---

23. **CRITICAL THINKING** Find the volume of the regular pentagonal pyramid. Round your answer to the nearest hundredth. In the diagram, $m\angle ABC = 35°$.

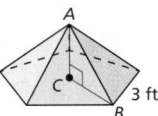

24. **THOUGHT PROVOKING** A *frustum* of a pyramid is the part of the pyramid that lies between the base and a plane parallel to the base, as shown. Write a formula for the volume of the frustum of a square pyramid in terms of a, b, and h. (*Hint*: Consider the "missing" top of the pyramid and use similar triangles.)

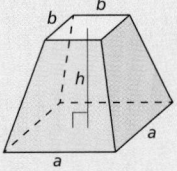

25. **MODELING WITH MATHEMATICS** Nautical deck prisms were used as a safe way to illuminate decks on ships. The deck prism shown here is composed of the following three solids: a regular hexagonal prism with an edge length of 3.5 inches and a height of 1.5 inches, a regular hexagonal prism with an edge length of 3.25 inches and a height of 0.25 inch, and a regular hexagonal pyramid with an edge length of 3 inches and a height of 3 inches. Find the volume of the deck prism.

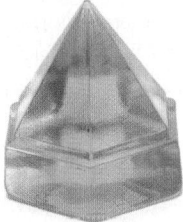

Laurie's Notes

Overview of Section 11.7

Introduction

- This is the third of four lessons on the volumes of solids. In this lesson, students will find the volume of a cone, which structurally is like a pyramid.
- A second topic presented in this lesson is the surface area of a cone.
- Students will also work with volumes of similar cones.

Teaching Strategy

- In the first exploration, students derive the formula for the surface area of a cone. Students begin with a circle of radius 3 inches. Then sectors of 60° are removed from the circle and a cone is formed. In the exploration, the students are gathering data about the radius, slant height, area of the base, lateral area, and total surface area.
- The one dimension that is not needed in the investigation is the height of the cone. As an extension to the exploration, have students solve for the height of each successive cone. Is there a pattern?
- Using a graphing calculator, store the base radius of the cone in L_1 and the slant height in L_2.
- Calculate the height of the cone $\left(L_3 = \sqrt{L_2^2 - L_1^2}\right)$ as shown in Figure 1, and store the height in L_3. (See Figure 2.)
- Figure 3 shows the graph of (L_1, L_3) or (radius of the base, height). As the radius increases, the height decreases.

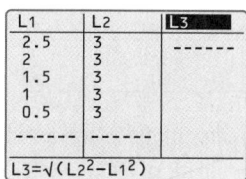

L1	L2	L3
2.5	3	------
2	3	
1.5	3	
1	3	
0.5	3	
------	------	

L3=√(L2²-L1²)

Figure 1

L1	L2	L3
2.5	3	1.6583
2	3	2.2361
1.5	3	2.5981
1	3	2.8284
0.5	3	2.958
------	------	------

L3(1)=1.658312395177

Figure 2

Figure 3

- Once students have the volume formula, they can also solve for the volume of the cone. Is there a pattern?
- Calculate the volume $\left(L_4 = (1/3)\pi L_1^2 L_3\right)$ as shown in Figure 4, and store the volume in L_4. (See Figure 5.)

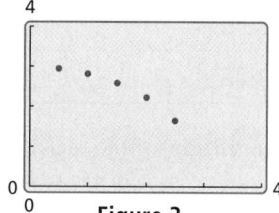

L1	L2	L3	L4
2.5	3	1.6583	------
2	3	2.2361	
1.5	3	2.5981	
1	3	2.8284	
0.5	3	2.958	
------	------	------	

L4=(1/3)πL1²L3

Figure 4

L1	L2	L3	L4
2.5	3	1.6583	10.854
2	3	2.2361	9.3664
1.5	3	2.5981	6.1216
1	3	2.8284	2.9619
0.5	3	2.958	.77441
------	------	------	------

L4(1)=10.853629245932

Figure 5

- Figure 6 shows the graph of (L_1, L_4) or (radius of the base, volume). As the radius increases, the volume increases.

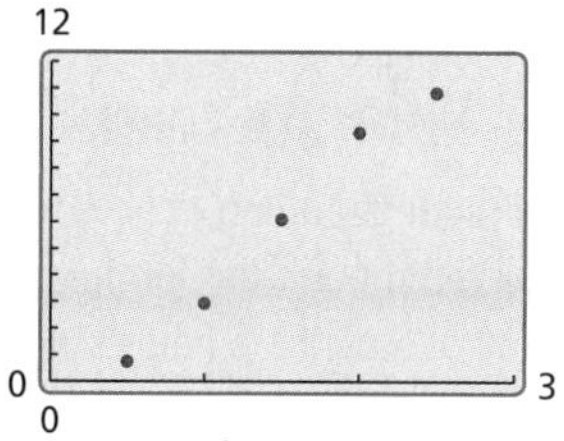

Figure 6

Pacing Suggestion

- Complete both explorations, the first of which takes a bit longer. Transition to the formal lesson by stating the *Core Concept*.

Dynamic Teaching Tools

- Dynamic Assessment & Progress Monitoring Tool
- Lesson Planning Tool
- Interactive Whiteboard Lesson Library
- Dynamic Classroom with Dynamic Investigations

**Common Core
State Standards**

HSG-GMD.A.1 Give an informal argument for the formulas for the ... volume of a ... cone.

HSG-GMD.A.3 Use volume formulas for ... cones, ... to solve problems.

Laurie's Notes

Exploration

Motivate
- "What does the net for a cone look like? Sketch it." Ask students to share their sketches. Many will have the lateral portion incorrect. Students will work with the net in the first exploration.

Exploration 1
- The first exploration focuses on the derivation of the formula for the surface area of a cone. It's cool that your students can derive a formula that generally is just given to students to use.
- Begin with a paper circle of radius 3 inches. A sector, $\frac{1}{6}$ of the original area of the circle, is removed each time. When taped, the remaining sector folds into a cone.
- Making a table to gather results will help facilitate this exploration.

Shape					
Radius of Base	$\frac{5}{2}$	2	$\frac{3}{2}$	1	$\frac{1}{2}$
Base Area	$\pi\left(\frac{5}{2}\right)^2$	$\pi(2)^2$	$\pi\left(\frac{3}{2}\right)^2$	$\pi(1)^2$	$\pi\left(\frac{1}{2}\right)^2$
Lateral Area	$\frac{5}{6}\pi(3)^2 = \frac{15}{2}\pi$	$\frac{2}{3}\pi(3)^2 = 6\pi$	$\frac{1}{2}\pi(3)^2 = \frac{9}{2}\pi$	$\frac{1}{3}\pi(3)^2 = 3\pi$	$\frac{1}{6}\pi(3)^2 = \frac{3}{2}\pi$
Total Area	$\frac{55}{4}\pi$	10π	$\frac{27}{4}\pi$	4π	$\frac{7}{4}\pi$

- **Observations:** The radius of the base is getting smaller. The radius of the lateral area is always 3 inches, and it is also the slant height of the cone when folded. To find the total area, you add the base area and the lateral area. Students will recognize that the area of the base is still πr^2. The pattern in the lateral area is that the coefficient of π is the radius of the base r times the slant height ℓ.
- So, the formula for the surface area of a cone is $\pi r^2 + r\ell\pi$.
- **Extension:** What is happening to the height of the cone? See the *Teaching Strategy* on page T-640.

Exploration 2
- If you have a set of clear plastic solids to demonstrate this relationship, it would be more engaging than a static picture. Alternately, an online search will result in videos that demonstrate this relationship.
- **?** "What do the images suggest in order to find the volume of a cone?" Multiply $\frac{1}{3}$ times the area of the base times the height.

Communicate Your Answer
- Listen for a general understanding of how to find the surface area of a cone (lateral surface area + base area) even though the formula may not be fully developed.
- Knowing the volume of a pyramid helps students gain an understanding of the formula for the volume of a cone.

Connecting to Next Step
- Students will be finding both the surface area and the volume of a cone in the lesson.

11.7 Surface Areas and Volumes of Cones

Essential Question
How can you find the surface area and the volume of a cone?

EXPLORATION 1   Finding the Surface Area of a Cone

Work with a partner. Construct a circle with a radius of 3 inches. Mark the circumference of the circle into six equal parts, and label the length of each part. Then cut out one sector of the circle and make a cone.

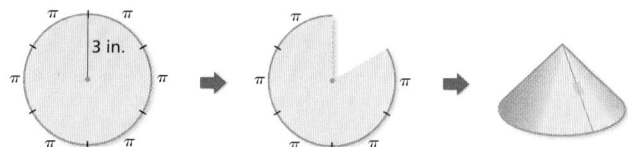

a. Explain why the base of the cone is a circle. What are the circumference and radius of the base?

b. What is the area of the original circle? What is the area with one sector missing?

c. Describe the surface area of the cone, including the base. Use your description to find the surface area.

EXPLORATION 2   Finding the Volume of a Cone

Work with a partner. The cone and the cylinder have the same height and the same circular base.

When the cone is filled with sand and poured into the cylinder, it takes three cones to fill the cylinder.

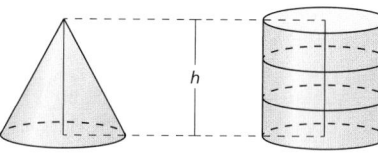

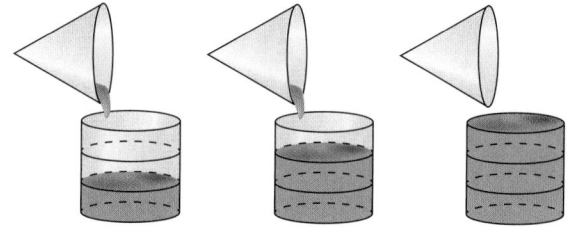

CONSTRUCTING VIABLE ARGUMENTS

To be proficient in math, you need to understand and use stated assumptions, definitions, and previously established results in constructing arguments.

Use this information to write a formula for the volume V of a cone.

Communicate Your Answer

3. How can you find the surface area and the volume of a cone?

4. In Exploration 1, cut another sector from the circle and make a cone. Find the radius of the base and the surface area of the cone. Repeat this three times, recording your results in a table. Describe the pattern.

Dynamic Teaching Tools

Dynamic Assessment & Progress Monitoring Tool

Lesson Planning Tool

Interactive Whiteboard Lesson Library

Dynamic Classroom with Dynamic Investigations

ANSWERS

1. a. *Sample answer:* The points on the edge of the base are all the same distance from the point on the same plane directly below the vertex of the cone; 5π in.; 2.5 in.

   b. 9π in.^{2}; 7.5π in.^{2}

   c. a circle with a radius of 2.5 in. and a sector which is $\frac{5}{6}$ of a circle with a radius of 3 in.; 13.75π in.^{2}

2. $V = \frac{1}{3}\pi r^2 h$

3. *Sample answer:* $S = \pi r^2 + \pi r \ell$; $V = \frac{1}{3}\pi r^2 h$

4. *Sample answer:* As the radius decreases, the total surface area decreases.

Auditory

Ask students to describe the types of figures for which they are finding lateral area and surface area in this section. Make sure students understand that the formulas for surface area and lateral area apply to right cones only. Draw a non-right cone on the board and label its radius and height. Ask students to explain why the formula $\pi r \ell$ does not work to find the lateral area of this figure.

Extra Example 1

Find the surface area of the right cone.

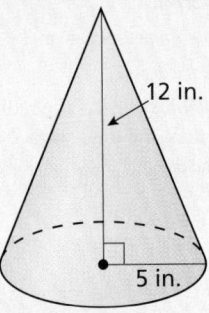

The surface area is 90π, or about 282.74 square inches.

MONITORING PROGRESS ANSWER

1. about 436.18 m^2

11.7 Lesson

Core Vocabulary

lateral surface of a cone, p. 642

Previous
cone
net
composite solid

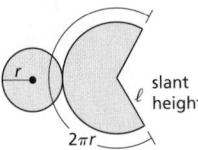

What You Will Learn

▶ Find surface areas of right cones.
▶ Find volumes of cones.
▶ Use volumes of cones.

Finding Surface Areas of Right Cones

Recall that a *circular cone*, or *cone*, has a circular *base* and a *vertex* that is not in the same plane as the base. The *altitude*, or *height*, is the perpendicular distance between the vertex and the base. In a *right cone*, the height meets the base at its center and the *slant height* is the distance between the vertex and a point on the base edge.

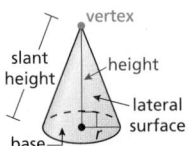

The **lateral surface of a cone** consists of all segments that connect the vertex with points on the base edge. When you cut along the slant height and lay the right cone flat, you get the net shown at the left. In the net, the circular base has an area of πr^2 and the lateral surface is a sector of a circle. You can find the area of this sector by using a proportion, as shown below.

$$\frac{\text{Area of sector}}{\text{Area of circle}} = \frac{\text{Arc length}}{\text{Circumference of circle}} \qquad \text{Set up proportion.}$$

$$\frac{\text{Area of sector}}{\pi \ell^2} = \frac{2\pi r}{2\pi \ell} \qquad \text{Substitute.}$$

$$\text{Area of sector} = \pi \ell^2 \cdot \frac{2\pi r}{2\pi \ell} \qquad \text{Multiply each side by } \pi \ell^2.$$

$$\text{Area of sector} = \pi r \ell \qquad \text{Simplify.}$$

The surface area of a right cone is the sum of the base area and the lateral area, $\pi r \ell$.

Core Concept

Surface Area of a Right Cone

The surface area S of a right cone is

$$S = \pi r^2 + \pi r \ell$$

where r is the radius of the base and ℓ is the slant height.

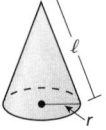

EXAMPLE 1 Finding Surface Areas of Right Cones

Find the surface area of the right cone.

SOLUTION

$$S = \pi r^2 + \pi r \ell = \pi \cdot 4^2 + \pi(4)(6) = 40\pi \approx 125.66$$

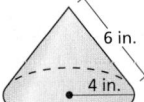

▶ The surface area is 40π, or about 125.66 square inches.

Monitoring Progress Help in English and Spanish at *BigIdeasMath.com*

1. Find the surface area of the right cone.

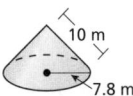

Laurie's Notes   Teacher Actions

- The introduction to this lesson defines the vocabulary associated with a cone.
- The formula for the surface area of a cone is then derived using the schematic of the net shown in the margin. If students did not complete the first exploration, work through the derivation.
- **? MP1 Make Sense of Problems and Persevere in Solving Them:** "What is the relationship between the slant height ℓ, the radius r, and the height of the cone h?" $r^2 + h^2 = \ell^2$
- Have students work independently on Example 1 and Question 1, if needed.

Finding Volumes of Cones

Consider a cone with a regular polygon inscribed in the base. The pyramid with the same vertex as the cone has volume $V = \frac{1}{3}Bh$. As you increase the number of sides of the polygon, it approaches the base of the cone and the pyramid approaches the cone. The volume approaches $\frac{1}{3}\pi r^2 h$ as the base area B approaches πr^2.

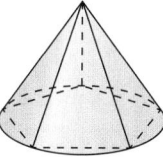 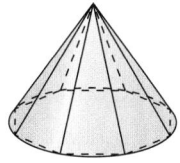 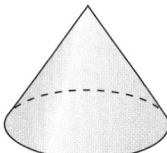

Core Concept

Volume of a Cone

The volume V of a cone is

$$V = \frac{1}{3}Bh = \frac{1}{3}\pi r^2 h$$

where B is the area of the base, h is the height, and r is the radius of the base.

 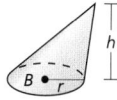

EXAMPLE 2 **Finding the Volume of a Cone**

Find the volume of the cone.

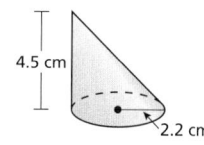

SOLUTION

$V = \frac{1}{3}\pi r^2 h$	Formula for volume of a cone
$= \frac{1}{3}\pi \cdot (2.2)^2 \cdot 4.5$	Substitute.
$= 7.26\pi$	Simplify.
≈ 22.81	Use a calculator.

▶ The volume is 7.26π, or about 22.81 cubic centimeters.

Monitoring Progress Help in English and Spanish at *BigIdeasMath.com*

Find the volume of the cone.

2.
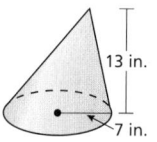

3.
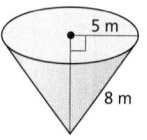

Extra Example 2

Find the volume of the cone.

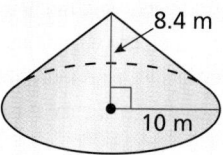

The volume is 280π, or about 879.65 cubic meters.

MONITORING PROGRESS ANSWERS

2. about 667.06 in.^{3}

3. about 163.49 m^3

Laurie's Notes   Teacher Actions

- Structurally, the cone is like a pyramid—a base and a lateral portion that converges to a vertex. It is not a surprise to students that the formula for the volume of a cone should be similar to the formula for the volume of a pyramid.
- Write the *Core Concept*. Note that the height of the cone is used in the formula, not the slant height.
- **Think-Pair-Share:** Have students answer Example 2, and then share and discuss as a class.

Extra Example 3

Cone A and cone B are similar. The height of cone A is 6 inches and the height of cone B is 2 inches The volume of cone B is 18π cubic inches. Find the volume of cone A. The volume of cone A is 486π cubic inches.

Extra Example 4

Find the volume of the composite solid.

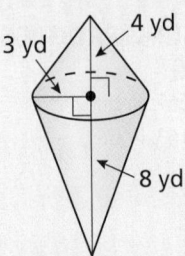

The volume is 36π, or about 113.10 cubic yards.

MONITORING PROGRESS ANSWERS

4. 6π cm³

5. about 329.87 cm³

Using Volumes of Cones

EXAMPLE 3   Finding the Volume of a Similar Solid

Cone A and cone B are similar. Find the volume of cone B.

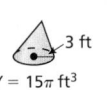
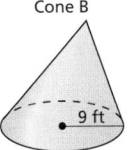

Cone A

Cone B

$V = 15\pi$ ft³

9 ft

SOLUTION

The scale factor is $k = \dfrac{\text{Radius of cone B}}{\text{Radius of cone A}} = \dfrac{9}{3} = 3$.

Use the scale factor to find the volume of cone B.

$\dfrac{\text{Volume of cone B}}{\text{Volume of cone A}} = k^3$ .... The ratio of the volumes is k^3.

$\dfrac{\text{Volume of cone B}}{15\pi} = 3^3$ .... Substitute.

Volume of cone B $= 405\pi$ .... Solve for volume of cone B.

▶ The volume of cone B is 405π cubic feet.

Monitoring Progress   🔊 Help in English and Spanish at *BigIdeasMath.com*

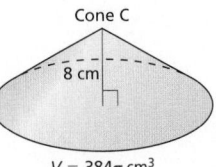

Cone C

8 cm

$V = 384\pi$ cm³

Cone D

2 cm

4. Cone C and cone D are similar. Find the volume of cone D.

EXAMPLE 4   Finding the Volume of a Composite Solid

Find the volume of the composite solid.

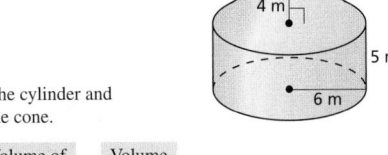

4 m

5 m

6 m

SOLUTION

Let h_1 be the height of the cylinder and let h_2 be the height of the cone.

Volume of solid	=	Volume of cylinder	+	Volume of cone

$= \pi r^2 h_1 + \frac{1}{3}\pi r^2 h_2$ .... Write formulas.

$= \pi \cdot 6^2 \cdot 5 + \frac{1}{3}\pi \cdot 6^2 \cdot 4$ .... Substitute.

$= 180\pi + 48\pi$ .... Simplify.

$= 228\pi$ .... Add.

≈ 716.28 .... Use a calculator.

▶ The volume is 228π, or about 716.28 cubic meters.

Monitoring Progress   🔊 Help in English and Spanish at *BigIdeasMath.com*

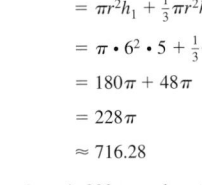
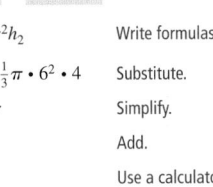

5 cm

10 cm

3 cm

5. Find the volume of the composite solid.

Laurie's Notes   Teacher Actions

❓ Pose Example 3. "What is the ratio of their linear measurements?" The radii are in the ratio of 3:1. "What is the ratio of their volumes?" The volumes are in the ratio of 3^3:1^3 or 27:1.

❓ **Extension:** "What is the ratio of their surface areas?" 3^2:1^2 or 9:1

• **Turn and Talk:** "How can you find the volume of the composite figure in Example 4?" Discuss and have partners find the volume.

Closure

• **Exit Ticket:** Find the surface area and volume of a cone with a diameter of 8 centimeters and height of 3 centimeters. The surface area is 36π, or about 113.10 square centimeters. The volume is 16π, or about 50.27 cubic centimeters.

Dynamic Solutions available at *BigIdeasMath.com*

Vocabulary and Core Concept Check

1. **WRITING** Describe the differences between pyramids and cones. Describe their similarities.

2. **COMPLETE THE SENTENCE** The volume of a cone with radius r and height h is $\frac{1}{3}$ the volume of a(n) _____ with radius r and height h.

Monitoring Progress and Modeling with Mathematics

In Exercises 3–6, find the surface area of the right cone. *(See Example 1.)*

3.
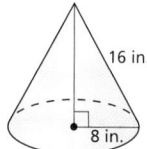
16 in.
8 in.

4.
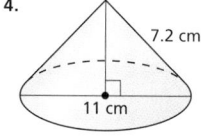
7.2 cm
11 cm

5. A right cone has a radius of 9 inches and a height of 12 inches.

6. A right cone has a diameter of 11.2 feet and a height of 9.2 feet.

In Exercises 7–10, find the volume of the cone. *(See Example 2.)*

7.
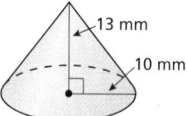
13 mm
10 mm

8.
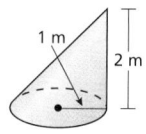
1 m
2 m

9. A cone has a diameter of 11.5 inches and a height of 15.2 inches.

10. A right cone has a radius of 3 feet and a slant height of 6 feet.

In Exercises 11 and 12, find the missing dimension(s).

11. Surface area = 75.4 cm²

h ℓ
3 cm

12. Volume = 216π in.³

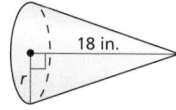
18 in.
r

In Exercises 13 and 14, the cones are similar. Find the volume of cone B. *(See Example 3.)*

13.
Cone A
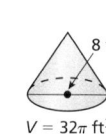
8 ft
$V = 32\pi$ ft³

Cone B
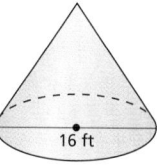
16 ft

14.
Cone A
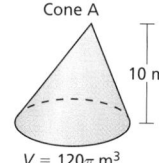
10 m
$V = 120\pi$ m³

Cone B

4 m

In Exercises 15 and 16, find the volume of the composite solid. *(See Example 4.)*

15.
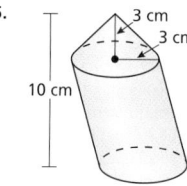
3 cm
3 cm
10 cm

16.
5.1 m
5.1 m
5.1 m

17. **ANALYZING RELATIONSHIPS** A cone has height h and a base with radius r. You want to change the cone so its volume is doubled. What is the new height if you change only the height? What is the new radius if you change only the radius? Explain.

Section 11.7 Surface Areas and Volumes of Cones **645**

Assignment Guide and Homework Check

ASSIGNMENT

Basic: 1, 2, 3–15 odd, 18, 25, 27–30

Average: 1, 2, 6–18 even, 19–22, 25, 27–30

Advanced: 1, 2, 6, 8, 12–20 even, 21–30

HOMEWORK CHECK

Basic: 3, 7, 11, 13, 15

Average: 6, 12, 14, 16, 20

Advanced: 14, 16, 20, 24, 26

ANSWERS

1. *Sample answer:* pyramids have a polygonal base, cones have a circular base; They both have sides that meet at a single vertex.

2. cylinder

3. about 603.19 in.²

4. about 219.44 cm²

5. about 678.58 in.²

6. about 288.00 ft²

7. about 1361.36 mm³

8. about 2.09 m³

9. about 526.27 in.³

10. about 48.97 ft³

11. $\ell \approx 5.00$ cm; $h \approx 4.00$ cm

12. 6 in.

13. 256π ft³

14. 7.68π m³

15. about 226.19 cm³

16. about 97.92 m³

17. $2h$; $r\sqrt{2}$; *Sample answer:* The original volume is $V = \frac{1}{3}\pi r^2 h$ and the new volume is $V = \frac{2}{3}\pi r^2 h$.

ANSWERS

18. a. 3; *Sample answer:* The volume of the cone-shaped container is $\frac{1}{3}$ the volume of the cylindrical container.

 b. the cylindrical container; *Sample answer:* Three cone-shaped containers cost $3.75.

19–30. See Additional Answers.

Mini-Assessment

1. Find the surface area of a right cone with height 9 meters and base radius 6 meters. $(36 + 18\sqrt{13})\pi$, or about 316.99 square meters

2. Find the volume of a cone with base diameter 30 centimeters and height 45 centimeters. 3375π, or about 10,603 cubic centimeters

3. An ice cream cone has a base radius of 2.1 centimeters and a volume of 56.4 cubic centimeters. Find the height of the cone.

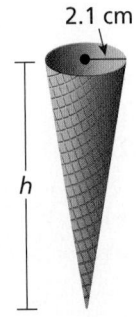

about 12.21 centimeters

4. Find the volume of the composite solid.

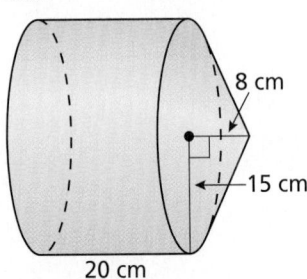

The volume is 5100π, or about 16,022 cubic meters.

646   Chapter 11

---

18. HOW DO YOU SEE IT A snack stand serves a small order of popcorn in a cone-shaped container and a large order of popcorn in a cylindrical container. Do not perform any calculations.

 a. How many small containers of popcorn do you have to buy to equal the amount of popcorn in a large container? Explain.

 b. Which container gives you more popcorn for your money? Explain.

In Exercises 19 and 20, find the volume of the right cone.

19.

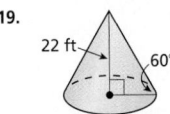

20.

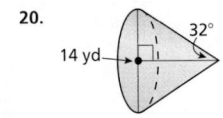

21. MODELING WITH MATHEMATICS A cat eats half a cup of food, twice per day. Will the automatic pet feeder hold enough food for 10 days? Explain your reasoning. (1 cup ≈ 14.4 in.³)

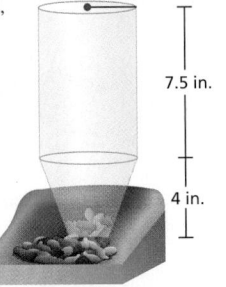

22. MODELING WITH MATHEMATICS During a chemistry lab, you use a funnel to pour a solvent into a flask. The radius of the funnel is 5 centimeters and its height is 10 centimeters. You pour the solvent into the funnel at a rate of 80 milliliters per second and the solvent flows out of the funnel at a rate of 65 milliliters per second. How long will it be before the funnel overflows? (1 mL = 1 cm³)

23. REASONING To make a paper drinking cup, start with a circular piece of paper that has a 3-inch radius, then follow the given steps. How does the surface area of the cup compare to the original paper circle? Find $m\angle ABC$.

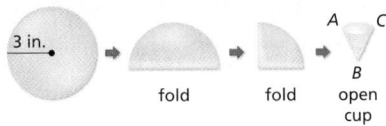

24. THOUGHT PROVOKING A *frustum* of a cone is the part of the cone that lies between the base and a plane parallel to the base, as shown. Write a formula for the volume of the frustum of a cone in terms of a, b, and h. (*Hint*: Consider the "missing" top of the cone and use similar triangles.)

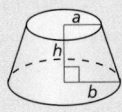

25. MAKING AN ARGUMENT In the figure, the two cylinders are congruent. The combined height of the two smaller cones equals the height of the larger cone. Your friend claims that this means the total volume of the two smaller cones is equal to the volume of the larger cone. Is your friend correct? Justify your answer.

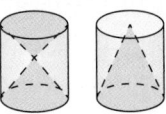

26. CRITICAL THINKING When the given triangle is rotated around each of its sides, solids of revolution are formed. Describe the three solids and find their volumes. Give your answers in terms of π.

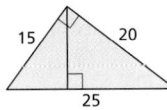

Maintaining Mathematical Proficiency   Reviewing what you learned in previous grades and lessons

Find the indicated measure. *(Section 11.2)*

27. area of a circle with a radius of 7 feet

28. area of a circle with a diameter of 22 centimeters

29. diameter of a circle with an area of 256π square meters

30. radius of a circle with an area of 529π square inches

If students need help...	If students got it...
Resources by Chapter • Practice A and Practice B • Puzzle Time	Resources by Chapter • Enrichment and Extension • Cumulative Review
Student Journal • Practice	Start the *next* Section
Differentiating the Lesson Skills Review Handbook	

Overview of Section 11.8

Introduction

- This is the fourth and final lesson on the volumes of solids. In this lesson, students will find the volume of a sphere.
- A second topic presented in this lesson is the surface area of a sphere.

Teaching Strategy

- The sphere is the only solid that has just one dimension, the radius. As the year comes to a close and students are preparing to take Algebra 2, have them discuss the formulas for surface area and volume of a sphere.
- **?** "What type of function is the surface area formula?" quadratic
- **?** "What type of function is the volume formula?" cubic
- **?** "What is the domain of each function?" the positive real numbers
- Use a graphing calculator to graph each function.

Pacing Suggestion

- Complete both explorations, the second of which takes a bit longer. Transition to the formal lesson by discussing the vocabulary of a sphere and stating the *Core Concept*.

Dynamic Teaching Tools

Dynamic Assessment & Progress Monitoring Tool
Lesson Planning Tool
Interactive Whiteboard Lesson Library
Dynamic Classroom with Dynamic Investigations

Common Core
State Standards

HSG-GMD.A.2 Give an informal argument using Cavalieri's principle for the formulas for the volume of a sphere ....

HSG-GMD.A.3 Use volume formulas for ... spheres to solve problems.

HSG-MG.A.1 Use geometric shapes, their measures, and their properties to describe objects (e.g., modeling a tree trunk or a human torso as a cylinder).

Laurie's Notes

Exploration

Motivate
- Have students describe the surface of a half sphere, and ask them how they might calculate its surface area.
- Discuss with students that the surface area consists of the flat, circular base, for which they can use the area formula $A = \pi r^2$, and half a ball-shaped surface.
- Tell students that in this lesson they will learn and apply formulas for the surface area and volume of a sphere.

Exploration 1
- This first exploration is a quick, visual way for students to estimate the surface area of a sphere. Students should estimate that to find the surface area they need to multiply 4 times πr^2.

Exploration 2
- If you have a set of clear plastic solids to demonstrate this relationship, it would be more engaging than a static picture. Alternately, an online search will result in videos that demonstrate this relationship.
- **?** "What does the exploration suggest is the formula for the volume of a sphere?" Multiply $\frac{4}{3}$ times πr^3.

Communicate Your Answer
- Listen for a general understanding of how to find the surface area and volume of a sphere even though the formulas may not be fully developed.

Connecting to Next Step
- Students will be finding both the surface area and the volume of a sphere in the lesson.

11.8 Surface Areas and Volumes of Spheres

Essential Question How can you find the surface area and the volume of a sphere?

EXPLORATION 1 **Finding the Surface Area of a Sphere**

Work with a partner. Remove the covering from a baseball or softball.

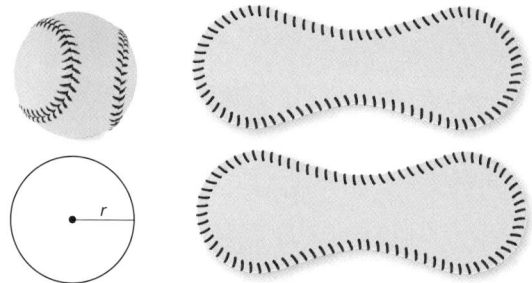

USING TOOLS STRATEGICALLY

To be proficient in math, you need to identify relevant external mathematical resources, such as content located on a website.

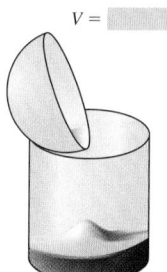

You will end up with two "figure 8" pieces of material, as shown above. From the amount of material it takes to cover the ball, what would you estimate the surface area S of the ball to be? Express your answer in terms of the radius r of the ball.

$S = $ ⬚   Surface area of a sphere

Use the Internet or some other resource to confirm that the formula you wrote for the surface area of a sphere is correct.

EXPLORATION 2 **Finding the Volume of a Sphere**

Work with a partner. A cylinder is circumscribed about a sphere, as shown. Write a formula for the volume V of the cylinder in terms of the radius r.

$V = $ ⬚   Volume of cylinder

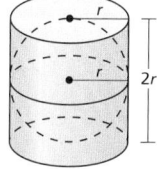

When half of the sphere (a *hemisphere*) is filled with sand and poured into the cylinder, it takes three hemispheres to fill the cylinder. Use this information to write a formula for the volume V of a sphere in terms of the radius r.

$V = $ ⬚   Volume of a sphere

Communicate Your Answer

3. How can you find the surface area and the volume of a sphere?

4. Use the results of Explorations 1 and 2 to find the surface area and the volume of a sphere with a radius of (a) 3 inches and (b) 2 centimeters.

ANSWERS

1. $4\pi r^2$

2. $2\pi r^3$; $\frac{4}{3}\pi r^3$

3. *Sample answer:* $S = 4\pi r^2$, $V = \frac{4}{3}\pi r^3$

4. **a.** about 113.10 in.^{2}; about 113.10 in.^{3}

   b. about 50.27 cm^2; about 33.51 cm^3

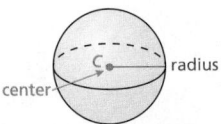

11.8 Lesson

What You Will Learn

▶ Find surface areas of spheres.
▶ Find volumes of spheres.

Core Vocabulary

chord of a sphere, *p. 648*
great circle, *p. 648*

Previous
sphere
center of a sphere
radius of a sphere
diameter of a sphere
hemisphere

Finding Surface Areas of Spheres

A *sphere* is the set of all points in space equidistant from a given point. This point is called the *center* of the sphere. A *radius* of a sphere is a segment from the center to a point on the sphere. A **chord of a sphere** is a segment whose endpoints are on the sphere. A *diameter* of a sphere is a chord that contains the center.

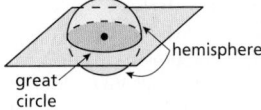

As with circles, the terms radius and diameter also represent distances, and the diameter is twice the radius.

If a plane intersects a sphere, then the intersection is either a single point or a circle. If the plane contains the center of the sphere, then the intersection is a **great circle** of the sphere. The circumference of a great circle is the circumference of the sphere. Every great circle of a sphere separates the sphere into two congruent halves called *hemispheres*.

Core Concept

Surface Area of a Sphere

The surface area S of a sphere is

$$S = 4\pi r^2$$

where r is the radius of the sphere.

$S = 4\pi r^2$

To understand the formula for the surface area of a sphere, think of a baseball. The surface area of a baseball is sewn from two congruent shapes, each of which resembles two joined circles.

So, the entire covering of the baseball consists of four circles, each with radius r. The area A of a circle with radius r is $A = \pi r^2$. So, the area of the covering can be approximated by $4\pi r^2$. This is the formula for the surface area of a sphere.

leather covering

Laurie's Notes — Teacher Actions

- **Teaching Tip:** If you have a globe, use it as a model as you discuss the vocabulary associated with a sphere. The globe is also useful in describing the role a great circle has in air travel. Traveling the path of a great circle is a shorter distance than traveling a latitude line.
- The baseball (or softball) cover has been the most visual way for my students to recall the formula for the surface area of a sphere.

EXAMPLE 1 **Finding the Surface Areas of Spheres**

Find the surface area of each sphere.

a.
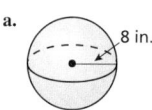
8 in.

b.
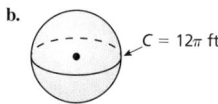
$C = 12\pi$ ft

SOLUTION

a. $S = 4\pi r^2$ Formula for surface area of a sphere

$\quad = 4\pi(8)^2$ Substitute 8 for r.

$\quad = 256\pi$ Simplify.

$\quad \approx 804.25$ Use a calculator.

▶ The surface area is 256π, or about 804.25 square inches.

b. The circumference of the sphere is 12π, so the radius of the sphere is $\dfrac{12\pi}{2\pi} = 6$ feet.

$\quad S = 4\pi r^2$ Formula for surface area of a sphere

$\quad\quad = 4\pi(6)^2$ Substitute 6 for r.

$\quad\quad = 144\pi$ Simplify.

$\quad\quad \approx 452.39$ Use a calculator.

▶ The surface area is 144π, or about 452.39 square feet.

EXAMPLE 2 **Finding the Diameter of a Sphere**

Find the diameter of the sphere.

SOLUTION

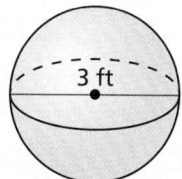
$S = 20.25\pi$ cm^2

$\quad S = 4\pi r^2$ Formula for surface area of a sphere

$20.25\pi = 4\pi r^2$ Substitute 20.25π for S.

$\quad 5.0625 = r^2$ Divide each side by 4π.

$\quad\quad 2.25 = r$ Find the positive square root.

COMMON ERROR

Be sure to multiply the value of r by 2 to find the diameter.

▶ The diameter is $2r = 2 \cdot 2.25 = 4.5$ centimeters.

Monitoring Progress Help in English and Spanish at *BigIdeasMath.com*

Find the surface area of the sphere.

1.
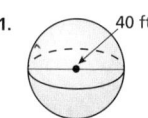
40 ft

2.

$C = 6\pi$ ft

3. Find the radius of the sphere.

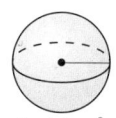
$S = 30\pi$ m^2

Extra Example 1
Find the surface area of each sphere.

a.

3 ft

The surface area is 9π, or about 28.27 square feet.

b.
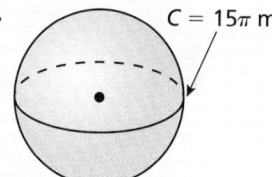
$C = 15\pi$ m

The surface area is 225π, or about 706.86 square meters.

Extra Example 2
Find the diameter of the sphere.

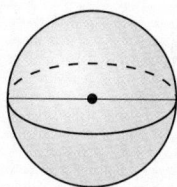
$S = 144\pi$ cm^2

The diameter is 12 centimeters.

MONITORING PROGRESS ANSWERS

1. about 5026.55 ft^2
2. about 113.10 ft^2
3. about 2.74 m

Laurie's Notes   **Teacher Actions**

❓MP2 Reason Abstractly and Quantitatively: "If you know the circumference of a sphere, can you find its surface area? Explain." yes; First solve for the radius using the formula for circumference, and then find the surface area.

• Have students solve parts (a) and (b) in Example 1.
• **Turn and Talk:** "Describe how to find the diameter of a sphere when you know the surface area." Circulate and listen to strategies.
• Have students work independently to solve Example 2.

Extra Example 3

Find the volume of the sphere.

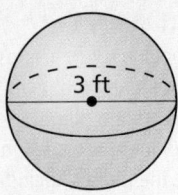

3 ft

The volume is $\frac{9}{2}\pi$, or about 14.14 cubic feet.

Finding Volumes of Spheres

The figure shows a hemisphere and a cylinder with a cone removed. A plane parallel to their bases intersects the solids z units above their bases.

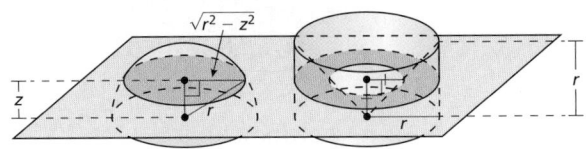

Using the AA Similarity Theorem (Theorem 8.3), you can show that the radius of the cross section of the cone at height z is z. The area of the cross section formed by the plane is $\pi(r^2 - z^2)$ for both solids. Because the solids have the same height and the same cross-sectional area at every level, they have the same volume by Cavalieri's Principle.

$$V_{hemisphere} = V_{cylinder} - V_{cone}$$

$$= \pi r^2(r) - \frac{1}{3}\pi r^2(r)$$

$$= \frac{2}{3}\pi r^3$$

So, the volume of a sphere of radius r is

$$2 \cdot V_{hemisphere} = 2 \cdot \frac{2}{3}\pi r^3 = \frac{4}{3}\pi r^3.$$

Core Concept

Volume of a Sphere

The volume V of a sphere is

$$V = \frac{4}{3}\pi r^3$$

where r is the radius of the sphere.

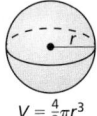

$V = \frac{4}{3}\pi r^3$

EXAMPLE 3 **Finding the Volume of a Sphere**

Find the volume of the soccer ball.

4.5 in.

SOLUTION

$V = \frac{4}{3}\pi r^3$ Formula for volume of a sphere

$= \frac{4}{3}\pi(4.5)^3$ Substitute 4.5 for r.

$= 121.5\pi$ Simplify.

≈ 381.70 Use a calculator.

▶ The volume of the soccer ball is 121.5π, or about 381.70 cubic inches.

Laurie's Notes **Teacher Actions**

- The formula for the volume of a sphere is developed using the graphics shown. If students did not complete the second exploration, work through the derivation.
- **Teaching Tip:** Draw the cross sections showing the right triangles.
- Write the *Core Concept*. Students sometimes have difficulty with this formula because of the fraction.
- **? MP2:** "How do you find the volume of the soccer ball?" Cube the radius and multiply by $\frac{4}{3}\pi$. Label the answer in cubic inches.

EXAMPLE 4 **Finding the Volume of a Sphere**

The surface area of a sphere is 324π square centimeters. Find the volume of the sphere.

SOLUTION

Step 1 Use the surface area to find the radius.

$$S = 4\pi r^2 \qquad \text{Formula for surface area of a sphere}$$
$$324\pi = 4\pi r^2 \qquad \text{Substitute } 324\pi \text{ for } S.$$
$$81 = r^2 \qquad \text{Divide each side by } 4\pi.$$
$$9 = r \qquad \text{Find the positive square root.}$$

The radius is 9 centimeters.

Step 2 Use the radius to find the volume.

$$V = \tfrac{4}{3}\pi r^3 \qquad \text{Formula for volume of a sphere}$$
$$= \tfrac{4}{3}\pi(9)^3 \qquad \text{Substitute 9 for } r.$$
$$= 972\pi \qquad \text{Simplify.}$$
$$\approx 3053.63 \qquad \text{Use a calculator.}$$

▶ The volume is 972π, or about 3053.63 cubic centimeters.

EXAMPLE 5 **Finding the Volume of a Composite Solid**

Find the volume of the composite solid.

SOLUTION

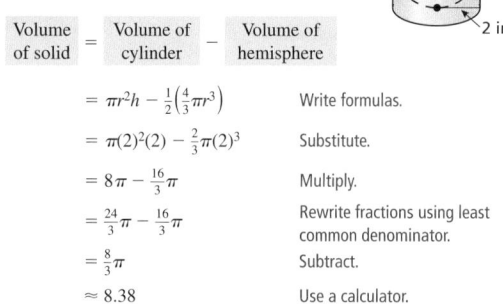

$$
\begin{array}{ccc}
\boxed{\begin{array}{c}\text{Volume} \\ \text{of solid}\end{array}} & = & \boxed{\begin{array}{c}\text{Volume of} \\ \text{cylinder}\end{array}} - \boxed{\begin{array}{c}\text{Volume of} \\ \text{hemisphere}\end{array}}
\end{array}
$$

$$= \pi r^2 h - \tfrac{1}{2}\left(\tfrac{4}{3}\pi r^3\right) \qquad \text{Write formulas.}$$
$$= \pi(2)^2(2) - \tfrac{2}{3}\pi(2)^3 \qquad \text{Substitute.}$$
$$= 8\pi - \tfrac{16}{3}\pi \qquad \text{Multiply.}$$
$$= \tfrac{24}{3}\pi - \tfrac{16}{3}\pi \qquad \begin{array}{l}\text{Rewrite fractions using least} \\ \text{common denominator.}\end{array}$$
$$= \tfrac{8}{3}\pi \qquad \text{Subtract.}$$
$$\approx 8.38 \qquad \text{Use a calculator.}$$

▶ The volume is $\tfrac{8}{3}\pi$, or about 8.38 cubic inches.

Monitoring Progress 🔊 Help in English and Spanish at *BigIdeasMath.com*

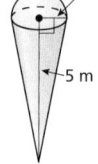

4. The radius of a sphere is 5 yards. Find the volume of the sphere.

5. The diameter of a sphere is 36 inches. Find the volume of the sphere.

6. The surface area of a sphere is 576π square centimeters. Find the volume of the sphere.

7. Find the volume of the composite solid at the left.

Section 11.8   Surface Areas and Volumes of Spheres   **651**

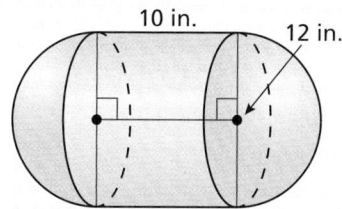

Extra Example 4
The surface area of a sphere is 676π square inches. Find the volume of the sphere.
The volume is about 2929.33π, or about 9202.77 cubic inches.

Extra Example 5
Find the volume of the composite solid.

The volume is 648π, or about 2036 cubic inches.

MONITORING PROGRESS ANSWERS

4. about 523.60 yd^3
5. about 24,429.02 in.^{3}
6. about 7238.23 cm^3
7. about 7.33 m^3

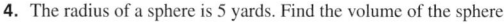

Laurie's Notes | **Teacher Actions**

- **Pass the Problem:** Review this technique. Pose Example 4, and say that each part of the problem is to be solved. Give partners a minute of discussion time (if needed) before they begin. Call "swap" and have partners continue to solve. Have partners debrief.
- **Turn and Talk:** "How can you find the volume of the composite figure in Example 5?" Discuss and have partners find the volume.

Closure

- **3-2-1:** Hand out a *3-2-1* reflection sheet as described on page T-214.

ANSWERS

1. The plane must contain the center of the sphere.

2. *Sample answer:* A hemisphere is one-half of a sphere.

3. about 201.06 ft²

4. about 706.86 cm²

5. about 1052.09 m²

6. about 50.27 ft²

7. 1 ft

8. 16 in.

9. 30 m

10. 14 cm

11. about 157.08 m²

12. about 226.19 in.²

13. about 2144.66 m³

14. about 268.08 ft³

15. about 5575.28 yd³

16. about 1436.76 ft³

17. about 4188.79 cm³

18. about 179.59 in.³

19. about 33.51 ft³

20. about 5575.28 cm³

21. The radius was squared instead of cubed;
$V = \frac{4}{3}\pi(6)^3 \approx 904.78$ ft³

Vocabulary and Core Concept Check

1. **VOCABULARY** When a plane intersects a sphere, what must be true for the intersection to be a great circle?

2. **WRITING** Explain the difference between a sphere and a hemisphere.

Monitoring Progress and Modeling with Mathematics

In Exercises 3–6, find the surface area of the sphere. *(See Example 1.)*

3.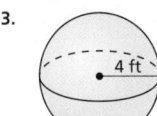

4.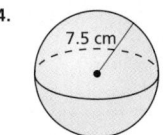

5.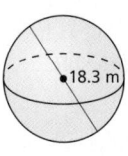

6.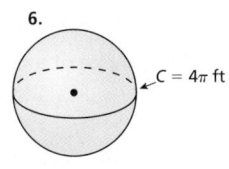

In Exercises 7–10, find the indicated measure. *(See Example 2.)*

7. Find the radius of a sphere with a surface area of 4π square feet.

8. Find the radius of a sphere with a surface area of 1024π square inches.

9. Find the diameter of a sphere with a surface area of 900π square meters.

10. Find the diameter of a sphere with a surface area of 196π square centimeters.

In Exercises 11 and 12, find the surface area of the hemisphere.

11.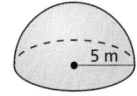

12.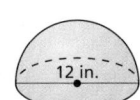

In Exercises 13–18, find the volume of the sphere. *(See Example 3.)*

13.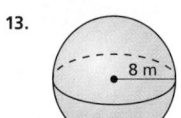

14.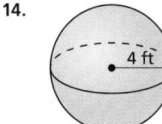

15.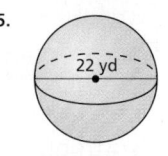

16.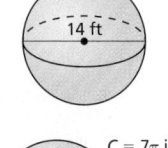

17.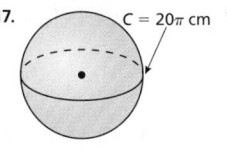

18.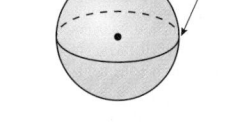

In Exercises 19 and 20, find the volume of the sphere with the given surface area. *(See Example 4.)*

19. Surface area = 16π ft²

20. Surface area = 484π cm²

21. **ERROR ANALYSIS** Describe and correct the error in finding the volume of the sphere.

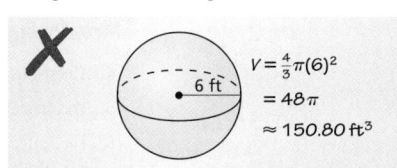

22. ERROR ANALYSIS Describe and correct the error in finding the volume of the sphere.

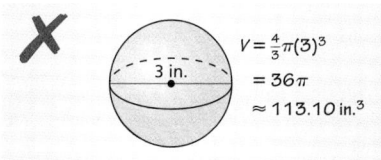

$$V = \frac{4}{3}\pi(3)^3$$
$$= 36\pi$$
$$\approx 113.10 \text{ in.}^3$$

In Exercises 23–26, find the volume of the composite solid. *(See Example 5.)*

23.

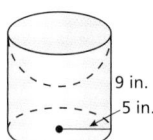

9 in.
5 in.

24.

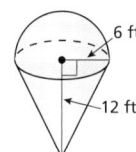

6 ft
12 ft

25.

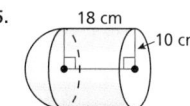

18 cm
10 cm

26.

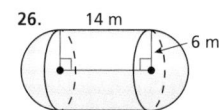

14 m
6 m

In Exercises 27–32, find the surface area and volume of the ball.

27. bowling ball

$d = 8.5$ in.

28. basketball

$C = 29.5$ in.

29. softball

$C = 12$ in.

30. golf ball

$d = 1.7$ in.

31. volleyball

$C = 26$ in.

32. baseball

$C = 9$ in.

33. MAKING AN ARGUMENT You friend claims that if the radius of a sphere is doubled, then the surface area of the sphere will also be doubled. Is your friend correct? Explain your reasoning.

34. REASONING A semicircle with a diameter of 18 inches is rotated about its diameter. Find the surface area and the volume of the solid formed.

35. MODELING WITH MATHEMATICS A silo has the dimensions shown. The top of the silo is a hemispherical shape. Find the volume of the silo.

60 ft
20 ft

36. MODELING WITH MATHEMATICS Three tennis balls are stored in a cylindrical container with a height of 8 inches and a radius of 1.43 inches. The circumference of a tennis ball is 8 inches.

a. Find the volume of a tennis ball.

b. Find the amount of space within the cylinder not taken up by the tennis balls.

37. ANALYZING RELATIONSHIPS Use the table shown for a sphere.

Radius	Surface area	Volume
3 in.	36π in.^{2}	36π in.^{3}
6 in.		
9 in.		
12 in.		

a. Copy and complete the table. Leave your answers in terms of π.

b. What happens to the surface area of the sphere when the radius is doubled? tripled? quadrupled?

c. What happens to the volume of the sphere when the radius is doubled? tripled? quadrupled?

38. MATHEMATICAL CONNECTIONS A sphere has a diameter of $4(x + 3)$ centimeters and a surface area of 784π square centimeters. Find the value of x.

Dynamic Teaching Tools

Dynamic Assessment & Progress Monitoring Tool

Interactive Whiteboard Lesson Library

Dynamic Classroom with Dynamic Investigations

ANSWERS

22. The diameter was used instead of the radius; $V = \frac{4}{3}\pi(1.5)^3 \approx 14.14$ in.^{3}

23. about 445.06 in.^{3}

24. about 904.78 ft^3

25. about 7749.26 cm^3

26. about 2488.14 m^3

27. $S \approx 226.98$ in.^{2}; $V \approx 321.56$ in.^{3}

28. $S \approx 277.01$ in.^{2}; $V \approx 433.53$ in.^{3}

29. $S \approx 45.84$ in.^{2}; $V \approx 29.18$ in.^{3}

30. $S \approx 9.08$ in.^{2}; $V \approx 2.57$ in.^{3}

31. $S \approx 215.18$ in.^{2}; $V \approx 296.80$ in.^{3}

32. $S \approx 25.78$ in.^{2}; $V \approx 12.31$ in.^{3}

33. no; The surface area is quadrupled.

34. about 1017.88 in.^{2}; about 3053.63 in.^{3}

35. about 20,944 ft^3

36. a. about 8.65 in.^{3}

b. about 25.46 in.^{3}

37. a. 144π in.^{2}, 288π in.^{3}; 324π in.^{2}, 972π in.^{3}; 576π in.^{2}, 2304π in.^{3}

b. It is multiplied by 4; It is multiplied by 9; It is multiplied by 16.

c. It is multiplied by 8; It is multiplied by 27; It is multiplied by 64.

38. 4

ANSWERS

39. a. Earth: about 197.1 million mi²; moon: about 14.7 million mi²

b. The surface area of the Earth is about 13.4 times greater than the surface area of the moon.

c. about 137.9 million mi²

40. a. about 80.9 million mi²

b. about 41%

41. about 50.27 in.²; *Sample answer:* The side length of the cube is the diameter of the sphere.

42. the hemisphere; *Sample answer:* The cone fits inside the hemisphere.

43. $V = \frac{1}{3}rS$

44. *Sample answer:* If θ is in radians, then $S = 2r^2\theta$.

45–51. See Additional Answers.

Mini-Assessment

1. Find the surface area and volume of a sphere with radius $\frac{3}{4}$ foot.

$S = \frac{9}{4}\pi$, or about 7.07 square feet;
$V = \frac{9}{16}\pi$, or about 1.77 cubic feet

2. The surface area of a sphere is 368.64π cubic centimeters. Find the diameter of the sphere.

19.2 centimeters

3. Find the surface area and volume of the sphere.

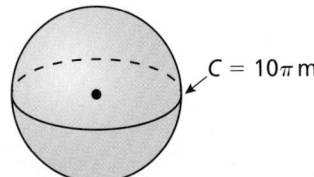

$S = 100\pi$, or about 314.16 square meters; $V = \frac{500}{3}\pi$, or about 523.60 cubic meters

4. Find the volume of the composite solid.

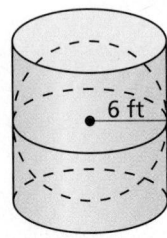

$432\pi - 288\pi = 144\pi$, or about 452.39 cubic feet

654   Chapter 11

---

39. MODELING WITH MATHEMATICS The radius of Earth is about 3960 miles. The radius of the moon is about 1080 miles.

a. Find the surface area of Earth and the moon.

b. Compare the surface areas of Earth and the moon.

c. About 70% of the surface of Earth is water. How many square miles of water are on Earth's surface?

40. MODELING WITH MATHEMATICS The Torrid Zone on Earth is the area between the Tropic of Cancer and the Tropic of Capricorn. The distance between these two tropics is about 3250 miles. You can estimate the distance as the height of a cylindrical belt around the Earth at the equator.

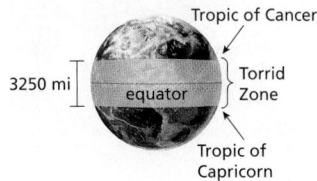

a. Estimate the surface area of the Torrid Zone. (The radius of Earth is about 3960 miles.)

b. A meteorite is equally likely to hit anywhere on Earth. Estimate the probability that a meteorite will land in the Torrid Zone.

41. ABSTRACT REASONING A sphere is inscribed in a cube with a volume of 64 cubic inches. What is the surface area of the sphere? Explain your reasoning.

42. HOW DO YOU SEE IT? The formula for the volume of a hemisphere and a cone are shown. If each solid has the same radius and $r = h$, which solid will have a greater volume? Explain your reasoning.

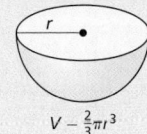   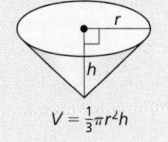

$V = \frac{2}{3}\pi r^3$ $V = \frac{1}{3}\pi r^2 h$

43. CRITICAL THINKING Let V be the volume of a sphere, S be the surface area of the sphere, and r be the radius of the sphere. Write an equation for V in terms of r and S. $\left(Hint:\text{ Start with the ratio } \frac{V}{S}.\right)$

44. THOUGHT PROVOKING A *spherical lune* is the region between two great circles of a sphere. Find the formula for the area of a lune.

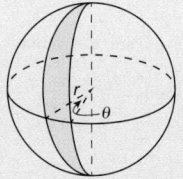

45. CRITICAL THINKING The volume of a right cylinder is the same as the volume of a sphere. The radius of the sphere is 1 inch. Give three possibilities for the dimensions of the cylinder.

46. PROBLEM SOLVING A *spherical cap* is a portion of a sphere cut off by a plane. The formula for the volume of a spherical cap is $V = \frac{\pi h}{6}(3a^2 + h^2)$, where a is the radius of the base of the cap and h is the height of the cap. Use the diagram and given information to find the volume of each spherical cap.

a. $r = 5$ ft, $a = 4$ ft

b. $r = 34$ cm, $a = 30$ cm

c. $r = 13$ m, $h = 8$ m

d. $r = 75$ in., $h = 54$ in.

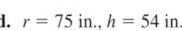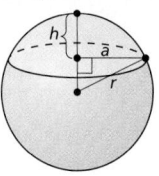

47. CRITICAL THINKING A sphere with a radius of 2 inches is inscribed in a right cone with a height of 6 inches. Find the surface area and the volume of the cone.

Maintaining Mathematical Proficiency   Reviewing what you learned in previous grades and lessons

Solve the triangle. Round decimal answers to the nearest tenth. *(Section 9.7)*

48. $A = 26°, C = 35°, b = 13$ **49.** $B = 102°, C = 43°, b = 21$

50. $a = 23, b = 24, c = 20$ **51.** $A = 103°, b = 15, c = 24$

If students need help...	If students got it...
Resources by Chapter • Practice A and Practice B • Puzzle Time	Resources by Chapter • Enrichment and Extension • Cumulative Review
Student Journal • Practice	Start the *next* Section
Differentiating the Lesson Skills Review Handbook	

Core Vocabulary

volume, *p. 626*

Cavalieri's Principle, *p. 626*

density, *p. 628*

similar solids, *p. 630*

lateral surface of a cone, *p. 642*

chord of a sphere, *p. 648*

great circle, *p. 648*

ANSWERS

1. *Sample answer:* yes; The larger container usually has a lesser unit cost.

2. *Sample answer:* The scale factor is $\frac{1}{4}$ and the ratio of the volumes is the scale factor cubed.

3. *Sample answer:* Substitute $r = 2x + 6$ into the surface area formula and set equal to 784π, then solve for x.

Core Concepts

Section 11.5

Cavalieri's Principle, *p. 626*

Volume of a Prism, *p. 626*

Volume of a Cylinder, *p. 627*

Density, *p. 628*

Similar Solids, *p. 630*

Section 11.6

Volume of a Pyramid, *p. 636*

Section 11.7

Surface Area of a Right Cone, *p. 642*

Volume of a Cone, *p. 643*

Section 11.8

Surface Area of a Sphere, *p. 648*

Volume of a Sphere, *p. 650*

Mathematical Practices

1. Search online for advertisements for products that come in different sizes. Then compare the unit prices, as done in Exercise 44 on page 633. Do you get results similar to Exercise 44? Explain.

2. In Exercise 15 on page 639, explain why the volume changed by a factor of $\frac{1}{64}$.

3. In Exercise 38 on page 653, explain the steps you used to find the value of x.

— — — — — Performance Task — — — — —

Water Park Renovation

The city council will consider reopening the closed water park if your team can come up with a cost analysis for painting some of the structures, filling the pool water reservoirs, and resurfacing some of the surfaces. What is your plan to convince the city council to open the water park?

To explore the answers to these questions and more, go to *BigIdeasMath.com*.

655

ANSWERS

1. about 30.00 ft
2. about 56.57 cm
3. about 26.09 in.
4. 218 ft
5. about 169.65 in.^{2}
6. about 17.72 in.^{2}
7. 173.166 ft^2

11.1 Circumference and Arc Length (pp. 593–600)

The arc length of $\overarc{QR}$ is 6.54 feet. Find the radius of $\odot P$.

$$\frac{\text{Arc length of } \overarc{QR}}{2\pi r} = \frac{m\overarc{QR}}{360°}$$ Formula for arc length

$$\frac{6.54}{2\pi r} = \frac{75°}{360°}$$ Substitute.

$$6.54(360) = 75(2\pi r)$$ Cross Products Property

$$5.00 \approx r$$ Solve for r.

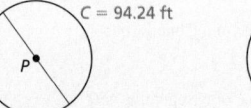

▶ The radius of $\odot P$ is about 5 feet.

Find the indicated measure.

1. diameter of $\odot P$ 2. circumference of $\odot F$ 3. arc length of $\overarc{AB}$

4. A mountain bike tire has a diameter of 26 inches. To the nearest foot, how far does the tire travel when it makes 32 revolutions?

11.2 Areas of Circles and Sectors (pp. 601–608)

Find the area of sector *ADB*.

$$\text{Area of sector } ADB = \frac{m\overarc{AB}}{360°} \cdot \pi r^2$$ Formula for area of a sector

$$= \frac{80°}{360°} \cdot \pi \cdot 10^2$$ Substitute.

$$\approx 69.81$$ Use a calculator.

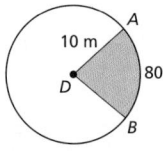

▶ The area of sector *ADB* is about 69.81 square meters.

Find the area of the blue shaded region.

5. 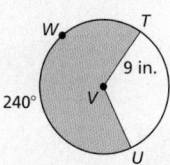 6. 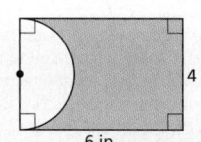 7.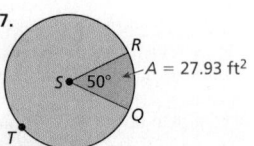

ANSWERS

8. 130 square units
9. 96 square units
10. 105 square units
11. about 201.20 square units
12. about 167.11 square units
13. about 37.30 square units
14. about 119.29 in.²

11.3 **Areas of Polygons** *(pp. 609–616)*

A regular hexagon is inscribed in ⊙*H*. Find
(a) *m∠EHG*, and (b) the area of the hexagon.

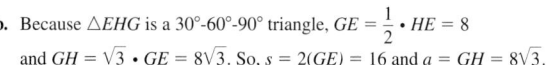

a. ∠*FHE* is a central angle, so $m\angle FHE = \frac{360°}{6} = 60°$.

   Apothem $\overline{GH}$ bisects ∠*FHE*.

   ▶ So, *m∠EHG* = 30°.

b. Because △*EHG* is a 30°-60°-90° triangle, $GE = \frac{1}{2} \cdot HE = 8$
   and $GH = \sqrt{3} \cdot GE = 8\sqrt{3}$. So, *s* = 2(*GE*) = 16 and *a* = *GH* = 8√3.

   ▶ The area is $A = \frac{1}{2}a \cdot ns = \frac{1}{2}(8\sqrt{3})(6)(16) \approx 665.1$ square units.

Find the area of the kite or rhombus.

8.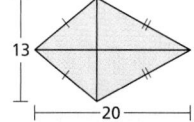

9.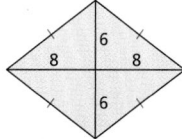

10.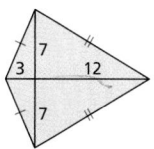

Find the area of the regular polygon.

11.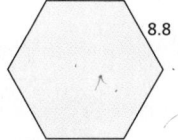

12.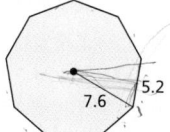

13.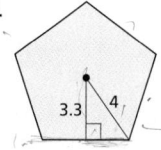

14. A platter is in the shape of a regular octagon with an apothem of 6 inches. Find the area of the platter.

11.4 **Three-Dimensional Figures** *(pp. 617–622)*

Sketch the solid produced by rotating the figure around
the given axis. Then identify and describe the solid.

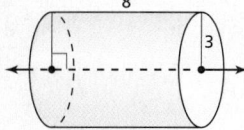

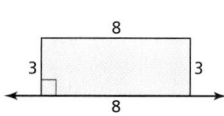

▶ The solid is a cylinder with a height of 8 and a radius of 3.

15.

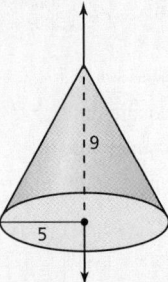

cone with height 9 and base radius 5

16.

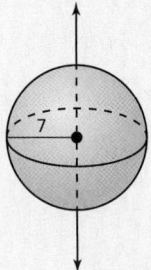

sphere with radius 7

17.

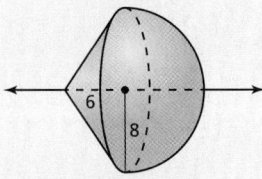

cone with height 6 and base radius 8
and hemisphere with radius 8

18. rectangle

19. square

20. triangle

21. 11.34 m³

22. about 100.53 mm³

23. about 27.53 yd³

Sketch the solid produced by rotating the figure around the given axis. Then identify and describe the solid.

15.

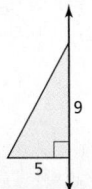

16.

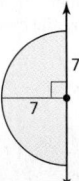

17.

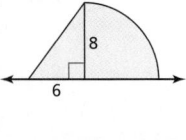

Describe the cross section formed by the intersection of the plane and the solid.

18.

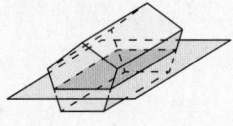

19.

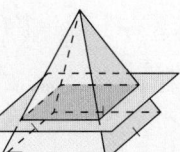

20.

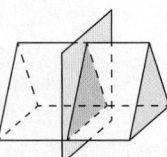

11.5 Volumes of Prisms and Cylinders *(pp. 625–634)*

Find the volume of the triangular prism.

The area of a base is $B = \frac{1}{2}(6)(8) = 24$ in.² and the height is $h = 5$ in.

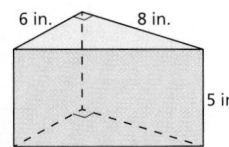

$V = Bh$ Formula for volume of a prism

$= 24(5)$ Substitute.

$= 120$ Simplify.

▶ The volume is 120 cubic inches.

Find the volume of the solid.

21.

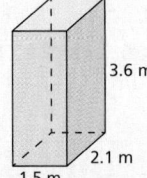

22.

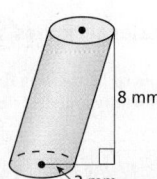

23.

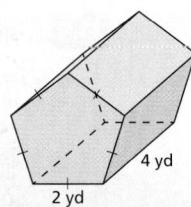

ANSWERS

24. 189 ft³
25. 400 yd³
26. 300 m³
27. about 3.46 in.
28. 12 in.

11.6 Volumes of Pyramids (pp. 635–640)

Find the volume of the pyramid.

$$V = \tfrac{1}{3}Bh \qquad \text{Formula for volume of a pyramid}$$

$$= \tfrac{1}{3}\left(\tfrac{1}{2} \cdot 5 \cdot 8\right)(12) \qquad \text{Substitute.}$$

$$= 80 \qquad \text{Simplify.}$$

▶ The volume is 80 cubic meters.

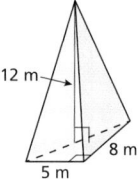

Find the volume of the pyramid.

24.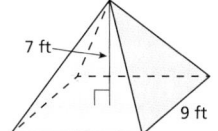

25.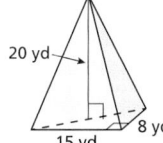

26.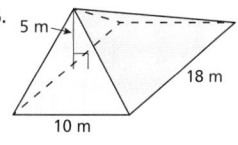

27. The volume of a square pyramid is 60 cubic inches and the height is 15 inches. Find the side length of the square base.

28. The volume of a square pyramid is 1024 cubic inches. The base has a side length of 16 inches. Find the height of the pyramid.

11.7 Surface Areas and Volumes of Cones (pp. 641–646)

Find the (a) surface area and (b) volume of the cone.

a. $S = \pi r^2 + \pi r \ell$ Formula for surface area of a cone

$$= \pi \cdot 5^2 + \pi(5)(13) \qquad \text{Substitute.}$$

$$= 90\pi \qquad \text{Simplify.}$$

$$\approx 282.74 \qquad \text{Use a calculator.}$$

▶ The surface area is 90π, or about 282.74 square centimeters.

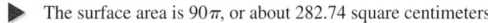

b. $V = \tfrac{1}{3}\pi r^2 h$ Formula for volume of a cone

$$= \tfrac{1}{3}\pi \cdot 5^2 \cdot 12 \qquad \text{Substitute.}$$

$$= 100\pi \qquad \text{Simplify.}$$

$$\approx 314.16 \qquad \text{Use a calculator.}$$

▶ The volume is 100π, or about 314.16 cubic centimeters.

Find the surface area and the volume of the cone.

29.
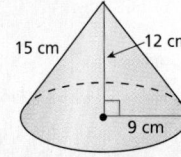
15 cm   12 cm
9 cm

30.
34 cm   30 cm
16 cm

31.
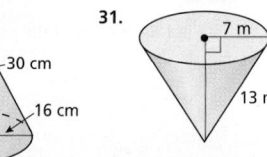
7 m
13 m

32. A cone with a diameter of 16 centimeters has a volume of 320π cubic centimeters. Find the height of the cone.

11.8   Surface Areas and Volumes of Spheres   *(pp. 647–654)*

Find the (a) surface area and (b) volume of the sphere.

a. $S = 4\pi r^2$ Formula for surface area of a sphere

    $= 4\pi(18)^2$ Substitute 18 for *r*.

    $= 1296\pi$ Simplify.

    ≈ 4071.50 Use a calculator.

18 in.

▶ The surface area is 1296π, or about 4071.50 square inches.

b. $V = \frac{4}{3}\pi r^3$ Formula for volume of a sphere

    $= \frac{4}{3}\pi(18)^3$ Substitute 18 for *r*.

    $= 7776\pi$ Simplify.

    $\approx 24,429.02$ Use a calculator.

▶ The volume is 7776π, or about 24,429.02 cubic inches.

Find the surface area and the volume of the sphere.

33.
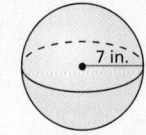
7 in.

34.
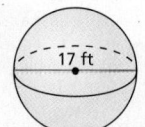
17 ft

35.
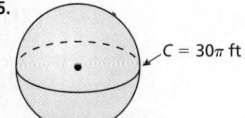
C = 30π ft

36. The shape of Mercury can be approximated by a sphere with a diameter of 4880 kilometers. Find the surface area and the volume of Mercury.

37. A solid is composed of a cube with a side length of 6 meters and a hemisphere with a diameter of 6 meters. Find the volume of the composite solid.

11 Chapter Test

Find the volume of the solid.

1.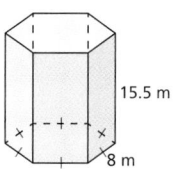
15.5 m
8 m

2.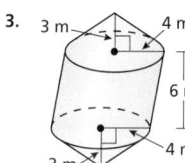
3.2 ft

3.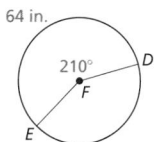
3 m   4 m
6 m
4 m
3 m

4.
4 ft
8 ft
5 ft 2 ft

Find the indicated measure.

5. circumference of ⊙F

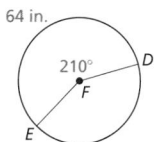
64 in.
210°
F   D
E

6. $m\widehat{GH}$

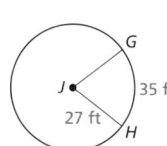
G
J   35 ft
27 ft
H

7. area of shaded sector

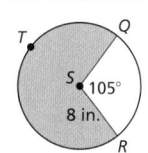
T   Q
S 105°
8 in.
R

8. Sketch the composite solid produced by rotating the figure around the given axis. Then identify and describe the composite solid.

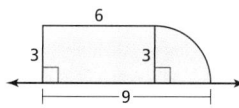
6
3   3
9

9. Find the surface area of a right cone with a diameter of 10 feet and a height of 12 feet.

10. You have a funnel with the dimensions shown.

   a. Find the approximate volume of the funnel.

   b. You use the funnel to put oil in a car. Oil flows out of the funnel at a rate of 45 milliliters per second. How long will it take to empty the funnel when it is full of oil? (1 mL = 1 cm³)

   c. How long would it take to empty a funnel with a radius of 10 centimeters and a height of 6 centimeters if oil flows out of the funnel at a rate of 45 milliliters per second?

   d. Explain why you can claim that the time calculated in part (c) is greater than the time calculated in part (b) without doing any calculations.

   6 cm
   10 cm

11. A water bottle in the shape of a cylinder has a volume of 500 cubic centimeters. The diameter of a base is 7.5 centimeters. What is the height of the bottle? Justify your answer.

12. Find the area of a dodecagon (12 sides) with a side length of 9 inches.

13. In general, a cardboard fan with a greater area does a better job of moving air and cooling you. The fan shown is a sector of a cardboard circle. Another fan has a radius of 6 centimeters and an intercepted arc of 150°. Which fan does a better job of cooling you?

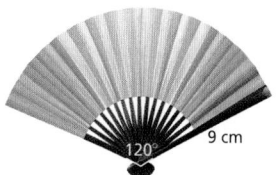
120°   9 cm

1. about 2577.29 m³
2. about 17.16 ft³
3. about 402.12 m³
4. $93\frac{1}{3}$ ft³
5. about 109.71 in.
6. about 74.27°
7. about 142.42 in.²
8.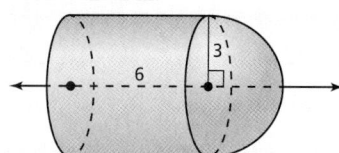
   6   3

   cylinder with height 6 and base radius 3, and hemisphere with radius 3
9. 90π ft² or about 282.74 ft²
10. a. about 376.99 cm³
    b. about 8.38 sec
    c. about 13.96 sec
    d. *Sample answer:* Changing the radius has a greater effect than changing the height.
11. about 11.32 cm; *Sample answer:* $500 = \pi(3.75)^3 h$, so $h \approx 11.32$.
12. about 906.89 in.²
13. the fan shown

If students need help...	If students got it...
Lesson Tutorials	Resources by Chapter • Enrichment and Extension • Cumulative Review
Skills Review Handbook	Performance Task
BigIdeasMath.com	Start the *next* Section

1. a. trapezoid
   b. pentagon
   c. rectangle
2. $\overline{PQ} \perp \overleftrightarrow{RS}$
3. a. about 4650 mm³
   b. about 75,267 mm³
4. A

11 Cumulative Assessment

1. Identify the shape of the cross section formed by the intersection of the plane and the solid.

   a.   b.   c.

   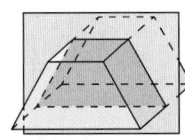   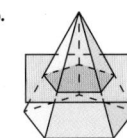   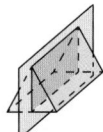

2. In the diagram, $\overleftrightarrow{RS}$ is tangent to $\odot P$ at Q and $\overline{PQ}$ is a radius of $\odot P$. What must be true about $\overleftrightarrow{RS}$ and $\overline{PQ}$? Select all that apply.

   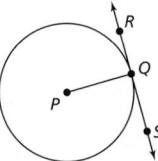

   | $PQ = \frac{1}{2}RS$ | $PQ = RS$ | $\overline{PQ}$ is tangent to $\odot P$. | $\overline{PQ} \perp \overleftrightarrow{RS}$ |

3. A crayon can be approximated by a composite solid made from a cylinder and a cone. A crayon box is a rectangular prism. The dimensions of a crayon and a crayon box containing 24 crayons are shown.

   a. Find the volume of a crayon.

   b. Find the amount of space within the crayon box not taken up by the crayons.

   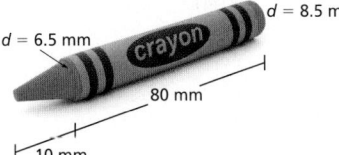

4. What is the equation of the line passing through the point (2, 5) that is parallel to the line $x + \frac{1}{2}y = -1$?

   Ⓐ $y = -2x + 9$ Ⓑ $y = 2x + 1$

   Ⓒ $y = \frac{1}{2}x + 4$ Ⓓ $y = -\frac{1}{2}x + 6$

5. The top of the Washington Monument in Washington, D.C., is a square pyramid, called a *pyramidion*. What is the volume of the pyramidion?

(A) 22,019.63 ft³

(B) 172,006.91 ft³

(C) 66,058.88 ft³

(D) 207,530.08 ft³

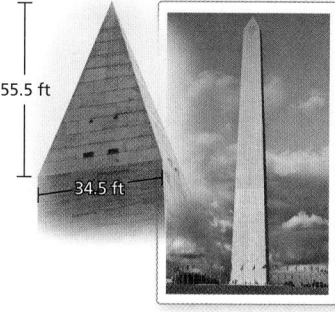

55.5 ft

34.5 ft

6. Prove or disprove that the point $(1, \sqrt{3})$ lies on the circle centered at the origin and containing the point $(0, 2)$.

7. Your friend claims that the house shown can be described as a composite solid made from a rectangular prism and a triangular prism. Do you support your friend's claim? Explain your reasoning.

8. The diagram shows a square pyramid and a cone. Both solids have the same height, h, and the base of the cone has radius r. According to Cavalieri's Principle, the solids will have the same volume if the square base has sides of length _____.

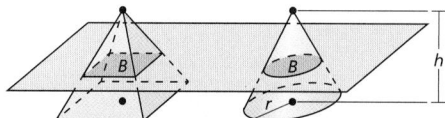

B B h r

9. About 19,400 people live in a region with a 5-mile radius. Find the population density in people per square mile.

Chapter 12 Pacing Guide	
Chapter Opener/ Mathematical Practices	0.5 Day
Section 1	1.5 Days
Section 2	2 Days
Section 3	2 Days
Quiz	0.5 Day
Section 4	1.5 Days
Section 5	2 Days
Section 6	2 Days
Chapter Review/ Chapter Tests	2 Days
Total Chapter 12	14 Days
Year-to-Date	160 Days

12 Probability

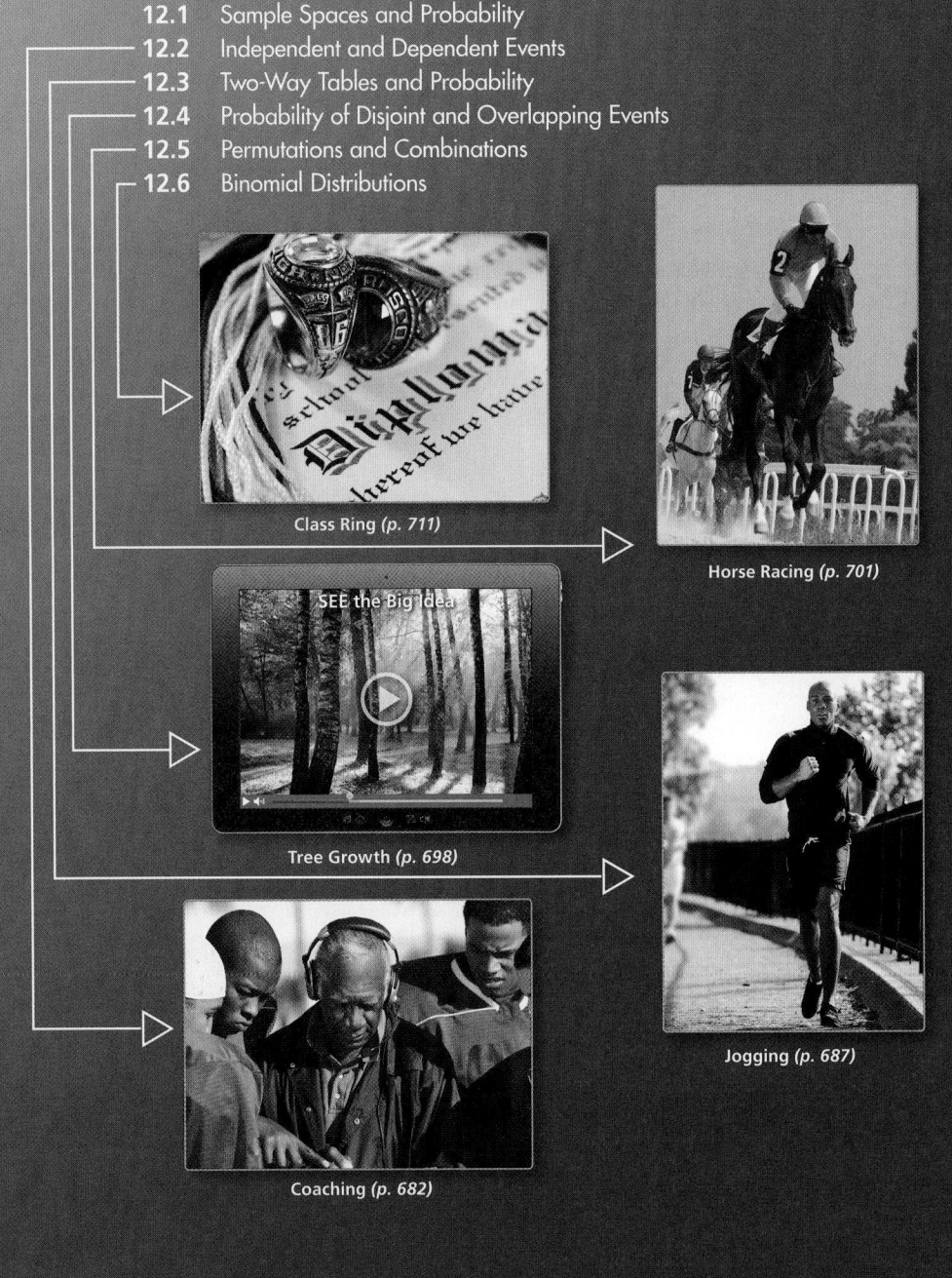

Class Ring (p. 711)

Horse Racing (p. 701)

SEE the Big Idea

Tree Growth (p. 698)

Jogging (p. 687)

Coaching (p. 682)

Chapter Summary

- This chapter on probability presumes knowledge of basic probability concepts from middle school and some data analysis techniques from Algebra 1.
- The chapter begins with finding sample spaces for a variety of classic contexts. The next three lessons focus on computing the probability of independent and dependent events, and compound events. Students construct and interpret two-way frequency tables of data and use the entries to compute joint and marginal relative frequencies.
- Permutations and combinations are introduced to allow students to compute probabilities of compound events and to solve real-life problems.
- The last lesson of the chapter introduces students to probability distributions. One type of probability distribution is a binomial distribution.

Scaffolding in the Classroom

Graphic Organizers: Y-Chart

A Y-Chart can be used to compare two topics. Students list differences between the two topics in the branches of the Y and similarities in the base of the Y. A Y-Chart serves as a good tool for assessing students' knowledge of a pair of topics that have subtle but important differences. You can include blank Y-Charts on tests or quizzes for this purpose.

 COMMON CORE PROGRESSION

Middle School
- Find outcomes of events.
- Understand that probability is the likelihood of an event occurring, expressed as a number from 0 to 1.
- Collect data to find experimental probability and use it to predict a frequency.
- Develop probability models and use them to find probabilities.
- Find probability of compound events.

Algebra 1
- Describe the shapes of data distributions.
- Make two-way tables.
- Recognize associations in data using two-way tables.
- Find and interpret marginal frequencies.

Geometry
- Find probabilities of independent and dependent events.
- Use conditional relative frequencies to find conditional probabilities.
- Use the formulas for the number of permutations and the number of combinations.
- Construct and interpret probability distributions and binomial distributions.

Standards Summary		
Section	**Common Core State Standards**	
12.1	Learning	HSS-CP.A.1
12.2	Learning	HSS-CP.A.1, HSS-CP.A.2, HSS-CP.A.3, HSS-CP.A.5, HSS-CP.B.6, HSS-CP.B.8
12.3	Learning	HSS-CP.A.4, HSS-CP.A.5
12.4	Learning	HSS-CP.A.1, HSS-CP.B.7
12.5	Learning	HSS-CP.B.9
12.6	Learning	HSS-CP.B.9

All students need to participate.
When a small group of students continually answers the questions in your classroom, no one else has to think. Try asking a different student whether they agree with the answer given, and then follow up with why or why not.

Laurie's Notes

Maintaining Mathematical Proficiency

Finding a Percent

- Review with students what each part of the percent proportion means.
- Tell students that they can also find the percent using an equation.

COMMON ERROR Students may invert the values for a and w.

Making a Histogram

- Review the differences between bar graphs and histograms.
- Discuss with students how individual pieces of data are not shown in a histogram.

COMMON ERROR Students may not use equal intervals for the bars in their histograms.

Mathematical Practices (continued on page 666)

- The eight *Mathematical Practices* focus attention on how mathematics is learned—process versus content. Page 666 demonstrates how mathematically proficient students apply the mathematics they know to solve real-life applications. Applying mathematics to solve everyday problems is an important skill.
- Use the *Mathematical Practices* page to help students develop mathematical habits of mind—how mathematics can be explored and how mathematics is thought about.

If students need help...	If students got it...
Student Journal • Maintaining Mathematical Proficiency	Game Closet at *BigIdeasMath.com*
Lesson Tutorials	Start the *next* Section
Skills Review Handbook	

Maintaining Mathematical Proficiency

Finding a Percent

Example 1 What percent of 12 is 9?

$$\frac{a}{w} = \frac{p}{100}$$ Write the percent proportion.

$$\frac{9}{12} = \frac{p}{100}$$ Substitute 9 for a and 12 for w.

$$100 \cdot \frac{9}{12} = 100 \cdot \frac{p}{100}$$ Multiplication Property of Equality.

$$75 = p$$ Simplify.

▶ So, 9 is 75% of 12.

Write and solve a proportion to answer the question.

1. What percent of 30 is 6?   **2.** What number is 68% of 25?   **3.** 34.4 is what percent of 86?

Making a Histogram

Example 2 The frequency table shows the ages of people at a gym. Display the data in a histogram.

Age	Frequency
10–19	7
20–29	12
30–39	6
40–49	4
50–59	0
60–69	3

Step 1 Draw and label the axes.

Step 2 Draw a bar to represent the frequency of each interval.

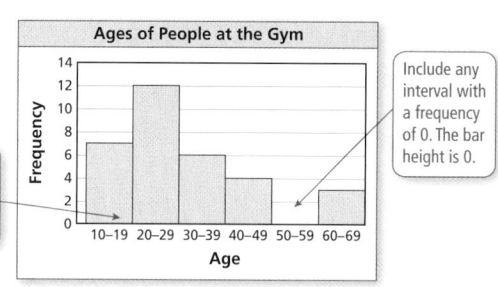

There is no space between the bars of a histogram.

Include any interval with a frequency of 0. The bar height is 0.

Display the data in a histogram.

4.

Movies Watched per Week			
Movies	0–1	2–3	4–5
Frequency	35	11	6

5. ABSTRACT REASONING You want to purchase either a sofa or an arm chair at a furniture store. Each item has the same retail price. The sofa is 20% off. The arm chair is 10% off, and you have a coupon to get an additional 10% off the discounted price of the chair. Are the items equally priced after the discounts are applied? Explain.

Dynamic Solutions available at *BigIdeasMath.com*

Common Core State Standards

7.RP.A.3 Use proportional relationships to solve … percent problems.

HSS-ID.A.1 Represent data with plots on the real number line (… histograms, …).

ANSWERS

1. $\frac{6}{30} = \frac{p}{100}$, 20%

2. $\frac{a}{25} = \frac{68}{100}$, 17

3. $\frac{34.4}{86} = \frac{p}{100}$, 40%

4.

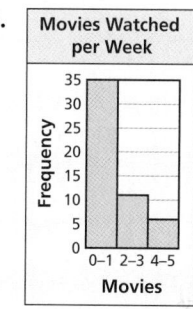

5. no; The sofa will cost 80% of the retail price and the arm chair will cost 81% of the retail price.

Vocabulary Review

Have students make a Notetaking Organizer for a histogram. Include the following words.

- Frequency
- Interval

1. equally likely to happen or not
   happen; The probability of the
   event is 0.5.

2. unlikely; The probability of the
   event is (0.5)(0.5) = 0.25.

3. *Sample answer:* rolling a number
   less than 7 on a six-sided die

Mathematical Practices

Mathematically proficient students apply the mathematics they know to solve real-life problems.

Modeling with Mathematics

🌀 Core Concept

Likelihoods and Probabilities

The **probability of an event** is a measure of the likelihood that the event will occur. Probability is a number from 0 to 1, including 0 and 1. The diagram relates *likelihoods* (described in words) and probabilities.

Words	Impossible	Unlikely	Equally likely to happen or not happen	Likely	Certain
Fraction	0	$\frac{1}{4}$	$\frac{1}{2}$	$\frac{3}{4}$	1
Decimal	0	0.25	0.5	0.75	1
Percent	0%	25%	50%	75%	100%

EXAMPLE 1 Describing Likelihoods

Describe the likelihood of each event.

Probability of an Asteroid or a Meteoroid Hitting Earth			
Name	Diameter	Probability of impact	Flyby date
a. Meteoroid	6 in.	0.75	Any day
b. Apophis	886 ft	0	2029
c. 2000 SG344	121 ft	$\frac{1}{435}$	2068–2110

SOLUTION

a. On any given day, it is *likely* that a meteoroid of this size will enter Earth's atmosphere. If you have ever seen a "shooting star," then you have seen a meteoroid.

b. A probability of 0 means this event is *impossible.*

c. With a probability of $\frac{1}{435} \approx 0.23\%$, this event is very *unlikely*. Of 435 identical asteroids, you would expect only one of them to hit Earth.

Monitoring Progress

In Exercises 1 and 2, describe the event as unlikely, equally likely to happen or not happen, or likely. Explain your reasoning.

1. The oldest child in a family is a girl.

2. The two oldest children in a family with three children are girls.

3. Give an example of an event that is certain to occur.

Laurie's Notes Mathematical Practices (continued from page T-665)

- Students will be working with probability in this chapter. In the *Core Concept*, the probability of an event is described. The likelihood that the event will occur is a number from 0 to 1, inclusive.

- **?** Pose Example 1. Ask, "What is the likelihood of an asteroid or meteoroid hitting Earth?" It depends on the size of the asteroid or meteoroid. Have students describe the likelihood of each event.

- Give time for students to work through the *Monitoring Progress* questions, and then discuss as a class.

Overview of Section 12.1

Introduction

- Students should have some beginning knowledge of probability from earlier grades.
- This lesson begins with finding sample spaces for a variety of events, a needed skill in finding theoretical and experimental probabilities.
- A geometric probability problem using area is included in the lesson.

Formative Assessment Tips

- **Predict, Explain, Observe (P-E-O Probe):** This technique provides students the opportunity to make a prediction or to select a prediction from a set of options. Students explain or give reasons why their prediction makes sense, and then they test out their prediction. Finally, they analyze the results against their prediction and make adjustments to their thinking.

- This technique gives students the opportunity to reason about a problem, situation, or concept that is being probed, and students are asked to make a prediction related to the probe. Explaining the reason for their prediction is an important step. Curiosity piqued, students think of how to investigate their prediction. Students carry out their investigation and analyze the results. If their prediction is correct and it was based on valid reasoning (versus an educated guess), then their reasoning has been confirmed. If the results are not exactly what they had predicted, then the cognitive dissonance created should lead to more discussion, rethinking, and a new prediction.

- This technique is best used when you want to probe students' ideas. This technique does not need to be done only with individuals. Partners or small groups can make predictions, discussing their reasoning and rethinking their prediction after an investigation.

Pacing Suggestion

- Each one of the explorations presents a classic context for exploring the concept of probability. If you sense that your students have little familiarity with these contexts, take time for all of the explorations. Students should be comfortable with finding the sample space of an experiment before beginning the formal lesson.

HSS-CP.A.1 Describe events as subsets of a sample space (the set of outcomes) using characteristics (or categories) of the outcomes, or as unions, intersections, or complements of other events ("or," "and," "not").

Exploration

Motivate

? Hold up a used lottery ticket and ask, "What do you think my chances are of holding a winning ticket?" Answers will vary.

• Most lottery or scratch-off tickets have a statement on them about the "odds of winning," which is quite close to the probability of winning.

• Explain to students that in this chapter they will learn more about probability and how the calculations are done.

Exploration Note

• The explorations on this page present four common contexts for introducing probability. It is important for students to work through each exploration so that they gain confidence and experience in determining possible outcomes in the sample space.

Exploration 1

• **Common Misconception:** Students may believe that HTT is the same outcome as THT because there is one head and two tails. One way to help students understand that these two outcomes are different is to use coins with three different dates. Using columns to list the outcomes of each coin will help as well.

• **Extension:** Look for patterns where you have 1 coin, 2 coins, 3 coins, 4 coins, and so on.

Exploration 2

• **Teaching Tip:** Use two colors of dice to help students distinguish 1-6 and 6-1.

• **MP5 Use Appropriate Tools Strategically:** A matrix is a common way to help students organize the possible outcomes.

Exploration 3

• Students may believe that the location of the numbers influences the outcomes, meaning two 5's adjacent to one another is different from two 5's that are nonadjacent.

? "Are each of the outcomes equally likely to occur? Explain." No; There are four 5's and only two 4's.

Exploration 4

• The numbers on the marbles will help students recognize that there are multiple ways (18) to draw two red marbles.

Communicate Your Answer

• Have students work independently to answer Questions 5 and 6, and then discuss as a whole class.

Connecting to Next Step

• Listing the possible outcomes in a sample space is necessary in finding a theoretical probability, the focus of the formal lesson.

12.1 Sample Spaces and Probability

Essential Question
How can you list the possible outcomes in the sample space of an experiment?

The **sample space** of an experiment is the set of all possible outcomes for that experiment.

EXPLORATION 1   Finding the Sample Space of an Experiment

Work with a partner. In an experiment, three coins are flipped. List the possible outcomes in the sample space of the experiment.

EXPLORATION 2   Finding the Sample Space of an Experiment

Work with a partner. List the possible outcomes in the sample space of the experiment.

a. One six-sided die is rolled.

b. Two six-sided dice are rolled.

EXPLORATION 3   Finding the Sample Space of an Experiment

Work with a partner. In an experiment, a spinner is spun.

a. How many ways can you spin a 1? 2? 3? 4? 5?

b. List the sample space.

c. What is the total number of outcomes?

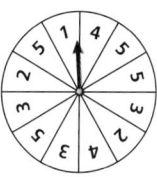

EXPLORATION 4   Finding the Sample Space of an Experiment

Work with a partner. In an experiment, a bag contains 2 blue marbles and 5 red marbles. Two marbles are drawn from the bag.

a. How many ways can you choose two blue? a red then blue? a blue then red? two red?

b. List the sample space.

c. What is the total number of outcomes?

> **LOOKING FOR A PATTERN**
>
> To be proficient in math, you need to look closely to discern a pattern or structure.

Communicate Your Answer

5. How can you list the possible outcomes in the sample space of an experiment?

6. For Exploration 3, find the ratio of the number of each possible outcome to the total number of outcomes. Then find the sum of these ratios. Repeat for Exploration 4. What do you observe?

ANSWERS

1. HHH, HHT, HTH, THH, HTT, THT, TTH, TTT

2. **a.** 1, 2, 3, 4, 5, 6

   b. 1-1, 1-2, 1-3, 1-4, 1-5, 1-6, 2-1, 2-2, 2-3, 2-4, 2-5, 2-6, 3-1, 3-2, 3-3, 3-4, 3-5, 3-6, 4-1, 4-2, 4-3, 4-4, 4-5, 4-6, 5-1, 5-2, 5-3, 5-4, 5-5, 5-6, 6-1, 6-2, 6-3, 6-4, 6-5, 6-6

3. **a.** 1; 2; 3; 2; 4

   b. 1, 2, 2, 3, 3, 3, 4, 4, 5, 5, 5, 5

   c. 12

4. **a.** 2; 10; 10; 20

   b. B1-B2, B2-B1, B1-R1, B1-R2, B1-R3, B1-R4, B1-R5, B2-R1, B2-R2, B2-R3, B2-R4, B2-R5, R1-B1, R1-B2, R2-B1, R2-B2, R3-B1, R3-B2, R4-B1, R4-B2, R5-B1, R5-B2, R1-R2, R1-R3, R1-R4, R1-R5, R2-R1, R2-R3, R2-R4, R2-R5, R3-R1, R3-R2, R3-R4, R3-R5, R4-R1, R4-R2, R4-R3, R4-R5, R5-R1, R5-R2, R5-R3, R5-R4

   c. 42

5. *Sample answer:* Make a table or diagram to show all of the possible outcomes.

6. The sum of the ratios is 1.

Extra Example 1

You spin this spinner and flip a coin. How many possible outcomes are in the sample space? List the possible outcomes.

The sample space has 8 possible outcomes. They are 1H, 1T, 2H, 2T, 3H, 3T, 4H, and 4T.

MONITORING PROGRESS ANSWERS

1. 4; HH, HT, TH, TT
2. 24; HH1, HH2, HH3, HH4, HH5, HH6, HT1, HT2, HT3, HT4, HT5, HT6, TH1, TH2, TH3, TH4, TH5, TH6, TT1, TT2, TT3, TT4, TT5, TT6

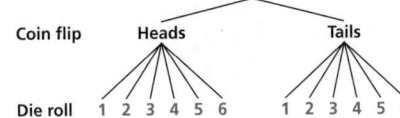

Core Vocabulary

probability experiment, *p. 668*
outcome, *p. 668*
event, *p. 668*
sample space, *p. 668*
probability of an event, *p. 668*
theoretical probability, *p. 669*
geometric probability, *p. 670*
experimental probability, *p. 671*

Previous
tree diagram

ANOTHER WAY

Using H for "heads" and T for "tails," you can list the outcomes as shown below.

H1 H2 H3 H4 H5 H6
T1 T2 T3 T4 T5 T6

What You Will Learn

▶ Find sample spaces.
▶ Find theoretical probabilities.
▶ Find experimental probabilities.

Sample Spaces

A **probability experiment** is an action, or trial, that has varying results. The possible results of a probability experiment are **outcomes**. For instance, when you roll a six-sided die, there are 6 possible outcomes: 1, 2, 3, 4, 5, or 6. A collection of one or more outcomes is an **event**, such as rolling an odd number. The set of all possible outcomes is called a **sample space**.

EXAMPLE 1 Finding a Sample Space

You flip a coin and roll a six-sided die. How many possible outcomes are in the sample space? List the possible outcomes.

SOLUTION

Use a tree diagram to find the outcomes in the sample space.

Coin flip	Heads	Tails
Die roll	1 2 3 4 5 6	1 2 3 4 5 6

▶ The sample space has 12 possible outcomes. They are listed below.

Heads, 1   Heads, 2   Heads, 3   Heads, 4   Heads, 5   Heads, 6

Tails, 1   Tails, 2   Tails, 3   Tails, 4   Tails, 5   Tails, 6

Monitoring Progress 🔊 Help in English and Spanish at *BigIdeasMath.com*

Find the number of possible outcomes in the sample space. Then list the possible outcomes.

1. You flip two coins.
2. You flip two coins and roll a six-sided die.

Theoretical Probabilities

The **probability of an event** is a measure of the likelihood, or chance, that the event will occur. Probability is a number from 0 to 1, including 0 and 1, and can be expressed as a decimal, fraction, or percent.

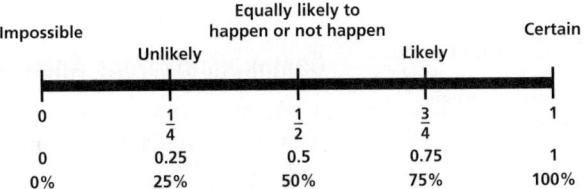

Laurie's Notes   Teacher Actions

- **Paired Verbal Fluency:** Have students pair up and follow the protocol described on page T-462. Ask students what they recall about probability from earlier courses. Expect to hear about theoretical versus experimental, sample spaces, likelihood, and outcomes.
- **Think-Pair-Share:** Have students work independently to solve Example 1. Share thinking with a neighbor.
- ❓ "How many outcomes were there?" 12
- ❓ "If it had been a ten-sided die, how many outcomes would you expect?" 20

The outcomes for a specified event are called *favorable outcomes*. When all outcomes are equally likely, the **theoretical probability** of the event can be found using the following.

$$\text{Theoretical probability} = \frac{\text{Number of favorable outcomes}}{\text{Total number of outcomes}}$$

The probability of event A is written as $P(A)$.

EXAMPLE 2 Finding a Theoretical Probability

A student taking a quiz randomly guesses the answers to four true-false questions. What is the probability of the student guessing exactly two correct answers?

SOLUTION

Step 1 Find the outcomes in the sample space. Let C represent a correct answer and I represent an incorrect answer. The possible outcomes are:

Number correct	Outcome
0	IIII
1	CIII ICII IICI IIIC
2	IICC ICIC ICCI CIIC CICI CCII
3	ICCC CICC CCIC CCCI
4	CCCC

exactly two correct → 2

Step 2 Identify the number of favorable outcomes and the total number of outcomes. There are 6 favorable outcomes with exactly two correct answers and the total number of outcomes is 16.

Step 3 Find the probability of the student guessing exactly two correct answers. Because the student is randomly guessing, the outcomes should be equally likely. So, use the theoretical probability formula.

$$P(\text{exactly two correct answers}) = \frac{\text{Number of favorable outcomes}}{\text{Total number of outcomes}}$$
$$= \frac{6}{16}$$
$$= \frac{3}{8}$$

▶ The probability of the student guessing exactly two correct answers is $\frac{3}{8}$, or 37.5%.

The sum of the probabilities of all outcomes in a sample space is 1. So, when you know the probability of event A, you can find the probability of the *complement* of event A. The *complement* of event A consists of all outcomes that are not in A and is denoted by $\overline{A}$. The notation $\overline{A}$ is read as "A bar." You can use the following formula to find $P(\overline{A})$.

Core Concept

Probability of the Complement of an Event

The probability of the complement of event A is

$$P(\overline{A}) = 1 - P(A).$$

Section 12.1 Sample Spaces and Probability 669

Vocabulary
Ask students to state the definitions of *complement* with which they are familiar. As students state the definitions, write on the board the spelling of the word that aligns to their definition. Explain that words that are spelled differently but sound the same are called *homophones*. Guide students to create a definition of the word *complement* in their own words as it relates to probability.

Extra Example 2
A coin is flipped four times. What is the probability that it lands on heads exactly three times?
The probability that the coin lands on heads exactly three times is $\frac{1}{4}$, or 25%.

ATTENTING TO PRECISION
Notice that the question uses the phrase "exactly two answers." This phrase is more precise than saying "two answers," which may be interpreted as "at least two" or as "exactly two."

Laurie's Notes **Teacher Actions**

• **Predict, Explain, Observe:** Group students and ask, "If you randomly guess on a four-question true-false quiz, what is the probability of answering exactly two questions correctly? Explain your reasoning." Give groups sufficient time to consider the question and to consider their reasoning. Often they predict a 50% chance of exactly two being correct. You want them to think about the sample space and the language of the question. The results are very different when asking about two or more questions being correct. Complements of events naturally arise in the discussion.

Extra Example 3

Use the diagram in Example 3. Find the probability of each event when two six-sided dice are rolled.

a. The sum is greater than 8.
$P(\text{sum} > 8) = \frac{10}{36} \approx 0.278$

b. The sum is not 2.
$P(\text{sum is not 2}) = 1 - \frac{1}{36} \approx 0.972$

Extra Example 4

You throw a dart at the board shown. Your dart is equally likely to hit any point inside the square board. What is the probability that your dart lands in one of the two yellow sectors in the smaller circle?

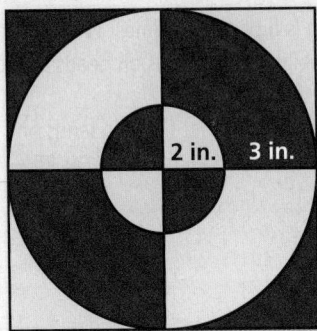

2 in.   3 in.

$P(\text{landing on one of the smaller yellow sectors}) = \frac{2\pi}{100} \approx 0.063$

MONITORING PROGRESS ANSWERS

3. $\frac{1}{12}$
4. 0.55
5. $\frac{3}{4}$
6. 0
7. 0.97
8. 5 points
9. score points

EXAMPLE 3   Finding Probabilities of Complements

When two six-sided dice are rolled, there are 36 possible outcomes, as shown. Find the probability of each event.

a. The sum is not 6.

b. The sum is less than or equal to 9.

SOLUTION

a. $P(\text{sum is not 6}) = 1 - P(\text{sum is 6}) = 1 - \frac{5}{36} = \frac{31}{36} \approx 0.861$

b. $P(\text{sum} \le 9) = 1 - P(\text{sum} > 9) = 1 - \frac{6}{36} = \frac{30}{36} = \frac{5}{6} \approx 0.833$

Some probabilities are found by calculating a ratio of two lengths, areas, or volumes. Such probabilities are called **geometric probabilities**.

EXAMPLE 4   Using Area to Find Probability

You throw a dart at the board shown. Your dart is equally likely to hit any point inside the square board. Are you more likely to get 10 points or 0 points?

3 in.

SOLUTION

The probability of getting 10 points is

$$P(10 \text{ points}) = \frac{\text{Area of smallest circle}}{\text{Area of entire board}} = \frac{\pi \cdot 3^2}{18^2} = \frac{9\pi}{324} = \frac{\pi}{36} \approx 0.0873.$$

The probability of getting 0 points is

$$P(0 \text{ points}) = \frac{\text{Area outside largest circle}}{\text{Area of entire board}}$$
$$= \frac{18^2 - (\pi \cdot 9^2)}{18^2}$$
$$= \frac{324 - 81\pi}{324}$$
$$= \frac{4 - \pi}{4}$$
$$\approx 0.215.$$

▶ You are more likely to get 0 points.

Monitoring Progress 🔊 Help in English and Spanish at *BigIdeasMath.com*

3. You flip a coin and roll a six-sided die. What is the probability that the coin shows tails and the die shows 4?

Find $P(\overline{A})$.

4. $P(A) = 0.45$ 5. $P(A) = \frac{1}{4}$

6. $P(A) = 1$ 7. $P(A) = 0.03$

8. In Example 4, are you more likely to get 10 points or 5 points?

9. In Example 4, are you more likely to score points (10, 5, or 2) or get 0 points?

Laurie's Notes   Teacher Actions

? MP2 Reason Abstractly and Quantitatively: "When is finding the probability of the complement of an event a helpful technique?" It is helpful when the probability of the complement can be found more easily than the probability of the event.

• Students often want to discuss the ability of the dart thrower in Example 4. Explain that you are considering someone whose dart is "equally likely to hit any point inside the square." Online simulators could be used to model this problem.

Experimental Probabilities

An **experimental probability** is based on repeated *trials* of a probability experiment. The number of trials is the number of times the probability experiment is performed. Each trial in which a favorable outcome occurs is called a *success*. The experimental probability can be found using the following.

$$\text{Experimental probability} = \frac{\text{Number of successes}}{\text{Number of trials}}$$

EXAMPLE 5 **Finding an Experimental Probability**

Spinner Results			
red	green	blue	yellow
5	9	3	3

Each section of the spinner shown has the same area. The spinner was spun 20 times. The table shows the results. For which color is the experimental probability of stopping on the color the same as the theoretical probability?

SOLUTION

The theoretical probability of stopping on each of the four colors is $\frac{1}{4}$. Use the outcomes in the table to find the experimental probabilities.

$$P(\text{red}) = \frac{5}{20} = \frac{1}{4} \qquad P(\text{green}) = \frac{9}{20}$$

$$P(\text{blue}) = \frac{3}{20} \qquad P(\text{yellow}) = \frac{3}{20}$$

▶ The experimental probability of stopping on red is the same as the theoretical probability.

EXAMPLE 6 **Solving a Real-Life Problem**

In the United States, a survey of 2184 adults ages 18 and over found that 1328 of them have at least one pet. The types of pets these adults have are shown in the figure. What is the probability that a pet-owning adult chosen at random has a dog?

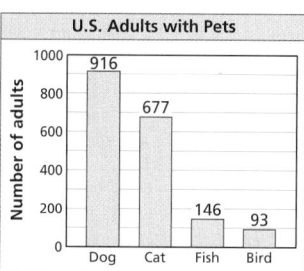

SOLUTION

The number of trials is the number of pet-owning adults, 1328. A success is a pet-owning adult who has a dog. From the graph, there are 916 adults who said that they have a dog.

$$P(\text{pet-owning adult has a dog}) = \frac{916}{1328} = \frac{229}{332} \approx 0.690$$

▶ The probability that a pet-owning adult chosen at random has a dog is about 69%.

Monitoring Progress Help in English and Spanish at *BigIdeasMath.com*

10. In Example 5, for which color is the experimental probability of stopping on the color greater than the theoretical probability?

11. In Example 6, what is the probability that a pet-owning adult chosen at random owns a fish?

Section 12.1   Sample Spaces and Probability   **671**

Section 12.1   671

Extra Example 5

A spinner has 5 sections, colored red, green, blue, yellow, and purple. Each section of the spinner has the same area. The table shows the results of 50 spins. For which color is the experimental probability of stopping on the color the same as the theoretical probability?

Spinner Results	
red	5
green	20
blue	3
yellow	10
purple	12

The experimental probability of stopping on yellow is the same as the theoretical probability.

Extra Example 6

Use the survey and data display in Example 6. What is the probability that a pet-owning adult chosen at random has a bird? The probability that a pet-owning adult chosen at random has a bird is ≈0.07003, or about 7%.

MONITORING PROGRESS ANSWERS

10. green

11. about 11%

Laurie's Notes   Teacher Actions

• Probe to ensure that students recognize the difference between experimental and theoretical probability. Example 5 assesses this.

? MP6 Attend to Precision: In Example 6, pet owners are the number of trials versus the 2184 adults that were initially surveyed. Ask, "What is the probability that an adult who was surveyed has a dog?" $\frac{916}{2184} \approx 0.419$

Closure

• **Exit Ticket:** You toss two dice. Find (a) P(sum is not 7) and (b) P(sum is more than 4).
(a) $\frac{5}{6} \approx 0.833$ (b) $\frac{5}{6} \approx 0.833$

ANSWERS

1. probability

2. Theoretical probability is based on the number of outcomes and experimental probability is based on repeated trials.

3. 48; 1HHH, 1HHT, 1HTH, 1THH, 1HTT, 1THT, 1TTH, 1TTT, 2HHH, 2HHT, 2HTH, 2THH, 2HTT, 2THT, 2TTH, 2TTT, 3HHH, 3HHT, 3HTH, 3THH, 3HTT, 3THT, 3TTH, 3TTT, 4HHH, 4HHT, 4HTH, 4THH, 4HTT, 4THT, 4TTH, 4TTT, 5HHH, 5HHT, 5HTH, 5THH, 5HTT, 5THT, 5TTH, 5TTT, 6HHH, 6HHT, 6HTH, 6THH, 6HTT, 6THT, 6TTH, 6TTT

4. 6; HP, HP, HW, TP, TP, TW

5. 12; R1, R2, R3, R4, W1, W2, W3, W4, B1, B2, B3, B4

6. 42; GG, GG, GG, GG, GG, GG, GB, GB, GB, GB, GB, GB, GB, GB, GB, GB, GB, GB, GB, BG, BG, BG, BG, BG, BG, BG, BG, BG, BG, BG, BG, BB, BB, BB, BB, BB, BB, BB, BB, BB, BB, BB, BB

7. $\frac{5}{16}$, or about 31.25%

8. $\frac{1}{16}$, or 6.25%

9. a. $\frac{11}{12}$, or about 92%
   b. $\frac{13}{18}$, or about 72%

10. a. 80%
    b. 26%

11. There are 4 outcomes, not 3; The probability is $\frac{1}{4}$.

12. The event should be that the number is less than or equal to 4; $\frac{13}{15}$

Vocabulary and Core Concept Check

1. **COMPLETE THE SENTENCE** A number that describes the likelihood of an event is the _____ of the event.

2. **WRITING** Describe the difference between theoretical probability and experimental probability.

Monitoring Progress and Modeling with Mathematics

In Exercises 3–6, find the number of possible outcomes in the sample space. Then list the possible outcomes. *(See Example 1.)*

3. You roll a die and flip three coins.

4. You flip a coin and draw a marble at random from a bag containing two purple marbles and one white marble.

5. A bag contains four red cards numbered 1 through 4, four white cards numbered 1 through 4, and four black cards numbered 1 through 4. You choose a card at random.

6. You draw two marbles without replacement from a bag containing three green marbles and four black marbles.

7. **PROBLEM SOLVING** A game show airs on television five days per week. Each day, a prize is randomly placed behind one of two doors. The contestant wins the prize by selecting the correct door. What is the probability that exactly two of the five contestants win a prize during a week? *(See Example 2.)*

8. **PROBLEM SOLVING** Your friend has two standard decks of 52 playing cards and asks you to randomly draw one card from each deck. What is the probability that you will draw two spades?

9. **PROBLEM SOLVING** When two six-sided dice are rolled, there are 36 possible outcomes. Find the probability that (a) the sum is not 4 and (b) the sum is greater than 5. *(See Example 3.)*

10. **PROBLEM SOLVING** The age distribution of a population is shown. Find the probability of each event.

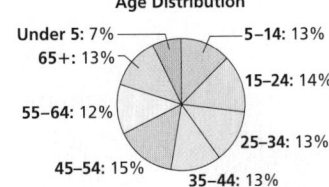

Age Distribution

Under 5: 7%
65+: 13%
55–64: 12%
45–54: 15%
35–44: 13%
25–34: 13%
15–24: 14%
5–14: 13%

a. A person chosen at random is at least 15 years old.

b. A person chosen at random is from 25 to 44 years old.

11. **ERROR ANALYSIS** A student randomly guesses the answers to two true-false questions. Describe and correct the error in finding the probability of the student guessing both answers correctly.

> The student can either guess two incorrect answers, two correct answers, or one of each. So the probability of guessing both answers correctly is $\frac{1}{3}$.

12. **ERROR ANALYSIS** A student randomly draws a number between 1 and 30. Describe and correct the error in finding the probability that the number drawn is greater than 4.

> The probability that the number is less than 4 is $\frac{3}{30}$, or $\frac{1}{10}$. So, the probability that the number is greater than 4 is $1 - \frac{1}{10}$, or $\frac{9}{10}$.

13. MATHEMATICAL CONNECTIONS
You throw a dart at the board shown. Your dart is equally likely to hit any point inside the square board. What is the probability your dart lands in the yellow region? *(See Example 4.)*

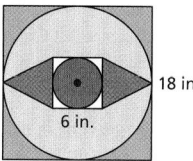
18 in.
6 in.
18 in.

14. MATHEMATICAL CONNECTIONS The map shows the length (in miles) of shoreline along the Gulf of Mexico for each state that borders the body of water. What is the probability that a ship coming ashore at a random point in the Gulf of Mexico lands in the given state?

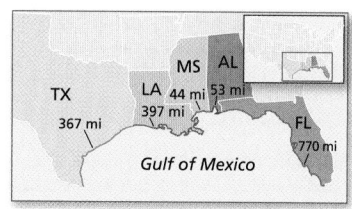
MS
AL
TX
LA 44 mi 53 mi
367 mi 397 mi
FL
770 mi
Gulf of Mexico

a. Texas
b. Alabama
c. Florida
d. Louisiana

15. DRAWING CONCLUSIONS You roll a six-sided die 60 times. The table shows the results. For which number is the experimental probability of rolling the number the same as the theoretical probability? *(See Example 5.)*

Six-sided Die Results					
⚀	⚁	⚂	⚃	⚄	⚅
11	14	7	10	6	12

16. DRAWING CONCLUSIONS A bag contains 5 marbles that are each a different color. A marble is drawn, its color is recorded, and then the marble is placed back in the bag. This process is repeated until 30 marbles have been drawn. The table shows the results. For which marble is the experimental probability of drawing the marble the same as the theoretical probability?

Drawing Results				
white	black	red	green	blue
5	6	8	2	9

17. REASONING Refer to the spinner shown. The spinner is divided into sections with the same area.

a. What is the theoretical probability that the spinner stops on a multiple of 3?

b. You spin the spinner 30 times. It stops on a multiple of 3 twenty times. What is the experimental probability of stopping on a multiple of 3?

c. Explain why the probability you found in part (b) is different than the probability you found in part (a).

30 4
27   6
24   9
21   12
18 15

18. OPEN-ENDED Describe a real-life event that has a probability of 0. Then describe a real-life event that has a probability of 1.

19. DRAWING CONCLUSIONS A survey of 2237 adults ages 18 and over asked which sport is their favorite. The results are shown in the figure. What is the probability that an adult chosen at random prefers auto racing? *(See Example 6.)*

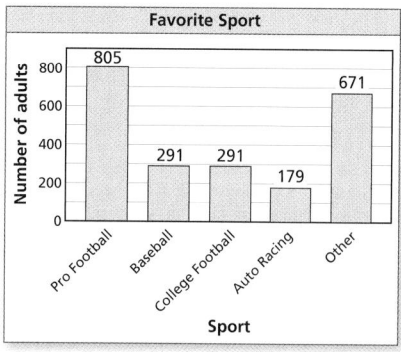
Favorite Sport
Number of adults
805
291 291
179
671
Pro Football Baseball College Football Auto Racing Other
Sport

20. DRAWING CONCLUSIONS A survey of 2392 adults ages 18 and over asked what type of food they would be most likely to choose at a restaurant. The results are shown in the figure. What is the probability that an adult chosen at random prefers Italian food?

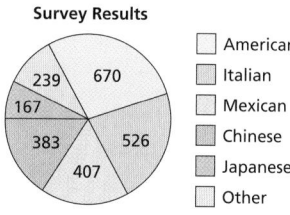
Survey Results
239 670
167
383 526
407
☐ American
☐ Italian
☐ Mexican
☐ Chinese
☐ Japanese
☐ Other

ANSWERS

13. about 0.56, or about 56%

14. a. about 0.23, or about 23%
b. about 0.03, or about 3%
c. about 0.47, or about 47%
d. about 0.24, or about 24%

15. 4

16. black

17. a. $\frac{9}{10}$, or 90%
b. $\frac{2}{3}$, or about 67%
c. The probability in part (b) is based on trials, not possible outcomes.

18. *Sample answer:* drawing an orange marble from a bag containing blue and green marbles; drawing a red marble from a bag containing red marbles

19. about 0.08, or about 8%

20. about 0.22, or about 22%

Mini-Assessment

A bag contains five cards numbered 1 through 5. You flip a coin and draw a card at random from the bag.

1. Find the number of possible outcomes in the sample space. Then list the outcomes. **10; H1, H2, H3, H4, H5, T1, T2, T3, T4, T5**

2. What is the probability that the coin lands on heads and you draw a card with an odd number on it? $\frac{3}{10}$, or 30%

3. You throw a dart at the board shown. Your dart is equally likely to hit any point inside the circular board. What is the probability that your dart does *not* land inside the square region?

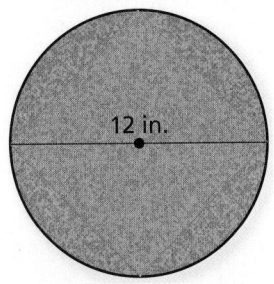

12 in.

P(not inside the square region)
$= 1 - \dfrac{2}{\pi} \approx 0.363$

4. A bag contains 5 red, 6 white, and 5 blue marbles. A marble is drawn from the bag and replaced 32 times. The table shows the results. For which color is the experimental probability of drawing the color the same as the theoretical probability?

red	white	blue
12	12	8

a white marble

5. Use the graph in Example 6. What is the probability that a pet-owning adult chosen at random has a cat? ≈0.5098, or about 51%

---

21. **ANALYZING RELATIONSHIPS** Refer to the board in Exercise 13. Order the likelihoods that the dart lands in the given region from least likely to most likely.

A. green
B. not blue
C. red
D. not yellow

22. **ANALYZING RELATIONSHIPS** Refer to the chart below. Order the following events from least likely to most likely.

Four-Day Forecast

Friday	Saturday	Sunday	Monday
Chance of Rain **5%**	Chance of Rain **30%**	Chance of Rain **80%**	Chance of Rain **90%**

A. It rains on Sunday.
B. It does not rain on Saturday.
C. It rains on Monday.
D. It does not rain on Friday.

23. **USING TOOLS** Use the figure in Example 3 to answer each question.

a. List the possible sums that result from rolling two six-sided dice.

b. Find the theoretical probability of rolling each sum.

c. The table below shows a simulation of rolling two six-sided dice three times. Use a random number generator to simulate rolling two six-sided dice 50 times. Compare the experimental probabilities of rolling each sum with the theoretical probabilities.

	A	B	C
	First Die	**Second Die**	**Sum**
1			
2	4	6	10
3	3	5	8
4	1	6	7
5			

Maintaining Mathematical Proficiency
Reviewing what you learned in previous grades and lessons

Simplify the expression. Write your answer using only positive exponents. *(Skills Review Handbook)*

29. $\dfrac{2x^3}{x^2}$

30. $\dfrac{2xy}{8y^2}$

31. $\dfrac{4x^9y}{3x^3y}$

32. $\dfrac{6y^0}{3x^{-6}}$

33. $(3pq)^4$

34. $\left(\dfrac{y^2}{x}\right)^{-2}$

---

24. **MAKING AN ARGUMENT** You flip a coin three times. It lands on heads twice and on tails once. Your friend concludes that the theoretical probability of the coin landing heads up is $P(\text{heads up}) = \frac{2}{3}$. Is your friend correct? Explain your reasoning.

25. **MATHEMATICAL CONNECTIONS** A sphere fits inside a cube so that it touches each side, as shown. What is the probability a point chosen at random inside the cube is also inside the sphere?

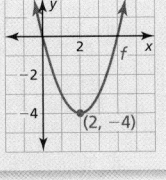

26. **HOW DO YOU SEE IT?** Consider the graph of f shown. What is the probability that the graph of $y = f(x) + c$ intersects the x-axis when c is a randomly chosen integer from 1 to 6? Explain.

(2, −4)

27. **DRAWING CONCLUSIONS** A manufacturer tests 1200 computers and finds that 9 of them have defects. Find the probability that a computer chosen at random has a defect. Predict the number of computers with defects in a shipment of 15,000 computers. Explain your reasoning.

28. **THOUGHT PROVOKING** The tree diagram shows a sample space. Write a probability problem that can be represented by the sample space. Then write the answer(s) to the problem.

Box A	Box B	Outcomes	Sum	Product
1	1	(1, 1)	2	1
	2	(1, 2)	3	2
2	1	(2, 1)	3	2
	2	(2, 2)	4	4
3	1	(3, 1)	4	3
	2	(3, 2)	5	6

If students need help...	If students got it...
Resources by Chapter • Practice A and Practice B • Puzzle Time	**Resources by Chapter** • Enrichment and Extension • Cumulative Review
Student Journal • Practice	Start the *next* Section
Differentiating the Lesson **Skills Review Handbook**	

Laurie's Notes

Overview of Section 12.2

Introduction

- In this lesson, the idea of independent and dependent events is introduced.
- Students will first prove whether events are independent or dependent by using the sample space. Students should use logical reasoning to confirm that their answer is correct.
- The probabilities of independent and dependent events are calculated, along with calculating conditional probabilities.

Teaching Strategy

- The graphing calculator can be used to simulate, and hence estimate, experimental probabilities. This strategy uses the random number generator to simulate events such as spinning a spinner.
- Example 3 in the lesson uses an eight-section spinner with the numbers 1–8. The problem asks students to calculate the probability of getting a 5 on the first spin and a number greater than 3 on the second spin.
- The steps below simulate 100 trials of each event, meaning spinning 100 times for the first spin, followed by another 100 spins for the second spin.
  - Generate two lists of 100 random integers from 1 to 8 by entering randInt(1,8,100) into lists L_1 and L_2. L_1 shows the outcomes of the first spin, and L_2 shows the outcomes of the second spin. (See Figure 1.)
  - To facilitate counting the number of outcomes with a 5 on the first spin, sort the two lists while keeping the paired data together by entering SortA(L_1,L_2) on the home screen. (See Figure 2.)
  - Scroll down L_1 to count the number of successful trials with 5 on the first spin and a number greater than 3 on the second spin. (See Figure 3.)

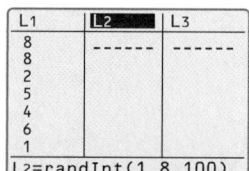   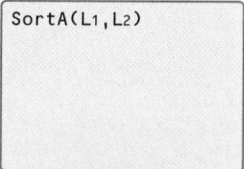   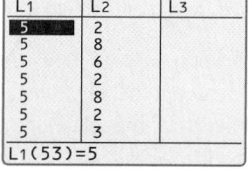

| Figure 1 | Figure 2 | Figure 3 |

- To calculate the experimental probability, divide the number of successes by 100.

Pacing Suggestion

- The explorations provide students the opportunity to explore the difference between independent and dependent events and to calculate probabilities of each.

Dynamic Teaching Tools

Dynamic Assessment & Progress Monitoring Tool

Lesson Planning Tool

Interactive Whiteboard Lesson Library

Dynamic Classroom with Dynamic Investigations

Common Core State Standards

HSS-CP.A.1 Describe events as subsets of a sample space (the set of outcomes) using characteristics (or categories) of the outcomes, or as unions, intersections, or complements of other events ("or," "and," "not").

HSS-CP.A.2 Understand that two events A and B are independent if the probability of A and B occurring together is the product of their probabilities, and use this characterization to determine if they are independent.

HSS-CP.A.3 Understand the conditional probability of A given B as $P(A$ and $B)/P(B)$, and interpret independence of A and B as saying that the conditional probability of A given B is the same as the probability of A, and the conditional probability of B given A is the same as the probability of B.

HSS-CP.A.5 Recognize and explain the concepts of conditional probability and independence in everyday language and everyday situations.

HSS-CP.B.6 Find the conditional probability of A given B as the fraction of B's outcomes that also belong to A, and interpret the answer in terms of the model.

HSS-CP.B.8 Apply the general Multiplication Rule in a uniform probability model, $P(A$ and $B) = P(A)P(B|A) = P(B)P(A|B)$, and interpret the answer in terms of the model.

Exploration

Motivate

- Before class, cut 25 pieces of paper. Because this motivator is to model Example 4 in the lesson, you could cut the paper to the size of dollar bills. Write $1 on 20 of the pieces of paper and $100 on the other 5 pieces of paper.
- Display the paper money to the students.
- Select one student and say, "If you select two slips of paper and end up with $200, there will be no homework tonight! If you end up with $101, you will do two extra homework problems. If you end up with $2, you will do five extra homework problems."
- **?** "What do you think your chances are of having no homework?" Answers will vary. Explain to students that in today's lesson they will calculate the probability of drawing $200.

Discuss

- Discuss independent and dependent events before students begin the explorations.

Exploration 1

- The two events may look very similar to students because they both involve the numbers 1 to 6.
- It is possible to end up with two 4s when rolling the dice. It is not possible when the pieces of paper are drawn from a bag without replacement.

Exploration 2

- Answers will vary in terms of the types of experiments students will design. If students are familiar with the random number generator on a graphing calculator, they may use it as part of the experiment.
- Have students share the description of their experiment and the results.

Exploration 3

- Before students find the two probabilities, ask them to make a guess as to which event has the greater probability, the dice or the paper.
- **?** "What is the probability of rolling a sum of 7?" $\frac{6}{36} = \frac{1}{6}$
- **?** "What is the probability of drawing two numbers that sum to 7?" $\frac{6}{30} = \frac{1}{5}$
- **Big Idea:** Students should recognize that the sample space is less for the dependent event than for the independent event.

Communicate Your Answer

- Have students work independently to answer Questions 4 and 5, and then discuss as a whole class.

Connecting to Next Step

- It should not take long for students to decide whether an event is independent or dependent. In the formal lesson, students will first prove whether an event is independent or dependent.

12.2 Independent and Dependent Events

Essential Question How can you determine whether two events are independent or dependent?

Two events are **independent events** when the occurrence of one event does not affect the occurrence of the other event. Two events are **dependent events** when the occurrence of one event *does* affect the occurrence of the other event.

EXPLORATION 1 **Identifying Independent and Dependent Events**

Work with a partner. Determine whether the events are independent or dependent. Explain your reasoning.

a. Two six-sided dice are rolled.

b. Six pieces of paper, numbered 1 through 6, are in a bag. Two pieces of paper are selected one at a time without replacement.

REASONING ABSTRACTLY
To be proficient in math, you need to make sense of quantities and their relationships in problem situations.

EXPLORATION 2 **Finding Experimental Probabilities**

Work with a partner.

a. In Exploration 1(a), experimentally estimate the probability that the sum of the two numbers rolled is 7. Describe your experiment.

b. In Exploration 1(b), experimentally estimate the probability that the sum of the two numbers selected is 7. Describe your experiment.

EXPLORATION 3 **Finding Theoretical Probabilities**

Work with a partner.

a. In Exploration 1(a), find the theoretical probability that the sum of the two numbers rolled is 7. Then compare your answer with the experimental probability you found in Exploration 2(a).

b. In Exploration 1(b), find the theoretical probability that the sum of the two numbers selected is 7. Then compare your answer with the experimental probability you found in Exploration 2(b).

c. Compare the probabilities you obtained in parts (a) and (b).

Communicate Your Answer

4. How can you determine whether two events are independent or dependent?

5. Determine whether the events are independent or dependent. Explain your reasoning.

a. You roll a 4 on a six-sided die and spin red on a spinner.

b. Your teacher chooses a student to lead a group, chooses another student to lead a second group, and chooses a third student to lead a third group.

ANSWERS

1. **a.** independent; The occurence of one event does not affect the occurence of the other event.

   b. dependent; The occurence of one event does affect the occurence of the other event.

2. **a.** *Sample answer:* 0.2; Two six-sided dice were rolled, and the sum of the numbers was recorded.

   b. *Sample answer:* 0.2; Two pieces of paper were selected one at a time from pieces numbered 1 through 6, and the sum of the numbers were recorded.

3. **a.** $\frac{6}{36} = \frac{1}{6} \approx 0.167$; *Sample answer:* This is less than the probability in Exploration 2(a).

   b. $\frac{6}{30} = \frac{1}{5} = 0.2$; *Sample answer:* This is the same as the probability in Exploration 2(b).

   c. The probability in part (a) is less than the probability in part (b).

4. Determine whether the occurence of one event affects the occurence of the other event.

5. **a.** independent; The occurence of one event does not affect the occurence of the other event.

   b. dependent; The occurence of one event does affect the occurence of the other event.

Extra Example 1
A bag contains six pieces of paper, numbered 1 through 6. A student randomly selects a piece of paper, replaces it, and randomly selects another piece of paper. Use a sample space to determine whether randomly selecting a 5 first and randomly selecting an odd number second are independent events.
$P(5) = \frac{1}{6}$; $P(\text{odd number}) = \frac{1}{2}$; $P(5, \text{then odd number}) = \frac{1}{12}$. Because $\frac{1}{6} \cdot \frac{1}{2} = \frac{1}{12}$, the events are independent.

Extra Example 2
A bag contains six pieces of paper, numbered 1 through 6. A student randomly selects a piece of paper, does not replace it, and randomly selects another piece of paper. Use a sample space to determine whether randomly selecting an even number first and randomly selecting a 4 second are independent events.
$P(\text{even number}) = \frac{1}{2}$; $P(4) = \frac{1}{6}$; $P(\text{even number, then 4}) = \frac{1}{15}$.
Because $\frac{1}{2} \cdot \frac{1}{6} \neq \frac{1}{15}$, the events are not independent.

12.2 Lesson

Core Vocabulary
independent events, *p. 676*
dependent events, *p. 677*
conditional probability, *p. 677*

Previous
probability
sample space

What You Will Learn

▶ Determine whether events are independent events.
▶ Find probabilities of independent and dependent events.
▶ Find conditional probabilities.

Determining Whether Events Are Independent
Two events are **independent events** when the occurrence of one event does not affect the occurrence of the other event.

🔎 Core Concept
Probability of Independent Events

Words Two events A and B are independent events if and only if the probability that both events occur is the product of the probabilities of the events.

Symbols $P(A \text{ and } B) = P(A) \cdot P(B)$

EXAMPLE 1 Determining Whether Events Are Independent

A student taking a quiz randomly guesses the answers to four true-false questions. Use a sample space to determine whether guessing Question 1 correctly and guessing Question 2 correctly are independent events.

SOLUTION

Using the sample space in Example 2 on page 669:

$$P(\text{correct on Question 1}) = \frac{8}{16} = \frac{1}{2} \qquad P(\text{correct on Question 2}) = \frac{8}{16} = \frac{1}{2}$$

$$P(\text{correct on Question 1 and correct on Question 2}) = \frac{4}{16} = \frac{1}{4}$$

▶ Because $\frac{1}{2} \cdot \frac{1}{2} = \frac{1}{4}$, the events are independent.

EXAMPLE 2 Determining Whether Events Are Independent

A group of four students includes one boy and three girls. The teacher randomly selects one of the students to be the speaker and a different student to be the recorder. Use a sample space to determine whether randomly selecting a girl first and randomly selecting a girl second are independent events.

SOLUTION

Let B represent the boy. Let G_1, G_2, and G_3 represent the three girls. Use a table to list the outcomes in the sample space.

Number of girls	Outcome	
1	G_1B	BG_1
1	G_2B	BG_2
1	G_3B	BG_3
2	G_1G_2	G_2G_1
2	G_1G_3	G_3G_1
2	G_2G_3	G_3G_2

Using the sample space:

$$P(\text{girl first}) = \frac{9}{12} = \frac{3}{4} \qquad P(\text{girl second}) = \frac{9}{12} = \frac{3}{4}$$

$$P(\text{girl first and girl second}) = \frac{6}{12} = \frac{1}{2}$$

▶ Because $\frac{3}{4} \cdot \frac{3}{4} \neq \frac{1}{2}$, the events are not independent.

Laurie's Notes Teacher Actions

? **MP6 Attend to Precision:** Write the *Core Concept* and ask, "What two statements result from the *if and only if* language?" If two events are independent, then $P(A \text{ and } B) = P(A) \cdot P(B)$, and if $P(A \text{ and } B) = P(A) \cdot P(B)$, then the events are independent.

• The probabilities can be used to test whether two events are independent or not. That is what Examples 1 and 2 do.

• **MP5 Use Appropriate Tools Strategically:** Have students write the sample space for Example 2. Coding the girls G_1, G_2, and G_3 is a helpful tool to organize and write results.

1. In Example 1, determine whether guessing Question 1 incorrectly and guessing Question 2 correctly are independent events.

2. In Example 2, determine whether randomly selecting a girl first and randomly selecting a boy second are independent events.

Finding Probabilities of Events

In Example 1, it makes sense that the events are independent because the second guess should not be affected by the first guess. In Example 2, however, the selection of the second person *depends* on the selection of the first person because the same person cannot be selected twice. These events are *dependent*. Two events are **dependent events** when the occurrence of one event *does* affect the occurrence of the other event.

The probability that event *B* occurs given that event *A* has occurred is called the **conditional probability** of *B* given *A* and is written as $P(B|A)$.

MAKING SENSE OF PROBLEMS

One way that you can find P(girl second | girl first) is to list the 9 outcomes in which a girl is chosen first and then find the fraction of these outcomes in which a girl is chosen second:

G_1B G_2B G_3B
G_1G_2 G_2G_1 G_3G_1
G_1G_3 G_2G_3 G_3G_2

Core Concept

Probability of Dependent Events

Words   If two events *A* and *B* are dependent events, then the probability that both events occur is the product of the probability of the first event and the conditional probability of the second event given the first event.

Symbols $P(A \text{ and } B) = P(A) \cdot P(B|A)$

Example   Using the information in Example 2:

$P(\text{girl first and girl second}) = P(\text{girl first}) \cdot P(\text{girl second} | \text{girl first})$

$$= \frac{9}{12} \cdot \frac{6}{9} = \frac{1}{2}$$

EXAMPLE 3   Finding the Probability of Independent Events

As part of a board game, you need to spin the spinner, which is divided into equal parts. Find the probability that you get a 5 on your first spin and a number greater than 3 on your second spin.

SOLUTION

Let event *A* be "5 on first spin" and let event *B* be "greater than 3 on second spin."

The events are independent because the outcome of your second spin is not affected by the outcome of your first spin. Find the probability of each event and then multiply the probabilities.

$P(A) = \frac{1}{8}$ 1 of the 8 sections is a "5."

$P(B) = \frac{5}{8}$ 5 of the 8 sections (4, 5, 6, 7, 8) are greater than 3.

$P(A \text{ and } B) = P(A) \cdot P(B) = \frac{1}{8} \cdot \frac{5}{8} = \frac{5}{64} \approx 0.078$

▶ So, the probability that you get a 5 on your first spin and a number greater than 3 on your second spin is about 7.8%.

Differentiated Instruction

Auditory

Write the formula from the *Core Concept* on the board. Read aloud the words for the probability of dependent events, and point to the symbols as you read the words that they represent. Be sure students understand what the vertical bar means. Ask students to describe the formula in their own words.

Extra Example 3

Use the spinner in Example 3. Find the probability that you get an even number on your first spin and a number less than 3 on your second spin. The probability is $\frac{1}{8}$, or 12.5%.

MONITORING PROGRESS ANSWERS

1. yes

2. no

Laurie's Notes   Teacher Actions

- Contrast Examples 1 and 2 to define *dependent events* and *conditional probability*. Introduce the notation $P(B|A)$.
- Write the *Core Concept*. Be careful with language and symbols, as students start to confuse both about now.
- **?** "Are the events of spinning a 5 on the first spin and spinning a number greater than 3 on the second spin independent? Explain." yes; The outcome of the first spin does not affect the outcome of the second spin. See the *Teaching Strategy* on page T-674 to simulate the events.

Extra Example 4

Nine women and six men are on a committee. Two people are randomly chosen from the committee members to serve as a chairperson and a treasurer. Find the probability that both events A and B will occur.

A: The chairperson is a man.
B: The treasurer is a woman.

The probability that the chairperson is a man and the treasurer is a woman is $\frac{9}{35}$, or about 25.7%.

Extra Example 5

A bag contains 10 red marbles and 5 blue marbles. You randomly select 3 marbles from the bag. What is the probability that all 3 marbles are blue when (a) you replace each marble before selecting the next one and (b) you do not replace each marble before selecting the next one? Compare the probabilities.

a. The probability that all three marbles are blue, with replacement, is $\frac{1}{27} \approx 0.037$.

b. The probability that all three marbles are blue, without replacement, is $\frac{2}{91} \approx 0.022$.

You are $\frac{1}{27} \div \frac{2}{91} \approx 1.7$ times more likely to select three blue marbles when you replace each marble before you select the next marble.

MONITORING PROGRESS ANSWERS

3. 25%

4. about 63.3%

5. **a.** about 42.2%

   b. about 41.4%

   You are about 1.02 times more likely to select 3 cards that are not hearts when you replace each card before you select the next card.

EXAMPLE 4 Finding the Probability of Dependent Events

A bag contains twenty \$1 bills and five \$100 bills. You randomly draw a bill from the bag, set it aside, and then randomly draw another bill from the bag. Find the probability that both events A and B will occur.

Event A: The first bill is \$100. **Event B:** The second bill is \$100.

SOLUTION

The events are dependent because there is one less bill in the bag on your second draw than on your first draw. Find $P(A)$ and $P(B\mid A)$. Then multiply the probabilities.

$P(A) = \frac{5}{25}$ 5 of the 25 bills are \$100 bills.

$P(B\mid A) = \frac{4}{24}$ 4 of the remaining 24 bills are \$100 bills.

$P(A \text{ and } B) = P(A) \cdot P(B\mid A) = \frac{5}{25} \cdot \frac{4}{24} = \frac{1}{5} \cdot \frac{1}{6} = \frac{1}{30} \approx 0.033.$

▶ So, the probability that you draw two \$100 bills is about 3.3%.

EXAMPLE 5 Comparing Independent and Dependent Events

You randomly select 3 cards from a standard deck of 52 playing cards. What is the probability that all 3 cards are hearts when (a) you replace each card before selecting the next card, and (b) you do not replace each card before selecting the next card? Compare the probabilities.

SOLUTION

Let event A be "first card is a heart," event B be "second card is a heart," and event C be "third card is a heart."

a. Because you replace each card before you select the next card, the events are independent. So, the probability is

$P(A \text{ and } B \text{ and } C) = P(A) \cdot P(B) \cdot P(C) = \frac{13}{52} \cdot \frac{13}{52} \cdot \frac{13}{52} = \frac{1}{64} \approx 0.016.$

b. Because you do not replace each card before you select the next card, the events are dependent. So, the probability is

$P(A \text{ and } B \text{ and } C) = P(A) \cdot P(B\mid A) \cdot P(C\mid A \text{ and } B)$

$= \frac{13}{52} \cdot \frac{12}{51} \cdot \frac{11}{50} = \frac{11}{850} \approx 0.013.$

▶ So, you are $\frac{1}{64} \div \frac{11}{850} \approx 1.2$ times more likely to select 3 hearts when you replace each card before you select the next card.

STUDY TIP

The formulas for finding probabilities of independent and dependent events can be extended to three or more events.

Monitoring Progress 🔊 Help in English and Spanish at *BigIdeasMath.com*

3. In Example 3, what is the probability that you spin an even number and then an odd number?

4. In Example 4, what is the probability that both bills are \$1 bills?

5. In Example 5, what is the probability that none of the cards drawn are hearts when (a) you replace each card, and (b) you do not replace each card? Compare the probabilities.

Laurie's Notes Teacher Actions

- **MP4 Model with Mathematics:** Model Example 4 as suggested in the *Motivate* on page T-675.
- Students find it difficult to trust the formula for finding the probability of dependent events. You do not want to write the sample space for Example 4, so referring back to a simpler example is helpful.
- Work through Example 5. Students find it intuitive that when you replace the cards each time, the probability of a success is greater.

Finding Conditional Probabilities

EXAMPLE 6   Using a Table to Find Conditional Probabilities

	Pass	Fail
Defective	3	36
Non-defective	450	11

A quality-control inspector checks for defective parts. The table shows the results of the inspector's work. Find (a) the probability that a defective part "passes," and (b) the probability that a non-defective part "fails."

SOLUTION

a. $P(\text{pass}|\text{defective}) = \dfrac{\text{Number of defective parts "passed"}}{\text{Total number of defective parts}}$

$= \dfrac{3}{3+36} = \dfrac{3}{39} = \dfrac{1}{13} \approx 0.077$, or about 7.7%

b. $P(\text{fail}|\text{non-defective}) = \dfrac{\text{Number of non-defective parts "failed"}}{\text{Total number of non-defective parts}}$

$= \dfrac{11}{450+11} = \dfrac{11}{461} \approx 0.024$, or about 2.4%

You can rewrite the formula for the probability of dependent events to write a rule for finding conditional probabilities.

$$P(A) \cdot P(B|A) = P(A \text{ and } B) \qquad \text{Write formula.}$$

$$P(B|A) = \dfrac{P(A \text{ and } B)}{P(A)} \qquad \text{Divide each side by } P(A).$$

> **STUDY TIP**
> Note that when A and B are independent, this rule still applies because $P(B) = P(B|A)$.

EXAMPLE 7   Finding a Conditional Probability

At a school, 60% of students buy a school lunch. Only 10% of students buy lunch and dessert. What is the probability that a student who buys lunch also buys dessert?

SOLUTION

Let event A be "buys lunch" and let event B be "buys dessert." You are given $P(A) = 0.6$ and $P(A \text{ and } B) = 0.1$. Use the formula to find $P(B|A)$.

$$P(B|A) = \dfrac{P(A \text{ and } B)}{P(A)} \qquad \text{Write formula for conditional probability.}$$

$$= \dfrac{0.1}{0.6} \qquad \text{Substitute 0.1 for } P(A \text{ and } B) \text{ and 0.6 for } P(A).$$

$$= \dfrac{1}{6} \approx 0.167 \qquad \text{Simplify.}$$

▶ So, the probability that a student who buys lunch also buys dessert is about 16.7%.

Monitoring Progress   🔊 Help in English and Spanish at *BigIdeasMath.com*

6. In Example 6, find (a) the probability that a non-defective part "passes," and (b) the probability that a defective part "fails."

7. At a coffee shop, 80% of customers order coffee. Only 15% of customers order coffee and a bagel. What is the probability that a customer who orders coffee also orders a bagel?

Extra Example 6

A quality-control inspector checks for defective parts. The table shows the results of the inspector's work.

	Pass	Fail
Defective	5	24
Non-defective	208	9

a. Find the probability that a defective part "passes."
$P(\text{pass} | \text{defective}) = \dfrac{5}{29} \approx 0.172$, or about 17.2%

b. Find the probability that a non-defective part "passes."
$P(\text{pass} | \text{non-defective}) = \dfrac{208}{217} \approx 0.959$, or about 95.9%

Extra Example 7

At a clothing store, 75% of the customers buy pants. Only 20% of the customers buy pants and a belt. What is the probability that a customer who buys pants also buys a belt? $\dfrac{4}{15}$, or about 26.7%

MONITORING PROGRESS ANSWERS

6. a. about 97.6%
   b. about 92.3%
7. 18.75%

Laurie's Notes   Teacher Actions

❓ Turn and Talk: "Look at the two-way table. How many parts were produced? What percent failed?" 500 were produced and 9.4% failed.

❓ "Why is the event *defective part passes* a conditional probability?" The event asks about a part passing, given that it was defective.

• **Think-Pair-Share:** Have students answer Questions 6 and 7, and then share and discuss as a class.

Closure

• **Muddiest Point:** Ask students to identify, aloud or on a paper, the muddiest point(s) about the lesson. What was difficult to understand?

Assignment Guide and Homework Check

ASSIGNMENT

Basic: 1, 2, 3–15 odd, 19–23 odd, 26, 27, 31–33

Average: 1, 2–26 even, 27, 31–33

Advanced: 1, 2, 8–26 even, 27–33

HOMEWORK CHECK

Basic: 7, 11, 13, 19, 21

Average: 8, 12, 14, 20, 22

Advanced: 10, 12, 14, 22, 24

ANSWERS

1. When two events are dependent, the occurrence of one event affects the other. When two events are independent, the occurrence of one event does not affect the other. *Sample answer:* choosing two marbles from a bag without replacement; rolling two dice

2. conditional probability; $P(B \mid A)$

3. dependent; The occurrence of event A affects the occurrence of event B.

4. independent; The occurrence of event A does not affect the occurrence of event B.

5. dependent; The occurrence of event A affects the occurrence of event B.

6. independent; The occurrence of event A does not affect the occurrence of event B.

7. yes

8. no

9. yes

10. no

11. about 2.8%

Vocabulary and Core Concept Check

1. **WRITING** Explain the difference between dependent events and independent events, and give an example of each.

2. **COMPLETE THE SENTENCE** The probability that event *B* will occur given that event *A* has occurred is called the _____ of *B* given *A* and is written as _____.

Monitoring Progress and Modeling with Mathematics

In Exercises 3–6, tell whether the events are independent or dependent. Explain your reasoning.

3. A box of granola bars contains an assortment of flavors. You randomly choose a granola bar and eat it. Then you randomly choose another bar.
   Event A: You choose a coconut almond bar first.
   Event B: You choose a cranberry almond bar second.

4. You roll a six-sided die and flip a coin.
   Event A: You get a 4 when rolling the die.
   Event B: You get tails when flipping the coin.

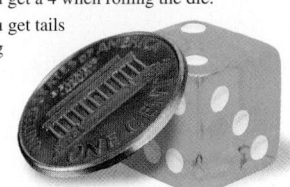

5. Your MP3 player contains hip-hop and rock songs. You randomly choose a song. Then you randomly choose another song without repeating song choices.
   Event A: You choose a hip-hop song first.
   Event B: You choose a rock song second.

6. There are 22 novels of various genres on a shelf. You randomly choose a novel and put it back. Then you randomly choose another novel.
   Event A: You choose a mystery novel.
   Event B: You choose a science fiction novel.

In Exercises 7–10, determine whether the events are independent. *(See Examples 1 and 2.)*

7. You play a game that involves spinning a wheel. Each section of the wheel shown has the same area. Use a sample space to determine whether randomly spinning blue and then green are independent events.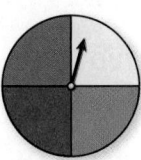

8. You have one red apple and three green apples in a bowl. You randomly select one apple to eat now and another apple for your lunch. Use a sample space to determine whether randomly selecting a green apple first and randomly selecting a green apple second are independent events.

9. A student is taking a multiple-choice test where each question has four choices. The student randomly guesses the answers to the five-question test. Use a sample space to determine whether guessing Question 1 correctly and Question 2 correctly are independent events.

10. A vase contains four white roses and one red rose. You randomly select two roses to take home. Use a sample space to determine whether randomly selecting a white rose first and randomly selecting a white rose second are independent events.

11. **PROBLEM SOLVING** You play a game that involves spinning the money wheel shown. You spin the wheel twice. Find the probability that you get more than $500 on your first spin and then go bankrupt on your second spin. *(See Example 3.)*

12. PROBLEM SOLVING You play a game that involves drawing two numbers from a hat. There are 25 pieces of paper numbered from 1 to 25 in the hat. Each number is replaced after it is drawn. Find the probability that you will draw the 3 on your first draw and a number greater than 10 on your second draw.

13. PROBLEM SOLVING A drawer contains 12 white socks and 8 black socks. You randomly choose 1 sock and do not replace it. Then you randomly choose another sock. Find the probability that both events A and B will occur. *(See Example 4.)*

Event A: The first sock is white.

Event B: The second sock is white.

14. PROBLEM SOLVING A word game has 100 tiles, 98 of which are letters and 2 of which are blank. The numbers of tiles of each letter are shown. You randomly draw 1 tile, set it aside, and then randomly draw another tile. Find the probability that both events A and B will occur.

Event A:
The first tile is a consonant.

Event B:
The second tile is a vowel.

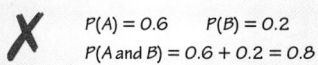

A – 9   H – 2   O – 8   V – 2
B – 2   I – 9   P – 2   W – 2
C – 2   J – 1   Q – 1   X – 1
D – 4   K – 1   R – 6   Y – 2
E – 12 L – 4   S – 4   Z – 1
F – 2   M – 2   T – 6   ▯ – 2
G – 3   N – 6   U – 4   Blank

15. ERROR ANALYSIS Events A and B are independent. Describe and correct the error in finding $P(A \text{ and } B)$.

> ✗ $P(A) = 0.6$ $P(B) = 0.2$
> $P(A \text{ and } B) = 0.6 + 0.2 = 0.8$

16. ERROR ANALYSIS A shelf contains 3 fashion magazines and 4 health magazines. You randomly choose one to read, set it aside, and randomly choose another for your friend to read. Describe and correct the error in finding the probability that both events A and B occur.

Event A: The first magazine is fashion.

Event B: The second magazine is health.

> ✗ $P(A) = \frac{3}{7}$ $P(B \mid A) = \frac{4}{7}$
> $P(A \text{ and } B) = \frac{3}{7} \cdot \frac{4}{7} = \frac{12}{49} \approx 0.245$

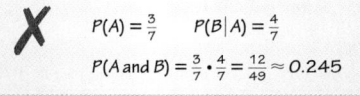

17. NUMBER SENSE Events A and B are independent. Suppose $P(B) = 0.4$ and $P(A \text{ and } B) = 0.13$. Find $P(A)$.

18. NUMBER SENSE Events A and B are dependent. Suppose $P(B \mid A) = 0.6$ and $P(A \text{ and } B) = 0.15$. Find $P(A)$.

19. ANALYZING RELATIONSHIPS You randomly select three cards from a standard deck of 52 playing cards. What is the probability that all three cards are face cards when (a) you replace each card before selecting the next card, and (b) you do not replace each card before selecting the next card? Compare the probabilities. *(See Example 5.)*

20. ANALYZING RELATIONSHIPS A bag contains 9 red marbles, 4 blue marbles, and 7 yellow marbles. You randomly select three marbles from the bag. What is the probability that all three marbles are red when (a) you replace each marble before selecting the next marble, and (b) you do not replace each marble before selecting the next marble? Compare the probabilities.

21. ATTEND TO PRECISION The table shows the number of species in the United States listed as endangered and threatened. Find (a) the probability that a randomly selected endangered species is a bird, and (b) the probability that a randomly selected mammal is endangered. *(See Example 6.)*

	Endangered	Threatened
Mammals	70	16
Birds	80	16
Other	318	142

22. ATTEND TO PRECISION The table shows the number of tropical cyclones that formed during the hurricane seasons over a 12-year period. Find (a) the probability to predict whether a future tropical cyclone in the Northern Hemisphere is a hurricane, and (b) the probability to predict whether a hurricane is in the Southern Hemisphere.

Type of Tropical Cyclone	Northern Hemisphere	Southern Hemisphere
tropical depression	100	107
tropical storm	342	487
hurricane	379	525

23. PROBLEM SOLVING At a school, 43% of students attend the homecoming football game. Only 23% of students go to the game and the homecoming dance. What is the probability that a student who attends the football game also attends the dance? *(See Example 7.)*

ANSWERS

12. 2.4%

13. about 34.7%

14. about 23.8%

15. The probabilities were added instead of multiplied;
$P(A \text{ and } B) = (0.6)(0.2) = 0.12$

16. $P(B \mid A)$ is incorrect; $P(B \mid A) = \frac{4}{6}$;
$P(A \text{ and } B) = \frac{2}{7} \approx 0.286$

17. 0.325

18. 0.25

19. **a.** about 1.2%
    b. about 1.0%
    You are about 1.2 times more likely to select 3 face cards when you replace each card before you select the next card.

20. **a.** about 9.1%
    b. about 7.4%
    You are about 1.23 times more likely to select 3 red marbles when you replace each marble before you select the next marble.

21. **a.** about 17.1%
    b. about 81.4%

22. **a.** about 46.2%
    b. about 58.1%

23. about 53.5%

Mini-Assessment

A bin contains 6 blue socks and 4 black socks.

1. You randomly select a sock, put it aside, and then randomly select a second sock from the bin. Use a sample space to determine whether selecting a black sock first and a blue sock second are independent events.

   $P(\text{black}) = \frac{2}{5}$; $P(\text{blue}) = \frac{3}{5}$; $P(\text{black, then blue}) = \frac{4}{15}$; not independent: $\frac{2}{5} \cdot \frac{3}{5} \neq \frac{4}{15}$

2. You randomly select 3 socks from the bin. What is the probability that all three socks are black for each situation?

   a. You replace each sock before selecting the next one.
   $\frac{8}{125} = 0.064$

   b. You do not replace each sock before selecting the next one.
   $\frac{1}{30} \approx 0.033$

3. At a school, all 9th and 10th grade students are required to take either band or chorus. The table shows the enrollments. Find the probability that a 10th grade student is taking band.

	9th grade	10th grade
Band	57	48
Chorus	63	77

   $\frac{48}{125}$, or 38.4%

4. In a science class, 27% of the students complete an extra-credit project. 18% of the students complete the extra-credit project and get an A in the class. What is the probability that a student who completes an extra-credit project also gets an A?
   $\frac{2}{3}$, or about 66.7%

24. **PROBLEM SOLVING** At a gas station, 84% of customers buy gasoline. Only 5% of customers buy gasoline and a beverage. What is the probability that a customer who buys gasoline also buys a beverage?

25. **PROBLEM SOLVING** You and 19 other students volunteer to present the "Best Teacher" award at a school banquet. One student volunteer will be chosen to present the award. Each student worked at least 1 hour in preparation for the banquet. You worked for 4 hours, and the group worked a combined total of 45 hours. For each situation, describe a process that gives you a "fair" chance to be chosen, and find the probability that you are chosen.

   a. "Fair" means equally likely.

   b. "Fair" means proportional to the number of hours each student worked in preparation.

26. **HOW DO YOU SEE IT?** A bag contains one red marble and one blue marble. The diagrams show the possible outcomes of randomly choosing two marbles using different methods. For each method, determine whether the marbles were selected with or without replacement.

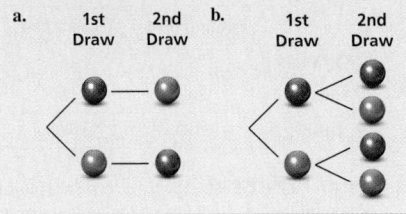

27. **MAKING AN ARGUMENT** A meteorologist claims that there is a 70% chance of rain. When it rains, there is a 75% chance that your softball game will be rescheduled. Your friend believes the game is more likely to be rescheduled than played. Is your friend correct? Explain your reasoning.

28. **THOUGHT PROVOKING** Two six-sided dice are rolled once. Events A and B are represented by the diagram. Describe each event. Are the two events dependent or independent? Justify your reasoning.

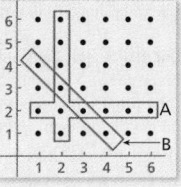

29. **MODELING WITH MATHEMATICS** A football team is losing by 14 points near the end of a game. The team scores two touchdowns (worth 6 points each) before the end of the game. After each touchdown, the coach must decide whether to go for 1 point with a kick (which is successful 99% of the time) or 2 points with a run or pass (which is successful 45% of the time).

   a. If the team goes for 1 point after each touchdown, what is the probability that the team wins? loses? ties?

   b. If the team goes for 2 points after each touchdown, what is the probability that the team wins? loses? ties?

   c. Can you develop a strategy so that the coach's team has a probability of winning the game that is greater than the probability of losing? If so, explain your strategy and calculate the probabilities of winning and losing the game.

30. **ABSTRACT REASONING** Assume that A and B are independent events.

   a. Explain why $P(B) = P(B|A)$ and $P(A) = P(A|B)$.

   b. Can $P(A \text{ and } B)$ also be defined as $P(B) \cdot P(A|B)$? Justify your reasoning.

Maintaining Mathematical Proficiency
Reviewing what you learned in previous grades and lessons

Solve the equation. Check your solution. *(Skills Review Handbook)*

31. $\frac{9}{10}x = 0.18$

32. $\frac{1}{4}x + 0.5x = 1.5$

33. $0.3x - \frac{3}{5}x + 1.6 = 1.555$

If students need help...	If students got it...
Resources by Chapter • Practice A and Practice B • Puzzle Time	Resources by Chapter • Enrichment and Extension • Cumulative Review
Student Journal • Practice	Start the *next* Section
Differentiating the Lesson Skills Review Handbook	

Overview of Section 12.3

Introduction
- Students were introduced to two-way tables in Algebra 1. In this lesson, the entries are converted to relative and conditional relative frequencies.
- This lesson connects to earlier work with conditional probabilities.

Formative Assessment Tips
- **Visitor Explanation:** This technique simulates what it would look like if a visitor were to enter your classroom during the middle of an exploration or activity. Could your students explain what they are doing and why they are doing it?
- This technique lets you know whether students understand the goal, or the essential question related to the exploration. Are students simply following directions or are they aware of the goal for today's exploration? Students are more engaged and their learning improves when the learning objective or purpose of the exploration is understood.
- This technique is best used when students are actively engaged in an exploration. This technique can be done as a *Think-Pair-Share* or as a *Writing Prompt*.
- The learning objective or essential question should have been made known to the students at the outset. This technique is not used to see whether students figured out the goal of the exploration or activity.

Pacing Suggestion
- The explorations are relatively short and serve to remind students of how two-way tables are constructed and analyzed. You may assign Exploration 3 as an out-of-class assignment.

Dynamic Teaching Tools
Dynamic Assessment & Progress Monitoring Tool
Lesson Planning Tool
Interactive Whiteboard Lesson Library
Dynamic Classroom with Dynamic Investigations

Common Core
State Standards

HSS-CP.A.4 Construct and interpret two-way frequency tables of data when two categories are associated with each object being classified. Use the two-way table as a sample space to decide if events are independent and to approximate conditional probabilities.

HSS-CP.A.5 Recognize and explain the concepts of conditional probability and independence in everyday language and everyday situations.

Laurie's Notes

Exploration

Motivate
- Ask whether there are any students who keep track of their training or practice routines. If there are serious athletes in the class, then chances are they do track their efforts.
- Explain to students that in this lesson they will study a structure that is used to calculate and compare when goals were met for different exercise options.

For Your Information
- Two-way tables are explained in the first exploration, although students should be familiar with these tables from Algebra 1.

Exploration 1
? "How many distinct regions are there in the Venn diagram? Name them." *four regions: play an instrument, speak a foreign language, do both, and do neither*
- **MP4 Model with Mathematics:** A Venn diagram is one way to represent the results of the survey. The two-way table is a second method.
? "What information is immediately known in the two-way table that is not displayed in the Venn diagram?" *the totals in each category*

Exploration 2
- Students should have little difficulty completing this exploration.
- Discuss the results as a class.

Exploration 3
- You might first ask students what categories they are curious to survey classmates about, though this can potentially lead to matters of privacy or discomfort for some students.
- Consider having safe yes-no questions ready to suggest: play video games, live more than x miles from school, and had a school-year job.

Communicate Your Answer
- Students should work independently to answer Questions 4 and 5. Discuss as a class.

Connecting to Next Step
- The explorations serve to quickly review how to construct and use a two-way table. Formal language describing the entries of the two-way table is presented in the formal lesson.

12.3 Two-Way Tables and Probability

Essential Question How can you construct and interpret a two-way table?

EXPLORATION 1 Completing and Using a Two-Way Table

Work with a partner. A *two-way table* displays the same information as a Venn diagram. In a two-way table, one category is represented by the rows and the other category is represented by the columns.

The Venn diagram shows the results of a survey in which 80 students were asked whether they play a musical instrument and whether they speak a foreign language. Use the Venn diagram to complete the two-way table. Then use the two-way table to answer each question.

Survey of 80 Students

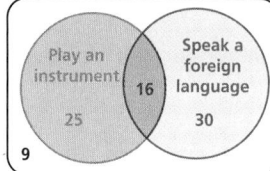

	Play an Instrument	Do Not Play an Instrument	Total
Speak a Foreign Language			
Do Not Speak a Foreign Language			
Total			

a. How many students play an instrument?

b. How many students speak a foreign language?

c. How many students play an instrument and speak a foreign language?

d. How many students do not play an instrument and do not speak a foreign language?

e. How many students play an instrument and do not speak a foreign language?

EXPLORATION 2 Two-Way Tables and Probability

Work with a partner. In Exploration 1, one student is selected at random from the 80 students who took the survey. Find the probability that the student

a. plays an instrument.

b. speaks a foreign language.

c. plays an instrument and speaks a foreign language.

d. does not play an instrument and does not speak a foreign language.

e. plays an instrument and does not speak a foreign language.

MODELING WITH MATHEMATICS

To be proficient in math, you need to identify important quantities in a practical situation and map their relationships using such tools as diagrams and two-way tables.

EXPLORATION 3 Conducting a Survey

Work with your class. Conduct a survey of the students in your class. Choose two categories that are different from those given in Explorations 1 and 2. Then summarize the results in both a Venn diagram and a two-way table. Discuss the results.

Communicate Your Answer

4. How can you construct and interpret a two-way table?

5. How can you use a two-way table to determine probabilities?

Section 12.3   Two-Way Tables and Probability   **683**

ANSWERS

1. See Additional Answers.

2. **a.** $\frac{41}{80}$

   b. $\frac{23}{40}$

   c. $\frac{1}{5}$

   d. $\frac{9}{80}$

   e. $\frac{5}{16}$

3. See Additional Answers.

4. *Sample answer:* You can use a Venn diagram to construct the two-way table. Each entry represents the number of people in each category.

5. Divide each number in each category by the total surveyed.

12.3 Lesson

Core Vocabulary

two-way table, *p. 684*
joint frequency, *p. 684*
marginal frequency, *p. 684*
joint relative frequency,
  p. 685
marginal relative frequency,
  p. 685
conditional relative frequency,
  p. 685

Previous
conditional probability

READING

A two-way table is also called a *contingency table*, or a *two-way frequency table*.

What You Will Learn

▶ Make two-way tables.
▶ Find relative and conditional relative frequencies.
▶ Use conditional relative frequencies to find conditional probabilities.

Making Two-Way Tables

A **two-way table** is a frequency table that displays data collected from one source that belong to two different categories. One category of data is represented by rows and the other is represented by columns. Suppose you randomly survey freshmen and sophomores about whether they are attending a school concert. A two-way table is one way to organize your results.

Each entry in the table is called a **joint frequency**. The sums of the rows and columns are called **marginal frequencies**, which you will find in Example 1.

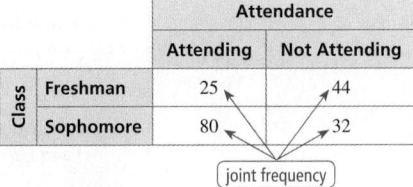

		Attendance	
		Attending	Not Attending
Class	Freshman	25	44
	Sophomore	80	32

joint frequency

EXAMPLE 1 Making a Two-Way Table

In another survey similar to the one above, 106 juniors and 114 seniors respond. Of those, 42 juniors and 77 seniors plan on attending. Organize these results in a two-way table. Then find and interpret the marginal frequencies.

SOLUTION

Step 1 Find the joint frequencies. Because 42 of the 106 juniors are attending, $106 - 42 = 64$ juniors are not attending. Because 77 of the 114 seniors are attending, $114 - 77 = 37$ seniors are not attending. Place each joint frequency in its corresponding cell.

Step 2 Find the marginal frequencies. Create a new column and row for the sums. Then add the entries and interpret the results.

		Attendance		
		Attending	Not Attending	Total
Class	Junior	42	64	106
	Senior	77	37	114
	Total	119	101	220

- 106 juniors responded.
- 114 seniors responded.
- 220 students were surveyed.
- 119 students are attending.
- 101 students are not attending.

Step 3 Find the sums of the marginal frequencies. Notice the sums $106 + 114 = 220$ and $119 + 101 = 220$ are equal. Place this value at the bottom right.

Monitoring Progress Help in English and Spanish at *BigIdeasMath.com*

1. You randomly survey students about whether they are in favor of planting a community garden at school. Of 96 boys surveyed, 61 are in favor. Of 88 girls surveyed, 17 are against. Organize the results in a two-way table. Then find and interpret the marginal frequencies.

Finding Relative and Conditional Relative Frequencies

You can display values in a two-way table as frequency counts (as in Example 1) or as *relative frequencies*.

STUDY TIP

Two-way tables can display relative frequencies based on the total number of observations, the row totals, or the column totals.

Core Concept

Relative and Conditional Relative Frequencies

A **joint relative frequency** is the ratio of a frequency that is not in the total row or the total column to the total number of values or observations.

A **marginal relative frequency** is the sum of the joint relative frequencies in a row or a column.

A **conditional relative frequency** is the ratio of a joint relative frequency to the marginal relative frequency. You can find a conditional relative frequency using a row total or a column total of a two-way table.

INTERPRETING MATHEMATICAL RESULTS

Relative frequencies can be interpreted as probabilities. The probability that a randomly selected student is a junior and is *not* attending the concert is 29.1%.

EXAMPLE 2   Finding Joint and Marginal Relative Frequencies

Use the survey results in Example 1 to make a two-way table that shows the joint and marginal relative frequencies.

SOLUTION

To find the joint relative frequencies, divide each frequency by the total number of students in the survey. Then find the sum of each row and each column to find the marginal relative frequencies.

		Attendance		
		Attending	**Not Attending**	**Total**
Class	**Junior**	$\frac{42}{220} \approx 0.191$	$\frac{64}{220} \approx 0.291$	0.482
	Senior	$\frac{77}{220} = 0.35$	$\frac{37}{220} \approx 0.168$	0.518
	Total	0.541	0.459	1

> About 29.1% of the students in the survey are juniors and are *not* attending the concert.

> About 51.8% of the students in the survey are seniors.

EXAMPLE 3   Finding Conditional Relative Frequencies

Use the survey results in Example 1 to make a two-way table that shows the conditional relative frequencies based on the row totals.

SOLUTION

Use the marginal relative frequency of each *row* to calculate the conditional relative frequencies.

		Attendance	
		Attending	**Not Attending**
Class	**Junior**	$\frac{0.191}{0.482} \approx 0.396$	$\frac{0.291}{0.482} \approx 0.604$
	Senior	$\frac{0.35}{0.518} \approx 0.676$	$\frac{0.168}{0.518} \approx 0.324$

> Given that a student is a senior, the conditional relative frequency that he or she is *not* attending the concert is about 32.4%.

Extra Example 2

Use the debate competition information in Extra Example 1 to make a two-way table that shows the joint and marginal relative frequencies.

Junior: $\frac{7}{40} = 0.175$, $\frac{9}{40} = 0.225$

Senior: $\frac{19}{40} = 0.475$, $\frac{5}{40} = 0.125$

	Qual.	**DNQ**	**Total**
Junior	0.175	0.225	0.4
Senior	0.475	0.125	0.6
Total	0.65	0.35	1

Extra Example 3

Use the debate competition information in Extra Example 1 to make a two-way table that shows the conditional relative frequencies based on the row totals.

Junior: $\frac{0.175}{0.4} \approx 0.438$, $\frac{0.225}{0.4} \approx 0.563$

Senior: $\frac{0.475}{0.6} \approx 0.792$, $\frac{0.125}{0.6} \approx 0.208$

	Qual.	**DNQ**
Junior	0.438	0.563
Senior	0.792	0.208

Laurie's Notes   **Teacher Actions**

- Discuss the difference between relative counts and relative frequencies. Write the *Core Concept*.
- **?** "In Example 1, there were 220 students surveyed. How do you calculate the joint relative frequencies?" Divide each entry by 220.
- **?** "What does the 0.396 entry in the two-way table mean in Example 3?" Given that the student is a junior, the conditional relative frequency that he or she is attending the concert is 39.6%.

Extra Example 4

A store surveys customers of different ages. The survey asks whether they would like to see the store expand its toy department. The results, given as joint relative frequencies, are shown in the two-way table.

	Age (in years)		
	< 10	10–20	> 20
Yes	0.27	0.06	0.23
No	0.09	0.17	0.18

a. What is the probability that a randomly selected customer whose age is between 10 and 20 would not like to see the toy department expanded?

$\dfrac{0.17}{0.17 + 0.06}$, or about 73.9%

b. What is the probability that a randomly selected customer who would like to see the toy department expanded is younger than 10?

$\dfrac{0.27}{0.27 + 0.06 + 0.23}$, or about 48.2%

c. Determine whether replying "Yes" and being younger than 10 are independent events.

P(younger than 10) = 0.36;
P(younger than 10 | Yes) ≈ 0.48;
Because 0.36 ≠ 0.48, the two events are not independent.

MONITORING PROGRESS ANSWERS

2.

		Response		
		In Favor	Against	Total
Gender	Boy	0.332	0.190	0.522
	Girl	0.386	0.092	0.478
	Total	0.718	0.282	1

3–4. See Additional Answers.

Chapter 12

  Help in English and Spanish at *BigIdeasMath.com*

2. Use the survey results in Monitoring Progress Question 1 to make a two-way table that shows the joint and marginal relative frequencies.

3. Use the survey results in Example 1 to make a two-way table that shows the conditional relative frequencies based on the column totals. Interpret the conditional relative frequencies in the context of the problem.

4. Use the survey results in Monitoring Progress Question 1 to make a two-way table that shows the conditional relative frequencies based on the row totals. Interpret the conditional relative frequencies in the context of the problem.

Finding Conditional Probabilities

You can use conditional relative frequencies to find conditional probabilities.

EXAMPLE 4 Finding Conditional Probabilities

A satellite TV provider surveys customers in three cities. The survey asks whether they would recommend the TV provider to a friend. The results, given as joint relative frequencies, are shown in the two-way table.

		Location		
		Glendale	Santa Monica	Long Beach
Response	Yes	0.29	0.27	0.32
	No	0.05	0.03	0.04

a. What is the probability that a randomly selected customer who is located in Glendale will recommend the provider?

b. What is the probability that a randomly selected customer who will not recommend the provider is located in Long Beach?

c. Determine whether recommending the provider to a friend and living in Long Beach are independent events.

SOLUTION

INTERPRETING MATHEMATICAL RESULTS

The probability 0.853 is a conditional relative frequency based on a column total. The condition is that the customer lives in Glendale.

a. $P(\text{yes} \mid \text{Glendale}) = \dfrac{P(\text{Glendale and yes})}{P(\text{Glendale})} = \dfrac{0.29}{0.29 + 0.05} \approx 0.853$

▶ So, the probability that a customer who is located in Glendale will recommend the provider is about 85.3%.

b. $P(\text{Long Beach} \mid \text{no}) = \dfrac{P(\text{no and Long Beach})}{P(\text{no})} = \dfrac{0.04}{0.05 + 0.03 + 0.04} \approx 0.333$

▶ So, the probability that a customer who will not recommend the provider is located in Long Beach is about 33.3%.

c. Use the formula $P(B) = P(B \mid A)$ and compare $P(\text{Long Beach})$ and $P(\text{Long Beach} \mid \text{yes})$.

$P(\text{Long Beach}) = 0.32 + 0.04 = 0.36$

$P(\text{Long Beach} \mid \text{yes}) = \dfrac{P(\text{Yes and Long Beach})}{P(\text{yes})} = \dfrac{0.32}{0.29 + 0.27 + 0.32} \approx 0.36$

▶ Because $P(\text{Long Beach}) \approx P(\text{Long Beach} \mid \text{yes})$, the two events are independent.

686   Chapter 12   Probability

Laurie's Notes   Teacher Actions

- **Think-Pair-Share:** Have students answer Questions 2–4, and then share and discuss as a class.
- Work through Example 4, finding conditional probabilities from the table of joint relative frequencies.
- **Visitor Explanation:** Ask, "If a visitor entered the room right now, how would you explain what you are doing and why are you doing it?" Students should practice explanations with partners. Solicit oral responses or do a one-minute write.

5. In Example 4, what is the probability that a randomly selected customer who is located in Santa Monica will not recommend the provider to a friend?

6. In Example 4, determine whether recommending the provider to a friend and living in Santa Monica are independent events. Explain your reasoning.

EXAMPLE 5 Comparing Conditional Probabilities

A jogger wants to burn a certain number of calories during his workout. He maps out three possible jogging routes. Before each workout, he randomly selects a route, and then determines the number of calories he burns and whether he reaches his goal. The table shows his findings. Which route should he use?

	Reaches Goal	Does Not Reach Goal
Route A	JHT JHT I	JHT I
Route B	JHT JHT I	IIII
Route C	JHT JHT II	JHT I

SOLUTION

Step 1 Use the findings to make a two-way table that shows the joint and marginal relative frequencies. There are a total of 50 observations in the table.

		Result		
		Reaches Goal	Does Not Reach Goal	Total
Route	A	0.22	0.12	0.34
	B	0.22	0.08	0.30
	C	0.24	0.12	0.36
	Total	0.68	0.32	1

Step 2 Find the conditional probabilities by dividing each joint relative frequency in the "Reaches Goal" column by the marginal relative frequency in its corresponding row.

$$P(\text{reaches goal}\,|\,\text{Route A}) = \frac{P(\text{Route A and reaches goal})}{P(\text{Route A})} = \frac{0.22}{0.34} \approx 0.647$$

$$P(\text{reaches goal}\,|\,\text{Route B}) = \frac{P(\text{Route B and reaches goal})}{P(\text{Route B})} = \frac{0.22}{0.30} \approx 0.733$$

$$P(\text{reaches goal}\,|\,\text{Route C}) = \frac{P(\text{Route C and reaches goal})}{P(\text{Route C})} = \frac{0.24}{0.36} \approx 0.667$$

▶ Based on the sample, the probability that he reaches his goal is greatest when he uses Route B. So, he should use Route B.

7. A manager is assessing three employees in order to offer one of them a promotion. Over a period of time, the manager records whether the employees meet or exceed expectations on their assigned tasks. The table shows the manager's results. Which employee should be offered the promotion? Explain.

	Exceed Expectations	Meet Expectations
Joy	JHT IIII	JHT I
Elena	JHT JHT II	JHT III
Sam	JHT JHT I	JHT II

Extra Example 5

An airline company strives not to lose luggage for passengers. A manager at the company randomly selects three flights to check on lost luggage. At the end of each day, the manager determines whether or not there was luggage lost on the flight that day. The table shows the findings. Which flight does the best at not losing luggage?

	Lost Luggage	No Lost Luggage
Flight 1	JHT JHT	III
Flight 2	JHT IIII	JHT
Flight 3	JHT JHT II	I

Based on the sample, the probability that a flight will not lose luggage is greatest for Flight 2. So, Flight 2 does the best at not losing luggage.

MONITORING PROGRESS ANSWERS

5. 0.1

6. The events are independent; $P(\text{Santa Monica}) \approx P(\text{Santa Monica} \mid \text{yes})$

7. Sam; Sam has the greatest probability of exceeding expectations.

Laurie's Notes Teacher Actions

- **MP7 Look For and Make Use of Structure:** Example 5 helps students recognize that the number of rows and columns in the table can be increased as needed for the context.
- Have students use the tally information to construct a two-way table of joint and marginal relative frequencies.
- **Turn and Talk:** "How do you now find the conditional probabilities of reaching his goal given a particular route?" Listen for correct reasoning.

Closure

- **Point of Most Significance:** Ask students to identify, aloud or on paper, the most significant point (or part) in the lesson that aided their learning.

Assignment Guide and Homework Check

ASSIGNMENT

Basic: 1, 2, 3–17 odd, 20, 21, 27–29

Average: 1, 2, 4–20 even, 21–23, 27–29

Advanced: 1, 2, 6–20 even, 21–29

HOMEWORK CHECK

Basic: 5, 9, 11, 13, 17

Average: 6, 10, 12, 14, 18

Advanced: 6, 10, 12, 14, 18

Vocabulary and Core Concept Check

1. **COMPLETE THE SENTENCE** A(n) _____ displays data collected from the same source that belongs to two different categories.

2. **WRITING** Compare the definitions of joint relative frequency, marginal relative frequency, and conditional relative frequency.

Monitoring Progress and Modeling with Mathematics

In Exercises 3 and 4, complete the two-way table.

3.

		Preparation		
		Studied	Did Not Study	Total
Grade	Pass		6	
	Fail			10
	Total	38		50

4.

		Response		
		Yes	No	Total
Role	Student	56		
	Teacher		7	10
	Total		49	

5. **MODELING WITH MATHEMATICS** You survey 171 males and 180 females at Grand Central Station in New York City. Of those, 132 males and 151 females wash their hands after using the public rest rooms. Organize these results in a two-way table. Then find and interpret the marginal frequencies. *(See Example 1.)*

6. **MODELING WITH MATHEMATICS** A survey asks 60 teachers and 48 parents whether school uniforms reduce distractions in school. Of those, 49 teachers and 18 parents say uniforms reduce distractions in school. Organize these results in a two-way table. Then find and interpret the marginal frequencies.

USING STRUCTURE In Exercises 7 and 8, use the two-way table to create a two-way table that shows the joint and marginal relative frequencies.

7.

		Dominant Hand		
		Left	Right	Total
Gender	Female	11	104	115
	Male	24	92	116
	Total	35	196	231

8.

		Gender		
		Male	Female	Total
Experience	Expert	62	6	68
	Average	275	24	299
	Novice	40	3	43
	Total	377	33	410

9. **MODELING WITH MATHEMATICS** Use the survey results from Exercise 5 to make a two-way table that shows the joint and marginal relative frequencies. *(See Example 2.)*

10. **MODELING WITH MATHEMATICS** In a survey, 49 people received a flu vaccine before the flu season and 63 people did not receive the vaccine. Of those who receive the flu vaccine, 16 people got the flu. Of those who did not receive the vaccine, 17 got the flu. Make a two-way table that shows the joint and marginal relative frequencies.

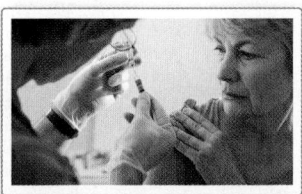

ANSWERS

1. two-way table

2. A joint relative frequency is the ratio of an entry in the table (that is not a total) to the survey total. A marginal relative frequency is the sum of the joint relative frequencies in any row or column. A conditional relative frequency is the ratio of the joint relative frequency to the marginal relative frequency.

3. 34; 40; 4; 6; 12

4. 42; 98; 3; 59; 108

5.

		Gender		
		Male	Female	Total
Response	Yes	132	151	283
	No	39	29	68
	Total	171	180	351

351 people were surveyed, 171 males were surveyed, 180 females were surveyed, 283 people said yes, 68 people said no.

6.

		Role		
		Teachers	Parents	Total
Response	Yes	49	18	67
	No	11	30	41
	Total	60	48	108

108 people were surveyed, 60 teachers were surveyed, 48 parents were surveyed, 67 people said yes, 41 people said no.

7.

		Dominant Hand		
		Left	Right	Total
Gender	Female	0.048	0.450	0.498
	Male	0.104	0.398	0.502
	Total	0.152	0.848	1

8.

		Gender		
		Male	Female	Total
Experience	Expert	0.151	0.015	0.166
	Average	0.670	0.059	0.729
	Novice	0.098	0.007	0.105
	Total	0.919	0.081	1

9–10. See Additional Answers.

11. MODELING WITH MATHEMATICS A survey finds that 110 people ate breakfast and 30 people skipped breakfast. Of those who ate breakfast, 10 people felt tired. Of those who skipped breakfast, 10 people felt tired. Make a two-way table that shows the conditional relative frequencies based on the breakfast totals. *(See Example 3.)*

12. MODELING WITH MATHEMATICS Use the survey results from Exercise 10 to make a two-way table that shows the conditional relative frequencies based on the flu vaccine totals.

13. PROBLEM SOLVING Three different local hospitals in New York surveyed their patients. The survey asked whether the patient's physician communicated efficiently. The results, given as joint relative frequencies, are shown in the two-way table. *(See Example 4.)*

		Location		
		Glens Falls	Saratoga	Albany
Response	Yes	0.123	0.288	0.338
	No	0.042	0.077	0.131

a. What is the probability that a randomly selected patient located in Saratoga was satisfied with the communication of the physician?

b. What is the probability that a randomly selected patient who was not satisfied with the physician's communication is located in Glens Falls?

c. Determine whether being satisfied with the communication of the physician and living in Saratoga are independent events.

14. PROBLEM SOLVING A researcher surveys a random sample of high school students in seven states. The survey asks whether students plan to stay in their home state after graduation. The results, given as joint relative frequencies, are shown in the two-way table.

		Location		
		Nebraska	North Carolina	Other States
Response	Yes	0.044	0.051	0.056
	No	0.400	0.193	0.256

a. What is the probability that a randomly selected student who lives in Nebraska plans to stay in his or her home state after graduation?

b. What is the probability that a randomly selected student who does not plan to stay in his or her home state after graduation lives in North Carolina?

c. Determine whether planning to stay in their home state and living in Nebraska are independent events.

ERROR ANALYSIS In Exercises 15 and 16, describe and correct the error in finding the given conditional probability.

		City			
		Tokyo	London	Washington, D.C.	Total
Response	Yes	0.049	0.136	0.171	0.356
	No	0.341	0.112	0.191	0.644
	Total	0.39	0.248	0.362	1

15. $P(\text{yes} \mid \text{Tokyo})$

$$✗ \quad P(\text{yes} \mid \text{Tokyo}) = \frac{P(\text{Tokyo and yes})}{P(\text{Tokyo})}$$
$$= \frac{0.049}{0.356} \approx 0.138$$

16. $P(\text{London} \mid \text{no})$

$$✗ \quad P(\text{London} \mid \text{no}) = \frac{P(\text{no and London})}{P(\text{London})}$$
$$= \frac{0.112}{0.248} \approx 0.452$$

17. PROBLEM SOLVING You want to find the quickest route to school. You map out three routes. Before school, you randomly select a route and record whether you are late or on time. The table shows your findings. Assuming you leave at the same time each morning, which route should you use? Explain. *(See Example 5.)*

	On Time	Late
Route A	卌 II	IIII
Route B	卌 卌 I	III
Route C	卌 卌 II	IIII

18. PROBLEM SOLVING A teacher is assessing three groups of students in order to offer one group a prize. Over a period of time, the teacher records whether the groups meet or exceed expectations on their assigned tasks. The table shows the teacher's results. Which group should be awarded the prize? Explain.

	Exceed Expectations	Meet Expectations
Group 1	卌 卌 II	IIII
Group 2	卌 III	卌
Group 3	卌 IIII	卌 I

ANSWERS

11.

		Breakfast	
		Ate	Did Not Eat
Feeling	Tired	0.091	0.333
	Not Tired	0.909	0.667

12.

		Vaccination	
		Received	Not Received
Health	Flu	0.327	0.270
	No Flu	0.673	0.730

13. a. about 0.789

   b. 0.168

   c. The events are independent.

14. a. about 0.10

   b. about 0.227

   c. The events are not independent.

15. The value for $P(\text{yes})$ was used in the denominator instead of the value for $P(\text{Tokyo})$; $\frac{0.049}{0.39} \approx 0.126$

16. The denominator should have been $P(\text{no})$; $\frac{0.112}{0.644} \approx 0.174$

17. Route B; It has the best probability of getting to school on time.

18. Group 1; It has the greatest probability of exceeding expectations.

Mini-Assessment

A radio station surveys listeners in three cities: Austin, Houston, and San Antonio. The survey asks whether they have installed the station's app on their mobile devices. The results are shown in the two-way table.

	AUS	HOU	SA
Yes	152	232	168
No	64	96	88

1. Use the survey results to make a two-way table that shows the joint and marginal relative frequencies.

	AUS	HOU	SA	Total
Yes	0.19	0.29	0.21	0.69
No	0.08	0.12	0.11	0.31
Total	0.27	0.41	0.32	1

2. Given that a listener downloaded the app, what is the conditional relative frequency that he or she lives in Austin? $\frac{0.19}{0.69}$, or about 27.5%

3. What is the probability that a randomly selected customer who is not located in Houston will not download the app? $\frac{0.19}{0.59}$, or about 32.2%

4. For a science project, a student plants seeds in 3 different soil mixes and observes whether the seeds sprout within 10 days. The table shows the results. Which soil mix has the highest probability of the seeds sprouting within 10 days?

	Sprouted	Did Not Sprout
Soil Mix 1	JHT JHT I	JHT IIII
Soil Mix 2	JHT JHT III	JHT JHT I
Soil Mix 3	JHT JHT	JHT I

Soil Mix 3

---

19. **OPEN-ENDED** Create and conduct a survey in your class. Organize the results in a two-way table. Then create a two-way table that shows the joint and marginal frequencies.

20. **HOW DO YOU SEE IT?** A research group surveys parents and coaches of high school students about whether competitive sports are important in school. The two-way table shows the results of the survey.

		Role		
		Parent	Coach	Total
Important	Yes	880	456	1336
	No	120	45	165
	Total	1000	501	1501

a. What does 120 represent?
b. What does 1336 represent?
c. What does 1501 represent?

21. **MAKING AN ARGUMENT** Your friend uses the table below to determine which workout routine is the best. Your friend decides that Routine B is the best option because it has the fewest tally marks in the "Does Not Reach Goal" column. Is your friend correct? Explain your reasoning.

	Reached Goal	Does Not Reach Goal
Routine A	JHT	III
Routine B	IIII	II
Routine C	JHT II	IIII

22. **MODELING WITH MATHEMATICS** A survey asks students whether they prefer math class or science class. Of the 150 male students surveyed, 62% prefer math class over science class. Of the female students surveyed, 74% prefer math. Construct a two-way table to show the number of students in each category if 350 students were surveyed.

Maintaining Mathematical Proficiency
Reviewing what you learned in previous grades and lessons

Draw a Venn diagram of the sets described. *(Skills Review Handbook)*

27. Of the positive integers less than 15, set *A* consists of the factors of 15 and set *B* consists of all odd numbers.

28. Of the positive integers less than 14, set *A* consists of all prime numbers and set *B* consists of all even numbers.

29. Of the positive integers less than 24, set *A* consists of the multiples of 2 and set *B* consists of all the multiples of 3.

---

23. **MULTIPLE REPRESENTATIONS** Use the Venn diagram to construct a two-way table. Then use your table to answer the questions.

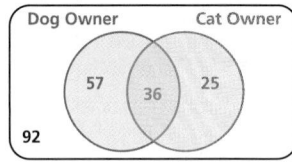

a. What is the probability that a randomly selected person does not own either pet?
b. What is the probability that a randomly selected person who owns a dog also owns a cat?

24. **WRITING** Compare two-way tables and Venn diagrams. Then describe the advantages and disadvantages of each.

25. **PROBLEM SOLVING** A company creates a new snack, N, and tests it against its current leader, L. The table shows the results.

	Prefer L	Prefer N
Current L Consumer	72	46
Not Current L Consumer	52	114

The company is deciding whether it should try to improve the snack before marketing it, and to whom the snack should be marketed. Use probability to explain the decisions the company should make when the total size of the snack's market is expected to (a) change very little, and (b) expand very rapidly.

26. **THOUGHT PROVOKING** Bayes' Theorem is given by

$$P(A|B) = \frac{P(B|A) \cdot P(A)}{P(B)}.$$

Use a two-way table to write an example of Bayes' Theorem.

If students need help...	If students got it...
Resources by Chapter • Practice A and Practice B • Puzzle Time	Resources by Chapter • Enrichment and Extension • Cumulative Review
Student Journal • Practice	Start the *next* Section
Differentiating the Lesson Skills Review Handbook	

Dynamic Teaching Tools

Dynamic Assessment & Progress Monitoring Tool

Interactive Whiteboard Lesson Library

Dynamic Classroom with Dynamic Investigations

Core Vocabulary

probability experiment, *p. 668*
outcome, *p. 668*
event, *p. 668*
sample space, *p. 668*
probability of an event, *p. 668*
theoretical probability, *p. 669*

geometric probability, *p. 670*
experimental probability, *p. 671*
independent events, *p. 676*
dependent events, *p. 677*
conditional probability, *p. 677*
two-way table, *p. 684*

joint frequency, *p. 684*
marginal frequency, *p. 684*
joint relative frequency, *p. 685*
marginal relative frequency, *p. 685*
conditional relative frequency,
    p. 685

ANSWERS

1. *Sample answer:* Draw a number line and then count the possibilities.

2. Create a table showing the conditional probability of each routine, and choose the routine with the highest probability of reaching the goal.

Core Concepts

Section 12.1

Theoretical Probabilities, *p. 668*
Probability of the Complement of an Event, *p. 669*
Experimental Probabilities, *p. 671*

Section 12.2

Probability of Independent Events, *p. 676*
Probability of Dependent Events, *p. 677*
Finding Conditional Probabilities, *p. 679*

Section 12.3

Making Two-Way Tables, *p. 684*
Relative and Conditional Relative Frequencies, *p. 685*

Mathematical Practices

1. How can you use a number line to analyze the error in Exercise 12 on page 672?

2. Explain how you used probability to correct the flawed logic of your friend in Exercise 21 on page 690.

------ Study Skills ------

Making a Mental Cheat Sheet

- Write down important information on note cards.
- Memorize the information on the note cards, placing the ones containing information you know in one stack and the ones containing information you do not know in another stack. Keep working on the information you do not know.

691

1. $\frac{11}{17}$
2. 0.68
3. $\frac{1}{9}$
4. 0.99
5. $\frac{1}{6}, \frac{4}{15}$
6. 0.2
7. 0.12
8. **a.** $\frac{1}{9}$, or about 0.11
   b. about 0.68
   c. about 0.21
9. **a.** 0.595
   b. 0.555
10.

		Vote		
		Friday	**Monday**	**Total**
Gender	**Boys**	6	8	14
	Girls	10	8	18
	Total	16	16	32

32 students were surveyed, 14 boys were surveyed, 18 girls were surveyed, 16 votes were for Friday, 16 votes were for Monday.

12.1–12.3   Quiz

1. You randomly draw a marble out of a bag containing 8 green marbles, 4 blue marbles, 12 yellow marbles, and 10 red marbles. Find the probability of drawing a marble that is not yellow. *(Section 12.1)*

Find $P(\overline{A})$. *(Section 12.1)*

2. $P(A) = 0.32$ 3. $P(A) = \frac{8}{9}$ 4. $P(A) = 0.01$

5. You roll a six-sided die 30 times. A 5 is rolled 8 times. What is the theoretical probability of rolling a 5? What is the experimental probability of rolling a 5? *(Section 12.1)*

6. Events A and B are independent. Find the missing probability. *(Section 12.2)*
   $P(A) = 0.25$
   $P(B) = \underline{\quad}$
   $P(A \text{ and } B) = 0.05$

7. Events A and B are dependent. Find the missing probability. *(Section 12.2)*
   $P(A) = 0.6$
   $P(B|A) = 0.2$
   $P(A \text{ and } B) = \underline{\quad}$

8. Find the probability that a dart thrown at the circular target shown will hit the given region. Assume the dart is equally likely to hit any point inside the target. *(Section 12.1)*
   a. the center circle
   b. outside the square
   c. inside the square but outside the center circle

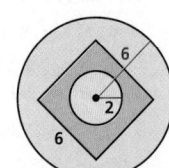

9. A survey asks 13-year-old and 15-year-old students about their eating habits. Four hundred students are surveyed, 100 male students and 100 female students from each age group. The bar graph shows the number of students who said they eat fruit every day. *(Section 12.2)*
   a. Find the probability that a female student, chosen at random from the students surveyed, eats fruit every day.
   b. Find the probability that a 15-year-old student, chosen at random from the students surveyed, eats fruit every day.

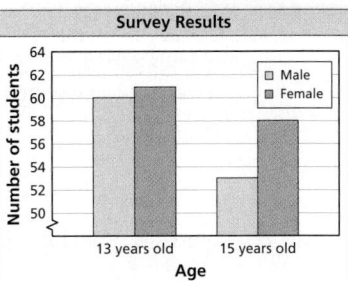

10. There are 14 boys and 18 girls in a class. The teacher allows the students to vote whether they want to take a test on Friday or on Monday. A total of 6 boys and 10 girls vote to take the test on Friday. Organize the information in a two-way table. Then find and interpret the marginal frequencies. *(Section 12.3)*

11. Three schools compete in a cross country invitational. Of the 15 athletes on your team, 9 achieve their goal times. Of the 20 athletes on the home team, 6 achieve their goal times. On your rival's team, 8 of the 13 athletes achieve their goal times. Organize the information in a two-way table. Then determine the probability that a randomly selected runner who achieves his or her goal time is from your school. *(Section 12.3)*

11.

		Goal		
		Achieved	**Not Achieved**	**Total**
School	**Your Team**	9	6	15
	Home Team	6	14	20
	Rival Team	8	5	13
	Total	23	25	48

about 0.391

Laurie's Notes

Overview of Section 12.4

Introduction

- Venn diagrams are used to introduce compound events. The events may be disjoint, or mutually exclusive. The events can also be overlapping.
- Probability rules are developed for both types of compound events, and students must first be able to distinguish between disjoint and overlapping events.
- Students will recognize that earlier skills such as determining the sample space of an event or finding the probability of a complement of an event are necessary skills in this lesson.
- In solving real-life applications, more than one type of probability rule may be needed.

Formative Assessment Tips

- **Partner Speaks:** This strategy provides a student the opportunity to share his or her thinking about a problem or concept with a partner. The partner then shares this thinking with the whole class.
- Thinking through a problem with a partner is less intimidating for many students than sharing it with an entire class. For the listener, he or she needs to pay attention to the thoughts of the speaker and set aside his or her own thinking about the problem. As students are engaged in this dialogue, circulate to hear the discussion and to gain an understanding of how students are thinking about the problem or concept. You will be able to judge appropriate next steps.
- The opportunity to speak to a partner and then have him or her share the student's thinking should not be used for simple, less challenging problems. It should be used as a way to pair students differently from the usual pairing of a student having a conversation with the person to his or her right.

Pacing Suggestion

- Have students work through all of the explorations before transitioning to the formal lesson.

Laurie's Notes

Exploration

Motivate

- Have students divide into two groups, girls and boys. Draw a Venn diagram of this relationship.
- Now ask students to divide into two more groups, those with female cousins and those without.
- **?** "What would the Venn diagram look like for this situation?" two intersecting circles where the overlapping region represents girls or boys in the class who have female cousins Draw the result.
- Explain to students that the two Venn diagrams represent the types of events they will study in this lesson.

Exploration Note

- Students should read the introduction, which describes new vocabulary about events: disjoint, mutually exclusive, and overlapping.

Exploration 1

- This exploration should not take students long to complete. Solicit a volunteer to draw the two Venn diagrams.
- **?** "Are the events in part (a) disjoint or overlapping?" overlapping
- **?** "Are the events in part (b) disjoint or overlapping?" disjoint

Exploration 2

- Students use the possible outcomes shown in the Venn diagrams in Exploration 1 to find probabilities. The same four questions are answered for parts (a) and (b).
- Students will use the results of this exploration to make a conjecture about a possible rule in the next exploration.
- Solicit responses for each part of the exploration.

Exploration 3

- **MP3 Construct Viable Arguments and Critique the Reasoning of Others:** Students may not yet have precise language to describe the rules, but listen for correct reasoning. The Venn diagram should be helpful in explaining why you need to subtract the probability of both events occurring.
- **Teaching Tip:** You could use the graphing calculator technique described in the *Teaching Strategy* on page T-674 to simulate the rolling of a six-sided die 50 times.

Communicate Your Answer

- Students should be able to describe disjoint events and overlapping events, along with how to find the probabilities of each type of event. Listen for reasoning discussed in Exploration 3.

Connecting to Next Step

- The explorations help students discover how to find the probability of compound events. The formula is stated in the formal lesson.

12.4 Probability of Disjoint and Overlapping Events

Essential Question
How can you find probabilities of disjoint and overlapping events?

Two events are **disjoint**, or **mutually exclusive**, when they have no outcomes in common. Two events are **overlapping** when they have one or more outcomes in common.

EXPLORATION 1 Disjoint Events and Overlapping Events

Work with a partner. A six-sided die is rolled. Draw a Venn diagram that relates the two events. Then decide whether the events are disjoint or overlapping.

> **MODELING WITH MATHEMATICS**
> To be proficient in math, you need to map the relationships between important quantities in a practical situation using such tools as diagrams.

a. Event A: The result is an even number.
   Event B: The result is a prime number.

b. Event A: The result is 2 or 4.
   Event B: The result is an odd number.

EXPLORATION 2 Finding the Probability that Two Events Occur

Work with a partner. A six-sided die is rolled. For each pair of events, find (a) P(A), (b) P(B), (c) P(A and B), and (d) P(A or B).

a. Event A: The result is an even number.
   Event B: The result is a prime number.

b. Event A: The result is 2 or 4.
   Event B: The result is an odd number.

EXPLORATION 3 Discovering Probability Formulas

Work with a partner.

a. In general, if event A and event B are disjoint, then what is the probability that event A or event B will occur? Use a Venn diagram to justify your conclusion.

b. In general, if event A and event B are overlapping, then what is the probability that event A or event B will occur? Use a Venn diagram to justify your conclusion.

c. Conduct an experiment using a six-sided die. Roll the die 50 times and record the results. Then use the results to find the probabilities described in Exploration 2. How closely do your experimental probabilities compare to the theoretical probabilities you found in Exploration 2?

Communicate Your Answer

4. How can you find probabilities of disjoint and overlapping events?

5. Give examples of disjoint events and overlapping events that do not involve dice.

ANSWERS

1. a.

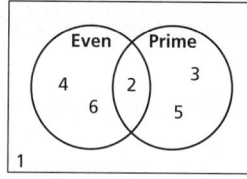

overlapping

b.

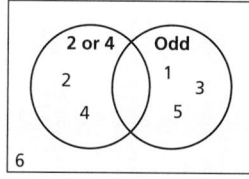

disjoint

2. a. $\frac{1}{2}; \frac{1}{2}; \frac{1}{6}; \frac{5}{6}$

b. $\frac{1}{3}; \frac{1}{2}; 0; \frac{5}{6}$

3. a. $P(A) + P(B)$; *Sample answer:*

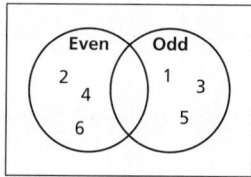

b. $P(A) + P(B) - P(A \text{ and } B)$; *Sample answer:*

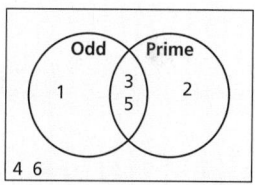

c. *Sample answer:*
$P(\text{even}) = \frac{25}{50} = \frac{1}{2}$, $P(\text{prime}) = \frac{19}{50}$,
$P(\text{even and prime}) = \frac{5}{50} = \frac{1}{10}$,
$P(\text{even or prime}) = \frac{39}{50}$,
$P(\text{odd}) = \frac{25}{50}$, $P(2 \text{ or } 4) = \frac{16}{50} = \frac{8}{25}$,
$P(\text{odd and 2 or 4}) = 0$,
$P(\text{odd or 2 or 4}) = \frac{41}{50}$;
The probabilities are similar.

4. For disjoint events, add the probabilities of each event. For overlapping events, add the probabilities of each event, and subtract the probability that both events occur.

5. *Sample answer:* disjoint events: picking an ace and picking a queen; overlapping events: picking an ace and picking a heart

Extra Example 1

Two six-sided dice are rolled. What is the probability that the sum of the numbers rolled is a multiple of 4 *or* is 5?

$\frac{9}{36} + \frac{4}{36} = \frac{13}{36} \approx 0.361$

12.4 Lesson

Core Vocabulary

compound event, *p. 694*
overlapping events, *p. 694*
disjoint or mutually exclusive events, *p. 694*

Previous
Venn diagram

STUDY TIP

If two events A and B are overlapping, then the outcomes in the intersection of A and B are counted *twice* when $P(A)$ and $P(B)$ are added. So, $P(A$ and $B)$ must be subtracted from the sum.

What You Will Learn

▶ Find probabilities of compound events.

▶ Use more than one probability rule to solve real-life problems.

Compound Events

When you consider all the outcomes for either of two events A and B, you form the *union* of A and B, as shown in the first diagram. When you consider only the outcomes shared by both A and B, you form the *intersection* of A and B, as shown in the second diagram. The union or intersection of two events is called a **compound event**.

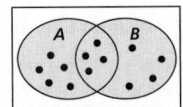
Union of A and B

Intersection of A and B

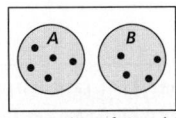
Intersection of A and B is empty.

To find $P(A$ or $B)$ you must consider what outcomes, if any, are in the intersection of A and B. Two events are **overlapping** when they have one or more outcomes in common, as shown in the first two diagrams. Two events are **disjoint**, or **mutually exclusive**, when they have no outcomes in common, as shown in the third diagram.

Core Concept

Probability of Compound Events

If A and B are any two events, then the probability of A or B is

$$P(A \text{ or } B) = P(A) + P(B) - P(A \text{ and } B).$$

If A and B are disjoint events, then the probability of A or B is

$$P(A \text{ or } B) = P(A) + P(B).$$

EXAMPLE 1 **Finding the Probability of Disjoint Events**

A card is randomly selected from a standard deck of 52 playing cards. What is the probability that it is a 10 *or* a face card?

SOLUTION

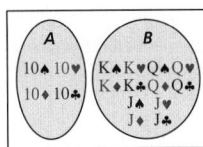

Let event A be selecting a 10 and event B be selecting a face card. From the diagram, A has 4 outcomes and B has 12 outcomes. Because A and B are disjoint, the probability is

$P(A \text{ or } B) = P(A) + P(B)$ Write disjoint probability formula.

$\qquad = \dfrac{4}{52} + \dfrac{12}{52}$ Substitute known probabilities.

$\qquad = \dfrac{16}{52}$ Add.

$\qquad = \dfrac{4}{13}$ Simplify.

$\qquad \approx 0.308.$ Use a calculator.

Laurie's Notes　Teacher Actions

- **MP4 Model with Mathematics:** Review union and intersection of sets by drawing Venn diagrams and relating them to disjoint and overlapping events.

- Write the *Core Concept*. Both formulas are used to find the probability of event A or event B occurring.

- ❓ "How are the formulas different?" If the events are not disjoint, you need to subtract the probability of both events occurring.

- ❓ "In Example 1, why are the two events disjoint?" A card cannot be both a 10 and a face card.

COMMON ERROR

When two events A and B overlap, as in Example 2, $P(A$ or $B)$ does not equal $P(A) + P(B)$.

EXAMPLE 2 Finding the Probability of Overlapping Events

A card is randomly selected from a standard deck of 52 playing cards. What is the probability that it is a face card *or* a spade?

SOLUTION

Let event A be selecting a face card and event B be selecting a spade. From the diagram, A has 12 outcomes and B has 13 outcomes. Of these, 3 outcomes are common to A and B. So, the probability of selecting a face card or a spade is

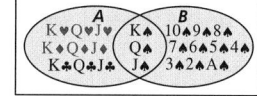

$$P(A \text{ or } B) = P(A) + P(B) - P(A \text{ and } B) \qquad \text{Write general formula.}$$

$$= \frac{12}{52} + \frac{13}{52} - \frac{3}{52} \qquad \text{Substitute known probabilities.}$$

$$= \frac{22}{52} \qquad \text{Add.}$$

$$= \frac{11}{26} \qquad \text{Simplify.}$$

$$\approx 0.423. \qquad \text{Use a calculator.}$$

EXAMPLE 3 Using a Formula to Find $P(A$ and $B)$

Out of 200 students in a senior class, 113 students are either varsity athletes or on the honor roll. There are 74 seniors who are varsity athletes and 51 seniors who are on the honor roll. What is the probability that a randomly selected senior is both a varsity athlete *and* on the honor roll?

SOLUTION

Let event A be selecting a senior who is a varsity athlete and event B be selecting a senior on the honor roll. From the given information, you know that $P(A) = \frac{74}{200}$, $P(B) = \frac{51}{200}$, and $P(A$ or $B) = \frac{113}{200}$. The probability that a randomly selected senior is both a varsity athlete *and* on the honor roll is $P(A$ and $B)$.

$$P(A \text{ or } B) = P(A) + P(B) - P(A \text{ and } B) \qquad \text{Write general formula.}$$

$$\frac{113}{200} = \frac{74}{200} + \frac{51}{200} - P(A \text{ and } B) \qquad \text{Substitute known probabilities.}$$

$$P(A \text{ and } B) = \frac{74}{200} + \frac{51}{200} - \frac{113}{200} \qquad \text{Solve for } P(A \text{ and } B).$$

$$P(A \text{ and } B) = \frac{12}{200} \qquad \text{Simplify.}$$

$$P(A \text{ and } B) = \frac{3}{50}, \text{ or } 0.06 \qquad \text{Simplify.}$$

Monitoring Progress 🔊 Help in English and Spanish at *BigIdeasMath.com*

A card is randomly selected from a standard deck of 52 playing cards. Find the probability of the event.

1. selecting an ace *or* an 8   2. selecting a 10 *or* a diamond

3. **WHAT IF?** In Example 3, suppose 32 seniors are in the band and 64 seniors are in the band or on the honor roll. What is the probability that a randomly selected senior is both in the band and on the honor roll?

Extra Example 2

A bag contains cards numbered 1 through 20. One card is randomly selected. What is the probability that the number on the card is a multiple of 3 *or* a multiple of 4?

$$\frac{6}{20} + \frac{5}{20} - \frac{1}{20} = \frac{10}{20} = 0.5$$

Extra Example 3

Out of 45 customers at a breakfast café, 42 customers bought either coffee or orange juice. There were 30 customers who bought orange juice and 40 customers who bought coffee. What is the probability that a randomly selected customer bought both coffee and orange juice?

$$\frac{30}{45} + \frac{40}{45} - \frac{42}{45} = \frac{28}{45} \approx 0.62$$

MONITORING PROGRESS ANSWERS

1. $\frac{2}{13}$

2. $\frac{4}{13}$

3. $\frac{19}{200}$, or 0.095

Laurie's Notes   **Teacher Actions**

- **Popsicle Sticks:** Pose Example 2, and have students work with their partners. Use *Popsicle Sticks* to solicit a solution.
- Have partners work independently on Example 3.
- Circulate and observe solution strategies. Students may draw a Venn diagram, or they may use mental math to determine the number that are athletes and on the honor roll. Others may use the formula for the probability of compound events.
- **MP3:** Have students share their approaches to increase the number of strategies students will be familiar with.

Extra Example 4

A medical association estimates that 10.9% of the people in the United States have a thyroid disorder. Suppose a medical lab has developed a simple diagnostic test that is 96% accurate for people who have the disorder and 99% accurate for people who do not have it. The medical lab gives the test to a randomly selected person. What is the probability that the diagnosis is correct? The probability that the diagnosis is correct is about 0.987, or 98.7%.

MONITORING PROGRESS ANSWERS

4. about 0.048, or 4.8%

5. 0.52, or 52%

Using More Than One Probability Rule

In the first four sections of this chapter, you have learned several probability rules. The solution to some real-life problems may require the use of two or more of these probability rules, as shown in the next example.

EXAMPLE 4   **Solving a Real-Life Problem**

The American Diabetes Association estimates that 8.3% of people in the United States have diabetes. Suppose that a medical lab has developed a simple diagnostic test for diabetes that is 98% accurate for people who have the disease and 95% accurate for people who do not have it. The medical lab gives the test to a randomly selected person. What is the probability that the diagnosis is correct?

SOLUTION

Let event A be "person has diabetes" and event B be "correct diagnosis." Notice that the probability of B depends on the occurrence of A, so the events are dependent. When A occurs, $P(B) = 0.98$. When A does not occur, $P(B) = 0.95$.

A probability tree diagram, where the probabilities are given along the branches, can help you see the different ways to obtain a correct diagnosis. Use the complements of events A and B to complete the diagram, where $\overline{A}$ is "person does not have diabetes" and $\overline{B}$ is "incorrect diagnosis." Notice that the probabilities for all branches from the same point must sum to 1.

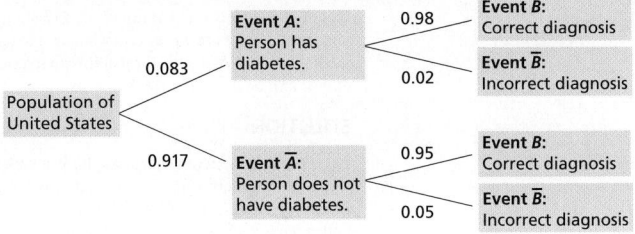

To find the probability that the diagnosis is correct, follow the branches leading to event B.

$$
\begin{aligned}
P(B) &= P(A \text{ and } B) + P(\overline{A} \text{ and } B) && \text{Use tree diagram.}\\
&= P(A) \cdot P(B\mid A) + P(\overline{A}) \cdot P(B\mid \overline{A}) && \text{Probability of dependent events}\\
&= (0.083)(0.98) + (0.917)(0.95) && \text{Substitute.}\\
&\approx 0.952 && \text{Use a calculator.}
\end{aligned}
$$

▶ The probability that the diagnosis is correct is about 0.952, or 95.2%.

Monitoring Progress Help in English and Spanish at *BigIdeasMath.com*

4. In Example 4, what is the probability that the diagnosis is *incorrect*?

5. A high school basketball team leads at halftime in 60% of the games in a season. The team wins 80% of the time when they have the halftime lead, but only 10% of the time when they do not. What is the probability that the team wins a particular game during the season?

Laurie's Notes   Teacher Actions

- Example 4 connects skills from earlier lessons.
- Pose the problem and say, "Work independently to answer the problem. Then you will have time to share your thinking with partners."
- **Partner Speaks:** After students have had sufficient time, pair students. Only one person speaks. The listener then asks for clarification or gives feedback. Have the listener describe the solution method or thinking used by his or her partner.

Closure

- **Exit Ticket:** A card is drawn from a standard deck of 52 playing cards. What is the probability of drawing a 4 *or* a red card? $\frac{28}{52} = \frac{7}{13} \approx 0.538$

12.4 Exercises

Dynamic Solutions available at *BigIdeasMath.com*

Vocabulary and Core Concept Check

1. **WRITING** Are the events A and $\bar{A}$ disjoint? Explain. Then give an example of a real-life event and its complement.

2. **DIFFERENT WORDS, SAME QUESTION** Which is different? Find "both" answers.

How many outcomes are in the intersection of A and B?

How many outcomes are shared by both A and B?

How many outcomes are in the union of A and B?

How many outcomes in B are also in A?

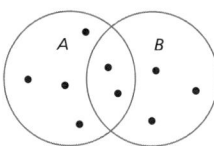

Monitoring Progress and Modeling with Mathematics

In Exercises 3–6, events A and B are disjoint.
Find $P(A \text{ or } B)$.

3. $P(A) = 0.3$, $P(B) = 0.1$
4. $P(A) = 0.55$, $P(B) = 0.2$

5. $P(A) = \frac{1}{3}$, $P(B) = \frac{1}{4}$
6. $P(A) = \frac{2}{3}$, $P(B) = \frac{1}{5}$

7. **PROBLEM SOLVING** Your dart is equally likely to hit any point inside the board shown. You throw a dart and pop a balloon. What is the probability that the balloon is red or blue? *(See Example 1.)*

8. **PROBLEM SOLVING** You and your friend are among several candidates running for class president. You estimate that there is a 45% chance you will win and a 25% chance your friend will win. What is the probability that you or your friend win the election?

9. **PROBLEM SOLVING** You are performing an experiment to determine how well plants grow under different light sources. Of the 30 plants in the experiment, 12 receive visible light, 15 receive ultraviolet light, and 6 receive both visible and ultraviolet light. What is the probability that a plant in the experiment receives visible or ultraviolet light? *(See Example 2.)*

10. **PROBLEM SOLVING** Of 162 students honored at an academic awards banquet, 48 won awards for mathematics and 78 won awards for English. There are 14 students who won awards for both mathematics and English. A newspaper chooses a student at random for an interview. What is the probability that the student interviewed won an award for English or mathematics?

ERROR ANALYSIS In Exercises 11 and 12, describe and correct the error in finding the probability of randomly drawing the given card from a standard deck of 52 playing cards.

11.

$$\begin{aligned} &P(\text{heart or face card}) \\ &\quad = P(\text{heart}) + P(\text{face card}) \\ &\quad = \frac{13}{52} + \frac{12}{52} = \frac{25}{52} \end{aligned}$$

12.

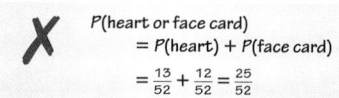

$$\begin{aligned} &P(\text{club or } 9) \\ &\quad = P(\text{club}) + P(9) + P(\text{club and } 9) \\ &\quad = \frac{13}{52} + \frac{4}{52} + \frac{1}{52} = \frac{9}{26} \end{aligned}$$

In Exercises 13 and 14, you roll a six-sided die. Find $P(A \text{ or } B)$.

13. Event A: Roll a 6.
    Event B: Roll a prime number.

14. Event A: Roll an odd number.
    Event B: Roll a number less than 5.

Assignment Guide and Homework Check

ASSIGNMENT

Basic: 1, 2, 3–17 odd, 20, 23–27

Average: 1, 2–20 even, 23–27

Advanced: 1, 2, 8–20 even, 21–27

HOMEWORK CHECK

Basic: 3, 7, 9, 15, 17

Average: 8, 10, 14, 16, 18

Advanced: 8, 10, 16, 18, 23

ANSWERS

1. yes; $\bar{A}$ is everything not in A; *Sample answer:* event A: you win the game, event $\bar{A}$: you do not win the game

2. How many outcomes are in the union of A and B?; 9; 2

3. 0.4

4. 0.75

5. $\frac{7}{12}$, or about 0.58

6. $\frac{13}{15}$, or about 0.87

7. $\frac{9}{20}$, or 0.45

8. 70%

9. $\frac{7}{10}$, or 0.7

10. $\frac{56}{81}$, or about 0.69

11. forgot to subtract $P(\text{heart and face card})$; $P(\text{heart}) + P(\text{face card}) - P(\text{heart and face card}) = \frac{11}{26}$

12. added instead of subtracted $P(\text{club and } 9)$; $P(\text{club}) + P(9) - P(\text{club and } 9) = \frac{4}{13}$

13. $\frac{2}{3}$

14. $\frac{5}{6}$

ANSWERS

15. 10%

16. $\frac{1}{6}$

17. 0.4742, or 47.42%

18. **a.** 0.09

    b. 0.12

    c. The coach should leave the goalie in the game.

19. $\frac{13}{18}$

20. no; The intersection of A and B is not empty.

21. $\frac{3}{20}$

22. See Additional Answers.

23. no; Until all cards, numbers, and colors are known, the conclusion cannot be made.

24. $n^2 - 24n + 144$

25. $4x^2 + 36x + 81$

26. $25z^2 - 60z + 36$

27. $9a^2 - 42ab + 49b^2$

Mini-Assessment

One card is randomly selected from a standard deck of 52 playing cards.

1. What is the probability that the card is a 4 *or* a queen? $\frac{2}{13} \approx 0.154$

2. What is the probability that the card is a diamond *or* a jack? $\frac{4}{13} \approx 0.308$

3. There are 63 cars in a used car lot, 60 of which have air conditioning or are silver. There are 18 silver cars and 57 cars with air conditioning. What is the probability that a car selected at random from the lot is silver *and* has air conditioning? $\frac{5}{21} \approx 0.238$

4. An airline estimates that 90% of its eastbound flights arrive on time and 72% of its westbound flights arrive on time. This morning, 42% of the airline's schedule is westbound flights. If a flight is chosen at random, what is the probability that the flight does not arrive on time? 0.1756, or about 17.6%

698   **Chapter 12**

---

15. **DRAWING CONCLUSIONS** A group of 40 trees in a forest are not growing properly. A botanist determines that 34 of the trees have a disease or are being damaged by insects, with 18 trees having a disease and 20 being damaged by insects. What is the probability that a randomly selected tree has both a disease and is being damaged by insects? (*See Example 3.*)

16. **DRAWING CONCLUSIONS** A company paid overtime wages or hired temporary help during 9 months of the year. Overtime wages were paid during 7 months, and temporary help was hired during 4 months. At the end of the year, an auditor examines the accounting records and randomly selects one month to check the payroll. What is the probability that the auditor will select a month in which the company paid overtime wages and hired temporary help?

17. **DRAWING CONCLUSIONS** A company is focus testing a new type of fruit drink. The focus group is 47% male. Of the responses, 40% of the males and 54% of the females said they would buy the fruit drink. What is the probability that a randomly selected person would buy the fruit drink? (*See Example 4.*)

18. **DRAWING CONCLUSIONS** The Redbirds trail the Bluebirds by one goal with 1 minute left in the hockey game. The Redbirds' coach must decide whether to remove the goalie and add a frontline player. The probabilities of each team scoring are shown in the table.

	Goalie	No goalie
Redbirds score	0.1	0.3
Bluebirds score	0.1	0.6

a. Find the probability that the Redbirds score and the Bluebirds do not score when the coach leaves the goalie in.

b. Find the probability that the Redbirds score and the Bluebirds do not score when the coach takes the goalie out.

c. Based on parts (a) and (b), what should the coach do?

Maintaining Mathematical Proficiency Reviewing what you learned in previous grades and lessons

Find the product. (*Skills Review Handbook*)

24. $(n - 12)^2$ 25. $(2x + 9)^2$ 26. $(-5z + 6)^2$ 27. $(3a - 7b)^2$

---

19. **PROBLEM SOLVING** You can win concert tickets from a radio station if you are the first person to call when the song of the day is played, or if you are the first person to correctly answer the trivia question. The song of the day is announced at a random time between 7:00 and 7:30 A.M. The trivia question is asked at a random time between 7:15 and 7:45 A.M. You begin listening to the radio station at 7:20. Find the probability that you miss the announcement of the song of the day or the trivia question.

20. **HOW DO YOU SEE IT?** Are events A and B disjoint events? Explain your reasoning.

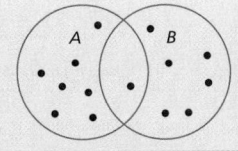

21. **PROBLEM SOLVING** You take a bus from your neighborhood to your school. The express bus arrives at your neighborhood at a random time between 7:30 and 7:36 A.M. The local bus arrives at your neighborhood at a random time between 7:30 and 7:40 A.M. You arrive at the bus stop at 7:33 A.M. Find the probability that you missed both the express bus and the local bus.

22. **THOUGHT PROVOKING** Write a general rule for finding $P(A$ or B or $C)$ for (a) disjoint and (b) overlapping events A, B, and C.

23. **MAKING AN ARGUMENT** A bag contains 40 cards numbered 1 through 40 that are either red or blue. A card is drawn at random and placed back in the bag. This is done four times. Two red cards are drawn, numbered 31 and 19, and two blue cards are drawn, numbered 22 and 7. Your friend concludes that red cards and even numbers must be mutually exclusive. Is your friend correct? Explain.

If students need help...	If students got it...
Resources by Chapter • Practice A and Practice B • Puzzle Time	Resources by Chapter • Enrichment and Extension • Cumulative Review
Student Journal • Practice	Start the *next* Section
Differentiating the Lesson Skills Review Handbook	

Laurie's Notes

Overview of Section 12.5

Introduction

- The Fundamental Counting Principle was introduced in grade 7 and is connected to the counting techniques students will learn in this lesson.
- Permutations (order matters) are introduced in contextual problems, and a formula is developed for calculating the number of ways n objects can be selected r at a time.
- Combinations (order does not matter) are introduced in contextual problems, and a formula is developed for calculating the number of ways n objects can be selected r at a time.

Teaching Strategy

- Formulas for permutations and combinations of n objects taken r at a time are presented in this lesson. Each of them involves finding factorials ($n!$) of a number.
- Most graphing calculators have built-in factorial, permutation, and combination functions.
- When you first introduce $n!$, students naturally want to know the largest factorial the calculator can compute before it reaches an overflow error. This exploration will not take students long. Students should also recognize that they can perform calculations with factorials.

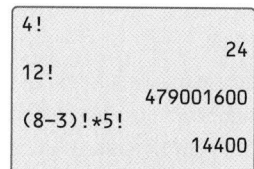

Factorials

- Permutations can be computed as well as combinations.

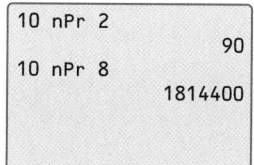

Permutations   **Combinations**

- If time permits, you might have students look at patterns with combinations, such as $_nC_r = {_nC_{n-r}}$.

Pacing Suggestion

- The explorations are a quick and fun way to help students recall how to determine the number of possible outcomes for a compound event. They provide a good introduction to permutations in the formal lesson.

**Common Core
State Standards**

HSS-CP.B.9 Use permutations and combinations to compute probabilities of compound events and solve problems.

Laurie's Notes

Exploration

Motivate
- **Story Time:** Tell students that your friend could not resist when the jackpot got really high, so she bought a lottery ticket. Your friend had to pick 6 numbers correctly out of the numbers from 1 to 40.
- **?** "What is the probability my friend will win the jackpot?" Students may be willing to take a guess. Many will say the probability is very small!
- Tell students that in today's lesson they will learn how to calculate the probability of winning the jackpot.

For Your Information
- Tree diagrams and the Fundamental Counting Principle were introduced in grade 7.

Exploration 1
- Students should be familiar with how to construct and read a tree diagram.
- **?** "How many events are there in this compound event?" three; flip a coin, flip a coin, and spin a spinner
- Students should be efficient with listing the outcomes, such as HH1 versus heads-heads-one.

Exploration 2
- Knowing how to read the tree diagram means it is not necessary to know what the actual events are in order to know the number of possible outcomes of the event.
- Discuss student responses and clarify any differences of opinion.

Exploration 3
- **MP3 Construct Viable Arguments and Critique the Reasoning of Others:** Students should recall what the Fundamental Counting Principle says, even if they have forgotten its name.
- A tree diagram is a helpful model in explaining why the number of possible outcomes of each event are multiplied together.

Communicate Your Answer
- Students should work independently to answer Questions 4 and 5 and then compare answers and language with their neighbor.

Connecting to Next Step
- The explorations will help students recall the use of tree diagrams to count outcomes of a compound event. Knowledge of the Fundamental Counting Principle is assumed in the formal lesson.

12.5 Permutations and Combinations

Essential Question How can a tree diagram help you visualize the number of ways in which two or more events can occur?

EXPLORATION 1   Reading a Tree Diagram

Work with a partner. Two coins are flipped and the spinner is spun. The tree diagram shows the possible outcomes.

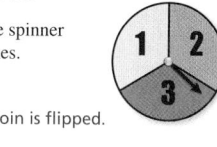

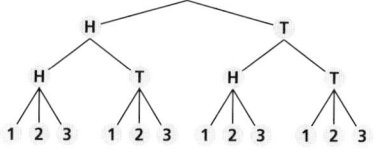

a. How many outcomes are possible?

b. List the possible outcomes.

EXPLORATION 2   Reading a Tree Diagram

Work with a partner. Consider the tree diagram below.

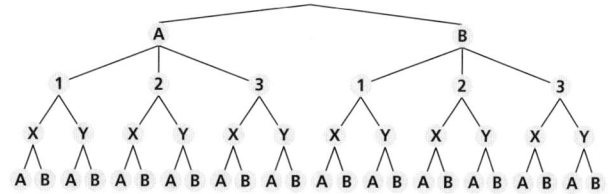

a. How many events are shown?   b. What outcomes are possible for each event?

c. How many outcomes are possible?   d. List the possible outcomes.

CONSTRUCTING VIABLE ARGUMENTS

To be proficient in math, you need to make conjectures and build a logical progression of statements to explore the truth of your conjectures.

EXPLORATION 3   Writing a Conjecture

Work with a partner.

a. Consider the following general problem: Event 1 can occur in m ways and event 2 can occur in n ways. Write a conjecture about the number of ways the two events can occur. Explain your reasoning.

b. Use the conjecture you wrote in part (a) to write a conjecture about the number of ways *more than* two events can occur. Explain your reasoning.

c. Use the results of Explorations 1(a) and 2(c) to verify your conjectures.

Communicate Your Answer

4. How can a tree diagram help you visualize the number of ways in which two or more events can occur?

5. In Exploration 1, the spinner is spun a second time. How many outcomes are possible?

Section 12.5   Permutations and Combinations   **699**

ANSWERS

1. **a.** 12

   b. HH1, HH2, HH3, HT1, HT2, HT3, TH1, TH2, TH3, TT1, TT2, TT3

2. **a.** 4

   b. event 1: A, B; event 2: 1, 2, 3; event 3: X, Y; event 4: A, B

   c. 24

   d. A1XA, A1XB, A1YA, A1YB, A2XA, A2XB, A2YA, A2YB, A3XA, A3XB, A3YA, A3YB, B1XA, B1XB, B1YA, B1YB, B2XA, B2XB, B2YA, B2YB, B3XA, B3XB, B3YA, B3YB

3. **a.** *Sample answer:* The two events can occur in mn ways; This is the Fundamental Counting Principle.

   b. *Sample answer:* Find the product of the number of ways each event can occur; The Fundamental Counting Principle works for more than two events.

   c. 1(a): $(2)(2)(3) = 12$; 2(c): $(2)(3)(2)(2) = 24$

4. *Sample answer:* Tree diagrams show all possibilities.

5. 36

12.5 Lesson

Core Vocabulary

permutation, *p. 700*
n factorial, *p. 700*
combination, *p. 702*

Previous
Fundamental Counting
   Principle

What You Will Learn

▶ Use the formula for the number of permutations.
▶ Use the formula for the number of combinations.

Permutations

A **permutation** is an arrangement of objects in which order is important. For instance, the 6 possible permutations of the letters A, B, and C are shown.

ABC   ACB   BAC   BCA   CAB   CBA

EXAMPLE 1   Counting Permutations

Consider the number of permutations of the letters in the word JULY. In how many ways can you arrange (a) all of the letters and (b) 2 of the letters?

SOLUTION

a. Use the Fundamental Counting Principle to find the number of permutations of the letters in the word JULY.

$$\text{Number of permutations} = \binom{\text{Choices for}}{\text{1st letter}}\binom{\text{Choices for}}{\text{2nd letter}}\binom{\text{Choices for}}{\text{3rd letter}}\binom{\text{Choices for}}{\text{4th letter}}$$

$$= 4 \cdot 3 \cdot 2 \cdot 1$$

$$= 24$$

▶ There are 24 ways you can arrange all of the letters in the word JULY.

b. When arranging 2 letters of the word JULY, you have 4 choices for the first letter and 3 choices for the second letter.

$$\text{Number of permutations} = \binom{\text{Choices for}}{\text{1st letter}}\binom{\text{Choices for}}{\text{2nd letter}}$$

$$= 4 \cdot 3$$

$$= 12$$

▶ There are 12 ways you can arrange 2 of the letters in the word JULY.

> **REMEMBER**
>
> *Fundamental Counting Principle*: If one event can occur in *m* ways and another event can occur in *n* ways, then the number of ways that both events can occur is *m* · *n*. The Fundamental Counting Principle can be extended to three or more events.

Monitoring Progress Help in English and Spanish at *BigIdeasMath.com*

1. In how many ways can you arrange the letters in the word HOUSE?

2. In how many ways can you arrange 3 of the letters in the word MARCH?

In Example 1(a), you evaluated the expression 4 · 3 · 2 · 1. This expression can be written as 4! and is read "4 *factorial*." For any positive integer *n*, the product of the integers from 1 to *n* is called *n* **factorial** and is written as

$$n! = n \cdot (n - 1) \cdot (n - 2) \cdot \cdots \cdot 3 \cdot 2 \cdot 1.$$

As a special case, the value of 0! is defined to be 1.

In Example 1(b), you found the permutations of 4 objects taken 2 at a time. You can find the number of permutations using the formulas on the next page.

Laurie's Notes   Teacher Actions

? "How can you tell that order is important for this example?" The word *arrange* means to put in order, so order is important.

? "Why are there 3 choices for the second letter?" There are 4 letters in the word JULY. Once one has been chosen for the first letter, there are 3 letters left.

• Introduce *n* factorial and the notation. See the *Teaching Strategy* on page T-698. Say, "When you have four objects taken four at a time and order matters, this is a permutation and can be found by multiplying 4 · 3 · 2 · 1 = 4!"

 **Core Concept**

Permutations

Formulas

The number of permutations of n objects is given by

$$_nP_n = n!.$$

The number of permutations of n objects taken r at a time, where $r \leq n$, is given by

$$_nP_r = \frac{n!}{(n-r)!}.$$

Examples

The number of permutations of 4 objects is

$$_4P_4 = 4! = 4 \cdot 3 \cdot 2 \cdot 1 = 24.$$

The number of permutations of 4 objects taken 2 at a time is

$$_4P_2 = \frac{4!}{(4-2)!} = \frac{4 \cdot 3 \cdot 2!}{2!} = 12.$$

USING A GRAPHING CALCULATOR

Most graphing calculators can calculate permutations.

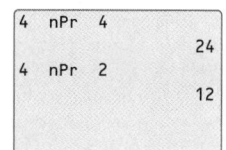

```
4  nPr  4
                24
4  nPr  2
                12
```

STUDY TIP

When you divide out common factors, remember that 7! is a factor of 10!.

EXAMPLE 2 Using a Permutations Formula

Ten horses are running in a race. In how many different ways can the horses finish first, second, and third? (Assume there are no ties.)

SOLUTION

To find the number of permutations of 3 horses chosen from 10, find $_{10}P_3$.

$$_{10}P_3 = \frac{10!}{(10-3)!} \qquad \text{Permutations formula}$$

$$= \frac{10!}{7!} \qquad \text{Subtract.}$$

$$= \frac{10 \cdot 9 \cdot 8 \cdot 7!}{7!} \qquad \text{Expand factorial. Divide out common factor, 7!.}$$

$$= 720 \qquad \text{Simplify.}$$

▶ There are 720 ways for the horses to finish first, second, and third.

EXAMPLE 3 Finding a Probability Using Permutations

For a town parade, you will ride on a float with your soccer team. There are 12 floats in the parade, and their order is chosen at random. Find the probability that your float is first and the float with the school chorus is second.

SOLUTION

Step 1 Write the number of possible outcomes as the number of permutations of the 12 floats in the parade. This is $_{12}P_{12} = 12!$.

Step 2 Write the number of favorable outcomes as the number of permutations of the other floats, given that the soccer team is first and the chorus is second. This is $_{10}P_{10} = 10!$.

Step 3 Find the probability.

$$P(\text{soccer team is 1st, chorus is 2nd}) = \frac{10!}{12!} \qquad \begin{array}{l}\text{Form a ratio of favorable} \\ \text{to possible outcomes.}\end{array}$$

$$= \frac{10!}{12 \cdot 11 \cdot 10!} \qquad \begin{array}{l}\text{Expand factorial. Divide} \\ \text{out common factor, 10!.}\end{array}$$

$$= \frac{1}{132} \qquad \text{Simplify.}$$

Section 12.5   Permutations and Combinations   **701**

Extra Example 2

Eight people serve on a committee. In how many different ways can a chairperson, a recorder, and a treasurer be chosen from the committee members?

There are 336 ways for a chairperson, a recorder, and a treasurer to be chosen from the committee members.

Extra Example 3

Drea and Bryan are auditioning for a part in the school play. There are 15 people auditioning, and the order of their auditions is chosen at random. Find the probability that Drea auditions last and Bryan auditions second to last.

$P(\text{Drea is last, Bryan is 2nd to last}) = \frac{13!}{15!} = \frac{1}{210}$

Laurie's Notes   Teacher Actions

? "How many ways can you arrange 10 objects taken 2 at a time?" $10 \cdot 9 = 90$

• Write the *Core Concept*. Explore the role of the denominator.

$$_{10}P_2 = \frac{10!}{(10-2)!} = \frac{10 \cdot 9 \cdot 8!}{8!} = 10 \cdot 9 = 90$$

Partially expanding the numerator allows common factors to divide out.

• **Another Way:** In Example 3, you could find that $_{12}P_2 = 132$, the number of permutations for the first two positions in the parade. Of those, only one has your team first followed by the school chorus, and therefore the probability is $\frac{1}{132}$.

Section 12.5   701

Extra Example 4

Count the possible combinations of 4 letters chosen from the list P, Q, R, S, T, U.
There are 15 possible combinations.

MONITORING PROGRESS ANSWERS

3. 336
4. $\frac{1}{182}$
5. 10

Monitoring Progress Help in English and Spanish at *BigIdeasMath.com*

3. **WHAT IF?** In Example 2, suppose there are 8 horses in the race. In how many different ways can the horses finish first, second, and third? (Assume there are no ties.)

4. **WHAT IF?** In Example 3, suppose there are 14 floats in the parade. Find the probability that the soccer team is first and the chorus is second.

Combinations

A **combination** is a selection of objects in which order is *not* important. For instance, in a drawing for 3 identical prizes, you would use combinations, because the order of the winners would not matter. If the prizes were different, then you would use permutations, because the order would matter.

EXAMPLE 4 Counting Combinations

Count the possible combinations of 2 letters chosen from the list A, B, C, D.

SOLUTION

List all of the permutations of 2 letters from the list A, B, C, D. Because order is not important in a combination, cross out any duplicate pairs.

AB	AC	AD	B̶A̶	BC	B̶D̶
C̶A̶	C̶B̶	CD	D̶A̶	D̶B̶	D̶C̶

> BD and DB are the same pair.

▶ There are 6 possible combinations of 2 letters from the list A, B, C, D.

Monitoring Progress Help in English and Spanish at *BigIdeasMath.com*

5. Count the possible combinations of 3 letters chosen from the list A, B, C, D, E.

In Example 4, you found the number of combinations of objects by making an organized list. You can also find the number of combinations using the following formula.

USING A GRAPHING CALCULATOR

Most graphing calculators can calculate combinations.

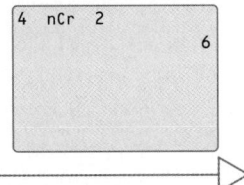

Core Concept

Combinations

Formula The number of combinations of n objects taken r at a time, where $r \le n$, is given by

$$_nC_r = \frac{n!}{(n-r)! \cdot r!}.$$

Example The number of combinations of 4 objects taken 2 at a time is

$$_4C_2 = \frac{4!}{(4-2)! \cdot 2!} = \frac{4 \cdot 3 \cdot 2!}{2! \cdot (2 \cdot 1)} = 6.$$

Laurie's Notes   Teacher Actions

? "Two players from a 12-person team are picked as co-captains. Does the order matter in terms of which player is picked first?" no
- Introduce combinations.
- **Predict, Explain, Observe:** Group students and ask, "If order does not matter in a combination, how will the number of outcomes compare to the permutation using the same numbers? Explain your reasoning." Give groups sufficient time to consider the question and their reasoning. Students often say that you need to subtract the arrangements of the lesser number. (For "12 take 2," students may say the number of combinations is the number of permutations minus the arrangements of 2 people.)

EXAMPLE 5   Using the Combinations Formula

You order a sandwich at a restaurant. You can choose 2 side dishes from a list of 8. How many combinations of side dishes are possible?

SOLUTION

The order in which you choose the side dishes is not important. So, to find the number of combinations of 8 side dishes taken 2 at a time, find $_8C_2$.

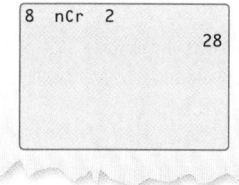

Check

8 nCr 2
              28

$$_8C_2 = \frac{8!}{(8-2)! \cdot 2!}$$ Combinations formula

$$= \frac{8!}{6! \cdot 2!}$$ Subtract.

$$= \frac{8 \cdot 7 \cdot 6!}{6! \cdot (2 \cdot 1)}$$ Expand factorials. Divide out common factor, 6!.

$$= 28$$ Multiply.

▶ There are 28 different combinations of side dishes you can order.

EXAMPLE 6   Finding a Probability Using Combinations

A yearbook editor has selected 14 photos, including one of you and one of your friend, to use in a collage for the yearbook. The photos are placed at random. There is room for 2 photos at the top of the page. What is the probability that your photo and your friend's photo are the 2 placed at the top of the page?

SOLUTION

Step 1   Write the number of possible outcomes as the number of combinations of 14 photos taken 2 at a time, or $_{14}C_2$, because the order in which the photos are chosen is not important.

$$_{14}C_2 = \frac{14!}{(14-2)! \cdot 2!}$$ Combinations formula

$$= \frac{14!}{12! \cdot 2!}$$ Subtract.

$$= \frac{14 \cdot 13 \cdot 12!}{12! \cdot (2 \cdot 1)}$$ Expand factorials. Divide out common factor, 12!.

$$= 91$$ Multiply.

Step 2   Find the number of favorable outcomes. Only one of the possible combinations includes your photo and your friend's photo.

Step 3   Find the probability.

$$P(\text{your photo and your friend's photos are chosen}) = \frac{1}{91}$$

Monitoring Progress 🔊)) Help in English and Spanish at *BigIdeasMath.com*

6. **WHAT IF?** In Example 5, suppose you can choose 3 side dishes out of the list of 8 side dishes. How many combinations are possible?

7. **WHAT IF?** In Example 6, suppose there are 20 photos in the collage. Find the probability that your photo and your friend's photo are the 2 placed at the top of the page.

Extra Example 5
You are listening to music. You have time to hear only 3 songs from your playlist of 16 songs. How many combinations of 3 songs are possible?
560 combinations

Extra Example 6
The art teacher has selected 13 projects, including one of yours and one of your friend's, to use in a display case in the hallway. The projects are placed at random. There is room for 2 projects in the middle row of the case. What is the probability that your project and your friend's project are the two placed in the middle row? $\frac{1}{78}$

MONITORING PROGRESS ANSWERS
6. 56
7. $\frac{1}{190}$

Laurie's Notes   **Teacher Actions**

❓ **Always-Sometimes-Never True:** "$_nP_r$ is always greater than $_nC_r$." Always true unless $r = 1$. If $r = 1$, then $_nP_r = _nC_r$.

• **Thumbs Up:** Work through Example 5 as shown. Have students self-assess with *Thumbs Up*.

❓ "How would you list the 28 combinations?" Answers will vary.

❓ "How can you tell order is not important for Example 6?" The problem does not specify that either picture must be first.

• **Predict, Explain, Observe:** "Which combination increases more, when you increase n by 1 or r by 1?" For example, for $_{14}C_2$, which combination increases more, $_{15}C_2$ or $_{14}C_3$?

Closure

• **Exit Ticket:** Calculate the probability of picking all 6 numbers out of 40 in a lottery. 3,838,380

Assignment Guide and Homework Check

ASSIGNMENT

Basic: 1, 2, 3–35 odd, 45, 52, 59, 60

Average: 1, 2–42 even, 46, 49, 52, 59, 60

Advanced: 1, 2, 8, 14–26 even, 34–44 even, 46–49, 53–60

HOMEWORK CHECK

Basic: 5, 13, 17, 27, 33

Average: 8, 18, 20, 34, 40

Advanced: 18, 20, 34, 46, 49

ANSWERS

1. permutation

2. $\dfrac{7!}{(7-2)!}$; It is the only expression that does not equal 21.

3. **a.** 2
   b. 2

4. **a.** 6
   b. 6

5. **a.** 24
   b. 12

6. **a.** 120
   b. 20

7. **a.** 720
   b. 30

8. **a.** 5040
   b. 42

9. 20

10. 210

11. 9

12. 720

13. 20,160

14. 1

15. 870

16. 6,375,600

17. 990

18. 720

19. $\frac{1}{56}$

20. $\frac{1}{720}$

21. 4

22. 6

23. 20

24. 5

25. 5

26. 56

27. 1

28. 28

29. 220

30. 330

31. 6435

32. 15,504

33. 635,376

12.5 Exercises

Dynamic Solutions available at *BigIdeasMath.com*

Vocabulary and Core Concept Check

1. **COMPLETE THE SENTENCE** An arrangement of objects in which order is important is called a(n) _____.

2. **WHICH ONE DOESN'T BELONG?** Which expression does *not* belong with the other three? Explain your reasoning.

   | $\dfrac{7!}{2! \cdot 5!}$ | $_7C_5$ | $_7C_2$ | $\dfrac{7!}{(7-2)!}$ |

Monitoring Progress and Modeling with Mathematics

In Exercises 3–8, find the number of ways you can arrange (a) all of the letters and (b) 2 of the letters in the given word. *(See Example 1.)*

3. AT   4. TRY

5. ROCK   6. WATER

7. FAMILY   8. FLOWERS

In Exercises 9–16, evaluate the expression.

9. $_5P_2$ 10. $_7P_3$

11. $_9P_1$ 12. $_6P_5$

13. $_8P_6$ 14. $_{12}P_0$

15. $_{30}P_2$ 16. $_{25}P_5$

17. **PROBLEM SOLVING** Eleven students are competing in an art contest. In how many different ways can the students finish first, second, and third? *(See Example 2.)*

18. **PROBLEM SOLVING** Six friends go to a movie theater. In how many different ways can they sit together in a row of 6 empty seats?

19. **PROBLEM SOLVING** You and your friend are 2 of 8 servers working a shift in a restaurant. At the beginning of the shift, the manager randomly assigns one section to each server. Find the probability that you are assigned Section 1 and your friend is assigned Section 2. *(See Example 3.)*

20. **PROBLEM SOLVING** You make 6 posters to hold up at a basketball game. Each poster has a letter of the word TIGERS. You and 5 friends sit next to each other in a row. The posters are distributed at random. Find the probability that TIGERS is spelled correctly when you hold up the posters.

In Exercises 21–24, count the possible combinations of *r* letters chosen from the given list. *(See Example 4.)*

21. A, B, C, D; *r* = 3   22. L, M, N, O; *r* = 2

23. U, V, W, X, Y, Z; *r* = 3   24. D, E, F, G, H; *r* = 4

In Exercises 25–32, evaluate the expression.

25. $_5C_1$ 26. $_8C_5$

27. $_9C_9$ 28. $_8C_6$

29. $_{12}C_3$ 30. $_{11}C_4$

31. $_{15}C_8$ 32. $_{20}C_5$

33. **PROBLEM SOLVING** Each year, 64 golfers participate in a golf tournament. The golfers play in groups of 4. How many groups of 4 golfers are possible? *(See Example 5.)*

34. PROBLEM SOLVING You want to purchase vegetable dip for a party. A grocery store sells 7 different flavors of vegetable dip. You have enough money to purchase 2 flavors. How many combinations of 2 flavors of vegetable dip are possible?

ERROR ANALYSIS In Exercises 35 and 36, describe and correct the error in evaluating the expression.

35.

✗ $_{11}P_7 = \dfrac{11!}{(11-7)} = \dfrac{11!}{4} = 9,979,200$

36.

✗ $_9C_4 = \dfrac{9!}{(9-4)!} = \dfrac{9!}{5!} = 3024$

REASONING In Exercises 37–40, tell whether the question can be answered using *permutations* or *combinations*. Explain your reasoning. Then answer the question.

37. To complete an exam, you must answer 8 questions from a list of 10 questions. In how many ways can you complete the exam?

38. Ten students are auditioning for 3 different roles in a play. In how many ways can the 3 roles be filled?

39. Fifty-two athletes are competing in a bicycle race. In how many orders can the bicyclists finish first, second, and third? (Assume there are no ties.)

40. An employee at a pet store needs to catch 5 tetras in an aquarium containing 27 tetras. In how many groupings can the employee capture 5 tetras?

41. CRITICAL THINKING Compare the quantities $_{50}C_9$ and $_{50}C_{41}$ without performing any calculations. Explain your reasoning.

42. CRITICAL THINKING Show that each identity is true for any whole numbers r and n, where $0 \le r \le n$.

    a. $_nC_n = 1$ **b.** $_nC_r = {_n}C_{n-r}$

    c. $_{n+1}C_r = {_n}C_r + {_n}C_{r-1}$

43. REASONING Complete the table for each given value of r. Then write an inequality relating $_nP_r$ and $_nC_r$. Explain your reasoning.

	r = 0	r = 1	r = 2	r = 3
$_3P_r$				
$_3C_r$				

44. REASONING Write an equation that relates $_nP_r$ and $_nC_r$. Then use your equation to find and interpret the value of $\dfrac{_{182}P_4}{_{182}C_4}$.

45. PROBLEM SOLVING You and your friend are in the studio audience on a television game show. From an audience of 300 people, 2 people are randomly selected as contestants. What is the probability that you and your friend are chosen? *(See Example 6.)*

46. PROBLEM SOLVING You work 5 evenings each week at a bookstore. Your supervisor assigns you 5 evenings at random from the 7 possibilities. What is the probability that your schedule does not include working on the weekend?

REASONING In Exercises 47 and 48, find the probability of winning a lottery using the given rules. Assume that lottery numbers are selected at random.

47. You must correctly select 6 numbers, each an integer from 0 to 49. The order is not important.

48. You must correctly select 4 numbers, each an integer from 0 to 9. The order is important.

49. MATHEMATICAL CONNECTIONS

A polygon is convex when no line that contains a side of the polygon contains a point in the interior of the polygon. Consider a convex polygon with n sides.

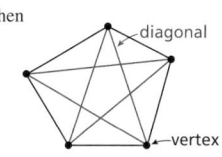

    a. Use the combinations formula to write an expression for the number of diagonals in an n-sided polygon.

    b. Use your result from part (a) to write a formula for the number of diagonals of an n-sided convex polygon.

50. PROBLEM SOLVING You are ordering a burrito with 2 main ingredients and 3 toppings. The menu below shows the possible choices. How many different burritos are possible?

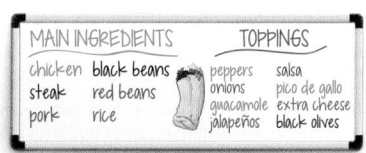

MAIN INGREDIENTS	TOPPINGS	
chicken black beans	peppers	salsa
steak red beans	onions	pico de gallo
pork rice	guacamole	extra cheese
	jalapeños	black olives

ANSWERS

34. 21

35. The factorial in the denominator was left out;

$$_{11}P_7 = \frac{11!}{(11-7)!} = 1,663,200$$

36. The permutations formula was used;

$$_9C_4 = \frac{9!}{(9-4)!4!} = 126$$

37. combinations; The order is not important; 45

38. permutations; The order is important; 720

39. permutations; The order is important; 132,600

40. combinations; The order is not important; 80,730

41. $_{50}C_9 = {_{50}}C_{41}$; For each combination of 9 objects, there is a corresponding combination of the 41 remaining objects.

42. a. $_nC_n = \dfrac{n!}{n!0!} = 1$

    b. $_nC_{n-r} = \dfrac{n!}{(n-(n-r))!(n-r)!}$

        $= \dfrac{n!}{(r)!(n-r)!} = {_n}C_r$

    c. $_nC_r + {_n}C_{r-1} = \dfrac{n!}{(n-r)!r!} +$

        $\dfrac{n!}{(n-r+1)!(r-1)!}$

        $= \dfrac{n!(n-r+1) + n!r}{(n-r+1)!r!}$

        $= \dfrac{n!n + n!}{(n-r+1)!r!}$

        $= \dfrac{n!(n+1)}{(n-r+1)!r!}$

        $= \dfrac{(n+1)!}{(n+1-r)!r!} = {_{n+1}}C_r$

43.

	r = 0	r = 1	r = 2	r = 3
$_3P_r$	1	3	6	6
$_3C_r$	1	3	3	1

$_nP_r \ge {_n}C_r$; Because $_nP_r = \dfrac{n!}{(n-r)!}$ and $_nC_r = \dfrac{n!}{(n-r)! \cdot r!}$,

$_nP_r > {_n}C_r$ when $r > 1$ and $_nP_r = {_n}C_r$ when $r = 0$ or $r = 1$.

44. $r! = \dfrac{_nP_r}{_nC_r}$; 24

45. $\dfrac{1}{44,850}$

46. $\dfrac{1}{21}$

47. $\dfrac{1}{15,890,700}$

48. $\dfrac{1}{5040}$

49. a. $_nC_{n-2} - n$

    b. $\dfrac{n(n-3)}{2}$

50. 840

51. 30

52. a. 1; Each outcome has the same three marbles.

    b. 6; Each outcome has a different permutation.

53. a. $\frac{1}{2}$

    b. $\frac{1}{2}$; The probabilities are the same.

54. $\frac{1061}{1250}$

55. a. $\frac{1}{90}$

    b. $\frac{9}{10}$

56. 376

57. $\frac{1}{406}$; There are $_{30}C_5$ possible groups. The number of groups that will have you and your two best friends is $_{27}C_2$.

58. a. about 0.04; about 0.12

    b. $1 - \dfrac{_{365}P_n}{365^n}$

    c. 23 people

59. $\frac{1}{5}$

60. TH

Mini-Assessment

1. Consider the letters in the word KINDLY.

    a. In how many ways can you arrange all the letters?
    720 ways

    b. In how many ways can you arrange 3 of the letters?
    120 ways

2. Nine people, including Becky and Samir, are being interviewed for a scholarship. If the order is chosen at random, what is the probability that Becky will be interviewed first and Samir will be interviewed second? $\frac{1}{72}$

3. You are preparing for a trip. You have a list of 7 books to read, but you can bring only 3 with you on the trip. How many combinations of books are possible?
35 different combinations

4. A restaurant is giving free pizzas to 2 customers selected at random from a group of 30. You and a friend enter the drawing. What is the probability that both of you win a free pizza? $\frac{1}{435}$

---

51. PROBLEM SOLVING You want to purchase 2 different types of contemporary music CDs and 1 classical music CD from the music collection shown. How many different sets of music types can you choose for your purchase?

52. HOW DO YOU SEE IT? A bag contains one green marble, one red marble, and one blue marble. The diagram shows the possible outcomes of randomly drawing three marbles from the bag without replacement.

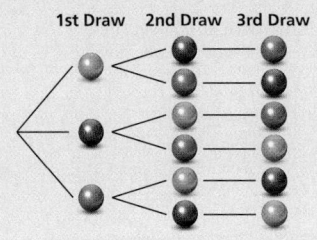

1st Draw 2nd Draw 3rd Draw

    a. How many combinations of three marbles can be drawn from the bag? Explain.

    b. How many permutations of three marbles can be drawn from the bag? Explain.

53. PROBLEM SOLVING Every student in your history class is required to present a project in front of the class. Each day, 4 students make their presentations in an order chosen at random by the teacher. You make your presentation on the first day.

    a. What is the probability that you are chosen to be the first or second presenter on the first day?

    b. What is the probability that you are chosen to be the second or third presenter on the first day? Compare your answer with that in part (a).

54. PROBLEM SOLVING The organizer of a cast party for a drama club asks each of the 6 cast members to bring 1 food item from a list of 10 items. Assuming each member randomly chooses a food item to bring, what is the probability that at least 2 of the 6 cast members bring the same item?

55. PROBLEM SOLVING You are one of 10 students performing in a school talent show. The order of the performances is determined at random. The first 5 performers go on stage before the intermission.

    a. What is the probability that you are the last performer before the intermission and your rival performs immediately before you?

    b. What is the probability that you are *not* the first performer?

56. THOUGHT PROVOKING How many integers, greater than 999 but not greater than 4000, can be formed with the digits 0, 1, 2, 3, and 4? Repetition of digits is allowed.

57. PROBLEM SOLVING There are 30 students in your class. Your science teacher chooses 5 students at random to complete a group project. Find the probability that you and your 2 best friends in the science class are chosen to work in the group. Explain how you found your answer.

58. PROBLEM SOLVING Follow the steps below to explore a famous probability problem called the *birthday problem*. (Assume there are 365 equally likely birthdays possible.)

    a. What is the probability that at least 2 people share the same birthday in a group of 6 randomly chosen people? in a group of 10 randomly chosen people?

    b. Generalize the results from part (a) by writing a formula for the probability $P(n)$ that at least 2 people in a group of n people share the same birthday. (*Hint*: Use $_nP_r$ notation in your formula.)

    c. Enter the formula from part (b) into a graphing calculator. Use the *table* feature to make a table of values. For what group size does the probability that at least 2 people share the same birthday first exceed 50%?

Maintaining Mathematical Proficiency
Reviewing what you learned in previous grades and lessons

59. A bag contains 12 white marbles and 3 black marbles. You pick 1 marble at random. What is the probability that you pick a black marble? *(Section 12.1)*

60. The table shows the result of flipping two coins 12 times. For what outcome is the experimental probability the same as the theoretical probability? *(Section 12.1)*

HH	HT	TH	TT
2	6	3	1

If students need help...	If students got it...
Resources by Chapter • Practice A and Practice B • Puzzle Time	Resources by Chapter • Enrichment and Extension • Cumulative Review
Student Journal • Practice	Start the *next* Section
Differentiating the Lesson Skills Review Handbook	

Dynamic Teaching Tools

Dynamic Assessment & Progress Monitoring Tool

Lesson Planning Tool

Interactive Whiteboard Lesson Library

Dynamic Classroom with Dynamic Investigations

Overview of Section 12.6

Introduction

- Students have worked with probability throughout this chapter. This last lesson introduces the probability distribution function that displays the probability of each possible value of a random variable.
- Students construct and interpret probability distributions.
- A special case of a probability distribution is a binomial distribution where the independent trials have only two possible outcomes: success and failure.
- Students construct and interpret binomial distributions.

Teaching Strategy

- The values of a binomial distribution can be calculated using a function (such as *binompdf*) found on most graphing calculators. This function is especially useful when there are numerous probabilities to calculate.
- Laurie's Notes on page 709 present a simple example for introducing the probability of a binomial experiment. The steps below correspond to this example.
  - Press 2ND VARS for the [DISTR] menu. Scroll down to *A:binompdf*. (See Figure 1.) Press ENTER.
  - The syntax for the binomial probability function will ask you to enter three values:
    - 3   the number of trials *n*,
    - 0.8 the probability of a success *p*, and
    - 2   the number of successes *k* (often *x* on the calculator).
    (See Figure 2.)
  - Paste the function to the home screen and press ENTER to calculate the probability of 2 successes. (See Figure 3.)

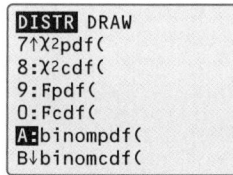

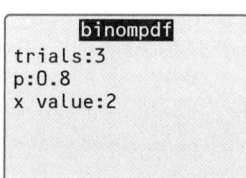

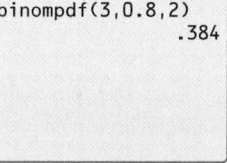

| Figure 1 | Figure 2 | Figure 3 |

- Probability distribution histograms can also be constructed using a graphing calculator.

Pacing Suggestion

- The explorations give students a chance to review skills from this chapter along with working with binomial distributions. Gaining a sense of what binomial distributions are will be helpful in the formal lesson. Begin the formal lesson with the definition.

**Common Core
State Standards**

HSS-CP.B.9 Use permutations and combinations to compute probabilities of compound events and solve problems.

Exploration

Motivate

? "What would be a reasonable free throw percentage for a professional basketball player?" Answers will vary.

• The NBA player with the highest career free throw percentage is Steve Nash, who over 18 years in the NBA has averaged 0.9043 at the free throw line.

• "If Nash goes to the free throw line 8 times in one game, what is the probability that he will make 6 of the 8 shots?" Students will have guesses about how to answer this question. Explain to students that at the end of this lesson they will be able to answer this question and others similar to it.

Exploration Note

• If you have two-color counters, students can use them to model the heads and tails that result when there are n coins flipped.

Exploration 1

• Give students time to study the histograms. They will be able to figure out what information is being conveyed without being told.

• Students will notice the symmetry of the histograms but may not recognize any patterns for the heights of each interval. When students get to part (b), they will find it a bit more challenging. Allow for productive struggle. You can also return to this problem after Exploration 2 when a numeric pattern may become evident.

? "What would the histograms look like for 'Number of Tails' when n coins are flipped?" The same as the histograms for number of heads when n coins are flipped.

? "How many different outcomes are there when n coins are flipped?" 2^n

Exploration 2

• Students should use the data from the histograms in Exploration 1 to complete this table.

? "If two coins are flipped, how many occurrences are there of 2 heads?" 1 This result could be added to the front of the table.

• Students will recognize the pattern of add 2, add 3, add 4, add 5, and so on.

? "Can you think of a way to generalize this in terms of n?" Answers will vary.

• Some students may recognize these numbers from working with combinations in the last lesson, or they may know that this set of numbers is known as the triangular numbers.

Communicate Your Answer

• Listen for valid reasoning as students discuss their answers.

Connecting to Next Step

• The explorations have students working with binomial distributions without naming or defining them. This will be done in the formal lesson.

12.6 Binomial Distributions

Essential Question How can you determine the frequency of each outcome of an event?

EXPLORATION 1 Analyzing Histograms

Work with a partner. The histograms show the results when n coins are flipped.

STUDY TIP

When 4 coins are flipped ($n = 4$), the possible outcomes are

TTTT TTTH TTHT TTHH

THTT THTH THHT THHH

HTTT HTTH HTHT HTHH

HHTT HHTH HHHT HHHH.

The histogram shows the numbers of outcomes having 0, 1, 2, 3, and 4 heads.

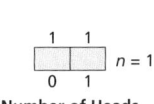

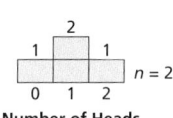

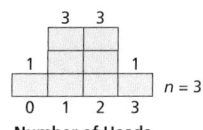

Number of Heads

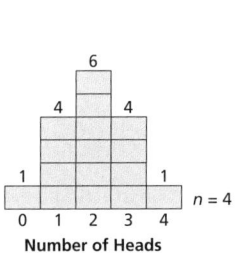

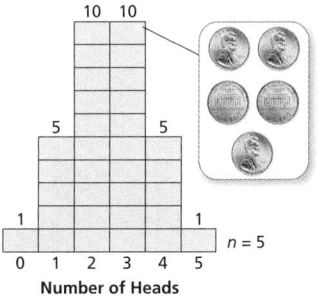

Number of Heads

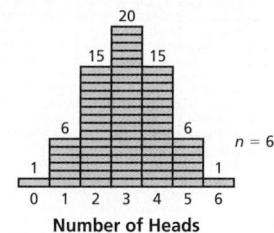

a. In how many ways can 3 heads occur when 5 coins are flipped?

b. Draw a histogram that shows the numbers of heads that can occur when 6 coins are flipped.

c. In how many ways can 3 heads occur when 6 coins are flipped?

EXPLORATION 2 Determining the Number of Occurrences

Work with a partner.

a. Complete the table showing the numbers of ways in which 2 heads can occur when n coins are flipped.

n	3	4	5	6	7
Occurrences of 2 heads					

LOOKING FOR A PATTERN

To be proficient in math, you need to look closely to discern a pattern or structure.

b. Determine the pattern shown in the table. Use your result to find the number of ways in which 2 heads can occur when 8 coins are flipped.

Communicate Your Answer

3. How can you determine the frequency of each outcome of an event?

4. How can you use a histogram to find the probability of an event?

ANSWERS

1. a. 10

   b.

   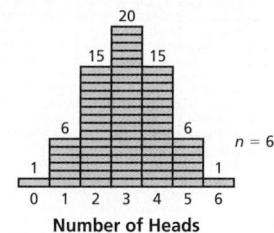

   Number of Heads

   c. 20

2. a. 3, 6, 10, 15, 21

   b. $_nC_2$; 28

3. List the possible outcomes, create a histogram, or use combinations.

4. Divide the total number of occurrences of an event by the total in the sample space.

Extra Example 1

The spinner is divided into equal three equal parts. Let *x* be a random variable that represents the sum when the spinner is spun twice. Make a table and draw a histogram showing the probability distribution for *x*.

x (sum)	0	1	2	3	4
Outcomes	1	2	3	2	1
P(x)	$\frac{1}{9}$	$\frac{2}{9}$	$\frac{1}{3}$	$\frac{2}{9}$	$\frac{1}{9}$

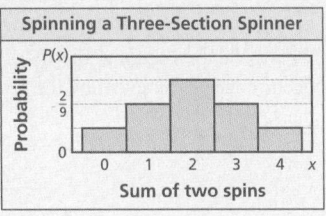

12.6 Lesson

What You Will Learn

▶ Construct and interpret probability distributions.
▶ Construct and interpret binomial distributions.

Probability Distributions

A **random variable** is a variable whose value is determined by the outcomes of a probability experiment. For example, when you roll a six-sided die, you can define a random variable *x* that represents the number showing on the die. So, the possible values of *x* are 1, 2, 3, 4, 5, and 6. For every random variable, a *probability distribution* can be defined.

⑤ Core Concept

Probability Distributions

A **probability distribution** is a function that gives the probability of each possible value of a random variable. The sum of all the probabilities in a probability distribution must equal 1.

Probability Distribution for Rolling a Six-Sided Die

x	1	2	3	4	5	6
P(x)	$\frac{1}{6}$	$\frac{1}{6}$	$\frac{1}{6}$	$\frac{1}{6}$	$\frac{1}{6}$	$\frac{1}{6}$

EXAMPLE 1   Constructing a Probability Distribution

Let *x* be a random variable that represents the sum when two six-sided dice are rolled. Make a table and draw a histogram showing the probability distribution for *x*.

SOLUTION

STUDY TIP

Recall that there are 36 possible outcomes when rolling two six-sided dice. These are listed in Example 3 on page 670.

Step 1 Make a table. The possible values of *x* are the integers from 2 to 12. The table shows how many outcomes of rolling two dice produce each value of *x*. Divide the number of outcomes for *x* by 36 to find *P(x)*.

x (sum)	2	3	4	5	6	7	8	9	10	11	12
Outcomes	1	2	3	4	5	6	5	4	3	2	1
P(x)	$\frac{1}{36}$	$\frac{1}{18}$	$\frac{1}{12}$	$\frac{1}{9}$	$\frac{5}{36}$	$\frac{1}{6}$	$\frac{5}{36}$	$\frac{1}{9}$	$\frac{1}{12}$	$\frac{1}{18}$	$\frac{1}{36}$

Step 2 Draw a histogram where the intervals are given by *x* and the frequencies are given by *P(x)*.

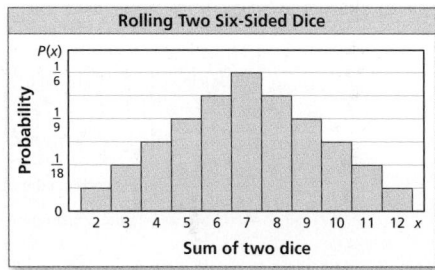

Laurie's Notes   Teacher Actions

- Use a context, such as the outcomes of a six-sided die, to discuss random variables. A probability distribution is a function.
- **?** "What are the possible sums when two six-sided dice are rolled?" 2, 3, 4, 5, 6, 7, 8, 9, 10, 11, 12
- There are many ways to simulate the sum of two dice. See the *Teaching Strategy* on page T-674, or search the Internet.
- The experimental probability should approximate the theoretical probability for large trials.
- **Connection:** The probability distribution shown has the same shape as the frequency distribution for the same event.

EXAMPLE 2   Interpreting a Probability Distribution

Use the probability distribution in Example 1 to answer each question.

a. What is the most likely sum when rolling two six-sided dice?

b. What is the probability that the sum of the two dice is at least 10?

SOLUTION

a. The most likely sum when rolling two six-sided dice is the value of x for which $P(x)$ is greatest. This probability is greatest for $x = 7$. So, when rolling the two dice, the most likely sum is 7.

b. The probability that the sum of the two dice is at least 10 is

$$P(x \geq 10) = P(x = 10) + P(x = 11) + P(x = 12)$$

$$= \frac{3}{36} + \frac{2}{36} + \frac{1}{36}$$

$$= \frac{6}{36}$$

$$= \frac{1}{6}$$

$$\approx 0.167.$$

▶ The probability is about 16.7%.

Monitoring Progress 🔊 Help in English and Spanish at *BigIdeasMath.com*

An octahedral die has eight sides numbered 1 through 8. Let x be a random variable that represents the sum when two such dice are rolled.

1. Make a table and draw a histogram showing the probability distribution for x.

2. What is the most likely sum when rolling the two dice?

3. What is the probability that the sum of the two dice is at most 3?

Binomial Distributions

One type of probability distribution is a **binomial distribution**. A binomial distribution shows the probabilities of the outcomes of a *binomial experiment*.

🔵 Core Concept

Binomial Experiments

A **binomial experiment** meets the following conditions.

- There are n independent trials.

- Each trial has only two possible outcomes: success and failure.

- The probability of success is the same for each trial. This probability is denoted by p. The probability of failure is $1 - p$.

For a binomial experiment, the probability of exactly k successes in n trials is

$$P(k \text{ successes}) = {}_nC_k \, p^k (1 - p)^{n-k}.$$

Section 12.6   Binomial Distributions   **709**

Laurie's Notes   **Teacher Actions**

- **Thumbs Up:** Have students work independently to answer Example 2. Students should self-assess with *Thumbs Up*.

- **Binomial Experiment:** Define a binomial experiment such as tossing a coin. Discuss the three parts of the formula $P(k \text{ successes}) = {}_nC_k \, p^k(1-p)^{n-k}$.  If the probability of a success is 0.8, then the probability of failure is 0.2. The event is repeated 3 times. Then $P(2 \text{ successes}) =$ $(0.8)(0.8)(0.2) + (0.8)(0.2)(0.8) + (0.2)(0.8)(0.8)$. There are ${}_3C_2 = 3$ combinations of 2 successes and 1 failure. See the *Teaching Strategy* on page T-706.

Differentiated Instruction

Inclusion

Students who struggle with the formula for the probability of k successes in n trials of a binomial experiment may benefit by having access to graphing calculators to compute the probabilities. Students can enter the number of trials and the probability of success and view a list of the coefficients given by the formula.

Extra Example 2

Use the probability distribution in Extra Example 1 to answer each question.

a. What is the most likely sum when spinning a 3-section spinner twice? The most likely sum is 2.

b. What is the probability that the sum of the two spins is odd? The probability is $\frac{4}{9}$, or about 44.4%.

MONITORING PROGRESS ANSWERS

1.

x (sum)	2	3	4	5	6	7	8	9
Outcomes	1	2	3	4	5	6	7	8
P(x)	$\frac{1}{64}$	$\frac{1}{32}$	$\frac{3}{64}$	$\frac{1}{16}$	$\frac{5}{64}$	$\frac{3}{32}$	$\frac{7}{64}$	$\frac{1}{8}$

x (sum)	10	11	12	13	14	15	16
Outcomes	7	6	5	4	3	2	1
P(x)	$\frac{7}{64}$	$\frac{3}{32}$	$\frac{5}{64}$	$\frac{1}{16}$	$\frac{3}{64}$	$\frac{1}{32}$	$\frac{1}{64}$

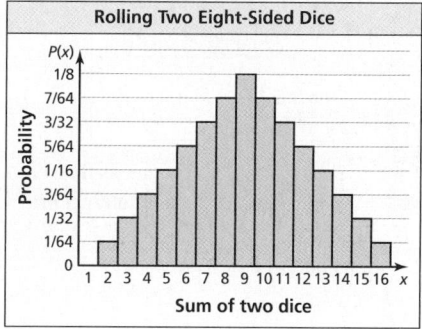

2. 9

3. $\frac{3}{64}$

Extra Example 3

According to a survey, about 62% of adults have visited a dentist in the past year. You ask 5 randomly selected adults whether they have had a dentist visit in the past year. Draw a histogram of the binomial distribution for your survey.

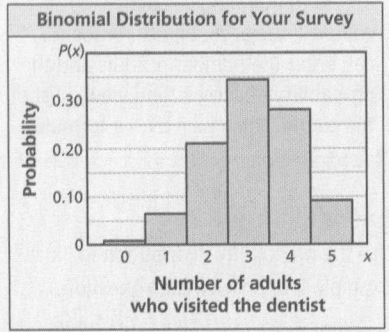

Extra Example 4

Use the binomial distribution in Extra Example 3 to answer each question.

a. What is the most likely outcome of the survey? The most likely outcome is that 3 of the 5 adults surveyed visited a dentist in the past year.

b. What is the probability that more than 3 people surveyed have visited a dentist in the past year? about 37.3%

MONITORING PROGRESS ANSWERS

4.

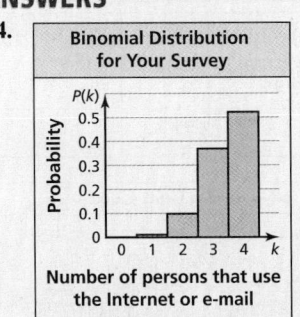

5. The most likely outcome is that 4 of the 4 people use the Internet or e-mail.

6. about 0.11

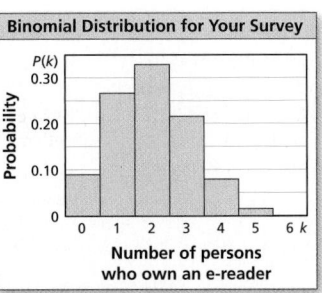

EXAMPLE 3 Constructing a Binomial Distribution

According to a survey, about 33% of people ages 16 and older in the U.S. own an electronic book reading device, or e-reader. You ask 6 randomly chosen people (ages 16 and older) whether they own an e-reader. Draw a histogram of the binomial distribution for your survey.

ATTENDING TO PRECISION

When probabilities are rounded, the sum of the probabilities may differ slightly from 1.

SOLUTION

The probability that a randomly selected person has an e-reader is $p = 0.33$. Because you survey 6 people, $n = 6$.

$P(k = 0) = {}_6C_0(0.33)^0(0.67)^6 \approx 0.090$

$P(k = 1) = {}_6C_1(0.33)^1(0.67)^5 \approx 0.267$

$P(k = 2) = {}_6C_2(0.33)^2(0.67)^4 \approx 0.329$

$P(k = 3) = {}_6C_3(0.33)^3(0.67)^3 \approx 0.216$

$P(k = 4) = {}_6C_4(0.33)^4(0.67)^2 \approx 0.080$

$P(k = 5) = {}_6C_5(0.33)^5(0.67)^1 \approx 0.016$

$P(k = 6) = {}_6C_6(0.33)^6(0.67)^0 \approx 0.001$

A histogram of the distribution is shown.

EXAMPLE 4 Interpreting a Binomial Distribution

Use the binomial distribution in Example 3 to answer each question.

a. What is the most likely outcome of the survey?

b. What is the probability that at most 2 people have an e-reader?

COMMON ERROR

Because a person may not have an e-reader, be sure you include $P(k = 0)$ when finding the probability that at most 2 people have an e-reader.

SOLUTION

a. The most likely outcome of the survey is the value of k for which $P(k)$ is greatest. This probability is greatest for $k = 2$. The most likely outcome is that 2 of the 6 people own an e-reader.

b. The probability that at most 2 people have an e-reader is

$$P(k \leq 2) = P(k = 0) + P(k = 1) + P(k = 2)$$

$$\approx 0.090 + 0.267 + 0.329$$

$$\approx 0.686.$$

▶ The probability is about 68.6%.

Monitoring Progress  Help in English and Spanish at *BigIdeasMath.com*

According to a survey, about 85% of people ages 18 and older in the U.S. use the Internet or e-mail. You ask 4 randomly chosen people (ages 18 and older) whether they use the Internet or e-mail.

4. Draw a histogram of the binomial distribution for your survey.

5. What is the most likely outcome of your survey?

6. What is the probability that at most 2 people you survey use the Internet or e-mail?

Laurie's Notes   Teacher Actions

- **MP5 Use Appropriate Tools Strategically:** Students should use calculators to generate the probability values for each possible outcome in Example 3. Students should be efficient in changing the parameters when editing the previous command.
- **Think-Pair-Share:** Have students answer Questions 4–6, and then share and discuss as a class.

Closure

- **Exit Ticket:** Have students answer the question posed at the end of the *Motivate* on page T-707. about 14%

12.6 Exercises

Dynamic Solutions available at *BigIdeasMath.com*

Vocabulary and Core Concept Check

1. **VOCABULARY** What is a random variable?

2. **WRITING** Give an example of a binomial experiment and describe how it meets the conditions of a binomial experiment.

Monitoring Progress and Modeling with Mathematics

In Exercises 3–6, make a table and draw a histogram showing the probability distribution for the random variable. *(See Example 1.)*

3. x = the number on a table tennis ball randomly chosen from a bag that contains 5 balls labeled "1," 3 balls labeled "2," and 2 balls labeled "3."

4. c = 1 when a randomly chosen card out of a standard deck of 52 playing cards is a heart and c = 2 otherwise.

5. w = 1 when a randomly chosen letter from the English alphabet is a vowel and w = 2 otherwise.

6. n = the number of digits in a random integer from 0 through 999.

In Exercises 7 and 8, use the probability distribution to determine (a) the number that is most likely to be spun on a spinner, and (b) the probability of spinning an even number. *(See Example 2.)*

7.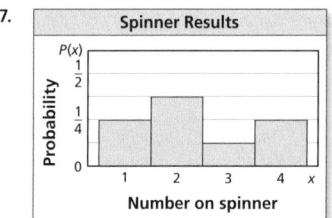

8.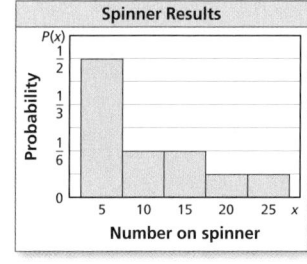

USING EQUATIONS In Exercises 9–12, calculate the probability of flipping a coin 20 times and getting the given number of heads.

9. 1   10. 4

11. 18   12. 20

13. **MODELING WITH MATHEMATICS** According to a survey, 27% of high school students in the United States buy a class ring. You ask 6 randomly chosen high school students whether they own a class ring. *(See Examples 3 and 4.)*

   a. Draw a histogram of the binomial distribution for your survey.
   b. What is the most likely outcome of your survey?
   c. What is the probability that at most 2 people have a class ring?

14. **MODELING WITH MATHEMATICS** According to a survey, 48% of adults in the United States believe that Unidentified Flying Objects (UFOs) are observing our planet. You ask 8 randomly chosen adults whether they believe UFOs are watching Earth.

   a. Draw a histogram of the binomial distribution for your survey.
   b. What is the most likely outcome of your survey?
   c. What is the probability that at most 3 people believe UFOs are watching Earth?

Section 12.6   Binomial Distributions   **711**

11. about 0.00018
12. about 0.000001
13. a.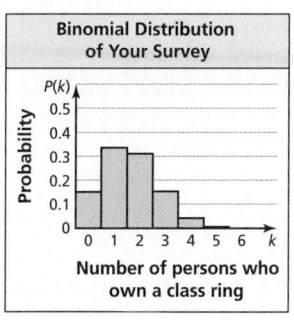

   b. The most likely outcome is that 1 of the 6 students owns a ring.
   c. about 0.798
14. a. See Additional Answers.
   b. The most likely outcome is that 4 of the 8 adults believe UFOs are watching Earth.
   c. about 0.407

Assignment Guide and Homework Check

ASSIGNMENT
Basic: 1, 2, 3–15 odd, 18, 19, 23, 24
Average: 1, 2–16 even, 17–19, 23, 24
Advanced: 1, 2–16 even, 17–24

HOMEWORK CHECK
Basic: 3, 5, 7, 13, 18
Average: 4, 8, 12, 14, 18
Advanced: 6, 8, 14, 18, 19

ANSWERS

1. a variable whose value is determined by the outcomes of a probability experiment
2. *Sample answer:* According to a survey, about 30% of households in America own at least one cat. You ask 5 randomly chosen people (who live in separate households) whether they own a cat. There are 5 independent trials, and each trial has only two possible outcomes.

3.
x (value)	1	2	3
Outcomes	5	3	2
$P(x)$	$\frac{1}{2}$	$\frac{3}{10}$	$\frac{1}{5}$

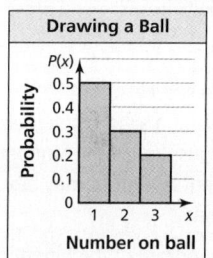

4.
c (value)	1	2
Outcomes	13	39
$P(c)$	$\frac{1}{4}$	$\frac{3}{4}$

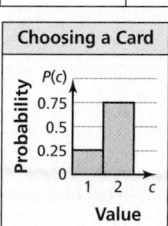

5–6. See Additional Answers.
7. a. 2   8. a. 5
   b. $\frac{5}{8}$ b. $\frac{1}{4}$
9. about 0.00002
10. about 0.0046

Section 12.6   **711**

ANSWERS

15. The exponents are switched;
$$P(k = 3) = {_5C_3}\left(\frac{1}{6}\right)^3\left(\frac{5}{6}\right)^{5-3} \approx 0.032$$

16. The combination part of the formula is missing;
$$P(k = 3) = {_5C_3}\left(\frac{1}{6}\right)^3\left(\frac{5}{6}\right)^{5-3} \approx 0.032$$

17–24. See Additional Answers.

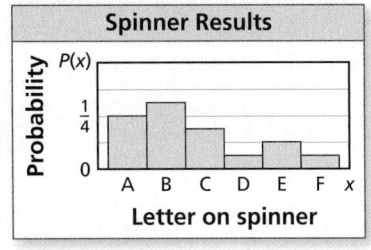
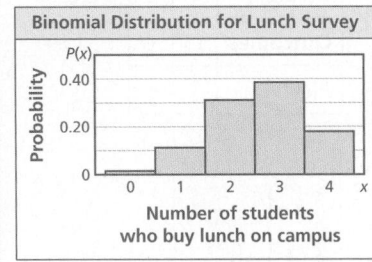

ERROR ANALYSIS In Exercises 15 and 16, describe and correct the error in calculating the probability of rolling a 1 exactly 3 times in 5 rolls of a six-sided die.

15.
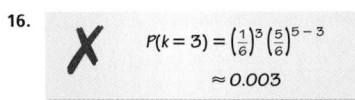
$$P(k = 3) = {_5C_3}\left(\frac{1}{6}\right)^{5-3}\left(\frac{5}{6}\right)^3$$
$$\approx 0.161$$

16.
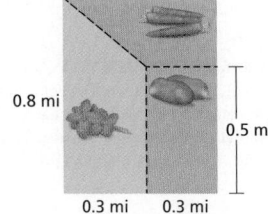
$$P(k = 3) = \left(\frac{1}{6}\right)^3\left(\frac{5}{6}\right)^{5-3}$$
$$\approx 0.003$$

17. **MATHEMATICAL CONNECTIONS** At most 7 gopher holes appear each week on the farm shown. Let x represent how many of the gopher holes appear in the carrot patch. Assume that a gopher hole has an equal chance of appearing at any point on the farm.

0.8 mi   0.5 mi   0.3 mi   0.3 mi

a. Find $P(x)$ for $x = 0, 1, 2, \ldots, 7$.

b. Make a table showing the probability distribution for x.

c. Make a histogram showing the probability distribution for x.

18. **HOW DO YOU SEE IT?** Complete the probability distribution for the random variable x. What is the probability the value of x is greater than 2?

x	1	2	3	4
$P(x)$	0.1	0.3	0.4	

Maintaining Mathematical Proficiency
Reviewing what you learned in previous grades and lessons

List the possible outcomes for the situation. *(Section 12.1)*

23. guessing the gender of three children

24. picking one of two doors and one of three curtains

---

19. **MAKING AN ARGUMENT** The binomial distribution shows the results of a binomial experiment. Your friend claims that the probability p of a success must be greater than the probability $1 - p$ of a failure. Is your friend correct? Explain your reasoning.

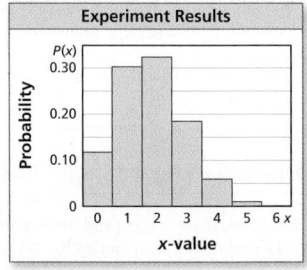

Experiment Results

20. **THOUGHT PROVOKING** There are 100 coins in a bag. Only one of them has a date of 2010. You choose a coin at random, check the date, and then put the coin back in the bag. You repeat this 100 times. Are you certain of choosing the 2010 coin at least once? Explain your reasoning.

21. **MODELING WITH MATHEMATICS** Assume that having a male and having a female child are independent events, and that the probability of each is 0.5.

a. A couple has 4 male children. Evaluate the validity of this statement: "The first 4 kids were all boys, so the next one will probably be a girl."

b. What is the probability of having 4 male children and then a female child?

c. Let x be a random variable that represents the number of children a couple already has when they have their first female child. Draw a histogram of the distribution of $P(x)$ for $0 \le x \le 10$. Describe the shape of the histogram.

22. **CRITICAL THINKING** An entertainment system has n speakers. Each speaker will function properly with probability p, independent of whether the other speakers are functioning. The system will operate effectively when at least 50% of its speakers are functioning. For what values of p is a 5-speaker system more likely to operate than a 3-speaker system?

Core Vocabulary

compound event, *p. 694*
overlapping events, *p. 694*
disjoint events, *p. 694*
mutually exclusive events, *p. 694*

permutation, *p. 700*
n factorial, *p. 700*
combination, *p. 702*
random variable, *p. 708*

probability distribution, *p. 708*
binomial distribution, *p. 709*
binomial experiment, *p. 709*

Core Concepts

Section 12.4
Probability of Compound Events, *p. 694*

Section 12.5
Permutations, *p. 701*
Combinations, *p. 702*

Section 12.6
Probability Distributions, *p. 708*
Binomial Experiments, *p. 709*

Mathematical Practices

1. How can you use diagrams to understand the situation in Exercise 22 on page 698?

2. Describe a relationship between the results in part (a) and part (b) in Exercise 52 on page 706.

3. Explain how you were able to break the situation into cases to evaluate the validity of the statement in part (a) of Exercise 21 on page 712.

- - - - - - - - - - - - - **Performance Task** - - - - - - - -

A New Dartboard

You are a graphic artist working for a company on a new design for the board in the game of darts. You are eager to begin the project, but the team cannot decide on the terms of the game. Everyone agrees that the board should have four colors. But some want the probabilities of hitting each color to be equal, while others want them to be different. You offer to design two boards, one for each group. How do you get started? How creative can you be with your designs?

To explore the answers to these questions and more, go to *BigIdeasMath.com*.

713

ANSWERS

1. Use a Venn diagram to show that when *A*, *B*, and *C* are disjoint, you must add the probability of each, and when *A*, *B*, and *C* are overlapping, you must subtract parts so you do not count anything more than once.

2. *Sample answer:* The same marbles are drawn in both parts.

3. The probability of having four boys and then a girl is equal to the probability of having four boys and then another boy, so the statement is invalid.

ANSWERS

1. $\frac{2}{9}$; $\frac{7}{9}$

2. 20 points

3. **a.** 0.15625

   b. about 0.1667

   You are about 1.07 times more likely to pick a red then a green if you do not replace the first marble.

4. **a.** about 0.0586

   b. 0.0625

   You are about 1.07 times more likely to pick a blue then a red if you do not replace the first marble.

5. **a.** 0.25

   b. about 0.2333

   You are about 1.07 times more likely to pick a green and then another green if you replace the first marble.

12 Chapter Review

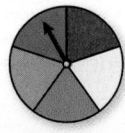

12.1 Sample Spaces and Probability (pp. 667–674)

Each section of the spinner shown has the same area. The spinner was spun 30 times. The table shows the results. For which color is the experimental probability of stopping on the color the same as the theoretical probability?

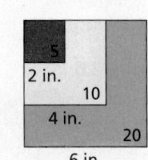

Spinner Results	
green	4
orange	6
red	9
blue	8
yellow	3

SOLUTION

The theoretical probability of stopping on each of the five colors is $\frac{1}{5}$. Use the outcomes in the table to find the experimental probabilities.

$P(\text{green}) = \frac{4}{30} = \frac{2}{15}$ $P(\text{orange}) = \frac{6}{30} = \frac{1}{5}$ $P(\text{red}) = \frac{9}{30} = \frac{3}{10}$ $P(\text{blue}) = \frac{8}{30} = \frac{4}{15}$ $P(\text{yellow}) = \frac{3}{30} = \frac{1}{10}$

▶ The experimental probability of stopping on orange is the same as the theoretical probability.

1. A bag contains 9 tiles, one for each letter in the word HAPPINESS. You choose a tile at random. What is the probability that you choose a tile with the letter S? What is the probability that you choose a tile with a letter other than P?

2. You throw a dart at the board shown. Your dart is equally likely to hit any point inside the square board. Are you most likely to get 5 points, 10 points, or 20 points?

12.2 Independent and Dependent Events (pp. 675–682)

You randomly select 2 cards from a standard deck of 52 playing cards. What is the probability that both cards are jacks when (a) you replace the first card before selecting the second, and (b) you do not replace the first card. Compare the probabilities.

SOLUTION

Let event A be "first card is a jack" and event B be "second card is a jack."

a. Because you replace the first card before you select the second card, the events are independent. So, the probability is

$$P(A \text{ and } B) = P(A) \cdot P(B) = \frac{4}{52} \cdot \frac{4}{52} = \frac{16}{2704} = \frac{1}{169} \approx 0.006.$$

b. Because you do not replace the first card before you select the second card, the events are dependent. So, the probability is

$$P(A \text{ and } B) = P(A) \cdot P(B \mid A) = \frac{4}{52} \cdot \frac{3}{51} = \frac{12}{2652} = \frac{1}{221} \approx 0.005.$$

▶ So, you are $\frac{1}{169} \div \frac{1}{221} \approx 1.3$ times more likely to select 2 jacks when you replace the first card before you select the second card.

Find the probability of randomly selecting the given marbles from a bag of 5 red, 8 green, and 3 blue marbles when (a) you replace the first marble before drawing the second, and (b) you do not replace the first marble. Compare the probabilities.

3. red, then green   4. blue, then red   5. green, then green

6. about 0.529

7.

		Gender		
		Men	Women	Total
Response	Yes	200	230	430
	No	20	40	60
	Total	220	270	490

About 44.9% of responders were men, about 55.1% of responders were women, about 87.8% of responders thought it was impactful, about 12.2% of responders thought it was not impactful.

8. 0.68

9. 0.02

12.3 **Two-Way Tables and Probability** (pp. 683–690)

A survey asks residents of the east and west sides of a city whether they support the construction of a bridge. The results, given as joint relative frequencies, are shown in the two-way table. What is the probability that a randomly selected resident from the east side will support the project?

		Location	
		East Side	West Side
Response	Yes	0.47	0.36
	No	0.08	0.09

SOLUTION

Find the joint and marginal relative frequencies. Then use these values to find the conditional probability.

$$P(\text{yes} \mid \text{east side}) = \frac{P(\text{east side and yes})}{P(\text{east side})} = \frac{0.47}{0.47 + 0.08} \approx 0.855$$

▶ So, the probability that a resident of the east side of the city will support the project is about 85.5%.

6. What is the probability that a randomly selected resident who does not support the project in the example above is from the west side?

7. After a conference, 220 men and 270 women respond to a survey. Of those, 200 men and 230 women say the conference was impactful. Organize these results in a two-way table. Then find and interpret the marginal frequencies.

12.4 **Probability of Disjoint and Overlapping Events** (pp. 693–698)

Let A and B be events such that $P(A) = \frac{2}{3}$, $P(B) = \frac{1}{2}$, and $P(A \text{ and } B) = \frac{1}{3}$. Find $P(A \text{ or } B)$.

SOLUTION

$P(A \text{ or } B) = P(A) + P(B) - P(A \text{ and } B)$	Write general formula.
$= \frac{2}{3} + \frac{1}{2} - \frac{1}{3}$	Substitute known probabilities.
$= \frac{5}{6}$	Simplify.
≈ 0.833	Use a calculator.

8. Let A and B be events such that $P(A) = 0.32$, $P(B) = 0.48$, and $P(A \text{ and } B) = 0.12$. Find $P(A \text{ or } B)$.

9. Out of 100 employees at a company, 92 employees either work part time or work 5 days each week. There are 14 employees who work part time and 80 employees who work 5 days each week. What is the probability that a randomly selected employee works both part time and 5 days each week?

10. 5040

11. 1,037,836,800

12. 15

13. 70

14. 40,320

15. $\frac{1}{84}$

16. about 0.12

17.

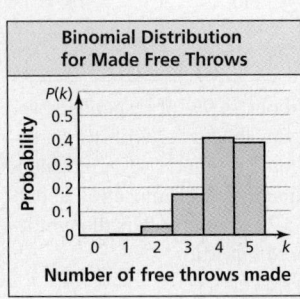

Binomial Distribution for Made Free Throws

The most likely outcome is that 4 of the 5 free throw shots will be made.

A 5-digit code consists of 5 different integers from 0 to 9. How many different codes are possible?

SOLUTION

To find the number of permutations of 5 integers chosen from 10, find $_{10}P_5$.

$$_{10}P_5 = \frac{10!}{(10-5)!}$$ Permutations formula

$$= \frac{10!}{5!}$$ Subtract.

$$= \frac{10 \cdot 9 \cdot 8 \cdot 7 \cdot 6 \cdot \cancel{5!}}{\cancel{5!}}$$ Expand factorials. Divide out common factor, 5!.

$$= 30{,}240$$ Simplify.

▶ There are 30,240 possible codes.

Evaluate the expression.

10. $_7P_6$ **11.** $_{13}P_{10}$ **12.** $_6C_2$ **13.** $_8C_4$

14. Eight sprinters are competing in a race. How many different ways can they finish the race? (Assume there are no ties.)

15. A random drawing will determine which 3 people in a group of 9 will win concert tickets. What is the probability that you and your 2 friends will win the tickets?

According to a survey, about 21% of adults in the U.S. visited an art museum last year. You ask 4 randomly chosen adults whether they visited an art museum last year. Draw a histogram of the binomial distribution for your survey.

SOLUTION

The probability that a randomly selected person visited an art museum is $p = 0.21$. Because you survey 4 people, $n = 4$.

$$P(k = 0) = {}_4C_0(0.21)^0(0.79)^4 \approx 0.390$$

$$P(k = 1) = {}_4C_1(0.21)^1(0.79)^3 \approx 0.414$$

$$P(k = 2) = {}_4C_2(0.21)^2(0.79)^2 \approx 0.165$$

$$P(k = 3) = {}_4C_3(0.21)^3(0.79)^1 \approx 0.029$$

$$P(k = 4) = {}_4C_4(0.21)^4(0.79)^0 \approx 0.002$$

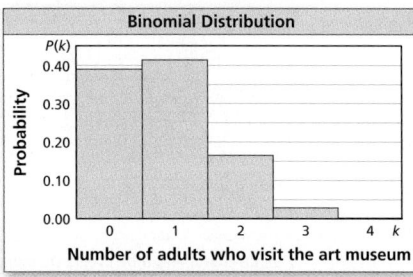

Binomial Distribution

16. Find the probability of flipping a coin 12 times and getting exactly 4 heads.

17. A basketball player makes a free throw 82.6% of the time. The player attempts 5 free throws. Draw a histogram of the binomial distribution of the number of successful free throws. What is the most likely outcome?

12 Chapter Test

You roll a six-sided die. Find the probability of the event described. Explain your reasoning.

1. You roll a number less than 5.

2. You roll a multiple of 3.

Evaluate the expression.

3. $_7P_2$

4. $_8P_3$

5. $_6C_3$

6. $_{12}C_7$

7. In the word PYRAMID, how many ways can you arrange (a) all of the letters and (b) 5 of the letters?

8. You find the probability $P(A \text{ or } B)$ by using the equation $P(A \text{ or } B) = P(A) + P(B) - P(A \text{ and } B)$. Describe why it is necessary to subtract $P(A \text{ and } B)$ when the events A and B are overlapping. Then describe why it is *not* necessary to subtract $P(A \text{ and } B)$ when the events A and B are disjoint.

9. Is it possible to use the formula $P(A \text{ and } B) = P(A) \cdot P(B|A)$ when events A and B are independent? Explain your reasoning.

10. According to a survey, about 58% of families sit down for a family dinner at least four times per week. You ask 5 randomly chosen families whether they have a family dinner at least four times per week.

    a. Draw a histogram of the binomial distribution for the survey.

    b. What is the most likely outcome of the survey?

    c. What is the probability that at least 3 families have a family dinner four times per week?

11. You are choosing a cell phone company to sign with for the next 2 years. The three plans you consider are equally priced. You ask several of your neighbors whether they are satisfied with their current cell phone company. The table shows the results. According to this survey, which company should you choose?

	Satisfied	Not Satisfied
Company A	IIII	II
Company B	IIII	III
Company C	IHT I	IHT

12. The surface area of Earth is about 196.9 million square miles. The land area is about 57.5 million square miles, and the rest is water. What is the probability that a meteorite that reaches the surface of Earth will hit land? What is the probability that it will hit water?

13. Consider a bag that contains all the chess pieces in a set, as shown in the diagram.

	King	Queen	Bishop	Rook	Knight	Pawn
Black	1	1	2	2	2	8
White	1	1	2	2	2	8

    a. You choose one piece at random. Find the probability that you choose a black piece or a queen.

    b. You choose one piece at random, do not replace it, then choose a second piece at random. Find the probability that you choose a king, then a pawn.

14. Three volunteers are chosen at random from a group of 12 to help at a summer camp.

    a. What is the probability that you, your brother, and your friend are chosen?

    b. The first person chosen will be a counselor, the second will be a lifeguard, and the third will be a cook. What is the probability that you are the cook, your brother is the lifeguard, and your friend is the counselor?

ANSWERS

1. $\frac{2}{3}$

2. $\frac{1}{3}$

3. 42

4. 336

5. 20

6. 792

7. a. 5040

    b. 2520

8. $P(A \text{ and } B)$ is counted twice when adding $P(A)$ and $P(B)$; When events A and B are disjoint, $P(A \text{ and } B) = 0$.

9. yes; If events A and B are independent, then $P(B \mid A) = P(B)$.

10. a.

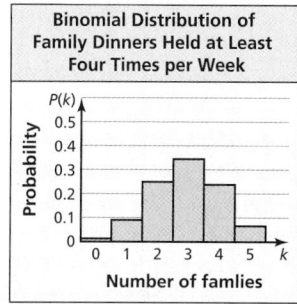

Binomial Distribution of Family Dinners Held at Least Four Times per Week

    b. The most likely outcome is that 3 of the 5 families will sit down for a family dinner at least 4 times per week.

    c. about 0.6474

11. Company A

12. about 29.2%; about 70.8%

13. a. $\frac{17}{32}$

    b. $\frac{1}{31}$

14. a. $\frac{1}{220}$

    b. $\frac{1}{1320}$

If students need help...	If students got it...
Lesson Tutorials	Resources by Chapter • Enrichment and Extension • Cumulative Review
Skills Review Handbook	Performance Task
BigIdeasMath.com	Start the *next* Section

1. a.

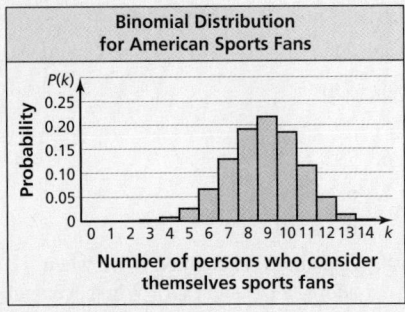

Binomial Distribution for American Sports Fans

Number of persons who consider themselves sports fans

b. 9

c. about 0.8988

2. B

3. 1800

4. $(x + 2)^2 + (y + 5)^2 = 100$

5. a. $\overline{AB} \approx 5.83$

b. $\overline{CD} \approx 5.39$

c. $\overline{EF} \approx 6.08$

d. $\overline{GH} = 6$

e. $\overline{JK} = 5$

f. $\overline{LM} \approx 8.06$

$\overline{JK}, \overline{CD}, \overline{AB}, \overline{GH}, \overline{EF}, \overline{LM}$

12 Cumulative Assessment

1. According to a survey, 63% of Americans consider themselves sports fans. You randomly select 14 Americans to survey.

    a. Draw a histogram of the binomial distribution of your survey.

    b. What is the most likely number of Americans who consider themselves sports fans?

    c. What is the probability at least 7 Americans consider themselves sports fans?

2. What is the arc length of $\overset{\frown}{AB}$?

    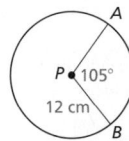

    Ⓐ 3.5π cm

    Ⓑ 7π cm

    Ⓒ 21π cm

    Ⓓ 42π cm

3. You order a fruit smoothie made with 2 liquid ingredients and 3 fruit ingredients from the menu shown. How many different fruit smoothies can you order?

    Liquids
    - Water
    - Tea
    - Coconut Water
    - Almond Milk
    - Apple Juice
    - Orange Juice

    Fruits
    - Orange
    - Watermelon
    - Banana
    - Kiwi
    - Pineapple
    - Peach
    - Cantaloupe
    - Blueberry
    - Strawberry
    - Pomegranate

4. The point $(4, 3)$ is on a circle with center $(-2, -5)$. What is the standard equation of the circle?

5. Find the length of each line segment with the given endpoints. Then order the line segments from shortest to longest.

    a. $A(1, -5), B(4, 0)$

    b. $C(-4, 2), D(1, 4)$

    c. $E(-1, 1), F(-2, 7)$

    d. $G(-1.5, 0), H(4.5, 0)$

    e. $J(-7, -8), K(-3, -5)$

    f. $L(10, -2), M(9, 6)$

6. Use the diagram to explain why the equation is true.

$$P(A) + P(B) = P(A \text{ or } B) + P(A \text{ and } B)$$

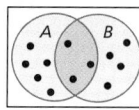

7. A plane intersects a cylinder. Which of the following cross sections cannot be formed by this intersection?

   Ⓐ line   Ⓑ triangle

   Ⓒ rectangle   Ⓓ circle

8. A survey asked male and female students about whether they prefer to take gym class or choir. The table shows the results of the survey.

		Class		
		Gym	Choir	Total
Gender	**Male**			50
	Female	23		
	Total		49	106

a. Complete the two-way table.

b. What is the probability that a randomly selected student is female and prefers choir?

c. What is the probability that a randomly selected male student prefers gym class?

9. The owner of a lawn-mowing business has three mowers. As long as one of the mowers is working, the owner can stay productive. One of the mowers is unusable 10% of the time, one is unusable 8% of the time, and one is unusable 18% of the time.

a. Find the probability that all three mowers are unusable on a given day.

b. Find the probability that at least one of the mowers is unusable on a given day.

c. Suppose the least-reliable mower stops working completely. How does this affect the probability that the lawn-mowing business can be productive on a given day?

10. You throw a dart at the board shown. Your dart is equally likely to hit any point inside the square board. What is the probability your dart lands in the yellow region?

   Ⓐ $\dfrac{\pi}{36}$ Ⓑ $\dfrac{\pi}{12}$

   Ⓒ $\dfrac{\pi}{9}$ Ⓓ $\dfrac{\pi}{4}$

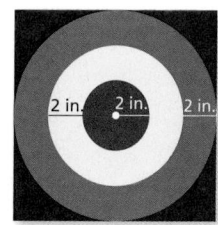

Chapter 12   Cumulative Assessment   **719**

ANSWERS

6. $P(A) + P(B)$ double counts the part that overlaps. $P(A \text{ or } B)$ counts all of the dots once, so adding $P(A \text{ and } B)$ makes sure the overlap is included again.

7. B

8. **a.** 34; 16; 33; 56; 57
   b. about 0.3113
   c. 0.68

9. **a.** 0.00144
   b. 0.32104
   c. It slightly decreases the probability.

10. B

Laurie's Notes

Overview of Additional Topic

For Your Information

- Use this Additional Topic, *Focus of a Parabola*, after Section 10.7.
- See Algebra 2, Section 2.3 for the additional resources that are available for *Focus of a Parabola*.
- You may want to review parabolas and associated terms: *vertex, axis of symmetry, vertex form, vertical stretch,* and *vertical shrink.*
- Students may need help with the term *cross section* in Exploration 1 and Example 5.
- Students will explore more characteristics of parabolas in Algebra 2.

Introduction

- Students have likely seen parabolic satellite dishes of different sizes: large transmission satellites, small dishes on a rooftop, or handheld dishes on the sideline of a sporting event. The cross section of each of these satellite dishes is a parabola.
- The explorations allow students to discover properties of the focus of a parabola. By sketching the reflected rays, students quickly discover the focus. The explorations do not take long and are important for students to experience.
- The formal lesson begins with the definition of the *focus* and the *directrix*. Careful sketches are needed to demonstrate what is meant by "Any point on the parabola is equidistant from the focus and directrix."
- Symbolic manipulation skills are necessary in this lesson as students write the equations of a parabola or as equations are rewritten in a general form.

Resources

- Dynamic geometry software can be used to graph a parabola given its focus and directrix. Clicking and dragging on the focus or directrix demonstrates the change in position and shape of the graph.
- Search the Internet for "parabola + focus + applet" to find dynamic geometry software.

Formative Assessment Tips

- **Exit Ticket:** This technique asks students to respond to a question at the end of the lesson, activity, or learning experience. The *Exit Ticket* allows you to collect evidence of student learning. I cut scrap paper into smaller pieces so that "exit tickets" can be distributed quickly to students.
- The *Exit Ticket* is helpful in planning instruction. During the class there may be students you have not heard from. They may not have raised their hands, or they may have been less vocal when working with partners. The *Exit Ticket* helps you gauge the ability of all students to answer a particular type of question.
- Students write their names on the exit tickets, which are then collected.
- If a subset of students has difficulty with the skill addressed by the *Exit Ticket*, instruction for the following day should address this problem.

Pacing Suggestion

- Use the *Motivate* and the two explorations before beginning the formal lesson.

Pacing Guide

Additional Topic	2 Days

HSF-IF.B.4 For a function that models
a relationship between two quantities,
interpret key features of graphs … in
terms of the quantities, … *Key features
include:* … *symmetries;* …

HSF-IF.C.7c Graph polynomial functions,
…

HSG-GPE.A.2 Derive the equation of a
parabola given a focus and directrix.

Laurie's Notes

Exploration

Motivate
- Display an image of a satellite dish. Have students share their knowledge of satellite dishes
  and how they work. The essential piece is that the satellite dish is an antenna that receives
  electromagnetic signals from an orbiting satellite. The shape of the satellite dish is parabolic.
- Discuss what it would mean to take a cross section of the satellite dish. The cross section is
  parabolic.
- Explain to students that in the exploration they will observe a new characteristic of the
  parabola.

Exploration 1
? "Have any of you played pool or billiards before?"
Answers will vary.
- Make a quick sketch of a pool table and its
  six pockets. Discuss what happens when a ball
  hits the edge of the table, namely the
  (angle of incidence) = (angle of reflection).
- Explain that a similar property is true for rays
  hitting a satellite dish.
- If students are accurate with estimating
  the outgoing angle, then the three rays they draw should be concurrent at the focus of
  the parabola.
- Students' reasoning of why this makes sense is connected to their knowledge of
  satellite dishes.

Angle of reflection | Angle of incidence

Exploration 2
- **Teaching Tip:** If you have a flashlight or overhead projector bulb, use it as a model for
  students to see as they begin this exploration. The bulb is located at the focus, and the rays
  are emanating from the bulb toward the parabolic surface.
- If students are accurate with estimating the outgoing angle, then the three rays they draw
  should be parallel.

Communicate Your Answer
- Students' understanding of a focus may be no more than knowing it is a point in the interior
  of the parabola. It may be necessary to ask a probing question for students to observe
  that the focus is on the line of symmetry. The properties of the focus are related to the
  observations made in the two explorations.

Connecting to Next Step
- The explorations should not take long to complete, and it is great for students to discover the
  properties of the focus. Begin the formal lesson with the definition of *focus* and *directrix*.

Additional Topic

Focus of a Parabola

Essential Question What is the focus of a parabola?

EXPLORATION 1 **Analyzing Satellite Dishes**

Work with a partner. Vertical rays enter a satellite dish whose cross section is a parabola. When the rays hit the parabola, they reflect at the same angle at which they entered. (See Ray 1 in the figure.)

a. Draw the reflected rays so that they intersect the y-axis.

b. What do the reflected rays have in common?

c. The optimal location for the receiver of the satellite dish is at a point called the *focus* of the parabola. Determine the location of the focus. Explain why this makes sense in this situation.

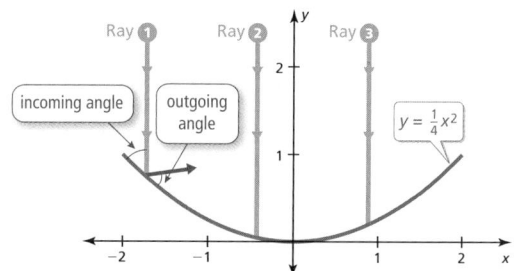

CONSTRUCTING VIABLE ARGUMENTS

To be proficient in math, you need to make conjectures and build logical progressions of statements to explore the truth of your conjectures.

EXPLORATION 2 **Analyzing Spotlights**

Work with a partner. Beams of light are coming from the bulb in a spotlight, located at the focus of the parabola. When the beams hit the parabola, they reflect at the same angle at which they hit. (See Beam 1 in the figure.) Draw the reflected beams. What do they have in common? Would you consider this to be the optimal result? Explain.

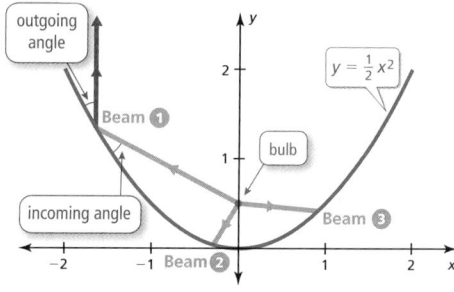

Communicate Your Answer

3. What is the focus of a parabola?

4. Describe some of the properties of the focus of a parabola.

Focus of a Parabola **721**

Dynamic Teaching Tools

Dynamic Assessment & Progress Monitoring Tool

Lesson Planning Tool

Interactive Whiteboard Lesson Library

Dynamic Classroom with Dynamic Investigations

ANSWERS

1–2. See Additional Answers.

3. a point on the inside of a parabola that lies on the axis of symmetry

4. The focus lies on the axis of symmetry, and all lines parallel to the axis of symmetry hit the parabola and reflect to intersect at the focus.

Extra Example 1

Use the Distance Formula to write an equation of the parabola with focus $F(0, 4)$ and directrix $y = -4$. $y = \frac{1}{16}x^2$

MONITORING PROGRESS ANSWER

1. $y = -\frac{1}{12}x^2$

Lesson

Core Vocabulary

focus, *p. 722*
directrix, *p. 722*

Previous
perpendicular
Distance Formula
congruent

REMEMBER

The distance from a point to a line is defined as the length of the perpendicular segment from the point to the line.

What You Will Learn

▶ Explore the focus and the directrix of a parabola.
▶ Write equations of parabolas.
▶ Solve real-life problems.

Exploring the Focus and Directrix

Previously, you learned that the graph of a quadratic function is a parabola that opens up or down. A parabola can also be defined as the set of all points (x, y) in a plane that are equidistant from a fixed point called the **focus** and a fixed line called the **directrix**.

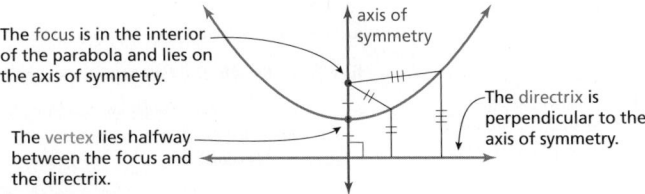

The focus is in the interior of the parabola and lies on the axis of symmetry.

The vertex lies halfway between the focus and the directrix.

The directrix is perpendicular to the axis of symmetry.

EXAMPLE 1 Using the Distance Formula to Write an Equation

Use the Distance Formula to write an equation of the parabola with focus $F(0, 2)$ and directrix $y = -2$.

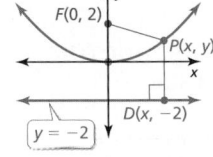

SOLUTION

Notice the line segments drawn from point F to point P and from point P to point D. By the definition of a parabola, these line segments must be congruent.

$PD = PF$	Definition of a parabola
$\sqrt{(x - x_1)^2 + (y - y_1)^2} = \sqrt{(x - x_2)^2 + (y - y_2)^2}$	Distance Formula
$\sqrt{(x - x)^2 + (y - (-2))^2} = \sqrt{(x - 0)^2 + (y - 2)^2}$	Substitute for x_1, y_1, x_2, and y_2.
$\sqrt{(y + 2)^2} = \sqrt{x^2 + (y - 2)^2}$	Simplify.
$(y + 2)^2 = x^2 + (y - 2)^2$	Square each side.
$y^2 + 4y + 4 = x^2 + y^2 - 4y + 4$	Expand.
$8y = x^2$	Combine like terms.
$y = \frac{1}{8}x^2$	Divide each side by 8.

Monitoring Progress Help in English and Spanish at *BigIdeasMath.com*

1. Use the Distance Formula to write an equation of the parabola with focus $F(0, -3)$ and directrix $y = 3$.

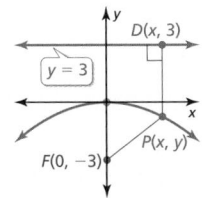

Laurie's Notes — Teacher Actions

- **Teaching Tip:** Demonstrate what is meant by the language "fixed point" and "fixed line" by drawing a line on the board and a point not on the line. "This line and this point define a set of points that we call a parabola."
- Discuss the sketch of the parabola, focus, and directrix. Demonstrate that any point on the parabola is equidistant to the focus and directrix. Mark the congruent segments. The focus and directrix are aids in graphing, but our sketches may not be exact; hence, marking the congruent segments is helpful.

- **Note:** The vertex is midway between the focus and directrix.
- The *Remember* note reminds students of how to find the distance between a point and a line.
- Review the technique of squaring both sides of an equation if students have forgotten.
- **Think-Pair-Share:** Before students begin work on Question 1, ask how this question differs from Example 1. Students should note that the parabola opens downward and therefore $a < 0$.

You can derive the equation of a parabola that opens up or down with vertex $(0, 0)$, focus $(0, p)$, and directrix $y = -p$ using the procedure in Example 1.

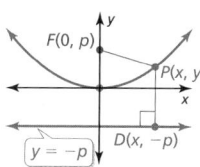

$$\sqrt{(x - x)^2 + (y - (-p))^2} = \sqrt{(x - 0)^2 + (y - p)^2}$$
$$(y + p)^2 = x^2 + (y - p)^2$$
$$y^2 + 2py + p^2 = x^2 + y^2 - 2py + p^2$$
$$4py = x^2$$
$$y = \frac{1}{4p}x^2$$

The focus and directrix each lie $|p|$ units from the vertex. Parabolas can also open left or right, in which case the equation has the form $x = \frac{1}{4p}y^2$ when the vertex is $(0, 0)$.

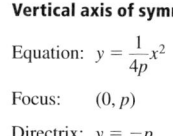 **Core Concept**

Standard Equations of a Parabola with Vertex at the Origin

Vertical axis of symmetry ($x = 0$)

Equation: $y = \frac{1}{4p}x^2$

Focus: $(0, p)$

Directrix: $y = -p$

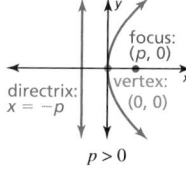

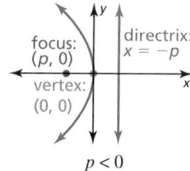

Horizontal axis of symmetry ($y = 0$)

Equation: $x = \frac{1}{4p}y^2$

Focus: $(p, 0)$

Directrix: $x = -p$

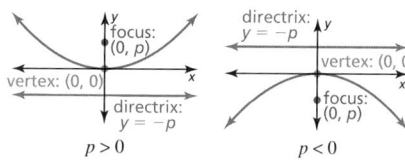

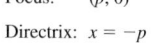

EXAMPLE 2 **Graphing an Equation of a Parabola**

Identify the focus, directrix, and axis of symmetry of $-4x = y^2$. Graph the equation.

SOLUTION

Step 1 Rewrite the equation in standard form.

$-4x = y^2$ Write the original equation.

$x = -\frac{1}{4}y^2$ Divide each side by -4.

Step 2 Identify the focus, directrix, and axis of symmetry. The equation has the form $x = \frac{1}{4p}y^2$, where $p = -1$. The focus is $(p, 0)$, or $(-1, 0)$. The directrix is $x = -p$, or $x = 1$. Because y is squared, the axis of symmetry is the x-axis.

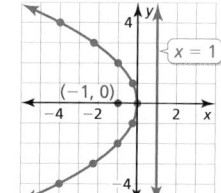

Step 3 Use a table of values to graph the equation. Notice that it is easier to substitute y-values and solve for x. Opposite y-values result in the same x-value.

y	0	±1	±2	±3	±4
x	0	−0.25	−1	−2.25	−4

Focus of a Parabola   **723**

LOOKING FOR STRUCTURE

Notice that $y = \frac{1}{4p}x^2$ is of the form $y = ax^2$. So, changing the value of p vertically stretches or shrinks the parabola.

STUDY TIP

Notice that parabolas opening left or right do *not* represent functions.

Extra Example 2

Identify the focus, directrix, and axis of symmetry of $-2x = y^2$. Graph the equation. The focus is $(-0.5, 0)$. The directrix is $x = 0.5$. The axis of symmetry is the x-axis, $y = 0$.

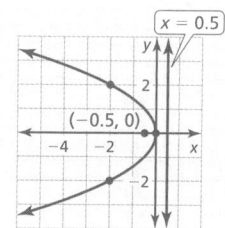

Laurie's Notes   Teacher Actions

- **MP7 Look For and Make Use of Structure:** Mathematically proficient students apply the practiced technique from the previous page to the general case. Relating this to the standard form of a quadratic, $y = ax^2$, students recognize that changing p will vertically stretch or shrink the parabola. When $p < 0$, the parabola will open downward.

- **?** "What if the directrix is a vertical line?" The parabola would open to the left or right.

- Write the *Core Concept,* which summarizes four cases of a parabola with the vertex at the origin.

- Students can be uncomfortable with having equations that are solved for x. Students should recognize that these parabolas are not functions. The simple vertical line test demonstrates this. Reassure students that the x- and y-axes are still horizontal and vertical, respectively, and ordered pairs are still written (x, y).

- **MP2 Reason Abstractly and Quantitatively:** In Example 2, where $x = -\frac{1}{4}y^2$ completing a table of values is easier when you substitute values of y and solve for x. Because y is squared, substituting $\pm y$ yields the same x-value.

Extra Example 3

Write an equation of the parabola shown.

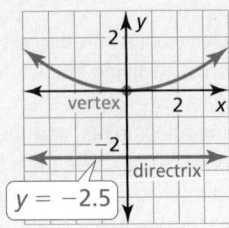

$y = 0.1x^2$

MONITORING PROGRESS ANSWERS

2. The focus is $\left(0, \frac{1}{2}\right)$, the directrix is $y = -\frac{1}{2}$, and the axis of symmetry is the y-axis.

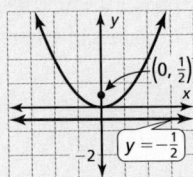

3. The focus is $\left(0, -\frac{1}{4}\right)$, the directrix is $y = \frac{1}{4}$, and the axis of symmetry is the y-axis.

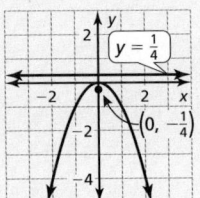

4. See Additional Answers.

5. $x = \frac{1}{12}y^2$
6. $x = -\frac{1}{8}y^2$
7. $y = \frac{1}{6}x^2$

Writing Equations of Parabolas

EXAMPLE 3 Writing an Equation of a Parabola

Write an equation of the parabola shown.

SOLUTION

Because the vertex is at the origin and the axis of symmetry is vertical, the equation has the form $y = \frac{1}{4p}x^2$. The directrix is $y = -p = 3$, so $p = -3$. Substitute -3 for p to write an equation of the parabola.

$$y = \frac{1}{4(-3)}x^2 = -\frac{1}{12}x^2$$

▶ So, an equation of the parabola is $y = -\frac{1}{12}x^2$.

Monitoring Progress ◀)) Help in English and Spanish at *BigIdeasMath.com*

Identify the focus, directrix, and axis of symmetry of the parabola. Then graph the equation.

2. $y = 0.5x^2$ 3. $-y = x^2$ 4. $y^2 = 6x$

Write an equation of the parabola with vertex at (0, 0) and the given directrix or focus.

5. directrix: $x = -3$ 6. focus: $(-2, 0)$ 7. focus: $\left(0, \frac{3}{2}\right)$

The vertex of a parabola is not always at the origin. As in previous transformations, adding a value to the input or output of a function translates its graph.

⨁ Core Concept

Standard Equations of a Parabola with Vertex at (h, k)

Vertical axis of symmetry (x = h)

Equation: $y = \frac{1}{4p}(x - h)^2 + k$

Focus: $(h, k + p)$

Directrix: $y = k - p$

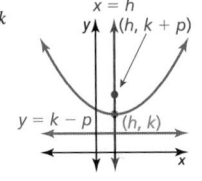
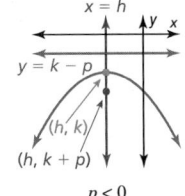

$p > 0$ $p < 0$

Horizontal axis of symmetry (y = k)

Equation: $x = \frac{1}{4p}(y - k)^2 + h$

Focus: $(h + p, k)$

Directrix: $x = h - p$

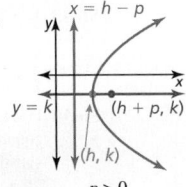
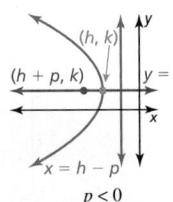

$p > 0$ $p < 0$

STUDY TIP

The standard form for a vertical axis of symmetry looks like vertex form. To remember the standard form for a horizontal axis of symmetry, switch x and y, and h and k.

Laurie's Notes   Teacher Actions

❓ "To write the equation of a parabola with its vertex at the origin, what information will you need?" The value of p and which way the parabola opens, vertically or horizontally. This could be determined by knowing the directrix or the focus.

• Work through the example as shown.

• **Thumbs Up:** Ask students to assess their level of understanding with a *Thumbs Up* signal. Have students work some or all of the *Monitoring Progress* questions based on their responses.

❓ Have students discuss the following question with their partners or in groups. "If the vertex of the parabola is translated to (h, k), what would the equations look like and what would happen to the directrix and focus?" Listen to student conversations before writing the *Core Concept* that summarizes this.

• **Note:** Be sure that students notice that with a horizontal axis of symmetry the general form is written in terms of "minus k" and "plus h," which is not what they are used to seeing.

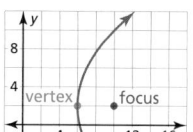

EXAMPLE 4 **Writing an Equation of a Translated Parabola**

Write an equation of the parabola shown.

SOLUTION

Because the vertex is not at the origin and the axis of symmetry is horizontal, the equation has the form $x = \frac{1}{4p}(y - k)^2 + h$. The vertex (h, k) is $(6, 2)$ and the focus $(h + p, k)$ is $(10, 2)$, so $h = 6$, $k = 2$, and $p = 4$. Substitute these values to write an equation of the parabola.

$$x = \frac{1}{4(4)}(y - 2)^2 + 6 = \frac{1}{16}(y - 2)^2 + 6$$

▶ So, an equation of the parabola is $x = \frac{1}{16}(y - 2)^2 + 6$.

Solving Real-Life Problems

Parabolic reflectors have cross sections that are parabolas. Incoming sound, light, or other energy that arrives at a parabolic reflector parallel to the axis of symmetry is directed to the focus (Diagram 1). Similarly, energy that is emitted from the focus of a parabolic reflector and then strikes the reflector is directed parallel to the axis of symmetry (Diagram 2).

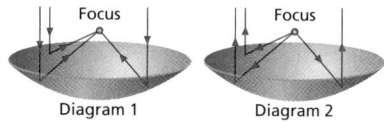

Diagram 1   Diagram 2

EXAMPLE 5 **Solving a Real-Life Problem**

An electricity-generating dish uses a parabolic reflector to concentrate sunlight onto a high-frequency engine located at the focus of the reflector. The sunlight heats helium to 650°C to power the engine. Write an equation that represents the cross section of the dish shown with its vertex at $(0, 0)$. What is the depth of the dish?

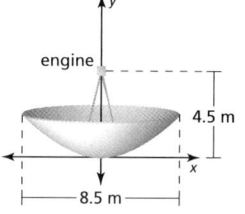

SOLUTION

Because the vertex is at the origin, and the axis of symmetry is vertical, the equation has the form $y = \frac{1}{4p}x^2$. The engine is at the focus, which is 4.5 meters above the vertex. So, $p = 4.5$. Substitute 4.5 for p to write the equation.

$$y = \frac{1}{4(4.5)}x^2 = \frac{1}{18}x^2$$

The depth of the dish is the y-value at the dish's outside edge. The dish extends $\frac{8.5}{2} = 4.25$ meters to either side of the vertex $(0, 0)$, so find y when $x = 4.25$.

$$y = \frac{1}{18}(4.25)^2 \approx 1$$

▶ The depth of the dish is about 1 meter.

Monitoring Progress Help in English and Spanish at *BigIdeasMath.com*

8. Write an equation of a parabola with vertex $(-1, 4)$ and focus $(-1, 2)$.

9. A parabolic microwave antenna is 16 feet in diameter. Write an equation that represents the cross section of the antenna with its vertex at $(0, 0)$ and its focus 10 feet to the right of the vertex. What is the depth of the antenna?

Extra Example 4

Write an equation of the parabola shown.

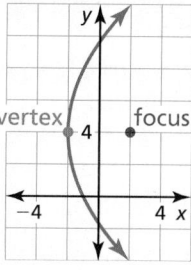

$$x = \frac{1}{16}(y - 4)^2 - 2$$

Extra Example 5

An archway in front of a school is in the shape of a parabola. The top of the arch is the vertex $(0, 0)$. The school seal is at the focus, 2.5 feet below the vertex, and the arch is 18 feet wide at the ground. Write an equation that represents a cross section of the arch. What is the height from the top of the arch to the ground?
$y = -0.1x^2$; 8.1 feet

MONITORING PROGRESS ANSWERS

8. $y = -\frac{1}{8}(x + 1)^2 + 4$

9. $x = \frac{1}{40}y^2$; 1.6 ft

Laurie's Notes   Teacher Actions

? "What is the vertex of the parabola?" $(6, 2)$
- Have students identify h, k, and p, and let them work through the example with partners.
- **Popsicle Sticks:** Use *Popsicle Sticks* to identify the student who volunteers his/her equation.
- The real-life example connects to the explorations and the *Motivate*.

COMMON ERROR Students think the depth of the dish is the distance from the engine (focus) to the vertex. Explain that the depth is the y-value at the outside edge of the dish.

Closure
- **Exit Ticket:** Identify the focus, directrix, and axis of symmetry for $4y = -x^2$. Graph.
  focus: $(0, -1)$, directrix: $y = 1$, axis of symmetry: $x = 0$

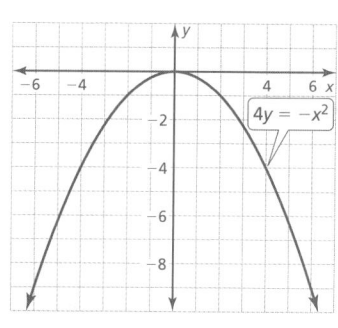

ANSWERS

1. focus; directrix

2. Using the equation for directrix $y = -p$, the result is $p = -5$. Since the focus is $(0, p)$, the focus must be $(0, -5)$.

3. $y = \frac{1}{4}x^2$

4. $y = -\frac{1}{16}x^2$

5. $y = -\frac{1}{8}x^2$

6. $y = -\frac{1}{28}x^2$

7. $y = \frac{1}{24}x^2$

8. $y = \frac{1}{20}x^2$

9. $y = -\frac{1}{40}x^2$

10. $y = \frac{1}{36}x^2$

11. A, B and D; Each has a value for p that is negative. Substituting in a negative value for p in $y = \frac{1}{4p}x^2$ results in a parabola that has been reflected across the x-axis.

12. B, C and E; Use the focus to create the equation $y = -\frac{1}{36}x^2$. Points B, C and E are the fourth quadrant points that satisfy the equation.

13. The focus is $(0, 2)$. The directrix is $y = -2$. The axis of symmetry is the y-axis.

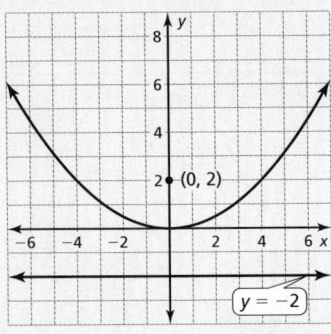

Exercises

Vocabulary and Core Concept Check

1. **COMPLETE THE SENTENCE** A parabola is the set of all points in a plane equidistant from a fixed point called the _____ and a fixed line called the _____ .

2. **WRITING** Explain how to find the coordinates of the focus of a parabola with vertex $(0, 0)$ and directrix $y = 5$.

Monitoring Progress and Modeling with Mathematics

In Exercises 3–10, use the Distance Formula to write an equation of the parabola. *(See Example 1.)*

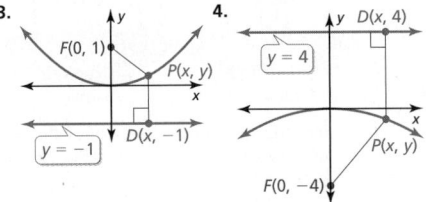

5. focus: $(0, -2)$
   directrix: $y = 2$

6. directrix: $y = 7$
   focus: $(0, -7)$

7. vertex: $(0, 0)$
   directrix: $y = -6$

8. vertex: $(0, 0)$
   focus: $(0, 5)$

9. vertex: $(0, 0)$
   focus: $(0, -10)$

10. vertex: $(0, 0)$
    directrix: $y = -9$

11. **ANALYZING RELATIONSHIPS** Which of the given characteristics describe parabolas that open down? Explain your reasoning.

    (A) focus: $(0, -6)$
        directrix: $y = 6$

    (B) focus: $(0, -2)$
        directrix: $y = 2$

    (C) focus: $(0, 6)$
        directrix: $y = -6$

    (D) focus: $(0, -1)$
        directrix: $y = 1$

12. **REASONING** Which of the following are possible coordinates of the point P in the graph shown? Explain.

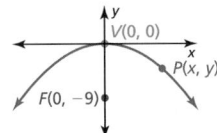

    (A) $(-6, -1)$ (B) $\left(3, -\frac{1}{4}\right)$ (C) $\left(4, -\frac{4}{9}\right)$

    (D) $\left(1, \frac{1}{36}\right)$ (E) $(6, -1)$ (F) $\left(2, -\frac{1}{18}\right)$

726   Additional Topic

In Exercises 13–20, identify the focus, directrix, and axis of symmetry of the parabola. Graph the equation. *(See Example 2.)*

13. $y = \frac{1}{8}x^2$

14. $y = -\frac{1}{12}x^2$

15. $x = -\frac{1}{20}y^2$

16. $x = \frac{1}{24}y^2$

17. $y^2 = 16x$

18. $-x^2 = 48y$

19. $6x^2 + 3y = 0$

20. $8x^2 - y = 0$

ERROR ANALYSIS In Exercises 21 and 22, describe and correct the error in graphing the parabola.

21.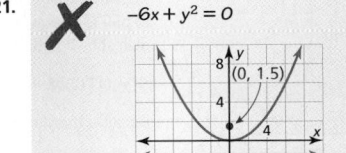

22.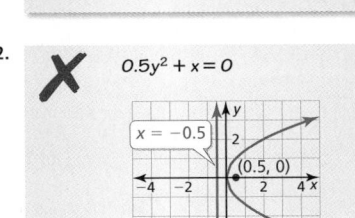

23. **ANALYZING EQUATIONS** The cross section (with units in inches) of a parabolic satellite dish can be modeled by the equation $y = \frac{1}{38}x^2$. How far is the receiver from the vertex of the cross section? Explain.

---

14. The focus is $(0, -3)$. The directrix is $y = 3$. The axis of symmetry is the y-axis.

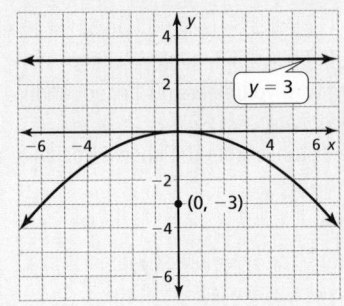

15. The focus is $(-5, 0)$. The directrix is $x = 5$. The axis of symmetry is the x-axis.

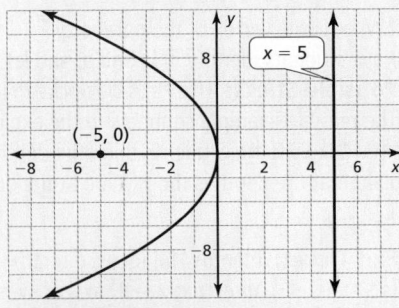

16–23. See Additional Answers.

24. ANALYZING EQUATIONS The cross section (with units in inches) of a parabolic spotlight can be modeled by the equation $x = \frac{1}{20}y^2$. How far is the bulb from the vertex of the cross section? Explain.

In Exercises 25–28, write an equation of the parabola shown. *(See Example 3.)*

25.

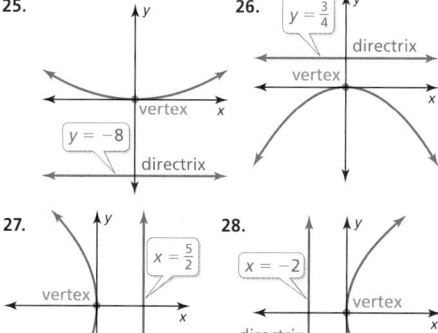

26.

27.

28.

In Exercises 29–36, write an equation of the parabola with the given characteristics.

29. focus: $(3, 0)$
directrix: $x = -3$

30. focus: $\left(\frac{2}{3}, 0\right)$
directrix: $x = -\frac{2}{3}$

31. directrix: $x = -10$
vertex: $(0, 0)$

32. directrix: $y = \frac{8}{3}$
vertex: $(0, 0)$

33. focus: $\left(0, -\frac{5}{3}\right)$
directrix: $y = \frac{5}{3}$

34. focus: $\left(0, \frac{5}{4}\right)$
directrix: $y = -\frac{5}{4}$

35. focus: $\left(0, \frac{6}{7}\right)$
vertex: $(0, 0)$

36. focus: $\left(-\frac{4}{5}, 0\right)$
vertex: $(0, 0)$

In Exercises 37–40, write an equation of the parabola shown. *(See Example 4.)*

37.

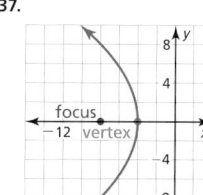

38.

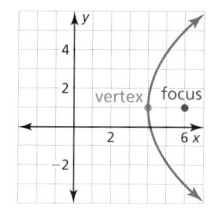

39.

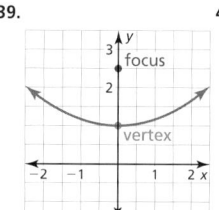

40.

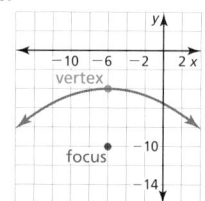

In Exercises 41–46, identify the vertex, focus, directrix, and axis of symmetry of the parabola. Describe the transformations of the graph of the standard equation with $p = 1$ and vertex $(0, 0)$.

41. $y = \frac{1}{8}(x - 3)^2 + 2$

42. $y = -\frac{1}{4}(x + 2)^2 + 1$

43. $x = \frac{1}{16}(y - 3)^2 + 1$

44. $y = (x + 3)^2 - 5$

45. $x = -3(y + 4)^2 + 2$

46. $x = 4(y + 5)^2 - 1$

47. MODELING WITH MATHEMATICS Scientists studying dolphin echolocation simulate the projection of a bottlenose dolphin's clicking sounds using computer models. The models originate the sounds at the focus of a parabolic reflector. The parabola in the graph shows the cross section of the reflector with focal length of 1.3 inches and aperture width of 8 inches. Write an equation to represent the cross section of the reflector. What is the depth of the reflector? *(See Example 5.)*

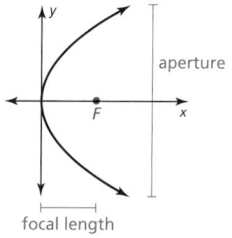

Focus of a Parabola **727**

ANSWERS

24. 5 in.; The bulb should be placed at the focus. The distance from the vertex to the focus is $p = \frac{20}{4} = 5$ in.

25. $y = \frac{1}{32}x^2$

26. $y = -\frac{1}{3}x^2$

27. $x = -\frac{1}{10}y^2$

28. $x = \frac{1}{8}y^2$

29. $x = \frac{1}{12}y^2$

30. $x = \frac{3}{8}y^2$

31. $x = \frac{1}{40}y^2$

32. $y = -\frac{3}{32}x^2$

33. $y = -\frac{3}{20}x^2$

34. $y = \frac{1}{5}x^2$

35. $y = \frac{7}{24}x^2$

36. $x = -\frac{5}{16}y^2$

37. $x = -\frac{1}{16}y^2 - 4$

38. $x = \frac{1}{8}(y - 1)^2 + 4$

39. $y = \frac{1}{6}x^2 + 1$

40. $y = -\frac{1}{24}(x + 6)^2 - 4$

41. The vertex is $(3, 2)$. The focus is $(3, 4)$. The directrix is $y = 0$. The axis of symmetry is $x = 3$. The graph is a vertical shrink by a factor of $\frac{1}{2}$ followed by a translation 3 units right and 2 units up.

42. The vertex is $(-2, 1)$. The focus is $(-2, 0)$. The directrix is $y = 2$. The axis of symmetry is $x = -2$. The graph is a reflection in the x-axis and a translation 2 units left and 1 unit up.

43. The vertex is $(1, 3)$. The focus is $(5, 3)$. The directrix is $x = -3$. The axis of symmetry is $y = 3$. The graph is a horizontal shrink by a factor of $\frac{1}{4}$ followed by a translation 1 unit right and 3 units up.

44. The vertex is $(-3, -5)$. The focus is $(-3, -4.75)$. The directrix is $y = -5.25$. The axis of symmetry is $x = -3$. The graph is a vertical stretch by a factor of 4 followed by a translation 3 units left and 5 units down.

45. The vertex is $(2, -4)$. The focus is $\left(\frac{23}{12}, -4\right)$. The directrix is $x = \frac{25}{12}$. The axis of symmetry is $y = -4$. The graph is a horizontal stretch by a factor of 12 followed by a reflection in the y-axis and a translation 2 units right and 4 units down.

46. The vertex is $(-1, -5)$. The focus is $\left(-\frac{15}{16}, -5\right)$. The directrix is $x = -\frac{17}{16}$. The axis of symmetry is $y = -5$. The graph is a horizontal stretch by a factor of 16 followed by a translation 1 unit left and 5 units down.

47. $x = \frac{1}{5.2}y^2$; about 3.08 in.

ANSWERS

48. $y = \frac{1}{6.8}x^2$; The domain is $-2.9 \leq x \leq 2.9$ and the range is $0 \leq y \leq 1.7$; The domain represents the width of the trough, and the range represents the height of the trough.

49. As $|p|$ increases, the graph gets wider; As $|p|$ increases, the constant in the function gets smaller which results in a vertical shrink, making the graph wider.

50. a. B is the vertex, C is the focus, and A is a point on the directrix.

    b. The focus and directrix will both be shifted up 3 units.

51. $y = \frac{1}{4}x^2$

52. *Sample answer:* One equation is $y = \frac{1}{8}(x - a)^2 + (b - 2)$ with a directrix of $y = b - 4$. Another equation is $y = -\frac{1}{8}(x - a)^2 + (b + 2)$ with a directrix of $y = b + 4$.

53. $x = \frac{1}{4p}y^2$ **54.** 8

Mini-Assessment

1. Use the Distance Formula to write an equation of the parabola with focus $F(0, 8)$ and directrix $y = -8$. $y = \frac{1}{32}x^2$

2. Identify the focus, directrix, and axis of symmetry of $8y = x^2$. Graph the equation. The focus is $F(0, 2)$. The directrix is $y = -2$. The axis of symmetry is the y-axis, $x = 0$.

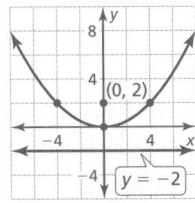

3. Write an equation of the parabola with vertex at $(0, 0)$ and directrix $y = 6$. $y = -\frac{1}{24}x^2$

4. Write an equation of the parabola with vertex $(2, 10)$ and focus $(2, 9.5)$. $y = -0.5(x - 2)^2 + 10$

5. An arch is 10 feet across at ground level. Write an equation that represents the cross section of the arch with its vertex at $(0, 0)$ and its focus 0.5 foot below the vertex. What is the height of the arch? $y = -0.5x^2$; 12.5 feet

48. MODELING WITH MATHEMATICS Solar energy can be concentrated using long troughs that have a parabolic cross section as shown in the figure. Write an equation to represent the cross section of the trough. What are the domain and range in this situation? What do they represent?

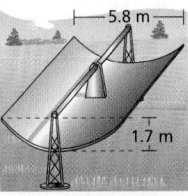

49. ABSTRACT REASONING As $|p|$ increases, how does the width of the graph of the equation $y = \frac{1}{4p}x^2$ change? Explain your reasoning.

50. HOW DO YOU SEE IT? The graph shows the path of a volleyball served from an initial height of 6 feet as it travels over a net.

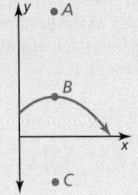

    a. Label the vertex, focus, and a point on the directrix.

    b. An underhand serve follows the same parabolic path but is hit from a height of 3 feet. How does this affect the focus? the directrix?

51. CRITICAL THINKING The distance from point P to the directrix is 2 units. Write an equation of the parabola.

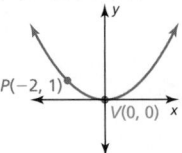

52. THOUGHT PROVOKING Two parabolas have the same focus (a, b) and focal length of 2 units. Write an equation of each parabola. Identify the directrix of each parabola.

53. REPEATED REASONING Use the Distance Formula to derive the equation of a parabola that opens to the right with vertex $(0, 0)$, focus $(p, 0)$, and directrix $x = -p$.

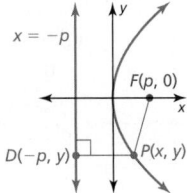

54. PROBLEM SOLVING The *latus rectum* of a parabola is the line segment that is parallel to the directrix, passes through the focus, and has endpoints that lie on the parabola. Find the length of the latus rectum of the parabola shown.

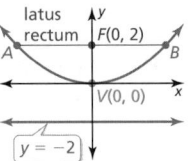

728   Additional Topic

If students need help...	If students got it...
Resources by Chapter • Practice A and Practice B • Puzzle Time	**Resources by Chapter** • Enrichment and Extension • Cumulative Review
Student Journal • Practice	Start the *next* Section
Differentiating the Lesson Skills Review Handbook	

Additional Answers

Chapter 1

1.1 Explorations

2. a. Two lines can intersect at a point, overlap, or not intersect.

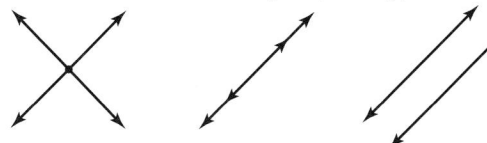

Sample answer: The line formed by the floor and front wall intersects the line formed by the front wall and side wall; The line formed by the bottom of the front wall overlaps the line formed by the front edge of the floor; The line formed by the front wall and the floor does not intersect the line formed by the side wall and back wall.

b. A line and a plane can intersect at a point, overlap, or not intersect.

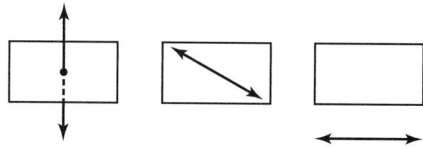

Sample answer: A line formed by two walls intersects the floor at a point; A line formed by a wall and the floor overlaps the floor; A line formed by a wall and the floor does not intersect the ceiling.

c. Two planes can intersect in a line, overlap, or not intersect.

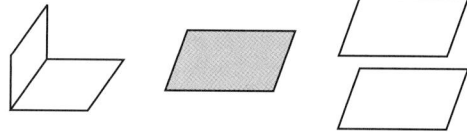

Sample answer: The floor and a wall intersect in a line; The door and the wall overlap; the floor and the ceiling do not intersect.

1.1 Monitoring Progress and Modeling with Mathematics

48. *Sample answer:*

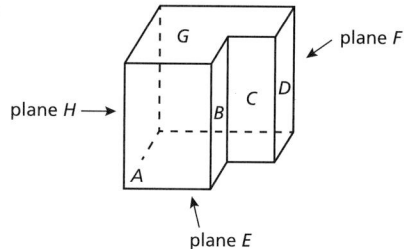

50. a. *Sample answer:* north on Cherry Court, south on Cherry Court; east on Apple Avenue, west on Apple Avenue

b. Opposite rays could not have been formed because both friends were not traveling along the same line (road).

51.

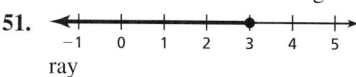

ray

52.

-8 -7 -6 -5 -4 -3 -2 -1 0 1 2 3 4 5 6

segment

53.

-4 -3 -2 -1 0 1 2 3 4 5 6 7

rays

54.

-2 -1 0 1 2

point

55. a. K, N

b. *Sample answer:* plane JKL, plane JQN

c. J, K, L, M, N, P, Q

56. never; A line extends without end.

57. sometimes; The point may be on the line.

58. sometimes; The point may be in the plane.

59. sometimes; The planes may not intersect.

60. always; There is exactly one line through any two points.

61. sometimes; The points may be collinear.

62. always; There is exactly one plane through any three points not on the same line.

63. sometimes; Lines in parallel planes do not intersect, and may not be parallel.

64. yes; yes; yes; *Sample answer:*

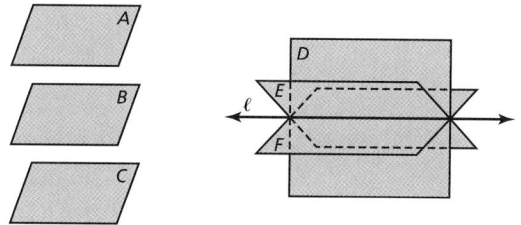

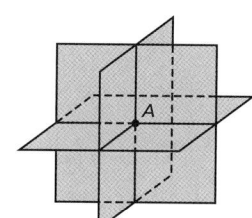

1.1 Maintaining Mathematical Proficiency

65. 8

66. 6

67. 10

68. 4

69. $x = 25$

70. $x = -16$

71. $x = 22$

72. $x = 42$

1.2 Monitoring Progress and Modeling with Mathematics

8.

14.

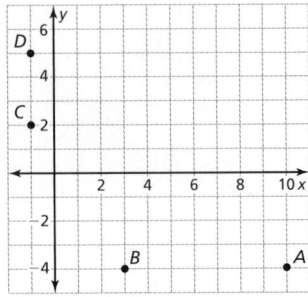

no

15. 22　　　　　　　**16.** 26

17. 23　　　　　　　**18.** 19

19. 24

30. yes; The legs could all be set at different angles with the table.

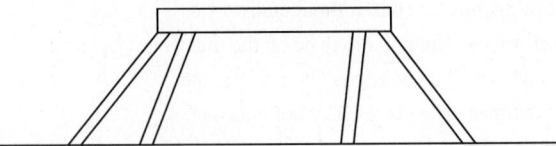

36. $AB = 3, BC = 3, BD = 9, AC = 6, CD = 6, AD = 12; \frac{2}{3}$; Two of the segments are 3 units long. The other four are longer than that.

37. yes, no; $FC + CB = FB$, so $FB > CB$.

$\overline{AC}$ and $\overline{DB}$ overlap but do not share an endpoint.

1.2 Maintaining Mathematical Proficiency

38. 1　　　　　　　**39.** 5

40. $\sqrt{34}$　　　　　**41.** $\frac{13}{2}$, or 6.5

42. $x = 6$　　　　　**43.** $y = 9$

44. $x = -13$　　　　**45.** $x = 2$

1.3 Monitoring Progress and Modeling with Mathematics

44. *Sample answer:* connect the midpoints of the lengths, connect the midpoints of the widths, connect opposite corners to create a diagonal; no

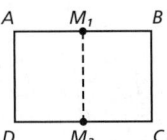

45. 13 cm

1.3 Maintaining Mathematical Proficiency

46. 20 cm, 25 cm²　　　　　　**47.** 26 ft, 30 ft²

48. 12 m, 6 m²　　　　　　　**49.** 36 yd, 60 yd²

50. $a < -11$

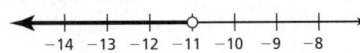

51. $y \geq 13$

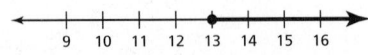

52. $x < -8$

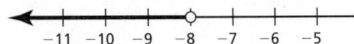

53. $z \leq 48$

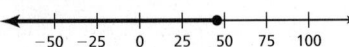

1.4 Monitoring Progress and Modeling with Mathematics

34. *Sample answer:*

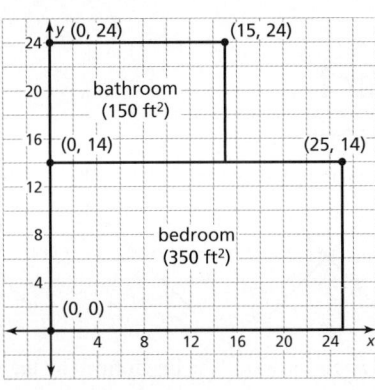

37. $x = 2$

1.4 Maintaining Mathematical Proficiency

38. $x = 3$　　　　　　**39.** $x = -1$

40. no solution　　　　**41.** $x = 14$

42. $x = 2$　　　　　　**43.** $x = 1$

44.

X •————————————→ Y

1.5 Monitoring Progress and Modeling with Mathematics

50. a. acute; Both angles would have to be greater than 0° and less than 90°, because the original angle is less than 90°.

b. acute; Both angles would have to be greater than 0° and less than 90°, because the angles are complimentary.

c. acute, right, obtuse; Possibilities include two acute angles, one right and one acute, or one obtuse and one acute. The sum of the measures is between 90° and 180°.

d. acute, right, obtuse; Possibilities are either two right angles, or one acute and one obtuse. The sum of the angle measures is 180°.

51. a. *Sample answer:* $(1, 2)$

b. *Sample answer:* $(0, 2)$

c. *Sample answer:* $(-2, 2)$

d. *Sample answer:* $(-2, 0)$

52. no; Each obtuse angle has to be greater than 90°, so their combined measure would be greater than 180°.

53. acute, right, or obtuse; The sum of the angles could be less than 90° (example: $30° + 20° = 50°$), equal to 90° (example: $60° + 30° = 90°$), or greater than 90° (example: $55° + 45° = 100°$).

54. a. no; $\angle WYV \cong \angle VYZ$, so $m\angle WYV = 46°$. $m\angle XYZ = m\angle XYW + m\angle WYV + m\angle VYZ = 90 + 46 + 46 = 182°$. $m\angle XYZ \neq 180°$, so it is not a straight angle.

b. *Sample answer:* $m\angle VYZ = 45°$

55. *Sample answer:* You draw a segment, ray, or line in the interior of an angle so that the two angles created are congruent to each other; Angle bisectors and segment bisectors can be segments, rays, or lines, but only a segment bisector can be a point. The two angles/segments created are congruent to each other, and their measures are each half the measure of the original angle/segment.

56. 68°; $m\angle RSP = 2(m\angle VSP) = 2(17°) = 34°$, $m\angle TSQ = m\angle RSQ = 2(m\angle RSP) = 2(34°) = 68°$

57. acute; It is likely that the angle with the horizontal is very small because levels are typically used when something appears to be horizontal but still needs to be checked.

1.5 Maintaining Mathematical Proficiency

58. $x = 113$ **59.** $x = 32$

60. $x = 74$ **61.** $x = 71$

62. $x = 8$ **63.** $x = 12$

64. $x = 3$ **65.** $x = 10$

1.6 Monitoring Progress and Modeling with Mathematics

46. e. yes; They appear to intersect at point A in the diagram.

  f. yes; They are adjacent, and $\angle BAD$ is marked as a right angle.

  g. yes; $\angle BAD$ and $\angle DAE$ are a linear pair, and $\angle BAD$ is marked as a right angle.

47. yes; Because $m\angle KJL + x° = 90°$ and $m\angle MJN + x° = 90°$, it must be that $m\angle KJL + x° = m\angle MJN + x°$. Subtracting $x°$ from each side of the equation results in the measures being equal. So, the angles are congruent.

48. yes; The angle of incidence is always congruent to the angle of reflection, so their complements will always be congruent.

49. a. $y°$, $(180 - y)°$, $(180 - y)°$

  b. They are always congruent; They are both supplementary to the same angle. So, their measures must be equal.

50. a. $y_1 = 90 - x$, $y_2 = 180 - x$; $D_{y_1}: 0 < x < 90$, $D_{y_2}: 0 < x < 90$; $\angle 1$ and $\angle 2$ are complementary, so the measures are between $0°$ and $90°$.

  b.

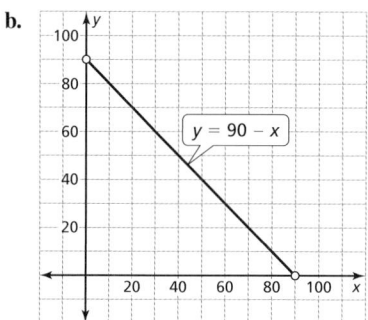

$R_{y_1}: 0 < y_1 < 90$

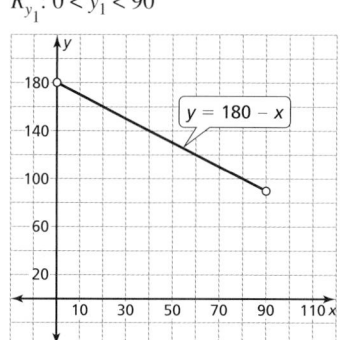

$R_{y_2}: 90 < y_2 < 180$

51. $37°$, $53°$; If two angles are complementary, then their sum is $90°$. If x is one of the angles, then $(90 - x)$ is the complement. Write and solve the equation $90 = (x - (90 - x)) + 74$. The solution is $x = 53$.

1.6 Maintaining Mathematical Proficiency

52. sometimes; Positive integers are whole numbers. Negative integers are not.

53. never; Integers are positive or negative whole numbers. Irrational numbers are decimals that never terminate and never repeat.

54. always; The real number set is made up of all rational and irrational numbers.

55. never; The whole numbers are positive or zero.

56. sometimes; The set of rational numbers includes integers, as well as fractions and decimals that terminate or repeat.

57. always; The set of integers includes all natural numbers and their opposites (and zero).

58. always; The set of rational numbers includes whole numbers.

59. sometimes; Irrational numbers can be positive or negative.

1.4–1.6 What Did You Learn?

1. Show your friend a graph of the lines and the written work for determining which sides are perpendicular and for finding the lengths of the sides and the perimeter and area of the triangle. Use arrows and labels, as shown.

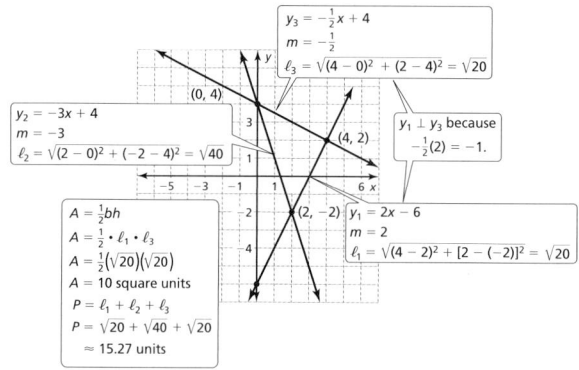

Chapter 1 Test

15.

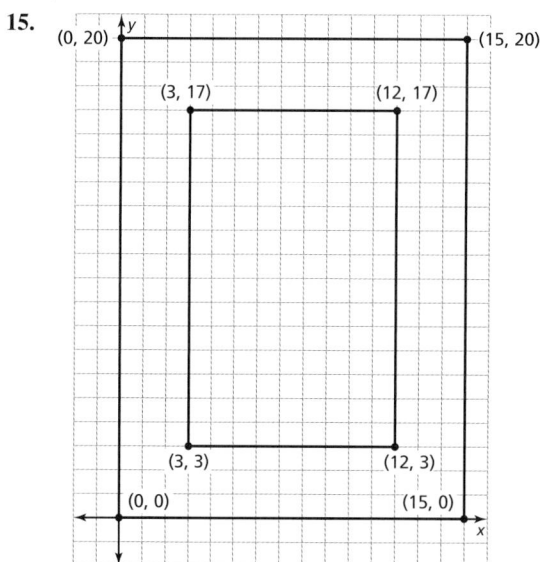

46 ft, 126 ft²

16. yellow; Because the green ball is the midpoint between the red ball and the pallino, it is equidistant from them. So, it is 10 inches from the pallino. Because the yellow ball is only 8 inches from the pallino, it is closer.

Chapter 2

2.1 Monitoring Progress and Modeling with Mathematics

20. conditional: If you are not an only child, then you have a sibling; true

converse: If you have a sibling, then you are not an only child; true

inverse: If you are an only child, then you do not have a sibling; true

contrapositive: If you do not have a sibling, then you are an only child; true

21. conditional: If it does not snow, then I will run outside; false

converse: If I run outside, then it is not snowing; true

inverse: If it snows, then I will not run outside; true

contrapositive: If I do not run outside, then it is snowing; false

22. conditional: If the Sun is out, then it is daytime; true

converse: If it is daytime, then the Sun is out; false

inverse: If the Sun is not out, then it is not daytime; false

contrapositive: If it is not daytime, then the Sun is not out; true

23. conditional: If $3x - 7 = 20$, then $x = 9$; true

converse: If $x = 9$, then $3x - 7 = 20$; true

inverse: If $3x - 7 \neq 20$, then $x \neq 9$; true

contrapositive: If $x \neq 9$, then $3x - 7 \neq 20$; true

24. conditional: If it is Valentine's Day, then it is February; true

converse: If it is February, then it is Valentine's Day; false

inverse: If it is not Valentine's Day, then it is not February; false

contrapositive: If it is not February, then it is not Valentine's Day; true

25. true; By definition of right angle, the measure of the right angle shown is 90°.

26. true; If intersecting lines form a right angle, then they are perpendicular.

27. true; If angles form a linear pair, then the sum of the measures of their angles is 180°.

28. false; The midpoint cannot be assumed unless $\overline{AM}$ and $\overline{MB}$ are marked as congruent.

41.

p	q	$\sim p$	$\sim q$	$\sim p \rightarrow \sim q$	$\sim(\sim p \rightarrow \sim q)$
T	T	F	F	T	F
T	F	F	T	T	F
F	T	T	F	F	T
F	F	T	T	T	F

42.

p	q	$\sim q$	$p \rightarrow \sim q$	$\sim(p \rightarrow \sim q)$
T	T	F	F	T
T	F	T	T	F
F	T	F	T	F
F	F	T	T	F

45. a. If a rock is igneous, then it is formed from the cooling of molten rock; If a rock is sedimentary, then it is formed from pieces of other rocks; If a rock is metamorphic, then it is formed by changing temperature, pressure, or chemistry.

  b. If a rock is formed from the cooling of molten rock, then it is igneous; true; All rocks formed from cooling molten rock are called igneous.

  If a rock is formed from pieces of other rocks, then it is sedimentary; true; All rocks formed from pieces of other rocks are called sedimentary.

  If a rock is formed by changing temperature, pressure, or chemistry, then it is metamorphic; true; All rocks formed by changing temperature, pressure, or chemistry are called metamorphic.

  c. *Sample answer:* If a rock is not sedimentary, then it was not formed from pieces of other rocks; This is the inverse of one of the conditional statements in part (a). So, the converse of this statement will be the contrapositive of the conditional statement. Because the contrapositive is equivalent to the conditional statement and the conditional statement was true, the contrapositive will also be true.

59. a.
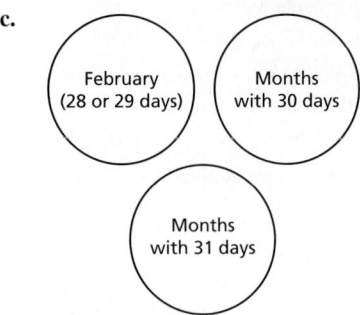
If you see a cat, then you went to the zoo to see a lion; The original statement is true, because a lion is a type of cat, but the converse is false, because you could see a cat without going to the zoo.

  b.
If you wear a helmet, then you play a sport; Both the original statement and the converse are false, because not all sports require helmets and sometimes helmets are worn for activities that are not considered a sport, such as construction work.

  c.

If this month is not February, then it has 31 days; The original statement is true, because February never has 31 days, but the converse is false, because a month that is not February could have 30 days.

60. a. true (as long as $x \neq y$)

  b. If the mean of the data is between x and y, then x and y are the least and greatest values in your data set. This converse is false, because x and y could be any two values in the set as long as one is higher and one is lower than the mean.

  c. mode; The mean is always a calculated value that is not necessarily equal to any of the data values, and the median is a calculated value when there are an even number of data values. The mode is the data value with the greatest frequency, so it is always a data value.

63. *Sample answer:* slogan: "This treadmill is a fat-burning machine!" conditional statement: If you use this treadmill, then you will burn fat quickly.

2.1 Maintaining Mathematical Proficiency

64. add a side;
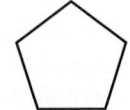 

65. add a square that connects the midpoints of the previously added square;
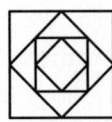 

66. add 2; 9, 11

67. add 11; 56, 67

68. multiply by $\frac{2}{3}$; $\frac{32}{81}$, $\frac{64}{243}$

69. $1^2, 2^2, 3^2, \ldots$; 25, 36

2.2 Monitoring Progress and Modeling with Mathematics

8. 5 blocks are added to each figure to get the next figure. One block is added to each of the four ends of the base and one block is added on top.

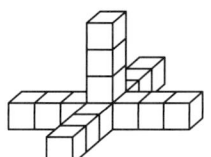 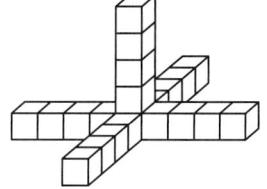

45. a. true; Based on the Law of Syllogism, if you went camping at Yellowstone, and Yellowstone is in Wyoming, then you went camping in Wyoming.

    b. false; When you go camping, you go canoeing, but even though your friend always goes camping when you do, he or she may not choose to go canoeing with you.

    c. true; It is known that if you go on a hike, your friend goes with you. It is also known that you went on a hike. So, based on the Law of Detachment, your friend went on a hike.

    d. false; It is known that you and your friend went on a hike, but it is not known where. It is only known that there is a 3-mile-long trail near where you are camping.

46. a. Mineral C must be Talc. Because it was scratched by all three of the other minerals, it must have the lowest hardness rating. Because Mineral B has a higher hardness rating than Mineral A, Mineral A could be either Gypsum or Calcite, and Mineral B could be either Calcite or Fluorite.

    b. Check Mineral B and Mineral D. If Mineral D scratches Mineral B, then Mineral D is Fluorite, Mineral B is Calcite, and Mineral A is Gypsum. If Mineral B scratches Mineral D, then Mineral B is Fluorite, and you have to check Mineral D and Mineral A. The one that scratches the other has the higher hardness rating and is therefore Calcite. The one that gets scratched is Gypsum.

2.3 Monitoring Progress and Modeling with Mathematics

26. Line Intersection Postulate (Post. 2.3)

27. a. If there are two points, then there exists exactly one line that passes through them.

    b. converse: If there exists exactly one line that passes through a given point or points, then there are two points; false; inverse: If there are not two points, then there is not exactly one line that passes through them; false; contrapositive: If there is not exactly one line that passes through a given point or points, then there are not two points; true

28. a. If a plane exists, then it contains at least three noncollinear points.

    b. converse: If a plane contains at least three noncollinear points, then the plane exists; true; inverse: If no plane exists, then there are not three noncollinear points; true; contrapositive: If there are not three noncollinear points, then a plane has not been defined; true

29. $<$

30. yes; Let two lines ℓ and m intersect at Point C. There must be a second point on each line, A on ℓ and B on m. Through the three nonlinear points A, B, and C, there exists exactly one plane R. Because A and C are in R, ℓ is in R. Because B and C are in R, m is in R.

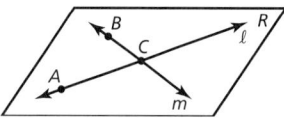

31. yes; For example, the ceiling and two walls of many rooms intersect in a point in the corner of the room.

32. no; The postulate says that if two planes intersect, they will intersect in a line. But planes can be parallel and never intersect. For example, the ceiling and floor of many rooms are parallel.

33. Points E, F, and G must be collinear. They must be on the line that intersects plane P and plane Q; Points E, F, and G can be either collinear or noncollinear.

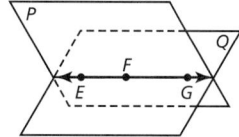 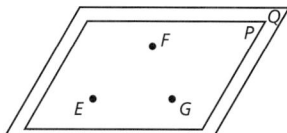

34. *Sample answer:* The Line Intersection Postulate (Post. 2.3) would have to be altered. In spherical geometry, if two lines intersect, then their intersection is exactly two points. The two points of intersection would be the endpoints of a diameter.

2.3 Maintaining Mathematical Proficiency

35. $t = 2$; Addition Property of Equality

36. $x = 7$; Division Property of Equality

37. $x = 4$; Subtraction Property of Equality

38. $x = 35$; Multiplication Property of Equality

2.4 Explorations

4.

Equation	Reason
$3(x + 1) - 1 = -13$	Write the equation.
$3x + 3 - 1 = -13$	Distributive Property
$3x + 2 = -13$	Simplify.
$3x + 2 - 2 = -13 - 2$	Subtraction Property of Equality
$3x = -15$	Simplify.
$\dfrac{3x}{3} = \dfrac{-15}{3}$	Division Property of Equality
$x = -5$	Simplify.

2.4 Lesson Monitoring Progress

1.

Equation	Explanation and Reason
$6x - 11 = -35$	Write the equation; Given
$6x - 11 + 11 = -35 + 11$	Add 11 to each side; Addition Property of Equality
$6x = -24$	Combine like terms; Simplify.
$x = -4$	Divide each side by 6; Division Property of Equality

2. Equation   **Explanation and Reason**

$-2p - 9 = 10p - 17$ Write the equation; Given

$-2p - 10p - 9 = 10p - 10p - 17$

     Subtract $10p$ from each side; Subtraction Property of Equality

$-12p - 9 = -17$ Combine like terms; Simplify.

$-12p - 9 + 9 = -17 + 9$ Add 9 to each side; Addition Property of Equality

$-12p = -8$ Combine like terms; Simplify.

$p = \frac{2}{3}$ Divide each side by -12; Division Property of Equality

3. Equation   **Explanation and Reason**

$39 - 5z = -1 + 5z$ Write the equation; Given

$39 - 5z - 5z = -1 + 5z - 5z$

     Subtract $5z$ from each side; Subtraction Property of Equality

$39 - 10z = -1$ Combine like terms; Simplify.

$39 - 39 - 10z = -1 - 39$ Subtract 39 from each side; Subtraction Property of Equality

$-10z = -40$ Combine like terms; Simplify.

$z = 4$ Divide each side by -10; Division Property of Equality

4. Equation   **Explanation and Reason**

$3(3x + 14) = -3$ Write the equation; Given

$9x + 42 = -3$ Multiply; Distributive Property

$9x = -45$ Subtract 42 from each side; Subtraction Property of Equality

$x = -5$ Divide each side by 9; Division Property of Equality

5. Equation   **Explanation and Reason**

$4 = -10b + 6(2 - b)$ Write the equation; Given

$4 = -10b + 12 - 6b$ Multiply; Distributive Property

$4 = -16b + 12$ Combine like terms; Simplify.

$-8 = -16b$ Subtract 12 from each side; Subtraction Property of Equality

$\frac{1}{2} = b$ Divide each side by -16; Division Property of Equality

$b = \frac{1}{2}$ Rewrite the equation; Symmetric Property of Equality

6. Equation   **Explanation and Reason**

$A = \frac{1}{2}bh$ Write the equation; Given

$2A = bh$ Multiply each side by 2; Multiplication Property of Equality

$\frac{2A}{h} = b$ Divide each side by h; Division Property of Equality

$b = \frac{2A}{h}$ Rewrite the equation; Symmetric Property of Equality

$b = 34$ feet

13.

$$\overset{\bullet}{P} \quad \overset{\bullet}{S} \; || \; \overset{\bullet}{H} \; || \; \overset{\bullet}{Z} \; || \; \overset{\bullet}{M}$$

Equation   **Explanation and Reason**

$SH = HZ$ Marked in diagram; Given

$PS = ZM$ Marked in diagram; Given

$PH = PS + SH$ Add lengths of adjacent segments; Segment Addition Postulate (Post. 1.2)

$HM = ZM + HZ$ Add lengths of adjacent segments; Segment Addition Postulate (Post. 1.2)

$PH = ZM + HZ$ Substitute ZM for PS and HZ for SH; Substitution Property of Equality

$PH = HM$ Substitute HM for $ZM + HZ$; Substitution Property of Equality

2.4 Monitoring Progress and Modeling with Mathematics

5. Equation   **Explanation and Reason**

$5x - 10 = -40$ Write the equation; Given

$5x = -30$ Add 10 to each side; Addition Property of Equality

$x = -6$ Divide each side by 5; Division Property of Equality

6. Equation   **Explanation and Reason**

$6x + 17 = -7$ Write the equation; Given

$6x = -24$ Subtract 17 from each side; Subtraction Property of Equality

$x = -4$ Divide each side by 6; Division Property of Equality

7. Equation   **Explanation and Reason**

$2x - 8 = 6x - 20$ Write the equation; Given

$-4x - 8 = -20$ Subtract $6x$ from each side; Subtraction Property of Equality

$-4x = -12$ Add 8 to each side; Addition Property of Equality

$x = 3$ Divide each side by -4; Division Property of Equality

8. Equation   **Explanation and Reason**

$4x + 9 = 16 - 3x$ Write the equation; Given

$7x + 9 = 16$ Add $3x$ to each side; Addition Property of Equality

$7x = 7$ Subtract 9 from each side; Subtraction Property of Equality

$x = 1$ Divide each side by 7; Division Property of Equality

9. Equation   **Explanation and Reason**

$5(3x - 20) = -10$ Write the equation; Given

$15x - 100 = -10$ Multiply; Distributive Property

$15x = 90$ Add 100 to each side; Addition Property of Equality

$x = 6$ Divide each side by 15; Division Property of Equality

10. Equation   **Explanation and Reason**

$3(2x + 11) = 9$ Write the equation; Given

$6x + 33 = 9$ Multiply; Distributive Property

$6x = -24$ Subtract 33 from each side; Subtraction Property of Equality

$x = -4$ Divide each side by 6; Division Property of Equality

11. Equation | **Explanation and Reason**

$2(-x - 5) = 12$ — Write the equation; Given

$-2x - 10 = 12$ — Multiply; Distributive Property

$-2x = 22$ — Add 10 to each side; Addition Property of Equality

$x = -11$ — Divide each side by -2; Division Property of Equality

12. Equation | **Explanation and Reason**

$44 - 2(3x + 4) = -18x$ — Write the equation; Given

$44 - 6x - 8 = -18x$ — Multiply; Distributive Property

$-6x + 36 = -18x$ — Combine like terms; Simplify.

$36 = -12x$ — Add $6x$ to each side; Addition Property of Equality

$-3 = x$ — Divide each side by -12; Division Property of Equality

$x = -3$ — Rewrite the solution; Symmetric Property of Equality

13. Equation | **Explanation and Reason**

$4(5x - 9) = -2(x + 7)$ — Write the equation; Given

$20x - 36 = -2x - 14$ — Multiply on each side; Distributive Property

$22x - 36 = -14$ — Add $2x$ to each side; Addition Property of Equality

$22x = 22$ — Add 36 to each side; Addition Property of Equality

$x = 1$ — Divide each side by 22; Division Property of Equality

14. Equation | **Explanation and Reason**

$3(4x + 7) = 5(3x + 3)$ — Write the equation; Given

$12x + 21 = 15x + 15$ — Multiply on each side; Distributive Property

$-3x + 21 = 15$ — Subtract $15x$ from each side; Subtraction Property of Equality

$-3x = -6$ — Subtract 21 from each side; Subtraction Property of Equality

$x = 2$ — Divide each side by -3; Division Property of Equality

15. Equation | **Explanation and Reason**

$5x + y = 18$ — Write the equation; Given

$y = -5x + 18$ — Subtract $5x$ from each side; Subtraction Property of Equality

16. Equation | **Explanation and Reason**

$-4x + 2y = 8$ — Write the equation; Given

$2y = 4x + 8$ — Add $4x$ to each side; Addition Property of Equality

$y = 2x + 4$ — Divide each side by 2; Division Property of Equality

17. Equation | **Explanation and Reason**

$2y + 0.5x = 16$ — Write the equation; Given

$2y = -0.5x + 16$ — Subtract $0.5x$ from each side; Subtraction Property of Equality

$y = -0.25x + 8$ — Divide each side by 2; Division Property of Equality

18. Equation | **Explanation and Reason**

$\frac{1}{2}x - \frac{3}{4}y = -2$ — Write the equation; Given

$-\frac{3}{4}y = -\frac{1}{2}x - 2$ — Subtract $\frac{1}{2}x$ from each side; Subtraction Property of Equality

$y = \frac{2}{3}x + \frac{8}{3}$ — Multiply each side by $-\frac{4}{3}$; Multiplication Property of Equality

19. Equation | **Explanation and Reason**

$12 - 3y = 30x + 6$ — Write the equation; Given

$-3y = 30x - 6$ — Subtract 12 from each side; Subtraction Property of Equality

$y = -10x + 2$ — Divide each side by -3; Division Property of Equality

20. Equation | **Explanation and Reason**

$3x + 7 = -7 + 9y$ — Write the equation; Given

$3x + 14 = 9y$ — Add 7 to each side; Addition Property of Equality

$\frac{1}{3}x + \frac{14}{9} = y$ — Divide each side by 9; Division Property of Equality

$y = \frac{1}{3}x + \frac{14}{9}$ — Rewrite the equation; Symmetric Property of Equality

21. Equation | **Explanation and Reason**

$C = 2\pi r$ — Write the equation; Given

$\frac{C}{2\pi} = r$ — Divide each side by 2π; Division Property of Equality

$r = \frac{C}{2\pi}$ — Rewrite the equation; Symmetric Property of Equality

22. Equation | **Explanation and Reason**

$I = Prt$ — Write the equation; Given

$\frac{I}{rt} = P$ — Divide each side by rt; Division Property of Equality

$P = \frac{I}{rt}$ — Rewrite the equation; Symmetric Property of Equality

23. Equation | **Explanation and Reason**

$S = 180(n - 2)$ — Write the equation; Given

$\frac{S}{180} = n - 2$ — Divide each side by 180; Division Property of Equality

$\frac{S}{180} + 2 = n$ — Add 2 to each side; Addition Property of Equality

$n = \frac{S}{180} + 2$ — Rewrite the equation; Symmetric Property of Equality

24. Equation | **Explanation and Reason**

$S = 2\pi r^2 + 2\pi rh$ — Write the equation; Given

$S - 2\pi r^2 = 2\pi rh$ — Subtract $2\pi r^2$ from each side; Subtraction Property of Equality

$\frac{S - 2\pi r^2}{2\pi r} = h$ — Divide each side by $2\pi r$; Division Property of Equality

$h = \frac{S - 2\pi r^2}{2\pi r}$ — Rewrite the equation; Symmetric Property of Equality

43.

Equation	Explanation and Reason
$P = 2\ell + 2w$	Write the equation; Given
$P - 2w = 2\ell$	Subtract $2w$ from each side; Subtraction Property of Equality
$\dfrac{P - 2w}{2} = \ell$	Divide each side by 2; Division Property of Equality
$\ell = \dfrac{P - 2w}{2}$	Rewrite the equation; Symmetric Property of Equality

$\ell = 11$ m

44.

Equation	Explanation and Reason
$A = \dfrac{1}{2}h(b_1 + b_2)$	Write the equation; Given
$\dfrac{2A}{h} = b_1 + b_2$	Divide each side by $\frac{1}{2}h$; Division Property of Equality
$\dfrac{2A}{h} - b_2 = b_1$	Subtract b_2 from each side; Subtraction Property of Equality
$b_1 = \dfrac{2A}{h} - b_2$	Rewrite the equation; Symmetric Property of Equality

$b_1 = 6$ m

45.

Equation	Explanation and Reason
$m\angle ABD = m\angle CBE$	Write the equation; Given
$m\angle ABD = m\angle 1 + m\angle 2$	Add measures of adjacent angles; Angle Addition Postulate (Post. 1.4)
$m\angle CBE = m\angle 2 + m\angle 3$	Add measures of adjacent angles; Angle Addition Postulate (Post. 1.4)
$m\angle ABD = m\angle 2 + m\angle 3$	Substitute $m\angle ABD$ for $m\angle CBE$; Substitution Property of Equality
$m\angle 1 + m\angle 2 = m\angle 2 + m\angle 3$	Substitute $m\angle 1 + m\angle 2$ for $m\angle ABD$; Substitution Property of Equality
$m\angle 1 = m\angle 3$	Subtract $m\angle 2$ from each side; Subtraction Property of Equality

46.

Equation	Explanation and Reason
$AC = BD$	Write the equation; Given
$AC = AB + BC$	Add measures of adjacent sides; Segment Addition Postulate (Post. 1.2)
$BD = BC + CD$	Add measures of adjacent sides; Segment Addition Postulate (Post. 1.2)
$AC = BC + CD$	Substitute AC for BD; Substitution Property of Equality
$AB + BC = BC + CD$	Substitute $AB + BC$ for AC; Substitution Property of Equality
$AB = CD$	Subtract BC from each side; Subtraction Property of Equality

49.

Equation	Explanation and Reason
$DC = BC, AD = AB$	Marked in diagram; Given
$AC = AC$	AC is equal to itself; Reflexive Property of Equality
$AC + AB + BC = AC + AB + BC$	Add $AB + BC$ to each side of $AC = AC$; Addition Property of Equality
$AC + AB + BC = AC + AD + DC$	Substitute AD for AB and DC for BC; Substitution Property of Equality

50.

Equation	Explanation and Reason
$BC = DA, CD = AB$	Marked in diagram; Given
$AC = AC$	AC is equal to itself; Reflexive Property of Equality
$AC + AB + BC = AC + AB + BC$	Add $AB + BC$ to each side of $AC = AC$; Addition Property of Equality
$AC + AB + BC = AC + CD + DA$	Substitute CD for AB, and DA for BC; Substitution Property of Equality

54. *Sample answer:* Reflexive: A student earns the same number of points as himself or herself on a video game. This is reflexive because a quantity is equal to itself. Symmetric: If Student A has the same score as Student B on a math quiz, then Student B has the same score as Student A. This is symmetric because the same two quantities are equal to each other. Transitive: If Student C has the same number of pets as Student D, and Student D has the same number of pets as Student E, then Student C has the same number of pets as Student E. This is transitive because two quantities are each equal to a third quantity.

55. a.

Equation	Explanation and Reason
$C = \dfrac{5}{9}(F - 32)$	Write the equation; Given
$\dfrac{9}{5}C = F - 32$	Multiply each side by $\frac{9}{5}$; Multiplication Property of Equality
$\dfrac{9}{5}C + 32 = F$	Add 32 to each side; Addition Property of Equality
$F = \dfrac{9}{5}C + 32$	Rewrite the equation; Symmetric Property of Equality

b.

Degrees Celsius (°C)	Degrees Fahrenheit (°F)
0	32
20	68
32	89.6
41	105.8

c.

Yes, it is a linear function.

56. A, B, F; The Addition and Subtraction Properties are true because if you add (or subtract) the same amount to each side of an inequality, the inequality is still true. For the Substitution Property, two equal quantities could be substituted for each other in an inequality, but if one quantity is less than (or greater than) another quantity, you cannot always substitute one for the other into another inequality. The Reflexive Property is not true because quantities are not less than (or greater than) themselves. In order for the Symmetric Property to be true, the sign must be flipped around, as in if $a < b$, then $b > a$. The Transitive Property is true as long as all signs are going in the same direction. For example, if quantity A is less than quantity B, and quantity B is less than quantity C, then quantity A is less than quantity C.

2.5 Monitoring Progress and Modeling with Mathematics

13.

STATEMENTS	REASONS
1. $\angle GFH \cong \angle GHF$	1. Given
2. $m\angle GFH = m\angle GHF$	2. Definition of congruent angles
3. $\angle EFG$ and $\angle GFH$ form a linear pair.	3. Given (diagram)
4. $\angle EFG$ and $\angle GFH$ are supplementary.	4. Definition of linear pair
5. $m\angle EFG + m\angle GFH = 180°$	5. Definition of supplementary angles
6. $m\angle EFG + m\angle GHF = 180°$	6. Substitution Property of Equality
7. $\angle EFG$ and $\angle GHF$ are supplementary.	7. Definition of supplementary angles

14.

STATEMENTS	REASONS
1. $\overline{AB} \cong \overline{FG}$	1. Given
2. $\overleftrightarrow{BF}$ bisects $\overline{AC}$ and $\overline{DG}$.	2. Given
3. $\overline{BC} \cong \overline{AB}, \overline{FG} \cong \overline{DF}$	3. Definition of segment bisector
4. $\overline{BC} \cong \overline{FG}$	4. Transitive Property of Equality
5. $\overline{BC} \cong \overline{DF}$	5. Transitive Property of Equality

16. a. Given: $RS = CF, SM = MC = FD$; Prove: $RM = CD$

b.

STATEMENTS	REASONS
1. $RS = CF,$ $SM = MC = FD$	1. Given
2. $RM = RS + SM$	2. Segment Addition Postulate (Post. 1.2)
3. $CF + FD = CD$	3. Segment Addition Postulate (Post. 1.2)
4. $RS + SM = CD$	4. Substitution Property of Equality
5. $RM = CD$	5. Substitution Property of Equality

17. equiangular; Because $\angle 1 \cong \angle 2$ and $\angle 2 \cong \angle 3$, $\angle 1 \cong \angle 3$ by the Transitive Property of Angle Congruence (Thm. 2.2). Because all three angles are congruent, the triangle is equiangular. (It is also equilateral and acute.)

18. no; The statements have to have one segment in common in order to use the Transitive Property of Segment Congruence (Thm. 2.1), but in this case, the statements are about four different segments. They may or may not all be congruent to each other.

19. The purpose of a proof is to ensure the truth of a statement with such certainty that the theorem or rule proved could be used as a justification in proving another statement or theorem. Because inductive reasoning relies on observations about patterns in specific cases, the pattern may not continue or may change. So, the ideas cannot be used to prove ideas for the general case.

20. a. Given: $\angle M$ is a right angle; Prove: $\angle J$ and $\angle L$ are complementary

b. Given: $\angle M$ is a right angle, N is the midpoint of $\overline{JM}$, and K is the midpoint of $\overline{JL}$; Prove: $NK = \frac{1}{2}ML$

21. a. It is a right angle.

b.

STATEMENTS	REASONS
1. $m\angle 1 + m\angle 1 + m\angle 2 + m\angle 2 = 180°$	1. Angle Addition Postulate (Post. 1.4)
2. $2(m\angle 1 + m\angle 2) = 180°$	2. Distributive Property
3. $m\angle 1 + m\angle 2 = 90°$	3. Division Property of Equality

22.

50 mi · · | · · 50 mi
M   L   S   B   J

23.

STATEMENTS	REASONS
1. $\overline{QR} \cong \overline{PQ}, \overline{RS} \cong \overline{PQ},$ $QR = 2x + 5, RS = 10 - 3x$	1. Given
2. $QR = PQ, RS = PQ$	2. Definition of congruent segments
3. $QR = RS$	3. Transitive Property of Equality
4. $2x + 5 = 10 - 3x$	4. Substitution Property of Equality
5. $5x + 5 = 10$	5. Addition Property of Equality
6. $5x = 5$	6. Subtraction Property of Equality
7. $x = 1$	7. Division Property of Equality

2.5 Maintaining Mathematical Proficiency

24. 57°   **25.** 33°

26. $\angle 1$ and $\angle 3$

2.6 Lesson Monitoring Progress

1. $\angle B$ and $\angle C$ are right angles; Right Angles Congruence Theorem (Thm. 2.3)

STATEMENTS	REASONS
1. $\overline{AB} \perp \overline{BC}$, $\overline{DC} \perp \overline{BC}$	**1.** Given
2. $\angle B$ and $\angle C$ are right angles.	**2.** Definition of $\perp$ lines
3. $\angle B \cong \angle C$	**3.** Right Angles Congruence Theorem (Thm. 2.3)

2. $AB + BC = CD + DE$; Segment Addition Postulate (Post. 1.2); $AC = CE$; Definition of congruent segments

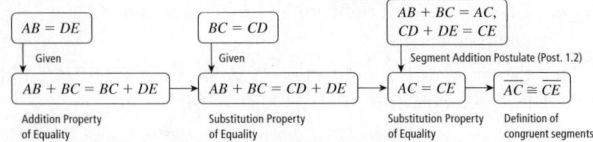

3.

STATEMENTS	REASONS
1. $\angle 5$ and $\angle 7$ are vertical angles.	**1.** Given
2. $\angle 5$ and $\angle 6$ are a linear pair. $\angle 6$ and $\angle 7$ are a linear pair.	**2.** Definition of linear pair, as shown in the diagram.
3. $\angle 5$ and $\angle 6$ are supplementary. $\angle 6$ and $\angle 7$ are supplementary.	**3.** Linear Pair Postulate (Post. 2.8)
4. $m\angle 5 + m\angle 6 = 180°$, $m\angle 6 + m\angle 7 = 180°$	**4.** Definition of supplementary angles
5. $m\angle 5 + m\angle 6 = m\angle 6 + m\angle 7$	**5.** Transitive Property of Equality
6. $m\angle 5 = m\angle 7$	**6.** Subtraction Property of Equality
7. $\angle 5 \cong \angle 7$	**7.** Definition of congruent angles

You save three steps.

2.6 Monitoring Progress and Modeling with Mathematics

16. Because the angles form a linear pair, the sum of their measures should be equal to 180°.

$$(13x + 45)° + (12x - 40)° = 180°$$
$$25x + 5 = 180$$
$$25x = 175$$
$$x = 7$$

17. Transitive Property of Angle Congruence (Thm. 2.2); Transitive Property of Angle Congruence (Thm. 2.2)

STATEMENTS	REASONS
1. $\angle 1 \cong \angle 3$	**1.** Given
2. $\angle 1 \cong \angle 2$, $\angle 3 \cong \angle 4$	**2.** Vertical Angles Congruence Theorem (Thm. 2.6)
3. $\angle 2 \cong \angle 3$	**3.** Transitive Property of Angle Congruence (Thm. 2.2)
4. $\angle 2 \cong \angle 4$	**4.** Transitive Property of Angle Congruence (Thm. 2.2)

18. Given; Definition of complementary angles; Congruent Complements Theorem (Thm. 2.5)

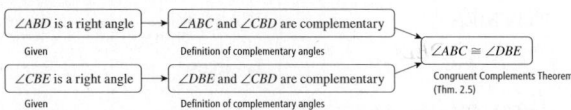

19. complementary; $m\angle 1 + m\angle 3$; Transitive Property of Equality; $m\angle 2 = m\angle 3$; congruent angles

STATEMENTS	REASONS
1. $\angle 1$ and $\angle 2$ are complementary. $\angle 1$ and $\angle 3$ are complementary.	**1.** Given
2. $m\angle 1 + m\angle 2 = 90°$, $m\angle 1 + m\angle 3 = 90°$	**2.** Definition of complementary angles
3. $m\angle 1 + m\angle 2 = m\angle 1 + m\angle 3$	**3.** Transitive Property of Equality
4. $m\angle 2 = m\angle 3$	**4.** Subtraction Property of Equality
5. $\angle 2 \cong \angle 3$	**5.** Definition of congruent angles

22.

STATEMENTS	REASONS
1. $\angle 1$ and $\angle 3$ are complementary. $\angle 2$ and $\angle 4$ are complementary.	**1.** Given
2. $m\angle 1 + m\angle 3 = 90°$, $m\angle 2 + m\angle 4 = 90°$	**2.** Definition of complementary angles
3. $m\angle 1 + m\angle 3 = m\angle 2 + m\angle 4$	**3.** Transitive Property of Equality
4. $\angle 2 \cong \angle 3$	**4.** Vertical Angles Congruence Theorem (Thm. 2.6)
5. $m\angle 2 = m\angle 3$	**5.** Definition of congruent angles
6. $m\angle 1 + m\angle 2 = m\angle 2 + m\angle 4$	**6.** Substitution Property of Equality
7. $m\angle 1 = m\angle 4$	**7.** Subtraction Property of Equality
8. $\angle 1 \cong \angle 4$	**8.** Definition of congruent angles

23.

STATEMENTS	REASONS
1. $\angle AEB \cong \angle DEC$	1. Given
2. $m\angle AEB = m\angle DEC$	2. Definition of congruent angles
3. $m\angle DEB = m\angle DEC + m\angle BEC$	3. Angle Addition Postulate (Post. 1.4)
4. $m\angle DEB = m\angle AEB + m\angle BEC$	4. Substitution Property of Equality
5. $m\angle AEC = m\angle AEB + m\angle BEC$	5. Angle Addition Postulate (Post. 1.4)
6. $m\angle AEC = m\angle DEB$	6. Transitive Property of Equality
7. $\angle AEC \cong \angle DEB$	7. Definition of congruent angles

25. your friend; $\angle 1$ and $\angle 4$ are not vertical angles because they do not form two pairs of opposite rays. So, the Vertical Angles Congruence Theorem (Thm. 2.6) does not apply.

26.

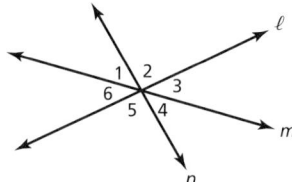

If the measures of any two angles that are not vertical, such as $\angle 1$ and $\angle 2$ were given, then you could find the other four angle measures. In this case, you could find $m\angle 1 + m\angle 2$ and subtract this sum from $180°$ in order to find $m\angle 3$ (or $m\angle 6$). You can find the measures of the other three angles because each is a vertical angle with one of the three angles you know. Because vertical angles are congruent, $m\angle 4 = m\angle 1$, $m\angle 5 = m\angle 2$, and $m\angle 6 = m\angle 3$.

27. no; The converse would be: "If two angles are supplementary, then they are a linear pair." This is false because angles can be supplementary without being adjacent.

28. You can use abbreviations and symbols instead of writing out the whole word. Also, when consecutive statements have the same reason, you can put them on the same line so that you only have to write the reason once.

29. $50°$; $130°$; $50°$; $130°$

30. **a.** $\angle 1$ and $\angle 2$ are right angles by definition of right angles.
b. no; $\angle 1 \cong \angle 2$ was one of the "Given" statements.

2.6 Maintaining Mathematical Proficiency

31. *Sample answer: B, I, and C*

32. $\overline{EF}$

2.6 Mini-Assessment

2. $\angle 2$ is congruent to $\angle 3$. $\angle 1 \cong \angle 2$ by the Vertical Angles Congruence Theorem (Thm. 2.6). By the Transitive Property of Congruence (Thm. 2.2), $\angle 1 \cong \angle 3$. It is given that $\angle 4$ is congruent to $\angle 5$. $\angle 3 \cong \angle 4$ by the Vertical Angles Congruence Theorem (Thm. 2.6). By the Transitive Property of Congruence (Thm. 2.2), $\angle 1 \cong \angle 4$. By the Transitive Property of Congruence (Thm. 2.2), $\angle 1 \cong \angle 5$.

2.4–2.6 What Did You Learn?

2.

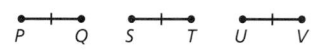

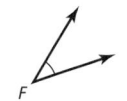 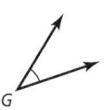 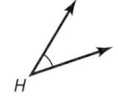

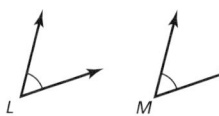 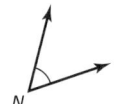

Chapter 2 Review

16.

Equation	Explanation and Reason
$-9x - 21 = -20x - 87$	Write the equation; Given
$11x - 21 = -87$	Add $20x$ to each side; Addition Property of Equality
$11x = -66$	Add 21 to each side; Addition Property of Equality
$x = -6$	Divide each side by 11; Division Property of Equality

17.

Equation	Explanation and Reason
$15x + 22 = 7x + 62$	Write the equation; Given
$8x + 22 = 62$	Subtract $7x$ from each side; Subtraction Property of Equality
$8x = 40$	Subtract 22 from each side; Subtraction Property of Equality
$x = 5$	Divide each side by 8; Division Property of Equality

18.

Equation	Explanation and Reason
$3(2x + 9) = 30$	Write the equation; Given
$6x + 27 = 30$	Multiply; Distributive Property
$6x = 3$	Subtract 27 from each side; Subtraction Property of Equality
$x = \frac{1}{2}$	Divide each side by 6; Division Property of Equality

19.

Equation	Explanation and Reason
$5x + 2(2x - 23) = -154$	Write the equation; Given
$5x + 4x - 46 = -154$	Multiply; Distributive Property
$9x - 46 = -154$	Combine like terms; Simplify.
$9x = -108$	Add 46 to each side; Addition Property of Equality
$x = -12$	Divide each side by 9; Division Property of Equality

25.

STATEMENTS	REASONS
1. An angle with vertex A exists.	1. Given
2. $m\angle A$ equals the measure of the angle with vertex A.	2. Protractor Postulate (Post. 1.3)
3. $m\angle A = m\angle A$	3. Reflexive Property of Equality
4. $\angle A \cong \angle A$	4. Definition of congruent angles

26.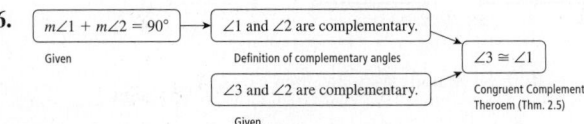

Chapter 2 Test

7.

Equation	Explanation and Reason
$9x + 31 = -23 + 3x$	Write the equation; Given
$6x + 31 = -23$	Subtract $3x$ from each side; Subtraction Property of Equality
$6x = -54$	Subtract 31 from each side; Subtraction Property of Equality
$x = -9$	Divide each side by 6; Division Property of Equality

8.

Equation	Explanation and Reason
$26 + 2(3x + 11) = -18$	Write the equation; Given
$26 + 6x + 22 = -18$	Multiply; Distributive Property
$6x + 48 = -18$	Combine like terms; Simplify.
$6x = -66$	Subtract 48 from each side; Subtraction Property of Equality
$x = -11$	Divide each side by 6; Division Property of Equality

9.

Equation	Explanation and Reason
$3(7x - 9) - 19x = -15$	Write the equation; Given
$21x - 27 - 19x = -15$	Multiply; Distributive Property
$2x - 27 = -15$	Combine like terms; Simplify.
$2x = 12$	Add 27 to each side; Addition Property of Equality
$x = 6$	Divide each side by 2; Division Property of Equality

13. The product of three even integers is a multiple of 8; Let m, n, and p be integers. Then, $2m$, $2n$, and $2p$ represent even integers because they are each the product of two and an integer. Their product, $(2m)(2n)(2p)$, equals $8mnp$ when it is simplified using the Associative and Commutative Properties of Equality. Because this is the product of 8 and integer mnp, the product is a multiple of 8.

14. *Sample answer:* If a figure is a rectangle, then it has four sides. *ABCD* has four sides.

15.

Equation	Explanation and Reason
$A = \dfrac{1}{2}bh$	Write the equation; Given
$2A = bh$	Multiply each side by 2; Multiplication Property of Equality
$\dfrac{2A}{b} = h$	Divide each side by b. Division Property of Equality
$h = 31$ in.	

16.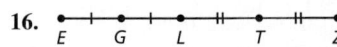

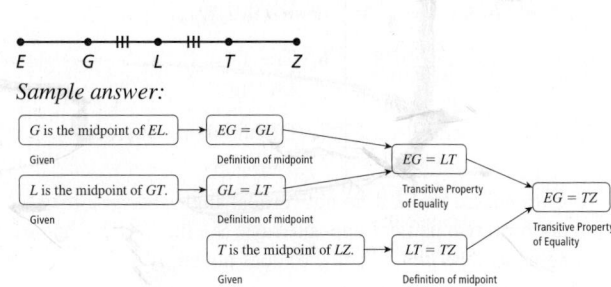

Sample answer:

17. *Sample answer:*

STATEMENTS	REASONS
1. $\angle 2 \cong \angle 3$, $\overrightarrow{TV}$ bisects $\angle UTW$	1. Given
2. $\angle 1 \cong \angle 2$	2. Definition of angle bisector
3. $\angle 1 \cong \angle 3$	3. Transitive Property of Angle Congruence (Thm. 2.2)

Chapter 3

3.1 Monitoring Progress and Modeling with Mathematics

20. There are infinitely many lines through a given point that intersect a given line, but only one is perpendicular; If there is a line and point not on the line, then there is exactly one line through the point that is perpendicular to the given line.

21.
 a. true; The floor is level with the horizontal just like the ground.

 b. false; The lines intersect the plane of the ground, so they intersect certain lines of that plane.

 c. true; The balusters appear to be vertical, and the floor of the tree house is horizontal. So, they are perpendicular.

22. no; All three lines could intersect at the same point.

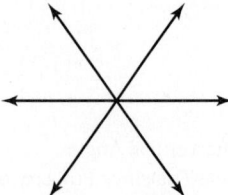

23. yes; If the original two lines are parallel, and the transversal is perpendicular to both lines, then all eight angles are right angles.

24. **a.** $\overleftrightarrow{KR}, \overleftrightarrow{LS}, \overleftrightarrow{MP}$
   b. $\overleftrightarrow{NK}, \overleftrightarrow{NM}, \overleftrightarrow{QR}, \overleftrightarrow{QP}$
   c. $\overleftrightarrow{KL}, \overleftrightarrow{RS}, \overleftrightarrow{PS}, \overleftrightarrow{LM}$
   d. yes; If lines do not intersect, then they are either parallel or skew depending on whether or not they are coplanar.

25. $\angle HJG, \angle CFJ$ **26.** $\angle HJC$

27. $\angle CFD, \angle HJC$ **28.** $\angle HJG$

29. no; They can both be in a plane that is slanted with respect to the horizontal.

3.2 Monitoring Progress and Modeling with Mathematics

12. $m\angle 1 = 47°$, $m\angle 2 = 133°$, $m\angle 3 = 47°$; Because $\angle 1$ is a consecutive interior angle with the angle that is a vertical angle with the $133°$ angle, they are supplementary by the Consecutive Interior Angles Theorem (Thm. 3.4). The vertical angle is also $133°$ by the Vertical Angles Congruence Theorem (Thm. 2.6). Because the $133°$ angle and $\angle 2$ are alternate interior angles, they are congruent by the Alternate Interior Angles Theorem (Thm. 3.2). Because the $133°$ angle and $\angle 3$ are consecutive interior angles, they are supplementary by the Consecutive Interior Angles Theorem (Thm. 3.4).

13. In order to use the Corresponding Angles Theorem (Thm. 3.1), the angles need to be formed by two parallel lines cut by a transversal, but none of the lines in this diagram appear to be parallel; $\angle 9$ and $\angle 10$ are corresponding angles.

15.

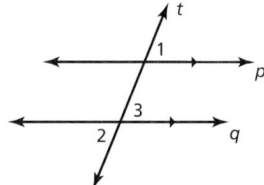

STATEMENTS	REASONS
1. $p \parallel q$	**1.** Given
2. $\angle 1 \cong \angle 3$	**2.** Corresponding Angles Theorem (Thm. 3.1)
3. $\angle 3 \cong \angle 2$	**3.** Vertical Angles Congruence Theorem (Thm. 2.6)
4. $\angle 1 \cong \angle 2$	**4.** Transitive Property of Congruence (Thm. 2.2)

16.

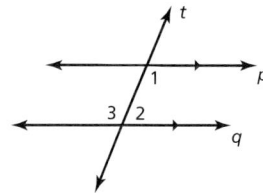

STATEMENTS	REASONS
1. $p \parallel q$	**1.** Given
2. $\angle 1 \cong \angle 3$	**2.** Alternate Interior Angles Theorem (Thm. 3.2)
3. $m\angle 1 = m\angle 3$	**3.** Definition of congruent angles
4. $m\angle 2 + m\angle 3 = 180°$	**4.** Linear Pair Postulate (Post. 2.8)
5. $m\angle 2 + m\angle 1 = 180°$	**5.** Substitution Property of Equality
6. $\angle 1$ and $\angle 2$ are supplementary angles.	**6.** Definition of supplementary angles

18. **a.** $m\angle 2 = 70°$, $m\angle 3 = 110°$
   b. $\angle 1$ and $\angle 2$ are congruent by the Alternate Interior Angles Theorem (Thm. 3.2). $\angle 1$ and $\angle 3$ are supplementary by the Consecutive Interior Angles Theorem (Thm. 3.4). By substitution, $\angle 2$ and $\angle 3$ are supplementary. So, $\angle ABC$ is a straight angle.
   c. yes; $m\angle 2$ will be $60°$ and $m\angle 3$ will be $120°$. The opening of the box will be more steep because $\angle 1$ is smaller.

19. yes; If two parallel lines are cut by a perpendicular transversal, then the consecutive interior angles will both be right angles.

20. no; It is impossible to have parallel lines in spherical geometry. Because all lines are circles with the same diameter, any two lines will always intersect in two points.

21. $19x - 10 = 180$
   $14x + 2y - 10 = 180$; $x = 10, y = 25$

22. $2x + 2y + 12 = 180$
   $4x + y + 6 = 180$; $x = 30, y = 54$

23. no; In order to make the shot, you must hit the cue ball so that $m\angle 1 = 65°$. The angle that is complementary to $\angle 1$ must have a measure of $25°$ because this angle is an alternate interior angle with the angle formed by the path of the cue ball and the vertical line drawn.

24. $60°$; $\angle 1 \cong \angle 5$ by the Corresponding Angles Theorem (Thm. 3.1), $\angle 2 \cong \angle 4$ by the Alternate Interior Angles Theorem (Thm 3.2), $\angle 2 \cong \angle 3$ by the definition of angle bisector, and $\angle 4 \cong \angle 5$ is given. So, by the Transitive Property of Congruence (Thm. 2.2), all five of the angles labeled must be congruent to each other. From the diagram, $m\angle 1 + m\angle 2 + m\angle 3 = 180°$, and because they all have the same measure, it must be that they each have a measure of $\dfrac{180°}{3} = 60°$.

3.2 Maintaining Mathematical Proficiency

25. If two angles are congruent, then they are vertical angles; false

26. If you see a tiger, then you went to the zoo; false

27. If two angles are supplementary, then they form a linear pair; false

28. If we go to the park, then it is warm outside; false

3.3 Monitoring Progress and Modeling with Mathematics

11.

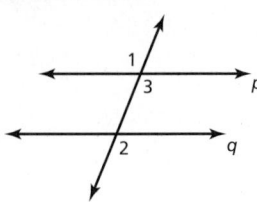

It is given that $\angle 1 \cong \angle 2$. By the Vertical Angles Congruence Theorem (Thm. 2.6), $\angle 1 \cong \angle 3$. Then by the Transitive Property of Congruence (Thm. 2.2), $\angle 2 \cong \angle 3$. So, by the Corresponding Angles Converse (Thm. 3.5), $p \parallel q$.

12.

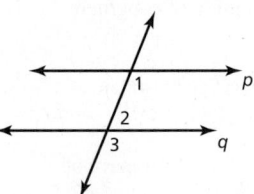

STATEMENTS	REASONS
1. $\angle 1$ and $\angle 2$ are supplementary.	**1.** Given
2. $\angle 2$ and $\angle 3$ are supplementary.	**2.** Linear Pair Postulate (Post. 2.8)
3. $m\angle 1 + m\angle 2 = 180°$, $m\angle 2 + m\angle 3 = 180°$	**3.** Definition of supplementary angles
4. $m\angle 1 + m\angle 2 = m\angle 2 + m\angle 3$	**4.** Transitive Property of Equality
5. $m\angle 1 = m\angle 3$	**5.** Subtraction Property of Equality
6. $\angle 1 \cong \angle 3$	**6.** Definition of congruent angles
7. $p \parallel q$	**7.** Corresponding Angles Converse (Thm. 3.5)

13. yes; Alternate Interior Angles Converse (Thm. 3.6)

14. yes; Alternate Exterior Angles Converse (Thm. 3.7)

15. no

16. yes; Corresponding Angles Converse (Thm. 3.5)

17. no

18. yes; Alternate Exterior Angles Converse (Thm. 3.7)

19. This diagram shows that vertical angles are always congruent. Lines a and b are not parallel unless $x = y$, and you cannot assume that they are equal.

20. It would be true that $a \parallel b$ if $\angle 1$ and $\angle 2$ were supplementary, but you cannot assume that they are supplementary unless it is stated or the diagram is marked as such. You can say that $\angle 1$ and $\angle 2$ are consecutive interior angles.

29. A, B, C, D; The Corresponding Angles Converse (Thm. 3.5) can be used because the angle marked at the intersection of line m and the transversal is a vertical angle with, and therefore congruent to, an angle that is corresponding with the other marked angle. The Alternate Interior Angles Converse (Thm. 3.6) can be used because the angles that are marked as congruent are alternate interior angles. The Alternate Exterior Angles Converse (Thm. 3.7) can be used because the angles that are vertical with, and therefore

congruent to, the marked angles are alternate exterior angles. The Consecutive Interior Angles Converse (Thm. 3.8) can be used because each of the marked angles forms a linear pair with, and is therefore supplementary to, an angle that is a consecutive interior angle with the other marked angle.

32. *Sample answer:*

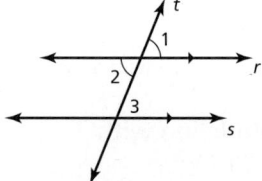

In this diagram, angles from only one intersection are marked as congruent. In order to prove that the two lines are parallel, you need to know something about at least one angle formed by each of the intersections that the transversal makes with the two other lines. For instance, if you knew something about the measure of $\angle 3$, you would be able to determine whether line r is parallel to line s.

33.

STATEMENTS	REASONS
1. $m\angle 1 = 115°$, $m\angle 2 = 65°$	**1.** Given
2. $m\angle 1 + m\angle 2 = m\angle 1 + m\angle 2$	**2.** Reflexive Property of Equality
3. $m\angle 1 + m\angle 2 = 115° + 65°$	**3.** Substitution Property of Equality
4. $m\angle 1 + m\angle 2 = 180°$	**4.** Simplify.
5. $\angle 1$ and $\angle 2$ are supplementary.	**5.** Definition of supplementary angles
6. $m \parallel n$	**6.** Consecutive Interior Angles Converse (Thm 3.8)

34.

STATEMENTS	REASONS
1. $\angle 1$ and $\angle 3$ are supplementary.	**1.** Given
2. $m\angle 1 + m\angle 3 = 180°$	**2.** Definition of supplementary angles
3. $\angle 1 \cong \angle 2$	**3.** Vertical Angles Congruence Theorem (Thm. 2.6)
4. $m\angle 1 = m\angle 2$	**4.** Definition of congruent angles
5. $m\angle 2 + m\angle 3 = 180°$	**5.** Substitution Property of Equality
6. $\angle 2$ and $\angle 3$ are supplementary.	**6.** Definition of supplementary angles
7. $m \parallel n$	**7.** Consecutive Interior Angles Converse (Thm. 3.8)

35.

STATEMENTS	REASONS
1. $\angle 1 \cong \angle 2$, $\angle 3 \cong \angle 4$	**1.** Given
2. $\angle 2 \cong \angle 3$	**2.** Vertical Angles Congruence Theorem (Thm. 2.6)
3. $\angle 1 \cong \angle 3$	**3.** Transitive Property of Congruence (Thm. 2.2)
4. $\angle 1 \cong \angle 4$	**4.** Transitive Property of Congruence (Thm. 2.2)
5. $\overline{AB} \parallel \overline{CD}$	**5.** Alternate Interior Angles Converse (Thm. 3.6)

36.

STATEMENTS	REASONS
1. $a \parallel b$, $\angle 2 \cong \angle 3$	**1.** Given
2. $\angle 3 \cong \angle 1$	**2.** Alternate Interior Angles Theorem (Thm. 3.2)
3. $\angle 1 \cong \angle 2$	**3.** Transitive Property of Congruence (Thm. 2.2)
4. $c \parallel d$	**4.** Corresponding Angles Converse (Thm. 3.5)

37. no; Based on the diagram $\overleftrightarrow{AB} \parallel \overleftrightarrow{CD}$ by the Alternate Interior Angles Converse (Thm. 3.6), but you cannot be sure that $\overleftrightarrow{AD} \parallel \overleftrightarrow{BC}$.

38. no; In order to conclude that $r \parallel s$, you would need to show that $\angle 1 \cong \angle 3$. In order to conclude that $p \parallel q$, you would need to show that either $\angle 1 \cong \angle 2$ or $\angle 3 \cong \angle 4$.

39. a.

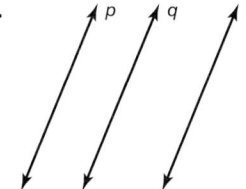

b. Given: $p \parallel q$, $q \parallel r$
Prove: $p \parallel r$

c.

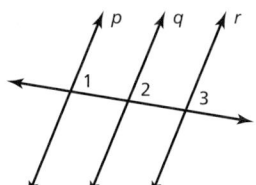

STATEMENTS	REASONS
1. $p \parallel q$, $q \parallel r$	**1.** Given
2. $\angle 1 \cong \angle 2$, $\angle 2 \cong \angle 3$	**2.** Corresponding Angles Theorem (Thm. 3.1)
3. $\angle 1 \cong \angle 3$	**3.** Transitive Property of Congruence (Thm. 2.2)
4. $p \parallel r$	**4.** Corresponding Angles Converse (Thm. 3.5)

40. a. $x = 54$

b. $y = 47.5$

c. no; If $x = 54$, then $(x + 56)° = 110°$. If $y = 47.5$, then $(y + 7)° = 54.5°$. Because these two angles form a linear pair, their sum should be 180°, but $110° + 54.5° = 164.5°$. So, both pairs of lines cannot be parallel at the same time.

3.3 Maintaining Mathematical Proficiency

41. about 6.71

42. about 17.03

43. 13

44. about 6.40

3.4 Lesson Monitoring Progress

2.

STATEMENTS	REASONS
1. $h \parallel k$, $j \perp h$	**1.** Given
2. $m\angle 2 = 90°$	**2.** Definition of perpendicular lines
3. $\angle 2 \cong \angle 7$	**3.** Alternate Exterior Angles Theorem (Thm. 3.3)
4. $m\angle 2 = m\angle 7$	**4.** Definition of congruent angles
5. $m\angle 7 = 90°$	**5.** Transitive Property of Equality
6. $j \perp k$	**6.** Definition of perpendicular lines

3.4 Monitoring Progress and Modeling with Mathematics

14.

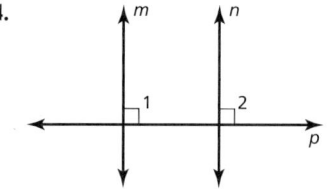

STATEMENTS	REASONS
1. $m \perp p$, $n \perp p$	**1.** Given
2. $\angle 1$ and $\angle 2$ are right angles.	**2.** Definition of perpendicular lines
3. $\angle 1 \cong \angle 2$	**3.** Right Angles Converse Theorem (Thm. 2.3)
4. $m \parallel n$	**4.** Corresponding Angles Converse (Thm. 3.5)

15.

STATEMENTS	REASONS
1. $a \perp b$	1. Given
2. $\angle 1$ is a right angle.	2. Definition of perpendicular lines
3. $\angle 1 \cong \angle 4$	3. Vertical Angles Congruence Theorem (Thm. 2.6)
4. $m\angle 1 = 90°$	4. Definition of right angle
5. $m\angle 4 = 90°$	5. Transitive Property of Equality
6. $\angle 1$ and $\angle 2$ form a linear pair.	6. Definition of linear pair
7. $\angle 1$ and $\angle 2$ are supplementary.	7. Linear Pair Postulate (Post. 2.8)
8. $m\angle 1 + m\angle 2 = 180°$	8. Definition of supplementary angles
9. $90° + m\angle 2 = 180°$	9. Substitution Property of Equality
10. $m\angle 2 = 90°$	10. Subtraction Property of Equality
11. $\angle 2 \cong \angle 3$	11. Vertical Angles Congruence Theorem (Thm. 2.6)
12. $m\angle 3 = 90°$	12. Transitive Property of Equality
13. $\angle 1, \angle 2, \angle 3,$ and $\angle 4$ are right angles.	13. Definition of right angle

16.

STATEMENTS	REASONS
1. $\overrightarrow{BA} \perp \overrightarrow{BC}$	1. Given
2. $\angle ABC$ is a right angle.	2. Definition of perpendicular lines
3. $m\angle ABC = 90°$	3. Definition of right angle
4. $m\angle 1 + m\angle 2 = m\angle ABC$	4. Angle Addition Postulate (Post. 1.4)
5. $m\angle 1 + m\angle 2 = 90°$	5. Transitive Property of Equality
6. $\angle 1$ and $\angle 2$ are complementary.	6. Definition of complementary angles

23. $m\angle 1 = 90°, m\angle 2 = 60°, m\angle 3 = 30°, m\angle 4 = 20°, m\angle 5 = 90°$;
$m\angle 1 = 90°$, because it is marked as a right angle.
$m\angle 2 = 90° - 30° = 60°$, because it is complementary to the 30° angle.
$m\angle 3 = 30°$, because it is a vertical angle with, and therefore congruent to, the 30° angle.
$m\angle 4 = 90° - (30° + 40°) = 20°$, because it forms a right angle with $\angle 3$ and the 40° angle.
$m\angle 5 = 90°$, because it is a vertical angle with, and therefore congruent to, $\angle 1$.

24. no; The shortest distance from a point on one line to the other line will be different for different points on the line unless the lines are parallel.

25. $x = 8$

29.

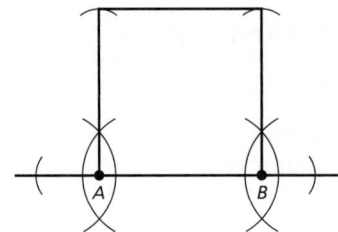

30.

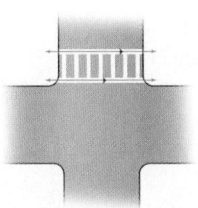

The line segments that are perpendicular to the crosswalk require less paint, because they represent the shortest distance from one side of the crosswalk to the other.

31. rectangle

32. about 2.5 units

33. Find the length of the segment that is perpendicular to the plane and that has one endpoint on the given point and one endpoint on the plane; You can find the distance from a line to a plane only if the line is parallel to the plane. Then you can pick any point on the line and find the distance from that point to the plane. If a line is not parallel to a plane, then the distance from the line to the plane is not defined because it would be different for each point on the line.

3.4 Maintaining Mathematical Proficiency

34. 2

35. $-\frac{2}{3}$

36. $\frac{11}{9}$

37. 3

38. $m = 3; b = 9$

39. $m = -\frac{1}{2}; b = 7$

40. $m = \frac{1}{6}; b = -8$

41. $m = -8; b = -6$

3.5 Monitoring Progress and Modeling with Mathematics

16. $y = \frac{1}{2}x - 2$

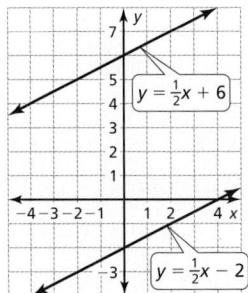

17. $y = \frac{1}{9}x$

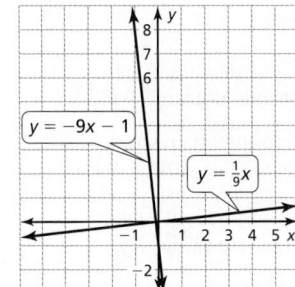

18. $x = 4$

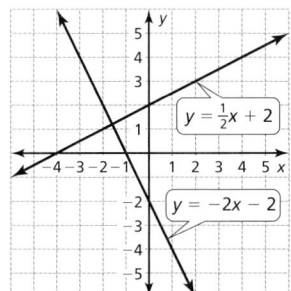

19. $y = \frac{1}{2}x + 2$

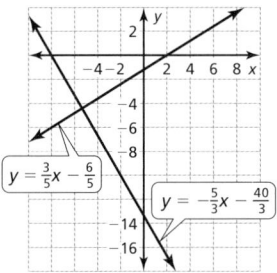

20. $y = -\frac{5}{3}x - \frac{40}{3}$

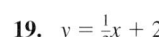

21. about 3.2 units **22.** about 8.5 units

23. about 5.4 units **24.** about 1.7 units

42. $\dfrac{|ax_0 + by_0|}{\sqrt{a^2 + b^2}}$; *Sample answer:* For Monitoring Progress Question 7

on page 159, $\dfrac{|ax_0 + by_0|}{\sqrt{a^2 + b^2}} = \dfrac{|(2)(-1) + (1)(6)|}{\sqrt{2^2 + 1^2}} \approx 1.8$ units.

45. Using points $A(3, 2)$ and $B(6, 8)$ find the coordinates of point P that lies beyond point B along $\overrightarrow{AB}$ so that the ratio of AB to BP is 3 to 2. In order to keep the ratio, $\dfrac{AB}{BP} = \dfrac{3}{2}$, solve this ratio for BP to get $BP = \dfrac{2}{3}AB$. Next, find the rise and run from point A to point B. Leave the slope in terms of rise and run and do not simplify.
$m_{\overline{AB}} = \dfrac{8 - 2}{6 - 3} = \dfrac{6}{3} = \dfrac{\text{rise}}{\text{run}}$. Add $\dfrac{2}{3}$ of the *run* to the x-coordinate of B, which is $\dfrac{2}{3} \cdot 3 + 6 = 8$. Add $\dfrac{2}{3}$ of the *rise* to the y-coordinate of B, which is $\dfrac{2}{3} \cdot 6 + 8 = 12$. So, the coordinates of P are $(8, 12)$.

46. about 2.2 units; The two lines have the same slope and are therefore parallel. So, the distance from a point on one line to the other line will be the same no matter which point is chosen. The line $y = -\frac{1}{2}x$ is perpendicular to both lines and intersects $y = 2x$ at $(-2, 1)$ and $y = 2x + 5$ at the origin. So, the distance between the lines is the same as the distance between these two points of intersection. $\sqrt{(-2 - 0)^2 + (1 - 0)^2} \approx 2.2$

47. If lines x and y are perpendicular to line z, then by the Slopes of Perpendicular Lines Theorem (Thm. 3.14), $m_x \cdot m_z = -1$ and $m_y \cdot m_z = -1$. By the Transitive Property of Equality, $m_x \cdot m_z = m_y \cdot m_z$, and by the Division Property of Equality, $m_x = m_y$. Therefore, by the Slopes of Parallel Lines Theorem (Thm. 3.13), $x \parallel y$.

48. If $x \parallel y$ and $y \parallel z$, then by the Slopes of Parallel Lines Theorem (Thm. 3.13), $m_x = m_y$ and $m_y = m_z$. Therefore, by the Transitive Property of Equality, $m_x = m_z$. So, by the Slopes of Parallel Lines Theorem (Thm. 3.13), $x \parallel z$.

49. If lines x and y are vertical lines and they are cut by any horizontal transversal z, then $x \perp z$ and $y \perp z$ by the Slopes of Perpendicular Lines Theorem (Thm. 3.14). Therefore, $x \parallel y$ by the Lines Perpendicular to a Transversal Theorem (Thm. 3.12).

50. If lines x and y are horizontal, then by definition $m_x = 0$ and $m_y = 0$. So, by the Transitive Property of Equality, $m_x = m_y$. Therefore, by the Slopes of Parallel Lines Theorem (Thm. 3.13), $x \parallel y$.

51. By definition, the x-axis is perpendicular to the y-axis. Let m be a horizontal line, and let n be a vertical line. Because any two horizontal lines are parallel, m is parallel to the x-axis. Because any two vertical lines are parallel, n is parallel to the y-axis. By the Perpendicular Transversal Theorem (Thm. 3.11), n is perpendicular to the x-axis. Then, by the Perpendicular Transversal Theorem (Thm. 3.11), n is perpendicular to m.

3.5 Maintaining Mathematical Proficiency

52.

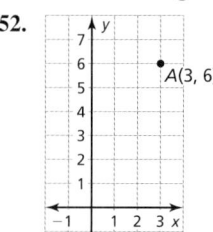

53.

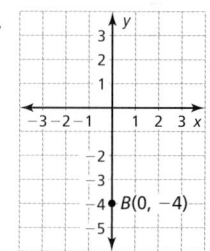

54.

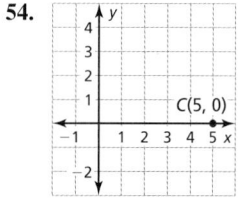

55.

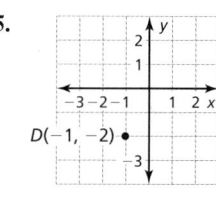

56.

x	-2	-1	0	1	2
$y = x + 9$	7	8	9	10	11

57.

x	-2	-1	0	1	2
$y = x - \frac{3}{4}$	$-\frac{11}{4}$	$-\frac{7}{4}$	$-\frac{3}{4}$	$\frac{1}{4}$	$\frac{5}{4}$

Chapter 4

Mathematical Practices Monitoring Progress

5.

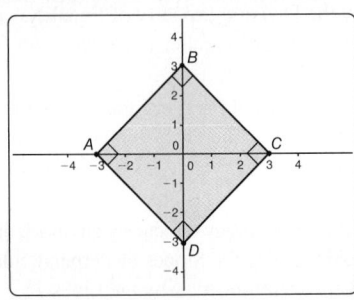

$AB \approx 4.24$; $BC \approx 4.24$; $CD \approx 4.24$; $AD \approx 4.24$;
$m\angle A = 90°$; $m\angle B = 90°$; $m\angle C = 90°$; $m\angle D = 90°$

6.

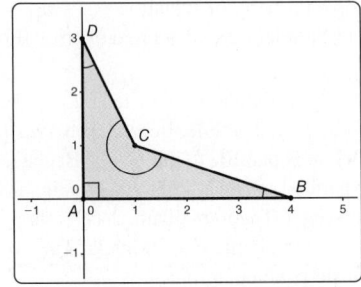

$AB = 4$; $BC \approx 3.16$; $CD \approx 2.24$; $AD = 3$; $m\angle A = 90°$;
$m\angle B \approx 18.43°$; $m\angle C = 225°$; $m\angle D \approx 26.57°$

4.1 Lesson Monitoring Progress

4. $R'(3, 4)$, $S'(6, 4)$, $T'(4, 7)$

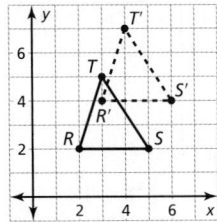

4.1 Monitoring Progress and Modeling with Mathematics

18.

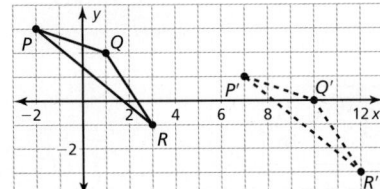

19.

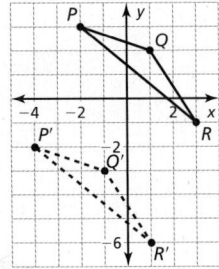

20.

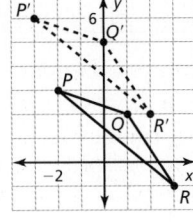

21.

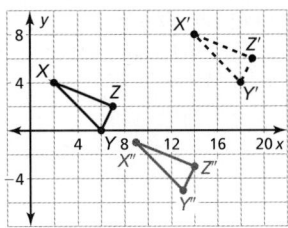

22.

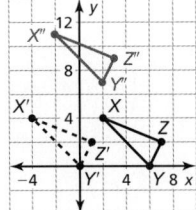

34. a. 21 square units; 21 square units

   b. They are equal; The preimage and image of a translation are congruent, so the areas are equal.

35. If a rigid motion is used to transform figure A to figure A', then by definition of rigid motion, every part of figure A is congruent to its corresponding part of figure A'. If another rigid motion is used to transform figure A' to figure A'', then by definition of rigid motion, every part of figure A' is congruent to its corresponding part of figure A''. So, by the Transitive Property of Congruence, every part of figure A is congruent to its corresponding part of figure A''. So by definition of rigid motion, the composition of two (or more) rigid motions is a rigid motion.

36. a.

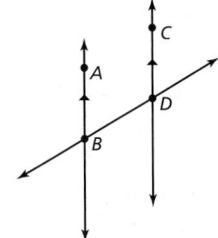

Because $\overleftrightarrow{AB} \parallel \overleftrightarrow{CD}$ and translations map lines to parallel lines, a translation along $\overrightarrow{BD}$ maps $\overleftrightarrow{AB}$ to $\overleftrightarrow{CD}$. Because translations are rigid motions, angle measures are preserved, which means the angles formed by $\overleftrightarrow{AB}$ and $\overleftrightarrow{BD}$ are congruent to the corresponding angles formed by $\overleftrightarrow{CD}$ and $\overleftrightarrow{BD}$.

   b.

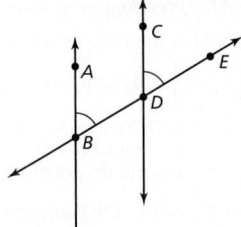

Because $\angle ABD \cong \angle CDE$, a translation along $\overrightarrow{BD}$ maps $\angle ABD$ onto $\angle CDE$. Because translations map lines to parallel lines, $\overleftrightarrow{AB} \parallel \overleftrightarrow{CD}$.

37. Draw a rectangle. Then draw a translation of the rectangle. Next, connect each vertex of the preimage with the corresponding vertex in the image. Finally, make the hidden lines dashed.

38. $w = 3, x = 1, y = 0, z = \frac{2}{3}$

39. yes; According to the definition of translation, the segments connecting corresponding vertices will be congruent and parallel. Also, because a translation is a rigid motion, $\overline{GH} \cong \overline{G'H'}$. So, the resulting figure is a parallelogram.

40. *Sample answer:*

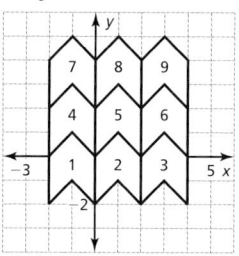

1 to 2: $(x, y) \rightarrow (x + 2, y)$
1 to 4: $(x, y) \rightarrow (x, y + 2)$
1 to 6: $(x, y) \rightarrow (x + 4, y + 2)$
1 to 8: $(x, y) \rightarrow (x + 2, y + 4)$

41. no; Because the value of y changes, you are not adding the same amount to each x-value.

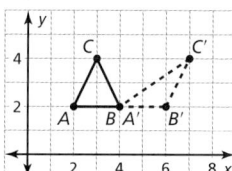

42.

STATEMENTS	REASONS
1. $\overline{MN}$ is perpendicular to line ℓ.	1. Given
2. $\overline{M'N'}$ is the translation of $\overline{MN}$ 2 units to the left.	2. Given
3. If $M(x_1, y_1)$ and $N(x_2, y_2)$, then $M'(x_1 - 2, y_1)$ and $N'(x_2 - 2, y_2)$.	3. Definition of translation
4. $m_{\overline{MN}} = \frac{y_2 - y_1}{x_2 - x_1}$ and $m_{\overline{M'N'}} = \frac{y_2 - y_1}{(x_2 - 2) - (x_1 - 2)}$ $= \frac{y_2 - y_1}{x_2 - x_1}$	4. Definition of slope
5. $m_{\overline{MN}} = m_{\overline{M'N'}}$	5. Transitive Property of Equality
6. $\overline{MN} \parallel \overline{M'N'}$	6. Slopes of Parallel Lines (Thm. 3.13)
7. $\overline{M'N'} \perp \ell$	7. Perpendicular Transversal Theorem (Thm. 3.11)

4.1 Maintaining Mathematical Proficiency

43. yes
44. no
45. no
46. yes
47. x
48. $-x - 3$
49. $6x - 12$
50. $3x - 4$

4.2 Lesson Monitoring Progress

2.

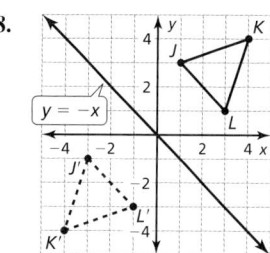

8.

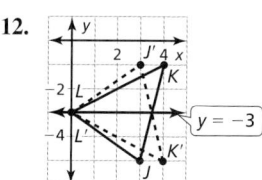

9. $m_{\overline{FF'}} = \frac{1 - 2}{-2 - (-1)} = 1$; The slope of $y = -x$ is -1; Because $1(-1) = -1$, the lines are perpendicular by Slopes of Perpendicular Lines (Thm. 3.14).

4.2 Monitoring Progress and Modeling with Mathematics

12.

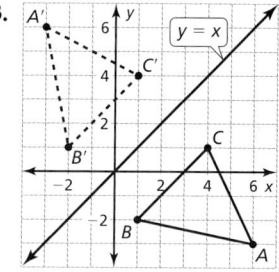

13.

14.

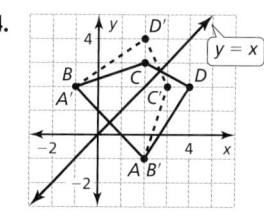

15.

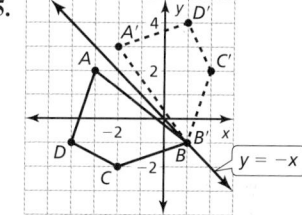

16.

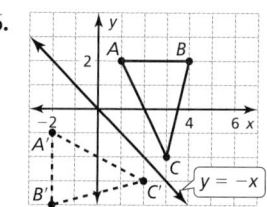

34. a. Figure 2; A reflection of Figure A will have the same y-values, and the x-values will be the same distance from the line of reflection, but on opposite sides.

b. Figure 4; A reflection of Figure A will have the same x-values, and the y-values will be the same distance from the line of reflection, but on opposite sides.

c. Figure 1; For each vertex (x, y) of Figure A, the corresponding vertex of Figure 1 is (y, x).

d. Figure 3; A glide transformation that maps Figure A to Figure 3 is as follows.
translation: $(x, y) \rightarrow (x, y - 2)$
reflection: in the line $x = 3.5$

35.

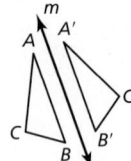

36. Line up the reflective device on line m to verify that $\triangle ABC$ reflects onto $\triangle A'B'C'$ and that $\triangle ABC \cong \triangle A'B'C'$.

37.

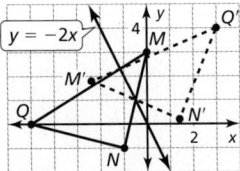

38. no; *Sample answer:* A counterexample would be as follows.

translation: $(x, y) \rightarrow (x, y - 2)$

reflection: in the x-axis

This composition is not commutative. However, all glide reflections are commutative because the line of reflection is parallel to the direction of the translation.

4.3 Lesson Monitoring Progress

5.

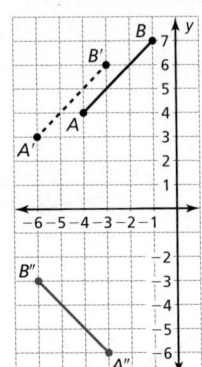

6.

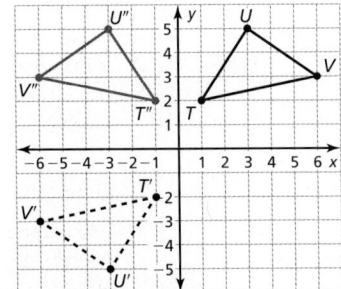

4.3 Monitoring Progress and Modeling with Mathematics

10.

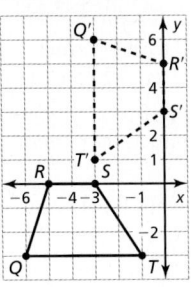

11.

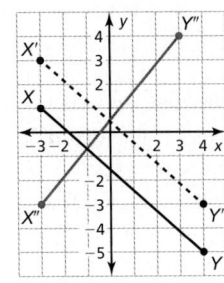

12.

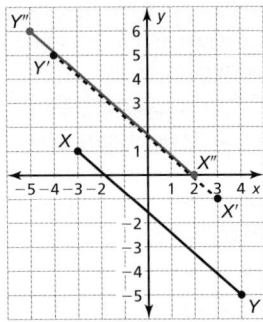

13.

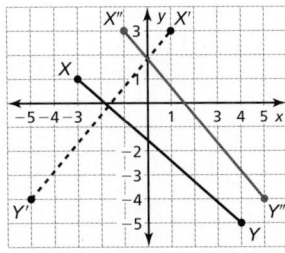

14.

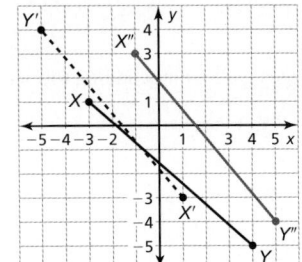

29. a. $90°: y = -\frac{1}{2}x + \frac{3}{2}$, $180°: y = 2x + 3$, $270°: y = -\frac{1}{2}x - \frac{3}{2}$, $360°$; $y = 2x - 3$; The slope of the line rotated $90°$ is the opposite reciprocal of the slope of the preimage, and the y-intercept is equal to the x-intercept of the preimage. The slope of the line rotated $180°$ is equal to the slope of the preimage, and the y-intercepts of the image and preimage are opposites. The slope of the line rotated $270°$ is the opposite reciprocal of the slope of the preimage, and the y-intercept is the opposite of the x-intercept of the preimage. The equation of the line rotated $360°$ is the same as the equation of the preimage.

b. yes; Because the coordinates of every point change in the same way with each rotation, the relationships described will be true for an equation with any slope and y-intercept.

34. yes; *Sample answer:*
$90°$: a reflection in $y = x$ followed by a reflection in the y-axis:
$(x, y) \rightarrow (y, x) \rightarrow (-y, x)$
$180°$: a reflection in the x-axis followed by a reflection in the y-axis: $(x, y) \rightarrow (x, -y) \rightarrow (-x, -y)$
$270°$: a reflection in $y = x$ followed by a reflection in the x-axis: $(x, y) \rightarrow (y, x) \rightarrow (y, -x)$
$360°$: a reflection in the x-axis twice: $(x, y) \rightarrow (x, -y) \rightarrow (x, y)$

37.

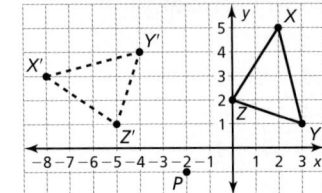

38. a. Pieces 1 and 2 each have 180° rotational symmetry when rotated about the center.

   b. two ways

   c. one way; When connected, the pieces can only fit into the puzzle one way because the combined shape does not have rotational symmetry.

39. (2, 120°); (2, 210°); (2, 300°); The radius remains the same. The angle increases in conjunction with the rotation.

4.3 Maintaining Mathematical Proficiency

40. $\angle P$ and $\angle W$, $\angle Q$ and $\angle V$, $\angle R$ and $\angle Z$, $\angle S$ and $\angle Y$, $\angle T$ and $\angle X$; $\overline{PQ}$ and $\overline{WV}$, $\overline{QR}$ and $\overline{VZ}$, $\overline{RS}$ and $\overline{ZY}$, $\overline{ST}$ and $\overline{YX}$, $\overline{TP}$ and $\overline{XW}$

41. $\angle A$ and $\angle J$, $\angle B$ and $\angle K$, $\angle C$ and $\angle L$, $\angle D$ and $\angle M$; $\overline{AB}$ and $\overline{JK}$, $\overline{BC}$ and $\overline{KL}$, $\overline{CD}$ and $\overline{LM}$, $\overline{DA}$ and $\overline{MJ}$

4.3 Mini-Assessment

1.

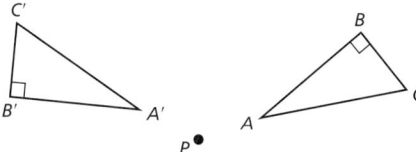

4.1–4.3 Quiz

7.

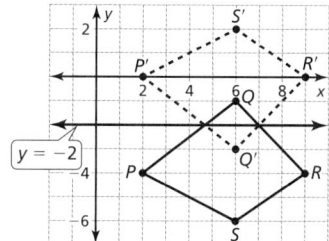

8.

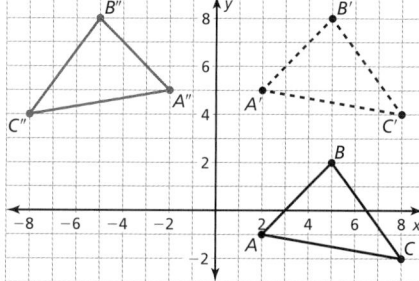

9.

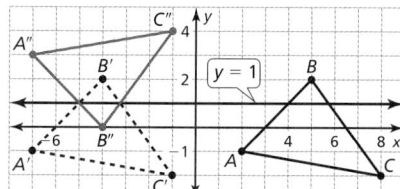

17.

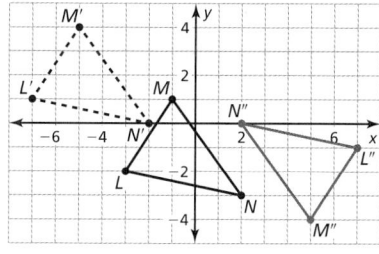

18.

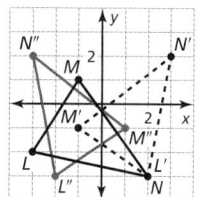

19. *Sample answer:* orange: rotate 90° around point (−2, 3), translate 4 units right and 5 units down; red: translate 7 units down and 3 units right; purple: rotate 90° around point (2, 3), translate 3 units left and 7 units down

4.4 Monitoring Progress and Modeling with Mathematics

30. a. reflections in parallel lines, or a translation

   b. reflection

   c. reflections in intersecting lines, or a rotation

   d. a glide reflection, or two reflections in parallel lines and then a reflection in a perpendicular line

31.

STATEMENTS	REASONS
1. A reflection in line ℓ maps $\overline{JK}$ to $\overline{J'K'}$, a reflection in line m maps $\overline{J'K'}$ to $\overline{J''K''}$, and $\ell \parallel m$.	**1.** Given
2. If $\overline{KK''}$ intersects line ℓ at L and line m at M, then L is the perpendicular bisector of $\overline{KK'}$, and M is the perpendicular bisector of $\overline{K'K''}$.	**2.** Definition of reflection
3. $\overline{KK'}$ is perpendicular to ℓ and m, and $KL = LK'$ and $K'M = MK''$.	**3.** Definition of perpendicular bisector
4. If d is the distance between ℓ and m, then $d = LM$.	**4.** Ruler Postulate (Post. 1.1)
5. $LM = LK' + K'M$ and $KK'' = KL + LK' + K'M + MK''$	**5.** Segment Addition Postulate (Post. 1.2)
6. $KK'' = LK' + LK' + K'M + K'M$	**6.** Substitution Property of Equality
7. $KK'' = 2(LK' + K'M)$	**7.** Distributive Property
8. $KK'' = 2(LM)$	**8.** Substitution Property of Equality
9. $KK'' = 2d$	**9.** Transitive Property of Equality

32. *Sample answer:*

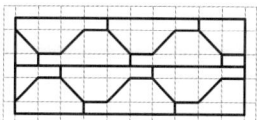

Translations and rotations are used.

33. the second classmate that says it is a 180° rotation;

reflections: $P(1, 3) \rightarrow P'(-1, 3) \rightarrow P''(-1, -3)$ and
$Q(3, 2) \rightarrow Q'(-3, 2) \rightarrow Q''(-3, -2)$

translation: $P(1, 3) \rightarrow (1 - 4, 3 - 5) \rightarrow (-3, -2)$ and
$Q(3, 2) \rightarrow (3 - 4, 2 - 5) \rightarrow Q''(-1, -3)$

180° rotation $P(1, 3) \rightarrow (-1, -3)$ and $Q(3, 2) \rightarrow (-3, -2)$

34. yes; no

35.

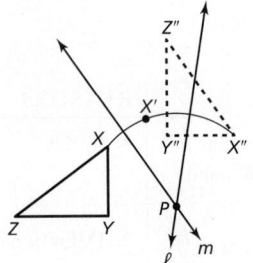

36.

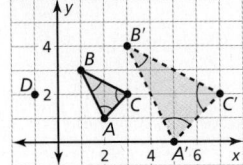

4.4 Maintaining Mathematical Proficiency

37. $x = -2$　　　　　**38.** $m = -3$

39. $b = 6$　　　　　**40.** $w = 2$

41. $n = -7.7$　　　　**42.** $y = 2$

43. 25%

4.4 Mini-Assessment

1. Rectangle *DEFG* is a translation of rectangle *JKLM* 1 unit left and 4 units up. So, they are congruent. $\triangle ABC$ is a 180° rotation of $\triangle TUS$ about the origin. So, they are congruent. $\triangle PQR$ is a reflection of $\triangle VWX$ in the *y*-axis. So, they are congruent.

2. *Sample answer:* A reflection over the *y*-axis followed by a translation 1 unit left

4.5 Explorations

4. The difference between the *x*-value of each vertex of $\triangle A'B'C'$ and the *x*-value of the center of dilation is equal to *k* times the difference between its corresponding *x*-value of $\triangle ABC$ and the *x*-value of the center of dilation. The difference between the *y*-value of each vertex of $\triangle A'B'C'$ and the *y*-value of the center of dilation is equal to *k* times the difference between its corresponding *y*-value of $\triangle ABC$ and the *y*-value of the center of dilation. Each side of $\triangle A'B'C'$ is *k* times as long as its corresponding side of $\triangle ABC$. Each angle of $\triangle A'B'C'$ is congruent to its corresponding angle of $\triangle ABC$.

Sample answer:

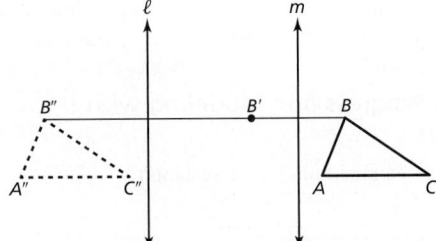

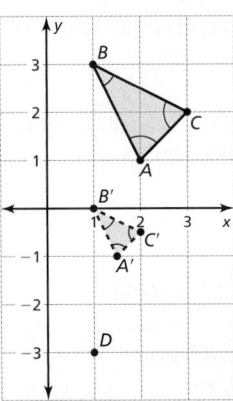

4.5 Lesson Monitoring Progress

3.

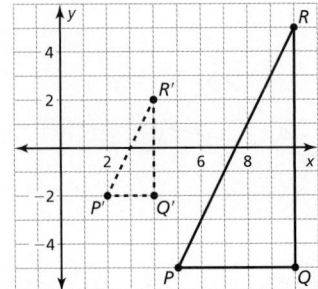

4.5 Monitoring Progress and Modeling with Mathematics

7.

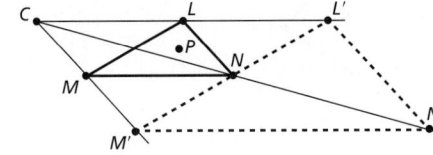

Not drawn to scale.

8.

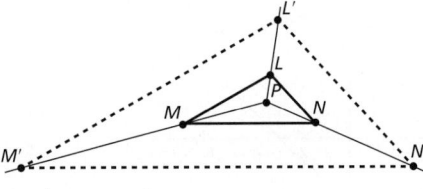

Not drawn to scale.

9.

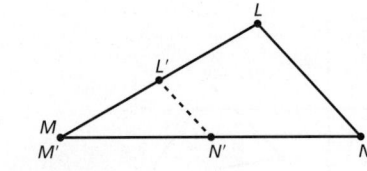

Not drawn to scale.

10.

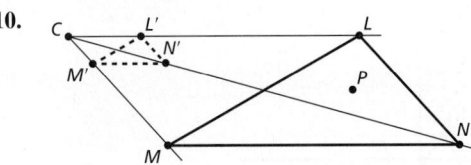

Not drawn to scale.

11.

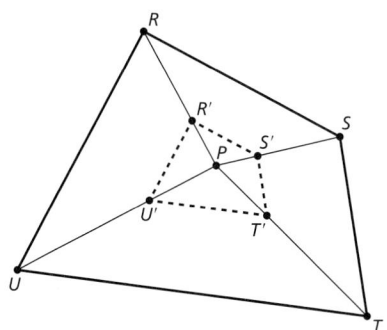

Not drawn to scale.

12.

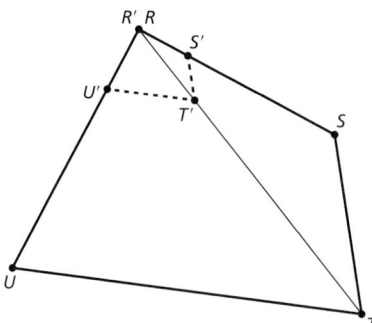

Not drawn to scale.

13.

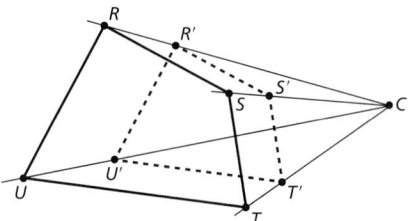

Not drawn to scale.

14.

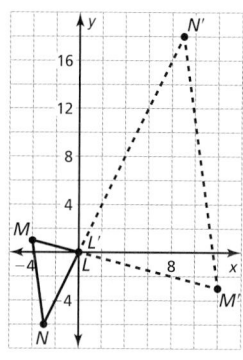

Not drawn to scale.

19.

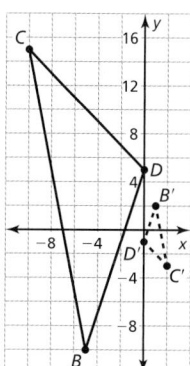

20.

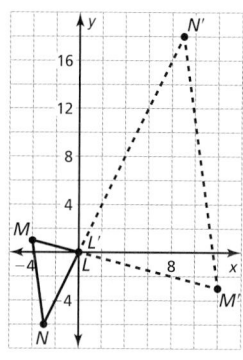

21.

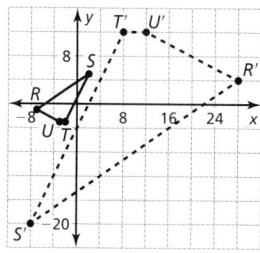

22.

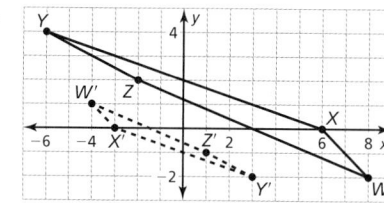

45.

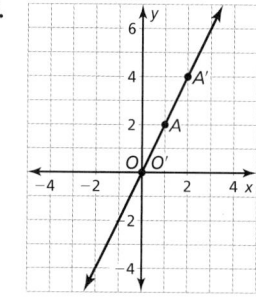

a. $O'A' = 2(OA)$

b. $\overleftrightarrow{O'A'}$ coincides with $\overleftrightarrow{OA}$.

46.

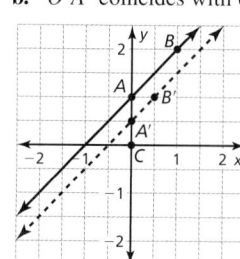

a. $A'B' = \frac{1}{2}(AB)$

b. $\overleftrightarrow{A'B'} \parallel \overleftrightarrow{AB}$ and the y-intercept of $\overleftrightarrow{A'B'}$ is half of the y-intercept of $\overleftrightarrow{AB}$.

47. $k = \frac{1}{16}$

48. no; It is true that dilating a figure with a scale factor of 1 will not enlarge or reduce the image nor will -1. However, by dilating with a scale factor that is negative, the image is rotated by 180°.

49. a. $P = 24$ units, $A = 32$ square units

b.

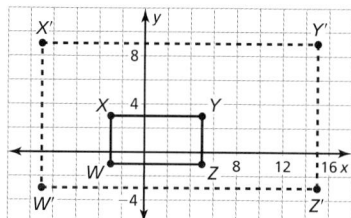

$P = 72$ units, $A = 288$ square units; The perimeter of the dilated rectangle is three times the perimeter of the original rectangle. The area of the dilated rectangle is nine times the area of the original rectangle.

c.

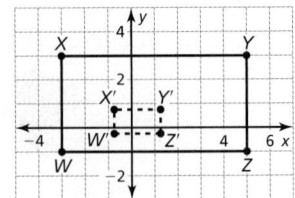

$P = 6$ units, $A = 2$ square units; The perimeter of the dilated rectangle is $\frac{1}{4}$ the perimeter of the original rectangle. The area of the dilated rectangle is $\frac{1}{16}$ the area of the original rectangle.

d. The perimeter changes by a factor of k. The area changes by a factor of k^2.

4.6 Explorations

2. c. *Sample answer:*

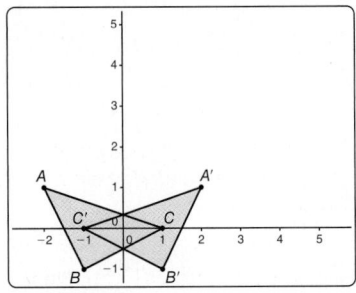

yes; Because the corresponding sides are congruent and the corresponding angles are congruent, the image is similar to the original triangle.

d. *Sample answer:*

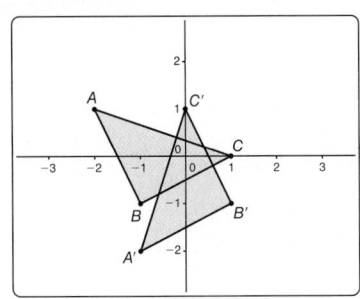

yes; Because the corresponding sides are congruent and the corresponding angles are congruent, the image is similar to the original triangle.

4.6 Extra Example 3

Translate square $ABCD$ so that point A maps to point E. Because translations map segments to parallel segments and $\overline{AD} \parallel \overline{EH}$, the image of $\overline{AD}$ lies on $\overline{EH}$.

Because translations preserve length and angle measure, the image of $ABCD$, $EB'C'D'$, is a square with side length s. Because all the interior angles of a square are right angles, $\angle B'ED' \cong \angle FEH$. When $\overrightarrow{ED'}$ coincides with $\overrightarrow{EH}$, $\overrightarrow{EB'}$ coincides with $\overrightarrow{EF}$. So $\overline{EB'}$ lies on $\overline{EF}$. Next, dilate square $EB'C'D'$ using center of dilation E. Choose the scale factor to be the ratio of the side lengths of $EFGH$ and $EB'C'D'$, which is $\frac{2s}{s} = 2$.

This dilation maps $\overline{ED'}$ to $\overline{EH}$ and $\overline{EB'}$ to $\overline{EF}$ because the images of $\overline{ED'}$ and $\overline{EB'}$ have side length $2(s) = 2s$ and the segments $\overline{ED'}$ and $\overline{EB'}$ lie on lines passing through the center of dilation. So, the dilation maps B' to F and D' to H. The image of C' lies $2(s) = 2s$ units to the right of the image of B' and $2(s) = 2s$ units above the image of D'. So, the image of C' is G.

A similarity transformation maps square $ABCD$ to square $EFGH$. So, square $ABCD$ is similar to square $EFGH$.

4.6 Lesson Monitoring Progress

5. Translate $\triangle JKL$ so that point L maps to point P. Because translations map segments to parallel segments and $\overline{LJ} \parallel \overline{PM}$, the image of $\overline{LJ}$ lies on $\overrightarrow{PM}$.

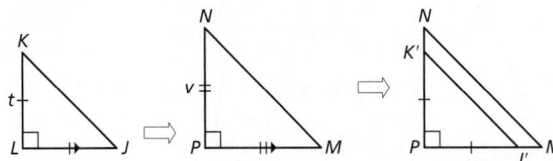

Because translations preserve side lengths and angle measures, the image of $\triangle JKL$, $\triangle J'K'P$, is a right isosceles triangle with leg length t. Because $\angle K'PJ'$ and $\angle NPM$ are right angles, they are congruent. When $\overrightarrow{PJ'}$ coincides with $\overrightarrow{PM}$, $\overrightarrow{PK'}$ coincides with $\overrightarrow{PN}$. So, $\overrightarrow{PK'}$ lies on $\overrightarrow{PN}$. Next, dilate $\triangle J'K'P$ using center of dilation P. Choose the scale factor to be the ratio of the side lengths of $\triangle MNP$ and $\triangle J'K'P$, which is $\frac{v}{t}$.

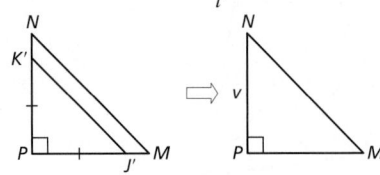

The dilation maps $\overline{PJ'}$ to $\overline{PM}$ and $\overline{PK'}$ to $\overline{PN}$ because the images of $\overline{PJ'}$ and $\overline{PK'}$ have side length $\frac{v}{t}(t) = v$ and the segments $\overline{PJ'}$ and $\overline{PK'}$ lie on lines passing through the center of dilation. So, the dilation maps K' to N and J' to M. A similarity transformation maps $\triangle JKL$ to $\triangle MNP$. So, $\triangle JKL$ is similar to $\triangle MNP$.

4.6 Monitoring Progress and Modeling with Mathematics

13. Reflect $\triangle ABC$ in $\overleftrightarrow{AB}$. Because reflections preserve side lengths and angle measures, the image of $\triangle ABC$, $\triangle ABC'$, is a right isosceles triangle with leg length j. Also because $\overline{AC} \perp \overleftrightarrow{BA}$, point C' is on $\overleftrightarrow{AC}$. So, $\overline{AC'}$ is parallel to $\overline{RT}$.

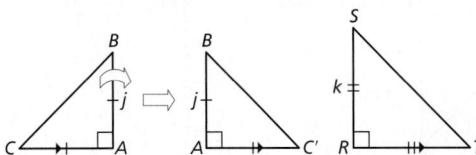

Then translate $\triangle ABC'$ so that point A maps to point R. Because translations map segments to parallel segments and $\overline{AC'} \parallel \overline{RT}$, the image of $\overline{AC'}$ lies on $\overline{RT}$.

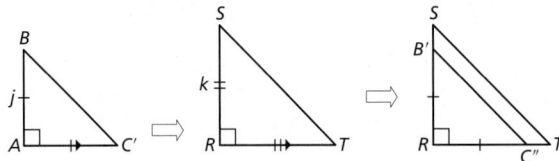

Because translations preserve side lengths and angle measures, the image of $\triangle ABC'$, $\triangle RB'C''$, is a right isosceles triangle with leg length j. Because $\angle B'RC''$ and $\angle SRT$ are right angles, they are congruent. When $\overrightarrow{RC''}$ coincides with $\overrightarrow{RT}$, $\overrightarrow{RB'}$ coincides with $\overrightarrow{RS}$. So, $\overrightarrow{RB'}$ lies on $\overrightarrow{RS}$. Next, dilate $\triangle RB'C''$ using center of dilation R. Choose the scale factor to be the ratio of the side lengths of $\triangle RST$ and $\triangle RB'C''$, which is $\dfrac{k}{j}$.

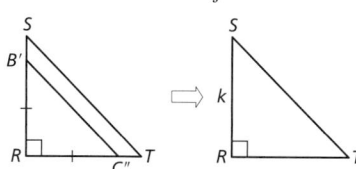

The dilation maps $\overline{RC''}$ to $\overline{RT}$ and $\overline{RB'}$ to $\overline{RS}$ because the images of $\overline{RC''}$ and $\overline{RB'}$ have side length $\dfrac{k}{j}(j) = k$ and the segments $\overline{RC''}$ and $\overline{RB'}$ lie on lines passing through the center of dilation. So, the dilation maps C' to T and B' to S. A similarity transformation maps $\triangle ABC$ to $\triangle RST$. So, $\triangle ABC$ is similar to $\triangle RST$.

14. If necessary, rotate $\square JKLM$ about point M so that $\overrightarrow{ML'} \parallel \overrightarrow{TS}$.

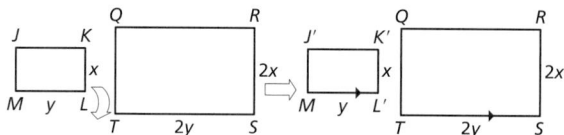

Note that because rotations are rigid motions, $\square J'K'L'M$ is congruent to $\square JKLM$. Translate $\square J'K'L'M$ so that point M maps to point T. Because translations map segments to parallel segments and $\overline{ML'} \parallel \overline{TS}$, the image of $\overline{ML'}$ lies on $\overline{TS}$.

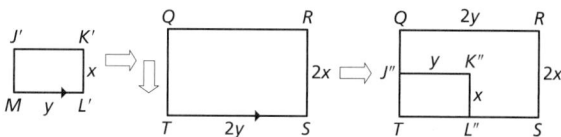

Because translations preserve side lengths and angle measures, the image of $\square J'K'L'M$, $\square J''K''L''T$, is a rectangle with side lengths x and y. Because all interior angles of a rectangle are right angles, $\angle J''TL''$ and $\angle QTS$ are congruent. When $\overrightarrow{TL''}$ coincides with $\overrightarrow{TS}$, $\overrightarrow{TJ''}$ coincides with $\overrightarrow{TQ}$. So, $\overrightarrow{TJ''}$ lies on $\overrightarrow{TQ}$. Next, dilate $\square J''K''L''T$ using center of dilation T. Choose the scale factor to be the ratio of the side lengths of $\square QRST$ and $\square J''K''L''T$, which is $\dfrac{2x}{x} = \dfrac{2y}{y} = 2$.

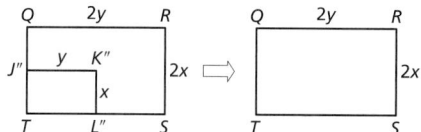

The dilation maps $\overline{TL''}$ to $\overline{TS}$ and $\overline{TJ''}$ to $\overline{TQ}$ because the images of $\overline{TL''}$ and $\overline{TJ''}$ have side lengths $y(2) = 2y$ and $x(2) = 2x$, and the segments $\overline{TL''}$ and $\overline{TJ''}$ lie on lines passing through the center of dilation. So, the dilation maps L'' to S and J'' to Q. The image of K'' lies $y(2) = 2y$ units to the right of the image of J'', and $x(2) = 2x$ units above the image of L''. So, the image of K'' is R. A similarity transformation maps $\square JKLM$ to $\square QRST$. So, $\square JKLM$ is similar to $\square QRST$.

16. Figure A is not similar to Figure B because the scale factor (A to B) of the shorter legs is $\dfrac{1}{2}$, and the scale factor (A to B) of the longer legs is $\dfrac{2}{3}$; Figure A is not similar to Figure B.

18. a. yes; The suns appear to be a dilation of one another.

   b. no; The hearts are about the same height but one is wider than the other.

19. *Sample answer:*

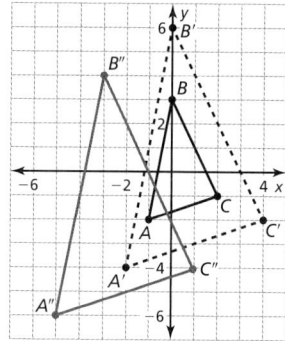

$\triangle A''B''C''$ can be mapped to $\triangle ABC$ by a translation 3 units right and 2 units up, followed by a dilation with center at the origin and a scale factor of $\dfrac{1}{2}$.

20. sometimes; As long as the center of dilation and the center of rotation are the same, rotations and dilations are commutative.

21. $J(-8, 0)$, $K(-8, 12)$, $L(-4, 12)$, $M(-4, 0)$; $J''(-9, -4)$, $K''(-9, 14)$, $L''(-3, 14)$, $M''(-3, -4)$; yes; A similarity transformation mapped quadrilateral $JKLM$ to quadrilateral $J''K''L''M''$.

22. a. yes; This triangle can be mapped to the larger one by a $180°$ rotation about the origin, followed by the translation $(x, y) \to (x + 5, y + 4)$, followed by a dilation with center $(1, 1)$ and a scale factor of 2. Because one can be mapped to the other by a similarity transformation, the triangles are similar.

   b. The triangle formed when the midpoints of a triangle are connected is always similar to the original triangle.

4.6 Maintaining Mathematical Proficiency

23. obtuse

24. straight

25. acute

26. right

Chapter 4 Test

10. *Sample answer:*

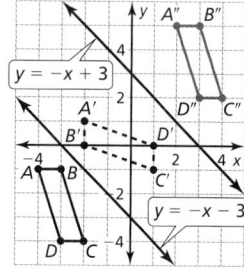

11. no; Each vertex has traded places with one other vertex.

12. *Sample answer:* reflection in the x-axis followed by the translation $(x, y) \to (x + 1, y + 2)$; yes; Both reflections and translations are rigid motions. So, according to the Composition Theorem (Thm. 4.1), this composition is a congruence transformation.

13. a. *Sample answer:* $270°$ rotation about the origin followed by a dilation with center at the origin and $k = \dfrac{1}{2}$, followed by the translation $(x, y) \to (x + 1, y - 1)$

   b. *Sample answer:* $k = \dfrac{3}{4}$; A medium slice would be between a small and a large, and $\dfrac{1}{2} < \dfrac{3}{4} < 1$.

14. a. reflection, reduction (dilation), and translation

   b. 2 in. by 3 in.

   c. no; The scale factor for the shorter sides is $\dfrac{17}{8}$, but the scale factor for the longer sides is $\dfrac{11}{6}$. So, the photo would have to be cropped or distorted in order to fit the frame.

Chapter 5

5.1 Monitoring Progress and Modeling with Mathematics

41.

STATEMENTS	REASONS
1. $\triangle ABC$ is a right triangle.	1. Given
2. $\angle C$ is a right angle.	2. Given (marked in diagram)
3. $m\angle C = 90°$	3. Definition of a right angle
4. $m\angle A + m\angle B + m\angle C = 180°$	4. Triangle Sum Theorem (Thm. 5.1)
5. $m\angle A + m\angle B + 90° = 180°$	5. Substitution Property of Equality
6. $m\angle A + m\angle B = 90°$	6. Subtraction Property of Equality
7. $\angle A$ and $\angle B$ are complementary.	7. Definition of complementary angles

42.

STATEMENTS	REASONS
1. $\triangle ABC$, exterior $\angle BCD$	1. Given
2. $m\angle A + m\angle B + m\angle BCA = 180°$	2. Triangle Sum Theorem (Thm. 5.1)
3. $\angle BCA$ and $\angle BCD$ form a linear pair.	3. Definition of linear pair
4. $m\angle BCA + m\angle BCD = 180°$	4. Linear Pair Postulate (Post. 2.8)
5. $m\angle A + m\angle B + m\angle BCA = m\angle BCA + m\angle BCD$	5. Transitive Property of Equality
6. $m\angle A + m\angle B = m\angle BCD$	6. Subtraction Property of Equality

47. A, B, F

48. no; According to the Exterior Angle Theorem (Thm. 5.2), the measure of an exterior angle of a triangle is always equal to the sum of the measures of the two nonadjacent interior angles.

49. $x = 43, y = 32$ **50.** $x = 118, y = 96$

51. $x = 85, y = 65$ **52.** $x = 26, y = 64$

53.

STATEMENTS	REASONS
1. $\overleftrightarrow{AB} \parallel \overleftrightarrow{CD}$	1. Given (marked in diagram)
2. $\angle ACD$ and $\angle 5$ form a linear pair.	2. Definition of linear pair
3. $m\angle ACD + m\angle 5 = 180°$	3. Linear Pair Postulate (Post. 2.8)
4. $m\angle 3 + m\angle 4 = m\angle ACD$	4. Angle Addition Postulate (Post. 1.4)
5. $m\angle 3 + m\angle 4 + m\angle 5 = 180°$	5. Substitution Property of Equality
6. $\angle 1 \cong \angle 5$	6. Corresponding Angles Theorem (Thm. 3.1)
7. $\angle 2 \cong \angle 4$	7. Alternate Interior Angles Theorem (Thm. 3.2)
8. $m\angle 1 = m\angle 5$, $m\angle 2 = m\angle 4$	8. Definition of congruent angles
9. $m\angle 3 + m\angle 2 + m\angle 1 = 180°$	9. Substitution Property of Equality

5.1 Maintaining Mathematical Proficiency

54. 43°   **55.** 86°

56. 12   **57.** 15

5.2 Monitoring Progress and Modeling with Mathematics

15.

STATEMENTS	REASONS
1. $\overline{AB} \parallel \overline{DC}$, $\overline{AB} \cong \overline{DC}$, E is the midpoint of $\overline{AC}$ and $\overline{BD}$.	1. Given
2. $\angle AEB \cong \angle CED$	2. Vertical Angles Congruence Theorem (Thm. 2.6)
3. $\angle BAE \cong \angle DCE$, $\angle ABE \cong \angle CDE$	3. Alternate Interior Angles Theorem (Thm. 3.2)
4. $\overline{AE} \cong \overline{CE}$, $\overline{BE} \cong \overline{DE}$	4. Definition of midpoint
5. $\triangle AEB \cong \triangle CED$	5. All corresponding parts are congruent.

A26   Additional Answers

16.

STATEMENTS	REASONS
1. $\overline{AB} \cong \overline{DC}$, $\overline{AF} \cong \overline{DG}$, $\overline{BE} \cong \overline{CE} \cong \overline{EF} \cong \overline{EG}$, $\angle B \cong \angle C$, $\angle A \cong \angle D$	1. Given
2. $\angle BGA \cong \angle CFD$	2. Third Angles Theorem (Thm. 5.4)
3. $AF + FG = AG$, $DG + FG = DF$, $BE + EG = BG$, $CE + EF = CF$	3. Segment Addition Postulate (Post. 1.2)
4. $AF = DG$, $BE = CE = EF = EG$	4. Definition of congruent segments
5. $DG + FG = AG$, $BE + EG = CF$	5. Substitution Property of Equality
6. $DF = AG$, $BG = CF$	6. Transitive Property of Equality
7. $\overline{DF} \cong \overline{AG}$, $\overline{BG} \cong \overline{CF}$	7. Definition of congruent segments
8. $\triangle ABG \cong \triangle DCF$	8. All corresponding parts are congruent.

19.

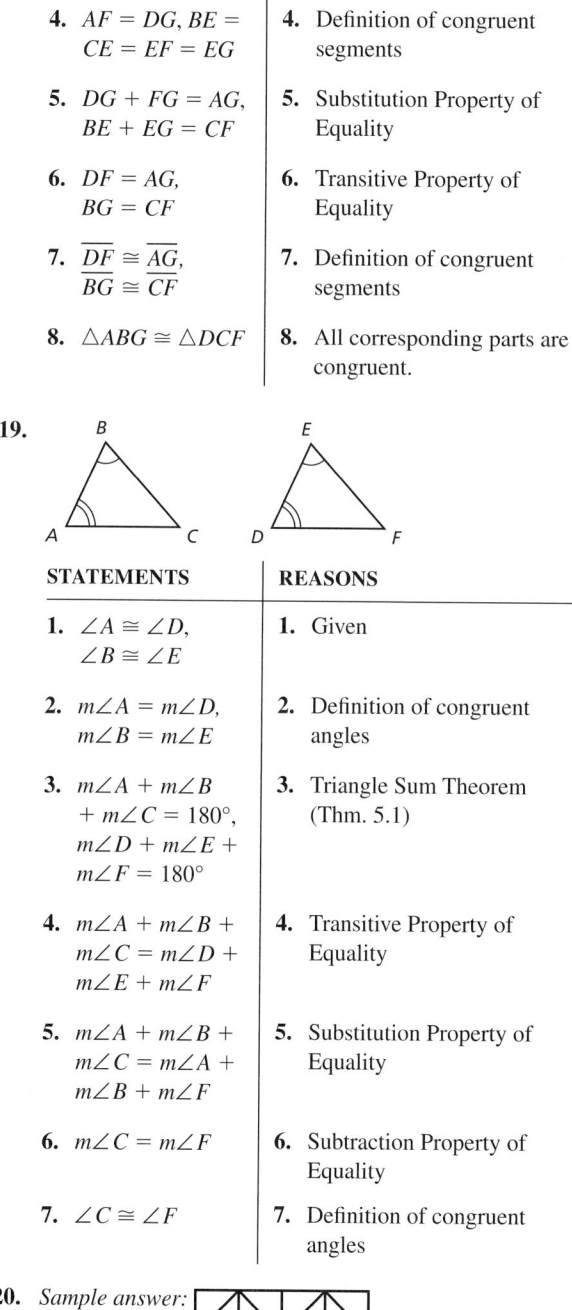

STATEMENTS	REASONS
1. $\angle A \cong \angle D$, $\angle B \cong \angle E$	1. Given
2. $m\angle A = m\angle D$, $m\angle B = m\angle E$	2. Definition of congruent angles
3. $m\angle A + m\angle B + m\angle C = 180°$, $m\angle D + m\angle E + m\angle F = 180°$	3. Triangle Sum Theorem (Thm. 5.1)
4. $m\angle A + m\angle B + m\angle C = m\angle D + m\angle E + m\angle F$	4. Transitive Property of Equality
5. $m\angle A + m\angle B + m\angle C = m\angle A + m\angle B + m\angle F$	5. Substitution Property of Equality
6. $m\angle C = m\angle F$	6. Subtraction Property of Equality
7. $\angle C \cong \angle F$	7. Definition of congruent angles

20. *Sample answer:*

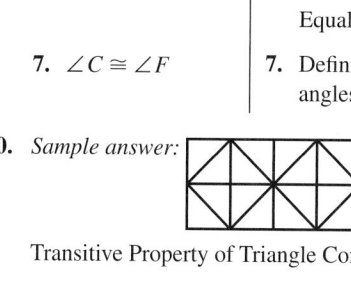

Transitive Property of Triangle Congruence (Thm. 5.3)

21. corresponding angles: $\angle J \cong \angle X$, $\angle K \cong \angle Y$, $\angle L \cong \angle Z$
corresponding sides: $\overline{JK} \cong \overline{XY}$, $\overline{KL} \cong \overline{YZ}$, $\overline{JL} \cong \overline{XZ}$

22. **a.** They are congruent because corresponding parts of congruent figures are congruent.

  b. They are congruent because they are both supplementary to congruent angles.

  c. $\angle GEB$ is also a right angle, and all right angles are congruent.

  d. yes; From parts (a)–(c), you know that $\overline{BE} \cong \overline{DE}$, $\angle ABE \cong \angle CDE$, $\angle GBE \cong \angle GDE$, and $\angle GEB \cong \angle GED$. Also, $\overline{GE} \cong \overline{GE}$ by the Reflexive Property of Congruence (Thm. 2.1), $\angle BGE \cong \angle DGE$ by the Third Angles Theorem (Thm. 5.4), and $\overline{BG} \cong \overline{DG}$ from the diagram markings. So, $\triangle BEG \cong \triangle DEG$ because all corresponding parts are congruent.

23. $\begin{cases} 17x - y = 40 \\ 2x + 4y = 50 \end{cases}$
$x = 3, y = 11$

24. $\begin{cases} 4x + y = 22 \\ 8x - 6y = 28 \end{cases}$
$x = 5, y = 2$

25. A rigid motion maps each part of a figure to a corresponding part of its image. Because rigid motions preserve length and angle measure, corresponding parts of congruent figures are congruent, which means that the corresponding sides and corresponding angles are congruent.

5.2 Maintaining Mathematical Proficiency

26. $\angle Z \cong \angle W$

27. $\overline{PQ} \cong \overline{RS}$, $\angle N \cong \angle T$

28. $\overline{JK} \cong \overline{MK}$, $\angle J \cong \angle M$, $m\angle LKM = 90°$

29. $\overline{DE} \cong \overline{HI}$, $\angle D \cong \angle H$, $\overline{DF} \parallel \overline{HG}$, $\angle DFE \cong \angle HGI$

5.3 Lesson Monitoring Progress

1.

STATEMENTS	REASONS
1. $\overline{SV} \cong \overline{VU}$, $\overline{RT} \perp \overline{SU}$	1. Given
2. $\overline{VR} \cong \overline{VR}$	2. Reflexive Property of Congruence (Thm. 2.1)
3. $\angle SVR$ and $\angle UVR$ are right angles.	3. Definition of perpendicular lines
4. $\angle SVR \cong \angle UVR$	4. Right Angles Congruence Theorem (Thm. 2.3)
5. $\triangle SVR \cong \triangle UVR$	5. SAS Congruence Theorem (Thm. 5.5)

2.

STATEMENTS	REASONS
1. $\angle B$ and $\angle D$ are right angles, $\overline{BA} \cong \overline{DA} \cong \overline{DC}$ $\cong \overline{BC}$, R is the midpoint of $\overline{BA}$, U is the midpoint of $\overline{DA}$, T is the midpoint of $\overline{DC}$, and S is the midpoint of $\overline{BC}$.	1. Given
2. $\angle B \cong \angle D$	2. Right Angles Congruence Theorem (Thm. 2.3)
3. $BA = DA = DC = BC$	3. Definition of congruent segments
4. $BA = BR + RA$, $DA = DU + UA$, $DC = DT + TC$, $BC = BS + SC$	4. Segment Addition Postulate (Post. 1.2)
5. $BR + RA = DU + UA$ $= DT + TC = BS + SC$	5. Transitive Property of Equality
6. $\overline{BR} \cong \overline{RA}$, $\overline{DU} \cong \overline{UA}$, $\overline{DT} \cong \overline{TC}$, $\overline{BS} \cong \overline{SC}$	6. Definition of midpoint
7. $BR = RA$, $DU = UA$, $DT = TC$, $BS = SC$	7. Definition of congruent segments
8. $BR + BR = DU + DU$ $= DT + DT = BS + BS$	8. Substitution Property of Equality
9. $2 \cdot BR = 2 \cdot DU = 2 \cdot DT = 2 \cdot BS$	9. Distributive Property
10. $BR = DU = DT = BS$	10. Division Property of Equality
11. $\overline{BR} \cong \overline{DU} \cong \overline{DT} \cong \overline{BS}$	11. Definition of congruent segments
12. $\triangle BSR \cong \triangle DUT$	12. SAS Congruence Theorem (Thm. 5.5)

3.

STATEMENTS	REASONS
1. $\overline{DA} \cong \overline{DG}$, $\angle ADR \cong \angle GDR$	1. Given
2. $\overline{DR} \cong \overline{DR}$	2. Reflexive Property of Congruence (Thm. 2.1)
3. $\triangle DRA \cong \triangle DRG$	3. SAS Congruence Theorem (Thm. 5.5)

5.3 Monitoring Progress and Modeling with Mathematics

15.

STATEMENTS	REASONS
1. $\overline{SP} \cong \overline{TP}$, $\overline{PQ}$ bisects $\angle SPT$.	1. Given
2. $\overline{PQ} \cong \overline{PQ}$	2. Reflexive Property of Congruence (Thm. 2.1)
3. $\angle SPQ \cong \angle TPQ$	3. Definition of angle bisector
4. $\triangle SPQ \cong \triangle TPQ$	4. SAS Congruence Theorem (Thm. 5.5)

16.

STATEMENTS	REASONS
1. $\overline{AB} \cong \overline{CD}$, $\overline{AB} \parallel \overline{CD}$	1. Given
2. $\overline{AC} \cong \overline{AC}$	2. Reflexive Property of Congruence (Thm. 2.1)
3. $\angle 1 \cong \angle 2$	3. Alternate Interior Angles Theorem (Thm. 3.2)
4. $\triangle ABC \cong \triangle CDA$	4. SAS Congruence Theorem (Thm. 5.5)

17.

STATEMENTS	REASONS
1. C is the midpoint of $\overline{AE}$ and $\overline{BD}$.	1. Given
2. $\angle ACB \cong \angle ECD$	2. Vertical Angles Congruence Theorem (Thm. 2.6)
3. $\overline{AC} \cong \overline{EC}$, $\overline{BC} \cong \overline{DC}$	3. Definition of midpoint
4. $\triangle ABC \cong \triangle EDC$	4. SAS Congruence Theorem (Thm. 5.5)

18.

STATEMENTS	REASONS
1. $\overline{PT} \cong \overline{RT}$, $\overline{QT} \cong \overline{ST}$	1. Given
2. $\angle PTQ \cong \angle RTS$	2. Vertical Angles Congruence Theorem (Thm. 2.6)
3. $\triangle PQT \cong \triangle RST$	3. SAS Congruence Theorem (Thm. 5.5)

19. $\triangle SRT \cong \triangle URT$; $\overline{RT} \cong \overline{RT}$ by the Reflexive Property of Congruence (Thm. 2.1). Also, because all points on a circle are the same distance from the center, $\overline{RS} \cong \overline{RU}$. It is given that $\angle SRT \cong \angle URT$. So, $\triangle SRT$ and $\triangle URT$ are congruent by the SAS Congruence Theorem (Thm. 5.5).

20. $\triangle BAD \cong \triangle DCB$; Because the sides of the square are congruent, $\overline{BA} \cong \overline{DC}$ and $\overline{AD} \cong \overline{CB}$. Also, because the angles of the square are congruent, $\angle A \cong \angle C$. So, $\triangle BAD$ and $\triangle DCB$ are congruent by the SAS Congruence Theorem (Thm. 5.5).

21. $\triangle STU \cong \triangle UVR$; Because the sides of the pentagon are congruent, $\overline{ST} \cong \overline{UV}$ and $\overline{TU} \cong \overline{VR}$. Also, because the angles of the pentagon are congruent, $\angle T \cong \angle V$. So, $\triangle STU$ and $\triangle UVR$ are congruent by the SAS Congruence Theorem (Thm. 5.5).

22. $\triangle NMK \cong \triangle NLK$; Because all points on a circle are the same distance from the center, $\overline{NM} \cong \overline{NL}$ and $\overline{KM} \cong \overline{KL}$. Because $\overline{MK} \perp \overline{MN}$ and $\overline{KL} \perp \overline{NL}$, $\angle M$ and $\angle L$ are right angles by definition of perpendicular lines, which means that $\angle M \cong \angle L$ by the Right Angles Congruence Theorem (Thm. 2.3). So, $\triangle NMK$ and $\triangle NLK$ are congruent by the SAS Congruence Theorem (Thm. 5.5).

23.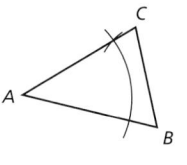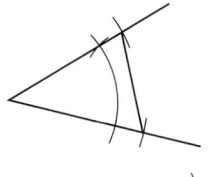

24.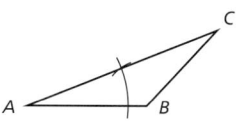

25. $\triangle XYZ$ and $\triangle WYZ$ are congruent so either the expressions for $\overline{XZ}$ and $\overline{WZ}$ or the expressions for $\overline{XY}$ and $\overline{WY}$ should be set equal to each other because they are corresponding sides.

$5x - 5 = 3x + 9$

$2x - 5 = 9$

$2x = 14$

$x = 7$

26. $\angle ACB \cong \angle DCB$

27. Because $\triangle ABC$, $\triangle BCD$, and $\triangle CDE$ are isosceles triangles, you know that $\overline{AB} \cong \overline{BC}$, $\overline{BC} \cong \overline{CD}$, and $\overline{CD} \cong \overline{DE}$. So, by the Transitive Property of Congruence (Thm. 2.1), $\overline{AB} \cong \overline{CD}$ and $\overline{BC} \cong \overline{DE}$. It is given that $\angle B \cong \angle D$, so $\triangle ABC \cong \triangle CDE$ by the SAS Congruence Theorem (Thm. 5.5).

28. SSS, SAS, ASA, and AAS;

Counterexample for SSA

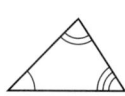 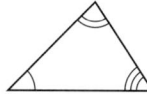

Counterexample for AAA

29.

STATEMENTS	REASONS
1. $\overline{AC} \cong \overline{DC}$, $\overline{BC} \cong \overline{EC}$	1. Given
2. $\angle ACB \cong \angle DCE$	2. Vertical Angles Congruence Theorem (Thm. 2.6)
3. $\triangle ABC \cong \triangle DEC$	3. SAS Congruence Theorem (Thm. 5.5)

$x = 4$, $y = 5$

30. no; When you construct $\overline{AB}$ and $\overline{AC}$, you have to construct them at an angle that is congruent to $\angle A$. Otherwise, when you construct an angle congruent to $\angle C$, you might not get a third segment that is congruent to $\overline{BC}$.

31.

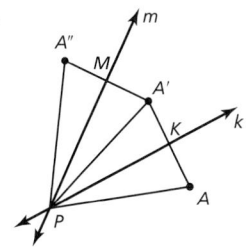

STATEMENTS	REASONS
1. A reflection in line k maps point A to A', a reflection in line m maps A' to A'', and $m\angle MPK = x°$.	1. Given
2. Line k is the perpendicular bisector of $\overline{AA'}$, and line m is the perpendicular bisector of $\overline{A'A''}$.	2. Definition of reflection
3. $\overline{AK} \cong \overline{KA'}$, $\angle AKP$ and $\angle A'KP$ are right angles, $\overline{A'M} \cong \overline{MA''}$, and $\angle A'MP$ and $\angle A''MP$ are right angles.	3. Definition of perpendicular bisector
4. $\angle AKP \cong \angle A'KP$, $\angle A'MP \cong \angle A''MP$	4. Right Angles Congruence Theorem (Thm. 2.3)
5. $\overline{KP} \cong \overline{KP}$	5. Reflexive Property of Congruence (Thm. 2.1)
6. $\triangle AKP \cong \triangle A'KP$, $\triangle A'MP \cong \triangle A''MP$	6. SAS Congruence Theorem (Thm. 5.5)
7. $\overline{AP} \cong \overline{A'P}$, $\overline{A'P} \cong \overline{A''P}$, $\angle APK \cong \angle A'PK$, $\angle A'PM \cong \angle A''PM$	7. Corresponding parts of congruent triangles are congruent.
8. $\overline{AP} \cong \overline{A''P}$	8. Transitive Property of Congruence (Thm. 2.1)
9. $m\angle APK = m\angle A'PK$, $m\angle A'PM = m\angle A''PM$	9. Definition of congruent angles
10. $m\angle MPK = m\angle A'PK + m\angle A'PM$, $m\angle APA'' = m\angle APK + m\angle A'PK + m\angle A'PM + m\angle A''PM$	10. Angle Addition Postulate (Post. 1.4)
11. $m\angle APA'' = m\angle A'PK + m\angle A'PK + m\angle A'PM + m\angle A'PM$	11. Substitution Property of Equality
12. $m\angle APA'' = 2(m\angle A'PK + m\angle A'PM)$	12. Distributive Property
13. $m\angle APA'' = 2(m\angle MPK)$	13. Substitution Property of Equality
14. $m\angle APA'' = 2(x°) = 2x°$	14. Substitution Property of Equality
15. A rotation about point P maps A to A'', and the angle of rotation is $2x°$.	15. Definition of rotation

5.3 Maintaining Mathematical Proficiency

32. right isosceles

33. obtuse isosceles

34. equiangular equilateral

35. obtuse scalene

5.3 Mini-Assessment

3. Statements (Reasons)

1. $\overline{PS} \cong \overline{PT}$ (Given)
2. $\overline{PQ}$ bisects $\angle SPT$. (Given)
3. $\angle SPQ \cong \angle TPQ$ (Def. of $\cong \angle$ bisector)
4. $\overline{PQ} \cong \overline{PQ}$ (Reflexive Prop. $\cong$ Thm. 2.1)
5. $\triangle PQS \cong \triangle PQT$ (SAS $\cong$ Thm. 5.5)

5.4 Monitoring Progress and Modeling with Mathematics

31. 6, 8, 10; If $3t = 5t - 12$, then $t = 6$. If $5t - 12 = t + 20$, then $t = 8$. If $3t = t + 20$, then $t = 10$.

32. $(180 - x)^\circ, \left(\dfrac{x}{2}\right)^\circ, \left(\dfrac{x}{2}\right)^\circ$ or $(180 - x)^\circ, (180 - x)^\circ, (2x - 180)^\circ$

33. If the base angles are x°, then the vertex angle is $(180 - 2x)^\circ$, or $[2(90 - x)]^\circ$. Because $2(90 - x)$ is divisible by 2, the vertex angle is even when the angles are whole numbers.

35. a. 2.1 mi; By the Exterior Angle Theorem (Thm. 5.2), $m\angle L = 70^\circ - 35^\circ = 35^\circ$. Because $m\angle SRL = 35^\circ = m\angle RLS$, by definition of congruent angles, $\angle SRL \cong \angle RLS$. So, by the Converse of the Base Angles Theorem (Thm. 5.7), $\overline{RS} \cong \overline{SL}$. So, $SL = RS = 2.1$ miles.

b. Find the point on the shore line that has an angle of 45° from the boat. Then, measure the distance that the boat travels until the angle is 90°. That distance is the same as the distance between the boat and the shore line because the triangle formed is an isosceles right triangle.

36. no; The sum of the angle measures of a very large spherical triangle will be greater than 180°, but for smaller spherical triangles, the sum will be closer to 180°.

37.

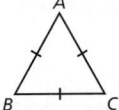

STATEMENTS	REASONS
1. $\triangle ABC$ is equilateral.	1. Given
2. $\overline{AB} \cong \overline{AC}, \overline{AB} \cong \overline{BC}, \overline{AC} \cong \overline{BC}$	2. Definition of equilateral triangle
3. $\angle B \cong \angle C, \angle A \cong \angle C, \angle A \cong \angle B$	3. Base Angles Theorem (Thm. 5.6)
4. $\triangle ABC$ is equiangular.	4. Definition of equiangular triangle

38. a. By the markings, $\overline{AE} \cong \overline{DE}, \overline{AB} \cong \overline{DC}$, and $\angle BAE \cong \angle CDE$. So, $\triangle ABE \cong \triangle DCE$ by the SAS Congruence Theorem (Thm. 5.5).

b. $\triangle AED, \triangle BEC$

c. $\angle EDA, \angle EBC, \angle ECB$

39.

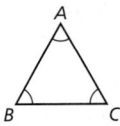

STATEMENTS	REASONS
1. $\triangle ABC$ is equiangular.	1. Given
2. $\angle B \cong \angle C, \angle A \cong \angle C, \angle A \cong \angle B$	2. Definition of equiangular triangle
3. $\overline{AB} \cong \overline{AC}, \overline{AB} \cong \overline{BC}, \overline{AC} \cong \overline{BC}$	3. Converse of the Base Angles Theorem (Thm. 5.7)
4. $\triangle ABC$ is equilateral.	4. Definition of equilateral triangle

40. no; T, U, and V will always be the vertices of an isosceles triangle except when V is collinear with T and U, which happens when the coordinates of V are $(3, 3)$.

41.

STATEMENTS	REASONS
1. $\triangle ABC$ is equilateral, $\angle CAD \cong \angle ABE \cong \angle BCF$	1. Given
2. $\triangle ABC$ is equiangular.	2. Corollary to the Base Angles Theorem (Cor. 5.2)
3. $\angle ABC \cong \angle BCA \cong \angle BAC$	3. Definition of equiangular triangle
4. $m\angle CAD = m\angle ABE = m\angle BCF$, $m\angle ABC = m\angle BCA = m\angle BAC$	4. Definition of congruent angles
5. $m\angle ABC = m\angle ABE + m\angle EBC$, $m\angle BCA = m\angle BCF + m\angle ACF$, $m\angle BAC = m\angle CAD + m\angle BAD$	5. Angle Addition Postulate (Post. 1.4)
6. $m\angle ABE + m\angle EBC = m\angle BCF + m\angle ACF = m\angle CAD + m\angle BAD$	6. Substitution Property of Equality
7. $m\angle ABE + m\angle EBC = m\angle ABE + m\angle ACF = m\angle ABE + m\angle BAD$	7. Substitution Property of Equality
8. $m\angle EBC = m\angle ACF = m\angle BAD$	8. Subtraction Property of Equality
9. $\angle EBC \cong \angle ACF \cong \angle BAD$	9. Definition of congruent angles
10. $\angle FEB \cong \angle DFC \cong \angle EDA$	10. Third Angles Theorem (Thm. 5.4)
11. $\angle FEB$ and $\angle FED$ are supplementary, $\angle DFC$ and $\angle EFD$ are supplementary, and $\angle EDA$ and $\angle FDE$ are supplementary.	11. Linear Pair Postulate (Post. 2.8)
12. $\angle FED \cong \angle EFD \cong \angle FDE$	12. Congruent Supplements Theorem (Thm. 2.4)
13. $\triangle DEF$ is equiangular.	13. Definition of equiangular triangle
14. $\triangle DEF$ is equilateral.	14. Corollary to the Converse of the Base Angles Theorem (Cor. 5.3)

5.4 Maintaining Mathematical Proficiency

42. $\overline{SE}$

43. $\overline{JK}, \overline{RS}$

44. $\overline{EF}, \overline{UV}$

5.1–5.4 Quiz

7. yes;

STATEMENTS	REASONS
1. $\overline{GH} \cong \overline{KH}$, $\overline{FH} \cong \overline{JH}$	1. Given
2. $\angle GHF \cong \angle KHJ$	2. Vertical Angles Congruence Theorem (Thm. 2.6)
3. $\triangle GHF \cong \triangle KHJ$	3. SAS Congruence Theorem (Thm. 5.5)

8. yes;

STATEMENTS	REASONS
1. $\overline{LM} \cong \overline{NM}$, $\angle LMP \cong \angle NMP$	1. Given
2. $\overline{MP} \cong \overline{MP}$	2. Reflexive Property of Congruence (Thm. 2.1)
3. $\triangle LMP \cong \triangle NMP$	3. SAS Congruence Theorem (Thm. 5.5)

16. c. yes;

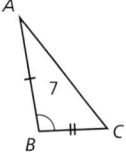 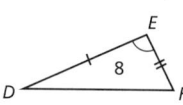

STATEMENTS	REASONS
1. $\overline{AB} \cong \overline{DE}, \overline{BC} \cong \overline{EF}$, $\angle B \cong \angle E$	1. Given
2. $\triangle ABC \cong \triangle DEF$	2. SAS Congruence Theorem (Thm. 5.5)

5.5 Lesson Monitoring Progress

2. no; $\overline{AB}$ corresponds with $\overline{CD}$, but they are not the same measure. In order for two triangles to be congruent, all pairs of corresponding sides must be congruent.

3. yes; From the diagram markings, $\overline{QP} \cong \overline{RS}, \overline{PT} \cong \overline{ST}$, and $\overline{QT} \cong \overline{RT}$. So, $\triangle QPT \cong \triangle RST$ by the SSS Congruence Theorem (Thm. 5.8).

4. not stable; This square is not stable because there are many possible quadrilaterals with the given side lengths.

5. stable; The diagonal support in this figure forms triangles with fixed side lengths. By the SSS Congruence Theorem (Thm. 5.8), these triangles cannot change shape, so the figure is stable.

6. not stable; The diagonal support in this figure forms a triangle and a quadrilateral. The triangle would be stable, but the quadrilateral is not because there are many possible quadrilaterals with the given side lengths.

8.

STATEMENTS	REASONS
1. $\overline{AC} \cong \overline{DB}$, $\angle ABC$ and $\angle DCB$ are right angles.	**1.** Given
2. $\overline{CB} \cong \overline{BC}$	**2.** Reflexive Property of Congruence (Thm. 2.1)
3. $\triangle ABC$ and $\triangle DCB$ are right triangles.	**3.** Definition of a right triangle
4. $\triangle ABC \cong \triangle DCB$	**4.** HL Congruence Theorem (Thm. 5.9)

5.5 Monitoring Progress and Modeling with Mathematics

13.

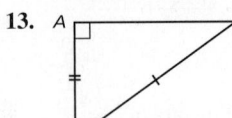 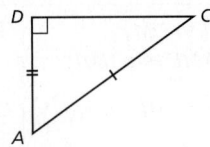

STATEMENTS	REASONS
1. $\overline{AC} \cong \overline{DB}$, $\overline{AB} \perp \overline{AD}$, $\overline{CD} \perp \overline{AD}$	**1.** Given
2. $\overline{AD} \cong \overline{AD}$	**2.** Reflexive Property of Congruence (Thm. 2.1)
3. $\angle BAD$ and $\angle CDA$ are right angles.	**3.** Definition of perpendicular lines
4. $\triangle BAD$ and $\triangle CDA$ are right triangles.	**4.** Definition of a right triangle
5. $\triangle BAD \cong \triangle CDA$	**5.** HL Congruence Theorem (Thm. 5.9)

14.

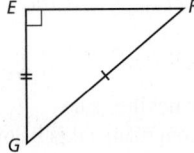 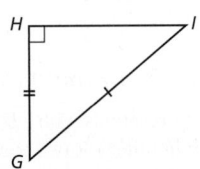

STATEMENTS	REASONS
1. G is the midpoint of $\overline{EH}$, $\overline{FG} \cong \overline{GI}$, $\angle A$ and $\angle H$ are right angles.	**1.** Given
2. $\overline{EG} \cong \overline{HG}$	**2.** Definition of midpoint
3. $\triangle EFG$ and $\triangle HIG$ are right triangles.	**3.** Definition of a right triangle
4. $\triangle EFG \cong \triangle HIG$	**4.** HL Congruence Theorem (Thm. 5.9)

15.

STATEMENTS	REASONS
1. $\overline{LM} \cong \overline{JK}$, $\overline{MJ} \cong \overline{KL}$	**1.** Given
2. $\overline{JL} \cong \overline{JL}$	**2.** Reflexive Property of Congruence (Thm. 2.1)
3. $\triangle LMJ \cong \triangle JKL$	**3.** SSS Congruence Theorem (Thm. 5.8)

16.

STATEMENTS	REASONS
1. $\overline{WX} \cong \overline{VZ}$, $\overline{WY} \cong \overline{VY}$, $\overline{YZ} \cong \overline{YX}$	**1.** Given
2. $\overline{WV} \cong \overline{WV}$	**2.** Reflexive Property of Congruence (Thm. 2.1)
3. $YZ = YX$, $WY = VY$	**3.** Definition of congruent segments
4. $VX = VY + YX$, $WZ = WY + YZ$	**4.** Segment Addition Postulate (Post. 1.2)
5. $VX = WY + YZ$	**5.** Substitution Property of Equality
6. $VX = WZ$	**6.** Transitive Property of Equality
7. $\overline{VX} \cong \overline{WZ}$	**7.** Definition of congruent segments
8. $\triangle VWX \cong \triangle WVZ$	**8.** SSS Congruence Theorem (Thm. 5.8)

22.

STATEMENTS	REASONS
1. $\overline{HF} \cong \overline{FS} \cong \overline{ST} \cong \overline{TH}$; $\overline{FT} \cong \overline{SH}$; $\angle H$, $\angle F$, $\angle S$, and $\angle T$ are right angles.	**1.** Given
2. $\overline{SH} \cong \overline{SH}$	**2.** Reflexive Property of Congruence (Thm. 2.1)
3. $\triangle HFS$, $\triangle FST$, and $\triangle STH$ are right triangles.	**3.** Definition of a right triangle
4. $\triangle HFS \cong \triangle FST \cong \triangle STH$	**4.** HL Congruence Theorem (Thm. 5.9)

30. *Sample answer:* SSS Congruence Theorem (Thm. 5.8), HL Congruence Theorem (Thm. 5.9)

31. both; $\overline{JL} \cong \overline{JL}$ by the Reflexive Property of Congruence (Thm. 2.1), and the other two pairs of sides are marked as congruent. So, the SSS Congruence Theorem (Thm. 5.8) can be used. Also, because $\angle M$ and $\angle K$ are right angles, they are both right triangles, and the legs and hypotenuses are congruent. So, the HL Congruence Theorem (Thm. 5.9) can be used.

32. yes; They would have to be formed from circles that were at the same angle with each other. So, all corresponding parts would be congruent.

33. *Sample answer:*

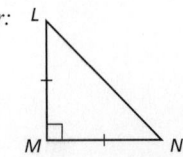 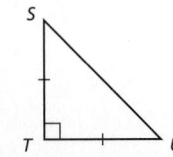

34. *Sample answer:*

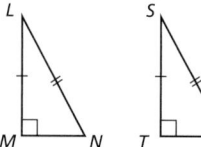

35. a. $\overline{BD} \cong \overline{BD}$ by the Reflexive Property of Congruence (Thm. 2.1). It is given that $\overline{AB} \cong \overline{CB}$ and that $\angle ADB$ and $\angle CDB$ are right angles. So, $\triangle ABC$ and $\triangle CBD$ are right triangles and are congruent by the HL Congruence Theorem (Thm. 5.9).

b. yes; Because $\overline{AB} \cong \overline{CB} \cong \overline{CE} \cong \overline{FE}$, $\overline{BD} \cong \overline{EG}$, and they are all right triangles, it can be shown that $\triangle ABD \cong \triangle CBD \cong \triangle CEG \cong \triangle FEG$ by the HL Congruence Theorem (Thm. 5.9).

36. $x = 5$; If $5x = 4x + 3$ and $5x - 2 = 3x + 10$, then $x = 3$ and $x = 6$, which is not possible. If $5x = 3x + 10$ and $5x - 2 = 4x + 3$, then $x = 5$ in both equations. So, when $x = 5$, $AB = CD = 25$ and $AC = BD = 23$, which means that $\overline{AB} \cong \overline{CD}$ and $\overline{AC} \cong \overline{BD}$. Because $\overline{BC} \cong \overline{BC}$, the triangles are congruent by the SSS Congruence Theorem (Thm. 5.8).

5.5 Maintaining Mathematical Proficiency

37. $\overline{DF}$

38. $\overline{BC}$

39. $\angle E$

40. $\angle C$

5.6 Explorations

2.

Possible congruence theorem	Valid or not valid?
SSS	Valid
SSA	Not valid
SAS	Valid
AAS	Valid
ASA	Valid
AAA	Not valid

Sample answer: A counterexample for SSA is given in Exploration 1. A counterexample for AAA is shown here.

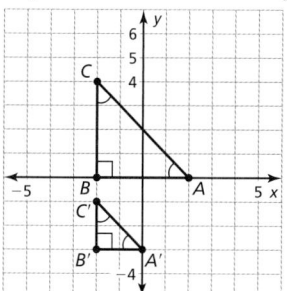

In this example, each pair of corresponding angles is congruent, but the corresponding sides are not congruent.

5.6 Lesson Monitoring Progress

2.

STATEMENTS	REASONS
1. $\overline{AB} \perp \overline{AD}$, $\overline{DE} \perp \overline{AD}$, $\overline{AC} \cong \overline{DC}$	**1.** Given
2. $\angle BAC$ and $\angle EDC$ are right angles.	**2.** Definition of perpendicular lines
3. $\angle BAC \cong \angle EDC$	**3.** Right Angles Congruence Theorem (Thm. 2.3)
4. $\angle ACB \cong \angle DCE$	**4.** Vertical Angles Congruence Theorem (Thm. 2.6)
5. $\triangle ABC \cong \triangle DEC$	**5.** ASA Congruence Theorem (Thm. 5.10)

3.

STATEMENTS	REASONS
1. $\angle S \cong \angle U$, $\overline{RS} \cong \overline{VU}$	**1.** Given
2. $\angle RTS \cong \angle VTU$	**2.** Vertical Angles Congruence Theorem (Thm. 2.6)
3. $\triangle RST \cong \triangle VUT$	**3.** AAS Congruence Theorem (Thm. 5.11)

5.6 Monitoring Progress and Modeling with Mathematics

17.

STATEMENTS	REASONS
1. M is the midpoint of $\overline{NL}$, $\overline{NL} \perp \overline{NQ}$, $\overline{NL} \perp \overline{MP}$, $\overline{QM} \parallel \overline{PL}$	**1.** Given
2. $\angle QNM$ and $\angle PML$ are right angles.	**2.** Definition of perpendicular lines
3. $\angle QNM \cong \angle PML$	**3.** Right Angles Congruence Theorem (Thm. 2.3)
4. $\angle QMN \cong \angle PLM$	**4.** Corresponding Angles Theorem (Thm. 3.1)
5. $\overline{NM} \cong \overline{ML}$	**5.** Definition of midpoint
6. $\triangle NQM \cong \triangle MPL$	**6.** ASA Congruence Theorem (Thm. 5.10)

18.

STATEMENTS	REASONS
1. $\overline{AJ} \cong \overline{KC}$, $\angle BJK \cong \angle BKJ$, $\angle A \cong \angle C$	1. Given
2. $AJ = KC$	2. Definition of congruent segments
3. $JC = JK + KC$, $AK = AJ + JK$	3. Segment Addition Postulate (Post. 1.2)
4. $AK = KC + JK$	4. Substitution Property of Equality
5. $AK = JK + KC$	5. Commutative Property of Addition
6. $AK = JC$	6. Transitive Property of Equality
7. $\overline{AK} \cong \overline{JC}$	7. Definition of congruent segments
8. $\triangle ABK \cong \triangle CBJ$	8. ASA Congruence Theorem (Thm. 5.10)

19.

STATEMENTS	REASONS
1. $\overline{VW} \cong \overline{UW}$, $\angle X \cong \angle Z$	1. Given
2. $\angle W \cong \angle W$	2. Reflexive Property of Congruence (Thm. 2.2)
3. $\triangle XWV \cong \triangle ZWU$	3. AAS Congruence Theorem (Thm. 5.11)

20.

STATEMENTS	REASONS
1. $\angle NKM \cong \angle LMK$, $\angle L \cong \angle N$	1. Given
2. $\overline{KM} \cong \overline{KM}$	2. Reflexive Property of Congruence (Thm. 2.1)
3. $\triangle NMK \cong \triangle LKM$	3. AAS Congruence Theorem (Thm. 5.11)

27.

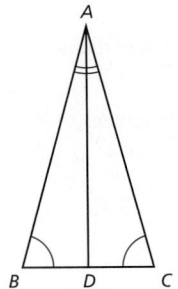

STATEMENTS	REASONS
1. Draw $\overline{AD}$, the angle bisector of $\angle ABC$.	1. Construction of angle bisector
2. $\angle CAD \cong \angle BAD$	2. Definition of angle bisector
3. $\angle B \cong \angle C$	3. Given
4. $\overline{AD} \cong \overline{AD}$	4. Reflexive Property of Congruence (Thm. 2.1)
5. $\triangle ABD \cong \triangle ACD$	5. AAS Congruence Theorem (Thm. 5.11)
6. $\overline{AB} \cong \overline{AC}$	6. Corresponding parts of congruent triangles are congruent.

29. a.

STATEMENTS	REASONS
1. $\angle CDB \cong \angle ADB$, $\overline{DB} \perp \overline{AC}$	1. Given
2. $\angle ABD$ and $\angle CBD$ are right angles.	2. Definition of perpendicular lines
3. $\angle ABD \cong \angle CBD$	3. Right Angles Congruence Theorem (Thm. 2.3)
4. $\overline{BD} \cong \overline{BD}$	4. Reflexive Property of Congruence (Thm. 2.1)
5. $\triangle ABD \cong \triangle CBD$	5. ASA Congruence Theorem (Thm. 5.10)

b. Because $\triangle ABD \cong \triangle CBD$ and corresponding parts of congruent triangles are congruent, you can conclude that $\overline{AD} \cong \overline{CD}$, which means that $\triangle ACD$ is isosceles by definition.

c. no; For instance, because $\triangle ACD$ is isosceles, the girl sees her toes in the bottom of the mirror. This remains true as she moves backwards because $\triangle ACD$ remains isosceles.

30. $\triangle PTS \cong \triangle RTQ$, $\triangle PTQ \cong \triangle RTS$, $\triangle SQR \cong \triangle QSP$, $\triangle SRP \cong \triangle QPR$; Because $\angle PTS \cong \angle RTQ$ by the Vertical Angles Congruence Theorem (Thm. 2.6), $\triangle PTS \cong \triangle RTQ$ by the SAS Congruence Theorem (Thm. 5.5); Because $\angle PTQ \cong \angle RTS$ by the Vertical Angles Congruence Theorem (Thm. 2.6), $\triangle PTQ \cong \triangle RTS$ by the SAS Congruence Theorem (Thm. 5.5); Transversal $\overline{SQ}$ intersects parallel sides $\overline{PS}$ and $\overline{QR}$ to create congruent alternate interior angles $\angle SQR$ and $\angle QSP$, and transversal $\overline{SQ}$ also intersects parallel sides $\overline{PQ}$ and $\overline{SR}$ to create congruent alternate interior angles $\angle QSR$ and $\angle SQP$. Also, $\overline{SQ} \cong \overline{SQ}$ by the Reflexive Property of Congruence (Thm. 2.1). So, $\triangle SQR \cong \triangle QSP$ by the ASA Congruence Theorem (Thm. 5.10); Transversal $\overline{PR}$ intersects parallel sides $\overline{PS}$ and $\overline{QR}$ to create congruent alternate interior angles $\angle SPR$ and $\angle QRP$, and transversal $\overline{PR}$ also intersects parallel sides $\overline{PQ}$ and $\overline{SR}$ to create congruent alternate interior angles $\angle QPR$ and $\angle SRP$. Also, $\overline{PR} \cong \overline{PR}$ by the Reflexive Property of Congruence (Thm. 2.1). So, $\triangle SRP \cong \triangle QPR$ by the ASA Congruence Theorem (Thm. 5.10).

33. a. $\overline{TU} \cong \overline{XY}, \overline{UV} \cong \overline{YZ}, \overline{TV} \cong \overline{XZ};$
$\overline{TU} \cong \overline{XY}, \angle U \cong \angle Y, \overline{UV} \cong \overline{YZ};$
$\overline{UV} \cong \overline{YZ}, \angle V \cong \angle Z, \overline{TV} \cong \overline{XZ};$
$\overline{TV} \cong \overline{XZ}, \angle T \cong \angle X, \overline{TU} \cong \overline{XY};$
$\angle T \cong \angle X, \overline{TU} \cong \overline{XY}, \angle U \cong \angle Y;$
$\angle U \cong \angle Y, \overline{UV} \cong \overline{YZ}, \angle V \cong \angle Z;$
$\angle V \cong \angle Z, \overline{TV} \cong \overline{XZ}, \angle T \cong \angle X;$
$\angle T \cong \angle X, \angle U \cong \angle Y, \overline{UV} \cong \overline{YZ};$
$\angle T \cong \angle X, \angle U \cong \angle Y, \overline{TV} \cong \overline{XZ};$
$\angle U \cong \angle Y, \angle V \cong \angle Z, \overline{TV} \cong \overline{XZ};$
$\angle U \cong \angle Y, \angle V \cong \angle Z, \overline{TU} \cong \overline{XY};$
$\angle V \cong \angle Z, \angle T \cong \angle X, \overline{TU} \cong \overline{XY};$
$\angle V \cong \angle Z, \angle T \cong \angle X, \overline{UV} \cong \overline{YZ}$

b. $\frac{13}{20}$, or 65%

5.6 Maintaining Mathematical Proficiency

34. (3, 2)

35. (1, 1)

36. $\left(-\frac{3}{2}, -\frac{11}{2}\right)$

37.

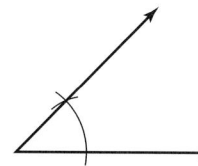

38.

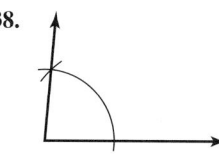

5.7 Explorations

1. a. The surveyor can measure $\overline{DE}$, which will have the same measure as the distance across the river ($\overline{AB}$). Because $\triangle ABC \cong \triangle DEC$ by the ASA Congruence Theorem (Thm. 5.10), the corresponding parts of the two triangles are also congruent.

b.

STATEMENTS	REASONS
1. $\overline{AC} \cong \overline{CD}$, $\angle A$ and $\angle D$ are right angles.	1. Given
2. $\angle A \cong \angle D$	2. Right Angles Congruence Theorem (Thm. 2.3)
3. $\angle ACB \cong \angle DCE$	3. Vertical Angles Congruence Theorem (Thm. 2.6)
4. $\triangle ABC \cong \triangle DEC$	4. ASA Congruence Theorem (Thm. 5.10)
5. $\overline{AB} \cong \overline{DE}$	5. Corresponding parts of congruent triangles are congruent.
6. $AB = DE$	6. Definition of congruent segments

c. By creating a triangle on land that is congruent to a triangle that crosses the river, you can find the distance across the river by measuring the distance of the corresponding congruent segment on land.

2. a. The officer's height stays the same, he is standing perpendicular to the ground the whole time, and he tipped his hat the same angle in both directions. So, $\triangle DEF \cong \triangle DEG$ by the ASA Congruence Theorem (Thm 5.10). Because corresponding parts of the two triangles are also congruent, $\overline{EG} \cong \overline{EF}$. By the definition of congruent segments, EG equals EF, which is the width of the river.

b.

STATEMENTS	REASONS
1. $\angle EDG \cong \angle EDF$, $\angle DEG$ and $\angle DEF$ are right angles.	1. Given
2. $\angle DEG \cong \angle DEF$	2. Right Angles Congruence Theorem (Thm. 2.3)
3. $\overline{DE} \cong \overline{DE}$	3. Reflexive Property of Congruence (Thm. 2.1)
4. $\triangle DEF \cong \triangle DEG$	4. ASA Congruence Theorem (Thm. 5.10)
5. $\overline{EG} \cong \overline{EF}$	5. Corresponding parts of congruent triangles are congruent.
6. $EG = EF$	6. Definition of congruent segments

c. By standing perpendicular to the ground and using the tip of your hat to gaze at two different points in such a way that the direction of your gaze makes the same angle with your body both times, you can create two congruent triangles, which ensures that you are the same distance from both points.

5.7 Monitoring Progress and Modeling with Mathematics

12. Use the ASA Congruence Theorem (Thm. 5.10) to prove that $\triangle ABE \cong \triangle CBE$. Then, state that $\overline{AE} \cong \overline{CE}$ and $\angle BCE \cong \angle BAE$ because corresponding parts of congruent triangles are congruent. Use the Congruent Complements Theorem (Thm. 2.5) to state that $\angle ECD \cong \angle EAF$. So, you can use the SAS Congruence Theorem (Thm. 5.5) to prove that $\triangle ECD \cong \triangle EAF$, so $\angle 1 \cong \angle 2$.

13.

STATEMENTS	REASONS
1. $\overline{AP} \cong \overline{BP}, \overline{AQ} \cong \overline{BQ}$	1. Given
2. $\overline{PQ} \cong \overline{PQ}$	2. Reflexive Property of Congruence (Thm. 2.1)
3. $\triangle APQ \cong \triangle BPQ$	3. SSS Congruence Theorem (Thm. 5.8)
4. $\angle APQ \cong \angle BPQ$	4. Corresponding parts of congruent triangles are congruent.
5. $\overline{PM} \cong \overline{PM}$	5. Reflexive Property of Congruence (Thm. 2.1)
6. $\triangle APM \cong \triangle BPM$	6. SAS Congruence Theorem (Thm. 5.5)
7. $\angle AMP \cong \angle BMP$	7. Corresponding parts of congruent triangles are congruent.
8. $\angle AMP$ and $\angle BMP$ form a linear pair.	8. Definition of a linear pair
9. $\overline{MP} \perp \overline{AB}$	9. Linear Pair Perpendicular Theorem (Thm. 3.10)
10. $\angle AMP$ and $\angle BMP$ are right angles.	10. Definition of perpendicular lines

14.

STATEMENTS	REASONS
1. $\overline{AP} \cong \overline{BP}, \overline{AQ} \cong \overline{BQ}$	1. Given
2. $\overline{PQ} \cong \overline{PQ}$	2. Reflexive Property of Congruence (Thm. 2.1)
3. $\triangle APQ \cong \triangle BPQ$	3. SSS Congruence Theorem (Thm. 5.8)
4. $\angle QPA \cong \angle QPB$	4. Corresponding parts of congruent triangles are congruent.
5. $\angle QPA$ and $\angle QPB$ form a linear pair.	5. Definition of a linear pair
6. $\overline{PQ} \perp \overline{AB}$	6. Linear Pair Perpendicular Theorem (Thm. 3.10)
7. $\angle QPA$ and $\angle QPB$ are right angles.	7. Definition of perpendicular lines

15.

STATEMENTS	REASONS
1. $\overline{FG} \cong \overline{GJ} \cong \overline{HG} \cong \overline{GK}, \overline{JM} \cong \overline{LM} \cong \overline{KM} \cong \overline{NM}$	1. Given
2. $\angle FGJ \cong \angle HGK, \angle JML \cong \angle KMN$	2. Vertical Angles Congruence Theorem (Thm. 2.6)
3. $\triangle FGJ \cong \triangle HGK, \triangle JML \cong \triangle KMN$	3. SAS Congruence Theorem (Thm. 5.5)
4. $\angle F \cong \angle H, \angle L \cong \angle N$	4. Corresponding parts of congruent triangles are congruent.
5. $FG = GJ = HG = GK$	5. Definition of congruent segments
6. $HJ = HG + GJ, FK = FG + GK$	6. Segment Addition Postulate (Post. 1.2)
7. $FK = HG + GJ$	7. Substitution Property of Equality
8. $FK = HJ$	8. Transitive Property of Equality
9. $\overline{FK} \cong \overline{HJ}$	9. Definition of congruent segments
10. $\triangle HJN \cong \triangle FKL$	10. AAS Congruence Theorem (Thm. 5.11)
11. $\overline{FL} \cong \overline{HN}$	11. Corresponding parts of congruent triangles are congruent.

16.

STATEMENTS	REASONS
1. $\angle PRU \cong \angle QVS, \angle PUR \cong \angle QSV \cong \angle RUX \cong \angle VSY, \overline{RS} \cong \overline{VU}$	1. Given
2. $RS = VU$	2. Definition of congruent segments
3. $RU = RS + SU, VS = VU + SU$	3. Segment Addition Postulate (Post. 1.2)
4. $VS = RS + SU$	4. Substitution Property of Equality
5. $RU = VS$	5. Transitive Property of Equality
6. $\overline{RU} \cong \overline{VS}$	6. Definition of congruent segments
7. $\triangle PUR \cong \triangle QSV$	7. ASA Congruence Theorem (Thm. 5.10)
8. $\angle P \cong \angle Q, \overline{PU} \cong \overline{QS}$	8. Corresponding parts of congruent triangles are congruent.
9. $m\angle PUR = m\angle QSV = m\angle RUX = m\angle VSY$	9. Definition of congruent angles
10. $m\angle PUX = m\angle PUR + m\angle RUX, m\angle QSY = m\angle QSV + m\angle VSY$	10. Angle Addition Postulate (Post. 1.4)
11. $m\angle QSY = m\angle PUR + m\angle RUX$	11. Substitution Property of Equality
12. $m\angle PUX = m\angle QSY$	12. Transitive Property of Equality
13. $\angle PUX \cong \angle QSY$	13. Definition of congruent angles
14. $\triangle PUX \cong \triangle QSY$	14. ASA Congruence Theorem (Thm. 5.10)

17. Because $\overline{AC} \perp \overline{BC}$ and $\overline{ED} \perp \overline{BD}$, $\angle ACB$ and $\angle EDB$ are congruent right angles. Because B is the midpoint of $\overline{CD}, \overline{BC} \cong \overline{BD}$. The vertical angles $\angle ABC$ and $\angle EBD$ are congruent. So, $\triangle ABC \cong \triangle EBD$ by the ASA Congruence Theorem (Thm. 5.10). Then, because corresponding parts of congruent triangles are congruent, $\overline{AC} \cong \overline{ED}$. So, you can find the distance AC across the canyon by measuring $\overline{ED}$.

19.

STATEMENTS	REASONS
1. $\overline{AD} \parallel \overline{BC}$, E is the midpoint of $\overline{AC}$.	1. Given
2. $\overline{AE} \cong \overline{CE}$	2. Definition of midpoint
3. $\angle AEB \cong \angle CED$, $\angle AED \cong \angle BEC$	3. Vertical Angles Congruence Theorem (Thm. 2.6)
4. $\angle DAE \cong \angle BCE$	4. Alternate Interior Angles Theorem (Thm. 3.2)
5. $\triangle DAE \cong \triangle BCE$	5. ASA Congruence Theorem (Thm. 5.10)
6. $\overline{DE} \cong \overline{BE}$	6. Corresponding parts of congruent triangles are congruent.
7. $\triangle AEB \cong \triangle CED$	7. SAS Congruence Theorem (Thm. 5.5)

21. yes; You can show that $WXYZ$ is a rectangle. This means that the opposite sides are congruent. Because $\triangle WZY$ and $\triangle YXW$ share a hypotenuse, the two triangles have congruent hypotenuses and corresponding legs, which allows you to use the HL Congruence Theorem (Thm. 5.9) to prove that the triangles are congruent.

22. a. false; If two triangles are congruent, then they have the same perimeter.

  b. true

23. $\triangle GHJ$, $\triangle NPQ$

5.7 Maintaining Mathematical Proficiency

24. 16 units   **25.** about 17.5 units

5.8 Lesson Monitoring Progress

1.

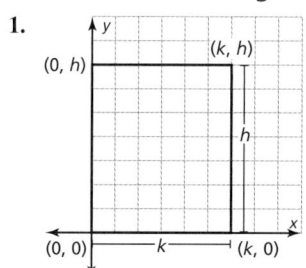

5.8 Monitoring Progress and Modeling with Mathematics

7. Find the lengths of $\overline{OP}$, $\overline{PM}$, $\overline{MN}$, and $\overline{NO}$ to show that $\overline{OP} \cong \overline{PM}$ and $\overline{MN} \cong \overline{NO}$.

8. Find the coordinates of G using the Midpoint Formula. Use these coordinates and the Distance Formula to show that $\overline{OG} \cong \overline{JG}$. Show that $\overline{HG} \cong \overline{FG}$ by the definition of midpoint, and $\angle HGL \cong \angle FGO$ by the Vertical Angles Congruence Theorem (Thm. 2.6). Then, use the SAS Congruence Theorem (Thm. 5.5) to conclude that $\triangle GHJ \cong \triangle GFO$.

9.

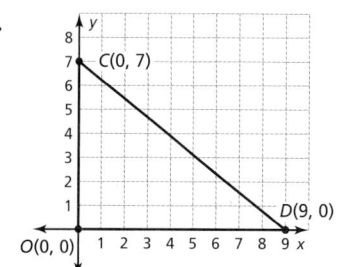

about 11.4 units

10.

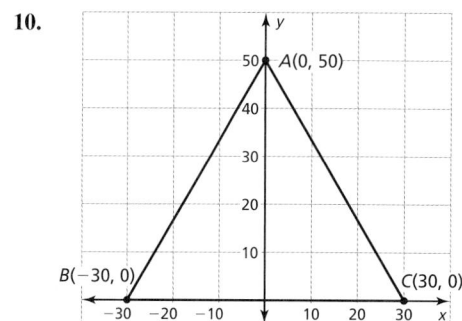

about 58.3 units

11.

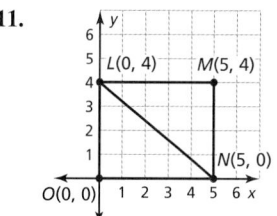

about 6.4 units

12.

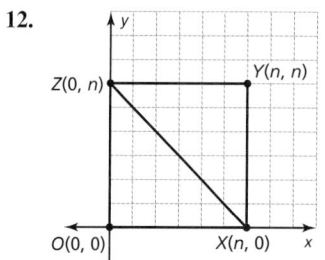

$n\sqrt{2}$ units

13.

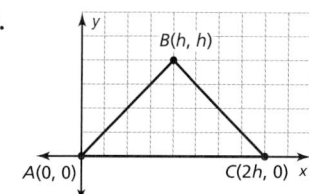

$AB = h\sqrt{2}$, $m_{\overline{AB}} = 1$, $M_{\overline{AB}}\left(\dfrac{h}{2}, \dfrac{h}{2}\right)$, $BC = h\sqrt{2}$, $m_{\overline{BC}} = -1$,

$M_{\overline{BC}}\left(\dfrac{3h}{2}, \dfrac{h}{2}\right)$, $AC = 2h$, $m_{\overline{AC}} = 0$, $M_{\overline{AC}}(h, 0)$; yes; yes; Because

$m_{\overline{AB}} \cdot m_{\overline{BC}} = -1$, $\overline{AB} \perp \overline{BC}$ by the Slopes of Perpendicular Lines Theorem (Thm. 3.14). So $\angle ABC$ is a right angle. $\overline{AB} \cong \overline{BC}$ because $AB = BC$. So, $\triangle ABC$ is a right isosceles triangle.

14.

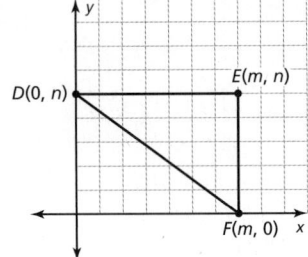

$DE = m$, $m_{\overline{DE}} = 0$, $M_{\overline{DE}}\left(\dfrac{m}{2}, n\right)$, $EF = n$, $m_{\overline{EF}} = $ undefined,

$M_{\overline{EF}}\left(m, \dfrac{n}{2}\right)$, $DF = \sqrt{m^2 + n^2}$, $m_{\overline{DF}} = -\dfrac{n}{m}$, $M_{\overline{DF}}\left(\dfrac{m}{2}, \dfrac{n}{2}\right)$; yes; no;

Because $m_{\overline{DE}} = 0$, $\overline{DE}$ is horizontal. Because $m_{\overline{EF}} = $ undefined, $\overline{EF}$ is vertical. So, $\overline{DE} \perp \overline{EF}$ by the Slopes of Perpendicular Lines Theorem (Thm 3.14), and $\angle DEF$ is a right angle by the definition of perpendicular lines. Also, none of the sides have the same length. So, $\triangle DEF$ is a right scalene triangle.

15. $N(h, k)$; $ON = \sqrt{h^2 + k^2}$, $MN = \sqrt{h^2 + k^2}$

16. $O(0, 0)$, $R(k, k)$, $S(k, 2k)$, $T(2k, 2k)$, $U(k, 0)$; $OT = 2k\sqrt{2}$

17. $DC = k$, $BC = k$, $DE = h$, $OB = h$, $EC = \sqrt{h^2 + k^2}$, $OC = \sqrt{h^2 + k^2}$

So, $\overline{DC} \cong \overline{BC}$, $\overline{DE} \cong \overline{OB}$, and $\overline{EC} \cong \overline{OC}$. By the SSS Congruence Theorem (Thm. 5.8), $\triangle DEC \cong \triangle BOC$.

18. Because H is the midpoint of $\overline{DA}$, and G is the midpoint of $\overline{EA}$, the coordinates of points H and G are $H(-h, k)$ and $G(h, k)$. Using these coordinates and the Distance Formula, you obtain $DG = \sqrt{9h^2 + k^2}$, and $EH = \sqrt{9h^2 + k^2}$. So, $\overline{DG} \cong \overline{EH}$.

19.

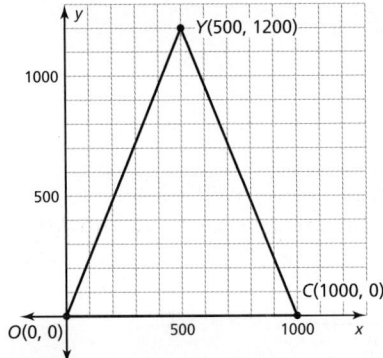

Using the Distance Formula, $OY = 1300$, and $CY = 1300$. Because $\overline{OY} \cong \overline{CY}$, $\triangle OYC$ is isosceles.

20. the friend that said it is a rectangle;

$PQ = 3\sqrt{5}$, $m_{\overline{PQ}} = -2$

$SR = 3\sqrt{5}$, $m_{\overline{SR}} = -2$

$SP = \sqrt{5}$, $m_{\overline{SP}} = \dfrac{1}{2}$

$RQ = \sqrt{5}$, $m_{\overline{RQ}} = \dfrac{1}{2}$

So, $\overline{PQ} \cong \overline{SR}$ and $\overline{SP} \cong \overline{RQ}$, which shows that opposite sides are congruent. Also, $m_{\overline{PQ}} \cdot m_{\overline{SP}} = -1$, $m_{\overline{PQ}} \cdot m_{\overline{RQ}} = -1$, $m_{\overline{SR}} \cdot m_{\overline{SP}} = -1$, and $m_{\overline{SR}} \cdot m_{\overline{RQ}} = -1$. So, $\overline{PQ} \perp \overline{SP}$, $\overline{PQ} \perp \overline{RQ}$, $\overline{SR} \perp \overline{SP}$, and $\overline{SR} \perp \overline{RQ}$ by the Slopes of Perpendicular Lines Theorem (Thm. 3.14). So, by definition of perpendicular lines, $\angle PSR$, $\angle SRQ$, $\angle RQP$, and $\angle QPS$ are right angles. So, the quadrilateral is a rectangle.

21. *Sample answer:* $(-k, -m)$ and (k, m)

24. *Sample answer:* It would be easy to prove the Base Angles Theorem (Thm. 5.6) with a coordinate proof. First, position the given isosceles triangle, $\triangle ABC$, on the coordinate plane so that the base is on the x-axis, and one vertex is at the origin.

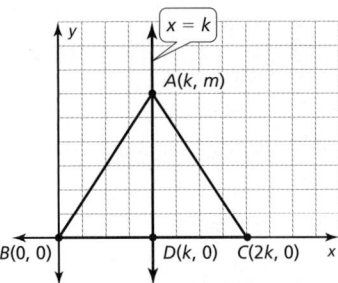

This is an isosceles triangle because $BA = \sqrt{k^2 + m^2}$ and $CA = \sqrt{k^2 + m^2}$. Draw the line $x = k$ that intersects $\triangle ABC$ in point $A(m, k)$ and the x-axis in the point $(k, 0)$. Call this point D. $\overline{BD}$ and $\overline{DC}$ are congruent because $BD = k$ and $DC = k$. $\overline{AD} \cong \overline{AD}$ by the Reflexive Property of Congruence (Thm. 2.1). Because $\overline{AD}$ is vertical and $\overline{BC}$ is horizontal, $\overline{AD} \perp \overline{BC}$ by the Slopes of Perpendicular Lines Theorem (Thm. 3.14). So, $\angle BDA$ and $\angle CDA$ are congruent right angles. By the SAS Congruence Theorem (Thm. 5.5), $\triangle ABD \cong \triangle ACD$. Because corresponding parts of congruent triangles are congruent, $\angle B \cong \angle C$.

25. $(0, 0)$, $(5d, 0)$, $(0, 5d)$

26. Diagonal $\overline{WU}$ is horizontal, and diagonal $\overline{TV}$ is vertical. So, by the Slopes of Perpendicular Lines Theorem (Thm. 3.14), $\overline{WU} \perp \overline{TV}$; Change the coordinates to $T(0, m)$, $U(m, 0)$, $V(0, -m)$, and $W(-m, 0)$. These coordinates can be used for any square, and the diagonals are still horizontal and vertical. So, the diagonals are perpendicular for any square.

27. a.

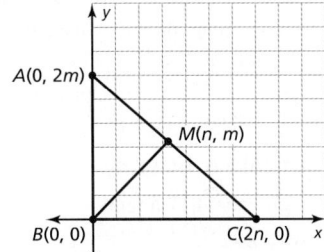

Because M is the midpoint of $\overline{AC}$, the coordinates of M are $M(n, m)$. Using the Distance Formula, $AM = \sqrt{n^2 + m^2}$, $BM = \sqrt{n^2 + m^2}$, and $CM = \sqrt{n^2 + m^2}$. So, the midpoint of the hypotenuse of a right triangle is the same distance from each vertex of the triangle.

b.

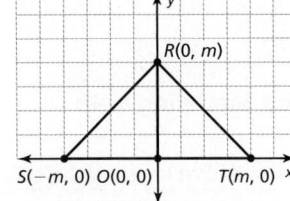

When any two congruent right isosceles triangles are positioned with the vertex opposite the hypotenuse on the origin and their legs on the axes as shown in the diagram, a triangle is formed and the hypotenuses of the original triangles make up two sides of the new triangle. $SR = m\sqrt{2}$ and $TR = m\sqrt{2}$ so these two sides are the same length. So, by definition, $\triangle SRT$ is isosceles.

5.8 Maintaining Mathematical Proficiency

28. $x = 8$

29. $34°$

Chapter 5 Review

9. yes;

STATEMENTS	REASONS
1. $\overline{WX} \cong \overline{YZ}, \overline{WZ} \parallel \overline{YX}$	1. Given
2. $\overline{XZ} \cong \overline{XZ}$	2. Reflexive Property of Congruence (Thm. 2.1)
3. $\angle WXZ \cong \angle YZX$	3. Alternate Interior Angles Theorem (Thm. 3.2)
4. $\triangle WXZ \cong \triangle YZX$	4. SAS Congruence Theorem (Thm. 5.5)

16. yes;

STATEMENTS	REASONS
1. $\overline{WX} \cong \overline{YZ}, \angle XWZ$ and $\angle ZYX$ are right angles.	1. Given
2. $\overline{XZ} \cong \overline{XZ}$	2. Reflexive Property of Congruence (Thm. 2.1)
3. $\triangle WXZ$ and $\triangle YZX$ are right triangles.	3. Definition of a right triangle
4. $\triangle WXZ \cong \triangle YZX$	4. HL Congruence Theorem (Thm. 5.9)

17. yes;

STATEMENTS	REASONS
1. $\angle E \cong \angle H,$ $\angle F \cong \angle J, \overline{FG} \cong \overline{JK}$	1. Given
2. $\triangle EFG \cong \triangle HJK$	2. AAS Congruence Theorem (Thm. 5.11)

19. yes;

STATEMENTS	REASONS
1. $\angle PLN \cong \angle MLN,$ $\angle PNL \cong \angle MNL$	1. Given
2. $\overline{LN} \cong \overline{LN}$	2. Reflexive Property of Congruence (Thm. 2.1)
3. $\triangle LPN \cong \triangle LMN$	3. ASA Congruence Theorem (Thm. 5.10)

Chapter 5 Test

1.

STATEMENTS	REASONS
1. $\overline{CA} \cong \overline{CB} \cong \overline{CD} \cong \overline{CE}$	1. Given
2. $\angle ACB \cong \angle ECD$	2. Vertical Angles Congruence Theorem (Thm. 2.6)
3. $\triangle ABC \cong \triangle EDC$	3. SAS Congruence Theorem (Thm. 5.5)

2.

STATEMENTS	REASONS
1. $\overline{JK} \parallel \overline{ML}, \overline{MJ} \parallel \overline{KL}$	1. Given
2. $\overline{MK} \cong \overline{KM}$	2. Reflexive Property of Congruence (Thm. 2.1)
3. $\angle JKM \cong \angle LMK,$ $\angle JMK \cong \angle LKM$	3. Alternate Interior Angles Theorem (Thm. 3.2)
4. $\triangle MJK \cong \triangle KLM$	4. ASA Congruence Theorem (Thm. 5.10)

3.

STATEMENTS	REASONS
1. $\overline{QR} \cong \overline{RS}, \angle P \cong \angle T$	1. Given
2. $\angle R \cong \angle R$	2. Reflexive Property of Congruence (Thm. 2.2)
3. $\triangle SRP \cong \triangle QRT$	3. AAS Congruence Theorem (Thm. 5.11)

11. a. isosceles

  b. $m\angle 1 = m\angle 2 = 70°$; By the Triangle Sum Theorem (Thm. 5.1), $m\angle 1 + m\angle 2 + m\angle 3 = 180°$. Because $m\angle 3 = 40°, m\angle 1 + m\angle 2 = 140°$. By the Base Angles Theorem (Thm. 5.6), $\angle 1 \cong \angle 2$, so $m\angle 1 = m\angle 2 = 140°/2 = 70°$.

Chapter 6

6.1 Lesson Monitoring Progress

1. 13.75   **2.** 27

3. 7.4

6.1 Monitoring Progress and Modeling with Mathematics

14. 16; $\overrightarrow{EG}$ is an angle bisector of $\angle FEH$, $\overrightarrow{FG} \perp \overrightarrow{EF}$, and $\overrightarrow{GH} \perp \overrightarrow{EH}$. So, by the Converse of the Angle Bisector Theorem (Thm. 6.4), $FG = GH$. This means that $x + 11 = 3x + 1$, and the solution is $x = 5$. So, $FG = x + 11 = 5 + 11 = 16$.

33. a.

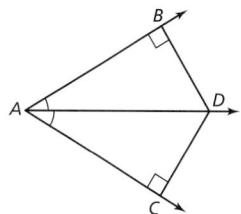

If $\overrightarrow{AD}$ bisects $\angle BAC$, then by definition of angle bisector, $\angle BAD \cong \angle CAD$. Also, because $\overrightarrow{DB} \perp \overrightarrow{AB}$ and $\overrightarrow{DC} \perp \overrightarrow{AC}$, by definition of perpendicular lines, $\angle ABD$ and $\angle ACD$ are right angles, and congruent to each other by the Right Angles Congruence Theorem (Thm. 2.3). Also, $\overline{AD} \cong \overline{AD}$ by the Reflexive Property of Congruence (Thm. 2.1). So, by the AAS Congruence Theorem (Thm. 5.11), $\triangle ADB \cong \triangle ADC$. Because corresponding parts of congruent triangles are congruent, $DB = DC$. This means that point D is equidistant from each side of $\angle BAC$.

b.

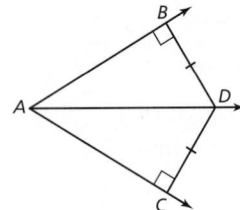

STATEMENTS	REASONS
1. $\overrightarrow{DC} \perp \overleftrightarrow{AC}$, $\overrightarrow{DB} \perp \overrightarrow{AB}$, $BD = CD$	1. Given
2. $\angle ABD$ and $\angle ACD$ are right angles.	2. Definition of perpendicular lines
3. $\triangle ABD$ and $\triangle ACD$ are right triangles.	3. Definition of a right triangle
4. $\overline{BD} \cong \overline{CD}$	4. Definition of congruent segments
5. $\overline{AD} \cong \overline{AD}$	5. Reflexive Property of Congruence (Thm. 2.1)
6. $\triangle ABD \cong \triangle ACD$	6. HL Congruence Theorem (Thm. 5.9)
7. $\angle BAD \cong \angle CAD$	7. Corresponding parts of congruent triangles are congruent.
8. $\overrightarrow{AD}$ bisects $\angle BAC$.	8. Definition of angle bisector

34. a. Roosevelt School; Because the corner of Main and 3rd is exactly 2 blocks of the same length from each hospital, and the two streets are perpendicular, 3rd Street is the perpendicular bisector of the segment that connects the two hospitals. Because Roosevelt school is on 3rd Street, it is the same distance from both hospitals by the Perpendicular Bisector Theorem (Thm. 6.1).

b. no; Because the corner of Maple and 2nd Street is approximately the midpoint of the segment that connects Wilson School to Roosevelt School, and 2nd Street is perpendicular to Maple, 2nd Street is the perpendicular bisector of the segment connecting Wilson and Roosevelt Schools. By the contrapositive of the Converse of the Perpendicular Bisector Theorem (Thm. 6.2), the Museum is not equidistant from the two schools because it is not on 2nd Street.

35. a. $y = x$

b. $y = -x$

c. $y = |x|$

36. no; In spherical geometry, all intersecting lines meet in two points which are equidistant from each other because they are the two endpoints of a diameter of the circle.

37. Because $\overline{AD} \cong \overline{CD}$ and $\overline{AE} \cong \overline{CE}$, by the Converse of the Perpendicular Bisector Theorem (Thm. 6.2), both points D and E are on the perpendicular bisector of $\overline{AC}$. So, $\overleftrightarrow{DE}$ is the perpendicular bisector of $\overline{AC}$. So, if $\overline{AB} \cong \overline{CB}$, then by the Converse of the Perpendicular Bisector Theorem (Thm. 6.2), point B is also on $\overleftrightarrow{DE}$. So, points D, E, and B are collinear. Conversely, if points D, E, and B are collinear, then by the Perpendicular Bisector Theorem (Thm. 6.2), point B is also on the perpendicular bisector of $\overline{AC}$. So, $\overline{AB} \cong \overline{CB}$.

38. a. Because $\overline{YW}$ is on plane P, and plane P is a perpendicular bisector of $\overline{XZ}$ at point Y, $\overline{YW}$ is a perpendicular bisector of $\overline{XZ}$ by definition of a plane perpendicular to a line. So, by the Perpendicular Bisector Theorem (Thm. 6.1), $\overline{XW} \cong \overline{ZW}$.

b. Because $\overline{YV}$ is on plane P, and plane P is a perpendicular bisector of $\overline{XZ}$ at point Y, $\overline{YV}$ is a perpendicular bisector of $\overline{XZ}$ by definition of a plane perpendicular to a line. So, by the Perpendicular Bisector Theorem (Thm. 6.1), $\overline{XV} \cong \overline{ZV}$.

c. First, $\overline{WV} \cong \overline{WV}$ by the Reflexive Property of Congruence (Thm. 2.1). Then, because $\overline{XW} \cong \overline{ZW}$ and $\overline{XV} \cong \overline{ZV}$, $\triangle WVX \cong \triangle WVZ$ by the SSS Congruence Theorem (Thm. 5.8). So, $\angle VXW \cong \angle VZW$ because corresponding parts of congruent triangles are congruent.

6.1 Maintaining Mathematical Proficiency

39. isosceles

40. scalene

41. equilateral

42. acute

43. right

44. obtuse

6.2 Monitoring Progress and Modeling with Mathematics

23. *Sample answer:*

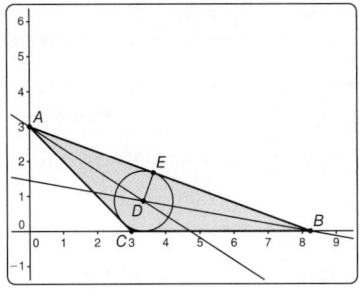

24. *Sample answer:*

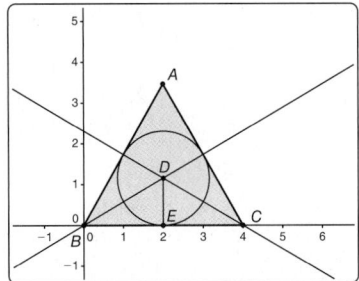

25. Because point G is the intersection of the angle bisectors, it is the incenter. But, because $\overline{GD}$ and $\overline{GF}$ are not necessarily perpendicular to a side of the triangle, there is not sufficient evidence to conclude that $\overline{GD}$ and $\overline{GF}$ are congruent; Point G is equidistant from the sides of the triangle.

26. Because point T is the intersection of the perpendicular bisectors, it is the circumcenter and is equidistant from the vertices of the triangle, not necessarily the sides; $TU = TW = TY$

27. You could copy the positions of the three houses, and connect the points to draw a triangle. Then draw the three perpendicular bisectors of the triangle. The point where the perpendicular bisectors meet, the circumcenter, should be the location of the meeting place.

28. You should place the fountain at the incenter of the pond because the incenter is equidistant from the sides of the triangle.

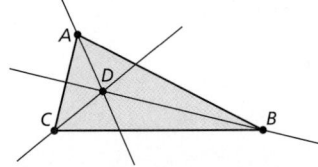

29. sometimes; If the scalene triangle is obtuse or right, then the circumcenter is outside or on the triangle, respectively. However, if the scalene triangle is acute, then the circumcenter is inside the triangle.

30. always; If the perpendicular bisector of one side of a triangle intersects the opposite vertex, then it divides the triangle into two congruent triangles. So, two sides of the original triangle are congruent because corresponding parts of congruent triangles are congruent.

31. sometimes; This only happens when the triangle is equilaterial.

32. always; This is the Incenter Theorem (Thm. 6.6).

42. b. $(7, 7)$

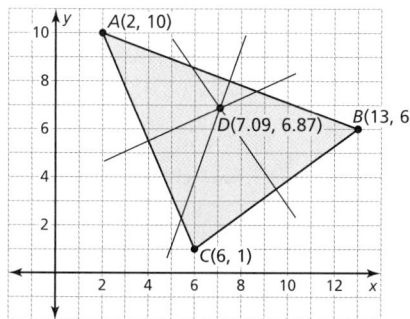

43. B

48. *Sample answer:*

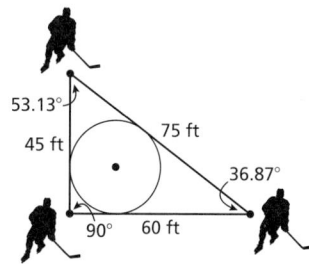

49. angle bisectors; about 2.83 in.

50. perpendicular bisectors; $(10, 10)$; 10

51. $x = \dfrac{AB + AC - BC}{2}$ or $x = \dfrac{AB \cdot AC}{AB + AC + BC}$

6.2 Maintaining Mathematical Proficiency

52. $M(0, 5)$; $AB = 6$

53. $M(6, 3)$; $AB \approx 11.3$

54. $M(-0.5, -2)$; $AB \approx 10.8$

55. $M(-1, 7)$; $AB \approx 12.6$

56. $y = -\frac{1}{2}x + 9$

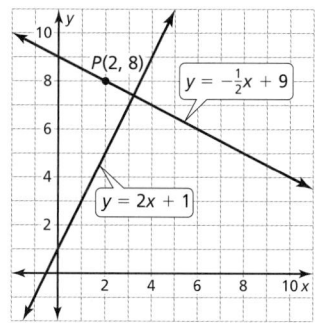

57. $x = 6$

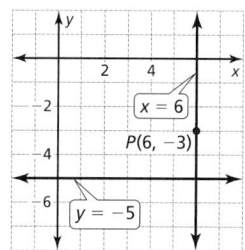

58. $y = \frac{3}{2}x + 6$

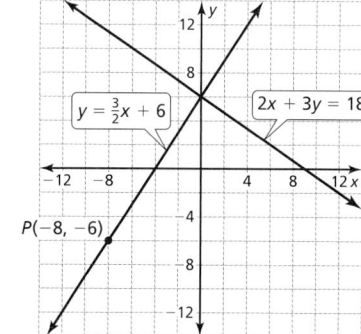

59. $y = \frac{1}{4}x + 2$

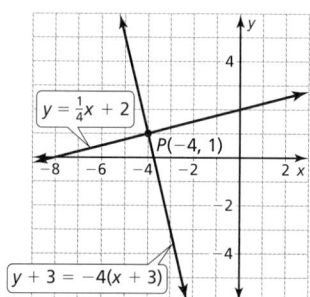

6.3 Monitoring Progress and Modeling with Mathematics

36. always; This is the definition of a centroid.

37. Both segments are perpendicular to a side of a triangle, and their point of intersection can fall either inside, on, or outside of the triangle. However, the altitude does not necessarily bisect the side, but the perpendicular bisector does. Also, the perpendicular bisector does not necessarily pass through the opposite vertex, but the altitude does.

38. All are segments that pass through the vertex of a triangle. A median connects a vertex with the midpoint of the opposite side. An altitude is perpendicular to the opposite side. An angle bisector bisects the angle through which it passes. The medians of a triangle intersect at a single point, and the same is true for the altitudes and angle bisectors of a triangle. Medians and angle bisectors always lie inside the triangle, but altitudes may be inside, on, or outside of the triangle.

39. 6.75 in.^{2}; altitude

40. a. $EJ = 3KJ$

   b. $DK = 2KH$

   c. $FG = \frac{3}{2}FK$

   d. $KG = \frac{1}{3}FG$

41. $x = 2.5$ **42.** $x = 9$

43. $x = 4$ **44.** $x = 3$

45.

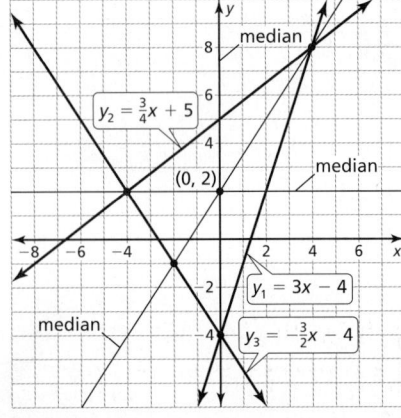

(0, 2)

46. right triangle; The orthocenter of a right triangle is the vertex of the right angle.

51.

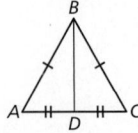

Sides $\overline{AB}$ and $\overline{BC}$ of equilateral $\triangle ABC$ are congruent. $\overline{AD} \cong \overline{CD}$ because $\overline{BD}$ is the median to $\overline{AC}$. Also, $\overline{BD} \cong \overline{BD}$ by the Reflexive Property of Congruence (Thm. 2.1). So, $\triangle ABD \cong \triangle CBD$ by the SSS Congruence Theorem (Thm. 5.8). $\angle ADB \cong \angle CDB$ and $\angle ABD \cong \angle CBD$ because corresponding parts of congruent triangles are congruent. Also, $\angle ADB$ and $\angle CDB$ are a linear pair. Because $\overline{BD}$ and $\overline{AC}$ intersect to form a linear pair of congruent angles, $\overline{BD} \perp \overline{AC}$. So, median $\overline{BD}$ is also an angle bisector, altitude, and perpendicular bisector of $\triangle ABC$.

52. *Sample answer:*

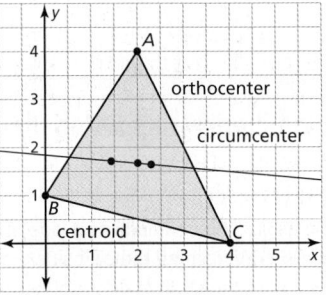

They are collinear.

53. *Sample answer:*

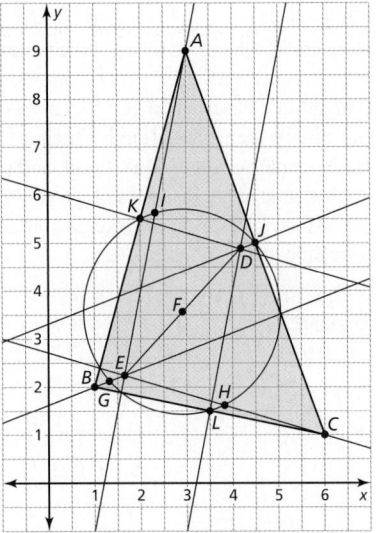

The circle passes through nine significant points of the triangle. They are the midpoints of the sides, the midpoints between each vertex and the orthocenter, and the points of intersection between the sides and the altitudes.

54. a.

STATEMENTS	REASONS
1. $\overline{LP}$ and $\overline{MQ}$ are medians of scalene $\triangle LMN$; $\overline{LP} \cong \overline{PR}$, $\overline{MQ} \cong \overline{QS}$	**1.** Given
2. $\overline{NP} \cong \overline{MP}, \overline{LQ} \cong \overline{NQ}$	**2.** Definition of median
3. $\angle LPM \cong \angle RPN$, $\angle MQL \cong \angle SQN$	**3.** Vertical Angles Congruence Theorem (Thm. 2.6)
4. $\triangle LPM \cong \triangle RPN$, $\triangle MQL \cong \triangle SQN$	**4.** SAS Congruence Theorem (Thm. 5.5)
5. $\overline{NR} \cong \overline{LM}, \overline{NS} \cong \overline{LM}$	**5.** Corresponding parts of congruent triangles are congruent.
6. $\overline{NS} \cong \overline{NR}$	**6.** Transitive Property of Congruence (Thm. 2.1)

b. It was shown in part (a) that $\triangle LPM \cong \triangle RPN$ and $\triangle MQL \cong \triangle SQN$. So, $\angle LMP \cong \angle RNP$ and $\angle MLQ \cong \angle SNQ$ because corresponding parts of congruent triangles are congruent. Then, $\overline{NS} \parallel \overline{LM}$ and $\overline{NR} \parallel \overline{LM}$ by the Alternate Interior Angles Converse (Thm. 3.6).

c. Because $\overline{NS}$ and $\overline{NR}$ are both parallel to the same segment, $\overline{LM}$, they would have to be parallel to each other by the Transitive Property of Parallel Lines (Thm. 3.9). However, because they intersect at point N, they cannot be parallel. So, they must be collinear.

6.3 Maintaining Mathematical Proficiency

55. yes

56. no

57. no

58. yes

6.4 Monitoring Progress and Modeling with Mathematics

22. The midpoint of $\overline{OC}$ is $F(p, 0)$. Because the slopes of $\overline{DF}$ and $\overline{BC}$ are the same $\left(-\dfrac{r}{p-q}\right)$, $\overline{DF} \parallel \overline{BC}$. $DF = \sqrt{p^2 - 2pq + q^2 + r^2}$ and $BC = 2\sqrt{p^2 - 2pq + q^2 + r^2}$. Because $\sqrt{p^2 - 2pq + q^2 + r^2} = \frac{1}{2}\left(2\sqrt{p^2 - 2pq + q^2 + r^2}\right)$, $DF = \frac{1}{2}BC$.

23. An eighth segment, $\overline{FG}$, would connect the midpoints of $\overline{DL}$ and $\overline{EN}$; $\overline{DE} \parallel \overline{LN} \parallel \overline{FG}$, $DE = \frac{3}{4}LN$, and $FG = \frac{7}{8}LN$; Because you are finding quarter segments and eighth segments, use $8p$, $8q$, and $8r$: $L(0, 0)$, $M(8q, 8r)$, and $N(8p, 0)$.

Find the coordinates of X, Y, D, E, F, and G.

$X(4q, 4r)$, $Y(4q + 4p, 4r)$, $D(2q, 2r)$, $E(2q + 6p, 2r)$, $F(q, r)$, and $G(q + 7p, r)$.

The y-coordinates of D and E are the same, so $\overline{DE}$ has a slope of 0. The y-coordinates of F and G are also the same, so $\overline{FG}$ also has a slope of 0. $\overline{LM}$ is on the x-axis, so its slope is 0. Because their slopes are the same, $\overline{DE} \parallel \overline{LM} \parallel \overline{FG}$.

Use the Ruler Postulate (Post. 1.1) to find DE, FG, and LM.

$DE = 6p$, $FG = 7p$, and $LN = 8p$.

Because $6p = \frac{3}{4}(8p)$, $DE = \frac{3}{4}LN$. Because $7p = \frac{7}{8}(8p)$, $FG = \frac{7}{8}LN$.

24. *Sample answer:*

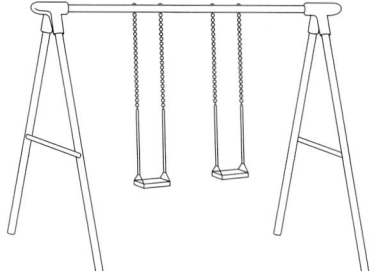

The crossbars on the ends of the swing set are midsegments.

25. a. 24 units

   b. 60 units

   c. 114 units

26. Two sides of the red triangle have a length of 4 tile widths. A yellow segment connects the midpoints, where there are two tile lengths on either side. The third red side has a length of 4 tile diagonals, and the other two yellow segments meet at the midpoint, where there are two tile diagonals on either side.

27. After graphing the midsegments, find the slope of each segment. Graph the line parallel to each midsegment passing through the opposite vertex. The intersections of these three lines will be the vertices of the original triangle: $(-1, 2)$, $(9, 8)$, and $(5, 0)$.

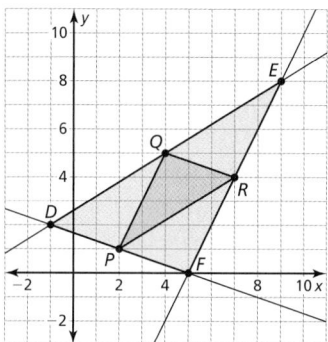

6.4 Maintaining Mathematical Proficiency

28. *Sample answer:* $-2 - (-7) = 5$, and $5 > -2$

29. *Sample answer:* An isosceles triangle whose sides are 5 centimeters, 5 centimeters, and 3 centimeters is not equilateral.

6.5 Explorations

1. c. *Sample answer:*

A(x, y)	B(x, y)	C(x, y)	AB	AC	BC
A(5, 1)	B(7, 4)	C(2, 4)	3.61	4.24	5
A(2, 4)	B(4, −2)	C(7, 6)	6.32	5.39	8.54
A(1, 0)	B(7, 0)	C(1, 7)	6	7	9.22

m∠A	m∠B	m∠C
78.69°	56.31°	45°
93.37°	38.99°	47.64°
90°	49.4°	40.6°

If one side of a triangle is longer than another side, then the angle opposite the longer side is larger than the angle opposite the shorter side. Similarly, if one angle of a triangle is larger than another angle, then the side opposite the larger angle is longer than the side opposite the smaller angle.

2. c. *Sample answer:*

A(x, y)	B(x, y)	C(x, y)	AB	AC + BC	AC
A(5, 1)	B(7, 4)	C(2, 4)	3.61	9.24	4.24
A(2, 4)	B(4, −2)	C(7, 6)	6.32	13.93	5.39
A(1, 0)	B(7, 0)	C(1, 7)	6	16.22	7
A(1, 0)	B(7, 0)	C(5, 1)	6	6.36	4.12

AB + BC	BC	AB + AC
8.61	5	7.85
14.86	8.54	11.71
15.22	9.22	13
8.24	2.24	10.12

The length of each side is less than the sum of the other two.

6.5 Monitoring Progress and Modeling with Mathematics

35. b. You could measure from distances that are closer together. In order to do this, you would have to use angle measures that are closer to 45°.

36. a. $x > 76$ km, $x < 1054$ km

   b. Because ∠2 is the smallest angle, the distance between Granite Peak and Fort Peck Lake must be the shortest side of the triangle. So, the second inequality becomes $x < 489$ kilometers.

37. ∠WXY, ∠Z, ∠YXZ, ∠WYX and ∠XYZ, ∠W; In △WXY, because $WY < WX < YX$, by the Triangle Longer Side Theorem (Thm. 6.9), $m∠WXY < m∠WYX < m∠W$. Similarly, in △XYZ, because $XY < YZ < XZ$, by the Triangle Longer Side Theorem (Thm. 6.9), $m∠Z < m∠YXZ < m∠XYZ$. Because $m∠WYX = m∠XYZ$ and ∠W is the only angle greater than either of them, you know that ∠W is the largest angle. Because △WXY has the largest angle and one of the congruent angles, the remaining angle, ∠WXY, is the smallest.

38. $EF < DF < DE$, $m∠D < m∠E < m∠F$

42. The shortest route is along Washington Avenue. By the Triangle Inequality Theorem (Thm. 6.11), the length of Washington Avenue must be shorter than the sum of the lengths of Eighth Street and View Street, as well as the sum of the lengths of Hill Street and Seventh Street.

43. It is given that $BC > AB$ and $BD = BA$. By the Base Angles Theorem (Thm. 5.6), $m∠1 = m∠2$. By the Angle Addition Postulate (Post. 1.4), $m∠BAC = m∠1 + m∠3$. So, $m∠BAC > m∠1$. Substituting $m∠2$ for $m∠1$ produces $m∠BAC > m∠2$. By the Exterior Angle Theorem (Thm. 5.2), $m∠2 = m∠3 + m∠C$. So, $m∠2 > m∠C$. Finally, because $m∠BAC > m∠2$ and $m∠2 > m∠C$, you can conclude that $m∠BAC > m∠C$.

44. Because the sum of the lengths of the legs must be greater than the length of the base, the length of a leg must be greater than $\frac{1}{2}\ell$.

45. no; The sum of the other two sides would be 11 inches, which is less than 13 inches.

46. *Sample answer:*

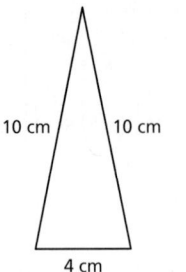

10 cm   10 cm

4 cm

acute

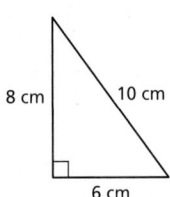

8 cm   10 cm

6 cm

right

47.

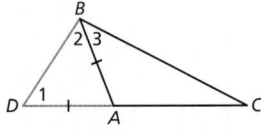

Assume $\overline{BC}$ is longer than or the same length as each of the other sides, $\overline{AB}$ and $\overline{AC}$. Then, $AB + BC > AC$ and $AC + BC > AB$. The proof for $AB + AC > BC$ follows.

STATEMENTS	REASONS
1. $\triangle ABC$	1. Given
2. Extend $\overline{AC}$ to D so that $\overline{AB} \cong \overline{AD}$.	2. Ruler Postulate (Post. 1.1)
3. $AB = AD$	3. Definition of segment congruence
4. $AD + AC = DC$	4. Segment Addition Postulate (Post. 1.2)
5. $\angle 1 \cong \angle 2$	5. Base Angles Theorem (Thm. 5.6)
6. $m\angle 1 = m\angle 2$	6. Definition of angle congruence
7. $m\angle DBC > m\angle 2$	7. Protractor Postulate (Post. 1.3)
8. $m\angle DBC > m\angle 1$	8. Substitution Property
9. $DC > BC$	9. Triangle Larger Angle Theorem (Thm. 6.10)
10. $AD + AC > BC$	10. Substitution Property
11. $AB + AC > BC$	11. Substitution Property

48. The perimeter of $\triangle HGF$ must be greater than 4 and less than 24; Because of the Triangle Inequality Theorem (Thm. 6.11), FG must be greater than 2 and less than 8, GH must be greater than 1 and less than 7, and FH must be greater than 1 and less than 9. So, the perimeter must be greater than $2 + 1 + 1 = 4$ and less than $8 + 7 + 9 = 24$.

49. Assume temporarily that another segment, $\overline{PA}$, where A is on plane M, is the shortest segment from P to plane M. By definition of the distance between a point and a plane, $\overline{PA} \perp$ plane M. This contradicts the given statement because there cannot be two different segments that share an endpoint and are both perpendicular to the same plane. So, the assumption is false, and because no other segment exists that is the shortest segment from P to plane M, it must be $\overline{PC}$ that is the shortest segment from P to plane M.

6.5 Maintaining Mathematical Proficiency

50. $\angle AEB$ **51.** $\angle ACD$

52. $\angle ADC$ **53.** $\angle CEB$

6.6 Explorations

1. f. *Sample answer:*

D	AC	BC	AB	BD	$m\angle ACB$	$m\angle BCD$
1. (4.75, 2.03)	2	3	3.61	2.68	90°	61.13°
2. (4.94, 2.5)	2	3	3.61	3.16	90°	75.6°
3. (5, 3)	2	3	3.61	3.61	90°	90°
4. (4.94, 3.5)	2	3	3.61	4	90°	104.45°
5. (3.85, 4.81)	2	3	3.61	4.89	90°	154.93°

6.6 Monitoring Progress and Modeling with Mathematics

18. The angle bisector of $\angle FEG$ will also pass through incenter H. Then, $m\angle HEG + m\angle HFG + m\angle HGF = \dfrac{180°}{2} = 90°$, because they are each half of the measure of an angle of a triangle. By subtracting $m\angle HEG$ from each side, you can conclude that $m\angle HFG + m\angle HGF < 90°$. Also, $m\angle FHG + m\angle HFG + m\angle HGF = 180°$ by the Triangle Sum Theorem (Thm. 5.1). So, $m\angle FHG > 90°$, which means that $m\angle FHG > m\angle HFG$ and $m\angle FHG > m\angle HGF$. So, $FG > FH$ and $FG > HG$.

19. Because $\overline{NR}$ is a median, $\overline{PR} \cong \overline{QR}$. $\overline{NR} \cong \overline{NR}$ by the Reflexive Property of Congruence (Thm. 2.1). So, by the Converse of the Hinge Theorem (Thm. 6.13), $\angle NRQ > \angle NRP$. Because $\angle NRQ$ and $\angle NRP$ form a linear pair, they are supplementary. So, $\angle NRQ$ must be obtuse and $\angle NRP$ must be acute.

20. $x > \dfrac{1}{2}$ **21.** $x > \dfrac{3}{2}$

22. $m\angle ACB < m\angle ACD$

23. $\triangle ABC$ is an obtuse triangle; If the altitudes intersect inside the triangle, then $m\angle BAC$ will always be less than $m\angle BDC$ because they both intercept the same segment, $\overline{CD}$. However, because $m\angle BAC > m\angle BDC$, $\angle A$ must be obtuse, and the altitudes must intersect outside of the triangle.

24. The sum of the measures of the angles of a triangle in spherical geometry must be greater than 180°; The area of spherical $\triangle ABC = \dfrac{\pi r^2}{180°}(m\angle A + m\angle B + m\angle C - 180°)$, where r is the radius of the sphere.

Chapter 6 Test

14. 9 mi; Because the path represents the shortest distance from the beach to Main Street, it must be perpendicular to Main Street, and you ended up at the midpoint between your house and the movie theater. So, the trail must be the perpendicular bisector of the portion of Main Street between your house and the movie theater. By the Perpendicular Bisector Theorem (Thm. 6.1), the beach must be the same distance from your house and the movie theater. So, Pine Avenue is the same length as the 9-mile portion of Hill Street between your house and the beach.

15.

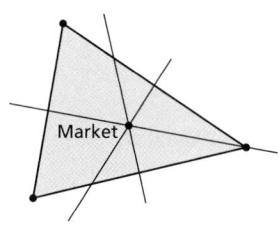

Chapter 6 Standards Assessment

2.

STATEMENTS	REASONS
1. $\overline{YG}$ is the perpendicular bisector of $\overline{DF}$.	1. Given
2. $\overline{DE} \cong \overline{FE}$, $\overline{YG} \perp \overline{DF}$	2. Definition of pependicular bisector
3. $\angle DEY$ and $\angle FEY$ are right angles.	3. Definition of perpendicular lines
4. $\angle DEY \cong \angle FEY$	4. Right Angles Congruence Theorem (Thm. 2.3)
5. $\overline{YE} \cong \overline{YE}$	5. Reflexive Property of Congruence (Thm. 2.1)
6. $\triangle DEY \cong \triangle FEY$	6. SAS Congruence Theorem (Thm. 5.5)

Chapter 7

Mathematical Practices

6.

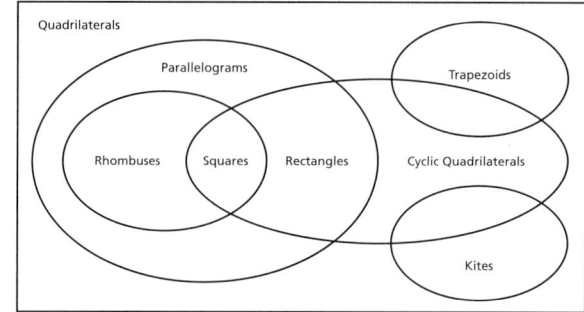

7.1 Monitoring Progress and Modeling with Mathematics

47. $(n - 2) \cdot 180°$; When diagonals are drawn from the vertex of the concave angle as shown, the polygon is divided into $n - 2$ triangles whose interior angle measures have the same total as the sum of the interior angle measures of the original polygon.

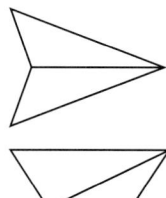
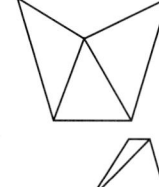
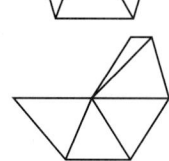

48. 90°; The base angles of $\triangle BPC$ are congruent exterior angles of the regular octagon, each with a measure of 45°. So, $m\angle BPC = 180° - 2(45°) = 90°$.

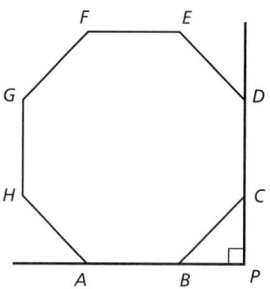

49. a. $h(n) = \dfrac{(n - 2) \cdot 180°}{n}$

   b. $h(9) = 140°$

   c. $n = 12$

   d.

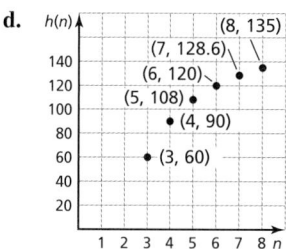

The value of $h(n)$ increases on a curve that gets less steep as n increases.

50. no; The interior angles are supplements of the adjacent exterior angles, and because the exterior angles have different values, the supplements will be different as well.

51. In a convex n-gon, the sum of the measures of the n interior angles is $(n - 2) \cdot 180°$ using the Polygon Interior Angles Theorem (Thm. 7.1). Because each of the n interior angles forms a linear pair with its corresponding exterior angle, you know that the sum of the measures of the n interior and exterior angles is $180n°$. Subtracting the sum of the interior angle measures from the sum of the measures of the linear pairs gives you $180n° - [(n - 2) \cdot 180°] = 360°$.

52. 3; In order to have $\dfrac{540°}{180°} = 3$ more triangles formed by the diagonals, the new polygon will need 3 more sides.

7.1 Maintaining Mathematical Proficiency

53. $x = 101$ **54.** $x = 67$

55. $x = 16$ **56.** $x = 21$

7.2 Lesson Monitoring Progress

4.

STATEMENTS	REASONS
1. *ABCD* and *GDEF* are parallelograms.	1. Given
2. ∠*C* and ∠*D* are supplementary angles.	2. Parallelogram Consecutive Angles Theorem (Thm. 7.5)
3. $m\angle C + m\angle D = 180°$	3. Definition of supplementary angles
4. ∠*D* ≅ ∠*F*	4. Parallelogram Opposite Angles Theorem (Thm. 7.4)
5. $m\angle D = m\angle F$	5. Definition of congruent angles
6. $m\angle C + m\angle F = 180°$	6. Substitution Property of Equality
7. ∠*C* and ∠*F* are supplementary angles.	7. Definition of supplementary angles

7.2 Monitoring Progress and Modeling with Mathematics

23.

STATEMENTS	REASONS
1. *ABCD* and *CEFD* are parallelograms.	1. Given
2. $\overline{AB} \cong \overline{DC}, \overline{DC} \cong \overline{FE}$	2. Parallelogram Opposite Sides Theorem (Thm. 7.3)
3. $\overline{AB} \cong \overline{FE}$	3. Transitive Property of Congruence (Thm. 2.1)

24.

STATEMENTS	REASONS
1. *ABCD*, *EBGF*, and *HJKD* are parallelograms.	1. Given
2. ∠1 ≅ ∠2, ∠3 ≅ ∠4, ∠1 ≅ ∠4	2. Parallelogram Opposite Angles Theorem (Thm. 7.4)
3. ∠2 ≅ ∠4	3. Transitive Property of Congruence (Thm. 2.2)
4. ∠2 ≅ ∠3	4. Transitive Property of Congruence (Thm. 2.2)

36. *Sample answer:*

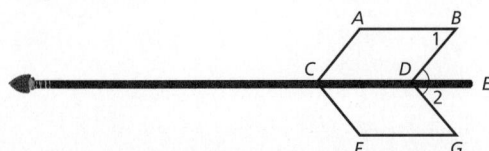

$m\angle 1 = m\angle G$ because corresponding parts of congruent figures are congruent. Note that $\overleftrightarrow{AB} \parallel \overleftrightarrow{CD} \parallel \overleftrightarrow{FG}$. So, $m\angle 1 = m\angle BDE$ and $m\angle GDE = m\angle G$ because they are pairs of alternate interior angles, and $m\angle 1 = m\angle GDE$ by the Transitive Property of Equality. Also, by the Angle Addition Postulate (Post. 1.4), $m\angle 2 = m\angle BDE + m\angle GDE$. By substituting, you get $m\angle 2 = m\angle 1 + m\angle 1 = 2m\angle 1$.

37.

STATEMENTS	REASONS
1. *ABCD* is a parallelogram.	1. Given
2. $\overline{AB} \parallel \overline{DC}, \overline{BC} \parallel \overline{AD}$	2. Definition of parallelogram
3. ∠*BDA* ≅ ∠*DBC*, ∠*DBA* ≅ ∠*BDC*	3. Alternate Interior Angles Theorem (Thm. 3.2)
4. $\overline{BD} \cong \overline{BD}$	4. Reflexive Property of Congruence (Thm. 2.1)
5. △*ABD* ≅ △*CDB*	5. ASA Congruence Theorem (Thm. 5.10)
6. ∠*A* ≅ ∠*C*, ∠*B* ≅ ∠*D*	6. Corresponding parts of congruent triangles are congruent.

38.

STATEMENTS	REASONS
1. *PQRS* is a parallelogram.	1. Given
2. $\overline{QR} \parallel \overline{PS}$	2. Definition of parallelogram
3. ∠*Q* and ∠*P* are supplementary.	3. Consecutive Interior Angles Theorem (Thm. 3.4)
4. $x° + y° = 180°$	4. Definition of supplementary angles

39.

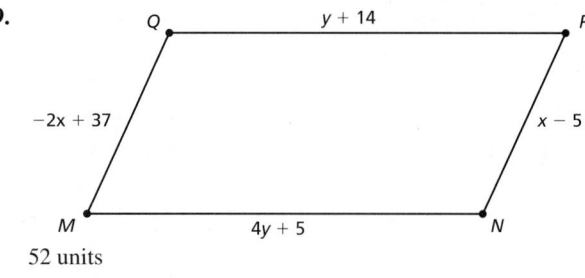

52 units

44. yes;

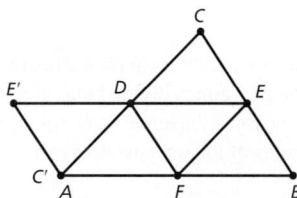

Any triangle, such as △*ABC*, can be partitioned into four congruent triangles by drawing the midsegment triangle, such as △*DEF*. Then, one triangle, such as △*CDE*, can be rotated 180° about a vertex, such as *D*, to create a parallelogram as shown.

45. 3; (4, 0), (−2, 4), (8, 8)

46.

STATEMENTS	REASONS
1. $\overline{EK}$ bisects $\angle FEH$ and $\overline{FJ}$ bisects $\angle EFG$. $EFGH$ is a parallelogram.	1. Given
2. $m\angle PEH = m\angle PEF$, $m\angle PFE = m\angle PFG$	2. Definition of angle bisector
3. $m\angle HEF = m\angle PEH + m\angle PEF$, $m\angle EFG = m\angle PFE + m\angle PFG$	3. Angle Addition Postulate (Post. 1.4)
4. $m\angle HEF = m\angle PEF + m\angle PEF$, $m\angle EFG = m\angle PFE + m\angle PFE$	4. Substitution Property of Equality
5. $m\angle HEF = 2(m\angle PEF)$, $m\angle EFG = 2(m\angle PFE)$	5. Distributive Property
6. $m\angle HEF + m\angle EFG = 180°$	6. Parallelogram Consecutive Angles Theorem (Thm 7.5)
7. $2(m\angle PEF) + 2(m\angle PFE) = 180°$	7. Substitution Property of Equality
8. $2(m\angle PEF + m\angle PFE) = 180°$	8. Distributive Property
9. $m\angle PEF + m\angle PFE = 90°$	9. Division Property of Equality
10. $m\angle PEF + m\angle PFE + m\angle EPF = 180°$	10. Triangle Sum Theorem (Thm. 5.1)
11. $90° + m\angle EPF = 180°$	11. Substitution Property of Equality
12. $m\angle EPF = 90°$	12. Subtraction Property of Equality
13. $\angle EPF$ is a right angle.	13. Definition of right angle
14. $\overline{EK} \perp \overline{FJ}$	14. Definition of perpendicular lines

47.

STATEMENTS	REASONS
1. $\overleftrightarrow{GH} \parallel \overrightarrow{JK} \parallel \overleftrightarrow{LM}$, $\overline{GJ} \cong \overline{JL}$	1. Given
2. Construct $\overline{PK}$ and $\overline{QM}$ such that $\overleftrightarrow{PK} \parallel \overleftrightarrow{GL} \parallel \overleftrightarrow{QM}$.	2. Construction
3. $GPKJ$ and $JQML$ are parallelograms.	3. Definition of parallelogram
4. $\angle GHK \cong \angle JKM$, $\angle PKQ \cong \angle QML$	4. Corresponding Angles Theorem (Thm. 3.1)
5. $\overline{GJ} \cong \overline{PK}$, $\overline{JL} \cong \overline{QM}$	5. Parallelogram Opposite Sides Theorem (Thm. 7.3)
6. $\overline{PK} \cong \overline{QM}$	6. Transitive Property of Congruence (Thm. 2.1)
7. $\angle HPK \cong \angle PKQ$, $\angle KQM \cong \angle QML$	7. Alternate Interior Angles Theorem (Thm. 3.2)
8. $\angle HPK \cong \angle QML$	8. Transitive Property of Congruence (Thm. 2.2)
9. $\angle HPK \cong \angle KQM$	9. Transitive Property of Congruence (Thm. 2.2)
10. $\triangle PHK \cong \triangle QKM$	10. AAS Congruence Theorem (Thm. 5.11)
11. $\overline{HK} \cong \overline{KM}$	11. Corresponding sides of congruent triangles are congruent.

7.2 Maintaining Mathematical Proficiency

48. yes; Alternate Interior Angles Converse (Thm. 3.6)

49. yes; Alternate Exterior Angles Converse (Thm. 3.7)

50. no; By the Consecutive Interior Angles Converse (Thm. 3.8), consecutive interior angles need to be supplementary for the lines to be parallel, and the consecutive interior angles are not supplementary.

7.3 Monitoring Progress and Modeling with Mathematics

18.

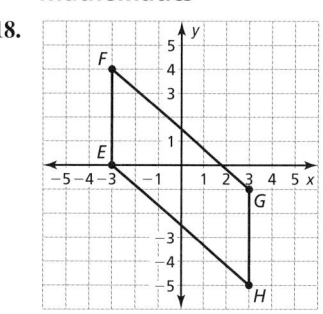

Because $EF = GH = 4$, $\overline{EF} \cong \overline{GH}$. Because both $\overline{EF}$ and $\overline{GH}$ are vertical lines with undefined slope, they are parallel. $\overline{EF}$ and $\overline{GH}$ are opposite sides that are both congruent and parallel. So, $EFGH$ is a parallelogram by the Opposite Sides Parallel and Congruent Theorem (Thm. 7.9).

19.

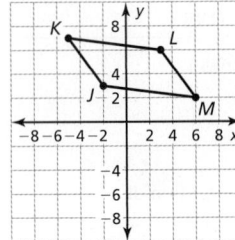

Because $JK = LM = 5$ and $KL = JM = \sqrt{65}$, $\overline{JK} \cong \overline{LM}$ and $\overline{KL} \cong \overline{JM}$. Because both pairs of opposite sides are congruent, quadrilateral *JKLM* is a parallelogram by the Parallelogram Opposite Sides Converse (Thm. 7.7).

20.

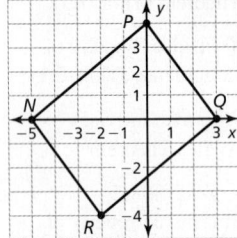

Because the slopes of $\overline{NP}$ and $\overline{QR}$ are both $\frac{4}{5}$, they are parallel. Because the slopes of $\overline{PQ}$ and $\overline{NR}$ are both $-\frac{4}{3}$, they are parallel. Because both pairs of opposite sides are parallel, *NPQR* is a parallelogram by definition.

39.

STATEMENTS	REASONS
1. $\angle A \cong \angle C$, $\angle B \cong \angle D$	**1.** Given
2. Let $m\angle A = m\angle C = x°$ and $m\angle B = m\angle D = y°$	**2.** Definition of congruent angles
3. $m\angle A + m\angle B + m\angle C + m\angle D = x° + y° + x° + y° = 360°$	**3.** Corollary to the Polygon Interior Angles Theorem (Cor. 7.1)
4. $2(x°) + 2(y°) = 360°$	**4.** Simplify
5. $2(x° + y°) = 360°$	**5.** Distributive Property
6. $x° + y° = 180°$	**6.** Division Property of Equality
7. $m\angle A + m\angle B = 180°$, $m\angle A + m\angle D = 180°$	**7.** Substitution Property of Equality
8. $\angle A$ and $\angle B$ are supplementary. $\angle A$ and $\angle D$ are supplementary.	**8.** Definition of supplementary angles
9. $\overline{BC} \parallel \overline{AD}$, $\overline{AB} \parallel \overline{DC}$	**9.** Consecutive Interior Angles Converse (Thm. 3.8)
10. *ABCD* is a parallelogram.	**10.** Definition of parallelogram

40.

STATEMENTS	REASONS
1. $\overline{QR} \parallel \overline{PS}$, $\overline{QR} \cong \overline{PS}$	**1.** Given
2. $\angle SQR \cong \angle QSP$	**2.** Alternate Interior Angles Theorem (Thm. 3.2)
3. $\overline{QS} \cong \overline{QS}$	**3.** Reflexive Property of Congruence (Thm. 2.1)
4. $\triangle QRS \cong \triangle SPQ$	**4.** SAS Congruence Theorem (Thm. 5.5)
5. $\angle QSR \cong \angle SQP$	**5.** Corresponding parts of congruent triangles are congruent.
6. $\overline{QP} \parallel \overline{RS}$	**6.** Alternate Interior Angles Converse (Thm. 3.6)
7. *PQRS* is a parallelogram.	**7.** Definition of parallelogram

41.

STATEMENTS	REASONS
1. Diagonals $\overline{JL}$ and $\overline{KM}$ bisect each other.	**1.** Given
2. $\overline{KP} \cong \overline{MP}$, $\overline{JP} \cong \overline{LP}$	**2.** Definition of segment bisector
3. $\angle KPL \cong \angle MPJ$	**3.** Reflexive Property of Congruence (Thm. 2.2)
4. $\triangle KPL \cong \triangle MPJ$	**4.** SAS Congruence Theorem (Thm. 5.5)
5. $\angle MKL \cong \angle KMJ$, $\overline{KL} \cong \overline{MJ}$	**5.** Corresponding parts of congruent triangles are congruent.
6. $\overline{KL} \parallel \overline{MJ}$	**6.** Alternate Interior Angles Converse (Thm. 3.6)
7. *JKLM* is a parallelogram.	**7.** Opposite Sides Parallel and Congruent Theorem (Thm. 7.9)

42.

STATEMENTS	REASONS
1. *DEBF* is a parallelogram, $AE = CF$	1. Given
2. $\overline{DE} \cong \overline{BF}, \overline{FD} \cong \overline{EB}$	2. Parallelogram Opposite Sides Theorem (Thm. 7.3)
3. $\angle DFB \cong \angle DEB$	3. Parallelogram Opposite Angles Theorem (Thm. 7.4)
4. $\angle AED$ and $\angle DEB$ form a linear pair. $\angle CFB$ and $\angle DFB$ form a linear pair.	4. Definition of linear pair
5. $\angle AED$ and $\angle DEB$ are supplementary. $\angle CFB$ and $\angle DFB$ are supplementary.	5. Linear Pair Postulate (Post. 2.8)
6. $\angle AED \cong \angle CFB$	6. Congruent Supplements Theorem (Thm. 2.4)
7. $\overline{AE} \cong \overline{CF}$	7. Definition of congruent segments
8. $\triangle AED \cong \triangle CFB$	8. SAS Congruence Theorem (Thm. 5.5)
9. $\overline{AD} \cong \overline{CB}$	9. Corresponding parts of congruent triangles are congruent.
10. $AB = AE + EB$, $DC = CF + FD$	10. Segment Addition Postulate (Post. 1.2)
11. $FD = EB$	11. Definition of congruent segments
12. $AB = CF + FD$	12. Substitution Property of Equality
13. $AB = DC$	13. Transitive Property of Equality
14. $\overline{AB} \cong \overline{DC}$	14. Definition of congruent segments
15. *ABCD* is a parallelogram.	15. Parallelogram Opposite Sides Converse (Thm. 7.7)

45. 8; By the Parallelogram Opposite Sides Theorem (Thm. 7.3), $\overline{AB} \cong \overline{CD}$. Also, $\angle ABE$ and $\angle CDF$ are congruent alternate interior angles of parallel segments $\overline{AB}$ and $\overline{CD}$. Then, you can use the Segment Addition Postulate (Post. 1.2), the Substitution Property of Equality, and the Reflexive Property of Congruence (Thm. 2.1) to show that $\overline{DF} \cong \overline{BE}$. So, $\triangle ABE \cong \triangle CDF$ by the SAS Congruence Theorem (Thm. 5.5), which means that $AE = CF = 8$ because corresponding parts of congruent triangles are congruent.

46. *Sample answer:*

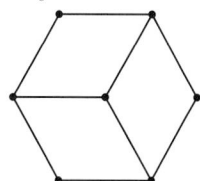

47. If every pair of consecutive angles of a quadrilateral is supplementary, then the quadrilateral is a parallelogram; In *ABCD*, you are given that $\angle A$ and $\angle B$ are supplementary, and $\angle B$ and $\angle C$ are supplementary. So, $m\angle A = m\angle C$. Also, $\angle B$ and $\angle C$ are supplementary, and $\angle C$ and $\angle D$ are supplementary. So, $m\angle B = m\angle D$. So, *ABCD* is a parallelogram by the Parallelogram Opposite Angles Converse (Thm. 7.8).

48. By the definition of a right angle, $m\angle A = 90°$. Because *ABCD* is a parallelogram, and opposite angles of a parallelogram are congruent, $m\angle A = m\angle C = 90°$. Because consecutive angles of a parallelogram are supplementary, $\angle C$ and $\angle B$ are supplementary, and $\angle C$ and $\angle D$ are supplementary. So, $90° + m\angle B = 180°$ and $90° + m\angle D = 180°$. This gives you $m\angle B = m\angle D = 90°$. So, $\angle B$, $\angle C$, and $\angle D$ are right angles.

49. Given quadrilateral *ABCD* with midpoints *E*, *F*, *G*, and *H* that are joined to form a quadrilateral, you can construct diagonal $\overline{BD}$. Then $\overline{FG}$ is a midsegment of $\triangle BCD$, and $\overline{EH}$ is a midsegment of $\triangle DAB$. So, by the Triangle Midsegment Theorem (Thm. 6.8), $\overline{FG} \parallel \overline{BD}$, $FG = \frac{1}{2}BD$, $\overline{EH} \parallel \overline{BD}$, and $EH = \frac{1}{2}BD$. So, by the Transitive Property of Parallel Lines (Thm. 3.9), $\overline{EH} \parallel \overline{FG}$ and by the Transitive Property of Equality, $EH = FG$. Because one pair of opposite sides is both congruent and parallel, *EFGH* is a parallelogram by the Opposite Sides Parallel and Congruent Theorem (Thm. 7.9).

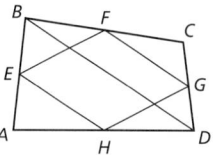

50. Based on the given information, $\overline{GH}$ is a midsegment of $\triangle EBC$, and $\overline{FJ}$ is a midsegment of $\triangle EAD$. So, by the Triangle Midsegment Theorem (Thm. 6.8), $\overline{GH} \parallel \overline{BC}$, $GH = \frac{1}{2}BC$, $\overline{FJ} \parallel \overline{AD}$, and $FJ = \frac{1}{2}AD$. Also, by the Parallelogram Opposite Sides Theorem (Thm. 7.3) and the definition of a parallelogram, $\overline{BC}$ and $\overline{AD}$ are congruent and parallel. So, by the Transitive Property of Parallel Lines (Thm. 3.9), $\overline{AD} \parallel \overline{FJ} \parallel \overline{GH} \parallel \overline{BC}$ and by the Transitive Property of Equality, $\frac{1}{2}BC = GH = FJ = \frac{1}{2}AD$. Because one pair of opposite sides is both congruent and parallel, *FGHJ* is a parallelogram by the Opposite Sides Parallel and Congruent Theorem (Thm. 7.9).

7.3 Maintaining Mathematical Proficiency

51. parallelogram

52. rectangle

53. square

54. rhombus

7.1–7.3 Quiz

22. **a.** $\overline{JK} \cong \overline{ML}$ by the Parallelogram Opposite Sides Theorem (Thm. 7.3), $\overline{JM} \cong \overline{KL}$ by the Parallelogram Opposite Sides Theorem (Thm. 7.3), $\angle J \cong \angle KLM$ by the Parallelogram Opposite Angles Theorem (Thm. 7.4), $\angle M \cong \angle JKL$ by the Parallelogram Opposite Angles Theorem (Thm. 7.4)

b. Opposite Sides Parallel and Congruent Theorem (Thm. 7.9)

c. 3 ft, 123°, 57°, 57°; $ST = QR$ by the Parallelogram Opposite Sides Theorem (Thm. 7.3), $m\angle QTS = m\angle QRS$ by the Parallelogram Opposite Angles Theorem (Thm. 7.4), $m\angle TQR = m\angle TSR = 180° - 123°$ by the Parallelogram Consecutive Angles Theorem (Thm. 7.5)

7.4 Monitoring Progress and Modeling with Mathematics

17. always; All angles of a rectangle are congruent.

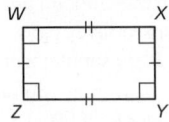

18. always; Opposite sides are congruent.

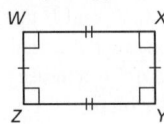

19. sometimes; Some rectangles are squares.

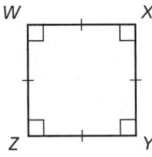

20. always; The diagonals of a rectangle are congruent.

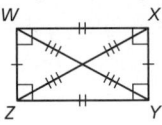

21. sometimes; Some rectangles are squares.

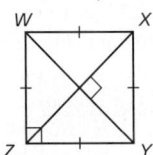

22. sometimes; Some rectangles are squares.

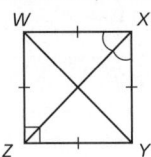

23. no; All four angles are not congruent.

24. yes; Opposite sides are congruent and the angles are 90°.

25. 11   **26.** 66

27. 4   **28.** 8.4

73.

STATEMENTS	REASONS
1. $PQRS$ is a parallelogram. $\overline{PR}$ bisects $\angle SPQ$ and $\angle QRS$. $\overline{SQ}$ bisects $\angle PSR$ and $\angle RQP$.	1. Given
2. $\angle SRT \cong \angle QRT$, $\angle RQT \cong \angle RST$	2. Definition of angle bisector
3. $\overline{TR} \cong \overline{TR}$	3. Reflexive Property of Congruence (Thm. 2.1)
4. $\triangle QRT \cong \triangle SRT$	4. AAS Congruence Theorem (Thm. 5.11)
5. $\overline{QR} \cong \overline{SR}$	5. Corresponding parts of congruent triangles are congruent.
6. $\overline{QR} \cong \overline{PS}$, $\overline{PQ} \cong \overline{SR}$	6. Parallelogram Opposite Sides Theorem (Thm. 7.3)
7. $\overline{PS} \cong \overline{QR} \cong \overline{SR} \cong \overline{PQ}$	7. Transitive Property of Congruence (Thm. 2.1)
8. $PQRS$ is a rhombus.	8. Definition of rhombus

74.

STATEMENTS	REASONS
1. $WXYZ$ is a rhombus.	1. Given
2. $\overline{WX} \cong \overline{XY} \cong \overline{YZ} \cong \overline{WZ}$	2. Definition of a rhombus
3. $\overline{XV} \cong \overline{XV}$, $\overline{YV} \cong \overline{YV}$, $\overline{ZV} \cong \overline{ZV}$, and $\overline{WV} \cong \overline{WV}$	3. Reflexive Property of Congruence (Thm. 2.1)
4. $WXYZ$ is a parallelogram.	4. Definition of a rhombus
5. $\overline{XZ}$ bisects $\overline{WY}$. $\overline{WY}$ bisects $\overline{XZ}$.	5. Parallelogram Diagonals Theorem (Thm. 7.6)
6. $\overline{WV} \cong \overline{YV}$, $\overline{XV} \cong \overline{ZV}$	6. Definition of segment bisector
7. $\triangle WXV \cong \triangle YXV \cong \triangle YZV \cong \triangle WZV$	7. SSS Congruence Theorem (Thm. 5.8)
8. $\angle WXV \cong \angle YXV$, $\angle XYV \cong \angle ZYV$, $\angle YZV \cong \angle WZV$, $\angle ZWV \cong \angle XWV$	8. Corresponding parts of congruent triangles are congruent.
9. $\overline{WY}$ bisects $\angle ZWX$ and $\angle XYZ$. $\overline{ZX}$ bisects $\angle WZY$ and $\angle YXW$.	9. Definition of angle bisector

81. If a quadrilateral is a rhombus, then it has four congruent sides; If a quadrilateral has four congruent sides, then it is a rhombus; The conditional statement is true by the definition of rhombus. The converse is true because if a quadrilateral has four congruent sides, then both pairs of opposite sides are congruent. So, by the Parallelogram Opposite Sides Converse (Thm. 7.7), it is a parallelogram with four congruent sides, which is the definition of a rhombus.

82. If a quadrilateral is a rectangle, then it has four right angles; If a quadrilateral has four right angles, then it is a rectangle; The conditional statement is true by definition of rectangle. The converse is true because if a quadrilateral has four right angles, then both pairs of opposite angles are congruent. So, by the Parallelogram Opposite Angles Converse (Thm. 7.8), it is a parallelogram with four right angles, which is the definition of a rectangle.

83. If a quadrilateral is a square, then it is a rhombus and a rectangle; If a quadrilateral is a rhombus and a rectangle, then it is a square; The conditional statement is true because if a quadrilateral is a square, then by definition of a square, it has four congruent sides, which makes it a rhombus by the Rhombus Corollary (Cor. 7.2), and it has four right angles, which makes it a rectangle by the Rectangle Corollary (Cor. 7.3); The converse is true because if a quadrilateral is a rhombus and a rectangle, then by the Rhombus Corollary (Cor. 7.2), it has four congruent sides, and by the Rectangle Corollary (Cor. 7.3), it has four right angles. So, by the definition, it is a square.

85.

STATEMENTS	REASONS
1. $\triangle XYZ \cong \triangle XWZ$, $\angle XYW \cong \angle ZWY$	1. Given
2. $\angle YXZ \cong \angle WXZ$, $\angle YZX \cong \angle WZX$, $\overline{XY} \cong \overline{XW}, \overline{YZ} \cong \overline{WZ}$	2. Corresponding parts of congruent triangles are congruent.
3. $\overline{XZ}$ bisects $\angle WXY$ and $\angle WZY$.	3. Definition of angle bisector
4. $\angle XWY \cong \angle XYW$, $\angle WYZ \cong \angle ZWY$	4. Base Angles Theorem (Thm. 5.6)
5. $\angle XYW \cong \angle WYZ$, $\angle XWY \cong \angle ZWY$	5. Transitive Property of Congruence (Thm. 2.2)
6. $\overline{WY}$ bisects $\angle XWZ$ and $\angle XYZ$.	6. Definition of angle bisector
7. $XYZW$ is a rhombus.	7. Rhombus Opposite Angles Theorem (Thm. 7.12)

86.

STATEMENTS	REASONS
1. $\overline{BC} \cong \overline{AD}, \overline{BC} \perp \overline{DC},$ $\overline{AD} \perp \overline{DC}$	1. Given
2. $\overline{BC} \parallel \overline{AD}$	2. Lines Perpendicular to a Transversal Theorem (Thm. 3.12)
3. $ABCD$ is a parallelogram.	3. Opposite Sides Parallel and Congruent Theorem (Thm. 7.9)
4. $m\angle DAB = m\angle BCD$, $m\angle ABC = m\angle ADC$	4. Parallelogram Opposite Angles Theorem (Thm. 7.4)
5. $m\angle BCD = m\angle ADC = 90°$	5. Definition of perpendicular lines
6. $m\angle DAB = m\angle BCD = m\angle ABC = m\angle ADC = 90°$	6. Transitive Property of Equality
7. $ABCD$ has four right angles.	7. Definition of a right angle
8. $ABCD$ is a rectangle.	8. Definition of a rectangle

87.

STATEMENTS	REASONS
1. $PQRS$ is a rectangle.	1. Given
2. $PQRS$ is a parallelogram.	2. Definition of a rectangle
3. $\overline{PS} \cong \overline{QR}$	3. Parallelogram Opposite Sides Theorem (Thm. 7.3)
4. $\angle PQR$ and $\angle QPS$ are right angles.	4. Definition of a rectangle
5. $\angle PQR \cong \angle QPS$	5. Right Angles Congruence Theorem (Thm. 2.3)
6. $\overline{PQ} \cong \overline{PQ}$	6. Reflexive Property of Congruence (Thm. 2.1)
7. $\triangle PQR \cong \triangle QPS$	7. SAS Congruence Theorem (Thm. 5.5)
8. $\overline{PR} \cong \overline{SQ}$	8. Corresponding parts of congruent triangles are congruent.

88.

STATEMENTS	REASONS
1. $PQRS$ is a parallelogram, $\overline{PR} \cong \overline{SQ}$	1. Given
2. $\overline{PS} \cong \overline{QR}$	2. Parallelogram Opposite Sides Theorem (Thm. 7.3)
3. $\overline{PQ} \cong \overline{PQ}$	3. Reflexive Property of Congruence (Thm. 2.1)
4. $\triangle PQR \cong \triangle QPS$	4. SSS Congruence Theorem (Thm. 5.8)
5. $\angle SPQ \cong \angle RQP$	5. Corresponding parts of congruent triangles are congruent.
6. $m\angle SPQ = m\angle RQP$	6. Definition of congruent angles
7. $m\angle SPQ + m\angle RQP = 180°$	7. Parallelogram Consecutive Angles Theorem (Thm. 7.5)
8. $2m\angle SPQ = 180°$ and $2m\angle RQP = 180°$	8. Substitution Property of Equality
9. $m\angle SPQ = 90°$ and $m\angle RQP = 90°$	9. Division Property of Equality
10. $m\angle RSP = 90°$ and $m\angle QRS = 90°$	10. Parallelogram Opposite Angles Theorem (Thm. 7.4)
11. $\angle SPQ, \angle RQP, \angle RSP,$ and $\angle QRS$ are right angles.	11. Definition of a right angle
12. $PQRS$ is a rectangle.	12. Definition of a rectangle

7.5 Monitoring Progress and Modeling with Mathematics

35.

STATEMENTS	REASONS
1. $\overline{JL} \cong \overline{LN}, \overline{KM}$ is a midsegment of $\triangle JLN$.	1. Given
2. $\overline{KM} \parallel \overline{JN}$	2. Triangle Midsegment Theorem (Thm. 6.8)
3. $JKMN$ is a trapezoid.	3. Definition of trapezoid
4. $\angle LJN \cong \angle LNJ$	4. Base Angles Theorem (Thm. 5.6)
5. $JKMN$ is an isosceles trapezoid.	5. Isosceles Trapezoid Base Angles Converse (Thm. 7.15)

36.

STATEMENTS	REASONS
1. $ABCD$ is a kite, $\overline{AB} \cong \overline{CB}, \overline{AD} \cong \overline{CD}$	1. Given
2. $\overline{BD} \cong \overline{BD}, \overline{ED} \cong \overline{ED}$	2. Reflexive Property of Congruence (Thm. 2.1)
3. $\triangle BCD \cong \triangle BAD$	3. SSS Congruence Theorem (Thm. 5.8)
4. $\angle CDE \cong \angle ADE$	4. Corresponding parts of congruent triangles are congruent.
5. $\triangle CED \cong \triangle AED$	5. SAS Congruence Theorem (Thm. 5.5)
6. $\overline{CE} \cong \overline{AE}$	6. Corresponding parts of congruent triangles are congruent.

44.

STATEMENTS	REASONS
1. $QRST$ is an isosceles trapezoid.	1. Given
2. $\angle QTS \cong \angle RST$	2. Isosceles Trapezoid Base Angles Theorem (Thm. 7.14)
3. $\overline{QT} \cong \overline{RS}$	3. Definition of an isosceles trapezoid
4. $\overline{TS} \cong \overline{TS}$	4. Reflexive Property of Congruence (Thm. 2.1)
5. $\triangle QST \cong \triangle RTS$	5. SAS Congruence Theorem (Thm. 5.5)
6. $\angle TQS \cong \angle SRT$	6. Corresponding parts of congruent triangles are congruent.

47. Given kite $EFGH$ with $\overline{EF} \cong \overline{FG}$ and $\overline{EH} \cong \overline{GH}$, construct diagonal $\overline{FH}$, which is congruent to itself by the Reflexive Property of Congruence (Thm. 2.1). So, $\triangle FGH \cong \triangle FEH$ by the SSS Congruence Theorem (Thm. 5.8), and $\angle E \cong \angle G$ because corresponding parts of congruent triangles are congruent. Next, assume temporarily that $\angle F \cong \angle H$. Then $EFGH$ is a parallelogram by the Parallelogram Opposite Angles Converse (Thm. 7.8), and opposite sides are congruent. However, this contradicts the definition of a kite, which says that opposite sides cannot be congruent. So, the assumption cannot be true and $\angle F$ is not congruent to $\angle H$.

50. no; A concave kite and a convex kite can have congruent corresponding sides and a pair of congruent corresponding angles, but the kites are not congruent.

51. **a.**

STATEMENTS	REASONS
1. *JKLM* is an isosceles trapezoid, $\overline{KL} \parallel \overline{JM}$, $\overline{JK} \cong \overline{LM}$	1. Given
2. $\angle JKL \cong \angle MLK$	2. Isosceles Trapezoid Base Angles Theorem (Thm. 7.14)
3. $\overline{KL} \cong \overline{KL}$	3. Reflexive Property of Congruence (Thm. 2.1)
4. $\triangle JKL \cong \triangle MLK$	4. SAS Congruence Theorem (Thm. 5.5)
5. $\overline{JL} \cong \overline{KM}$	5. Corresponding parts of congruent triangles are congruent.

b. If the diagonals of a trapezoid are congruent, then the trapezoid is isosceles. Let *JKLM* be a trapezoid, $\overline{KL} \parallel \overline{JM}$ and $\overline{JL} \cong \overline{KM}.$ Construct line segments through *K* and *L* perpendicular to $\overline{JM}$ as shown below.

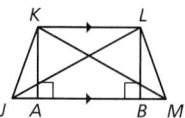

Because $\overline{KL} \parallel \overline{JM}$, $\angle AKL$ and $\angle KLB$ are right angles, so *KLBA* is a rectangle and $\overline{AK} \cong \overline{BL}$. Then $\triangle JLB \cong \triangle MKA$ by the HL Congruence Theorem (Thm. 5.9). So, $\angle LJB \cong \angle KMA$. $\overline{JM} \cong \overline{JM}$ by the Reflexive Property of Congruence (Thm. 2.1). So, $\triangle KJM \cong \triangle LMJ$ by the SAS Congruence Theorem (Thm. 5.5). Then $\angle KJM \cong \angle LMJ$, and the trapezoid is isosceles by the Isosceles Trapezoid Base Angles Converse (Thm. 7.15).

52. rhombus

STATEMENTS	REASONS
1. $\overline{JK} \cong \overline{LM}$, *E* is the midpoint of $\overline{JL}$, *F* is the midpoint of $\overline{KL}$, *G* is the midpoint of $\overline{KM}$, *H* is the midpoint of $\overline{JM}$	1. Given
2. $\overline{EF}$ is a midsegment of $\triangle JKL$, $\overline{FG}$ is a midsegment of $\triangle KML$, $\overline{GH}$ is a midsegment of $\triangle KMJ$, $\overline{EH}$ is a midsegment of $\triangle JML$.	2. Definition of midsegment
3. $\overline{EF} \parallel \overline{JK}, \overline{FG} \parallel \overline{LM}, \overline{GH} \parallel \overline{JK}, \overline{EH} \parallel \overline{LM}$	3. Triangle Midsegment Theorem (Thm. 6.8)
4. $\overline{EF} \parallel \overline{GH}, \overline{FG} \parallel \overline{EH}$	4. Transitive Property of Parallel Lines (Thm. 3.9)
5. *EFGH* is a parallelogram.	5. Definition of parallelogram
6. $EF = \frac{1}{2}JK, FG = \frac{1}{2}LM, GH = \frac{1}{2}JK, EH = \frac{1}{2}LM$	6. Trapezoid Midsegment Theorem (Thm. 7.17)
7. $JK = LM$	7. Definition of congruent segments
8. $FG = \frac{1}{2}JK, EH = \frac{1}{2}JK$	8. Substitution Property of Equality
9. $EF = FG = GH = EH$	9. Transitive Property of Equality
10. $\overline{EF} \cong \overline{FG} \cong \overline{GH} \cong \overline{EH}$	10. Definition of congruent segments
11. *EFGH* is a rhombus.	11. Definition of a rhombus

7.5 Maintaining Mathematical Proficiency

53. *Sample answer:* translation 1 unit right followed by a dilation with a scale factor of 2

54. *Sample answer:* reflection in the *y*-axis followed by a dilation with a scale factor of $\frac{1}{3}$

6.

STATEMENTS	REASONS
1. $\overline{BC} \parallel \overline{AD}$, $\angle EBC \cong$ $\angle ECB$, $\angle ABE \cong \angle DCE$	1. Given
2. $ABCD$ is a trapezoid.	2. Definition of trapezoid
3. $m\angle EBC = m\angle ECB$, $m\angle ABE = m\angle DCE$	3. Definition of congruent angles
4. $m\angle ABE + m\angle EBC =$ $m\angle ABC$, $m\angle DCE +$ $m\angle ECB = m\angle DCB$	4. Angle Addition Postulate (Post. 1.4)
5. $m\angle ABE + m\angle EBC =$ $m\angle ABE + m\angle EBC$	5. Reflexive Property of Equality
6. $m\angle ABE + m\angle EBC =$ $m\angle DCE + m\angle ECB$	6. Substitution Property of Equality
7. $m\angle ABC = m\angle DCB$	7. Transitive Property of Equality
8. $\angle ABC \cong \angle DCB$	8. Definition of congruent angles
9. $ABCD$ is an isosceles trapezoid.	9. Isosceles Trapezoid Base Angles Converse (Thm. 7.15)

Chapter 8

8.1 Monitoring Progress and Modeling with Mathematics

46. always

47. sometimes

48. never

49. yes; All four angles of each rectangle will always be congruent right angles.

50. yes; The light, object, and image form similar triangles.

51. about 1116 mi

52.

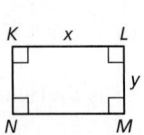 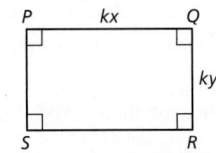

Let $KLMN$ and $PQRS$ be similar rectangles as shown. The ratio of corresponding side lengths is $\dfrac{KL}{PQ} = \dfrac{x}{kx} = \dfrac{1}{k}$. The perimeter of $KLMN$ is $2x + 2y$ and the perimeter of $PQRS$ is $2kx + 2ky$. So, the ratio of the perimeters is $\dfrac{2x + 2y}{2kx + 2ky} = \dfrac{2x + 2y}{k(2x + 2y)} = \dfrac{1}{k}$. Because both ratios equal $\dfrac{1}{k}$, the ratios are equal. So, $\dfrac{KL + LM + MN + NK}{PQ + QR + RS + SP} = \dfrac{KL}{PQ} = \dfrac{LM}{QR} = \dfrac{MN}{RS} = \dfrac{NK}{SP}$.

53.

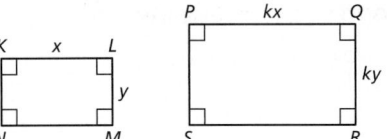

Let $KLMN$ and $PQRS$ be similar rectangles as shown. The ratio of corresponding side lengths is $\dfrac{KL}{PQ} = \dfrac{x}{kx} = \dfrac{1}{k}$. The area of $KLMN$ is xy and the area of $PQRS$ is $(kx)(ky) = k^2xy$. So, the ratio of the areas is $\dfrac{xy}{k^2xy} = \dfrac{1}{k^2} = \left(\dfrac{1}{k}\right)^2$. Because the ratio of corresponding side lengths is $\dfrac{1}{k}$, any pair of corresponding side lengths can be substituted for $\dfrac{1}{k}$. So, $\dfrac{\text{Area of } KLMN}{\text{Area of } PQRS} = \left(\dfrac{KL}{PQ}\right)^2 = \left(\dfrac{LM}{QR}\right)^2 = \left(\dfrac{MN}{RS}\right)^2 = \left(\dfrac{NK}{SP}\right)^2$.

54. no; Three angles determine a unique triangle on a sphere.

55. $x = \dfrac{1 + \sqrt{5}}{2}$; $x = \dfrac{1 + \sqrt{5}}{2}$ satisfies the proportion $\dfrac{1}{x} = \dfrac{x - 1}{1}$.

56. The coordinates of the points are $A(-3, 0)$, $B(0, 4)$, $C(6, 0)$, $D(0, -8)$, and $O(0, 0)$. The side lengths are $OA = 3$, $OB = 4$, $AB = 5$, $OC = 6$, $OD = 8$, and $CD = 10$. Corresponding side lengths are proportional with a scale factor of 2, so the triangles are proportional.

8.1 Maintaining Mathematical Proficiency

57. $x = 63$

58. $x = 66$

59. $x = 64$

60. $x = 60$

8.2 Explorations

1. a. Check students' work.

b, d, and e. *Sample answer for columns 4, 5, and 6:*

	1.	2.	3.	4.	5.	6.
$m\angle A$, $m\angle D$	106°	88°	40°	45°	90°	15°
$m\angle B$, $m\angle E$	31°	42°	65°	90°	60°	150°
$m\angle C$	43°	50°	75°	45°	30°	15°
$m\angle F$	43°	50°	75°	45°	30°	15°
AB	2	2	3	2	2	2
DE	4	3	5	6	4	3.16
BC	2.82	2.61	2	2	4	2
EF	5.64	3.91	3.33	6	8	3.16
AC	1.51	1.75	2.81	2.83	3.46	3.86
DF	3.02	2.62	4.69	8.49	6.93	6.11

c. yes; Corresponding angles are congruent, and the corresponding side lengths are proportional.

e. no

f. Two triangles with two pairs of congruent corresponding angles are similar.

8.2 Monitoring Progress and Modeling with Mathematics

22. yes;

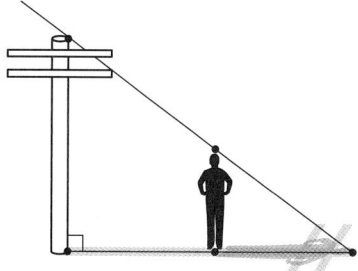

If you and the telephone are both standing at right angles with the ground, then two similar triangles are formed, and you can use a proportion to estimate the height.

23. yes; Corresponding angles are congruent.

24. yes; The angle measures could be 30°, 60°, and 90°.

25. no; $94° + 87° > 180°$

26. no; $m\angle X = 100°$ and $100° + 85° > 180°$

27. *Sample answer:* Because the triangles are similar, the ratios of the vertical sides to the horizontal sides are equal.

28. *Sample answer:* $\triangle KLM$ and $\triangle JLN$; The triangles are similar, so you can use the proportion $\dfrac{x}{x + 20} = \dfrac{100}{125}$.

29. The angle measures are 60°.

30. **a.** no; Not all rectangles are similar.

   b. no; Not all rectangles are similar.

31.

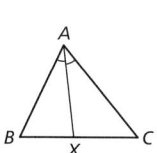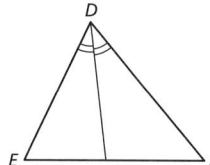

Let $\triangle ABC \sim \triangle DEF$ with a scale factor of k, and $\overline{AX}$ and $\overline{DY}$ be angle bisectors as shown. Then $\angle C \cong \angle F$, $m\angle CAB = m\angle FDE$, $2m\angle CAX = m\angle CAB$ and $2m\angle FDY = m\angle FDE$. By the Substitution Property of Equality, $2m\angle CAX = 2m\angle FDY$, so $m\angle CAX = m\angle FDY$. Then $\triangle ACX \sim \triangle DFY$ by the AA Similarity Theorem (Thm. 8.3), and because corresponding side lengths are proportional, $\dfrac{AX}{DY} = \dfrac{AC}{DF} = k$.

32. Let $\triangle XYZ$ be any triangle such that $a = XY$ and $b = XZ$, and the altitudes to $\overline{XY}$ and $\overline{XZ}$ are $\overline{AZ}$ and $\overline{BY}$, respectively. Then, $\angle XAZ$ and $\angle XBY$ are congruent right angles and $\angle YXB \cong \angle ZXA$, so $\triangle BXY \sim \triangle AXZ$ by the AA Similarity Theorem (Thm. 8.3). Because corresponding side lengths of similar figures are proportional, $\dfrac{AZ}{BY} = \dfrac{XZ}{XY} = \dfrac{b}{a}$. Note: When $m\angle X = 90°$, $XY = BY$ and $XZ = AZ$, so the ratio is still $\dfrac{b}{a}$.

33. about 17.1 ft; $\triangle AED \sim \triangle CEB$, so $\dfrac{DE}{BE} = \dfrac{4}{3}$. $\triangle DEF \sim \triangle DBC$, so $\dfrac{EF}{30} = \dfrac{DE}{DB} = \dfrac{4}{7}$ and $EF = \dfrac{120}{7}$.

8.2 Maintaining Mathematical Proficiency

34. yes; Use the SAS Congruence Theorem (Thm. 5.5).

35. yes; Use the SSS Congruence Theorem (Thm. 5.8).

36. no; $\angle PSQ$ is not necessarily a right angle.

8.3 Explorations

1. b, d, and g. *Sample answer for column 7:*

	1.	2.	3.	4.
AB	5	5	6	15
BC	8	8	8	20
AC	10	10	10	10
DE	10	15	9	12
EF	16	24	12	16
DF	20	30	15	8
$m\angle A$	52.41°	52.41°	53.13°	104.48°
$m\angle B$	97.9°	97.9°	90°	28.96°
$m\angle C$	29.69°	29.69°	36.87°	46.57°
$m\angle D$	52.41°	52.41°	53.13°	104.48°
$m\angle E$	97.9°	97.9°	90°	28.96°
$m\angle F$	29.69°	29.69°	36.87°	46.57°

	5.	6.	7.
AB	9	24	3
BC	12	18	5
AC	8	16	6
DE	12	8	9
EF	15	6	15
DF	10	8	18
$m\angle A$	89.6°	48.59°	56.25°
$m\angle B$	41.81°	41.81°	93.82°
$m\angle C$	48.59°	89.6°	29.93°
$m\angle D$	85.46°	44.05°	56.25°
$m\angle E$	41.65°	67.98°	93.82°
$m\angle F$	52.89°	67.98°	29.93°

8.3 Monitoring Progress and Modeling with Mathematics

33.

STATEMENTS	REASONS
1. $\angle A \cong \angle D$, $\dfrac{AB}{DE} = \dfrac{AC}{DF}$	1. Given
2. Draw $\overline{PQ}$ so that P is on $\overline{AB}$, Q is on $\overline{AC}$, $\overline{PQ} \parallel \overline{BC}$, and $AP = DE$.	2. Parallel Postulate (Post. 3.1)
3. $\angle APQ \cong \angle ABC$	3. Corresponding Angles Theorem (Thm. 3.1)
4. $\angle A \cong \angle A$	4. Reflexive Property of Congruence (Thm. 2.2)
5. $\triangle APQ \sim \triangle ABC$	5. AA Similarity Theorem (Thm. 8.3)
6. $\dfrac{AB}{AP} = \dfrac{AC}{AQ} = \dfrac{BC}{PQ}$	6. Corresponding sides of similar figures are proportional.
7. $\dfrac{AB}{DE} = \dfrac{AC}{AQ}$	7. Substitution Property of Equality
8. $AQ \cdot \dfrac{AB}{DE} = AC$, $DF \cdot \dfrac{AB}{DE} = AC$	8. Multiplication Property of Equality
9. $AQ = AC \cdot \dfrac{DE}{AB}$, $DF = AC \cdot \dfrac{DE}{AB}$	9. Multiplication Property of Equality
10. $AQ = DF$	10. Transitive Property of Equality
11. $\overline{AQ} \cong \overline{DF}$, $\overline{AP} \cong \overline{DE}$	11. Definition of congruent segments
12. $\triangle APQ \cong \triangle DEF$	12. SAS Congruence Theorem (Thm. 5.5)
13. $\overline{PQ} \cong \overline{EF}$	13. Corresponding parts of congruent triangles are congruent.
14. $PQ = EF$	14. Definition of congruent segments
15. $\dfrac{AB}{DE} = \dfrac{AC}{DF} = \dfrac{BC}{EF}$	15. Substitution Property of Equality
16. $\triangle ABC \sim \triangle DEF$	16. SSS Similarity Theorem (Thm. 8.4)

39. *Sample answer:*

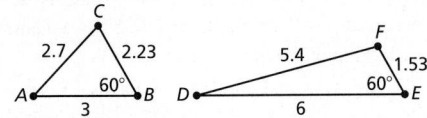

40. *Sample answer:*

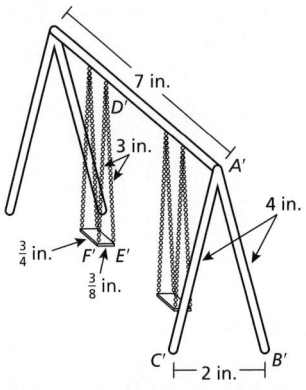

$\triangle ABC \sim \triangle A'B'C'$, $\triangle DEF \sim \triangle D'E'F'$; $k = \frac{1}{24}$

42. Substitution Property of Equality; $\dfrac{AD}{AB}$; $\angle ABC \cong \angle ADE$; SAS Similarity Theorem (Thm. 8.5); Definition of congruent angles; Triangle Sum Theorem (Thm. 5.1); $m\angle BAC + m\angle BCA = 90°$; Transitive Property of Equality; $\ell \perp n$

8.4 Monitoring Progress and Modeling with Mathematics

27.

STATEMENTS	REASONS
1. $\overline{QS} \parallel \overline{TU}$	1. Given
2. $\angle RQS \cong \angle RTU$, $\angle RSQ \cong \angle RUT$	2. Corresponding Angles Theorem (Thm. 3.1)
3. $\triangle RQS \sim \triangle RTU$	3. AA Similarity Theorem (Thm. 8.3)
4. $\dfrac{QR}{TR} = \dfrac{SR}{UR}$	4. Corresponding side lengths of similar figures are proportional.
5. $QR = QT + TR$, $SR = SU + UR$	5. Segment Addition Postulate (Post. 1.2)
6. $\dfrac{QT + TR}{TR} = \dfrac{SU + UR}{UR}$	6. Substitution Property of Equality
7. $\dfrac{QT}{TR} + \dfrac{TR}{TR} = \dfrac{SU}{UR} + \dfrac{UR}{UR}$	7. Rewrite the proportion.
8. $\dfrac{QT}{TR} + 1 = \dfrac{SU}{UR} + 1$	8. Simplify.
9. $\dfrac{QT}{TR} = \dfrac{SU}{UR}$	9. Subtraction Property of Equality

28.

STATEMENTS	REASONS
1. $\dfrac{ZY}{YW} = \dfrac{ZX}{XV}$	1. Given
2. $\dfrac{YW}{ZY} = \dfrac{XV}{ZX}$	2. Rewrite the proportion.
3. $\dfrac{YW}{ZY} + 1 = \dfrac{XV}{ZX} + 1$	3. Addition Property of Equality
4. $\dfrac{YW}{ZY} + \dfrac{ZY}{ZY} = \dfrac{XV}{ZX} + \dfrac{ZX}{ZX}$	4. Substitution Property of Equality
5. $\dfrac{YW + ZY}{ZY} = \dfrac{XV + ZX}{ZX}$	5. Add fractions.
6. $ZW = YW + ZY$, $ZV = XV + ZX$	6. Segment Addition Postulate (Post. 1.2)
7. $\dfrac{ZW}{ZY} = \dfrac{ZV}{ZX}$	7. Substitution Property of Equality
8. $\angle Z \cong \angle Z$	8. Reflexive Property of Congruence (Thm. 2.2)
9. $\triangle ZWV \sim \triangle ZYX$	9. SAS Similarity Theorem (Thm. 8.5)
10. $\angle ZYX \cong \angle ZWV$	10. Corresponding angles of similar triangles are congruent.
11. $\overline{YX} \parallel \overline{WV}$	11. Corresponding Angles Converse (Thm. 3.5)

33. isosceles; By the Triangle Angle Bisector Theorem (Thm. 8.9), the ratio of the lengths of the segments of $\overline{LN}$ equals the ratio of the other two side lengths. Because $\overline{LN}$ is bisected, the ratio is 1, and $ML = MN$.

34. Player 1; The angle is bisected, so the lengths are proportional.

35. Because $\overline{WX} \parallel \overline{ZA}$, $\angle XAZ \cong \angle YXW$ by the Corresponding Angles Theorem (Thm. 3.1) and $\angle WXZ \cong \angle XZA$ by the Alternate Interior Angles Theorem (Thm. 3.2). So, by the Transitive Property of Congruence (Thm. 2.2), $\angle XAZ \cong \angle XZA$. Then $\overline{XA} \cong \overline{XZ}$ by the Converse of the Base Angles Theorem (Thm. 5.7), and by the Triangle Proportionality Theorem (Thm. 8.6), $\dfrac{YW}{WZ} = \dfrac{XY}{XA}$. Because $XA = XZ$, $\dfrac{YW}{WZ} = \dfrac{XY}{XZ}$.

36. If a ray that passes through a vertex of a triangle divides the opposite side into segments whose lengths are proportional to the lengths of the other two sides, then the ray bisects the angle through which it passes; yes; The ray divides the triangle into proportional parts. So, the angles must be congruent.

37. The Triangle Midsegment Theorem (Thm. 6.8) is a specific case of the Triangle Proportionality Theorem (Thm. 8.6) when the segment parallel to one side of a triangle that connects the other two sides also happens to pass through the midpoints of those two sides.

38. no; You can use the ratio of AD and BE to find the rate.

39.
•————————————•
      x

40. By the Vertical Angles Congruence Theorem (Thm. 2.6), $\angle NPA \cong \angle CPM$, $\angle BXP \cong \angle CXM$, and $\angle PZB \cong \angle NZA$. By the Alternate Interior Angles Theorem (Thm. 3.2), $\angle M \cong \angle PAN$, $\angle M \cong \angle BPX$, and $\angle N \cong \angle ZPB$. So, $\triangle APN \sim \triangle MPC$, $\triangle CXM \sim \triangle BXP$, and $\triangle BZP \sim \triangle AZN$ by the AA Similarity Theorem (Thm. 8.3). Then $\dfrac{CX}{XB} = \dfrac{CM}{BP}$, $\dfrac{AP}{PM} = \dfrac{AN}{CM}$, and $\dfrac{BZ}{ZA} = \dfrac{BP}{AN}$, and by the Triangle Proportionality Theorem (Thm. 8.6) $\dfrac{AY}{YC} = \dfrac{AP}{PM}$. So, $\dfrac{AY}{YC} = \dfrac{AN}{CM}$ by the Transitive Property of Equality. Then $\dfrac{AY}{YC} \cdot \dfrac{CX}{XB} \cdot \dfrac{BZ}{ZA} = \dfrac{AN}{CM} \cdot \dfrac{CM}{BP} \cdot \dfrac{BP}{AN} = 1$.

8.4 Maintaining Mathematical Proficiency

41. a, b **42.** c

43. $x = \pm 11$ **44.** $x = \pm 3$

45. $x = \pm 7$

Chapter 9

9.1 Explorations

2. c.

STATEMENTS	REASONS
1. $\triangle ABC \sim \triangle ACD \sim \triangle CBD$	1. Given
2. $\dfrac{c}{b} = \dfrac{b}{c - d}, \dfrac{c}{a} = \dfrac{a}{d}$	2. Corresponding sides of similar figures are proportional.
3. $c(c - d) = b^2, cd = a^2$	3. Cross Products Property
4. $c^2 - cd = b^2$	4. Distributive Property
5. $c^2 - a^2 = b^2$	5. Substitution Property of Equality
6. $c^2 = a^2 + b^2$	6. Addition Property of Equality
7. $a^2 + b^2 = c^2$	7. Symmetric Property of Equality

9.1 Monitoring Progress and Modeling with Mathematics

38. Let the sides of the first triangle be represented by a_1, b_1, and c_1, and the sides of the second triangle be represented by a_2, b_2, and c_2. By using the Subtraction Property of Equality on $c^2 = a^2 + b^2$, you can say $b^2 = c^2 - a^2$. So, $b_1^2 = c_1^2 - a_1^2$ and $b_2^2 = c_2^2 - a_2^2$. We are given that $c_1 = c_2$, and one pair of legs are congruent. Because a and b are interchangeable in the Pythagorean Theorem (Thm. 9.1), we can say that either $a_1 = a_2$ or $b_1 = b_2$. For simplicity, let's use $a_1 = a_2$. By the Substitution Property of Equality, we get $b_1^2 = c_2^2 - a_2^2$. So, by the Transitive Property, $b_1^2 = b_2^2$. Then, by taking the positive square root of each side, you get $b_1 = b_2$. So, the two right triangles are congruent by the SSS Congruence Theorem (Thm. 5.8).

39.

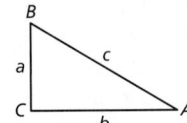 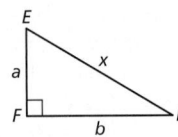

Let $\triangle ABC$ be any triangle so that the square of the length, c, of the longest side of the triangle is equal to the sum of the squares of the lengths, a and b, of the other two sides: $c^2 = a^2 + b^2$. Let $\triangle DEF$ be any right triangle with leg lengths of a and b. Let x represent the length of its hypotenuse. Because $\triangle DEF$ is a right triangle, by the Pythagorean Theorem (Thm. 9.1), $a^2 + b^2 = x^2$. So, by the Transitive Property, $c^2 = x^2$. By taking the positive square root of each side, you get $c = x$. So, $\triangle ABC \cong \triangle DEF$ by the SSS Congruence Theorem (Thm. 5.8).

40. no; Let $m = 2$ and $n = -1$. The resulting integers are -4, 3, and 5. The integers in a Pythagorean triple must be positive.

41. no; They can be part of a Pythagorean triple if 75 is the hypotenuse: $21^2 + 72^2 = 75^2$

42. given; Pythagorean Theorem (Thm. 9.1); Substitution Property; definition of a right angle; Substitution Property; definition of acute angle; definition of acute triangle

43.

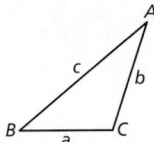 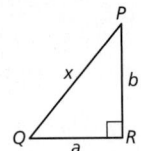

STATEMENTS	REASONS
1. In $\triangle ABC$, $c^2 > a^2 + b^2$, where c is the length of the longest side. $\triangle PQR$ has side lengths a, b, and x, where x is the length of the hypotenuse and $\angle R$ is a right angle.	1. Given
2. $a^2 + b^2 = x^2$	2. Pythagorean Theorem (Thm. 9.1)
3. $c^2 > x^2$	3. Substitution Property
4. $c > x$	4. Take the positive square root of each side.
5. $m\angle R = 90°$	5. Definition of a right angle
6. $m\angle C > m\angle R$	6. Converse of the Hinge Theorem (Thm. 6.13)
7. $m\angle C > 90°$	7. Substitution Property
8. $\angle C$ is an obtuse angle.	8. Definition of obtuse angle
9. $\triangle ABC$ is an obtuse triangle.	9. Definition of obtuse triangle

9.1 Maintaining Mathematical Proficiency

44. $\dfrac{7\sqrt{2}}{2}$

45. $\dfrac{14\sqrt{3}}{3}$

46. $4\sqrt{2}$

47. $4\sqrt{3}$

9.2 Monitoring Progress and Modeling with Mathematics

20. a. the triangle farthest to the left with legs that are each 1 unit

b. the third triangle from the left with legs that are 1 unit and $\sqrt{3}$ units, and a hypotenuse that is $\sqrt{4} = 2$ units

21. Given $\triangle JKL$, which is a 30°-60°-90° triangle, whose shorter leg, $\overline{KL}$, has length x, construct $\triangle JML$, which is congruent and adjacent to $\triangle JKL$. Because corresponding parts of congruent triangles are congruent, $LM = KL = x$, $m\angle M = m\angle K = 60°$, $m\angle MJL = m\angle KJL = 30°$, and $JM = JK$.
Also, by the Angle Addition Postulate (Post. 1.4), $m\angle KJM = m\angle KJL + m\angle MJL$, and by substituting, $m\angle KJM = 30° + 30° = 60°$. So, $\triangle JKM$ has three 60° angles, which means that it is equiangular by definition, and by the Corollary to the Converse of the Base Angles Theorem (Cor. 5.3), it is also equilateral. By the Segment Addition Postulate (Post. 1.2), $KM = KL + LM$, and by substituting, $KM = x + x = 2x$. So, by the definition of an equilateral triangle, $JM = JK = KM = 2x$. By the Pythagorean Theorem (Thm. 9.1), $(JL)^2 + (KL)^2 = (JK)^2$. By substituting, we get $(JL)^2 + x^2 = (2x)^2$, which is equivalent to $(JL)^2 + x^2 = 4x^2$, when simplified. When the Subtraction Property of Equality is applied, we get $(JL)^2 = 4x^2 - x^2$, which is equivalent to $(JL)^2 = 3x^2$. By taking the positive square root of each side, $JL = x\sqrt{3}$. So, the hypotenuse of the 30°-60°-90° triangle, $\triangle JKL$, is twice as long as the shorter leg, and the longer leg is $\sqrt{3}$ times as long as the shorter leg.

22.

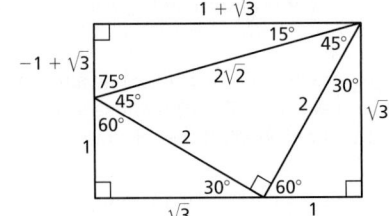

This rectangle contains two 30°-60°-90° triangles with side lengths of 1, 2, and $\sqrt{3}$ units, one 45°-45°-90° triangle with side lengths of 2, 2, and $2\sqrt{2}$ units, and one 15°-75°-90° triangle with side lengths of $1 + \sqrt{3}$, $-1 + \sqrt{3}$, and $2\sqrt{2}$ units.

23. *Sample answer:* Because all isosceles right triangles are 45°-45°-90° triangles, they are similar by the AA Similarity Theorem (Thm. 8.3). Because both legs of an isosceles right triangle are congruent, the legs will always be proportional. So, 45°-45°-90° triangles are all similar by the SAS Similarity Theorem (Thm. 8.5) also.

24. no; The length of the legs of the triangles added are divided by $\sqrt{2}$ in each stage. The triangles that are added in stage 1, for example, have a hypotenuse that is 1 unit long. So, the legs must be $\dfrac{1}{\sqrt{2}} = \dfrac{\sqrt{2}}{2}$. So, the length of the legs in stage 8 will be $\dfrac{1}{(\sqrt{2})^8} = \dfrac{1}{16}$.

25. $T(1.5, 1.6)$

9.3 Monitoring Progress and Modeling with Mathematics

41.

STATEMENTS	REASONS
1. Draw $\triangle ABC$, $\angle BCA$ is a right angle.	1. Given
2. Draw a perpendicular segment (altitude) from C to $\overline{AB}$, and label the new point on $\overline{AB}$ as D.	2. Perpendicular Postulate (Post. 3.2)
3. $\triangle ADC \sim \triangle CDB$	3. Right Triangle Similarity Theorem (Thm. 9.6)
4. $\dfrac{BD}{CD} = \dfrac{CD}{AD}$	4. Corresponding sides of similar figures are proportional.
5. $CD^2 = AD \cdot BD$	5. Cross Products Property

42.

STATEMENTS	REASONS
1. Draw $\triangle ABC$, $\angle BCA$ is a right angle.	1. Given
2. Draw a perpendicular segment (altitude) from C to $\overline{AB}$, and label the new point on $\overline{AB}$ as D.	2. Perpendicular Postulate (Post. 3.2)
3. $\triangle ADC \sim \triangle CDB$	3. Right Triangle Similarity Theorem (Thm. 9.6)
4. $\dfrac{DB}{CB} = \dfrac{CB}{AB}$, $\dfrac{AD}{AC} = \dfrac{AC}{AB}$	4. Corresponding sides of similar figures are proportional.
5. $CB^2 = DB \cdot AB$, $AC^2 = AD \cdot AB$	5. Cross Products Property

43.

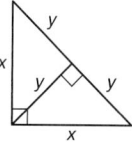
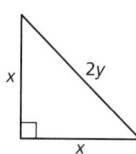
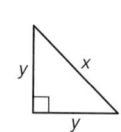
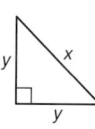

The two smaller triangles are congruent; Their corresponding sides lengths are represented by the same variables. So, they are congruent by the SSS Congruence Theorem (Thm. 5.8).

45.

STATEMENTS	REASONS
1. $\triangle ABC$ is a right triangle. Altitude $\overline{CD}$ is drawn to hypotenuse $\overline{AB}$.	1. Given
2. $\angle BCA$ is a right angle.	2. Definition of right triangle
3. $\angle ADC$ and $\angle BDC$ are right angles.	3. Definition of perpendicular lines
4. $\angle BCA \cong \angle ADC \cong \angle BDC$	4. Right Angles Congruence Theorem (Thm. 2.3)
5. $\angle A$ and $\angle ACD$ are complementary. $\angle B$ and $\angle BCD$ are complementary.	5. Corollary to the Triangle Sum Theorem (Cor. 5.1)
6. $\angle ACD$ and $\angle BCD$ are complementary.	6. Definition of complementary angles
7. $\angle A \cong \angle BCD$, $\angle B \cong \angle ACD$	7. Congruent Complements Theorem (Thm. 2.5)
8. $\triangle CBD \sim \triangle ABC$, $\triangle ACD \sim \triangle ABC$, $\triangle CBD \sim \triangle ACD$	8. AA Similarity Theorem (Thm. 8.3)

9.3 Maintaining Mathematical Proficiency

46. $x = 65$

47. $x = 116$

48. $x = \dfrac{26}{3} \approx 8.7$

49. $x = \dfrac{23}{6} \approx 3.8$

9.4 Monitoring Progress and Modeling with Mathematics

20. 45°; greater than 45°; less than 45°; If the ratio of the legs is equal to 1, then the legs are congruent, and all isosceles right triangles are 45°-45°-90° triangles. If one acute angle measure of a right triangle is less than 45°, then the other acute angle is greater than 45°. So, the side opposite the smaller acute angle will be the shorter leg, which means the ratio will be less than 1, and the leg opposite the larger acute angle will be the longer leg, which means the ratio will be greater than 1.

21. no; The Sun's rays form a right triangle with the length of the awning and the height of the door. The tangent of the angle of elevation equals the height of the door divided by the length of the awning, so the length of the awning equals the quotient of the height of the door, 8 feet, and the tangent of the angle of elevation, 70°: $x = \dfrac{8}{\tan 70°} \approx 6.5$ ft

22. $\tan A = \dfrac{a}{b}$; $\tan B = \dfrac{b}{a}$; They are reciprocals of each other; complementary

23. You cannot find the tangent of a right angle, because each right angle has two adjacent legs, and the opposite side is the hypotenuse. So, you do not have an opposite leg and an adjacent leg. If a triangle has an obtuse angle, then it cannot be a right triangle, and the tangent ratio only works for right triangles.

24.

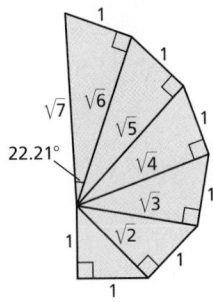

about 22.2°

25. a. about 33.4 ft

b. 3 students at each end; The triangle formed by the 60°
angle has an opposite leg that is about 7.5 feet longer than
the opposite leg of the triangle formed by the 50° angle.
Because each student needs 2 feet of space, 3 more students
can fit on each end with about 1.5 feet of space left over.

9.5 Monitoring Progress and Modeling with Mathematics

37. a.

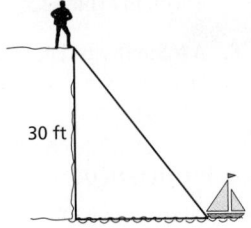

30 ft

b.

Angle of depression	40°	50°	60°	70°	80°
Approximate length of line of sight (feet)	46.7	39.2	34.6	31.9	30.5

c.

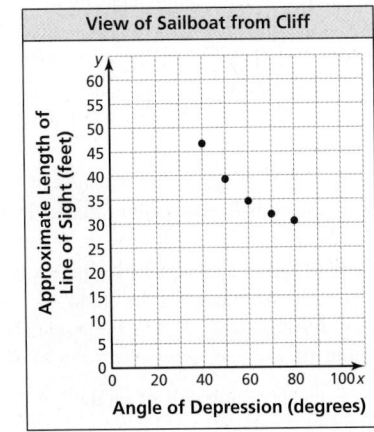

View of Sailboat from Cliff

Approximate Length of Line of Sight (feet) vs. Angle of Depression (degrees)

d. 60 ft

38. (a) represesents $\sin x$ and (b) represents $\cos x$; $\sin 0 = 0$ and
$\cos 0 = 1$. Substitute 0 for x in each series. Part (a) yields
0 and part (b) yields 1, so (a) represents $\sin x$ and (b)
represents $\cos x$; $\sin \frac{\pi}{6} \approx 0.5$, $\cos \frac{\pi}{6} \approx 0.87$

39. a. $\dfrac{\sin A}{\cos A} = \dfrac{\dfrac{\text{length of side opposite } A}{\text{length of hypotenuse}}}{\dfrac{\text{length of side adjacent to } A}{\text{length of hypotenuse}}} \cdot \dfrac{\text{length of hypotenuse}}{\text{length of hypotenuse}}$

$= \dfrac{\text{length of side opposite } A}{\text{length of side adjacent to } A}$

$= \tan A$

b. $(\sin A)^2 + (\cos A)^2$

$= \left(\dfrac{\text{length of side opposite } A}{\text{length of hypotenuse}}\right)^2 + \left(\dfrac{\text{length of side adjacent to } A}{\text{length of hypotenuse}}\right)^2$

$= \dfrac{(\text{length of side opposite } A)^2 + (\text{length of side adjacent to } A)^2}{(\text{length of hypotenuse})^2}.$

By the Pythagorean Theorem (Thm. 9.1),
(length of side opposite A)^2 + (length of side adjacent to A)^2
= (length of hypotenuse)^2.

So, $(\sin A)^2 + (\cos A)^2 = \dfrac{(\text{length of hypotenuse})^2}{(\text{length of hypotenuse})^2} = 1$.

40. In $\triangle ABC$, $\sin C = \dfrac{h}{a}$. So, $h = a \sin C$. When you substitute
this into the formula for the area of a triangle, you get

$A = \dfrac{1}{2}bh = \dfrac{1}{2}b(a \sin C) = \dfrac{1}{2}ab \sin C$; about 9.0 square units

9.5 Maintaining Mathematical Proficiency

41. $x = 8$; yes   **42.** $x = 12\sqrt{2} \approx 17.0$; no

43. $x = 45$; yes   **44.** $x = 6\sqrt{2} \approx 8.5$; no

9.6 Monitoring Progress and Modeling with Mathematics

23. 4.76°, 96.4 in., 8 in., 96.1 in.

24. a. about 32.5°

b. *Sample answer:* The ratio is 8 inches to 15 inches; about 28.1°

25. about 36.9°; $PQ = 3$ centimeters and $PR = 4$ centimeters, so

$m\angle R = \tan^{-1}\left(\frac{3}{4}\right) \approx 36.9°$.

26. no; *Sample answer:* Measures from a 30°-60°-90° triangle
illustrate a counterexample: $\tan^{-1}\sqrt{3} = 60°$, but $\dfrac{1}{\tan\sqrt{3}} \approx 33.1$.

27. $KM \approx 7.8$ ft, $JK \approx 11.9$ ft, $m\angle JKM = 49°$; $ML \approx 19.5$ ft,
$m\angle MKL \approx 68.2°$, $m\angle L \approx 21.8°$

28. $TS \approx 9.1$ m, $TU \approx 8.2$ m , $m\angle UTS = 26°$; $TV \approx 14.1$ m,
$TW \approx 10.9$ m, $m\angle V \approx 50.5°$, $m\angle VTW \approx 39.5°$

29. a. *Sample answer:* $\tan^{-1}\frac{3}{1}$; about 71.6°

b. *Sample answer:* $\tan^{-1}\frac{4}{3}$; about 53.1°

30. a. $\sin^{-1}(\sin x) = x$; Inverse operations cancel each other out.

b. $\tan(\tan^{-1} y) = y$; Inverse operations cancel each other out.

c. $\cos(\cos^{-1} z) = z$; Inverse operations cancel each other out.

31. Because the sine is the ratio of the length of a leg to the length of
the hypotenuse, and the hypotenuse is always longer than either of
the legs, the sine cannot have a value greater than 1.

32. $AB = CD = 6$ cm, $BD = 2\sqrt{10}$ cm, $AD = BC = 2$ cm;
$m\angle A = m\angle C = 90°$, $m\angle ADB = m\angle CBD \approx 71.6°$,
$m\angle BDC = m\angle DBA \approx 18.4°$

9.6 Maintaining Mathematical Proficiency

33. $x = 8$ **34.** $x = 26$

35. $x = 2.46$ **36.** $x = 11.1125$

9.7 Monitoring Progress and Modeling with Mathematics

51. a.

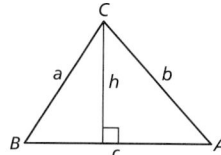

The formula for the area of $\triangle ABC$ with altitude h drawn from C to $\overline{AB}$ as shown is Area $= \frac{1}{2}ch$. Because

$\sin A = \dfrac{h}{b}$, $h = b \sin A$. By substituting, you get

Area $= \dfrac{1}{2}c(b \sin A) = \dfrac{1}{2}bc \sin A$.

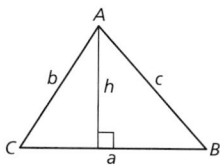

The formula for the area of $\triangle ABC$ with altitude h drawn from A to $\overline{BC}$ as shown is Area $= \frac{1}{2}ah$. Because

$\sin B = \dfrac{h}{c}$, $h = c \sin B$. By substituting, you get

Area $= \dfrac{1}{2}a(c \sin B) = \dfrac{1}{2}ac \sin B$. See Exercise 50 for

Area $= \dfrac{1}{2}ab \sin C$.

b. They are all expressions for the area of the same triangle, so they are all equal to each other by the Transitive Property.

c. By the Multiplication Property of Equality, multiply all three expressions by 2 to get $bc \sin A = ac \sin B = ab \sin C$. By the Division Property of Equality, divide all three expressions by abc to get $\dfrac{\sin A}{a} = \dfrac{\sin B}{b} = \dfrac{\sin C}{c}$.

52. definition of altitude; Pythagorean Theorem (Thm. 9.1); $a^2 = b^2 - 2bx + x^2 + h^2$; Pythagorean Theorem (Thm. 9.1); $a^2 = b^2 - 2bx + c^2$; definition of cosine ratio; Multiplication Property of Equality; Substitution Property of Equality

9.7 Maintaining Mathematical Proficiency

53. $r = 4$ ft, $d = 8$ ft   **54.** $r = 10$ in., $d = 20$ in.

55. $r = 1$ ft, $d = 2$ ft   **56.** $r = 50$ in., $d = 100$ in.

Chapter 9 Standards Assessment

6.

STATEMENTS	REASONS
1. $\overline{HE} \cong \overline{HG}$, $\overline{EG} \perp \overline{DF}$	1. Given
2. $\overline{HF} \cong \overline{HF}$, $\overline{DH} \cong \overline{DH}$	2. Reflexive Property of Congruence (Thm. 2.1)
3. $\angle EHF$, $\angle GHF$, $\angle GHD$, and $\angle EHD$ are right angles.	3. Definition of perpendicular lines
4. $\angle EHF \cong \angle GHF$, $\angle GHD \cong \angle EHD$	4. Right Angles Congruence Theorem (Thm. 2.3)
5. $\triangle EHF \cong \triangle GHF$, $\triangle EHD \cong \triangle GHD$	5. SAS Congruence Theorem (Thm 5.5)
6. $\overline{FE} \cong \overline{FG}$, $\overline{DE} \cong \overline{DG}$	6. Corresponding parts of congruent triangles are congruent.

Chapter 10

10.1 Lesson Monitoring Progress

5. 0

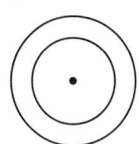

10.1 Monitoring Progress and Modeling with Mathematics

42. $\overline{PA} \cong \overline{PB}$ and $\overline{PB} \cong \overline{PC}$ by the External Tangent Congruency Theorem (Thm. 10.2).

43. $\angle ARC \cong \angle BSC$ and $\angle ACR \cong \angle BCS$, so $\triangle ARC \sim \triangle BSC$ by the AA Similarity Theorem (Thm. 8.3). Because corresponding sides of similar figures are proportional, $\dfrac{AC}{BC} = \dfrac{RC}{SC}$.

44. yes; $\overline{AZ} = \overline{AW}$, $\overline{BW} = \overline{BX}$, $\overline{CX} = \overline{CY}$, and $\overline{DY} = \overline{DZ}$, so, $(AW + WB) + (CY + YD) = (AZ + DZ) + (BX + CX)$.

45. $x = 13$, $y = 5$; $2x - 5 = x + 8$ and $2x + 4y - 6 = 2x + 14$.

46. By the Tangent Line to Circles Theorem (Thm. 10.1), $m\angle PRS = m\angle PTS = 90°$. $\overline{PT} \cong \overline{PR}$ and $\overline{PS} \cong \overline{PS}$, so $\triangle PTS \cong \triangle PRS$ by the HL Congruence Theorem (Thm. 5.9). So, $\overline{SR} \cong \overline{ST}$.

47. a. Assume m is not perpendicular to $\overline{QP}$. The perpendicular segment from Q to m intersects m at some other point R. Then $QR < QP$, so R must be inside $\odot Q$, and m must be a secant line. This is a contradiction, so m must be perpendicular to $\overline{QP}$.

b. Assume m is not tangent to $\odot Q$. Then m must intersect $\odot Q$ at a second point R. $\overline{QP}$ and $\overline{QR}$ are both radii of $\odot Q$, so $\overline{QP} \cong \overline{QR}$. Because $m \perp \overline{QP}$, $QP < QR$. This is a contradiction, so m must be tangent to $\odot Q$.

48. $2\sqrt{2}$; *Sample answer:* Use the given lengths and the Pythagorean Theorem (Thm. 9.1) to find $AE = 8\sqrt{2}$. So, $PF = 2\sqrt{2}$.

10.1 Maintaining Mathematical Proficiency

49. $43°$ **50.** 3

10.2 Monitoring Progress and Modeling with Mathematics

35. a. Translate $\odot B$ so that point B maps to point A. The image of $\odot B$ is $\odot B'$ with center A. Because $\overline{AC} \cong \overline{BD}$, this translation maps $\odot B'$ to $\odot A$. A rigid motion maps $\odot B$ to $\odot A$, so $\odot A \cong \odot B$.

b. Because $\odot A \cong \odot B$, the distance from the center of the circle to a point on the circle is the same for each circle. So, $\overline{AC} \cong \overline{BD}$.

36. similar; The circles each have different radii.

37. a. $m\widehat{BC} = m\angle BAC$, $m\widehat{DE} = m\angle DAE$ and $m\angle BAC = m\angle DAE$, so $m\widehat{BC} = m\widehat{DE}$. Because $\widehat{BC}$ and $\widehat{DE}$ are in the same circle, $\widehat{BC} \cong \widehat{DE}$.

b. $m\widehat{BC} = m\angle BAC$ and $m\widehat{DE} = m\angle DAE$. Because $\widehat{BC} \cong \widehat{DE}$, $\angle BAC \cong \angle DAE$.

38. $s = \dfrac{\pi r\theta}{180}$; The circumference $= 2\pi r$, so the arc length

$$s = 2\pi r \cdot \dfrac{\theta}{360}.$$

10.3 Monitoring Progress and Modeling with Mathematics

18. a. $\overline{AB}$ is a diameter; Perpendicular Chord Bisector Converse (Thm. 10.8)

b. $\overline{AB} \cong \overline{CD}$; Congruent Corresponding Chords Theorem (Thm. 10.6)

c. $\overline{JH}$ bisects $\overline{FG}$ and $\widehat{FG}$; Perpendicular Chord Bisector Theorem (Thm. 10.7)

d. $\overline{NP} \cong \overline{LM}$; Equidistant Chords Theorem (Thm. 10.9)

19. a. Because $PA = PB = PC = PD$, $\triangle PDC \cong \triangle PAB$ by the SSS Congruence Theorem (Thm. 5.8). So, $\angle DPC \cong \angle APB$ and $\widehat{AB} \cong \widehat{CD}$.

b. $PA = PB = PC = PD$, and because $\widehat{AB} \cong \widehat{CD}$, $\angle DPC \cong \angle APB$. By the SAS Congruence Theorem (Thm. 5.5), $\triangle PDC \cong \triangle PAB$, so $\overline{AB} \cong \overline{CD}$.

20. *Sample answer:* $\overline{AC} \cong \overline{BC}$, so $\widehat{AC} \cong \widehat{BC}$ and $m\widehat{AB} = 360 - 2m\widehat{AC}$. $m\widehat{AC}$ is an integer, so $2m\widehat{AC}$ is even and $360 - 2m\widehat{AC}$ is even.

21. about $16.26°$; *Sample answer:* $AB = 2\sqrt{2}$ and $PA = PB = 10$, so $m\angle APB \approx 16.26°$ by the Law of Cosines (Thm. 9.10).

22. $\overline{LD} \cong \overline{LF}$ and $\overline{LC} \cong \overline{LC}$, so $\triangle LDC \cong \triangle LFC$ by the HL Congruence Theorem (Thm. 5.9). Then $\overline{DC} \cong \overline{FC}$ and $\angle DLC \cong \angle FLC$. So, $\widehat{DG} \cong \widehat{FG}$.

23. $\overline{TP} \cong \overline{PR}$, $\overline{LP} \cong \overline{LP}$, and $\overline{LT} \cong \overline{LR}$, so $\triangle LPR \cong \triangle LPT$ by the SSS Congruence Theorem (Thm. 5.8). Then $\angle LPT \cong \angle LPR$, so $m\angle LPT = m\angle LPR = 90°$. By definition, $\overline{LP}$ is a perpendicular bisector of $\overline{RT}$, so L lies on $\overline{QS}$. Because $\overline{QS}$ contains the center, $\overline{QS}$ is a diameter of $\odot L$.

24. yes; *Sample answer:* Draw several pairs of chords to see that the segment lengths are proportional.

25. If $\overline{AB} \cong \overline{CD}$, then $\overline{GC} \cong \overline{FA}$. Because $\overline{EC} \cong \overline{EA}$, $\triangle ECG \cong \triangle EAF$ by the HL Congruence Theorem (Thm. 5.9), so $\overline{EF} \cong \overline{EG}$ and $EF = EG$. If $EF = EG$, then because $\overline{EC} \cong \overline{ED} \cong \overline{EA} \cong \overline{EB}$, $\triangle AEF \cong \triangle BEF \cong \triangle DEG \cong \triangle CEG$ by the HL Congruence Theorem (Thm. 5.9). Then $\overline{AF} \cong \overline{BF} \cong \overline{DG} \cong \overline{CG}$, so $\overline{AB} \cong \overline{CD}$.

10.4 Monitoring Progress and Modeling with Mathematics

37. a. $\overline{QB} \cong \overline{QA}$, so $\triangle ABC$ is isosceles. By the Base Angles Theorem (Thm. 5.6), $\angle QBA \cong \angle QAB$, so $m\angle BAQ = x°$. By the Exterior Angles Theorem (Thm. 5.2), $m\angle AQC = 2x°$. Then $m\widehat{AC} = 2x°$, so $m\angle ABC = x° = \frac{1}{2}(2x)° = \frac{1}{2}m\widehat{AC}$.

b. Given: $\angle ABC$ is inscribed in $\odot Q$. $\overline{DB}$ is a diameter; Prove: $m\angle ABC = \frac{1}{2}m\widehat{AC}$; By Case 1, proved in part (a), $m\angle ABD = \frac{1}{2}m\widehat{AD}$ and $m\angle CBD = \frac{1}{2}m\widehat{CD}$. By the Arc Addition Postulate (Post. 10.1), $m\widehat{AD} + m\widehat{CD} = m\widehat{AC}$. By the Angle Addition Postulate (Post. 1.4), $m\angle ABD + m\angle CBD = m\angle ABC$. Then $m\angle ABC = \frac{1}{2}m\widehat{AD} + \frac{1}{2}m\widehat{CD}$

$$= \tfrac{1}{2}\left(m\widehat{AD} + m\widehat{CD}\right)$$

$$= \tfrac{1}{2}m\widehat{AC}.$$

c. Given: $\angle ABC$ is inscribed in $\odot Q$. $\overline{DB}$ is a diameter; Prove: $m\angle ABC = \frac{1}{2}m\widehat{AC}$; By Case 1, proved in part (a), $m\angle DBA = \frac{1}{2}m\widehat{AD}$ and $m\angle DBC = \frac{1}{2}m\widehat{CD}$. By the Arc Addition Postulate (Post. 10.1), $m\widehat{AC} + m\widehat{CD} = m\widehat{AD}$, so $m\widehat{AC} = m\widehat{AD} - m\widehat{CD}$. By the Angle Addition Postulate (Post. 1.4), $m\angle DBC + m\angle ABC = m\angle DBA$, so $m\angle ABC = m\angle DBA - m\angle DBC$. Then $m\angle ABC = \frac{1}{2}m\widehat{AD} - \frac{1}{2}m\widehat{CD}$

$$= \tfrac{1}{2}\left(m\widehat{AD} - m\widehat{CD}\right)$$

$$= \tfrac{1}{2}m\widehat{AC}.$$

38.

Given: $\angle ABC$ and $\angle ADC$ are inscribed angles intercepting $\widehat{AC}$; Prove: $\angle ABC \cong \angle ADC$; By the Measure of an Inscribed Angle Theorem (Thm. 10.10), $m\angle ABC = \frac{1}{2}m\widehat{AC}$ and $m\angle ADC = \frac{1}{2}m\widehat{AC}$. By the Transitive Property of Equality, $m\angle ABC = m\angle ADC$. So, $\angle ABC \cong \angle ADC$.

39. To prove the conditional, find the measure of the intercepted arc of the right angle and the definition of a semicircle to show the hypotenuse of the right triangle must be the diameter of the circle. To prove the converse, use the definition of a semicircle to find the measure of the angle opposite the diameter.

40. $m\widehat{EDG}$; Measure of an Inscribed Angle; $2m\angle F$; $m\angle D + m\angle F = 180°$; $m\angle E + m\angle G = 180°$

10.5 Monitoring Progress and Modeling with Mathematics

33. a. By the Tangent Line to Circle Theorem (Thm. 10.1), $m\angle BAC$ is 90°, which is half the measure of the semicircular arc.

b.

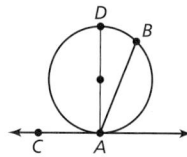

By the Tangent Line to Circle Theorem (Thm. 10.1), $m\angle CAD = 90°$. $m\angle DAB = \frac{1}{2}m\widehat{DB}$ and by part (a), $m\angle CAD = \frac{1}{2}m\widehat{AD}$. By the Angle Addition Postulate (Post. 1.4), $m\angle BAC = m\angle BAD + m\angle CAD$. So, $m\angle BAC = \frac{1}{2}m\widehat{DB} + \frac{1}{2}m\widehat{AD} = \frac{1}{2}(m\widehat{DB} + m\widehat{AD})$. By the Arc Addition Postulate (Post. 10.1), $m\widehat{DB} + m\widehat{AD} = m\widehat{ADB}$, so $m\angle BAC = \frac{1}{2}(m\widehat{ADB})$.

c.

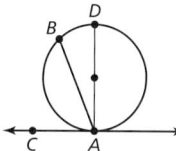

By the Tangent Line to Circle Theorem (Thm. 10.1), $m\angle CAD = 90°$. $m\angle DAB = \frac{1}{2}m\widehat{DB}$ and by part (a), $m\angle DAC = \frac{1}{2}m\widehat{ABD}$. By the Angle Addition Postulate (Post. 1.4), $m\angle BAC = m\angle DAC - m\angle DAB$. So, $m\angle BAC = \frac{1}{2}m\widehat{ABD} - \frac{1}{2}m\widehat{DB} = \frac{1}{2}(m\widehat{ABD} - m\widehat{DB})$. By the Arc Addition Postulate (Post. 10.1), $m\widehat{ABD} - m\widehat{DB} = m\widehat{AB}$, so $m\angle BAC = \frac{1}{2}(m\widehat{AB})$.

34. closer; The smaller arc needs to be 20°.

35.

STATEMENTS	REASONS
1. Chords $\overline{AC}$ and $\overline{BD}$ intersect.	1. Given
2. $m\angle ACB = \frac{1}{2}m\widehat{AB}$ and $m\angle DBC = \frac{1}{2}m\widehat{DC}$	2. Measure of an Inscribed Angle Theorem (Thm. 10.10)
3. $m\angle 1 = m\angle DBC + m\angle ACB$	3. Exterior Angle Theorem (Thm. 5.2)
4. $m\angle 1 = \frac{1}{2}m\widehat{DC} + \frac{1}{2}m\widehat{AB}$	4. Substitution Property of Equality
5. $m\angle 1 = \frac{1}{2}(m\widehat{DC} + m\widehat{AB})$	5. Distributive Property

36.

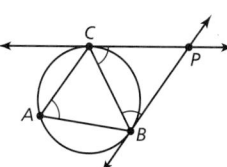

$\angle PCB$, $\angle PBC$, and $\angle CAB$ intercept $\widehat{BC}$.

37. By the Exterior Angle Theorem (Thm. 5.2), $m\angle 2 = m\angle 1 + m\angle ABC$, so $m\angle 1 = m\angle 2 - m\angle ABC$. By the Tangent and Intersected Chord Theorem (Thm. 10.14), $m\angle 2 = \frac{1}{2}m\widehat{BC}$ and by the Measure of an Inscribed Angle Theorem (Thm. 10.10), $m\angle ABC = \frac{1}{2}m\widehat{AC}$. By the Substitution Property, $m\angle 1 = \frac{1}{2}m\widehat{BC} - \frac{1}{2}m\widehat{AC} = \frac{1}{2}(m\widehat{BC} - m\widehat{AC})$;

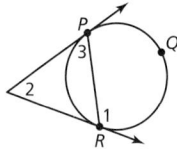

By the Exterior Angle Theorem (Thm. 5.2), $m\angle 1 = m\angle 2 + m\angle 3$, so $m\angle 2 = m\angle 1 - m\angle 3$. By the Tangent and Intersected Chord Theorem (Thm. 10.14), $m\angle 1 = \frac{1}{2}m\widehat{PQR}$ and $m\angle 3 = \frac{1}{2}m\widehat{PR}$. By the Substitution Property, $m\angle 2 = \frac{1}{2}m\widehat{PQR} - \frac{1}{2}m\widehat{PR} = \frac{1}{2}(m\widehat{PQR} - m\widehat{PR})$;

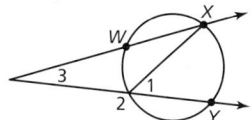

By the Exterior Angle Theorem (Thm. 5.2), $m\angle 1 = m\angle 3 + m\angle WXZ$, so $m\angle 3 = m\angle 1 - m\angle WXZ$. By the Measure of an Inscribed Angle Theorem (Thm. 10.10), $m\angle 1 = \frac{1}{2}m\widehat{XY}$ and $m\angle WXZ = \frac{1}{2}m\widehat{WZ}$. By the Substitution Property, $m\angle 3 = \frac{1}{2}m\widehat{XY} - \frac{1}{2}m\widehat{WZ} = \frac{1}{2}(m\widehat{XY} - m\widehat{WZ})$.

38.

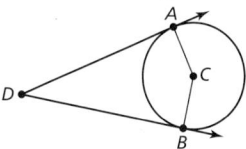

By the Angles Outside the Circle Theorem (Thm. 10.16),
$$m\angle ADB = \frac{1}{2}\left((360° - m\widehat{AB}) - m\widehat{AB}\right)$$
$$= \frac{1}{2}(360° - 2m\widehat{AB})$$
$$= 180° - m\widehat{AB}$$
$$= 180° - m\angle ACB.$$

39. 20°; *Sample answer:* $m\widehat{WY} = 160°$ and $m\widehat{WX} = m\widehat{ZY}$, so
$$m\angle P = \frac{1}{2}(m\widehat{WZ} - m\widehat{XY})$$
$$= \frac{1}{2}\left((200° - m\widehat{ZY}) - (160° - m\widehat{WX})\right)$$
$$= \frac{1}{2}(40°).$$

10.6 Monitoring Progress and Modeling with Mathematics

18. It takes the sparkles 3 seconds to move from point C to point D. Because $CN = 12$ centimeters and the sparkles have 3 seconds to move from point C to point N, the sparkles need to move at a speed of 4 centimeters per second from point C to point N.

19.

STATEMENTS	REASONS
1. $\overline{AB}$ and $\overline{CD}$ are chords intersecting in the interior of the circle.	1. Given
2. $\angle AEC \cong \angle DEB$	2. Vertical Angles Congruence Theorem (Thm. 2.6)
3. $\angle ACD \cong \angle ABD$	3. Inscribed Angles of a Circle Theorem (Thm. 10.11)
4. $\triangle AEC \sim \triangle DEB$	4. AA Similarity Theorem (Thm. 8.3)
5. $\dfrac{EA}{ED} = \dfrac{EC}{EB}$	5. Corresponding side lengths of similar triangles are proportional.
6. $EB \cdot EA = EC \cdot ED$	6. Cross Products Property

20.

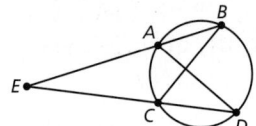

STATEMENTS	REASONS
1. $\overline{EB}$ and $\overline{ED}$ are secant segments.	1. Given
2. $\angle BEC \cong \angle DEA$	2. Reflexive Property of Congruence (Thm. 2.2)
3. $\angle ABC \cong \angle ADC$	3. Inscribed Angles of a Circle Theorem (Thm. 10.11)
4. $\triangle BCE \sim \triangle DAE$	4. AA Similarity Theorem (Thm. 8.3)
5. $\dfrac{EA}{EC} = \dfrac{ED}{EB}$	5. Corresponding side lengths of similar triangles are proportional.
6. $EA \cdot EB = EC \cdot ED$	6. Cross Products Property

21.

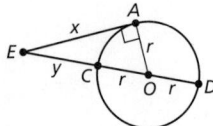

By the Tangent Line to Circle Theorem (Thm. 10.1), $\angle EAO$ is a right angle, which makes $\triangle AEO$ a right triangle. By the Pythagorean Theorem (Thm. 9.1), $(r + y)^2 = r^2 + x^2$. So, $r^2 + 2yr + y^2 = r^2 + x^2$. By the Subtraction Property of Equality, $2yr + y^2 = x^2$. Then $y(2r + y) = x^2$, so $EC \cdot ED = EA^2$.

22.

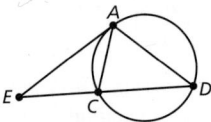

STATEMENTS	REASONS
1. $\overline{EA}$ is a tangent segment and $\overline{ED}$ is a secant segment.	1. Given
2. $\angle E \cong \angle E$	2. Reflexive Property of Congruence (Thm. 2.2)
3. $m\angle EAC = \frac{1}{2}m\widehat{AC}$	3. Tangent and Intersected Chord Theorem (Thm. 10.14)
4. $m\angle ADC = \frac{1}{2}m\widehat{AC}$	4. Measure of an Inscribed Angle Theorem (Thm. 10.10)
5. $m\angle EAC = m\angle ADC$	5. Transitive Property of Equality
6. $\angle EAC \cong \angle ADC$	6. Definition of congruence
7. $\triangle EAC \sim \triangle EDA$	7. AA Similarity Theorem (Thm. 8.3)
8. $\dfrac{EA}{ED} = \dfrac{EC}{EA}$	8. Corresponding side lengths of similar triangles are proportional.
9. $EA^2 = EC \cdot ED$	9. Cross Products Property

23. $BC = \dfrac{AD^2 + (AD)(DE) - AB^2}{AB}$

24. *Sample answer:* Segments of Secants and Tangents Theorem (Thm. 10.20), Pythagorean Theorem (Thm. 9.1); Use the equation $RQ^2 = RS \cdot RP$ to find RQ. Then use the Pythagorean Theorem (Thm. 9.1) to find PQ.

25. $2\sqrt{10}$

26. no; The side lengths are not proportional.

10.6 Maintaining Mathematical Proficiency

27. $x = -9, x = 5$ **28.** $x = 1 \pm \sqrt{10}$

29. $x = -7, x = 1$ **30.** $x = 1 \pm 2\sqrt{2}$

10.7 Monitoring Progress and Modeling with Mathematics

17. center: $(4, 1)$, radius: 1

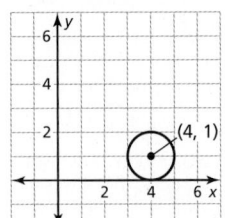

18. center: $(-2, -6)$, radius: 5

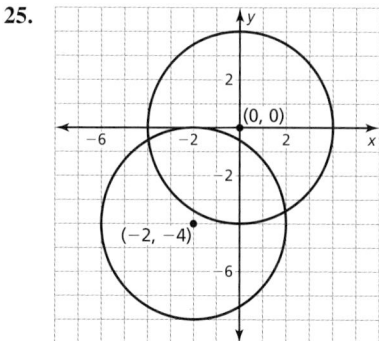

19. The radius of the circle is 8. $\sqrt{(2-0)^2 + (3-0)^2} = \sqrt{13}$, so $(2, 3)$ does not lie on the circle.

20. The radius of the circle is 3. $\sqrt{(4-0)^2 + (\sqrt{5}-0)^2} = \sqrt{21}$, so $(4, \sqrt{5})$ does not lie on the circle.

21. The radius of the circle is $\sqrt{10}$.
$\sqrt{(\sqrt{6}-0)^2 + (2-0)^2} = \sqrt{10}$, so $(\sqrt{6}, 2)$ does lie on the circle.

22. The radius of the circle is $\sqrt{29}$.
$\sqrt{(\sqrt{7}-0)^2 + (5-0)^2} = \sqrt{32}$, so $(\sqrt{7}, 5)$ does not lie on the circle.

23. **a.**

(graph showing Zone 1, Zone 2, Zone 3 concentric circles)

b. zone 2, zone 3, zone 1, zone 1, zone 2

25.

(graph with circles centered at $(0,0)$ and $(-2, -4)$)

The equation of the image is $(x + 2)^2 + (y + 4)^2 = 16$;
The equation of the image of a circle after a translation m units to the left and n units down is $(x + m)^2 + (y + n)^2 = r^2$.

26. **a.** C **b.** D **c.** B **d.** A

27. $(x - 4)^2 + (y - 9)^2 = 16$; $m\angle Z = 90°$, so $\overline{XY}$ is a diameter.

28. $y - b = \dfrac{h - a}{b - k}(x - a)$

29. tangent; The system has one solution.

30. none of these; The system has no solution.

31. secant; The system has two solutions, and $(5, -1)$ is not on the line.

32. secant that contains the diameter; The system has two solutions, and $(-3, 6)$ is on the line.

33. yes; The diameter perpendicularly bisects the chord from $(-1, 0)$ to $(1, 0)$, so the center is on the y-axis at $(0, k)$ and the radius is $k^2 + 1$.

34. $(x - 15)^2 + y^2 = 100$; *Sample answer:* If r is the radius of $\odot O$, C is at $(15r, 0)$, and the distance to $(63, 16)$ is $4r$.

10.7 Maintaining Mathematical Proficiency

35. minor arc; 53° **36.** minor arc; 90°

37. major arc; 270° **38.** minor arc, 127°

39. semicircle; 180° **40.** minor arc; 78°

Chapter 11

11.1 Monitoring Progress and Modeling with Mathematics

40. no; *Sample answer:* The values are the same to 6 decimal places; $\dfrac{104{,}348}{33{,}215}$

41. *Sample answer:*

STATEMENTS	REASONS
1. $\overline{FG} \cong \overline{GH}$, $\angle JFK \cong \angle KLF$	**1.** Given
2. $FG = GH$	**2.** Definition of congruent segments
3. $FH = FG + GH$	**3.** Segment Addition Postulate (Post. 1.2)
4. $FH = 2FG$	**4.** Substitution Property of Equality
5. $m\angle JFK = m\angle KFL$	**5.** Definition of congruent angles
6. $m\angle JFL = m\angle JFK + m\angle KFL$	**6.** Angle Addition Postulate (Post. 1.4)
7. $m\angle JFL = 2m\angle JFK$	**7.** Substitution Property of Equality
8. $\angle NFG \cong \angle JFL$	**8.** Vertical Angles Congruence Theorem (Thm. 2.6)
9. $m\angle NFG = m\angle JFL$	**9.** Definition of congruent angles
10. $m\angle NFG = 2m\angle JFK$	**10.** Substitution Property of Equality
11. arc length of $\overset{\frown}{JK}$ $= \dfrac{m\angle JFK}{360°} \cdot 2\pi FH$, arc length of $\overset{\frown}{NG}$ $= \dfrac{m\angle NFG}{360°} \cdot 2\pi FG$	**11.** Formula for arc length
12. arc length of $\overset{\frown}{JK}$ $= \dfrac{m\angle JFK}{360°} \cdot 2\pi(2FG)$, arc length of $\overset{\frown}{NG}$ $= \dfrac{2m\angle JFK}{360°} \cdot 2\pi FG$	**12.** Substitution Property of Equality
13. arc length of $\overset{\frown}{NG}$ $=$ arc length of $\overset{\frown}{JK}$	**13.** Transitive Property of Equality

42. a. $4\pi r$

  b. $4\pi r$; $4\pi r$; $4\pi r$; The total length of the segments is the same.

11.1 Maintaining Mathematical Proficiency

43. 15 square units   **44.** 42 square units

11.2 Monitoring Progress and Modeling with Mathematics

35. a. *Sample answer:* The total is 100%.

  b. bus 234°; walk 90°; other 36°

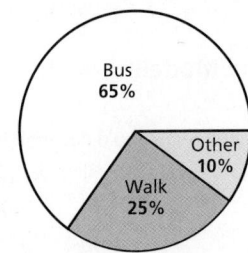

  c. bus: about 8.17 in.^{2}; walk: about 3.14 in.^{2}; other: about 1.26 in.^{2}

36. yes; *Sample answer:* The side length of each of the small squares is $\frac{1}{8}$ the side length of the outer square, and each small square is either completely colored or has a quarter circle colored.

37. a. You should buy two 14-inch pizzas; *Sample answer:* The area is 98π square inches and the cost is $25.98.

  b. You should buy two 10-inch pizzas and one 14-inch pizza; *Sample answer:* Buying three 10-inch pizzas is the only cheaper option, and it would not be enough pizza.

  c. You should buy four 10-inch pizzas; *Sample answer:* The total circumference is 20π inches.

38. πab

39. a. 2.4 in.^{2}; 4.7 in.^{2}; 7.1 in.^{2}; 9.4 in.^{2}; 11.8 in.^{2}; 14.1 in.^{2}

  b.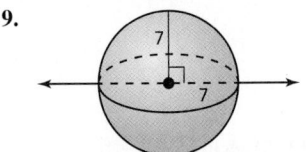

  c. yes; *Sample answer:* The rate of change is constant.

  d. yes; no; *Sample answer:* The rate of change will still be constant.

40. about 5.81 in.^{2}

41. *Sample answer:* Let $2a$ and $2b$ represent the lengths of the legs of the triangle. The areas of the semicircles are $\frac{1}{2}\pi a^2$, $\frac{1}{2}\pi b^2$, and $\frac{1}{2}\pi(a^2+b^2)$. $\frac{1}{2}\pi a^2 + \frac{1}{2}\pi b^2 = \frac{1}{2}\pi(a^2+b^2)$, and subtracting the areas of the unshaded regions from both sides leaves the area of the crescents on the left and the area of the triangle on the right.

11.4 Lesson Monitoring Progress

9.

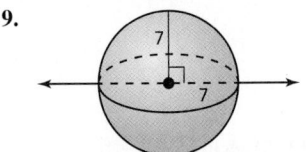

sphere with radius 7

11.4 Monitoring Progress and Modeling with Mathematics

21. 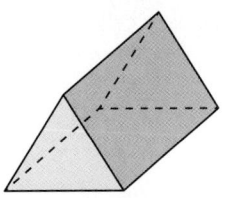   **22.**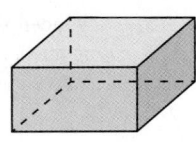

23. 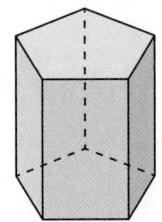   **24.**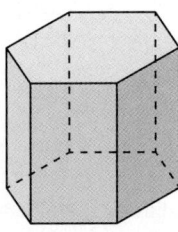

25. 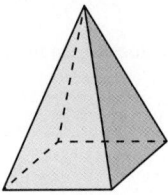   **26.**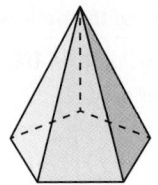

28. a. rectangle

  b. about 28.97 in.

  c. about 50.91 in.^{2}

29. no

30. yes; *Sample answer:* The plane passes through five faces.

31. yes; *Sample answer:* The plane is parallel to a face.

32. yes; *Sample answer:* The plane passes through three edges from a common vertex and two points are the same distance from the vertex.

33. yes; *Sample answer:* The plane passes through six faces.

34. yes; *Sample answer:* The plane passes through three edges from a common vertex and the three points are different distances from the vertex.

35. a.

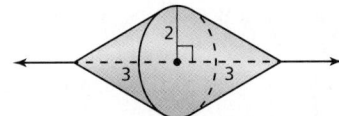

two cones with heights 3 and base radii 2

  b.

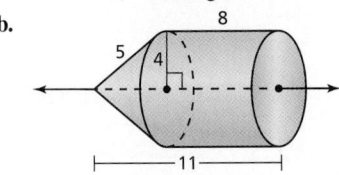

cone with height 3 and base radius 4 and cylinder with height 8 and base radius 4

36. *Sample answer:* At least three angles meet at a vertex, so the sum of the measures must be less than 360°. There can be three, four, or five triangles, three squares, or three pentagons at each vertex.

11.4 Maintaining Mathematical Proficiency

37. yes; SSS Congruence Theorem (Thm. 5.8)

38. yes; SAS Congruence Theorem (Thm. 5.5)

39. yes; ASA Congruence Theorem (Thm. 5.10)

11.5 Monitoring Progress and Modeling with Mathematics

46. The volume of cylinder X is half the volume of cylinder Y. *Sample answer:* Doubling the height doubles the volume and halving the radius multiplies the volume by $\frac{1}{4}$.

47. about 7.33 in.^{3} **48.** $r = \dfrac{R\sqrt{2}}{2}$

49. Increase the height by 25%.

50. Reduce the edge length by about 15.66%.

51. yes; *Sample answer:* Density is proportional to mass when the volume is constant.

52. no; *Sample answer:* The bases are the same but the sides of the other faces change.

53. 36 ft, 15 ft   **54.** 218.0 cm^3

11.5 Maintaining Mathematical Proficiency

55. 16 m^2 **56.** 406.3 cm^2

57. 680.4 in.^{2}

11.6 Maintaining Mathematical Proficiency

26. 12.9   **27.** 12.6

28. 5.8   **29.** 16.0

11.7 Monitoring Progress and Modeling with Mathematics

19. about 3716.85 ft^3 **20.** about 574.82 yd^3

21. yes; *Sample answer:* The automatic pet feeder holds about 12 cups of food.

22. about 17.45 sec   **23.** It is half; about 60°

24. $V = \frac{1}{3}\pi h(a^2 + ab + b^2)$

25. yes; *Sample answer:* The base areas are the same and the total heights are the same.

26. cone with height 15 and base radius 20, 2000π; cone with height 20 and base radius 15, 1500π; two cones, one with base radius 12 and height 9, the other with base radius 12 and height 16, 1200π

11.7 Maintaining Mathematical Proficiency

27. about 153.94 ft^2 **28.** about 380.13 cm^2

29. 32 m   **30.** 23 in.

11.8 Monitoring Progress and Modeling with Mathematics

45. *Sample answer:* radius 1 in. and height $\frac{4}{3}$ in.; radius $\frac{1}{3}$ in. and height 12 in.; radius 2 in. and height $\frac{1}{3}$ in.

46. a. about 54.45 ft^3

   b. about 28,500.53 cm^3

   c. about 2077.64 m^3

   d. about 522,170.40 in.^{3}

47. $S \approx 113.10$ in.^{2}, $V \approx 75.40$ in.^{3}

11.8 Maintaining Mathematical Proficiency

48. $B = 119°$, $a \approx 6.5$, $c \approx 8.5$

49. $A = 35°$, $a \approx 12.3$, $c \approx 14.6$

50. $A \approx 62.2°$, $B \approx 67.4°$, $C \approx 50.4°$

51. $a \approx 31.0$, $B \approx 28.1°$, $C \approx 48.9°$

Chapter 12

12.1 Monitoring Progress and Modeling with Mathematics

23. a. 2, 3, 4, 5, 6, 7, 8, 9, 10, 11, 12

   b. 2: $\frac{1}{36}$, 3: $\frac{1}{18}$, 4: $\frac{1}{12}$, 5: $\frac{1}{9}$, 6: $\frac{5}{36}$, 7: $\frac{1}{6}$, 8: $\frac{5}{36}$, 9: $\frac{1}{9}$, 10: $\frac{1}{12}$, 11: $\frac{1}{18}$, 12: $\frac{1}{36}$

   c. *Sample answer:* The probabilities are similar.

24. no; Your friend calculated the experimental probability. The theoretical probability of the coin landing heads up is $\frac{1}{2}$.

25. $\frac{\pi}{6}$, or about 52%

26. $\frac{2}{3}$; $f(x) + c$ intersects the x-axis when c is 1, 2, 3, or 4.

27. $\frac{3}{400}$, or 0.75%; about 113; $(0.0075)15,000 = 112.5$

28. *Sample answer:* Box A contains three cards numbered 1, 2, and 3. Box B contains 2 cards numbered 1 and 2. One card is removed at random from each box. Find the probability that the product of the two numbers is at least 5; $\frac{1}{6}$

12.1 Maintaining Mathematical Proficiency

29. $2x$ **30.** $\dfrac{x}{4y}$

31. $\dfrac{4x^6}{3}$ **32.** $2x^6$

33. $81p^4q^4$ **34.** $\dfrac{x^2}{y^4}$

12.2 Monitoring Progress and Modeling with Mathematics

25. a. *Sample answer:* Put 20 pieces of paper with each of the 20 students' names in a hat and pick one; 5%

   b. *Sample answer:* Put 45 pieces of paper in a hat with each student's name appearing once for each hour the student worked. Pick one piece; about 8.9%

26. a. without

   b. with

27. yes; The chance that it will be rescheduled is $(0.7)(0.75) = 0.525$, which is a greater than a 50% chance.

28. Event A represents rolling at least one 2. Event B represents the dice summing to 5; dependent; $P(A \text{ and } B) = \frac{2}{36}$ and $P(A)P(B) = \frac{11}{324}$

29. a. wins: 0%; loses: 1.99%; ties: 98.01%

   b. wins: 20.25%; loses: 30.25%; ties: 49.5%

   c. yes; Go for 2 points after the first touchdown, and then go for 1 point if they were successful the first time or 2 points if they were unsuccessful the first time; winning: 44.55%; losing: 30.25%

30. a. The occurrence of one event does not affect the occurrence of the other, so the probability of each event is the same whether or not the other event has occurred.

   b. yes; $P(A \text{ and } B) = P(A) \cdot P(B)$ and $P(A) = P(A \mid B)$.

12.2 Maintaining Mathematical Proficiency

31. $x = 0.2$

32. $x = 2$

33. $x = 0.15$

12.3 Explorations

1.

	Play an Instrument	Do Not Play an Instrument	Total
Speak a Foreign Language	16	30	46
Do Not Speak a Foreign Language	25	9	34
Total	41	39	80

- **a.** 41
- **b.** 46
- **c.** 16
- **d.** 9
- **e.** 25

3. *Sample answer:*

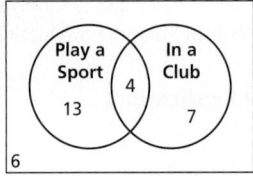

	Play a Sport	Do Not Play a Sport	Total
In a Club	4	7	11
Not in a Club	13	6	19
Total	17	13	30

Of the students in the class, 43.33% only play a sport, 13.33% play a sport and are in a club, 23.33% are only in a club, and 20% do neither activity. A total of 36.67% are in a club, and a total of 56.67% play a sport.

12.3 Lesson Monitoring Progress

3.

		Attendance	
		Attending	Not Attending
Class	Junior	0.353	0.634
	Senior	0.647	0.366

Given that a student is attending, the conditional relative frequency that he or she is a junior is about 35.3%. Given that a student is attending, the conditional relative frequency that he or she is a senior is about 64.7%. Given that a student is not attending, the conditional relative frequency that he or she is a junior is about 63.4%. Given that a student is not attending, the conditional relative frequency that he or she is a senior is about 36.6%.

4.

		Response	
		In Favor	Against
Gender	Boy	0.636	0.364
	Girl	0.808	0.192

Given that a student is a boy, the conditional relative frequency that he is in favor is about 63.6%. Given that a student is a girl, the conditional relative frequency that she is in favor is about 80.8%. Given that a student is a boy, the conditional relative frequency that he is against is about 36.4%. Given that a student is a girl, the conditional relative frequency that she is against is about 19.2%.

12.3 Monitoring Progress and Modeling with Mathematics

9.

		Gender		
		Male	Female	Total
Response	Yes	0.376	0.430	0.806
	No	0.111	0.083	0.194
	Total	0.487	0.513	1

10.

		Vaccination		
		Received	Not Received	Total
Health	Flu	0.1429	0.1518	0.2947
	No Flu	0.2946	0.4107	0.7053
	Total	0.4375	0.5625	1

19. *Sample answer:*

		Transportation to School			
		Rides Bus	Walks	Car	Total
Gender	Male	6	9	4	19
	Female	5	2	4	11
	Total	11	11	8	30

		Transportation to School			
		Rides Bus	Walks	Car	Total
Gender	Male	0.2	0.3	0.133	0.633
	Female	0.167	0.067	0.133	0.367
	Total	0.367	0.367	0.266	1

20. a. the parents surveyed that said no

   b. the total people that said yes

   c. the total people surveyed

21. Routine B is the best option, but your friend's reasoning of why is incorrect; Routine B is the best choice because there is a 66.7% chance of reaching the goal, which is higher than the chances of Routine A (62.5%) and Routine C (63.6%).

22.

		Preference		
		Math	Science	Total
Gender	Male	93	57	150
	Female	148	52	200
	Total	241	109	350

23. **a.** about 0.438
b. about 0.387

24. *Sample answer:* Venn diagrams show a visual representation of the data, and two-way tables organize the information into rows and columns; An advantage of a Venn diagram is that people who learn visually will easily understand them. A disadvantage is that as more categories are used, the Venn diagram becomes harder to draw and interpret. An advantage of a two-way table is that it is very easy to read and interpret, even with many categories. A disadvantage is that they are not as visual as Venn diagrams.

25. **a.** More of the current consumers prefer the leader, so they should improve the new snack before marketing it.
b. More of the new consumers prefer the new snack than the leading snack, so there is no need to improve the snack.

26. *Sample answer:*

		Owns a Dog		
		Yes	No	Total
Gender	Male	5	3	8
	Female	7	5	12
	Total	12	8	20

$$P(A \mid B) = \frac{P(B \mid A) \cdot P(A)}{P(B)}$$

$$P(\text{Male} \mid \text{yes}) = \frac{P(\text{yes} \mid \text{Male}) \cdot P(\text{Male})}{P(\text{yes})}$$

$$= \frac{\frac{5}{8} \cdot \frac{8}{20}}{\frac{12}{20}}$$

$$= \frac{5}{12}$$

12.3 Maintaining Mathematical Proficiency

27.

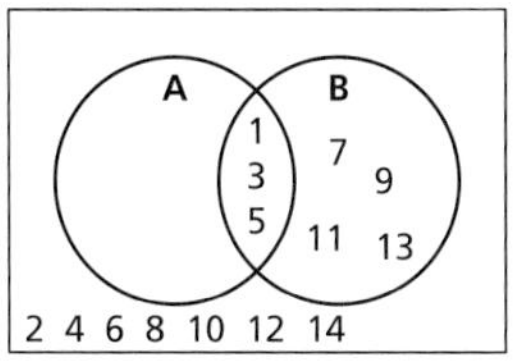

28.

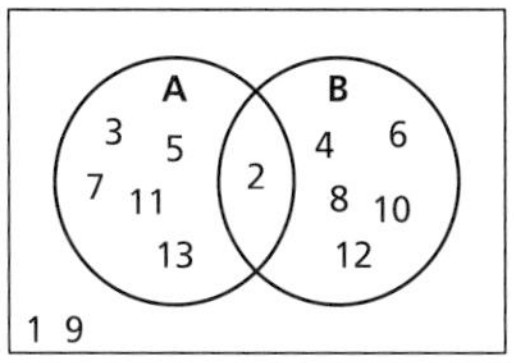

29.

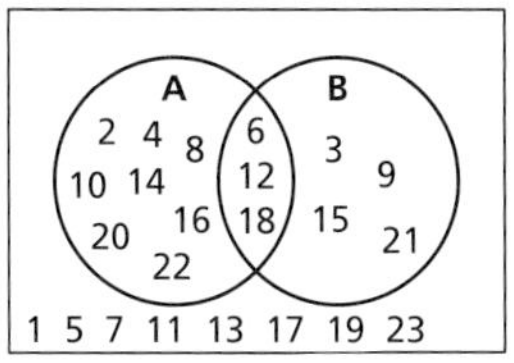

12.4 Monitoring Progress and Modeling with Mathematics

22. **a.** $P(A \text{ or } B \text{ or } C) = P(A) + P(B) + P(C)$
b. $P(A \text{ or } B \text{ or } C) = P(A) + P(B) + P(C) - P(A \text{ and } B) - P(A \text{ and } C) - P(B \text{ and } C) + P(A \text{ and } B \text{ and } C)$

12.6 Monitoring Progress and Modeling with Mathematics

5.

w (value)	1	2
Outcomes	5	21
P(*w*)	$\frac{5}{26}$	$\frac{21}{26}$

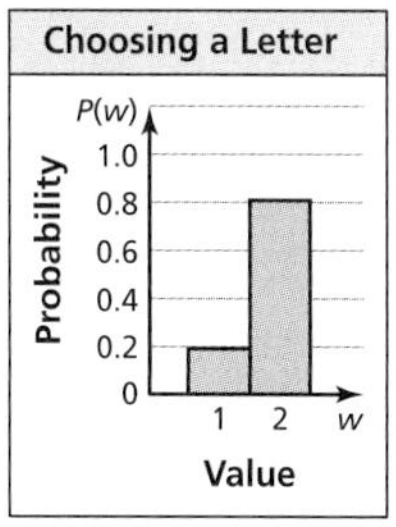

6.

n (value)	1	2	3
Outcomes	10	90	900
P(*n*)	$\frac{1}{100}$	$\frac{9}{100}$	$\frac{9}{10}$

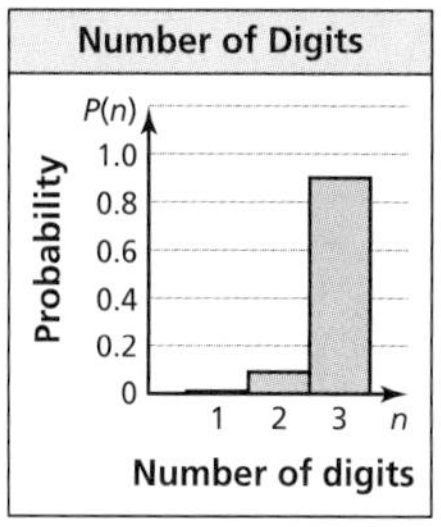

14. **a.**

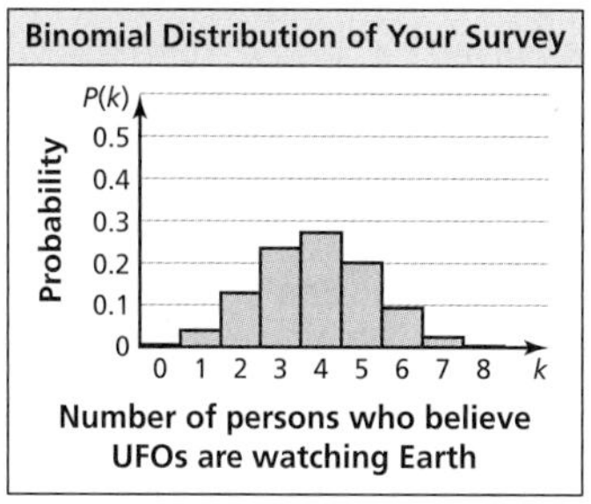

17. a. $P(0) \approx 0.099$, $P(1) \approx 0.271$, $P(2) \approx 0.319$,
$P(3) \approx 0.208$, $P(4) \approx 0.081$, $P(5) \approx 0.019$,
$P(6) \approx 0.0025$, $P(7) \approx 0.00014$

b.

x	0	1	2	3	4
$P(x)$	0.099	0.271	0.319	0.208	0.081

x	5	6	7
$P(x)$	0.019	0.0025	0.00014

c.

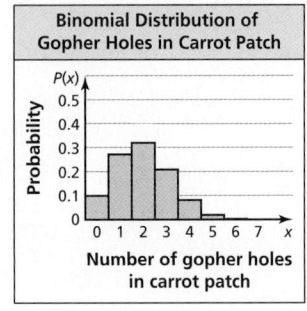

18. 0.2; 0.6

19. no; The data is skewed right, so the probability of failure is greater.

20. no; The probability of not choosing the coin 100 times
is $\left(\frac{99}{100}\right)^{100} \approx 0.366$.

21. a. The statement is not valid, because having a male and having a female are independent events.

b. 0.03125

c.

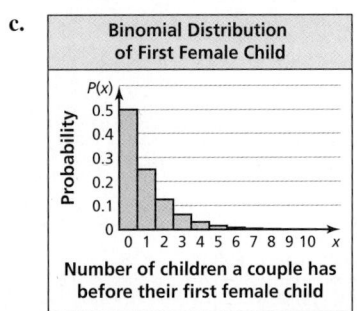

skewed right

22. $p > 0.5$

12.6 Maintaining Mathematical Proficiency

23. FFF, FFM FMF, FMM, MMM, MMF, MFM, MFF

24. D_1C_1, D_1C_2, D_1C_3, D_2C_1, D_2C_2, D_2C_3

Additional Topic
Additional Topic Explorations

1. a.

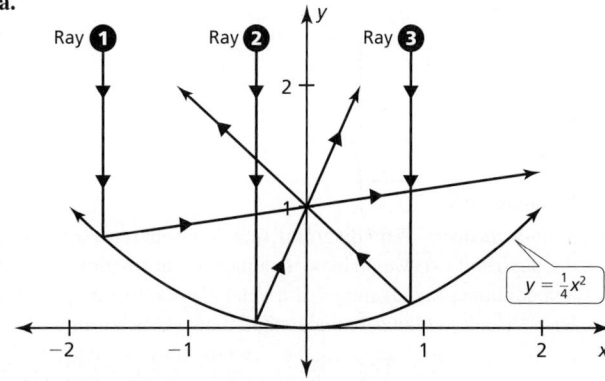

b. All the reflected rays cross through the point $(0, 1)$.

c. $(0,1)$; This is the best place for the receiver because any ray entering the satellite dish will hit the receiver.

2.

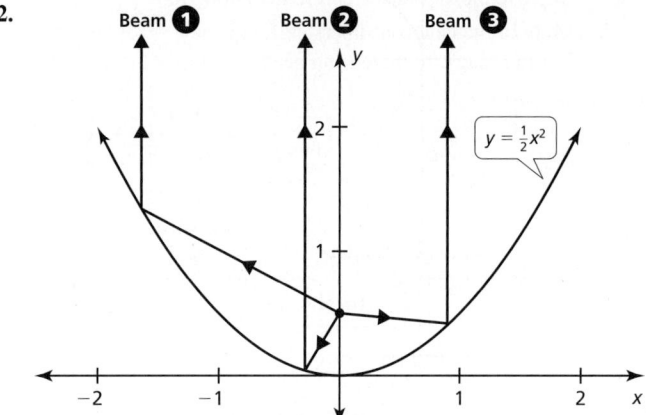

All beams leaving the parabola are parallel; yes; With a spotlight, all beams of light should be pointed at the same object.

Additional Topic Lesson Monitoring Progress

4. The focus is $\left(\frac{3}{2}, 0\right)$, the directrix is $x = -\frac{3}{2}$, and the axis of symmetry is the x-axis.

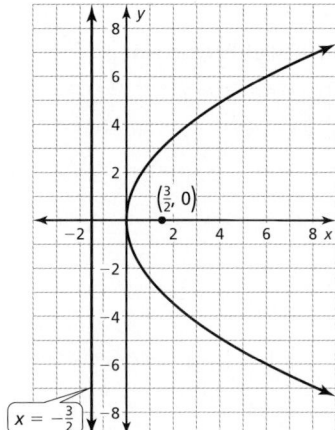

Additional Topic Monitoring Progress and Modeling with Mathematics

16. The focus is $(6, 0)$. The directrix is $x = -6$. The axis of symmetry is the x-axis.

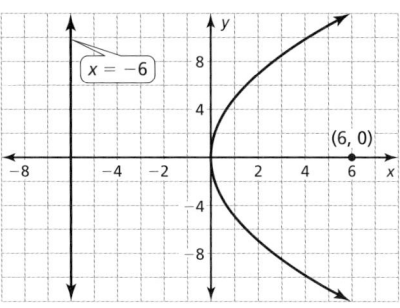

17. The focus is $(4, 0)$. The directrix is $x = -4$. The axis of symmetry is the x-axis.

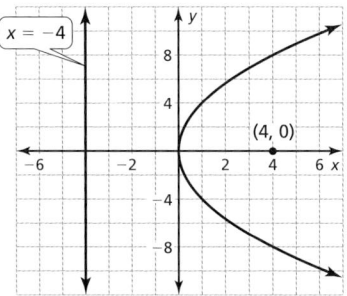

18. The focus is $(0, -12)$. The directrix is $y = 12$. The axis of symmetry is the y-axis.

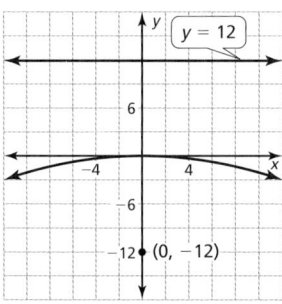

19. The focus is $\left(0, -\frac{1}{8}\right)$. The directrix is $y = \frac{1}{8}$. The axis of symmetry is the y-axis.

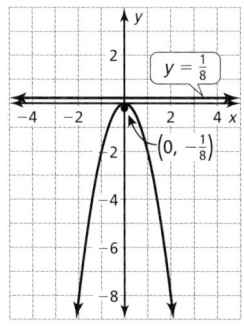

20. The focus is $\left(0, \frac{1}{32}\right)$. The directrix is $y = -\frac{1}{32}$. The axis of symmetry is the y-axis.

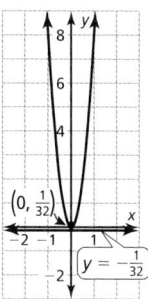

21. Instead of a vertical axis of symmetry, the graph should have a horizontal axis of symmetry.

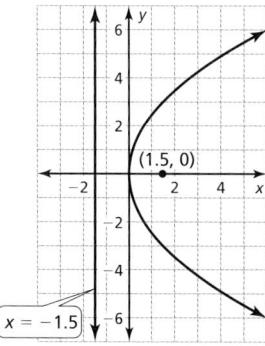

22. Because $p = -0.5$, the focus is $(-0.5, 0)$, and the directrix is $x = 0.5$.

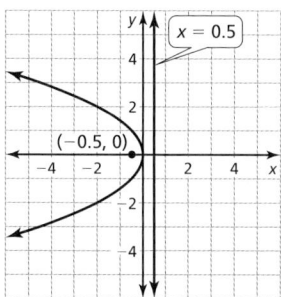

23. 9.5 in.; The receiver should be placed at the focus. The distance from the vertex to the focus is $p = \frac{38}{4} = 9.5$ in.

Additional Answers

English-Spanish Glossary

English

Spanish

acute angle *(p. 39)* An angle that has a measure greater than 0° and less than 90°

ángulo agudo *(p. 39)* Un ángulo que tiene una medida mayor que 0° y menor que 90°

adjacent angles *(p. 48)* Two angles that share a common vertex and side, but have no common interior points

ángulos adyacentes *(p. 48)* Dos ángulos que comparten un vértice y lado en común, pero que no tienen puntos interiores en común

adjacent arcs *(p. 539)* Arcs of a circle that have exactly one point in common

arcos adyacentes *(p. 539)* Arcos de un círculo que tienen exactamente un punto en común

alternate exterior angles *(p. 128)* Two angles that are formed by two lines and a transversal that are outside the two lines and on opposite sides of the transversal

ángulos exteriores alternos *(p. 128)* Dos ángulos que son formados por dos rectas y una transversal que están fuera de las dos rectas y en lados opuestos de la transversal

alternate interior angles *(p. 128)* Two angles that are formed by two lines and a transversal that are between the two lines and on opposite sides of the transversal

ángulos interiores alternos *(p. 128)* Dos ángulos que son formados por dos rectas y una transversal que están entre las dos rectas y en lados opuestos de la transversal

altitude of a triangle *(p. 321)* The perpendicular segment from a vertex of a triangle to the opposite side or to the line that contains the opposite side

altitud de un triángulo *(p. 321)* El segmento perpendicular desde el vértice de un triángulo al lado opuesto o a la recta que contiene el lado opuesto

angle *(p. 38)* A set of points consisting of two different rays that have the same endpoint

ángulo *(p. 38)* Un conjunto de puntos que consiste en dos rayos distintos que tienen el mismo punto extremo

angle bisector *(p. 42)* A ray that divides an angle into two angles that are congruent

bisectriz de un ángulo *(p. 42)* Un rayo que divide un ángulo en dos ángulos congruentes

angle of depression *(p. 497)* The angle that a downward line of sight makes with a horizontal line

ángulo de depresión *(p. 497)* El ángulo formado entre una recta de vista descendente y una recta horizontal

angle of elevation *(p. 490)* The angle that an upward line of sight makes with a horizontal line

ángulo de elevación *(p. 490)* El ángulo formado entre una recta de vista ascendente y una recta horizontal

angle of rotation *(p. 190)* The angle that is formed by rays drawn from the center of rotation to a point and its image

ángulo de rotación *(p. 190)* El ángulo que está formado por rayos dibujados desde el centro de rotación hacia un punto y su imagen

apothem of a regular polygon *(p. 611)* The distance from the center to any side of a regular polygon

apotema de un polígono regular *(p. 611)* La distancia desde el centro a cualquier lado de un polígono regular

arc length *(p. 595)* A portion of the circumference of a circle

longitud de arco *(p. 595)* Una porción de la circunferencia de un círculo

axiom *(p. 12)* A rule that is accepted without proof

axioma *(p. 12)* Una regla que es aceptada sin demostración

axis of revolution (p. 620) The line around which a two-dimensional shape is rotated to form a three-dimensional figure

eje de revolución (p. 620) La recta alrededor de la cual una forma bidimensional rota para formar una figura tridimensional

---

B

base angles of an isosceles triangle (p. 252) The two angles adjacent to the base of an isosceles triangle

ángulos de la base de un triángulo isósceles (p. 252) Los dos ángulos adyacentes a la base de un triángulo isósceles

base angles of a trapezoid (p. 398) Either pair of consecutive angles whose common side is a base of a trapezoid

ángulos de la base de un trapecio (p. 398) Cualquier par de ángulos consecutivos cuyo lado común es la base de un trapezoide

base of an isosceles triangle (p. 252) The side of an isosceles triangle that is not one of the legs

base de un triángulo isósceles (p. 252) El lado de un triángulo isósceles que no es uno de los catetos

bases of a trapezoid (p. 398) The parallel sides of a trapezoid

bases de un trapecio (p. 398) Los lados paralelos de un trapezoide

between (p. 14) When three points are collinear, one point is between the other two.

entre (p. 14) Cuando tres puntos son colineales, un punto está entre los otros dos.

biconditional statement (p. 69) A statement that contains the phrase "if and only if"

enunciado bicondicional (p. 69) Un enunciado que contiene la frase "si y sólo si"

binomial distribution (p. 709) A type of probability distribution that shows the probabilities of the outcomes of a binomial experiment

distribución del binomio (p. 709) Un tipo de distributión de probabilidades que muestra las probabilidades de los resultados posibles de un experimento del binomio

binomial experiment (p. 709) An experiment in which there are a fixed number of independent trials, exactly two possible outcomes for each trial, and the probability of success is the same for each trial.

experimento del binomio (p. 709) Un experimento en el que hay un número fijo de pruebas independientes, exactamente dos resultados posibles para cada prueba, y la probabilidad de éxito es la misma para cada prueba

---

C

Cavalieri's Principle (p. 626) If two solids have the same height and the same cross-sectional area at every level, then they have the same volume.

Principio de Cavalieri (p. 626) Si dos sólidos tienen la misma altura y la misma área transversal en todo nivel, entonces tienen el mismo volumen.

center of a circle (p. 530) The point from which all points on a circle are equidistant

centro de un círculo (p. 530) El punto desde donde todos los puntos en un círculo son equidistantes

center of dilation (p. 208) The fixed point in a dilation

centro de dilatación (p. 208) El punto fijo en una dilatación

center of a regular polygon (p. 611) The center of a polygon's circumscribed circle

centro de un polígono regular (p. 611) El centro del círculo circunscrito de un polígono

center of rotation (p. 190) The fixed point in a rotation

centro de rotación (p. 190) El punto fijo en una rotación

center of symmetry (p. 193) The center of rotation in a figure that has rotational symmetry

centro de simetría (p. 193) El centro de rotación en una figura que tiene simetría rotacional

central angle of a circle (p. 538) An angle whose vertex is the center of a circle

ángulo central de un círculo (p. 538) Un ángulo cuyo vértice es el centro de un círculo

central angle of a regular polygon *(p. 611)* An angle formed by two radii drawn to consecutive vertices of a polygon

centroid *(p. 320)* The point of concurrency of the three medians of a triangle

chord of a circle *(p. 530)* A segment whose endpoints are on a circle

chord of a sphere *(p. 648)* A segment whose endpoints are on a sphere

circle *(p. 530)* The set of all points in a plane that are equidistant from a given point

circumcenter *(p. 310)* The point of concurrency of the three perpendicular bisectors of a triangle

circumference *(p. 594)* The distance around a circle

circumscribed angle *(p. 564)* An angle whose sides are tangent to a circle

circumscribed circle *(p. 556)* A circle that contains all the vertices of an inscribed polygon

collinear points *(p. 4)* Points that lie on the same line

combination *(p. 702)* A selection of objects in which order is not important

common tangent *(p. 531)* A line or segment that is tangent to two coplanar circles

complementary angles *(p. 48)* Two angles whose measures have a sum of 90°

component form *(p. 174)* A form of a vector that combines the horizontal and vertical components

composition of transformations *(p. 176)* The combination of two or more transformations to form a single transformation

compound event *(p. 694)* The union or intersection of two events

concentric circles *(p. 531)* Coplanar circles that have a common center

conclusion *(p. 66)* The "then" part of a conditional statement written in if-then form

concurrent *(p. 310)* Three or more lines, rays, or segments that intersect in the same point

ángulo central de un polígono regular *(p. 611)* Un ángulo formado por dos radios extendidos a vértices consecutivos de un polígono

centroide *(p. 320)* El punto de concurrencia de las tres medianas de un triángulo

cuerda de un círculo *(p. 530)* Un segmento cuyos puntos extremos están en un círculo

cuerda de una esfera *(p. 648)* Un segmento cuyos puntos extremos están en una esfera

círculo *(p. 530)* El conjunto de todos los puntos en un plano que son equidistantes de un punto dado

circuncentro *(p. 310)* El punto de concurrencia de las tres bisectrices perpendiculares de un triángulo

circunferencia *(p. 594)* La distancia alrededor de un círculo

ángulo circunscrito *(p. 564)* Un ángulo cuyos lados son tangentes a un círculo

círculo circunscrito *(p. 556)* Un círculo que contiene todos los vértices de un polígono inscrito

puntos colineales *(p. 4)* Puntos que descansan en la misma recta

combinación *(p. 702)* Una selección de objetos en la que el orden no es importante

tangente común *(p. 531)* Una recta o segmento que es tangente a dos círculos coplanarios

ángulos complementarios *(p. 48)* Dos ángulos cuyas medidas suman 90°

forma componente *(p. 174)* Una forma de un vector que combina los componentes horizontales y verticales

composición de transformaciones *(p. 176)* La combinación de dos o más transformaciones para formar una transformación única

evento compuesto *(p. 694)* la unión o intersección de dos eventos

círculos concéntricos *(p. 531)* Círculos coplanarios que tienen un centro en común

conclusión *(p. 66)* La parte después de "entonces" en un enunciado condicional escrito de la forma "si..., entonces..."

concurrente *(p. 310)* Tres o más rectas, rayos o segmentos que se intersectan en el mismo punto

conditional probability *(p. 677)* The probability that event *B* occurs given that event *A* has occurred, written as $P(B|A)$

conditional relative frequency *(p. 685)* The ratio of a joint relative frequency to the marginal relative frequency in a two-way table

conditional statement *(p. 66)* A logical statement that has a hypothesis and a conclusion

congruence transformation *(p. 201)* A transformation that preserves length and angle measure
See rigid motion.

congruent angles *(p. 40)* Two angles that have the same measure

congruent arcs *(p. 540)* Arcs that have the same measure and are of the same circle or of congruent circles

congruent circles *(p. 540)* Circles that can be mapped onto each other by a rigid motion or a composition of rigid motions

congruent figures *(p. 200)* Geometric figures that have the same size and shape

congruent segments *(p. 13)* Line segments that have the same length

conjecture *(p. 76)* An unproven statement that is based on observations

consecutive interior angles *(p. 128)* Two angles that are formed by two lines and a transversal that lie between the two lines and on the same side of the transversal

construction *(p. 13)* A geometric drawing that uses a limited set of tools, usually a compass and a straightedge

contrapositive *(p. 67)* The statement formed by negating both the hypothesis and conclusion of the converse of a conditional statement

converse *(p. 67)* The statement formed by exchanging the hypothesis and conclusion of a conditional statement

coordinate *(p. 12)* A real number that corresponds to a point on a line

coordinate proof *(p. 284)* A style of proof that involves placing geometric figures in a coordinate plane

probabilidad condicional *(p. 677)* La probabilidad de que el evento *B* ocurra dado que el evento *A* ha ocurrido, escrito como $P(B|A)$

frecuencia relativa condicional *(p. 685)* La razón de una frecuencia relativa conjunta a la frecuencia relativa marginal en una tabla de doble entrada

enunciado condicional *(p. 66)* Un enunciado lógico que tiene una hipótesis y una conclusión

transformación de congruencia *(p. 201)* Una transformación que preserva la longitud y medida del ángulo
Ver movimiento rígida.

ángulos congruentes *(p. 40)* Dos ángulos que tienen la misma medida

arcos congruentes *(p. 540)* Arcos que tienen la misma medida y que son del mismo círculo o de círculos congruentes

círculos congruentes *(p. 540)* Círculos que pueden superponerse sobre sí mismos mediante un movimiento rígido o una composición de movimientos rígidos

figuras congruentes *(p. 200)* Figuras geométricas que tienen el mismo tamaño y forma

segmentos congruentes *(p. 13)* Segmentos de rectas que tienen la misma longitud

conjetura *(p. 76)* Una afirmación no comprobada que se basa en observaciones

ángulos interiores consecutivos *(p. 128)* Dos ángulos que son formados por dos rectas y una transversal que descansan entre las dos rectas y en el mismo lado de la transversal

construcción *(p. 13)* Un dibujo geométrico que usa un conjunto limitado de herramientas, generalmente una regla y compás

contrapositivo *(p. 67)* El enunciado formado por la negación de la hipótesis y conclusión del converso de un enunciado condicional

converso *(p. 67)* El enunciado formado por el intercambio de la hipótesis y conclusión de un enunciado condicional

coordenada *(p. 12)* Un número real que corresponde a un punto en una línea

prueba de coordenadas *(p. 284)* Un estilo de prueba que implica colocar figuras geométricas en un plano coordenado

coplanar points *(p. 4)* Points that lie in the same plane

corollary to a theorem *(p. 235)* A statement that can be proved easily using the theorem

corresponding angles *(p. 128)* Two angles that are formed by two lines and a transversal that are in corresponding positions

corresponding parts *(p. 240)* A pair of sides or angles that have the same relative position in two congruent figures

cosine *(p. 494)* For an acute angle of a right triangle, the ratio of the length of the leg adjacent to the acute angle to the length of the hypotenuse

counterexample *(p. 77)* A specific case for which a conjecture is false

cross section *(p. 619)* The intersection of a plane and a solid

———————— **D** ————————

deductive reasoning *(p. 78)* A process that uses facts, definitions, accepted properties, and the laws of logic to form a logical argument

defined terms *(p. 5)* Terms that can be described using known words, such as *point* or *line*

density *(p. 628)* The amount of matter that an object has in a given unit of volume

dependent events *(p. 677)* Two events in which the occurrence of one event does affect the occurrence of the other event

diagonal *(p. 360)* A segment that joins two nonconsecutive vertices of a polygon

diameter *(p. 530)* A chord that contains the center of a circle

dilation *(p. 208)* A transformation in which a figure is enlarged or reduced with respect to a fixed point

directed line segment *(p. 156)* A segment that represents moving from point A to point B is called the directed line segment AB.

directrix *(p. 722)* A fixed line perpendicular to the axis of symmetry, such that the set of all points (x, y) of the parabola are equidistant from the focus and the directrix

disjoint events *(p. 694)* Two events that have no outcomes in common

puntos coplanarios *(p. 4)* Puntos que descansan en el mismo plano

corolario de un teorema *(p. 235)* Un enunciado que puede comprobarse fácilmente usando el teorema

ángulos correspondientes *(p. 128)* Dos ángulos que están formados por dos líneas y una transversal que están en las posiciones correspondientes

partes correspondientes *(p. 240)* Un par de lados o ángulos que tienen la misma posición relativa en dos figuras congruentes

coseno *(p. 494)* Para un ángulo agudo de un triángulo rectángulo, la razón de la longitud del cateto adyacente al ángulo agudo a la longitud de la hipotenusa

contraejemplo *(p. 77)* Un caso específico para el que una conjetura es falsa

sección transversal *(p. 619)* La intersección de un plano y un sólido

razonamiento deductivo *(p. 78)* Un proceso que usa hechos, definiciones, propiedades aceptadas y las leyes de la lógica para formar un argumento lógico

términos definidos *(p. 5)* Términos que pueden describirse usando palabras conocidas, como *punto* o *línea*

densidad *(p. 628)* La cantidad de materia que tiene un objeto en una unidad de volumen dada

eventos dependientes *(p. 677)* Dos eventos en los que la ocurrencia de un evento afecta la ocurrencia del otro evento

diagonal *(p. 360)* Un segmento que une dos vértices no consecutivos de un polígono

diámetro *(p. 530)* Una cuerda que contiene el centro de un círculo

dilatación *(p. 208)* Una transformación en la cual una figura se agranda o reduce con respecto a un punto fijo

segmento de línea dirigido *(p. 156)* Un segmento que representa el moverse del punto A al punto B se llama el segmento de línea dirigido AB.

directriz *(p. 722)* Una recta fija perpendicular al eje de simetría de modo tal, que el conjunto de todos los puntos (x, y) de la parábola sean equidistantes del foco y la directriz

eventos disjunto *(p. 694)* Dos eventos que no tienen resultados en común

distance *(p. 12)* The absolute value of the difference of two coordinates on a line

distance from a point to a line *(p. 148)* The length of the perpendicular segment from the point to the line

distancia *(p. 12)* El valor absoluto de la diferencia de dos coordenadas en una línea

distancia desde un punto a una línea *(p. 148)* La longitud del segmento perpendicular desde el punto a la línea

---

E

---

edge *(p. 618)* A line segment formed by the intersection of two faces of a polyhedron

endpoints *(p. 5)* Points that represent the ends of a line segment or ray

enlargement *(p. 208)* A dilation in which the scale factor is greater than 1

equiangular polygon *(p. 361)* A polygon in which all angles are congruent

equidistant *(p. 302)* A point is equidistant from two figures when it is the same distance from each figure.

equilateral polygon *(p. 361)* A polygon in which all sides are congruent

equivalent statements *(p. 67)* Two related conditional statements that are both true or both false

event *(p. 668)* A collection of one or more outcomes in a probability experiment.

experimental probability *(p. 671)* The ratio of the number of successes, or favorable outcomes, to the number of trials in a probability experiment

exterior of an angle *(p. 38)* The region that contains all the points outside of an angle

exterior angles *(p. 233)* Angles that form linear pairs with the interior angles of a polygon

external segment *(p. 571)* The part of a secant segment that is outside the circle

borde *(p. 618)* Un segmento de línea formado por la intersección de dos caras de un poliedro

puntos extremos *(p. 5)* Punto que representan los extremos de un rayo o segmento de línea

agrandamiento *(p. 208)* Una dilatación en donde el factor de escala es mayor que 1

polígono equiangular *(p. 361)* Un polígono en donde todos los ángulos son congruentes

equidistante *(p. 302)* Un punto es equidistante desde dos figuras cuando está a la misma distancia de cada figura.

polígono equilátero *(p. 361)* Un polígono en donde todos los lados son congruentes

enunciados equivalentes *(p. 67)* Dos enunciados condicionales relacionados que son ambos verdaderos, o ambos falsos

evento *(p. 668)* Una colección de uno o más resultados en un experimento de probabilidades

probabilidad experimental *(p. 671)* La razón del número de éxitos, o resultados favorables, con respecto al número de pruebas en un experimento de probabilidades

exterior de un ángulo *(p. 38)* La región que contiene todos los puntos fuera de un ángulo

ángulos exteriores *(p. 233)* Ángulos que forman pares lineales con los ángulos interiores de un polígono

segmento externo *(p. 571)* La parte de un segmento secante que está fuera del círculo

---

F

---

face *(p. 618)* A flat surface of a polyhedron

flowchart proof (flow proof) *(p. 106)* A type of proof that uses boxes and arrows to show the flow of a logical argument

focus *(p. 722)* A fixed point in the interior of a parabola, such that the set of all points (x, y) of the parabola are equidistant from the focus and the directrix

cara *(p. 618)* Una superficie plana de un poliedro

prueba de organigrama (prueba de flujo) *(p. 106)* Un tipo de prueba que usa casillas y flechas para mostrar el flujo de un argumento lógico

foco *(p. 722)* Un punto fijo en el interior de una parábola, de tal forma que el conjunto de todos los puntos (x, y) de la parábola sean equidistantes del foco y la directriz

geometric mean *(p. 480)* The positive number x that satisfies $\dfrac{a}{x} = \dfrac{x}{b}$

So, $x^2 = ab$ and $x = \sqrt{ab}$.

media geométrica *(p. 480)* El número positivo x que satisface $\dfrac{a}{x} = \dfrac{x}{b}$

Entonces, $x^2 = ab$ and $x = \sqrt{ab}$.

geometric probability *(p. 670)* A probability found by calculating a ratio of two lengths, areas, or volumes

probabilidad geométrica *(p. 670)* Una probabilidad hallada al calcular la razón de dos longitudes, áreas o volúmenes

glide reflection *(p. 184)* A transformation involving a translation followed by a reflection

reflexión por deslizamiento *(p. 184)* Una transformación que implica una traslación seguida de una reflexión

great circle *(p. 648)* The intersection of a plane and a sphere such that the plane contains the center of the sphere

gran círculo *(p. 648)* La intersección de un plano y una esfera, de tal forma que el plano contiene el centro de la esfera

horizontal component *(p. 174)* The horizontal change from the starting point of a vector to the ending point

componente horizontal *(p. 174)* El cambio horizontal desde el punto de inicio de un vector hasta el punto final

hypotenuse *(p. 264)* The side opposite the right angle of a right triangle

hipotenusa *(p. 264)* El lado opuesto al ángulo recto de un triángulo recto

hypothesis *(p. 66)* The "if" part of a conditional statement written in if-then form

hipótesis *(p. 66)* La parte después de "si" en un enunciado condicional escrito de la forma "si..., entonces..."

if-then form *(p. 66)* A conditional statement in the form "if p, then q"

forma "si..., entonces..." *(p. 66)* Un enunciado condicional en la forma de "si p, entonces q"

image *(p. 174)* A figure that results from the transformation of a geometric figure

imagen *(p. 174)* Una figura que resulta de la transformación de una figura geométrica

incenter *(p. 313)* The point of concurrency of the angle bisectors of a triangle

incentro *(p. 313)* El punto de concurrencia de las bisectrices de los ángulos de un triángulo

independent events *(p. 676)* Two events in which the occurrence of one event does not affect the occurrence of another event

eventos independientes *(p. 676)* Dos eventos en los que la ocurrencia de un evento no afecta la ocurrencia de otro evento

indirect proof *(p. 336)* A style of proof in which you temporarily assume that the desired conclusion is false, then reason logically to a contradiction
This proves that the original statement is true.

prueba indirecta *(p. 336)* Un estilo de prueba en donde uno asume temporalmente que la conclusión deseada es falsa, luego se razona de forma lógica hasta llegar a una contradicción
Esto prueba que el enunciado original es verdadero.

inductive reasoning *(p. 76)* A process that includes looking for patterns and making conjectures

razonamiento inductivo *(p. 76)* Un proceso que incluye buscar patrones y hacer conjeturas

initial point *(p. 174)* The starting point of a vector

punto inicial *(p. 174)* El punto de inicio de un vector

English-Spanish Glossary

inscribed angle *(p. 554)* An angle whose vertex is on a circle and whose sides contain chords of the circle

inscribed polygon *(p. 556)* A polygon in which all the vertices lie on a circle

intercepted arc *(p. 554)* An arc that lies between two lines, rays, or segments

interior of an angle *(p. 38)* The region that contains all the points between the sides of an angle

interior angles *(p. 233)* Angles of a polygon

intersection *(p. 6)* The set of points two or more geometric figures have in common

inverse *(p. 67)* The statement formed by negating both the hypothesis and conclusion of a conditional statement

inverse cosine *(p. 502)* An inverse trigonometric ratio, abbreviated as $\cos^{-1}$
For acute angle A, if $\cos A = z$, then $\cos^{-1} z = m\angle A$.

inverse sine *(p. 502)* An inverse trigonometric ratio, abbreviated as $\sin^{-1}$
For acute angle A, if $\sin A = y$, then $\sin^{-1} y = m\angle A$.

inverse tangent *(p. 502)* An inverse trigonometric ratio, abbreviated as $\tan^{-1}$
For acute angle A, if $\tan A = x$, then $\tan^{-1} x = m\angle A$.

isosceles trapezoid *(p. 398)* A trapezoid with congruent legs

ángulo inscrito *(p. 554)* Un ángulo cuyo vértice está en un círculo y cuyos lados contienen cuerdas del círculo

polígono inscrito *(p. 556)* Un polígono en donde todos los vértices descansan sobre un círculo

arco interceptado *(p. 554)* Un arco que descansa entre dos rectas, rayos o segmentos

interior de un ángulo *(p. 38)* La región que contiene todos los puntos entre los lados de un ángulo

ángulos interiores *(p. 233)* Los ángulos de un polígono

intersección *(p. 6)* El conjunto de puntos que dos o más figuras geométricas tienen en común

inverso *(p. 67)* El enunciado formado por la negación de la hipótesis y conclusión de un enunciado condicional

coseno inverso *(p. 502)* Una razón trigonométrica inversa, abreviada como $\cos^{-1}$
Para un ángulo agudo A, si $\cos A = z$, entonces $\cos^{-1} z = m\angle A$.

seno inverso *(p. 502)* Una razón trigonométrica inversa, abreviada como $\sin^{-1}$
Para un ángulo agudo A, si $\sin A = y$, entonces $\sin^{-1} y = m\angle A$.

tangente inversa *(p. 502)* Una razón trigonométrica inversa, abreviada como $\tan^{-1}$
Para un ángulo agudo A, si $\tan A = x$, entonces $\tan^{-1} x = m\angle A$.

trapecio isósceles *(p. 398)* Un trapecio con catetos congruentes

---

---

joint frequency *(p. 684)* Each entry in a two-way table

joint relative frequency *(p. 685)* The ratio of a frequency that is not in the total row or the total column to the total number of values or observations in a two-way table

frecuencia conjunta *(p. 684)* Cada valor en una tabla de doble entrada

frecuencia relativa conjunta *(p. 685)* La razón de una frecuencia que no está en la hilera total o columna total del número total de valores u observaciones en una tabla de doble entrada

---

---

kite *(p. 401)* A quadrilateral that has two pairs of consecutive congruent sides, but opposite sides are not congruent

papalote *(p. 401)* Un cuadrilátero que tiene dos pares de lados congruentes consecutivos, pero los lados opuestos no son congruentes

lateral surface of a cone *(p. 642)* Consists of all segments that connect the vertex with points on the base edge of a cone

Law of Cosines *(p. 511)* For $\triangle ABC$ with side lengths of a, b, and c,

$$a^2 = b^2 + c^2 - 2bc \cos A,$$
$$b^2 = a^2 + c^2 - 2ac \cos B, \text{ and}$$
$$c^2 = a^2 + b^2 - 2ab \cos C.$$

Law of Sines *(p. 509)* For $\triangle ABC$ with side lengths of a, b, and c,

$$\frac{\sin A}{a} = \frac{\sin B}{b} = \frac{\sin C}{c} \text{ and}$$
$$\frac{a}{\sin A} = \frac{b}{\sin B} = \frac{c}{\sin C}.$$

legs of an isosceles triangle *(p. 252)* The two congruent sides of an isosceles triangle

legs of a right triangle *(p. 264)* The sides adjacent to the right angle of a right triangle

legs of a trapezoid *(p. 398)* The nonparallel sides of a trapezoid

line *(p. 4)* A line has one dimension. It is represented by a line with two arrowheads, but it extends without end.

line perpendicular to a plane *(p. 86)* A line that intersects the plane in a point and is perpendicular to every line in the plane that intersects it at that point

line of reflection *(p. 182)* A line that acts as a mirror for a reflection

line segment *(p. 5)* Consists of two endpoints and all the points between them
See segment.

line symmetry *(p. 185)* A figure in the plane has line symmetry when the figure can be mapped onto itself by a reflection in a line.

line of symmetry *(p. 185)* A line of reflection that maps a figure onto itself

linear pair *(p. 50)* Two adjacent angles whose noncommon sides are opposite rays

superficie lateral de un cono *(p. 642)* Consta los segmentos que conectan el vértice con puntos en borde base de un cono

Ley de cosenos *(p. 511)* Para $\triangle ABC$ con longitudes de lados de a, b, y c,

$$a^2 = b^2 + c^2 - 2bc \cos A,$$
$$b^2 = a^2 + c^2 - 2ac \cos B, \text{ y}$$
$$c^2 = a^2 + b^2 - 2ab \cos C.$$

Ley de senos *(p. 509)* Para $\triangle ABC$ con longitudes de lados de a, b, y c,

$$\frac{\sin A}{a} = \frac{\sin B}{b} = \frac{\sin C}{c} \text{ y}$$
$$\frac{a}{\sin A} = \frac{b}{\sin B} = \frac{c}{\sin C}.$$

catetos de un triángulo isósceles *(p. 252)* Los dos lados congruentes de un triángulo isósceles

catetos de un triángulo recto *(p. 264)* Los lados adyacentes al ángulo recto de un triángulo recto

catetos de un trapecio *(p. 398)* Los lados no paralelos de un trapezoide

recta *(p. 4)* Una recta tiene una dimensión. Se representa por una línea con dos flechas, pero se extiende sin fin.

recta perpendicular a un plano *(p. 86)* Una recta que intersecta el plano en un punto y es perpendicular a cada recta en el plano que la intersecta en ese punto

recta de reflexión *(p. 182)* Una recta que actúa como un espejo para una reflexión

segmento de recta *(p. 5)* Consiste en dos puntos extremos y todos los puntos entre ellos
Ver segmento.

simetría de recta *(p. 185)* Una figura en el plano tiene simetría de recta cuando la figura puede superponerse sobre sí misma por una reflexión en una recta.

recta de simetría *(p. 185)* Una recta de reflexión que superpone una figura sobre sí misma

par lineal *(p. 50)* Dos ángulos adyacentes cuyos lados no comunes son rayos opuestos

English-Spanish Glossary

major arc *(p. 538)* An arc with a measure greater than 180°

marginal frequency *(p. 684)* The sums of the rows and columns in a two-way table

marginal relative frequency *(p. 685)* The sum of the joint relative frequencies in a row or a column in a two-way table

measure of an angle *(p. 39)* The absolute value of the difference between the real numbers matched with the two rays that form the angle on a protractor

measure of a major arc *(p. 538)* The measure of a major arc's central angle

measure of a minor arc *(p. 538)* The measure of a minor arc's central angle

median of a triangle *(p. 320)* A segment from a vertex of a triangle to the midpoint of the opposite side

midpoint *(p. 20)* The point that divides a segment into two congruent segments

midsegment of a trapezoid *(p. 400)* The segment that connects the midpoints of the legs of a trapezoid

midsegment of a triangle *(p. 330)* A segment that connects the midpoints of two sides of a triangle

minor arc *(p. 538)* An arc with a measure less than 180°

mutually exclusive events *(p. 694)* Two events that have no outcomes in common

arco mayor *(p. 538)* Un arco con una medida mayor de 180°

frecuencia marginal *(p. 684)* Las sumas de las hileras y columnas en una tabla de doble entrada

frecuencia relativa marginal *(p. 685)* La suma de las frecuencias relativas conjuntas en una hilera o columna en una tabla de doble entrada

medida de un ángulo *(p. 39)* El valor absoluto de la diferencia entre los números reales asociados con los dos rayos que forman el ángulo en un transportador

medida de arco mayor *(p. 538)* La medida del ángulo central de un arco mayor

medida de arco menor *(p. 538)* La medida del ángulo central de un arco menor

mediana de un triángulo *(p. 320)* Un segmento desde el vértice de un triángulo hasta el punto medio del lado opuesto

punto medio *(p. 20)* El punto que divide un segmento en dos segmentos congruentes

segmento medio de un trapezoide *(p. 400)* El segmento que conecta los puntos medios de los catetos de un trapezoide

segmento medio de un triángulo *(p. 330)* Un segmento que conecta los puntos medios de dos lados de un triángulo

arco menor *(p. 538)* Un arco con una medida menor de 180°

eventos mutuamente exclusivos *(p. 694)* Dos eventos que no tienen resultados en común

***n* factorial** *(p. 700)* The product of the integers from 1 to n, for any positive integer n

negation *(p. 66)* The opposite of a statement
If a statement is p, then the negation is "not p," written $\sim p$.

net *(p. 592)* A two-dimensional pattern than can be folded to form a three-dimensional figure

factorial de *n* *(p. 700)* El producto de los números enteros de 1 a n, para cualquier número entero positivo n

negación *(p. 66)* Lo opuesto de un enunciado o afirmación
Si un enunciado es p, entonces la negación es "no p," y se escribe $\sim p$.

desarrollo de poliedros *(p. 592)* Un patrón bidimensional que puede doblarse para formar una figura tridimensional

obtuse angle *(p. 39)* An angle that has a measure greater than 90° and less than 180°

ángulo obtuso *(p. 39)* Un ángulo que tiene una medida mayor que 90° y menor que 180°

opposite rays *(p. 5)* If point *C* lies on $\overleftrightarrow{AB}$ between *A* and *B*, then $\overrightarrow{CA}$ and $\overrightarrow{CB}$ are opposite rays.

rayos opuestos *(p. 5)* Si el punto *C* descansa en $\overleftrightarrow{AB}$ entre *A* y *B*, entonces $\overrightarrow{CA}$ y $\overrightarrow{CB}$ son rayos opuestos.

orthocenter *(p. 321)* The point of concurrency of the lines containing the altitudes of a triangle

ortocentro *(p. 321)* El punto de concurrencia de las líneas que contienen las alturas de un triángulo

outcome *(p. 668)* The possible result of a probability experiment

resultado *(p. 668)* El resultado posible de un experimento de probabilidad

overlapping events *(p. 694)* Two events that have one or more outcomes in common

eventos superpuestos *(p. 694)* Dos eventos que tienen uno o más resultados en común

paragraph proof *(p. 108)* A style of proof that presents the statements and reasons as sentences in a paragraph, using words to explain the logical flow of an argument

prueba en forma de párrafo *(p. 108)* Un estilo de prueba que presenta los enunciados y motivos como oraciones en un párrafo, usando palabras para explicar el flujo lógico de un argumento

parallel lines *(p. 126)* Coplanar lines that do not intersect

rectas paralelas *(p. 126)* Rectas coplanarias que no se intersectan

parallel planes *(p. 126)* Planes that do not intersect

planos paralelos *(p. 126)* Planos que no se intersectan

parallelogram *(p. 368)* A quadrilateral with both pairs of opposite sides parallel

paralelogramo *(p. 368)* Un cuadrilátero con ambos pares de lados opuestos paralelos

permutation *(p. 700)* An arrangement of objects in which order is important

permutación *(p. 700)* Una disposición de objetos en la que el orden es importante

perpendicular bisector *(p. 149)* A line that is perpendicular to a segment at its midpoint

bisectriz perpendicular *(p. 149)* Una recta que es perpendicular a un segmento en su punto medio

perpendicular lines *(p. 68)* Two lines that intersect to form a right angle

rectas perpendiculares *(p. 68)* Dos líneas que se intersectan para formar un ángulo recto

plane *(p. 4)* A flat surface made up of points that has two dimensions and extends without end and is represented by a shape that looks like a floor or wall

plano *(p. 4)* Una superficie plana formada por puntos que tiene dos dimensiones y se extiende sin fin y que está representada por una forma que parece un piso o una pared

point *(p. 4)* A location in space that is represented by a dot and has no dimension

punto *(p. 4)* Un lugar en el espacio que está representado por un punto y no tiene dimensión

point of concurrency *(p. 310)* The point of intersection of concurrent lines, rays, or segments

punto de concurrencia *(p. 310)* El punto de intersección de rectas, rayos o segmentos concurrentes

point of tangency *(p. 530)* The point at which a tangent line intersects a circle

punto de tangencia *(p. 530)* El punto en donde una recta tangente intersecta a un círculo

polyhedron *(p. 618)* A solid that is bounded by polygons

poliedro *(p. 618)* Un sólido que está encerrado por polígonos

English-Spanish Glossary

population density *(p. 603)* A measure of how many people live within a given area

densidad de población *(p. 603)* Medición de la cantidad de personas que habitan un área dada

postulate *(p. 12)* A rule that is accepted without proof

postulado *(p. 12)* Una regla que es aceptada sin demostración

preimage *(p. 174)* The original figure before a transformation

preimagen *(p. 174)* La figura original antes de una transformación

probability distribution *(p. 708)* A function that gives the probability of each possible value of a random variable

distribución de probabilidad *(p. 708)* Una función que da la probabilidad de cada valor posible de una variable aleatoria

probability of an event *(p. 668)* A measure of the likelihood, or chance, that an event will occur

probabilidad de un evento *(p. 668)* Una medida de la probabilidad o posibilidad de que ocurrirá un evento

probability experiment *(p. 668)* An action, or trial, that has varying results

experimento de probabilidad *(p. 668)* Una acción o prueba que tiene resultados variables

proof *(p. 100)* A logical argument that uses deductive reasoning to show that a statement is true

prueba *(p. 100)* Un argumento lógico que usa el razonamiento deductivo para mostrar que un enunciado es verdadero

Pythagorean triple *(p. 464)* A set of three positive integers a, b, and c that satisfy the equation $c^2 = a^2 + b^2$

triple pitagórico *(p. 464)* Un conjunto de tres números enteros positivos a, b, y c que satisfacen la ecuación $c^2 = a^2 + b^2$

R

---

radian *(p. 597)* A unit of measurement for angles

radián *(p. 597)* Una unidad de medida para ángulos

radius of a circle *(p. 530)* A segment whose endpoints are the center and any point on a circle

radio de un círculo *(p. 530)* Un segmento cuyos puntos extremos son el centro y cualquier punto en un círculo

radius of a regular polygon *(p. 611)* The radius of a polygon's circumscribed circle

radio de un polígono regular *(p. 611)* El radio del círculo circunscrito de un polígono

random variable *(p. 708)* A variable whose value is determined by the outcomes of a probability experiment

variable aleatoria *(p. 708)* Una variable cuyo valor está determinado por los resultados de un experimento de probabilidad

ray *(p. 5)* $\overrightarrow{AB}$ is a ray if it consists of the endpoint A and all points on $\overleftrightarrow{AB}$ that lie on the same side of A as B.

rayo *(p. 5)* $\overrightarrow{AB}$ es un rayo, si consiste del punto extremo A y todos los puntos en $\overleftrightarrow{AB}$ que descansan en el mismo lado de A como B.

rectangle *(p. 388)* A parallelogram with four right angles

rectángulo *(p. 388)* Un paralelogramo con cuatro ángulos rectos

reduction *(p. 208)* A dilation in which the scale factor is greater than 0 and less than 1

reducción *(p. 208)* Una dilatación en donde el factor de escala es mayor que 0 y menor que 1

reflection *(p. 182)* A transformation that uses a line like a mirror to reflect a figure

reflexión *(p. 182)* Una transformación que usa una recta como un espejo para reflejar una figura

regular polygon *(p. 361)* A convex polygon that is both equilateral and equiangular

polígono regular *(p. 361)* Un polígono convexo que es tanto equilátero como equiángulo

rhombus *(p. 388)* A parallelogram with four congruent sides

right angle *(p. 39)* An angle that has a measure of 90°

rigid motion *(p. 176)* A transformation that preserves length and angle measure
See congruence transformation.

rotation *(p. 190)* A transformation in which a figure is turned about a fixed point

rotational symmetry *(p. 193)* A figure has rotational symmetry when the figure can be mapped onto itself by a rotation of 180° or less about the center of the figure.

rombo *(p. 388)* Un paralelogramo con cuatro lados congruentes

ángulo recto *(p. 39)* Un ángulo que tiene una medida de 90°

movimiento rígido *(p. 176)* Una transformación que preserva la longitud y medida del ángulo
Ver transformación de congruencia.

rotación *(p. 190)* Una transformación en la cual una figura gira sobre un punto fijo

simetría de rotación *(p. 193)* Una figura tiene simetría de rotación cuando la figura puede superponerse sobre sí misma mediante una rotación de 180° o menos en el centro de la figura.

S

---

sample space *(p. 668)* The set of all possible outcomes for an experiment

scale factor *(p. 208)* The ratio of the lengths of the corresponding sides of the image and the preimage of a dilation

secant *(p. 530)* A line that intersects a circle in two points

secant segment *(p. 571)* A segment that contains a chord of a circle and has exactly one endpoint outside the circle

sector of a circle *(p. 604)* The region bounded by two radii of the circle and their intercepted arc

segment *(p. 5)* Consists of two endpoints and all the points between them
See line segment.

segment bisector *(p. 20)* A point, ray, line, line segment, or plane that intersects the segment at its midpoint

segments of a chord *(p. 570)* The segments formed from two chords that intersect in the interior of a circle

semicircle *(p. 538)* An arc with endpoints that are the endpoints of a diameter

sides of an angle *(p. 38)* The rays of an angle

similar arcs *(p. 541)* Arcs that have the same measure

espacio de muestra *(p. 668)* El conjunto de todos los resultados posibles de un experimento

factor de escala *(p. 208)* La razón de las longitudes de los lados correspondientes de la imagen y la preimagen de una dilatación

secante *(p. 530)* Una recta que intersecta a un círculo en dos puntos

segmento de secante *(p. 571)* Un segmento que contiene una cuerda de un círculo y que tiene exactamente un punto extremo fuera del círculo

sector de un círculo *(p. 604)* La región encerrada por dos radios del círculo y su arco interceptado

segmento *(p. 5)* Consiste en dos puntos extremos y todos los puntos entre ellos
Ver segmento de recta.

bisectriz de segmento *(p. 20)* Un punto, rayo, recta, segmento de recta o plano que intersecta el segmento en su punto medio

segmentos de una cuerda *(p. 570)* Los segmentos formados a partir de dos cuerdas que se intersectan en el interior de un círculo

semicírculo *(p. 538)* Un arco con puntos extremos que son los puntos extremos de un diámetro

lados de un ángulo *(p. 38)* Los rayos de un ángulo

arcos similares *(p. 541)* Arcos que tienen la misma medida

similar figures *(p. 216)* Geometric figures that have the same shape but not necessarily the same size

similar solids *(p. 630)* Two solids of the same type with equal ratios of corresponding linear measures

similarity transformation *(p. 216)* A dilation or a composition of rigid motions and dilations

sine *(p. 494)* For an acute angle of a right triangle, the ratio of the length of the leg opposite the acute angle to the length of the hypotenuse

skew lines *(p. 126)* Lines that do not intersect and are not coplanar

solid of revolution *(p. 620)* A three-dimensional figure that is formed by rotating a two-dimensional shape around an axis

solve a right triangle *(p. 503)* To find all unknown side lengths and angle measures of a right triangle

square *(p. 388)* A parallelogram with four congruent sides and four right angles

standard equation of a circle *(p. 576)*
$(x - h)^2 + (y - k)^2 = r^2$, where r is the radius and (h, k) is the center

standard position *(p. 462)* A right triangle is in standard position when the hypotenuse is a radius of the circle of radius 1 with center at the origin, one leg lies on the x-axis, and the other leg is perpendicular to the x-axis.

straight angle *(p. 39)* An angle that has a measure of $180°$

subtend *(p. 554)* If the endpoints of a chord or arc lie on the sides of an inscribed angle, the chord or arc is said to subtend the angle.

supplementary angles *(p. 48)* Two angles whose measures have a sum of $180°$

figuras similares *(p. 216)* Figuras geométricas que tienen la misma forma pero no necesariamente el mismo tamaño

sólidos similares *(p. 630)* Dos sólidos del mismo tipo con razones iguales de medidas lineales correspondientes

transformación de similitud *(p. 216)* Una dilatación o composición de movimientos rígidos y dilataciones

seno *(p. 494)* Para un ángulo agudo de un triángulo rectángulo, la razón de la longitud del cateto enfrente del ángulo agudo a la longitud de la hipotenusa

rectas sesgadas *(p. 126)* Rectas que no se intersectan y que no son coplanarias

sólido de revolución *(p. 620)* Una figura tridimensional que se forma por la rotación de una forma bidimensional alrededor de un eje

resolver un triángulo recto *(p. 503)* Para encontrar todas las longitudes de los lados y las medidas de los ángulos desconocidas de un triángulo recto

cuadrado *(p. 388)* Un paralelogramo con cuatro lados congruentes y cuatro ángulos rectos

ecuación estándar de un círculo *(p. 576)*
$(x - h)^2 + (y - k)^2 = r^2$, donde r es el radio y (h, k) es el centro

posición estándar *(p. 462)* Un triángulo recto se encuentra en posición estándar cuando la hipotenusa es un radio del círculo de radio 1 con centro en el origen, un cateto descansa en el eje x y el otro cateto es perpendicular al eje x.

ángulo llano *(p. 39)* Un ángulo que tiene una medida de $180°$

subtender *(p. 554)* Si los puntos extremos de una cuerda o arco descansan en los lados de un ángulo inscrito, se dice que la cuerda o arco subtiende el ángulo.

ángulos suplementarios *(p. 48)* Dos ángulos cuyas medidas suman $180°$

——————————————— **T** ———————————————

tangent *(p. 488)* For an acute angle of a right triangle, the ratio of the length of the leg opposite the acute angle to the length of the leg adjacent to the acute angle

tangent of a circle *(p. 530)* A line in the plane of a circle that intersects the circle at exactly one point

tangente *(p. 488)* Para un ángulo agudo de un triángulo rectángulo, la razón de la longitud del cateto enfrente del ángulo agudo a la longitud del cateto adyacente al ángulo agudo

tangente de un círculo *(p. 530)* Una recta en el plano de un círculo que intersecta el círculo en exactamente un punto

tangent circles *(p. 531)* Coplanar circles that intersect in one point

tangent segment *(p. 571)* A segment that is tangent to a circle at an endpoint

terminal point *(p. 174)* The ending point of a vector

theorem *(p. 101)* A statement that can be proven

theoretical probability *(p. 669)* The ratio of the number of favorable outcomes to the total number of outcomes when all outcomes are equally likely

transformation *(p. 174)* A function that moves or changes a figure in some way to produce a new figure

translation *(p. 174)* A transformation that moves every point of a figure the same distance in the same direction

transversal *(p. 128)* A line that intersects two or more coplanar lines at different points

trapezoid *(p. 398)* A quadrilateral with exactly one pair of parallel sides

trigonometric ratio *(p. 488)* A ratio of the lengths of two sides in a right triangle

truth table *(p. 70)* A table that shows the truth values for a hypothesis, conclusion, and conditional statement

truth value *(p. 70)* True (T) or false (F)

two-column proof *(p. 100)* A type of proof that has numbered statements and corresponding reasons that show an argument in a logical order

two-way table *(p. 684)* A frequency table that displays data collected from one source that belong to two different categories

círculos tangentes *(p. 531)* Círculos coplanarios que se intersectan en un punto

segmento de tangente *(p. 571)* Un segmento que es tangente a un círculo en un punto extremo

punto terminal *(p. 174)* El punto final de un vector

teorema *(p. 101)* Un enunciado que puede comprobarse

probabilidad teórica *(p. 669)* La razón del número de resultados favorables con respecto al número total de resultados cuando todos los resultados son igualmente probables

transformación *(p. 174)* Una función que mueve o cambia una figura de cierta manera para producir una nueva figura

traslación *(p. 174)* Una transformación que mueve cada punto de una figura la misma distancia en la misma dirección

transversal *(p. 128)* Una recta que intersecta dos o más rectas coplanarias en puntos distintos

trapecio *(p. 398)* Un cuadrilátero con exactamente un par de lados paralelos

razón trigonométrica *(p. 488)* Una razón de las longitudes de dos lados en un triángulo recto

tabla de verdad *(p. 70)* Una tabla que muestra los verdaderos valores para una hipótesis, conclusión y enunciado condicional

valor de verdad *(p. 70)* Verdadero (V) o falso (F)

prueba de dos columnas *(p. 100)* Un tipo de prueba que tiene enunciados numerados y motivos correspondientes que muestran un argumento en un orden lógico

tabla de doble entrada *(p. 684)* Una tabla de frecuencia que muestra los datos recogidos de una fuente que pertenece a dos categorías distintas

undefined terms *(p. 4)* Words that do not have formal definitions, but there is agreement about what they mean

In geometry, the words *point*, *line*, and *plane* are undefined terms.

términos no definidos *(p. 4)* Palabras que no tienen definiciones formales, pero hay un consenso acerca de lo que significan

En geometría, las palabras *punto*, *línea* y *plano* son términos no definidos.

vector *(p. 174)* A quantity that has both direction and magnitude and is represented in the coordinate plane by an arrow drawn from one point to another

vector *(p. 174)* Una cantidad que tiene tanto dirección como magnitud y que está representada en el plano coordenado por una flecha dibujada de un punto a otro

vertex angle *(p. 252)* The angle formed by the legs of an isosceles triangle

ángulo del vértice *(p. 252)* El ángulo formado por los catetos de un triángulo isósceles

vertex of an angle *(p. 38)* The common endpoint of two rays

vértice de un ángulo *(p. 38)* El punto extremo que dos rayos tienen en común

vertex of a polyhedron *(p. 618)* A point of a polyhedron where three or more edges meet

vértice de un poliedro *(p. 618)* Un punto de un poliedro donde se encuentran tres o más bordes

vertical angles *(p. 50)* Two angles whose sides form two pairs of opposite rays

ángulos verticales *(p. 50)* Dos ángulos cuyos lados forman dos pares de rayos opuestos

vertical component *(p. 174)* The vertical change from the starting point of a vector to the ending point

componente vertical *(p. 174)* El cambio vertical desde el punto de inicio de un vector hasta el punto final

volume *(p. 626)* The number of cubic units contained in the interior of a solid

volumen *(p. 626)* El número de unidades cúbicas contenidas en el interior de u sólido

Index

A

30°-60°-90° right triangles
  finding sine and cosine of 30°, 496
  finding tangent with, 489
  side lengths of, 471, 473
30°-60°-90° Triangle Theorem
  (Thm. 9.5), 473
45°-45°-90° (isosceles) right triangles
  finding sine and cosine of 30°, 496
  side lengths, 471, 472
  in standard position, 462
45°-45°-90° Triangle Theorem
  (Thm. 9.4), 472
AA, *See* **Angle-Angle (AA) Similarity**
  Theorem (Thm. 8.3)
AAS, *See* **Angle-Angle-Side (AAS)**
Absolute value, finding, 1
Acute angle, 39
Acute triangle
  in circumscribed circle, 311
  classifying by angles, 232
  classifying by Pythagorean
    inequalities, 467
  orthocenter of, 322
Addition Property of Equality, 92
Adjacent angles, 48–49
Adjacent arcs, 539
Ailles rectangle, 476
Algebraic Properties of Equality, 92
Algebraic reasoning, 91–95, 117
  distributive property, 93
  other properties of equality, 94
  properties of equality, 92
Alternate exterior angles, 128
Alternate Exterior Angles Converse
  (Thm. 3.7), 139
Alternate Exterior Angles Theorem
  (Thm. 3.3), 132
  exploring converses, 137
Alternate interior angles, 128
Alternate Interior Angles Converse
  (Thm. 3.6), 139
  proving theorems about parallel
    lines, 140
Alternate Interior Angles Theorem
  (Thm. 3.2), 132
  exploring converses, 137
  proof of, 134
Altitude of cone, 642
Altitude of triangle
  defined, 321
  examples of segments and points in
    triangles, 300, 323

using, 319, 321–323, 351
"and" (intersection), 694–695
Angle(s)
  and arc measures in circles, 561–563
  circumscribed, 564
  classifying, and types of, 39
  congruent, 40
  construction, copying an angle, 40
  corresponding (*See* Corresponding
    angles)
  defined, 38
  diagram interpretation, 51
  finding angle measures, 47, 49, 50
    (*See also* Angle measures)
  inscribed, 553–555, 584
  measuring and constructing, 37–42,
    58
  naming, 38
  pairs of, describing, 47–51, 58
    adjacent angles, 48–49
    complementary angles, 48–49
    linear pair, 50
    supplementary angles, 48–49
    vertical angles, 50
  pairs of, formed by transversals, 128
    alternate exterior angles, 128
    alternate interior angles, 128
    consecutive interior angles, 128
    corresponding angles, 128
  proof of Symmetric Property of
    Angle Congruence, 102, 110
  Properties of Angle Congruence
    (Thm. 2.2), 101
  of triangles, 231–235, 290
    angle measures of triangles,
      233–235
    classifying triangles by sides and
      angles, 232–233
    relating to sides, 335, 337–338
Angle Addition Postulate
  (Post. 1.4), 41
Angle-Angle-Side (AAS)
  congruence, 271, 273
    identifying congruent triangles,
      271
  using Law of Sines to solve triangle,
    510
Angle-Angle-Side (AAS) Congruence
  Theorem (Thm. 5.11), 271
Angle-Angle (AA) Similarity
  Theorem (Thm. 8.3), 428
  proof of, 428
  triangle similarity theorems
    compared, 439

using, 429–430
Angle bisector(s)
  construction, bisecting an angle, 42
  defined, 42
  examples of segments and points in
    triangles, 300, 323
  finding angle measures, 42
  points on, 301
  proportionality in triangle, 449
  using, 304–305
Angle Bisector Theorem
  (Thm. 6.3), 304
  converse of, 304
Angle measures
  in kite, 401
  of polygons
    exterior, 362–363
    interior, 360–362
  in regular polygons, 611
  in rhombus, 390
  of triangles, 233–235
  types of angles, 39
  using properties of equality with, 94
Angle of depression, 497
Angle of elevation, 490
Angle of rotation, 190
Angle-Side-Angle (ASA)
  congruence, 270, 272, 273
    copying a triangle using ASA,
      272
  using Law of Sines to solve triangle,
    510
Angle-Side-Angle (ASA) Congruence
  Theorem (Thm. 5.10), 270
Angles Inside the Circle Theorem
  (Thm. 10.15), 563
Angles Outside the Circle Theorem
  (Thm. 10.16), 563
Another Way
  corresponding angles, 132
  probability, sample space and
    outcomes, 668
  segments of secants and tangents,
    572
  sketching a diagram, 86
  solving right triangle, 503
  Table of Trigonometric Ratios, 502
  triangles and Laws of Cosines or
    Sines, 511
Another Way
  alternate proofs, T-146
  coordinate proofs, T-282
  exterior angles of triangles, T-231
  inscribed angles, T-552

proving without words, 463
using, 464–465
using converse of, 466
Pythagorean Theorem (Thm. 9.1),
464
Pythagorean triple, 464

Q

Quadratic equations, solving by
completing the square, 527
Quadrilateral
area of, 29
classifications of, 358, 389, 402
identifying special, 402
with inscribed angles, 553
Quadrilaterals and other polygons,
356
angles of polygons, 359–363, 408
properties of parallelograms,
367–371, 408
properties of special parallelograms,
387–392, 409–410
properties of trapezoids and kites,
397–402, 410
proving quadrilateral is a
parallelogram, 375–380, 409
Questioning in the Classroom, T-1,
T-63, T-123, T-171, T-229,
T-299, T-357, T-415, T-461,
T-527, T-591, T-665

R

Radians, measuring angles in, 597
Radicals, using properties of, 461
Radius
of arc, 40
of circle
defined, 530
finding with congruent chords,
548
finding with segments, 572
of regular polygon, 611
of sphere, 648
Random variable, 708
Ratios, forming a proportionality, 415
Ray(s), and naming, 5
Reading
abbreviations: sin, cos, hyp., 494
abbreviations: tan, opp., adj., 488
approximately equal to, 23
biconditionals, 390
bisect, 20
bisector of circle arc, 546
circles, radius and diameter, 530
circum- prefix, 311
compound inequality, 339
contradiction, 336

corresponding lengths, 419
dilation scale factor, 208
inverse tangent, 502
negative reciprocals, 157
parallelogram notation, 201
raked stage, 504
scale factors, 211
statement of proportionality, 418
trapezoid midsegment, 400
triangle altitudes, 322
triangle area formula, 321
triangle classifications, 232
triangle notation, 31
two-way table, 684
Reading Diagrams
center of circle circumscribed about
polygon, 612
congruent angles, 40
congruent segments, 13
rely on marked information, 402
right angle and right triangle, 23
Real-life problems, *Throughout. See*
for example:
basics of geometry
angles in ball-return net, 49
planes in sulfur hexafluoride, 7
circles, graphs of, earthquake and
seismograph, 578
circumference and distance traveled,
596
congruent triangles
bench with diagonal support, 263
sign on barn, 248
parallel and perpendicular lines
in neighborhood layout, 151
sunlight angles, 134
probability
adults with pets, 671
diagnostic test for diabetes, 696
reasoning and proofs, percent raise,
93
relationships within triangles
biking, 346
bridge, 303
circumcenter or incenter for
lamppost placement, 314
distance in city, 311
soccer goal, 305
right triangles and trigonometry
angle of depression and skiing on
mountain, 497
angle of elevation and height of
tree, 490
equilateral triangle road sign, 474
roof height, 479
skyscrapers and support beams,
465

solving right triangles and raked
stage, 504
step angle of dinosaurs, 512
similarity
height of flagpole, 430
triangles and shoe rack, 447
three-dimensional figures,
rectangular dresser, 629
transformations
finding minimum distance, 185
golf website, 177
scale factor and length of image,
211
Reasoning and proofs, 62
algebraic reasoning, 91–95
conditional statements, 65–70, 116
inductive and deductive reasoning,
75–79, 116
postulates and diagrams, 83–86, 117
proving geometric relationships,
105–110, 118
proving statements about segments
and angles, 99–102, 118
Reasoning, visual, of similar triangles,
429
Rectangle
defined, 388
diagonal lengths in, 391
perimeter and area, 31
Rectangle Corollary (Cor. 7.3), 388
Rectangle Diagonals Theorem
(Thm. 7.13), 391
Reduction, 208
Reflection(s), 181–185, 222
coordinate rules for, 183
defined, 182
glide reflections, 184
in horizontal and vertical lines, 182
in line $y = x$ or $y = -x$, 183
performing, 182–183
triangle in coordinate plane, 181
triangle using reflective device, 181
Reflection Postulate (Post. 4.2), 184
Reflections in Intersecting Lines
Theorem (Thm. 4.3), 203
Reflections in Parallel Lines Theorem
(Thm. 4.2), 202
Reflexive Property, 94
triangle congruence, 241
Regular polygon
angle measures in, 611
areas of, 609–610, 612–613, 657
defined, 361
Related conditional statements, 67
Relationships between special
parallelograms, 389
Relationships within triangles, 298
bisectors of triangles, 309–341, 350

Postulates

1.1 Ruler Postulate

The points on a line can be matched one to one with the real numbers. The real number that corresponds to a point is the coordinate of the point. The distance between points A and B, written as AB, is the absolute value of the difference of the coordinates of A and B.

1.2 Segment Addition Postulate

If B is between A and C, then $AB + BC = AC$.
If $AB + BC = AC$, then B is between A and C.

1.3 Protractor Postulate

Consider $\overleftrightarrow{OB}$ and a point A on one side of $\overleftrightarrow{OB}$. The rays of the form $\overrightarrow{OA}$ can be matched one to one with the real numbers from 0 to 180. The measure of $\angle AOB$, which can be written as $m\angle AOB$, is equal to the absolute value of the difference between the real numbers matched with $\overrightarrow{OA}$ and $\overleftrightarrow{OB}$ on a protractor.

1.4 Angle Addition Postulate

If P is in the interior of $\angle RST$, then the measure of $\angle RST$ is equal to the sum of the measures of $\angle RSP$ and $\angle PST$.

2.1 Two Point Postulate

Through any two points, there exists exactly one line.

2.2 Line-Point Postulate

A line contains at least two points.

2.3 Line Intersection Postulate

If two lines intersect, then their intersection is exactly one point.

2.4 Three Point Postulate

Through any three noncollinear points, there exists exactly one plane.

2.5 Plane-Point Postulate

A plane contains at least three noncollinear points.

2.6 Plane-Line Postulate

If two points lie in a plane, then the line containing them lies in the plane.

2.7 Plane Intersection Postulate

If two planes intersect, then their intersection is a line.

2.8 Linear Pair Postulate

If two angles form a linear pair, then they are supplementary.

3.1 Parallel Postulate

If there is a line and a point not on the line, then there is exactly one line through the point parallel to the given line.

3.2 Perpendicular Postulate

If there is a line and a point not on the line, then there is exactly one line through the point perpendicular to the given line.

4.1 Translation Postulate

A translation is a rigid motion.

4.2 Reflection Postulate

A reflection is a rigid motion.

4.3 Rotation Postulate

A rotation is a rigid motion.

10.1 Arc Addition Postulate

The measure of an arc formed by two adjacent arcs is the sum of the measures of the two arcs.

Theorems

2.1 Properties of Segment Congruence

Segment congruence is reflexive, symmetric, and transitive.

Reflexive For any segment AB, $\overline{AB} \cong \overline{AB}$.

Symmetric If $\overline{AB} \cong \overline{CD}$, then $\overline{CD} \cong \overline{AB}$.

Transitive If $\overline{AB} \cong \overline{CD}$ and $\overline{CD} \cong \overline{EF}$, then $\overline{AB} \cong \overline{EF}$.

2.2 Properties of Angle Congruence

Angle congruence is reflexive, symmetric, and transitive.

Reflexive For any angle A, $\angle A \cong \angle A$.

Symmetric If $\angle A \cong \angle B$, then $\angle B \cong \angle A$.

Transitive If $\angle A \cong \angle B$ and $\angle B \cong \angle C$, then $\angle A \cong \angle C$.

2.3 Right Angles Congruence Theorem

All right angles are congruent.

2.4 Congruent Supplements Theorem

If two angles are supplementary to the same angle (or to congruent angles), then they are congruent.

2.5 Congruent Complements Theorem

If two angles are complementary to the same angle (or to congruent angles), then they are congruent.

2.6 Vertical Angles Congruence Theorem

Vertical angles are congruent.

3.1 Corresponding Angles Theorem

If two parallel lines are cut by a transversal, then the pairs of corresponding angles are congruent.

3.2 Alternate Interior Angles Theorem

If two parallel lines are cut by a transversal, then the pairs of alternate interior angles are congruent.

3.3 Alternate Exterior Angles Theorem

If two parallel lines are cut by a transversal, then the pairs of alternate exterior angles are congruent.

3.4 Consecutive Interior Angles Theorem

If two parallel lines are cut by a transversal, then the pairs of consecutive interior angles are supplementary.

3.5 Corresponding Angles Converse

If two lines are cut by a transversal so the corresponding angles are congruent, then the lines are parallel.

3.6 Alternate Interior Angles Converse

If two lines are cut by a transversal so the alternate interior angles are congruent, then the lines are parallel.

3.7 Alternate Exterior Angles Converse

If two lines are cut by a transversal so the alternate exterior angles are congruent, then the lines are parallel.

3.8 Consecutive Interior Angles Converse

If two lines are cut by a transversal so the consecutive interior angles are supplementary, then the lines are parallel.

3.9 Transitive Property of Parallel Lines

If two lines are parallel to the same line, then they are parallel to each other.

3.10 Linear Pair Perpendicular Theorem

If two lines intersect to form a linear pair of congruent angles, then the lines are perpendicular.

3.11 Perpendicular Transversal Theorem

In a plane, if a transversal is perpendicular to one of two parallel lines, then it is perpendicular to the other line.

3.12 Lines Perpendicular to a Transversal Theorem

In a plane, if two lines are perpendicular to the same line, then they are parallel to each other.

3.13 Slopes of Parallel Lines

In a coordinate plane, two nonvertical lines are parallel if and only if they have the same slope. Any two vertical lines are parallel.

3.14 Slopes of Perpendicular Lines

In a coordinate plane, two nonvertical lines are perpendicular if and only if the product of their slopes is -1. Horizontal lines are perpendicular to vertical lines.

4.1 Composition Theorem

The composition of two (or more) rigid motions is a rigid motion.

4.2 Reflections in Parallel Lines Theorem

If lines k and m are parallel, then a reflection in line k followed by a reflection in line m is the same as a translation. If A'' is the image of A, then

1. $\overline{AA''}$ is perpendicular to k and m, and
2. $AA'' = 2d$, where d is the distance between k and m.

4.3 Reflections in Intersecting Lines Theorem

If lines k and m intersect at point P, then a reflection in line k followed by a reflection in line m is the same as a rotation about point P. The angle of rotation is $2x°$, where $x°$ is the measure of the acute or right angle formed by lines k and m.

5.1 Triangle Sum Theorem

The sum of the measures of the interior angles of a triangle is 180°.

5.2 Exterior Angle Theorem

The measure of an exterior angle of a triangle is equal to the sum of the measures of the two nonadjacent interior angles

Corollary 5.1 Corollary to the Triangle Sum Theorem

The acute angles of a right triangle are complementary.

5.3 Properties of Triangle Congruence

Triangle congruence is reflexive, symmetric, and transitive.

Reflexive For any triangle $\triangle ABC$, $\triangle ABC \cong \triangle ABC$.

Symmetric If $\triangle ABC \cong \triangle DEF$, then $\triangle DEF \cong \triangle ABC$.

Transitive If $\triangle ABC \cong \triangle DEF$ and $\triangle DEF \cong \triangle JKL$, then $\triangle ABC \cong \triangle JKL$.

5.4 Third Angles Theorem

If two angles of one triangle are congruent to two angles of another triangle, then the third angles are also congruent.

5.5 Side-Angle-Side (SAS) Congruence Theorem

If two sides and the included angle of one triangle are congruent to two sides and the included angle of a second triangle, then the two triangles are congruent.

5.6 Base Angles Theorem

If two sides of a triangle are congruent, then the angles opposite them are congruent.

5.7 Converse of the Base Angles Theorem

If two angles of a triangle are congruent, then the sides opposite them are congruent.

Corollary 5.2 Corollary to the Base Angles Theorem

If a triangle is equilateral, then it is equiangular.

Corollary 5.3 Corollary to the Converse of the Base Angles Theorem

If a triangle is equiangular, then it is equilateral.

5.8 Side-Side-Side (SSS) Congruence Theorem

If three sides of one triangle are congruent to three sides of a second triangle, then the two triangles are congruent.

5.9 Hypotenuse-Leg (HL) Congruence Theorem

If the hypotenuse and a leg of a right triangle are congruent to the hypotenuse and a leg of a second right triangle, then the two triangles are congruent.

5.10 Angle-Side-Angle (ASA) Congruence Theorem

If two angles and the included side of one triangle are congruent to two angles and the included side of a second triangle, then the two triangles are congruent.

5.11 Angle-Angle-Side (AAS) Congruence Theorem

If two angles and a non-included side of one triangle are congruent to two angles and the corresponding non-included side of a second triangle, then the two triangles are congruent.

6.1 Perpendicular Bisector Theorem

In a plane, if a point lies on the perpendicular bisector of a segment, then it is equidistant from the endpoints of the segment.

6.2 Converse of the Perpendicular Bisector Theorem

In a plane, if a point is equidistant from the endpoints of a segment, then it lies on the perpendicular bisector of the segment.

6.3 Angle Bisector Theorem

If a point lies on the bisector of an angle, then it is equidistant from the two sides of the angle.

6.4 Converse of the Angle Bisector Theorem

If a point is in the interior of an angle and is equidistant from the two sides of the angle, then it lies on the bisector of the angle.

6.5 Circumcenter Theorem

The circumcenter of a triangle is equidistant from the vertices of the triangle.

6.6 Incenter Theorem

The incenter of a triangle is equidistant from the sides of the triangle.

6.7 Centroid Theorem

The centroid of a triangle is two-thirds of the distance from each vertex to the midpoint of the opposite side.

6.8 Triangle Midsegment Theorem

The segment connecting the midpoints of two sides of a triangle is parallel to the third side and is half as long as that side.

6.9 Triangle Longer Side Theorem

If one side of a triangle is longer than another side, then the angle opposite the longer side is larger than the angle opposite the shorter side.

6.10 Triangle Larger Angle Theorem

If one angle of a triangle is larger than another angle, then the side opposite the larger angle is longer than the side opposite the smaller angle.

6.11 Triangle Inequality Theorem

The sum of the lengths of any two sides of a triangle is greater than the length of the third side.

6.12 Hinge Theorem

If two sides of one triangle are congruent to two sides of another triangle, and the included angle of the first is larger than the included angle of the second, then the third side of the first is longer than the third side of the second.

6.13 Converse of the Hinge Theorem

If two sides of one triangle are congruent to two sides of another triangle, and the third side of the first is longer than the third side of the second, then the included angle of the first is larger than the included angle of the second.

7.1 Polygon Interior Angles Theorem

The sum of the measures of the interior angles of a convex n-gon is $(n - 2) \cdot 180°$.

Corollary 7.1 Corollary to the Polygon Interior Angles Theorem

The sum of the measures of the interior angles of a quadrilateral is $360°$.

7.2 Polygon Exterior Angles Theorem

The sum of the measures of the exterior angles of a convex polygon, one angle at each vertex, is $360°$.

7.3 Parallelogram Opposite Sides Theorem

If a quadrilateral is a parallelogram, then its opposite sides are congruent.

7.4 Parallelogram Opposite Angles Theorem

If a quadrilateral is a parallelogram, then its opposite angles are congruent.

7.5 Parallelogram Consecutive Angles Theorem

If a quadrilateral is a parallelogram, then its consecutive angles are supplementary.

7.6 Parallelogram Diagonals Theorem

If a quadrilateral is a parallelogram, then its diagonals bisect each other.

7.7 Parallelogram Opposite Sides Converse

If both pairs of opposite sides of a quadrilateral are congruent, then the quadrilateral is a parallelogram.

7.8 Parallelogram Opposite Angles Converse

If both pairs of opposite angles of a quadrilateral are congruent, then the quadrilateral is a parallelogram.

7.9 Opposite Sides Parallel and Congruent Theorem

If one pair of opposite sides of a quadrilateral are congruent and parallel, then the quadrilateral is a parallelogram.

7.10 Parallelogram Diagonals Converse

If the diagonals of a quadrilateral bisect each other, then the quadrilateral is a parallelogram.

Corollary 7.2 Rhombus Corollary

A quadrilateral is a rhombus if and only if it has four congruent sides.

Corollary 7.3 Rectangle Corollary

A quadrilateral is a rectangle if and only if it has four right angles.

Corollary 7.4 Square Corollary

A quadrilateral is a square if and only if it is a rhombus and a rectangle.

7.11 Rhombus Diagonals Theorem

A parallelogram is a rhombus if and only if its diagonals are perpendicular.

7.12 Rhombus Opposite Angles Theorem

A parallelogram is a rhombus if and only if each diagonal bisects a pair of opposite angles.

7.13 Rectangle Diagonals Theorem

A parallelogram is a rectangle if and only if its diagonals are congruent.

7.14 Isosceles Trapezoid Base Angles Theorem

If a trapezoid is isosceles, then each pair of base angles is congruent.

7.15 Isosceles Trapezoid Base Angles Converse

If a trapezoid has a pair of congruent base angles, then it is an isosceles trapezoid.

7.16 Isosceles Trapezoid Diagonals Theorem

A trapezoid is isosceles if and only if its diagonals are congruent.

7.17 Trapezoid Midsegment Theorem

The midsegment of a trapezoid is parallel to each base, and its length is one-half the sum of the lengths of the bases.

7.18 Kite Diagonals Theorem

If a quadrilateral is a kite, then its diagonals are perpendicular.

7.19 Kite Opposite Angles Theorem

If a quadrilateral is a kite, then exactly one pair of opposite angles are congruent.

8.1 Perimeters of Similar Polygons

If two polygons are similar, then the ratio of their perimeters is equal to the ratios of their corresponding side lengths.

8.2 Areas of Similar Polygons

If two polygons are similar, then the ratio of their areas is equal to the squares of the ratios of their corresponding side lengths.

8.3 Angle-Angle (AA) Similarity Theorem

If two angles of one triangle are congruent to two angles of another triangle, then the two triangles are similar.

8.4 Side-Side-Side (SSS) Similarity Theorem

If the corresponding side lengths of two triangles are proportional, then the triangles are similar.

8.5 Side-Angle-Side (SAS) Similarity Theorem

If an angle of one triangle is congruent to an angle of a second triangle and the lengths of the sides including these angles are proportional, then the triangles are similar.

8.6 Triangle Proportionality Theorem

If a line parallel to one side of a triangle intersects the other two sides, then it divides the two sides proportionally.

8.7 Converse of the Triangle Proportionality Theorem

If a line divides two sides of a triangle proportionally, then it is parallel to the third side.

8.8 Three Parallel Lines Theorem

If three parallel lines intersect two transversals, then they divide the transversals proportionally.

8.9 Triangle Angle Bisector Theorem

If a ray bisects an angle of a triangle, then it divides the opposite side into segments whose lengths are proportional to the lengths of the other two sides.

9.1 Pythagorean Theorem

In a right triangle, the square of the length of the hypotenuse is equal to the sum of the squares of the lengths of the legs.

9.2 Converse of the Pythagorean Theorem

If the square of the length of the longest side of a triangle is equal to the sum of the squares of the lengths of the other two sides, then the triangle is a right triangle.

9.3 Pythagorean Inequalities Theorem

For any $\triangle ABC$, where c is the length of the longest side, the following statements are true.
If $c^2 < a^2 + b^2$, then $\triangle ABC$ is acute.
If $c^2 > a^2 + b^2$, then $\triangle ABC$ is obtuse.

9.4 45°-45°-90° Triangle Theorem

In a 45°-45°-90° triangle, the hypotenuse is $\sqrt{2}$ times as long as each leg.

9.5 30°-60°-90° Triangle Theorem

In a 30°-60°-90° triangle, the hypotenuse is twice as long as the shorter leg, and the longer leg is $\sqrt{3}$ times as long as the shorter leg.

9.6 Right Triangle Similarity Theorem

If the altitude is drawn to the hypotenuse of a right triangle, then the two triangles formed are similar to the original triangle and to each other.

9.7 Geometric Mean (Altitude) Theorem

In a right triangle, the altitude from the right angle to the hypotenuse divides the hypotenuse into two segments. The length of the altitude is the geometric mean of the lengths of the two segments of the hypotenuse.

9.8 Geometric Mean (Leg) Theorem

In a right triangle, the altitude from the right angle to the hypotenuse divides the hypotenuse into two segments. The length of each leg of the right triangle is the geometric mean of the lengths of the hypotenuse and the segment of the hypotenuse that is adjacent to the leg.

9.9 Law of Sines

The Law of Sines can be written in either of the following forms for $\triangle ABC$ with sides of length a, b, and c.

$$\frac{\sin A}{a} = \frac{\sin B}{b} = \frac{\sin C}{c}$$

$$\frac{a}{\sin A} = \frac{b}{\sin B} = \frac{c}{\sin C}$$

9.10 Law of Cosines

If $\triangle ABC$ has sides of length a, b, and c, then the following are true.

$a^2 = b^2 + c^2 - 2bc \cos A$
$b^2 = a^2 + c^2 - 2ac \cos B$
$c^2 = a^2 + b^2 - 2ab \cos C$

10.1 Tangent Line to Circle Theorem

In a plane, a line is tangent to a circle if and only if the line is perpendicular to a radius of the circle at its endpoint on the circle.

10.2 External Tangent Congruence Theorem

Tangent segments from a common external point are congruent.

10.3 Congruent Circles Theorem

Two circles are congruent circles if and only if they have the same radius.

10.4 Congruent Central Angles Theorem

In the same circle, or in congruent circles, two minor arcs are congruent if and only if their corresponding central angles are congruent.

10.5 Similar Circles Theorem

All circles are similar.

10.6 Congruent Corresponding Chords Theorem

In the same circle, or in congruent circles, two minor arcs are congruent if and only if their corresponding chords are congruent.

10.7 Perpendicular Chord Bisector Theorem

If a diameter of a circle is perpendicular to a chord, then the diameter bisects the chord and its arc.

10.8 Perpendicular Chord Bisector Converse

If one chord of a circle is a perpendicular bisector of another chord, then the first chord is a diameter.

10.9 Equidistant Chords Theorem

In the same circle, or in congruent circles, two chords are congruent if and only if they are equidistant from the center.

10.10 Measure of an Inscribed Angle Theorem

The measure of an inscribed angle is one-half the measure of its intercepted arc.

10.11 Inscribed Angles of a Circle Theorem

If two inscribed angles of a circle intercept the same arc, then the angles are congruent.

10.12 Inscribed Right Triangle Theorem

If a right triangle is inscribed in a circle, then the hypotenuse is a diameter of the circle. Conversely, if one side of an inscribed triangle is a diameter of the circle, then the triangle is a right triangle and the angle opposite the diameter is the right angle.

10.13 Inscribed Quadrilateral Theorem

A quadrilateral can be inscribed in a circle if and only if its opposite angles are supplementary.

10.14 Tangent and Intersected Chord Theorem

If a tangent and a chord intersect at a point on a circle, then the measure of each angle formed is one-half the measure of its intercepted arc.

10.15 Angles Inside the Circle Theorem

If two chords intersect inside a circle, then the measure of each angle is one-half the sum of the measures of the arcs intercepted by the angle and its vertical angle.

10.16 Angles Outside the Circle Theorem

If a tangent and a secant, two tangents, or two secants intersect outside a circle, then the measure of the angle formed is one-half the difference of the measures of the intercepted arcs.

10.17 Circumscribed Angle Theorem

The measure of a circumscribed angle is equal to $180°$ minus the measure of the central angle that intercepts the same arc.

10.18 Segments of Chords Theorem

If two chords intersect in the interior of a circle, then the product of the lengths of the segments of one chord is equal to the product of the lengths of the segments of the other chord.

10.19 Segments of Secants Theorem

If two secant segments share the same endpoint outside a circle, then the product of the lengths of one secant segment and its external segment equals the product of the lengths of the other secant segment and its external segment.

10.20 Segments of Secants and Tangents Theorem

If a secant segment and a tangent segment share an endpoint outside a circle, then the product of the lengths of the secant segment and its external segment equals the square of the length of the tangent segment.

Reference

Properties

Properties of Equality

Addition Property of Equality
If $a = b$, then $a + c = b + c$.

Subtraction Property of Equality
If $a = b$, then $a - c = b - c$.

Multiplication Property of Equality
If $a = b$, then $a \cdot c = b \cdot c, c \neq 0$.

Division Property of Equality
If $a = b$, then $\dfrac{a}{c} = \dfrac{b}{c}, c \neq 0$.

Reflexive Property of Equality
$a = a$

Symmetric Property of Equality
If $a = b$, then $b = a$.

Transitive Property of Equality
If $a = b$ and $b = c$, then $a = c$.

Substitution Property of Equality
If $a = b$, then a can be substituted for b (or b for a) in any equation or expression.

Properties of Segment and Angle Congruence

Reflexive Property of Congruence
For any segment $AB, \overline{AB} \cong \overline{AB}$.

For any angle $A, \angle A \cong \angle A$.

Symmetric Property of Congruence
If $\overline{AB} \cong \overline{CD}$, then $\overline{CD} \cong \overline{AB}$.

If $\angle A \cong \angle B$, then $\angle B \cong \angle A$.

Transitive Property of Congruence
If $\overline{AB} \cong \overline{CD}$ and $\overline{CD} \cong \overline{EF}$, then $\overline{AB} \cong \overline{EF}$.

If $\angle A \cong \angle B$ and $\angle B \cong \angle C$, then $\angle A \cong \angle C$.

Other Properties

Transitive Property of Parallel Lines
If $p \parallel q$ and $q \parallel r$, then $p \parallel r$.

Distributive Property
Sum
$a(b + c) = ab + ac$
Difference
$a(b - c) = ab - ac$

Triangle Inequalities

Triangle Inequality Theorem

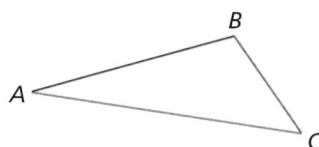

$AB + BC > AC$
$AC + BC > AB$
$AB + AC > BC$

Pythagorean Inequalities Theorem

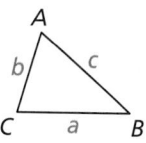

If $c^2 < a^2 + b^2$, then $\triangle ABC$ is acute.

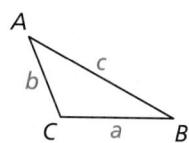

If $c^2 > a^2 + b^2$, then $\triangle ABC$ is obtuse.

Formulas

Coordinate Geometry

Slope

$m = \dfrac{y_2 - y_1}{x_2 - x_1}$

Slope-intercept form

$y = mx + b$

Point-slope form

$y - y_1 = m(x - x_1)$

Standard form of a linear equation

$Ax + By = C$

Standard equation of a circle

$(x - h)^2 + (y - k)^2 = r^2$, with center (h, k) and radius r

Midpoint Formula

$\left(\dfrac{x_1 + x_2}{2}, \dfrac{y_1 + y_2}{2} \right)$

Distance Formula

$d = \sqrt{(x_2 - x_1)^2 + (y_2 - y_1)^2}$

Polygons

Triangle Sum Theorem

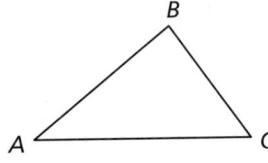

$m\angle A + m\angle B + m\angle C = 180°$

Exterior Angle Theorem

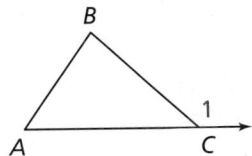

$m\angle 1 = m\angle A + m\angle B$

Triangle Midsegment Theorem

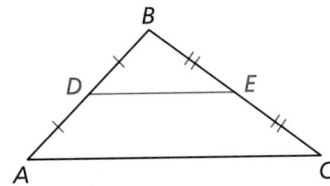

$\overline{DE} \parallel \overline{AC},\ DE = \frac{1}{2}AC$

Trapezoid Midsegment Theorem

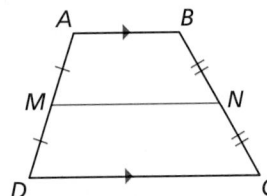

$\overline{MN} \parallel \overline{AB}, \overline{MN} \parallel \overline{DC},\ MN = \frac{1}{2}(AB + CD)$

Polygon Interior Angles Theorem

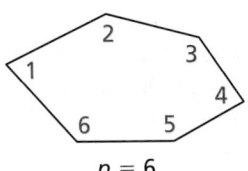

$n = 6$

$m\angle 1 + m\angle 2 + \cdots + m\angle n = (n - 2) \cdot 180°$

Polygon Exterior Angles Theorem

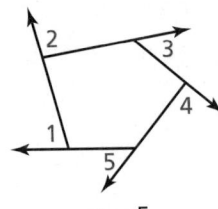

$n = 5$

$m\angle 1 + m\angle 2 + \cdots + m\angle n = 360°$

Geometric Mean (Altitude) Theorem

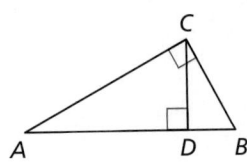

$CD^2 = AD \cdot BD$

Geometric Mean (Leg) Theorem

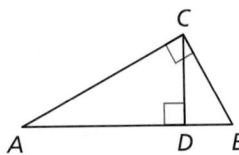

$CB^2 = DB \cdot AB$ $AC^2 = AD \cdot AB$

Right Triangles

Pythagorean Theorem

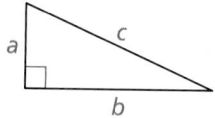

$a^2 + b^2 = c^2$

45°-45°-90° Triangles

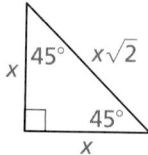

hypotenuse = leg $\cdot \sqrt{2}$

30°-60°-90° Triangles

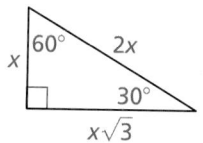

hypotenuse = shorter leg $\cdot$ 2
longer leg = shorter leg $\cdot \sqrt{3}$

Trigonometry

Ratios

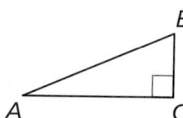

$\sin A = \dfrac{BC}{AB}$

$\sin^{-1} \dfrac{BC}{AB} = m\angle A$

$\cos A = \dfrac{AC}{AB}$

$\cos^{-1} \dfrac{AC}{AB} = m\angle A$

$\tan A = \dfrac{BC}{AC}$

$\tan^{-1} \dfrac{BC}{AC} = m\angle A$

Conversion between degrees and radians
$180° = \pi$ radians

Sine and cosine of complementary angles
Let A and B be complementary angles. Then the following statements are true.
$\sin A = \cos(90° - A) = \cos B$ $\sin B = \cos(90° - B) = \cos A$
$\cos A = \sin(90° - A) = \sin B$ $\cos B = \sin(90° - B) = \sin A$

Any Triangle

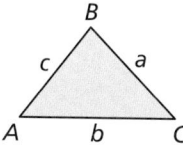

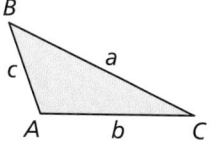

Area

Area $= \dfrac{1}{2}bc \sin A$

Area $= \dfrac{1}{2}ac \sin B$

Area $= \dfrac{1}{2}ab \sin C$

Law of Sines

$\dfrac{\sin A}{a} = \dfrac{\sin B}{b} = \dfrac{\sin C}{c}$

$\dfrac{a}{\sin A} = \dfrac{b}{\sin B} = \dfrac{c}{\sin C}$

Law of Cosines

$a^2 = b^2 + c^2 - 2bc \cos A$
$b^2 = a^2 + c^2 - 2ac \cos B$
$c^2 = a^2 + b^2 - 2ab \cos C$

Circles

Arc length

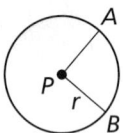

Arc length of $\widehat{AB} = \dfrac{m\widehat{AB}}{360°} \cdot 2\pi r$

Area of a sector

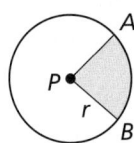

Area of sector $APB = \dfrac{m\widehat{AB}}{360°} \cdot \pi r^2$

Central angles

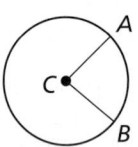

$m\angle ACB = m\widehat{AB}$

Inscribed angles

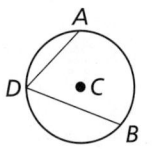

$m\angle ADB = \frac{1}{2}m\widehat{AB}$

Tangent and intersected chord

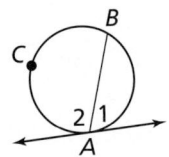

$m\angle 1 = \frac{1}{2}m\widehat{AB}$

$m\angle 2 = \frac{1}{2}m\widehat{BCA}$

Angles and Segments of Circles

Two chords

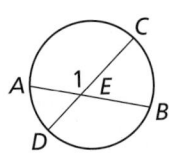

$m\angle 1 = \frac{1}{2}\left(m\widehat{AC} + m\widehat{DB}\right)$

$EA \cdot EB = EC \cdot ED$

Two secants

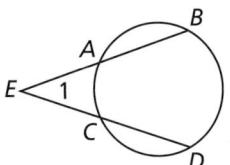

$m\angle 1 = \frac{1}{2}\left(m\widehat{BD} - m\widehat{AC}\right)$

$EA \cdot EB = EC \cdot ED$

Tangent and secant

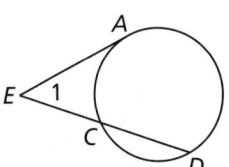

$m\angle 1 = \frac{1}{2}\left(m\widehat{AD} - m\widehat{AC}\right)$

$EA^2 = EC \cdot ED$

Two tangents

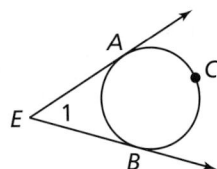

$m\angle 1 = \frac{1}{2}\left(m\widehat{ACB} - m\widehat{AB}\right)$

$EA = EB$

Probability and Combinatorics

Theoretical Probability $= \dfrac{\text{Number of favorable outcomes}}{\text{Total number of outcomes}}$

Experimental Probability $= \dfrac{\text{Number of successes}}{\text{Number of trials}}$

Probability of the complement of an event
$P(\overline{A}) = 1 - P(A)$

Probability of independent events
$P(A \text{ and } B) = P(A) \cdot P(B)$

Probability of dependent events
$P(A \text{ and } B) = P(A) \cdot P(B \mid A)$

Probability of compound events
$P(A \text{ or } B) = P(A) + P(B) - P(A \text{ and } B)$

Permutations

$_nP_r = \dfrac{n!}{(n-r)!}$

Combinations

$_nC_r = \dfrac{n!}{(n-r)! \cdot r!}$

Binomial experiments

$P(k \text{ successes}) = {_nC_k}\,p^k(1-p)^{n-k}$

Perimeter, Area, and Volume Formulas

Square

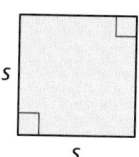

$P = 4s$
$A = s^2$

Rectangle

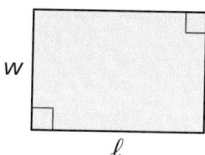

$P = 2\ell + 2w$
$A = \ell w$

Triangle

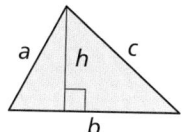

$P = a + b + c$
$A = \frac{1}{2}bh$

Circle

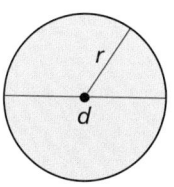

$C = \pi d$ or $C = 2\pi r$
$A = \pi r^2$

Parallelogram

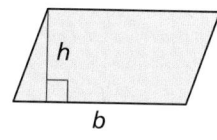

$A = bh$

Trapezoid

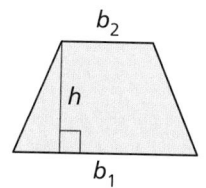

$A = \frac{1}{2}h(b_1 + b_2)$

Rhombus/Kite

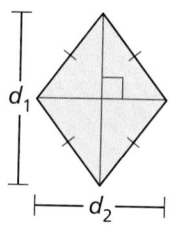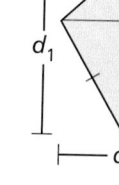

$A = \frac{1}{2}d_1 d_2$

Regular *n*-gon

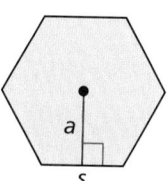

$A = \frac{1}{2}aP$ or $A = \frac{1}{2}a \cdot ns$

Prism

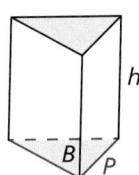

$L = Ph$
$S = 2B + Ph$
$V = Bh$

Cylinder

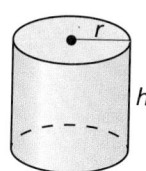

$L = 2\pi rh$
$S = 2\pi r^2 + 2\pi rh$
$V = \pi r^2 h$

Pyramid

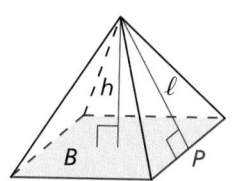

$L = \frac{1}{2}P\ell$
$S = B + \frac{1}{2}P\ell$
$V = \frac{1}{3}Bh$

Cone

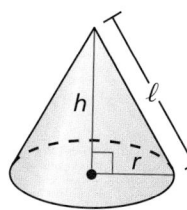

$L = \pi r\ell$
$S = \pi r^2 + \pi r\ell$
$V = \frac{1}{3}\pi r^2 h$

Sphere

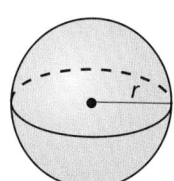

$S = 4\pi r^2$
$V = \frac{4}{3}\pi r^3$

Other Formulas

Geometric mean

$x = \sqrt{a \cdot b}$

Quadratic Formula

$x = \dfrac{-b \pm \sqrt{b^2 - 4ac}}{2a}$,

where $a \neq 0$ and $b^2 - 4ac \geq 0$

Density

$\text{Density} = \dfrac{\text{Mass}}{\text{Volume}}$

Similar polygons or similar solids with scale factor $a : b$

Ratio of perimeters $= a : b$

Ratio of areas $= a^2 : b^2$

Ratio of volumes $= a^3 : b^3$

Conversions

U.S. Customary

1 foot = 12 inches

1 yard = 3 feet

1 mile = 5280 feet

1 mile = 1760 yards

1 acre = 43,560 square feet

1 cup = 8 fluid ounces

1 pint = 2 cups

1 quart = 2 pints

1 gallon = 4 quarts

1 gallon = 231 cubic inches

1 pound = 16 ounces

1 ton = 2000 pounds

U.S. Customary to Metric

1 inch = 2.54 centimeters

1 foot ≈ 0.3 meter

1 mile ≈ 1.61 kilometers

1 quart ≈ 0.95 liter

1 gallon ≈ 3.79 liters

1 cup ≈ 237 milliliters

1 pound ≈ 0.45 kilogram

1 ounce ≈ 28.3 grams

1 gallon ≈ 3785 cubic centimeters

Time

1 minute = 60 seconds

1 hour = 60 minutes

1 hour = 3600 seconds

1 year = 52 weeks

Temperature

$C = \frac{5}{9}(F - 32)$

$F = \frac{9}{5}C + 32$

Metric

1 centimeter = 10 millimeters

1 meter = 100 centimeters

1 kilometer = 1000 meters

1 liter = 1000 milliliters

1 kiloliter = 1000 liters

1 milliliter = 1 cubic centimeter

1 liter = 1000 cubic centimeters

1 cubic millimeter = 0.001 milliliter

1 gram = 1000 milligrams

1 kilogram = 1000 grams

Metric to U.S. Customary

1 centimeter ≈ 0.39 inch

1 meter ≈ 3.28 feet

1 meter ≈ 39.37 inches

1 kilometer ≈ 0.62 mile

1 liter ≈ 1.06 quarts

1 liter ≈ 0.26 gallon

1 kilogram ≈ 2.2 pounds

1 gram ≈ 0.035 ounce

1 cubic meter ≈ 264 gallons

Credits

Front Matter

viii © Francisco Javier Alcerreca Gomez | Dreamstime.com; **ix** Colette3/Shutterstock.com; **x** © Kaehub | Dreamstime.com; **xi** ©iStockphoto.com/bradwieland; **xii** Edimur/Shutterstock.com; **xiii** sculpies/Shutterstock.com; **xiv** FreshPaint/Shutterstock.com; **xv** koh sze kiat/Shutterstock.com; **xvi** ©iStockphoto.com/Pamela Moore; **xvii** ©iStockphoto.com/-hakusan-; **xviii** CristinaMuraca/Shutterstock.com; **xix** Nadiia Gerbish/Shutterstock.com; **xxi** Monkey Business Images/Shutterstock.com; **xxv** Tyler Olson/Shutterstock.com; **xxix** Goodluz/Shutterstock.com

Chapter 1

0 *top left* © Francisco Javier Alcerreca Gomez | Dreamstime.com; *top right* CHEN WS/Shutterstock.com; *center left* Dimitar Kunev/Shutterstock.com; *bottom right* Maxim Blinkov/Shutterstock.com; *bottom left* Sukpaiboonwat/Shutterstock.com; **7** *top right* Benjah-bmm27; *top left* Sukpaiboonwat/Shutterstock.com; *bottom right* Benjah-bmm27; **9** *Exercise 35* koosen/Shutterstock.com; *Exercise 36* Vladru/Shutterstock.com, Jeff Schultes/Shutterstock.com; *Exercise 37* Winston Link/Shutterstock.com; *Exercise 38* Nyord/Shutterstock.com; **17** paulrommer/Shutterstock.com; **20** Maxim Blinkov/Shutterstock.com; **25** Mark Herreid/Shutterstock.com; **27** Aleksander Erin/Shutterstock.com; **33** Dimitar Kunev/Shutterstock.com; **40** malamalama/Shutterstock.com; **45** Lewis Calvert Cooper (*gonzoshots.com*); **46** Ruslan Gi/Shutterstock.com; **49** CHEN WS/Shutterstock.com; **53** *center left* © Francisco Javier Alcerreca Gomez | Dreamstime.com; *bottom left* Shane Trotter/Shutterstock.com; **55** pirita/Shutterstock.com

Chapter 2

62 *top left* Josef Hanus/Shutterstock.com; *top right* 60 Degrees, sculpture by Kevin O'Dwyer, Sculpture in the Parklands, Ireland; *center left* spirit of america/Shutterstock.com; *bottom right* Colette3/Shutterstock.com; *bottom left* sint/Shutterstock.com; **67** sint/Shutterstock.com; **72** *Exercise 45 top* mikeledray/Shutterstock.com; *Exercise 45 center and bottom* Tyler Boyes/Shutterstock.com; **73** Darren J. Bradley/Shutterstock.com; **81** BMCL/Shutterstock.com; **82** Siim Sepp/Shutterstock.com, © Vevesoran | Dreamstime.com; **89** Aleksander Erin/Shutterstock.com; **90** Kolopach/Shutterstock.com; **95** spirit of america/Shutterstock.com; **104** *top left* keko-ka/Shutterstock.com, tele52/Shutterstock.com; *bottom left* 60 Degrees, sculpture by Kevin O'Dwyer, Sculpture in the Parklands, Ireland; **108** Josef Hanus/Shutterstock.com; **113** kastianz/Shutterstock.com; **115** TsuneoMP/Shutterstock.com; **119** Natykach Nataliia/Shutterstock.com; **121** JeniFoto/Shutterstock.com

Chapter 3

122 *top left* gyn9037/Shutterstock.com; *top right* CC BY-NC-SA/ElizabethGarbee; *center left* EpicStockMedia/Shutterstock.com; *bottom right* © Kaehub | Dreamstime.com; *bottom left* ©iStockphoto.com/Brian McEntire; **129** Iraidak/Shutterstock.com; **130** *center left* © Kaehub | Dreamstime.com; *bottom right* ©iStockphoto.com/skynesher; **141** bikeriderlondon/Shutterstock.com; **143** *center left* Aleksangel/Shutterstock.com; *bottom left* EpicStockMedia/Shutterstock.com; **145** Aleksander Erin/Shutterstock.com; **146** © Bingram | Dreamstime.com; **151** *top* ©iStockphoto.com/Renphoto; *bottom* ©iStockphoto.com/kokouu; **153** *Exercise 21* Palto/Shutterstock.com; *Exercise 22* Mircea Maties/Shutterstock.com; **161** gyn9037/Shutterstock.com; **163** Irmairma/Shutterstock.com; **167** © Chris Eriksson | Dreamstime.com

Chapter 4

170 *top left* Roman Gorielov/Shutterstock.com; *top right* Odua Images/Shutterstock.com; *center left* Sybille Yates/Shutterstock.com; *bottom right* ©iStockphoto.com/bradwieland; *bottom left* Dima Sobko/Shutterstock.com; **179** Tribalium/Shutterstock.com; **181** Big Ideas Learning, LLC; **185** *top left* Butterfly Hunter/Shutterstock.com; *bottom right* Melinda Fawver/Shutterstock.com; **195** ©iStockphoto.com/bradwieland; **196** *Exercise 35a* Laura Mountainspring/Shutterstock.com; *Exercise 35b* Sybille Yates/Shutterstock.com; *top right* nito/Shutterstock.com; **197** Aleksander Erin/Shutterstock.com; **205** Dario Sabljak/Shutterstock.com; **211** *top right* Odua Images/Shutterstock.com; *center right and bottom left* Henrik Larsson/Shutterstock.com; **213** *Exercise 31* sarra22/Shutterstock.com; *Exercise 32* irin-k/Shutterstock.com; *Exercise 33* paulrommer/Shutterstock.com; *Exercise 34 and Exercise 35 top and bottom left* Evgeniy Ayupov/Shutterstock.com; *Exercise 35 top right* irin-k/Shutterstock.com; *Exercise 35 bottom right* Ambient Ideas/Shutterstock.com; **221** ©iStockphoto.com/OlgaChertova; **225** *Exercise 7* serg_dibrova/Shutterstock.com; *Exercise 8* Africa Studio/Shutterstock.com; *bottom right* greggsphoto/Shutterstock.com

Chapter 5

228 *top left* © Edimur/Shutterstock.com; *top right* Andrey Smirnov/Shutterstock.com; *center left* MaxyM/Shutterstock.com; *bottom right* racorn/Shutterstock.com; *bottom left* clivewa/Shutterstock.com; **232** © Ralf Broskvar | Dreamstime.com; **235** clivewa/Shutterstock.com; **241** racorn/Shutterstock.com; **248** MaxyM/Shutterstock.com; **255** Andrey Smirnov/Shutterstock.com; **257** *top left* Jeff Whyte/Shutterstock.com; *Exercise 23* Lucie Lang/Shutterstock.com; *Exercise 24* Yezepchyk Oleksandr/Shutterstock.com; **259** Aleksander Erin/Shutterstock.com; **268** *center left* Victoria Kalinina/Shutterstock.com; *center right* Koksharov Dmitry/Shutterstock.com; **276** szefei/Shutterstock.com; **278** Edimur/Shutterstock.com; **279** Kert/Shutterstock.com; **282** *top left* pisaphotography/Shutterstock.com; *top right* MarcelClemens/Shutterstock.com; **288** Mikael Damkier/Shutterstock.com; **289** wanpatsorn/Shutterstock.com; **295** Viacheslav Lopatin/Shutterstock.com

Chapter 6

298 *top left* Warren Goldswain/Shutterstock.com; *top right* puttsk/Shutterstock.com; *center left* sculpies/Shutterstock.com; *bottom right* Olena Mykhaylova/Shutterstock.com; *bottom left* Nikonaft/Shutterstock.com; **303** Nikonaft/Shutterstock.com; **305** sababa66/Shutterstock.com; **307** Tobias W/Shutterstock.com; **311** filip robert/Shutterstock.com, John T Takai/Shutterstock.com; **316** *top right* Matthew Cole/Shutterstock.com; *center right* artkamalov/Shutterstock.com, anton_novik/Shutterstock.com; **318** *center left* Olena Mykhaylova/Shutterstock.com; *top right* Lonely/Shutterstock.com; **325** Laschon Maximilian/Shutterstock.com; **327** Aleksander Erin/Shutterstock.com; **331** sculpies/Shutterstock.com; **332** Shumo4ka/Shutterstock.com; **333** Alexandra Lande/Shutterstock.com, Dan Kosmayer/Shutterstock.com; **334** clearviewstock/Shutterstock.com; **338** Dzm1try/Shutterstock.com; **344** ©iStockphoto.com/enchanted_glass; **346** Warren Goldswain/Shutterstock.com; **349** Portokalis/Shutterstock.com

Chapter 7

356 *top left* FreshPaint/Shutterstock.com; *top right* © Swinnerrr | Dreamstime.com; *center left* CC-PD by Ppntori; *bottom right* nacroba/Shutterstock.com; *bottom left* Reprinted with permission of The Photo News.; **360** © Peter Spirer | Dreamstime.com; **365** Reprinted with permission of The Photo News.; **370** Marco Prati/Shutterstock.com; **377** ©iStockphoto.com/A-Digit; **378** Ann Paterson; **383** kokandr/Shutterstock.com; **385** Aleksander Erin/Shutterstock.com; **386** Matthew Cole/Shutterstock.com; **393** *Exercise 9* Ksenia Palimski/Shutterstock.com; *Exercise 10* Sundraw Photography/Shutterstock.com; *Exercise 11* EvenEzer/Shutterstock.com; *Exercise 12* donatas1205/Shutterstock.com; **395** © Swinnerrr | Dreamstime.com; **407** © Dmitry Kalinovsky | Dreamstime.com